Pocket Oxford Russian Dictionary

Third edition

Edited by
Della Thompson

OXFORD
UNIVERSITY PRESS

Great Clarendon Street, Oxford OX2 6DP

Oxford University Press is a department of the University of Oxford.
It furthers the University's objective of excellence in research, scholarship, and education by publishing worldwide in

Oxford New York

Auckland Cape Town Dar es Salaam Hong Kong Karachi
Kuala Lumpur Madrid Melbourne Mexico City Nairobi
New Delhi Shanghai Taipei Toronto

with offices in

Argentina Austria Brazil Chile Czech Republic France Greece
Guatemala Hungary Italy Japan Poland Portugal Singapore
South Korea Switzerland Thailand Turkey Ukraine Vietnam

Oxford is a registered trade mark of Oxford University Press in the UK and in certain other countries

Published in the United States by Oxford University Press Inc., New York

First published 2006

British Library Cataloguing in Publication Data

Data available

Library of Congress Cataloging in Publication Data

Data available

Typeset in Nimrod, Arial, and Meta
by Interactive Sciences Ltd, Gloucester
Printed in Great Britain by Clays Ltd, Bungay, Suffolk

ISBN 0-19-861006-8
ISBN 9-78-019-861006-9

2

Contents

Project team ... vi

Preface ... vii

Предисловие ... vii

Guide to the use of the Dictionary ... viii

О пользовании словарём ... xv

Символы фонетической транскрипции, используемые в Словаре ... xxiii

О произношении звуков английского языка ... xxiv

Russian pronunciation guide ... xxxii

Abbreviations used in the Dictionary ... xxxvi

Russian–English ... 1

Russian life and culture ... 412

Британские и американские культурные реалии ... 418

Correspondence and CVs ... 432

English–Russian ... 449

Glossary of grammatical terms ... 868

Russian declensions and conjugations ... 878

Russian verbs ... 887

Заметки об английской грамматике ... 896

Английские неправильные глаголы ... 917

The Russian alphabet ... 920

Английский алфавит ... 920

Editors and contributors

Managing Editor
Della Thompson

Subeditor/Proofreader
Mikhaïl Pirozhok

Editors
Alexander Stoliarchuk
Pat Bulhosen

Supplementary material
Mikhaïl Pirozhok
Albina Ozieva
Terence Wade
Alexander Levtov

Preface

This 3rd edition of the *Pocket Oxford Russian Dictionary* is a completely new text, based on the much larger *Oxford Russian Dictionary*. It includes the most important new words that have entered Russian and English in recent years, especially as reflected in the areas of most rapid development such as IT, finance and commerce, medicine, and popular culture.

The dictionary has been made more useful to the Russian native speaker by the addition of sense indicators in Russian in the Russian–English section, the clear labelling of US and British terms and spellings, a guide to English pronunciation, a summary of English grammar, and a table of English irregular verbs. The English native speaker is now aided by tables of Russian declensions and conjugations, a guide to Russian pronunciation, and a glossary of grammatical terms.

Other new features include sections on how to write letters and CVs in both languages, and sections about life and culture in Britain, the US, and Russia.

The whole of the dictionary has been checked by Russian and English native speakers, ensuring that the information given is accurate and up to date.

Предисловие

Настоящее, третье издание *Pocket Oxford Russian Dictionary* представляет собой совершенно новый словарь, в основу которого легли материалы большого *Oxford Russian Dictionary*. В Словарь вошли наиболее значимые новые слова, пополнившие лексику русского и английского языков в последние годы, в особенности это справедливо в отношении таких стремительно развивающихся областей жизнедеятельности, как информационные технологии, финансы и торговля, медицина и популярная культура.

В новом издании Словаря в значительной мере были учтены интересы русскоязычных пользователей. Для нужд последних смысловые указатели в русско-английской части Словаря теперь даются на русском языке, а колебания в семантике и орфографии слов британского и американского вариантов английского последовательно разграничиваются путём приведения соответствующих помет. Специально для русскоязычной аудитории в Словарь были включены краткое руководство по английскому произношению, приложение английской грамматики и таблица неправильных глаголов. В помощь англоязычным пользователям предлагаются таблицы парадигм русского склонения и спряжения, краткое руководство по русскому произношению и глоссарий терминов русской грамматики.

Среди других важных новшеств Словаря приложения по написанию писем и резюме на обоих языках и обзорные статьи по культурным реалиям Великобритании, США и России.

Текст Словаря был полностью проверен носителями русского и английского языков, что позволяет утверждать, что информация, представленная в нём, точна и в полной мере соответствует современной речи.

Guide to the use of the Dictionary

Russian–English Section

Presentation

1 The following devices are used to save space:

(i) The first letter of the headword, followed by a full point, represents the whole headword, e.g.

автомоби́л|ь ... **води́ть а.** (= **води́ть автомоби́ль**)

(ii) The swung dash, in conjunction with a vertical stroke, represents that part of the headword which is to the left of the vertical stroke, e.g.

ава́ри|я ... **потерпе́ть ~ю** (= **потерпе́ть ава́рию**)

Exceptions: the swung dash is not used in indicating the genitive singular of nouns or the 1st and 2nd persons singular of the present tense of verbs with unchanged stress (for examples, see below: *Grammatical Information*: *Nouns* and *Verbs*); and, in cross-references from the imperfective to the perfective verbal aspect, it may, when preceded by a prefix, represent the entire headword, e.g.

беле́|ть, ю *impf.* (*of* **по~**) ... (= **побеле́ть**)

Pronunciation

2 With the general exception of monosyllables, stress is indicated for every Russian word. A stress mark above the swung dash, where this sign represents two or more syllables, indicates shift of stress to the syllables immediately preceding the vertical stroke dividing the headword, e.g.

запи|са́ть, шу́, ~́шешь ... (= **запишу́, запи́шешь**)

3 Conversely, a stress mark above a syllable to the right of the swung dash indicates shift of stress away from the syllables(s) represented by the swung dash, e.g.

а́дрес, а, *pl.* **~а́** ... (= **адреса́**)

4 Where a variant stress is permissible, both variants are shown, e.g.

зап|ере́ться ... **~́ерся́** ... (= **за́перся** *or* **заперся́**)

Meaning

5 Separate meanings of a word are indicated by means of Arabic numerals. Shades of meaning, represented by translations not considered strictly synonymous, are indicated by the means of a semicolon, whereas translations considered synonymous are indicated by a comma, e.g.

ава́нс ... **1** (*деньги*) advance.
2 (*pl. only*; *fig.*) advances, overtures.

авантю́ра ... **1** (*приключение*) adventure; escapade.
2 (*coll.*) shady enterprise.

6 Homonyms are indicated by repetition of the headword as a separate entry, followed by a superscript Arabic numeral, e.g.

блок[1] ... (*tech.*) block, pulley.

блок[2] ... (*pol.*) bloc.

Explanation

7 Where necessary for the avoidance of ambiguity, explanatory glosses are given in brackets in italic type. This device is used in particular in the case of words denoting specifically Russian or Soviet concepts (e.g. **ка́ша, микрорайо́н**) and makes it possible to use one-word transliterations rather than clumsy paraphrases as a substitute for translation.

8 Indications of style or usage are given, where appropriate, in brackets, e.g.

(*coll.*), (*fig.*), (*joc.*), (*agric.*), (*pol.*), etc.

Grammatical Information

9 The following grammatical information is given:

Nouns

The genitive singular ending and gender of all nouns are shown, e.g.

мо́лот, а *m.* hammer.
мо́лни|я, и *f.* lightning.
молок|о́, а́ *nt.* milk.
пья́ниц|а, ы *c.g.* drunkard.

Other case endings are shown where declension or stress is, in relation to generally accepted systems of classification, irregular, e.g.

англича́н|ин, ина, *pl.* **~е, ~** *m.* Englishman.
бор|ода́, оды́, *a.* **~̀оду,** *pl.* **~̀оды, ~о́д, ~ода́м** *f.* beard.

(But the inserted vowel in the genitive plural ending of numerous feminine nouns with nominative singular ending **-ка** is *not* regarded as irregular, e.g. **англича́нка,** *g. pl.* **англича́нок.**)

Adjectives

Only the masculine nominative singular of the full form of the adjective is shown. Endings of the short forms, where these are found, are shown in brackets in most cases, e.g.

глу́|пый (~, ~а́, ~о, ~̀ы)

The neuter and plural short form endings are omitted where stress is as for the feminine, e.g.

нау́ч|ный (~ен, ~на)

Verbs

Endings are shown of the 1st and 2nd persons singular of the present tense (or of the 1st person only of verbs with infinitive ending **-ать, -ова́ть, -ять, -еть** which retain stem and stress unchanged throughout the present tense), e.g.

говор|и́ть, ю́, и́шь ...
чита́|ть, ю ...

Other endings of the present tense and endings of the past tense are shown where formation or stress is irregular, e.g.

ид|ти́, у́, ёшь, *past* **шёл, шла** ...
бер|е́чь, егу́, ежёшь, егу́т, *past* **~ёг, ~егла́** ...

Participles and gerunds, and forms of the passive voice, are not shown unless they have special semantic of syntactical features.

If a past participle passive has an adjectival homonym with the same or similar meaning (as a rule, a participle has a word or words syntactically related to it, whereas an adjective does not), these homonyms are given as a single entry. In such cases, if the endings of the short forms of the participle and adjective differ, this is shown, e.g.

запу́тан|ный (**~**, **~а**) *p.p.p. of* **запу́тать** *and adj.* (**~**, **~на**) ...

Verbal aspects: the imperfective aspect is normally treated as the basic form of the simple verb, a cross-reference to the relevant form being shown in brackets, e.g.

чита́|ть, ю *impf.* (*of* **про~**, **прочéсть**) ...

The corresponding entries are:

прочита́|ть, ю *pf. of* **чита́ть**
про|чéсть, чту́, чтёшь, *past* **~чёл**, **~чла́** = **~чита́ть**

In the case, however, of compound verbs formed by means of a prefix, the perfective aspect is treated as the basic form, e.g.

заш|и́ть, ью́, ьёшь *pf.* (*of* **~ива́ть**) ...

Prefixes and Combining Forms

A number of prefixes and combining forms are shown as separate entries, e.g.

без... *pref.* in-, un-, -less.
гидро... *comb. form* hydro-.

English–Russian Section

Orthography

1 English spelling follows British usage, with American variations also noted, e.g. **honour...** (*US* **honor**).

Pronunciation

2 For the convenience of readers whose native language is not English, the pronunciation of headwords is given, using the International Phonetic Alphabet.

A key to the phonetic symbols used is given on p. xxiii.

Presentation

3 Headwords are printed in **bold roman** type except for non-naturalized foreign words and expressions, for which ***bold italic*** is used.

Alternative spellings (including American variants) are presented alongside the preferred spelling in full or abbreviated form, or shown in brackets; these variants appear again in alphabetical sequence (unless adjacent to the main entry), as cross-references, e.g.

cosy (*US* **cozy**) **cozy** = **cosy**
hicc|up, -ough
curts(e)y

Similar treatment is applied to words in which an alternative termination can be used without affecting the sense, e.g.

cyclic(al)

4 Also presented as headwords are a few two-word expressions of which the first element does not qualify for an individual entry, e.g. **Boxing Day**, **Parkinson's disease**.

5 Separate headword entries with superscript numerals are created for words which, though identical in spelling, differ in basic meaning and origin (**fine** as noun and verb; **fine** as adjective and adverb), or in pronunciation and/or stress (**house** and **supplement** as nouns and as verbs), or both (**tear** meaning 'teardrop' and **tear** meaning 'rip').

6 Separate entries for adverbs in '-ly' are made only when they have meanings or usage (idiom, compounds, etc.) which cannot conveniently be treated under the corresponding adjective. Examples are **hardly**, **really**, and **surely**. When there is no separate entry, and no instance of the adverb in the adjectival entry, it can be assumed that the corresponding Russian adverb is also formed regularly from the adjective. Thus, **clumsy** неуклю́жий, нело́вкий implies that the Russian for 'clumsily' is неуклю́же and нело́вко; **critical** крити́ческий implies that 'critically' can be translated крити́чески, and so on.

7 Gerundial and participial forms of English verbs, used as nouns or adjectives, are often accommodated within the verb entry (transitive or intransitive as appropriate), e.g.

revolving doors is found under **revolve** *v.i.*
a retarded child is found under **retard** *v.t.*

but in certain cases, for the sake of clarity, such forms have been treated as independent headwords, e.g.

barbed *adj.*; **flying** *n.* and *adj.*

8 Some headwords are divided by a vertical stroke in order that the unchanging letters preceding the stroke may subsequently be replaced, in inflected forms, by a swung dash. Where there is no divider, the swung dash represents the whole headword, e.g.

house ... **full ~** ... **~hold** ... **~hold word** ...

9 The vertical divider is also used in both English and Russian to separate the main part of a word from its termination when it is necessary to show modifications or alternative forms of the latter: e.g. paragraphs 3, 24 (c), and 25.

10 Within the headword entry each grammatical function has its own paragraph, introduced by a part-of-speech indicator: *n.*, *pron.*, *adj.*, *adv.*, *v.t.*, *v.i.*, *prep.*, *conj.*, *int.* A combined heading, e.g. **adagio** *n.*, *adj. & adv.*, may sometimes be used for convenience; the most common instance is *v.t. & i.* when the two uses are not clearly distinguishable, or when the Russian intransitive is expressed by means of the suffix -ся.

11 Verb-adverb combinations forming phrasal verbs normally appear in a separate paragraph headed '*with advs.*', immediately following simple verb usage; they are given in alphabetical order of the adverb.

12 There are also a few verbs (e.g. **go**) where idiomatic usage with prepositions is extensive and complex enough to call for a separate paragraph headed '*with preps.*'.

13 Compounds in which the headword forms the first element (including those that are written as two words rather than being hyphenated or written as one word), are mostly brought together or 'nested' under the headword in a final paragraph headed '*cpds.*'.

14 Adjective-noun expressions generally appear under the adjective unless this has relatively little weight, as in '**good riddance**'.

15 Within an entry, differences of meaning or application are defined by a synonym, context, or other means. Major differences may be distinguished by numerals in bold type, e.g.

gag *n.* **1** (*to prevent speech etc.*) ... **2** (*joke*) ...

16 A second type of label indicates status or level of usage, e.g.: *arch*(aic), *liter*(ary), *coll*(oquial), *sl*(ang), *vulg*(ar). It may apply to the headword as a whole, to one of its functions or meanings, or to a single phrase or sentence, and is placed accordingly, e.g.

gym *n.* (*coll.*) ...
bell *n.* ... **that rings a ~** (*fig., coll.*) ...
bung ... *v.t.* ... **2** (*Br. sl., throw*) ...

17 Russian expressions, especially idioms or proverbs, which parallel rather than translate their English equivalents are preceded by the symbol ≈.

18 The use of the comma or the semicolon to separate Russian words offered as translations of the same English word reflects a greater or lesser degree of equivalence; in the latter case an auxiliary English gloss is often used to express the nuance of difference, e.g.

ineligible *adj.* (*for office*) ...; (*for a benefit*) ...

19 To avoid ambiguity the semicolon is used when the alternatives are complete phrases or sentences, and also in most cases between synonymous verbs, e.g.

what is he getting at? что он хо́чет сказа́ть?; куда́ он кло́нит?
allow *v.t.* ... позв|оля́ть, -о́лить; разреш|а́ть, -и́ть ...

Idiom and Illustration

20 The examples of usage in both languages may consist of phrases or finite sentences.

21 In both English and Russian there are many instances when one word in a phrase or sentence may be replaced by a synonymous alternative. This is shown by means of a comma or oblique stroke in English, and an oblique stroke in Russian, e.g.

I'll knock a pound off the price я сбро́шу/ски́ну/сба́влю фунт с цены́.

22 Non-synonymous alternatives are linked by the oblique stroke in both languages, e.g.

carry on a conversation/business вести́ разгово́р/де́ло.

23 In most cases the oblique stroke expresses an alternative regarding only one word on either side of it. Other alternatives are generally shown in the form (*or* ...), e.g.

I could do with a drink я охо́тно (*or* с удово́льствием) вы́пил бы.

Grammatical Information

24 The following grammatical information is given in respect of words offered as translations of headwords:

a) the gender of *masculine* nouns ending in -ь, except when this is made clear by an accompanying adjective (e.g. **polar bear** бéлый медвéдь) or by the existence of a corresponding female form (see (*e*) below).

b) the gender of nouns (e.g. neuters in -мя, masculines in -а and -я, foreign borrowings in -и and -у) whose final letter does not serve as an indicator of gender. Nouns of common gender are designated (*c.g.*). Indeclinable nouns are designated (*indecl.*), preceded by a gender indicator if required. The many adjectives used as nouns (e.g. портнóй) are not specially marked.

c) the gender (or, for *pluralia tantum*, the genitive plural termination) and number (*pl.*) of all plural nouns which translate a headword or compound, e.g.

> **timpani, tympani** *n.* литáвры (*f. pl.*).
> **pliers** *n.* клéщ|и (*pl.*, *g.* -éй).

This information, however, is not given if the singular form has already appeared in the same entry, nor in the case of neuter plurals with an accompanying adjective, where the number and gender are self-evident from the terminations. Plurals of adjectives used substantively are shown as (*pl.*).

d) the nominative plural termination (-á or -я́) of certain masculine nouns when this form denotes a meaning different from that of the plural in -ы or -и, e.g.

> **fur** ... мех (*pl.* -á)

e) the forms of nouns used where Russian differs from English in making a verbal distinction between male and female, e.g.

> **teacher** учи́тель (*fem.* -ница)

f) aspectual information: see paragraphs 25–27 below.

g) case usage with prepositions, e.g. **before** до + *g*.

h) the case, with or without preposition, required to provide an equivalent to an English transitive verb, e.g.

> **attack** *v.t.* нап|адáть, -áсть на + a.

If no case is indicated, it is to be taken that the Russian verb is transitive.

i) Use is also made of oblique cases of the Russian pronouns кто and что (in brackets and italics) to indicate case/preposition usage after a verb, e.g.

> **apologize** *v.i.* извин|я́ться, -и́ться (*перед кем за что*)

Aspects

25 Aspectual information is given on all verbs (except быть) offered as renderings in infinitive form (except when they are subordinate to the finite verb in a sentence). If the verb is mono-aspectual, or used in a phrase to which only one aspect applies, it is designated either imperfective (*impf.*) or perfective (*pf.*) as the case may be.

With verbs of motion a distinction is made between determinate (*det.*) and indeterminate (*indet.*) forms, the imperfective aspect being assumed unless otherwise stated. Bi-aspectual infinitives are shown as (*impf.*, *pf.*). In all other cases both aspects are indicated (the imperfective always preceding the perfective) as in the following examples:

> **(i)** получ|áть, -и́ть; возра|жáть, -зи́ть; сн|оси́ть, -ести́.
> **(ii)** позв|оля́ть, -óлить; встр|ечáть, -éтить.

(iii) пока́з|ывать, -а́ть (i.e. *pf.* показа́ть); очаро́в|ывать, -а́ть.
(iv) гоня́ть, гнать; брать, взять; вынужда́ть, вы́нудить.
(v) смотре́ть, по-; звать, по- (i.e. *pf.* позва́ть); мости́ть, вы́- (i.e. *pf.* вы́мостить); жа́рить, за-/из-/по-.
(vi) и|мити́ровать, сы-.

26 It will be seen from the above that

i) when the first two or more letters of both aspects are identical, a vertical divider in the imperfective separates these letters from those which undergo change in the perfective. The perfective is then represented by the changed letters, preceded by a hyphen.

ii) a 'change' includes change of stress only if the stress shifts *back* in the perfective to the previous vowel: the divider then precedes this vowel in the imperfective.

iii) if it shifts *forward*, only the stressed syllable of the perfective is shown.

iv) when the two aspects have only their first letter in common, or are in fact different verbs, or both begin with вы- (which is always accented in the perfective), both are given in full.

v) perfectives of the type prefix + imperfective are shown by giving the prefix only, followed by a hyphen. Prefixes are unstressed except for вы́-.

Alternative prefixes are separated by an oblique stroke.

27 When two or three verbs separated by an oblique stroke are followed by the indication (*pf.*) or (*impf.*) this applies to both or all of them.

28 The following grammatical information is given in respect of English headwords.

a) Irregular or difficult plural forms of nouns, e.g.

child ... (*pl.* **children**) ...
leaf ... (*pl.* **leaves**) ...
monkey ... (*pl.* **~s**) ...
referend|um ... (*pl.* **~ums** or **~a**) ...

b) The comparative and superlative forms of adjectives which take **-er**, **-est**, e.g.

chic ... (**chicer, chicest**) ...
glib ... (**glibber, glibbest**) ...
tatty ... (**tattier, tattiest**) ...

c) Irregular or difficult forms of verbs, e.g.

eat ... (*past* **ate;** *p.p.* **eaten**) ...
go ... (*3rd pers. sg. pres.* **goes;** *past* **went;** *p.p.* **gone**) ...
hold ... (*past and p.p.* **held**) ...
run ... (**running;** *past* **ran;** *p.p.* **run**) ...
tattoo ... (**tattoos, tattooed**) ...
taxi ... (**taxis, taxied, taxiing**) ...
tip ... (**tipped, tipping**) ...

In the case of compound verbs, e.g. **foretell**, irregular or difficult forms follow those of the base verb, in this case **tell**.

О пользовании словарём

Русско-английская часть

Заглавное слово

1 В целях экономии места в отношении заглавного слова, повторяющегося в тексте словарной статьи, используются следующие приёмы:

1) начальная буква заглавного слова с последующей точкой заменяет всё слово целиком в его неизменной форме. Например:

автомоби́л|ь ... **води́ть а.** (= **води́ть автомоби́ль**)

2) т. н. тильда (знак ~) заменяет часть заглавного слова, расположенную до сплошной вертикальной черты. Например:

ава́ри|я ... **потерпе́ть ~ю** (= **потерпе́ть ава́рию**)

Исключения. Тильда не применяется для обозначения форм родительного падежа единственного числа существительных и форм 1-го и 2-го лица единственного числа глаголов настоящего времени с неподвижным ударением (см. об этом ниже: *Грамматический комментарий*: *Существительные* и *Глаголы*).

В статьях о глаголах несовершенного вида приводятся перекрёстные ссылки на формы совершенного вида. В таких случаях тильда, употребляемая с предшествующей приставкой, может заменять заглавное слово полностью, например:

беле́|ть, ю *impf.* (*of* **по~**) ... (= **побеле́ть**)

Ударение

2 Ударение последовательно отмечается во всех русских словах за исключением односложных. Знак ударения над тильдой (если та обозначает часть слова, состоящую из двух или более слогов) показывает перенос ударения на слог, ближайший к сплошной вертикальной черте в заглавном слове. Например:

запи|са́ть, шу́, ~́шешь ... (= **запишу́, запи́шешь**)

3 Напротив, знак ударения над слогом правее тильды показывает перенос ударения на этот слог со слога или слогов, заменяемых этим знаком. Например:

а́дрес, а, *pl.* **~а́** ... (= **адреса́**)

4 Допустимые вариантные (в отношении постановки ударения) формы приводятся. Например:

зап|ере́ться ... **~́ерся́** ... (= **за́перся** *или* **заперся́**)

Значения слова

5 Самостоятельные значения слова обозначаются арабскими цифрами. Оттенки значения, представленные переводами, которые не являются близкими синонимами, отделяются точкой с запятой, в то время как тождественные или близкие по значению переводы отделяются запятой. Например:

ава́нс ...**1** (*деньги*) advance.
2 (*pl. only*; *fig.*) advances, overtures.

авантю́ра ...**1** (*приключение*) adventure; escapade.
2 (*coll.*) shady enterprise.

6 Каждый омоним выделяется в отдельную статью и нумеруется при помощи надстрочной цифры, которая помещается сразу после заглавного слова. Например:

блок[1] ... (*tech.*) block, pulley.

блок[2] ... (*pol.*) bloc.

Пометы и пояснения

7 Во избежание неясности, в скобках приводятся пояснения, набранные курсивом. В особенности этот приём применяется в отношении слов, обозначающих типично русские или советские понятия (как, например, **ка́ша**, **микрорайо́н**), что позволяет использовать транслитерацию в качестве замены неудачным описательным переводам.

8 В необходимых случаях в скобках приводятся стилистические, а также отраслевые и некоторые другие пометы, которые могут относиться как ко всему слову, так и к отдельным его значениям. Примеры таких помет: (*coll.*), (*fig.*), (*joc.*), (*agric.*), (*pol.*) и т. п.

Грамматический комментарий

9 Грамматический комментарий включает в себя следующее:

Существительные

У всех существительных отмечается форма родительного падежа единственного числа, например:

мо́лот, а *m.* hammer.

мо́лни|я, и *f.* lightning.

молок|о́, а́ *nt.* milk.

пья́ниц|а, ы *c.g.* drunkard.

Окончания других падежей приводятся только у существительных, которые имеют особенности в склонении или постановке ударения, и эти особенности не определяются общими правилами. Например:

англича́н|ин, ина, *pl.* **~е, ~** *m.* Englishman.

бор|ода́, оды́, *a.* **~́оду,** *pl.* **~́оды, ~о́д, ~ода́м** *f.* beard.

Прилагательные

Прилагательные даются в форме именительного падежа единственного числа мужского рода. Окончания большинства кратких форм, если такие имеются, приводятся в скобках. Например:

глу́|пый (~, ~а́, ~о, ~́ы)

Окончания кратких прилагательных среднего рода и множественного числа не указываются, если постановка ударения в этих формах не отличается от формы женского рода. Например:

нау́ч|ный (~ен, ~на)

Глаголы

У глаголов приводятся формы 1-го и 2-го лица единственного числа настоящего времени (исключение составляют глаголы, оканчивающиеся в инфинитиве на **-ать**, **-ова́ть**, **-ять**, **-еть**, у которых приводится только форма 1-го лица единственного числа настоящего времени, так как основа этих глаголов и место постановки ударения не меняются во всех формах настоящего времени). Например:

говор|и́ть, ю́, и́шь ...
чита́|ть, ю ...

Другие формы настоящего времени, а также формы прошедшего времени даются только у глаголов, имеющих особенности в спряжении или постановке ударения. Например:

ид|ти́, у́, ёшь, *past* **шёл, шла** ...
бер|е́чь, егу́, ежёшь, егу́т, *past* **~ёг, ~егла́** ...

Формы причастий (в т. ч. страдательных) и деепричастий опускаются, если они не обладают особыми семантическими или морфологическими чертами.

Если страдательное причастие прошедшего времени совпадает в полной форме с близким или тождественным по значению прилагательным, оба омонима даются в одной словарной статье, причём, если их краткие формы отличаются, это отмечается в статье. Например:

запу́тан|ный (**~, ~а**) *p.p.p. of* **запу́тать** *and adj.* (**~, ~на**) ...

При подаче глаголов, образующих пары глагол несовершенного вида – глагол совершенного вида, используются следующие принципы:

1) если в названной паре глагол несовершенного вида — бесприставочный, то основной *словарной* формой глагола признаётся форма инфинитива несовершенного вида, возле которой и помещается перевод, а в скобках помещается ссылка на соответствующий глагол совершенного вида. При этом словарные статьи глаголов совершенного вида, в случае тождественности значений/переводов глаголов в видовой паре, представляют собой перекрёстные ссылки на статьи о соответствующих глаголах несовершенного вида. Например:

   чита́|ть, ю *impf.* (*of* **про~, проче́сть**) ...
   прочита́|ть, ю *pf. of* **чита́ть**
   про|че́сть, чту́, чтёшь, *past* **~чёл, ~чла́** = **~чита́ть**

2) если же в видовой паре глагол несовершенного вида – приставочный глагол, то основной *словарной* формой считается форма инфинитива совершенного вида, и перевод следует искать в статье о глаголе совершенного вида. Например:

   заш|и́ть, ью́, ьёшь *pf.* (*of* **~ива́ть**) ...

Приставки и составные части сложных слов

Ряд приставок и составных частей сложных слов выделяется в отдельные статьи, например:

без ... *pref.* in-, un-, -less.
гидро ... *comb. form* hydro-.

Англо-русская часть

Орфография

1 Слова английского языка даются в соответствии с британскими правилами орфографии. Американский вариант правописания, в случае расхождения с британским, указывается в скобках, например **honour**… (*US* **honor**).

Произношение

2 В Словаре рассматривается произношение, характерное для жителей южной Англии и известное как *Received Pronunciation* или *RP* (буквально «общепринятое/нормативное произношение»). Для удобства русскоязычной читательской аудитории все заглавные слова приводятся в фонетической транскрипции. Исключение составляют аббревиатуры типа **BBC**, которые произносятся по буквам: отдельно каждая буква в соответствии с её названием. Названия букв английского алфавита см. на с. 920. У сложных слов, у которых вторая составная часть слова представлена в Словаре в качестве отдельной статьи, приводится транскрипция только первой части.

Перечень используемых транскрипционных символов с примерами слов, содержащих тот или иной звук, см. на с. xxiii.

Заглавное слово и подача информации в словарной статье

3 Заглавные слова печатаются **полужирным** шрифтом. Исключение сделано для иностранных слов и выражений, не в полной мере освоенных английским языком: такие слова отображаются ***полужирным курсивом***.

Вариантные орфографические формы (включая те, которые свойственны американскому английскому) фиксируются наряду с нормативным/преобладающим правописанием слова и могут приводиться как в полном, так и в сокращённом виде, а также в скобках после главного слова. Такие формы даются повторно, согласно их положению в алфавитном порядке, с обязательной отсылкой к основному варианту (кроме тех случаев, когда альтернативный вариант примыкает по алфавиту непосредственно к основному). Например:

cosy (*US* **cozy**)   **cozy** = **cosy**
hicc|up, -ough
curts(e)y

4 Некоторые выражения, состоящие из двух слов, приводятся в качестве заглавных, при условии что словарная статья для первого слова такого выражения отсутствует, например: **Boxing Day, Parkinson's disease**.

5 В отдельные словарные статьи, нумерующиеся надстрочными цифрами после заглавного слова, выделяются слова, которые, хотя и имеют одинаковое написание, но отличаются:

1) значением и происхождением (например, **fine** существительное и глагол и **fine** прилагательное и наречие);
2) произношением и/или ударением (например, **house** существительное и **house** глагол);
3) всем вышеперечисленным (например, **tear** в значении «слеза» и **tear** в значении «разрывать, рвать»).

6 Отдельные словарные статьи о наречиях на -ly приводятся только для слов, значение которых не может быть безошибочно определено исходя из значения соответствующего прилагательного. Примеры: **hardly**, **really** и **surely**.

7 Формы герундия и причастий английских глаголов, перешедшие в разряд существительных или прилагательных, нередко помещаются внутри статьи о глаголе (переходном или непереходном, в зависимости от значения). Например:

> **revolving doors** следует искать в статье **revolve** *v.i.*
> **a retarded child** следует искать в статье **retard** *v.t.*

Но в некоторых случаях, во избежание неясности, подобные существительные и прилагательные выделяются в самостоятельные статьи. Например:

> **barbed** *adj.*; **flying** *n.* и *adj.*

8 Некоторые заглавные слова делит сплошная вертикальная черта. Это указывает на то, что неизменяемая часть слова, находящаяся до вертикальной черты, в изменяемых формах этого слова может заменяться тильдой. При отсутствии разделительной вертикальной линии в заглавном слове, тильда обозначает всё заглавное слово целиком, например:

> **house** ... **full ~** ... **~hold** ... **~hold word** ...

9 Сплошная вертикальная черта, отделяющая неизменяемую часть слова от изменяемой, используется также в английских и русских словах, когда необходимо отобразить словоизменение или привести вариантные формы. См. примеры в пунктах 3 и 26.

10 Внутри словарной статьи, для каждого лексико-грамматического разряда (части речи) отводится отдельный параграф, начинающийся с указателя части речи: *n.*, *pron.*, *adj.*, *adv.*, *v.t.*, *v.i.*, *prep.*, *conj.*, *int.* При необходимости такие указатели объединяются в одну запись, например: **adagio** *n.*, *adj. & adv.* Наиболее часто встречается объединение указателей переходного и непереходного глаголов: *v.t. & i.* Последнее наблюдается, когда отличие переходного глагола от непереходного не усматривается явно и когда в переводе русский непереходный глагол образуется при помощи постфикса -ся.

11 Сочетания типа «глагол-наречие», образующие фразовые глаголы, обыкновенно даются отдельным параграфом под заголовком *with advs.*, непосредственно вслед за примерами простого употребления глагола, и размещаются внутри параграфа в алфавитном порядке входящих в эти сочетания наречий.

12 У некоторых глаголов (например **go**), образующих многочисленные идиоматические выражения с предлогами, устойчивые сочетания «глагол-предлог» выделяются в отдельный параграф под заголовком *with preps.*

13 Сложные слова, первая составная часть которых образует заглавное слово словарной статьи, объединяются в заключительном параграфе этой статьи под заголовком *cpds.* (включая те, которые по правилам английского языка пишутся раздельно).

14 Сочетания типа «прилагательное-существительное» приводятся преимущественно в статье о прилагательном, за исключением случаев, когда прилагательное не оказывает определяющего влияния на значение всего выражения, как например в идиоме **good riddance**.

15 Различия в значении или употреблении слова помечаются пояснительными комментариями в виде синонимов или контекстного окружения слова. Такие пояснения даются курсивом в скобках. Для обозначения существенных различий в значении или употреблении слова используются набранные полужирным шрифтом цифры, которые нумеруют самостоятельные значения слова. Например:

gag *n.* **1** (*to prevent speech etc.*) … **2** (*joke*) …

16 Другой тип пояснений в скобках — стилистические пометы, а также пометы, определяющие или ограничивающие область (географический ареал, профессиональную сферу и пр.) употребления слова. Такие пометы, в зависимости от их местоположения в статье, могут относиться как ко всему слову, так и к отдельным его значениям и случаям употребления в конкретном словосочетании или предложении. Например:

gym *n.* (*coll.*) …
bell *n.* … **that rings a ~** (*fig., coll.*) …
bung … *v.t.* … **2** (*Br. sl., throw*) …
positive … *adj.* … **5** (*gram., math., elec.*)

17 Выражения русского языка, в особенности идиомы и пословицы, которые являются скорее переводными аналогами, нежели точными эквивалентами, помечаются предшествующим знаком приблизительного равенства ≈.

18 Употребление запятой либо точки с запятой для разграничения переводов одного и того же слова указывает на степень тождественности/синонимичности этих переводов: большую для переводов, разделяемых запятой, и меньшую для разделяемых точкой с запятой. В последнем случае для уточнения оттенка значения нередко используется вспомогательный комментарий на английском языке, например:

ineligible *adj.* (*for office*) …; (*for a benefit*) …

19 Во избежание неясности, точка с запятой применяется для разграничения альтернативных переводов словосочетаний или предложений и большинства видовых пар синонимичных глаголов. Например:

what is he getting at? что он хо́чет сказа́ть?; куда́ он кло́нит?
allow *v.t.* … позв|оля́ть, -о́лить; разреш|а́ть, -и́ть …

Устойчивые выражения и примеры употребления слова

20 Примеры употребления на обоих языках могут представлять собой как словосочетания, так и законченные предложения.

21 И в английском, и в русском языках существует немало примеров того, как то или иное слово в словосочетании или предложении может быть заменено синонимом без ущерба для смысла высказывания. Такие синонимы отделяются друг от друга при помощи запятой или косой черты в английских примерах, и посредством косой черты в примерах на русском языке. Например:

I'll knock a pound off the price я сбро́шу/ски́ну/сба́влю фунт с цены́.

22 Переводные варианты, не являющиеся синонимами, отделяются косой чертой в примерах на обоих языках, например:

carry on a conversation/business вести́ разгово́р/де́ло.

23 Косая черта, как правило, не применяется, если один из переводов, примыкающий непосредственно к косой черте, состоит из двух и более слов. В таком случае вариант(ы) перевода даются в скобках после слова *or* («или»), например:

I could do with a drink я охо́тно (*or* с удово́льствием) вы́пил бы.

Грамматический комментарий

24 В грамматическом комментарии к заглавным словам содержится следующая информация:

а) образуемые не по общим правилам либо вызывающие затруднения в образовании формы множественного числа существительных, например:

child ... (*pl.* **children**) ...
leaf ... (*pl.* **leaves**) ...
monkey ... (*pl.* **~s**) ...
referend|um ... (*pl.* **~ums** or **~a**) ...

б) сравнительная и превосходная степень прилагательных, образующих указанные формы путём прибавления -er, -est, например:

chic ... (**chicer, chicest**) ...
glib ... (**glibber, glibbest**) ...
tatty ... (**tattier, tattiest**) ...

в) формы неправильных глаголов и сложные случаи образования основных форм у прочих глаголов, например:

eat ... (*past* **ate**; *p.p.* **eaten**) ...
go ... (*3rd pers. sg. pres.* **goes**; *past* **went**; *p.p.* **gone**) ...
hold ... (*past and p.p.* **held**) ...
run ... (**running**; *past* **ran**; *p.p.* **run**) ...
tattoo ... (**tattoos, tattooed**) ...
taxi ... (**taxis, taxied, taxiing**) ...
tip ... (**tipped, tipping**) ...

Неправильные и трудные формы сложных глаголов, таких как **foretell**, образуются по модели основного в смысловом отношении глагола, в нашем случае **tell**. Иными словами, если известно, что глагол **tell** образует неправильные формы **told, told**, то формами простого прошедшего времени и причастия прошедшего времени глагола **foretell** будут **foretold**, **foretold**.

25 Русскоязычным пользователям следует обратить внимание на следующие основные моменты в грамматическом комментарии к русским переводам заглавных слов:

а) у некоторых существительных мужского рода в скобках приводится окончание именительного падежа множественного числа (-а́ или -я́), если слово с этим окончанием принимает значение, отличное от значения с окончанием -ы или -и, например:

fur ... мех (*pl.* -а́)

б) у предлогов приводится управление, например **before** до + *g*.

в) для более точного перевода английских переходных глаголов, в необходимых случаях, у русских глаголов даётся предложное (или беспредложное) управление, например:

attack *v.t.* нап|ада́ть, -а́сть на + а.

Если русский глагол не имеет при себе уточнения в виде падежа с предлогом или без, то этот глагол — переходный.

г) управление также может объясняться при помощи местоимений «кто» и «что», приводимых в скобках в соответствующих падежных формах с предлогами или без и выделяемых курсивом, например:

apologize *v.i.* извин|я́ться, -и́ться (*перед кем за что*)

Вид глагола

26 Информация о виде даётся последовательно у всех глаголов в форме инфинитива (за исключением глагола «быть»). У одновидовых глаголов (глаголов, не имеющих соотносительной пары другого вида) категория вида отмечается соответствующей пометой: (*impf.*) или (*pf.*).

Т. н. глаголы движения, подразделяющиеся на глаголы *определённого* (однонаправленного) движения и глаголы *неопределённого* (разнонаправленного) движения, снабжаются пометами, соответственно, (*det.*) и (*indet.*). При этом, если категория вида этих глаголов не указывается, предполагается, что они несовершенного вида.

Инфинитивы двувидовых глаголов помечаются (*impf., pf.*). Во всех остальных случаях указываются оба вида (форма несовершенного вида всегда предшествует форме совершенного вида), что можно проследить на следующих примерах:

(1) получ|а́ть, -и́ть; возра|жа́ть, -зи́ть; сн|оси́ть, -ести́.

(2) позв|оля́ть, -о́лить; встр|еча́ть, -е́тить.

(3) пока́з|ывать, -а́ть (т. е. *pf.* показа́ть); очаро́в|ывать, -а́ть.

(4) гоня́ть, гнать; брать, взять; вынужда́ть, вы́нудить.

(5) смотре́ть, по-; звать, по-; (т. е. *pf.* позва́ть); мости́ть, вы́- (т. е. *pf.* вы́мостить); жа́рить, за-/из-/по-.

(6) и|мити́ровать, сы-.

Символы фонетической транскрипции, используемые в Словаре

Согласные

b	*b*ut	s	*s*it
d	*d*og	t	*t*op
f	*f*ew	v	*v*oice
g	*g*et	w	*w*e
h	*h*e	z	*z*oo
j	*y*es	ʃ	*sh*e
k	*c*at	ʒ	deci*s*ion
l	*l*eg	θ	*th*in
m	*m*an	ð	*th*is
n	*n*o	ŋ	ri*ng*
p	*p*en	ʧ	*ch*ip
r	*r*ed	ʤ	*j*ar

Гласные

æ	c*a*t	aɪ	m*y*
ɑː	*a*rm	aʊ	h*ow*
e	b*e*d	eɪ	d*ay*
əː	h*er*	əʊ	n*o*
ɪ	s*i*t	eə	h*air*
iː	s*ee*	ɪə	n*ear*
ɒ	h*o*t	ɔɪ	b*oy*
ɔː	s*aw*	ʊə	p*oor*
ʌ	r*u*n	aɪə	f*ire*
ʊ	p*u*t	aʊə	s*our*
uː	t*oo*		
ə	*a*go		

(ə) обозначает безударный беглый гласный, который слышится в таких словах, как gard*e*n, carn*a*l и rhyth*m*.

(r) в конце слова обозначает согласный r, который произносится в случае, если следующее слово начинается с гласного звука, как, например, в *clutter up* и *an acre of land*.

Тильда ~ обозначает носовой гласный звук, как в некоторых заимствованиях из французского языка, например ɑ̃ (*en* masse).

Основное ударение в слове отмечается знаком ' перед ударным слогом.

О произношении звуков английского языка

Произношение английских слов, приводимое в Словаре в транскрипции, соответствует британской норме. Именно о звуках британского английского и пойдёт речь ниже.

Гласные звуки

Среди *гласных звуков* современного английского языка выделяют три основные группы: **монофтонги** (гласные, состоящие из одного звука), **дифтонги** (гласные, состоящие из двух звуков, которые произносятся в пределах одного слога) и **трифтонги** (гласные, состоящие из трёх звуков, произносимых в пределах одного слога).

В современном английском языке 12 монофтонгов, 8 дифтонгов и 2 трифтонга. Особенности их произношения (артикуляции) будут рассмотрены по группам: в отдельности для каждого звука.

Монофтонги

Исторически английские *монофтонги* подразделяются на **краткие** (ɪ, e, æ, ʌ, ɒ, ʊ, ə) и **долгие** (iː, ɑː, ɔː, uː, ɜː). Долгота последних обозначается в транскрипции двоеточием (ː) после символа соответствующего гласного.

/ɪ/ Краткий гласный звук, произносится без напряжения. Качественно (по месту и способу артикуляции) и количественно (по долготе) противопоставляется долгому /iː/ (см. ниже). Английский /ɪ/ слегка напоминает безударный русский /и/ в слове *игра* и ударный русский /и/ после шипящих. Для правильной артикуляции /ɪ/ язык следует располагать во рту ниже, чем при произношении русского /и/. Согласные перед /ɪ/ не смягчаются, на что нужно обращать особое внимание. В то же время английский /ɪ/ не должен походить на русский /ы/.

Примеры: s*i*t, h*i*s, *i*n.

/e/ Краткий гласный звук, произносится без напряжения. Английский /e/ отчасти напоминает русский звук /э/ в словах *свет* и *эти*, если его произносить очень кратко. Следует, однако, помнить о том, что согласные перед английским /e/ не смягчаются. При произнесении английского /e/ средняя часть языка поднята к нёбу выше, чем при произнесении русского /э/, а расстояние между челюстями уже.

Примеры: dr*e*ss, b*e*d, m*e*n.

/æ/ Краткий гласный звук, произносится с ощутимым напряжением. Качественно противопоставляется звуку /æ/. Во избежание ошибочного произношения русского /э/ вместо /æ/ язык следует располагать низко во рту, как при произнесении русского /а/. Нижняя челюсть должна быть заметно опущена. При этом основная масса языка должна оставаться в передней части рта, а его кончик должен быть прижат к нижним зубам.

Примеры: c*a*t, b*a*d, m*a*n.

/ʌ/ Краткий гласный звук, произносится напряжённо. Положение языка во ртy, как при молчании. Английский /ʌ/ похож на русский /а/, произносимый в первом предударном слоге после твёрдых согласных на месте русских букв ***а*** и ***о***, как, например, в словах *ск**а**ла* и *к**о**ра*. По сравнению с русским ударным /а/ при произнесении английского /ʌ/ язык отодвинут назад, а задняя его часть приподнята. Чрезмерно отодвинутый назад язык приведёт к образованию звука, близкого к английскому /ɑː/, что будет являться грубой фонематической ошибкой, так как данные звуки нередко выполняют смыслоразличительную функцию (d*u*ck и d*a*rk, l*u*st и l*a*st).

Примеры: b*u*t, c*u*p, r*u*n.

/ɒ/ Краткий гласный звук, произносится без напряжения. Английский /ɒ/ отчасти похож на русский /о/ в слове *к**о**нь*, если его произносить не округляя и не выпячивая губы. При произнесении /ɒ/ необходимо максимально отодвинуть назад язык, как при произнесении /ɑː/ (см. ниже), и, широко раскрывая рот, попытаться добиться минимального округления губ.

Примеры: h*o*t, wh*a*t, w*a*nt.

/ʊ/ Краткий гласный звук, произносится без напряжения. Качественно и количественно противопоставляется долгому /uː/ (см. ниже). Основное отличие от русского /у/ в том, что при произнесении /ʊ/ губы почти не округляются и не выпячиваются.

Примеры: p*u*t, g*oo*d, b*oo*k.

/ə/ Краткий нейтральный (образуемый языком в нейтральном положении) гласный звук, произносится без напряжения. Как и русский язык, английский язык характеризуется сильной качественной редукцией (ослабленным произношением гласных в безударных слогах). Так, звук, близкий английскому /ə/, можно встретить во втором предударном и в двух заударных слогах в русских словах на месте гласных букв ***о***, ***а*** и ***е*** после твёрдых согласных, например: *с**а**довод, дар**о**м, ц**е**ликом*.

Ошибка при артикуляции английского /ə/ возникает вследствие смешения парадигм редукции в английском и русском языках. Нейтральный гласный звук /ə/ в английском встречается преимущественно в первом предударном и первом заударном слогах. Носители русского языка в первом и втором предударных слогах и втором заударном нередко произносят гласные, по степени качественной редукции близкие к русским. Частой ошибкой является произношение в первом предударном слоге английских слов русского /э/ вместо /ə/. Для устранения этой ошибки необходимо не смещать язык в переднюю часть рта, сохраняя его в нейтральном срединном положении.

Примеры: *a*go, fath*er*, comm*o*n.

/iː/ Долгий гласный звук, произносится напряжённо. Качественно и количественно противопоставляется краткому /ɪ/ (см. выше). Английский /iː/ несколько напоминает русский /и/ в слове ***и**ва*, если произнести его напряжённо и протяжно. Согласные перед /iː/ не смягчаются. Помимо долготы английский /iː/ отличается неоднородностью звучания на всем протяжении. При произнесении /iː/ язык движется в полости рта вперёд и вверх.

Примеры: s*ee*, ch*ee*se, m*ea*t.

/ɑː/ Долгий гласный звук, произносится напряжённо. Своей протяжностью, характерной придавленностью корня языка во рту и низким тембром английский /ɑː/ напоминает звук, издаваемый при показе горла врачу. Для того чтобы правильно произносить английский /ɑː/, не делая его похожим на русский /а/, следует как можно дальше отводить корень языка назад и вниз.

Примеры: *a*rm, c*a*r, p*a*rk.

/ɔː/ Долгий гласный звук. Английский /ɔː/ произносится напряжённо, при оттянутом назад языке и сильно округлённых губах. Следует избегать характерного для артикуляции русского /о/ выпячивания губ, которое приводит к образованию несвойственного английскому /ɔː/ призвука /у/.

Примеры: s*aw*, *a*ll, s*o*rt.

/uː/ Долгий гласный звук, произносится напряжённо. Качественно и количественно противопоставляется краткому /ʊ/ (см. выше). Помимо долготы, английский /uː/, как и /iː/, отличается неоднородностью звучания на всем протяжении. При произнесении /uː/ язык движется в полости рта назад и вверх. Губы в начальный момент заметно округлены и, по мере движения языка, округляются ещё сильнее. Во избежание замены английского /uː/ русским /у/ при округлении губ не следует их выпячивать.

Примеры: t*oo*, f*oo*d, bl*ue*.

/ɜː/ Долгий гласный звук, произносится напряжённо. Губы при произнесении /ɜː/ растянуты, зубы слегка обнажены. Согласные перед /ɜː/ не смягчаются. Английский /ɜː/ не должен напоминать русские /о/ и /э/. Именно звук /ɜː/, как правило, произносится носителями английского языка при обдумывании ответа или подборе нужного слова.

Примеры: h*e*r, f*i*rst, w*o*rk.

Дифтонги

Дифтонги — это особые гласные звуки, произносимые без паузы в пределах одного слога. У английских дифтонгов основным, ударным элементом — **ядром** — всегда является первый из двух его составляющих. Второй элемент — **скольжение** или **глайд** — всегда безударный, произносится без напряжения.

Интонационно все английские дифтонги — нисходящие, т. е. их произношение сопровождается понижением интонации к конечному элементу.

/eɪ/ Сочетание сильного первого элемента /е/ и ослабленного второго /ɪ/ (см. выше). Следует избегать превращения глайда дифтонга /ɪ/ в английский согласный /j/ или русский /й/.

Примеры: d*ay*, th*ey*, br*ea*k.

/aɪ/ Сочетание сильного первого элемента /а/ и ослабленного второго /ɪ/. Английский звук /а/ — ядро дифтонга /aɪ/ — отличается от русского /а/ передним положением языка при его артикуляции. К тому же в начальной стадии звучания английского /а/ язык располагается ниже. Глайд дифтонга /ɪ/ не должен заменяться английским согласным /j/ или русским /й/.

Примеры: m*y*, s*i*de, h*igh*.

/ɔɪ/ Сочетание сильного первого элемента /ɔ/ и ослабленного второго /ɪ/. Английский звук /ɔ/ — ядро дифтонга /ɔɪ/ — представляет собой нечто среднее между английскими звуками /ɔː/ и /ɒ/ (см. выше). Превращение глайда дифтонга /ɪ/ в английский согласный /j/ или русский /й/ является ошибкой.

Примеры: b*oy*, s*oi*l, n*oi*se.

/əʊ/ Сочетание сильного первого элемента /ə/ и незначительно ослабленного второго /ʊ/. Ядро дифтонга /əʊ/ — звук /ə/ — произносится как английский /əː/ (см. выше), но с раскрытым шире, чем для /əː/, ртом, и с округлёнными (но не выпяченными) губами. Дифтонг /əʊ/ — единственный английский дифтонг, второй элемент которого произносится отчётливо, без заметного расслабления органов речи.

Примеры: n*o*, sh*ow*, h*o*me.

/aʊ/ Сочетание сильного первого элемента /a/ и ослабленного второго /ʊ/. При произнесении ядра дифтонга /aʊ/ — звука /a/ — язык не настолько продвигается вперёд, как при произнесении ядра /aɪ/, и первый элемент /aʊ/ во многом схож с русским /а/. В отличие от глайда /əʊ/ второй элемент дифтонга /aʊ/ звучит неясно. Следует помнить об этом и не превращать неясный глайд /ʊ/ в самостоятельный гласный /ʊ/ или /uː/, а также русский /у/, который произносится с характерным выпячиванием губ, не свойственным гласным звукам английского языка в целом.

Примеры: h*ow*, t*ow*n, m*ou*th.

/ɪə/ Сочетание сильного первого элемента /ɪ/ и ослабленного второго /ə/ (см. выше). В открытом конечном положении (на конце слова) глайд /ə/ может переходить в звук, близкий к английскому /ʌ/ (см. выше).

Примеры: b*eer*, n*ear*, h*ere*.

/eə/ Сочетание сильного первого элемента /e/ и ослабленного второго /ə/. Рот при произнесении ядра дифтонга /eə/ — звука /e/ — раскрыт намного шире, чем при произнесении самостоятельного английского гласного /e/, что делает похожим ядро дифтонга /eə/ на русский /э/ в слове *этот* (но не *эти*).

Примеры: h*air*, c*are*, th*ere*.

/ʊə/ Сочетание сильного первого элемента /ʊ/ и ослабленного второго /ə/ (см. выше).

Примеры: p*oor*, s*ure*, t*our*.

Трифтонги

В английском языке сочетания дифтонгов /aɪ/ и /aʊ/ с безударным нейтральным неслоговым гласным /ə/ называются *трифтонгами*. Как и дифтонги, английские трифтонги имеют в своём составе **ядро** — сильный ударный элемент — и **глайд** или **скольжение**, которое включает в себя два безударных элемента.

/aɪə/ Сочетание дифтонга /aɪ/ и нейтрального гласного /ə/. Элемент /ɪ/ не должен превращаться в согласный /j/.

Примеры: f*ire*, l*iar*, *iro*n.

/aʊə/ Сочетание дифтонга /aʊ/ и нейтрального гласного /ə/. Элемент /ʊ/ не должен превращаться в согласный /w/.

Примеры: s*our*, fl*ower*, t*owe*l.

Согласные звуки

Английские *согласные* имеют следующие характерные отличительные черты по сравнению с согласными русского языка:

1) «звонкость-глухость» не является основным различительным признаком английских согласных, напротив, применительно к английскому согласному важно знать: является ли он **сильным** или **слабым**, а не звонким или глухим. В русском языке глухие согласные, как правило, слабые, а звонкие — сильные. В английском языке, наоборот, звонкие /b/, /d/, /g/, /j/, /l/, /m/, /n/, /r/, /v/, /w/, /z/, /ʒ/, /ð/, /ŋ/ и /ʤ/ — в большинстве случаев слабые, а глухие /f/, /h/, /k/, /p/, /s/, /t/, /ʃ/, /θ/ и /ʧ/ — сильные;

2) сильные глухие /k/, /p/ и /t/ отличаются от соответствующих русских согласных тем, что они произносятся с сильным **придыханием**, — промежуток между одним из этих согласных и следующим за ним гласным заполняется порцией резко выдыхаемого воздуха, причём воздух этот выходит не из ротовой полости, как в случае с русскими /к/, /п/ и /т/, а непосредственно из лёгких;

3) отличительной чертой системы русских согласных является наличие палатализации (смягчения). За исключением всегда мягких /ч/ и /щ/ и всегда твёрдых /ц/, /ш/ и /ж/ (не путать с двойным «долгим» мягким /жʲжʲ/, как в слове *вожжи*), остальные русские согласные встречаются как в мягкой, так и в твёрдой разновидностях. Согласные английского языка полностью лишены такой артикуляционной особенности, поэтому следует уделять особое внимание тому, чтобы английские согласные не смягчались перед гласными /e/, /ɪ/, /iː/;

4) английские звонкие согласные на конце слов не оглушаются, как русские;

5) удвоенные английские согласные читаются как один звук.

В современном английском языке 24 согласных звука. Особенности их произношения (артикуляции) будут рассмотрены отдельно для каждого звука.

/b/ Произносится как ослабленный русский /б/. Перед гласными /e/, /ɪ/, /iː/, /əː/ и согласным /j/ не смягчается.

Примеры: *b*ut, *b*ig, *b*est.

/d/ Произносится как ослабленный русский /д/. Перед гласными /e/, /ɪ/, /iː/, /əː/ и согласным /j/ не смягчается. Следует избегать призвука /ə/ перед сочетаниями с /n/ и /l/, для чего образующейся между /d/ и /n/ мгновенной паузе надлежит придавать носовую артикуляцию, а мгновенной паузе между /d/ и /l/ соответственно боковую (по месту образования — между опущенным в одну сторону боковым краем языка и щекой).

Примеры: *d*og, *d*ay, *d*oor.

/f/ Произносится как русский /ф/, но энергичнее и без участия верхней губы. Перед гласными /e/, /ɪ/, /iː/, /əː/ и согласным /j/ не смягчается.

Примеры: *f*ew, *f*it, *f*eel.

/g/ Произносится как ослабленный русский /г/. Перед гласными /e/, /ɪ/, /iː/, /əː/ и согласным /j/ не смягчается.

Примеры: *g*et, *g*o, *g*ive.

/h/ Аналогов этому звуку в русском языке нет. Согласный /h/ представляет собой простой выдох без участия языка и округления губ — как при дуновении на стекло с целью почистить его. Звук /h/ не является шумным и ни в коем случае не должен напоминать русский /х/.

Примеры: *h*e, *h*ill, *h*air.

/j/ Произносится как заметно ослабленный русский /й/.

Примеры: *y*es, *y*ou, *y*ear.

/k/ Произносится как русский /к/, но энергичнее и с придыханием перед гласными. Перед гласными /e/, /ɪ/, /iː/, /əː/ и согласным /j/ не смягчается.

Примеры: *c*at, *k*ind, *q*ui*ck*.

/l/ В отличие от русского /л/ английский /l/ произносится с участием кончика языка, который касается тканей непосредственно за передними верхними зубами. Перед гласными звучит несколько мягче, но не так, как русский мягкий /ль/. В то же время в положении не перед гласными английский /l/ никогда не звучит так твёрдо, как русский /л/.

Примеры: *l*eg, *l*ike, *l*ook.

/m/ Произносится как ослабленный русский /м/. Перед гласными /e/, /ɪ/, /iː/, /əː/ и согласным /j/ не смягчается.

Примеры: *m*an, *m*e, *m*ilk.

/n/ В отличие от русского /н/, который произносится при помощи языка, упирающегося в передние верхние зубы, английский /n/ произносится с участием кончика языка, который касается тканей за передними верхними зубами, но не самих зубов. Английский /n/ звучит менее энергично, чем русский /н/. Перед гласными /e/, /ɪ/, /iː/, /əː/ и согласным /j/ не смягчается.

Примеры: *n*o, *n*ew, *n*iece.

/p/ Произносится как русский /п/, но энергичнее и с придыханием перед гласными. Перед гласными /e/, /ɪ/, /iː/, /əː/ и согласным /j/ не смягчается.

Примеры: *p*en, *p*ut, *p*lease.

/r/ Очень слабый согласный звук, лишь условно сравниваемый с русским /р/. Произносится он с положением органов речи, как для русского /ж/, но щель, образуемая между поднятым кончиком языка и передней частью твёрдого нёба, несколько шире, чем для /ж/. Кончик языка загнут назад и не должен вибрировать. Вибрируют при произнесении английского /r/ только голосовые связки. Средняя и задняя части языка остаются плоскими. Во избежание замены английского /r/ русским /р/ следует помнить о том, что при образовании английского /r/ язык не ударяется ни о зубы, ни о верхние ткани полости рта, оставаясь неподвижным.

Примеры: *r*ed, *r*eal, *r*oot.

/s/ Напоминает русский /с/, но произносится энергичнее. Язык, по сравнению с русским /с/, при произнесении английского /s/ поднят кверху, и струя воздуха проходит между кончиком языка и тканями позади передних верхних зубов, а не между языком и самими зубами. Перед гласными /e/, /ɪ/, /iː/, /ɜː/ и согласным /j/ не смягчается.

Примеры: *s*it, *s*ame, *s*o.

/t/ Напоминает русский /т/, но произносится энергичнее и с придыханием перед гласными. По сравнению с русским /т/ при произнесении английского /t/ кончик языка приподнят к тканям, расположенным позади передних верхних зубов. Перед гласными /e/, /ɪ/, /iː/, /ɜː/ и согласным /j/ не смягчается. Следует избегать призвука /ə/ перед сочетаниями с /n/ и /l/, для чего образующейся между /t/ и /n/ мгновенной паузе надлежит придавать носовую артикуляцию, а мгновенной паузе между /t/ и /l/ соответственно боковую (по месту образования — между опущенным в одну сторону боковым краем языка и щекой).

Примеры: *t*op, *t*ea, *t*ime.

/v/ Произносится как ослабленный русский /в/, но без участия верхней губы. Перед гласными /e/, /ɪ/, /iː/, /ɜː/ и согласным /j/ не смягчается.

Примеры: *v*oice, *v*ery, *v*iew.

/w/ Аналогов этому звуку в русском языке нет. Английский /w/ получается мгновенным пропусканием струи воздуха через щель, образуемую сильно округлёнными и слегка выпяченными губами. Зубы не касаются нижней губы. Звук /w/ произносится очень кратко и слабо, губы совершают движение, как при задувании свечи.

Примеры: *w*e, *w*hat, *w*ill.

/z/ Произносится как ослабленный русский /з/. Отличается от русского /з/ тем же, чем английский /s/ от русского /с/ (см. выше). Перед гласными /e/, /ɪ/, /iː/, /ɜː/ и согласным /j/ не смягчается.

Примеры: *z*oo, ea*s*y, ro*s*e.

/ʃ/ Произносится как смягчённый русский /ш/, но не настолько мягкий, как /щ/. Положение кончика языка, как при произнесении английского /s/ (см. выше), но щель, в которую пропускается воздух, более широкая, а органы речи напряжены меньше.

Примеры: *sh*e, *sh*all, *sh*op.

/ʒ/ Произносится как смягчённый русский /ж/, но не настолько мягкий, как в слове *вожжи*. Отличается от /ʃ/ только использованием голоса при его произнесении.

Примеры: deci*s*ion, plea*s*ure, u*s*ual.

/θ/ Аналогов этому звуку в русском языке нет. При произнесении сильного английского согласного /θ/ язык лежит плоско во рту, и его кончик находится между передними верхними и нижними зубами.
В образуемую таким образом между краем верхних зубов и кончиком языка щель выдыхается воздух. Во избежание образования звука /f/ зубы должны быть обнажены так, чтобы нижняя губа не касалась верхних зубов. Во избежание образования звука /s/ кончик языка должен

находиться между зубами, а сам язык оставаться плоским, особенно его передняя часть.

Примеры: *th*in, *th*ree, *th*rough.

/ð/ Аналогов этому звуку в русском языке нет. Произносится так же, как /θ/, но с голосом и менее энергично. Во избежание образования звука /v/ зубы должны быть обнажены так, чтобы нижняя губа не касалась верхних зубов. Во избежание образования звука /z/ кончик языка должен находиться между зубами, а сам язык оставаться плоским, особенно его передняя часть.

Примеры: *th*is, *th*ere, *th*at.

/ŋ/ Аналогов этому звуку в русском языке нет. Упрощённо, английский /ŋ/ представляет собой /g/, если произносить его через нос при полностью опущенном мягком нёбе. Так же, как и для /g/, для произношения /ŋ/ задняя часть языка смыкается с мягким нёбом, но последнее при артикуляции /ŋ/ полностью опущено, и воздух проходит не через рот, а через нос. Кончик языка при произнесении /ŋ/ обязательно должен находиться у нижних зубов, а передняя и средняя части языка не касаться нёба. Следует избегать призвука /g/ после /ŋ/ и не подменять /ŋ/ звуком /n/.

Примеры: ri*ng*, so*ng*, wro*ng*.

/ʧ/ Произносится как русский /ч/, но энергично и твёрдо, без какого бы то ни было смягчения. Для правильной артикуляции английского /ʧ/ второй элемент /ʃ/ следует произносить так же твёрдо, как русский /ш/.

Примеры: *ch*ip, *ch*eese, *ch*ild.

/ʤ/ Произносится так же, как /ʧ/, но с голосом, менее энергично и всегда со вторым мягким элементом /ʒ/.

Примеры: *j*ar, *j*am, *g*in.

Russian pronunciation guide

The pronunciation of Russian headwords is not given in the dictionary because, with the help of the additional information given below, it can be worked out from the spelling.

Russian letter	Approximate English sound and phonetic transcription	
а	like the English *a* in calm, but slightly shorter, as in French *la* or German *Mann*, e.g. **ра́дио, мать**; transcribed /a/	! See Note 5 below
б	like an English *b*, but with the expulsion of less breath, e.g. **ба́бушка, буты́лка**; transcribed /b/	! See Note 4 below
в	like an English *v*, e.g. **вино́, вот**; transcribed /v/	! See Note 4 below
г	like the English *g* in go, but with the expulsion of less breath, e.g. **газе́та, гара́ж**; transcribed /g/	! See Notes 4, 6 below
д	like an English *d*, but with the expulsion of less breath, e.g. **да, дом**; transcribed /d/	! See Note 4 below
е	like the English *ye* in yes, e.g. **е́сли, обе́д**; transcribed /je/	! See Notes 2, 3 below
ё	like the English *yo* in yonder, e.g. **её, ёлка**; transcribed /jo/	! See Note 2 below
ж	like the English *s* in measure, e.g. **ждать, жена́**; transcribed /zh/	! See Notes 3, 4 below
з	like an English *z*, e.g. **за́пад, зо́нтик**; transcribed /z/	! See Note 4 below
и	like the English *ee* in see, e.g. **игра́ть, и́ли**; transcribed /i/	! See Notes 2, 3 below
й	like the English *y* in boy, e.g. **мой, трамва́й**; transcribed /j/	
к	like an English *k*, but with the expulsion of less breath, e.g. **кто, ма́рка**; transcribed /k/	! See Note 4 below
л	like an English *l*, but harder, pronounced with the tongue behind the front teeth, e.g. **ла́мпа, луна́**; transcribed /l/	
м	like an English *m*, e.g. **ма́ма, молоко́**; transcribed /m/	
н	like an English *n*, but harder, pronounced with the tongue behind the front teeth, e.g. **на́до, нога́**; transcribed /n/	
о	like the English *o* in for, but pronounced with more rounded lips, e.g. **о́чень, мо́ре**; transcribed /o/	! See Note 5 below
п	like an English *p*, but with the expulsion of less breath, e.g. **па́па, по́сле**; transcribed /p/	! See Note 4 below

Russian letter	Approximate English sound and phonetic transcription	
р	like an English *r*, but rolled at the front of the mouth, e.g. **ры́ба, пора́**; transcribed /r/	
с	like an English *s*, e.g. **сала́т, соба́ка**; transcribed /s/	! See Note 4 below
т	like an English *t*, but with the expulsion of less breath, e.g. **таре́лка, то́лько**; transcribed /t/	! See Note 4 below
у	like the English *oo* in p**oo**l, but pronounced with more rounded lips, e.g. **муж, у́лица**; transcribed /u/	
ф	like an English *f*, e.g. **футбо́л, фле́йта**; transcribed /f/	! See Note 4 below
х	like the Scottish *ch* in lo**ch**, e.g. **хлеб, хо́лодно**; transcribed /kh/	
ц	like the English *ts* in nu**ts**, e.g. **центр, цирк**; transcribed /ts/	! See Note 3 below
ч	like the English *ch* in **ch**urch, e.g. **чай, час**; transcribed /ch/	! See Notes 3, 7 below
ш	like the English *sh* in **sh**op, but harder, pronounced with the tongue lower, e.g. **шко́ла, наш**; transcribed /sh/	! See Notes 3, 4 below
щ	either like a long soft English *sh*, similar to the *sh* in **sh**ould, or like an English *shch*, as in fre**sh** **ch**eese, e.g. **щи, ещё**; transcribed /shch/	! See Note 3 below
ъ	hard sign (hardens the preceding consonant), e.g. **объясня́ть**; transcribed /"/	
ы	like the English *i* in b**i**t, but with the tongue further back in the mouth, e.g. **вы, ты**; transcribed /y/	
ь	soft sign (softens the preceding consonant), e.g. **мать, говори́ть**; transcribed /'/	
э	like the English *e* in th**e**re, e.g. **э́то, эта́ж**; transcribed /e/	
ю	like the English *u* in **u**nit, but pronounced with more rounded lips, e.g. **ю́бка, юг**; transcribed /ju:/	! See Note 2 below
я	like the English *ya* in **ya**rd, but slightly shorter, e.g. **я́блоко, моя́**; transcribed /ja/	! See Notes 2, 5 below

Notes

1. Stress

Russian words have one main stress. In this dictionary this is indicated by an acute accent placed over the vowel of the stressed syllable. The vowel ё is never marked as it is almost always stressed.

2. Hard and soft consonants

An important feature of Russian consonants is that they may be hard or soft. At the end of a word or before a consonant, the soft sign (ь) indicates that the preceding consonant is soft, e.g. день, брать, де́ньги. In addition, the vowels е, ё, и, ю, and я coming after a consonant indicate that the consonant is soft, e.g. нет, нёс, лить, тюрьма́, ряд. A soft consonant is pronounced by placing the tongue closer to the roof of the mouth than in the pronunciation of the equivalent hard consonant. Soft consonants are particularly discernible in the case of the sounds /d, t, n, l/. In British English they can be heard in the words due, tune, new, and illuminate.

In the transcriptions below, a soft consonant is indicated by a /j/ immediately after the consonant, e.g. нет /njet/, except when represented by a soft sign which is transcribed /'/, e.g. лить /ljit'/.

3. Consonants that are always hard or always soft

The consonants ж, ш, and ц are always hard.

If the letter и follows one of these consonants, it is pronounced as if it were ы, e.g. жир /zhyr/, маши́на /mashýnə/, цирк /tsyrk/.

If a stressed е follows one of these consonants, it is pronounced as if it were э, e.g. жечь /zhech'/, шесть /shest'/, це́лый /tsélyj/.

If ё follows ж or ш, it is pronounced /o/, e.g. жёлтый /zhóltyj/, шёл /shol/.

The consonants ч and щ are always soft.

This means that following these consonants the vowels а, о, and у are pronounced /ja/, /jo/, and /ju/, e.g. ча́сто /chjástə/, чуло́к /chjulók/.

4. Unvoicing of voiced consonants and voicing of unvoiced consonants

Voiced consonant sounds (/b, v, g, d, zh, z/) become unvoiced (/p, f, k, t, sh, s/) when they occur

a) at the end of a word, e.g.

хлеб	/khljep/
рука́в	/rukáf/
снег	/snjek/
муж	/mush/
моро́з	/marós/

or

b) before an unvoiced consonant, e.g.

во́дка	/vótkə/
авто́бус	/aftóbus/

Conversely, unvoiced consonant sounds (/p, f, k, t, sh, s/) become voiced (/b, v, g, d, zh, z/) when they occur before another voiced consonant, except before в, e.g.

ждать /zhdat'/
отда́ть /addát'/
but
отве́т /atvjét/ (no voicing before в)

5. Unstressed vowels

The Russian vowels о, е, а, and я change their pronunciation when they are not stressed:

о is pronounced like the stressed Russian а, transcribed /a/, when it appears in the syllable before the stressed syllable, and like the indeterminate vowel in the first syllable of *amaze*, transcribed as /ə/, when it appears after the stressed syllable or more than one syllable before the stressed syllable, e.g.

окно́ /aknó/
нога́ /nagá/
мно́го /mnógə/
хорошо́ /khərashó/

е is pronounced like the Russian и, transcribed /i/, when it is unstressed, unless it follows a hard consonant (ж, ц, ш) when it is pronounced like ы, e.g.

пе́рец /pjérjits/
стена́ /stjiná/
жена́ /zhyná/
на у́лице /na úljitsy/

а is pronounced like a stressed Russian а, transcribed /a/, when it appears in the syllable before the stressed syllable, but like the indeterminate vowel in the first syllable of *amaze*, transcribed /ə/, when it appears after the stressed syllable or more than one syllable before the stressed syllable, e.g.

маши́на /mashýnə/
кассе́та /kasjétə/
магнитофо́н /məgnjitafón/

я is pronounced like the Russian и, transcribed /i/, when it occurs in the syllable before the stressed syllable, and like the indeterminate vowel in the first syllable of *amaze*, transcribed /ə/, when it appears after the stressed syllable or more than one syllable before the stressed syllable, e.g.

пяти́ /pjitjí/
язы́к /jizýk/
языка́ /jəzyká/
тётя /tjótjə/

6.

г is pronounced as if it were в in the words его́, сего́дня, and other words with the genitive ending -ого, -его, e.g. ма́ленького, си́него, всего́, ничего́.

7.

ч is pronounced as if it were ш in the words что, что́бы, and коне́чно.

Abbreviations used in the Dictionary

a.	accusative (case)	винительный падеж
abbr.	abbreviat|ion, -ed (to)	сокращение, сокращённо
abstr.	abstract	абстрактный
acad.	academic	академический термин
acc.	according	согласно
act.	active (voice)	действительный (залог)
adj., adjs.	adjectiv|e, -al, -es	имя прилагательное, адъективное, имена прилагательные
admin.	administration	управление
adv., advs.	adverb, -ial, -s	наречие, наречное, наречия
aeron.	aeronautics	авиация
agric.	agriculture	сельское хозяйство
anat.	anatomy	анатомия
approx.	approximate(ly)	приблизительн|ый, -о
arch.	archaic	архаичное слово/выражение
archaeol.	archaeology	археология
archit.	architecture	архитектура
astrol.	astrology	астрология
astron.	astronomy	астрономия
attr.	attributive	определительное, атрибутивное
aux.	auxiliary	вспомогательный глагол
bibl.	biblical	библейский термин
biol.	biology	биология
bot.	botany	ботаника
Br.	British; British usage	британский английский; употребительно в Великобритании
c.g.	common gender	общий род
chem.	chemistry	химия
cin.	cinema(tography)	кинематография
coll.	colloquial	разговорное
collect.	collective	собирательное (существительное)
comb.	combin|ation, -ing	сочетание
comm.	commerc|e, -ial	коммерческий термин
comp.	comparative	сравнительная степень
comput.	computing	вычислительная техника
concr.	concrete	конкретный
conj., conjs.	conjunction, -s	союз, -ы
cpd., cpds.	compound, -s	сложн|ое слов|о, -ые -а
cul.	culinary	кулинария
d.	dative (case)	дательный падеж

Abbreviations used in the Dictionary

decl.	declin|able, -ed	склоняемое, склоняется
def. art.	definite article	определённый артикль
det.	determinate	определённый
dial.	dialect	диалектизм
dim.	diminutive	уменьшительное
dipl.	diploma|cy, -tic	дипломатический термин
disp.	disputed	спорное
eccl.	ecclesiastical	церковный термин
econ.	economics	экономика
educ.	education, -al	образование
elec.	electric|al, -ity	электротехника
ellipt.	elliptical	эллиптический
emph.	empha|size(s), -sizing; -tic	подчёркива|ть, -ет, -ющее; усилительное
equ., eqvs.	equivalent, -s	эквивалент, -но(е), -ы
esp.	especially	особенно
ethnol.	ethnology	этнология
euph.	euphemis|m, -tic	эвфеми|зм, -стическое
exc.	except	исключая
excl.	exclamation	междометие
expr.	express|ed, -es, -ing; -ion	выраж|енный, -ает, -ающее; выражение
f.	feminine	женский род
fem.	female	форма женского рода
fig.	figurative	в переносном смысле
fin.	financ|e, -ial	финансы, финансовый термин
freq.	frequentative	многократный (глагол)
fut.	future (tense)	будущее время
g.	genitive (case)	родительный падеж
geog.	geography	география
geol.	geology	геология
geom.	geometry	геометрия
ger.	gerund	герундий
gram.	grammar	грамматика
her.	heraldry	геральдика
hist.	histor|y, -ical	история
hort.	horticulture	садоводство
i.	instrumental (case); intransitive in *v.i.*	творительный падеж; непереходный глагол
imper.	imperative	повелительное наклонение
impers.	impersonal	безличное
impf.	imperfective	несовершенный вид
ind.	indirect	косвенный
indecl.	indeclinable	несклоняемое

indef. art.	indefinite	неопределённый артикль
indet.	indeterminate	неопределённый
inf.	infinitive	инфинитив
inst.	instantaneous	однократный (глагол)
int.	interjection	междометие
interrog.	interrogative	вопросительный
intrans.	intransitive	непереходный глагол
iron.	ironical	ироническое
joc.	jocular	шутливое
journ.	journalism	журналистика
leg.	legal	юридический термин
ling.	linguistics	лингвистика
lit.	literal	буквально
liter.	literary	книжное
m.	masculine	мужской род
math.	mathematics	математика
mech.	mechanics	механика
med.	medic|ine, -al	медицин|а, -ский термин
metall.	metallurgy	металлургия
meteor.	meteorology	метеорология
mil.	military	военное дело
min.	mineralogy	минералогия
mus.	music(al)	музыка, -льный термин
myth.	mythology	мифология
n.	noun	имя существительное
naut.	nautical	морское дело
nav.	naval	военно-морской термин
neg.	negative	отрицательный
nn.	nouns	имена существительные
nom.	nominative (case)	именительный падеж
nt.	neuter	средний род
num., nums.	numer|al, -ical, -als	числительное, числовой, числительные
obj.	object	дополнение
obs.	obsolete	устаревшее слово/выражение
offens.	offensive	оскорбительное
oft.	often	часто
opp.	opposite (to); as opposed to	противоположное
opt.	optics	оптика
o.s.	oneself	себя

Abbreviations used in the Dictionary

p.	prepositional (case). *See also p.p. and p.p.p.*	предложный падеж
parl.	parliamentary	парламентский термин
part.	participle	причастие
pass.	passive (voice)	страдательный (залог)
pej.	pejorative	пренебрежительное
pers.	person(s); personal	лиц|о, -а; личный
pert.	pertaining	относительно
pf.	perfective	совершенный вид
pharm.	pharmaceutical	фармакология, фармацевтика
phil.	philosophy	философия
philol.	philology	языкознание
phon.	phonetics	фонетика
phot.	photography	фотография
phr., phrr.	phrase, -s	фраз|а, -ы
phys.	physic|s, -al	физика, физический
physiol.	physiology	физиология
pl.	plural	множественное число
poet.	poet|ical, -ry	поэтическое, поэзия
pol.	political	политический термин
poss.	possessive	притяжательное
p.p.	past participle	причастие второе, причастие прошедшего времени
p.p.p.	past participle passive	страдательное причастие прошедшего времени
pr.	pronounce(d); pronunciation	произносит|ь, -ся; произношение
pred.	predicate; predicative	сказуемое; предикативный
pref.	prefix	префикс
prep., preps.	preposition, -s	предлог, -и
pres.	present (tense)	настоящее время
pres. part.	present participle	причастие первое, действительное причастие настоящего времени
pron., prons.	pronoun, -s	местоимени|е, -я
pronunc.	pronunciation	произношение
propr.	proprietary term	фирменное название
prov.	proverb	пословица
psych.	psychology	психология
rail.	railway	железнодорожный термин
refl.	reflexive (verb)	возвратный (глагол)
rel.	relative (pronoun)	относительное (местоимение)
relig.	religion	религия
rhet.	rhetorical	высокого стиля
Sc.	Scottish	шотландский (английский) язык
sc.	scilicet	а именно
sg.	singular	единственное число

sl.	slang	сленг
s.o.	someone	кто-нибудь
sth.	something	что-нибудь
subj.	subject	подлежащее
suff.	suffix	суффикс
superl.	superlative	превосходная степень
t.	transitive in *v.t.*	переходный (глагол)
tech.	technical	техника
teleph.	telephony	телефония
text.	textiles	текстильный термин
theatr.	theatr|e, -ical	театр, театральный термин
theol.	theology	богословие
trans.	transitive	переходный глагол
TV	television	телевидение
typ.	typography	типографский термин
univ.	university	университетский жаргон
US	United States; United States usage	американский английский; употребительно в США
usu.	usually	обычно
v.	verb	глагол
var.	variant	вариант
v. aux.	auxiliary verb	вспомогательный глагол
vbl.	verbal	отглагольное
v.i.	intransitive verb	непереходный глагол
voc.	vocative (case)	звательный падеж
v.t.	transitive verb	переходный глагол
vulg.	vulgar(ism)	грубое
vv.	verbs	глаголы
zool.	zoology	зоология

The Russian -н. or -л. in illustrative phrases within entries stands for -нибудь or -либо (in the words кто-нибудь, что-нибудь, что-либо, etc.).

This dictionary includes some words which are, or are asserted to be, proprietary names or trade marks. These words are labelled (*propr.*). The presence or absence of this label should not be regarded as affecting the legal status of any proprietary name or trade mark.

Aa

а¹ *conj.*
[1] (*и*) and; **вот ма́рки, а вот три рубля́ сда́чи** here are the stamps and here is three roubles change.
[2] (*но*) but (*or not translated*); **я иду́ не в кино́, а в теа́тр** I am not going to the cinema, but to the theatre (*Br.*), theater (*US*); **пиши́ карандашо́м, а не ру́чкой** write in pencil, not pen.
[3]: **а как же!** (*coll.*) of course!; **а то** or (else), otherwise; **дава́й быстре́е, а то мы опозда́ем** hurry up or (else) we'll be late.
а² *interrog. particle* (*coll.*) eh?; what('s that)?; huh?
а³ *int.* (*coll.*) ah, oh.
абажу́р, а *m.* lampshade.
абба́тств|о, а *nt.* abbey.
аббревиату́р|а, ы *f.* abbreviation.
абза́ц, а *m.*
[1] (*typ.*) indention; **сде́лать а.** to indent; **нача́ть с но́вого ~а** to begin a new line, new paragraph.
[2] (*часть текста*) paragraph.
абитурие́нт, а *m.* (*university, college*) entrant.
абитурие́нт|ка, ки *f. of* ▸ ~
абонеме́нт, а *m.* (*право пользования чем-н.*) subscription; (*многоразовый билет*) season ticket.
абоне́нт, а *m.* (*телефона*) subscriber; (*библиотеки*) borrower, reader; (*театра*) season-ticket holder.
абоне́нтск|ий *adj.* subscription; **~ая пла́та** subscription fee.
аборите́н, а *m.* aboriginal.
або́рт, а *m.* abortion; **сде́лать а.** (*о пациентке*) to have an abortion.
абрико́с, а *m.* apricot.
абсолю́т|ный (~ен, ~на) *adj.* absolute.
абстра́кт|ный (~ен, ~на) *adj.* abstract.
абстра́кци|я, и *f.* abstraction.
абсу́рд, а *m.* absurdity; **довести́ до ~а** to carry to the point of absurdity.
абсу́рд|ный (~ен, ~на) *adj.* absurd.
абха́з, а *m.* Abkhaz(ian).
абха́з|ка, ки *f. of* ▸ ~
абха́зский *adj.* Abkhazian.
аванга́рд, а *m.* the avant-garde.
авангарди́зм, а *m.* avant-gardism.
авангарди́ст, а *m.* avant-gardist.
авангарди́стский = **аванга́рдный**
аванга́рд|ный *adj. of* ▸ ~
ава́нс, а *m.*
[1] (*деньги*) advance.
[2] (*pl. only; fig.*) advances, overtures.
ава́нсом *adv.* in advance, on account.
авантю́р|а, ы *f.*
[1] (*приключение*) adventure; escapade.
[2] (*coll.*) shady enterprise.
авантюри́ст, а *m.* adventurist.
авантюри́стк|а, и *f.* adventuress.
авантю́р|ный (~ен, ~на) *adj.* adventurous; **а. рома́н** adventure story.
авари́йно-спаса́тельный *adj.* (emergency-)rescue, life-saving.
авари́йн|ый *adj.*
[1] *adj. of* ▸ **ава́рия; ~ая поса́дка** crash landing; **а. сигна́л** distress signal.
[2] (*запасной*) emergency, spare.
ава́ри|я, и *f.*
[1] (*несчастный случай*) crash, accident.
[2] (*поломка*) breakdown; **потерпе́ть ~ю** to crash, have an accident.
а́вгуст, а *m.* August.
а́вгуст|овский *adj. of* ▸ ~
а́виа (*abbr. of* **авиапо́чтой**) '(by) airmail'.
авиа... *comb. form, abbr. of* **авиацио́нный**
авиаба́з|а, ы *f.* air base.
авиабиле́т, а *m.* airline ticket.
авиадиспе́тчер, а *m.* air traffic controller.
авиака́сс|а, ы *f.* air tickets booking office.
авиакатастро́ф|а, ы *f.* air crash.
авиакомпа́ни|я, и *f.* airline.
авиаконстру́ктор, а *m.* aircraft designer.
авиала́йнер, а *m.* airliner.
авиали́ни|я, и *f.* airway, air route.
авиано́с|ец, ца *m.* aircraft carrier.
авиапо́чт|а, ы *f.* air mail.
авиасало́н, а *m.* air show.
авиацио́нно-косми́ческ|ий *adj.* aerospace; **~ая промы́шленность** the aerospace industry.
авиацио́нный *adj. of* ▸ **авиа́ция**
авиа́ци|я, и *f.*
[1] aviation.
[2] (*collect.*) aircraft.
ави́зо *nt. indecl.* (*fin.*) advice note.
аво́сь *particle*: **на а.** on the off-chance.
аво́ськ|а, и *f.* (*coll.*) string bag.
австрали́|ец, йца *m.* Australian.
австрали́|йка, йки *f. of* ▸ **~ец**
австрали́йский *adj.* Australian.
Австра́ли|я, и *f.* Australia.
австри́|ец, йца *m.* Austrian.
австри́|йка, йки *f. of* ▸ **~ец**
австри́йский *adj.* Austrian.
А́встри|я, и *f.* Austria.
авто... *comb. form*
[1] self-, auto-.
[2] *abbr. of* (*i*) **автомати́ческий** *and* (*ii*) **автомоби́льный**
автоба́з|а, ы *f.* motor-transport depot.
автобиографи́ческий *adj.* autobiographical.
автобиогра́фи|я, и *f.*
[1] (*описание своей жизни*) autobiography.

а

2 (*описание своей карьеры*) curriculum vitae, CV.
автóбус, а *m.* bus; (*междугородный*) coach (*Br.*), bus (*US*).
автóбусн|ый *adj.* bus; **~ая остановка** bus stop; **~ая стáнция** bus station.
автовокзáл, а *m.* bus terminal; coach station (*Br.*).
автогóл, а *m.* (*sport*) own goal.
автогóнк|а, и *f.* car race; (*pl.*) motor racing (*Br.*), automobile racing (*US*).
автогóнщик, а *m.* racing driver.
автóграф, а *m.* (*in var. senses*) autograph.
автодорóг|а, и *f.* road; highway.
автозавóд, а *m.* car factory.
автозаправóчн|ый *adj.* filling, refuelling; **~ая стáнция** petrol *or* filling station.
автоинспéктор, а *m.* traffic inspector.
автоинспéкци|я, и *f.* traffic inspectorate.
автокáр, а *m.* motor trolley.
автокатастрóф|а, ы *f.* road accident.
автоколóнн|а, ы *f.* motorcade; (*mil.*) convoy.
автолюбúтел|ь, я *m.* (private) motorist.
автомагистрáл|ь, и *f.* motorway (*Br.*), interstate (highway) (*US*).
автомастерск|áя, óй *f.* car repair garage.
автомáт, а *m.*
1 automatic machine, slot machine; **билéтный а.** ticket machine; **игровóй а.** one-armed bandit; **телефóн-а.** pay phone; (*fig.*) automaton, robot.
2 (*mil.*) submachine gun.
автоматизáци|я, и *f.* automation.
автоматизúрованн|ый *adj.* computer-aided; **~ое проектúрование** CAD, computer-aided design.
автоматизúр|овать, ую *impf. and pf.* to automate.
автомáтик|а, и *f.*
1 (*отрасль науки*) automation.
2 (*автоматические механизмы*) automatic equipment.
автоматúческ|ий *adj.*
1 (*tech.*) automatic.
2 (*fig.*) automatic, involuntary.
автомáтчик, а *m.* (*mil.*) soldier armed with a submachine gun.
автомашúн|а, ы *f.* motor vehicle.
автомехáник, а *m.* car mechanic.
автомобилúст, а *m.* motorist.
автомобúл|ь, я *m.* motor vehicle; (motor)car; **легковóй а.** car; **грузовóй а.** lorry; **водúть а.** to drive a car.
автомобúльн|ый *adj. of* ▸ ~
автонóми|я, и *f.* autonomy.
автонóм|ный (~ен, ~на) *adj.* autonomous; (*comput.*) stand-alone.
автоотвéтчик, а *m.* answering machine.
автопилóт, а *m.* autopilot.
автопортрéт, а *m.* self-portrait.
автоприцéп, а *m.* trailer; **жилóй а.** caravan (*Br.*), mobile home; **турúстский а.** caravan (*Br.*), camper (*US*).
áвтор, а *m.* author.
авторизóванный *adj.* (*издание, перевод*) authorized.
авторитáр|ный (~ен, ~на) *adj.* authoritarian.
авторитéт, а *m.* authority; **пóльзоваться ~ом** to enjoy authority, command respect.
авторитéт|ный (~ен, ~на) *adj.* authoritative.
áвтор|ский *adj. of* ▸ ~; **а. гонорáр** royalty, royalties; **~ское прáво** copyright.
áвторств|о, а *nt.* authorship.
авторýчк|а, и *f.* fountain pen.
автосалóн, а *m.*
1 (*магазин*) car showroom.
2 (*выставка*) motor show.
автосéрвис, а *m.* garage (*usu. one that repairs cars, but sometimes one that sells petrol etc.*).
автостóп, а *m.* (*способ путешествия*) hitch-hiking; **путешéствовать** (*impf.*) **~ом** to hitch-hike.
автостоя́нк|а, и *f.* car park.
автострáд|а, ы *f.* motorway (*Br.*), interstate (highway) (*US*).
автотрáнспорт, а *m.* motor transport.
автошкóл|а, ы *f.* driving school; **преподавáтель** (*m.*) **~ы** driving instructor.
агá *int.* (*coll.*) (*expr. (i) comprehension, (ii) malicious pleasure*) ah!; aha!
агéнт, а *m.* (*in var. senses*) agent.
агéнтств|о, а *nt.* agency; **а. печáти** news agency, press agency; **информациóнное/телеграфное а.** news agency.
агентýр|а, ы *f.*
1 (*служба*) secret service.
2 (*collect.*) agents.
агитáтор, а *m.* (*pol.*) agitator; campaigner.
агитациóнн|ый *adj.* (*pol.*) agitation; **~ая речь** campaign speech.
агитáци|я, и *f.* (*pol.*) agitation; campaign; **вестú ~ю** to campaign; **предвы́борная а.** electioneering.
агитúр|овать, ую *impf. only* (*pol.*) (**за** + *a.*) to agitate, campaign (for).
агóни|я, и *f.* (*med. and fig.*) death throes.
агорафóбия, и *f.* agoraphobia.
агрáри|й, я *m.* landowner.
агрáрный *adj.* agrarian.
агрегáт, а *m.*
1 (*часть машины*) unit.
2 (*соединение нескольких машин*) assembly.
агрессúв|ный (~ен, ~на) *adj.* aggressive.
агрéсси|я, и *f.* (*pol.*) aggression.
агрéссор, а *m.* aggressor.
агро... *comb. form* agro-, agricultural, farm.
агронóм, а *m.* agronomist.
агронóми|я, и *f.* agronomy; agricultural science.
агропромы́шленный *adj.* agro-industrial.
ад, а *m.* hell.
адаптáци|я, и *f.* (*in var. senses*) adaptation.
адáптер, а *m.* (*tech.*) adapter.
адаптúр|овать, ую *impf. and pf.* to adapt.
адаптúр|оваться, уюсь *impf. and pf.* to

adapt; to get used to sth.

адвока́т, а *m.* (*поверенный*) solicitor, lawyer; (*выступающий в суде*) barrister (*Br.*), attorney (*US*); (*fig.*) advocate.

адвокату́р|а, ы *f.*
1 (*деятельность адвоката*) the legal profession; practising law.
2 (*collect.*) lawyers; the Bar (*Br.*).

адеква́т|ный (~ен, ~на) *adj.* identical, coincident; adequate.

аджа́р|ец, ца *m.* Adzharian.

аджа́р|ка, ки *f. of* ▸ **~ец**

аджа́рский *adj.* Adzharian.

администрати́вн|ый *adj.* administrative; **в ~ом поря́дке** by administrative order.

администра́тор, а *m.* administrator; manager (*of hotel, theatre, etc.*).

администра́ци|я, и *f.* administration; management.

адмира́л, а *m.* admiral.

адренали́н, а *m.* adrenalin.

а́дрес, а, *pl.* **~а́, ~о́в** *m.* (*in var. senses*) address; **в а.** (+ *g.*) addressed to; (*fig.*) directed at; **не по ~у** (*fig.*) to the wrong quarter.

адреса́т, а *m.* addressee; **в слу́чае ненахожде́ния ~а** 'if undelivered'; **за ненахожде́нием ~а** 'not known' (*on letters*).

а́дрес|ный *adj. of* ▸ **~; ~ная кни́га** directory; **а. стол** address bureau.

адрес|ова́ть, у́ю *impf. and pf.* (*письмо*) to address; (*критику, вопрос*) to direct.

Адриати́ческ|ое мо́р|е, ~ого ~я *nt.* the Adriatic (Sea).

а́дский *adj.* infernal, diabolical; (*fig.*) hellish, intolerable.

адъюта́нт, а *m.* (*mil.*) aide-de-camp.

аза́рт|ный (~ен, ~на) *adj.* excited, ardent; **~ная игра́** game of chance.

а́збук|а, и *f.* alphabet; the ABC (*also fig.*).

Азербайджа́н, а *m.* Azerbaijan.

азербайджа́н|ец, ца *m.* Azerbaijani.

азербайджа́н|ка, ки *f. of* ▸ **~ец**

азербайджа́нский *adj.* Azerbaijani.

азиа́т, а *m.* Asian.

азиа́т|ка, ки *f. of* ▸ **~**

азиа́тский *adj.* Asian.

А́зи|я, и *f.* Asia.

Азо́вск|ое мо́р|е, ~ого ~я *nt.* the Sea of Azov.

азо́т, а *m.* (*chem.*) nitrogen.

а́ист, а *m.* (*zool.*) stork.

ай *int.* (*expr.* (*i*) *fear,* (*ii*) *surprise and/or pleasure*) oh!; ow!, ouch!

а́йсберг, а *m.* iceberg.

акаде́мик, а *m.* academician (*member of a specific academy*).

академи́ческий *adj.* academic; **а. о́тпуск** sabbatical (leave) (*for undergraduates or postgraduates*).

академи́ч|ный (~ен, ~на) *adj.* academic, theoretical.

акаде́ми|я, и *f.* academy.

аквала́нг, а *m.* aqualung.

аквалангѝст, а *m.* (skin *or* scuba) diver.

аквалангѝст|ка, ки *f. of* ▸ **~**

аквар́ел|ь, и *f.* (*краски*) watercolours (*Br.*), watercolors (*US*); **писа́ть ~ью** to paint in watercolours; (*картина*) watercolour (*Br.*), watercolor (*US*).

аква́риум, а *m.* fish tank, aquarium.

аквато́ри|я, и *f.* (*defined*) waters.

акклиматиза́ци|я, и *f.* acclimatization.

акклиматизи́р|овать, ую *impf. and pf.* to acclimatize.

акклиматизи́р|оваться, уюсь *impf. and pf.* to become acclimatized, to acclimatize.

аккомпанеме́нт, а *m.* (*mus.*) accompaniment (*also fig.*); **под а.** (+ *g.*) to the accompaniment of.

аккомпани́р|овать, ую *impf.* (+ *d.*, **на** + *p.*; *mus.*) to accompany.

акко́рд, а *m.* (*mus.*) chord.

аккордео́н, а *m.* accordion.

аккордеони́ст, а *m.* accordionist.

аккордеони́ст|ка, ки *f. of* ▸ **~**

аккумули́р|овать, ую *impf. and pf.* to accumulate.

аккумуля́тор, а *m.* (*tech.*) accumulator; (*elec.*) accumulator (*Br.*), storage battery (*US*).

аккура́тност|ь, и *f.*
1 (*тщательность*) exactness, thoroughness.
2 (*опрятность*) tidiness, neatness.

аккура́т|ный (~ен, ~на) *adj.*
1 (*тщательный*) exact, thorough.
2 (*опрятный*) tidy, neat.
3 (*регулярный*) regular, punctual.

акри́л, а *m.* acrylic.

акри́л|овый *adj. of* ▸ **~**

акроба́т, а *m.* acrobat.

акселера́тор, а *m.* accelerator.

аксессуа́р, а *m.*
1 accessory.
2 *pl.* (*theatr.*) props.

аксио́м|а, ы *f.* axiom.

акт, а *m.*
1 act; **полово́й а.** sexual intercourse.
2 (*theatr.*) act.
3 (*leg.*) deed, document; **обвини́тельный а.** indictment.

актёр, а *m.* actor.

актёр|ский *adj. of* ▸ **~**

активизи́р|овать, ую *impf. and pf.* (*приводить в действие*) to activate; (*оживлять*) to stimulate, enliven.

активи́ст, а *m.* (*pol.*) activist.

акти́в|ный (~ен, ~на) *adj.* active, energetic.

актри́с|а, ы *f.* actress.

актуа́л|ьный (~ен, ~ьна) *adj.* topical, current.

аку́л|а, ы *f.* (*zool.*) shark (*also fig.*).

аку́стик|а, и *f.* acoustics.

акусти́ческий *adj.* acoustic.

акуше́р, а *m.* obstetrician.

акуше́рк|а, и *f.* midwife.

акуше́рский *adj.* obstetric(al).

акце́нт, а *m.* accent.

акценти́р|овать, ую *impf. and pf.* to accentuate.

акционе́р, а *m.* shareholder, stockholder.

акционе́р|ный *adj. of* ▸ **~; ~ное**

a

общество joint-stock company.
áкци|я¹, и *f.* (*fin.*) share.
áкци|я², и *f.* action.
албáн|ец, ца *m.* Albanian.
Албáни|я, и *f.* Albania.
албáн|ка, ки *f. of* ▸ **~ец**
албáнский *adj.* Albanian.
áлгебр|а, ы *f.* algebra.
алгори́тм, а *m.* algorithm.
алебáстр, а *m.* alabaster.
Алжи́р, а *m.*
1 (*страна*) Algeria.
2 (*столица*) Algiers.
алжи́р|ец, ца *m.* Algerian.
алжи́р|ка, ки *f. of* ▸ **~ец**
алжи́рский *adj.* Algerian.
áлиби *nt. indecl.* (*leg.*) alibi.
алимéнт|ы, ов *no sg.* (*leg.*) alimony.
алкоголи́зм, а *m.* alcoholism.
алкогóлик, а *m.* alcoholic; (*coll.*) drunkard.
алкогóл|ь, я *m.* alcohol; **провéрить на а.** to breathalyse (*Br.*), breathalyze (*US*).
алкогóльный *adj.* alcoholic.
Аллáх, а *m.* Allah.
аллегóри|я, и *f.* allegory.
аллерги́ческий *adj.* allergic.
аллерги́|я, и *f.* allergy; **а. на клубни́ку** an allergy to strawberries.
аллé|я, и *f.* tree-lined path, avenue.
аллигáтор, а *m.* alligator.
аллó *int.* hello!
алмáз, а *m.* (uncut) diamond.
алтáр|ь, я́ *m.*
1 (*жертвенник*) altar.
2 (*восточная часть церкви*) chancel.
алфави́т, а *m.* alphabet; (*comput.*, *typ.*) character set.
алфави́тный *adj.* alphabetical; **а. указáтель** index.
алхи́мик, а *m.* alchemist.
алхи́ми|я, и *f.* alchemy.
áлч|ный (~ен, ~на) *adj.* greedy, grasping.
áл|ый (~, ~а) *adj.* scarlet.
альбóм, а *m.* (*книга; грампластинка*) album.
альманáх, а *m.* anthology.
альпи́йский *adj.* alpine.
альпини́зм, а *m.* mountaineering.
альпини́ст, а *m.* mountain-climber, mountaineer.
альпини́ст|ка, ки *f. of* ▸ **~**
Áльп|ы, ~ *no sg.* the Alps.
альт, á *m.* (*mus.*)
1 (*певец, голос*) alto.
2 (*инструмент*) viola.
альтернати́в|а, ы *f.* alternative.
альтернати́в|ный (~ен, ~на) *adj.* alternative.
альти́ст, а *m.* viola player.
альти́ст|ка, ки *f. of* ▸ **~**
альт|óвый *adj. of* ▸ **~; ~óвая пáртия** alto part; **а. концéрт** viola concerto.
альтруи́зм, а *m.* altruism.
алья́нс, а *m.* alliance.
алюми́ниевый *adj.* aluminium (*Br.*), aluminum (*US*).
алюми́ни|й, я *m.* aluminium (*Br.*), aluminum (*US*).
Аля́ск|а, и *f.* Alaska.
амбициóз|ный (~ен, ~на) *adj.* arrogant, conceited.
амби́ци|я, и *f.*
1 arrogance.
2 *pl.* claims (to) (**на** + *a.*).
амбулатóри|я, и *f.* (*med.*) (*в больнице*) outpatient department; (*кабинет врача*) doctor's surgery (*Br.*), doctor's office (*US*).
амбулатóр|ный *adj. of* ▸ **~ия; а. больнóй** out-patient; **а. приём** out-patient reception hours; surgery hours.
Амéрик|а, и *f.* America.
америкáн|ец, ца *m.* American.
америкáн|ка, ки *f. of* ▸ **~ец**
америкáнский *adj.* American.
аммиáк, а *m.* (*chem.*) ammonia.
амнисти́р|овать, ую *impf. and pf.* to amnesty.
амни́сти|я, и *f.* amnesty.
аморáл|ьный (~ен, ~ьна) *adj.* (*нейтральный в отношении морали*) amoral; (*безнравственный*) immoral.
амортизáтор, а *m.* (*tech.*) shock absorber.
амортизáци|я, и *f.*
1 (*econ.*) amortization.
2 (*tech.*) shock-absorption.
амортизи́р|овать, ую *impf. and pf.* (*econ.*) to amortize.
амóрф|ный (~ен, ~на) *adj.* amorphous.
ампéр, а, *g. pl.* **а.** *m.* (*phys.*) ampere.
ампи́р, а *m.* Empire style (*of furniture, etc.*).
амплиту́д|а, ы *f.* amplitude.
амплуá *nt. indecl.* (*theatr.*) type; (*fig.*) role.
áмпул|а, ы *f.* ampoule (*Br.*), ampule (*US*).
ампутáци|я, и *f.* amputation.
ампути́р|овать, ую *impf. and pf.* to amputate.
Амстердáм, а *m.* Amsterdam.
амулéт, а *m.* amulet.
амуни́ци|я, и *f.* (*collect.*) (*mil.*, *hist.*) accoutrements (*Br.*), accouterments (*US*).
амфи́би|я, и *f.* amphibian.
амфитеáтр, а *m.* (*hist.*) amphitheatre (*Br.*), amphitheater (*US*); (*theatr.*) circle.
анáлиз, а *m.* analysis; **а. крóви** blood test.
анализи́р|овать, ую *impf. and pf.* (*pf. also* ▸ **про~**) to analyse (*Br.*), analyze (*US*).
анали́тик, а *m.* analyst.
аналити́ческий *adj.* analytic(al).
анáлог, а *m.* analogue.
аналоги́ч|ный (~ен, ~на) *adj.* analogous.
аналóги|я, и *f.* analogy; **по ~и (с** + *i.*) by analogy (with), on the analogy (of); **проводи́ть ~ю** to draw an analogy.
ананáс, а *m.* pineapple.
анархи́ст, а *m.* anarchist.
анархи́ческий *adj.* anarchic(al).
анáрхи|я, и *f.* anarchy.

анатоми́ческий *adj.* anatomical.
анато́ми|я, и *f.* anatomy.
анахрони́зм, а *m.* anachronism.
анаш|а́, и́ *f.* (*sl.*) pot, hash.
анга́р, а *m.* (*aeron.*) hangar.
а́нгел, а *m.* angel; **а.-храни́тель** guardian angel; **день ~а** name day.
а́нгельский *adj.* angelic (*also fig.*).
анги́н|а, ы *f.* (*med.*) quinsy; tonsillitis.
англи́йск|ий *adj.*
1 English; **~ая була́вка** safety pin.
2 (*британский*) British.
англика́н|ец, ца *m.* Anglican.
англика́н|ка, ки *f. of* ▸ **~ец**
англика́нский *adj.* (*eccl.*) Anglican.
англича́н|ин, ина, *pl.* **~е, ~** *m.* Englishman.
англича́нк|а, и *f.* Englishwoman.
А́нгли|я, и *f.*
1 England.
2 (*Британия*) Britain.
англоса́кс, а *m.* Anglo-Saxon.
англосаксо́нский *adj.* Anglo-Saxon.
англоязы́чный *adj.*
1 (*англоговорящий*) English-speaking, anglophone.
2 (*на английском языке*) English-language.
Анго́л|а, ы *f.* Angola.
анго́л|ец, ьца *m.* Angolan.
анго́л|ка, ки *f. of* ▸ **~ец**
анго́льский *adj.* Angolan.
андегра́унд, а *m.* (*sl.*) underground.
А́нд|ы, ~ *no sg.* the Andes.
анекдо́т, а *m.*
1 (*рассказ*) anecdote, story.
2 (*шутка*) joke.
анеми́|я, и *f.* anaemia (*Br.*), anemia (*US*).
анестезио́лог, а *m.* anaesthetist (*Br.*), anesthesiologist (*US*).
анестези́|я, и *f.* (*med.*) anaesthesia (*Br.*), anesthesia (*US*).
ани́с, а *m.*
1 (*растение*) anise.
2 (*семя*) aniseed.
Анкар|а́, ы́ *m.* Ankara.
анке́т|а, ы *f.* (*опросный лист*) questionnaire; (*бланк*) form.
анке́т|ный *adj. of* ▸ **~а; ~ные да́нные** biographical details.
аннекси́р|овать, ую *impf. and pf.* (*pol.*) to annex.
аннота́ци|я, и *f.* abstract, precis.
аннули́р|овать, ую *impf. and pf.* (*договор*) to annul, nullify; (*долг*) to cancel; (*закон*) to abrogate.
анома́ли|я, и *f.* anomaly.
анони́мк|а, и *f.* (*coll.*) (*письмо*) poison pen letter.
анони́м|ный (~ен, ~на) *adj.* anonymous.
ано́нс, а *m.* announcement, notice; (*cin.*) trailer.
анса́мбл|ь, я *m.* ensemble.
Антаркти́д|а, ы *f.* Antarctica.
Анта́рктик|а, и *f.* the Antarctic.
антаркти́ческий *adj.* Antarctic.
анте́нн|а, ы *f.* aerial, antenna.
анти... *pref.* anti-.
антиалкого́льный *adj.* anti-alcohol.
антибио́тик, а *m.* (*med.*) antibiotic.
антивое́нный *adj.* anti-war.
антидепресса́нт, а *m.* (*med.*) antidepressant.
антиква́р, а *m.* (*любитель антикварных предметов*) antiquary; (*дилер*) antique dealer.
антиквариа́т, а *m.* (*collect.*) antiques.
антиква́рный *adj.* (*книга*) antiquarian; (*ваза; магазин*) antique.
антило́п|а, ы *f.* (*zool.*) antelope.
антипа́ти|я, и *f.* antipathy.
антисеми́т, а *m.* anti-Semite.
антисемити́зм, а *m.* anti-Semitism.
антисеми́т|ка, ки *f. of* ▸ **~**
антисеми́тский *adj.* anti-Semitic.
антисе́птик, а *m.* antiseptic.
антицикло́н, а *m.* (*meteor.*) anticyclone.
анти́чный *adj.* ancient; classical.
антра́кт, а *m.* (*theatr.*) interval.
антраци́т, а *m.* (*min.*) anthracite.
антреко́т, а *m.* entrecôte, steak.
антрепри́з|а, ы *f.* (*theatr.*) private theatrical concern.
антресо́л|ь, и *f.* (*usu. pl.*)
1 (*полуэтаж*) mezzanine.
2 (*полка*) shelf.
антропо́лог, а *m.* anthropologist.
антрополо́ги|я, и *f.* anthropology.
антура́ж, а *m.* environment; (*collect.*) entourage, associates.
анчо́ус, а *m.* anchovy.
аншла́г, а *m.* (*theatr.*) sell-out notice; **спекта́кль идёт с ~ом** the show is sold out.
АО (*abbr. of* **акционе́рное о́бщество**) joint-stock company.
апартаме́нт|ы, ов *pl.* (*sg.* **~, ~а** *m.*) large apartment.
апартеи́д, а *m.* apartheid.
апа́ти|я, и *f.* apathy.
апелли́р|овать, ую *impf. and pf.* (**к** + *d.*) to appeal (to).
апелл|яцио́нный *adj. of* ▸ **~я́ция; а. суд** Court of Appeal (*in England and Wales*), court of appeals (*US*).
апелля́ци|я, и *f.*
1 (*обращение*) (**к** + *d.*) appeal (to).
2 (*обжалование*) (**на** + *a.*) appeal (against).
апельси́н, а *m.* orange.
апельси́новый *adj.* orange.
Апенни́н|ы, ~ *no sg.* the Apennines.
аперити́в, а *m.* aperitif.
аплоди́р|овать, ую *impf.* (+ *d.*) to applaud.
аплодисме́нт|ы, ов *m. pl.* applause.
апоге́|й, я *m.* (*astron.*) apogee; (*fig.*) climax.
апока́липсис, а *m.* apocalypse.
апокалипти́ческий *adj.* apocalyptic.
аполити́ч|ный (~ен, ~на) *adj.*

apolitical; politically indifferent.

апо́стол, а *m.* apostle (*also fig.*).

апостро́ф, а *m.* apostrophe.

апофео́з, а *m.* apotheosis.

Аппала́ч|и, ей *no sg.* the Appalachians.

аппара́т, а *m.*
1 (*прибор*) apparatus; appliance; **копирова́льный а.** photocopier; **косми́ческий аппара́т** spacecraft; **ка́ссовый а.** cash register; **слухово́й а.** hearing aid; **телефо́нный а.** telephone.
2 (*admin.*): **госуда́рственный а.** machinery of State.
3 (*штат*) staff, personnel.

аппара́тн|ый *adj.* (*comput.*) hardware; **~ые сре́дства** hardware.

аппарату́р|а, ы *f.* (*tech., collect.*) apparatus, equipment; (*comput.*) hardware.

аппе́ндикс, а *m.* appendix.

аппендици́т, а *m.* appendicitis.

аппети́т, а *m.* appetite; **прия́тного ~а!** bon appétit!

аппети́т|ный (~ен, ~на) *adj.* appetizing, mouth-watering.

апплика́ци|я, и *f.* appliqué.

апре́л|ь, я *m.* April.

апре́ль|ский *adj. of* ▸ **~**

апте́к|а, и *f.* chemist's (shop) (*Br.*), pharmacy.

апте́кар|ь, я *m.* chemist (*Br.*); pharmacist.

апте́чк|а, и *f.* (*первой помощи*) first-aid kit; (*коробка*) medicine chest.

ара́б, а *m.* Arab.

ара́б|ка, ки *f. of* ▸ **~**

ара́бск|ий *adj.* Arab; Arabian; Arabic; **~ие ци́фры** Arabic numerals; **а. язы́к** Arabic.

арави́йский *adj.* Arabian.

аранжиро́вк|а, и *f.* arrangement.

ара́хис, а *m.* peanut, groundnut.

арбале́т, а *m.* arbalest, crossbow.

арби́тр, а *m.* (*в споре*) arbiter, arbitrator; (*в спорте*) umpire, referee.

арбитра́ж, а *m.* arbitration.

арбу́з, а *m.* watermelon.

Аргенти́н|а, ы *f.* Argentina.

аргенти́н|ец, ца *m.* Argentinian.

аргенти́н|ка, ки *f. of* ▸ **~ец**

аргенти́нский *adj.* Argentinian, Argentine.

аргуме́нт, а *m.* argument.

аргумента́ци|я, и *f.* reasoning, argumentation.

аргументи́р|овать, ую *impf. and pf.* to argue; (*pf. only*) to prove.

ареа́л, а *m.* (*bot. and zool.*) natural habitat; (*fig.*) region.

аре́н|а, ы *f.* arena, ring; (*fig.*) arena.

аре́нд|а, ы *f.* lease; **сдать в ~у** to rent, lease (*of owner, landlord*); **взять в ~у** to rent, lease (*of tenant*).

арендáтор, а *m.* tenant, lessee.

аре́нд|ный *adj. of* ▸ **~а; ~ная пла́та** rent; **а. подря́д** contract for lease (*of land*).

аренд|ова́ть, у́ю *impf. and pf.* to rent, lease (*of tenant*).

аре́ст, а *m.* (*человека*) arrest; (*имущества*) seizure, sequestration; **взять под а.** to place under arrest; **сиде́ть, находи́ться под ~ом** to be under arrest, in custody; **наложи́ть а. на** (+ *a.*) to sequestrate.

ареста́нт, а *m.* prisoner.

арест|ова́ть, у́ю *pf.* (*of* ▸ **~о́вывать**) (*человека*) to arrest; (*имущество*) to sequestrate.

аресто́выва|ть, ю *impf. of* ▸ **арестова́ть**

аристокра́т, а *m.* aristocrat.

аристократи́ческий *adj.* aristocratic.

аристокра́ти|я, и *f.* aristocracy.

арифме́тик|а, и *f.* arithmetic.

арифмети́ческий *adj.* arithmetical.

а́ри|я, и *f.* aria.

а́рк|а, и *f.* arch.

арка́н, а *m.* lasso.

А́рктик|а, и *f.* the Arctic.

аркти́ческий *adj.* arctic.

арме́йский *adj. of* ▸ **а́рмия**

Арме́ни|я, и *f.* Armenia.

а́рми|я, и *f.* army; **А. Спасе́ния** Salvation Army; **де́йствующая а.** front-line forces.

армян|и́н, и́на, *pl.* **~́е, ~́** *m.* Armenian.

армя́н|ка, ки *f. of* ▸ **~и́н**

армя́нский *adj.* Armenian.

арома́т, а *m.* (*цветов*) scent, fragrance; (*пищи*) aroma.

ароматиза́тор, а *m.* (*cul.*) flavouring (*Br.*), flavoring (*US*).

арома́т|ный (~ен, ~на) *adj.* aromatic, fragrant.

арсена́л, а *m.* arsenal.

арт... *comb. form*
1 *abbr. of* **артиллери́йский** artillery.
2 (*искусство*) art.

арте́ри|я, и, *f.* artery.

арти́кл|ь, я *m.* (*gram.*) article.

артиллери́йский *adj.* (*mil.*) artillery; **а. обстре́л** bombardment, shelling; **а. склад** ordnance depot.

артилле́ри|я, и *f.* artillery.

арти́ст, а *m.* artist(e); **а. бале́та** ballet dancer; **а. кино́** film actor.

артисти́ческ|ий *adj.* artistic; *as n.* **~ая, ~ой** *f.* (*theatr.*) dressing room.

арти́ст|ка, ки *f. of* ▸ **~**

артри́т, а *m.* arthritis.

а́рф|а, ы *f.* harp.

арфи́ст, а *m.* harpist.

арфи́ст|ка, ки *f. of* ▸ **~**

архаи́ч|ный (~ен, ~на) *adj.* archaic.

архео́лог, а *m.* archaeologist (*Br.*), archeologist (*US*).

археологи́ческий *adj.* archaeological (*Br.*), archeological (*US*).

археоло́ги|я, и *f.* archaeology (*Br.*), archeology (*US*).

архи́в, а *m.* archive; (*collect.*) archives; **сдать в а.** (*coll., fig.*) to shelve, leave out of account.

архи́в|ный *adj. of* ▸ **~**

архиепи́скоп, а *m.* archbishop.

архиере́|й, я *m.* member of higher orders of

clergy (*bishop, archbishop, or metropolitan*).
архипела́г, а *m.* archipelago.
архите́ктор, а *m.* architect.
архитекту́р|а, ы *f.* architecture.
архитекту́рный *adj.* architectural.
арьерга́рд, а *m.* (*mil.*) rearguard.
асбе́ст, а *m.* asbestos.
асоциа́льный *adj.* antisocial.
аспе́кт, а *m.* (*сторона*) aspect; (*точка зрения*) viewpoint, perspective.
аспира́нт, а *m.* postgraduate student.
аспира́нт|ка, ки *f. of* ▸ ~
аспиранту́р|а, ы *f.* postgraduate study.
аспири́н, а *m.* (*med.*) aspirin; **табле́тка ~а** an aspirin.
ассамбле́|я, и *f.* assembly.
ассигн|ова́ть, у́ю *impf. and pf.* (*fin.*) to assign, allocate.
ассимиля́ци|я, и *f.* assimilation.
ассисте́нт, а *m.*
1 (*помощник*) assistant.
2 (*в вузе*) junior member of teaching or research staff.
ассисти́р|овать, ую *impf.* (*med.*) (+ *d.*) to assist.
ассортиме́нт, а *m.* assortment; range (*of goods*).
ассоциа́ци|я, и *f.* association.
ассоции́р|овать, ую *impf. and pf.* (**с** + *i.*) to associate (with).
астеро́ид, а *m.* asteroid.
а́стм|а, ы *f.* asthma.
астма́тик, а *m.* asthmatic.
а́стр|а, ы *f.* aster.
астро́лог, а *m.* astrologer.
астрологи́ческий *f.* astrological.
астроло́ги|я, и *f.* astrology.
астрона́вт, а *m.* astronaut.
астроно́м, а *m.* astronomer.
астрономи́ческий *adj.* astronomic(al) (*also fig.*).
астроно́ми|я, и *f.* astronomy.
астрофи́зик|а, и *f.* astrophysics.
асфа́льт, а *m.* asphalt.
ата́к|а, и *f.* attack.
атак|ова́ть, у́ю *impf. and pf.* to attack, charge, assault.
атама́н, а *m.* ataman (*Cossack chieftain*).
атеи́зм, а *m.* atheism.
атеи́ст, а *m.* atheist.
атеи́ст|ка, ки *f. of* ▸ ~
ателье́ *nt. indecl.* studio; **а. мод** tailor's shop.
Атланти́ческ|ий океа́н, ~ого ~а *m.* the Atlantic Ocean; the Atlantic.
а́тлас, а *m.* atlas.
атла́с, а *m.* satin.
атле́т, а *m.* (*спортсмен*) athlete; (*в цирке*) strongman.
атле́тик|а, и *f.* athletics; **лёгкая а.** (track and field) athletics; **тяжёлая а.** weightlifting.
атлети́ческ|ий *adj.* athletic; **~ое телосложе́ние** athletic build.
атмосфе́р|а, ы *f.* atmosphere.
атмосфе́рн|ый *adj.* atmospheric; **~ые оса́дки** atmospheric precipitation, rainfall.
а́том, а *m.* atom.
а́томн|ый *adj.* atomic; nuclear; **~ая бо́мба** atomic bomb; **~ая электроста́нция** nuclear power station.
атрибу́т, а *m.* attribute.
АТС *f. indecl.* (*abbr. of* **автомати́ческая телефо́нная ста́нция**) automatic telephone exchange.
атташе́ *m. indecl.* (*dipl.*) attaché.
аттеста́т, а *m.* certificate.
аттестацио́нн|ый *adj.*: **~ая коми́ссия** examination board.
аттеста́ци|я, и *f.* attestation.
аттест|ова́ть, у́ю *impf. and pf.* (*присвоить звание*) to confer a rank on; (*оценить знания*) to grade.
аттракцио́н, а *m.* (*theatr.*) attraction; (*fairground*) sideshow, ride; **парк ~ов** amusement park.
аудие́нци|я, и *f.* audience.
ауди́т, а *m.* audit.
ауди́тор, а *m.* auditor.
аудито́ри|я, и *f.*
1 auditorium; lecture hall.
2 (*collect.*) audience.
аукцио́н, а *m.* auction, auction sale; **продава́ть с ~а** to auction.
а́ут, а *m.* (*sport*) out (*also as int.*).
аутенти́ч|ный (~ен, ~на) *adj.* authentic.
ути́зм, а *m.* autism.
афга́н|ец, ца *m.* Afghan; **«а.»** Afghan war vet(eran).
Афганиста́н, а *m.* Afghanistan.
афга́н|ка, ки *f. of* ▸ **~ец**
афе́р|а, ы *f.* swindle, trickery.
афери́ст, а *m.* swindler; trickster.
афери́ст|ка, ки *f. of* ▸ ~
Афи́н|ы, ~ *no sg.* Athens.
афи́ш|а, и *f.* poster, placard; **театра́льная а.** playbill.
афори́зм, а *m.* aphorism.
А́фрик|а, и *f.* Africa.
африка́н|ец, ца *m.* African.
африка́н|ка, ки *f. of* ▸ **~ец**
африка́нский *adj.* African.
афроамерика́н|ец, ца *m.* African American.
афроамерика́н|ка, ки *f. of* ▸ **~ец**
афроамерика́нский *adj.* African American.
ах *int.* ah! oh!
аэро... *comb. form* aero-; air-, aerial.
аэро́бик|а, и *f.* aerobics.
аэровокза́л, а *m.* air terminal.
аэродина́мик|а, и *f.* aerodynamics.
аэродинами́ческий *adj.* aerodynamic.
аэродро́м, а *m.* aerodrome.
аэрозо́л|ь, я *m.* aerosol, spray.
аэрона́втик|а, и *f.* aeronautics.
аэропо́рт, а, об ~е, в ~у́ *m.* airport.
АЭС *f. indecl.* (*abbr. of* **а́томная электроста́нция**) atomic power station.
а/я *m. indecl.* (*abbr. of* **абоне́нтский я́щик**) PO (*abbr. of* Post Office) Box.

Бб

б *particle* = **бы** (*after words ending in vowel*).
ба́б|а, ы *f.* (*coll.*) (*женщина*) woman; **сне́жная б.** snowman.
ба́бк|а, и *f.* = **ба́бушка**
ба́б|ки, ок *f. pl.* (*coll.*) money.
ба́бочк|а, и *f.* butterfly; **ночна́я б.** moth.
ба́бушк|а, и *f.* grandmother; (*coll.*) old woman; gran(ny) (*as mode of address*).
бага́ж, а́ *m.* luggage; **сдать свои́ ве́щи в б.** to register one's luggage.
бага́жник, а *m.* (*в автомобиле*) boot (*Br.*), trunk (*US*); (*на крыше*) roof rack; (*велосипеда*) carrier.
бага́ж|ный *adj. of* ▶ **~**; **б. ваго́н** luggage van (*Br.*), baggage car (*US*).
Багда́д, а *m.* Baghdad.
багро́в|ый (~, ~а) *adj.* crimson, purple.
бадминто́н, а *m.* badminton.
бадминтони́ст, а *m.* badminton player.
бадминтони́ст|ка, ки *f. of* ▶ **~**
бад|ья́, ьи́, *g. pl.* **~е́й** *f.* tub.
ба́з|а, ы *f.*
1 (*mil., archit.*) base; (*склад*) depot; (*туристов*) centre (*Br.*), center (*US*); **б. да́нных** database.
2 (*основание*) basis; **на ~е** (+ *g.*) on the basis (of);
база́р, а *m.* (*coll.*) market.
база́р|ный *adj. of* ▶ **~**; (*coll.*) of the marketplace, rough, crude.
бази́р|оваться, уюсь *impf.* (**на** + *p.*)
1 to be based (on).
2 (*mil.*) to be based (at).
ба́зис, а *m.* (*archit.*) base; (*основание*) basis.
ба́зовый *adj.*
1 basic; **б. курс** foundation course.
2: **б. ла́герь** base camp.
базу́к|а, и *f.* bazooka.
байда́рк|а, и *f.* kayak; canoe.
ба́йт, а *m.* (*comput.*) byte.
бак, а *m.* cistern; tank; **му́сорный б.** dustbin (*Br.*), garbage can (*US*).
бакала́вр, а *m.* bachelor (*holder of degree*).
бакале́йный *adj.* grocery; **б. магази́н** grocer's shop (*Br.*), grocery store (*US*).
бакале́|я, и *f.*
1 (*collect.*) dry goods, groceries.
2 (*в магазине*) grocery section; (*магазин*) grocer's (shop).
ба́кен, а *m.* (*буй*) buoy.
бакенба́рд|ы, ~ *pl.* (*sg.* **~а, ~ы** *f.*) side whiskers.
баклажа́н, а *m.* aubergine (*Br.*), eggplant (*US*).
бакла́н, а *m.* cormorant.
ба́кс|ы, ов *pl.* (*sl.*) bucks, American dollars.
бактериологи́ческ|ий *adj.* bacteriological; **~ая война́** germ warfare.
бактериоло́ги|я, и *f.* bacteriology.
бактерици́дный *adj.* germicidal.
бакте́ри|я, и *f.* bacterium.
Баку́ *m. indecl.* Baku.
бал, а, о ~е, на ~у́, *pl.* **~ы́** *m.* ball, dance.
балала́йк|а, и *f.* balalaika.
бала́нс, а *m.* (*econ., tech.*) balance; **платёжный б.** balance of payments.
баланси́р|овать, ую *impf.* (*сохранять равновесие*) to balance.
балери́н|а, ы *f.* ballerina.
бале́т, а *m.* ballet; **б. на льду́** ice review *or* show.
бале́т|ный *adj. of* ▶ **~**
ба́лк|а, и *f.* (*брус*) beam, girder.
балка́нский *adj.* Balkan.
Балка́н|ы, ~ *no sg.* the Balkans.
балко́н, а *m.* balcony.
балл, а *m.*
1 (*meteor.*) number; **ве́тер в пять ~ов** wind force 5.
2 (*в школе*) mark; **вы́сший б.** an 'A'; **проходно́й б.** pass mark; (*sport*) point; score.
балла́д|а, ы *f.* ballad.
балли́стик|а, и *f.* ballistics.
баллисти́ческий *adj.* ballistic.
балло́н, а *m.*
1 (*сосуд*) container (*of glass, metal, or rubber*); carboy; **аэрозо́льный б.** spray can; **кислоро́дный б.** oxygen cylinder.
2 (*шина*) balloon tyre (*Br.*), tire (*US*).
баллоти́р|оваться, уюсь *impf.* (**в** + *a.*, **на** + *a.*) to stand (*Br.*), run (*US*) (for), be a candidate (for).
бал|ова́ть, у́ю *impf.* (*of* ▶ **из~**) (*детей*) to spoil; to pamper.
бал|ова́ться, у́юсь *impf.* (*coll.*)
1 (*шалить*) to get up to mischief.
2 (**с** + *i.*) (*со спичками*) to play, fool about (with).
3 (*позволять себе что-л.*) to indulge (in).
баловств|о́, а́ *nt.*
1 (*шалости*) mischief.
2 (*причуда*) folly, extravagance.
балти́йский *adj.* Baltic; **Балти́йское мо́ре** Baltic Sea.
Ба́лтик|а, и *f.* (*море*) the Baltic (Sea); (*район*) the Baltic coast.
бальза́м, а *m.* balsam; (*fig.*) balm; **б. для воло́с** hair conditioner.
ба́л|ьный *adj. of* ▶ **~**; **~ьные та́нцы** ballroom dancing.
бамбу́к, а *m.* bamboo.
ба́мпер, а *m.* bumper.
бана́льност|ь, и *f.*
1 (*свойство*) banality.
2 (*замечание*) banal remark; platitude.
бана́л|ьный (~ен, ~ьна) *adj.* banal, trite.

бана́н, а *m.* banana.
Бангко́к, а *m.* Bangkok.
Бангладе́ш, а *m.* Bangladesh.
бангладе́ш|ец, ца *m.* Bangladeshi.
бангладе́ш|ка, ки *f. of* ▸ **~ец**
бангладе́шский *adj.* Bangladeshi.
ба́нд|а, ы *f.* band, gang.
бандеро́л|ь, и *f.* (*почтовое отправление*) small package.
банди́т, а *m.* bandit; thug; armed robber.
бандити́зм, а *m.* banditry; thuggery.
банди́т|ский *adj. of* ▸ **~**
банк, а *m.* bank (*also fig.*); **б. да́нных** databank.
ба́нк|а, и *f.* (*стеклянная*) jar; (*жестяная*) tin (*Br.*), can (*US*).
банке́т, а *m.* banquet.
банки́р, а *m.* banker.
банкно́т|а, ы *f.* banknote.
ба́нк|овский *adj. of* ▸ **~; б. биле́т** banknote; **~овская кни́жка** passbook, bank book.
банкома́т, а *m.* cash machine.
банкро́т, а *m.* bankrupt; **объявля́ть (кого́-л.) ~ом** to declare (s.o.) bankrupt.
банкро́тств|о, а *nt.* bankruptcy.
бант, а *m.* bow.
ба́н|я, и *f.* (Russian) baths; bathhouse; **фи́нская б.** sauna.
бапти́ст, а *m.* Baptist.
бапти́ст|ка, ки *f. of* ▸ **~**
бар, а *m.* bar; **пивно́й б.** pub.
бараба́н, а *m.* drum.
бараба́н|ить, ю, ишь *impf.* to drum.
бараба́н|ный *adj. of* ▸ **~; ~ная дробь** drum roll; **~ная перепо́нка** (*anat.*) ear drum, tympanum.
бараба́нщик, а *m.* drummer.
бараба́нщи|ца, цы *f. of* ▸ **~к**
бара́к, а *m.* hut.
бара́н, а *m.* ram; (wild) sheep.
бара́н|ий *adj.*
1 sheep's; ram's.
2 (*из кожи барана*) sheepskin.
3 (*о еде*) mutton; **~ья котле́та** mutton chop.
бара́нин|а, ы *f.* mutton; (*молодая*) lamb.
барахл|о́, а́ *nt.* (*collect.*; *coll.*) trash, junk.
барда́к, а́ *m.* (*coll.*) chaos.
бардач|о́к, ка́ *m.* (*coll.*) glove compartment (*in car*).
Ба́ренцев|о мо́р|е, ~а ~я *nt.* the Barents Sea.
ба́рж|а, и *f.* barge.
барито́н, а *m.* baritone.
ба́рмен, а *m.* barman, bartender.
баро́кко *nt. indecl.* baroque.
баро́метр, а *m.* barometer.
баро́н, а *m.* baron.
барон́есс|а, ы *f.* baroness.
баррика́д|а, ы *f.* barricade.
барс, а *m.* (*zool.*) snow leopard (*Uncia uncia*).
барсу́к, а́ *m.* badger.
ба́ртер, а *m.* barter.
ба́рхат, а *m.* velvet.
ба́рхатный *adj.*
1 velvet; **б. сезо́н** autumn season, autumn months (*in the south of Russia*).
2 (*fig.*) velvety.
ба́рхат|цы, цев *pl.* (*sg.* **~ец, ~ца** *m.*) (African/French) marigold (*genus Tagetes*).
барье́р, а *m.* barrier (*also fig.*); **звуково́й б.** sound barrier; **языково́й б.** language barrier; (*sport*) hurdle; **взять б.** to clear a hurdle.
бас, а, *pl.* **~ы́** *m.* (*mus.*) bass.
бас-гита́р|а, ы *f.* bass guitar.
баск, а *m.* Basque.
баскетбо́л, а *m.* basketball (*sport*).
баскетболи́ст, а *m.* basketball player.
баскетболи́ст|ка, ки *f. of* ▸ **~**
баск|о́нка, о́нки *f. of* ▸ **~**
ба́скский *adj.* Basque.
баснослó́в|ный (~ен, ~на) *adj.* (*fig.*, *coll.*) fabulous.
ба́с|ня, ни, *g. pl.* **~ен** *f.*
1 fable.
2 (*fig.*, *coll.*) fable, fabrication.
бассе́йн, а *m.*
1 (*man-made*) pool; **пла́вательный б.** swimming pool.
2 (*geog.*) basin; **каменноу́гольный б.** coalfield.
бастио́н, а *m.* (*mil. and fig.*) bastion.
баст|ова́ть, у́ю *impf.* to strike, go on strike; to be on strike.
батальо́н, а *m.* battalion.
батаре́йк|а, и *f.* (*electric*) battery.
батаре́|я, и *f.* (*mil. and tech.*) battery; (*отопительная*) radiator.
бато́н, а *m.* (*long*) white loaf.
бату́т, а *m.* trampoline.
ба́тюшк|а, и *m.* (*священник*) father.
бахром|а́, ы́ *f.* fringe.
башк|а́, и́ *no g. pl.*, *f.* (*coll.*) head.
башма́к, а́ *m.* (*ботинок*) boot; (*туфля*) shoe.
ба́ш|ня, ни, *g. pl.* **~ен** *f.* tower; turret.
бая́н, а *m.* (*mus.*) bayan (*kind of accordion*).
бди́тельност|ь, и *f.* vigilance, watchfulness.
бди́тел|ьный (~ен, ~ьна) *adj.* vigilant, watchful.
бег, а, о, ~е, на ~у́, *pl.* **~а́, ~о́в** *m.*
1 run, running; jogging; **~о́м, на ~у́** running; at the double; **на всём ~у́** at full speed; **б. на ме́сте** running on the spot; marking time (*also fig.*).
2 (*sport*) (*состязание*) race.
3 *pl.* (*гонки упряжных лошадей*) harness races; trotting races.
4 : **быть в ~а́х** to be on the run.
бе́га|ть, ю *impf.* (*indet. of* ▸ **бежа́ть**)
1 to run (about); (**за** + *i.*; *coll.*) to run (after), chase (after).
2 (*о глазах*) to rove, roam.
бегемо́т, а *m.* hippopotamus.
бегле́ц, а́ *m.* fugitive.
бе́глый *adj.*
1 (*убежавший*) fugitive, runaway.
2 (*свободный*) fluent, quick.
бегля́нк|а, и *f. of* ▸ **бегле́ц**
бег|ово́й *adj. of* ▸ **~; ~ова́я доро́жка**

racetrack, running track; **~ова́я ло́шадь** racehorse.

беготн|я́, и́ *f.* (*coll.*) running about; bustle.

бе́гств|о, а *nt.* flight; escape; **обрати́ть в б.** to put to flight; **обрати́ться в б., спаса́ться ~ом** to take to flight.

бе|гу́, ~жи́шь *see* ▸ **~жа́ть**

бегу́н, а́ *m.* runner.

бед|а́, ы́, *pl.* **~ы** *f.*

1 (*несчастье*) misfortune; calamity; **на свою́ ~у́** to one's cost.

2 *as pred.* it is awful!; it is a trouble; **б. в том, что** the trouble is (that); **не б.!** it doesn't matter.

бе́дност|ь, и *f.* poverty (*also fig.*).

бе́д|ный (~ен, ~на́, ~но, ~ны́) *adj.* poor; meagre (*Br.*), meager (*US*); (*fig.*) barren.

бедня́г|а, и *m.* (*coll.*) poor devil, poor thing.

бедня́к, а́ *m.* pauper.

бед|ро́, ра́, *pl.* **~ра, ~ер, ~рам** *nt.* (*верхняя часть ноги*) thigh; (*таз*) hip.

бе́дстви|е, я *nt.* calamity, disaster; **райо́н ~я** disaster area; **сигна́л ~я** distress signal.

бе́дств|овать, ую *impf.* to live in poverty.

бе|жа́ть, гу́, жи́шь, гу́т *impf.* (*det. of* ▸ **бе́гать**)

1 to run; (*fig.*) (*о воде*) to run; (*о крови*) to flow.

2 (*impf. and pf.*) (*спасаться*) to escape.

бе́жевый *adj.* beige.

бе́жен|ец, ца *m.* refugee.

бе́жен|ка, ки *f. of* ▸ **~ец**

без *prep.* + *g.* without; in the absence of; minus, less; **не б.** not without; **б. вас** in your absence; **б. пяти́ (мину́т) три** five (minutes) to three; **б. че́тверти час** a quarter to one; **б. ма́лого** (*coll.*) almost, all but; **быть б. ума́ (от** + *g.*) to be crazy (about).

без... *pref.* in-, un-, -less.

безалкого́льный *adj.* non-alcoholic; **б. напи́ток** non-alcoholic drink, soft drink.

безапелляцио́н|ный (~ен, ~на) *adj.* peremptory, categorical.

безбиле́тный *adj.* ticketless; **б. пассажи́р** fare dodger; (*on ship*) stowaway.

безбо́жный *adj.*

1 irreligious, anti-religious.

2 (*coll.*) (*бессовестный*) outrageous.

безбо́лезнен|ный (~, ~на) *adj.* painless.

безбра́чный *adj.* celibate.

безбре́ж|ный (~ен, ~на) *adj.* boundless.

безве́трен|ный (~, ~на) *adj.* calm, windless.

безве́три|е, я *nt.* calm.

безвку́с|ный (~ен, ~на) *adj.* tasteless.

безво́д|ный (~ен, ~на) *adj.* arid; waterless.

безвозвра́т|ный (~ен, ~на) *adj.* irrevocable; irretrievable; **~ная ссу́да** permanent loan.

безвозме́здный *adj.* free (of charge); **б. труд** unpaid work.

безво́ли|е, я *nt.* lack of will; weak will.

безво́л|ьный (~ен, ~ьна) *adj.* weak-willed.

безвре́д|ный (~ен, ~на) *adj.* harmless.

безвре́менн|ый *adj.* untimely, premature; **~ая конч́ина** untimely end, untimely death.

безвы́ездно *adv.* uninterruptedly, without a break.

безвы́ездн|ый *adj.* uninterrupted; **~ое пребыва́ние** continuous residence.

безвы́ход|ный (~ен, ~на) *adj.* hopeless, desperate.

безгра́мот|ный (~ен, ~на) *adj.* illiterate (*also fig.*); ignorant.

безграни́ч|ный (~ен, ~на) *adj.* infinite, limitless, boundless.

безгре́ш|ный (~ен, ~на) *adj.* innocent, sinless.

безда́рност|ь, и *f.*

1 (*свойство*) lack of talent.

2 (*человек*) person without talent.

безда́р|ный (~ен, ~на) *adj.* (*человек*) talentless, undistinguished; (*произведение*) third-rate.

безде́йстви|е, я *nt.* inaction, idleness; (*leg.*) (criminal) negligence.

безделу́шк|а, и *f.* knick-knack.

безде́ль|е, я *nt.* idleness.

безде́льник, а *m.* idler, loafer.

безде́льнича|ть, ю *impf.* to idle, loaf about.

безде́т|ный (~ен, ~на) *adj.* childless.

бе́здн|а, ы *f.* abyss, chasm.

бездоказа́тел|ьный (~ен, ~ьна) *adj.* unsubstantiated.

бездо́м|ный (~ен, ~на) *adj.* homeless; (*о кошке, собаке*) stray.

бездоро́ж|е, я *nt.*

1 (*отсутствие дорог*) absence of roads.

2 (*распутица*) bad condition of roads; season when roads are impassable.

безду́м|ный (~ен, ~на) *adj.* unthinking; feckless.

безе́ *nt. indecl.* meringue.

безжа́лост|ный (~ен, ~на) *adj.* ruthless, pitiless.

безжи́знен|ный (~, ~на) *adj.* lifeless, inanimate; (*fig.*) spiritless.

беззабо́т|ный (~ен, ~на) *adj.* carefree, light-hearted; (*бездумный*) careless.

беззако́ни|е, я *nt.*

1 (*отсутствие законности*) lawlessness.

2 (*поступок*) unlawful act.

беззащи́т|ный (~ен, ~на) *adj.* defenceless (*Br.*), defenseless (*US*), unprotected.

беззву́ч|ный (~ен, ~на) *adj.* soundless, noiseless.

беззло́б|ный (~ен, ~на) *adj.* good-natured.

беззу́б|ый (~, ~а) *adj.* toothless; (*fig.*) weak, impotent.

безли́кий *adj.* featureless; faceless, impersonal.

безли́ч|ный (~ен, ~на) *adj.*

1 without personality, characterless, impersonal.

2 (*gram.*) impersonal.

безлю́д|ный (~ен, ~на) *adj.* (*малонаселённый*) uninhabited; sparsely populated; (*улица*) empty, deserted.

безмо́згл|ый (~, ~а) *adj.* (*coll.*)

brainless.

безмо́лви|е, я *nt.* silence; **цари́т б.** silence reigns.

безмо́лв|ный (~ен, ~на) *adj.* silent, mute; **~ное согла́сие** tacit consent.

безмяте́ж|ный (~ен, ~на) *adj.* serene, placid.

безнадёж|ный (~ен, ~на) *adj.* hopeless; despairing.

безнака́занно *adv.* with impunity; **э́то ему́ не пройдёт б.** he won't get away with this.

безнака́занност|ь, и *f.* impunity.

безнали́чный *adj.* (*fin.*) cashless.

безно́г|ий (~, ~а) *adj.* (*без ног*) legless; (*без ноги*) one-legged.

безнра́вственност|ь, и *f.* immorality.

безнра́вствен|ный (~, ~на) *adj.* immoral.

безоби́д|ный (~ен, ~на) *adj.* inoffensive.

безо́блач|ный (~ен, ~на) *adj.* cloudless; (*fig.*) serene, unclouded.

безобра́зи|е, я *nt.*
1 (*уродство*) ugliness.
2 (*поступок*) outrage.
3 (*as pred; coll.*) it is disgraceful.

безобра́знича|ть, ю *impf.* (*coll.*) to behave disgracefully; to make a nuisance of o.s.

безобра́з|ный (~ен, ~на) *adj.*
1 (*уродливый*) ugly.
2 (*поступок*) disgraceful, outrageous.

безоговоро́роч|ный (~ен, ~на) *adj.* unconditional, unreserved, absolute.

безопа́сност|ь, и *f.* safety, security; **по́яс/реме́нь ~и** seat belt; **Сове́т Безопа́сности** Security Council.

безопа́с|ный (~ен, ~на) *adj.* safe, secure; **б. секс** safe sex.

безору́ж|ный (~ен, ~на) *adj.* unarmed; (*fig.*) defenceless (*Br.*), defenseless (*US*).

безоснова́тел|ьный (~ен, ~ьна) *adj.* groundless.

безотве́тствен|ный (~, ~на) *adj.* irresponsible.

безотка́з|ный (~ен, ~на) *adj.*
1 (*человек*) dependable.
2 (*работа машины*) trouble-free.

безотноси́тельно *adv.* (**к** + *d.*) irrespective (of).

безотчёт|ный (~ен, ~на) *adj.*
1 (*бесконтрольный*) not subject to control.
2 (*бессознательный*) unconscious, instinctive.

безоши́боч|ный (~ен, ~на) *adj.* correct.

безрабо́тиц|а, ы *f.* unemployment.

безрабо́тн|ый *adj.* unemployed; *as n.* **~ые, ~ых** *pl.* the unemployed.

безра́дост|ный (~ен, ~на) *adj.* joyless; dismal.

безразде́л|ьный (~ен, ~ьна) *adj.* (*внимание*) undivided; **~ьная власть** complete sway.

безразли́чи|е, я *nt.* indifference.

безразли́чно *adv.* indifferently; **относи́ться б.** (**к** + *d.*) to be indifferent (to).

безразли́ч|ный (~ен, ~на) *adj.* indifferent; **мне ~но** it's all the same to me.

безрассу́д|ный (~ен, ~на) *adj.* reckless; foolhardy.

безрезульта́т|ный (~ен, ~на) *adj.* futile; unsuccessful.

безру́к|ий (~, ~а) *adj.*
1 (*без рук*) armless.
2 (*без руки*) one-armed.
3 (*fig.*) clumsy.

безуда́р|ный (~ен, ~на) *adj.* (*ling.*) unstressed.

безукори́зннен|ный (~, ~на) *adj.* irreproachable; impeccable.

безу́м|ец, ца *m.* madman.

безу́ми|е, я *nt.* madness; **довести́ до ~я** to drive crazy; **люби́ть до ~я** to love to distraction.

безу́м|ный (~ен, ~на) *adj.*
1 (*план*) mad, crazy.
2 (*fig., coll.*) (*страсть*) wild; **~ные це́ны** absurd, crazy prices.

безупре́ч|ный (~ен, ~на) *adj.* (*человек*) irreproachable; (*работа*) flawless.

безусло́вно *adv.*
1 (*повиноваться, доверять*) unconditionally, absolutely.
2 (*coll.*) (*несомненно*) of course, it goes without saying, undoubtedly.

безусло́в|ный (~ен, ~на) *adj.*
1 (*повиновение, доверие*) unconditional, absolute.
2 (*успех*) undoubted, indisputable.

безуспе́ш|ный (~ен, ~на) *adj.* unsuccessful.

безуте́ш|ный (~ен, ~на) *adj.* inconsolable.

безуча́ст|ный (~ен, ~на) *adj.* apathetic, indifferent.

безъя́дерный *adj.* nuclear-free.

безымя́нный *adj.* (*не имеющий названия*) nameless; (*анонимный*) anonymous; **б. па́лец** third finger, ring finger.

Бейру́т, а *m.* Beirut.

бейсбо́л, а *m.* baseball.

бейсболи́ст, а *m.* baseball player.

бе́й(те) *imper. of* ▶ **бить**

бeко́н, а *m.* bacon.

Белару́с|ь, и *f.* Belarus.

Белгра́д, а *m.* Belgrade.

беле́|ть, ю *impf.* (*of* ▶ **по~**)
1 (*становиться белым*) to grow white.
2 (*no pf.*) (*виднеться*) to show up white.

белизн|а́, ы́ *f.* whiteness.

бели́л|а, ~ *no sg.* whitewash.

бел|и́ть, ю́, ~́ишь *impf.* (*pf.* **по~**) to whitewash.

бе́лк|а, и *f.* squirrel; **верте́ться, крути́ться как б. в колесе́** to run round in circles.

беллетри́ст, а *m.* fiction writer.

беллетри́стик|а, и *f.* (*liter.*) fiction.

бело... *comb. form* white-.

белогварде́|ец, йца *m.* (*pol.*) White Guard.

бел|о́к[1], ка́ *m.* (*chem.*) protein.

б

бел|óк², **кá** *m.* (*яйца*) white (of egg).
бел|óк³, **кá** *m.* (*глаза*) white (of the eye).
белокýр|ый (~, ~а) *adj.* blond(e), fair(-haired).
белорýс, а *m.* B(y)elorussian.
белорýс|ка, ки *f. of* ▸ **~**
белорýсский *adj.* B(y)elorussian.
белоснéж|ный (~ен, ~на) *adj.* snow-white.
белýг|а, и *f.* beluga, white sturgeon (*Huso huso*).
бéл|ый (~, ~á) *adj.*
1 white; **~ая берёза** silver birch; **Б. дом** White House (*in Washington and Moscow*); **б. медвéдь** polar bear.
2 (*светлый*) white; fair; **б. билéт** 'white chit' (*certificate of exemption from mil. service*); **~ое винó** white wine; **б. хлеб** white bread; **на ~ом свéте** in all the world; **средь ~а дня** in broad daylight; *as n.* **~ые, ~ых** *pl.* white(-skinned) people.
3 (*чистый*) clean; blank; **б. лист** clean sheet (*of paper*).
4 : **б. гриб** cep (*wild mushroom, Boletus edulis*).
бельги́|ец, йца *m.* Belgian.
бельги́|йка, йки *f. of* ▸ **~ец**
бельги́йский *adj.* Belgian.
Бéльги|я, и *f.* Belgium.
бель|ё, я́ *nt.* (*collect.*) linen; **дáмское б.** lingerie; **ни́жнее б.** underclothes; **постéльное б.** bedlinen.
бемóл|ь, я *m.* (*also as indecl. adj.*) (*mus.*) flat.
бензи́н, а *m.* benzine; (*для автомобиля*) petrol (*Br.*), gas (*US*).
бензи́н|овый *adj. of* ▸ **~**; petrol (*Br.*), gas (*US*).
бензо... *comb. form, abbr. of* **бензи́новый**
бензобáк, а *m.* petrol tank (*Br.*), gas tank (*US*).
бензовóз, а *m.* petrol tanker (*Br.*), gasoline truck (*US*).
бензоколóнк|а, и *f.* petrol pump (*Br.*), gas(oline) pump (*US*).
бер|ёг, ~еглá *see* ▸ **берéчь**
бéрег, а, о ~е, на ~ý, *pl.* **~á** *m.* (*реки*) bank; (*моря, озера*) shore; (*суша*) land (*opp.* sea); **на ~ý мóря** at the seaside; **вы́броситься на б.** to run aground; **вы́йти из ~óв** to burst its banks; **сойти́ на б.** to go ashore.
берегов|óй *adj.* coastal; waterside; **~áя оборóна** coastal defence (*Br.*), defense (*US*).
бере|гý, ~жёшь, ~гýт *see* ▸ **берéчь**
бережли́в|ый (~, ~а) *adj.* thrifty, economical.
бéреж|ный (~ен, ~на) *adj.* (*осторожный*) careful; cautious; (*заботливый*) solicitous.
берёз|а, ы *f.* birch.
берéмене|ть, ю, ешь *impf.* (*of* ▸ **за~**) to become pregnant.
берéме|нная (~нна) *adj.* (+ *i.*) pregnant (with).
берéменност|ь, и *f.* (*состояние*) pregnancy; (*процесс*) gestation.
берéт, а *m.* beret.
бер|éчь, егý, ежёшь, егýт, *past* **~ёг, ~еглá** *impf.*
1 (*человека, здоровье, предмет*) to take care (of), look after.
2 (*не тратить*) to be careful with; **б. кáждую копéйку** to count every penny.
бер|éчься, егýсь, ежёшься, егýтся, *past* **~ёгся, ~еглáсь** *impf.*
1 (*быть осторожным*) to be careful, take care.
2 (+ *g. or* + *inf.*) (*остерегаться*) to beware (of).
Бéрингов|о мóр|е, ~а ~я *nt.* the Bering Sea.
Берли́н, а *m.* Berlin.
берлóг|а, и *f.* den, lair.
Бермýдск|ие óстров|á, ~их ~óв *no sg.* the Bermudas (*islands*), Bermuda.
бер|ý, ёшь *see* ▸ **брать**
бес, а *m.* demon, devil, evil spirit.
бесéд|а, ы *f.*
1 talk, conversation.
2 (*дискуссия*) discussion; **провести́ ~у** to give a talk.
бесéдк|а, и *f.* summer house.
бесéд|овать, ую *impf.* (**с** + *i.*) to talk, converse (with).
бе|си́ть, шý, ^~сишь *impf.* (*of* ▸ **вз~**) (*coll.*) to enrage, madden, infuriate.
бе|си́ться, шýсь, ^~сишься *impf.* (*of* ▸ **вз~**)
1 to go mad (*of animals*).
2 (*fig.*) to rage, be furious; **с жи́ру б.** (*coll.*) to grow fastidious, fussy; to be too well off.
бескомпроми́сс|ный (~ен, ~на) *adj.* uncompromising.
бесконéчно *adv.* infinitely, endlessly; (*coll.*) extremely.
бесконéчност|ь, и *f.* endlessness; infinity; **до ~и** endlessly.
бесконéч|ный (~ен, ~на) *adj.* (*дорога*) endless; (*время, удовольствие*) infinite; (*слишком длинный*) interminable.
бескоры́ст|ный (~ен, ~на) *adj.* disinterested; (*альтруистичный*) unselfish.
бескрáйний *adj.* boundless.
бескрóв|ный (~ен, ~на) *adj.* (*без кровопролития*) bloodless.
бесперебóйный *adj.* uninterrupted; (*регулярный*) regular.
беспересáдочный *adj.* direct; **б. пóезд** through train.
бесперспекти́в|ный (~ен, ~на) *adj.* having no prospects; (*безнадёжный*) hopeless.
беспéчност|ь, и *f.* carelessness, unconcern.
беспéч|ный (~ен, ~на) *adj.* carefree.
беспилóтный *adj.* unmanned.
бесплáтно *adv.* free of charge, gratis.
бесплáт|ный (~ен, ~на) *adj.* free, gratuitous.
бесплóди|е, я *nt.* (*почвы*) barrenness; (*женщины*) infertility.
бесплóд|ный (~ен, ~на) *adj.*
1 (*почва*) barren; (*женщина*) infertile; (*брак*) childless.
2 (*fig.*) fruitless, futile.
бесподóб|ный (~ен, ~на) *adj.* matchless; incomparable.

беспозвоно́ч|ный *adj.* (*zool.*) invertebrate; *as n.* **~ое, ~ого** *nt.* invertebrate.

беспоко́|ить, ю, ишь *impf.* 1 (*волновать*) to concern, worry. 2 (*pf.* **по~**) (*мешать*) to disturb, worry.

беспоко́|иться, юсь, ишься *impf.* 1 (**о** + *p.*) to worry, be worried *or* anxious (about). 2 (*pf.* **по~**) to trouble o.s., put o.s. out; **не ~йтесь!** don't worry!

беспоко́|йный (~ен, ~йна) *adj.* 1 (*человек, вид, состояние*) agitated, disturbed; anxious; uneasy; (*ребёнок*) fidgety. 2 (*сон*) restless, disturbed; (*поездка*) uncomfortable.

беспоко́йств|о, а *nt.* 1 (*волнение*) agitation; anxiety; unrest; **с ~ом** anxiously. 2 (*нарушение покоя*) disturbance.

бесполе́з|ный (~ен, ~на) *adj.* useless.

беспо́мощ|ный (~ен, ~на) *adj.* helpless, powerless; (*fig.*) feeble.

беспоря́д|ок, ка *m.* disorder, confusion; (*pl. only*; *pol.*) disturbances, riots.

беспоря́доч|ный (~ен, ~на) *adj.* disorderly; untidy.

беспоса́дочный *adj.*: **б. перелёт** non-stop flight.

беспо́чвен|ный (~, ~на) *adj.* groundless; unfounded.

беспо́шлинн|ый *adj.* (*econ.*) duty-free; **~ая торго́вля** free trade.

беспоща́д|ный (~ен, ~на) *adj.* merciless, relentless.

бесправи|е, я *nt.* 1 (*отсутствие законности*) lawlessness, arbitrariness. 2 (*отсутствие прав*) lack of rights.

беспра́в|ный (~ен, ~на) *adj.* without rights.

беспреде́л, а *m.* (*coll.*) lawlessness, scandalous practices; chaos, mayhem.

беспреде́л|ьный (~ен, ~ьна) *adj.* boundless, infinite.

беспрепя́тствен|ный (~, ~на) *adj.* free, clear, unimpeded.

беспрецеде́нт|ный (~ен, ~на) *adj.* unprecedented.

беспризо́рн|ый *adj.* (*бездомный*) homeless; *as n.* **б., ~ого** *m.* waif, urchin.

беспринци́п|ный (~ен, ~на) *adj.* unscrupulous, unprincipled.

беспристра́сти|е, я *nt.* impartiality.

беспристра́ст|ный (~ен, ~на) *adj.* impartial, unbias(s)ed.

беспро́игрыш|ный (~ен, ~на) *adj.* safe; risk-free.

беспросве́т|ный (~ен, ~на) *adj.* 1 pitch-dark; **~ная тьма** thick darkness. 2 (*fig.*) hopeless; unrelieved.

беспроце́нтный *adj.* (*fin.*) interest-free.

бессерде́ч|ный (~ен, ~на) *adj.* heartless; callous.

бесси́ли|е, я *nt.* (*слабость*) weakness; debility; (*fig.*) impotence.

бесси́л|ьный (~ен, ~ьна) *adj.* (*слабый*) weak; (*fig.*) impotent, powerless.

бессисте́м|ный (~ен, ~на) *adj.* unsystematic.

бесcла́в|ный (~ен, ~на) *adj.* ignominious; inglorious.

бессле́дно *adv.* without leaving a trace; completely.

бессле́д|ный (~ен, ~на) *adj.* without leaving a trace; **~ное исчезнове́ние** complete disappearance.

бесслове́с|ный (~ен, ~на) *adj.* dumb, speechless; (*fig.*) silent.

бессме́н|ный (~ен, ~на) *adj.* permanent; continuous.

бессме́рти|е, я *nt.* immortality.

бессме́рт|ный (~ен, ~на) *adj.* immortal; undying.

бессмы́слен|ный (~, ~на) *adj.* (*поступок*) senseless; foolish; (*слова*) meaningless, nonsensical; (*взгляд*) vacant.

бессо́вест|ный (~ен, ~на) *adj.* 1 (*нечестный*) unscrupulous, dishonest. 2 (*бесстыдный*) shameless, brazen.

бессодержа́тел|ьный (~ен, ~ьна) *adj.* (*жизнь*) empty; (*слова*) tame; dull.

бессозна́тел|ьный (~ен, ~ьна) *adj.* 1 unconscious. 2 (*непроизвольный*) involuntary.

бессо́нниц|а, ы *f.* insomnia, sleeplessness.

бессо́нный *adj.* sleepless.

бесспо́рно *adv.* indisputably; undoubtedly.

бесспо́р|ный (~ен, ~на) *adj.* indisputable, incontrovertible.

бессро́чный *adj.* without time limit; **б. о́тпуск** indefinite leave.

бесстра́ст|ный (~ен, ~на) *adj.* impassive.

бесстра́ш|ный (~ен, ~на) *adj.* fearless, intrepid.

бессты́д|ный (~ен, ~на) *adj.* shameless.

бессчёт|ный (~ен, ~на) *adj.* innumerable.

беста́ктност|ь, и *f.* 1 (*свойство*) tactlessness. 2 (*поступок*) tactless action, faux pas.

беста́кт|ный (~ен, ~на) *adj.* tactless.

бестолко́в|ый (~, ~а) *adj.* 1 (*человек*) slow-witted, muddle-headed. 2 (*объяснение*) disconnected, incoherent.

бестсе́ллер, а *m.* best-seller (*book*).

бесфо́рмен|ный (~, ~на) *adj.* shapeless, formless.

бесхара́ктер|ный (~ен, ~на) *adj.* weak-willed; spineless.

бесхи́трост|ный (~ен, ~на) *adj.* (*человек*) artless; (*слова*) ingenuous.

бесцве́т|ный (~ен, ~на) *adj.* colourless (*Br.*), colorless (*US*).

бесце́л|ьный (~ен, ~ьна) *adj.* aimless; idle.

бесце́н|ный (~ен, ~на) *adj.* 1 (*сокровища*) priceless. 2 (*опыт, совет*) invaluable.

бесцеремо́н|ный (~ен, ~на) *adj.* unceremonious; familiar; cavalier.

бесчелове́ч|ный (~ен, ~на) *adj.*

inhuman.

бесчéст|ный (~ен, ~на) *adj.* dishonourable (*Br.*), dishonorable (*US*); disgraceful.

бесчéсть|е, я *nt.* dishonour (*Br.*), dishonor (*US*); disgrace.

бесчíслен|ный (~, ~на) *adj.* innumerable.

бесчýвствен|ный (~, ~на) *adj.* 1 (*лишённый сознания*) insensible. 2 (*равнодушный*) insensitive, unfeeling.

бесшýм|ный (~ен, ~на) *adj.* noiseless.

бетóн, а *m.* (*tech.*) concrete.

бетóнный *adj.* (*tech.*) concrete.

бéшенств|о, а *nt.* 1 (*med.*) hydrophobia; rabies; **корóвье б.** mad cow disease. 2 (*fig.*) fury, rage; **довестí до ~а** to enrage.

бéшен|ый *adj.* 1 (*med.*) rabid, mad; **~ая собáка** mad dog. 2 (*fig.*) furious; violent; **~ая скóрость** furious pace; **~ые цéны** (*coll.*) exorbitant prices.

биатлóн, а *m.* biathlon.

биатлонíст, а *m.* biathlete, biathlon competitor.

биатлонíст|ка, ки *f.* *of* ▸ ~

библéйский *adj.* biblical.

библиогрáфи|я, и *f.* bibliography.

библиотéк|а, и *f.* library.

библиотéкар|ь, я *m.* librarian.

бíбли|я, и *f.* bible; **(Б.)** the Bible.

бигуд|í, éй *no sg.* (*also indecl.*) (hair) curlers.

бидé *nt. indecl.* bidet.

бидóн, а *m.* can; **б. для молокá** milk can, (milk) churn (*Br.*).

биéни|е, я *nt.* beating; throb; **б. сéрдца** heartbeat; **б. пýльса** pulse.

бижутéри|я, и *f.* costume jewellery.

бíзнес, а *m.* business; **реклáмный б.** advertising.

бизнесмéн, а *m.* businessman.

бикíни *nt. indecl.* bikini.

билéт, а *m.* ticket; (*удостоверение*) card; **входнóй б.** entrance ticket, permit; **едíный б.** rover ticket; **обрáтный б.** return ticket; **экзаменациóнный б.** examination question(-paper) (*at oral examination*).

биллиóн, а *m.* trillion (*one million million*).

бильярд, а *m.* 1 (*стол*) billiard table. 2 (*игра*) billiards.

бинóкл|ь, я *m.* binoculars; **полевóй б.** field glasses.

бинт, á *m.* bandage.

бинт|овáть, ýю *impf.* to bandage.

био... *comb. form* bio-.

биóграф, а *m.* biographer.

биографíческий *adj.* biographical.

биогрáфи|я, и *f.* biography; (*жизнь*) life story.

биóлог, а *m.* biologist.

биологíческий *adj.* biological.

биолóги|я, и *f.* biology.

биосфéр|а, ы *f.* biosphere.

биохíмик, а *m.* biochemist.

биохíми|я, и *f.* biochemistry.

бíрж|а, и *f.* exchange; **фóндовая б.** stock exchange; **б. трудá** jobcentre.

биржевíк, á *m.* (*fin., coll.*) stockbroker.

бирж|евóй *adj. of* ▸ **~а; б. мáклер** stockbroker.

бíрк|а, и *f.* tag, label.

Бíрм|а, ы *f.* (*hist.*) Burma.

бирюз|á, ы́ *no pl., f.* turquoise.

бирюзóвый *adj.* turquoise.

бисексуáльный *adj.* bisexual.

бисквíт, а *m.* sponge cake.

бит, а *m.* (*comput.*) bit.

бíт|а, ы *f.* (*sport*) bat.

бíтв|а, ы *f.* battle.

бить, бью, бьёшь *impf.* 1 (*pf.* **по~**) (*избивать*) to beat (*a person, an animal, etc.*). 2 (**удáрить** *used in place of pf.*) (*ударять*) to strike, hit; **б. в лицó** to strike, hit in the face (*also fig.*). 3 (*impf. only*) (*убивать*) to kill, slaughter (*animals*). 4 (*pf.* **раз~**) (*ломать*) to break, smash (*crockery, etc.*). 5 (*pf.* **про~**) (*издавать звуки*) to strike, sound; **б. отбóй** to beat a retreat (*also fig.*); **часы́ бьют пять** the clock is striking five. 6 (*impf. only*) (*вытекать*) to spurt, gush; **б. ключóм** to gush out, well up; (*fig.*) to be in full swing. 7 (*impf. only*) (*стрелять*) to shoot, fire; (*with firearms; also fig.*) to hit; to have a range (of); **б. в цель** to hit the target (*also fig.*); **б. навернякá** (*fig.*) to take no chances.

бíться, бьюсь, бьёшься *impf.* 1 (**с** + *i.*) (*драться*) to fight (with, against). 2 (*о сердце*) to beat; **сéрдце егó перестáло б.** his heart stopped beating. 3 (**о** + *a.*) (*ударяться*) to knock (against), hit (against), strike; **б. головóй об стéну** to bang one's head against a brick wall. 4 (*метаться*) to writhe, struggle; **б. в истéрике** to writhe in hysterics. 5 (**над** + *i.*; *fig.*) (*стараться изо всех сил*) to struggle (with), exercise o.s. (over); **б. над задáчей** to rack one's brains over a problem. 6 (*о стекле*) to break, smash; **легкó б.** to be very fragile. 7 : **б. об заклáд** to bet, wager.

бифштéкс, а *m.* beefsteak.

бíцепс, а *m.* (*anat.*) biceps.

бич, á *m.* whip; (*fig.*) scourge.

блáг|о[1], а *nt.* good, the good; blessing; **óбщее б.** the common weal; **всех благ!** (*coll.*) all the best!

блáго[2] *conj.* (*coll.*) since; seeing that; **скажíте емý сейчáс, б. он здесь** tell him now since he is here.

благовíд|ный (~ен, ~на) *adj.* plausible.

благодар|íть, ю́, íшь *impf.* (*of* ▸ **по~**) to thank; **~ю́ вас (за** + *a.*) thank you (for).

благодáрност|ь, и *f.* 1 gratitude; **не стóит ~и** don't mention it. 2 (*usu. pl.*) (*выражение благодарности*) thanks.

благода́р|ный (~ен, ~на) *adj.* 1 grateful. 2 (*стоящий*) rewarding; worthwhile.

благода́рственн|ый *adj.* expressing thanks; **~ое письмо́** letter of thanks.

благодаря́ *prep.* + *d.* thanks to, owing to, because of; **б. тому́, что** owing to the fact that.

благоде́тел|ь, я *m.* benefactor.

благоде́тельниц|а, ы *f.* benefactress.

благоду́ш|ный (~ен, ~на) *adj.* (*спокойный*) placid, equable; (*добродушный*) good-humoured (*Br.*), -humored (*US*).

благожела́тельност|ь, и *f.* goodwill; benevolence.

благожела́тел|ьный (~ен, ~ьна) *adj.* (*человек*) kind; well-disposed; (*приём, улыбка*) friendly, cordial; (*рецензия*) favourable (*Br.*), favorable (*US*).

благозву́ч|ный (~ен, ~на) *adj.* euphonious; (*голос*) melodious.

благ|о́й *adj.* good; **~ие наме́рения** good intentions.

благонадёжност|ь, и *f.* reliability, trustworthiness.

благонадёж|ный (~ен, ~на) *adj.* reliable, trustworthy.

благополу́чи|е, я *nt.* well-being; prosperity.

благополу́чно *adv.* well, all right; happily; (*в целости и сохранности*) safely.

благополу́ч|ный (~ен, ~на) *adj.* (*удачный*) successful; (*прибытие*) safe; **б. коне́ц** happy ending.

благоприя́т|ный (~ен, ~на) *adj.* favourable (*Br.*), favorable (*US*); **~ные ве́сти** good news.

благоприя́тств|овать, ую *impf.* (+ *d.*) to favour (*Br.*), favor (*US*).

благоразу́ми|е, я *nt.* prudence; sense.

благоразу́м|ный (~ен, ~на) *adj.* prudent; sensible.

благоро́д|ный (~ен, ~на) *adj.* noble; **б. мета́лл** precious metal.

благоро́дств|о, а *nt.* nobleness; nobility.

благоскло́нност|ь, и *f.* favour (*Br.*), favor (*US*); **по́льзоваться чьей-н. ~ью** to be in s.o.'s good graces.

благоскло́н|ный (~ен, ~на) *adj.* favourable (*Br.*), favorable (*US*); gracious.

благослове́ни|е, я *nt.* (*eccl. and fig.*) blessing; **с ~я** (+ *g.*) with the blessing (of).

благослов|и́ть, лю́, и́шь *pf.* (*of* ▸ **~ля́ть**) 1 (*перекрестить*) to bless; (*выразить одобрение*) to give one's blessing (to). 2 (*воздать благодарность*) to be grateful to; **б. свою́ судьбу́** to thank one's stars.

благослов|ля́ть, ля́ю *impf. of* ▸ **~и́ть**

благосостоя́ни|е, я *nt.* well-being, welfare.

благотвори́тел|ь, я *m.* (*лицо*) philanthropist; (*организация*) charity.

благотвори́тельниц|а, ы *f. of* ▸ **благотвори́тель**

благотвори́тельност|ь, и *f.* charity, philanthropy.

благотвори́тельный *adj.* charitable, philanthropic; **б. спекта́кль** charity performance.

благотво́р|ный (~ен, ~на) *adj.* beneficial; wholesome, salutary.

благоустра́ива|ть, ю *impf. of* ▸ **благоустро́ить**

благоустро́ен|ный (~, ~на) *adj. and* (**~, ~а**) *p.p.p. of* ▸ **благоустро́ить** well-equipped; comfortable; **б. дом** house with all modern conveniences.

благоустро́|ить, ю, ишь *pf.* (*of* ▸ **благоустра́ивать**) to equip with services and utilities.

благоустро́йств|о, а *nt.* equipping with services and utilities.

благочести́в|ый (~, ~а) *adj.* pious, devout.

благоче́сти|е, я *nt.* piety.

блаже́нств|о, а *nt.* bliss.

бланк, а *m.* form; **анке́тный б.** questionnaire; **фи́рменный б.** sheet of headed notepaper; **запо́лнить б.** to fill in a form.

блат, а *m.* (*coll.*) pull, string-pulling; **получи́ть по ~́у** to obtain through connections.

блатн|о́й *adj.* (*coll.*) (*достающийся по блату*) obtained through string-pulling; (*человек*) string-pulling; (*язык, музыка*) criminal, thieves'; *as n.* (**б., ~о́го**) (*пользующийся блатом*) string-puller; (*связанный с преступным миром*) criminal.

бл|ева́ть, ю́ю, юёшь *impf.* (*sl.*) to puke, spew (*both coll.*).

бледне́|ть, ю, ешь *impf.* (*of* ▸ **по~**) to grow pale; to pale.

бле́дност|ь, и *f.* paleness, pallor; (*fig.*) dullness.

бле́д|ный (~ен, ~на́, ~но) *adj.* pale, pallid; **б. как полотно́** white as a sheet; (*fig.*) colourless (*Br.*), colorless (*US*), insipid, dull.

блеск, а *m.* brightness, brilliance, shine; (*fig.*) splendour (*Br.*), splendor (*US*), magnificence; (*as int., sl.*) **б.!** brilliant!; great!; super!; **во всём ~́е** in all (one's) glory.

блесн|у́ть, у́, ёшь *pf.* to flash; **в моей голове́ ~у́ла мысль** a thought flashed across my mind.

бле|сте́ть, щу́, сти́шь *and* **~́щешь** *impf.* to shine; to glitter; to sparkle; **её глаза́ ~сте́ли ра́достью** her eyes shone with joy; **он не ~́щет умо́м** he's no genius.

блестя́щ|ий (~, ~а, ~е) *pres. part. of* ▸ **блесте́ть** *and adj.* shining, bright; (*fig.*) brilliant.

бле|щу́, ~́щешь *see* ▸ **~сте́ть**

бле́|ять, ю, ешь *impf.* to bleat.

ближа́йш|ий *superl. of* ▸ **бли́зкий;** (*город, почта*) nearest; (*день, год*) next; (*задача*) immediate; **в ~ем бу́дущем** in the near future; **б. друг** closest friend; **б. ро́дственник** next of kin; **при ~ем рассмотре́нии** on closer examination.

бли́|же *comp. of* ▸ **~зкий, ~зко** nearer; (*fig.*) closer.

ближневосто́чный *adj.* Middle East; Middle Eastern.

бли́жн|ий *adj.*
1 (*близкий*) near; (*соседний*) neighbouring (*Br.*), neighboring (*US*); **Б. Восто́к** Middle East.
2 (*mil.*) short range, close range.
3 (*родственник*) close; *as n.* **б., ~его** *m.* (*fig.*) one's neighbour (*Br.*), neighbor (*US*).
4 (*путь*) shortest.

бли́з|иться, ится *impf.* to approach, draw near.

бли́з|кий (~ок, ~ка́, ~ко, ~ки́) *adj.*
1 (*место*) nearby, close; **на ~ком расстоя́нии** a short way off; at close range.
2 (*конец*) near; imminent.
3 (*в тесных отношениях*) intimate, close; **б. друг** close friend; **быть ~ким с кем-н.** to be on intimate terms with s.o.; **быть ~ким** (+ *d.*) to be dear (to); *as n.* **~кие, ~ких** one's nearest and dearest.
4 (*похожий*) (**к** + *d.*) like; similar (to); close (to); **б. нам по ду́ху челове́к** kindred spirit.

бли́зко *adv.*
1 (**от** + *g.*) near close (to); close by.
2 *as pred.* it is not far.

близлежа́щий *adj.* neighbouring (*Br.*), neighboring (*US*), nearby.

близне́ц, а́ *m.* twin (*also triplet, etc.*); **Б~ы́** (*созвездие*) Gemini.

близору́к|ий (~, ~а) *adj.* short-sighted (*Br.*), nearsighted (*US*) (*also fig.*).

бли́зост|ь, и *f.* nearness, proximity; (*близкие отношения*) intimacy.

блик, а *m.* spot/speck/patch of light; **со́лнечный б.** patch of sunlight.

блин, а́ *m.* pancake; **пе́рвый б. ко́мом** (*prov.*) practice makes perfect; *excl.* (*sl.*) damn!; shit! (*vulg.*).

блиста́тел|ьный (~ен, ~ьна) *adj.* brilliant, splendid.

блиста́|ть, ю *impf.* to shine.

блог, а *m.* (*comput.*) blog, weblog.

бло́ггер, а *m.* (*comput.*) blogger, weblogger.

блок[1], а *m.* (*tech.*) block, pulley.

блок[2], а *m.* (*pol.*) bloc.

блок[3], а *m.* carton (of cigarettes); unit; **б. пита́ния** power supply (unit).

блока́д|а, ы *f.* blockade; **снять ~у** to raise the blockade.

блоки́р|овать, ую *impf. and pf.*
1 to blockade.
2 (*sport*) to block.

блокно́т, а *m.* notebook, notepad.

блокпо́ст, а́, о ~е́, на ~у́ *m.* checkpoint.

блонди́н, а *m.* fair-haired man.

блонди́нк|а, и *f.* blonde (woman).

блох|а́, и́, *pl.* **~̂и,** *d.* **~а́м** *and* **~ам** *f.* flea; **иска́ть ~** to nit-pick (*fig.*).

бло́чный *adj.* modular.

блужда́|ть, ю *impf.* to roam, wander; to rove; **б. по у́лицам** to roam the streets.

блужда́|ющий *pres. part. of* ▸ **~ть; б. огонёк** will-o'-the-wisp.

блу́зк|а, и *f.* blouse.

блю́д|о, а *nt.* dish; **обе́д из трёх ~** three-course dinner; **вку́сное б.** a tasty dish.

блю́д|це, ца, *g. pl.* **~ец** *nt.* saucer.

блюз, а *m.* (*mus.*) the blues.

блю|сти́, ду́, дёшь, *past* **~л, ~ла́** *impf.* to guard, watch over; **б. поря́док** to keep order.

блюсти́тел|ь, я *m.* keeper, guardian; **б. поря́дка** (*coll.*, *iron.*) arm of the law.

бляд|ь, и, *g. pl.* **~е́й** *n.* (*vulg.*) (*женщина*) whore; (*мужчина*) bastard; (*as int.*) fuck!

боб, а́ *m.* bean.

боб|ёр, ра́ *m.* (*мех*) beaver (fur).

бобр, а́ *m.* beaver.

Бог, а, *voc. sg.* **Бо́же** *m.* God; god; **бо́же мой!** good God!, my God!; **б. зна́ет!, б. весть!** God knows!; **б. его́ зна́ет!** who knows!; **не дай б.!** God forbid!; **ра́ди ~̂а!** for God's sake!; **б. с ним!** blow it; **сла́ва ~̂у** thank God!

богате́|ть, ю, ешь *impf.* (*of* ▸ **раз~**) to grow rich.

бога́тств|о, а *nt.*
1 riches, wealth; **есте́ственные ~а** natural resources.
2 (*fig.*) richness, wealth.

бога́т|ый (~, ~а) *adj.* (+ *i.*) rich (in), wealthy; **~ая расти́тельность** luxuriant vegetation; **б. о́пыт** wide experience; *as n.* **б., ~ого** *m.* rich man.

богаты́р|ь, я́ *m.*
1 bogatyr (*hero in Russian folklore*).
2 (*fig.*) Hercules; hero.

бога́ч, а́ *m.* rich man; **~и́** (*collect.*) the rich.

боге́м|а, ы *f.* (*collect.*) Bohemians; (*образ жизни*) Bohemianism.

боге́м|ный *adj. of* ▸ **~а**

боги́н|я, и *f.* goddess (*also fig.*).

Богоро́диц|а, ы *f.* the Virgin, Our Lady.

богосло́ви|е, я *nt.* theology.

богосло́вский *adj.* theological.

богослуже́ни|е, я *nt.* divine service, worship; liturgy.

боготвор|и́ть, ю́, и́шь *impf.* to worship, idolize.

богоху́льств|о, а *nt.* blasphemy.

бо́дрост|ь, и *f.* cheerfulness; good spirits; (*мужество*) courage.

бо́дрствовани|е, я *nt.* keeping awake; vigilance.

бо́дрств|овать, ую *impf.* to stay awake; to keep vigil.

бо́др|ый (~, ~а́, ~о, ~ы́) *adj.* cheerful, bright; (*старик*) hale and hearty.

боеви́к, а́ *m.*
1 (*солдат*) fighter; militant.
2 (*coll.*) (*остросюжетный фильм*) action movie, thriller.

боев|о́й *adj.*
1 military, fighting, battle; **~ы́е де́йствия** operations; **б. дух** fighting spirit; **~о́е креще́ние** baptism of fire; **б. патро́н** live cartridge.
2 (*coll.*) (*воинственный*) militant; energetic.

боеголо́вк|а, и *f.* (*mil.*) warhead.

боеприпа́с|ы, ов *no sg.* ammunition.

боеспосо́б|ный (~ен, ~на) *adj.* (*mil.*) battle-worthy.

бо|е́ц, йца́ *m.* (*участник боя*) fighter; (*солдат*) private soldier.

Бо́же *see* ▶ **Бог**

боже́ствен|ный (~, ~на) *adj.* divine (*also fig.*).

божеств|о́, а́ *nt.* deity, divine being.

бо́ж|ий, ья, ье *adj.* God's; **я́сно как б. день** it is as clear as could be; **~ья коро́вка** (*zool.*) ladybird.

бо|й, я, *pl.* **~и́, ~ёв** *m.*
1 (*сражение*) battle, fight, action, combat; **~и́** fighting; **в ~ю́** in action.
2 (*часов*) striking, strike; **бараба́нный б.** drumbeat.
3 (*убой*) killing, slaughtering; **б. кито́в** whaling.

бо́|йкий (~ек, ~йка́, ~йко) *adj.*
1 (*дерзкий*) bold, spry, smart; **б. ум** ready wit; **б. язы́к** glib tongue.
2 (*живой*) lively, animated; **~йкая торго́вля** brisk trade; **~йкая у́лица** busy street.

бойко́т, а *m.* boycott; **объяви́ть б.** (+ *d.*) to declare a boycott (of).

бойкоти́р|овать, ую *impf.* to boycott.

бо́йн|я, и, *g. pl.* **бо́ен** *f.* slaughterhouse, abattoir; (*fig.*) slaughter, butchery, carnage.

бо́йче *comp. of* ▶ **бо́йкий, бо́йко**

бойче́е = **бо́йче**

бок, а, о ~е, на ~у́, *pl.* **~а́** *m.* side; flank; **в б.** sideways; **схвати́ться за ~а́ (от сме́ха)** to split one's sides (with laughter); **на́ б.** sideways, to the side; **на ~у́** on one side; **б. о́ б.** side by side; **под ~ом** nearby, close at hand; **с ~у** from the side, from the flank.

бока́л, а *m.* (wine)glass, goblet; **подня́ть б.** (**за** + *a.*) to drink the health (of), raise one's glass (to).

боков|о́й *adj.* side, flank, lateral, sidelong; **~а́я у́лица** side street.

бо́ком *adv.* sideways; **ходи́ть б.** to sidle.

бокс[1]**, а** *m.* (*sport*) boxing.

бокс[2]**, а** *m.* (*в больнице*) cubicle.

боксёр, а *m.* (*спортсмен; собака*) boxer.

болва́нк|а, и *f.*
1 (*tech.*) pig (*of iron, etc.*).
2 (*компактный диск*) blank CD, DVD.

болга́р|ин, ина, *pl.* **~ы, ~** *m.* Bulgarian.

Болга́ри|я, и *f.* Bulgaria.

болга́р|ка, ки *f. of* ▶ **~ин**

болга́рский *adj.* Bulgarian.

болев|о́й *adj. of* ▶ **боль; ~о́е ощуще́ние** sensation of pain.

бо́лее *adv.* more; **б. то́лстый** thicker; **б. того́** and what is more; **б. и́ли ме́нее** more or less; **не б. и не ме́нее, как** neither more nor less than; **б. всего́** most of all; **тем б., что** especially as.

боле́знен|ный (~, ~на) *adj.*
1 (*нездоровый*) sickly; unhealthy; (*fig.*) abnormal, morbid; **~ное любопы́тство** morbid curiosity.
2 (*вызывающий боль*) painful.

боле́зн|ь, и *f.* illness; disease; (*fig.*) abnormality; **б. Да́уна** Down's syndrome; **б. Паркинсо́на** Parkinson's disease; **б. ро́ста** growing pains; **морска́я б.** seasickness.

боле́льщик, а *m.* (*coll.*) fan, supporter.

боле́льщи|ца, цы *f. of* ▶ **~к**

боле́|ть[1]**, ю, ешь** *impf.*
1 (+ *i.*) to be ill, be down (with); (*intrans.*) to ail; **она́ с де́тства ~ет а́стмой** she has suffered from asthma ever since she was a child; **б. душо́й** (**за** + *a.*) to be worried (about).
2 (**за** + *a.*; *coll.*) to be a fan (of), support.

бол|е́ть[2]**,** *1st and 2nd persons not used,* **~и́т** *impf.* to ache, hurt; **у меня́ зу́бы ~я́т** I have toothache.

болеутоля́ющ|ий *adj.* soothing, analgesic; **~ее сре́дство** (*med.*) painkiller, analgesic.

боливи́|ец, йца *m.* Bolivian.

боливи́|йка, йки *f. of* ▶ **~ец**

боливи́йский *adj.* Bolivian.

Боли́ви|я, и *f.* Bolivia.

боло́тист|ый (~, ~а) *adj.* marshy, boggy, swampy.

боло́тн|ый *adj.* marsh; **~ая лихора́дка** marsh fever, malaria.

боло́т|о, а *nt.* marsh, bog, swamp; **торфяно́е б.** peat bog; (*fig.*) mire, slough.

болт, а́ *m.* (*tech.*) bolt.

болта́|ть[1]**, ю** *impf.*
1 (*мешать*) to stir; (*взбалтывать*) to shake.
2 (+ *i.*) (*ногами*) to dangle.

болта́|ть[2]**, ю** *impf.* (*coll.*) to chatter, jabber (away); **б. глу́пости** to talk nonsense; **б. по-францу́зски** to jabber away in French.

болта́|ться, юсь *impf.* (*coll.*)
1 (*качаться*) to dangle, swing; to hang loosely.
2 (*слоняться*) to hang about, loaf.

болтли́в|ый (~, ~а) *adj.* garrulous, talkative; (*бестактный*) indiscreet.

болтовн|я́, и́ *f.* (*coll.*) chatter; (*сплетня*) gossip.

болту́н, а́ *m.* (*coll.*)
1 (*пустослов*) chatterbox; gasbag.
2 (*сплетник*) gossip.

бол|ь, и *f.* pain; ache; **б. в боку́** stitch; **зубна́я б.** toothache; **душе́вная б.** mental anguish.

больни́ц|а, ы *f.* hospital; **лечь в ~у** to go to hospital; **лежа́ть в ~е** to be in hospital.

больни́|чный *adj. of* ▶ **~ца; б. лист** medical certificate.

бо́льно *adv.*
1 painfully, badly; **б. ушиби́ться** to be badly bruised.
2 *as pred.* it is painful (*also fig.*); **мне б. дыша́ть** it hurts me to breathe.

бол|ьно́й (~ен, ~ьна́) *adj.* (*человек*) ill, sick; (*орган*) diseased; (*часть тела*) sore (*also fig.*); **~ьны́е дёсны** sore gums; **б. зуб** bad tooth; **он тяжело́ ~ен** he is seriously ill; **б. вопро́с** sore subject; **~ьно́е ме́сто** sore spot; *as n.* **б., ~ьно́го** *m.*, **~ьна́я, ~ьно́й** *f.* patient, invalid; **амбулато́рный б.** outpatient; **стациона́рный б.** inpatient.

бо́льше
1 (*comp. of* ▶ **большо́й** *and* ▶ **вели́кий**) bigger, larger; (*об отвлечённых понятиях*) greater; **Ло́ндон б. Пари́жа** London is larger than Paris.
2 (*comp. of* ▶ **мно́го**) more; **чем б. ..., тем б.** the more ... the more; **б. не** no more, no

б

longer; **он б. не живёт на той у́лице** he does not live in that street any longer; **б. не бу́ду!** I won't do it again!; **б. нет вопро́сов?** any more questions?; **б. у** (+ *g.*) (*tennis*) advantage.

большеви́к, а́ *m.* Bolshevik.

бо́льш|ий *comp. of* ▸ **~о́й** *and* ▸ **вели́кий;** greater, larger; **по ~ей ча́сти** for the most part; **са́мое ~ее** at most.

большинств|о́, а́ *nt.* majority; most (of); **в ~е́ слу́чаев** in most cases; **б. голосо́в** a majority vote.

больш|о́й *adj.* (*по величине*) big, large; (*значительный; важный*) great; (*coll.*) (*взрослый*) grown-up; **~а́я бу́ква** capital (letter); **~а́я доро́га** high road; **б. па́лец** thumb; **б. па́лец ноги́** big toe; **б. свет** haut monde, society; **когда́ я бу́ду б.** when I grow up.

боля́чк|а, и *f.* sore; scab; (*fig.*) defect.

бо́мб|а, ы *f.* bomb; **кассе́тная б.** cluster bomb.

бомбардиро́вк|а, и *f.* bombardment; bombing; **ковро́вая б.** carpet bombing.

бомбардиро́вщик, а *m.*
1 (*самолёт*) bomber; **пики́рующий б.** dive-bomber.
2 (*coll.*) (*лётчик*) bomber pilot.

бомб|и́ть, лю́, и́шь *impf.* to bomb.

бомбоубе́жищ|е, а *nt.* air-raid shelter, bomb shelter.

бомж, а *m.* (*abbr. of* **без определённого ме́ста жи́тельства**) homeless person, vagrant.

бор, а, о ~е, в ~у́, *pl.* **~ы́, ~о́в** *m.* coniferous forest (*usu. pine*).

борде́л|ь, я *m.* (*coll.*) brothel.

бордо́вый *adj.* claret-coloured (*Br.*), -colored (*US*).

бордю́р, а *m.* border.

бор|е́ц, ца́ *m.*
1 (**за** + *a.*) fighter (for); campaigner; activist; **б. за права́ же́нщин** women's liberationist.
2 (*sport*) wrestler.

борз|а́я, о́й *f.*: **англи́йская б.** greyhound; **ру́сская б.** borzoi, Russian wolfhound.

бормаши́н|а, ы *f.* (dentist's) drill.

бормота́ни|е, я *nt.* muttering.

бормо|та́ть, чу́, ~чешь *impf.* (*of* ▸ **про~**) to mutter.

борм|очу́, о́чешь *see* ▸ **~ота́ть**

Борне́о *nt. indecl.* Borneo.

бо́ров, а *m.* hog.

бор|ода́, о́ды, *a.* **~оду,** *pl.* **~оды, ~о́д, ~ода́м** *f.* beard.

борода́вк|а, и *f.* wart.

борода́т|ый (~, ~а) *adj.* bearded.

бор|озда́, озды́, *a.* **~озду** *and* **~озду́,** *pl.* **~озды, ~о́зд, ~озда́м** *f.* furrow.

бороз|ди́ть, жу́, ди́шь *impf.* (*of* ▸ **из~**) to furrow.

бор|о́ться, ю́сь, ~ешься *impf.* (**с** + *i.*; **за** + *a.*; **про́тив** + *g.*) to wrestle; (*fig.*) to struggle, fight (with; for; against).

борт, а, о ~е, на ~у́, *pl.* **~а́, ~о́в** *m.* (*судна, грузовика*) side; **на ~у́** on board (*ship or aircraft*); **вы́бросить за́ б.** to throw overboard (*also fig.*).

борт|ово́й *adj. of* ▸ **~; б. журна́л** (ship's) logbook.

бортпроводни́к, а́ *m.* air steward.

бортпроводни́ц|а, ы *f.* stewardess; air hostess (*Br.*).

борщ, а́ *m.* (*cul.*) bor(t)sch.

борьб|а́, ы́ *f.*
1 (*sport*) wrestling.
2 (*fig.*) (**с** + *i.*; **за** + *a.*; **про́тив** + *g.*) struggle, fight (with; for; against); conflict; **душе́вная б.** mental strife; **кампа́ния по ~е́ с престу́пностью** crime-prevention campaign.

босано́в|а, ы *f.* (*танец, музыка*) bossa nova.

босико́м *adv.* barefoot; **ходи́ть б.** to go barefoot.

Бо́сни|я и Герцегови́н|а, ~и и ~ы *f.* Bosnia–Herzegovina, Bosnia and Herzegovina.

бос|о́й (~, ~а́, ~о) *adj.* barefooted; **на ~у но́гу** with bare feet, barefoot.

босоно́ж|ки, ек *pl.* (*sg.* **~а, ~и** *f.*) sandals; (*без задников*) mules.

босс, а *m.* boss.

Босфо́р, а *m.* the Bosporus.

бота́ник, а *m.* botanist.

бота́ник|а, и *f.* botany.

ботани́ческий *adj.* botanical; **б. сад** botanical gardens.

боти́н|ок, ка, *g. pl.* **б.** *m.* (*ankle-high*) boot.

бо́цман, а *m.* (*naut.*) boatswain.

бо́чк|а, и *f.* barrel, cask.

бочо́н|ок, ка *m.* small barrel, keg.

боязли́в|ый (~, ~а) *adj.* timid, timorous.

боя́зн|ь, и *f.* (+ *g.*) fear (of), dread of; **б. темноты́** fear of the dark; **из ~и** for fear of, lest.

боя́рышник, а *m.* (*bot.*) hawthorn.

бо|я́ться, ю́сь, и́шься *impf.* (+ *g.*)
1 (*испытывать страх*) to fear, be afraid (of); **она́ ~и́тся темноты́** she is afraid of the dark; **он ~и́тся пойти́ к врачу́** he is afraid to go to the doctor; **~ю́сь, что он (не) прие́дет** I am afraid that he will (not) come; **~ю́сь, как бы он не прие́хал** I am afraid that he may come.
2 (*не переносить*) to be afraid of, suffer from; **э́ти расте́ния ~я́тся хо́лода** these plants do not like the cold.

бра́вый *adj.* gallant; manly.

брази́л|ец, ьца *m.* Brazilian.

Брази́ли|я, и *f.* Brazil.

брази́льский *adj.* Brazilian.

бразил|ья́нка, ья́нки *f. of* ▸ **~ец**

брак[1]**, а** *m.* (*супружество*) marriage; matrimony; **свиде́тельство о ~е** certificate of marriage.

брак[2]**, а** *m.* (*продукция*) rejects; (*изъян*) defect.

брако́ван|ный (~, ~а) *p.p.p. of* ▸ **бракова́ть** *and adj.* rejected; defective.

брак|ова́ть, у́ю *impf.* (*of* ▸ **за~**) to reject.

браконье́р, а *m.* poacher.

браконье́рств|о, а *nt.* poaching.

бракоразво́дный *adj.* divorce; **б. проце́сс** divorce suit.

бракосочета́ни|е, я *nt.* wedding, wedding ceremony.

бра́нн|ый *adj.* abusive; **~ое сло́во** swear word.

бран|ь, и *f.* swearing; abuse; bad language.

брасле́т, а *m.* bracelet.

брасс, а *m.* (*sport*) breast stroke.

брат, а, *pl.* **~ья, ~ьев** *m.*
1 brother; **сво́дный б.** stepbrother; **единокро́вный б.** half-brother (*by father*); **единоутро́бный б.** half-brother (*by mother*); **двою́родный б.** cousin.
2 (*fig.*) brother; comrade; **~ья-писа́тели** fellow-writers.

бра́тск|ий *adj.* brotherly, fraternal; **~ая моги́ла** communal grave (*esp. of war dead*).

бра́тств|о, а *nt.* (*abstr. and concr.*) brotherhood, fraternity.

бра|ть, беру́, берёшь, *past* **~л, ~ла́, ~ло** *impf.* (*of* ▶ **взять**)
1 (*in var. senses*) to take; **б. наза́д** to take back; **б. курс (на** + *a.*) to make (for), head (for); **б. нача́ло (в** + *p.*) to originate (in); **б. но́ту** to sing, play a note; **б. приме́р (с** + *g.*) to follow the example (of); **б. сло́во** to take the floor; **б. в плен** to take prisoner; **б. на себя́** to take upon o.s.; **б. под аре́ст** to put under arrest.
2 (*получить*) to get, obtain; (*принимать*) to take on; **б. верх** to get the upper hand; **б. такси́** to take a taxi; **б. своё** to get one's way; to make itself felt; **го́ды беру́т своё** age tells; **б. взаймы́** to borrow; **б. в аре́нду** to rent; **б. напрока́т** to hire.
3 (**в** + *nom.-a.*) to take (as); **б. в жёны** to take to wife.
4 (*захватить*) to seize; to grip; **б. власть** to seize power.
5 (*требовать*) to exact; to take (= *to demand, require*); **б. штраф** to exact a fine.
6 (*преодолевать*) to take; to surmount; **б. барье́р** to clear a hurdle.
7 (+ *adv. of place*; *coll.*) to bear; **б. вле́во** to bear left.

бра́|ться, беру́сь, берёшься, *past* **~лся, ~ла́сь, ~ло́сь** *impf.* (*of* ▶ **взя́ться**)
1 *pass. of* ▶ **~ть.**
2 (**за** + *a.*) (*трогать*) to touch, lay hands (upon); **б. за́ руки** to link arms.
3 (**за** + *a.*) (*приниматься*) to take up; to get down (to); **б. за де́ло** to get down to business.
4 (**за** + *a. or* + *inf.*) (*принимать на себя*) to undertake; to take upon o.s.; **б. за поруче́ние** to undertake a commission; **б. вы́полнить рабо́ту** to undertake a job; **не беру́сь суди́ть** I do not presume to judge.
5 (*3rd person only*) (*coll.*) (*появляться*) to appear, arise; **не зна́ю, отку́да у них де́ньги беру́тся** I don't know where they get their money from.
6 : **б. за ум** (*coll.*) to come to one's senses.

бра́т|ья *see* ▶ **~**

бра́узер, а *m.* (*comput.*) browser.

бра́чн|ый *adj.* marriage; conjugal; **б. во́зраст** marriageable age; **~ая конто́ра** marriage bureau; **~ое свиде́тельство** marriage certificate.

брев|но́, на́, *pl.* **~на, ~ен, ~нам** *nt.* log, beam; (*sport*) caber; (*fig.*) (*тупой человек*) dullard, insensitive person.

бред, а, о ~е, в ~у́, *m.* delirium; ravings; (*fig.*) gibberish; **быть в ~у́** to be delirious.

бре́|дить, жу, дишь *impf.* to be delirious, rave.

бредо́вый *adj.* crackpot, crazy.

бре́|жу, дишь *see* ▶ **~дить**

брезгли́в|ый (~, ~а) *adj.* squeamish, fastidious; **~ое чу́вство** feeling of disgust.

брезе́нт, а *m.* tarpaulin.

брело́к, а *m.* (*bracelet*) charm; **б. для ключе́й** key ring.

бре́м|я, ~ени, *i.* **~енем, о ~ени** *nt.* burden; load.

бренд, а *m.* (*comm.*) brand.

бре́ндинг, а *m.* (*comm.*) branding.

бренч|а́ть, у́, и́шь *impf.*
1 (+ *i.*) to jingle.
2 (*coll.*) (*играть*) to strum.

бре́|ю, ешь *see* ▶ **бри́ть**

брига́д|а, ы *f.*
1 (*mil.*) brigade; (*naut.*) subdivision.
2 (*группа рабочих*) brigade, (work) team.

бригади́р, а *m.* team leader; foreman.

брига́д|ный *adj. of* ▶ **~а**

бридж, а *m.* bridge (*card game*).

брике́т, а *m.* briquette.

бриллиа́нт, а *m.* (cut) diamond.

бриллиа́нт|овый *adj. of* ▶ **~**

брита́н|ец, ца *m.* Briton; **~цы** the British.

Брита́ни|я, и *f.* Britain.

брита́н|ка, ки *f. of* ▶ **~ец**

Брита́нск|ие остров|а́, ~их ~о́в *no sg.* the British Isles.

брита́нский *adj.* British.

бри́тв|а, ы *f.* razor.

бри́твенн|ый *adj.* shaving; **~ые принадле́жности** shaving things.

бритоголо́в|ый *adj.* shaven-headed; *as n.* **б., ~ого** *m.* skinhead.

бри́т|ый (~, ~а) *p.p.p. of* ▶ **~ь** *and adj.* clean-shaven.

бр|ить, е́ю, е́ешь *impf.* (*of* ▶ **по~**) to shave.

брить|ё, я́ *nt.* shave; (*процесс*) shaving; **лосьо́н по́сле ~я́** aftershave.

бр|и́ться, е́юсь, е́ешься *impf.* (*of* ▶ **по~**) to shave, have a shave.

бров|ь, и, *pl.* **~и, ~е́й** *f.* eyebrow; brow; **хму́рить ~и** to knit one's brows, frown.

брод, а *m.* ford.

бро|ди́ть[1], жу́, ~дишь *impf.* (*гулять*) to wander, roam.

бро|ди́ть[2], ~дит *impf.* (*о пиве*) to ferment.

бродя́г|а, и *c.g.* tramp, vagrant; down-and-out.

бродя́ч|ий *adj.* vagrant; wandering, roving; (*fig.*) restless; **~ая соба́ка** stray dog.

броже́ни|е, я *nt.* fermentation.

бро|жу́, ~дишь *see* ▶ **~ди́ть[1]**

бро́кер, а *m.* broker; **биржево́й б.** stockbroker.

бро́кколи *f. indecl.* broccoli.

броне... *comb. form* (*mil.*) armoured- (*Br.*), armored- (*US*).

б

броневи́к, а́ *m.* armoured car (*Br.*), armored car (*US*).
бронев|о́й *adj.* armoured (*Br.*), armored (*US*); **~ые пли́ты** (*mil.*) armour plating (*Br.*), armor plating (*US*).
бронежиле́т, а *m.* bulletproof vest.
броненó́с|ец, ца *m.* (*naut.*) battleship.
бронетранспортёр, а *m.* armoured (*Br.*), armored (*US*) personnel carrier.
бро́нз|а, ы *f.* bronze.
бро́нзовый *adj.* bronze; (*загорелый*) tanned; **б. век** the Bronze Age; **б. зага́р** sunburn, suntan.
брони́рова|нный *p.p.p. of* ▸ **~ть** *and adj.* reserved.
брониро́в|анный *p.p.p. of* ▸ **~а́ть** *and adj.* armoured (*Br.*), armored (*US*).
брони́р|овать, ую *impf.* (*of* ▸ **за~**) to reserve, book.
бронир|ова́ть, у́ю *impf. and pf.* to armour (*Br.*), armor (*US*).
бронхи́т, а *m.* bronchitis.
брон|ь, и *f.* (*coll.*) reservation.
брон|я́, и́ *f.* armour (*Br.*), armor (*US*); armour plating (*Br.*), armor plating (*US*).
броса́|ть, ю *impf.* (*of* ▸ **бро́сить**)
1 (*метать*) to throw, cast, fling; **б. взгляд** to dart a glance; **б. обвине́ния** to hurl accusations; **б. тень** to cast a shadow; **б. на ве́тер** to throw away, waste.
2 (*покинуть*) to leave, abandon, desert; **б. му́жа** to desert one's husband; **б. рабо́ту** to give up, throw up one's work.
3 (+ *inf.*) (*переставать*) to give up, leave off; **он бро́сил кури́ть** he gave up smoking.
брос|а́ться, а́юсь *impf.*
1 (*impf. only*) (+ *i.*) to throw at one another, pelt one another (with).
2 (*impf. only*) (+ *i.*) to throw away; **б. деньга́ми** to throw away, squander one's money.
3 (*pf.* **~́иться**) **(на, в** + *a.*) to throw o.s. (on, upon), rush (to); **б. на коле́ни** to fall on one's knees; **б. в объя́тия** (+ *d.*) to fall into the arms (of); **б. на по́мощь** to rush to assistance.
4 (*pf.* **~́иться**): **б. в глаза́** to be striking, arrest attention.
5 (*pf.* **~́иться**) (+ *inf.*) to begin, start.
бро́|сить, шу, сишь *pf. of* ▸ **~са́ть; ~сь(те)!** stop it!
бро́|ситься, шусь, сишься *pf. of* ▸ **~са́ться**
брос|о́к, ка́ *m.*
1 (*взмах руки*) throw; **штрафно́й б.** (*sport*) free throw.
2 (*скачок*) bound; spurt.
бро́|шу, сишь *see* ▸ **~сить**
брош|ь, и *f.* brooch.
брошю́р|а, ы *f.* pamphlet; (*рекламная*) brochure.
брус, а, *pl.* **~́ья, ~́ьев** *m.* beam; **паралле́льные ~́ья** (*sport*) parallel bars.
брусни́к|а, и *f.* cowberry (*Vaccinium vitis-idaea*).
брус|о́к, ка́ *m.* bar; ingot; **точи́льный б.** whetstone.
бру́тто *adj. indecl.* gross; **вес б.** gross weight.
бры́з|гать, жу, жешь *impf.* (*of* ▸ **~нуть**) (+ *i.*)
1 to splash, spatter; (*забить струёй*) to gush, spurt.
2 (*pres.* **~жу** *or* **~гаю**) (*окроплять*) to sprinkle.
бры́зга|ться, юсь *impf.* (*coll.*) to splash; to splash o.s., one another.
бры́зг|и, ~ *no sg.* spray, splashes.
бры́з|жу, жешь *see* ▸ **~гать**
бры́з|нуть, ну, нешь *inst. pf. of* ▸ **~гать**
брыка́|ться, юсь *impf.* (*ребёнок*) to kick; (*лошадь*) to buck; (*fig.*) to kick, rebel.
брюзж|а́ть, у́, и́шь *impf.* to grumble.
брю́к|и, ~ *no sg.* trousers; **б.-ю́бка** culottes.
брюне́т, а *m.* dark-haired man.
брюне́тк|а, и *f.* brunette.
Брюссе́л|ь, я *m.* Brussels.
брюссе́льск|ий *adj.* Brussels; **~ая капу́ста** Brussels sprouts.
брю́х|о, а, *pl.* **~и** *nt.* (*coll.*) belly; (*большой живот*) paunch.
брюшно́й *adj.* abdominal; **б. тиф** typhoid (fever).
БТР (*abbr. of* ▸ **бронетранспортёр**) APC (*armoured personnel carrier*).
бу́б|ен, на *m.* tambourine.
бу́б|ны[1] *pl. of* ▸ **~ен**
бу́б|ны[2], **ен** *pl.* (*sg. coll.* **~на, ~ны** *f.*) (*в картах*)
1 diamonds; **дво́йка ~ен** the two of diamonds.
2 (*sg.*) a diamond.
бу́ги-ву́ги *nt. indecl.* boogie-woogie.
Будапе́шт, а *m.* Budapest.
будди́зм, а *m.* Buddhism.
будди́йский *adj.* Buddhist.
будди́ст, а *m.* Buddhist.
будди́ст|ка, ки *f. of* ▸ **~**
бу́дет
1 *3rd person sg. fut. of* ▸ **быть; б. ему́ за э́то!** he'll catch it.
2 *as pred.* (*coll.*) that's enough; that'll do; **б. вам писа́ть** it's time you stopped writing.
буди́льник, а *m.* alarm clock.
бу|ди́ть, жу́, ~́дишь *impf.*
1 (*pf.* **раз~**) to wake, awaken, call.
2 (*pf.* **про~**) (*fig.*) (*возбуждать*) to rouse, arouse; to stir up; **б. мысль** to set (one) thinking.
бу́дк|а, и *f.* (*сторожа*) box, booth; (*ларёк*) stall; **карау́льная б.** sentry box; **соба́чья б.** dog kennel; **телефо́нная б.** telephone booth.
бу́дни|и, ей *pl.*
1 weekdays; working days, workdays; **по ~ям** on weekdays.
2 (*однообразная жизнь*) humdrum life; colourless existence.
бу́дний *adj.*: **б. день** weekday.
бу́дто
1 *conj.* as if, as though.
2 *conj.* that (*implying doubt as to the truth of a statement*); **он утвержда́ет, б. свобо́дно говори́т на десяти́ языка́х** he claims that he speaks ten languages fluently.
3 (*also* **б. бы, как б.**) *particle* (*coll.*)

(*кажется*) apparently.

бу́д|у, ешь *fut. of* ▶ **быть**

бу́дучи *pres. ger. of* ▶ **быть** being.

бу́дущ|ий *adj.* future; next; ... to be; **~ее вре́мя** (*gram.*) future tense; **в ~ем году́** next year; **~ая мать** expectant mother; *as n.* **~ее, ~его** *nt.* (*i*) the future; **в ближа́йшем ~ем** in the near future, (*ii*) (*gram.*) future tense.

бу́дь(те) *imper. of* ▶ **быть** (*sg. also used in place of* **е́сли** + *main v. to form clause expressing condition in conditional sentences*): **бу́дьте добры́, бу́дьте любе́зны** (+ *inf. or imper.*) please; would you be good enough (to), kind enough (to); **будь, что бу́дет** come what may; **не будь вас, всё бы пропа́ло** but for you, all would have been lost; **будь он бога́т, будь он бе́ден, мне всё равно́** be he rich or be he poor, it is all one to me.

бужени́н|а, ы *f.* boiled salted pork.

бу|жу́, ~́дишь *see* ▶ **~ди́ть**

бузин|а́, ы́ *f.* (*bot.*) (*красная; чёрная*) elder.

бу́|йный (~ен, ~йна́, ~́йно) *adj.*
1 (*непокорный*) wild; tempestuous; **б. сумасше́дший** violent, dangerous lunatic.
2 (*обильный*) luxuriant, lush; **б. рост** luxuriant growth.

бу́йств|о, а *nt.* unruly conduct.

бук, а *m.* beech.

бу́кв|а, ы, *g. pl.* **~** *f.* letter (*of the alphabet*); **б. зако́на** (*fig.*) the letter of the law.

буква́льно *adv.* literally; (*дословно*) word for word.

буква́льн|ый *adj.* literal; **~ое значе́ние** literal meaning; **б. перево́д** word-for-word translation.

буква́р|ь, я́ *m.* ABC; primer.

буке́т, а *m.*
1 bouquet; bunch of flowers.
2 (*аромат*) bouquet; aroma.

букинисти́ческий *adj.*: **б. магазин** second-hand bookshop.

букле́т, а *m.* (fold-out) leaflet.

букме́кер, а *m.* bookmaker; bookie.

букси́р, а *m.*
1 (*судно*) tug, tugboat.
2 (*канат*) tow rope; **взять на б.** to take in tow; (*fig.*) to give a helping hand.

букси́р|овать, ую *impf.* to tow, have in tow.

букс|ова́ть, у́ю *impf.* to skid.

була́вк|а, и *f.* pin; **англи́йская б.** safety pin.

бу́лк|а, и *f.* (*булочка*) roll; (*белый хлеб*) white bread; **сдо́бная б.** bun.

бу́лочн|ая, ой *f.* bakery; baker's shop.

булы́жник, а *m.* cobblestone (*also collect.*).

бульва́р, а *m.* avenue; boulevard.

бульва́р|ный *adj. of* ▶ **~; ~ная литерату́ра** pulp fiction; **~ная пре́сса** the tabloids; gutter press.

бульдо́г, а *m.* bulldog.

бульдо́зер, а *m.* bulldozer.

бульо́н, а *m.* broth; stock.

бум, а *m.* (*econ.*) boom.

бума́г|а, и *f.*
1 (*материал*) paper; **газе́тная б.** newsprint.
2 (*документ*) document; (*pl.*) (official) papers; **це́нные ~и** (*fin.*) securities.

бума́жник, а *m.* wallet.

бума́|жный *adj. of* ▶ **~га;** (*fig.*) (existing only on) paper; **~жная волоки́та** red tape; **~жные де́ньги** paper money; **б. змей** kite; **~жная фа́брика** paper mill.

бумера́нг, а *m.* boomerang.

бу́нгало *nt. indecl.* bungalow (*in tropical countries*).

бу́нкер, а *m.* bunker.

бунт, а *m.* revolt; riot.

бунта́рский *adj.*
1 seditious; mutinous.
2 (*fig.*) rebellious; turbulent; **б. дух** rebellious spirit.

бунта́р|ь, я́ *m.* rebel (*also fig.*); insurgent; mutineer; rioter.

бунт|ова́ть, у́ю *impf.* (*pf.* **взбунтова́ться**) to revolt, rebel; to mutiny; to riot; (*fig.*) to rage, go berserk.

бунтовщи́к, а́ *m.* rebel, insurgent; mutineer; rioter.

буреве́стник, а *m.* stormy petrel.

буре́ни|е, я *nt.* (*tech.*) boring, drilling.

буржуази́|я, и *f.* bourgeoisie; **ме́лкая б.** petty bourgeoisie.

буржуа́з|ный (~ен, ~на) *adj.* bourgeois.

бур|и́ть, ю́, и́шь *impf.* (*of* ▶ **про~**) (*tech.*) to bore; to drill.

бурл|и́ть, ю́, и́шь *impf.* to seethe, boil up (*also fig.*).

бу́р|ный (~ен, ~на́, ~но) *adj.*
1 (*погода, море*) stormy, rough; (*спор*) heated; (*жизнь, восторг, аплодисменты*) wild.
2 (*рост*) rapid.

буров|о́й *adj.* boring; **~а́я вы́шка** derrick; **~а́я сква́жина** bore, borehole, well.

бу́р|ый (~, ~а́, ~о) *adj.* brown; **б. медве́дь** brown bear.

бу́р|я, и *f.* storm (*also fig.*); **б. в стака́не воды́** storm in a teacup.

буря́т, а, *g. pl.* **б.** *m.* Buryat.

буря́т|ка, ки *f. of* ▶ **~**

буря́тский *adj.* Buryat.

бу́с|ы, ~ *no sg.* beads.

бутербро́д, а *m.* slice of bread and butter; sandwich; **зако́н ~а** Sod's Law, Murphy's Law.

бути́к, а *m.* boutique.

буто́н, а *m.* bud.

бу́тс|ы, ~ *pl.* (*sg.* **~а, ~ы** *f.*) football boots.

буты́лк|а, и *f.* bottle.

бу́фер, а, *pl.* **~а́** *m.* (*rail.*; *comput.*; *fig.*) buffer.

буфе́т, а *m.*
1 (*шкаф*) sideboard.
2 (*закусочная*) buffet, snack bar; (*стойка*) (refreshment) bar, counter.

буха́нк|а, и *f.* loaf.

Бухаре́ст, а *m.* Bucharest.

бу́х|ать, аю *impf.* (*of* ▶ **~нуть**)
1 (*ударять*) to thump, bang.
2 (*о выстреле*) to thud, thunder.

бухга́лтер, а, *pl.* **~ы** *m.* bookkeeper, accountant.

бухгалте́ри|я, и *f.*
[1] bookkeeping, accountancy.
[2] (*отдел*) counting house.

бухга́лтерск|ий *adj.* bookkeeping, account; **~ая кни́га** account book.

бу́х|нуть, ну, нешь, *past* **~нул** *pf. of* ▸ **~ать**

бу́хт|а, ы *f.* (*geog.*) bay.

буш|ева́ть, у́ю *impf.* to rage; (*fig.*) to rage, storm.

Буэ́нос-А́йрес, а *m.* Buenos Aires.

бы (*abbr.* **б**) *particle*
[1] (*выражает предположительную возможность*) (*see also* ▸ **е́сли**): **я мог бы об э́том догада́ться** I might have guessed it; **бы́ло бы о́чень прия́тно вас ви́деть** it would be very nice to see you.
[2] (+ **ни**) *forms indef. prons.*: **кто бы ни** whoever; **что бы ни** whatever; **как бы ни** however; **кто бы ни пришёл** whoever comes; **что бы ни случи́лось** whatever happens; **как бы то ни́ было** however that may be, be that as it may.
[3] (*выражает пожелание*): **я бы вы́пил пи́ва** I should like a drink of beer.
[4] (*выражает предложение*): **вы бы отдохну́ли** you should take a rest.

быва́|ло *see* ▸ **~ть**

быва́л|ый *adj.* experienced; worldly-wise.

быва́|ть, ю *impf.*
[1] (*случаться*) to happen; (*происходить*) to take place; **~ет, что поезда́ с се́вера опа́здывают** trains from the north are sometimes late.
[2] (*быть*) to be; (*находиться*) to be present; (*посещать*) to frequent; **они́ ре́дко ~ют в теа́тре** they seldom go to the theatre.
[3] (*быть склонным*) to be inclined to be, tend to be; **он ~ет раздражи́тельным** he is inclined to be irritable.
[4] : **как ни в чём не ~ло** (*coll.*) as if nothing had happened; **как не ~ло** (+ *g.*) to have completely disappeared; **головно́й бо́ли у меня́ как не ~ло** my headache has completely gone.

бы́вший *p.p. of* ▸ **быть** *and adj.* former, ex-; one-time; **б. президе́нт** former president, ex-president.

бык, а́ *m.* bull; ox; **здоро́в как б.** as strong as an ox.

бы́ло *particle* (*indicates that an action was impending or had just begun, but was not completed*): **он отпра́вился б. с ни́ми, но верну́лся** he started out with them but turned back; **чуть б.** very nearly; **они́ чуть б. не уби́ли его́** they all but killed him.

быстроде́йстви|е, я *nt.* (*tech.*) speed, response time.

быстрот|а́, ы́ *f.* rapidity, quickness; (*скорость*) speed.

быстрохо́д|ный (~ен, ~на) *adj.* fast, high-speed.

бы́стр|ый (~, ~а́, ~о) *adj.* rapid, fast, quick; (*немедленный*) prompt.

быт, а, о ~е, в ~у́, *no pl., m.* way of life; life; **солда́тский б.** army life.

быти|е́, я́ *nt.* (*phil.*) being, existence, objective reality; **кни́га Б~я́** (*bibl.*) Genesis.

быт|ово́й *adj. of* ▸ **~; ~овы́е прибо́ры** domestic appliances; **~ово́е обслу́живание населе́ния** consumer services; **~ово́е явле́ние** everyday occurrence.

быть *pres. not used exc. 3rd person sg.* **есть** *fut.* **бу́ду, бу́дешь,** *past* **был, была́, бы́ло (не́ был, не была́, не́ было)** *imper.* **бу́дь(те)** (*see also* ▸ **бу́дет, бу́дь(те), бы́ло, есть**[2])
▪ **I.**
[1] (*существовать*) to be; **есть таки́е лю́ди** there are such people, such people do exist.
[2] : **б. у** (*see also* ▸ **есть**) (*иметь*) to be in the possession (of); **у них была́ прекра́сная да́ча** they had a lovely dacha.
[3] (*находиться*) to be; **где вы бы́ли вчера́?** where were you yesterday?; **он тут был не при чём** he had nothing to do with it; **на ней была́ ро́зовая ко́фточка** she had on a pink blouse.
[4] (*случаться*) to be, happen, take place; **э́того не мо́жет б.!** it cannot be!; **так и б.** so be it, all right, very well, have it your own way.
▪ **II.** *as v. aux.* to be.

быч|о́к[1]**, ка́** *m.* (*бык*) steer.

быч|о́к[2]**, ка́** *m.* (*рыба*) goby.

бью, бьёшь *see* ▸ **бить**

бюдже́т, а *m.* budget.

бюдже́тник, а *m.* (*coll.*) person who is paid from the State budget (*e.g. a teacher*).

бюдже́тный *adj.* budgetary; **б. год** fiscal year.

бюллете́н|ь, я *m.*
[1] bulletin; **информацио́нный б.** newsletter.
[2] **(избира́тельный) б.** ballot paper.
[3] **(больни́чный) б.** medical certificate; **быть на ~е** (*coll.*) to be on sick leave.

бюро́ *nt. indecl.*
[1] (*контора*) bureau, office; **б. нахо́док** lost-property office; **б. по трудоустро́йству** employment agency; **спра́вочное б.** inquiry office, information office; **туристи́ческое б.** travel agency.
[2] (*стол*) bureau, writing desk.

бюрокра́т, а *m.* bureaucrat.

бюрократи́ческий *adj.* bureaucratic.

бюрокра́ти|я, и *f.* bureaucracy (*also collect.*).

бюст, а *m.* (*скульптура*) bust; (*женский*) bust, bosom.

бюстга́льтер, а *m.* bra(ssiere).

Вв

в *prep.*
■ I. + *a. and p.*
[1] (+ *a., denoting direction*) into, to; (+ *p., denoting position*) in, at; **поéхать в Москвý** to go to Moscow; **роди́ться в Москвé** to be born in Moscow; **сесть в вагóн** to get into the carriage; **сидéть в вагóне** to be in the carriage.
[2] *in reference to external attributes*: **рубáшка в клéтку** check(ed) shirt; **ходи́ть в шýбе** to wear a fur coat.
[3] (+ *nom.-a. pl. and p. pl.*) *in reference to occupation*: **пойти́ в учителя́** to become a teacher.
[4] *in reference to calendar units and periods of time*: **в понедéльник** on Monday; **в январé** in January; **в 1899 годý** in 1899; **в двадцáтом вéке** in the twentieth century; **в четы́ре часá** at four o'clock; **в четвёртом часý** between three and four; **в нáши дни** in our day; **в течéние** (+ *g.*) during, in the course (of).
■ II. + *a.*
[1] *in reference to objects through which vision is directed*: **смотрéть в окнó** to look out of the window.
[2] *in attribution of resemblance*: **быть в когó-н.** to take after s.o.; to be like s.o.; **онá вся в тётю** she is just like her aunt.
[3] *indicating aim or purpose*: for, as; **сказáть в шýтку** to say for a joke.
[4] (+ **раз** *and comp. adv.*) *indicates comparison in numerical terms*: **в два рáза бóльше** twice as big, twice the size; **в два рáза мéньше** half as big, half the size.
[5] *indicates game or sport played*: **игрáть в кáрты, шáхматы, футбóл** to play cards, chess, football.
■ III. + *p.*
[1] at a distance of; **в трёх киломéтрах от гóрода** three kilometres from the town; **они́ живýт в десяти́ минýтах ходьбы́ отсю́да** they live ten minutes' walk from here.
[2] in; of (= *consisting of, amounting to*); **пьéса в трёх дéйствиях** play in three acts.

в. (*abbr. of* **век**) c., century.

вагóн, а *m.*
[1] carriage (*Br.*), coach (*Br.*), car (*US*); **мя́гкий, жёсткий в.** soft-seated, hard-seated carriage (*Br.*), car (*US*); **багáжный в.** luggage van; **в.-ресторáн** dining car, restaurant car; **спáльный в.** sleeping car.
[2] (*груз*) wagonload; (*fig., coll.*) loads, lots.

вагонéтк|а, и *f.* truck; trolley.

вáжност|ь, и *f.*
[1] importance; significance.
[2] (*надменность*) pomposity, pretentiousness.

вáж|ный (~ен, ~нá, ~но, ~ны́) *adj.*
[1] (*short form pl.* **~ны́**) important; weighty, consequential; **сáмое ~ное** the (important) thing (is); **~ная пти́ца/ши́шка** (*coll.*) bigwig.
[2] (*short form pl.* **~ны**) (*гордый*) pompous, pretentious.

вáз|а, ы *f.* vase, bowl.

вакáнси|я, и *f.* vacancy; **я́рмарка ~й** jobs fair.

вакáнт|ный (~ен, ~на) *adj.* vacant, unfilled; **~ная дóлжность** vacancy.

вáкс|а, ы *f.* black (shoe) polish.

вáкуум, а *m.* vacuum.

вакци́н|а, ы *f.* vaccine.

вал[1], а, *pl.* **~ы́** *m.* (*волна*) billow, roller.

вал[2], а, *pl.* **~ы́** *m.* (*насыпь*) bank, earthen wall; (*mil.*) rampart.

вал[3], а, *pl.* **~ы́** *m.* (*tech.*) shaft.

валéжник, а *no pl., m.* (*collect.*) windfallen trees, branches.

вáлен|ки, ок *pl.* (*sg.* **~ок, ~ка** *m.*) valenki (*felt boots*).

валéт, а *m.* (*cards*) jack.

вал|и́ть[1], ю́, ~ишь *impf.*
[1] (*pf.* **по~** *and* **с~**) (*заставлять падать*) to throw down, bring down; to overthrow; **в. когó-н. с ног** to knock s.o. off his feet; **в. дерéвья** to fell trees.
[2] (*pf.* **с~**) (*в кучу*) to heap up, pile up.
[3] (*pf.* **с~**) (*coll.*): **в. винý** (**на** + *a.*) to lump the blame (on).

вал|и́ть[2], и́т *impf.* (*coll.*) (*двигаться массой*) to flock, throng, pour; **снег ~и́т крýпными хлóпьями** the snow is coming down in large flakes.

вал|и́ться, ю́сь, ~ишься *impf.* (*of* ▸**по~** *and* ▸**с~**) to fall, collapse; to topple over; **в. от устáлости** to drop from tiredness;

валли́|ец, йца *m.* Welshman.

валли́йк|а, и *f.* Welshwoman.

валли́йский *adj.* Welsh.

валовóй *adj.* (*econ.*) gross; wholesale; **в. внýтренний продýкт** gross domestic product; **в. национáльный продýкт** gross national product.

валтóрн|а, ы *f.* (*mus.*) French horn.

валторни́ст, а *m.* hornist, (French) horn player.

валторни́ст|ка, ки *f. of* ▸**~**

валýн, á *m.* boulder.

вальс, а *m.* waltz.

валю́т|а, ы *f.* (*fin., econ.*)
[1] (*денежная система*) currency; **курс ~ы** rate of exchange.
[2] (*collect.*) (*иностранные деньги*) foreign currency; **твёрдая/свобóдно конверти́руемая в.** hard currency.

валю́тно-финáнсов|ый *adj.*: **~ая би́ржа** foreign exchange market.

валю́т|ный *adj. of* ▸**~а;** currency; **в. фонд** monetary fund.

валя́|ть, ю *impf.*
[1] (*pf.* **вы~**) (*валяя, покрыть чем-н.*) to roll,

drag; **в. в грязи́** to drag in the mire.
[2]: **в. дурака́** (*coll.*) to play the fool.

валя́|ться, юсь *impf.*
[1] (*кататься*) to roll.
[2] (*coll.*) (*бездельничать*) to lie about.

вам *d. of* ▸ **вы**

ва́ми *i. of* ▸ **вы**

вампи́р, а *m.* vampire.

ванда́л, а *m.* vandal.

вандали́зм, а *m.* vandalism.

вани́л|ь, и *f.* vanilla.

вани́ль|ный *adj. of* ▸ **~**

ва́нн|а, ы *f.* bath; **приня́ть ~у** to take a bath.

ва́нн|ая, ой *f.* bathroom.

ва́рварский *adj.* barbaric.

ва́рварств|о, а *nt.* barbarity.

ва́режк|а, и *f.* mitten.

варе́ник, а *m.* varenik (*curd or fruit dumpling*).

варёный *adj.* boiled.

варе́нь|е, я *nt.* preserve(s) (*containing whole fruit*), jam (*Br.*).

вариа́нт, а *m.* (*разновидность*) variant; version; (*возможность*) option; (*сценарий*) scenario; model.

вар|и́ть, ю́, ~́ишь *impf.* (*of* ▸ **с~ 1**)
[1] to boil; to cook; **в. карто́фель** to boil potatoes; **в. обе́д** to cook dinner; **в. пи́во** to brew beer.
[2] (*о голове*): **голова́/башка́ у него́ ва́рит** (*coll.*) he's quick on the uptake.

вар|и́ться, ~́ится *impf.* (*of* ▸ **с~**)
[1] (*в кипятке*) to boil (*intrans.*); (*приготовляться на огне*) to cook (*intrans.*).
[2] *pass. of* ▸ **~и́ть**

Варша́в|а, ы *f.* Warsaw.

варьи́р|овать, ую *impf.* to vary, modify.

вас *g., a., and p. of* ▸ **вы**

васил|ёк, ька́ *m.* (*bot.*) cornflower.

ва́т|а, ы *f.* cotton wool (*Br.*), absorbent cotton (*US*); (*для подкладки*) wadding.

Ватика́н, а *m.* the Vatican.

ва́тник, а *m.* quilted jacket.

ва́тн|ый *adj.* wadded, quilted; **~ое одея́ло** quilt.

ватру́шк|а, и *f.* curd tart; cheesecake.

ватт, а, *g. pl.* **в.** *m.* watt.

ва́учер, а *m.* voucher.

ва́ф|ля, ли, *g. pl.* **~ель** *f.* waffle; wafer.

ва́хт|а, ы *f.* (*сменная работа*) shift; **нести́ ~у** to be on duty; (*naut.*) watch; **стоя́ть на ~е** to keep watch.

вахтёр, а *m.* janitor, porter.

ва́хтовый *adj.* shift-based.

ваш, ~́его; *f.* **~́а, ~́ей;** *nt.* **~́е, ~́его;** *pl.* **~́и, ~́их** *possessive pron.* (*при существительном*) your; (*без существительного*) yours; **э́то в. каранда́ш** this is your pencil; **э́тот каранда́ш в.** this pencil is yours; *as n.* **~́и, ~́их** your people, your folk.

Вашингто́н, а *m.* Washington.

ва́я|ть, ю *impf.* (*of* ▸ **из~**) to sculpt; (*из камня, дерева*) to carve, chisel.

вбега́|ть, ю *impf.* (**в** + *a.*) to run (into).

вбе|жа́ть, гу́, жи́шь, гу́т *pf. of* ▸ **~га́ть**

вбива́|ть, ю *impf. of* ▸ **вбить**

вбить, вобью́, вобьёшь *pf.* (*of* ▸ **вбива́ть**) to drive in, hammer in.

вблизи́ *adv.* (**от** + *g.*) close by; not far (from); **рассма́тривать в.** to examine closely.

вбок *adv.* sideways, to one side.

вбра́сывани|е, я *nt.* **в. (мяча́)** throw-in (*in football*); **в. (ша́йбы)** face-off (*in ice hockey*).

вбра́сыва|ть, ю *impf. of* ▸ **вбро́сить**

вбро́|сить, шу, сишь *pf.* (*of* ▸ **вбра́сывать**) to throw in(to).

вва́лива|ться, юсь *impf. of* ▸ **ввали́ться**

ввал|и́ться, ю́сь, ~́ишься *pf.*
[1] (*fig., coll.*) (*входить*) to burst into.
[2] (*стать впалым*) to become hollow, sunken; **с ~ившимися щека́ми** hollow-cheeked.

введе́ни|е, я *nt.* introduction.

вве|ду́, дёшь *see* ▸ **~сти́**

ввез|ти́, у́, ёшь, *past* **~̈, ~ла́** *pf.* (*of* ▸ **ввози́ть**) to import.

вверх *adv.* up, upward(s); **идти́ в. по ле́стнице** to go upstairs; **в. по тече́нию** upstream; **в. дном** upside down; **в. нога́ми** head over heels.

вверху́ *adv. and prep.* + *g.* above, overhead; **в. страни́цы** at the top of the page.

вве|сти́, ду́, дёшь, *past* **~̈л, ~ла́** *pf.* (*of* ▸ **вводи́ть**) (*человека, животное*) to lead in, bring in, take in; (*закон, пошлины*) to introduce, bring in; (*поместить внутрь*) to introduce, put into; (*данные*) to enter, key in; **в. в заблужде́ние** to mislead; **в. в курс чего́-н.** to acquaint with (the facts of) sth.

ввиду́ *prep.* + *g.* in view (of); **в. того́, что** as.

ввин|ти́ть, чу́, ти́шь *pf.* (*of* ▸ **~́чивать**) (**в** + *a.*) to screw (in).

вви́нчива|ть, ю *impf. of* ▸ **ввинти́ть**

вво|ди́ть, жу́, ~́дишь *impf. of* ▸ **ввести́**

вво́дн|ый *adj.* introductory; (*gram.*) **~ое сло́во** parenthetic word, parenthesis.

вво|жу́[1]**, ~́дишь** *see* ▸ **вводи́ть**

вво|жу́[2]**, ~́зишь** *see* ▸ **ввози́ть**

ввоз, а *no pl., m.*
[1] (*действие*) importation.
[2] (*импорт*) import.

вво|зи́ть, жу́, ~́зишь *impf. of* ▸ **ввезти́**

ввозн|о́й *adj.* (*товар*) imported; (*attr.*) import; **~а́я по́шлина** import duty.

ВВП *m. indecl.* (*abbr. of* **валово́й вну́тренний проду́кт**) GDP (*gross domestic product*).

ВВС *no sg., indecl.* (*abbr. of* **вое́нно-возду́шные си́лы**) Air Force.

ввя|за́ться, жу́сь, ~́жешься *pf.* (*of* ▸ **ввя́зываться**) (**в** + *a.*; *coll.*) (*вмешаться*) to meddle (in); (*впутаться*) to get involved (in), mixed up (in).

ввя́зыва|ться, юсь *impf. of* ▸ **ввяза́ться**

вглубь *adv. and prep.* + *g.* deep down; deep into, into the depths.

вдалеке́ *adv.* in the distance; **в. от** (+ *g.*) a long way from.

вдали́ *adv.* in the distance, far off; **в. от го́рода** a long way from the city; **исчеза́ть в.** to vanish into the distance.

вдаль *adv.* afar, at a distance; **гляде́ть в.** to look into the distance.

вдво́е *adv.* twice; double; **в. лу́чше** twice as good; **сложи́ть в.** to fold double.

вдвоём *adv.* the two together; **они́ написа́ли статью́ в.** the two of them together wrote the article.

вдвойне́ *adv.* twice, double; doubly (*also fig.*); **плати́ть в.** to pay double; **он в. винова́т** he is doubly to blame.

вдева́|ть, ю *impf. of* ▸ **вдеть**

вде|ть, ~ну, ~нешь *pf.* (*of* ▸ **~ва́ть**) (**в** + *a.*) to put in(to); **в. ни́тку в иго́лку** to thread a needle.

вдоба́вок *adv.* (*coll.*) in addition; moreover; into the bargain; **в. к** (+ *d.*) in addition to.

вдов|а́, ы́, *pl.* **~ы** *f.* widow.

вдов|е́ц, ца́ *m.* widower.

вдо́воль *adv.*
1 (*в изоби́лии*) in abundance.
2 (*вполне́ доста́точно*) enough; **он нае́лся в.** he ate his fill.

вдого́нку *adv.* (*coll.*) after, in pursuit of; **бро́ситься в.** (**за** + *i.*) to rush (after).

вдоль
1 *prep.* (+ *g. or* **по** + *d.*) along; **в. бе́рега** along the bank.
2 *adv.* lengthwise, longways; **в. и поперёк** (*повсю́ду*) in all directions, far and wide.

вдох, а *m.* breath; **сде́лать глубо́кий в.** to take a deep breath.

вдохнове́ни|е, я *nt.* inspiration.

вдохнов|и́ть, лю́, и́шь *pf.* (*of* ▸ **~ля́ть**) (+ *a. or* **на** + *a.*) to inspire (to).

вдохновля́|ть, ю *impf. of* ▸ **вдохнови́ть**

вдохн|у́ть, у́, ёшь *pf.* (*of* ▸ **вдыха́ть**) (**в** + *a.*)
1 (*во́здух*) to breathe in; (*дым*) inhale.
2 (*настрое́ние*) to inspire (with), instil (into).

вдре́безги *adv.* (*на ме́лкие ча́сти*) to pieces, to smithereens.

вдруг *adv.*
1 (*неожи́данно*) suddenly, all of a sudden.
2 *as interrog. particle* (*coll.*) (*а что е́сли*) what if, suppose; **(а) в. они́ узна́ют?** but suppose they find out?

вду́м|аться, аюсь *pf.* (*of* ▸ **~ываться**) (**в** + *a.*) to think over, ponder, meditate (on).

вду́мыва|ться, юсь *impf. of* ▸ **вду́маться**

вдыха́ни|е, я *nt.* inhalation.

вдыха́|ть, ю *impf. of* ▸ **вдохну́ть**

веб-са́йт, а *m.* (*comput.*) website.

веб-страни́ц|а, ы *f.* (*comput.*) web page.

вегетариа́н|ец, ца *m.* vegetarian.

вегетариа́н|ка, ки *f. of* ▸ **~ец**

вегетариа́нский *adj.* vegetarian.

ве́да|ть, ю *impf.*
1 (*знать*) to know.
2 (+ *i.*) (*заве́довать*) to manage, be in charge of.

ве́дени|е, я *nt.* authority; jurisdiction; **э́ти дела́ в моём ~и** I am in charge of these things.

веде́ни|е, я *nt.* conducting, conduct; **в. хозя́йства** the running of a household.

ве́дома *only in phrr.*: **без в., с в.; без моего́ в.** unknown to me; **с моего́ в.** with my knowledge, with my consent.

ве́домост|ь, и *f.* list, register; **платёжная в.** payroll.

ве́домственный *adj.* departmental.

ве́домств|о, а *nt.* department.

вед|ро́, ра́, *pl.* **~ра, ~ер** *nt.* bucket, pail.

вед|у́, ёшь *see* ▸ **вести́**

веду́щ|ий *pres. part. act. of* ▸ **вести́** *and adj.* leading; (*tech.*) **~ее колесо́** driving wheel; *as n.* **в., ~его** *m.* presenter; compère.

ведь *conj.*
1 (*де́ло в том, что*) you see, you know (*but oft. requires no translation*); **она́ всё вре́мя покупа́ет но́вые пла́тья: в. она́ о́чень бога́та** she is always buying new dresses — she is very rich, you know.
2 (*particle*) (*не пра́вда ли?*) is it not?; is it?; **в. э́то пра́вда?** it's the truth, isn't it?

ве́дьм|а, ы *f.* witch.

ве́ер, а, *pl.* **~а́** *m.* fan.

ве́жливост|ь, и *f.* politeness, courtesy.

ве́жлив|ый (~, ~а) *adj.* polite, courteous.

везде́ *adv.* everywhere; **в. и всю́ду** here, there, and everywhere.

вездесу́щ|ий (~, ~а) *adj.* (*челове́к*) ubiquitous; (*Бог*) omnipresent.

вездехо́д, а *m.* four-wheel drive (vehicle).

везе́ни|е, я *nt.* luck.

вез|ти́, у́, ёшь, *past* **~, ~ла́** *impf.* (*of* ▸ **по~**) (*det. of* ▸ **вози́ть**)
1 (*перемеща́ть*) to take, convey, carry (*of beasts of burden, mechanical transport, or people when on transport*).
2 (*coll.*) (*impers.* + *d.*) (*об уда́че*) to have luck; **ему́ не ~ёт в ка́рты** he has no luck at cards.

везу́чий *adj.* (*coll.*) lucky.

век, а, о ~е, на ~у́, *pl.* **~а́** (*obs.* **~и**) *m.*
1 (*столе́тие*) century.
2 (*эпо́ха*) age; **ка́менный в.** Stone Age; **Сре́дние ~а́** the Middle Ages; **испоко́н ~о́в** from time immemorial; **в ко́и-то ~и** once in a blue moon.
3 (*жизнь*) life, lifetime; **на моём ~у́** in my lifetime.

ве́к|о, а, *pl.* **~и, ~** *nt.* eyelid.

веково́й *adj.* ancient, age-old.

вёл, ~а́ *see* ▸ **вести́**

вел|е́ть, ю́, и́шь *impf. and pf.* (+ *d. and inf. or* **что́бы**) to order; **я ~е́л ему́ сде́лать э́то** *or* **что́бы он сде́лал э́то** I ordered him to do this.

велика́н, а *m.* giant.

вели́к|ий (~, ~а́) *adj.*
1 (*short form* **~а, ~о,** *pl.* **~и**) (*выдаю́щийся*) great; **~ие держа́вы** the Great Powers.
2 (*short form* **~а́, ~о́,** *pl.* **~и́**) (*большо́й*) big, large; **~ое мно́жество** a lot, a great deal.
3 (*short form only*; **~а́, ~о́,** *pl.* **~и́**) (+ *d. or* **для** + *g.*) (*сли́шком большо́й*) too big; **э́ти брю́ки мне ~и́** these trousers are too big for me.

Великобрита́ни|я, и *f.* Great Britain.

великоду́ши|е, я *nt.* magnanimity,

generosity.
великоду́ш|ный (~ен, ~на) *adj.* magnanimous, generous.
великоле́пи|е, я *nt.* magnificence.
великоле́п|ный (~ен, ~на) *adj.* 1 (*роскошный*) splendid, magnificent. 2 (*отличный*) excellent; **~но!** (*int.*) splendid!; excellent!
великому́ченик, а *m.* (*relig.*) great martyr.
великосве́тский *adj.* high-society (*attr.*).
велича́йший *adj.* (*superl. of* ▸ **вели́кий**) greatest, extreme, supreme.
вели́чественност|ь, и *f.* majesty, grandeur.
вели́чествен|ный (~, ~на) *adj.* majestic, grand.
вели́честв|о, а *nt.* majesty; **Ва́ше В.** Your Majesty.
вели́чи|е, я *nt.* greatness; grandeur; **ма́ния ~я** megalomania.
величин|а́, ины́, *pl.* **~и́ны, ~и́н, ~и́нам** *f.* 1 size. 2 (*math.*) quantity, magnitude; (*значение*) value.
вело... *comb. form* bicycle-, cycle-.
велого́нк|а, и *f.* cycle race.
велого́нщик, а *m.* racing cyclist.
велосипе́д, а *m.* bicycle.
велосипеди́ст, а *m.* cyclist.
велоспо́рт, а *m.* cycling.
велотренажёр, а *m.* exercise bicycle.
вельве́т, а *m.* corduroy.
вельве́товый *adj.* corduroy.
велю́р, а *m.* velour.
Ве́н|а, ы *f.* Vienna.
ве́н|а, ы *f.* (*anat.*) vein.
венге́р|ка, ки *f. of* ▸ **венгр**
венге́рский *adj.* Hungarian.
венгр, а *m.* Hungarian.
Ве́нгри|я, и *f.* Hungary.
венери́ческий *adj.* (*med.*) venereal.
Венесуэ́л|а, ы *f.* Venezuela.
венесуэ́л|ец, ца *m.* Venezuelan.
венесуэ́л|ка, ки *f. of* ▸ **~ец**
венесуэ́льский *adj.* Venezuelan.
вен|е́ц, ца́ *m.* (*корона*) crown.
венециа́нский *adj.* Venetian.
Вене́ци|я, и *f.* Venice.
ве́ник, а *m.* 1 (*из прутьев*) besom, broom. 2 (*в бане*) birch twigs (*used in Russian baths*).
вен|о́к, ка́ *m.* wreath.
ве́нский *adj.* Viennese.
ве́нтил|ь, я *m.* valve.
вентиля́тор, а *m.* extractor (fan).
вентиля́ци|я, и *f.* ventilation.
венча́ни|е, я *nt.* (*бракосочетание*) wedding ceremony.
венча́|ть, ю *impf.* 1 (*pf.* **в.** *and* **у~**) (*находиться наверху*) to crown. 2 (*pf.* **у~**) (*fig.*) to crown. 3 (*pf.* **об~** *and* **по~**) (*соединять браком*) to marry (*of officiating priest*).
венча́|ться, юсь *impf.* (*pf.* **об~** *and* **по~**) to be married, marry.
ве́нчурный *adj.* (*fin.*) venture; **в. капита́л** venture capital.
ве́р|а, ы *f.* (**в** + *a.*) faith, belief (in); (*уверенность*) trust, confidence; **приня́ть на ~у** to take on trust.
вера́нд|а, ы *f.* veranda.
ве́рб|а, ы *f.* willow.
верблю́д, а *m.* camel.
верб|ова́ть, у́ю *impf.* (*of* **за~**) to recruit, enlist.
верди́кт, а *m.* verdict.
верёвк|а, и *f.* cord, rope; string.
верени́ц|а, ы *f.* file, line.
ве́реск, а *m.* (*bot.*) heather.
веретен|о́, а́, *pl.* **веретёна, веретён** *nt.* spindle.
ве́р|ить, ю, ишь *impf.* (*of* ▸ **по~**) (+ *d. or* **в** + *a.*) to believe, have faith (in); (+ *d.*) (*доверять*) to trust (in), rely (upon); **в. в Бо́га** to believe in God; **в. на́ слово** to take on trust; **я не ~ил своим уша́м, своим глаза́м** I could not believe my ears, eyes.
ве́р|иться, ится *impf.* (*impers.* + *d.*): **(мне) ~ится с трудо́м** I find it hard to believe.
вермише́л|ь, и *f.* vermicelli.
верн|е́е *adv.* (*comp. of* ▸ **~́о**) rather; **в. (сказа́ть)** to be more exact.
верниса́ж, а *m.* (*art*) 1 (*закрытый просмотр*) private viewing. 2 (*день открытия*) opening-day (*of an exhibition*).
ве́рн|о *adv. of* ▸ **~ый**
ве́рност|ь, и *f.* 1 (*преданность*) faithfulness, loyalty. 2 (*правильность*) truth, correctness.
верн|у́ть, у́, ёшь *pf.* (*of* ▸ **возвраща́ть**) 1 (*отдать обратно*) to give back, return. 2 (*получить обратно*) to get back, recover, retrieve.
верн|у́ться, у́сь, ёшься *pf.* (*of* ▸ **возвраща́ться**) to return (*also fig.*); **в. домо́й** to return home.
ве́р|ный (~ен, ~на́, ~но, ~́ны) *adj.* 1 (*правильный*) true, correct. 2 (*преданный*) faithful, loyal, true; **в. свои́м убежде́ниям** true to one's convictions. 3 (*надёжный*) sure, reliable; **в. при́знак** sure sign. 4 (*несомненный*) certain, sure; **~ная смерть** certain death.
ве́ровани|е, я *nt.* belief, creed.
ве́р|овать, ую *impf.* (**в** + *a.*) to believe (in).
вероисповеда́ни|е, я *nt.* creed, denomination; **свобо́да ~я** freedom of religion.
вероло́м|ный (~ен, ~на) *adj.* treacherous, perfidious.
вероуче́ни|е, я *nt.* (*relig.*) dogma, teachings.
вероя́тно *adv.* probably.
вероя́тност|ь, и *f.* probability; **по всей ~и** in all probability.
вероя́т|ный (~ен, ~на) *adj.* probable, likely; **~нее всего́** most probably.

ве́рси|я, и *f.* version.

верст|а́, ы́, *a.* **~у́** *pl.* **~ы, ~** *f.* (*мера*) verst (*old Russian measurement, equivalent to approx. 1.07 kilometres*); **за ~у́** (*coll.*) from far off.

верста́к, а́ *m.* (*tech.*) (work)bench.

ве́ртел, а, *pl.* **~а́** *m.* spit; skewer.

вер|те́ть, чу́, ~тишь *impf.* (+ *a. or i.*) (*рукоятку, колесо*) to turn; (*быстро*) to twirl; **в. голово́й** to shake one's head; **в. что-н. в рука́х** to fiddle with sth.

вер|те́ться, чу́сь, ~тишься *impf.*
1 (*вращаться*) to rotate, turn (round), revolve (*also fig.*); **его́ фами́лия весь день ~те́лась у меня на языке́** his name was on the tip of my tongue all day; **в. под нога́ми, пе́ред глаза́ми** (*coll.*) to be under one's feet, in the way.
2 (*coll.*) (*ёрзать*) to fidget.

вертика́л|ь, и *f.* (*линия*) vertical line; (*в кроссворде*) down.

вертика́л|ьный (~ен, ~ьна) *adj.* vertical.

вертолёт, а *m.* helicopter.

вертолётчик, а *m.* helicopter pilot.

ве́рующ|ий *adj.* religious; *as n.* **в., ~его** *m.* believer.

верф|ь, и *f.* dockyard; shipyard.

верх, а, *pl.* **~и́** *m.*
1 (*верхняя часть*) top, (*горы*) summit (*also fig.*); **встре́ча в ~а́х** (*pol.*) summit conference; (*крайняя степень*) height; **в. глу́пости** the height of folly.
2 (*автомашины*) hood (*Br.*), folding top (*US*); **«верх!»** (*sign*) 'this side up'; **взять в.** (**над** + *i.*) to gain the upper hand (over).
3 (*лицевая сторона*) outside, top; right side (*of material*).

ве́рхн|ий *adj.* upper; **~яя оде́жда** outer clothing; **~яя пала́та** (*pol.*) upper chamber.

верхо́вн|ый *adj.* supreme; **~ое кома́ндование** high command; **В. Сове́т** (*hist.*) Supreme Soviet; **В. суд** Supreme Court.

верх|ово́й *adj.*: **~ова́я езда́** riding (*Br.*), horseback riding (*US*); **~ова́я ло́шадь** mount; *as n.* **в., ~ово́го** *m.* rider.

верхо́вь|е, я, *g. pl.* **~ев** *nt.* upper reaches.

верхо́м *adv.* astride; on horseback; **е́здить в.** to ride.

верху́шк|а, и *f.*
1 top; **~ а́йсберга** (*fig.*) tip of the iceberg.
2 (*fig., coll.*) (*организации*) elite, top.

вер|чу́, ~тишь *see* ▶ **~те́ть**

верши́н|а, ы *f.*
1 (*дерева, холма*) top; (*горы*) summit, peak; (*fig.*) peak, acme.
2 (*math.*) vertex; apex.

вес, а, *pl.* (*special use only*) **~а́** *m.* weight; **ли́шний в.** excess baggage; (*fig.*) (*значение*) weight, authority; **на в.** by weight; **на ~у́** balanced, hanging, suspended; **приба́вить, уба́вить в ~е** to put on, lose weight.

весел|и́ть, ю́, и́шь *impf.* (*of* ▶ **раз~**) to amuse.

весел|и́ться, ю́сь, и́шься *impf.* to enjoy o.s.; to have fun.

ве́село *adv.* gaily, merrily; *as pred.* (+ *d.*) to enjoy o.s.; **бы́ло в.** it was fun.

весёл|ый (ве́сел, ~а́, ве́село) *adj.*
1 cheerful, merry.
2 (*no short form*) (*фильм, рассказ*) cheerful, feel-good; (*краски, обои*) bright, cheerful.

вес|е́нний *adj. of* ▶ **~на́**

ве́|сить, шу, сишь *impf.* (*иметь тот или иной вес*) to weigh; **груз ~сит три то́нны** the cargo weighs three tons.

ве́с|кий (~ок, ~ка) *adj.* weighty.

вес|ло́, ла́, *pl.* **~ла, ~ел, ~лам** *nt.* oar.

вес|на́, ны́, *pl.* **~ны, ~ен, ~нам** *f.* spring (*season*).

весно́й *adv.* in the spring.

весну́ш|ки, ек *pl.* (*sg.* **~ка, ~ки** *f.*) freckles.

весну́шчатый *adj.* freckled.

вес|ово́й
1 *adj. of* ▶ **~; ~ова́я катего́рия** (*sport*) weight category.
2 (*продаваемый на вес*) sold by weight.

весо́м|ый (~, ~а) *adj.* (*fig.*) weighty; substantial.

ве́стерн, а *m.* western (*film*).

ве|сти́, ду́, дёшь, *past* **~л, ~ла́** *impf.* (*det. of* ▶ **води́ть**)
1 (*pf.* **по~**) (*сопровождать*) to lead; to take; (*войска*) to lead.
2 (*pf.* **про~**) (+ *i.* **по** + *d.*) to run (over), pass (over, across).
3 (*pf.* **про~**) (*осуществлять, делать*) to conduct; to carry on; **в. войну́** to wage war; **в. ого́нь** (**по** + *d., impf. only*) to fire (on); **в. перегово́ры** to carry on negotiations; **в. перепи́ску** (**с** + *i., impf. only*) to correspond (with); **в. проце́сс** to carry on a lawsuit.
4 (*impf. only*) (*машину*) to drive; **в. кора́бль** to navigate a ship; **в. самолёт** to pilot an aircraft.
5 (*impf. only*) (*руководить*) to conduct, direct, run; (*передачу*) to present; (*собрание*) to chair; **в. де́ло** to run a business; **в. хозя́йство** to keep house.
6 (*impf. only*) (*учёт*) to keep; **в. дневни́к** to keep a diary; **в. протоко́л** to keep minutes.
7 (*impf. only*): **в. себя́** to behave.
8 (*pf.* **при~**) (*служить путём куда-нибудь*) to lead (*also fig.*); **куда́ ~дёт э́та доро́га?** where does this road lead (to)?

вестибю́л|ь, я *m.* entrance hall, lobby.

Вест-И́нди|я, и *f.* the West Indies.

ве́стник, а *m.* messenger, herald.

ве́стни|ца, цы *f. of* ▶ **~к**

вест|ь, и, *pl.* **~и, ~е́й** *f.* news; piece of news; **пропа́сть бе́з ~и** (*mil.*) to be missing.

вес|ы́, о́в *no sg.*
1 scales, balance.
2 **В.** (*созвездие*) the Scales, Libra.

весь, вся, всё, *g.* **всего́, всей, всего́,** *pl.* **все, всех** *pron.* all; **весь день** all day; **вся страна́** the whole country; **вся Фра́нция** the whole of France; **по всему́ го́роду** all over the town; **он весь в отца́** he is the (very) image of his father; **во весь го́лос** at the top of one's voice; **от всего́ се́рдца** from the bottom of one's heart; **пре́жде всего́** before all, first and foremost; **вот и всё** that's all; there's nothing more to it; **всего́ хоро́шего!** goodbye!, all the best!; *as n.* **всё, всего́** *nt.* everything; **все, всех** *no sg.* all, everyone.

весьма́ *adv.* very, highly.
ветви́ст|ый (~, ~а) *adj.* branchy, spreading.
ветв|ь, и, *pl.* **~и, ~е́й** *f.* branch; (*fig.*) branch.
ве́т|ер, ра *m.* wind; (*fig.*) **у него́ в. в голове́** he is a thoughtless fellow.
ветера́н, а *m.* veteran.
ветерина́р, а *m.* veterinary surgeon (*Br.*), veterinarian (*US*).
ветерина́рный *adj.* veterinary.
ве́тк|а, и *f.* branch; (*мелкая*) twig; **железнодоро́жная в.** branch line.
вет|ла́, лы́, *pl.* **~лы, ~ел** *f.* (*bot.*) (*белая/серебристая ива*) white willow.
ве́то *nt. indecl.* veto; **наложи́ть в. (на** + *a.*) to veto.
ве́тош|ь, и *f.* old clothes, rags.
ве́трен|ый (~, ~а) *adj.*
1 windy.
2 (*fig.*) (*человек*) empty-headed.
ветров|о́й *adj. of* ▸ **ве́тер**; **~о́е стекло́** windscreen (*Br.*), windshield (*US*).
ветря́нк|а, и *f.* (*med.*) chickenpox.
ветрян|о́й *adj.* wind(-powered); **~а́я ме́льница** windmill.
ве́тх|ий (~, ~а́, ~о) *adj.* (*очень старый*) old, ancient; (*здание*) dilapidated, tumbledown, decrepit; **В. Заве́т** the Old Testament.
ветчин|а́, ы́ *no pl.*, *f.* ham.
ветша́|ть, ю *impf.* (*of* ▸ **об~**) to decay; to become dilapidated.
ве́х|а, и *f.* landmark (*also fig.*); milestone.
ве́чер, а, *pl.* **~а́** *m.*
1 (*время*) evening; **по ~а́м** in the evenings; **под в., к ~у** towards evening.
2 (*собрание*) party; evening, soirée.
вечере́|ть, ет *impf.* (*impers.*) to grow dark; **~ет** night is falling.
вечери́нк|а, и *f.* party.
вече́рн|ий *adj. of* ▸ **ве́чер; ~яя заря́** twilight, dusk; **~ие ку́рсы** evening classes; **~ее пла́тье** evening dress.
ве́чером *adv.* in the evening.
ве́чно *adv.* (*всегда*) for ever, eternally; (*coll.*) (*постоянно*) always; **они́ в. ссо́рятся** they are always quarrelling.
вечнозелёный *adj.* (*bot.*) evergreen.
ве́чност|ь, и *f.* eternity; **це́лую в.** (*coll.*) for ages.
ве́ч|ный (~ен, ~на) *adj.*
1 (*льды, слава*) eternal, everlasting; **~ная мерзлота́** permafrost.
2 (*бессрочный*) indefinite, perpetual.
3 (*coll.*) (*постоянный*) perpetual, continual.
ве́шалк|а, и *f.*
1 (*крючок*) peg, (*планка*) rack, (*стойка*) stand.
2 (*петля*) tab (*on clothes for hanging on pegs*).
3 (*плечики*) (coat) hanger.
ве́ша|ть[1]**, ю** *impf.* (*of* ▸ **пове́сить**) to hang; **в. бельё на верёвку** to hang washing on a line; **в. уби́йцу** to hang a murderer.
ве́ша|ть[2]**, ю** *impf.* (*of* ▸ **взве́сить**) to weigh, weigh out.
ве́ша|ться , юсь *impf.* (*of* ▸ **пове́ситься**)
1 *pass. of* ▸ **~ть**[1]; (*картина*) to be hung.
2 (*кончать свою жизнь*) to hang o.s.
ве́|шу, сишь *see* ▸ **~сить**
веща́ни|е, я *nt.* broadcasting.
веща́|ть, ю *impf.*
1 (*по радио, телевидению*) to broadcast.
2 (*говорить высокопарно*) to pontificate, lay down the law.
вещ|ево́й *adj. of* ▸ **~ь; в. мешо́к** holdall; kitbag; **в. ры́нок** merchandise market; **в. склад** storage warehouse, store; (*mil.*) stores.
веще́ственн|ый *adj.* substantial, material; **~ые доказа́тельства** material evidence.
веществ|о́, а́ *nt.* substance.
вещ|ь, и, *pl.* **~и, ~е́й** *f.*
1 (*in var. senses*) thing.
2 (*pl.*) things (= (*i*) *belongings*; *baggage*; (*ii*) *clothes*); **э́то ва́ши ~и?** are these things yours?
3 (*произведение*) work; piece, thing.
ве́яни|е, я *nt.* (*fig.*) (*тенденция*) current, tendency, trend; **в. вре́мени** spirit of the times.
ве́|ять, ю, ешь *impf.* (*о ветре*) to blow; **~ял прохла́дный ветеро́к** a cool breeze was blowing; (*impers.*, + *i.*): **~ет весно́й** spring is in the air.
взаи́мност|ь, и *f.* reciprocity; return (*of affection*); **отвеча́ть кому́-н. ~ью** to reciprocate s.o.'s feelings, return s.o.'s love; **любо́вь без ~и** unrequited love.
взаи́м|ный (~ен, ~на) *adj.* mutual, reciprocal.
взаимовы́год|ный (~ен, ~на) *adj.* mutually beneficial.
взаимоде́йстви|е, я *nt.* (*связь*) interaction; (*mil.*) cooperation, coordination.
взаимоде́йств|овать, ую *impf.* to interact; (*mil.*) to cooperate.
взаимозачёт, а *m.* (*fin.*) offsetting of debts.
взаимоотноше́ни|е, я *nt.* (*pl.*) relationship(s), relation(s).
взаимопо́мощ|ь, и *f.* mutual aid; mutual assistance.
взаиморасчёт|ы, ов *m. pl.* (*fin.*) mutual settlement of accounts.
взаимосвя́з|ь, и *f.* interrelationship.
взаймы́ *adv.*: **взять в.** to borrow; **дать в.** to lend, loan.
взаме́н *prep.* + *g.* (*вместо*) instead (of); (*в обмен на что-н.*) in return (for), in exchange (for).
взаперти́ *adv.*
1 (*под замком*) under lock and key.
2 (*в уединении*) (*coll.*) in seclusion.
взба́лтыва|ть, ю *impf. of* ▸ **взболта́ть**
взбега́|ть, ю *impf.* (*of* ▸ **взбежа́ть**) to run up; **в. на́ гору** to run up a hill; **в. по ле́стнице** to run upstairs.
взбе|жа́ть, гу́, жи́шь, гу́т *pf. of* ▸ **~га́ть**
взбе|си́ть(ся), шу́(сь), ~сишь(ся) *pf. of* ▸ **беси́ть(ся)**
взбива́|ть, ю *impf. of* ▸ **взбить**
взбира́|ться, юсь *impf. of* ▸ **взобра́ться**
вз|би́ть, обью́, обьёшь *pf.* (*of* ▸ **~бива́ть**)

1 (*яйца*) to beat (up); **в. сли́вки** to whip cream.
2 (*подушку*) to fluff up.
взболта́|ть, ю *pf.* (*of* ▸ **взба́лтывать**) to shake (up) (*liquids*).
взбунт|ова́ться, у́юсь *pf. of* ▸ **бунтова́ть**
взбу́чк|а, и *f.* (*coll.*)
1 (*побои*) thrashing, beating.
2 (*выговор*) dressing-down.
взва́лива|ть, ю *impf. of* ▸ **взвали́ть**
взвал|и́ть, ю́, ~́ишь *pf.* (*of* ▸ **~́ивать**) to load, lift (onto); **в. мешо́к на́ спину** to hoist a pack onto one's back; **всю вину́ ~или на него́** he was made to shoulder all the blame.
взве́|сить, шу, сишь *pf.* (*of* ▸ **~шивать** *and* ▸ **ве́шать**[2]) (*груз*) to weigh; (*fig.*) (*варианты*) to weigh, consider.
взве́шен|ный (~, ~на) *adj.* (*решение, ответ*) carefully thought out, balanced.
взве́шива|ть, ю *impf. of* ▸ **взве́сить**
взвива́|ться, юсь *impf. of* ▸ **взви́ться**
взви́згива|ть, ю *impf. and freq. of* ▸ **взви́згнуть**
взви́згн|уть, у, ешь *pf.* to scream, cry out; (*собака*) to yelp.
взви́ться, взовью́сь, взовьёшься *pf.* (*of* ▸ **взвива́ться**) to fly up, soar; (*о флагах*) to be raised, go up.
взвод, а *m.* (*mil.*) platoon.
взволно́ван|ный (~, ~на) *adj.* anxious, worried; (*от счастья*) excited.
взволн|ова́ть, у́ю *pf. of* ▸ **волнова́ть**
взгляд, а *m.*
1 (*выражение глаз*) look; (*быстрый*) glance; (*пристальный*) gaze, stare; **бро́сить в.** (**на** + *a.*) to glance (at); **на пе́рвый в., с пе́рвого ~́а** at first sight.
2 (*мнение*) view; opinion; **на мой в.** in my opinion, as I see it.
взгллян|у́ть, у́, ~́ешь *pf.* (**на** + *a.*) to look (at); (*быстро*) to cast a glance (at).
вздор, а *no pl., m.* (*coll.*) nonsense; **говори́ть, нести́ в.** to talk nonsense.
вздо́р|ный (~ен, ~на) *adj.*
1 (*нелепый*) foolish, stupid.
2 (*coll.*) (*сварливый*) cantankerous, quarrelsome.
вздох, а *m.* sigh; deep breath; **испусти́ть после́дний в.** to breathe one's last.
вздохн|у́ть, у́, ёшь *pf.* (*of* ▸ **вздыха́ть**)
1 to sigh.
2 : **в. свобо́дно** to breathe freely; to relax (*after having been frightened or after exertion*).
вздра́гива|ть, ю *impf. of* ▸ **вздро́гнуть**
вздремн|у́ть, у́, ёшь *pf.* (*coll.*) to have a nap, doze.
вздро́гн|уть, у, ешь *pf.* (*of* ▸ **вздра́гивать**) (*от неожиданности*) to start; (*от боли*) to wince, flinch; (*дрожать*) tremble, shudder.
вздыха́|ть, ю *impf.* (*of* ▸ **вздохну́ть**)
1 to breathe; to sigh.
2 (**о** + *p.*, **по** + *d.*) (*тосковать*) to pine (for); to long, sigh (for); (*по девушке*) to be in love (with).
взима́|ть, ю *impf.* (*налог, штраф*) to levy, collect, raise.
взла́мыва|ть, ю *impf. of* ▸ **взлома́ть**
взлёт, а *m.* (*самолёта*) take-off.
взлета́|ть, ю *impf. of* ▸ **взлете́ть**
взле|те́ть, чу́, ти́шь *pf.* (*of* ▸ **~та́ть**) (*птица*) to fly up; (*самолёт*) to take off; **в. на во́здух** to explode, blow up.
взлёт|ный *adj. of* ▸ **~**; (*aeron.*): **~ная доро́жка** runway; **~но-поса́дочная полоса́** landing strip.
взлом, а *m.* (*сейфа*) breaking (into); (*двери*) forcing; **кра́жа со ~́ом** housebreaking; (*в ночное время*) burglary.
взлома́|ть, ю *pf.* (*of* ▸ **взла́мывать**) to break open, force; (*разворотить*) to smash; **в. замо́к** to force a lock; (*comput.*) to hack into.
взло́мщик, а *m.* burglar; **компью́терный в.** hacker.
взмах, а *m.* (*руки*) wave; (*крыльев*) flap, flapping; (*весла*) stroke; **одни́м ~́ом** at one stroke.
взма́хива|ть, ю *impf. of* ▸ **взмахну́ть**
взмахн|у́ть, у́, ёшь *pf.* (+*i.*) (*рукой*) to wave; (*крылом*) flap.
взметн|у́ть, у́, ёшь *pf.* (+ *i.*) to throw up, fling up; **в. рука́ми** to throw up one's hands.
взметн|у́ться, у́сь, ёшься *pf.* to leap up, fly up.
взмо́рь|е, я *nt.* seashore; seaside.
взмыва́|ть, ю *impf. of* ▸ **взмыть**
взм|ыть, о́ю, о́ешь *pf.* (*of* ▸ **~ыва́ть**) to soar (up).
взнос, а *m.* (*платёж*) payment; (*членский*) fee, dues; **вступи́тельный в.** membership fee; **очередно́й в.** instalment.
взобра́|ться, взберу́сь, взберёшься, *past* **~лся, ~ла́сь** *pf.* (*of* ▸ **взбира́ться**) (**на** + *a.*) to climb (up).
взобь|ю, ёшь *see* ▸ **взбить**
взо|йти́, йду́, йдёшь, *past* **~шёл, ~шла́,** *p.p.* **~ше́дший** *pf.* (*of* ▸ **всходи́ть** *and* ▸ **восходи́ть 1**)
1 (**на** + *a.*) to ascend, mount.
2 (*солнце; тесто*) to rise.
3 (*семена*) to come up.
взорв|а́ть, у́, ёшь *pf.* (*of* ▸ **взрыва́ть**) (*здание*) to blow up; (*бомбу*) to detonate.
взорв|а́ться, у́сь, ёшься, *past* **~а́лся, ~ала́сь** *pf.* (*of* ▸ **взрыва́ться**) (*о бомбе, газе*) to explode; (*о здании*) to blow up; (*fig.*) (*о человеке*) to blow up, explode.
взо|шёл, шла́ *see* ▸ **~йти́**
взрев|е́ть, у́, ёшь *pf.* to let out a roar.
взро́сл|ый *adj.* grown-up, adult; *also as n.* **в., ~ого** *m.*; **~ая, ~ой** *f.*
взрыв, а *m.* explosion; (*fig.*) burst, outburst; **«Большо́й в.»** the Big Bang.
взрыва́тел|ь, я *m.* detonator.
взрыва́|ть, ю *impf. of* ▸ **взорва́ть**
взрыва́|ться, юсь *impf. of* ▸ **взорва́ться**
взрывни́к, а́ *m.* explosives expert; shotfirer.
взрывн|о́й *adj.* explosive; **~а́я волна́** blast.
взрывоопа́с|ный (~ен, ~на) *adj.* explosive (*also fig.*).
взрывча́тк|а, и *f.* (*coll.*) explosive.
взры́вчат|ый *adj.* explosive; **~ое**

вещество́ explosive.

взыска́ни|е, я *nt.*
1 (*выговор*) reprimand; (*наказание*) penalty; punishment.
2 (*штрафа*) exaction; (*долга*) recovery.

взы|ска́ть, щу́, ~́щешь *pf.* (*of* ▸ **~́скивать**)
1 (*штраф*) to exact; (*долг*) to recover.
2 (**с** + *g.*) to call to account.

взы́скива|ть, ю *impf. of* ▸ **взыска́ть**

взы|щу́, ~́щешь *see* ▸ **~ска́ть**

взя́ти|е, я *nt.* taking; (*крепости*) capture; (*власти*) seizure.

взя́тк|а, и *f.*
1 bribe; backhander.
2 (*cards*) trick; **с него́ ~и гла́дки** (*coll.*) he isn't going to take responsibility.

взя́точник, а *m.* bribe-taker.

взя́точни|ца, цы *f. of* ▸ **~к**

взя́точничеств|о, а *nt.* bribery, bribe-taking.

взя|ть, возьму́, возьмёшь, *past* **~л, ~ла́, ~́ло** *pf.* (*of* ▸ **брать**)
1 *see* ▸ **брать.**
2 (*coll.*) (*думать*): **с чего́ ты взял?** what makes you think so?
3 : **в. да, в. и, в. да и...** (*coll.*) to do sth. suddenly; **он ~л да убежа́л** he upped and ran off.
4 : **чёрт возьми́!** (*coll.*) damn it!

взя́|ться, возьму́сь, возьмёшься, *past* **~лся, ~ла́сь** *pf.* (*of* ▸ **бра́ться**): **отку́да ни возьми́сь** (*coll.*) from nowhere, out of the blue.

вибрафо́н, а *m.* (*mus.*) vibraphone.

вибра́ци|я, и *f.* vibration.

вибри́р|овать, ую *impf.* to vibrate.

вигва́м, а *m.* wigwam.

вид[1], а *m.*
1 (*внешность*) air, look; appearance; aspect; **у него́ был мра́чный в.** he looked gloomy; **сде́лать в., бу́дто** to make it appear that, pretend that; **для ~́а** for the sake of appearances; **под ~́ом** (+ *g.*) under the guise (of).
2 (*состояние*) shape, form; condition.
3 (*панорама*) view; **ко́мната с ~́ом на го́ры** room with a view of the mountains.
4 (*pl.*) (*перспективы*) prospect; **~́ы на бу́дущее** prospects for the future; **име́ть ~́ы на** (+ *a.*) to have designs on.
5 (*поле зрения*) sight; **упусти́ть из ~́у** to lose sight (of); **на ~у́ у** (+ *g.*) within sight of; **быть на ~у́** to be in the public eye; **при ~́е** (+ *g.*) at the sight (of); **име́ть в ~у́** (*i*) to plan, intend, (*ii*) to mean; **что вы име́ли в ~у́, говоря́ э́то?** what did you mean when you said that?, (*iii*) to bear in mind; **име́й(те) в ~у́** bear in mind, don't forget; **име́ться в ~у́** (*i*) to be intended, be envisaged, (*ii*) to be meant.

вид[2], а *m.*
1 (*biol.*) species; **исчеза́ющий в.** endangered *or* threatened species.
2 (*mun*) type, kind.
3 (*gram.*) aspect; **соверше́нный, несоверше́нный в.** perfective, imperfective aspect.

ви́дени|е, я *nt.* (*способность видеть*) vision; (*восприятие, подход*) vision, outlook.

виде́ни|е, я *nt.* (*призрак*) vision, apparition.

ви́део *nt. indecl.* video (recorder, film, cassette).

видео... *comb. form* video-.

видеоза́пис|ь, и *f.* video recording.

видеоигр|а́, ы́, *pl.* **~́ы** *f.* video game.

видеока́мер|а, ы *f.* video camera, camcorder.

видеокассе́т|а, ы *f.* video cassette.

видеокли́п, а *m.* video clip, music video.

видеомагнитофо́н, а *m.* video recorder.

видеонаблюде́ни|е, я *nt.* (*оборудование*) CCTV.

видеофи́льм, а *m.* video (film).

ви́|деть, жу, дишь *impf.* (*of* ▸ **у~ 1**) to see; **в. кого́-н. наскво́зь** to see through s.o.; **в. во сне** to dream (of); **~дишь (ли); ~дите (ли)** you see; **вот уви́дишь** (*coll.*) you'll see.

ви́|деться, жусь, дишься *impf.*
1 (*встречаться*) to see one another; (**с** + *i.*) to meet with.
2 (*pf.* **при~**) to appear; **ему́ ~делся стра́шный сон** he had a terrifying dream.

ви́димо *adv.* evidently, apparently.

ви́димост|ь, и *f.*
1 (*различаемость*) visibility.
2 (*внешность*) outward appearance; **для ~и** (*coll.*) for show.
3 : **по всей ~и** to all appearances.

ви́дим|ый (~, ~а) *p.p.p. of* ▸ **ви́деть** *and adj.*
1 visible.
2 (*очевидный*) apparent, evident; **без ~ой причи́ны** for no apparent reason.
3 (*кажущийся*) apparent, seeming.

видне́|ться, ется, ются *impf.* to be visible.

ви́дно
1 *adv.* obviously, evidently; *as pred.* it is obvious, it is apparent; **в. было, как она́ расстро́илась** you could see how upset she was; **там в. бу́дет** (*coll.*) we'll see.
2 *adv. as pred.* visible; in sight; **бе́рега ещё не́ было в.** the coast was not yet visible.

ви́д|ный *adj.*
1 **(~ен, ~на́, ~но, ~ны́)** (*заметный*) visible; conspicuous.
2 (*важный*) distinguished, prominent.

видово́й *adj.* (*of* ▸ **вид[2]**)
1 (*biol.*) species.
2 (*gram.*) aspectual.

видоизмен|и́ть, ю́, и́шь *pf.* (*of* ▸ **~я́ть**) to modify, alter.

видоизмен|и́ться, ю́сь, и́шься *pf.* (*of* ▸ **~я́ться**) to alter (*intrans.*).

видоизмен|я́ть(ся), я́ю(сь) *impf. of* ▸ **~и́ть(ся)**

ви́з|а, ы *f.*
1 visa.
2 (*пометка*) official signature.

визажи́ст, а *m.* make-up artist.

Виза́нти|й, я *m.* (*hist.*) Byzantium.

византи́йский *adj.* Byzantine.

Византи́|я, и *f.* (*hist.*) Byzantine Empire.

визг, а *m.* (*человека*) scream, (*поросёнка*)

squeal, (*собаки*) yelp, (*тормозов*) screech.
визгли́в|ый (~, ~а) *adj.*
1 (*голос*) shrill.
2 (*крикливый*) given to screaming, squealing, yelping.
визж|а́ть, у́, и́шь *impf.* to scream; to squeal; to yelp.
визи́т, а *m.* visit; call; **нанести́ в.** to make an (official) visit; **прийти́ с ~ом к кому́-н.** to visit s.o., pay s.o. a call.
визи́тк|а, и *f.* (*карточка*) (business) card.
визи́т|ный *adj. of* ▸ **~; ~ная ка́рточка** (business) card.
визуа́л|ьный (~ен, ~ьна) *adj.* visual.
вика́ри|й, я *m.* (*eccl.*) vicar.
виктори́н|а, ы *f.* quiz.
ви́лк|а, и *f.*
1 fork.
2 (*elec.*) plug.
ви́лл|а, ы *f.* villa.
вильн|у́ть, у́, ёшь *pf. of* ▸ **виля́ть**
Ви́льнюс, а *m.* Vilnius.
виля́|ть, ю *impf. of* ▸ **вильну́ть**
1 **в. хвосто́м** to wag one's tail;
2 (*coll.*) (*дорога*) to wind, turn sharply.
вин|а́, ы́, *pl.* **~́ы** *f.* fault, guilt; (*причина*) blame; **моя́ в.** it is my fault; **не по их ~е́** through no fault of theirs; **поста́вить кому́-н. в ~у́** to accuse s.o. of, blame s.o. for; **свали́ть ~у́ (на** + *a.*) to lay the blame (on); **по ~е́** + *g.* because of.
виндсёрф(ер), а *m.* (*coll.*) sailboard.
виндсёрфинг, а *m.* windsurfing.
винегре́т, а *m.* beetroot salad (*of diced cooked beetroot, potato, and carrot, pickled cucumber, and vegetable oil dressing*); (*fig.*) (*смесь*) mishmash.
вини́л, а *m.* vinyl.
вини́тельный *adj.* (*gram.*): **в. паде́ж** accusative case.
вин|и́ть, ю́, и́шь *impf.* (**в** + *p.*) (*обвинять*) to accuse (of); (*считать виноватым*) to blame; **я ~ю́ его́ за наш прова́л** I blame him for our failure.
ви́нный *adj.* wine; winey; **в. спирт** alcohol.
вин|о́, а́, *pl.* **~́а** *nt.* wine.
винова́т|ый (~, ~а) *adj.*
1 (*взгляд*) guilty; (*человек*) guilty; to blame; **мы все ~ы в э́том** we are all to blame for this.
2 **~!** sorry!
вино́вник, а *m.* culprit; (*торжества, праздника*) cause, reason.
вино́вност|ь, и *f.* guilt.
вино́в|ный (~ен, ~на) *adj.* (**в** + *p.*) guilty (of); **призна́ть себя́ ~ным** to plead guilty.
виногра́д, а *m.*
1 (*растение*) vine.
2 (*collect.*) (*ягоды*) grapes.
виногра́дник, а *m.* vineyard.
винт, а́ *m.*
1 (*стержень*) screw.
2 (*самолёта*) propeller.
3 (*спираль*) spiral.
винто́вк|а, и *f.* rifle.
винт|ово́й *adj. of* ▸ **~;** spiral; **~ова́я ле́стница** spiral staircase.
виолончели́ст, а *m.* cellist.
виолончели́ст|ка, ки *f. of* ▸ **~**
виолонче́л|ь, и *f.* cello.
вира́ж, а́ *m.* (*поворот*) turn; **круто́й в.** steep turn.
виртуа́л|ьный (~ен, ~ьна) *adj.* virtual; **~ьная реа́льность** (*comput.*) virtual reality.
виртуо́з, а *m.* virtuoso.
виртуо́з|ный (~ен, ~на) *adj.* masterly, virtuosic.
ви́рус, а *m.* (*med.*) virus; bug; (*comput.*) virus.
ви́рус|ный *adj. of* ▸ **~**
ви́селиц|а, ы *f.* gallows, gibbet.
ви|се́ть, шу́, си́шь *impf.* to hang; to be suspended; **в. над** (+ *i.*) (*fig.*) to hang over; **в. на телефо́не** (*coll.*) to talk a lot on the phone.
ви́ски *nt. indecl.* whisky (*Br.*), whiskey (*US*).
ви́сн|уть, ет *impf.* (*comput.*) to crash.
вис|о́к, ка́ *m.* (*anat.*) temple.
високо́сный *adj.*: **в. год** leap year.
вися́чий *adj.* hanging; **в. замо́к** padlock; **в. мост** suspension bridge.
витами́н, а *m.* vitamin.
витами́н|ный *adj.*
1 *adj. of* ▸ **~; ~ная недоста́точность** vitamin deficiency.
2 vitamin-rich *or* -packed.
вит|о́к, ка́ *m.*
1 (*спирали*) turn, twist.
2 (*проволоки*) coil.
3 (*при полёте*) orbit.
4 (*fig.*) (*цикл*) round.
витра́ж, а́ *m.* stained-glass window.
витри́н|а, ы *f.*
1 (*в магазине*) (shop) window.
2 (*в музее*) showcase.
ви|ть, вью, вьёшь, *past* **~л, ~ла́, ~́ло** *impf.* (*of* ▸ **с~**) to weave.
ви́|ться, вьётся, *past* **~лся, ~ла́сь** *impf.* (*of* ▸ **с~**)
1 (*растение*) to wind, twine.
2 (*волосы*) to curl, wave.
3 (*птица*) to hover, circle.
4 (*змея*) to writhe, twist.
5 (*пыль, дым*) to spiral up.
вихр|ь, я *m.* whirlwind; **сне́жный в.** blizzard; (*fig.*) whirlwind, maelstrom.
ви́це-... *comb. form* vice-.
вице-президе́нт, а *m.* vice-president.
ВИЧ *m. indecl.* (*abbr. of* **ви́рус иммунодефици́та челове́ка**) (*med.*) HIV (*human immunodeficiency virus*); **ВИЧ-инфици́рованный** HIV-positive.
вишнёвый *adj.*
1 cherry; **в. сад** cherry orchard.
2 (*о цвете*) cherry-coloured, burgundy.
ви́ш|ня, ни, *g. pl.* **~ен** *f.*
1 (*дерево*) cherry tree.
2 (*плод*) cherry; (*collect.*) cherries.
вка́лыва|ть, ю *impf. of* ▸ **вколо́ть**
вка́пыва|ть, ю *impf. of* ▸ **вкопа́ть**
вка|ти́ть, чу́, ~́тишь *pf.* (*of* ▸ **~́тывать**) to roll into, onto; (*на колёсах*) to wheel in, into.

вка́тыва|ть, ю *impf. of* ▸ **вкати́ть**

вклад, а *m.*
1 (*в банке*) deposit.
2 (*действие*) investment.
3 (*fig.*) contribution.

В

вкла́дк|а, и *f.* supplementary sheet, insert.

вкла́дчик, а *m.* depositor, investor.

вкла́дчи|ца, цы *f. of* ▸ **~к**

вкла́дыва|ть, ю *impf. of* ▸ **вложи́ть**

вкла́дыш, а *m.* = **вкла́дка**

включ|а́ть(ся), а́ю(сь) *impf. of* ▸ **~и́ть(ся)**

включа́|я *pres. ger. of* ▸ **~ть;** *as prep.* + *a.* including.

включе́ни|е, я *nt.*
1 (**в** + *a.*) inclusion (in).
2 (*лампы, станка*) switching on, turning on.

включи́тельно *adv.* inclusive; **с пя́того по девя́тое в.** from the 5th to the 9th inclusive.

включ|и́ть, у́, и́шь *pf.* (*of* ▸ **~а́ть**)
1 (**в** + *a.*) to include (in); **в. в себя́** to include, comprise, take in; **в. в спи́сок** to enter on a list.
2 (*tech.*) to switch on, turn on; (*в розетку*) to plug in; **в. ра́дио** to switch on the radio; **в. ско́рость** to engage a gear.

включ|и́ться, у́сь, и́шься *pf.* (*of* ▸ **~а́ться**)
1 (**в** + *a.*) to join (in), enter (into).
2 (*о свете, радио*) to come on.

вкола́чива|ть, ю *impf. of* ▸ **вколоти́ть**

вкол|оти́ть, очу́, о́тишь *pf.* (*of* ▸ **~а́чивать**) to knock in, hammer in (*also fig.*).

вкол|о́ть, ю́, ~́ешь *pf.* (*of* ▸ **вка́лывать**) (**в** + *a.*) to stick (in, into).

вкопа́|ть, ю *pf.* (*of* ▸ **вка́пывать**) to dig in.

вкра́дчив|ый (~, ~а) *adj.* insinuating, ingratiating.

вкра́тце *adv.* briefly; succinctly.

вкру|ти́ть, чу́, ~́тишь *pf.* (*of* ▸ **~́чивать**) to screw in.

вкру́чива|ть, ю *impf. of* ▸ **вкрути́ть**

вкру|чу́, ~́тишь *see* ▸ **~ти́ть**

вкус, а *m.* taste (*also fig.*); **в чьём-н. ~́е** to s.o.'s taste; **э́то де́ло ~́а** it is a matter of taste; **челове́к со ~́ом** a man of taste; **одева́ться со ~́ом** to dress tastefully.

вку́с|ный (~ен, ~на́, ~но) *adj.* tasty, delicious, good.

вла́г|а, и *no pl., f.* moisture.

влага́лищ|е, а *nt.* vagina.

владе́л|ец, ьца *m.* owner.

владе́л|ица, ицы *f. of* ▸ **~ец**

владе́ни|е, я *nt.*
1 ownership; possession.
2 (*территория в собственности*) estate.

владе́|ть, ю, ешь *impf.* (+ *i.*)
1 (*иметь*) to own, possess.
2 (*подчинять себе*) to control; to be in possession (of); **в. собо́й** to control o.s.
3 (*fig.*) (*уметь пользоваться*) to have (a) command (of); to have the use (of); **она́ ~ет шестью́ языка́ми** she has a command of six languages.

вла́жност|ь, и *f.* (*воздуха*) humidity; (*почвы*) dampness.

вла́ж|ный (~ен, ~на́, ~но) *adj.* (*воздух, климат*) humid, damp; (*простыня*) damp; (*глаза, лоб*) moist.

вла́мыва|ться, юсь *impf. of* ▸ **вломи́ться**

вла́ст|ный (~ен, ~на) *adj.*
1 (*характер, жест*) imperious, commanding; **~ные структу́ры** authorities.
2 (**над** + *i., or inf.*) authoritative, competent.

вла́ст|ь, и, *pl.* **~́и, ~е́й** *f.*
1 (*политическая*) power; (*pl.*) authorities; **прийти́ к ~́и** to come to power; **у ~́и** in power.
2 (*родительская*) power, authority; **во ~́и** (+ *g.*) at the mercy (of), in the power (of); (*над чувствами*) control.

вле́во *adv.* to the left (*also fig., pol.*).

влеза́|ть, ю *impf. of* ▸ **влезть**

влез|ть, у, ешь, *past* **~, ~́ла** *pf.* (*of* ▸ **~а́ть**)
1 (*в окно*) to climb in(to); (*на дерево*) to climb (up); (*на крышу*) to climb onto; **в. в долги́** (*fig.*) to get into debt.
2 (*coll.*) (*уместиться*) to fit in, go in, go on; **все э́ти ве́щи не ~́ут в мою́ су́мку** these things will not all go into my bag.

влет|а́ть, а́ю *impf. of* ▸ **~е́ть**

вле|те́ть, чу́, ти́шь *pf.* (*of* ▸ **~та́ть**) to fly in, into; (*fig., coll.*) to rush in, into; (*impers.*): **ему́ опя́ть ~те́ло** he is in trouble again.

влече́ни|е, я *nt.* (**к** + *d.*) attraction (to).

вле|чь, ку́, чёшь, ку́т, *past* **влёк, ~кла́** *impf.* (*тащить*) to draw, drag; (*привлекать*) to attract; **в. за собо́й** to involve, entail.

влива́ни|я, й *nt. pl.* (*econ.*) investment, (financial) aid.

влива́|ть, ю *impf. of* ▸ **влить**

вли|ть, волью́, вольёшь, *past* **~л, ~ла́, ~́ло** *pf.* (*of* ▸ **~ва́ть**) to pour in; (*med.*) to infuse.

влия́ни|е, я *nt.* influence; **под ~м** (+ *g.*) under the influence of; **оказа́ть в. на** (+ *a.*) to influence; **по́льзоваться ~ем** to have influence, be influential.

влия́тел|ьный (~ен, ~ьна) *adj.* influential.

влия́|ть, ю *impf.* (*of* ▸ **по~**) (**на** + *a.*) to influence, have an influence on; (*действовать*) to affect.

вложе́ни|е, я *nt.*
1 enclosure.
2 (*fin.*) investment.

влож|и́ть, у́, ~́ишь *pf.* (*of* ▸ **вкла́дывать**)
1 to put in, insert; (*в письмо*) to enclose (*with a letter*).
2 (*fin.*) to invest.

влом|и́ться, лю́сь, ~́ишься *pf.* (*of* ▸ **вла́мываться**) to break in, into.

влюб|и́ться, лю́сь, ~́ишься *pf.* (*of* ▸ **~ля́ться**) (**в** + *a.*) to fall in love (with).

влюблён|ный (~, ~а́) *adj.* (*человек*) in love; (*no short form*) (*взгляд*) loving; tender.

влюбля́|ться, юсь *impf. of* ▸ **влюби́ться**

вмен|и́ть, ю́, и́шь *pf.* (*of* ▸ **~я́ть**): **в. (что́-н.) в вину́** (+ *d.*) to blame (sth.) on (s.o.); **в. в**

обязанность кому́-н. to impose as a duty on (s.o.).

вменя́ем|ый (~, ~а) *adj.* (*leg.*) sane, of sound mind.

вменя́|ть, ю *impf. of* ▶ **вмени́ть**

вме́сте *adv.* together; at the same time; **в. с** (+ *i.*) together with; **в. с тем** at the same time, also; **но/а в. с тем** but.

вмести́мост|ь, и *f.* capacity.

вмести́тел|ьный (~ен, ~ьна) *adj.* capacious; roomy.

вме|сти́ть(ся), щу́(сь), сти́шь(ся) *pf. of* ▶ **~ща́ть(ся)**

вме́сто *prep.* + *g.* instead of; in place of.

вмеша́тельств|о, а *nt.* interference; (*pol., mil., med.*) intervention.

вмеш|а́ться, а́юсь *pf.* (*of* ▶ **~иваться**) (**в** + *a.*) (*вторгнуться*) to interfere (in), meddle (with); (*для пресечения нежелательных последствий*) to intervene (in).

вме́шива|ться, юсь *impf. of* ▶ **вмеша́ться**

вмеща́|ть, ю *impf.* (*of* ▶ **вмести́ть**)
1 (*контейнер*) to contain; to hold; (*дом, зал*) to accommodate; **э́та бо́чка ~ет пятьдеся́т ли́тров** this barrel holds fifty litres.
2 (**в** + *a.*) to put, place (in, into).

вмеща́|ться, юсь *impf.* (*of* ▶ **вмести́ться**)
1 to fit, go in.
2 *pass. of* ▶ **~ть 2**

вмиг *adv.* in an instant; in a flash.

ВМФ *m. indecl.* (*abbr. of* **вое́нно-морско́й флот**) Navy.

вмя́тин|а, ы *f.* dent.

внаём, внаймы́ *adv.*: **отда́ть в.** to let, hire out, rent; **взять в.** to hire, rent; **сдаётся в.** 'to let'.

внача́ле *adv.* at first, in the beginning.

вне *prep.* + *g.* outside; out of; **объяви́ть в. зако́на** to outlaw; **в. о́череди** out of turn; **в. себя́** beside o.s.; **в. вся́ких сомне́ний** beyond any doubt.

вне... *comb. form* extra-.

внебра́чный *adj.* extramarital; **в. ребёнок** illegitimate child.

внедоро́жник, а *m.* four-wheel drive (vehicle).

внедре́ни|е, я *nt.* (*методов*) introduction; (*идей*) inculcation.

внедр|и́ть, ю́, и́шь *pf.* (*of* ▶ **~я́ть**)
1 (*методы*) to introduce.
2 (*идеи*) to inculcate, instil.

внедр|и́ться, ю́сь, и́шься *pf.* (*of* ▶ **~я́ться**) to take root.

внедря́|ть(ся), ю(сь) *impf. of* ▶ **внедри́ть(ся)**

внеза́пно *adv.* suddenly, all of a sudden.

внеза́пный *adj.* sudden.

внеочередно́й *adj.*
1 out of turn; **зада́ть в. вопро́с** to ask a question out of order.
2 (*заседание*) extraordinary; (*рейс*) extra.

внепла́новый *adj.* (*econ.*) not provided for by the plan; extraordinary.

внесе́ни|е, я *nt.*
1 (*денег*) paying in, deposit.
2 (*предложения*) moving, submission.

внес|ти́, у́, ёшь, *past* **~̀, ~ла́** *pf.* (*of* ▶ **вноси́ть**)
1 (*принести внутрь*) to bring in, carry in.
2 (*fig.*) to introduce, put in; **в. я́сность в де́ло** to clarify a matter; **в. свой вклад в де́ло** to do one's bit; to make one's contribution.
3 (*деньги*) to pay in, deposit.
4 (*предложение*) to make, move, table.
5 (*вписать*) to insert, enter.

внешнеторго́вый *adj.* foreign-trade (*attr.*).

вне́шн|ий *adj.*
1 outer, exterior; outward, external; outside; **в. вид** appearance.
2 (*иностранный*) foreign; **~яя поли́тика** foreign policy.

вне́шност|ь, и *f.* appearance; exterior.

внешта́тный *adj.* freelance; casual.

вниз *adv.* down, downwards; **в. голово́й** head first; **идти́ в. по ле́стнице** to go downstairs; **в. по тече́нию** downstream; **в. по Во́лге** down the Volga.

внизу́ *adv.* below; downstairs; *prep.* + *g.*: **в. страни́цы** at the foot of the page.

вник|а́ть, а́ю *impf. of* ▶ **~̀нуть**

вни́к|нуть, ну, нешь, *past* **~, ~ла** *pf.* (*of* ▶ **~а́ть**) (**в** + *a.*) (*изучить*) to go carefully (into), investigate thoroughly; (*понять*) to understand, penetrate.

внима́ни|е, я *nt.*
1 (*сосредоточенность*) attention; heed; notice, note; **обраща́ть в.** (**на** + *a.*) (*i*) to pay attention (to); (*ii*) to draw attention (to); **удели́ть в. кому́-н.** to give s.o. attention; **принима́я во в.** taking into account.
2 (*забота*) kindness, consideration.
3 (*int.*): **в.!** look out! mind out!

внима́тельност|ь, и *f.* attentiveness.

внима́тел|ьный (~ен, ~ьна) *adj.*
1 attentive.
2 (**к** + *d.*) (*заботливый*) thoughtful, considerate (towards).

вничью́ *adv.* (*sport*): **па́ртия око́нчилась в.** the game ended in a draw; **на́ша кома́нда сыгра́ла сего́дня в.** our team drew today.

вновь *adv.*
1 (*опять*) afresh, anew; again.
2 (*недавно*) newly; **в. прибы́вший** newcomer.

вно|си́ть, шу́, ~̀сишь *impf. of* ▶ **внести́**

ВНП *m. indecl.* (*abbr. of* **валово́й национа́льный проду́кт**) GNP (*Gross National Product*).

внук, а *m.* grandson; grandchild.

вну́тренн|ий *adj.*
1 inner, interior; internal; intrinsic; **в. мир** inner life, private world.
2 (*в государстве*) domestic, inland; **~ие дохо́ды** inland revenue; **~яя поли́тика** internal politics; **Министе́рство ~их дел** Ministry of Internal Affairs.

вну́тренност|ь, и *f.* interior; (*pl. only*) entrails, intestines; internal organs.

внутри́ *adv. and prep.* + *g.* inside, within; **в. до́ма** inside the house.

внутри... *comb. form* intra-.

внутриве́нный *adj.* (*med.*) intravenous.
внутрь *adv. and prep.* + *g.* within, inside; inwards; **открыва́ться в.** to open inwards; **войти́ в. до́ма** to go inside the house.
вну́чк|а, и *f.* granddaughter.
внуш|а́ть, а́ю *impf. of* ▶ **~и́ть**
внуше́ни|е, я *nt.*
1 (*выговор*) reprimand.
2 (*psych.*) suggestion.
внуши́тел|ьный (~ен, ~ьна) *adj.* imposing, impressive.
внуш|и́ть, у́, и́шь *pf.* (*of* ▶ **~а́ть**) (+ *a.* and *d.*) to inspire (with); to instil (*Br.*), instill (*US*); to suggest; **его́ вид ~и́л мне страх** the sight of him inspired me with fear.
вня́т|ный (~ен, ~на) *adj.* distinct.
во *prep.* = **в**
вовлека́|ть, ю *impf. of* ▶ **вовле́чь**
вовл|е́чь, еку́, ечёшь, еку́т, *past* **~ёк, ~екла́** *pf.* to draw in, involve.
вовну́трь *adv. and prep.* + *g.* (*coll.*) inside.
во́время *adv.* in time, on time; **не в.** at the wrong time.
во́все *adv.* (*coll.*) completely; (+ *neg.*) at all; **он в. не бога́тый челове́к** he is not at all a rich man.
во-вторы́х *adv.* secondly, in the second place.
во́гнут|ый (~, ~а) *adj.* concave.
вод|а́, ы́, *a.* **~́у,** *pl.* **~́ы, ~, ~́ам** *f.*
1 water; **выводи́ть на чи́стую ~́у** to show up, unmask; **похо́жи как две ка́пли ~ы́** as like as two peas.
2 (*pl.*) (*минеральные*) the waters; (*курорт*) spa.
води́тел|ь, я *m.* driver.
води́тельск|ий *adj.*: **~ие права́** driving licence (*Br.*), driver's license (*US*).
во|ди́ть, жу́, ~́дишь *impf.* (*indet. of* ▶ **вести́**)
1 (*see also* ▶ **вести́**) (*сопровождать*) to take; to lead; to conduct; (*машину*) to drive.
2 (*coll.*) (*see also* ▶ **вести́**): **в. дру́жбу (с** + *i.*) to be friends with; **в. знако́мство (с** + *i.*) to keep up an acquaintance (with).
3 (+ *i.*, **по** + *d.*; *see also* ▶ **вести́**) to pass (over, across).
во|ди́ться, жу́сь, ~́дишься *impf.*
1 (**с** + *i.*) to associate (with); (*о детях*) to play (with).
2 (*обитать*) to be, be found; **львы́ не ~́дятся в Евро́пе** lions are not found in Europe.
3 (*быть принятым*) to be the custom; to happen; **как ~́дится** as usually happens.
4 (*быть в наличии, иметься*) (*coll.*) be abundant; **де́ньги у него́ ~́дятся** he's always in the money.
во́дк|а, и *f.* vodka.
во́дн|ый *adj.* water; **~ые лы́жи** (*вид спорта*) waterskiing, (*экипировка*) waterskis.
водоворо́т, а *m.* whirlpool; (*fig.*) maelstrom.
водоём, а *m.* reservoir.
водола́з, а *m.* diver; (*ныряльщик с аквалангом*) frogman.
водола́зк|а, и *f.* thin polo-necked sweater.
водола́з|ный *adj. of* ▶ **~; в. костю́м** diving suit.
Водоле́|й, я *m.* (*созвездие*) Aquarius.
водонепроница́ем|ый (~, ~а) *adj.* watertight; waterproof.
водопа́д, а *m.* waterfall.
водопрово́д, а *m.* water supply system; plumbing.
водопрово́дчик, а *m.* plumber.
водоро́д, а *m.* (*chem.*) hydrogen.
во́доросл|ь, и *f.* (*bot.*) water plant; **морска́я в.** seaweed.
водосто́к, а *m.* drain; (*на улице, крыше*) gutter.
водосто́|чный *adj. of* ▶ **~к; ~чная труба́** drainpipe.
водохрани́лищ|е, а *nt.* reservoir.
во́д|очный *adj. of* ▶ **~ка**
водян|о́й *adj.*
1 *adj. of* ▶ **вода́.**
2 (*живущий, растущий в воде*) water, aquatic.
3 (*приводимый в движение водой*) water-driven.
во|ева́ть, ю́ю, ю́ешь *impf.* (**с** + *i.*) to wage war (with), make war (upon); to be at war.
воен... *comb. form, abbr. of* **вое́нный**
военача́льник, а *m.* commander.
военкома́т, а *m.* (*abbr. of* **вое́нный комисса́риат**) military recruitment office.
вое́нно-... *comb. form, abbr. of* **вое́нный**
вое́нно-возду́шн|ый *adj.*: **~ые си́лы** Air Force(s).
вое́нно-морско́й *adj.* naval; **в. флот** the Navy.
военнообя́занн|ый, ого *m.* man liable for call-up (*including reservists*).
военнопле́нн|ый, ого *m.* prisoner of war.
вое́нно-полево́й *adj.* (*mil.*) field; **в. суд** court-martial.
вое́нно-промы́шленный *adj.* military-industrial.
военнослу́жащ|ий, его *m.* serviceman.
вое́нн|ый *adj.* military; war; (*форма*) army; **в. врач** (army) medical officer; **~ое вре́мя** wartime; **~ое положе́ние** martial law; **~ое учи́лище** military college; *as n.* **в., ~ого** *m.* soldier, serviceman; **~ые** (*collect.*) the military.
вожделе́ни|е, я *nt.* desire, lust (*also fig.*).
вожд|ь, я́ *m.* (*организации*) leader; (*племени*) chief.
во́жж|и, е́й *pl.* (*sg.* **~а́, ~и́** *f.*) reins.
во|жу́[1], **~́дишь** *see* ▶ **~ди́ть**
во|жу́[2], **~́зишь** *see* ▶ **~зи́ть**
воз, а, о ~́е, на ~у́, *pl.* **~ы́** *m.* cart, wagon.
возбуди́м|ый (~, ~а) *adj.* excitable.
возбу|ди́ть, жу́, ди́шь *pf.* (*of* ▶ **~жда́ть**)
1 to excite, rouse, arouse; **в. аппети́т** to whet the appetite.
2 (*leg.*) to institute; **в. де́ло (про́тив** + *g.*) to institute proceedings (against), bring an action (against); **в. иск (про́тив** + *g.*) to bring a suit (against).
возбу|ди́ться, жу́сь, ди́шься *pf.* (*of* ▶ **~жда́ться**) (*о человеке*) to get excited.
возбужда́|ть(ся), ю(сь) *impf. of* ▶ **возбуди́ть(ся)**

возбужде́ни|е, я *nt.* excitement.
возбу|ждённый *p.p.p. of* ▶ **~ди́ть** *and adj.* excited.
возбу|жу́(сь), ди́шь(ся) *see* ▶ **~ди́ть(ся)**
возве|сти́, ду́, дёшь, *past* **~л, ~ла́** *pf.* (*of* ▶ **возводи́ть**)
1 (*возвысить*) to elevate; **в. в сан патриа́рха** to elect to the patriarchate.
2 (*строить*) to erect, put up.
3 (*math.*) to raise; **в. в куб** to cube.
возво|ди́ть, жу́, ~дишь *impf. of* ▶ **возвести́**
возвра́т, а *m.* return; repayment, reimbursement; **без ~а** irrevocably.
возвра|ти́ть, щу́, ти́шь *pf.* (*of* ▶ **~ща́ть**)
1 (*отдать обратно*) to return, give back; (*деньги*) to pay back.
2 (*получить обратно*) to recover, retrieve; **в. де́ньги, о́тданные взаймы́** to recover a loan.
возвра|ти́ться, щу́сь, ти́шься *pf.* (*of* ▶ **~ща́ться**) to return; (*fig.*) to revert.
возвраща́|ть(ся), ю(сь) *impf. of* ▶ **возврати́ть(ся)** *and* ▶ **верну́ть(ся)**
возвраще́ни|е, я *nt.* return; **в. домо́й** homecoming.
возвра|щу́, ти́шь *see* ▶ **~ти́ть**
возвы́|ситься, шусь, сишься *pf.* (*of* ▶ **~ша́ться**) to rise, go up.
возвыша́|ться, юсь *impf.*
1 *impf. of* ▶ **возвы́ситься.**
2 (*impf. only*) (**над** + *i.*) to tower (above) (*also fig.*).
возвыше́ни|е, я *nt.*
1 (*действие*) rise; raising.
2 (*место*) elevation; raised place.
возвы́шенност|ь, и *f.* (*geog.*) height; elevation.
возвы́шен|ный (~, ~на) *adj.*
1 (*высокий*) high; elevated.
2 (*благородный*) lofty, sublime, elevated; **~ные идеа́лы** lofty ideals.
возгла́в|ить, лю, ишь *pf.* (*of* ▶ **~ля́ть**) to head, be at the head of.
возглавля́|ть, ю *impf. of* ▶ **возгла́вить**
во́зглас, а *m.* cry, exclamation.
воздвига́|ть, ю *impf.* (*of* ▶ **воздви́гнуть**) to raise, erect.
воздви́г|нуть, ну, нешь, *past* **~, ~ла** *pf. of* ▶ **~а́ть**
возде́йстви|е, я *nt.* influence; **он э́то сде́лал под физи́ческим ~ем** he did it under coercion.
возде́йств|овать, ую *impf. and pf.* (**на** + *a.*) to influence, affect; to exert influence.
возде́л|ать, аю *pf.* (*of* ▶ **~ывать**) to cultivate, till.
возде́лыва|ть, ю *impf. of* ▶ **возде́лать**
воздержа́вш|ийся *p.p. of* ▶ **воздержа́ться;** *as n.* **в., ~егося** *m.* abstainer; **предложе́ние бы́ло при́нято при трёх ~ихся** the motion was carried with three abstentions.
воздержа́ни|е, я *nt.*
1 abstinence.
2 (**от** + *g.*) abstention (from).
воз|держа́ться, держу́сь, де́ржишься *pf.* (*of* ▶ **~де́рживаться**) (**от** + *g.*)
1 (*от замечания, курения*) to refrain (from); (*от алкоголя, курения, мяса*) to abstain (from).
2 (*от голосования*) to abstain.
возде́ржива|ться, юсь *impf. of* ▶ **воздержа́ться**
во́здух, а *no pl., m.*
1 air; **на (откры́том) ~е** out of doors; **вы́йти на в.** to go out of doors; **в ~е** (*fig.*) in the air.
2 (*атмосфера*) atmosphere.
возду́ш|ный *adj.*
1 air, aerial; **в. змей** kite; **~ная трево́га** air-raid warning; **в. шар** balloon.
2 (*приводимый в движение воздухом*) air-driven.
3 (**~ен, ~на**) (*очень лёгкий*) airy, light; flimsy.
воззва́ни|е, я *nt.* appeal.
во|зи́ть, жу́, ~зишь *impf.* (*indet. of* ▶ **везти́**) to take, convey; to carry; (*тянуть*) to draw.
во|зи́ться, жу́сь, ~зишься *impf.* (**с** + *i.*) (*с чем-н. трудным*) to take trouble (over); (*с детьми*) to spend time, busy o.s. (with); (*coll.*) (*копаться*) to potter; **он лю́бит в. в саду́** he likes pottering about in the garden.
возлага́|ть, ю *impf. of* ▶ **возложи́ть**
во́зле *prep.* + *g.* by, near; *adv.* nearby.
возлож|и́ть, у́, ~ишь *pf.* (*of* ▶ **возлага́ть**)
1 (*положить*) to lay; **в. вено́к на моги́лу** to lay a wreath on a grave.
2 (*поручить*) (**на** + *a.*) to entrust (to); **в. вину́/отве́тственность на** (+ *a.*) to lay the blame/responsibility on.
возлю́бленн|ый, ого *m.* (*n. decl. as an adj.*; *f.* **~ая, ~ой**) beloved, sweetheart; (*любовник*) lover; (*любовница*) mistress.
возме́зди|е, я *nt.* retribution.
возме|сти́ть, щу́, сти́шь *pf.* (*of* ▶ **~ща́ть**) to compensate (for), make up (for); **в. расхо́ды** to refund expenses.
возмеща́|ть, ю *impf. of* ▶ **возмести́ть**
возмеще́ни|е, я *nt.*
1 (*сумма*) compensation; (*leg.*) damages.
2 (*расходов*) reimbursement.
возме|щу́, сти́шь *see* ▶ **~сти́ть**
возмо́жно *adv.*
1 possibly.
2 *as pred.* it is possible; **в., что мы за́втра уе́дем** we may possibly go away tomorrow.
возмо́жност|ь, и *f.*
1 possibility; **по (ме́ре) ~и** as far as possible.
2 (*удобный случай*) opportunity; **при пе́рвой ~и** at the first opportunity.
3 (*pl.*) (*средства*) means, resources.
возмо́ж|ный (~ен, ~на) *adj.*
1 possible; **врач сде́лал для неё всё ~ное** the doctor did all in his power for her.
2 (*наибольший*) the greatest possible.
возмути́тел|ьный (~ен, ~ьна) *adj.* disgraceful, outrageous, scandalous.
возму|ти́ть, щу́, ти́шь *pf.* to anger, outrage.

возму|ти́ться, щу́сь, ти́шься *pf.* (+ *i.*) to be indignant (at); to be outraged (at).

возмуща́|ть, ю *impf. of* ▸ **возмути́ть**

возмуща́|ться, юсь *impf. of* ▸ **возмути́ться**

возмуще́ни|е, я *nt.* indignation, outrage.

возму|щу́, ти́шь *see* ▸ **~ти́ть**

вознагражде́ни|е, я *nt.*
1 (*за труд, за подвиг*) reward, recompense; (*компенсация*) compensation.
2 (*оплата*) fee, remuneration.

возник|а́ть, а́ю *impf.* (*of* ▸ **~нуть**)
1 (*трудности, подозрение*) to arise, spring up; **у меня́ ~ла мысль** the thought occurred to me.
2 (*coll.*) (*появляться*) to appear, pop up.
3 (*начинаться*) to begin.

возникнове́ни|е, я *m.* rise, beginning, origin.

возни́к|нуть, ну, нешь, *past* **~, ~ла** *pf. of* ▸ **~а́ть**

возн|я́, и́ *no pl., f.* (*coll.*)
1 (*шум*) row, noise.
2 (*хлопоты*) bother, trouble.

возоблада́|ть, ю *pf.* (**над** + *i.*) to prevail (over).

возобнов|и́ть, лю́, и́шь *pf.* (*of* ▸ **~ля́ть**) (*переговоры, отношения*) to resume; (*абонемент, контракт*) to renew.

возобновле́ни|е, я *nt.* resumption, renewal.

возобновля́|ть, ю *impf. of* ▸ **возобнови́ть**

возража́|ть, ю *impf. of* ▸ **возрази́ть; не ~ю** I have no objection.

возраже́ни|е, я *nt.* objection; (*резкий ответ*) retort.

возра|зи́ть, жу́, зи́шь *pf.* (*of* ▸ **~жа́ть**)
1 (**про́тив** + *g. or* **на** + *a.*) to object (to); to take exception (to); **про́тив э́того не́чего в.** nothing can be said against it.
2 (*pf. only*) (*ответить резко*) to retort.

во́зраст, а *m.* age; **ребёнок в ~е двена́дцати лет** a twelve-year-old child.

возраста́ни|е, я *nt.* growth, increase.

возраст|а́ть, а́ю *impf. of* ▸ **~и́**

возраст|и́, у́, ёшь, *past* **возро́с, возросла́** *pf.* (*of* ▸ **~а́ть**) to grow, increase.

возраст|но́й *adj. of* ▸ **во́зраст; ~на́я гру́ппа** age group.

возро|ди́ть, жу́, ди́шь *pf.* (*of* ▸ **~жда́ть**) (*хозяйство, город*) to regenerate; (*надежду, культуру*) to revive.

возро|ди́ться, жу́сь, ди́шься *pf.* (*of* ▸ **~жда́ться**) to revive (*intrans.*).

возрожда́|ть, ю *impf. of* ▸ **возроди́ть**

возрожда́|ться, юсь *impf. of* ▸ **возроди́ться**

возрожде́ни|е, я *nt.* regeneration; revival; **эпо́ха Возрожде́ния** Renaissance.

возьм|у́(сь), ёшь(ся) *see* ▸ **взя́ть(ся)**

во́ин, а *m.* warrior; fighter.

во́инск|ий *adj.*
1 military; **~ая пови́нность** conscription.
2 (*свойственный военному*) martial, warlike.

во́инствен|ный (~, ~на) *adj.*
1 (*народ*) warlike.
2 (*вид, тон*) bellicose.

во|й, я *no pl., m.* howl, howling; wail, wailing.

вой|ду́, дёшь *see* ▸ **~ти́**

во́йлок, а *m.* felt.

войн|а́, ы́, *pl.* **~ы** *f.* war; (*ведение войны*) warfare; **вести́ ~у́** to wage war; **объяви́ть ~у́** to declare war.

войск|а́, ~ *pl.* (*sg.* **~о, ~а** *nt.*) troops; forces; **наёмные в.** mercenaries.

войсково́й *adj.* military.

во|йти́, йду́, йдёшь, *past* **~шёл, ~шла́** *pf.* (*of* ▸ **входи́ть**) (**в.** + *a.*) (*вступить*) to enter; (*из данного места внутрь*) to go in(to); (*извне в данное место*) to come in(to); (*уместиться*) to go in, fit in; (*в состав чего-н.*) to enter; **в. в исто́рию** to go down in history; **в. в мо́ду** to become fashionable; **в. в систе́му** (*comput.*) to log on.

вокали́ст, а *m.* (*mus.*) vocalist.

вокали́ст|ка, ки *f. of* ▸ **~**

вока́льный *adj.* vocal.

вокза́л, а *m.* (large) station; **железнодоро́жный в.** railway (*esp. main or terminus*) station; **морско́й в.** port arrival and departure building.

вокру́г *adv. and prep.* + *g.* round, around; (*по поводу*) about; **в. све́та** round the world.

вол, а́ *m.* ox, bullock.

Во́лг|а, и *f.* the Volga (*river*).

волды́р|ь, я́ *m.* (*пузырь*) blister.

волево́й *adj.* (*человек, натура*) strong-willed; (*лицо, голос*) determined.

волейбо́л, а *m.* volleyball.

волейболи́ст, а *m.* volleyball player.

волейболи́ст|ка, ки *f. of* ▸ **~**

волк, а, *pl.* **~и, ~о́в** *m.* wolf.

волкода́в, а *m.* wolfhound.

волн|а́, ы́, *pl.* **~ы, ~, ~а́м** *f.* wave.

волне́ни|е, я *nt.*
1 (*на воде*) choppiness.
2 (*fig.*) (*нервное*) agitation; (*радостное*) excitement; (*душевное*) emotion; **прийти́ в в.** to become agitated, excited.
3 (*usu. pl.*; *pol.*) disturbance(s); unrest.

волни́ст|ый (~, ~а) *adj.* wavy.

волн|ова́ть, у́ю, *impf.* (*of* ▸ **вз~**) (*возбуждать*) to excite; (*беспокоить*) to worry; (*воду*) to disturb, agitate (*also fig.*).

волн|ова́ться, у́юсь *impf.*
1 (*нервно*) to worry, be nervous; (*радостно*) to be excited; **она́ ~у́ется о де́тях/за дете́й** she worries about her children.
2 (*вода*) to be agitated, choppy.

волноре́з, а *m.* breakwater.

волн|у́ющий *pres. part. act. of* ▸ **~ова́ть** *and adj.* (*беспокоящий*) disturbing, worrying; (*захватывающий*) exciting, thrilling.

волоки́т|а, ы[1] *f.* (*coll.*) (*бюрократизм*) red tape.

волоки́т|а, ы[2] *m.* (*coll.*) (*мужчина*) philanderer.

волок|но́, на́, *pl.* **~на, ~он, ~нам** *nt.* fibre (*Br.*), fiber (*US*).

волонтёр, а *m.* volunteer.

во́лос, а, *pl.* **~ы, воло́с, ~а́м** *m.* hair; (*pl.*) hair (*of the head*); **рвать на себе́ ~ы** to tear one's hair.

волоса́т|ый (~, ~а) *adj.* hairy.
волос|о́к, ка́ *m. dim. of* ▶**во́лос; на в.** (**от** + *g.*) within a hair's breadth (of); **висе́ть, держа́ться на ~ке́** to hang by a thread.
волоч|и́ть, у́, ~ишь *impf.* to drag; **в. но́ги** to shuffle one's feet.
вол|о́чь, оку́, очёшь, оку́т, *past* **~о́к, ~окла́** *impf.* (*coll.*) to drag.
волше́бник, а *m.* magician; wizard.
волше́бниц|а, ы *f.* enchantress.
волше́б|ный (~ен, ~на) *adj.*
1 magic (*attr.*); magical; **~ная па́лочка** magic wand.
2 (*fig.*) magical, bewitching; enchanting.
волшебств|о́, а́ *nt.* magic.
волы́нк|а, и *f.* bagpipes.
волье́р, а *m.* cage; enclosure.
волье́р|а, ы *f.* = ~
вольнонаёмный *adj.* (*рабочий, труд*) hired; freelance.
во́льност|ь, и *f.* freedom; liberty; **поэти́ческая в.** poetic licence (*Br.*), poetic license (*US*).
во́л|ьный *adj.*
1 free.
2 (*sport*) free, freestyle; **~ьная борьба́** freestyle wrestling.
3 **(~ен, ~ьна́, ~ьно,** *pl.* **~ьны́)** (*short forms only*) free, at liberty; **вы ~ьны́ де́лать, что хоти́те** you are at liberty to do as you wish.
вольт, а, *g. pl.* **в.** *m.* (*elec.*) volt.
воль|ю́, ёшь *see* ▶**влить**
во́л|я, и *no pl., f.*
1 (*in var. senses*) will; **после́дняя в.** last will; **си́ла ~и** willpower; **по до́брой ~е** of one's own free will; **не по свое́й ~е** against one's will.
2 (*свобода*) freedom, liberty; **на ~е** at liberty; **дать ~ю** (+ *d.*) to give free rein (to).
вон[1] *adv.* out; off, away; **вы́йти в.** to go away; **в. отсю́да!** get out!
вон[2] *particle* (*на отдалении*) there, over there; **в. он идёт** there he goes.
вон|жу́, зи́шь *see* ▶**~зи́ть**
вонза́|ть, ю *impf. of* ▶**вонзи́ть**
вонза́|ться, юсь
1 *impf. of* ▶**вонзи́ться.**
2 *pass. of* ▶**~ть**
вон|зи́ть, жу́, зи́шь *pf.* (*of* ▶**~за́ть**) (**в** + *a.*) to plunge, thrust (into).
вон|зи́ться, жу́сь, зи́шься *pf.* (*of* ▶**~за́ться 1**) to pierce, penetrate; **стрела́ ~зи́лась ему́ в се́рдце** the arrow pierced his heart.
вон|ь, и *no pl., f.* stink, stench.
воня́|ть, ю *impf.* (*coll.*) (+ *i.*) to stink, reek (of).
вообража́|емый *pres. part. pass. of* ▶**~ть** *and adj.* imaginary; fictitious.
вообража́|ть, ю *impf.* (*of* ▶**вообрази́ть**) to imagine.
воображе́ни|е, я *nt.* imagination.
вообра|зи́ть, жу́, зи́шь *pf. of* ▶**~жа́ть; ~зи́(те)!** (just) imagine!
вообще́ *adv.*
1 (*в общем*) in general; on the whole; **в. говоря́** generally speaking.
2 (*всегда*) always.
3 (*with neg.*) at all.
воодушев|и́ть, лю́, и́шь *pf.* (*of* ▶**~ля́ть**) (**кого́-н. на** + *a.*) to inspire (to), rouse (to).
воодушевле́ни|е, я *nt.*
1 (*действие*) rousing.
2 (*увлечение*) enthusiasm, fervour (*Br.*), fervor (*US*).
воодушевля́|ть, ю *impf. of* ▶**воодушеви́ть**
вооруж|а́ть(ся), а́ю(сь) *impf. of* ▶**~и́ть(ся)**
вооруже́ни|е, я *nt.*
1 (*действие*) arming.
2 (*оружие*) arms, armament; **быть на ~и** to be deployed.
3 (*принадлежности*) equipment.
вооружён|ный (~, ~а́) *p.p.p. of* ▶**вооружи́ть** *and adj.* armed; **~ные си́лы** armed forces.
вооруж|и́ть, у́, и́шь *pf.* (*of* ▶**~а́ть**) (+ *i.*) to arm; to equip (with) (*also fig.*).
вооруж|и́ться, у́сь, и́шься *pf.* (*of* ▶**~а́ться**) to arm o.s.; (*fig.*) to equip o.s.
во-пе́рвых *adv.* first, first of all, in the first place.
вопло|ти́ть, щу́, ти́шь *pf.* (*of* ▶**~ща́ть**) to embody, personify; **в. в себе́** to be the embodiment (of); **в. в жизнь** (*планы*) to realize.
вопло|ти́ться, щу́сь, ти́шься *pf.* (*of* ▶**~ща́ться**) to be realized; to be fulfilled.
вопloща́|ть(ся), ю(сь) *impf. of* ▶**воплоти́ть(ся)**
воплоще́ни|е, я *nt.* embodiment.
вопл|ь, я *m.* cry, wail; wailing, howling.
вопреки́ *prep.* + *d.* (*несмотря на*) despite, in spite of; (*наперекор*) against, contrary to.
вопро́с, а *m.*
1 question; **зада́ть в.** to ask, put a question; **отве́тить на в.** to answer a question.
2 (*проблема*) question, problem; (*дело*) matter; **подня́ть, поста́вить в.** (**о** + *p.*) to raise the question (of); **в. жи́зни и сме́рти** matter of life and death; **спо́рный в.** moot point.
вопроси́тельный *adj.* interrogative; **в. знак** question mark; **в. взгляд** inquiring look.
вор, а, *pl.* **~ы, ~о́в** *m.* thief.
ворв|а́ться, у́сь, ёшься, *past* **~а́лся, ~ала́сь** *pf.* (*of* ▶**врыва́ться**) to burst (into).
вороб|е́й, ья́ *m.* sparrow.
воро́ванный *adj.* stolen.
вор|ова́ть, у́ю *impf.* (*coll. pf.* **с~**) to steal; **в. де́ньги у кого́-н.** to steal money from s.o.
воро́вк|а, и *f. of* ▶**вор**
воровств|о́, а́ *nt.* stealing; theft.
во́рон, а *m.* raven.
воро́н|а, ы *f.* crow.
воро́нк|а, и *f.*
1 (*для переливания*) funnel (*for pouring liquids*).
2 (*mil.*) (*яма*) crater.

В

ворóт|а, ~ *no sg.*
[1] gate, gates; (*вход*) gateway.
[2] (*sport*) goal.

воротúл|а, ы *m.* (*coll.*) big shot.

воротнúк, á *m.* collar.

вóрох, а, *pl.* **~á** *m.* heap, pile.

ворóча|ться, юсь *impf.* (*coll.*) to turn, move (*intrans.*); **в. с бóку нá бок** to toss and turn.

ворч|áть, ý, úшь *impf.* **(на** + *a.*) to grumble (at); (*о собаке*) to growl (at).

ворчлúв|ый (~, ~а) *adj.* querulous.

восемнáдцатый *adj.* eighteenth.

восемнáдцат|ь, и *num.* eighteen.

вóс|емь, ьмú, *i.* **емью́** *and* **ьмью́** *num.* eight.

вóс|емьдесят, ьмúдесяти *num.* eighty.

вос|емьсóт, ьмисóт, *i.* **емьюстáми** *and* **ьмьюстáми** *num.* eight hundred.

воск, а *m.* wax.

воскли́кн|уть, у, ешь *pf. of* ▸ **восклицáть**

восклицáни|е, я *nt.* exclamation.

восклицáтельный *adj.* exclamatory; **в. знак** exclamation mark.

восклицá|ть, ю *impf.* (*of* ▸ **воскли́кнуть**) to exclaim.

восковóй *adj.* wax; (*цвет*) waxen.

воскрес|áть, áю *impf.* (*of* ▸ **~нуть**) to rise again, rise from the dead; (*fig.*) to revive.

воскресéни|е, я *nt.* resurrection.

воскресéнь|е, я *nt.* Sunday.

воскре|сúть, шý, сúшь *pf.* (*of* ▸ **~шáть**) to raise from the dead, resurrect; (*fig.*) to revive.

воскрéс|нуть, ну, нешь, *past* **~, ~ла** *pf. of* ▸ **~áть**

воскрéсный *adj.* Sunday.

воскрешá|ть, ю *impf. of* ▸ **воскресúть**

воскрешéни|е, я *nt.* resurrection; (*fig.*) revival.

воспалéни|е, я *nt.* (*med.*) inflammation; **в. лёгких** pneumonia.

воспалён|ный (~, ~á) *adj.* sore; inflamed.

воспал|úться, ю́сь, úшься *pf.* (*of* ▸ **~я́ться**) to become inflamed.

воспал|я́ть(ся), я́ю(сь) *impf. of* ▸ **~úть(ся)**

воспитáни|е, я *nt.*
[1] upbringing; (*образование*) education.
[2] (*воспитанность*) (good) breeding.

воспи́танник, а *m.*
[1] (*школьник*) pupil.
[2] (*приёмыш*) ward.

воспи́танный *p.p.p. of* ▸ **воспитáть** *and adj.* well brought up.

воспитáтел|ь, я *m.* teacher; (*приёмыша*) guardian.

воспитáтель|ница, ницы *f. of* ▸ **~**

воспит|áть, áю *pf.* (*of* ▸ **~ывать**) (*вырастить*) to bring up; (*дать образование*) to educate.

воспи́тыва|ть, ю *impf. of* ▸ **воспитáть**

воспламен|úться, ю́сь, úшься *pf.* (*of* ▸ **~я́ться**) to catch fire, ignite; (*fig.*) to flare up.

воспламеня́|ть(ся), ю(сь) *impf. of* ▸ **воспламенúть(ся)**

воспóлн|ить, ю, ишь *pf.* to fill in.

восполня́|ть, ю *impf. of* ▸ **воспóлнить**

воспóльз|оваться, уюсь *pf. of* ▸ **пóльзоваться 1, 2**

воспоминáни|е, я *nt.*
[1] recollection, memory.
[2] *pl.* (*liter.*) memoirs; reminiscences.

воспрепя́тств|овать, ую *pf. of* ▸ **препя́тствовать**

воспрещá|ться, ется *impf.* to be prohibited.

восприи́мчив|ый (~, ~а) *adj.*
[1] (*ум, натура*) receptive; impressionable.
[2] (*подверженный*) susceptible.

восприм|ý, ~ешь *see* ▸ **восприня́ть**

воспринимá|ть, ю *impf. of* ▸ **восприня́ть**

воспри|ня́ть, мý, ~мешь, *past* **~нял, ~нялá, ~няло** *pf.* (*of* ▸ **~нимáть**)
[1] (*ощутить*) to perceive, apprehend; (*понять*) to grasp, take in.
[2] (*понять как*) to take (for), interpret.

восприя́ти|е, я *nt.* (*phil., psych.*) perception.

воспроизведéни|е, я *nt.*
[1] reproduction; **в. человéческого рóда** reproduction of the human species; **вéрное в. карти́ны Рýбенса** faithful reproduction of a painting by Rubens.
[2] (*electronics*) playback, replay; **замéдленное/ускóренное в.** slow-motion/high-speed playback.

воспроизве|сти́, дý, дёшь, *past* **~л, ~лá** *pf.* (*of* ▸ **воспроизводи́ть**) (*in var. senses*) to reproduce; **в. в пáмяти** to recall.

воспроизво|ди́ть, жý, ~дишь *impf. of* ▸ **воспроизвести́**

воссоединéни|е, я *nt.* reunification.

воссоедин|и́ть, ю́, и́шь *pf.* (*of* ▸ **~я́ть**) to reunite.

воссоединя́|ть, ю *impf. of* ▸ **воссоедини́ть**

воссозда|вáть, ю́, ёшь *impf. of* ▸ **~ть**

воссоздáни|е, я *nt.* reconstruction.

воссоз|дáть, дáм, дáшь, дáст, дади́м, дади́те, дадýт, *past* **~дáл, ~далá, ~дáло** *pf.* (*of* ▸ **~давáть**) to reconstruct, reconstitute.

восста|вáть, ю́, ёшь *impf. of* ▸ **~ть**

восстанáвлива|ть, ю *impf. of* ▸ **восстанови́ть**

восстáни|е, я *nt.* uprising, insurrection.

восстанови́тельн|ый *adj.* restorative; **в. перио́д** period of reconstruction; **~ые рабóты** restoration work.

восстанов|и́ть, лю́, ~ишь *pf.* (*of* ▸ **восстанáвливать**)
[1] to restore; **в. в пáмяти** to recall, recollect.
[2] **(прóтив** + *g.*) to set (against), antagonize.

восстановлéни|е, я *nt.* restoration, renewal; **в. в дóлжности** reinstatement.

восстá|ть, ну, нешь, *imper.* **~нь** *pf.* (*of* ▸ **~вáть**) **(прóтив** + *g.*) to rise (against); (*fig.*) to be up in arms (against), revolt against.

восто́к, а *m.*
[1] east; **на в., с ~а** to, from the east.
[2] **В.** the East; the Orient; **Бли́жний В.** the Middle East; **Да́льний В.** the Far East.

восто́рг, а *m.* delight; rapture; **быть в ~е (от** + *g.*) to be delighted (with); **приходи́ть в в. от** (+ *g.*) to go into raptures (over).

восто́рžен|ный (~, ~на) *adj.* (*поклонник*) enthusiastic; (*приём, отзыв*) rapturous.

восторжеств|ова́ть, у́ю *pf. of* ▸ **торжествова́ть**

восто́чный *adj.* east, eastern; (*направление, ветер*) easterly; (*культура*) oriental.

востре́бовани|е, я *nt.* claiming, demand; **до ~я** poste restante.

восхити́тел|ьный (~ен, ~ьна) *adj.* (*женщина, красота*) ravishing; (*вечер, музыка*) delightful; (*вкус, запах*) delicious.

восхи|ти́ть, щу́, ти́шь *pf.* to delight, captivate.

восхи|ти́ться, щу́сь, ти́шься *pf.* (+ *i.*) to be delighted (by); to be carried away (by); to admire.

восхища́|ть(ся), ю(сь) *impf. of* ▸ **восхити́ть(ся)**

восхище́ни|е, я *nt.* admiration; (*восторг*) delight, rapture; **прийти́ в в. от** (+ *g.*) to be delighted with.

восхи|щу́(сь), ти́шь(ся) *see* ▸ **~ти́ть(ся)**

восхо́д, а *m.* rising; **в. со́лнца** sunrise.

восхо|ди́ть, жу́, ~́дишь *impf.*
[1] *impf. of* ▸ **взойти́.**
[2] (*impf. only*) (**к** + *d.*) to go back (to), date (from); **в. к дре́вности** to go back to antiquity.

восход|я́щий *pres. part. of* ▸ **~и́ть** *and adj.* **~я́щая звезда́** (*fig.*) rising star.

восхожде́ни|е, я *nt.* ascent; **в. на Монбла́н** the ascent of Mont Blanc.

восьм|а́я *see* ▸ **~о́й**

восьмёрк|а, и *f.*
[1] (*цифра, игральная карта*) eight.
[2] (*coll.*) (*автобус, трамвай*) No. 8 (*bus, tram, etc.*).
[3] (*группа из восьмерых*) (group of) eight.
[4] (*фигура*) (figure of) eight.

восьми... *comb. form* eight-, octo-.

восьмиуго́льный *adj.* octagonal.

восьмичасово́й *adj.* eight-hour; **в. рабо́чий день** eight-hour (working) day.

восьм|о́й *adj.* eighth; *as n.* **~а́я, ~о́й** *f.* an eighth.

вот *particle*
[1] (*здесь*) here (is), (*там*) there (is); (*это*) this is; **в. мой дом** here is my house, this is my house; **в. идёт авто́бус** here comes the bus; **в. мы пришли́** here we are; **в. где я живу́** this is where I live.
[2] (*emph. prons.*; *unstressed*): **в. э́ти ту́фли ей нра́вились** *these* are the shoes she liked.
[3] (*in excl.*) here's a ..., there's a ... (for you); **во́т так исто́рия!** here's a pretty kettle of fish!; **в. и всё** I've said it all, that's that; (*expr. surprise*) **во́т как!, во́т (оно) что!** really? you don't mean to say so!; **в. тебе на́!** well!; well, I never!; (*surprise and disapproval*) **в. ещё!** no way!; what(ever) next!; (*approval and/ or encouragement*) **в. та́к!, в.-в.!** that's right!; that's it!; **в. та́к** and that's that; **вот тебе́ и...** so much for ...; **вот тебе́ и пое́здка в Пари́ж!** so much for the trip to Paris!; **в. и** (*указывает на завершение чего-н.*): **в. и пришли́** here we are.

вот-во́т *adv.* (*coll.*) just, on the point of, any minute; **по́езд в.-в. придёт** the train is just coming.

воткн|у́ть, у́, ёшь *pf.* (*of* ▸ **втыка́ть**) (**в** + *a.*) to stick (into); (*с большим усилием*) to drive (into).

вотр|у́, ёшь *see* ▸ **втере́ть**

во́тум, а *no pl., m.* vote; **в. (не)дове́рия** (+ *d.*) vote of (no) confidence (in).

воцар|и́ться, ю́сь, и́шься *pf.* (*of* ▸ **~я́ться**)
[1] to come to power.
[2] (*fig.*) to set in; to be established.

воцаря́|ться, юсь *impf. of* ▸ **воцари́ться**

вош|ёл, ла́ *see* ▸ **войти́**

вошь, вши, *i.* **~́ю,** *pl.* **вши, вшей** *f.* louse.

во́|ю, ешь *see* ▸ **выть**

вою́|ю, ешь *see* ▸ **воева́ть**

впада́|ть, ю *impf.*
[1] *impf. of* ▸ **впасть.**
[2] (*impf. only*) (*of rivers*) (**в** + *a.*) flow (into).

впа́дин|а, ы *f.* cavity, hollow.

впад|у́, ёшь *see* ▸ **впасть**

впа|сть, ду́, дёшь, *past* **~л, ~́ла** *pf.* (*of* ▸ **~да́ть 1**) (**в** + *a.*) to fall (into), lapse (into), sink (into).

впервы́е *adv.* for the first time, first; **в. слы́шу об э́том** it's the first I've heard of it.

вперёд *adv.*
[1] forward(s), ahead; **взад и в.** (*coll.*) back and forth.
[2] (*авансом*) in advance.

впереди́
[1] *adv.* in front, ahead.
[2] *adv.* (*в будущем*) in (the) future; ahead; **у него́ всё в.** he has his whole life in front of him.
[3] *prep.* + *g.* in front of, before.

впечатле́ни|е, я *nt.* impression; **произвести́ в.** (**на** + *a.*) to make an impression (upon).

впечатли́тел|ьный (~ен, ~ьна) *adj.* impressionable.

впечатля́|ть, ю *impf.* to impress.

впечатля́ющий *adj.* impressive.

впива́|ться, юсь *impf. of* ▸ **впи́ться**

впи|са́ть, шу́, ~́шешь *pf.* (*of* ▸ **~́сывать**) to enter; to insert; **в. своё и́мя в спи́сок** to enter one's name on a list.

впи|са́ться, шу́сь, ~́шешься *pf.* (*of* ▸ **~́сываться**) (*гармонировать*) to fit in, blend in.

впи́сыва|ть(ся), ю(сь) *impf. of* ▸ **вписа́ть(ся)**

впит|а́ть, а́ю *pf.* (*of* ▸ **~́ывать**) to absorb; (*fig.*) to absorb, take in.

впит|а́ться, а́юсь *pf.* (*of* ▸ **~́ываться**) (**в** + *a.*) to soak (into).

впи́тыва|ть(ся), ю(сь) *impf. of*

В

▶ **впита́ть(ся)**

впи́|ться, вопью́сь, вопьёшься, *past* **~лся, ~ла́сь** *pf.* (*of* ▶ **~ва́ться**) (**в** + *a.*) (*вонзиться*) to stick (into); (*укусить*) to bite; (*ужалить*) to sting; **гвоздь ~лся мне в но́гу** a nail stuck into my foot.

ВПК *m. indecl.* (*abbr. of* **вое́нно-промы́шленный ко́мплекс**) military-industrial complex.

вплавь *adv.* by swimming.

вплотну́ю *adv.* close; (*fig.*) in earnest; **в. к стене́** right up against the wall.

вплоть *adv.*: **в. до** (+ *g.*) (*до предела*) (right) up to; until; (*включая*) including.

вплыва́|ть, ю *impf. of* ▶ **вплыть**

вплы|ть, ву́, вёшь, *past* **~л, ~ла́, ~́ло** *pf.* (*of* ▶ **~ва́ть**) (*о человеке*) to swim in; (*о корабле*) to sail in.

вполго́лоса *adv.* in an undertone, under one's breath.

вполз|а́ть, а́ю *impf. of* ▶ **~ти́**

вполз|ти́, у́, ёшь, *past* **~, ~ла́** *pf.* (*of* ▶ **~а́ть**) to creep in, crawl in; (*подняться вверх*) to creep up, crawl up.

вполне́ *adv.* fully, entirely; quite.

впосле́дствии *adv.* subsequently; afterwards.

впра́ве *as pred.*: **быть в.** (+ *inf.*) to have a right (to).

впра́в|ить, лю, ишь *pf.* (*of* ▶ **~ля́ть**) (*med.*) (*кость*) to set.

вправля́|ть, ю *impf. of* ▶ **впра́вить**

впра́во *adv.* (**от** + *g.*) to the right (of).

впредь *adv.* in future, henceforth; **в. до** until.

впрок *adv.*
1 (*про запас*) for future use; **загото́вить в.** to stock up on.
2 *as pred.* (*на пользу*) to advantage; **э́то не пойдёт ему́ в.** it will do him no good.

впро́чем *adv. and conj.*
1 (*однако, но*) however, but.
2 (*выражает нерешимость*) or rather; but then again; **приезжа́йте за́втра, в., лу́чше да́же послеза́втра** come tomorrow, or, even better, the day after.

впряга́|ть(ся), ю(сь) *impf. of* ▶ **впря́чь(ся)**

впря|чь, гу́, жёшь, гу́т, *past* **впряг, ~гла́** *pf.* (*of* ▶ **~га́ть**) (**в** + *a.*) to harness (to).

впря́|чься, гу́сь, жёшься, гу́тся, *past* **впря́гся, ~гла́сь** *pf.* (*of* ▶ **~га́ться**) (**в** + *a.*) to harness o.s. (to).

впуска́|ть, ю *impf. of* ▶ **впусти́ть**

впу|сти́ть, щу́, ~́стишь *pf.* (*of* ▶ **~ска́ть**) to admit, let in.

впусту́ю *adv.* (*coll.*) for nothing, to no purpose.

впу|щу́, ~́стишь *see* ▶ **~сти́ть**

впятеро́м *adv.* five (together).

враг, а́ *m.* enemy; (*collect.*) the enemy.

вражд|а́, ы *f.* enmity, hostility.

вражде́б|ный (~ен, ~на) *adj.* hostile.

вражд|ова́ть, у́ю *impf.* (**с** + *i.*) to be at enmity (with), at odds (with).

вра́жеский *adj.* (*mil.*) enemy; hostile.

вран|ьё, я́ *nt.* (*coll.*) (*ложь*) lies; (*вздор*) nonsense.

врасплóх *adv.* (*coll.*): **заста́ть, захвати́ть, засти́гнуть в.** to take unawares; to catch off guard.

враст|а́ть, а́ю *impf.* (*of* ▶ **~и́**) to grow in(to); **~а́ющий но́готь** ingrowing nail.

враст|и́, у́, ёшь, *past* **врос, вросла́** *pf. of* ▶ **~а́ть**

врата́р|ь, я́ *m.* (*sport*) goalkeeper.

вр|ать, у, ёшь, *past* **~ал, ~ала́, ~а́ло** *impf.* (*of* ▶ **на~** *and* ▶ **со~**) (*coll.*)
1 (*лгать*) to lie, tell lies.
2 (*говорить вздор*) to talk nonsense.
3 (*быть неточным*) to be wrong (*of inanimate objects only*).

врач, а́ *m.* doctor, physician; **де́тский в.** paediatrician (*Br.*), pediatrician (*US*); **зубно́й в.** dentist.

враче́бный *adj.* medical.

враща́|ть, ю *impf.* to revolve, rotate; **в. глаза́ми** to roll one's eyes.

враща́|ться, юсь *impf.* to revolve, rotate (*intrans.*); **он ~ется в худо́жественных круга́х** he moves in artistic circles.

враще́ни|е, я *nt.* rotation; revolution.

вред, а́ *no pl., m.* (*человеку*) harm, injury; (*здоровью, зданию*) damage; **без ~а́ (для** + *g.*) without detriment (to); **во ~** (+ *d.*) to the detriment of.

вреди́тел|ь, я *m.* (*agric.*) pest.

вре|ди́ть, жу́, ди́шь *impf.* (*of* ▶ **на~** *and* ▶ **по~ 1**) (+ *d.*) (*человеку*) to injure, harm, hurt; (*здоровью, зданию*) to damage.

вре́дно *adv. as pred.* it is harmful; **в. для здоро́вья** it is bad for one's health.

вре́д|ный (~ен, ~на́, ~но, ~́ны) *adj.* harmful, unhealthy; (*производство*) hazardous; (*no short form*) (*человек*) (*coll.*) nasty.

вре|жу́, ди́шь *see* ▶ **~ди́ть**

вре́|жу(сь), жешь(ся) *see* ▶ **~зать(ся)**

врез|а́ть, а́ю *impf. of* ▶ **~́ать 1**

вре́|зать, жу, жешь *pf.* (*of* ▶ **~за́ть**)
1 to cut in; (*вставить*) to set in.
2 (*pf. only*) (*coll.*) (+ *d.*) (*ударить*) to whack (s.o.).

врез|а́ться, а́юсь *impf. of* ▶ **~́аться**

вре́|заться, жусь, жешься *pf.* (*of* ▶ **~за́ться**) (**в** + *a.*) (*удариться*) to smash (into).

времена́ми *adv.* at times, now and then, now and again.

вре́менный *adj.* temporary; provisional.

вре́м|я, ени, *i.* **~енем, о ~ени,** *pl.* **~ена́, ~ён, ~ена́м** *nt.*
1 time; **в. от ~ени** from time to time; **в да́нное в.** at present, at the present moment; **(в) пе́рвое в.** at first; **(в) после́днее в.** lately, of late; **в своё в.** (*i*) (*in ref. to past*) in one's time, once, at one time, (*ii*) (*in ref. to future*) in due course; in one's own time; **за после́днее в.** lately; **на в.** for a while; **на пе́рвое в.** for the time being; **одно́ в.** once (*in the past*); **с тече́нием ~ени** in the course of time; **всё в.** all the time, continually; **ско́лько ~ени?** what is the time?; **тем ~енем** meanwhile.
2: **в. го́да** season.
3 (*gram.*) tense.

4 : **в то в. как** while, whereas.
5 : **во в.** (+ *g.*) during, in.

время(пре)провожде́ни|е, я *nt.* pastime; way of spending one's time.

вро́вень *adv.* (**с** + *i.*) level (with); **в. с края́ми** to the brim.

вро́де
1 *prep.* + *g.* like; **не́что в.** (*coll.*) a sort of, a kind of.
2 *particle* (*coll.*) (*кажется*) it looks as if.

врождён|ный (~, ~на) *adj.* (*способность*) innate; (*недостаток*) congenital.

врозь *adv.* separately, apart.

врун, а́ *m.* (*coll.*) liar.

вруч|а́ть, а́ю *impf. of* ▶ **~и́ть**

вруч|и́ть, у́, и́шь *pf.* (*of* ▶ **~а́ть**) (*письмо, посылку*) to hand, deliver; (*медаль*) to present.

вручну́ю *adv.* by hand.

врыва́|ться, юсь *impf. of* ▶ **ворва́ться**

вряд (ли) *adv.* (*coll.*) hardly, it is unlikely; **в. ли сто́ит** it is hardly worth it; **они́ в. ли приду́т** they are unlikely to come.

вса́дник, а *m.* rider, horseman.

вса́дниц|а, ы *f.* rider, horsewoman.

все *see* ▶ **весь**

все... *comb. form* all-, omni-, pan-; most (*gracious etc.*).

всё
1 *pron. see* ▶ **весь.**
2 *adv.* (*coll.*) always; all the time.
3 **в. (ещё)** still; **дождь в. (ещё) идёт** it is still raining; **в. же** after all, nevertheless.
4 (*coll.*) only, all; **э́то в. из-за тебя́!** it is all because of you!
5 *as conj.* (*всё равно*) however, nevertheless.
6 *as particle* (*strengthening comp.*): **в. бо́лее и бо́лее** more and more; **он в. толсте́ет** he is getting fatter and fatter.
7 *pred.* (*coll.*) (*кончено*) that's it!

всевозмо́жн|ый *adj.* all kinds of; every possible; **~ые това́ры** goods of all kinds.

Всевы́шн|ий, ~его *n.* (*relig.*) the Almighty.

всегда́ *adv.* always.

всего́
1 *pron. see* ▶ **весь; бо́льше в.** (the) most; **лу́чше в.** (the) best; **ча́ще в.** most often.
2 *adv.* (*итого*) in all, all told; (*лишь*) only; **в. лишь** (*coll.*) only; **в.-на́всего** only, all in all; **то́лько и в.** (*coll.*) that's all.

вседозво́ленност|ь, и *f.* permissiveness.

Вселе́нн|ая, ой *no pl., f.* (*космос*) the universe.

вселе́нский *adj.* universal; (*eccl.*) ecumenical; **в. собо́р** ecumenical council.

всел|и́ть, ю́, и́шь *pf.* (*of* ▶ **~я́ть**)
1 (*жильца*) to move (s.o.) in; to install.
2 (*fig., rhet.*) to instil (*Br.*), instill (*US*) (in); **в. страх** (**в** + *a.*) to strike fear (into).

всел|и́ться, ю́сь, и́шься *pf.* (*of* ▶ **~я́ться**) (**в** + *a.*)
1 (*в дом*) to move in(to).
2 (*fig.*) to be implanted (in).

вселя́|ть(ся), ю(сь) *impf. of* ▶ **всели́ть(ся)**

всем *see* ▶ **весь**

всеме́рный *adj.* all possible.

всеми́рный *adj.* world (*attr.*); worldwide.

всемогу́щ|ий (~, ~а) *adj.* omnipotent, all-powerful; **В.** (*of God*) Almighty.

всенаро́дно *adv.* publicly.

всенаро́дный *adj.* national; nationwide.

все́нощн|ая, ой *f.* (*eccl.*) vespers.

всео́бщ|ий *adj.* universal; general; **~ая во́инская пови́нность** universal military service; **~ая забасто́вка** general strike; **~ие вы́боры** general election.

всеобъе́млющ|ий (~, ~а) *adj.* all-embracing, comprehensive.

всеросси́йский *adj.* all-Russian.

всерьёз *adv.* seriously, in earnest.

всеси́л|ьный (~ен, ~ьна) *adj.* all-powerful.

всесторо́нний *adj.* (*образование*) all-round; (*анализ*) thorough, detailed.

всё-таки *conj. and particle* still, all the same.

всех *see* ▶ **весь**

всеце́ло *adv.* completely.

всея́дный *adj.* omnivorous.

вска́кива|ть, ю *impf. of* ▶ **вскочи́ть**

вска́пыва|ть, ю *impf. of* ▶ **вскопа́ть**

вскара́бк|аться, аюсь *pf. of* ▶ **кара́бкаться**

вски́дыва|ть, ю *impf. of* ▶ **вски́нуть**

вски́|нуть, ну, нешь *pf.* (*of* ▶ **~дывать**) (*кинуть*) to throw up; **в. на пле́чи** to shoulder; (*поднять*) to raise (*suddenly*); **в. глаза́** to look up suddenly.

вскипа́|ть, ю *impf. of* ▶ **вскипе́ть**

вскип|е́ть, лю́, и́шь *pf.* (*of* ▶ **~а́ть**)
1 (*вода*) to boil up.
2 (*fig.*) to flare up, fly into a rage.

вскипя|ти́ть, чу́, ти́шь *pf. of* ▶ **кипяти́ть**

вскользь *adv.* slightly; in passing; **упомяну́ть в.** to mention in passing.

вскопа́|ть, ю *pf.* (*of* ▶ **вска́пывать** *and* ▶ **копа́ть 1**) to dig over.

вско́ре *adv.* soon, shortly after.

вскоч|и́ть, у́, ~ишь *pf.* (*of* ▶ **вска́кивать**)
1 (**в, на** + *a.*; **с** + *g.*) to leap up (into, on to; from).
2 (*coll.*) (*шишка*) to come up (*of bumps, boils, etc.*).

вскро́|ю, ешь *see* ▶ **вскрыть**

вскрыва́|ть(ся), ю(сь) *impf. of* ▶ **вскры́ть(ся)**

вскры́ти|е, я *nt.*
1 (*письма*) opening, unsealing; (*сейфа*) unlocking.
2 (*med.*) (*нарыва*) lancing.
3 (*med.*) (*трупа*) autopsy, post-mortem.

вскр|ыть, о́ю, о́ешь *pf.* (*of* ▶ **~ыва́ть**)
1 (*письмо*) to open, unseal; (*сейф*) to unlock.
2 (*med.*) (*нарыв*) to lance.

вскр|ы́ться, о́юсь, о́ешься *pf.* (*of* ▶ **~ыва́ться**)
1 (*река*) to become clear (of ice); become open.
2 (*med.*) to break, burst.

вслед
1 *adv.* (**за** + *i.*) after.
2 *prep.* + *d.* after; **смотре́ть в.** to follow with one's eyes.

В

вслéдствие *prep.* + *g.* in consequence of, owing to, due to.
вслух *adv.* aloud, out loud.
вслýш|аться, аюсь *pf.* (*of* ▸ **~иваться**) (**в** + *a.*) to listen attentively (to).
вслýшива|ться, юсь *impf. of* ▸ **вслýшаться**
всмятку *adv.*: **яйцó в.** soft-boiled, lightly-boiled egg.
вспа|хáть, шý, ~шешь *pf.* (*of* ▸ **~хивать** *and* ▸ **пахáть 1**) to plough up (*Br.*), plow up (*US*).
вспáхива|ть, ю *impf. of* ▸ **вспахáть**
всплеск, а *m.* splash.
всплывá|ть, ю *impf. of* ▸ **всплыть**
всплы|ть, вý, вёшь, *past* **~л, ~лá, ~ло** *pf.* (*of* ▸ **~вáть**) to rise to the surface, surface; (*fig.*) (*факт*) to come to light; (*вопрос*) to arise.
вспоминá|ть, ю *impf. of* ▸ **вспóмнить**
вспóм|нить, ню, нишь *pf.* (*of* ▸ **~инáть**) (*детство*) to remember, recall, recollect; (**о** + *p.*, **что**) to remember.
вспомогáтельный *adj.* auxiliary; subsidiary; (*gram.*) auxiliary.
вспотé|ть, ю *pf.* (*of* ▸ **потéть**) to come out in a sweat.
вспýгива|ть, ю *impf. of* ▸ **вспугнýть**
вспуг|нýть, нý, нёшь *pf.* (*of* ▸ **~ивать**) to scare away; (*дичь*) to put up.
вспыл|ить, ю́, и́шь *pf.* to flare up; **в.** (**на** + *a.*) to fly into a rage (with).
вспы́льчив|ый (~, ~а) *adj.* hot-tempered; irascible.
вспы́хива|ть, ю *impf. of* ▸ **вспы́хнуть**
вспы́х|нуть, ну, нешь *pf.* (*of* ▸ **~ивать**) (*огонь, свет*) to flash; (*бумага*) to burst into flames, blaze up; (*пожар*) to break out; (*fig.*) (*ссора, конфликт*) to flare up; (*паника, война*) to break out.
вспы́шк|а, и *f.* flash; (*phot.*) flash (attachment); (*fig.*) (*гнева*) outburst, (*энергии*) burst; (*болезни*) outbreak.
вста|вáть, ю́, ёшь *impf. of* ▸ **~ть**
встáв|ить, лю, ишь *pf.* (*of* ▸ **~лять**) to put in, insert; **в. в рáму** to frame; **в. себé зýбы** to have false teeth, dentures made.
встáвк|а, и *f.*
1 (*действие*) fixing, insertion.
2 (*в одежде*) inset.
3 (*в тексте*) insertion.
вставля́|ть, ю *impf. of* ▸ **встáвить**
вставн|óй *adj.* inserted; **~ы́е зýбы** false teeth, dentures; **~ы́е рáмы** removable window frames.
вста|ть, ну, нешь *pf.* (*of* ▸ **~вáть**)
1 (*с постели*) to get up, rise; (*на ноги*) to stand up, rise, get up; (*солнце*) to rise.
2 (**в** + *a.*) (*coll.*) to go (into), fit (into); **большóй шкаф не ~нет в э́ту кóмнату** the large cupboard will not go into this room.
3 (*вопрос, образ*) to appear, arise.
4 (*impf. only*) (*coll.*) (*часы*) to stop (working).
встревóжен|ный *adj.* (*выражающий тревогу*) **(~, ~на)** anxious; (*испытывающий тревогу*) **(~, ~а)** anxious.
встрé|тить, чу, тишь *pf.* (*of* ▸ **~чáть**)
1 (*запланированно*) to meet; to meet; (*случайно*) to come across; (*сопротивление*) to meet with, encounter; (*обнаружить*) to come across.
2 (*оказать приём*) to receive, greet; (*Новый год, Пасху*) to celebrate.
встрé|титься, чусь, тишься *pf.* (*of* ▸ **~чáться 1**) (**с** + *i.*)
1 to meet (with), encounter, come across; **в. с затруднéниями** to encounter difficulties.
2 (*на пути*) to be found, occur.
3 (*собраться*) to gather, congregate.
встрéч|а, и *f.*
1 meeting; (*приём*) reception; **в. в верхáх** (*pol.*) summit; **в. Нóвого гóда** New Year's Eve party.
2 (*sport*) match, meeting.
встречá|ть, ю *impf. of* ▸ **встрéтить**
встречá|ться, юсь *impf.*
1 *impf. of* ▸ **встрéтиться.**
2 (*impf. only*) (*ареал распространения*) to be found; **в Шотлáндии ещё ~ются ди́кие кóшки** wild cats are still to be found in Scotland.
встрéчный *adj.*
1 (*поезд, машина*) proceeding from opposite direction; oncoming; *as n.* **пéрвый в.** the first person you meet, anyone.
2 (*предложение*) counter; **в. иск** (*leg.*) counterclaim.
встрóенный *adj.* built-in.
встря́хива|ть, ю *impf. of* ▸ **встряхнýть**
встрях|нýть, нý, нёшь *pf.* (*of* ▸ **~ивать**) to shake; (*fig.*) to shake up, rouse.
вступá|ть(ся), ю(сь) *impf. of* ▸ **вступи́ть(ся)**
вступи́тельный *adj.* introductory; **в. взнос** entrance fee; **в. экзáмен** entrance exam.
вступ|и́ть, лю́, ~ишь *pf.* (*of* ▸ **~áть**)
1 (**в** + *a.*) (*войти, въехать*) to enter; (*стать членом*) to join; (*в спор, переговоры*) to enter into; **в. в бой** to join battle; **в. в дéйствие** (*договор, закон*) to come into force; **в. в брак** to marry.
2 (**на** + *a.*) to mount, go up; **в. на престóл** to ascend the throne.
вступ|и́ться, лю́сь, ~ишься *pf.* (*of* ▸ **~áться**) (**за** + *a.*) to stand up (for).
вступлéни|е, я *nt.*
1 (*в клуб*) joining; (*в должность*) assumption (of).
2 (*в музыке*) prelude; (*в книге*) introduction.
всхли́п|нуть, ну, нешь *pf.* (*of* ▸ **~ывать**) to sob.
всхли́пывани|е, я *nt.* (*действие*) sobbing; (*звуки*) sobs.
всхли́пыва|ть, ю *impf. of* ▸ **всхли́пнуть**
всхо|ди́ть, жý, ~дишь *impf. of* ▸ **взойти́**
всхóд|ы, ов *no sg.* shoots.
всю́ду *adv.* everywhere.
вся *see* ▸ **весь**
вся́к|ий *pron.*
1 any; **во ~ом слýчае** in any case, at any rate; *as n.* anyone.
2 (*разнообразный*) all sorts of; every; **на в. слýчай** just in case.
Вт (*abbr. of* **ватт**) W, watt.

вта́йне *adv.* secretly, in secret.
вта́лкива|ть, ю *impf. of* ▸ **втолкну́ть**
втека́|ть, ет, ют *impf. of* ▸ **втечь**
втер|е́ть, вотру́, вотрёшь, *past* **~̃, ~̃ла** *pf.* (*of* ▸ **втира́ть**) (**в** + *a.*) to rub in(to).
вте|чь, чёт, ку́т, *past* **~̃к, ~кла́** *pf.* (*of* ▸ **~ка́ть**) to flow in(to).
втира́|ть, ю *impf. of* ▸ **втере́ть**
втолкн|у́ть, у́, ёшь *pf.* (*of* ▸ **вта́лкивать**) (**в** + *a.*) to push in(to), shove in(to).
вторг|а́ться, а́юсь *impf. of* ▸ **~̃нуться**
вто́рг|нуться, нусь, нешься, *past* **~ся, ~лась** *pf.* (*of* ▸ **~а́ться**) (**в** + *a.*) (*в страну*) to invade; (*в чужие дела*) to interfere (in).
вторже́ни|е, я *nt.* invasion; interference.
втори́чн|ый *adj.*
1 (*второй*) second.
2 (*второстепенный*) secondary.
3 : **~ое сырьё** recyclable material.
вто́рник, а *m.* Tuesday; **во в.** on Tuesday; **на в.** for Tuesday; **в сле́дующий/про́шлый в.** next/last Tuesday.
втор|о́й *adj.*
1 second; **в. час** (it is) past one; (*не главный*) secondary; **на ~о́м пла́не** (*fig.*) in the background.
2 *as n.* **~о́е, ~о́го** *nt.* main course (*of meal*).
второсо́ртный *adj.* of the second-best quality; second-rate.
второстепе́н|ный (~ен, ~на) *adj.* secondary; minor.
в-тре́тьих *adv.* thirdly, in the third place.
втро́е *adv.* three times; **в. бо́льше** three times as big; **увели́чить в.** to triple.
втроём *adv.* three (together); **мы в.** the three of us.
втройне́ *adv.* three times as much, treble.
втыка́|ть, ю *impf. of* ▸ **воткну́ть**
втя́гива|ть(ся), ю(сь) *impf. of* ▸ **втяну́ть(ся)**
втя|ну́ть, ну́, ~̃нешь *pf.* (*of* ▸ **~̃гивать**)
1 (*лодку; щёки, живот*) to draw (in, into, up), pull (in, into, up); (*воздух, жидкость*) to absorb, take in.
2 (*fig.*) (**в** + *a.*) to draw (into), involve (in); **в. в спор** to draw into an argument.
втя|ну́ться, ну́сь, ~̃нешься *pf.* (*of* ▸ **~̃гиваться**) (**в** + *a.*)
1 (*постепенно войти*) to draw (into), enter.
2 (*щёки*) to sag, fall in.
3 (*привыкнуть*) (*coll.*) to get accustomed (to), used (to).
вуа́л|ь, и *f.* veil.
вуз, а *m.* (*abbr. of* **вы́сшее учёбное заведе́ние**) institution of higher education.
вулка́н, а *m.* volcano.
вульга́р|ный (~ен, ~на) *adj.* (*in var. senses*) vulgar.
вход, а *m.*
1 (*действие*) entry.
2 (*место*) entrance.
вхо|ди́ть, жу́, ~̃дишь *impf. of* ▸ **войти́**
вход|но́й *adj. of* ▸ **~; в. биле́т** entrance ticket; **~на́я пла́та** entrance fee.
вход|я́щий *pres. part. of* ▸ **~и́ть** *and adj.* (*почта, звонок*) incoming.

вцеп|и́ться, лю́сь, ~̃ишься *impf.* (*of* ▸ **~ля́ться**) (**в** + *a.*) to seize hold of.
вцепля́|ться, юсь *impf. of* ▸ **вцепи́ться**
вчера́ *adv.* yesterday.
вчера́шн|ий *adj.* (*дождь, суп*) yesterday's; **в. день** yesterday; (*fig.*) yesterday, the past; **жить ~им днём** to live in the past.
вче́тверо *adv.* four times.
въезд, а *m.*
1 (*действие*) entry; «**В. запрещён**» 'No entry' (*official notice and road sign*).
2 (*место*) entrance.
въезд|но́й *adj. of* ▸ **~; ~на́я ви́за** entry visa.
въезжа́|ть, ю *impf. of* ▸ **въе́хать**
въе́|хать, ду, дешь *pf.* (*of* ▸ **~зжа́ть**)
1 (**в** + *a.*) to enter, ride in(to), drive in(to); (**на** + *a.*) (*наверх*) to ride up, drive up.
2 (*в дом*) to move in.
3 (*sl.*) to understand.
вы, вас, вам, ва́ми, вас *pron.* (*pl. and formal or respectful mode of address to one person*) you; **быть на в.** (**с** + *i.*) to be on formal terms (with).
вы... *pref. indicating*
1 motion outwards.
2 action directed outwards.
3 acquisition (*as outcome of a series of actions*).
4 completion of a process.
выбега́|ть, ю *impf. of* ▸ **вы́бежать**
вы́бе|жать, гу, жишь, гут *pf.* (*of* ▸ **~га́ть**) to run out.
вы́бер|у, ешь *see* ▸ **вы́брать**
выбива́|ть(ся), ю(сь) *impf. of* ▸ **вы́бить(ся)**
выбира́|ть(ся), ю(сь) *impf. of* ▸ **вы́брать(ся)**
вы́б|ить, ью, ьешь *pf.* (*of* ▸ **~ива́ть**)
1 (*заставить выпасть*) to knock out; (*врага*) to drive out; to dislodge.
2 (*очистить*) to beat (clean); **в. ковёр** to beat a carpet.
вы́б|иться, ьюсь, ьешься *pf.* (*of* ▸ **~ива́ться**): **в. в лю́ди** to make one's way in the world; **в. из сил** to wear o.s. out; to be exhausted.
вы́бор, а *m.*
1 choice; option.
2 (*ассортимент*) selection; assortment; **по своему́ ~у** of one's choice.
3 (*pl. only*) (*pol.*) election(s); **дополни́тельные ~ы** by-election.
вы́борк|а, и *f.*
1 (*статистическая*) selection; sample.
2 (*usu. in pl.*) (*цитата*) excerpt.
вы́борн|ый *adj.*
1 (*кампания*) election (*attr.*); **в. бюллете́нь** ballot paper.
2 (*орган, должность*) elective.
вы́борочный *adj.* selective.
вы́борщик, а *m.* (*pol.*) elector (*in indirect elections*); **колле́гия ~ов** electoral college.
вы́бор|ы, ов *see* ▸ **~**
выбра́сыва|ть, ю *impf. of* ▸ **вы́бросить**
вы́б|рать, еру, ерешь *pf.* (*of* ▸ **~ира́ть**)
1 to choose, select, pick out.
2 (*голосованием*) to elect.

В

вы́б|раться, ерусь, ерешься *pf.* (*of* ▶ **~ира́ться**)
1 (**из** + *g.*) to get out (of).
2 (*coll.*) (*найти возможность*) to (find time to) get to; **в. в о́перу** to manage to get to the opera.

вы́брос, а *m.* discharge, emission; spillage; (*in pl.*) emissions.

вы́бро|сить, шу, сишь *pf.* (*of* ▶ **выбра́сывать**)
1 (*за пределы чего-н., наружу*) to throw out.
2 (*старые вещи*) discard, throw away; (*отходы*) to discharge.

выбыва́|ть, ю *impf. of* ▶ **вы́быть**

вы́б|ыть, уду, удешь *pf.* (*of* ▶ **~ыва́ть**) (**из** + *g.*) (*из города*) to leave; (*из соревнования*) to quit.

выва́лива|ть(ся), ю(сь) *impf. of* ▶ **вы́валить(ся)**

вы́вал|ить, ю, ишь *pf.* (*of* ▶ **~́ивать**) (**из** + *g.*)
1 to empty out (of).
2 (*coll.*) (*толпа*) to pour out (of).

вы́вал|иться, юсь, ишься *pf.* (*of* ▶ **~́иваться**) (**из** + *g.*) to fall out (of), tumble out (of).

вы́валя|ть, ю *pf. of* ▶ **валя́ть 1**

выведе́ни|е, я *nt.*
1 leading out, bringing out.
2 (*формулы*) deduction, conclusion.
3 (*цыплят*) hatching (out); (*растений*) growing; (*животных*) breeding, raising.
4 (*пятен*) removal (*of stains*); (*вредителей*) extermination (*of pests*).

вы́вез|ти, у, ешь, *past* **~, ~ла** *pf.* (*of* ▶ **вывози́ть**)
1 (*везя, удалить*) to take out, remove; (*везя, отправить*) to take; (*привезти с собой*) to bring.
2 (*econ.*) (*за границу*) to export.

вы́вер|нуть, ну, нешь *pf.* (*of* ▶ **вывора́чивать**)
1 (*винт*) to unscrew; (*пробку*) to pull out.
2 (*coll.*) (*ногу*) to twist, wrench.
3 (*карман*) to turn (inside) out.

вы́ве|сить, шу, сишь *pf.* (*of* ▶ **~́шивать**)
1 (*объявление*) to put up; to post up.
2 (*бельё, флаг*) to hang out.

вы́веск|а, и *f.*
1 sign, signboard.
2 (*fig.*) screen, pretext; **под ~ой** (+ *g.*) under the guise of.

вы́ве|сти, ду, дешь, *past* **~л, ~ла** *pf.* (*of* ▶ **выводи́ть**)
1 to lead out, bring out; (*войска*) to withdraw; **в. кого́-н. в лю́ди** to help s.o. on in life; **в. кого́-н. из себя́** to drive s.o. out of his wits; **в. из стро́я** to disable, put out of action (*also fig.*); **в. из терпе́ния** to exasperate.
2 (*исключить*) to force out, expel.
3 (*пятна*) to remove; (*вредителей*) to exterminate.
4 (*заключить*) to deduce, conclude.
5 (*птенцов*) to hatch (out); (*растения*) to grow; (*животных*) to breed, raise.

вы́ве|стись, дется, *past* **~лся, ~лась** *pf.* (*of* ▶ **выводи́ться**) (*цыплята*) to hatch out (*intrans.*).

выве́шива|ть, ю *impf. of* ▶ **вы́весить**

вы́вин|тить, чу, тишь *pf.* (*of* ▶ **~́чивать**) to unscrew.

выви́нчива|ть, ю *impf. of* ▶ **вы́винтить**

вы́вих, а *m.* dislocation.

выви́хива|ть, ю *impf. of* ▶ **вы́вихнуть**

вы́вих|нуть, ну, нешь *pf.* (*of* ▶ **~́ивать**) to dislocate, put out (of joint).

вы́вод, а *m.*
1 (*заключение*) deduction, conclusion.
2 (*выведение*) leading out, bringing out; **в. войск** withdrawal of troops; **в. да́нных** (*comput.*) output.

выво|ди́ть(ся), жу́, ~́дит(ся) *impf. of* ▶ **вы́вести(сь)**

выво|жу́[1], ~́дишь *see* ▶ **~ди́ть**

выво|жу́[2], ~́зишь *see* ▶ **~зи́ть**

вы́воз, а *m.*
1 (*отправление*) sending, dispatch.
2 (*экспорт*) export.

выво|зи́ть, жу́, ~́зишь *impf. of* ▶ **вы́везти**

вывозн|о́й *adj.* (*товар*) exported; (*attr.*) export; **~а́я по́шлина** export duty.

вывора́чива|ть, ю *impf. of* ▶ **вы́вернуть**

выгиба́|ть(ся), ю(сь) *impf. of* ▶ **вы́гнуть(ся)**

вы́гла|дить, жу, дишь *pf. of* ▶ **гла́дить 1**

вы́гля|деть, жу, дишь *impf.* (*человек*) to look (like); **он ~дит о́чень мо́лодо** he looks very young; **она́ пло́хо ~дит** she does not look well; (*показания*) to appear (to be).

выгля́дыва|ть, ю *impf. of* ▶ **вы́глянуть**

вы́гля|нуть, ну, нешь *pf.* (*of* ▶ **~́дывать**)
1 (*из окна*) to look out.
2 (*показаться*) to peep out, emerge.

вы́г|нать, оню, онишь *pf.* (*of* ▶ **~оня́ть**)
1 (*удалить*) to drive out; to expel; **в. с рабо́ты** (*coll.*) to sack (*Br.*), fire (*US*).
2 (*скот*) to send out to pasture.

вы́гнут|ый (~, ~а) *adj.* curved; convex.

вы́гн|уть, у, ешь *pf.* (*of* ▶ **выгиба́ть**) to bend.

вы́гн|уться, усь, ешься *pf.* (*of* ▶ **выгиба́ться**) to bend (*intrans.*).

выгова́рива|ть, ю *impf. of* ▶ **вы́говорить**

вы́говор, а *m.*
1 (*произношение*) accent; pronunciation.
2 (*порицание*) reprimand; rebuke.

вы́говор|ить, ю, ишь *pf.* (*of* ▶ **выгова́ривать**) to articulate, speak.

вы́год|а, ы *f.* (*польза*) advantage, benefit; (*прибыль*) profit, gain.

вы́годно *adv.*
1 advantageously.
2 *as pred.* it is profitable, it pays.

вы́год|ный (~ен, ~на) *adj.* (*дающий пользу*) advantageous, beneficial; (*прибыльный*) profitable.

выгоня́|ть, ю *impf. of* ▶ **вы́гнать**

вы́гравир|овать, ую *pf. of* ▶ **гравирова́ть**

выгружа́|ть(ся), ю(сь) *impf. of* ▶ **вы́грузить(ся)**

вы́гру|зить, жу, зишь *pf.* (*of* ▶ **~жа́ть**) to unload.

вы́гру|зиться, жусь, зишься *pf.* (*of* ▶ **~жа́ться**) (*люди*) to disembark; (*корабль*) to unload.

вы́грузк|а, и *f.* unloading; (*людей*) disembarkation.

выгу́лива|ть, аю *impf. of* ▶ **вы́гулять**

вы́гуля|ть, ю *pf.* (*of* ▶ **выгу́ливать**) to walk (*a dog, etc.*).

выда|ва́ть(ся), ю́(сь), ёшь(ся) *impf. of* ▶ **вы́дать(ся)**

вы́дав|ить, лю, ишь *pf.* (*of* ▶ **~́ливать**)
1 (*выжать*) to press out, squeeze out (*also fig.*); **в. улы́бку** to force a smile.
2 (*выломать*) to break, knock out.

выда́влива|ть, ю *impf. of* ▶ **вы́давить**

вы́да|ть, м, шь, ст, дим, дите, дут *pf.* (*of* ▶ **~ва́ть**)
1 (*дать*) to give (out), issue; (*изготовить*) to produce; **в. зарпла́ту** to pay out wages; **в. про́пуск** to issue a pass; **в. кого́-н. за́муж** (**за** + *a.*) to give s.o. in marriage (to).
2 (*предать*) to give away, betray; (*в чужую страну*) to extradite.
3 (**за** + *a.*) to pass off (as), give out to be; **в. (себя́)** to pose (as).

вы́да|ться, мся, шься, стся, димся, дитесь, дутся *pf.* (*of* ▶ **~ва́ться**)
1 to protrude, project, jut out.
2 (*coll.*) (*случиться*) to happen.

вы́дач|а, и *f.*
1 (*предоставление*) giving, issuing; (*изготовление*) production.
2 (*преступника*) extradition.

выдаю́щийся *pres. part. of* ▶ **выдава́ться** *and adj.* prominent, salient; (*fig.*) (*замечательный*) outstanding, eminent; prominent.

выдвига́|ть(ся), ю(сь) *impf. of* ▶ **вы́двинуть(ся)**

вы́дви|нуть, ну, нешь *pf.* (*of* ▶ **~га́ть**)
1 (*стол, шкаф*) to move out, pull out; (*ящик*) to pull open.
2 (*fig.*) (*предложить*) to put forward, advance; **в. обвине́ние** to bring an accusation.
3 (*по работе*) to promote.
4 (*кандидата*) to nominate, propose.

вы́дви|нуться, нусь, нешься *pf.* (*of* ▶ **~га́ться**)
1 (*вперёд*) to move forward; (*наружу*) to move, move out; (*ящик*) to slide in and out.
2 (*работник*) to rise, get on (in the world).

выделе́ни|е, я *nt.*
1 (*средств*) allocation, assignment.
2 (*physiol.*) secretion; (*обработанных веществ*) excretion.

вы́дел|ить, ю, ишь *pf.* (*of* ▶ **~я́ть**)
1 (*средства*) to allocate, assign, earmark; (*время*) to allot.
2 (*отобрать*) to pick out, single out; (*mil.*) to detach, detail; (*comput.*) to highlight; (*typ.*) **в. курси́вом** to italicize.

вы́дел|иться, юсь, ишься *pf.* (*of* ▶ **~я́ться**)
1 (*отделиться от целого*) to split off, separate.
2 (+ *i.*) to stand out (on account of).
3 (*пот*) to ooze out, exude; (*газ*) to be emitted.

вы́делк|а, и *f.*
1 (*качество*) workmanship.
2 (*кожи*) dressing, currying.

выделя́|ть(ся), ю(сь) *impf. of* ▶ **вы́делить(ся)**

выдёргива|ть, ю *impf. of* ▶ **вы́дернуть**

вы́держа|нный (~н, ~на) *p.p.p. of* ▶ **~ть** *and* **(~н, ~нна)** *adj.*
1 (*последовательный*) consistent.
2 (*умеющий владеть собой*) self-possessed; (*стойкий*) firm.
3 (*сыр, вино*) mature; (*дерево*) seasoned.

вы́держ|ать, у, ишь *pf.* (*of* ▶ **~́ивать**)
1 (*под тяжестью, давлением*) to bear, hold; **(э́тот) лёд вас не ~ит** the ice will not hold you.
2 (*fig.*) (*вытерпеть*) to bear, stand (up to), endure; **не в.** to give in, break down; **я не мог э́того бо́льше в.** I could stand it no longer.
3: **в. не́сколько изда́ний** to run into several editions.
4 (*сыр, вино*) to mature; (*дерево*) to season.
5 (*соблюсти*) to maintain, sustain; **в. па́узу** to pause.

выде́ржива|ть, ю *impf. of* ▶ **вы́держать**

вы́держк|а[1], и *f.*
1 (*самообладание*) self-possession; (*терпение*) endurance.
2 (*phot.*) exposure.

вы́держк|а[2], и *f.* (*цитата*) excerpt, quotation.

вы́дер|нуть, ну, нешь *pf.* (*of* ▶ **~́гивать**) to pull out.

вы́дох, а *m.* exhalation.

вы́дохн|уть, у, ешь *pf.* (*of* ▶ **выдыха́ть**) to breathe out.

вы́дрессир|овать, ую *pf. of* ▶ **дрессирова́ть**

вы́думан|ный (~, ~а) *p.p.p. of* ▶ **вы́думать** *and* **(~, ~на)** *adj.* made-up, fabricated; **~ная исто́рия** fabrication, fiction.

вы́дум|ать, аю *pf.* (*of* ▶ **~́ывать**) to invent; to make up, fabricate.

вы́думк|а, и *f.*
1 invention.
2 (*изобретательность*) inventiveness.
3 (*вымысел*) invention, fabrication (*lie*).

выду́мыва|ть, ю *impf. of* ▶ **вы́думать**

выдыха́|ть, ю *impf. of* ▶ **вы́дохнуть**

вы́еб|ать, у, ешь *pf. of* ▶ **еба́ть**

вы́езд, а *m.*
1 (*отъезд*) departure.
2 (*место*) exit.

выезжа́|ть, ю *impf. of* ▶ **вы́ехать**

вы́е|хать, ду, дешь *pf.* (*of* ▶ **~зжа́ть**)
1 (*уехать*) to depart, leave (*in or on a vehicle or on an animal*); (*из города, из ворот*) (*на машине*) to drive out.
2 (*из квартиры*) to leave, move (out).

вы́ж|ать, му, мешь *pf.* (*of* ▶ **~има́ть**) (*бельё*) to wring (out); (*лимон*) to squeeze; (*сок*) to squeeze out; **~атый лимо́н** (*fig.*) a has-been; (*fig.*) (*извлечь*) to wring (out), squeeze (out).

вы́жд|ать, у, ешь *pf.* (*of* ▶ **выжида́ть**) to wait (for); to bide one's time.

В

вы́ж|ечь, гу, жешь *pf.* (*of* ▸ **~ига́ть**)
1 (*сжечь целиком*) to burn down; to burn out; (*солнце*) to scorch.
2 (*сделать знак*) to make a mark, *etc.*, by burning; **в. клеймо́ (на** + *p.*) to brand.
выжива́ни|е, я *nt.* survival.
выжива́|ть, ю *impf. of* ▸ **вы́жить**
выжига́|ть, ю *impf. of* ▸ **вы́жечь**
выжида́|ть, ю *impf. of* ▸ **вы́ждать**
выжима́|ть, ю *impf. of* ▸ **вы́жать**
вы́жи|ть, ву, вешь *pf.* (*of* ▸ **~ва́ть**)
1 (*остаться в живых*) to survive.
2 : **в. из ума́** to lose possession of one's faculties.
вы́з|вать, ову, овешь *pf.* (*of* ▸ **~ыва́ть**)
1 (*пригласить*) to call (out); to send for; (*потребовать явиться*) to summon; **в. врача́** to send for a doctor.
2 (*гнев, любопытство*) to provoke, arouse; (*пожар, болезнь*) to cause; (*интерес*) to stimulate; (*спор*) to provoke.
выздора́влива|ть, ю *impf. of* ▸ **вы́здороветь**
вы́здорове|ть, ю, ешь *pf.* (*of* ▸ **выздора́вливать**) to recover, get better.
выздоровле́ни|е, я *nt.* recovery; convalescence.
вы́зов, а *m.*
1 (*приглашение*) call.
2 (*требование явиться*) summons.
3 (*предложение вступить в борьбу*) challenge; **бро́сить в. кому́-н.** to throw down a challenge to s.o.
вызыва́|ть, ю *impf. of* ▸ **вы́звать**
вызыва́|ющий *pres. part. act. of* ▸ **~ть** *and adj.* defiant; provocative.
вы́игр|ать, аю *pf.* (*of* ▸ **~́ывать**) (*войну, партию; много денег*) to win; (*получить пользу*) to gain; **в. вре́мя** to gain time.
вы́игрыва|ть, ю *impf. of* ▸ **вы́играть**
вы́игрыш, а *m.*
1 (*победа*) win; winning.
2 (*деньги*) winnings; (*премия*) prize; (*выгода*) gain; **быть в ~е** (*в игре*) to be the winner; (*fig.*) to stand to gain.
вы́игрышный *adj.*
1 winning; **в. ход** winning move.
2 (*выгодный*) advantageous.
вы́|йти, йду, йдешь, *past* **~шел, ~шла** *pf.* (*of* ▸ **~ходи́ть 1**)
1 to go out; to come out; **она́ ~шла из ко́мнаты** she went out of/left the room; **в. в отста́вку** to retire; **в. в фина́л** (*sport*) to reach the final; **в. из грани́ц** (+ *g.*), **из преде́лов** (+ *g.*) (*fig.*) to exceed the bounds (of); **в. из себя́** to lose one's temper; **в. из систе́мы** (*comput.*) to log off; **в. из терпе́ния** to lose patience; **в. на прогу́лку** to go out for a walk.
2 : **в. (в свет)** (*быть изданным*) to come out, appear.
3 : **в. (за́муж) (за** + *a.*) (*о женщине*) to marry.
4 (*получаться*) to come (out); to turn out (*also impers.*); to ensue; (*произойти*) to happen, occur; **в. победи́телем** to come out victor; **из э́того ничего́ не ~йдет** nothing will come of it; **~шло, что он винова́т** it turned out that he was to blame.
5 (*быть родом*) to be by origin; **она́ ~шла из крестья́н** she is of peasant origin.
6 (*израсходоваться*) to be used up; (*of a period of time*) to have expired; **срок уже́ ~шел** time is up.
выка́лыва|ть, ю *impf. of* ▸ **вы́колоть**
выка́пыва|ть, ю *impf. of* ▸ **вы́копать**
выки́дыва|ть, ю *impf. of* ▸ **вы́кинуть**
вы́кидыш, а *m.* (*med.*) miscarriage.
вы́ки|нуть, ну, нешь *pf.* (*of* ▸ **~́дывать**)
1 (*выбросить*) to throw out.
2 (*вывесить*) to put out; **в. флаг** to hoist a flag.
3 (*coll., pej.*): **в. фо́кус** to play a trick.
выкипа́|ть, ет *impf. of* ▸ **вы́кипеть**
вы́кип|еть, ит *pf.* (*of* ▸ **~а́ть**) to boil away.
выкла́дыва|ть, ю *impf. of* ▸ **вы́ложить**
выключа́тел|ь, я *m.* switch.
выключа́|ть(ся), ю(сь) *impf. of* ▸ **вы́ключить(ся)**
вы́ключ|ить, у, ишь *pf.* (*of* ▸ **~а́ть**)
1 (*свет, радио*) to turn off, switch off.
2 (*исключить*) to remove, exclude.
вы́ключ|иться, усь, ишься *pf.* (*of* ▸ **~а́ться**)
1 (*о свете*) to go off.
2 (*о человеке*) to switch off.
вы́к|овать, ую, уешь *pf. of* ▸ **кова́ть 1**
вы́кол|оть, ю, ешь *pf.* (*of* ▸ **выка́лывать**) to poke out.
вы́копа|ть, ю *pf.* (*of* ▸ **выка́пывать** *and* ▸ **копа́ть 2**) (*яму*) to dig; (*картофель*) to dig up; (*тело*) to exhume.
выкра́ива|ть, ю *impf. of* ▸ **вы́кроить**
вы́кра|сить, шу, сишь *pf.* (*of* ▸ **~́шивать**) (*стену*) to paint; (*ткань, волосы*) to dye.
выкра́шива|ть, ю *impf. of* ▸ **вы́красить**
вы́кро|ить, ю, ишь *pf.* (*of* ▸ **выкра́ивать**)
1 (*вырезать*) to cut out.
2 (*fig.*) (*уделить*) to find; **в. вре́мя** to find time.
вы́кройк|а, и *f.* pattern.
вы́кру|тить, чу, тишь *pf.* (*of* ▸ **~́чивать**)
1 (*лампочку, винт*) to unscrew.
2 (*руку*) to twist, wrench.
вы́кру|титься, чусь, тишься *pf.* (*of* ▸ **~́чиваться**)
1 (*винт*) to come unscrewed.
2 (*fig., coll.*) (*выпутаться*) to extricate o.s., get o.s. out (of).
выкру́чива|ть(ся), ю(сь) *impf. of* ▸ **вы́крутить(ся)**
вы́куп, а *m.*
1 (*leg.*) redemption.
2 (*плата*) ransom.
выкуп|а́ть, а́ю *impf. of* ▸ **вы́купить**
вы́купа|ть(ся), ю(сь) *pf. of* ▸ **купа́ть(ся)**
вы́куп|ить, лю, ишь *pf.* (*of* ▸ **~а́ть**)
1 (*заложника*) to ransom.
2 (*вещи*) to redeem.
вы́лазк|а, и *f.* (*mil.*) sortie (*also fig.*).
выла́мыва|ть, ю *impf. of* ▸ **вы́ломать**
вылеза́|ть, ю *impf. of* ▸ **вы́лезти**
вы́лез|ти, у, ешь, *past* **~, ~ла** *pf.* (*of*

▶ **~а́ть**)
[1] (*ползком*) to crawl out; (*карабкаясь*) to climb out; (*coll.*) (*выйти*) to get out, alight.
[2] (*coll.*) (*выпасть*) to fall out, come out.

вы́лет, а *m.* (*самолёта*) take-off; **зал ~а** departure lounge.

вылета́|ть, ю *impf. of* ▶ **вы́лететь**

вы́ле|теть, чу, тишь *pf.* (*of* ▶ **~та́ть**) (*птица*) to fly out; (*самолёт*) to take off; (*fig., coll.*) to rush out; **в. из головы́** to slip one's mind.

выле́чива|ть(ся), ю(сь) *impf. of* ▶ **вы́лечить(ся)**

вы́леч|ить, у, ишь *pf.* (*of* ▶ **~́ивать**) (**от** + *g.*) to cure (of) (*also fig.*).

вы́леч|иться, усь, ишься *pf.* (*of* ▶ **~́иваться**) (**от** + *g.*) to be cured (of); to get over (*also fig.*).

вы́леч|у[1], **ишь** *see* ▶ **~ить**

вы́ле|чу[2], **тишь** *see* ▶ **~теть**

вылива́|ть(ся), ю, ет(ся) *impf. of* ▶ **вы́лить(ся)**

вы́л|ить, ью, ьешь *pf.* (*of* ▶ **~ива́ть**) to pour out; (*ведро*) to empty (out).

вы́л|иться, ьется *pf.* (*of* ▶ **~ива́ться**) (*жидкость*) to run out, flow out; (*fig.*) to flow (from), spring (from).

вы́лож|ить, у, ишь *pf.* (*of* ▶ **выкла́дывать**)
[1] (*товар, вещи*) to lay out, spread out; (*fig., coll.*) (*сказать*) to tell; to reveal.
[2] (+ *i.*) (*покрыть*) to cover, lay (with); **в. дёрном** to turf; **в. ка́мнем** to face with masonry.

вы́ломa|ть, ю *pf.* (*of* ▶ **выла́мывать**) (*замок*) to break open; (*дверь*) to break down.

вы́луп|иться, ится *pf.* (*of* ▶ **~ля́ться**) to hatch (out).

вылупля́|ться, ется *impf. of* ▶ **вы́лупиться**

вы́л|ью, ьешь *see* ▶ **~ить**

выма́нива|ть, ю *impf. of* ▶ **вы́манить**

вы́ман|ить, ю, ишь *pf.* (*of* ▶ **~́ивать**)
[1] (**у** + *g.*) (*получить обманом*) to cheat (out of); (*получить лестью*) to wheedle (out of).
[2] (**из** + *g.*) to lure (out of, from).

вы́м|ереть, рет, рут, *past* **~ер, ~ерла** *pf.* (*of* ▶ **~ира́ть**)
[1] (*исчезнуть*) to die out, become extinct.
[2] (*опустеть*) to become desolate, deserted.

вы́мер|ший *p.p. act. of* ▶ **~еть** *and adj.* extinct.

вымира́ни|е, я *nt.* dying out, extinction.

вымира́|ть, ю *impf. of* ▶ **вы́мереть**

вымога́тел|ь, я *m.* extortionist.

вымога́тельств|о, а *nt.* extortion.

вымога́|ть, ю *impf.* to extort; **в. де́ньги у кого́-н.** to extort money from s.o.

вымока́|ть, ю *impf. of* ▶ **вы́мокнуть**

вы́мок|нуть, ну, нешь, *past* **~, ~ла** *pf.* (*of* ▶ **~а́ть**) to be drenched, be soaked; **мы ~ли до ни́тки** we are soaked to the skin.

вы́м|ою, оешь *see* ▶ **~ыть**

вы́мпел, а *m.* pennant.

вы́мр|ет, ут *see* ▶ **вы́мереть**

вымыва́|ть, ю *impf. of* ▶ **вы́мыть**

вы́мыс|ел, ла *m.*
[1] (*ложь*) invention, fabrication.
[2] (*фантазия*) fantasy.

вы́м|ыть, ою, оешь *pf.* (*of* ▶ **мыть** *and* ▶ **~ыва́ть**)
[1] (*сделать чистым*) to wash; **в. посу́ду** to wash up.
[2] (*размыть*) to wash away.

вы́м|ыться, оюсь, оешься *pf.* (*of* ▶ **мы́ться**) to wash o.s.

вымышлен|ный (~, ~а) *adj.* fictitious, imaginary, invented.

вына́шива|ть, ю *impf. of* ▶ **вы́носить**

вынесе́ни|е, я *nt.*
[1] (*решения*) taking.
[2] (*благодарности*) giving, expressing.
[3] (*на рассмотрение*) submitting.
[4] (*приговора*) pronouncement.

вы́нес|ти, у, ешь, *past* **~, ~ла** *pf.* (*of* ▶ **выноси́ть 1**)
[1] (*удалить за пределы*) to carry out, take out; to take way; (*убрать*) to carry away; (*доставить*) to bring; **в. на бе́рег** to wash ashore.
[2] (*fig.*) (*получить*) to take away, receive, derive; **в. прия́тное впечатле́ние** to be favourably impressed.
[3]: **в. вопро́с (на собра́ние, на обсужде́ние)** to put, submit a question (to a meeting, for discussion).
[4] (*вытерпеть*) to bear, stand, endure. **в. на свои́х плеча́х** (*fig.*) to shoulder, take the full weight (of), bear the full brunt (of).
[5]: **в. благода́рность** to express gratitude; **в. пригово́р** (+ *d.*) to pass sentence (on), pronounce sentence (on); **в. реше́ние** to decide; (*leg.*) to pronounce judgement.

вынима́|ть, ю *impf. of* ▶ **вы́нуть**

вы́нос, а *m.* (*покойника*) bearing-out; **на в.** (*о еде*) to take away (*Br.*), to take out (*US*).

выно|си́ть, шу́, ~́сишь *impf.*
[1] *impf. of* ▶ **вы́нести.**
[2] (*impf. only*) (+ *neg.*) to be unable to bear/stand **я его́ не ~шу́** I can't stand him.

вы́но|сить, шу, сишь *pf.* (*of* ▶ **вына́шивать**) (*ребёнка*) to bear, bring forth (*a child at full term*); (*план, мысль*) to nurture.

выно́сливост|ь, и *f.* (power of) endurance; staying power.

выно́слив|ый (~, ~а) *adj.* (*человек, растение*) hardy.

выно|шу́, ~́сишь *see* ▶ **~си́ть**

вы́но|шу, сишь *see* ▶ **~сить**

вы́ну|дить, жу, дишь *pf.* (*of* ▶ **~жда́ть**) (+ *inf.*) to force, compel.

вынужда́|ть, ю *impf. of* ▶ **вы́нудить**

вы́нужден|ный (~, ~а) *p.p.p. of* ▶ **вы́нудить** *and* **(~, ~на)** *adj.* forced; **~ная поса́дка** (*aeron.*) forced landing.

вы́н|уть, у, ешь *pf.* (*of* ▶ **~има́ть**) to take out; to pull out, extract.

вы́пад, а *m.* (*враждебное выступление*) attack.

выпада́|ть, ю *impf. of* ▶ **вы́пасть**

вы́па|сть, ду, дешь, *past* **~л** *pf.* (*of* ▶ **~да́ть**)
[1] (*упасть наружу*) to fall out.
[2] (*дождь, снег*) to fall.

В

3 (+ *d.*) (*задача*) to befall, fall (to); **мне ~ло сча́стье** (+ *inf.*) I had the luck (to).
4 (*случиться*) to occur, turn out; **ночь ~ла звёздная** it turned out a starry night.

вы́пе|к *see* ▸ **~чь**

выпека́|ть, ю *impf. of* ▸ **вы́печь**

вы́печк|а, и *f.* baking.

вы́пе|чь, ку, чешь, кут, *past* **~к, ~кла** *pf.* (*of* ▸ **~ка́ть**) to bake.

выпива́|ть, ю *impf.*
1 *impf. of* ▸ **вы́пить.**
2 (*impf. only; coll.*) to be fond of the bottle.

вы́пивк|а, и *f.* (*coll., collect.*) drinks.

вы́пи|сать, шу, шешь *pf.* (*of* ▸ **~́сывать**)
1 (*переписать*) to copy out; to excerpt.
2 (*документ*) to write out; **в. квита́нцию** to write out a receipt.
3 (*сделать заказ*) to send for (*in writing*).
4 (*из больницы*) to discharge.
5 (*газету, журнал*) to subscribe to.

вы́пи|саться, шусь, шешься *pf.* (*of* ▸ **~́сываться**) (*из больницы*) to be discharged; **он уже́ ~сался из больни́цы** he is already out of hospital; (*из квартиры*) to officially change one's place of residence.

вы́писк|а, и *f.*
1 (*списывание*) copying, excerpting.
2 (*цитата*) extract, excerpt.
3 (*книг, газет*) subscription.
4 (*из больницы*) discharge.

выпи́сыва|ть(ся), ю(сь) *impf. of* ▸ **вы́писать(ся)**

вы́п|ить, ью, ьешь *pf.* (*of* ▸ **выпива́ть 1** *and* ▸ **пить**) to drink.

вы́пи|шу, шешь *see* ▸ **~сать**

вы́плат|а, ы *f.* payment.

вы́пла|тить, чу, тишь *pf.* (*of* ▸ **~́чивать**)
1 to pay (out).
2 (*долг*) to pay off.

выпла́чива|ть, ю *impf. of* ▸ **вы́платить**

вы́пла|чу, тишь *see* ▸ **~тить**

выплёвыва|ть, ю *impf. of* ▸ **вы́плюнуть**

выплёскива|ть, ю *impf. of* ▸ **вы́плеснуть**

вы́плес|нуть, ну, нешь *pf.* (*of* ▸ **~̈кивать**) to pour out.

вы́плюн|уть, у, ешь *pf.* (*of* ▸ **выплёвывать**) to spit out.

выполза́|ть, ю *impf. of* ▸ **вы́ползти**

вы́полз|ти, у, ешь, *past* **~, ~ла** *pf.* (*of* ▸ **~а́ть**) (**из** + *g.*) to crawl out, creep out (from); (*змея*) to slither out.

выполне́ни|е, я *nt.* (*работы, приказа*) execution, carrying-out; (*желания*) fulfilment.

выполни́м|ый (~, ~а) *adj.* practicable, feasible.

вы́полн|ить, ю, ишь *pf.* (*of* ▸ **~я́ть**) (*приказание, работу*) to carry out; (*обязанность, желание, план*) to fulfil (*Br.*), fulfill (*US*); (*рисунок*) to execute.

выполня́|ть, ю *impf. of* ▸ **вы́полнить**

вы́прав|ить, лю, ишь *pf.* (*of* ▸ **~ля́ть**)
1 (*сделать прямым*) to straighten (out).
2 (*исправить*) to correct; (*улучшить*) to improve.

вы́прав|иться, люсь, ишься *pf.* (*of* ▸ **~ля́ться**)
1 (*выпрямиться*) to become straight.
2 (*стать лучше*) to improve (*intrans.*).

выправля́|ть(ся), ю(сь) *impf. of* ▸ **вы́править(ся)**

выпра́шива|ть, ю *impf.*
1 *impf. of* ▸ **вы́просить.**
2 (*impf. only*) to try to get, beg for.

вы́про|сить, шу, сишь *pf.* (*of* ▸ **выпра́шивать 1**) (**у** + *g.*) to get (out of), obtain, elicit (by begging).

вы́про|шу, сишь *see* ▸ **~сить**

выпры́гива|ть, ю *impf. of* ▸ **вы́прыгнуть**

вы́прыг|нуть, ну, нешь *pf.* (*of* ▸ **~́ивать**) to jump out, spring out.

вы́прям|ить, лю, ишь *pf.* (*of* ▸ **~ля́ть**) to straighten (out).

вы́прям|иться, люсь, ишься *pf.* (*of* ▸ **~ля́ться**) to become straight; **в. во весь рост** to draw o.s. up to one's full height.

выпрямля́|ть(ся), ю(сь) *impf. of* ▸ **вы́прямить(ся)**

вы́пуклост|ь, и *f.* (*неровность*) protuberance; bulge.

вы́пукл|ый (~, ~а) *adj.* (*неровный*) protuberant; prominent, bulging.

вы́пуск, а *m.*
1 (*товаров*) output; (*денег, акций*) issue; **в. новосте́й** newscast; **сро́чный в. новосте́й** newsflash.
2 (*романа*) part, instalment (*Br.*), installment (*US*).
3 (*в школе, институте*) leavers; graduates.

выпуска́|ть, ю *impf. of* ▸ **вы́пустить**

выпускни́к, а́ *m.*
1 (*окончивший учебное заведение*) graduate; **бы́вший в.** old boy.
2 (*на последнем курсе*) final-year student.

выпускни́|ца, цы *f. of* ▸ **~к**

выпускно́й *adj. of* ▸ **вы́пуск; в. экза́мен** final examination, finals.

вы́пу|стить, щу, стишь *pf.* (*of* ▸ **~ска́ть**)
1 (*дать выйти*) to let out; (*заключённого, фильм*) to release; (*из учебного заведения*) to turn out; **в. из рук** to let go of; **в. из тюрьмы́** to release from prison.
2 (*деньги, акции*) to issue; (*продукцию*) to turn out, produce; **в. в прода́жу** to put on the market; **в. (в свет)** to publish.

вы́пя|тить, чу, тишь *pf.* (*of* ▸ **~́чивать**) (*coll.*) to stick out; **в. грудь** to stick out one's chest.

выпя́чива|ть, ю *impf. of* ▸ **вы́пятить**

выраба́тыва|ть, ю *impf. of* ▸ **вы́работать**

вы́работа|ть, ю *pf.* (*of* ▸ **выраба́тывать**)
1 (*произвести*) to manufacture; to produce, make.
2 (*план*) to work out, draw up; (*привычку*) to develop.

вы́работк|а, и *f.* (*производство*) manufacture; production, making.

выра́внива|ть(ся), ю(сь) *impf. of* ▸ **вы́ровнять(ся)**

выража́|ть, ю *impf. of* ▸ **вы́разить**

выража́|ться, юсь *impf. of*

▶ **вы́разиться; мя́гко ~ясь** to put it mildly.

выраже́ни|е, я *nt.* expression.

вы́ражен|ный (~, ~а) *p.p.p. of* ▶ **вы́разить** *and* **(~, ~на)** *adj.* pronounced, marked.

вырази́тел|ьный (~ен, ~ьна) *adj.* expressive.

вы́ра|зить, жу, зишь *pf.* (*of* ▶ **~жа́ть**) to express.

вы́ра|зиться, жусь, зишься *pf.* (*of* ▶ **~жа́ться**)
1 (*сказать словами*) to express o.s.
2 (*обнаружиться*) (**в** + *p.*) to manifest itself (in).

выраста́|ть, ю *impf. of* ▶ **вы́расти**

вы́р|асти, асту, астешь, *past* **~ос, ~осла** *pf.* (*of* ▶ **~аста́ть** *and* ▶ **расти́**)
1 to grow (up).
2 (**в** + *a. or* + *i.*) (*стать*) to grow (into), develop (into), become.
3 (**из** + *g.*) to grow (out of) (*clothing*).
4 (*увеличиться*) to increase.
5 (*появиться*) to appear, rise up.

вы́ра|стить, щу, стишь *pf.* (*of* ▶ **~́щивать**) (*детей*) to bring up; (*животных*) to rear, breed; (*растения*) to grow, cultivate.

выра́щива|ть, ю *impf. of* ▶ **вы́растить**

вы́рв|ать¹, у, ешь *pf.* (*of* ▶ **вырыва́ть¹**)
1 to pull out, tear out; **в. зуб** to pull out a tooth; (*отнять*) to snatch.
2 (*fig.*) (*добиться*) to extort, wring; **в. призна́ние у кого́-н.** to wring a confession out of s.o.

вы́рв|ать², у, ешь *pf. of* ▶ **рвать²**

вы́рв|аться, усь, ешься *pf.* (*of* ▶ **вырыва́ться**)
1 (**из** + *g.*) (*освободиться*) to tear o.s. away (from); to break out (from), break loose (from), break free (from); **в. из чьих-н. объя́тий** to tear o.s. away from s.o.'s embrace; (*уехать*) to get away (from).
2 (*стон, замечание*) to burst (from), escape.
3 (*3rd pers. only*) (*стремительно устремиться наружу*) to shoot up, shoot out.

вы́рез, а *m.* (*выемка*) cut; notch; (*в одежде*) neck; **пла́тье с больши́м ~ом** low-necked dress.

вы́ре|зать, жу, жешь *pf.* (*of* ▶ **~за́ть**)
1 (*опухоль; заметку из газеты*) to cut out; (*comput.*) to cut.
2 (*из дерева*) to cut, carve; (*на металле, на камне*) to engrave.
3 (*fig., coll.*) (*убить*) to slaughter, butcher.

выреза́|ть, ю *impf. of* ▶ **вы́резать**

вы́резк|а, и *f.*
1 : **газе́тная в.** press cutting.
2 (*говяжья*) sirloin steak; (*свиная, баранья и т. д.*) fillet steak.

вы́рис|оваться, уется *pf.* (*of* ▶ **~о́вываться**) to appear (in outline); to stand out; (*fig.*) (*ситуация*) to emerge.

вырисо́выва|ться, ется *impf. of* ▶ **вы́рисовать(ся)**

вы́ровня|ть, ю *pf.* (*of* ▶ **выра́внивать**)
1 (*шероховатое*) to smooth (out), level; (*шаг, дыхание*) to regulate.
2 (*по прямой линии*) to align.

вы́ровня|ться, юсь *pf.* (*of* ▶ **выра́вниваться**) to become level; to become even.

вы́род|иться, ится *pf.* (*of* ▶ **вырожда́ться**) to degenerate.

вырожда́|ться, ется *impf. of* ▶ **вы́родиться**

вырожде́ни|е, я *nt.* degeneration.

вы́рон|ить, ю, ишь *pf.* to drop.

вы́р|ою, оешь *see* ▶ **~ыть**

вы́рубк|а, и *f.*
1 cutting down, felling; **в. ле́са** *or* **лесо́в** deforestation.
2 (*вырубленное место*) clearing.

вы́руга|ть(ся), ю(сь) *pf. of* ▶ **руга́ть(ся)**

выруча́|ть, ю *impf. of* ▶ **вы́ручить**

вы́руч|ить, у, ишь *pf.* (*of* ▶ **~а́ть**) (*помочь*) to help out; to come to the help, aid (of).

вы́ручк|а, и *f.*
1 help, assistance; **прийти́ на ~у** to come to the rescue.
2 (*деньги*) takings; earnings.

вырыва́|ть¹, ю *impf. of* ▶ **вы́рвать¹**

вырыва́|ть², ю *impf. of* ▶ **вы́рыть**

вырыва́|ться, юсь *impf. of* ▶ **вы́рваться**

вы́р|ыть, ою, оешь *pf.* (*of* ▶ **~ыва́ть²**) (*землю, яму*) to dig; (*предмет*) to dig up, dig out.

вы́са|дить, жу, дишь *pf.* (*of* ▶ **~́живать**)
1 (*пассажира*) to drop off, set down; **в. на бе́рег** to put ashore; (*заставить выйти*) to throw off, out.
2 (*растение*) to plant out.

вы́са|диться, жусь, дишься *pf.* (*of* ▶ **~́живаться**) (**из, с** + *g.*) to alight (from), get off; (*с судна, самолёта*) to disembark.

вы́садк|а, и *f.*
1 (*с судна*) debarkation, disembarkation; (*из автобуса*) alighting, getting off.
2 (*растения*) planting out.

выса́жива|ть(ся), ю(сь) *impf. of* ▶ **вы́садить(ся)**

вы́са|жу, дишь *see* ▶ **~дить**

вы́свобо|дить, жу, дишь *pf.* (*of* ▶ **высвобожда́ть**)
1 (*вынуть, освободить*) to free.
2 (*средства, рабочих*) to free up, release.

высвобожда́|ть, ю *impf. of* ▶ **вы́свободить**

выселе́ни|е, я *nt.* eviction.

вы́сел|ить, ю, ишь *pf.* (*of* ▶ **~я́ть**)
1 (*из квартиры*) to evict.
2 (*переселить*) to evacuate, move.

вы́сел|иться, юсь, ишься *pf.* (*of* ▶ **~я́ться**) to move.

выселя́|ть(ся), ю(сь) *impf. of* ▶ **вы́селить(ся)**

вы́с|иться, ится *impf.* to tower (up), rise.

вы́ска|зать, жу, жешь *pf.* (*of* ▶ **~́зывать**) to express; to state; **в. предположе́ние** to come out with a suggestion.

вы́ска|заться, жусь, жешься *pf.* (*of* ▶ **~́зываться**)

В

1 to speak out; to speak one's mind; to have one's say.
2 (**за** + *a. or* **против** + *g.*) to speak (for *or* against).

высказывани|е, я *nt.* (*суждение*) pronouncement; (*мнение*) opinion.

высказыва|ть(ся), ю(сь) *impf. of* ▸ **высказать(ся)**

выскакива|ть, ю *impf. of* ▸ **выскочить**

выскальзыва|ть, ю *impf. of* ▸ **выскользнуть**

выскользн|уть, у, ешь *pf.* (*of* ▸ **выскальзывать**) to slip out (*also fig.*).

выскоч|ить, у, ишь *pf.* (*of* ▸ **выскакивать**) (*выпрыгнуть*) to jump out; to leap out, spring out; (*выбежать*) to run out.

вы|слать, шлю, шлешь *pf.* (*of* ▸ **~сылать**)
1 (*посылку, помощь*) to send, send out, dispatch.
2 (*pol.*) to exile; (*иностранца*) to deport.

высле|дить, жу, дишь *pf.* (*of* ▸ **выслеживать 1**) to trace; to track down.

выслежива|ть, ю *impf.*
1 *impf. of* ▸ **выследить.**
2 (*impf. only*) to be on the track of; to shadow.

высле|жу, дишь *see* ▸ **~дить**

выслуша|ть, ю *pf.* (*of* ▸ **выслушивать**) to hear out.

выслушива|ть, ю *impf. of* ▸ **выслушать**

высматрива|ть, ю *impf. of* ▸ **высмотреть**

высмеива|ть, ю *impf. of* ▸ **высмеять**

высме|ять, ю, ешь *pf.* (*of* ▸ **~ивать**) to ridicule.

высморка|ть(ся), ю(сь) *pf. of* ▸ **сморкать(ся)**

высмотр|еть, ю, ишь *pf.* (*of* ▸ **высматривать**) (*найти*) to spy out; to locate (*by eye*).

высовыва|ть(ся), ю(сь) *impf. of* ▸ **высунуть(ся)**

высок|ий (~, ~а) *adj.* (*дом, гора; цена, температура; качество, мнение*) high; (*человек*) tall; (*мысль, стиль*) lofty; (*гость*) distinguished; (*честь*) great; **в ~ой степени** highly.

высоко *adv.*
1 (*располагаться*) high (up).
2 *as pred.* it is high (up); it is a long way up; **окно было в. от земли** the window was high up off the ground.
3 : **оценить в.** to value highly.

высоко... *comb. form* high-, highly-.

высокогорный *adj.* alpine, mountain.

высококачественный *adj.* high-quality.

высококвалифицированный *adj.* highly qualified.

высокомери|е, я *nt.* haughtiness, arrogance.

высокомер|ный (~ен, ~на) *adj.* haughty, arrogant.

высокооплачиваемый *adj.* highly-paid.

высокопоставленный *adj.* high-ranking.

высот|а, ы, *pl.* **~ы, ~** *f.*
1 (*здания, столба*) height; (*над земной поверхностью*) altitude; (*температуры, давления*) level; (*mus.*) pitch; **набрать ~у** (*aeron.*) to gain altitude.
2 (*возвышенность*) height; **командные ~ы** commanding heights (*also fig.*).
3 (*искусства, мастерства*) high level; **достигнуть новых высот** to reach new heights.
4 (*fig.*): **оказаться на ~е положения** to rise to the occasion.

высотк|а, и *f.* (*coll.*) tower block.

высотн|ый *adj.*
1 high-altitude.
2 : **~ое здание** high-rise building, tower block.

высох|нуть, ну, нешь, *past* **~, ~ла** *pf.* (*of* ▸ **высыхать**)
1 (*бельё*) to dry (out); (*река*) to dry up.
2 (*растение*) to wither, fade; (*fig.*) (*исхудать*) to waste away, fade away.

высох|ший *p.p. act. of* ▸ **~нуть** *and adj.* dried-up; shrivelled; wizened.

Высочеств|о, а *nt.*: **(Ваше) В.** (your) Highness.

высп|аться, люсь, ишься *pf.* (*of* ▸ **высыпаться²**) to have a good sleep.

выстав|ить, лю, ишь *pf.* (*of* ▸ **~лять**)
1 (*поставить наружу*) to put out, move out; (*картины, товары*) to exhibit, display; **в. на продажу** to put on sale; **в. напоказ** to show off, parade.
2 (*часовых*) to post.
3 (+ *i.*) (*представить*) to represent (as), make out (as); **в. в плохом свете** to represent in an unfavourable light; **его ~или трусом** he was made out to be a coward.
4 (*предложить*) to put forward; **в. свою кандидатуру** to come forward as a candidate.

выстав|иться, люсь, ишься *pf.* (*of* ▸ **~ляться**) (*о художнике*) to exhibit.

выставк|а, и *f.* exhibition, show.

выставля|ть, ю *impf. of* ▸ **выставить**

выставля|ться, юсь *impf. of* ▸ **выставиться**

выстав|очный *adj. of* ▸ **~ка**

выстаива|ть, ю, ешь *impf. of* ▸ **выстоять 1**

выст|елю, елешь *see* ▸ **~лать**

выстила|ть, ю *impf. of* ▸ **выстлать**

выстира|ть, ю *pf. of* ▸ **стирать²**

выст|лать, елю, елешь *pf.* (*покрыть*) to cover; (*вымостить*) to pave.

высто|ять, ю, ишь *pf.* (*of* ▸ **выстаивать**)
1 (*долго простоять*) to stand.
2 (*pf. only*) (*не сдаться*) to stand one's ground.

выстрада|ть, ю *pf.*
1 (*пережить много страданий*) to suffer; to go through.
2 (*достигнуть страданиями*) to gain, achieve through suffering.

выстраива|ть(ся), ю(сь) *impf. of* ▸ **выстроить(ся)**

выстрел, а *m.* shot; **произвести в.** to fire a shot; **раздался в.** a shot rang out.

выстрел|ить, ю, ишь *pf.* to shoot, fire; **я ~ил в него три раза** I fired three shots at him.

вы́стро|ить, ю, ишь *pf.* (*of* ▸ **выстра́ивать**)
[1] to build.
[2] (*mil.*) to draw up, form up.

вы́стро|иться, юсь, ишься *pf.* (*of* ▸ **выстра́иваться**)
[1] (*mil.*) to form up (*intrans.*).
[2] (*стоять рядами*) to stand in rows.

вы́ступ, а *m.* projection, ledge.

выступа́|ть, ю *impf.*
[1] *impf. of* ▸ **вы́ступить.**
[2] (*impf. only*) to project, jut out, stick out.

вы́ступ|ить, лю, ишь *pf.* (*of* ▸ **~а́ть 1**)
[1] (*выйти вперёд*) to come forward; to come out.
[2] (*публично*) to appear (*publicly*); (**за** + *a.*, **про́тив** + *g.*) to come out (for, against); **в. в печа́ти** to appear in print; **в. с ре́чью** to make a speech; **в. по телеви́дению** to appear on television.

выступле́ни|е, я *nt.* (*публичное*) appearance; (*речь*) speech; (*актёра*) performance.

вы́сун|уть, у, ешь *pf.* (*of* ▸ **высо́вывать**) to put out, thrust out, stick out; **в. язы́к** to put/stick one's tongue out.

вы́сун|уться, усь, ешься *pf.* (*of* ▸ **высо́вываться**)
[1] (*о человеке*) to show o.s., thrust o.s. forward; **в. из окна́** to lean out of the window.
[2] (*о ноге, руке*) to stick out.

высу́шива|ть, ю *impf. of* ▸ **вы́сушить**

вы́суш|ить(ся), у(сь), ишь(ся) *pf. of* ▸ **суши́ть(ся)**

вы́счита|ть, ю *pf.* (*of* ▸ **высчи́тывать**) to calculate.

высчи́тыва|ть, ю *impf. of* ▸ **вы́считать**

вы́с|ший *adj.* (*comp. and superl. of* ▸ **высо́кий**) (*самый высокий*) highest; (*самый главный*) supreme; (*более высокий*) higher; **~шего ка́чества** of the highest quality; **~шая ме́ра наказа́ния** capital punishment; **~шее образова́ние** higher education; **~шее уче́бное заведе́ние** *see* ▸ **вуз**; **в ~шей сте́пени** in the highest degree.

высыла́|ть, ю *impf. of* ▸ **вы́слать**

вы́сып|ать, лю, лешь *pf.* (*of* ▸ **высыпа́ть**)
[1] to pour out (*trans.*); (*нечаянно*) to spill.
[2] (*coll.*) to pour out (*intrans.*).

высыпа́|ть, ю *impf. of* ▸ **вы́сыпать**

высыпа́|ться[1]**, ется** *impf. of* ▸ **вы́сыпаться**

высыпа́|ться[2]**, юсь** *impf. of* ▸ **вы́спаться**

вы́сып|аться, лется, лются *pf.* (*of* ▸ **высыпа́ться**[1]) to pour out; (*нечаянно*) to spill (*intrans.*).

высыха́|ть, ю *impf. of* ▸ **вы́сохнуть**

выта́лкива|ть, ю *impf. of* ▸ **вы́толкнуть**

выта́скива|ть, ю *impf. of* ▸ **вы́тащить**

вы́тащ|ить, у, ишь *pf.* (*of* ▸ **выта́скивать**) (*из кармана, из сумки*) to pull out, extract.

вытека́|ть, ю *impf.*
[1] *impf. of* ▸ **вы́течь.**
[2] (*impf. only*) (*река*) to flow (from, out of).
[3] (*impf. only*) (*fig.*) (*вывод*) to result, follow (from).

вы́те|кут *see* ▸ **~чь**

вы́т|ереть, ру, решь, *past* **~ер, ~ерла** *pf.* (*of* ▸ **~ира́ть**) (*руки, глаза, посуду, стол*) to wipe; (*грязь*) to wipe up; **в. пыль** to dust.

вы́терп|еть, лю, ишь *pf.* to bear, endure.

вытесне́ни|е, я *nt.* ousting; (*замена собой*) displacing, supplanting.

вы́тесн|ить, ю, ишь *pf.* (*of* ▸ **~я́ть**) (*врага*) to force out; to oust; (*заменить собой*) to displace, supplant.

вытесня́|ть, ю *impf. of* ▸ **вы́теснить**

вы́те|чь, чет, кут, *past* **~к, ~кла** *pf.* (*of* ▸ **~ка́ть 1**) to flow out, run out.

вытира́|ть, ю *impf. of* ▸ **вы́тереть**

вы́толкн|уть, у, ешь *pf.* (*of* ▸ **выта́лкивать**)
[1] to throw out.
[2] (*пробку*) to push out, force out.

вы́торг|овать, ую *pf.* (*of* ▸ **~о́вывать**) (*coll.*) (*получить уступку*) to get a reduction (of); (*fig., coll.*) to manage to get.

выторго́выва|ть, ю *impf.* (*coll.*)
[1] *impf. of* ▸ **вы́торговать.**
[2] to try to get (*by bargaining*); to haggle over.

вы́трав|ить, лю, ишь *pf. of* ▸ **трави́ть**

вы́т|ру, решь *see* ▸ **~ереть**

вытряса́|ть, ю *impf. of* ▸ **вы́трясти**

вы́тряс|ти, у, ешь, *past* **~, ~ла** *pf.* (*песок, мусор*) to shake out.

вытря́хива|ть, ю *impf. of* ▸ **вы́тряхнуть**

вы́тряхн|уть, у, ешь *pf.* (*of* ▸ **вытря́хивать**) (*песок, мусор; скатерть*) to shake out.

выть, во́ю, во́ешь *impf.* (*собака, волк, ветер*) to howl; (*сирена*) to wail.

вытя́гива|ть(ся), ю(сь) *impf. of* ▸ **вы́тянуть(ся)**

вы́тян|уть, у, ешь *pf.* (*of* ▸ **вытя́гивать**)
[1] (*вытащить*) to pull out.
[2] (*ноги, руки*) to stretch (out); (*сделать длиннее*) to extend.
[3] (*дым, гной*) to draw out, extract (*also fig.*); (*impers.*): **газ ~уло в окно́** the gas had escaped through the window.

вы́тян|уться, усь, ешься *pf.* (*of* ▸ **вытя́гиваться**)
[1] (*растянуться*) to stretch (*intrans.*); (*вдоль реки; на полу*) to stretch out; **лицо́ у неё ~улось** (*coll.*) her face fell.
[2] (*выпрямиться*) to stand erect.

выу́чива|ть, ю *impf. of* ▸ **вы́учить**

вы́уч|ить, у, ишь *pf.* (*of* ▸ **учи́ть 1, 4** *and* ▸ **~ивать**)
[1] to learn.
[2] (+ *a. and d. or* + *inf.*) to teach; **он ~ил нас испа́нскому языку́** he taught us Spanish.

вы́уч|иться, усь, ишься *pf.* (*of* ▸ **учи́ться 1, 3**) (+ *d. or inf.*) to learn; (*coll., на кого-н.*) to learn (to be).

вы́хва|тить, чу, тишь *pf.*
[1] (*отнять*) to snatch out; to grab.
[2] (*вытащить*) to pull out, draw; **в. нож** to draw a knife.

выхва́тыва|ть, ю *impf. of* ▸ **вы́хватить**

вы́хва|чу, тишь *see* ▸ **~тить**
выхлопн|о́й *adj.* (*tech.*) exhaust; **~а́я труба́** exhaust pipe; **~ы́е га́зы** exhaust (fumes).
вы́ход, а *m.*
1 (*на улицу*) going out; (*с целью уйти*) leaving, departure; (*из партии*) leaving; (*поезда, корабля*) departure; **в. в отста́вку** retirement.
2 (*место выхода*) way out, exit; (*трубки*) outlet; (*способ*) way out; **дать в.** (+ *d.*) to give vent (to).
3 (*издания*) appearance; (*фильма*) release; (*theatr.*) entrance.
4 (*comput.*) exit; logoff.
вы́ход|ец, ца *m.*
1 (*из другой страны*) immigrant.
2 (*из другой социальной среды*) person moving from one social group to another; **он — в. из крестья́н** he is of peasant origin.
выхо|ди́ть, жу́, ~дишь *impf.*
1 *impf. of* ▸ **вы́йти.**
2 (*impf. only*) to look out (on), give (on), face; **его́ ко́мната ~дит о́кнами на у́лицу** his room looks onto the street.
3 : **не в. из головы́, из ума́** to be unforgettable, stick in one's mind.
4 *as pred.* **~дит (, что)** (*coll.*) it turns out that.
вы́ходк|а, и *f.* (*pej.*) trick; escapade.
выходн|о́й *adj.*
1 exit; **~а́я дверь** street door.
2 : **в. день** day off; **~а́я оде́жда** 'best' clothes; *as n.* (*i*) **в., ~о́го** *m.* (*день*) day off; (*ii*) **в., ~о́го** *m.*, **~а́я, ~о́й** *f.* (*coll.*) (*человек*) person having day off; **он сего́дня в.** it is his day off today.
3 : **~о́е посо́бие** severance pay.
выхо|жу́, ~дишь *see* ▸ **~ди́ть**
вы́ч|ел, ла *see* ▸ **~есть**
вычёркива|ть, ю *impf. of* ▸ **вы́черкнуть**
вы́черкн|уть, у, ешь *pf.* (*слова*) to cross out; (*из списка*) to cross off; **в. из па́мяти** to erase from one's memory.
вы́черпа|ть, ю *pf.* (*of* ▸ **вычёрпывать**) (**из** + *g.*) (*содержимое*) to take out; (*из лодки*) to bail (out); **в. во́ду из ло́дки** to bail out a boat.
вычёрпыва|ть, ю *impf. of* ▸ **вы́черпать**
вы́ч|есть, ту, тешь, *past* **~ел, ~ла,** *pres. ger.* **~тя** *pf.* (*of* ▸ **~ита́ть**)
1 (*math.*) to subtract.
2 (*удержать*) to deduct, keep back.
вычисле́ни|е, я *nt.* calculation.
вычисли́тельн|ый *adj.* calculating, computing; **~ая те́хника** computers.
вы́числ|ить, ю, ишь *pf.* (*of* ▸ **~я́ть**) to calculate, compute.
вычисля́|ть, ю *impf. of* ▸ **вы́числить**
вы́чи|стить, щу, стишь *pf.* (*of* ▸ **чи́стить 1, 2** *and* ▸ **~ща́ть**) to clean (up, out).
вычита́ни|е, я, *nt.* (*math.*) subtraction.
вычита́|ть, ю *impf. of* ▸ **вы́честь**
вычища́|ть, ю *impf. of* ▸ **вы́чистить**
вы́чи|щу, стишь *see* ▸ **~стить**
вы́ч|ту, тешь *see* ▸ **~есть**

вы́ше
1 *comp. of* ▸ **высо́кий** *and* ▸ **высоко́;** higher, taller.
2 *prep.* + *g.* (*вверх от*) above, beyond; (*больше*) over; **в. нуля́** above zero; (*за пределами*) beyond; **э́то в. моего́ понима́ния** it is beyond my comprehension.
3 *adv.* (*liter.*) above; **смотри́ в.** see above.
выше... *comb. form* above-, afore-.
вы́|шел, шла *see* ▸ **~йти**
вышеска́занный *adj.* aforesaid.
вышестоя́щий *adj.* higher.
вышеука́занный *adj.* foregoing.
вышеупомя́нутый *adj.* aforementioned.
вышива́ни|е, я *nt.* embroidery, needlework.
вышива́|ть, ю *impf. of* ▸ **вы́шить**
вы́шивк|а, и *f.* embroidery, needlework.
вы́ш|ить, ью, ьешь, *imper.* **~ей** *pf.* (*of* ▸ **~ива́ть**) to embroider.
вы́шк|а, и *f.* (*башня*) (watch)tower; **сторожева́я в.** watchtower; **бурова́я в.** derrick.
вы́|шлю, шлешь *see* ▸ **~слать**
вы́щип|ать, лю, лешь *pf.* (*of* ▸ **выщи́пывать**) to pull out, pluck; **в. пе́рья у ку́рицы** to pluck a chicken.
выщи́пыва|ть, ю *impf. of* ▸ **вы́щипать**
вы́яв|ить, лю, ишь *pf.* (*of* ▸ **~ля́ть**)
1 (*предать гласности*) to bring out; to make known.
2 (*недостатки*) to expose.
вы́яв|иться, люсь, ишься *pf.* (*of* ▸ **~ля́ться**) (*недостатки*) to come to light, be revealed, be exposed.
выявля́|ть(ся), ю(сь) *impf. of* ▸ **вы́явить(ся)**
выясне́ни|е, я *nt.* clarification; explanation.
вы́ясн|ить, ю, ишь *pf.* (*of* ▸ **выясня́ть**) (*сделать понятным*) to clarify, clear up, explain; (*установить*) to find out, ascertain.
вы́ясн|иться, ится *pf.* (*of* ▸ **выясня́ться**) (*объясниться*) to become clear; (*стать явным*) to turn out, prove (*intrans.*).
выясн|я́ть(ся), я́ю, я́ет(ся) *impf. of* ▸ **вы́яснить(ся)**
Вьетна́м, а *m.* Vietnam.
вьетна́м|ец, ца *m.* Vietnamese.
вьетна́м|ка, ки *f. of* ▸ **~ец**
вьетна́мский *adj.* Vietnamese.
вью, вьёшь *see* ▸ **вить**
вью́г|а, и *f.* snowstorm, blizzard.
вью́щ|ийся *pres. part. of* ▸ **ви́ться** *and adj.*: **~иеся во́лосы** curly hair; **~ееся расте́ние** (*bot.*) creeper, climber.
вя|жу́, ~жешь *see* ▸ **~за́ть**
вяз, а *m.* elm (tree).
вяза́ни|е, я *nt.* knitting, crocheting.
вяза́нк|а, и *f.* bundle.
вя́заный *adj.* knitted.
вя|за́ть, жу́, ~жешь *impf.*
1 (*pf.* **с~**) to tie, bind.
2 (*pf.* **с~**) (*спицами*) to knit; (*крючком*) to crochet.
3 (*impf. only*) to be astringent; (*impers.*): **у меня́ ~жет во рту** my mouth feels

constricted.

вя|за́ться, жу́сь, ~́жешься *impf.* (*coll.*) (**с** + *i.*) to agree, tally (with).

вя́з|кий (~ок, ~ка́, ~ко) *adj.*
[1] (*клейкий*) viscous, sticky.
[2] (*топкий*) boggy.

вя́з|нуть, ну, нешь, *past* **~, ~ла** *impf.* (**в** + *p.*) to get stuck (in).

вя́лост|ь, и *f.* (*кожи, мышц*) flabbiness; limpness; (*fig.*) sluggishness; inertia; slackness.

вя́л|ый *adj.*
[1] (*растение*) faded.
[2] **(~, ~а)** (*кожа, тело*) flabby; limp; (*fig.*) sluggish, inert; slack.

вя́н|уть, у, ешь, *past* **вял/вя́нул, вя́ла, вя́ло, вя́ли** *impf.* (*of* ▶ **за~**) (*растение*) to fade, wither; (*fig.*) (*красота, способности*) to fade.

г. *abbr. of*
[1] **год** yr (year).
[2] **го́род** city, town.
[3] **гора́** Mt (Mount).

габари́т, а *m.* (*usu. in pl.*) (*tech.*) size, dimensions.

габари́т|ный *adj. of* ▶ **~; ~ные огни́** sidelights (*Br.*), sidemarker lights (*US*).

Гава́й|и, ев *m. pl.* Hawaii.

га́вань, и *f.* harbour (*Br.*), harbor (*US*).

га́вка|ть, ю *impf.* (*coll.*) to bark.

гага́р|а, ы *f.* (*zool.*) diver (*Br.*), loon (*US*).

гад, а *m.* (*fig., coll.*) louse, rat, skunk.

гада́лк|а, и *f.* fortune-teller.

гада́ни|е, я *nt.* (*догадка*) guesswork.

гада́|ть, ю *impf.*
[1] (*pf.* **по~**) (**на** + *p. or* **по** + *d.*) (*предсказывать*) to tell fortunes (by).
[2] (*impf. only*) (**о** + *p.*) (*предполагать*) to guess.

га́дин|а, ы *f.* = **гад**

га́|дить, жу, дишь *impf.* (*of* ▶ **на~**) (*coll.*)
[1] (*о животных*) to defecate.
[2] (**на** + *a. or p.*, **в** + *p.*) (*пачкать*) to foul.
[3] (+ *d.*) (*вредить*) to play dirty tricks (on).

га́д|кий (~ок, ~ка́, ~ко) *adj.* nasty, vile, repulsive; **г. утёнок** ugly duckling.

га́дост|ь, и *f.*
[1] (*coll.*) (*дрянь*) filth, muck.
[2] (*поступок*) dirty trick; **говори́ть ~и** to say foul things.

гадю́к|а, и *f.* adder, viper.

га́ечный *adj. of* ▶ **га́йка; г. ключ** spanner, wrench.

га́же *comp. of* ▶ **га́дкий**

газ, а *m.*
[1] gas.
[2] (*coll.*): **педа́ль ~́а** accelerator, gas pedal; **да́ть ~́у** to step on the gas; **сба́вить г.** to reduce speed.
[3] (*pl.*) (*в кишечнике*) wind.

газе́т|а, ы *f.* newspaper.

газиро́ванный *adj.* carbonated.

газиро́вк|а, и *f.* (*coll.*) carbonated water, soda (water).

газовщи́к, а́ *m.* gasman.

га́зов|ый *adj. of* ▶ **газ; ~ая плита́** gas cooker, gas stove; **г. счётчик** gas-meter; **~ая ка́мера** gas chamber.

газо́н, а *m.* grassed area, lawn.

газонокоси́лк|а, и *f.* lawnmower.

газопрово́д, а *m.* gas pipeline; gas main.

ГАИ *f. indecl.* (*abbr. of* **Госуда́рственная автомоби́льная инспе́кция**) State Motor Vehicle Inspectorate; traffic police.

Гаи́ти *indecl.* (*государство*) Haiti; (*m.*) (*остров*) Hispaniola.

гаитя́н|ин, ина, *pl.* **~е, ~** *m.* Haitian.

гаитя́н|ка, ки *f. of* ▶ **~ин**

гаитя́нский *adj.* Haitian.

гаи́шник, а *m.* (*coll.*) traffic cop.

Гайа́н|а, ы *f.* Guyana.

гайа́н|ец, ца *m.* Guyanese.

гайа́н|ка, ки *f. of* ▶ **~ец**

гайа́нский *adj.* Guyanese.

га́йк|а, и *f.* nut; **закрути́ть ~и** (*fig.*) to put the screws on.

гаймори́т, а *m.* (*med.*) sinusitis.

гала́ктик|а, и *f.* (*astron.*) galaxy.

галантере́|йный *adj. of* ▶ **~я; г. магази́н** haberdashery, fancy goods shop.

галантере́|я, и *f.* haberdashery, fancy goods.

гала́нт|ный (~ен, ~на) *adj.* chivalrous.

гале́р|а, ы *f.* galley.

галере́|я, и *f.* (*in var. senses*) gallery.

га́лк|а, и *f.* jackdaw.

галло́н, а *m.* gallon.

галлюцина́ци|я, и *f.* hallucination.

галлюциноге́н, а *m.* hallucinogen.

га́лочк|а, и *f.* tick, check (*US*).

га́лстук, а *m.* tie; **г.-ба́бочка** bow tie.

га́л|ька, ьки *f.* (*g. pl.* **~ек**) pebble; (*collect.*) pebbles, shingle.

гам, а *m.* (*coll.*) din, uproar.

гама́к, а́ *m.* hammock.

Га́мби|я, и *f.* Gambia.

га́мбургер, а *m.* (ham)burger.

га́мм|а, ы *f.* (*mus.*) scale; gamut (*also fig.*).

Га́н|а, ы *f.* Ghana.

га́нгстер, а *m.* gangster.

гандбо́л, а *m.* handball.

гандболи́ст, а *m.* handball player.

гандболи́ст|ка, ки *f. of* ▶ **~**

га́н|ец, ца *m.* Ghanaian.

га́нк|а, и *f. of* ▶ **~ец**

га́нский *adj.* Ghanaian.

Г

гара́ж, а́ *m.* garage.
гара́нт, а *m.* guarantor.
гаранти́йный *adj.* guarantee.
гаранти́р|овать, ую *impf. and pf.* to guarantee, vouch for.
гара́нти|я, и *f.* guarantee; (*охрана*) safeguard.
гардеро́б, а *m.*
1 (*шкаф*) wardrobe.
2 (*помещение*) cloakroom.
3 (*collect.*) (*одежда*) wardrobe.
гардеро́бщик, а *m.* cloakroom attendant.
гардеро́бщи|ца, цы *f. of* ▶ **~к**
гаре́м, а *m.* harem.
гармони́р|овать, ую *impf.* (**с** + *i.*) to be in harmony (with); (*о красках*) to tone (with), go (with).
гармони́ст, а *m.* accordion player.
гармони́ч|ный (~ен, ~на) *adj.* harmonious.
гармо́ни|я, и *f.*
1 (*mus.*) harmony.
2 (*fig.*) harmony, concord.
гармо́н|ь, и *f.* accordion, concertina.
гарнизо́н, а *m.* garrison.
гарни́р, а *m.* (*cul.*) garnish; (*из овощей*) vegetables; **на г.** as a side dish.
гарниту́р, а *m.* set; (*мебели*) suite.
гарпу́н, а́ *m.* harpoon.
га|си́ть, шу́, ~́сишь *impf.* (*of* ▶ **по~**)
1 (*pf. also* **за~**) (*пожар, свет*) to put out, extinguish; **г. свет** to put out the light.
2 (*погашать*) to cancel; **г. задо́лженность** to liquidate a debt.
га́с|нуть, ну, нешь, *past* **~, ~ла** *impf.* (*of* ▶ **по~**) (*переставать гореть*) to be extinguished, go out; (*слабеть*) to grow feeble; (*о чувствах*) to fade, weaken.
гастри́т, а *m.* gastritis.
гастроли́р|овать, ую *impf.* to tour, be on tour (*of an artiste*).
гастро́л|ь, и *f.* (*usu. in pl.*) tour; engagement (*of touring artiste*).
гастроно́м, а *m.* grocer's (shop) (*Br.*), grocery store (*US*).
гастроно́ми|я, и *f.*
1 (*продукты*) high-quality cooked meats, fish, cheeses, etc.
2 (*гастрономический отдел*) delicatessen counter.
гаши́ш, а *m.* hashish.
ГБ (*abbr. of* **орга́ны госуда́рственной безопа́сности**) (organs of) State security.
гвалт, а *m.* (*coll.*) row, uproar, rumpus.
гварде́|ец, йца *m.* (*mil.*) guardsman.
гва́рди|я, и *f.* (*mil.*) Guards; **~и** (*preceding* **капита́н** *etc., in titles of rank*) Guards.
Гватема́л|а, ы *f.* Guatemala.
гватема́л|ец, ьца *m.* Guatemalan.
гватема́л|ка, ки *f. of* ▶ **~ец**
гватема́льский *adj.* Guatemalan.
гвине́|ец, йца *m.* Guinean.
гвине́|йка, йки *f. of* ▶ **~ец**
гвине́йский *adj.* Guinean.
Гвине́|я, и *f.* Guinea.
гвозди́к|а[1]**, и** *f.* (*bot.*) pink(s); carnation(s).
гвозди́к|а[2]**, и** *f.* (*collect.*) (*пряность*) cloves.
гвозд|ь, я́, *pl.* **~́и, ~е́й** *m.*
1 nail.
2 (+ *g.*; *fig., coll.*) (*самое главное*) crux; highlight; (*программы*) highlight, main attraction.
где *adv.*
1 (*interrog. and rel. adv.*) where; **г. бы ни** wherever; **г. бы то ни́ было** no matter where.
2 (*coll.*) (*где-нибудь*) somewhere; anywhere.
где́-либо *adv.* anywhere.
где́-нибудь *adv.* somewhere; anywhere.
где́-то *adv.* somewhere.
ге|й, я *m.* (*sl.*) gay (*homosexual*); **г.-клуб** gay club.
гекта́р, а *m.* hectare (*10,000 square metres*).
гел|ь, я *m.* gel.
геморро́|й, я *m.* (*med.*) haemorrhoids (*Br.*), hemorrhoids (*US*), piles.
гемофи́лик, а *m.* (*med.*) haemophiliac (*Br.*), hemophiliac (*US*).
гемофили́|я, и *f.* (*med.*) haemophilia (*Br.*), hemophilia (*US*).
ген, а *m.* (*physiol.*) gene.
ген... *comb. form, abbr. of* **генера́льный**
генеалоги́ческий *adj.* genealogical.
генеало́ги|я, и *f.* genealogy.
генера́л, а *m.* general; **г.-майо́р** major general; **г.-губерна́тор** governor general.
генера́льн|ый *adv.* (*in var. senses*) general; **г. констру́ктор** chief designer; **~ая репети́ция** dress rehearsal; **г. секрета́рь** general secretary; **~ая убо́рка** spring-clean; **г. штаб** general staff.
генера́льский *adj.* general's; **г. чин** rank of general.
генера́тор, а *m.* (*tech.*) generator.
гене́тик|а, и *f.* genetics.
генети́ческий *adj.* genetic.
гениа́л|ьный (~ен, ~ьна) *adj.* (*поэт, произведение*) brilliant; (*решение*) ingenious.
ге́ни|й, я *m.* (*талант, способность*) genius; (*человек*) a genius.
генита́ли|и, й *no sg.* (*med.*) genitalia, genitals.
ге́н|ный *adj. of* ▶ **~; ~ная инжене́рия** genetic engineering.
гено́м, а *m.* genome; **~ челове́ка** human genome.
генофо́нд, а *m.* gene pool.
геноци́д, а *m.* genocide.
генсе́к, а *m.* (*abbr. of* **генера́льный секрета́рь**) (*coll.*) general secretary.
гео... *comb. form, abbr. of* **географи́ческий**
гео́граф, а *m.* geographer.
географи́ческий *adj.* geographical.
геогра́фи|я, и *f.* geography.
геодези́ст, а *m.* land surveyor.
геоде́зи|я, и *f.* geodesy, (land) surveying.
гео́лог, а *m.* geologist.
геологи́ческий *adj.* geological.
геоло́ги|я, и *f.* geology.
геометри́ческий *adj.* geometric(al).
геоме́три|я, и *f.* geometry.

геополити́ческий *adj.* geopolitical.
георги́н, а *m.* dahlia.
гепати́т, а *m.* hepatitis.
гера́н|ь, и *f.* geranium.
герб, а́ *m.* arms, coat of arms.
геркуле́с, а *m.* (*sg. only*) (*крупа*) rolled oats; porridge.
Герма́ни|я, и *f.* Germany.
герма́нский *adj.* Germanic.
герои́зм, а *m.* heroism.
герои́н, а *m.* heroin.
герои́н|я, и *f.* heroine.
герои́ческий *adj.* heroic.
геро́|й, я *m.* hero; (*liter.*) (*действующее лицо*) character; **гла́вный г.** protagonist.
геро́йский *adj.* heroic.
ге́рпес, а *m.* herpes.
герц, а, *g. pl.* **г.** *m.* (*phys.*) hertz.
ге́рцог, а *m.* duke; **г. Эдинбу́ргский** the Duke of Edinburgh.
герцоги́н|я, и *f.* duchess.
гетеросексуа́льный *adj.* heterosexual.
ге́тр|ы, гетр *pl.* (*sg.* **~а, ~ы** *f.*)
1 gaiters.
2 (*sport*) football socks.
ге́тто *nt. indecl.* ghetto.
г-жа (*abbr. of* **госпожа́**) (*замужняя*) Mrs; (*незамужняя*) Miss; (*замужняя или незамужняя*) Ms.
гиаци́нт, а *m.* hyacinth.
ГИБДД (*abbr. of* **Госуда́рственная инспе́кция безопа́сности доро́жного движе́ния**) State road safety inspectorate.
ги́бел|ь, и *f.* (*смерть*) death; (*уничтожение*) destruction, ruin; (*потеря*) loss; (*государства*) downfall.
ги́б|кий (~ок, ~ка́, ~ко) *adj.*
1 flexible; (*тело*) supple; **г. диск** (*comput.*) floppy (disk).
2 (*ум*) adaptable, versatile.
ги́бкост|ь, и *f.*
1 flexibility; (*тела*) suppleness.
2 (*ума*) versatility, resourcefulness.
ги́блый *adj.* (*coll.*) (*место*) godforsaken; (*безнадёжный*) hopeless.
ги́б|нуть, ну, нешь, *past* **~** *and* **~нул, ~ла** *impf.* (*of* ▸**по~**) to perish.
Гибралта́р, а *m.* Gibraltar.
гибри́д, а *m.* hybrid.
гига... *comb. form* giga-.
гигаба́йт, а *m.* (*comput.*) gigabyte.
гига́нт, а *m.* giant.
гига́нтский *adj.* gigantic.
гигие́н|а, ы *f.* hygiene.
гигиени́ческ|ий *adj.* hygienic, sanitary; **~ая прокла́дка** sanitary towel (*Br.*), napkin (*US*).
гид, а *m.* guide.
гидро... *comb. form* hydro-.
гидроста́нци|я, и *f.* hydroelectric (power) station.
гидроэлектроста́нци|я, и *f.* hydroelectric power station.
ги́льз|а, ы *f.* cartridge case.
Гимала́|и, ев *no sg.* the Himalayas.
гимн, а *m.* hymn; **госуда́рственный г.** national anthem.
гимна́зи|я, и *f.* grammar school (*Br.*), high school.
гимна́ст, а *m.* gymnast.
гимна́стик|а, и *f.* gymnastics; **спорти́вная г.** artistic gymnastics; **худо́жественная г.** rhythmic gymnastics.
гимнасти́ческий *adj.* gymnastic; **г. зал** gymnasium.
гимна́ст|ка, ки *f. of* ▸**~**
гинеко́лог, а *m.* gynaecologist (*Br.*), gynecologist (*US*).
гинекологи́ческий *adj.* gynaecological (*Br.*), gynecological (*US*).
гинеколо́ги|я, и *f.* gynaecology (*Br.*), gynecology (*US*).
гиперма́ркет, а *m.* hypermarket (*Br.*).
гиперссы́лк|а, и *f.* (*comput.*) hyperlink.
гипертони́|я, и *f.* (*med.*) hypertension, high blood pressure.
гипно́з, а *m.* hypnosis.
гипнотизёр, а *m.* hypnotist.
гипнотизи́р|овать, ую *impf.* (*of* ▸**за~**) to hypnotize.
гипноти́ческий *adj.* hypnotic.
гипо́тез|а, ы *f.* hypothesis.
гипотети́ческий *adj.* hypothetical.
гипс, а *m.*
1 (*min.*) gypsum.
2 (*art*) (*материал*) plaster of Paris.
3 (*хирургическая повязка*) plaster cast, plaster.
гирля́нд|а, ы *f.* garland, wreath.
ги́р|я, и *f.* (*для весов*) weight; (*sport*) weight, dumb-bell.
гита́р|а, ы *f.* guitar.
гитари́ст, а *m.* guitarist.
гитари́ст|ка, ки *f. of* ▸**~**
глав... *comb. form, abbr. of* **гла́вный**
глав|а́[1]**, ы́,** *pl.* **~ы** *c.g.* (*начальник*) head, chief; **г. делега́ции** head of a delegation; **быть/стоя́ть во ~е́** (+ *g.*) to be at the head (of), lead; **во ~е́ (с** + *i.*) under the leadership (of), led (by).
глав|а́[2]**, ы́,** *pl.* **~ы** *f.* (*раздел книги*) chapter.
главнокома́ндующ|ий, его *m.* commander-in-chief; **Верхо́вный г.** Supreme Commander.
гла́вн|ый *adj.* (*самый важный*) chief, main, principal; (*старший*) head, senior; **г. врач** head physician; **г. инжене́р** chief engineer; **~ое управле́ние** central directorate; **~ым о́бразом** chiefly, mainly, for the most part; *as n.* **~ое, ~ого** *nt.* the chief thing, the main thing; the essentials.
глаго́л, а *m.* verb.
глади́льн|ый *adj.* ironing; **~ая доска́** ironing board.
гладио́лус, а *m.* gladiolus.
гла́|дить, жу, дишь *impf.* (*of* ▸**по~**)
1 (*pf. also* **вы́~**) (*выравнивать утюгом*) to iron, press.
2 (*ласково проводить рукой по чему-н.*) to stroke.
гла́д|кий (~ок, ~ка́, ~ко) *adj.* (*дорога*) smooth; (*волосы*) straight; (*ткань*) plain.
гла́д|ко *adv. of* ▸**~кий;** smoothly.

Г

гла́же *comp. of* ▸ **гла́дкий, гла́дко**
гла́жень|е, я *nt.* ironing.
глаз, а, о ~́е, в ~у́, *pl.* **~а́, ~, ~а́м** *m.* (*орган зрения*) eye; (*зрение*) eyesight; **в ~а́** to one's face; **в ~а́х** (+ *g.*) in the eyes (of); **я его́ в ~а́ не ви́дел** I have never seen him; **руга́ть кого́-н. за ~а́** to abuse s.o. behind his back; **на ~а́х** before one's eyes; **не попада́йся мне на ~а́!** keep out of my sight!; **на г.** approximately, by eye; **с ~у на́ г.** tête-à-tête, cheek by jowl; **с г. доло́й** out of sight; **смотре́ть во все ~а́** to be all eyes; **закрыва́ть ~а́** (**на** + *a.*) to close one's eyes (to); **открыва́ть кому́-н. ~а́** (**на** + *a.*) to open s.o.'s eyes (to); **идти́ куда́ ~а́ глядя́т** to follow one's nose.
глазн|о́й *adj. of* ▸ **глаз; г. врач** ophthalmologist; **~о́е я́блоко** eyeball.
глаз|о́к, ка́, *pl.* **~́ки, ~́ок** *and* **~ки́, ~ко́в** *m.*
1 (*pl.* **~́ки**) *dim. of* ▸ **~; стро́ить ~́ки кому́-н.** to make eyes at s.o.
2 (*pl.* **~ки́**) (*coll.*) peephole.
глазу́н|ья, ьи, *g. pl.* **~ий** *f.* fried eggs (*with yolk and white unmixed*).
глазу́р|ь, и *f.*
1 (*на посуде*) glaze.
2 (*cul.*) icing.
гламу́р|ный (~ен, ~на) *adj.* (*coll.*) glamorous, glitzy.
гла́нд|а, ы *f.* (*anat.*) tonsil; **удали́ть ~ы** to take out tonsils; **воспале́ние гланд** glandular fever.
гла|си́ть, шу́, си́шь *impf.* to say, run; **докуме́нт ~си́т сле́дующее** the paper runs as follows; **как ~си́т погово́рка** as the saying goes.
гла́сно *adv.* openly, publicly.
гла́сност|ь, и *f.*
1 (*известность*) publicity; **преда́ть ~и** to make public, make known, publish.
2 (*pol.*) *glasnost*, openness.
гла́сный[1] *adj.* (*открытый*) open, public; **г. суд** public trial.
гла́сн|ый[2] *adj.* (*ling.*) vowel, vocalic; *as n.* **г., ~ого** *m.* vowel.
глауко́м|а, ы *f.* glaucoma.
гли́н|а, ы *f.* clay.
глинobи́тный *adj.* adobe; mud.
глинтве́йн, а *m.* mulled wine.
гли́нян|ый *adj.* (*сделанный из глины*) clay; earthenware; **~ая посу́да** earthenware crockery.
глобализа́ци|я, и *f.* globalization.
глоба́льный *adj.* global; (*fig.*) extensive.
гло́бус, а *m.* globe.
гло|да́ть, жу́, ~́жешь *impf.* to gnaw (at) (*also fig.*).
глота́|ть, ю *impf.* (*of* ▸ **проглоти́ть**) to swallow.
гло́тк|а, и *f.*
1 (*anat.*) gullet.
2 (*coll.*) (*горло*) throat.
глот|о́к, ка́ *m.* gulp, mouthful; (*небольшое количество*) drop.
гло́х|нуть, ну, нешь, *past* **~нул** *and* **~, ~ла** *impf.*
1 (*pf.* **о~**) (*становиться глухим*) to become deaf.
2 (*pf.* **за~**) (*о звуках*) to die away, subside; (*о моторе*) to stall.
глу́б|же *comp. of* ▸ **~о́кий** *and* ▸ **~око́**
глубин|а́, ы́, *pl.* **~́ы** *f.*
1 depth; **на ~е́ трёхсо́т ме́тров** at a depth of 300 metres.
2 (*pl.*) (the) depths.
3 (+ *g.*) heart, interior (*also fig.*); **в ~е́ ле́са** in the heart of the forest; **в ~е́ души́** at heart, in one's heart of hearts.
глуби́нный *adj.* deep.
глубо́к|ий (~, ~а́) *adj.*
1 (*in var. senses*) deep; **г. сон** deep sleep; **~ая таре́лка** soup plate.
2 (*основательный*) profound; thorough; (*серьёзный*) serious.
3 (*время, возраст*) late; advanced; extreme; **до ~ой но́чи** (until) far into the night; **~ая ста́рость** extreme old age.
4 (*очень сильный*) deep, profound, intense; **с ~им приско́рбием** (*in obituary formula*) with deep regret.
глубоко́[1] *adv.* deep; (*fig.*) deeply, profoundly.
глубоко́[2] *as pred.* it is deep.
глубоково́д|ный (~ен, ~на) *adj.* deep-water.
глубокоуважа́емый *adj.* (*в письмах*) dear.
глубоча́йший *superl. of* ▸ **глубо́кий**
глум|и́ться, лю́сь, и́шься *impf.* (**над** + *i.*) to mock (at).
глу́пост|ь, и *f.*
1 (*свойство*) foolishness, stupidity.
2 (*поступок*) foolish, stupid action; foolish, stupid thing.
3 (*usu. pl.*) (*вздор*) nonsense; **~и!** nonsense!
глу́п|ый (~, ~а́, ~о, ~́ы) *adj.* foolish, stupid; silly.
глуха́р|ь, я́ *m.* (*zool.*) capercailzie, woodgrouse.
глух|о́й (~, ~а́, ~́о) *adj.*
1 (*лишенный слуха*) deaf (*also fig.*); *as n.* **г., ~о́го** *m.* deaf person.
2 (*звук*) muffled, indistinct.
3 (*густо заросший*) thick, dense; **г. лес** dense forest.
4 (*отдалённый*) remote; godforsaken.
5 (*затаённый, скрытый*) concealed, hidden.
6 (*закрытый*) sealed; blank, blind; **~а́я стена́** blind wall.
7 (*время, сезон*) quiet, dead; **~а́я ночь** dead of night.
глухонем|о́й *adj.* deaf and dumb; *as n.* **г., ~о́го** *m.* deaf mute.
глухот|а́, ы́ *f.* deafness.
глу́|ше *comp. of* ▸ **~хо́й** *and* ▸ **~хо**
глуши́тел|ь, я *m.* (*tech.*) silencer, muffler (*US*).
глуш|и́ть, у́, ~и́шь *impf.*
1 (*pf.* **о~**) (*рыбу*) to stun, stupefy.
2 (*pf.* **за~**) (*звуки*) to muffle; **г. боль** to dull pain; **г. мото́р** to stop the engine.
3 (*pf.* **за~**) (*растения*) to choke, stifle.
глуш|ь, и́ *f.* (*заросшая часть*) overgrown part; (*пустынное место*) backwoods (*also fig.*); **жить в ~и́** to live in the back of beyond.
глюк, а *m.* (*sl.*)

1 (*oft. pl.*) (*галлюцинация*) trip (*effect of drugs*) (*coll.*).
2 (*comput.*) glitch (*coll.*).

глюкóз|а, ы *f.* glucose.

гля|дéть, жý, дúшь *impf.* (*of* ▸ **по~ 1**) (**на** + *a.*) to look (at); to peer (at); to gaze (upon).

гля́н|ец, ца *m.* gloss, lustre (*Br.*), luster (*US*).

гля́|нуть, ну, нешь *pf.* (**на** + *a.*) glance (at).

гля́нцев|ый *adj.* glossy, lustrous; **~ая крáска** gloss paint; **г. журнáл** glossy magazine, glossy (*coll.*).

г-н (*abbr. of* **господúн**) Mr.

гна|ть, гоню́, гóнишь, *past* **~л, ~лá, ~ло** *impf.*
1 (*det. of* ▸ **гоня́ть**) (*стадо*) to drive.
2 (*торопить*) to urge (on); (*coll.*) (*автомобиль*) to drive hard.
3 (*coll.*) (*быстро ехать*) to dash, tear.
4 (*преследовать*) to hunt, chase.
5 (*выгонять*) to throw out, turf out.
6 (*водку*) to distil (*Br.*), distill (*US*).

гнá|ться, гоню́сь, гóнишься, *past* **~лся, ~лáсь** *impf.* (*det. of* ▸ **гоня́ться**) (**за** + *i.*) (*преследовать*) to pursue; (*стремиться*) to strive (for, after); (*fig.*) (*стараться быть не хуже*) to (try to) keep up with.

гнев, а *m.* anger, rage, wrath.

гнéв|ный (~ен, ~нá, ~но) *adj.* angry, irate.

гнез|дúться, дúтся *impf.* to nest.

гнезд|ó, á, *pl.* **гнёзда** *nt.*
1 (*птицы*) nest; **осúное г.** wasps' nest, (*fig.*) hornets' nest.
2 (*животного*) den, lair (*also fig.*).
3 (*tech.*) socket; seat; housing.

гнёт, а *m.* (*fig.*) oppression, yoke; **г. рáбства** the yoke of slavery.

гниéни|е, я *nt.* decay, putrefaction, rot.

гнил|óй (~, ~á, ~о) *adj.* rotten (*also fig.*).

гнил|ь, и *f.*
1 (*что-н. гнилое*) rotten stuff.
2 (*плесень*) mould.

гни|ть, ю, ёшь *impf.* (*of* ▸ **с~**) to rot, decay.

гно|úться, ю́сь, úшься *impf.* to suppurate, fester.

гно|й, я, в ~е *or* **в ~ю́** *m.* pus.

гнойнúк, á *m.* (*нарыв*) abscess; (*язва*) ulcer.

гнóйный *adj.* purulent.

гнýс|ный (~ен, ~нá, ~но) *adj.* vile, foul.

гнуть, гну, гнёшь *impf.* (*of* ▸ **со~**) (*проволоку*) to bend; (*деревья*) to bow; **г. спúну, шéю (пéред** + *i.*) (*coll.*) to cringe (before), kowtow (to).

гнýться, гнусь, гнёшься *impf.* (*of* ▸ **со~**) (*о материале, палке*) to bend; (*о деревьях*) to be bowed.

гобелéн, а *m.* tapestry.

гобоúст, а *m.* oboist.

гобоúст|ка, ки *f. of* ▸ **~**

гобó|й, я *m.* oboe.

говн|ó, á *nt.* (*vulg.*) shit.

говор|úть, ю́, úшь *impf.*
1 (*impf. only*) (*владеть устной речью*) to speak, talk; **он ещё не ~úт** he can't speak yet; **г. по-францýзски** to speak French.
2 (*pf.* ▸ **сказáть**) (*выражать, сообщать*) to say; to tell; to speak, talk; **г. прáвду** to tell the truth; **~я́т** they say, it is said; **стрóго ~я́** strictly speaking; **не ~я́ ужé (о** + *p.*) not to mention.
3 (*pf.* ▸ **по~ 1**) (**о** + *p.*) (*беседовать*) to talk (about), discuss.
4 (*impf. only*) (*значить*) to mean, convey, signify; **э́то úмя мне ничегó не ~úт** this name means nothing to me.
5 (*impf. only*) (**о** + *p.*) (*свидетельствовать*) to point (to), indicate, testify (to); **всё ~úт о том, что он покóнчил с собóй** everything points to his having committed suicide.

говор|úться, úтся *impf. pass. of* ▸ **~úть; как ~úтся** as they say, as the saying goes.

говя́дин|а, ы *f.* beef.

говя́жий *adj.* beef.

гóгот, а *m.* (*крик гусей*) cackle; (*coll.*) (*хохот*) loud laughter.

гого|тáть, чý, ~чешь *impf.* to cackle.

год, а, о ~е, в ~ý, *pl.* **~ы** *and* **~á,** *g.* **~óв** *and* **лет** *m.*
1 (*g. pl.* **лет**) year; **високóсный г.** leap year; **крýглый г.** (*as adv.*) the whole year round; **в бýдущем, прóшлом ~ý** next, last year; **в г.** a year, per annum; **спустя́ три ~а** three years later; **чéрез три ~а** in three years' time; **ей пошёл пятнáдцатый г.** she is in her fifteenth year.
2 : **двадцáтые, тридцáтые,** *etc.*, **~ы** (*g.* **~óв**) the twenties, the thirties etc.
3 **~á** *and* **~ы, ~óв** (*pl. only*) years, age, time; **в ~ы** (+ *g.*) in the days (of); during; **в те ~ы** in those days; **не по ~áм** beyond one's years, precocious(ly).

годáми *adv.* for years (on end).

го|дúться, жýсь, дúшься *impf.*
1 (**на** + *a.*, **для** + *g.*, *or* + *d.*) (*быть полезным*) to be fit (for), be suitable (for), do (for).
2 (**в** + *nom.-a.*) (*быть впору*) to serve (as), be suited to be.
3 (**в** + *nom.-a.*) (*подходить по возрасту*) to be old enough to be; **онá ~дúтся тебé в мáтери** she is old enough to be your mother.
4 : **не ~дúтся** (+ *inf.*) it does not do (to), one should not.

гóдност|ь, и *f.* fitness, suitability; (*билета*) validity; **срок ~и** expiry date.

гóд|ный (~ен, ~нá, ~но, ~ны́) *adj.* fit, suitable, (*о билете*) valid; **г. к вoéнной слýжбе** fit for military service.

годовáлый *adj.* one-year-old, yearling.

годовóй *adj.* annual, yearly.

годовщúн|а, ы *f.* anniversary.

гол, а *m.* (*sport*) goal; **забúть г.** to score a goal.

голенúщ|е, а *nt.* top (*of a boot*).

гóлен|ь, и *f.* shin.

голкúпер, а *m.* (*sport*) goalkeeper.

голлáнд|ец, ца *m.* Dutchman.

Голлáнди|я, и *f.* Holland.

голлáндк|а, и *f.* Dutchwoman.

голлáндский *adj.* Dutch.

Г

голов|а́, ы́, *a.* **го́лову,** *pl.* **го́ловы, голо́в, ~а́м** *f.*
1 head (*also fig.*); **на све́жую го́лову** while one is fresh; **быть на́ голову вы́ше кого́-н.** (*fig.*) to be head and shoulders above s.o.; **с ~ы до ног** from head to foot; **у неё г. шла кру́гом** her head was going round and round; **у меня́ г. кру́жится** I feel giddy.
2 (*единица счёта скота*) head (*of cattle*).
3 (*fig.*) (*ум*) head; brain, mind; wits; **ей пришла́ в го́лову мысль** it occurred to her, it struck her.
4 (*fig.*) (*человек, как носитель каких-либо свойств*) head (= *person*); **горя́чая г.** hothead.
5 (*fig.*) (*жизнь*) head, life; **на свою́ го́лову** to one's cost; **отвеча́ть ~о́й за что-н.** to stake one's life on sth.

голова́стик, а *m.* tadpole.

голо́вк|а, и *f.* (*булавки, спички, цветка*) head; **г. лу́ка** an onion, onion bulb; **г. чеснока́** head of garlic.

головн|о́й *adj.*
1 *adj. of* ▸ **голова́; ~а́я боль** headache; **г. плато́к** headscarf; **г. убо́р** headgear, headdress.
2 (*anat.*): **г. мозг** brain, cerebrum.
3 (*fig.*) head, leading.

головокруже́ни|е, я *nt.* giddiness.

головокружи́тельн|ый *adj.* dizzy, giddy (*also fig.*); **~ая высота́** dizzy height.

головоло́мк|а, и *f.* puzzle, conundrum.

го́лод, а (у) *m.*
1 hunger; (*длительное недоедание*) starvation; **умира́ть с ~у** to die of starvation; **мори́ть ~ом** to starve (*trans.*).
2 (*народное бедствие*) famine.
3 (*недостаток продуктов питания*) dearth, acute shortage.

голода́ни|е, я *nt.*
1 (*недоедание*) starvation.
2 (*воздержание*) fasting.

голод|а́ть, а́ю *impf.*
1 (*скудно питаться*) to starve.
2 (*воздерживаться от пищи*) to fast, go without food.
3 (*быть на диете*) to diet.

голода́|ющий *pres. part. act. of* ▸ **~ть** *and adj.* starving, hungry; *as n.* **г., ~ющего** *m.*, **~ющая, ~ющей** *f.* starving person.

гол|о́дный (~́оден, ~одна́, ~́одно, ~́одны́) *adj.*
1 (*желающий есть*) hungry.
2 (*вызванный голодом*) hunger, starvation.
3 (*скудный*) meagre, scanty, poor; **г. год** lean year.

голодо́вк|а, и *f.* (*в знак протеста*) hunger strike.

гололёд, а *m.* = **гололе́дица**

гололе́диц|а, ы *f.* black ice.

го́лос, а, *pl.* **~а́** *m.*
1 voice; **во весь г.** at the top of one's voice.
2 (*mus.*) voice, part.
3 (*fig.*) (*мнение*) voice, word, opinion.
4 (*pol.*) vote; **пра́во ~а** the vote, suffrage; **пода́ть г. (за** + *a.*) to vote (for).

голосло́в|ный (~ен, ~на) *adj.* unsubstantiated.

голосова́ни|е, я *nt.* voting; poll.

голос|ова́ть, у́ю *impf.* (*of* ▸ **про~**)
1 (**за** + *a.*, **про́тив** + *g.*) to vote (for, against).
2 (*ставить на голосование*) to put to the vote, vote on.

голосов|о́й *adj.* vocal; (*anat.*) **~ые свя́зки** vocal chords; **~а́я по́чта** voice mail.

голуби́к|а, и *f.* great bilberry, bog whortleberry (*Vaccinium uliginosum*).

голу́бк|а, и *f.* (*самка голубя*) female pigeon, dove.

голуб|о́й *adj.* pale blue, sky blue; **~а́я кровь** (*fig.*) blue blood; *as n.* **голуб|о́й, о́го** *m.* (*sl.*) gay (= *homosexual*).

го́луб|ь, я, *g. pl.* **~е́й** *m.* pigeon, dove.

голубя́т|ня, ни, *g. pl.* **~ен** *f.* dovecot(e), pigeon loft.

го́л|ый (~, ~а́, ~о) *adj.* naked, bare (*also fig.*); **~ыми рука́ми** with one's bare hands.

гольф, а *m.* golf; **игро́к в г.** golfer.

го́льф|ы, ов (*sg.* **~, ~а**) *m.pl.* (*coll.*) knee-length socks.

гомеопа́ти|я, и *f.* homoeopathy (*Br.*), homeopathy (*US*).

го́мик, а *m.* (*coll., pej.*) queer, poof(ter) (*coll., pej.*), gay.

гомосексуали́зм, а *m.* homosexuality.

гомосексуали́ст, а *m.* homosexual; gay.

гомосексуа́льный *adj.* homosexual; gay.

гонг, а *m.* gong.

гондо́л|а, ы *f.*
1 (*лодка*) gondola.
2 (*aeron.*) car (*of balloon*).

Гондура́с, а *m.* Honduras.

гондура́с|ец, ца *m.* Honduran.

гондура́с|ка, ки *f. of* ▸ **~ец**

гондура́сский *adj.* Honduran.

гоне́ни|е, я *nt.* persecution.

го́нк|а, и *f.* (*sport*; *usu. pl.*) race; **г. вооруже́ний** arms race.

Гонко́нг, а *m.* Hong Kong.

гонора́р, а *m.* fee; **а́вторский г.** royalties.

гоноре́|я, и *f.* gonorrhoea (*Br.*), gonorrhea (*US*).

го́ночный *adj. of* ▸ **го́нка; г. автомоби́ль** racing car.

гонча́р, а́ *m.* potter.

го́нщик, а *m.* racing driver.

гоню́(сь), го́нишь(ся) *see* ▸ **гна́ть(ся)**

гоня́|ть, ю *impf.* (*indet. of* ▸ **гнать**) (*стада*) to drive; (*птиц*) to chase off.

гоня́|ться, юсь *impf.* (*indet. of* ▸ **гна́ться**) (**за** + *i.*) to chase, pursue; (*на охоте*) to hunt.

гор... *comb. form, abbr. of*
1 **городско́й.**
2 **го́рный**

гор|а́, ы́, *a.* **~́у́,** *pl.* **~́ы,** *d.* **~а́м** *f.* mountain; hill; **г. Эвере́ст** Mount Everest; **в ~́у** uphill (*also fig.*); **по́д ~у** downhill (*also fig.*).

гора́здо *adv.* (+ *comp. adjs. and advs.*) much, far, by far; **г. лу́чше** far better.

горб, а́, о ~е́, на ~у́ *m.* hump.

горба́т|ый (~, ~а) *adj.* hunchbacked; **г. нос** hooked nose.

го́рб|иться, люсь, ишься *impf.* (*of* ▸ **с~**) (*о человеке*) to stoop; (*о спине*) to become bent.

горбу́ш|а, и *f.* humpback salmon.

гор|ди́ться, жу́сь, ди́шься *impf.* (+ *i.*) to be proud (of), pride o.s. (on).
го́рдост|ь, и *f.* pride.
го́рд|ый (~, ~а́, ~о, ~ы) *adj.* proud.
го́р|е, я *nt.*
1 (*печаль*) grief, sorrow, woe; **на своё г.** to one's sorrow.
2 (*беда*) misfortune, trouble.
3 *as pred.* (+ *d.*; *coll.*) woe (unto), woe betide.
гор|ева́ть, ю́ю, ю́ешь *impf.* (**о** + *p.*) to grieve (for).
горе́лк|а, и *f.* burner; **при́мусная г.** Primus (*propr.*) stove.
горе́ни|е, я *nt.* burning, combustion; (*fig.*) enthusiasm.
гор|е́ть, ю́, и́шь *impf.*
1 (*о доме*) to burn, be on fire.
2 (*о дровах, свете*) to burn, be alight; **в ку́хне у них ~е́л свет** the lights were burning in their kitchen.
3 (+ *i.*; *fig.*) to burn (with); **г. жела́нием** (+ *inf.*) to be itching (to), be impatient (to).
го́р|ец, ца *m.* mountain-dweller.
го́реч|ь, и *f.*
1 (*вкус*) bitter taste.
2 (*горькое чувство*) bitterness.
горизо́нт, а *m.* horizon (*also fig.*); skyline.
горизонта́л|ь, и *f.*
1 horizontal; **по ~и** across (*in crossword*).
2 (*geog.*) contour line.
горизонта́л|ьный (~ен, ~ьна) *adj.* horizontal.
гори́лл|а, ы *f.* gorilla.
гори́ст|ый (~, ~а) *adj.* mountainous, hilly.
го́рк|а, и *f.*
1 hill, hillock.
2 (*для детей*) slide.
го́рлиц|а, ы *f.* turtle dove.
го́рл|о, а *nt.*
1 throat; **дыха́тельное г.** windpipe; **во всё г.** at the top of one's voice; **сыт по г.** full up; (*fig.*) fed up.
2 (*сосуда*) neck.
горлови́н|а, ы *f.* mouth, orifice; **г. вулка́на** crater.
гормо́н, а *m.* hormone.
гормона́льный *adj.* hormone, hormonal.
горн, а *m.* (*печь*) furnace, forge.
го́рничн|ая, ой *f.* (*в гостинице*) chambermaid; (*в доме*) maid.
горнолы́жник, а *m.* Alpine skier.
горнолы́жный *adj.*: **г. спорт** Alpine skiing.
горноста́|й, я *m.* ermine.
го́рн|ый *adj.*
1 *adj. of* ▸ **гора́;** mountain; (*гористый*) mountainous; **~ые лы́жи** downhill skis; **~ая цепь** mountain range.
2 (*минеральный*) mineral; **~ая поро́да** rock; **г. хруста́ль** rock crystal.
3 (*относящийся к разработке недр*) mining; **~ое де́ло** mining.
го́род, а, *pl.* **~а́** *m.* town; city; **вы́ехать за́ г.** to go out of town; **жить за́ ~ом** to live out of town.
город|о́к, ка́ *m.* small town; **университе́тский г.** campus.
городск|о́й *adj.* urban; city; municipal; (*coll.*) *as n.* **г., ~о́го** *m.* city-dweller, town-dweller.
горожа́н|ин, ина, *pl.* **~е, ~** *m.* city-dweller, town-dweller; townsman.
горожа́н|ка, ки *f. of* ▸ **~ин;** townswoman.
гороско́п, а *m.* horoscope.
горо́х, а *no pl., m.*
1 pea.
2 (*collect.*) peas.
горо́ш|ек, ка *m.*
1 *dim. of* ▸ **горо́х; души́стый г.** (*bot.*) sweet peas.
2 (*collect.*) polka dots; **пла́тье в г.** polka-dot dress.
горо́шин|а, ы *f.* a pea.
горст|ь, и, *g. pl.* **~е́й** *f.*
1 (*ладонь с согнутыми пальцами*) cupped hand.
2 (*находящееся на/в ладони*) handful (*also fig.*).
го́рче *comp. of* ▸ **го́рький 1**
горч|и́ть, и́т *impf.* (*impers.*) to have a bitter taste.
горчи́ц|а, ы *f.* mustard.
го́рше *comp. of* ▸ **го́рький 2**
горш|о́к, ка́ *m.* pot; **ночно́й г.** chamber pot; (*ребёнка*) potty.
го́р|ький (~ек, ~ька́, ~ько, ~ьки́) *adj.*
1 (*comp.* **~че**) bitter.
2 (*comp.* **~ше**) (*fig.*) bitter; hard; **~ькие слёзы** bitter tears.
го́рько[1] *adv.* bitterly.
го́рько[2] *as pred.*
1 : **у меня́ г. во рту** I have a bitter taste in my mouth.
2 it is bitter; **мне г.** I am sorry, I am grieved.
горю́ч|ее, его *nt.* fuel.
горю́чий *adj.* combustible, inflammable.
горя́ч|ий (~, ~а́) *adj.*
1 hot (*also fig.*); **~ая ли́ния** hotline.
2 (*любовь, желание*) passionate.
3 (*человек*) hot-tempered.
4 (*спор*) heated; (*речь*) impassioned.
5 (*время*) busy, hectic.
горячо́[1] *adv.* hot.
горячо́[2] *as pred.* it is hot.
гос... *comb. form, abbr. of* **госуда́рственный**
Госду́м|а, ы *f.* State Duma (*lower house of the Russian parliament*).
госпитализи́р|овать, ую *impf. and pf.* to hospitalize.
го́спитал|ь, я *m.* hospital (*esp. mil.*).
госпита́льный *adj. of* ▸ **го́спиталь**
го́споди *int.* good heavens!; good Lord!
господ|и́н, и́на, *pl.* **~а́, ~, ~а́м** *m.* (*при фамилии*) Mr; **~а́** (*при обращении*) (*i*) gentlemen, (*ii*) (*coll.*) ladies and gentlemen.
госпо́дств|о, а *nt.*
1 (*власть*) supremacy.
2 (*преобладание*) predominance.
госпо́дств|овать, ую *impf.*
1 (*обладать властью*) to hold sway.
2 (*преобладать*) to predominate, prevail.
3 (**над** + *i.*) (*возвышаться*) to command,

dominate; to tower (above).
госпо́дств|ующий *pres. part. act. of* ▶ **~овать** *and adj.*
1 (*властвующий*) ruling.
2 (*преобладающий*) predominant, prevailing.
3 (*возвышающийся*) commanding.
Госпо́дь, Го́спода, *voc.* **Го́споди** *m.* God, the Lord.
госпож|а́, и́ *f.* (*при фамилии; замужняя*) Mrs, Ms; (*незамужняя*) Miss, Ms.
гостеприи́м|ный (~ен, ~на) *adj.* hospitable.
гостеприи́мств|о, а *nt.* hospitality.
гости́н|ая, ой *f.* living room, sitting room.
гости́н|ец, ца *m.* (*coll.*) present.
гости́ниц|а, ы *f.* hotel.
гости́ть, гощу́, гости́шь *impf.* (**у** + *g.*) to stay (with), be on a visit (to).
гост|ь, я, *g. pl.* **~е́й** *m.* guest, visitor; **пойти́ в ~и** (**к** + *d.*) to visit; **быть в гостя́х** (**у** + *g.*) to be a guest (at, of), be visiting.
го́ст|ья, ьи, *g. pl.* **~ий** *f. of* ▶ **~ь**
госуда́рственник, а *m.* supporter of a powerful State.
госуда́рственн|ый *adj.* state, public; **г. переворо́т** coup d'état; **~ая изме́на** high treason; **~ая слу́жба** public service; **г. слу́жащий** civil servant.
госуда́рств|о, а *nt.* state.
госуда́р|ь, я *m.* sovereign; **Г.** (*as form of address*) Your Majesty, Sire.
го́тик|а, и *f.* Gothic (style).
готи́ческий *adj.* Gothic.
гото́в|ить, лю, ишь *impf.*
1 to prepare, make ready; (*обучать*) to train.
2 (*пищу*) to cook.
гото́в|иться, люсь, ишься *impf.*
1 (**к** + *d. or* + *inf.*) to get ready (for, to); to prepare (o.s.) (for).
2 (*предстоять*) to be at hand, in the offing.
гото́вност|ь, и *f.*
1 readiness, preparedness; **в боево́й ~и** ready for action.
2 (*согласие*) readiness, willingness.
гото́в|ый (~, ~а) *adj.*
1 (**к** + *d.*) ready (for), prepared (for).
2 (**на** + *a. or* + *inf.*) (*согласный*) ready (for, to), prepared (for, to); willing (to); **мы ~ы на всё** we are prepared for anything; **она́ не ~а идти́** she is not willing to go.
3 (+ *inf.*) (*находящийся в состоянии близком к чему-либо*) on the point (of), on the verge (of), ready (to).
4 (*окончательно сделанный*) ready-made, finished; ready-to-wear; **~ые изде́лия** finished articles, the finished product.
граб, а *m.* (*bot.*) hornbeam.
грабёж, а́ *m.* robbery (*also fig., coll.*).
граби́тел|ь, я *m.* robber; (*дома*) burglar.
гра́б|ить, лю, ишь *impf.*
1 (*pf.* **о~**) (*человека*) to rob; (*дом*) burgle; (*fig.*) to rob.
2 (*pf.* **раз~**) (*город*) to loot, pillage.
гра́б|ли, лей *or* **~ель** *no sg.* rake.
гра́ви|й, я *m.* gravel.
гравир|ова́ть, у́ю, у́ешь *impf.* (*of* ▶ **вы́~**) to engrave.
гравиро́вк|а, и *f.* engraving.
гравита́ци|я, и *f.* (*phys.*) gravitation.
гравю́р|а, ы *f.* engraving, print; (*офорт*) etching.
град, а *m.*
1 hail.
2 (*fig.*) (*поток*) hail, shower, torrent.
града́ци|я, и *f.* gradation, scale.
гра́дус, а *m.* degree; **у́гол в 40 ~ов** angle of 40 degrees; **сего́дня 20 ~ов тепла́, моро́за** it is twenty degrees above, below zero today.
гра́дусник, а *m.* thermometer.
граждани́н, а, *pl.* **гра́ждане, гра́ждан** *m.* citizen.
гражда́н|ка, ки *f. of* ▶ **~и́н**
гражда́нск|ий *adj.*
1 (*leg., etc.*) civil; citizen's; civic; **г. иск** civil suit; **~ое пра́во** civil law.
2 (*нецерковный, светский*) civil, secular; **г. брак** civil marriage.
3 (*невоенный*) civilian; **~ое пла́тье** civilian clothes.
4 (*подобающий гражданину*) civic, befitting a citizen.
5 : **~ая война́** civil war.
гражда́нств|о, а *nt.* citizenship, nationality; **права́ ~а** civic rights.
грамм, а *m.* gramme, gram.
грамма́тик|а, и *f.*
1 (*раздел языкознания*) grammar.
2 (*учебник*) grammar (book).
граммати́ческий *adj.* grammatical.
граммофо́н, а *m.* gramophone.
гра́мотност|ь, и *f.*
1 (*умение читать и писать*) literacy (*also fig.*).
2 (*отсутствие грамматических ошибок*) grammatical correctness.
3 (*умелость*) competence.
гра́мот|ный (~ен, ~на) *adj.*
1 (*умеющий читать и писать*) literate; able to read and write.
2 (*без ошибок*) grammatically correct.
3 (*умелый*) competent.
грампласти́нк|а, и *f.* gramophone record (*Br.*), phonograph record (*US*).
грана́т, а *m.* pomegranate.
грана́т|а, ы *f.* (*mil.*) shell, grenade; **ручна́я г.** hand grenade.
гранатомёт, а *m.* (*mil.*) grenade launcher.
грандио́з|ный (~ен, ~на) *adj.* grandiose; mighty; vast.
гранён|ый *adj.* (*алмаз*) cut, faceted; (*стакан*) cut-glass; **~ое стекло́** cut glass.
грани́т, а *m.* granite.
грани́тный *adj.* granite.
грани́ц|а, ы *f.*
1 frontier, border; **за ~ей** abroad; **е́хать за ~у** to go abroad.
2 (*fig.*) boundary, limit.
грани́ч|ить, у, ишь *impf.* (**с** + *i.*)
1 to border (on).
2 (*fig.*) to border (on), verge (on).
грант, а *m.* grant.
гран|ь, и *f.*
1 border, verge, brink; **на ~и безу́мия** on

the verge of insanity.
[2] (*geom.*) face; (*алмаза*) facet.

граф, а *m.* count.

граф|а́, ы *f.* (*столбец*) column; (*раздел*) section.

гра́фик, а *m.*
[1] (*диаграмма*) graph, chart.
[2] (*расписание*) schedule; **плотный г.** packed schedule; **скользя́щий г.** flexible working hours; flexitime.

гра́фик|а, и *f.* (*art*) graphic art; (*comput.*) graphics.

графи́н, а *m.* carafe; (*с пробкой*) decanter.

графи́н|я, и *f.* countess.

графи́т, а *m.*
[1] (*min.*) graphite.
[2] (*карандаша*) pencil lead.

графи́ческий *adj.* graphic; **г. паке́т** (*comput.*) graphics package.

гра́фств|о, а *nt.* county.

грацио́з|ный (∼ен, ∼на) *adj.* graceful.

гра́ци|я, и *f.* grace, gracefulness.

грач, а́ *m.* (*zool.*) rook.

гре́б|ень, ня *m.*
[1] (*для расчёсывания волос*) comb.
[2] (*птицы*) comb, crest.
[3] (*волны, горы*) crest.

гре́бл|я, и *f.* rowing.

грейпфру́т, а *m.* grapefruit.

грек, а *m.* Greek.

гре́лк|а, и *f.* hot-water bottle.

грем|е́ть, лю́, и́шь *impf.* (*of* **про∼**) to thunder, roar; (*о колоколах*) to peal; (*посудой*) to clatter; (*ключами*) to jangle; (*fig.*) to resound, ring out.

гре́нк|а, и *f.* toast; (*для супа, салата*) crouton.

Гренла́нди|я, и *f.* Greenland.

гре|сти́, бу́, бёшь, *past* **∼̈б, ∼бла́** *impf.*
[1] to row; (*веслом, руками*) to paddle.
[2] (*граблями*) to rake.

греть, гре́ю, гре́ешь *impf.*
[1] (*intrans.*) to give out warmth.
[2] (*trans.*) to warm, heat (up); (*предохранять от холода*) to keep warm.

гре́|ться, юсь, ешься *impf.* (*человек*) to warm o.s.; (*вода, обед*) to warm, heat (up).

грех, а́ *m.*
[1] (*relig. or fig.*) sin.
[2] *as pred.* (+ *inf.*; *coll.*) it is a sin, it is sinful; **не г.** (+ *inf.*) there is no harm (in).
[3] : **с ∼о́м попола́м** (only) just.

Гре́ци|я, и *f.* Greece.

гре́цкий *adj.*: **г. оре́х** walnut.

греча́нк|а, и *f. of* ▸ **грек**

гре́ческий *adj.* Greek.

гречи́х|а, и *f.* buckwheat.

гре́чк|а, и *f.* (*coll.*) buckwheat.

гре́чнев|ый *adj.* buckwheat; **∼ая ка́ша** buckwheat porridge.

греш|и́ть, у́, и́шь *impf.*
[1] (*pf.* **со∼**) to sin.
[2] (*pf.* **по∼**) (**про́тив** + *g.*; *fig.*) to sin (against).

гре́шник, а *m.* sinner.

гре́шни|ца, цы *f. of* ▸ **∼к**

гре́ш|ный (∼ен, ∼на́, ∼но, ∼́ны) *adj.* sinful.

гриб, а́ *m.* fungus; (*съедобный*) mushroom; (*поганка*) toadstool.

грибн|о́й *adj. of* ▸ **гриб;** mushroom; **г. дождь** rain while the sun is shining.

гриб|о́к, ка́ *m.*
[1] *dim. of* ▸ **гриб.**
[2] (*biol.*) fungus, micro-organism.

гри́в|а, ы *f.* mane.

гри́зли *m. indecl.* grizzly (bear).

грил|ь, я *m.* grill (*Br.*), broiler (*US*).

грим, а *m.* (*theatr.*) make-up; greasepaint.

грима́с|а, ы *f.* grimace; **стро́ить ∼ы** to make *or* pull faces.

гримёр, а *m.* (*theatr.*) make-up artist.

гримёрн|ая, ой *f.* (*theatr.*) make-up (room).

гримир|ова́ть, у́ю *impf.* (*of* ▸ **за∼**) (*theatr.*) to make up.

гримир|ова́ться, у́юсь *impf.* (*of* ▸ **за∼**) (*theatr.*) to make up (*intrans.*); (+ *i. or* **под** + *a.*; *fig.*) to make o.s. out.

грипп, а *m.* influenza; flu.

гриф[1], а *m.* (*zool.*) vulture.

гриф[2], а *m.* (*mus.*) fingerboard.

гриф[3], а *m.* (*штемпель*) seal, stamp.

гри́фел|ь, я *m.* (*карандаша*) lead.

гроб, а, о/на ∼́е, в ∼у́, *pl.* **∼ы́** *m.*
[1] coffin.
[2] (*fig.*) the grave; **вогна́ть в г.** to drive to the grave; **до ∼́а, по г. жи́зни** (*coll.*) until the end of one's days.

гробни́ц|а, ы *f.* tomb.

гробов|о́й *adj.*
[1] *adj. of* ▸ **гроб; ∼а́я доска́** (*fig.*) the grave; **ве́рный до ∼о́й доски́** faithful unto death.
[2] (*мрачный*) sepulchral, deathly; **∼а́я тишина́** deathly silence.

гроз|а́, ы́, *pl.* **∼́ы** *f.*
[1] (thunder)storm.
[2] (*fig.*) (+ *g.*) threat (to).

грозд|ь, и, *pl.* **∼́и, ∼е́й** *and* **∼́ья, ∼́ьев** *f.* cluster, bunch (*of fruit or flowers*).

гро|зи́ть, жу́, зи́шь *impf.*
[1] (*pf.* **при∼**) (+ *d. and i. or* + *inf.*) (*предупреждать с угрозой*) to threaten.
[2] (*pf.* **по∼**) (*делать угрожающий жест*) to make threatening gestures.
[3] (*no pf.*) (*предстоять*) to threaten; **ему́ ∼зи́т банкро́тство** he is threatened with bankruptcy.

гро́з|ный (∼ен, ∼на́, ∼но) *adj.*
[1] (*угрожающий*) menacing, threatening.
[2] (*ужасный*) terrible; formidable.

гроз|ово́й *adj. of* ▸ **∼а́; ∼ова́я ту́ча** storm cloud, thundercloud.

гром, а, *pl.* **∼́ы, ∼о́в** *m.* thunder (*also fig.*); **уда́р ∼́а** thunderclap.

грома́д|ный (∼ен, ∼на) *adj.* huge, vast, enormous.

гром|и́ть, лю́, и́шь *impf.* (*of* ▸ **раз∼**) to destroy; (*mil.*) to smash, rout.

гро́м|кий (∼ок, ∼ка́, ∼ко) *adj.*
[1] loud.
[2] (*известный*) famous; (*пресловутый*) notorious.
[3] (*напыщенный*) fine-sounding; **∼кие слова́** (*iron.*) big words.

грóмко *adv.* loud(ly); (*вслух*) aloud.
громкоговори́тел|ь, я *m.* loudspeaker.
грóмкост|ь, и *f.* (*звука*) loudness, volume.
громов|óй *adj.*
1 *adj. of* ▸ **гром; ~ы́е раскáты** peals of thunder.
2 (*громкий*) thunderous, deafening.
громоглáс|ный (~ен, ~на) *adj.*
1 (*громкий*) loud; (*о человеке*) loud-voiced.
2 (*открытый*) public, open.
громóзд|кий (~ок, ~ка) *adj.* cumbersome, unwieldy.
грóм|че *comp. of* ▸ **~кий** *and* ▸ **~ко**
гроссмéйстер, а *m.* grandmaster (*at chess*).
гротéск, а *m.* (*art*) grotesque.
грóхот, а *m.* crash, din.
грох|отáть, очý, óчешь *impf.* to crash; roll, rumble; roar.
грош, á, *pl.* **~и́, ~éй** *m.* (*fig., coll.*) penny, cent; **рабóтать за ~и́** to work for peanuts.
груб|и́ть, лю́, и́шь *impf.* (*of* ▸ **на~**) (+ *d.*) to be rude (to).
грýбо *adv.*
1 (*неискусно*) crudely.
2 (*невежливо*) rudely.
3 (*приблизительно*) roughly; **г. говоря́** roughly speaking.
грýбост|ь, и *f.*
1 (*невежливость*) rudeness.
2 (*замечание*) rude remark; **говори́ть ~и** to be rude.
грýб|ый (~, ~á, ~о, ~́ы) *adj.*
1 (*без изящества*) coarse, rough.
2 (*недопустимый*) gross, flagrant; **г. обмáн** gross deception.
3 (*человек, слово*) rude; coarse, crude.
4 (*приблизительный*) rough.
грудн|óй *adj. of* ▸ **грудь; ~áя клéтка** (*anat.*) thorax; **г. ребёнок** baby.
груд|ь, и́, *i.* **~́ю, в/на/о ~и́,** *pl.* **~́и, ~éй** *f.*
1 (*anat.*) chest.
2 (*женщины*) breast; bosom, bust; **корми́ть ~́ью** to breastfeed.
груз, а *m.*
1 (*тяжесть*) weight; (*кладь*) load, cargo, freight.
2 (*fig.*) weight, burden.
грузи́н, а, *g. pl.* **г.** *m.* Georgian.
грузи́н|ка, ки *f. of* ▸ **~**
грузи́нский *adj.* Georgian.
гру|зи́ть, жý, ~́зишь *impf.*
1 (*pf.* **за~** *and* **на~**) (*судно*) to load.
2 (*pf.* **по~**) (*товар*) to load.
гру|зи́ться, жýсь, ~́зишься *impf.* (*of* ▸ **по~ 2**) (*о судне*) to load (*intrans.*), take on cargo; (*о людях*) to board.
Грýзи|я, и *f.* Georgia.
грузови́к, á *m.* lorry (*Br.*), truck.
грузов|óй *adj.* goods, cargo, freight; **~óе сýдно** cargo boat, freighter.
грузоподъёмност|ь, и *f.* payload capacity; freight-carrying capacity.
грýзчик, а *m.* loader; (*в порту*) docker (*Br.*), stevedore.
грунт, а *m.* (*почва*) soil, earth; (*дно*) bottom.
грунтов|óй *adj. of* ▸ **грунт; ~ы́е вóды** subsoil waters; **~áя дорóга** dirt road.
грýпп|а, ы *f.* (*in var. senses*) group; **г. крóви** (*med.*) blood group; **операти́вная г.** task force; **рабóчая г.** working party.
группир|овáть, ýю *impf.* (*of* ▸ **с~**) to group; (*классифицировать*) to classify.
группирóвк|а, и *f.*
1 grouping; (*классификация*) classification; **г. сил** (*mil.*) distribution of forces.
2 (*совокупность лиц*) group, grouping.
3 (*бандитская*) (criminal) gang.
группов|óй *adj.* group; **~ы́е заня́тия** group study, group work.
гру|сти́ть, щý, сти́шь *impf.* to grieve, mourn; (**о** + *p.*, **по** + *d.*) to pine (for).
грýстно[1] *adv.* sadly, sorrowfully.
грýстно[2] *as pred.* it is sad; **ей г.** she feels sad.
грýст|ный (~ен, ~нá, ~но) *adj.* sad, melancholy.
груст|ь, и *f.* sadness, melancholy.
грýш|а, и *f.*
1 pear.
2 : **боксёрская г.** punchball.
гры́ж|а, и *f.* (*med.*) hernia.
грыз|ть, ý, ёшь, *past* **~, ~́ла** *impf.* to gnaw; to nibble; **г. нóгти** to bite one's nails.
грызýн, á *m.* rodent.
гряд|á, ы́, *pl.* **~́ы, ~, ~́áм** *f.*
1 *pl.* **~ы́, ~, ~áм** (*гор*) ridge.
2 *pl.* **~́ы, ~, ~́ам** (*в огороде*) bed.
3 *pl.* **~ы́, ~, ~áм** (*ряд*) row, series.
гря́дк|а, и *f. dim. of* ▸ **грядá 2**
грядýщ|ий *adj.* coming, future; **~ие гóды** years to come; *as n.* **~ее, ~его** *nt.* the future.
гря́зн|о[1] *adv. of* ▸ **~ый**
гря́зно[2] *as pred.* it is dirty.
гря́з|ный (~ен, ~нá, ~но, ~́ны) *adj.*
1 (*покрытый грязью*) muddy.
2 (*нечистый*) dirty; **~ное бельё** dirty washing (*also fig.*).
3 (*неопрятный*) untidy.
4 (*fig.*) (*непристойный*) dirty, filthy; **~ное дéло** dirty business.
гряз|ь, и, о ~́и, в ~и́ *f.*
1 mud (*also fig.*).
2 (*pl.*) (*лечебное средство*) mud baths.
3 (*отсутствие чистоты*) dirt, filth (*also fig.*).
губ|á, ы́, *pl.* **~́ы, ~, ~áм** *f.* lip; **надýть ~́ы** to pout.
губернáтор, а *m.* governor.
губ|и́ть, лю́, ~́ишь *impf.* (*of* ▸ **по~**) (*разрушать*) to destroy; (*портить*) to ruin, spoil.
гýбк|а, и *f.* sponge; **мыть ~ой** to sponge.
губн|óй *adj.* lip; **~áя помáда** lipstick.
гувернáнтк|а, и *f.* governess.
гувернёр, а *m.* tutor.
гудéни|е, я *nt.* drone; hum; (*об автомобильном гудке*) honk.
гу|дéть, жý, ди́шь *impf.*
1 to drone; to hum; (*impers.*): **у меня́ ~дéло в ушáх** there was a buzzing in my ears.
2 (*о гудке*) to hoot; to honk.
гуд|óк, кá *m.*
1 (*устройство*) (*автомобиля*) horn;

(*фабрики*) siren.
2 (*звук*) hoot(ing); honk; toot.
3 (*teleph.*) tone.

гул, а *m.* (*машин, голосов*) drone, hum; (*орудий*) rumble.

гуля́н|ье, ья, *g. pl.* **~ий** *nt.* (*празднество*) outdoor party.

гуля́|ть, ю *impf.* (*of* ▸ **по~**)
1 to walk, stroll; go for a walk.
2 (*coll.*) (*веселиться*) to make merry, have a good time.

гуля́ш, а́ *m.* (*cul.*) goulash.

гумани́зм, а *m.* humanism.

гуманита́рн|ый *adj.*
1 pertaining to the humanities; **~ые нау́ки** the humanities, the liberal arts; **~ое образова́ние** liberal education.
2 (*гуманный*) humane; **~ая по́мощь** humanitarian aid.

гума́нност|ь, и *f.* humanity, humaneness.

гума́н|ный (~ен, ~на) *adj.* humane.

гурма́н, а *m.* gourmet.

гу́ру *m. indecl.* guru.

гуса́р, а *m.* hussar.

гу́сениц|а, ы *f.*
1 (*zool.*) caterpillar.
2 (*трактора*) (caterpillar) track.

гус|ёнок, ёнка, *pl.* **~я́та** *m.* gosling.

гу́сто *adv.* thickly, densely.

густ|о́й (~, ~а́, ~́о, ~ы́) *adj.*
1 thick, dense; **~ые бро́ви** bushy eyebrows.
2 (*о цвете*) deep, rich.

густонаселённый *adj.* densely populated.

густот|а́, ы *f.*
1 thickness, density.
2 (*цвета*) deepness, richness.

гус|ь, я, *pl.* **~́и, ~е́й** *m.* goose.

гу́щ|а, и *f.*
1 (*осадок*) sediment; **кофе́йная г.** coffee grounds.
2 (*чаща*) thicket; (*fig.*) thick, centre; **в са́мой ~е собы́тий** in the thick of things.

гу́ще *comp. of* ▸ **густо́й, гу́сто**

Гц (*abbr. of* **герц**) Hz (= hertz).

гэ́льский *adj.* Gaelic.

ГЭС *f. indecl.* (*abbr. of* **гидроэлектроста́нция**) hydroelectric power station.

Дд

да¹ *particle*
1 yes.
2 (*interrog.*) yes?, is that so?, really?
3 (*emph.*) why; well; **да нет!** of course not!; not likely!
4 *emph. pred.*: **когда́-н. э́то да ко́нчится** it must end some time.
5 : **вот э́то да!** (*coll.*) splendid!

да² *particle* (+ *3rd pers. pres. or fut. of v.*) (*пусть*) may, let; **да здра́вствует..!** long live ... !

да³ *conj.*
1 (*mainly in conventional phrr.*) (*и*) and; **ко́жа да ко́сти** skin and bone.
2 : **да ещё** (*к тому же*) and (besides); and what is more.
3 : **да и то́лько** and that's all.
4 but; **я охо́тно проводи́л бы тебя́, да вре́мени нет** I would gladly come with you but I haven't the time.

дава́й(те) *as particle*
1 (+ *inf. or 1st pers. pl. of fut.*) let's.
2 (+ *imper.*; *coll.*) come on; **дава́й, расскажи́ что-н.** come on, tell us a story.

да|ва́ть, ю́, ёшь *impf. of* ▸ **дать**

да|ва́ться, ю́сь, ёшься *impf.* (*of* ▸ **~́ться**)
1 *pass. of* ▸ **дава́ть.**
2 : **легко́ д.** to come easily, naturally; **ру́сский язы́к ему́ даётся легко́** Russian comes easily to him.

дав|и́ть, лю́, ~́ишь *impf.*
1 (*also* **на** + *a.*) to press (upon); (*о сапоге*) to pinch; (*fig.*) (*угнетать*) to oppress, weigh (upon).
2 (*насекомых*) to crush; to trample; (*о машине*) to run over.
3 (*лимон, сок*) to squeeze.

дав|и́ться, лю́сь, ~́ишься *impf.* (*of* ▸ **по~**) (+ *i. or* **от** + *g.*) to choke (with).

да́вк|а, и *f.* (*coll.*) throng, crush.

давле́ни|е, я *nt.* pressure.

да́вн|ий *adj.*
1 ancient.
2 (*существующий издавна*) of long standing; **с ~их пор, времён** for a long time.

давно́ *adv.*
1 (*много времени тому назад*) long ago.
2 (*в течение долгого времени*) for a long time.

давны́м-давно́ *adv.* (*coll.*) ages ago.

Дагеста́н, а *m.* Dagestan.

дагеста́н|ец, ца *m.* Dagestani.

дагеста́н|ка, ки *f. of* ▸ **~ец**

дагеста́нский *adj.* Dagestani.

да́же *particle* even; **е́сли д.** even if; **о́чень д. пло́хо** extremely bad.

дактилоскопи́|я, и *f.* identification by means of fingerprints; **ге́нная д.** genetic fingerprinting.

дала́й-ла́м|а, ы *m.* Dalai Lama.

да́лее *adv.* further; **и так д.** (*abbr.* **и т. д.**) and so on, et cetera.

далёк|ий (~, ~а́, ~о́) *adj.* (*страна, выстрел*) distant; **д. путь** long journey; **~ое про́шлое** distant past; **я ~ от того́, что́бы**

жела́ть I am far from wishing.

далеко́[1] *adv.*
1 (*о расстоянии*) far, far off; (**от** + *g.*) far (from).
2 (*fig.*) far, by a long way, by much; **д. за** (*of time*) long after; **д. не** far from.

далеко́[2] *as pred.* it is far, it is a long way; (+ *d.* **до** + *g.*, *fig.*) to be far (from); **ему́ д. до соверше́нства** he is far from perfect.

дал|ь, и, о ~́и, в ~и́ *f.*
1 (*далёкое пространство*) distance; distant prospect.
2 (*coll.*) (*далёкое место*) distant spot.

дальневосто́чный *adj.* Far Eastern.

дальне́йш|ий *adj.* further, furthest; **в ~ем** (*в будущем*) in future, henceforth.

да́льн|ий *adj.*
1 (*далёкий*) distant, remote; **Д. Восто́к** the Far East; **~ее пла́вание** long voyage; **~его де́йствия** long-range; **~его сле́дования** (*of a train*) long-distance.
2 (*о родстве*) distant.

дальнови́д|ный (~ен, ~на) *adj.* far-sighted.

дальнозо́р|кий (~ок, ~ка) *adj.* long-sighted (*Br.*), far-sighted (*US*); (*fig.*) far-sighted.

да́льност|ь, и *f.* distance; range.

дальто́ник, а *m.* colour-blind (*Br.*), color-blind (*US*) person.

да́льше *adj. and adv.*
1 *comp. of* ▶ **далёкий.**
2 (*adv.*) further; **д. не́куда** (*coll.*) that's the limit; **ти́ше е́дешь, д. бу́дешь** (*prov.*) more haste, less speed.
3 (*adv.*) (*продолжая начатое*) further; **д.!** go on!
4 (*adv.*) (*затем*) then, next.
5 (*adv.*) (*долее*) longer.

да́м|а, ы *f.*
1 (*женщина*) lady.
2 (*игральная карта*) queen.

да́мб|а, ы *f.* dike.

да́м|ский *adj. of* ▶ **~а; ~ская су́мка** ladies' handbag.

Да́ни|я, и *f.* Denmark.

да́нн|ые, ых *no sg.*
1 (*also comput.*) data; (*факты*) facts, information.
2 (*свойства*) qualities, gifts.

да́нн|ый *p.p.p. of* ▶ **дать** *and adj.* given; present; in question; **в д. моме́нт** at present; **в ~ом слу́чае** in this case.

дан|ь, и *f.* (*fig.*) (*моде, традиции*) tribute; debt; **отда́ть д.** (+ *d.*) to pay tribute to, recognize.

дар, а, *pl.* **~ы́** *m.*
1 (*подарок*) gift, donation.
2 (+ *g.*) (*талант, способность*) gift (of).

дари́тел|ь, я *m.* donor.

дар|и́ть, ю, ~́ишь *impf.* (*of* ▶ **по~**) (+ *d.* and *a.*) (*давать*) to give.

дарова́ни|е, я *nt.* gift, talent.

даровО́й *adj.* free (of charge), gratuitous.

да́ром *adv.*
1 (*бесплатно*) free (of charge), gratis.
2 (*напрасно*) in vain, to no purpose; **пропа́сть д.** to be wasted.

да́т|а, ы *f.* date.

да́тельный *adj.* (*gram.*) dative.

дати́р|овать, ую *impf. and pf.* to date.

да́тский *adj.* Danish.

да́тчик, а *m.* sensor.

дать, дам, дашь, даст, дади́м, дади́те, даду́т, *past* **дал, дала́, да́ло́, да́ли** *pf.* (*of* ▶ **дава́ть**)
1 to give; **д. взаймы́** to lend (*money*); **на чай** to tip; **д. конце́рт** to give a concert.
2 to give, administer; **д. лека́рство** to give medicine.
3 (**по** + *d.*, **в** + *a.*; *coll.*) (*ударить*) to give (it); to hit.
4 (*fig.*) to give; **д. сло́во** to give one's word.
5 (*fig.*) to give, grant; **д. во́лю** (+ *d.*) to give (free) rein (to), give vent (to); **д. доро́гу** (+ *d.*) to make way (for).
6 *with certain nn. expr. action related to meaning of n.*; **д. звоно́к** to ring (*a bell*); **д. тре́щину** to crack (*on telephone*).
7 (+ *inf.*) (*позволить*) to let; **д. поня́ть** to give to understand; **да́йте ему́ сказа́ть** let him speak.

да́ться, да́мся, да́шься, *etc.*, *past* **да́лся, дала́сь** *pf. of* ▶ **дава́ться**

да́ч|а, и *f.*
1 (*загородный дом*) dacha.
2 : **быть на ~е** to be in the country; **пое́хать на ~у** to go to the country.

да́чник, а *m.* (holiday) visitor (*in the country*).

дБ (*abbr. of* **децибе́л**) dB, decibel(s).

два (*f.* **две**), **двух, двум, двумя́, о двух** *num.* two; **в двух слова́х** briefly, in short; **в д. счёта** in no time; **в двух шага́х** a short step away; **ка́ждые д. дня** every other day.

двадцати... *comb. form* twenty-.

двадцатиле́тний *adj.*
1 (*срок*) twenty-year, of twenty years.
2 (*человек*) twenty-year-old.

двадца́т|ый *adj.* twentieth; **одна́ ~ая** a twentieth; **~ое января́** the twentieth of January; **~ые го́ды** the twenties.

два́дцат|ь, и́, *i.* **ью** *num.* twenty; **д. оди́н,** *etc.*, twenty-one, *etc.*

два́жды *adv.* twice; **д. два — четы́ре** twice two is four.

двена́дцатый *adj.* twelfth.

двена́дцат|ь, и *num.* twelve.

двер|но́й *adj. of* ▶ **~ь**

две́р|ца, ы, *g. pl.* **~ец** *f.* door (*of car, cupboard, etc.*).

двер|ь, и, о ~́и, в ~и́, *pl.* **~́и, ~е́й,** *i.* **~я́ми** *and* **~ьми́** *f.* door; **в ~я́х** in the doorway.

две́сти, двухсо́т, двумста́м, двумяста́ми, о двухста́х *num.* two hundred.

дви́гател|ь, я *m.* motor, engine; (*fig.*) motive force.

дви́га|ть, ю *and* **дви́жу** *impf.* (*of* ▶ **дви́нуть**)
1 **(~ю)** to move.
2 **(~ю)** (+ *i.*) (*шевелить*) to move (*part of the body*); to make a movement (of).
3 **(дви́жу)** (*приводить в движение*) to set in motion, get going (*also fig.*).

дви́га|ться, юсь *and* **дви́жусь** *impf.* (*of*

▸ дви́нуться)
[1] to move (*intrans.*); **д. вперёд** to advance (*also fig.*).
[2] (*отправляться*) to start, get going.
[3] *pass. of* **▸ ~ть**

движе́ни|е, я *nt.*
[1] (*in var. senses*) movement; motion; **привести́ в д.** to set in motion; **д. «зелёных»** the green movement.
[2] (*физическое*) movement, exercise.
[3] (*дорожное*) traffic; **односторо́ннее д.** one-way traffic.

дви́|нуть, ну, нешь *pf. of* **▸ ~гать**

дви́|нуться, нусь, нешься *pf. of* **▸ ~гаться**

дво́е, двои́х *num.*
[1] (+ *m. nn. denoting persons, pers. prons. in pl. or nn. used only in pl.*) two; **нас бы́ло д.** there were two of us; **д. су́ток** forty-eight hours.
[2] (+ *nn. denoting objects usu. found in pairs*) two pairs; **д. чуло́к** two pairs of stockings.

двоето́чи|е, я *nt.* (*gram.*) colon.

дво|и́ться, ю́сь, и́шься *impf.* (*казаться двойным*) to appear double; **у него́ ~и́лось в глаза́х** he saw (objects) double.

двоичн|ый *adj.* (*math.*) binary.

дво́йк|а, и *f.*
[1] (*цифра, игральная карта*) two.
[2] (*отметка*) 'two' (*out of five*).
[3] (*coll.*) (*автобус, трамвай*) No. 2 (*bus, tram, etc.*).

двойни́к, а́ *m.* (*кого-н.*) double.

двойн|о́й *adj.* double; **~а́я фами́лия** double-barrelled (*Br.*), double-barreled (*US*) surname.

дво́|йня, йни, *g. pl.* **~ен** *f.* twins.

двор, а́ *m.*
[1] (*при одном доме*) yard; (*между домами*) courtyard.
[2] : **ско́тный д.** farmyard.
[3] : **на ~е́** out of doors, outside.
[4] (*королевский*) court; **при ~е́** at court.

двор|е́ц, ца́ *m.* palace.

дворе́цк|ий, ого *m.* butler.

дво́рник, а *m.*
[1] (*работник*) caretaker.
[2] (*coll.*) (*в машине*) windscreen wiper (*Br.*), windshield wiper (*US*).

дворян|и́н, и́на, *pl.* **~е, ~** *m.* nobleman.

дворя́н|ка, ки *f. of* **▸ дворяни́н**

дворя́нский *adj.* of the nobility.

дворя́нств|о, а *nt.* (*collect.*) nobility.

двою́родный *adj.* related through grandparent; **д. брат** (first) cousin (*male*); **д. дя́дя** (first) cousin once removed.

дву..., двух... *comb. form* bi-, di-, two-, double-.

двузна́чный *adj.* two-digit.

двули́ч|ный (~ен, ~на) *adj.* (*fig.*) two-faced.

двуро́г|ий *adj.* two-horned; **~ая луна́** crescent moon.

двуру́чный *adj.* two-handled.

двусмы́слен|ный (~, ~на) *adj.* ambiguous.

двуспа́льный *adj.* double (*of beds*).

двуство́лк|а, и *f.* double-barrelled gun (*Br.*), double-barreled gun (*US*).

двусторо́н|ний (~ен, ~ня) *adj.*
[1] double-sided; **~нее воспале́ние лёгких** double pneumonia.
[2] (*движение*) two-way.
[3] (*соглашение*) bilateral.

двухдне́вный *adj.* two-day.

двухколёсный *adj.* two-wheeled.

двухме́стный *adj.* two-seater; **д. но́мер** double room.

двухмото́рный *adj.* twin-engined.

двухсо́тый *adj.* two-hundredth.

двухчасово́й *adj.*
[1] (*фильм*) two-hour.
[2] (*поезд*) two o'clock.

двухэта́жный *adj.* two-storey (*Br.*), two-story (*US*); (*автобус*) double-decker.

двуязы́ч|ный (~ен, ~на) *adj.* bilingual.

деба́т|ы, ов *no sg.* debate.

деби́л, а *m.*
[1] mentally handicapped person.
[2] (*coll., pej.*) moron.

де́бр|и, ей *no sg.*
[1] jungle; thickets.
[2] (*fig.*) maze, labyrinth.

дебю́т, а *m.* debut.

дебюта́нт, а *m.* debutant.

дебюта́нтк|а, и *f.* debutante.

дебюти́р|овать, ую *impf. and pf.* to make one's debut.

де́в|а, ы *f.*
[1] (*obs.*) girl, maiden; **ста́рая д.** (*coll.*) old maid.
[2] **Д.** (*созвездие*) Virgo.

девальва́ци|я, и *f.* devaluation.

дева́|ть, ю *impf. of* **▸ деть**

дева́|ться, юсь *impf. of* **▸ де́ться**

де́вер|ь, я, *pl.* **~ья́, ~е́й** *m.* brother-in-law (*husband's brother*).

деви́з, а *m.* motto.

деви́честв|о, а *nt.* girlhood; **в ~е Ивано́ва** née Ivanova.

де́вич|ий *adj.* girlish; **~ья фами́лия** maiden name.

де́вочк|а, и *f.* (little) girl.

де́вственник, а *m.* virgin.

де́вственниц|а, ы *f.* virgin.

де́вственност|ь, и *f.* virginity; chastity.

де́вствен|ный (~, ~на) *adj.*
[1] (*целомудренный*) virgin.
[2] (*невинный*) virginal; innocent.
[3] (*fig.*) virgin; **д. лес** virgin forest.

де́вушк|а, и *f.*
[1] (unmarried) girl.
[2] (*coll.*) (*обращение*) miss.

девяно́ст|о, *g., d., i., and p.* **а** *num.* ninety.

девяно́стый *adj.* ninetieth.

де́вятер|о, ы́х *num.* (+ *m. nn. denoting persons, pers. prons. in pl. or nn. used only in pl.*) nine; **нас д.** there are nine of us.

девятисо́тый *adj.* nine-hundredth.

девя́тк|а, и *f.*
[1] (*цифра, игральная карта*) nine.
[2] (*coll.*) (*автобус, трамвай*) No. 9 (*bus, tram, etc.*).
[3] (*группа из девятерых*) (group of) nine.

девятна́дцатый *adj.* nineteenth.
девятна́дцат|ь, и *num.* nineteen.
девя́тый *adj.* ninth.
де́вят|ь, и́, *i.* **ью** *num.* nine.
девятьсо́т, девятисо́т, девятиста́м, девятьюста́ми, о девятиста́х *num.* nine hundred.
дёг|оть, тя *no pl., m.* tar.
деграда́ци|я, и *f.* degradation.
деградир|овать, ую *impf. and pf.* to become degraded.
дегуста́ци|я, и *f.* tasting; **д. вин** wine tasting.
дед, а *m.*
1 grandfather; (*pl.*; *fig.*) grandfathers, forefathers.
2 (*coll.*) (*старик*) grandad, grandpa.
3: **Д. Моро́з** Father Christmas, Santa Claus.
дедовщи́н|а, ы *f.* (*mil., sl.*) bullying, harassment (*of subordinates*).
деду́кци|я, и *f.* deduction.
де́душк|а, и *m.* grandfather, grandpa.
дееприча́сти|е, я *nt.* (*gram.*) gerund (*e.g.* **чита́я, прочита́в**).
дееспосо́б|ный (~ен, ~на) *adj.*
1 able to function, active.
2 (*leg.*) capable.
дежу́р|ить, ю, ишь *impf.*
1 (*быть дежурным*) to be on duty.
2 (*неотлучно находиться*) to be in constant attendance.
дежу́рн|ый *adj.*
1 duty; on duty; **д. офице́р** (*mil.*) orderly officer; **~ая апте́ка** chemist's shop open outside normal opening hours.
2 *as n.* **д., ~ого** *m.*, **~ая, ~ой** *f.* man, woman on duty; **кто д.?** who is on duty?
дежу́рств|о, а *nt.* (being on) duty; **гра́фик ~** rota; (*mil.*) roster.
дезерти́р, а *m.* deserter.
дезерти́р|овать, ую *impf. and pf.* to desert.
дезинфе́кци|я, и *f.* disinfection.
дезинфици́р|овать, ую *impf. and pf.* to disinfect.
дезинформа́ци|я, и *f.* misinformation; (*намеренная*) disinformation.
дезинформи́р|овать, ую *impf. and pf.* to misinform.
дезодора́нт, а *m.* deodorant.
дезорганиз|ова́ть, у́ю *impf. and pf.* to disrupt.
дезориенти́р|овать, ую *impf. and pf.* to disorient.
де́йстви|е, я *nt.*
1 (*деятельность*) action, operation; activity; **ввести́ в д.** to bring into operation, bring into force.
2 (*функционирование*) functioning (*of a machine etc.*).
3 (*влияние*) effect; action; **под ~ем** (+ *g.*) under the influence (of).
4 (*события, о которых идёт речь*) action (*of a story, etc.*).
5 (*часть пьесы*) act.
6 (*pl.*) (*поступки*) actions; (*mil.*) operations.
действи́тельно *adv.* really; indeed.
действи́тельност|ь, и *f.* reality; **в ~и** in reality, in fact.
действи́тел|ьный (~ен, ~ьна) *adj.*
1 (*настоящий*) real, actual; true, authentic; **~ьное положе́ние веще́й** the true state of affairs; **~ьная слу́жба** (*mil.*) active service.
2 (*имеющий силу*) valid.
де́йств|овать, ую *impf.*
1 (*impf. only*) (*совершать действия*) to act; (*функционировать*) to work, function; to operate.
2 (*pf.* **по~**) (**на** + *a.*) (*влиять*) to affect, have an effect (upon), act (upon); **лека́рство ~ует** the medicine is taking effect.
де́йствующ|ий *pres. part. act. of* ▸**де́йствовать** *and adj.*: **~ая а́рмия** army in the field; **д. вулка́н** active volcano; **~ие ли́ца** (*theatr.*) characters.
дека́бр|ь, я́ *m.* December.
дека́брь|ский *adj. of* ▸**~**
дека́д|а, ы *f.* (*срок*) ten-day period.
деклара́ци|я, и *f.* declaration; **нало́говая д.** tax return.
деклари́р|овать, ую *impf. and pf.* to declare, proclaim.
декоди́р|овать, ую *impf. and pf.* to decode.
декольте́ *nt. indecl.* décolleté (*also as adj.*); décolletage.
декорати́в|ный (~ен, ~на) *adj.* decorative, ornamental.
декора́тор, а *m.* (*помещения*) interior decorator; (*theatr.*) scene-painter.
декора́ци|я, и *f.* (*theatr.*) set, scenery.
декре́тный *adj.*: **д. о́тпуск** maternity leave.
де́ланный *adj.* artificial, forced, affected.
де́ла|ть, ю *impf.* (*of* ▸**с~**)
1 (*производить*) to make.
2 (*приводить в какое-н. состояние*) to make; **д. кого́-н. несча́стным** to make s.o. unhappy.
3 (*поступать*) to do; **д. не́чего** it can't be helped.
4 (+ *var. nn.*) to make, do, give; **д. вид** to pretend, feign; **д. вы́воды** to draw conclusions.
де́ла|ться, юсь *impf.* (*of* ▸**с~**)
1 (*становиться*) to become, get, grow.
2 (*происходить*) to happen; **что там ~ется?** what is going on?
делега́т, а *m.* delegate.
делега́ци|я, и *f.* delegation; group.
делеги́р|овать, ую *impf. and pf.* to delegate.
деле́ни|е, я *nt.*
1 division.
2 (*на шкале*) point, degree, unit.
Де́ли *m. indecl.* Delhi.
деликате́с, а *m.* delicacy; **магази́н ~ов** delicatessen.
делика́тност|ь, и *f.* (*in var. senses*) delicacy.
делика́т|ный (~ен, ~на) *adj.* (*in var. senses*) delicate.
дел|и́ть, ю́, ~́ишь *impf.*
1 (*pf.* **раз~**) to divide; **д. шесть на́ три** to divide six by three.
2 (*pf.* **по~**) (**с** + *i.*) to share (with); **д. с кем-**

н. горе и радость to share s.o.'s sorrows and joys.

дел|иться, юсь, ~ишься *impf.*
1 (*pf.* **раз~**) (**на** + *a.*) to divide (into).
2 (*pf.* **по~**) (+ *i.*, **с** + *i.*) to share (with); to communicate (to); **д. куском хлеба с кем-н.** to share a crust of bread with s.o.
3 (*impf. only*) (**на** + *a.*) to be divisible (by); **число сорок девять ~ится на семь** forty-nine is divisible by seven.

дел|о, а, *pl.* **~а, ~, ~ам** *nt.*
1 (*работа, занятие*) business, affair(s); **по ~у, по ~ам** on business; **это моё д.** that is my affair; **иметь д.** (**с** + *i.*) to have to do (with), deal (with); **не вмешивайтесь не в своё д.** mind your own business; **как (ваши) ~а?** how are things going (with you)?, how are you getting on?; **привести свой ~а в порядок** to put one's affairs in order; **какое мне до этого д.?** what has this to do with me?; **первым ~ом** in the first instance, first of all.
2 (*идеи*) cause; **д. мира** the cause of peace.
3 (+ *adj.*) (*специальность*) occupation; (*предприятие*) business, concern; **горное д.** mining.
4 matter, point; **д. вкуса** matter of taste; **д. чести** point of honour; **д. в том, что...** the point is that ...; **в том-то и д.** that's (just) the point; **не в этом д.** that's not the point.
5 (*факт*) fact, deed; thing; **на самом ~е** in actual fact, as a matter of fact; **в самом ~е** really, indeed.
6 (*поступок*) act, deed.
7 (*leg.*) (*судебное*) case; cause; **вести д.** to plead a cause; **возбудить д.** (**против** + *g.*) to bring an action (against), institute proceedings (against).
8 (*досье*) file, dossier; **личное д.** personal file.

деловит|ый (~, ~а) *adj.* businesslike, efficient.

делов|ой *adj.*
1 business; work; **~ое письмо** business letter; **~ая поездка** business trip.
2 (*человек, тон*) businesslike.

дельт|а, ы *f.* delta.

дельтаплан, а *m.* hang-glider (*craft*).

дельтапланерист, а *m.* hang-glider (*person*).

дельтапланерист|ка, ки *f. of* ▸ ~

дельфин, а *m.* dolphin.

демагог, а *m.* demagogue.

демагоги|я, и *f.* demagogy.

демилитариз|овать, ую *impf.* and *pf.* to demilitarize.

демисезонн|ый *adj.*: **~ое пальто** light overcoat (*for spring and autumn wear*).

демобилиз|овать, ую *impf.* and *pf.* to demobilize.

демобилиз|оваться, уюсь *impf.* and *pf.* to be demobilized.

демографический *adj.* demographic; **д. взрыв** population explosion.

демократ, а *m.* democrat.

демократический *adj.* democratic.

демократи|я, и *f.* democracy.

демон, а *m.* demon.

демонстрант, а *m.* (*pol.*) demonstrator.

демонстрант|ка, ки *f. of* ▸ ~

демонстратив|ный (~ен, ~на) *adj.* (*вызывающий*) demonstrative, done for effect.

демонстраци|я, и *f.*
1 (*in var. senses*) demonstration.
2 (*публичный показ*) showing (*of a film, etc.*).

демонстрир|овать, ую *impf.* and *pf.* (*pf. also* **про~**) to show, display; to give a demonstration (of).

демонтир|овать, ую *impf.* and *pf.* (*tech.*) to dismantle.

деморализ|овать, ую *impf.* and *pf.* to demoralize.

денежный *adj.*
1 monetary; money; **д. автомат** cash dispenser; **д. знак** banknote; **д. перевод** money order.
2 (*coll.*) (*богатый*) rich; **д. мешок** moneybags.

день, дня *m.*
1 day; afternoon; **в 4 ч дня** at 4 p.m.; **днём** in the afternoon; **д. рождения** birthday; **д. ото дня** with every passing day, day by day; **в один прекрасный д.** one fine day; **изо дня в д.** day after day; **на другой, следующий д.** next day; **на днях** (*i*) the other day, (*ii*) one of these days, any day now; **со дня на д.** daily, from day to day; **через д.** every other day.
2 (*pl.*) (*время; жизнь*) days; **его дни сочтены** his days are numbered.

ден|ьги, ег, ьгам *pl.* money; **мелкие д.** small change; **наличные д.** cash, ready money.

департамент, а *m.* department.

депеш|а, и *f.* dispatch.

депо *nt. indecl.* (*rail.*) depot.

депозит, а *m.* (*fin.*) deposit.

депортаци|я, и *f.* deportation.

депортир|овать, ую *impf.* and *pf.* to deport.

депрессивный *adj. of* ▸ **депрессия**

депресси|я, и *f.* (*econ., psych.*) depression.

депутат, а *m.* deputy; delegate.

депутат|ский *adj. of* ▸ ~

дёрга|ть, ю *impf.* (*of* ▸ **дёрнуть**) (*тянуть*) to pull, tug.

дёрга|ться, юсь *impf.* (*of* ▸ **дёрнуться**)
1 *pass. of* ▸ **~ть.**
2 to twitch.

деревенский *adj.*
1 (*магазин*) village.
2 (*тишина, пейзаж*) rural; (*житель, воздух*) country.

дерев|ня, ни, *g. pl.* **~ень** *f.*
1 (*селение*) village.
2 (*местность*) (the) country (*opp. the town*).

дерев|о, а, *pl.* **~ья, ~ьев** *nt.*
1 (*растение*) tree.
2 (*sg. only*) (*древесина*) wood (*as material*).

деревообработк|а, и *f.* woodworking.

деревушк|а, и *f.* hamlet.

деревянный *adj.* wood; wooden.

держав|а, ы *f.* (*pol.*) power.

держател|ь, я *m.*
1 (*fin.*) holder.

2 (*приспособление*) holder.
держ|а́ть, у́, ~ишь *impf.*
1 (*в руках*) to hold; (*не отпускать*) to hold on to; **~и́те во́ра!** stop thief!
2 (*поддерживать*) to hold up, support.
3 (*in var. senses*) (*заставлять находиться в каком-н. состоянии*) to keep, hold; **д. путь (к, на** + *a.*) to head (for), make (for); **д. пари́** to bet; **д. чью-н. сто́рону** to take s.o.'s side.
4 (*животных*) to keep; **д. лошаде́й** to keep horses.
5 + *certain nn.* = *to carry out*; **д. ре́чь** to make a speech.
держ|а́ться, у́сь, ~ишься *impf.*
1 (**за** + *a.*) to hold (on to); **~и́тесь за пери́ла** hold on to the banister.
2 (**на** + *p.*) to be held up (by), be supported (by).
3 (*находиться где-либо*) to keep, stay, be; **д. вме́сте** to stick together; **д. в стороне́** to hold aloof.
4 (*стоять*) to hold o.s.; (*fig.*) (*вести себя*) to behave.
5 (*сохраняться*) to last.
6 (*не сдаваться*) to hold out, stand firm.
7 (+ *g.*) (*придерживаться определённого направления*) to keep (to); **д. ле́вой стороны́** to keep to the left.
8 (+ *g.*) (*следовать чему-либо*) to adhere (to), stick (to).
де́рз|кий (~ок, ~ка́, ~ко) *adj.*
1 (*грубый*) impertinent, cheeky.
2 (*смелый*) audacious.
де́рзост|ь, и *f.*
1 (*грубость*) impertinence; cheek; **говори́ть ~и** to be impertinent.
2 (*смелость*) audacity.
дермати́н, а *m.* leatherette.
дермати́т, а *m.* dermatitis.
дермато́лог, а *m.* dermatologist.
дерматоло́ги|я, и *f.* dermatology.
дёрн, а *m.* turf.
дёрн|уть, у, ешь *pf. of* ▸ **дёргать**
дёрн|уться, усь, ешься *pf.* (*of* ▸ **дёргаться**) to start up (with a jerk); to dart.
дер|у́, ёшь *see* ▸ **драть**
дерьм|о́, а́ *nt.* (*vulg.*) (*животных*) dung; (*человека*) crap; (*fig.*) crap.
деса́нт, а *m.* (*mil.*)
1 (*высадка войск*) landing.
2 (*войска*) landing force; **вы́садить, вы́бросить д.** to make a landing.
деса́нтник, а *m.* paratrooper.
десе́рт, а *m.* dessert.
десн|а́, ы́, *pl.* **~ы, дёсен** *f.* (*anat.*) gum.
де́сятер|о, ы́х *num.* (+ *m. nn. denoting persons, pers. prons. in pl. or nn. used only in pl.*) ten.
десятибо́рь|е, я *nt.* (*sport*) decathlon.
десятикра́тный *adj.* tenfold.
десятиле́ти|е, я *nt.*
1 (*срок*) decade.
2 (*годовщина*) tenth anniversary.
десяти́чн|ый *adj.* decimal; **~ая дробь** decimal fraction.
деся́тка, и *f.*
1 (*цифра, игральная карта*) ten.
2 (*coll.*) (*автобус, трамвай*) No. 10 (*bus, tram, etc.*).
3 (*группа из десятерых*) (group of) ten.
4 (*coll.*) (*десять рублей*) ten-rouble note, tenner.
деся́т|ок, ка *m.*
1 (*десять*) ten.
2 (*десять лет*) ten years, decade (*of life*).
3 (*pl.*) (*math.*) tens.
4 (*pl.*) tens; **~ки люде́й** scores of people.
деся́тый *num.* tenth.
де́сят|ь, и́, *i.* **ью** *num.* ten.
дета́л|ь, и *f.*
1 (*подробность*) detail.
2 (*часть машины*) part, component.
детдо́м, а *m.* children's home.
детекти́в, а *m.*
1 (*человек*) detective.
2 (*роман*) detective story.
3 (*фильм*) detective film.
детекти́вный *adj.* detective (*attr.*).
детёныш, а *m.* young (*of animals*).
де́т|и, ~е́й, ~ям, ~ьми́, о ~ях *pl.* (*sg.* **дитя́** *nt.*; *oblique cases in singular not used*) children.
детса́д, а *m.* kindergarten, nursery school.
де́тск|ая, ой *f.* playroom; nursery.
де́тский *adj.*
1 child's, children's; **д. дом** children's home; **д. сад** kindergarten, nursery school.
2 (*ребяческий*) childish; **д. язы́к** baby talk.
де́тств|о, а *nt.* childhood.
деть, де́ну, де́нешь *pf.* (*of* ▸ **дева́ть**) (*coll.*) to put, do (with); **куда́ ты дел мою ру́чку?** what have you done with my pen?
де́|ться, нусь, нешься *pf.* (*of* ▸ **дева́ться**) to get to, disappear; **куда́ ~лись мои часы́?** where has my watch got to?
дефе́кт, а *m.* defect.
дефи́с, а *m.* hyphen.
дефици́т, а *m.*
1 (*econ.*) deficit.
2 (*нехватка*) shortage, deficiency.
дефици́т|ный (~ен, ~на) *adj.* in short supply; scarce.
дефо́лт, а *m.* (*fin.*) default (in payment).
деформа́ци|я, и *f.* deformation.
деформи́р|овать, ую *impf. and pf.* (*исказить*) to deform; (*изменить форму чего-н.*) to change the form of.
деформи́р|оваться, уюсь *impf. and pf.* to change one's shape; to become deformed.
деци... *comb. form* deci-.
децибе́л, а, *g. pl.* **д.** *m.* decibel.
дециме́тр, а *m.* decimetre (*Br.*), decimeter (*US*).
дешеве́|ть, ю *impf.* (*of* ▸ **по~**) to fall in price, become cheaper.
дешеви́зн|а, ы *f.* cheapness; low price.
деше́вле *comp. of* ▸ **дешёвый** *or* ▸ **дёшево.**
дёшево *adv.* cheap, cheaply; (*fig.*) cheaply, lightly.
дешёвый (дёшев, дешева́, дёшево) *adj.* cheap; (*fig.*) cheap; empty, worthless.
дешифр|ова́ть, у́ю *impf. and pf.* to decipher, decode.

де́ятел|ь, я *m.* agent; **госуда́рственный д.** statesman; **обще́ственный д.** public figure.
де́ятельност|ь, и *f.*
1 activity, activities; work; **обще́ственная д.** public work.
2 (*physiol., psych., etc.*) activity, operation.
де́ятел|ьный (~ен, ~ьна) *adj.* active, energetic.
джаз, а *m.* jazz.
джаз-ба́нд, а *m.* jazz band.
джази́ст, а *m.* jazzman, jazz musician.
джазме́н, а *m.* = **джази́ст**
джем, а *m.* jam (*Br.*), jelly (*US*).
дже́мпер, а *m.* jumper.
джентльме́н, а *m.* gentleman.
джентльме́нский *adj.* gentlemanly.
джин, а *m.* gin (*liquor*); **д. с то́ником** gin and tonic.
джинсо́вый *adj.* denim.
джи́нс|ы, ов *no sg.* jeans.
джип, а *m.* jeep (*propr.*).
джиха́д, а *m.* (*relig.*) jihad.
джо́йстик, а *m.* (*comput.*) joystick.
джо́кер, а *m.* (*cards*) joker.
джу́нгл|и, ей *no sg.* jungle.
джут, а *m.* (*bot.*) jute.
дзюдо́ *nt. indecl.* judo.
дзюдои́ст, а *m.* judoist, judoka.
дзюдои́ст|ка, ки *f. of* ▶ ~
диабе́т, а *m.* diabetes.
диабе́тик, а *nt.* diabetic.
диа́гноз, а *nt.* diagnosis.
диагности́р|овать, ую *impf. and pf.* to diagnose; (*tech.*) to check.
диагона́л|ь, и *f.* diagonal; **по ~и** diagonally.
диагра́мм|а, ы *f.* diagram; chart.
диаде́м|а, ы *f.* diadem.
диале́кт, а *m.* dialect.
диало́г, а *m.* dialogue (*Br.*), dialog (*US*).
диало́гов|ый *adj.* (*comput.*) interactive; **~ое окно́** dialog box.
диа́метр, а *m.* diameter.
диапазо́н, а *m.*
1 (*mus.*) diapason, range.
2 (*fig.*) range, compass.
3 (*tech.*; *fig.*) range; **д. волн** (*radio*) waveband.
диа́спор|а, ы *f.* diaspora.
дива́н, а *m.* divan (*couch*); sofa; **д.-крова́ть** sofa bed.
диверса́нт, а *m.* saboteur.
диве́рси|я, и *f.*
1 (*mil.*) diversion.
2 sabotage.
dividéнд **дивиде́нд, а** *m.* dividend.
Ди-ви-ди́ (*usu. spelt* **DVD**) *m. indecl.* DVD.
диви́зи|я, и *f.* (*mil.*) division.
дие́з, а *m.* (*also as indecl. adj.*) (*mus.*) sharp.
дие́т|а, ы *f.* diet; **сиде́ть на ~е** to be on a diet; **соблюда́ть ~у** to keep to a diet.
диети́ческий *adj.* dietetic.
диза́йн, а *m.* design.
диза́йнер, а *m.* designer.
ди́зел|ь, я *m.* diesel engine.
ди́зельный *adj.* diesel.
дизентери́|я, и *f.* dysentery.
дика́р|ь, я́ *m.* savage; (*некультурный человек*) barbarian.
ди́к|ий (~, ~а́, ~о) *adj.*
1 (*животное, растение*) wild; **~ая ко́шка** wild cat.
2 (*племя*) savage.
3 (*необузданный*) wild; **~ие кри́ки** wild cries; **д. восто́рг** wild delight.
4 (*абсурдный*) ridiculous.
5 (*застенчивый*) shy; unsociable.
6 (*страшный*) terrible, awful.
ди́к|о[1] *adv.*
1 *adv. of* ▶ **~ий.**
2 (*в испуге*) in fright; startled; **д. озира́ться** to look around wildly.
ди́ко[2] *as pred.* it is ridiculous.
дикобра́з, а *m.* porcupine.
дикорасту́щий *adj.* wild.
ди́кост|ь, и *f.* absurdity; **э́то соверше́нная д.** it is quite absurd.
дикта́нт, а *m.* dictation.
дикта́тор, а *m.* dictator.
диктату́р|а, ы *f.* dictatorship.
дикт|ова́ть, у́ю, у́ешь *impf.* (*of* ▶ **про~**) to dictate.
ди́ктор, а *m.* announcer; (*программы новостей*) newscaster.
диктофо́н, а *m.* Dictaphone (*propr.*).
ди́кци|я, и *f.* diction; enunciation.
ди́лер, а *m.* dealer.
дилета́нт, а *m.* amateur, dilettante, dabbler.
дина́мик, а *m.* loudspeaker.
дина́мик|а, и *f.* dynamics.
динами́т, а *m.* dynamite.
динами́ческий *adj.* dynamic.
динами́чный *adj.* dynamic.
дина́сти|я, и *f.* dynasty.
ди́нго *m. indecl.* (*zool.*) dingo.
диноза́вр, а *m.* dinosaur.
дио́д, а *m.*: **светоизлуча́ющий д.** light-emitting diode, LED.
дипло́м, а *m.*
1 (*документ*) diploma, certificate; degree.
2 (*coll.*) (*работа*) degree work, research.
диплома́т, а *m.*
1 diplomat.
2 (*coll.*) attaché case, (rigid) briefcase.
дипломати́ческий *adj.* diplomatic.
дипломати́ч|ный (~ен, ~на) *adj.* (*fig.*) diplomatic.
диплома́ти|я, и *f.* diplomacy.
дипло́м|ный *adj. of* ▶ **~; ~ная рабо́та** degree work, degree thesis.
директи́в|а, ы *f.* directive.
дире́ктор, а, *pl.* **~а́** *m.* director, manager; **д. шко́лы** head (master, mistress); principal.
дире́кци|я, и *f.* management; board (of directors).
дирижа́бл|ь, я *m.* airship, dirigible.
дирижёр, а *m.* (*mus.*) conductor.
дирижи́р|овать, ую *impf.* (+ *i.*; *mus.*) to conduct.
диск, а *m.*
1 disk; (*телефонный*) telephone dial.

2 (*sport*) discus.
3 (*грампластинка*) disc, record.
4 (*компьютерный, музыкальный*) disk, CD, DVD.

дисквалифика́ци|я, и *f.* disqualification.
диске́т|а, ы *f.* (*comput.*) diskette.
ди́ско *nt. indecl.* disco music.
дисково́д, а *m.* (*comput.*) disk drive.
дискомфо́рт, а *m.* discomfort.
диско́нтн|ый *adj.*: **~ая ка́рта** discount card.
дискоте́к|а, и *f.* disco(theque) (*place*).
дискредити́р|овать, ую *impf. and pf.* to discredit.
дискримина́ци|я, и *f.* discrimination; **д. же́нщин** sexism; **д. по во́зрасту** ageism.
дискримини́р|овать, ую *impf. and pf.* to discriminate against.
диску́сси|я, и *f.* discussion.
дискути́р|овать, ую *impf. and pf.* (+ *a. or* **о** + *p.*) to discuss.
дислока́ци|я, и *f.* (*mil.*) deployment, distribution (*of troops*).
диспансе́р, а *m.* (*med.*) clinic, (health) centre.
диспе́тчер, а *m.* controller (*of movement of transport, etc.*); (*comput.*) manager.
диспе́тчер|ский *adj. of* ▸ **~**; (*aeron.*): **~ская слу́жба** flying control organization; *as n.* **~ская, ~ской** *f.* controller's office; (*aeron.*) control tower.
диспле́|й, я *m.* (*comput.*) display, VDU (*visual display unit*).
диспропо́рци|я, и *f.* disproportion.
ди́спут, а *m.* (public) debate.
диссерта́ци|я, и *f.* dissertation, thesis.
диссиде́нт, а *m.* dissident.
диссона́нс, а *m.* (*mus. and fig.*) dissonance, discord.
дистанцио́нн|ый *adj.*: **~ое управле́ние** remote control.
диста́нци|я, и *f.*
1 distance; **на большо́й, ма́лой ~и** at a great, short distance.
2 (*sport*) distance; **сойти́ с ~и** to withdraw.
3 (*mil.*) range.

дистрибью́тор, а *m.* distributor, supplier.
дисципли́н|а, ы *f.* discipline.
дисциплини́рованный *adj.* disciplined.
дитя́, *pl.* **де́ти** (*oblique cases not used in sg.*) *nt.* child; baby.
дифтери́|я, и *f.* diphtheria.
дифференциа́л, а *m.*
1 (*math.*) differential.
2 (*tech.*) differential gear.

дифференциа́льн|ый *adj.* differential; **~ое исчисле́ние** (*math.*) differential calculus.
дича́|ть, ю *impf.* (*of* ▸ **о~**) to run wild, become wild; (*fig.*) to become unsociable.
дич|ь, и *f.* (*collect.*) game; wildfowl.
длин|а́, ы́ *f.* length; **в ~у́** longways, lengthwise; **во всю ~у́** at full length; **~о́й (в) шесть ме́тров** six metres long (*Br.*), six meters long (*US*).
длинно... *comb. form* long-.
дли́н|ный (~ен, ~на́, ~но) *adj.* long; lengthy.
дли́тельност|ь, и *f.* duration.
дли́тел|ьный (~ен, ~ьна) *adj.* long, protracted.
дл|и́ться, и́тся *impf.* (*of* ▸ **про~**) to last.
для *prep.* + *g.*
1 (*в пользу кого, чего*) for (the sake of); **э́то д. тебя́** this is for you.
2 (*выражает цель*) for; **д. того́, что́бы...** in order to ... .
3 (*по отношению к*) for, to; **вре́дно д. дете́й** bad for children.
4 (*по отношению к норме*) for, of; **он о́чень высо́к д. свои́х лет** he is very tall for his age.

дневни́к, а́ *m.* diary, journal; **вести́ д.** to keep a diary.
дневн|о́й *adj.*
1 day; **в ~о́е вре́мя** during daylight hours; **д. свет** daylight.
2 (*одного дня*) day's, daily.

днём *adv.*
1 in the daytime, by day.
2 (*после обеда*) in the afternoon; **сего́дня д.** this afternoon.

дни́щ|е, а *nt.* bottom (*of vessel or barrel*).
ДНК *f. indecl.* (*abbr. of* **дезоксирибонуклеи́новая кислота́**) (*chem.*) DNA (*deoxyribonucleic acid*).
дно, дна, *pl.* **до́нья, до́ньев** *nt.*
1 (*сосуда*) bottom; **вверх дном** upside down; **(пей) до дна!** bottoms up!
2 (*no pl.*) (*моря, реки*) bottom, bed.

до[1] *prep.* + *g.*
1 (*о пределе, границе*) to, up to; as far as; **от Ло́ндона до Москвы́** from London to Moscow.
2 (*о временном пределе*) to, up to; until, till; **до сих пор** up to now, till now, hitherto; **до тех пор** till then, before; **до тех пор, пока́** until; **до свида́ния!** goodbye!
3 (*перед*) before; **до войны́** before the war; **до на́шей э́ры (до н. э.)** before Christ (*abbr.* BC); **до того́ как** before.
4 (*о пределе состояния*) to, up to, to the point of; **до бо́ли** until it hurt(s); **до того́..., что** to the point where.
5 (*о количественном пределе*) under, up to (= *not over, not more than*); **де́ти до пяти́ лет** children under five; **до ты́сячи рубле́й** up to a thousand roubles.
6 (*приблизительно*) about, approximately.
7 (*относительно*) with regard to, concerning; **что до меня́** as far as I am concerned; **мне,** *etc.*, **не до** (*coll.*) I, *etc.*, don't feel like; **мне не до разгово́ра** I don't feel like talking.

до[2] *nt. indecl.* (*mus.*) C.
до...[1] *vbl. pref.*
1 *expr. completion of action*: **дочита́ть кни́гу** to finish (reading) a book.
2 *indicates that action is carried to a certain point*: **дочита́ть до страни́цы 270** to read as far as page 270.
3 *expr. supplementary action*: **докупи́ть** to buy in addition.
4 (+ *refl. vv.*) *expr. eventual attainment of object*: **дозвони́ться** to ring until one gets an answer.

до...² *pref. of nn. and adjs., used to indicate priority in chronological sequence* pre-.

добáв|ить, лю, ишь *pf.* (*of* ▸ **~ля́ть**) (+ *a. or g.*) to add.

добáвк|а, и *f.*
1 (*пищевая*) additive.
2 (*дополнительная порция*) second helping.

добавлéни|е, я *nt.* addition.

добавля́|ть, ю *impf. of* ▸ **добáвить**

добáвочн|ый *adj.*
1 additional, extra; **~ое врéмя** (*sport*) extra time.
2 (*teleph.*) extension; **д. три́дцать** extension 30.

добегá|ть, ю *impf. of* ▸ **добежáть**

добе|жáть, гу́, жи́шь, гу́т *pf.* (*of* ▸ **~гáть**) (**до** + *g.*) to run (to, as far as); (*достигнуть*) to reach (*also fig.*).

добермáн(-пи́нчер), добермáна(-пи́нчера) *m.* Dobermann (pinscher).

добивá|ть, ю *impf. of* ▸ **доби́ть**

добивá|ться, юсь *impf.*
1 *impf. of* ▸ **доби́ться.**
2 (+ *g.*) to try to get, strive (for), aim (at).

добирá|ться, юсь *impf. of* ▸ **добрáться**

до|би́ть, бью́, бьёшь *pf.* (*of* ▸ **~бивáть**) to finish off, do for.

до|би́ться, бью́сь, бьёшься *pf.* (*of* ▸ **добивáться**) (+ *g.*) to get, obtain, secure; **д. своегó** to get one's way.

дóблест|ь, и *f.* valour (*Br.*), valor (*US*), gallantry.

до|брáться, беру́сь, берёшься, *past* **~брáлся, ~бралáсь** *pf.* (*of* ▸ **~бирáться**)
1 (**до** + *g.*) to get (to), reach.
2 (*coll.*) to get (one's hands on); **я до тебя́ ~беру́сь!** I'll get you!

добр|ó, á *nt.*
1 good; (*поступок*) good deed; **не к ~у́ э́то** it is a bad omen.
2 (*collect.*; *coll.*) (*имущество*) goods, property.
3 : **д. пожáловать!** welcome!

доброво́л|ец, ьца *m.* volunteer.

доброво́льно *adv.* voluntarily.

доброво́л|ьный (~ен, ~ьна) *adj.* voluntary.

добродéтел|ь, и *f.* virtue.

доброду́ш|ный (~ен, ~на) *adj.* good-natured.

доброжелáтел|ьный (~ен, ~ьна) *adj.* benevolent.

доброкáчествен|ный (~, ~на) *adj.*
1 of good quality.
2 (*med.*) benign.

добросо́вест|ный (~ен, ~на) *adj.* conscientious.

доброт|á, ы́ *f.* goodness, kindness.

добро́т|ный (~ен, ~на) *adj.* of good, high quality; durable.

дóбр|ый (~, ~á, ~о, ~ы́) *adj.*
1 (*хороший*) good; **~ое и́мя** good name; **~ое у́тро!** good morning!; **всегó ~ого!** goodbye!; all the best!; **по ~ой вóле** of one's own free will.
2 (*отзывчивый*) kind, good; **бу́дьте ~ы** (+ *imper.*) please, would you be so kind as to.
3 (*coll.*) (*не меньше чем*) a good; **д. час** a good hour.

добывá|ть, ю *impf. of* ▸ **добы́ть**

до|бы́ть, бу́ду, бу́дешь, *past* **~бы́л, ~былá, ~бы́ло** *pf.* (*of* ▸ **~бывáть**)
1 (*достать*) to get, obtain, procure.
2 (*из земли*) to extract, mine, quarry.

добы́ч|а, и *f.*
1 (*действие*) extraction (*of minerals*), mining, quarrying.
2 (*захваченное*) booty, spoils, loot.
3 (*охотника*) bag; (*рыболова*) catch.
4 (*добытое из недр земли*) mineral products; output.

довез|ти́, у́, ёшь, *past* **~̈, ~лá** *pf.* (*of* ▸ **довози́ть**) to take (to).

довéренност|ь, и *f.* warrant, power of attorney; **по ~и** by proxy.

довéр|енный *p.p.p. of* ▸ **~ить** *and adj.* trusted; **~енное лицó;** *as n.* **д., ~енного** *m.* agent, proxy.

довéри|е, я *nt.* trust, confidence; **слу́жба/телефóн ~я** helpline.

довери́тельный *adj.* confiding, trusting.

довéр|ить, ю, ишь *pf.* (*of* ▸ **~я́ть 1**) (+ *d.*) to entrust (to).

довéр|иться, юсь, ишься *pf.* (*of* ▸ **~я́ться**) (+ *d.*) to trust (in), confide (in).

дóверху *adv.* to the top; to the brim.

довéрчив|ый (~, ~а) *adj.* trustful, credulous.

довер|я́ть, я́ю *impf.*
1 *impf. of* ▸ **~́ить.**
2 (*impf. only*) (+ *d.*) to trust, confide (in).

довер|я́ться, я́юсь *impf. of* ▸ **~́иться**

довéс|ок, ка *m.* makeweight.

дове|сти́, ду́, дёшь, *past* **~̈л, ~лá** *pf.* (*of* ▸ **доводи́ть**)
1 (*до какого-то места*) to lead (to), take (to), accompany (to).
2 (*до какого-то состояния*) to bring (to); to drive (to), reduce (to); **д. до совершéнства** to perfect; **д. до свéдения** (+ *g.*) to inform, let know.

дóвод, а *m.* argument.

дово|ди́ть, жу́, ~́дишь *impf. of* ▸ **довести́**

довоéнный *adj.* pre-war.

дово|зи́ть, жу́, ~́зишь *impf. of* ▸ **довезти́**

довóльно¹ *adv.* (*достаточно*) quite, fairly; rather, pretty; **д. хорóший фильм** quite a good film.

довóльно² *adv.* (*с удовлетворением*) contentedly.

довóл|ьный (~ен, ~ьна) *adj.*
1 contented, satisfied; **д. вид** contented expression.
2 (+ *i.*) contented (with), satisfied (with), pleased (with); **д. собóй** pleased with o.s., self-satisfied.

довóльств|оваться, уюсь *impf.* (+ *i.*) to be content (with), be satisfied (with).

дог, а *m.* mastiff; **далмáтский д.** Dalmatian.

догад|áться, áюсь *pf.* (*of* ▸ **~́ываться 1**) to guess.

догáдк|а, и *f.* surmise, conjecture; (*pl.*) guesswork; **теря́ться в ~ах** to be lost in conjecture.

догáдлив|ый (~, ~а) *adj.* quick-witted, bright.

догáдыва|ться, юсь *impf.*
1 *impf. of* ▶ **догадáться.**
2 (*impf. only*) to suspect.

дóгм|а, ы *f.* dogma.

дóгмат, а *m.*
1 (*relig.*) doctrine, dogma.
2 (*принцип*) tenet, foundation.

до|гнáть, гоню́, гóнишь, *past* **~гнáл, ~гналá, ~гнáло** *pf.* (*of* ▶ **~гоня́ть**) to catch up (with) (*also fig.*).

договáрива|ть, ю *impf. of* ▶ **договори́ть**

договáрива|ться, юсь *impf.*
1 *impf. of* ▶ **договори́ться.**
2 (*impf. only*) (**о** + *p.*) to negotiate (about).

договóр, а *m.* agreement; (*pol.*) treaty, pact.

договорённост|ь, и *f.* agreement, understanding; (*pol.*) accord.

договор|и́ть, ю́, и́шь *pf.* (*of* ▶ **договáривать**) to finish saying; to finish telling.

договор|и́ться, ю́сь, и́шься *pf.* (*of* ▶ **договáриваться 1**)
1 (**о** + *p.*) to come to an agreement, understanding (about); to arrange; **~и́лись!** agreed!; it's a deal!
2 (**до** + *g.*) to come (to); to talk (to the point of).

договóрн|ый *adj.* agreed; contractual; **~ая ценá** agreed price.

доголá *adv.* stark naked; **раздéться д.** to strip to the skin.

догоня́|ть, ю *impf. of* ▶ **догнáть**

догор|áть, áю *impf. of* ▶ **~éть**

догор|éть, ю́, и́шь *pf.* (*of* ▶ **~áть**) (*сгореть до какого-либо предела*) to burn down; (*сгореть до конца*) to burn out.

дода|вáть, ю́, ёшь *impf. of* ▶ **~́ть**

додá|ть, м, шь, ст, ди́м, ди́те, ду́т, *past* **дóдал, ~лá, дóдало** *pf.* (*of* ▶ **~вáть**) to make up (the rest of); to pay up.

додéл|ать, аю *pf.* (*of* ▶ **~ывать**) to finish.

додéлыва|ть, ю *impf. of* ▶ **додéлать**

доду́м|аться, аюсь *pf.* (*of* ▶ **~ываться**) (**до** + *g.*) to hit (upon) (*afterthought*).

доду́мыва|ться, юсь *impf. of* ▶ **доду́маться**

доедá|ть, ю *impf. of* ▶ **доéсть**

доезжá|ть, ю *impf. of* ▶ **доéхать**

до|éсть, éм, éшь, éст, еди́м, еди́те, едя́т *pf.* (*of* ▶ **~едáть**) to eat up, finish eating.

до|éхать, éду, éдешь *pf.* (*of* ▶ **~езжáть**) (**до** + *g.*) to reach, arrive (at).

дожд|áться, у́сь, ёшься, *past* **~áлся, ~алáсь** *pf.*
1 (+ *g.*) to wait (for); **д. концá спектáкля** to wait until the end of the show.
2 : **д. тогó, что** to end up (by); **он ~áлся тогó, что емý указáли на дверь** he ended up by being shown the door.

дождеви́к, á *m.* (*coll.*) raincoat.

дождевóй *adj. of* ▶ **дождь**

дóждик, а *m.* shower.

дождли́в|ый (~, ~а) *adj.* rainy.

дожд|ь, я́ *m.*
1 rain (*also fig.*); **под ~ём** in the rain; **мéлкий д.** drizzle; **проливнóй д.** downpour; **идёт д.** it is raining.
2 (*fig.*) cascade.

доживá|ть, ю *impf.*
1 *impf. of* ▶ **дожи́ть.**
2 (*impf. only*) to live out; **д. свой век** to live out one's days.

дожидá|ться, юсь *impf.* (*of* ▶ **дождáться**) (+ *g.*) to wait (for).

до|жи́ть, живу́, живёшь, *past* **~́жил, ~жилá, ~́жило** *pf.* (*of* ▶ **~живáть 1**)
1 (**до** + *g.*) (*прожить*) to live (till); to attain the age (of); **онá ~жилá до концá войны́** she lived to see the end of the war.
2 (**до** + *g.*) (*дойти до какого-либо состояния*) to come (to), be reduced (to); **до чегó мы ~́жили!** what have we come to!

дóз|а, ы *f.* dose.

дозапрáвк|а, и *f.* refuelling (*Br.*), refueling (*US*).

дозвон|и́ться, ю́сь, и́шься *pf.* (**до** + *g.*, **к** + *d.*) to ring until one gets an answer; to get through (*on telephone*); **я не мог к тебé/до тебя́ д.** I rang you but could not get through.

дозирóвк|а, и *f.* dosage.

дознáни|е, я *nt.* (*leg.*) inquiry; inquest.

дозóр, а *m.* patrol.

дозóр|ный *adj. of* ▶ **~**; *as n.* **д., ~ного** *m.* (*mil.*) scout.

дозревá|ть, ю *impf. of* ▶ **дозрéть**

дозр|éть, éю *pf.* (*of* ▶ **~евáть**) to ripen.

доигр|áть, áю *pf.* (*of* ▶ **~́ывать**) to finish (playing).

доигрыва|ть, ю *impf. of* ▶ **доигрáть**

доистори́ческий *adj.* prehistoric.

до|и́ть, ю́, ~́ишь *impf.* (*of* ▶ **по~**) to milk.

до|йти́, йду́, йдёшь, *past* **~шёл, ~шлá** *pf.* (*of* ▶ **~ходи́ть**)
1 (**до** + *g.*) (*in var. senses*) to reach; **д. до тогó, что...** to reach a point where ...; **ру́ки не ~ходи́ли** (**до** + *g.*) I, *etc.*, had no time (for).
2 (*coll.*) (**до** + *g.*) (*произвести впечатление*) to make an impression (upon); (*стать понятным в ходе объяснения*) to get through (to).
3 (*impers.*; *also* **дéло ~йдёт, ~шлó до** + *g.*) to come (to); **(дéло) чуть не ~шлó до дрáки** it nearly came to blows.

док, а *m.* dock.

доказáтельств|о, а *nt.* proof, evidence.

док|азáть, ажу́, áжешь *pf.* (*of* ▶ **~áзывать 1**) to demonstrate, prove; **считáть ~áзанным** to take for granted.

докáзыва|ть, ю *impf.*
1 *impf. of* ▶ **доказáть.**
2 (*impf. only*) to argue, try to prove.

докáпыва|ться, юсь *impf. of* ▶ **докопáться**

док|ати́ться, ачу́сь, áтишься *pf.* (*of* ▶ **~áтываться**)
1 (**до** + *g.*) to roll (to).
2 (*о звуках*) to roll, thunder, boom.

докáтыва|ться, юсь *impf. of* ▶ **докати́ться**

дóкер, а *m.* docker.

доклáд, а *m.* report; lecture; paper; talk; **читáть д.** to give a report; to read a paper.
доклáдчик, а *m.* speaker.
доклáдчи|ца, цы *f. of* ▸ **~к**
доклáдыва|ть, ю *impf. of* ▸ **доложи́ть**
докопá|ться, юсь *pf.* (*of* ▸ **докáпываться**) (**до** + *g.*)
1 to dig down (to).
2 (*fig.*) to get to the bottom (of); to find out, discover.
дóктор, а, *pl.* **~á** *m.* doctor.
дóктор|ский *adj. of* ▸ **~; ~ская диссертáция** doctoral thesis.
доктри́н|а, ы *f.* doctrine.
докумéнт, а *m.* document.
документáльный *adj.* documentary; **д. фильм** documentary (film).
документáци|я, и *f.* (*collect.*) documentation.
долб|и́ть, лю́, и́шь *impf.* to hollow out; to gouge.
долг, а, о ~е, в ~ý, *pl.* **~и́** *m.*
1 (*обязанность*) duty.
2 (*одолженное*) debt; **в д.** on credit; **быть у когó-н. в ~ý** to be indebted to s.o.
дóл|гий (~ог, ~гá, ~го) *adj.* long.
дóлго *adv.* long, (for) a long time.
долговéч|ный (~ен, ~на) *adj.* lasting; durable.
долгов|óй *adj. of* ▸ **долг 2; ~óе обязáтельство** promissory note.
долговрéмен|ный (~, ~на) *adj.* of long duration, prolonged.
долговя́з|ый (~, ~а) *adj.* (*coll.*) lanky.
долгождáнный *adj.* long-awaited.
долгожи́тел|ь, я *m.* long-lived person.
долгожи́тель|ница, ницы *f. of* ▸ **~**
долголéти|е, я *nt.* longevity.
долголéтний *adj.* of many years; long-standing.
долгосрóчн|ый (~ен, ~на) *adj.* (*кредит*) long-term; (*отпуск*) of long duration.
долгот|á, ы́, *pl.* **~ы** *f.*
1 (*sg. only*) (*дня*) duration.
2 (*geog.*) longitude.
долет|áть, áю *impf. of* ▸ **~éть**
доле|тéть, чý, ти́шь, *pf.* (*of* ▸ **~тáть**) (**до** + *g.*) to fly (to, as far as); to reach.
дóлж|ен (~нá, ~нó) *pred. adj.*
1 owing; **он д. мне три рубля́** he owes me three roubles.
2 (+ *inf.*) (*обязан, вынужден*): **я д. идти́** I must go, I have to go.
3 (+ *inf.*) (*вероятно*): **онá ~нá скóро прийти́** she should be here soon; **~нó быть** probably.
должни́к, á *m.* debtor.
должностн|óй *adj.* official; **~óе лицó** official, functionary, public servant.
дóлжност|ь, и, *g. pl.* **~éй** *f.* post, office.
дóлжн|ый *adj.* due, fitting, proper; **~ым óбразом** properly; *as n.* **~ое, ~ого** due.
доливá|ть, ю *impf. of* ▸ **доли́ть**
доли́н|а, ы *f.* valley.
дол|и́ть, ью́, ьёшь, *past* **~и́л, ~илá, ~и́ло** *pf.* (*of* ▸ **~ивáть**)
1 (*жидкость*) to add; to pour in addition.
2 (*сосуд*) to fill (up); to refill.
дóллар, а *m.* dollar.
долож|и́ть[1], ý, ~ишь *pf.* (*of* ▸ **доклáдывать**)
1 (+ *a. or* **о** + *p.*) (*сделать доклад*) to report; to give a report (on).
2 (**о** + *p.*) (*сообщить о приходе посетителя*) to announce (*a guest, etc.*).
долож|и́ть[2], ý, ~ишь *pf.* (*of* ▸ **доклáдывать**) (*добавить*) to add.
долóй *adv.* (+ *a.*; *coll.*) down (with), away (with); **д. измéнников!** down with the traitors!
долот|ó, á, *pl.* **~а, ~** *nt.* chisel.
дóльше *adv.* longer.
дóл|я, и, *g. pl.* **~éй** *f.*
1 (*часть*) part, portion; share; quota; **войти́ в ~ю** (**с** + *i.*) to go shares (with).
2 (*судьба*) lot, fate; **вы́пасть на чью-н. ~ю** to fall to s.o.'s lot.
дом, а (у), *pl.* **~á** *m.*
1 (*жилое здание*) house; (*многоквартирный*) block (of flats) (*Br.*), apartment block (*US*); (*здание учреждения*) building; **д. культýры** palace of culture; ≈ arts (and leisure) centre; **д. óтдыха** holiday home; **д.-музéй...** ... House; **Д.-музéй Пýшкина** Pushkin House.
2 (*своё жильё*) home; (*семья*) household.
дом... *comb. form, abbr. of* **домáшний**
дóма *adv.* at home, in; **быть как д.** to feel at home; **бýдьте как д.** make yourself at home; **у негó не все д.** he's not all there.
домáшн|ий *adj.*
1 house; home; domestic; **д. áдрес** home address; **~яя страни́ца** (*comput.*) home page; **под ~им арéстом** under house arrest.
2 (*самодельный*) home-made.
3 (*не дикий*) domestic; **~ие живóтные** domestic animals; **~яя пти́ца** (*collect.*) poultry.
домéн *m.* (*comput.*) domain.
Доминикáнск|ая Респýблик|а, ~ой ~и *f.* the Dominican Republic.
домини́р|овать, ую *impf.* to dominate, prevail (*fig.*).
доминó *nt. indecl.* (*игра*) dominoes.
домкрáт, а *m.* (*tech.*) jack.
домо... *comb. form*
1 home-.
2 *abbr. of* **домáшний**
домовладéл|ец, ьца *m.* house-owner; (*по отношению к нанимателю*) landlord.
домогáтельств|о, а *nt.* solicitation, demand, bid; **сексуáльное д.** sexual harassment.
домóй *adv.* home, homewards; **нам порá д.** it's time for us to go home.
домофóн, а *m.* electronic security system (*at entrance to building*); entryphone (*Br., propr.*).
домохозя́йк|а, и *f.* housewife.
домрабóтниц|а, ы *f.* domestic (servant), maid; **приходя́щая д.** home help.
дóмыс|ел, ла *m.* conjecture.
донáшива|ть, ю *impf. of* ▸ **доноси́ть[1]**
донесéни|е, я *nt.* report, message.
донес|ти́[1], ý, ёшь, *past* **~, ~лá** *pf.* (*of*

▸**доноси́ть**[2]) (**до** + *g.*) to carry (to, as far as); (*звук, запах*) to carry, bear.

донес|ти́[2], **у́, ёшь,** *past* **~̈, ~ла́** *pf.* (*of* ▸**доноси́ть**[3])
1 to report, announce; (+ *d.*) to inform.
2 (**на** + *a.*) (*сделать донос*) to inform (on, against), denounce.

донес|ти́сь, у́сь, ёшься, *past* **~̈ся, ~ла́сь** *pf.* (*of* ▸**доноси́ться**[2])
1 (*о звуках, запахах, новостях*) to reach.
2 (*coll.*) (*быстро доехать, добежать*) to reach quickly.

до́низу *adv.* to the bottom.

до́нор, а *m.* donor.

доно́с, а *m.* denunciation.

дон|оси́ть[1], **ошу́, ~о́сишь** *pf.* (*of* ▸**дона́шивать**)
1 to wear out.
2 : (*usu. with neg.*) **д. ребёнка** to bear at full term.

дон|оси́ть[2,3], **ошу́, ~о́сишь** *impf. of* ▸**донести́**[1,2]

дон|оси́ться[1], **~о́сится** *pf.* to wear out, be worn out.

дон|оси́ться[2], **~о́сится** *impf. of* ▸**донести́сь**

доно́счик, а *m.* informer.

доно́счи|ца, цы *f. of* ▸**~к**

допива́|ть, ю *impf. of* ▸**допи́ть**

до́пинг, а *m.* drugs, dope.

дописа́ть, шу́, ~́шешь *pf.* (*of* ▸**~́сывать**)
1 (*письмо*) to finish writing; (*картину*) to finish painting.
2 (*приписать*) to add.

допи́сыва|ть, ю *impf. of* ▸**дописа́ть**

доп|и́ть, ью́, ьёшь, *past* **~и́л, ~ила́, ~и́ло** *pf.* (*of* ▸**~ива́ть**) to drink (up).

допла́т|а, ы *f.* additional payment; surcharge.

допл|ати́ть, ачу́, ~а́тишь *pf.* (*of* ▸**~а́чивать**) to pay in addition, pay the remainder.

допла́чива|ть, ю *impf. of* ▸**доплати́ть**

доплыва́|ть, ю *impf. of* ▸**доплы́ть**

доплы́|ть, ву́, вёшь, *past* **~л, ~ла́, ~ло** *pf.* (*of* ▸**~ва́ть**) (**до** + *g.*) (*вплавь*) to swim (to, as far as); (*на корабле*) to sail (to, as far as); (*fig.*) to reach.

допоздна́ *adv.* (*coll.*) till late.

дополне́ни|е, я *nt.* supplement, addition; addendum.

дополни́тельно *adv.* in addition.

дополни́тельн|ый *adj.* supplementary, additional, extra; **~ое вре́мя** (*sport*) extra time.

допо́лн|ить, ю, ишь *pf.* (*of* ▸**~я́ть**) to supplement, add to.

дополн|я́ть, я́ю *impf. of* ▸**~́ить**

допото́пный *adj.* antediluvian.

допра́шива|ть, ю *impf. of* ▸**допроси́ть**

допро́с, а *m.* (*leg.*) interrogation.

допр|оси́ть, ошу́, о́сишь *pf.* (*of* ▸**~а́шивать**) (*leg.*) to interrogate, question.

до́пуск, а *m.* (**к** + *d.*) access (to); (**в** + *a.*) right of entry, admittance.

допуска́|ть, ю *impf. of* ▸**допусти́ть**

допусти́м|ый (~, ~а) *adj.* permissible, admissible.

допу|сти́ть, щу́, ~́стишь *pf.* (*of* ▸**~ска́ть**)
1 (**до** + *g.*, **к** + *d.*) to admit (to); give access (to) **д. к ко́нкурсу** to allow to compete.
2 (*позволить*) to allow, permit.
3 (*предположить*) to grant, assume; **~́стим** let us assume.
4 (*сделать*): **д. оши́бку** to make a mistake.

допуще́ни|е, я *nt.* (*предположение*) assumption.

допыт|а́ться, а́юсь *pf.* (*of* ▸**~́ываться**) to find out.

допы́тыва|ться, юсь *impf. of* ▸**допыта́ться;** (*impf. only*) to try to find out, try to elicit.

дораба́тыва|ть, ю *impf. of* ▸**дорабо́тать**

дорабо́та|ть, ю *pf.* (*of* ▸**дораба́тывать**)
1 (*усовершенствовать*) to refine.
2 (**до** + *g.*) to work (until).

дораст|а́ть, а́ю *impf. of* ▸**~и́**

дораст|и́, у́, ёшь, *past* **доро́с, доросла́** *pf.* (*of* ▸**дораста́ть**) (**до** + *g.*) to grow (to); (*fig.*) to attain (to), come up (to).

дорв|а́ться, у́сь, ёшься, *past* **~а́лся, ~ала́сь, ~а́ло́сь** *pf.* (**до** + *g.*; *coll.*) to fall upon, seize upon.

дореволюцио́нный *adj.* pre-revolutionary.

доро́г|а, и *f.*
1 (*путь сообщения*) road; (*путь следования*) way (*also fig.*); **желе́зная д.** railway (*Br.*), railroad (*US*); **дать, уступи́ть кому́-н. ~у** to make way for s.o. (*also fig.*).
2 (*путешествие*) journey; **отпра́виться в ~у** to set out; **в ~е** on the journey, en route.
3 (*направление пути, маршрут*) (the) way, route; **показа́ть ~у** to show the way; **сби́ться с ~и** to lose one's way.

до́рого *adv.* dear, dearly; **д. обойти́сь** (+ *d.*) to cost one dear.

дорогови́зн|а, ы *f.* high prices.

доро́гой *adv.* on the way, en route.

дорог|о́й (до́рог, дорога́, до́рого) *adj.*
1 dear, expensive.
2 (*близкий сердцу*) dear; precious; *as n.* **д., ~о́го** *m.*, **~а́я, ~о́й** *f.* (my) dear.

дорожа́|ть, ет *impf.* (*of* ▸**по~**) to rise (in price), go up.

доро́же *comp. of* ▸**дорого́й** *and* ▸**до́рого**

дорож|и́ть, у́, и́шь *impf.* (+ *i.*) to value.

доро́жк|а, и *f.*
1 path.
2 (*sport*) track; lane.
3 (*коврик*) runner.
4 (*магнитофона*) track.

доро́жн|ый *adj.*
1 *adj. of* ▸**доро́га; д. знак** road sign; **~ая поли́ция** traffic police.
2 (*для путешествия*) travel, travelling (*Br.*), traveling (*US*); **д. чек** traveller's cheque (*Br.*), traveler's check (*US*).

доса́д|а, ы *f.* annoyance; **кака́я д.!** what a nuisance!

доса|ди́ть, жу́, ди́шь *pf.* (*of* ▸**~жда́ть**)

(+ *d.*) (*раздражить*) to annoy, vex.
доса́д|ный (~ен, ~на) *adj.* annoying.
досажда́|ть, ю *impf. of* ▶**досади́ть**
доск|а́, и́, *a.* **~у,** *pl.* **~и, досо́к, ~а́м** *f.*
1 board, plank; **д. объявле́ний** noticeboard.
2 (*мраморная*) slab; (*металлическая*) plaque, plate.
3 (*для сёрфинга, скейтбординга и т. п.*) board.
доскона́л|ьный (~ен, ~ьна) *adj.* thorough.
до|сла́ть, шлю́, шлёшь *pf.* (*of* ▶**~сыла́ть**) to send in addition; to send the remainder.
досло́вно *adv.* verbatim, word for word.
досло́вный *adj.* literal, verbatim; **д. перево́д** literal translation.
дослу́ша|ть, ю *pf.* (*of* ▶**дослу́шивать**) to listen to (sth.) till the end.
дослу́шива|ть, ю *impf. of* ▶**дослу́шать**
досма́трива|ть, ю, *impf. of* ▶**досмотре́ть**
досмо́тр, а *m.* examination; inspection.
досмотр|е́ть, ю́, ~ишь *pf.* (*of* ▶**досма́тривать**) (**до** + *g.*) to watch, look at (to, as far as); **мы ~е́ли пье́су до тре́тьего а́кта** we saw the play as far as the third act.
доспе́х|и, ов *pl.* (*sg.* **~, ~а** *m.*) armour (*Br.*), armor (*US*).
досро́ч|ный (~ен, ~на) *adj.* ahead of schedule, early.
доста|ва́ть(ся), ю́(сь), ёшь(ся) *impf. of* ▶**~ть(ся)**
доста́в|ить, лю, ишь *pf.* (*of* ▶**~ля́ть**)
1 (*груз, посылку*) to deliver; (*пассажиров*) to transport, convey.
2 (*удовольствие*) to give; (*трудности*) to cause.
доста́вк|а, и *f.* delivery.
доставля́|ть, ю *impf. of* ▶**доста́вить**
доста́т|ок, ка *m.* prosperity.
доста́точно[1] *adv.* sufficiently, enough; (*значительно*) considerably.
доста́точно[2] *as pred.* it is enough; **д. сказа́ть** suffice it to say.
доста́точ|ный (~ен, ~на) *adj.* sufficient.
доста́|ть, ну, нешь *pf.* (*of* ▶**~ва́ть**)
1 (*взять*) to fetch; to take out; **д. плато́к из карма́на** to take a handkerchief out of one's pocket.
2 (+ *g. or* **до** + *g.*) (*коснуться*) to touch; to reach.
3 (*получить*) to get, obtain.
доста́|ться, нусь, нешься *pf.* (*of* ▶**~ва́ться**) (+ *d.*)
1 (*перейти в собственность*) to pass (to) (by inheritance).
2 (*выпасть на долю*) to fall to one's lot.
достига́|ть, ю *impf. of* ▶**дости́гнуть** *and* ▶**дости́чь**
дости́г|нуть, ну, нешь, *past* **~, ~ла** *pf.* (*of* ▶**~а́ть**) (+ *g.*)
1 (*дойти, доехать*) to reach.
2 (*добиться*) to attain, achieve.
достиже́ни|е, я *nt.* achievement, attainment.
достижи́м|ый (~, ~а) *adj.* achievable, attainable.
дости́чь = **дости́гнуть**
достове́рност|ь, и *f.* (*правдивость*) trustworthiness, reliability; (*о документе*) authenticity.
достове́р|ный (~ен, ~на) *adj.* (*правдивый*) reliable, trustworthy; (*о документе*) authentic.
досто́инств|о, а *nt.*
1 (*хорошее качество*) merit, virtue.
2 (*sg. only*) (*уважение*) dignity; **чу́вство со́бственного ~а** self-respect.
3 (*стоимость*) value; **моне́та ~ом в пять рубле́й, моне́та пятирублёвого ~а** a five-rouble coin.
досто́йно *adv.* suitably, fittingly.
досто́|йный (~ин, ~йна) *adj.*
1 (+ *g.*) (*стоящий*) worthy (of), deserving; **д. внима́ния** worthy of note.
2 (*заслуженный*) deserved; fitting, adequate.
3 (*соответствующий*) suitable, fit.
достопримеча́тельност|ь, и *f.* sight; place, object of note; **осма́тривать ~и** to see the sights.
до́ступ, а *m.* access, admittance.
досту́п|ный (~ен, ~на) *adj.*
1 (*место*) accessible.
2 (**для** + *g.*) open (to); available (to).
3 (*книга*) easily understood; intelligible.
4 (*цены*) moderate, reasonable.
досу́г, а *m.* leisure, leisure time; **на ~е** at leisure, in one's spare time.
до́суха *adv.* (until) dry; **вы́тереть д.** to rub dry.
досчита́|ть, ю *pf.* (*of* ▶**досчи́тывать**)
1 to finish counting.
2 (**до** + *g.*) to count (up to); **д. до ста** to count up to a hundred.
досчи́тыва|ть, ю *impf. of* ▶**досчита́ть**
досыла́|ть, ю *impf. of* ▶**досла́ть**
досье́ *nt. indecl.* dossier, file.
досяга́емост|ь, и *f.* reach; (*mil.*) range; **вне преде́лов ~и** beyond reach.
дота́скива|ть, ю *impf. of* ▶**дотащи́ть**
дота́ци|я, и *f.* grant, subsidy.
дотащ|и́ть, у́, ~ишь *pf.* (*of* ▶**дота́скивать**) (*coll.*) (**до** + *g.*) to carry, drag (to).
дотла́ *adv.* utterly, completely; **сгоре́ть д.** to burn to the ground.
дотра́гива|ться, юсь *impf. of* ▶**дотро́нуться**
дотро́н|уться, усь, ешься *pf.* (*of* ▶**дотра́гиваться**) (**до** + *g.*) to touch.
дотя́гива|ть(ся), ю(сь), ешь(ся) *impf. of* ▶**дотяну́ть(ся)**
дотян|у́ть, у́, ~ешь *pf.* (*of* ▶**дотя́гивать**) (**до** + *g.*)
1 to draw, drag (to, as far as).
2 (*coll.*) (*дойти, доехать*) to reach, make.
3 (*coll.*) (*выдержать*) to hold out (till); (*дожить*) to live (till).
дотян|у́ться, у́сь, ~ешься *pf.* (*of* ▶**дотя́гиваться**) (**до** + *g.*) to reach; to touch.
до́хл|ый (~а́, ~о) *adj.* (*мёртвый*) dead (*of animals*).
до́х|нуть, ну, нешь, *past* **~, ~ла** *impf.*

(*of* ▸ **из~**, ▸ **по~**, ▸ **с~**)
1 (*о животных*) to die.
2 (*coll., pej.*) (*о людях*) to peg out, kick the bucket.

дохо́д, а *m.* income; receipts; revenue.

дохо|ди́ть, жу́, ~́дишь *impf. of* ▸ **дойти**

дохо́д|ный (~ен, ~на) *adj.*
1 profitable, lucrative, paying.
2 *adj. of* ▸ **~**

дохо́дчив|ый (~, ~а) *adj.* intelligible, easy to understand.

доце́нт, а *m.* reader (*Br.*), associate professor (*US*).

до́чери, до́черью *see* ▸ **дочь**

доче́рний *adj.* (*о компании, предприятии*) daughter; branch.

дочит|а́ть, а́ю *pf.* (*of* ▸ **~́ывать**)
1 (*окончить чтение чего-н.*) to finish reading.
2 (**до** + *g.*) to read (to, as far as).

дочи́тыва|ть, ю *impf. of* ▸ **дочита́ть**

до́чк|а, и *f.* (*coll.*) = **дочь**

доч|ь, ~́ери, *i.* **~́ерью,** *pl.* **~́ери, ~ере́й, ~еря́м, ~ерьми́, о ~еря́х** *f.* daughter.

дошко́льник, а *m.* pre-schooler.

дошко́льни|ца, цы *f. of* ▸ **~к**

дошко́льный *adj.* preschool.

доща́тый *adj.* made of planks, boards; **д. насти́л** duckboards.

доя́рк|а, и *f.* milkmaid.

д-р *abbr. of* **до́ктор** Dr, Doctor.

др.: и ~ (*abbr. of* **и други́е**) & Co.; *et al.*

драгоце́нност|ь, и *f.* jewel; gem; (*pl.*) jewellery.

драгоце́н|ный (~ен, ~на) *adj.* precious.

дразн|и́ть, ю́, ~́ишь *impf.*
1 (*собаку*) to tease.
2 (*аппетит, любопытство*) to stimulate.

дра́йвер, а *m.* (*comput.*) driver.

дра́к|а, и *f.* fight.

драко́н, а *m.* dragon.

дра́м|а, ы *f.*
1 drama.
2 (*fig.*) crisis, calamity.

драматизи́р|овать, ую *impf. and pf.* to dramatize.

драмати́ческий *adj.*
1 dramatic; drama; **д. теа́тр** theatre (*Br.*), theater (*US*).
2 (*напыщенный*) dramatic, theatrical.

драмати́ч|ный (~ен, ~на) *adj.* (*fig.*) dramatic.

драмату́рг, а *m.* playwright, dramatist.

драп, а *m.* thick woollen cloth.

дра|ть, деру́, дерёшь, *past* **~л, ~ла́, ~́ло** *impf.*
1 (*impf. only*) (*рвать*) to tear (up, to pieces).
2 (*pf.* **со~**) (*снимать*) to tear off.

дра́|ться, деру́сь, дерёшься, *past* **~лся, ~ла́сь, ~́ло́сь** *impf.*
1 (*pf.* **по~**) (**с** + *i.*) to fight (with).
2 (*fig.*) (**за** + *a.*) to fight, struggle (for).

дребезж|а́ть, и́т *impf.* to jingle, tinkle.

древеси́н|а, ы *f.*
1 (*плотная часть дерева*) wood.
2 (*лесоматериалы*) timber.

древнегре́ческий *adj.* ancient, classical Greek.

древнеевре́йский *adj.* ancient, classical Hebrew.

древнеру́сский *adj.* Old Russian.

дре́в|ний (~ен, ~няя) *adj.* ancient; **~няя исто́рия** ancient history.

дре́вност|ь, и *f.*
1 (*sg. only*) (*далёкое прошлое*) antiquity.
2 (*pl.*; *archaeol.*) antiquities.

дрези́н|а, ы *f.* (*rail.*) trolley (*Br.*), handcar (*US*).

дрейф|ова́ть, у́ю *impf.* (*naut.*) to drift.

дрел|ь, и *f.* (*tech.*) drill.

дрем|а́ть, лю́, ~́лешь *impf.* to doze; **не д.** (*also fig.*) to be watchful; to be wide awake.

дрена́ж, а *and* **а́** *m.* drainage.

дрена́ж|ный *adj. of* ▸ **~**; **~ная труба́** drainpipe.

дрессиро́ванн|ый *p.p.p. of* ▸ **дрессирова́ть** *and adj.*: **~ые живо́тные** performing animals.

дрессир|ова́ть, у́ю *impf.* (*of* ▸ **вы~**) to train.

дрессиро́вщик, а *m.* trainer.

дресс-ко́д, а *m.* dress code.

дробови́к, а́ *m.* shotgun.

дроб|ь, и, *pl.* **~́и, ~е́й** *f.*
1 (*collect.*) (*для стрельбы*) small shot.
2 (*звуки*) drumming; tapping; patter; **бараба́нная ~** drum roll.
3 (*math.*) fraction.
4 (*черта*) slash.

дров|а́, ~, ~а́м *no sg.* firewood.

дровосе́к, а *m.* woodcutter.

дро́гн|уть, у, ешь, *past* **~ул, ~ула** *pf.*
1 to shake, move; (*о свете*) to flicker.
2 (*о человеке*) to waver, falter.

дрож|а́ть, у́, и́шь *impf.*
1 to tremble; to shiver, shake; to quiver; to vibrate; (*о свете*) to flicker.
2 (**за** + *a. or* **пе́ред** + *i.*; *fig.*) to tremble (for; before).
3 (**над** + *i.*) to grudge; **д. над ка́ждой копе́йкой** to count every penny.

дро́жж|и, е́й *no sg.* yeast, leaven.

дрож|ь, и *f.* shivering, trembling; (*в голосе*) tremor, quaver.

дрозд, а́ *m.* thrush; **чёрный д.** blackbird.

дро́тик, а *m.*
1 (*оружие*) spear, javelin.
2 (*в игре*) dart.

друг[1]**, а,** *pl.* **друзья́, друзе́й** *m.* friend.

друг[2] (*short form of* ▸ **~о́й**) **д. ~́а** each other, one another; **д. за ~́ом** one after another; **д. с ~́ом** with each other.

друг|о́й *adj.*
1 other, another; different; **и тот и д.** both; **ни тот ни д.** neither; **(э́то) совсе́м ~о́е де́ло** (that is) quite another matter; **~и́ми слова́ми** in other words; **с ~о́й стороны́** on the other hand; **на д. день** the next day; *as n.* **~и́е, ~и́х** others.
2 (*второй*) second.

дру́жб|а, ы *f.* friendship.

дружелю́б|ный (~ен, ~на) *adj.* friendly, amicable.

дру́жеский *adj.* friendly.
дру́жественный *adj.* friendly, amicable; (*comput.*) user-friendly.
друж|и́ть, у́, ~́ишь *impf.* (**с** + *i.*) to be friends (with).
дру́жно *adv.*
1 harmoniously, in concord.
2 (*вместе*) (all) together, in concert.
дру́ж|ный (~ен, ~на́, ~но, ~́ны) *adj.*
1 (*единодушный*) amicable; harmonious.
2 (*одновременный*) simultaneous, concerted.
друзья́ *see* ▶ **друг**
дря́бл|ый (~, ~́а, ~о) *adj.* flabby.
дрян|но́й (~́ен, ~на́, ~́но, ~ны́) *adj.* (*coll.*) worthless, rotten; good-for-nothing.
дрян|ь, и *f.* (*coll.*) trash, rubbish.
дря́хл|ый (~, ~а́, ~о) *adj.* decrepit, senile.
ДТП *nt. indecl.* (*abbr. of* **доро́жно-тра́нспортное происше́ствие**) road accident.
дуб, а, *pl.* **~ы́** *m.* oak.
дуби́нк|а, и *f.* cudgel, truncheon.
дублёнк|а, и *f.* (*coll.*) sheepskin coat.
дублёр, а *m.* (*theatr.*) understudy; (*cin.*) stand-in.
Ду́блин, а *m.* Dublin.
дубли́р|овать, ую *impf.* to duplicate; **д. роль** (*theatr.*) to understudy a part.
дубо́вый *adj.*
1 oak.
2 (*fig., coll.*) (*глупый*) thick.
дуг|а́, и́, *pl.* **~́и** *f.* arc.
ду́дк|а, и *f.* pipe, fife; **плясა́ть под чью-н. ~у** (*fig.*) to dance to s.o.'s tune.
ду́л|о, а *nt.* (*отверстие ствола*) muzzle; (*ствол*) barrel.
Ду́м|а, ы *f.* Duma (*lower house of the Russian parliament*).
ду́ма|ть, ю *impf.* (*of* ▶ **по~ 1**)
1 (**о** + *p. or* **над** + *i.*) to think (about); to be concerned (about).
2 (*impf. only*) **д. что...** to think, suppose that ... .
3 (+ *inf.*) to think of, plan to; **он ~ет поéхать в Ло́ндон** he is thinking of going to London.
ду́ма|ться, ется *impf.* (*impers.*, + *d.*) to seem; **мне ~ется** I think, I fancy; **~ется** it seems.
ду́м|ец, ца *m.* (*coll.*) member of Duma.
ду́мский *adj. of* ▶ **Ду́ма**
ду́н|уть, у, ешь *pf.* to blow.
дупл|о́, а́, *pl.* **~́а, ду́пел** *nt.*
1 (*в стволе дерева*) hollow.
2 (*в зубе*) cavity.
ду́р|а, ы *f. of* ▶ **дура́к**
дура́к, а́ *m.* fool, ass; **оста́вить в ~а́х** to make a fool of.
дура́цкий *adj.* (*coll.*) stupid, foolish, idiotic.
дура́ч|ить, у, ишь *impf.* (*of* ▶ **о~**) to fool, dupe.
дура́ч|иться, усь, ишься *impf.* to play the fool.
дурдо́м, а *m.* (*coll., lit. & fig.*) madhouse.
ду́рно *as pred.* (*impers.*, + *d.*): **мне,** *etc.*, **д.** I, *etc.*, feel faint, bad.
дур|но́й (~ён, ~на́, ~́но, ~́ны) *adj.*
1 (*плохой*) bad, evil; nasty; **д. вкус** nasty taste; **~ные мы́сли** evil thoughts; **~ные привы́чки** bad habits.
2 : **д. (собо́ю)** (*некрасивый*) ugly.
дуршла́г, а *m.* (*cul.*) colander.
дуть, ду́ю, ду́ешь *impf.* (*of* ▶ **по~ 1**) to blow; **сего́дня ду́ет за́падный ве́тер** there is a west wind today.
дух, а *m.*
1 (*relig., phil., and fig.*) spirit; **Свято́й Д.** the Holy Spirit.
2 (*моральное состояние*) spirit(s); heart; mind; **быть в ~́е** to be in good (high) spirits; **не в ~́е** in low spirits.
3 (*дыхание*) breath; (*coll.*) air; **перевести́ д.** to take breath.
4 (*призрак*) spectre (*Br.*), specter (*US*), ghost.
дух|и́, о́в *no sg.* perfume, scent.
духове́нств|о, а *nt.* (*collect.*) clergy, priesthood.
духо́вк|а, и *f.* oven.
духовни́к, а́ *m.* (*eccl.*) confessor.
духо́вност|ь, и *f.* spirituality.
духо́вный *adj.*
1 spiritual; inner; **д. мир** inner world.
2 (*церковный*) ecclesiastical, church; religious; **д. сан** holy orders.
духово́й *adj.* (*mus.*) wind; **д. инструме́нт** wind instrument; **д. орке́стр** brass band.
духот|а́, ы *f.* stuffiness, closeness.
душ, а *m.* shower; **приня́ть д.** to take a shower.
душ|а́, и́, *a.* **~́у,** *pl.* **~́и** *f.*
1 soul; (*fig.*) heart; **д. в ~́у** at one, in harmony; **в ~е́** (*i*) inwardly, secretly, (*ii*) at heart.
2 (*чувства*) feelings, spirit.
3 (*fig.*) (*человек, при указании количества*) soul; **на ~́у** per head.
душев|а́я, о́й *f.* shower room.
душевнобольн|о́й *adj.* insane; mentally ill; *as n.* **д., ~о́го** *m.*, **~а́я, ~о́й** *f.* insane person; psychiatric patient.
душе́вн|ый *adj.*
1 mental; **~ая боле́знь** mental illness.
2 (*искренний*) sincere, heartfelt; **д. челове́к** understanding person.
души́ст|ый (~, ~а) *adj.* fragrant, sweet-scented.
душ|и́ть[1], у́, ~́ишь *impf.* (*of* ▶ **за~**)
1 (*убивать*) to strangle; to stifle, smother, suffocate; (*fig.*) (*угнетать*) to stifle, suppress.
2 (*impf. only*) (*лишать возможности дышать*) to choke; **его́ ~и́л гнёв** he choked with rage.
душ|и́ть[2], у́, ~́ишь *impf.* (*of* ▶ **на~**) to scent, perfume.
душ|и́ться[2], у́сь, ~́ишься *impf.* (*of* ▶ **на~**) (+ *i.*) to perfume o.s. (with).
душ|и́ться[1], у́сь, ~́ишься *impf.*, *pass. of* ▶ **~и́ть[1]**
ду́шно *as pred.* it is stuffy; it is stifling, suffocating; **мне ста́ло д.** I felt suffocated.
ду́ш|ный (~ен, ~на́, ~но) *adj.* stuffy, close, sultry; stifling.
дуэ́л|ь, и *f.* duel.
дуэ́т, а *m.* duet.

ды́бом *adv.* on end; **во́лосы у него́ вста́ли д.** his hair stood on end.
дым, а (у), о ~е, в ~у́, *pl.* **~ы́** *m.* smoke.
дым|и́ться, и́тся *impf.* to smoke (*intrans.*); (*of fog*) to billow.
ды́мк|а, и *f.* haze (*also fig.*).
дымово́й *adj. of* ▸ **дым**
дымохо́д, а *m.* flue.
ды́мчат|ый (~, ~а) *adj.* smoke-coloured (*Br.*), smoke-colored (*US*); (*очки*) tinted.
ды́н|я, и *f.* melon.
дыр|а́, ы́, *pl.* **~ы** *f.* hole (*also fig., coll.*).
ды́рк|а, и *f.* hole.
дыроко́л, а *m.* hole-puncher, punch.
дыря́в|ый (~, ~а) *adj.* full of holes, holey.
дыха́ни|е, я *nt.* breathing; breath; **иску́сственное д.** artificial respiration.
дыха́тельн|ый *adj.* respiratory; **~ые пути́** respiratory tract.
дыш|а́ть, у́, ~ишь *impf.* (+ *i.*) to breathe; (*быть проникнутым чем-либо*) to exude.
дья́вол, а *m.* devil.
дья́вольский *adj.* devilish, diabolical.
дья́кон, а *m.* (*eccl.*) deacon.
дю́жин|а, ы *f.* dozen.
дюйм, а *m.* inch.
дю́н|а, ы *f.* dune.
дюра́л|ь, я *m.* = **~юми́ний**
дюралюми́ни|й, я *m.* (*tech.*) Duralumin (*propr.*).
дя́д|я, и *m.*
1 (*родственник*) uncle.
2 (*coll.*) (*обращение*) mister (*as term of address*).
3 (*coll.*) (*мужчина*) guy.
дя́т|ел, ла *m.* woodpecker.

Ее

ёбаный *adj.* (*vulg.*) fucking.
еб|а́ть, у́, ёшь *impf.* (*of* ▸ **вы́~**) (*vulg.*) to fuck; **ёб твою́ мать!** fuck you!; (*as int.*) (*чёрт возьми!*) fuck!; fucking hell!
Ева́нгели|е, я *nt.* (*collect.*) the Gospels; gospel (*also fig.*).
еврази́йский *adj.* Eurasian.
Евра́зи|я, и *f.* Eurasia.
евре́|й, я *m.* Jew; (*древний*) Hebrew.
евре́йк|а, и *f.* Jewish woman, girl.
евре́йский *adj.* Jewish; **~ язы́к** (*иврит*) Hebrew.
е́вро *m. indecl.* euro (*currency unit*).
евро... *comb. form* Euro-.
Еврозо́н|а, ы *f.* eurozone.
Евро́п|а, ы *f.* Europe.
Европарла́мент, а *m.* Europarliament.
европе́|ец, йца *m.* European.
европе́|йка, йки *f. of* ▸ **~ец**
европе́йский *adj.* European.
евроремо́нт, а *m.* restoration carried out to Western standards.
Евросою́з, а *m.* European Union.
Еги́п|ет, та *m.* Egypt.
еги́петский *adj.* Egyptian.
египтя́н|ин, ина, *pl.* **~е, ~** *m.* Egyptian.
египтя́н|ка, ки *f. of* ▸ **~ин**
его́
1 *g. and a. sg. of* ▸ **он, оно́.**
2 (*possessive pron.*) (*относящийся к человеку*) his; (*относящийся к предмету*) its.
ед|а́, ы́ *f.*
1 (*пища*) food.
2 (*трапеза*) meal; **во вре́мя ~ы́** at mealtimes, while eating.
едва́ *adv. and conj.*
1 (*adv.*) (*с трудом*) hardly, barely.
2 (*adv.*) (*чуть*) hardly, scarcely.
3 : **е. ли** (*adv.*) hardly, scarcely (*in judgements of probability*).
4 : **е. (ли) не** (*adv.*) nearly, almost, all but; **я е. не по́мер со́ смеху** I nearly died laughing.
5 (*conj.*) hardly, scarcely, barely; **е. ..., как** scarcely ... when; no sooner ... than; **е. самолёт взлете́л, как отказа́л оди́н из двигателе́й** no sooner had the plane taken off than one of the engines seized up.
еди́м *see* ▸ **есть**[1]
едини́ц|а, ы *f.*
1 (*цифра*) one; figure 1; (*math.*) unity.
2 (*in var. senses*) unit; **е. мо́щности** unit of power; **боевы́е ~ы фло́та** naval units; **15 ~ боево́й те́хники** 15 military vehicles.
3 (*отметка*) 'one' (*lowest mark in Russian school marking system*).
едини́чный *adj.* single; **е. слу́чай** isolated case.
единобо́жи|е, я *nt.* monotheism.
единобо́рств|о, а *nt.* single combat.
единовла́сти|е, я *nt.* autocracy, absolute rule.
единовре́мен|ный (~ен, ~на) *adj.* extraordinary, unique; **~ное посо́бие** extraordinary grant.
единогла́сно *adv.* unanimously.
единогла́с|ный (~ен, ~на) *adj.* unanimous.
единоду́ши|е, я *adj.* unanimity.
единоду́ш|ный (~ен, ~на) *adj.* unanimous.
единомы́шленник, а *m.* person who holds the same views; like-minded person.
единообра́з|ный (~ен, ~на) *adj.* uniform.
единоро́г, а *m.* (*myth.*) unicorn.
еди́нственно *adv.* only, solely; **е.**

возмо́жный ход the only possible move.
еди́нствен|ный (~ *and* ~ен, ~на) *adj.* only, sole; **е. сын** only son; **он е. оста́лся в живы́х** he was the sole survivor; **~ное число́** (*gram.*) singular (number).
еди́нств|о, а *nt.* (*in var. senses*) unity.
еди́н|ый (~, ~а) *adj.*
1 (*единственный*) one; single, sole; **там не́ было ни ~ой души́** there was not a soul there; **все до ~ого** to a man.
2 (*один*) united, unified.
3 (*общий*) common, single; **~ая во́ля** single will/purpose.
еди́те *see* ▶ **есть**[1]
е́д|кий (~ок, ~ка́, ~ко) *adj.*
1 caustic; acrid, pungent.
2 (*fig.*) caustic, sarcastic.
е́д|у, ешь *see* ▶ **е́хать**
едя́т *see* ▶ **есть**[1]
её
1 *g. and a. of* ▶ **она́.**
2 (*possessive pron.*) (*относящийся к человеку*) (*при существительном*) her; (*без существительного*) hers; (*относящийся к предмету*) its.
ёж, ежа́ *m.* hedgehog.
ежеви́к|а, и *f.*
1 (*collect.*) blackberries.
2 (*кустарник*) bramble, blackberry bush.
ежего́дный *adj.* annual, yearly.
ежедне́в|ный (~ен, ~на) *adj.* daily; everyday.
ежеме́сячный *adj.* monthly.
ежемину́т|ный (~ен, ~на) *adj.*
1 occurring every minute, at intervals of a minute.
2 (*непрерывный*) incessant, continual.
еженеде́льный *adj.* weekly.
ежеча́сный *adj.* hourly.
езд|а́, ы *f.*
1 ride, riding; (*на машине*) drive.
2 *in phrr. indicating distance from one point to another* journey, drive; **отсю́да до о́зера — до́брых три часа́ ~ы́** from here to the lake is a good three hours' journey.
е́з|дить, жу, дишь *impf.*
1 (*indet. of* ▶ **е́хать**) to go (*in or on a vehicle or on an animal*); to ride, drive; **е. верхо́м** to ride (on horseback).
2 (*уметь ездить*) to (be able to) ride, drive.
3 (**к** + *d.*) (*посещать*) to visit.
езжа́|ть (*coll.*): **~й(те)** (*as imper. of* ▶ **е́хать**) go!; get going!
ей *d. and i. of* ▶ **она́**
ел, е́ла *see* ▶ **есть**[1]
е́ле *adv.*
1 (*с трудом*) hardly, barely, only just.
2 (*почти не*) hardly, scarcely, barely, only just; **по́езд е. дви́гался** the train was scarcely moving.
ёлк|а, и *f.*
1 fir (tree), spruce; **новогодняя ё.** Christmas tree.
2 (*coll.*) (*праздник*) Christmas, New Year's party.
ёлочн|ый *adj. of* ▶ **ёлка; ~ые украше́ния** Christmas-tree decorations.
ел|ь, и *f.* spruce (*Picea*); fir (tree).
ем *see* ▶ **есть**[1]
ём|кий (~ок, ~ка) *adj.* capacious.
ёмкост|ь, и *f.* (*вместимость*) capacity, cubic content; (*вместилище*) container.
ему́ *d. of* ▶ **он, оно́**
ено́т *m.* raccoon.
епа́рхи|я, и *f.* (*eccl.*) diocese.
епи́скоп, а *m.* bishop.
ерала́ш, а *m.* (*coll.*) jumble, muddle.
е́рес|ь, и, *pl.* **~и, ~ей** *f.* heresy.
ёрза|ть, ю *impf.* (*coll.*) to fidget.
ерунд|а́, ы *f.* (*coll.*)
1 (*чепуха*) nonsense, rubbish; **говори́ть ~у́** to talk nonsense.
2 (*пустяк*) trifle, trifling matter; child's play.
ЕС *nt. indecl.* (*abbr. of* **Европе́йское соо́бщество, Европе́йский сою́з**) EC, EU (*European Community, European Union*).
е́сли *conj.* if; **е. не** unless; **е. то́лько** provided; **е. бы не** but for, if it were not for; **е. бы** (*in exclamations*) if only; **что е. ...?** what if ...?
ест *see* ▶ **есть**[1]
есте́ственно[1] *adv.*
1 naturally.
2 *as particle* naturally, of course.
есте́ственно[2] *as pred.* it is natural.
есте́ствен|ный (~, ~на) *adj.* (*in var. senses*) natural; **~ные нау́ки** natural sciences; **е. отбо́р** (*biol.*) natural selection.
естествозна́ни|е, я *nt.* (natural) science.
есть[1]**, ем, ешь, ест, еди́м, еди́те, едя́т,** *past* **ел, е́ла,** *imper.* **ешь,** *impf.* (*of* ▶ **съ~**)
1 (*принимать пищу*) to eat.
2 (*impf. only*) (*металл*) to corrode, eat away.
3 (*impf. only*) (*о дыме*) to sting, cause to smart.
есть[2]
1 *3rd pers. sg.* (*also, rarely, substituted for all persons*) *pres. of* ▶ **быть.**
2 there is; there are; **у меня́, него́** *etc.*, **е.** I have, he has, *etc.*
е́хать, е́ду, е́дешь *impf.* (*of* ▶ **по~**) (*det. of* ▶ **е́здить**) to go (*in or on a vehicle or on an animal*); to ride, drive; **е. верхо́м** to ride (*on horseback*); **е. по́ездом, на по́езде** to go by train.
ехи́д|ный (~ен, ~на) *adj.* (*coll.*) malicious, spiteful; **~ные замеча́ния** snide remarks, taunts.
ешь *see* ▶ **есть**[1]
ещё *adv.*
1 (*по-прежнему*) still; yet; **е. не, нет е.** not yet; **всё е.** still.
2 (*больше*) some more; any more; yet, further; again; **вам нали́ть е. (вина́** *etc.*)? may I pour you some more (wine, *etc.*)?; **е. оди́н** one more, yet another; **е. раз** once more, again.
3 (*уже*) already; as long ago as, as far back as; **е. в 1900 году́** in 1900 already; as long ago as 1900.
4 (*дополнительно*) else; **кто е. хо́чет ко́фе?** who else wants coffee?; **вы хоти́те е. что-нибу́дь?** do you want anything else?
5 (+ *comp.*) still, yet, even; **е. гро́мче** even louder; **е. и е.** more and more.
6 (+ *prons. and advs.*) *as emph. particle*; **ты не ви́дел кота́? — како́го е. кота́?** have you seen the cat? — what cat, for heaven's sake?

[7] : **е. бы** (*coll.*) (*конечно, безусловно*) yes, rather!; you bet!, of course!
ЕЭС *nt. indecl.* (*abbr. of* **Европе́йское экономи́ческое соо́бщество**) EEC (*European Economic Community*).
е́ю *i. of* ▶ **она́**

Жж

ж = **же**
жа́б|а, ы *f.* (*zool.*) toad.
жа́ворон|ок, ка *m.* (*zool.*) lark; (*fig.*) early riser.
жа́дност|ь, и *f.*
[1] (*к деньгам, еде, действию*) greed (for); greediness.
[2] (*скупость*) avarice, meanness.
жа́д|ный (~ен, ~на́, ~но) *adj.*
[1] (**к** + *d.*; (*coll.*) **до** + *g.*) greedy (for); avid (for).
[2] (*скупой*) avaricious, mean.
жа́жд|а, ы *no pl., f.* thirst; (+ *g.*; *fig.*) thirst, craving (for); **ж. зна́ний** thirst for knowledge.
жа́жд|ать, у *impf.* (+ *g. or inf.*; *fig.*) to thirst (for, after), crave.
жаке́т, а *m.* (*ladies'*) jacket.
жале́|ть, ю *impf.* (*of* ▶ **по~**)
[1] (*чувствовать жалость*) to pity, feel sorry (for).
[2] (**о** + *p. or* + *g.*; **что**) (*сожалеть*) to regret, be sorry (for, about).
[3] (+ *a. or g.*) (*скупиться*) to spare; to grudge; **не ~я сил** not sparing o.s., unsparingly.
жа́л|ить, ю, ишь *impf.* (*of* ▶ **у~**) to sting; to bite.
жа́л|кий (~ок, ~ка́, ~ко) *adj.* pitiful, pathetic, wretched; **име́ть ж. вид** to be a sorry sight.
жа́лк|о¹ *adv. of* ▶ **~ий**
жа́лко² *as pred.* (*impers.*)
[1] (+ *d. and a.*) (*о чувстве сострадания*) to pity, feel sorry (for); **мне ж. бра́та** I feel sorry for my brother.
[2] (*о чувстве грусти*) (it is) a pity, a shame; (+ *d. and g. or a.*) it grieves (me, *etc.*); to regret.
[3] (+ *g. or* + *inf.*) (*скупиться*) to grudge.
жа́л|о, а *nt.* (*пчелы*) sting (*also fig.*).
жа́лоб|а, ы *f.* complaint; **пода́ть ~у (на** + *a.*) to make, lodge a complaint (about).
жа́лоб|ный (~ен, ~на) *adj.* plaintive; mournful.
жа́лованье|е, я *nt.* salary.
жа́л|оваться, уюсь *impf.* (*of* ▶ **по~**) (**на** + *a.*) to complain (of, about).
жа́лост|ь, и *f.* pity, compassion; **из ~и (к** + *d.*) out of pity (for); **кака́я ж.!** what a pity!
жаль *as pred.* (*impers.*)
[1] (+ *d. and a.*) (*о чувстве сострадания*) to pity, feel sorry (for); **мне ж. тебя́** I pity you.
[2] (*о чувстве грусти*) (it is) a pity, a shame; (+ *d.*) it grieves (me, *etc.*); to regret, feel sorry.
[3] (+ *g. or* + *inf.*) (*скупиться*) to grudge; **(мне) ж. де́нег** I begrudge the money.
жалюзи́ *pl. indecl.* Venetian blinds.
жанда́рм, а *m.* gendarme.
жанр, а *m.* genre.
жар, а (у), о ~е, в ~у́ *no pl., m.*
[1] heat; heat of the day; hot place.
[2] (*лихорадка*) fever; (high) temperature.
жар|а́, ы́ *f.* heat; hot weather; **в са́мую ~у́** in the heat of the day.
жарго́н, а *m.* jargon; slang.
жа́реный *adj.* (*на сковороде*) fried; (*в духовке*) roast; (*на решётке*) grilled (*Br.*), broiled (*US*).
жа́р|ить, ю, ишь *impf.* (*pf.* **за~** *or* **из~** *or* **по~**) (*на сковороде*) to fry; (*в духовке*) to roast; (*на решётке*) to grill (*Br.*), broil (*US*).
жа́р|иться, юсь, ишься *impf.*
[1] (*pf.* **за~** *or* **из~**) to roast, fry (*intrans.*).
[2] : **ж. на солнце** (*coll.*) to bask in the sun, sun o.s.
[3] *pass. of* ▶ **~ить**
жа́р|кий (~ок, ~ка́, ~ко) *adj.*
[1] hot; (*тропический*) tropical.
[2] (*fig.*) hot, heated; ardent; passionate; **ж. спор** heated argument.
жа́р|ко¹ *adv. of* ▶ **~кий**
жа́рко² *as pred.* it is hot; **мне,** *etc.*, **ж.** I am, *etc.*, hot.
жарк|о́е, о́го *nt.* (fried) meat.
жаропро́ч|ный (~ен, ~на) *adj.* ovenproof; **~ная кастрю́ля** casserole (dish).
жар-пти́ц|а, ы *f.* (*folklore*) the Firebird.
жа́р|че *comp. of* ▶ **~кий** *and* ▶ **~ко**
жасми́н, а *m.* jasmine.
жа́тв|а, ы *no pl., f.* reaping, harvesting; harvest (*also fig.*).
жа́тк|а, и *f.* harvester, reaping machine.
жать¹, жму, жмёшь *impf.* (*no pf.*)
[1] (*руку*) to press, squeeze; **ж. ру́ку** to shake (s.o.) by the hand.
[2] (*о платье, обуви*) to pinch, be tight; (*impers.*): **в плеча́х жмёт** it is tight on the shoulders.
жать², жну, жнёшь *impf.* (*of* ▶ **с~ 2**) to reap, cut, mow.
жва́чк|а, и *f.* (*coll.*) chewing gum.
жва́чн|ый *adj.* (*zool.*) ruminant; *as n.* **~ое, ~ого** *nt.* ruminant.
жгу, жжёшь, жгут *see* ▶ **жечь**
жгут, а́ *m.*
[1] plait (*Br.*); braid.
[2] (*med.*) tourniquet.
жгу́ч|ий (~, ~а, ~е) *adj.* burning hot (*also fig.*); **~ая боль** smart, smarting pain; **ж. брюне́т** person with jet-black hair and eyes.
ж. д. (*abbr. of* **желе́зная доро́га**) railway

(*Br.*), railroad (*US*).

ждать, жду, ждёшь, *past* **ждал, ждала́, ждало́** *impf.* (+ *g.*)
1 to wait (for); to await; **заста́вить ж.** to keep waiting; **не заста́вить себя́ ж.** to come quickly; **что нас ждёт?** what is in store for us?
2 (*надеяться на, предполагать*) to expect.

же[1] *conj.*
1 (*при противопоставлении*) but; **иди́, е́сли тебе́ охо́та, я же оста́нусь здесь** you go, if you feel like it, but I shall stay here.
2 (*для присоединения*) and; **Ока́ впада́ет в Во́лгу, Во́лга же в Каспи́йское мо́ре** the Oka flows into the Volga, and the Volga flows into the Caspian Sea.
3 (*ведь*) after all; **расскажи́ ей: она́ же твоя́ мать** tell her — she's your mother, after all.

же[2] *emph. particle*: **что же ты де́лаешь?** whatever are you doing, what *are* you doing?

же[3] *particle expr. identity*: **тот же, тако́й же** the same, idem; **тогда́ же** at the same time.

жева́тельн|ый *adj.*: **~ая рези́нка** chewing gum.

жева́ть, жую́, жуёшь *impf.* to chew.

жёг, жгла *see* ▸ **жечь**

жезл, а́ *m.* (*символ власти*) rod, staff (of office); (*милиционера*) baton.

жела́ни|е, я *nt.*
1 (+ *g.*) wish (for), desire (for); **при всём ~и** with the best will in the world.
2 (*просьба*) request.
3 (*вожделение*) desire, lust.

жела́|нный *p.p.p. of* ▸ **~ть** *and adj.* wished for, longed for, desired, beloved; **ж. гость** welcome visitor.

жела́тельно[1] *adv.* preferably.

жела́тельно[2] *as pred.* it is desirable; it is advisable, preferable.

жела́тел|ьный (~ен, ~ьна) *adj.* desirable; advisable.

жела́|ть, ю *impf.* (*of* ▸ **по~**)
1 (+ *g.*) to wish (for), desire.
2 (**что́бы** *or* + *inf.*) to wish, want.
3 (+ *d. and g. or inf.*) to wish (*s.o. sth.*); **~ю вам успе́ха/уда́чи** good luck!; **э́то оставля́ет ж. лу́чшего** it leaves much to be desired.

жела́|ющий *pres. part. act. of* ▸ **~ть; ~ющие** persons interested, those who so desire.

желе́ *nt. indecl.* jelly.

желез|а́, ы́, *pl.* **же́лезы, желёз, ~а́м** *f.* (*anat.*) gland; (*pl.*) (*coll.*) tonsils.

железнодоро́жник, а *m.* railway worker.

железнодоро́жный *adj.* rail, railway, railroad (*US*); **ж. путь** (railway) track; **ж. у́зел** (railway) junction.

желе́зн|ый *adj.*
1 iron (*also fig.*); (*chem.*) ferric, ferrous; **ж. век** the Iron Age; **ж. за́навес** the 'Iron Curtain'.
2: **~ая доро́га** railway (*Br.*), railroad (*US*); **по ~ой доро́ге** by rail.

желе́з|о, а *nt.* iron.

железобето́н, а *m.* (*tech.*) reinforced concrete, ferroconcrete.

жёлоб, а, *pl.* **~а́, ~о́в** *m.* (*водосточный*) gutter; (*для ссыпания чего-л.*) chute.

желте́|ть, ю *impf.* (*pf.* ▸ **по~**) (*становиться жёлтым*) to turn yellow.

желт|о́к, ка́ *m.* yolk.

желту́х|а, и *f.* (*med.*) jaundice.

жёлт|ый (~, ~а́, ~о) *adj.* yellow; **~ая пре́сса** the yellow press, the tabloids; **Жёлтые страни́цы** Yellow Pages (*propr.*).

желу́д|ок, ка *m.* stomach; **несваре́ние ~ка** indigestion.

желу́дочный *adj.* stomach; gastric; **ж. сок** gastric juice.

жёлуд|ь, я, *g. pl.* **~е́й** *m.* acorn.

жёлч|ь (*coll.* **желчь**), **и** *no pl.*, *f.* bile, gall (*also fig.*).

жема́н|ный (~ен, ~на) *adj.* affected.

же́мчуг, а, *pl.* **~а́** *m.* (*collect.*) pearl(s).

жемчу́жин|а, ы *f.* pearl (*also fig.*).

жемчу́жн|ый *adj. of* ▸ **же́мчуг;** (*fig.*) pearly(-white); **~ое ожере́лье** pearl necklace.

жен|а́, ы́, *pl.* **~́ы, ~́, ~́ам** *f.* wife; **быть у ~ы́ под каблуко́м** to be henpecked.

жена́т|ый (~) *adj.* married; **ж.** (**на** + *p.*) (*о мужчине*) married (to).

жени́тьб|а, ы *f.* marriage.

жен|и́ться, ю́сь, ~́ишься *impf. and pf.* (**на** + *p.*) (*о мужчине*) to marry, get married (to).

жени́х, а́ *m.*
1 fiancé.
2 (*на свадьбе*) bridegroom.

женоподо́б|ный (~ен, ~на) *adj.* effeminate.

же́нский *adj.* woman's; female; feminine.

же́нствен|ный (~ and ~ен, ~на) *adj.* feminine, womanly.

же́нщин|а, ы *f.* woman.

женьше́н|ь, я *m.* (*bot., med.*) ginseng.

жереб|ёнок, ёнка, *pl.* **~я́та, ~я́т** *m.* foal, colt.

жереб|е́ц, ца́ *m.* stallion.

жеребьёвк|а, и *f.* casting of lots; (*sport*) draw (*for play-off*).

жёрнов, а, *pl.* **~а́, ~о́в** *m.* millstone.

же́ртв|а, ы *f.*
1 sacrifice (*also fig.*); **принести́ ~у** (+ *d.*) to make a sacrifice (to); **принести́ в ~у** to sacrifice.
2 (*пострадавший*) victim; **пасть ~ой** (+ *g.*) to fall victim (to).

же́ртв|овать, ую, *impf.* (*of* ▸ **по~**)
1 (*дарить*) to make a donation (of), present.
2 (+ *i.*) (*подвергать опасности*) to sacrifice, give up.

жертвоприноше́ни|е, я *nt.* sacrifice.

жест, а *m.* gesture (*also fig.*).

жестикули́р|овать, ую *impf.* to gesticulate.

жестикуля́ци|я, и *f.* gesticulation.

жёст|кий (~ок, ~ка́, ~ко) *adj.* hard; tough; (*fig.*) rigid, strict; **ж. диск** (*comput.*) hard disk.

жёст|ко[1] *adv. of* ▸ **~кий**

жёстко[2] *as pred.* it is hard.
жесто́к|ий (~, ~а) *adj.* cruel; brutal; (*fig.*) severe, sharp.
жесто́кост|ь, и *f.* cruelty, brutality.
жёст|че *comp. of* ▶ **~кий** *and* ▶ **~ко**
жест|ь, и *f.* tinplate.
жест|яно́й *adj. of* ▶ **~ь; ~яна́я посу́да** tinware.
жестя́нщик, а *m.* tinman, tinsmith.
жето́н, а *m.*
1 (*награда*) medal; (*опознавательный знак*) badge (*of police officer, porter, etc.*).
2 (*средство оплаты*) token.
жечь, жгу, жжёшь, жгут, *past* **жёг, жгла** *impf.*
1 (*pf.* **с~**) to burn; (*дотла*) to burn down.
2 (*impf. only*) to burn, sting; (*impers.*): **от э́того ликёра жжёт в го́рле** this liqueur burns one's throat.
же́чься, жгусь, жжёшься, жгу́тся, *past* **жёгся, жглась** *impf.* to burn, sting (*intrans.*).
жжёшь *see* ▶ **жечь**
жи́во *adv.*
1 (*ярко*) vividly.
2 (*оживлённо*) with animation.
3 (*остро*) keenly.
4 (*coll.*) (*быстро*) quickly, promptly.
жив|о́й (~, ~а́, ~́о) *adj.*
1 (*обладающий жизнью*) living, live, alive; **оста́ться в ~ы́х** to survive.
2 (*энергичный*) lively; keen; active.
3 (*выразительный*) lively, vivacious; bright; **~ы́е глаза́** bright eyes.
4 (*без предварительной записи*) live; **~а́я му́зыка** live music; **ж. эфи́р** live broadcast.
живопи́с|ец, ца *m.* painter.
живопи́с|ный (~ен, ~на) *adj.*
1 (*относящийся к живописи*) pictorial.
2 (*красивый*) picturesque (*also fig.*); **~ное ме́сто** beauty spot.
жи́вопис|ь, и *f.*
1 painting.
2 (*collect.*) paintings.
жи́вост|ь, и *f.* liveliness, vivacity; animation.
живо́т, а *m.* abdomen, belly; stomach; (*coll.*) tummy.
животново́дств|о, а *nt.* stockbreeding, animal husbandry.
живо́тно|е, го *nt.* animal; **дома́шнее ж.** pet.
живо́тный *adj.*
1 animal.
2 (*грубый*) bestial, brute.
живу́ч|ий (~, ~а) *adj.*
1 tenacious of life; (*bot.*) hardy; **он ~ как ко́шка** he has nine lives like a cat.
2 (*fig.*) (*обычай*) deep-rooted, enduring.
живьём *adv.* (*coll.*) alive; **петь ж.** to sing live; **постара́йтесь взять его́ ж.** try to catch him alive.
жи́голо *m. indecl.* gigolo.
жи́д|кий (~ок, ~ка́, ~ко) *adj.*
1 (*имеющий свойство течь*) liquid; fluid.
2 (*водянистый*) watery; weak, thin; **ж. суп** thin soup.
3 (*о волосах*) sparse, scanty; **~кая борода́** straggly beard.
жидкокристалли́ческий *adj.*: **ж. диспле́й** liquid crystal display (*abbr.* LCD).
жи́дкост|ь, и *f.* liquid; fluid.
жи́ж|а, и *no pl., f.* liquid; swill; slush.
жи́|же *comp. of* ▶ **~дкий**
жизнедея́тельност|ь, и *f.* (*biol.*) vital activity.
жи́знен|ный (~, ~на) *adj.*
1 (of) life; (*biol.*) vital; **ж. у́ровень** standard of living.
2 (*близкий к жизни, реальный*) close to life; lifelike.
3 (*fig.*) vital, vitally important.
жизнеобеспе́чени|е, я *nt.*: **систе́ма ~я** life-support system.
жизнеописа́ни|е, я *nt.* biography.
жизнера́дост|ный (~ен, ~на) *adj.* cheerful; vivacious.
жизнеспосо́б|ный (~ен, ~на) *adj.* capable of living; (*biol.*) viable; (*fig.*) vigorous, flourishing.
жизн|ь, и *f.* life; (*существование*) existence; **зараба́тывать на ж.** to earn one's living; **как ж.?** (*coll.*) how is life?; **лиши́ть себя́ ~́и** to take one's life; **о́браз ~́и** way of life; lifestyle.
жи́л|а, ы *f.*
1 (*сухожилие*) tendon, sinew; (*coll.*) (*кровеносный сосуд*) vein.
2 (*min.*) vein.
жиле́т, а *m.* waistcoat (*Br.*), vest (*US*); **спаса́тельный ж.** life jacket.
жил|е́ц, ьца́ *m.* tenant.
жи́лист|ый (~, ~а) *adj.*
1 (*руки*) having prominent veins.
2 (*тело*) sinewy; (*старик*) wiry; **~ое мя́со** stringy meat.
жили́щ|е, а *nt.* dwelling, abode, (living) quarters.
жили́щ|ный *adj. of* ▶ **~е; ~ные усло́вия** housing conditions.
жил|о́й *adj.*
1 dwelling; residential; **ж. дом** dwelling house, block of flats; **ж. кварта́л** residential area; **~а́я пло́щадь = жилпло́щадь.**
2 (*обитаемый*) inhabited.
жилпло́щад|ь, и *f.* housing, accommodation.
жиль|ё, я́ *nt.*
1 (*селение*) habitation; dwelling.
2 (*жилище*) lodging; (living) accommodation.
жи́молост|ь, и *f.* (*bot.*) honeysuckle.
жир, а (у), о ~́е, в ~у́, *pl.* **~ы́** *m.* fat; grease.
жира́ф, а *m.* giraffe.
жи́р|ный (~ен, ~на́, ~но) *adj.*
1 (*пища, мясо*) fatty; (*руки, волосы*) greasy.
2 (*человек*) fat, plump.
3 (*земля*) rich.
4 (*typ.*) bold.
жиров|о́й *adj.* fatty, aliphatic; (*anat.*) adipose; **~а́я ткань** adipose tissue.
жите́йск|ий *adj.*
1 worldly; of life; **~ая му́дрость** worldly wisdom;
2 (*обыденный*) everyday.
жи́тел|ь, я *m.* inhabitant; dweller; **ми́рные ~и** civilians.

жи́тель|ница, ницы *f. of* ▶ **~**
жи́тельств|о, а *nt.* residence; **вид на ж.** residence permit.
жить, живу́, живёшь, *past* **жил, жила́, жи́ло (не́ жил, не жила́, не́ жило)** *impf.*
[1] to live; **ж. в Москве́** to live in Moscow.
[2] (+ *i. or* **на** + *a.*) to live (on); (+ *i.*; *fig.*) to live (in, for); **нам не́ на что ж.** we have nothing to live on.
жи́ться, живётся, *past* **жило́сь** *impf.* (*impers.*, + *d.*; *coll.*) to live, get on; **ей ве́село живётся** she enjoys her life.
ЖК-диспле́|й, я (*abbr. of* **жидкокристалли́ческий диспле́й**) liquid-crystal display.
жму, жмёшь *see* ▶ **жать[1]**
жму́р|ки, ок *no sg.* blind man's buff.
жнец, а́ *m.* reaper.
жни́ц|а, ы *f. of* ▶ **жнец**
жну, жнёшь *see* ▶ **жать[2]**
жоке́|й, я *m.* jockey.
жongли́р|овать, ую *impf.* (+ *i.*) to juggle (with) (*also fig.*).
жо́п|а, ы *f.* (*vulg.*) arse (*Br.*), ass (*US*); **иди́** *or* **пошёл ты в ~у!** piss off!; **пья́ный в ~у** pissed as a newt (*Br.*), pissed off (*US*).
жр|ать, у́, ёшь, *past* **~а́л, ~ала́, ~а́ло** *impf.* (*of* ▶ **со~**)
[1] (*о живо́тных*) to eat.
[2] (*sl.*) (*о челове́ке*) to guzzle, gobble.
жре́би|й, я *m.*
[1] lot; **броса́ть ж.** to cast lots; **тяну́ть ж.** to draw lots.
[2] (*fig.*) lot, fate, destiny; **ж. бро́шен** the die is cast.
жрец, а́ *m.* (*pagan*) priest; (*fig.*) devotee.
жри́ц|а, ы *f.* priestess.
жу́желиц|а, ы *f.* (*zool.*) ground beetle.
жужжа́ни|е, я *nt.* hum, buzz, drone; humming, buzzing, droning.
жужж|а́ть, у́, и́шь *impf.* to hum, buzz, drone; (*о пу́лях*) to whizz.
жук, а́ *m.*
[1] beetle; **ма́йский ж.** May bug, cockchafer.
[2] (*coll.*) (*плут*) rogue, swindler.
жу́лик, а *m.* petty thief; cheat, swindler.
жура́вл|ь, я́ *m.* (*zool.*) crane.
журна́л, а *m.*
[1] (*периоди́ческое изда́ние*) magazine; periodical; journal.
[2] (*кни́га для за́писи*) journal, diary; (*кла́ссный*) register.
журнали́ст, а *m.* journalist.
журнали́стик|а, и *f.* journalism.
журч|а́ть, и́т *impf.* to babble, murmur (*of water; also fig., poet.*).
жу́т|кий (~ок, ~ка́, ~ко) *adj.* terrible, terrifying; awe-inspiring, eerie.
жу́тко[1] *adv.* terrifyingly; (*coll.*) terribly, awfully.
жу́тко[2] *as pred.* **ж. поду́мать об э́том** it's terrible to think about it; (*impers.*, + *d.*): **мне,** *etc.*, **ж.** I, *etc.*, am terrified.
жут|ь, и *f.* (*coll.*)
[1] (*страх*) terror; awe.
[2] *as pred.*: **~!** it is terrible!
жуч|о́к, ка́ *m.*
[1] *dim. of* ▶ **жук 1.**
[2] (*coll.*) (*про́бка*) makeshift fuse.
[3] (*coll.*) (*подслу́шивающее устро́йство*) bug.
жу|ю́, ёшь *see* ▶ **жева́ть**
ЖЭК, а *or* **жэк, а** *m.* (*abbr. of* **жили́щно-эксплуатацио́нная конто́ра**) housing office.
жюри́ *indecl. nt.* (*collect.*) judges (*of competition, etc.*).

Зз

за *prep.* **I.** + *a. and i.* (+ *a.*: *indicates motion or action*; + *i.*: *indicates rest or state*).
[1] (*позади́*) behind; **за крова́ть, за крова́тью** behind the bed.
[2] (*вне*) beyond; across, the other side of; **за́ борт, за бо́ртом** overboard; **за́ угол, за угло́м** round the corner; **за́ городом** out of town.
[3] (*у*) at; **сесть за роя́ль** to sit down at the piano.
[4] (*занима́ясь да́нным предме́том*) at, to (*or translated by part.*); **приня́ться за рабо́ту** get down to work; **заста́ть кого́-н. за рабо́той** to find s.o. at work, working; **проводи́ть всё своё вре́мя за чте́нием** to spend all one's time reading.
[5]: **вы́йти за́муж за** (+ *a.*) to marry (*of a woman*); **(быть) за́мужем за** (+ *i.*) (to be) married (to).
■ **II.** + *a.*
[1] (*свы́ше*) after (*of time*); over (*of age*); **далеко́ за́ полночь** long after midnight; **ему́ уже́ за со́рок** he is already over forty.
[2] (*на расстоя́нии*): **самолёт разби́лся за ми́лю от дере́вни** the aeroplane crashed a mile from the village; **за час** an hour before, an hour early.
[3] (*в тече́ние*) during, in the space of; **за́ ночь** during the night, overnight; **за су́тки** in (the space of) twenty-four hours.
[4] (*ука́зывает на предме́т, кото́рый охва́тывается*) by; **вести́ за́ руку** to lead by the hand.
[5] (*in var. senses*) for; **плати́ть за биле́т** to pay for a ticket; **подписа́ть за дире́ктора** to sign for the director; **боя́ться, ра́доваться за кого́-н.** to fear, be glad for s.o.
■ **III.** + *i.*
[1] (*по́сле*) after; **друг за дру́гом** one after

another; **год за го́дом** year after year; **сле́довать за кем-н.** to follow s.o.
2 (*заботясь*) after; **следи́ть за детьми́** to look after children.
3 (*чтобы достать, получить*) for; **идти́ за молоко́м** to go for milk; **зайти́ за кем-н.** to call for s.o.
4 (*во время*) at, during; **за за́втраком** at breakfast.
5 (*по причине*) for, on account of, because of; **за неиме́нием** (+ *g.*) for want of.
6 (+ *prons.*) (*указывает на ответственного должника*): **за тобо́й пять рубле́й** you are owing five roubles.
■ **IV.** *as pred.* (*согласен*) for, in favour (*Br.*), favor (*US*).

за... *pref.* **I.** (*of vv.*)
1 *indicates commencement of action*: **заля́ять** to start barking.
2 *indicates direction of action beyond given point*: **заверну́ть за́ угол** to turn a corner.
3 *indicates continuation of action to excess*: **закорми́ть** to overfeed.
4 *forms pf. aspect of some vv.*
■ **II.** (*of nn. and adjs.*) trans-; **Закавка́зье** Transcaucasia.

3

заба́в|а, ы *f.*
1 (*игра*) game; (*развлечение*) pastime.
2 (*потеха*) amusement, fun; **он э́то сде́лал для ~ы** he did it for fun.

заба́вн|о[1] *adv. of* ▸ **~ый**

заба́вно[2] *as pred.* it is amusing, funny; **(мне) з.** I find it amusing, funny; **з.!** how funny!

заба́в|ный (~ен, ~на) *adj.* amusing; funny.

забасто́вк|а, и *f.* strike; **всео́бщая з.** general strike; **голо́дная з.** hunger strike.

забасто́вщик, а *m.* striker.

забасто́вщи|ца, цы *f. of* ▸ **~к**

забве́ни|е, я *nt.* oblivion; **преда́ть ~ю** to consign to oblivion.

забе́г, а *m.* (*sport*) race.

забега́ловк|а, и *f.* (*coll.*) snack bar.

забега́|ть, ю *impf. of* ▸ **забежа́ть**

забе́га|ть, ю *pf.*
1 (*начать бегать*) to start running.
2 (*о глазах*) to become shifty.

забе|жа́ть, гу́, жи́шь, гу́т *pf.* (*of* ▸ **~га́ть**)
1 (**в** + *a.*) to run in(to).
2 (**к** + *d.*; *coll.*) to drop in (to see).
3 (*далеко*) to run off; (*неизвестно куда*) to stray.
4 : **з. вперёд** to run ahead; (*fig., coll.*) to rush ahead.

забеле́|ть, ет *pf.*
1 (*начать белеть*) to begin to turn white.
2 (*показаться*) to appear white (in the distance).

забере́мене|ть, ю *pf.* (*of* ▸ **бере́менеть**) to become pregnant.

забеспоко́|иться, юсь, ишься *pf.* to begin to worry.

забива́|ть, ю *impf. of* ▸ **заби́ть**[1]

забива́|ться, юсь *impf. of* ▸ **заби́ться**

забинт|ова́ть, у́ю *pf.* (*of* ▸ **~о́вывать**) to bandage.

забинто́выва|ть, ю *impf. of* ▸ **забинтова́ть**

забира́ть(ся), ю(сь) *impf. of* ▸ **забра́ть(ся)**

заб|и́ть[1]**, ью́, ьёшь** *pf.* (*of* ▸ **~ива́ть**)
1 (*вбить*) to drive in, hammer in, ram in.
2 (*sport*) to score; **з. мяч** to kick the ball into the goal.
3 (*заделать*) to seal, block up.
4 (*закрыть проход*) to obstruct.
5 (+ *i.*; *coll.*) (*наполнить*) to cram, stuff (with).
6 (*избить*) to beat up; **з. до́ смерти** to beat to death; (*fig.*) to render defenceless (*Br.*), defenseless (*US*).
7 (*убить*) to slaughter (*cattle*).

заб|и́ть[2]**, ью́, ьёшь** *pf.* (*in var. senses; trans. and intrans.*) to begin to beat (*in some cases forms pf. aspect of* ▸ **бить**).

заб|и́ться, ью́сь, ьёшься *pf.* (*of* ▸ **~ива́ться**)
1 (**в** + *a.*) (*спрятаться*) to hide (in), take refuge (in).
2 (**в** + *a.*) (*проникнуть*) to get (into), penetrate.
3 (+ *i.*) (*засоряться*) to become cluttered (with), clogged (with).

заблаговре́менно *adv.* in good time; well in advance.

забле|сте́ть, щу́, сти́шь *pf.* to begin to shine, glitter, glow.

заблу|ди́ться, жу́сь, ~дишься *pf.* to lose one's way, get lost.

заблужда́|ться, юсь *impf.* to be mistaken.

заблужде́ни|е, я *nt.* error; delusion; **ввести́ в з.** to delude, mislead.

забо́|й, я *m.* (*mining*) (pit-)face.

заболева́ни|е, я *nt.* sickness, illness.

заболева́|ть[1]**, ю** *impf. of* ▸ **заболе́ть**[1]

заболева́|ть[2]**, ет** *impf. of* ▸ **заболе́ть**[2]

заболе́|ть[1]**, ю, ешь** *pf.* (*of* ▸ **~ва́ть**[1]) (*заразиться*) to fall ill, fall sick; (+ *i.*) to be taken ill (with), go down (with).

забол|е́ть[2]**, и́т** *pf.* (*of* ▸ **~ева́ть**[2]) (*о появившейся боли*) to (begin to) ache, hurt; **у меня́ ~е́л зуб** my tooth has started to ache.

забо́р, а *m.* fence.

забо́т|а, ы *f.*
1 (*беспокойство*) care(s), trouble(s); **без ~** carefree.
2 (*уход*) care, attention(s); concern.

забо́|титься, чусь, тишься *impf.* (*of* ▸ **по~**) (**о** + *p.*)
1 (*беспокоиться*) to worry, be troubled (about).
2 (*ухаживать*) to take care (of); to take trouble (about); to care (about).

забо́тлив|ый (~, ~а) *adj.* solicitous, thoughtful; caring.

забрако́в|анный *p.p.p. of* ▸ **~а́ть; з. това́р** rejects.

забрак|ова́ть, у́ю *pf. of* ▸ **бракова́ть**

забра́л|о, а *nt.* visor.

забра́сыва|ть, ю *impf. of* ▸ **заброса́ть** *and* ▸ **забро́сить**

забра́|ть, заберу́, заберёшь, *past* **~л, ~ла́, ~ло** *pf.* (*of* ▸ **забира́ть**)

[1] (*взять*) to take (*in one's hands*); (*человека*) to take (with one); **з. с собо́й ве́щи** to take one's things with one.
[2] (*арестовать*) to arrest; (*отнять*) to take away; to seize, appropriate.

забра́|ться, заберу́сь, заберёшься, *past* **~лся, ~ла́сь, ~ло́сь** *pf.* (*of* ▸ **забира́ться**)
[1] (**в** + *a.*) to get (into); (**в, на** + *a.*) to climb (into, on to).
[2] (*уйти, уехать*) to get to; (*спрятаться*) to hide out, go into hiding.

заброни́р|овать, ую *pf.* (*of* ▸ **брони́ровать**) to reserve.

заброса́|ть, ю *pf.* (*of* ▸ **забра́сывать**) (+ *a.* and *i.*) (*заполнить*) to fill (up) (with).

забро́|сить, шу, сишь *pf.* (*of* ▸ **забра́сывать**)
[1] (*метнуть*) to throw (*with force or to a distance*).
[2] (*оставить*) to throw up, give up, abandon; to neglect, let go; **з. дете́й** to neglect children.
[3] (*доставить в определённое место*) to take, bring.

забро́|шенный *p.p.p. of* ▸ **~сить** *and adj.*
[1] (*сад, человек*) neglected.
[2] (*место*) deserted, desolate.

забры́зг|ать, аю *pf.* (+ *i.*) to splash (with).

заб|у́ду, у́дешь *see* ▸ **~ы́ть**

забыва́|ть(ся), ю(сь) *impf. of* ▸ **забы́ть(ся)**

забы́вчив|ый (~, ~а) *adj.* forgetful; absent-minded.

заб|ы́ть, у́ду, у́дешь *pf.* (*of* ▸ **~ыва́ть**)
[1] (+ *a. or* **о** + *p. or inf.*) to forget.
[2] (*случайно оставить*) to leave behind, forget (to bring).

заб|ы́ться, у́дусь, у́дешься *pf.* (*of* ▸ **~ыва́ться**)
[1] (*задремать*) to doze off, drop off.
[2] (*замечтаться*) to sink into a reverie.
[3] (*coll.*) (*выйти из границ приличия*) to forget o.s.

зава́л, а *m.* obstruction, blockage.

зава́лива|ть(ся), ю(сь) *impf. of* ▸ **завали́ть(ся)**

завал|и́ть, ю́, ~́ишь *pf.* (*of* ▸ **~́ивать**)
[1] (*загромоздить*) to block up, obstruct; to fill (*so as to block up*); **з. вход мешка́ми с песко́м** to block up the entrance with sandbags.
[2] (+ *i.*; *coll.*) (*заполнить*) to pile (with); to fill cram-full (with); (*fig.*) (*переобременить*) to overload with; **реда́кция ~́ена рабо́той** the editors are snowed under with work.

завал|и́ться, ю́сь, ~́ишься *pf.* (*of* ▸ **~́иваться**)
[1] (*упасть*) to fall; to collapse; **нож ~и́лся за шкаф** the knife has fallen behind the cupboard.
[2] (*coll.*) (*лечь*) to lie down; **з. спать** to fall into bed.
[3] (*coll.*) (*опрокинуться*) to overturn, tip up.

зава́рива|ть(ся), ет(ся) *impf. of* ▸ **завари́ть(ся)**

завар|и́ть, ю́, ~́ишь *pf.* (*of* ▸ **~́ивать**) to make (*drinks, etc., by pouring on boiling water*); **з. чай** to brew tea.

завар|и́ться, ю́, ~́ится *pf.* (*of* ▸ **~́иваться**) (*о напитках*) to brew.

зава́рк|а, и *f.*
[1] (*действие*) brewing (*of tea, etc.*).
[2] (*coll.*) (*сухой чай*) enough tea for one brew; (*заваренный чай*) brew.

заведе́ни|е, я *nt.* establishment, institution.

заве́д|овать, ую *impf.* (+ *i.*) to manage, superintend; to be in charge (of).

заве́домо *adv.* wittingly; (+ *adj.*) known to be; **з. зна́я** being fully aware.

заве|ду́, дёшь *see* ▸ **~сти́**

заве́дующ|ий, его *m.* (+ *i.*) manager (of); head (of); person in charge (of); **з. отде́лом** head of a department.

завез|ти́, у́, ёшь, *past* **~́, ~ла́** *pf.* (*of* ▸ **завози́ть**)
[1] (*привезти*) to deliver, drop off; **з. запи́ску по доро́ге домо́й** to deliver a note on the way home.
[2] (*увезти*) to take (to a distance *or* out of one's way).

заверб|ова́ть, у́ю *pf. of* ▸ **вербова́ть**

заве́р|ить, ю, ишь *pf.* (*of* ▸ **~я́ть**)
[1] (**в** + *p.*) (*убедить*) to assure (of).
[2] (*удостоверить*) to certify; **з. по́дпись** to witness a signature.

заверн|у́ть, у́, ёшь *pf.* (*of* ▸ **завора́чивать**)
[1] (**в** + *a.*) (*обернуть*) to wrap (in).
[2] (*загнуть*) to tuck up, roll up (*sleeve, etc.*).
[3] (*свернуть в сторону*) to turn (*intrans.*); **з. напра́во** to turn to the right.
[4] (*завинтить*) to screw tight; (*закрыть*) to turn off (*by screwing*); **з. кран** to turn off a tap.

заверн|у́ться, у́сь, ёшься *pf.* (*of* ▸ **завора́чиваться**)
[1] (**в** + *a.*) to wrap o.s. up (in), muffle o.s. (in).
[2] *pass. of* ▸ **~у́ть**

заверш|а́ть, а́ю *impf. of* ▸ **~и́ть**

заверше́ни|е, я *nt.* completion; end; **в з.** in conclusion.

заверш|и́ть, у́, и́шь *pf.* (*of* ▸ **~а́ть**) to complete, conclude, crown.

завер|я́ть, я́ю *impf. of* ▸ **~́ить**

заве́с|а, ы *f.* (*fig.*) veil, screen; **дымова́я з.** (*mil.*) smokescreen.

заве́|сить, шу, сишь *pf.* (*of* ▸ **~шивать**) to curtain (off).

заве|сти́, ду́, дёшь, *past* **~́л, ~ла́** *pf.* (*of* ▸ **заводи́ть**)
[1] (*привести*) to take, bring (*to a place*); to leave, drop off (*at a place*).
[2] (*увести*) to take (to a distance *or* out of one's way).
[3] (*основать*) to set up; to start; **з. семью́** to start a family.
[4] (*приобрести*) to acquire.
[5] (*ввести*) to institute, introduce (*as a custom*); **з. привы́чку** (+ *inf.*) to get into the habit (of).
[6] (*часы*) to wind (up); (*машину*) to start; **з. мото́р** to start an engine.

заве|сти́сь, ду́сь, дёшься, *past* **~́лся, ~ла́сь** *pf.* (*of* ▸ **заводи́ться**)
[1] (*появиться*) to be; to appear; **в по́гребе ~ли́сь кры́сы** there are rats in the cellar.

2 (*о механизме*) to start (*intrans.*).
заве́т, а *m.* : **Ве́тхий, Но́вый з.** the Old, the New Testament.
заве́тный *adj.* (*мечты*) cherished.
заве́шива|ть, ю *impf. of* ▸ **заве́сить**
завеща́ни|е, я *nt.* will, testament.
завеща́|ть, ю *impf. and pf.* (+ *a. and d.*) to leave (to), bequeath (to); (+ *d.* + *inf.*) (*поручить*) to instruct.
завива́|ть(ся), ю(сь) *impf. of* ▸ **зави́ть(ся)**
зави́дно *as pred.* (*impers.*, + *d.*) to feel envious; **мне з.** I feel envious.
зави́д|ный (~ен, ~на) *adj.* enviable.
зави́д|овать, ую *impf.* (*of* ▸ **по~**) (+ *d.*) to envy; be jealous of.
завизж|а́ть, у́, и́шь *pf.* to begin to scream, squeal.
завин|ти́ть, чу́, ти́шь *pf.* (*of* ▸ **~чивать**) to screw up.
зави́нчива|ть, ю *impf. of* ▸ **завинти́ть**
зав|иса́ть, иса́ет *impf. of* ▸ **~и́снуть**
зависа́|ть, ю *impf. of* ▸ **зави́снуть**
зави́|сеть, шу, сишь *impf.* (**от** + *g.*) to depend (on).
зави́симост|ь, и *f.* dependence; **з. от нарко́тиков** dependence on drugs, drug dependence; **в ~и** (**от** + *g.*) depending (on), subject (to).
зави́сим|ый (~, ~а) *adj.* (**от** + *g.*) dependent (on).
зави́сн|уть, ет *pf.* (*of* ▸ **зависа́ть**) (*comput.*) to crash.
зави́с|нуть, ну, нешь, *past* **~, ~ла** *pf.* (*of* ▸ **~а́ть**)
1 (*о вертолёте и т. д.*) to hover, hang (in the air).
2 (*comput.*) to crash.
3 (*coll.*) (*о вопросе, ситуации*) to be in limbo, unresolved, up in the air.
зави́стлив|ый (~, ~а) *adj.* envious.
за́вист|ь, и *f.* envy; jealousy.
завит|о́к, ка́ *m.*
1 (*локон*) curl, lock.
2 (*почерка*) flourish.
зав|и́ть, ью́, ьёшь, *past* **~и́л, ~ила́, ~и́ло** *pf.* (*of* ▸ **~ива́ть**) to curl, to wave, to twist, wind.
зав|и́ться, ью́сь, ьёшься, *past* **~и́лся, ~ила́сь, ~и́ло́сь** *pf.* (*of* ▸ **~ива́ться**)
1 (*виться*) to curl, wave, twine (*intrans.*).
2 (*завить себе волосы*) to curl, wave one's hair; (*у парикмахера*) to have one's hair curled, waved.
завладева́|ть, ю *impf. of* ▸ **завладе́ть**
завладе́|ть, ю *pf.* (*of* ▸ **~ва́ть**) (+ *i.*) to take possession (of); to seize, capture (*also fig.*); **он ~л внима́нием слу́шателей** he captured the audience's attention.
завлека́|ть, ю *impf. of* ▸ **завле́чь**
завле́|чь, ку́, чёшь, ку́т, *past* **~̈к, ~кла́** *pf.* (*of* ▸ **~ка́ть**)
1 (*заманить*) to lure, entice.
2 (*соблазнить*) to fascinate, captivate.
заво́д¹, а *m.*
1 factory, mill; works.
2 (**ко́нный**) **з.** stud (farm).
заво́д², а *m.* (*у часов*) winding mechanism; **игру́шка с ~ом** clockwork toy.
заво|ди́ть, жу́, ~́дишь *impf. of* ▸ **завести́**
завод|и́ться, ~́ится *impf. of* ▸ **завести́сь**
заводско́й *adj. of* ▸ **заво́д¹**
завоева́ни|е, я *nt.*
1 (*действие*) conquest; winning.
2 (*захваченная территория*) conquest; (*fig.*) (*достижение*) achievement.
завоева́тел|ь, я *m.* conqueror.
заво|ева́ть, ю́ю, ю́ешь *pf.* (*of* ▸ **~ёвывать**) to conquer; (*fig.*) to win, gain; **з. симпа́тии** to gain sympathy.
завоёвыва|ть, ю *impf. of* ▸ **завоева́ть;** to try to get.
заво|зи́ть, жу́, ~́зишь *impf. of* ▸ **завезти́**
завола́кива|ть(ся), ю, ет(ся) *impf. of* ▸ **заволо́чь(ся)**
заволн|ова́ться, у́юсь *pf.* to become agitated.
заволо́|чь, ку́, чёшь, ку́т, *past* **~к, ~кла́** *pf.* (*of* ▸ **завола́кивать**) to cloud; to obscure; **тума́н ~к со́лнце** the sun was obscured by fog; **её глаза́ ~кло́ слеза́ми** her eyes were clouded with tears.
заволо́|чься, чётся, ку́тся, *past* **~кся, ~кла́сь** *pf.* (*of* ▸ **завола́киваться**) to cloud over, become clouded.
завоп|и́ть, лю́, и́шь *pf.* (*coll.*) to cry out, yell; to give a cry.
завора́чива|ть(ся), ю(сь) *impf. of* ▸ **заверну́ть(ся)**
за́втра *adv.* tomorrow; **до з.!** see you tomorrow!
за́втрак, а *m.* breakfast; **второ́й з.** elevenses, mid-morning snack.
за́втрака|ть, ю *impf.* (*of* ▸ **по~**) to (have) breakfast; (*среди дня*) to (have) lunch.
за́втрашний *adj.* tomorrow's; **з. день** tomorrow.
за́вуч, а *m.* (*abbr. of* **заве́дующий уче́бной ча́стью**) director of studies.
завхо́з, а *m.* (*abbr. of* **заве́дующий хозя́йством**) bursar, steward.
завыва́|ть, ю *impf.* to howl.
завы́|сить, шу, сишь *pf.* (*of* ▸ **~ша́ть**) to raise too high; **з. отме́тку на экза́мене** to give too high a mark in an examination.
зав|ы́ть, о́ю, о́ешь *pf.* to begin to howl.
завыша́|ть, ю *impf. of* ▸ **завы́сить**
завя|за́ть¹, жу́, ~́шешь *pf.* (*of* ▸ **~́зывать**)
1 (*узел, шнурки*) to tie; (*пакет*) to tie up; (*галстук*) to knot.
2 (*палец*) to bind (up).
3 (*fig.*) (*начать*) to start; **з. разгово́р** to strike up a conversation.
завяза́|ть², ю *impf. of* ▸ **завя́знуть**
завя|за́ться, ~́жется *pf.* (*of* ▸ **~́зываться**)
1 *pass. of* ▸ **~за́ть.**
2 (*начаться*) to start; to arise.
завя́з|нуть, ну, нешь, *past* **~, ~ла** *pf.*

(*of* ▸ ~а́ть²) to stick, get stuck.
завя́зыва|ть(ся), ет(ся) *impf. of* ▸ **завяза́ть(ся)**
завя́|нуть, ну, нешь, *past* ~л *pf. of* ▸ **вя́нуть**
загад|а́ть, а́ю *pf.* (*of* ▸ ~́ывать)
1 : **з. зага́дки** to ask riddles.
2 (*задумать*) to think of; **~а́йте число́** think of a number.
зага́дк|а, и *f.* riddle; (*fig.*) enigma; mystery.
зага́доч|ный (~ен, ~на) *adj.* enigmatic; mysterious.
зага́дыва|ть, ю *impf. of* ▸ **загада́ть**
загазо́ванност|ь, и *f.* pollution (*with gases*).
загазо́ван|ный (~, ~а) *adj.* polluted (*with gases*).
зага́р, а *m.* sunburn, (sun)tan.
зага|си́ть, шу́, ~́сишь *pf. of* ▸ **гаси́ть 1**
загиба́|ть(ся), ю(сь) *impf. of* ▸ **загну́ть(ся)**
загипнотизи́р|овать, ую *pf. of* ▸ **гипнотизи́ровать**
загла́ви|е, я *nt.* title; heading; **под ~ем** entitled, headed.
загла́в|ный *adj. of* ▸ **~ие**
загла́|дить, жу, дишь *pf.* (*of* ▸ **~живать**)
1 (*сделать гладким*) to iron (out), press.
2 (*fig.*) (*смягчить*) to make up (for), make amends (for).
загла́жива|ть, ю *impf. of* ▸ **загла́дить**
загла́тыва|ть, ю *impf. of* ▸ **заглота́ть**
заглота́|ть, ю *pf.* (*of* ▸ **загла́тывать**) to swallow.
загло́хн|уть, у, ешь *pf. of* ▸ **гло́хнуть 2**
заглуш|а́ть, а́ю *impf. of* ▸ **~и́ть**
заглуш|и́ть, у́, и́шь *pf.* (*of* ▸ **глуши́ть 2, 3** *and* ▸ **~а́ть**)
1 (*звуки*) to drown, deaden, muffle.
2 (*передачи*) to jam.
3 (*растения*) to choke.
загля|де́ться, жу́сь, ди́шься *pf.* (*of* ▸ **~́дываться**) (**на** + *a.*; *coll.*) to stare (at); to be lost in admiration (of).
загля́дыва|ть, ю *impf. of* ▸ **загляну́ть**
загля́дыва|ться, юсь *impf. of* ▸ **загляде́ться**
загляну|́ть, у́, ~́ешь *pf.* (*of* ▸ **загля́дывать**)
1 (*взглянуть*) to peep; to glance.
2 (*coll.*) (*зайти*) to look in, drop in.
загна́ива|ться, ется *impf. of* ▸ **загнои́ться**
загна́|ть, загоню́, заго́нишь, *past* **~л, ~ла́, ~ло** *pf.* (*of* ▸ **загоня́ть**)
1 to drive in; **з. коро́в в хлев** to drive the cows into the shed, get the cows in.
2 (*coll.*) (*вбить*) to drive home.
3 (*coll.*) (*продать*) to sell, flog (*Br.*).
загнива́|ть, ю *impf. of* ▸ **загни́ть**
загни́|ть, ю́, ёшь, *past* **~л, ~ла́, ~ло** *pf.* (*of* ▸ **~ва́ть**) to begin to rot; to rot, decay (*also fig.*).
загно|и́ться, и́тся *pf.* (*of* ▸ **загна́иваться**) to fester.
загн|у́ть, у́, ёшь *pf.* (*of* ▸ **загиба́ть**) (*вверх*) to turn up; (*вниз*) to turn down; (*сгибать*) to bend, fold; to crease.
загн|у́ться, у́сь, ёшься *pf.* (*of* ▸ **загиба́ться**)
1 (*вверх*) to turn up, stick up; (*вниз*) to turn down.
2 (*sl.*) (*умереть*) to turn up one's toes.
загова́рива|ться, юсь *impf.* (*of* ▸ **заговори́ться**)
1 (*увлечься разговором*) to be carried away by a conversation.
2 (*impf. only*) (*говорить бессмыслицу*) to rave; to ramble (*in speech*).
за́говор, а¹ *m.* plot, conspiracy.
загово́р, а² *m.* (*заклинание*) charm, spell.
заговор|и́ть, ю́, и́шь *pf.* (*начать говорить*) to begin to speak.
заговор|и́ться, ю́сь, и́шься *pf. of* ▸ **загова́риваться**
загово́рщик, а *m.* conspirator, plotter.
загово́рщи|ца, цы *f. of* ▸ **~к**
заголо́в|ок, ка *m.*
1 (*заглавие*) title; heading.
2 (*газетный*) headline.
заго́н, а *m.* (*для скота*) enclosure; (*для овец*) pen.
за|гоню́, го́нишь *see* ▸ **~гна́ть**
загоня́|ть, ю *impf. of* ▸ **загна́ть**
загора́жива|ть, ю *impf. of* ▸ **загороди́ть**
загора́|ть(ся), ю(сь) *impf. of* ▸ **загоре́ть(ся)**
загоре́лый *adj.* sunburnt; brown, bronzed.
загор|е́ть, ю́, и́шь *pf.* (*of* ▸ **~а́ть**) to become sunburnt; to acquire a tan.
загор|е́ться, ю́сь, и́шься *pf.* (*of* ▸ **~а́ться**) (*начать гореть*) to catch fire; to begin to burn.
загоро|ди́ть, жу́, ~ди́шь *pf.* (*of* ▸ **загора́живать**)
1 (*огородить*) to enclose, fence in.
2 (*преградить*) to barricade; to obstruct; **з. кому́-н. свет** to stand in s.o.'s light.
загоро́дк|а, и *f.* (*coll.*) fence.
за́городный *adj.* out-of-town; country.
загота́влива|ть, ю *impf. of* ▸ **загото́вить**
загото́в|ить, лю, ишь *pf.* (*of* ▸ **загота́вливать** *and* ▸ **~ля́ть**) (*создать запас чего-либо*) to lay in; to stockpile.
загото́вк|а, и *f.*
1 (*закупка*) procurement.
2 (*зерна, корма*) laying in; stockpiling.
заготовля́|ть, ю *impf. of* ▸ **загото́вить**
загражде́ни|е, я *nt.* obstacle, barrier, obstruction.
заграни́ц|а, ы *f.* (*coll.*) foreign countries (*see also* ▸ **грани́ца**).
заграни́чный *adj.* foreign.
За́греб, а *n.* Zagreb.
загреба́|ть, ю *impf. of* ▸ **загрести́**
загре|сти́, бу́, бёшь, *past* **~́б, ~бла́** *pf.* (*of* ▸ **~ба́ть**) (*coll.*) to rake up; (*fig.*) to rake in.
загримир|ова́ть(ся), у́ю(сь) *pf. of* ▸ **гримирова́ть(ся)**
загро́бн|ый *adj.* beyond the grave; **~ая жизнь** life after death.

загружá|ть, ю *impf. of* ▸ **загрузи́ть 2, 3**

загр|узи́ть, ужý, ýзишь *pf.*
[1] (*impf.* **грузи́ть**) to load.
[2] (*impf.* **∼ужáть**) (*tech.*) to feed, charge, prime; (*comput.*) (*компьютер*) to boot; (*программу, данные*) to load; (*скопировать*) (*откуда*) to download; (*куда*) to upload.
[3] (*impf.* **∼ужáть**) (*coll.*) (*занять работой*) to keep fully occupied.

загрýзк|а, и *f.*
[1] (*действие*) loading.
[2] (*объём работы*) capacity, workload.

загру|сти́ть, щý, сти́шь *pf.* to grow sad.

загрызá|ть, ю *impf. of* ▸ **загры́зть**

загры́з|ть, ý, ёшь *past* **∼, ∼ла** *pf.* (*of* ▸ **∼áть**) (*убить*) to kill.

загрязнéни|е, я *nt.* soiling; (*природы*) pollution.

загрязн|и́ть, ю́, и́шь *pf.* (*of* ▸ **∼я́ть**) to soil, make dirty; (*природу*) to pollute.

загрязня́|ть, ю *impf. of* ▸ **загрязни́ть**

ЗАГС, а *or* **загс, а** *m.* (*abbr. of* **(отдéл) зáписи áктов граждáнского состоя́ния**) registry office.

загуб|и́ть, лю́, ∼́ишь *pf.* (*погубить*) to ruin; **з. чью-н. жизнь** to make s.o.'s life a misery.

зад, а, о ∼́е, на (в) ∼ý, *pl.* **∼ы́** *m.*
[1] (*машины, дома*) back; **∼́ом наперёд** back to front.
[2] (*животного*) hind quarters; rump; (*человека*) behind, buttocks.

зада|вáть, ю́, ёшь *impf. of* ▸ **∼́ть**

задав|и́ть, лю́, ∼́ишь *pf.* to crush; (*о машине*) to run over, knock down.

задáни|е, я *nt.* task, job.

задáром *adv.* (*coll.*) (*бесплатно*) for nothing; very cheaply; **купи́ть з.** to buy for a song.

задáт|ок, ка *m.* deposit.

за|дáть, дáм, дáшь, дáст, дади́м, дади́те, дадýт, *past* **∼́дал, ∼далá, ∼́дало** *pf.* (*of* ▸ **∼давáть**) to set; to give; **з. вопрóс** to put a question.

задáч|а, и *f.*
[1] (*math., etc.*) problem.
[2] (*цель*) task; mission.

задáчник, а *m.* book of (mathematical) problems.

задви́га|ть, ю *pf.* to begin to move.

задвигá|ть, ю *impf. of* ▸ **задви́нуть**

задви́н|уть, у, ешь *pf.* (*of* ▸ **задвигáть**)
[1] (*переместить*) to push.
[2]: **з. зáнавески** to draw the curtains.

задвóр|ки, ок *no sg.* backyard; (*fig.*) out-of-the-way place, backwoods.

задевá|ть, ю *impf. of* ▸ **задéть**

задéл|ать, аю *pf.* (*of* ▸ **∼ывать**) (*дыру, щель*) to block up, close up; **з. течь** to stop up a leak.

задéлыва|ть, ю *impf. of* ▸ **задéлать**

задёргива|ть, ю *impf. of* ▸ **задёрнуть**

задержáни|е, я *nt.* (*преступника*) detention, arrest.

задéржанн|ый, ого *m.* detainee.

задерж|áть, ý, ∼́ишь *pf.* (*of* ▸ **∼́ивать**)
[1] (*остановить*) to stop, hold back, delay, detain; (*отсрочить*) to delay.
[2] (*удержать*) to withhold, keep back; **з. зарплáту** to stop wages; **з. дыхáние** to hold one's breath.
[3] (*арестовать*) to detain, arrest.

задерж|áться, ýсь, ∼́ишься *pf.* (*of* ▸ **∼́иваться**)
[1] (*на работе, в гостях*) to be held up, delayed; to stay too long.
[2] (*у входа, перед магазином*) to linger.
[3] (*не сделать вовремя*) to be late.

задéржива|ть(ся), ю(сь) *impf. of* ▸ **задержáть(ся)**

задéржк|а, и *f.* delay; hold-up.

задёрн|уть, у, ешь *pf.* (*of* ▸ **задёргивать**) to pull; to draw; **з. занавéски** to draw the curtains.

задé|ть, ну, нешь *pf.* (*of* ▸ **∼вáть**) (*коснуться*) to touch, brush (against); (*fig.*) (*обидеть*) to offend, wound; **егó ∼ло за живóе** he was stung to the quick.

задирá|ть(ся), ю, ет(ся) *impf. of* ▸ **задрáть(ся)**

зáдн|ий *adj.* (*сиденье*) back, rear; (*ноги*) hind; **∼яя мысль** ulterior motive; **з. прохóд** (*anat.*) anus; **дать з. ход** to go into reverse; to back up; **∼им числóм** later, with hindsight.

зáдник, а *m.*
[1] back, counter (*of shoe*).
[2] (*theatr.*) backdrop.

зáдниц|а, ы *f.* (*coll.*) backside, butt (*US*).

задóлго *adv.* long before.

задóлженност|ь, и *f.* debts; **погаси́ть з.** to pay off one's debts.

зáдом *adv.* backwards.

задóр, а *m.* fervour, ardour (*Br.*) frevor, ardor (*US*); passion.

задóр|ный (∼ен, ∼на) *adj.* fervent, ardent; impassioned.

задох|нýться, нýсь, нёшься *pf.* (*of* ▸ **задыхáться**)
[1] (*умереть*) to suffocate; to choke.
[2] (*тяжело дышать*) to pant; to gasp for breath.

зад|рáть, ерý, ерёшь, *past* **∼рáл, ∼ралá, ∼рáло** *pf.* (*of* ▸ **∼ирáть**) (*coll.*) (*поднять кверху*) to lift up; to pull up; **з. гóлову** to crane one's neck; **з. нос** (*fig.*) to cock one's nose.

зад|рáться, ерётся, *past* **∼рáлся, ∼ралáсь** *pf.* (*of* ▸ **∼ирáться**) (*coll.*) (*о платье*) to ride up.

задрем|áть, лю́, ∼́лешь *pf.* to doze off, begin to nod.

задрож|áть, ý, и́шь *pf.* to begin to tremble; (*от холода*) to begin to shiver.

задувá|ть, ю *impf. of* ▸ **задýть**

задýма|ть, ю *pf.* (*of* ▸ **задýмывать**)
[1] (+ *a. or inf.*) (*решить*) to plan; to intend; to conceive the idea (of).
[2] (*число*) to think of.

задýма|ться, юсь *pf.* to become thoughtful, pensive; to fall to thinking.

задýмчив|ый (∼, ∼а) *adj.* thoughtful, pensive.

задýмыва|ть, ю *impf. of* ▸ **задýмать**

задýмыва|ться, юсь *impf.* (*погружаться в свои мысли*) to be thoughtful, be pensive; (*размышлять*) to meditate; to ponder; **з. о** +

p. to think about.
задý|ть, ю, ешь *pf.* (*of* ▶ **~вáть**)
1 (*погасить*) to blow out.
2 (*начать дуть*) to begin to blow.
задуш|и́ть, ý, ~́ишь *pf. of* ▶ **души́ть**[1]
задыхá|ться, юсь *impf. of* ▶ **задохнýться**
заедá|ть, ю *impf. of* ▶ **заéсть**
заезжá|ть, ю *impf. of* ▶ **заéхать**
заём, зáйма *m.* loan.
заёмщик, а *m.* borrower, debtor.
заé|сть[1]**, м, шь, ст, ди́м, ди́те, дя́т,** *past* **~л** *pf.* (*of* ▶ **~дáть**)
1 (*укусами*) to bite to death; (*загрызть*) to kill; (*fig., coll.*) (*измучить*) to torment, oppress; **егó ~ла тоскá** he fell a prey to melancholy.
2 (*impers.*; *tech.*) to jam; (*naut.*) to foul; **канáт ~ло** the cable has fouled.
заé|сть[2]**, м, шь, ст, ди́м, ди́те, дя́т,** *past* **~л** *pf.* (*of* ▶ **~дáть**) (+ *a. and i.*) to take (with); **он ~л лекáрство сáхаром** he took the medicine with sugar.
заé|хать, ду, дешь *pf.* (*of* ▶ **~зжáть**)
1 (**к** + *d.*) to call in (at); to drop in (on); (**в** + *a.*) to enter, ride into, drive into; (**за** + *a.*) to go beyond, past; (**за** + *i.*) to call for; to fetch, pick up.
2 (*уехать или попасть куда-н. далеко или куда не следует*) to get (to), go; **он ~хал в канáву** he landed in the ditch.
зажáр|ить(ся), ю, ит(ся) *pf. of* ▶ **жáрить(ся)**
зажáт|ый *p.p.p. of* ▶ **~ь** *and adj.* **(~, ~а)** (*coll.*) (*о человеке*) tense, uptight.
заж|áть, мý, мёшь *pf.* (*of* ▶ **~имáть**) (*стиснуть*) to squeeze; to press; to clutch; (*заткнуть*) to stop up; **з. в рукé** to grip; **з. рот комý-н.** (*fig.*) to stop s.o.'s mouth.
заж|гý, жёшь, гýт *see* ▶ **~éчь**
заж|éчь, гý, жёшь, гýт, *past* **~ёг, ~глá** *pf.* (*of* ▶ **~игáть**) (*огонь, лампу*) to light; (*свет*) to turn on; **з. спи́чку** to strike a match.
заж|éчься, гýсь, жёшься, гýтся, *past* **зажёгся, зажглáсь** *pf.* (*of* ▶ **~игáться**) (*об огне*) to begin to burn; (*о фонарях*) to go on, light up.
заживá|ть, ю *impf. of* ▶ **зажи́ть**
зажигáлк|а, и *f.* (cigarette) lighter.
зажигáни|е, я *nt.* (*в машине*) ignition.
зажигá|ть(ся), ю(сь) *impf. of* ▶ **зажéчь(ся)**
зажи́м, а *m.*
1 (*tech.*) clamp; clip.
2 (*elec.*) terminal.
зажимá|ть, ю *impf. of* ▶ **зажáть**
зажи́точ|ный (~ен, ~на) *adj.* well-to-do; prosperous; affluent.
зажи́|ть, вý, вёшь, *past* **зáжил, ~лá, зáжило** *pf.* (*of* ▶ **~вáть**)
1 (*о ране*) to heal (*intrans.*); to close up.
2 (*начать жить*) to begin to live; **з. по-нóвому** to begin a new life.
зазвен|éть, ю́, и́шь *pf.* to begin to ring.
зазвон|и́ть, ю́, и́шь *pf.* to begin to ring.
зазвуч|áть, ý, и́шь *pf.* to begin to sound; to begin to resound.
заземлéни|е, я *nt.* (*elec.*)
1 (*действие*) earthing (*Br.*), grounding (*US*).
2 (*устройство*) earth (*Br.*), ground (*US*).
заземл|и́ть, ю́, и́шь *pf.* (*elec.*) to earth.
зазим|овáть, ýю *pf.* to winter; to pass the winter.
зазна|вáться, ю́сь, ёшься *impf. of* ▶ **~́ться**
зазнá|ться, юсь *pf.* (*of* ▶ **~вáться**) (*coll.*) to give o.s. airs, become conceited.
зазóр, а *m.* gap.
зазóр|ный (~ен, ~на) *adj.* (*coll.*) shameful, disgraceful.
заигрá|ть, ю *pf.* (*начать играть*) to begin to play.
заигрá|ться, юсь *pf.* (*of* ▶ **заи́грываться**) to become absorbed in playing.
заи́грыва|ть, ю *impf.* (**с** + *i.*; *coll.*) to flirt (with); to make advances (to) (*also fig.*).
заи́грыва|ться, юсь *impf. of* ▶ **заигрáться**
заикáни|е, я *nt.* stammer(ing), stutter(ing).
заикá|ться, юсь *impf.* to stammer, stutter; (*нерешительно говорить*) to falter (*in speech*).
заи́мств|овать, ую *impf.* (*of* ▶ **по~**) to borrow.
заинтересóван|ный (~, ~а) *p.p.p. of* ▶ **заинтересовáть** *and adj.* **(~, ~на)** (**в** + *p.*) interested (in); **~ная сторонá** interested party.
заинтерес|овáть, ýю *pf.* to interest; to excite the curiosity (of).
заинтерес|овáться, ýюсь *pf.* (+ *i.*) to become interested; to take an interest (in).
заи́скива|ть, ю *impf.* (**пéред** + *i.*) to try to ingratiate o.s. (with).
зай|дý, дёшь *see* ▶ **~ти́**
зáйма *see* ▶ **заём**
займ|ý, ёшь *see* ▶ **заня́ть**
за|йти́, йдý, йдёшь, *past* **~шёл, ~шлá** *pf.* (*of* ▶ **~ходи́ть**)
1 (**к** + *d.*, **в** + *a.*) (*посетить*) to call (on); to look in (at); to drop in (at).
2 (**за** + *i.*) (*чтобы взять*) to call for, fetch.
3 (**в** + *a.*) (*войти*) to go into, get into; (*попасть*) to get (*to a place*); to find o.s. (*in a place*).
4 (*о разговоре*) to turn to.
5 (**за** + *a.*) (*скрыться за чем-н.*) to go behind; (*продолжаться*) to go on, continue (after); (*закатиться*) to set (*of sun, etc.*); **з. зá угол** to turn a corner; **з. сли́шком далекó** (*fig.*) to go too far.
Закавкáзь|е, я *nt.* Transcaucasia.
закáдровый *adj.*: **з. комментáрий** (*TV, cin.*) voice-over.
закáз, а *m.* order; (*билетов, стола*) reservation; (*портрета*) commission; **на з.** to order; **как по ~у** as if to order.
зака|зáть, жý, ~́жешь *pf.* (*of* ▶ **~́зывать**) to order; (*билеты, стол*) to reserve; (*портрет*) to commission.
закáзник, а *m.* (*game*) reserve.
заказн|óй *adj.*
1 done or made to order; **~áя статья́** article written to order; **~áя журнали́стика** chequebook journalism; **~óе уби́йство**

contract killing.
2 : **~óe письмó** registered letter.
закáзчик, а *m.* customer, client.
закáзыва|ть, ю *impf. of* ▸ **заказáть**
закалён|ный (~, ~á) *p.p.p. of* ▸ **закалúть** *and adj.* **(~, ~на)** hardened, hard.
закал|úть, ю́, и́шь *pf.* (*of* ▸ **~я́ть**) (*tech.*) to temper; to case-harden; (*fig.*) to temper, harden; to make hard, hardy.
закáлк|а, и *f.* tempering; hardening; (*sport*) conditioning.
закáлыва|ть, ю *impf. of* ▸ **заколóть**
закаля́|ть, ю *impf. of* ▸ **закалúть**
закáнчива|ть(ся), ю, ет(ся) *impf. of* ▸ **закóнчить(ся)**
закáп|ать, аю *pf.* (*impf.* **~ывать**) to spot, stain.
закáпыва|ть, ю *impf. of* ▸ **закопáть** *and* ▸ **закáпать**
закáрмлива|ть, ю *impf. of* ▸ **закормúть**
закáт, а *m.* setting; **з. (сóлнца)** sunset; (*fig.*) decline.
закатá|ть, ю *pf.* (*of* ▸ **закáтывать**)
1 (*coll.*) (*рукава*) to roll up.
2 (*банку, крышку*) to close, hermetically seal.
зака|тúть, чу́, ~тишь *pf.* (*of* ▸ **~тывать**) (*мяч*) to roll; **з. истéрику** (*coll.*) to go off into hysterics; **з. глазá** to roll one's eyes.
зака|тúться, чу́сь, ~тишься *pf.* (*of* ▸ **~тываться**)
1 (*мяч*) to roll (*intrans.*).
2 (*солнце*) to set (*of heavenly bodies*); (*fig.*) (*слава*) to wane; to vanish.
закáтыва|ть, ю *impf. of* ▸ **закатáть** *and* ▸ **закатúть**
закáтыва|ться, юсь *impf. of* ▸ **закатúться**
закáшля|ться, юсь *pf.* to have a fit of coughing.
заквáск|а, и *f.* (*для теста*) leaven; (*для кефира*) culture.
закидá|ть, ю *pf.* (*of* ▸ **закúдывать**) (+ *a. and i.*)
1 (*осыпать*) to bespatter (with); to shower (with); **з. камня́ми** to stone.
2 (*заполнить*) to fill up (with); (*сверху*) to cover (with).
закúдыва|ть, ю *impf. of* ▸ **закидáть** *and* ▸ **закúнуть**
закúн|уть, у, ешь *pf.* (*мяч в сетку, майку под кровать*) to throw; (*невод, удочку*) to cast.
закипá|ть, ет *impf. of* ▸ **закипéть**
закип|éть, úт *pf.* (*of* ▸ **закипáть**) (*начать кипеть*) to begin to boil; (*кипеть*) to be on the boil; (*fig.*) (*о работе*) to be in full swing.
заклáд, а *m.* (*залог*) pawning; (*недвижимости*) mortgaging.
заклáдк|а, и *f.* (*в книге*) bookmark (*also comput.*).
заклáдыва|ть, ю *impf. of* ▸ **заложúть**
заклéива|ть, ю, ет *impf. of* ▸ **заклéить**
заклé|ить, ю, ишь *pf.* (*of* ▸ **~ивать**) to glue up; to stick up; **з. конвéрт** to seal an envelope.
заклинáни|е, я *nt.*
1 (*магические слова*) incantation; spell.
2 (*мольба*) entreaty.
заклинáтел|ь, я *m.* exorcist; **з. змей** snake charmer.
заклинáтель|ница, ницы *f. of* ▸ **~**
заклúнива|ть, ю *impf. of* ▸ **заклúнить**
заклú|нить, ю, ишь *pf.* (*of* ▸ **заклúнивать**)
1 (*закрепить*) to wedge, fasten with a wedge.
2 (*лишить возможности вращаться*) to jam; (*also. impers.*): **дверь ~ило** the door jammed.
заключá|ть, ю *impf. of* ▸ **заключúть**
заключ|áться, áется *impf.*
1 *pass. of* ▸ **~áть.**
2 (*impf. only*) (**в** + *p.*) to consist (of, in); to lie (in).
заключéни|е, я *nt.*
1 (*конец*) conclusion, end; (*завершение*) conclusion, ending; **в з.** in conclusion.
2 (*вывод*) conclusion, inference.
3 (*договора, сделки*) conclusion, signing.
4 (*лишение свободы*) confinement, detention; **тюрéмное з.** imprisonment.
заключён|ный (~, ~á) *p.p.p. of* ▸ **заключúть;** *as n.* **з., ~ного** *m., and* **~ная, ~ной** *f.* (*leg.*) prisoner, convict.
заключúтельный *adj.* final, concluding.
заключ|úть, у́, úшь *pf.* (*of* ▸ **~áть**)
1 (*сделать вывод*) to conclude, infer.
2 (*принять*) to conclude, enter into; **з. брак** to contract marriage; **з. договóр** to conclude a treaty; **з. сдéлку** to strike a bargain.
3 : **з. в себé** to contain, enclose; to comprise; **з. в скóбки** to enclose in brackets.
4 (*лишить свободы*) to confine; **з. в тюрьму́** to imprison.
зак|овáть, ую́, уёшь *pf.* (*of* ▸ **~óвывать**) to chain; **з. в кандалы́** to shackle, put in irons.
закóвыва|ть, ю *impf. of* ▸ **заковáть**
заколáчива|ть, ю *impf. of* ▸ **заколотúть**
заколдóванный *p.p.p. of* ▸ **заколдовáть** *and adj.* enchanted; spellbound; (*fig.*) **з. круг** vicious circle.
заколд|овáть, у́ю *pf.* (*of* ▸ **заколдóвывать**) to bewitch, enchant; to lay a spell (on).
заколдóвыва|ть, ю *impf. of* ▸ **заколдовáть**
заколеб|áться, ~люсь, ~лешься *pf.* to begin to shake; (*fig.*) to begin to waver, begin to vacillate.
закóлк|а, и *f.* hairgrip (*Br.*), bobby pin (*US*).
заколо|тúть, чу́, ~тишь *pf.* (*of* ▸ **заколáчивать**) (*досками*) to board up; (*гвоздями*) to nail up.
закол|óть, ю́, ~ешь *pf.* (*of* ▸ **закáлывать** *and* ▸ **колóть**[2] ▸ **2, 3**)
1 (*убить*) to stab (to death); (*животное*) to slaughter.
2 (*прикрепить*) to pin (up).
3 (*impers.*): **у меня́,** *etc.*, **~óло в боку́** I, *etc.*, have a stitch in my side.
закóн, а *m.* law; **свод ~ов** code, statute book; **объявúть вне ~а** to outlaw.
закóнност|ь, и *f.*
1 (*документа, постановления*) lawfulness,

legality.
[2] (*соблюдение законов*) law and order.
зако́н|ный (~ен, ~на) *adj.*
[1] (*действия*) lawful, legal; (*документ, договор*) legal; **з. брак** lawful wedlock; **з. владе́лец** rightful owner.
[2] (*fig.*) (*возмущение*) legitimate, understandable, natural.
законода́тел|ь, я *m.* legislator; lawgiver; **з. мод/мо́ды** trendsetter.
законода́тельный *adj.* legislative.
законода́тельств|о, а *nt.* legislation.
закономе́рност|ь, и *f.* regularity; conformity with a law; normality.
закономе́р|ный (~ен, ~на) *adj.*
[1] (*развитие, успех*) natural, logical.
[2] (*fig.*) (*понятный*) legitimate, understandable, natural.
законопослу́ш|ный (~ен, ~на) *adj.* law-abiding.
законопрое́кт, а *m.* (*pol., leg.*) bill.
законсерви́р|овать, ую *pf. of* ▸ **консерви́ровать**
зако́нчен|ный (**~, ~а**) *p.p.p. of* ▸ **зако́нчить** *and adj.* (**~, ~на**) (*дело*) finished; (*мысль, фраза*) complete; (*негодяй*) consummate; **з. лгун** consummate liar.
зако́нч|ить, у, ишь *pf.* (*of* ▸ **зака́нчивать**) to end, finish.
зако́нч|иться, у, ится *pf.* (*of* ▸ **зака́нчиваться**) to end, finish (*intrans.*).
закопа́|ть, ю *pf.* (*of* ▸ **зака́пывать**) (*спрятать в земле*) to bury.
закоп|ти́ть, чу́, ти́шь *pf.* (*of* ▸ **копти́ть**)
[1] (*рыбу, окорок*) to smoke.
[2] (*покрыть копотью*) to blacken with smoke.
закоп|ти́ться, чу́сь, ти́шься *pf.* (*покрыться копотью*) to become covered with soot.
закорм|и́ть, лю́, ~́ишь *pf.* (*of* ▸ **зака́рмливать**) to overfeed; to stuff.
закра́|сить, шу, сишь *pf.* (*of* ▸ **~шивать**) to paint over, paint out.
закра́шива|ть, ю *impf. of* ▸ **закра́сить**
закреп|и́ть, лю́, и́шь *pf.* (*of* ▸ **~ля́ть**)
[1] to fasten, secure; (*naut.*) to make fast; (*phot.*) to fix.
[2] (*fig.*) to consolidate.
[3] (+ *a.* **за** + *i.*) (*помещение*) to allot, assign (to); (*человека*) to appoint, attach (to); **з. за собо́й** to secure.
закреп|и́ться, лю́сь, и́шься *pf.* (*of* ▸ **~ля́ться**)
[1] (*о войсках*) (**на** + *a.*) to consolidate one's hold (on).
[2] (*о слове, привычке*) to establish itself.
закрепля́|ть(ся), ю(сь) *impf. of* ▸ **закрепи́ть(ся)**
закрич|а́ть, у́, и́шь *pf.*
[1] (*начать кричать*) to begin to shout.
[2] (*однократно*) to give a shout, cry out.
закро́йщик, а *m.* cutter.
закро́йщи|ца, цы *f. of* ▸ **~к**
закругл|и́ть, ю́, и́шь *pf.* (*of* ▸ **~я́ть**) to make round; to round off.
закругл|и́ться, ю́сь, и́шься *pf.* (*of* ▸ **~я́ться**) (*coll.*) to round off, conclude.
закругля́|ть(ся), ю(сь) *impf. of* ▸ **закругли́ть(ся)**
закруж|и́ться, у́сь, ~́ишься *pf. of* ▸ **кружи́ться**
закру|ти́ть, чу́, ~́тишь *pf.* (*of* ▸ **закру́чивать** *and* ▸ **крути́ть 2**)
[1] (*верёвку*) to twist; (*усы*) to twirl; (*вокруг*) to wind round.
[2] (*кран*) to turn; (*гайку*) to screw in.
закру|ти́ться, чу́сь, ~́тишься *pf.* (*of* ▸ **закру́чиваться**) to twist; to twirl; to wind round (*intrans.*).
закру́чива|ть(ся), ю(сь) *impf. of* ▸ **закрути́ть(ся)**
закрыва́|ть(ся), ю(сь) *impf. of* ▸ **закры́ть(ся)**
закры́ти|е, я *nt.* closing; shutting; (*конец*) close.
закры́т|ый (~, ~а) *p.p.p. of* ▸ **~ь** *and adj.* closed, shut; (*не для всех*) private; **с ~ыми глаза́ми** (*fig.*) blindly; **в ~ом помеще́нии** indoors.
закр|ы́ть, о́ю, о́ешь *pf.* (*of* ▸ **~ыва́ть**)
[1] (*сделать недоступным*) to close, shut; **з. глаза́** (**на** + *a.*) to shut one's eyes (to); **з. счёт** to close an account.
[2] (*выключить*) to shut off, turn off.
[3] (*ликвидировать*) to close down, shut down.
[4] (*покрыть*) to cover.
закр|ы́ться, о́юсь, о́ешься *pf.* (*of* ▸ **~ыва́ться**)
[1] (*стать недоступным*) to close, shut; (*окончиться*) to end; (*перестать существовать*) to close down.
[2] (*покрыть себя*) to cover o.s.; to take cover.
закули́сный *adj.* (*fig.*) secret; underhand, undercover.
закупа́|ть, ю *impf. of* ▸ **закупи́ть**
закуп|и́ть, лю́, ~́ишь *pf.* (*of* ▸ **~а́ть**)
[1] (*скупить*) to buy up (wholesale).
[2] (*запастись*) to lay in; to stock up with.
заку́порива|ть, ю *impf. of* ▸ **заку́порить**
заку́пор|ить, ю, ишь *pf.* (*of* ▸ **заку́поривать**) to cork; to stop up.
заку́рива|ть, ю *impf. of* ▸ **закури́ть**
закур|и́ть, ю́, ~́ишь *pf.* (*of* ▸ **заку́ривать**)
[1] (*сигарету*) to light up.
[2] (*стать курильщиком*) to begin to smoke.
заку|си́ть, шу́, ~́сишь *pf.* (*of* ▸ **~́сывать**)
[1] (*поесть*) to have a snack, have a bite.
[2] (+ *a. and i.*) to take (with); **з. во́дку ры́бой** to drink vodka with fish hors d'oeuvres.
заку́ск|а, и *f.* (*usu. pl.*) hors d'oeuvre; snack; **на ~у** for a titbit; (*fig., coll.*) as a special treat.
заку́сыва|ть, ю *impf. of* ▸ **закуси́ть**
заку́та|ть, ю *pf.* (*of* ▸ **заку́тывать**) to wrap up, muffle; **з. в одея́ло** to tuck up (in bed).
заку́та|ться, юсь *pf.* (*of* ▸ **заку́тываться**) to wrap o.s. up, muffle o.s.
заку́тыва|ть(ся), ю(сь) *impf. of* ▸ **заку́тать(ся)**
зал, а *m.* hall; **з. ожида́ния** waiting room; **з. вы́лета** (*airport*) departure lounge.
залега́|ть, ю *impf. of* ▸ **зале́чь**

3

залеза́|ть, ю *impf. of* ▶ **зале́зть**

зале́з|ть, у, ешь, *past* ~, ~**ла** *pf.*
1 (**на** + *a.*) (*на дерево, крышу*) to climb (up, on to).
2 (**в** + *a.*; *coll.*) (*в комнату*) to get (into); to break into.

залета́|ть, ю *impf. of* ▶ **залете́ть**

зале|те́ть, чу́, ти́шь *pf.*
1 (**в** + *a.*) to fly (into); (**за** + *a.*) to fly (over, beyond).
2 (**в** + *a.*) to make a stopover (at), call in (at).

зал|е́чь, я́гу, я́жешь, я́гут, *past* ~**ёг,** ~**егла́** *pf.* (*of* ▶ ~**ега́ть**)
1 (*лечь*) to lie down; (*притаиться*) to lie low.
2 (*geol.*) to lie, be deposited.

зали́в, а *m.* bay; (*длинный*) gulf; (*маленький*) cove.

залива́|ть(ся), ю(сь) *impf. of* ▶ **зали́ть(ся)**

заливн|о́е, о́го *nt.* fish or meat in aspic.

зал|и́ть, ью́, ьёшь, *past* ~**ил,** ~**ила́,** ~**и́ло** *pf.* (*of* ▶ ~**ива́ть**)
1 (*покрыть жидкостью*) to flood, inundate.
2 (*испачкать жидким*) (+ *a. and i.*) to pour (over); to spill (on).
3 (*потушить водой*) to quench, extinguish (*with water*); **з. пожа́р** to put out a fire.
4 (*наполнить, покрыть жидким*) to fill, cover with.
5 (*налить, наполнив что-н.*): **з. бензи́н в бак** to fill up with petrol (*Br.*), gas (*US*).

зал|и́ться, ью́сь, ьёшься, *past* ~**и́лся,** ~**ила́сь** *pf.* (*of* ▶ ~**ива́ться**)
1 (*попасть*) to pour; to spill (*intrans.*); **вода́ ~ила́сь мне за воротни́к** water has gone down my neck.
2 (+ *i.*) (*зазвучать*) to break into, burst out (into); **соба́ка ~ила́сь ла́ем** the dog began to bark furiously.

зало́г, а *m.*
1 deposit; pledge; security; (*leg.*) bail; **под з.** (+ *g.*) on the security of; **отда́ть в з.** (*в ломбарде*) to pawn; (*дом*) to mortgage; **вы́купить из ~а** to redeem; to pay off mortgage (on); **з. успе́ха** guarantee of success.
2 (*fig.*) (*доказательство*) pledge, token.

залож|и́ть, у́, ~ишь *pf.* (*of* ▶ **закла́дывать**)
1 (*положить за*) to put (behind); **он ~и́л ру́ки за́ спину** he put his hands behind his back.
2 (*положить основание чему-л.*) to lay (the foundation of).
3 (+ *i.*) (*загромоздить*) to pile up, heap up (with); to block up (with); (*impers.*, + *d.*): **мне ~и́ло нос** my nose is blocked up.
4 (*место в книге*) to mark, put a marker in.
5 (*для хранения*) to lay in, store, put by.
6 (*часы*) to pawn; (*дом*) to mortgage.

зало́жник, а *m.* hostage.

зало́жни|ца, цы *f. of* ▶ ~**к**

залп, а *m.* volley; salvo; ~**ом** (*fig., coll.*) without pausing for breath; **вы́пить ~ом** to drain at one draught.

зама́|зать, жу, жешь *pf.* (*of* ▶ **ма́зать 3** *and* ▶ ~**зывать**)
1 (*покрыть краской*) to paint over; (*зачеркнуть*) to efface; (*fig.*) to slur over.
2 (*залепить*) to putty.
3 (*запачкать*) to daub, smear, to soil.

зама́|заться, жусь, жешься *pf.* (*of* ▶ **ма́заться 1** *and* ▶ ~**зываться**) to smear o.s.; to get dirty.

зама́зк|а, и *f.*
1 (*вещество*) putty.
2 (*действие*) puttying.

зама́зыва|ть(ся), ю(сь) *impf. of* ▶ **зама́зать(ся)**

зама́нива|ть, ю *impf. of* ▶ **замани́ть**

заман|и́ть, ю́, ~ишь *pf.* (*of* ▶ ~**ивать**) to entice, lure; (*обманом*) to decoy.

зама́нчив|ый (~, ~а) *adj.* tempting, alluring.

замарин|ова́ть, у́ю *pf. of* ▶ **маринова́ть**

замаскир|ова́ть, у́ю *pf. of* ▶ **маскирова́ть**

замаскир|ова́ться, у́юсь *pf. of* ▶ **маскирова́ться**

зама́тыва|ть, ю *impf. of* ▶ **замота́ть**

зама|ха́ть, шу́, ~шешь *pf.* to begin to wave.

зама́хива|ться, юсь *impf. of* ▶ **замахну́ться**

замахн|у́ться, у́сь, ёшься *pf.*
1 (+ *i. and* **на** + *a.*) to raise (sth.) threateningly (at s.o.).
2 (*поднять руку*) (**на** + *a.*) to raise a hand against.
3 (**на** + *a.*) (*fig., coll.*) to set one's sights on.

зама́чива|ть, ю *impf. of* ▶ **замочи́ть 1**

замби́|ец, йца *m.* Zambian.

замби́йк|а, и *f.* Zambian.

замби́йский *adj.* Zambian.

За́мби|я, и *f.* Zambia.

заме́дленн|ый *p.p.p. of* ▶ **заме́длить** *and adj.* retarded; delayed; **бо́мба ~ого де́йствия** delayed-action bomb, time bomb; (*fig.*) time bomb; ~**ое воспроизведе́ние** slow-motion replay.

заме́дл|ить, ю, ишь *pf.* (*of* ▶ ~**я́ть**) to slow down, retard; **з. шаг** to slacken one's pace; **з. ход** to reduce speed.

заме́дл|иться, юсь, ишься *pf.* (*of* ▶ ~**я́ться**) to slow down; to slacken, become slower.

замедля́|ть(ся), ю(сь) *impf. of* ▶ **заме́длить(ся)**

заме́н|а, ы *f.*
1 (*действие*) substitution; replacement.
2 (*тот, кто* (*или то, что*) *заменяет*) substitute.

замени́тел|ь, я *m.* (+ *g.*) substitute; **з. са́хара** sweetener.

замен|и́ть, ю́, ~ишь *pf.* (*of* ▶ ~**я́ть**)
1 (+ *a. and i.*) to replace (by), substitute (for); **з. ма́сло маргари́ном** to use margarine instead of butter.
2 (*занять место кого-то, чего-то*) to take the place of; **тру́дно бу́дет з. его́** it will be hard to replace him.

замен|я́ть, я́ю *impf. of* ▶ ~**и́ть**

зам|ере́ть, ру́, рёшь, *past* ~**ер,** ~**ерла́,** ~**ерло** *pf.* (*of* ▶ ~**ира́ть**)
1 (*стать неподвижным*) to stand still; to freeze, be rooted to the spot; to die (*fig.*).

[2] (*о звуках*) to die down, die away.

замерзá|ть, ю *impf. of* ▶ **замёрзнуть**

замёрз|нуть, ну, нешь, *past* **~, ~ла** *pf.* (*of* ▶ **замерзáть**) (*о реке, окне*) to freeze (up); (*умереть от мороза*) to freeze to death; (*о растениях*) to be killed by frost; **я ~** I'm frozen.

зáмертво *adv.* like one dead; **онá упáла з.** she collapsed in a dead faint.

зам|есúть, ешý, éсишь *pf. of* ▶ **месить**

заме|стú, тý, тёшь, *past* **~л, ~лá** *pf.* (*of* ▶ **~тáть**)
[1] (*подмести*) to sweep up.
[2] (*покрыть*) to cover (up); (*impers.*): **дорóгу ~лó снéгом** the road is covered with snow.

заместúтел|ь, я *m.* substitute; deputy; **з. дирéктора** deputy director.

заме|стúть, щý, стúшь *pf.* (*of* ▶ **~щáть**)
[1] (+ *a. and i.*) (*заменить*) to replace (by); to substitute (for).
[2] (*должность*) to fill.
[3] (*заменить собой*) to deputize for, act for.

заметá|ть, ю *impf. of* ▶ **замести́**

заме|тáться, чýсь, ~чешься *pf.* to begin to rush about; (*в постели*) to begin to toss.

замé|тить, чу, тишь *pf.* (*of* ▶ **~чáть**)
[1] (*увидеть*) to notice.
[2] (*обратить внимание* (*на*)) to take notice (of); (*пометить*) to make a note (of).
[3] (*сказать*) to remark, observe.

замéтк|а, и *f.*
[1] (*запись*) note.
[2] (*краткое сообщение*) notice; paragraph.

замéт|ный (~ен, ~на) *adj.* (*видимый*) noticeable; (*ощутимый*) appreciable; **~но** (*as pred.*) it is noticeable.

замечáни|е, я *nt.*
[1] remark, observation.
[2] (*упрёк*) reprimand; reproof.

замечáтельно *adv.*
[1] (*with verbs*) splendidly, brilliantly, wonderfully.
[2] (*with adjectives, adverbs*) remarkably.
[3] *pred.*: **з.!** (it's) splendid!, wonderful!

замечáтел|ьный (~ен, ~ьна) *adj.* remarkable; splendid, wonderful.

замечá|ть, ю *impf. of* ▶ **замéтить**

замешáтельств|о, а *nt.* confusion; embarrassment; **привестú в з.** to throw into confusion; **прийтú в з.** to be confused, be embarrassed.

замéшка|ться, юсь *pf.* (*coll.*) to linger, dawdle.

замещá|ть, ю *impf. of* ▶ **заместúть**

заминúр|овать, ую *pf. of* ▶ **минúровать**

замирá|ть, ю *impf. of* ▶ **замерéть**

зáмкнут|ый (~, ~а) *adj.*
[1] (*no short forms*) (*среда, жизнь*) isolated, secluded.
[2] (*человек*) reserved, withdrawn.

замкн|ýть, ý, ёшь *pf.* (*of* ▶ **замыкáть**) to lock; to close; **з. шéствие, з. колóнну** to bring up the rear.

замкн|ýться, ýсь, ёшься *pf.* (*of* ▶ **замыкáться**)
[1] (*цепь*) to be joined at the ends; **круг ~ýлся** (*fig.*) everything fell into place.
[2] to shut o.s. up; (*fig.*) **з. в себé** to become reserved, retire into o.s.

зáм|ок, ка *m.* castle.

зам|óк, кá *m.*
[1] lock; **висячий з.** padlock.
[2] (*браслета*) clasp; (*серьги*) clip.

замолч|áть, ý, úшь *pf.* to fall silent; (*fig.*) to cease corresponding.

заморáжива|ть, ю *impf. of* ▶ **заморóзить**

заморó|женный *p.p.p. of* ▶ **~зить** *and adj.* frozen; iced; **~женное мя́со** frozen meat.

заморó|зить, жу, зишь *pf.* (*of* ▶ **заморáживать**) to freeze.

зáмороз|ок, ка *m.* (*usu. pl.*) (light) frost.

заморóч|ить, у, ишь *pf. of* ▶ **морóчить**

замóтан|ный (~, ~а) *adj.* (*coll.*) worn out, shattered.

замотá|ть, ю *pf.* (*of* ▶ **замáтывать**)
[1] to wind, twist; (+ *i.*) (*обмотать*) to wrap (in, with).
[2] (*fig., coll.*) (*утомить*) to tire out.

замоч|úть, ý, ~ишь
[1] *pf.* (*of* ▶ **замáчивать**) (*слегка*) to wet; (*погрузить в воду*) to soak.
[2] *pf. of* ▶ **мочúть**

зáмуж *adv.*: **вы́йти з. за когó-н.** to marry s.o. (*of woman*); **вы́дать когó-н. з.** (**за** + *a.*) to give s.o. in marriage (to); to marry off (to).

зáмужем *adv.*: **быть з.** (**за** + *i.*) to be married (to) (*of woman*).

замур|овáть, ýю *pf.* to brick up; (*человека*) to immure.

замурóвыва|ть, ю *impf. of* ▶ **замуровáть**

замýч|ить, у, ишь *pf.* (*of* ▶ **мýчить**) to torment; (*утомить*) to wear out; (*разговорами*) to bore to tears; (*убить*) to torture to death.

замýч|иться, усь, ишься *pf.* (*of* ▶ **мýчиться**) to be worn out.

зáмш|а, и *f.* chamois (leather); suede.

замыкáни|е, я *nt.* locking; **корóткое з.** (*elec.*) short circuit.

замыкá|ть(ся), ю(сь) *impf. of* ▶ **замкнýть(ся)**

зáмыс|ел, ла *m.* (*план*) project, plan; design, scheme; (*смысл*) idea.

замы́сл|ить, ю, ишь *pf.* (*of* ▶ **замышля́ть**) (+ *a. or inf.*) to plan; to contemplate; **он ~ил самоубúйство** he contemplated suicide.

замысловáт|ый (~, ~а) *adj.* intricate, complicated.

замышля́|ть, ю *impf. of* ▶ **замы́слить**

зáнавес, а *m.* curtain.

занавé|сить, шу, сишь *pf.* (*of* ▶ **~шивать**) to curtain; to cover.

занавéск|а, и *f.* curtain (*of light material*).

занавéшива|ть, ю *impf. of* ▶ **занавéсить**

занес|тú, ý, ёшь, *past* **~, ~лá** *pf.* (*of* ▶ **заносúть**)
[1] (*принести*) to bring; (*доставить мимоходом*) to drop off.

2 (*поднять*) to raise, lift.
3 (*записать*) to note down; **з. в протокол/список** to enter in the minutes/list.
4 (*impers.*): **з. снéгом** to cover with snow; **дорóгу ~лó снéгом** the road is snowed up.

занимáтел|ьный (~ен, ~ьна) *adj.* entertaining, diverting; absorbing.

занимá|ть[1]**, ю** *impf.* (*of* ▸ **занять**)
1 (*город, квартиру*) to occupy; **кровáть ~ет мнóго мéста** the bed takes up a lot of room; **он ~ет высóкое положéние** (*fig.*) he occupies a high post.
2 (*увлекать*) to occupy; to interest; **бóльше всегó егó ~ют вопрóсы филосóфии** his chief interest is in philosophy.
3 (*время*) to take; **éто ~ет мнóго врéмени** this takes a lot of time.
4 (*пост, должность*) to take up.
5 : **з. мéсто комý-н./для когó-н.** to reserve a seat for s.o.; **з. пéрвое мéсто** to take first place.

занимá|ть[2]**, ю** *impf.* (*of* ▸ **занять**) (*деньги*) to borrow.

занимá|ться, юсь *impf.* (*of* ▸ **заняться**) (+ *i.*)
1 to be occupied (with), be engaged (in); (*работать*) to work (at, on); (*учиться*) to study; to practise; **чем он ~ется?** what does he do? (*for a living*).
2 (*посвящать себя*) to devote o.s. (to); **з. естéственными наýками** to devote o.s. to the natural sciences; **з. собóй** to devote time to o.s.
3 (**с** + *i.*) (*помогать в учении*) to assist with (*study*).

зáново *adv.* anew.

занóз|а, ы *f.* splinter.

зано|зить, жý, зишь *pf.* to get a splinter into.

занóс, а *m.* drift; **снéжные ~ы** snowdrifts; **песчáный з.** sand drift.

зано|сить, шý, ~сишь *impf. of* ▸ **занести**

занóсчив|ый (~, ~а) *adj.* arrogant, haughty.

занýд|а, ы *c.g.* (*coll.*) tiresome person, pain in the neck.

занýд|ный (~ен, ~на) *adj.* (*coll.*) tiresome.

занáти|е, я *nt.*
1 (*дело*) occupation; pursuit.
2 (*pl.*) studies; (*usu. pl.*) (*урок*) lesson, class.

занáт|ный (~ен, ~на) *adj.* (*coll.*) entertaining, amusing.

занятóй *adj.* busy.

зáнятост|ь, и *f.*
1 busyness, lack of time
2 (*econ.*) employment; **пóлная з.** full employment; **центр ~и** jobcentre (*Br.*), employment agency.

зáнят|ый (~, ~á, ~о) *p.p.p. of* ▸ **~ь** *and adj.*
1 occupied; **~о** (*телефон, туалет*) engaged.
2 (*only short forms*) (*человек*) busy; **он сейчáс ~** he is busy at the moment.

зан|ять, займý, займёшь, *past* **~ял, ~ялá, ~яло** *pf. of* ▸ **занимáть**

зан|яться, займýсь, займёшься, *past* **~ялся, ~ялáсь** *pf. of* ▸ **занимáться**

заоднó *adv.* in concert, at one; **дéйствовать з.** to act in concert.

заокеáнский *adj.* transoceanic.

заор|áть, ý, ёшь *pf.* (*coll.*) to begin to bawl, begin to yell.

заострённый *p.p.p. of* ▸ **заострить** *and adj.* pointed, sharp.

заóчно *adv.*
1 (*в отсутствие кого-н.*) in one's absence.
2 (*об обучении*) by correspondence course, externally.

заóчн|ый *adj.*: **з. курс** correspondence course; **~ое обучéние** distance learning.

зáпад, а *m.*
1 west.
2 (**З.**) (*pol.*) the West.

зáпадный *adj.* west, western; (*направление, ветер*) westerly.

западн|я, и, *g. pl.* **~éй** *f.* trap, snare; **попáсть в ~ю** to fall into a trap (*also fig.*).

запак|овáть, ýю *pf.* (*of* ▸ **~óвывать**) to pack (up); to wrap up, do up.

запакóвыва|ть, ю *impf. of* ▸ **запаковáть**

запáл, а *m.* fuse.

запáс, а *m.*
1 supply, stock; reserve; **про з.** for an emergency; **отложить про з.** to put by; **словáрный з.** vocabulary; **у меня день в ~е** I have one day in reserve, to spare.
2 (*mil.*) reserve; **егó увóлили в з.** he has been transferred to the reserve.

запасá|ть(ся), ю(сь) *impf. of* ▸ **запасти(сь)**

запаснóй *adj.* spare; (*игрок*) reserve; **з. выход** emergency exit; *as n.* **з., ~óго** *m.* (*mil.*) reservist; (*sport*) reserve.

запас|ти, ý, ёшь, *past* **~, ~лá** *pf.* (*of* ▸ **~áть**) (+ *a. or g.*) to stock, store; to lay in a stock of.

запас|тись, ýсь, ёшься, *past* **~ся, ~лáсь** *pf.* (*of* ▸ **~áться**) (+ *i.*) to provide o.s. (with); to stock up (on, with); **з. терпéнием** (*fig.*) to arm o.s. with patience.

запатентовáть *pf. of* ▸ **патентовáть**

зáпах, а *m.* smell.

запáчка|ть(ся), ю(сь) *pf. of* ▸ **пáчкать(ся)**

запевá|ть, ю *impf. of* ▸ **запéть**

запекá|ть, ю *impf. of* ▸ **запéчь**

зап|ерéть, рý, рёшь, *past* **~ер, ерлá, ~ерло** *pf.* (*of* ▸ **~ирáть**)
1 (*дверь*) to lock; **з. на засóв** to bolt.
2 (*человека*) to lock in; to shut up.
3 (*преградить доступ*) to bar; to block up.

зап|ерéться, рýсь, рёшься, *past* **~ерся, ~ерлáсь, ~ерлóсь** *pf.* (*of* ▸ **~ирáться**)
1 to lock o.s. in.
2 (*дверь*) to lock.

зап|éть, ою, оёшь *pf.* (*of* ▸ **~евáть**) (*начать петь*) to begin to sing; **з. пéсню** to break into a song.

запечáт|ать, аю *pf.* (*of* ▸ **~ывать**) to seal.

запечáтыва|ть, ю *impf. of* ▸ **запечáтать**

запé|чь, кý, чёшь, кýт, *past* **~к, ~клá** *pf.* (*of* ▸ **~кáть**) to bake.
запивá|ть, ю *impf. of* ▸ **запи́ть**
запинá|ться, юсь *impf.* (*of* ▸ **запнýться**) to stumble.
запирá|ть(ся), ю(сь) *impf. of* ▸ **заперéть(ся)**
запи|сáть, шý, ~шешь *pf.* (*of* ▸ **~сывать**)
1 (*занести на бумагу*) to note, make a note (of); to take down (in writing); (*концерт, фильм*) to record (*with apparatus*); **з. (на плёнку)** to tape; **з. (на ви́део)** to video.
2 (*включить в состав чего-либо*) to enter, register, enrol.
запи|сáться, шýсь, ~шешься *pf.* (*of* ▸ **~сываться**) to register, enter one's name, enrol; **з. в клуб** to join a club; **з. к врачý** to make an appointment with the doctor.
запи́ск|а, и *f.* note; **деловáя з.** memorandum, minute.
записн|óй *adj.*: **~áя кни́жка** notebook.
запи́сыва|ть(ся), ю(сь) *impf. of* ▸ **записáть(ся)**
зáпис|ь, и *f.*
1 (*действие*) writing down; recording; registration.
2 (*в дневнике*) entry; (*comput.*) record; (*заметка*) note; (*на плёнку*) recording; (*leg.*) deed.
зап|и́ть, ью́, ьёшь *pf.* (*of* ▸ **~ивáть**)
1 (*past* **~и́л, ~илá, ~и́ло** + *a. and i.*) to wash down (with); to take (with, after); **з. таблéтку водóй** to take a tablet with water.
2 (*past* **~ил, ~илá, ~ило**) to begin to drink heavily.
запи|шý, ~шешь *see* ▸ **~сáть**
заплáкан|ный (~, ~а) *adj.* tear-stained; in tears.
заплá|кать, чу, чешь *pf.* to begin to cry.
запланир|овать, ую *pf. of* ▸ **плани́ровать**
заплáт|а, ы *f.* patch (*in garments*); **наложи́ть ~у (на** + *a.*) to patch.
запла|ти́ть, чý, ~тишь *pf. of* ▸ **плати́ть**
запла|чý, ~тишь *see* ▸ **~ти́ть**
запла́|чу, чешь *see* ▸ **~кать**
запле|сти́, тý, тёшь, *past* **~л, ~лá** *pf.* (*of* ▸ **заплетáть**) (*волосы*) to braid, plait.
заплетá|ть, ю *impf. of* ▸ **заплести́**
запломбир|овáть, ýю *pf.* (*of* ▸ **пломбировáть**)
1 (*зуб*) to fill.
2 (*вагон, избирательную урну*) to seal.
заплывá|ть, ю *impf. of* ▸ **заплы́ть**[1,2]
заплы́|ть[1]**, вý, вёшь,** *past* **~л, ~лá, ~ло** *pf.* (*of* ▸ **~вáть**) (*о пловце*) to swim far out; (*о судне*) to sail away.
заплы́|ть[2]**, вý, вёшь,** *past* **~л, ~лá, ~ло** *pf.* (*of* ▸ **~вáть**) to be swollen; to be bloated; **~вшие жи́ром глазá** bloated eyes.
запн|ýться, ýсь, ёшься *pf. of* ▸ **запинáться**
заповéдник, а *m.* reserve; preserve; sanctuary; **госудáрственный з.** national park.
зáповед|ь, и *f.* precept; (*relig. and fig.*) commandment; **дéсять ~ей** the Ten Commandments.
заподáзрива|ть, ю *impf. of* ▸ **заподóзрить**
заподóзр|ить, ю, ишь *pf.* (*of* ▸ **заподáзривать**) (+ *a. and* **в** + *p.*) to suspect (of).
запоздáлый *adj.* belated.
заползá|ть, ю *impf. of* ▸ **заползти́**
заполз|ти́, ý, ёшь, *past* **~, ~лá** *pf.* (*of* ▸ **~áть**) **(в, под** + *a.*) to creep, crawl (into, under).
запóлн|ить, ю, ишь *pf.* (*of* ▸ **~я́ть**) to fill in, fill up; **з. бланк** to fill in (*Br.*), out (*US*) a form.
запóлн|иться, ится *pf.* (*of* ▸ **~я́ться**) to fill up (*intrans.*).
заполня́|ть(ся), ю, ет(ся) *impf. of* ▸ **запóлнить(ся)**
заполя́рь|е, я *nt.* (*geog.*) polar regions.
запоминá|ть(ся), ю(сь) *impf. of* ▸ **запóмнить(ся)**
запóмн|ить, ю, ишь *pf.* (*of* ▸ **запоминáть**)
1 (*текст, номер*) to memorize.
2 (*человека, картину, событие*) to remember.
запóмн|иться, юсь, ишься *pf.* (*of* ▸ **запоминáться**) to stick, remain in one's memory.
зáпонк|а, и *f.* cufflink; stud.
запóр, а *m.* (*med.*) constipation.
запотевá|ть, ю *impf. of* ▸ **запотéть**
запотé|ть, ю *pf.* (*of* ▸ **потéть** *and* ▸ **~вáть**) to mist over.
зап|ою́, оёшь *see* ▸ **~éть**
запрáв|ить, лю, ишь *pf.* (*of* ▸ **~ля́ть**)
1 (*вставить*) to insert; **з. брю́ки в сапоги́** to tuck one's trousers into one's boots.
2 (*приготовить*) to prepare; **з. автомоби́ль бензи́ном** to fill a car up with petrol.
3 (+ *i.*) (*добавить*) to mix in; (*сдобрить*) to season (with).
запрáв|иться, люсь, ишься *pf.* (*of* ▸ **~ля́ться**) (*горючим*) to refuel (*intrans.*).
запрáвк|а, и *f.*
1 (*приправа*) seasoning; **з. для салáта** salad dressing.
2 (*машины*) refuelling (*Br.*), refueling (*US*).
3 (*coll.*) (*заправочная станция*) filling station.
заправля́|ть, ю *impf. of* ▸ **заправить;** (+ *i.*) (*coll.*) to be in charge (of).
заправля́|ться, юсь *impf. of* ▸ **запрáвиться**
запрáвочн|ый *adj.*: **~ая стáнция** filling station.
запрáшива|ть, ю *impf. of* ▸ **запроси́ть**
запрéт, а *m.* prohibition, ban; **быть под ~ом** to be banned; **наложи́ть з. (на** + *a.*) to place a ban (on).
запре|ти́ть, щý, ти́шь *pf.* (*of* ▸ **~щáть**) (*не позволять*) to prohibit, forbid; **«въезд запрещён»** 'No Entry'; (*книгу, наркотики, оружие*) to ban.
запрéтн|ый *adj.* forbidden; **~ая тéма** taboo subject.
запрещá|ть, ю *impf. of* ▸ **запрети́ть**

запреща́|ться, ется *impf.* to be forbidden, to be prohibited.

запрограмми́р|овать, ую *pf. of* ▶ **программи́ровать**

запроки́дыва|ть, ю *impf. of* ▶ **запроки́нуть**

запроки́н|уть, у, ешь *pf.* to throw back.

запро́с, а *m.*
1 inquiry; (*pol.*) question.
2 (*pl. only*) (*потребности*) needs, requirements.

запро|си́ть, шу́, ~́сишь *pf.* (*of* ▶ **запра́шивать**)
1 (**о** + *p.*) to inquire (about); (+ *a.*) (*попросить*) to request.
2: **з. сли́шком высо́кую це́ну** (*coll.*) to ask an exorbitant price.

3

за́просто *adv.* (*coll.*) (*без формальностей*) without ceremony, without formality; (*coll.*) (*легко*) without any problem, easily.

зап|ру́, рёшь *see* ▶ **~ере́ть**

запры́гива|ть, ю *impf. of* ▶ **запры́гнуть**

запры́гн|уть, у, ешь *pf.* (*of* ▶ **запры́гивать**) (**за** + *a.*) to leap (over); (**на** + *a.*) to jump (onto).

запряга́|ть, ю *impf. of* ▶ **запря́чь**

запря́|чь, гу́, жёшь, гу́т, *past* **~г, ~гла́** *pf.* (*of* ▶ **~га́ть**) to harness (*also fig.*).

запу́ганный *p.p.p. of* ▶ **запуга́ть** *and adj.* broken-spirited; frightened.

запуга́|ть, ю *pf.* (*of* ▶ **запу́гивать**) to intimidate, cow; to frighten.

запу́гива|ть, ю *impf. of* ▶ **запуга́ть**

за́пуск, а *m.* (*мотора*) starting; (*ракеты*) launch, launching; (*comput.*) running.

запус|ка́ть, ка́ю *impf. of* ▶ **~ти́ть**

запусте́ни|е, я *nt.* neglect; desolation.

запу|сти́ть¹, щу́, ~́стишь *pf.* (*of* ▶ **~ска́ть**)
1 (+ *i. and* **в** + *a.*; *coll.*) (*бросить*) to throw (at), fling (at).
2 (**в** + *a.*) (*засунуть*) to thrust (*hands, etc.*, into); **з. ко́гти, ла́пы, ру́ки** (**в** + *a.*; *fig.*) to get one's hands on.
3 (*привести в действие*) to start (up); (*comput.*) to run; **з. мото́р** to start up the engine; **з. раке́ту** to launch a rocket.

запу|сти́ть², щу́, ~́стишь *pf.* (*of* ▶ **~ска́ть**)
1 (*оставить без ухода*) to neglect, allow to fall into neglect; **з. дела́** to neglect one's affairs; **з. сад** to neglect a garden.
2 (*дать развиться*) to allow to develop unchecked.

запу́тан|ный (~, ~а) *p.p.p. of* ▶ **запу́тать** *and adj.* (**~, ~на**) tangled; (*fig.*) intricate, involved; **з. вопро́с** knotty question.

запу́та|ть, ю *pf.* (*of* ▶ **запу́тывать** *and* ▶ **пу́тать**)
1 (*нитки, волосы*) to tangle (up).
2 (*fig.*) (*человека*) to confuse; (*дело*) to complicate; to muddle.

запу́та|ться, юсь *pf.* (*of* ▶ **запу́тываться** *and* ▶ **пу́таться**)
1 (*нитки, волосы*) to become entangled; to foul (*intrans.*); (**в** + *p.*) (*в сетях*) to entangle o.s. (in), be caught (in).
2 (**в** + *p.*; *fig.*) (*в деле*) to become entangled (in), become involved (in); (*дело, речь*) to become confused, complicated; (*сбиться с толку*) to get in a muddle.

запу́тыва|ть(ся), ю(сь) *impf. of* ▶ **запу́тать(ся)**

запу́щен|ный (~, ~а) *p.p.p. of* ▶ **запусти́ть²** *and adj.* (**~, ~на**) neglected.

запча́ст|и, е́й *pl.* (*sg.* **~ь, ~и** *f.*; *abbr. of* **запасны́е ча́сти**) spare parts; spares.

запыха́|ться, юсь *pf.* (*coll.*) to be out of breath.

запя́сть|е, я *nt.* wrist.

запят|а́я, о́й *f.* comma.

зараба́тыва|ть, ю *impf. of* ▶ **зарабо́тать 1**

зарабо́та|ть, ю *pf.* (*of* ▶ **зараба́тывать**)
1 (*приобрести работой*) to earn.
2 (*no impf.*) (*начать работать*) to begin to work; to start (up).

за́работн|ый *adj.*: **~ая пла́та** wages, pay, salary.

за́работ|ок, ка *m.* earnings; **лёгкий з.** easy money.

зара́внива|ть, ю *impf. of* ▶ **заровня́ть**

заража́|ть(ся), ю(сь) *impf. of* ▶ **зарази́ть(ся)**

зараже́ни|е, я *nt.* infection; (*местности*) contamination.

зара|жу́, зи́шь *see* ▶ **~зи́ть**

зара́з|а, ы *f.*
1 infection, contagion.
2 (*fig., coll.*) (*негодяй*) pest.

зарази́тел|ьный (~ен, ~ьна) *adj.* infectious; catching; **з. смех** infectious laughter.

зара|зи́ть, жу́, зи́шь *pf.* (*of* ▶ **~жа́ть**) (+ *i.*) to infect (with) (*also fig.*); (*местность*) to contaminate.

зара|зи́ться, жу́сь, зи́шься *pf.* (*of* ▶ **~жа́ться**) (+ *i.*) to be infected (with); catch (*also fig.*).

зара́з|ный (~ен, ~на) *adj.* infectious; contagious; **з. больно́й** infectious case; *as n.* **з., ~ного** *m.*, **~ная, ~ной** *f.* infectious case.

зара́нее *adv.* beforehand; in good time; **заплати́ть з.** to pay in advance.

зараста́|ть, ю *impf. of* ▶ **зарасти́**

зараст|и́, у́, ёшь, *past* **заро́с, заросла́** *pf.* (*of* ▶ **~а́ть**)
1 (+ *i.*) to be overgrown (with); **тропа́ заросла́ мхом** the path was overgrown with moss.
2 (*о ране*) to heal.

зарегистри́р|овать, ую *pf.* (*of* ▶ **регистри́ровать**) to register.

зарегистри́р|оваться, уюсь *pf.* (*of* ▶ **регистри́роваться**) to register o.s.

заре́|зать, жу, жешь *pf.* (*of* ▶ **ре́зать 3**) (*человека*) to murder; to knife; (*животное*) to slaughter; (*coll.*) (*о волке*) to devour, kill.

зарезерви́р|овать, ую *pf. of* ▶ **резерви́ровать**

зарекоменд|ова́ть, у́ю *pf. only in phr.*: **з. себя́** (+ *i.*) to prove o.s., show o.s. (to be); **хорошо́ з. себя́** to show to advantage.

заржаве́|ть, ет *pf.* (*of* ▸ **ржаве́ть**) to rust; to have got rusty.
зарис|ова́ть, у́ю *pf.* (*of* ▸ **~о́вывать**) to sketch.
зарисо́вк|а, и *f.* sketch.
зарисо́выва|ть, ю *impf. of* ▸ **зарисова́ть**
заровня́|ть, ю *pf.* (*of* ▸ **зара́внивать**) to level, even up; **з. я́му** to fill up a hole.
заро|ди́ться, жу́сь, ди́шься *pf.* (*of* ▸ **~жда́ться**) (*возникнуть*) to arise, come into being; **у него́ ~ди́лось сомне́ние** a doubt arose in his mind.
заро́дыш, а *m.* (*biol.*) embryo; (*fig.*) embryo, germ; **подави́ть в ~е** to nip in the bud.
заро́дышевый *adj.* embryonic.
зарожда́|ться, юсь *impf. of* ▸ **зароди́ться**
за́росл|ь, и *f.* (*usu. pl.*) thicket.
зар|о́ю, о́ешь *see* ▸ **~ы́ть**
зарпла́т|а, ы *f.* (*abbr. of* **за́работная пла́та**) wages, pay, salary; **сего́дня з.** today is pay day.
заруба́|ть, ю *impf. of* ▸ **заруби́ть**
зарубе́жный *adj.* foreign.
зарубе́жь|е, я *nt.* foreign countries; **бли́жнее з.** the countries of the former Soviet Union; **да́льнее з.** abroad (*excluding the countries of the former Soviet Union*).
заруб|и́ть, лю́, ~ишь *pf.* (*of* ▸ **~а́ть**)
1 (*убить*) to hack to death.
2 (*сделать зарубку*) to notch, make an incision (on).
зарыва́|ть, ю *impf. of* ▸ **зары́ть**
зарыва́|ться, юсь *impf. of* ▸ **зары́ться**
зар|ы́ть, о́ю, о́ешь *pf.* (*of* ▸ **~ыва́ть**) to bury.
зар|ы́ться, о́юсь, о́ешься *pf.* (*of* ▸ **~ыва́ться**) to bury o.s.
зар|я́, и́, *pl.* **зо́ри, зорь, зо́рям** *f.* daybreak, dawn (*also fig.*).
заря|ди́ть, жу́, ~ди́шь *pf.* (*of* ▸ **~жа́ть**)
1 (*орудие, фотоаппарат*) to load.
2 (*elec.*) (*батарею*) to charge.
заря́дк|а, и *f.*
1 (*ружья*) loading; (*elec.*) charging.
2 (*упражнения*) exercises; drill.
заря́дн|ый *adj.*: **~ое устро́йство** charger, charging unit (*for battery*).
заряжа́|ть, ю *impf. of* ▸ **заряди́ть**
заря|жу́, ~ди́шь *see* ▸ **~ди́ть**
заса́д|а, ы *f.* ambush.
заса́лива|ть, ю *impf. of* ▸ **засоли́ть**
заса́сыва|ть, ю *impf. of* ▸ **засоса́ть**
засверка́|ть, ю *pf.* to begin to sparkle, begin to twinkle.
засве|ти́ться, ~тится *pf.* to light up (*also fig.*).
заседа́ни|е, я *nt.* (*собрание*) meeting; (*совещание*) conference; (*суда*) session, sitting.
заседа́|ть, ю *impf.* to sit; to meet.
засе́ива|ть, ю *impf. of* ▸ **засе́ять**
засекре́|тить, чу, тишь *pf.* (*of* ▸ **~чивать**) to place on secret list; to classify as secret, restrict.
засекре́|ченный *p.p.p. of* ▸ **~тить** *and adj.* secret; (*документы, сведения*) classified.
засекре́чива|ть, ю *impf. of* ▸ **засекре́тить**
засел|и́ть, ю́, и́шь *pf.* (*of* ▸ **~я́ть**) (*землю*) to settle; to colonize; **з. но́вый дом** to occupy a new house.
засел|я́ть, я́ю *impf. of* ▸ **~и́ть**
засе́|ять, ю, ешь *pf.* (*of* ▸ **~ивать**) to sow.
заска́кива|ть, ю *impf. of* ▸ **заскочи́ть**
заскоч|и́ть, у́, ~ишь *pf.* (*of* ▸ **заска́кивать**)
1 (**за** + *a.*, **на** + *a.*) to jump, spring (behind, onto).
2 (**в** + *a.*; *fig.*) to drop in (to, at).
заскуча́|ть, ю *pf.*
1 to get bored.
2 (**по** + *d.*) to begin to miss.
за|сла́ть, шлю́, шлёшь *pf.* (*of* ▸ **~сыла́ть**) to send, dispatch; **з. шпио́на** to send out a spy.
заслон|и́ть, ю́, и́шь *pf.* (*of* ▸ **~я́ть**) (*закрыть*) to hide, cover; (*защитить*) to shield, screen.
заслон|и́ться, ю́сь, и́шься *pf.* (*of* ▸ **~я́ться**) (**от** + *g.*) to shield o.s., screen o.s. (from).
засло́нк|а, и *f.* oven door; (*регулятор тяги*) damper.
заслон|я́ть(ся), я́ю(сь) *impf. of* ▸ **~и́ть(ся)**
заслу́г|а, и *f.* service; contribution; **они́ получи́ли по ~ам** they got what they deserved.
заслу́жива|ть, ю *impf.* (*of* ▸ **заслужи́ть**) (+ *g.*) to deserve, merit.
заслуж|и́ть, у́, ~ишь *pf.* (*of* ▸ **~ивать**) (+ *a.*) to deserve, merit; (*выслужить*) to win, earn.
засме|я́ться, ю́сь, ёшься *pf.* to begin to laugh.
засне́жен|ный (~, ~а) *adj.* snow-covered.
засн|у́ть, у́, ёшь *pf.* (*of* ▸ **засыпа́ть**[1]) to go to sleep, fall asleep.
засо́в, а *m.* bolt, bar.
засо́выва|ть, ю *impf. of* ▸ **засу́нуть**
засол|и́ть, ю́, ~ишь *pf.* (*of* ▸ **заса́ливать**) to salt; to pickle.
засор|и́ть, ю́, и́шь *pf.* (*of* ▸ **~я́ть**)
1 (*трубу*) to clog, block up, stop.
2 (*глаза*) to get dirt into; **з. желу́док** to have constipation.
засор|и́ться, и́тся *pf.* (*of* ▸ **~я́ться**) to become obstructed, blocked up.
засоря́|ть(ся), ю, ет(ся) *impf. of* ▸ **засори́ть(ся)**
засос|а́ть, у́, ёшь *pf.* (*of* ▸ **заса́сывать**) to suck in, engulf, swallow up (*also fig.*).
засо́х|нуть, ну, нешь, *past* **~, ~ла** *pf.* (*of* ▸ **засыха́ть**)
1 (*о булке, красках*) to dry (up).
2 (*о траве*) to wither.
заста́в|а, ы *f.*
1 (*пограничная застава*) border post.
2 (*mil.*) picket; outpost.
заста|ва́ть, ю́, ёшь *impf. of* ▸ **~ть**
заста́в|ить[1]**, лю, ишь** *pf.* (*of* ▸ **~ля́ть**[1])
1 (*загромоздить*) to cram, fill; **з. ко́мнату**

мéбелью to cram a room with furniture.
[2] (*загородить*) to block up, obstruct.

застáв|ить², лю, ишь *pf.* (*of* ▸ **∼лять²**) (+ *a. and inf.*) (*принудить*) to compel, force, make.

застáвк|а, и *f.* (*TV*) repeated image at the start of TV programme; logo; **музыкáльная з.** signature tune.

заставля́|ть¹˒², ю *impf. of* ▸ **застáвить¹˒²**

застá|ну, нешь *see* ▸ **∼ть**

застá|ть, ну, нешь *pf.* (*of* ▸ **∼вáть**) to find; **вы ∼ли егó дóма?** did you find him in?; **з. врасплóх** to catch napping; **з. на мéсте преступлéния** to catch red-handed.

заста|ю́, ёшь *see* ▸ **∼вáть**

застёгива|ть, ю *impf. of* ▸ **застегнýть**

застёгива|ться, юсь *impf.* (*of* ▸ **застегнýться**)
[1] to fasten, do up (*intrans.*); **воротни́к ∼ется на пýговицу** the collar does up with a button.
[2] to button o.s. up; **з. на все пýговицы** to do up all one's buttons.

застег|нýть, нý, нёшь *pf.* (*of* ▸ **∼̃ивать**) to fasten, do up; **з. (на пýговицы)** to button up.

застег|нýться, нýсь, нёшься *pf. of* ▸ **∼̃иваться**

застёжк|а, и *f.* fastening; clasp.

застекл|и́ть, ю́, и́шь *pf.* (*of* ▸ **∼я́ть** *and* ▸ **стекли́ть**) to glaze, fit with glass; **з. портрéт** to frame a portrait.

застекл|я́ть, я́ю *impf. of* ▸ **∼и́ть**

застел|и́ть, ю́, ∼́ешь *pf.* = **застлáть 1**

застéнчив|ый (∼, ∼а) *adj.* shy; bashful.

засти́|г, гла *see* ▸ **∼чь**

засти|гáть, гáю *impf. of* ▸ **∼́гнуть** *and* ▸ **∼́чь**

засти́|гнуть = **∼чь**

застилá|ть, ю *impf. of* ▸ **застлáть**

засти́|чь, гну, гнешь, *past* **∼г, ∼гла** *pf.* (*of* ▸ **∼гáть**) to catch; to take unawares; **нас ∼гла грозá** we were caught by the storm.

заст|лáть, елю́, éлешь *pf.* (*of* ▸ **∼илáть**)
[1] (+ *i.*) to cover (with); **з. коврóм** to carpet, lay a carpet (over).
[2] (*fig.*) to hide from view; to cloud; **слёзы ∼лáли её глазá** tears dimmed her eyes.
[3] (*кровать*) to make.

застó|й, я *m.* stagnation (*fig.*); **в ∼е** at a standstill; (*econ.*) depression.

застóль|е, я *nt.* (*coll.*) celebratory meal.

застóльн|ый *adj.* table-, occurring at table; **∼ая бесéда** table talk; **∼ая пéсня** drinking song.

застрáива|ть, ю *impf. of* ▸ **застрóить**

застрахóван|ный *p.p.p. of* ▸ **застраховáть** *and adj.* insured; *as n.* **з., ∼ного** *m.* insured person.

застрах|овáть, ýю *pf.* (*of* ▸ **страховáть**) (**от** + *g.*) to insure (against).

застрах|овáться, ýюсь *pf.* (*of* ▸ **страховáться**) to insure o.s.

застревá|ть, ю *impf. of* ▸ **застря́ть**

застрéлива|ть(ся), ю(сь) *impf. of* ▸ **застрели́ть(ся)**

застрел|и́ть, ю́, ∼́ишь *pf.* (*of* ▸ **∼́ивать**) to shoot (dead).

застрел|и́ться, ю́сь, ∼́ишься *pf.* (*of* ▸ **∼́иваться**) to shoot o.s.; to blow one's brains out.

застрóенный *p.p.p. of* ▸ **застрóить** *and adj.* built-up.

застрó|ить, ю, ишь *pf.* (*of* ▸ **застрáивать**) to build on, develop.

застрóйк|а, и *f.* building; development; **прáво ∼и** building permit.

застря́|ну, нешь *see* ▸ **∼ть**

застря́|ть, ну, нешь *pf.* (*of* ▸ **застревáть**)
[1] to stick; **з. в грязи́** to get stuck in the mud; **словá ∼ли у негó в гóрле** the words stuck in his throat.
[2] (*fig., coll.*) (*задержаться*) to be held up; to become bogged down.

зáступ, а *m.* spade.

заступá|ться, юсь *impf. of* ▸ **заступи́ться**

заступ|и́ться, лю́сь, ∼́ишься *pf.* (**за** + *a.*) to stand up for; to plead (for).

застывá|ть, ю *impf. of* ▸ **засты́ть**

засты́|ну, нешь *see* ▸ **∼ть**

засты́|ть *pf.* (*of* ▸ **∼вáть**)
[1] (*о желе, цементе*) to set; (*о лаве*) to harden.
[2] (*coll.*) (*о руках*) to become stiff; (*fig.*): **з. от ýжаса** to be paralysed with fright.
[3] (*coll.*) (*о воде*) to freeze (*also fig.*).

засýн|уть, у, ешь *pf.* (*of* ▸ **засóвывать**) to stick in, thrust in; **з. рýки в кармáны** to thrust one's hands into one's pockets.

зáсух|а, и *f.* drought.

засýчива|ть, ю *impf. of* ▸ **засучи́ть**

засуч|и́ть, ý, ∼́ишь *pf.* (*of* ▸ **∼́ивать**) (**рукавá**, *etc.*) to roll up (*sleeves, etc.*).

засýшива|ть(ся), ю, ет(ся) *impf. of* ▸ **засуши́ть(ся)**

засуш|и́ть, ý, ∼́ишь *pf.* (*of* ▸ **∼́ивать**) to dry up (*plants; also fig.*).

засуш|и́ться, ∼́ится *pf.* (*of* ▸ **∼́иваться**) to dry up (*intrans.*), shrivel.

засýшлив|ый (∼, ∼а) *adj.* dry, droughty.

засчит|áть, áю *pf.* (*of* ▸ **∼́ывать**) to take into consideration; **з. в уплáту дóлга** to reckon towards payment of a debt.

засчи́тыва|ть, ю *impf. of* ▸ **засчитáть**

засылá|ть, ю *impf. of* ▸ **заслáть**

засыпá|ть¹, ю *impf. of* ▸ **заснýть**

засыпá|ть², ю *impf. of* ▸ **засы́пать**

засы́п|ать, лю, лешь *pf.* (*of* ▸ **∼áть²**)
[1] (*яму*) to fill up.
[2] (+ *i.*) (*покрыть*) to cover (with), strew (with).
[3] (+ *i.; fig., coll.*): **з. вопрóсами** to bombard with questions.
[4] (+ *a. or g.* **в** + *a.; coll.*) to put (into).

засыхá|ть, ю *impf. of* ▸ **засóхнуть**

затáива|ть(ся), ю(сь) *impf. of* ▸ **затаи́ть(ся)**

зата|и́ть, ю́, и́шь *pf.* (*of* ▸ **∼́ивать**) (*мечту, злобу*) to harbour (*Br.*), harbor (*US*), cherish; **з. оби́ду (на** + *a.*) to nurse a grievance (against); **з. дыхáние** to hold one's breath.

зата|и́ться, ю́сь, и́шься *pf.* (*of*

▸ ~иваться) (*coll.*) to hide (*intrans.*).
заталкива|ть, ю *impf. of* ▸ **затолкать** *and* ▸ **затолкнуть**
затаплива|ть, ю *impf. of* ▸ **затопить**[1]
затаптыва|ть, ю *impf. of* ▸ **затоптать**
затаскива|ть, ю *impf. of* ▸ **затащить**
затачива|ть, ю *impf. of* ▸ **заточить**
затащ|ить, у, ~ишь *pf.* (*of* ▸ **затаскивать**) (*coll.*) to drag off, drag away (*also fig.*).
затвердева|ть, ет *impf. of* ▸ **затвердеть**
затверде|ть, ет *pf.* (*of* ▸ **~вать** *and* ▸ **твердеть**) (*о земле, цементе*) to harden, become hard; (*о жидкости*) to set.
затвор, а *m.*
1 (*винтовки*) bolt; breechblock; (*плотины*) floodgate.
2 (*phot.*) shutter.
затева|ть, ю *impf. of* ▸ **затеять**
затека|ть, ю *impf. of* ▸ **затечь**
затем *adv.*
1 (*после этого*) after that, then, next.
2 (*для этого*) for that reason; **з. что** because, since, as; **она приехала з., чтобы ухаживать за тобой** she has come (in order) to look after you.
зате|чь, чёт, кут, *past* **~к, ~кла** *pf.* (*of* ▸ **~кать**) (*онеметь*) to become numb; **у меня нога ~кла** my foot's gone numb.
зате|я, и *f.* undertaking, enterprise, venture.
зате|ять, ю *pf.* (*of* ▸ **~вать**) (*coll.*) (*путешествие*) to undertake; (*игру*) to organize; (*разговор, драку, спор*) to start.
затих|ать, аю *impf. of* ▸ **~нуть**
затих|нуть, ну, нешь, *past* **~, ~ла** *pf.* (*of* ▸ **~ать**) (*о звуке, ветре, буре*) to die down, abate; (*о человеке*) to quieten down (*Br.*), quiet down (*US*).
затишь|е, я *nt.* calm; lull.
заткн|уть, у, ёшь *pf.* (*of* ▸ **затыкать**)
1 (+ *a. and i.*) to stop up; to plug; **з. бутылку пробкой** to cork a bottle; **з. рот, глотку кому-н.** (*coll.*) to shut s.o. up.
2 (*засунуть*) to stick, thrust; **з. кого-н. за пояс** (*fig., coll.*) to outdo s.o.
заткн|уться, усь, ёшься *pf.* (*coll.*) to shut up; **~ись!** shut up!
затмева|ть, ю *impf. of* ▸ **затмить**
затмени|е, я *nt.*
1 (*astron.*) eclipse.
2 (*fig., coll.*) blackout.
затм|ить, ишь *pf.* (*of* ▸ **~евать**)
1 to obscure.
2 (*fig.*) to eclipse; to overshadow.
зато *conj.* (*coll.*) but then, but on the other hand; but to make up for it; **дорого, з. хорошая вещь** it is expensive, but then it is good stuff.
затолка|ть, ю *pf.* (*of* ▸ **заталкивать**) to jostle.
затолкн|уть, у, ёшь *pf.* (*of* ▸ **заталкивать**) (*coll.*) to shove in.
затон|уть, у, ~ешь *pf. of* ▸ **тонуть 1**
затоп|ить[1]**, лю, ~ишь** *pf.* (*of* ▸ **затапливать**) (*печь*) to light; (*включить отопление*) to turn on the heating.
затоп|ить[2]**, лю, ~ишь** *pf.* (*of* ▸ **~лять**)
1 (*остров, окрестности*) to flood; to submerge.
2 (*судно*) to sink; **з. корабль** to scuttle a ship.
затоплять, ю *impf. of* ▸ **затопить**[2]
затоп|тать, чу, ~чешь *pf.* (*of* ▸ **затаптывать**) (*траву, цветы*) to trample down; (*костёр, папиросу*) to stamp out
затоп|чу, ~чешь *see* ▸ **~тать**
затор, а *m.* blocking, obstruction; **з. уличного движения** traffic jam, congestion.
затормо|зить, жу, зишь *pf. of* ▸ **тормозить**
заточ|ить, у, ~ишь *pf.* (*of* ▸ **затачивать**) to sharpen.
затрагива|ть, ю *impf. of* ▸ **затронуть**
затрат|а, ы *f.*
1 (*действие*) expenditure.
2 (*usu. pl.*) (*расходы*) expenses, outlay.
затра|тить, чу, тишь *pf.* (*of* ▸ **~чивать**) to expend, spend.
затрачива|ть, ю *impf. of* ▸ **затратить**
затрещин|а, ы *f.* (*coll.*) box on the ears.
затрон|уть, у, ешь *pf.* (*of* ▸ **затрагивать**)
1 to affect.
2 (*fig.*) to touch (on); **з. вопрос** to broach a question.
затруднени|е, я *nt.* difficulty.
затруднённый *p.p.p. of* ▸ **затруднить** *and adj.* laboured (*Br.*), labored (*US*).
затруднител|ьный (~ен, ~ьна) *adj.* difficult; embarrassing.
затрудн|ить, ю, ишь *pf.* (*of* ▸ **~ять**)
1 (*кого-н.*) to trouble; to cause trouble (to); to embarrass.
2 (*что-н.*) to make difficult; to hamper.
затрудн|ять, яю *impf. of* ▸ **~ить**
затуп|ить, лю, ~ишь *pf.* (*of* ▸ **~лять**) to blunt; to dull.
затуп|иться, ~ится *pf.* (*of* ▸ **~ляться**) to become blunt(ed).
затупля|ть(ся), ю, ет(ся) *impf. of* ▸ **затупить(ся)**
затух|ать, ает *impf. of* ▸ **~нуть**
затух|нуть, нет, *past* **~, ~ла** *pf.* (*of* ▸ **~ать**)
1 (*перестать гореть*) to go out, be extinguished.
2 (*fig., coll.*) (*о звуке*) to die away.
затуш|ить, у, ~ишь *pf.* to put out, extinguish; (*fig.*) to suppress.
затхл|ый (~а) *adj.* (*запах*) musty; (*воздух*) stale, stuffy; (*fig.*) stagnant.
затыка|ть, ю *impf. of* ▸ **заткнуть**
затыл|ок, ка *m.*
1 back of the head.
2 : **становиться в з.** to form up in file.
затычк|а, и *f.* (*coll.*) stopper; plug.
затягива|ть(ся), ю(сь) *impf. of* ▸ **затянуть(ся)**
затяжн|ой, *adj.* long drawn-out, protracted; **~ая болезнь** protracted, lingering illness; **~ые дожди** long periods of rain.
затя|нуть, ну, ~нешь *pf.* (*of* ▸ **~гивать**)

1 (*узел, пояс*) to tighten; (*naut.*) to haul taut.
2 (*покрыть*) to cover; to close; (*impers.*): **не́бо ~нуло ту́чами** it has clouded over.
3 (*засосать*) to drag down, drag in; (*fig., coll.*) (*вовлечь*) to inveigle.
4 (*coll.*) (*продлить*) to drag out, spin out.

затя|ну́ться, ну́сь, ~́нешься *pf.* (*of* ▸ **~́гиваться**)
1 (*затянуть на себе*) to lace o.s. up; (*туго завязаться*) to tighten; **у́зел ~ну́лся** the knot tightened.
2 (*покрыться*) to be covered; to close (*intrans.*), heal over (of a wound).
3 (*coll.*) (*продлиться*) to drag on (*intrans.*).
4 (*при курении*) to inhale.

зау́м|ный (~ен, ~на) *adj.* abstruse, esoteric, unintelligible.

зауны́в|ный (~ен, ~на) *adj.* doleful, plaintive.

заупоко́йн|ый *adj.* for the repose of the soul; **~ая слу́жба** requiem.

зауря́д|ный (~ен, ~на) *adj.* (*обыкновенный*) ordinary, commonplace; (*посредственный*) mediocre.

зау́ченный *p.p.p. of* ▸ **заучи́ть** *and adj.* studied.

зау́чива|ть, ю *impf. of* ▸ **заучи́ть**

зау|чи́ть, чу́, ~́чишь *pf.* (*of* ▸ **~́чивать**) (*твёрдо выучить*) to learn by heart.

зафарши|рова́ть, у́ю *pf. of* ▸ **фарширова́ть**

зафикси́р|овать, ую *pf. of* ▸ **фикси́ровать**

зафрахт|ова́ть, у́ю *pf. of* ▸ **фрахтова́ть**

захва́т, а *m.* seizure, capture; (*власти*) seizure; **з. зало́жников** hostage-taking.

захва|ти́ть, чу́, ~́тишь *pf.* (*of* ▸ **~́тывать**)
1 (*взять*) to take; **они́ ~ти́ли с собо́й дете́й** they have taken the children with them.
2 (*завладеть*) to seize; to capture; **з. власть** to seize power; **мы ~ти́ли три́ста пле́нных** we took three hundred prisoners.
3 (*fig.*) (*увлечь*) to carry away; to thrill, excite.

захва́тчик, а *m.* invader; aggressor.

захва́тыва|ть, ю *impf. of* ▸ **захвати́ть**

захва́тыва|ющий *pres. part. act. of* ▸ **~ть** *and adj.* (*fig.*) gripping.

захлеб|ну́ться, ну́сь, нёшься *pf.* (*of* ▸ **~́ываться**)
1 to choke (*intrans.*); to swallow the wrong way.
2 (*fig., coll.*): **з. от восто́рга** to be breathless with delight; **ата́ка ~ну́лась** (*mil.*) the attack misfired.

захлёбыва|ться, юсь *impf.* (*of* ▸ **захлебну́ться**) to choke (*intrans.*).

захло́п|нуть, ну, нешь *pf.* (*of* ▸ **~ывать**) (*дверь*) to slam.

захло́п|нуться, нется *pf.* (*of* ▸ **~ываться**) to slam to; to close with a bang.

захло́пыва|ть(ся), ю, ет(ся) *impf. of* ▸ **захло́пнуть(ся)**

захо́д, а *m.*
1 (*also* **з. со́лнца**) sunset.
2 (*куда-н.*) stopping (at), putting in (at); **без ~а в Ло́ндон** without calling at London.

захо|ди́ть, жу́, ~́дишь *impf. of* ▸ **зайти́**

захороне́ни|е, я *nt.* burial.

захорон|и́ть, ю́, ~́ишь *pf. of* ▸ **хорони́ть**

захо|те́ть(ся), чу́, ~́чешь, ~́чет(ся), ти́м, ти́те, тя́т *pf. of* ▸ **хоте́ть(ся)**

зацве|сти́, ту́, тёшь, *past* **~́л, ~ла́** *pf.* (*of* ▸ **~та́ть**) to break into blossom.

зацвета́|ть, ю *impf. of* ▸ **зацвести́**

зацве|ту́, тёшь *see* ▸ **~сти́**

зацеп|и́ть, лю́, ~́ишь *pf.* (*of* ▸ **~ля́ть**) to hook.

зацеп|и́ться, лю́сь, ~́ишься *pf.* (*of* ▸ **~ля́ться**) (**за** + *a.*)
1 to catch (on); **чуло́к у неё ~и́лся за гвоздь** her stocking caught on a nail.
2 (*coll.*) (*ухватиться*) to catch hold (of).

зацепля́|ть(ся), ю(сь) *impf. of* ▸ **зацепи́ть(ся)**

заци́клива|ться, юсь *impf. of* ▸ **заци́клиться**

заци́кл|иться, юсь, ишься *pf.* (*of* ▸ **заци́кливаться**) (**на** + *p.*) (*coll.*) to become obsessed (with).

зачаро́ванный *p.p.p. of* ▸ **зачарова́ть** *and adj.* spellbound.

зачар|ова́ть, у́ю *pf.* (*of* ▸ **~о́вывать**) to bewitch, enchant, captivate.

зачаро́выва|ть, ю *impf. of* ▸ **зачарова́ть**

зача́ти|е, я *nt.* (*physiol.*) conception.

зач|а́ть, ну́, нёшь, *past.* **~а́л, ~ала́, ~а́ло** *pf.* (*of* ▸ **~ина́ть**) to conceive (*trans. and intrans.*).

зача́х|нуть, ну, нешь, *past* **~, ~ла** *pf. of* ▸ **ча́хнуть**

заче́м *interrog. and rel. adv.* why; what for; **з. ты пришла́?** why did you come? **так *вот* з. пришла́** so that's why you came.

заче́м-то *adv.* for some reason or other.

зачёркива|ть, ю *impf. of* ▸ **зачеркну́ть**

зачерк|ну́ть, ну́, нёшь *pf.* (*of* ▸ **~́ивать**) to cross out, strike out.

зачерп|ну́ть, ну́, нёшь *pf.* (*of* ▸ **~́ывать**) to scoop up; (*ложкой*) to ladle out.

заче́рпыва|ть, ю *impf. of* ▸ **зачерпну́ть**

зачёт, а *m.*
1 reckoning; **в з. пла́ты** in payment.
2 (*экзамен*) test; **получи́ть з., сдать з. (по** + *d.*) to pass a test (in); **поста́вить** (+ *d.*) **з. (по** + *d.*) to pass (in); **мне поста́вили з. по исто́рии** they have passed me in history.

зачина́|ть, ю *impf. of* ▸ **зача́ть**

зачи́нщик, а *m.* (*pej.*) instigator, ringleader.

зачисле́ни|е, я *nt.* enrolment.

зачи́сл|ить, ю, ишь *pf.* (*of* ▸ **~я́ть**)
1 (*записать*) to include; **з. на счёт** to enter in an account.
2 (*включить в состав*) to enrol, enlist; **з. в штат** to take on the staff.

зачи́сл|иться, юсь, ишься *pf.* (*of* ▸ **~я́ться**) (**в** + *a.*) to join, enter.

зачисл|я́ть(ся), я́ю(сь) *impf. of* ▸ **~́ить(ся)**

зашива́|ть, ю *impf. of* ▸ **заши́ть**

заш|и́ть, ью́, ьёшь *pf.* (*of* ▸ **~ива́ть**)
1 (*дыру, пальто*) to mend.
2 (*med.*) to stitch (up).

зашифр|овáть, ýю *pf.* (*of* ▸ **шифровáть** *and* ▸ **~óвывать**) to encipher, put into code.
зашифрóвыва|ть, ю *impf. of* ▸ **зашифровáть**
за|шлю́, шлёшь *see* ▸ **~слáть**
зашнур|овáть, ýю *pf. of* ▸ **шнуровáть**
заштóпа|ть, ю *pf.* (*of* ▸ **штóпать**) to darn.
защёлк|а, и *f.* (*в двери*) latch; (*в механизме*) catch.
защёлкива|ть, ю *impf. of* ▸ **защёлкнуть**
защёлк|нуть, ну, нешь *pf.* (*of* ▸ **~ивать**) (*coll.*) to latch.
защи́т|а, ы *no pl., f.* defence (*Br.*), defense (*US*); (**от, прóтив** + *g.*) protection (from, against); (*collect.*) the defence (*Br.*), defense (*US*) (*leg. and sport*); **в ~у** (+ *g.*) in defence (*Br.*), defense (*US*) (of); **под ~ой** (+ *g.*) under the protection (of); **з. окружáющей среды́** *or* **прирóды** environmentalism, conservation.
защи|ти́ть(ся), щý(сь), ти́шь(ся) *pf. of* ▸ **~щáть(ся)**
защи́тник, а *m.*
1 defender, protector; (*leg.*) counsel for the defence (*Br.*), defense attorney (*US*).
2 (*sport*) (full)back; **лéвый, прáвый з.** left, right back.
защи́тн|ый *adj.* protective; **~ые очки́** goggles; **з. цвет** khaki.
защищá|ть, ю *impf.* (*impf. of* ▸ **защити́ть**)
1 to defend, protect.
2 (*leg.*) to defend; **з. диссертáцию** to defend a thesis (*before examiners*).
защищá|ться, юсь *impf.* (*of* ▸ **защити́ться**)
1 to defend o.s., protect o.s.
2 *pass. of* ▸ **~ть**
защищённост|ь, и *f.* protection.
заяв|и́ть, лю́, ~́ишь *pf.* (*of* ▸ **~ля́ть**) (+ *a. or* **о** + *p. or* **что**) to announce, declare; **з. свои́ правá** (**на** + *a.*) to claim one's rights (to); **з. об ухóде со слýжбы** to announce one's resignation.
зая́вк|а, и *f.* (**на** + *a.*) (*просьба*) application (for); (*о своих правах*) claim (for); demand (for); (*заказ*) order (for); **з. на изобретéние** patent application; **бланк ~и** application form.
заявлéни|е, я *nt.*
1 (*сообщение*) statement, declaration.
2 (*просьба*) application; **подáть з.** to put in an application.
заявля́|ть, ю *impf. of* ▸ **заяви́ть**
зá|яц, йца *m.*
1 hare; (*prov.*) **одни́м удáром уби́ть двух ~йцев** to kill two birds with one stone.
2 (*coll.*) (*пассажир*) stowaway; fare-dodger; **éхать ~йцем** to travel without paying for a ticket.
звáни|е, я *nt.* rank; title; **ры́царское з.** knighthood.
зва|ть, зовý, зовёшь, *past* **~л, ~лá, ~́ло** *impf.* (*of* ▸ **по~́**)
1 to call; **з. на пóмощь** to call for help.
2 (*приглашать*) to ask, invite.
3 (*impf. only*) (*называть*) to call; **как вас зовýт?** what is your name? **меня́ зовýт Влади́мир** my name is Vladimir.
звезд|á, ы́, *pl.* **~́ы, ~́, ~́ам** *f.*
1 star; **нóвая з.** (*astron.*) nova; (*fig.*): **з. экрáна** film star.
2 (*zool.*): **морскáя з.** starfish.
звёздн|ый *adj. of* ▸ **звездá; з. дождь** meteor shower; shooting stars; **~ая ночь** starlit night; **з. час** finest hour.
звёздочк|а, и *f.*
1 *dim. of* ▸ **звездá.**
2 (*typ.*) asterisk.
звен|éть, ю́, и́шь *impf.*
1 to ring; **у неё ~éло в ушáх** there was a ringing in her ears.
2 (+ *i.*): **з. монéтами** to jingle coins.
звен|ó, á, *pl.* **~́ья, ~́ьев** *nt.*
1 (*цепи*) link (*also fig.*).
2 (*fig.*) (*на предприятии*) team, section; (*aeron.*) flight.
зверé|ть, ю, ешь *impf.* (*of* ▸ **о~**) to become brutalized.
звери́н|ец, ца *m.* menagerie.
звер|и́ный *adj. of* ▸ **~ь;** animal; savage.
звéрски *adv.*
1 brutally, bestially.
2 (*coll.*) terribly, awfully.
звéрский *adj.*
1 brutal, bestial.
2 (*coll.*) (*чрезвычайный*) terrific, tremendous; **у негó з. аппети́т** he has a tremendous appetite.
звéрств|о, а *nt.* brutality; atrocity; **~а** atrocities (*in war, etc.*).
звер|ь, я, *pl.* **~́и, ~éй** *m.*
1 wild animal, wild beast; **пушнóй з.** fur-bearing animal.
2 (*fig.*) (*человек*) brute, beast.
звон, а *m.* (ringing) sound, peal.
звон|и́ть, ю́, и́шь *impf.* (*pf. of* ▸ **по~**) (**в** + *a.*) to ring; **з. комý-н. (по телефóну)** to phone s.o., call s.o.; **вы не тудá ~и́те** you've got the wrong number; **~я́т** s.o. is ringing.
звóн|кий (~ок, ~кá, ~ко) *adj.* ringing, clear; **~кая монéта** hard cash, coin.
звон|óк, кá *m.* bell; **дать з.** to ring; **з. (по телефóну)** (phone) call.
звóн|че *comp. of* ▸ **~кий, ~ко**
звук, а *m.* sound; **пустóй звук** (*fig.*) (mere) name, empty phrase; (*ling.*) **глáсный з.** vowel; **соглáсный з.** consonant.
звук|овóй *adj. of* ▸ **~; з. барьéр** sound barrier; **~овáя кáрта** (*comput.*) sound card.
звукозáпис|ь, и *f.* sound recording.
звукоизоля́ци|я, и *f.* soundproofing.
звуконепроницáем|ый (~, ~а) *adj.* soundproof.
звукорежиссёр, а *m.* sound engineer.
звуч|áть, ý, и́шь *impf.* (*of* ▸ **про~**)
1 (*раздаваться*) to be heard; to sound; **вдали́ ~áли голосá** voices could be heard in the distance.
2 (+ *adv. or i.*; *fig.*) (*выражаться*) to sound; to express, convey; **з. и́скренно** to ring true.
звýч|ный (~ен, ~нá, ~но) *adj.* sonorous.
звя́к|ать, аю *impf. of* ▸ **~нуть 1**
звя́к|нуть, ну, нешь *pf.* (*of* ▸ **~ать**)
1 (+ *i.*) to jingle; to tinkle.
2 (*pf. only*) (+ *d.*): **з. (по телефóну)** (*coll.*)

to ring up; to give s.o. a buzz.
здáни|е, я *nt.* building.
здесь *adv.*
1 here.
2 (*coll.*) here, at this point (*of time*); in this; **з. мы засмеялись** here we burst out laughing; **з. нет ничегó смешнóго** there is nothing funny in this.
здéшний *adj.* local; of this place; **вы з.? нет, я не з.** are you a local? no, I am a stranger here.
здорóва|ться, юсь *impf.* (*of* ▸ **по~**) (**с** + *i.*) to greet; to say hello (to); **з. зá руку** to shake hands (*in greeting*).
здóрово (*coll.*)
1 (*adv.*) (*отлично*) splendidly, magnificently; **ты з. поработáл** you have worked splendidly.
2 (*adv.*) (*очень сильно*) very, very much; **вчерá онú з. вы́пили** they had a great deal to drink yesterday.
3 (*int.*) great!; well done!
здорóво *int.* (*coll.*) hello!, hi!
здорóв|ый[1] **(~, ~а)** *adj.*
1 healthy; **бýдь(те) ~(ы)!** (*on parting*) take care!; (*to s.o. sneezing*) bless you!
2 (*полезный*) health-giving, wholesome; (*fig.*) sound, healthy; **з. клúмат** healthy climate.
здорóв|ый[2] **(~, ~á, ~ó)** *adj.* (*coll.*)
1 (*большой, сильный: о человеке*) robust, sturdy.
2 (*большой, сильный: о предметах, явлениях*) strong, powerful; sound.
здорóвь|е, я *no pl., nt.* health; **пить за чьё-н. з.** to drink s.o.'s health; **(за) вáше з.!** your health!; **как вáше з.?** how are you?; **на з.** to your heart's content, as you please.
здравоохранéни|е, я *nt.* health care; public health; **Министéрство ~я** Ministry of Health.
здрáвств|овать, ую *impf.* to be healthy; (*процветать*) to thrive, prosper; **~уй(те)!** how do you do; how are you; **да ~ует!** long live!
здрáв|ый (~, ~а) *adj.* sensible; **з. смысл** common sense; **быть в ~ом умé** to be in one's right mind.
зéбр|а, ы *f.*
1 (*zool.*) zebra.
2 (*место перехода*) zebra crossing (*Br.*).
зев|áть, áю *impf.*
1 (*pf.* **~нýть**) to yawn.
2 (*no pf.*) (*coll.*) to gape, stand gaping; **не ~áй!** keep your wits about you!
3 (*pf.* **про~**) (*coll.*) to miss opportunities.
зев|нýть, нý, нёшь *pf. of* ▸ **~áть 1**
зеленé|ть, ю *impf.*
1 (*pf.* **по~**) (*становиться зелёным*) to turn green, come out green.
2 (*виднеться*) to show green.
зеленоглáз|ый (~, ~а) *adj.* green-eyed.
зелёный (зéлен, ~á, зéлено) *adj.* green (*also fig.*); **з. горóшек** green peas; **з. лук** spring onions (*Br.*), green onions (*US*)
зéлен|ь, и *no pl., f.*
1 (*зелёный цвет*) green colour (*Br.*), color (*US*).
2 (*collect.*) (*растительность*) greenery.
3 (*collect.*) (*овощи*) greens.
землевладéл|ец, ьца *m.* landowner.
земледéл|ец, ьца *m.* arable farmer.
землéдéли|е, я *nt.* arable farming.
землéдéльческий *adj.* agricultural.
землекóп, а *m.* navvy.
землемéр, а *m.* land surveyor.
землерóйк|а, и *f.* (*zool.*) shrew.
землетрясéни|е, я *nt.* earthquake.
землечерпáлк|а, и *f.* (*tech.*) dredger, excavator.
зем|ля́, лú, *a.* **~лю,** *pl.* **~ли, ~éль, ~лям** *f.*
1 **(З.)** (*планета*) Earth.
2 (*суша*) (dry) land; **увúдеть ~лю** to sight land; **упáсть на ~лю** to fall to the ground.
3 (*владение*) land; soil (*fig.*).
4 (*почва*) earth, soil.
земля́к, á *m.* fellow-countryman, compatriot.
землянúк|а, и *no pl., f.* (*collect.*) wild strawberries.
земля́н|ин, ина, *pl.* **~е, ~** *m.* earth-dweller, earthling.
земля́нк|а, и *f.* dugout.
землян|óй *adj.*
1 earthen, of earth; **~ы́е рабóты** excavations.
2 earth-; **з. орéх** peanut.
земля́чк|а, и *f.* fellow-countrywoman, compatriot.
земновóдн|ый *adj.* amphibious; *as n.* (*zool.*) **~ые, ~ых** amphibia; *sg.* **~ое, ~ого** *nt.* amphibian.
земн|óй *adj.*
1 earthly; terrestrial; **~áя корá** (earth's) crust; **з. шар** the globe.
2 (*мирской*) mundane.
зенúт, а *m.* zenith (*also fig.*).
зéркал|о, а, *pl.* **~á, зеркáл, ~áм** *nt.* mirror (*also fig.*); **кривóе з.** distorting mirror.
зеркáльн|ый *adj. of* ▸ **зéркало;** (*fig.*) smooth; **~ое стеклó** plate glass; **~ое oкнó** plate-glass window; **~ая повéрхность** smooth surface.
зер|нó, нá, *pl.* **~на, ~ен, ~нам** *nt.*
1 (*пшеницы*) grain; (*мака*) seed; (*fig.*) grain; (*ядро*) kernel, core; **кóфе в ~нах** coffee beans.
2 (*collect., sg. only*) grain, cereal.
зернов|óй *adj.* grain, cereal; **~ы́е злáки** cereals.
зернохранúлищ|е, а *nt.* granary.
зигзáг, а *m.* zigzag.
зим|á, ы́, *a.* **~у,** *pl.* **~ы,** *d.* **~ам** *f.* winter; **нá ~у** for the winter; **всю ~у** all winter.
зúмн|ий *adj. of* ▸ **~á;** winter; (*погода*) wintry.
зим|овáть, ýю *impf.* (*of* ▸ **пере~**) to winter, pass the winter.
зимóй *adv.* in winter.
злак, а *m.* (*bot.*) grass; **хлéбные ~и** cereals.
злéйший *superl. of* ▸ **злой**
зл|ить, ю, ишь *impf.* (*of* ▸ **разо~**) to anger; to vex; to irritate.
зл|úться, юсь, úшься *impf.* (*of*

▶**разо~**) (**на** + *a.*) to be in a bad temper; to be angry (with).

зло[1], **зла,** *no pl. except g.* **зол** *nt.*
1 (*нечто дурное*) evil; harm; **отплатить ~м за добро** to repay good with evil.
2 (*беда*) evil, misfortune, disaster; **желать кому-н. зла** to bear s.o. malice.
3 (*sg. only*) (*досада*) malice, spite; vexation; **меня з. берёт** it annoys me, I feel annoyed.

зло[2] *adv. of* ▶**~й**

злоб|а, ы *f.* malice; spite; anger; **по ~е** out of spite; **со ~ой** maliciously.

злоб|ный (~ен, ~на) *adj.* malicious, spiteful; bad-tempered.

зловещ|ий (~, ~а) *adj.* ominous, ill-omened; sinister.

зловон|ный (~ен, ~на) *adj.* fetid, stinking.

зловред|ный (~ен, ~на) *adj.* harmful, pernicious.

злоде|й, я *m.* villain, scoundrel (*also joc.*).

злодей|ка, ки *f. of* ▶**~**

злодеяни|е, я *nt.* crime, evil deed.

злой (зол, зла, зло) *adj.*
1 (*о человеке*) evil; bad; **з. гений** evil genius.
2 (*выражающий злобу*) wicked; malicious; malevolent; vicious; **злая улыбка** malevolent smile; **со злым умыслом** with malicious intent; (*leg.*) of malice prepense.
3 (*short form only*) (**на** + *a.*) (*сердит*) angry; **она зла на всех** she is angry with everybody.
4 (*о животных*) fierce, savage; «**осторожно, злая собака**» 'beware of the dog!'

злокачествен|ный (~, ~на) *adj.* (*med.*) malignant; **~ная опухоль** malignant tumour (*Br.*), tumor (*US*).

злопамят|ный (~ен, ~на) *adj.* rancorous, unforgiving.

злорад|ный (~ен, ~на) *adj.* gloating.

злост|ный (~ен, ~на) *adj.*
1 (*сознательно недобросовестный*) conscious, intentional; **~ное банкротство** fraudulent bankruptcy; **з. неплательщик** persistent defaulter (*in payment of debt*).
2 (*закоренелый*) inveterate, hardened.

злост|ь, и *f.* malice, fury.

злоумышленник, а *m.* plotter; criminal.

злоупотреб|ить, лю, ишь *pf.* (*of* ▶**~лять**) (+ *i.*) to abuse; (*сладким*) to indulge in to excess; **з. властью** to abuse power; **з. чьим-н. вниманием** to take up too much of s.o.'s time.

злоупотреблени|е, я *nt.* (+ *i.*) abuse (of); **з. доверием** breach of confidence.

злоупотреб|лять, ляю *impf. of* ▶**~ить**

змей, змея *m.*: **(бумажный) з.** kite; **запустить змея** to fly a kite.

зме|я, и, *pl.* **~и, ~й** *f.* snake (*also fig.*).

знак, а *m.*
1 (*in var. senses*) sign; (*след*) mark; (*символ*) token, symbol; (*comput.*) character; **номерной з.** licence plate; **~и препинания** punctuation marks; **~и отличия** decorations (and medals); **в з.** (+ *g.*) as a mark (of), as a token (of), to show.
2 (*предзнаменование*) omen.
3 (*сигнал*) signal; **подать з.** to give a signal.

знаком|ить, лю, ишь *impf.* (*of* ▶**по~**) (+ *a. and* **с** + *i.*) to acquaint s.o. (with); to introduce s.o. (to).

знаком|иться, люсь, ишься *impf.* (*of* ▶**по~**) (**с** + *i.*)
1 (*с человеком*) to meet, make the acquaintance (*of a person*).
2 (*представляться*) to introduce o.s.; **~ьтесь!** (*informal mode of introduction*) may I introduce you?
3 (*с вещью*) to become acquainted (with), familiarize o.s. (with); to study, investigate.

знакомств|о, а *nt.*
1 (**с** + *i.*) (*между людьми*) acquaintance (with); **служба ~** dating service.
2 (*collect.*) (circle of) acquaintances; **по ~у** by exploiting one's personal connections, by pulling strings.
3 (**с** + *i.*) (*знание*) familiarity (with), knowledge (of).

знаком|ый (~, ~а) *adj.*
1 familiar; **его лицо мне ~о** his face is familiar (to me).
2 (**с** + *i.*) familiar (with); **быть ~ым (с** + *i.*) to be acquainted (with), know.
3 *as n.* **з., ~ого** *m.*, **~ая, ~ой** *f.* acquaintance, friend.

знам|ени, енем, *etc., see* ▶**~я**

знаменитост|ь, и *f.* celebrity.

знаменит|ый (~, ~а) *adj.* celebrated, famous, renowned; **печально з.** infamous, notorious.

знаменос|ец, ца *m.* standard-bearer (*also fig.*).

знам|я, *g., d., and p.* **~ени,** *i.* **~енем,** *pl.* **~ёна, ~ён** *nt.* banner; standard; **под ~енем** (+ *g.*; *fig.*, *rhet.*) in the name of.

знани|е, я *nt.*
1 knowledge; **со ~ем дела** capably, competently.
2 (*pl. only*) learning; accomplishments.

знат|ный (~ен, ~на, ~но) *adj.* (*аристократический*) noble.

знаток, а *m.* expert; connoisseur.

зна|ть[1], **~ю** *impf.* to know, have a knowledge of; **вы ~ете Александрова?** do you know Alexandrov?; **з. в лицо** to know by sight; **з. меру** to know when to stop; **не з. покоя** to know no peace; **дать кому-н. з.** to let s.o. know; **кто его ~ет, бог его ~ет, чёрт его ~ет** (*coll.*) goodness knows!; God knows!; the devil (only) knows!; **вам лучше з.** you know best; **~ешь (ли), ~ете (ли)** (*coll.*) you know, do you know what.

знат|ь[2], **и** *no pl., f.* (*collect.*) the nobility, the aristocracy.

значени|е, я *nt.*
1 (*смысл*) meaning, significance.
2 (*важность*) importance, significance; **придавать большое з.** (+ *d.*) to attach great importance (to); **это не имеет ~я** it is of no importance.
3 (*math.*) value.

значимост|ь, и *f.* significance.

значит (*coll.*) so, then; well then; **он умер до войны? з., вы не были с ним знакомы** he died before the war? then you didn't know him.

значи́тел|ьный (~ен, ~ьна) *adj.* 1 (*большой*) considerable, sizeable; **в ~ьной сте́пени** to a considerable extent. 2 (*важный*) important. 3 (*выразительный*) significant, meaningful.

зна́ч|ить, у, ишь *impf.* 1 (*иметь смысл*) to mean, signify. 2 (*иметь значение*) to mean, have significance, be of importance; **ничего́ не ~ит** it is of no importance; **э́то о́чень мно́го ~ит для неё** it means a great deal to her.

знач|о́к, ка́ *m.* 1 badge. 2 (*пометка*) mark.

зна́|ющий *pres. part. act. of* ▶ **~ть¹** *and adj.* expert; learned, erudite.

зно|й, я *m.* intense heat; sultriness.

зно́|йный (~ен, ~йна) *adj.* hot, sultry; torrid; burning (*also fig.*).

зоб, а, *pl.* **~ы́, ~о́в** *m.* 1 (*птицы*) crop, craw. 2 (*med.*) goitre (*Br.*), goiter (*US*).

зов, а *m.* call, summons.

зов|у́, ёшь *see* ▶ **звать**

зодиа́к, а *m.* (*astron.*) zodiac; **зна́ки ~а** signs of the zodiac.

зол¹ *see* ▶ **злой**

зол² *g. pl. of* ▶ **зло¹**

зол|а́, ы *no pl., f.* ashes, cinders.

золо́вк|а, и *f.* sister-in-law (*husband's sister*).

золоти́ст|ый (~, ~а) *adj.* golden (*of colour*).

зо́лот|о, а *no pl., nt.* gold; (*collect.*) gold (*coins, ware*); (*fig.*): **она́ — настоя́щее з.** she is pure gold, a treasure; **на вес ~а** worth its weight in gold.

золот|о́й *adj.* gold; golden (*also fig.*); **~ы́х дел ма́стер** goldsmith; **з. песо́к** gold dust; **з. запа́с** (*econ.*) gold reserves; **~а́я ры́бка** goldfish; **з. век** the Golden Age; **~а́я молодёжь** gilded youth; **~а́я середи́на** golden mean.

золочёный *adj.* gilded, gilt.

зо́н|а, ы *f.* 1 zone; area. 2 (*geol.*) stratum, layer. 3 (*sl.*) (*тюрьма*) prison; (*лагерь*) prison camp.

зонд, а *m.* 1 (*med.*) probe. 2 (*meteor.*) weather balloon.

зонт, а́ *m.* 1 umbrella. 2 (*навес*) awning.

зо́нтик, а *m.* umbrella; (*от солнца*) sunshade, parasol.

зоо... *comb. form, abbr. of* **зоологи́ческий**

зоо́лог, а *m.* zoologist.

зоологи́ческий *adj.* zoological; **з. парк, з. сад** zoological garden(s).

зооло́ги|я, и *f.* zoology.

зоомагази́н, а *m.* pet shop.

зоопа́рк, а *m.* zoo.

зо́ри *see* ▶ **заря́**

зо́р|кий (~ок, ~ка́, ~ко) *adj.* 1 sharp-sighted. 2 (*fig.*) (*проницательный*) perspicacious, penetrating; (*бдительный*) vigilant.

зрач|о́к, ка́ *m.* pupil (*of the eye*).

зре́лищ|е, а *nt.* 1 (*предмет наблюдения*) sight. 2 (*представление*) spectacle; show; pageant.

зре́лост|ь, и *f.* (*винограда*) ripeness; (*человека*) maturity (*also fig.*); **полова́я з.** puberty.

зре́л|ый (~, ~а́, ~о) *adj.* (*виноград*) ripe; (*человек*) mature (*also fig.*); **дости́гнуть ~ого во́зраста** to reach maturity; **з. ум** mature mind.

зре́ни|е, я *nt.* (eye)sight; **по́ле ~я** (*phys.*) field of vision; **обма́н ~я** optical illusion; **то́чка ~я** point of view.

зре|ть, ю, ешь *impf. of* ▶ **со~**

зри́тел|ь, я *m.* spectator, observer; **быть ~ем** to look on.

зри́тельный *adj.* 1 visual; optic; **з. нерв** optic nerve. 2: **з. зал** hall, auditorium.

зря *adv.* (*coll.*) to no purpose, for nothing; **болта́ть з.** to chatter idly; **рабо́тать з.** to work in vain.

зуб, а *m.* 1 (*pl.* **~ы, ~о́в**) (*во рту*) tooth; **з. му́дрости** wisdom tooth; **вооружённый до ~о́в** armed to the teeth; **не по ~а́м** beyond one's capacity. 2 (*pl.* **~ья, ~ьев**) (*зубец*) tooth, cog.

зуба́ст|ый (~, ~а) *adj.* (*coll.*) sharp-toothed; (*fig.*) sharp-tongued.

зуб|е́ц, ца́ *m.* tooth, cog.

зуби́л|о, а *nt.* (*tech.*) chisel.

зубн|о́й *adj.* dental; **~а́я боль** toothache; **з. врач** dentist; **~а́я па́ста** toothpaste; **~а́я щётка** toothbrush.

зубочи́стк|а, и *f.* toothpick.

зубр, а *m.* (*zool.*) (European) bison.

зуд, а *m.* itch; (*fig.*) itch, urge.

зы́б|кий (~ок, ~ка́, ~ко) *adj.* (*поверхность*) rippling; (*почва*) unsteady, shaky; (*fig.*) unstable, vacillating.

зэк, а *m.* (*sl.*) prisoner, convict.

зя́блик, а *m.* chaffinch.

зят|ь, я, *pl.* **~ья́, ~ьёв** *m.* (*муж дочери*) son-in-law; (*муж сестры, муж сестры мужа*) brother-in-law.

Ии

и *conj.*
1 and.
2 : **и... и** both ... and; **и тот и друго́й** both.
3 (*тоже*) too; (*with negation*) either; **она́ сказа́ла, что и муж придёт** she said that her husband would come too.
4 (*даже*) even; **и знатоки́ ошиба́ются** even experts may be mistaken.

и́бо *conj.* for.

и́в|а, ы *f.* willow.

иври́т, а *m.* (modern) Hebrew.

игл|á, ы́, *pl.* ~ы, ~ *f.*
1 (*для шитья*) needle.
2 (*bot.*) (*у хвойных деревьев*) needle; (*у растения*) thorn, prickle.
3 (*ежа*) quill, spine.
4 (*проигрывателя*) needle, stylus.

иглоука́лывани|е, я *nt.* acupuncture.

игнори́р|овать, ую *impf. and pf.* to ignore; to disregard.

иго́лк|а, и *f.* needle; **сиде́ть как на ~ах** to be on tenterhooks.

иго́рный *adj.* gambling, gaming; **и. дом** casino.

игр|á, ы́, *pl.* ~́ы *f.*
1 (*действие*) play, playing; **и. слов** play on words.
2 (*занятие*) game.

игра́льн|ый *adj.* playing; **~ые ка́рты** playing cards.

игра́|ть, ю *impf.* (*of* ▸ **сыгра́ть**)
1 to play; **и. пье́су** to put on a play; **и. роль** to play a part; **э́то не ~ет ро́ли** it is of no importance; **и. в ка́рты, те́ннис, футбо́л, ша́хматы** to play cards, tennis, football, chess; **и. на роя́ле, скри́пке** to play the piano, the violin.
2 (*impf. only*) (+ *i. or* **с** + *i.*) (*относиться несерьёзно*) to play with, toy with, trifle with (*also fig.*); **и. с огнём** (*fig.*) to play with fire.
3 (*impf. only*) (*сверкать*) to play; to sparkle (*of wine, jewellery, etc.*); **улы́бка ~ла на её лице́** a smile played on her face.

игри́в|ый (~, ~а) *adj.* playful; (*coll.*) naughty, ribald.

игри́ст|ый (~, ~а) *adj.* sparkling (*of wine*).

игр|ово́й *adj. of* ▸ **~á; и. автома́т** one-armed bandit, fruit machine (*Br.*); **~ова́я приста́вка** (*comput.*) game(s) console.

игро́к, á *m.*
1 (**в** + *a.*, **на** + *p.*) player (of).
2 (*в азартные игры*) gambler.

игру́шечный *adj.* toy; **и. парово́з** toy engine.

игру́шк|а, и *f.* toy; (*fig.*) plaything; **ёлочные ~и** Christmas tree decorations.

идеа́л, а *m.* ideal.

идеализи́р|овать, ую *impf. and pf.* to idealize.

идеали́зм, а *m.* idealism.

идеали́ст, а *m.* idealist.

идеа́л|ьный (~ен, ~ьна) *adj.* ideal (*also phil.*); perfect; **~ьное состоя́ние** perfect condition.

иде́|йный (~ен, ~йна) *adj.*
1 (*идеологический*) ideological.
2 (*преданный какой-н. идее*) expressing an idea *or* ideas; committed, engagé.
3 (*принципиальный*) high-principled, acting on principle.

идентифика́ци|я, и *f.* identification.

идентифици́р|овать, ую *impf. and pf.* to identify.

иденти́чност|ь, и *f.* identity.

иденти́ч|ный (~ен, ~на) *adj.* identical.

идео́лог, а *m.* ideologist.

идеологи́ческий *adj.* ideological.

идеоло́ги|я, и *f.* ideology.

иде́|я, и *f.*
1 idea (*also coll.*); notion, concept; (*phil.*) Idea.
2 (*главная мысль*) point, purport (*of a work of art*); **по ~е** (*coll.*) in principle.

идио́м|а, ы *f.* idiom.

идиосинкрази́|я, и *f.* (*med.*) allergy.

идио́т, а *m.* (*med. and coll.*) idiot, imbecile.

идиоти́зм, а *m.* (*med. and coll.*) idiocy, imbecility.

идио́тский *adj.* idiotic, imbecile.

и́диш *m. indecl.* Yiddish (*language*).

и́дол, а *m.* idol (*also fig.*).

ид|ти́, у́, ёшь, *past* **шёл, шла** *impf.* (*of* ▸ **пойти́ 1;** *det. of* ▸ **ходи́ть**)
1 to go; (*impf. only*) (*приближаться*) to come; **и. в го́ру** to go uphill; **авто́бус ~ёт** the bus is coming.
2 (**на** + *a.*) (*поступать*) to enter; (**в** + *nom.-a.*) to become; **и. на госуда́рственную слу́жбу** to enter government service.
3 (**в** + *a.*) (*использоваться*) to be used (for); (**на** + *a.*) to go to make.
4 (**из, от** + *g.*) (*о дыме, воде*) to come (from), proceed (from); **из трубы́ шёл чёрный дым** black smoke was coming from the chimney.
5 (*coll.*) (*находить сбыт*) to sell, be sold; **хорошо́ и.** to be selling well.
6 (*о механизме*) to go, run, work.
7 (*о дожде, снеге*) to fall; **дождь, снег ~ёт** it is raining, snowing.
8 (*о времени*) to pass; **шли го́ды** years passed; **ей пошёл тридца́тый год** she is in her thirtieth year.
9 (*происходить*) to go on, be in progress; (*о спектакле*) to be on, be showing; **перегово́ры ~у́т** talks are in progress; **сего́дня ~ёт «Дя́дя Ва́ня»** 'Uncle Vanya' is on today.
10 (+ *d. or* **к** + *d.*) (*быть к лицу*) to suit, become; **э́та шля́па ей не ~ёт** this hat does not become her.
11 (**о** + *p.*) (*о разговоре*) to be (about); **речь**

~ёт о том, что... the point is that ..., it is a matter of ... .
иезуи́т, а *m.* (*eccl.*) Jesuit.
ие́н|а, ы *f.* yen (*Japanese currency*).
иерархи́ческий *adj.* hierarchic(al).
иера́рхи|я, и *f.* hierarchy.
иеро́глиф, а *m.* (*египетский*) hieroglyph; (*китайский, японский*) character.
Иерусали́м, а *m.* Jerusalem.
иждиве́н|ец, ца *m.* dependant; (*нахлебник*) sponger.
иждиве́ни|е, я *nt.* maintenance; **на чьём-н. ~и** at s.o.'s expense.
иждиве́н|ка, ки *f. of* ▸ **~ец**
из (изо) *prep.* + *g.* from, out of; of.
1 (*обозначает источник действия*): **прие́хать из Ло́ндона** to come from London; **пить из ча́шки** to drink out of a cup.
2 (*обозначает часть целого*): **оди́н из её покло́нников** one of her admirers; **(ни) оди́н из ста** (not) one in a hundred.
3 (*обозначает состав, компоненты*): **из чего́ э́то сде́лано?** what is it made of?; **варе́нье из абрико́сов** apricot jam; **обе́д из трёх блюд** a three-course dinner.
4 (*обозначает средство*): **изо всех сил** with all one's might.
5 (*обозначает причину*): **из благода́рности** in gratitude.
из... (*also* **изо..., изъ...,** *and* **ис...**) *vbl. pref. indicating*:
1 motion outwards.
2 action over entire surface of object, in all directions.
3 expenditure of instrument *or* object in course of action; continuation *or* repetition of action to extreme point; exhaustiveness of action.
изб|а́, ы́, *pl.* **~́ы** *f.* izba (*peasant's hut or cottage*).
изба́в|ить, лю, ишь *pf.* (*of* ▸ **~ля́ть**) (**от** + *g.*) to save, deliver (from); **~ьте меня́ от ва́ших замеча́ний** spare me your remarks.
изба́в|иться, люсь, ишься *pf.* (*of* ▸ **~ля́ться**) (**от** + *g.*) to be saved (from), escape; to get out (of); to get rid (of); **и. от привы́чки** to get out of a habit.
избавля́|ть(ся), ю(сь) *impf. of* ▸ **изба́вить(ся)**
избало́ванный *p.p.p. of* ▸ **избалова́ть** *and adj.* spoilt.
избал|ова́ть, у́ю *pf.* (*of* ▸ **балова́ть** *and* ▸ **~о́вывать**) to spoil (*a child, etc.*).
избало́выва|ть, ю *impf. of* ▸ **избалова́ть**
избег|а́ть, а́ю *impf.* (*of* ▸ **~́нуть** *and* ▸ **избежа́ть**) (+ *g. or inf.*) (*сторониться*) to avoid; (*избавиться*) to escape, evade.
избе́г|нуть, ну, нешь, *past* **~нул** *and* **~, ~ла** *pf. of* ▸ **~а́ть**
избе|жа́ть, гу́, жи́шь, гу́т *pf. of* ▸ **~га́ть**
избива́|ть, ю *impf. of* ▸ **изби́ть**
избие́ни|е, я *nt.* (*убийство*) slaughter, massacre.
избира́тел|ь, я *m.* elector, voter.
избира́тельн|ый *adj.*
1 electoral; **и. бюллете́нь** voting-paper; **~ая кампа́ния** election campaign.
2 (*tech.*) selective.
избира́|ть, ю *impf. of* ▸ **избра́ть**
изби́т|ый *p.p.p. of* ▸ **~ь** *and adj.*; (*fig.*) hackneyed, trite.
из|би́ть, обью́, обьёшь *pf.* (*of* ▸ **~бива́ть**) (*человека*) beat up.
избороз|ди́ть, жу́, ди́шь *pf. of* ▸ **борозди́ть**
избра́ни|е, я *nt.* election.
и́збран|ный *p.p.p. of* ▸ **избра́ть** *and adj.*
1 (*отобранный*) selected; **~ные сочине́ния Пу́шкина** selected works of Pushkin.
2 (*лучший*) select; *as n.* **~ные, ~ных** *no sg.*, elite.
из|бра́ть, беру́, берёшь, *past* **~бра́л, ~брала́, ~бра́ло** *pf.* (*of* ▸ **~бира́ть**) (+ *a. and i.*) to elect (as, for); to choose; **его́ ~бра́ли чле́ном парла́мента** he has been elected a Member of Parliament.
избы́т|ок, ка *m.* (*излишек*) surplus, excess; (*обилие*) abundance, plenty; **в ~ке** in plenty; **от ~ка чувств** from a fullness of heart.
избы́точ|ный (~ен, ~на) *adj.* surplus.
изваяни|е, я *nt.* statue, sculpture; graven image.
изва́я|ть, ю *pf. of* ▸ **ва́ять**
и́зверг, а *m.* monster, fiend.
изверг|а́ться, а́ется *impf.* to erupt (*of volcanoes*).
изверже́ни|е, я *nt.*
1 (*вулкана*) eruption.
2 (*fig.*) ejection, expulsion.
изверн|у́ться, у́сь, ёшься *pf.* (*of* ▸ **извора́чиваться**) (*coll.*) to dodge, take evasive action (*also fig.*).
изве́сти|е, я *nt.* (**о** + *p.*) news (of); **после́дние ~я** the latest news.
изве|сти́ть, щу́, сти́шь *pf.* (*of* ▸ **~ща́ть**) to inform, notify.
извёстк|а, и *f.* (slaked) lime.
изве́стно *as pred.* it is (well) known; **как и.** as is well known; **наско́лько мне и.** as far as I know.
изве́стност|ь, и *f.* (*слава*) fame, reputation; (*лгуна, преступника*) notoriety; **приноси́ть и.** (+ *d.*) to bring fame (to); **поста́вить кого́-н. в и.** to inform, notify.
изве́ст|ный (~ен, ~на) *adj.*
1 (+ *d.*) well-known (to); (+ *i.*) (well-)known (for); (**за** + *a.*) (well-)known (as).
2 (*лгун, преступник*) infamous, notorious.
3 (*некоторый*) (a) certain; **до ~ной сте́пени, в ~ной ме́ре** to a certain extent.
известня́к, а́ *m.* limestone.
и́звест|ь, и *f.* lime.
извеща́|ть, ю *impf. of* ▸ **извести́ть**
извеще́ни|е, я *nt.* notification, notice; (*comm.*) advice.
извива́|ться, юсь *impf.*
1 (*о змее, канате*) to coil (*intrans.*); (*о черве*) to wriggle.
2 (*impf. only*) (*о дороге, реке*) to twist, wind (*intrans.*); to meander.
изви́лист|ый (~, ~а) *adj.* winding, twisting, tortuous.

извинéни|е, я *nt.*
1 (*оправдание*) excuse.
2 (*просьба о прощении*) apology; **приня́ть ~я** to accept an apology.
3 (*прощение*) pardon.

извин|и́ть, ю́, и́шь *pf.* (*of* ▸ **~я́ть**)
1 (*простить*) to excuse; **~и́те (меня́)!** I beg your pardon; excuse me!; (I'm) sorry!; **~и́те, что я опозда́л** sorry I'm late; **прошу́ и. меня́ за бестáктное замечáние** I apologize for my tactless remark.
2 (*оправдать*) to excuse; **э́то ниче́м нельзя́ и.** this is inexcusable.

извин|и́ться, ю́сь, и́шься *pf.* (*of* ▸ **~я́ться**)
1 (**пе́ред** + *i.*) (*попросить прощения*) to apologize (to); **~и́тесь за меня́** present my apologies, make my excuses.
2 (+ *i.*) (*оправдаться*) to excuse o.s. (on account of, on the ground of); to make excuses.

извин|я́ть, я́ю *impf. of* ▸ **~и́ть**

извин|я́ться, я́юсь *impf. of* ▸ **~и́ться; ~я́юсь** (*coll.*) I apologize; (I'm) sorry!

извлекá|ть, ю *impf. of* ▸ **извлéчь**

извлé|чь, кý, чёшь, кýт, *past* **~̈к, ~клá** *pf.* (*of* ▸ **~кáть**) to extract; (*fig.*) to derive, elicit; **и. урóк** (**из** + *g.*) to learn a lesson (from); **и. пóльзу** (**из** + *g.*) to derive benefit (from); **и. кóрень** (*math.*) to find the root.

извнé *adv.* from without.

изворáчива|ться, юсь *impf. of* ▸ **извернýться**

изворóтлив|ый (**~, ~а**) *adj.* (*спорщик, ум*) versatile, resourceful; (*человек*) wily, shrewd.

извра|ти́ть, щý, ти́шь *pf.* (*of* ▸ **~щáть**)
1 (*испортить*) to pervert.
2 (*ложно истолковать*) to misinterpret, misconstrue; **и. и́стину** to distort the truth; **и. чью-н. мысль** to misinterpret s.o.

извращá|ть, ю *impf. of* ▸ **изврати́ть**

извращéн|ец, ца *m.* pervert.

извращéни|е, я *nt.*
1 (*ненормальность*) perversion.
2 (*искажение*) misinterpretation, distortion (*fig.*).

изги́б, а *m.* bend, twist.

изгибá|ть(ся), ю(сь) *impf. of* ▸ **изогнýть(ся)**

изгнáни|е, я *nt.*
1 (*действие*) banishment; expulsion.
2 (*ссылка*) exile.

изгнáнник, а *m.* exile (*person*).

из|гнáть, гоню́, гóнишь, *past* **~гнáл, ~гналá, ~гнáло** *pf.* (*of* ▸ **~гоня́ть**) to banish, expel; (*сослать*) to exile.

из|гоню́, гóнишь *see* ▸ **~гнáть**

изгоня́|ть, ю *impf. of* ▸ **изгнáть**

и́згород|ь, и *f.* fence; **живáя и.** hedge.

изготáвлива|ть, ю *impf.* = **изготовля́ть**

изготови́тел|ь, я *m.* manufacturer, producer.

изготóв|ить, лю, ишь *pf.* (*of* ▸ **~ля́ть**) to manufacture.

изготовлéни|е, я *nt.* manufacture.

изготовля́|ть, ю *impf. of* ▸ **изготóвить**

изда|вáть, ю́, ёшь *impf. of* ▸ **~́ть**

изда|вáться, ю́сь, ёшься *impf. of* ▸ **~́ться**

и́здавна *adv.* for a long time; from time immemorial.

издалекá *adv.* from afar; from a distance; **гóрод ви́ден и.** the town is visible from afar; **приéхать и.** to come from a distance.

и́здал|и *adv.* = **~екá**

издáни|е, я *nt.*
1 (*книг*) publication; (*закона*) promulgation.
2 (*то, что издано*) edition.

издáтел|ь, я *m.* publisher.

издáтель|ский *adj. of* ▸ **~** *and* ▸ **~ство; ~ское дéло** publishing.

издáтельств|о, а *nt.* publishing house, publisher.

издá|ть, м, шь, ст, ди́м, ди́те, дýт, *past* **~л, ~лá, ~ло** *pf.* (*of* ▸ **~вáть**)
1 (*опубликовать*) to publish; **и. укáз** to issue an edict.
2 (*запах*) to produce, emit; (*звук*) to let out; **и. крик** to let out a cry.

издá|ться, мся, шься, стся, ди́мся, ди́тесь, дýтся, *past* **~лся, ~лáсь, ~лось** *pf.* to be published.

издевáтельский *adj.* mocking.

издевáтельств|о, а *nt.* (*действие*) mockery; (*насмешка*) taunt, insult.

издевá|ться, юсь *impf.* (**над** + *i.*) to mock (at), scoff (at).

издéли|е, я *nt.* (manufactured) article; (*pl.*) wares.

издéрж|ки, ек *pl.* (*sg.* **~ка, ~ки** *f.*) expenses; costs; **судéбные и.** (*leg.*) costs; **и. произвóдства** production costs.

издóх|нуть, ну, нешь *past* **~, ~ла** *pf.* (*of* ▸ **дóхнуть, издыхáть**) to die (*of animals*).

издыхá|ть, ю *impf. of* ▸ **издóхнуть**

изжáр|ить(ся), ю(сь), ишь(ся) *pf. of* ▸ **жáрить(ся)**

изживá|ть, ю *impf. of* ▸ **изжи́ть**

изжи́|ть, вý, вёшь, *past* **~л, ~лá, ~ло** *pf.* (*of* ▸ **~вáть**)
1 (*искоренить*) to eliminate.
2 : **и. себя́** to become obsolete.

из-за *prep.* + *g.*
1 from behind; **из-за двéри** from behind the door; **встать из-за столá** to rise from the table.
2 (*по причине*) because of, through.
3 (*ради*) for; **жени́ться из-за дéнег** to marry for money.

излагá|ть, ю *impf. of* ▸ **изложи́ть**

излечéни|е, я *nt.*
1 (*лечение*) medical treatment.
2 (*выздоровление*) recovery.

излéчива|ть(ся), ю(сь) *impf. of* ▸ **излечи́ть(ся)**

излечи́м|ый (**~, ~а**) *adj.* curable.

излеч|и́ть, ý, ~́ишь *pf.* (*of* ▸ **~́ивать**) to cure.

излеч|и́ться, ýсь, ~́ишься *pf.* (*of* ▸ **~́иваться**) (**от** + *g.*) to make a complete recovery (from); to be cured (of); (*fig.*) to rid o.s. (of), shake off.

изли́ш|ек, ка *m.* surplus; remainder.

изли́шеств|о, а *nt.* excess; overindulgence.
изложе́ни|е, я *nt.* exposition, account; **кра́ткое и.** synopsis, outline.
излож|и́ть, у́, ~́ишь *pf.* (*of* ▸ **излага́ть**) to expound, state; to set forth; **и. на бума́ге** to commit to paper.
изло́м, а *m.*
1 (*место перелома*) break, fracture.
2 (*изгиб*) sharp bend.
излуч|а́ть, а́ю *impf.* to radiate (*also fig.*); **её глаза́ ~а́ли не́жность** her eyes radiated tenderness.
излуч|а́ться, а́ется *impf.*
1 (**из** + *g.*) to emanate (from).
2 *pass. of* ▸ **~а́ть**
излуче́ни|е, я *nt.* radiation; emanation.
излю́бленный *adj.* favourite (*Br.*), favorite (*US*).
изма́|зать, жу, жешь *pf.* (*of* ▸ **ма́зать 3** *and* ▸ **~зывать**) (*coll.*) to make dirty, smear; **и. пальто́ кра́ской** to get paint all over one's coat.
изма́|заться, жусь, жешься *pf.* (*of* ▸ **ма́заться 1** *and* ▸ **~зываться**) (*coll.*) to get dirty; **он весь ~зался в кра́ске** he has got paint all over himself.
изма́зыва|ть(ся), ю(сь) *impf. of* ▸ **изма́зать(ся)**
изма́тыва|ть, ю *impf. of* ▸ **измота́ть**
изме́н|а, ы *f.* betrayal; treachery; **госуда́рственная и.** high treason; **супру́жеская и.** unfaithfulness, (conjugal) infidelity.
измене́ни|е, я *nt.* change, alteration.
измен|и́ть[1], ю, ~́ишь *pf.* (*of* ▸ **~я́ть**) to change, alter; (*pol.*) **и. законопрое́кт** to amend a bill.
измен|и́ть[2], ю, ~́ишь *pf.* (*of* ▸ **~я́ть**) (+ *d.*) (*родине, другу*) to betray; (*мужу*) to be unfaithful (to); (*fig.*) **зре́ние ~и́ло ему́** his eyesight had failed him.
измен|и́ться, ю́сь, ~́ишься *pf.* (*of* ▸ **~я́ться**) to change, alter (*intrans.*); **и. к лу́чшему, к ху́дшему** to change for the better, for the worse.
изме́нник, а *m.* traitor.
изме́нни|ца, цы *f. of* ▸ **~к**
изме́нчивост|ь, и *f.* changeableness; (*непостоянство*) inconstancy, fickleness.
измен|я́ть(ся), я́ю(сь) *impf. of* ▸ **~и́ть(ся)**
измере́ни|е, я *nt.*
1 measurement, measuring; (*глубины моря*) sounding, fathoming; (*температуры*) taking.
2 (*math.*) dimension.
измери́тельный *adj.* (for) measuring.
изме́р|ить, ю, ишь *pf.* (*of* ▸ **~я́ть**) to measure; **и. кому́-н. температу́ру** to take s.o.'s temperature.
измер|я́ть, я́ю *impf. of* ▸ **~́ить**
и́зморо|зь, и *f.* hoar frost.
и́зморос|ь, и *f.* drizzle.
измота́|ть, ю *pf.* (*of* ▸ **изма́тывать**) (*coll.*) to exhaust, wear out.
изму́ч|аться, аюсь *pf.* = **~иться**
изму́ченный *adj.* worn out, tired out.
изму́чива|ть(ся), ю(сь) *impf. of* ▸ **изму́чить(ся)**
изму́ч|ить, у, ишь *pf.* (*pf. of* ▸ **~ивать**) to torment; to tire out, exhaust.
изму́ч|иться, усь, ишься *pf. pf.* (*of* ▸ **~иваться**) to be tired out, be exhausted.
измышле́ни|е, я *nt.* fabrication, invention.
из|мя́ть(ся), омну́, омнёт(ся) *pf. of* ▸ **мя́ть(ся)**
изна́нк|а, и *f.* the wrong side (*of material, clothing*); **с ~и** on the inner side; **и. жи́зни** the seamy side of life.
изнаси́ловани|е, я *nt.* rape.
изнаси́л|овать, ую *pf.* (*of* ▸ **наси́ловать 2**) to rape.
изна́шива|ть(ся), ю(сь) *impf. of* ▸ **износи́ть(ся)**
изне́женный *adj.* pampered; soft, effete.
изнеможе́ни|е, я *nt.* exhaustion; **рабо́тать до ~я** to work to the point of exhaustion.
изно́с, а (у) *m.* (*coll.*) wear; wear and tear.
износ|и́ть, шу́, ~́сишь *pf.* (*of* ▸ **изна́шивать**) to wear out.
износ|и́ться, шу́сь, ~́сишься *pf.* (*of* ▸ **изна́шиваться**) to wear out (*intrans.*); (*fig., coll.*) to be used up, be played out.
изно́шенный *p.p.p. of* ▸ **износи́ть** *and adj.* worn out.
изнури́тел|ьный (~ен, ~ьна) *adj.* exhausting; gruelling; **~ьная боле́знь** wasting disease.
изнутри́ *adv.* from within; **дверь запира́ется и.** the door fastens on the inside.
изо *prep.* = **из**
изо...[1] *pref.* = **из...**
изо...[2] *comb. form*
1 iso-.
2 = *abbr. of* **изобрази́тельный**
изоби́ли|е, я *nt.* abundance, plenty.
изоби́л|овать, ует *impf.* (+ *i.*) to abound (in), be rich (in).
изоблич|а́ть, а́ю *impf.*
1 *impf. of* ▸ **~и́ть.**
2 (*no pf.*) (**в** + *p. and a.*) to show (to be), point to (as being); **все его́ посту́пки ~а́ли в нём моше́нника** his every action pointed to his being a swindler.
изоблич|и́ть, у́, и́шь *pf.* (*of* ▸ **~а́ть 1**) (+ *a. and* **в** + *p.*) to expose (as); to unmask; **его́ ~и́ли во лжи** he stands exposed as a liar.
изобража́|ть, ю *impf. of* ▸ **изобрази́ть**
изображе́ни|е, я *nt.* representation, portrayal; image.
изобрази́тельный *adj.* graphic; decorative.
изобра|зи́ть, жу́, зи́шь *pf.* (*of* ▸ **~жа́ть**)
1 (+ *i.*) to depict, portray, represent (as); **и. из себя́** (+ *a.*; *coll.*) to make o.s. out (to be), represent o.s. (as).
2 (*копировать*) to imitate, take off.
3 (*выразить*) to express, show.
изобре|сти́, ту́, тёшь *past* **~̈л, ~ла́** *pf.* (*of* ▸ **~та́ть**) (*создать что-либо новое*) to invent; (*придумать*) to devise, contrive.
изобрета́тел|ь, я *m.* inventor.

изобретáтел|ьный (~ен, ~ьна) *adj.* inventive; resourceful.
изобретá|ть, ю *impf. of* ▶ **изобрести́**
изобретéни|е, я *nt.* invention.
изóгнут|ый *p.p.p. of* ▶ **~ь** *and adj.* bent, curved, winding.
изогн|ýть, ý, ёшь *pf.* (*of* ▶ **изгибáть**) to bend, curve.
изогн|ýться, ýсь, ёшься *pf.* (*of* ▶ **изгибáться**) to bend, curve (*intrans.*).
изо|йти́, йдý, йдёшь, *past* **~шёл, ~шлá** *pf. of* ▶ **исходи́ть 3**
изоли́рованный *p.p.p. of* ▶ **изоли́ровать** *and adj.* isolated; separate.
изоли́р|овать, ую *impf. and pf.* to isolate.
изоля́тор, а *m.*
1 (*med.*) isolation ward.
2 (*в тюрьме*) solitary confinement cell.
изорв|áть, ý, ёшь, *past* **~áл, ~алá, ~áло** *pf.* (*of* ▶ **изрывáть**[1]) to tear (to shreds).
изощрённый *adj.* (*ум, вкус*) refined; (*слух*) keen, acute.
из-под *prep.* + *g.*
1 from under.
2 (*города*) from near.
3 (*о вместилище*) for (*or not translated*); **бáнка из-под варéнья** jam jar.
изразé|ц, цá *m.* tile.
Изрáил|ь, я *m.* Israel.
изрáильский *adj.* Israeli.
израильтя́н|ин, ина, *pl.* **~е, ~** *m.* Israeli.
израильтя́н|ка, ки *f. of* ▶ **~ин**
изрáн|ить, ю, ишь *pf.* to cover with wounds.
израсхóд|овать, ую *pf. of* ▶ **расхóдовать**
и́зредка *adv.* now and then; from time to time.
изрé|зать, жу, жешь *pf.* (*of* ▶ **~зывать**)
1 (*на много частей*) to cut into pieces; to cut up; (*сделать на чём-н. много надрезов*) to make cuts in.
2 (*geog.*) to cut across.
изрéзыва|ть, ю *impf. of* ▶ **изрéзать**
изрис|овáть, ýю *pf.* (*of* ▶ **~óвывать**) to cover with drawings.
изрисóвыва|ть, ю *impf. of* ▶ **изрисовáть**
изрывá|ть[1]**, ю** *impf. of* ▶ **изорвáть**
изрывá|ть[2]**, ю** *impf. of* ▶ **изры́ть**
изр|ы́ть, óю, óешь *pf.* (*of* ▶ **~ывáть**[2]) to dig up; to dig through.
изря́д|ный (~ен, ~на) *adj.* (*coll.*) fair, handsome; fairly large, tolerable; **~ное коли́чество** a fair amount.
изувéчива|ть, ю *impf. of* ▶ **изувéчить**
изувéч|ить, у, ишь *pf.* (*of* ▶ **~ивать**) to maim, mutilate.
изуми́тел|ьный (~ен, ~ьна) *adj.* amazing, astounding.
изум|и́ть, лю́, и́шь *pf.* (*of* ▶ **~ля́ть**) to amaze, astound.
изум|и́ться, лю́сь, и́шься *pf.* (*of* ▶ **~ля́ться**) to be amazed, astounded.
изумлéни|е, я *nt.* amazement.
изумлённый *p.p.p. of* ▶ **изуми́ть** *and adj.* amazed, astounded; dumbfounded.
изумля́|ть(ся), ю(сь) *impf. of* ▶ **изуми́ть(ся)**
изумрýд, а *m.* emerald.
изумрýдный *adj.*
1 emerald.
2 (*цвет*) emerald(-green).
изурóд|овать, ую *pf. of* ▶ **урóдовать**
изуч|áть, áю *impf.* (*of* ▶ **~и́ть**) to learn; (*impf. only*) to study.
изучéни|е, я *nt.* study, studying.
изуч|и́ть, ý, ~ишь *pf.* (*of* ▶ **~áть**)
1 to learn.
2 (*понять*) to come to know (very well), come to understand.
изъ... *pref.* = **из...**
изъéз|дить, жу, дишь *pf.* (*of* ▶ **~живать**) to travel all over, round; **мы ~дили весь свет** we have been all round the world.
изъéзжива|ть, ю *impf. of* ▶ **изъéздить**
изъяв|и́ть, лю́, ~ишь *pf.* (*of* ▶ **~ля́ть**) to indicate, express; **и. своё соглáсие** to give one's consent.
изъявля́|ть, ю *impf. of* ▶ **изъяви́ть**
изъя́н, а *m.* defect, flaw.
изъя́ти|е, я *nt.* withdrawal; removal.
из|ъя́ть, ымý, ы́мешь *pf.* (*of* ▶ **~ымáть**) to withdraw; to remove; **и. из обращéния** to withdraw from circulation; **и. в пóльзу госудáрства** to confiscate.
изымá|ть, ю *impf. of* ▶ **изъя́ть**
из|ымý, ы́мешь *see* ▶ **~ъя́ть**
изы́скан|ный (~, ~на) *adj.* refined.
изы|скáть, щý, ~щешь *pf.* (*of* ▶ **~скивать**) to find; to search out; **и. срéдства на пострóйку домóв** to find funds for house-building.
изы́скива|ть, ю *impf.* (*of* ▶ **изыскáть**) to search out; to try to find.
изю́м, а (у) *no pl., m.* raisins.
изя́ществ|о, а *nt.* elegance, grace.
изя́щ|ный (~ен, ~на) *adj.* elegant, graceful.
Иисýс, а *m.* (*bibl.*): **И. (Христóс)** Jesus Christ.
ик|áть, áю *impf.* (*of* ▶ **~нýть**) to hiccup.
ик|нýть, нý, нёшь *pf. of* ▶ **~áть**
икóн|а, ы *f.* (*relig., comput.*) icon.
икóнк|а, и *f.* (*comput.*) icon.
икóт|а, ы *f.* hiccups.
икр|á[1]**, ы́** *no pl., f.*
1 (hard) roe; spawn; **метáть ~ý** to spawn; (*fig., coll.*) to rage.
2 (*рыбный деликатес*) caviar; (*из овощей*) pâté; **баклажáнная и.** aubergine pâté.
икр|á[2]**, ы́,** *pl.* **~ы** *f.* (*anat.*) calf.
икри́нк|а, и *f.* grain of caviar.
ил, а *m.* silt.
и́ли *conj.* or; **и. ... и.** either ... or.
иллю́зи|я, и *f.* illusion.
иллюзóр|ный (~ен, ~на) *adj.* illusory.
иллюминáтор, а *m.* (*naut., aeron.*) porthole.

иллюмина́ци|я, и *f.* illuminations.
иллюстра́тор, а *m.* illustrator.
иллюстра́ци|я, и *f.* illustration.
иллюстри́р|ованный *p.p.p. of* ▸ **~овать** *and adj.* illustrated.
иллюстри́р|овать, ую *impf. and pf.* (*pf. also* ▸ **про~**) to illustrate (*also fig.*).
им
1 *i. of prons.* ▸ **он, оно́.**
2 *d. of pron.* ▸ **они́**
им. (*abbr. of* **и́мени**) named after; **музе́й им. Пу́шкина** Pushkin Museum.
има́м, а *nt.* imam (*Muslim priest or leader*).
имби́р|ь, я́ *m.* ginger.
и́м|ени, енем *see* ▸ **~я**
име́ни|е, я *nt.* estate.
имени́нник, а *m.* person whose birthday it is; birthday boy; (*relig.*) person whose name day it is.
имени́нни|ца, цы *f. of* ▸ **~к**
имени́т|ый (~, ~а) *adj.* distinguished.
и́менно *adv.*
1 **(а) и.** (*перед перечислением*) namely; to wit.
2 (*как раз, точно*) just, exactly; to be exact; **где и. она́ живёт?** where exactly does she live?; **вот и.!** exactly!; precisely!
имен|ова́ть, у́ю *impf.* (*of* ▸ **на~**) to name.
имен|ова́ться, у́юсь *impf.* (+ *i.*) to be called; to be termed.
име́|ть, ю, ешь *impf.* to have (*of abstract possession*); **и. возмо́жность** (+ *inf.*) to have an opportunity (to), be in a position (to); **и. де́ло (с** + *i.*) to have dealings (with), have to do (with); **и. значе́ние (для** + *g.*) to matter (to), be important (to); **и. ме́сто** to take place; **и. в виду́** (*не забывать*) to bear in mind, think of, (*подразумевать*) mean.
име́|ться, ется *impf.* to be; to be present, be available (**~ется у, ~ются у** *are equivalent to* **есть у**); **в на́шем го́роде ~ется два кинотеа́тра** there are two cinemas in our town.
име́|ющийся *pres. part. of* ▸ **~ться** *and adj.* available; present.
и́ми *i. of pron.* ▸ **они́**
и́мидж, а *m.* image.
имиджме́йкер, а *m.* image-maker.
имита́ци|я, и *f.* mimicry; mimicking; imitation.
имити́р|овать, ую *impf.* (*of* ▸ **сымити́ровать**) to mimic, imitate.
иммигра́нт, а *m.* immigrant.
иммигра́нт|ка, ки *f. of* ▸ **~**
иммигра́ци|я, и *f.*
1 immigration.
2 (*collect.*) (*иммигранты*) immigrants.
иммигри́р|овать, ую *impf. and pf.* to immigrate.
иммуните́т, а *m.* (*med., leg.*) immunity.
импера́тор, а *m.* emperor.
императри́ц|а, ы *f.* empress.
империали́зм, а *m.* imperialism.
импе́ри|я, и *f.* empire.
импе́рский *adj.* imperial.
импи́чмент *m.* (*pol.*) impeachment.
и́мпорт, а *m.*
1 (*ввоз товаров*) import.
2 (*collect., coll.*) (*товары*) foreign goods.
импорти́р|овать, ую *impf. and pf.* (*econ.*) to import.
и́мпорт|ный *adj. of* ▸ **~; ~ные по́шлины** import duties.
импрессиони́зм, а *m.* (*art*) Impressionism.
импрессиони́ст, а *m.* (*art*) Impressionist.
импровиза́ци|я, и *f.* improvisation.
импровизи́р|овать, ую *impf.* (*of* ▸ **сымпровизи́ровать**) to improvise; to extemporize.
и́мпульс, а *m.* (**к** + *d.*) impulse, impetus (for).
иму́ществ|о, а *nt.* property, belongings; **дви́жимое и.** (*leg.*) personalty, personal estate; **недви́жимое и.** (*leg.*) realty, real estate.
и́м|я, *g., d., and p.* **~ени,** *i.* **~енем,** *pl.* **~ена́, ~ён, ~ена́м** *nt.*
1 name; (*личное название*) first, Christian name; **вы́мышленное и.** alias, false name; **во и.** (+ *g.*) in the name of; **от ~ени** (+ *g.*) on behalf of.
2 (*fig.*) (*репутация*) name, reputation.
3 (*gram.*) noun (*any part of speech declined, as opposed to conjugated*); **и. прилага́тельное** adjective; **и. существи́тельное** noun, substantive; **и. числи́тельное** numeral.
ин... (*also* **ино...**) *comb. form, abbr. of* **иностра́нный**
инакомы́сли|е, я *nt.* dissidence; nonconformism.
инакомы́слящ|ий *adj.* dissident; nonconformist; *as n.* **и., ~его** *m.* dissident.
ина́че
1 (*adv.*) differently, otherwise; **так и́ли и.** in either event, at all events.
2 (*conj.*) otherwise, or (else); **потороп́итесь, и. вы опозда́ете** hurry up, or you will be late.
инвали́д, а *m.* invalid; disabled person.
инвали́дност|ь, и *f.* disablement; invalidity (*Br.*).
инвентариза́ци|я, и *f.* inventory making, stocktaking.
инвента́р|ь, я́ *m.* stock; equipment, appliances; **сельскохозя́йственный и.** agricultural implements.
инвести́р|овать, ую *impf. and pf.* to invest.
инвести́ци|я, и *f.* investment.
инве́стор, а *m.* (*fin.*) investor.
ингаля́ци|я, и *f.* (*med.*) inhaling.
ингредие́нт, а *m.* ingredient.
ингу́ш, а́, *g. pl.* **~е́й** *m.* Ingush.
Ингуше́ти|я, и *f.* Ingushetia.
ингу́ш|ка, ки *f. of* ▸ **~**
ингу́шский *adj.* Ingush.
инде́|ец, йца, *pl.* **~йцы, ~йцев** *m.* American Indian, Native American.
инде́йк|а, и *f.* turkey(-hen).
инде́|йский *adj. of* ▸ **~ец**
и́ндекс, а *m.* index; **и. цен** (*econ.*) price index; **почто́вый и.** postcode (*Br.*), zip code

(*US*).

индекса́ци|я, и *f.* (*econ.*) indexation.

инд|иа́нка, иа́нки *f. of* ▸ **~е́ец** *and* ▸ **~и́ец**

индивидуа́льност|ь, и *f.* individuality.

индивидуа́л|ьный (~ен, ~ьна) *adj.* individual.

индиви́дуум, а *m.* individual.

инди́го *nt. indecl.* indigo; **пла́тье цве́та и.** indigo dress.

инди́|ец, йца, *pl.* **~йцы, ~йцев** *m.* Indian.

инди́йский *adj.* Indian.

Инди́йск|ий океа́н, ~ого ~а *m.* the Indian Ocean.

индика́тор, а *m.* (*tech.*) indicator.

И́нди|я, и *f.* India.

индонези́|ец, йца, *pl.* **~йцы, ~йцев** *m.* Indonesian.

индонези́|йка, йки *f. of* ▸ **~ец**

индонези́йский *adj.* Indonesian.

Индоне́зи|я, и *f.* Indonesia.

индуи́зм, а *m.* Hinduism.

инду́кци|я, и *f.* (*phil., phys.*) induction.

инду́с, а *m.* Hindu.

инду́с|ка, ки *f. of* ▸ **~**

инду́сский *adj.* Hindu.

индустриализа́ци|я, и *f.* industrialization.

индустриа́льный *adj.* industrial.

индустри́|я, и *f.* industry.

индю́к, а́ *m.* turkey(-cock).

и́не|й, я *no pl., m.* hoar frost.

ине́рт|ный (~ен, ~на) *adj.* inert (*phys. and fig.*); (*fig.*) sluggish, inactive.

ине́рци|я, и *f.* (*phys. and fig.*) inertia; momentum; **дви́гаться по ~и** to move under its own momentum; (*fig.*): **де́лать что-н. по ~и** to do sth. from force of inertia, mechanically.

инжене́р, а *m.* engineer; **и.-меха́ник** mechanical engineer.

инжи́р, а *no pl., m.* (*дерево; плод*) fig.

инициа́л|ы, ов *pl.* (*sg.* **~, ~а** *m.*) initials.

инициати́в|а, ы *f.* initiative; **по со́бственной ~е** on one's own initiative.

инициати́в|ный (~ен, ~на) *adj.* full of initiative, enterprising; dynamic, go-getting.

инициа́тор, а *m.* initiator.

инкасса́тор, а *m.* (*fin.*) security guard (*delivering money to a bank*).

инквизи́ци|я, и *f.* inquisition.

инко́гнито
1 *adv.* incognito.
2 *n.; c.g. indecl.* incognito (*person*).

инкримини́р|овать, ую *impf. and pf.* (+ *d. and a.*) to charge (with); **ему́ ~уют поджо́г** he is being charged with arson.

инкруста́ци|я, и *f.* inlaid work, inlay.

инкуба́тор, а *m.* incubator.

инкубацио́нный *adj.* incubative, incubatory; **и. пери́од** (*med.*) incubation.

ино... *see* ▸ **ин...**

инове́р|ец, ца *m.* (*relig.*) adherent of different faith, creed.

иногда́ *adv.* sometimes.

иногоро́дний *adj.* of, from another town.

инозе́мный *adj.* foreign.

ин|о́й *adj.*
1 (*другой*) different; other; **~ы́ми слова́ми** in other words; **не кто и., как; не что ~о́е, как** none other than.
2 (*некоторый*) some; **и. раз** sometimes.

инома́рк|а, и *f.* foreign car, foreign make of car.

инопланё́тный *adj.* alien, extraterrestrial.

инопланетя́н|ин, ина, *pl.* **~е, ~** *m.* alien, extraterrestrial.

иноро́д|ный (~ен, ~на) *adj.* alien; **~ное те́ло** (*med. or fig.*) foreign body.

иностра́н|ец, ца *m.* foreigner.

иностра́н|ка, ки *f. of* ▸ **~ец**

иностра́нный *adj.* foreign.

иноязы́чный *adj.*
1 (*население*) speaking another language.
2 (*слово*) belonging to another language.

инсектици́д, а *m.* insecticide.

инсинуа́ци|я, и *f.* insinuation.

инспе́ктор, а, *m.* inspector; (*mil.*) inspecting officer.

инспе́кци|я, и *f.*
1 (*действие*) inspection; **и. на ме́сте** (*mil.*) on-site inspection.
2 (*организация*) inspectorate.

инсти́нкт, а *m.* instinct.

инстинкти́в|ный (~ен, ~на) *adj.* instinctive.

институ́т, а *m.*
1 (*общественное установление*) institution; **и. бра́ка** the institution of marriage.
2 (*учебное или научное заведение*) institute; school; **медици́нский и.** medical school.

инструкта́ж, а *m.* instructing; (*mil., aeron.*) briefing.

инструкти́р|овать, ую *impf. and pf.* (*pf. also* ▸ **про~**) to instruct, brief.

инстру́ктор, а *m.* instructor.

инстру́кци|я, и *f.* instructions, directions.

инструме́нт, а *m.* (*mus.; tech.*) instrument; (*tech.*) tool, implement; (*sg.; collect.*) tools.

инсули́н, а *m.* insulin.

инсу́льт, а *m.* (*med.*) stroke.

инсцени́р|овать, ую *impf. and pf.*
1 (*роман*) to dramatize, adapt (for stage *or* screen).
2 (*fig.*) to feign, stage; **и. о́бморок** to stage a faint.

интегра́ци|я, и *f.* integration.

интелле́кт, а *m.* intellect; **иску́сственный и.** (*comput.*) artificial intelligence.

интеллектуа́л, а *m.* intellectual.

интеллектуа́л|ьный (~ен, ~ьна) *adj.* intellectual.

интеллиге́нт, а *m.* member of the intelligentsia, intellectual.

интеллиге́нт|ный (~ен, ~на) *adj.* cultured, educated.

интеллиге́нци|я, и *f.* (*collect.*) intelligentsia.

интенси́в|ный (~ен, ~на) *adj.* intensive.

интеракти́вный *adj.* interactive.

И

интерва́л, а *m.* (*in var. senses*) interval.

интерве́нци|я, и *f.* (*pol.*) intervention.

интервью́ *nt. indecl.* (*press*) interview; **взять ~ у** + *g.* to interview (*a person*).

интере́с, а *m.*
1 interest; **представля́ть и.** to be of interest; **прояви́ть и.** (**к** + *d.*) to show interest (in).
2 (*выгода*) interest; (*pl.*) interests; **в ва́ших ~ах пое́хать** it is in your interest to go.

интере́сно *as pred.* it is, would be interesting; **и., что из него́ вы́йдет** I wonder how he will turn out.

интере́с|ный (~ен, ~на) *adj.* interesting.

интерес|ова́ть, у́ю *impf.* to interest.

интерес|ова́ться, у́юсь *impf.* (+ *i.*) to be interested (in); (*coll.*) (*осведомляться*) to enquire.

интерна́т, а *m.*
1 (*школа*) boarding school.
2 (*общежитие*) boarding house (*at private school*).

интернациона́льный *adj.* international.

Интерне́т, а *m.* the Internet; **путеше́ствовать по ~у** to surf the Internet.

интерне́т-са́йт, а *m.* website.

интерпрета́ци|я, и *f.* interpretation.

интерпрети́р|овать, ую *impf. and pf.* to interpret.

интерфе́йс, а *m.* (*comput.*) interface.

интерфере́нци|я, и *f.* (*phys.*) interference.

интерье́р, а *m.* (*art*) interior.

инти́м|ный (~ен, ~на) *adj.* intimate; **~ные места́** private parts.

интоксика́ци|я, и *f.* (*med.*) intoxication; **алкого́льная и.** alcoholic poisoning.

интона́ци|я, и *f.* intonation.

интри́г|а, и *f.* intrigue.

интрове́рт, а *m.* introvert.

интуити́в|ный (~ен, ~на) *adj.* intuitive.

интуи́ци|я, и *f.* intuition.

инфанти́л|ьный (~ен, ~ьна) *adj.* infantile.

инфа́ркт, а *m.* (*med.*) heart attack; infarction.

инфекцио́нн|ый *adj.* infectious; **~ая больни́ца** isolation hospital.

инфе́кци|я, и *f.* infection.

инфля́ци|я, и *f.* (*econ.*) inflation.

информати́в|ный (~ен, ~на) *adj.* informative.

информа́тик|а, и *f.* information science, information technology.

информа́тор, а *m.* informant.

информ|ацио́нный *adj. of* ▸ **~а́ция**

информа́ци|я, и *f.* information.

информи́р|овать, ую *impf. and pf.* (*pf. also* ▸ **про~**) to inform.

инфраструкту́р|а, ы *f.* infrastructure.

инциде́нт, а *m.* incident; **пограни́чный и.** frontier incident.

инъе́кци|я, и *f.* injection.

и. о. (*abbr. of* **исполня́ющий обя́занности**) + *g.* acting … .

Иорда́н, а *m.* Jordan (*river*).

иорда́н|ец, ца *m.* Jordanian.

Иорда́ни|я, и *f.* Jordan (*country*).

иорда́н|ка, ки *f. of* ▸ **~ец**

иорда́нский *adj.* Jordanian.

ипоте́к|а, и *f.* mortgage.

ипоте́|чный *adj. of* ▸ **~ка**; **и. банк** mortgage bank; ≈ building society.

ипподро́м, а *m.* racecourse.

Ира́к, а *m.* Iraq.

ира́к|ец, ца *m.* Iraqi.

ира́кский *adj.* Iraqi.

Ира́н, а *m.* Iran.

ира́н|ец, ца *m.* Iranian.

ира́н|ка, ки *f. of* ▸ **~ец**

ира́нский *adj.* Iranian.

и́рис, а *m.* (*bot.*) iris.

ири́с, а *m.* toffee.

ирла́нд|ец, ца *m.* Irishman.

Ирла́нди|я, и *f.* Ireland.

ирла́нд|ка, ки *f.* Irishwoman.

ирла́ндский *adj.* Irish.

иронизи́р|овать, ую *impf.* (**над** + *i.*) to speak ironically (about).

ирони́ческий *adj.* ironic(al).

ирони́ч|ный (~ен, ~на) *adj.* = **~еский**

иро́ни|я, и *f.* irony.

иррациона́л|ьный (~ен, ~ьна) *adj.* irrational.

ирригáци|я, и *f.* (*agric. and med.*) irrigation.

ис... *pref.* = **из...**

иск, а *m.* (*leg.*) suit, action; **предъяви́ть и. (к) кому́-н.** to sue, prosecute s.o., bring an action against s.o.

искажа́|ть, ю *impf. of* ▸ **искази́ть**

искаже́ни|е, я *nt.* distortion, perversion.

искажённый *p.p.p. of* ▸ **искази́ть** *and adj.* distorted, perverted.

иска|зи́ть, жу́, зи́шь *pf.* (*of* ▸ **~жа́ть**) to distort, pervert, twist; to misrepresent; **и. чьи-н. слова́** to twist s.o.'s words; **и. фа́кты** to misrepresent the facts.

искале́ч|енный *p.p.p. of* ▸ **~ить** *and adj.* crippled, maimed.

искале́ч|ить, у, ишь *pf.* (*of* ▸ **кале́чить**) to cripple, maim.

искале́ч|иться, усь, ишься *pf. of* ▸ **кале́читься**

иска́тел|ь, я *m.* seeker, searcher; **и. же́мчуга** pearl diver.

иска́ть, ищу́, и́щешь *impf.*
1 (+ *a.*) to look for, search for; to seek (*sth. concr.*).
2 (+ *g.*) to seek, look for, try to obtain (*sth. abstr.*); **и. слу́чая, сове́та** to seek an opportunity, seek advice.

исключ|а́ть, а́ю *impf. of* ▸ **~и́ть**

исключа́|я *pres. ger. of* ▸ **~ть** *and prep.* + *g.* excepting, with the exception of; **и. прису́тствующих** the present company excepted.

исключе́ни|е, я *nt.*
1 (*отклонение от нормы*) exception; **за ~ем** (+ *g.*) with the exception (of).

2 (*из списка*) exclusion; (*из организации*) expulsion; **ме́тодом ~я** by process of elimination.

исключи́тельно *adv.*
1 (*необыкновенно*) exceptionally.
2 (*только*) exclusively, solely.

исключи́тел|ьный (~ен, ~ьна) *adj.*
1 (*необыкновенный*) exceptional.
2 (*не для всех*) exclusive; **~ьное пра́во** exclusive right, sole right.

исключ|и́ть, у́, и́шь *pf.* (*of* ▸ **~а́ть**)
1 (*удалить*) to exclude; to eliminate; **и. из спи́ска** to strike off a list.
2 (*из организации*) to expel; to dismiss.
3 (*не допустить*) to rule out; **не ~ено́, что́ на́ши проигра́ют** our side could conceivably lose.

иско́нный *adj.* (*права*) immemorial, age-old; (*население*) native, indigenous.

ископа́ем|ое, ого *nt.*
1 fossil (*also fig., iron.*).
2 (*also* **поле́зное ~**) (*usu. pl.*) mineral.

искорен|и́ть, ю́, и́шь *pf.* (*of* ▸ **~я́ть**) to eradicate.

искорен|я́ть, я́ю *impf. of* ▸ **~и́ть**

и́скр|а, ы *f.* spark; (*fig.*) flash.

и́скренне *adv.* sincerely, candidly; **и. ваш** (*epistolary formula*) Yours sincerely; Yours faithfully.

и́скрен|ний (~ен, ~на, ~не *or* **~но,** *pl.* **~ни** *or* **~ны)** *adj.* sincere, candid.

и́скренност|ь, и *f.* sincerity, candour.

искрив|и́ть, лю́, и́шь *pf.* (*of* ▸ **~ля́ть**) to bend; (*fig.*) to distort.

искривля́|ть, ю *impf. of* ▸ **искриви́ть**

и́скр|иться, ~́ится *impf.* to sparkle; to scintillate (*also fig.*).

искупа́|ть[1]**, ю** *pf.* to bath.

искуп|а́ть[2]**, а́ю** *impf. of* ▸ **~и́ть**

искупа́|ться, юсь *pf.* (*of* ▸ **купа́ться**) to bathe; to take a bath.

искуп|и́ть, лю́, ~́ишь *pf.* (*of* ▸ **~а́ть**[2]) (*theol. and fig.*) (*вину, грех*) to expiate, atone for.

искупле́ни|е, я *nt.* redemption, expiation, atonement.

искус|а́ть, а́ю *pf.* (*of* ▸ **~́ывать**) (*о комарах*) to bite badly, all over; (*о пчёлах*) to sting badly, all over.

иску|си́ть, шу́, си́шь *pf. of* ▸ **~ша́ть**

иску́с|ный (~ен, ~на) *adj.* skilful (*Br.*), skillful (*US*); expert.

иску́сствен|ный *adj.*
1 artificial; (*ткань, волокно*) synthetic, man-made; **~ное дыха́ние** artificial respiration.
2 **(~, ~на)** (*fig.*) (*смех*) artificial, feigned.

иску́сств|о, а *nt.*
1 art; **изобрази́тельные, изя́щные ~а** fine arts.
2 (*умение*) craftsmanship, skill; **и. верхово́й езды́** horsemanship.

искусствове́д, а *m.* art historian.

искусствове́дени|е, я *nt.* history of art, art history.

иску́сыва|ть, ю *impf. of* ▸ **искуса́ть**

искуша́|ть, ю *impf.* (*of* ▸ **искуси́ть**) to tempt; to seduce; **и. судьбу́** to tempt fate.

искуше́ни|е, я *nt.* temptation; seduction; **подда́ться ~ю, впасть в и.** to yield to temptation.

искушённый *p.p.p. of* ▸ **искуси́ть** *and adj.* (*политик*) experienced; (*публика*) sophisticated.

исла́м, а *m.* Islam.

исла́мский *adj.* Islamic.

Исла́нди|я, и *f.* Iceland.

испа́н|ец, ца *m.* Spaniard, Spanish man.

Испа́ни|я, и *f.* Spain.

испа́нк|а, и *f.* Spaniard, Spanish woman.

испа́нский *adj.* Spanish.

испаре́ни|е, я *nt.*
1 (*действие*) evaporation.
2 (*usu. pl.*) (*пар*) fumes.

испар|и́ться, ю́сь, и́шься *pf.* (*of* ▸ **~я́ться**) to evaporate; (*fig., joc.*) (*исчезнуть*) to vanish into thin air.

испар|я́ться, я́юсь *impf. of* ▸ **~и́ться**

испа́чка|ть(ся), ю(сь) *pf. of* ▸ **па́чкать(ся)**

испепел|и́ть, ю́, и́шь *pf.* (*of* ▸ **~я́ть**) to reduce to ashes, incinerate.

испепел|я́ть, я́ю *impf. of* ▸ **~и́ть**

испе́|чь, ку́, чёшь, ку́т, *past* **~̈к, ~кла́** *pf. of* ▸ **печь**[1]

испе́|чься, чётся, ку́тся, *past* **~̈кся, ~кла́сь** *pf. of* ▸ **пе́чься**

испещр|и́ть, ю́, и́шь *pf.* (*of* ▸ **~я́ть**) (+ *a. and i.*) to spot (with); to mark all over (with).

испещр|я́ть, я́ю *impf. of* ▸ **~и́ть**

испи|са́ть, шу́, ~́шешь *pf.* (*of* ▸ **~́сывать**)
1 (*тетрадь*) to cover with writing; **он уже́ ~са́л два́дцать тетра́дей** he has already filled up twenty exercise books.
2 (*карандаш, бумагу*) to use up (in writing).

испи́сыва|ть, ю *impf. of* ▸ **исписа́ть**

испове́д|ать, аю *pf.* (*coll.*) = **~овать**[1]

испове́д|аться, аюсь *pf.* (*coll.*) = **~оваться**[1]

испове́д|овать[1]**, ую** *impf. and pf.* (*eccl.*) to hear the confession (of).

испове́д|овать[2]**, ую** *impf.* (*веру*) to profess.

испове́д|оваться, уюсь *impf. and pf.*
1 (+ *d. or* **у** + *g.*; *eccl.*) to confess, make one's confession (to).
2 (+ *d. or* **пе́ред** + *i.*; *fig., coll.*) to confess; to unburden o.s. of; **он ~овался мне в свои́х сомне́ниях** he confessed his doubts to me.

и́споведь, и *f.* (*eccl.*) confession.

исподло́бья *adv.* from under the brows (*distrustfully, sullenly*).

исподтишка́ *adv.* (*coll., pej.*) in an underhand way; on the quiet, on the sly; **смея́ться и.** to laugh in one's sleeve.

исполне́ни|е, я *nt.*
1 (*желания*) fulfilment (*Br.*), fulfillment (*US*); (*приказа*) execution; (*долгов*) discharge; **привести́ в и.** to carry out, execute.
2 (*роли, музыки*) performance; (*theatr., mus.*) **в ~и** (+ *g.*) (as) played (by), (as) performed (by).

исполни́тел|ь, я *m.*
1 executor; **суде́бный и.** bailiff.
2 (*theatr., mus., etc.*) performer; **соста́в ~ей** cast.

исполни́тель|ница, ницы *f. of* ▸ **~**
исполни́тел|ьный *adj.*
1 (*власть, директор, комитет*) executive.
2 **(~ен, ~ьна)** (*человек*) efficient and dependable.
испо́лн|ить, ю, ишь *pf.* (*of* ▸ **~я́ть**)
1 (*заказ*) to carry out, execute; (*желание*) to fulfil (*Br.*), fulfill (*US*); **и. обеща́ние** to keep a promise; **и. про́сьбу** to grant a request.
2 (*роль, танец*) to perform; **и. роль** (+ *g.*) to take the part (of).
испо́лн|иться, юсь, ишься *pf.* (*of* ▸ **~я́ться**)
1 (*осуществиться*) to be fulfilled.
2 (*impers.,* + *d.*; *expr. passage of time*): **ему́ ~илось семь лет** he is seven, he was seven last birthday.
исполн|я́ть(ся), я́ю(сь) *impf. of* ▸ **~́ить(ся)**; **~я́ющий обя́занности** (+ *g.*) acting.
испо́льзовани|е, я *nt.* use; (*сырья*) utilization.
испо́льз|овать, ую *impf. and pf.* to use, make use of, utilize.
испо́р|тить(ся), чу(сь), тишь(ся) *pf. of* ▸ **по́ртить(ся)**
испо́рченн|ый *p.p.p. of* ▸ **испо́ртить** *and adj.*
1 (*человек*) depraved; corrupted.
2 (*настроение, день*) ruined; (*товары*) spoiled; bad, rotten; **~ое мя́со** tainted meat.
3 (*coll.*) (*ребёнок*) spoiled.
4 (*comput.*) corrupt.
испра́в|ить, лю, ишь *pf.* (*of* ▸ **~ля́ть**)
1 (*ошибку*) to rectify, correct, emend.
2 (*починить*) to repair, mend.
испра́в|иться, люсь, ишься *pf.* (*of* ▸ **~ля́ться**) to improve (*intrans.*); to reform (*intrans.*), turn over a new leaf.
исправле́ни|е, я *nt.* correcting; repairing; correction.
исправля́|ть, ю *impf. of* ▸ **испра́вить**
исправля́|ться, юсь *impf. of* ▸ **испра́виться**
испра́в|ный (~ен, ~на) *adj.* (*механизм*) in good order.
испражне́ни|е, я *nt.*
1 (*действие*) defecation.
2 (*pl.*) (*экскременты*) faeces.
испражн|и́ться, ю́сь, и́шься *pf. of* ▸ **~я́ться**
испражн|я́ться, я́юсь *impf.* (*of* ▸ **~и́ться**) to defecate.
испу́г, а (у) *m.* fright; alarm; **с ~у/~а** from fright.
испу́ганный *p.p.p. of* ▸ **испуга́ть** *and adj.* frightened, scared, startled.
испуга́|ть(ся), ю(сь) *pf. of* ▸ **пуга́ть(ся)**
испуска́|ть, ю *impf. of* ▸ **испусти́ть**
испу|сти́ть, щу́, ~́стишь *pf.* (*of* ▸ **~ска́ть**) (*свет, лучи*) to emit; (*стон*) to let out; **и. дух** to breathe one's last.
испыта́ни|е, я *nt.* test, trial; (*fig.*) ordeal.
испы́т|анный *p.p.p. of* ▸ **~а́ть** *and adj.* tried, well-tried.
испыта́тел|ь, я *m.* tester; **лётчик-и.** test pilot.
испыт|а́ть, а́ю *pf.* (*of* ▸ **~́ывать**)
1 (*проверить*) to test, put to the test.
2 (*ощутить*) to feel, experience.
испы́тыва|ть, ю *impf. of* ▸ **испыта́ть**
иссле́довани|е, я *nt.*
1 (*темы*) research; (*местности*) exploration; (*проблемы*) examination; (*крови, состава*) analysis.
2 (*научный труд*) paper; study.
иссле́довател|ь, я *m.* researcher; (*страны*) explorer.
иссле́дователь|ница, ницы *f. of* ▸ **~**
иссле́довательский *adj.* research.
иссле́д|овать, ую *impf. and pf.* (*ситуацию, проблему*) to investigate; (*тему*) to research into; (*страну*) to explore; (*кровь*) to analyse.
иссяк|а́ть, а́ю *impf. of* ▸ **~́нуть**
исся́к|нуть, ну, нешь, *past* **~, ~ла** *pf.* (*of* ▸ **~а́ть**) to run dry, dry up; (*fig.*) (*терпение, силы*) to run out.
истека́|ть, ю *impf. of* ▸ **исте́чь**
исте́|кший *p.p. of* ▸ **~чь 1** *and adj.* past, preceding; **в тече́ние ~кшего го́да** during the past year.
истерза́|ть, ю *pf.*
1 (*разорвать на части*) to tear in pieces; to mutilate.
2 (*измучить*) to torment.
исте́рик|а, и *f.* hysterics.
истери́ческий *adj.* hysterical; **и. припа́док** fit of hysterics.
истери́|я, и *f.* (*med.*) hysteria; (*fig.*): **ма́ссовая и.** mass hysteria.
ист|е́ц, ца́ *m.* (*leg.*) plaintiff.
истече́ни|е, я *nt.*
1 outflow; **и. кро́ви** haemorrhage (*Br.*), hemorrhage (*US*).
2 (*окончание*) expiry, expiration; **по ~и сро́ка гара́нтии** on the expiry of the guarantee period.
исте́|чь, ку́, чёшь, ку́т, *past* **~̈к, ~кла́** *pf.* (*of* ▸ **~ка́ть**)
1: **и. кро́вью** to bleed profusely.
2 (*окончиться*) to expire, elapse; **вре́мя ~кло́** time is up.
и́стин|а, ы *f.* truth; **изби́тая и.** truism.
и́стин|ный (~ен, ~на) *adj.* true, veritable.
ист|и́ца, и́цы *f. of* ▸ **~е́ц**
исто́к, а *m.* source (*also fig.*).
истолк|ова́ть, у́ю *pf.* (*of* ▸ **~о́вывать**) (*смысл, слово*) to interpret; (*письменный памятник*) to comment upon; **и. замеча́ние в дурну́ю сто́рону** to put a nasty construction on a remark.
истолко́выва|ть, ю *impf. of* ▸ **истолкова́ть**
исто́м|а, ы *f.* languor.
истопни́к, а́ *m.* stoker; (*котлов*) boilerman.
исто́рик, а *m.* historian.
истори́ческ|ий *adj.*
1 historical; **~ое лицо́** historical figure.
2 (*важный*) historic; **~ое реше́ние** historic decision.
исто́ри|я, и *f.*
1 history; **и. боле́зни** case history.
2 (*coll.*) (*рассказ*) story.
3 (*coll.*) (*событие*) incident, event; scene;

вчера́ со мной произошла́ заба́вная и. a funny thing happened to me yesterday.

исто́чник, а *m.*
1 spring.
2 (*fig.*) source; **и. информа́ции** source of information; **и. све́та** source of light; **служи́ть ~ом** (+ *g.*) to be a source (of).

истоще́ни|е, я *nt.* exhaustion.

истощённый *adj.* exhausted; (*исхудалый*) emaciated.

истра́|тить, чу, тишь *pf. of* ▸ **тра́тить**

истреби́тел|ь, я *m.*
1 (*человек*) destroyer.
2 (*самолёт*) fighter.
3 (*лётчик*) fighter pilot.

истреб|и́ть, лю́, и́шь *pf.* (*of* ▸ **~ля́ть**) (*посевы*) to destroy; (*крыс*) to exterminate.

истребле́ни|е, я *nt.* (*посевов*) destruction; (*крыс*) extermination.

истребля́|ть, ю *impf. of* ▸ **истреби́ть**

истука́н, а *m.* idol, statue.

истяза́ни|е, я *nt.* torture.

истяза́|ть, ю *impf.* to torture.

исхо́д, а *m.* (*итог*) outcome; (*конец*) end; **быть на ~е** to be nearing the end, be coming to an end; **на ~е дня** towards evening.

исхо|ди́ть, жу́, ~́дишь *impf.* (*of* ▸ **изойти́**)
1 (*impf. only*) (**из** + *g.*) (*происходить*) to come (from); to emanate (from); **отку́да исхо́дит э́тот слух?** where does this rumour (*Br.*), rumor (*US*) come from?
2 (*impf. only*) (**из** + *g.*) (*основываться*) to proceed (from), base o.s. (on).
3 : **и. кро́вью** to become weak through loss of blood.

исхо́дн|ый *adj.* initial; **~ое положе́ние** point of departure.

исходя́щий *adj.* outgoing.

исхуда́|ть, ю *pf.* to become emaciated, become wasted.

исцеле́ни|е, я *nt.*
1 (*действие*) healing, cure.
2 (*выздоровление*) recovery.

исцел|и́ть, ю́, и́шь *pf.* (*of* ▸ **~я́ть**) to heal, cure.

исцел|я́ть, я́ю *impf. of* ▸ **~и́ть**

исчез|а́ть, а́ю *impf.* (*of* ▸ **~́нуть**) to disappear, vanish.

исчезнове́ни|е, я *nt.* disappearance.

исче́з|нуть, ну, нешь, *past* **~, ~ла** *pf. of* ▸ **~а́ть**

исче́рп|ать, аю *pf.* (*of* ▸ **~ывать**)
1 to exhaust, drain.
2 (*довести до конца*) to settle, conclude; **и. вопро́с** to settle a question.

исче́рпыва|ть, ю *impf. of* ▸ **исче́рпать**

исче́рпыва|ющий *pres. part. act. of* ▸ **~ть** *and adj.* exhaustive.

исчисле́ни|е, я *nt.* calculation; (*math.*) calculus.

ита́к *conj.* thus; so then.

Ита́ли|я, и *f.* Italy.

италья́н|ец, ца *nt.* Italian.

италья́н|ка, ки *f. of* ▸ **~ец**

италья́нский *adj.* Italian.

и т. д. (*abbr. of* **и так да́лее**) etc., et cetera, and so on.

ито́г, а *m.*
1 (*общая сумма*) sum, total; **о́бщий и.** grand total.
2 (*fig.*) (*результат*) result; **подвести́ и.** to sum up; **в ~е** (*в конце концов*) in the end; (*в результате*) as a result.

итого́ *adv.* in all, altogether; (sub)total.

ито́говый *adj.* (*сумма*) total; (*завершающий*) final, concluding.

и т. п. (*abbr. of* **и тому́ подо́бное**) etc., et cetera, and so on.

иудаи́зм, а *m.* Judaism.

иуде́|й, я *m.* (*liter.*) Jew.

иуде́й|ка, ки *f. of* ▸ **~**

иуде́йский *adj.* (*hist. and relig.*) Judaic.

их[1] *a. and g. of* ▸ **они́**

их[2] *possessive pron.* (*при существительном*) their; (*без существительного*) theirs; **их маши́на ме́ньше, чем на́ша** their car is smaller than ours.

иша́к, а́ *m.* donkey, ass; (*fig., coll.*) dogsbody (*Br.*), gofer (*US*).

ишь *int.* (*coll.*) *expr. surprise or disgust*: look!; just look!; well I never!; **и. ты!** = **и.!** *or expr. disagreement or objection.*

ище́йк|а, и *f.* bloodhound.

и́щущий *pres. part. act. of* ▸ **иска́ть** *and adj.*: **и. взгляд** searching look.

ию́л|ь, я *m.* July.

ию́ль|ский *adj. of* ▸ **~**

ию́н|ь, я *m.* June.

ию́нь|ский *adj. of* ▸ **~**

Йй

Йе́мен, а *m.* Yemen.

йе́мен|ец, ца *m.* Yemeni.

йе́мен|ка, ки *f. of* ▸ **~ец**

йе́менский *adj.* Yemeni.

йо́г|а, и *f.* yoga.

йо́гурт, а *m.* yog(h)urt.

йод, а *m.* iodine.

Кк

к, ко *prep. + d.*
[1] (*при обозначении места*) to, towards; **мы подъезжа́ли к Москве́** we were nearing Moscow; **прислони́те ле́стницу к стене́** place the ladder against the wall; (*fig.*): **лицо́м к лицу́** face to face; **к лу́чшему** for the better; **к (не)сча́стью** (un)fortunately; **к тому́ же** besides, moreover.
[2] (*при обозначении предельного срока*) to, towards; by; **зима́ подходи́ла к концу́** winter was drawing to a close; **к пе́рвому января́** by the first of January; **к тому́ вре́мени** by then, by that time; **к сро́ку** on time.
[3] (*при указании назначения*) for; **к чему́?** what for?; **э́то ни к чему́** it is no use.

-ка *particle* (*coll.*)
[1] *modifying force of imper.*: **скажи́-ка мне** come on now, tell me; **да́й-ка мне посмотре́ть** come on, let me take a look; **ну́-ка** well; **ну́-ка, спо́йте что-н.!** come on, give us a song!
[2] *with 1st pers. sg. of fut., expr. tentative decision*: **напишу́-ка ей письмо́** I think I'll write to her; **куплю́-ка тот га́лстук** maybe I'll buy that tie.

каба́к, а́ *m.* tavern; (*coll., fig.*) noisy place.
кабал|а́, ы́ *f.* servitude, bondage.
каба́н, а́ *m.* (wild) boar.
кабаре́ *nt. indecl.* cabaret.
кабач|о́к, ка́ *m.* (*растение*) (vegetable) marrow (*Br.*), squash (*US*).
ка́бел|ь, я *m.* cable; **о́птико-волоко́нный к.** (*or* **волоко́нно-опти́ческий к.**) fibre-optic cable (*Br.*), fiber-optic cable (*US*).
ка́бель|ный *adj. of* ▸ **~; ~ное телеви́дение** cable television.
каби́н|а, ы *f.* (*в самолёте, для пассажиров*) cabin; (*в самолёте, для лётчика*) cockpit; (*грузовика*) cab; (*в туалете*) cubicle; (*телефонная; для голосования*) booth; (*для купальщиков*) bathing hut; (*лифта*) cage.
кабине́т[1], а *m.*
[1] (*в доме*) study; (*на работе*) office; (*врача*) surgery (*Br.*), office (*US*).
[2] (*комплект мебели*) suite.
кабине́т[2], а *m.* (*also* **к. мини́стров**; *often* **к.**) (*pol.*) cabinet.
каблу́к, а́ *m.* heel (*of footwear*).
кабриоле́т, а *m.* cabriolet.
Кабу́л, а *m.* Kabul.
кавале́р[1], а *m.*
[1] (*в танце*) partner; (*мужчина*) (gentle)man.
[2] (*coll.*) (*поклонник*) admirer, suitor.
кавале́р[2], а *m.*: **к. (о́рдена)** knight, holder (of an order).
кавалери́ст, а *m.* cavalryman.
кавале́ри|я, и *f.* cavalry.
ка́вер-ве́рси|я, и *f.* cover version (*of a song*).
Кавка́з, а *m.* Caucasus.
кавка́з|ец, ца *m.* Caucasian.
кавка́з|ка, ки *f. of* ▸ **~ец**
кавка́зский *adj.* Caucasian.
кавы́ч|ки, ек *pl.* (*sg.* **~ка, ~ки** *f.*) inverted commas, quotation marks; **в ~ках** in inverted commas, in quotes; (*fig., iron.*) so-called.
каде́т, а *m.* cadet.
ка́дк|а, и *f.* tub, vat.
кадр, а *m.* (*cinema*) (*снимок*) frame; (*эпизод*) shot; **го́лос за ~́ом** voice-over.
кадри́л|ь, и *f.* quadrille (*dance*).
ка́дровый *adj.*
[1] (*mil.*) (*офицер*) regular.
[2] (*рабочий*) skilled; best.
ка́др|ы, ов *pl.* (*collect.*)
[1] (*mil.*) (regular, peacetime) establishment.
[2] (*работники*) personnel; **отде́л ~́ов** personnel department (*of institution, factory, etc.*).
[3] (*pol.*) cadres.
кады́к, а́ *m.* (*coll.*) Adam's apple.
каждодне́вный *adj.* daily.
ка́ждый *adj.*
[1] every, each; **к. день** every day; **к. из них получи́л по пять фу́нтов** they received five pounds each.
[2] *as n.* everyone.
ка́жущийся *adj.* apparent.
каза́к, а́, *pl.* **~и́** *m.* Cossack.
каза́рм|а, ы *f.* barracks.
ка|за́ться, жу́сь, ~́жешься *impf.* (*of* ▸ **показа́ться 1**)
[1] to seem, appear; **она́ ~́жется ста́рше свои́х лет** she looks older than she is.
[2] (*impers.*): **(мне, *etc.*) ~́жется, ~за́лось** it seems, seemed (to me, *etc.*); apparently; **мне ~́жется, что он был прав** I think he was right; **вы, ~́жется, из Москвы́?** you are from Moscow, I believe?; **~за́лось бы** it would seem, one would think.
каза́х, а *m.* Kazakh.
каза́хский *adj.* Kazakh.
Казахста́н, а *m.* Kazakhstan.
каза́честв|о, а *nt.* (*collect.*) the Cossacks.
каза́чий *adj.* Cossack.
каза́|чка, чки *f. of* ▸ **~к**
каза́|шка, шки *f. of* ▸ **~х**
казема́т, а *m.* casemate; (*камера*) (prison) cell (*for one person*).
казённ|ый *adj.*
[1] (*государственный*) State, public; **~ое иму́щество** State property; **на к. счёт** at public cost.
[2] (*fig.*) (*бюрократический*) bureaucratic, formal; **к. язы́к** language of officialdom, official jargon.
казино́ *nt. indecl.* casino.
казн|а́, ы́ *no pl., f.* (*государственное имущество*) Exchequer, Treasury.
казначе́|й, я *m.*

1 (*кассир*) treasurer, bursar (*Br.*).
2 (*mil.*) paymaster; (*naut.*) purser.

казначе́йств|о, а *nt.* Treasury, Exchequer.

казн|и́ть, ю́, и́шь *impf. and pf.* to execute, put to death.

казнокра́дств|о, а *nt.* embezzlement of public funds.

казн|ь, и *f.* execution, capital punishment; **сме́ртная к.** death penalty.

Каи́р, а *m.* Cairo.

ка|йма́, йм́ы, *pl.* **~и́мы, ~ём, ~и́мам** *f.* edging, border.

кайма́н, а *m.* (*zool.*) cayman.

кайф, а *m.* (*coll.*) kicks, 'high'; turn-on; buzz; **быть под ~ом** to be high *or* spaced out.

как[1] *adv. and particle*
1 how; **к. вам нра́вится Москва́?** how do you like Moscow?; **к. (ва́ши) дела́?** how are you getting on?; **забы́л, к. э́то де́лается** I have forgotten how to do this; **к. вам не сты́дно!** you ought to be ashamed!; **к. его́ фами́лия, к. его́ зову́т?** what is his name?, what is he called?; **к. называ́ется э́тот цвето́к?** what is this flower called?; **к. вы ду́маете?** what do you think?; *expr. surprise and/or displeasure*: **к.! ты опя́ть здесь** what! are you here again?; **к. же так?** how is that?; (*coll.*): **к. сказа́ть** it all depends; **кому́ к.** it depends on the person.
2 (*о внезапном действии*) (*coll.*): **она́ к. закричи́т!** she suddenly cried out.
3: **к. ни, к. ... ни** however; **к. ни стара́йтесь** however hard you may try, try as you may.

как[2] *conj.*
1 (*выражает сравнение*) as; like; **бе́лый к. снег** white as snow; **бу́дьте к. до́ма** make yourself at home; (*with comp.*): **к. мо́жно, к. нельзя́** as ... as possible; **к. мо́жно скоре́е** as soon as possible.
2: **к. ..., так и** both ... and; **к. ма́льчики, так и де́вочки** both the boys and the girls.
3 (*что*) *following vv. of perceiving not translated*: **я ви́дел, к. она́ ушла́** I saw her go out.
4 (*когда*) when; (*с тех пор, как*) since; **прошло́ два го́да, к. мы встре́тились** it is two years since we met; **к. то́лько** as soon as, when.
5 (+ *neg.*) but, except, than; **что ему́ остава́лось де́лать, к. не созна́ться?** what could he do but confess?; **кому́, к. не мне знать э́то!** if anyone knows, I do!
6: **в то вре́мя к.; до того́ к.; ме́жду тем к.; тогда́ к.** *see* ▸ **вре́мя, до, ме́жду, тогда́.**

какаду́ *m. indecl.* (*zool.*) cockatoo.

кака́о *nt. indecl.* cocoa.

ка́ка|ть, аю *impf.* (*baby talk*) to (do a) poo.

как бу́дто (бы)
1 *conj.* as if, as though; **к. б. вы не зна́ете!** as if you didn't know!
2 *particle* (*coll.*) (*кажется*) it would seem.

как бы
1 (+ *inf.*) how; **к. б. э́то сде́лать?** how is it to be done, I wonder.
2: **к. б. ни** however; **к. б. то ни́ было** however that may be, be that as it may.
3 as if, as though.
4: **к. б. не** (*expr. anxious expectation*) what if, supposing; (*following v.*) (that, lest); **к. б. он не опозда́л** what if he is late!

ка́к-либо *adv.* somehow.

ка́к-нибудь *adv.*
1 (*так или иначе*) somehow (or other).
2 (*coll.*) (*когда-нибудь*) some time; **загляни́те к.-н.** look in some time.

как-ника́к *adv.* (*coll.*) nevertheless, for all that.

како́в (~а́, ~о́, ~ы́) *pron.* (*interrog., and in exclamations expr. strong feeling*) what; of what sort; **к. результа́т?** what is the result?; **к. он?** what is he like?; **к. он собо́й?** what does he look like?; **а пого́да-то ~а́** what (*splendid, filthy*) weather!

как|о́й *pron.*
1 (*interrog. and rel.; and in exclamations*) what; **~о́е сего́дня число́?** what is today's date?; **~и́м о́бразом?** how?
2: **(тако́й) к.** such as; **гнев, ~о́го он никогда́ не испы́тывал** anger such as he had never felt.
3: **к. ни** whatever, whichever.

како́й-либо *pron.* = **како́й-нибудь**

како́й-нибудь *pron.* some; any.

как|о́й-то *pron.*
1 (*неизвестно какой*) some, a.
2 (*напоминающий*) a kind of; **э́то ~а́я-то боле́знь** it is a kind of disease.

как ра́з *adv.* just, exactly; **к. р. то, что мне ну́жно** just what I need; *as pred.*: **э́ти ту́фли мне к. р.** these shoes are just right.

ка́к-то *adv.*
1 somehow; **он к.-то ухитри́лся сде́лать э́то** he managed to do it somehow.
2 (*coll.*): **к.-то (раз)** once.

ка́ктус, а *m.* (*bot.*) cactus.

кал, а *m.* faeces, excrement.

каламбу́р, а *m.* pun.

каланч|а́, и́, *g. pl.* **~е́й** *f.* watchtower; **пожа́рная к.** fire observation tower.

калейдоско́п, а *m.* kaleidoscope.

кале́к|а, и *c.g.* cripple.

календа́р|ь, я́ *m.* calendar.

кале́ч|ить, у, ишь *impf.* (*of* ▸ **искале́чить**) to cripple, maim, mutilate; (*fig.*) to twist, pervert.

кале́ч|иться, усь, ишься *impf.* (*of* ▸ **искале́читься**)
1 to become a cripple.
2 *pass. of* ▸ **~ить**

кали́бр, а *m.*
1 calibre (*Br.*), caliber (*US*).
2 (*tech.*) gauge.

ка́ли|й, я *m.* (*chem.*) potassium.

кали́н|а, ы *no pl., f.* (*bot.*) guelder rose, viburnum.

кали́тк|а, и *f.* (wicket) gate.

кали́ф, а *m.* caliph; **к. на час** (*iron.*) king for a day.

Калифо́рни|я, и *f.* California.

ка́лл|а, ы *f.* (*bot.*) arum lily (*Br.*), calla lily (*US*).

каллигра́фи|я, и *f.* calligraphy.

калмы́к, а *m.* Kalmyk.

калмы́цкий *adj.* Kalmyk.

калмы́|чка, чки *f. of* ▶ **~к**
калори́йност|ь, и *f.*
1 (*пищи*) calorie content.
2 (*phys.*) calorific value.
калори́|йный (~ен, ~йна) *adj.* high-calorie; fattening.
кало́ри|я, и *f.* calorie.
ка́л|ька, ьки, *g. pl.* **~ек** *f.*
1 (*бумага*) tracing paper.
2 (*копия*) (tracing paper) copy.
3 (*ling.*) loan translation, calque.
калькуля́тор, а *m.* calculator.
Кальку́тт|а, ы *f.* Calcutta, Kolkata.
кальма́р, а *m.* (*zool.*) squid.
кальсо́н|ы, ~ *no sg.* long johns.
ка́льци|й, я *m.* (*chem.*) calcium.
калья́н, а *m.* hookah.
ка́мбал|а, ы *f.* plaice; flounder.
Камбо́дж|а, и *f.* Cambodia.
камбоджи́|ец, йца *m.* Cambodian.
камбоджи́|йка, йки *f. of* ▶ **~ец**
камбоджи́йский *adj.* Cambodian.
каме́ли|я, и *f.* (*bot.*) camellia.
К
камене́|ть, ю *impf.* (*of* ▶ **о~**) (*становиться твёрдым*) to become petrified, turn to stone; (*fig.*) (*о сердце*) to harden; (*от страха*) to be petrified.
камени́ст|ый (~, ~а) *adj.* stony.
ка́менн|ый *adj.*
1 stone-; stony; **к. век** the Stone Age; **~ая кла́дка** stonework.
2 (*fig.*) stony; **~ое се́рдце** stony heart.
каменоло́м|ня, ни, *g. pl.* **~ен** *f.* quarry.
ка́менщик, а *m.* bricklayer.
ка́м|ень, ня, *pl.* **~ни, ~не́й** *m.* stone; (*зубной*) tartar; **драгоце́нный к.** precious stone, gem.
ка́мер|а, ы *f.*
1 chamber (*in var. senses*); (*в тюрьме*) cell; **морози́льная к.** freezer compartment (*of refrigerator*); **к. хране́ния (багажа́)** left-luggage office (*Br.*), baggage room (*US*).
2 (*фото*) camera; (*видео*) camcorder.
3 (*шины*) inner tube; (*мяча*) bladder.
ка́мерн|ый *adj.* (*mus.*): **~ая му́зыка** chamber music.
камерто́н, а *m.* tuning fork.
каме́|я, и *f.* cameo.
камика́дзе *m. indecl.* kamikaze pilot.
ками́н, а *m.* fireplace.
камнепа́д, а *m.* rockfall.
камо́рк|а, и *f.* (*coll.*) closet, tiny room; box room.
кампа́ни|я, и *f.* campaign.
камуфля́ж, а *no pl., m.* camouflage.
Камча́тк|а, и *f.* Kamchatka.
камы́ш, а́ *m.* reed, rush (*also collect.*).
кана́в|а, ы *f.* ditch; **сто́чная к.** gutter.
Кана́д|а, ы *f.* Canada.
кана́д|ец, ца, *g. pl.* **~цев** *m.* Canadian.
кана́д|ка, ки *f. of* ▶ **~ец**
кана́дский *adj.* Canadian.
кана́л, а *m.*
1 (*искусственное русло*) canal; (*морской*) channel.
2 (*fig.*) (*путь*) channel; **дипломати́ческие ~ы** diplomatic channels.
3 (*anat.*) duct, canal.
4 (*телевизионный*) channel.
канализа|цио́нный *adj. of* ▶ **~ция; ~цио́нная труба́** sewer (pipe).
канализа́ци|я, и *f.* sewerage system.
канаре́йк|а, и *f.* canary.
Кана́рск|ие острова́, ~их ~о́в *no sg.* Canary Islands.
кана́т, а *m.* rope; cable.
кандал|ы́, о́в *no sg.* shackles, fetters; **ручны́е к.** manacles; **закова́ть в к.** to put into irons.
кандида́т, а *m.* candidate; **~ нау́к** (*educ.*) Doctor.
кандидату́р|а, ы *f.* candidature; **вы́ставить чью-н. ~у** to nominate s.o. for election; (*кандидат*) candidate.
кани́кул|ы, ~ *no sg.* (*школьные*) holidays (*Br.*), vacation (*US*); (*университетские*) vacation.
кани́стр|а, ы *f.* jerrycan.
канифо́л|ь, и *f.* rosin.
ка́нн|а, ы *f.* (*bot.*) canna (lily).
канниба́л, а *m.* cannibal.
каннибали́зм, а *m.* cannibalism.
кано́н, а *m.* canon.
канона́д|а, ы *f.* cannonade.
канониза́ци|я, и *f.* (*eccl.*) canonization.
канонизи́р|овать, ую *impf. and pf.* (*eccl. and fig.*) to canonize.
кано́э *nt. indecl.* canoe.
ка́нтор, а *m.* cantor.
кану́н, а *m.* eve; **к. Но́вого го́да** New Year's Eve; **к. Рождества́** Christmas Eve.
канцеля́ри|я, и *f.* clerical office.
канцеля́р|ский *adj. of* ▶ **~ия; ~ские принадле́жности/това́ры** stationery, office supplies.
канцероге́н, а *m.* carcinogen.
ка́нцлер, а *m.* chancellor.
каньо́н, а *m.* (*geog.*) canyon.
ка́п|ать, аю *impf.* (*of* ▶ **на~**)
1 (*no pf., 3rd pers. only*) (*падать каплями*) to drip, drop; to trickle; to dribble; to fall (in drops); **слёзы ~али у неё из глаз** teardrops were falling from her eyes.
2 (*наливать каплями*) to pour out (*in drops*); **к. лека́рство в рю́мку** to pour medicine into a glass.
3 (+ *i.*) (*проливать*) to spill; **ты ~аешь водо́й на ска́терть** you are spilling water on the cloth.
капе́лл|а, ы *f.*
1 (*хор*) choir.
2 (*часовня*) chapel.
капелла́н, а *m.* chaplain.
ка́пельниц|а, ы *f.* (*med.*) drip.
ка́перс, а *m.* (*pl. only; cul.*) capers.
капита́л, а *m.* (*fin.*) capital; (*fig.*): **полити́ческий к.** political capital.
капитали́зм, а *m.* capitalism.
капитали́ст, а *m.* capitalist.
капиталисти́ческий *adj.* capitalist.
капиталовложе́ни|е, я *nt.* capital investment.

капита́льный *adj.* (*fin.*) capital; (*основной*) main, fundamental; (*самый важный*) most important; **к. ремо́нт** major repairs, refurbishment.
капита́н, а *m.* captain.
капитуля́ци|я, и *f.* capitulation.
капка́н, а *m.* trap; **попа́сться в к.** to fall into a trap (*also fig.*).
ка́п|ля, ли, *g. pl.* **~ель** *f.*
1 drop; **похо́жи как две ~ли воды́** as like as two peas; (*fig.*): **к. в мо́ре** a drop in the ocean (*Br.*), bucket (*US*).
2 (*pl.*; *med.*) drops.
3 (*fig.*, *coll.*) drop, bit; **в нём (нет) ни ~ли благоразу́мия** he hasn't a drop of sense.
ка́п|нуть, ну, нешь *pf.* to drop, let fall a drop.
капо́т, а *m.* (*машины*) bonnet (*Br.*), hood (*US*).
капри́з, а *m.* caprice, whim; **к. судьбы́** twist of fate.
капри́знича|ть, ю *impf.* to behave capriciously; (*о ребёнке*) to play up.
капри́з|ный (~ен, ~на) *adj.* capricious.
капро́н, а *m.* kapron (*synthetic fibre, similar to nylon*).
ка́псул|а, ы *f.* capsule.
капу́ст|а, ы *f.* cabbage; **брюссе́льская к.** Brussels sprouts; **цветна́я к.** cauliflower.
капу́ст|ный *adj. of* ▸ **~а**
капюшо́н, а *m.* hood.
ка́р|а, ы *f.* (*rhet.*) punishment, retribution.
караби́н, а *m.* (*винтовка*) carbine.
кара́бка|ться, юсь *impf.* (*of* ▸ **вс~**) to clamber.
карава́|й, я *m.* cottage loaf.
карава́н, а *m.*
1 (*верблюдов*) caravan.
2 (*судов*) convoy.
карака́тиц|а, ы *f.* (*zool.*) cuttlefish.
кара́кул|ь, я *no pl., m.* Persian lamb; astrakhan.
кара́кул|я, и, *g. pl.* **~ей** *and* **~ь** *f.* scrawl, scribble.
караме́л|ь, и *no pl., f.*
1 (*collect.*) (*конфеты*) caramels.
2 (*жжёный сахар*) caramel.
каранда́ш, а́ *m.* pencil.
каранти́н, а *m.* quarantine.
карао́ке *nt. indecl.* karaoke.
кара́т, а *m.* carat.
карате́ *nt. indecl.* karate.
кара́тельный *adj.* punitive; **к. отря́д** death squad.
кара́|ть, ю *impf.* (*of* ▸ **по~**) to punish.
карау́л, а *m.* guard; watch; **нести́ к.** to be on guard duty; **смени́ть к.** to relieve the guard.
карау́л|ить, ю, ишь *impf.* to guard.
карбюра́тор, а *m.* (*tech.*, *chem.*) carburettor (*Br.*), carburetor (*US*).
кардина́л, а *m.* (*eccl.*) cardinal.
кардина́л|ьный (~ен, ~ьна) *adj.* cardinal; fundamental.
кардиогра́мм|а, ы *f.* cardiogram.
кардио́лог, а *m.* cardiologist.
кардиоло́ги|я, и *f.* cardiology.
кардиохиру́рг, а *m.* heart surgeon.
каре́т|а, ы *f.* carriage, coach.
кари́бский *adj.* Caribbean.
Кари́бск|ое мо́р|е, ~ого ~я *m.* the Caribbean Sea; the Caribbean.
ка́риес, а *m.* (*med.*) caries.
ка́рий *adj.* (*глаза*) brown, hazel.
карикату́р|а, ы *f.* caricature, cartoon; (*fig.*) caricature.
карка́с, а *m.* (*tech.*) frame; (*fig.*) framework.
ка́рк|ать, аю *impf.* to caw.
ка́рк|нуть, ну, нешь *pf.* to give a caw.
ка́рлик, а *m.* dwarf.
ка́рликовый *adj.* dwarf.
ка́рли|ца, цы *f. of* ▸ **~к**
карма́н, а *m.* pocket; (*fig.*, *coll.*): **э́то мне не по ~у** I can't afford it.
карма́нник, а *m.* pickpocket.
карма́н|ный *adj. of* ▸ **~; к. вор** pickpocket; **~ные де́ньги** pocket money.
карнава́л, а *m.* carnival.
карни́з, а *m.* (*archit.*; *mountaineering*) cornice.
карп, а *m.* carp (*fish*).
ка́рри *nt. indecl.* curry.
ка́рт|а, ы *f.*
1 (*geog.*) map.
2 (*игральная*) (playing) card; **игра́ть в ~ы** to play cards; **поста́вить на ~у** to stake, risk.
3 (*бланк*) form.
4 = **ка́рточка 1; магни́тная к.** swipe card.
карт-бла́нш *m. indecl.* carte blanche.
ка́ртер, а *m.* (*tech.*) crankcase.
карте́ч|ь, и *f.*
1 (*mil.*) case-shot; grapeshot.
2 (*для охотничьего ружья*) buckshot.
карти́н|а, ы *f.*
1 (*in var. senses*) picture.
2 (*theatr.*) scene.
карти́н|ный (~ен, ~на) *adj.*
1 *adj. of* ▸ **~а; ~ная галере́я** art gallery, picture gallery.
2 (*жест, поза*) theatrical, mannered.
карто́граф, а *m.* cartographer.
картогра́фи|я, и *f.* cartography.
карто́н, а *m.* card, cardboard.
картоте́к|а, и *f.* card index.
карто́фелин|а, ы *f.* (*coll.*) potato.
карто́фел|ь, я *no pl., m.*
1 (*collect.*) potatoes; **жа́реный к.** fried potatoes; **молодо́й к.** new potatoes.
2 (*растение*) potato plant.
карто́фель|ный *adj. of* ▸ **~; ~ное пюре́** mashed potatoes.
ка́рточк|а, и *f.*
1 card; **визи́тная к.** visiting card, business card; **пла́стиковая к.** credit card.
2 (*проездной билет*) season ticket.
ка́рточ|ный *adj.*
1 *adj. of* ▸ **ка́рта; к. долг** gambling debt; (*coll.*): **к. до́мик** house of cards (*also fig.*); **к. фо́кус** card trick.
2 *adj. of* ▸ **~ка; ~ная систе́ма** rationing system.
карто́шк|а, и *f.* (*coll.*)
1 (*collect.*) (*картофель*) potatoes.
2 (*картофелина*) potato.

ка́ртридж, а *m.* cartridge.
карусе́л|ь, и *f.* merry-go-round, carousel.
ка́рцер, а *m.* isolation cell.
карье́р[1], а *m.* (*галоп*) career, full gallop; (*fig.*): **с ме́ста в к.** straight away, without more ado.
карье́р[2], а *m.* (*каменоломня*) quarry; (*песочный*) sandpit; **у́гольный к.** open-cast mine.
карье́р|а, ы *f.* career; **сде́лать ~у** to make good, get on.
карьери́ст, а *m.* careerist.
каса́ни|е, я *nt.* contact.
каса́тельно *prep.* + *g.* touching, concerning.
каса́|ться, юсь *impf.* (*of* ▸**косну́ться**)
1 (+ *g.*) to touch.
2 (+ *g.*; *fig.*) (*вопроса, темы*) to touch (on, upon).
3 (+ *g.*; *fig.*) (*иметь отношение*) to concern, relate (to); **э́то тебя́ не ~ется** it is no concern of yours; **что ~ется** as to, as regards, with regard to.
ка́ск|а, и *f.* helmet.
каска́д, а *m.* cascade.
каскадёр, а *m.* stunt man.
Каспи́йск|ое мо́р|е, ~ого ~я *nt.* the Caspian Sea.
ка́сс|а, ы *f.*
1 (*ящик*) cash box; (*аппарат в магазине*) till, cash register; (*место в магазине*) cash desk.
2 (*деньги*) cash.
3 (*железнодорожная*) booking office; (*театральная*) box office; **сберега́тельная к.** savings bank.
касса|цио́нный *adj.*: **~цио́нная жа́лоба** appeal; **к. суд** Court of Appeal.
кассе́т|а, ы *f.* cassette.
кассе́т|ный *adj. of* ▸**~а; к. магнитофо́н** cassette recorder.
касси́р, а *m.* cashier.
ка́сс|овый *adj.*
1 *adj. of* ▸**~а; ~овая кни́га** cash book.
2: **к. спекта́кль, фильм** a box office success.
касте́т, а *m.* knuckleduster.
кастри́р|овать, ую *impf. and pf.* to castrate.
кастрю́л|я, и *f.* saucepan.
катало́г, а *m.* catalogue (*Br.*), catalog (*US*).
катамара́н, а *m.* catamaran.
ката́ни|е, я *nt.*
1 (*мяча*) rolling.
2: **к. в экипа́же** driving; **к. верхо́м** riding; **к. на ло́дке** boating; **к. на конька́х** skating; **к. на ро́ликах** roller skating.
катапу́льт|а, ы *f.* catapult.
катапультиро́|ваться, уюсь *impf. and pf.* (*о лётчике*) to eject.
Ка́тар, а *m.* Qatar.
ката́р, а *m.* (*med.*) catarrh.
катара́кт|а, ы *f.* (*med.*) cataract.
катастро́ф|а, ы *f.* catastrophe, disaster; (*авария*) accident.
катастрофи́ческий *adj.* catastrophic.
кат|а́ть, а́ю *impf.*
1 (*indet. of* ▸**~и́ть**) (*мяч*) to roll; (*велосипед, тачку*) to wheel, trundle.
2 (*человека*) to drive, take for a drive; (*на санках*) to take for a ride.
3 (*pf.* **с~**) (*из глины, теста*) to roll.
кат|а́ться, а́юсь *impf.*
1 (*indet. of* ▸**~и́ться**) (*о мяче*) to roll (*intrans.*); **к. с горы́** to slide down a hill.
2 (*на машине*) to go for a drive; **к. верхо́м** to ride, go riding; **к. на велосипе́де** to cycle, go cycling; **к. на конька́х** to skate, go skating; **к. на ло́дке** to go boating.
катафа́лк, а *m.* hearse.
категори́чески *adv.* categorically; **к. отказа́ться** to flatly refuse.
катего́ри|я, и *f.* category.
ка́тер, а, *pl.* **~а́** *m.* (*naut.*) boat; **сторожево́й к.** patrol boat.
кате́тер, а *m.* (*med.*) catheter.
ка|ти́ть, чу́, ~́тишь *impf.* (*of* ▸**по~ 1**)
1 *det. of* ▸**~та́ть.**
2 (*coll.*) (*быстро ехать*) to bowl along, tear.
ка|ти́ться, чу́сь, ~́тишься *impf.* (*of* ▸**по~ 1**)
1 *det. of* ▸**~та́ться; к. по́д гору** (*fig.*) to go downhill.
2 (*течь*) to flow, stream; (*fig.*) to roll; **слёзы ~ти́лись по её щека́м** tears were rolling down her cheeks.
3 (*coll.*): **~ти́сь; ~ти́сь отсю́да!** get out!; clear off!
кат|о́к[1], ка́ *m.* (*ледяная площадка*) skating rink.
кат|о́к[2], ка́ *m.* (*машина*) roller.
като́лик, а *m.* (Roman) Catholic.
католици́зм, а *m.* (Roman) Catholicism.
католи́ческий *adj.* (Roman) Catholic.
католи́честв|о, а *nt.* (Roman) Catholicism.
католи́чк|а, и *f. of* ▸**като́лик**
ка́торг|а, и *no pl., f.* penal servitude, hard labour (*Br.*), labor (*US*).
ка́торжник, а *m.* convict.
кату́шк|а, и *f.*
1 reel, spool.
2 (*elec.*) coil.
каучу́к, а *m.* (India) rubber, caoutchouc.
каучу́к|овый *adj. of* ▸**~;** rubber.
кафе́ *nt. indecl.* café; **к.-моро́женое** ice-cream parlour (*Br.*), parlor (*US*).
ка́федр|а, ы *f.*
1 (*в церкви*) pulpit; (*для оратора*) rostrum, platform.
2 (*профессорство*) chair; **получи́ть ~у** to obtain a chair.
3 (*в университете*) department, sub-faculty.
кафедра́льный *adj.*: **к. собо́р** cathedral.
ка́фел|ь, я *m.* (*collect.*) Dutch tiles.
ка́фель|ный *adj. of* ▸**~; ~ная печь** tiled stove; **~ная пли́тка** Dutch tile.
кафете́ри|й, я *m.* cafeteria.
кач|а́ть, а́ю *impf.* (*of* ▸**~ну́ть**)
1 (+ *a.*) (*ребёнка, колыбель*) to rock; (+ *i.*) (*головой, ногой*) to shake; (*impers.*): **ло́дку ~а́ет** the boat is rolling.
2 (*coll.*) (*подбрасывать вверх*) to lift up, chair (*as mark of esteem or congratulation*).
3 (*pf.* ▸**на~[1,2]**) (*насосом*) to pump.
4 (*pf.* ▸**на~[3]**) (*coll.*): **к. му́скулы** to do bodybuilding exercises; to work out; to pump iron.

кач|а́ться, а́юсь *impf.* (*of* ▸ **~ну́ться**)
1 to rock, swing (*intrans.*); (*о лодке*) to roll, pitch.
2 (*при ходьбе*) to reel, stagger.
3 (*pf.* ▸ **на~**) (*coll.*) to practise bodybuilding; to work out; to pump iron.

каче́л|и, ей *no sg.* (*child's*) swing; (*доска-качели*) see-saw.

ка́чествен|ный (~, ~на) *adj.*
1 (*различие, изменение*) qualitative.
2 (*товар*) quality.

ка́честв|о, а *nt.* quality; **ни́зкого ~а** poor quality; low-grade; **в ~е** (+ *g.*) in the capacity (of); **в ~е исключе́ния** as a special concession.

кач|ну́ть(ся), ну́(сь), нёшь(ся) *pf. of* ▸ **~а́ть(ся)**

ка|чу́, ~тишь *see* ▸ **~ти́ть**

ка́ш|а, и *f.*
1 kasha (*dish of cooked grain or groats*); porridge; **ма́нная к.** semolina; **ри́совая к.** boiled rice.
2 (*fig., coll.*) (*месиво*) jumble; (*путаница*) muddle; **расхлёбывать ~у** to put things right.

кашало́т, а *m.* (*zool.*) sperm whale.

ка́ш|ель, ля *m.* cough.

ка́шлян|уть, у, ешь *pf.* to give a cough.

ка́шля|ть, ю *impf.*
1 to cough.
2 (*как болезнь*) to have a cough.

кашне́ *nt. indecl.* scarf, muffler.

кашпо́ *nt. indecl.* decorative flowerpot holder.

кашта́н, а *m.*
1 (*орех*) chestnut.
2 (*дерево*) chestnut tree; **ко́нский к.** horse chestnut.

кашта́н|овый *adj.*
1 *adj. of* ▸ **~.**
2 (*цвет*) chestnut(-coloured).

каю́т|а, ы *f.* cabin.

каяк, а *m.* kayak.

ка́|яться, юсь, ешься *impf.* (*of* ▸ **по~**) (**в** + *p.*)
1 (*сожалеть*) to repent (of); **он сам тепе́рь ~ется** he is sorry himself now.
2 (*признаться*) to confess.

КБ (*abbr. of* **констру́кторское бюро́**) construction office.

кв. (*abbr. of* **кварти́ра**) flat, apartment.

квадра́т, а *m.* (*math.*) square; **возвести́ в к.** to square; **в ~е** squared.

квадра́тный *adj.* square; **к. ко́рень** square root; **к. метр** square metre (*Br.*), meter (*US*).

ква́ка|ть, ю *impf.* to croak.

ква́кн|уть, у, ешь *pf.* to give a croak.

квалифика́ци|я, и *f.* qualification; (*профессия*) profession.

квалифици́рова|нный (~н, ~на) *p.p.p. of* ▸ **~ть** *and* **(~н, ~нна)** *adj.*
1 (*работник*) qualified, skilled.
2 (*труд*) skilled.

квалифици́р|овать, ую *impf. and pf.*
1 (*специалиста, спортсмена*) to rank, test.
2 (*оценить*) to categorize; **как к. тако́е поведе́ние?** how should one describe such conduct?

кварта́л, а *m.*
1 (*домов*) block.
2 (*часть города*) quarter; **кита́йский к.** Chinatown.
3 (*года*) quarter.

кварте́т, а *m.* (*mus.*) quartet.

кварти́р|а, ы *f.*
1 flat (*Br.*), apartment (*US*).
2 (*снимаемое жильё*) lodgings; **жить на ~е** to live in lodgings.

квартира́нт, а *m.* lodger, tenant.

квартира́нт|ка, ки *f. of* ▸ **~**

кварти́р|ный *adj. of* ▸ **~а; ~ная пла́та** rent.

квартпла́т|а, ы *f.* (*abbr. of* **кварти́рная пла́та**) rent.

кварц, а *m.* (*min.*) quartz.

ква́рц|евый *adj. of* ▸ **~**

квас, а, *pl.* **~ы́** *m.* kvass.

кве́рху *adv.* up, upwards.

квита́нци|я, и *f.* receipt; **бага́жная к.** luggage ticket (*Br.*), baggage check (*US*).

кво́т|а, ы *f.* quota.

кВт (*abbr. of* **килова́тт**) kW, kilowatt(s).

кг (*abbr. of* **килогра́мм**) k, kg, kilo(s), kilogram(s).

КГБ *m. indecl.* (*abbr. of* **Комите́т госуда́рственной безопа́сности**) (*hist.*) KGB, State Security Committee.

ке́гл|и, ей *pl.* (*sg.* **~я, ~и** *f.*)
1 skittles, ninepins; **спорти́вные к.** bowls.
2 (*sg.*) skittle; pin.

кедр, а *m.* cedar; **сиби́рский к.** Siberian pine.

кедр|о́вый *adj. of* ▸ **~**

ке́д|ы, ов *or* **~** *pl.* (*sg.* **кед, а**) *m.* trainers (*Br.*), sneakers (*US*).

кекс, а *m.* fruit cake.

кельт, а *m.* Celt.

ке́льтский *adj.* Celtic.

кем *i. of* ▸ **кто**

Ке́мбридж, а *m.* Cambridge.

ке́мпинг, а *m.* campsite.

кенгуру́ *m. indecl.* kangaroo.

кени́|ец, йца *m.* Kenyan.

кени́йк|а, и *f.* Kenyan.

кени́йский *adj.* Kenyan.

Ке́ни|я, и *f.* Kenya.

ке́пк|а, и *f.* cloth cap.

кера́мик|а, и *f.* ceramics.

керами́ческий *adj.* ceramic.

кероси́н, а *m.* paraffin (*Br.*), kerosene (*US*).

ке́тчуп, а *m.* ketchup.

кефа́л|ь, и *f.* grey mullet.

кефи́р, а *m.* kefir (*thin yoghurt drink*).

киберне́тик|а, и *f.* cybernetics.

киберпреступле́ни|е, я *nt.* (*comput.*) cybercrime (*offence*).

киберпресту́пност|ь, и *f.* (*comput.*) cybercrime (*collect.*).

кив|а́ть, а́ю *impf.* (*of* ▸ **~ну́ть**) **к. (голово́й)** to nod (one's head); (*в знак согласия*) to nod assent.

ки́ви *m. & nt. indecl.*
1 (*m.*) (*zool.*) kiwi.
2 (*m. & nt.*) kiwi fruit.

кив|ну́ть, ну́, нёшь *pf. of* ▸ **~а́ть**

кив|óк, кá *m.* nod.
ки|дáть, дáю *impf.* (*of* ▸ **~нуть**)
1 to throw, fling, cast (*usage as for* **бросáть**); **кудá ни кинь** whichever way you turn.
2 (*sl.*) (*обманывать*) to cheat, con.
ки|дáться, дáюсь *impf.* (*of* ▸ **~нуться**)
1 to throw o.s., fling o.s.; (*устремиться куда-н.*) to rush.
2 (+ *i.*) to throw, fling.
3 *pass. of* ▸ **~дáть**
киднéппинг, а *m.* kidnapping.
Кúев, а *m.* Kiev.
киевля́н|ин, ина, *pl.* **~е, ~** *m.* Kievan.
киевля́н|ка, ки *f. of* ▸ **~ин**
ки|й, я́, *pl.* **~и́, ~ёв** *m.* (*sport*) cue.
ки́ллер, а *m.* contract killer, hit man.
килобáйт, а *m.* (*comput.*) kilobyte.
киловáтт, а *m.*, *g. pl.* **~** (*elec.*) kilowatt.
килогрáмм, а *m.* kilogram.
киломéтр, а *m.* kilometre (*Br.*), kilometer (*US*).
кил|ь, я *m.* (*naut.*) keel.
ки́льк|а, и *f.* sprat.
кимонó *nt. indecl.* kimono.
кинематóграф, а *m.* cinematography.
кинематографи́ст, а *m.* cinematographer, film-maker.
кинематографи́|я, и *f.* cinematography.
кинжáл, а *m.* dagger.
кинó *nt. indecl.*
1 (*как искусство*) the cinema.
2 (*coll.*) (*здание*) cinema (*Br.*), movie theater (*US*).
3 (*coll.*) (*фильм*) film, movie.
кино... *comb. form, abbr. of* **кинó, кинематографи́ческий**
киноактёр, а *m.* film actor (*Br.*), movie actor (*US*).
киноактри́с|а, ы *f.* film actress (*Br.*), movie actress (*US*).
кинозáл, а *m.*
1 (*здание*) cinema (*Br.*), movie theater (*US*).
2 (*зал*) auditorium.
кинозвезд|á, ы́, *pl.* **~ы, ~, ~ам** *f.* film star (*Br.*), movie star (*US*).
кинозри́тел|ь, я *m.* cinema-goer.
кинокáмер|а, ы *f.* movie camera.
кинокомéди|я, и *f.* comedy film, movie.
кинокри́тик, а *m.* film critic.
кинооперáтор, а *m.* cameraman.
киноплёнк|а, и *f.* cine film (*Br.*), movie film (*US*).
кинорежиссёр, а *m.* film director.
киносеáнс, а *m.* (cinema) performance, showing.
киностýди|я, и *f.* film studio (*Br.*), movie studio (*US*).
киносценáри|й, я *m.* screenplay.
киносъёмк|а, и *f.* filming, shooting.
кинотеáтр, а *m.* cinema (*Br.*), movie theater (*US*).
кинофи́льм, а *m.* film, movie.
кинохрóник|а, и *f.* newsreel.
ки́|нуть(ся), ну(сь), нешь(ся) *pf. of* ▸ **~дáть(ся)**
киóск, а *m.* kiosk, stall; **газéтный к.** news-stand.
ки́п|а, ы *f.* pile, stack.
кипари́с, а *m.* (*bot.*) cypress.
кипéни|е, я *nt.* boiling; **тóчка ~я** boiling point.
кип|éть, лю́, и́шь *impf.* to boil, seethe; **рабóта ~éла** work was in full swing.
Кипр, а *m.* Cyprus.
киприóт, а *m.* Cypriot.
киприóт|ка, ки *f. of* ▸ **~**
ки́прский *adj.* Cypriot.
кипяти́льник, а *m.* kettle, boiler.
кипя|ти́ть, чý, ти́шь *impf.* (*of* ▸ **вс~**) to boil.
кипят|óк, кá *m.* boiling water.
кипячёный *adj.* boiled.
кирги́з, а *m.* Kyrgyz.
Киргизи́|я, и *f.* Kyrgyzstan.
киргиз|ка, ки *f. of* ▸ **~**
кирги́зский *adj.* Kyrgyz.
кири́ллиц|а, ы *f.* Cyrillic alphabet.
кирилли́ческий *adj.* Cyrillic.
кирк|á, и́ *f.* pick(axe).
кирпи́ч, á *m.*
1 brick.
2 (*collect.*) bricks.
3 (*coll.*) (*дорожный знак*) no-entry sign.
кисéл|ь, я́ *m.* kissel (*kind of blancmange*).
кислорóд, а *m.* oxygen.
ки́сло-слáд|кий (~ок, ~ка) *adj.* sweet-and-sour.
кислот|á, ы́, *pl.* **~ы** *f.*
1 sourness; acidity.
2 (*chem.*) acid.
кислóтный *adj.* (*chem.*) acid; **к. дождь** acid rain.
ки́с|лый (~ел, ~лá, ~ло) *adj.*
1 (*яблоко*) sour; (*fig.*): **~лое настроéние** sour mood.
2 (*закисший*) sour, fermented; **~лая капýста** sauerkraut.
3 (*chem.*) acid.
кист|ь[1], и, *pl.* **~и, ~éй** *f.*
1 (*bot.*) cluster, bunch; **к. виногрáда** bunch of grapes.
2 (*для рисования*) brush; **маля́рная к.** paintbrush.
3 (*на скатерти*) tassel.
кист|ь[2], и, *pl.* **~и, ~éй** *f.* hand.
кит, á *m.* whale.
китá|ец, йца, *pl.* **~йцы, ~йцев** *m.* Chinese.
Китá|й, я *m.* China.
китáйск|ий *adj.* Chinese; **~ая грáмота** double Dutch.
китая́нк|а, и *f. of* ▸ **китáец**
китч, а *m.* kitsch.
киш|éть, и́т *impf.* (+ *i.*) to swarm (with), teem (with).
кишéчник, а *m.* (*anat.*) bowels, intestines.
киш|кá, ки́, *g. pl.* **~óк** *f.* (*anat.*) gut, intestine.
клавеси́н, а *m.* (*mus.*) harpsichord.
клавиатýр|а, ы *f.* keyboard.
клáвиш|а, и *f.* key (*of piano, computer, etc.*).
клáвишны|е, х *pl.* keyboard(s) (*musical*

instrument).

клад, а *m.* treasure; (*fig., coll.*) treasure(-house).

кла́дбищ|е, а *nt.* cemetery, graveyard; (*при церкви*) churchyard.

кладов|а́я, о́й *f.* (*для провизии*) pantry, larder; (*для товаров*) storeroom.

кла|ду́, дёшь *see* ▶ **~сть**

клад|ь, и *f.* (*sg. only*) load; **ручна́я к.** hand luggage (*Br.*), baggage (*US*).

клан, а *m.* clan.

кла́ня|ться, юсь *impf.* (*of* ▶ **поклони́ться**)
1 (+ *d. or* **с** + *i.*) to bow (to); (*приветствовать*) to greet.
2 (*передавать привет*) to send, convey greetings; **~йтесь ему́ от меня́** give him my regards.
3 (+ *d. or* **пе́ред** + *i.*; *coll.*) (*униженно просить*) to cringe (before); to humiliate o.s. (before).

кла́пан, а *m.* valve.

кларне́т, а *m.* clarinet.

кларнети́ст, а *m.* clarinettist.

кларнети́ст|ка, ки *f. of* ▶ **~**

класс, а *m.*
1 class.
2 (*комната*) classroom.

кла́ссик|а, и *f.* the classics.

классифика́ци|я, и *f.* classification.

классифици́р|овать, ую *impf. and pf.* to classify.

классици́зм, а *m.* classicism.

класси́ческий *adj.* (*музыка, образование, язык*) classical; (*работа, пример, одежда*) classic.

кла́сс|ный *adj.* (*of* ▶ **~**)
1: **~ная рабо́та** class work.
2 (*coll.*) (*отличный*) excellent, great.

кла́ссов|ый *adj.* (*pol.*) class; **~ая борьба́** class struggle.

кла|сть, ду́, дёшь, *past* **~л, ~́ла** *impf.*
1 (*pf.* **положи́ть**) (*помещать*) to lay; to put; to place.
2 (*pf.* **сложи́ть** [1] **4**) (*строить*) to build.

клаустрофо́би|я, и *f.* claustrophobia.

клёв, а *m.* biting, bite; **сего́дня хоро́ший к.** the fish are biting well today.

кл|ева́ть, юю́, юёшь *impf.* (*of* ▶ **~ю́нуть**)
1 (*о птице*) to peck.
2 (*о рыбе*) to bite.

кле́вер, а *m.* (*bot.*) clover.

клевет|а́, ы́ *f.* slander; (*в печати*) libel.

клеве|та́ть, щу́, ~́щешь *impf.* (*of* ▶ **о~** (*кого*) *and* ▶ **на~** (*на кого* + *d.*)) to slander, malign; (*в печати*) to libel; **он оклевета́л меня́, он наклевета́л на меня́** he slandered me; **он клевета́л нача́льнику на всех сотру́дников в тече́ние двух лет** he made slanderous remarks/complained to the boss about all the staff over a period of two years; **он наклевета́л мне на вас** he made slanderous remarks/complained to me about you.

клеве|щу́, ~́щешь *see* ▶ **~та́ть**

клёвый *adj.* (*sl.*) brill, knockout, fantastic.

клеёнк|а, и *f.* oilcloth.

кле́|ить, ю, ишь *impf.* (*of* ▶ **с~**) to glue; to gum; to paste.

кле|й, я, о ~́е, в ~́е/~ю́, на ~ю́ *m.* glue.

кле́йк|ий *adj.* sticky; **~ая ле́нта** adhesive tape.

клейм|о́, а́, *pl.* **~́а** *nt.* brand, stamp.

кле́йстер, а *m.* paste.

клён, а *m.* maple.

клено́вый *adj. of* ▶ **клён**

кле́тк|а, и *f.*
1 cage; (*для кур*) coop; (*для кроликов*) hutch.
2 (*на бумаге*) square; (*на ткани*) check.
3 (*anat.*): **грудна́я к.** thorax.
4 (*biol.*) cell.

кле́тчатый *adj.* checked; **к. плато́к** checked headscarf.

клёш, а *m.* (*and indecl. adj.*) flare; **брю́ки к.** flared trousers, bell-bottom trousers.

клещ, а́ *m.* (*zool.*) tick.

клещ|и, е́й *no sg.* pincers, pliers, tongs.

клие́нт, а *m.* client.

клие́нт|ка, ки *f. of* ▶ **~**

клиенту́р|а, ы *f.* (*collect.*) clientele.

кли́зм|а, ы *f.* (*med.*) enema.

кли́макс, а *m.* menopause.

кли́мат, а *m.* climate.

климати́ческий *adj.* climatic.

клин, а, *pl.* **~́ья, ~́ьев** *m.* wedge.

кли́ник|а, и *f.* clinic.

клини́ческий *adj.* clinical.

клин|о́к, ка́ *m.* blade.

клип, а *m.* video clip.

кли́пс|ы, ~ *or* **~ов** *pl.* (*sg.* **~а, ~ы** *f. or* **~, ~а** *m.*) clip-on earrings.

клич, а *m.* (*rhet.*) call; **боево́й к.** war cry.

кли́чк|а, и *f.*
1 (*животного*) name.
2 (*человека*) nickname.

клише́ *nt. indecl.* (*typ. and fig.*) cliché.

клозе́т, а *m.* (*coll.*) water closet, W.C.

клок, а́ *pl.* **кло́чья, кло́чьев** *and* **~и́, ~о́в** *m.* rag, shred; **разорва́ть в кло́чья** to tear to shreds.

клоко|та́ть, чу́, ~́чешь *impf.* to bubble; to gurgle; (*кипеть*) to boil up (*also fig.*).

клон, а *m.* (*biol. etc.*) clone.

клони́р|овать, ую *impf. and pf.* (*biol. etc.*) to clone.

клон|и́ть, ю́, ~́ишь *impf.*
1 to bend; to incline; (*impers.*): **старика́ уже́ ~и́ло ко сну́** the old man was already nodding off.
2 (*fig., coll.*) to lead (*conversation*); **куда́ ты ~́ишь?** what are you driving at?

клон|и́ться, ю́сь, ~́ишься *impf.*
1 to bow, bend (*intrans.*).
2 (**к** + *d., fig.*): to be nearing; to be leading up (to).

клоп, а́ *m.* bedbug.

кло́ун, а *m.* clown.

клуб[1]**, а** *m.*
1 (*общество*) club.
2 (*здание*) clubhouse.

клуб[2]**, а,** *pl.* **~ы́, ~о́в** *m.* (*дыма*) puff; **~ы́**

пы́ли clouds of dust.

клуб|и́ться, и́тся *impf.* to swirl; to curl, wreathe.

клубни́к|а, и *f.* (cultivated) strawberry.

клуб|о́к, ка́ *m.*
[1] ball; **сверну́ться ~ко́м, в к.** to roll o.s. up into a ball.
[2] (*fig.*) (*запутанное сцепление чего-н.*) tangle, mass; **к. противоре́чий** a mass of contradictions.

клу́мб|а, ы *f.* (flower) bed.

клык, а́ *m.*
[1] (*у человека*) canine (tooth).
[2] (*у животного*) fang; (*бивень*) tusk.

клюв, а *m.* beak; bill.

клю́кв|а, ы *f.* cranberry.

клю́н|уть, у, ешь *pf. of* ▸ **клева́ть**

ключ[1]**, а́** *m.* (*in var. senses*) key; **запере́ть на к.** to lock; **га́ечный к.** spanner, wrench.

ключ[2]**, а́** *m.* (*источник*) spring; source; **бить ~о́м** to spout, jet; (*fig.*) to be in full swing.

ключ|ево́й *adj. of* ▸ **~**[1]; **~евы́е о́трасли промы́шленности** key industries.

ключи́ц|а, ы *f.* (*anat.*) collarbone.

клю́шк|а, и *f.* (*гольф*) (golf) club; (*хоккей*) (hockey) stick.

кл|юю́, юёшь *see* ▸ **~ева́ть**

кля́кс|а, ы *f.* blot, smudge.

кля́нч|ить, у, ишь *impf.* (*coll.*) (**у** + *g.*) to pester, nag (*s.o. for*); **к. де́ньги у кого́-н.** to pester s.o. for money.

кляп, а *m.* gag; **засу́нуть к. в рот** (+ *d.*) to gag.

кля́|сться, ну́сь, нёшься, *past* **~лся, ~ла́сь** *impf.* (*of* ▸ **по~**) (**в** + *p.*, + *inf. or* **что**) to swear, vow; **к. отомсти́ть** to vow vengeance; **к. че́стью** to swear on one's honour (*Br.*), honor (*US*).

кля́тв|а, ы *f.* oath, vow; **дать ~у** to take an oath.

кля́уз|а, ы *f.* (*coll.*) petty slander, malicious gossip.

км (*abbr. of* **киломе́тр**) km, kilometre(s) (*Br.*), kilometer(s) (*US*).

КНДР *f. indecl.* (*abbr. of* **Коре́йская Наро́дно-Демократи́ческая Респу́блика**) Democratic People's Republic of Korea.

кни́г|а, и *f.* book.

книгоизда́тел|ь, я *m.* publisher.

книготорго́в|ец, ца *m.* bookseller.

книготорго́вл|я, и *f.* book trade.

кни́жк|а, и *f.*
[1] *dim. of* ▸ **кни́га; записна́я к.** notebook.
[2] (*документ*) book, card; **че́ковая к.** chequebook (*Br.*), checkbook (*US*).

кни́жн|ый *adj.*
[1] *adj. of* ▸ **кни́га; ~ая по́лка** bookshelf; **к. шкаф** bookcase.
[2] (*отвлечённый*) bookish; **к. червь** bookworm.

кни́зу *adv.* downwards.

кно́пк|а, и *f.*
[1] (*гвоздик*) drawing pin (*Br.*), thumbtack (*US*); **прикрепи́ть ~ой** to pin.
[2] (*застёжка*) press stud, popper (*Br.*), snap (*US*).
[3] (*elec.*) button; knob.

КНР *f. indecl.* (*abbr. of* **Кита́йская Наро́дная Респу́блика**) PRC (People's Republic of China).

кнут, а́ *m.* whip.

княги́н|я, и *f.* princess (*wife of prince*).

княз|ь, я, *pl.* **~ья́, ~е́й** *m.* prince; **вели́кий к.** grand duke.

ко *see* ▸ **к**

коали́ци|я, и *f.* (*pol.*) coalition.

ко́бр|а, ы *f.* cobra.

кобур|а́, ы́ *f.* holster.

кобы́л|а, ы *f.* (*лошадь*) mare.

ко́ваный *adj.*
[1] forged; hammered.
[2] (*fig.*) terse.

кова́р|ный (~ен, ~на) *adj.* crafty; treacherous.

кова́ть, кую́, куёшь *impf.*
[1] (*pf.* **вы~**) to forge (*also fig.*); (*железо*) to hammer.
[2] (*pf.* **под~**) to shoe (*horses*).

ковбо́|й, я *m.* cowboy.

ков|ёр, ра́ *m.* carpet; (*маленький*) rug; mat.

ко́врик, а *m.* rug; mat; **к. для мы́ши** mouse mat (*Br.*), mouse pad (*US*).

ковче́г, а *m.* ark; **Но́ев к.** Noah's ark.

ковш, а́ *m.*
[1] scoop, ladle.
[2] (*tech.*) bucket.

ковыля́|ть, ю *impf.* (*coll.*) to hobble.

ковыр|ну́ть, ну́, нёшь *pf. of* ▸ **~я́ть**

ковыр|я́ть, я́ю *impf.* (*of* ▸ **~ну́ть**) to dig into; (**в** + *p.*) to pick (at); **к. в зуба́х/носу́** to pick one's teeth/nose.

когда́[1] *adv.*
[1] (*interrog. and rel.*) when.
[2]: **к. (бы) ни** whenever; **к. бы вы ни пришли́** whenever you come.
[3] (*coll.*): **к. ..., к.** sometimes ... sometimes; **я занима́юсь к. у́тром, к. ве́чером** sometimes I work in the morning, sometimes in the evening.
[4] (*coll.*): **к. как** it depends.

когда́[2] *conj.* when; while, as; **я встре́тил её, к. шёл домо́й** I met her as I was going home.

когда́-либо *adv.* = **когда́-нибудь**

когда́-нибудь *adv.*
[1] (*в будущем*) some time, some day.
[2] (*в вопросах*) ever; **вы бы́ли к.-н. в Кита́е?** have you ever been to China?

когда́-то *adv.* once; some time; formerly.

кого́ *a. and g. of* ▸ **кто**

ко́г|оть, тя, *pl.* **~ти, ~те́й** *m.* claw.

код, а *m.* code.

ко́декс, а *m.* (*leg. and fig.*) code; **гражда́нский к.** civil code; **уголо́вный к.** criminal code.

ко́дов|ый *adj. of* ▸ **код; ~ое назва́ние** code name.

ко́е-где́ *adv.* here and there, in places.

ко́е-ка́к *adv.*
[1] (*плохо, небрежно*) anyhow.
[2] (*с трудом*) somehow (or other), just; **к.-к. мы доплы́ли до того́ бе́рега** somehow we managed to swim to the other side.

ко́е-како́й, ко́е-како́го *pron.* some.
ко́е-кто́, ко́е-кого́ *pron.* somebody; some people.
ко́е-что́, ко́е-чего́ *pron.* something; (*немного*) a little.
ко́ж|а, и *f.*
1 (*у человека и животных*) skin; (*у крупных животных*) hide.
2 (*материал*) leather.
ко́жаный *adj.* leather.
кожур|а́, ы́ *f.* rind, peel, skin.
коз|а́, ы́, *pl.* **~ы** *f.*
1 (*вид*) goat.
2 (*самка козла*) nanny goat.
коз|ёл, ла́ *m.* (*животное*) billy goat.
Козеро́г, а *m.* (*созвездие*) Capricorn; **тро́пик К~а** (*geog.*) Tropic of Capricorn.
ко́з|ий *adj. of* ▸ **~а́; ~ье молоко́** goat's milk.
козл|ёнок, ёнка, *pl.* **~я́та, ~я́т** *m.* kid.
коз|ли́ный *adj. of* ▸ **~ёл; ~ли́ная боро́дка** goatee.
козл|я́та, я́т *see* ▸ **~ёнок**
козыр|ёк, ька́ *m.* (cap) peak; **взять под к.** (+ *d.*) to salute.
ко́зыр|ь, я, *pl.* **~и, ~е́й** *m.* (*cards and fig.*) trump.
ко́йк|а, и *f.*
1 (*на судне*) berth, bunk.
2 (*в больнице*) bed.
койо́т, а *m.* coyote.
кокаи́н, а *m.* cocaine.
кока́рд|а, ы *f.* cockade.
ко́кер-спание́л|ь, я *m.* cocker spaniel.
коке́тк|а, и *f.* coquette, flirt.
коке́тлив|ый (~, ~а) *adj.* coquettish, flirtatious.
коклю́ш, а *m.* whooping cough.
ко́кон, а *m.* cocoon.
коко́с, а *m.*
1 (*дерево*) coconut palm.
2 (*плод*) coconut.
кокте́йл|ь, я *m.* cocktail; (*встреча*) cocktail party; **моло́чный к.** milk shake.
кол, а́ *m.*
1 (*pl.* **~ья, ~ьев**) stake, picket.
2 (*pl.* **~ы́, ~о́в**) (*coll.*) (*низшая школьная отметка*) a 'very poor' (*mark*).
ко́лб|а, ы *f.* (*chem.*) flask.
колбас|а́, ы́, *pl.* **~ы** *f.* sausage.
колго́т|ки, ок *no sg.* tights.
колд|ова́ть, у́ю *impf.* to practise witchcraft.
колдовств|о́, а́ *nt.* witchcraft, sorcery, magic.
колду́н, а́ *m.* sorcerer, magician, wizard.
колду́н|ья, ьи, *g. pl.* **~ий** *f.* witch, sorceress.
колеба́ни|е, я *nt.*
1 (*phys.*) oscillation, vibration; **к. ма́ятника** swing of the pendulum.
2 (*изменение*) fluctuation, variation.
3 (*fig.*) (*сомнение*) hesitation, wavering, vacillation.
колеб|а́ть, ~лю, ~лешь *impf.* (*of* ▸ **по~**) to shake.
колеб|а́ться, ~люсь, ~лешься *impf.* (*of* ▸ **по~ 1**)
1 to shake to and fro, sway; (*phys.*) to oscillate.
2 (*изменяться*) to fluctuate, vary.
3 (*fig.*) (*не решаться*) to hesitate; to waver, vacillate.
коле́н|о, а *nt.*
1 (*pl.* **~и, ~ей, ~ям**) knee; **стать на ~и (пе́ред)** to kneel (to); **по к., по ~и** knee-deep, up to one's knees.
2 (*pl. only*; **~и, ~ей, ~ям**) lap; **сиде́ть у кого́-н. на ~ях** to sit on s.o.'s lap.
3 (*pl.* **~ья, ~ьев**) (*tech.*) knee, joint.
колесни́ц|а, ы *f.* chariot.
колес|о́, а́, *pl.* **~а** *nt.* wheel; **запасно́е к.** spare wheel; **рулево́е к.** driving wheel.
коле|я́, и́ *f.*
1 rut; (*fig.*): **войти́ в ~ю́** to settle down (again); **вы́битый из ~и́** unsettled.
2 (*rail.*) track; gauge.
коли́бри *f. and m. indecl.* (*zool.*) hummingbird.
коли́т, а *m.* (*med.*) colitis.
коли́чественн|ый *adj.* quantitative; **~ое числи́тельное** cardinal number.
коли́честв|о, а *nt.* quantity, amount; number.
коллабораციони́ст, а *m.* (*pol.*; *pej.*) collaborator.
колла́ж, а *m.* collage.
колла́пс, а *m.* collapse.
колле́г|а, и *c.g.* colleague.
колле́ги|я, и *f.* board; **к. адвока́тов** the Bar; **к. вы́борщиков** electoral college.
ко́лледж, а *m.* college.
коллекти́в, а *m.* collective, team; (*in many phrr. does not require separate translation*) **нау́чный к.** (the) scientists.
коллекти́в|ный (~ен, ~на) *adj.* collective; joint; **~ное владе́ние** joint ownership.
коллекционе́р, а *m.* collector.
коллекциони́р|овать, ую *impf.* to collect.
колле́кци|я, и *f.* collection.
ко́лли *f. indecl.* collie (*dog*).
коло́д|а[1], ы *f.* block, log.
коло́д|а[2], ы *f.* (*карт*) pack (*of cards*).
коло́д|ец, ца *m.*
1 well.
2 (*tech.*) shaft.
ко́локол, а, *pl.* **~а́, ~о́в** *m.* bell.
колоко́л|ьня, ьни, *g. pl.* **~ен** *f.* bell tower.
колоко́льчик, а *m.*
1 small bell.
2 (*bot.*) campanula.
колониа́льный *adj.* colonial.
колониза́ци|я, и *f.* colonization.
колонизи́р|овать, ую *impf. and pf.* to colonize.
коло́ни|я, и *f.* colony; settlement.
коло́нк|а, и *f.*
1 *dim. of* ▸ **коло́нна.**
2 (*для нагрева воды*) geyser (*Br.*), water heater.
3 (*на улице*) standpipe; water pump.
4 : **бензи́новая к.** petrol pump (*Br.*), gas pump (*US*).

К

5 (*столбец*) column (*in a table, in a newspaper*).
6 (*coll.*) (*громкоговоритель*) (loud)speaker.

колóнн|а, ы *f.* column; (*mil.*) **тáнковая к.** tank column.

колори́т, а *m.* colouring, colour (*Br.*); coloring, color (*US*); (*fig.*): **мéстный к.** local colour (*Br.*), color (*US*).

колори́т|ный (~ен, ~на) *adj.* colourful (*Br.*), colorful (*US*); graphic (*also fig.*).

кóлос, а, *pl.* **~ья, ~ьев** *m.* (*agric.*) ear, spike.

колóсс, а *m.* colossus.

колоссáл|ьный (~ен, ~ьна) *adj.* colossal; (*coll.*) terrific, great.

коло|ти́ть, чý, ~тишь *impf.* (*of* ▸ **поколоти́ть**)
1 (*impf. only*) (**по** + *d.*, **в** + *a.*) to strike (on); to batter (on), pound (on); **к. в дверь** to bang on the door.
2 (*coll.*) (*бить*) to thrash, beat.

кол|óть¹, ю, ~ешь *impf.* (*of* ▸ **расколóть 1**) to break, chop, split; **к. дровá** to chop wood; **к. орéхи** to crack nuts.

кол|óть², ю, ~ешь *impf.*
1 (*pf.* **у~**) (*булавкой*) to prick.
2 (*pf.* **за~**) (*ранить, убивать чем-нибудь острым*) to stab; (*impers.*): **у меня́ ~ет в бокý** I've got a stitch in my side.
3 (*pf.* **за~**) (*животных*) to slaughter.

кол|óться², ю́сь, ~ешься *impf.*
1 (*причинять укол*) to be prickly (*intrans.*).
2 (*pf.* **у~ 2**) (*coll.*) (*о наркомане*) to inject o.s.; to be on drugs.

кол|óться¹, ю́сь, ~ешься *impf., pass. of* ▸ **~óть¹**

колпáк, á *m.*
1 cap.
2 (*лампы*) lampshade; (*tech.*) cowl.

колумби́|ец, йца *m.* Colombian.

колумби́|йка, йки *f. of* ▸ **~ец**

колумби́йский *adj.* Colombian.

Колýмби|я, и *f.* Colombia.

колýн, á *m.* (wood-)chopper, hatchet.

колхóз, а *m.* (*abbr. of* **коллекти́вное хозя́йство**) collective farm.

колхóзник, а *m.* member of collective farm.

колхóзн|ица, ицы *f. of* ▸ **~ик**

колыбéл|ь, и *f.* cradle; (*fig.*): **с ~и** from the cradle.

колыбéль|ный *adj. of* ▸ **~**; **~ная (пéсня)** lullaby.

колы|хáться, ~шется *impf.* (*of* ▸ **~хнýться**) (*о ветках*) to sway; (*о море*) to heave; (*о флагах*) to flutter.

колых|нýться, нýсь, нёшься *pf. of* ▸ **~áться**

кольé *m. indecl.* necklace.

кол|ьнýть, ьнý, ьнёшь *inst. pf. of* ▸ **~óть²**

кольрáби *f. indecl.* (*bot.*) kohlrabi.

кольцев|óй *adj.* annular; circular; **~áя дорóга** ring road; **~áя развя́зка** roundabout.

кол|ьцó ~ьцá, *pl.* **~ьца, ~éц, ~ьцам** *nt.* ring; **обручáльное к.** wedding ring.

колю́ч|ий (~, ~а) *adj.* prickly; thorny; (*fig.*) sharp, biting; **~ая прóволока** barbed wire.

колю́чк|а, и *f.* (*coll.*) prickle; thorn; (*у ежа*) quill.

коля́ск|а, и *f.*
1 (*экипаж*) carriage.
2 : **(дéтская) к.** pram (*Br.*), baby carriage (*US*); (*раскладная*) pushchair (*Br.*), stroller (*US*); **инвали́дная к.** wheelchair.
3 (*у мотоцикла*) sidecar.

ком¹, а, *pl.* **~ья, ~ьев** *m.* lump; ball; (*fig.*): **к. в гóрле** lump in the throat.

ком² *p. of* ▸ **кто**

ком... *comb. form, abbr. of*
1 **коммунисти́ческий.**
2 **комáндный.**
3 **команди́р**

кóм|а, ы *f.* (*med.*) coma.

комáнд|а, ы *f.*
1 (*приказ*) command, order; **дáть ~у** to give a command.
2 (*mil.*) (*отряд*) party, detachment, crew; (*naut.*) crew; **пожáрная к.** fire brigade.
3 (*sport*) team.

команди́р, а *m.* (*mil.*) commander, commanding officer.

командирóвк|а, и *f.* business trip; **éхать в ~у** to go on a business trip; **он в ~е** he is away on business;

комáндовани|е, я *nt.*
1 commanding, command; **приня́ть к. (над** + *i.*) to take command (of, over).
2 (*collect.*) command.

комáнд|овать, ую *impf.*
1 (*pf.* ▸ **с~**) to give orders.
2 (*no pf.*) (+ *i.*) (*быть командиром*) to command, be in command (of).

комáндующ|ий, его *m.* commander.

комáр, á *m.* mosquito.

комбáйн, а *m.* (*tech.*) combine; **зерновóй к.** combine harvester; **кýхонный к.** food processor.

комбинáт, а *m.* industrial complex; plant.

комбинáци|я¹, и *f.*
1 combination.
2 (*fig.*) scheme, system; (*pol., sport*) manoeuvre (*Br.*), maneuver (*US*).

комбинáци|я², и *f.* (*женское бельё*) slip.

комбинезóн, а *m.* overalls; dungarees.

комбини́р|овать, ую *impf.* (*of* ▸ **с~**) to combine, arrange.

комéди|я, и *f.*
1 comedy.
2 (*fig.*) farce; **ломáть ~ю** to put on an act.

комендáнт, а *m.*
1 (*mil*) commandant.
2 (*общественного здания*) manager; warden; **к. общежи́тия** warden of a hostel.

комендáнт|ский *adj. of* ▸ **~**; **к. час** (*mil.*) curfew.

комéт|а, ы *f.* comet.

кóмик, а *m.*
1 comic actor.
2 (*fig.*) comedian.

кóмикс, а *m.* (*книжка*) comic (book); (*серия рисунков*) comic strip.

комиссáр, а *m.* commissar, commissioner;

верхо́вный к. high commissioner.
комиссариа́т, а *m.* commissariat.
комисс|ио́нный *adj.*: **к. магази́н** second-hand shop (*where goods are sold on commission*); *as n.* **~ио́нные, ~ио́нных** (*comm.*) commission.
коми́сси|я, и *f.* commission, committee.
комите́т, а *m.* committee.
коми́ческий *adj.*
1 comic.
2 (*смешной*) comical, funny.
ко́мка|ть, ю *impf.* (*of* ▸ **с~**) to crumple.
коммента́ри|й, я *m.*
1 (*разъяснительные замечания*) commentary.
2 (*pl.*) (*рассуждения*) comment; **~и изли́шни** comment is superfluous.
коммента́тор, а *m.* commentator.
коммента́р|овать, ую *impf. and pf.* to comment (upon).
коммерса́нт, а *m.* businessman.
комме́рци|я, и *f.* commerce, trade.
комме́рческий *adj.*
1 commercial; **к. флот** merchant navy.
2 (*негосударственный*) private.
коммивояжёр, а *m.* commercial traveller, travelling salesman (*Br.*), traveling salesman (*US*).
комму́н|а, ы *f.* commune.
коммуна́льн|ый *adj.*
1 communal; municipal; **~ые услу́ги** public utilities.
2 *adj. of* ▸ **комму́на**
коммуни́зм, а *m.* communism.
коммуника́бел|ьный (~ен, ~ьна) *adj.* sociable, communicative.
коммуника́ци|я, и *f.* communication; (*mil.*) line of communication.
коммуни́ст, а *m.* communist.
коммунисти́ческий *adj.* communist.
коммуни́ст|ка, ки *f. of* ▸ **~**
коммута́тор, а *m.*
1 (*elec.*) commutator.
2 (*teleph.*) switchboard.
коммюнике́ *nt. indecl.* communiqué.
ко́мнат|а, ы *f.* room.
ко́мнатн|ый *adj.*
1 *adj. of* ▸ **ко́мната.**
2 (*домашний*) indoor; **~ые расте́ния** house plants; **~ая температу́ра** room temperature.
компа́кт-ди́ск, а *m.* compact disc, CD; **проигрыватель** (*m.*) **~ов** compact disc *or* CD player.
компа́кт|ный (~ен, ~на) *adj.* compact; (*fig.*) concise.
компа́ни|я, и *f.* (*in var. senses*) company; **соста́вить кому́-н. ~ю** to keep s.o. company; **за ~ю** for company.
компаньо́н, а *m.*
1 (*comm.*) partner.
2 (*товарищ*) companion.
компаньо́н|ка, ки *f.*
1 *f. of* ▸ **~.**
2 (lady's) companion; chaperone.
компа́рти|я, и *f.* Communist Party.
компенса́ци|я, и *f.* compensation.
компенси́р|овать, ую *impf. and pf.* to compensate.
компете́нт|ный (~ен, ~на) *adj.* competent; **к. исто́чник** reliable source.
компете́нци|я, и *f.* (*область знания*) competence; (*круг полномочий*) jurisdiction; **э́то не в моéй ~и** it is beyond my scope.
ко́мплекс, а *m.* (*in var. senses*) complex; (*набор*) set; **к. неполноце́нности** inferiority complex; **к. мероприя́тий** package of measures.
ко́мплексный *adj.* all-embracing, all-in; **к. обе́д** table d'hôte dinner.
комплекс|ова́ть, у́ю *impf.* (*coll.*) to suffer from complexes; to feel inadequate, insecure.
компле́кт, а *m.* set; kit; **к. белья́** bedding, bedclothes.
компле́кци|я, и *f.* build.
комплиме́нт, а *m.* compliment; **сде́лать к.** (+ *d.*) to pay a compliment (to).
компози́тор, а *m.* (*mus.*) composer.
компози́ци|я, и *f.* composition.
компоне́нт, а *m.* component.
компо́т, а *m.* compote, stewed fruit.
компре́сс, а *m.* (*med.*) compress; **поста́вить к.** to apply a compress.
компре́ссор, а *m.* (*tech., med.*) compressor.
компрома́т, а *m.* (*abbr. of* **компромети́рующий материа́л**) compromising material.
компромети́р|овать, ую *impf.* (*of* ▸ **с~**) to compromise.
компроми́сс, а *m.* compromise; **идти́ на к.** to make a compromise, meet halfway.
компью́тер, а *m.* computer; **портати́вный к.** laptop (computer); **со зна́нием ~а** computer literate.
компью́терщик, а *m.* (*coll.*) computer specialist; computer buff.
кому́ *d. of* ▸ **кто**
комфо́рт, а *m.* comfort.
комфорта́бел|ьный (~ен, ~ьна) *adj.* comfortable.
конве́йер, а *m.* (*tech.*) conveyor (*belt*); **сбо́рочный к.** assembly line.
конве́рси|я, и *f.* (*econ., fin.*) conversion.
конве́рт, а *m.*
1 (*для писем*) envelope.
2 (*для грампластинки*) sleeve.
конверти́р|овать, ую *impf. and pf.* (*fin.*) to convert.
конверти́руемый *adj.* (*fin.*) convertible.
конво́ир, а *m.* escort.
конво́|й, я *m.* escort.
конву́льси|я, и *f.* (*med.*) convulsion.
Ко́нго *nt. indecl.* Congo; **Демократи́ческая Респу́блика Ко́нго** Democratic Republic of the Congo (*formerly Zaire*).
конголе́з|ец, ца *m.* Congolese.
конголе́з|ка, ки *f. of* ▸ **~ец**
конголе́зский *adj.* Congolese.
конгре́сс, а *m.* congress; (*в США*) Congress.
конгрессме́н, а *m.* congressman.
конденса́т, а *m.* condensate.

конденса́ци|я, и *f.* condensation.
конди́тер, а *m.* confectioner, pastry cook.
конди́терск|ая, ой *f.* (*продающая конфеты*) confectioner's, sweet shop (*Br.*), candy store (*US*); (*продающая торты*) cake shop, pastry shop.
кондиционе́р, а *m.* air conditioner.
ко́ндор, а *m.* (*zool.*) condor.
конду́ктор, а, *pl.* **~а́, ~о́в** *m.* (*человек*) (*bus, tram*) conductor; (*rail.*) guard.
кон|ёк, ька́ *m.*
1 *dim. of* ▸ **~ь; морско́й к.** (*zool.*) sea horse.
2 (*fig., coll.*) hobby horse; hobby; **сесть на своего́ ~ька́** to mount one's hobby horse.
3 *see* ▸ **~ьки́**
кон|е́ц, ца́ *m.*
1 end; **в ~це́ ~цо́в** in the end, after all; **положи́ть к.** (+ *d.*) to put an end to; **своди́ть ~цы́ с ~ца́ми** (*coll.*) to make both ends meet.
2 (*coll.*) (*расстояние, путь*) distance, way; **в оди́н к.** one way; **в о́ба ~ца́** there and back.
коне́чно *adv.* of course, certainly.
коне́чност|ь, и *f.* (*anat.*) extremity.
коне́ч|ный (~ен, ~на) *adj.*
1 final, last; ultimate; **~ная ста́нция** terminus; **~ная цель** ultimate aim; **в ~ном ито́ге, счёте** ultimately, in the last analysis.
2 (*имеющий конец*) finite.
кони́н|а, ы *no pl., f.* horseflesh.
конкре́т|ный (~ен, ~на) *adj.* concrete; specific.
конкуре́нт, а *m.* competitor; rival.
конкуре́нт|ка, ки *f. of* ▸ **~**
конкурентоспосо́бност|ь, и *f.* competitiveness.
конкурентоспосо́б|ный (~ен, ~на) *adj.* competitive.
конкуре́нци|я, и *f.* competition; **вне ~и** unrivalled.
конкури́р|овать, ую *impf.* (**с** + *i.*) to compete (with).
ко́нкурс, а *m.* competition; contest.
конкурса́нт, а *m.* competitor; contestant.
конкурса́нт|ка, ки *f. of* ▸ **~**
ко́нкурс|ный *adj. of* ▸ **~; к. экза́мен** competitive examination.
ко́нник, а *m.* cavalryman.
ко́нниц|а, ы *f.* cavalry.
ко́н|ный *adj. of* ▸ **~ь;** horse; mounted; equestrian; **к. спорт** equestrianism.
конопл|я́, и́ *f.* (*bot.*) hemp; (*наркотик*) cannabis.
консерва́нт, а *m.* preservative.
консервати́в|ный (~ен, ~на) *adj.* conservative.
консервати́зм, а *m.* conservatism.
консерва́тор, а *m.* (*esp. pol.*) conservative.
консервато́ри|я, и *f.* conservatoire, music college.
консерви́рован|ный (~, ~а) *p.p.p. of* ▸ **консерви́ровать** *and adj.*; **~ные фру́кты** bottled fruit, canned fruit.
консерви́р|овать, ую *impf. and pf.* (*pf. also* **за~**) to preserve; to can; to bottle.
консе́рв|ный *adj. of* ▸ **~ы; ~ная ба́нка** tin can; **к. нож** can-opener.
консе́рв|ы, ов *no sg.* canned food.
консолида́ци|я, и *f.* consolidation.
консо́л|ь, и *f.* (*comput.*) console.
конспе́кт, а *m.* outline, summary.
конспирати́в|ный (~ен, ~на) *adj.* secret, clandestine.
конспира́тор, а *m.* conspirator.
констати́р|овать, ую *impf. and pf.* to ascertain; to establish; **к. смерть** to certify death; **к. факт** to establish a fact.
конституцио́нный *adj.* (*pol.*) constitutional.
конститу́ци|я, и *f.* (*pol., med.*) constitution.
конструи́р|овать, ую *impf. and pf.* (*pf. also* **с~**) (*строить*) to construct; (*проектировать*) to design.
конструктиви́зм, а *m.* (*art*) constructivism.
конструкти́в|ный (~ен, ~на) *adj.*
1 structural; construction.
2 (*критика*) constructive.
констру́ктор, а *m.* designer.
констру́ктор|ский *adj. of* ▸ **~; ~ское бюро́** design office.
констру́кци|я, и *f.*
1 (*состав*) construction; design.
2 (*сооружение*) structure.
ко́нсул, а *m.* consul.
ко́нсульств|о, а *nt.* consulate.
консульта́нт, а *m.* consultant, adviser; (*в вузе*) tutor.
консульта́ци|я, и *f.*
1 consultation; specialist advice.
2 (*учреждение*) advice bureau; **же́нская к.** antenatal (*Br.*), prenatal (*US*) clinic; gynaecological (*Br.*), gynecological (*US*) clinic; **юриди́ческиая к.** legal advice office.
консульти́р|овать, ую *impf.* (*pf.* **про~**) to advise; (*в вузе*) to act as tutor (to).
консульти́р|оваться, уюсь *impf.* (*of* ▸ **про~**) (**с** + *i.*) to consult.
конта́кт, а *m.* contact; **вступи́ть в к. с кем-н.** to come into contact, get in touch with s.o.
конта́кт|ный (~ен, ~на) *adj.*
1 contact; **к. телефо́н** contact number; **~ные ли́нзы** (*med.*) contact lenses.
2 (*coll.*) (*о человеке*) sociable.
конте́йнер, а *m.* container.
конте́кст, а *m.* context.
континге́нт, а *m.* contingent; batch; **к. во́йск** a military force; **к. новобра́нцев** batch, squad of recruits.
контине́нт, а *m.* continent.
континента́льный *adj.* continental.
конто́р|а, ы *f.* office, bureau.
контраба́нд|а, ы *f.*
1 (*действие*) contraband, smuggling; **занима́ться ~ой** to smuggle.
2 (*товары*) contraband.
контрабанди́ст, а *m.* smuggler.
контрабанди́ст|ка, ки *f. of* ▸ **~**
контраба́с, а *m.* (*mus.*) double bass.
контрабаси́ст, а *m.* double bass player.
контрабаси́ст|ка, ки *f. of* ▸ **~**

контра́кт, а *m.* contract.
контра́ктник, а *m.* (*coll.*) contract worker.
контра́льто *nt. indecl.* (*voice*) & *f. indecl.* (*singer*) (*mus.*) contralto.
контра́ст, а *m.* contrast; **по ~у (с** + *i.*) by contrast (with).
контра́ст|ный (~ен, ~на) *adj.* contrasting.
контрата́к|а, и *f.* (*mil.*, *sport*) counter-attack.
контрацепти́в, а *m.* contraceptive.
контролёр, а *m.* inspector; (*билетов*) ticket collector.
контроли́р|овать, ую *impf.* (*of* ▸ **про~**) (*проверять*) to check; (*держать под своим контролем*) to control.
контро́л|ь, я *m.*
1 control.
2 (*проверка*) check(ing); inspection; (*tech.*, *mil.*) monitoring; (*mil.*) verification.
контро́льно-пропускно́й *adj.*: **к. пункт** checkpoint.
контро́ль|ный *adj. of* ▸ **~**; **~ная рабо́та** test.
контрразве́дк|а, и *f.* counter-espionage; counter-intelligence.
контрреволю́ци|я, и *f.* counter-revolution.
конту́зи|я, и *f.* contusion, bruising; (*при разрыве снаряда*) shell shock.
ко́нтур, а *m.*
1 contour.
2 (*elec.*) circuit.
конур|а́, ы́ *f.* kennel; (*fig.*) hovel, dump.
ко́нус, а *m.* cone.
конфедера́ци|я, и *f.* confederation.
конферансье́ *m. indecl.* (*theatr.*) compère, master of ceremonies (*abbr.* MC).
конфере́нц-за́л, а *m.* conference hall.
конфере́нци|я, и *f.* conference.
конфе́сси|я, и *f.* confession, faith.
конфе́т|а, ы *f.* sweet; **шокола́дная к.** chocolate.
конфигура́ци|я, и *f.* configuration.
конфиденциа́льност|ь, и *f.* confidentiality.
конфиденциа́л|ьный (~ен, ~ьна) *adj.* confidential.
конфиска́ци|я, и *f.* confiscation, seizure.
конфиск|ова́ть, у́ю *impf. and pf.* to confiscate.
конфли́кт, а *m.* conflict.
конфликт|ова́ть, у́ю *impf.* (**с** + *i.*) (*coll.*) to clash (with), come up (against).
конфо́рк|а, и *f.* ring (*on cooker*).
конфронта́ци|я, и *f.* confrontation, showdown.
конфу́з, а *m.* (*coll.*) discomfiture, embarrassment.
концентра́т, а *m.* concentrate.
концентрацио́нный *adj.*: **к. ла́герь** concentration camp.
концентра́ци|я, и *f.* (*in var. senses*) concentration.
концентри́рова|нный *p.p.p. of* ▸ **~ть** *and adj.* concentrated.
концентри́р|овать, ую *impf.* (*of* ▸ **с~**) (*in var. senses*) to concentrate; (*mil.*) to mass.
концентри́р|оваться, уюсь *impf.* (*of* ▸ **с~**)
1 to mass, collect (*intrans.*).
2 (*fig.*; **на** + *p.*) to concentrate.
концептуа́л|ьный (~ен, ~ьна) *adj.* conceptual.
конце́пци|я, и *f.* conception, idea.
конце́рн, а *m.* (*econ.*) concern.
конце́рт, а *m.* (*mus.*)
1 concert; recital; **симфони́ческий к.** symphony concert; **быть на ~е** to be at a concert.
2 (*произведение*) concerto.
конце́сси|я, и *f.* (*econ.*) concession.
концла́гер|ь, я *m.* (*abbr. of* **концентрацио́нный ла́герь**) concentration camp.
концо́вк|а, и *f.* ending.
конч|а́ть(ся), а́ю(сь) *impf. of* ▸ **~́ить(ся)**
ко́нч|енный *p.p.p. of* ▸ **~ить;** *as int.* **~ено!** enough!; **всё ~ено!** it's all over!
ко́нчик, а *m.* tip; point; **на ~е языка́** on the tip of one's tongue.
кончи́н|а, ы *f.* (*rhet.*) decease, demise.
ко́нч|ить, у, ишь *pf.* (*of* ▸ **~а́ть**)
1 to finish, end; **на э́том он ~ил** here he stopped; **к. шко́лу** to finish/leave school; **к. университе́т** to graduate; **к. (жизнь) самоуби́йством** to commit suicide; **пло́хо к.** to come to a bad end.
2 (**с** + *i.*) to be finished (with), give up.
3 (+ *inf.*) to stop.
4 (*coll.*) to come (= *have an orgasm*).
ко́нч|иться, усь, ишься *pf.* (*of* ▸ **~а́ться**) (+ *i.*) to end (in), finish (by); to come to an end; **де́ло ~илось ниче́м** it came to nothing.
конъюнкту́р|а, ы *f.*
1 state of affairs, juncture; **междунаро́дная к.** international situation.
2 (*econ.*) state of the market.
конъюнкту́р|ный
1 *adj. of* ▸ **~а 2; ~ные це́ны** (free) market prices.
2 (*pej.*) (*поведение, человек*) ready to compromise; opportunistic.
кон|ь, я́, *pl.* **~́и, ~е́й** *m.*
1 horse.
2 (*шахматы*) knight.
кон|ьки́, ько́в *pl.* (*sg.* **~ёк, ~ька́** *m.*) skates; **ро́ликовые к.** roller skates; **ката́ться на ~ька́х** to skate.
конькобе́ж|ец, ца *m.* skater.
конькобе́жный *adj.* skating; **к. спорт** skating.
конья́к, а́ (у́) *m.* brandy.
ко́нюх, а *m.* groom, stableman.
коню́ш|ня, ни, *g. pl.* **~ен** *f.* stable.
кооперати́в, а *m.*
1 (*организация*) cooperative society.
2 (*coll.*) (*магазин*) cooperative store; (*квартира*) flat in housing cooperative.
кооперати́вный *adj.* cooperative.
координа́т|а, ы *f.* (*math.*) coordinate; *pl.* (*coll.*) contact details (*address, telephone number, etc.*).

координа́ци|я, и *f.* coordination.
коп|а́ть, а́ю *impf.*
1 (*pf.* **вс~**) to dig.
2 (*pf.* **вы́~**) to dig up, dig out.
копа́|ться, юсь *impf.*
1 (**в** + *p.*) (*в сундуке*) to rummage (in); (*в песке*) to root around (in); (*fig.*): **к. в душе́** to be given to soul-searching.
2 (*coll.*; **с** + *i.*) (*канителиться*) to dawdle (over).
3 *pass. of* ▸ **~ть**
копе́йк|а, и, *g. pl.* **копе́ек** *f.* kopek.
Копенга́ген, а *m.* Copenhagen.
ко́п|и, ей *pl.* (*sg.* **~ь, ~и** *f.*) mines.
копи́лк|а, и *f.* money box.
копира́йт, а *m.* copyright.
копи́р|овать, ую *impf.* (*of* ▸ **с~**) to copy; to imitate, mimic.
коп|и́ть, лю́, ~́ишь *impf.* (*of* ▸ **на~**) to accumulate, amass; to store up; **к. де́ньги** to save up; (*fig.*): **к. си́лы** to save one's strength.
коп|и́ться, ~́ится *impf.* (*of* ▸ **на~**) to accumulate (*intrans.*).
ко́пи|я, и *f.* copy; **печа́тная к.** (*comput.*) hard copy; **резе́рвная к.** (*comput.*) backup; **снять ~ю** (**с** + *g.*) to copy, make a copy (of).
коп|на́, ны́, *pl.* **~́ны, ~ён, ~на́м** *f.* shock, stook (*of corn*); **к. се́на** haycock; **к. воло́с** shock of hair.
ко́пот|ь, и *f.* soot; lampblack.
копош|и́ться, у́сь, и́шься *impf.*
1 (*о насекомых*) to swarm.
2 (*fig., coll.*) (*о мыслях*) to stir, creep in.
3 (*coll.*) (*возиться*) to potter about.
коп|ти́ть, чу́, ти́шь *impf. of* ▸ **за~**
копчёный *adj.* smoked.
коп|чу́, ти́шь *see* ▸ **~ти́ть**
копы́тн|ый *adj.* (*zool.*) hoofed, ungulate; *as n.* **~ые, ~ых** ungulates.
копы́т|о, а *nt.* hoof.
коп|ь *see* ▸ **~́и**
коп|ьё, ья́, *pl.* **~́ья, ~́ий, ~́ьям** *nt.* spear, lance.
кор|а́, ы́ *f.*
1 (*bot.*) bark.
2 (*anat.*): **к. головно́го мо́зга** cerebral cortex.
3 (*Земли*) crust; **земна́я к.** the earth's crust.
кораблекруше́ни|е, я *nt.* shipwreck; **потерпе́ть к.** to be shipwrecked.
кораблестрое́ни|е, я *nt.* shipbuilding.
кора́бл|ь, я́ *m.* ship, vessel; **лине́йный к.** battleship; **косми́ческий к.** spaceship; **сади́ться на к.** to go on board (ship).
кора́лл, а *m.* coral.
Кора́н, а *m.* the Koran.
коре́|ец, йца *m.* Korean.
коре́йк|а, и *f.* smoked back bacon.
коре́йский *adj.* Korean.
корена́ст|ый (~, ~а) *adj.* thickset, stocky.
коренн|о́й *adj.* radical, fundamental; **к. зуб** molar (tooth); **к. жи́тель** native; **~о́е населе́ние** indigenous population.
ко́р|ень, ня, *pl.* **~ни, ~не́й** *m.* (*in var. senses*) root; **вы́рвать с ~нем** to uproot (*also fig.*).
Коре́|я, и *f.* Korea.
коре|я́нка, я́нки *f. of* ▸ **~́ец**
корзи́н|а, ы *f.* basket.
кориа́ндр, а *m.* coriander.
коридо́р, а *m.* corridor, passage.
кори́ц|а, ы *f.* cinnamon.
кори́чневый *adj.* brown.
ко́рк|а, и *f.*
1 (*хлеба*) crust.
2 (*апельсина*) peel, rind.
корм, а, о ~́е, на ~́е *and* **на ~у́,** *pl.* **~а́, ~о́в** *m.*
1 (*пища*) food, fodder; **пти́чий к.** birdseed.
2 (*действие*) feeding.
корм|а́, ы́ *f.* (*naut.*) stern.
корм|и́ть, лю́, ~́ишь *impf.*
1 (*pf.* **на~** *and* **по~**) (*давать корм*) to feed; **к. гру́дью** to nurse, (breast)feed.
2 (*pf.* **про~**) (*содержать*) to keep, maintain.
корм|и́ться, лю́сь, ~́ишься *impf.* (*pf.* **про~**) (+ *i.*) (*содержать себя*) to live (on); **к. уро́ками** to make a living by giving tuition.
кормле́ни|е, я *nt.* feeding.
корму́шк|а, и *f.* (*agric.*) (feeding) trough; (*для птиц*) bird table, bird feeder.
корнепло́д, а *m.* root vegetable.
корнишо́н, а *m.* (*cul.*) gherkin.
коро́бк|а, и *f.* box, case; **к. скоросте́й** (*tech.*) gearbox; **черепна́я к.** (*anat.*) cranium.
короб|о́к, ка́ *m.* (small) box.
коро́в|а, ы *f.* cow.
коро́в|ий *adj. of* ▸ **~а; ~ье ма́сло** butter.
коро́в|ка, ки *f. affectionate dim. of* ▸ **~а; бо́жья к.** ladybird.
коро́вник, а *m.* cowshed.
короле́в|а, ы *f.* queen.
короле́вский *adj.* royal.
короле́вств|о, а *nt.* kingdom.
коро́л|ь, я́ *m.* king; (*fig.*) baron.
коро́н|а, ы *f.* crown (*also fig.*).
корона́ци|я, и *f.* coronation.
коро́нк|а, и *f.* crown (*of tooth*).
корон|ова́ть, у́ю *impf. and pf.* to crown.
коро́ст|а, ы *f.* scab.
коро́т|кий (ко́роток, коротка́, ко́ротко, *pl.* **ко́ротки́)** *adj.* short; **э́то пальто́ тебе́ ко́ротко** this coat is too short for you.
ко́ротк|о[1] *see* ▸ **~ий**
ко́ротко[2] *adv.* briefly.
короткометра́жный *adj.*: **к. фильм** short (film).
кор|о́че *comp. of* ▸ **~о́ткий** *and* ▸ **~́отко** shorter; **к. говоря́** in short, to cut a long story short.
корпорати́в|ный (~ен, ~на) *adj.* corporate.
корпора́ци|я, и *f.* corporation.
ко́рпус[1], а, *pl.* **~ы** *m.*
1 (*туловище*) body.
2 (*мера*) length (*of animal, as unit of measurement*).
ко́рпус[2], а, *pl.* **~а́, ~о́в** *m.*
1 (*mil.*) corps; **каде́тский, морско́й к.** military school, naval college; **дипломати́ческий к.** diplomatic corps.

2 (*здание*) building; block.
3 (*корабля*) hull; (*tech.*) frame, body, case.

корректир|овать, ую *impf.* (*of* ▶ **с~**) to correct.

корре́кт|ный (~ен, ~на) *adj.* correct, proper.

корре́ктор, а *m.* proofreader.

корре́кци|я, и *f.* correction.

корреспонде́нт, а *m.* correspondent.

корреспонде́нт|ка, ки *f. of* ▶ **~**

корреспонде́нци|я, и *f.*
1 (*переписка; письма*) correspondence.
2 (*сообщение*) dispatch, report.

корри́д|а, ы *f.* bullfight.

корро́зи|я, и *f.* (*chem.*) corrosion.

коррумпи́рован|ный (~, ~а) *adj.* corrupt.

корру́пци|я, и *f.* (*pol.*) corruption.

корса́ж, а *m.* bodice.

корсе́т, а *m.* corset.

корт, а *m.* (tennis) court.

корте́ж, а *m.* procession, cortège; (*автомобилей*) motorcade.

ко́ртик, а *m.* dagger.

ко́рточ|ки, ек *no sg.*: **сиде́ть на ~ках, сесть на к.** to squat.

корч|ева́ть, у́ю *impf.* to uproot, root out.

ко́ршун, а *m.* (*zool.*) kite.

коры́ст|ный (~ен, ~на) *adj.* mercenary, selfish.

коры́т|о, а *nt.* tub; trough.

кор|ь, и *f.* measles.

коря́в|ый (~, ~а) *adj.* (*coll.*)
1 (*дуб, пальцы*) gnarled.
2 (*почерк, речь, стиль*) clumsy.

коря́г|а, и *f.* (*ветвь*) dead branch, (*пень*) dead tree stump (*oft. submerged under water*).

кос|а́[1], ы́, *a.* **~́у,** *pl.* **~́ы** *f.* (*волосы*) plait, pigtail, braid.

кос|а́[2], ы́, *pl.* **~́ы** *f.* (*орудие*) scythe.

коса́тк|а, и *f.* killer whale.

ко́свенн|ый *adj.* indirect, oblique; **~ые у́лики** circumstantial evidence; (*gram.*): **~ая речь** indirect speech.

коси́лк|а, и *f.* mowing-machine, mower; **газо́нная к.** lawn mower.

ко|си́ть[1], шу́, ~́сишь *impf.* (*of* ▶ **с~[1]**) (*траву*) to mow; to cut.

ко|си́ть[2], шу́, си́шь *impf.* (*of* ▶ **с~[2]**
1 (*глаза при косоглазии*) to squint.
2 (*рот, глаза*) to twist, slant.
3 (*no pf.*) (*быть косоглазым*) to have a squint.

ко|си́ться, шу́сь, си́шься *impf.* (*of* ▶ **по~**)
1 (*о доме*) to slant.
2 (*coll.*) (**на** + *a.*) to cast a sidelong look (at); (*fig.*) to look askance (at).

коси́чк|а, и *f. dim. of* ▶ **коса́[1]**

косма́т|ый (~, ~а) *adj.* shaggy.

косме́тик|а, и *f.* cosmetics, make-up.

космети́ческ|ий *adj.* cosmetic; **к. кабине́т** beauty salon; **~ая ма́ска** face pack; **к. ремо́нт** redecoration.

космети́чк|а, и *f.* (*coll.*) make-up bag.

космето́лог, а *m.*
1 (*врач в клинике*) cosmetic surgeon.
2 (*специалист в салоне*) beautician.

косми́ческий *adj.*
1 space (*attr.*).
2 (*пыль, радиация*) cosmic; **к. кора́бль** spaceship.

космодро́м, а *m.* cosmodrome, space centre (*Br.*), center (*US*).

космона́вт, а *m.* astronaut, cosmonaut, spaceman.

космона́втик|а, и *f.* astronautics, space exploration.

космополи́т, а *m.* cosmopolitan.

космополити́ческий *adj.* cosmopolitan.

ко́смос, а *m.* cosmos; outer space.

косноязы́ч|ный (~ен, ~на) *adj.* speaking thickly.

косн|у́ться, у́сь, ёшься *pf. of* ▶ **каса́ться**

ко́с|ный (~ен, ~на) *adj.* (*ум*) inert, sluggish; (*образ жизни, общество*) stagnant.

ко́со *adv.* slantwise, askew; obliquely; **смотре́ть к.** to look askance, scowl.

Ко́сово *nt., decl. and indecl.* Kosovo.

косогла́зи|е, я *nt.* squint, cast in the eye.

косогла́з|ый (~, ~а) *adj.* cross-eyed, squint-eyed.

кос|о́й (~, ~а́, ~́о) *adj.*
1 slanting; oblique.
2 (*косоглазый*) squinting; cross-eyed.

косола́п|ый (~, ~а) *adj.* pigeon-toed; (*fig.*) clumsy.

косте́л, а *m.* (Roman Catholic) church.

кост|ёр, ра́ *m.* bonfire; (*походный*) campfire; **зажéчь/развести́ к.** to make a fire.

костля́в|ый (~, ~а) *adj.* bony.

ко́стный *adj.* osseous; (*anat.*): **к. мозг** marrow.

ко́сточк|а, и *f.*
1 *dim. of* ▶ **кость.**
2 (*сливы, абрикоса*) stone; (*лимона, винограда*) pip.

косты́л|ь, я́ *m.* crutch; **ходи́ть на ~я́х** to walk on crutches.

кост|ь, и, *pl.* **~́и, ~е́й** *f.*
1 bone; **слоно́вая к.** ivory.
2 (*pl.*) (*в игре*) dice.

костю́м, а *m.*
1 (*одежда*) dress, clothes; **маскара́дный к.** fancy dress.
2 (*пиджак и брюки; жакет и юбка*) suit; **вече́рний к.** dress suit; **купа́льный к.** swimsuit.
3 (*theatr.*) costume.

костюме́р, а *m.* (*theatr.*) wardrobe master.

костя́к, а́ *m.* (*fig.*) (+ *g.*) backbone (of).

косу́л|я, и *f.* roe deer.

косы́нк|а, и *f.* (triangular) kerchief, scarf.

кося́к[1], а́ *m.* (*дверной*) (door-)post; jamb.

кося́к[2], а́ *m.*
1 (*лошадей*) herd.
2 (*рыб*) shoal, school; (*птиц*) flock.

кося́к[3], а́ *m.* (*sl.*) (*с марихуаной*) joint.

кот, а́ *m.* tomcat.

Кот-д'Ивуа́р, а *m.* the Ivory Coast.

кот|ёл, ла́ *m.*
1 pot, cauldron; **о́бщий к.** communal pot.

[2] (*tech.*) boiler.
котел|óк, кá *m.*
[1] pot.
[2] (*mil.*) mess tin.
[3] (*шляпа*) bowler (hat).
котéльн|ая, ой *f.* boiler house.
кот|ёнок, ёнка, *pl.* **~ята, ~ят** *m.* kitten.
кóтик, а *m.*
[1] (*тюлень*) fur seal.
[2] (*мех*) sealskin.
котúр|овать, ую *impf. and pf.* (*fin.*) to quote.
котúр|оваться, уюсь *impf. and pf.*
[1] (*fin.*) to be quoted.
[2] (*fig.*) to be rated.
котлéт|а, ы *f.* burger; rissole; **(отбивнáя) к.** chop.
котловáн, а *m.* (*tech.*) foundation pit.
котóмк|а, и *f.* knapsack.
котóрый *pron.*
[1] *interrog. and rel.* (*о предметах*) which; **к. час?** what time is it?
[2] (*coll.*) (*не один*) some, quite a few; **к. год он не пúшет** he hasn't been writing for some years.
[3] *rel.* (*о людях*) who.
коттéдж, а *m.* cottage.
кот|ята, ят *see* ▶ **~ёнок**
кóфе *m. indecl.* coffee; **растворúмый к.** instant coffee; **к. в зёрнах** coffee beans.
кофевáрк|а, и *f.* coffee-maker.
кофеин, а *m.* caffeine.
кофéйник, а *m.* coffee pot.
коф|éйный *adj. of* ▶ **~е**
кофé|йня, йни, *g. pl.* **~ен** *f.* coffee house.
кофемóлк|а, и *f.* coffee grinder.
кóфт|а, ы *f.* (*woman's*) jacket, cardigan.
кóфточк|а, и *f.* blouse.
кочáн, á *m.*: **к. капýсты** head of cabbage.
коч|евáть, ýю *impf.*
[1] (*о племенах*) to be a nomad, to roam from place to place; (*fig.*) (*передвигаться*) to wander.
[2] (*о животных*) to migrate.
кочéвник, а *m.* nomad.
кочевóй *adj.*
[1] (*люди*) nomadic.
[2] (*животные*) migratory.
кочегáр, а *m.* stoker, fireman.
кочер|гá, гú, *g. pl.* **~ёг** *f.* poker.
кóчк|а, и *f.* hummock; tussock.
кошел|ёк, ькá *m.* purse.
кошёлк|а, и *f.* (*coll.*) small basket.
кóшк|а, и *f.* cat; (*fig., coll.*): **игрáть в ~и-мышки** to play cat-and-mouse; **жить как к. с собáкой** to lead a cat-and-dog life.
кошмáр, а *m.*
[1] nightmare (*also fig.*).
[2] *as pred.* (*coll.*) it is a nightmare.
кошмáр|ный (~ен, ~на) *adj.* nightmarish; (*fig.*) horrible, awful.
ко|шý, ~сúшь *see* ▶ **~сúть**[1,2]
кощýнств|о, а *nt.* blasphemy.
коэффициéнт, а *m.* (*math.*) coefficient; (*tech.*): **к. полéзного дéйствия** efficiency (*also fig.*); **к. ýмственных спосóбностей** intelligence quotient, IQ.

КПП *m. indecl.* (*abbr. of* **контрóльно-пропускнóй пункт**) checkpoint.
краб, а *m.* (*zool.*) crab.
крáден|ый *adj.* stolen; **~ое** (*collect.*) stolen goods.
кра|дý, дёшь *see* ▶ **~сть**
крáж|а, и *f.* theft; **к. со взлóмом** burglary; **магазúнная к.** shoplifting.
кра|й, я, о ~е, в ~ю́, *pl.* **~я́, ~ёв** *m.*
[1] (*поля, одежды*) edge; (*сосуда*) brim; (*пропасти*) brink (*also fig.*); **на ~ю́ свéта** at the world's end.
[2] (*страна, область*) land, country; **в нáших ~я́х** in our part of the world; **в чужúх ~я́х** in foreign parts.
крáйне *adv.* extremely.
крáйн|ий *adj.*
[1] (*in var. senses*) extreme; (*последний*) last; **К. Сéвер** the Far North; **в ~ем слýчае** in the last resort; **к. срок** deadline; **по ~ей мéре** at least.
[2] (*sport*) outside, wing.
крáйност|ь, и *f.* (*крайняя степень*) extreme; (*тяжёлое положение*) (*no pl.*) extremity.
крал, а *see* ▶ **красть**
кран[1]**, а** *m.* (*водопроводный*) tap, faucet (*US*); (*на трубопроводах*) valve.
кран[2]**, а** *m.* (*машина*) crane.
крапúв|а, ы *f.* (stinging) nettle; (*collect.*) nettles.
красáв|ец, ца *m.* handsome man; good-looker (*male*).
красáвиц|а, ы *f.* beauty; good-looker (*female*).
красúв|ый (~, ~а) *adj.* beautiful; (*мужчина*) handsome; (*поступок, слова*) fine.
красúтел|ь, я *m.* dye(-stuff); **пищевóй к.** food colouring.
крá|сить, шу, сишь *impf.* (*of* ▶ **по~**)
[1] (*стену, губы*) to paint.
[2] (*ткань, волосы*) to dye; (*дерево, стекло*) to stain.
крá|ситься, шусь, сишься *impf.*
[1] (*pf.* **на~**) to make up one's face.
[2] (*pf.* **по~**) to dye one's hair.
[3] (*no pf.*) (*пачкать собой*) to run.
[4] *pass. of* ▶ **~сить**
крáск|а, и *f.*
[1] (*материал*) paint; (*для ткани*) dye; **акварéльная к.** watercolour (*Br.*), watercolor (*US*); **мáсляная к.** oil paint.
[2] (*pl., fig.*) (*колорит*) colours (*Br.*), colors (*US*); **сгущáть ~и** (*coll.*) to lay it on thick.
краснé|ть, ю *impf.* (*of* ▶ **по~**)
[1] (*становиться красным*) to redden, become red.
[2] (*от стыда*) to blush; (*fig.*): **к. за** + *a.* to blush for.
красноречúв|ый (~, ~а) *adj.* eloquent.
красноречи|е, я *nt.* eloquence.
краснýх|а, и *f.* (*med.*) German measles.
крáс|ный (~ен, ~нá, ~но) *adj.* red (*also fig., pol.*); **~ное дéрево** mahogany; **К. Крест** Red Cross; (*fig.*): **~ная строкá** (first line of) new paragraph.
красот|á, ы́, *pl.* **~ы** *f.* beauty.
красóтк|а, и *f.* (*coll.*) good-looking girl;

beauty.

кра́с|очный *adj.*
1 *adj. of* ▶ **~ка.**
2 **(~очен, ~очна)** colourful (*Br.*), colorful (*US*).

кра|сть, ду́, дёшь, *past* **~л, ~́ла** *impf.* (*of* ▶ **у~́**) to steal.

кра́|сться, ду́сь, дёшься, *past* **~лся, ~лась** *impf.* to steal, creep, sneak.

кра́тер, а *m.* crater.

кра́т|кий (~ок, ~ка́, ~ко) *adj.* short; brief; **я бу́ду ~ок** I'll be brief; (*сжатый*) concise; **«и» ~кое** *Russian letter* **й**.

кра́тко *adv.* briefly.

кратковре́мен|ный (~ *and* **~ен, ~на**) *adj.* of short duration, brief; **к. дождь** shower.

краткосро́ч|ный (~ен, ~на) *adj.* (*ссуда*) short-term; (*отпуск*) short.

крат|ча́йший *superl. of* ▶ **~́кий**

крах, а *m.* (*fin. and fig.*) crash, collapse; (*fig.*) (*провал*) failure; **потерпе́ть к.** to fail.

крахма́л, а *m.* starch.

кра́шен|ый *adj.*
1 (*стена*) painted; **~ое яйцо́** (decorated) Easter egg.
2 (*ткань*) dyed.

креве́тк|а, и *f.* (*zool.*) (*мелкая*) shrimp; (*крупная*) prawn.

креди́т, а *m.* credit; **в к.** on credit.

креди́тк|а, и *f.* (*coll.*) credit card.

креди́т|ный *adj. of* ▶ **~; к. биле́т** banknote; **~ная ка́рточка/ка́рта** credit card.

кредито́р, а *m.* creditor.

кредитоспосо́бность, и *f.* creditworthiness, credit rating.

кредитоспосо́б|ный (~ен, ~на) *adj.* creditworthy.

кре́йсер, а, *pl.* **~ы** *and* **~а́** (*mil.*) cruiser; **лине́йный к.** battle cruiser.

кре́кер, а *m.* cracker.

крем, а *m.* (*in var. senses*) cream; **к. для о́буви** shoe polish.

кремато́ри|й, я *m.* crematorium.

крема́ци|я, и *f.* cremation.

крем|е́нь, ня́ *m.* flint.

кремл|ёвский *adj. of* ▶ **~ь**

кремл|ь, я́ *m.* citadel; **(моско́вский) К.** the Kremlin.

кре́мни|й, я *m.* (*chem.*) silicon.

кре́мовый *adj.* cream(-coloured).

креп|и́ть, лю́, и́шь *impf.*
1 (*прочно прикреплять*) to fasten.
2 (*усиливать*) to strengthen.

креп|и́ться, лю́сь, и́шься *impf.*
1 to hold out.
2 *pass. of* ▶ **~и́ть**

кре́п|кий (~ок, ~ка́, ~ко, ~́ки́) *adj.* (*чай, кофе; запах; ветер; организм; ткань*) strong; (*сон*) sound; (*забор*) sturdy, robust; (*мороз, удар*) hard; (*fig.*) (*стойкий*) firm; **~кие напи́тки** spirits; **~кое словцо́** (*coll.*) swear word, strong language.

кре́пко *adv.* (*держать; завязать*) tight; (*построенный*) strongly; (*спать*) soundly.

крепле́ни|е, я *nt.*
1 (*naut.*) lashing; furling.
2 (*лыжное*) binding.

кре́пн|уть, у, ешь *impf.* (*of* ▶ **о~**) to get stronger.

кре́пост|ь[1]**, и** *f.* (*свойство*) strength.

кре́пост|ь[2]**, и** *f.* (*mil.*) fortress.

кре́п|че *comp. of* ▶ **~кий** *and* ▶ **~ко**

кре́с|ло, ла, *g. pl.* **~ел** *nt.* armchair, easy chair; (*fig.*) (*должность*) post, office; **инвали́дное к.** wheelchair; **к.-кача́лка** rocking chair; **к.-крова́ть** sofa bed; (*theatr.*) seat.

крест, а́ *m.*
1 cross; **поста́вить к.** (**на** + *p.*) to give up for lost.
2 (*жест*) the sign of the cross.

кре|сти́ть, щу́, ~́стишь *impf.*
1 (*pf.* **к.** *or* **о~**) to baptize, christen.
2 (*no pf.*) (+ *a. and* **у** + *g.*) to be godfather, godmother (*to the child of*); **я у них ~сти́ла дочь** I was godmother to their daughter.
3 (*pf.* **пере~**) to make the sign of the cross over.

кре|сти́ться, щу́сь, ~́стишься *impf.*
1 (*pf.* **к.**) to be baptized, be christened.
2 (*pf.* **пере~**) to cross o.s.

крест-на́крест *adv.* crosswise.

кре́стник, а *m.* godson, godchild.

кре́стниц|а, ы *f.* goddaughter, godchild.

крёстн|ый *adj.*: **к. оте́ц** (*also as n.* **к., ~ого** *m.*) godfather; **~ая мать** (*also as n.* **~ая, ~ой** *f.*) godmother; **~ые де́ти** godchildren.

крестоно́с|ец, ца *m.* crusader.

крестья́н|ин, ина, *pl.* **~е, ~** *m.* peasant.

крестья́нк|а, и *f.* peasant (woman).

крестья́нский *adj.* peasant.

крестья́нств|о, а *nt.* (*collect.*) the peasants, peasantry.

крети́н, а *m.* cretin; (*fig., coll.*) idiot, imbecile.

креще́ни|е, я *nt.* baptism, christening; **боево́е к.** (*fig.*) baptism of fire.

кре|щу́, ~́стишь *see* ▶ **~сти́ть**

крив|а́я, о́й *f.* (*math., econ., etc.*) curve.

кривля́|ться, юсь *impf.* to behave affectedly; to show off.

крив|о́й (~, ~а́, ~́о) *adj.* crooked; **~о́е зе́ркало** (*also fig.*) distorting mirror.

кривоно́г|ий (~, ~а) *adj.* bandy-legged, bow-legged.

кри́зис, а *m.* crisis.

кри́зис|ный *adj. of* ▶ **~; ~ная ситуа́ция** crisis situation, crisis.

крик, а *m.* cry, shout; *pl.* clamour (*Br.*), clamor (*US*), outcry; **к. души́** emotional outpouring.

кри́кет, а *m.* cricket; **игро́к в к.** cricketer.

крикли́в|ый (~, ~а) *adj.*
1 (*ребёнок*) clamorous, bawling.
2 (*голос*) loud, penetrating.

кри́кн|уть, у, ешь *inst. pf. of* ▶ **крича́ть**

кримина́л, а *m.* (*coll.*)
1 (*плохое поведение*) foul play.
2 (*преступление*) crime.

криминали́ст, а *m.* (*leg.*) specialist in crime detection.

криминали́стик|а, и *f.* (*science of*) crime

detection.

криминáл|ьный (~ен, ~ьна) *adj.* criminal.

криминогéн|ный (~ен, ~на) *adj.* criminogenic, conducive to crime.

кристáлл, а *m.* crystal.

критéри|й, я *m.* criterion.

кри́тик, а *m.* critic.

кри́тик|а, и *f.*
1 criticism.
2 (*отрицательное суждение*) critique.

критик|овáть, ýю *impf.* to criticize.

крити́ческий *adj.* critical; **к. момéнт** (*fig.*) crucial moment.

кри|чáть, чý, чи́шь *impf.* (*of* ▸ **~кнуть**)
1 to cry, shout; to yell, scream; **к. (на** + *a.*) to shout (at); **к. о пóмощи** to call for help.
2 (**о** + *p.*) (*coll.*) to make a song and dance (about), talk a lot (about).

кричá|щий *pres. part. act. of* ▸ **~ть** *and adj.* (*fig.*) loud; blatant.

кровáвый *adj.* (*режим, события*) bloody.

кровáтк|а, и *f.*: **дéтская к.** cot (*Br.*), crib (*US*).

кровáт|ь, и *f.* bed; **двухъя́русная к.** bunk bed.

крóв|ля, ли, *g. pl.* **~ель** *f.* roof.

крóвн|ый *adj.* blood; **~ая месть** blood feud.

кровожáд|ный (~ен, ~на) *adj.* bloodthirsty.

кровоизлия́ни|е, я *nt.* (*med.*) haemorrhage (*Br.*), hemorrhage (*US*).

кровообращéни|е, я *nt.* circulation of the blood.

кровопроли́ти|е, я *nt.* bloodshed.

кровотечéни|е, я *nt.* bleeding; (*сильное*) haemorrhage (*Br.*), hemorrhage (*US*).

кровоточ|и́ть, ~и́т *impf.* to bleed.

кров|ь, и, о ~и, в ~и́, *g. pl.* **~éй** *f.* blood (*also fig.*); **в к., до ~и** till it bleeds; **пусти́ть к.** (+ *d.*) to bleed (*trans.*); (*fig.*): **по ~и** by birth.

кров|янóй *adj. of* ▸ **~ь**

кро|и́ть, ю́, и́шь *impf.* (*of* ▸ **с~**) to cut (out).

кро|й, я *m.*
1 cutting (out).
2 (*фасон*) cut (*of dress etc.*).

крóйк|а, и *f.* cutting (out).

крокéт, а *m.* (*игра*) croquet.

крокоди́л, а *m.* crocodile.

крóкус, а *m.* (*bot.*) crocus.

крóлик, а *m.*
1 (*животное*) rabbit.
2 (*мех*) rabbit fur.

крóме *prep.* + *g.*
1 (*за исключением*) except.
2 (*в добавление*) besides, in addition to; **к. тогó** besides, moreover, furthermore; (*coll.*): **к. шýток** joking apart.

крóмк|а, и *f.* edge; (*ткани*) selvage; **к. тротуáра** kerb.

крóн|а, ы *f.* (*дерева*) crown.

кронштéйн, а *m.* (*tech.*) (*полки*) bracket; (*балкона*) corbel.

кропотли́в|ый (~, ~а) *adj.* painstaking, precise.

кроссвóрд, а *m.* crossword.

кроссóв|ки, ок *pl.* (*sg.* **~ка, ~ки** *f.*) trainers (*Br.*), sneakers (*US*).

крот, á *m.* mole.

крóт|кий (~ок, ~кá, ~ко) *adj.* meek, mild.

крóхотный *adj.* (*coll.*) tiny, minute.

крóшеч|ный (~ен, ~на) *adj.* (*coll.*) tiny, minute.

крош|и́ть, ý, ~ишь *impf.*
1 (*pf.* **на~** *or* **рас~**) (*хлеб*) to crumb, crumble; (*нарезать*) to dice; (*fig.*) to hack to pieces.
2 (*pf.* **на~**) (+ *i.*) (*сорить*) to drop, spill crumbs (of).

крош|и́ться, ~ится *impf.* (*of* ▸ **рас~**) to crumble.

крóшк|а, и *f.* (*хлеба*) crumb.

круассáн, а *m.* (*cul.*) croissant.

круг, а, *pl.* **~и́** *m.*
1 (*p. sg.* **в, на ~ý** = *circular area*; **в, на ~е** = *circumference*) circle; **движéние по ~у** movement in a circle.
2 (*круглый предмет*) ring; **спасáтельный к.** lifebelt; **~и́ под глазáми** rings round the eyes.
3 (*sport*; *p. sg.* **на ~е**) **беговóй к.** racecourse, ring; **к. почёта** lap of honour (*Br.*), honor (*US*).
4 (*fig.*; *p. sg.* **в ~ý**) (*сфера, область*) sphere, range; compass; **к. вопрóсов** range of questions.
5 (*fig.*; *p. sg.* **в ~ý**) (*группа людей*) circle (*of persons*); **официáльные ~и́** official quarters; **в семéйном ~ý** in the family circle.

круглогоди́чный *adj.* year-round.

круглоли́ц|ый (~, ~а) *adj.* round-faced.

круглосýточный *adj.* round-the-clock, twenty-four-hour.

крýгл|ый (~, ~á, ~о, ~лы) *adj.*
1 round; **к. год** all the year round; **~ая дáта** 10th, 20th, 30th, etc. anniversary; **~ые скóбки** round brackets; **~ые сýтки** day and night; **~ая сýмма** round sum.
2 (*no short forms*) (*coll.*) complete, utter, perfect; **к. дурáк** utter fool; **к., ~ая сиротá** orphan (*having neither father nor mother*).

круговорóт, а *m.* (*цикличность*) cycle; (*событий*) flow.

кругозóр, а *m.*
1 prospect.
2 (*fig.*) horizon, range of interests.

кругóм[1] *adv.*
1 round, around.
2 (*вокруг*) (all) round, round about; **к. всё бы́ло ти́хо** all around was still.
3 (*coll.*) (*совершенно*) completely, entirely; **вы к. винавáты** you are entirely to blame.

кругóм[2] *prep.* + *g.* round, around.

кругообрáз|ный (~ен, ~на) *adj.* circular.

кругосвéтный *adj.* round-the-world.

круж|евá, ~ев, ~евáм = **~ево**

кружев|нóй *adj. of* ▸ **~á** *and* ▸ **крýжево**

крýжев|о, а *nt.* lace.

круж|и́ть, ý, ~ишь *impf.*

[1] (*заставлять двигаться по кругу*) to whirl, spin round.
[2] (*кружиться*) to circle.

круж|и́ться, у́сь, ⁓и́шься *impf.* (*of* ▸ **за⁓**) to whirl, spin round; (*о птицах*) to circle; **у меня́ ⁓ится голова́** my head is going round, I feel giddy.

кру́жк|а, и *f.* mug.

круж|о́к, ка́ *m.*
[1] *dim. of* ▸ **круг.**
[2] (*группа*) circle, club; (*учебный*) study group.

круи́з, а *m.* cruise.

круп|а́, ы́, *pl.* **⁓ы** *f.* (*collect.*) groats; **гре́чневая к.** buckwheat; **ма́нная к.** semolina; **овся́ная к.** oatmeal.

крупномасшта́б|ный (⁓ен, ⁓на) *adj.* large-scale; (*fig.*) ambitious.

кру́п|ный (⁓ен, ⁓на́, ⁓но, ⁓ны́) *adj.*
[1] (*большой*) large, big; (*крупномасштабный*) large-scale; (*fig.*) (*значительный*) prominent, outstanding; **к. рога́тый скот** cattle; **⁓ный план** (*cinema*) close-up.
[2] (*песок*) coarse.
[3] (*важный*) important; (*серьёзный*) serious; **⁓ная неприя́тность** serious trouble.

крупье́ *m. indecl.* croupier.

кру|ти́ть, чу́, ⁓тишь *impf.*
[1] (*pf.* **с⁓**) to twist; to twirl.
[2] (*pf.* **за⁓**) (*кран, ручку*) to turn, wind.

кру|ти́ться, чу́сь, ⁓тишься *impf.*
[1] (*вращаться*) to turn, spin, revolve.
[2] (*кружиться*) to whirl.
[3] (*fig., coll.*) (*быть в хлопотах*) to be in a whirl.

кру́то *adv.*
[1] (*вверх, вниз*) steeply.
[2] (*внезапно*) suddenly; abruptly, sharply; **к. поверну́ть** to turn round sharply.
[3] (*coll.*) harshly; **к. распра́виться с кем-н.** to give s.o. short shrift.
[4] (*туго*) tightly.

крут|о́й (⁓, ⁓а́, ⁓о) adj.
[1] (*подъём*) steep.
[2] (*внезапный*) sudden; abrupt, sharp.
[3] (*coll.*) (*характер*) severe; (*меры*) drastic.
[4] (*cul.*) (*каша*) thick; **⁓о́е яйцо́** hard-boiled egg.
[5] (*sl.*) (*отличный*) cool; (*сильный и властный*) tough; (*влиятельный*) influential; (*богатый*) well-off.

кру́|че *comp. of* ▸ **⁓то́й** *and* ▸ **⁓то**

кру|чу́, ⁓тишь *see* ▸ **⁓ти́ть**

круше́ни|е, я *nt.*
[1] (*авария*) crash; (*судна*) wreck; **потерпе́ть к.** (*поезд, самолёт*) to crash; (*корабль*) to be wrecked.
[2] (*fig.*) (*надежд; коммунизма*) collapse.

круш|и́ть, у́, и́шь *impf.* to destroy (*also fig.*).

крыжо́вник, а *m.* gooseberry.

крыла́т|ый *adj.* winged (*also fig.*): **⁓ые слова́** pithy saying(s); **⁓ая раке́та** cruise missile.

крыл|о́, а́, *pl.* **⁓ья, ⁓ьев** *nt.* (*птицы, самолёта, дома*) wing; (*мельницы*) sail, vane; (*автомобиля*) wing, mudguard (*Br.*), fender (*US*).

крыл|ьцо́, ьца́, *pl.* **⁓ьца, ⁓е́ц, ⁓ьца́м** *nt.* porch.

Крым, а, о ⁓е, в ⁓у́ *m.* the Crimea.

кры́с|а, ы *f.* rat.

кры́тый *adj.* covered; sheltered; **к. ры́нок** covered market.

кры́ш|а, и *f.* roof; (*coll.*) (*преступная группировка, охранное предприятие и т. п., обеспечивающие защиту или покровительсвтво*) protection, front.

кры́шк|а, и *f.*
[1] (*кастрюли, банки, чемодана*) lid; (*люка*) cover.
[2] (*coll.*) death, end; **ему́ к.** he's done for; he's finished.

крю|к, ка́ *m.* (*pl.* **⁓ки́, ⁓ко́в**) hook.

крюч|о́к, ка́ *m.* hook; **спусково́й к.** trigger.

кря́ду *adv.* (*coll.*) running; in a row.

кряж, а *m.*
[1] (*горный*) (mountain) ridge.
[2] (*дубовый*) block, log.

кря́к|ать, аю *impf.* to quack.

кря́к|нуть, ну, нешь *pf.* to give a quack.

крях|те́ть, чу́, ти́шь *impf.* to groan.

ксёндз, а́ *m.* Roman Catholic (*esp. Polish*) priest.

ксенофо́б, а *m.* xenophobe.

ксенофо́би|я, и *f.* xenophobia.

ксероко́пи|я, и *f.* Xerox (*propr.*), photocopy.

ксе́рокс, а *m.*
[1] (*ксерография*) xerography.
[2] (*устройство*) Xerox (machine) (*propr.*), photocopier.
[3] (*coll.*) (*копия*) xerox, photocopy.

ксилофо́н, а *m.* (*mus.*) xylophone.

кста́ти *adv.*
[1] (*уместно*) to the point, apropos.
[2] (*своевременно*) opportunely; **э́тот пода́рок оказа́лся о́чень к.** the present has proved most welcome.
[3] (*coll.*) (*заодно*) at the same time, incidentally; **к., зайди́те, пожа́луйста, в апте́ку** will you please call at the chemist's at the same time.
[4] : **к. (сказа́ть)** by the way.

к/т (*abbr. of* **кинотеа́тр**) cinema.

кто, кого́, кому́, кем, о ком *pron.*
[1] (*interrog.*) (*какой человек?*) who; **к. э́то тако́й?** who is that?
[2] (*rel.*) (*в придаточных*) who (*normally after pron. antecedent*); **тот, к.** he who; **те, к.** those who.
[3] (*indef.*): **к. (бы) ни** who(so)ever; **к. бы то ни был** whoever it may be.
[4] (*indef.*): **к. ... к.** some ... others; (+ *adv.*): **разбежа́лись к. куда́** they scattered in all directions; **как они́ устро́ились? — к. как** how did they settle in? — in all sorts of ways.

кто́-либо, кого́-либо *pron.* = **кто́-нибудь**

кто́-нибудь, кого́-нибудь *pron.* (*в вопросах*) anyone, anybody; (*в утверждениях*) someone, somebody.

кто́-то, кого́-то *pron.* someone, somebody.

куб, а, *pl.* **⁓ы** *m.*
[1] (*math.*) cube; **два в ⁓е** two cubed.
[2] (*coll.*) (*кубический метр*) cubic metre (*Br.*), meter (*US*).

Ку́б|а, ы *f.* Cuba.
куби́зм, а *m.* (*art*) cubism.
ку́бик, а *m.* (*pl.*) (*игрушка*) blocks, bricks.
куби́н|ец, ца *m.* Cuban.
куби́н|ка, ки *f. of* ▸ **~ец**
куби́нский *adj.* Cuban.
ку́б|ок, ка *m.*
1 (*бокал*) goblet.
2 (*sport*) cup.
кубоме́тр, а *m.* cubic metre (*Br.*), meter (*US*).
кува́лд|а, ы *f.* sledgehammer.
Куве́йт, а *m.* Kuwait.
куве́йт|ец, ца *m.* Kuwaiti.
куве́йт|ка, ки *f. of* ▸ **~ец**
куве́йтский *adj.* Kuwaiti.
кувши́н, а *m.* jug; pitcher.
кувши́нк|а, и *f.* (*bot.*) water lily.
кувырк|а́ться, а́юсь *impf.* (*of* ▸ **~ну́ться**) to turn somersaults, go head over heels.
кувырк|ну́ться, ну́сь, нёшься *inst. pf. of* ▸ **~а́ться**
кувырко́м *adv.* (*coll.*) head over heels; topsy-turvy; **полете́ть к.** to go head over heels; **всё пошло́ к.** everything went haywire.
кугуа́р, а *m.* (*zool.*) puma, cougar.
куда́ *adv.*
1 (*interrog. and rel.*) where, whither; **к. ты идёшь?** where are you going?
2 : **к. (бы) ни** wherever.
3 (*coll.*) (*для чего*) what for; **к. вам сто́лько багажа́?** what do you want so much luggage for?
4 (+ *comp.*; *coll.*) (*гораздо*) much, far; **сего́дня мне к. лу́чше** I am much better today.
куда́-либо *adv.* = **куда́-нибудь**
куда́-нибудь *adv.* anywhere; somewhere.
куда́-то *adv.* somewhere.
куда́х|тать, чу, чешь *impf.* to cackle, cluck.
ку́др|и, е́й *no sg.* curls.
кудря́в|ый (~, ~а) *adj.* (*волосы*) curly; (*человек*) curly-headed.
кузе́н, а *m.* cousin.
кузи́н|а, ы *f.* cousin.
кузне́ц, а́ *m.* (black)smith; farrier.
кузне́чик, а *m.* grasshopper.
ку́зниц|а, ы *f.* forge, smithy.
ку́зов, а, *pl.* **~а́** *and* **~ы** *m.* (*автомобиля*) body.
кукаре́ка|ть, ю *impf.* to crow.
ку́киш, а *m.* (*coll.*) fig (*gesture of derision or contempt, consisting of thumb placed between index and middle fingers*); **показа́ть кому́-н. к.** *to make this gesture* (*cf.* to cock a snook, give the V-sign).
ку́к|ла, лы, *g. pl.* **~ол** *f.* doll; (*в театре*) puppet.
ку́колк|а, и *f.* (*zool.*) chrysalis, pupa.
ку́кольный *adj.* doll's; **к. теа́тр** puppet theatre (*Br.*), theater (*US*).
кукуру́з|а, ы *f.* maize, (sweet)corn; **возду́шная к.** popcorn.
кукуру́з|ный *adj. of* ▸ **~а**
куку́шк|а, и *f.* cuckoo; **часы́ с ~ой** cuckoo clock.
кула́к, а́ *m.* fist.
кул|ёк, ька́ *m.* (*paper*) bag.
кули́к, а́ *m.* (*zool.*) stint; sandpiper (*Calidris*).
кулинари́|я, и *f.*
1 (*искусство*) cookery.
2 (*магазин*) delicatessen.
кулина́рн|ый *adj.* culinary; **~ая кни́га** cookery book (*Br.*), cookbook (*US*); **к. отде́л** delicatessen counter.
кули́с|ы, ~ *pl.* (*sg.* **~а, ~ы** *f.*) (*theatr.*) wings; **за ~ами** behind the scenes (*also fig.*).
кули́ч, а́ *m.* Easter cake.
куло́н, а *m.* pendant.
кульби́т, а *m.* somersault.
ку́льман, а *m.* drawing-board.
кульмина́ци|я, и *f.* culmination.
культ, а *m.* cult; **к. ли́чности** personality cult; cult of personality.
культ... *comb. form, abbr. of* **культу́рный**
культиви́р|овать, ую *impf.* to cultivate (*also fig.*).
ку́льт|овый *adj. of* ▸ **~; ~овый режиссёр** cult filmmaker.
культу́р|а, ы *f.*
1 culture; **Министе́рство ~ы** Ministry of Culture.
2 (*уровень*) standard, level; **к. ре́чи** standard of speech.
3 (*usu. pl.*) (*agric.*) (*растение*) crop; **зерновы́е ~ы** cereals; **кормовы́е ~ы** forage crops.
4 : **физи́ческая к.** physical education.
культури́зм, а *m.* bodybuilding.
культу́р|ный (~ен, ~на) *adj.*
1 (*человек, общество*) cultured, cultivated.
2 (*уровень, связи, обмен*) cultural.
3 (*agric., hort.*) (*не дикий*) cultured; cultivated.
кум, а, *pl.* **~овья́, ~овьёв** *m.* godfather of one's child; father of one's godchild.
кум|а́, ы́ *f.* godmother of one's child; mother of one's godchild.
куми́р, а *m.* idol (*also fig.*).
кунжу́т, а *m.* (*bot.*) sesame.
куни́ц|а, ы *f.* (*zool.*) marten.
купа́льник, а *m.* bathing costume (*Br.*), bathing suit (*US*), swimsuit.
купа́льный *adj.* bathing, swimming; **к. костю́м** bathing costume (*Br.*), bathing suit (*US*), swimsuit.
купа́|ть, ю *impf.* (*of* ▸ **вы́~** *and* ▸ **ис~**[1]) to bathe; to bath.
купа́|ться, юсь *impf.* (*of* ▸ **вы́~** *and* ▸ **ис~**) (*плавать*) to swim, bathe; (*в ванне*) to have, take a bath; **к. в луча́х сла́вы** to bask in glory.
купе́ *nt. indecl.* compartment (*of railway carriage*).
куп|е́ц, ца́ *m.* merchant.
куп|и́ть, лю́, ~́ишь *pf.* (*of* ▸ **покупа́ть**) to buy, purchase.
купле́т, а *m.*
1 (*строфа*) stanza, strophe, verse.
2 (*pl.*) (*сатирические песенки*) satirical ballad(s), song(s).
ку́пол, а, *pl.* **~а́** *m.* cupola, dome.

купóн, а *m.* coupon.
купю́р|а, ы *f.*
1 (*сокращение*) cut.
2 (*fin.*) (*деньги*) banknote; (*облигация*) band.
кураг|á, и́ *f.* (*collect.*) dried apricots.
курáнт|ы, ов *no sg.* chiming clock; chimes.
курáтор, а *m.*
1 (*попечитель*) curator.
2 (*студента*) (academic) supervisor.
кургáн, а *m.* burial mound.
курд, а *m.* Kurd.
кýрдский *adj.* Kurdish.
курдя́нк|а, и *f. of* ▶ **курд**
курéни|е, я *nt.*
1 (*действие*) smoking.
2 (*ладан*) incense.
кури́льщик, а *m.* smoker.
кури́льщи|ца, цы *f. of* ▶ **~к**
кури́ный *adj.* (*яйцо*) hen's; (*бульон*) chicken.
кури́р|овать, ую *impf.* to supervise.
кури́тельн|ый *adj.* smoking; **~ая (кóмната)** smoking room.
кур|и́ть, ю́, ~́ишь *impf.* (*of* ▶ **по~ 1**)
1 to smoke; **к. трýбку** to smoke a pipe.
2 (+ *a.* or *i.*) to burn.
кýр|ица, ицы, *pl.* **~ы, ~** *f.* hen.
курнóс|ый (~, ~а) *adj.* snub-nosed.
кур|óк, кá *m.* hammer; **взвести́ к.** to cock; **спусти́ть к.** to pull the trigger.
куропáтк|а, и *f.* (*zool.*): **(сéрая) к.** partridge; **бéлая к.** willow grouse.
курóрт, а *m.* holiday resort; **водолечéбный к.** spa.
курóрт|ный *adj. of* ▶ **~**
курс, а *m.*
1 course; **взять к. на сéвер** to steer northwards; (*pol.*) policy; **к. лéкций/обучéния** course of lectures/instruction; **быть на трéтьем ~́е** to be in the third year (*of a course of studies*); **держáть к. (на** + *a.*) to head (for); **быть в ~́е (дéла)** to be au courant, be in the know.
2 (*fin.*) exchange rate; **рáзница кýрсов (валю́т)** difference in exchange rates.
курсáнт, а *m.* (*mil.*) cadet.
курси́в, а *m.* italic type, italics; **~ом** in italics.
курс|овóй *adj. of* ▶ **~**; **~овáя рабóта** project; short dissertation.
курсóр, а *m.* (*comput.*) cursor.
кýртк|а, и *f.* jacket; anorak.
курчáв|ый (~, ~а) *adj.* (*волосы*) curly; (*человек*) curly-haired.
кýр|ы *see* ▶ **~ица**
курьёз|ный (~ен, ~на) *adj.* curious; funny.
курьéр, а *m.* (*в учреждении*) messenger; (*дипломатический*) courier.
курьéр|ский *adj.*
1 *adj. of* ▶ **~.**
2 fast; **к. пóезд** express.
куря́тин|а, ы *f.* (*coll.*) chicken (*as meat*).
куря́тник, а *m.* henhouse.
кур|я́щий *pres. part. act. of* ▶ **~и́ть;** *as n.* **к., ~я́щего** smoker.
кусá|ть, ю *impf.* (*о собаке, о человеке*) to bite; (*о пчеле*) to sting.
кусá|ться, юсь *impf.*
1 (*о собаке*) to bite; (*о крапиве, о пчеле*) to sting.
2 (*кусать друг друга*) to bite one another.
кусáч|ки, ек *no sg.* pliers; wire-cutters.
кус|óк, кá *m.* piece, bit; (*хлеба*) slice; (*сахара*) lump; (*мыла*) cake.
куст, á *m.* bush, shrub; **спря́татся в ~ы́** (*fig.*) to scarper, make o.s. scarce.
кустáрник, а *m.* (*collect.*) bushes, shrubs; shrubbery.
кустáрн|ый *adj.*
1 handicraft; **~ые издéлия** craftwork.
2 (*fig., pej.*) amateurish, primitive.
кустáр|ь, я́ *m.* craftsman.
ку|ти́ть, чý, ~́тишь *impf.* (*of* ▶ **~тнýть**) to carouse; to go on the booze.
кут|нýть, нý, нёшь *inst. pf. of* ▶ **~и́ть**
кухáрк|а, и *f.* cook.
кýх|ня, ни, *g. pl.* **~онь** *f.*
1 (*помещение*) kitchen.
2 (*кушанья*) cooking, cuisine.
кýхонн|ый *adj.* kitchen; **~ая плитá** kitchen range.
кýц|ый (~, ~а, ~е) *adj.*
1 (*животное*) tailless; bob-tailed.
2 (*одежда*) skimpy; (*fig.*) limited, abbreviated.
кýч|а, и *f.*
1 heap, pile; (*людей*) group; (*coll.*): **вали́ть всё в однý ~у** to lump everything together.
2 (*coll.*; + *g.*) heaps (of), piles (of); **у негó к. дéнег** he has heaps of money.
кýчер, а, *pl.* **~á, ~óв** *m.* coachman.
кýша|ть, ю *impf.* (*of* ▶ **по~** *and* ▶ **с~**) (*in polite invitation to eat*) to eat, have.
кушéтк|а, и *f.* couch.
ку|ю́, ёшь *see* ▶ **ковáть**
к/ф (*abbr. of* **кинофи́льм**) (cinema) film, movie.
Кыргызстáн, а *m.* Kyrgyzstan.
кювéт, а *m.* ditch (*at side of road*).

Лл

л (*abbr. of* **литр**) l, litre(s) (*Br.*), liter(s) (*US*).
лабири́нт, а *m.* (*in var. senses*) labyrinth, maze.
лабора́нт, а *m.* laboratory assistant.
лабора́нт|ка, ки *f. of* ▸**~**
лаборато́ри|я, и *f.* laboratory.
лабрадо́р, а *m.* labrador (*dog*).
ла́в|а, ы *f.* (*вулканическая*) lava.
лава́нд|а, ы *f.* (*bot.*) lavender.
лава́ш, а *m.* lavash (*flat white loaf*).
лави́н|а, ы *f.* avalanche (*also fig.*).
лави́р|овать, ую *impf.*
1 (*naut.*) to tack.
2 (*fig.*) to manoeuvre (*Br.*), maneuver (*US*).
ла́вк|а¹, и *f.* (*скамья*) bench.
ла́вк|а², и *f.* (*магазин*) small shop.
лавр, а *m.*
1 (*bot.*) laurel; bay (tree).
2 (*pl., fig.*) laurels.
ла́вр|о́вый *adj. of* ▸**~**; **~о́вый вено́к** laurel wreath; (*fig.*) laurels; **~о́вый лист** bay leaf.
ла́гер|ный *adj. of* ▸**~ь**
ла́гер|ь, я *m.*
1 (*pl.* **~я́, ~е́й**) camp; (*mil.*): **располага́ться, стоя́ть ~ем** to camp, be encamped.
2 (*pl.* **~и, ~ей**) (*fig.*) camp.
лагу́н|а, ы *f.* lagoon.
лад, а, о ~́е, в ~у́, *pl.* **~ы́, ~о́в** *m.*
1 (*mus. and fig.*) (*согласие*) harmony, concord; **жить в ~у́ (с +** *i.*) to live in harmony (with); **быть не в ~а́х (с +** *i.*) to be at odds (with); (*coll.*) **идти́, пойти́ на л.** to go well, be successful.
2 (*способ*) manner, way; **на свой л.** in one's own way.
ла́дан, а *m.* incense; **дыша́ть на л.** (*fig., coll.*) to have one foot in the grave.
ла́|дить, жу, дишь *impf.* (**с** + *i.*) to get on (with), be on good terms (with); **они́ не ~дят** they don't get on.
ла́дно *particle* (*coll.*) all right! OK!
ладо́н|ь, и *f.* palm (*of hand*); **быть (ви́дным) как на ~и** to be clearly visible.
лазаре́т, а *m.* (*mil.*) field hospital; (*naut.*) sickbay.
ла́з|ать, аю *impf.* (*coll.*) = **~ить**
лазе́йк|а, и *f.* hole, gap; (*fig., coll.*) loophole.
ла́зер, а *m.* (*phys., tech.*) laser.
ла́зер|ный *adj. of* ▸**~**; **л. при́нтер** laser printer.
ла́|зить, жу, зишь *impf.* (*indet. of* ▸**лезть**)
1 (**на** + *a.*, **по** + *d.*) to climb, clamber (on to, up); **л. по дере́вьям** to climb trees.
2 (**в** + *a.*) to climb (into), get (into).
лазу́р|ный (~ен, ~на) *adj.* sky blue, azure; **Л. Бе́рег** French Riviera.
ла|й, я *m.* bark(ing).
ла́йк|а¹, и *f.* (*собака*) husky.
ла́йк|а², и *f.* (*кожа*) kidskin.
ла́йнер, а *m.* (*naut., aeron.*) liner.
лак, а *m.* varnish, lacquer; **л. для воло́с** hair spray.
лаке́|й, я *m.* footman; lackey, flunkey (*also fig., pej.*).
лакиро́в|анный *p.p.p. of* ▸**~а́ть** *and adj.* varnished, lacquered; **~анная ко́жа** patent leather.
лакир|ова́ть, у́ю *impf.* (*of* ▸**от~**) to varnish, lacquer; (*fig., pej.*) to varnish.
ла́к|овый *adj. of* ▸**~**; varnished, lacquered; **~овые ту́фли** patent leather shoes.
ла́ком|ый (~, ~а) *adj.* tasty, delicious; **л. кусо́(че)к** tasty morsel (*also fig.*).
лакони́ч|ный (~ен, ~на) *adj.* laconic.
лакри́ц|а, ы *f.* (*bot.*) liquorice.
ла́м|а, ы *m.* llama.
Ла-Ма́нш, а *m.* the (English) Channel.
ла́мп|а, ы *f.*
1 lamp; **л. дневно́го све́та** fluorescent lamp.
2 (*radio*) valve; tube.
лампа́д|а, ы *f.* icon lamp.
лампа́с, а *m.* stripe (*down side of trousers*).
ла́мпочк|а, и *f.*
1 *dim. of* ▸**ла́мпа.**
2 (electric light) bulb; **стова́ттная л.** 100-watt bulb.
3: **мне э́то до ~и** (*sl.*) I couldn't care less about it.
лангу́ст, а *m.* spiny lobster.
ландша́фт, а *m.* landscape.
ла́ндыш, а *m.* lily of the valley.
ланце́т, а *m.* (*med.*) lancet; **вскрыть ~ом** to lance.
ланч, а *m.* lunch.
Лао́с, а *m.* Laos.
лао́с|ец, ца *m.* Laotian.
лао́с|ка, ки *f. of* ▸**~ец**
лао́сский *adj.* Laotian.
ла́п|а, ы *f.* (*животного*) paw; (*птицы*) foot; (*fig., coll.*): (*нога*) big foot; (*рука*) big hand; **попа́сть в ~ы к кому́-н.** to fall into s.o.'s clutches;
лапида́р|ный (~ен, ~на) *adj.* lapidary, terse.
ла́п|оть, тя, *pl.* **~ти, ~те́й** *m.*
1 (*обувь*) bast shoe.
2 (*coll.*) (*о человеке*) oaf, bumpkin.
лапш|а́, и́ *f.*
1 noodles.
2 (*суп*) noodle soup.
лар|ёк, ька́ *m.* stall.
лар|е́ц, ца́ *m.* casket.
ларинги́т, а *m.* laryngitis.
ла́ск|а, и *f.*
1 caress, endearment; (*pl.*) petting.

2 (*доброе отношение*) kindness.
ласка́|ть, ю *impf.* to caress, fondle, pet; (*о ветре, о воде*) to caress.
ласка́|ться, юсь *impf.* (**к** + *d.*) to show affection (towards); to snuggle up to; (*о собаке*) to fawn (on).
ла́сков|ый (~, ~а) *adj.* affectionate, tender; (*fig.*) gentle; **л. ве́тер** gentle wind.
лассо́ *nt. indecl.* lasso.
ласт, а *m.* flipper.
ла́стик, а *m.* (*coll.*) (*для стирания написанного*) rubber (*Br.*), eraser.
ла́сточк|а, и *f.* swallow; **берегова́я л.** sand martin; **городска́я л.** (house) martin.
латви́|ец, йца *m.* Latvian.
латви́|йка, йки *f. of* ▶ **~ец**
латви́йский *adj.* Latvian.
Ла́тви|я, и *f.* Latvia.
ла́текс, а *m.* latex.
лати́ниц|а, ы *f.* Roman alphabet, Roman letters.
латиноамерика́н|ец, ца *m.* Latin American.
латиноамерика́н|ка, ки *f. of* ▶ **~ец**
латиноамерика́нский *adj.* Latin American.
лати́нский *adj.* Latin; **Лати́нская Аме́рика** Latin America.
лату́к, а *m.* (*bot.*) lettuce.
лату́н|ь, и *f.* brass.
латы́н|ь, и *f.* Latin (*language*).
латы́ш, а́, *pl.* **~и́, ~е́й** *m.* Latvian.
латы́ш|ка, ки *f. of* ▶ **~**
латы́шский *adj.* Latvian.
лауреа́т, а *m.* prizewinner; laureate; **л. Но́белевской пре́мии** Nobel prizewinner.
ла́цкан, а, *pl.* **~ы, ~ов** *m.* lapel.
лачу́г|а, и *f.* (*coll.*) hovel, shack.
ла́|ять, ю, ешь *impf.* to bark; (*о гончих*) to bay.
лба, лбу *etc., see* ▶ **лоб**
лгать, лгу, лжёшь, лгут, *past* **лгал, лгала́, лга́ло** *impf.* (*of* **со~**) to lie; to tell lies.
лгун, а́ *m.* liar.
лгу́н|ья, ьи, *g. pl.* **~ий** *f. of* ▶ **~**
лебёдк|а, и *f.* (*tech.*) winch, windlass.
ле́бед|ь, я, *pl.* **~и, ~е́й** *m.* swan.
лев, льва *m.*
1 (*животное*) lion; **морско́й л.** sea lion.
2 **Л.** (*созвездие*) Leo.
левита́ци|я, и *f.* levitation.
левобере́жный *adj.* left-bank.
левш|а́, и́, *i.* **~о́й,** *g. pl.* **~е́й** *c.g.* left-hander.
ле́в|ый *adj.*
1 left; (*со стороны левой руки*) left-hand; (*naut.*) port; **л. борт** port side; **~ая сторона́** left-hand side.
2 (*coll.*) (*незаконный*) illegal, unofficial; **~ая рабо́та** work on the side.
3 (*pol.*) left-wing; *as n.* **л., ~ого** *m.* left-winger; (*pl.*; *collect.*) the left.
лега́в|ая, ой *f.*: **(длинношёрст(н)ая) л.** setter; **(короткошёрст(н)ая) л.** pointer.
легализа́ци|я, и *f.* legalization.
легализ|ова́ть, у́ю *impf. and pf.* to legalize.
лега́л|ьный (~ен, ~ьна) *adj.* legal.
леге́нд|а, ы *f.* legend; (*на карте*) key, legend.
легенда́р|ный (~ен, ~на) *adj.* legendary.
легио́н, а *m.* legion; (*fig.*) (*очень много*) plethora.
легионе́р, а *m.*
1 (*hist.*) legionary.
2 (*sport*) (*игрок-иностранец*) foreign player.
легити́м|ный (~ен, ~на) *adj.* (*власть*) legitimate.
лёг|кий (~ок, ~ка́, ~ко́, *pl.* **~ки́)** *adj.*
1 (*на вес*) light; **л. за́втрак** light breakfast; **~ая промы́шленность** light industry.
2 (*нетрудный*) easy; **у него́ л. хара́ктер** he is easy to get on with; **~кая атле́тика** (*sport*) athletics (*Br.*), track and field (*US*).
3 (*незначительный*) light; slight; **~кая просту́да** slight cold.
легко́ *adv.* (*несильно*) lightly; (*без труда*) easily; (*слегка*) slightly; **э́то ему́ л. даётся** it comes easily to him; *as pred.* it is easy; **л. сказа́ть** easier said than done!
легкоатле́т, а *m.* (track and field) athlete.
легкове́р|ный (~ен, ~на) *adj.* credulous, gullible.
легково́й *adj.* passenger (*conveyance*); **л. автомоби́ль** (motor) car.
лёгк|ое, ого *nt.* (*anat.*) lung; **односторо́ннее, двусторо́ннее воспале́ние ~их** single, double pneumonia.
легкомы́слен|ный (~, ~на) *adj.* thoughtless; flippant, frivolous.
лёгкост|ь, и *f.*
1 (*веса*) lightness.
2 (*нетрудность*) easiness.
3 (*свобода*) ease; **с ~ью** with ease.
ле́г|че *comp. of* ▶ **~кий** *and* ▶ **~ко́;** (*as pred.*): **больно́му л.** the patient is feeling better; **мне от э́того не л.** I am none the better for it.
лёд, льда, о льде́, во/на льду́ *m.* ice; **л. сло́ман** (*fig.*) the ice is broken.
ледене́|ть, ю *impf.* (*of* ▶ **о~**) to freeze (*intrans.*).
леден|е́ц, ца́ *m.* fruit drop.
ледни́к, а́ *m.* glacier.
леднико́вый *adj.* glacial; **л. пери́од** ice age.
ледо́в|ый *adj.* ice; **~ое пла́вание** Arctic voyage; **Ледо́вое побо́ище** the Battle on the Ice (*fought on 5 April 1242 between the army of Alexander Nevsky and the Teutonic Knights*).
ледоко́л, а *m.* ice-breaker.
ледору́б, а *m.* ice axe.
ледохо́д, а *m.* drifting of ice.
лед|яно́й *adj.*
1 *adj. of* ▶ **~;** **~яна́я гора́/го́рка** ice slope (*for tobogganing*).
2 (*ветер; взгляд*) icy; ice-cold.
лёжа *adv.* lying down, in lying position.
леж|а́ть, у́, и́шь *impf.* (*in var. senses*) to lie; (*о предметах*) to be (situated); **л. в больни́це** to be in hospital; **на нём ~и́т отве́тственность за э́то** it is his responsibility.

лежа́ч|ий *adj.* lying, recumbent; **л. больно́й** bed patient.
ле́зви|е, я *nt.* blade.
лез|ть, у, ешь, *past* **~, ~ла** *impf.* (*of* ▶**по~ 1**), *det. of* ▶**ла́зить**
1 (**на** + *a.*, **по** + *d.*) (*взбираться вверх*) to climb (up, on to); **л. на де́рево** to climb a tree.
2 (**в** + *a.*, **под** + *a.*) (*проникать*) to climb, clamber, crawl (through, into, under).
3 (*тайком*) to sneak.
4 (**в** + *a.*) (*проникать рукой*) to thrust the hand (into).
5 (*coll.*) (*вмешиваться*) to interfere; **л. не в своё де́ло** to poke one's nose into s.o. else's affairs.
лейбл, а *m.* (*comm.*, *mus.*) label.
лейбори́ст, а *m.* (*pol.*) Labourite (*Br.*), Laborite (*US*); labour supporter (*Br.*), labor supporter (*US*).
лейбори́стск|ий *adj.* (*pol.*) Labour (*Br.*), Labor (*US*); **~ая па́ртия** Labour Party (*Br.*), Labor Party (*US*).
ле́йк|а, и *f.*
1 (*для поливки*) watering can.
2 (*coll.*) (*воронка*) funnel.
лейкеми́|я, и *f.* (*med.*) leukaemia (*Br.*), leukemia (*US*).
лейкопла́стыр|ь, я *m.* sticking plaster (*Br.*), adhesive tape (*US*), Band-Aid (*propr.*) (*US*).
лейкоци́т, а *m.* (*physiol.*) leucocyte.
лейтена́нт, а *m.* lieutenant.
лека́л|о, а *nt.* (*чертёжный инструмент*) French curve.
лека́рственный *adj.* (*растение*, *настой*) medicinal; **л. препара́т** medicine, drug.
лека́рств|о, а *nt.* medicine; **л. от ка́шля** cough medicine.
ле́ксик|а, и *f.* vocabulary; (*всего языка*) lexis.
ле́ктор, а *m.* (*в учебном заведении*) lecturer; (*выступающий*) speaker.
ле́кци|я, и *f.* lecture; **чита́ть ~ю** to lecture, deliver a lecture.
леле́|ять, ю *impf.*
1 to coddle, pamper.
2 (*fig.*) to cherish, foster; **л. мечту́** to cherish a hope.
ле́мминг, а *m.* (*zool.*) lemming.
лён, льна *m.* (*bot.*) flax.
лени́в|ец, ца *m.* (*zool.*) sloth.
лени́в|ый (~, ~а) *adj.* lazy, idle; (*походка*, *вид*) sluggish.
Ленингра́д, а *m.* (*hist.*) Leningrad.
лен|и́ться, ю́сь, ~ишься *impf.*
1 to be lazy, idle.
2 (+ *inf.*) to be too lazy (to).
ле́нт|а, ы *f.* (*украшение*; *орденская*) ribbon; (*магнитная*) tape; (*фильм*) film.
лентя́|й, я *m.* lazybones.
лен|ь, и *f.*
1 laziness.
2 *as pred.* (+ *d. and inf.*; *coll.*) to feel too lazy (to), not to feel like; **ему́ бы́ло л. вы́ключить ра́дио** he was too lazy to turn the radio off.
леопа́рд, а *m.* leopard.
лепест|о́к, ка́ *m.* petal.
лепе|та́ть, чу́, ~чешь *impf.* to babble.
лепёшк|а, и *f.* flat cake.
леп|и́ть, лю́, ~ишь *impf.*
1 (*pf.* **с~**²) to model, fashion; to mould.
2 (*pf.* **на~**¹) (*coll.*) (*наклеить*) to stick (on).
ле́пк|а, и *f.* modelling (*Br.*), modeling (*US*).
лепни́н|а, ы *f.* (*collect.*) moulding(s) (*Br.*), molding(s) (*US*).
лес, а (у), *pl.* **~а́** *m.*
1 (**в ~у́**) (*большой*) forest, (*небольшой*) wood(s); **вы́йти из ~а (и́з ~у)** to come out of the wood; **тропи́ческий л.** rainforest.
2 (**в ~е**) (*sg. only*; *collect.*) timber (*Br.*), lumber (*US*).
лес|а́¹ *pl. of* ▶**~**
лес|а́², **о́в** (*строительные*) scaffolding.
лесбия́нк|а, и *f.* lesbian.
ле́ск|а, и *f.* fishing line.
лесни́ч|ий, его *m.* forestry officer; forest warden.
лесн|о́й *adj. of* ▶**~**; **л. двор, склад** timber yard; **~о́е хозя́йство** forestry.
лесопа́рк, а *m.* wooded park.
лесопи́лк|а, и *f.* sawmill.
лесопова́л, а *m.* tree felling.
лесору́б, а *m.* lumberjack.
ле́стниц|а, ы *f.* stairs, staircase; (*приставная*) ladder; **пожа́рная л.** fire escape; **складна́я л.** steps, stepladder; **служе́бная л.** career ladder.
ле́стни|чный *adj. of* ▶**~ца; ~чная кле́тка** stairwell; **~чная площа́дка** landing.
ле́ст|ный (~ен, ~на) *adj.* flattering.
лест|ь, и *f.* flattery.
лет|а́, ~ *pl.*
1 years; age; **с де́тских лет** from childhood; **сре́дних лет** middle-aged.
2 *g. pl.* (*as g. pl. of* ▶**год**) years; **ско́лько вам ~?** how old are you?; **ему́ бо́льше, ме́ньше сорока́ ~** he is over, under forty.
лет|а́ть, а́ю *indet. of* ▶**~е́ть**
лета́ющ|ий *adj.*: **~ая таре́лка** (*coll.*) flying saucer.
ле|те́ть, чу́, ти́шь *impf.* (*of* ▶**по~ 1**), *det. of* ▶**лета́ть**
1 to fly.
2 (*fig.*) (*мчаться*) to fly; to rush, tear.
3 (*fig.*, *coll.*) (*падать*) to fall, drop (*intrans.*).
ле́тний *adj.* summer; **л. сад** pleasure garden(s).
ле́т|о, а, *nt.* summer; **ба́бье л.** Indian summer; **ско́лько ~, ско́лько зим** it's been ages!
лето(и)счисле́ни|е, я *nt.* chronology.
ле́том *adv.* in summer.
ле́топис|ь, и *f.* chronicle, annals.
лету́ч|ий *adj.*
1 flying; **~ая мышь** bat.
2 (*chem.*) volatile.
лётчик, а *m.* pilot; **л.-испыта́тель** test pilot; **л.-истреби́тель** fighter pilot.
лече́бниц|а, ы *f.* clinic (*usu. psychiatric or veterinary*).
лече́бный *adj.*
1 (*учреждение*; *средства*) medical.

2 (*свойства; мазь*) medicinal; **л. препарат** medicine, drug.
лечени|е, я *nt.* (medical) treatment; **амбулаторное л.** outpatient treatment.
леч|ить, у, ~ишь *impf.* to treat (*medically*).
леч|иться, усь, ~ишься *impf.*
1 (**от** + *g.*) to receive, undergo (medical) treatment (for).
2 (**у** + *g.*) to be s.o.'s patient.
ле|чу[1], **тишь** *see* ▶ **~теть**
леч|у[2], **~ишь** *see* ▶ **~ить**
лечь, лягу, ляжешь, лягут, *past* **лёг, легла,** *imper.* **ляг, лягте** *pf.* (*of* ▶ **ложиться**) to lie (down); **л. в постель, л. спать** to go to bed; **л. в больницу** to go into hospital.
леш|ий, его *m.* wood goblin.
лещ, а *m.* bream (*fish*).
лжец, а *m.* liar.
лжёшь *see* ▶ **лгать**
лжив|ый (~, ~а) *adj.*
1 (*человек*) lying; mendacious.
2 (*улыбка*) false, deceitful.
ли (ль)
1 *interrog. particle* **возможно ли?** is it possible?
2 *conj.* whether, if; **не знаю, придёт ли он** I don't know whether he is coming.
3 : **ли... ли** whether ... or; **сегодня ли, завтра ли** whether today or tomorrow.
лиан|а, ы *f.* (*bot.*) liana.
либерал, а *m.* liberal; **л.-демократ** Liberal Democrat.
либерализаци|я, и *n.* liberalization.
либерализм, а *m.* liberalism.
либерализ|овать, ую *impf. and pf.* to liberalize.
либерал|ьный (~ен, ~ьна) *adj.* liberal.
либери|ец, йца *m.* Liberian.
либери|йка, йки *f. of* ▶ **~ец**
либерийский *adj.* Liberian.
Либери|я, и *f.* Liberia.
либо *conj.* or; **л. ... л.** (either) ... or.
либретто *nt. indecl.* libretto.
Ливан, а *m.* (the) Lebanon.
ливан|ец, ца *m.* Lebanese.
ливан|ка, ки *f. of* ▶ **~ец**
ливанский *adj.* Lebanese.
лив|ень, ня *m.* heavy shower, downpour.
ливер, а *m.* (*cul.*) offal.
ливер|ный *adj. of* ▶ **~; ~ная колбаса** offal sausage.
ливи|ец, йца *m.* Libyan.
ливи|йка, йки *f. of* ▶ **~ец**
ливийский *adj.* Libyan.
Ливи|я, и *f.* Libya.
лиг|а, и *f.* league.
лидер, а *m.* leader.
лидир|овать, ую *impf.* to lead, be in the lead.
ли|зать, жу, ~жешь *impf.* (*of* ▶ **~знуть**) to lick.
лизинг, а *m.* (*econ.*) leasing.
лиз|нуть, ну, нёшь *inst. pf. of* ▶ **~ать**
лизоблюд, а *m.* (*coll., pej.*) lickspittle, bootlicker.
ликвидаци|я, и *f.*
1 (*comm.*) liquidation.
2 (*pol., etc.*) (*отмена*) liquidation; elimination, abolition.
ликвидир|овать, ую *impf. and pf.*
1 (*comm.*) to liquidate, wind up.
2 (*отменять*) to liquidate; to eliminate, abolish.
ликвид|ный (~ен, ~на) *adj.* (*fin.*) liquid; **~ные активы, средства** liquid assets.
ликёр, а *m.* liqueur.
ликёроводочный *adj.*: **~ завод** distillery.
лик|овать, ую *impf.* to rejoice, exult.
лилипут, а *m.* Lilliputian, midget.
лили|я, и *f.* lily.
лиловый *adj.* purple.
лиман, а *m.* estuary; (*солёное озеро*) salt marshes.
лимит, а *m.* (*норма*) quota; (**на** + *a.*) (*ограничение*) limit (on).
лимон, а *m.* lemon.
лимонад, а *m.*
1 lemonade; lemon squash.
2 (*любой газированный напиток*) fizzy drink.
лимузин, а *m.* limousine.
лимф|а, ы *f.* (*physiol.*) lymph.
лингвист, а *m.* linguist.
лингвистик|а, и *f.* linguistics.
лингвистический *adj.* linguistic.
линейк|а, и *f.*
1 (*на бумаге*) (ruled) line.
2 (*инструмент*) ruler.
3 (*строй в шеренгу*) line; parade.
линз|а, ы *f.* lens.
лини|я, и *f.* line; (*fig.*): policy.
линолеум, а *m.* linoleum.
линя|ть, ет *impf.* (*of* ▶ **по~**)
1 (*о материи*) to fade; (*о краске*) to run.
2 (*о животных*) to moult (*Br.*), molt (*US*).
лип|а, ы *f.* lime (tree).
лип|кий (~ок, ~ка, ~ко) *adj.* sticky, adhesive.
лир|а, ы *f.* (*музыкальный инструмент*) lyre.
лирик|а, и *f.* lyric poetry.
лирический *adj.*
1 (*поэзия, сопрано*) lyric.
2 (*настроение*) lyrical.
лис|а, ы, *pl.* **~ы** *f.* fox; **чернобурая л.** silver fox.
лис|ёнок, ёнка, *pl.* **~ята, ~ят** *m.* fox cub.
лис|ий *adj. of* ▶ **~а**
лисиц|а, ы *f.* fox; vixen.
Лиссабон, а *m.* Lisbon.
лист[1], **а,** *pl.* **~ья, ~ьев** *m.* (*растения*) leaf.
лист[2], **а,** *pl.* **~ы, ~ов** *m.*
1 (*бумаги*) sheet.
2 : **опросный л.** questionnaire; **охранный л.** safe conduct.
листа|ть, ю *impf.* (*coll.*) to leaf through.
листв|а, ы *f.* (*collect.*) leaves, foliage.
лиственниц|а, ы *f.* (*bot.*) larch.
лиственный *adj.* (*bot.*) deciduous.

листо́вк|а, и *f.* leaflet.

лист|о́к, ка́ *m.*
1 *dim. of* ▸ **~**[1,2].
2 (*листовка*) leaflet.
3 (*бланк*) form.

листопа́д, а *m.* fall of the leaves.

лита́вр|ы, ~ *pl.* (*sg.* **~а, ~ы** *f.*) kettledrum.

Литв|а́, ы́ *f.* Lithuania.

лите́йный *adj.* founding, casting.

литера́тор, а *m.* man of letters.

литерату́р|а, ы *f.* literature; **худо́жественная л.** fiction.

литерату́р|ный (~ен, ~на) *adj.* literary.

литературове́д, а *m.* literary critic.

лито́в|ец, ца *m.* Lithuanian.

лито́в|ка, ки *f. of* ▸ **~ец**

лито́вский *adj.* Lithuanian.

лит|о́й *adj.* cast; **~а́я сталь** cast steel.

литр, а *m.* litre (*Br.*), liter (*US*).

литурги́|я, и *f.* liturgy.

лить, лью, льёшь, *past* **лил, лила́, ли́ло,** *imper.* **лей** *impf.*
1 to pour (*trans. and intrans.*); **л. слёзы** to shed tears; **дождь льёт как из ведра́** it is raining cats and dogs.
2 (*tech.*) to found, cast, mould (*Br.*), mold (*US*).

ли́|ться, льётся, *past* **~лся, ~ла́сь** *impf.*
1 to flow; to stream, pour.
2 *pass. of* ▸ **~ть**

лифт, а *m.* lift, elevator.

лифтёр, а *m.* lift operator.

ли́фчик, а *m.* bra.

лих|о́й (~, ~а́, ~о, ~и́) *adj.* (*coll.*) dashing, spirited; jaunty.

лихора́дк|а, и *f.*
1 fever (*also fig.*); **сенна́я л.** hay fever.
2 (*на губах*) cold sore.

лицев|о́й *adj.*
1 (*anat.*) facial.
2 exterior; **~а́я сторона́** (*здания*) facade, front; (*материи*) right side; (*монеты*) obverse.
3 (*bookkeeping*): **л. счёт** personal account.

лице́|й, я *m.* lycée.

лицеме́р, а *m.* hypocrite.

лицеме́ри|е, я *nt.* hypocrisy.

лицеме́р|ный (~ен, ~на) *adj.* hypocritical.

лицензио́нный *adj.* (*econ.*) (*сделка*) licensing; (*произведённый по лицензии*) licensed.

лицензи́р|овать, ую *impf. and pf.* (*econ.*) to license.

лице́нзи|я, и *f.* (*econ.*) licence (*Br.*), license (*US*).

лиц|о́, а́, *pl.* **~а** *nt.*
1 face; **черты́ ~а́** features; **сказа́ть в л. кому́-н.** to say to s.o.'s face; **знать кого́-н. в л.** to know s.o. by sight; **быть к ~у́** (+ *d.*) to suit, become; (*fig.*) to become, befit; **~о́м к ~у́** face to face; **пе́ред ~о́м** (+ *g.*) in the face (of).
2 (*наружная сторона*) exterior; (*материи*) right side; (*fig.*): **показа́ть това́р ~о́м** to show sth. to advantage; to make the best of sth.
3 (*человек*) person; **гражда́нское л.** civilian; **должностно́е л.** official; **духо́вное л.** clergyman; **в ~е́** (+ *g.*) in the person (of); **от ~а́** (+ *g.*) in the name (of), on behalf (of).
4 (*индивидуальный облик*) identity.

личи́нк|а, и *f.* larva, grub; maggot.

ли́чно *adv.* personally, in person.

ли́чност|ь, и *f.*
1 (*индивидуальность*) personality.
2 (*человек*) person, individual; **удостовере́ние ~и** identity card; **установи́ть чью-н. л.** to establish s.o.'s identity.

ли́чн|ый *adj.* personal; (*частный*) private; **~ая охра́на** bodyguard; **~ая со́бственность** personal property; **л. соста́в** staff.

лиша́йник, а *m.* (*bot.*) lichen.

лиш|а́ть(ся), а́ю(сь) *impf. of* ▸ **~и́ть(ся)**

лише́ни|е, я *nt.*
1 (*действие*) deprivation; **л. гражда́нских прав** (*leg.*) disenfranchisement.
2 (*usu. pl.*) (*недостаток*) privation, hardship.

лишён|ный (~, ~а́, ~о́) *p.p.p. of* ▸ **лиши́ть** *and adj.* (+ *g.*) lacking (in), devoid (of).

лиш|и́ть, у́, и́шь *pf.* (*of* ▸ **~а́ть**) (+ *g.*) to deprive (of); **л. кого́-н. насле́дства** to disinherit s.o.; **л. себя́ жи́зни** to take one's life.

лиш|и́ться, у́сь, и́шься *pf.* (*of* ▸ **~а́ться**) (+ *g.*) to lose, be deprived (of); **л. зре́ния** to lose one's sight.

ли́шн|ий *adj.*
1 (*избыточный*) superfluous; unnecessary; unwanted.
2 (*запасной*) spare, odd; **л. раз** once more; **с ~им** (*coll.*) and more, odd.

лишь *adj. and conj.* only; **не хвата́ет л. одного́** one thing only is lacking; **л. то́лько** as soon as; **л. бы** if only, provided that; **л. бы он мог прие́хать** provided that he can come.

лоб, лба, о лбе́, во (на) лбу́, *pl.* **лбы, лбов** *m.* forehead, brow.

ло́бби *nt. indecl.* (*pol.*) lobby.

лобби́р|овать, ую *impf. and pf.* (*pol.*)
1 (*кого*) to lobby (*s.o.*).
2 (*что*) to lobby for (*sth.*).

ло́бзик, а *m.* fretsaw.

лобов|о́й *adj.* frontal; **~а́я ата́ка** (*mil.*) frontal attack; **~о́е стекло́** windscreen (*Br.*), windshield (*US*).

лоб|о́к, ка́ *m.* (*anat.*) pubis.

лов|и́ть, лю́, ~ишь *impf.* (*of* ▸ **пойма́ть**) to (try to) catch; (*fig.*) **л. (удо́бный) моме́нт** to (try to) seize an opportunity; to look for an opportunity; **л. себя́ на чём-н.** to catch o.s. at sth.; **л. ста́нцию** (*radio*) to try to pick up a station.

ло́в|кий (~ок, ~ка́, ~ко) *adj.*
1 (*искусный*) adroit, dexterous, deft; **л. ход** master stroke.
2 (*хитрый*) cunning, smart.

ло́вко *adv.* (*искусно*) adroitly; **он л. устро́ился** he fixed himself up with a good job.

ло́вкост|ь, и *f.*
1 (*искусность*) adroitness, dexterity, deftness;

л. рук sleight of hand.
[2] (*хитрость*) cunning, smartness.
ло́в|ля, ли, *g. pl.* **~ель** *f.* catching, hunting; **ры́бная л.** fishing.
лову́шк|а, и *f.* snare, trap (*also fig.*).
ло́в|че (*and* **~че́е**) *comp. of* ▶ **~кий** *and* ▶ **~ко**
логари́фм, а *m.* (*math.*) logarithm.
ло́гик|а, и *f.* logic.
логи́ческий *adj.* logical.
логи́ч|ный (~ен, ~на) *adj.* = **~еский**
ло́гов|о, а *nt.* den, lair.
логопе́д, а *m.* speech therapist.
логоти́п, а *m.* (*эмблема*) logo.
ло́дк|а, и *f.* boat; **подво́дная л.** submarine; **спаса́тельная л.** lifeboat; **ката́ться на ~е** to go boating.
ло́дочник, а *m.* boatman.
лоды́жк|а, и *f.* (*anat.*) ankle bone.
ло́ж|а, и *f.*
[1] (*theatr.*) box.
[2] (*масонская*) lodge.
ложби́н|а, ы *f.* (*geog.*) hollow, dip.
лож|и́ться, у́сь, и́шься *impf. of* ▶ **лечь**
ло́жк|а, и *f.*
[1] spoon; **столо́вая л.** tablespoon; **ча́йная л.** teaspoon.
[2] (*количество*) spoonful.
ло́ж|ный (~ен, ~на) *adj.* false; **~ная трево́га** false alarm.
ложь, лжи *f.* lie.
лоз|а́, ы́, *pl.* **~ы** *f.* vine.
ло́зунг, а *m.*
[1] (*призыв*) slogan.
[2] (*плакат*) banner.
лока́л|ьный (~ен, ~ьна) *adj.* local; **~ьная сеть** (*comput.*) local area network.
лока́тор, а *m.* locator.
локомоти́в, а *m.* locomotive.
ло́кон, а *m.* lock, curl, ringlet.
ло́к|оть, тя, *pl.* **~ти, ~те́й** *m.* elbow.
лом, а, *pl.* **~ы, ~о́в** *m.*
[1] (*инструмент*) crowbar.
[2] (*sg. only*; *collect.*) (*ломаные предметы*) scrap, waste; **желе́зный л.** scrap-iron.
ло́маный *adj.* broken; **л. англи́йский язы́к** broken English.
лома́|ть, ю *impf.* (*of* ▶ **с~**)
[1] to break.
[2] (*no pf.*) (*fig.*): **л. себе́ го́лову** (**над** + *i.*) to rack one's brains (over); **л. ру́ки** to wring one's hands;
лома́|ться, юсь *impf.*
[1] (*pf.* **с~**) to break (*intrans.*).
[2] (*pf.* **с~**) (*о голосе*) to crack, break.
[3] (*pf.* **по~**) (*coll.*) (*кривляться*) to pose, put on airs.
ломба́рд, а *m.* pawnshop; **заложи́ть в л.** to pawn.
лом|и́ть, лю́, ~ишь *impf.*
[1] (*impers.*) to cause to ache; **у меня́ ~ит спи́ну** my back aches.
[2] (*coll.*) (*пробиваться*) to break through, rush.
лом|и́ться, лю́сь, ~ишься *impf.*
[1] (*быть переполненным*) to be (near to) breaking; (**от** + *g.*) to burst (with), be crammed (with); **ве́тви ~ятся от плодо́в** the boughs are groaning with fruit.
[2] (*coll.*) (*стремиться проникнуть*) to force one's way; (*идти толпами*) (**на** + *a.*) to flock (to).
ло́м|кий (~ок, ~ка́, ~ко) *adj.* fragile, brittle.
ло́мтик, а *m.* slice; **ре́зать ~ами** to slice.
Ло́ндон, а *m.* London.
ло́ндон|ец, ца *m.* Londoner.
ло́ндон|ка, ки *f. of* ▶ **~ец**
ло́ндонский *adj.* London.
лопа́т|а, ы *f.* spade, shovel.
лопа́тк|а, и *f.*
[1] (*лопата*) shovel; (*садовника*) trowel; (*cul.*) spatula; blade (*of turbine*).
[2] (*anat.*) shoulder blade; (*часть туши*) shoulder.
ло́п|аться, аюсь *impf. of* ▶ **~нуть**
ло́п|нуть, ну, нешь *pf.* (*of* ▶ **~аться**)
[1] (*о пузыре, шине, почке*) burst; (*о стекле*) to break, crack; (*о верёвке, струне*) to snap, break; (*fig., coll.*): **чуть не л. от сме́ха** to split one's sides with laughter, burst with laughter; **моё терпе́ние ~нуло** my patience is exhausted.
[2] (*fig., coll.*) (*потерпеть неудачу*) to fail, be a failure; (*fin.*) to go bankrupt, crash.
лопу́х, а́ *m.*
[1] (*bot.*) burdock.
[2] (*sl.*) fool.
лорд, а *m.* lord; **пала́та ~ов** House of Lords.
Лос-А́нджелес, а *m.* Los Angeles.
лоск, а *m.* lustre (*Br.*), luster (*US*), gloss, shine (*also fig.*).
лоску́т, а́, *pl.* **~ы́, ~о́в** *and* **~ья, ~ьев** *m.* rag, shred, scrap.
лосн|и́ться, ю́сь, и́шься *impf.* to be glossy, shine.
лосо́с|ь, я, *pl.* **~и, ~ей** *m.* salmon.
лос|ь, я, *pl.* **~и, ~е́й** *m.* elk (*Br.*), moose (*US*).
лосьо́н, а *m.* lotion; (*после бритья*) aftershave.
лот, а *m.* (*на аукционе*) lot.
лотере́|йный *adj. of* ▶ **~я; л. биле́т** lottery ticket.
лотере́|я, и *f.* lottery, raffle.
лот|о́к, ка́ *m.*
[1] (*прилавок*) hawker's stand; (*ящик для торговли*) hawker's tray.
[2] (*для ссыпания*) chute; (*для стока*) gutter.
ло́тос, а *m.* (*bot.*) lotus.
лото́чник, а *m.* hawker.
лох, а *m.* (*sl.*) simpleton, halfwit.
лохма́т|ый (~, ~а) *adj.*
[1] (*животное*) shaggy(-haired).
[2] (*человек, волосы*) dishevelled (*Br.*), disheveled (*US*), tousled.
лохмо́ть|я, ев *no sg.* rags; **в ~ях** in rags, ragged.
лошади́н|ый *adj.* of horses; equine; **~ая си́ла** horsepower.
ло́шад|ь, и, *pl.* **~и, ~е́й, ~я́м, ~ьми́, о ~я́х** *f.* horse; **бегова́я, скакова́я л.** racehorse; **чистокро́вная л.** thoroughbred; **сади́ться на л.** to mount.

лоя́льност|ь, и *f.* loyalty.
лоя́л|ьный (~ен, ~ьна) *adj.* loyal (*to the State authorities*).
ЛСД *m. indecl.* (*abbr. of* **диэтилами́д лизерги́новой кислоты́**) LSD.
луг, а, о ~́е, на ~у́, *pl.* **~а́, ~о́в** *m.* meadow; **заливно́й л.** water meadow.
лу́ж|а, и *f.* puddle, pool; **сесть в ~у** (*fig., coll.*) to get into a mess; to slip up.
лужа́йк|а, и *f.* (*полянка*) (forest) glade; (*газон*) lawn.
лу́з|а, ы *f.* (billiard) pocket.
лук[1], а *m.* (*collect.*) (*растение*) onions; **голо́вка ~́а** (*a single*) onion; **зелёный л.** spring onion(s) (*Br.*), scallion(s).
лук[2], а *m.* (*оружие*) bow.
лука́в|ый (~, ~а) *adj.*
1 (*хитрый*) crafty, sly, cunning.
2 (*игривый*) arch.
лу́ковиц|а, ы *f.*
1 (*головка лука*) onion.
2 (*bot.*) bulb.
лун|а́, ы́, *pl.* **~́ы** *f.* moon; (**Л.**) the Moon.
луна́тик, а *m.* sleepwalker, somnambulist.
лу́нк|а, и *f.* hole.
лу́н|ный *adj. of* ▸ **~а́;** (*astron.*) lunar; **~ное затме́ние** lunar eclipse; **~ная ночь** moonlit night; **л. свет** moonlight.
лу́п|а, ы *f.* magnifying glass.
луч, а́ *m.* ray; beam; **рентге́новские ~и́** X-rays.
луч|ево́й *adj.*
1 *adj. of* ▸ **~.**
2 radial.
3 (*med.*): **~ева́я боле́знь** radiation sickness.
лу́чник, а *m.* archer.
лу́чше *adj. and adv.*
1 (*comp. of* ▸ **хоро́ший** *and* ▸ **хорошо́**) better; **тем л.** so much the better; **л. всего́, л. всех** best of all; **как мо́жно л.** as well as possible; **нам л. верну́ться** we had better go back.
2 *as particle* (*предпочтительнее*) rather, instead; **давайте л. поговори́м об э́том** let's talk it over instead.
лу́чш|ий *adj.* (*comp. and superl. of* ▸ **хоро́ший**) better; best; **к ~ему** for the better; **в ~ем слу́чае** at best.
лы́ж|а, и *f.* ski; **го́рные ~́и** alpine skis; **бе́гать, ходи́ть на ~ах** to ski.
лы́жник, а *m.* skier.
лы́жни|ца, цы *f. of* ▸ **~к**
лыжн|я́, и́ *f.* ski track.
лысе́|ть, ю *impf.* (*of* ▸ **об~** *and* ▸ **по~**) to go bald.
лы́син|а, ы *f.* bald patch.
лы́с|ый (~, ~а́, ~о) *adj.* bald; (*гора*) bare.
ль = **ли**
льв|ёнок, ёнка, *pl.* **~я́та, ~я́т** *m.* lion cub.
льви́н|ый *adj. of* ▸ **лев; ~ая до́ля** (*fig.*) the lion's share.
льви́ц|а, ы *f.* lioness.
льв|я́та *see* ▸ **~ёнок**
льго́т|а, ы *f.* (*блокадникам, инвалидам*) privilege; advantage; benefit; (*при оплате*) discount.
льго́тный *adj.* privileged; favourable; **л. биле́т** concessionary ticket.
льда *g. sg. of* ▸ **лёд**
льди́н|а, ы *f.* block of ice, ice floe.
льна, льну *see* ▸ **лён**
льнян|о́й *adj.*
1 of flax; **~о́го цве́та** flaxen.
2 (*платье*) linen.
льстец, а́ *m.* flatterer.
льсти́в|ый (~, ~а) *adj.* (*слова*) flattering; (*человек*) smooth-tongued.
льстить, льщу, льстишь *impf.* (*of* ▸ **по~́**)
1 (+ *d.*) to flatter; to gratify; **э́то льстит его́ самолю́бию** it flatters his self-esteem.
2 (+ *a., with refl. pron. only*) to delude; **л. себя́ наде́ждой** to flatter o.s. with the hope.
лью, льёшь *see* ▸ **лить**
лэпто́п, а *m.* laptop (computer).
любе́зност|ь, и *f.*
1 (*свойство*) courtesy; politeness, civility.
2 (*услуга*) kindness; **оказа́ть, сде́лать кому́-н. л.** to do s.o. a kindness.
любе́з|ный (~ен, ~на) *adj.*
1 (*вежливый*) courteous; polite; obliging.
2 (*милый*) kind, amiable; **бу́дьте ~ны...** (*polite form of request*) be so kind as ....
люби́м|ец, ца *m.* favourite (*Br.*), favorite (*US*), darling.
люби́м|ица, ицы *f. of* ▸ **~ец**
люби́мчик, а *m.* (*pej.*) pet, blue-eyed boy.
люби́м|ый (~, ~а) *adj.*
1 (*дорогой*) beloved, loved.
2 (*предпочитаемый*) favourite (*Br.*), favorite (*US*).
люби́тел|ь, я *m.*
1 (+ *g. or* + *inf.*) lover; **л. му́зыки** music-lover; **л. соба́к** dog-lover; **он л. сплё́тничать** he loves gossiping.
2 (*непрофессионал*) amateur.
люби́тель|ница, ницы *f. of* ▸ **~**
люби́тельский *adj.*
1 amateur; **л. спекта́кль** amateur performance.
2 (*pej.*) amateurish.
люб|и́ть, лю́, ~́ишь *impf.*
1 (*мать, родину*) to love.
2 (*читать, музыку*) to like, be fond (of).
3 (*о растениях*) (*coll.*) to like; **фиа́лки ~́ят тень** violets like shade.
люб|ова́ться, у́юсь *impf.* (*of* ▸ **по~**) (+ *i.*, **на** + *a.*) to admire.
любо́вник, а *m.* lover.
любо́вниц|а, ы *f.* lover, mistress.
любо́вн|ый *adj.*
1 love-; **~ая исто́рия** love affair.
2 (*отношение*) loving.
люб|о́вь, ви́, *i.* **~о́вью** *f.* (**к** + *d.*) love (for, of); **занима́ться ~о́вью** to make love.
любозна́тел|ьный (~ен, ~ьна) *adj.* inquisitive.
любо́й
1 *adj.* any; (*из двоих*) either; **л. ціно́й** at any price.
2 *as n.* anyone; (*из двоих*) either.
любопы́т|ный (~ен, ~на) *adj.* curious;

interesting; (*impers.*; + *d. and inf.*): **~но, придёт ли она́** I wonder if she will come.
любопы́тств|о, а *nt.* curiosity.
лю́д|и, е́й, ~́ям, ~ьми́, о ~́ях *no sg.*
1 (*pl. of* ▸ **челове́к**) people.
2 (*mil.*) men.
3 (*кадры*) staff, people.
людое́д, а *m.*
1 (*человек*) cannibal; (*животное*) maneater; **тигр-л.** man-eating tiger.
2 (*в сказках*) ogre.
люк, а *m.*
1 (*naut., aeron.*) hatch, hatchway.
2 (*theatr.*) trap.
3 : **светово́й л.** skylight.
люкс *adj. indecl.* de luxe, luxury.
Люксембу́рг, а *m.* Luxembourg.
люксембу́ргский *m.* Luxembourg.
люксембу́рж|ец, ца *m.* Luxembourger.
лю́тик, а *m.* (*bot.*) buttercup.
лю́т|ня, ни, *g. pl.* **~ен** *and* **~ней** *f.* (*mus.*) lute.
лю́т|ый (~, ~а́, ~́о) *adj.* ferocious, fierce, cruel; (*мороз*) sharp; (*ненависть*) intense.
ля *nt. indecl.* (*mus.*) A; **л. бемо́ль** A flat.
ляг(те) *imper. of* ▸ **лечь**
ляг|а́ть, а́ю *impf.* (*of* ▸ **~ну́ть**) to kick.
ляга́|ться, юсь *impf.* to kick (*intrans*); (*друг друга*) to kick one another.
ляг|ну́ть, ну́, нёшь *inst. pf. of* ▸ **~а́ть**
ля́|гу, жешь, гут *see* ▸ **лечь**
лягу́шк|а, и *f.* frog.
ля́жк|а, и *f.* (*coll.*) thigh, haunch.
лязг, а *no pl., m.* clank, clang.
ля́зга|ть, ю *impf.* (+ *i.*) to clank, clang; **он ~л зуба́ми** his teeth were chattering.
ля́мк|а, и *f.* strap.
ля́п|нуть, ну, нешь *pf.* (*coll.*) to blurt out.

Мм

м (*abbr. of* **метр**) m, metre(s) (*Br.*), meter(s) (*US*).
мавзоле́|й, я *m.* mausoleum.
Маврита́ни|я, и *f.* Mauritania.
маг, а *m.* magician, wizard.
магази́н, а *m.*
1 shop; **гастрономи́ческий/продово́льственный м.** grocer's (shop) (*Br.*), grocery store (*US*); **универса́льный м.** department store.
2 (*у стрелкового оружия*) magazine.
МАГАТЭ́ *nt. indecl.* (*abbr. of* **Междунаро́дное аге́нтство по а́томной эне́ргии**) IAEA (*International Atomic Energy Agency*).
маги́стр, а *m.*
1 (*лицо*) holder of a master's degree.
2 (*учёная степень*) master's degree.
магистра́л|ь, и *f.*
1 (*водная, газовая*) main; (*железнодорожная*) main line.
2 (*улица*) arterial road, main road.
маги́ческий *adj.* magic(al).
ма́ги|я, и *f.* magic.
магна́т, а *m.* magnate, tycoon.
магнети́зм, а *m.* magnetism.
магнети́ческий *adj.* magnetic.
ма́гни|й, я *m.* (*chem.*) magnesium.
магни́т, а *m.* magnet.
магни́тн|ый *adj.* magnetic; **~ая ка́рточка** smart card, swipe card.
магнито́л|а, ы *f.* radio cassette player.
магнитофо́н, а *m.* tape recorder; **видео~** video (cassette) recorder, VCR.
магно́ли|я, и *f.* (*bot.*) magnolia.
маде́р|а, ы *f.* Madeira (wine).
мадо́нн|а, ы *f.* madonna.
Мадри́д, а *m.* Madrid.
мажо́р, а *m.* (*mus.*) major key.
ма́|зать, жу, жешь *impf.*
1 (*pf.* **на~, по~**) (*смазывать*) to oil, grease, lubricate.
2 (*pf.* **на~, по~**) (*намазывать*) to smear (with); **м. хлеб ма́слом** to spread butter on bread, butter bread.
3 (*pf.* **из~, за~;** *coll.*) (*пачкать*) to soil, stain.
4 (*pf.* **про~;** *coll.*) (*не попадать*) to miss.
ма́|заться, жусь, жешься *impf.*
1 (*pf.* **из~, за~**) (*пачкаться*) to soil o.s., stain o.s.
2 (*pf.* **на~**) to make up.
3 (*pf.* **на~**) (+ *i.*) to apply (*ointment, cream, etc.*).
мазохи́ст, а *m.* masochist.
мазу́т, а *m.* (*tech.*) fuel oil.
маз|ь, и *f.*
1 (*лекарство*) ointment.
2 (*для смазки*) grease.
ма|й, я *m.* May.
ма́йк|а, и *f.* sleeveless top; (*нижняя*) vest (*Br.*), undershirt (*US*).
майоне́з, а *m.* (*cul.*) mayonnaise.
майо́р, а *m.* major (*mil. rank*).
майора́н, а *m.* (*bot.*) marjoram.
ма́й|ский *adj. of* ▸ **~; м. жук** cockchafer.
мак, а *m.* (*растение*) poppy; (*семена*) poppy seed(s).
мака́к|а, и *f.* (*zool.*) macaque.
макаро́н|ы, ~ *pl.* pasta.
мак|а́ть, а́ю *impf.* (*of* ▸ **~ну́ть**) to dip.
македо́н|ец, ца *m.* Macedonian.
Македо́ни|я, и *f.* Macedonia.
македо́н|ка, ки *f. of* ▸ **~ец**

македо́нский *adj.* Macedonian; **Алекса́ндр М.** Alexander the Great.
маке́т, а *m.* model; (*книги*) dummy.
макия́ж, а *m.* make-up.
ма́клер, а *m.* (*comm.*) broker.
мак|ну́ть, ну́, нёшь *inst. pf. of* ▶ **~а́ть**
максимали́зм, а *m.* uncompromisingness.
максимали́ст, а *m.* uncompromising person.
максима́л|ьный (~ен, ~ьна) *adj.* maximum.
ма́ксимум, а *m.*
1 maximum.
2 *as adv.* at most; **м. сто рубле́й** a hundred roubles at most.
макулату́р|а, ы *f.* paper for recycling.
маку́шк|а, и *f.*
1 (*дерева*) top.
2 (*головы*) crown.
мала́|ец, йца *m.* Malay.
Мала́йзи|я, и *f.* Malaysia.
мала́|йка, йки *f. of* ▶ **~ец**
мала́йский *adj.* Malay, Malayan.
Мала́й|я, и *f.* Malaya.
малахи́т, а *m.* (*min.*) malachite.
мале́йший *adj.* (*superl. of* ▶ **ма́лый**) least, slightest.
мал|ёк, ька́ *m.* young fish; (*collect.*) fry.
ма́леньк|ий *adj.*
1 little, small.
2 (*незначительный*) slight.
3 (*малолетний*) young; *as n.* **м., ~ого** *m.*, **~ая, ~ой** *f.* the baby, the child; **~ие** the young.
мали́н|а, ы *no pl.*, *f.* (*кустарник*) raspberry bush; (*ягоды*) raspberries.
мали́новый *adj.*
1 (*варенье*) raspberry.
2 (*цвет*) crimson.
ма́ло *adv.* (*времени, денег*) little, not much; (*книг, людей*) few; (*недостаточно*) not enough; (*читать*) not much; **э́того ма́ло** this is not enough; **я м. где быва́л** I have hardly been anywhere; **м. того́** moreover; **м. того́, что...** not only ..., it is not enough that ...; **м. того́, что он сам прие́хал, он привёз всех това́рищей** it was not enough that he came himself, but he had to bring all his friends.
малова́ж|ный (~ен, ~на) *adj.* of little importance, insignificant.
малова́т (~а, ~о) *adj.* (*coll.*) on the small side.
малоду́ш|ный (~ен, ~на) *adj.* faint-hearted.
малоиму́щ|ий (~, ~а) *adj.* needy, indigent.
малокро́ви|е, я *nt.* anaemia (*Br.*), anemia (*US*).
малоле́тн|ий *adj.*
1 young; juvenile.
2 *as n.* **м., ~его** *m.*, **~яя, ~ей** *f.* (*ребёнок*) infant; (*подросток*) juvenile, minor.
малолитра́жк|а, и *f.* (*coll.*) compact (car); mini.
маломо́щ|ный (~ен, ~на) *adj.* low-powered; weak.
малоподви́ж|ный (~ен, ~на) *adj.* not mobile, slow-moving.
малоро́сл|ый (~, ~а) *adj.* undersized, stunted.
малоупотреби́тел|ьный (~ен, ~ьна) *adj.* infrequent, rarely used.
малочи́слен|ный (~, ~на) *adj.* small (in numbers); scanty.
ма́л|ый (~, ~а́, ~о́) *adj.* little, (too) small; **э́ти сапоги́ мне ~ы́** these boots are too small for me; *as n.* **~ое, ~ого** *nt.* little; **са́мое ~ое** (*coll.*) at the least; **без ~ого** almost, all but.
малы́ш, а́ *m.* (*coll.*) child, kid; little boy.
ма́льв|а, ы *f.* (*bot.*) mallow.
Мальо́рк|а, и *f.* Majorca.
Ма́льт|а, ы *f.* Malta.
мальти́|ец, йца *m.* Maltese.
мальти́|йка, йки *f. of* ▶ **~ец**
мальти́йский *adj.* Maltese.
ма́льчик, а *m.* boy.
мальчи́шеский *adj.* boyish.
маля́р, а́ *m.* (house-)painter, decorator.
маляри́|я, и *f.* (*med.*) malaria.
маля́р|ный *adj. of* ▶ **~; ~ная кисть** paintbrush.
ма́м|а, ы *f.* mum, mummy (*Br.*), mom, mommy (*US*).
ма́мин *adj.* mother's.
ма́монт, а *m.* mammoth.
ма́нго *nt. indecl.* (*bot.*) mango.
мангу́ст, а *m.* (*zool.*) mongoose.
мандари́н, а *m.* (*дерево, плод*) mandarin, tangerine.
манда́т, а *m.* mandate.
мандоли́н|а, ы *f.* (*mus.*) mandolin.
манёвр, а *m.*
1 manoeuvre (*Br.*), maneuver (*US*); manoeuvres (*Br.*), maneuvers (*US*).
2 (*pl.*) (*rail.*) shunting.
маневри́р|овать, ую *impf.* (*of* ▶ **с~**) to manoeuvre (*Br.*), maneuver (*US*).
мане́ж, а *m.*
1 riding school, manège.
2 (*цирка*) ring.
3 : **спорти́вный м.** sports hall.
4 : **(де́тский) м.** playpen.
манеке́н, а *m.* mannequin; dummy.
манеке́нщик, а *m.* male model.
манеке́нщиц|а, ы *f.* model.
мане́р|а, ы *f.*
1 manner, style; **м. вести́ себя́** way of behaving; **м. держа́ть себя́** bearing, carriage; **петь в ~е Кару́зо** to sing in the style of Caruso.
2 (*pl.*) manners; **у него́ плохи́е ~ы** he has no manners.
мане́р|ный (~ен, ~на) *adj.* affected.
манже́т|а, ы *f.* cuff.
маникю́р, а *m.* manicure.
маникю́рш|а, и *f.* manicurist.
манипули́р|овать, ую *impf.* (+ *i.*) to manipulate.
манипуля́ци|я, и *f.*
1 manipulation.

[2] (*fig.*) machination, intrigue.
ман|и́ть, ю́, ~ишь *impf.* (*of* **по~**) to beckon.
манифе́ст, а *m.* manifesto; proclamation.
манифеста́ци|я, и *f.* (street) demonstration.
мани́шк|а, и *f.* (false) shirt front, dicky.
ма́ни|я, и *f.*
[1] mania; **м. вели́чия** megalomania.
[2] (*fig.*) passion, craze.
ма́нк|а, и *f.* (*coll.*) semolina.
манса́рд|а, ы *f.* attic, garret.
ма́нти|я, и *f.* cloak, mantle; robe, gown.
манто́ *nt. indecl.* (*lady's*) fur coat.
манускри́пт, а *m.* manuscript.
манья́к, а *m.* maniac.
мара́зм, а *m.* (*med.*) marasmus; **ста́рческий м.** senility; (*fig.*) decay.
марафо́н, а *m.* marathon.
маргари́н, а *m.* margarine.
маргари́тк|а, и *f.* (*bot.*) daisy.
маргина́л, а *m.* person living on the fringes of society.
маргина́л|ьный (~ен, ~ьна) *adj.* marginal.
марина́д, а *m.* marinade.
марини́ст, а *m.* painter of seascapes.
марино́в|анный *p.p.p. of* ▸ **~а́ть** *and adj.* (*cul.*) pickled.
марин|ова́ть, у́ю *impf.* (*pf.* **за~**) to pickle.
марионе́т|ка, ки *f.* marionette; puppet (*also fig.*).
марионе́т|очный *adj. of* ▸ **~ка; ~очное госуда́рство** puppet state.
марихуа́н|а, ы *f.* marijuana.
ма́рк|а, и *f.*
[1] (*почтовая*) (postage) stamp.
[2] (*сорт*) brand, make; **фабри́чная м.** trademark.
ма́ркер, а *m.* (*фломастер*) marker (pen).
ма́рке́тинг, а *m.* marketing.
марки́з|а, ы *f.* marchioness.
маркси́зм, а *m.* Marxism.
ма́рл|я, и *f.* gauze.
мармела́д, а *m.* (*конфеты*) fruit jellies.
мародёр, а *m.* marauder, pillager.
мародёрств|о, а *nt.* pillage, looting.
марокка́н|ец, ца *m.* Moroccan.
марокка́н|ка, ки *f. of* ▸ **~ец**
марокка́нский *adj.* Moroccan.
Маро́кко *nt. indecl.* Morocco.
Марс, а *m.* (*astron., myth.*) Mars.
марсиа́н|ин, ина, *pl.* **~е, ~** *m.* Martian.
март, а *m.* March.
ма́рт|овский *adj. of* ▸ **~**
марты́шк|а, и *f.* marmoset; (*fig., coll.*) monkey.
марципа́н, а *m.* (*кондитерское изделие*) (*из теста*) marzipan cake; (*не из теста*) marzipan sweet; (*начинка, глазурь*) marzipan.
марш, а *m.* march; **м. проте́ста** protest march.
ма́ршал, а *m.* marshal.
марши́р|ова́ть, у́ю *impf.* (*of* ▸ **про~**) to march.
маршру́т, а *m.* route.
ма́ск|а, и *f.* mask; (*fig.*): **сбро́сить с себя́ ~у** to throw off the mask.
маскара́д, а *m.* masked ball; (*fig.*) masquerade.
маскара́д|ный *adj. of* ▸ **~; м. костю́м** fancy dress.
маскир|ова́ть, у́ю *impf.* (*of* ▸ **за~**) to mask, disguise; (*mil.*) to camouflage.
маскир|ова́ться, у́юсь *impf.* (*of* ▸ **за~**) to disguise o.s.; (*mil.*) to camouflage o.s.
Ма́слениц|а, ы *f.* Shrovetide; carnival.
маслёнк|а, и *f.*
[1] (*посуда для сливочного масла*) butter dish.
[2] (*tech.*) oilcan.
масли́н|а, ы *f.*
[1] (*дерево*) olive tree.
[2] (*плод*) olive.
ма́с|ло, ла, *pl.* **~ла́, ~ел, ~ла́м** *nt.*
[1] : **(сли́вочное) м.** butter.
[2] (*растительное*) oil; **как по ~лу** (*fig., coll.*) swimmingly.
[3] (*краски*) oil (paints); **писа́ть ~лом** to paint in oils.
масляни́ст|ый (~, ~а) *adj.* oily.
масо́н, а *m.* Freemason, Mason.
масо́нский *adj.* Masonic.
ма́сс|а, ы *f.*
[1] mass; *pl.* (*pol.*) the masses; **в (о́бщей) ~е** on the whole.
[2] (*coll.*) (*множество*) a lot, lots.
масса́ж, а *m.* massage; **то́чечный м.** shiatsu, acupressure.
массажи́ст, а *m.* masseur.
массажи́стк|а, и *f.* masseuse.
масси́в, а *m.* (*geog.*) massif; (*fig.*) expanse; **жило́й м.** housing development.
масси́в|ный (~ен, ~на) *adj.* massive.
масси́ровани|е, я *nt.* massing, concentration.
масси́рованный *adj.* intensive.
масс(-)ме́диа *pl. indecl.* mass media.
ма́ссов|ый *adj.* mass; **~ое произво́дство** mass production; **м. чита́тель** general reader.
ма́стер, а, *pl.* **~а́** *m.*
[1] (*цеха*) foreman.
[2] (*ремесленник*) craftsman, skilled workman.
[3] (**на** + *a., or* + *inf.*) (*знаток*) expert, master (at, of); (*sport*) vet(eran); **м. (по ремо́нту)** repairman; **телевизио́нный м.** TV repairman.
ма́стер-кла́сс, а *m.* masterclass.
мастерск|а́я, о́й *f.* (*столяра*) workshop; (*художника*) studio; (*на заводе*) shop; **авторемо́нтная м.** car repair garage.
ма́стерски́ *adv.* skilfully; in masterly fashion.
мастерств|о́, а́ *nt.*
[1] (*ремесло*) trade, craft.
[2] (*умение*) skill, craftsmanship.
масти́к|а, и *f.*
[1] (*смола*) mastic.
[2] (*замазка*) putty.
[3] (*для натирания полов*) floor polish.
мастурба́ци|я, и *f.* masturbation.
мастурби́р|овать, ую *impf.* to masturbate.

М

маст|ь, и, *pl.* **~и, ~éй** *f.*
1 (*цвет шерсти*) colour (*Br.*), color (*US*).
2 (*cards*) suit; **ходи́ть в м.** to follow suit.

масшта́б, а *m.* scale; **конфли́кт большо́го ~а** large-scale conflict.

масшта́б|ный (~ен, ~на) *adj.*
1 scale; **~ная моде́ль** scale model.
2 (*большой*) large-scale.

мат[1], а *m.* (*chess*) checkmate, mate; **объяви́ть м.** (+ *d.*) to mate.

мат[2], а *m.* (*половик, тюфяк*) mat.

мат[3], а *m.* (*брань*) foul language, abuse; **руга́ться ~ом** to use foul language.

матема́тик, а *m.* mathematician.

матема́тик|а, и *f.* mathematics.

математи́ческий *adj.* mathematical.

материа́л, а *m.* material; (*для публикации в прессе*) copy.

материали́зм, а *m.* materialism.

материализ|ова́ться, у́юсь *impf. and pf.* to materialize.

материали́ст, а *m.* materialist.

материа́л|ьный (~ен, ~ьна) *adj.* material; **~ьные затрудне́ния** financial difficulties; **~ьное положе́ние** economic conditions.

матери́к, а́ *m.*
1 (*континент*) continent.
2 (*суша*) mainland.

материко́вый *adj.* continental.

матери́нск|ий *adj.* maternal, motherly; **~ая пла́та** (*comput.*) motherboard.

матер|и́ться, ю́сь, и́шься *impf.* (*coll.*) to swear.

мате́ри|я[1], и *f.* (*phil.*) matter.

мате́ри|я[2], и *f.* (*text.*) material, cloth.

мате́рчатый *adj.* made of cloth.

матёр|ый (~, ~а) *adj.*
1 (*достигший полной зрелости*) full-grown, mature (*of animal*).
2 (*опытный*) experienced, practised.
3 (*неисправимый*) inveterate, out-and-out.

ма́тк|а, и *f.*
1 (*anat.*) uterus, womb.
2 (*самка*) female; (*пчелиная*) queen (bee).

ма́тов|ый *adj.* matt; **~ое стекло́** frosted glass.

матра́с, а *m.* mattress; **надувно́й м.** air bed, inflatable mattress.

матра́|ц, ца = **~с**

матрёшк|а, и *f.* matryoshka, (set of) nested Russian dolls.

ма́триц|а, ы *f.*
1 (*typ.*) matrix.
2 (*tech.*) die, mould (*Br.*), mold (*US*).

матро́с, а *m.* sailor, seaman.

матч, а *m.* (*sport*) match; **междунаро́дный м.** (*cricket, rugby*) test (match).

мат|ь, *g., d., p.* **~ери, ~ерью,** *pl.* **~ери, ~ерéй** *f.*
1 mother; **бу́дущая м.** expectant mother, mother-to-be; **м.-одино́чка** single mother.
2 (*coll.*) *familiar term of address to a woman.*

мафио́зи *m. indecl.* Mafioso.

мафио́зный *adj. of* ▸ **ма́фия**

ма́фи|я, и *f.* Mafia.

мах, а (у) *m.* (*рукой*) swing, stroke; (*крыла*) flap; **одни́м ~ом** at one stroke, in a trice; **с ~у** (*coll.*) rashly, without thinking.

ма|ха́ть, шу́, ~шешь *impf.* (*of* ▸ **~хну́ть 1**) (+ *i.*) (*рукой*) to wave; (*веткой*) to brandish; (*хвостом*) to wag; (*крыльями*) to flap.

махи́н|а, ы *f.* (*coll.*) bulky and cumbersome object.

махина́ци|я, и *f.* machination, intrigue.

мах|ну́ть, ну́, нёшь *pf.*
1 *pf. of* ▸ **~а́ть; м. руко́й (на** + *a.*) (*fig., coll.*) to give up as a bad job.
2 (*coll.*) (*поехать*) to go, travel.

махови́к, а́ *m.* flywheel.

махро́вый *adj.* (*ткань*) terry.

мац|а́, ы́ *no pl., f.* matzos (*Jewish biscuits for Passover*).

маче́те *nt. indecl.* machete.

ма́чех|а, и *f.* stepmother.

ма́чт|а, ы *f.* mast.

маши́н|а, ы *f.*
1 (*механическое устройство*) machine (*also fig.*); **посудомо́ечная м.** dishwasher.
2 (*автомобиль*) car; vehicle; **м. «ско́рой по́мощи»** ambulance.

машина́л|ьный (~ен, ~ьна) *adj.* mechanical (*fig.*); **м. отве́т** an automatic response.

машини́ст, а *m.*
1 (*комбайна*) driver, operator (*workman in charge of machinery*).
2 (*локомотива*) engine driver (*Br.*), engineer (*US*).

машини́стк|а, и *f.* typist; **м.-стенографи́стка** shorthand typist.

маши́н|ка, ки *f. dim. of* ▸ **~а; (пи́шущая) м.** typewriter.

машинопи́сный *adj.* typewritten; **м. текст** typescript.

машинострое́ни|е, я *nt.* mechanical engineering, machinery construction.

машиностро|и́тельный *adj. of* ▸ **~е́ние**

мая́к, а́ *m.* lighthouse; beacon (*also fig.*).

ма́ятник, а *m.* pendulum.

ма́|яться, юсь, ешься *impf.* (*coll.*)
1 (**с** + *i.*) (*трудиться*) to toil (with, over).
2 (*томиться*) to pine, suffer.

мая́ч|ить, у, ишь *impf.* (*coll.*) to loom (up), appear indistinctly.

МВД *nt. indecl.* (*abbr. of* **Министе́рство вну́тренних дел**) Ministry of Internal Affairs; ≈ Home Office.

МВФ *m. indecl.* (*abbr. of* **Междунаро́дный валю́тный фонд**) IMF (*International Monetary Fund*).

мг (*abbr. of* **миллигра́мм**) mg, milligram(s).

мгл|а, ы *f.*
1 (*туман*) haze; mist.
2 (*темнота*) gloom, darkness.

мгнове́ни|е, я *nt.* instant, moment; **в м. о́ка** in the twinkling of an eye.

мгнове́н|ный (~ен, ~на) *adj.*
1 (*сразу возникающий*) instantaneous.
2 (*быстро проходящий*) momentary.

МГУ *m. indecl.* (*abbr. of* **Моско́вский госуда́рственный университе́т**)

Moscow State University.
ме́бел|ь, и *f.* furniture.
ме́бельщик, а *m.* furniture maker.
меблир|ова́ть, у́ю *impf. and pf.* to furnish.
мегаба́йт, а *m.* (*comput.*) megabyte.
мегафо́н, а *m.* megaphone.
мед... *comb. form, abbr. of* **медици́нский**
мёд, а, о ~е, в ~у́/~е, на ~у́, *pl.* **~ы́, ~о́в** *m.*
1 honey.
2 (*старинный напиток*) mead.
медали́ст, а *m.* medallist (*Br.*), medalist (*US*); medal winner.
медали́ст|ка, и *f. of* ▶ **~**
меда́л|ь, и *f.* medal.
медальо́н, а *m.* medallion, locket.
медве́диц|а, ы *f.* she-bear; (*astron.*): **Большая М.** the Great Bear (Ursa Major).
медве́д|ь, я *m.* bear (*also fig.*); **бе́лый м.** polar bear.
медвеж|а́та *pl. of* ▶ **~о́нок**
медве́|жий *adj. of* ▶ **~дь; ~жья услу́га** well-meant action having opposite effect.
медвеж|о́нок, о́нка, *pl.* **~а́та, ~а́т** *m.* bear cub.
меди́йный *adj.* media.
ме́дик, а *m.*
1 (*врач*) physician, doctor.
2 (*студент*) medical student.
медикаме́нт, а *m.* (*usu. pl.*) medicine.
медита́ци|я, и *f.* meditation.
медити́р|овать, ую *impf.* to meditate.
ме́диум, а *m.* medium, spiritualist.
медици́н|а, ы *f.* medicine.
медици́нский *adj.* medical.
ме́дленно *adv.* slowly.
ме́длен|ный (~/~ен, ~на) *adj.* slow.
медли́тел|ьный (~ен, ~ьна) *adj.* sluggish; slow.
ме́дл|ить, ю, ишь *impf.* to linger; to tarry; (**с** + *i.*) to be slow (in); **он ~ит с отве́том** he is a long time replying.
ме́дный *adj.*
1 copper.
2 (*chem.*) cupric, cuprous; **м. купоро́с** copper sulphate, bluestone.
3 (*mus.*) brass.
медо́вый *adj. of* ▶ **мёд; м. ме́сяц** honeymoon.
медосмо́тр, а *m.* medical (examination), checkup; **пройти́ м.** to have a checkup.
медпу́нкт, а *m.* first-aid station.
медсестр|а́, ы́ *f.* (*medical*) nurse.
меду́з|а, ы *f.* (*zool.*) jellyfish.
мед|ь, и *f.*
1 copper; **жёлтая м.** brass.
2 (*collect.*) (*монеты*) coppers.
меж (*coll.*) = **ме́жду**
меж... *comb. form* inter-.
межгосуда́рственный *adj.* interstate.
междоме́ти|е, я *nt.* (*gram.*) interjection.
междоусо́бный *adj.* internecine.
ме́жду *prep.* + *i.* (+ *g. pl., obs.*)
1 between; **м. про́чим** incidentally; **м. тем** meanwhile; **м. тем как** while, whereas.
2 (*среди*) among, amongst.
междугоро́дний = **междугоро́дный**
междугоро́дный *adj.* intercity; long-distance.
междунаро́дный *adj.* international; **М. валю́тный фонд** International Monetary Fund.
межконтинента́льн|ый *adj.* intercontinental; **~ая баллисти́ческая раке́та** intercontinental ballistic missile.
межправи́тельственный *adj.* intergovernmental.
межрегиона́льный *adj.* inter-regional.
межэтни́ческий *adj.* interethnic.
мейнстри́м, а *m.* (*coll.*) the mainstream (*of culture, music*).
Ме́кк|а, и *f.* Mecca.
Ме́ксик|а, и *f.* Mexico.
мексика́н|ец, ца *m.* Mexican.
мексика́н|ка, ки *f. of* ▶ **~ец**
мексика́нский *adj.* Mexican.
мел, а, о ~е, в ~у́ *m.* chalk.
меланхо́ли|я, и *f.* melancholy; (*med.*) melancholia.
мелиора́ци|я, и *f.* (*agric.*) land improvement, reclamation.
ме́л|кий (~ок, ~ка́, ~ко) *adj.*
1 (*небольшой*) small.
2 (*неглубокий*) shallow.
3 (*дождь; песок*) fine.
4 (*fig.*) (*человек*) petty, small-minded; **~кая со́шка** small fry.
ме́лко *adv.*
1 (*некрупно*) fine, into small particles.
2 (*неглубоко*) not deep.
мелково́д|ный (~ен, ~на) *adj.* shallow.
мелоди́ч|ный (~ен, ~на) *adj.* melodious, melodic.
мело́ди|я, и *f.* melody, tune.
мелодра́м|а, ы *f.* melodrama.
мелома́н, а *m.* music-lover.
ме́лоч|ный (~ен, ~на) *adj.*
1 petty, trifling.
2 (*pej.*) (*человек*) petty, small-minded.
ме́лоч|ь, и, *pl.* **~и, ~е́й** *f.*
1 (*collect.*) (*мелкие предметы*) small items; small fry.
2 (*collect.*) (*монеты*) (small) change.
3 (*pl.*) (*пустяки*) trifles, trivialities.
мел|ь, и, о ~и, на ~и́ *f.* shoal; bank; **песча́ная м.** sandbank; **на ~и́** aground; (*fig.*) on the rocks, high and dry; **сесть на м.** to run aground.
мельк|а́ть, а́ю *impf.* (*of* ▶ **~ну́ть**)
1 (*являться и исчезать*) to flash (past).
2 (*мерцать*) to twinkle.
3 (*о мыслях*) to flash.
мельк|ну́ть, ну́, нёшь *inst. pf. of* ▶ **~а́ть; у меня́ ~ну́ла мысль** I had a sudden idea.
ме́льком *adv.* in passing, cursorily.
ме́льник, а *m.* miller.
ме́льниц|а, ы *f.* mill.
мельхио́р, а *m.* cupro-nickel.
мельча́йший *superl. of* ▶ **ме́лкий**
ме́л|ьче *comp. of* ▶ **~кий** *and* ▶ **~ко**
мелю́, ме́лешь *see* ▶ **моло́ть**
мембра́н|а, ы *f.* (*tech.*) diaphragm.

меморáндум, а *m.* (*dipl.*) memorandum.
мемориáл, а *m.* memorial.
мемориáльный *adj.* memorial.
мемуáр|ы, ов *no sg.* memoirs.
мéнеджер, а *m.* manager; **м. по сбы́ту** sales manager.
мéнеджмент, а *m.* management.
мéнее *adv.* (*comp. of* ▶ **мáло**) less; **тем не м.** none the less.
менестрéл|ь, я *m.* (*hist.*) minstrel.
мензу́рк|а, и *f.* (*pharm.*) measuring glass.
менинги́т, а *m.* (*med.*) meningitis.
мени́ск, а *m.* (*math., phys.*) meniscus.
менструáльный *adj.* menstrual.
менструáци|я, и *f.* menstruation.
мент, á *m.* (*sl.*) police officer, cop.
менталитéт, а *m.* mentality.
ментóл, а *m.* (*chem.*) menthol.
менуэ́т, а *m.* minuet.
мéньше *comp.* (*of* ▶ **мáленький** *and* ▶ **мáло**) smaller; less.
мéньш|ий *adj.* (*comp. of* ▶ **мáленький, мáлый**) lesser, smaller; younger; **по ~ей мéре** at least; **сáмое ~ее** at the least.
меньшинств|ó, á *nt.* minority.
меню́ *nt. indecl.* menu.
меня́ *a. and g. of* ▶ **я**
меня́|ть, ю *impf.*
1 (*no pf.*) to change.
2 (+ *a. and* **на** + *a.*; *pf.* **об~, по~**) to exchange (for).
меня́|ться, юсь *impf.*
1 (*no pf.*) to change; **м. в лицé** to change countenance.
2 (+ *i.*; *pf.* **об~, по~**) to exchange; **м. с кем-н. кóмнатами** to exchange rooms with s.o.
мéр|а, ы *f.* measure; **вы́сшая м. наказáния** capital punishment; **по ~е возмóжности, по ~е сил** as far as possible; **по ~е тогó, как** as, (in proportion) as; **по крáйней, мéньшей ~е** at least; **в ~у** fairly; **сверх ~ы** excessively, immoderately; **знать ~у** *see* ▶ **знать**[1]
мерзáв|ец, ца *m.* (*coll.*) swine, bastard.
мéрз|кий (~ок, ~кá, ~ко) *adj.* disgusting, loathsome; abominable, foul.
мерзлот|á, ы́ *f.* frozen condition of ground; **вéчная м.** permafrost.
мёрз|нуть, ну, нешь, *past* **~, ~ла** *impf.* (*of* ▶ **за~**) to freeze.
мéрзост|ь, и *f.*
1 (*свойство*) vileness, loathsomeness.
2 (*мерзкая вещь*) abomination.
меридиáн, а *m.* meridian; **Гри́нвичский м.** Greenwich meridian.
мéрин, а *m.* gelding.
мéр|ить, ю, ишь *impf.*
1 (*pf.* **с~**) to measure; **м. взгля́дом** to look up and down.
2 (*pf.* **по~, при~**) (*примерять*) to try on (*clothing, footwear*).
мéр|иться, юсь, ишься *impf.* (*of* ▶ **по~**) (+ *i.*) to measure (against); **м. рóстом с кем-н.** to compare heights with s.o.
мéрк|а, и *f.*
1 (*определённый размер*) measurements.
2 (*предмет для измерения*) measure; (*fig.*) yardstick.
меркантíл|ьный (~ен, ~ьна) *adj.* (*fig., pej.*) mercenary.
мéрк|нуть, нет, *past* **~нул** *and* **~, ~ла** *impf.* (*of* ▶ **по~**) to grow dark, grow dim; (*fig.*) to fade.
Меркý́ри|й, я *m.* (*myth., astron.*) Mercury.
мероприя́ти|е, я *nt.*
1 (*мера*) measure.
2 (*событие*) event, function.
мертвéц, á *m.* corpse, dead person.
мёртв|ый (~, ~á, ~ó) *adj.* dead; **спать ~ым сном** (*coll.*) to sleep like the dead; **~ая хвáтка** mortal grip.
мерцá|ть, ю *impf.* to twinkle, glimmer, flicker.
мéсив|о, а *nt.* (*мешанина*) medley, jumble, mishmash; (*корм*) mash; (*на дороге*) slush.
ме|си́ть, шу́, ~сишь *impf.* (*of* ▶ **за~**) to knead.
мéсс|а, ы *f.* (*relig., mus.*) Mass.
месси́|я, и *m.* Messiah.
местáми *adv.* here and there, in places.
ме|сти́, ту́, тёшь, *past* **мёл, ~лá** *impf.*
1 (*пол, двор*) to sweep; (*cop*) to sweep up.
2 (*развевать*) to whirl; (*impers.*): **~тёт** there is a snowstorm.
мéстност|ь, и *f.*
1 (*дачная, сельская*) locality, district; area.
2 (*mil.*) (*гористая, открытая*) ground, country, terrain.
мéстный *adj.* local.
-мéстный *comb. form* -seated, -seater.
мéст|о, а, *pl.* **~á, ~, ~áм** *nt.*
1 place; site; **больнóе м.** (*fig.*) tender spot, sensitive point; **óбщее м.** platitude; **имéть м.** to take place; **не к ~у** (*fig.*) out of place; **ни с ~а!** don't move!; stay put!
2 (*в театре*) seat; (*на пароходе, поезде*) berth, seat.
3 (*свободное пространство*) space; room; **нет ~а** there is no room.
4 (*должность*) post, situation; job.
5 (*часть текста*) passage.
6 (*о багаже*) piece (*of luggage*).
местоимéни|е, я *nt.* (*gram.*) pronoun.
местонахождéни|е, я *nt.* location, the whereabouts.
месторождéни|е, я *nt.* (*geol.*) deposit.
мест|ь, и *f.* vengeance, revenge.
мéсяц, а *m.*
1 month; **медóвый м.** honeymoon.
2 (*луна*) moon; **молодóй м.** new moon.
мéсячн|ый *adj.* monthly; *as n.* **~ые, ~ых** *no sg.* (*coll.*) (menstrual) period.
метаболи́зм, а *m.* metabolism.
метáлл, а *m.* metal.
металли́ческий *adj.* metal; (*звук, привкус*) metallic.
металлоискáтел|ь, я *m.* metal detector.
металлу́рг, а *m.* metallurgist.
металлурги́ческий *adj.* metallurgical; **м. завóд** metal works, iron and steel works.
металлурги́|я, и *f.* metallurgy.
метáн, а *m.* (*chem.*) methane.
ме|тáть, чу́, ~чешь *impf.* (*of* ▶ **~тну́ть**) (*бросать*) to throw, cast, fling.

ме|та́ться, чу́сь, ~чешься *impf.* (*по комнате*) to rush about; (*в постели*) to toss.
метафи́зик|а, и *f.* metaphysics.
мета́фор|а, ы *f.* metaphor.
мете́л|ь, и *f.* snowstorm; blizzard.
метеори́т, а *m.* (*astron.*) meteorite.
метеоро́лог, а *m.* meteorologist; weather forecaster; (*coll.*) weatherman.
метеорологи́ческ|ий *adj.* meteorological; **~ая ста́нция** weather station.
метеороло́ги|я, и *f.* meteorology.
метеосво́дк|а, и *f.* weather report.
ме́|тить[1], чу, тишь *impf.* (*of* ▸ **по~**) (*ставить знак на*) to mark.
ме́|тить[2], чу, тишь *impf.* (**в** + *a.*) (*стараться попасть*) to aim at; (*fig., coll.*; **в** + *nom.-a. pl.*) to aim (at), aspire (to).
ме́тк|а, и *f.* mark.
ме́т|кий (~ок, ~ка́, ~ко) *adj.* well-aimed, accurate; **м. стрело́к** a good shot; (*fig.*): **~кое замеча́ние** apt remark.
ме́ткост|ь, и *f.* marksmanship; accuracy; (*fig.*) aptness.
мет|ла́, лы́, *pl.* **~лы, ~ел, ~лам** *f.* broom.
мет|ну́ть, ну́, нёшь *inst. pf. of* ▸ **~а́ть**
ме́тод, а *m.* method.
мето́дик|а, и *f.* method(s), system; principles; **м. преподава́ния ру́сского языка́** methods of teaching Russian.
методи́ч|ный (~ен, ~на) *adj.* methodical, orderly.
метр, а *m.*
1 (*единица длины*; *в стихе*) metre (*Br.*), meter (*US*).
2 (*линейка такой длины*) metre (*Br.*), meter (*US*) rule.
метра́ж, а́ *m.* (*квартиры*) metric area; (*ткани*) length in metres (*Br.*), meters (*US*).
метрдоте́л|ь, я *m.* head waiter.
ме́трик|а, и *f.* birth certificate.
метри́ческий *adj.* metric.
метро́ *nt. indecl.* (*abbr. of* **~полите́н**)
1 (*железная дорога*) underground (railway system) (*Br.*); the tube (*Br.*), subway (*US*).
2 (*coll.*) (*станция*) metro station; tube station (*Br.*), subway station (*US*).
метрополите́н, а *m.* underground (railway) (*Br.*), subway (*US*).
метропо́ли|я, и *f.* mother country, centre (*of empire*).
ме|ту́, тёшь *see* ▸ **~сти́**
ме́т|че *comp. of* ▸ **~кий, ~ко**
мех[1], а, о ~е, в ~у́ (~е), на ~у́, *pl.* **~а́, ~о́в** *m.* fur; **на ~у́** fur-lined.
мех[2], а, *pl.* **~и́, ~о́в** *m.* (*pl.*) bellows.
механи́зм, а *m.* mechanism, gear(ing); (*pl.*; *collect.*) machinery (*also fig.*).
меха́ник, а *m.* mechanic.
меха́ник|а, и *f.* mechanics.
механи́ческий *adj.* mechanical; **м. цех** machine shop.
Ме́хико *m. indecl.* Mexico City.
мехово́й *adj. of* ▸ **мех[1]**; **м. магази́н** furrier's.
мецена́т, а *m.* patron.
ме́ццо-сопра́но *nt. indecl.* (*voice*) & *f. indecl.* (*singer*) (*mus.*) mezzo-soprano.
меч, а́ *m.* sword.
мечёт|ь, и *f.* mosque.
меч-ры́б|а, ы *f.* swordfish.
мечт|а́, ы́ (*g. pl. not used*) *f.*
1 dream, daydream.
2 (*предмет желаний*) dream, ambition.
мечта́тел|ь, я *m.* dreamer; daydreamer.
мечта́тель|ница, ницы *f. of* ▸ **~**
мечта́тел|ьный (~ен, ~ьна) *adj.* dreamy.
мечта́|ть, ю *impf.* (**о** + *p.*) to dream (of, about).
ме|чу́, ~чешь *see* ▸ **~та́ть**
ме́|чу, тишь *see* ▸ **~тить[1,2]**
меша́|ть[1], ю *impf.* (*of* ▸ **по~**)
1 (+ *d.* + *inf.*) (*препятствовать*) to prevent (from); to hinder, impede, hamper; **что ~ет вам прие́хать в Москву́?** what prevents you from coming to Moscow?
2 (+ *d.*) (*беспокоить*) to disturb; **не ~ло бы** (+ *inf.*) (*coll.*) it would not hurt (to).
меша́|ть[2], ю *impf.*
1 (*pf.* **по~**) (*чай, кашу*) to stir; **м. в котле́** to stir the pot.
2 (*pf.* **с~**) (**с** + *i.*) (*вино с водой*) to mix (with), blend (with).
3 (*pf.* **с~**) (*путать*) to confuse, mix up.
ме́шка|ть, ю *impf.* (*coll.*; **с** + *i.*) to linger, dawdle, be slow.
мешкови́н|а, ы *f.* sacking, hessian.
меш|о́к, ка́ *m.* bag; sack.
мещан|и́н, и́на, *pl.* **~е, ~** *m.*
1 (*hist.*) petty bourgeois.
2 (*fig.*) Philistine.
меща́н|ский *adj. of* ▸ **~и́н**; (*fig.*) Philistine; bourgeois, narrow-minded.
ми *nt. indecl.* (*mus.*) E.
миг, а *m.* moment, instant.
миг|а́ть, а́ю *impf.* (*of* ▸ **~ну́ть**)
1 (*непроизвольно*) to blink.
2 (+ *d.*) (*подавать знак*) to wink (at); (*fig.*) (*мерцать*) to wink, twinkle.
миг|ну́ть, ну́, нёшь *inst. pf. of* ▸ **~а́ть**
мигра́нт, а *m.* migrant.
миграцио́нный *adj. of* ▸ **мигра́ция**
мигра́ци|я, и *f.* migration.
мигре́н|ь, и *f.* migraine.
мигри́р|овать, ую *impf.* to migrate.
МИД, а *m.* (*abbr. of* **Министе́рство иностра́нных дел**) Ministry of Foreign Affairs; Foreign Office (*Br.*), State Department (*US*).
ми́ди|я, и *f.* mussel.
мизантро́п, а *m.* misanthrope.
мизи́н|ец, ца *m.* (*на руке*) little finger; (*на ноге*) little toe.
микро... *comb. form* micro-.
микроавто́бус, а *m.* minibus.
микро́б, а *m.* microbe.
микробио́лог, а *m.* microbiologist.
микробиоло́ги|я, и *f.* microbiology.
микроволно́в|ый *adj.*: **~ая пе́чь** microwave (oven).

микрокли́мат, а *m.* microclimate.
микро́н, а *m.* (*phys.*) micron.
микроорганизм, а *m.* (*biol.*) micro-organism; **разлага́емый ~ами** biodegradable.
микроплёнк|а, и *f.* microfilm.
микропроце́ссор, а *m.* microprocessor.
микрорайо́н, а *m.* microrayon (*administrative subdivision of urban area*).
микроско́п, а *m.* microscope.
микросхе́м|а, ы *f.* microcircuit, microchip.
микрофо́н, а *m.* microphone.
микрохирурги́|я, и *f.* microsurgery.
микрочи́п, а *m.* microchip.
ми́ксер, а *m.* (*cul.*) mixer, blender, liquidizer.
миксту́р|а, ы *f.* (liquid) medicine, mixture.
милитари́зм, а *m.* militarism.
милиц|е́йский *adj. of* ▸ **~́ия**
милицио́не́р, а *m.* policeman (*in Russia*).
мили́ци|я, и *f.* police (*in Russia*).
миллиа́рд, а *m.* billion (= *thousand million*).
миллиарде́р, а *m.* billionaire.
миллиа́рдный *adj.* billionth.
миллигра́мм, а *m.* milligram(me).
миллили́тр, а *m.* millilitre (*Br.*), milliliter (*US*).
миллиме́тр, а *m.* millimetre (*Br.*), millimeter (*US*).
миллио́н, а *m.* million.
миллионе́р, а *m.* millionaire.
миллио́нный *adj.* millionth.
ми́л|овать, ую *impf.* (*of* ▸ **по~**) to pardon, spare.
милови́д|ный (~ен, ~на) *adj.* pretty, nice-looking.
милосе́рди|е, я *nt.* mercy, charity.
милосе́рд|ный (~ен, ~на) *adj.* merciful, charitable.
ми́лостын|я, и *f.* alms.
ми́лост|ь, и *f.*
1 (*благодеяние*) favour (*Br.*), favor (*US*).
2 (*доброта*) kindness; charity; **из ~и** out of charity.
ми́л|ый (~, ~á, ~o, ~́лы́) *adj.*
1 nice, sweet; lovable; **э́то о́чень ~о с ва́шей стороны́** it is very nice of you.
2 dear; *as n.* **м., ~ого** *m.*, **~ая, ~ой** *f.* dear, darling.
ми́л|я, и *f.* mile.
ми́мик|а, и *f.* facial expressions.
ми́мо *adv. and prep.* + *g.* by, past; **пройти́, прое́хать м.** to pass by, to pass; **м.!** miss(ed)!
мимо́з|а, ы *f.* (*bot.*) mimosa.
мимолёт|ный (~ен, ~на) *adj.* fleeting, transient.
мимохо́дом *adv.* in passing; **м. упомяну́ть** (*fig., coll.*) to mention in passing.
мин. (*abbr. of* **мину́та**) min., minute(s).
ми́н|а¹, ы *f.*
1 (*mil., naut.*) mine.
2 (*mil.*) (*снаряд миномёта*) mortar shell, mortar bomb.
ми́н|а², ы *f.* (*выражение лица*) expression, mien.
минаре́т, а *m.* minaret.
минда́л|ь, я́ *m.*
1 (*дерево*) almond tree.
2 (*collect.*) (*орехи*) almonds.
минера́л, а *m.* mineral.
минера́лк|а, и *f.* (*coll.*) mineral water.
Минздра́в, а *m.* (*abbr. of* **Министе́рство здравоохране́ния**) Ministry of Health.
ми́ни *nt. indecl.* mini (*garment*).
миниатю́р|а, ы *f.* (*art, mus.*) miniature; (*theatr.*) short piece, play.
миниатю́р|ный (~ен, ~на) *adj.*
1 *adj. of* ▸ **~а.**
2 (*fig.*) diminutive, tiny, dainty.
ми́ни-ди́ск, а *m.* minidisc.
минима́л|ьный (~ен, ~ьна) *adj.* minimum.
ми́нимум, а *m.*
1 minimum; **прожи́точный м.** living wage.
2 (*as adv.*) at the least, at the minimum.
мини́р|овать, ую *impf. and pf.* (*pf. also* **за~**) (*mil., naut.*) to mine.
министе́рский *adj.* ministerial.
министе́рств|о, а *nt.* (*pol.*) ministry.
мини́стр, а *m.* (*pol.*) minister; **премье́р-м.** Prime Minister, premier.
мин|ова́ть, у́ю *impf. and pf.*
1 (*пройти/проехать мимо*) to pass (by); **~у́я подро́бности** omitting details.
2 (*pf. only*) (*окончиться*) to be over, be past; **опа́сность ~ова́ла** the danger is past.
3 (*only with* **не** + *g.*) (*избежать*) to escape, avoid; **не м. тебе́ тюрьмы́** you cannot escape being sent to prison.
мино́г|а, и *f.* (*zool.*) lamprey.
миномёт, а *m.* (*mil.*) mortar.
миноно́с|ец, ца *m.* (*naut.*) torpedo boat; **эска́дренный м.** destroyer.
мино́р, а *m.* (*mus.*) minor key.
Минск, а *m.* Minsk.
мину́вш|ий *adj.* past; *as n.* **~ее, ~его** *nt.* the past.
ми́нус, а *m.*
1 (*math.*) minus.
2 (*fig., coll.*) (*недостаток*) shortcoming, drawback.
мину́т|а, ы *f.* minute.
мину́т|ный *adj.*
1 *adj. of* ▸ **~а; ~ная стре́лка** minute hand.
2 momentary; **~ная встре́ча** brief encounter.
мир¹, а *m.* (*согласие*) peace; **заключи́ть м.** to make peace.
мир², а, *pl.* **~ы́** *m.* (*вселенная*) world (*also fig.*); universe; **живо́тный м.** fauna; **расти́тельный м.** flora.
мира́ж, á *m.* mirage (*also fig.*); optical illusion.
мир|и́ть, ю́, и́шь *impf.*
1 (*pf.* **по~**) (*враждующих*) to reconcile.
2 (*pf.* **при~**) (**с** + *i.*) (*заставлять терпимо относиться*) to reconcile (to).
мир|и́ться, ю́сь, и́шься *impf.* (**с** + *i.*)
1 (*pf.* **по~**) (*прекращать вражду*) to be reconciled (with), make it up (with).
2 (*pf.* **при~**) (*терпимо относиться*) to reconcile o.s. (to); **м. со свои́м**

положе́нием to accept the situation.
ми́р|ный (~ен, ~на) *adj.*
[1] *adj. of* ▸ **~**[1].
[2] peaceful; peaceable.
мировоззре́ни|е, я *nt.* (world-)outlook, Weltanschauung; (one's) philosophy (of life).
мир|ово́й *adj. of* ▸ **~**[2]; **~ова́я война́** world war.
мирозда́ни|е, я *nt.* the universe.
миролюби́в|ый (~, ~а) *adj.* peaceable.
миротво́р|ец, ца *m.* peacemaker.
мирско́й *adj.* secular, lay; mundane, worldly.
мирт, а *m.* (*bot.*) myrtle.
ми́ск|а, и *f.* basin, bowl.
ми́сс *f. indecl.* Miss.
миссионе́р, а *m.* missionary.
ми́ссис *nt. indecl.* Mrs.
ми́сси|я, и *f.* mission.
ми́стер, а *m.* mister, Mr.
ми́стик|а, и *f.* mysticism; (*coll.*) mystery.
мистифика́ци|я, и *f.* hoax, leg-pull.
мистифици́р|овать, ую *impf. and pf.* to hoax, mystify.
мисти́ческий *adj.* mystic(al).
ми́тинг, а *m.* (political) mass meeting; rally.
митрополи́т, а *m.* (*eccl.*) metropolitan.
миф, а *m.* myth (*also fig.*).
мифи́ческий *adj.* mythical.
мифологи́ческий *adj.* mythological.
мифоло́ги|я, и *f.* mythology.
мише́н|ь, и *f.* target (*also fig.*).
ми́шка, и *m.*: **плю́шевый м.** teddy (bear).
младе́н|ец, ца *m.* baby, infant.
младе́нческий *adj.* infantile.
мла́дший *adj.* (*comp. and superl. of* ▸ **молодо́й**)
[1] (*более молодой*) younger.
[2] (*самый молодой*) the youngest.
[3] (*по служебному положению*) junior; **м. лейтена́нт** second lieutenant.
млекопита́ющ|ее, его *nt.* (*zool.*) mammal.
мле|ть, ю *impf.* (**от** + *g.*) to be overcome (*with delight, fright, etc.*).
млн. (*abbr. of* **миллио́н**) m, million(s).
млрд. (*abbr. of* **миллиа́рд**) b., billion(s) (= *thousand million*).
мм (*abbr. of* **миллиме́тр**) mm, millimetre(s) (*Br.*), millimeter(s) (*US*).
мне *d. and p. of* ▸ **я**
мне́ни|е, я *nt.* opinion.
мни́мый *adj.*
[1] (*воображаемый*) imaginary.
[2] (*притворный*) sham, pretended; **м. больно́й** hypochondriac.
мни́тел|ьный (~ен, ~ьна) *adj.*
[1] (*ипохондрический*) hypochondriac.
[2] (*подозрительный*) mistrustful, suspicious.
мно́г|ие, их *adj. and n.* many; **во ~их отноше́ниях** in many respects.
мно́го *adv.* (+ *g.*) much; many; a lot (of); **м. вре́мени** much time; **м. лет** many years.
много... *comb. form* many-, poly-, multi-.
многобо́р|ец, ца *m.* all-round athlete, multi-eventer.
многобо́рь|е, я *nt.* multi-discipline event *or* competition.
многогра́н|ный (~ен, ~на) *adj.* (*math.*) polyhedral; (*fig.*) many-sided; multi-faceted.
многоде́т|ный (~ен, ~на) *adj.* having many children.
многодне́вный *adj.*: **м. путь** a journey lasting several days.
мно́г|ое, ого *nt.* much, a great deal; **во ~ом** in many respects.
многожё́нств|о, а *nt.* polygamy.
многозначи́тел|ьный (~ен, ~ьна) *adj.* significant.
многозна́ч|ный (~ен, ~на) *adj.*
[1] (*math.*) multi-digit.
[2] (*ling.*) polysemantic.
многокра́т|ный (~ен, ~на) *adj.* repeated; frequent.
многоле́тний *adj.*
[1] lasting *or* living many years; of many years' standing.
[2] (*bot.*) perennial.
многоли́к|ий (~, ~а) *adj.* many-sided.
многолю́д|ный (~ен, ~на) *adj.* (*район*) populous; (*улица*) crowded.
многонациона́л|ьный (~ен, ~ьна) *adj.* multinational.
многообеща́ющий *adj.*
[1] (*ученик*) promising, hopeful.
[2] (*взгляд*) significant.
многообра́зи|е, я *nt.* variety, diversity.
многоparти́йный *adj.* multiparty.
многосери́йный *adj.* serial.
многосло́в|ный (~ен, ~на) *adj.* verbose.
многосторо́н|ний (~ен, ~ня) *adj.*
[1] (*no short forms*) (*math.*) polygonal.
[2] (*договор*) multilateral.
[3] (*человек*) many-sided, versatile.
многострада́л|ьный (~ен, ~ьна) *adj.* long-suffering.
многоуго́льник, а *m.* (*math.*) polygon.
многоцелево́й *adj.* multipurpose.
многочи́слен|ный (~, ~на) *adj.* numerous.
многоэта́жный *adj.* multi-storey (*Br.*), multistory (*US*), high-rise.
мно́жественн|ый *adj.* plural; **~ое число́** (*gram.*) plural (number).
мно́жеств|о, а *nt.* a great number, a quantity; multitude; (*math.*) set.
мно́ж|ить, у, ишь *impf.* (*of* ▸ **по~** *and* ▸ **у~**) (*math.*) to multiply.
мной, мно́ю *i. of* ▸ **я**
мобилиза́ци|я, и *f.* mobilization.
мобилиз|ова́ть, у́ю *impf. and pf.* (**на** + *a.*) to mobilize (for).
моби́л|ьник, а *m.* (*coll.*) mobile (phone) (*Br.*), cellphone.
моби́л|ьный (~ен, ~ьна) *adj.* mobile; *as n.* (*coll.*) (= **м. телефо́н**) mobile (phone) (*Br.*), cellphone.
моги́л|а, ы *f.* grave.
моги́льщик, а *m.* gravedigger.
мо|гу́, ~́гут *see* ▸ **мочь**
могу́ч|ий (~, ~а) *adj.* mighty, powerful.
могу́ществен|ный (~, ~на) *adj.*

powerful; potent.
могу́ществ|о, а *nt.* power, might.
мо́д|а, ы *f.* fashion, vogue; **выходи́ть из ~ы** to go out of fashion.
моде́л|ь, и *f.* model; (*платья*) design; (*для отливки*) pattern.
моделье́р, а *m.* fashion designer, couturier.
моде́м, а *m.* (*comput.*) modem.
моде́рн, а *m.* modernist style, art nouveau.
модерниза́ци|я, и *f.* modernization; updating.
модернизи́р|овать, ую *impf.* and *pf.* to modernize; to update.
модерни́зм, а *m.* (*art*) modernism.
модифика́ци|я, и *f.* modification.
модифици́р|овать, ую *impf.* and *pf.* to modify.
мо́д|ный (~ен, ~на́, ~но) *adj.*
1 fashionable, stylish.
2 *adj. of* ▸ **~а; м. журна́л** fashion magazine.
мо́дул|ь, я *m.* (*math.*) modulus; (*tech.*) module.
мо́жет *see* ▸ **мочь**
можжеве́льник, а *m.* (*bot.*) juniper.
мо́жно *pred.* (*impers.* + *inf.*)
1 (*возможно*) it is possible; **м. было э́то предви́деть** it could have been foreseen; **как м.** + *comp.* as ... as possible; **как м. скоре́е** as soon as possible.
2 (*разрешается*) it is permissible, one may; **м. (мне/нам) идти́?** may I/we go?
моза́ик|а, и *f.* mosaic; (*искусство*) mosaic work.
Мозамби́к, а *m.* Mozambique.
мозамби́к|ец, ца *m.* Mozambican.
мозамби́кский *adj.* Mozambican.
мозг, а, в ~у́, *pl.* **~и́, ~о́в** *m.*
1 brain (*also fig.*); (*fig.*) nerve centre (*Br.*), center (*US*); **головно́й м.** brain, cerebrum; **спинно́й м.** spinal cord.
2 (*anat.*) marrow; **до ~а косте́й** (*fig., coll.*) to the core.
мозо́л|ь, и *f.* corn; callus; **ру́ки в ~ях** calloused hands.
мой *possessive pron.* (*при существительном*) my; (*без существительного*) mine; *as n.* **мои́, мои́х** my people; **по-мо́ему** (*по моему мнению*) in my opinion; (*так, как я считаю правильным*) as I think right.
мо́йк|а, и *f.*
1 (*действие*) washing.
2 (*машина*) washer.
3 (*раковина*) sink.
мо́йщик, а *m.* washer; cleaner.
мокри́ц|а, ы *f.*
1 (*zool.*) woodlouse.
2 (*bot.*) chickweed (*Stellaria media*).
мо́кр|ый (~, ~а́, ~о) *adj.* wet; **м. снег** sleet; (*impers., pred.*): **~о** it is wet.
мол[1], а *m.* mole, pier.
мол[2] (*contraction of* **мо́лвил**) (*coll.*) he says (said), they say (said), *etc.* (*indicating reported speech*); **он, м., никогда́ там не́ был** he said he had never been there.
молдава́н|ин, ина, *pl.* **~е, ~** *m.* Moldovan.
молдава́н|ка, ки *f. of* ▸ **~ин**
молда́вский *adj.* Moldovan; (*язык*) Moldavian.
Молдо́в|а, ы *f.* Moldova.
моле́кул|а, ы *f.* (*phys.*) molecule.
моли́тв|а, ы *f.* prayer.
мол|и́ть, ю́, ~ишь *impf.* (*a. and* **о** + *p.*) to pray (for), implore (for), beseech; **~ю́ вас о по́мощи** I beg you to help me.
мол|и́ться, ю́сь, ~ишься *impf.*
1 (*pf.* **по~;** + *d.*) to pray (to).
2 (*fig.*; **на** + *a.*) to idolize.
моллю́ск, а *m.* mollusc; shellfish.
молниено́с|ный (~ен, ~на) *adj.* (quick as) lightning; **~ная война́** blitzkrieg.
мо́лни|я, и *f.*
1 lightning.
2: **(застёжка-)м.** zip (*Br.*), zipper (*US*).
молодёж|ный *adj. of* ▸ **~ь**
молодёж|ь, и *f.* (*collect.*) youth; young people.
молод|е́ц, ца́ *m.* fine fellow; (*о женщине*) fine girl; *as int.*: **м.!** well done!
молодожён|ы, ов *pl.* (*sg.* **~, ~а** *m.*) newly-married couple, newly-weds.
молод|о́й (мо́лод, ~а́, мо́лодо) *adj.*
1 young; (*свойственный молодости*) youthful.
2 *as n.* (*coll.*) **м., ~о́го** *m.* bridegroom; **~а́я, ~о́й** *f.* bride; **~ы́е, ~ы́х** newly-married couple, newly-weds.
мо́лодост|ь, и *f.* youth; youthfulness.
моложа́в|ый (~, ~а) *adj.* (*человек*) young-looking; (*вид*) youthful.
моло́|же *comp. of* ▸ **~до́й**
молок|о́, а́ *no pl., nt.* milk.
мо́лот, а *m.* hammer; **кузне́чный м.** sledgehammer.
молот|о́к, ка́ *m.* hammer; **отбо́йный м.** pneumatic drill; **прода́ть с ~ка́** to sell by auction, auction.
мо́лот|ый (~, ~а) *p.p.p. of* ▸ **моло́ть** *and adj.* ground.
моло́ть, мелю́, ме́лешь *impf.* (*of* ▸ **с~**) to grind; **м. вздор** (*no pf.*; *fig., coll.*) to talk nonsense.
моло́чн|ый *adj.*
1 *adj. of* ▸ **молоко́; м. брат** foster-brother; **~ые проду́кты** dairy products; **~ое хозя́йство** dairy farm(ing).
2 milky; lactic.
мо́лча *adv.* silently, in silence.
молчали́в|ый (~, ~а) *adj.*
1 (*человек*) taciturn, silent.
2 (*одобрение*) tacit, unspoken.
молча́ни|е, я *nt.* silence.
молч|а́ть, у́, и́шь *impf.* to be silent; (**о** + *p.*) to keep silent (about).
мол|ь, и *f.* (clothes) moth.
мольб|а́, ы́ *f.* entreaty, supplication.
мольбе́рт, а *m.* easel.
моме́нт, а *m.*
1 (*миг*) moment; instant; **в да́нный м.** at the present time; at the moment.
2 (*черта*) feature, element, factor.
момента́льно *adv.* in a moment, instantly.
момента́л|ьный (~ен, ~ьна) *adj.*

instantaneous; **м. снúмок** snapshot.
монáрх, а *m.* monarch.
монархúзм, а *m.* monarchism.
монáрхи|я, и *f.* monarchy.
монастыр|ь, я́ *m.* monastery; **(жéнский) м.** convent, nunnery.
монáх, а *m.* monk.
монáхин|я, и *f.* nun.
монгóл, а *m.* Mongol, Mongolian.
Монгóли|я, и *f.* Mongolia.
монгóл|ка, ки *f. of* ▶ **~**
монгóльский *adj.* Mongolian.
монéт|а, ы *f.* coin; **размéнная м.** change; **принять за чúстую ~у** (*fig., coll.*) to take at face value, take in good faith.
монитóр, а *m.* (*TV, comput.*) monitor.
мóно *nt. indecl.* mono.
монográфи|я, и *f.* monograph.
монолúт, а *m.* monolith.
монолúт|ный (~ен, ~на) *adj.* monolithic (*also fig.*; *pol.*); (*fig.*) solid.
монолóг, а *m.* monologue, soliloquy.
монопóли|я, и *f.* (*econ. and fig.*) monopoly.
монотеúзм, а *m.* monotheism.
монотóн|ный (~ен, ~на) *adj.* monotonous.
монстр, а *m.* monster.
монтáж, á *m.*
1 (*tech.*) (*действие*) assembling, mounting, installation.
2 (*cin.*) editing, montage; (*art, mus., liter.*) arrangement.
монтáжник, а *m.* (*на стройке*) rigger; (*на заводе*) fitter.
монтёр, а *m.*
1 fitter.
2 (*электромонтёр*) electrician.
монтúр|овать, ую *impf.* (*of* ▶ **с~**)
1 (*tech.*) to assemble, mount, fit.
2 (*cin.*) to edit; (*art, mus., liter.*) to arrange.
монумéнт, а *m.* monument.
монументáл|ьный (~ен, ~ьна) *adj.* monumental (*also fig.*).
мопéд, а *m.* moped.
морáл|ь, и *f.*
1 (*нормы поведения*) (code of) morals, ethics.
2 (*coll.*) (*нравоучение*) moralizing; **читáть м.** to moralize, preach.
морáл|ьный (~ен, ~ьна) *adj.* moral; ethical.
моратóри|й, я *m.* (*leg., comm.*) moratorium.
морг, а *m.* morgue, mortuary.
морг|áть, áю *impf.* (*of* ▶ **~нýть**) to blink; to wink.
морг|нýть, нý, нёшь *pf. of* ▶ **~áть; глáзом не ~нýв** (*coll.*) without batting an eyelid.
мордв|á, ы́ *f.* (*collect.*) the Mordva, the Mordvins.
мордвúн, а *m.* Mordvin.
мордвúн|ка, ки *f. of* ▶ **~**
Мордóви|я, и *f.* Mordvinia.
мордóвский *adj.* Mordvinian.
мóр|е, я, *pl.* **~я́, ~éй** *nt.*: **зá ~ем** overseas; **из-за ~я** from overseas; **нá м./на ~е** at sea; **у ~я** by the sea.
мореплáвани|е, я *nt.* navigation, seafaring.
морж, á *m.* walrus; (*coll.*) (*open-air*) winter bather.
моркóвк|а, и *f.* (*coll.*) a carrot.
моркóв|ь, и *f.* carrot; (*collect.*) carrot(s).
морóжен|ое, ого *nt.* ice (cream).
морóженый *adj.* frozen; (*картофель*) frost-damaged.
морóз, а *m.*
1 frost; **(у) меня́ м. по кóже подирáет (*or* пошёл)** it makes (made) my flesh creep.
2 (*usu. in pl.*) intensely cold weather.
морозúлк|а, и *f.* (*coll.*) freezer compartment; freezer.
морозúльник, а *m.* freezer.
морóзн|ый *adj.* frosty; (*impers., pred.*): **~о** it is freezing.
морозостó|йкий (~ек, ~йка) *adj.* (*bot.*) frost-resistant.
морос|úть, úт *impf.* to drizzle.
морóч|ить, у, ишь *impf.* (*of* ▶ **за~**) (*coll.*) to fool; **м. гóлову комý-н.** to take s.o. in.
морс, а *m.* fruit drink.
морск|óй *adj.*
1 sea; maritime; marine, nautical; **м. волк** (*coll.*) old salt; **~áя звездá** starfish; **м. конёк** (*zool.*) sea horse; **~áя свúнка** guinea pig.
2 naval; **~áя пехóта** marines; **м. флот** navy, fleet.
мóрфи|й, я *m.* (*pharm.*) morphine.
морфолóги|я, и *f.* morphology.
морщúн|а, ы *f.* wrinkle.
морщúнист|ый (~, ~а) *adj.* wrinkled.
мóрщ|иться, усь, ишься *impf.* (*of* **с~**)
1 (*делать гримасы*) to make a wry face, wince.
2 (*об одежде*) to crease, wrinkle.
моря́к, á *m.* sailor.
Москв|á, ы́ *f.*
1 (*город*) Moscow.
2 (*река*) the Moskva.
москвúч, á *m.* Muscovite.
москвúч|ка, ки *f. of* ▶ **~**
москúт, а *m.* mosquito.
москúт|ный *adj. of* ▶ **~; ~ная сéтка** mosquito net.
москóвский *adj.* (of) Moscow.
мост, ~á, о ~é, на ~ý, *pl.* **~ы́** *m.*
1 (*через реку*) bridge.
2 (*автомобиля*) axle.
мóстик, а *m.*
1 *dim. of* ▶ **мост.**
2 : **капитáнский м.** (*naut.*) (*captain's*) bridge.
мостк|ú, óв *no sg.*
1 (*для перехода*) planked walkway.
2 (*площадка*) wooden platform.
мостов|áя, óй *f.* road(way), carriageway.
мот|áть, áю *impf.*
1 (*pf.* **на~**) (*нитки, шерсть*) to wind, reel.
2 (*pf.* **~нýть**) (+ *i.*; *coll.*) (*головой*) to shake (*head, etc.*).
мотá|ться¹, ется *impf.* (*coll.*) to dangle.
мотá|ться², юсь *impf.* (*coll.*) to rush about.
мотéл|ь, я *m.* motel.

моти́в[1], **а** *m.*
1 (*повод*) motive.
2 (*довод*) reason.
моти́в[2], **а** *m.*
1 (*mus.*) tune, motif.
2 (*fig.*) motif.
мотиви́р|овать, ую *impf. and pf.* to give reasons (for), justify.
мот|ну́ть, ну́, нёшь *inst. pf. of* ▸ **~а́ть**
мотого́н|ки, ок *no sg.* motorcycle races.
мотого́нщик, а *m.* motorcycle racer.
мотого́нщи|ца, цы *f. of* ▸ **~к**
мот|о́к, ка́ *m.* skein, hank.
мото́р, а *m.* motor; (*автомобиля, самолёта*) engine.
моторо́ллер, а *m.* (motor) scooter.
мотоспо́рт, а *m.* motorcycle racing.
мотоци́кл, а *m.* motorcycle.
мотоцикли́ст, а *m.* motorcyclist; biker.
мотоцикли́ст|ка, ки *f. of* ▸ **~**
моты́г|а, и *f.* hoe.
мотыл|ёк, ька́ *m.* moth.
мох, мха *and* **мо́ха, о мхе** *and* **о мо́хе, во (на) мху́,** *pl.* **мхи, мхов** *m.* moss.
мохе́р, а *m.* mohair.
мохна́т|ый (~, ~а) *adj.* hairy, shaggy.
моч|а́, и́ *f.* urine.
моча́лк|а, и *f.* bath sponge, loofah.
мочево́й *adj.* urinary, uric; **м. пузы́рь** (*anat.*) bladder.
моч|и́ть, у́, ~́ишь *impf.*
1 (*pf.* **на~, за~**) (*делать мокрым*) to wet, moisten.
2 (*pf.* **на~, за~**) (*бельё*) to soak; (*лён*) to ret.
3 (*pf.* **за~**) (*sl.*) (*убивать*) to kill.
мочь, могу́, мо́жешь, мо́гут, *past* **мог, могла́** *impf.* (*of* ▸ **с~**) to be able; **мо́жет быть, быть мо́жет** perhaps, maybe; **мо́жет** (*coll.*) = **мо́жет быть; не мо́жет быть!** impossible!
моше́нник, а *m.* swindler, crook.
моше́ннича|ть, ю *impf.* (*of* ▸ **с~**) to swindle.
моше́нничеств|о, а *nt.* swindling; cheating.
мо́шк|а, и *f.* midge.
мощёный *adj.* paved.
мо́щ|и, е́й *no sg.* (*relig.*) relics.
мо́щност|ь, и *f.* power; (*tech.*) capacity, rating; output; **двигатель ~ью в сто лошади́ных сил** hundred horsepower engine.
мо́щ|ный (~ен, ~на́, ~но) *adj.* powerful, mighty; (*рост*) vigorous.
мощ|ь, и *f.* power, might.
мо́|ю, ешь *see* ▸ **мыть**
мо́ющ|ий *pres. part. act. of* ▸ **мыть** *and adj.* detergent; **~ие сре́дства** detergents.
мо́ющ|ийся *adj.* washable; **~иеся обо́и** washable wallpaper.
мраз|ь, и *no pl., f.* (*coll.*) dregs, scum.
мрак, а *m.* darkness, gloom (*also fig., rhet.*).
мра́мор, а *m.* marble.
мра́морный *adj.* marble; (*fig.*) (white as) marble; (*бумага*) marbled.
мра́ч|ный (~ен, ~на́, ~но, ~́ны) *adj.*
1 dark, sombre (*Br.*), somber (*US*).
2 (*fig.*) gloomy, dismal.
мсти́ть, мщу, мстишь *impf.* (*of* ▸ **ото~**)
1 (+ *d.*) to take revenge/vengeance (on s.o.).
2 (**за** + *a.*) to avenge; **м. за дру́га** to avenge one's friend.
3 (+ *d. and* **за** + *a.*) to take revenge on s.o. for sth.; to avenge o.s. on s.o. for sth.
мудре́ц, а́ *m.* (*rhet.*) sage, wise man.
му́дрост|ь, и *f.* wisdom.
му́др|ый (~, ~а́, ~о, ~́ы) *adj.* wise.
муж, а *m.*
1 (*pl.* **~ья́, ~е́й, ~ья́м**) husband.
2 (*pl.* **~и́, ~е́й, ~а́м**) (*rhet.*) (*мужчина*) man; **госуда́рственный м.** statesman; **учёный м.** scholar.
мужа́|ться, юсь *impf.* to take heart, take courage; **~йтесь!** courage!
му́жествен|ный (~, ~на) *adj.* manly, steadfast.
му́жеств|о, а *nt.* courage, fortitude.
мужи́к, а́ *m.*
1 (*крестьянин*) muzhik (*Russian peasant*).
2 (*coll.*) (*мужчина*) bloke, guy.
мужско́й *adj.* (*голос, рукопожатие*) masculine; (*пол, клетка*) male; (*туалет, платье*) men's; **м. род** (*gram.*) masculine gender.
мужчи́н|а, ы *m.* man.
му́з|а, ы *f.* muse.
музе́|й, я *m.* museum.
му́зык|а, и *f.* music.
музыка́л|ьный (~ен, ~ьна) *adj.* music (*attr.*); musical.
музыка́нт, а *m.* musician.
музыкове́д, а *m.* musicologist.
му́к|а, и *f.* torment; torture; (*pl.*) pangs, throes; **родовы́е ~и** labour (*Br.*), labor (*US*) pains.
мук|а́, и́ *f.* (*пшеничная, кукурузная*) flour; (*костяная, рыбная*) meal.
мулл|а́, ы *m.* mullah.
мультиме́диа *pl. indecl.* multimedia.
мультимеди́йный *adj.* multimedia.
мультипликаци|я, и *f.* (film) animation.
мультфи́льм, а *m.* cartoon, animation.
му́ми|я, и *f.* mummy (*corpse*).
мунди́р, а *m.* full dress uniform.
мундшту́к, а́ *m.*
1 (*сигареты, трубки*) mouthpiece; (*трубочка, в которую вставляют сигарету*) cigarette holder.
2 (*mus.*) mouthpiece.
муниципалите́т, а *m.* municipality; town council; **зда́ние ~а** town hall.
муниципа́льн|ый *adj.* municipal; **~ая кварти́ра** council flat.
мурав|е́й, ья́ *m.* ant.
мураве́йник, а *m.* anthill.
муравье́д, а *m.* (*zool.*) anteater.
мурлы́|кать, чу, чешь *impf.*
1 (*о кошке*) to purr.
2 (*coll.*) (*о человеке*) to hum.
муска́т, а *m.*
1 (*орех*) nutmeg.
2 (*виноград*) muscadine, muscat.

3 (*вино*) muscatel, muscat.

му́скул, а *m.* muscle.

мускулату́р|а, ы *f.* (*collect.*) muscular system, musculature.

мускули́ст|ый (~, ~а) *adj.* muscular, brawny.

му́сор, а *m.* rubbish (*Br.*), garbage (*US*).

му́сор|ный *adj. of* ▸ **~; м. я́щик** dustbin (*Br.*), garbage can (*US*).

мусорово́з, а *m.* dustcart (*Br.*), garbage truck (*US*).

мусоропрово́д, а *m.* refuse chute.

му́сорщик, а *m.* dustman (*Br.*), garbage collector (*US*).

мусульма́н|ин, ина, *pl.* **~е, ~** *m.* Muslim.

мусульма́н|ка, ки *f. of* ▸ **~ин**

мусульма́нский *adj.* Muslim.

мусульма́нств|о, а *nt.* Islam.

мута́нт, а *m.* (*biol.*) mutant.

мута́ци|я, и *f.* (*biol.*) mutation.

мути́р|овать, ую *impf. and pf.* (*biol.*) mutate.

му́т|ный (~ен, ~на́, ~но, ~ны) *adj.*
1 cloudy, turbid.
2 (*fig.*) dull(ed); confused.

му́фт|а, ы *f.*
1 (*для рук*) muff.
2 (*tech.*) coupling; (*elec.*) connecting box; **м. сцепле́ния** clutch.

му́фти|й, я *m.* (*relig.*) mufti.

му́х|а, и *f.* fly; **де́лать из ~и слона́** (*fig.*) to make a mountain out of a molehill.

мухомо́р, а *m.* (*гриб*) fly agaric (*mushroom*).

муче́ни|е, я *nt.* torment, torture.

му́ченик, а *m.* martyr.

му́чени|ца, цы *f. of* ▸ **~к**

мучи́тел|ьный (~ен, ~ьна) *adj.* excruciating; agonizing.

му́ч|ить, у, ишь *impf.* (*of* ▸ **за~**) to torment; to worry, harass.

му́ч|иться, усь, ишься *impf.* (*of* ▸ **за~**)
1 (+ *i.*, **от** + *g.*) *pass. of* ▸ **~ить; м. от бо́ли** to be racked with pain.
2 (**из-за** + *g.*) to worry (about), feel unhappy.
3 (**над** + *i.*) to torment o.s. (over, about).

мха, мху *see* ▸ **мох**

мч|а́ться, усь, и́шься *impf.* to rush, race, tear along; **м. во весь опо́р** to go at full speed; **вре́мя ~и́тся** time flies.

МЧС *m.* (*abbr. of* **Министе́рство по чрезвыча́йным ситуа́циям**) Ministry of Emergency Situations.

мы, *a.*, *g.*, *p.* **нас,** *d.* **нам,** *i.* **на́ми** *pron.* we; **мы с ва́ми** you and I.

мы́л|о, а *nt.*
1 soap.
2 (*у лошади*) foam, lather.

мы́льниц|а, ы *f.* soap dish.

мы́л|ьный *adj. of* ▸ **~о; ~ьная о́пера** soap opera.

мыс, а *m.* (*geog.*) cape, promontory.

мы́сленный *adj.* mental; **м. о́браз** mental image.

мысли́м|ый (~, ~а) *adj.* conceivable, thinkable.

мысли́тел|ь, я *m.* thinker.

мысли́тельный *adj.* intellectual, of thought; **м. проце́сс** thought process.

мы́сл|ить, ю, ишь *impf.*
1 (*думать*) to think; to reason.
2 (*представлять себе*) to conceive, imagine.

мысл|ь, и *f.* (**о** + *p.*) thought (of, about); (*идея*) idea; **о́браз ~ей** way of thinking, views; **собира́ться с ~ями** to collect one's thoughts.

мыть, мо́ю, мо́ешь *impf.* (*of* ▸ **вы́~, по~**) to wash.

мы́ться, мо́юсь, мо́ешься *impf.* (*of* ▸ **вы́~, по~**)
1 to wash (o.s.).
2 *pass. of* ▸ **мыть**

мыч|а́ть, у́, и́шь *impf.*
1 (*о корове*) to moo; (*о быке*) to bellow.
2 (*fig., coll.*) (*о человеке*) to mumble.

мышело́вк|а, и *f.* mousetrap.

мыш|и́ный *adj. of* ▸ **~ь; ~и́ная возня́** pointless fussing over trifles.

мы́шк|а[1], и *f. dim. of* ▸ **мышь**

мы́шк|а[2], и *f.* armpit; **под ~у, под ~ой** under one's arm; **нести́ под ~ой** to carry under one's arm.

мышле́ни|е, я *nt.* thinking, thought.

мы́шц|а, ы *f.* muscle.

мыш|ь, и, *pl.* **~и, ~е́й** *f.*
1 (*also comput.*) mouse.
2 : **летучая м.** bat.

мышья́к, а́ *m.* (*chem., pharm.*) arsenic.

Мья́нм|а, ы *f.* Myanmar.

мэр, а *m.* mayor.

мэ́ри|я, и *f.*
1 (*управление*) town council.
2 (*здание*) town hall.

мю́зикл, а *m.* musical.

мю́зик-хо́лл, а *m.* music hall.

мю́сли *pl. and nt. indecl.* muesli.

мя́г|кий (~ок, ~ка́, ~ко) *adj.* soft; (*fig.*) mild, gentle; (*о приговоре*) lenient; **м. ваго́н** (*rail.*) soft-(seated) carriage (*Br.*), sleeping car; **м. знак** (*ling.*) soft sign (*name of Russian letter* «ь»); **~кое кре́сло** easy chair.

мя́гко *adv.* softly; (*fig.*) mildly, gently.

мя́г|че *comp. of* ▸ **~кий** *and* ▸ **~ко**

мя́кот|ь, и *f.*
1 (*мяса*) flesh.
2 (*плода*) pulp (*of fruit*).

мяси́ст|ый (~, ~а) *adj.* fleshy; meaty.

мясни́к, а́ *m.* butcher.

мяс|но́й *adj. of* ▸ **~о; ~ны́е консе́рвы** tinned meat.

мя́с|о, а *nt.* meat; **пу́шечное м.** (*fig.*) cannon fodder.

мясору́бк|а, и *f.* mincer.

мя́т|а, ы *f.* (*bot.*) mint; **пе́речная м.** peppermint.

мяте́ж, а́ *m.* mutiny, revolt.

мяте́жник, а *m.* mutineer, rebel.

мяте́ж|ный (~ен, ~на) *adj.*
1 rebellious, mutinous.
2 (*fig.*) restless; stormy.

мя́т|ный *adj.* mint; **~ые леденцы́** peppermints.

мя́т|ый *p.p.p. of* ▸ **~ь** *and adj.* creased.

мять, мну, мнёшь *impf.*
1 (*pf.* **раз~**) (*глину*) to work up, knead.
2 (*pf.* **из~** *and* **с~**) (*бумагу, платье*) to crumple; **м. траву́** to trample grass.

мя́ться, мнётся *impf.* (*of* ▸ **из~, по~** *and* ▸ **с~**) to become crumpled; to crease easily.

мяу́ка|ть, ю *impf.* to mew, miaow.

мяч, а́ *m.* ball.

Нн

на́[1] *int.* (*coll.*) here; here you are; here, take it; **на́ кни́гу!** here, take the book!

на[2] *prep.* **I.** + *a.*
1 on (to); to; into; over, through; **положи́те кни́гу на стол** put the book on the table; **сесть на авто́бус, по́езд** to board a bus, a train; **на се́вер** to the north; **на заво́д** to the factory; **перевести́ на англи́йский** to translate into English.
2 (*о времени деятельности*) at; on; until, to (*or untranslated*); **на друго́й день, на сле́дующий день** (the) next day; **на э́тот раз** this time, for this once.
3 (*при обозначении срока*) for; **на два дня** for two days; **собра́ние назна́чено на понеде́льник** the meeting is fixed for Monday; (*при обозначении цели, назначения*) for; **на́ зиму** for the winter; **ко́мната на двои́х** a room for two.
4 (*при обозначении меры*) by (*or untranslated*); **коро́че на дюйм** shorter by an inch; **опозда́ть на час** to be an hour late; **ста́рше на три го́да** three years older; **четы́ре ме́тра (в длину́) на два (в ширину́)** four metres (long) by two (broad); (*при умножении, делении*) **помно́жить пять на́ три** to multiply five by three; **дели́ть на́ два** to divide into two.
5 (*при обозначении стоимости*) worth (*of sth.*); **ма́рок на рубль** a rouble's worth of stamps.
■ **II.** + *p.*
1 on, upon; in; at; **на столе́** on the table; **на бума́ге** on paper (*also fig.*); **на се́вере** in the north; **на заво́де** at the factory; **на со́лнце** in the sun; **на во́здухе** in the open air; **на дворе́, на у́лице** out of doors; **на рабо́те** at work; **игра́ть на роя́ле** to play the piano; **писа́ть на неме́цком языке́** to write in German.
2 (*во время чего-н.*) in (*or untranslated*); during; **на э́той неде́ле** this week.
3 (*при помощи чего-н.*) on (*or untranslated*); **на ва́те** padded; **э́тот дви́гатель рабо́тает на не́фти** this engine runs on oil.
4 (*о транспорте*) by; **е́хать на по́езде/авто́бусе** to go by train/bus.

на... *as vbl. pref.* **I.** *forms pf. aspect.*
■ **II.** *indicates*
1 action continued to sufficiency, to point of satisfaction or exhaustion.
2 action relating to determinate quantity or number of objects.

набалда́шник, а *m.* knob.

набе́г, а *m.* raid; foray.

набега́|ть, ю *impf. of* ▸ **набежа́ть**

набе|гу́, жи́шь, гу́т *see* ▸ **~жа́ть**

набе|жа́ть, гу́, жи́шь, гу́т *pf.* (*of* ▸ **~га́ть**)
1 (*натолкнуться*) (**на** + *a.*) to run into, smash into; (*о волнах*) to lap against.
2 (*сбежаться*) to come running (*together*).

на́бережн|ая, ой *f.* embankment.

набива́|ть, ю *impf. of* ▸ **наби́ть**

набира́|ть(ся), ю(сь) *impf. of* ▸ **набра́ть(ся)**

наб|и́ть, ью́, ьёшь *pf.* (*of* ▸ **~ива́ть**) (+ *a. and i.*) to stuff (with), pack (with), fill (with); **н. тру́бку** to fill one's pipe.

наблюда́тел|ь, я *m.* observer.

наблюда́тел|ьный *adj.*
1 **(~ен, ~ьна)** (*внимательный*) observant.
2 (*для наблюдения*) observation (*attr.*); **н. пункт** (*mil.*) observation post.

наблюда́|ть, ю *impf.*
1 (*следить глазами; изучать*) to observe; to watch.
2 (**за** + *i.*) (*за детьми*) to take care (of), look after.
3 (**за** + *i.*) to supervise, superintend; **н. за у́личным движе́нием** to control traffic.

наблюде́ни|е, я *nt.*
1 observation.
2 (*надзор*) supervision, superintendence.

на́бок *adv.* on one side, awry.

набо́р, а *m.*
1 (*рабочих*) recruitment; (*скорости, высоты*) gaining, gathering.
2 (*typ.*) composition, typesetting.
3 (*комплект*) set, collection.

набра́сыва|ть, ю *impf. of* ▸ **наброса́ть**[1] *and* ▸ **набро́сить**

набра́сыва|ться, юсь *impf. of* ▸ **набро́ситься**

набра́|ть, наберу́, наберёшь, *past* **~л, ~ла́, ~ло** *pf.* (*of* ▸ **набира́ть**)
1 (+ *g. or a.*) (*собрать*) to gather; to collect, assemble; **н. угля́** to take on coal; **н. но́мер** to dial a (*telephone*) number; **н. ско́рость** to pick up, gather speed; **н. высоту́** (*aeron.*) to gain height; to climb.
2 (*рабочих*) to recruit, enrol, engage.
3 (*typ.*) to compose, set up.

набра́|ться, наберу́сь, наберёшься, *past* **~лся, ~ла́сь ~ло́сь** *pf.* (*of* ▸ **набира́ться**)

1 (*usu. impers.*) (*скопиться*) (*о людях*) to assemble, gather, collect; (*о пыли, деньгах, работе*) to accumulate.
2 (+ *g.*) (*храбрости, сил*) to find, muster; (*знаний*) to acquire.
набросá|ть¹, ю *pf.* (*of* ▸ **набрáсывать**) (*рисунок и т. п.*) to sketch, outline.
набросá|ть², ю *pf.* (*накидать*) to throw about; to throw (*in successive instalments*).
набрó|сить, шу, сишь *pf.* (*of* ▸ **набрáсывать**) to throw (on, over).
набрó|ситься, шусь, сишься *pf.* (*of* ▸ **набрáсываться**) (**на** + *a.*) to fall upon; to go for; **собáка ~силась на меня** the dog went for me; (*на работу, на еду*) (*coll.*) to attack, get stuck into.
набрóс|ок, ка *m.* (*рисунок*) sketch; (*статьи*) draft.
набух|áть, áю *impf. of* ▸ **~нуть**
набýх|нуть, ну, нешь, *past* **~, ~ла** *pf.* (*of* ▸ **~áть**) to swell.
наб|ью, ьёшь *see* ▸ **~ить**
наваждéни|е, я *nt.* delusion; (*призрак*) hallucination.
навáлива|ть(ся), ю(сь) *impf. of* ▸ **навалить(ся)**
навал|ить, ю, ~ишь *pf.* (*of* ▸ **~ивать**) (*наложить наверх*) to heap, pile; (*возложить*) to load (*also fig.*); *impers.*: **снéгу ~ило по колéно** the snow had piled up knee deep.
навал|иться, юсь, ~ишься *pf.* (*of* ▸ **~иваться**) (**на** + *a.*)
1 (*coll.*) (*на еду, на работу*) to attack, get stuck into.
2 (*на дверь, на человека*) to lean (on, upon); to bring all one's weight to bear (on).
3 (*насыпаться*) to pile up (on).
наве|дý, дёшь *see* ▸ **~сти**
навéк *adv.* for ever.
навéк|и = ~
навéрно(е) *adv.* (*вводное слово*) probably, most likely; **он, н., не позвонит** he probably won't phone.
наверняка *adv.* (*coll.*)
1 (*несомненно*) for sure, certainly.
2 (*безошибочно*) safely, without taking risks; **бить н.** to take no chances.
наверстá|ть, ю *pf.* (*of* ▸ **навёрстывать**) to make up (for); **н. потéрянное врéмя** to make up for lost time; **н. упýщенное** to repair an omission.
навёрстыва|ть, ю *impf. of* ▸ **наверстáть**
навéрх *adv.* (*вверх*) up, upward; (*по лестнице*) upstairs; (*на поверхность*) to the top.
наверхý *adv.* above; (*в верхнем этаже*) upstairs; (*fig.*) (*в руководстве*) at the top.
навéс, а *m.*
1 (*крыша*) roof; (*тент*) awning.
2 (*скалы*) overhang.
3 (*sport*) lob.
навé|сить, шу, сишь *pf.* (*of* ▸ **~шивать¹**)
1 (+ *a. or g.*) (*дверь, замок*) to hang; (*повесить много*) to hang (*a number of*) pictures.
2 (*sport*) to lob.
наве|сти, дý, дёшь, *past* **~л, ~лá** *pf.* (*of* ▸ **наводить**)
1 (**на** + *a.*) (*указать направление*) to direct (at); (*орудие, прожектор*) to aim (at); **н. когó-н. на мысль** to suggest an idea to s.o.; **н. на след** to put on the track.
2 (*устроить, сделать*) to lay, put, make; **н. порядок** to introduce order, establish order; **н. справку** to make an inquiry.
наве|стить, щý, стишь *pf.* (*of* ▸ **~щáть**) to visit, call on.
навéтренный *adj.* windward.
навéчно *adv.* for ever.
навéш|ать, аю *pf.* (*of* ▸ **~ивать²**) (+ *a. or g.*) to hang (up), suspend.
навéшива|ть¹, ю *impf. of* ▸ **навéсить**
навéшива|ть², ю *impf. of* ▸ **навéшать**
навещá|ть, ю *impf. of* ▸ **навестить**
нáвзничь *adv.* backwards, on one's back.
навигáци|я, и *f.* navigation.
навис|áть, áю *impf.* (*of* ▸ **~нуть**) (**на** + *a.*, **над** + *i.*) to hang (over), overhang; (*fig.*) to impend, threaten; **над нáми ~ла опáсность** danger threatened us.
навис|нуть, ну, нешь, *past* **~, ~ла** *pf.* *of* ▸ **~áть**
навлекá|ть, ю *impf. of* ▸ **навлéчь**
навле|кý, чёшь, кýт *see* ▸ **~чь**
навлé|чь, кý, чёшь, кýт, *past* **~к, ~клá** *pf.* (*of* ▸ **~кáть**) (**на** + *a.*) to bring (on); **н. на себя гнев** to incur anger.
наво|дить, жý, ~дишь *impf. of* ▸ **навести**
наводнéни|е, я *nt.* flood, flooding; (*товарами*) flooding, inundation.
наводн|ить, ю, ишь *pf.* (*of* ▸ **~ять**) (+ *a. and i.*) to flood (with), inundate (with); (*fig.*): **н. рынок дешёвыми товáрами** to flood the market with cheap goods.
наводн|ять, яю *impf. of* ▸ **~ить**
наво|жý, ~дишь *see* ▸ **~дить**
навóз, а *m.* manure.
нáволочк|а, и *f.* pillowcase, pillowslip.
навор|овáть, ýю *pf.* (*coll.*) to steal (*a quantity of*).
наворóчен|ный (~, ~а) *adj.* (*coll.*) fancy.
навр|áть, ý, ёшь, *past* **~áл, ~алá, ~áло** *pf.* (*of* ▸ **врать**) (*coll.*)
1 to tell lies.
2 (**в** + *p.*) to make mistakes (in); **н. в рассказе** to get the story wrong.
навре|дить, жý, дишь *pf. of* ▸ **вредить**
наврядли *adv.* scarcely, hardly.
навсегдá *adv.* for ever, for good; **раз и н.** once (and) for all.
навстрéчу *adv. and prep.* (+ *d.*) to meet; towards; **он вышел н. гостям** he went out to meet the guests; (*fig.*) to help, show sympathy towards; **идти н. чьим-н. пожелáниям** to meet s.o.'s wishes.
нáвык, а *m.* skill.
навынос *adv.* to take away (*Br.*), to go (*US*); for consumption off the premises.
навя|зáть, жý, ~жешь *pf.* (*of* ▸ **~зывать**)
1 (**на** + *a.*) (*привязать*) to tie on (to), fasten (to).
2 (*fig.*; + *d. and a.*) (*заставить принять*) to thrust (on); to foist (on); **н. комý-н. совéт** to

thrust advice on s.o.

навя|за́ться, жу́сь, ~́жешься *pf.* (*of* ▸ **~́зываться**) (*coll.*; + *d.*) to thrust o.s. (upon), intrude (upon).

навя́зчив|ый (~, ~а) *adj.*
1 (*человек*) importunate; annoying.
2 (*мысль*) persistent; **~ая иде́я** idée fixe, obsession.

навя́зыва|ть(ся), ю(сь) *impf. of* ▸ **навяза́ть(ся)**

нага́|дить, жу, дишь *pf. of* ▸ **га́дить**

нагиба́|ть(ся), ю(сь) *impf. of* ▸ **нагну́ть(ся)**

нагишо́м *adv.* (*coll.*) stark naked.

нагле́ц, а́ *m.* impudent fellow, insolent fellow.

на́глост|ь, и *f.* impudence, insolence, impertinence.

на́гл|ый (~, ~а́, ~о) *adj.* impudent, insolent, impertinent.

нагля́д|ный (~ен, ~на) *adj.*
1 (*очевидный*) clear; graphic, obvious.
2 (*no short forms*) (*в обучении*) visual.

наг|на́ть, оню́, о́нишь, *past* **~на́л, ~нала́, ~на́ло** *pf.* (*of* ▸ **~оня́ть**)
1 (*догнать*) to overtake, catch up (with).
2 (*наверстать*) to make up (for).
3 (+ *a. or g.*) to herd together (*a number of*).
4 (*fig., coll.*) (*внушить*) to inspire, arouse, occasion.

нагн|у́ть, у́, ёшь *pf.* (*of* ▸ **нагиба́ть**) to bend.

нагн|у́ться, у́сь, ёшься *pf.* (*of* ▸ **нагиба́ться**) to bend (down), stoop.

нагова́рива|ть, ю *impf. of* ▸ **наговори́ть**[1]

наговор|и́ть[1]**, ю́, и́шь** *pf.* (*of* ▸ **нагова́ривать**) (*coll.*; **на** + *a.*) to slander, calumniate.

наговор|и́ть[2]**, ю́, и́шь** *pf.* (+ *a. or g.*) to talk, say a lot (of); **н. чепухи́** to talk a lot of nonsense.

наг|о́й (~, ~а́, ~́о) *adj.* (*о человеке*) naked, nude; (*о части тела*) bare.

нагоня́|ть, ю *impf. of* ▸ **нагна́ть**

наго́рь|е, я *nt.* tableland, plateau.

нагот|а́, ы́ *f.* nakedness, nudity.

наготове *adv.* in readiness; ready to hand; **быть н.** to hold o.s. in readiness, be on call.

награ́б|ить, лю, ишь *pf.* (+ *a. or g.*) to amass by robbery.

награ́д|а, ы *f.*
1 reward, recompense; **в ~у** as a reward.
2 (*почётный знак, орден*) award; decoration; (*в школе*) prize.

награ|ди́ть, жу́, ди́шь *pf.* (*of* ▸ **~жда́ть**) (+ *a. and i.*)
1 to reward (with).
2 (*орденом, медалью*) to decorate (with); to award, confer; (*fig.*) to endow (with).

награжда́|ть, ю *impf. of* ▸ **награди́ть**

награждённ|ый *p.p.p. of* ▸ **награди́ть;** *as n.* **н., ~ого** *m.* recipient (*of an award*).

нагрева́ни|е, я *nt.* heating.

нагрева́тел|ь, я *m.* (*tech.*) heater.

нагрева́|ть(ся), ю(сь) *impf. of* ▸ **нагре́ть(ся)**

нагре́|ть, ю *pf.* (*of* ▸ **~ва́ть**) to warm, heat.

нагре́|ться, юсь *pf.* (*of* ▸ **нагрева́ться**) (*стать тёплым*) to become warm; (*стать горячим*) to become hot; to warm up, heat up.

нагромождени|е, я *nt.* pile, heap.

нагруб|и́ть, лю́, и́шь *pf. of* ▸ **груби́ть**

нагру́дник, а *m.* (*детский*) bib.

нагружа́|ть, ю *impf. of* ▸ **нагрузи́ть**

нагру|зи́ть, жу́, ~́зишь *pf.* (*of* ▸ **грузи́ть 1** *and* ▸ **~жа́ть**) (+ *a. and i.*) to load (with).

нагру́зк|а, и *f.*
1 (*груз*) load.
2 (*fig.*) work; commitments.

нагря́н|уть, у, ешь *pf.* (*вдруг появиться*) to appear unexpectedly; (**на** + *a.*) to descend (on).

над *prep.* + *i.*
1 (*выше*) over, above.
2 (*при обозначении предмета труда*) on; at; **рабо́тать над диссерта́цией** to be working on a dissertation; **смея́ться над** to laugh at.

над... *comb. form* super-, over-.

нада|ва́ть, ю́, ёшь *pf.* (*coll.*)
1 (+ *d. and a. or g.*) to give (*a large quantity of*).
2 (*побить*) (+ *d.*) to thrash.

надав|и́ть, лю́, ~́ишь *pf.* (*of* ▸ **~́ливать**) (**на** + *a.*) (*кнопку*) to press (on).

нада́влива|ть, ю *impf. of* ▸ **надави́ть**

надба́вк|а, и *f.* (*повышение*) addition, increase; (*о цене*) extra charge; **н. к зарпла́те** rise (*Br.*), raise (*US*) (*in wages*).

надвига́|ть(ся), ю(сь) *impf. of* ▸ **надви́нуть(ся)**

надви́н|уть, у, ешь *pf.* (*of* ▸ **надвига́ть**) to move, pull (up to, over).

надви́н|уться, усь, ешься *pf.* (*of* ▸ **надвига́ться**) to approach, draw near.

на́двое *adv.* in two.

надева́|ть, ю *impf. of* ▸ **наде́ть**

наде́жд|а, ы *f.* hope; **в ~е на** (+ *a.*) in the hope of; **подава́ть ~ы** to promise well.

надёж|ный (~ен, ~на) *adj.* (*человек*) reliable, trustworthy; (*замок, фундамент*) solid, secure; (*средство*) safe.

наде́ла|ть, ю *pf.* (+ *a. or g.*)
1 (*пельменей*) to make (*a quantity of*).
2 (*coll.*; + *g.*) (*неприятностей*) to cause (*a lot of*), (*ошибок*) to make (*a lot of*).
3 (*coll.*) (*сделать что-то плохое*) to do (*sth. wrong*); **что ты ~л?** what have you done?

надел|и́ть, ю́, и́шь *pf.* (*of* ▸ **~я́ть**) (+ *a. and i.*) to provide (with); (*fig.*) to endow (with).

наделя́|ть, ю *impf. of* ▸ **надели́ть**

наде́|ну, нешь *see* ▸ **~ть**

наде́|ть, ну, нешь *pf.* (*of* ▸ **~ва́ть**) to put on (*clothes, etc.*).

наде́|яться, юсь, ешься *impf.* (*of* ▸ **по~**)
1 (**на** + *a.*) (*успех*) to hope (for); **н. на лу́чшее** to hope for the best.
2 (**на** + *a.*) (*друга, помощь*) to rely (on), count on.
3 (+ *inf.*) to hope to.

надзе́мный *adj.* (*над поверхностью*)

overground; (*на поверхности*) surface.

надзира́тел|ь, я *m.* overseer, supervisor; **тюре́мный н.** prison guard.

надзира́|ть, ю *impf.* (**за** + *i.*) to oversee, supervise.

надзо́р, а *m.*
1 supervision; (*за подозреваемым*) surveillance.
2 (*collect.*) (*орган*) inspectorate.

надлежа́щий *adj.* appropriate; fitting, proper.

надме́н|ный (~ен, ~на) *adj.* haughty, arrogant.

на́до¹ = **над**

на́до² + *d. and inf.* it is necessary; one must, one ought; (+ *a. or g.*) there is need of; **не н.** (*i*) (*не нужно*) one need not, (*ii*) (*нельзя*) one must not; **мне н. идти́** I must go, I ought to go; **так ему́ и н.** serves him right!; **н. же!** well, I never!

надоеда́|ть, ю *impf. of* ▸ **надое́сть**

надое́длив|ый (~, ~а) *adj.* annoying, boring, tiresome.

надое́|сть, м, шь, ст, ди́м, ди́те, дя́т *pf.* (*of* ▸ **~да́ть**)
1 (+ *d. and i.*) to get on the nerves (of), (*просьбами*) to pester (with), plague (with); to bore (with).
2 (*impers.*, + *d. and inf.*): **мне**, *etc.*, **~ло** I, *etc.*, am tired (of), sick (of); **нам ~ло гуля́ть** we are tired of walking.

надо́лго *adv.* for a long time.

надорв|а́ться, у́сь, ёшься, *past* **~а́лся, ~ала́сь, ~а́ло́сь** *pf.* (*of* ▸ **надрыва́ться 1**) to (over)strain o.s.; (*переутомиться*) to tire o.s. out.

надпи|са́ть, шу́, ~́шешь *pf.* (*of* ▸ **~́сывать**) (*книгу*) to inscribe.

надпи́сыва|ть, ю *impf. of* ▸ **надписа́ть**

на́дпис|ь, и *f.* inscription.

надре́з, а *m.* cut, incision; (*зарубка*) notch.

надрез|а́ть, а́ю *impf. of* ▸ **~́ать**

надре́|зать, жу, жешь *pf.* (*of* ▸ **~за́ть**) to make an incision (in).

надруга́|ться, юсь *pf.* (**над** + *i.*) to commit an outrage (against).

надры́в, а *m.*
1 (*надорванное место*) slight tear, rent.
2 (*физический*) strain.
3 (*fig.*) (*нервный*) breakdown.
4 (*возбуждённость*) hysteria.

надрыва́|ться, юсь *impf.*
1 *impf. of* ▸ **надорва́ть(ся).**
2 (*no pf.*) (*стараться*) to exert o.s.; to break one's neck.
3 (*no pf.*) (*кричать*) to yell, bellow.

надсмо́трщик, а *m.* overseer, supervisor; (*тюремный*) jailer.

надстра́ива|ть, ю *impf. of* ▸ **надстро́ить**

надстро́|ить, ю, ишь *pf.* (*of* ▸ **надстра́ивать**)
1 (*этаж*) to build on.
2 (*здание*) to raise the height (of).

надстро́йк|а, и *f.*
1 (*действие*) building on; raising.
2 (*надстроенная часть*) superstructure (*also phil.*).

надува́|ть(ся), ю(сь) *impf. of* ▸ **наду́ть(ся)**

надувн|о́й *adj.* pneumatic; **н. матра́с** air bed; **~а́я/рези́новая ло́дка** inflatable/rubber dinghy.

наду́ман|ный (~, ~на) *adj.* far-fetched, forced.

наду́|ть, ю, ешь *pf.* (*of* ▸ **~ва́ть**)
1 (*шар, мяч, колесо*) to inflate, blow up; (*паруса*) to puff out; **н. велосипе́дную ка́меру** to inflate, blow up a bicycle tyre; **н. гу́бы** (*coll.*) to pout one's lips.
2 (*coll.*) (*обмануть*) to dupe; to swindle.

наду́|ться, юсь, ешься *pf.* (*of* ▸ **~ва́ться**) (*шар, мяч, колесо*) to inflate; (*паруса*) to fill out, swell out; (*вена, почка*) to swell.

надуш|и́ть(ся), у́(сь), ~́ишь(ся) *pf. of* ▸ **души́ть(ся)²**

наеда́|ться, юсь *impf. of* ▸ **нае́сться**

наедине́ *adv.* privately, in private; **н. с** (+ *i.*) alone (with); **н. с собо́й** alone, by oneself.

нае́|ду, дешь *see* ▸ **~хать**

нае́зд, а *m.*
1 (*столкновение*) collision; **маши́на соверши́ла н. на пешехо́да** the car hit a pedestrian.
2 (*визит*) flying visit; **быва́ть ~ом/~ами** to pay short, infrequent visits.

нае́здник, а *m.* horseman, rider.

нае́здни|ца, цы *f. of* ▸ **~к**

наезжа́|ть, ю *impf. of* ▸ **нае́хать**

на|ём, ~́йма *m.* (*на короткий период, рабочих*) hire; (*в длительное пользование, квартиры*) renting; **взять в н.** to rent; **сдать в н.** to let.

наёмник, а *m.*
1 (*mil.*) mercenary.
2 (*наёмный работник*) hireling; (*fig.*) mercenary.

наёмный *adj.* hired; rented; **н. уби́йца** hit man.

нае́|сться, мся, шься, стся, ди́мся, ди́тесь, дя́тся, *past* **~лся, ~лась** *pf.* (*of* ▸ **~да́ться**)
1 to eat one's fill.
2 (+ *g. or i.*) to eat (a large quantity of), stuff o.s. (with).

нае́|хать, ду, дешь *pf.* (*of* ▸ **~зжа́ть**)
1 (**на** + *a.*) to run (into, over), collide (with); **на нас ~хал авто́бус** a bus ran into us, hit us.
2 (*coll.*) (*приехать*) to come, arrive (*unexpectedly or in numbers*).
3 (*sl.*) (**на** + *a.*) (*придраться; выругать*) to go on at, give (s.o.) a hard time; (*о рэкете*) to try to blackmail (s.o).

наж|а́ть, му́, мёшь *pf.* (*of* ▸ **~има́ть**)
1 (+ *a. or* **на** + *a.*) to press (on); **н. (на) кно́пку** to press the button.
2 (*fig., coll.*; **на** + *a.*) (*понудить*) to put pressure (upon).

нажи́в|а, ы *f.* gain, profit.

нажива́|ть(ся), ю(сь) *impf. of* ▸ **нажи́ть(ся)**

нажи́вк|а, и *f.* bait.

нажи|ву́, вёшь *see* ▸ **~́ть**

нажи́м, а *m.* pressure (*also fig.*); **сде́лать что-н. под ~ом** to do sth. under pressure.

нажима́|ть, ю *impf. of* ▸ **нажа́ть**

наж|и́ть, иву́, ивёшь, *past* **~́ил, ~ила́, ~́ило** *pf.* (*of* ▸ **~ива́ть**) (*богатство*) to acquire, gain; (*fig., coll.*) (*болезнь*) to contract, get.

наж|и́ться, иву́сь, ивёшься, *past* **~и́лся́, ~ила́сь** *pf.* (*of* ▸ **~ива́ться**) (**на** + *p.*) to become rich (from), make a fortune (from).

наж|му́, мёшь *see* ▸ **~а́ть**

наза́д *adv.*
1 (*оглянуться*) back; (*катиться*) backwards; (*на прежнее место*) back; **н.!** back!; stand back!
2 **(тому́) н.** ago.

назва́ни|е, я *nt.* name; **под ~ем** named.

наз|ва́ть, ову́, овёшь, *past* **~ва́л, ~вала́, ~ва́ло** *pf.* (*of* ▸ **~ыва́ть**) (+ *a.* and *i.*) to call; to name.

наз|ва́ться, ову́сь, овёшься, *past* **~ва́лся, ~вала́сь** *pf.* (*of* ▸ **~ыва́ться**) (+ *i.*)
1 (*получить какое-н. имя*) to call o.s.; to be named.
2 (*представиться*) to give one's name.
3 (*журналистом*) to claim to be.

назе́мн|ый *adj.* ground, surface; **~ые войска́** (*mil.*) ground troops; **~ая по́чта** surface mail.

назида́тел|ьный (~ен, ~ьна) *adj.* edifying.

назло́
1 *adv.* (*сделать*) out of spite.
2 *prep.* (+ *d.*) (*родителям*) to spite.

назнач|а́ть, а́ю *impf. of* ▸ **~́ить**

назначе́ни|е, я *nt.*
1 (*на работу*) appointment.
2 (*med.*) prescription.
3 (*цель*) purpose; **испо́льзовать что́-н. по ~ю** to use sth. properly, appropriately; **отря́д осо́бого ~я** special task force.
4 : **ме́сто ~я** destination.

назна́ч|ить, у, ишь *pf.* (*of* ▸ **~а́ть**)
1 (*дату, место, размер*) to fix, set, appoint; **н. день встре́чи** to fix, appoint a day for a meeting; **н. кому́-н. свида́ние** to make a date with s.o.
2 (+ *a.* and *i.*) to appoint, nominate; **его́ ~или дире́ктором** he has been appointed director.
3 (*med.*) to prescribe.

назо́йлив|ый (~, ~а) *adj.* importunate, troublesome.

назрева́|ть, ю *impf.* (*of* ▸ **назре́ть**) to become imminent; **кри́зис ~л** a crisis was brewing.

назре́|ть, ю, ешь *pf. of* ▸ **~ва́ть**

называ́|емый *pres. part. pass. of* ▸ **~ть; так н.** so-called.

называ́|ть, ю *impf. of* ▸ **назва́ть; н. ве́щи свои́ми имена́ми** to call a spade a spade.

называ́|ться, юсь *impf.* (*of* ▸ **назва́ться**) (*носить какое-н. наименование, имя*) to be called; **как ~ется э́то село́?** what is this village called?

наибо́лее *adv.* (the) most.

наибо́льший *adj.* the greatest; (*по величине*) the largest.

наи́вност|ь, и *f.* naivety.

наи́в|ный (~ен, ~на) *adj.* naive; (*простой*) artless.

наивы́сш|ий *adj.* the highest; **в ~ей сте́пени** to the utmost.

наизна́нку *adv.* inside out; **вы́вернуть н.** to turn inside out.

наизу́сть *adv.* by heart; from memory.

наилу́чший *adj.* (the) best.

наиме́нее *adv.* (the) least.

наимен|ова́ть, у́ю *pf. of* ▸ **именова́ть**

наиме́ньший *adj.* (the) least; (*по величине*) the smallest.

наискосо́к *adv.* = **на́искось**

на́искось *adv.* obliquely, slantwise.

наиху́дший *adj.* (the) worst.

на|йти́[1]**, йду́, йдёшь,** *past* **~шёл, ~шла́** *pf.* (*of* ▸ **~ходи́ть**) to find; **н. иде́ю интере́сной** to find the idea interesting.

на|йти́[2]**, йду́, йдёшь,** *past* **~шёл, ~шла́** *pf.* (*of* ▸ **~ходи́ть**) (**на** + *a.*) (*натолкнуться*) to come (across, upon); (*о чувствах*) to come over; **что э́то на неё ~шло́?** what has come over her?; (*закрыть собой*) to cover.

на|йти́сь, йду́сь, йдёшься, *past* **~шёлся, ~шла́сь** *pf.* (*of* ▸ **~ходи́ться**[1])
1 (*обнаружиться*) (*после поисков*) to be found; to turn up; (*вызваться*) to volunteer.
2 (*не растеряться*) not to be at a loss; **я не ~шёлся, что сказа́ть** I was at a loss for what to say.

наказа́ни|е, я *nt.* punishment.

нака|за́ть, жу́, ~́жешь *pf.* (*of* ▸ **~́зывать**) to punish.

нака́зыва|ть, ю *impf. of* ▸ **наказа́ть**

нака́лива|ть(ся), ю(сь) *impf. of* ▸ **накали́ть(ся)**

накал|и́ть, ю́, и́шь *pf.* (*of* ▸ **~́ивать**) to heat, incandesce; (*fig.*) (*ситуацию*) to inflame.

накал|и́ться, ю́сь, и́шься *pf.* (*of* ▸ **~́иваться** and ▸ **~я́ться**) to glow, incandesce; (*fig.*) (*обстановка*) to become inflamed; **стра́сти ~и́лись** passions were running high.

накаля́|ть(ся), ю(сь) *impf. of* ▸ **накали́ть(ся)**

накану́не
1 (*adv.*) the day before.
2 (*prep.* + *g.*) on the eve (of); **н. Рождества́** on Christmas Eve.

нака́п|ать, аю *pf. of* ▸ **ка́пать**

нака́пливать(ся) *impf. of* ▸ **накопи́ть(ся)**

накач|а́ть[1]**, а́ю** *pf.* (*of* ▸ **~́ивать**) (*шину, камеру*) to pump up, pump full.

накач|а́ть[2]**, а́ю** *pf.* (*of* ▸ **~́ивать** and ▸ **кача́ть 3**) (*воды*) to pump (*a quantity of*).

накач|а́ть[3]**, а́ю** *pf.* (*of* ▸ **кача́ть 4** and ▸ **~́ивать**) (*coll.*) to be muscly from pumping iron.

накача́|ться, юсь *pf. of* ▸ **кача́ться 3**

нака́чива|ть, ю *impf. of* ▸ **накача́ть**[1,2,3]

наки́дк|а, и *f.* cloak, mantle; wrap.

наки́дыва|ться, юсь *impf. of* ▸ **наки́нуться**

наки́|нуться, нусь, нешься *pf.* (*of*

▶ **~дываться**) (**на** + *a.*) to fall (on, upon); (*на еду, на работу*) to attack, get stuck into.

накладн|а́я, о́й *f.* invoice, waybill.

накладн|о́й *adj.*
1 (*прикреплённый поверх чего-н.*) superimposed; **н. карма́н** patch pocket; **~ые расхо́ды** overheads.
2 (*искусственный*) false; **~а́я борода́** false beard.

накла́дыва|ть, ю *impf. of* ▶ **наложи́ть**

наклеве|та́ть, щу́, ~́щешь *pf. of* ▶ **клевета́ть**

накле́ива|ть, ю *impf. of* ▶ **накле́ить**

накле́|ить, ю, ишь *pf.* (*of* ▶ **~ивать**) to stick on, paste on.

накле́йк|а, и *f.* sticker.

накло́н, а *m.* (*головы*) inclination; (*почерка*) slope, slant; (*покатая поверхность*) slope, incline.

наклон|и́ть, ю́, ~́ишь *pf.* (*of* ▶ **~я́ть**) to incline, bend.

наклон|и́ться, ю́сь, ~́ишься *pf.* (*of* ▶ **~я́ться**) to stoop, bend.

накло́нност|ь, и *f.* (**к** + *d.*) inclination (towards), tendency (towards), propensity (for).

накло́нн|ый *adj.* inclined, sloping; **~ая пло́скость** inclined plane.

наклон|я́ть(ся), я́ю(сь) *impf. of* ▶ **~и́ть(ся)**

накова́л|ьня, ьни, *g. pl.* **~ен** *f.* anvil.

наконе́ц *adv.* at last, finally, in the end; **н.-то!** at last!, about time too!; (*ещё, кроме всего*) after all; (*выражает недовольство*) ever; **переста́ньте, н., спо́рить!** will you ever stop arguing!

наконе́чник, а *m.* tip, point.

накоп|и́ть, лю́, ~́ишь *pf.* (*of* ▶ **копи́ть** *and* ▶ **нака́пливать**) (+ *a. or g.*) to accumulate, amass.

накоп|и́ться, ~́ится *pf.* (*of* ▶ **нака́пливаться** *and* ▶ **копи́ться**) to accumulate.

накопле́ни|е, я *nt.*
1 accumulation.
2 (*pl.*) (*сбережения*) savings.

накорм|и́ть, лю́, ~́ишь *pf. of* ▶ **корми́ть 1**

накра́|сить, шу, сишь *pf.* (*of* ▶ **~шивать**)
1 (*ногти, губы*) to paint.
2 (*лицо*) to make up.

накра́|ситься, шусь, сишься *pf. of* ▶ **кра́ситься 1**

накра́шива|ть, ю *impf. of* ▶ **накра́сить**

накрош|и́ть, у́, ~́ишь *pf.* (*of* ▶ **кроши́ть**)
1 to crumble, shred (*a quantity of*).
2 (*насорить крошками*) to spill crumbs.

накр|о́ю, о́ешь *see* ▶ **~ы́ть**

накру|ти́ть, чу́, ~́тишь *pf.* (*of* ▶ **~́чивать**)
1 (*намотать*) (**на** + *a.*) to wind (around, onto).
2 (*верёвок*) to twist (*a quantity of*).

накру́чива|ть, ю *impf. of* ▶ **накрути́ть**

накрыва́|ть(ся), ю(сь) *impf. of* ▶ **накры́ть(ся)**

накр|ы́ть, о́ю, о́ешь *pf.* (*of* ▶ **~ыва́ть**) to cover; **н. (на) стол** to lay the table; **н. к у́жину** to lay supper.

накр|ы́ться, о́юсь, о́ешься *pf.* (*of* ▶ **~ыва́ться**) (+ *i.*) to cover o.s. (with).

накуп|а́ть, а́ю *impf. of* ▶ **~и́ть**

накуп|и́ть, лю́, ~́ишь *pf.* (*of* ▶ **~а́ть**) (+ *a. or g.*) to buy up (*a number or quantity of*).

нал, а *m.* (*coll.*) cash.

налага́|ть, ю *impf. of* ▶ **наложи́ть[1]** ▶ **2, 4**

нала́|дить, жу, дишь *pf.* (*of* ▶ **~живать**)
1 (*отрегулировать*) to regulate, adjust; (*исправить*) to repair, put right.
2 (*организовать*) to set going, arrange; **н. дела́** to get things going.

нала́|диться, дится *pf.* (*of* ▶ **~живаться**) to go right; **рабо́та ~дилась** the work is well in hand.

нала́жива|ть(ся), ю, ет(ся) *impf. of* ▶ **нала́дить(ся)**

нале́во *adv.*
1 (**от** + *g.*) to the left (of); **н.!** (*mil.*) left turn!
2 (*coll.*) (*продавать*) on the side (= *illicitly*); **рабо́тать н.** to moonlight.

налеп|и́ть[1], лю́, ~́ишь *pf.* (*of* ▶ **лепи́ть 2**) to stick on.

налеп|и́ть[2], лю́, ~́ишь *pf.* (+ *a. or g.*) to model (*a number of*).

налёт[1], а *m.* (*нападение*) raid; (*на квартиру, на магазин*) robbery, burglary; **возду́шный н.** air raid.

налёт[2], а *m.* (*тонкий слой*) deposit; thin coating; (*на бронзе*) patina; **зубно́й н.** dental plaque; (*fig.*) touch, soupçon; **с ~ом иро́нии** with a touch of irony.

налет|а́ть, а́ю *impf. of* ▶ **~е́ть[1,2]**

нале|те́ть[1], чу́, ти́шь *pf.* (*of* ▶ **~та́ть**)
1 (**на** + *a.*) (*наброситься*) to fall (upon); (*о птице*) to swoop down (on); to fly (upon, against); (*натолкнуться*) to run (into).
2 (*о ветре, буре*) to spring up.

нале|те́ть[2], чу́, ти́шь *pf.* (*of* ▶ **~та́ть**) (*прилететь*) to fly in, drift in (*in quantities, in large numbers*).

налива́|ть, ю *impf. of* ▶ **нали́ть**

нал|и́ть, ью́, ьёшь, *past* **~́ил, ~ила́, ~́ило** *pf.* (*of* ▶ **~ива́ть**)
1 (*влить*) to pour out; (*наполнить*) (+ *i.*) to fill (with).
2 (*пролить*) to spill.

налицо́ *adv.* present, available, on hand.

нали́чи|е, я *nt.* presence; **быть, оказа́ться в ~и** to be present, be available.

нали́чник, а *m.* (*двери, окна*) casing, jambs and lintel.

нали́чн|ый *adj.* on hand, available; **~ые (де́ньги)** ready money, cash; **плати́ть ~ыми** to pay in cash.

налов|и́ть, лю́, ~́ишь *pf.* (+ *a or g.*) to catch (*a number of*).

нало́г, а *m.* tax; **подохо́дный н.** income tax; **н. на доба́вленную сто́имость** value added tax, VAT; **н. на при́быль** profits tax.

нало́г|овый *adj. of* ▶ **~; ~овая деклара́ция** tax return; **н. инспе́ктор** tax inspector.

налогообложе́ни|е, я *nt.* taxation.

налогоплате́льщик, а *m.* taxpayer.

налож|и́ть[1], у́, ~́ишь *pf.*
1 (*impf.* **накла́дывать**) (*повязку; лак*) to apply; (*положить сверху*) to put on, over.
2 (*impf.* **накла́дывать, налага́ть**) (*печать, визу*) affix; **н. отпеча́ток на** + *a.* (*fig.*) to have a great influence (on).
3 (*impf.* **накла́дывать**) (*навалить*) to load, pack.
4 (*impf.* **налага́ть**) (**на** + *a.*) (*подвергнуть*) to lay (on), impose; **н. штраф** to impose a fine; **н. аре́ст на чьё-н. иму́щество** (*leg.*) to seize s.o.'s property.

налож|и́ть[2], у́, ~́ишь *pf.* (*of* ▸**накла́дывать**) (+ *a. or g.*) to put, lay (*a quantity of*).

нал|ью́, ьёшь *see* ▸**~и́ть**

нам *d. of* ▸**мы**

нама́з, а *m.* Muslim prayer.

нама́|зать, жу, жешь *pf. of* ▸**ма́зать 1, 2** *and* ▸**~зывать**

нама́|заться, жусь, жешься *pf.*
1 (*impf.* **~зываться**) (+ *i.*) to rub o.s. (with).
2 *pf. of* ▸**ма́заться 2, 3**

нама́зыва|ть(ся), ю(сь) *impf. of* ▸**нама́зать(ся)**

нама́тыва|ть, ю *impf.* (*of* ▸**намота́ть**) to wind, reel.

нама́чива|ть, ю *impf. of* ▸**намочи́ть**

намёк, а *m.* hint; **сде́лать н.** to drop a hint.

намек|а́ть, а́ю *impf.* (*of* ▸**~ну́ть**) (**на** + *a.*, **о** + *p.*) to hint (at), allude (to).

намек|ну́ть, ну́, нёшь *pf. of* ▸**~а́ть**

намерева́|ться, юсь *impf.* (+ *inf.*) to intend (to), mean (to).

наме́рен (~а, ~о) *adj. as pred.* (+ *inf.*) intending; **я н. за́втра е́хать** I intend to go tomorrow; **что вы ~ы де́лать?** what do you intend to do?

наме́рени|е, я *nt.* intention; purpose; **без вся́кого ~я** unintentionally.

наме́ренно *adv.* intentionally, deliberately.

наме́рен|ный (~, ~на) *adj.* intentional, deliberate.

наме́|тить[1], чу, тишь *pf.* (*of* ▸**~ча́ть[1]**) (*изобразить*) to sketch, outline.

наме́|тить[2], чу, тишь *pf.*
1 (*impf.* **~ча́ть[2]**) (*планировать*) to plan, project; to have in view; **н. пое́здку в Росси́ю** to plan a visit to Russia.
2 (*impf.* **~ча́ть[2]**) (*предположить*) to nominate; (*назначить*) to select; **н. зда́ние к разруше́нию** to designate a building for demolition.

наме́|титься, тится *pf.* (*of* ▸**~ча́ться**) to begin to appear; to take shape.

намеча́|ть[1], ю *impf. of* ▸**наме́тить[1]**

намеча́|ть[2], ю *impf. of* ▸**наме́тить[2]**

намеча́|ться, ется *impf. of* ▸**наме́титься**

на́ми *i. of* ▸**мы**

намиби́|ец, йца *m.* Namibian.

намиби́|йка, йки *f. of* ▸**~ец**

намиби́йский *adj.* Namibian.

Нами́би|я, и *f.* Namibia.

намно́го *adv.* much, far (*with comparatives*); **н. лу́чше** much, far better; greatly, considerably (*with verbs*).

намок|а́ть, а́ю *impf.* (*of* ▸**~́нуть**) to become wet, get wet.

намо́к|нуть, ну, нешь, *past* **~, ~ла** *pf. of* ▸**~а́ть**

намо́рдник, а *m.* muzzle.

намота́|ть, ю *pf. of* ▸**мота́ть 1** *and* ▸**нама́тывать**

намоч|и́ть, у́, ~́ишь *pf. of* ▸**нама́чивать** *and* ▸**мочи́ть 1, 2** to wet, moisten.

нанес|ти́, у́, ёшь, *past* **~̈, ~ла́** *pf.* (*of* ▸**наноси́ть**)
1 (+ *a. or g.*) to bring (*a quantity of*); to pile up (*a quantity of*); (*о снеге, песке*) (*usu. impers.*) to drift.
2 (*начертить*) (**на** + *a.*) to draw, plot (*on a map etc.*).
3 (*причинить*) to cause; to inflict; **н. оскорбле́ние** to insult; **н. уще́рб** to inflict damage.
4 (*лак, краску*) to apply.

нани|за́ть, жу́, ~́жешь *pf. of* ▸**~́зывать**

нани́зыва|ть, ю *impf.* to string, thread.

нанима́тел|ь, я *m.*
1 (*квартиры*) tenant.
2 (*рабочей силы*) employer.

нанима́тель|ница, ницы *f. of* ▸**~**

нанима́|ть(ся), ю(сь) *impf. of* ▸**наня́ть(ся)**

нано|си́ть, шу́, ~́сишь *impf. of* ▸**нанести́**

нан|я́ть, найму́, наймёшь, *past* **~́ял, ~яла́, ~́яло** *pf.* (*of* ▸**~има́ть**) (*квартиру*) to rent; (*машину, рабочих*) to hire; **н. на рабо́ту** to engage, take on.

нан|я́ться, найму́сь, наймёшься, *past* **~я́лся́, ~яла́сь** *pf.* (*of* ▸**~има́ться**) to get a job.

наоборо́т *adv.*
1 (*обратной стороной*) back to front; **проче́сть сло́во н.** to read a word backwards.
2 (*не так*) the other way round; the wrong way (round).
3 (*при противопоставлении*) on the contrary; **как раз н.** quite the contrary; **и н.** and vice versa.

наобу́м *adv.* (*не подумав*) without thinking; (*наудачу*) at random.

наор|а́ть, у́, ёшь *pf.* (**на** + *a.*; *coll.*) to shout (at).

наотре́з *adv.* flatly, point-blank.

напада́|ть, ю *impf. of* ▸**напа́сть**

напада́ющ|ий, его *m.* (*sport*) forward.

нападе́ни|е, я *nt.* attack, assault; (*sport; collect.*) forwards, forward line.

напа|ду́, дёшь *see* ▸**~́сть**

напа́рник, а *m.* fellow worker, mate.

напа́|сть, ду́, дёшь, *past* **~л** *pf.* (*of* ▸**~да́ть**) (**на** + *a.*)
1 to attack; to descend (on).
2 (*о чувстве*) to come (over); to grip, seize; **на нас ~л страх** fear seized us.

напева́|ть, ю *impf.*
1 *impf. of* ▸**напе́ть.**

[2] (*тихо, вполголоса*) to hum; to croon.

напереpéз *adv.* (*and prep.* + *d.*) so as to cross one's path; **бежáть комý-н. н.** to run to head s.o. off.

напёрст|ок, ка *m.* thimble.

нап|éть, ою́, оёшь *pf.* (*of* ▸ **~евáть 1**) to hum, sing sketchily.

напечáта|ть(ся), ю(сь) *pf. of* ▸ **печáтать(ся)**

напивá|ться, юсь *impf. of* ▸ **напи́ться**

напи́льник, а *m.* (*tech.*) file.

напи|сáть, шу́, ~́шешь *pf. of* ▸ **писáть**

напи́т|ок, ка *m.* drink, beverage.

нап|и́ться, ью́сь, ьёшься, *past* **~и́лся, ~илáсь, ~и́лóсь** *pf.* (*of* ▸ **~ивáться**)
[1] (+ *g.*) (*утолить жажду*) to slake one's thirst (with, on); (*выпить*) to have a drink (of).
[2] (*coll.*) (*стать пьяным*) to get drunk.

напих|áть, áю *pf.* (*of* ▸ **~́ивать**) (**в** + *a.*) to cram (into), stuff (into).

напи́хива|ть, ю *impf. of* ▸ **напихáть**

напи|шу́, ~́шешь *see* ▸ **~сáть**

напл|евáть, юю́, юёшь *pf.*
[1] (+ *g.*) to spit (out).
[2] (*fig., coll.*; **на** + *a.*) to wash one's hands (of); **н.!** to hell with it! who cares!; **мне н.!** I couldn't care less!

нап|ои́ть, ою́, о́ишь *pf.* (*of* ▸ **пои́ть**)
[1] (*дать попить*) to give to drink; to water (*an animal*).
[2] (*довести до опьянения*) to make drunk.

напокáз *adv.* for show; **вы́ставить н.** to show off (*also fig.*).

напóлн|ить, ю, ишь *pf.* (*of* ▸ **~я́ть**) (+ *i.*) to fill (with).

напóлн|иться, юсь, ишься *pf.* (*of* ▸ **~я́ться**) (+ *i.*) to fill (with) (*intrans.*)

наполн|я́ть(ся), я́ю(сь) *impf. of* ▸ **~́ить(ся)**

наполови́ну *adv.* half; **зал ещё н. пуст** the hall is still half empty.

напоминáни|е, я *nt.*
[1] (*действие*) reminding.
[2] (*что-н. напоминающее*) reminder.

напоминá|ть, ю *impf. of* ▸ **напóмнить**

напóмн|ить, ю, ишь *pf.* (*of* ▸ **напоминáть**)
[1] (+ *d. and* **о** + *p. or* + *d. and a.*) (*заставить вспомнить*) to remind (of); **портрéт ~ил мне о прóшлом** the portrait reminded me of the past.
[2] (*иметь сходство*) to remind (of), recall (= *to resemble*); **он ~ил мне моегó дéда** he reminded me of my grandfather.

напóр, а *m.* (*воздуха, воды*) pressure (*also fig.*); **под ~ом** under pressure.

напóрист|ый (~, ~а) *adj.* energetic; pushy.

напослéдок *adv.* (*coll.*) in the end, finally, after all.

нап|ою́[1]**, оёшь** *see* ▸ **~éть**

напо|ю́[2]**, и́шь** *see* ▸ **~и́ть**

напрáв|ить, лю, ишь *pf.* (*of* ▸ **~ля́ть**)
[1] (**на** + *a.*) (*устремить*) to direct (to, at); **н. внимáние (на** + *a.*) to direct one's attention (to); **н. удáр** to aim a blow (at).
[2] (*отправить*) to send; **н. заявлéние** to send in an application; (*к врачу, к юристу*) to refer.

напрáв|иться, люсь, ишься *pf.* (*of* ▸ **~ля́ться**) (**к** + *d.*, **в** + *a.*, **на** + *a.*) (*двинуться куда-н.*) to make (for).

направлéни|е, я *nt.*
[1] (*линия, путь*) direction; **по ~ю (к** + *d.*) in the direction (of), towards;
[2] (*fig.*) (*в экономике, в политике*) trend, tendency; **либерáльное н.** liberal tendency; (*группировка*) movement.
[3] (*документ*) order, warrant.

напрáвленност|ь, и *f.* direction, focus, purposefulness.

направля́|ть, ю *impf. of* ▸ **напрáвить**

направля́|ться, юсь *impf. of* ▸ **напрáвиться; ~емся в Мýрманск** we are bound for Murmansk.

направля́ющ|ая, ей *f.* (*tech.*) guide.

напрáво *adv.* (**от** + *g.*) to the right (of).

напрáсно *adv.*
[1] (*бесполезно*) vainly, in vain; to no purpose.
[2] (*несправедливо*) wrong, unjustly, mistakenly.

напрáс|ный (~ен, ~на) *adj.*
[1] (*бесполезный*) vain, idle; **~ная надéжда** vain hope.
[2] (*ненужный*) needless.

напрáшива|ться, юсь *impf. of* ▸ **напроси́ться;** (*impf. only*) to arise, suggest itself; **~ется вопрóс** the question arises.

напримéр for example, for instance.

напрокáт *adv.* for hire, on hire; **взять н.** to hire, rent; **дать н.** to hire out, let.

напролóм *adv.* straight, regardless of obstacles (*also fig.*).

напрорóч|ить, у, ишь *pf. of* ▸ **пророчить**

напро|си́ться, шу́сь, ~́сишься *pf.* (*of* ▸ **напрáшиваться**) (*coll.*) to thrust o.s. upon; (**на** + *a.*) to provoke; **н. на комплимéнты** to fish for compliments.

напрóтив *adv. and prep.* + *g.*
[1] opposite; **он живёт н. (нáшего дóма)** he lives opposite (our house).
[2] (*при противопоставлении*) on the contrary.

нáпрочь *adv.* (*coll.*) completely.

напря́г, а *m.* (*sl.*) pressure.

напрягá|ть(ся), ю(сь) *impf. of* ▸ **напря́чь(ся)**

напря|гу́, жёшь *see* ▸ **~́чь**

напряжéни|е, я *nt.*
[1] (*затрата усилий*) effort, exertion; **рабóтать с ~ем** to exert o.s.; (*трудное положение*) strain, tension.
[2] (*phys., tech.*) strain; stress; (*elec.*) voltage.

напряжённост|ь, и *f.* tension, strain.

напряжён|ный (~, ~на) *adj.* tense, strained; **~ные отношéния** strained relations; **~ная рабóта** intensive work.

напрями́к *adv.*
[1] (*пойти*) straight.
[2] (*fig.*) (*сказать*) straight out, bluntly.

напря́|чь, гу́, жёшь, гу́т, *past* **~г, ~глá** *pf.* (*of* ▸ **~гáть**) (*мускулы*) to tense; (*голос, слух, внимание*) to strain (*also fig.*).

напря́|чься, гу́сь, жёшься, гу́тся, *past* **~гся, ~глáсь** *pf.* (*of* ▸ **~гáться**)

Н

1 (*о мускулах*) to become tense.
2 (*о человеке*) to exert o.s., strain o.s.
3 (*о взгляде, силах*) to be concentrated.

напуга|ть, ю *pf. of* ▶ **пугать**

напудр|ить(ся), ю(сь), ишь(ся) *pf. of* ▶ **пудрить(ся)**

напуска|ть, ю *impf. of* ▶ **напустить**

напускной *adj.* assumed, put on.

напу|стить, щу, ́стишь *pf.* (*of* ▶ **~скать**)
1 (+ *g.*) (*дыма, мух*) to let in; **н. воды в ванну** to fill a bath.
2 (*направить для нападения*) (**на** + *a.*) to let loose on, set on.
3 (**на себя** + *a.*) to affect, put on; **н. на себя важность** to assume an air of importance.

напута|ть, ю *pf.* (*coll.*; **в** + *p.*) to make a mess (of), make a hash (of); (*ошибиться*) to confuse, get wrong.

напу|щу, ́стишь *see* ▶ **~стить**

наравне *adv.* (**с** + *i.*) equally (with); on an equal footing (with); together (with).

нараст|ать, аю *impf. of* ▶ **~и**

нарас|ти, ту, тёшь, *past* **нарос, наросла** *pf.* (*of* ▶ **~тать**)
1 (**на** + *p.*) to grow (on), form (on); **мох нарос на камнях** moss has grown on the stones.
2 (*увеличиться*) to increase; (*о звуке*) to swell.
3 (*накопиться*) to accumulate.

нара|стить, щу, стишь *pf.* (*of* ▶ **~щивать**)
1 (*мускулы*) to develop.
2 (*удлинить*) to lengthen; (*fig.*) (*увеличить*) to increase, augment.

наращивани|е, я *nt.* increase; build-up; **н. вооружений** arms build-up.

наращива|ть, ю *impf. of* ▶ **нарастить**

нард|ы, ов *pl.* backgammon.

наре|жу, жешь *see* ▶ **~зать**

нарез|ать, аю *impf. of* ▶ **~ать**

наре|зать, жу, жешь *pf.* (*of* ▶ **~зать**)
1 (+ *a. or g.*) (*хлеба, сыр*) to cut; to slice.
2 (*tech.*) to thread.

нарекани|е, я *nt.* censure; reprimand.

наречи|е, я *nt.* (*gram.*) adverb.

нарис|овать, ую *pf. of* ▶ **рисовать**

наркобизнес, а *m.* drug trafficking.

наркоз, а *m.* anaesthetic (*Br.*), anesthetic (*US*); **местный н.** local anaesthetic; **общий н.** general anaesthetic.

нарколог, а *m.* expert in drug and alcohol abuse.

наркоман, а *m.* drug addict.

наркомани|я, и *f.* drug addiction.

наркоман|ка, ки *f. of* ▶ **~**

наркотик, а *m.* narcotic; drug; **торговля ~ами** drug trafficking.

наркотическ|ий *adj.* narcotic; **~ие средства** narcotics, drugs.

наркоторгов|ец, ца *m.* drug dealer.

народ, а (у) *m.* (*все жители*) people; (*нация*) nation; **~ы мира** nations of the world; **английский н.** the English people, the people of England; **человек из ~а** a man of the people; **на митинге было мало ~у** there were not many people at the meeting.

народност|ь, и *f.*
1 (*народ*) nationality.
2 (*sg. only*) (*искусства*) national character; national traits.

народн|ый *adj.*
1 (*национальный*) national; **~ое хозяйство** national economy.
2 (*песня, искусство*) folk.
3 (*восстание, движение*) of the (*sc. common, working*) people, popular.
4 *forms part of the official designation of certain Communist and former Communist states*; **Китайская Н~ая Республика** the People's Republic of China.

нарост, а *m.*
1 (*грязи*) layer.
2 (*на растении*) excrescence, growth.

нарочно *adv.*
1 (*намеренно*) on purpose, purposely; **как н.** (*coll.*) to make things worse; **н. не придумаешь** it is quite something.
2 (*coll.*) (*в шутку*) for fun, pretending.

наруб|ить, лю, ́ишь *pf.* (+ *a. or g.*) to chop (*a quantity of*).

наружност|ь, и *f.* exterior; (outward) appearance; **н. обманчива** appearances are deceptive.

наружн|ый *adj.* (*стена, дверь*) external, exterior; (*изменение*) external; (*спокойствие*) outward; (*tech.*) male (*of screw thread*); **~ое (лекарство)** medicine for external application.

наружу *adv.* outside, on the outside; **выйти н.** to come out; (*fig.*) to come to light, transpire.

нарукавник, а *m.* oversleeve; armlet.

нарукавн|ый *adj.* (worn on the) sleeve; **~ая повязка** armband.

наручник, а *m.* (*usu. pl.*) handcuff, manacle.

наручн|ый *adj.* worn on the arm; **~ые часы** wristwatch.

наруш|ать(ся), аю, ает(ся) *impf. of* ▶ **~ить(ся)**

нарушени|е, я *nt.*
1 (*закона, дисциплины*) breach; violation; (*обещания*) breaking.
2 (*покоя*) disturbance.

нарушител|ь, я *m.* (*правила, закона*) transgressor, infringer.

нарушитель|ница, ницы *f. of* ▶ **~**

наруш|ить, у, ишь *pf.* (*of* ▶ **~ать**)
1 (*сон, покой*) to break, disturb.
2 (*закон, обещание*) to break; **н. границу** to cross a border illegally.

наруш|иться, ится *pf.* (*of* ▶ **~аться**) (*сон, покой, связь*) to be broken.

нарцисс, а *m.* narcissus; (*жёлтый*) daffodil.

нар|ы, ~ *no sg.* plank-bed; bunk.

нарыв, а *m.* abscess; boil.

наряд, а *m.* (*одежда*) attire, apparel, costume.

наря|дить, жу, ́дишь *pf.* (*of* ▶ **~жать**)
1 (**в** + *a.*) to dress (in), array (in); **н. ёлку** to decorate a Christmas tree.
2 (+ *i.*) to dress up (as).

наря|диться, жусь, ́дишься *pf.* (*of* ▶ **~жаться**)

[1] (**в** + *a.*) to array o.s. (in).
[2] (+ *i.*) to dress up (as).

наря́д|ный (~ен, ~на) *adj.* (*человек*) well-dressed; elegant; (*одежда*) smart; (*комната*) well decorated.

наряду́ *adv.* (**с** + *i.*) side by side (with), equally (with); together (with); **н. с э́тим** at the same time.

наряжа́|ть(ся), ю(сь) *impf. of* ▸**наряди́ть(ся)**

нас *a., g., and p. of* ▸**мы**

наса|ди́ть[1], **жу́, ~́дишь** *pf.* (*of* ▸**~́живать**) (*надеть*) to put; to stick, pin; **н. червяка́ на крючо́к** to fix a worm on to a hook.

наса|ди́ть[2], **жу́, ~́дишь** *pf.* (*of* ▸**~жда́ть**) (*fig.*) to inculcate; to propagate.

насажда́|ть, ю *impf. of* ▸**насади́ть**[2]

насажде́ни|е, я *nt.*
[1] (*действие*) planting; (*fig.*) propagation, dissemination.
[2] (*деревья*) plantation.

наса́жива|ть, ю *impf. of* ▸**насади́ть**[1]

наса́лива|ть, ю *impf. of* ▸**насоли́ть**

насви́стыва|ть, ю *impf.* to whistle (*a tune*).

наседа́|ть, ю *impf.* (*of* ▸**насе́сть**) (**на** + *a.*) to press.

насе́дк|а, и *f.* sitting hen.

насеко́м|ое, ого *nt.* insect.

населе́ни|е, я *nt.* population; (*города, деревни*) inhabitants.

насел|ённый *p.p.p. of* ▸**~и́ть** *and adj.* (*район*) densely populated; **н. пункт** (*official designation*) locality, place.

насел|и́ть, ю́, и́шь *pf.* (*of* ▸**~я́ть**) to people, settle.

населя́|ть, ю, ешь *impf. of* ▸**насели́ть**

нас|е́сть, я́ду, я́дешь, *past* **~е́л** *pf. of* ▸**~еда́ть**

наси́ли|е, я *nt.* (*физическое*) violence; (*принуждение*) force.

наси́л|овать, ую *impf.*
[1] (*принуждать*) to coerce, constrain.
[2] (*pf.* **из~**) (*женщину*) to rape.

наси́льник, а *m.*
[1] tyrant; aggressor.
[2] (*сексуальный*) rapist.

наси́льно *adv.* by force, forcibly.

наси́льственн|ый *adj.* (*меры*) violent; (*выселение*) forcible; **~ая смерть** murder.

наска́кива|ть, ю *impf. of* ▸**наскочи́ть**

насквозь *adv.* (*полностью*) through (and through); throughout; **промо́кнуть н.** to get wet through; (*пробить, прострелить*) through.

наско́лько *adv.*
[1] (*interrog.*) how?; **н. э́то серьёзно?** how serious is it?; (*in clauses*) **я не зна́ю, н. э́то сро́чно** I don't know how urgent it is.
[2] (*rel.*) (*помню, знаю*) as far as; **н. мне изве́стно** as far as I know.
[3] (*в такой степени*) so; **н. э́то трудне́е** it is so much more difficult.

наскоч|и́ть, у́, ~́ишь *pf.* (*of* ▸**наска́кивать**) (**на** + *a.*)
[1] (*столкнуться*) to run (against), collide (with).
[2] (*fig., coll.*) (*с упрёками*) to fly (at).

наску́ч|ить, у, ишь *pf.* (+ *d.*) to bore; **мне э́то ~ило** I am sick of it.

насла|ди́ться, жу́сь, ди́шься *pf.* (*of* ▸**~жда́ться**) (+ *i.*) to enjoy; to take pleasure (in), delight (in).

наслажда́|ться, юсь *impf. of* ▸**наслади́ться**

наслажде́ни|е, я *nt.* enjoyment, delight.

насле́ди|е, я *nt.* legacy; (*культурное*) heritage.

насле́дник, а *m.* heir; (*fig.*) successor, inheritor.

насле́дниц|а, ы *f.* heiress.

насле́д|овать, ую *impf. and pf.*
[1] (*pf. also* **у~**) to inherit.
[2] (+ *d.*) to succeed (to).

насле́дственност|ь, и *f.* heredity.

насле́дств|о, а *nt.*
[1] inheritance, legacy; **получи́ть в н., по ~у** to inherit.
[2] (*fig.*) heritage.

наслу́ша|ться, юсь *pf.* (+ *g.*)
[1] (*услышать много*) to hear (a lot of).
[2] (*вдоволь послушать*) to hear enough, listen to long enough.

на́смерть *adv.* to death; **испуга́ть н.** (*fig.*) to frighten to death.

насмеха́|ться, юсь *impf.* (**над** + *i.*) to mock, ridicule.

насмеш|и́ть, у́, и́шь *pf. of* ▸**смеши́ть**

насме́шк|а, и *f.* jibe, taunt; (*pl.*) mockery; **сказа́ть что-н. в ~у** to say sth. to hurt s.o.

насме́шлив|ый (~, ~а) *adj.* mocking.

на́сморк, а *m.* cold (*in the head*); **схвати́ть, получи́ть н.** to catch a cold.

насмотр|е́ться, ю́сь, ~́ишься *pf.*
[1] (+ *g.*) (*увидеть много*) to see a lot (of).
[2] (**на** + *a.*) to have looked enough (at), to see enough (of); **не н.** not to tire of looking (at).

насол|и́ть, ю́, ~и́шь *pf.* (*of* ▸**наса́ливать**)
[1] (*usu.* **~́ишь**) (+ *a. or g.*) (*огурцов, грибов*) to salt, pickle (*a quantity of*).
[2] (*usu.* **~и́шь**) (*fig.*; + *d.*) (*сделать неприятность*) to spite; to do a bad turn (to).

насор|и́ть, ю́, и́шь *pf. of* ▸**сори́ть**

насо́с, а *m.* pump.

на́спех *adv.* hastily; carelessly.

наср|а́ть, у́, ёшь *pf. of* ▸**срать**

наста|ва́ть, ёт, ю́т *impf. of* ▸**~́ть**

наста́в|ить[1], **лю, ишь** *pf.* (*of* ▸**~ля́ть**)
[1] (*платье*) to lengthen; (*кусок ткани*) to put on, add on.
[2] (**на** + *a.*) (*нацелить*) to aim (at), point (at); **н. револьве́р на кого́-н.** to point a revolver at s.o.

наста́в|ить[2], **лю, ишь** *pf.* (*of* ▸**~ля́ть**) (*научить*) to edify; to exhort, admonish; **н. на путь и́стинный** to set on the right path.

наста́в|ить[3], **лю, ишь** *pf.* (+ *a. or g.*) (*стульев*) to set up, place (*a quantity of*); (*синяков*) to cause.

наставля́|ть, ю *impf. of* ▸**наста́вить**[1,2]

наста́вник, а *m.* (*воспитатель*) mentor; (*преподаватель*) teacher, instructor.

наста|ёт *see* ▸**~ва́ть**

Н

настáива|ть, ю *impf. of* ▸ **настоя́ть**

настáива|ться, ется *impf. of* ▸ **настоя́ться**

настá|ть, нет, нут *pf.* (*of* ▸ **~вáть**) (*of times or seasons*) to come, begin.

нáстежь *adv.* wide open; **откры́ть н.** to open wide.

настéнный *adj.* wall (*attr.*).

настиг|áть, áю *impf. of* ▸ **~́нуть** *and* ▸ **насти́чь**

насти́гн|уть, у, ешь *pf.* = **насти́чь**

насти́л, а *m.* flooring; planking.

насти́|чь, гну, гнешь, *past.* **~г, ~гла** *pf.* (*of* ▸ **~гáть**) to overtake (*also fig.*).

настóйк|а, и *f.*
1 (*спиртной напиток*) liqueur.
2 (*pharm.*) tincture.

настóйчив|ый (~, ~а) *adj.*
1 (*человек*) persistent.
2 (*просьба, тон*) urgent, insistent.

настóлько *adv.* so; so much; **н., наскóлько** as much as.

настóльн|ый *adj.*
1 table, desk; desktop; **~ая игрá** board game; **~ая издáтельская систéма** desktop publishing system; **н. тéннис** table tennis.
2 (*fig.*) for constant reference, in constant use; **~ая кни́га** bible.

насторáжива|ться, юсь *impf. of* ▸ **насторожи́ться**

настораж|и́ться, ýсь, и́шься *pf.* (*of* ▸ **насторáживаться**) to prick up one's ears.

настоя́тел|ь, я *m.* (*eccl.*)
1 (*монастыря*) prior, superior.
2 (*церкви*) senior priest.

настоя́тельниц|а, ы *f.* (*eccl.*) prioress, mother superior.

настоя́тел|ьный (~ен, ~ьна) *adj.*
1 (*требование*) persistent; insistent; **~ьная прóсьба** urgent request.
2 (*необходимость*) urgent, pressing.

насто|я́ть, ю́, и́шь *pf.* (*of* ▸ **настáивать**) (**на** + *p.*) to insist (on); **н. на своём** to insist on having it one's own way; **он ~я́л на том, чтóбы пойти́ самомý** he insisted on going himself.

насто|я́ться, и́тся, я́тся *pf.* (*of* ▸ **настáиваться**) (*о чае, травах*) to infuse, draw, brew.

настоя́щ|ий *adj.*
1 (*теперешний*) present; this; **в ~ее врéмя** at present, now; *as n.* **~ее, ~его** *nt.* the present (time); **жить ~им** to live in the present.
2 (*подлинный*) real, genuine; **н. друг** real friend.
3 (*coll.*) (*совершенный*) complete, utter, absolute; **он н. дурáк** he is an absolute fool.

настрадá|ться, юсь *pf.* (*coll.*) to suffer much.

настрáива|ть, ю *impf. of* ▸ **настрóить**

настроéни|е, я *nt.*
1 (*душевное состояние*) mood, temper, humour (*Br.*), humor (*US*); **припóднятое/ подáвленное н.** high/low spirits; **быть в плохóм,** *etc.* **~и** to be in a bad, *etc.* mood; **не в ~и** in a bad mood.
2 (+ *inf.*) mood (for); **у меня́ нет ~я танцевáть** I don't feel like dancing.

настрó|ить, ю, ишь *pf.* (*of* ▸ **настрáивать**)
1 (*mus.*) (*пианино, рояль*) to tune; (*скрипку, флейту*) to tune up, tune.
2 (*приёмник*) to tune.
3 (*механизм*) to tune, adjust.
4 (*fig.*; **на** + *a.*) to dispose (to), incline (to); to incite; **н. когó-н. (прóтив** + *g.*) to incite s.o. (against).

настрóйк|а, и *f.* (*mus., radio*) tuning.

настрóйщик, а *m.* tuner.

наступá|ть[2], ю *impf.* (*mil.*) to advance, be on the offensive.

наступ|áть[1], áю *impf. of* ▸ **~и́ть[1,2]**

наступá|ющий *pres. part. act. of* ▸ **~ть[1]** *and adj.* coming.

наступ|и́ть[1], лю́, ~́ишь *pf.* (*of* ▸ **~áть[1]**) (**на** + *a.*) to tread (on).

наступ|и́ть[2], ~́ит *pf.* (*of* ▸ **~áть[1]**) (*о времени, состоянии*) to come, begin; (*о молчании, тишине*) to ensue; to set in; **~́ит врéмя, когдá...** there will come a time, when ... .

наступлéни|е[1], я *nt.* (*mil.*) offensive; attack; **перейти́ в н.** to assume the offensive.

наступлéни|е[2], я *nt.* (*зимы*) coming, approach; onset.

настуч|áть, ý, и́шь *pf. of* ▸ **стучáть 3**

насýщ|ный (~ен, ~на) *adj.* vital, urgent; **хлеб н.** daily bread (*also fig.*).

насчёт *prep.* + *g.* about; as regards, concerning.

насып|áть, áю *impf. of* ▸ **~́ать**

насы́п|ать, лю, лешь *pf.* (*of* ▸ **~áть**)
1 (+ *a. or g.*) to pour (in, into); to fill (with); **н. муки́ в мешóк** to pour flour into a bag.
2 (+ *a. or g.* **на** + *a.*) (*посыпать*) to spread (on).
3 (*холм*) to raise (*a heap or pile of sand, etc.*).

нáсып|ь, и *f.* embankment.

насы́|титься, щусь, тишься *pf.* (*of* ▸ **~щáться**)
1 (*наесться*) to be full; to be sated.
2 (*chem.*) to become saturated.

насыщá|ться, юсь *impf. of* ▸ **насы́титься**

насы́щен|ный *adj.*
1 **(~, ~а)** saturated.
2 **(~, ~на)** (*fig.*) (*содержательный*) rich.

натáлкива|ться, юсь *impf. of* ▸ **натолкнýться**

натáплива|ть, ю *impf. of* ▸ **натопи́ть**

натвор|и́ть, ю́, и́шь *pf.* (+ *g.*; *coll., pej.*) to do, get up to; **н. вся́ких глýпостей** to get up to every sort of stupid trick; **что ты ~и́л!** what ever have you done?

на|терéть, трý, трёшь, *past* **~тёр, ~тёрла** *pf.* (*of* ▸ **~тирáть**)
1 (*намазать*) to rub (in, on).
2 (*пол*) to polish.
3 (*повредить*) to rub sore; to chafe; **н. себé мозóль** to get a corn.
4 (+ *a. or g.*) (*сыру*) to grate (*a quantity of*).

на|терéться, трýсь, трёшься, *past* **~тёрся, ~тёрлась** *pf.* (*of* ▸ **~тирáться**) (+ *i.*) to rub o.s. (with).

натирá|ть(ся), ю(сь) *impf. of*

▶ **натерéть(ся)**

наткн|ýться, ýсь, ёшься *pf.* (*of* ▶ **натыкáться**) (**на** + *a.*)
1 to run (against), strike; to stumble (upon); **н. на гвоздь** to run against a nail.
2 (*fig.*) to stumble (upon, across), come (across); **н. на интерéсную мысль** to stumble across an interesting idea.

НÁТО *nt. indecl.* NATO (*abbr. of* North Atlantic Treaty Organization — *Организáция Североатлантúческого договóра*).

нáтовский *adj. of* ▶ **НÁТО**

натолкн|ýться, ýсь, ёшься *pf.* (*of* ▶ **натáлкиваться**) (**на** + *a.*) to run (against); (*fig.*) to run across.

натоп|úть, лю́, ~ишь *pf.* (*of* ▶ **натáпливать**) to heat well, heat up.

наточ|úть, ý, ~ишь *pf. of* ▶ **точúть 1**

натрав|úть, лю́, ~ишь *pf.* (*of* ▶ **~ливать**) (**на** + *a.*) (*собаку*) to set (on); (*fig.*) to set (against).

натрáвлива|ть, ю *impf. of* ▶ **натравúть**

нáтри|й, я *m.* (*chem.*) sodium.

нáтрое *adv.* in three.

нат|рý, рёшь *see* ▶ **~ерéть**

натýр|а, ы *f.*
1 (*характер*) nature.
2 (*натурщик*) (artist's) model, sitter.
3 (*econ.*) kind; **платúть ~ой** to pay in kind.
4 (*естественная обстановка*) natural setting; **рисовáть с ~ы** to paint from life.

натурализáци|я, и *f.* naturalization.

натурализ|овáть, ýю *impf. and pf.* to naturalize.

натурализ|овáться, ýюсь *impf. and pf.* to become naturalized.

натуралúст, а *m.* naturalist.

натурáл|ьный (~ен, ~ьна) *adj.*
1 natural; **в ~ьную величинý** life-size.
2 (*настоящий*) (*мех, кожа, кофе*) real; (*смех*) genuine.
3 (*econ.*) in kind; **н. обмéн** barter.

натýрщик, а *m.* (artist's) model, sitter.

натýрщи|ца, цы *f. of* ▶ **~к**

натыкá|ться, юсь *impf. of* ▶ **наткнýться**

натюрмóрт, а *m.* (*art*) still life.

натягива|ть(ся), ю, ет(ся) *impf. of* ▶ **натянýть(ся)**

натяжк|а, и *f.* strained interpretation; **с ~ой** (*fig.*) at a stretch.

натян|утый *p.p.p. of* ▶ **~ýть** *and adj.*
1 tight.
2 (*fig.*) strained; forced; **~утые отношéния** strained relations.

натя|нýть, нý, ~нешь *pf.* (*of* ▶ **~гивать**)
1 (*сделать тугим*) to stretch; to draw (tight); **н. лук** to draw a bow.
2 (*надеть*) to pull on; **н. шáпку нá уши** to pull a cap over one's ears.

натя|нýться, ~нется, ~нутся *pf.* (*of* ▶ **~гиваться**) to stretch (*intrans.*).

наугáд *adv.* at random, by guesswork.

наудáчу *adv.* at random, by guesswork.

наýк|а, и *f.* (*система знаний*) science; (*учение*) learning; scholarship; **естéственные ~и** science.

наукоём|кий (~ок, ~ка) *adj.* high-technology, high-tech.

наýтро *adv.* next morning.

науч|úть, ý, ~ишь *pf.* (*of* ▶ **учúть 1**) (+ *a. and d. or* + *inf.*) to teach; **н. когó-н. рýсскому языкý** to teach s.o. Russian; **н. когó-н. водúть машúну** to teach s.o. to drive (a car).

науч|úться, ýсь, ~ишься *pf.* (*of* ▶ **учúться 1**) (+ *d. or inf.*) to learn.

наýчно-исслéдовательск|ий *adj.* scientific research; **~ая рабóта** (scientific) research work.

наýчно-фантастúческий *adj.* science fiction.

наýч|ный (~ен, ~на) *adj.* scientific; **н. рабóтник** researcher; **~ная фантáстика** science fiction.

наýшник, а *m.* (*in pl.*) headphones.

нахáл, а *m.* (*coll.*) impudent fellow, cheeky fellow.

нахáлк|а, и *f.* (*coll.*) impudent woman, cheeky woman.

нахáл|ьный (~ен, ~ьна) *adj.* impudent, cheeky.

нахам|úть, лю́, úшь *pf. of* ▶ **хамúть**

нахват|áть, áю *pf.* (*of* ▶ **~ывать**) (*coll.*; + *a. or g.*) to pick up, get hold (of); (*fig.*) (*знаний*) to pick up, come by.

нахват|áться, áюсь *pf.* (*of* ▶ **~ываться**) (*coll., fig.*; + *g.*) (*слов, привычек, знаний*) to pick up.

нахвáтыва|ть(ся), ю(сь) *impf. of* ▶ **нахватáть(ся)**

нахлéбник, а *m.* parasite, hanger-on.

нахлобýчива|ть, ю *impf. of* ▶ **нахлобýчить**

нахлобýч|ить, у, ишь *pf.* (*of* ▶ **~ивать**) (*coll.*) to pull down (over one's head *or* eyes).

нахмýр|ить(ся), ю(сь), ишь(ся) *pf. of* ▶ **хмýрить(ся)**

нахо|дúть, жý, ~дишь *impf. of* ▶ **найтú**[1,2]

нахо|дúться[1]**, жýсь, ~дишься** *impf. of* ▶ **найтúсь**

нахо|дúться[2]**, жýсь, ~дишься** *impf.* to be (situated); **где ~дится стáнция?** where is the station?; (*под наблюдением, стрессом*) to be.

нахóдк|а, и *f.*
1 find.
2 (*fig.*) (*подходящее*) godsend; (*приём*) device.

нахóдчив|ый (~, ~а) *adj.*
1 (*человек*) resourceful.
2 (*ответ*) quick-witted.

наце|дúть, жý, ~дишь *pf.* (+ *a. or g.*) to strain.

нацéлива|ть(ся), ю(сь) *impf. of* ▶ **нацéлить(ся)**

нацéл|ить, ю, ишь *pf.*
1 (*impf.* **цéлить** *and* **~ивать**) (*оружие*) to aim, level.
2 (*impf.* **~ивать**) (*fig.*) (**на** + *a.*) (*на выполнение*) to aim, direct.

нацéл|иться, юсь, ишься *pf.* (*of* ▶ **~иваться**)
1 (**в** + *a.*) to aim (at), take aim (at).
2 (*fig.*; **на** + *a.*) to aim (at, for), strive (for).

Н

3 (*fig.*, + *inf.*) to aim, strive (to do).

наце́нк|а, и *f.* markup.

нацеп|и́ть, лю́, ⁓ишь *pf.* (*of* ▸ **⁓ля́ть**)
1 to fasten on; to attach (*by means of hook or pin*).
2 (*coll.*) (*надеть*) to put on.

нацеп|ля́ть, ля́ю *impf. of* ▸ **⁓и́ть**

наци́зм, а *m.* Nazism.

национализа́ци|я, и *f.* nationalization.

национализи́р|овать, ую *impf. and pf.* to nationalize.

национали́зм, а *m.* nationalism.

национали́ст, а *m.* nationalist.

националисти́ческий *adj.* nationalist(ic).

национали́ст|ка, ки *f. of* ▸ **⁓**

национа́льност|ь, и *f.*
1 (*принадлежность к нации*) nationality.
2 (*нация*) nation.

национа́льн|ый *adj.* national; **⁓ое меньшинство́** national minority.

наци́ст, а *m.* Nazi.

наци́стский *adj.* Nazi.

на́ци|я, и *f.* nation.

нача́л|о, а *nt.*
1 beginning; start; **в ⁓е четвёртого** soon after three (o'clock); **по ⁓у** at first; **положи́ть, дать н.** (+ *d.*) to begin, commence; (*традиции, партии*) to establish.
2 (*источник*) origin, source; **брать н.** (**в** + *p.*) to originate (from, in).

нача́льник, а *m.* head, chief; superior; **н. отде́ла** head of a department, section.

нача́льн|ый *adj.*
1 (*находящийся в начале*) initial, first.
2 (*первоначальный*) primary, elementary; **⁓ая шко́ла** primary school (*Br.*), elementary school (*US*).

нача́льств|о, а *nt.*
1 (*collect.*) (the) authorities, management.
2 (*coll.*) (*начальник*) chief, boss.

нач|а́ть, ну́, нёшь, *past* **⁓ал, ⁓ала́, ⁓ало** *pf.* (*of* ▸ **⁓ина́ть**)
1 to begin, start, commence; **н. с нача́ла** to begin at the beginning; **н. всё снача́ла** to start all over again, start afresh.
2 (*новую пачку, тетрадь*) to start.

нач|а́ться, нётся, *past* **⁓алс́я, ⁓ала́сь** *pf.* (*of* ▸ **⁓ина́ться**) to begin, start.

начеку́ *adv.* on the alert, on one's guard.

начер|ти́ть, чу́, ⁓тишь *pf. of* ▸ **черти́ть**

начина́ни|е, я *nt.* undertaking, initiative.

начина́|ть(ся), ю, ет(ся) *impf. of* ▸ **нача́ть(ся)**

начина́|ющий *pres. part. act. of* ▸ **⁓ть** *and adj.* (*писатель*) fledgling; *as n.* **н., ⁓ющего** *m.* beginner.

начина́я *as prep.*
1 (**с** + *g.*) (*о времени*) as from, starting from; (*в том числе*) starting with, including.
2 (**от** + *g.*) starting with, including.

начи́нк|а, и *f.* (*cul.*) (*курицы, утки*) stuffing; (*пирожка*) filling.

начи́|стить, щу, стишь *pf.* (*of* ▸ **⁓ща́ть**) (*сапоги, кастрюлю*) to polish, shine (*trans.*).

на́чисто *adv.*
1 clean, fair; **переписа́ть н.** to make a fair copy (of).
2 (*coll.*) (*совсем*) completely, thoroughly.

начи́тан|ный (⁓, ⁓на) *adj.* well-read, widely-read.

начита́|ться, юсь *pf.*
1 (+*g.*) (*прочитать много*) to have read (*a lot of*).
2 (*почитать вдоволь*) to have read one's fill.

начища́|ть, ю *impf. of* ▸ **начи́стить**

нач|ну́, нёшь *see* ▸ **⁓а́ть**

наш, ⁓его; *f.* **⁓а, ⁓ей;** *nt.* **⁓е, ⁓его;** *pl.* **⁓и, ⁓их** *possessive pron.* (*при существительном*) our; (*без существительного*) ours; *as n.* **⁓и, ⁓их** our people, people on our side; **его́ счита́ют одни́м из ⁓их** they regard him as one of us.

наше́стви|е, я *nt.* (*also fig.*) invasion, descent.

наши́вк|а, и *f.* stripe, chevron.

нашинк|ова́ть, у́ю *pf. of* ▸ **шинкова́ть**

нащу́п|ать, аю *pf.* (*of* ▸ **⁓ывать**) to find, discover (*by groping*).

нащу́пыва|ть, ю *impf.* (*of* ▸ **нащу́пать**) to grope (for, after); to fumble (for, after); to feel about (for) (*also fig.*).

наяву́ *adv.* waking; in reality.

НДС *m. indecl.* (*abbr. of* **нало́г на доба́вленную сто́имость**) VAT (*Value Added Tax*).

не[1] not; **я не зна́ю** I do not know; **я не могу́ не сказа́ть** I can't but say; I must say; **не без волне́ния** with some excitement; **не до** (+ *g.*) not time for; **мне не до шу́ток** I have no time for jokes; **не..., не** neither ... nor; **не то** otherwise, or else.

не[2] *separable component of prons.* ▸ **не́кого** *and* ▸ **не́чего; не́ о чем бы́ло говори́ть** there was nothing to talk about.

не... *pref.* un-, in-, non-, mis-, dis-, *etc.*

неаккура́т|ный (⁓ен, ⁓на) *adj.*
1 (*небрежный*) careless; inaccurate.
2 (*неопрятный*) untidy.

неаппети́т|ный (⁓ен, ⁓на) *adj.* unappetizing (*also fig.*).

небезопа́с|ный (⁓ен, ⁓на) *adj.* unsafe, insecure.

небезоснова́тел|ьный (⁓ен, ⁓ьна) *adj.* not unfounded.

небезразли́ч|ный (⁓ен, ⁓на) *adj.* not indifferent.

небезуспе́ш|ный (⁓ен, ⁓на) *adj.* not unsuccessful.

небезызве́ст|ный (⁓ен, ⁓на) *adj.* not unknown; (*iron.*) notorious; **⁓но, что...** it is no secret that ... .

небезынтере́с|ный (⁓ен, ⁓на) *adj.* not without interest.

неб|еса́ *pl. of* ▸ **⁓о**

небе́сн|ый *adj.* heavenly, celestial; **⁓ые свети́ла** heavenly bodies; **Ца́рство Н⁓ое** the Kingdom of Heaven; **⁓ого цве́та** sky blue.

неблагови́д|ный (⁓ен, ⁓на) *adj.* unseemly, improper.

неблагода́рност|ь, и *f.* ingratitude.

неблагода́р|ный (⁓ен, ⁓на) *adj.*
1 (*человек*) ungrateful.

2 (*задача*) thankless.

неблагозву́ч|ный (~ен, ~на) *adj.* inharmonious, disharmonious.

неблагополу́ч|ный (~ен, ~на) *adj.* unfavourable (*Br.*), unfavorable (*US*), bad; unsuccessful.

неблагоприя́т|ный (~ен, ~на) *adj.* unfavourable (*Br.*), unfavorable (*US*), inauspicious.

неблагоскло́н|ный (~ен, ~на) *adj.* unfavourable (*Br.*), unfavorable (*US*); (**к** + *d.*) ill-disposed (towards).

нёб|о, а *nt.* (*anat.*) palate.

не́б|о, а, *pl.* **~еса́, ~е́с, ~еса́м** *nt.* sky; (*relig.*) heaven; **под откры́тым ~ом** in the open (air).

небольш|о́й *adj.* small; not great; **о́чень ~о́е расстоя́ние** a very short distance; **ты́сяча с ~и́м** a thousand odd.

небосво́д, а *m.* firmament; the vault of heaven.

небоскло́н, а *m.* horizon (*strictly, sky immediately over the horizon*).

небоскрёб, а *m.* skyscraper.

небре́жност|ь, и *f.* carelessness, negligence.

небре́ж|ный (~ен, ~на) *adj.* (*человек, работа*) careless; (*одежда, почерк*) untidy; (*тон, манера*) offhand.

небри́т|ый (~, ~а) *adj.* unshaven.

небыва́л|ый (~, ~а) *adj.* unprecedented.

небыли́ц|а, ы *f.* (*сказка*) fable; (*выдумка*) cock-and-bull story.

небыти|е́, я́ *nt.* non-existence.

небью́щийся *adj.* unbreakable.

Нев|а́, ы́ *f.* the Neva (*river*).

нева́жно *adv.* not too well, indifferently; **дела́ иду́т н.** things are not going too well.

нева́ж|ный (~ен, ~на́, ~но) *adj.*
1 (*незначительный*) unimportant.
2 (*coll.*) (*посредственный*) poor, indifferent.

невдалеке́ *adv.* not far away, not far off.

неве́дени|е, я *nt.* ignorance; **пребыва́ть в блаже́нном ~и** (*iron.*) to be in a state of blissful ignorance.

неве́домо *adv.* (*coll.*; + **что, как, когда́, куда́** *etc.*) God knows, no one knows; **он так и появи́лся, н. отку́да** he just turned up, God knows where from.

неве́дом|ый (~, ~а) *adj.*
1 unknown.
2 (*fig.*) (*таинственный*) mysterious.

неве́ж|а, и *c.g.* boor, lout.

неве́жд|а, ы *c.g.* ignoramus.

неве́жествен|ный (~, ~на) *adj.* ignorant.

неве́жеств|о, а *nt.* ignorance.

неве́жлив|ый (~, ~а) *adj.* rude, impolite.

невезе́ни|е, я *nt.* (*coll.*) bad luck.

неве́ри|е, я *nt.* unbelief; lack of faith.

неве́рност|ь, и *f.*
1 (*неправильность*) incorrectness.
2 (*друга*) disloyalty; (*супруга*) infidelity, unfaithfulness.

неве́р|ный (~ен, ~на́, ~но) *adj.*
1 (*ошибочный*) incorrect; **~ная но́та** false note.
2 (*друг*) faithless, disloyal; (*муж, жена*) unfaithful.

невероя́тно *adv.* incredibly, unbelievably.

невероя́т|ный (~ен, ~на) *adj.*
1 (*неправдоподобный*) improbable, unlikely.
2 (*чрезвычайный*) incredible, unbelievable (*also fig.*); (*impers., as pred.*): **~но** it is incredible, it is unbelievable; it is beyond belief.

неве́рующ|ий *adj.* (*relig.*) unbelieving; *as n.* **н., ~его** *m.*, **~ая, ~ей** *f.* unbeliever.

невес|ёлый (~́ел, ~ела́, ~́ело) *adj.* sad, gloomy, melancholy.

невесо́мост|ь, и *f.* weightlessness.

неве́ст|а, ы *f.* fiancée; (*в день свадьбы*) bride.

неве́стк|а, и *f.*
1 (*жена сына*) daughter-in-law.
2 (*жена брата*) sister-in-law.

невзира́я *prep.* (**на** + *a.*) in spite of, regardless of.

невзра́ч|ный (~ен, ~на) *adj.* unprepossessing, unattractive; plain.

неви́дан|ный (~, ~на) *adj.* unprecedented.

неви́дим|ый (~, ~а) *adj.* invisible.

неви́нност|ь, и *f.* innocence; (*девственность*) virginity.

неви́н|ный (~ен, ~на) *adj.* innocent; (*девственный*) virgin(al); **~ная жéртва** innocent victim.

невино́в|ный (~ен, ~на) *adj.* (**в** + *p.*) innocent (of); (*leg.*) not guilty; **призна́ть ~ным** to acquit.

невку́с|ный (~ен, ~́на́, ~но) *adj.* unpalatable.

невменя́ем|ый (~, ~а) *adj.*
1 (*leg.*) irresponsible.
2 (*coll.*) beside o.s.

невмеша́тельств|о, а *m.* (*pol.*) non-intervention, non-interference.

невнима́ни|е, я *nt.*
1 (*рассеянность*) inattention; carelessness.
2 (**к** + *d.*) (*пренебрежение*) lack of consideration (for).

невнима́тельност|ь, и *f.* inattention; (*небрежность*) thoughtlessness.

невнима́тел|ьный (~ен, ~ьна) *adj.* (*рассеянный*) inattentive; (*незаботливый*) thoughtless.

невня́т|ный (~ен, ~на) *adj.* indistinct, incomprehensible.

не́вод, а, *pl.* **~а́, ~о́в** *m.* seine, sweep net.

невозмо́ж|ный (~ен, ~на) *adj.* impossible; (*impers., pred.*): **~но** it is impossible; *as n.* **~ное, ~ного** *nt.* the impossible.

невозмути́м|ый (~, ~а) *adj.*
1 (*человек*) imperturbable.
2 (*тон*) calm, unruffled.

невозобновля́емый *adj.* non-renewable.

нево́льно *adv.* involuntarily; unintentionally, unwittingly.

нево́льный *adj.*
1 (*вздох, трепет*) involuntary; (*ложь, обида*) unintentional.
2 (*вынужденный*) forced.

Н

невóл|я, и *f.* bondage; captivity.
невообрази́м|ый (~, ~а) *adj.* unimaginable, inconceivable; **н. шум** (*fig.*) unimaginable din.
невооружённ|ый *adj.* unarmed; **~ым глáзом** with the naked eye.
невоспи́тан|ный (~, ~на) *adj.* ill-bred; bad-mannered.
невосполни́м|ый (~, ~а) *adj.* irreplaceable.
невосприи́мчив|ый (~, ~а) *adj.* 1 (*к знаниям*) unreceptive. 2 (*med.*) (**к** + *d.*) immune (to).
невразуми́тел|ьный (~ен, ~ьна) *adj.* unintelligible, incomprehensible.
невралги́|я, и *f.* neuralgia.
неврастéник, а *m.* neurasthenic.
неврастени́|я, и *f.* neurasthenia.
невреди́м|ый (~, ~а) *adj.* unharmed, intact; **цел и ~** safe and sound.
неврóз, а *m.* neurosis.
невропатóлог, а *m.* neuropathologist.
невы́год|ный (~ен, ~на) *adj.* 1 (*положение*) disadvantageous, unfavourable (*Br.*), unfavorable (*US*); **показáть себя́ с ~ной стороны́** to show o.s. at a disadvantage. 2 (*сделка*) unprofitable, unremunerative; (*impers., pred.*): **~но** it does not pay.
невыноси́м|ый (~, ~а) *adj.* unbearable, insufferable, intolerable.
невыполни́м|ый (~, ~а) *adj.* impracticable; unrealizable.
невырази́м|ый (~, ~а) *adj.* inexpressible, beyond expression.
невырази́тел|ьный (~ен, ~ьна) *adj.* inexpressive, expressionless.
невысóк|ий (~, ~á, ~о *and* **ó, ~и** *and* **и́)** *adj.* (*забор, потолок, голос*) rather low; (*человек*) rather short; **~ого кáчества** of poor quality; **быть ~ого мнéния** (**о** + *p.*) to have a low opinion (of).
негати́в, а *m.* (*phot.*) negative.
негати́в|ный (~ен, ~на) *adj.* negative.
нéгде *adv.* (+ *inf.*) there is nowhere; **н. достáть э́ту кни́гу** this book is nowhere to be had.
неглáс|ный (~ен, ~на) *adj.* secret.
неглу́п|ый (~, ~á, ~о) *adj.* quite intelligent; **он óчень ~** he is no fool.
негó *a. and g. of* ▸ **он** *when governed by preps.*
негóд|ный (~ен, ~на) *adj.* unfit, unsuitable.
негодовáни|е, я *nt.* indignation.
негод|овáть, у́ю *impf.* (**на** + *a.*, **прóтив** + *g.*) to be indignant (with).
негрáмотност|ь, и *f.* illiteracy (*also fig.*).
негрáмот|ный (~ен, ~на) *adj.* illiterate (*also fig.*); *as n.* **н., ~ного** *m.*, **~ная, ~ной** *f.* illiterate (*person*).
негрóм|кий (~ок, ~кá, ~ко) *adj.* quiet, low.
негумáн|ный (~ен, ~на) *adj.* inhumane.
недáвний *adj.* recent.
недáвно *adv.* recently.
недалёк|ий *adj.* 1 (**~, ~á, ~о** *or* **~ó**) *место*) nearby, not far off, near; (*путешествие, прогулка, расстояние*) short. 2 (**~, ~а, ~о**) (*fig.*) (*глуповатый*) not bright, dull-witted.
недалекó *adv.* not far, near.
недальнови́д|ный (~ен, ~на) *adj.* short-sighted (*fig.*).
недáром *adv.* not for nothing; for good reason.
недви́жимост|ь, и *f.* (*leg.*) (immovable) property, real estate.
недви́жим|ый *adj.*: **~ое иму́щество** = **~ость**
недееспосóбност|ь, и *f.* (*leg.*) incapacity.
недееспосóб|ный (~ен, ~на) *adj.* (*leg.*) (*человек*) incapacitated.
недействи́тел|ьный (~ен, ~ьна) *adj.* (*leg.*) invalid.
недели́м|ый (~, ~а) *adj.* indivisible.
недéльный *adj.* of a week's duration.
недéл|я, и *f.* week; **на э́той ~е** this week.
недоброжелáтел|ь, я *m.* ill-wisher.
недоброжелáтел|ьный (~ен, ~ьна) *adj.* malevolent, ill-disposed.
недобросóвест|ный (~ен, ~на) *adj.* 1 (*нечестный*) unscrupulous. 2 (*небрежный*) lacking in conscientiousness; careless.
недóбр|ый *adj.* 1 (*человек, взгляд*) unkind; unfriendly. 2 (*намерение, чувство*) evil; **~ая весть** bad news.
недовéри|е, я *nt.* distrust; mistrust; **вóтум ~я** vote of no confidence.
недовéрчив|ый (~, ~а) *adj.* distrustful; mistrustful.
недовóл|ьный (~ен, ~ьна) *adj.* (+ *i.*) dissatisfied, discontented, displeased (with); *as n.* **н., ~ьного** *m.*, **~ьная, ~ьной** *f.* malcontent.
недовóльств|о, а *nt.* dissatisfaction, discontent, displeasure.
недогáдлив|ый (~, ~а) *adj.* slow(-witted).
недогля|дéть, жу́, ди́шь *pf.* to overlook, miss.
недода|вáть, ю́, ёшь *impf. of* ▸ **~́ть**
недо|дáть, дáм, дáшь, дáст, дади́м, дади́те, даду́т, *past* **~́дал, ~далá, ~́дало** *pf.* (*of* ▸ **~давáть**) to give short; to deliver short; **он мне ~́дал пятьдеся́т рублéй** he gave me fifty roubles short.
недоедá|ть, ю *impf.* to be undernourished, be underfed.
недозвóлен|ный (~, ~а) *adj.* illicit, unlawful.
недозрéлый *adj.* (*яблоко*) unripe; (*fig.*) (*человек*) immature.
недóл|гий (~ог, ~гá, ~го) *adj.* short, brief.
недóлго *adv.* 1 not long; **н. ду́мая** without hesitation. 2 (*coll.*): (*легко*) **н. и** (+ *inf.*) one can easily; it is easy (to).
недолговéч|ный (~ен, ~на) *adj.* short-lived, ephemeral.

недолю́бливa|ть, ю *impf.* (+ *a. or g.*; *coll.*) not to be overfond of; **они́ ~ли друг дру́га** there was no love lost between them.
недомога́ни|е, я *nt.* indisposition.
недоно́шен|ный (~, ~а) *adj.* (*med.*) premature.
недооце́нива|ть, ю *impf. of* ▸ **недооцени́ть**
недооцен|и́ть, ю́, ~́ишь *pf.* (*of* ▸ **~́ивать**) to underestimate, underrate.
недополуч|а́ть, а́ю *impf. of* ▸ **~и́ть**
недополуч|и́ть, у́, ~́ишь *pf.* (*of* ▸ **~а́ть**) to receive less (than one's due).
недопусти́м|ый (~, ~а) *adj.* inadmissible, intolerable.
недора́звит|ый (~, ~а) *adj.* underdeveloped, backward.
недоразуме́ни|е, я *nt.* misunderstanding.
недо́рого *adv.* not dear, cheaply.
недор|ого́й (~́ог, ~ога́, ~́ого) *adj.* inexpensive; reasonable (*of price*).
недоса́лива|ть, ю *impf. of* ▸ **недосоли́ть**
недосмотр|е́ть, ю́, ~́ишь *pf.*
1 (+ *g.*) to overlook, miss.
2 (**за** + *i.*) not to look after properly.
недосол|и́ть, ю́, ~́ишь *pf.* (*of* ▸ **недоса́ливать**) to put too little salt in.
недос|па́ть, плю́, пи́шь *pf.* (*of* ▸ **~ыпа́ть**) not to get enough sleep.
недоста|ва́ть, ёт *impf.* (*of* ▸ **~́ть**) (*impers.*, + *g.*) to be missing, be lacking, be wanting; **ему́ ~ёт о́пыта** he lacks experience.
недоста́т|ок, ка *m.*
1 (+ *g. or* **в** + *p.*) shortage (of), lack (of); **име́ть н. в рабо́чей си́ле** to be short-handed.
2 (*несовершенство*) shortcoming, imperfection; defect; **н. зре́ния** defective eyesight.
недоста́точно *adv.*
1 insufficiently.
2 (*pred.* + *g.*) (*не хватает*) not enough.
недоста́точ|ный (~ен, ~на) *adj.* insufficient; inadequate.
недоста́|ть, нет *pf. of* ▸ **~ва́ть**
недостижи́м|ый (~, ~а) *adj.* unattainable.
недостове́р|ный (~ен, ~на) *adj.* unreliable, apocryphal.
недосто́|йный (~ин, ~йна) *adj.* unworthy.
недосту́п|ный (~ен, ~на) *adj.* inaccessible (*also fig.*); **э́то ~но моему́ понима́нию** it is beyond my comprehension.
недосчит|а́ться, а́юсь *pf.* (*of* ▸ **~́ываться**) (+ *g.*) to find missing, miss; to be out (in one's accounts); **он ~а́лся десяти́ рубле́й** he found he was ten roubles short.
недосчи́тыва|ться, юсь *impf. of* ▸ **недосчита́ться**
недосыпа́|ть, ю *impf. of* ▸ **недоспа́ть**
недосяга́ем|ый (~, ~а) *adj.* unattainable.
недоумева́|ть, ю *impf.* to be perplexed, be at a loss.
недоуме́ни|е, я *nt.* perplexity, bewilderment; **быть в ~и** to be in a quandary.
недочёт, а *m.* (*usu. pl.*) defect, shortcoming.
не́др|а, ~ *no sg.*
1 depths (*of the earth*); **н. земли́** bowels of the earth; **разве́дка ~** prospecting of mineral wealth.
2 (*fig.*) depths, heart.
не́друг, а *m.* enemy, foe.
недружелю́б|ный (~ен, ~на) *adj.* unfriendly.
неду́г, а *m.* ailment, disease.
неё *a. and g. of* ▸ **она́** *when governed by preps.*
нeесте́ствен|ный (~, ~на) *adj.* unnatural.
нежда́нный *adj.* unexpected.
нежела́тел|ьный (~ен, ~ьна) *adj.* undesirable.
нежена́т|ый (~) *adj.* (*of a man*) unmarried.
нежив́ой *adj.*
1 (*мёртвый*) lifeless, dead.
2 (*неорганический*) inanimate, inorganic.
3 (*fig.*) (*вялый*) dull, lifeless.
нежило́й *adj.*
1 (*необитаемый*) uninhabited.
2 (*негодный для жилья*) not fit for habitation; uninhabitable.
не́ж|иться, усь, ишься *impf.* to luxuriate; **н. на со́лнце** to bask in the sun.
не́жност|ь, и *f.*
1 (*ласковость*) tenderness.
2 (*тонкость*) delicacy.
не́ж|ный (~ен, ~на́, ~но) *adj.*
1 tender; affectionate; **~ный во́зраст** tender age.
2 (*тонкий*) delicate (= *soft, fine*; *of colours, taste, skin, etc.*).
3 (*хрупкий*) delicate.
незабу́дк|а, и *f.* (*bot.*) forget-me-not.
незабыва́ем|ый (~, ~а) *adj.* unforgettable.
незави́симо *adv.* independently; **н. от** irrespective of.
незави́симост|ь, и *f.* independence.
незави́сим|ый (~, ~а) *adj.* independent.
незадо́лго *adv.* (**до** + *g.*, **пе́ред** + *i.*) shortly (before), not long (before).
незако́н|ный (~ен, ~на) *adj.* illegal, unlawful.
незако́нчен|ный (~, ~на) *adj.* incomplete, unfinished.
незамедли́тельно *adv.* without delay.
незамени́м|ый (~, ~а) *adj.*
1 irreplaceable.
2 (*очень нужный*) indispensable.
незаме́тно *adv.* imperceptibly; **н., что́бы …** you cannot tell that … .
незаме́т|ный (~ен, ~на) *adj.*
1 (*следы*) imperceptible.
2 (*человек*) unremarkable.
незаму́жняя *adj.* unmarried, single.
незаслу́жен|ный (~, ~на) *adj.* undeserved, unmerited.
незауря́д|ный (~ен, ~на) *adj.* outstanding, exceptional.

нéзачем *adv.* (+ *inf.*) there is no point (in), it is pointless; there is no need (to).
нездéшний *adj.* (*coll.*) not of these parts; **я н.** I am a stranger here.
нездорóвит|ься, ~ся *impf.* (*impers.*, + *d.*) to feel unwell.
нездорóв|ый (~, ~а) *adj.*
1 unhealthy (*also fig.*).
2 *as pred.* unwell, poorly.
неземнóй *adj.* unearthly.
незнакóм|ец, ца *m.* stranger.
незнакóм|ка, ки *f. of* ▶ **~ец**
незнакóм|ый (~, ~а) *adj.*
1 unknown, unfamiliar.
2 (**с** + *i.*) unacquainted (with).
незнáни|е, я *nt.* ignorance.
незначи́тел|ьный (~ен, ~ьна) *adj.* insignificant, negligible, trivial.
незрéлост|ь, и *f.* unripeness; (*fig.*) immaturity.
незрéл|ый (~, ~а) *adj.* unripe (*also fig.*); (*fig.*) immature.
незри́м|ый (~, ~а) *adj.* invisible.
незы́блем|ый (~, ~а) *adj.* unshakeable, stable.
неизбéж|ный (~ен, ~на) *adj.* inevitable, unavoidable; inescapable.
неизвéстност|ь, и *f.*
1 (*отсутствие сведений*) uncertainty; **быть в ~и** (**о** + *p.*) to be uncertain (about), be in the dark (about).
2 (*незаметное существование*) obscurity; **жить в ~и** to live in obscurity.
неизвéст|ный (~ен, ~на) *adj.* unknown; **~но где, когдá,** *etc.*, no one knows where, when, *etc.* (= *somewhere, at some time, etc.*); *as n.* **н., ~ного** *m.*, **~ная, ~ной** *f.* unknown person; **~ное, ~ного** *nt.* (*math.*) unknown (quantity).
неизлечи́м|ый (~, ~а) *adj.* incurable.
неизмéн|ный (~ен, ~на) *adj.* (*постоянный*) invariable, immutable.
неимéни|е, я *nt.* lack, want; **за ~ем лу́чшего** for want of sth. better.
неимовéр|ный (~ен, ~на) *adj.* incredible, unbelievable.
неиму́щий *adj.* indigent, poor.
неинтерéс|ный (~ен, ~на) *adj.* uninteresting.
нeи́скрен|ний (~ен, ~на) *adj.* insincere.
неисправи́м|ый (~, ~а) *adj.*
1 (*человек*) incorrigible.
2 (*недостаток, ошибка*) irremediable, irreparable.
неисправност|ь, и *f.* (*машины*) disrepair; fault, defect.
неисправ|ный (~ен, ~на) *adj.* (*машина*) out of order; faulty, defective.
неиссякáем|ый (~, ~а) *adj.* inexhaustible.
неи́стов|ый (~, ~а) *adj.* furious, frenzied.
неистощи́м|ый (~, ~а) *adj.* inexhaustible.
неистреби́м|ый (~, ~а) *adj.* ineradicable; undying.
неисчерпáем|ый (~, ~а) *adj.* inexhaustible.
неисчисли́м|ый (~, ~а) *adj.* innumerable; incalculable.
ней *d., i., and p. of* ▶ **онá** *when governed by preps.*
нейлóн, а *m.* nylon.
нейлóновый *adj.* nylon, made of nylon.
нейрохиру́рг, а *m.* neurosurgeon.
нейтрализáци|я, и *f.* neutralization.
нейтрализ|овáть, у́ю *impf. and pf.* to neutralize.
нейтралитéт, а *m.* (*pol.*) neutrality.
нейтрáл|ьный (~ен, ~ьна) *adj.* neutral.
нейтрóн, а *m.* (*phys.*) neutron.
некáчествен|ный (~, ~на) *adj.* poor-quality.
неквалифици́рован|ный (~, ~на) *adj.* unqualified; **н. рабóчий** unskilled labourer (*Br.*), laborer (*US*).
нéкий *pron.* a certain; a kind of; **вас спрáшивал н. господи́н Пáвлов** a (certain) Mr Pavlov was asking for you.
нéкогда[1] *adv.* once, formerly; in the old days.
нéкогда[2] *adv.* there is no time; **мне сегóдня н. разговáривать** I have no time to chat today.
нéкого, нéкому, нéкем, нé о ком *pron.* (+ *inf.*) there is nobody (to); **н. вини́ть** nobody is to blame; **ей нé с кем пойти́** she has nobody to go with (her).
некомпетéнт|ный (~ен, ~на) *adj.* incompetent, unqualified.
неконкурентоспосóб|ный (~ен, ~на) *adj.* uncompetitive.
неконституциóн|ный (~ен, ~на) *adj.* unconstitutional.
некоррéкт|ный (~ен, ~на) *adj.* discourteous, impolite.
нéкотор|ый *pron.* some; **мы с ~ых пор живём здесь** we have been living here for some time; **~ым óбразом** somehow, in some way; **в, до ~ой стéпени** to some extent, to a certain extent; *as n.* **~ые, ~ых** (*coll.*) some; some people.
некраси́в|ый (~, ~а) *adj.*
1 ugly, unattractive.
2 (*coll.*) (*поведение*) unseemly, not nice.
некредитоспосóб|ный (~ен, ~на) *adj.* insolvent.
некролóг, а *m.* obituary (notice).
некстáти *adv.* (*прийти, сказать*) at the wrong moment, inopportunely; (*о замечании*) inopportune, inappropriate.
нектáр, а *m.* nectar.
нéкто *pron.* someone; **н. Петрóв** one Petrov, a certain Petrov.
нéкуда *adv.* (+ *inf.*) there is nowhere (to); **мне н. пойти́** I have nowhere to go.
некульту́р|ный (~ен, ~на) *adj.*
1 (*нецивилизованный*) uncivilized; backward.
2 (*грубый*) rough(-mannered), boorish.
некуря́щ|ий *adj.* non-smoking; *as n.* **н., ~его** *m.* non-smoker; **вагóн для ~их** non-smoking carriage.
нелегáл, а *m.* (*coll.*) illegal person (*person living somewhere illegally or doing sth. illegally*).

нелега́л|ьный (~ен, ~ьна) *adj.* illegal.
нелёг|кий (~ок, ~ка́) *adj.*
1 (*трудный*) difficult, not easy.
2 (*тяжёлый*) heavy, not light (*also fig.*).
нелéп|ый (~, ~а) *adj.* absurd, ridiculous.
нело́в|кий (~ок, ~ка́, ~ко) *adj.*
1 (*неуклюжий*) awkward; clumsy.
2 (*fig.*) awkward; embarrassing; **~кое молча́ние** awkward silence.
нело́вко *adv.* awkwardly; uncomfortably; **чу́вствовать себя́ н.** to feel ill at ease, feel awkward, feel uncomfortable.
нело́вкост|ь, и *f.*
1 (*свойство*) awkwardness, clumsiness (*also fig.*).
2 (*поступок*) blunder, gaffe.
нелоги́ч|ный (~ен, ~на) *adj.* illogical.
нельзя́ *adv.* (+ *inf.*)
1 (*нет возможности*) it is impossible; **н. не призна́ть** it is impossible not to admit, one cannot but admit.
2 (*запрещается*) it is not allowed; **здесь н. кури́ть** smoking is not allowed here.
3 (*нехорошо*) one ought not, one should not; **н. ложи́ться (спать) так по́здно** you ought not to go to bed so late.
нём *p. of* ▶ **он, оно́**
нема́ло *adv.*
1 (+ *g.*) (*времени, денег*) not a little; a good deal of; (*людей*) quite a few.
2 (*читать, гордиться*) a good deal, quite a lot.
немалова́ж|ный (~ен, ~на) *adj.* of no small importance.
нема́л|ый (~, ~а́) *adj.* considerable.
неме́дленно *adv.* immediately.
неме́|ть, ю *impf.* (*of* ▶ **о~**)
1 (*становиться немым*) to become dumb, grow dumb.
2 (*цепенеть*) to become numb, grow numb.
не́м|ец, ца *m.* German.
неме́цк|ий *adj.* German; **~ая овча́рка** Alsatian (dog) (*Br.*), German shepherd.
немину́ем|ый (~, ~а) *adj.* inevitable, unavoidable.
не́м|ка, ки *f. of* ▶ **~ец**
немно́г|ие *adj.* few, a few; *as n.* **н., ~их** few.
немно́го *adv.*
1 (+ *g.*) (*времени, денег*) a little, some, not much; (*людей*) a few, not many.
2 (*слегка*) a little, somewhat, slightly; **я н. уста́л** I am a little tired.
немно́г|ое, ого *nt.* few things, little.
немно́жко *adv.* (*coll.*) a little; a bit.
нем|о́й (~, ~а́, ~̀о) *adj.*
1 dumb; *as n.* **н., ~о́го** *m.* mute; **~ы́е** (*collect.*) the mute.
2 (*fig.*) silent; **н. фильм** silent film.
не|молодо́й (~мо́лод, ~молода́, ~мо́лодо) *adj.* not young, elderly.
немот|а́, ы́ *f.* dumbness; muteness.
нему́ *d. of* **он, оно́** *after preps.*
немы́слим|ый (~, ~а) *adj.* unthinkable, inconceivable.
ненави́|деть, жу, дишь *impf.* to hate, detest, loathe.
ненави́ст|ный (~ен, ~на) *adj.* hated; hateful.
не́навист|ь, и *f.* hatred, detestation.
ненавя́зчив|ый (~, ~а) *adj.* unobtrusive.
ненадёж|ный (~ен, ~на) *adj.* (*человек; сведение*) unreliable, untrustworthy; (*защита; лёд*) insecure.
ненадо́лго *adv.* for a short while, not for long.
ненаме́ренно *adv.* unintentionally, unwittingly, accidentally.
ненаме́рен|ный (~, ~на) *adj.* unintentional, accidental.
нена́ст|ный (~ен, ~на) *adj.* (*погода*) bad, foul.
ненастоя́щий *adj.* (*мех*) artificial; (*деньги*) counterfeit.
нена́ст|е, я *nt.* bad, foul weather.
ненорма́л|ьный (~ен, ~ьна) *adj.*
1 abnormal.
2 (*сумасшедший*) mad.
нену́ж|ный (~ен, ~на́, ~но) *adj.* (*мягкость*) unnecessary; (*книга, человек*) superfluous.
необду́ман|ный (~, ~на) *adj.* thoughtless, precipitate.
необита́ем|ый (~, ~а) *adj.* uninhabited; **н. о́стров** desert island.
необозри́м|ый (~, ~а) *adj.* boundless, immense.
необосно́ван|ный (~, ~на) *adj.* unfounded, groundless.
необрабо́тан|ный (~, ~а) *adj.*
1 (*земля*) uncultivated, untilled.
2 (*минерал*) raw, crude.
необразо́ван|ный (~, ~на) *adj.* uneducated.
необрати́м|ый (~, ~а) *adj.* irreversible.
необу́здан|ный (~, ~на) *adj.* (*фантазия*) unbridled; (*нрав*) ungovernable.
необходи́мост|ь, и *f.* necessity; **по ~и** out of necessity; **при~и** if necessary.
необходи́м|ый (~, ~а) *adj.* necessary, essential; (*impers., as pred.*): **~о** it is necessary *or* imperative.
необщи́тел|ьный (~ен, ~ьна) *adj.* unsociable.
необъекти́в|ный (~ен, ~на) *adj.* not objective; biased.
необъясни́м|ый (~, ~а) *adj.* inexplicable, unaccountable.
необъя́т|ный (~ен, ~на) *adj.* immense, unbounded.
необыкнове́н|ный (~ен, ~на) *adj.* unusual, uncommon.
необыча́|йный (~ен, ~йна) *adj.* extraordinary, exceptional.
необы́ч|ный (~ен, ~на) *adj.* unusual.
необяза́тел|ьный (~ен, ~ьна) *adj.*
1 (*предмет, курс*) not obligatory, optional.
2 (*человек*) unreliable.
неограни́чен|ный (~, ~на) *adj.* unlimited, unbounded.
неоднозна́ч|ный (~ен, ~на) *adj.*
1 ambiguous, equivocal.
2 (*сложный*) complex, complicated.
неоднокра́тно *adv.* repeatedly.

неоднокра́т|ный (~ен, ~на) *adj.* repeated.

неоднoро́д|ный (~ен, ~на) *adj.* heterogeneous; dissimilar.

неодобре́ни|е, я *nt.* disapproval.

неодоли́м|ый (~, ~а) *adj.* insuperable.

неодушевлённый *adj.* inanimate.

неожи́данност|ь, и *f.*
1 unexpectedness, suddenness.
2 (*событие*) surprise.

неожи́дан|ный (~, ~на) *adj.* unexpected, sudden.

неоко́нченный *adj.* unfinished.

нео́н, а *m.* (*chem.*) neon.

неонаци́ст, а *m.* neo-Nazi.

неонаци́ст|ка, ки *f. of* ▸ ~

нео́новый *adj.*: **~ свет** neon light.

неопа́с|ный (~ен, ~на) *adj.* (*место, путешествие*) safe; (*болезнь, собака*) harmless.

неопису́ем|ый (~, ~а) *adj.* indescribable.

неопо́знан|ный (~, ~а) *adj.* unidentified.

неопра́вдан|ный (~, ~на) *adj.* unjustified, unwarranted.

неопределённост|ь, и *f.* vagueness, uncertainty.

неопределён|ный (~ен, ~на) *adj.*
1 indefinite; **~ная фо́рма глаго́ла** (*gram.*) infinitive.
2 indeterminate; vague, uncertain.

неопровержи́м|ый (~, ~а) *adj.* irrefutable.

неопря́т|ный (~ен, ~на) *adj.* slovenly; untidy, sloppy.

нео́пыт|ный (~ен, ~на) *adj.* inexperienced.

неосмотри́тел|ьный (~ен, ~ьна) *adj.* imprudent, incautious.

неоспори́м|ый (~, ~а) *adj.* unquestionable, incontestable, indisputable.

неосторо́жност|ь, и *f.* carelessness; imprudence.

неосторо́ж|ный (~ен, ~на) *adj.* careless; imprudent, incautious.

неотврати́м|ый (~, ~а) *adj.* inevitable.

не́откуда *adv.* there is nowhere; **мне н. э́то получи́ть** there is nowhere I can get it from.

неотло́ж|ный (~ен, ~на) *adj.* urgent, pressing; **~ная медици́нская по́мощь** emergency medical service.

неотрази́м|ый (~, ~а) *adj.* irresistible (*also fig.*).

неотъе́млем|ый (~, ~а) *adj.* inalienable; **~ое пра́во** inalienable right; **~ая часть** integral part.

неофаши́зм, а *m.* neo-fascism.

неофаши́ст, а *m.* neo-fascist.

неофаши́стский *adj.* neo-fascist.

неофициа́л|ьный (~ен, ~ьна) *adj.* unofficial.

неохо́т|а, ы *f.*
1 reluctance.
2 (+ *d.*, *as pred.*; *coll.*): **мне,** *etc.* **н. идти́** I, *etc.* have no wish to go, don't feel like going.

неохо́тно *adv.* reluctantly; unwillingly.

неоцени́м|ый (~, ~а) *adj.* inestimable, priceless, invaluable.

Непа́л, а *m.* Nepal.

непа́л|ец, ьца *m.* Nepalese.

непа́л|ка, ки *fem. of* ▸ **~ец**

непа́льский *adj.* Nepalese.

непереводи́м|ый (~, ~а) *adj.* untranslatable.

непередава́ем|ый (~, ~а) *adj.* inexpressible, indescribable.

непереxо́дный *adj.* (*gram.*) intransitive.

неплатёжеспосо́б|ный (~ен, ~на) *adj.* (*fin.*) insolvent.

неплате́льщик, а *m.* defaulter; person in arrears with payment (*of taxes, etc.*).

непло́хо *adv.* not badly, quite well.

неплох|о́й (~́, ~а́, ~́о) *adj.* not bad, quite good.

непобеди́м|ый (~, ~а) *adj.* invincible.

неповоро́тлив|ый (~, ~а) *adj.* (*неуклюжий*) clumsy, awkward; (*медлительный*) sluggish, slow.

неповтори́м|ый (~, ~а) *adj.* unique.

непого́д|а, ы *f.* bad weather.

неподалёку *adv.* not far off.

неподви́жност|ь, и *f.* immobility.

неподви́ж|ный (~ен, ~на) *adj.* motionless, immobile, immovable (*also fig.*); fixed, stationary.

неподде́л|ьный (~ен, ~ьна) *adj.* genuine; unfeigned, sincere.

неподку́п|ный (~ен, ~на) *adj.* incorruptible.

неподража́ем|ый (~, ~а) *adj.* inimitable.

непозволи́тел|ьный (~ен, ~ьна) *adj.* inadmissible, impermissible.

непоколеби́м|ый (~, ~а) *adj.* steadfast, unshakeable.

непоко́р|ный (~ен, ~на) *adj.* recalcitrant; unruly.

непола́дк|а, и *f.* defect, fault.

неполноце́нност|ь, и *f.* inferiority; **ко́мплекс ~и** inferiority complex.

неполноце́н|ный (~ен, ~на) *adj.* inferior; substandard; **у́мственно н.** mentally deficient; **физи́чески н.** physically handicapped.

непо́л|ный (~он, ~на́, ~но, ~́ны) *adj.* (*ведро, корзина*) not full; (*знания, перечень*) incomplete; **~ная семья́** single-parent family; **рабо́тать ~ную неде́лю** to work part-time.

непонима́ни|е, я *nt.* incomprehension.

непоня́тлив|ый (~, ~а) *adj.* slow (to grasp things), dim.

непоня́т|ный (~ен, ~на) *adj.* unintelligible, incomprehensible; (*impers., as pred.*): **~но** it is incomprehensible; **мне ~но, как он мог э́то сде́лать** I cannot understand how he could do it.

непоправи́м|ый (~, ~а) *adj.* irreparable, irremediable; irretrievable.

непоря́доч|ный (~ен, ~на) *adj.* dishonourable (*Br.*), dishonorable (*US*).

непосе́длив|ый (~, ~а) *adj.* fidgety,

restless.

непосле́довательност|ь, и *f.* inconsistency; inconsequence.

непосле́довател|ьный (~ен, ~ьна) *adj.* inconsistent; inconsequent.

непослу́ш|ный (~ен, ~на) *adj.* disobedient, naughty.

непосре́дственност|ь, и *f.* spontaneity, ingenuousness.

непосре́дствен|ный (~, ~на) *adj.* 1 (*результат*) immediate, direct; **в ~ной бли́зости** (**от** + *g.*) in the immediate vicinity (of). 2 (*fig.*) (*натура*) direct; spontaneous, ingenuous.

непостижи́м|ый (~, ~а) *adj.* incomprehensible, inscrutable; **уму́ ~о** it passes understanding.

непостоя́н|ный (~ен, ~на) *adj.* inconstant, changeable.

непостоя́нств|о, а *nt.* inconstancy.

непра́вд|а, ы *f.* untruth, lie.

неправдоподо́б|ный (~ен, ~на) *adj.* improbable, unlikely; implausible.

непра́вильно *adv.* incorrectly, erroneously; *in conjunction with vv. frequently* = mis-, *e.g.* **н. истолкова́ть** to misinterpret.

непра́вил|ьный (~ен, ~ьна) *adj.* 1 (*развитие, черты, форма*) irregular; **н. глаго́л** irregular verb. 2 (*расчёт, суждение*) incorrect, erroneous, wrong, mistaken.

неправоме́р|ный (~ен, ~на) *adj.* illegal.

непра́в|ый (~, ~á, ~о) *adj.* 1 (*заблуждающийся*) wrong, mistaken. 2 (*несправедливый*) unjust.

непредвзя́т|ый (~, ~а) *adj.* unbiased.

непредви́денный *adj.* unforeseen.

непреднаме́рен|ный (~, ~на) *adj.* unpremeditated.

непредсказу́ем|ый (~, ~а) *adj.* unpredictable.

непредумы́шленн|ый *adj.* unpremeditated; **~ое уби́йство** manslaughter.

непрекло́н|ный (~ен, ~на) *adj.* inflexible, unbending; inexorable, adamant.

непреме́нно *adv.* 1 (*обязательно*) without fail; certainly; **они́ н. приду́т за́втра** they are sure to come tomorrow. 2 (*очень*) absolutely; **мне н. ну́жно поговори́ть с ним** it is absolutely essential that I speak to him.

непреме́н|ный (~ен, ~на) *adj.* (*условие*) necessary; (*следствие*) unavoidable; (*черта*) indispensable.

непреодоли́м|ый (~, ~а) *adj.* insuperable, insurmountable; (*желание*) irresistible; **~ая си́ла** (*leg.*) force majeure.

непреры́вно *adv.* uninterruptedly, continuously.

непреры́вност|ь, и *f.* continuity.

непреры́в|ный (~ен, ~на) *adj.* uninterrupted, unbroken; continuous.

непреста́нно *adv.* incessantly, continually.

неприве́тлив|ый (~, ~а) *adj.* (*человек, взгляд*) unfriendly, ungracious; (*местность*) bleak, forbidding.

непривлека́тел|ьный (~ен, ~ьна) *adj.* unattractive.

непривы́ч|ный (~ен, ~на) *adj.* unaccustomed, unwonted; unusual.

непригля́д|ный (~ен, ~на) *adj.* unattractive, unsightly.

пригó

неприго́д|ный (~ен, ~на) *adj.* unfit, useless; unserviceable; (*для военной службы*) ineligible.

неприе́млем|ый (~, ~а) *adj.* unacceptable.

непри́знан|ный (~, ~а) *adj.* unrecognized, unacknowledged.

неприкоснове́нност|ь, и *f.* inviolability; **дипломати́ческая н.** diplomatic immunity.

неприкоснове́н|ный (~ен, ~на) *adj.* inviolable; **н. запа́с** (*mil.*) emergency ration, iron ration.

неприли́ч|ный (~ен, ~на) *adj.* indecent, improper; unseemly, unbecoming.

неприме́т|ный (~ен, ~на) *adj.* 1 (*разница*) imperceptible. 2 (*fig.*) (*человек*) unremarkable, undistinguished.

непримири́м|ый (~, ~а) *adj.* (*противоречия*) irreconcilable; (*характер*) intransigent, uncompromising.

непринуждён|ный (~, ~на) *adj.* natural, relaxed; laid-back.

непристо́йност|ь, и *f.* obscenity; indecency.

непристо́|йный (~ен, ~йна) *adj.* obscene; indecent.

непристу́п|ный (~ен, ~на) *adj.* 1 (*скала*) inaccessible; (*крепость*) unassailable, impregnable. 2 (*fig.*) (*начальник*) inaccessible, unapproachable.

неприхотли́в|ый (~, ~а) *adj.* 1 (*человек*) unpretentious; modest; (*растение, животное*) undemanding. 2 (*рисунок*) simple, plain; **~ая пи́ща** frugal meal.

непричá́ст|ный (~ен, ~на) *adj.* (**к** + *d.*) not implicated (in), not involved (in).

неприя́тел|ь, я *m.* enemy; (*mil.*) the enemy.

неприя́тност|ь, и *f.* unpleasantness; trouble.

неприя́т|ный (~ен, ~на) *adj.* unpleasant, disagreeable.

непродолжи́тел|ьный (~ен, ~ьна) *adj.* of short duration, short-lived.

непроду́ман|ный (~, ~на) *adj.* ill-considered.

непрозра́ч|ный (~ен, ~на) *adj.* opaque.

непроизво́л|ьный (~ен, ~ьна) *adj.* involuntary.

непромока́ем|ый (~, ~а) *adj.* waterproof; **н. плащ** waterproof (coat), raincoat.

непроница́ем|ый (~, ~а) *adj.* (*мрак, ночь; тайна*) impenetrable; (*для жидкостей, газов*) impermeable; **н. для зву́ка** soundproof.

непрости́тел|ьный (~ен, ~ьна) *adj.* unforgivable, unpardonable, inexcusable.
непроходи́м|ый (~, ~а) *adj.* impassable.
непро́ч|ный (~ен, ~на́, ~но) *adj.* fragile, flimsy; (*fig.*) precarious, unstable.
неработоспосо́б|ный (~ен, ~на) *adj.* unable to work, disabled.
нерабо́ч|ий *adj.* non-working; **~ее вре́мя** time off, free time.
нера́венств|о, а *nt.* inequality, disparity.
неравноду́ш|ный (~ен, ~на) *adj.* (**к** + *d.*) not indifferent (to).
неравноме́р|ный (~ен, ~на) *adj.* uneven, irregular.
нера́в|ный (~ен, ~на́) *adj.* unequal.
неради́в|ый (~, ~а) *adj.* negligent, careless.
неразбо́рчив|ый (~, ~а) *adj.*
1 (*почерк*) illegible, indecipherable.
2 (*fig.*) (*читатель, вкус*) undiscriminating; not fastidious; **н. в сре́дствах** unscrupulous; **сексуа́льно н.** promiscuous.
неразгово́рчив|ый (~, ~а) *adj.* taciturn, not talkative.
неразличи́м|ый (~, ~а) *adj.* indistinguishable; indiscernible.
неразлу́ч|ный (~ен, ~на) *adj.* inseparable.
неразреши́м|ый (~, ~а) *adj.* insoluble.
неразу́м|ный (~ен, ~на) *adj.* unreasonable; unwise; foolish.
нерасторо́п|ный (~ен, ~на) *adj.* sluggish, slow.
нерв, а *m.* (*anat. and fig.*) nerve; **де́йствовать кому́-н. на ~́ы** to get on s.o.'s nerves.
не́рвнича|ть, ю *impf.* to be *or* become fidgety; fret; be *or* become irritable.
не́рв|ный (~ен, ~́на́, ~но) *adj.*
1 (*болезнь, тик, походка, жест, состояние*) nervous; **~ная систе́ма** the nervous system; **н. центр** (*fig.*) nerve centre (*Br.*), -center (*US*).
2 (*человек*) nervous, highly strung.
3 (*работа*) nerve-racking.
нерво́з|ный (~ен, ~на) *adj.* nervy, irritable.
нереа́л|ьный (~ен, ~ьна) *adj.*
1 (*местность*) unreal.
2 (*предложение*) impracticable.
нере́дко *adv.* not infrequently, quite often.
нерезиде́нт, а *m.* non-resident.
нерента́бел|ьный (~ен, ~ьна) *adj.* unprofitable.
не́рест, а *m.* (*zool.*) spawning.
нереши́тельност|ь, и *f.* indecision; indecisiveness; **быть в ~и** to be undecided.
нереши́тел|ьный (~ен, ~ьна) *adj.* indecisive, irresolute.
нержаве́ющ|ий *adj.* non-rusting; **~ая сталь** stainless steel.
неро́в|ный (~ен, ~на́, ~но) *adj.*
1 (*поверхность*) uneven, rough.
2 (*пульс, дыхание*) irregular.
3 (*линия*) crooked.
не́рп|а, ы *f.* (*zool.*) ringed seal.
несве́дущ|ий (~, ~а) *adj.* (**в** + *p.*) ignorant (about), not well-informed (about).
несве́ж|ий (~, ~а́, ~е) *adj.*
1 (*еда*) not fresh, stale.
2 (*бельё; воздух*) dirty.
несвоевре́мен|ный (~, ~на) *adj.* inopportune, untimely, unseasonable.
несгиба́ем|ый (~, ~а) *adj.* unbending, inflexible.
несгово́рчив|ый (~, ~а) *adj.* intractable.
несде́ржан|ный (~, ~на) *adj.* unrestrained.
несерьёз|ный (~ен, ~на, ~но) *adj.*
1 (*человек*) frivolous.
2 (*замечание*) flippant.
3 (*дело, рана*) trivial.
нескла́д|ный (~ен, ~на) *adj.* ungainly, awkward; absurd.
несклоня́ем|ый (~, ~а) *adj.* (*gram.*) indeclinable.
не́скольк|о[1], их *num.* some, several; a few; **в ~их слова́х** in a few words; **н. челове́к** several people.
не́сколько[2] *adv.* somewhat, rather, slightly; **они́ н. разочаро́ваны** they are rather disillusioned.
нескро́м|ный (~ен, ~на́, ~но) *adj.*
1 (*человек*) immodest; vain.
2 (*вопрос*) indiscreet.
3 (*жест*) indecent.
нескрыва́ем|ый (~, ~а) *adj.* undisguised.
несло́ж|ный (~ен, ~на́, ~но) *adj.* simple, uncomplicated.
несы́хан|ный (~, ~на) *adj.* unheard-of, unprecedented.
неслы́ш|ный (~ен, ~на) *adj.* inaudible.
несмолка́ем|ый (~, ~а) *adj.* ceaseless, unremitting.
несмотря́ *prep.* (**на** + *a.*) in spite of, despite; notwithstanding; **н. ни на что** in spite of everything.
несовершеннолéтн|ий *adj.* under-age; *as n.* **н., ~его** *m.*, **~яя, ~ей** *f.* minor.
несоверше́н|ный (~ен, ~на) *adj.* imperfect, incomplete.
несовмести́м|ый (~, ~а) *adj.* incompatible.
несогла́си|е, я *nt.*
1 disagreement.
2 (*разлад*) discord.
3 (*sg. only*) (*отказ*) refusal.
несоизмери́м|ый (~, ~а) *adj.* incommensurable, incommensurate.
несокруши́м|ый (~, ~а) *adj.* unshakeable.
несомне́нно *adv.* undoubtedly, doubtless.
несомне́н|ный (~ен, ~на) *adj.* undoubted, indubitable, unquestionable.
несостоя́тел|ьный (~ен, ~ьна) *adj.*
1 (*обанкротившийся*) insolvent, bankrupt; (*бедный*) poor.
2 (*необоснованный*) groundless, unsupported.
неспе́л|ый (~, ~а́, ~о) *adj.* unripe.
неспе́ш|ный (~ен, ~на) *adj.* unhurried.
неспоко́|йный (~ен, ~йна) *adj.* (*сон,*

характер) restless; (*жизнь*) troubled; (*море, погода*) rough.

неспосóбност|ь, и *f.* incapacity, inability.

неспосóб|ный (~ен, ~на) *adj.* dull, not able; (**к** + *d.*, **на** + *a.*) incapable (of); **онá ~на к языкáм** she has no aptitude for languages; **н. на ложь** incapable of a lie.

несправедлúвост|ь, и *f.* injustice, unfairness.

несправедлúв|ый (~, ~а) *adj.*
1 (*человек, суд*) unjust, unfair.
2 (*мнение*) incorrect, unfounded.

неспростá *adv.* (*coll.*) not without purpose; with an ulterior motive.

несравнéнно *adv.*
1 incomparably.
2 (+ *comp.*) far, by far; **н. лýчше** far better.

несравнéн|ный (~ен, ~на) *adj.* incomparable.

нестабúльност|ь, и *f.* instability.

нестабúл|ьный (~ен, ~ьна) *adj.* unstable.

нестерпúм|ый (~, ~а) *adj.* unbearable, intolerable.

нес|тú[1], ý, ёшь, *past* **~̈, ~лá** *impf.* (*of* ▶**по~ 1**), *det.*
1 (*перемещать на себе*) to carry.
2 (*поддерживать*) to bear; to support.
3 (*fig.*) (*терпеть*) to bear; to suffer; to incur; **н. убы́тки** (*fin.*) to incur losses.
4 (*выполнять*) to perform; **н. дежýрство** to be on duty.
5 (*fig.*) (*причинять*) to bear, bring; **н. гúбель** to bring destruction.
6 (*coll.*) (**вздор, чепухý,** *etc.*) to talk (nonsense).

нес|тú[2], ёт, *past* **~̈, ~лá** *impf.* (*of* ▶**с~[2]**) (*яйцо*) to lay.

нес|тúсь, ýсь, ёшься, *past* **~̈ся, ~лáсь** *impf.* (*of* ▶**по~ 1**), *det.*
1 (*о человеке, машине*) to rush, tear, fly; (*по воздуху, воде*) to float, drift; (**по** + *d.*, **вдоль** + *g.*, **над** + *i.*) to skim (along; over).
2 (*о звуке, запахе*) to spread, be diffused.

несурáз|ный (~ен, ~на) *adj.*
1 (*глупый*) absurd, senseless.
2 (*неуклюжий*) awkward.

несущéствен|ный (~, ~на) *adj.* inessential, immaterial.

несчáст|ный (~ен, ~на) *adj.*
1 unhappy; unfortunate, unlucky; **н. слýчай** accident.
2 *as n.* **н., ~ного** *m.* wretch; an unfortunate.

несчáсть|е, я *nt.*
1 (*беда*) misfortune; **к ~ю** unfortunately.
2 (*несчастный случай*) accident.

несъедóб|ный (~ен, ~на) *adj.* inedible.

нет[1]
1 (*при отрицании*) no; not; **вы егó вúдели? н.** you saw him? No; **вы не вúдели егó? н., вúдел** you didn't see him? Yes, I did.
2 nothing, naught; **свестú на н.** to bring to naught; **свестúсь (сойтú) на н.** to come to naught.

нет[2] (+ *g.*) (*не имеется*) (there) is no, (there) are no; **у меня́ н. врéмени** I have no time.

нетактúч|ный (~ен, ~на) *adj.* tactless.

нетвёрдо *adv.*
1 (*ходить*) unsteadily, not firmly.
2 (*fig.*) not definitely; **знать н.** to have a shaky knowledge of.

нетерпелúв|ый (~, ~а) *adj.* impatient.

нетерпéни|е, я *nt.* impatience.

нетерпúмост|ь, и *f.* intolerance.

нетерпúм|ый (~, ~а) *adj.*
1 (*поступок*) intolerable.
2 (*человек*) intolerant.

нетороплúв|ый (~, ~а) *adj.* leisurely, unhurried.

нетóчност|ь, и *f.*
1 (*свойство*) inaccuracy, inexactitude.
2 (*ошибка*) error, slip.

нетóч|ный (~ен, ~нá, ~но, ~́ны́) *adj.* inaccurate, inexact.

нетрадициóн|ный (~ен, ~на) *adj.* unconventional.

нетрéзв|ый (~, ~á, ~о) *adj.* not sober, drunk; **в ~ом вúде** in a state of intoxication.

нетривиáл|ьный (~ен, ~ьна) *adj.* not trivial; outstanding, exceptional.

нетрóнут|ый (~, ~а) *adj.* (*почва, снег*) virgin; (*обед*) untouched; (*fig.*) (*целомудренный*) unsullied, virginal.

нетрудоспосóб|ный (~ен, ~на) *adj.* disabled; invalid.

неубедúтел|ьный (~ен, ~ьна) *adj.* unconvincing.

неуважéни|е, я *nt.* disrespect, lack of respect; (*leg.*): **н. к судý** contempt of court.

неуважúтел|ьный (~ен, ~ьна) *adj.*
1 (*причина*) inadequate; not acceptable.
2 (*coll.*) (*непочтительный*) disrespectful.

неувéренност|ь, и *f.* uncertainty; **н. в себé** lack of self-confidence.

неувéрен|ный (~, ~на *and* (*with syntactically related word(s)*) **~а)** *adj.*
1 (*человек*) lacking confidence, unsure; **н. в себé** lacking self-confidence, unsure of o.s.
2 (*походка, движение*) uncertain.

неувя́зк|а, и *f.* (*coll.*) (*в расчётах*) discrepancy; (*недоразумение*) misunderstanding.

неудáч|а, и *f.* failure.

неудáчник, а *m.* unlucky person, failure, loser.

неудáчни|ца, цы *f. of* ▶**~к**

неудáч|ный (~ен, ~на) *adj.* unsuccessful; (*несчастливый*) unfortunate; (*плохой*) bad; **~ное начáло** bad start.

неудержúм|ый (~, ~а) *adj.* irrepressible.

неудóб|ный (~ен, ~на) *adj.*
1 (*одежда, постель*) uncomfortable.
2 (*fig.*) (*время*) inconvenient; (*положение*) awkward; embarrassing.

неудóбств|о, а *nt.*
1 (*постели*) discomfort.
2 (*положения*) awkwardness; embarrassment.

неудовлетворúтел|ьный (~ен, ~ьна) *adj.* unsatisfactory.

неудовóльстви|е, я *nt.* dissatisfaction, displeasure.

неужéли *interrog. particle* really? is it

possible?; **н. он так ду́мает?** does he really think that?; **н. ты не знал, что мы здесь?** did you really not know that we were here?; surely you knew that we were here?

неузнава́ем|ый (~, ~а) *adj.* unrecognizable.

неуклю́ж|ий (~, ~а, ~е) *adj.* clumsy, awkward.

неулови́м|ый (~, ~а) *adj.*
[1] (*человек*) elusive, difficult to catch.
[2] (*fig.*) (*звук*) imperceptible.

неуме́л|ый (~, ~а) *adj.* clumsy; unskilful (*Br.*), unskillful (*US*).

неуме́рен|ный (~, ~на) *adj.* (*аппетит, восторг*) immoderate; excessive.

неуме́ст|ный (~ен, ~на) *adj.*
[1] (*шутка*) inappropriate.
[2] (*факт, информация*) irrelevant.

неу́м|ный (~ён, ~на́) *adj.* foolish; (*решение*) unwise.

неумоли́м|ый (~, ~а) *adj.* implacable; inexorable.

неуравнове́шен|ный (~, ~на) *adj.* (*psych.*) unbalanced.

неурожа́|й, я *m.* bad harvest, crop failure.

неусто́йчив|ый (~, ~а) *adj.* unstable, unsteady.

неустраши́м|ый (~, ~а) *adj.* fearless, intrepid.

неутеши́тел|ьный (~ен, ~ьна) *adj.* not comforting, depressing; **~ьные ве́сти** distressing news.

Н

неутоми́м|ый (~, ~а) *adj.* tireless, indefatigable.

неучти́в|ый (~, ~а) *adj.* discourteous, impolite, uncivil.

неую́т|ный (~ен, ~на) *adj.* bleak, comfortless.

неуязви́м|ый (~, ~а) *adj.*
[1] (*позиция, человек, подводная лодка*) invulnerable.
[2] (*доказательство*) unassailable.

неформа́л, а *m.* (*coll.*) member of an unofficial organization.

неформа́л|ьный (~ен, ~ьна) *adj.* unofficial; informal.

нефтедо́ллар, а *m.* petrodollar.

нефтеперераба́тывающий *adj.* oil-refining; **н. заво́д** oil refinery.

нефтепрово́д, а *m.* oil pipeline.

нефт|ь, и *f.* oil, petroleum; **сыра́я н.** crude oil.

нефтя́ник, а *m.* oil (industry) worker.

нефтян|о́й *adj.* oil; **~а́я вы́шка** derrick.

нехва́тк|а, и *f.* (*coll.*) shortage.

нехоро́ш|ий (~, ~а́) *adj.* bad.

не́хотя *adv.* reluctantly, unwillingly.

нецелесообра́з|ный (~ен, ~на) *adj.* inexpedient; pointless.

нецензу́р|ный (~ен, ~на) *adj.* unprintable; **~ные слова́** swear words, obscenities.

нечая́нный *adj.* accidental; unintentional.

не́чего, не́чему, не́чем, не́ о чем
[1] *pron.* (+ *inf.*) there is nothing (to); **мне н. чита́ть** I have nothing to read; **не́ о чем бы́ло говори́ть** there was nothing to talk about; **от н. де́лать** for want of sth. better to do, to while away the time.
[2] *as pred.* (*impers.*; + *inf.*) (*незачем*) it's no good, it's no use; there is no need; **н. жа́ловаться** it's no use complaining.

нечелове́ческий *adj.*
[1] (*усилия*) superhuman.
[2] (*отношения*) inhuman.

нече́стност|ь, и *f.* dishonesty.

нече́ст|ный (~ен, ~на́, ~но, ~ны́) *adj.*
[1] (*человек*) dishonest.
[2] (*поступок*) dishonourable (*Br.*), dishonorable (*US*); **~ная игра́** (*sport*) foul play.

нечёт|кий (~ок, ~ка) *adj.* (*почерк*) illegible; (*рисунок*) indistinct; (*изложение*) unclear.

нечётный *adj.* odd.

нечистопло́т|ный (~ен, ~на) *adj.*
[1] (*грязный*) dirty; (*неопрятный*) untidy, slovenly.
[2] (*fig.*) (*нечестный*) unscrupulous.

нечистот|а́, ы́, *pl.* **~ы, ~** *f.*
[1] *sg. only* dirtiness.
[2] *pl. only* (*отбросы*) sewage, garbage.

нечи́ст|ый (~, ~а́, ~о, ~ы́) *adj.*
[1] (*грязный*) unclean, dirty (*also fig.*); **~ое де́ло** suspicious affair.
[2] (*с примесью чего-л.*) impure, adulterated.
[3] (*неаккуратный*) careless, inaccurate.
[4] (*нечестный*) dishonourable (*Br.*), dishonorable (*US*); dishonest; **быть ~ым на́ руку** to be light-fingered.
[5]: **~ая си́ла** evil spirits.

не́что *pron.* (*nom. and a. cases only*) something.

нечувстви́тел|ьный (~ен, ~ьна) *adj.* (**к** + *d.*) insensitive (to).

нешу́точ|ный (~ен, ~на) *adj.* grave, serious; **де́ло ~ное** it is no joke; it is no laughing matter.

неэффекти́в|ный (~ен, ~на) *adj.* ineffective; inefficient.

нея́с|ный (~ен, ~на́, ~но) *adj.* vague, obscure.

ни
[1] *correlative conj.* **ни... ни** neither ... nor; **ни тот ни друго́й** neither (the one nor the other).
[2] *particle* not a; **ни оди́н, ни одна́, ни одно́** not a, not one, not a single; **на у́лице не́ было ни души́** there was not a soul about.
[3] *separable component of prons.* **никако́й, никто́, ничто́** *following preps.*; **ни в како́м (ни в ко́ем) слу́чае** on no account; **ни за что (на све́те!)** in no circumstances; not for the world!
[4] (*particle, in comb. with* **как, кто, куда́** *etc.*) = -ever; **как бы мы ни стара́лись** however hard we tried; **что бы он ни говори́л** whatever he might say.

нигде́ *adv.* nowhere.

Ни́гер, а *m.*
[1] (*страна*) Niger.
[2] (*река*) the Niger.

нигери́|ец, йца *m.* Nigerian.

нигери́|йка, йки *f. of* ▸ **~ец**
нигери́йский *adj.* Nigerian.
Нигéри|я, и *f.* Nigeria.
нидерлáндский *adj.* Dutch, Netherlands; (*язык*) Dutch.
Нидерлáнд|ы, ов *no sg.* the Netherlands.
ни́же
1 *comp. of* ▸ **ни́зкий, ни́зко.**
2 *prep.* (+ *g.*) *and adv.* below, beneath.
ни́жн|ий *adj.* lower; **~ее бельё** underclothes, underwear; **~яя палáта** Lower Chamber, Lower House; **~яя ю́бка** slip.
низ, а, *pl.* **~ы́** *m.*
1 bottom.
2 (*pl.*) (*общества*) lower classes.
низи́н|а, ы *f.* low-lying area.
ни́з|кий (~ок, ~кá, ~ко) *adj.*
1 low; **~кого происхождéния** of humble origin; **быть ~кого мнéния о** + *p.* to have a low opinion of.
2 (*подлый*) base, mean; **н. посту́пок** shabby act.
низкокáчествен|ный (~, ~на) *adj.* low-quality.
низкооплáчиваем|ый (~, ~а) *adj.* poorly-paid.
низкоро́сл|ый (~, ~а) *adj.* (*человек*) short; (*дерево*) undersized, stunted.
ни́зменност|ь, и *f.* (*geog.*) lowland (*not exceeding 200 m above sea level*).
ни́змен|ный (~, ~на) *adj.*
1 low-lying.
2 (*подлый*) low; base, vile; **~ные инсти́нкты** basic instincts.
низо́в|ье, ья, *g. pl.* **~ьев** *nt.* the lower reaches (*of a river*).
ни́зост|ь, и *f.* lowness; (*подлость*) baseness, meanness.
ни́зший *superl. of* ▸ **ни́зкий;** lowest.
НИИ *m. indecl.* (*abbr. of* **нау́чно-исслéдовательский институ́т**) research institute.
никáк *adv.* (*никаким образом*) by no means, in no way; **он н. не мог узнáть её áдрес** in no way could he discover her address.
никак|о́й *pron.* no; **не... ~о́го, ~о́й, ~и́х** no ... whatever; **я не имéю ~о́го представлéния (поня́тия)** I have no idea, no conception; **~и́х возражéний!** no objections!
Никарáгуа *nt. & f. indecl.* Nicaragua.
никарагуáн|ец, ца *m.* Nicaraguan.
никарагуáн|ка, ки *f. of* ▸ **~ец**
никарагуáнский *adj.* Nicaraguan.
ни́кел|ь, я *m.* nickel.
никогдá *adv.* never; **как н.** as never before.
нико́|й *pron.*: **~им о́бразом** by no means, in no way; **ни в ко́ем слу́чае** on no account, in no circumstances.
никоти́н, а *m.* nicotine.
никоти́н|овый *adj. of* ▸ **~**
никто́, никого́, никому́, нике́м, ни о ком *pron.* nobody, no one; **ни у кого́ нет э́того** no one has it.
никудá *adv.* nowhere; **э́то н. не годи́тся** (*fig.*) this won't do; it is no good at all.
никчёмн|ый (~ен, ~на) *adj.* (*coll.*) useless, good-for-nothing.
Нил, а *m.* the Nile (*river*).
ним *i. of* ▸ **он, оно́;** *d. of* ▸ **они́** *after preps.*
нимáло *adv.* not in the least, not at all.
ни́ми *i. of* ▸ **они́** *after preps.*
ни́мф|а, ы *f.* nymph.
ниоткýда *adv.* from nowhere; **н. не слéдует, что...** it in no way follows that ... .
нирвáн|а, ы *f.* nirvana.
ниско́лько *adv.* not at all, not in the least; **ей от э́того бы́ло н. не лу́чше** she was none the better for it.
ни́тк|а, и *f.* thread; **н. жéмчуга** string of pearls; **промо́кнуть до ~и** (*fig.*) to get soaked to the skin.
нитрáт, а *m.* (*chem.*) nitrate.
нитроглицери́н, а *m.* (*chem.*) nitroglycerine.
нит|ь, и *f.*
1 thread.
2 (*bot., elec.*) filament.
3 (*med.*) suture.
них *a. and g. of* ▸ **они́** *when governed by preps.*
ничего́[1] *g. of* ▸ **ничто́**
ничего́[2] *adv.* (*coll.*)
1 (*also* **н. себé**) so-so; passably, not (too) badly; all right; **как вы чу́вствуете себя́? н.** how do you feel? all right.
2 *as indecl. adj.* not (too) bad, passable, tolerable; **пáрень он н.** he is not a bad chap.
нич|е́й (~ья́, ~ьё) *pron.* nobody's, no one's; **~ья́ земля́** no man's land; *as n.* **~ья́,** *g., d., i., p.* **~ье́й** *f.* (*sport*) draw, drawn game.
ничко́м *adv.* prone, face downwards.
ничто́, ничего́, ничему́, ниче́м, ни о чём *pron.* nothing; **э́то ничего́ не знáчит** it means nothing; **ничего́ подо́бного!** nothing of the kind!; **ничего́!** (*coll.*) that's all right!; never mind!
ничто́жеств|о, а *nt.*
1 (*убожество*) poverty.
2 (*человек*) a nonentity, a nobody.
ничто́ж|ный (~ен, ~на) *adj.* (*незначительный*) insignificant; (*человек*) paltry, worthless.
ничу́ть *adv.* (*coll.*) not at all, not in the least, not a bit; **н. не бывáло** not at all.
ничь|я́, е́й *f. see* ▸ **ниче́й**
ни́ш|а, и *f.* niche, recess; (*archit.*) alcove, bay.
ни́щенский *adj.* beggarly.
ни́щенств|овать, ую *impf.*
1 (*заниматься нищенством*) to beg, go begging.
2 (*жить в нищете*) to be destitute.
нищет|á, ы́ *f.* poverty (*also fig.*).
ни́щ|ий *adj.*
1 destitute; poverty-stricken.
2 *as n.* **н., ~его** *m.* beggar; pauper.
НЛО *m. indecl.* (*abbr. of* **неопо́знанный летáющий объе́кт**) UFO (*unidentified flying object*).
но *conj.* but; *after concessive clause not translated or* still, nevertheless; **хотя́ он и бо́лен, но намéрен прийти́** although he is ill, he (still) intends to come.
Но́в|ая Зелáнди|я, ~ой ~и *f.* New Zealand.
нове́йший *superl. of* ▸ **но́вый;** newest;

(*последний*) latest.
новéлл|а, ы *f.* novella.
новизн|á, ы́ *f.* novelty; newness.
нови́нк|а, и *f.* new thing, novelty; **кни́жные ~и** new books.
новичіо́к, кá *m.*
1 (**в** + *p.*) novice (at), beginner (at).
2 (*в школе*) new boy; new girl.
новобрáн|ец, ца *m.* recruit.
новобрáчн|ые, ых *pl.* newly-weds.
нововведéни|е, я *nt.* innovation.
новогóдн|ий *adj.* New Year's; **~яя ночь** New Year's Eve.
новозелáнд|ец, ца *m.* New Zealander.
новозелáнд|ка, ки *f. of* ▸ **~ец**
новозелáндский *adj.* New Zealand.
новолýни|е, я *nt.* new moon.
новорождённ|ый *adj.* newborn; *as n.* **н., ~ого** *m.*, **~ая, ~ой** *f* .the baby; (*med.*) neonate.
новосéль|е, я *nt.* house-warming; **справля́ть н.** to give a house-warming party.
новостнóй *adj.* news (*attr.*).
новострóйк|а, и *f.* (*здание*) newly erected building.
нóвост|ь, и, *g. pl.* **~éй** *f.* news.
нóвшеств|о, а *nt.* innovation, novelty.
нóв|ый (~, ~á, ~о, ~ы́) *adj.*
1 new; **совершéнно н.** brand new; **Н. год** New Year's Day; **Н. Завéт** the New Testament; **что ~ого?** what's the news?; what's new?
2 (*современный*) modern; recent; **~ая истóрия** modern history.
ног|á, и́, *a.* **~у,** *pl.* **~и, ~, ~áм** *f.* (*ступня*) foot; (*до ступни*) leg; **вверх ~áми** head over heels; **положи́ть ~у на́ ~у** to cross one's legs.
ноготк|и́, óв *m. pl.* (common *or* pot) marigold (*genus Calendula*).
нóг|оть, тя, *pl.* **~ти, ~тéй** *m.* (finger-, toe-) nail.
нож, á *m.* knife; **перочи́нный н.** penknife; **садóвый н.** pruning knife; **н. в спи́ну** (*fig.*) stab in the back.
нóжик, а *m.* (small) knife.
нóжк|а, и *f.*
1 *dim. of* ▸ **ногá; подстáвить ~у** (+ *d.*) to trip up.
2 (*мебели, утвари*) leg; (*рюмки*) stem.
3 (*bot.*) stalk; (*гриба*) stem.
нóжниц|ы, ~ *pl.*
1 scissors, pair of scissors; (*большие*) shears.
2 (*econ.*) (*расхождение*) discrepancy.
ножнóй *adj. of* ▸ **ногá; н. тóрмоз** foot brake.
нóж|ны, ~ен, ~нам *pl.* sheath; scabbard.
ножóвк|а, и *f.* hacksaw.
ноздр|я́, и́, *pl.* **~и, ~éй** *f.* nostril.
нол|ь, я́ *m.* = **нуль**
нóмер, а, *pl.* **~á** *m.*
1 (*телефона, машины, дома*) number; (*газеты, журнала*) number, issue.
2 (*размер*) size.
3 (*в гостинице*) room.
4 (*концерта*) item on the programme (*Br.*), program (*US*); number, turn; **сóльный н.** solo (number).
номер|óк, кá *m.* (*в гардеробе*) ticket.
номинáльн|ый *adj.* nominal; **~ая ценá** face value.
номинáнт, а *m.* nominee.
номинáнт|ка, ки *f. of* ▸ **~**
номинáци|я, и *f.* nomination.
номини́р|овать, ую *impf. and pf.* nominate.
нор|á, ы́, *pl.* **~ы, ~, ~ам** *f.* (*зайца*) burrow, hole; (*лисы*) lair.
Норвéги|я, и *f.* Norway.
норвéж|ец, ца *m.* Norwegian.
норвéж|ка, ки *f. of* ▸ **~ец**
норвéжский *adj.* Norwegian.
нóрк|а, и *f.* mink.
нóрм|а, ы *f.*
1 (*поведения*) standard, norm.
2 (*величина*) rate; **н. вы́работки** rate of output.
нормáльно *as pred.* (*coll.*) it is all right, fine, OK.
нормáл|ьный (~ен, ~ьна) *adj.* normal.
нос, а, о ~е, в/на ~ý, *pl.* **~ы́** *m.*
1 nose; **остáться с ~ом** (*coll.*) to be duped, be left looking a fool; **совáть н. не в своё дéло** (*coll.*) to poke one's nose into other people's affairs.
2 (*птицы*) beak.
3 (*naut.*) bow, head; prow.
носáт|ый (~, ~а) *adj.* big-nosed.
нóсик, а *m.* (*чайника*) spout.
носи́л|ки, ок *no sg.* stretcher.
носи́льщик, а *m.* porter.
носи́тел|ь, я *m.*
1 (*fig.*) (*идей*) bearer; repository.
2 (*инфекции, гриппа*) carrier.
но|си́ть, шý, ~сишь *impf.*
1 *indet. of* ▸ **нести́**[1].
2 (*indet. only*) (*вещи; ребёнка*) to carry; (*большую тяжесть*) to bear (*also fig.*); **н. свою́ дéвичью фами́лию** to use one's maiden name.
3 (*indet. only*) (*одежду, украшения*) to wear.
4 (*indet. only*) (*характер*) to have (*a certain character*), to be of (*a certain nature*).
но|си́ться, шýсь, ~сишься *impf.*
1 *indet. of* ▸ **нести́сь; э́то ~сится в вóздухе** (*fig.*) it is in the air, it is rumoured (*Br.*), rumored (*US*).
2 (**с** + *i.*) (*с человеком*) to make a fuss (of); **н. с мы́слью** to be obsessed with an idea.
3 (*intr.*) (*одежда*) to wear; **э́та матéрия хорошó ~сится** this material wears well.
нос|овóй *adj. of* ▸ **~; н. платóк** (pocket) handkerchief.
носоглóтк|а, и *f.* (*anat.*) nasopharynx.
нос|óк[1]**, кá** *m.* (*ботинка, чулка*) toe.
нос|óк[2]**, кá,** *pl.* **~ки́, ~кóв** *or* **~óк** *m.* (*чулок*) sock.
носорóг, а *m.* rhinoceros.
ностальги́|я, и *f.* homesickness; (*о прошлом*) nostalgia.
нóт|а[1]**, ы** *f.* (*mus.*)
1 note.
2 (*pl.*) (*текст*) (sheet) music; **игрáть по**

~ам (без нот) to play from music (without music).
нóт|а², ы *f.* (*dipl.*) (diplomatic) note.
нотáриус, а *m.* notary.
ноутбýк, а *m.* notebook (computer).
нóу-xáу *nt. indecl.* know-how.
ноч|евáть, ýю *impf.* (*of* ▸**пере~**) to spend, pass the night.
ночни́к, á *m.* night light.
ночн|óй *adj.* night; **н. пóезд** overnight train; **~áя рубáшка** (*мужская*) nightshirt; (*женская*) nightdress.
ноч|ь, и, о ~и, в ~и́, pl. ~и, ~éй *f.* night; **спокóйной ~и!** goodnight!; **по ~áм** by night, at night.
нóчью *adv.* by night.
нóш|а, и, *f.* burden.
нóшеный *adj.* second-hand.
нó|ю, ешь *see* ▸**ныть**
нoя́бр|ь, я́ *m.* November.
нoя́бр|ьский *adj. of* ▸**~**
нрав, а *m.*
1 (*характер*) disposition, temper; **быть** (+ *d.*) **по ~у** to please.
2 (*pl.*) (*обычаи*) customs, ways.
нрáв|иться, люсь, ишься *impf.* (*of* ▸**по~**) (+ *d.*) to please; **мне, емý,** *etc.*, **~ится** I like, he likes, *etc.*; **мне óчень ~ится э́та пьéса** I like this play very much; (*impers.*): **ей не ~ится катáться на лóдке** she does not like going in boats.
нрáвственност|ь, и *f.* morality; morals.
нрáвствен|ный (~, ~на) *adj.* moral.
ну *int. and particle* (*coll.*)
1 well!; well ... then!; come on!; **ну, ну!** come, come!; come now!
2 : **(да) ну!** not really?; you don't mean to say so!
3 *выражает удивление, восхищение, негодование, иронию* well; what; why; **ну и...** what (a) ...!; here's ... (for you)!; there's ... (for you)!; **ну вот и..!** there you are, you see ...!
4 *выражает согласие, уступку, примирение, облегчение* well; **ну вот** (*в повествовании*) well, well then; **ну что ж, нý так** well then; **ну хорошó** all right then.
нуди́ст, а *m.* nudist, naturist.
нуди́ст|ка, ки *f. of* ▸**~**
нýд|ный (~ен, ~нá, ~но, ~ны́) *adj.* (*coll.*) tedious.
нужд|á, ы́, *pl.* **~ы** *f.*
1 *sg. only* (*бедность*) want, poverty.
2 (*необходимость*) need; necessity.
нуждá|ться, юсь *impf.*
1 (*жить в бедности*) to be in want; to be needy, hard up.
2 (**в** + *p.*) to need, require; to be in need (of).
нýжно (+ *d.*)
1 (*impers.*; + *inf.* *or* + **чтóбы**) it is necessary; (one) ought, (one) should, (one) must, (one) need(s); **н. бы́ло (бы) взять такси́** you should have taken a taxi; **н., чтóбы онá реши́лась** she ought to make up her mind.
2 (*impers.*, + *a.* *or* *g.*; *coll.*) I, *etc.*, need; **мне н. пять рублéй** I need five roubles.
3 *see* ▸**нýжный**
нýж|ный (~ен, ~нá, ~но, ~ны́) *adj.* necessary; requisite; (*pred. forms* + *d.*) I, *etc.*, need; **что вам ~но?** what do you need?, what do you want?
нý-ка *int.* (*coll.*) now then!; come on!
нул|евóй *adj. of* ▸**~ь;** (*math.*) zero; **н. вариáнт** (*pol.*) zero option.
нул|ь, я́ *m.* nought; (*о температуре*) zero; (*в играх*) nil.
нумизмáтик|а, и *f.* numismatics.
нýтри|я, и *f.* (*zool.*) coypu; (*мех*) nutria.
ны́нешний *adj.* (*coll.*) present; present-day; **н. президéнт** the incumbent president.
нырн|ýть, нý, нёшь *pf. of* ▸**~я́ть**
ныря́льщик, а *m.* diver.
ныря́льщи|ца, цы *f. of* ▸**~к**
ныр|я́ть, я́ю *impf.* (*of* ▸**~нýть**) to dive.
ныть, нóю, нóешь *impf.*
1 (*болеть*) to ache.
2 (*coll.*) (*жаловаться*) to moan.
Нью-Йóрк, а *m.* New York.
н. э. (*abbr. of* **нáшей э́ры**) AD; **до н. э.** (*abbr. of* **до нáшей э́ры**) BC.
нюáнс, а *m.* nuance.
нюх, а *m.* scent; (*fig.*) (**на** + *a.*) a nose (for).
ню́ха|ть, ю *impf.* (*of* ▸**по~**) (*цветок*) to smell; (*воздух; наркотик*) to sniff.
ня́нч|ить, у, ишь *impf.* to look after, mind.
ня́н|я, и *f.*
1 nanny; childminder; **приходя́щая н.** babysitter.
2 (*coll.*) (*в больнице*) auxiliary nurse.

Оо

о (об, обо) *prep.*
1 (+ *p.*) (*указывает на предмет речи, мысли*) of, about, concerning; on; **о чём вы дýмаете?** what are you thinking about?
2 (+ *a.*) (*указывает на соприкосновение, столкновение*) against; on, upon; over; **оперéться о стéну** to lean against the wall; **споткнýться о кáмень** to stumble on, over a stone; **бок ó бок** side by side; **рукá óб руку** hand in hand.
оáзис, а *m.* oasis (*also fig.*).
об *prep. see* ▸**о**
óба, обóих *m. and nt.*; **óбе, обéих** *f. num.* both; **обéими рукáми** with both hands (*fig.*,

coll.); very willingly, readily.

обанкро́|титься, чусь, тишься *pf.* go bankrupt.

обая́ни|е, я *nt.* fascination, charm.

обая́тел|ьный (~ен, ~ьна) *adj.* fascinating, charming.

обва́л, а *m.* (*стены*) collapse; caving-in; (*камней*) rockfall; (*снежный*) avalanche; (*econ.*) collapse, dive.

обва́лива|ться, ется *impf. of* ▶ **обвали́ться**

обвал|и́ться, ~́ится *pf.* (*of* ▶ **~́иваться**) to fall, collapse, cave in.

обве|ду́, дёшь *see* ▶ **~сти́**

обвенча́|ть(ся), ю(сь) *pf. of* ▶ **венча́ть(ся)**

обве|сти́, ду́, дёшь, *past* **~̈л, ~ла́** *pf.* (*of* ▶ **обводи́ть**)
1 (*провести вокруг*) to lead round, take round; **о. вокру́г па́льца** (*fig., coll.*) to twist round one's little finger.
2 (*очертить*) to outline; **о. чертёж ту́шью** to outline a sketch in ink.

обве́тренный *adj.* (*скалы, лицо*) weather-beaten; (*губы*) chapped.

обветша́|ть, ю *pf. of* ▶ **ветша́ть**

обвива́|ть(ся), ю(сь) *impf. of* ▶ **обви́ть(ся)**

обвине́ни|е, я *nt.*
1 charge, accusation; **по ~ю (в** + *p.*) on a charge (of).
2 (*leg.*) (*collect.*) the prosecution.

обвини́тел|ь, я *m.* accuser; (*leg.*) prosecutor.

обвини́тельный *adj.*: **о. пригово́р** verdict of 'guilty'.

обвин|и́ть, ю́, и́шь *pf.* (*of* ▶ **~я́ть**)
1 (**в** + *p.*) to accuse (of), charge (with).
2 (*leg.*) to prosecute, indict.

обвиня́ем|ый, ого *m.* (*leg.*) the accused; defendant.

обвин|я́ть, я́ю *impf. of* ▶ **~и́ть**

обви́|ть, обовью́, обовьёшь, *past* **~л, ~ла́, ~ло** *pf.* (*of* ▶ **~ва́ть**) to wind (round), entwine; **о. ше́ю рука́ми** to throw one's arms round s.o.'s neck.

обви́|ться, обовью́сь, обовьёшься, *past* **~лся, ~ла́сь** *pf.* (*of* ▶ **~ва́ться**) to wind round, twine round.

обво|ди́ть, жу́, ~́дишь *impf. of* ▶ **обвести́**

обвола́кива|ть, ю *impf. of* ▶ **обволо́чь**

обволо́|чь, ку́, чёшь, ку́т, *past* **~к, ~кла́** *pf.* (*of* ▶ **обвола́кивать**) to cover; to envelop (*also fig.*).

обвор|ова́ть, у́ю *pf.* (*of* ▶ **~о́вывать**) (*coll.*) to rob.

обворо́выва|ть, ю *impf. of* ▶ **обворова́ть**

обворожи́тел|ьный (~ен, ~ьна) *adj.* fascinating, charming, enchanting.

обвя|за́ться, жу́сь, ~́жешься *pf.* (*of* ▶ **~́зываться**) (+ *i.*) to tie round o.s.; **о. верёвкой** to tie a rope round o.s.

обвя́зыва|ться, юсь *impf. of* ▶ **обвяза́ться**

огла́дыва|ть, ю *impf. of* ▶ **обглода́ть**

обгло|да́ть, жу́, ~́жешь *pf.* (*of* ▶ **огла́дывать**) to pick, gnaw round.

обгова́рива|ть, ю *impf. of* ▶ **обговори́ть**

обговор|и́ть, ю́, и́шь *pf.* (*of* ▶ **обгова́ривать**) (*coll.*) to discuss.

обго́н, а *m.* passing, overtaking.

обгон|ю́, ~́ишь *see* ▶ **обогна́ть**

обгоня́|ть, ю *impf. of* ▶ **обогна́ть**

обгор|а́ть, а́ю *impf. of* ▶ **~е́ть**

обгор|е́ть, ю́, и́шь *pf.* (*of* ▶ **~а́ть**) to be burnt; (*на солнце*) to get burnt.

обда|ва́ть, ю́, ёшь *impf. of* ▶ **обда́ть**

обд|а́ть, а́м, а́шь, а́ст, ади́м, ади́те, аду́т, *past* **~́ал, ~ала́, ~́ало** *pf.* (*of* ▶ **~ава́ть**) (+ *i.*)
1 to pour over; **о. кого́-н. кипятко́м** to pour boiling water over s.o.
2 (*fig.*) to seize, cover; **меня́ ~́ало хо́лодом** (*impers.*) I came over cold.

обде́л|ать, аю *pf.* (*of* ▶ **~ывать**) (*coll.*)
1 to finish; to dress (*leather, stone, etc.*); **о. драгоце́нные ка́мни** to set precious stones.
2 (*fig.*) to manage, arrange; **о. свои́ дели́шки** to manage one's affairs with profit.

обдел|и́ть, ю́, ~́ишь *pf.* (*of* ▶ **~я́ть**) (+ *a. and i.*) to do out of one's (fair) share (of); **он ~и́л сестёр насле́дством** he did his sisters out of their share of the legacy.

обде́лыва|ть, ю *impf. of* ▶ **обде́лать**

обдел|я́ть, я́ю *impf. of* ▶ **~и́ть**

обдер|у́, ёшь *see* ▶ **ободра́ть**

обдира́|ть, ю *impf. of* ▶ **ободра́ть**

обду́ман|ный
1 **(~, ~а)** *p.p.p. of* ▶ **обду́мать.**
2 **(~, ~на)** *adj.* well-considered, carefully thought out.

обду́м|ать, аю *pf.* (*of* ▶ **~ывать**) to consider, think over.

обду́мыва|ть, ю *impf. of* ▶ **обду́мать**

о́бе *see* ▶ **о́ба**

обега́|ть, ю *impf. of* ▶ **обежа́ть**

обе́д, а *m.*
1 lunch, dinner.
2 (*время*) lunchtime, dinner time (= *midday*); **пе́ред ~ом** before lunch, dinner; in the morning; **по́сле ~а** after lunch, dinner; in the afternoon.

обе́да|ть, ю *impf.* (*of* ▶ **по~**) to have lunch, dinner.

обе́д|енный *adj. of* ▶ **~; ~енное вре́мя** lunch, dinner time; **о. переры́в** lunch hour, lunch break; **о. стол** dinner table.

обе|жа́ть, гу́, жи́шь, гу́т *pf.* (*of* ▶ **~га́ть**) to run round.

обезбо́ливани|е, я *nt.* anaesthetization (*Br.*), anesthetization (*US*).

обезбо́лива|ть, ю *impf. of* ▶ **обезбо́лить**

обезбо́лива|ющий *pres. part. act. of* ▶ **~ть; ~ющее сре́дство** anaesthetic (*Br.*), anesthetic (*US*).

обезбо́л|ить, ю, ишь *pf.* (*of* ▶ **~ивать**) to anaesthetize (*Br.*), anesthetize (*US*).

обезво́жен|ный (~, ~а) *adj.* dehydrated.

обезвре́|дить, жу, дишь *pf.* (*of*

▸ ~живать) (*человека*) to render harmless; (*бомбу*) to defuse; (*мину*) to deactivate.

обезврéжива|ть, ю *impf. of* ▸ **обезврéдить**

обезглáв|ить, лю, ишь *pf.* (*of* ▸ **~ливать**)
1 to behead, decapitate.
2 (*fig.*) (*лишить главы*) to deprive of a head, of a leader.

обезглáвлива|ть, ю *impf. of* ▸ **обезглáвить**

обездóлен|ный (~, ~а) *adj.* unfortunate, hapless.

обезжúренный *adj.* fat-free; skimmed.

обезопá|сить, шу, сишь *pf.* (**от** + *g.*) to protect (against).

обезопá|ситься, шусь, сишься *pf.* (**от** + *g.*) to secure o.s., protect o.s. (against).

обезорýжива|ть, ю *impf. of* ▸ **обезорýжить**

обезорýж|ить, у, ишь *pf.* (*of* ▸ **~ивать**) to disarm (*also fig.*).

обезýме|ть, ю *pf.* to lose one's senses, lose one's head; **о. от испýга** to become panic-stricken.

обезья́н|а, ы *f.* monkey; (*бесхвостая*) ape.

обелúск, а *m.* obelisk.

оберегá|ться, юсь *impf. of* ▸ **оберéчься**

оберé|чься, гýсь, жёшься, гýтся, *past* **~гся, ~глáсь** *pf.* (*of* ▸ **~гáться**) (**от** + *g.*) to guard o.s. (from, against), protect o.s. (from).

обернý|ть, ý, ёшь *pf.* (*of* ▸ **оборáчивать**)
1 (*шарф вокруг шеи*) to wind (round), twist (round).
2 (*посылку*) to wrap up.

обернý|ться, ýсь, ёшься *pf.* (*of* ▸ **оборáчиваться**)
1 (*повернуться*) to turn; **о. лицóм** to turn one's head.
2 (*о делах*) to turn out; **собы́тия ~ýлись инáче, чем мы ожидáли** events turned out otherwise than we expected.
3 (*coll.*) (*сходить, съездить туда и обратно*) to (go and) come back; **я ~ýсь за два часá** I shall be back in two hours.

обёртк|а, и *f.* wrapper; (*книги*) dust jacket, dust cover.

обеспéчени|е, я *nt.*
1 (*мира, успеха*) securing, guaranteeing; ensuring.
2 (+ *i.*) (*углём*) providing (with), provision (of, with), supplying (of, with).
3 (*гарантия*) guarantee; security (= *pledge*).
4 (*материальные средства к жизни*) security; safeguard(s); **социáльное о.** social security.
5 : (*comput.*) **аппарáтное о.** hardware; **прогрáммное о.** software.

обеспéч|енный *p.p.p. of* ▸ **~ить (~ен, ~ена)** *and adj.* **(~ен, ~енна)** well-to-do; well provided for.

обеспéчива|ть, ю *impf. of* ▸ **обеспéчить**

обеспéч|ить, у, ишь *pf.* (*of* ▸ **~ивать**)
1 (*семью; старость*) to provide for.
2 (+ *i.*) (*снабдить чем-н.*) to provide (with), guarantee supply (of).
3 (*успех*) to secure, guarantee; to ensure.

обеспокóенный *adj.* worried, concerned.

обессúле|ть, ю *pf.* to grow weak, lose one's strength.

обессúлива|ть, ю *impf. of* ▸ **обессúлить**

обессúл|ить, ю, ишь *pf.* (*of* ▸ **~ивать**) to weaken.

обесцéн|енный *p.p.p. of* ▸ **~ить** *and adj.* depreciated.

обесцéнива|ть(ся), ю, ет(ся) *impf. of* ▸ **обесцéнить(ся)**

обесцéн|ить, ю, ишь *pf.* (*of* ▸ **~ивать**) to depreciate, cheapen.

обесцéн|иться, ится *pf.* (*of* ▸ **~иваться**) (*intrans.*) to depreciate.

обещáни|е, я *nt.* promise; **дать, сдержáть, нарушúть о.** to give, keep, break a promise (*or* one's word).

обещá|ть, ю *impf. and pf.* (*pf. also* ▸ **по~**) to promise.

обжáл|овать, ую *pf.* (*leg.*) to appeal (against).

обжáрива|ть, ю *impf. of* ▸ **обжáрить**

обжáр|ить, ю, ишь *pf.* (*of* ▸ **~ивать**) (*cul.*) to fry on both sides, to brown all over.

обжéчь, обожгý, обожжёшь, обожгýт, *past* **обжёг, обожглá** *pf.* (*of* ▸ **обжигáть**)
1 to burn, scorch; **о. себé пáльцы** to burn one's fingers (*also fig.*).
2 (*кирпич*) to fire, bake.
3 (*о крапиве*) to sting.

обжéчься, обожгýсь, обожжёшься, обожгýтся, *past* **обжёгся, обожглáсь** *pf.* (*of* ▸ **обжигáться**) (+ *i. or* **на** + *p.*) to burn o.s. (on, with); **о. горя́чим чáем** to scald o.s. with hot tea.

обжигá|ть(ся), ю(сь) *impf. of* ▸ **обжéчь(ся)**

обжóр|а, ы *c.g.* (*coll.*) glutton.

обжóрств|о, а *nt.* gluttony.

обзаве|стúсь, дýсь, дёшься, *past* **~лся, ~лáсь** *pf.* (*of* ▸ **обзаводúться**) (+ *i.*; *coll.*) to get o.s.; to set up; **о. семьёй** to start a family; **о. хозя́йством** to set up home.

обзаво|дúться, жýсь, ~дишься *impf. of* ▸ **обзавестúсь**

обзóр, а *m.*
1 (*сжатое сообщение*) survey, review, overview.
2 (*mil.*) field of view.

обзóр|ный *adj.* giving an overall view; **~ная лéкция, ~ная статья́** survey.

обзывá|ть, ю *impf. of* ▸ **обозвáть**

обивá|ть, ю *impf. of* ▸ **обúть**

обúвк|а, и *f.* upholstery.

обúд|а, ы *f.* insult; (*чувство*) offence, (sense of) grievance, resentment; **затаúть ~у** to nurse a grievance; **не давáть себя́ в ~у** to (be able to) stick up for o.s.

обú|деть, жу, дишь *pf.* (*of* ▸ **~жáть**)
1 to offend; to hurt (the feelings of), wound.
2 (*причинить ущерб*) to hurt; to do damage

(to); **мухи не ~дит** (*fig.*) he would not harm a fly.
3 (+ *i.*; *following* **Бог, природа,** *etc.*) to stint, begrudge; **природа не ~дела его талантом** he has plenty of natural ability.

оби|деться, жусь, дишься *pf.* (*of* ▸ **~жаться**) (**на** + *a.*) to take offence (at); to feel hurt (by), resent.

обид|ный (~ен, ~на) *adj.*
1 offensive; **мне ~но** I feel hurt, it pains me.
2 (*досадный*) annoying; **~но** (*impers.*) it is a pity, it is a nuisance; **~но, что мы опоздали** it is a pity that we are late.

обидчив|ый (~, ~а) *adj.* touchy, sensitive.

обидчик, а *m.* offender.

обижа|ть, ю *impf. of* ▸ **обидеть**

обижа|ться, юсь *impf. of* ▸ **обидеться; не ~йтесь** don't be offended.

оби|женный *p.p.p of* ▸ **~деть** *and adj.* offended, aggrieved; **быть ~женным (на** + *a.*) to have a grudge (against); **о. Богом, о. природой** (*joc.*) not over-blessed (with talents); ill-starred.

обили|е, я *nt.* abundance, plenty.

обиль|ный (~ен, ~ьна) *adj.* abundant, plentiful; (+ *i.*) rich (in); **~ьное угощение** lavish entertainment.

обира|ть, ю *impf. of* ▸ **обобрать**

обитаем|ый (~, ~а) *adj.* inhabited.

обитател|ь, я *m.* inhabitant.

обита|ть, ю *impf.* (**в** + *p.*) to live (in).

оби|ть, обобью, обобьёшь *pf.* (*of* ▸ **~вать**) (+ *i.*) to cover (with); **о. гвоздями** to stud; **о. железом** to bind with iron.

обиход, а *m.* (*употребление*) use; **войти в о.** to come into (general) use; **выйти из ~а** to go out of use, fall into disuse.

обиход|ный (~ен, ~на) *adj.* everyday; **~ное выражение** colloquial expression.

обкладыва|ть, ю *impf. of* ▸ **обложить 1, 2, 3**

обкрадыва|ть, ю *impf. of* ▸ **обокрасть**

обкурен|ный (~, ~а) *adj.* (*sl.*) stoned (*from smoking marijuana etc.*).

облав|а, ы *f.* (*на преступников*) raid; round-up.

облага|ть, ю *impf. of* ▸ **обложить 4**

обладател|ь, я *m.* possessor.

облада|ть, ю *impf.* (+ *i.*) to possess, have; **о. правом** to have the right.

облак|о, а, *pl.* **~а, ~ов** *nt.* cloud; **витать в ~ах** (*fig.*) to live in the clouds.

обламыва|ть(ся), ю(сь) *impf. of* ▸ **обломать(ся)**

област|ь, и, *g. pl.* **~ей** *f.*
1 (*административная единица*) oblast; province.
2 (*часть страны*) region, district; belt.
3 (*fig.*) (*отрасль*) field, sphere, realm, domain.

облачност|ь, и *f.* cloudiness; **переменная о.** overcast with sunny periods.

облач|ный (~ен, ~на) *adj.* cloudy.

облега|ть, ю *impf.* (*об одежде*) to fit tightly; to cling to.

облегающий *adj.* tight-fitting.

облегч|ать(ся), аю(сь) *impf. of* ▸ **~ить(ся)**

облегчени|е, я *nt.*
1 (*действие*) facilitation, lightening, easing.
2 (*чувство успокоения*) relief; **вздохнуть с ~ем** to heave a sigh of relief.

облегч|ить, у, ишь *pf.* (*of* ▸ **~ать**)
1 (*груз, вес*) to lighten.
2 (*сделать менее трудным*) to make easier.
3 (*упростить*) to simplify.

облегч|иться, усь, ишься *pf.* (*of* ▸ **~аться**) (*стать более лёгким*) to become easier; to become lighter.

обледене|ть, ю *pf.* to ice over, become covered with ice.

облезл|ый (~, ~а) *adj.* (*coll.*) shabby, bare; **~ая кошка** mangy cat.

обленива|ться, юсь *impf. of* ▸ **облениться**

облен|иться, юсь, ~ишься *pf.* (*of* ▸ **~иваться**) to grow lazy.

облеп|ить, лю, ~ишь *pf.* (*of* ▸ **~лять**)
1 (*прилипнуть*) to stick (to); (*fig.*) to cling (to); (*окружить*) to surround, throng; **нас ~ила куча мальчишек** we were surrounded by a swarm of small boys.
2 (+ *a. and i.*) (*заклеить*) to paste all over (with), plaster (with).

облепля|ть, ю *impf. of* ▸ **облепить**

облет|ать, аю *impf. of* ▸ **~еть**

обле|теть, чу, тишь *pf.* (*of* ▸ **~тать**)
1 (+ *a. or* **вокруг** + *g.*) to fly (round).
2 (*о новостях*) to spread (round, all over); **за полчаса весть о победе ~тела весь город** in half an hour the news of the victory had spread round the town.
3 (*о листьях*) to fall.

облива|ть, ю *impf. of* ▸ **облить**

облива|ться, юсь *impf. of* ▸ **облиться; сердце у меня кровью ~ется** my heart bleeds.

облигаци|я, и *f.* (*fin.*) bond, debenture.

обли|зать, жу, ~жешь *pf.* (*of* ▸ **~зывать**) to lick (all over); to lick clean.

обли|заться, жусь, ~жешься *pf.* (*of* ▸ **~зываться**)
1 (*о человеке*) to smack one's lips (*also fig.*).
2 (*о животном*) to lick itself.

облизыва|ть, ю *impf. of* ▸ **облизать; о. губы** (*fig., coll.*) to smack one's lips.

облизыва|ться, юсь *impf. of* ▸ **облизаться**

облик, а *m.* look, appearance.

обл|ить, оболью, обольёшь, *past* **~ил, ~ила, ~ило** *and* **~ил, ~ила, ~ило** *pf.* (*of* ▸ **~ивать**) (*намеренно*) to pour (over); (*случайно*) to spill (over); **о. грязью** (*fig., coll.*) to vilify.

обли|ться, оболью́сь, обольёшься, *past* **~лся, ~лась, ~лось** *pf.* (*of* ▸ **~ваться**) (+ *i.*)
1 to have a shower; to sponge down; **о. холодной водой** to have a cold shower.
2 (*случайно*) to spill over o.s.

облицовк|а, и *f.* facing, cladding.

облич|ать, аю *impf.* (*of* ▸ **~ить**)
1 (*разоблачать*) to expose, unmask, denounce.
2 (*impf. only*) (*показывать*) to reveal, display, manifest; to point (to).

облич|и́ть, у́, и́шь *pf. of* ▸ **~а́ть**

облож|и́ть, у́, ~ишь *pf.*
1 (*impf.* **обкла́дывать**) (*положить вокруг*) to put (round); to edge; **о. больно́го поду́шками** to surround a patient with pillows.
2 (*impf.* **обкла́дывать**) (*покрыть*) to cover.
3 (*impf.* **обкла́дывать**) (*окружить*) to surround.
4 (*impf.* **облага́ть**) to assess; **о. нало́гом** to tax.

обло́жк|а, и *f.* (dust) cover; (*для бумаг*) folder.

облока́чива|ться, юсь *impf. of* ▸ **облокоти́ться**

облоко|ти́ться, чу́сь, ти́шься *pf.* (*of* ▸ **облока́чиваться**) (**на** + *a.*) to lean one's elbow(s) (on, against).

обло́м, а *m.*
1 (*действие*) breaking off.
2 (*место*) break.
3 (*sl.*) (*неудача*) failure, misfortune.

облома́|ть, ю *pf.* (*of* ▸ **обла́мывать**) to break off, snap.

облома́|ться, юсь *pf.* (*of* ▸ **обла́мываться**)
1 (*ветка*) to break off, snap.
2 (*sl.*) to fail.

облом|и́ть, лю́, ~ишь *pf.* to break off.

облом|и́ться, лю́сь, ~ишься *pf.* = **~а́ться**

обло́м|ок, ка *m.*
1 fragment.
2 (*pl.*) debris, wreckage.

облуче́ни|е, я *nt.* (*med.*) irradiation.

облысе́|ть, ю, ешь *pf. of* ▸ **лысе́ть**

облюб|ова́ть, у́ю *pf.* (*of* ▸ **~о́вывать**) to pick, choose.

облюбо́выва|ть, ю *impf. of* ▸ **облюбова́ть**

обма́|зать, жу, жешь *pf.* (*of* ▸ **~зывать**) to coat (with).

обма́зыва|ть, ю *impf. of* ▸ **обма́зать**

обма́кива|ть, ю *impf. of* ▸ **обмакну́ть**

обмак|ну́ть, ну́, нёшь, *past* **~ну́л** *pf.* (*of* ▸ **~ивать**) to dip.

обма́н, а *m.* fraud, deception; **о. зре́ния** optical illusion.

обман|у́ть, у́, ~ешь *pf.* (*of* ▸ **~ывать**) to deceive; (*мошеннически*) to cheat, swindle; (*нарушить обещание*) to fail; to let s.o. down; **о. чьи-н. наде́жды** to disappoint s.o.'s hopes.

обман|у́ться, у́сь, ~ешься *pf.* (*of* ▸ **~ываться**) to be deceived; **о. в свои́х ожида́ниях** to be disappointed in one's expectations.

обма́нчив|ый (~, ~а) *adj.* deceptive, delusive; **вне́шность ~а** appearances are deceptive.

обма́нщик, а *m.* deceiver; cheat, fraud.

обма́нщи|ца, цы *f. of* ▸ **~к**

обма́ныва|ть(ся), ю(сь) *impf. of* ▸ **обману́ть(ся)**

обма́тыва|ть(ся), ю(сь) *impf. of* ▸ **обмота́ть(ся)**

обме́н, а *m.* (+ *i.*) exchange (of); **о. мне́ниями** exchange of opinions; **о. веще́ств** (*biol.*) metabolism; **в о.** (**на** + *a.*) in exchange (for).

обме́нива|ть(ся), ю(сь) *impf. of* ▸ **обменя́ть(ся)**

обме́н|ный *adj. of* ▸ **~**

обмен|я́ть, я́ю *pf.* (*of* ▸ **меня́ть 2** *and* ▸ **~ивать**) (+ *a.* **на** + *a.*) to exchange (sth. for sth.).

обмен|я́ться, я́юсь *pf.* (*of* ▸ **меня́ться 2** *and* ▸ **~иваться**) (+ *i.*) to exchange; to swap; **о. впечатле́ниями** to compare notes.

обме́рива|ть, ю *impf. of* ▸ **обме́рить**

обме́р|ить, ю, ишь *pf.* (*of* ▸ **~ивать**) (*измерить*) to measure.

обмо́лв|иться, люсь, ишься *pf.* (*coll.*)
1 (*оговориться*) to make a slip in speaking.
2 (+ *i.*) (*сказать*) to say; to utter; **не о. ни сло́вом** (**о** + *p.*) to say not a word (about).

обмороже́ни|е, я *nt.* frostbite.

обморо́|зить, жу, зишь *pf.*: **я ~зил себе́ нос, ру́ки** my nose is, hands are, frost-bitten.

о́бморок, а *m.* fainting fit; **упа́сть в о.** to faint.

обмота́|ть, ю *pf.* (*of* ▸ **обма́тывать**) (+ *a. and i. or a.* **вокру́г** + *g.*) to wind (round); **о. ше́ю ша́рфом** to wind a scarf round one's neck.

обмота́|ться, юсь *pf.* (*of* ▸ **обма́тываться**)
1 (+ *i.*) to wrap o.s. (in).
2 *pass. of* ▸ **~ть**

обмундирова́ни|е, я *nt.* uniform.

обнадёжива|ть, ю *impf. of* ▸ **обнадёжить**

обнадёж|ить, у, ишь *pf.* (*of* ▸ **~ивать**) to reassure.

обнаж|а́ть(ся), а́ю(сь) *impf. of* ▸ **~и́ть(ся)**

обнаж|ённый *p.p.p. of* ▸ **~и́ть** *and adj.* naked, bare; nude.

обнаж|и́ть, у́, и́шь *pf.* (*of* ▸ **~а́ть**)
1 to bare, uncover; **о. го́лову** to bare one's head; **о. шпа́гу** to draw the sword.
2 (*fig.*) (*раскрыть*) to lay bare, reveal.

обнаж|и́ться, у́сь, и́шься *pf.* (*of* ▸ **~а́ться**)
1 to bare o.s., uncover o.s.
2 (*fig.*) (*стать явным*) to be revealed.

обнаро́д|овать, ую *impf. and pf.* (*liter.*) to publish, promulgate (*esp. official documents*).

обнаруже́ни|е, я *nt.*
1 displaying, revealing.
2 discovery; detection.

обнару́жива|ть(ся), ю(сь) *impf. of* ▸ **обнару́жить(ся)**

обнару́ж|ить, у, ишь *pf.* (*of* ▸ **~ивать**)
1 (*показать*) to display, reveal; **о. свою́ ра́дость** to betray one's joy.
2 (*найти*) to discover; to detect.

обнару́ж|иться, усь, ишься *pf.* (*of* ▸ **~иваться**)
1 (*оказаться*) to be revealed; to come to light.
2 (*найтись*) to turn up, be found.

обнес|ти́, у́, ёшь, *past* **~̈, ~ла́** *pf.* (*of* ▸ **обноси́ть**) (+ *i.*) to enclose (with); **о. и́згородью** to fence (in).

обнима́|ть(ся), ю(сь) *impf. of*

▶ **обнять(ся)**

обнов|ить, лю, ишь *pf.* (*of* ▶ **~лять**) 1 (*памятник*) to renovate; (*жизнь, душу*) to revitalize; (*горечь*) to renew; (*гардероб, репертуар*) (*also comput.*) to update; to replenish.
2: **о. свой знания** (*fig.*) to refresh one's knowledge.

обнов|иться, люсь, ишься *pf.* (*of* ▶ **~ляться**) to revive, be restored.

обновлени|е, я *nt.* renovation; revitalization; renewal; replenishment; (*comput.*) update; **внешнее о.** facelift.

обновля|ть(ся), ю(сь) *impf. of* ▶ **обновить(ся)**

обно|сить, шу, ~сишь *impf. of* ▶ **обнести**

обнюх|ать, аю *pf.* (*of* ▶ **~ивать**) to sniff (around).

обнюхива|ть, ю *impf. of* ▶ **обнюхать**

обн|ять, иму, имешь, *past* **~ял, ~яла, ~яло** *pf.* (*of* ▶ **~имать**) to embrace; to clasp in one's arms; (*fig.*) to envelop; **он шёл, ~яв её за талию** he was walking with his arm round her waist.

обн|яться, имусь, имешься, *past* **~ялся, ~ялась, ~ялось** *pf.* (*of* ▶ **~иматься**) to embrace; to hug (one another).

обо *prep.* = **о**

обобра|ть, оберу, оберёшь, *past* **~л, ~ла, ~ло** *pf.* (*of* ▶ **обирать**) (*coll.*) to rob, to clean out (*coll.*).

обобщ|ать, аю *impf. of* ▶ **~ить**

обобщени|е, я *nt.* generalization.

обобщ|ить, у, ишь *pf.* (*of* ▶ **~ать**) to generalize (from).

обога|тить, щу, тишь *pf.* (*of* ▶ **~щать**) to enrich.

обога|титься, щусь, тишься *pf.* (*of* ▶ **~щаться**) to become rich; (+ *i.*) to enrich o.s. (with).

обогаща|ть(ся), ю(сь) *impf. of* ▶ **обогатить(ся)**

обогащени|е, я *nt.* enrichment.

обогна|ть, обгоню, обгонишь, *past* **~л, ~ла, ~ло** *pf.* (*of* ▶ **обгонять**) to pass, overtake; (*fig.*) to outstrip, outdistance.

обогн|уть, у, ёшь *pf.* (*of* ▶ **огибать**) to round; to skirt.

обогревател|ь, я *m.* (*tech.*) heater.

обогрева|ть(ся), ю(сь) *impf. of* ▶ **обогреть(ся)**

обогре|ть, ю, ешь *pf.* (*of* ▶ **~вать**) (*помещение*) to heat; (*человека*) to warm.

обогре|ться, юсь, ешься *pf.* (*of* ▶ **~ваться**) to warm o.s.; (*о помещении*) to warm up.

обод, а, *pl.* **~ья, ~ьев** *m.* (*колеса*) rim; (*бочки*) hoop.

ободрать, обдеру, обдерёшь, *past* **ободрал, ободрала, ободрало** *pf.* (*of* ▶ **обдирать**)
1 (*стену, прутик*) to strip; (*убитого зверя*) to skin; (*coll.*) (*лицо, руку*) to scratch; **о. кору с дерева** to bark a tree.
2 (*fig., coll.*) to fleece.

ободр|ить, ю, ишь *pf.* (*of* ▶ **~ять**) to cheer up; to encourage, reassure.

ободр|ять, яю *impf. of* ▶ **~ить**

обожа|ть, ю *impf.* to adore, worship.

обож|гу, жёшь, гут *see* ▶ **обжечь**

обожжённый *p.p.p. of* ▶ **обжечь**

обоз, а *m.* convoy.

обозва|ть, обзову, обзовёшь, *past* **~л, ~ла, ~ло** *pf.* (*of* ▶ **обзывать**) (+ *a. and i.*) to call; **о. кого-н. дураком** to call s.o. a fool.

обозна|ваться, юсь, ёшься *impf. of* ▶ **~ться**

обозна|ться, юсь, ешься *pf.* (*of* ▶ **~ваться**) (*coll.*) to take s.o. for s.o. else; to be mistaken.

обознач|ать, аю *impf.*
1 (*no pf.*) (*значить*) to mean.
2 (*pf.* **~ить**) (*отмечать*) to mark.
3 (*pf.* **~ить**) (*делать заметным*) to reveal; to emphasize.

обозначени|е, я *nt.*
1 (*действие*) marking.
2 (*знак*) sign, symbol; **условные ~я** conventional signs, legend (*on maps, etc.*).

обознач|ить, у, ишь *pf. of* ▶ **~ать 2, 3**

обозревател|ь, я *m.* commentator; columnist.

обозрени|е, я *nt.*
1 (*действие*) surveying, viewing; looking round.
2 (*обзор*) survey; overview.

обо|и, ев *no sg.* (*also comput.*) wallpaper; **оклеить ~ями** to paper.

обойм|а, ы, *g. pl.* **~** *f.* (*mil.*) cartridge clip.

обо|йти, йду, йдёшь, *past* **~шёл, ~шла** *pf.* (*of* ▶ **обходить**[1])
1 (*пройти, окружая, минуя*) to go round.
2 (*пройти по всему пространству чего-л.*) to make the round (of), go (all) round; (*о враче*) to make (go) one's round(s); **слух ~шёл весь город** the rumour spread all over the town.
3 (*избежать*) to avoid; to leave out; to pass over; **о. закон** to get round (evade) a law.

обо|йтись, йдусь, йдёшься, *past* **~шёлся, ~шлась** *pf.* (*of* ▶ **обходиться**)
1 (**с** + *i.*) to treat; **плохо о. с кем-н.** to treat s.o. badly.
2 (*coll.*) to cost, come to.
3 (+ *i.*) to manage (with, on), make do (with, on).
4 (*закончиться*) to turn out, end; **всё ~шлось** everything worked out; **всё ~шлось благополучно** everything turned out all right.

обокра|сть, обкраду, обкрадёшь, *past* **~л, ~ла** *pf.* (*of* ▶ **обкрадывать**) to rob.

обо|лгать, лгу, лжёшь, *past* **~лгал, ~лгала, ~лгало** *pf.* to slander.

оболочк|а, и *f.*
1 (*скорлупа*) shell; (*tech.*) casing.
2 (*anat.*) membrane; **радужная о.** iris.

оболь|ститься, щусь, стишься *pf.* (*of* ▶ **~щаться**) to be *or* labour (*Br.*), labor (*US*) under a delusion; (+ *i.*) to flatter o.s. (with).

обольща|ться, юсь *impf. of* ▶ **обольститься**

оболь|ю́, ёшь *see* ▶ **обли́ть**

обоня́ни|е, я *nt.* sense of smell; **име́ть то́нкое о.** to have a fine sense of smell.

обора́чива|ть(ся), ю(сь) *impf. of* ▶ **оберну́ть(ся)**

оборв|а́ть, у́, ёшь, *past* **~а́л, ~ала́, ~а́ло** *pf.* (*of* ▶ **обрыва́ть**)
1 (*цветы, яблоки*) to tear off, pluck.
2 (*нитку*) to break; to snap.
3 (*fig.*) (*разговор; человека*) to cut short, interrupt.

оборв|а́ться, у́сь, ёшься, *past* **~а́лся, ~ала́сь, ~ало́сь** *pf.* (*of* ▶ **обрыва́ться**)
1 (*о верёвке*) to break; to snap.
2 (*о человеке*) to fall; (*о вещах*) to come away.
3 (*о жизни, песне*) to be cut short, come abruptly to an end.

обо́рк|а, и *f.* frill, flounce.

оборо́н|а, ы *no pl., f.* defence (*Br.*), defense (*US*).

оборони́тельный *adj.* defensive.

оборон|и́ть, ю́, и́шь *pf.* (*of* ▶ **~я́ть**) to defend.

оборон|и́ться, ю́сь, и́шься *pf.* (*of* ▶ **~я́ться**) (**от** + *g.*) to defend o.s. (from).

оборон|я́ть(ся), я́ю(сь) *impf. of* ▶ **~и́ть(ся)**

оборо́т, а *m.*
1 turn.
2 (*употребление*) circulation; (*fin., comm.*) turnover; **ввести́ в о.** to put into circulation.
3 (*обратная сторона*) back; **смотри́ на ~е** please turn over.

о́борот|ень, ня *m.* werewolf.

оборо́т|ный *adj. of* ▶ **~; о. капита́л** (*fin., comm.*) working capital; **~ная сторона́** verso; reverse side (*also fig.*).

обору́довани|е, я *nt.*
1 (*действие*) equipping.
2 (*приборы*) equipment.

обору́д|овать, ую *impf. and pf.* to equip, fit out.

обоснова́ни|е, я *nt.*
1 (*действие*) substantiation.
2 (*довод*) basis, ground.

обосно́в|анный *p.p.p. of* ▶ **~а́ть** *and adj.* well founded, well grounded.

обосн|ова́ть, у́ю, у́ешь *pf.* (*of* ▶ **~о́вывать**) to substantiate.

обосн|ова́ться, у́юсь, у́ешься *pf.* (*of* ▶ **~о́вываться**) to settle.

обосно́выва|ть(ся), ю(сь) *impf. of* ▶ **обоснова́ть(ся)**

обосо́бленный *adj.* isolated, solitary.

обостре́ни|е, я *nt.*
1 (*чувств*) sharpening, intensification.
2 (*боли*) aggravation, exacerbation; (*отношений*) straining; (*кризиса, конфликта*) worsening, deepening.

обостр|и́ться, ю́сь, и́шься *pf.* (*of* ▶ **~я́ться**)
1 (*об ощущениях*) to become more sensitive, become keener.
2 (*о боли*) to become aggravated, become exacerbated; (*об отношениях*) to become strained; (*о кризисе, конфликте*) to worsen, deepen.

обостр|я́ться, я́юсь *impf. of* ▶ **~и́ться**

обо́чин|а, ы *f.* (*дороги*) edge, side; (*тротуара*) kerb (*Br.*), curb (*US*).

обою́д|ный (~ен, ~на) *adj.* mutual, reciprocal; **по ~ному согла́сию** by mutual consent.

обраба́тыва|ть, ю *impf. of* ▶ **обрабо́тать**

обрабо́та|ть, ю *pf.* (*of* ▶ **обраба́тывать**)
1 (*кожу*) to treat, process; **о. зе́млю** to work the land; **о. ра́ну** to dress a wound.
2 (*статью; голос*) to polish, perfect.

обрабо́тк|а, и *f.*
1 (*кожи*) treatment, processing; **о. земли́** cultivation of land.
2 (*статьи*) polishing.

обра́д|овать(ся), ую(сь) *pf. of* ▶ **ра́довать(ся)**

о́браз, а *m.*
1 (*вид*) shape, form; appearance.
2 (*представление*) image; **мы́слить ~ами** to think in images.
3 (*liter.*) (*тип*) type; figure; **о. Га́млета** the Hamlet type.
4 (*порядок*) mode, manner; way; **о. жи́зни** way of life, lifestyle; **каки́м ~ом?** how?; **таки́м ~ом** thus; **гла́вным ~ом** mainly, chiefly, largely.

образ|е́ц, ца́ *nt.*
1 model, pattern.
2 (*товарный*) specimen, sample; (*материи*) pattern.

о́браз|ный (~ен, ~на) *adj.* picturesque, vivid; (*liter.*) figurative; employing images.

образова́ни|е[1], я *nt.* (*действие*) formation.

образова́ни|е[2], я *nt.* (*обучение*) education.

образо́в|анный *p.p.p. of* ▶ **~а́ть** *and adj.*; **о. челове́к** educated person.

образова́тельный *adj.* educational.

образ|ова́ть, у́ю *impf.* (*in pres. tense*) *and pf.* (*of* ▶ **~о́вывать**) to form; to make up.

образ|ова́ться, у́ется *pf.* (*of* ▶ **~о́вываться**) to form; to arise.

образо́выва|ть(ся), ю, ет(ся) *impf. of* ▶ **образова́ть(ся)**

образцо́вый *adj.* model; exemplary.

обраст|а́ть, а́ю *impf. of* ▶ **~и́**

обраст|и́, у́, ёшь, *past* **обро́с, обросла́** *pf.* (*of* ▶ **~а́ть**) (+ *i.*)
1 (*покрыться растительностью*) to become (be) overgrown (with).
2 (*fig.*) (*создать вокруг себя*) to become (be) surrounded (by); to acquire, accumulate.

обрати́м|ый (~, ~а) *adj.* reversible.

обра|ти́ть, щу́, ти́шь *pf.* (*of* ▶ **~ща́ть**) to turn; (**в** + *a.*) to turn (into); **о. внима́ние (на** + *a.*) to pay attention (to), take notice (of); **о. чьё-н. внима́ние (на** + *a.*) to call, draw s.o.'s attention (to); **о. на себя́ внима́ние** to attract attention (to o.s.).

обра|ти́ться, щу́сь, ти́шься *pf.* (*of* ▶ **~ща́ться 1**)
1 to turn; **о. в бе́гство** to take to flight.
2 (**к** + *d.*) to turn (to), appeal (to); to apply (to); to accost; **она́ не зна́ла, к кому́ о. за по́мощью** she did not know to whom to turn for help.

обра́тно *adv.*
1 back; **туда́ и о.** there and back; **пое́здка**

туда́ и о. round trip.
2 (*наоборот*) conversely; inversely.
обра́тн|ый *adj.*
1 reverse; **о. а́дрес** sender's address; **о. биле́т** return (*Br.*), round trip (*US*) ticket; **о. путь** return journey; **на ~ом пути́** on the way back.
2 (*противоположный*) opposite; **в ~ую сто́рону** in the opposite direction.
3 (*math.*) inverse; **~ое отноше́ние** inverse ratio.
обраща́|ть, ю *impf. of* ▸ **обрати́ть**
обраща́|ться, юсь *impf.*
1 *impf. of* ▸ **обрати́ться.**
2 (*physiol., econ., etc.*) to circulate.
3 (**с** + *i.*) to treat; **пло́хо о. с кем-н.** to treat s.o. badly, maltreat s.o.
4 (**с** + *i.*) (*пользоваться*) to handle, manage (*an inanimate object*).
обраще́ни|е, я *nt.*
1 (**к** + *d.*) appeal (to), address (to).
2 (**в** + *a.*) conversion (to, into).
3 (*econ.*) circulation.
4 (**с** + *i.*) treatment (of); **плохо́е о.** ill-treatment.
5 (**с** + *i.*) (*пользование*) handling (of), use (of).
обреза́ни|е, я *nt.* (*relig.*) circumcision.
обрез|а́ть, а́ю *impf. of* ▸ **~ать**
обре́|зать, жу, жешь *pf.* (*of* ▸ **~за́ть**) to clip, trim; cut.
обрез|а́ться, а́юсь *impf. of* ▸ **~аться**
обре́|заться, жусь, жешься *pf.* (*of* ▸ **~за́ться**) (*поранить себя*) to cut o.s.
обрека́|ть, ю *impf. of* ▸ **обре́чь**
обре|ку́, чёшь, ку́т *see* ▸ **~чь**
обремени́тел|ьный (~ен, ~ьна) *adj.* burdensome, onerous.
обречённый *adj.* doomed.
обре́|чь, ку́, чёшь, ку́т, *past* **~к, ~кла́** *pf.* (*of* ▸ **~ка́ть**) (**на** + *a.*) to condemn, doom (to).
обрис|ова́ть, у́ю *pf.* (*of* ▸ **~о́вывать**) to outline, delineate, depict (*also fig.*).
обрисо́выва|ть, ю *impf. of* ▸ **обрисова́ть**
обр|и́ть, е́ю, е́ешь *pf.* (*голову*) to shave; (*усы*) to shave off.
обр|и́ться, е́юсь, е́ешься *pf.* to shave one's head.
обруга́|ть, ю *pf. of* ▸ **руга́ть 2, 3**
обрусе́|ть, ю *pf.* to become Russified, become Russianized.
о́бруч, а, *pl.* **~и, ~е́й** *m.* (*на бочке; гимнастический*) hoop; (*для волос*) hairband.
обруча́льн|ый *adj.*: **~ое кольцо́** wedding ring.
обруч|а́ться, а́юсь *impf. of* ▸ **~и́ться**
обруч|и́ться, у́сь, и́шься *pf.* (*of* ▸ **~а́ться**) (**с** + *i.*) to become engaged (to).
обру́шива|ть(ся), ю(сь) *impf. of* ▸ **обру́шить(ся)**
обру́ш|ить, у, ишь *pf.* (*of* ▸ **~ивать**) to bring down, rain down.
обру́ш|иться, усь, ишься *pf.* (*of* ▸ **~иваться**)
1 (*о здании, крыше*) to come down, collapse, cave in.
2 (*fig.*) (**на** + *a.*) to come down (upon), fall (upon).
обры́в, а *m.*
1 precipice.
2 (*tech.*) break, rupture.
обрыва́|ть(ся), ю(сь) *impf. of* ▸ **оборва́ть(ся)**
обры́в|ок, ка *m.* (*бумаги; разговора*) scrap; (*верёвки*) piece; (*песни, мелодии*) snatch.
обры́зг|ать, аю *pf.* (*of* ▸ **~ивать**) (+ *i.*) (*водой*) to besprinkle (with); (*грязью*) to splash; to bespatter (with).
обры́згива|ть, ю *impf. of* ▸ **обры́згать**
обря́д, а *m.* rite, ceremony.
обса|ди́ть, жу́, ~дишь *pf.* (*of* ▸ **~живать**) to plant round.
обса́жива|ть, ю *impf. of* ▸ **обсади́ть**
обсервато́ри|я, и *f.* observatory.
обсле́довани|е, я *nt.* (+ *g.*) (*осмотр*) inspection (of); (*в больнице*) observation, tests.
обсле́д|овать, ую *impf. and pf.* (*произвести осмотр*) to inspect; (*исследовать*) to investigate; **о. больно́го** to examine a patient.
обслу́живани|е, я *nt.* service; (*tech.*) servicing, maintenance; **медици́нское о.** health service.
обслу́жива|ть, ю *impf. of* ▸ **обслужи́ть**
обслуж|и́ть, у́, ~ишь *pf.* (*of* ▸ **~ивать**) to serve; **о. потреби́теля** to serve a customer.
обсо́х|нуть, ну, нешь, *past* **~, ~ла** *pf.* (*of* ▸ **обсыха́ть**) to dry (off).
обстано́вк|а, и *f.*
1 (*квартиры*) furniture; decor.
2 (*theatr.*) set.
3 (*положение*) situation.
4 (*атмосфера*) atmosphere, environment.
обстоя́тел|ьный (~ен, ~ьна) *adj.* thorough, detailed.
обстоя́тельств|о, а *nt.* circumstance; **по незави́сящим от меня́ ~ам** for reasons beyond my control; **ни при каки́х ~ах** in no circumstances.
обсто|я́ть, и́т *impf.* to be; to get on; **как ~и́т де́ло?** how is it going?; **вот как ~я́т дела́** that is the way it is; that's how matters stand.
обстре́л, а *m.* firing, fire; **артиллери́йский о.** bombardment, shelling; **попа́сть под о.** to come under fire.
обстре́лива|ть, ю *impf. of* ▸ **обстреля́ть**
обстрел|я́ть, я́ю *pf.* (*of* ▸ **~ивать**) to fire (at, on); to bombard.
обступ|а́ть, а́ю *impf. of* ▸ **~и́ть**
обступ|и́ть, лю́, ~ишь *pf.* (*of* ▸ **~а́ть**) to surround; to cluster (round).
обсу|ди́ть, жу́, ~дишь *pf.* (*of* ▸ **~жда́ть**) to discuss; to consider.
обсужда́|ть, ю *impf. of* ▸ **обсуди́ть**
обсужде́ни|е, я *nt.* discussion.
обсу́шива|ть(ся), ю(сь) *impf. of* ▸ **обсуши́ть(ся)**
обсуш|и́ть, у́, ~ишь *pf.* (*of* ▸ **~ивать**) to dry (out).
обсуш|и́ться, у́сь, ~ишься *pf.* (*of* ▸ **~иваться**) to dry o.s., get dry.
обсчит|а́ть, а́ю *pf.* (*of* ▸ **~ывать**) to

shortchange.

обсчит|а́ться, а́юсь *pf.* (*of* ▶ **~ываться**) to make a mistake (*in counting*).

обсчи́тыва|ть(ся), ю(сь) *impf. of* ▶ **обсчита́ть(ся)**

обсыха́|ть, ю *impf. of* ▶ **обсо́хнуть**

обта́чива|ть, ю *impf. of* ▶ **обточи́ть**

обтека́ем|ый (~, ~а) *adj.*
1 (*tech.*) streamlined.
2 (*fig., coll.*) evasive.

обтека́|ть, ю *impf. of* ▶ **обте́чь**

обтер|е́ть, оботру́, оботрёшь, *past* **~, ~ла** *pf.* (*of* ▶ **обтира́ть**)
1 (*высушить*) to wipe; to wipe dry.
2 (+ *i.*) (*натереть*) to rub all over (with).

обтер|е́ться, оботру́сь, оботрёшься, *past* **~ся, ~лась** *pf.* (*of* ▶ **обтира́ться**)
1 (*обтереть себя*) to wipe o.s. dry, dry o.s.
2 (*водой*) to sponge down.

обте́|чь, ку́, чёшь, ку́т, *past* **~к, ~кла́** *pf.* (*of* ▶ **~ка́ть**)
1 to flow round.
2 (*mil.*) to by-pass.

обтира́ни|е, я *nt.*
1 sponge-down.
2 (*coll.*) (*жидкость*) lotion.

обтира́|ть(ся), ю(сь) *impf. of* ▶ **обтере́ть(ся)**

обточ|и́ть, у́, ~ишь *pf.* (*of* ▶ **обта́чивать**) to grind smooth; (*на станке*) to turn.

обтя́гивающий *adj.* skin-tight, figure-hugging.

обува́|ть(ся), ю(сь) *impf. of* ▶ **обу́ть(ся)**

обувно́й *adj. of* ▶ **о́бувь; о. магази́н** shoe shop.

о́був|ь, и *no pl., f.* footwear; shoes.

обу́глива|ться, юсь *impf. of* ▶ **обу́глиться**

обу́гл|иться, юсь, ишься *pf.* (*of* ▶ **~иваться**) to become charred, char.

обусло́влива|ться, ется *impf.* (+ *i.*) to be conditional (upon); to depend (on); **разме́р ~ется тре́бованиями** the size is conditioned by the requirements.

обу́|ть, ю, ешь *pf.* (*of* ▶ **~ва́ть**)
1 : **о. кого́-н.** to put on s.o.'s boots (shoes) for him.
2 (*coll.*) (*снабдить обувью*) to provide with boots *or* shoes.
3 (*сапоги*) to put on.

обу́|ться, юсь, ешься *pf.* (*of* ▶ **~ва́ться**)
1 (*надеть обувь*) to put on one's boots, shoes.
2 (*coll.*) (*снабдить себя обувью*) to provide o.s. with boots *or* shoes.

обуч|а́ть(ся), а́ю(сь) *impf. of* ▶ **~и́ть(ся)**

обуче́ни|е, я *nt.* teaching; instruction, training.

обуч|и́ть, у́, ~ишь *pf.* (*of* ▶ **учи́ть 1** *and* ▶ **~а́ть**) (*кого́-н. чему́-н.*) to teach (s.o. sth.); to instruct, train (s.o. in).

обуч|и́ться, у́сь, ~ишься *pf.* (*of* ▶ **учи́ться 1** *and* ▶ **~а́ться**) (+ *d. or* + *inf.*) to learn.

обхо́д, а *m.*
1 (*врача, почтальона*) round.
2 (*кружной путь*) roundabout way; bypass.
3 (*уклонение*) evasion, circumvention (*of law, etc.*); **в о.** (+ *g.*) round, bypassing; (*минуя*) evading.

обхо|ди́ть[1], жу́, ~дишь *impf. of* ▶ **обойти́**

обхо|ди́ть[2], жу́, ~дишь *pf.* (*город, друзей*) to go all round.

обхо|ди́ться, жу́сь, ~дишься *impf. of* ▶ **обойти́сь**

обша́рива|ть, ю *impf. of* ▶ **обша́рить**

обша́р|ить, ю, ишь *pf.* (*of* ▶ **~ивать**) (*coll.*) to ransack.

обшива́|ть, ю *impf. of* ▶ **обши́ть**

обши́вк|а, и *f.*
1 (*воротника*) trim.
2 (*корабля*) plating.
3 (*дома*) cladding; (*стен*) panelling (*Br.*) paneling (*US*).

обши́р|ный (~ен, ~на) *adj.* extensive (*also fig.*); (*комната*) spacious; (*пространство*) vast.

об|ши́ть, ошью́, ошьёшь *pf.* (*of* ▶ **~шива́ть**)
1 (*одежду*) to edge, trim.
2 (*корабль*) to plate; (*дом*) to clad; (*стены*) to panel.

обща́|ться, юсь *impf.* (**с** + *i.*) to associate (with), mix (with).

общедосту́п|ный (~ен, ~на) *adj.*
1 available to all.
2 (*цены*) moderate.
3 (*книга, лекция*) accessible, popular.

общежи́ти|е, я *nt.* (*рабочее*) hostel; (*студенческое*) hall of residence (*Br.*), dormitory (*US*).

общеизве́ст|ный (~ен, ~на) *adj.* well-known, generally known; (*преступник*) notorious.

общенаро́д|ный (~ен, ~на) *adj.* national; public; **о. пра́здник** public holiday.

обще́ни|е, я *nt.* relations, links; **ли́чное о.** personal contact.

общеобразова́тельный *adj.* of general education.

общепри́знан|ный (~, ~а) *adj.* universally recognized.

общепри́нят|ый (~, ~а) *adj.* generally accepted.

обще́ственност|ь, и *f.* (*collect.*) (the) public, the community; **англи́йская о.** the British public; **нау́чная о.** the scientific community.

обще́ственн|ый *adj.*
1 social, public; **~ая жизнь** public life; **~ое мне́ние** public opinion.
2 (*добровольный*) voluntary, unpaid; **~ые организа́ции** voluntary organizations.

о́бществ|о, а *nt.*
1 society.
2 (*компания*) company; **в ~е кого́-н.** in s.o.'s company; **попа́сть в дурно́е о.** to fall into bad company.

обществове́дени|е, я *nt.* social science.

общеупотреби́тел|ьный (~ен, ~ьна) *adj.* in general use.

общечелове́ческий *adj.* common to all mankind.

о́бщ|ий *adj.* general; common; **о. знако́мый** mutual acquaintance; **~ее собра́ние** general meeting; **~ая су́мма** sum total.

общи́н|а, ы *f.* (*общество*) community; (*коммуна*) commune.

общи́тел|ьный (~ен, ~ьна) *adj.* sociable.

объеда́|ться, юсь *impf. of* ▸ **объе́сться**

объедине́ни|е, я *nt.*
1 (*действие*) unification; amalgamation.
2 (*союз*) union, association.

объедин|ённый *p.p.p. of* ▸ **~и́ть** *and adj.* united; **Организа́ция Объединённых На́ций** United Nations (Organization).

объедин|и́ть, ю́, и́шь *pf.* (*of* ▸ **~я́ть**) (*людей*) to unite; (*организации*) to amalgamate; **о. уси́лия** to combine efforts.

объедин|и́ться, ю́сь, и́шься *pf.* (*of* ▸ **~я́ться**) (**с** + *i.*) to unite (with); amalgamate (with).

объедин|я́ть(ся), я́ю(сь) *impf. of* ▸ **~и́ть(ся)**

объе́д|ки, ков *pl.* (*sg.* **~ок, ~ка** *m.*) (*coll.*) leftovers, scraps.

объе́зд, а *m.*
1 (*действие*) travelling (*Br.*), traveling (*US*) round, riding round, going round.
2 (*место*) detour, diversion (*Br.*); **пое́хать в о.** to make a detour.

объе́з|дить[1], жу, дишь *pf.* (*of* ▸ **~жа́ть[1]**) (*страну*) to travel all over; (*друзей*) to go round visiting.

объе́з|дить[2], жу, дишь *pf.* (*of* ▸ **~жа́ть[2]**) (*лошадей*) to break in.

объезжа́|ть[1], ю *impf. of* ▸ **объе́здить[1]** *and* ▸ **объе́хать**

объезжа́|ть[2], ю *impf. of* ▸ **объе́здить[2]**

объе́кт, а *m.*
1 object.
2 (*mil.*) objective.
3 (*предприятие*) establishment; **строи́тельный о.** building site.

объекти́в, а *m.* (*opt.*) lens.

объекти́вност|ь, и *f.* objectivity.

объекти́в|ный (~ен, ~на) *adj.* objective.

объём, а *m.* volume (*also fig.*); (*величина*) size.

объём|ный (~ен, ~на) *adj.*
1 by volume, volumetric; (*изображение*) three-dimensional.
2 (*большой по объёму*) voluminous, bulky.

объе́|сться, мся, шься, стся, ди́мся, ди́тесь, дя́тся, *past* **~лся** *pf.* (*of* ▸ **~да́ться**) to overeat.

объе́|хать, ду, дешь *pf.* (*of* ▸ **~зжа́ть[1]**)
1 (*болото*) to go round, skirt.
2 (*всю страну*) to travel over.

объяв|и́ть, лю́, ~ишь *pf.* (*of* ▸ **~ля́ть**) to declare, announce; **о. войну́** to declare war.

объявле́ни|е, я *nt.*
1 declaration, announcement; (*вывеска*) notice.
2 (*рекламное*) advertisement; **дать о. в газе́ту, помести́ть о. в газе́те** to put an advertisement in a paper.

объявля́|ть, ю *impf. of* ▸ **объяви́ть**

объясне́ни|е, я *nt.* explanation.

объясн|и́ть, ю́, и́шь *pf.* (*of* ▸ **~я́ть**) to explain.

объясн|и́ться, ю́сь, и́шься *pf.* (*of* ▸ **~я́ться**)
1 to explain o.s.; (**с** + *i.*) to have a talk (with); to have it out (with); **о. в любви́** (+ *d.*) to make a declaration of love (to).
2 (*найти себе объяснение*) to become clear, be explained.

объясн|я́ть, я́ю *impf. of* ▸ **~и́ть**

объясн|я́ться, я́юсь *impf.*
1 *impf. of* ▸ **~и́ться.**
2 to speak; to make o.s. understood; **о. же́стами и зна́ками** to use sign language.
3 (+ *i.*) to be explained (by), be accounted for (by); **э́тим ~я́ется его́ стра́нное поведе́ние** that accounts for his strange behaviour.

объя́ти|е, я *nt.* embrace; **с распростёртыми ~ями** with open arms.

обыва́тел|ь, я *m.* philistine.

обыва́тельский *adj.* philistine; narrow-minded.

обыгр|а́ть, а́ю *pf.* (*of* ▸ **~ывать**)
1 (*соперника*) to beat (*at a game*).
2 (*theatr.*) to use with (good) effect, play up; (*fig.*) (*ошибку*) to turn to advantage, turn to account.

обы́грыва|ть, ю *impf. of* ▸ **обыгра́ть**

обы́ден|ный (~, ~на) *adj.* ordinary; commonplace, everyday.

обыкнове́нно *adv.* usually, as a rule.

обыкнове́н|ный (~ен, ~на) *adj.* usual; ordinary; commonplace; **~ная исто́рия** everyday occurrence.

о́быск, а *m.* search; **о́рдер на о.** search warrant.

обы|ска́ть, щу́, ~щешь *pf.* (*of* ▸ **~скивать**) to search.

обы́скива|ть, ю *impf. of* ▸ **обыска́ть**

обы́ча|й, я *m.* custom.

обы́чно *adv.* usually; as a rule; **как о.** as usual.

обы́ч|ный (~ен, ~на) *adj.* usual; ordinary.

обя́занност|ь, и *f.* duty; responsibility; **во́инская о.** military service; **исполня́ть ~и дире́ктора** to act as director; **исполня́ющий ~и дире́ктора** acting director.

обя́зан|ный (~, ~а) *adj.*
1 (+ *inf.*) obliged, bound; **он ~ верну́ться** he is obliged to go back; it is his duty to go back.
2 (+ *d.*) obliged, indebted (to); **она́ вам ~а свое́й жи́знью** she owes her life to you.

обяза́тельно *adv.* without fail; definitely; **он о. там бу́дет** he is sure to be there, he is bound to be there; **не о.** not necessarily.

обяза́тел|ьный (~ен, ~ьна) *adj.*
1 obligatory; compulsory; binding; **~ьное обуче́ние** compulsory education.
2 (*человек*) reliable.

обязáтельств|о, а *nt.*
1 obligation; **взять на себя́ о.** (+ *inf.*) to commit o.s. (to), undertake (to).
2 (*pl.*; *leg.*) liabilities.

обя|зáться, жу́сь, ~́жешься *pf.* (*of* ▸**~́зываться**) to bind o.s., pledge o.s., undertake.

обя́зыва|ться, юсь *impf. of* ▸**обязáться**

овáл, а *m.* oval.

овáл|ьный (~ен, ~ьна) *adj.* oval.

овáци|я, и *f.* ovation.

Óвéн, Óвнá *m.* Aries.

ов|ёс, сá *m.* oats.

овладевá|ть, ю *impf. of* ▸**овладéть**

овладé|ть, ю *pf.* (*of* ▸**~вáть**) (+ *i.*)
1 (*взять*) to seize; to take possession (of); **о. собóй** to get control of o.s., regain self-control.
2 (*fig.*) (*усвоить*) master.

óвод, а, *pl.* **~ы, ~ов** (*and* **~á, ~óв**) gadfly.

óвощ|и, éй *pl.* (*sg.* **~, ~а** *m.*) vegetables.

овощнóй *adj.* vegetable; **о. магази́н** greengrocer's (shop).

oврáг, а *m.* ravine, gully.

овся́нк|а, и *f.* (*coll.*)
1 (*крупа*) oatmeal.
2 (*каша*) porridge (*Br.*), oatmeal (*US*).

овся́н|ый *adj.* made of oats; oatmeal; **~ая кáша** (oatmeal) porridge (*Br.*), oatmeal (*US*); **~ая крупá** oatmeal.

овц|á, ы, *pl.* **~́ы, овéц, ~́ам** *f.* sheep; (*самка*) ewe.

овчáрк|а, и *f.* sheepdog; **немéцкая о.** Alsatian (*Br.*), German shepherd (*dog*).

огибá|ть, ю *impf. of* ▸**обогну́ть**

оглавлéни|е, я *nt.* table of contents.

огла|си́ть, шу́, си́шь *pf.* (*of* ▸**~шáть**) (*объявить*) to proclaim, announce; **о. резолю́цию** to read out a resolution.

оглáск|а, и *f.* publicity; **избегáть ~и** to shun publicity; **предáть ~е** to make public, make known.

оглашá|ть, ю *impf. of* ▸**огласи́ть**

оглóх|нуть, ну, нешь, *past* **~, ~ла** *pf. of* ▸**глóхнуть 1**

оглуш|áть, áю *impf. of* ▸**~и́ть 2**

оглуши́тел|ьный (~ен, ~ьна) *adj.* deafening.

оглуш|и́ть, у́, и́шь *pf.*
1 *pf. of* ▸**глуши́ть 1.**
2 (*impf.* **~áть**) to deafen; (*ударом*) to stun (*also fig.*).

огля́дыва|ться, юсь *impf. of* ▸**огляну́ться**

огля|ну́ться, ну́сь, ~́нешься *pf.* (*of* ▸**~́дываться**) to turn (back) to look at sth.; to glance back.

óгнен|ный (~, ~на) *adj.* fiery (*also fig.*).

огнеопáс|ный (~ен, ~на) *adj.* inflammable.

огнетуши́тел|ь, я *m.* fire extinguisher.

огнеупóр|ный (~ен, ~на) *adj.* fire-resistant, fireproof.

оговáрива|ть(ся), ю(сь) *impf. of* ▸**оговори́ть(ся)**

оговор|и́ть[1], ю, и́шь *pf.* (*of* ▸**оговáривать**) (*оклеветать*) to slander.

оговор|и́ть[2], ю, и́шь *pf.* (*of* ▸**оговáривать**)
1 (*заранее условиться о чём-л.*) to stipulate (for); to fix, agree (on); **мы ~и́ли услóвия рабóты** we have fixed the conditions of work.
2 (*сделать оговорку*) to spell out; to specify.

оговор|и́ться, ю́сь, и́шься *pf.* (*of* ▸**оговáриваться**)
1 (*сделать оговорку*) to make a reservation, make a proviso.
2 (*в речи*) to make a slip in speaking.

оговóр|ка, ки *f.*
1 reservation, proviso; **он согласи́лся, но с нéкоторыми ~ками** he agreed but made certain reservations.
2 (*в речи*) slip of the tongue.

огол|и́ть, ю́, и́шь *pf.* (*of* ▸**~я́ть**) to bare; (*провод*) to strip; (*шашку*) to draw; **о. фланг** (*mil.*) to expose one's flank.

огол|и́ться, ю́сь, и́шься *pf.* (*of* ▸**~я́ться**)
1 to strip (o.s.).
2 (*о проводе*) to become exposed; (*о дереве*) to become bare.

огол|я́ть(ся), я́ю(сь) *impf. of* ▸**~и́ть(ся)**

ог|óнь, ня́ *m.*
1 (*пламя*) fire (*also fig.*).
2 (*свет*) light.

огорáжива|ть, ю *impf. of* ▸**огороди́ть**

огорóд, а *m.* kitchen garden, vegetable garden.

огоро|ди́ть, жу́, ~́дишь *pf.* (*of* ▸**огорáживать**) to fence in, enclose.

огорч|áть(ся), áю(сь) *impf. of* ▸**~и́ть(ся)**

огорчéни|е, я *nt.* distress; chagrin.

огорч|и́ть, у́, и́шь *pf.* (*of* ▸**~áть**) to distress, upset.

огорч|и́ться, у́сь, и́шься *pf.* (*of* ▸**~áться**) to be distressed; **не ~áйтесь!** cheer up!

огрáб|ить, лю, ишь *pf. of* ▸**грáбить**

ограблéни|е, я *nt.* robbery; (*дома*) burglary.

огрáд|а, ы *f.* (*забор*) fence; (*решётка*) railings.

огра|ди́ть, жу́, ди́шь *pf.* (*of* ▸**~ждáть**) (**от** + *g.*) to guard (against, from), protect (against).

огра|ди́ться, жу́сь, ди́шься *pf.* (*of* ▸**~ждáться**) (**от** + *g.*) to defend o.s. (against); to protect o.s. (against).

ограждá|ть(ся), ю(сь) *impf. of* ▸**огради́ть(ся)**

ограждéни|е, я *nt.* barrier.

ограничéни|е, я *nt.* limitation, restriction.

ограни́ч|енный *p.p.p. of* ▸**~ить** *and adj.* limited; **о. человéк** (*fig.*) narrow(-minded) person.

ограни́чива|ть(ся), ю(сь) *impf. of* ▸**ограни́чить(ся)**

ограничи́тельный *adj.* restrictive, limiting.

ограни́ч|ить, у, ишь *pf.* (*of* ▸**~ивать**) to limit, restrict, cut down; **о. себя́ в расхóдах** to cut down one's expenditure.

ограни́ч|иться, усь, ишься *pf.* (*of*

▸ ~иваться) (+ *i.*)
[1] (*удовлетвориться*) to limit o.s. (to), confine o.s. (to).
[2] (*остаться в каких-л. пределах*) to be limited (to), be confined (to).

огро́м|ный (~ен, ~на) *adj.* huge; vast; enormous.

огрыз|а́ться, а́юсь *impf.* (*of* **▸ ~ну́ться**) (*coll.*) (**на** + *a.*) to snap (at).

огрыз|ну́ться, ну́сь, нёшься *pf. of* **▸ ~а́ться**

огры́з|ок, ка *m.* (*coll.*) (*яблока, сосиски*) leftover bit; (*карандаша*) stub.

огур|е́ц, ца́ *m.* cucumber.

о́д|а, ы *f.* ode.

ода́лжива|ть, ю *impf. of* **▸ одолжи́ть**

одарённый *adj.* gifted, talented.

одева́|ть(ся), ю(сь) *impf. of* **▸ оде́ть(ся)**

оде́жд|а, ы *f.* clothes; clothing; **ве́рхняя о.** outer clothing, overcoat; **мужска́я о.** menswear; **фо́рменная о.** uniform.

одеколо́н, а *m.* eau de cologne.

одёргива|ть, ю *impf. of* **▸ одёрнуть**

одержи́м|ый (~, ~а) *adj.* (+ *i.*) possessed (by); afflicted (by); **о. стра́хом** consumed with fear.

одёр|нуть, ну, нешь *pf.* (*of* **▸ ~гивать**)
[1] (*рубашку, юбку*) to pull down, straighten.
[2] (*fig., coll.*) (*человека*) to call to order; to silence; to snub.

оде́т|ый *p.p.p. of* **▸ ~ь** *and adj.* (+ *i. or* **в** + *a.*) dressed (in), clothed (in); with one's clothes on; **хорошо́ о.** well-dressed.

O

оде́|ть, ну, нешь *pf.* (*of* **▸ ~ва́ть**)
[1] (**в** + *a.*) to dress (in), clothe (in); **о. ребёнка в брю́ки** to dress a child in trousers; (+ *i.*) (*покрыть*) to cover (with), wrap (in).
[2] (*снабдить одеждой*) to clothe.

оде́|ться, нусь, нешься *pf.* (*of* **▸ ~ва́ться**)
[1] to dress (o.s.); to clothe o.s.; **о. в вече́рнее пла́тье** to put on an evening dress.
[2] (*покрыться*) (+ *i.*) to be covered with.

одея́л|о, а *nt.* blanket.

оди́н, одного́ *m.*; **одна́, одно́й** *f.*; **одно́, одного́** *nt.*; *pl.* **одни́, одни́х** *num. and pron.*
[1] (*число*) one; **одно́** one thing; **о. за други́м** one after the other, one by one; **одни́... други́е** some ..., (while) others; **с одно́й стороны́... с друго́й (стороны́)** on the one hand ... on the other hand; **одно́ вре́мя** at one time; **о. раз** once; **одни́м сло́вом** in a word.
[2] (*некий*) a, an; a certain; **я встре́тил одного́ моего́ бы́вшего колле́гу** I met an old colleague of mine.
[3] (*без других*) alone; by o.s.; **я живу́ о.** I live alone.
[4] (*без супруги*) single.
[5] (*coll.*) (*только*) only; **она́ чита́ет одни́ детекти́вные рома́ны** she reads nothing but detective stories.
[6]: **о., о. и тот же** the same, one and the same; **мы с ней одного́ во́зраста** she and I are the same age.

одина́ково *adv.* equally, alike.

одина́ков|ый (~, ~а) *adj.* (**с** + *i.*) identical (with), the same (as).

оди́ннадцатый *adj.* eleventh.

оди́ннадцат|ь, и *num.* eleven.

одино́к|ий (~, ~а) *adj.*
[1] solitary; lonely; lone.
[2] *as n.* **о., ~ого** *m.* single man, bachelor; **~ая, ~ой** *f.* single woman.

одино́ко *adv.* lonely; **чу́вствовать себя́ о.** to feel lonely.

одино́честв|о, а *nt.* solitude; loneliness.

одино́чк|а, и *c.g.* lone person; **мать-о.** single mother; **оте́ц-о.** single father.

одино́чн|ый *adj.*
[1] (*одного человека*) individual; one-man; **~ое заключе́ние** solitary confinement.
[2] (*отдельный*) solitary; single.

одича́|ть, ю *pf. of* **▸ дича́ть**

одна́жды *adv.* once; one day; **о. у́тром (ве́чером, но́чью)** one morning (evening, night).

одна́ко *adv. and conj.* however; but; though.

одновре́ме́нно *adv.* simultaneously, at the same time.

одновр|е́ме́нный (~е́ме́нен, ~е́ме́нна) *adj.* simultaneous.

одногла́зый *adj.* one-eyed.

одноднев́ный *adj.* one-day.

однозна́ч|ный (~ен, ~на) *adj.*
[1] (*тождественный*) synonymous.
[2] (*fig.*) (*недвусмысленный*) unambiguous; simple, straightforward.

одноимён|ный (~ен, ~на) *adj.* of the same name.

однокла́ссник, а *m.* classmate.

однокла́ссни|ца, цы *f. of* **▸ ~к**

одноку́рсник, а *m.* person in the same year of study.

одноку́рсни|ца, цы *f. of* **▸ ~к**

одноме́стный *adj.* single-seated, single-seater.

одноно́гий *adj.* one-legged.

однообра́з|ный (~ен, ~на) *adj.* monotonous.

однора́зовый *adj.* (*шприц*) disposable; (*пропуск*) temporary, valid only once.

одноро́д|ный (~ен, ~на) *adj.* (*одинаковый во всех частях*) homogeneous.

однору́кий *adj.* one-armed.

односельча́н|ин, ина, *pl.* **~е, ~** *m.* fellow villager.

односельча́н|ка, ки *f. of* **▸ ~ин**

односло́ж|ный *adj.*
[1] monosyllabic.
[2] **(~ен, ~на)** (*fig.*) terse, abrupt.

односторо́нн|ий *adj.*
[1] (*ткань*) one-sided (*also fig.*); (*разоружение, договор*) unilateral.
[2] (*ток*) one-way; **~ее движе́ние** one-way traffic; **о. ум** (*fig.*) one-track mind.

одноти́п|ный (~ен, ~на) *adj.* of the same type, of the same kind; **о. кора́бль** sister ship.

однофами́л|ец, ьца *m.* (**с** + *i.*) person having the same surname (as), namesake.

однофами́л|ица, ицы *f. of* **▸ ~ец**

одноцве́т|ный (~ен, ~на) *adj.* (*ткань*) plain; (*fig.*) monochrome.

одноэта́жный *adj.* single-storey (*Br.*), single-story (*US*).

одобре́ни|е, я *nt.* approval.

одобри́тел|ьный (~ен, ~ьна) *adj.* approving; (*отзыв*) favourable (*Br.*), favorable (*US*).

одо́бр|ить, ю, ишь *pf.* (*of* ▸ **~я́ть**) to approve (of); **не о.** to disapprove (of).

одобр|я́ть, я́ю *impf. of* ▸ **~ить**

одолева́|ть, ю *impf. of* ▸ **одоле́ть**

одоле́|ть, ю *pf.* (*of* ▸ **~ва́ть**)
1 to overcome, conquer; **его́ ~л сон** he was overcome by sleepiness.
2 (*fig.*) to master; to cope (with); to get through.

одолже́ни|е, я *nt.* favour (*Br.*), favor (*US*), service; **сде́лайте мне о.** do me a favour (*Br.*), favor (*US*).

одолж|и́ть, у́, и́шь *pf.* (*of* ▸ **ода́лживать**)
1 (+ *d.*) to lend.
2 (*coll.*; **у** + *g.*) to borrow (from).

одува́нчик, а *m.* (*bot.*) dandelion.

оду́м|аться, аюсь *pf.* (*of* ▸ **~ываться**) to change one's mind; to think better of it.

оду́мыва|ться, юсь *impf. of* ▸ **оду́маться**

одура́чива|ть, ю *impf. of* ▸ **одура́чить**

одура́ч|ить, у, ишь *pf.* (*of* ▸ **дура́чить** *and* ▸ **~ивать**) (*coll.*) to make a fool (of), fool.

одухотворённый *adj.* inspired; (*лицо*) spiritual.

одышк|а, и *f.* short breath; **страда́ть ~ой** to be short-winded.

ожере́ль|е, я *nt.* necklace.

ожесточ|а́ть(ся), а́ю(сь) *impf. of* ▸ **~и́ть(ся)**

ожесточе́ни|е, я *nt.* bitterness.

ожесточённый *p.p.p. of* ▸ **ожесточи́ть** *and adj.* (*бой, спор*) bitter; (*человек*) embittered; hardened.

ожесточ|и́ть, у́, и́шь *pf.* (*of* ▸ **~а́ть**) to embitter; to harden.

ожесточ|и́ться, у́сь, и́шься *pf.* (*of* ▸ **~а́ться**) to become embittered; to become hardened.

ожива́|ть, ю *impf. of* ▸ **ожи́ть**

оживи́|ть, лю́, и́шь *pf.* (*of* ▸ **~ля́ть**)
1 (*человека; воспоминание*) to revive.
2 (*fig.*) (*общество, вечер*) to liven up, enliven; (*торговлю*) to revitalize; (*лицо, картину*) to brighten up.

оживи́|ться, лю́сь, и́шься *pf.* (*of* ▸ **~ля́ться**)
1 (*человек, разговор*) to become animated, liven (up); (*взгляд*) to brighten up.
2 (*улица*) to come to life.

оживле́ни|е, я *nt.*
1 (*состояние*) animation, gusto.
2 (*действие*) reviving; enlivening.

оживлённый *p.p.p. of* ▸ **оживи́ть** *and adj.* animated; lively.

оживля́|ть(ся), ю(сь) *impf. of* ▸ **оживи́ть(ся)**

ожида́ни|е, я *nt.* expectation; waiting; **обману́ть ~я** to disappoint; **в ~и** (+ *g.*) pending; **сверх ~я** beyond expectation.

ожида́|ть, ю *impf.* (+ *g.*) to wait (for); (*предвидеть*) to expect, anticipate; **как я и ~л** just as I expected.

ожире́ни|е, я *nt.* obesity.

ож|и́ть, иву́, ивёшь, *past* **~ил, ~ила́, ~ило** *pf.* (*of* ▸ **~ива́ть**) to come to life, revive (*also fig.*).

ожо́г, а *m.* burn; (*жидкостью, паром*) scald.

озабо́|тить, чу, тишь *pf.* to trouble, worry.

озабо́ченност|ь, и *f.* anxiety.

озабо́чен|ный (~, ~а) *p.p.p. of* ▸ **озабо́тить** *and adj.* **(~, ~на)** anxious, worried.

озагла́в|ить, лю, ишь *pf.* (*of* ▸ **~ливать**) to entitle; (*главу, раздел*) to head.

озагла́влива|ть, ю *impf. of* ▸ **озагла́вить**

озада́ч|енный (~ен, ~ена) *p.p.p. of* ▸ **~ить** *and adj.* **(~ен, ~енна)** perplexed, puzzled.

озада́чива|ть, ю *impf. of* ▸ **озада́чить**

озада́ч|ить, у, ишь *pf.* (*of* ▸ **~ивать**) to perplex, puzzle, take aback.

озвере́|ть, ю *pf. of* ▸ **звере́ть**

озву́чива|ть, ю *impf. of* ▸ **озву́чить**

озву́ч|ить, у, ишь *pf.* (*of* ▸ **~ивать**)
1 (*cin.*) to add a soundtrack to.
2 (*coll.*) (*высказать*) to state, to formulate.

о́зер|о, а, *pl.* **озёра, озёр** *nt.* lake.

ози́м|ый *adj.* winter; *as n.* **~ые, ~ых** winter crops.

означа́|ть, ет *impf.* to mean, signify, stand for; **что ~ют э́ти бу́квы?** what do these letters stand for?

озно́б, а *m.* shivering; chill; **почу́вствовать о.** to feel shivery.

озо́н, а *m.* ozone.

озо́н|овый *adj. of* ▸ **~; ~овая дыра́** ozone hole; **о. слой** ozone layer.

озорно́й *adj.* (*coll.*) mischievous.

озорств|о́, а́ *nt.* (*coll.*) mischief.

озя́б|нуть, ну, нешь, *past* **~, ~ла** *pf.* (*coll.*) to be cold; **я ~!** I am frozen!

ой (*or* **ой-ой-ой)** *int. expr. surprise or pleasure* oh, (*pain*) ow, ouch!, (*recognition of a mistake*) oops!

ока|за́ть, жу́, ~жешь *pf.* (*of* ▸ **~зывать**) to render, show; **о. влия́ние (на** + *a.*) to influence, exert influence (upon); **о. де́йствие (на** + *a.*) to have an effect (upon); to take effect; **о. по́мощь** (+ *d.*) to help, give (s.o.) help; **о. услу́гу** (+ *d.*) to do, render (s.o.) a service; to do (s.o.) a good turn.

ока|за́ться, жу́сь, ~жешься *pf.* (*of* ▸ **~зываться**)
1 to turn out (to be), prove (to be).
2 (*очутиться*) to find o.s.; to be found; **я ~за́лся в больни́це** I found myself in hospital.

ока́зыва|ть(ся), ю(сь) *impf. of* ▸ **оказа́ть(ся)**

окайм|и́ть, лю́, и́шь *pf.* (*of* ▸ **~ля́ть**) (+ *i.*) to border (with), edge (with).

окаймля́|ть, ю *impf. of* ▸ **окайми́ть**

окамене́|ть, ю *pf. of* ▸ **камене́ть**

ока́нчива|ть(ся), ю, ет(ся) *impf. of* ▸ **око́нчить(ся)**

О

ока|ти́ть, чу́, ~тишь *pf.* (*of* ▶ ~чивать) to pour (over); **о. холо́дной водо́й** to pour cold water (over) (*also fig.*).
ока|ти́ться, чу́сь, ~тишься *pf.* (*of* ▶ ~чиваться) to pour over o.s.
ока́чива|ть(ся), ю(сь) *impf. of* ▶ **окати́ть(ся)**
окая́нный *adj.* damned, cursed.
океа́н, а *m.* ocean.
Океа́ни|я, и *f.* Oceania (*the islands of the Pacific and adjacent seas*).
океа́нский *adj.* ocean; oceanic; **о. парохо́д** ocean(-going) liner.
о́кис|ь, и *f.* (*chem.*) oxide.
оккупа́ци|я, и *f.* (*mil.*) occupation.
оккупи́р|овать, ую *impf. and pf.* (*mil.*) to occupy.
окла́д, а *m.* salary.
оклеве|та́ть, щу́, ~щешь *pf. of* ▶ **клевета́ть**
окле́ива|ть, ю *impf. of* ▶ **окле́ить**
окле́|ить, ю, ишь *pf.* (*of* ▶ ~ивать) (+ *i.*) to cover (with); to paste over (with); **о. ко́мнату обо́ями** to paper a room.
оклик|а́ть, а́ю *impf. of* ▶ ~нуть
окли́к|нуть, ну, нешь *pf.* (*of* ▶ ~а́ть) to hail, call (to).
окн|о́, а́, *pl.* **~а, о́кон, ~ам** *nt.*
1 (*also comput.*) window; **диало́говое о.** (*comput.*) dialog box.
2 (*fig.*) (*отверстие*) gap, break.
око́в|ы, ~ *no sg.* fetters (*also fig.*).
о́коло *prep.* + *g. and adv.*
1 (*рядом, возле*) by; (*вблизи*) close (to), near; (*вокруг*) around, about.
2 (*приблизительно*) about; **о. полу́ночи** about midnight.
око́нн|ый *adj. of* ▶ **окно́; ~ая ра́ма** window frame; **~ое стекло́** windowpane.
оконча́ни|е, я *nt.* (*завершение*) completion, conclusion; (*конец*) end; **о. сро́ка** expiration; **по ~и университе́та** on graduating; (*gram.*) ending.
оконча́тельно *adv.* (*бесповоротно*) finally, definitively; (*совершенно*) completely.
оконча́тел|ьный (~ен, ~ьна) *adj.* (*бесповоротный*) final, definitive; (*совершенный*) complete.
око́нч|ить, у, ишь *pf.* (*of* ▶ **ока́нчивать**) to finish, end; **о. шко́лу** to leave school (*Br.*), to graduate from high school (*US*); **о. университе́т** to graduate.
око́нч|иться, ится *pf.* (*of* ▶ **ока́нчиваться**) to finish, end; to be over.
око́п, а *m.* (*mil.*) trench; entrenchment.
о́коро|к, ка, *pl.* **~ка́** *m.* ham; (*баранины, телятины*) leg.
окра́ин|а, ы *f.*
1 (*города*) outskirts; outlying districts; (*леса, деревни*) edge.
2 *pl.* (*страны*) border areas.
окра́|сить, шу, сишь *pf.* (*of* ▶ ~шивать) (*стену, крышу*) to paint; (*ткань, волосы*) to dye; (*жизнь*) to colour (*Br.*), color (*US*); **слегка́ о.** to tinge, tint.
окра́ск|а, и *f.*
1 (*действие*) painting; dyeing.
2 (*цвет*) colouring (*Br.*), coloring (*US*), coloration; **защи́тная о.** (*zool.*) protective coloration.
3 (*fig.*) tinge, tint; (*pol.*) slant.
окра́шива|ть, ю *impf. of* ▶ **окра́сить**
окре́п|нуть, ну, нешь, *past* **~, ~ла** *pf. of* ▶ **кре́пнуть**
окре|сти́ть, щу́, ~стишь *pf. of* ▶ **крести́ть 1**
окре́стност|ь, и *f.* (*usu. pl.*)
1 (*столицы, деревни*) environs.
2 (*окружающее пространство*) neighbourhood (*Br.*), neighborhood (*US*), vicinity.
о́крик, а *m.* shout, cry.
окрова́влен|ный (~, ~а) *adj.* bloodstained; bloody.
о́круг, а, *pl.* **~а́** *m.* region, district; circuit; **избира́тельный о.** electoral district.
окру́г|а, и *f.* (*coll.*) neighbourhood (*Br.*), neighborhood (*US*).
округл|и́ть, ю́, и́шь *pf.* (*of* ▶ ~я́ть) (*счёт, цифры*) to express in round numbers.
окру́гл|ый (~, ~а) *adj.* rounded; (*лицо*) round.
округл|я́ть, я́ю *impf. of* ▶ ~и́ть
окруж|а́ть, а́ю *impf. of* ▶ ~и́ть
окружа́|ющий *pres. part. act. of* ▶ ~ть *and adj.* surrounding; *as n.* **~ющее, ~ющего** *nt.* environment; **~ющие, ~ющих** the people around/surrounding one.
окруже́ни|е, я *nt.*
1 (*действие*) encirclement.
2 (*среда*) surroundings; environment; milieu; **в ~и** (+ *g.*) surrounded (by), in the midst (of); (*люди*) the people around/surrounding one.
окруж|и́ть, у́, и́шь *pf.* (*of* ▶ ~а́ть) to surround; to encircle; **о. кого́-н. забо́тами** to lavish attentions on s.o.
окружн|о́й *adj.*
1 *adj. of* ▶ **о́круг; о. суд** circuit court.
2 operating (situated) about a circle; **~а́я желе́зная доро́га** circle line.
окру́жност|ь, и *f.* circumference; (*замкнутая кривая*) circle.
О́ксфорд, а *m.* Oxford.
октя́бр|ь, я́ *m.* October (*fig.* = *Russian revolution of October 1917*).
октя́бр|ьский *adj. of* ▶ ~
окули́ст, а *m.* ophthalmic optician.
окуля́р, а *m.* eyepiece.
окун|а́ть(ся), а́ю(сь) *impf. of* ▶ ~у́ть(ся)
окун|у́ть, у́, ёшь *pf.* (*of* ▶ ~а́ть) to dip.
окун|у́ться, у́сь, ёшься *pf.* (*of* ▶ ~а́ться)
1 to dip (o.s.).
2 (*fig.*; **в** + *a.*) to plunge (into), become (utterly) absorbed (in), engrossed (in).
о́кун|ь, я, *pl.* **~и, ~е́й** *m.* (*zool.*) perch; **морско́й о.** redfish, North Atlantic rockfish.
окуп|а́ть(ся), а́ю(сь) *impf. of* ▶ ~и́ть(ся)
окуп|и́ть, лю́, ~ишь *pf.* (*of* ▶ ~а́ть) to compensate, repay, make up (for); **о. расхо́ды** to cover one's outlay.
окуп|и́ться, лю́сь, ~ишься *pf.* (*of* ▶ ~а́ться) to be compensated, be repaid; (*fig.*) to pay; to be justified, be requited, be rewarded;

затрáченные нáми усилия ~ились our efforts were rewarded.
окýр|ок, ка *m.* (*сигареты*) butt.
окýт|ать, аю *pf.* (*of* ▶ **~ывать**) (+ *i.*)
1 to wrap up (in).
2 (*fig.*) to shroud, cloak (in).
окýт|аться, аюсь *pf.* (*of* ▶ **~ываться**) (+ *i.*)
1 to wrap o.s. up (in).
2 (*fig.*) to shroud, cloak o.s. (in); **о. тáйной** to shroud o.s. in mystery.
окýтыва|ть(ся), ю(сь) *impf. of* ▶ **окýтать(ся)**
олáд|ья, ьи, *pl.* **~ьи, ~ий** *f.* fritter; **картóфельная о.** potato cake.
оледенé|ть, ю *pf. of* ▶ **леденéть**
оленин|а, ы *f.* venison.
олéн|ь, я *m.* deer; **благорóдный о.** stag, red deer; **сéверный о.** reindeer.
олúвк|а, и *f.* olive.
олúвков|ый *adj.*
1 olive; **~ое мáсло** olive oil.
2 (*цвет*) olive-green.
олигáрх, а *m.* oligarch.
олимпиáд|а, ы *f.*
1 (**О.**) (*олимпийские игры*) Olympics.
2 (*соревнования*) Olympiad.
олимпúйски|й *adj.* Olympic; **О~е игры** Olympic Games, Olympics.
олúф|а, ы *f.* drying oil.
олицетворéни|е, я *nt.* personification.
олицетвор|úть, ю́, úшь *pf.* (*of* ▶ **~я́ть**) to personify.
олицетвор|я́ть, я́ю *impf. of* ▶ **~úть**
óлов|о, а *nt.* tin.
оловя́нн|ый *adj.* tin; **~ая фóльга** tin foil.
Óльстер, а *m.* Ulster.
ольх|á, ú, *pl.* **~́и** *f.* alder (tree).
омáр, а *m.* lobster.
омерзúтел|ьный (~ен, ~ьна) *adj.* loathsome, disgusting.
омлéт, а *m.* omelette (*Br.*), omelet (*US*).
ОМÓН *m. indecl.* (*abbr. of* **отря́д милúции осóбого назначéния**) special forces unit; riot squad.
омóнов|ец, ца *m.* member of the special force.
ОМП (*abbr. of* **орýжие мáссового поражéния**) WMD (*weapons of mass destruction*).
омрач|áть(ся), áю(сь) *impf. of* ▶ **~úть(ся)**
омрач|úть, ý, úшь *pf.* (*of* ▶ **~áть**) to darken, cloud.
омрач|úться, ýсь, úшься *pf.* (*of* ▶ **~áться**) to darken, become clouded (*also fig.*).
óмут, а *m.*
1 (*водоворот*) whirlpool; (*fig.*) maelstrom.
2 (*глубокое место*) deep place (*in river or lake*).
он, егó, емý, им, о нём *pron.* he.
онá, её, ей, ей (éю), о ней *pron.* she.
онанúзм, а *m.* masturbation.
ондáтр|а, ы *f.* muskrat, musquash.
онемé|ть, ю *pf. of* ▶ **немéть**
онú, их, им, úми, о них *pron.* they.
óникс, а *m.* (*min.*) onyx.
онкóлог, а *m.* oncologist.
онкологúческий *adj.* oncological.
онколóги|я, и *f.* (*med.*) oncology.
онлáйновый *adj.* (*comput.*) online.
онó, егó, емý, им, о нём *pron.*
1 it.
2 (*это*) this, that; **о. и вúдно** that is evident.
3 *as emph. particle* **вот о. что!** oh, I see!
ООН *f. indecl.* (*abbr. of* **Организáция Объединённых Нáций**) UN (*United Nations Organization*).
опадá|ть, ет *impf. of* ▶ **опáсть**
опáздыва|ть, ю *impf.*
1 *impf. of* ▶ **опоздáть.**
2 (*impf. only*) (*coll.*) (*о часах*) to be slow.
опáл, а *m.* opal.
опáлива|ть, ю *impf. of* ▶ **опалúть**
опал|úть, ю́, úшь *pf.* (*of* ▶ **~́ивать**) to singe.
опасá|ться, юсь *impf.*
1 (+ *g.*) (*бояться*) to fear, be afraid (of).
2 (+ *g. or inf.*) (*избегать*) to beware (of); to avoid, keep off.
опасéни|е, я *nt.* fear; apprehension.
опáсност|ь, и *f.* danger; peril; **вне ~и** out of danger.
опáс|ный (~ен, ~на) *adj.* dangerous, perilous.
опá|сть, дёт *pf.* (*of* ▶ **~дáть**)
1 (*о листьях*) to fall (off).
2 (*об опухоли*) to go down; (*о суфле*) to sink.
ОПÉК *f. indecl.* OPEC (*abbr. of* Organization of Petroleum Exporting Countries — *Организáция стран – экспортёров нéфти*).
опéк|а, и *f.* guardianship (*also fig.*); (*над имуществом*) trusteeship; **взять под ~у** to take into one's care; (*fig.*) to take charge (of).
опекá|ть, ю *impf.*
1 (*сирот*) to be guardian (to).
2 (*fig.*) (*младших*) to take care (of).
опекýн, á *m.* (*leg.*) guardian; (*над имуществом*) trustee.
опекýн|ша, ши *f.* (*coll.*) *of* ▶ **~**
óпер|а, ы *f.* opera; «**мы́льная о.**» soap (opera).
оперативник, а *m.* detective.
оператúв|ный *adj.*
1 **(~ен, ~на)** (*руководство*) efficient.
2 (*штаб, работа*) executive.
3 (*med.*) surgical.
4 (*comput.*): **~ная пáмять** random-access memory.
оперáтор, а *m.*
1 (*оборудования*) operator.
2 (*кинооператор*) cameraman.
3 (*comput.*) computer operator.
опера|циóнный *adj. of* ▶ **~́ция; ~циóнная системá** (*comput.*) operating system; **о. стол** operating table; **о. зал (на бúрже)** (*fin.*) trading floor; *as n.* **~циóнная, ~циóнной** *f.* operating theatre (*Br.*), operating room (*US*).
оперáци|я, и *f.* (*med., mil., etc.*) operation; **перенестú ~ю** to have an operation; to be operated (upon); **сдéлать ~ю** to perform an

operation.

опере|ди́ть, жу́, ди́шь *pf.* (*of* ▸ **~жа́ть**)
[1] (*в беге, в развитии*) to outstrip, leave behind.
[2] (*успеть раньше*) to forestall.

опережа́|ть, ю *impf. of* ▸ **опереди́ть**

опере́ни|е, я *nt.* plumage.

опере́тт|а, ы *f.* musical comedy, operetta.

опере́ться, обопру́сь, обопрёшься, *past* **опёрся, оперла́сь** *pf.* (*of* ▸ **опира́ться**) (**на** + *a.*; **о** + *a.*)
[1] to lean (on; against); **о. о подоко́нник** to lean against the window sill.
[2] (*fig.*) to rely on; to depend on.

опери́р|овать, ую *impf. and pf.*
[1] (*med.*) to operate (upon).
[2] (*mil.*) to operate, act.
[3] (+ *i.*) (*fin.*) to deal (in); (*fig.*) to use, handle; **о. недоста́точными да́нными** to operate with inadequate data.

опеча́т|ка, ки *f.* misprint; **спи́сок ~ок** (list of) errata.

опира́|ться, юсь *impf. of* ▸ **опере́ться**

описа́ни|е, я *nt.* description; account; **э́то не поддаётся ~ю** it is beyond description.

опи|са́ть, шу́, ~́шешь *pf.* (*of* ▸ **~́сывать**)
[1] to describe.
[2] (*сделать опись*) to list, inventory; **о. иму́щество** (*leg.*) to distrain property.

опи́ск|а, и *f.* slip of the pen.

опи́сыва|ть, ю *impf. of* ▸ **описа́ть**

о́пис|ь, и *f.* list; inventory; **о. иму́щества** (*leg.*) distraint.

о́пиум, а *m.* opium.

опла́|кать, чу, чешь *pf.* (*of* ▸ **~кивать**) to mourn (over); to bewail, bemoan.

опла́кива|ть, ю *impf. of* ▸ **опла́кать**

опла́т|а, ы *f.* pay, payment.

опла|ти́ть, чу́, ~́тишь *pf.* to pay (for); **о. счёт** to settle the account, pay the bill; **о. убы́тки** to pay damages.

опла́чива|ть, ю *impf. of* ▸ **оплати́ть**

опла|чу́, ~́тишь *see* ▸ **~ти́ть**

опла́|чу, чешь *see* ▸ **~кать**

оплеу́х|а, и *f.* (*coll.*) slap in the face.

оплодотворе́ни|е, я *nt.* fertilization.

оплодотвор|и́ть, ю́, и́шь *pf.* (*of* ▸ **~я́ть**) to fertilize.

оплодотвор|я́ть, я́ю *impf. of* ▸ **~и́ть**

опломбир|ова́ть, у́ю *pf. of* ▸ **пломбирова́ть 1**

опло́шност|ь, и *f.* blunder.

опове|сти́ть, щу́, сти́шь *pf.* (*of* ▸ **~ща́ть**) to notify, inform.

оповеща́|ть, ю *impf. of* ▸ **оповести́ть**

опозда́ни|е, я *nt.* lateness; delay; **без ~я** on time; **с ~ем на де́сять мину́т** ten minutes late.

опозда́|ть, ю *pf.* (*of* ▸ **опа́здывать 1**) to be late; **о. на ле́кцию** to be late for the lecture; **о. на полчаса́** to be half an hour late.

опозна|ва́ть, ю́, ёшь *impf. of* ▸ **~́ть**

опозна́ни|е, я *nt.* (*leg.*) identification.

опозна́|ть, ю *pf.* (*of* ▸ **~ва́ть**) to identify.

опозо́р|ить(ся), ю(сь), ишь(ся) *pf. of* ▸ **позо́рить(ся)**

ополáскива|ть, ю *impf. of* ▸ **ополосну́ть**

о́полз|ень, ня *m.* landslide, landslip.

ополосн|у́ть, у́, ёшь *pf.* (*of* ▸ **ополáскивать**) to rinse.

ополче́н|ец, ца *m.* militiaman; home guard.

ополче́ни|е, я *nt.*
[1] militia; home guard.
[2] (*collect.*; *hist.*) irregulars; levies.

опо́мн|иться, юсь, ишься *pf.* (*прийти в сознание*) to come round; (*одуматься*) to come to one's senses.

опо́р|а, ы *f.* support (*also fig.*); (*моста*) pier.

опорожн|и́ть, ю́, и́шь *pf.* (*of* ▸ **опорожня́ть**) to empty.

опорожня́|ть, ю *impf. of* ▸ **опорожни́ть**

опо́ссум, а *m.* (*zool.*) opossum.

оппози́ци|я, и *f.* opposition.

оппоне́нт, а *m.* opponent.

опра́в|а, ы *f.* frame; (*очков*) frames.

оправда́ни|е, я *nt.*
[1] justification.
[2] (*извинение*) excuse.
[3] (*leg.*) acquittal, discharge.

оправда́тельный *adj.*: **о. пригово́р** verdict of 'not guilty'.

оправд|а́ть, а́ю *pf.* (*of* ▸ **~́ывать**)
[1] (*показать себя достойным*) to justify, warrant; **о. ожида́ния** to come up to expectations.
[2] (*извинить*) to excuse.
[3] (*leg.*) to acquit, discharge.

оправд|а́ться, а́юсь *pf.* (*of* ▸ **~́ываться 1**)
[1] to justify o.s.
[2] to be justified; **на́ши опасе́ния ~да́лись** our fears have been confirmed.

опра́вдыва|ть, ю *impf. of* ▸ **оправда́ть; о. незна́нием** (*leg.*) to plead ignorance.

опра́вдыва|ться, юсь *impf.*
[1] *impf. of* ▸ **оправда́ться.**
[2] to try to justify *or* vindicate o.s.

опра́шива|ть, ю *impf. of* ▸ **опроси́ть**

определе́ни|е, я *nt.* (*понятия*) definition; (*chem., phys., etc.*) determination.

определён|ный (~ен, ~на) *adj.*
[1] (*точно установленный*) definite; fixed.
[2] (*некоторый*) certain; **в ~ных слу́чаях** in certain cases.

определ|и́ть, ю́, и́шь *pf.* (*of* ▸ **~я́ть**) (*понятие*) to define; (*установить*) to determine; (*назначить*) to fix, appoint.

определ|и́ться, ю́сь, и́шься *pf.* (*of* ▸ **~я́ться**) to be formed; to take shape; to be determined.

определ|я́ть(ся), я́ю(сь) *impf. of* ▸ **~и́ть(ся)**

опро́б|овать, ую *pf.* to test.

опроверг|а́ть, а́ю *impf. of* ▸ **~́нуть**

опрове́рг|нуть, ну, нешь, *past* **~** *and* **~нул, ~ла** *pf.* (*of* ▸ **~а́ть**) to refute, disprove.

опроверже́ни|е, я *nt.* refutation; disproof; denial.

опроки́дыва|ть(ся), ю(сь) *impf. of*

▸ **опроки́нуть(ся)**

опроки́|нуть, ну, нешь *pf.* (*of* ▸ **~дывать**) (*чашку*) to knock over; (*лодку*) to overturn.

опроки́|нуться, нусь, нешься *pf.* (*of* ▸ **~дываться**) (*о стакане*) to fall over, topple over; (*о лодке*) to capsize.

опроме́тчив|ый (~, ~а) *adj.* precipitate, hasty.

опро́с, а *m.* (*свидетелей*) questioning; **о. обще́ственного мне́ния** opinion poll.

опро|си́ть, шу́, ~́сишь *pf.* (*of* ▸ **опра́шивать**) (*свидетелей*) to question; (*общественное мнение*) to canvass, survey.

опроти́ве|ть, ю *pf.* to become loathsome, become repulsive.

опры́ск|ать, ю *pf.* (*of* ▸ **~ивать**) (+ *i.*) to sprinkle (with); to spray (with).

опры́ск|аться, аюсь *pf.* (*of* ▸ **~иваться**) (+ *i.*) to sprinkle o.s. (with); to spray o.s. (with).

опры́скива|ть(ся), ю(сь) *impf. of* ▸ **опры́скать(ся)**

опря́т|ный (~ен, ~на) *adj.* neat, tidy.

о́птик|а, и *f.*
1 (*раздел физики*) optics.
2 (*collect.*) optical instruments.

оптима́л|ьный (~ен, ~на) *adj.* optimum, optimal.

оптими́зм, а *m.* optimism.

оптими́ст, а *m.* optimist.

оптимисти́ч|ный (~ен, ~на) *adj.* optimistic.

опти́ческ|ий *adj.* optic, optical; **~ое волокно́** optical fibre (*Br.*), fiber (*US*); **о. обма́н** optical illusion.

оптови́к, а́ *m.* wholesaler.

опто́вый *adj.* wholesale.

о́птом *adv.* wholesale; **о. и в ро́зницу** wholesale and retail.

опублик|ова́ть, у́ю *pf.* (*of* ▸ **публикова́ть** *and* ▸ **~о́вывать**) to publish; **о. зако́н** to promulgate a law.

опублико́выва|ть, ю *impf. of* ▸ **опубликова́ть**

опуска́|ть(ся), ю(сь) *impf. of* ▸ **опусти́ть(ся)**

опусте́|ть, ет *pf. of* ▸ **пусте́ть**

опу|сти́ть, щу́, ~́стишь *pf.* (*of* ▸ **~ска́ть**)
1 (*шторы*) to lower; to let down; **о. глаза́** to look down; **о. ру́ки** (*fig.*) to lose heart.
2 (*воротник*) to turn down.

опу|сти́ться, щу́сь, ~́стишься *pf.* (*of* ▸ **~ска́ться**)
1 to lower o.s.; **о. в кре́сло** to sink into a chair; **о. на коле́ни** to go down on one's knees.
2 (*о солнце*) to sink, go down.
3 (*fig.*) (*внешне, морально*) to let o.s. go; to go to pieces.

опустош|а́ть, а́ю *impf. of* ▸ **~и́ть**

опустош|и́ть, у́, и́шь *pf.* (*of* ▸ **~а́ть**) to devastate, lay waste, ravage.

опу́т|ать, аю *pf.* (*of* ▸ **~ывать**) to enmesh, entangle (*also fig.*); (*fig.*) to ensnare.

опу́тыва|ть, ю *impf. of* ▸ **опу́тать**

опух|а́ть, а́ю *impf. of* ▸ **~́нуть**

опу́х|нуть, ну, нешь, *past* **~, ~ла** *pf.* (*of* ▸ **~а́ть**) to swell (up).

о́пухол|ь, и *f.* swelling; (*med.*) tumour (*Br.*), tumor (*US*); **~ мо́зга** brain tumour (*Br.*), tumor (*US*)

о́пыт, а *m.*
1 experience; **на ~е, по ~у** by experience.
2 (*эксперимент*) experiment; test, trial; (*попытка*) attempt.

о́пытност|ь, и *f.* experience.

о́пыт|ный *adj.*
1 **(~ен, ~на)** (*человек*) experienced.
2 (*экспериментальный*) experimental; **узна́ть ~ным путём** to learn by means of experiment.

опьяне́ни|е, я *nt.* intoxication.

опьяне́|ть, ю *pf. of* ▸ **пьяне́ть**

опя́ть *adv.* again.

ора́кул, а *m.* oracle.

орангута́н(г), а *m.* orang-utan.

ора́нжевый *adj.* orange (*colour*).

оранжере́|я, и *f.* hothouse, greenhouse, conservatory.

ора́тор, а *m.* orator, (public) speaker.

ор|а́ть, у́, ёшь *impf.* (*coll.*) to bawl, yell.

орби́т|а, ы *f.* (*astron. and fig.*) orbit; **вы́вести на ~у** to put into orbit.

орга́зм, а *m.* orgasm, climax.

о́рган, а *m.* (*biol., pol., etc.*) organ; **~ы вла́сти** organs of government; **половы́е ~ы** genitals.

орга́н, а *m.* (*mus.*) organ.

организа́тор, а *m.* organizer.

организа́ци|я, и *f.* organization; **О. Объединённых На́ций** United Nations Organization.

органи́зм, а *m.* organism.

организо́ван|ный (~, ~а) *p.p.p. of* ▸ **организова́ть** *and adj.* (**~, ~на**) organized; **~ная престу́пность** organized crime.

организ|ова́ть, у́ю *impf. and pf.* to organize.

организо́выва|ть, ю *impf. of* ▸ **организова́ть**

органи́ст, а *m.* organist.

органи́ч|ный (~ен, ~на) *adj.* organic.

о́рги|я, и *f.* orgy.

оргте́хник|а, и *f.* (*abbr. of* **организацио́нная те́хника**) office equipment.

о́рден[1], а, *pl.* **~а́, ~о́в** *m.* (*знак отличия*) order; decoration.

о́рден[2], а, *pl.* **~ы, ~ов** *m.* (*организация*) order; **иезуи́тский о.** Society of Jesus.

о́рдер, а, *pl.* **~а́, ~о́в** *m.* order, warrant; (*leg.*) writ; **о. на о́быск** search warrant.

ор|ёл, ла́ *m.* eagle; **о. или ре́шка?** heads or tails?

орео́л, а *m.* halo, aureole.

оре́х, а *m.*
1 (*плод*) nut; **гре́цкий о.** walnut; **коко́совый о.** coconut; **лесно́й о.** hazelnut.
2 (*дерево*) nut tree.
3 (*древесина*) walnut.

оригина́льност|ь, и *f.* originality.

оригина́л|ьный (~ен, ~ьна) *adj.* original.

ориента́ци|я, и *f.* (**на** + *a.*) orientation (towards).

ориенти́р, а *m.* reference point; guiding line; **(есте́ственный) о.** landmark.

ориенти́р|овать, ую *impf. and pf.* (*pf. also* ▸ **с~**) to orient, orientate.

ориенти́р|оваться, уюсь *impf. and pf.* (*pf. also* ▸ **с~**) to orient o.s.; to find one's bearings (*also fig.*).

ориентиро́вочно *adv.* tentatively; approximately.

орке́стр, а *m.* orchestra; (*духовой, джазовый*) band.

оркестро́вк|а, и *f.* orchestration.

оркестро́вый *adj.* orchestral.

орна́мент, а *m.* ornament.

орнито́лог, а *m.* ornithologist.

орнитоло́ги|я, и *f.* ornithology.

ороше́ни|е, я *nt.* irrigation; **поля́ ~я** sewage farm (*Br.*), sewage plant (*US*)

ортодокса́л|ьный (~ен, ~ьна) *adj.* orthodox.

ортопе́д, а *m.* orthopaedist (*Br.*), orthopedist (*US*).

ортопеди́ческий *adj.* orthopaedic (*Br.*), orthopedic (*US*).

ору́ди|е, я *nt.*
1 instrument; implement; tool (*also fig.*).
2 (*артиллерийское*) gun.

оруженос|ец, ца *m.* armour-bearer, sword-bearer; (*fig.*) henchman.

О

ору́жи|е, я *nt.* weapon; (*collect.*) arms, weapons.

орфогра́фи|я, и *f.* orthography, spelling.

орхиде́|я, и *f.* (*bot.*) orchid.

ос|а́, ы́, *pl.* **~́ы** *f.* wasp.

оса́д|а, ы *f.* siege; **снять ~у** to raise a siege.

оса|ди́ть, жу́, ди́шь *pf.* (*of* ▸ **~жда́ть**) to besiege, lay siege to; to beleaguer; **о. про́сьбами** to bombard with requests.

оса́д|ок, ка *m.*
1 *pl.* (*атмосферные*) precipitation.
2 (*частицы*) sediment, deposit.

осажда́|ть, ю *impf. of* ▸ **осади́ть**

оса́нк|а, и *f.* carriage, bearing.

осва́ива|ть(ся), ю(сь) *impf. of* ▸ **осво́ить(ся)**

осве́дом|ить, лю, ишь *pf.* (*of* ▸ **~ля́ть**) to inform.

осве́дом|иться, люсь, ишься *pf.* (*of* ▸ **~ля́ться**) (**о** + *p.*) to inquire (about).

осведом|ля́ть(ся), ля́ю(сь) *impf. of* ▸ **осве́домить(ся)**

освеж|а́ть, а́ю *impf. of* ▸ **~и́ть**

освежи́тел|ьный (~ен, ~ьна) *adj.* refreshing.

освеж|и́ть, у́, и́шь *pf.* (*of* ▸ **~а́ть**) to refresh, revive.

освети́тел|ь, я *m.* lighting technician.

освети́тельный *adj.* lighting, illuminating; **о. прибо́р** light.

осве|ти́ть, щу́, ти́шь *pf.* (*of* ▸ **~ща́ть**) to light up; to illuminate; (*fig.*) to throw light on; (*в прессе*) to cover, report.

осве|ти́ться, щу́сь, ти́шься *pf.* (*of* ▸ **~ща́ться**) to light up; to brighten.

освеща́|ть(ся), ю(сь) *impf. of* ▸ **освети́ть(ся)**

освеще́ни|е, я *nt.* light, lighting, illumination; (*в прессе*) coverage; **электри́ческое о.** electric light.

осве|щённый *p.p.p. of* ▸ **~ти́ть; о. луно́й** moonlit.

освободи́тел|ь, я *m.* liberator.

освобо|ди́ть, жу́, ди́шь *pf.* (*of* ▸ **~жда́ть**)
1 (*город, страну, человека*) to free, liberate; (*заключённого; животное*) to release, set free.
2 (*от должности*) to dismiss.
3 (*квартиру*) to vacate; (*место; полку от книг*) to clear, empty.

освобо|ди́ться, жу́сь, ди́шься *pf.* (*of* ▸ **~жда́ться**)
1 (**от** + *g.*) to free o.s. (of, from); to become free.
2 *pass. of* ▸ **~ди́ть**

освобожда́|ть(ся), ю(сь) *impf. of* ▸ **освободи́ть(ся)**

освобожде́ни|е, я *nt.* (*города*) liberation; (*заключённого*) release.

освобо|ждённый *p.p.p. of* ▸ **~ди́ть; о. от нало́га** tax-free, exempt from tax.

осво́|ить, ю, ишь *pf.* (*of* ▸ **осва́ивать**) to assimilate, master; to cope (with); to become familiar (with).

осво́|иться, юсь, ишься *pf.* (*of* ▸ **осва́иваться**)
1 (**с** + *i.*) to familiarize o.s. (with).
2 to feel at home; **о. в но́вой среде́** to get the feel of new surroundings.

освя|ти́ть, щу́, ти́шь *pf.* (*of* ▸ **~ща́ть**) (*eccl.*) to bless.

освяща́|ть, ю *impf. of* ▸ **освяти́ть**

оседа́|ть, ю *impf. of* ▸ **осе́сть**

ос|ёл, ла́ *m.* donkey; ass (*also fig.*).

осе́нний *adj. of* ▸ **о́сень;** autumnal.

о́сен|ь, и *f.* autumn.

о́сенью *adv.* in autumn.

ос|е́сть, я́ду, я́дешь, *past* **~е́л, ~е́ла** *pf.* (*of* ▸ **~еда́ть**)
1 (*о здании*) to subside; (*о пыли, осадке*) to settle.
2 (*о людях*) to settle.

осети́н, а, *g. pl.* **о.** *m.* Ossetian, Ossete.

осети́н|ка, ки *f. of* ▸ **~**

осети́нский *adj.* Ossetian.

осётр, а́ *m.* sturgeon.

осетри́н|а, ы *f.* (flesh of) sturgeon.

осе́чк|а, и *f.* misfire; **дать ~у** to misfire (*also fig.*).

оси́н|а, ы *f.* aspen.

оска́лива|ть(ся), ю(сь) *impf. of* ▸ **оска́лить(ся)**

оска́л|ить, ю, ишь *pf.* (*of* ▸ **~ивать**): **о. зу́бы** to bare one's teeth.

оска́л|иться, юсь, ишься *pf.* (*of* ▸ **~иваться**) to bare one's teeth.

оскверн|и́ть, ю́, и́шь *pf.* (*of* ▸ **~я́ть**) to defile; to profane.

оскверн|я́ть, я́ю *impf. of* ▸ **~и́ть**

оско́л|ок, ка *m.* splinter; fragment.

оскорби́тел|ьный (~ен, ~ьна) *adj.* insulting, abusive.

оскорб|и́ть, лю́, и́шь *pf.* (*of* ▸**~ля́ть**) to insult, offend.

оскорбле́ни|е, я *nt.* insult.

оскорбля́|ть, ю *impf. of* ▸**оскорби́ть**

ослабева́|ть, ю *impf. of* ▸**ослабе́ть**

ослабе́|ть, ю *pf.* (*of* ▸**слабе́ть** *and* ▸**~ва́ть**) (*о человеке, стране, решительности*) to weaken, grow weaker, become weak; (*о внимании, канате, напряжении*) to slacken; (*о шуме, ветре*) to abate.

осла́б|ить, лю, ишь *pf.* (*of* ▸**~ля́ть**)
1 to weaken.
2 (*сделать менее натянутым*) to slacken, relax; to loosen; **о. внима́ние** to relax one's attention; **о. по́яс** to loosen a belt.

ослабля́|ть, ю *impf. of* ▸**осла́бить**

осла́б|нуть, ну, нешь, *past* **~, ~ла** *pf.* = **~е́ть**

ослепи́тел|ьный (~ен, ~ьна) *adj.* blinding, dazzling.

ослеп|и́ть, лю́, и́шь *pf.* (*of* ▸**~ля́ть**) to blind, dazzle (*also fig.*).

ослепле́ни|е, я *nt.*
1 blinding, dazzling.
2 (*fig.*) blindness.

ослепля́|ть, ю *impf. of* ▸**ослепи́ть**

осле́п|нуть, ну, нешь, *past* **~, ~ла** *pf. of* ▸**сле́пнуть**

О́сло *m. indecl.* Oslo.

осложне́ни|е, я *nt.* complication.

осложн|и́ть, ю́, и́шь *pf.* (*of* ▸**~я́ть**) to complicate.

осложн|и́ться, и́тся *pf.* (*of* ▸**~я́ться**) to become complicated; (*о болезни*) to develop complications.

осложн|я́ть(ся), я́ю, я́ет(ся) *impf. of* ▸**~и́ть(ся)**

ослу́ш|аться, аюсь *pf.* (*of* ▸**~иваться**) to disobey.

ослу́шива|ться, юсь *impf. of* ▸**ослу́шаться**

ослы́ш|аться, усь, ишься *pf.* to mishear.

осма́трива|ть(ся), ю(сь) *impf. of* ▸**осмотре́ть(ся)**

осме́ива|ть, ю *impf. of* ▸**осмея́ть**

осме́лива|ться, юсь *impf. of* ▸**осме́литься**

осме́л|иться, юсь, ишься *pf.* (*of* ▸**~иваться**) (+ *inf.*) to dare; to take the liberty (of).

осме|я́ть, ю́, ёшь *pf.* (*of* ▸**~́ивать**) to mock, ridicule.

осмо́тр, а *m.* (*багажа*) examination, inspection; (*школы*) inspection; **медици́нский о.** medical (examination); check-up.

осмотр|е́ть, ю́, ~́ишь *pf.* (*of* ▸**осма́тривать**) (*багаж, больного*) to examine; (*школу*) to inspect; (*выставку*) to look round, look over.

осмотр|е́ться, ю́сь, ~́ишься *pf.* (*of* ▸**осма́триваться**)
1 to look round.
2 (*fig.*) to take one's bearings, see how the land lies.

осмотри́тел|ьный (~ен, ~ьна) *adj.* circumspect, cautious.

осмы́слен|ный (~, ~а) *p.p.p. of* ▸**осмы́слить** *and adj.* **(~, ~на)** intelligent, sensible.

осмы́слива|ть, ю *impf. of* ▸**осмы́слить**

осмы́сл|ить, ю, ишь *pf.* (*of* ▸**~ивать** *and* ▸**~я́ть**) (*истолковать*) to interpret; (*понять*) to comprehend.

осмысл|я́ть, я́ю *impf.* = **~́ивать**

осна|сти́ть, щу́, сти́шь *pf.* (*of* ▸**~ща́ть**) (*naut.*) to rig; (*fig.*) to fit out, equip.

оснаща́|ть, ю *impf. of* ▸**оснасти́ть**

оснаще́ни|е, я *nt.*
1 (*действие*) rigging; fitting out.
2 (*оборудование*) equipment.

осно́в|а, ы *f.* (*здания*) foundation; (*fig.*) basis, foundation; *pl.* fundamentals; **лежа́ть в ~е** (+ *g.*) to be the basis (of).

основа́ни|е, я *nt.*
1 (*действие*) founding, foundation.
2 (*chem., math., etc.*) base; (*здания*) foundation; **о. горы́** foot of a mountain; **разру́шить до ~я** to raze to the ground.
3 (*fig.*) foundation, basis; ground, reason; **на како́м ~и вы э́то утвержда́ете?** on what grounds do you assert this?; **име́ть о. предполага́ть** to have reason to suppose.

основа́тел|ь, я *m.* founder.

основа́тель|ница, ницы *f. of* ▸**~**

основа́тел|ьный (~ен, ~ьна) *adj.*
1 (*совет, причина*) well-founded; just.
2 (*постройка*) solid, sound; (*человек*) solid; (*осмотр*) thorough; **~ьные до́воды** sound arguments.

осн|ова́ть, ую́, уёшь *pf.* (*of* ▸**~о́вывать**)
1 (*учредить*) to found.
2 **(на** + *p.*) to base (on).

основн|о́й *adj.* (*причина, цель*) main; (*принцип*) fundamental, basic; **~а́я мысль** keynote; **~ы́е цвета́** primary colours; **в ~о́м** on the whole; basically.

основополо́жник, а *m.* founder, initiator.

осно́выва|ть, ю *impf. of* ▸**основа́ть**

осно́выва|ться, юсь *impf.* **(на** + *p.*) to base o.s. (on); to be based, founded (on).

осо́б|а, ы *f.* person, individual, personage; **ва́жная о.** (*iron.*) bigwig.

осо́бенно *adv.* especially; particularly; unusually; **не о.** not very, not particularly.

осо́бенност|ь, и *f.* peculiarity; **в ~и** especially, in particular, (more) particularly.

осо́бенн|ый *adj.* (e)special, particular, peculiar; **ничего́ ~ого** nothing in particular; nothing much.

особня́к, а́ *m.* private residence; mansion, manor house.

осо́б|ый *adj.* special; particular; peculiar; **удели́ть ~ое внима́ние** (+ *d.*) to give special attention (to).

осозна|ва́ть, ю́, ёшь *impf. of* ▸**~́ть**

осо́знанный *adj.* deliberate; conscious.

осозна́|ть, ю *pf.* (*of* ▸**~ва́ть**) to realize.

осо́к|а, и *f.* (*bot.*) sedge.

óсп|а, ы *f.* smallpox; **ве́тряная о.** chicken pox.

оспа́рива|ть, ю *impf.*
1 *impf. of* ▶ **оспо́рить.**
2 (*impf. only*) to contend (for).

оспо́р|ить, ю, ишь *pf.* (*of* ▶ **оспа́ривать 1**) to dispute, question; **о. завеща́ние** to dispute a will.

оста|ва́ться, ю́сь, ёшься *impf. of* ▶ **оста́ться**

оста́в|ить, лю, ишь *pf.* (*of* ▶ **~ля́ть**)
1 to leave; (*покинуть*) to abandon; (*надежду*) to give up; (*перестать, бросить*) to stop, give up; **о. в поко́е** to leave alone, let alone; **о. госте́й ночева́ть/обе́дать** to ask guests to stay the night/stay to dinner.
2 (*сохранить*) to reserve; to keep; **о. за собо́й пра́во** to reserve the right.

оставля́|ть, ю *impf. of* ▶ **оста́вить; ~ет жела́ть лу́чшего** it leaves much to be desired.

остальн|о́й *adj.* the rest of; **в ~о́м** in other respects; *as n.* **~ы́е** *pl.* the others; **~о́е** *nt.* the rest; **всё ~о́е** everything else.

остана́влива|ть(ся), ю(сь) *impf. of* ▶ **останови́ть(ся)**

оста́нк|и, ов *no sg.* remains.

останов|и́ть, лю́, ~ишь *pf.* (*of* ▶ **остана́вливать**)
1 to stop.
2 (*сдержать*) to stop short, restrain.
3 (**на** + *p.*) (*направить*) to direct (to), concentrate (on); **о. взгляд** to rest one's gaze (on).

останов|и́ться, лю́сь, ~ишься *pf.* (*of* ▶ **остана́вливаться**)
1 to stop; to come to a stop, come to a halt.
2 (*переночевать*) to stay, put up, (*coll.*) stop; **о. у знако́мых** to stay with friends.
3 (**на** + *p.*) (*fig.*) (*в речи, докладе*) to dwell (on); (*о взгляде*) to settle (on), rest (on).

остано́вк|а, и *f.*
1 (*в пути, работе*) stop; (*задержка*) stoppage.
2 (*автобусная*) stop; **коне́чная о.** terminus; **мне на́до прое́хать ещё одну́ ~у** I have to go one stop further.

оста́т|ок, ка *m.*
1 remainder; rest; (*ткани*) remnant; *pl.* remains; (*еды*) leftovers.
2 (*fin., comm.*) rest, balance.

оста́|ться, нусь, нешься *pf.* (*of* ▶ **~ва́ться**) to remain; to stay; to be left (over); **о. в живы́х** to survive, come through; **о. на́ ночь** to stay the night; **от обе́да ничего́ не ~лось** there is nothing left over from dinner; (*impers.*): **~ётся, ~лось** (+ *d.*) it remains (remained), it is (was) necessary; **~лось то́лько заплати́ть** it remained only to pay.

остекл|и́ть, ю́, и́шь *pf.* (*of* ▶ **~я́ть**) to glaze.

остекл|я́ть, я́ю *impf. of* ▶ **~и́ть**

остерега́|ться, юсь *impf.* (*of* ▶ **остере́чься**) (+ *g. or inf.*) to beware (of); to be careful (of); **~йтесь соба́ки!** beware of the dog!

остере́|чься, гу́сь, жёшься, гу́тся, *past* **~гся, ~гла́сь** *pf. of* ▶ **~га́ться**

óстов, а *m.* frame, framework (*also fig.*).

осторо́жно *adv.* carefully; cautiously; **о.!** look out!

осторо́жност|ь, и *f.* care; caution.

осторо́ж|ный (~ен, ~на) *adj.* careful; cautious; **бу́дьте ~ны!** take care!

остри|ё, я́ *nt.*
1 (*иголки, штыка*) point.
2 (*ножа, бритвы*) (cutting) edge.

остр|и́ть, ю́, и́шь *impf.* (*of* ▶ **с~**) (*говорить остроты*) to be witty; to make witticisms, crack jokes.

остри́|чь, гу́, жёшь, гу́т, *past* **~г, ~гла** *pf. of* ▶ **стричь 1, 2**

óстров, а, *pl.* **~а́** *m.* island; isle.

островитя́н|ин, ина, *pl.* **~е, ~** *m.* islander.

островитя́н|ка, ки *f. of* ▶ **~ин**

остроконе́ч|ный (~ен, ~на) *adj.* pointed.

остро́т|а, ы *f.* witticism, joke; **пло́ская о.** stupid joke; **то́нкая о.** subtle crack.

острот|а́, ы́ *f.* (*ножа, ума*) sharpness; (*зрения, слуха*) keenness; (*ситуации; боли*) acuteness; (*запаха*) pungency; (*чувства*) poignancy.

остроу́ми|е, я *nt.*
1 wit; wittiness.
2 (*изобретательность*) ingenuity.

остроу́м|ный (~ен, ~на) *adj.*
1 witty.
2 (*изобретательный*) ingenious.

óстр|ый (остёр *and* **~, ~а́, ~о** (*in fig. sense* **~о́**), **~ы** (*in fig. sense* **~ы́**)) *adj.* (*нож, ум*) sharp; (*нос*) pointed (*also fig.*); (*ситуация, боль*) acute; (*зрение, слух*) keen; **~ое зре́ние** keen eyesight; **о. интере́с** (**к** + *d.*) keen interest (in); **о. у́гол** (*math.*) acute angle.

остря́к, а́ *m.* wit.

осту|ди́ть, жу́, ~дишь *pf.* (*of* ▶ **~жа́ть**) to cool.

остужа́|ть, ю *impf. of* ▶ **остуди́ть**

оступ|а́ться, а́юсь *impf. of* ▶ **~и́ться**

оступ|и́ться, лю́сь, ~ишься *pf.* (*of* ▶ **~а́ться**) to stumble.

остыва́|ть, ю *impf. of* ▶ **осты́ть**

осты́|ть, ну, нешь *pf.* (*of* ▶ **~ва́ть**) to get cold; (*fig.*) to cool (down); **у вас чай ~л** your tea is cold.

осу|ди́ть, жу́, ~дишь *pf.* (*of* ▶ **~жда́ть**)
1 (*порицать*) to censure, condemn.
2 (*leg.*) (*на смерть*) to condemn, sentence; (**за** + *a.*) to convict (of).
3 (**на** + *a.*) (*fig.*) (*обречь*) to condemn.

осужда́|ть, ю *impf. of* ▶ **осуди́ть**

осужде́ни|е, я *nt.*
1 censure, condemnation.
2 (*leg.*) conviction.

осуждённ|ый *p.p.p. of* ▶ **осуди́ть** *and adj.* condemned; convicted; *as n.* **о., ~ого** *m.*, **~ая, ~ой** *f.* convict.

осу́н|уться, усь, ешься *pf.* (*о лице*) to grow thin, get pinched(-looking).

осуш|а́ть, а́ю *impf. of* ▶ **~и́ть**

осуш|и́ть, у́, ~ишь *pf.* (*of* ▶ **~а́ть**) (*болото, луга; стакан*) to drain; (*помещение*) to dry.

осуществи́м|ый (~, ~а) *adj.*

practicable, feasible.

осуществ|и́ть, лю́, и́шь *pf.* (*of* ▸ **~ля́ть**) (*мечту*) to realize, bring about; (*намерение*) to carry out; (*решение*) to implement; (*контроль, руководство*) to exercise.

осуществ|и́ться, и́тся *pf.* (*of* ▸ **~ля́ться**) to be fulfilled, come true.

осуществле́ни|е, я *nt.* realization; accomplishment; implementation.

осуществля́|ть(ся), ю, ет(ся) *impf. of* ▸ **осуществи́ть(ся)**

осчастли́в|ить, лю, ишь *pf.* (*of* ▸ **~ливать**) to make happy.

осчастли́влива|ть, ю *impf. of* ▸ **осчастли́вить**

осы́п|ать, лю, лешь *pf.* (*of* ▸ **~а́ть**) (+ *a. and i.*) (*покрыть*) to strew (with); to shower (on); (*fig.*) to heap (on); **о. поцелу́ями** to smother with kisses.

осып|а́ть(ся), а́ю(сь) *impf. of* ▸ **~́ать(ся)**

осы́п|аться, люсь, лешься *pf.* (*of* ▸ **~а́ться**) (*о насыпи*) to crumble; (*о листьях*) to fall.

ос|ь, и, *pl.* **~́и, ~е́й** *f.*
1 (*geom.*) axis; **земна́я о.** axis of the equator.
2 (*колеса*) axle.

осьмино́г, а *m.* (*zool.*) octopus.

осяза́ем|ый (~, ~а) *adj.* tangible; **~ые результа́ты** tangible results.

осяза́ние, я *nt.* touch; **чу́вство ~я** a sense of touch.

от (ото) *prep.* + *g.* from; of; for.
1 (*указывает на исходную точку, источник чего-н.*): **от це́нтра го́рода** from the centre of the town; **от нача́ла до конца́** from beginning to end; **де́ти от пяти́ до десяти́ лет** children from five to ten (years); **бли́зко от го́рода** near the town; **на се́вер от Москвы́** to the north of Moscow; **от всей души́** with all one's heart; **от и́мени** (+ *g.*) on behalf (of); **я получи́л письмо́ от до́чери** I have received a letter from my daughter; **сын от пре́жнего бра́ка** a son by a previous marriage.
2 (*указывает на причину чего-н.*): **вскри́кнуть от ра́дости** to cry out for joy; **дрожа́ть от стра́ха** to tremble with fear; **умере́ть от го́лода** to die of hunger; **глаза́, кра́сные от слёз** eyes red with weeping.
3 (*указывает на дату документа*): **ва́ше письмо́ от пе́рвого а́вгуста** your letter of the first of August.
4 (*указывает на целое, которому принадлежит часть*): **ключ от две́ри** door key; **пу́говица от пиджака́** coat button.
5 (*против*) for; against; **миксту́ра от ка́шля** cough mixture; **защища́ть глаза́ от со́лнца** to shield one's eyes from the sun; **застрахова́ть от огня́** to insure against fire.

ота́плива|ть, ю *impf. of* ▸ **отопи́ть**

ота́р|а, ы *f.* large flock (*of sheep*).

отбега́|ть, ю *impf. of* ▸ **отбежа́ть**

отбе|жа́ть, гу́, жи́шь, гу́т *pf.* (*of* ▸ **~га́ть**) to run off.

отбе́ливател|ь, я *m.* bleach.

отбе́лива|ть, ю *impf. of* ▸ **отбели́ть**

отбел|и́ть, ю́, ~́ишь *pf.* (*of* ▸ **~́ивать**) to bleach.

отбива́|ть(ся), ю(сь) *impf. of* ▸ **отби́ть(ся)**

отбивн|о́й *adj.*: **~а́я котле́та** (*cul.*) chop.

отбира́|ть, ю *impf. of* ▸ **отобра́ть**

отби́|ть, отобью́, отобьёшь *pf.* (*of* ▸ **~ва́ть**)
1 to beat off, repel; **о. ата́ку** to beat off an attack; **о. уда́р** to parry a blow.
2 (*вернуть себе силой*) to retake, recapture; (*привлечь к себе*) to win over; (*coll.*): **о.** *кого/что* **у кого́-н.** to take *s.o./sth.* off s.o., do s.o. out of *s.o./sth.*
3 (*удалить*) to remove, dispel; **о. у кого́-н. охо́ту к чему́-н.** to discourage s.o. from sth., take away s.o.'s inclination for sth.
4 (*отколоть*) to break off, knock off; **о. но́сик у ча́йника** to knock the spout off a teapot.
5 : **о. такт** to beat (out) time.
6 (*повредить ударами*) to damage by blows, by knocks; **о. ру́ку нело́вким уда́ром** to hurt one's hand with a clumsy blow.

отби́|ться, отобью́сь, отобьёшься *pf.* (*of* ▸ **~ва́ться**)
1 (**от** + *g.*) to defend o.s. (against); to repel, beat off.
2 (*отстать*) to drop behind, straggle; **о. от ста́да** to stray from the herd.

отблагодар|и́ть, ю́, и́шь *pf.* to show one's gratitude (to).

отбо́р, а *m.* selection; **есте́ственный о.** (*biol.*) natural selection.

отбо́рный *adj.* choice, select(ed).

отбра́сыва|ть, ю *impf. of* ▸ **отбро́сить**

отбро́|сить, шу, сишь *pf.* (*of* ▸ **отбра́сывать**)
1 to throw off; to cast away; **о. тень** to cast a shadow.
2 (*mil.*) to repel.
3 (*отвергнуть*) to give up, reject, discard; **о. мысль** to give up an idea.

отбро́с|ы, ов *pl.* (*sg.* **~, ~а** *m.*) garbage, refuse; **о. произво́дства** industrial waste; **о. о́бщества** (*fig.*) dregs of society.

отва́г|а, и *f.* courage, bravery.

отва́ж|ный (~ен, ~на) *adj.* courageous, brave.

отва́лива|ться, юсь *impf. of* ▸ **отвали́ться**

отвал|и́ться, ю́сь, ~́ишься *pf.* (*of* ▸ **~́иваться**) to fall off.

отва́рива|ть, ю *impf. of* ▸ **отвари́ть**

отвар|и́ть, ю́, ~́ишь *pf.* (*of* ▸ **~́ивать**) to boil.

отвез|ти́, у́, ёшь, *past* **~̈, ~ла́** *pf.* (*of* ▸ **отвози́ть**) (*везя, доставить*) to take; (*везя, убрать*) to take away.

отверг|а́ть, а́ю *impf. of* ▸ **~́нуть**

отве́рг|нуть, ну, нешь, *past* **~/~нул, ~ла** *pf.* (*of* ▸ **~а́ть**) to reject, turn down.

отвер|ну́ться, ну́сь, нёшься *pf.* (*of* ▸ **отвора́чиваться**) to turn away, turn aside; **о. от кого́-н.** (*fig.*) to turn one's back upon s.o.

отве́рсти|е, я *nt.* opening; (*дыра*) hole; (*в торговом/игровом автомате*) slot.

отвёртк|а, и *f.* screwdriver.

отве́с|ный (~ен, ~на) *adj.* (*линия*) perpendicular; (*скала*) steep.

отве|сти́, ду́, дёшь, *past* **~л, ~ла́** *pf.* (*of* ▸ **отводи́ть**)
1 (*ведя, доставить*) to lead, take, conduct.
2 (*ведя, направить в сторону*) to draw aside, take aside.
3 (*изменить направление движения чего-либо*) to deflect; **он не мог о. от неё глаз** he could not take his eyes off her.
4 (*выделить*) to allot, assign.

отве́т, а *m.*
1 answer, reply, response; **в о.** (**на** + *a.*) in reply (to), in response (to).
2 : **быть в ~е** (**за** + *a.*) to be answerable (for); **призва́ть к ~у** to call to account.

ответвле́ни|е, я *nt.* branch, offshoot (*also fig.*).

отве́|тить, чу, тишь *pf.* (*of* ▸ **~ча́ть 1**)
1 (**на** + *a.*) to answer, reply (to); **о. на письмо́** to answer a letter; **о. уро́к** to repeat one's lesson.
2 (**на** + *a. and i.*) to answer (with), return; **о. на чьё-н. чу́вство** to return s.o.'s feelings.
3 (**за** + *a.*) to answer (for), pay (for); **вы ~тите за э́ти слова́!** you will pay for these words!

отве́тный *adj.* given in reply; (*визит*) return; (*меры*) retaliatory.

отве́тственност|ь, и *f.* responsibility; **привле́чь к ~и** (**за** + *a.*) to call to account, bring to book.

отве́тствен|ный (~, ~на) *adj.*
1 (*человек; работа*) responsible.
2 (*решающий*) crucial; **о. моме́нт** crucial point.

отве́тчик, а *m.* (*leg.*) defendant.

отве́тчи|ца, цы *f. of* ▸ **~к**

отвеча́|ть, ю *impf.*
1 *impf. of* ▸ **отве́тить.**
2 (**за** + *a.*) to answer (for), be answerable (for).
3 (+ *d.*) to answer (to), meet, be up (to); **о. тре́бованиям** to meet requirements.

отвин|ти́ть, чу́, ти́шь *pf.* (*of* ▸ **~чивать**) to unscrew.

отвин|ти́ться, ти́тся *pf.* (*of* ▸ **~чиваться**) to unscrew, come unscrewed.

отви́нчива|ть(ся), ю, ет(ся) *impf. of* ▸ **отвинти́ть(ся)**

отвлека́|ть(ся), ю(сь) *impf. of* ▸ **отвле́чь(ся)**

отвлечён|ный (~, ~на) *adj.* abstract.

отвле́|чь, ку́, чёшь, ку́т, *past* **~к, ~кла́** *pf.* (*of* ▸ **~ка́ть**) to distract, divert; **о. чьё-н. внима́ние** to divert s.o.'s attention.

отвле́|чься, ку́сь, чёшься, ку́тся, *past* **~кся, ~кла́сь** *pf.* (*of* ▸ **~ка́ться**)
1 to be distracted; **о. от те́мы** to digress.
2 (**от** + *g.*) (*абстрагироваться*) to abstract o.s. (from).

отво|ди́ть, жу́, ~дишь *impf. of* ▸ **отвести́**

отво|ева́ть[1], ю́ю, ю́ешь *pf.* (*of* ▸ **~ёвывать**) (**у** + *g.*) (*вернуть войной*) to win back (from), retake (from).

отво|ева́ть[2], ю́ю, ю́ешь *pf.* (*coll.*)
1 (*какое-н. время*) to fight, spend in fighting; **мы де́сять лет ~ева́ли** we have fought for ten years.
2 (*кончить воевать*) to finish fighting.

отвоёвыва|ть, ю *impf. of* ▸ **отвоева́ть[1]**

отво|зи́ть, жу́, ~зишь *impf. of* ▸ **отвезти́**

отвора́чива|ться, юсь *impf. of* ▸ **отверну́ться**

отвор|и́ть, ю́, ~ишь *pf.* (*of* ▸ **~я́ть**) to open.

отвор|и́ться, ~ится *pf.* (*of* ▸ **~я́ться**) to open.

отворо́т, а *m.* (*на пиджаке*) lapel; (*на брюках*) turn-up (*Br.*), cuff (*US*); (*сапога, рукава*) cuff.

отвор|я́ть(ся), я́ю, я́ет(ся) *impf. of* ▸ **~и́ть(ся)**

отврати́тел|ьный (~ен, ~ьна) *adj.* repulsive, disgusting.

отвраще́ни|е, я *nt.* disgust, repugnance; **пита́ть о.** (**к** + *d.*) to have an aversion (for), loathe.

отвык|а́ть, а́ю *impf. of* ▸ **~нуть**

отвы́к|нуть, ну, нешь, *past* **~, ~ла** *pf.* (*of* ▸ **~а́ть**) (**от** + *g.*, *or* + *inf.*) (*от плохой привычки*) to break o.s. (of the habit of), give up; (*от работы, ходьбы*) to get out of the habit of, become unaccustomed to; (*от друзей, своей страны*) to become estranged from.

отвя|за́ть, жу́, ~жешь *pf.* (*of* ▸ **~зывать**) to untie, unfasten.

отвя|за́ться, жу́сь, ~жешься *pf.* (*of* ▸ **~зываться**)
1 (*освободиться от привязи*) to come untied, come loose.
2 (*fig., coll.*; **от** + *g.*) (*отделаться*) to get rid (of), shake off.
3 (*fig., coll.*; **от** + *g.*) (*перестать надоедать*) to leave alone, leave in peace; stop nagging; **~жи́сь от меня́!** leave me alone!

отвя́зыва|ть(ся), ю(сь) *impf. of* ▸ **отвяза́ть(ся)**

отгад|а́ть, а́ю *pf.* (*of* ▸ **~ывать**) to guess.

отга́дк|а, и *f.* answer, solution (*to a riddle*).

отга́дыва|ть, ю *impf. of* ▸ **отгада́ть**

отгиба́|ть(ся), ю, ет(ся) *impf. of* ▸ **отогну́ть(ся)**

отгова́рива|ть, ю *impf. of* ▸ **отговори́ть**

отговор|и́ть, ю́, и́шь *pf.* (*of* ▸ **отгова́ривать**) (**от** + *g.*, *or* + *inf.*) to dissuade (from); **я ~и́л его́ е́хать** I have talked him out of going.

отгово́рк|а, и *f.* excuse.

отгоня́|ть, ю *impf. of* ▸ **отогна́ть**

отгора́жива|ть(ся), ю(сь) *impf. of* ▸ **отгороди́ть(ся)**

отгоро|ди́ть, жу́, ~и́шь *pf.* (*of* ▸ **отгора́живать**) to fence off, partition off.

отгоро|ди́ться, жу́сь, ~ди́шься *pf.* (*of* ▸ **отгора́живаться**) to fence o.s. off; (*fig., coll.*; **от** + *g.*) to shut *or* cut o.s. off (from).

отгрыз|а́ть, а́ю *impf. of* ▸ **~ть**

отгры́з|ть, у́, ёшь, *past* **~, ~ла** *pf.* (*of* ▸ **~а́ть**) to bite off, gnaw off.

отда|ва́ть(ся), ю́(сь), ёшь(ся) *impf. of* ▸ **отда́ть(ся)**

отдав|и́ть, лю́, ~́ишь *pf.* to crush; **о. кому́-н. но́гу** to tread on s.o.'s foot.

отдалён|ный (~, ~на) *adj.* distant, remote.

отд|а́ть, а́м, а́шь, а́ст, ади́м, ади́те, аду́т, *past* **~́ал, ~ала́, ~́ало** *pf.* (*of* ▸ **~ава́ть**)
[1] (*дать обратно*) to give back, return; **о. себе́ отчёт** (**в** + *p.*) to be aware (of), realize.
[2] (*посвятить*) to devote; **о. жизнь нау́ке** to devote one's life to scholarship.
[3] (+ *a. and d.*, *or* + *a.* **за** + *a.*) (*выдать замуж*) to give in marriage (to), give away.
[4] (**в** + *a.*, **под** + *a.*) (*вручить*) to give, put (= *hand over for certain purpose*); **о. кни́гу в переплёт** to send a book to be bound; **о. под суд** to prosecute.
[5] (*in comb. with certain nn.*) to give; to make (*or not requiring separate translation*); **о. прика́з** (+ *d.*) to issue an order (to).

отд|а́ться, а́мся, а́шься, а́стся, ади́мся, ади́тесь, аду́тся, *past* **~а́лся, ~ала́сь** *pf.* (*of* ▸ **~ава́ться**)
[1] (+ *d.*) (*победителю*) to give o.s. up (to); (*науке*) to devote o.s. (to); (*о женщине*) to give o.s. (to).
[2] (*о голосе, об эхе*) to resound; to reverberate; to ring.

отда́ч|а, и *f.*
[1] (*от вложенного*) return.
[2] (*эффективность*) efficiency, performance.
[3] (*при выстреле*) recoil.

отде́л, а *m.* department; **о. ка́дров** personnel department.

отде́л|ать, аю *pf.* (*of* ▸ **~ывать**) to finish, put the finishing touches (to); to decorate.

отде́л|аться, аюсь *pf.* (*of* ▸ **~ываться**) (*coll.*)
[1] (**от** + *g.*) to get rid (of), get shot (of).
[2] (+ *i.*) to escape (with); **легко́ о.** to have a lucky escape.

отделе́ни|е, я *nt.*
[1] (*действие*) separation; **о. це́ркви от госуда́рства** separation of church and state, secularization; (*с обретением независимости*) secession.
[2] (*учреждение*) department, branch; **о. мили́ции** local police station.
[3] (*вместилища*) compartment, section; (*представления*) part.
[4] (*mil.*) section.

отдел|и́ть, ю́, ~́ишь *pf.* (*of* ▸ **~я́ть**)
[1] (*отнять*) to separate.
[2] (*отграничить*) to separate off; **о. перегоро́дкой** to partition off.

отдел|и́ться, ю́сь, ~́ишься *pf.* (*of* ▸ **~я́ться**) (*отодвинуться*) to move away, separate; (*оторваться*) to get detached; to come off; (*быть отграниченным от чего-л.*) to be separated.

отде́лк|а, и *f.*
[1] (*действие*) finishing; trimming.
[2] (*украшение*) finish, decoration; (*в комнате*) decor.

отде́лыва|ть(ся), ю(сь) *impf. of* ▸ **отде́лать(ся)**

отде́льно *adv.* separately.

отде́льный *adj.*
[1] separate, (*некоторый*) individual, (*единичный*) isolated.
[2] (*mil.*) independent.

отдел|я́ть(ся), я́ю(сь) *impf. of* ▸ **~и́ть(ся)**

отдёргива|ть, ю *impf. of* ▸ **отдёрнуть**

отдёр|нуть, ну, нешь *pf.* (*of* ▸ **~гивать**)
[1] (*в сторону*) to draw aside, pull aside.
[2] (*руку*) to pull back, withdraw.

отдира́|ть, ю *impf. of* ▸ **отодра́ть**

отдохн|у́ть, у́, ёшь *pf.* (*of* ▸ **отдыха́ть**) to rest; to have a rest.

отду́шин|а, ы *f.* air hole, (air) vent; (*fig.*) outlet.

о́тдых, а *m.* rest; relaxation; (*отпуск*) holiday (*Br.*), vacation (*US*).

отдыха́|ть, ю *impf.* (*of* ▸ **отдохну́ть**) to be resting; (*быть в отпуске*) to be on holiday (*Br.*), vacation (*US*); (*проводить отпуск*) to holiday (*Br.*), vacation (*US*).

отдыха́|ющий *pres. part. of* ▸ **~ть;** *as n.* **о., ~ющего** *m.*; **~ющая, ~ющей** *f.* holidaymaker (*Br.*), vacationer (*US*).

отдыш|а́ться, у́сь, ~́ишься *pf.* to recover one's breath.

отёк, а *m.* (*med.*) oedema (*Br.*), edema (*US*); **о. лёгких** emphysema.

оте́л|ь, я *m.* hotel.

от|е́ц, ца́ *m.* father (*also fig.*); **О. Небе́сный** (*relig.*) the heavenly Father.

оте́честв|енный *adj. of* ▸ **~о; Вели́кая Оте́чественная война́** the Great Patriotic War (*1941-45*).

оте́честв|о, а *nt.* native land, fatherland, homeland.

от|жа́ть, ожму́, ожмёшь *pf.* (*of* ▸ **~жима́ть**) to wring out.

отжима́|ть, ю *impf. of* ▸ **отжа́ть**

о́тзвук, а *m.* echo (*also fig.*).

о́тзыв, а *m.*
[1] (*мнение*) opinion, judgement.
[2] (*рекомендация*) reference; testimonial; **дать хоро́ший о. о ко́м-н.** to give s.o. a good reference.
[3] (*рецензия*) review.

отзыва́|ться, юсь *impf. of* ▸ **отозва́ться**

отзы́вчив|ый (~, ~а) *adj.* responsive.

оти́т, а *m.* (*med.*) otitis (*inflammation of the ear*).

отка́з, а *m.*
[1] refusal; **получи́ть о.** to be refused, be turned down; **до ~а** to overflowing.
[2] (**от** + *g.*) renunciation (of), giving up (of).
[3] (*механизма*) failure.

отка|за́ть, жу́, ~́жешь *pf.* (*of* ▸ **~́зывать**)
[1] (+ *d. and* **в** + *p.*) to refuse, deny; **она́ ~за́ла ему́ в про́сьбе** she refused his request; **ему́ нельзя́ о. в тала́нте** there is no denying that he has talent.
[2] (*о механизме*) to fail, break down.

отка|за́ться, жу́сь, ~́жешься *pf.* (*of* ▸ **~́зываться**)
[1] (**от** + *g. or* + *inf.*) to refuse, decline; to turn down; **о. от предложе́ния** to turn down a proposal; **о. от свои́х слов** to retract one's words.

[2] (*отречься*) to renounce, give up; (*от права*) to relinquish; (*от власти*) to abdicate; **о. от борьбы́** to give up the struggle.

отка́зыва|ть(ся), ю(сь) *impf. of* ▸ **отказа́ть(ся)**

отка́лыва|ть(ся), ю(сь) *impf. of* ▸ **отколо́ть(ся)**

отка́пыва|ть, ю *impf. of* ▸ **откопа́ть**

отка́рмлива|ть, ю *impf. of* ▸ **откорми́ть**

отка|ти́ть, чу́, ~́тишь *pf.* (*of* ▸ **~́тывать**) (*бревно*) to roll away.

отка|ти́ться, чу́сь, ~́тишься *pf.* (*of* ▸ **~́тываться**) to roll away.

отка́тыва|ть(ся), ю(сь) *impf. of* ▸ **откати́ть(ся)**

откач|а́ть, а́ю *pf.* (*of* ▸ **~ивать**)
[1] (*воздух, воду*) to pump out.
[2] (*человека*) to resuscitate.

отка́чива|ть, ю *impf. of* ▸ **откача́ть**

отка́шл|иваться, иваюсь *impf. of* ▸ **~яться**

отка́шл|яться, яюсь *pf.* (*of* ▸ **~иваться**) to clear one's throat.

отки́дыва|ться, юсь *impf. of* ▸ **отки́нуться**

отки́|нуться, нусь, нешься *pf.* (*of* ▸ **~дываться**) to lean back; to recline, settle back.

откла́дыва|ть, ю *impf. of* ▸ **отложи́ть**

откле́ива|ть(ся), ю, ет(ся) *impf. of* ▸ **откле́ить(ся)**

откле́|ить, ю, ишь *pf.* (*of* ▸ **~ивать**) to peel off.

откле́|иться, ится *pf.* (*of* ▸ **~иваться**) to come unstuck.

о́тклик, а *m.* (*ответ на зов*) response; (*fig.*) (*в печати*) comment.

отклик|а́ться, а́юсь *impf.* (*of* ▸ **~́нуться**) (**на** + *a.*) to answer, respond (to) (*also fig.*).

откли́к|нуться, нусь, нешься *pf. of* ▸ **~а́ться**

отклоне́ни|е, я *nt.*
[1] (*отход в сторону; от нормы*) deviation; divergence.
[2] (*отказ*) declining, refusal.

отклон|и́ть, ю́, ~́ишь *pf.* (*of* ▸ **~я́ть**)
[1] (*в сторону*) to deflect.
[2] (*отказать*) to decline; **о. предложе́ние** to decline an offer.

отклон|и́ться, ю́сь, ~́ишься *pf.* (*of* ▸ **~я́ться**) (*от курса*) to deviate; (*от удара*) to dodge; (*отодвинуться*) to move aside; **о. от те́мы** to digress.

отклоня́|ть(ся), ю(сь) *impf. of* ▸ **отклони́ть(ся)**

отключ|а́ть(ся), а́ю(сь) *impf. of* ▸ **~и́ть(ся)**

отключ|и́ть, у́, и́шь *pf.* (*of* ▸ **~а́ть**) (*elec.*) to cut off, disconnect.

отключ|и́ться, у́сь, и́шься *pf.* (*of* ▸ **~а́ться**)
[1] to become disconnected.
[2] (*coll.*) (*о человеке*) to switch off.

откол|о́ть, ю́, ~́ешь *pf.* (*of* ▸ **отка́лывать**)
[1] (*отломать*) to break off; (*отбить*) to chop off; (*от семьи*) to cut off.
[2] (*булавку, чепец*) to unpin.

откол|о́ться, ю́сь, ~́ешься *pf.* (*of* ▸ **отка́лываться**)
[1] (*отломаться*) to break off.
[2] (*о булавке, чепце*) to come unpinned *or* undone.
[3] (*fig.*) (*от семьи*) to break away; to cut o.s. off.

откопа́|ть, ю *pf.* (*of* ▸ **отка́пывать**)
[1] to dig out; (*труп*) to exhume, disinter.
[2] (*fig., coll.*) (*найти*) to dig up, unearth.

откорм|и́ть, лю́, ~́ишь *pf.* (*of* ▸ **отка́рмливать**) to fatten (up).

отко́с, а *m.*
[1] (*покатый спуск*) slope, side (*of embankment etc.*); **о. холма́** hillside.
[2] (*rail.*) embankment; **пусти́ть по́езд под о.** to derail a train.

открове́ни|е, я *nt.* revelation.

открове́нност|ь, и *f.* candour (*Br.*), candor (*US*), frankness; *pl.* (*coll.*) candid revelations.

открове́н|ный (~ен, ~на) *adj.*
[1] (*искренний*) candid, frank.
[2] (*нескрываемый*) open, unconcealed; **~ная непри́язнь** unconcealed hostility.
[3] (*coll.*) (*о платье*) revealing.

откру|ти́ть, чу́, ~́тишь *pf.* (*of* ▸ **~́чивать**) to untwist; **о. кран** to turn off a tap.

откру́чива|ть, ю *impf. of* ▸ **открути́ть**

открыва́лк|а, и *f.* (*coll.*)
[1] (*для банок*) can opener.
[2] (*для бутылок*) bottle opener.

открыва́|ть(ся), ю(сь) *impf. of* ▸ **откры́ть(ся)**

откры́ти|е, я *nt.*
[1] (*действие*) opening.
[2] (*научное*) discovery.

откры́тк|а, и *f.* postcard.

откры́то *adv.* openly.

откры́т|ый *p.p.p. of* ▸ **~ь** *and adj.* open; **на ~ом во́здухе, под ~ым не́бом** out of doors, in the open (air); **~ое мо́ре** the open sea; **~ое пла́тье** low-necked dress.

откр|ы́ть, о́ю, о́ешь *pf.* (*of* ▸ **~ыва́ть**)
[1] to open; **о. кому́-н. глаза́ на что-н.** (*fig.*) to open s.o.'s eyes to sth.; **о. ого́нь** (*mil.*) to open fire; **о. счёт** to open an account.
[2] (*обнажить*) to uncover, reveal (*also fig.*); **о. секре́т** to reveal a secret.
[3] (*обнаружить*) to discover; **о. Аме́рику** (*fig., iron.*) to retail stale news.
[4] (*воду, газ*) to turn on.

откр|ы́ться, о́юсь, о́ешься *pf.* (*of* ▸ **~ыва́ться**)
[1] (*дверь, глаза*) to open.
[2] (*обнаружиться*) to come to light, be revealed; **пе́ред на́ми ~ы́лся великоле́пный вид а** magnificent view unfolded before us.

отку́да *adv.* (*interrog.*) where from; (*rel.*) whence, from which; **о. вы?** where are you from?; **о. вы об э́том зна́ете?** how come you know about it?

отку́да-нибудь *adv.* from somewhere or other.

отку́да-то *adv.* from somewhere.

откуп|а́ться, а́юсь *impf. of* ▸ **~и́ться**
откуп|и́ться, лю́сь, ~́ишься *pf.* (*of* ▸ **~а́ться**) (**от** + *g.*) to pay off.
отку́порива|ть, ю *impf. of* ▸ **отку́порить**
отку́пор|ить, ю, ишь *pf.* (*of* ▸ **~ивать**) (*бутылку*) to uncork; (*банку*) to open.
отку|си́ть, шу́, ~́сишь *pf.* (*of* ▸ **~́сывать**) to bite off; (*щипцами*) to cut off.
отку́сыва|ть, ю *impf. of* ▸ **откуси́ть**
отла́дчик, а *m.* (*comput.*) (*программа*) debugger.
отлакир|ова́ть, у́ю *pf. of* ▸ **лакирова́ть**
отла́мыва|ть(ся), ю, ет(ся) *impf. of* ▸ **отлома́ть(ся)** *and* ▸ **отломи́ть(ся)**
отлет|а́ть, а́ю *impf. of* ▸ **~е́ть**
отле|те́ть, чу́, ти́шь *pf.* (*of* ▸ **~та́ть**)
1 (*улететь*) to fly (away, off); (*fig.*) (*исчезнуть*) to fly, vanish.
2 (*о мяче*) to rebound, bounce back.
3 (*coll.*) (*о пуговице*) to come off.
отли́в, а *m.* ebb, ebb tide.
отлива́|ть, ю *impf. of* ▸ **отли́ть**
отли́ть, отолью́, отольёшь, *past* **о́тли́л, отлила́, о́тли́ло** *pf.* (*of* ▸ **отлива́ть**)
1 (+ *a. or g.*) (*молока*) to pour off; (*отхлынуть*) to flood back.
2 (*tech.*) to cast, found.
отлич|а́ть, а́ю *impf. of* ▸ **~и́ть**
отлич|а́ться, а́юсь *impf.*
1 (*pf.* **~и́ться**) to distinguish o.s., excel (*also joc., iron.*).
2 (*impf. only*) (**от** + *g.*) to differ (from).
3 (*impf. only*) (+ *i.*) to be notable (for).
отли́чи|е, я *nt.*
1 difference, distinction; **в о. от** (+ *g.*) unlike, in contrast to.
2 (*оценка*) distinction; (*заслуга*) distinguished services.
отличи́тельный *adj.* distinctive; distinguishing; **о. при́знак** distinguishing feature.
отлич|и́ть, у́, и́шь *pf.* (*of* ▸ **~а́ть**)
1 to distinguish; **о. одно́ от друго́го** to tell one thing from another.
2 (*выделить из числа других*) to single out.
отлич|и́ться, у́сь, и́шься *pf. of* ▸ **~а́ться 1**
отли́чно
1 *adv.* excellently; perfectly; extremely well; **о. знать** to know perfectly well.
2 *n.*; *nt. indecl.* 'excellent' mark (*in school, etc.*).
отли́ч|ный (~ен, ~на) *adj.*
1 (**от** + *g.*) (*иной*) different (from).
2 (*превосходный*) excellent; perfect; extremely good; **~но!** excellent!
отло́г|ий (~, ~а) *adj.* sloping.
отлож|и́ть, у́, ~́ишь *pf.* (*of* ▸ **откла́дывать**)
1 (*положить в сторону*) to put aside, set aside; (*сохранить*) to put away, put by; **о. на чёрный день** to put by for a rainy day.
2 (*отсрочить*) to put off, postpone.
3 (*о птицах*) to lay.
отлома́|ть, ю *pf.* (*of* ▸ **отла́мывать**) to break off.
отлома́|ться, ю, ет(ся) *pf.* (*of* ▸ **отла́мываться**) to break off.
отлом|и́ть(ся), лю́, ~́ит(ся) *pf.* = **~а́ть(ся)**
отлуч|а́ться, а́юсь *impf. of* ▸ **отлучи́ться**
отлуч|и́ться, у́сь, и́шься *pf.* (*of* ▸ **~а́ться**) to absent o.s.
отма́хива|ть(ся), ю(сь) *impf. of* ▸ **отмахну́ть(ся)**
отмах|ну́ть, ну́, нёшь *pf.* (*of* ▸ **~́ивать**) to wave away, brush off (*with one's hand*).
отмах|ну́ться, ну́сь, нёшься *pf.* (*of* ▸ **~́иваться**) (**от** + *g.*)
1 = **~ну́ть; о. от комаро́в** to brush mosquitoes off.
2 (*fig.*) to brush aside.
о́тмел|ь, и *f.* sandbank.
отме́н|а, ы *f.* abolition; repeal; cancellation.
отмен|и́ть, ю́, ~́ишь *pf.* (*of* ▸ **~я́ть**) (*налог*) to abolish; (*закон*) to repeal; (*решение, приказание*) to revoke; (*заседание*) to cancel.
отме́н|ный (~ен, ~на) *adj.* excellent.
отмен|я́ть, я́ю *impf. of* ▸ **~и́ть**
отмер|е́ть, отомрёт, *past* **о́тмер, ~ла́, о́тмерло** *pf.* (*of* ▸ **отмира́ть**) to die off; (*fig.*) to die out, die away.
отмерз|а́ть, а́ет *impf. of* ▸ **~̈нуть**
отмёрз|нуть, нет, *past* **~, ~ла** *pf.* (*of* ▸ **~а́ть**) (*coll.*) to freeze; **ру́ки у меня́ ~ли** my hands are frozen.
отме́рива|ть, ю *impf. of* ▸ **отме́рить**
отме́р|ить, ю, ишь *pf.* (*of* ▸ **~ивать** *and* ▸ **~я́ть**) to measure off.
отмер|я́ть, я́ю *impf.* = **~́ивать**
отме|сти́, ту́, тёшь, *past* **~̈л, ~ла́** *pf.* (*of* ▸ **~та́ть**) to sweep aside (*also fig.*).
отмета́|ть, ю *impf. of* ▸ **отмести́**
отме́|тить, чу, тишь *pf.* (*of* ▸ **~ча́ть**)
1 (*место в книге*) to mark, note; (*присутствующих; высоту*) to make a note (of); **о. пти́чкой** to tick off.
2 (*достоинства*) to point to, mention, record; **о. чьи-н. по́двиги** to point to s.o.'s feats.
3 (*день рождения*) to celebrate.
отме́тк|а, и *f.*
1 (*знак*) mark; (*запись*) note.
2 (*оценка*) mark.
отмеча́|ть, ю *impf. of* ▸ **отме́тить**
отмира́|ть, ет *impf. of* ▸ **отмере́ть**
отмора́жива|ть, ю *impf. of* ▸ **отморо́зить**
отморо́|зить, жу, зишь *pf.* (*of* ▸ **отмора́живать**) to injure by frostbite; **я ~зил себе́ у́ши** my ears are frostbitten.
отмыва́ни|е, я *nt.*: **о. де́нег** money laundering.
отмыва́|ть(ся), ю(сь) *impf. of* ▸ **отмы́ть(ся)**
отм|ы́ть, о́ю, о́ешь *pf.* (*of* ▸ **~ыва́ть**)
1 (*руки*) to wash clean.
2 (*грязь*) to wash off, wash away.
3 (*fig., coll.*): **о. де́ньги** to launder money.
отм|ы́ться, о́юсь, о́ешься *pf.* (*of* ▸ **~ыва́ться**)
1 (*о человеке*) to wash o.s. clean.
2 (*о руках*) to become/get clean.
3 (*о грязи*) to come out, come off.
отнес|ти́, у́, ёшь, *past* **~̈, ~ла́** *pf.* (*of* ▸ **относи́ть**)

О

1 (**в** + *a.*, **к** + *d.*) (*доставить*) to take (to).
2 to carry away, carry off; (*impers.*): **ло́дку ~ло́ тече́нием** the boat was carried away by the current; (*переместить*) to move.
3 (**к** + *d.*) to ascribe (to), attribute (to), refer (to); **мы ~ли́ его́ раздражи́тельность на счёт глухоты́** we put his irritability down to his deafness.

отнес|ти́сь, у́сь, ёшься, *past* **~ся, ~ла́сь** *pf.* (*of* ▸ **относи́ться 1**) (**к** + *d.*) to treat; to regard; **хорошо́ о. к кому́-н.** to treat s.o. well, be nice to s.o.; **как вы ~ли́сь к его́ слова́м?** what did you think of what he said?

отнима́|ть, ю *impf. of* ▸ **отня́ть**

относи́тельно
1 *adv.* relatively.
2 *prep.* (+ *g.*) concerning, about, with regard to.

относи́тельност|ь, и *f.* relativity; **тео́рия ~и Эйнште́йна** Einstein's Theory of Relativity.

относи́тел|ьный (~ен, ~ьна) *adj.* relative.

отно|си́ть, шу́, ~сишь *impf. of* ▸ **отнести́**

отно|си́ться, шу́сь, ~сишься *impf.*
1 *impf. of* ▸ **отнести́сь.**
2 (*impf. only*) (**к** + *d.*) to concern, have to do (with), relate (to); **э́то к де́лу не ~сится** that's beside the point, that is irrelevant.
3 (*impf. only*) (**к** + *d.*) to date (from); **э́тот храм ~сится к двена́дцатому ве́ку** this church dates from the twelfth century.

отноше́ни|е, я *nt.*
1 (**к** + *d.*) attitude (to); treatment (of).
2 (*связь*) relation; respect; **име́ть о. к чему́-н.** to bear a relation to sth., have a bearing on sth.; **не име́ть ~я** (**к** + *d.*) to bear no relation (to), have nothing to do (with); **в ~и** (+ *g.*), **по ~ю** (**к** + *d.*) with respect (to), with regard (to).
3 (*pl.*) (*связи между людьми*) relations; terms; **быть в дру́жеских ~ях** (**с** + *i.*) to be on friendly terms (with); **вы́яснить ~я** (**с** + *i.*) to have it out (with).
4 (*math.*) ratio; **в прямо́м (обра́тном) ~и** in direct (inverse) ratio.

отны́не *adv.* (*rhet.*) henceforth.

отню́дь *adv.* by no means, not at all.

от|ня́ть, ниму́, ни́мешь, *past* **~нял, ~няла́, ~няло** *pf.* (*of* ▸ **~нима́ть**) to take (away); **о. жизнь у кого́-н.** to take s.o.'s life; **от шести́ о. три** to take away three from six.

ото *prep.* = **от**

отобража́|ть, ю *impf. of* ▸ **отобрази́ть**

отобра|зи́ть, жу́, зи́шь *pf.* (*of* ▸ **~жа́ть**) to reflect; to represent.

от|обра́ть, беру́, берёшь, *past* **~обра́л, ~обрала́, ~обра́ло** *pf.* (*of* ▸ **отбира́ть**)
1 (*отнять*) to take (away).
2 (*выбрать*) to select, pick out.

отовсю́ду *adv.* from everywhere, from every quarter.

от|огна́ть, гоню́, го́нишь, *past* **~огна́л, ~огнала́, ~огна́ло** *pf.* (*of* ▸ **~гоня́ть**) to drive away, chase away.

отогн|у́ть, у́, ёшь *pf.* (*of* ▸ **отгиба́ть**) to bend back.

отогн|у́ться, ётся *pf.* (*of* ▸ **отгиба́ться**) to bend back.

отогрева́|ть(ся), ю(сь) *impf. of* ▸ **отогре́ть(ся)**

отогре́|ть, ю *pf.* (*of* ▸ **~ва́ть**) to warm.

отогре́|ться, юсь *pf.* (*of* ▸ **~ва́ться**) to warm o.s.

отодвига́|ть(ся), ю(сь) *impf. of* ▸ **отодви́нуть(ся)**

отодви́|нуть, ну, нешь *pf.* (*of* ▸ **~га́ть**)
1 to move aside.
2 (*fig., coll.*) (*отсрочить*) to put off, put back.

отодви́|нуться, нусь, нешься *pf.* (*of* ▸ **~га́ться**)
1 to move aside.
2 (*coll.*) (*о сроке*) to be postponed.

от|одра́ть, деру́, дерёшь, *past* **~одра́л, ~одрала́, ~одра́ло** *pf.* (*of* ▸ **~дира́ть**) to tear off, rip off.

от|озва́ться, зову́сь, зовёшься, *past* **~озва́лся, ~озвала́сь** *pf.* (*of* ▸ **~зыва́ться**)
1 (**на** + *a.*) to answer; to respond (to).
2 (**о** + *p.*) to speak (of).
3 (**на** + *a.*) (*сказаться*) to tell (on, upon).

ото|йти́, йду́, йдёшь, *past* **~шёл, ~шла́** *pf.* (*of* ▸ **отходи́ть**)
1 to move away; to move off; (*о поезде*) to leave, depart.
2 (*оставить свою прежнюю позицию*) to withdraw; to recede; (*mil.*) to withdraw, fall back; (*fig.*; **от** + *g.*) to move away (from); to digress (from), diverge (from).
3 (*о пятнах*) to come out; (**от** + *g.*) to come away (from), come off; **обо́и ~шли́ от стены́** the paper has come off (the wall).
4 (*прийти в обычное состояние*) to recover (normal state).
5 (**к** + *d.*) (*перейти в чью-л. собственность*) to pass (to), go (to).

отом|сти́ть, щу́, сти́шь *pf. of* ▸ **мстить**

отоп|и́ть, лю́, ~ишь *pf.* (*of* ▸ **ота́пливать**) to heat.

отопле́ни|е, я *nt.* heating.

оторв|а́ть, у́, ёшь, *past* **~а́л, ~ала́, ~а́ло** *pf.* (*of* ▸ **отрыва́ть**) (*пуговицу*) to tear off; (*отвлечь*) to tear away (*fig.*); **о. кого́-н. от рабо́ты** to tear s.o. away from his work.

оторв|а́ться, у́сь, ёшься, *past* **~а́лся, ~ала́сь** *pf.* (*of* ▸ **отрыва́ться**)
1 (*о пуговице*) to come off, be torn off.
2 (*aeron.*): **о. от земли́** to take off.
3 (*fig.*; **от** + *g.*) (*от друзей*) to be cut off (from), lose touch (with); (*от соперников*; *от отряда*) to break away (from).
4 (*fig.*; **от** + *g.*) to tear o.s. away (from); **я не мог о. от э́той кни́ги** I could not tear myself away from this book.

ото|сла́ть, шлю́, шлёшь *pf.* (*of* ▸ **отсыла́ть**)
1 to send off, dispatch.
2 (**к** + *d.*) to refer (to).

ото|шёл, шла́ *see* ▸ **~йти́**

ото|шлю́, шлёшь *see* ▸ **~сла́ть**

отпада́|ть, ю *impf. of* ▸ **отпа́сть**

отпа́рыва|ть, ю *impf. of* ▸ **отпоро́ть**

отпа́|сть, ду́, дёшь, *past* **~л** *pf.* (*of* ▸ **~да́ть**)

1 (*отделиться*) to fall off, drop off.
2 (*fig.*; **от** + *g.*) to drop out (of).
3 (*fig.*) (*утратить силу*) to pass, fade; **вопро́с об э́том ~л** the question no longer arises.

от|пере́ть, опру́, опрёшь, *past* **~пер, ~перла́, ~перло** *pf.* (*of* ▸ **~пира́ть**) to unlock; to open.

от|пере́ться, опрётся, *past* **~перся́, ~перла́сь** *pf.* (*of* ▸ **~пира́ться**) to open.

отпеча́т|ать, аю *pf.*
1 (*impf.* **печа́тать**) to print (off).
2 (*impf.* **~ывать**) to imprint.
3 (*impf.* **~ывать**) (*помещение*) to open (up).

отпеча́т|аться, ается *pf.* to leave an imprint; to be imprinted.

отпеча́т|ок, ка *m.* imprint (*also fig.*); **о. па́льца** fingerprint.

отпеча́тыва|ть(ся), ю, ет(ся) *impf. of* ▸ **отпеча́тать(ся)**

отпива́|ть, ю *impf. of* ▸ **отпи́ть**

отпи́лива|ть, ю *impf. of* ▸ **отпили́ть**

отпил|и́ть, ю́, ~ишь *pf.* (*of* ▸ **~ивать**) to saw off.

отпира́|ть(ся), ю, ет(ся) *impf. of* ▸ **отпере́ть(ся)**

от|пи́ть, опью́, опьёшь, *past* **~пи́л, ~пила́, ~пи́ло** *pf.* (*of* ▸ **~пива́ть**) (+ *a. or g.*) to take a sip (of).

отпла|ти́ть, чу́, ~тишь *pf.* (*of* ▸ **~чивать**) (+ *d.*) to pay back (to); repay; **о. кому́-н. той же моне́той** to pay s.o. in his own coin.

отпла́чива|ть, ю *impf. of* ▸ **отплати́ть**

отплыва́|ть, ю *impf. of* ▸ **отплы́ть**

отплы́ти|е, я *nt.* sailing, departure.

отплы́|ть, ву́, вёшь, *past* **~л, ~ла́, ~ло** *pf.* (*of* ▸ **~ва́ть**) (*о корабле*) to sail, set sail; (*о плывущих людях*) to swim off.

отполз|а́ть, а́ю *impf. of* ▸ **~ти́**

отполз|ти́, у́, ёшь, *past* **~, ~ла́** *pf.* (*of* ▸ **~а́ть**) to crawl away.

отполир|ова́ть, у́ю *pf. of* ▸ **полирова́ть**

отпо́р, а *m.* repulse; rebuff; **дать о.** (+ *d.*) to repulse; **встре́тить о.** to be repulsed; to meet with a rebuff.

отпор|о́ть, ю́, ~ешь *pf.* (*of* ▸ **отпа́рывать**) to rip off.

отпра́в|ить, лю, ишь *pf.* (*of* ▸ **~ля́ть**) to send; (*по почте*) to post (*Br.*), mail (*US*); to send off; **о. на тот свет** to send to kingdom come.

отпра́в|иться, люсь, ишься *pf.* (*of* ▸ **~ля́ться**) to set out, set off, start; (*о поезде*) to leave, depart.

отправле́ни|е, я *nt.*
1 (*действие*) sending.
2 (*почтовое, заказное*) item.
3 (*поезда*) departure.

отправля́|ть, ю *impf. of* ▸ **отпра́вить**

отправля́|ться, юсь *impf. of* ▸ **отпра́виться**

отпра́здн|овать, ую *pf. of* ▸ **пра́здновать**

отпра́шива|ться, юсь *impf.* (*of* ▸ **отпроси́ться**) (*просить разрешения*) to ask (for) leave.

отпро|си́ться, шу́сь, ~сишься *pf.* (*of* ▸ **отпра́шиваться**) (*получить разрешение*) to obtain leave.

отпры́гива|ть, ю *impf. of* ▸ **отпры́гнуть**

отпры́г|нуть, ну, нешь *pf.* (*of* ▸ **~ивать**) (*назад*) to jump back; (*в сторону*) to jump aside.

отпу́гива|ть, ю *impf. of* ▸ **отпугну́ть**

отпуг|ну́ть, ну́, нёшь *pf.* (*of* ▸ **~ивать**) to frighten off, scare away.

о́тпуск, а, в ~е, *pl.* **~а́, ~о́в** *m.* leave, holiday(s) (*Br.*), vacation (*US*); (*mil.*) leave, furlough; **в ~е** on leave.

отпуска́|ть, ю *impf. of* ▸ **отпусти́ть**

отпу|сти́ть, щу́, ~стишь *pf.* (*of* ▸ **~ска́ть**)
1 (*позволить кому-н. уйти*; *перестать держать*) to let go; (*в сад, во двор*) to let out; (*освободить*) to set free; to release; (*дать отпуск*) to give leave (of absence).
2 (*ослабить*) to relax, slacken.
3 (*бороду*) to (let) grow; (*платье*) let down.
4 (*выдать*) to issue, give out; (*продать*) to sell.

отраба́тыва|ть, ю *impf. of* ▸ **отрабо́тать**

отрабо́та|нный *p.p.p. of* ▸ **~ть** *and adj.* (*tech.*) worked out; spent; **о. газ** waste gas.

отрабо́та|ть, ю *pf.* (*of* ▸ **отраба́тывать**)
1 (*долг*) to work off.
2 (*какое-н. время*) to work.
3 (*придать окончательный вид*) to put the finishing touches to.
4 (*упражнение, приём*) to work through, give a workout to.

отра́в|а, ы *f.* poison.

отрав|и́ть, лю́, ~ишь *pf.* (*of* ▸ **~ля́ть**) to poison (*also fig.*).

отрав|и́ться, лю́сь, ~ишься *pf.* (*of* ▸ **~ля́ться**) to poison o.s.

отравле́ни|е, я *nt.* poisoning.

отравля́|ть(ся), ю(сь) *impf. of* ▸ **отрави́ться**

отра́д|ный (~ен, ~на) *adj.* gratifying, pleasing; comforting.

отража́|ть(ся), ю(сь) *impf. of* ▸ **отрази́ть(ся)**

отраже́ни|е, я *nt.*
1 reflection.
2 (*нападения*) repelling; warding off.

отра|зи́ть, жу́, зи́шь *pf.* (*of* ▸ **~жа́ть**)
1 to reflect (*also fig.*).
2 (*нападение*) to repel; to ward off.

отра|зи́ться, жу́сь, зи́шься *pf.* (*of* ▸ **~жа́ться**)
1 to be reflected.
2 (*fig.*; **на** + *p.*) to affect; to tell (on); **пое́здка в го́ры благоприя́тно ~зи́лась на его́ рабо́те** the mountain trip had a beneficial effect on his work.

о́трасл|ь, и *f.* branch; **о. промы́шленности** branch of industry.

отраст|а́ть, а́ю *impf. of* ▸ **~и́**

отраст|и́, у́, ёшь, *past* **отро́с, отросла́** *pf.* (*of* ▸ **~а́ть**) to grow.

отра|сти́ть, щу́, сти́шь *pf.* (*of* ▸ **~щивать**) to (let) grow; **о. во́лосы** to grow one's hair long.

отра́щива|ть, ю *impf. of* ▸ **отрасти́ть**

отреаги́р|овать, ую *pf.* (*coll.*) *of*

▸ **реаги́ровать 2**
отрегули́р|овать, ую *pf. of* ▸ **регули́ровать 3**
отредакти́р|овать, ую *pf. of* ▸ **редакти́ровать 1**
отрез|а́ть, а́ю *impf. of* ▸ **~́ать**
отре́|зать, жу, жешь *pf.* (*of* ▸ **~за́ть**)
1 to cut off (*also fig.*).
2 (*coll.*) (*резко ответить*) to snap back.
отре́з|ок, ка *m.* (*ткани*) piece, cut; (*пути*) section; (*math.*) segment; **о. вре́мени** stretch of time.
отрека́|ться, юсь *impf. of* ▸ **отре́чься**
отремонти́р|овать, ую *pf. of* ▸ **ремонти́ровать**
отрепети́р|овать, ую *pf. of* ▸ **репети́ровать**
отреставри́р|овать, ую *pf. of* ▸ **реставри́ровать**
отре́|чься, ку́сь, чёшься, ку́тся, *past* **~́кся, ~кла́сь** *pf.* (*of* ▸ **~ка́ться**) (**от** + *g.*) to renounce, disavow, give up; **о. от престо́ла** to abdicate.
отрица́ни|е, я *nt.* denial; negation.
отрица́тел|ьный (~ен, ~ьна) *adj.* negative.
отрица́|ть, ю *impf.* to deny; to disclaim; **о. вино́вность** (*leg.*) to plead not guilty.
отруб|а́ть, а́ю *impf. of* ▸ **~и́ть**
отруб|и́ть, лю́, ~́ишь *pf.* (*of* ▸ **~а́ть**) (*сук*) to chop off.
отруга́|ть, ю *pf. of* ▸ **руга́ть 1, 2**
отры́в, а *m.*
1 tearing off.
2 (*fig.*) alienation, isolation; loss of contact; **в ~е** (**от** + *g.*) out of touch (with).
отрыва́|ть, ю *impf. of* ▸ **оторва́ть**
отрыва́|ться, юсь *impf. of* ▸ **оторва́ться**
отры́вист|ый (~, ~а) *adj.* jerky, abrupt; (*речь*) curt.
отры́в|ок, ка *m.* (*разговора*) fragment; (*книги*) excerpt; passage; **о. из фи́льма** film clip.
отры́жк|а, и *f.* belch.
отря́д, а *m.* (*mil.*) detachment; (*группа*) group, party, brigade; **передово́й о.** (*fig.*) vanguard.
отря́хива|ть(ся), ю(сь) *impf. of* ▸ **отряхну́ть(ся)**
отрях|ну́ть, ну́, нёшь *pf.* (*of* ▸ **~́ивать**) to shake down, shake off.
отрях|ну́ться, ну́сь, нёшься *pf.* (*of* ▸ **~́иваться**) to shake o.s. down.
о́тсвет, а *m.* reflection; reflected light.
отсе́ива|ть(ся), ю(сь) *impf. of* ▸ **отсе́ять(ся)**
отсе́к, а *m.*
1 (*naut., etc.*) compartment.
2 (*astronautics*) module.
отсека́|ть, ю *impf. of* ▸ **отсе́чь**
отсе́|чь, ку́, чёшь, ку́т, *past* **~к, ~кла́** *pf.* (*of* ▸ **~ка́ть**) to cut off, chop off.
отсе́|ять, ю, ешь *pf.* (*of* ▸ **~ивать**)
1 to sift, screen.
2 (*fig.*) to eliminate, screen out.
отсе́|яться, юсь, ешься *pf.* (*of* ▸ **~иваться**)
1 to be separated.
2 (*fig.*) to fall off, fall away.
отси|де́ть, жу́, ди́шь *pf.* (*of* ▸ **~́живать**)
1 (*просидеть*) to stay (for); to sit out; **он ~де́л де́сять лет в тюрьме́** he has done ten years (in prison).
2 (*вызвать онемение части тела*) to make numb by sitting; **я ~де́л себе́ но́гу** I have pins and needles in my leg.
отси|де́ться, жу́сь, ди́шься *pf.* (*of* ▸ **~́живаться**) (*coll.*) to sit tight.
отси́жива|ть(ся), ю(сь) *impf. of* ▸ **отсиде́ть(ся)**
отска́кива|ть, ю *impf. of* ▸ **отскочи́ть**
отскоч|и́ть, у́, ~́ишь *pf.* (*of* ▸ **отска́кивать**)
1 (*отпрыгнуть*) to jump (aside, away); (*о мяче*) to rebound, bounce back.
2 (*coll.*) (*отделиться*) to come off, break off.
отскреба́|ть, ю *impf. of* ▸ **отскрести́**
отскре|сти́, бу́, бёшь, *past* **~̈б, ~бла́** *pf.* (*of* ▸ **~ба́ть**) to scrape off.
отслуж|и́ть, у́, ~́ишь *pf. of* ▸ **служи́ть 5**
отсоедин|и́ть, ю́, и́шь *pf.* ▸ **~я́ть**) to disconnect.
отсоединя́|ть, ю *impf. of* ▸ **отсоедини́ть**
отсортир|ова́ть, у́ю *pf.* (*of* ▸ **~о́вывать**) to sort (out).
отсортиро́выва|ть, ю *impf. of* ▸ **отсортирова́ть**
отсро́чива|ть, ю *impf. of* ▸ **отсро́чить**
отсро́ч|ить, у, ишь *pf.* (*of* ▸ **~ивать**) to postpone, defer.
отсро́чк|а, и *f.* postponement, deferment.
отстава́ни|е, я *nt.* lag.
отста|ва́ть, ю́, ёшь *impf. of* ▸ **~́ть**
отста́вк|а, и *f.* (*mil.*) retirement; (*hist.*) (*с государственной службы*) resignation; **вы́йти в ~у** to retire; to resign.
отставно́й *adj.* (*mil.*) retired.
отста́ива|ть, ю *impf. of* ▸ **отстоя́ть**
отста́лый *adj.* (*fig.*) backward; **у́мственно о.** mentally retarded.
отста́|ть, ну, нешь *pf.* (*of* ▸ **~ва́ть**)
1 (**от** + *g.*) (*оказаться позади*) to fall behind; to lag behind; (*умственно*) to be backward, be retarded.
2 (**от** + *g.*) (*отделиться*) to become detached (from); **о. от по́езда** to be left behind by the train (*sc., at a station en route*); **обо́и ~ли от стены́** the wallpaper came off.
3 (*о часах*) to be slow; **о. на полчаса́** to be half an hour slow.
4 (*coll.*; **от** + *g.*) (*перестать надоедать*) to leave alone; **~нь от меня́!** leave me alone!
отстёгива|ть, ю *impf. of* ▸ **отстегну́ть**
отстег|ну́ть, ну́, нёшь *pf.* (*of* ▸ **~̈ивать**) (*крючок*) to unfasten, undo; (*пуговицы*) to unbutton.
отстир|а́ть, а́ю *pf.* (*of* ▸ **~́ывать**) to wash off.
отстир|а́ться, а́ется *pf.* (*of* ▸ **~́ываться**) to wash off, come out in the wash.
отсти́рыва|ть(ся), ю, ет(ся) *impf. of* ▸ **отстира́ть(ся)**

отсто|я́ть, ю́, и́шь *pf.* (*of* ▸ **отста́ивать**) to defend.

отстра́ива|ть, ю *impf. of* ▸ **отстро́ить**

отстран|и́ть, ю́, и́шь *pf.* (*of* ▸ **~я́ть**)
1 (*отодвинуть*) to push aside.
2 (*уволить*) to dismiss, discharge.

отстран|я́ть, я́ю *impf. of* ▸ **~и́ть**

отстре́лива|ться, юсь *impf. of* ▸ **отстреля́ться**

отстрел|я́ться, я́юсь *pf.* (*of* ▸ **~̂иваться**)
1 (**от** + *g.*) to defend o.s. (against) (by shooting).
2 (*ответить стрельбой на стрельбу*) to return fire, fire back.

отстрига́|ть, ю *impf. of* ▸ **отстри́чь**

отстри́|чь, гу́, жёшь, гу́т, *past* **~г, ~гла** *pf.* (*of* ▸ **~га́ть**) to cut off, clip.

отстр|о́ить, о́ю, о́ишь *pf.* (*of* ▸ **~а́ивать**) to complete the construction of, finish building.

о́тступ, а *m.* (*typ.*) indentation.

отступ|а́ть(ся), а́ю(сь) *impf. of* ▸ **~и́ть(ся)**

отступ|и́ть, лю́, ~̂ишь *pf.* (*of* ▸ **~а́ть**)
1 (*отойти назад*) to step back; to recede.
2 (*mil.*) to retreat, fall back.
3 (*fig.*; **от** + *g.*) (*от чего-н. установленного*) to deviate (from); **о. от те́мы** to digress.

отступ|и́ться, лю́сь, ~̂ишься *pf.* (*of* ▸ **~а́ться**) (*coll.*; **от** + *g.*) to give up, renounce; **о. от своего́ сло́ва** to go back on one's word.

отступле́ни|е, я *nt.*
1 (*mil. and fig.*) retreat.
2 (*от темы*) deviation; digression.

отсу́тстви|е, я *nt.* absence; (+ *g.*) lack (of); **в его́ о.** in his absence; **за ~ем** (+ *g.*) (*кого-н.*) in the absence (of); (*чего-н.*) for lack (of), for want (of).

отсу́тств|овать, ую *impf.* (*о человеке*) to be absent; (*о доказательстве*) to be lacking.

отсу́тств|ующий *pres. part. of* ▸ **~овать** *and adj.* absent (*also fig.*); **о. вид** blank expression; *as n.* **о., ~ующего** *m.* absentee.

отсчит|а́ть, а́ю *pf.* (*of* ▸ **~̂ывать**) to count out, count off; **о. кому́-н. пятьсо́т рубле́й** to count out five hundred roubles to s.o.

отсчи́тыва|ть, ю *impf. of* ▸ **отсчита́ть**

отсыла́|ть, ю *impf. of* ▸ **отосла́ть**

отсып|а́ть, а́ю *impf. of* ▸ **~̂ать**

отсы́п|ать, лю, лешь *pf.* (*of* ▸ **~а́ть**) (+ *a. or g.*) to pour off; to measure off.

отсыре́|ть, ю *pf. of* ▸ **сыре́ть**

отсю́да *adv.* from here; hence (*also fig.*); (*fig.*) from this; **о. сле́дует, что...** from this it follows that ... .

Отта́в|а, ы *f.* Ottawa.

отта́ива|ть, ю *impf. of* ▸ **оття́ять**

отта́лкива|ть(ся), ю(сь) *impf. of* ▸ **оттолкну́ть(ся)**

отта́скива|ть, ю *impf. of* ▸ **оттащи́ть**

оттащ|и́ть, у́, ~̂ишь *pf.* (*of* ▸ **отта́скивать**) to drag aside (away), pull aside (away).

отта́|ять, ю, ешь *pf.* (*of* ▸ **~ивать**) (*trans. and intrans.*) to thaw out.

отте́н|ок, ка *m.* (*цвета*) shade, hue; (*fig.*) shade, nuance; **он говори́л с ~ком иро́нии** there was a note of irony in his voice.

о́ттепел|ь, и *f.* thaw.

оттер|е́ть, ототру́, ототрёшь, *past* **~̂, ~̂ла** *pf.* (*of* ▸ **оттира́ть**) (*грязь*) to rub off, rub out.

оттесн|и́ть, ю́, и́шь *pf.* (*of* ▸ **~я́ть**) to drive back; press back; to push aside, shove aside (*also fig.*); **о. проти́вника** (*mil.*) to force the enemy back.

оттесн|я́ть, я́ю *impf. of* ▸ **~и́ть**

оттира́|ть, ю *impf. of* ▸ **оттере́ть**

оттого́ *adv.* = **потому́**

отто́к, а *m.* mass departure (*of specialists, sportsmen, etc.*).

оттолкн|у́ть, у́, ёшь *pf.* (*of* ▸ **отта́лкивать**)
1 (*стул*) to push away, push aside.
2 (*fig.*) (*друзей*) to antagonize, alienate.

оттолкн|у́ться, у́сь, ёшься *pf.* (*of* ▸ **отта́лкиваться**)
1 (**от** + *g.*) to push off (from).
2 (*fig.*; **от** + *g.*) to take as a starting point.

оттопы́рен|ный (~, ~а) *adj.* (*coll.*) protruding, sticking out; (*карманы*) bulging.

отторже́ни|е, я *nt.* tearing away, seizure; (*med.*) rejection (*of a transplanted organ*).

отту́да *adv.* from there.

оття́гива|ть, ю *impf. of* ▸ **оттяну́ть**

оття|ну́ть, ну́, ~̂нешь *pf.* (*of* ▸ **~̂гивать**)
1 to pull, drag (away).
2 (*mil.*) (*отряд*) to draw off.
3 (*карман*) to stretch, weigh down.

отупе́ни|е, я *nt.* stupefaction, dullness, torpor.

отуч|а́ть(ся), а́ю(сь) *impf. of* ▸ **~и́ть** *and* ▸ **~и́ться**[1]

оту́чива|ться, юсь *impf. of* ▸ **отучи́ться**[2]

отуч|и́ть, у́, ~̂ишь *pf.* (*of* ▸ **~а́ть**) (**от** + *g. or* + *inf.*) to break (of); **о. от груди́** to wean.

отуч|и́ться[1]**, у́сь, ~̂ишься** *pf.* (*of* ▸ **~а́ться**) (**от** + *g. or* + *inf.*) (*отвыкнуть*) to break o.s. (of).

отуч|и́ться[2]**, у́сь, ~̂ишься** *pf.* (*of* ▸ **~̂иваться**) (*кончить учиться*) to have finished one's lessons; to finish learning.

отфильтр|ова́ть, у́ю *pf.* (*of* ▸ **фильтрова́ть**)

отформати́р|овать, ую *pf.* (*of* ▸ **формати́ровать**)

отхва|ти́ть, чу́, ~̂тишь *pf.* (*of* ▸ **~̂тывать**) (*coll.*)
1 (*отрезать*) to snip off; (*отрубить*) to chop off.
2 (*достать*) to get hold of.

отхва́тыва|ть, ю *impf. of* ▸ **отхвати́ть**

отхлеб|ну́ть, ну́, нёшь *pf.* (*of* ▸ **~̂ывать**) (*coll.*; + *a. or g.*) to take a sip (of); to take a mouthful (of).

отхлёбыва|ть, ю *impf. of* ▸ **отхлебну́ть**

отхлы́н|уть, у, ешь *pf.* to rush back, flood back (*also fig.*).

отхо́д, а *m.*
1 departure.
2 (*mil.*) withdrawal.

3 (**от** + *g.*) (*отклонение*) deviation (from); (*разрыв*) break (with).
4 *see* ▸ **~ы**

отхо|ди́ть, жу́, ~́дишь *impf. of* ▸ **отойти́**

отхо́д|ы, ов (*tech.*) waste (products).

отцеп|и́ть, лю́, ~́ишь *pf.* (*of* ▸ **~ля́ть**) to unhook; to uncouple.

отцеп|и́ться, лю́сь, ~́ишься *pf.* (*of* ▸ **~ля́ться**) to come unhooked; to come uncoupled.

отцепля́|ть(ся), ю(сь) *impf. of* ▸ **отцепи́ть(ся)**

отцо́вский *adj.* one's father's; paternal.

отча́ива|ться, юсь *impf. of* ▸ **отча́яться**

отча́сти *adv.* partly.

отча́яни|е, я *nt.* despair.

отча́ян|ный (~, ~на) *adj.* (*положение, взор, крик*) desperate; (*смелый до безрассудности*) daring, reckless; (*coll.*) (*ужасный*) terrible, awful.

отча́|яться, юсь, ешься *pf.* (*of* ▸ **~иваться**) (+ *inf. or* **в** + *p.*) to despair (of).

отчего́ *adv.* why; **вот о.** that's why.

отчего́-нибудь *adv.* for some reason or other.

отчего́-то *adv.* for some reason.

о́честв|о, а *nt.* patronymic; **как его́ по ~у** what is his patronymic?

отчёт, а *m.* account; **дать о.** (**в** + *p.*) to give an account (of), report (on); **отдава́ть себе́ о.** (**в** + *p.*) to be aware (of), realize.

отчётлив|ый (~, ~а) *adj.* intelligible, clear, distinct.

отчёт|ный *adj. of* ▸ **~; о. год** financial year, current year; **о. докла́д** report.

о́тчим, а *m.* stepfather.

отчи́|стить, щу, стишь *pf.* (*of* ▸ **~ща́ть**)
1 (*пятно*) to clean off; to brush off.
2 (*одежду*) to clean.

отчи́|ститься, щусь, стишься *pf.* (*of* ▸ **~ща́ться**)
1 (*о грязи*) to come off, come out.
2 (*об одежде*) to become clean.

отчит|а́ться, а́юсь *pf.* (*of* ▸ **~́ываться**) (**в** + *p.*) to give an account (of), report (on); **о. пе́ред избира́телями** to report back to the electors.

отчи́тыва|ться, юсь *impf. of* ▸ **отчита́ться**

отчища́|ть(ся), ю(сь) *impf. of* ▸ **отчи́стить(ся)**

отшатн|у́ться, у́сь, ёшься *pf.* (*of* ▸ **отша́тываться**) (**от** + *g.*)
1 (*от удара*) to start back (from); to recoil (from).
2 (*fig.*) (*прекратить общение*) to give up; to break (with).

отша́тыва|ться, юсь *impf. of* ▸ **отшатну́ться**

отшвы́рива|ть, ю *impf. of* ▸ **отшвырну́ть**

отшвыр|ну́ть, ну́, нёшь *pf.* (*of* ▸ **~́ивать**) to fling away; to throw off.

отше́льник, а *m.* hermit; recluse.

отшлёпа|ть, ю *pf. of* ▸ **шлёпать**

отшлиф|ова́ть, у́ю *pf.* (*of* ▸ **~о́вывать** *and* ▸ **шлифова́ть**)
1 (*tech.*) to polish; to grind.
2 (*fig.*) (*совершенствовать*) to polish, perfect.

отшлифо́выва|ть, ю *impf. of* ▸ **отшлифова́ть**

отъеда́|ть(ся), ю(сь) *impf. of* ▸ **отъе́сть(ся)**

отъе́зд, а *m.* departure; **быть в ~е** to be away.

отъезжа́|ть, ю *impf. of* ▸ **отъе́хать**

отъе́|сть, м, шь, ст, ди́м, ди́те, дя́т, *past* **~л, ~ла** *pf.* (*of* ▸ **~да́ть**) to bite off and eat.

отъе́|сться, мся, шься, стся, ди́мся, ди́тесь, дя́тся, *past* **~лся, ~лась** *pf.* (*of* ▸ **~да́ться**) to put on weight; to feed well.

отъе́|хать, ду, дешь *pf.* (*of* ▸ **~зжа́ть**) to depart.

отъя́вленный *adj.* (*coll., pej.*) thorough, inveterate, out-and-out.

отыгр|а́ться, а́юсь *pf.* (*of* ▸ **~́ываться**) to win (having lost); to get back what one has lost.

оты́грыва|ться, юсь *impf. of* ▸ **отыгра́ться**

оты|ска́ть, щу́, ~́щешь *pf.* (*of* ▸ **~́скивать 1**) to find; to track down, run to earth.

оты|ска́ться, щу́сь, ~́щешься *pf.* (*of* ▸ **~́скиваться**) to turn up, appear.

оты́скива|ть, ю *impf.*
1 *impf. of* ▸ **отыска́ть.**
2 (*impf. only*) to look for, try to find.

оты́скива|ться, юсь *impf. of* ▸ **отыска́ться**

отяжеле́|ть, ю *pf.* to become heavy.

о́фис, а *m.* office.

о́фисный *adj.* office (*attr.*).

офице́р, а *m.* officer.

офице́р|ский *adj. of* ▸ **~; ~ское собра́ние** officers' mess.

официа́льн|ый *adj.* official; **~ое лицо́** an official.

официа́нт, а *m.* waiter.

официа́нтк|а, и *f.* waitress.

офла́йновый *adj.* (*comput.*) offline.

оформи́тел|ь, я *m.* designer; **о. спекта́кля** set designer.

оформи́тель|ница, ницы *f. of* ▸ **~**

офо́рм|ить, лю, ишь *pf.* (*of* ▸ **~ля́ть**)
1 to design; **о. витри́ну** to dress a window.
2 (*узаконить*) to register officially, legalize; **о. догово́р** to draw up an agreement.
3 (*на работу*) to enrol, take on.

офо́рм|иться, люсь, ишься *pf.* (*of* ▸ **~ля́ться**)
1 (*об идеях*) to take shape.
2 (*узакониться*) to be registered; to legalize one's position.
3 (*на работу*) to be taken on, join the staff.

оформле́ни|е, я *nt.*
1 design; **сцени́ческое о.** staging.
2 (*узаконение*) registration, legalization.

оформля́|ть(ся), ю(сь) *impf. of* ▸ **офо́рмить(ся)**

офо́рт, а *m.* (*вид гравюры на металле*)

etching.

офтальмо́лог, а *m.* ophthalmologist.

офтальмоло́ги|я, и *f.* ophthalmology.

офшо́рный *adj.* (*fin.*) offshore.

о́х|ать, аю *impf.* (*of* ▶ **~нуть**) (*от боли*) to moan, groan; (*от печали*) to sigh.

охва|ти́ть, чу́, ~́тишь *pf.* (*of* ▶ **~́тывать**)
1 (*обхватить*) to envelop; to enclose; **дом ~ти́ло пла́менем** the house was enveloped in flames.
2 (*о чувстве*) to grip, seize; **их ~ти́л у́жас** they were seized with panic.

охва́тыва|ть, ю *impf. of* ▶ **охвати́ть**

охва́|ченный *p.p.p. of* ▶ **~ти́ть; о. у́жасом** terror-stricken.

охла|ди́ть, жу́, ди́шь *pf.* (*of* ▶ **~жда́ть**) to cool, cool off (*also fig.*).

охла|ди́ться, жу́сь, ди́шься *pf.* (*of* ▶ **~жда́ться**) to become cool, cool down (*also fig.*).

охлажда́|ть(ся), ю(сь) *impf. of* ▶ **охлади́ть(ся)**

охлажда́|ющий *pres. part. act. of* ▶ **~ть** *and adj.* cooling, refrigerating; **~ющая жи́дкость** coolant.

охлажде́ни|е, я *nt.*
1 cooling (off); **с возду́шным ~ем** air-cooled.
2 (*fig.*) coolness.

о́х|нуть, ну, нешь *pf. of* ▶ **~ать**

охо́т|а[1], ы *f.* hunt, hunting; chase.

охо́т|а[2], ы *f.* (**к** + *d. or* + *inf.*) desire, wish, inclination; **о. тебе́ спо́рить с ним!** (*coll.*) what makes you argue with him!

охо́|титься, чусь, тишься *impf.* (**на** + *a. or* **за** + *i.*) to hunt; (*fig.*; **за** + *i.*) to hunt for.

охо́тник, а *m.* hunter.

охо́тничий *adj.* hunting.

охо́тно *adv.* willingly, gladly, readily.

о́хр|а, ы *f.* ochre (*Br.*), ocher (*US*).

охра́н|а, ы *f.*
1 (*помещения*) guarding; (*природы*) protection; **о. труда́** health and safety measures.
2 (*группа людей*) guard; **ли́чная о.** bodyguard; **пограни́чная о.** frontier guard.

охран|и́ть, ю́, и́шь *pf.* (*of* ▶ **~я́ть**) (*границу, помещение*) to guard; (*природу, интересы*) to protect.

охра́нник, а *m.* guard.

охран|я́ть, я́ю *impf. of* ▶ **~и́ть**

охри́п|нуть, ну, нешь, *past* **~, ~ла** *pf.* (*of* ▶ **хри́пнуть**) to become hoarse.

оцара́па|ть, ю *pf.* (*of* ▶ **цара́пать**) to scratch.

оце́нива|ть, ю *impf. of* ▶ **оцени́ть**

оцен|и́ть, ю́, ~́ишь *pf.* (*of* ▶ **~́ивать**)
1 (*определить цену чего-н.*) to estimate the value of, value; (*назначить цену чему-н.*) to price; (*определить ценность, значительность чего-н.*) to evaluate, appraise.
2 (*признать достоинства чего-н.*) to appreciate; **о. что-н. по досто́инству** to appreciate sth. at its true value.

оце́нк|а, и *f.*
1 (*имущества*) valuation; (*работы*) evaluation, appraisal.
2 (*мнение о ценности*) appreciation.
3 (*отметка*) mark, grade.

оцепене́ни|е, я *nt.* stupor.

оцеп|и́ть, лю́, ~́ишь *pf.* (*of* ▶ **~ля́ть**) to surround; to cordon off.

оцепле́ни|е, я *nt.*
1 (*действие*) surrounding; cordoning off.
2 (*люди*) cordon.

оцепля́|ть, ю *impf. of* ▶ **оцепи́ть**

оча́г, а́ *m.*
1 hearth (*also fig.*); **дома́шний о.** (*fig.*) hearth, home.
2 (*fig.*) centre, seat.

очарова́тел|ьный (~ен, ~ьна) *adj.* charming, fascinating.

очар|ова́ть, у́ю *pf.* (*of* ▶ **~о́вывать**) to charm, fascinate.

очаро́выва|ть, ю *impf. of* ▶ **очарова́ть**

очеви́д|ец, ца *m.* eyewitness.

очеви́дно *adv.* obviously, evidently; **вы, о., не согла́сны** you obviously do not agree.

очеви́д|ный (~ен, ~на) *adj.* obvious, evident.

о́чень *adv.* (*при прилагательных и наречиях*) very; (*при глаголах*) very much.

очередно́й *adj.*
1 next; next in turn; **о. вопро́с** the next question; **о. вы́пуск** latest issue (*of a journal, etc.*).
2 usual; regular; **о. о́тпуск** regular holidays.

о́черед|ь, и, *pl.* **~и, ~е́й** *f.*
1 turn; **о. за ва́ми** it is your turn; **в свою́ о.** in one's turn; **по ~и** in turn, in order; **в пе́рвую о.** in the first place/instance.
2 (*ряд*) queue (*Br.*), line (*US*); **стоя́ть в ~и (за** + *i.*) to queue (for) (*Br.*), stand in line (for) (*US*); **стать в о́чередь** to queue (up) (*Br.*), stand in line (*US*).
3 (*mil.*): **(пулемётная) о.** burst.

о́черк, а *m.* essay, sketch, study; (*контур*) outline; **~и ру́сской исто́рии** studies in Russian history.

очерта́ни|е, я *nt.* (*usu. pl.*) outline.

очи́|стить, щу, стишь *pf.* (*of* ▶ **~ща́ть, чи́стить 3**)
1 (*тарелку, обувь*) to clean; (*воду, спирт*) to purify; (*совесть*) to salve, clear; (*душу*) to cleanse, purify.
2 (**от** + *g.*) (*стол*) to clear (of); to free; **о. кише́чник** to open bowels.
3 (*картофелину, яблоко*) to peel.

очи́|ститься, щусь, стишься *pf.* (*of* ▶ **~ща́ться**) (**от** + *g.*) to become clear (of).

очи́стк|а, и *f.*
1 (*обуви*) cleaning; (*души*) cleansing, purification; (*воды*) purification; (*овощей*) peeling.
2 (**от** + *g.*) clearing, clearance (of); freeing (of).

очи́стк|и, ов *no sg.* peelings.

очища́|ть(ся), ю(сь) *impf. of* ▶ **очи́стить(ся)**

очк|и́, о́в *no sg.* glasses, spectacles (*Br.*), eyeglasses (*US*); (*защитные*) goggles.

очк|о́, а́, *pl.* **~и́, ~о́в** *nt.* (*sport*) point.

очн|у́ться, у́сь, ёшься *pf.*
1 (*после сна*) to wake.

2 (*после обморока*) to come to, regain consciousness.

о́чн|ый *adj.*
1 (*opp.* **заóчный**) internal (*instruction, student, etc., as opposed to* external, extra-mural).
2 : **~ая ста́вка** (*leg.*) confrontation.

очут|и́ться, ~ишься *pf.* to find o.s.; to come to be; **как вы здесь ~и́лись?** how did you come to be here?

оше́йник, а *m.* (*animal's*) collar.

ошелом|и́ть, лю́, и́шь *pf.* (*of* ▸ **~ля́ть**) to stun.

ошеломля́|ть, ю *impf. of* ▸ **ошеломи́ть**

ошиб|а́ться, а́юсь *impf. of* ▸ **~и́ться**

ошиб|и́ться, у́сь, ёшься, *past* **~ся, ~лась** *pf.* (*of* ▸ **~а́ться**) to be mistaken, make a mistake, make mistakes.

оши́бк|а, и *f.* mistake; error; **по ~е** by mistake.

оши́боч|ный (~ен, ~на) *adj.* erroneous, mistaken.

ошпа́рива|ть, ю *impf. of* ▸ **ошпа́рить**

ошпа́р|ить, ю, ишь *pf.* (*of* ▸ **~ивать** *and* ▸ **шпа́рить 1**) (*coll.*) to scald.

оштраф|ова́ть, у́ю *pf. of* ▸ **штрафова́ть**

оштукату́р|ить, ю, ишь *pf. of* ▸ **штукату́рить**

ощети́нива|ться, юсь *impf. of* ▸ **ощети́ниться**

ощети́н|иться, юсь, ишься *pf.* (*of* ▸ **~иваться** *and* ▸ **щети́ниться**) to bristle (*also fig.*).

ощип|а́ть, лю́, ~лешь *pf.* (*of* ▸ **щипа́ть 3** *and* ▸ **~ывать**) to pluck.

ощи́пыва|ть, ю *impf. of* ▸ **ощипа́ть**

ощу́п|ать, аю *pf.* (*of* ▸ **~ывать**) to feel.

ощу́пыва|ть, ю *impf. of* ▸ **ощу́пать**

о́щуп|ь, и *f.*: **на о.** to the touch; by touch; **идти́ на о.** to grope one's way.

ощути́м|ый (~, ~а) *adj.*
1 (*запах, похолодание*) perceptible, noticeable.
2 (*fig.*) (*недостатки, расходы*) appreciable.

ощу|ти́ть, щу́, ти́шь *pf.* (*of* ▸ **~ща́ть**) to feel, sense; **о. го́лод** to feel hunger.

ощуща́|ть, ю *impf. of* ▸ **ощути́ть**

ощуще́ни|е, я *nt.*
1 (*physiol.*) sensation.
2 (*страха, радости*) feeling, sense.

Пп

павильо́н, а *m.*
1 pavilion.
2 (*cin.*) film studio.

павли́н, а *m.* peacock.

па́вод|ок, ка *m.* flood (*esp. resulting from melting of snow*).

па́год|а, ы *f.* pagoda.

па́дал|ь, и *f.* (*usu. collect.*) carrion.

па́да|ть, ю *impf.*
1 (*pf.* **пасть**[1] ▸ **1** *and* **упа́сть**) to fall; (*о настроении*) to sink; (*о нравах*) to decline; **п. в о́бморок** to faint.
2 (*pf.* **пасть**[1] ▸ **1**) (*fig.*; **на** + *a.*) to fall (on, to); **отве́тственность ~ет на вас** the responsibility falls on you.

паде́ж, а́ *m.* (*gram.*) case.

паде́ни|е, я *nt.* fall; (*нравов*) decline.

па́дчериц|а, ы *f.* stepdaughter.

па|ёк, йка́ *m.* ration.

пазл, а *m.* jigsaw puzzle.

па́зух|а, и *f.* bosom; **за ~ой** in one's bosom.

паке́т, а *m.*
1 (*свёрток*) parcel, package.
2 (*письмо*) (official) letter.
3 (*мешок*) (paper) bag.
4 (*comput.*) package.

Пакиста́н, а *m.* Pakistan.

пакиста́н|ец, ца *m.* Pakistani.

пакиста́н|ка, ки *f. of* ▸ **~ец**

пакиста́нский *adj.* Pakistani.

пак|ова́ть, у́ю *impf.* (*of* ▸ **у~**) to pack.

па́кост|ь, и *f.*
1 (*о поступке*) dirty trick; **де́лать ~и** (+ *d.*) to play dirty tricks (on).
2 (*дрянь*) filth.

пакт, а *m.* pact; **п. о ненападе́нии** non-aggression pact.

пала́т|а, ы *f.*
1 (*в больнице*) ward.
2 (*pol.*) chamber, house; **ве́рхняя, ни́жняя п.** Upper, Lower Chamber; **п. ло́рдов** House of Lords; **п. о́бщин** House of Commons.
3 (*название некоторых государственных учреждений*): **Торго́вая п.** Chamber of Commerce.

пала́тк|а, и *f.*
1 tent; (*большая*) marquee.
2 (*ларёк*) stall, booth.

пала́ч, а́ *m.* executioner; (*fig.*) butcher.

палеоли́т, а *m.* (*archaeol.*) palaeolithic period (*Br.*), paleolithic period (*US*).

палеонто́лог, а *m.* palaeontologist (*Br.*), paleontologist (*US*).

палеонтоло́ги|я, и *f.* palaeontology (*Br.*), paleontology (*US*).

Палести́н|а, ы *f.* Palestine.

палести́н|ец, ца *m.* Palestinian.

палести́н|ка, ки *f. of* ▸ **~ец**

палести́нский *adj.* Palestinian.

па́л|ец, ьца *m.* finger; **п. ноги́** toe; **большо́й п.** thumb; **смотре́ть сквозь ~ьцы на что-н.** (*coll.*) to shut one's eyes to sth.

палиса́дник, а *m.* small front garden.
пали́тр|а, ы *f.* palette.
пал|и́ть, ю́, и́шь *impf.* (*coll.*) (*стрелять*) to fire (*from gun*).
па́лк|а, и *f.* stick; **вставля́ть кому́-н. ~и в колёса** to put a spoke in s.o.'s wheel.
пало́мник, а *m.* pilgrim (*also fig.*).
па́лочк|а, и *f. dim. of* ▸ **па́лка; бараба́нная п.** drumstick; **волше́бная п.** magic wand; **дирижёрская п.** conductor's baton.
па́лтус, а *m.* halibut; (*в рыболовстве также, ошибочно*) turbot.
па́луб|а, ы *f.* deck.
па́льм|а, ы *f.* palm (tree).
пал|ьну́ть, ьну́, ьнёшь *inst. pf.* (*of* ▸ **~и́ть**) (*coll.*) to fire a shot.
пальто́ *nt. indecl.* (over)coat.
пампа́с|ы, ов *no sg.* (*geog.*) pampas.
памфле́т, а *m.* lampoon.
па́мятк|а, и *f.* (list of) instructions, guidelines.
па́мятник, а *m.* monument; (*на могиле*) tombstone; (*статуя*) statue; (*археологический*) relic.
па́мят|ный (~ен, ~на) *adj.* memorable.
па́мят|ь, и *f.*
1 (*also comput.*) memory; **на мое́й ~и** within my memory; **по ~и** from memory.
2 (*воспоминание*) memory, recollection, remembrance; **в п.** (+ *g.*) in memory (of); **подари́ть на п.** to give as a keepsake.
3 (*сознание*) mind, consciousness; **быть без ~и** to be unconscious; **быть от кого́-н. без ~и** (*coll.*) be crazy about s.o.
Пана́м|а, ы *f.* Panama.
пана́м|а, ы *f.* panama (hat).
па́нд|а, ы *f.* panda.
пане́л|ь, и *f.*
1 (*тротуар*) pavement (*Br.*), sidewalk (*US*).
2 (*обшивка*) panel, panelling (*Br.*), paneling (*US*).
3: **прибо́рная п.** instrument panel; dashboard.
па́ник|а, и *f.* panic.
паник|ова́ть, у́ю *impf.* (*no pf.*) (*coll.*) to panic.
панихи́д|а, ы *f.* funeral service; requiem; **гражда́нская п.** civil funeral.
пани́ческий *adj.* panic-stricken; **п. страх** utter terror.
панк, а *m.* (*also as indecl. adj.*) punk.
панно́ *nt. indecl.* panel.
панора́м|а, ы *f.* panorama.
панора́мный *adj.* panoramic.
пансио́н, а *m.*: **по́лный ~** (full) board and lodging.
пансиона́т, а *m.* boarding house, guest house.
пантеи́зм, а *m.* pantheism.
пантео́н, а *m.* pantheon.
панте́р|а, ы *f.* panther.
пантоми́м|а, ы *f.* mime.
па́нцир|ь, я *m.* (*zool.*) shell.
па́п|а[1], ы *m.* (*coll.*) dad, daddy, papa (*US*).
па́п|а[2], ы *m.*: **П. Ри́мский** pope; the Pope.
папа́й|я, и *f.* papaya, pawpaw.
папара́цци *c.g. indecl.* paparazzo.
па́перт|ь, и *f.* church porch, parvis.
папиро́с|а, ы *f.* cigarette (*of Russian type, with cardboard mouthpiece*).
папи́рус, а *m.* papyrus.
па́пк|а, и *f.* folder, file; (*comput.*) file.
па́поротник, а *m.* fern.
па́прик|а, и *f.* paprika.
Па́пуа – Но́вая Гвине́я, – Но́вой Гвине́и *f.* Papua New Guinea.
папуа́с, а *m.* Papuan.
папуа́с|ка, ки *f. of* ▸ **~**
папуа́сский *adj.* Papuan.
папье́-маше́ *nt. indecl.* papier mâché.
пар, а, о ~е, в ~у́, *pl.* **~ы́** *m.*
1 steam.
2 (*видимое испарение*) vapour (*Br.*), vapor (*US*).
па́р|а, ы *f.* (*сапог, чулок, ножниц*) pair; (*два предмета, двое людей*) couple; **супру́жеская п.** married couple; **она́ ему́ не п.** she is no match for him.
Парагва́|й, я *m.* Paraguay.
пара́граф, а *m.* paragraph.
пара́д, а *m.* (*шествие*) parade; (*mil.*) review.
паради́гм|а, ы *f.* paradigm.
пара́д|ный (~ен, ~на) *adj.*
1 (*торжественный*) ceremonial; **~ная фо́рма** full dress (uniform).
2 (*пышный*) gala.
3 (*главный*) main, front; **п. подъе́зд** main entrance; *as n.* **~ная, ~ной** *f.* front door.
парадо́кс, а *m.* paradox.
парази́т, а *m.* (*biol. and fig.*) parasite.
парализо́в|анный *p.p.p. of* ▸ **~а́ть** *and adj.* paralysed (*also fig.*).
парализ|ова́ть, у́ю *impf. and pf.* to paralyse (*also fig.*).
парали́ч, а́ *m.* paralysis; **он разби́т ~о́м** he is completely paralysed.
паралле́л|ь, и *f.* parallel; **провести́ п.** (**ме́жду** + *i.*) to draw a parallel (between).
паралле́льно *adv.* (+ *d.*; **с** + *i.*)
1 parallel (with).
2 (*одновременно*) simultaneously (with), at the same time (as).
паралле́л|ьный (~ен, ~ьна) *adj.* parallel.
пара́метр, а *m.* parameter.
парано́ик, а *m.* (*med.*) paranoid.
парано́й|я, и *f.* (*med.*) paranoia.
паранорма́льный *adj.* paranormal.
параолимпи́йски|й *adj.* Paralympic; **П~е и́гры** Paralympics.
парапе́т, а *m.* parapet.
парафи́н, а *m.* paraffin (wax).
парашю́т, а *m.* parachute.
парашюти́ст, а *m.* parachutist; skydiver.
па́р|ень, ня, *pl.* **~ни, ~не́й** *m.*
1 (*юноша*) boy, lad.
2 (*coll.*) (*мужчина*) chap (*Br.*), fellow, guy; **свой п.** a good guy.
пари́ *nt. indecl.* bet; **держа́ть п.** to bet, lay a bet; **держу́ п., что...** I bet that ... .
Пари́ж, а *m.* Paris.

парижа́н|ин, ина, *pl.* **~е, ~** *m.* Parisian.
парижа́н|ка, ки *f. of* ▸ **~ин;** Parisienne.
пари́жский *adj.* Parisian.
пари́к, а́ *m.* wig.
парикма́хер, а *m.* hairdresser; (*мужской*) barber.
парикма́херск|ая, ой *f.* hairdresser's; hairdressing salon; (*мужская*) barber's (shop).
парите́т, а *m.* parity.
пар|и́ть, ю́, и́шь *impf.* (*no pf.*) to soar, swoop, hover; **п. в облака́х** (*fig.*) to live in the clouds.
па́р|иться, юсь, ишься *impf. of* ▸ **по~**
парк, а *m.*
1 (*сад*) park; **разби́ть п.** to lay out a park.
2 (*место стоянки*) yard, depot.
3 (*подвижной состав*) fleet; stock; pool.
парке́т, а *m.* parquet; parquetry.
парк|ова́ть(ся), у́ю(сь) *impf. of* ▸ **припаркова́ть(ся)**
парко́вк|а, и *f.* parking.
парла́мент, а *m.* parliament.
парламента́ри|й, я *m.* parliamentarian.
парла́ментский *adj.* parliamentary; **п. запро́с** interpellation.
парни́к, а́ *m.* hotbed, polytunnel; (*из стекла*) greenhouse.
парн|о́й *adj.* fresh; **~о́е мя́со** fresh meat.
па́рн|ый *adj.* pair; forming a pair; twin; **п. носо́к, п. сапо́г,** *etc.*, pair, fellow (*other one of pair of socks, boots, etc.*); **~ое ката́ние** (*на коньках*) pair skating.
парово́з, а *m.* (steam) engine, locomotive.
паров|о́й *adj.*
1 *adj. of* ▸ **пар; ~а́я маши́на** steam engine.
2 (*cul.*) steamed.
пароди́ст, а *m.* impressionist, mimic.
паро́ди|я, и *f.*
1 (*произведение*) parody.
2 (**на** + *a.*) (*на справедливость*) travesty, caricature.
паро́л|ь, я *m.* password.
паро́м, а *m.* ferry (boat); **перепра́вить на ~е** to ferry.
парохо́д, а *m.* steamship.
па́рт|а, ы *f.* (school) desk.
парте́р, а *m.* (*theatr.*) the stalls.
партиза́н, а, *g. pl.* **~** *m.* (*на войне*) partisan; (*против режима*) guerrilla.
партиту́р|а, ы *f.* (*mus.*) score.
па́рти|я[1], и *f.* (*pol.*) party.
па́рти|я[2], и *f.*
1 (*группа лиц*) party, group.
2 (*в производстве*) batch; lot; (*груза*) consignment; (*отправленных товаров*) shipment.
3 (*sport*) game; set.
4 (*mus.*) part.
партнёр, а *m.* partner.
па́рус, а, *pl.* **~а́** *m.* sail; **на всех ~а́х** in full sail (*also fig.*).
паруси́н|а, ы *f.* canvas, sailcloth.
па́русник, а *m.* sailing vessel.
па́рус|ный *adj. of* ▸ **~; п. спорт** sailing.
парфюме́р, а *m.* perfumer.
парфюме́ри|я, и *f.* (*промышленность*) perfumery; (*духи*) perfumes; (*косметика*) cosmetics; (*отдел духов*) perfume department; (*отдел косметики*) cosmetics department.
парфюме́р|ный *adj. of* ▸ **~ия; п. магази́н** (*только духи*) perfumery, perfumer's shop; (*косметика*) cosmetics shop.
парч|а́, и́, *g. pl.* **~е́й** *f.* brocade.
парши́в|ый (~, ~а) *adj.* (*coll., fig.*) rotten, lousy.
пас, а *m.* (*sport*) pass.
па́смур|ный (~ен, ~на) *adj.*
1 (*день*) dull, cloudy; overcast.
2 (*fig.*) (*лицо*) gloomy, sullen.
пас|ова́ть, у́ю *impf. and pf.* (*sport*) to pass.
па́спорт, а, *pl.* **~а́** *m.*
1 passport.
2 (*машины, аппарата*) registration certificate.
пасса́ж, а *m.*
1 (*галерея*) arcade.
2 (*mus.*) passage.
пассажи́р, а *m.* passenger.
пассажи́р|ка, ки *f. of* ▸ **~**
пассажи́р|ский *adj. of* ▸ **~**
пасса́т, а *m.* (*meteor.*) trade wind.
пасси́в|ный (~ен, ~на) *adj.* passive.
па́ст|а, ы *f.* paste; **зубна́я п.** toothpaste; **тома́тная п.** tomato purée.
па́стбищ|е, а *nt.* pasture.
па́ств|а, ы *f.* (*eccl.*) flock, congregation.
пасте́л|ь, и *f.*
1 (*collect.*) (*карандаши*) pastel(s).
2 (*рисунок ~ью*) pastel (drawing).
пастериз|ова́ть, у́ю *impf. and pf.* to pasteurize.
пастерна́к, а *m.* parsnip.
пас|ти́, у́, ёшь, *past* **~, ~ла́** *impf.* (*no pf.*) (*скот*) to graze, pasture; (*гусей*) to tend.
пас|ти́сь, ётся, *past* **~ся, ~ла́сь** *impf.* (*no pf.*) to graze; to browse; (*coll., fig.*) to hang about.
па́стор, а *m.* (*Protestant*) minister, pastor.
пасту́х, а́ *m.* (*коров*) herdsman; (*овец*) shepherd.
пасту́шк|а, и *f.* shepherdess.
па́стыр|ь, я *m.* (*eccl.*) pastor.
па|сть[1], ду́, дёшь, *past* **~л, ~ла**
1 *pf. of* ▸ **~да́ть**
2 (*pf. only*) (*погибнуть*) to die, fall; **п. же́ртвой чего́-н.** to fall victim to.
3 (*pf. only*) (*о крепости, о городе*) to fall, surrender.
4 : **п. ду́хом** to despair.
паст|ь[2], и *f.* (*зверя*) mouth; jaws.
Па́сх|а, и *f.*
1 (*в иудаизме*) Passover.
2 (*в христианстве*) Easter.
3 **п.** (*cul.*) paskha (*sweet cream cheese dish eaten at Easter*).
па́сын|ок, ка *m.* stepson, stepchild.
пате́нт, а *m.* (**на** + *a.*) (*на изобретение*) patent (for); (*торговый*) licence (*Br.*), license (*US*) (for).
патент|ова́ть, у́ю *impf.* (*of* ▸ **за~**) to patent; to take out a patent for.
патети́ческий *adj.* passionate; emotional.

пато́лог, а *m.* pathologist.
патологи́ческ|ий *adj.* pathological; **~ая анато́мия** (anatomical) pathology.
патоло́ги|я, и *f.* pathology.
патологоана́том, а *m.* (anatomical) pathologist.
патриа́рх, а *m.* (*ethnol. and eccl.*) patriarch.
патриарха́л|ьный (~ен, ~ьна) *adj.* patriarchal.
патриархи́|я, и *f.* (*eccl.*) patriarchate.
патрио́т, а *m.* patriot.
патриоти́зм, а *m.* patriotism.
патриоти́ческий *adj.* patriotic.
патрио́т|ка, ки *f. of* ▸**~**
патро́н[1]**, а** *m.*
1 (*покровитель*) patron.
2 (*хозяин*) (*coll.*) boss.
патро́н[2]**, а** *m.*
1 (*mil.*) cartridge.
2 (*tech.*) chuck (*of drill, lathe*), holder.
3 (*лампочки*) socket.
патрули́р|овать, ую *impf.* (*no pf.*) (*mil.*) to patrol.
патру́л|ь, я́ *m.* patrol.
патч, а *m.* (*comput.*) patch.
па́уз|а, ы *f.* pause; interval; (*mus.*) rest.
пау́к, а́ *m.* spider.
паути́н|а, ы *f.* cobweb, spider's web; (*fig.*) web; **Всеми́рная п.** (*comput.*) the Web.
па́фос, а *m.*
1 (+ *g.*) enthusiasm (for), zeal (for).
2 (*сущность*) spirit; emotional content.
пах, а, о ~́е, в ~у́ *m.* (*anat.*) groin.
па́хар|ь, я *m.* ploughman (*Br.*), plowman (*US*).
па|ха́ть, шу́, ~́шешь *impf.*
1 (*pf.* **вс~**) to plough (*Br.*), plow (*US*), till.
2 (*coll.*) (*работать*) to slave (away).
па́х|нуть, ну, нешь, *past* **~** *or* **~нул, ~ла** *impf.* (*no pf.*) (+ *i.*) to smell (of); **~нет лу́ком** there is a smell of onions; (*fig.*; *usu. impers.*) to savour (*Br.*), savor (*US*) (of), smack (of); **~ло ссо́рой** a quarrel was in the air.
паху́ч|ий (~, ~а) *adj.* strong-smelling.
паца́н, а́ *m.* (*coll.*) boy, lad.
пацие́нт, а *m.* patient.
пацие́нт|ка, ки *f. of* ▸**~**
пацифи́зм, а *m.* pacifism.
пацифи́ст, а *m.* pacifist.
па́чк|а, и *f.*
1 (*писем, газет*) bundle; (*сигарет, чая, печенья*) packet (*Br.*), pack.
2 (*балерины*) tutu.
па́чка|ть, ю *impf.* (*of* ▸**за~** *and* ▸**ис~**) to dirty, soil, stain, sully (*also fig.*); **п. ру́ки** (*fig.*) to soil one's hands.
па́чка|ться, юсь *impf.* (*of* ▸**за~** *and* ▸**ис~**)
1 (*человек*) to make o.s. dirty; to soil o.s.
2 (*вещь*) to become dirty.
па́ш|ня, ни, *g. pl.* **~ен** *f.* arable land; ploughland (*Br.*), plowland (*US*).
паште́т, а *m.* pâté.
пая́льник, а *m.* soldering iron.
пая́снича|ть, ю *impf.* (*no pf.*) (*coll.*) to clown, play the fool.
пая́|ть, ю *impf.* (*no pf.*) to solder.
пая́ц, а *m.* (*fig., pej.*) clown.
пев|е́ц, ца́ *m.* singer.
певи́ц|а, ы *f. of* ▸**пев́ец**
пе́вч|ий
1 *adj.* singing; **~ая пти́ца** songbird.
2 *as n.* **п., ~его** *m.* chorister.
педаго́г, а *m.* teacher.
педагоги́ческий *adj.* pedagogic(al); educational; **п. институ́т** college of education (*Br.*), teachers' college (*US*).
педа́л|ь, и *f.* pedal.
педа́нт, а *m.* pedant.
педанти́ч|ный (~ен, ~на) *adj.* pedantic.
педиа́тр, а *m.* paediatrician (*Br.*), pediatrician (*US*).
педиатри́ческий *adj.* paediatric (*Br.*), pediatric (*US*).
педиатри́|я, и *f.* paediatrics (*Br.*), pediatrics (*US*).
пе́дик, а *m.* (*coll., pej.*) queer, poof (*Br.*).
педикю́р, а *m.* pedicure.
педофи́л, а *m.* paedophile (*Br.*), pedophile (*US*).
педофили́|я, и *f.* paedophilia (*Br.*), pedophilia (*US*).
пе́йджер, а *m.* pager.
пейза́ж, а *m.*
1 landscape; scenery.
2 (*картина*) landscape.
пёк, пекла́ *see* ▸**печь**[1]
пека́р|ня, ни, *g. pl.* **~ен** *f.* bakery, bakehouse.
пе́кар|ь, я, *pl.* **~и, ~ей** *m.* baker.
Пеки́н, а *m.* Beijing; Peking.
пе́кл|о, а *nt.*
1 (*сильный жар*) scorching heat.
2 (*ад*) hell, hellfire.
пеку́, пеку́т *see* ▸**печь**[1]
пелен|а́, ы́, *pl.* **~ы́, ~̈, ~а́м** *f.* shroud; **у него́ сло́вно п. с глаз упа́ла** the scales fell from his eyes.
пелён|ка, ки *f.* (*usu. pl.*) swaddling clothes; **с пелёнок** (*fig.*) from the cradle.
пелика́н, а *m.* pelican.
пельме́н|и, ей *pl.* (*sg.* **~ь, ~я** *m.*) (*cul.*) pelmeni (*a kind of ravioli*).
пе́н|а, ы *f.* (*на море*) foam; (*на бульоне*) scum; (*на пиве*) froth.
пена́л, а *m.* pencil case.
пе́ни|е, я *nt.* singing.
пе́нист|ый (~, ~а) *adj.* foamy; frothy.
пе́н|иться, ится *impf.* to foam; to froth (up) (*intrans.*).
пеницилли́н, а *m.* penicillin.
пе́н|ный *adj.* = **~истый**
пенопла́ст, а *m.* foam plastic.
пенс, а *m.* penny.
пенсионе́р, а *m.* pensioner.
пенсионе́р|ка, ки *f. of* ▸**~**
пенсио́нный *adj. of* ▸**пе́нсия; п. во́зраст** retirement age; **п. фонд** pension fund.
пе́нси|я, и *f.* pension; **он на ~и** he is retired; **вы́йти на ~ю** to retire.
пенсне́ *nt. indecl.* pince-nez.

пентха́ус, а *m.* penthouse.
пень, пня *m.* stump.
пеньк|а́, и́ *f.* hemp.
пенько́вый *adj.* hempen.
пеньюа́р, а *m.* peignoir, negligée.
пе́н|я, и *f.* fine.
пе́п|ел, ла *m.* ash(es).
пе́пельниц|а, ы *f.* ashtray.
пе́пельн|ый *adj.* ashy; **~ого цве́та** ash-grey.
пе́рвенств|о, а *nt.* first place; (*sport*) championship.
перви́чный *adj.* (*главный*) primary; (*первоначальный*) initial.
первобы́т|ный (~ен, ~на) *adj.* (*ethnol. and fig.*) primitive; primordial; primeval.
пе́рв|ое, ого *nt.* first course (*of a meal*).
первозда́нный *adj.* primordial; (*geol.*) primitive, primary; **п. ха́ос** primordial chaos (*also fig., iron.*).
первоисто́чник, а *m.* (*сведений*) primary source; (*основа*) origin.
первокла́сс|ный (~ен, ~на) *adj.* first-class, first-rate.
первонача́л|ьный (~ен, ~ьна) *adj.*
1 (*самый первый*) original.
2 (*являющийся началом*) initial.
первооткрыва́тел|ь, я *m.* discoverer.
первоочередн|о́й *adj.* immediate; **~а́я зада́ча** immediate task.
первопрохо́д|ец, ца *m.* (*also fig., rhet.*) pioneer; trailblazer.
первосо́рт|ный (~ен, ~на) *adj.*
1 top-quality.
2 (*coll.*) (*превосходный*) first-class, first-rate.
пе́рв|ый *adj.*
1 first; (*по времени*) earliest, first; **~ого января́** on the first of January; **быть ~ым, идти́ ~ым** to come first, lead; **~ое вре́мя** at first; **~ая скри́пка** first violin; **п. эта́ж** ground floor (*Br.*), first floor (*US*); **в ~ую о́чередь** in the first place; **на п. взгляд, с ~ого взгля́да** at first sight.
2 (*лучший*) best.
перга́мент, а *m.* parchment.
пер|де́ть, ди́шь *impf.* (*vulg.*) to fart.
пере... *vbl. pref. indicating*
1 *action across or through sth.* (trans-).
2 *repetition of action* (re-).
3 *superiority, excess, etc.* (over-, out-).
4 *extension of action to encompass many or all objects or cases of a given kind.*
5 *division into two or more parts.*
6 (*reflexives*) reciprocity of action.
переадрес|ова́ть, у́ю *pf.* (*of* ▸ **~о́вывать**) to re-address; to forward.
переадресо́выва|ть, ю *impf. of* ▸ **переадресова́ть**
перебази́р|оваться, уюсь *pf.* to relocate.
переба́рщива|ть, ю *impf. of* ▸ **переборщи́ть**
перебега́|ть, ю *impf. of* ▸ **перебежа́ть**
перебе|жа́ть, гу́, жи́шь, гу́т *pf.* (*of* ▸ **~га́ть**)
1 (**че́рез** + *a.*) to cross (running); **п. (че́рез) у́лицу** to run across the street.
2 (*fig., coll.*; **к** + *d.*) (*к противнику*) to go over (to), desert (to).
перебе́жчик, а *m.* deserter; (*fig.*) turncoat.
перебе́жчи|ца, цы *f. of* ▸ **~к**
перебива́|ть, ю *impf. of* ▸ **переби́ть**
перебинт|ова́ть, у́ю *pf.* (*of* ▸ **~о́вывать**) (*поменять повязку*) to change the dressing (on), put a new dressing (on).
перебинто́выва|ть, ю *impf. of* ▸ **перебинтова́ть**
перебира́|ть[1](ся), ю(сь) *impf. of* ▸ **перебра́ть(ся)**
перебира́|ть[2], ю *impf.*
1 (*касаться пальцами*) to finger; **п. стру́ны** to run one's fingers over the strings.
2 (+ *i.*) (*ногами, пальцами*) to move (*in turn or in a regular manner*).
переб|и́ть, ью́, ьёшь *pf.* (*of* ▸ **~ива́ть**) (*говорящего*) to interrupt.
перебо́|й, я *m.* (*перерыв*) interruption; (*задержка*) hold-up; (*двигателя*) misfire; (*сердца*) irregularity; **пульс с ~ями** irregular pulse.
переболе́|ть, ю *pf.* (+ *i.*) to have had, have been down (*with an illness*); **де́ти все ~ли ветря́нкой** the children have all been down with chickenpox.
перебо́рк|а, и *f.* (*перегородка*) partition; (*naut.*) bulkhead.
перебор|о́ть, ю́, ~́ешь *pf.* (*no impf.*) to overcome.
переборщ|и́ть, у́, и́шь *pf.* (*of* ▸ **переба́рщивать**) (**в** + *p.*; *coll.*) to go too far; to overdo it; to go over the top.
перебра́сыва|ть, ю *impf. of* ▸ **перебро́сить**
пере|бра́ть, беру́, берёшь, *past* **~бра́л, ~брала́, ~бра́ло** *pf.* (*of* ▸ **~бира́ть[1]**)
1 (*сортировать*) to sort; (*пересмотреть*) to look through.
2 (*fig.*) (*в уме*) to turn over (in one's mind).
3 (*взять слишком много*) to take too much.
пере|бра́ться, беру́сь, берёшься, *past* **~бра́лся, ~брала́сь, ~бра́ло́сь** *pf.* (*coll.*)
1 (*перейти*) to get over, cross.
2 (*переселиться*) to move.
перебро́|сить, шу, сишь *pf.* (*of* ▸ **перебра́сывать**)
1 (*мяч*) to throw over.
2 (*переместить*) to transfer (*troops, etc.*).
перева́л, а *m.* (*geog.*) pass.
перева́лива|ть, ю *impf. of* ▸ **перевали́ть**
перева́лива|ться[1], юсь *impf. of* ▸ **перевали́ться**
перева́лива|ться[2], юсь *impf.* (*no pf.*) to waddle.
перевал|и́ть, ю́, ~́ишь *pf.* (*of* ▸ **~́ивать**)
1 (*переместить*) to transfer, shift.
2 (*перейти*) to cross; (*impers.*; *coll.*) (*о пределе*) to be past; **~и́ло за́ полночь** it is past midnight.
перевал|и́ться, ю́сь, ~́ишься *pf.* (*of* ▸ **~́иваться[1]**) to roll over.
перева́рива|ть, ю *impf. of*

▶ **переварить**

перевар|ить, ю, ~ишь *pf.* (*of* ▶ **~ивать**) to digest.

перевез|ти, у, ёшь, *past* **~, ~ла** *pf.* (*of* ▶ **перевозить**)
1 (*переместить*) (*людей через реку*) to take across, transport across.
2 (*везя, доставить*) (*детей на дачу*) to transport, take (*from A to B*).

переверн|уть, у, ёшь *pf.* (*of* ▶ **переворачивать**)
1 (*с одной стороны на другую*) to turn over; (*вверх дном*) to turn upside down.
2 (*изменить*) to change radically, transform.
3 (*потрясти*) to shake, stun.

переверн|уться, усь, ёшься *pf.* (*of* ▶ **переворачиваться**) to turn over.

переве|сить[1], шу, сишь *pf.* (*of* ▶ **~шивать**) (*пальто*) to hang somewhere else; **п. картину с одной стены на другую** to move a picture from one wall to another.

переве|сить[2], шу, сишь *pf.* (*of* ▶ **~шивать**) to outweigh, outbalance (*also fig.*); (*fig.*) (*оказаться более весомым*) to tip the scales.

переве|сти, ду, дёшь, *past* **~л, ~ла** *pf.* (*of* ▶ **переводить**)
1 (*ведя, переместить*) to take across; **п. детей через улицу** to take children across the road.
2 (*в другое место*) to transfer, move, switch, shift; **п. на другую работу** to transfer to another post; **п. деньги** to transfer money.
3 (**с** + *g.* **на** + *a.*) to translate (from into); (**в, на** + *a.*) (*в другие единицы*) to convert (to), express (as, in); **п. с русского языка на английский** to translate from Russian into English; **п. в метрические меры** to convert to metric units.
4 (*взгляд, разговор*) to shift; **п. разговор на другую тему** to change the subject.

перевешива|ть, ю *impf. of* ▶ **перевесить**

перевива|ть, ю *impf. of* ▶ **перевить**

перевира|ть, ю *impf. of* ▶ **переврать**

перев|ить, ью, ьёшь, *past* **~ил, ~ила, ~ило** *pf.* (*of* ▶ **~ивать**) (+ *i.*) to interweave (with), intertwine (with).

перевод, а *m.*
1 (*в другое место*) transfer, move, switch, shift; **денежный п.** remittance; **почтовый п.** postal order.
2 (*с одного языка на другой*) translation; (*в другие единицы*) conversion.

перево|дить, жу, ~дишь *impf. of* ▶ **перевести**

переводчик, а *m.* translator; (*устный*) interpreter.

переводчи|ца, цы *f. of* ▶ **~к**

перево|зить, жу, ~зишь *impf. of* ▶ **перевезти**

перевозк|а, и *f.* transportation, conveyance.

перевоплощени|е, я *nt.* reincarnation; (*fig.*) transformation.

переворачива|ть(ся), ю(сь) *impf. of* ▶ **перевернуть(ся)**

переворот, а *m.* revolution; **государственный п.** coup d'état.

перевоспитани|е, я *nt.* re-education; rehabilitation.

перевр|ать, у, ёшь, *past* **~ал, ~ала, ~ало** *pf.* (*of* ▶ **перевирать**) (*coll.*) to garble, confuse; to misinterpret; **п. цитату** to misquote.

перевыбор|ы, ов *no sg.* re-election.

перевя|зать, жу, ~жешь *pf.* (*of* ▶ **~зывать**)
1 (*рану*) to dress, bandage.
2 (*коробку*) to tie up, cord.

перевязк|а, и *f.* dressing, bandage.

перевяз|очный *adj. of* ▶ **~ка; п. материал** dressing; **п. пункт** dressing station.

перевязыва|ть, ю *impf. of* ▶ **перевязать**

перегиб, а *m.*
1 bend, twist; (*линия*) fold.
2 (*fig.*) (*преувеличение*) exaggeration; (*в политике, в руководстве*): **допустить п. в чём-н.** to carry sth. too far.

перегиба|ть(ся), ю(сь) *impf. of* ▶ **перегнуть(ся)**

перегляд|ыва|ться, юсь *impf. of* ▶ **переглянуться**

перегля|нуться, нусь, ~нешься *pf.* (*of* ▶ **~дываться**) (**с** + *i.*) to exchange glances (with).

пере|гнать, гоню, гонишь, *past* **~гнал, ~гнала, ~гнало** *pf.* (*of* ▶ **~гонять**)
1 (*обогнать*) to outdistance, leave behind; (*fig.*) to overtake, surpass.
2 (*скот*) to drive (*somewhere else; from A to B*).
3 (*chem.*) to distil (*Br.*), distill (*US*).

перегно|й, я *m.* humus.

перег|нуть, ну, нёшь *pf.* (*of* ▶ **~ибать**) to bend; (*fig., coll.*) to go too far; **п. палку** (*fig.*) to go too far.

перег|нуться, нусь, нёшься *pf.* (*of* ▶ **~ибаться**)
1 (*о человеке*) to lean over, bend over.
2 (*о ветви*) to bend.

переговарива|ться, юсь *impf.* (**с** + *i.*) to exchange remarks (with).

переговор|ы, ов *no sg.* negotiations, talks; **вести п.** (**с** + *i.*) to negotiate, hold talks (with).

перегоня|ть, ю *impf. of* ▶ **перегнать**

перегоражива|ть, ю *impf. of* ▶ **перегородить**

перегор|ать, аю *impf. of* ▶ **~еть**

перегор|еть, ит *pf.* (*of* ▶ **~ать**)
1 (*о лампочке*) to burn out.
2 (*о балке*) to burn through.

перегоро|дить, жу, ~дишь *pf.* (*of* ▶ **перегораживать**) to partition off.

перегородк|а, и *f.*
1 partition.
2 (*fig.*) barrier.

перегрев, а *m.* overheating.

перегрева|ть(ся), ю(сь) *impf. of* ▶ **перегреть(ся)**

перегре|ть, ю *pf.* (*of* ▶ **~вать**) to overheat.

перегре|ться, юсь *pf.* (*of* ▶ **~ваться**) to overheat; (*на солнце*) to spend too long in the sun.

перегружа́|ть, ю *impf. of* ▸ **перегрузи́ть**

перегру|зи́ть[1]**, жу́, ~́зишь** *pf.* (*of* ▸ **~жа́ть**) to overload; **п. рабо́той** to overwork.

перегру|зи́ть[2]**, жу́, ~́зишь** *pf.* (*of* ▸ **~жа́ть**) to load (*somewhere else*; *from A to B*); to trans-ship; **п. с по́езда на парохо́д** to load from a train on to a ship.

перегру́зк|а, и *f.* overloading; (*usu. pl.*) strain, stress.

перегрыза́|ть, ю *impf. of* ▸ **перегры́зть**

перегры́з|ть, у́, ёшь, *past* **~, ~ла** *pf.* (*of* ▸ **~а́ть**) to gnaw through, bite through.

перегры́з|ться, у́сь, ёшься, *past* **~ся, ~лась** *pf.* (*no impf.*) (**из-за** + *g.*; *coll.*; *of dogs*) to fight (over); (*fig.*) to quarrel (over), wrangle (about).

пе́ред *and* **пе́редо** *prep.* + *i.*
1 (*при обозначении места*) in front of; before; **п. до́мом** in front of the house; (*also fig.*): **п. опа́сностью/тру́дностями** in the face of danger/difficulties.
2 (*раньше*) before; **п. обе́дом** before dinner; **п. тем, как** (*conj.*) before.
3 (*в присутствии*) in the presence of, in front of; **п. учи́телем** in front of the teacher.
4 (*в отношении*; *по сравнению*) to; **извини́ться п. кем-н.** to apologize to s.o.

переда|ва́ть(ся), ю́(сь), ёшь(ся) *impf. of* ▸ **переда́ть(ся)**

переда́тчик, а *m.* transmitter.

переда́|ть, м, шь, ст, ди́м, ди́те, ду́т, *past* **пе́редал, ~ла́, пе́редало** *pf.* (*of* ▸ **~ва́ть**)
1 (*отдать через кого-н.*) to pass; (*вручить*) to hand; (*свои права, коллекцию*) to hand over; to transfer.
2 (*сообщить*) to tell; to communicate; **переда́йте ему́, что я приезжа́ю за́втра** tell him I shall be arriving tomorrow; (*распространить*) to transmit, convey; **п. по ра́дио/телеви́дению** to broadcast (on the radio/television); **п. приве́т** to send one's regards.
3 (*воспроизвести*) to reproduce (*a sound, a thought, etc.*).

переда́|ться, стся, ду́тся, *past* **~лся, ~ла́сь** *pf.* (*of* ▸ **~ва́ться**) to pass; (*о тревоге, болезни*) to be transmitted, be communicated; (*по наследству*) to be inherited; **корь ~ла́сь ему́ от сосе́дских дете́й** he picked up measles from the children next door.

переда́ч|а, и *f.*
1 (*действие*) passing; transmission; communication; transfer, transference.
2 (*больному, заключённому*) parcel.
3 (*по телевидению, по радио*) broadcast; **пряма́я п.** live broadcast; (*программа*) programme (*Br.*), program (*US*).
4 (*tech.*) drive; gear(ing); transmission; **ремённая п.** belt drive.

передвига́|ть(ся), ю(сь) *impf. of* ▸ **передви́нуть(ся)**

передвижно́й *adj.*
1 (*перегородка*) movable.
2 (*библиотека*) mobile, travelling (*Br.*), traveling (*US*).

передви́|нуть, ну, нешь *pf.* (*of* ▸ **~га́ть**) to move, shift (*also fig.*); **п. сро́ки экза́менов** to alter the date of examinations.

передви́|нуться, нусь, нешься *pf.* (*of* ▸ **~га́ться**) to move, shift.

переде́л|ать, аю *pf.* (*of* ▸ **~ывать**) (*сделать заново*) to redo; (*сделать по-иному*) to alter; (*fig.*) to refashion, recast; **п. пла́тье** to alter a dress.

переде́лыва|ть, ю *impf. of* ▸ **переде́лать**

передерж|а́ть, у́, ~́ишь *pf.* (*of* ▸ **~́ивать**)
1 (*кушанье*) to overdo; to overcook.
2 (*phot.*) to overexpose.

переде́ржива|ть, ю *impf. of* ▸ **передержа́ть**

пере́дн|ий *adj.* front; **~ие коне́чности** forelegs; **п. план** foreground.

пере́дник, а *m.* apron.

пере́дн|яя, ей *f.* (entrance) hall, lobby.

пе́редо = **пе́ред**

передово́й *adj.* (*отряд*) forward; (*технология*) advanced; (*взгляды*) progressive.

передозиро́вк|а, и *f.* (*med.*) overdose.

передохн|у́ть, у́, ёшь *pf.* (*of* ▸ **передыха́ть**) (*coll.*) to pause for breath, take a short rest.

передра́знива|ть, ю *impf. of* ▸ **передразни́ть**

передразн|и́ть, ю́, ~́ишь *pf.* (*of* ▸ **~́ивать**) to take off, mimic.

пере|дра́ться, деру́сь, дерёшься, *past* **~дра́лся, ~драла́сь, ~драло́сь** *pf.* (*no impf.*) (*coll.*) to fight, brawl (*of many people, etc.*).

переду́м|ать, аю *pf.* (*of* ▸ **~ывать**) to change one's mind.

переду́мыва|ть, ю *impf. of* ▸ **переду́мать**

передыха́|ть, ю *impf. of* ▸ **передохну́ть**

перееда́|ть, ю *impf. of* ▸ **перее́сть**

перее́зд[1]**, а** *m.* (*место*) crossing.

перее́зд[2]**, а** *m.* (*переселение*) move.

переезжа́|ть, ю *impf. of* ▸ **перее́хать**

перее́|сть, м, шь, ст, ди́м, ди́те, дя́т, *past* **~л** *pf.* (*of* ▸ **~да́ть**) to overeat.

перее́|хать, ду, дешь *pf.* (*of* ▸ **~зжа́ть**)
1 (+ *a.* or **че́рез** + *a.*) (*дорогу*) to cross.
2 (*задавить*) to run over, knock down.
3 (*переселиться*) to move.

пережд|а́ть, у́, ёшь, *past* **~а́л, ~ала́, ~а́ло** *pf.* (*of* ▸ **пережида́ть**) to wait through; **мы ~а́ли грозу́** we waited till the storm was over.

переж|ева́ть, ую́, уёшь *pf.* (*of* ▸ **~ёвывать**) to masticate, chew.

пережёвыва|ть, ю *impf. of* ▸ **пережева́ть**

пережива́ни|е, я *nt.* (*события*) experience; (*душевное состояние*) feeling.

пережива́|ть, ю *impf.*
1 *impf. of* ▸ **пережи́ть.**
2 (*impf. only*) (**за** + *a.*) (*coll.*) to be upset, worry (for, on behalf of).

пережида́|ть, ю *impf. of* ▸ **пережда́ть**

пережи́т|ок, ка *m.* relic, vestige, survival.

пережи́|ть, ву́, вёшь, *past* **пе́режил,**

~лá, пéрежило *pf.* (*of* ▸ **~вáть 1**)
1 (*испытать*) to experience; to go/live through; (*выдержать*) to endure, suffer; **тяжелó п. что-н.** to take sth. hard; (*остаться в живых*) to survive.
2 (*прожить дольше*) to outlive, survive.

перезагру|жáть, жáю *impf. of* ▸ **~зúть**

перезагр|узúть, ужý, ýзишь *pf.* (*of* ▸ **~ужáть**) (*comput.*) to reboot.

перезаря|дúть, жý, ~́дишь *pf.* (*of* ▸ **~жáть**)
1 (*аккумулятор*) to recharge.
2 (*револьвер, фотоаппарат*) to reload.

перезаряжá|ть, ю *impf. of* ▸ **перезарядúть**

перезвáнива|ть, ю *impf. of* ▸ **перезвонúть**

перезвон|úть, ю́, úшь *pf.* (*of* ▸ **перезвáнивать**) to ring back (*Br.*), call back (*US*).

перезим|овáть, ýю *pf.* (*of* ▸ **зимовáть**) to winter, pass the winter.

перезревá|ть, ю *impf. of* ▸ **перезрéть**

перезрéлый *adj.* overripe; (*fig.*) passé, past one's prime.

перезрé|ть, ю *pf.* (*of* ▸ **~вáть**)
1 to become overripe.
2 (*fig.*) to be past one's prime.

переигр|áть[1], áю *pf.* (*of* ▸ **~́ывать**)
1 (*партию*) to play again.
2 (*coll.*) (*изменить*) to change; to reconsider.

переигр|áть[2], áю *pf.* (*of* ▸ **~́ывать**) (*theatr.*; *coll.*) to overact, overdo.

переигр|áть[3], áю *pf.* (*of* ▸ **~́ывать**) (*сыграть многое*) to play, act, perform (*all or a number of*).

переигр|áть[4], áю *pf.* (*of* ▸ **~́ывать**) (*coll., sport*) to outplay; to beat.

переигрыва|ть, ю *impf. of* ▸ **переигрáть[1,2,3,4]**

переизбирá|ть, ю *impf. of* ▸ **переизбрáть**

переиз|брáть, берý, берёшь, *past* **~брáл, ~бралá, ~брáло** *pf.* (*of* ▸ **~бирáть**) to re-elect.

переизда|вáть, ю́, ёшь *impf. of* ▸ **~́ть**

переиздá|ть, м, шь, ст, дúм, дúте, дýт, *past* **~л, ~лá, ~ло** *pf.* (*of* ▸ **~вáть**) to republish, reprint.

переимен|овáть, ýю *pf.* (*of* ▸ **~óвывать**) (**в** + *a.*) to rename.

переименóвыва|ть, ю *impf. of* ▸ **переименовáть**

пере|йтú, йдý, йдёшь, *past* **~шёл, ~шлá** *pf.* (*of* ▸ **~ходúть**)
1 (+ *a. or* **чéрез** + *a.*) (*переправляться*) to cross; to get across, get over, go over; **п. границу** to cross the frontier; **п. чéрез мóст** to go across a bridge.
2 (**в, на** + *a. or* **к** + *d.*) (*в другое место*) to pass (to); **п. в сосéднюю кóмнату** to go into the next room; **п. на другýю рабóту** to change one's job.
3 (**в** + *a.*) (*превратиться*) to turn (into); **их ссóра ~шлá в дрáку** their quarrel turned into a fight.

перекáпыва|ть, ю *impf. of* ▸ **перекопáть**

перекáрмлива|ть, ю *impf. of* ▸ **перекормúть**

перека|тúть, чý, ~́тишь *pf.* (*of* ▸ **~́тывать**) (*бочку*) to roll; (*велосипед*) to wheel.

перека|тúться, чýсь, ~́тишься *pf.* (*of* ▸ **~́тываться**) to roll.

перекáтыва|ть(ся), ю(сь) *impf. of* ▸ **перекатúть(ся)**

перекач|áть, áю *pf.* (*of* ▸ **~́ивать**) to pump over, pump across.

перекáчива|ть, ю *impf. of* ▸ **перекачáть**

перекид|áть, áю *pf.* (*of* ▸ **~́ывать**) to throw (one after another).

перекúдыва|ть(ся), ю(сь) *impf. of* ▸ **перекидáть** *and* ▸ **перекúнуть(ся)**

перекú|нуть, ну, нешь *pf.* (*of* ▸ **~дывать**) to throw (over).

перекú|нуться, нусь, нешься *pf.* (*of* ▸ **~дываться**)
1 (*быстро переместиться*) to leap (over).
2 (*огонь*) to spread.
3 (+ *i.*) (*мячом*) to throw (one to another); (*словами*) to bandy, exchange.

переклáдин|а, ы *f.*
1 (*брус*) cross-beam, crosspiece, transom.
2 (*sport*) horizontal bar.

переклáдыва|ть, ю *impf. of* ▸ **переложúть**

переклик|áться, áюсь *impf.* (**с** + *i.*)
1 (*pf.* **~́нуться**) to call to one another.
2 (*no pf.*) (*fig.*) (*быть подобным*) to have sth. in common (with).

переклúк|нуться, нусь, нешься *pf. of* ▸ **~áться 1**

переклúчк|а, и *f.* roll-call; **дéлать ~у** to call the roll.

переключáтел|ь, я *m.* (*tech.*) switch.

переключ|áть(ся), áю(сь) *impf. of* ▸ **~úть(ся)**

переключ|úть, ý, úшь *pf.* (*of* ▸ **~áть**) (*tech. and fig.*; **на** + *a.*) to switch (over to); **п. скóрость** to change gear (*Br.*), shift gears (*US*); **п. телевúзор/рáдио на другýю прогрáмму** to switch over, change channels (*on the TV/radio*).

переключ|úться, ýсь, úшься *pf.* (*of* ▸ **~áться**) (*tech. and fig.*; **на** + *a.*) to switch (over to); **внимáние пýблики ~úлось на говорящего** attention switched to the speaker.

перекопá|ть, ю *pf.* (*of* ▸ **перекáпывать**)
1 (*картофель; огород*) to dig up.
2 (*чемодан*) to rummage through.
3 (*дорогу*) to dig a ditch across.

перекорм|úть, лю́, ~́ишь *pf.* (*of* ▸ **перекáрмливать**) to overfeed.

перекóс, а *m.*
1 (*искривление*) warping.
2 (*fig.*) (*тенденциозность*) slant.

перекóшен|ный (~, ~а) *adj.* distorted, twisted.

перекрáива|ть, ю *impf. of* ▸ **перекроúть**

перекрá|сить, шу, сишь *pf.* (*of* ▸ **~шивать**) (*стену*) to repaint; (*в другой цвет*) to paint another colour (*Br.*), color (*US*); (*волосы*) to re-dye.

перекра́шива|ть, ю *impf. of* ▸ **перекра́сить**

перекре|сти́ть, щу́, ∼́стишь *pf.* (*of* ▸ **крести́ть 3**) to make the sign of the cross over.

перекре|сти́ться, щу́сь, ∼́стишься *pf.* (*of* ▸ **крести́ться 2**) (*о человеке*) to cross o.s.

перекрёстн|ый *adj.* cross; **п. ого́нь** (*mil.*) crossfire; **∼ая ссы́лка** cross reference.

перекрёст|ок, ка *m.* crossroads, crossing.

перекри́кива|ть, ю *impf. of* ▸ **перекрича́ть**

перекри|ча́ть, чу́, чи́шь *pf.* (*of* ▸ **∼́кивать**) (*шум*) to shout above; (*человека*) to shout down.

перекро|и́ть, ю́, и́шь *pf.* (*of* ▸ **перекра́ивать**) to cut out again; (*fig.*) (*статью, план*) to rehash; to re-shape.

перекрыва́|ть, ю *impf. of* ▸ **перекры́ть**

перекр|ы́ть[1], **о́ю, о́ешь** *pf.* (*of* ▸ **∼ыва́ть**) (*покрыть заново*) to re-cover.

перекр|ы́ть[2], **о́ю, о́ешь** *pf.* (*of* ▸ **∼ыва́ть**) (*дорогу*) to close; (*воду, доступ*) to cut off; (*реку*) to dam.

перекувы́ркива|ться, юсь *impf. of* ▸ **перекувырну́ться**

перекувыр|ну́ться, ну́сь, нёшься *pf.* (*of* ▸ **∼́киваться**) (*coll.*)
1 (*упасть*) to topple over.
2 (*перевернуться кувырком*) to turn a somersault.

переку́р, а *m.* (*coll.*) smoking break; (*перерыв вообще*) break; **пойдём на п.** let's take five.

переку|си́ть, шу́, ∼́сишь *pf.* (*of* ▸ **∼́сывать**) (*coll.*) (*поесть*) to have a bite, have a snack.

переку́сыва|ть, ю *impf. of* ▸ **перекуси́ть**

перела́мыва|ть(ся), ю, ет(ся) *impf. of* ▸ **переломи́ть(ся)**

перелез|а́ть, а́ю *impf. of* ▸ **∼́ть**

переле́з|ть, у, ешь, *past* **∼, ∼ла** *pf.* (*of* ▸ **∼а́ть**) to climb over, get over.

переле́с|ок, ка *m.* copse, coppice.

перелёт, а *m.*
1 (*самолёта*) flight.
2 (*птиц*) migration.

перелет|а́ть, а́ю *impf. of* ▸ **∼е́ть**

переле|те́ть, чу́, ти́шь *pf.* (*of* ▸ **∼та́ть**)
1 (+ *a. or* **че́рез** + *a.*) to fly over.
2 (*дальше нужного*) to fly too far; to overshoot (the mark).

перелётн|ый *adj.*: **∼ая пти́ца** bird of passage (*also fig.*); migratory bird.

пере|ле́чь, ля́гу, ля́жешь, ля́гут, *past* **∼лёг, ∼легла́** *pf.* (*no impf.*) to lie somewhere else; to move; **п. с дива́на на крова́ть** to move from the sofa to the bed.

перели́в, а *m.* (*цвета*) tint, tinge; (*цветов*) play (of colours (*Br.*), colors (*US*)); (*голоса*) modulation.

перелива́|ть, ю *impf. of* ▸ **перели́ть**

перелива́|ться, ется *impf. of* ▸ **перели́ться**

перелист|а́ть, а́ю *pf.* (*of* ▸ **∼́ывать**)
1 to leaf through.
2 (*бегло просмотреть*) to look through, flick through.

перели́стыва|ть, ю *impf. of* ▸ **перелиста́ть**

перел|и́ть, ью́, ьёшь, *past* **∼и́л, ∼ила́, ∼и́ло** *pf.* (*of* ▸ **∼ива́ть**)
1 to pour (*somewhere else; from A into B*); to decant; **п. молоко́ из кастрю́ли в кувши́н** to pour milk from a saucepan into a jug.
2 (*med.*) to transfuse; **п. кровь** (+ *d.*) to administer a blood transfusion (to).
3 (*через край*) to let overflow.

перел|и́ться, ьётся, *past* **∼и́лся, ∼ила́сь** *pf.* (*of* ▸ **∼ива́ться**)
1 (*литься в другое место*) to flow.
2 (*вылиться*) to overflow, run over.

перелож|и́ть, у́, ∼́ишь *pf.* (*of* ▸ **перекла́дывать**)
1 to put somewhere else; to shift, move; (*fig.*) to shift, transfer; **п. отве́тственность на кого́-н.** to shift the responsibility on to s.o.
2 (+ *a. and i.*) to interlay (with); **п. посу́ду соло́мой** to interlay crockery with straw.

перело́м, а *m.* break, breaking; (*кости*) fracture.

перелом|и́ть, лю́, ∼́ишь *pf.* (*of* ▸ **перела́мывать**)
1 to break in two.
2 (*fig.*) to break, master; **п. ход собы́тий** to turn events around.

перелом|и́ться, ∼́ится *pf.* (*of* ▸ **перела́мываться**) to break in two; to be fractured.

перело́мн|ый *adj. of* ▸ **∼; п. моме́нт** critical moment, crucial moment.

перема́лыва|ть(ся), ю, ет(ся) *impf. of* ▸ **перемоло́ть(ся)**

перема́нива|ть, ю *impf. of* ▸ **перемани́ть**

переман|и́ть, ю́, ∼́ишь *pf.* (*of* ▸ **∼́ивать**) (*coll.*) to entice; **п. на свою́ сто́рону** to win over.

перема́тыва|ть, ю *impf. of* ▸ **перемота́ть**

перемежа́|ть, ю *impf.* (*no pf.*) (+ *a. and i.* or **с** + *i.*) to alternate; **он ∼л угро́зы (с) обеща́ниями** he alternated threats and promises.

перемежа́|ться, ется *impf.* (*no pf.*) (+ *i. or* **с** + *i.*) to alternate; **снег ∼лся (с) дождём** snow alternated with rain, it snowed and rained by turns.

переме́н|а, ы *f.*
1 change.
2 (*в школе*) break (*Br.*), recess (*US*).

перемен|и́ть, ю́, ∼́ишь *pf.* (*of* ▸ **∼я́ть**) to change; **п. пози́цию** to shift one's ground (*also fig.*); **п. тон** (*fig.*) to change one's tune.

перемен|и́ться, ю́сь, ∼́ишься *pf.* (*of* ▸ **∼я́ться**) to change; **п. в лице́** to change countenance; **п. к кому́-н.** to change (one's attitude) towards s.o.

переме́нн|ый *adj.* variable; **∼ая величина́** (*math.*) variable (quantity); **п. ток** (*elec.*) alternating current; **с ∼ым успе́хом** with varying success.

перемен|я́ть(ся), я́ю(сь) *impf. of* ▶ **~и́ть(ся)**

переме|сти́ть, щу́, сти́шь *pf.* (*of* ▶ **~ща́ть**) to move (*somewhere else*); (*на другую работу*) to transfer.

переме|сти́ться, щу́сь, сти́шься *pf.* (*of* ▶ **~ща́ться**) to move.

перемеш|а́ть, а́ю *pf.* (*of* ▶ **~́ивать**) to (inter)mix, intermingle; **п. у́гли в пе́чке** to poke the fire.

перемеш|а́ться, а́юсь *pf.* (*of* ▶ **~́иваться**) to get mixed (up); **всё у него́ в голове́ ~а́лось** he has got everything mixed up.

переме́шива|ть(ся), ю(сь) *impf. of* ▶ **перемеша́ть(ся)**

перемеща́|ть(ся), ю(сь) *impf. of* ▶ **перемести́ть(ся)**

перемеще́ни|е, я *nt.* (*изменение положения*) transference, shift; (*движение*) movement; (*по службе*) transfer.

переми́ри|е, я *nt.* armistice, truce.

перемнож|а́ть, а́ю *impf. of* ▶ **~́ить**

перемно́ж|ить, у, ишь *pf.* (*of* ▶ **~а́ть**) to multiply.

перем|оло́ть, елю́, е́лешь *pf.* (*of* ▶ **~а́лывать**) (*кофе, зерно*) to grind, mill; (*fig.*) (*разрушить*) to pulverize.

перем|оло́ться, е́лется *pf.* (*of* ▶ **~а́лываться**): **~е́лется — мука́ бу́дет** (*prov.*) it will all come right in the end.

перемота́|ть, ю *pf.* (*of* ▶ **перема́тывать**)
1 (*на что-н. другое*) to wind; to reel; **п. наза́д** to rewind; **п. вперёд** to fast forward.
2 (*намотать заново*) to re-wind.

перемыва́|ть, ю *impf. of* ▶ **перемы́ть**

перем|ы́ть, о́ю, о́ешь *pf.* (*of* ▶ **~ыва́ть**)
1 (*вымыть заново*) to wash up again.
2 (*вымыть многое*) to wash (up) (*all or a quantity of*).

перемы́чк|а, и *f.* (*tech.*)
1 (*соединение*) crosspiece.
2 (*заграждение*) cofferdam.

перенапряга́|ться, юсь *impf. of* ▶ **перенапря́чься**

перенапря́|чься, гу́сь, жёшься, *past* **~гся, ~гла́сь** *pf.* (*of* ▶ **~га́ться**) to overstrain o.s.

перенес|ти́[1]**, у́, ёшь,** *past* **~̈, ~ла́** *pf.* (*of* ▶ **переноси́ть**)
1 (*через пространство*) to carry (*somewhere else*); (*поместить в другое место*) to move, transfer.
2: **п. сло́во** (*typ.*) to carry over (*part of word*) to the next line.
3 (*отсрочить*) to put off, postpone; to carry over.

перенес|ти́[2]**, у́, ёшь,** *past* **~̈, ~ла́** *pf.* (*of* ▶ **переноси́ть**) (*выдержать*) to endure, bear, stand; **п. боле́знь** to have an illness; **я э́того не мог п.** I couldn't stand that.

перенес|ти́сь, у́сь, ёшься, *past* **~̈ся, ~ла́сь** *pf.* (*of* ▶ **переноси́ться**) to be carried, be borne.

перено́с, а *m.*
1 transfer; moving.
2 (*typ.*) hyphenation at the end of a line; word division; (*знак*) hyphen (*at the end of a line*); **знак ~а** hyphen.
3 (*заседания*) postponement.

перено|си́ть(ся), шу́(сь), ~́сишь(ся) *impf. of* ▶ **перенести́(сь)**

перено́сиц|а, ы *f.* bridge of the nose.

переносно́й *adj.* (*приёмник*) portable.

перено́сный *adj.* (*ling.*) figurative.

переноч|ева́ть, у́ю *pf.* (*of* ▶ **ночева́ть**) to spend the night.

переобува́|ть(ся), ю(сь) *impf. of* ▶ **переобу́ть(ся)**

переобу́|ть, ю, ешь *pf.* (*of* ▶ **~ва́ть**) to change s.o.'s shoes; **п. ту́фли** to change one's shoes.

переобу́|ться, юсь, ешься *pf.* (*of* ▶ **~ва́ться**) to change one's shoes, boots, *etc.*

переобуча́|ть, ю *impf. of* ▶ **переобучи́ть**

переобуче́ни|е, я *nt.* retraining.

переобу|чи́ть, чу́, ~́чишь *pf.* (*of* ▶ **~ча́ть**) to retrain.

переодева́|ть(ся), ю(сь) *impf. of* ▶ **переоде́ть(ся)**

переоде́тый *adj.* disguised.

переоде́|ть, ну, нешь *pf.* (*of* ▶ **~ва́ть**)
1 (*платье, свитер*) to change; (*ребёнка, больного*) to change s.o.'s clothes; **п. пла́тье** to change one's dress.
2 (+ *i. or* **в** + *a.*) to dress up, disguise (as, in).

переоде́|ться, нусь, нешься *pf.* (*of* ▶ **~ва́ться**)
1 to change (one's clothes).
2 (+ *i. or* **в** + *a.*) to disguise o.s. *or* dress up (as, in); **она ~лась в ма́льчика** she disguised herself as a boy.

переосмы́сл|ить, ю, ишь *pf.* (*of* ▶ **~я́ть**) to re-examine.

переосмысля́|ть, ю *impf. of* ▶ **переосмы́слить**

переоце́нива|ть, ю *impf. of* ▶ **переоцени́ть**

переоцен|и́ть, ю́, ~́ишь *pf.* (*of* ▶ **~́ивать**) to overestimate, overrate.

перепа́д, а *m.* (*температур, давления*) differential, difference.

перепа́чка|ть, ю *pf.* to make all dirty.

перепа́чка|ться, юсь *pf.* to make o.s. dirty (all over).

пе́репел, а, *pl.* **~а́** *m.* (*zool.*) quail.

перепелен|а́ть, а́ю *pf.* (*of* ▶ **~̈ывать**): **п. ребёнка** to change a baby.

перепелёныва|ть, ю *impf. of* ▶ **перепелена́ть**

перепи́лива|ть, ю *impf. of* ▶ **перепили́ть**

перепил|и́ть, ю́, ~́ишь *pf.* (*of* ▶ **~́ивать**) to saw in two.

перепи|са́ть[1]**, шу́, ~́шешь** *pf.* (*of* ▶ **~́сывать**)
1 (*заново*) to rewrite; **п. на́бело** to make a fair copy (of).
2 (*списать*) to copy.

перепи|са́ть[2]**, шу́, ~́шешь** *pf.* (*of* ▶ **~́сывать**) (*сделать список*) to make a list (of), list; **п. всех прису́тствующих** to take the names of all those present.

перепи́ск|а, и *f.*

1 (*действие*) copying.
2 (*корреспонденция*) correspondence; **быть в ~е** (**с** + *i.*) to be in correspondence (with).
3 (*collect.*) (*все письма*) correspondence, letters.

перепи́сыва|ть, ю *impf. of* ▸ **переписа́ть**

перепи́сыва|ться, юсь *impf.* (**с** + *i.*) to correspond (with).

пе́репис|ь, и *f.* census.

перепла́в|ить, лю, ишь *pf.* (*of* ▸ **~ля́ть**) (*руду*) to smelt.

переплавля́|ть, ю *impf. of* ▸ **перепла́вить**

перепланиро́вк|а, и *f.* replanning.

перепла́т|а, ы *f.* overpayment.

перепле|сти́, ту́, тёшь, *past* **~л, ~ла́** *pf.* (*of* ▸ **~та́ть**)
1 (*книгу*) to bind.
2 (+ *i.*) (*нити, верёвки*) to interlace (with), interknit (with).

перепле|сти́сь, тётся, *past* **~лся, ~ла́сь** *pf.* (*of* ▸ **~та́ться**)
1 (*стебли, верёвки*) to interlace, interweave.
2 (*fig.*) (*события*) to be interwoven.

переплёт, а *m.*
1 (*действие*) binding; **отда́ть кни́гу в п.** to have a book bound.
2 (*обложка*) binding, book cover.

переплета́|ть(ся), ю, ет(ся) *impf. of* ▸ **переплести́сь**

переплете́ни|е, я *nt.*
1 (*нитей*) weave.
2 (*событий*) interweaving.

переплыва́|ть, ю *impf. of* ▸ **переплы́ть**

переплы́|ть, ву́, вёшь, *past* **~л, ~ла́, ~ло** *pf.* (*of* ▸ **~ва́ть**) (*вплавь*) to swim (across); (*на пароходе*) to sail (across).

переподгото́вк|а, и *f.* retraining.

переполз|а́ть, а́ю *impf. of* ▸ **~ти́**

переполз|ти́, у́, ёшь, *past* **~, ~ла́** *pf.* (*of* ▸ **~а́ть**) to crawl across.

перепо́лн|ить, ю, ишь *pf.* (*of* ▸ **~я́ть**) (*сосуд*) to overfill; (*автобус*) to overcrowd.

перепо́лн|иться, юсь *pf.* (*of* ▸ **~я́ться**) (*о сосуде*) to be overfilled; (*о сердце, душе*) to overflow; (*об автобусе*) to be overcrowded; **её се́рдце ~илось ра́достью** her heart overflowed with joy.

переполн|я́ть(ся), я́ю(сь) *impf. of* ▸ **~ить(ся)**

перепо́нк|а, и *f.* membrane; **бараба́нная п.** (*anat.*) eardrum, tympanum.

перепоруч|а́ть, а́ю *impf. of* ▸ **~и́ть**

перепоруч|и́ть, у́, ~ишь *pf.* (*of* ▸ **~а́ть**) (+ *d.*) to turn over (to), reassign (to).

перепра́в|а, ы *f.* (*действие*) crossing; (*место*) crossing (place); (*брод*) ford.

перепра́в|ить[1], лю, ишь *pf.* (*of* ▸ **~ля́ть**)
1 (*перевезти*) to convey, transport; to take across.
2 (*письмо*) to forward (*mail*).

перепра́в|ить[2], лю, ишь *pf.* (*of* ▸ **~ля́ть**) (*исправить*) to correct.

перепра́в|иться, люсь, ишься *pf.* (*of* ▸ **~ля́ться**) to cross, get across; (*вплавь*) to swim across; (*на пароходе*) to sail across.

переправля́|ть(ся), ю(сь) *impf. of* ▸ **перепра́вить(ся)**

перепро́б|овать, ую *pf.* (*еду*) to taste (*all or a quantity of*); (*fig.*) (*средства*) to try.

перепрода|ва́ть, ю́, ёшь *impf. of* ▸ **~ть**

перепрода́|ть, м, шь, ст, ди́м, ди́те, ду́т, *past* **перепро́дал, ~ла́, перепро́дало** *pf.* (*of* ▸ **~ва́ть**) to resell.

перепроизво́дств|о, а *nt.* overproduction.

перепры́гива|ть, ю *impf. of* ▸ **перепры́гнуть**

перепры́г|нуть, ну, нешь *pf.* (*of* ▸ **~ивать**) (+ *a. or* **че́рез** + *a.*) to jump (over).

перепуга́|ть, ю *pf.* (*no impf.*) to frighten, give a fright.

перепуга́|ться, юсь *pf.* (*no impf.*) to get a fright.

перепу́т|ать, аю *pf.* (*of* ▸ **~ывать**)
1 (*нити*) to entangle.
2 (*fig.*) (*имена, факты*) to confuse, mix up, muddle up.

перепу́т|аться, ается *pf.* (*of* ▸ **~ываться**)
1 (*нити*) to get entangled.
2 (*fig.*) (*мысли*) to get confused, get mixed up.

перепу́тыва|ть(ся), ю, ет(ся) *impf. of* ▸ **перепу́тать(ся)**

перераба́тыва|ть, ю *impf. of* ▸ **перерабо́тать**

перерабо́та|ть[1], ю *pf.* (*of* ▸ **перераба́тывать**)
1 (*сырьё*) to process; (*преобразовать*) to convert (to); to treat; **п. свёклу в са́хар** to convert beet to sugar.
2 (*переделать*) to remake; (*fig.*) (*статью*) to revise, recast, reshape.

перерабо́та|ть[2], ю *pf.* (*of* ▸ **перераба́тывать**) to exceed fixed hours of work, work overtime; (*coll.*) (*переутомиться*) to overwork.

перерабо́тк|а[1], и *f.*
1 (*сырья*) processing, treatment.
2 (*переделка*) remaking; (*вторичное использование*) recycling.

перерабо́тк|а[2], и *f.* (*время*) overtime work.

перераспределе́ни|е, я *nt.* redistribution.

перераспредел|и́ть, ю́, и́шь *pf.* (*of* ▸ **~я́ть**) to redistribute.

перераспредел|я́ть, я́ю *impf. of* ▸ **~и́ть**

перераст|а́ть, а́ю *impf. of* ▸ **~и́**

перераст|и́, у́, ёшь, *past* **перерóс, переросла́** *pf.* (*of* ▸ **~а́ть**)
1 (*стать выше*) to outgrow, (over)top; (*превзойти*) to outstrip (*in height, also fig.*); **п. своего́ учи́теля** to outstrip one's teacher.
2 (*fig.*; **в** + *a.*) (*превратиться*) to grow (into), develop (into), turn (into).
3 (*оказаться по возрасту старше, чем нужно*) to be too old (for).

перерасхо́д, а *m.*
1 (*денег, энергии*) overspending, overexpenditure.
2 (*fin.*) (*в банковском счёте*) overdraft.

перерасхо́д|овать, ую *pf.* (*no impf.*)

1 (*деньги, энергию*) to overspend, spend to excess.
2 (*fin.*) (*в банковском счёте*) to overdraw.

перерасчёт, а *m.* recalculation; (*в другие единицы*) conversion.

перерез|áть, áю *impf. of* ▸ **~́ать**

перерé|зать, жу, жешь *pf.* (*of* ▸ **~зáть**)
1 (*верёвку*) to cut (in two).
2 (*fig.*) (*путь*) to cut off.

переруб|áть, áю *impf. of* ▸ **~и́ть**

переруб|и́ть, лю́, ~́ишь *pf.* (*of* ▸ **~áть**) to chop in two.

переры́в, а *m.* break; **обéденный п.** lunch break; **без ~а** without a break; **с ~ами** off and on.

перерывá|ть, ю *impf. of* ▸ **переры́ть**

перер|ы́ть, óю, óешь *pf.* (*of* ▸ **~ывáть**) (*fig., coll.*) to rummage (*through*).

переса|ди́ть, жу́, ~́дишь *pf.* (*of* ▸ **~́живать**)
1 (*заставить пересесть*) to move, make s.o. change his seat; (*на другой поезд*) to transfer.
2 (*bot.*) to transplant.
3 (*med.*) (*сердце*) to transplant; (*кожу*) to graft.

пересáдк|а, и *f.*
1 (*bot.*) transplantation.
2 (*med.*) transplant; grafting; **операция по ~е сéрдца** heart transplant operation.
3 (*переход на другой поезд, автобус*) change; **сдéлать ~у** to change (*trains, buses, etc.*).

пересáжива|ть, ю *impf. of* ▸ **пересади́ть**

пересáжива|ться, юсь *impf. of* ▸ **пересéсть**

пересáлива|ть, ю *impf. of* ▸ **пересоли́ть**

пересда|вáть, ю́, ёшь *impf. of* ▸ **~́ть**

пересдá|ть, м, шь, ст, ди́м, ди́те, ду́т, *past* **~л, ~лá, ~́ло** *pf.* (*of* ▸ **~вáть**)
1 (*помещение*) to relet; to sublet.
2 (*cards*) to redeal.
3 (*экзамен*) to resit (*Br.*), retake.

пересекá|ть(ся), ю, ет(ся) *impf. of* ▸ **пересéчь(ся)**

переселéн|ец, ца *m.* settler.

переселéни|е, я *nt.* migration; resettlement.

пересел|и́ть, ю́, и́шь *pf.* (*of* ▸ **~я́ть**) to move; (*на новую территорию*) to resettle.

пересел|и́ться, ю́сь, и́шься *pf.* (*of* ▸ **~я́ться**) to move; (*на новую территорию*) to migrate.

пересел|я́ть(ся), я́ю(сь) *impf. of* ▸ **~и́ть(ся)**

перес|éсть, я́ду, я́дешь *pf.* (*of* ▸ **~áживаться**)
1 (*на другое место*) to change one's seat.
2 (*сделать пересадку*) to change (*trains, etc.*).

пересечéни|е, я *nt.* crossing, intersection.

пересé|чь, кý, чёшь, кýт, *past* **~̈к, ~клá** *pf.* (*of* ▸ **~кáть**)
1 (*перейти*) to cross; to traverse; **п. ýлицу** to cross the road.
2 (*город, местность*) to cross, cut across.

пересé|чься, чётся, кýтся, *past* **~̈кся, ~клáсь** *pf.* (*of* ▸ **~кáться**) to cross, intersect.

переси́лива|ть, ю *impf. of* ▸ **переси́лить**

переси́л|ить, ю, ишь *pf.* (*of* ▸ **~ивать**) to overcome, master.

перескáз, а *m.*
1 (*содержания романа*) retelling, narration.
2 (*изложение*) exposition.

переска|зáть, жý, ~́жешь *pf.* (*of* ▸ **~́зывать**)
1 to retell, narrate.
2 (*рассказать подробно*) to retail, relate; **п. слýхи** to retail rumours (*Br.*), rumors (*US*).

перескáзыва|ть, ю *impf. of* ▸ **пересказáть**

перескáкива|ть, ю *impf. of* ▸ **перескочи́ть**

перескоч|и́ть, ý, ~́ишь *pf.* (*of* ▸ **перескáкивать**)
1 (+ *a. or* **чéрез** + *a.*) to jump (over); (*fig.*) (*пропустить*) to skip (over).
2 (*fig.*) to skip; **п. с однóй тéмы на другýю** to skip from one topic to another.

пере|слáть, шлю́, шлёшь *pf.* (*of* ▸ **~сылáть**) (*отправить*) to send; (*деньги*) to remit; (*по другому адресу*) to forward.

пересмáтрива|ть, ю *impf. of* ▸ **пересмотрéть**

пересмотр|éть, ю́, ~́ишь *pf.* (*of* ▸ **пересмáтривать**)
1 (*книгу, документ*) to look through; to go over again.
2 (*решение*) to reconsider; (*leg.*) to review.
3 (*ища что-л.*) to go through (*in search of sth.*).

переснимá|ть, ю *impf. of* ▸ **переснять**

пересн|я́ть, иму́, и́мешь, *past* **~я́л, ~ялá, ~я́ло** *pf.* (*of* ▸ **~имáть**)
1 (*фотографировать заново*) to photograph again.
2 (*копировать*) (*coll.*) to make a copy of.

пересол|и́ть, ю́, ~́ишь *pf.* (*of* ▸ **пересáливать**) to put too much salt (into).

пересóх|нуть, нет, *past* **~, ~ла** *pf.* (*of* ▸ **пересыхáть**) (*о белье*) to dry out; (*о земле, речке*) to dry up, become parched.

пересп|áть, лю́, и́шь, *past* **~áл, ~алá, ~áло** *pf.* (*coll.*)
1 (*проспать слишком долго*) to oversleep.
2 (**с** + *i.*; *euph.*) to sleep (with).

переспóр|ить, ю, ишь *pf.* to defeat in argument.

переспрáшива|ть, ю *impf. of* ▸ **переспроси́ть**

переспро|си́ть, шý, ~́сишь *pf.* (*of* ▸ **переспрáшивать**) (*повторить вопрос*) to ask again; (*просить повторить*) to ask to repeat.

пересta|вáть, ю́, ёшь *impf. of* ▸ **~́ть**

перестáв|ить, лю, ишь *pf.* (*of* ▸ **~ля́ть**) to move, shift; **п. мéбель** to rearrange the furniture.

переставля́|ть, ю *impf. of* ▸ **перестáвить**

перестанóвк|а, и *f.*
1 rearrangement, transposition.
2 (*math.*) permutation.

перестá|ть, ну, нешь *pf.* (*of* ▸ **~вáть**) (+ *inf.*) to stop, cease; **они́ ~ли**

разгова́ривать they stopped talking; **~ньте!** stop it!
перестел|и́ть, ю́, ~ешь *pf.* (*of* ▸**перестила́ть**) to re-lay; **п. посте́ль** to remake a bed.
перестила́|ть, ю *impf. of* ▸**перестели́ть**
перестра́ива|ть(ся), ю(сь) *impf. of* ▸**перестро́ить(ся)**
перестрах|ова́ться, у́юсь *pf.* (*of* ▸**~о́вываться**)
1 to reinsure o.s.
2 (*fig., pej.*) to play safe.
перестрахо́выва|ться, юсь *impf. of* ▸**перестрахова́ться**
перестре́лк|а, и *f.* exchange of fire, shoot-out.
перестро́|ить, ю, ишь *pf.* (*of* ▸**перестра́ивать**)
1 (*дом*) to rebuild, reconstruct.
2 (*план, работу*) to redesign, refashion, reshape; to reorganize; **п. фра́зу** to reshape a sentence.
перестро́|иться, юсь, ишься *pf.* (*of* ▸**перестра́иваться**) to re-form; to reorganize o.s.; to restructure.
перестро́йк|а, и *f.*
1 (*здания*) rebuilding, reconstruction; (*pol., econ.*) perestroika.
2 (*реорганизация*) reorganization.
переступ|а́ть, а́ю *impf. of* ▸**~и́ть**
переступ|и́ть, лю́, ~ишь *pf.* (*of* ▸**~а́ть**) (+ *a.* or **че́рез** + *a.*) to step over; (*fig.*) to overstep; **п. поро́г** to cross the threshold; **п. зако́н** to break the law.
пересу́шива|ть, ю *impf. of* ▸**пересуши́ть**
пересуш|и́ть, у́, ~ишь *pf.* (*of* ▸**~ивать**) to overdry.
пересчит|а́ть[1], а́ю *pf.* (*of* ▸**~ывать**)
1 to recount.
2 (**в** + *p.*) to convert (to), express (in terms of).
пересчит|а́ть[2], а́ю *pf.* (*no impf.*) (*многое*) to count.
пересчи́тыва|ть, ю *impf. of* ▸**пересчита́ть[1]**
пересыла́|ть, ю *impf. of* ▸**пересла́ть**
пересып|а́ть, а́ю *impf. of* ▸**~ать**
пересы́п|ать, лю, лешь *pf.* (*of* ▸**~а́ть**) to pour (*dry substance*) into another container; **п. зерно́ в мешки́** to pour off grain into bags.
пересыха́|ть, ет *impf. of* ▸**пересо́хнуть**
перета́скива|ть, ю *impf. of* ▸**перетащи́ть**
перетас|ова́ть, у́ю *pf. of* ▸**тасова́ть**
перетащ|и́ть, у́, ~ишь *pf.* (*of* ▸**перета́скивать**) (*волоча*) to drag over; (*неся*) to carry over; (*переместить*) to move, shift; **п. сунду́к на черда́к** to move a trunk into the attic.
перетека́|ть, ю *impf. of* ▸**перете́чь**
перете́|чь, ку́, чёшь, ку́т, *past* **~к, ~кла́** *pf.* (*of* ▸**~ка́ть**) to overflow.
перетя́гива|ть, ю *impf. of* ▸**перетяну́ть**
перетя|ну́ть, ну́, ~нешь *pf.* (*of* ▸**~гивать**)
1 to pull, draw (*somewhere else; from A to B*); **п. ло́дку от одного́ бе́рега к друго́му** to pull the boat from one bank to the other.
2 (*fig., coll.*) to pull over, attract; **п. на свою́ сто́рону** to win over, gain support of.
3 (*крепко стянуть*) to tighten.
переубе|ди́ть, ди́шь *pf.* (*of* ▸**~жда́ть**) to make (*s.o.*) change his, her, *etc.* mind.
переубежда́|ть, ю *impf. of* ▸**переубеди́ть**
переу́л|ок, ка *m.* lane, side street.
переутом|и́ть, лю́, и́шь *pf.* (*of* ▸**~ля́ть**) to tire out; to overwork.
переутом|и́ться, лю́сь, и́шься *pf.* (*of* ▸**~ля́ться**) to tire o.s. out; to overwork; (*pf. only*) to be run down.
переутомле́ни|е, я *nt.* exhaustion; overwork.
переутомля́|ть(ся), ю(сь) *impf. of* ▸**переутоми́ть(ся)**
перефрази́р|овать, ую *impf. and pf.* to paraphrase.
перехва|ти́ть, чу́, ~тишь *pf.* (*of* ▸**~тывать**) to intercept, catch; **я ~ти́л его́ по доро́ге на рабо́ту** I caught him on the way to work.
перехва́тыва|ть, ю *impf. of* ▸**перехвати́ть**
перехитр|и́ть, ю́, и́шь *pf.* to outwit.
перехо́д, а *m.*
1 (*действие; место*) crossing; (*к другому состоянию, к другой системе*) transition, switch(-over); **подзе́мный п.** underpass, subway.
2 (*mil.*) (day's) march.
перехо|ди́ть, жу́, ~дишь *impf. of* ▸**перейти́**
переходни́к, а́ *m.* adaptor.
перехо́дный *adj.* (*период*) transitional; transient.
пе́р|ец, ца *m.* pepper.
пе́реч|ень, ня *m.* (*список*) list; (*перечисление*) enumeration.
перечёркива|ть, ю *impf. of* ▸**перечеркну́ть**
перечерк|ну́ть, ну́, нёшь *pf.* (*of* ▸**~ивать**) to cross (out); (*fig.*) (*уничтожить*) to cancel.
перечи́сл|ить, ю, ишь *pf.* (*of* ▸**~я́ть**)
1 to enumerate.
2 (*перевести*) to transfer; **п. на теку́щий счёт** (*fin.*) to transfer to one's current account.
перечисл|я́ть, я́ю *impf. of* ▸**~ить**
перечит|а́ть[1], а́ю *pf.* (*of* ▸**~ывать**) (*заново*) to reread.
перечит|а́ть[2], а́ю *pf.* (*всё или многое*) to read (*all or a quantity of*); **он ~а́л все кни́ги в библиоте́ке** he has read all the books in the library.
перечи́тыва|ть, ю *impf. of* ▸**перечита́ть[1]**
пе́речниц|а, ы *f.* (*для молотого перца*) pepper pot.
переша́гива|ть, ю *impf. of* ▸**перешагну́ть**
перешаг|ну́ть, ну́, нёшь *pf.* (*of* ▸**~ивать**) to step over; **п. (че́рез) поро́г** to cross the threshold.

переше́|ек, йка *m.* isthmus.
перешива́|ть, ю *impf. of* ▸ **переши́ть**
переш|и́ть, ью́, ьёшь *pf.* (*of* ▸ **~ива́ть**) to alter; to have altered.
пери́л|а, ~ *no sg.* rail(ing); handrail; (*лестницы*) banisters.
пери́метр, а *m.* (*math.*) perimeter.
пери́н|а, ы *f.* feather bed.
пери́од, а *m.* period; **леднико́вый п.** (*geol.*) ice age.
перио́дик|а, и *f.* (*collect.*) periodicals.
периоди́ческ|ий *adj.* periodic(al); recurring; **п. журна́л** periodical, magazine; **~ое явле́ние** recurrent phenomenon.
периско́п, а *m.* periscope.
перифери́|я, и *f.*
1 periphery.
2 (*collect.*) (*местность, удалённая от центра*) the provinces; the outlying districts.
3 (*comput.*) peripherals, peripheral devices.
перламу́тр, а *m.* mother-of-pearl.
перламу́тр|овый *adj. of* ▸ **~**
перманéнт|ный (~ен, ~на) *adj.* permanent.
перна́т|ый (~, ~а) *adj.* feathered; *as n. pl.* **~ые, ~ых** birds.
пёр|нуть, ну, нешь (*inst. pf. of* ▸ **~де́ть**) (*vulg.*) to fart.
пер|о́, а́, *pl.* **~ья, ~ьев** *nt.*
1 (*птицы*) feather.
2 (*hist.*) quill; (*стальное*) nib.
перочи́нный *adj.*: **п. нож** penknife.
перпендикуля́р|ный (~ен, ~на) *adj.* perpendicular.
перро́н, а *m.* platform (*at railway station*).
перс, а *m.* Persian.
перси́дский *adj.*: **П. зали́в** the Persian Gulf.
пе́рсик, а *m.*
1 (*плод*) peach.
2 (*дерево*) peach tree.
персия́нк|а, и *f. of* ▸ **перс**
персо́н|а, ы *f.* person; **обе́д на́ шесть ~** dinner for six.
персона́ж, а *m.* (*liter.*) character; (*fig.*) personage.
персона́л, а *m.* personnel, staff.
персона́льный *adj.* personal; individual; **п. компью́тер** personal computer.
перспекти́в|а, ы *f.*
1 (*art*) perspective.
2 (*fig.*) prospect, outlook; **име́ть ~у** to have prospects, have a future (before one).
перспекти́в|ный *adj.*
1 (*art*) perspective.
2 (*план*) long-term.
3 **(~ен, ~на)** (*многообещающий*) having prospects; promising.
пе́рст|ень, ня *m.* ring.
Перу́ *nt. & f. indecl.* Peru.
перуа́н|ец, ца *m.* Peruvian.
перуа́н|ка, ки *f. of* ▸ **~ец**
перуа́нский *adj.* Peruvian.
перфе́кт, а *m.* (*gram.*) perfect (tense).
пе́рхот|ь, и *f.* dandruff.
перча́тк|а, и *f.* glove; **бро́сить ~у** (*fig.*) to throw down the gauntlet.
пе́рч|ить, ~у́, ~ишь *impf.* (*of* ▸ **попе́рчить**) to pepper.
пёс, пса *m.* dog.
пес|е́ц, ца́ *m.* Arctic fox.
пе́с|ня, ни, *g. pl.* **~ен** *f.* song.
пес|о́к, ка́ *m.*
1 sand; **са́харный п.** granulated sugar.
2 (*pl.*) sands.
песо́чн|ый *adj.*
1 *adj. of* ▸ **песо́к;** sandy; **~ые часы́** sandglass, hourglass.
2 (*cul.*) short; **~ое пече́нье** shortbread.
пессими́зм, а *m.* pessimism.
пессими́ст, а *m.* pessimist.
пессимисти́ческий *adj.* pessimistic.
пессимисти́ч|ный (~ен, ~на) *adj.* = **~еский**
пессими́ст|ка, ки *f. of* ▸ **~**
пёстр|ый (~, ~а́, ~о *and* **~о́)** *adj.*
1 variegated, multicoloured (*Br.*), -colored (*US*).
2 (*fig., coll.*) mixed; **п. соста́в населе́ния** mixed population.
песча́н|ый *adj.* sandy; **~ая коса́** sandbar; **п. холм** dune.
песчи́нк|а, и *f.* grain of sand.
петáрд|а, ы *f.* banger (*Br.*), firecracker.
петербу́ргский *adj.* St Petersburg.
петербу́рж|ец, ца *m.* St Petersburger.
пети́ци|я, и *f.* petition.
петли́ц|а, ы *f.* buttonhole; tab.
пет|ля́, ли́, *pl.* **~ли, ~ель** *f.*
1 loop.
2 (*fig.*) noose.
3 (*для пуговицы*) buttonhole.
4 (*в вязании*) stitch.
5 (*двери*) hinge.
петля́|ть, ю *impf.* (*coll.*) to dodge.
петру́шк|а, и *f.* parsley.
пету́х, а́ *m.* cock; **встава́ть с ~а́ми** to rise with the lark.
петь, пою́, поёшь *impf.* (*of* ▸ **с~**^{2}) to sing; **п. ба́сом** to have a bass voice; **п. вполго́лоса** to hum.
пехо́т|а, ы *f.* infantry; **морска́я п.** (the) marines.
пехоти́н|ец, ца *m.* infantryman.
печа́л|ь, и *f.* grief, sorrow.
печа́л|ьный (~ен, ~ьна) *adj.*
1 sad, doleful.
2 (*прискорбный*) bad, regrettable; **п. коне́ц** bad end.
печа́та|ть, ю *impf.* (*of* ▸ **на~** *and* ▸ **от~ 1**) to print; (*на машинке*) to type.
печа́та|ться, юсь *impf.* (*of* ▸ **на~**)
1 to have (*literary compositions, etc.*) published; **в три́дцать лет он ещё нигде́ не ~лся** at thirty he had not yet had anything published.
2 (*находиться в печати*) to be at the printer's.
печа́тн|ый *adj.*
1 printing; **п. лист** quire, printer's sheet.
2 (*напечатанный*) printed; in the press; **~ая кни́га** printed book (*opp. manuscript*).
3 : **писа́ть ~ыми бу́квами** to (write in)

print; to write in block capitals.

печáт|ь[1], **и** *f.* (*для получения оттиска*) seal, stamp (*also fig.*); **на мои́х устáх п. молчáния** my lips are sealed.

печáть[2], **и** *f.*
1 (*печатание*) print(ing); **вы́йти из ~и** to come out, be published.
2 (*вид напечатанного*) print, type; **мéлкая п.** small print; **кру́пная п.** large print.
3 (*пресса*) (the) press; **свобóда ~и** freedom of the press.

печёнк|а, и *f.* liver (*of animal, as food*).

печёный *adj.* (*cul.*) baked.

пéчен|ь, и *f.* liver.

печéнь|е, я *nt.* biscuit (*Br.*), cookie (*US*).

пéчк|а, и *f.* stove.

печь[1], **пеку́, печёшь, пеку́т,** *past* **пёк, пеклá** *impf.* (*of* ▶ **ис~**) to bake; **сóлнце пеклó** there was a scorching sun.

печ|ь[2], **и, о ~́и, в ~и́,** *pl.* **~́и, ~éй** *f.*
1 stove; (*духовка*) oven.
2 (*tech.*) furnace; (*обжиговая*) kiln.

пéчься, печётся, пеку́тся, *past* **пёкся, пеклáсь** *impf.* (*of* ▶ **ис~**) to bake.

пешехóд, а *m.* pedestrian.

пешехóдный *adj.* pedestrian; **п. мост** footbridge.

пéший *adj.*
1 pedestrian.
2 (*mil.*) unmounted, foot.

пéшк|а, и *f.* (*in chess, also fig.*) pawn.

пешкóм *adv.* on foot.

пещéр|а, ы *f.* cave.

пиани́но *nt. indecl.* (upright) piano.

пиани́ст, а *m.* pianist.

пиани́ст|ка, ки *f. of* ▶ **~**

пиáр, а *m.* PR (*Public Relations*).

пивн|áя, óй *f.* pub.

пи́в|о, а *nt.* beer.

пивовáр, а *m.* brewer.

пивоварéни|е, я *nt.* brewing.

пивовáренн|ый *adj.*: **п. завóд** brewery; **~ая промы́шленность** brewing.

пигмéнт, а *m.* pigment.

пиджáк, á *m.* jacket, coat.

пижáм|а, ы *f.* pyjamas.

пижóн, а *m.* (*coll.*) fop.

пизд|á, ы́, *pl. not used or disp.* (*oft. joc.*) **пёзды, пёзд** *f.* (*vulg.*) cunt.

пик[1], **а** *m.* (*geog.*) peak; (*fig.*) pinnacle.

пик[2], **а**
1 *m.* peak (*of work, traffic, etc.*); **п. нагру́зки** (*elec.*) peak load.
2 *adj. indecl.*: **часы́ пик** rush hour.

пи́к|а[1], **и** *f.* (*оружие*) pike, lance.

пи́к|а[2], **и** *f.* (*cards*) spade.

пикáп, а *m.* pickup (truck).

пикéт, а *m.* (*группа бастующих*) picket.

пикети́р|овать, ую *impf.* to picket.

пи́кколо *nt. indecl.* piccolo.

пикни́к, á *m.* picnic.

пи́ксел|ь, я *m.* (*comput.*) pixel.

пиктогрáмм|а, ы *f.* pictogram; (*comput.*) icon.

пил|á, ы́, *pl.* **~́ы, ~** *f.* saw.

пилá-ры́ба, пилы́-ры́бы *f.* sawfish.

пилигри́м, а *m.* pilgrim.

пил|и́ть, ю́, ~́ишь *impf.* to saw.

пилóт, а *m.* pilot.

пилóтк|а, и *f.* (*mil.*) forage cap.

пилю́л|я, и *f.* pill (*also fig.*).

пинá|ть, ю *impf. of* ▶ **пнуть**

пингви́н, а *m.* penguin.

пинг-пóнг, а *m.* ping-pong.

пинцéт, а *m.* (*tech.*) pincers; (*med.*) tweezers.

пи́нчер, а *m.* (*собака*) pinscher.

пиóн, а *m.* (*bot.*) peony.

пионéр, а *m.* pioneer.

пипéтк|а, и *f.* pipette; medicine dropper.

пир, а, о ~́е, на ~у́, *pl.* **~ы́** *m.* feast, banquet.

пирами́д|а, ы *f.* (*also fin.*) pyramid.

пирáт, а *m.* pirate.

пирáтский *adj.* (*судно*) pirate; (*обычаи*) piratical; (*издание*) pirated.

пирáтств|о, а *nt.* piracy.

Пиренé|и, ев *no sg.* the Pyrenees.

пирóг, á *m.* pie; **п. с мя́сом** meat pie.

пирóг|а, и *f.* pirogue, canoe.

пирóжн|ое, ого *nt.* (fancy) cake, pastry.

пирож|óк, кá *m.* pasty (*Br.*), patty, pie.

пи́рсинг, а *m.* body piercing.

пи́ршеств|о, а *nt.* feast, banquet.

писáтел|ь, я *m.* writer, author.

писáтель|ница, ницы *f. of* ▶ **~**

пи|сáть, шу́, ~́шешь *impf.* (*of* ▶ **на~**)
1 to write; (*на машинке*) to type.
2 (+ *i.*) (*красками*) to paint (in).

пи́са|ть, ю *impf.* (*of* ▶ **по~**) (*coll.*) to pee, have a pee.

писк, а *m.* (*ребёнка, мыши*) squeak; (*цыплят*) cheep.

пи́скн|уть, у, ешь *inst. pf.* (*of* ▶ **пищáть**) (*coll.*) to give a squeak, cheep.

пистолéт, а *m.* pistol.

пи́сьменност|ь, и *f.*
1 (*литературные памятники*) literature; (*collect.*) literary texts.
2 (*средства письменного общения*) the written language.

пи́сьменн|ый *adj.*
1 (*для письма*) writing; **п. стол** writing table, bureau.
2 (*написанный*) written; **в ~ом ви́де, в ~ой фóрме** in writing, in written form; **п. экзáмен** written examination.

письм|ó, á, *pl.* **~́а, пи́сем, ~́ам** *nt.*
1 letter; **заказнóе п.** registered letter.
2 (*система графических знаков*) script; **арáбское п.** Arabic script.

питáни|е, я *nt.*
1 (*действие*) feeding, nutrition; (*характер пищи*) diet; **недостáточное п.** malnutrition; (*пища*) food.
2 (*tech.*) feed, supply.
3 (*elec.*) power supply.

питáтел|ьный (~ен, ~ьна) *adj.* nourishing, nutritious; **~ьная средá** (*biol.*) culture medium; (*fig.*) breeding ground.

питá|ться, юсь *impf.* (+ *i.*) to feed (on), live (on); **хорошó п.** to be well fed, eat well.

Пи́тер, а *m.* (*coll.*) St. Petersburg.

пи́тер|ский *adj. of* ▶ **П~**
питóмник, а *m.* nursery (*for plants or animals; also fig.*).
питóн, а *m.* python.
пить, пью, пьёшь, *past* **пил, пила́, пи́ло** *impf.* (*of* ▶ **вы́~**) to drink; **мне хóчется п.** I am thirsty; **п. за** (+ *a.*), **за здорóвье** (+ *g.*) to drink to, to the health (of).
пить|ё, я́ *nt.* drink.
пих|а́ть, а́ю *impf.* (*of* ▶ **~ну́ть**) (*coll.*)
1 (*толкать*) to push; shove, jostle.
2 (*запихивать*) to shove, cram.
пих|ну́ть, ну́, нёшь *pf. of* ▶ **~а́ть**
пи́хт|а, ы *f.* fir (tree).
пи́цц|а, ы *f.* pizza.
пи́щ|а, и *no pl., f.* food.
пищ|а́ть, у́, и́шь *impf.* (*of* ▶ **пи́скнуть**) (*о мыши, о двери*) to squeak; (*о цыплятах*) to cheep.
пищеваре́ни|е, я *nt.* digestion; **расстрóйство ~я** indigestion.
пищ|евóй *adj. of* ▶ **~́а; ~евы́е продýкты** foodstuffs.
пия́вк|а, и *f.* leech.
ПК *m. indecl.* (*abbr. of* **персона́льный компью́тер**) PC (*personal computer*).
пла́вани|е, я *nt.*
1 swimming.
2 (*на судне*) sailing; navigation; **отпра́виться в п.** to put out to sea.
пла́вательный *adj.* swimming; **п. бассéйн** swimming pool.
пла́ва|ть, ю *impf.*
1 *indet. of* ▶ **плыть.**
2 (*держаться на воде*) to float.
пла́в|ить, лю, ишь *impf.* to smelt.
пла́в|иться, ится *impf.* to melt.
пла́вк|а, и *f.* fusing; fusion.
пла́в|ки, ок *no sg.* swimming trunks.
плавни́к, а́ *m.* (*рыбы*) fin; (*дельфина, тюленя*) flipper.
пла́в|ный (~ен, ~на) *adj.* smooth; **~ная речь** flowing speech.
плавýчий *adj.* floating.
плагиа́т, а *m.* plagiarism.
пла́зм|а, ы *f.* (*biol., phys.*) plasma.
пла́зменный *adj.*: **~ экра́н** (*TV, comput.*) plasma screen.
плака́т, а *m.* poster.
пла́|кать, чу, чешь *impf.* to cry, weep; **п. навзры́д** to sob.
плакси́в|ый (~, ~а) *adj.* (*coll.*) (*ребёнок*) given to crying; whining; (*голос, лицо, улыбка*) pathetic.
пла́мен|ный (~ен, ~на) *adj.* ardent, burning.
пла́м|я, ени *nt.* flame; (*яркое*) blaze.
план, а *m.*
1 (*намерение; чертёж, карта*) plan; **по ~́у** according to plan.
2 (*место*): **пере́дний п.** foreground; **за́дний п.** background; **крýпный п.** close-up (*in filming*).
пла́нер, а *m.* (*aeron.*) glider.
плане́т|а, ы *f.*
1 planet.
2 (*Земля*) (the) planet (= *Earth*).
плани́ровани|е, я *nt.* planning.
плани́р|овать, ую *impf.* (*of* ▶ **за~**) to plan.
планирóвк|а, и *f.* layout.
пла́нк|а, и *f.* lath, slat.
планктóн, а *m.* (*biol.*) plankton.
пла́нов|ый *adj.* planned, systematic; **~ое хозя́йство** planned economy.
планоме́р|ный (~ен, ~на) *adj.* systematic, planned.
планта́ци|я, и *f.* plantation.
пласт, а́ *m.* layer; sheet; (*archit.*) course; (*geol.*) stratum, bed.
пла́стик, а *m.* plastic (*material*).
пла́стиковый *adj.* plastic.
пластили́н, а *m.* plasticine (*propr.*).
пласти́н|а, ы *f.* plate.
пласти́нк|а, и *f.*
1 plate; **(вини́ловая) п.** (vinyl) record.
2 (*coll.*) (*зубной протез*) plate.
пласти́ческ|ий *adj.* plastic; **~ая хирурги́я** plastic surgery.
пласти́ч|ный (~ен, ~на) *adj.*
1 (*материал, вещество*) plastic; pliant.
2 (*плавный*) rhythmical; fluent, flowing; (*изящный*) graceful; (*гармоничный*) harmonious.
пластма́сс|а, ы *f.* plastic.
пластма́сс|овый *adj. of* ▶ **~а**
пла́стыр|ь, я *m.* (*med.*) plaster.
пла́т|а[1]**, ы** *f.*
1 (*за труд*) pay; salary; **за́работная п.** wages.
2 (*за получение, использование чего-н.*) payment, charge; fee; **входна́я п.** entrance fee; **кварти́рная п.** rent; **п. за проéзд** fare.
пла́т|а[2]**, ы** *f.* (*comput.*) card, board; **монта́жная п.** circuit board.
плата́н, а *m.* plane (tree).
плат|ёж, ежа́ *m.* payment.
платёжеспосóб|ный (~ен, ~на) *adj.* solvent.
платёж|ный *adj. of* ▶ **~; ~ная ве́домость** payroll; **~ное поручéние** payment order.
пла́тин|а, ы *f.* (*min.*) platinum.
пла|ти́ть, чý, ~́тишь *impf.* (*of* ▶ **за~**)
1 to pay; **п. нали́чными** to pay in cash, pay in ready money.
2 (*fig.*; + *i.* **за** + *a.*) to pay back, return.
пла́тн|ый *adj.*
1 paid; requiring payment, chargeable; **~ая дорóга** toll road.
2 paying; (*школа*) fee-paying; (*больница*) private.
платó *nt. indecl.* (*geog.*) plateau.
плат|óк, ка́ *m.* (*на плечи*) shawl; (*на голову*) headscarf; **носовóй п.** (pocket) handkerchief.
платфóрм|а, ы *f.*
1 (*перрон*) platform.
2 (*вагон*) (open) goods truck (*Br.*), flatcar (*US*).
3 (*fig., pol.*) platform.
пла́ть|е, я, *g. pl.* **~ев** *nt.*
1 (*женское*) dress; (*длинное*) gown; **вечéрнее п.** evening dress.
2 (*одежда*) clothes, clothing.
плач, а *m.* weeping, crying.

плачéв|ный (~ен, ~на) *adj.* lamentable, deplorable, sorry; **в ~ном состоя́нии** in a sorry state.

плашмя́ *adv.* flat; flatways; prone.

плащ, á *m.*
1 (*непромокаемое пальто*) raincoat.
2 (*накидка*) cloak.

плевáть, плюю́, плюёшь *impf.* (*of* ▸ **плю́нуть**)
1 to spit.
2 (**на** + *a.*; *coll.*) to spit (upon); to not care a rap about; **им п. на всё** they don't give a damn about anything.

плев|óк, кá *m.* spit(tle).

плед, а *m.* travelling rug (*Br.*), lap robe (*US*).

плéер, а *m.* (*аудиокассет, аудиодисков*) personal stereo, Walkman (*propr.*); (*MP3, DVD и т. п.*) (MP3, DVD, *etc.*) player.

плéм|я, ени, *pl.* **~енá, ~ён, ~енáм** *nt.* tribe.

племя́нник, а *m.* nephew.

племя́нниц|а, ы *f.* niece.

плен, а, о ~е, в ~ý *m.* captivity; **попáсть в п.** (**к** + *d.*) to be taken prisoner (by).

плени́тел|ьный (~ен, ~ьна) *adj.* captivating, charming.

плёнк|а, и *f.* (*тонкий слой*) film (*also phot.*); (*магнитофонная*) tape.

плéнник, а *m.* prisoner, captive.

плéнни|ца, цы *f. of* ▸ **~к**

плéнн|ый *adj.* captive; *as n.* **п., ~ого** *m.* captive, prisoner.

плéнум, а *m.* plenum, plenary session.

плéсен|ь, и *f.* mould (*Br.*), mold (*US*).

плеск, а *m.* splash; **п. волн** lapping of waves.

пле|скáть, щý, ~щешь *impf.* (*of* ▸ **~сну́ть**) to splash; **п. на когó-н. водóй** to splash s.o. (with water).

пле|скáться, щýсь, ~щешься *impf.* to splash; (*о волнах*) to lap.

плес|нýть, нý, нёшь *inst. pf. of* ▸ **~кáть**

пле|сти́, тý, тёшь, *past* **~л, ~лá**
1 *impf. of* ▸ **с~.**
2 (*pf.* ▸ **за~**) (*волосы*) to braid, plait.

пле|сти́сь, тýсь, тёшься, *past* **~лся, ~лáсь** *impf.* (*coll.*) to trudge, plod (along).

плет|ь, и, *pl.* **~и, ~éй** *f.* lash.

плечи́ст|ый (~, ~а) *adj.* broad-shouldered.

плеч|ó, á, *pl.* **~и, ~, ~áм** *nt.* shoulder; **имéть гóлову на ~áх** to have a good head on one's shoulders; **э́то емý не по ~ý** he is not up to it; **пожáть ~áми** to shrug one's shoulders.

плеши́в|ый (~, ~а) *adj.* bald.

плеш|ь, и *f.* bald patch.

пли́нтус, а *m.*
1 (*archit.*) plinth.
2 (*между стеной и полом*) skirting board (*Br.*), baseboard (*US*).

плит|á, ы́, *pl.* **~ы** *f.*
1 (*металлическая*) plate; (*каменная*) slab; (*для настилки полов*) flag(stone); **моги́льная п.** gravestone, tombstone; **мрáморная п.** marble slab.
2 (*печь*) stove; cooker.

пли́тк|а, и *f.*
1 *dim. of* ▸ **плитá;** (*облицовочная*) tile, (thin) slab; **п. шоколáда** bar of chocolate.
2 (*печь*) small stove.

плов, а *m.* (*cul.*) pilaf.

плов|éц, цá *m.* swimmer.

плов|чи́ха, чи́хи *f. of* ▸ **~éц**

плод, á *m.*
1 fruit (*also fig.*); **приноси́ть ~ы́** to bear fruit; **запрéтный п.** (*fig.*) forbidden fruit.
2 (*biol.*) fetus.

плодóв|ый *adj. of* ▸ **плод; ~ое дéрево** fruit tree.

плодорóди|е, я *nt.* fertility.

плодорóд|ный (~ен, ~на) *adj.* fertile.

плодотвóр|ный (~ен, ~на) *adj.* fruitful.

плóмб|а, ы *f.*
1 (*на вагоне*) seal.
2 (*в зубе*) filling; **стáвить ~у** to fill a tooth.

пломбир|овáть, ýю *impf.*
1 (*pf.* **о~, за~**) (*вагон, избирательную урну*) to seal.
2 (*pf.* **за~**) (*зуб*) to fill.

плóс|кий (~ок, ~кá, ~ко) *adj.*
1 flat; plane; **~кая повéрхность** plane surface.
2 (*fig.*) (*пошлый*) trivial, tame; **~кая шýтка** feeble joke.

плоскогóрь|е, я *nt.* plateau; tableland.

плоскогýбц|ы, ев *no sg.* pliers.

плóскост|ь, и, *pl.* **~и, ~éй** *f.* (*поверхность*) plane (*also fig.*); **наклóнная п.** inclined plane.

плот, á, о ~é, на ~ý *m.* raft.

плотв|á, ы́ *f.* (*fish*) roach.

плоти́н|а, ы *f.* dam.

плóтник, а *m.* carpenter.

плóтно *adv.*
1 close(ly), tightly; **п. заколоти́ть дверь** to board up a door.
2: **п. поéсть** to eat heartily.

плóтност|ь, и *f.*
1 (*тумана, населения*) density (*also phys.*).
2 (*человека*) solidity.

плóт|ный (~ен, ~нá, ~но, ~ны́) *adj.*
1 (*туман, население*) dense (*also phys.*).
2 (*бумага*) thick, solid, strong; (*человек*) thickset, solidly built.
3 (*папка*) tightly-filled.
4 (*coll.*) (*завтрак*) hearty.

плотоя́д|ный (~ен, ~на) *adj.*
1 carnivorous.
2 (*fig.*) (*сладострастный*) lustful; voluptuous.

плот|ь, и *f.* flesh; **во ~и́** in the flesh.

плóхо *adv.* bad(ly); ill; **чýвствовать себя́ п.** to feel unwell; **п. пáхнуть** to smell bad.

плох|óй (~, ~á, ~о) *adj.* bad; poor; **~óе настроéние** bad mood; *as pred.*: **емý óчень ~о** he is in a very bad way.

площáдк|а, и *f.*
1 ground, area; **дéтская п.** children's playground; **спорти́вная п.** sports ground; **строи́тельная п.** building site; **тéннисная п.** tennis court; **киносъёмочная п.** (film) set; **п. для**

игры́ в гольф golf course.
[2] (*лестничная*) landing (*on staircase*).
[3] (*в вагоне*) platform; **пусковая п.** launch pad (*of rocket*).

пло́щад|ь, и, *pl.* **~и, ~ей** *f.*
[1] (*в городе*) square.
[2] (*пространство*) area; space; **жилая п.** living space.
[3] (*math.*) area.

плуг, а, *pl.* **~и́** *m.* plough (*Br.*), plow (*US*).

плут, а́ *m.* cheat; rogue.

плы|ть, ву́, вёшь, *past* **~л, ~ла́, ~́ло** *impf.* (*det. of* ▸ **пла́вать 1**)
[1] (*о человеке, о животном*) to swim; (*об облаках, о звуках*) to float.
[2] (*ехать на судне*) to sail; **п. на вёслах** to row; **п. под паруса́ми** to sail.

плю́н|уть, у, ешь *pf. of* ▸ **плева́ть**

плюрали́зм, а *m.* (*phil. & pol.*) pluralism.

плюс, а *m.*
[1] plus; *as connective in math. expressions*: **два п. два равно́ четырём** two plus two equals four.
[2] (*fig., coll.*) (*преимущество*) advantage.

плю́х|аться, аюсь *impf. of* ▸ **~нуться**

плю́х|нуться, нусь, нешься *pf.* (*of* ▸ **~аться**) (*coll.*) to flop (down).

плюш, а *m.* plush.

плю́ш|евый *adj. of* ▸ **~**

плющ, а́ *m.* ivy.

пляж, а *m.* beach.

пля|са́ть, шу́, ~́шешь *impf.* (*of* ▸ **с~**) to dance.

пля́ск|а, и *f.* (*действие*) dancing; (*танец*) dance (*esp. folk dance*).

пневмати́ческий *adj.* pneumatic.

пневмони́|я, и *f.* pneumonia; **атипи́чная п.** SARS (*severe acute respiratory syndrome*).

пнуть, пну, пнёшь *inst. pf.* (*of* ▸ **пина́ть**) (*coll.*) to kick.

по *prep.* **I.** + *d.*
[1] (*на поверхности*) on; (*вдоль*) along; **идти́ по траве́** to walk on the grass; **е́хать по у́лице** to go along the street; **идти́ по следа́м** (+ *g.*) to follow in the tracks (of); **по всему́, по всей** all over.
[2] (*в разные места*) round, about; **ходи́ть по магази́нам** to go round the shops.
[3] (*посредством*) by, on, over; **по желе́зной доро́ге** by rail; **по по́чте** by post; **по ра́дио** over the radio; **по телефо́ну** on, over the telephone.
[4] (*в соответствии, согласно*) according to; by; in accordance with; **по пра́ву** by right(s); **по расписа́нию** according to schedule; **звать по и́мени** to call by first name.
[5] (*в отношении*) by, in (= *in respect of*); **по профе́ссии** by profession; **по происхожде́нию он армяни́н** he is of Armenian origin; **лу́чший по ка́честву** better in quality; **това́рищ по шко́ле** schoolmate.
[6] (*в области*) at, on, in (= *in the field of*); **ле́кции по европе́йской исто́рии** lectures on European history; **специали́ст по я́дерной фи́зике** specialist in nuclear physics.
[7] (*из-за*) by (reason of); on account of; from; **по боле́зни** on account of sickness; **по рассе́янности** from absent-mindedness.
[8] (*указывает на предмет действия*) at, for (*or not translated*); **скуча́ть по де́тям** to miss one's children.
[9] (*указывает время*) on; in; **по пра́здникам** on holidays.
■ **II.** (*в распределительном значении*) (+ *d.*: **по одному́; по ты́сяче, по миллио́ну, по миллиа́рду;** *with other numerals* + *a.*) **по́ два (две), по́ три, по четы́ре, по две́сти, по три́ста, по четы́реста; да́йте им по** (*sc.* **одному́**) **я́блоку** give them an apple each; **мы получи́ли по три фу́нта** we received three pounds each; **по рублю́ шту́ка** one rouble each.
■ **III.** + *a.* (*до*) to, up to; **по по́яс в воде́** up to the waist in water.
■ **IV.** + *p.* (*после*) on, after; **по прибы́тии** on arrival.

по- + *d. of adj. or ending* **...ски** *forms adv. indicating*
[1] *manner of action, conduct, etc., as* **жить по-ста́рому** to live in the old manner.
[2] *use of given language, as* **говори́ть по-ру́сски** to speak Russian.
[3] *accordance with opinion or wish, as* **по-мо́ему** in my opinion.

по...[1] *as vbl. pref.*
[1] *forms pf. aspect.*
[2] *indicates action of short duration or of incomplete character, as* **порабо́тать** to do a little work; **поспа́ть** to have a sleep.
[3] (+ *suff.* **...ыва..., ...ива...**) *indicates action repeated at intervals or of indet. duration, as* **позва́нивать** to keep ringing.

по...[2] *pref. modifying comp. adj. or adv., as* **погро́мче** a little louder.

поба́ива|ться, юсь *impf.* (+ *g. or inf.*; *coll.*) to be rather afraid.

поба́лива|ть, ю *impf.* (*coll.*) (*немного*) to ache a little; (*иногда*) to ache on and off.

побе́г, а *m.* flight; escape.

побе́д|а, ы *f.* victory; **одержа́ть ~у** to gain a victory.

победи́тел|ь, я *m.* victor; (*sport*) winner.

победи́тель|ница, ницы *f. of* ▸ **~**

побед|и́ть, и́шь *pf.* (*of* ▸ **побежда́ть**) (*врага*) to conquer; (*соперника*) to defeat, beat; **на́ша кома́нда победи́ла** our team won; (*fig.*) to master, overcome.

побе́дный *adj.* victorious, triumphant; **п. гол** winning goal.

побе|жа́ть, гу́, жи́шь, гу́т *pf.*
[1] *pf. of* ▸ **бежа́ть 1.**
[2] to break into a run.

побежда́|ть, ю *impf. of* ▸ **победи́ть**

побеле́|ть, ю *pf. of* ▸ **беле́ть 1**

побел|и́ть, ю́, ~́ишь *pf. of* ▸ **бели́ть**

побе́лк|а, и *f.* whitewashing.

побере́жь|е, я *nt.* coast, seaboard.

побесе́д|овать, ую *pf.* to have a (little) talk, have a chat.

побеспоко́|ить, ю, ишь *pf. of* ▸ **беспоко́ить 2; позво́льте вас п.** may I trouble you?

побеспоко́|иться, юсь, ишься *pf. of* ▸ **беспоко́иться 2**

побива́|ть, ю *impf.* (*of* ▸ **поби́ть 2**) (*противника*) to beat; (*рекорд*) to break.

поб|и́ть, ью́, ьёшь *pf.*
[1] *pf. of* ▸ **бить 1.**
[2] *pf. of* ▸ **побива́ть.**
[3] (*pf. only*) (*растения*) to beat down, damage; (*о морозе*) to nip.
[4] (*pf. only*) (*посуду*) to break, smash.

поб|и́ться, ью́сь, ьёшься *pf.* (*coll.*)
[1] (*1st and 2nd pers. not used*) (*получить повреждения*) to get damaged; (*о фруктах и овощах*) to bruise; (*о посуде, яйцах*) to break, smash.
[2] (**над** + *i.*; *fig.*) to struggle (with) (for some time).

поблагодар|и́ть, ю́, и́шь *pf. of* ▸ **благодари́ть**

побледне́|ть, ю *pf. of* ▸ **бледне́ть**

поблёскива|ть, ю *impf.* to gleam.

побли́зости *adv.* nearby; **п.** (**от** + *g.*) near (to).

поболта́|ть, ю *pf.* (*coll.*) to have a chat.

побор|о́ть, ю́, ~́ешь *pf.* to overcome.

побо́чный *adj.* secondary; **п. эффе́кт** side effect; **п. проду́кт** by-product.

побо|я́ться, ю́сь, и́шься *pf.* (+ *g. or inf.*) to be afraid.

побр|и́ть(ся), е́ю(сь) *pf. of* ▸ **бри́ть(ся)**

поброса́|ть, ю *pf.*
[1] (*бросить как попало*) to throw.
[2] (*покинуть*) to desert, abandon.

побыва́|ть, ю *pf.*
[1] (*посетить*) to have been, have visited; **в про́шлом году́ мы ~ли в Норве́гии и Шве́ции** last year we were in Norway and Sweden.
[2] (*зайти*) to drop in, call in; **он ~л у друзе́й** he dropped in to see some friends.

по|бы́ть, бу́ду, бу́дешь, *past* **~́был, ~была́, ~́было** *pf.* to stay (*for a short time*); **мы ~́были в Ло́ндоне два дня** we stayed in London for two days.

пова́дк|а, и *f.* (*coll.*) habit.

повал|и́ть[1], ю́, ~́ишь *pf. of* ▸ **вали́ть[1] 1**

повал|и́ть[2], ю́, ~́ишь *pf.* to begin to throng, begin to pour; **дым ~и́л из трубы́** smoke began to pour from the chimney.

повал|и́ться, ю́сь, ~́ишься *pf. of* ▸ **вали́ться**

пова́льный *adj.* general, mass.

по́вар, а, *pl.* **~а́** *m.* cook.

по-ва́шему *adv.*
[1] (*по вашему мнению*) in your opinion.
[2] (*как вы хотите*) as you wish.

поведе́ни|е, я *nt.* behaviour (*Br.*), behavior (*US*).

повез|ти́, у́, ёшь, *past* **~̈, ~ла́** *pf. of* ▸ **везти́**

повели́тельн|ый *adj.*: **~ое наклоне́ние** (*gram.*) imperative mood, the imperative.

повенча́|ть(ся), ю(сь) *pf. of* ▸ **венча́ть(ся)**

поверг|а́ть, а́ю *impf. of* ▸ **~́нуть**

пове́рг|нуть, ну, нешь, *past* **~** *and* **~нул, ~ла** *pf.* (*of* ▸ **~а́ть**) (**в** + *a.*) to plunge (into); **п. в отча́яние** to plunge into despair.

пове́р|ить, ю, ишь *pf. of* ▸ **ве́рить**

повер|ну́ть, ну́, нёшь *pf.* (*of* ▸ **повора́чивать**) to turn; (*fig.*) to change.

повер|ну́ться, ну́сь, нёшься *pf.* (*of* ▸ **повора́чиваться**) to turn; **п. круго́м** to turn round, turn about; **п. спино́й** (**к** + *d.*) to turn one's back (upon).

пове́рх *prep.* + *g.* over, above; on top of; **смотре́ть п. очко́в** to look over the top of one's spectacles.

пове́рхност|ный *adj.*
[1] surface, superficial; **~ное натяже́ние** (*tech.*) surface tension.
[2] (**~ен, ~на**) (*fig.*) superficial.

пове́рхност|ь, и *f.* surface.

по́верху *adv.* on the surface, on top.

повеселе́|ть, ю *pf.* to cheer up, become cheerful.

по-весе́ннему *adv.* as in spring.

пове́|сить, шу, сишь *pf. of* ▸ **ве́шать[1]**

пове́|ситься, шусь, сишься *pf. of* ▸ **ве́шаться 2**

повествова́ни|е, я *nt.* narrative, narration.

повеств|ова́ть, у́ю *impf.* (**о** + *p.*) to narrate, recount, relate.

пове|сти́, ду́, дёшь, *past* **~̈л, ~ла́** *pf. of* ▸ **вести́ 1**

пове́стк|а, и *f.* notice, notification; **п. в суд** summons, writ, subpoena; **на ~е дня** on the agenda (*also fig.*).

по́вест|ь, и, *pl.* **~и, ~е́й** *f.* story, tale.

повзросле́|ть, ю *pf.* to grow up.

повида́|ть, ю *pf.* (*coll.*) to see.

повида́|ться, юсь *pf.* (*coll.*) (**с**+ *i.*) to meet; to see one another.

по-ви́димому *adv.* apparently, seemingly.

пови́дл|о, а *nt.* jam.

пови́нност|ь, и *f.* duty, obligation; **во́инская п.** compulsory military service, conscription.

повин|ова́ться, у́юсь *impf.* (*in past tense also pf.*) (+ *d.*) to obey.

повинове́ни|е, я *nt.* obedience.

повис|а́ть, а́ю *impf. of* ▸ **~́нуть**

пови́с|нуть, ну, нешь, *past* **~, ~ла** *pf.* (*of* ▸ **~а́ть**)
[1] (**на** + *p.*) to hang (by).
[2] (*склониться*) to hang down, droop; **п. в во́здухе** (*fig.*) to hang in mid-air; (*о шутке*) to fall flat.

повле́|чь, ку́, чёшь, ку́т, *past* **~̈к, ~кла́** *pf.* **(за собо́й)** to entail, bring in one's train; **п. за собо́й неприя́тные после́дствия** to have unpleasant consequences.

повлия́|ть, ю *pf. of* ▸ **влия́ть**

по́вод, а, *pl.* **~ы** *m.* (**к** + *d.*) occasion, cause, ground (for, of); **дать п.** (+ *d.*) to give occasion (to), give cause (for); **без вся́кого ~а** without cause; **по ~у** (+ *g.*) apropos (of), as regards, concerning.

повод|о́к, ка́ *m.* lead (*Br.*), leash (*US*).

пово́зк|а, и *f.* cart.

повора́чива|ть(ся), ю(сь) *impf. of* ▸ **поверну́ть(ся); ~йся!, ~йтесь!** (*coll.*) get a move on!, look sharp!

поворóт, а *m.* turn(ing); **указáтели ~а** direction indicator lamps (*of car*); (*fig.*) turning point; **на ~е дорóги** at the turn of the road.

повре|дить, жý, дишь *pf.*
1 *pf. of* ▸ **вредить.**
2 (*pf. of* ▸ **~ждáть**) (*испортить*) to damage; (*поранить*) to injure, hurt.

повре|диться, жýсь, дишься *pf.* (*of* ▸ **~ждáться**) (*испортиться*) to be damaged.

повреждá|ть(ся), ю(сь) *impf. of* ▸ **повредить(ся)**

повреждéни|е, я *nt.* damage; injury.

повседнéвный *adj.* daily; everyday.

повсемéстно *adv.* everywhere.

повстáн|ец, ца *m.* rebel, insurgent.

повстречá|ть, ю *pf.* (*coll.*) to meet, run into.

повстречá|ться, юсь *pf.* (*coll.*) (+ *d.* or **с** + *i.*) to meet, run into; **я ~лся со знакóмым** I met an acquaintance.

повсюду *adv.* everywhere.

повтóр, а *m.* replay.

повторéни|е, я *nt.*
1 (*действия*) repetition.
2 (*события*) recurrence.
3 (*урока*) revision.

повтор|ить, ю, ишь *pf.* (*of* ▸ **~ять**)
1 to repeat.
2 (*уроки*) to revise.

повтор|иться, юсь, ишься *pf.* (*of* ▸ **~яться**)
1 (*повторить сказанное*) to repeat o.s.
2 (*о событиях*) to reoccur; (*о болезни*) to recur.

повтóр|ный (~ен, ~на) *adj.* (*визит*) second, repeated; (*заболевание*) recurring.

повтор|ять(ся), яю(сь) *impf. of* ▸ **~ить(ся)**

повы|сить, шу, сишь *pf.* (*of* ▸ **~шáть**)
1 to raise, heighten; **п. вдвóе, втрóе** to double, treble; **п. в пять раз,** *etc.* to raise fivefold, *etc.*; **п. давлéние** to increase pressure; **п. гóлос** to raise one's voice (*also fig., in anger*); (*улучшить*) to improve.
2 (*работника*) to promote, advance; **п. когó-н. по слýжбе** to give s.o. promotion.

повы|ситься, шусь, сишься *pf.* (*of* ▸ **~шáться**) to rise; (*увеличиться*) to increase; (*улучшиться*) to improve; **нáши áкции ~сились** our shares have gone up; (*fig.*) our stock has risen.

повышá|ть(ся), ю(сь) *impf. of* ▸ **повысить(ся)**

повыше *comp. adj. and adv.* a little higher (up); (*о росте человека*) a little taller.

повышéни|е, я *nt.* rise, increase; **п. по слýжбе** advancement, promotion.

повя|зáть, жý, ~жешь *pf.* (*of* ▸ **~зывать**) to tie; **п. гáлстук** to tie a tie.

повя́зк|а, и *f.*
1 (*лента*) band.
2 (*бинт*) bandage.

повя́зыва|ть, ю *impf. of* ▸ **повязáть**

погадá|ть, ю *pf. of* ▸ **гадáть 1**

погáнк|а, и *f.* (*гриб*) toadstool.

пога|сить, шý, ~сишь *pf.* (*of* ▸ **гасить** *and* ▸ **~шáть**) to liquidate, cancel; **п. долг** to clear a debt.

погáс|нуть, ну, нешь, *past* **~, ~ла** *pf. of* ▸ **гáснуть**

погашá|ть, ю *impf. of* ▸ **погасить**

погиб|áть, áю *impf. of* ▸ **~нуть**

погиб|нуть, ну, нешь, *past* **~, ~ла** *pf.* (*of* ▸ **гибнуть** *and* ▸ **~áть**) to perish; (*naut. and fig.*) to be lost; **корáбль ~ со всей комáндой** the ship was lost with all hands.

погиб|ший *p.p. of* ▸ **~нуть** *and adj.* lost, ruined.

поглá|дить, жу, дишь *pf. of* ▸ **глáдить**

поглáжива|ть, ю *impf.* to stroke (*every so often*).

погло|тить, щý, ~тишь *pf.* (*of* ▸ **~щáть**) to soak up, absorb (*also fig.*); **п. вóду** to absorb water.

поглощá|ть, ю *impf. of* ▸ **поглотить**

погля|дéть, жý, дишь *pf.*
1 *pf. of* ▸ **глядéть.**
2 (*взглянуть*) to have a look.
3 (*некоторое время*) to look for a while.

поглядыва|ть, ю *impf.*
1 (**на** + *a.*) to glance from time to time (at).
2 (**за** + *i.*; *coll.*) to keep an eye (on).

по|гнáть, гоню, гóнишь, *past* **~гнáл, ~гналá, ~гнáло** *pf.* to drive; (*начать гнать*) to begin to drive.

по|гнáться, гонюсь, гóнишься, *past* **~гнáлся, ~гналáсь, ~гнáлось** *pf.* (**за** + *i.*) to run (after); to give chase; (*fig.*) to strive (after, for).

погн|ýть, ý, ёшь *pf.* to bend.

погн|ýться, ётся *pf.* to bend (*intrans.*).

поговáрива|ть, ю *impf.* (**о** + *p.*) to talk (of); **~ют** there is talk (of).

поговор|ить, ю, ишь
1 *pf. of* ▸ **говорить 3.**
2 (*pf. only*) to have a talk.

поговóрк|а, и *f.* saying.

погóд|а, ы *f.* weather.

поголóвный *adj.* general, universal.

погóн, а, *g. pl.* **~** *m.* (*mil.*) shoulder strap.

погóн|я, и *f.* pursuit, chase.

погоня́|ть, ю *impf.* (*торопить*) to urge on, drive (*also fig.*).

пого|стить, щý, стишь *pf.* (**у** + *g.*) to stay for a while (at, with).

пограничник, а *m.* border guard, frontier guard.

погранич|ный *adj.* (*страны*) border, frontier; (*участки*) boundary; **~ая стрáжа** border guards.

пóгреб, а, *pl.* **~á** *m.* cellar (*also fig.*); **винный п.** wine cellar.

погребéни|е, я *nt.* burial, interment.

погремýшк|а, и *f.* rattle.

погрé|ть, ю *pf.* to warm.

погрé|ться, юсь *pf.* to warm o.s.

погреш|ить, ý, ишь *pf. of* ▸ **грешить 2**

погрéшност|ь, и *f.* error, mistake.

погро|зить, жý, зишь *pf. of* ▸ **грозить 2**

погрóм, а *m.* pogrom; (*coll.*) chaos.

погружá|ть(ся), ю(сь) *impf. of* ▸ **погрузить(ся)**

погружéни|е, я *nt.* submergence;

immersion; (*подводной лодки*) dive, diving.

погру|зи́ть, жу́, ~̑зишь *pf.* (*of* ▸ **~жа́ть**)
1 (**в** + *a.*) to immerse; (*в темноту*) to plunge.
2 *pf. of* ▸ **грузи́ть 2**

погру|зи́ться, жу́сь, ~̑зишься *pf.*
1 (**в** + *a.*) to sink (into), plunge (into); (*о подводной лодке*) to submerge, dive; (*fig.*) to be plunged (in); to be absorbed (in), be buried (in), be lost (in); **п. в темноту́** to be plunged into darkness; **п. в размышле́ния** to be deep in thought.
2 *pf. of* ▸ **грузи́ться**

погру́зк|а, и *f.* loading.

погряз|а́ть, а́ю *impf. of* ▸ **~̑нуть**

погря́з|нуть, ну, нешь, *past* **~, ~ла** *pf.* (*of* ▸ **~а́ть**) (**в** + *p.*) to be stuck (in); to be bogged down (in); (*в разврате*) to wallow (in); **п. в долга́х** to be up to one's eyes in debt.

погуб|и́ть, лю́, ~̑ишь *pf. of* ▸ **губи́ть**

погуля́|ть, ю *pf. of* ▸ **гуля́ть**

под (*also* **подо**) *prep.*
1 (+ *a. and i.*) (*ниже*) under; **поста́вить п. стол** to put under the table; **п. ви́дом** (+ *g.*) in the guise (of); **п. влия́нием** (+ *g.*) under the influence (of); **п. вопро́сом** open to question; **п. землёй** underground; **взять кого́-н. по́д руку** to take s.o.'s arm; **п. руко́й** (close) at hand, to hand; **отда́ть п. суд** to prosecute.
2 (+ *a. and i.*) (*около*) in the environs of, near; **жить п. Москво́й** to live near Moscow.
3 (+ *a.*) (*для*) for; (to serve) as; **отвести́ помеще́ние п. шко́лу** to earmark premises for a school.
4 (+ *a.*) (*о времени*) towards; on the eve of; **п. ве́чер** towards evening; **п. Но́вый год** on New Year's Eve; **ему́ п. пятьдеся́т (лет)** he is getting on for fifty.
5 (+ *a.*) (*в сопровождении*) to (the accompaniment of); **танцева́ть п. му́зыку** to dance to music.
6 (+ *i.*) (*при обозначении понятия*) by; **что на́до понима́ть п. э́тим выраже́нием?** what is meant by this expression?; **что п. э́тим подразумева́ется?** what is implied by this?
7 (+*a.*) (*в обмен*) on (= *in exchange for*); **п. зало́г** (+ *g.*) on security (of); **п. распи́ску** on receipt.

под...[1] (*also* **подо...** *and* **подъ...**) *as vbl. pref. indicates*
1 *action from beneath or affecting lower part of sth., as* **подчеркну́ть** to underline.
2 *motion upwards, as* **подня́ть** to raise.
3 *motion towards, as* **подъе́хать** to approach.

под...[2] (*also* **подо...** *and* **подъ...**) *as pref. of nn. and adjs.* under-, sub-.

пода|ва́ть, ю́, ёшь *impf. of* ▸ **пода́ть**

подав|и́ть, лю́, ~̑ишь *pf.* (*of* ▸ **~ля́ть**)
1 (*восстание; стон*) to suppress; to repress.
2 (*fig.*) (*ослабить, угнетать*) to depress; to crush, overwhelm.

под|ави́ться, авлю́сь, а́вишься *pf. of* ▸ **дави́ться**

пода́в|ленный *p.p.p. of* ▸ **~и́ть** *and adj.*
1 (*стон, смех*) suppressed, stifled.
2 (*человек, настроение*) depressed, dispirited.

подавля́|ть, ю *impf. of* ▸ **подави́ть**

подавля́|ющий *pres. part. act. of* ▸ **~ть** *and adj.* overwhelming.

пода́гр|а, ы *f.* gout.

пода́льше *adv.* (*coll.*) a little farther.

подар|и́ть, ю́, ~̑ишь *pf. of* ▸ **дари́ть**

пода́р|ок, ка *m.* present, gift; **получи́ть в п.** to receive as a present.

пода́тлив|ый (~, ~а) *adj.*
1 pliant, pliable.
2 (*fig.*) (*уступчивый*) complaisant.

по|да́ть, да́м, да́шь, да́ст, дади́м, дади́те, даду́т, *past* **~̑дал, ~дала́, ~̑дало** *pf.* (*of* ▸ **~дава́ть**)
1 to give; **п. приме́р** to set an example; **п. ру́ку** (+ *d.*) to offer one's hand; **п. сигна́л** to give the signal.
2 (*еду*) to serve; **обе́д ~̑дан** dinner is served.
3 (*sport*): **п. мяч** to serve.
4 (*заявление, жалобу*) to serve, present, hand in; **п. заявле́ние** to hand in an application; **п. в отста́вку** to tender one's resignation; **п. в суд** (**на** + *a.*) to bring an action (against).

пода́ч|а, и *f.*
1 giving, presenting; **п. заявле́ния** sending in of application.
2 (*в теннисе, волейболе*) service, serve; (*в футболе*) pass.

подбега́|ть, ю *impf. of* ▸ **подбежа́ть**

подбе|жа́ть, гу́, жи́шь, гу́т *pf.* (*of* ▸ **~га́ть**) (**к** + *d.*) to run up (to), come running up (to).

подбива́|ть, ю *impf. of* ▸ **подби́ть**

подбира́|ть(ся), ю(сь) *impf. of* ▸ **подобра́ть(ся)**

под|би́ть, обью́, обьёшь *pf.* (*of* ▸ **~бива́ть**)
1 (+ *i.*) (*пальто*) to line (with).
2 (*обувь*) to resole.
3 (*ушибить*) to injure; **п. кому́-н. глаз** to give s.o. a black eye.
4 (*самолёт, утку*) to shoot down.
5 (+ *inf. or* **на** + *a.*; *coll.*) (*подстрекать*) to incite (to).

подбодр|и́ть, ю́, и́шь *pf.* (*of* ▸ **~я́ть**) to cheer up.

подбодр|я́ть, я́ю *impf. of* ▸ **~и́ть**

подбо́р, а *m.* selection, assortment.

подбо́рк|а, и *f.* set, selection.

подборо́д|ок, ка *m.* chin.

подбра́сыва|ть, ю *impf. of* ▸ **подбро́сить**

подбро́|сить, шу, сишь *pf.* (*of* ▸ **подбра́сывать**)
1 to throw up, toss up; (**под** + *a.*) to throw (under); **п. моне́ту** to toss up.
2 (+ *a. or g.*) to throw in, throw on; **п. дров в печь** to throw more wood on the fire.
3 (*положить скрытно*) to place surreptitiously.

подва́л, а *m.* cellar; basement.

подвез|ти́, у́, ёшь, *past* **~̈, ~ла́** *pf.* (*of* ▸ **подвози́ть**)
1 (*довезти*) to bring, take (with one); to give a lift (*on the road*).
2 (+ *a. or g.*) (*доставить*) to bring up, transport.

подверг|а́ть(ся), а́ю(сь) *impf. of*

▶ ~́нуть(ся)

подве́рг|нуть, ну, нешь, *past* ~ *and* ~**нул,** ~**ла** *pf.* (*of* ▶ ~**а́ть**) (+ *d.*) to subject (to); to expose (to); **п. испыта́нию** to put to the test; **п. опа́сности** to expose to danger, endanger.

подве́рг|нуться, нусь, нешься, *past* ~**ся** *and* ~**нулся,** ~**лась** *pf.* (*of* ▶ ~**а́ться**) (+ *d.*) to undergo, be subjected to.

подве́ржен|ный (~, ~а) *adj.* (+ *d.*) (*влиянию ветров*) subject (to); (*простуде*) prone (to), susceptible (to).

подвер|ну́ть, ну́, нёшь *pf.* (*of* ▶ ~̈**тывать**)
1 (*подвинтить*) to screw up a little.
2 (*подоткнуть*) to tuck in, tuck up; **п. брю́ки** to tuck up one's trousers.
3 (*повредить*) to twist, sprain; **п. но́гу** to sprain one's ankle.

подвер|ну́ться, ну́сь, нёшься *pf.* (*of* ▶ ~̈**тываться**)
1 to be twisted, sprained.
2 (*fig., coll.*) (*попасться*) to turn up, show up; **он кста́ти** ~**ну́лся** he turned up just at the right moment.

подвёртыва|ть(ся), ю(сь) *impf. of* ▶ **подверну́ть(ся)**

подве́|сить, шу, сишь *pf.* (*of* ▶ ~**шивать**) to hang up, suspend.

подве́ск|а, и *f.*
1 (*действие*) hanging up, suspension.
2 (*украшение*) pendant.

подве|сти́, ду́, дёшь, *past* ~̈**л,** ~**ла́** *pf.* (*of* ▶ **подводи́ть**)
1 (**к** + *d.*) (*человека*) to lead up (to); (*поезд*) to bring up (to); (*дорогу*) to extend (to).
2 (**под** + *a.*) to place (under).
3 (*coll.*) (*поставить в трудное положение*) to let down; to put in a spot.

подве́тренный *adj.* leeward.

подве́шива|ть, ю *impf. of* ▶ **подве́сить**

по́двиг, а *m.* exploit, feat; heroic deed.

подвига́|ть(ся), ю(сь) *impf. of* ▶ **подви́нуть(ся)**

подви́д, а *m.* (*biol.*) subspecies.

подви́ж|ный (~ен, ~на) *adj.*
1 (*группа войск*) mobile.
2 (*ребёнок*) lively; ~**ное лицо́** mobile features.

подви́|нуть, ну, нешь *pf.* (*of* ▶ ~**га́ть**) to move; to push; ~**ньте стул!** pull up a chair!

подви́|нуться, нусь, нешься *pf.* (*of* ▶ ~**га́ться**) to move; ~**ньтесь и да́йте мне сесть!** move up and let me sit down!

подвла́ст|ный (~ен, ~на) *adj.* (+ *d.*) subject to, under the control of.

подво|ди́ть, жу́, ~́дишь *impf. of* ▶ **подвести́**

подво́дн|ый *adj.* submarine; underwater; ~**ая ло́дка** submarine.

подво|зи́ть, жу́, ~́зишь *impf. of* ▶ **подвезти́**

подгиба́|ть, ю *impf. of* ▶ **подогну́ть**

подгля|де́ть, жу́, ди́шь *pf.* (*of* ▶ ~́**дывать**) (**за** + *i.*; *coll.*) to peep (at); to spy (on), watch furtively.

подгля́дыва|ть, ю *impf. of* ▶ **подгляде́ть**

подгова́рива|ть, ю *impf. of* ▶ **подговори́ть**

подговор|и́ть, ю, и́шь *pf.* (*of* ▶ **подгова́ривать**) (**на** + *a. or* + *inf.*) to put up (to), incite (to).

подголо́вник, а *m.* headrest.

подгоня́|ть, ю *impf. of* ▶ **подогна́ть**

подгор|а́ть, а́ет *impf. of* ▶ ~**е́ть**

подгор|е́ть, и́т *pf.* (*of* ▶ ~**а́ть**) to burn slightly.

подгота́влива|ть(ся), ю(сь) *impf. of* ▶ **подгото́вить(ся)**

подготови́тельный *adj.* preparatory.

подгото́в|ить, лю, ишь *pf.* (*of* ▶ **подгота́вливать**) (**для** + *g.*, **к** + *d.*) to prepare (for); **п. по́чву** (*fig.*) to pave the way.

подгото́в|иться, люсь, ишься *pf.* (*of* ▶ **подгота́вливаться**) (**к** + *d.*) to prepare (for), get ready (for).

подгото́вк|а, и *f.*
1 (**к** + *d.*) preparation (for), training (for).
2 (**в** + *p. or* **по** + *d.*) grounding (in), schooling (in).

подгру́пп|а, ы *f.* subgroup.

подгу́зник, а *m.* nappy (*Br.*), diaper (*US*).

подда|ва́ться, ю́сь, ёшься *impf. of* ▶ **подда́ться**

по́дданн|ый *as n.* **п.,** ~**ого** *m., and* ~**ая,** ~**ой** *f.* subject, national.

по́дданств|о, а *nt.* citizenship, nationality.

под|да́ться, да́мся, да́шься, да́стся, дади́мся, дади́тесь, даду́тся, *past* ~**да́лся,** ~**дала́сь** *pf.* (*of* ▶ ~**дава́ться**) (+ *d.*) to yield (to), give way (to), give in (to); **дверь не** ~**дала́сь** the door would not give; **п. искуше́нию** to yield to temptation; **не** ~**дава́ться описа́нию** to beggar description.

поддева́|ть, ю *impf. of* ▶ **подде́ть**

подде́л|ать, аю *pf.* (*of* ▶ ~**ывать**) to forge; to counterfeit.

подде́лк|а, и *f.* forgery; counterfeit, fake; **п. под же́мчуг** imitation pearls.

подде́лыва|ть, ю *impf. of* ▶ **подде́лать**

подде́льный *adj.* forged, counterfeit; (*неискренний*) sham; **п. па́спорт** forged passport.

поддерж|а́ть, у́, ~́ишь *pf.* (*of* ▶ ~́**ивать 1**)
1 to support (*also fig.*); to back, second; **п. резолю́цию** to second a resolution.
2 (*не дать прекратиться*) to keep up, maintain; **п. разгово́р** to keep up a conversation.

подде́ржива|ть, ю *impf.*
1 *impf. of* ▶ **поддержа́ть; подде́рживать отноше́ния** (**с** + *i.*) to keep in touch (with).
2 (*impf. only*) to bear, support.

подде́ржк|а, и *f.* support; backing; seconding.

подде́|ть, ну, нешь *pf.* (*of* ▶ ~**ва́ть**)
1 (**под** + *a.*; *coll.*) to put on under, wear under; ~**нь(те) сви́тер под ку́ртку** put a sweater on under your jacket.
2 (*зацепить*) to hook; to catch up.
3 (*fig., coll.*) (*человека*) to catch out; to have a dig at s.o.

поддо́н, а *m.* (*для кирпичей*) pallet;

(*подставка*) stand, tray.

подéйств|овать, ую *pf. of* ▶**дéйствовать 2**

подел|ить(ся), ю(сь), ⁓ишь(ся) *pf. of* ▶**делить(ся) 2**

подéлк|а, и *f.* handmade article; **⁓и из дéрева** handmade wooden articles.

подéржанный *adj.* second-hand.

подерж|áть, ý, ⁓ишь *pf.* (*в руках*) to hold for some time; (*у себя*) to keep for some time.

под|ержáться, ержýсь, éржишься *pf.*
1 (**за** + *a.*) to hold (on to) for some time.
2 (*сохраниться*) to hold (out), last.

подешевé|ть, ет *pf. of* ▶**дешевéть**

поджáрива|ть, ю *impf. of* ▶**поджáрить**

поджáр|ить, ю, ишь *pf.* (*of* ▶**⁓ивать**) (*на сковороде*) to fry; (*в духовке*) to roast; **п. хлеб** to toast bread.

под|жáть, ожмý, ожмёшь *pf.* (*of* ▶**⁓жимáть**) to draw in; **п. гýбы** to purse one's lips.

под|жéчь, ожгý, ожжёшь, ожгýт, *past* **⁓жёг, ⁓ожглá** *pf.* (*of* ▶**⁓жигать**) to set fire (to), set on fire.

поджигá|ть, ю *impf. of* ▶**поджéчь**

поджидá|ть, ю *impf.* to wait (for).

поджимá|ть, ю *impf. of* ▶**поджáть**

поджóг, а *m.* arson; arson attack.

подзаголóв|ок, ка *m.* subtitle, subheading.

подзатыльник, а *m.* (*coll.*) clip round the ear.

подзащитн|ый, ого *m.* (*leg.*) client.

подземéл|ье, ья, *g. pl.* **⁓ий** *nt.* cave; (*тюрьма*) dungeon.

подзéмк|а, и *f.* (*coll.*) underground (railway), tube.

подзéмный *adj.* underground, subterranean.

подзывá|ть, ю *impf. of* ▶**подозвáть**

подкáпыва|ться, юсь *impf. of* ▶**подкопáться**

подкáрмлива|ть, ю *impf. of* ▶**подкормить**

подка|тить, чý, ⁓тишь *pf.* (*of* ▶**⁓тывать**)
1 (*мяч*) to roll; (*велосипед*) to wheel.
2 (*intrans., coll.*) (*об автомобиле, экипаже*) to roll up, drive up.

подка|титься, чýсь, ⁓тишься *pf.* (*of* ▶**⁓тываться**) (**под** + *a.*) to roll (under).

подкáтыва|ть(ся), ю(сь) *impf. of* ▶**подкатить(ся)**

подкидыва|ть, ю *impf. of* ▶**подкинуть**

подки|нуть, ну, нешь *pf.* (*of* ▶**⁓дывать**) = **подбрóсить**

подклáдк|а, и *f.* lining.

подклáдыва|ть, ю *impf. of* ▶**подложить**

подклéива|ть, ю *impf. of* ▶**подклéить**

подклé|ить, ю, ишь *pf.* (*of* ▶**⁓ивать**) to glue up, paste up.

подключ|áть(ся), áю(сь) *impf. of* ▶**⁓ить(ся)**

подключ|ить, ý, ишь *pf.* (*of* ▶**⁓áть**) (**к** + *d.*)
1 (*tech.*) to link up (to), connect up (to).
2 (*fig.*) to attach (to); to involve; **к рабóте ⁓или специалистов** specialists were involved in the work.

подключ|иться, ýсь, ишься *pf.* (*of* ▶**⁓áться**)
1 (*tech.*) to be connected up.
2 (*fig.*) to get involved, become a participant.

подкóв|а, ы *f.* (horse)shoe.

подк|овáть, ую, уёшь *pf.* (*of* ▶**⁓óвывать**) to shoe.

подкóвыва|ть, ю *impf. of* ▶**подковáть**

подкол|óть, ю, ⁓ешь *pf.* (*of* ▶**подкáлывать**)
1 (*волосы*) to pin up.
2 (*документ к делу*) to attach, append.

подкопá|ться, юсь *pf.* (*of* ▶**подкáпываться**) (**под** + *a.*)
1 (*о животных*) to burrow (under).
2 (*fig., coll.*) to undermine.

подкорм|ить, лю, ⁓ишь *pf.* (*of* ▶**подкáрмливать**) to feed up; to fatten (up).

подкрáдыва|ться, юсь *impf. of* ▶**подкрáсться**

подкрá|сить, шу, сишь *pf.* (*of* ▶**⁓шивать**) (*стену*) to tint, colour (*Br.*), color (*US*); (*губы*) to touch up.

подкрá|сться, дýсь, дёшься *pf.* (*of* ▶**⁓дываться**) (**к** + *d.*) to steal up (to), sneak up (to).

подкрáшива|ть, ю *impf. of* ▶**подкрáсить**

подкреп|иться, люсь, ишься *pf.* (*of* ▶**⁓ляться**) to fortify o.s. (*with food and/or drink*).

подкрепля|ться, юсь *impf. of* ▶**подкрепиться**

пóдкуп, а *m.* bribery; corruption.

подкуп|áть, áю *impf. of* ▶**⁓ить**

подкуп|ить, лю, ⁓ишь *pf.* (*of* ▶**⁓áть**)
1 (*деньгами*) to bribe.
2 (*fig.*) (*добротой*) to win over.

подлáмыва|ться, ется *impf. of* ▶**подломиться**

пóдле *prep.* + *g.* by the side of, beside.

подлеж|áть, ý, ишь *impf.* (+ *d.*) to be liable (to), be subject (to); **этот дом ⁓ит снóсу** this house is to be pulled down.

подлежáщ|ее, его *nt.* (*gram.*) subject.

подлез|áть, áю *impf. of* ▶**⁓ть**

подлéз|ть, у, ешь *pf.* (*of* ▶**⁓áть**) (**под** + *a.*) to crawl (under), creep (under).

подлет|áть, áю *impf. of* ▶**⁓éть**

подле|тéть, чý, тишь *pf.* (*of* ▶**⁓тáть**) (**к** + *d.*) to fly up (to); (*fig.*) to rush up (to).

подлéц, á *m.* scoundrel, villain, rascal.

подлéчива|ть(ся), ю(сь) *impf. of* ▶**подлечить(ся)**

подлеч|ить, ý, ⁓ишь *pf.* (*of* ▶**⁓ивать**) (*coll.*) to treat.

подлеч|иться, ýсь, ⁓ишься *pf.* (*of* ▶**⁓иваться**) (*coll.*) to take medical treatment.

подливá|ть, ю *impf. of* ▶**подлить**

подливк|а, и *f.* sauce; (*салатная*) dressing; (*мясная*) gravy.

пóдлинник, а *m.* original (*opp. copy*).

пóдлин|ный (⁓ен, ⁓на) *adj.*

1 (*не поддельный*) genuine; authentic; (*не копия*) original.
2 (*истинный*) true, real; **п. учёный** a true scholar.

под|ли́ть, олью́, ольёшь, *past* **~ли́л, ~лила́, ~ли́ло** *pf.* (*of* ▸ **~лива́ть**) (+ *a. or g.* **в** + *a.*) to add (to); **п. ма́сла в ого́нь** (*fig.*) to add fuel to the fire.

подлож|и́ть, у́, ~́ишь *pf.* (*of* ▸ **подкла́дывать**)
1 (**под** + *a.*) to lay under.
2 (+ *a. or g.*) (*добавить*) to add; **~и́те дров** put some more wood on.
3 (*скрытно*) to put furtively; **п. кому́-н. свинью́** to play a dirty trick on s.o.

подлоко́тник, а *m.* elbow rest; arm (*of chair*).

подлом|и́ться, ~́ится *pf.* (*of* ▸ **подла́мываться**) (**под** + *i.*) to break (under).

по́длост|ь, и *f.*
1 (*свойство*) meanness, baseness.
2 (*поступок*) mean trick, low-down trick.

по́дл|ый (~, ~а́, ~о) *adj.* mean, base, despicable.

подма́нива|ть, ю *impf. of* ▸ **подмани́ть**

подман|и́ть, ю́, ~́ишь *pf.* (*of* ▸ **~́ивать**) to call (to); to beckon.

подме́н|а, ы *f.* substitution (*of sth. false for sth. real*).

подмен|и́ть, ю́, ~́ишь *pf.* (*of* ▸ **~я́ть**) (+ *a. and i.*) to substitute (for) (*intentionally*); **кто́-то на вечери́нке ~и́л мне шля́пу** s.o. at the party took my hat (and left his instead).

подмен|я́ть, я́ю *impf. of* ▸ **~и́ть**

подме|сти́, ту́, тёшь, *past* **~̈л, ~ла́** *pf.* (*of* ▸ **~та́ть**)
1 (*место*) to sweep.
2 (*мусор*) to sweep up.

подмета́|ть, ю *impf. of* ▸ **подмести́**

подмётк|а, и *f.* sole.

подмеш|а́ть, а́ю *pf.* (*of* ▸ **~́ивать**) to stir in, mix in.

подме́шива|ть, ю *impf. of* ▸ **подмеша́ть**

подми́гива|ть, ю *impf. of* ▸ **подмигну́ть**

подмиг|ну́ть, ну́, нёшь *pf.* (*of* ▸ **~́ивать**) (+ *d.*) to wink (at).

подмина́|ть, ю *impf. of* ▸ **подмя́ть**

подмоско́вный *adj.* (situated) near Moscow.

подмыва́|ть, ю *impf. impf. of* ▸ **подмы́ть**

подм|ы́ть, о́ю, о́ешь *pf.* (*of* ▸ **~ыва́ть**)
1 (*ребёнка*) to wash s.o.'s bottom.
2 (*берег*) to wash away, undermine.

подмы́шк|а, и *f.* armpit.

под|мя́ть, омну́, омнёшь *pf.* (*of* ▸ **~мина́ть**) to crush.

поднес|ти́, у́, ёшь, *past* **~̈, ~ла́** *pf.* (*of* ▸ **подноси́ть**)
1 (*нести*) (**к** + *d.*) to take (to), bring (to).
2 (+ *d. and a.*) (*подарить*) to present (with); to take (as a present); (*угостить*) to treat (to); **п. кому́-н. буке́т цвето́в** to present s.o. with a bouquet.

поднима́|ть(ся), ю(сь) *impf. of* ▸ **подня́ть(ся)**

поднов|и́ть, лю́, и́шь *pf.* (*of* ▸ **~ля́ть**) (*краску*) to freshen up, touch up; (*мебель*) to renovate.

подно́жи|е, я *nt.*
1 (*горы, башни*) foot.
2 (*пьедестал*) pedestal.

подно́жк|а[1], и *f.* (*автобуса*) step, footboard.

подно́жк|а[2], и *f.* (*в борьбе*) backheel; **дать кому́-н. ~у** to trip s.o. up.

подно́с, а *m.* tray.

подно|си́ть, шу́, ~́сишь *impf. of* ▸ **поднести́**

под|ня́ть, ниму́, ни́мешь, *past* **~́нял, ~няла́, ~́няло** *pf.* (*of* ▸ **~нима́ть**)
1 to raise; to lift; **п. настрое́ние** (+ *g. or d.*) to cheer up, raise the spirits (of); **п. паруса́** to set sail; **п. флаг** to hoist a flag.
2 (*подобрать*) to pick up.
3 (*возбудить*) to rouse, stir up; **п. восста́ние** to stir up rebellion; **п. ссо́ру** to pick a quarrel; **п. на́ ноги** to rouse.

под|ня́ться, ниму́сь, ни́мешься, *past* **~ня́лся, ~няла́сь** *pf.* (*of* ▸ **~нима́ться**)
1 (*о температуре, ценах, солнце*) to rise; (*по лестнице*) to go up; (*встать*) to get up; **п. на́ ноги** to rise to one's feet.
2 (**на** + *a.*) (*гору*) to climb, ascend, go up.
3 (*возникнуть*) to arise; to break out, develop; **~ня́лся ве́тер** a wind got up.
4 (*econ.*; *fig.*) (*улучшиться*) to improve; to recover.

подо *prep.* = **под**

подо...[1] *as vbl. pref.* = **под...[1]**

подо...[2] *as pref. of nn. and adjs.* = **под...[2]**

подо́би|е, я *nt.*
1 likeness; **по своему́ о́бразу и ~ю** in one's own image.
2 (*math.*) similarity.

подо́бно *adv.* (+ *d.*) like; **п. тому́, как** just as.

подо́б|ный (~ен, ~на) *adj.* like; similar; **~ное поведе́ние** such behaviour (*Br.*), behavior (*US*); **ничего́ ~ного!** (*coll.*) nothing of the kind!; **и тому́ ~ное** (*abbr.* **и т. п.**) and so on, and such like.

под|обра́ть, беру́, берёшь, *past* **~обра́л, ~обрала́, ~обра́ло** *pf.* (*of* ▸ **~бира́ть**)
1 (*поднять*) to pick up.
2 (*ноги*) to tuck up; (*вожжи*) to take up.
3 (*выбрать*) to select, pick; **п. дже́мпер под цвет костю́ма** to choose a jumper to match a suit.

под|обра́ться, беру́сь, берёшься, *past* **~обра́лся, ~обрала́сь, ~обра́ло́сь** *pf.* (*of* ▸ **~бира́ться**)
1 (*составиться, образоваться*) to get together, be formed.
2 (**к** + *d.*) (*незаметно подойти*) to steal up (to), approach stealthily.

под|огна́ть, гоню́, го́нишь, *past* **~огна́л, ~огнала́, ~огна́ло** *pf.* (*of* ▸ **~гоня́ть**)
1 (**к** + *d.*) (*приблизить*) to drive (to).
2 (*coll.*) (*заставить идти быстрее*) to drive on, urge on, hurry.
3 (**к** + *d.*) (*приспособить*) to adjust (to), fit (to).

под|огну́ть, огну́, огнёшь *pf.* (*of* ▸ **~гиба́ть**) to tuck in; to bend under.

подогрева́|ть, ю *impf. of* ▸ **подогре́ть**

П

подогре́|ть, ю *pf.* (*of* ▸ **~ва́ть**) to warm up, heat up.
пододвига́|ть, ю *impf. of* ▸ **пододви́нуть**
пододви́|нуть, ну, нешь *pf.* (*of* ▸ **~га́ть**) (**к** + *d.*) to move up (to), push up (to).
пододея́льник, а *m.* blanket cover, duvet cover.
подожд|а́ть, у́, ёшь, *past* **~а́л, ~ала́, ~а́ло** *pf.* (+ *a. or g.*) to wait (for).
под|озва́ть, зову́, зовёшь, *past* **~озва́л, ~озвала́, ~озва́ло** *pf.* (*of* ▸ **~зыва́ть**) to call over; (*жестом*) to beckon.
подозрева́|ть, ю *impf.* (*no pf.*) to suspect (*s.o. or that sth. is the case*); **я ~ю его́ в преступле́нии** I suspect him of a crime.
подозре́ни|е, я *nt.* suspicion; **по ~ю** (**в** + *p.*) on suspicion (of); **быть под ~ем, на ~и** to be under suspicion.
подозри́тел|ьный (~ен, ~ьна) *adj.* suspicious.
подо|и́ть, ю́, ~́ишь *pf. of* ▸ **дои́ть**
подо|йти́, йду́, йдёшь, *past* **~шёл, ~шла́** *pf.* (*of* ▸ **подходи́ть**)
1 (**к** + *d.*) (*приблизиться*) to approach (*also fig.*); to come up (to), go up (to); **по́езд ~шёл к ста́нции** the train pulled in to the station.
2 (*годиться*) (+ *d.*) to do (for); to suit; (*по размеру*) to fit.
подоко́нник, а *m.* window sill.
подо́лгу *adv.* for a long time; for ages; for long periods of time; **они́ п. не разгова́ривали друг с дру́гом** they had long periods of not speaking to each other.
подо́н|ки, ков *pl.* (*sg. coll.* **~ок, ~ка** *m.*) (*fig.*) scum, riff-raff, dregs (*fig.*).
подорв|а́ть, у́, ёшь, *past* **~а́л, ~ала́, ~а́ло** *pf.* (*of* ▸ **подрыва́ть**)
1 to blow up.
2 (*fig.*) to undermine; to damage severely; **п. здоро́вье** to damage one's health.
подорожа́|ть, ю *pf. of* ▸ **дорожа́ть**
подо|сла́ть, шлю́, шлёшь *pf.* (*of* ▸ **подсыла́ть**) to send, dispatch (*secretly*).
под|остла́ть, стелю́, сте́лешь *pf.* (*of* ▸ **~стила́ть**) (**под** + *a.*) to lay (under), stretch (under).
подоткн|у́ть, у́, ёшь *pf.* (*of* ▸ **подтыка́ть**) (*coll.*) to tuck in, tuck up; **п. ю́бку** to tuck up one's skirt.
подо́х|нуть, ну, нешь, *past* **~, ~ла** *pf.* (*of* ▸ **до́хнуть, подыха́ть**)
1 (*о животных*) to die.
2 (*sl., pej.*) (*о людях*) to peg out, kick the bucket.
подохо́дный *adj.*: **п. нало́г** income tax.
подо́шв|а, ы *f.* sole.
подпада́|ть, ю *impf. of* ▸ **подпа́сть**
подпа́|сть, ду́, дёшь, *past* **~л** *pf.* (*of* ▸ **~да́ть**) (**под** + *a.*) to fall (under); **п. под чьё-н. влия́ние** to fall under s.o.'s influence.
подпева́|ть, ю *impf.* (+ *d.*) to join (in singing); (*fig.*) to echo.
под|пере́ть, опру́, опрёшь, *past* **~пёр, ~пёрла** *pf.* (*of* ▸ **~пира́ть**) to prop up.
подпи́лива|ть, ю *impf. of* ▸ **подпили́ть**
подпил|и́ть, ю́, ~́ишь *pf.* (*of* ▸ **~́ивать**)
1 (*подрезать пилой*) to saw; (*напильником*) to file.
2 (*укоротить пилой*) to saw a little off; (*напильником*) to file down.
подпира́|ть, ю *impf. of* ▸ **подпере́ть**
подпи|са́ть, шу́, ~́шешь *pf.* (*of* ▸ **~́сывать**)
1 (*поставить подпись* (*на*)) to sign.
2 (*включить в число подписчиков*) to subscribe.
подпи|са́ться, шу́сь, ~́шешься *pf.* (*of* ▸ **~́сываться**)
1 (**под** + *i.*) to sign; (*fig.*) (*согласиться*) to subscribe (to).
2 (**на** + *a.*) to subscribe (to, for); **п. на журна́л** to subscribe to a magazine.
подпи́ск|а, и *f.*
1 (*на журнал*) subscription.
2 (*письменное обязательство*) written undertaking; signed statement.
подпи́счик, а *m.* (+ *g.*) subscriber (to).
подпи́сыва|ть(ся), ю(сь) *impf. of* ▸ **подписа́ть(ся)**
по́дпис|ь, и *f.*
1 signature; **поста́вить свою́ п.** (**под** + *i.*) to put one's signature (to).
2 (*надпись*) caption; inscription.
подплыва́|ть, ю *impf. of* ▸ **подплы́ть**
подплы́|ть, ву́, вёшь, *past* **~л, ~ла́, ~ло** *pf.* (*of* ▸ **~ва́ть**)
1 (**к** + *d.*) (*вплавь*) to swim up (to); (*на лодке*) to sail up (to).
2 (**под** + *a.*) to swim under.
подполз|а́ть, а́ю *impf. of* ▸ **~ти́**
подполз|ти́, у́, ёшь, *past* **~́, ~ла́** *pf.* (*of* ▸ **~а́ть**) (**к** + *d.*) to creep up (to); to crawl up (to); (**под** + *a.*) to creep (under); to crawl (under).
подполко́вник, а *m.* lieutenant colonel.
подпо́ль|е, я *nt.* (*fig.*) underground (*organization, activities*); **уйти́ в п.** to go underground.
подпо́льный *adj.* underground (*also fig.*).
подпо́рк|а, и *f.* prop, support.
подпо́р|тить, чу, тишь *pf.* (*coll.*) to spoil slightly.
подпоя́|саться, шусь, шешься *pf.* (*of* ▸ **~сываться**) to belt o.s.; to put on a belt.
подпоя́сыва|ться, юсь *impf. of* ▸ **подпоя́саться**
подпра́в|ить, лю, ишь *pf.* (*of* ▸ **~ля́ть**) to touch up.
подправля́|ть, ю *impf. of* ▸ **подпра́вить**
подпры́гива|ть, ю *impf. of* ▸ **подпры́гнуть**
подпры́г|нуть, ну, нешь *pf.* (*of* ▸ **~ивать**) to leap up, jump up.
подпуска́|ть, ю *impf. of* ▸ **подпусти́ть**
подпу|сти́ть, щу́, ~́стишь *pf.* (*of* ▸ **~ска́ть**) to allow to approach; **п. на расстоя́ние вы́стрела** to allow to come within range.
подраба́тыва|ть, ю *impf. of* ▸ **подрабо́тать**
подрабо́та|ть, ю *pf.* (*of* ▸ **подраба́тывать**) (*coll.*) (*ради дополнительного заработка*) to earn additionally.
подра́внива|ть, ю *impf. of* ▸ **подровня́ть**

подража́|ть, ю *impf.* (*no pf.*) (+ *d.*) to imitate.

подразде́л, а *m.* subsection.

подраздел|и́ть, ю́, и́шь *pf.* (*of* ▸ **~я́ть**) to subdivide.

подраздел|я́ть, я́ю *impf. of* ▸ **~и́ть**

подразумева́|ть, ю *impf.* to mean.

подразумева́|ться, ется *impf.* to be implied, be meant.

подраст|а́ть, а́ю *impf. of* ▸ **~и́; ~а́ющее поколе́ние** the rising generation.

подраст|и́, у́, ёшь, *past* **подро́с, подросла́** *pf.* to grow (a little).

по|дра́ться, деру́сь, дерёшься, *past* **~дра́лся, ~драла́сь, ~дра́ло́сь** *pf. of* ▸ **дра́ться 1**

подре́|зать, жу, жешь *pf.* (*of* ▸ **~за́ть**) (*волосы*) to cut; (*ногти, куст*) to clip, trim; (*деревья*) to prune, lop.

подреза́|ть, ю *impf. of* ▸ **подре́зать**

подрис|ова́ть, у́ю *pf.* (*of* ▸ **~о́вывать**)
1 (*подправить*) to touch up.
2 (*добавить*) to add, put in (*on a painting, etc.*).

подрисо́выва|ть, ю *impf. of* ▸ **подрисова́ть**

подро́бно *adv.* minutely, in detail; at (great) length.

подро́бност|ь, и *f.* detail; **вдава́ться в ~и** to go into detail; **во всех ~ях** in every detail.

подро́б|ный (~ен, ~на) *adj.* detailed, minute.

подровня́|ть, ю *pf.* (*of* ▸ **подра́внивать**) (*сделать более ровным*) to level; (*бороду, волосы*) to trim.

подро́ст|ок, ка *m.* adolescent, teenager.

подру́г|а, и *f.* (*female*) friend; **п. по шко́ле** school friend.

по-дру́жески *adv.* in a friendly way; as a friend.

подр|ужи́ться, ужу́сь, у́жишься *pf.* (**с** + *i.*) to make friends (with).

подру́жк|а, и *f. affectionate dim. of* ▸ **подру́га; п. неве́сты** bridesmaid.

подру́чн|ый *adj.*
1 (*инструмент*) at hand, to hand; (*средства*) improvised, makeshift.
2 *as n.* **п., ~ого** *m.* assistant, mate.

подрыва́|ть, ю *impf. of* ▸ **подорва́ть**

подря́д[1] *adv.* in succession; running; on end; **три го́да п.** three years running; **не́сколько дней п. шёл дождь** it rained for days on end.

подря́д[2], **а** *m.* contract; **взять п. на постро́йку плоти́ны** to contract to build a dam.

подря́дчик, а *m.* contractor.

подса|ди́ть, жу́, ~́дишь *pf.* (*of* ▸ **~́живать**)
1 (**в, на** + *a.*) to help (into, on to); **п. кого́-н. на ло́шадь** to help s.o. on to a horse.
2 (**к** + *d.*) to place next (to).

подса́жива|ть, ю *impf. of* ▸ **подсади́ть**

подса́жива|ться, юсь *impf. of* ▸ **подсе́сть**

подсве́чник, а *m.* candlestick.

под|се́сть, ся́ду, ся́дешь, *past* **~се́л** *pf.* (*of* ▸ **~са́живаться**) (**к** + *d.*) to sit down (near, next to), take a seat (near, next to).

подска|за́ть, жу́, ~́жешь *pf.* (*of* ▸ **~́зывать**) (+ *d. and a.*)
1 (*напомнить*) to prompt (s.o. with sth.) (*also fig.*).
2 (*решение*) to suggest.

подска́зк|а, и *f.* prompt(ing).

подска́зыва|ть, ю *impf. of* ▸ **подсказа́ть**

подска́кива|ть, ю *impf. of* ▸ **подскочи́ть**

подскоч|и́ть, у́, ~́ишь *pf.* (*of* ▸ **подска́кивать**)
1 (**к** + *d.*) to run up (to), come running (to).
2 to jump up, leap up; **п. от ра́дости** to jump with joy; **це́ны ~и́ли** (*coll.*) prices soared.

подслу́ш|ать, аю *pf.* (*of* ▸ **~ивать**) to overhear; to eavesdrop (on).

подслу́шива|ть, ю *impf. of* ▸ **подслу́шать**

подсма́трива|ть, ю *impf. of* ▸ **подсмотре́ть**

подсме́ива|ться, юсь *impf.* (**над** + *i.*) to laugh (at), make fun (of).

подсмотр|е́ть, ю́, ~́ишь *pf.* (*of* ▸ **подсма́тривать**) to spy.

подсне́жник, а *m.* (*bot.*) snowdrop.

подсо́выва|ть, ю *impf. of* ▸ **подсу́нуть**

подсоедин|и́ть, ю́, и́шь *pf.* (*of* ▸ **~я́ть**) (*телефон*) to connect up; (*стиральную машину*) to plumb in.

подсоедин|я́ть, я́ю *impf. of* ▸ **~и́ть**

подсозна́ни|е, я *nt.* the subconscious.

подсозна́тел|ьный (~ен, ~ьна) *adj.* subconscious.

подсо́лнечник, а *m.* sunflower.

подсо́лнечн|ый *adj. of* ▸ **~ик; ~ое ма́сло** sunflower oil.

подсо́лнух, а *m.* (*coll.*)
1 (*цветок*) sunflower.
2 (*семена*) sunflower seeds.

подста́в|ить, лю, ишь *pf.* (*of* ▸ **~ля́ть**)
1 (**под** + *a.*) to put (under), place (under); **п. го́лову под струю́ воды́ из кра́на** to put one's head under a tap.
2 (*fig.*) to expose; (*coll.*) (*поставить кого-л. в неприятное положение*) to leave s.o. holding the baby (*Br.*), bag (*US*).

подста́вк|а, и *f.* stand; (*для бутылки, стакана*) coaster.

подставля́|ть, ю *impf. of* ▸ **подста́вить**

подстерега́|ть, ю *impf. of* ▸ **подстере́чь**

подстере́|чь, гу́, жёшь, гу́т, *past* **~̈г, ~гла́** *pf.* (*of* ▸ **~га́ть**) to be on the watch (for), lie in wait (for).

подстила́|ть, ю *impf. of* ▸ **подостла́ть**

подсти́лк|а, и *f.* bedding.

подстра́ива|ть, ю *impf. of* ▸ **подстро́ить**

подстрах|ова́ть, у́ю *pf.* (*of* ▸ **подстрахо́вывать**)
1 (*гимнаста*) to stand by ready to help.
2 (*fig.*) to (take measures to) protect; to provide with additional insurance.

подстрахо́выва|ть, ю *impf. of* ▸ **подстрахова́ть**

П

подстрек|а́ть, а́ю *impf.* (**к** + *d.*) to incite (to).

подстре́лива|ть, ю *impf. of* ▸ **подстрели́ть**

подстрел|и́ть, ю́, ~́ишь *pf.* (*of* ▸ **~́ивать**) to wound (*by a shot*); to wing.

подстрига́|ть(ся), ю(сь) *impf. of* ▸ **подстри́чь(ся)**

подстри́|чь, гу́, жёшь, гу́т, *past* **~г, ~гла** *pf.* (*of* ▸ **~га́ть**) (*волосы, ногти, газон*) to cut, trim; (*дерево*) to prune.

подстри́|чься, гу́сь, жёшься, гу́тся, *past* **~гся, ~глась** *pf.* (*of* ▸ **~га́ться**) to trim one's hair; to have a haircut.

подстро́|ить, ю, ишь *pf.* (*of* ▸ **подстра́ивать**) (*coll.*) to contrive; (*pej.*) to arrange; **э́то де́ло ~ено** it's a put-up job.

подступ|а́ть(ся), а́ю(сь) *impf. of* ▸ **~и́ть(ся)**

подступ|и́ть, лю́, ~́ишь *pf.* (*of* ▸ **~а́ть**) (**к** + *d.*) to approach, come up (to), come near; **слёзы ~и́ли к её глаза́м** tears came to her eyes.

подступ|и́ться, лю́сь, ~́ишься *pf.* (*of* ▸ **~а́ться**) (**к** + *d.*) to approach.

подсуди́м|ый, ого *m.* (*leg.*) defendant; the accused.

подсу́н|уть, у, ешь *pf.* (*of* ▸ **подсо́вывать**)
1 (**под** + *a.*) to shove (under).
2 (+ *d. and a.*; *coll.*) to slip (into); to palm off (on, upon); **они́ мне ~ули не ту кни́гу** they palmed off the wrong book on me.

подсу́шива|ть, ю *impf. of* ▸ **подсуши́ть**

подсуш|и́ть, у́, ~́ишь *pf.* (*of* ▸ **~́ивать**) to dry a little.

подсчёт, а *m.* calculation; count.

подсыла́|ть, ю *impf. of* ▸ **подосла́ть**

подсы́п|ать, лю, лешь *pf.* (*of* ▸ **~а́ть**) (+ *a. or g.*) to add, pour in.

подта́скива|ть, ю *impf. of* ▸ **подтащи́ть**

подтащ|и́ть, у́, ~́ишь *pf.* (*of* ▸ **подта́скивать**) (**к** + *d.*) to drag up (to).

подтвер|ди́ть, жу́, ди́шь *pf.* (*of* ▸ **~жда́ть**) to confirm; to corroborate, bear out; **п. получе́ние чего́-н.** to acknowledge receipt of sth.

подтвер|ди́ться, ди́тся *pf.* (*of* ▸ **~жда́ться**) to be confirmed.

подтвержда́|ть(ся), ю, ет(ся) *impf. of* ▸ **подтверди́ть(ся)**

подтвержде́ни|е, я *nt.* confirmation; corroboration.

подтыка́|ть, ю *impf. of* ▸ **подоткну́ть**

подтя́гива|ть(ся), ю(сь) *impf. of* ▸ **подтяну́ть(ся)**

подтя́ж|ки, ек *no sg.* braces (*Br.*), suspenders (*US*).

подтя|ну́ть, ну́, ~́нешь *pf.* (*of* ▸ **~́гивать**)
1 (*пояс*) to tighten.
2 (**к** + *d.*) (*подтащить*) to pull up (to), haul up (to); **п. ло́дку к бе́регу** to haul up a boat on shore.
3 (*mil.*) to bring up, move up.
4 (*fig., coll.*) (*ученика*) to take in hand, pull up, chase up.

подтя|ну́ться, ну́сь, ~́нешься *pf.* (*of* ▸ **~́гиваться**)
1 to gird o.s. more tightly; **п. по́ясом** to tighten one's belt.
2 (*на перекладине*) to pull o.s. up (*on gymnastic apparatus, etc.*).
3 (*mil.*) to move up, move in.
4 (*fig., coll.*) (*об ученике*) to pull o.s. together, take o.s. in hand.

поду́ма|ть, ю *pf.*
1 *pf. of* ▸ **ду́мать; п. (то́лько)!** just think!; **~ешь** (*as iron. int.*; *coll.*) I say!; what do you know?; **мо́жно п.** one might think.
2 (*немного*) to think a little, for a while.

по-дура́цки *adv.* (*coll.*) foolishly, like a fool.

поду́|ть, ю, ешь *pf.*
1 *pf. of* ▸ **дуть.**
2 (*начать дуть*) to begin to blow.

подуш|и́ться, у́сь, ~́ишься *pf.* to put some perfume on.

поду́шк|а, и *f.* (*в постели*) pillow; (*диванная*) cushion.

подхали́м, а *m.* toady.

подхва|ти́ть, чу́, ~́тишь *pf.* (*of* ▸ **~́тывать**) to catch (up); to pick up; to take up; **п. на́сморк** to catch, pick up a cold; **п. пе́сню** to catch up a melody, join in a song.

подхва́тыва|ть, ю *impf. of* ▸ **подхвати́ть**

подхлест|ну́ть, ну́, нёшь *pf.* (*of* ▸ **~̈ывать**) to whip up (*also fig., coll.*).

подхлёстыва|ть, ю *impf. of* ▸ **подхлестну́ть**

подхо́д, а *m.* approach.

подхо|ди́ть, жу́, ~́дишь *impf. of* ▸ **подойти́**

подход|я́щий *pres. part. of* ▸ **~и́ть** *and adj.* suitable, appropriate; **п. моме́нт** the right moment.

подцеп|и́ть, лю́, ~́ишь *pf.* (*of* ▸ **~ля́ть**) (*coll.*) to hook on, couple on; (*fig., joc.*) (*в т. ч. девушку*) to pick up; **п. на́сморк** to pick up a cold.

подцепля́|ть, ю *impf. of* ▸ **подцепи́ть**

подча́с *adv.* sometimes, at times.

подчёркива|ть, ю *impf. of* ▸ **подчеркну́ть**

подчерк|ну́ть, ну́, нёшь *pf.* (*of* ▸ **~̈ивать**)
1 to underline.
2 (*fig.*) to emphasize, stress.

подчине́ни|е, я *nt.* subordination; submission, subjection; **быть в ~и (у)** to be subordinate (to).

подчин|ённый
1 *p.p.p. of* ▸ **~и́ть;** (+ *d.*) under, under the command (of).
2 *adj.* subordinate; *as n.* **п., ~ённого** *m.* subordinate.

подчин|и́ть, ю́, и́шь *pf.* (*of* ▸ **~я́ть**) (+ *d.*) to subordinate (to), subject (to); to place under the command (of); **п. свое́й во́ле** to bend to one's will.

подчин|и́ться, ю́сь, и́шься *pf.* (*of* ▸ **~я́ться**) (+ *d.*) to submit (to); **п. прика́зу** to obey an order.

подчин|я́ть(ся), я́ю(сь) *impf. of* ▸ **~и́ть(ся)**

подшива́|ть, ю *impf. of* ▸ **подши́ть**

подши́пник, а *m.* (*tech.*) bearing.

подјши́ть, ошью́, ошьёшь *pf.* (*of* ▸ **~шива́ть**)
1 (*пришить*) to sew on, in; (*платье, платок*) to hem; (*с изнанки*) to line; (*обувь*) to sole.
2 (*бумаги*) to file.

подшу|ти́ть, чу́, ~тишь *pf.* (*of* ▸ **~чивать**) (**над** + *i.*) to make fun of; to mock; to play a trick (on).

подшу́чива|ть, ю *impf. of* ▸ **подшути́ть**

подъ...[1] *as vbl. pref.* = **под...**[1]

подъ...[2] *as pref. of nn. and adjs.* = **под...**[2]

подъе́зд, а *m.*
1 (*вход*) entrance, doorway.
2 (*к реке*) approach(es).

подъезжа́|ть, ю *impf. of* ▸ **подъе́хать**

подъём, а *m.*
1 (*груза*) lifting; (*флага*) raising.
2 (*в гору*) ascent.
3 (*aeron.*) climb.
4 (*fig.*) (*рост, развитие*) development; rise; **промы́шленный п.** boom, upsurge.
5 (*fig.*) elan; enthusiasm, animation; **говори́ть с больши́м ~ом** to speak with great animation.

подъёмник, а *m.* lift (*Br.*), elevator (*US*), hoist.

подъёмн|ый *adj.*
1 lifting; **п. кран** crane; **~ое окно́** sash window.
2 : **п. мост** drawbridge.

подъе́|хать, ду, дешь *pf.* (*of* ▸ **~зжа́ть**) (**к** + *d.*) to drive up (to), draw up (to).

подыгр|а́ть, а́ю *pf.* (*of* ▸ **~ывать**) (+ *d.*; *coll.*)
1 (*mus.*) to accompany.
2 (*theatr.*) to play up (to).

поды́грыва|ть, ю *impf. of* ▸ **подыгра́ть**

поды|ска́ть, щу́, ~щешь *pf.* (*of* ▸ **~скивать 1**) to seek out, find.

поды́скива|ть, ю *impf.*
1 *impf. of* ▸ **подыска́ть.**
2 (*impf. only*) to seek, try to find.

подыха́|ть, ю *impf. of* ▸ **подо́хнуть**

подыш|а́ть, у́, ~ишь *pf.* to breathe; **вы́йти п. све́жим во́здухом** to go out for a breath of fresh air.

поеда́|ть, ю *impf. of* ▸ **пое́сть 3**

поеди́н|ок, ка *m.* duel.

по́езд, а, *pl.* **~а́** *m.* train; **~ом** by train; **п. да́льнего сле́дования** long-distance train.

пое́здк|а, и *f.* trip, excursion, outing, tour.

по|е́сть, е́м, е́шь, е́ст, еди́м, еди́те, едя́т, *past* **~е́л** *pf.*
1 (*pf. only*) to eat (up).
2 (*pf. only*) (*немного*) to eat a little; to take some food, have a bite.
3 (*impf.* **поеда́ть**) (*о кроликах, насекомых*) to eat, devour.

пое́|хать, ду, дешь *pf.* (*of* ▸ **е́хать**) to go (*in or on a vehicle or on an animal*); (*отправиться*) to set off, depart; **~хали!** (*coll.*) let's go!

пожале́|ть, ю *pf. of* ▸ **жале́ть**

пожа́л|оваться, уюсь *pf. of* ▸ **жа́ловаться**

пожа́луй *adv.* perhaps; very likely; it may be.

пожа́луйста *particle*
1 (*при просьбе*) please; **сади́тесь, п.** please sit down.
2 (*при согласии*) certainly!, by all means!, with pleasure! (*or not translated*); **переда́йте мне, п., кни́гу. — п.** would you mind passing me the book? — there you are.
3 (*в ответ на «спасибо»*) don't mention it; not at all.

пожа́р, а *m.* fire.

пожа́рить *pf. of* ▸ **жа́рить**

пожа́рник, а *m.* (*coll.*) fireman, firefighter.

пожа́р|ный *adj. of* ▸ **~; ~ная кома́нда** fire brigade; **~ная ле́стница** fire escape; **~ная маши́на** fire engine; *as n.* **п., ~ного** *m.* fireman, firefighter.

по|жа́ть, жму́, жмёшь *pf.* (*of* ▸ **~жима́ть**) to press, squeeze; **п. ру́ку** (+ *d.*) to shake hands (with); **п. плеча́ми** to shrug one's shoulders.

пожела́ни|е, я *nt.* wish, desire.

пожела́|ть, ю *pf. of* ▸ **жела́ть**

пожелте́|ть, ю *pf. of* ▸ **желте́ть**

пожен|и́ться, ~имся *pf.* (*pl. used only*; *of two people*) to get married.

поже́ртвовани|е, я *nt.* donation.

поже́ртв|овать, ую *pf. of* ▸ **же́ртвовать**

пожива́|ть, ю *impf.*: **как (вы) ~ете?** how are you (getting on)?

пожи́знен|ный (~, ~на) *adj.* life(long); for life; **~ное заключе́ние** life imprisonment.

пожило́й *adj.* elderly.

пожима́|ть, ю *impf. of* ▸ **пожа́ть**

пожира́|ть, ю *impf. of* ▸ **пожра́ть**

пожи́тк|и, ов *no sg.* (*coll.*) belongings; (one's) things.

по|жи́ть, живу́, живёшь, *past* **~жил, ~жила́, ~жило** *pf.* to live (*for a time*); to stay; **мы ~жили три го́да в Ки́еве** we lived for three years in Kiev.

пожм|у́, ёшь *see* ▸ **пожа́ть**

пожр|а́ть, у́, ёшь, *past* **~а́л, ~ала́, ~а́ло** *pf.* (*of* ▸ **пожира́ть**) to devour.

по́з|а, ы *f.* pose, attitude, posture; (*fig.*) pose; **приня́ть каку́ю-н. ~у** to strike an attitude, adopt a pose.

позаба́в|ить, лю, ишь *pf.* to amuse a little.

позаба́в|иться, люсь, ишься *pf.* to amuse o.s. a little.

позабо́|титься, чусь, тишься *pf. of* ▸ **забо́титься**

позабыва́|ть, ю *impf. of* ▸ **позабы́ть**

позаб|ы́ть, у́ду, у́дешь *pf.* (*of* ▸ **~ыва́ть**) (+ *a. or* **о** + *p.*; *coll.*) to forget (about).

позави́д|овать, ую *pf. of* ▸ **зави́довать**

поза́втрака|ть, ю *pf. of* ▸ **за́втракать**

позавчера́ *adv.* the day before yesterday.

позади́[1] *adv.* (*of place*; *fig. of time*) behind; **оста́вить п.** to leave behind.

позади́[2] *prep.* + *g.* behind.

позаимств|овать, ую *pf. of* ▸ **заимствовать**

позапро́шлый *adj.* before last; **п. год** the year before last.

по|зва́ть, зову́, зовёшь, *past* **~зва́л, ~звала́, ~зва́ло** *pf. of* ▸ **звать 1, 2**

позво́л|ить, ю, ишь *pf.* (*of* ▸ **~я́ть**) (+ *d. of person and inf.*, + *a. of inanimate object*) to allow, permit; **п. себе́** (+ *inf.*) to venture, take the liberty (of); (+ *a.*) to be able to afford; **п. себе́ сде́лать замеча́ние** to venture a remark; **~ь(те)** (*i*) *polite form of request* **~ьте предста́вить до́ктора Х.** allow me to introduce Doctor X., (*ii*) *expr. of disagreement or objection* **~ьте, что э́то зна́чит?** excuse me, what does that mean?

позвол|я́ть, я́ю *impf. of* ▸ **~́ить**

позвон|и́ть, ю́, и́шь *pf. of* ▸ **звони́ть**

позвоно́чник, а *m.* (*anat.*) spine, backbone.

поздн|е́е *comp. of* ▸ **~́ий** *and* ▸ **~́о** later.

позднейший *adj.* (*более поздний*) later; (*самый поздний*) latest.

по́здн|ий *adj.* late; **до ~ей но́чи** until late at night, late into the night; **~о** it is late.

по́здно *adv.* late.

поздоро́ва|ться, юсь *pf. of* ▸ **здоро́ваться**

поздра́в|ить, лю, ишь *pf.* (*of* ▸ **~ля́ть**) (**с** + *i.*) to congratulate (on, upon); **п. кого́-н. с Но́вым го́дом** to wish s.o. a happy New Year.

поздравле́ни|е, я *nt.* congratulation, greeting(s).

поздравля́|ть, ю *impf. of* ▸ **поздра́вить**

позелене́|ть, ю *pf. of* ▸ **зелене́ть 1**

по́з|же *comp. of* ▸ **~дний** *and* ▸ **~дно;** later (on).

пози́р|овать, ую *impf.* (+ *d.*) to pose (for).

пози́ци|я, и *f.* position.

познако́м|ить(ся), лю(сь), ишь(ся) *pf. of* ▸ **знако́мить(ся)**

позна́ни|е, я *nt.*
1 (*phil.*) cognition; **тео́рия ~я** epistemology.
2 (*pl.*) knowledge.

позоло́т|а, ы *f.* gilding, gilt.

позо́р, а *m.* shame, disgrace.

позо́р|ить, ю, ишь *impf.* (*of* ▸ **о~**) to disgrace.

позо́р|иться, юсь, ишься *impf.* (*of* ▸ **о~**) to disgrace o.s.

позо́р|ный (~ен, ~на) *adj.* shameful, disgraceful; ignominious.

поигра́|ть, ю *pf.* to have a game, play a little.

поимк|а, и *f.* capture.

по-ино́му *adv.* differently, in a different way.

по́иск, а *m.* (*comput.*) search; (*pl.*) search; **в ~ах** (+ *g.*) in search (of), in quest (of).

поис|ка́ть, щу́, ~́щешь *pf.* to look for, search for; **~щи́те хороше́нько** have a good look.

поиско́в|ый *adj.*: **~ая систе́ма/маши́на** (*comput.*) search engine.

пои́стине *adv.* indeed, in truth.

по|и́ть, ю́, ~́ишь *impf.* (*of* ▸ **на~**) to give to drink; (*скот*) to water; **п. вино́м** to treat to wine.

по|ищу́, и́щешь *see* ▸ **~иска́ть**

пой|ду́, дёшь *see* ▸ **~ти́**

по́йм|а, ы, *g. pl.* **~** *f.* floodlands; water meadow.

пойма́|ть, ю *pf. of* ▸ **лови́ть**

пойм|у́, ёшь *see* ▸ **поня́ть**

пой|ти́, ду́, дёшь, *past* **пошёл, пошла́** *pf.*
1 *pf. of* ▸ **идти́** *and* ▸ **ходи́ть; пошёл вон!** be off!; off with you!
2 (*начать ходить*) to begin to (be able to) walk.
3 (**в** + *a.*) to take after; **он пошёл в отца́** he takes after his father.

пока́[1] *adv.* for the present, for the time being; **п. что** (*coll.*) in the meanwhile; **п.!** (*coll.*) bye!

пока́[2] *conj.*
1 while; **нам на́до попроси́ть его́, п. он тут** we must ask him while he is here.
2 : **п. не** until, till, before; **п. (ещё) не по́здно** before it's too late.

показа́тел|ь, я *m.*
1 indicator; index.
2 (*math.*) exponent, index.

показа́тел|ьный (~ен, ~ьна) *adj.*
1 (*характерный*) significant; instructive, revealing.
2 (*образцовый*) model; demonstration; **п. проце́сс** show trial; **п. уро́к** object lesson.
3 (*math.*) exponential.

пока|за́ть, жу́, ~́жешь *pf.* (*of* ▸ **~́зывать**)
1 to show; to display, reveal; **п. свои́ зна́ния** to display one's knowledge.
2 (*о приборе*) to show, register, read.
3 (**на** + *a.*) to point (at, to).

пока|за́ться, жу́сь, ~́жешься *pf.*
1 *pf. of* ▸ **каза́ться.**
2 (*pf. of* ▸ **~́зываться**) to show o.s.; to appear; to come in sight; **из-за облако́в ~за́лась луна́** the moon appeared from behind the clouds; **п. врачу́** to see a doctor.
3 *pass. of* ▸ **~за́ть**

показно́й *adj.* (*сочувствие*) affected; (*роскошь*) ostentatious.

пока́зыва|ть(ся), ю(сь) *impf. of* ▸ **показа́ть(ся)**

покара́|ть, ю *pf. of* ▸ **кара́ть**

score пока́та|ть[1]**, ю** *pf.* to roll.

поката́|ть[2]**, ю** *pf.* to take for a drive; **п. дете́й** to take children out.

поката́|ться, юсь *pf.* to go for a drive; **п. на ло́дке** to go out boating.

пока|ти́ть, чу́, ~́тишь *pf.*
1 *pf. of* ▸ **кати́ть.**
2 (*мяч*) to start (rolling), set rolling.

пока|ти́ться, чу́сь, ~́тишься *pf.*
1 *pf. of* ▸ **кати́ться.**
2 (*начать катиться*) to start rolling.

пока́чива|ться, юсь *impf.* to rock slightly; **идти́ ~ясь** to walk unsteadily.

пока́шлива|ть, ю *impf.* to have a slight cough; to cough intermittently.

покая́ни|е, я *nt.*
1 (*eccl.*) (*исповедь*) confession.
2 (*раскаяние*) penitence, repentance; **принести́ п.** (**в** + *p.*) to repent (of).

пока́|яться, юсь, ешься *pf. of* ▸ **ка́яться**

по́кер, а *m.* poker (*card game*).

покида́|ть, ю *impf. of* ▸ **поки́нуть**

поки́нут|ый *p.p.p. of* ▸ **~ь** *and adj.* deserted, abandoned.

поки́|нуть, ну, нешь *pf.* (*of* ▸ **~да́ть**) to

leave; to desert, abandon, forsake.
покла́дист|ый (~, ~а) *adj.* complaisant, obliging.
покло́н, а *m.* bow.
поклон|и́ться, ю́сь, ~́ишься *pf. of* ▶ **кла́няться**
покло́нник, а *m.* admirer; fan.
покло́нни|ца, цы *f. of* ▶ **~к**
покло́ня́|ться, юсь *impf.* (+ *d.*) to worship.
покля́|сться, ну́сь, нёшься *pf. of* ▶ **кля́сться**
поко́|й, я *m.* rest, peace; **оста́вить в ~е** to leave in peace; **уйти́ на п., удали́ться на п.** to retire.
поко́йник, а *m.* the deceased.
поко́йни|ца, цы *f. of* ▶ **~к**
поко́йн|ый *adj.* (*умерший*) (the) late; *as n.* **п., ~ого** *m.*, **~ая, ~ой** *f.* the deceased.
поколеб|а́ть, ~́лю, ~́лешь *pf. of* ▶ **колеба́ть**
поколеб|а́ться, ~́люсь, ~́лешься *pf.*
1 *pf. of* ▶ **колеба́ться.**
2 to waver (for a time), hesitate (for a time).
поколе́ни|е, я *nt.* generation.
поколо|ти́ть, чу́, ~́тишь *pf. of* ▶ **колоти́ть 2**
поко́нч|ить, у, ишь *pf.* (**с** + *i.*)
1 (*завершить*) to finish off; to finish (with), be through (with), have done (with); **с э́тим ~ено** that's done with.
2 (*уничтожить*) to put an end (to); to do away (with); **п. жизнь самоуби́йством** to commit suicide.
покоре́ни|е, я *nt.* conquest.
покори́тел|ь, я *m.* conqueror.
покор|и́ть, ю́, и́шь *pf.* (*of* ▶ **~я́ть**) to conquer, subdue.
покор|и́ться, ю́сь, и́шься *pf.* (*of* ▶ **~я́ться**) (+ *d.*) to submit (to); to resign o.s. (to); **п. свое́й у́части** to resign o.s. to one's lot.
покорм|и́ть, лю́, ~́ишь *pf. of* ▶ **корми́ть 1**
поко́р|ный (~ен, ~на) *adj.* (+ *d.*) submissive (to), obedient; **п. судьбе́** resigned to one's fate.
покор|я́ть(ся), я́ю(сь) *impf. of* ▶ **~и́ть(ся)**
поко|си́ться, шу́сь, си́шься *pf. of* ▶ **коси́ться**
покра́|сить(ся), шу(сь), сишь(ся) *pf. of* ▶ **кра́сить(ся)**
покрасне́|ть, ю *pf. of* ▶ **красне́ть**
покрови́тел|ь, я *m.* patron, protector.
покрови́тельниц|а, ы *f.* patroness, protectress.
покрови́тельствен|ный (~, ~на) *adj.*
1 protective; **~ная окра́ска** (*zool.*) protective colouring.
2 (*снисходительный*) condescending, patronizing.
покрови́тельств|о, а *nt.* protection, patronage; **под ~ом** (+ *g.*) under the patronage (of), under the auspices (of).
покрыва́л|о, а *nt.*
1 (*кусок ткани*) cover; (*на кровать*) bedspread, counterpane.
2 shawl; (*вуаль*) veil.
покрыва́|ть(ся), ю(сь) *impf. of* ▶ **покры́ть(ся)**
покры́ти|е, я *nt.*
1 covering; **п. доро́ги** road surfacing; **п. кры́ши** roofing.
2 (*возмещение*) covering, discharge, payment; **п. расхо́дов** defrayment of expenses.
покр|ы́ть, о́ю, о́ешь *pf.* (*of* ▶ **~ыва́ть**)
1 to cover; **п. кра́ской** to coat with paint; **п. ла́ком** to varnish, lacquer; **п. позо́ром** to cover with shame.
2 (*возместить*) to meet, pay off; **п. расхо́ды** to cover expenses, defray expenses.
3 (*расстояние*) to cover.
покр|ы́ться, о́юсь, о́ешься *pf.* (*of* ▶ **~ыва́ться**) (+ *i.*)
1 (*накрыть себя*) to cover s.o. (with).
2 (*заполниться, усеяться*) to be, get covered (with).
покры́шк|а, и *f.* tyre (*Br.*), tire (*US*).
покупа́тел|ь, я *m.* (*дома, машины*) buyer, purchaser; (*в магазине*) customer.
покупа́тель|ница, ницы *f. of* ▶ **~**
покупа́|ть, ю *impf. of* ▶ **купи́ть**
поку́пк|а, и *f.*
1 (*действие*) buying; purchasing, purchase.
2 (*вещь*) purchase; **вы́годная п.** bargain; **де́лать ~и** to go shopping.
покур|и́ть, ю́, ~́ишь *pf.*
1 *pf. of* ▶ **кури́ть.**
2 to have a smoke; **дава́й ~́им** let's have a smoke.
покуса́|ть, ю *pf.* to bite; (*о пчёлах*) to sting.
поку|си́ться, шу́сь, си́шься *pf.* (*of* ▶ **~ша́ться**) (**на** + *a.*)
1 (*попытаться сделать что-н.*) to attempt, make an attempt (upon).
2 (*попытаться завладеть чем-н.*) to encroach (on, upon).
поку́ша|ть, ю *pf. of* ▶ **ку́шать**
покуша́|ться, юсь *impf. of* ▶ **покуси́ться**
покуше́ни|е, я *nt.* attempt; **п. на жизнь** (+ *g.*) *or* **п. на** (+ *a.*) attempt upon the life (of).
пол[1], а, о ~́е, на/в ~у́, *pl.* **~ы́** *m.* floor.
пол[2], а, *pl.* **~́ы, ~о́в** *m.* sex; **обо́его ~́а** of both sexes.
пол... *comb. form, abbr. of* **полови́на;** half (*as in* **полчаса́** half an hour; **полдеся́того** half past nine, *etc.*).
полага́|ть, ю *impf.* to suppose, think; **на́до п.** it is to be supposed; one must suppose.
полага́|ться, юсь *impf.*
1 *impf. of* ▶ **положи́ться.**
2 (*impers.*): **~ется** one is supposed (to).
3 : **~ется** (+ *d.*) to be due (to).
пола́|дить, жу, дишь *pf.* (**с** + *i.*) to come to an understanding (with); to get on (with).
полве́ка, полуве́ка *m.* half a century.
полго́да, полуго́да *m.* half a year, six months.
по́лдень, полу́дня *and* **по́лдня** *m.* noon, midday; **за́ полдень** past noon; **к полу́дню** towards noon.
по́лдник, а *m.* (afternoon) snack.
полдоро́г|и *f.* halfway; **остановиться на**

~е to stop halfway (*also fig.*).

по́л|е, я, *pl.* **~я́, ~е́й** *nt.*
1 field; **п. би́твы, п. сраже́ния** battlefield; **п. зре́ния** field of vision.
2 (*art*) ground; (*heraldry*) field.
3 (*pl.*) (*чистая полоса*) margin.
4 (*pl.*) (*шляпы*) brim.

полев|о́й *adj.* (*bot., mil.*) field; **п. команди́р** warlord; **~ы́е усло́вия** field conditions; **~ы́е цветы́** wild flowers.

поле́з|ный (~ен, ~на) *adj.* useful; helpful; (*пища*) wholesome, health-giving; **чем могу́ быть ~ен?** can I help you?

поле́з|ть, у, ешь, *past* **~, ~ла** *pf.*
1 *pf. of* ▸ **лезть.**
2 (*начать лезть*) to start to climb.

поле́мик|а, и *f.* polemic(s); dispute, controversy.

полен|и́ться, ю́сь, ~́ишься *pf.* (+ *inf.*) to be too lazy to.

поле́н|о, а, *pl.* **~ья, ~ьев** *nt.* log.

полёт, а *m.* flight; flying; **вид с высоты́ пти́чьего ~а** bird's-eye view; **п. фанта́зии** flight of fancy.

поле|те́ть, чу́, ти́шь *pf.*
1 *pf. of* ▸ **лете́ть.**
2 (*начать лететь*) to start to fly; to fly off.

по-ле́тнему *adv.* as in summer, as for summer; **оде́т п.** (dressed) in summer clothes.

полеч|и́ть, у́, ~́ишь *pf.* to treat (*for a while*).

полеч|и́ться, у́сь, ~́ишься *pf.* to undergo treatment (*for a while*).

пол|е́чь, я́гу, я́жешь, я́гут, *past* **~ёг, ~егла́** *pf.*
1 to lie down (*in numbers*).
2 (*fig.*) (*погибнуть*) to fall, be killed (*in numbers*).

по́лз|ать, аю *impf., indet. of* ▸ **~ти́**

полз|ти́, у́, ёшь, *past* **~, ~ла́** *impf.*
1 to crawl, creep (along); **по́езд ~** the train was crawling.
2 (*о жидкости*) to ooze (out).

полиартри́т, а *m.* (*med.*) polyarthritis.

полива́|ть(ся), ю(сь) *impf. of* ▸ **поли́ть 1, поли́ться**

поли́вк|а, и *f.* watering.

полигло́т, а *m.* polyglot.

полиго́н, а *m.* (*mil.*) (artillery *or* bombing) range; **испыта́тельный п.** proving ground, testing area.

полиграфи́|я, и *f.* printing.

поликли́ник|а, и *f.* clinic; health centre (*Br.*), center (*US*).

полинези́|ец, йца *m.* Polynesian.

полинези́|йка, йки *f. of* ▸ **~ец**

полинези́йский *adj.* Polynesian.

Полине́зи|я, и *f.* Polynesia.

полиня́|ть, ет *pf. of* ▸ **линя́ть**

поли́п, а *m.* (*zool., med.*) polyp.

полир|ова́ть, у́ю *impf.* (*of* ▸ **от~**) to polish.

по́лис, а *m.* policy; **страхово́й п.** insurance policy.

политеи́зм, а *m.* polytheism.

политехни́ческий *adj.*: **п. институ́т** polytechnic.

политзаключённ|ый, ого *m.* political prisoner.

поли́тик, а *m.* politician.

поли́тик|а, и *f.*
1 policy; **проводи́ть ~у** to carry out a policy.
2 (*наука*) politics; **п. си́лы** power politics.

полити́ческ|ий *adj.* political; **п. де́ятель** political figure, politician; **~ая корре́ктность** political correctness; **~ое убе́жище** political asylum.

полито́лог, а *m.* political scientist.

политоло́ги|я, и *f.* political science.

политтехно́лог, а *m.* spin doctor.

пол|и́ть, ью́, ьёшь, *past* **~и́л, ~ила́, ~и́ло** *pf.*
1 (*impf.* ▸ **~ива́ть**) (+ *a. and i.*) (*смочить*) to pour (on, upon); **п. цветы́** to water the flowers.
2 (*no impf.*) (*начать лить*) to begin to pour.

пол|и́ться, ью́сь, ьёшься, *past* **~и́лся, ~ила́сь** *pf.* (*of* ▸ **~ива́ться**)
1 (+ *i.*) (*полить себя*) to pour over o.s.
2 (*начать литься*) to begin to flow.

полице́йск|ий *adj.* police; **п. уча́сток** police station; *as n.* **п., ~ого** *m.* policeman, police officer.

поли́ци|я, и *f.* police.

полиэтиле́н, а *m.* polythene.

полк, а́, о ~е́, в ~у́ *m.* regiment.

по́лк|а, и *f.*
1 shelf; **кни́жная п.** bookshelf.
2 (*в поезде*) berth.

полко́вник, а *m.* colonel.

полково́д|ец, ца *m.* commander; military leader.

поллино́з, а *m.* hay fever.

пол-ли́тра, полули́тра *m.* half a litre (*Br.*), liter (*US*).

полне́йший *adj.* sheer, utter(most).

полне́|ть, ю *impf.* (*of* ▸ **по~**) to grow stout, put on weight.

полно́ *adv.* (+ *g.*) (*coll.*) lots; **в ко́мнате полно́ наро́ду** the room is packed with people.

полнолу́ни|е, я *nt.* full moon.

полномо́чи|е, я *nt.* authority, power; (*leg.*) proxy; **превыше́ние ~й** exceeding one's commission; **дать ~я** (+ *d.*) to empower.

полнопра́в|ный (~ен, ~на) *adj.* enjoying full rights; **п. член** full member.

по́лностью *adv.* fully, in full; completely.

полнот|а́, ы́ *no pl., f.*
1 fullness, completeness; **п. вла́сти** absolute power.
2 (*тучность*) stoutness, corpulence.

полноце́н|ный (~ен, ~на) *adj.* proper; fully fledged (*Br.*), full fledged (*US*).

по́лночь, полу́ночи *and* **по́лночи** *f.* midnight; **за́ п.** after midnight.

по́л|ный (~он, ~на́, ~́но́) *adj.*
1 (+ *g. or i.*) (*наполненный*) full (of); (*совершенный*) complete, entire, total; absolute; **п. карма́н** (+ *g.*) a pocketful (of); **~ное собра́ние сочине́ний** complete works; **в ~ной ме́ре** fully, in full measure; **на ~ном ходу́** at full speed.

2 (*толстый*) stout, portly; plump.

по́ло *nt. indecl.* (*sport*) polo; **во́дное п.** water polo.

полови́к, а́ *m.* mat; long narrow carpet, runner.

полови́н|а, ы *f.* half; **два с ~ой** two and a half; **п. шесто́го** half past five; **во второ́й ~е дня** in the afternoon.

поло́вник, а *m.* ladle.

полово́дь|е, я *nt.* flood, high water (*at time of spring thaw*).

полов|о́й *adj.* sexual; **~а́я зре́лость** puberty; **~ы́е о́рганы** genitals, sexual organs; **~а́я связь** sexual intercourse.

поло́г|ий (~, ~а) *adj.* gently sloping.

положе́ни|е, я *nt.*
1 (*местонахождение*) position; whereabouts.
2 (*тела*) position; posture; attitude; **в сидя́чем ~и** in a sitting position.
3 (*состояние*) position; condition, state; situation; (*социальное*) status; (*обстоятельство*) circumstances; **семе́йное п.** marital status; **вое́нное п.** martial law; **чрезвыча́йное п.** state of emergency; **п. веще́й** state of affairs; **выходи́ть из ~я** to find a way out.

поло́жено *pred.* (*coll., impers.*) one is supposed to, it is customary; **э́того де́лать не п.** one is not supposed to do that.

поло́жим let us assume; **п., что вы пра́вы** let us assume that you are right.

положи́тел|ьный (~ен, ~ьна) *adj.*
1 positive.
2 (*утвердительный*) affirmative; **п. отве́т** affirmative reply.
3 (*благоприятный*) favourable (*Br.*), favorable (*US*).

полож|и́ть, у́, ~́ишь *pf. of* ▸ **класть 1**

полож|и́ться, у́сь, ~́ишься *pf.* (*of* ▸ **полага́ться 1**) (**на** + *a.*) to rely (upon), count (upon).

полома́|ть, ю *pf.* (*coll.*) to break, put out of action.

полома́|ться, юсь *pf. of* ▸ **лома́ться 3**

поло́мк|а, и *f.*
1 (*машины*) breakdown.
2 (*место*) damaged part; damage.

полоне́з, а *m.* polonaise.

полос|а́, ы́, *a.* **по́лосу́,** *pl.* **по́лосы, поло́с, ~а́м** *f.*
1 (*какого-н. цвета*) stripe; streak.
2 (*воды, бумаги*) strip.
3 (*период*) period; phase.
4 (*газеты*) page.

полоса́т|ый (~, ~а) *adj.* striped.

поло́ск|а, и *f. dim. of* ▸ **полоса́; в ~у** striped.

поло|ска́ть, щу́, ~́щешь *impf. of* ▸ **про~**

полоте́н|це, ца, *g. pl.* **~ец** *nt.* towel.

полотёр, а *m.* floor polisher.

полот|но́, на́, *pl.* **~́на, ~́ен, ~́нам** *nt.*
1 (*ткань*) linen; **бле́дный как п.** white as a sheet.
2 (*картина*) canvas.
3 (*дороги*) roadbed.
4 (*tech.*) (*пилы*) blade.

полотня́ный *adj.* linen.

полоу́м|ный (~ен, ~на) *adj.* (*coll.*) crazy.

полпути́ *m. indecl.*: **на п.** halfway; **останови́ться на п.** (*fig.*) to stop halfway.

полста́вки *pl. indecl.*: **на п.** part-time.

полтора́, полу́тора (*used with m. and nt. nouns*) one and a half; **в п. ра́за бо́льше** half as much again.

полтора́ста, полу́тораста *num.* a hundred and fifty.

полтор|ы́ (*used with f. nouns*) = **~а́; п. ты́сячи** one and a half thousand.

полу... *comb. form* half-, semi-, demi-.

полуго́ди|е, я *nt.* half-year, six months.

полугодова́лый *adj.* six-month-old.

полужив|о́й (~́, ~а́, ~́о) *adj.* half dead; more dead than alive.

полузащи́тник, а *m.* (*sport*) halfback, midfield player; **центра́льный п.** centre half (*Br.*), center half (*US*).

полукру́г, а *m.* semicircle.

полукру́глый *adj.* semicircular.

полулеж|а́ть, у́, и́шь *impf.* to recline.

полуме́сяц, а *m.* half moon; crescent.

полумра́к, а *m.* semi-darkness.

полуоде́т|ый (~, ~а) *adj.* half-dressed, half-clothed.

полуо́стров, а *m.* peninsula.

полуоткры́т|ый (~, ~а) *adj.* half-open; (*дверь, окно*) ajar (*pred.*).

полупроводни́к, а́ *m.* (*phys.*) semiconductor.

полуразру́шен|ный (~, ~а) *adj.* tumbledown, dilapidated.

полуфабрика́т, а *m.* (*изделие*) semi-finished product; (*пищевой*) semi-prepared foodstuff, convenience food.

полуфина́л, а *m.* semi-final.

получ|а́ть(ся), а́ю, ет(ся) *impf. of* ▸ **~и́ть(ся)**

получе́ни|е, я *nt.* receipt; obtaining; **распи́ска в ~и** receipt.

получ|и́ть, у́, ~́ишь *pf.* (*of* ▸ **~а́ть**) to get, receive, obtain; **п. на́сморк** to catch a cold; **п. удово́льствие** to derive pleasure.

получ|и́ться, ~́ится *pf.* (*of* ▸ **~а́ться**)
1 (*оказаться*) to turn out, prove, be; **~и́лось, что он был прав** it turned out that he was right, he proved right.
2 (*coll.*) (*оказаться удачным*) to work out; (*о снимке*) to come out.

полу́чше *adv.* (*coll.*) a little better.

полуша́ри|е, я *nt.* hemisphere.

полушу́б|ок, ка *m.* (knee-length) sheepskin coat.

полцены́ *f. indecl.*: **за п.** at half price; for half its value.

полчаса́, получа́са *pl.* half an hour; **ка́ждые п.** every half-hour.

по́лый *adj.* hollow.

полы́н|ь, и *f.* wormwood.

полысе́|ть, ю *pf. of* ▸ **лысе́ть**

по́льз|а, ы *f.* use; advantage, benefit, profit; **извлека́ть из чего́-н. ~у** to benefit from sth; to profit by sth.; **принести́ ~у** (+ *d.*) to be of benefit (to); **в ~у** (+ *g.*) in favour (*Br.*), favor (*US*) (of), on behalf (of); **два-ноль в**

~у Дина́мо (*sport*) 2–0 to Dynamo; **пойти́ на ~у кому́-н.** to be of benefit to s.o.
пóльзовани|е, я *nt.* (+ *i.*) use (of).
пóльзовател|ь, я *m.* user.
пóльз|оваться, уюсь *impf.* (+ *i.*)
1 (*pf.* **вос~**) to make use (of), use, utilize.
2 (*pf.* **вос~**) (*извлекать выгоду*) to profit (by); **п. слу́чаем** to take an opportunity.
3 (*обладать*) to enjoy; **п. успéхом** to enjoy success, be a success.
пóльк|а[1], и *f.* (*женщина*) Pole, Polish woman.
пóльк|а[2], и *f.* (*танец*) polka.
пóльский *adj.* Polish.
поль|сти́ть, щу́, сти́шь *pf. of* ▸ **льсти́ть**
Пóльш|а, и *f.* Poland.
полюб|и́ть, лю́, ~ишь *pf.* to come to like, grow fond (of); (*влюбиться*) to fall in love (with).
полюб|ова́ться, у́юсь *pf. of* ▸ **любова́ться; ~у́йся, ~у́йтесь (на** + *a.*; *coll., iron.*) just look; **~у́йся на э́того дурака́!** just look at that fool!
пóлюс, а *m.* (*geog., phys., and fig.*) pole; **Сéверный п.** North Pole.
поля́к, а *m.* Pole.
поля́н|а, ы *f.* glade, clearing.
поля́рник, а *m.* polar explorer.
поля́рн|ый *adj.*
1 polar, arctic; **П~ая звезда́** Pole star, North Star; **Сéверный п. круг** Arctic Circle.
2 (*fig.*) polar, diametrically opposed.
пома́д|а, ы *f.* pomade; **губна́я п.** lipstick.
пома́|зать, жу, жешь *pf. of* ▸ **ма́зать 1, 2**
помаз|óк, ка́ *m.* (small) brush.
пома́лкива|ть, ю *impf.* (*coll.*) to hold one's tongue, keep quiet.
поман|и́ть, ю́, ~ишь *pf. of* ▸ **мани́ть**
пома́рк|а, и *f.* (*исправление*) correction (*by hand*); (*вычеркнутое место*) crossing-out.
пома|ха́ть, шу́, ~шешь *pf.* (+ *i.*) to wave (*for a while, a few times*).
пома́хива|ть, ю *impf.* (+ *i.*) to wave, brandish, swing (*from time to time*); **соба́ка ~ла хвостóм** the dog would wag his tail.
помéньше *comp. of* ▸ **ма́ленький** *and* ▸ **ма́ло** (*coll.*) (*по размеру*) somewhat smaller, a little smaller; (*по количеству*) somewhat less, a little less.
поменя́|ть(ся), ю(сь) *pf. of* ▸ **меня́ть(ся) 2**
по|мерéть, мру́, мрёшь, *past* **~мер, ~мерла́, ~мерло** *pf.* (*of* ▸ **~мира́ть**) (*coll.*) to die; **п. сó смеху** to split one's sides (with laughing).
помéр|ить(ся), ю(сь), ишь(ся) *pf. of* ▸ **мéрить(ся)**
помéрк|нуть, ну, нешь, *past* **~, ~ла** *pf. of* ▸ **мéркнуть**
поме|сти́ть, щу́, сти́шь *pf.* (*of* ▸ **~ща́ть**)
1 (*поселить*) to lodge, accommodate; to put up.
2 (*поставить*) to put, place; (*fin.*) to invest; **п. объявлéние в газéте** to put an advertisement in a paper.
поме|сти́ться, щу́сь, сти́шься *pf.* (*of* ▸ **~ща́ться 3**)
1 (*жить*) to find room; to put up; (*о вещах*) to go in; **в э́тот я́щик мои́ вéщи не ~стя́тся** my things will not go into this drawer.
2 *pass. of* ▸ **~сти́ть**
помéст|ье, ья, *g. pl.* **~ий** *nt.* estate.
пóмес|ь, и *f.*
1 hybrid; cross; **п. терьéра и овча́рки, п. терьéра с овча́ркой** a cross between a terrier and a sheepdog.
2 (*fig.*) mixture, hotchpotch.
помé|тить, чу, тишь *pf.* (*of* ▸ **~ча́ть** *and* ▸ **мéтить[1]**) to mark; to date; **п. га́лочкой** to tick.
помéх|а, и *f.*
1 hindrance; obstacle; **быть ~ой** (+ *d.*) to hinder, impede.
2 (*usu. pl.*) (*radio, TV*) interference.
помеча́|ть, ю *impf. of* ▸ **помéтить**
помéшан|ный (~, ~а) *adj.*
1 mad, crazy; insane; *as n.* **п., ~ного** *m.* madman; **~ная, ~ной** *f.* madwoman.
2 (**на** + *p.*; *fig., coll.*) mad (on, about), crazy (about).
помеша́|ть[1,2], ю *pf. of* ▸ **меша́ть[1,2]**
помеща́|ть, ю *impf. of* ▸ **помести́ть**
помеща́|ться, юсь *impf.*
1 (*impf. only*) (*находиться*) to be; to be located, be situated; (*храниться*) to be housed.
2 (*impf. only*): **на э́том стадиóне ~ется сéмьдесят ты́сяч человéк** this stadium holds seventy thousand people.
3 *impf. of* ▸ **помести́ться**
помещéни|е, я *nt.*
1 (*действие*) placing, location; (*капитала*) investment.
2 (*жильё*) room, lodging, apartment; (*для учреждения*) premises; **жилóе п.** housing.
помéщик, а *m.* landowner.
помидóр, а, *g. pl.* **~ов** *m.* tomato.
поми́ловани|е, я *nt.* (*leg.*) pardon, forgiveness; **прóсьба/прошéние о ~и** appeal (for pardon).
поми́л|овать, ую *pf.* (*of* ▸ **ми́ловать**) to pardon, forgive.
поми́мо *prep.* + *g.*
1 (*кроме*) apart from; besides; **п. всегó прóчего** apart from anything else.
2 (*минуя*) without the knowledge (of), unbeknown (to); **всё э́то реши́лось п. меня́** all this was decided without my knowledge.
поми́н|ки, ок *no sg.* funeral repast, wake.
помину́т|ный (~ен, ~на) *adj.*
1 occurring every minute; (*fig., coll.*) (*очень частый*) continual, constant.
2 (*оплата*) by the minute.
помира́|ть, ю *impf. of* ▸ **померéть**
помир|и́ть(ся), ю́(сь), и́шь(ся) *pf. of* ▸ **мири́ть(ся) 1**
пóмн|ить, ю, ишь *impf.* (+ *a. or* **о** + *p.*) to remember.
пóмн|иться, ится *impf.* (*impers.* + *d.*) I, *etc.*, remember; **наскóлько мне ~ится** as far as I can remember.
помнóгу *adv.* (*coll.*) in plenty, in large quantities; in large numbers.
помнóж|ить, у, ишь *pf. of* ▸ **мнóжить**
помога́|ть, ю *impf. of* ▸ **помóчь**
пом|огу́, óжешь, óгут *see* ▸ **~óчь**

по-мо́ему *adv.*
1 (*по моему мнению*) in my opinion.
2 (*как я хочу*) as I wish.

помо́|и, ев *no sg.* slops; **обли́ть кого́-н. ~ями** (*fig., coll.*) to fling mud at s.o.

помо́й|ка, ки, *g. pl.* **помо́ек** *f.* rubbish dump (*Br.*), garbage dump (*US*); (*яма*) cesspit.

помо́|йный *adj.*: **~йное ведро́** slop bucket; **~йная я́ма** cesspit.

помо́лвк|а, и *f.* betrothal, engagement.

помол|и́ться, ю́сь, ~́ишься *pf. of* ▶ **моли́ться 1**

помолч|а́ть, у́, и́шь *pf.* to be silent for a while.

помо́ст, а *m.* platform, rostrum.

помо́|чь, гу́, жешь, гут, *past* **~г, ~гла́** *pf.* (*of* ▶ **~га́ть**)
1 (+ *d.*) to help, aid, assist; **~ги́(те) ей наде́ть пальто́** help her on with her coat.
2 (*о лекарстве*) to relieve, bring relief; **уко́лы ~гли́ от бо́ли** the injections relieved the pain.

помо́щник, а *m.*
1 helper.
2 (*заместитель*) assistant; **п. дире́ктора** assistant director; **п. капита́на** (*naut.*) mate.

помо́щни|ца, цы *f. of* ▶ **~к 1**

по́мощ|ь, и *f.* help, assistance; **оказа́ть п.** to help, assist; **позва́ть на п.** to call for help; **прийти́ на п.** (+ *d.*) to come to the aid (of); **на п.!** help!; **с ~ью** (+ *g.*), **при ~и** (+ *g.*) with the help (of), by means (of); **ско́рая п.** ambulance; **пе́рвая п.** first aid.

по́мп|а, ы *f.* pump.

помпе́з|ный (~ен, ~на) *adj.* pompous.

помýч|ить, у, ишь *pf.* to make suffer, torment (*for a time*).

помýч|иться, усь, ишься *pf.* to suffer (*for a while*).

помч|а́ться, ýсь, и́шься *pf.* to begin to rush, begin to tear along.

пом|ы́ть(ся), о́ю(сь), о́ешь(ся) *pf. of* ▶ **мы́ть(ся)**

пом|я́ть, нý, нёшь *pf.* to rumple slightly; to crumple slightly.

пом|я́ться, нётся *pf. of* ▶ **мя́ться**

понаде́|яться, юсь, ешься *pf. of* ▶ **наде́яться**

пона́доб|иться, люсь, ишься *pf.* to be, become necessary; **е́сли ~ится** if necessary.

по-настоя́щему *adv.* properly.

по-на́шему *adv.*
1 (*по нашему мнению*) in our opinion.
2 (*как мы хотим*) as we wish.

понево́ле *adv.* against one's will.

понеде́льник, а *m.* Monday.

понемно́гу *adv.*
1 (*немного*) little, a little at a time.
2 (*постепенно*) little by little.

понес|ти́, ý, ёшь, *past* **~̈, ~ла́** *pf.*
1 *pf. of* ▶ **нести́**[1].
2 (*о лошадях*) to bolt.

понес|ти́сь, ýсь, ёшься, *past* **~̈ся, ~ла́сь** *pf.*
1 *pf. of* ▶ **нести́сь.**
2 to rush off, tear off, dash off.

по́ни *m. indecl.* pony.

понижа́|ть(ся), ю, ет(ся) *impf. of* ▶ **пони́зить(ся)**

пониже́ни|е, я *nt.* fall, drop; lowering; reduction; **п. цен** reduction, fall in prices; **п. по слýжбе** demotion.

пони́|зить, жу, зишь *pf.* (*of* ▶ **~жа́ть**) (*голос*) to lower; (*цены*) to reduce; **п. по слýжбе** to demote.

пони́|зиться, зится *pf.* (*of* ▶ **~жа́ться**) to fall, drop, go down, be reduced.

по́низу *adv.* (*coll.*) low; along the ground.

поника́|ть, ю *impf. of* ▶ **пони́кнуть**

пони́к|нуть, ну, нешь, *past* **~, ~ла** *pf.* (*of* ▶ **~а́ть**) to droop; **п. голово́й** to hang one's head.

понима́ни|е, я *nt.*
1 understanding, comprehension; **э́то вы́ше моего́ ~я** it is beyond me.
2 (*толкование*) interpretation, conception.

понима́|ть, ю *impf.* (*of* ▶ **поня́ть**)
1 to understand; to comprehend; to realize; **~ю!** I see!
2 (*толковать*) to interpret; **непра́вильно п.** to misunderstand; **как вы ~ете э́тот постýпок?** what do you make of this action?
3 (*impf. only*) (+ *a. or* **в** + *p.*) (*знать толк*) to be a (good) judge (of), know (about); **я ничего́ не ~ю в мýзыке** I know nothing about music.

по-но́вому *adv.* in a new fashion; **нача́ть жить п.** to start life afresh, turn over a new leaf.

поно́с, а *m.* diarrhoea (*Br.*), diarrhea (*US*).

поно|си́ть, шý, ~́сишь *pf.*
1 (*ребёнка*) to carry (*for a while*).
2 (*свитер*) to wear (*for a while*).

поно́|шенный *p.p.p. of* ▶ **~си́ть** *and adj.* worn, shabby, threadbare.

понра́в|иться, люсь, ишься *pf. of* ▶ **нра́виться**

понто́н, а *m.* pontoon.

понýр|ый (~, ~а) *adj.* downcast.

по́нчик, а *m.* doughnut (*Br.*), donut (*US*).

по́нчо *nt. indecl.* poncho.

понюха|ть, ю *pf. of* ▶ **ню́хать**

поня́ти|е, я *nt.*
1 (*общая мысль*) conception.
2 (*представление*) notion, idea; **~я не име́ю!** (*coll.*) I've no idea!; I haven't a clue!
3 (*usu. pl.*) (*понимание*) notions; level (of understanding).

поня́тлив|ый (~, ~а) *adj.* sharp, quick (on the uptake).

поня́т|ный (~ен, ~на) *adj.*
1 (*обоснованный*) understandable; **~но, что...** it is understandable that ...; it is natural that ...; **~ное де́ло** (*coll.*) of course, naturally.
2 (*ясный*) clear, intelligible; **~но?** (*coll.*) (do you) see?; is that clear?; **~но!** (*coll.*) I see!; I understand!

пон|я́ть, пойму́, поймёшь, *past* **~́ял, ~яла́, ~́яло** *pf.* (*of* ▶ **~има́ть 1, 2**) to understand; to comprehend; (*осознать*) to realize; **дать п.** to give to understand.

пообе́да|ть, ю *pf. of* ▶ **обе́дать**

пообеща́|ть, ю *pf.* (*of* ▶ **обеща́ть**) to

П

promise.

поочерёдно *adv.* in turn, by turns.

поощр|и́ть, ю́, и́шь *pf.* (*of* ▸ **~я́ть**) to encourage.

поощр|я́ть, я́ю *impf. of* ▸ **~и́ть**

попада́ни|е, я *nt.* hit (*on target*); **прямо́е п.** direct hit.

попада́|ть(ся), ю(сь) *impf. of* ▸ **попа́сть(ся)**

попа́р|иться, юсь, ишься *pf.* (*impf.* **па́риться**) (*в бане*) to steam, sweat.

поп-а́рт, а *m.* pop art.

попа́|сть, ду́, дёшь, *past* **~л** *pf.* (*of* ▸ **~да́ть**)

1 (**в** + *a.*) to hit; **п. в цель** to hit the target; **не п. в цель** to miss.

2 (**в** + *a.*) (*оказаться*) to get (to), find o.s. (in); (**на** + *a.*) to hit (upon), come (upon); **п. домо́й** to get home; **п. в плен** to be taken prisoner; **п. кому́-н. в ру́ки** to fall into s.o.'s hands; **не туда́ п.** to get the wrong number (*on telephone*); **п. в беду́** to get into trouble, come to grief.

попа́|сться, ду́сь, дёшься, *past* **~лся** *pf.* (*of* ▸ **~да́ться**)

1 (+ *d.*) to come across; **он мне ~лся навстре́чу на у́лице** I ran into him in the street; **п. кому́-н. на глаза́** to catch s.o.'s eye; **пе́рвый ~вшийся** the first person one happens to meet.

2 (*быть пойманным*) to be caught; (**в** + *a.*) to get (into); **п. с поли́чным** to be taken red-handed.

попа́хива|ть, ет *impf.* (*coll.*) (+ *i.*) to smell slightly (of).

попере́к *adv. and prep.* + *g.* across; **де́рево упа́ло п. доро́ги** the tree fell across the road; **стоя́ть у кого́-н. п. доро́ги** to be in s.o.'s way; **знать что-н. вдоль и п.** to know sth. inside out.

попере́чн|ый *adj.* transverse, cross-; **~ая ба́лка** cross-beam; **п. разре́з, ~ое сече́ние** cross section.

поперхн|у́ться, у́сь, ёшься *pf.* (+ *i.*) to choke (over).

поп|ерчи́ть, е́рчу́, е́рчи́шь *pf. of* ▸ **перчи́ть**

пописа́|ть, ю *pf. of* ▸ **писа́ть**

по|пи́ть, пью́, пьёшь, *past* **~пи́л, ~пила́, ~пи́ло** *pf.* to have a drink.

попко́рн, а *m.* popcorn.

попла́ва|ть, ю *pf.* to have, take a swim.

поплав|о́к, ка́ *m.* float.

попла́|кать, чу, чешь *pf.* to cry (*a little, for a while*); to shed a few tears.

попла|ти́ться, чу́сь, ~́тишься *pf.* (+ *i.*, **за** + *a.*) to pay (*with, for*).

поплы́|ть, ву́, вёшь, *past* **~л, ~ла́, ~ло** *pf.* (*о человеке*) to strike out, start swimming; (*о судне*) to set sail.

поп-му́зык|а, и *f.* pop music.

попола́м *adv.* in two, in half; half-and-half; **раздели́ть п.** to divide in two, divide in half, halve; **ви́ски п. с водо́й** whisky and water half-and-half.

пополне́|ть, ю *pf. of* ▸ **полне́ть**

попо́лн|ить, ю, ишь *pf.* (*of* ▸ **~я́ть**) to replenish, fill up; to restock; (*коллекцию*) to enlarge; (*mil.*) to reinforce; **п. горю́чим** to refuel; **п. свой зна́ния** to supplement one's knowledge.

попо́лн|иться, ится *pf.* (*of* ▸ **~я́ться**)

1 to increase.

2 *pass. of* ▸ **~ить**

пополн|я́ть(ся), я́ю, я́ет(ся) *impf. of* ▸ **~́ить(ся)**

пополу́дни *adv.* in the afternoon, p.m.; **в два часа́ п.** at 2 p.m.

пополу́ночи *adv.* after midnight, a.m.; **в два часа́ п.** at 2 a.m.

попо́н|а, ы *f.* horse cloth.

попра́в|ить, лю, ишь *pf.* (*of* ▸ **~ля́ть**)

1 (*починить*) to mend, repair.

2 (*ошибку, ученика*) to correct, set right, put right.

3 (*шляпу*) to adjust, set straight; **п. приче́ску** to tidy one's hair.

4 (*улучшить*) to improve, better.

попра́в|иться, люсь, ишься *pf.* (*of* ▸ **~ля́ться**)

1 (*исправить свою ошибку*) to correct o.s.

2 (*выздороветь*) to get better, recover; **я совсе́м ~ился** I am completely recovered.

3 (*пополнеть*) to put on weight; to look better; **он о́чень ~ился** he has put on a lot of weight; he looks much better.

4 (*о делах*) to improve.

попра́вк|а, и *f.*

1 (*починка*) mending, repairing.

2 (*ошибки*) correction; amendment; **внести́ ~и в законопрое́кт** to amend a bill.

поправля́|ть(ся), ю(сь) *impf. of* ▸ **попра́вить(ся)**

по-пре́жнему *adv.* as before; as usual.

попро́б|овать, ую *pf. of* ▸ **про́бовать**

попро|си́ть(ся), шу́(сь), ~́сишь(ся) *pf. of* ▸ **проси́ть(ся)**

попроща́|ться, юсь *pf.* (**с** + *i.*) to take leave (of), say goodbye (to).

попря́|тать, чу, чешь *pf.* (*coll.*) to hide (*many objects*).

попря́|таться, чемся, чутся *pf.* (*coll.*) (*о многих*) to hide (o.s.).

попс|а́, ы́ *f.* (*coll.*)

1 popular culture; sth. trendy.

2 (*mus.*) pop music.

попсо́вый *adj.* (*coll.*) pop.

попуга́|й, я *m.* parrot; **волни́стый ~й(чик)** budgie, budgerigar.

попу́др|ить, ю, ишь *pf.* to powder.

попу́др|иться, юсь, ишься *pf.* to powder one's face.

попули́ст, а *m.* populist.

популяризи́р|овать, ую *impf. and pf.* to popularize.

популяриз|ова́ть, у́ю *impf. and pf.* = **~и́ровать**

популя́рност|ь, и *f.* popularity.

популя́р|ный (~ен, ~на) *adj.* popular.

попу́тн|ый *adj.*

1 accompanying; (*машина*) passing; **п. ве́тер** fair wind, favourable (*Br.*), favorable (*US*) wind; **~ая струя́** backwash.

2 (*fig.*) passing, incidental; **~ое замеча́ние** passing remark.

попу́тчик, а *m.* fellow-traveller (*Br.*),

-traveler (*US*) (*also fig., pol.*).

попу́тчи|ца, цы *f. of* ▸ **~к** (*lit. only*).

попыта́|ться, юсь *pf. of* ▸ **пыта́ться**

попы́тк|а, и *f.* attempt, try; **предприня́ть ~у** to make an attempt; **со второ́й ~и** at the second attempt.

попя́|титься, чусь, тишься *pf. of* ▸ **пя́титься**

по́р|а, ы *f.* pore.

пор|а́, ы́, *a.* **~у** *f.*
1 time, season; **весе́нняя п.** springtime; **осе́нняя п.** autumn; **до каки́х ~?** till when?, till what time?; **до каки́х ~ вы пробу́дете здесь?** how long will you be here?; **до сих ~** till now, up to now; **с да́вних ~** long, for a long time, for ages; **с тех ~, как...** (ever) since ...; **с э́тих ~** since then, since that time.
2 *as pred.* it is time; **давно́ п.** it is high time; **п. спать!** (it is) bedtime!

порабо́та|ть, ю *pf.* to do some work.

поравня́|ться, юсь *pf.* (**с** + *i.*) to pull alongside (of).

пора́д|овать(ся), ую(сь) *pf. of* ▸ **ра́довать(ся)**

поража́|ть(ся), ю(сь) *impf. of* ▸ **порази́ть(ся)**

пораже́ни|е, я *nt.* defeat.

порази́тел|ьный (~ен, ~ьна) *adj.* striking; staggering, startling.

пора|зи́ть, жу́, зи́шь *pf.* (*of* ▸ **~жа́ть**)
1 to hit, strike; **п. кинжа́лом** to stab with a dagger.
2 (*fig.*) (*удивить*) to strike; to stagger; **меня́ ~зи́л её мра́чный вид** I was struck by her gloomy appearance.

пора|зи́ться, жу́сь, зи́шься *pf.* (*of* ▸ **~жа́ться**) to be staggered, be astounded.

по-ра́зному *adv.* differently, in different ways.

пора́н|ить, ю, ишь *pf.* to wound, injure, hurt (*slightly*).

пора́н|иться, юсь, ишься *pf.* to injure, hurt o.s. (*slightly*).

порв|а́ть, у́, ёшь, *past* **~а́л, ~ала́, ~а́ло** *pf.*
1 to tear slightly.
2 (*impf.* **порыва́ть**) (**с** + *i.*; *fig.*) to break (with); to break off (with); **она́ давно́ ~ала́ с ним** she broke with him long ago.

порв|а́ться, ётся, *past* **~а́лся, ~ала́сь, ~а́ло́сь** *pf.*
1 (*о верёвке*) to break (off), snap.
2 (*об одежде*) to tear.

пореде́|ть, ет *pf. of* ▸ **реде́ть**

поре́з, а *m.* cut.

поре́|зать, жу, жешь *pf.*
1 (*поранить*) to cut; **п. себе́ па́лец** to cut one's finger.
2 (+ *a. or g.*) (*нарезать*) to cut (*a quantity of*).

поре́|заться, жусь, жешься *pf.* to cut o.s.

порекоменд|ова́ть, у́ю *pf. of* ▸ **рекомендова́ть**

порица́|ть, ю *impf.* to censure; to reprimand.

по́рно *nt. indecl.* (*coll.*) porn.

порнографи́ческий *adj.* pornographic.

порногра́фи|я, и *f.* pornography.

порнофи́льм, а *m.* porno film, blue movie.

по́ровну *adv.* equally, in equal parts; **раздели́ть п.** to divide equally, into equal parts.

поро́г, а *m.*
1 threshold (*also fig.*); **переступи́ть п.** to cross the threshold.
2 (*geog., usu. pl.*) rapids.

поро́д|а, ы *f.*
1 (*животных*) breed; (*деревьев*) species; (*fig.*) (*людей*) kind, sort, type.
2 (*geol.*) rock; **го́рная п.** rock; (*пласт*) layer, stratum.

поро́дист|ый (~, ~а) *adj.* thoroughbred, pedigree.

поро|ди́ть, жу́, ди́шь *pf.* (*of* ▸ **~жда́ть**) to give rise (to), spawn, engender.

порожда́|ть, ю *impf. of* ▸ **породи́ть**

поро́й (*and* **поро́ю**) *adv.* at times, now and then.

поро́к, а *m.*
1 (*человека*) vice.
2 (*вещи*) defect; flaw, blemish; **п. се́рдца** heart disease.

пороло́н, а *m.* foam rubber.

порос|ёнок, ёнка, *pl.* **~я́та, ~я́т** *m.* piglet.

по́росл|ь, и *f.* verdure, shoots.

по́рох, а (у), *pl.* **~а́, ~о́в** *m.* gunpowder; powder.

поро́ч|ный (~ен, ~на) *adj.*
1 (*безнравственный*) depraved; wanton.
2 (*неправильный*) faulty; fallacious; **п. круг** vicious circle.

порош|о́к, ка́ *m.* powder.

порт, а, о ~е, в ~у́, *pl.* **~ы́, ~о́в** *m.* port; (*гавань*) harbour; (*comput.*) port; **возду́шный п.** airport; **морско́й п.** seaport.

порта́л, а *m.* (*comput.*) portal.

портати́в|ный (~ен, ~на) *adj.* portable.

портве́йн, а *m.* port (*wine*).

по́ртик, а *m.* portico.

по́р|тить, чу, тишь *impf.* (*of* ▸ **ис~**)
1 (*аппетит, вечер, настроение, ребёнка*) to spoil; (*машину, здоровье, зрение*) to damage.
2 (*развращать*) to corrupt.

по́р|титься, чусь, тишься *impf.* (*of* ▸ **ис~**)
1 (*о здоровье, погоде, отношениях*) to deteriorate; (*о продуктах*) to go off; (*о зубах*) to decay; to rot; **отноше́ния ста́ли п.** relations have begun to deteriorate.
2 (*о механизме*) to get out of order.
3 (*нравственно*) to become corrupt.

портни́х|а, и *f.* dressmaker.

портн|о́й, о́го *m.* tailor.

портре́т, а *m.* portrait.

портсига́р, а *m.* cigarette case.

португа́л|ец, ьца *m.* Portuguese.

Португа́ли|я, и *f.* Portugal.

португа́л|ка, ки *f. of* ▸ **~ец**

португа́льский *adj.* Portuguese.

портфе́л|ь, я *m.*
1 briefcase.
2 (*pol., comm.*) portfolio.

портье́ *m. indecl.* (*hotel*) porter, doorman.
портье́р|а, ы *f.* portière; (*heavy*) curtain.
портя́нк|а, и *f.* foot binding; puttee.
поруб|и́ть, лю́, ~́ишь *pf.* to chop down (*all or a large number of*).
поруга́|ться, юсь *pf.*
1 to swear, curse.
2 (**с** + *i.*; *coll.*) to fall out (with).
по-ру́сски *adv.* (in) Russian; **говори́ть п.** to speak Russian.
поруч|а́ть, а́ю *impf. of* ▸ **~и́ть**
поруче́ни|е, я *nt.* (*задание*) errand; (*весомое*) mission, assignment; **по ~ю** (+ *g.*) on the instructions (of); (*от имени*) per procurationem (p.p.).
по́руч|ень, ня *m.* handrail.
поруч|и́ть, у́, ~́ишь *pf.* (*of* ▸ **~а́ть**)
1 (*возложить на кого-н. исполнение чего-н.*) to charge, commission; to instruct; **он ~и́л мне переда́ть вам де́ньги** he charged me to hand you the money.
2 (*вверить кого-, что-н. заботе кого-н.*) to entrust.
поруч|и́ться, у́сь, ~́ишься *pf. of* ▸ **руча́ться**
порх|а́ть, а́ю *impf.* (*of* ▸ **~ну́ть**) to flutter, fly about.
порх|ну́ть, ну́, нёшь *pf. of* ▸ **~а́ть**
по́рци|я, и *f.* portion.
по́рш|ень, ня *m.* (*tech.*) (*двигателя*) piston; (*насоса*) plunger.
поры́в, а *m.*
1 (*ветра*) gust; rush.
2 (*fig.*) (*чувства*) fit; upsurge; **п. гне́ва** fit of temper.
порыва́|ть, ю *impf. of* ▸ **порва́ть 2**
поры́вист|ый (~, ~а) *adj.*
1 (*ветер*) gusty.
2 (*движение*) jerky.
3 (*fig.*) (*характер*) impetuous, violent.
пор|ы́ться, о́юсь, о́ешься *pf.* (**в** + *p.*; *coll.*) to rummage (in, among); **п. в па́мяти** to give one's memory a jog.
поря́дков|ый *adj.* ordinal; **~ое числи́тельное** ordinal numeral.
поря́д|ок, ка *m.* order.
1 (*правильное состояние, расположение*): **привести́ в п.** to put in order; **привести́ себя́ в п.** to tidy o.s. up; **всё в ~ке!** everything is all right!; **не в ~ке** out of order, not right.
2 (*последовательность*): **алфави́тный п.** alphabetical order; **по ~ку** in order, in succession.
3 (*способ*) manner, way; procedure; **в обяза́тельном ~ке** without fail.
4 (*mil.*) (*построение*): **боево́й п.** battle order.
5 (*pl.*) (*обычаи*) customs, usages, observances.
поря́доч|ный (~ен, ~на) *adj.*
1 (*честный*) decent; honest; **~ные лю́ди** decent folk.
2 (*coll.*) (*значительный*) fair, considerable; **он п. плут** he is pretty much of a rogue.
поса|ди́ть, жу́, ~́дишь *pf. of* ▸ **сажа́ть**
поса́дк|а, и *f.*
1 (*семян*) planting.
2 (*на судно*) embarkation; (*на поезд, автобус*) boarding.
3 (*aeron.*) landing; **вы́нужденная п.** forced landing.
поса́дочный *adj.* (*aeron.*) landing; **п. биле́т** boarding pass.
поса́хар|ить, ю, ишь *pf. of* ▸ **са́харить**
посве|ти́ть, чу́, ~́тишь *pf.*
1 to shine for a while.
2 (+ *d.*) to hold a light (for).
посви|сте́ть, щу́, сти́шь *pf.* to whistle, give a whistle.
посви́стыва|ть, ю *impf.* to whistle (*softly, from time to time*).
по-сво́ему *adv.* in one's own way; **де́лайте п., поступа́йте п.** have it your own way.
посвя|ти́ть, щу́, ти́шь *pf.* (*of* ▸ **~ща́ть**)
1 (+ *a.* **в** + *a.*) to let (into); **мы вас ~ти́м в на́шу та́йну** we will let you into our secret.
2 (+ *a. and d.*) (*жизнь*) to devote (to), give up (to); (*книгу*) to dedicate (to); **п. себя́ нау́ке** to devote o.s. to (the cause of) learning; **он ~ти́л пе́рвую кни́гу свое́й ма́тери** he dedicated his first book to his mother.
3 (+ *a.* **в** + *nom.-a.*) (*в сан*) to ordain, consecrate; **п. в ры́цари** to knight.
посвяща́|ть, ю *impf. of* ▸ **посвяти́ть**
посе́в, а *m.*
1 (*действие*) sowing.
2 (*то, что посеяно*) crops; **пло́щадь ~ов** sown area, area under crops.
поседе́|ть, ю *pf. of* ▸ **седе́ть**
поселе́н|ец, ца *m.* settler.
поселе́ни|е, я *nt.* settlement.
поселе́н|ка, ~ки *f. of* ▸ **~ец**
посел|и́ть, ю́, и́шь *pf.* (*of* ▸ **~я́ть** *and* ▸ **сели́ть**) to settle; to lodge.
посел|и́ться, ю́сь, и́шься *pf.* (*of* ▸ **~я́ться** *and* ▸ **сели́ться**) to settle, take up residence.
посёл|ок, ка *m.* village; settlement.
посел|я́ть(ся), я́ю(сь) *impf. of* ▸ **~и́ть(ся)**
посереди́не *adv. and prep.* + *g.* in the middle (of).
посети́тел|ь, я *m.* visitor.
посети́тель|ница, ницы *f. of* ▸ **~**
посе|ти́ть, щу́, ти́шь *pf.* (*of* ▸ **~ща́ть**) to visit; **п. ле́кции** to attend lectures.
посеща́|ть, ю *impf. of* ▸ **посети́ть**
посеще́ни|е, я *nt.* visit; (*лекций*) attendance.
посе́|ять, ю *pf. of* ▸ **се́ять**
поси|де́ть, жу́, ди́шь *pf.* to sit awhile.
поска|ка́ть, чу́, ~́чешь *pf. of* ▸ **скака́ть 1, 2**
поскользн|у́ться, у́сь, ёшься *pf.* to slip.
поско́льку *conj.*
1 as far as; **мы путеше́ствуем посто́льку, п. позволя́ют сре́дства** we travel (just) as much as we can afford.
2 (*так как*) in so far as, since; so long as.
поскоре́е *adv.* (*coll.*) somewhat quicker; *int.* **п.!** quick!
посла́ни|е, я *nt.*
1 (*официальное*) dispatch; (*дружеское*) message.
2 (*liter.*) epistle; **Посла́ния** (*bibl.*) the

Epistles.

послáнник, а *m.* envoy, minister.

по|слáть, шлю́, шлёшь *pf.* (*of* ▸ **~сылáть**) to send; **п. по пóчте** to post; **п. привéт** to send one's regards; **п. когó-н. к чёрту** (*fig., coll.*) to tell s.o. to go to hell.

пóсле *adv. and prep.* + *g.* after; afterwards, later (on); (*after a neg.*) since; **п. войны́** after the war; **п. чегó** whereupon; **п. тогó, как** after.

послевоéнный *adj.* post-war.

послéдн|ий *adj.*
1 last; (*решение, слово*) final; **(в) ~ее врéмя, за ~ее врéмя** lately, of late, recently; **(в) п. раз** for the last time.
2 (*самый новый*) (the) latest; **~ие извéстия** the latest news.
3 (*из упомянутых*) the latter.
4 (*coll.*) (*самый плохой*) worst, lowest; **~яя кáпля** the last straw.

послéдовател|ь, я *m.* follower.

послéдовательност|ь, и *f.* succession, sequence.

послéдовател|ьный (~ен, ~ьна) *adj.*
1 (*следующий один за другим*) successive, consecutive.
2 (*логичный*) consistent, logical.

послéд|овать, ую *pf. of* ▸ **слéдовать**[1] ▸ **1, 2**

послéдстви|е, я *nt.* consequence.

послéдующий *adj.* subsequent.

послезáвтра *adv.* the day after tomorrow.

послеобéденный *adj.* after-dinner.

послеродовóй *adj.* post-natal.

послеслóви|е, я *nt.* afterword, postface; concluding remarks.

послóвиц|а, ы *f.* proverb.

послуж|и́ть, ý, ~ишь *pf. of* ▸ **служи́ть 1, 3, 4**

послýша|ть(ся), ю(сь) *pf. of* ▸ **слýшать(ся)**

послýш|ный (~ен, ~на) *adj.* obedient.

послы́ш|аться, ится *pf. of* ▸ **слы́шаться**

посмáтрива|ть, ю *impf.* (**на** + *a.*) to look (at) from time to time.

посмéива|ться, юсь *impf.* to chuckle, laugh softly; **п. в кулáк** to laugh up one's sleeve.

посмéртный *adj.* posthumous.

посмé|ть, ю *pf. of* ▸ **сметь**

посмотр|éть(ся), ю́(сь), ~ишь(ся) *pf. of* ▸ **смотрéть(ся)**

посóби|е, я *nt.*
1 (*денежная помощь*) allowance, benefit; **п. по безрабóтице** unemployment benefit; **п. на детéй** child benefit.
2 (*учебник*) textbook; (*учебный предмет*) (educational) aid; **учéбные ~я** educational supplies; school textbooks.

посовéт|овать(ся), ую(сь) *pf. of* ▸ **совéтовать(ся)**

пос|óл, лá *m.* (*дипломатический представитель*) ambassador.

посол|и́ть, ю́, ~ишь *pf. of* ▸ **соли́ть**

посóльств|о, а *nt.* embassy.

пóсох, а *m.*
1 (*пастуха*) staff, crook.
2 (*епископа, монарха*) crozier.

посп|áть, лю́, и́шь, *past* **~áл, ~алá, ~áло** *pf.* to have a sleep, have a nap.

поспевá|ть, ет *impf. of* ▸ **поспéть**

поспé|ть, ет *pf.* (*of* ▸ **~вáть**) (*coll.*) to ripen.

поспеш|и́ть, ý, и́шь *pf. of* ▸ **спеши́ть 1**

поспéш|ный (~ен, ~на) *adj.* hasty, hurried.

поспóр|ить, ю, ишь *pf.*
1 *pf. of* ▸ **спóрить.**
2 (*заключить пари*) to bet, have a bet.

посреди́ *adv. and prep.* + *g.* in the middle (of), in the midst (of).

посрéдник, а *m.*
1 mediator, intermediary; go-between.
2 (*comm.*) middleman.

посрéдственно *adv.* so-so, mediocrely, not particularly well; **он игрáет в тéннис п.** he is not particularly good at tennis.

посрéдственност|ь, и *f.* (*свойство, о человеке*) mediocrity.

посрéдствен|ный (~, ~на) *adj.*
1 mediocre, middling.
2 (*отметка*) fair, satisfactory.

посрéдством *prep.* + *g.* by means of; with the aid of.

поссóр|ить(ся), ю(сь), ишь(ся) *pf. of* ▸ **ссóрить(ся)**

пост[1]**, á, о ~é, на ~ý,** *pl.* **~ы́** *m.* post; **наблюдáтельный п.** observation post; **занимáть высóкий п.** to hold a high post.

пост[2]**, á, о ~é** *m.*
1 **(в ~é)** (*воздержание от пищи*) fasting; (*fig., coll.*) abstinence.
2 **(в ~ý)** (*eccl.*) fast; **Вели́кий п.** Lent.

постáв|ить[1]**, лю, ишь** *pf. of* ▸ **стáвить**

постáв|ить[2]**, лю, ишь** *pf.* (*of* ▸ **~ля́ть**) (*снабдить*) to supply.

постáвк|а, и *f.* supply; delivery; **мáссовая п.** bulk delivery.

поставля́|ть, ю *impf. of* ▸ **постáвить**[2]

поставщи́к, á *m.* supplier.

постамéнт, а *m.* pedestal, base.

постанов|и́ть, лю́, ~ишь *pf.* to decide, resolve; to decree.

постанóвк|а, и *f.*
1 (*дела, работы*) arrangement, organization.
2 (*theatr.*) staging, production.

постановлéни|е, я *nt.*
1 (*решение*) decision, resolution; **вы́нести п.** to pass a resolution.
2 (*распоряжение*) decree; **издáть п.** to issue a decree.

постарá|ться, юсь *pf. of* ▸ **старáться**

постарé|ть, ю *pf. of* ▸ **старéть 1**

по-стáрому *adv.*
1 (*как раньше*) as before.
2 (*как в старые времена*) as of old.

постел|и́ть, ю́, ~ешь *pf. of* ▸ **стели́ть**

постéл|ь, и *f.* bed; **лечь в п.** to get into bed; **встать с ~и** to get out of bed.

постепéнно *adv.* gradually, little by little.

постепéн|ный (~ен, ~на) *adj.* gradual.

постеснý|ться, юсь *pf. of* ▸ **стесня́ться**

постиг|áть, áю *impf. of* ▸ **~́нуть** *and* ▸ **пости́чь**

пости́гнуть = **пости́чь**

постилá|ть, ю *impf. of* ▸ **постлáть**

постимпрессиони́зм, а *m.* post-Impressionism.

постирá|ть, ю *pf.* to wash.

по|сти́ться, щу́сь, сти́шься *impf.* to fast.

пости́|чь, гну, гнешь, *past* **~г** *pf.* (*of* ▸ **~гáть**)
1 (*понять*) to comprehend, grasp.
2 (*о горе, о несчастье*) to befall, strike; **их ~гло ещё однó несчáстье** yet another misfortune has befallen them.

пост|лáть, елю́, éлешь *pf.* (*of* ▸ **стлать** *and* ▸ **~илáть**) to spread, lay; **п. ковёр** to lay a carpet; **п. постéль** to make one's bed.

постмодерни́зм, а *m.* postmodernism.

постмодерни́стский *adj.* postmodern.

пóст|ный (~ен, ~нá, ~но) *adj.*
1 Lenten; **п. день** (*eccl.*) fast day; **п. обéд** meatless dinner.
2 (*coll.*) (*о мясе*) lean.

постóльку *conj.*: **п., поскóльку** in so far as … .

посторóнн|ий *adj.*
1 (*побочный*) extraneous, outside; **без ~ей пóмощи** unaided.
2 (*чужой*) strange; *as n.* **п., ~его** *m.* stranger; outsider; «**~им вход воспрещён**» 'unauthorized persons not admitted'.

постоя́нно *adv.* constantly, continually.

постоя́н|ный *adj.*
1 constant, continual; **п. посети́тель** constant visitor.
2 (*не временный*) constant; permanent, invariable; **п. áдрес** permanent address; **~ная рабóта** a permanent job; **п. ток** (*elec.*) direct current.
3 **(~ен, ~на)** (*не изменчивый*) constant, unchanging.

посто|я́ть[1], ю́, и́шь *pf.* (*некоторое время*) to stand (*for a while*).

посто|я́ть[2], ю́, и́шь *pf.* (**за** + *a.*) (*защитить*) to stand up (for).

пострадá|вший *p.p. of* ▸ **~ть;** *as n.* **п., ~вшего** *m.* victim.

пострадá|ть, ю *pf. of* ▸ **страдáть 3**

пострéлива|ть, ю *impf.* to fire intermittently.

постреля́|ть, ю *pf.*
1 (*некоторое время*) to do some shooting.
2 (+ *a. or g.*; *coll.*) (*застрелить многих*) to shoot, bag (*a number of*).

пострú|чь, гу́, жёшь, гу́т, *past* **~г, ~гла** *pf. of* ▸ **стричь**

постри́|чься, гу́сь, жёшься, гу́тся, *past* **~гся, ~глась** *pf. of* ▸ **стри́чься 1**

построéни|е, я *nt.* construction.

пострó|ить(ся), ю(сь), ишь(ся) *pf. of* ▸ **стрóить(ся)**

пострóйк|а, и *f.*
1 (*действие*) building, erection, construction.
2 (*здание*) building.

постскри́птум, а *m.* postscript.

поступ|áть(ся), áю(сь) *impf. of* ▸ **~и́ть(ся)**

поступ|и́ть, лю́, ~́ишь *pf.* (*of* ▸ **~áть**)
1 to act; **они́ с ним плóхо ~и́ли** they have treated him badly.
2 (**в, на** + *a.*) (*зачислиться*) to enter, join; **п. в университéт** to enter the university; **п. на рабóту** to start work.
3 (*о посланном*) (*дойти*) to come through; to be received; **~и́ла жáлоба** a complaint has been received, has come in; **п. в продáжу** to go on sale, come on the market.

поступ|и́ться, лю́сь, ~́ишься *pf.* (*of* ▸ **~áться**) (+ *i.*) to waive, forgo; to give up.

поступлéни|е, я *nt.*
1 (*в университет*) entering; (*в партию, клуб*) joining; **п. на воéнную слу́жбу** enlisting, joining up.
2 (*денежное*) receipt; (*в библиотеке*) acquisition.

постýп|ок, ка *m.* action; deed; (*pl., collect.*) behaviour (*Br.*), behavior (*US*).

постуч|áть(ся), ý(сь), и́шь(ся) *pf. of* ▸ **стучáть(ся)**

посты|ди́ться, жу́сь, ди́шься *pf. of* ▸ **стыди́ться**

посты́д|ный (~ен, ~на) *adj.* shameful.

посу́д|а, ы *f.* (*collect.*) crockery; **гли́няная п., фая́нсовая п.** earthenware; **ку́хонная п.** kitchen utensils.

посудомóечн|ый *adj.*: **~ая маши́на** dishwasher, dishwashing machine.

посчастли́в|иться, ится *pf.* (*impers.* + *d.*) to have the luck (to); to be lucky enough (to).

посчитá|ть, ю *pf. of* ▸ **считáть**

посылá|ть, ю *impf. of* ▸ **послáть**

посы́лк|а, и *f.* parcel.

посып|áть, áю *impf. of* ▸ **~́ать**

посы́п|ать, лю, лешь *pf.* (*of* ▸ **~áть**) (+ *i.*) to sprinkle (with).

посы́п|аться, лется *pf.* to begin to fall; (*fig.*) to rain down.

посяг|áть, áю *impf. of* ▸ **~нýть**

посяг|нýть, нý, нёшь *pf.* (*of* ▸ **~áть**) (**на** + *a.*) to encroach (on, upon), infringe (on, upon).

пот, а, о ~́е, в ~ý, *pl.* **~ы́, ~óв** *m.* sweat, perspiration; **весь в ~ý** all of a sweat, bathed in sweat.

по-твóему *adv.*
1 (*по твоему мнению*) in your opinion.
2 (*как ты хочешь*) as you wish.

потемнé|ть, ю *pf. of* ▸ **темнéть 1**

потенциáл, а *m.* potential.

потенциáл|ьный (~ен, ~ьна) *adj.* potential.

потеплéни|е, я *nt.* warm(er) spell.

потеплé|ть, ет *pf. of* ▸ **теплéть**

потерп|éть, лю́, ~́ишь *pf. of* ▸ **терпéть 1**

потёрт|ый (~, ~а) *adj.* shabby, threadbare.

потéр|я, и *f.* loss; *pl.* (*mil.*) losses.

потеря́|ть(ся), ю(сь) *pf. of* ▸ **теря́ть(ся)**

потé|ть, ю *impf.*
1 to sweat, perspire.
2 *impf. of* ▸ **за~**

потé|чь, ку́, чёшь, ку́т, *past* **~́к, ~клá**

pf. to begin to flow.

потихо́ньку *adv.* (*coll.*)
1 (*медленно*) slowly.
2 (*тихо*) softly, noiselessly.
3 (*тайно*) on the sly, secretly.

по́т|ный (~ен, ~на́, ~но) *adj.* sweaty, damp with perspiration.

пото́к, а *m.* stream; flow; **п. слов** flow of words.

потол|о́к, ка́ *m.* ceiling.

потолсте́|ть, ю *pf. of* ▶**толсте́ть**

пото́м *adv.* (*после*) afterwards; (*позже*) later (on); (*затем*) then, after that; **мы п. придём** we shall come later.

пото́м|ок, ка *m.* descendant; (*pl.*) offspring, progeny.

пото́мств|о, а *nt.* (*collect.*) posterity, descendants.

потому́
1 *adv.* that is why.
2 *conj.* **п. что; п. ..., что** because, as; **я не знал об э́том, п. что был в о́тпуске** I did not know about it because I was on leave.

пото́п, а *m.* flood, deluge; **Всеми́рный п.** (*bibl.*) the Flood.

потоп|и́ть, лю́, ~ишь *pf.* (*of* ▶**~ля́ть** *and* ▶**топи́ть**[3] **1**) to sink.

потопля́|ть, ю *impf. of* ▶**потопи́ть**

потороп|и́ть(ся), лю́(сь), ~ишь(ся) *pf. of* ▶**торопи́ть(ся)**

потра́|тить, чу, тишь *pf. of* ▶**тра́тить**

потреби́тел|ь, я *m.* consumer, user.

потреб|и́ть, лю́, и́шь *pf.* (*of* ▶**~ля́ть**) to consume, use.

потребля́|ть, ю *impf. of* ▶**потреби́ть**

потре́бност|ь, и *f.* need, requirement; **испы́тывать п. в чём-н.** to feel a need for sth.

потре́б|овать(ся), ую(сь) *pf. of* ▶**тре́бовать(ся)**

потрево́ж|ить(ся), у(сь), ишь(ся) *pf. of* ▶**трево́жить(ся)**

потр|ёпанный *p.p.p. of* ▶**~епа́ть** *and adj.*
1 (*рубаха, книга*) shabby; tattered.
2 (*fig.*) (*вид*) worn, seedy.

потреп|а́ть(ся), лю́(сь), ~лешь(ся) *pf. of* ▶**трепа́ть(ся)**

потре́ска|ться, ется *pf. of* ▶**тре́скаться**

потро́га|ть, ю *pf.* to touch, run one's hand over; **п. па́льцем** to finger.

потрох|а́, о́в *no sg.* giblets.

потру|ди́ться, жу́сь, ~дишься *pf.* to take pains; to do some work.

потряс|а́ть, а́ю *impf. of* ▶**~ти́**[1]

потряса́|ющий *pres. part. act. of* ▶**~ть** *and adj.* (*coll.*) staggering, stupendous, tremendous.

потрясе́ни|е, я *nt.* shock; (*социальное*) upheaval.

потряс|ти́[1]**, у́, ёшь,** *past* **~, ~ла́** *pf.* (*of* ▶**~а́ть**)
1 to shake; to rock; **п. до основа́ния** to rock to its foundations.
2 (+ *i.*) (*взмахнуть*) to brandish, shake; **п. кулако́м** to shake one's fist.
3 (*fig.*) (*удивить*) to shake; to stagger, stun.

потряс|ти́[2]**, у́, ёшь,** *past* **~, ~ла́** *pf.* to shake (*a little, a few times*).

потускне́|ть, ет *pf. of* ▶**тускне́ть**

потух|а́ть, а́ю *impf. of* ▶**~нуть**

поту́х|нуть, ну, нешь, *past* **~, ~ла** *pf.* (*of* ▶**ту́хнуть**[1] *and* ▶**~а́ть**) to go out; (*fig.*) to be extinguished, die out.

потуш|и́ть[1]**, у́, ~ишь** *pf. of* ▶**туши́ть**[1]

потуш|и́ть[2]**, у́, ~ишь** *pf.* (*мясо*) to stew (*for a while*).

потя́гива|ться, юсь *impf. of* ▶**потяну́ться**

потян|у́ть, у́, ~ешь *pf.* to begin to pull.

потян|у́ться, у́сь, ~ешься *pf.* (*of* ▶**потя́гиваться**) to stretch o.s.; (*растянуться*) to stretch out.

поу́жина|ть, ю *pf. of* ▶**у́жинать**

поумне́|ть, ю *pf. of* ▶**умне́ть**

поуча́|ть, ю *impf.* (*coll., iron.*) to preach (at), lecture.

поучи́тел|ьный (~ен, ~ьна) *adj.* instructive.

поуч|и́ться, у́сь, ~ишься *pf.* to study (*for a while*); to do a bit of studying.

похвал|а́, ы́ *f.* praise; **отозва́ться с ~о́й** (**о** + *p.*) to praise, speak favourably (of).

похвал|и́ть, ю́, ~ишь *pf. of* ▶**хвали́ть**

похва́л|ьный (~ен, ~ьна) *adj.*
1 (*заслуживающий похвалы*) praiseworthy, commendable.
2 (*содержащий похвалу*) laudatory; **~ьная гра́мота** certificate of merit.

похва́ста|ть(ся), ю(сь) *pf. of* ▶**хва́стать(ся)**

похити́тел|ь, я *m.* thief; kidnapper; abductor; hijacker.

похити́тель|ница, ницы *f. of* ▶**~**

похи́|тить, щу, тишь *pf.* (*of* ▶**~ща́ть**) (*вещь*) to steal; (*человека*) to kidnap; to abduct; (*самолёт*) to hijack.

похища́|ть, ю *impf. of* ▶**похи́тить**

похище́ни|е, я *nt.* theft; kidnapping; abduction; hijacking.

похлёбк|а, и *f.* soup, broth.

похло́па|ть, ю *pf.* to slap, clap (a few times).

похме́ль|е, я *nt.* hangover; **быть с ~я** to have a hangover.

похо́д, а *m.*
1 (*mil.*) march; (*naut.*) cruise.
2 (*mil.; fig.*) campaign; **кресто́вый п.** (*also fig.*) crusade.
3 (*прогулка*) walking tour, hike.

похо|ди́ть[1]**, жу́, ~дишь** *impf.* (**на** + *a.*) to resemble, look like.

похо|ди́ть[2]**, жу́, ~дишь** *pf.* to walk (*for a while*).

похо́дк|а, и *f.* gait, walk, step.

похожде́ни|е, я *nt.* adventure, escapade.

похо́ж|ий (~, ~а) *adj.*
1 resembling, alike; (**на** + *a.*) like; **он ~ на де́да** he is like his grandfather; **они́ о́чень ~и друг на дру́га** they are very much alike.
2 (*coll.*): **~е** it appears, it would appear; **~е на то, что...** it looks as if ...; **он, ~е, бо́лен** it would appear he is ill.

похолода́ни|е, я *nt.* fall of temperature, cold spell.

похолода́|ть, ет *pf. of* ▸ **холода́ть**

похолоде́|ть, ю *pf. of* ▸ **холоде́ть**

похорон|и́ть, ю́, ~́ишь *pf. of* ▸ **хорони́ть**

похоро́нн|ый *adj.* funeral; **~ое бюро́** undertaker's.

по́хор|оны, о́н, она́м *no sg.* funeral; burial.

по-хоро́шему *adv.* in an amicable way.

похотли́в|ый (~, ~а) *adj.* lustful, lewd, lascivious.

похуде́|ть, ю *pf. of* ▸ **худе́ть**

поцара́па|ть, ю *pf.* to scratch (slightly).

поцара́па|ться, юсь *pf.* to get slightly scratched.

поцел|ова́ть(ся), у́ю(сь) *pf. of* ▸ **целова́ть(ся)**

поцелу́|й, я *m.* kiss.

по́чв|а, ы *f.*
1 soil, ground, earth.
2 (*fig.*) (*основа*) foundation, basis; **на ~е** (+ *g.*) owing (to), because (of).

почём *interrog. and rel. adv.* (*coll.*) how much; **п. сего́дня я́блоки?** how much are apples today?

почему́
1 *interrog. and rel. adv.* why; **п. вы так ду́маете?** why do you think that?
2 *as conj.* (and) so; which is why; **она́ простуди́лась, п. и оста́лась до́ма** she has caught a cold, which is why she has stayed at home.

почему́-либо = **почему́-нибудь**

почему́-нибудь *adv.* for some reason or other.

почему́-то *adv.* for some reason.

по́черк, а *m.* handwriting; (*fig.*) hallmark.

почерне́|ть, ю *pf. of* ▸ **черне́ть 1**

поче|са́ть(ся), шу́(сь), ~́шешь(ся) *pf. of* ▸ **чеса́ть(ся)**

почёт, а *m.* honour (*Br.*), honor (*US*); respect, esteem; **быть в ~е у кого́-н.** to stand high in s.o.'s esteem.

почёт|ный *adj.*
1 (*пользующийся почётом*) honoured (*Br.*), honored (*US*); **п. гость** guest of honour (*Br.*), honor (*US*).
2 (*избираемый в знак почёта*) honorary; **п. член** honorary member.
3 **(~ен, ~на)** (*являющийся проявлением почёта; доставляющий почёт*) honourable (*Br.*), honorable (*US*).

почин|и́ть, ю́, ~́ишь *pf.* (*of* ▸ **чини́ть**) to repair, mend.

почи́нк|а, и *f.* repairing, mending; **отда́ть что́-н. в ~у** to have sth. repaired, mended.

почи́|стить, щу, стишь *pf. of* ▸ **чи́стить**

почита́|ть, ю *pf.* to read (*a little, for a while*).

по́чк|а[1]**, и** *f.* (*bot.*) bud.

по́чк|а[2]**, и** *f.* (*anat.*) kidney; **иску́сственная п.** (*med.*) kidney machine.

по́чт|а, ы *f.*
1 (*система*) post; **возду́шная п.** airmail; **электро́нная п.** email; **посла́ть по ~е, ~ой** to send by post, post.
2 (*письма*) (the) post, (the) mail; **пришла́ ли п.?** has the post come?
3 (*учреждение*) post office.

почтальо́н, а *m.* postman, postwoman (*Br.*), letter carrier (*US*).

почтальо́нк|а, и *f.* (*coll.*) postwoman (*Br.*), letter carrier (*US*).

почта́мт, а *m.* main post office (*of city or town*).

почте́ни|е, я *nt.* respect, esteem; deference.

почти́ *adv.* almost, nearly; **п. ничего́** next to nothing; **п. что** = **п.**

почти́тел|ьный (~ен, ~ьна) *adj.* respectful, deferential.

почт|о́вый *adj. of* ▸ **~́а; п. и́ндекс** postcode (*Br.*), Zip code (*US*); **~о́вая ка́рточка** postcard; **~о́вая ма́рка** (postage) stamp; **~о́вое отделе́ние** post office; **п. я́щик** letter box, postbox (*Br.*), mailbox (*US*); (*comput.*) mailbox.

почу́вств|овать, ую *pf. of* ▸ **чу́вствовать**

пошатн|у́ться, у́сь, ёшься *pf.*
1 to sway, totter, stagger.
2 (*fig.*) to be shaken; **её здоро́вье ~у́лось** her health has suffered.

пошевел|и́ть(ся), ю́(сь), ~и́шь(ся) *pf. of* ▸ **шевели́ть(ся)**

пошевельн|у́ть(ся), у́(сь), ёшь(ся) *pf.* (*coll.*) = **пошевели́ть(ся)**

пош|ёл, ла́ *see* ▸ **пойти́**

по́шлин|а, ы *f.* duty; **и́мпортная п.** import duty; **э́кспортная п.** export duty.

по́шлост|ь, и *f.*
1 (*свойство*) vulgarity, commonness.
2 (*замечание*) trite remark, banality; **говори́ть ~и** to utter banalities.

по́шл|ый (~, ~á, ~о) *adj.*
1 (*низкий*) vulgar; **у него́ о́чень ~ые вку́сы** he has very vulgar tastes.
2 (*банальный*) trite, banal; **~ая по́весть** banal story.

пошум|е́ть, лю́, и́шь *pf.* to make a bit of a noise.

пошу|ти́ть, чу́, ~́тишь *pf. of* ▸ **шути́ть**

поща|ди́ть, жу́, ди́шь *pf. of* ▸ **щади́ть**

пощеко|та́ть, чу́, ~́чешь *pf. of* ▸ **щекота́ть**

пощёчин|а, ы *f.* slap in the face (*also fig.*); **дать ~у** (+ *d.*) to slap in the face.

пощу́па|ть, ю *pf. of* ▸ **щу́пать**

поэ́зи|я, и *f.* poetry.

поэ́м|а, ы *f.* (narrative) poem (*usu. of large proportions*).

поэ́т, а *m.* poet.

поэте́сс|а, ы *f.* poetess.

поэ́тому *adv.* therefore, and so.

по|ю́[1]**, ёшь** *see* ▸ **петь**

по|ю́[2]**, ~́ишь** *see* ▸ **пои́ть**

появ|и́ться, лю́сь, ~́ишься *pf.* (*of* ▸ **~ля́ться**) to appear.

появле́ни|е, я *nt.* appearance.

появля́|ться, юсь *impf. of* ▸ **появи́ться**

по́яс, а, *pl.* **~á, ~о́в** *m.*

1 belt; **спаса́тельный п.** lifebelt.
2 (*талия*) waist; **по п.** up to the waist, waist-deep, waist-high.
3 (*geog., econ.*) zone, belt.

поясне́ни|е, я *nt.* explanation.

поясн|и́ть, ю́, и́шь *pf.* (*of* ▸ **~я́ть**) to explain, elucidate.

поясни́ц|а, ы *f.* small of the back; **боль в ~е** lumbago.

поясн|я́ть, я́ю *impf. of* ▸ **~и́ть**

праба́бушк|а, и *f.* great-grandmother.

пра́вд|а, ы *f.*
1 truth; the truth; **су́щая п.** the honest truth; **э́то п.** it is true; it is the truth; **по ~е сказа́ть, говоря́** to tell the truth.
2 (*справедливость*) justice; **иска́ть ~ы** to seek justice.
3 : **п.?** is that so?; really?; **п. (ли), что он умира́ет?** is it true that he is dying?; **не п. ли?** *in interrog. sentences indicates that affirmative answer is expected*; **вы погаси́ли свет, не п. ли?** you (did) put out the light, didn't you?
4 (*as concessive conj.*) true; **п., я ему́ не написа́л, но я вот-во́т собира́лся позвони́ть** true I had not written to him, but I was on the point of phoning.

правди́в|ый (~, ~а) *adj.*
1 true; veracious; **п. расска́з** true story.
2 (*человек*) truthful; upright; **п. отве́т** honest answer.

правдоподо́б|ный (~ен, ~на) *adj.* probable, likely; plausible.

пра́вед|ный (~ен, ~на) *adj.*
1 (*благочестивый*) righteous; upright.
2 (*справедливый*) just.

пра́вил|о, а *nt.*
1 rule; regulation; **~а у́личного движе́ния** traffic regulations; **как п.** as a rule.
2 (*принцип*) rule, principle; **взять за п.** to make it a rule; **взять себе́ за п.** (+ *inf.*) to make a point (of).

пра́вильно *adv.*
1 (*верно*) rightly; correctly; **п. ли иду́т ва́ши часы́?** is your watch right?
2 (*регулярно*) regularly.

пра́вил|ьный (~ен, ~ьна) *adj.*
1 (*верный*) right, correct; **п. отве́т** the right answer; **~ьно** (*as pred.*) it is correct; **~ьно!** that's right!
2 (*регулярный*) regular; **~ьные черты́ лица́** regular features.

прави́тел|ь, я *m.* ruler.

прави́тельственн|ый *adj.* governmental; government; **~ое учрежде́ние** government establishment.

прави́тельств|о, а *nt.* government.

пра́в|ить[1], лю, ишь *impf.* (+ *i.*) to rule (over), govern.

пра́в|ить[2], лю, ишь *impf.* to correct; **п. корректу́ру** (*typ.*) to read, correct proofs.

пра́вк|а, и *f.* correcting; **п. корректу́ры** (*typ.*) proofreading.

правле́ни|е, я *nt.*
1 (*действие*) government; **фо́рма ~я** form of government.
2 (*орган*) board, governing body.

пра́внук, а *m.* great-grandson.

пра́внучк|а, и *f.* great-granddaughter.

пра́в|о, а, *pl.* **~а́** *nt.*
1 (*наука*) law; **гражда́нское п.** civil law; **уголо́вное п.** criminal law.
2 (*свобода*) right; **(води́тельские) ~а́** driving licence (*Br.*), driver's license (*US*); **п. го́лоса, избира́тельное п.** the vote, suffrage; **~а́ челове́ка** human rights; **по ~у** by rights; **име́ть п. (на** + *a.*) to have the right (to), be entitled (to).

правове́р|ный (~ен, ~на) *adj.* (*relig.*) orthodox.

правозащи́тник, а *m.* human rights activist.

правозащи́тни|ца, цы *f. of* ▸ **~к**

правоме́р|ный (~ен, ~на) *adj.* (*действие, поступок*) lawful, rightful; (*вопрос, сомнение*) legitimate.

правомо́ч|ный (~ен, ~на) *adj.* competent, authorized.

правонаруше́ни|е, я *nt.* infringement of the law, offence.

правонаруши́тел|ь, я *m.* offender.

правоохрани́тельн|ый *adj.* law enforcement; **~ые о́рганы** law enforcement agencies.

правописа́ни|е, я *nt.* spelling, orthography.

правопоря́д|ок, ка *m.* law and order.

правосла́ви|е, я *nt.* (*relig.*) Orthodoxy.

правосла́вн|ый *adj.* (*relig.*) orthodox; **~ая це́рковь** Orthodox Church; *as n.* **п., ~ого** *m.*, **~ая, ~ой** *f.* member of the Orthodox Church.

правосу́ди|е, я *nt.* justice.

правот|а́, ы́ *f.* rightness; (*leg.*) innocence.

пра́в|ый[1] *adj.*
1 (*по направлению*) right; right-hand; (*naut.*) starboard; **~ая рука́** (*fig.*) right-hand man.
2 (*pol.*) right-wing, right; **~ая па́ртия** party of the right.

пра́в|ый[2] (~, ~а́, ~о) *adj.* right, correct; **вы не совсе́м ~ы** you are not quite right.

Пра́г|а, и *f.* Prague.

прагмати́зм, а *m.* pragmatism.

прагмати́ческий *adj.* pragmatic.

пра́дед, а *m.*
1 great-grandfather.
2 (*pl.*) ancestors, forefathers.

праде́душк|а, и *m. dim. of* ▸ **пра́дед 1**

пра́здник, а *m.*
1 (public) holiday; (*религиозный*) (religious) feast, festival; **по ~ам** on high days and holidays.
2 (*день радости, торжества*) festive occasion; **по слу́чаю ~а** to celebrate the occasion.

пра́здничн|ый *adj.* holiday; festive; **п. день** holiday; **~ое настрое́ние** festive mood.

пра́здн|овать, ую *impf.* (*of* ▸ **от~**) to celebrate.

пра́зд|ный (~ен, ~на) *adj.* idle, inactive; empty; **~ное любопы́тство** idle curiosity.

пра́ктик|а, и *f.*

1 practice; **на ~е** in practice; **вам не хвата́ет разгово́рной ~и** you need more conversational practice.
2 (*форма обучения*) practical work.
3 (*работа врача, юриста*) practice.

практика́нт, а *m.* trainee.

практика́нт|ка, ки *f. of* ▸ ~

практик|ова́ть, у́ю *impf.*
1 to practise (*Br.*), practice (*US*).
2 (*о враче, юристе*) to practise (*Br.*), practice (*US*).

практик|ова́ться, у́юсь *impf.*
1 (**в** + *p.*) to practise (*Br.*), practice (*US*); **п. в игре́ на скри́пке** to practise the violin.
2 *pass. of* ▸ **~ова́ть; э́тот приём бо́льше не ~у́ется** this method is no longer used.

практи́ческ|ий *adj.* practical; **~ие заня́тия** practical training.

практи́ч|ный (~ен, ~на) *adj.* practical.

прах, а *no pl., m.*
1 (*liter.*) (*пыль*) dust, earth; **обрати́ть в п., пове́ргнуть в п.**
2 (*rhet.*) (*умершего*) ashes, remains; **мир ~́у его́** may he rest in peace.

пра́чечн|ая, ой *f.* laundry; **п. самообслу́живания** (*автоматическая*) launderette.

пра́чк|а, и *f.* laundress.

пращ|а́, и́, *g. pl.* **~е́й** *f.* sling (*weapon*).

пре...[1] *adj. pref. indicating superl. degree* very, most, exceedingly.

пре...[2] *vbl. pref. indicating action in extreme degree or superior measure* sur-, over-, out- (*cf.* ▸ **пере...**).

превали́р|овать, ую *impf.* (**над** + *i.*) to prevail (over).

превзо|йти́, йду́, йдёшь, *past* **~шёл, ~шла́** *pf.* (*of* ▸ **превосходи́ть**) (**в** + *p. or* + *i.*) to surpass (in); to excel (in); **п. все ожида́ния** to exceed all expectations.

превозмога́|ть, ю *impf. of* ▸ **превозмо́чь**

превозмо́|чь, гу́, ~́жешь, ~́гут, *past* **~г, ~гла́** *pf.* (*of* ▸ **~га́ть**) to overcome, surmount.

превознес|ти́, у́, ёшь, *past* **~̈, ~ла́** *pf.* (*of* ▸ **превозноси́ть**) to extol.

превозно|си́ть, шу́, ~́сишь *impf. of* ▸ **превознести́**

превосхо|ди́ть, жу́, ~́дишь *impf. of* ▸ **превзойти́**

превосхо́д|ный (~ен, ~на) *adj.*
1 superb, outstanding.
2 : **~ная сте́пень** (*gram.*) superlative degree.

превосхо́дств|о, а *nt.* superiority.

превра|ти́ть, щу́, ти́шь *pf.* (*of* ▸ **~ща́ть**) (**в** + *a.*) to turn (to, into), convert (into); **п. в ка́мень** to turn to stone.

превра|ти́ться, щу́сь, ти́шься *pf.* (*of* ▸ **~ща́ться**) (**в** + *a.*) to turn (into), change (into).

превра́т|ный (~ен, ~на) *adj.* wrong, false.

превраща́|ть(ся), ю(сь) *impf. of* ▸ **преврати́ть(ся)**

превраще́ни|е, я *nt.* transformation, conversion.

превы́|сить, шу, сишь *pf.* (*of* ▸ **~ша́ть**) to exceed; **п. полномо́чия** to exceed one's authority.

превыша́|ть, ю *impf. of* ▸ **превы́сить**

превы́ше *adv.* far above; **п. всего́** above all.

прегра́д|а, ы *f.* barrier; obstacle.

прегра|ди́ть, жу́, ди́шь *pf.* (*of* ▸ **~жда́ть**) to bar, obstruct, block; **п. путь кому́-н.** to bar s.o.'s way.

прегражда́|ть, ю *impf. of* ▸ **прегради́ть**

преда|ва́ть(ся), ю́(сь), ёшь(ся) *impf. of* ▸ **преда́ть(ся)**

пре́данност|ь, и *f.* devotion.

пре́дан|ный (~, а) *p.p.p. of* ▸ **преда́ть** *and adj.* **(~, ~на)** (+ *d.*) devoted (to); (*делу*) dedicated (to); **п. друг** staunch friend.

преда́тел|ь, я *m.* traitor.

преда́тель|ница, ницы *f. of* ▸ ~

преда́тельский *adj.* treacherous (*also fig.*).

преда́тельств|о, а *nt.* treachery, betrayal.

пре|да́ть, да́м, да́шь, да́ст, дади́м, дади́те, даду́т, *past* **~́дал, ~дала́, ~́дало** *pf.* (*of* ▸ **~дава́ть**)
1 (+ *d.*) (*отдать*) to hand over (to), commit (to); **п. забве́нию** to consign to oblivion; **п. земле́** to commit to the earth.
2 (*изменить*) to betray.

пре|да́ться, да́мся, да́шься, да́стся, дади́мся, дади́тесь, даду́тся, *past* **~да́лся, ~дала́сь** *pf.* (*of* ▸ **~дава́ться**) (+ *d.*) to give o.s. up (to); **п. отча́янию** to give way to despair.

предвари́тельно *adv.* in advance, beforehand.

предвари́тел|ьный (~ен, ~ьна) *adj.* (*замечания, работа*) preliminary; (*продажа, заказ*) advance; **п. пока́з** preview; **~ьное усло́вие** precondition.

предвеща́|ть, ю *impf.* (*no pf.*) herald, presage, portend; **ту́чи ~ли грозу́** the clouds heralded a storm.

предвзя́т|ый (~, ~а) *adj.* prejudiced, biased.

предви́дени|е, я *nt.* foresight; (*предсказание*) prediction.

предви́|деть, жу, дишь *impf.* (*no pf.*) to foresee; (*предсказать*) to predict.

предвкуша́|ть, ю *impf.* to look forward (to).

предвкуше́ни|е, я *nt.* (*pleasurable*) anticipation; **в ~и** (+ *g.*) in anticipation (of).

предводи́тел|ь, я *m.* leader.

предвое́нный *adj.* pre-war.

предвосхи́|тить, щу, тишь *pf.* (*of* ▸ **~ща́ть**) to anticipate.

предвосхища́|ть, ю *impf. of* ▸ **предвосхи́тить**

предвы́борн|ый *adj.* (pre-)election; **~ая кампа́ния** election campaign.

предго́р|ье, ья, *g. pl.* **~ий** *nt.* (*often pl.*) foothills.

преде́л, а *m.* limit; bound; **в ~ах** (+ *g.*) within, within the limits (of), within the bounds (of); **за ~ами** (+ *g.*) outside, beyond; **в ~ах досяга́емости** within reach.

преде́л|ьный *adj.*
1 *adj. of* ▸ **~; п. во́зраст** age limit; **п. срок** time limit, deadline.

2 (*крайний*) maximum; utmost; **с ~ьной я́сностью** with the utmost clarity.

предзнаменова́ни|е, я *nt.* omen, augury.

предисло́ви|е, я *nt.* preface, foreword.

предлага́|ть, ю *impf. of* ▸ **предложи́ть**

предло́г[1], а *m.* pretext; **под ~ом** (+ *g.*) on the pretext (of).

предло́г[2], а *m.* (*gram.*) preposition.

предложе́ни|е[1], я *nt.*
1 (*помощи*) offer; (*идея*) suggestion, proposition; (*брака*) proposal (of marriage); **сде́лать п. кому́-н.** to propose (marriage) to s.o.
2 (*на заседании*) proposal, motion; **внести́ п.** to introduce a motion; **отклони́ть п.** to turn down a proposal.
3 (*econ.*) supply; **зако́н спро́са и ~я** law of supply and demand.

предложе́ни|е[2], я *nt.* (*gram.*) sentence.

предлож|и́ть, у́, ~́ишь *pf.* (*of* ▸ **предлага́ть**)
1 (*помощь, услуги*) to offer.
2 (*решение, проект*) to propose; to suggest; **мы ~и́ли ей обрати́ться к врачу́** we suggested that she should see a doctor.
3 (*задать*) to put, set; **п. зада́чу** to set a problem.
4 (*потребовать*) to order, require; **им ~и́ли освободи́ть кварти́ру** they have been ordered to vacate their apartment.

предме́ст|ье, ья, *g. pl.* **~ий** *nt.* suburb.

предме́т, а *m.*
1 object; (*вещь*) article, item; (*pl.*) goods; **~ы пе́рвой необходи́мости** necessities.
2 (*тема*) subject, topic, theme; (+ *g.*) object (of); **п. спо́ра** point at issue.
3 (*в школе*) subject.
4 (*цель*) object; **на п.** (+ *g.*) with the object (of).

предназнач|а́ть, а́ю *impf. of* ▸ **~́ить**

предназна́ч|ить, у, ишь *pf.* (*of* ▸ **~а́ть**) (**для** + *g. or* **на** + *a.*) intend (for); **мы ~или э́ти де́ньги для поку́пки автомоби́ля** we set aside this money to buy a car.

преднаме́рен|ный (~, ~на) *adj.* premeditated; deliberate.

пре́д|ок, ка *m.* forefather, ancestor; (*pl.*) forbears.

предопределе́ни|е, я *nt.* predestination.

предоста́в|ить, лю, ишь *pf.* (*of* ▸ **~ля́ть**)
1 (+ *d. and inf.*) (*дать право*) to let; to leave; **нам ~или сами́м реши́ть де́ло** we were left to decide the matter for ourselves.
2 (*дать*) to give, grant; **п. креди́т** to give credit; **п. пра́во** to concede a right; **п. возмо́жность** to afford an opportunity, give a chance.

предоставля́|ть, ю *impf. of* ▸ **предоста́вить**

предостерега́|ть, ю *impf. of* ▸ **предостере́чь**

предостереже́ни|е, я *nt.* warning, caution.

предостере́|чь, гу́, жёшь, гу́т, *past* **~́г, ~гла́** *pf.* (*of* ▸ **~га́ть**) (**от** + *g.*) to warn (against), caution (against).

предосторо́жност|ь, и *f.*
1 (*осторожное поведение*) caution; **ме́ры ~и** precautionary measures, precautions.
2 (*мера*) precaution.

предотвра|ти́ть, щу́, ти́шь *pf.* (*of* ▸ **~ща́ть**) to prevent, avert; to stave off; **п. войну́** to avert a war; **п. опа́сность** to stave off, avert danger.

предотвраща́|ть, ю *impf. of* ▸ **предотврати́ть**

предохрани́тел|ь, я *m.* guard, safety device; (*elec.*) fuse.

предохрани́тельный *adj.* (*tech.*) safety; protective; **п. кла́пан** safety valve.

предохран|и́ть, ю́, и́шь *pf.* (*of* ▸ **~я́ть**) (**от** + *g.*) to protect (from, against).

предохран|и́ться, ю́сь, и́шься *pf.* (*of* ▸ **~я́ться**) (**от** + *g.*) to protect o.s. (from, against).

предохран|я́ть(ся), я́ю(сь) *impf. of* ▸ **~и́ть(ся)**

предписа́ни|е, я *nt.* order, injunction; (*pl.*) directions, instructions; (*med.*) prescription; **по ~ю врача́** on doctor's orders.

предпле́ч|ье, ья, *g. pl.* **~ий** *nt.* (*anat.*) forearm.

предполага́емый *pres. part. pass. of* ▸ **предполага́ть** *and adj.* proposed.

предполага́|ть, ю *impf.*
1 *impf. of* ▸ **предположи́ть.**
2 (*impf. only*) (*намереваться*) to intend, propose.
3 (*impf. only*) (*иметь своим условием*) to presuppose.

предполага́|ться, ется *impf.*
1 to be planned; **сва́дьба ~лась ле́том** the wedding was planned for the summer.
2 (*impers.*): **~ется** it is proposed, it is intended.

предположе́ни|е, я *nt.* supposition, assumption.

предположи́тельно *adv.*
1 hypothetically; supposedly, presumably.
2 (*in parenthesis*) (*вероятно*) probably.

предположи́тельный *adj.* (*дата, результат*) hypothetical; (*доход*) estimated, anticipated.

предполож|и́ть, у́, ~́ишь *pf.* (*of* ▸ **предполага́ть 1**) to suppose, assume; **~́им, что он опозда́л на по́езд** (let us) suppose he missed the train.

предпосле́дний *adj.* penultimate, last but one, next to last; one from the bottom (*on list*).

предпосы́лк|а, и *f.*
1 prerequisite, precondition.
2 (*phil.*) premise.

предпоч|е́сть, ту́, тёшь, *past* **~ёл, ~ла́** *pf.* (*of* ▸ **~ита́ть**) (+ *a. and d.*) to prefer; **п. говя́дину бара́нине** to prefer beef to lamb; **я ~ёл бы идти́ пешко́м** I would rather walk; (+ *inf.*) to choose to; **он ~ёл уйти́** he chose to leave.

предпочита́|ть, ю *impf. of* ▸ **предпоче́сть**

предпочте́ни|е, я *nt.* preference; **отда́ть п.** (+ *d.*) to show a preference (for), give preference.

предпочти́тел|ьный (~ен, ~ьна) *adj.* preferable.

предприи́мчивост|ь, и *f.* enterprise.
предприи́мчив|ый (~, ~а) *adj.* enterprising.
предпринима́тел|ь, я *m.* entrepreneur; businessman.
предпринима́тельств|о, а *no pl., nt.* enterprise; **свобо́дное п.** free enterprise.
предпринима́|ть, ю *impf. of* ▸ **предприня́ть**
предпри|ня́ть, му́, ~́мешь, *past* **~́нял, ~няла́, ~́няло** *pf.* (*of* ▸ **~нима́ть**) to undertake; (*mil., etc.*) to launch; **п. шаги́** to take steps.
предприя́ти|е, я *nt.*
1 (*предпринятое дело*) undertaking, enterprise; (*инициатива*) venture; **риско́ванное п.** risky undertaking, venture.
2 (*econ.*) enterprise, concern, business; (*завод, фабрика*) works; **совме́стное п.** joint venture.
предрасполо́женност|ь, и *f.* (**к** + *d.*) predisposition (to).
предрассу́д|ок, ка *m.* prejudice.
предрека́|ть, ю *impf. of* ▸ **предре́чь**
предре́|чь, ку́, чёшь, ку́т, *past* **~̈к, ~кла́** *pf.* (*of* ▸ **~ка́ть**) to foretell.
предреш|а́ть, а́ю *impf. of* ▸ **~и́ть**
предреш|и́ть, у́, и́шь *pf.* (*of* ▸ **~а́ть**) to predetermine.
председа́тел|ь, я *m.* (*собрания, правления*) chairman; (*общества*) president.
предсказа́ни|е, я *nt.* prediction.
предска|за́ть, жу́, ~́жешь *pf.* (*of* ▸ **~́зывать**) to foretell, predict.
предска́зыва|ть, ю *impf. of* ▸ **предсказа́ть**
представи́тел|ь, я *m.*
1 representative; (*должностное лицо*) (+ *g.*) spokesman (for); **полномо́чный п.** plenipotentiary.
2 (*bot., etc.*) specimen.
представи́тель|ница, ницы *f. of* ▸ **~ 1**
представи́тельств|о, а *nt.*
1 representation, representing.
2 (*collect.*) representation, representatives; **торго́вое п.** trade mission.
предста́в|ить, лю, ишь *pf.* (*of* ▸ **~ля́ть 1**)
1 (*причинить*) to present; **п. интере́с** to be of interest.
2 (*предъявить*) to produce, submit; **п. доказа́тельства** to produce evidence.
3 (+ *a. and d.*) (*познакомить*) to introduce (to), present (to).
4 : **п. (себе́)** to imagine.
5 (*изобразить*) to represent, display.
предста́в|иться, люсь, ишься *pf.* (*of* ▸ **~ля́ться**)
1 (*возникнуть*) to present itself, arise; **~ился слу́чай пое́хать в Москву́** a chance arose to go to Moscow.
2 (+ *d.*) (*познакомиться*) to introduce o.s. (to).
представле́ни|е, я *nt.*
1 introduction; **п. но́вого сотру́дника** introduction of a new colleague.
2 (*theatr.*) performance.
3 (*psych., math.*) representation.
4 (*понимание*) idea, notion, conception; **дать п.** (**о** + *p.*) to give an idea (of); **я не име́ю ни мале́йшего ~я** I have not the faintest idea.
представля́|ть, ю *impf.*
1 *impf. of* ▸ **предста́вить.**
2 (*impf. only*) (*страну, интересы*) to represent.
3 (*являться*) to represent, be, constitute; **п. угро́зу** to represent a threat.
4 : **п. собо́й** (*являться*) to represent, be; to constitute; **э́то ~ет собо́й исключе́ние** this constitutes an exception.
представля́|ться, юсь *impf. of* ▸ **предста́виться**
предсто|я́ть, и́т *impf.* (+ *d.*) to be in prospect (for), lie ahead (of), be at hand; to be in store (for); **~я́ла суро́вая зима́** a hard winter lay ahead; **нам ~и́т столкну́ться со мно́гими неприя́тностями** we are in for a lot of trouble.
предстоя́|щий *pres. part. of* ▸ **~ть** *and adj.* forthcoming; impending; **~щие вы́боры** the forthcoming elections.
предубежде́ни|е, я *nt.* prejudice, bias.
предубежд|ённый (~ён, ~ена́) *adj.* prejudiced, biased (**про́тив** + *g.*: against).
предупреди́тельный *adj.* (*меры*) preventive, precautionary.
предупре|ди́ть, жу́, ди́шь *pf.* (*of* ▸ **~жда́ть**)
1 (**о** + *p.*) to let know beforehand (about), notify in advance (about), warn (about); to give notice (of, about); **п. об увольне́нии за неде́лю** to give a week's notice (*of dismissal*).
2 (*предотвратить*) to prevent, avert; **п. ава́рию** to prevent an accident.
предупрежда́|ть, ю *impf. of* ▸ **предупреди́ть**
предупрежде́ни|е, я *nt.*
1 (*извещение*) notice; notification.
2 (*предотвращение*) prevention.
3 (*предостережение*) warning; (*взыскание*) caution.
предусма́трива|ть, ю *impf. of* ▸ **предусмотре́ть**
предусмотр|е́ть, ю́, ~́ишь *pf.* (*of* ▸ **предусма́тривать**) (*предвидеть*) to envisage, foresee; (*обеспечить*) to provide (for), make provision (for).
предусмотри́тел|ьный (~ен, ~ьна) *adj.* prudent; far-sighted.
предчу́встви|е, я *nt.* presentiment; (*дурного*) foreboding, premonition.
предчу́вств|овать, ую *impf.* to have a presentiment (of, about), have a premonition (of, about).
предше́ственник, а *m.* predecessor; forerunner, precursor.
предше́ственни|ца, цы *f. of* ▸ **~к**
предше́ств|овать, ую *impf.* (+ *d.*) to go in front (of); to precede; **её сме́рти ~овала дли́тельная боле́знь** her death was preceded by a long illness.
предъяв|и́ть, лю́, ~́ишь *pf.* (*of* ▸ **~ля́ть**)
1 to show, produce, present; **п. биле́т** to show one's ticket; **п. доказа́тельства** to produce evidence, present proofs.
2 (*leg., etc.*) to bring (forward); **ему́ ~и́ли**

обвине́ние в поджо́ге he is charged with arson.
предъявля́|ть, ю *impf. of* ▸ **предъяви́ть**
предыду́щ|ий *adj.* previous, preceding; *as n.* **~ее, ~его** *nt.* the foregoing.
прее́мник, а *m.* successor.
прее́мственност|ь, и *f.* succession; (*традиций, культуры*) continuity.
пре́жде
1 *adv.* (*opp.* **пото́м**) (*сначала*) before; first; **п. чем** *as conj.* before.
2 *adv.* (*opp.* **тепе́рь**) (*раньше*) formerly, in former times; before.
3 *prep.* + *g.* before; **они́ пришли́ п. нас** they arrived before us; **п. всего́** first of all, to begin with; (*самое важное*) first and foremost.
преждевре́менно *adv.* prematurely; (*умереть*) before one's time.
преждевре́мен|ный (~ *and* **~ен, ~на)** *adj.* premature, untimely; **~ные ро́ды** (*med.*) premature birth.
пре́жний *adj.* previous, former.
презента́ци|я, и *f.* presentation; launch; **п. кни́ги** book launch.
презервати́в, а *m.* condom.
президе́нт, а *m.* president.
президе́нт|ский *adj. of* ▸ **~; ~ские вы́боры** presidential elections.
президе́нтств|о, а *nt.* presidency.
прези́диум, а *m.* presidium.
презира́|ть, ю *impf.* to despise, hold in contempt.
презре́ни|е, я *nt.* contempt, scorn.
презри́тел|ьный (~ен, ~ьна) *adj.* contemptuous, scornful.
преиму́ществ|о, а *nt.* advantage; **получи́ть п. (пе́ред** + *i.*) to gain an advantage (over).
прейскура́нт, а *m.* price list.
преклон|и́ться, ю́сь, и́шься *pf.* (*of* ▸ **~я́ться**) (**пе́ред** + *i.*) to admire, worship.
преклон|я́ться, я́юсь *impf. of* ▸ **~и́ться**
прекра́сно *adv.*
1 excellently; (*знать, понимать*) perfectly well; **они́ п. зна́ют, что э́то запрещено́** they know perfectly well that it is forbidden.
2 *as int.* excellent!; splendid!
прекра́с|ный (~ен, ~на) *adj.*
1 (*красивый*) beautiful, fine; **в оди́н п. день** one fine day, once upon a time; *as n.* **~ное, ~ного** *nt.* the beautiful.
2 (*отличный*) excellent, capital, first-rate.
прекра|ти́ть, щу́, ти́шь *pf.* (*of* ▸ **~ща́ть**) to stop; (*положить конец*) to put a stop (to), put an end (to); (*отношения*) to break off; **п. войну́** to end the war.
прекра|ти́ться, ти́тся *pf.* (*of* ▸ **~ща́ться**) to cease, end.
прекраща́|ть(ся), ю, ет(ся) *impf. of* ▸ **прекрати́ть(ся)**
прекраще́ни|е, я *nt.* stopping, cessation; **п. вое́нных де́йствий** cessation of hostilities; **п. огня́** ceasefire.
преле́ст|ный (~ен, ~на) *adj.* charming, delightful, lovely.
пре́лест|ь, и *f.* charm, delight; **кака́я п.!** how lovely!
преломле́ни|е, я *nt.*
1 (*phys.*) refraction.
2 (*fig.*) interpretation, construction.
пре́л|ый (~, ~а) *adj.* rotten, fusty.
прель|сти́ться, щу́сь, сти́шься *pf.* (*of* ▸ **~ща́ться**) (+ *i.*) to be attracted (by); to be tempted (by), fall (for).
прельща́|ться, юсь *impf. of* ▸ **прельсти́ться**
прелюбодея́ни|е, я *nt.* adultery.
прелю́ди|я, и *f.* (*mus. and fig.*) prelude.
пре́ми|я, и *f.*
1 (*победителю*) prize; (*работнику*) bonus; **Но́белевская п.** Nobel Prize; **п. О́скар** Oscar.
2 (*fin.*) (*в страховании*) premium; **страхова́я п.** insurance premium.
премье́р|а, ы *f.* (*theatr.*) premiere, opening night.
премье́р-мини́стр, а *m.* prime minister, premier.
пренебрега́|ть, ю *impf. of* ▸ **пренебре́чь**
пренебреже́ни|е, я *nt.*
1 (*презрение*) scorn, contempt, disdain.
2 (*невнимание*) neglect, disregard; **п. свои́ми обя́занностями** neglect of one's duties, dereliction of duty.
пренебрежи́тел|ьный (~ен, ~ьна) *adj.* scornful, disdainful.
пренебре́|чь, гу́, жёшь, гу́т, *past* **~̈г, ~гла́** *pf.* (*of* ▸ **~га́ть**) (+ *i.*)
1 (*презреть*) to scorn, despise; **п. сове́том** to scorn advice.
2 (*обязанностями*) to neglect, disregard.
преоблада́|ть, ет *impf.* to predominate; to prevail.
преобража́|ть(ся), ю(сь) *impf. of* ▸ **преобрази́ть(ся)**
преобра|зи́ть, жу́, зи́шь *pf.* (*of* ▸ **~жа́ть**) to transform.
преобра|зи́ться, жу́сь, зи́шься *pf.* (*of* ▸ **~жа́ться**) to be transformed.
преобразова́ни|е, я *nt.*
1 (*в что-н. другое*) transformation.
2 (*реформа*) reform; reorganization.
преобраз|ова́ть, у́ю *pf.* (*of* ▸ **~о́вывать**)
1 to transform (*also phys., tech.*).
2 (*реформировать*) to reform; (*реорганизовать*) to reorganize.
преобразо́выва|ть, ю *impf. of* ▸ **преобразова́ть**
преодолева́|ть, ю *impf. of* ▸ **преодоле́ть**
преодоле́|ть, ю *pf.* (*of* ▸ **~ва́ть**) to overcome, get over; **п. препя́тствия** to surmount obstacles; **п. тру́дности** to overcome difficulties.
препара́т, а *m.* (*chem., pharm.*) preparation.
препина́ни|е, я *nt.*: **зна́ки ~я** (*gram.*) punctuation marks.
препира́|ться, юсь *impf.* (**с** + *i.*) to wrangle (with), squabble (with).
преподава́тел|ь, я *m.* teacher; (*вуза*) lecturer, instructor.
преподава́тель|ница, ницы *coll. f. of* ▸ **~**

препода|ва́ть, ю́, ёшь *impf.* to teach.

преподнес|ти́, у́, ёшь, *past* **~̈, ~ла́** *pf.* (*of* ▸ **преподноси́ть**) (+ *a. and d.*) to present (with); (*сведения*) to convey; (*сюрприз*) to give.

преподно|си́ть, шу́, ~́сишь *impf. of* ▸ **преподнести́**

препя́тстви|е, я *nt.*
1 obstacle, impediment, hindrance.
2 (*sport*) obstacle; **бег с ~ями, ска́чки с ~ями** steeplechase; **взять п.** to clear an obstacle; (*fig.*) to clear a hurdle.

препя́тств|овать, ую *impf.* (*of* ▸ **вос~**) (+ *d.*) to hinder, impede; to stand in the way (of).

прерв|а́ть, у́, ёшь, *past* **~а́л, ~ала́, ~а́ло** *pf.* (*of* ▸ **прерыва́ть**) (*прекратить*) to break off, sever; (*перебить*) to interrupt, to cut short; **п. молча́ние** to break a silence; **п. ора́тора** to interrupt a speaker; **нас ~а́ли** (*of telephone conversation*) we have been cut off.

прерв|а́ться, ётся, *past* **~а́лся, ~ала́сь, ~а́ло́сь** *pf.* (*of* ▸ **прерыва́ться**)
1 (*приостановиться*) to be interrupted; (*оборваться*) to be broken off.
2 (*о голосе, от волнения*) to break.

препека́|ться, юсь *impf.* (**с** + *i.*) to argue (with).

прерогати́в|а, ы *f.* prerogative.

прерыва́|ть(ся), ю, ет(ся) *impf. of* ▸ **прерва́ть(ся)**

преры́вист|ый (~, ~а) *adj.* (*дыхание, звук*) intermittent; (*линия*) broken, dotted.

пресека́|ть, ю, ешь *impf. of* ▸ **пресе́чь**

пресе́|чь, ку́, чёшь, ку́т, *past* **~̈к, ~кла́** *pf.* (*of* ▸ **~ка́ть**) to cut short, stop; **п. в ко́рне** to nip in the bud.

пресле́довани|е, я *nt.*
1 (*погоня*) pursuit.
2 (*притеснение*) persecution, victimization; **ма́ния ~я** persecution complex.
3 (*leg.*): **суде́бное п.** prosecution.

пресле́дovател|ь, я *m.*
1 (*тот, кто гонится за кем-н.*) pursuer.
2 (*тот, кто притесняет кого-н.*) persecutor.

пресле́д|овать, ую *impf.*
1 (*врага, зверя*) to pursue; (*fig.*) (*о мыслях, чувствах*) to haunt.
2 (*fig.*) (*интересы, замысел, женщину*) to pursue; **п. цель** to pursue an end.
3 (*притеснить*) to persecute.
4 (*leg.*) to prosecute.

пресмыка́ющ|ееся, егося *nt.* reptile.

пресново́дный *adj.* freshwater.

пре́с|ный (~ен, ~на́, ~но) *adj.*
1 (*вода*) fresh, sweet.
2 (*хлеб*) unleavened.
3 (*пища*) flavourless (*Br.*), flavorless (*US*), tasteless; (*fig.*) insipid, vapid.

пресс, а *m.* press.

пре́сс|а, ы *f.* (*collect.*) the press; **ло́жа ~ы** press gallery.

пресс-конфере́нци|я, и *f.* press conference.

пресс|ова́ть, у́ю *impf.* (*of* ▸ **с~**) to press, compress.

пресс-рели́з, а *m.* press release.

пресс-секрета́р|ь, я́ *m.* press secretary.

пресс-це́нтр, а *m.* press office.

престаре́л|ый *adj.* aged, old; **дом ~ых** old people's home.

прести́ж, а *m.* prestige.

прести́ж|ный (~ен, ~на) *adj.* prestigious.

престо́л, а *m.*
1 throne; **взойти́ на п.** to come to the throne; **отре́чься от ~а** to abdicate.
2 (*eccl.*) altar.

преступле́ни|е, я *nt.* crime, offence.

престу́пник, а *m.* criminal; **вое́нный п.** war criminal.

престу́пни|ца, цы *f. of* ▸ **~к**

престу́пност|ь, и *f.* (*collect.*) crime; **организо́ванная п.** organized crime.

престу́п|ный (~ен, ~на) *adj.* criminal.

претенде́нт, а *m.* (**на** + *a.*) (*на престол*) pretender, claimant (to); (*на наследство*) claimant (to); (*на должность*) candidate (for); (*sport*) contender.

претенде́нт|ка, ки *f. of* ▸ **~**

претенд|ова́ть, у́ю *impf.* (**на** + *a.*) (*на престол, на остроумие*) to have pretensions (to); (*на наследство*) to lay claim (to); (*на должность*) to aspire (to); **он ~у́ет на пост мини́стра** he aspires to the position of minister.

прете́нзи|я, и *f.*
1 (*заявление прав*) claim; **заявля́ть ~ю** (**на** + *a.*) to claim, lay claim (to), make claims (on).
2 (*на остроумие*) pretension; **быть в ~и на кого́-н.** to have a grievance against s.o.
3 (*жалоба*) complaint.

претенцио́з|ный (~ен, ~на) *adj.* pretentious, affected.

претерпева́|ть, ю *impf. of* ▸ **претерпе́ть**

претерп|е́ть, лю́, ~́ишь *pf.* (*of* ▸ **~ева́ть**) (*подвергнуться*) to undergo; (*вытерпеть*) to suffer, endure; **план ~е́л измене́ния** the plan has undergone changes.

преувеличе́ни|е, я *nt.* exaggeration; overstatement.

преувели́чива|ть, ю *impf. of* ▸ **преувели́чить**

преувели́ч|ить, у, ишь *pf.* (*of* ▸ **~ивать**) to exaggerate; to overstate.

преуменьш|а́ть, а́ю *impf. of* ▸ **~́ить**

преуме́ньш|ить, у, ишь *pf.* (*of* ▸ **~а́ть**) (*представить меньшим*) to underestimate, minimize; (*представить менее важным*) to belittle; to understate; **п. опа́сность** to underestimate the danger.

преуспева́|ть, ю *impf.*
1 *impf. of* ▸ **преуспе́ть.**
2 (*impf. only*) to thrive, prosper, flourish.

преуспева́|ющий *pres. part. act. of* ▸ **~ть** *and adj.* successful, prosperous.

преуспе́|ть, ю *pf.* (*of* ▸ **~ва́ть 1**) (**в** + *p.*) to succeed (in), be successful (in); **п. в жи́зни** to get on in life.

прецеде́нт, а *m.* precedent.

при *prep.* + *p.*
1 (*около*) by, at; (*в присутствии*) in the presence of; **би́тва при Ватерло́о** the Battle of Waterloo; **письмо́ бы́ло подпи́сано при мне** the letter was signed in my presence.
2 (*под эгидой*) attached to, affiliated to, under

the auspices of (*usu. not translated*); **при магази́не есть кафе́** there is a cafe attached to the shop.
3 (*с собой*) by, with; about, on; **у него́ не́ было при себе́ де́нег** he had no money on him.
4 (*при наличии*) with; (*несмотря на*) for, notwithstanding; **при таки́х тала́нтах он далеко́ пойдёт** with such talent he will go far; **при уча́стии** (+ *g.*) with the participation (of); **при всём том** (*i*) with it all, moreover, (*ii*) for all that; **при чём тут я?** what has it to do with me?
5 (*во время, в эпоху*) in the time of, in the days of; under (*sc.* the rule of); during; **при Ива́не Гро́зном** during the reign of, in the time of Ivan the Terrible.
6 (*указывает на обстоятельства*) by; **при све́те ла́мпы** by lamplight.
7 (*когда*) when; on; in case of; **при перехо́де че́рез у́лицу** when crossing the street; **при усло́вии(, что)** under the condition (that).

при...[1] *vbl. pref. indicating*
1 *completion of action or motion up to given terminal point, as* **прие́хать** to arrive.
2 *action of attaching, as* **пристро́ить** to build on.
3 *direction of action towards speaker, as* **пригласи́ть** to invite.
4 *direction of action from above downward, as* **придави́ть** to press down.
5 *incompleteness or tentativeness of action, as* **приоткры́ть** to open slightly.
6 *exhaustiveness of action, as* **приучи́ть** to train.

при...[2] *as pref. of nn. and adjs. (esp. geog.) indicates juxtaposition or proximity, as* **приозе́рье** lakeside; **прибре́жный, примо́рский** coastal.

приба́в|ить, лю, ишь *pf.* (*of* ▸ **~ля́ть**)
1 (+ *a. or g.*) to add; **к пяти́ п. три** to add three to five; **п. (в ве́се)** to put on (weight).
2 (+ *g.*) (*увеличить*) to increase; **п. ша́гу** to hasten one's steps.

приба́в|иться, ится *pf.* (*of* ▸ **~ля́ться**) to increase; (*о воде*) to rise; (*о луне*) to wax.

прибавле́ни|е, я *nt.* addition; **п. семе́йства** addition to the family; **сказа́ть в п.** to say in addition, add.

прибавля́|ть(ся), ю, ет(ся) *impf. of* ▸ **приба́вить(ся)**

прибалти́йский *adj.* Baltic (= *adjacent to the Baltic Sea, esp. of former Soviet republics*).

Приба́лтик|а, и *f.* the Baltic States (*esp. the former Soviet republics*).

прибега́|ть[1]**, ю** *impf. of* ▸ **прибе́гнуть**

прибега́|ть[2]**, ю** *impf. of* ▸ **прибежа́ть**

прибе́г|нуть, ну, нешь, *past* **~(нул), ~ла** *pf.* (*of* ▸ **~а́ть**[1]) (**к** + *d.*) to resort (to), have resort (to); **п. к си́ле** to resort to force.

прибе|жа́ть, гу́, жи́шь, гу́т *pf.* (*of* ▸ **~га́ть**[2]) (*бегом или в спешке*) to come running.

прибе́жищ|е, а *nt.* refuge; **после́днее п.** (*fig.*) last resort; **найти́ п.** (**в** + *p.*) to take refuge (in).

приберега́|ть, ю *impf. of* ▸ **прибере́чь**

прибере́|чь, гу́, жёшь, гу́т, *past* **~г, ~гла́** *pf.* (*of* ▸ **~га́ть**) to save up.

прибива́|ть, ю *impf. of* ▸ **приби́ть**

прибира́|ть(ся), ю(сь) *impf. of* ▸ **прибра́ть(ся)**

приб|и́ть, ью́, ьёшь *pf.* (*of* ▸ **~ива́ть**)
1 (*гвоздями*) to nail; **п. до́ску к стене́** to nail a board to a wall.
2 (*usu. impers.*) (*волной, течением*) to wash up; **труп ~и́ло к бе́регу** a body was washed ashore.

приближа́|ть, ю *impf. of* ▸ **прибли́зить**

приближа́|ться, юсь *impf. of* ▸ **прибли́зиться**

приближе́ни|е, я *nt.* approach; approaching, drawing near.

приблизи́тельно *adv.* approximately, roughly.

приблизи́тел|ьный (~ен, ~ьна) *adj.* approximate, rough.

прибли́|зить, жу, зишь *pf.* (*of* ▸ **~жа́ть**)
1 (*придвинуть ближе*) to bring nearer, move nearer; (*сделать близким*) to bring closer.
2 (*ускорить*) to hasten, advance.

прибли́|зиться, жусь, зишься *pf.* (*of* ▸ **~жа́ться**) (**к** + *d.*) to approach, draw near; to draw nearer (to), come nearer (to).

прибо́|й, я *m.* surf, breakers.

прибо́р, а *m.*
1 instrument, device, apparatus, appliance.
2 (*комплект*) set; **бри́твенный п.** shaving things.

при|бра́ть, беру́, берёшь, *past* **~бра́л, ~брала́, ~бра́ло** *pf.* (*of* ▸ **~бира́ть**) (*coll.*)
1 (*привести в порядок*) to clear up, clean up, tidy (up); **п. ко́мнату, п. в ко́мнате** to do a room; **п. что-н. к рука́м** to lay one's hands on sth.
2 (*убрать*) to put away.

при|бра́ться, беру́сь, берёшься, *past* **~бра́лся, ~брала́сь, ~бра́ло́сь** *pf.* (*of* ▸ **~бира́ться**) (*coll.*) to tidy o.s. up; to have a clear-up of one's things.

прибре́жн|ый *adj.*
1 (*у берега моря*) coastal; **~ая полоса́** coastal strip.
2 (*у берега реки*) riverside.

прибыва́|ть, ю *impf. of* ▸ **прибы́ть**

при́был|ь, и *f.* profit; **чи́стая п.** net profit.

при́был|ьный (~ен, ~ьна) *adj.* profitable, lucrative.

прибы́ти|е, я *nt.* arrival.

при|бы́ть, бу́ду, бу́дешь, *past* **~́был, ~была́, ~́было** *pf.* (*of* ▸ **~быва́ть**) (*прийти, приехать*) to arrive.

прива́л, а *m.*
1 (*остановка*) halt, stop.
2 (*место остановки*) stopping place.

прива́рива|ть, ю *impf. of* ▸ **привари́ть**

привар|и́ть, ю́, ~́ишь *pf.* (*of* ▸ **~́ивать**) (**к** + *d.*) to weld on (to).

приватиза́ци|я, и *f.* privatization.

приватизи́р|овать, ую *impf.* & *pf.* to privatize.

привез|ти́, у́, ёшь, *past* **~́, ~ла́** *pf.* (*of* ▸ **привози́ть**) to bring (*not on foot*); (*товар, почту*) to deliver.

приверéдлив|ый (~, ~а) *adj.* fussy, finicky.
привéржен|ный (~, ~а) *adj.* (+ *d.*) attached (to), devoted (to).
приве|стú, дý, дёшь, *past* **~л, ~лá** *pf.* (*of* ▸ **приводúть** *and* ▸ **вестú 8**)
1 to bring; (*о дороге*) to lead, take; **он ~л с собóй невéсту** he has brought his fiancée (with him).
2 (**к** + *d.*; *fig.*) to lead (to), bring (to), result (in); **э́то к добрý не ~дёт** no good will come of it.
3 (**в** + *a.*) to put, set (*or translated by v. corresponding to n. governed by* **в**); **п. в бéшенство** to throw into a rage, drive mad; **п. в движéние, в дéйствие** to set in motion, set going; **п. в отчáяние** to reduce to despair; **п. в порядок** to put in order, tidy (up); to arrange, fix.
4 (*слова, доказательства*) to adduce, cite; **п. примéр** to give an example.
привéт, а *m.* greeting(s); regards; **п.!** (*coll.*) hi!; **передáть п.** to send one's regards.
привéтлив|ый (~, ~а) *adj.* friendly; affable; cordial.
привéтстви|е, я *nt.*
1 greeting, salutation.
2 (*речь*) speech of welcome.
привéтств|овать, ую *impf.*
1 (*in past tense also pf.*) to greet; to welcome.
2 (*fig.*) to welcome.
прививá|ть(ся), ю, ет(ся) *impf. of* ▸ **привúть(ся)**
привúвк|а, и *f.* (**от, прóтив** + *g.*; *med.*) inoculation (against); vaccination.
привидéни|е, я *nt.* ghost, spectre (*Br.*), specter (*US*); apparition.
привú|деться, дится *pf. of* ▸ **вúдеться 2**
привилегирóванный *adj.* privileged.
привилéги|я, и *f.* privilege; (*для ветеранов, инвалидов*) benefit.
привин|тúть, чý, тúшь *pf.* (*of* ▸ **~чивать**) to screw on.
привúнчива|ть, ю *impf. of* ▸ **привинтúть**
прив|úть, ью́, ьёшь, *past* **~úл, ~илá, ~úло** *pf.* (*of* ▸ **~ивáть**) (+ *a. and d.*) (*med.*) to inoculate (with); **п. комý-н. óспу** to vaccinate s.o. against smallpox.
прив|úться, ьётся, *past* **~úлся, ~илáсь** *pf.* (*of* ▸ **~ивáться**)
1 (*о вакцине, черенке*) to take.
2 (*fig.*) (*идеи, теория*) to find acceptance; (*мода, интерес*) to catch on.
прúвкус, а *m.* (*посторонний вкус*) aftertaste; (*характерный вкус*) flavour (*Br.*), flavor (*US*).
привлекáтел|ьный (~ен, ~ьна) *adj.* attractive.
привлекá|ть, ю *impf. of* ▸ **привлéчь**
привлé|чь, кý, чёшь, кýт, *past* **~к, ~клá** *pf.* (*of* ▸ **~кáть**)
1 to attract; **п. внимáние** to attract attention.
2 (*сделать участником*) to draw in, involve; **п. на свою́ стóрону** to win over (*to one's side*).
3 (*leg.*) to have up; **п. к судý** to take to court; to put on trial; **п. к отвéтственности/отвéту (за** + *a.*) to make answer (for), call to account (for).
прúвод, а *m.* (*comput., mech.*) drive.
приво|дúть, жý, ~дишь *impf. of* ▸ **привестú**
приво|жý[1], ~дишь *see* ▸ **~дúть**
приво|жý[2], ~зишь *see* ▸ **~зúть**
приво|зúть, жý, ~зишь *impf. of* ▸ **привезтú**
привра́тник, а *m.* doorman, porter.
привста|вáть, ю́, ёшь *impf. of* ▸ **~ть**
привстá|ть, ну, нешь *pf.* (*of* ▸ **~вáть**) to half-rise.
привык|áть, áю *impf. of* ▸ **~нуть**
привы́к|нуть, ну, нешь, *past* **~, ~ла** *pf.* (*of* ▸ **~áть**) (**к** + *d. or* + *inf.*)
1 (*освоиться*) to get accustomed (to), get used (to).
2 (*получить привычку*) to get into the habit (of); **он ~ ругáться** he has got into the habit of swearing.
привы́чк|а, и *f.* habit; **войтú в ~у** to become a habit; **имéть ~у (к** + *d.*) to be accustomed (to); to be in the habit (of); **приобрестú ~у** (+ *inf.*) to get into the habit (of); **сдéлать что-н. по ~е** to do sth. out of habit.
привы́ч|ный (~ен, ~на) *adj.* habitual, usual, customary.
привя́занност|ь, и *f.* (**к** + *d.*) attachment (to); affection (for, towards).
привя|зáть, жý, ~жешь *pf.* (*of* ▸ **~зывать**) (**к** + *d.*) to tie (to), fasten (to), attach (to); **п. верёвку/собáку к забóру** to tie a rope/the dog to the fence.
привя|зáться, жýсь, ~жешься *pf.* (*of* ▸ **~зываться**) (**к** + *d.*)
1 to become attached (to); **онá óчень к вам ~зáлась** she has become very attached to you.
2 to attach o.s. (to); **на дорóге к нам ~зáлся какóй-то нúщий** a beggar attached himself to us on the road.
привя́зыва|ть(ся), ю(сь) *impf. of* ▸ **привязáть(ся)**
приглá|дить, жу, дишь *pf.* (*of* ▸ **~живать**) to smooth.
приглáжива|ть, ю *impf. of* ▸ **приглáдить**
пригла|сúть, шý, сúшь *pf.* (*of* ▸ **~шáть**)
1 to invite, ask; **п. когó-н. на тáнец** to ask s.o. to dance, ask s.o. for a dance; **п. в гóсти** to invite, ask round.
2 (*врача*) to call.
приглашá|ть, ю *impf. of* ▸ **пригласúть**
приглашéни|е, я *nt.*
1 invitation; **по ~ю** by invitation; **разослáть ~я** to send out invitations.
2 (*на работу*) offer (*of employment*).
приглуш|áть, áю *impf. of* ▸ **~úть**
приглуш|úть, ý, úшь *pf.* (*of* ▸ **~áть**) (*звук*) to muffle, deaden; (*голос, речь*) to mute; (*свет, радио*) to turn down; (*огонь*) to choke, damp; (*тоску*) to relieve.
пригля|дéть, жý, дúшь *pf.* (*of*

▶ **~́дывать**) (*coll.*)
[1] (*подыскать*) to find, look out (*Br.*).
[2] (**за** + *i.*) to look after; **п. за детьми́** to look after children.

пригля|де́ться, жу́сь, ди́шься *pf.* (*of* ▶ **~́дываться**) (*coll.*) (**к** + *d.*)
[1] (*внимательно посмотреть*) to look closely (at), scrutinize.
[2] (*привыкнуть*) to get accustomed (to), get used (to); **п. к темноте́** to get accustomed to darkness.

пригля́дыва|ть(ся), ю(сь) *impf. of* ▶ **пригляде́ть(ся)**

приглян|у́ться, у́сь, ~́ешься *pf.* (+ *d.*; *coll.*) to take one's fancy, attract; **она́ сра́зу ~у́лась ему́** he was attracted by her instantly.

при|гна́ть[1], гоню́, го́нишь, *past* **~гна́л, ~гнала́, ~гна́ло** *pf.* (*of* ▶ **~гоня́ть**) (*гоня, доставить*) to drive.

при|гна́ть[2], гоню́, го́нишь, *past* **~гна́л, ~гнала́, ~гна́ло** *pf.* (*of* ▶ **~гоня́ть**) (*приладить*) to fit, adjust.

пригова́рива|ть, ю *impf. of* ▶ **приговори́ть**

пригово́р, а *m.* (*судьи*) sentence; **вы́нести п.** to pass sentence; **отмени́ть п.** to quash a sentence; (*присяжных*) verdict.

приговор|и́ть, ю́, и́шь *pf.* (*of* ▶ **пригова́ривать**) (**к** + *d.*) to sentence (to), condemn (to).

приго|ди́ться, жу́сь, ди́шься *pf.* (+ *d.*) to prove useful (to), come in handy; to stand in good stead.

приго́д|ный (~ен, ~на) *adj.* (**к** + *d.*) fit (for), suitable (for), good (for).

пригоня́|ть, ю *impf. of* ▶ **пригна́ть[1,2]**

пригор|а́ть, а́ет *impf. of* ▶ **~е́ть**

пригор|е́ть, и́т *pf.* (*of* ▶ **~а́ть**) to be burnt.

при́город, а *m.* suburb.

при́городный *adj.* suburban; **п. по́езд** local train.

пригота́влива|ть(ся), ю(сь) *impf.* = **приготовля́ть(ся)**

пригото́в|ить, лю, ишь *pf.* (*of* ▶ **пригота́вливать** *and* ▶ **~ля́ть**) to prepare; **п. обе́д** to cook, prepare a dinner.

пригото́в|иться, люсь, ишься *pf.* (*of* ▶ **пригота́вливаться** *and* ▶ **~ля́ться**) (+ *inf.*) to prepare (to); (**к** + *d.*) to prepare (o.s.) (for).

приготовля́|ть(ся), ю(сь) *impf. of* ▶ **пригото́вить(ся)**

пригро|зи́ть, жу́, зи́шь *pf. of* ▶ **грози́ть 1**

прида|ва́ть, ю́, ёшь *impf. of* ▶ **прида́ть**

прида́|ть, м, шь, ст, ди́м, ди́те, ду́т, *past* **~л, ~ла́, ~ло** *pf.* (*of* ▶ **~ва́ть**)
[1] to add.
[2] (*усилить*) to increase, strengthen; **п. бо́дрости** (+ *d.*) to hearten, put heart (into).
[3] (+ *a. and d.*) (*свойство, состояние*) to give (to), impart (to); (*fig.*) to attach (to); **п. значе́ние** to attach importance (to); **п. фо́рму** to shape (to).

придвига́|ть(ся), ю(сь) *impf. of* ▶ **придви́нуть(ся)**

придви́|нуть, ну, нешь *pf.* (*of* ▶ **~га́ть**) to move (up), draw (up); **~нь(те) кре́сло к пе́чке** draw your chair up to the stove.

придви́|нуться, нусь, нешься *pf.* (*of* ▶ **~га́ться**) (**к** + *d.*) to move.

придво́рн|ый *adj.* court; **п. шут** court jester; *as n.* **п., ~ого** *m.* courtier.

приде́л|ать, аю *pf.* (*of* ▶ **~ывать**) (**к** + *d.*) to fix (to), attach (to).

приде́лыва|ть, ю *impf. of* ▶ **приде́лать**

приде́ржива|ться, юсь *impf.*
[1] (**за** + *a.*) to hold on (to).
[2] (+ *g.*) to hold (to), keep (to) (*also fig.*); (*fig.*) to stick (to), adhere (to); (*моды, советов*) to follow; **п. пра́вой стороны́** to keep to the right; **п. догово́ра** to adhere to an agreement; **п. мне́ния** to hold the opinion, be of the opinion; **п. пра́вил** to stick to, follow the rules.

придира́|ться, юсь *impf. of* ▶ **придра́ться**

при|дра́ться, деру́сь, дерёшься, *past* **~дра́лся, ~драла́сь, ~дра́ло́сь** *pf.* (*of* ▶ **~дира́ться**) (**к** + *d.*) to find fault (with), carp (at); to nag (at), pick (on); **п. к кому́-н. из-за пустяко́в/по пустяка́м** to find fault with s.o. over trifles.

при|ду́ *see* ▶ **~йти́**

приду́м|ать, аю *pf.* (*of* ▶ **~ывать**)
[1] (*отговорку, выход*) to think of, think up; (*приспособление*) to devise, invent; (*сказку, песню*) to make up; (*музыку*) to compose, make up; **наконе́ц я ~ал, что де́лать** at last I have thought of what to do.
[2] (*вообразить*) to imagine.

приду́мыва|ть, ю *impf. of* ▶ **приду́мать**

приду́р|ок, ка *m.* (*coll.*) idiot, fool.

прие́зд, а *m.* arrival, coming; **с ~ом!** welcome!

приезжа́|ть, ю *impf. of* ▶ **прие́хать**

прие́зж|ий *adj.* newly arrived; visiting; *as n.* **п., ~его** *m.*, **~ая, ~ей** *f.* newcomer; (*гость*) visitor.

приём, а *m.*
[1] (*действие*) receiving; reception; **часы́ ~а** (reception) hours, calling hours; (*врача*) surgery (hours) (*Br.*), office hours (*US*).
[2] (*гостей*) reception, welcome; **оказа́ть кому́-н. раду́шный п.** to accord s.o. a hearty welcome.
[3] (*в партию, клуб*) admittance.
[4] (*собрание приглашённых*) reception.
[5] (*лекарства*) dose.
[6] (*отдельное действие*) go; motion, movement; **в оди́н п.** at one go; **испо́лнить кома́нду в три ~а** to execute a command in three movements.
[7] (*способ*) method, way, mode; (*уловка*) device, trick (*also pej.*); (*sport*) hold, grip; **лече́бный п.** method of treatment.
[8] (*radio, TV*) reception.

прие́млем|ый (~, ~а) *adj.* acceptable; admissible.

приёмн|ая, ой *f.*
[1] (*для ожидания*) waiting room.
[2] (*где принимают гостей*) reception room.

приёмник, а *m.* (*радиоприёмник*) radio (set); (*для приёма сигналов*) receiver.

приёмн|ый *adj.*
1 receiving; reception; **п. день** visiting day; **~ые часы́** (reception) hours; (*врача*) surgery (hours) (*Br.*), office hours (*US*); **п. поко́й** casualty ward.
2 selection; entrance; **~ая коми́ссия** selection committee.
3 foster, adoptive; **п. оте́ц** foster-father; **п. сын** adopted son, foster-son.

прие́|хать, ду, дешь *pf.* (*of* ▸ **~зжа́ть**) to arrive, come (*not on foot*).

приж|а́ть, му́, мёшь *pf.* (*of* ▸ **~има́ть**) (**к** + *d.*) to press (to), clasp (to); **п. к груди́** to clasp to one's bosom; **п. к стене́** (*fig.*) to drive into a corner.

приж|а́ться, му́сь, мёшься *pf.* (*of* ▸ **~има́ться**) (**к** + *d.*) (*прислони́ться*) to press o.s. (to, against); (*к матери*) to cuddle up (to), snuggle up (to), nestle up (to); **п. к стене́** to flatten o.s. against the wall.

при|же́чь, жгу́, жжёшь, жгу́т, *past* **~жёг, ~жгла́** *pf.* (*of* ▸ **~жига́ть**) to cauterize, sear.

прижива́|ться, юсь *impf. of* ▸ **прижи́ться**

прижига́|ть, ю *impf. of* ▸ **прижéчь**

прижима́|ть(ся), ю(сь) *impf. of* ▸ **прижа́ть(ся)**

приж|и́ться, иву́сь, ивёшься, *past* **~и́лся, ~ила́сь** *pf.* (*of* ▸ **~ива́ться**)
1 (*прожив, привыкнуть*) to settle down, get acclimatized (*Br.*), acclimated (*US*).
2 (*о растениях*) to take root.

приз, а, *pl.* **~ы́** *m.* prize; **получи́ть п.** to win a prize; **присуди́ть п.** (+ *d.*) to award a prize (to).

призва́ни|е, я *nt.* (*назначение*) vocation, calling; **сле́довать своему́ ~ю** to follow one's vocation; (*склонность*) aptitude; (*музыки, театра*) mission, purpose.

при|зва́ть, зову́, зовёшь, *past* **~зва́л, ~звала́, ~зва́ло** *pf.* (*of* ▸ **~зыва́ть**) (*позвать явиться*) to call, summon; (*позвать делать что-н.*) to call upon, appeal; **п. на вое́нную слу́жбу** to call up (*for mil. service*); **п. к поря́дку** to call to order.

призе́мист|ый (~, ~а) *adj.* stocky, squat; thickset.

приземле́ни|е, я *nt.* (*aeron.*) landing, touchdown.

приземл|и́ться, ю́сь, и́шься *pf.* (*of* ▸ **~я́ться**) (*aeron.*) to land, touch down.

приземля́|ться, юсь *impf. of* ▸ **приземли́ться**

призёр, а *m.* prizewinner.

при́зм|а, ы *f.* prism.

призна|ва́ть(ся), ю́(сь), ёшь(ся) *impf. of* ▸ **призна́ть(ся)**

при́знак, а *m.* sign; indication; **служи́ть ~ом** (+ *g.*) to be a sign (of); **обнару́живать ~и** (+ *g.*) to show signs (of); **не подава́ть ~ов жи́зни** to show no sign of life.

призна́ни|е, я *nt.*
1 (*заявление*) confession, declaration; admission, acknowledgement; **п. вины́** (*обвиняемым*) admission of guilt; **п. вино́вным** (*судом*) guilty verdict; **п. в любви́** declaration of love.
2 (*оценка по достоинству*) recognition; **получи́ть п.** to obtain, win recognition.

при́зн|анный *p.p.p. of* ▸ **~а́ть** *and adj.* acknowledged, recognized.

призна́тел|ьный (~ен, ~ьна) *adj.* grateful.

призна́|ть, ю *pf.* (*of* ▸ **~ва́ть**)
1 (*leg., pol.*) to recognize; **п. прави́тельство** to recognize a government.
2 (*сознать*) to admit, acknowledge; **п. себя́ вино́вным** (*leg.*) to plead guilty; **п. свою́ оши́бку** to admit one's mistake.
3 (*считать*) to deem; **п. недействи́тельным** to declare invalid; **п. (не)вино́вным** to find (not) guilty.

призна́|ться, юсь *pf.* (*of* ▸ **~ва́ться**) (**в** + *p.*) to confess (to).

при́зрак, а *m.* spectre (*Br.*), specter (*US*), ghost, apparition.

призы́в, а *m.*
1 (*просьба*) call, appeal; **откли́кнуться на чей-н. п.** to respond to s.o.'s call.
2 (*mil.*) call-up, conscription.

призыва́|ть, ю *impf. of* ▸ **призва́ть**

призывни́к, а́ *m.* conscript.

при́иск, а *m.* mine; **золоты́е ~и** gold field(s).

при|йти́, ду́, дёшь, *past* **~шёл, ~шла́** *pf.* (*of* ▸ **~ходи́ть**) to come; to arrive; **п. пе́рвым** to come first; **п. в восто́рг** (**от** + *g.*) to go into raptures (over); **п. в у́жас** to be horrified; **п. в я́рость** to fly into a rage; **п. в го́лову кому́-н.** to occur to s.o., strike s.o., cross one's mind; **п. в себя́, п. в чу́вство** to come round, regain consciousness; (*fig.*) to come to one's senses; **п. к соглаше́нию** to come to an agreement.

при|йти́сь, ду́сь, дёшься, *past* **~шёлся, ~шла́сь** *pf.* (*of* ▸ **~ходи́ться 1**)
1 (**по** + *d.*) to fit; **п. кому́-н. по вку́су, по нра́ву** to be to s.o.'s taste, liking.
2 (**на** + *a.*; *о датах, событиях*) to fall (on); **Па́сха ~шла́сь на 28-е ма́рта** Easter fell on the 28th of March.
3 (*impers.* + *d.*) (*оказаться нужным*) to have (to); **ей ~дётся неме́дленно верну́ться в Москву́** she will have to return to Moscow immediately.
4 (*impers.* + *d.*) (*выпасть на долю*) to happen (to), fall to the lot (of); **мне ~шло́сь быть ря́дом в тот моме́нт, когда́ он упа́л в о́бморок** I happened to be standing by when he fainted; **ему́ ~шло́сь тяжело́** he had a hard time; **как ~дётся** (*coll.*) anyhow; **что ~дётся** anything; whatever comes along.

прика́з, а *m.* order, command; **вы́полнить п.** to carry out an order; **отда́ть п.** to give an order; **по ~у** by order.

прика|за́ть, жу́, ~́жешь *pf.* (*of* ▸ **~́зывать**) (+ *d.*) to order; to give orders; **дире́ктор ~за́л соста́вить но́вый гра́фик** the director ordered a new schedule to be worked out.

прика́зыва|ть, ю *impf. of* ▸ **приказа́ть**

прика́лыва|ть, ю *impf. of* ▸ **приколо́ть**

прика́нчива|ть, ю *impf. of* ▸ **прико́нчить**

прикаса́|ться, юсь *impf. of* ▸ **прикосну́ться**

прики́дыва|ться, юсь *impf. of* ▸ **прики́нуться**

прики́|нуться, нусь, нешься *pf.* (*of* ▸ **~дываться**) (+ *i.*; *coll.*) to pretend (to be), feign; **п. больны́м** to pretend to be ill, feign illness.

прикла́д, а *m.* (*ружья*) butt.

прикладн|о́й *adj.* applied; **~о́е иску́сство** applied arts; **~а́я програ́мма** (*comput.*) application (program).

прикла́дыва|ть, ю *impf. of* ▸ **приложи́ть 1, 2**

прикле́ива|ть(ся), ю, ет(ся) *impf. of* ▸ **прикле́ить(ся)**

прикле́|ить, ю, ишь *pf.* (*of* ▸ **~ивать**) to stick; to glue; **п. ма́рку** to stick on a stamp; **п. афи́шу к стене́** to stick (up) a bill on a wall.

прикле́|иться, ится *pf.* (*of* ▸ **~иваться**) (**к** + *d.*) to stick (to), adhere (to).

приключ|а́ться, а́ется *impf. of* ▸ **~и́ться**

приключе́ни|е, я *nt.* adventure.

приключ|и́ться, и́тся *pf.* (*of* ▸ **~а́ться**) (*coll.*) to happen, occur.

прик|ова́ть, ую́, уёшь *pf.* (*of* ▸ **~о́вывать**) (**к** + *d.*)
1 to chain (to).
2 (*fig.*) (*взгляд*) to fix; (*внимание*) to rivet; **боле́знь ~ова́ла его́ к посте́ли** illness confined him to his bed.

прико́выва|ть, ю *impf. of* ▸ **прикова́ть**

прикола́чива|ть, ю *impf. of* ▸ **приколоти́ть**

приколо|ти́ть, чу́, ~́тишь *pf.* (*of* ▸ **прикола́чивать**) to nail, fasten with nails.

прикол|о́ть, ю́, ~́ешь *pf.* (*of* ▸ **прика́лывать**) to pin, fasten with a pin.

прико́нч|ить, у, ишь *pf.* (*of* ▸ **прика́нчивать**) (*coll.*)
1 (*израсходовать*) to use up.
2 (*fig.*) (*умертвить*) to finish off.

прикоснове́ни|е, я *nt.* touch.

прикосн|у́ться, у́сь, ёшься *pf.* (*of* ▸ **прикаса́ться**) (**к** + *d.*) to touch (lightly).

прикреп|и́ть, лю́, и́шь *pf.* (*of* ▸ **~ля́ть**) (**к** + *d.*) to fasten (to).

прикрепля́|ть, ю *impf. of* ▸ **прикрепи́ть**

прикру|ти́ть, чу́, ~́тишь *pf.* (*of* ▸ **~́чивать**) (**к** + *d.*) to tie (to), bind (to), fasten (to).

прикру́чива|ть, ю *impf. of* ▸ **прикрути́ть**

прикрыва́|ть(ся), ю(сь) *impf. of* ▸ **прикры́ть(ся)**

прикр|ы́ть, о́ю, о́ешь *pf.* (*of* ▸ **~ыва́ть**)
1 (+ *i.*) (*покрыть*) to cover (with); to screen.
2 (*защитить*) to protect, shield; **п. глаза́ руко́й** to shade, shield one's eyes (with one's hand); (*о войсках*) to cover.
3 (*coll.*) (*ликвидировать*) to close down, wind up.
4 (*coll.*) (*закрыть неплотно*) to close (*a door, etc.*) to.

прикр|ы́ться, о́юсь, о́ешься *pf.* (*of* ▸ **~ыва́ться**)
1 (+*i.*) to cover o.s. (with); (*fig.*) to use as a cover, take refuge (in), shelter (behind); **он ~ы́лся боле́знью** he took refuge in being ill.
2 (*coll.*) (*ликвидироваться*) to close down, go out of business.
3 (*coll.*) (*закрыться неплотно*) to close to.

прику́рива|ть, ю *impf. of* ▸ **прикури́ть**

прикур|и́ть, ю́, ~́ишь *pf.* (*of* ▸ **~́ивать**) (**у кого́-н.**) to get a light (*from s.o.'s cigarette*).

прила́в|ок, ка *m.* counter; (*на рынке*) stall.

прилага́тельн|ое *adj.*: **и́мя ~ое** (*or as n.* **~ое, ~ого** *nt.*) adjective.

прилага́|ть, ю *impf. of* ▸ **приложи́ть 2, 3**

приласка́|ть, ю *pf.* to caress, pet; (*отнестись хорошо*) to show kindness to.

приласка́|ться, юсь *pf.* (**к** + *d.*) to snuggle up (to).

приле́ж|ный (~ен, ~на) *adj.* diligent, assiduous.

прилеп|и́ть, лю́, ~́ишь *pf.* (*of* ▸ **~ля́ть**) (**к** + *d.*) to stick (to, on).

прилеп|и́ться, лю́сь, ~́ишься *pf.* (*of* ▸ **~ля́ться**) (**к** + *d.*) to stick (to, on).

прилепля́|ть(ся), ю(сь) *impf. of* ▸ **прилепи́ть(ся)**

прилёт, а *m.* arrival (*by air*).

прилет|а́ть, а́ю *impf. of* ▸ **~е́ть**

приле|те́ть, чу́, ти́шь *pf.* (*of* ▸ **~та́ть**)
1 to arrive (*by air*), fly in.
2 (*fig., coll.*) (*быстро прибыть*) to fly, come flying.

при|ле́чь, ля́гу, ля́жешь, ля́гут, *past* **~лёг, ~легла́** *pf.* to lie down, have a lie-down (*Br.*).

прили́в, а *m.*
1 rising tide; (*fig.*) (*людей, денег*) influx; **п. и отли́в** ebb and flow.
2 (*med.*) congestion; (*fig.*): **п. эне́ргии, негодова́ния** surge of energy, indignation.

прилип|а́ть, а́ет *impf. of* ▸ **~́нуть**

прили́п|нуть, нет, *past* **~, ~ла** *pf.* (*of* ▸ **~а́ть**) (**к** + *d.*) to stick (to), adhere (to).

прили́ч|ный (~ен, ~на) *adj.*
1 decent, proper; decorous, seemly.
2 (*coll.*) (*достаточно хороший*) decent, fair; **~ная зарпла́та** a decent wage; (*достаточно большой*) sizeable.

приложе́ни|е, я *nt.*
1 (*документов к письму*) enclosure; (*comput.*) (*к электронному письму*) attachment.
2 (*к журналу, газете*) supplement.
3 (*к книге*) appendix; (*к документу*) addendum.
4 (*comput.*) (*прикладная программа*) application; (*небольшое*) applet.

прилож|и́ть, у́, ~́ишь *pf.*
1 (*impf.* **прикла́дывать**) (**к** + *d.*) (*положить*) to put (to), hold (to); **п. ру́ку ко лбу** to put one's hand to one's head.
2 (*impf.* **прикла́дывать** *and* **прилага́ть**) (*прибавить*) to add; (*к письму*) to enclose; (*печать*) to affix.
3 (*impf.* **прилага́ть**) (*использовать*) to apply; **п. все уси́лия** to make every effort.

прима́нива|ть, ю *impf. of* ▸ **примани́ть**

приман|и́ть, ю́, ~́ишь *pf.* (*of* ▸ **~́ивать**) (*coll.*) to lure; to entice.

прима́нк|а, и *f.* bait; (*fig.*) enticement, allurement.

прима́т, а *m.* (*zool.*) primate.

примене́ни|е, я *nt.* application;

П

(*употребление*) use, employment; **на́ши ме́тоды получи́ли широ́кое п.** our methods have been widely adopted; **непра́вильное п.** misuse; **в ~и** (**к** + *d.*) in application (to).

примен|и́ть, ю́, ~́ишь *pf.* (*of* ▸ **~я́ть**) to apply; to employ, use; **п. свои́ зна́ния** to apply one's knowledge; **п. на пра́ктике** to put into practice.

примен|и́ться, ю́сь, ~́ишься *pf.* (*of* ▸ **~я́ться**) (**к** + *d.*) to be used, to be applied.

применя́|ть(ся), ю(сь) *impf. of* ▸ **примени́ть(ся)**

приме́р, а *m.*
1 example, instance; **привести́ п.** to give an example; **к ~у** for example.
2 (*образец*) example; model; **брать п. с кого́-н., сле́довать чьему́-н. ~у** to follow s.o.'s example; **показа́ть п.** to give an example, give the lead; **по ~у** (+ *g.*) after the example (of), on the pattern (of).

приме́р|ить, ю, ишь *pf.* (*of* ▸ **ме́рить 2** *and* ▸ **~я́ть**) to try on.

приме́рно *adv.* approximately, roughly.

приме́р|ный (~ен, ~на) *adj.*
1 (*отличный*) exemplary, model.
2 (*приблизительный*) approximate, rough.

приме́рочн|ая, ой *f.* fitting room.

пример|я́ть, я́ю *impf. of* ▸ **~́ить**

при́мес|ь, и *f.* admixture; dash; (*fig.*) touch; **без ~ей** unadulterated.

приме́т|а, ы *f.* (*признак*) sign, token; mark; (*суеверие*) omen; **осо́бые ~ы** distinguishing marks.

приме́т|ный (~ен, ~на) *adj.*
1 (*след, волнение*) perceptible, noticeable.
2 (*человек, внешность*) conspicuous, prominent.

примеча́ни|е, я *nt.* note, comment; (*сноска*) footnote.

примеча́тел|ьный (~ен, ~ьна) *adj.* noteworthy, notable, remarkable.

примина́|ть, ю *impf. of* ▸ **примя́ть**

примире́ни|е, я *nt.* reconciliation.

примир|и́ть, ю́, и́шь *pf.* (*of* ▸ **~я́ть** *and* ▸ **мири́ть 2**) to reconcile; **п. супру́гов** to reconcile a husband and wife.

примир|и́ться, ю́сь, и́шься *pf.* (*of* ▸ **~я́ться** *and* ▸ **мири́ться 2**) (*с чем-н.*) to reconcile o.s. (to); **п. с неудо́бствами** to reconcile o.s. to discomforts.

примир|я́ть(ся), я́ю(сь) *impf. of* ▸ **~и́ть(ся)**

примити́в|ный (~ен, ~на) *adj.* primitive.

примкн|у́ть, у́, ёшь *pf.* (*of* ▸ **примыка́ть 1**) (**к** + *d.*)
1 (*плотно придвинуть, присоединить*) to fix (to), attach (to).
2 (*fig.*) (*присоединиться*) to join, attach o.s. (to); to side (with).

примо́рский *adj.* seaside; (*растение, климат*) maritime.

примо́чк|а, и *f.* wash, lotion.

при́мус, а *m.* Primus (*propr.*) (stove).

примч|а́ться, у́сь, и́шься *pf.* to come tearing along.

примыка́|ть, ю *impf.*
1 *impf. of* ▸ **примкну́ть.**
2 (*impf. only*) (**к** + *d.*) to adjoin, abut (upon).

при|мя́ть, мну́, мнёшь *pf.* (*of* ▸ **~мина́ть**) to crush, flatten; (*ногами*) to trample down, tread down.

принадлеж|а́ть, у́, и́шь *impf.*
1 (+ *d.*) to belong (to).
2 (**к** + *d.*) (*быть членом*) to belong (to), be a member (of); (*входить в состав*) to be among; to be one/some of.
3 : **Герма́нии ~и́т веду́щая роль в хими́ческой промы́шленности** Germany plays a leading role in the chemical industry.
4 : **п. ки́сти/перу́** (+ *g.*) to be the work of.

принадле́жност|ь, и *f.*
1 (**к** + *d.*) belonging (to), membership (of).
2 (*pl.*) accessories; equipment; gear; **канцеля́рские ~и** stationery.

принес|ти́, у́, ёшь, *past* **~́, ~ла́** *pf.* (*of* ▸ **приноси́ть**)
1 (*неся, доставить*) to bring (*also fig.*); to fetch; **п. обра́тно** to bring back; **п. в же́ртву** to sacrifice; **п. извине́ния** to apologize.
2 (*приплод, урожай*) to bear, yield; **п. результа́т** to yield/give results; (*причинить*) to bring in; **п. большо́й дохо́д** to bring in big revenues, show a large return; **п. по́льзу** to be of use, be of benefit; (*о чём-н. нежелательном*): **отку́да тебя́ ~ло́ в тако́й час?** where have you come from at this hour?

приник|а́ть, а́ю *impf. of* ▸ **~́нуть**

прини́к|нуть, ну, нешь, *past* **~, ~ла** *pf.* (*of* ▸ **~а́ть**) (**к** + *d.*) to press o.s. (against, to); (*прильнуть*) to nestle up (against, to); **мы ~ли к земле́** we pressed ourselves to the ground.

принима́|ть, ю *impf. of* ▸ **приня́ть**

принима́|ться, юсь *impf. of* ▸ **приня́ться**

принора́влива|ться, юсь *impf. of* ▸ **приноровиться**

приноров|и́ться, лю́сь, и́шься *pf.* (*of* ▸ **принора́вливаться**) (**к** + *d.*) to adapt o.s. (to), accommodate o.s. (to).

прино|си́ть, шу́, ~́сишь *impf. of* ▸ **принести́**

при́нтер, а *m.* (*comput.*) printer.

принуди́тел|ьный (~ен, ~ьна) *adj.* compulsory, forced; **~ьные рабо́ты** forced labour (*Br.*), labor (*US*).

прину́|дить, жу, дишь *pf.* (*of* ▸ **~жда́ть**) to force, compel, coerce.

принужда́|ть, ю *impf. of* ▸ **прину́дить**

принужде́ни|е, я *nt.* compulsion, coercion; **по ~ю** under duress.

принц, а *m.* prince.

принце́сс|а, ы *f.* princess.

при́нцип, а *m.* principle; **в ~е** in principle.

принципиа́л|ьный (~ен, ~ьна) *adj.*
1 of principle; based on, guided by principle; **п. челове́к** man of principle; **име́ть ~ьное значе́ние** to be a matter of principle.
2 (*в основном*) in principle; general; **они́ да́ли ~ьное согла́сие** they consented in

principle.
3 (*коренной*): **~ьное различие** fundamental difference.

принюх|аться, аюсь *pf.* (*of* ▸ **~иваться**) (*coll.*) to sniff.

принюхива|ться, юсь *impf. of* ▸ **принюхаться**

принят|ый *p.p.p. of* ▸ **принять; ~о** (+ *inf.*) it is accepted, it is usual (*to do sth.*); **не ~о** it is not done, it is not accepted.

при|нять, му, ~мешь, *past* **~нял, ~няла, ~няло** *pf.* (*of* ▸ **~нимать**)
1 to take; (*взять как дар; согласиться*) to accept; **п. ванну/душ** to take, have a bath/shower; **п. лекарство** to take medicine; **п. меры** to take measures; **п. подарок** to accept a present; **п. решение** to take, reach a decision; **п. участие (в** + *p.*) to take part (in); participate (in); **п. во внимание** to take into consideration; **не п. во внимание** to disregard.
2 (*пост*) to take up; **п. дела (от** + *g.*) to take over duties (from).
3 (*через голосование*) to accept; **п. резолюцию** to pass, adopt, carry a resolution.
4 **(в, на** + *a.*) (*зачислить*) to admit (to); to accept (for); **п. на службу** to accept for a job.
5 (*посетителей, пациентов, заказ*) to receive; **они ~няли нас радушно** they gave us a warm welcome, a cordial reception.
6 (*приобрести*) to assume, take (on); **переговоры ~няли благоприятный оборот** the talks took a favourable turn.
7 (+ *a.* **за** + *a.*) (*счесть по ошибке*) to take (for); **я ~нял вас за шотландца** I took you for a Scotsman.

при|няться, мусь, ~мешься, *past* **~нялся, ~нялась** *pf.* (*of* ▸ **~ниматься**)
1 (+ *inf.*) (*начать*) to begin; to start.
2 **(за** + *a.*) to set (to), get down (to); **п. за работу** to set to work.

приободр|ить, ю, ишь *pf.* (*of* ▸ **~ять**) to cheer up, encourage, hearten.

приободр|ять, яю *impf. of* ▸ **~ить**

приобре|сти, ту, тёшь, *past* **~л, ~ла** *pf.* (*of* ▸ **~тать**)
1 (*дом, друзей, машину*) to acquire; (*авторитет, репутацию*) to gain; **п. опыт** to gain experience.
2 (*свойство*) to take on, assume; **проблема ~ла особое значение** the problem took on a special significance.

приобрета|ть, ю *impf. of* ▸ **приобрести**

приобретени|е, я *nt.* acquisition.

приобщ|ать(ся), аю(сь) *impf. of* ▸ **~ить(ся)**

приобщ|ить, у, ишь *pf.* (*of* ▸ **~ать**)
1 **(к** + *d.*) (*познакомить*) to introduce (to); **п. ребёнка к искусству** to introduce a child to art.
2 (*присоединить*) to join, attach; **п. к делу** to file.

приобщ|иться, усь, ишься *pf.* (*of* ▸ **~аться**) **(к** + *d.*) to join (in), become involved (in).

приоде|ть, ну, нешь *pf.* (*coll.*) to dress up, smarten up.

приоде|ться, нусь, нешься *pf.* (*coll.*) to dress up; to get dressed up; to smarten o.s. up.

приоритет, а *m.* priority.

приосанива|ться, юсь *impf. of* ▸ **приосаниться**

приосан|иться, юсь, ишься *pf.* (*coll.*) to assume a dignified air.

приостанавлива|ть(ся), ю(сь) *impf. of* ▸ **приостановить(ся)**

приостанов|ить, лю, ~ишь *pf.* (*of* ▸ **приостанавливать**) to halt, suspend.

приостанов|иться, люсь, ~ишься *pf.* (*of* ▸ **приостанавливаться**) to halt, come to a halt; (*о человеке*) to pause.

приоткрыва|ть(ся), ю(сь) *impf. of* ▸ **приоткрыть(ся)**

приоткр|ыть(ся), ою(сь), оешь(ся) *pf.* (*of* ▸ **~ываться**) to open slightly, half-open; **п. дверь** to half-open the door, set the door ajar.

припада|ть, ю *impf. of* ▸ **припасть**

припад|ок, ка *m.* fit; attack; **нервный п.** attack of nerves.

припаива|ть, ю *impf. of* ▸ **припаять**

припарк|овать, ую *pf.* (*of* ▸ **парковать**) to park (*v.t.*).

припарк|оваться, уюсь *pf.* (*of* ▸ **парковаться**) to park (*v.i.*).

припа|сть, ду, дёшь, *past* **~л** *pf.* (*of* ▸ **~дать**) **(к** + *d.*) (*к земле, к груди*) to press o.s. (to); (*склониться*) to fall down (before); **п. ухом** to press one's ear (to).

припая|ть, ю *pf.* (*of* ▸ **припаивать**) **(к** + *d.*) to solder (to).

припи|сать, шу, ~шешь *pf.* (*of* ▸ **~сывать**)
1 (*написать в добавление*) to add.
2 **(к** + *d.*) (*причислить, записать*) to register (at).
3 (+ *d.*) to attribute (to); to ascribe (to); to put down (to); **п. стихотворение Пушкину** to attribute a poem to Pushkin; **п. неудачу лени** to put a failure down to laziness.

приписыва|ть, ю *impf. of* ▸ **приписать**

приплыва|ть, ю *impf. of* ▸ **приплыть**

приплы|ть, ву, вёшь, *past* **~л, ~ла, ~ло** *pf.* (*of* **~вать**) (*вплавь*) to swim up; (*на лодке*) to sail up.

приплюснут|ый (~, ~а) *adj.* flattened; **п. нос** flat nose.

приподнима|ть(ся), ю(сь) *impf. of* ▸ **приподнять(ся)**

приподн|ятый *p.p.p. of* ▸ **~ять** *and adj.* (*оживленный*) elated; animated; (*торжественный*) elevated.

приподн|ять, иму, имешь, *past* **~ял, ~яла, ~яло** *pf.* (*of* ▸ **~имать**) to raise slightly; to lift slightly.

приподн|яться, имусь, имешься, *past* **~ялся, ~ялась** *pf.* (*of* ▸ **~иматься**) to raise o.s. (a little); **п. на носки** to rise on one's toes.

приполз|ать, аю *impf. of* ▸ **~ти**

приполз|ти, у, ёшь, *past* **~, ~ла** *pf.* (*of* ▸ **~ать**) to creep up, crawl up.

припомина|ть, ю *impf. of* ▸ **припомнить**

припом|нить, ню, нишь *pf.* (*of*

П

▸ ∼ина́ть)
1 to remember, recollect, recall.
2 (+ *d.*) to remind; **я это тебе́ ∼ню!** (*coll.*) you won't forget this!; I'll get even with you for this!

припра́в|а, ы *f.* flavouring (*Br.*), flavoring (*US*), seasoning; (*соус*) dressing; **п. к сала́ту** salad dressing.

припра́в|ить, лю, ишь *pf.* (*of* ▸ ∼ля́ть) (+ *i.*) to season (with), flavour (*Br.*), flavor (*US*) (with); (*соусом*) to dress (with).

приправля́|ть, ю *impf. of* ▸ **припра́вить**

припря́|тать, чу, чешь *pf.* (*of* ▸ ∼тывать) (*coll.*) to put by, store up (*for future use*).

припря́тыва|ть, ю *impf. of* ▸ **припря́тать**

припу́гива|ть, ю *impf. of* ▸ **припугну́ть**

припуг|ну́ть, ну́, нёшь *pf.* (*of* ▸ ∽ивать) (*coll.*) to intimidate, scare.

приравнива|ть, ю *impf. of* ▸ **приравня́ть**

приравн|я́ть, я́ю *pf.* (*of* ▸ ∽ивать) (**к** + *d.*) to equate (with).

прираст|а́ть, а́ю *impf. of* ▸ ∼и́

прираст|и́, у́, ёшь, *past* **приро́с, приросла́** *pf.* (*of* ▸ ∼а́ть)
1 (**к** + *d.*) to adhere (to); (*о пересаженной ткани, о черенке*) to take.
2 (*увеличиться*) to increase; (*проценты*) to accrue.

приро́д|а, ы *f.*
1 nature.
2 (*характер*) nature, character; **от ∼ы** by nature, congenitally; **по ∼е** by nature, naturally.

приро́дн|ый *adj.*
1 (*созданный природой*) natural; **∼ые бога́тства** natural resources; **п. газ** natural gas.
2 (*врождённый*) inborn, innate; **п. ум** native wit.

природове́дени|е, я *nt.* natural history.

прирождённый *adj.*
1 (*о способностях*) inborn, innate.
2 (*о человеке*) a born; **п. лгун** a born liar.

приро́ст, а *m.* increase, growth.

прируч|а́ть, а́ю *impf. of* ▸ ∼и́ть

прируче́ни|е, я *nt.* taming; domestication.

прируч|и́ть, у́, и́шь *pf.* (*of* ▸ ∼а́ть) to tame (*also fig.*); to domesticate.

приса́жива|ться, юсь *impf. of* ▸ **присе́сть 1**

приса́сыва|ться, юсь *impf. of* ▸ **присоса́ться**

присва́ива|ть, ю *impf. of* ▸ **присво́ить**

присво́|ить, ю, ишь *pf.* (*of* ▸ **присва́ивать**)
1 (*завладеть*) to appropriate; **незако́нно п. сре́дства** to misappropriate funds.
2 (+ *a. and d.*) (*дать*) to give, award, confer; **ему́ ∼или сте́пень до́ктора нау́к** he has been given the degree of Doctor.

приседа́|ть, ю *impf. of* ▸ **присе́сть 2**

при|се́сть, ся́ду, ся́дешь, *past* **∼се́л** *pf.*
1 (*impf.* **∼са́живаться**) (*сесть*) to sit down, take a seat.
2 (*impf.* **∼седа́ть**) (*на корточки*) to squat; (*от страха*) to cower.

приска|ка́ть, чу́, ∽чешь *pf.* to come galloping, arrive at a gallop; (*fig., coll.*) to rush, tear.

приско́рб|ный (∼ен, ∼на) *adj.* regrettable, deplorable.

при|сла́ть, шлю́, шлёшь *pf.* (*of* ▸ ∼сыла́ть) to send.

прислон|и́ть, ю́, ∽ишь *pf.* (*of* ▸ ∼я́ть) (**к** + *d.*) to lean (against), rest (against).

прислон|и́ться, ю́сь, и́шься *pf.* (*of* ▸ ∼я́ться) (**к** + *d.*) to lean (against), rest (against).

прислон|я́ть(ся), я́ю(сь) *impf. of* ▸ ∼и́ть(ся)

прислу́г|а, и *f.*
1 maid, servant.
2 (*collect.*) servants, domestics.

прислу́ш|аться, аюсь *pf.* (*of* ▸ ∼иваться) (**к** + *d.*)
1 to listen (to).
2 (*fig.*) (*принять во внимание*) to listen (to); to heed; **п. к чьему́-н. сове́ту** to listen to s.o.'s advice.

прислу́шива|ться, юсь *impf. of* ▸ **прислу́шаться**

присма́трива|ть(ся), ю(сь) *impf. of* ▸ **присмотре́ть(ся)**

присмире́|ть, ю *pf.* to grow quiet, calm down.

присмир|и́ть, ю́, и́шь *pf.* (*of* ▸ ∼я́ть) to quieten (*Br.*), quiet (*US*).

присмир|я́ть, я́ю *impf. of* ▸ ∼и́ть

присмотр|е́ть, ю́, ∽ишь *pf.* (*of* ▸ **присма́тривать**)
1 (**за** + *i.*) to look after, keep an eye (on); **п. за ребёнком** to mind the baby.
2 (*coll.*) (*подыскать*) to look for; **п. себе́ рабо́ту** to look for a job.

присмотр|е́ться, ю́сь, ∽ишься *pf.* (*of* ▸ **присма́триваться**) (**к** + *d.*) to look closely (at); **п. к кому́-н.** to size s.o. up.

присн|и́ться, ю́сь, и́шься *pf. of* ▸ **сни́ться**

присоедине́ни|е, я *nt.*
1 addition.
2 (*pol.*) annexation.

присоедин|и́ть, ю́, и́шь *pf.* (*of* ▸ ∼я́ть)
1 to add; to join.
2 (*pol.*) to annex.
3 (*elec.*) to connect.

присоедин|и́ться, ю́сь, и́шься *pf.* (*of* ▸ ∼я́ться) (**к** + *d.*)
1 to join; **пора́ нам п. к остальны́м** it is time we joined the others.
2 (*согласиться*) to endorse, associate o.s. (with); **п. к мне́нию** to subscribe to an opinion.

присоедин|я́ть(ся), я́ю(сь) *impf. of* ▸ ∼и́ть(ся)

присос|а́ться, у́сь, ёшься *pf.* (*of* ▸ **приса́сываться**) (**к** + *d.*) to stick (to), adhere to (*by suction*).

приспоса́блива|ть(ся), ю(сь) *impf. of* ▸ **приспосо́бить(ся)**

приспосо́б|ить, лю, ишь *pf.* (*of* ▸ **приспоса́бливать**) to adapt, convert; **п.**

шко́лу под больни́цу to convert a school into a hospital.
приспосо́б|иться, люсь, ишься *pf.* (*of* ▸ **приспоса́бливаться**) (**к** + *d.*) to adapt o.s. (to).
приспособле́ни|е, я *nt.* device; appliance.
приспуска́|ть, ю *impf. of* ▸ **приспусти́ть**
приспу|сти́ть, щу́, ~́стишь *pf.* (*of* ▸ **~ска́ть**) to lower a little; **п. флаг** to lower a flag to half-mast.
приста|ва́ть, ю, ёшь *impf. of* ▸ **приста́ть**
приста́в|ить, лю, ишь *pf.* (*of* ▸ **~ля́ть**) (**к** + *d.*) to put (to, against), lean (against); **п. ле́стницу к стене́** to put a ladder against the wall.
приста́вк|а, и *f.* attachment; (*gram.*) prefix.
приставля́|ть, ю *impf. of* ▸ **приста́вить**
при́стально *adv.* intently; **п. смотре́ть** (**на** + *a.*) to look intently (at); to stare (at), gaze (at).
при́стал|ьный (~ен, ~ьна) *adj.* fixed, intent; **п. взгляд** intent look; stare, gaze.
при́стан|ь, и, *pl.* **~и, ~е́й** *f.* landing stage, jetty; pier; wharf.
приста́|ть, ну, нешь *pf.* (*of* ▸ **~ва́ть**) (**к** + *d.*)
1 (*прилипнуть*) to stick (to), adhere (to).
2 (*присоединиться*) to join; to attach o.s. (to); **п. к гру́ппе экскурса́нтов** to join a party of tourists.
3 (*надоесть*) to pester, bother; **п. с предложе́ниями** to pester with suggestions.
4 (*naut.*) to put in (to), come alongside.
пристёгива|ть, ю *impf. of* ▸ **пристегну́ть**
пристег|ну́ть, ну́, нёшь *pf.* (*of* ▸ **~́ивать**) to fasten; to button up.
пристра́ива|ть, ю *impf. of* ▸ **пристро́ить**
пристра|сти́ться, щу́сь, сти́шься *pf.* (**к** + *d.*) to develop a passion (for).
пристра́ст|ный (~ен, ~на) *adj.* partial, biased.
пристре́лива|ть, ю *impf. of* ▸ **пристрели́ть**
пристрел|и́ть, ю́, ~́ишь *pf.* (*of* ▸ **~́ивать**) to shoot (down).
пристро́|ить, ю, ишь *pf.* (*of* ▸ **пристра́ивать**) (**к** + *d.*) to add (*to a building*), build on (to).
пристро́йк|а, и *f.* annex, extension.
при́ступ, а *m.*
1 (*mil.*) assault, storm; **пойти́ на п.** to go in to the assault.
2 (*припадок*) fit, attack; **п. гне́ва/ка́шля** fit of temper/coughing; **серде́чный п.** heart attack.
приступ|а́ть, а́ю *impf. of* ▸ **~и́ть**
приступ|и́ть, лю́, ~́ишь *pf.* (*of* ▸ **~а́ть**) (**к** + *d.*) to set about, get down (to), start; **п. к де́лу** to set to work, get down to business.
присты|ди́ть, жу́, ди́шь *pf. of* ▸ **стыди́ть**
прису|ди́ть, жу́, ~́дишь *pf.* (*of* ▸ **~жда́ть**)
1 (+ *a. and* **к** + *d. or* + *a. and d.*) to sentence (to), condemn (to); **п. к штра́фу, п. штраф** (+ *d.*) to fine, impose a fine (on).
2 (+ *d.*) to award; to confer (on); **ему́ ~ди́ли сте́пень до́ктора** a doctorate has been conferred on him.
присужда́|ть, ю *impf. of* ▸ **присуди́ть**
прису́тстви|е, я *nt.* presence; **в ~и дете́й** in the presence of the children, in front of the children.
прису́тств|овать, ую *impf.* (**на** + *p.*) to be present (at), attend.
прису́тств|ующий *pres. part. act. of* ▸ **~овать** *and adj.* present; *as n.* **~ующие, ~ующих** (*pl.*) those present.
прису́щ|ий (~, ~а) *adj.* (+ *d.*) inherent (in); characteristic; **~ая ей ще́дрость** her characteristic generosity.
присыла́|ть, ю *impf. of* ▸ **присла́ть**
прися́г|а, и *f.* oath; **под ~ой** on oath, under oath.
прися́жн|ый *adj.*: **п. заседа́тель** juror; *as n.* **п., ~ого** *m.* = **п. заседа́тель; суд ~ых** jury.
прита́скива|ть, ю *impf. of* ▸ **притащи́ть**
притащ|и́ть, у́, ~́ишь *pf.* (*of* ▸ **прита́скивать**) to bring, drag, haul.
притвор|и́ться, ю́сь, и́шься *pf.* (*of* ▸ **~я́ться**) (+ *i.*) to pretend (to be); to feign; **п. больны́м** to pretend to be ill, feign illness.
притвор|я́ться, я́юсь *impf. of* ▸ **~и́ться**
притесне́ни|е, я *nt.* oppression.
притесн|и́ть, ю́, и́шь *pf.* (*of* ▸ **~я́ть**) to oppress, keep down.
притесн|я́ть, я́ю *impf. of* ▸ **~и́ть**
притих|а́ть, а́ю *impf. of* ▸ **~́нуть**
прити́х|нуть, ну, нешь, *past* **~, ~ла** *pf.* (*of* ▸ **~а́ть**) to quieten (*Br.*), quiet (*US*) down; to grow quiet.
прито́к, а *m.*
1 (*geog.*) tributary.
2 (*воздуха, воды, денег*) inflow; (*людей*) influx.
прито́м *conj.* (and) besides; and what's more.
прито́н, а *m.* den; **воровско́й п.** den of thieves.
при́тор|ный (~ен, ~на) *adj.* sickly sweet, cloying (*also fig.*); **~ная улы́бка** unctuous smile.
притра́гива|ться, юсь *impf. of* ▸ **притро́нуться**
притро́н|уться, усь, ешься *pf.* (*of* ▸ **притра́гиваться**) (**к** + *d.*) to touch; **они́ не ~улись к у́жину** they have not touched their supper.
притуп|и́ть, лю́, ~́ишь *pf.* (*of* ▸ **~ля́ть**) to blunt; (*fig.*) to dull, deaden.
притуп|и́ться, лю́, ~́ится *pf.* (*of* ▸ **~ля́ться**) to become blunt; (*fig.*) (*о памяти, зрении*) to fail.
притупля́|ть(ся), ю, ет(ся) *impf. of* ▸ **притупи́ть(ся)**
притуш|и́ть, у́, ~́ишь *pf.* (*coll.*) (*огонь*) to damp; **п. фа́ры** to dip lights.
при́тч|а, и *f.* parable.
притя́гива|ть, ю *impf. of* ▸ **притяну́ть**
притяжа́тельный *adj.* (*gram.*) possessive.
притяже́ни|е, я *nt.* (*phys.*) attraction; **зако́н земно́го ~я** law of gravity.
притяза́ни|е, я *nt.* claim, pretension;

име́ть ~я (на + *a.*) to have claims (to, on).
притя|ну́ть, ну́, ~́нешь *pf.* (*of* ▸ **~́гивать**)
1 to drag (up), pull (up).
2 (*fig.*) (*привлечь*) to draw, attract; **п. как магни́т** to attract like a magnet.
приукра́|сить, шу, сишь *pf.* (*of* ▸ **~шивать**) (*coll.*) (*успехи*) to exaggerate; (*рассказ*) to embellish, embroider.
приукра́шива|ть, ю *impf. of* ▸ **приукра́сить**
приуменьш|а́ть, а́ю *impf. of* ▸ **~́ить**
приуме́ньш|ить, у, ишь *pf.* (*of* ▸ **~а́ть**) to diminish, lessen, reduce.
приуч|а́ть(ся), а́ю(сь) *impf. of* ▸ **~и́ть(ся)**
приуч|и́ть, у́, ~́ишь *pf.* (*of* ▸ **~а́ть**) (**к** + *d. or* + *inf.*) to train (to), school (to, in); **п. кого́-н. к дисципли́не** to inculcate discipline in s.o.
приуч|и́ться, у́сь, ~́ишься *pf.* (*of* ▸ **~а́ться**) (+ *inf.*) to train o.s. (to); to accustom o.s. (to).
прихва|ти́ть, чу́, ~́тишь *pf.* (*of* ▸ **~́тывать**) (*coll.*) to catch up, seize up.
прихва́тыва|ть, ю *impf. of* ▸ **прихвати́ть**
прихо́д[1], а *m.* (*прибытие*) coming, arrival.
прихо́д[2], а *m.* (*eccl.*) parish.
прихо|ди́ть, жу́, ~́дишь *impf. of* ▸ **прийти́**
прихо|ди́ться, жу́сь, ~́дишься *impf.*
1 *impf. of* ▸ **прийти́сь.**
2 (*impf. only*) (+ *d. and i.*) to be (*in a given degree of relationship to*); **я ей ~жу́сь дя́дей** I am her uncle.
прихожа́н|ин, ина, *pl.* **~е** *m.* parishioner.
прихожа́н|ка, ки *f. of* ▸ **~ин**
прихо́ж|ая, ей *f.* (entrance) hall, lobby.
прихотли́в|ый (~, ~а) intricate.
при́хот|ь, и *f.* whim, caprice, fancy.
прице́л, а *m.* (back)sight; **взять на п.** to take aim (at), aim (at); (*fig.*) to keep a watch on.
прице́лива|ться, юсь *impf. of* ▸ **прице́литься**
прице́л|иться, юсь, ишься *pf.* (*of* ▸ **~иваться**) to take aim.
прице́п, а *m.* trailer.
прицеп|и́ть, лю́, ~́ишь *pf.* (*of* ▸ **~ля́ть**) (**к** + *d.*)
1 to hitch (to), hook on (to); (*вагоны*) to couple (to).
2 (*coll.*) (*брошку, бант*) to pin on (to), fasten (to).
прицеп|и́ться, лю́сь, ~́ишься *pf.* (*of* ▸ **~ля́ться**) (**к** + *d.*)
1 to stick (to), cling (to).
2 (*fig., coll.*) (*пристать*) to pester; to nag (at).
прицепля́|ть(ся), ю(сь) *impf. of* ▸ **прицепи́ть(ся)**
прича́л, а *m.* berth, moorage.
прича́лива|ть, ю *impf. of* ▸ **прича́лить**
прича́л|ить, ю, ишь *pf.* (*of* ▸ **~ивать**)
1 (**к** + *d.*) to moor (to).
2 (*intrans.*) to moor.
прича́сти|е[1], я *nt.* (*gram.*) participle.
прича́сти|е[2], я *nt.* (*eccl.*)
1 communion; the Eucharist.
2 (*причащение*) making one's communion, communicating.
прича|сти́ться, щу́сь, сти́шься *pf.* (*of* ▸ **~ща́ться**) (*eccl.*) to receive communion.
прича́ст|ный (~ен, ~на) *adj.* (**к** + *d.*) connected (with), involved (in); **быть ~ным** (**к** + *d.*) to be connected (with), be involved (in).
причаща́|ться, юсь *impf. of* ▸ **причасти́ться**
причём *conj.* moreover, and (*or translated by means of participial clause*); **бы́ло о́чень темно́, п. я пло́хо ориенти́ровалась на ме́стности** it was very dark and I didn't know the area well.
приче|са́ть, шу́, ~́шешь *pf.* (*of* ▸ **~́сывать**) to comb; **п. кого́-н.** to brush, comb s.o.'s hair.
приче|са́ться, шу́сь, ~́шешься *pf.* (*of* ▸ **~́сываться**) to brush, comb one's hair; (*у парикмахера*) to have one's hair done.
приче́ск|а, и *f.* hair style, hairdo.
приче́сыва|ть(ся), ю(сь) *impf. of* ▸ **причеса́ть(ся)**
причи́н|а, ы *f.* (*пожара, болезни*) cause; (*основание*) reason; **по той просто́й ~е, что** for the simple reason that; **по ~е** (+ *g.*) by reason (of), on account (of), owing (to), because (of).
причин|и́ть, ю́, и́шь *pf.* (*of* ▸ **~я́ть**) to cause.
причин|я́ть, я́ю *impf. of* ▸ **~и́ть**
причита́|ть, ю *impf.* (**по** + *p.*) to lament (for); to bewail.
пришварт|ова́ть(ся), у́ю(сь) *pf. of* ▸ **швартова́ть(ся)**
прише́л|ец, ьца *m.* alien.
пришива́|ть, ю *impf. of* ▸ **приши́ть**
приш|и́ть, ью́, ьёшь *pf.* (*of* ▸ **~ива́ть**) to sew on.
прищем|и́ть, лю́, и́шь *pf.* (*of* ▸ **~ля́ть**) to pinch, catch; **п. себе́ па́лец две́рью** to pinch one's finger in the door.
прищемля́|ть, ю *impf. of* ▸ **прищеми́ть**
прище́пк|а, и *f.* (clothes) peg (*Br.*), clothespin (*US*).
прищу́рива|ться, юсь *impf. of* ▸ **прищу́риться**
прищу́р|иться, юсь, ишься *pf.* (*of* ▸ **~иваться**) to screw up one's eyes, squint.
прию́т, а *m.*
1 shelter, refuge.
2 : **де́тский п.** orphanage.
прия́тел|ь, я *m.* friend.
прия́тельниц|а, ы *f.* (*female*) friend.
прия́т|ный (~ен, ~на) *adj.* nice, pleasant, pleasing; (*impers., pred.*): **~но** it is pleasant; it is nice; **о́чень ~но** pleased to meet you; how do you do?
про *prep.* + *a.*
1 (*о*) about.
2 : **про себя́** to o.s.; **чита́ть про себя́** to read to o.s.
про...[1] *vbl. pref. indicating*
1 *action through, across or past object, as* **прострели́ть** to shoot through; **прое́хать** to pass (by).

[2] *overall or exhaustive action, as* **прогре́ть** to warm thoroughly.
[3] *duration of action throughout given period of time, as* **просиде́ть всю ночь** to sit up all night.
[4] *loss or failure, as* **проигра́ть** to lose (*a game*).

про...[2] *as pref. of nn. and adjs.* pro-.

проанализи́р|овать, ую *pf. of* ▶ **анализи́ровать**

про́б|а, ы *f.*
[1] (*машины*) trial, test; try-out; (*металла*) assay; (*theatr.*) audition; **п. сил** trial of strength.
[2] (*для анализа*) sample.
[3] (*драгоценного металла*) standard (*measure of purity of gold*); **зо́лото 96-й ~ы** pure gold, 24 carat gold.
[4] (*клеймо*) hallmark.

проба́лтыва|ться, юсь *impf. of* ▶ **проболта́ться**

пробега́|ть, ю *impf. of* ▶ **пробежа́ть**

пробе|жа́ть, гу́, жи́шь, гу́т *pf.* (*of* ▶ **~га́ть**)
[1] (*мимо*) to run past; (*через*) to run through; (*по*) to run along; **п. па́льцами по клавиату́ре** to run one's fingers over the keyboard.
[2] (*fig.*) (*пронестись*) to run, flit (over, down, across); **хо́лод ~жа́л по её спине́** a chill ran down her spine.

пробе́жк|а, и *f.* run, jog.

пробе́л, а *m.*
[1] blank, gap; **запо́лнить ~ы** to fill in the blanks.
[2] (*недостаток*) deficiency, gap; **~ы в зна́ниях** gaps in one's knowledge.

пробива́|ть(ся), ю(сь) *impf. of* ▶ **проби́ть(ся)**

пробира́|ться, юсь *impf. of* ▶ **пробра́ться**

проби́рк|а, и *f.* test tube.

про|би́ть[1], **бью́, бьёшь,** *past* **~́би́л, ~би́ла, ~́би́ло** *pf. of* ▶ **бить 5**

про|би́ть[2], **бью́, бьёшь** *pf.* (*of* ▶ **~бива́ть**) to make a hole (in); to pierce; to punch; **п. сте́ну** to breach a wall.

про|би́ться, бью́сь, бьёшься *pf.* (*of* ▶ **~бива́ться**)
[1] to fight one's way through; to break, strike through; **п. сквозь толпу́** to fight one's way through the crowd.
[2] (*о растениях*) to appear, push up.

про́бк|а, и *f.*
[1] (*материал*) cork (*substance*).
[2] (*для бутылок*) cork; stopper; (*в раковину*) plug; **глуп как п.** (*coll.*) daft as a brush.
[3] (*elec.*) fuse.
[4] (*fig.*) (*на улице*) traffic jam; congestion.

пробле́м|а, ы *f.* problem.

проблемати́чный *adj.* problematic(al).

про́блеск, а *m.* flash; ray, gleam (*also fig.*); **п. наде́жды** ray of hope.

про́бный *adj.* trial, test; **п. ка́мень** touchstone; **п. полёт** test flight.

про́б|овать, ую *impf.* (*of* ▶ **по~**)
[1] (*проверять*) to test; **п. пи́щу** to taste, try food.
[2] (+ *inf.*) (*стараться*) to try (to), attempt (to).

проболта́|ться, юсь *pf.* (*of* ▶ **проба́лтываться**) (*coll.*) to shoot one's mouth off, let the cat out of the bag.

пробо́р, а *m.* parting (*Br.*), part (*US*) (*of the hair*); **прямо́й п.** middle part(ing); **косо́й п.** side part(ing).

пробормо|та́ть, чу́, ~́чешь *pf. of* ▶ **бормота́ть**

про|бра́ться, беру́сь, берёшься, *past* **~бра́лся, ~брала́сь, ~брало́сь** *pf.* (*of* ▶ **~бира́ться**)
[1] (*с трудом*) to fight, force one's way.
[2] (*тихо*) to steal (through, past); **п. о́щупью** to feel one's way; **п. на цы́почках** to tiptoe (through).

пробу|ди́ть, жу́, ~́дишь *pf.* (*of* ▶ **буди́ть 2** *and* ▶ **~жда́ть**) to wake; to awaken, rouse, arouse (*also fig.*).

пробу|ди́ться, жу́сь, ~́дишься *pf.* (*of* ▶ **~жда́ться**) to wake up, awake (*also fig.*).

пробужда́|ть(ся), ю(сь) *impf. of* ▶ **пробуди́ть(ся)**

пробужде́ни|е, я *nt.* waking up, awakening.

пробур|и́ть, ю́, и́шь *pf. of* ▶ **бури́ть**

проб|ы́ть, у́ду, у́дешь, *past* **~́ыл, ~ыла́, ~́ыло** *pf.* to stay, remain; to be (*for a certain time*); **он ~́ыл у нас три неде́ли** he stayed with us for three weeks.

прова́йдер, а *m.* Internet service provider (*abbr.* ISP).

прова́л, а *m.*
[1] (*действие*) collapse.
[2] (*geog.*) gap; hole.
[3] (*неудача*) failure; **по́лный п.** a complete flop.

прова́лива|ться, юсь *impf. of* ▶ **провали́ться**

провал|и́ться, ю́сь, ~́ишься *pf.* (*of* ▶ **~́иваться**)
[1] to collapse, fall through; **потоло́к ~и́лся** the ceiling has come down.
[2] (*fig., coll.*) (*потерпеть неудачу*) to fail, fall through; (*на экзамене*) to fail.

провез|ти́, у́, ёшь, *past* **~̈, ~ла́** *pf.* (*of* ▶ **провози́ть**)
[1] (*везя, доставить*) to convey, transport; **п. контраба́ндой** to smuggle.
[2] (*перевезти с собой*) to bring (with one).

прове́р|ить, ю, ишь *pf.* (*of* ▶ **~я́ть**)
[1] to check; to verify; **п. биле́ты** to examine tickets.
[2] (*на практике*) to test; **п. свои́ си́лы** to try one's strength.

прове́рк|а, и *f.*
[1] checking; examination; verification; check-up.
[2] (*на практике*) testing.

провер|я́ть, я́ю *impf. of* ▶ **~́ить**

прове|сти́, ду́, дёшь, *past* **~̈л, ~ла́** *pf.* (*of* ▶ **проводи́ть**[1] **1, вести́ 2, 3**)
[1] (*человека*) to lead, take; (*машину*) to take; (*судно*) to pilot.
[2] (*дорогу*) to build; (*электричество*) to install.
[3] (*реформы, опыты*) to carry out; (*кампанию*) to carry on; (*урок, заседание*) to conduct, hold; **п. бесе́ду** to give a talk.

4 (*черту*) to draw; **п. границу** to draw a boundary line.
5 (+ *i.*) (*рукой*) to pass over, run over; **она ~ла рукой по лбу** she passed her hand over her forehead.
6 (*время*) to spend, pass; **чтобы п. время** to pass the time.
7 (*coll.*) (*обмануть*) to take in, trick, fool.

провéтрива|ть, ю *impf. of* ▸ **провéтрить**

провéтр|ить, ю, ишь *pf.* (*of* ▸ **~ивать**) to air; to ventilate.

провизи|я, и *no pl., f.* provisions.

провин|иться, юсь, ишься *pf.* (**в** + *p.*) to be guilty (of); to commit an offence; **п. перед кем-н.** to wrong s.o.; **в чём мы ~ились?** what have we done wrong?

провинциáл|ьный (~ен, ~ьна) *adj.* provincial (*also fig.*).

провинци|я, и *f.*
1 (*область*) province.
2 (*удалённая местность*) the provinces; **жить в глухóй ~и** to live in the depths of the country.

прóвод, а, *pl.* **~á** *m.* wire, lead; **п. под напряжéнием** live wire.

прово|дить[1], жý, ~дишь *impf.*
1 *impf. of* ▸ **провести.**
2 (*impf. only*) (*phys., elec.*) to conduct.

прово|дить[2], жý, ~дишь *pf.* (*of* ▸ **~жáть**) to accompany; to see off; **п. когó-н. домóй** to take, see s.o. home; **п. когó-н. до дверéй** to see s.o. to the door; **п. глазáми** to follow with one's eyes.

провóдк|а, и *f.* (*collect.*; *elec.*) wiring, wires.

проводни́к[1], á *m.*
1 (*провожатый*) guide.
2 (*в поезде*) conductor; guard (*Br.*).

проводни́к[2], á *m.* (*phys., elec.*) conductor.

проводни́|ца, цы *f. of* ▸ **~к[1]**

прóвод|ы, ов *no sg.* seeing-off; send-off.

провожá|ть, ю *impf. of* ▸ **проводить[2]**

провóз, а *m.* carriage, conveyance, transport; **плáта за п.** payment for carriage.

провозгла|сить, шý, сишь *pf.* (*of* ▸ **~шáть**) to proclaim; **егó ~сили королём** he was proclaimed king.

провозглашá|ть, ю *impf. of* ▸ **провозгласить**

прово|зить, жý, ~зишь *impf. of* ▸ **провезти**

провокáтор, а *m.*
1 agent provocateur.
2 (*fig.*) instigator, provoker.

провокáци|я, и *f.* provocation.

прóволок|а, и *f.* wire; **колючая п.** barbed wire.

провóр|ный (~ен, ~на) *adj.*
1 (*быстрый*) quick, swift, expeditious.
2 (*ловкий*) agile, nimble, adroit, dexterous.

провоци́р|овать, ую *impf. and pf.* (*pf. also* **с~**) to provoke.

прогибá|ться, юсь *impf. of* ▸ **прогнýться**

проглáтыва|ть, ю *impf. of* ▸ **проглоти́ть; говори́ть, ~я словá** to swallow one's words.

прогло|ти́ть, чý, ~тишь *pf.* (*of* ▸ **проглáтывать** *and* ▸ **глотáть**) to swallow (*also fig.*); **п. язы́к** to lose one's tongue; **п. кни́гу** to devour a book.

прогля|дéть, жý, ди́шь *pf.* (*of* ▸ **~дывать**)
1 (*просмотреть*) to look through, skim through.
2 (*pf. only*) (*не заметить*) to overlook.

проглядыва|ть, ю *impf. of* ▸ **проглядéть**

про|гнáть, гоню́, гóнишь, *past* **~гнáл, ~гналá, ~гнáло** *pf.* (*of* ▸ **~гоня́ть**)
1 (*заставить уйти*) to drive away (*also fig.*); (*fig.*) to banish.
2 (*coll.*) (*с работы*) to sack, fire.

прогнивá|ть, ет *impf. of* ▸ **прогни́ть**

прогн|и́ть, иёт, *past* **~и́л, ~илá, ~и́ло** *pf.* (*of* ▸ **~ивáть**) to rot through.

прогнóз, а *m.* prognosis; forecast; **п. погóды** weather forecast.

прогн|ýться, ýсь, ёшься *pf.* (*of* ▸ **прогибáться**) to cave in, sag.

проговáрива|ть(ся), ю(сь) *impf. of* ▸ **проговори́ть(ся)**

проговор|и́ть, ю́, и́шь *pf.* (*of* ▸ **проговáривать**)
1 (*сказать*) to say, utter; **п. сквозь зýбы** to mutter.
2 (*некоторое время*) to speak, talk.

проговор|и́ться, ю́сь, и́шься *pf.* (*of* ▸ **проговáриваться**) to shoot one's mouth off, let the cat out of the bag.

проголодá|ться, юсь *pf.* to get hungry, grow hungry.

проголос|овáть, ýю *pf. of* ▸ **голосовáть**

прогоня́|ть, ю *impf. of* ▸ **прогнáть**

прогор|áть, áю *impf. of* ▸ **~éть**

прогор|éть, ю́, и́шь *pf.* (*of* ▸ **~áть**)
1 (*сгореть совсем*) to burn through; to burn to a cinder.
2 (*coll.*) (*разориться*) to go bankrupt, go bust.

прогрáмм|а, ы *f.* programme (*Br.*), program (*US*); (*comput.*) program, application.

программи́р|овать, ую *impf.* (*of* ▸ **за~**) to programme (*Br.*), program (*US*); (*comput.*) to program.

программи́ст, а *m.* (computer) programmer.

программи́ст|ка, ки *f. of* ▸ **~**

прогрáмм|ный *adj. of* ▸ **~а; ~ное обеспéчение** (*comput.*) software.

прогревá|ть(ся), ю(сь) *impf. of* ▸ **прогрéть(ся)**

прогрем|éть, лю́, и́шь *pf. of* ▸ **гремéть**

прогрéсс, а *m.* progress.

прогресси́в|ный (~ен, ~на) *adj.* progressive.

прогрé|ть, ю *pf.* (*of* ▸ **~вáть**) to heat, warm up.

прогрé|ться, юсь *pf.* (*of* ▸ **~вáться**) to warm up.

прогýл, а *m.* (*на работе*) absence; (*в школе*) truancy.

прогýлива|ть, ю *impf. of* ▸ **прогуля́ть**

прогýлива|ться, юсь *impf.*
1 *impf. of* ▸ **прогуля́ться.**
2 (*impf. only*) to stroll, saunter.

прогу́лк|а, и *f.*
[1] (*хождение*) walk; stroll.
[2] (*поездка*) outing; (*в автомобиле*) drive; (*верхом*) ride.

прогуля́|ть, ю *pf.* (*of* ▸ **прогу́ливать**) (*на работе*) to be absent from work; (*школу*) to play truant.

прогуля́|ться, юсь *pf.* (*of* ▸ **прогу́ливаться 1**) to take a walk, stroll.

прода|ва́ть, ю́, ёшь *impf. of* ▸ **~́ть**

прода|ва́ться, ю́сь, ёшься *impf.*
[1] (*impf. only*) to be on sale, be for sale; **дом ~ётся** the house is for sale; **~ётся мотоци́кл** (*formula of advertisement of sale*) 'motorcycle for sale'.
[2] (*impf. only*) to sell; **дёшево п.** to sell cheap, go cheap; **его́ но́вый рома́н хорошо́ ~ётся** his new novel is selling well.
[3] *impf. of* ▸ **~́ться**

продав|е́ц, ца́ *m.*
[1] seller; vendor.
[2] (*в магазине*) salesman, shop assistant.

продавщи́ц|а, ы *f.*
[1] seller; vendor.
[2] (*в магазине*) saleswoman, shop assistant.

прода́ж|а, и *f.* sale; **опто́вая п.** wholesale; **п. в ро́зницу/ро́зничная п.** retail; **нет в ~е** out of stock; sold out.

прода́ж|ный *adj.*
[1] sale; selling; **~ная цена́** selling price.
[2] **(~ен, ~на)** (*fig.*) corrupt; **~ная же́нщина** prostitute.

прода́лблива|ть, ю *impf. of* ▸ **продолби́ть**

прода́|ть, м, шь, ст, ди́м, ди́те, ду́т, *past* **про́дал, ~ла́, про́дало** *pf.* (*of* ▸ **~ва́ть**) to sell; **п. о́птом** to sell wholesale; **п. в ро́зницу** to sell retail.

прода́|ться, мся, шься, стся, ди́мся, ди́тесь, ду́тся, *past* **~лся, ~ла́сь** *pf.* (*of* ▸ **~ва́ться 3**) (*о человеке*) to sell o.s.

продвига́|ться, юсь *impf. of* ▸ **продви́нуться**

продвиже́ни|е, я *nt.*
[1] advancement.
[2] (*mil., fig.*) progress, advance.

продви́нут|ый (~, ~а) (*coll.*) *adj.* advanced.

продви́|нуться, нусь, нешься *pf.* (*of* ▸ **~га́ться**)
[1] to advance (*also fig.*); to move on, move forward; to push on.
[2] (*по службе*) to be promoted.

продева́|ть, ю *impf. of* ▸ **проде́ть**

проде́л|ать, аю *pf.* (*of* ▸ **~ывать**)
[1] (*отверстие, проход*) to make.
[2] (*работу, упражнения*) to do, perform, accomplish.

проде́лыва|ть, ю *impf. of* ▸ **проде́лать**

продемонстри́р|овать, ую *pf. of* ▸ **демонстри́ровать**

продерж|а́ть, у́, ~́ишь *pf.* (*чемодан*) to hold (*for a certain time*); (*человека*) to keep (*for a certain time*); **его́ ~а́ли два ме́сяца в больни́це** he was kept in hospital for two months.

продерж|а́ться, у́сь, ~́ишься *pf.* to hold out.

проде́|ть, ну, нешь *pf.* (*of* ▸ **~ва́ть**) to pass, run; **п. ни́тку в иго́лку** to thread a needle.

продикт|ова́ть, у́ю *pf. of* ▸ **диктова́ть**

продира́|ться, юсь *impf. of* ▸ **продра́ться**

продлева́|ть, ю *impf. of* ▸ **продли́ть**

продле́ни|е, я *nt.* extension, prolongation.

продл|и́ть, ю́, и́шь *pf.* (*of* ▸ **~ева́ть**) to extend, prolong; **п. срок де́йствия ви́зы** to extend a visa.

продл|и́ться, и́тся *pf. of* ▸ **дли́ться**

продово́льств|енный *adj. of* ▸ **~ие; п. магази́н** grocery (store); **п. склад** food store; (*mil.*) ration store, ration dump; **~енные това́ры** foodstuffs.

продово́льстви|е, я *nt.* foodstuffs, provisions; (*mil.*) rations.

продолб|и́ть, лю́, и́шь *pf.* (*of* ▸ **прода́лбливать**) to make a hole (in), chisel through.

продолгова́т|ый (~, ~а) *adj.* oblong.

продолж|а́ть, а́ю *impf.*
[1] to continue, go on; **п. рабо́тать** to continue to work, go on working.
[2] *impf. of* ▸ **~́ить**

продолж|а́ться, а́ется *impf.* (*of* ▸ **~́иться**) to continue, last, go on; **восста́ние ~а́ется уже́ второ́й год** the insurrection is now in its second year.

продолже́ни|е, я *nt.*
[1] continuation.
[2] (*рассказа*) continuation; sequel; **п. сле́дует** to be continued.
[3] : **в п.** (+ *g.*) in the course (of), during, for, throughout; **в п. почти́ двух лет я ни ра́зу её не ви́дел** for almost two years I did not see her once.

продолжи́тельност|ь, и *f.* duration, length.

продолжи́тел|ьный (~ен, ~ьна) *adj.* long; prolonged, protracted.

продо́лж|ить, у, ишь *pf.* (*of* ▸ **~а́ть**) to extend, prolong.

продо́лж|иться, ится *pf. of* ▸ **~а́ться**

продо́льн|ый *adj.* longitudinal; **~ая ось** longitudinal axis.

про|дра́ться, деру́сь, дерёшься, *past* **~дра́лся, ~драла́сь, ~дра́ло́сь** *pf.* (*of* ▸ **~дира́ться**) (*coll.*) to squeeze through, force one's way through.

продрем|а́ть, лю́, ~́лешь *pf.* to doze (*for a certain time*).

продро́г|нуть, ну, нешь, *past* **~, ~ла** *pf.* to be chilled to the marrow.

продува́|ть, ю *impf. impf. of* ▸ **проду́ть**

проду́кт, а *m.*
[1] product; **побо́чный п.** by-product.
[2] (*pl.*) produce; provisions, foodstuffs; **моло́чные ~ы** dairy produce.

продукти́в|ный (~ен, ~на) *adj.* productive; (*fig.*) fruitful.

продукто́вый *adj.* food; **п. магази́н** grocery (store).

проду́кци|я, и *f.* production, output.

проду́м|ать, аю *pf.* (*of* ▸ **~ывать**) (*вопрос*) to think over; (*план*) to think out.

продумыва|ть, ю *impf. of* ▸ **продумать**

проду|ть, ю, ешь *pf.* (*of* ▸ **~вать**)
1 (*прочистить*) to blow through; to clean by blowing.
2 (*impers.* + *a.*) to be in a draught (*Br.*), draft (*US*); **меня** *etc.* **~ло** I *etc.* have caught a cold from being in a draught (*Br.*), draft (*US*).
3 (*coll.*) (*проиграть*) to lose (*at games*).

продыряв|ить, лю, ишь *pf.* (*of* ▸ **~ливать**) to make a hole (in), pierce.

продырявлива|ть, ю *impf. of* ▸ **продырявить**

продюсер, а *m.* producer.

проезд, а *m.*
1 (*место*) passage, thoroughfare; «**~а нет!**» 'no thoroughfare!'
2 (*в транспорте*) trip, journey.

проездной *adj.* travelling (*Br.*), traveling (*US*); **п. (билет)** travel card.

проезжа|ть, ю *impf. of* ▸ **проехать**

проект, а *m.*
1 (*здания*) design.
2 (*предварительный текст*) draft; **п. договора** draft treaty.
3 (*замысел*) plan, project.

проектировани|е, я *nt.* designing; **автоматизированное п.** CAD, computer-aided design.

проектир|овать, ую *impf.* (*of* **с~**) to design; **п. театр** to design a theatre (*Br.*), theater (*US*).

проектировщик, а *m.* designer.

проектн|ый *adj.*
1 planning, designing; **~ое бюро** planning office.
2 (*предусмотренный*) planned; **~ая мощность** (*tech.*) rated capacity.

проектор, а *m.* projector.

проекци|я, и *f.* projection.

проём, а *m.* (*archit.*) aperture; embrasure; **дверной п.** doorway.

прое|хать, ду, дешь *pf.* (*of* ▸ **~зжать**)
1 (*на транспорте*) to pass (by, through); to drive (by, through), ride (by, through).
2 (*по ошибке*) to pass, go past.
3 (*расстояние*) to go, do, make, cover.

проецир|овать, ую *impf. and pf.* (*изображение*) to project.

прожарива|ть(ся), ю, ет(ся) *impf. of* ▸ **прожарить(ся)**

прожар|ить, ю, ишь *pf.* (*of* ▸ **~ивать**) to fry, roast thoroughly.

прожар|иться, ится *pf.* (*of* ▸ **~иваться**) to fry, roast thoroughly.

прожд|ать, у, ёшь, *past* **~ал, ~ала, ~ало** *pf.* (+ *a. or g.*) to wait (for), spend (*a certain time*) waiting (for).

прож|евать, ую, уёшь *pf.* (*of* ▸ **~ёвывать**) to chew well.

прожёвыва|ть, ю *impf. of* ▸ **прожевать**

прожектор, а, *pl.* **~ы** *and* **~а** *m.* searchlight, floodlight.

про|жечь, жгу, жжёшь, жгут, *past* **~жёг, ~жгла** *pf.* (*of* ▸ **~жигать**) to burn a hole in.

прожива|ть, ю *impf.*
1 (*иметь жилище*) to live, reside.
2 *impf. of* ▸ **прожить**

прожига|ть, ю *impf. of* ▸ **прожечь**

про|жить, живу, живёшь, *past* **~жил, ~жила, ~жило** *pf.* (*of* ▸ **~живать 2**)
1 (*пробыть живым*) to live; **он ~жил сто лет** he lived to be a hundred (*years of age*).
2 (*провести*) to spend; **мы ~жили месяц август на берегу моря** we spent the month of August at the seaside.

прожорлив|ый (~, ~а) *adj.* voracious, gluttonous.

проз|а, ы *f.* prose.

прозаик, а *m.* prose writer.

про|звать, зову, зовёшь, *past* **~звал, ~звала, ~звало** *pf.* (*of* ▸ **~зывать**) to nickname.

проз|вать, ову, овёшь *pf.* (+ *a. and i.*) to nickname (s.o. sth.).

прозвищ|е, а *nt.* nickname.

прозвуч|ать, ит *pf. of* ▸ **звучать**

прозева|ть, ю *pf. of* ▸ **зевать 3;** (*coll.*) to miss.

прозорлив|ый (~, ~а) *adj.* sagacious, perspicacious.

прозрачност|ь, и *f.* transparency.

прозрач|ный (~ен, ~на) *adj.* transparent (*also fig.*); (*вода, воздух*) clear, pellucid; (*ткань, одежда*) see-through, transparent; **п. намёк** transparent hint.

прозрева|ть, ю *impf. of* ▸ **прозреть**

прозрени|е, я *nt.*
1 recovery of sight.
2 (*fig.*) insight.

прозре|ть, ю, ешь *pf.* (*of* ▸ **прозревать**)
1 to recover one's sight.
2 (*fig.*) to see the light.

прозыва|ть, ю *impf. of* ▸ **прозвать**

проигнорир|овать, ую *pf.* to ignore.

проигр|ать, аю *pf.* (*of* ▸ **~ывать**)
1 (*потерпеть неудачу*) to lose; **п. судебный процесс** to lose a case.
2 (*сыграть*) to play (through, over); **п. концерт** to play through a concerto.
3 (*pf. only*) (*некоторое время*) to play.

проигрывател|ь, я *m.* record player; **п. компакт-дисков** CD player.

проигрыва|ть, ю *impf. of* ▸ **проиграть 1, 2**

проигрыш, а *m.* loss; **остаться в ~е** to be the loser, come off loser.

произведени|е, я *nt.*
1 (*искусства, литературы*) work; **избранные ~я Л. Н. Толстого** selected works of L. N. Tolstoy.
2 (*math.*) product.

произве|сти, ду, дёшь, *past* **~л, ~ла** *pf.* (*of* ▸ **производить 1**)
1 (*сделать*) to make; (*ремонт, опыты*) to carry out; **п. выстрел** to fire a shot.
2 (*вызвать*) to cause, produce; **п. впечатление (на** + *a.*) to create an impression (on, upon); **п. сенсацию** to cause a sensation.

производител|ь, я *m.* producer; **мелкие ~и** small producers.

производительност|ь, и *f.* productivity.

произво|дить, жу, ~дишь *impf.*
1 *impf. of* ▸ **произвести.**
2 (*impf. only*) (*изготовлять*) to produce.

произво́дн|ый *adj.* derivative, derived; *as n.* **~ая, ~ой** *f. (math.)* derivative.

произво́дств|енный *adj. of* ▸ **~о;** production; industrial.

произво́дств|о, а *nt.*
1 *(товаров)* production, manufacture; **япо́нского ~а** Japanese-made.
2 *(завод)* factory, works.

произво́л, а *m.*
1 *(необоснованность)* arbitrariness.
2 *(своеволие)* arbitrary rule.

произво́льно *adv.*
1 *(необоснованно)* arbitrarily.
2 *(по желанию)* at will.

произво́л|ьный (~ен, ~ьна) *adj.* arbitrary.

произнес|ти́, у́, ёшь, *past* **~̈, ~ла́** *pf. (of* ▸ **произноси́ть)**
1 *(выговорить)* to pronounce; to articulate.
2 *(сказать)* to pronounce, say, utter; **п. речь** to deliver a speech.

произно|си́ть, шу́, ~́сишь *impf. of* ▸ **произнести́**

произноше́ни|е, я *nt.* pronunciation.

произо|йти́, йду́, йдёшь, *past* **~шёл, ~шла́** *pf. (of* ▸ **происходи́ть 1)**
1 *(случиться)* to happen, occur, take place.
2 **(от, из-за** + *g.*) *(по причине)* to arise (from), result (from).
3 **(из, от** + *g.*) *(родиться)* to come (from, of), be descended (from).

произраст|а́ть, а́ет *impf. of* ▸ **~и́**

произраст|и́, ёт, *past* **произро́с, произросла́** *pf. (of* ▸ **~а́ть)** to grow, spring up.

проиллюстри́р|овать, ую *pf. (of* ▸ **иллюстри́ровать)** to illustrate.

проинструкти́р|овать, ую *pf. (of* ▸ **инструкти́ровать)** to instruct, give instructions (to).

проинформи́р|овать, ую *pf. (of* ▸ **информи́ровать)** to inform.

про́иск|и, ов *no sg.* intrigues; machinations.

происхо|ди́ть, жу́, ~́дишь *impf.*
1 *impf. of* ▸ **произойти́.**
2 *(impf. only)* to go on, be going on; **что тут ~́дит?** what is going on here?

происхожде́ни|е, я *nt.* origin; *(по рождению)* birth; **по ~ю он армяни́н** he is (an) Armenian by birth.

происше́стви|е, я *nt.* event, incident, happening, occurrence; *(авария)* accident.

про|йти́, йду́, йдёшь, *past* **~шёл, ~шла́** *pf. (of* ▸ **~ходи́ть[1] 1)**
1 *(передвинуться)* to pass (by, through); to go (by, through); **п. ми́мо** to pass by, go by, go past.
2 *(по ошибке)* to pass, go past.
3 *(расстояние)* to go, do, cover; **п. две ты́сячи миль за неде́лю** to do two thousand miles in a week.
4 *(о новостях, слухах)* to travel, spread.
5 *(о дожде, снеге)* to fall.
6 *(о времени)* to pass, elapse, go, go by; **~шёл це́лый год** a whole year had passed.
7 *(миновать)* to be over; *(прекратиться)* to pass (off), stop, let up; **~шло́ ле́то** summer was over; **дождь ~шёл** the rain stopped.
8 (+ *a. or* **че́рез** + *a.*) to pass, go through, get through.
9 *(завершиться)* to go, go off; **заседа́ние ~шло́ уда́чно** the meeting went off successfully.
10 *(курсы)* to do, take; **п. ку́рс лече́ния** to take a course of treatment.

про|йти́сь, йду́сь, йдёшься, *past* **~шёлся, ~шла́сь** *pf. (of* ▸ **~ха́живаться)** to walk, stroll; *(прогуляться)* to take a stroll; **п. по ко́мнате** to pace up and down the room.

прока́з|а[1], ы *f. (болезнь)* leprosy.

прока́з|а[2], ы *f. (шалость)* mischief, prank, trick.

прока́зник, а *m.* mischief-maker; prankster.

прока́зни|ца, цы *f. of* ▸ **~к**

прока́лыва|ть, ю *impf. of* ▸ **проколо́ть**

прока́т, а *m. (аренда)* hire.

прока|ти́ться, чу́сь, ~́тишься *pf. (of* ▸ **~́тываться)**
1 *(о мяче)* to roll (*also fig., of thunder, etc.*).
2 *(для развлечения)* to go for a drive, go for a spin.

прока́тыва|ться, юсь *impf. of* ▸ **прокати́ться**

прока́шлива|ться, юсь *impf. of* ▸ **прока́шляться**

прока́шл|яться, яюсь *pf. (of* ▸ **~иваться)** to clear one's throat.

прокипя|ти́ть, чу́, ти́шь *pf.* to boil thoroughly.

прокис|а́ть, а́ет *impf. of* ▸ **~́нуть**

проќис|нуть, нет *pf. (of* ▸ **~а́ть)** to turn (sour).

прокла́дк|а, и *f.*
1 *(действие)* laying; building, construction; **п. трубопрово́да** pipe laying.
2 *(tech.) (деталь)* washer, gasket; packing, padding.
3 *(coll.) (гигиеническая)* sanitary towel.

прокла́дыва|ть, ю *impf. of* ▸ **проложи́ть**

проклина́|ть, ю *impf. of* ▸ **прокля́сть**

прокл|я́сть, яну́, янёшь, *past* **~́ял, ~яла́, ~́яло** *pf. (of* ▸ **~ина́ть)** to curse, damn.

прокля́ти|е, я *nt.*
1 *(осуждение)* damnation.
2 *(слово, выражение)* curse.

прокля́тый *adj.* damned; cursed.

проко́л, а *m.*
1 *(в шине)* puncture.
2 *(на билете; на ухе)* hole.
3 *(coll.) (неудача)* failure; *(оплошность)* blunder.

прокол|о́ть, ю́, ~́ешь *pf. (of* ▸ **прока́лывать)**
1 *(шину)* to puncture.
2 *(уши)* to pierce.
3 *(дыру)* to pierce, prick.

проконсульти́р|овать(ся), ую(сь) *pf. of* ▸ **консульти́ровать(ся)**

проконтроли́р|овать, ую *pf. of* ▸ **контроли́ровать**

прокорм|и́ть(ся), лю́(сь), ~́ишь(ся) *pf. of* ▸ **корми́ть(ся)**

прокра́дыва|ться, юсь *impf. of* ▶ **прокра́сться**

прокра́|сться, ду́сь, дёшься *pf.* (*of* ▶ **~дываться**) to steal; **п. ми́мо** to steal by, past.

прокрич|а́ть, у́, и́шь *pf.*
1 to shout, cry; to give a shout, raise a cry.
2 (**о** + *p.*; *coll.*) to trumpet.

прокурату́р|а, ы *f.* office of public prosecutor.

прокуро́р, а *m.* public prosecutor.

проку|си́ть, шу́, ~́сишь *pf.* (*of* ▶ **~́сывать**) to bite through.

проку́сыва|ть, ю *impf. of* ▶ **прокуси́ть**

прола́мыва|ть(ся), ю, ет(ся) *impf. of* ▶ **проломи́ть(ся)**

пролега́|ть, ет *impf.* to lie, run; **доро́га ~ла вдоль бе́рега кана́ла** the path lay by the canal.

пролез|а́ть, а́ю *impf. of* ▶ **~́ть**

проле́з|ть, у, ешь, *past* **~, ~ла** *pf.* (*of* ▶ **~а́ть**)
1 (*проникнуть куда-н.*) to get through, climb through.
2 (**в** + *a.*; *fig., coll., pej.*) (*хитростью*) to worm o.s. (into, on to).

пролетариа́т, а *m.* proletariat.

пролет|а́ть[1]**, а́ю** *impf. of* ▶ **~е́ть**

пролет|а́ть[2]**, а́ю** *pf.* to fly (*for a certain time*).

проле|те́ть, чу́, ти́шь *pf.* (*of* ▶ **~та́ть**[1])
1 (*какое-н. расстояние*) to fly, cover.
2 (*мимо*) to fly (by, through, past) (*also fig.*); **кани́кулы ~те́ли** the holidays flew by.
3 (*fig.*) (*мелькнуть*) to flash, flit.

проли́в, а *m.* (*geog.*) strait, sound.

пролива́|ть, ю *impf. of* ▶ **проли́ть**

проливно́й *adj.*: **п. дождь** pouring rain; **шёл п. дождь** it was pouring.

прол|и́ть, ью́, ьёшь, *past* **~́ил, ~ила́, ~́ило** *pf.* (*of* ▶ **~ива́ть**) to spill, shed; **п. чью-н. кровь** to shed s.o.'s blood; **п. свет** (**на** + *a.*; *fig.*) to shed light (on).

проло́г, а *m.* prologue (*Br.*), prolog (*US*).

пролож|и́ть, у́, ~́ишь *pf.* (*of* ▶ **прокла́дывать**)
1 to lay; to build, construct; **п. путь** (*fig.*) to pave the way.
2 (**ме́жду** + *i. or* + *a. and i.*) to interlay; to insert (between).

проло́м, а *m.* break; gap.

пролом|и́ть, лю́, ~́ишь *pf.* (*of* ▶ **прола́мывать**) to break (through); **п. че́реп** to fracture one's skull.

пролом|и́ться, ~́ится *pf.* (*of* ▶ **прола́мываться**) to break, give way.

прома́|зать, жу, жешь *pf. of* ▶ **ма́зать 4**

промаршир|ова́ть, у́ю *pf. of* ▶ **марширова́ть**

про́мах, а *m.* miss; (*fig.*) slip, blunder.

прома́хива|ться, юсь *impf. of* ▶ **промахну́ться**

промах|ну́ться, ну́сь, нёшься *pf.* (*of* ▶ **~́иваться**) to miss.

прома́чива|ть, ю *impf. of* ▶ **промочи́ть**

промедле́ни|е, я *nt.* delay; procrastination.

промежу́т|ок, ка *m.* (*между событий*) interval; (*между предметами*) space; **п. вре́мени** period, stretch of time.

промежу́точный *adj.* (*положение*) intermediate; (*период*) intervening.

промелькн|у́ть, у́, ёшь *pf.*
1 to flash; (*о времени*) to fly by.
2 (*появиться*) to be faintly perceptible; **в его́ слова́х ~у́ло разочарова́ние** there was a shade of disappointment in his words.

проме́нива|ть, ю *impf. of* ▶ **променя́ть**

промен|я́ть, я́ю *pf.* (*of* ▶ **~́ивать**) (**на** + *a.*) to exchange, swap (for); to trade (for), barter (for).

промерз|а́ть, а́ю *impf. of* ▶ **~̈нуть**

промёрз|нуть, ну, нешь, *past* **~, ~ла** *pf.* (*of* ▶ **~а́ть**) to freeze through.

промо́зглый *adj.* dank.

промок|а́ть, а́ю *impf.*
1 *impf. of* ▶ **~́нуть.**
2 (*impf. only*) to let water through, not be waterproof; **э́ти боти́нки ~а́ют** these boots are not waterproof.

промо́к|нуть, ну, нешь *pf.* (*of* ▶ **~а́ть 1**) to get soaked, get drenched.

промолч|а́ть, у́, и́шь *pf.* to keep silent, say nothing.

промо́утер, а *m.* promoter.

промо́ушен, а *m.* promotion.

промоч|и́ть, у́, ~́ишь *pf.* (*of* ▶ **прома́чивать**) to get wet (through); to soak, drench; **п. но́ги** to get one's feet wet.

промч|а́ться, у́сь, и́шься *pf.*
1 to tear (by, past, through); **п. стрело́й** to dart (by, past), flash (by, past).
2 (*о времени*) to fly (by).

промыва́|ть, ю *impf. of* ▶ **промы́ть**

про́мыс|ел, ла *m.*
1 (*охота*) hunting, catching; **пушно́й п.** trapping.
2 (*занятие*) trade, business; **го́рный п.** mining.
3 *pl.* (*предприятие*) fields, mines; **нефтяны́е ~лы** oilfields.

пром|ы́ть, о́ю, о́ешь *pf.* (*of* ▶ **~ыва́ть**)
1 to wash well, thoroughly; **п. мозги́** (+ *d.*, *fig.*) to brainwash.
2 (*med.*) to bathe.

промы́шленник, а *m.* manufacturer, industrialist.

промы́шленност|ь, и *f.* industry.

промы́шленный *adj.* industrial.

пронес|ти́, у́, ёшь, *past* **~̈, ~ла́** *pf.* (*of* ▶ **проноси́ть**)
1 to carry (by, past, through).
2: **~ло́!** (*coll.*) the danger is over!

пронес|ти́сь, у́сь, ёшься, *past* **~̈ся, ~ла́сь** *pf.* (*of* ▶ **проноси́ться**)
1 to rush (by, past, through); (*об облаках*) to scud (past).
2 (*о времени*) to fly by.

пронз|а́ть, а́ю *impf. of* ▶ **~и́ть**

пронзи́тел|ьный (~ен, ~ьна) *adj.* piercing.

прон|зи́ть, жу́, зи́шь *pf.* (*of* ▶ **~за́ть**) to pierce.

прони|за́ть, жу́, ~́жешь *pf.* (*of*

▸ ~́зывать) to pierce; to permeate, penetrate; (*fig.*) to run through; **свет ~за́л темноту́** the light pierced the darkness; **одна́ иде́я ~за́ла все его́ произведе́ния** one idea ran through all his works.

прони́зыва|ть, ю *impf. of* ▸ **прониза́ть**

прони́зыва|ющий *pres. part. act. of* ▸ **~ть** *and adj.* piercing.

проник|а́ть, а́ю *impf. of* ▸ **~́нуть**

прони́к|нуть, ну, нешь, *past* **~, ~ла** *pf.* (*of* ▸ **~а́ть**) (**в** + *a.*) to penetrate (*also fig.*); (**че́рез** + *a.*) to percolate (through).

проница́тел|ьный (~ен, ~ьна) *adj.* perspicacious; shrewd; penetrating, piercing.

проно|си́ть, шу́, ~́сишь *impf. of* ▸ **пронести́**

проно|си́ться, шу́сь, ~́сишься *impf. of* ▸ **пронести́сь**

прообраз, а *m.* prototype.

пропага́нд|а, ы *f.* propaganda; promotion, advocacy.

пропаганди́р|овать, ую *impf.* to propagandize; to advocate.

пропада́|ть, ю *impf. of* ▸ **пропа́сть**

пропа́ж|а, и *f.* loss.

пропа́лыва|ть, ю *impf. of* ▸ **пропо́лоть**

пропа́н, а *m.* propane.

пропа́|сть, ду́, дёшь, *past* **~л** *pf.* (*of* ▸ **~да́ть**)
1 (*потеряться*) to be missing; to be lost; **п. бе́з вести** (*mil.*) to be missing.
2 (*исчезнуть*) to disappear, vanish; **куда́ вы ~ли?** where did you vanish to?
3 (*погибнуть*) to be lost, be done for; (*о цветах*) to die; **тепе́рь мы ~ли!** now we're done for!

про́паст|ь, и *f.* precipice (*also fig.*); abyss; **на краю́ ~и** (*fig.*) on the brink of disaster.

пропа́х|нуть, ну, нешь, *past* **~, ~ла** *pf.* to become permeated with the smell (of).

пропека́|ть(ся), ю, ет(ся) *impf. of* ▸ **пропе́чь(ся)**

пропе́ллер, а *m.* propeller.

пропе́|чь, ку́, чёшь, ку́т, *past* **~̈к, ~кла́** *pf.* (*of* ▸ **~ка́ть**) to bake well, thoroughly.

пропе́|чься, чётся, ку́тся, *past* **~̈кся, ~кла́сь** *pf.* (*of* ▸ **~ка́ться**) to bake well, get baked through.

пропива́|ть, ю *impf. of* ▸ **пропи́ть**

пропи́лива|ть, ю *impf. of* ▸ **пропили́ть**

пропил|и́ть, ю́, ~́ишь *pf.* (*of* ▸ **~́ивать**) to saw through.

пропи|са́ть, шу́, ~́шешь *pf.* (*of* ▸ **~́сывать**)
1 (*лекарство*) to prescribe.
2 (*жильца*) to register.

пропи|са́ться, шу́сь, ~́шешься *pf.* (*of* ▸ **~́сываться**) to register (*intrans.*).

пропи́ск|а, и *f.*
1 (*регистрация*) registration.
2 (*отметка в паспорте*) residence permit.

прописно́й *adj.* (*буква*) capital; **писа́ться с п. бу́квы** to be written with a capital letter.

прописыва|ть(ся), ю(сь) *impf. of* ▸ **прописа́ть(ся)**

пропит|а́ть, а́ю *pf.* (*of* ▸ **~́ывать**) (+ *i.*) to impregnate (with), steep (in); **п. ма́слом** to oil.

пропит|а́ться, а́юсь *pf.* (*of* ▸ **~́ываться**) (+ *i.*) to become saturated (with).

пропи́тыва|ть(ся), ю(сь) *impf. of* ▸ **пропита́ть(ся)**

про|пи́ть, пью, пьёшь, *past* **~́пил, ~пила́, ~́пило** *pf.* (*of* ▸ **~пива́ть**)
1 (*деньги*) to spend on drink, squander on drink.
2 (*coll.*) (*талант*) to ruin (*through excessive drinking*).

пропла́ва|ть, ю *pf.* (*вплавь*) to swim (*for a certain time*); (*на судне*) to sail (*for a certain time*).

пропла́|кать, чу, чешь *pf.* to cry, weep (*for a certain time*).

проплыва́|ть, ю *impf. of* ▸ **проплы́ть**

проплы́|ть, ву́, вёшь, *past* **~л, ~ла́, ~ло** *pf.* (*of* ▸ **~ва́ть**)
1 (*вплавь*) to swim (by, past, through); (*на судне*) to sail (by, past, through); (*о предмете*) to float, drift (by, past, through).
2 (*расстояние*) to cover (*a certain distance*).

пропове́дник, а *m.*
1 preacher.
2 (+ *g.*; *fig.*) advocate (of).

пропове́д|овать, ую *impf.*
1 to preach.
2 (*fig.*) to advocate, propagate.

про́поведь, и *f.* sermon; homily.

пропolz|а́ть, а́ю *impf. of* ▸ **~ти́**

пропolz|ти́, у́, ёшь, *past* **~, ~ла́** *pf.* (*of* ▸ **~а́ть**) to creep, crawl (by, past, through).

прополо|ска́ть, щу́, ~́щешь *pf.* (*of* ▸ **полоска́ть**) to rinse, swill; **п. го́рло** to gargle.

пропол|о́ть, ю́, ~́ешь *pf.* (*of* ▸ **пропа́лывать**) to weed.

пропорциона́л|ьный (~ен, ~ьна) *adj.*
1 proportional; proportionate.
2 (*обладающий правильными пропорциями*) well-proportioned.

пропо́рци|я, и *f.* proportion.

про́пуск, а *m.*
1 *no pl.* (*действие*) admission.
2 (*pl.* **~а́**) (*документ*) pass, permit.
3 (*pl.* **~а́**) (*mil.*) password.
4 (*pl.* **~и**) (+ *g.*) (*непосещение*) non-attendance (at), absence (from).
5 (*pl.* **~и**) (*пустое место*) blank, gap.

пропуска́|ть, ю *impf.*
1 *impf. of* ▸ **пропусти́ть.**
2 (*impf. only*) to let pass; **п. во́ду** to leak; **не п. воды́** to be waterproof.

пропускн|о́й *adj.*: **п. пункт** checkpoint; **~а́я спосо́бность** capacity; (*comput.*) bandwidth.

пропу|сти́ть, щу́, ~́стишь *pf.* (*of* ▸ **~ска́ть 1**)
1 (*дать пройти*) to let pass, let through; to make way (for); (*впустить*) to let in, admit; (*обслужить*) to put through, deal with; **п. на перро́н** to let on to the platform.
2 (**че́рез** + *a.*) to run (through), pass (through); **п. че́рез фильтр** to filter.

3 (*при чтении, письме*) to omit, leave out; to skip.
4 (*не явиться*) to miss; **п. ле́кцию** to miss a lecture.

пропылесо́с|ить, ишь *pf. of* ▸**пылесо́сить**

прораба́тыва|ть, ю *impf. of* ▸**прорабо́тать**[1]

прорабо́та|ть[1], **ю** *pf.* (*of* ▸**прораба́тывать**) (*coll.*)
1 (*изучить*) to work (at), study.
2 (*критиковать*) to pick holes (in).

прорабо́та|ть[2], **ю** *pf.* (*некоторое время*) to work (*for a while*).

прораст|а́ть, а́ет *impf. of* ▸**~и́**

прораст|и́, ёт, *past* **проро́с, проросла́** *pf.* (*of* ▸**~а́ть**) to germinate, sprout, shoot (*of plant*).

прорв|а́ть, у́, ёшь, *past* **~а́л, ~ала́, ~а́ло** *pf.* (*of* ▸**прорыва́ть**[1])
1 to break through; to tear, make a hole (in); **п. ли́нию оборо́ны проти́вника** to break through the enemy's defence line; (*impers.*): **плоти́ну ~а́ло** the dam has burst.
2 (*impers.*; *coll.*) to lose patience.

прорв|а́ться, у́сь, ёшься, *past* **~а́лся, ~ала́сь, ~а́ло́сь** *pf.* (*of* ▸**прорыва́ться**)
1 (*сломаться*) to break, burst (open).
2 (*разорваться*) to tear.
3 (*силой проложить себе путь*) to break (out, through); to force one's way (through).

прореаги́р|овать, ую *pf. of* ▸**реаги́ровать 2**

проре́|зать, жу, жешь *pf.* (*of* ▸**~зывать** *and* ▸**~за́ть**) to cut through (*also fig.*).

прореза́|ть, ю *impf. of* ▸**проре́зать**

проре́зыва|ть, ю *impf. of* ▸**проре́зать**

про́резь, и *f.* opening, aperture.

проржаве́|ть, ет *pf.* to rust through.

проро́к, а *m.* prophet.

проро́ч|ить, у, ишь *impf.* (*of* **на~**) to prophesy, predict.

проруб|а́ть, а́ю *impf. of* ▸**~и́ть**

проруб|и́ть, лю́, ~́ишь *pf.* (*of* ▸**~а́ть**) to hack through, cut through.

про́рубь, и *f.* ice hole.

проры́в, а *m.* break; (*mil.*) breakthrough, breach.

прорыва́|ть[1], **ю** *impf. of* ▸**прорва́ть**

прорыва́|ть[2], **ю** *impf. of* ▸**проры́ть**

прорыва́|ться, юсь *impf. of* ▸**прорва́ться**

прор|ы́ть, о́ю, о́ешь *pf.* (*of* ▸**~ыва́ть**[2]) to dig through.

проса́чива|ться, ется *impf. of* ▸**просочи́ться**

просверл|и́ть, ю́, и́шь *pf. of* ▸**сверли́ть**

просве́т, а *m.* shaft of light; (*fig.*) ray of hope.

просве|ти́ть[1], **щу́, ти́шь** *pf.* (*of* ▸**~ща́ть**) to educate; to enlighten.

просве|ти́ть[2], **чу́, ~́тишь** *pf.* (*of* ▸**~́чивать**[1]) (*med.*) to X-ray.

просве́чива|ть[1], **ю** *impf. of* ▸**просвети́ть**[2]

просве́чива|ть[2], **ю** *impf.*
1 (*быть прозрачным*) to be translucent; (*одежда, занавески*) to be see-through.
2 (**че́рез, сквозь** + *a.*) (*быть видным*) to be visible (through), show (through), appear (through); (*о солнце*) to shine (through).

просвеща́|ть, ю *impf. of* ▸**просвети́ть**[1]

просвеще́ни|е, я *nt.*
1 (*образование*) education; **наро́дное п.** public education.
2 enlightenment; **эпо́ха П~я** (*hist.*) the Age of the Enlightenment.

просве|щённый *p.p.p. of* ▸**~ти́ть**[1] *and adj.* enlightened; educated, cultured; **~щённое мне́ние** expert opinion; **п. челове́к** educated person.

про́сек|а, и *f.* cutting (*in a forest*).

проси|де́ть, жу́, ди́шь *pf.* (*of* ▸**~́живать**) to sit (*for a certain time*); **п. ночь у посте́ли больно́го** to sit up all night with a patient.

проси́жива|ть, ю *impf. of* ▸**просиде́ть**

про|си́ть, шу́, ~́сишь *impf.* (*of* ▸**по~**)
1 (+ *a. of person asked*; + *a. or g. of thing sought, or* **о** + *p.*) to ask (for), beg; **~шу́ (вас)** please; **п. кого́-н. о по́мощи** to ask s.o. for help, ask s.o.'s assistance; **п. разреше́ния** to ask permission; **п. сове́та** to ask (for) advice; **п. извине́ния у кого́-н.** to apologize to s.o.
2 (**за** + *a.*) (*вступаться*) to intercede (for).
3 (*приглашать*) to invite; **вас ~́сят к столу́** please take your places at the table.

про|си́ться, шу́сь, ~́сишься *impf.* (*of* ▸**по~**) (+ *inf. or* **в** + *a.*, **на** + *a.*) to ask (for); to apply (for); **п. в о́тпуск** to apply for leave.

проска́кива|ть, ю *impf. of* ▸**проскочи́ть**

проска́льзыва|ть, ю *impf. of* ▸**проскользну́ть**

проскользн|у́ть, у́, ёшь *pf.* (*of* ▸**проска́льзывать**) (*coll.*) to slip in, creep in (*also fig.*); **~у́ло мно́го оши́бок** many errors have crept in.

проскоч|и́ть, у́, ~́ишь *pf.* (*of* ▸**проска́кивать**)
1 (*пробежать*) to rush by, tear by.
2 (**че́рез** + *a.*) to slip (through).
3 (**сквозь** + *a.*, **ме́жду** + *i.*) to fall (through, between); **п. ме́жду па́льцами** to fall through one's fingers.
4 (*не остановиться, где нужно*) to overshoot.

просла́в|иться, люсь, ишься *pf.* (*of* ▸**~ля́ться**) (+ *i.*) to become famous (for).

прославля́|ться, юсь *impf. of* ▸**просла́виться**

просле|ди́ть, жу́, ди́шь *pf.* (*of* ▸**~́живать**)
1 (*выследить*) to track (down).
2 (*исследовать*) to trace (through); to trace back, retrace.

просле́жива|ть, ю *impf. of* ▸**проследи́ть**

просло́йк|а, и *f.* layer, stratum (*also fig.*).

прослуж|и́ть, у́, ~́ишь *pf.*
1 to work, serve (*for a certain time*).
2 (*пробыть в употреблении*) to last (*for a certain time*); **э́то пальто́ ~́ит мне ещё оди́н год** this coat will last me another year.

прослу́ш|ать, аю *pf.*
[1] (*impf.* **слу́шать**) to hear (through); **п. курс ле́кций** to attend a course of lectures.
[2] (*impf.* **~ивать**) (*med.*) to listen to; **п. чьё-н. се́рдце** to listen to s.o.'s heart.
[3] (*impf.* **~ивать**) (*coll.*) to miss, not to catch; **прости́те, я ~ал, что вы сказа́ли** I am sorry, I did not catch what you said.

прослу́шивани|е, я *nt.* audition.

прослу́шива|ть, ю *impf. of* ▸ **прослу́шать 2, 3**

просма́трива|ть, ю *impf. of* ▸ **просмотре́ть**

просмо́тр, а *m.* survey; view, viewing; **предвари́тельный п.** preview.

просмотр|е́ть, ю́, ~ишь *pf.* (*of* ▸ **просма́тривать**)
[1] to survey; to view.
[2] (*читая*) to look over, look through; (*бегло*) to glance over, glance through; **п. ру́копись** to glance through a manuscript.
[3] (*пропустить*) to overlook, miss.

прос|ну́ться, ну́сь, нёшься *pf.* (*of* ▸ **~ыпа́ться**[1]) to wake up, awake.

просо́выва|ть(ся), ю(сь) *impf. of* ▸ **просу́нуть(ся)**

просо́х|нуть, ну, нешь, *past* **~, ~ла** *pf.* (*of* ▸ **просыха́ть**) to get dry, dry out.

просоч|и́ться, и́тся *pf.* (*of* ▸ **проса́чиваться**)
[1] to percolate; to filter; to leak; to seep out.
[2] (*fig.*) to filter through; to leak out.

просп|а́ть[2]**, лю́, и́шь,** *past* **~а́л, ~ала́, ~а́ло** *pf.* (*некоторое время*) to sleep (*for a certain time*).

просп|а́ть[1]**, лю́, и́шь,** *past* **~а́л, ~ала́, ~а́ло** *pf.* (*of* ▸ **просыпа́ть**[2])
[1] (*не проснуться вовремя*) to oversleep.
[2] (*пропустить*) to miss, pass (*due to being asleep*).

проспе́кт[1]**, а** *m.* (*улица*) avenue.

проспе́кт[2]**, а** *m.*
[1] (*справочное издание*) brochure, prospectus.
[2] (*план*) outline, résumé.

проспо́рива|ть, ю *impf. of* ▸ **проспо́рить**

проспо́р|ить, ю, ишь *pf.* (*of* ▸ **~ивать**) (*деньги*) to lose (*in a bet*).

проспряга́|ть, ю *pf. of* ▸ **спряга́ть**

просро́ч|енный *p.p.p. of* ▸ **~ить** *and adj.* overdue.

просро́чива|ть, ю *impf. of* ▸ **просро́чить**

просро́ч|ить, у, ишь *pf.* (*of* ▸ **~ивать**) to exceed the time limit; **п. платёж** to fail to pay in time.

воста́ива|ть, ю *impf. of* ▸ **просто́ять**

проста́к, а́ *m.* simpleton.

проста́т|а, ы *f.* (*anat.*) prostate (gland).

проститу́тк|а, и *f.* prostitute.

проститу́ци|я, и *f.* prostitution.

про|сти́ть, щу́, сти́шь *pf.* (*of* ▸ **~ща́ть**)
[1] to forgive, pardon; **~сти́те (меня́)!** excuse me!; I beg your pardon!
[2] (*долг*) to remit; **п. долг кому́-н.** to remit s.o.'s debt.

про|сти́ться, щу́сь, сти́шься *pf.* (*of* ▸ **~ща́ться**) (**с** + *i.*) to say goodbye (to), bid farewell (to).

про́сто *adv.* simply; **п. так** for no particular reason; **э́то п. невероя́тно** it is simply incredible.

простоду́ш|ный (~ен, ~на) *adj.* simple-hearted; ingenuous, artless.

прост|о́й (~, ~а́, ~о, ~ы) *adj.*
[1] (*нетрудный*) simple; easy; **вам ~о критикова́ть** it is easy (*or* all very well) for you to criticize.
[2] (*однородный*) simple (= *unitary*); **~о́е число́** (*math.*) prime number.
[3] (*обыкновенный*) simple; ordinary; **п. наро́д** the common people.
[4] (*без претензий*) simple, plain; unaffected, unpretentious; **~ы́е лю́ди** ordinary people; homely people.
[5] (*не более как*) mere; **п. сме́ртный** a mere mortal; **по той ~о́й причи́не, что** for the simple reason that.

простон|а́ть, у́, ~ешь *pf.* to groan.

просто́р, а *m.*
[1] (*пространство*) spaciousness; space, expanse.
[2] (*свобода*) freedom, scope.

просто́р|ный (~ен, ~на) *adj.* spacious, roomy; (*об одежде*) loose-fitting.

простот|а́, ы *f.* simplicity.

просто|я́ть, ю́, и́шь *pf.* (*of* ▸ **проста́ивать**)
[1] (*некоторое время*) to stay, stand; **по́езд ~я́л на запасно́м пути́ всю ночь** the train stood in a siding all night.
[2] (*бездействовать*) to stand idle, lie idle.
[3] (*о здании*) to stand, last.

простра́н|ный (~ен, ~на) *adj.* verbose.

простра́нственный *adj.* spatial.

простра́нств|о, а *nt.* space; (*неограниченная протяжённость*) expanse; **возду́шное п.** air space; **пусто́е п.** void.

простра́ци|я, и *f.* prostration.

простре́лива|ть, ю *impf. impf. of* ▸ **прострели́ть**

прострел|и́ть, ю́, ~ишь *pf.* (*of* ▸ **~ивать**)
[1] (*выстрелом пробить насквозь*) to shoot through.
[2] (*sport*) to cross low.

просту́д|а, ы *f.* (chest) cold; **схвати́ть/подхвати́ть ~у** (*coll.*) to catch (a) cold.

просту|ди́ть, жу́, ~дишь *pf.* (*of* ▸ **~жа́ть**) to let catch cold; **п. себе́ го́рло** to get a sore throat.

просту|ди́ться, жу́сь, ~дишься *pf.* (*of* ▸ **~жа́ться**) to catch (a) cold.

простужа́|ть(ся), ю(сь) *impf. of* ▸ **простуди́ть(ся)**

проступ|а́ть, а́ет *impf. of* ▸ **~и́ть**

проступ|и́ть, ~ит *pf.* (*of* ▸ **~а́ть**) to appear, show through, come through; **сыры́е пя́тна ~и́ли на сте́нах** damp patches have appeared on the walls.

просту́п|ок, ка *m.* misdeed; (*leg.*) misdemeanour (*Br.*), misdemeanor (*US*).

простыва́|ть, ю *impf. of* ▸ **просты́ть**

простын|я́, и́, *pl.* **про́стыни, ~е́й/~ь, ~я́м** *f.* sheet.

просты́|ть, ну, нешь *pf.* (*of* ▸ **~ва́ть**)

(*coll.*) to catch cold.

просу́н|уть, у, ешь *pf.* (*of* ▸ **просо́вывать**) (**в** + *a.*) to push (through, in), shove (through, in), thrust (through, in).

просу́н|уться, усь, ешься *pf.* (*of* ▸ **просо́вываться**) to push through, force one's way through.

просу́шива|ть(ся), ю(сь) *impf. of* ▸ **просуши́ть(ся)**

просуш|и́ть, у́, ~ишь *pf.* (*of* ▸ **~ивать**) to dry thoroughly, properly.

просуш|и́ться, у́сь, ~ишься *pf.* (*of* ▸ **~иваться**) to (get) dry.

просуществ|ова́ть, у́ю *pf.* (*прожить*) to exist; (*продлиться*) to last, endure.

просчёт, а *m.*
[1] (*действие*) counting (up), reckoning (up).
[2] (*ошибка*) error (*in counting, reckoning*).

просчит|а́ться, а́юсь *pf.* (*of* ▸ **~ываться**) to miscalculate.

просчи́тыва|ться, юсь *impf. of* ▸ **просчита́ться**

просып|а́ть[1], а́ю *impf. of* ▸ **~ать**

просып|а́ть[2], а́ю *impf. of* ▸ **проспа́ть[1]**

просы́п|ать, лю, лешь *pf.* (*of* ▸ **~а́ть[1]**) to spill.

просы́п|аться, лется *pf.* (*of* ▸ **~а́ться[2]**) to spill, get spilled.

просып|а́ться[1], а́юсь *impf. of* ▸ **просну́ться**

просып|а́ться[2], а́ется *impf. of* ▸ **~аться**

просыха́|ть, ю *impf. of* ▸ **просо́хнуть**

про́сьб|а, ы *f.* request; **обраща́ться с ~ой** to make a request; **у меня́ к вам п.** I have a favour (*Br.*), favor (*US*) to ask you; **по мое́й ~е** at my request; «**п. не кури́ть!**» 'no smoking, please!'

прота́лкива|ть, ю *impf. of* ▸ **протолкну́ть**

прота́птыва|ть, ю *impf. of* ▸ **протопта́ть**

прота́скива|ть, ю *impf. of* ▸ **протащи́ть**

протащ|и́ть, у́, ~ишь *pf.* (*of* ▸ **прота́скивать**) to pull (through, along), drag (through, along), trail.

проте́з, а *m.* prosthesis; artificial limb; **зубно́й п.** false tooth, denture.

протеи́н, а *m.* (*chem.*) protein.

протека́|ть, ю *impf.*
[1] *impf. of* ▸ **протéчь.**
[2] (*impf. only*) (*о реке, струе*) to flow, run.
[3] (*impf. only*) (*о крыше*) to leak, be leaky.

про|тере́ть, тру́, трёшь, *past* **~тёр, ~тёрла** *pf.* (*of* ▸ **~тира́ть**)
[1] (*окна*) to rub over, wipe over.
[2] : **п. глаза́** (*coll.*) to rub one's eyes.

проте́ст, а *m*
[1] protest; **заяви́ть п.** to make a protest.
[2] (*leg.*) objection.

протеста́нт, а *m.* (*relig.*) Protestant.

протеста́нт|ка, ки *f. of* ▸ **~**

протеста́нтский *adj.* (*relig.*) Protestant.

протест|ова́ть, у́ю *impf.* (**про́тив** + *g.*) to protest (against).

проте́|чь, чёт, ку́т, *past* **~к, ~кла́** *pf.* (*of* ▸ **~ка́ть**)
[1] to ooze, seep.
[2] (*о времени*) to elapse, pass.
[3] (*о болезни*) to take its course.

про́тив *prep.* + *g.*
[1] against; **п. тече́ния** against the current; **за и п.** for and against, pro and con; **име́ть что-н. п.** to have sth. against; to mind, object; **вы ничего́ не име́ете п. того́, что я курю́?** do you mind my smoking?
[2] (*прямо перед*) opposite; facing; **друг п. дру́га** facing one another.
[3] (*вопреки*) contrary to; **п. на́ших ожида́ний** contrary to our expectations.

про́тив|ень, ня *m.* (*неглубокий*) baking sheet, baking tray; (*глубокий*) roasting pan.

проти́вник, а *m.*
[1] opponent, adversary.
[2] (*collect.*; *mil.*) the enemy.

проти́вн|ый[1] *adj.* opposite; contrary; **в ~ом слу́чае** otherwise; **доказа́тельство от ~ого** the rule of contraries.

проти́в|ный[2] (~ен, ~на) *adj.* (*отвратительный*) nasty, disgusting; **п. за́пах** nasty smell; **он мне ~ен** I find him offensive.

противове́с, а *m.* (*tech. and fig.*) counterbalance, counterpoise.

противога́з, а *m.* gas mask.

противоде́йстви|е, я *nt.* opposition, counteraction.

противоде́йств|овать, ую *impf.* (+ *d.*) to oppose, counteract.

противоесте́ствен|ный (~, ~на) *adj.* unnatural.

противозако́н|ный (~ен, ~на) *adj.* unlawful; (*leg.*) illegal.

противозача́точн|ый *adj.* contraceptive; **~ое сре́дство** contraceptive.

противопожа́рн|ый *adj.* anti-fire; **~ая дверь** fire door.

противополо́жност|ь, и *f.*
[1] (*несходство*) opposition; contrast; **в п.** (+ *d.*) as opposed (to), by contrast (with).
[2] (*что-н. противоположное*) opposite, antithesis; **пряма́я п.** exact opposite.

противополо́ж|ный (~ен, ~на) *adj.*
[1] (*берег*) opposite.
[2] (*мнение*) opposed, contrary.

противопоста́в|ить, лю, ишь *pf.* (*of* ▸ **~ля́ть**) (+ *d.*)
[1] (*направить против*) to oppose (with), counter (with); **си́ле п. си́лу** to oppose force with force.
[2] (*сравнить*) to contrast (with), set off (against).

противопоставля́|ть, ю *impf. of* ▸ **противопоста́вить**

противопра́в|ный (~ен, ~на) *adj.* unlawful, illegal.

противоречи́в|ый (~, ~а) *adj.* contradictory; conflicting; **~ые сообще́ния** conflicting reports.

противоре́чи|е, я *nt.*
[1] (*несоответствие*) contradiction; inconsistency.
[2] (*возражение*) contrariness; defiance.
[3] (*конфликт*) conflict, clash; **находи́ться в ~и (с** + *i.*) to be at variance (with), conflict (with).

противоре́ч|ить, у, ишь *impf.* (+ *d.*)

1 (*возражать*) to contradict.
2 (*несоответствовать*) to be at variance (with), conflict (with), be contrary (to); **их показа́ния ~ат друг дру́гу** their evidence is conflicting.

противостоя́ни|е, я *nt.*
1 (*astron.*) opposition.
2 (*pol.*) confrontation.

противоя́ди|е, я *nt.* antidote.

протира́|ть, ю *impf. of* ▶ **протере́ть**

прокн|у́ть, у́, ёшь *pf.* (*of* ▶ **протыка́ть**) to pierce.

прото́к, а *m.*
1 channel.
2 (*anat.*) duct.

протоко́л, а *m.*
1 (*заседания*) minutes; report; **вести́ п.** to take the minutes.
2 (*leg.*) statement; charge sheet; **соста́вить п.** to draw up a report.
3 (*dipl., comput.*) protocol.

протолкн|у́ть, у́, ёшь *pf.* (*of* ▶ **прота́лкивать**) to push through, press through.

прото́н, а *m.* (*phys.*) proton.

протоп|та́ть, чу́, ~́чешь *pf.* (*of* ▶ **прота́птывать**) to beat, make (*by walking*); **п. тропи́нку** to make a path.

прототи́п, а *m.* prototype.

прото́чн|ый *adj.* flowing, running; **~ая вода́** running water; **п. пруд** pond fed by springs.

протрезве́|ть, ю *pf. of* ▶ **трезве́ть**

протрезв|и́ться, лю́сь, и́шься *pf.* (*of* ▶ **~ля́ться**) to sober up.

протрезвля́|ться, юсь *impf. of* ▶ **протрезви́ться**

протух|а́ть, а́ет *impf. of* ▶ **~́нуть**

проту́х|нуть, нет, *past* **~, ~ла** *pf.* (*of* ▶ **~а́ть**) (*мясо, рыба*) to go bad.

проту́х|ший *p.p. act. of* ▶ **~нуть** *and adj.* rotten; bad.

протыка́|ть, ю *impf. of* ▶ **проткну́ть**

протя́гива|ть(ся), ю(сь) *impf. of* ▶ **протяну́ть(ся)**

протяже́ни|е, я *nt.*
1 extent; (*пространство*) expanse, area; **на всём ~и** (+ *g.*) along the whole length (of), all along.
2 : **на ~и** (+ *g.*) during, for the duration (of).

протя́ж|ный (~ен, ~на) *adj.* long drawn-out.

прот|яну́ть, яну́, ~я́нешь *pf.* (*of* ▶ **~я́гивать**)
1 (*верёвку*) to stretch; (*линию связи*) to extend.
2 (*руки, ноги*) to stretch out; (*газету, книгу*) to hold out; **п. ру́ку по́мощи** to extend a helping hand.

прот|яну́ться, яну́сь, ~я́нешься *pf.* (*of* ▶ **~я́гиваться**)
1 (*о дороге, о пространстве*) to extend, stretch, reach.
2 (*pf. only*) (*продлиться*) to last, go on.

проу́чива|ть, ю *impf. of* ▶ **проучи́ть**

проуч|и́ть, у́, ~́ишь *pf.* (*of* ▶ **~́ивать**) (*coll.*) (*наказать*) to teach (a lesson).

профа́н, а *m.* ignoramus; (*неспециалист*) layman.

профессиона́л, а *m.* professional.

профессионали́зм, а *m.* professionalism.

профессиона́льный *adj.*
1 professional, occupational; **п. диплома́т** career diplomat; **п. секре́т** trade secret; **п. сою́з** trade union.
2 (*компетентный*) professional (*opp. amateur*).

профе́сси|я, и *f.* profession, occupation, trade; **по ~и** by profession, by trade.

профе́ссор, а, *pl.* **~а́** *m.* professor.

про́фи *c.g. indecl.* (*coll.*) professional; pro (*coll.*).

профила́ктик|а, и *f.*
1 (*med.*) prophylaxis.
2 (*collect.*) preventive measures, precautions.

профилакто́ри|й, я *m.* sanatorium, health farm.

про́фил|ь, я *m.*
1 (*вид сбоку*) profile; side view; **в п.** in profile.
2 (*специфический характер*) type; **шко́лы ра́зного ~я** schools of various types.

профильтр|ова́ть, у́ю *pf.* (*of* ▶ **фильтрова́ть**)

профсою́з, а *m.* trade union.

проха́жива|ться, юсь *impf. of* ▶ **пройти́сь**

прохла́д|а, ы *f.* coolness.

прохла́д|ный (~ен, ~на) *adj.*
1 cool; (*impers., pred.*): **~но** it is cool.
2 (*fig.*) cool.

прохо́д, а *m.*
1 (*действие*) passage; **не дава́ть ~а** (+ *d.*) to give no peace, pester.
2 (*место*) passageway; (*между рядами*) gangway, aisle.

проходи́м|ец, ца *m.* (*coll.*) rogue, rascal.

проходи́м|ый (~, ~а) *adj.* passable.

прохо|ди́ть[1], жу́, ~́дишь *impf.*
1 *impf. of* ▶ **пройти́.**
2 (*impf. only*) (**че́рез** + *a.*) to lie (through), go (through), pass (through).

прохо|ди́ть[2], жу́, ~́дишь *pf.* (*некоторое время*) to walk; **мы ~ди́ли весь день** we have spent the whole day walking.

прохо́ж|ий *adj.* passing, in transit; *as n.* **п., ~его** *m.*, **~ая, ~ей** *f.* passer-by.

процвета́ни|е, я *nt.* prosperity, well-being; flourishing.

процвета́|ть, ю *impf.* to prosper, flourish, thrive.

проце|ди́ть, жу́, ~́дишь *pf.* (*of* ▶ **~́живать**)
1 to filter, strain.
2 : **п. сквозь зу́бы** to say through clenched teeth.

процеду́р|а, ы *f.*
1 procedure.
2 (*usu. pl.*) (*med.*) treatment.

проце́жива|ть, ю *impf. of* ▶ **процеди́ть**

проце́нт, а *m.*
1 percentage; per cent; **сто ~ов** one hundred per cent.
2 (*доход с капитала*) interest.

проце́сс, а *m.*
1 process.
2 (*leg.*) trial; legal proceedings; lawsuit.

процéсси|я, и *f.* procession.
процéссор, а *m.* (*comput.*) processor; **центрáльный п.** central processing unit.
процитúр|овать, ую *pf. of* ▸ **цитúровать**
прóчерк, а *m.* dash, line.
про|чéсть, чтý, чтёшь, *past* **~чёл, ~члá** *pf.* = **~читáть**
прóч|ий *adj.* other; **и ~ее** (*abbr.* **и пр., и проч.**) et cetera, and so on; **~ие** (the) others; **мéжду ~им** by the way; **помúмо (всегó) ~его** in addition.
прочú|стить, щу, стишь *pf.* (*of* ▸ **~щáть**) to clean out.
прочитá|ть, ю *pf. of* ▸ **читáть**
прочищá|ть, ю *impf. of* ▸ **прочúстить**
прóчно *adv.* firmly, soundly, solidly, well.
прóчност|ь, и *f.* firmness, soundness, stability, solidity; durability; strength; **запáс ~и, коэффициéнт ~и** safety factor, safety margin.
прóч|ный (~ен, ~нá, ~но, ~нЫ) *adj.* firm, sound, stable, solid; durable, lasting; **~ные знáния** sound knowledge; **~ная ткань** durable fabric.
прочь *adv.*
1 away, off; **(подú) п.!** go away!; be off!; **п. с дорóги!** (get) out of the way!, make way!; **рýки п.!** hands off!
2 *as pred.* averse (to); **не п.** (+ *inf.*; *coll.*) to have no objection (to); to be not averse (to).
прошéдш|ий *p.p. act. of* ▸ **пройтú** *and adj.* past; last; **~ее врéмя** (*gram.*) past tense; *as n.* **~ее, ~его** *nt.* the past.
прошеп|тáть, чý, ~чешь *pf. of* ▸ **шептáть**
прошивá|ть, ю *impf. of* ▸ **прошúть**
прош|úть, ью, ьёшь *pf.* (*of* ▸ **~ивáть**) to sew, stitch (on).
прошлогóдний *adj.* last year's; of last year.
прóшл|ый *adj.*
1 (*происходивший ранее*) past; former; *as n.* **~ое, ~ого** *nt.* the past; **далёкое ~ое** the distant past.
2 (*предшествовавший настоящему*) last; **в ~ом годý** last year; **на ~ой недéле** last week.
прошмы́гива|ть, ю *impf. of* ▸ **прошмыгнýть**
прошмыг|нýть, нý, нёшь *pf.* (*of* ▸ **~ивать**) (*coll.*) (*человек*) to slip (by, past, through); (*животное*) to scurry past.
прощáй(те) goodbye!; farewell!
прощáни|е, я *nt.* farewell; parting, leave-taking; **на п.** at parting.
прощá|ть(ся), ю(сь) *impf. of* ▸ **простúть(ся)**
прóще *comp. of* ▸ **простóй** *and* ▸ **прóсто;** simpler; plainer; easier.
прощéни|е, я *nt.* forgiveness; (*преступника*) pardon; (*грехов*) absolution; **просúть ~я у когó-н.** to ask s.o.'s pardon; **прошý ~я!** I beg your pardon!; (I am) sorry!
проэкзамен|овáть, ýю *pf. of* ▸ **экзаменовáть**
прояв|úть, лю, ~ишь *pf.* (*of* ▸ **~лять**)
1 to show, display; **п. интерéс (к** + *d.*) to show interest (in); **п. себя́** (+ *i.*) to show o.s., prove (to be).
2 (*phot.*) to develop.
прояв|úться, ~ится *pf.* (*of* ▸ **~ля́ться**) to show (itself), reveal itself, manifest itself.
проявлéни|е, я *nt.* display, manifestation.
проявля́|ть(ся), ю, ет(ся) *impf. of* ▸ **проявúть(ся)**
проясн|úть, ю́, úшь *pf.* (*of* ▸ **~я́ть**) to clarify.
проясн|úться, úтся *pf.* (*of* ▸ **~я́ться**)
1 (*о погоде*) to clear (up); **днём ~úлось** in the afternoon it cleared up.
2 (*о мыслях, о положении*) to become clear.
проясн|я́ть, я́ю *impf. of* ▸ **~úть**
проясн|я́ться, я́ется *impf. of* ▸ **~úться**
пруд, á, в ~ý, *pl.* **~ы́** *m.* pond.
пружúн|а, ы *f.* spring.
Прýсси|я, и *f.* Prussia.
прут, á *m.* (*pl.* **~ья, ~ьев**) twig; switch; **úвовый п.** withe, withy.
пры́гал|ки, ок *no sg., f.* (*coll.*) skipping-rope (*Br.*), jump rope (*US*).
пры́г|ать, аю *impf.* (*of* ▸ **~нуть**)
1 to jump, leap, spring; to bound; **п. на однóй ногé** to hop on one leg; **п. со скакáлкой** to skip.
2 (*о мяче*) to bounce.
пры́г|нуть, ну, нешь *inst. pf. of* ▸ **~ать**
прыгýн, á *m.* (*sport*) jumper; **п. в вóду** diver; **п. в длинý** long jumper.
прыгýн|ья, ьи, *g. pl.* **~ий** *f. of* ▸ **~**
прыж|óк, кá *m.*
1 jump, leap, spring.
2 (*sport*) jump; **~кú** jumping; **~кú в вóду** diving; **п. в высотý** high jump; **п. в длинý** long jump.
пры́ска|ть, ю *impf. of* ▸ **пры́снуть**
пры́с|нуть, ну, нешь *pf.* (*of* ▸ **~кать**) (*coll.*)
1 (+ *i.*) to sprinkle (with); to spray (with).
2 (*политься струёй*) to spurt, gush.
пры́т|кий (~ок, ~ка) *adj.* quick, lively, sharp (*oft. disapproving*).
прыщ, á *m.* pimple, spot.
пряд|ь, и *f.* lock (*of hair*).
пря́ж|а, и *no pl., f.* yarn.
пря́жк|а, и *f.* buckle.
пря́лк|а, и *f.* spinning wheel.
прям|áя, óй *f.* straight line; **провестú ~ýю** to draw a straight line; **расстоя́ние по ~óй** distance as the crow flies.
прямикóм *adv.* (*coll.*) straight.
пря́мо *adv.*
1 straight (on); **идúте п.!** (go) straight on!; **держáться п.** to hold o.s. straight *or* erect.
2 (*непосредственно*) straight, directly; **смотрéть п. в глазá комý-н.** to look s.o. straight in the face.
3 (*fig.*) (*откровенно*) straight; frankly, openly; **сказáть что-н. комý-н. п. в лицó** to say sth. to s.o.'s face.
прям|óй (~, ~á, ~о, ~ы) *adj.*
1 (*без изгибов*) straight; (*вертикальный*) upright, erect; **п. ýгол** (*math.*) right angle.
2 (*без промежуточных пунктов*) through; direct; **~áя лúния** direct (*telephone*) line.

3 (*непосредственный*) direct; **~ые вы́боры** direct elections; **~а́я противополо́жность** direct opposite.
4 (*откровенный*) straightforward, frank.

прямолине́|йный (~ен, ~йна) *adj.*
1 rectilinear.
2 (*fig.*) straightforward; direct.

прямоуго́льник, а *m.* (*math.*) rectangle.

пря́ник, а *m.* spice cake; gingerbread; **медо́вый п.** honey cake.

пря́ност|ь, и *f.* spice.

пря|сть, ду́, дёшь, *past* **~л, ~ла́, ~ло** *impf.* (*of* ▸ **с~**) to spin.

пря́|тать, чу, чешь *impf.* (*of* ▸ **с~**) to hide, conceal.

пря́|таться, чусь, чешься *impf.* (*of* ▸ **с~**) to hide; to conceal o.s.; to take refuge.

прят|ки, ок *no sg.* hide-and-seek; **игра́ть в п.** to play hide-and-seek.

пря́х|а, и *f.* spinner.

псал|о́м, ма́ *m.* psalm.

псевдони́м, а *m.* pseudonym; (*comput.*) alias.

псих, а *m.* (*coll.*) loony, nutcase.

психиа́тр, а *m.* psychiatrist.

психиатри́ческий *adj.* psychiatric.

психиатри́|я, и *f.* psychiatry.

пси́хик|а, и *f.* state of mind; psyche; **вре́дно де́йствовать на ~у** to have a harmful effect on the psyche.

психи́чески *adv.* mentally, psychically, psychologically; **п. больно́й** mentally ill; *as n.* **п. больно́й, п. больно́го** *m.* mental patient.

психи́ческ|ий *adj.* mental; **~ая боле́знь** mental illness.

психоана́лиз, а *m.* psychoanalysis.

психоанали́тик, а *m.* psychoanalyst.

психо́з, а *m.* (*med.*) psychosis; **вое́нный п.** war hysteria.

психо́лог, а *m.* psychologist.

психологи́ческий *adj.* psychological.

психоло́ги|я, и *f.* psychology.

психопа́т, а *m.* psychopath; (*coll.*) lunatic.

психотерапе́вт, а *m.* psychotherapist.

психотерапи́|я, и *f.* psychotherapy.

псориа́з, а *m.* (*med.*) psoriasis.

птен|е́ц, ца́ *m.* chick; fledgling (*also fig.*).

пти́ц|а, ы *f.* bird; **дома́шняя п.** (*collect.*) poultry; **хи́щные ~ы** birds of prey; **ва́жная п.** (*fig., coll.*) big noise.

птицефе́рм|а, ы *f.* poultry farm.

ПТУ *nt. indecl.* (*abbr. of* **профессиона́льно-техни́ческое учи́лище**) vocational technical school.

пу́блик|а, и *f.* (*collect.*) (the) public; (*зрители, слушатели*) (the) audience.

публика́ци|я, и *f.*
1 (*действие*) publication.
2 (*объявление*) advertisement, notice.

публик|ова́ть, у́ю *impf.* (*of* ▸ **о~**) to publish.

публици́стик|а, и *f.* sociopolitical journalism.

публи́чно *adv.* publicly; in public; openly.

публи́чн|ый *adj.* public; **~ая библиоте́ка** public library; **п. дом** brothel.

пу́гал|о, а *nt.* scarecrow.

пуга́|ть, ю *impf.* (*of* ▸ **ис~, на~**)
1 to frighten, scare.
2 (+ *i.*) to threaten (with).

пуга́|ться, юсь *impf.* (*of* ▸ **ис~**) (+ *g.*) to be frightened (of), be scared (of); to take fright (at); (*о лошади*) to shy (at).

пугли́в|ый (~, ~а) *adj.* fearful, timid.

пу́говиц|а, ы *f.* button.

пу́дел|ь, я, *pl.* **~и, ~ей** *or* **~я́, ~е́й** *m.* poodle.

пу́динг, а *m.* pudding.

пу́др|а, ы *f.* powder.

пу́др|ить, ю, ишь *impf.* (*of* ▸ **на~**) to powder.

пу́др|иться, юсь, ишься *impf.* (*of* ▸ **на~**) to use powder, powder one's face.

пуза́т|ый (~, ~а) *adj.* (*coll.*) pot-bellied.

пу́з|о, а *nt.* (*coll.*) belly, paunch.

пузы́р|ь, я́ *m.*
1 (*шарик*) bubble; **мы́льный п.** soap bubble.
2 (*anat.*) bladder.

пулемёт, а *m.* machine gun.

пулемётчик, а *m.* machine-gunner.

пуленепробива́емый *adj.* bulletproof.

пуло́вер, а *m.* pullover.

пульвериза́тор, а *m.* atomizer, sprayer.

пульс, а *m.* pulse.

пульси́р|овать, ую *impf.* to pulsate; (*о боли*) to throb.

пульт, а *m.*
1 (*пюпитр*) desk, stand.
2 (*диспетчерский*) control panel; **п. ДУ, п. дистанцио́нного управле́ния** (*TV etc.*) remote control.

пу́л|я, и *f.* bullet.

пункт, а *m.*
1 point; spot; **населённый п.** inhabited area.
2 (*организационный центр*) station, centre (*Br.*), center (*US*); post, point; **медици́нский п.** first-aid station; **наблюда́тельный п.** observation post, point.
3 (*документа*) point; paragraph, item; **соглаше́ние из трёх ~ов** a three-point agreement.

пункти́р, а *m.* dotted line.

пунктуа́л|ьный (~ен, ~ьна) *adj.* punctual.

пунктуа́ци|я, и *f.* punctuation.

пунцо́в|ый (~, ~а) *adj.* crimson.

пунш, а *m.* punch (*drink*).

пупови́н|а, ы *f.* (*anat.*) umbilical cord.

пуп|о́к, ка́ *m.* navel.

пурпу́рный *adj.* purple.

пуск, а *m.* starting (up); setting in motion.

пуска́й *particle and conj.* (*coll.*) = **пусть**

пуска́|ть(ся), ю(сь) *impf. of* ▸ **пусти́ть(ся)**

пусте́|ть, ет *impf.* (*of* ▸ **о~**) to (become) empty; to become deserted.

пу|сти́ть, щу́, ~стишь *pf.* (*of* ▸ **~ска́ть**)
1 (*дать свободу*) to let go.

П

2 (*разрешить идти*) to let; to allow, permit; **нас не ~сти́ли в пала́ту** they would not let us into the ward.
3 (*разрешить войти*) to let in, allow to enter; **не п.** to keep out.
4 (*привести в движение*) to start, set in motion, set going; to set working; **п. во́ду** to turn on water; **п. слух** to start a rumour (*Br.*), rumor (*US*).
5 (*заставить или дать возможность двигаться*) to set, put; to send; **п. в ход** to start, launch, set going, set in train; **п. кора́бль ко дну** to send a ship to the bottom.

пу|сти́ться, щу́сь, ~́стишься *pf.* (*of* ▶ **~ска́ться**) (**в** + *a. or* + *inf.*; *coll.*)
1 (*отправиться*) to set out, start; **п. в путь** to set out, get on the way.
2 (*начать*) to begin, start; to set to; **п. в пляс** to break into a dance.

пуст|ова́ть, у́ю *impf.* to be empty, stand empty; (*о земле*) to lie fallow.

пуст|о́й (~, ~а́, ~́о, ~ы́) *adj.*
1 empty; **п. взгляд** vacant look; **~о́е ме́сто** blank space.
2 (*fig.*) (*несерьёзный*) idle; shallow; frivolous; **п. челове́к** shallow person.
3 (*fig.*) (*напрасный*) vain, ungrounded; **~ы́е слова́** mere words; **~ы́е угро́зы** empty threats, bluster.

пустот|а́, ы́, *pl.* **~́ы** *f.*
1 emptiness; void; (*phys.*) vacuum.
2 (*fig.*) emptiness, shallowness.
3 (*полое место*) cavity.

пу́стош|ь, и *f.* waste (plot of) land, waste ground.

пусты́н|ный (~ен, ~на) *adj.*
1 (*необитаемый*) uninhabited; **п. о́стров** desert island.
2 (*безлюдный*) deserted.

пусты́н|я, и *f.* desert, wilderness.

пусты́р|ь, я́ *m.* wasteland, vacant plot (of land).

пусты́шк|а, и *f.* (*coll.*) (*у младенца*) dummy (*Br.*), pacifier (*US*).

пусть
1 *particle* let; **п. она́ сама́ реши́т** let her decide herself.
2 *as conj.* though, even if; **п. им бу́дет проти́вно, но я до́лжен вы́сказать своё мне́ние** even if they hate it, I must express my opinion.
3 *particle* (*coll.*) (*ладно*) all right, very well.

пустя́к, а́ *m.* (*coll.*) trifle; **~и́!** (*ничего*) it's nothing!; never mind!; (*вздор*) nonsense!; rubbish!

пу́таниц|а, ы *f.* muddle, confusion; mess, tangle.

пу́та|ть, ю *impf.* (*of* ▶ **с~, за~**)
1 (*нитки*) to tangle.
2 (*сбивать с толку*) to confuse, muddle.
3 (*смешивать*) to confuse, mix up; **ты (всё) ещё ~ешь на́ши имена́** you are still mixing our names up.

пу́та|ться, юсь *impf.* (*of* ▶ **с~, за~**)
1 (*о нитках*) to get tangled.
2 (*о мыслях*) to get confused.
3 (*сбиваться с толку*) to get mixed up, get muddled; **п. в расска́зе** to give a muddled account.

путёвк|а, и *f.*
1 (*удостоверение*) pass, authorization; **пода́ть зая́вку на ~у в санато́рий** to apply for a place in a sanatorium.
2 place on a package holiday; **я купи́л ~у в Ита́лию** I have booked a package holiday to Italy.
3 (*водителя транспорта*) schedule of duties.

путеводи́тел|ь, я *m.* guide, guidebook.

путепрово́д, а *m.* (*над дорогой*) overpass, flyover; (*под дорогой*) underpass.

путеше́ственник, а *m.* traveller (*Br.*), traveler (*US*).

путеше́ственни|ца, цы *f. of* ▶ **~к**

путеше́стви|е, я *nt.*
1 journey; trip; (*морской*) voyage; cruise.
2 *pl.* (*liter.*) travels.

путеше́ств|овать, ую *impf.* to travel, go on travels; (*по морю*) to voyage.

путч, а *m.* (*pol.*) putsch.

пут|ь, и́, *i.* **ём, о ~и́,** *pl.* **~и́, ~е́й, ~я́м** *m.*
1 (*дорога*) way, track, path; (*aeron.*) track; (*astron.*) race; (*fig.*) road, course; **~и́ сообще́ния** communications; **на пра́вильном ~и́** on the right track.
2 (*rail.*) track.
3 (*путешествие*) journey; voyage; **в ~и́** on one's way, en route; **в четырёх днях ~и́ (от** + *g.*) four days' journey (from); **на обра́тном ~и́** on the way back; **по ~и́** on the way.
4 (*fig.*) (*средство*) way, means; **ми́рным ~ём** amicably, peaceably; **пойти́ по ~и́** (+ *g.*) to take the path (of).

пух, а, о ~́е, в ~у́ *m.* down; fluff; **ни ~а ни пера́!** (*coll.*) good luck!

пу́хл|ый (~, ~а́, ~о) *adj.* (*человек*) chubby, plump; (*книга, досье*) fat.

пу́х|нуть, ну, нешь, *past* **~** *and* **~нул, ~ла** *impf.* to swell.

пучегла́з|ый (~, ~а) *adj.* (*coll.*) goggle-eyed.

пучи́н|а, ы *f.* gulf, abyss (*also fig.*); (*морская бездна*) the deep.

пуши́ст|ый (~, ~а) *adj.* fluffy, downy.

пу́шк|а, и *f.* gun, cannon.

пуэрторика́н|ец, ца *m.* Puerto Rican.

пуэрторика́н|ка, ки *f. of* ▶ **~ец**

пуэ́рто-рика́нский *adj.* Puerto Rican.

Пуэ́рто-Ри́ко *nt. indecl.* Puerto Rico.

пчел|а́, ы́, *pl.* **~̈ы** *f.* bee.

пшени́ц|а, ы *f.* wheat.

пшени́чный *adj.* wheat(en).

пшён|ный *adj. of* ▶ **~о́**

пшен|о́, а́ *nt.* millet.

пыла́|ть, ю *impf.*
1 to blaze, flame.
2 (*о лице*) to glow.
3 (+ *i.*; *fig.*) to burn (with); **п. стра́стью** to be burning with passion.

пылесо́с, а *m.* vacuum cleaner, Hoover (*propr.*).

пылесо́с|ить, ишь *impf.* (*of* ▶ **про~**) to vacuum(-clean), hoover.

пыли́нк|а, и *f.* speck of dust.

пы́л|кий (~ок, ~ка́, ~ко) *adj.* (*желание, речь*) ardent, passionate; (*воображение*) fervid.

пыл|ь, и, о ~и, в ~и́ *f.* dust.

пы́л|ьный (~ен, ~ьна́, ~ьно) *adj.* dusty.

пыльц|а́, ы́ *f.* (*bot.*) pollen.

пыта́|ть, ю *impf.* to torture (*also fig.*); (*fig.*) to torment.

пыта́|ться, юсь *impf.* (*of* ▶ **по~**) to try, attempt.

пы́тк|а, и *f.* torture, torment (*also fig.*); **ору́дие ~и** instrument of torture.

пытли́в|ый (~, ~а) *adj.* inquisitive.

пых|те́ть, чу́, ти́шь *impf.* to puff, pant.

пы́ш|ный (~ен, ~на́, ~но) *adj.*
1 (*великолепный*) splendid, magnificent.
2 (*пушистый*) fluffy; light; luxuriant; **~ные во́лосы** fluffy hair.

пьедеста́л, а *m.* pedestal (*also fig.*).

пье́с|а, ы *f.*
1 (*theatr.*) play.
2 (*mus.*) piece.

пьяне́|ть, ю, ешь *impf.* (*of* ▶ **о~**) to get drunk, get intoxicated.

пья́ниц|а, ы *c.g.* drunkard.

пья́нк|а, и *f.* (*coll.*) drinking bout, binge, booze-up.

пья́нств|о, а *nt.* drunkenness.

пья́н|ый (~, ~а́, ~о, ~ы́) *adj.* drunk; drunken; intoxicated; *as n.* **п., ~ого** *m.* (a) drunk.

пюре́ *nt. indecl.* (*cul.*) purée; **карто́фельное п.** mashed potatoes.

пятёрк|а, и *f.*
1 (*цифра, игральная карта*) five.
2 (*отметка*) five (*highest mark in Russian educational marking system*).
3 (*coll.*) (*автобус, трамвай*) No. 5 (*bus, tram, etc.*).
4 (*группа из пятерых*) (group of) five.
5 (*coll.*) (*пять рублей*) five-rouble note, fiver.

пя́тер|о, ы́х *num.* (*collect.*) five.

пятидеся́т|ый *adj.* fiftieth; **~ые го́ды** the fifties.

пятизвёздочный *adj.* five-star.

пятикра́тный *adj.* fivefold.

пятисо́тый *adj.* five-hundredth.

пя́|титься, чусь, тишься *impf.* (*of* ▶ **по~**) to back, move backward(s); (*о лошади*) to jib.

пя́тк|а, и *f.* heel (*also of sock or stocking*).

пятна́дцатый *adj.* fifteenth.

пятна́дцат|ь, и *num.* fifteen.

пятни́ст|ый (~, ~а) *adj.* spotted, dappled; **п. оле́нь** spotted deer.

пя́тниц|а, ы *f.* Friday.

пят|но́, на́, *pl.* **~на, ~ен, ~нам** *nt.*
1 (*место иной окраски*) spot; patch; (*запачканное место*) stain; **роди́мое п.** birthmark.
2 (*fig.*) blot, stain; blemish.

пя́т|ый *adj.* fifth; **глава́ ~ая** chapter five; **в ~ом часу́** after four (o'clock).

пят|ь, и́, *i.* **ью́** *num.* five.

пятьдеся́т, пяти́десяти, *i.* **пятью́десятью** *num.* fifty.

пятьсо́т, пятисо́т, пятиста́м, пятьюста́ми *num.* five hundred.

пя́тью *adv.* five times; **п. шесть** five times six.

Рр

раб, а́ *m.* slave.

рабо́т|а, ы *f.*
1 (*действие*) work, working; (*функционирование*) functioning, running.
2 (*занятие, труд*) work; labour (*Br.*), labor (*US*); **дома́шняя р.** homework; **сельскохозя́йственные ~ы** agricultural work.
3 (*как источник заработка*) work, job; **постоя́нная р.** regular work; **случа́йная р.** casual work, odd job(s); **иска́ть ~у** to look for a job.

рабо́та|ть, ю *impf.*
1 (**на** + *a.*; **над** + *i.*) to work (for; on); **он ~ет над но́вым рома́ном** he is working on a new novel.
2 (*функционировать*) to work, run, function; **не р.** not to work, be out of order.
3 (*быть открытым*) to be open; **галере́я не ~ет по воскресе́ньям** the gallery is not open on Sundays.
4 (+ *i.*) (*управлять*) to work, operate; **р. вёслами** to ply the oars.

рабо́тник, а *m.* worker; (*учреждения*) employee.

рабо́тниц|а, ы *f.* (*female*) worker; (*учреждения*) (*female*) employee.

работода́тел|ь, я *m.* employer.

работоспосо́б|ный (~ен, ~на) *adj.*
1 (*могущий работать*) able to work, able-bodied.
2 (*способный много работать*) able to work hard, hardworking.

работя́щий *adj.* (*coll.*) hard-working, industrious.

рабо́ч|ий[1], его *m.* worker; workman; **~ие** (*collect.*; *as social class*) the workers.

рабо́ч|ий[2] *adj.*
1 (*относящийся к рабочим*) workers', working-class; **р. класс** the working class.
2 (*выполняющий работу*) work, working; **~ая си́ла** manpower.
3 (*предназначенный для работы*) working;

∼ее врéмя working time, working hours; **р. день** working day (*Br.*), workday (*US*); **∼ее мéсто** (*i*) (*помещение*) working place, workplace, (*ii*) (*пост*) job.
4 : **в ∼ем поря́дке** while working, without breaking off from work.

рáб|ский *adj.*
1 *adj. of* ▶ **∼; р. труд** slave labour (*Br.*), labor (*US*).
2 (*fig.*) (*раболепный*) servile.

рáбств|о, а *nt.* slavery, servitude.

рабы́н|я, и, *g. pl.* **∼ь** *f.* (*female*) slave.

раввúн, а *m.* rabbi.

рáвенств|о, а *nt.* equality; parity; **знак ∼а** (*math.*) equals sign.

равиóл|и, ей *m. pl.* ravioli.

равнúн|а, ы *f.* plain.

равнó *nt. pred. form of* ▶ **рáвный**
1 (*math.*) make(s), equals, is; **три плюс три р. шести́** three plus three equals six.
2 : **всё р.** it is all the same, it makes no difference; *as adv.* all the same; **всё р., что** it is just the same as, it is equivalent to; **мне всё р.** I don't care; it's all the same, all one to me; **я всё р. вам позвоню́** I will ring you all the same.

равновéси|е, я *nt.* equilibrium (*also fig.*); balance; **душéвное р.** mental equilibrium; **сохраня́ть р.** to keep one's balance.

равнодéнстви|е, я *nt.*: **весéннее, осéннее р.** spring, autumn equinox.

равноду́ши|е, я *nt.* indifference.

равноду́ш|ный (∼ен, ∼на) *adj.* (**к** + *d.*) indifferent (to).

равнозначн|ный (∼ен, ∼на) *adj.* equivalent.

равномéр|ный (∼ен, ∼на) *adj.* even; uniform.

Р

равнопрáви|е, я *nt.* (possession of) equal rights; equality.

равносúл|ьный (∼ен, ∼ьна) *adj.* (+ *d.*) equal (to), equivalent (to), tantamount (to); **э́то ∼ьно измéне** it is tantamount to treachery; it amounts to treachery.

равноцéн|ный (∼ен, ∼на) *adj.* of equal value, of equal worth; equivalent.

рáв|ный (∼ен, ∼нá, ∼нó) *adj.* equal; **ему́ нет ∼ных** he has no equal.

равня́|ться, юсь *impf.*
1 (**по** + *d.*) (*mil.*) to dress; **∼йсь!** (*word of command*) eyes right!
2 (*impf. only*) (+ *d.*) to equal, be equal (to); (*fig.*) to be equivalent (to); **двáжды пять ∼ется десяти́** twice five is ten.

рагу́ *nt. indecl.* (*cul.*) stew.

рад (∼а, ∼о) *pred. adj.* (+ *d.*; + *inf.*; **что**) glad (of; to; that); **(óчень) р. познакóмиться с вáми!** pleased to meet you!

радáр, а *m.* radar.

рáди *prep.* + *g.* for the sake of; **чегó р.?** what for?; **р. бóга** (*coll.*) for God's sake.

радиáтор, а *m.* radiator.

радиáци|я, и *f.* radiation.

рáди|й, я *m.* (*chem.*) radium.

радикáл, а *m.* (*pol.*) radical.

радикáл|ьный (∼ен, ∼ьна) *adj.*
1 (*pol.*) radical.
2 (*решительный*) radical, drastic; **∼ьное срéдство** drastic remedy.

радикулúт, а *m.* radiculitis; back pain.

рáдио *nt. indecl.*
1 (*средство связи*) radio; **по р.** by radio, over the air; **передáть по р.** to broadcast; **слу́шать р.** to listen in.
2 (*радиоприёмник*) radio.

радиоактúвност|ь, и *f.* radioactivity.

радиоактúв|ный (∼ен, ∼на) *adj.* radioactive.

радиовещáни|е, я *nt.* (radio) broadcasting.

радиолокáтор, а *m.* radar set.

радиоприёмник, а *m.* radio (set).

радиостáнци|я, и *f.* radio station.

радиотелефóн, а *m.* cordless (tele)phone.

радиотерапú|я, и *f.* radiotherapy.

радúст, а *m.* radio operator.

радúст|ка, ки *f. of* ▶ **∼**

рáдиус, а *m.* radius; **р. дéйствия** range.

рáд|овать, ую *impf.* (*of* ▶ **об∼, по∼**) to gladden, make happy.

рáд|оваться, уюсь *impf.* (*of* ▶ **об∼, по∼**) (+ *d.*) to be glad (at), be happy (at), rejoice (in).

рáдост|ный (∼ен, ∼на) *adj.* glad, joyous, joyful; **∼ное извéстие** glad tidings, good news.

рáдост|ь, и *f.* gladness, joy; **к всеóбщей ∼и** to everybody's delight; **с ∼ью** with pleasure, gladly.

рáдуг|а, и *f.* rainbow.

рáдужн|ый *adj.*
1 (*переливчатый*) iridescent, opalescent; **∼ая оболóчка (глáза)** (*anat.*) iris.
2 (*светлый, радостный*) cheerful; optimistic; **∼ые надéжды** high hopes.

раду́ш|ный (∼ен, ∼на) *adj.* cordial.

раз[1]**, а,** *pl.* **∼ы́, ∼, ∼áм** *m.*
1 time; occasion; **оди́н р., кáк-то р.** once; **два ∽а** twice; **мнóго р.** many times; **ещё р.** once again, once more; **не р.** more than once; time and again; **ни ∽у** not once, never; **р. (и) навсегдá** once (and) for all; **р. в день** once a day; **вся́кий р.** every time, each time; **вся́кий р., когдá** whenever; **в другóй р.** another time, some other time; **на э́тот р.** this time, on this occasion, for (this) once; **с пéрвого ∽а** from the very first; **как р.** just, exactly.
2 (*num.*) one.

раз[2] *conj.* if; since; **р. вы бу́дете во Фрáнции, не смóжете ли вы приéхать и сюдá?** if you are going to be in France, can't you come here too?

раз[1]**...** (*also* **разо..., разъ...** *and* **рас...**) *vbl. pref. indicating*
1 *division into parts* (dis-, un-).
2 *distribution, direction of action in different directions* (dis-).
3 *action in reverse* (un-).
4 *termination of action or state.*
5 *intensification of action.*

раз[2]**...** (*also* **разо..., разъ...** *and* **рас...**) (*coll.*) *adj. pref. indicating high degree of a quality.*

разба́в|ить, лю, ишь *pf.* (*of* ▶ **~ля́ть**) to dilute.

разбавля́|ть, ю *impf. of* ▶ **разба́вить**

разба́лива|ться, юсь *impf. of* ▶ **разболе́ться**

разба́лтыва|ть(ся), ю(сь) *impf. of* ▶ **разболта́ть(ся)**

разбе́г, а *m.* run, running start; **пры́гнуть с ~а** to take a running jump; **р. при взлёте** (*aeron.*) take-off run.

разбега́|ться, юсь *impf. of* ▶ **разбежа́ться**

разбе|жа́ться, гу́сь, жи́шься, гу́тся *pf.* (*of* ▶ **~га́ться**)
1 (*взять разбег*) to take a run, run up.
2 (*в разные стороны*) to scatter, disperse.
3 (*о мыслях*) to be scattered; **глаза́ у меня́ ~жа́лись** I was dazzled.

разбива́|ть(ся), ю(сь) *impf. of* ▶ **разби́ть(ся)**

разбинт|ова́ть, у́ю *pf.* (*of* ▶ **~о́вывать**) to remove a bandage (from).

разбинто́выва|ть, ю *impf. of* ▶ **разбинтова́ть**

разбира́тельств|о, а *nt.* (*leg.*) examination, investigation; **суде́бное р.** court examination.

разбира́|ть, ю *impf. of* ▶ **разобра́ть**

разбира́|ться, юсь *impf. of* ▶ **разобра́ться**

раз|би́ть, обью́, обьёшь *pf.* (*of* ▶ **~бива́ть**)
1 (*impf. also* **бить 4**) (*окно, чашку*) to break, smash.
2 (*разделить*) to divide (up); to break up; **р. на гру́ппы** to divide up into groups.
3 (*расположить*) to lay out, mark out; **р. ла́герь** to pitch a camp.
4 (*повредить*) to damage severely, hurt badly; to fracture; **р. кому́-н. нос в кровь** to make s.o.'s nose bleed.
5 (*победить*) to beat, defeat, smash (*also fig.*).

раз|би́ться, обью́сь, обьёшься *pf.* (*of* ▶ **~бива́ться**)
1 (*расколоться*) to break, get broken, get smashed.
2 (*разделиться*) to divide; to break up.
3 (*пораниться*) to hurt o.s. badly; to smash o.s. up.

разбогате́|ть, ю, ешь *pf. of* ▶ **богате́ть**

разбо́|й, я *m.* robbery; **морско́й р.** piracy.

разбо́йник, а *m.* robber; **морско́й р.** pirate.

разболе́|ться[1], юсь, ешься *pf.* (*of* ▶ **разба́ливаться**) (*coll.*) to become ill; **он совсе́м ~лся** his health has completely cracked.

разбол|е́ться[2], и́тся *pf.* (*of* ▶ **разба́ливаться**) to begin to ache badly.

разболта́|ть[1], ю *pf.* (*of* ▶ **разба́лтывать**) (*размешать*) to mix in.

разболта́|ть[2], ю *pf.* (*of* ▶ **разба́лтывать**) (*coll.*) (*секрет*) to blab out, give away.

разболта́|ться, юсь *pf.* (*of* ▶ **разба́лтываться**)
1 (*о муке*) to mix in (*as result of stirring*).
2 (*о гайке*) to come loose, work loose.
3 (*fig.*) (*об ученике*) to get out of hand; to come unstuck.

разбомб|и́ть, лю́, и́шь *pf.* (*no impf.*) to destroy by bombing.

разбо́рк|а, и *f.*
1 (*бумаг*) sorting out.
2 (*механизма*) stripping, dismantling.
3 (*coll.*) (*ссора*) quarrel, fight, argument.

разбо́рчив|ый (~, ~а) *adj.*
1 (*требовательный*) fastidious, exacting; discriminating; scrupulous.
2 (*чёткий*) legible.

разбра́сыва|ть, ю *impf. of* ▶ **разброса́ть**

разбреда́|ться, юсь *impf. of* ▶ **разбрести́сь**

разбре|сти́сь, ду́сь, дёшься, *past* **~лся, ~ла́сь** *pf.* (*of* ▶ **~да́ться**) to disperse; **р. по дома́м** to disperse and go home.

разбро́д, а *m.* disorder.

разброса́|ть, ю *pf.* (*of* ▶ **разбра́сывать**) to scatter, spread.

разбры́зг|ать, аю *pf.* (*of* ▶ **~ивать**) to splash; to spray.

разбры́згивател|ь, я *m.* sprinkler.

разбры́згива|ть, ю *impf. of* ▶ **разбры́згать**

разбу|ди́ть, жу́, ~дишь *pf. of* ▶ **буди́ть 1**

разбух|а́ть, а́ет *impf. of* ▶ **~нуть**

разбу́х|нуть, нет, *past* **~, ~ла** *pf.* (*of* ▶ **~а́ть**) to swell (*also fig.*).

разбуш|ева́ться, у́юсь *pf.* (*о буре*) to rage; to blow up; (*о море*) to run high.

разва́л, а *m.*
1 (*распад*) breakdown, disintegration; (*беспорядок*) disorder.
2 (*рынок*) flea market.

разва́лива|ть(ся), ю(сь) *impf. of* ▶ **развали́ть(ся)**

разва́лин|а, ы *f. pl.* ruins; **лежа́ть в ~ах** to be in ruins; **преврати́ть в ~ы** to reduce to ruins.

развал|и́ть, ю́, ~ишь *pf.* (*of* ▶ **~ивать**)
1 to pull down (*a building, etc.*).
2 (*fig.*) (*хозяйство*) to ruin.

развал|и́ться, ю́сь, ~ишься *pf.* (*of* ▶ **~иваться**)
1 (*распасться*) to fall down, collapse.
2 (*fig.*) (*прийти в упадок*) to go to pieces, fall to pieces, break down.
3 (*coll.*) (*сидеть, раскинувшись*) to lounge, sprawl.

ра́зве
1 *interrog. particle, neutral or indicating that neg. answer is expected; + neg. indicates that affirmative answer is expected* **р. они́ все поме́стятся в э́той маши́не?** will they (really) all get in this car?; **р. ты не знал, что он ру́сский?** didn't you know that he is Russian?; surely you knew that he is Russian?
2 **р. (что), р. (то́лько)** *as adv.* only; perhaps; *as conj.* except that, only; **он вы́глядит так же как всегда́, р. что похуде́л** he looks the same as ever, except that he has lost weight.

развева́|ться, ется *impf.* (*флаг*) to flutter; (*волосы, плащ*) to blow about.

разве́д|ать, аю *pf.* (*of* ▶ **~ывать**)
1 (*coll.*) to find out (about).
2 (*mil.*) to reconnoitre (*Br.*), reconnoiter (*US*).
3 (*geol.*) to prospect (for); (*pf. only*) to locate; **р. нефть** to prospect for oil.

разведе́ни|е, я *nt.* (*скота*) breeding, rearing; (*сада*) cultivation; (*костра*) making.

разведённ|ый *p.p.p. of* ▶ **развести́** *and adj.* divorced; *as n.* **р., ~ого** *m.*, **~ая, ~ой** *f.* divorcee.

разве́дк|а, и *f.*
1 (*geol., etc.*) prospecting.
2 (*mil.*) (*для получения сведений*) reconnaissance.
3 (*pol.*) intelligence service.

разве́дчик, а *m.*
1 (*mil.*) scout.
2 (*pol.*) intelligence officer.

разве́дывательный *adj.*
1 (*mil.*) reconnaissance; **р. бой** probing attack; **р. отря́д** reconnaissance detachment.
2 (*pol.*) intelligence; **р. отде́л** intelligence section.

разве́дыва|ть, ю *impf. of* ▶ **разве́дать**

развез|ти́, у́, ёшь, *past* **~̈, ~ла́** *pf.* (*of* ▶ **развози́ть**) (*доставить*) to deliver.

разве́ива|ть(ся), ю(сь) *impf. of* ▶ **разве́ять(ся)**

разв|ёрнутый *p.p.p. of* ▶ **~ерну́ть** *and adj.*
1 (*предпринятый в широких масштабах*) extensive.
2 (*подробный*) detailed.

развер|ну́ть, ну́, нёшь *pf.* (*of* ▶ **развора́чивать**)
1 (*бумагу*) to unfold; (*ковёр*) to unroll; (*свёрток*) to unwrap; (*знамя*) to unfurl.
2 (*mil.*) (*перестроить*) to deploy.
3 (*fig.*) (*проявить*) to show, display.
4 (*fig.*) (*стройку, торговлю, работу*) to develop; to expand.
5 (*машину*) to turn (around).

развер|ну́ться, ну́сь, нёшься *pf.* (*of* ▶ **развора́чиваться**)
1 (*о бумаге*) to come unfolded; (*о ковре*) to come unrolled; (*о свёртке*) to come undone.
2 (*mil.*) (*перестроиться*) to deploy.
3 (*fig.*) (*проявиться*) to show *or* display o.s.
4 (*fig.*) (*о стройке, торговле, работе*) to develop; to expand.
5 (*о машине*) to turn (around).

развесел|и́ть, ю́, и́шь *pf. of* ▶ **веселить**

развесел|и́ться, ю́сь, и́шься *pf.* to cheer up.

разве́|сить¹, шу, сишь *pf.* (*of* ▶ **~шивать**)
1 (*картины*) to hang.
2 (*ветви*) to spread.

разве́|сить², шу, сишь *pf.* (*of* ▶ **~шивать**) (*бельё*) to hang out.

разве|сти́¹, ду́, дёшь, *past* **~̈л, ~ла́** *pf.* (*of* ▶ **разводи́ть**)
1 (*ведя, доставить*) to take, conduct; **р. дете́й по дома́м** to take the children to their homes.
2 (*в разные стороны*) to part, separate; **р. мост** to raise a bridge; **р. рука́ми** to shrug one's shoulders.
3 (*сок*) to dilute; (*порошок*) to dissolve.

разве|сти́², ду́, дёшь, *past* **~̈л, ~ла́** *pf.* (*of* ▶ **разводи́ть**)
1 (*животных*) to breed, rear; (*сад*) to cultivate; **р. парк** to lay out a park.
2 (*разжечь*) to start; **р. костёр** to make a campfire.

разве|сти́сь¹, ду́сь, дёшься, *past* **~̈лся, ~ла́сь** *pf.* (*of* ▶ **разводи́ться**) (**с** + *i.*) to divorce, get divorced (from).

разве|сти́сь², дётся, *past* **~̈лся, ~ла́сь** *pf.* (*of* ▶ **разводи́ться**) (*о животных*) to breed, multiply.

разветвле́ни|е, я *nt.*
1 (*действие*) branching; forking.
2 (*место*) branch; fork (*of road, etc.*).

разве́ш|ать, аю *pf.* (*of* ▶ **~ивать**) to hang.

разве́шива|ть, ю *impf. of* ▶ **разве́сить** *and* ▶ **разве́шать**

разве́|ять, ю, ешь *pf.* (*of* ▶ **~ивать**) to scatter, disperse; (*fig.*) (*грусть, сомнения*) to dispel; **р. миф** to shatter a myth.

разве́|яться, юсь, ешься *pf.* (*of* ▶ **~иваться**)
1 (*о тумане*) to disperse; (*fig.*) (*о тоске*) to be dispelled.
2 (*coll.*) (*о человеке*) to relax.

развива́|ть(ся), ю(сь) *impf. of* ▶ **разви́ть(ся)**

развин|ти́ть, чу́, ти́шь *pf.* (*of* ▶ **~́чивать**) to unscrew.

развин|ти́ться, чу́сь, ти́шься *pf.* (*of* ▶ **~́чиваться**) to come unscrewed.

разви́нчива|ть(ся), ю(сь) *impf. of* ▶ **развинти́ть(ся)**

разви́ти|е, я *nt.* development; evolution.

развит|о́й (ра́звит, ~а́, ра́звито) *adj.*
1 developed.
2 (*умственно*) (intellectually) mature; adult.

раз|ви́ть, овью́, овьёшь, *past* **~ви́л, ~вила́, ~ви́ло** *pf.* (*of* ▶ **~вива́ть**) to develop; **р. мускулату́ру** to develop one's muscles; **р. ско́рость** to gather speed.

раз|ви́ться, овью́сь, овьёшься, *past* **~ви́лся, ~вила́сь** *pf.* (*of* ▶ **~вива́ться**) (*о мускулах, о таланте*) to develop.

развлека́тел|ьный (~ен, ~ьна) *adj.* entertaining; **~ьное чте́ние** light reading.

развлека́|ть(ся), ю(сь) *impf. of* ▶ **развле́чь(ся)**

развлече́ни|е, я *nt.* entertainment; amusement.

развле́|чь, ку́, чёшь, ку́т, *past* **~̈к, ~кла́** *pf.* (*of* ▶ **~ка́ть**)
1 (*повеселить*) to entertain, amuse.
2 (*отвлечь*) to divert.

развле́|чься, ку́сь, чёшься, ку́тся, *past* **~̈кся, ~кла́сь** *pf.* (*of* ▶ **~ка́ться**)
1 (*повеселиться*) to have a good time; to amuse o.s.
2 (*отвлечься*) to be distracted.

разво́д, а *m.* divorce; **они́ в ~е** they are divorced.

разво|ди́ть(ся), жу́(сь), ~́дишь(ся) *impf. of* ▶ **развести́(сь)**

разво|зи́ть, жу́, ~́зишь *impf. of* ▶ **развезти́**

разволн|ова́ться, у́юсь *pf.* to get

excited, get agitated.

развора́чива|ть, ю *impf. of* ▶ **разверну́ть**

развора́чива|ться, юсь *impf. of* ▶ **разверну́ться**

развор|ова́ть, у́ю *pf.* (*of* ▶ **~о́вывать**) to loot, clean out.

разворо́выва|ть, ю *impf. of* ▶ **разворова́ть**

разворо́т, а *m.*
1 (*машины*) U-turn.
2 (*в книге*) double page.

разворош|и́ть, у́, и́шь *pf.* to turn upside down, scatter.

развра́т, а *m.* (*половой*) debauchery; (*духовный*) depravity.

развра|ти́ть, щу́, ти́шь *pf.* (*of* ▶ **~ща́ть**) to corrupt.

развра́т|ный (~ен, ~на) *adj.* debauched; corrupt.

развраща́|ть, ю *impf. of* ▶ **разврати́ть**

развя|за́ть, жу́, ~́жешь *pf.* (*of* ▶ **~́зывать**) to untie, undo; to unleash; **р. кому́-н. ру́ки** to untie s.o.'s hands (*also fig.*); **р. войну́** to unleash war.

развя|за́ться, жу́сь, ~́жешься *pf.* (*of* ▶ **~́зываться**) to come untied, come undone.

развя́зк|а, и *f.*
1 (*liter.*) denouement.
2 (*завершение*) outcome, upshot; **де́ло идёт к ~е** things are coming to a head.
3 : **(тра́нспортная) р.** (traffic) roundabout.

развя́з|ный (~ен, ~на) *adj.* (unduly) familiar; free-and-easy.

развя́зыва|ть(ся), ю(сь) *impf. of* ▶ **развяза́ть(ся)**

разгад|а́ть, а́ю *pf.* (*of* ▶ **~́ывать**) (*тайну, замысел*) to guess; (*загадку*) to solve; (*сны*) to interpret; (*шифр*) to break; (*человека*) to figure out.

разга́дк|а, и *f.* solution (*of a riddle, etc.*).

разга́дыва|ть, ю *impf. of* ▶ **разгада́ть**

разга́р, а *m.*: **в ~е** (+ *g.*) at the height (of); **в по́лном ~е** in full swing; **в ~е бо́я** in the heat of the battle; **р. сезо́на** peak season.

разгиба́|ть(ся), ю(сь) *impf. of* ▶ **разогну́ть(ся)**

разглаго́льств|овать, ую *impf.* (*coll.*) to hold forth; to talk big.

разгла́|дить, жу, дишь *pf.* (*of* ▶ **~живать**) to smooth out; to iron out, press.

разгла́|диться, дится *pf.* (*of* ▶ **~живаться**) (*платье*) to become smoothed out; (*морщины*) to drop out.

разгла́жива|ть(ся), ю, ет(ся) *impf. of* ▶ **разгла́дить(ся)**

разгла|си́ть, шу́, си́шь *pf.* (*of* ▶ **~ша́ть**) to divulge, give away, let out.

разглаша́|ть, ю *impf. of* ▶ **разгласи́ть**

разгля|де́ть, жу́, ди́шь *pf.* to make out, discern.

разгля́дыва|ть, ю *impf.* to examine closely, scrutinize.

разгова́рива|ть, ю *impf.* (**с** + *i.*) to talk (to, with), speak (to, with); **переста́ньте р.!** stop talking!; **они́ друг с дру́гом не ~ют** they are not on speaking terms.

разгово́р, а *m.*
1 talk, conversation; **без ~ов!** and no argument!
2 *pl.* (*coll.*) (*толки*) gossip.

разговор|и́ть, ю́, и́шь *pf.* (*coll.*) to dissuade.

разговор|и́ться, ю́сь, и́шься *pf.*
1 (**с** + *i.*) to get into conversation (with).
2 (*увлечься разговором*) to warm to one's theme.

разгово́рник, а *m.* phrase book.

разгово́рный *adj.* colloquial.

разгово́рчив|ый (~, ~а) *adj.* talkative.

разго́н, а *m.*
1 (*толпы*) dispersal; **р. собра́ния** breaking up of a meeting.
2 (*sport*) running start.
3 (*машины*) acceleration.

разгоня́|ть(ся), ю(сь) *impf. of* ▶ **разогна́ть(ся)**

разгор|а́ться, а́ется *impf. of* ▶ **~е́ться**

разгор|е́ться, и́тся *pf.* (*of* ▶ **~а́ться**)
1 (*об огне*) to flare up.
2 (*fig.*) (*о битве, о споре*) to flare up.

разгра́б|ить, лю, ишь *pf.* to plunder, loot.

разграниче́ни|е, я *nt.*
1 (*размежевание*) demarcation, delimitation.
2 (*определение*) differentiation.

разграни́чива|ть, ю *impf. of* ▶ **разграни́чить**

разграни́ч|ить, у, ишь *pf.* (*of* ▶ **~ивать**)
1 (*размежевать*) to delimit, demarcate.
2 (*точно определить*) to differentiate, distinguish.

разгреба́|ть, ю *impf. of* ▶ **разгрести́**

разгре|сти́, бу́, бёшь, *past* **~̈б, ~бла́** *pf.* (*of* ▶ **~ба́ть**) to rake (aside); to shovel (aside).

разгро́м, а *m.* (*неприятеля*) crushing defeat, rout.

разгром|и́ть, лю́, и́шь *pf. of* ▶ **громи́ть**

разгружа́|ть(ся), ю(сь) *impf. of* ▶ **разгрузи́ть(ся)**

разгру|зи́ть, жу́, ~́зишь *pf.* (*of* ▶ **~жа́ть**)
1 to unload.
2 (**от** + *g.*; *fig., coll.*) to relieve (of).

разгру|зи́ться, жу́сь, ~́зишься *pf.* (*of* ▶ **~жа́ться**) to unload.

разгру́зк|а, и *f.* unloading.

разгрыза́|ть, ю *impf. of* ▶ **разгры́зть**

разгры́з|ть, у́, ёшь, *past* **~, ~ла** *pf.* (*of* ▶ **~а́ть**) to crack (*with one's teeth*).

разгу́л, а *m.*
1 (*веселье*) revelry.
2 (+ *g.*; *fig.*) wave (of); outburst (of); **р. антисемити́зма** a wave of anti-semitism.

разгу́лива|ть, ю *impf.* to stroll about, walk about.

разда|ва́ть(ся), ю́, ёшь(ся) *impf. of* ▶ **разда́ть(ся)**

раздав|и́ть, лю́, ~́ишь *pf.* (*of* ▶ **~́ливать**) (*насекомых*) to crush, squash; (*о машине*) to run over.

разда́влива|ть, ю *impf. of* ▶ **раздави́ть**

разда́|ть, м, шь, ст, ди́м, ди́те, ду́т,

past **~л, ~лá, ~ло** *pf.* (*of* ▸**~вáть**) to distribute, give out, serve out, dispense; **р. кни́ги** to give out books.

раздá|ться, стся, дýтся, *past* **~лся, ~лáсь, ~лóсь** *pf.* (*of* ▸**~вáться**) to be heard; to resound; to ring (out); **~лся вы́стрел** a shot rang out; **~лся стук (в дверь)** a knock at the door was heard.

раздáч|а, и *f.* distribution.

раздвáива|ться, юсь *impf. of* ▸**раздвои́ться**

раздвигá|ть(ся), ю, ет(ся) *impf. of* ▸**раздви́нуть(ся)**

раздви́|нуть, ну, нешь *pf.* (*of* ▸**~гáть**) to move apart, slide apart; **р. занавéски** to draw back the curtains; **р. стол** to extend a table.

раздви́|нуться, нется *pf.* (*of* ▸**~гáться**) to move apart; **зáнавес ~нулся** the curtain was drawn back; (*в театре*) the curtain rose; **толпá ~нулась** the crowd made way.

раздвоéни|е , я *nt.* division into two; bifurcation; **р. ли́чности** (*med.*) split personality.

раздво|и́ться, ю́сь, и́шься *pf.* (*of* ▸**раздвáиваться**) to bifurcate, fork, split, become double.

раздевáлк|а, и *f.* (*coll.*)
1 (*гардероб*) cloakroom.
2 (*в банях*) changing room.

раздевáни|е, я *nt.* undressing.

раздевá|ть(ся), ю(сь) *impf. of* ▸**раздéть(ся)**

раздéл, а *m.*
1 (*имущества*) division; (*земли*) allotment.
2 (*часть*) section, part (*of book, etc.*).

Р

раздéл|ать, аю *pf.* (*of* ▸**~ывать**) (*тушу*) to dress, prepare.

раздéл|аться, аюсь *pf.* (*of* ▸**~ываться**) (**с** + *i.*)
1 (*с поручениями*) to be through (with); (*с кредиторами*) to settle (accounts) (with); **р. с долгáми** to pay off debts.
2 (*fig.*) (*расправиться*) to settle accounts (with), get even (with), make short work of.

разделéни|е, я *nt.* division; **р. трудá** division of labour.

раздел|и́ть, ю́, ~̃ишь *pf.* (*of* ▸**~я́ть** *and* ▸**дели́ть 1**)
1 (*деньги*) to divide.
2 (*разъединить*) to separate, part.
3 (*мнение, убеждение*) to share.

раздел|и́ться, ю́сь, ~̃ишься *pf.* (*of* ▸**~я́ться** *and* ▸**дели́ться 1**) (**на** + *a.*) to divide (into); to be divided; **мнéния ~и́лись** opinions were divided.

раздéлыва|ть(ся), ю(сь) *impf. of* ▸**раздéлать(ся)**

раздéльн|ый *adj.* separate; **~ое обучéние** separate education for boys and girls.

раздел|я́ть, я́ю *impf. of* ▸**~и́ть**

раздел|я́ться, я́юсь *impf. of* ▸**~и́ться**

раздé|ть, ну, нешь *pf.* (*of* ▸**~вáть**) to undress.

раздé|ться, нусь, нешься *pf.* (*of* ▸**~вáться**) to undress, get undressed; (*снять пальто, шапку*) to take off one's things.

раздирá|ть, ю *impf.*
1 *impf. of* ▸**разодрáть.**
2 (*impf. only*) (*fig.*) to rend, tear, lacerate, harrow.

раздобывá|ть, ю *impf. of* ▸**раздобы́ть**

раздо|бы́ть, бýду, бýдешь, *past* **~бы́л** *pf.* (*of* ▸**~бывáть**) (*coll.*) get, procure, get hold of.

раздраж|áть(ся), áю(сь) *impf. of* ▸**~и́ть(ся)**

раздражá|ющий *pres. part. act. of* ▸**~ть** *and adj.* irritating, annoying.

раздражéни|е, я *nt.* irritation.

раздражи́тел|ьный (~ен, ~ьна) *adj.* irritable; short-tempered.

раздраж|и́ть, ý, и́шь *pf.* (*of* ▸**~áть**)
1 to irritate, annoy.
2 (*med.*) to irritate.

раздраж|и́ться, ýсь, и́шься *pf.* (*of* ▸**~áться**)
1 to get irritated, get annoyed.
2 (*med.*) to become inflamed.

раздувá|ть(ся), ю(сь) *impf. of* ▸**раздýть(ся)**

раздýм|ать, аю *pf.* (*of* ▸**~ывать 1**) to change one's mind; (+ *inf.*) to decide not (to); **я ~ал подавáть заявлéние на э́то мéсто** I decided not to apply for that job; I changed my mind about applying for that job.

раздýмыва|ть, ю *impf.*
1 *impf. of* ▸**раздýмать.**
2 (*impf. only*) (**о** + *p.*) to ponder (on, over), consider; **не ~я** without a moment's thought.

раздý|ть, ю, ешь *pf.* (*of* ▸**~вáть**)
1 (*разжечь*) to blow; to fan; **р. плáмя** (*fig.*) to fan the flames.
2 (*надуть*) to blow (out); **р. щёки** to blow out one's cheeks.
3 (*fig., coll.*) (*преувеличить*) to exaggerate; to inflate, swell; **р. потéри** to exaggerate losses.
4 (*развеять*) to blow about; (*impers.*): **бумáги ~ло пó полу** the papers had blown all over the floor.

раздý|ться, юсь, ешься *pf.* (*of* ▸**~вáться**) to swell.

разевáть, ю *impf. of* ▸**рази́нуть**

разжáлоб|ить, лю, ишь *pf.* to move (to pity).

разжáл|овать, ую *pf.* (*mil.*) to demote; **р. в солдáты** to reduce to the ranks.

раз|жáть, ожмý, ожмёшь *pf.* (*of* ▸**~жимáть**) (*руки*) to unclasp; (*пружину*) to release; (*кулак, зубы*) to unclench.

раз|жáться, ожмётся *pf.* (*of* ▸**~жимáться**) (*о пружине*) to come loose; (*о кулаке, губах*) to relax.

разж|евáть, ую́, уёшь *pf.* (*of* ▸**~ёвывать**)
1 to chew.
2 (*fig., coll.*) (*разъяснить*) to spell out.

разжёвыва|ть, ю *impf. of* ▸**разжевáть**

раз|жéчь, ожгý, ожжёшь, ожгýт, *past* **~жёг, ~ожглá** *pf.* (*of* ▸**~жигáть**)
1 (*заставить гореть*) to kindle.
2 (*fig.*) to kindle, rouse, stir up; **р. стрáсти** to arouse passion.

разжигá|ть, ю *impf. of* ▸**разжéчь**

разжимá|ть(ся), ю, ет(ся) *impf. of* ▶ **разжáть(ся)**

разúн|уть, у, ешь *pf.* (*of* ▶ **разевáть**) (*coll.*) to open wide (*the mouth*); to gape; **слýшать, ~ув рот** to listen open-mouthed.

разлагá|ть(ся), ю(сь) *impf. of* ▶ **разложúть(ся)**[2]

разлáд, а *m.* discord, dissension.

разлáмыва|ть(ся), ю, ет(ся) *impf. of* ▶ **разломáть(ся)** *and* ▶ **разломúть(ся)**

разлез|áться, áется *impf. of* ▶ **~ться**

разлéз|ться, ется, *past* **~ся, ~лась** *pf.* (*of* ▶ **~áться**) (*coll.*) to come to pieces; to fall apart.

разлéнива|ться, юсь *impf. of* ▶ **разленúться**

разлен|úться, юсь, ~ишься *pf.* (*of* ▶ **~иваться**) (*coll.*) to become sunk in sloth.

разлет|áться, áюсь *impf. of* ▶ **~éться**

разле|тéться, чýсь, тúшься *pf.* (*of* ▶ **~тáться**)
1 (*о птицах*) to fly away; to scatter (*in the air*); (*о людях*) to scatter.
2 (*coll.*) (*разбиться*) to smash, shatter.
3 (*fig., coll.*) (*о мечтах*) to vanish, be shattered.
4 (*о новостях*) to spread.

разл|éчься, ягусь, яжешься, *past* **~ёгся, ~еглáсь** *pf.* (*coll.*) to sprawl; to stretch o.s. out.

разлúв, а *m.*
1 (*вина*) bottling.
2 (*реки*) flood; overflow.

разливá|ть(ся), ю, ет(ся) *impf. of* ▶ **разлúть(ся)**

разливнóй *adj.* (*пиво*) on tap; draught (*Br.*), draft (*US*).

раз|лúть, олью, ольёшь, *past* **~лúл, ~лилá, ~лúло** *pf.* (*of* ▶ **~ливáть**) to pour out; **р. по бутылкам** to bottle; **р. чай** to pour out tea.

раз|лúться, ольётся, *past* **~лúлся, ~лилáсь** *pf.* (*of* ▶ **~ливáться**)
1 (*пролиться*) to spill; **суп ~лúлся по скáтерти** the soup has spilled over the tablecloth.
2 (*о реке*) to overflow.
3 (*fig.*) (*распространиться*) to spread; **по её лицý ~лилáсь улыбка** a smile spread across her face.

различ|áть, áю *impf. of* ▶ **~úть**

различá|ться, юсь *impf.* to differ.

разлúчи|е, я *nt.* distinction; difference; **дéлать р.** (**мéжду** + *i.*) to make distinctions (between); **без ~я** without distinction.

различ|úть, ý, úшь *pf.* (*of* ▶ **~áть**)
1 (*установить различие*) to distinguish; to tell the difference (between).
2 (*воспринять*) to discern, make out.

разлúч|ный (~ен, ~на) *adj.*
1 (*несходный*) different; **у нас бы́ли ~ные мнéния** our opinions differed.
2 (*разнообразный*) various, diverse; **по ~ным соображéниям** for various reasons.

разложéни|е, я *nt.*
1 (*на составные части*) breaking down.
2 (*гниение*) decomposition, decay.
3 (*fig.*) (*деморализация*) demoralization; disintegration.

разлож|úть[1]**, ý, ~ишь** *pf.* (*of* ▶ **раскладывать**)
1 (*положить по разным местам*) to put; **р. свой вéщи по ящикам** to put one's things in their respective drawers.
2 (*в определённом порядке*) to lay out, to spread (out).

разлож|úть[2]**, ý, ~ишь** *pf.* (*of* ▶ **разлагáть**)
1 (*на составные части*) to break down; **р. веществó на составныe чáсти** to break a substance down into its component parts.
2 (*fig.*) (*деморализовать*) to break down, demoralize.

разлож|úться[1]**, ýсь, ~ишься** *pf.* (*of* ▶ **раскладываться**) (*coll.*) (*разместить свои вещи*) to lay one's things out.

разлож|úться[2]**, ýсь, ~ишься** *pf.* (*of* ▶ **разлагáться**)
1 (*сгнить*) to decompose, rot; **труп ужé ~úлся** the body has already decomposed.
2 (*fig.*) (*деморализоваться*) to become demoralized; to go to pieces.

разлóм, а *m.* (*место*) break.

разломá|ть, ю *pf.* (*of* ▶ **разлáмывать**) to break (in pieces).

разломá|ться, ется *pf.* (*of* ▶ **разлáмываться**) to break (in pieces); to break up.

разлом|úть, лю́, ~ишь *pf.* (*of* ▶ **разлáмывать**) to break (in pieces).

разлом|úться, ~ится *pf.* (*of* ▶ **разлáмываться**) to break in pieces.

разлýк|а, и *f.*
1 separation; **жить в ~е** (**с** + *i.*) to live apart (from), be separated (from).
2 (*расставание*) parting; **час ~и** hour of parting.

разлуч|áть(ся), áю(сь) *impf. of* ▶ **~úть(ся)**

разлуч|úть, ý, úшь *pf.* (*of* ▶ **~áть**) (+ *a.* and **с** + *i.*) to separate (from), part (from).

разлуч|úться, ýсь, úшься *pf.* (*of* ▶ **~áться**) (**с** + *i.*) to separate, part (from).

разлюб|úть, лю́, ~ишь *pf.* (*человека*) to cease to love, stop loving; (*гулять; Москву*) to cease to like.

размá|зать, жу, жешь *pf.* (*of* ▶ **~зывать**) to spread, smear; **р. варéнье по всемý лицý** to get jam all over one's face.

размá|заться, жется *pf.* (*of* ▶ **~зываться**) to spread; to get smeared.

размáзыва|ть(ся), ю, ет(ся) *impf. of* ▶ **размáзать(ся)**

размáлыва|ть, ю *impf. of* ▶ **размолóть**

размáтыва|ть(ся), ю, ет(ся) *impf. of* ▶ **размотáть(ся)**

размáх, а *m.* (*рук, крыльев*) span; (*fig.*) scope, range.

размáхива|ть, ю *impf.* (+ *i.*) to swing; to brandish; **р. рукáми** to gesticulate.

размáхива|ться, юсь *impf. of* ▶ **размахнýться**

размах|нýться, нýсь, нёшься *pf.* (*of* ▶ **~иваться**) to swing one's arm (*to strike or as if to strike*).

размáчива|ть, ю *impf. of* ▶ **размочúть**

Р

размельч|а́ть, а́ю *impf. of* ▶ **~и́ть**

размельч|и́ть, у́, и́шь *pf.* (*of* ▶ **~а́ть**) to divide into particles; to pulverize.

разме́н, а *m.* exchange; **р. де́нег** changing of money.

разме́нива|ть, ю *impf. of* ▶ **разменя́ть**

разме́нн|ый *adj.*: **~ая моне́та** small change.

размен|я́ть, я́ю *pf.* (*of* ▶ **~́ивать**) to change; **р. сторублёвку** to change a hundred-rouble note.

разме́р, а *m.*

1 (*масштаб*) dimensions; **воро́нка ~ом в де́сять квадра́тных ме́тров** a crater measuring ten square metres.

2 (*одежды, обуви*) size (in); (*pl.*) measurements; **како́й у вас р.?** what size do you take?

3 (*зарплаты, процентов*) rate, amount; **получа́ть зарпла́ту в ~е ты́сячи рубле́й в день** to be paid at the rate of a thousand roubles per day.

4 (*степень*) scale, extent; (*pl.*) proportions; **увели́читься до огро́мных ~ов** to assume enormous proportions.

5 (*ритм стиха, музыки*) rhythm.

разме́ренн|ый *adj.* measured; **~ая похо́дка** measured tread.

разме|сти́, ту́, тёшь, *past* **~̈л, ~ла́** *pf.* (*of* ▶ **~та́ть**[1])

1 (*дорожку*) to sweep clean.

2 (*снег*) to shovel, sweep away.

разме|сти́ть, щу́, сти́шь *pf.* (*of* ▶ **~ща́ть**) (*поместить по местам*) to place, accommodate; **р. делега́тов по гости́ницам** to accommodate the delegates in hotels.

разме|сти́ться, щу́сь, сти́шься *pf.* (*of* ▶ **~ща́ться**)

1 (*занять места*) to take one's seat.

2 (*поместиться*) to be housed, located.

размета́|ть[1]**, ю** *impf. of* ▶ **размести́**

разме|та́ть[2]**, чу́, ~́чешь** *pf.* (*of* ▶ **~̈тывать**) to scatter, disperse.

разме́|тить, чу, тишь *pf.* (*of* ▶ **~ча́ть**) to mark.

размётыва|ть, ю *impf. of* ▶ **разметать**[2]

размеча́|ть, ю *impf. of* ▶ **разме́тить**

размеш|а́ть, а́ю *pf.* (*of* ▶ **~́ивать**) to stir.

разме́шива|ть, ю *impf. of* ▶ **размеша́ть**

размеща́|ть(ся), ю(сь) *impf. of* ▶ **размести́ть(ся)**

размеще́ни|е, я *nt.*

1 (*по местам*) placing, accommodation; **р. промы́шленности** location of industry.

2 (*fin.*) (*капитала*) placing, investment.

размина́|ть(ся), ю(сь) *impf. of* ▶ **размя́ть(ся)**

размини́р|овать, ую *pf.* to clear of mines.

разми́нк|а, и *f.* (*sport*) limbering-up; warm-up.

размин|у́ться, у́сь, ёшься *pf.* (*coll.*)

1 (**с** + *i.*) to pass (*without meeting*); to miss; **мы, должно́ быть, ~у́лись с ним на доро́ге** we must have passed one another on the road.

2 (*о письмах*) to cross.

размнож|а́ть(ся), а́ю, ает(ся) *impf. of* ▶ **~́ить(ся)**

размноже́ни|е, я *nt.*

1 duplicating; photocopying.

2 (*biol.*) reproduction, propagation.

размно́ж|ить, у, ишь *pf.* (*of* ▶ **~а́ть**) to duplicate; to photocopy.

размно́ж|иться, ится *pf.* (*of* ▶ **~а́ться**) (*biol.*) to reproduce; to breed.

размок|а́ть, а́ет *impf. of* ▶ **~́нуть**

размо́к|нуть, нет, *past* **~, ~ла** *pf.* (*of* ▶ **~а́ть**) to get soaked; to get sodden.

размо́лвк|а, и *f.* tiff, disagreement.

раз|моло́ть, мелю́, ме́лешь *pf.* (*of* ▶ **разма́лывать**) to grind.

размора́жива|ть(ся), ю, ет(ся) *impf. of* ▶ **разморо́зить(ся)**

разморо́|зить, жу, зишь *pf.* (*of* ▶ **размора́живать**) to defrost.

разморо́|зиться, зится *pf.* (*of* ▶ **размора́живаться**) to defrost.

размота́|ть, ю *pf.* (*of* ▶ **разма́тывать**) to unwind, uncoil, unreel.

размота́|ться, ется *pf.* (*of* ▶ **разма́тываться**) to unwind, uncoil, unreel; to come unwound.

размоч|и́ть, у́, ~́ишь *pf.* (*of* ▶ **разма́чивать**) to soak, steep.

размыва́|ть, ю *impf. of* ▶ **размы́ть**

размыка́|ть, ю *impf. of* ▶ **разомкну́ть**

разм|ы́ть, о́ю, о́ешь *pf.* (*of* ▶ **~ыва́ть**) to wash away; (*geol.*) to erode.

размышле́ни|е, я *nt.* reflection, meditation, thought; **быть погружённым в ~я** to be lost in thought.

размышля́|ть, ю *impf.* (**о** + *p.*) to reflect (on, upon), meditate (on, upon), ponder (over).

размягч|а́ть, а́ю *impf. of* ▶ **~и́ть**

размягч|и́ть, у́, и́шь *pf.* (*of* ▶ **~а́ть**) to soften.

раз|мя́ть, омну́, омнёшь *pf.* (*of* ▶ **мять 1** *and* ▶ **~мина́ть**) (*глину*) to knead; (*картошку*) to mash.

раз|мя́ться, омну́сь, омнёшься *pf.* (*of* ▶ **~мина́ться**)

1 to grow soft (*as result of kneading*).

2 (*coll.*) to stretch one's legs; (*sport*) to limber up, loosen up.

разне́рвнича|ться, юсь *pf.* (*coll.*) to become very nervous.

разнес|ти́, у́, ёшь, *past* **~̈, ~ла́** *pf.* (*of* ▶ **разноси́ть**)

1 to carry, convey; to take round; **р. газе́ты** to deliver newspapers; (*слух*) to spread.

2 (*coll.*) (*разбить*) to smash, break up.

3 (*рассеять*) to scatter, disperse.

разнес|ти́сь, ётся, *past* **~̈ся, ~ла́сь** *pf.* (*of* ▶ **разноси́ться**)

1 (*о слухах*) to spread.

2 (*о звуках*) to resound.

разнима́|ть, ю *impf. of* ▶ **разня́ть**

ра́зниц|а, ы *f.* difference; disparity; **кака́я р.?** (*coll.*) what difference does it make?

разнови́дност|ь, и *f.* variety.

разногла́си|е, я *nt.*

1 (*во мнениях*) difference, disagreement; **~я во взгля́дах** difference of opinion.

2 (*противоречие*) discrepancy; **р. в**

показа́ниях conflicting evidence.

разнообра́зи|е, я *nt.* variety, diversity; **для ~я** for a change.

разнообра́з|ный (~ен, ~на) *adj.* various, varied, diverse.

разноро́д|ный (~ен, ~на) *adj.* heterogeneous.

разно|си́ть, шу́, ~́сишь *impf. of* ▸ **разнести́**

разно|си́ться, ~́сится *impf. of* ▸ **разнести́сь**

разносторо́н|ний (~ен, ~ня) *adj.* many-sided; versatile.

ра́зност|ь, и *f.* difference.

разно́счик, а *m.* (*газет, телеграмм*) delivery man; (*новостей*) bearer; (*инфекции*) carrier.

разноцве́т|ный (~ен, ~на) *adj.* of different colours (*Br.*), colors (*US*); multicoloured (*Br.*), multicolored (*US*).

ра́зн|ый *adj.*
1 (*взгляды*) different, differing.
2 (*разнообразный*) various, diverse; **~ого ро́да** of various kinds; *as n.* **~ое, ~ого** *nt.* (*на повестке дня*) miscellaneous.

раз|ня́ть, ниму́, ни́мешь, *past* **~ня́л, ~няла́, ~ня́ло** *pf.* (*of* ▸ **~нима́ть**) to part, separate.

разо... *vbl. pref.* = **раз...**

разоблача́|ть, а́ю *impf. of* ▸ **~и́ть**

разоблаче́ни|е, я *nt.* exposure, unmasking.

разоблач|и́ть, у́, и́шь *pf.* (*of* ▸ **~а́ть**) to expose, unmask.

раз|обра́ть, беру́, берёшь, *past* **~обра́л, ~обрала́, ~обра́ло** *pf.* (*of* ▸ **~бира́ть**)
1 (*механизм*) to take to pieces, dismantle.
2 (*раскупить*) to buy up; (*взять*) to take.
3 (*привести в порядок*) to sort out.
4 (*ссору, дело*) to investigate, look into.
5 (*понять*) to make out, understand.

раз|обра́ться, беру́сь, берёшься, *past* **~обра́лся, ~обрала́сь** *pf.* (*of* ▸ **~бира́ться**) (**в** + *p. or coll.* **с** + *i.*) (*исследовать*) to investigate, look into; (*понимать*) to understand.

разобщённо *adv.* apart, separately; **де́йствовать р.** to act independently.

ра́зов|ый *adj.* valid for one occasion (only); **~ого по́льзования** disposable.

раз|огна́ть, гоню́, го́нишь, *past* **~огна́л, ~огнала́, ~огна́ло** *pf.* (*of* ▸ **~гоня́ть**)
1 to drive away; to disperse; (*fig.*) to dispel; **р. демонстра́цию** to break up a demonstration.
2 (*coll.*) (*автомобиль*) to drive at high speed, race.

раз|огна́ться, гоню́сь, го́нишься, *past* **~огна́лся, ~огнала́сь, ~огна́ло́сь** *pf.* (*of* ▸ **~гоня́ться**) to gather speed; to gather momentum.

разогн|у́ть, у́, ёшь *pf.* (*of* ▸ **разгиба́ть**) to unbend, straighten; **р. спи́ну** to straighten one's back.

разогн|у́ться, у́сь, ёшься *pf.* (*of* ▸ **разгиба́ться**) to straighten o.s. up.

разогрева́|ть(ся), ю(сь) *impf. of* ▸ **разогре́ть(ся)**

разогре́|ть, ю *pf.* (*of* ▸ **~ва́ть**) to warm up.

разогре́|ться, юсь *pf.* (*of* ▸ **~ва́ться**) to warm up, grow warm.

разоде́|ть, ну, нешь *pf.* (*coll.*) to dress up.

разоде́|ться, нусь, нешься *pf.* (*coll.*) to dress up.

раз|одра́ть, деру́, дерёшь, *past* **~одра́л, ~одрала́, ~одра́ло** *pf.* (*of* ▸ **~дира́ть 1**) to tear up.

разозл|и́ть, ю, и́шь *pf.* (*of* ▸ **злить**) to make angry, enrage.

разозл|и́ться, ю́сь, и́шься *pf.* (*of* ▸ **зли́ться**) to get angry, get in a rage.

раз|ойти́сь, ойду́сь, ойдёшься, *past* **~ошёлся, ~ошла́сь** *pf.* (*of* ▸ **расходи́ться**)
1 (*уйти*) to go away; (*рассеяться*) to disperse; **толпа́ ~ошла́сь** the crowd broke up.
2 (**с** + *i.*) (*расстаться*) to part (from); (*о супругах*) to separate (from); **он ~ошёлся с жено́й** he has separated from his wife.
3 (*о линиях, о дорогах*) to branch off, diverge; (*о лучах*) to radiate.
4 (*разминуться*) to pass (*without meeting*).
5 (**с** + *i.*) (*обнаружить разногласие*) to conflict (with); **р. во мне́нии с кем-н.** to disagree with s.o.
6 (*раствориться*) to dissolve; (*растаять*) to melt.
7 (*coll.*) (*дать волю себе*) to get going; **бу́ря ~ошла́сь** the storm raged.

разомкн|у́ть, у́, ёшь *pf.* (*of* ▸ **размыка́ть**) to open, unfasten; (*tech.*) to break, disconnect.

разонра́в|иться, люсь, ишься *pf.* (*coll.*; + *d.*) to cease to please, lose its attraction (for).

разор|а́ться, у́сь, ёшься *pf.* (*coll.*) to start shouting.

разорв|а́ть, у́, ёшь, *past* **~а́л, ~ала́, ~а́ло** *pf.* (*of* ▸ **разрыва́ть**[1])
1 (*письмо*) to tear up; (*пакет, конверт*) to tear open; (*одежду*) to tear.
2 (*impers.*) (*взорвать*) to blow up, burst; **котёл ~а́ло** the boiler has blown up.
3 (*fig.*) (*прекратить*) to break (off), sever; **р. дипломати́ческие отноше́ния** to break off diplomatic relations.

разорв|а́ться, у́сь, ёшься, *past* **~а́лся, ~ала́сь, ~а́ло́сь** *pf.* (*of* ▸ **разрыва́ться**)
1 (*о верёвке*) to break, snap; (*об одежде*) to tear, become torn.
2 (*взорваться*) to blow up; to explode.
3 (*об отношениях*) to be broken off, severed.

разоре́ни|е, я *nt.* (*города*) destruction, ravage; (*народа*) ruin.

разор|и́ть, ю́, и́шь *pf.* (*of* ▸ **~я́ть**)
1 (*опустошить*) to destroy, ravage.
2 (*довести до нищеты*) to ruin, bring to ruin.

разор|и́ться, ю́сь, и́шься *pf.* (*of* ▸ **~я́ться**)
1 (*прийти в упадок*) to be ruined.
2 (*впасть в нищету*) to go broke, ruin o.s.

разоруж|а́ть(ся), а́ю(сь) *impf. of* ▸ **~и́ть(ся)**

разоруже́ни|е, я *nt.* (*действие*)

Р

disarming; (*политика*) disarmament.

разоруж|и́ть, у́, и́шь *pf.* (*of* ▸ **~а́ть**) to disarm.

разоруж|и́ться, у́сь, и́шься *pf.* (*of* ▸ **~а́ться**) to disarm.

разор|я́ть(ся), я́ю(сь) *impf. of* ▸ **~и́ть(ся)**

разо|сла́ть, шлю́, шлёшь *pf.* (*of* ▸ **рассыла́ть**) to send out.

разостла́ть, расстелю́, рассте́лешь = ▸ **расстила́ть**

разостла́|ться, рассте́лется *pf.* = **расстила́ться**

разочарова́ни|е, я *nt.* disappointment.

разочар|ова́ть, у́ю *pf.* (*of* ▸ **~о́вывать**) to disappoint.

разочар|ова́ться, у́юсь *pf.* (*of* ▸ **~о́вываться**) (**в** + *p.*) to be disappointed (in s.o., with sth.).

разочаро́выва|ть(ся), ю(сь) *impf. of* ▸ **разочарова́ть(ся)**

разраба́тыва|ть, ю *impf. of* ▸ **разрабо́тать**

разрабо́та|ть, ю *pf.* (*of* ▸ **разраба́тывать**)
1 (*подготовить*) to develop; to elaborate; **р. пла́н** to work out a plan.
2 (*mining*) to work, exploit.

разрабо́тк|а, и *f.*
1 (*проекта*) working out; development; elaboration.
2 (*mining*) working, exploitation; **откры́тая р.** opencast mining.
3 : **нефтяна́я р.** oilfield.

разра́внива|ть, ю *impf. of* ▸ **разровня́ть**

разража́|ться, юсь *impf. of* ▸ **разрази́ться**

Р

разра|зи́ться, жу́сь, зи́шься *pf.* (*of* ▸ **~жа́ться**) (*о грозе, о катастрофе*) to break out, burst out; **р. слеза́ми** to burst into tears; **р. сме́хом** to burst out laughing.

разраст|а́ться, а́ется *impf. of* ▸ **~и́сь**

разраст|и́сь, ётся, *past* **разро́сся, разросла́сь** *pf.* (*of* ▸ **~а́ться**) to grow; to spread; **де́ло разросло́сь** the business has grown; **сире́нь разросла́сь** the lilac has spread.

разре́з, а *m.*
1 (*отверстие*) cut; slit; **ю́бка с ~ом** slit skirt.
2 (*сечение*) section; **попере́чный р.** cross section; **р. глаз** shape of one's eyes.

разрез|а́ть, а́ю *impf. of* ▸ **~́ать**

разре́|зать, жу, жешь *pf.* (*of* ▸ **~за́ть**) to cut; to slit.

разреш|а́ть, а́ю *impf. of* ▸ **~и́ть**

разреш|а́ться, а́ется *impf.*
1 *impf. of* ▸ **~и́ться.**
2 (*impf. only*) to be allowed; **здесь кури́ть не ~а́ется** smoking is not allowed here.

разреше́ни|е, я *nt.*
1 (*право*) permission; **с ва́шего ~я** with your permission, by your leave.
2 (*документ*) permit, authorization; **р. на въезд** entry permit.
3 (*проблемы*) solution.
4 (*спора*) settlement.
5 (*tech.*) (*степень детализации*) resolution.

разреши́м|ый (~, ~а) *adj.* solvable.

разреш|и́ть, у́, и́шь *pf.* (*of* ▸ **~а́ть**)
1 (+ *d.*) to allow, permit; **~и́те пройти́** do you mind letting me pass?
2 (*книгу, фильм*) to authorize; **р. кни́гу к печа́ти** to authorize the printing of a book.
3 (*проблему*) to solve.
4 (*конфликт*) to settle; **р. сомне́ния** to resolve doubts.

разреш|и́ться, и́тся *pf.* (*of* ▸ **~а́ться 1**)
1 (*о проблеме*) to be solved.
2 (*о конфликте*) to be settled.

разрис|ова́ть, у́ю *pf.* (*of* ▸ **~о́вывать**) to cover with drawings.

разрисо́выва|ть, ю *impf. of* ▸ **разрисова́ть**

разровня́|ть, ю *pf.* (*of* ▸ **разра́внивать**) to level.

разро́знен|ный (~, ~на) *adj.*
1 (*лишенный единства*) uncoordinated.
2 : **р. компле́кт** incomplete set; **~ные тома́** odd volumes.

разруб|а́ть, а́ю *impf. of* ▸ **~и́ть**

разруб|и́ть, лю́, ~́ишь *pf.* (*of* ▸ **~а́ть**) to cut, cleave.

разру́х|а, и *f.* ruin, collapse.

разруш|а́ть(ся), а́ю, а́ет(ся) *impf. of* ▸ **~́ить(ся)**

разруше́ни|е, я *nt.* destruction; (*pl.*) havoc.

разруши́тел|ьный (~ен, ~ьна) *adj.* destructive.

разру́ш|ить, у, ишь *pf.* (*of* ▸ **~а́ть**)
1 to destroy; to ruin.
2 (*fig.*) to ruin; **р. чьи-н. наде́жды** to ruin s.o.'s hopes.

разру́ш|иться, ится *pf.* (*of* ▸ **~а́ться**) to go to ruin, be destroyed, collapse.

разры́в, а *m.*
1 (*пространство*) break; gap; (*прореха*) tear; (*отношений*) breaking, severance; (*с кем-н.*) break-up; (*несоответствие*) gap; **р. ме́жду поколе́ниями** generation gap.
2 (*снаряда*) burst, explosion.

разрыва́|ть[1]**, ю** *impf. of* ▸ **разорва́ть**

разрыва́|ть[2]**, ю** *impf. of* ▸ **разры́ть**

разрыва́|ться, юсь *impf. of* ▸ **разорва́ться**

разр|ы́ть, о́ю, о́ешь *pf.* (*of* ▸ **~ыва́ть**[2])
1 to dig up.
2 (*fig., coll.*) (*раскидать*) to turn upside-down, rummage through.

разря́д[1]**, а** *m.* (*электричества*) discharge.

разря́д[2]**, а** *m.* (*категория*) category, sort; (*в профессии, в спорте*) rank, class; **пе́рвого ~а** first class.

разря|ди́ть, жу́, ди́шь *pf.* (*of* ▸ **~жа́ть**)
1 (*elec.*) to discharge; **р. атмосфе́ру** (*fig.*) to clear the air.
2 (*ружьё*) to unload; (*стреляя*) to discharge.

разря|ди́ться, ди́тся *pf.* (*of* ▸ **~жа́ться**)
1 (*elec.*) to run down; (*fig.*) to clear, ease.
2 (*об оружии*) to be unloaded; (*стреляя*) to be discharged.

разряжа́|ть(ся), ю, ет(ся) *impf. of* ▸ **разряди́ть(ся)**

разубе|ди́ть, жу́, ди́шь *pf.* (*of* ▶ **~жда́ть**) (**в** + *p.*) to dissuade (from).
разубе|ди́ться, жу́сь, ди́шься *pf.* (*of* ▶ **~жда́ться**) (**в** + *p.*) to change one's mind (about).
разубежда́|ть(ся), ю(сь) *impf. of* ▶ **разубеди́ть(ся)**
разува́|ть(ся), ю(сь) *impf. of* ▶ **разу́ть(ся)**
разуве́р|ить, ю, ишь *pf.* (*of* ▶ **~я́ть**) (**в** + *p.*) to cause s.o. to lose faith, stop believing (in); to persuade to the contrary; **он меня́ ~ил в том, что э́того мо́жно доби́ться** he persuaded me that it could not be achieved.
разуве́р|иться, юсь, ишься *pf.* (*of* ▶ **~я́ться**) (**в** + *p.*) to lose faith (in).
разуверя́|ть(ся), ю(сь) *impf. of* ▶ **разуве́рить(ся)**
разузна|ва́ть, ю́, ёшь *impf.*
1 *impf. of* ▶ **разузна́ть.**
2 (*impf. only*) to make inquiries (about).
разузна́|ть, ю *pf.* (*of* ▶ **~ва́ть 1**) to find out.
разукра́|сить, шу, сишь *pf.* (*of* ▶ **~шивать**) to adorn; to decorate; to embellish.
разукра́шива|ть, ю *impf. of* ▶ **разукра́сить**
ра́зум, а *m.* reason; (*интеллект*) intellect.
разуме́|ться, ется *impf.* (**под** + *i.*) to be understood (by), be meant (by); **под э́тим ~ется...** by this is meant ...; **(са́мо собо́й) ~ется** it goes without saying, of course; **он, ~ется, не знал, что вы уже́ пришли́** he, of course, did not know that you were already here.
разу́м|ный (~ен, ~на) *adj.*
1 (*существо*) rational, intelligent.
2 (*парень*) intelligent, clever.
3 (*поступок*) reasonable; **э́то (вполне́) ~но** it is (perfectly) reasonable.
разу́|ть, ю, ешь *pf.* (*of* ▶ **~ва́ть**); **р. кого́-н.** to take s.o.'s shoes off.
разу́|ться, юсь, ешься *pf.* (*of* ▶ **~ва́ться**) to take one's shoes off.
разу́чива|ть(ся), ю(сь) *impf. of* ▶ **разучи́ть(ся)**
разуч|и́ть, у́, ~́ишь *pf.* (*of* ▶ **~́ивать**) to learn (up); **р. роль** to learn, study one's part.
разуч|и́ться, у́сь, ~́ишься *pf.* (*of* ▶ **~́иваться**) (+ *inf.*) to forget (how to); **я ~и́лся ходи́ть на лы́жах** I have forgotten how to ski.
разъ... *vbl. pref.* = **раз...**
разъеда́|ть, ю *impf. of* ▶ **разъе́сть**
разъедине́ни|е, я *nt.*
1 separation.
2 (*elec.*) disconnection, breaking.
разъедин|и́ть, ю́, и́шь *pf.* (*of* ▶ **~я́ть**)
1 (*друзей*) to separate.
2 (*elec.*) to disconnect; **нас ~и́ли** we were cut off (*on telephone*).
разъедин|и́ться, и́тся *pf.* (*of* ▶ **~я́ться**) to separate, part; (*о проводах*) to come apart, be disconnected.
разъедин|я́ть(ся), я́ет(ся) *impf. of* ▶ **~и́ть(ся)**
разъе́зд, а *m.*
1 (*людей*) departure.
2 (*pl.*) (*поездки*) travels.
3 (*mil.*) mounted patrol.
4 (*rail.*) siding.
разъезжа́|ть, ю *impf.* to drive (about, around), ride (about, around); to travel; **р. по дела́м** to travel about on business.
разъезжа́|ться, юсь *impf. of* ▶ **разъе́хаться**
разъе́|сть, ст, дя́т, *past* **~л** *pf.* (*of* ▶ **~да́ть**) to eat away; to corrode (*also fig.*).
разъе́|хаться, дусь, дешься *pf.* (*of* ▶ **~зжа́ться**)
1 (*уехать*) to depart; to disperse.
2 (*о супругах*) to separate, stop living together.
3 (*о машинах*) to (be able to) pass.
4 (*разминуться*) to pass one another (*without meeting*); to miss one another.
разъяр|и́ться, ю́сь, и́шься *pf.* (*of* ▶ **~я́ться**) to fly into a rage.
разъяр|я́ться, я́юсь *impf. of* ▶ **~и́ться**
разъясне́ни|е, я *nt.* explanation.
разъясн|и́ть, ю́, и́шь *pf.* (*of* ▶ **~я́ть**) to explain.
разъясн|и́ться, и́тся *pf.* (*of* ▶ **~я́ться**) to become clear, be cleared up.
разъясн|я́ть(ся), я́ю, я́ет(ся) *impf. of* ▶ **~и́ть(ся)**
разыгр|а́ть, а́ю *pf.* (*of* ▶ **~́ывать**)
1 (*исполнить*) to play (through); to perform; **р. дурака́** to play the fool.
2 (*игру, карту*) to play.
3 (*в лотерее*) to raffle.
4 (*coll.*) (*одурачить*) to play a trick (on).
разыгр|а́ться, а́юсь *pf.* (*of* ▶ **~́ываться**)
1 (*увлечься игрой*) to be carried away by a game, by play.
2 (*о музыканте, об актёре*) to warm up.
3 (*о ветре, буре*) to get up; (*о чувствах*) to run high.
разы́грыва|ть(ся), ю(сь) *impf. of* ▶ **разыгра́ть(ся)**
разы|ска́ть, щу́, ~́щешь *pf.* to find (after searching).
разы́скива|ть, ю *impf.* to hunt, search for.
разы́скива|ться, юсь *impf.* to be searched, hunted for; **р. поли́цией** to be wanted by the police.
ра|й, я, о ~́е, в ~ю́ *m.* paradise.
райо́н, а *m.*
1 region.
2 (*административная единица*) district.
райо́н|ный *adj. of* ▶ **~**
рак, а *m.*
1 (*zool.*) (*речной*) crayfish (*Br.*), crawfish (*US*); (*морской*) spiny lobster.
2 (*med.*) cancer.
3 **Р.** (*astrol., astron.*) Crab, Cancer.
раке́т|а, ы *f.*
1 (*для сигналов; фейерверк; космическая*) rocket; **пусти́ть ~у** to let off a rocket.
2 (*mil.*) rocket, ballistic missile; **крыла́тая р.** cruise missile.
раке́т|ка, ки *f.* (*sport*) racket.
раке́тчик, а *m.* missile specialist.
ра́ковин|а, ы *f.*
1 (*моллюска*) shell.

2 (*для умывания*) sink; washbasin.
раку́шк|а, и *f.* shell; seashell.
ра́лли *nt. indecl.* rally.
ра́м|а, ы *f.*
1 frame; **вста́вить в ~у** to frame.
2 (*машины*) chassis.
Рамада́н, а *m.* = **Рамаза́н**
Рамаза́н, а *m.* (*relig.*) Ramadan.
ра́мк|а, и *f.* frame; (*текста*) border.
ра́м|ки, ок (*pl. only*) framework; limits; **в ~ках** (+ *g.*) within the framework (of), within the limits (of); **вы́йти за р.** (+ *g.*) to exceed the limits (of).
ра́мп|а, ы *f.* (*theatr.*) footlights.
ра́н|а, ы *f.* wound.
ранг, а *m.* class, rank.
ра́нее *adv.* = **ра́ньше**
ране́ни|е, я *nt.*
1 (*действие*) wounding; injuring.
2 (*рана*) wound; injury.
ра́нен|ый *adj.* wounded; injured; *as n.* **р., ~ого** *m.* injured man; wounded man; casualty; *pl.* the injured; the wounded.
ра́н|ец, ца *m.* (*походный, солдатский*) knapsack, pack; (*ученический*) satchel.
рани́м|ый (~, а) *adj.* vulnerable.
ра́н|ить, ю, ишь *impf. and pf.* to wound; to injure.
ра́нн|ий *adj.* early; **~им у́тром** early in the morning; **с ~его де́тства** from early childhood.
ра́но[1] *pred.* it is early; **ещё р. ложи́ться спать** it is too early for bed.
ра́но[2] *adv.* early; **р. и́ли по́здно** sooner or later.
рантье́ *m. indecl.* rentier.
ра́нчо *nt. indecl.* ranch.
ра́ньше *adv.*
1 earlier; **как мо́жно р.** as early as possible; as soon as possible.
2 (+ *g.*) (*прежде*) before; **до Ло́ндона он р. ве́чера не дое́дет** he will not reach London before evening.
3 (*прежде*) before, formerly; **р. мы жи́ли в дере́вне** we used to live in the country.
ра́порт, а *m.* report.
рапорт|ова́ть, у́ю *impf. and pf.* to report.
рапс, а *m.* (*bot.*) rape.
рарите́т, а *m.* rarity, curiosity.
рас... *vbl. pref.* = **раз...**
ра́с|а, ы *f.* race.
раси́зм, а *m.* racism.
раси́ст, а *m.* racist.
раси́ст|ка, ки *f. of* ▸ **~**
раси́стский *adj.* racist.
раска́ива|ться, юсь *impf. of* ▸ **раска́яться**
раскал|ённый *p.p.p. of* ▸ **~и́ть** *and adj.* scorching, burning hot.
раскал|и́ть, ю́, и́шь *pf.* (*of* ▸ **~я́ть**) to bring to a great heat.
раскал|и́ться, ю́сь, и́шься *pf.* (*of* ▸ **~я́ться**) to glow, become hot.
раска́лыва|ть(ся), ю(сь) *impf. of* ▸ **расколо́ть(ся)**
раскал|я́ть(ся), я́ю(сь) *impf. of* ▸ **~и́ть(ся)**
раска́пыва|ть, ю *impf. of* ▸ **раскопа́ть**
раска́т, а *m.* roll, peal; **р. гро́ма** peal of thunder.
раскат|а́ть, а́ю *pf.* (*of* ▸ **~́ывать**)
1 (*ковёр*) to unroll.
2 (*тесто*) to roll (out); (*дорогу*) to level.
раска́тыва|ть, ю *impf. of* ▸ **раската́ть**
раскач|а́ть, а́ю *pf.* (*of* ▸ **~́ивать**)
1 (*качели*) to swing; to rock.
2 (*расшатать*) to loosen, shake loose.
раскач|а́ться, а́юсь *pf.* (*of* ▸ **~́иваться**)
1 (*на качелях*) to swing (back and forth); (*о лодке*) to rock.
2 (*расшататься*) to shake loose.
раска́чива|ть(ся), ю(сь) *impf. of* ▸ **раскача́ть(ся)**
раска́яни|е, я *nt.* repentance.
раска́|яться, юсь *pf.* (*of* ▸ **~иваться**) (**в** + *p.*) to repent (of).
расквартир|ова́ть, у́ю *pf.* (*of* ▸ **~о́вывать**) to quarter, billet.
расквартиро́выва|ть, ю *impf. of* ▸ **расквартирова́ть**
раскид|а́ть, а́ю *pf.* (*of* ▸ **~́ывать**) to scatter.
раски́дыва|ть, ю *impf. of* ▸ **раскида́ть** *and* ▸ **раски́нуть**
раски́дыва|ться, юсь *impf. of* ▸ **раски́нуться**
раски́|нуть, ну, нешь *pf.* (*of* ▸ **~дывать**)
1 (*руки*) to stretch (out).
2 (*ковёр*) to spread (out); (*лагерь*) to set up; (*палатку*) to pitch.
раски́|нуться, нусь, нешься *pf.* (*of* ▸ **~дываться**)
1 to spread out, stretch out.
2 (*coll.*) to sprawl.
раскла́д, а *m.* (*расположение*) disposition, arrangement; (*сил, средств*) apportionment; (*положение дел*) state of affairs.
раскладн|о́й *adj.* folding; **~а́я крова́ть** camp bed (*Br.*), cot (*US*).
раскладу́шк|а, и *f.* (*coll.*) camp bed (*Br.*), cot (*US*).
раскла́дыва|ть(ся), ю(сь) *impf. of* ▸ **разложи́ть(ся)**[1]
раскла́нива|ться, юсь *impf. of* ▸ **раскла́няться**
раскла́н|яться, яюсь *pf.* (*of* ▸ **~иваться**)
1 to exchange bows (*on meeting or leave-taking*).
2 (*об актёре*) to take a bow.
раскле́ива|ть(ся), ю(сь) *impf. of* ▸ **раскле́ить(ся)**
раскле́|ить, ю, ишь *pf.* (*of* ▸ **~ивать**)
1 (*конверт*) to unstick.
2 (*афиши*) to stick, paste (*in various places*).
раскле́|иться, юсь, ишься *pf.* (*of* ▸ **~иваться**)
1 to come unstuck.
2 (*fig., coll.*) (*о планах*) to fall through.
3 (*fig., coll.*) (*о человеке*) to be feel unwell; **он совсе́м ~ился** he has gone to pieces.
раско́ванный *adj.* relaxed, uninhibited.
раско́л, а *m.*

1 (*relig., hist.*) schism, dissent.
2 (*pol., etc.*) split, division.

раскол|о́ть, ю́, ~́ешь *pf.*
1 *pf. of* ▶ **коло́ть**[1].
2 (*impf.* **раска́лывать**) (*fig.*) to disrupt, break up.

раскол|о́ться, ю́сь, ~́ешься *pf.* (*of* ▶ **раска́лываться**) to split (*also fig.*).

раскопа́|ть, ю *pf.* (*of* ▶ **раска́пывать**) to dig up, unearth (*also fig.*); (*archaeol.*) to excavate.

раско́пк|а, и *f.* (*действие*) digging up; *pl.* (*archaeol.*) excavations.

раскра́ива|ть, ю *impf. of* ▶ **раскрои́ть**

раскра́|сить, шу, сишь *pf.* (*of* ▶ **~шивать**) to paint, colour (*Br.*), color (*US*).

раскра́ск|а, и *f.*
1 (*действие*) painting, colouring (*Br.*), coloring (*US*).
2 (*расцветка*) colours (*Br.*), colors (*US*), colour scheme (*Br.*), color scheme (*US*).

раскра́шива|ть, ю *impf. of* ▶ **раскра́сить**

раскрепо|сти́ться, щу́сь, сти́шься *pf.* (*of* ▶ **~ща́ться**) to free *or* liberate o.s.

раскрепоща́|ться, юсь *impf. of* ▶ **раскрепости́ться**

раскритик|ова́ть, у́ю *pf.* to criticize severely, slam.

раскрич|а́ться, у́сь, и́шься *pf.*
1 to start shouting, start crying.
2 (**на** + *a.*) to shout (at).

раскро|и́ть, ю́, и́шь *pf.* (*of* ▶ **раскра́ивать**)
1 (*ткань*) to cut out.
2 (*fig., coll.*) to cut open; **р. кому́-н. че́реп** to split s.o.'s skull.

раскрош|и́ть(ся), у́, ~́ит(ся) *pf. of* ▶ **кроши́ть(ся)**

раскру|ти́ть, чу́, ~́тишь *pf.* (*of* ▶ **~́чивать**)
1 (*развить*) to untwist, undo.
2 (*колесо*) to spin, rotate.
3 (*coll.*) (*заставить развиваться*) to develop, establish; (*рекламировать*) promote, popularize.

раскру|ти́ться, чу́сь, ~́тишься *pf.* (*of* ▶ **~́чиваться**)
1 (*развиться*) to come untwisted, come undone.
2 (*начать крутиться*) to start spinning, rotating.
3 (*coll.*) (*начать действовать*) to develop, get established; (*получить известность*) to become famous, popular.

раскру́чива|ть(ся), ю(сь) *impf. of* ▶ **раскрути́ть(ся)**

раскрыва́|ть(ся), ю(сь) *impf. of* ▶ **раскры́ть(ся)**

раскр|ы́ть, о́ю, о́ешь *pf.* (*of* ▶ **~ыва́ть**)
1 (*открыть*) to open (wide); **р. зо́нтик** to put up an umbrella; **р. кни́гу** to open a book.
2 (*сделать видным*) to expose, bare.
3 (*обнаружить*) to reveal, disclose, lay bare; (*найти*) to discover; **р. секре́т** to disclose a secret.

раскр|ы́ться, о́юсь, о́ешься *pf.* (*of* ▶ **~ыва́ться**)
1 to open.
2 (*раскрыть себя*) to uncover o.s.
3 (*обнаружиться*) to come out; to come to light.

раскуп|а́ть, а́ю *impf. of* ▶ **~и́ть**

раскуп|и́ть, лю́, ~́ишь *pf.* (*of* ▶ **~а́ть**) to buy up.

раску́рива|ть, ю, ет *impf. of* ▶ **раскури́ть**

раскур|и́ть, ю́, ~́ишь *pf.* (*of* ▶ **~́ивать**)
1 (*заставить куриться*) to puff at (*a pipe or cigarette*).
2 (*зажечь*) to light up.

расску|си́ть, шу́, ~́сишь *pf.* (*of* ▶ **~́сывать**)
1 (*конфету*) to bite into.
2 (*pf. only*) (*coll.*) (*узнать, понять*) to suss out.

раску́сыва|ть, ю *impf. of* ▶ **раскуси́ть**

ра́совый *adj.* racial.

распа́д, а *m.*
1 disintegration, break-up; (*fig.*) collapse.
2 (*chem.*) decomposition.

распада́|ться, ется *impf. of* ▶ **распа́сться**

распак|ова́ть, у́ю *pf.* (*of* ▶ **~о́вывать**) to unpack.

распако́выва|ть, ю *impf. of* ▶ **распакова́ть**

распа́рыва|ть, ет *impf. of* ▶ **распоро́ть**

распа́|сться, дётся, *past* **~лся** *pf.* (*of* ▶ **~да́ться**)
1 to disintegrate; (*fig.*) to break up; to collapse; **коали́ция ~лась** the coalition broke up.
2 (*chem.*) to decompose.

распа|ха́ть, шу́, ~́шешь *pf.* (*of* ▶ **~́хивать**) to plough up (*Br.*), plow up (*US*).

распа́хива|ть, ю *impf. of* ▶ **распаха́ть** *and* ▶ **распахну́ть**

распа́хива|ться, юсь *impf. of* ▶ **распахну́ться**

распах|ну́ть, ну́, нёшь *pf.* (*of* ▶ **~́ивать**) to open wide; to throw open; **широко́ р. две́ри** (+ *d.*) to open wide the doors (to) (*also fig.*).

распах|ну́ться, ну́сь, нёшься *pf.* (*of* ▶ **~́иваться**)
1 (*о двери, об окне*) to fly open, swing open.
2 (*распахнуть полы своей одежды*) to throw open one's coat.

распере́ть, разопру́, разопрёшь, *past* **распёр, распёрла** *pf.* (*of* ▶ **распира́ть**) (*coll.*) to burst open, cause to burst.

распеча́т|ать, аю *pf.* (*of* ▶ **~ывать**)
1 (*вскрыть*) to unseal; **р. письмо́** to open a letter.
2 (*напечатать во многих экземплярах*) to print off.
3 (*comput.*) to print (out).

распеча́тк|а, и *f.* printout; (*действие*) printing out.

распеча́тыва|ть, ю *impf. of* ▶ **распеча́тать**

распи́лива|ть, ю *impf. of* ▶ **распили́ть**

распил|и́ть, ю́, ~́ишь *pf.* (*of* ▶ **~́ивать**) to saw up.

распира́|ть, ю *impf. of* ▶ **распере́ть**

расписа́ни|е, я *nt.* timetable, schedule.
распи|са́ть, шу́, ~́шешь *pf.* (*of* ▸ **~́сывать**)
1 (*сведения*) to enter; to note down; **р. счета́ по кни́гам** to enter bills in the account book.
2 (*распределить*) to assign, allot.
3 (*разрисовать*) to paint.
распи|са́ться, шу́сь, ~́шешься *pf.* (*of* ▸ **~́сываться**)
1 to sign (one's name); (**в** + *p.*) to sign (for); **р. в получе́нии заказно́го письма́** to sign for a registered letter.
2 (*coll.*) (*регистрировать брак*) to register one's marriage.
3 (**в** + *p.*; *fig.*) (*признаться*) to acknowledge; **р. в со́бственном неве́жестве** to acknowledge one's own ignorance.
распи́ск|а, и *f.* receipt; **р. в получе́нии** (+ *g.*) receipt (for).
распи́сыва|ть(ся), ю(сь) *impf. of* ▸ **расписа́ть(ся)**
распих|а́ть, а́ю *pf.* (*of* ▸ **~́ивать**) (*coll.*)
1 (*растолкать*) to push aside.
2 (*рассовать*) to shove; **р. я́блоки по карма́нам** to stuff apples into one's pockets.
распи́хива|ть, ю *impf. of* ▸ **распиха́ть**
распла́в|ить, лю, ишь *pf.* (*of* ▸ **~ля́ть**) to melt, fuse.
распла́в|иться, ится *pf.* (*of* ▸ **~ля́ться**) to melt, fuse.
расплавля́|ть(ся), ю, ет(ся) *impf. of* ▸ **распла́вить(ся)**
распла́|каться, чусь, чешься *pf.* to burst into tears.
распла́т|а, ы *f.* payment; (*fig.*) retribution; **час ~ы** day of reckoning.
распла|ти́ться, чу́сь, ~́тишься *pf.* (*of* ▸ **~́чиваться**)
1 (**с** + *i.*) to pay off; to settle accounts (with), get even (with) (*also fig.*); **р. с долга́ми** to pay off one's debts.
2 (**за** + *a.*; *fig.*) to pay (for).
распла́чива|ться, юсь *impf. of* ▸ **расплати́ться**
распле|ска́ть, щу́, ~́щешь *pf.* (*of* ▸ **~́скивать**) to spill.
распле|ска́ться, ~́щется *pf.* (*of* ▸ **~́скиваться**) to spill.
расплёскива|ть(ся), ю, ет(ся) *impf. of* ▸ **расплеска́ть(ся)**
распле|сти́, ту́, тёшь, *past* **~̈л, ~ла́** *pf.* (*of* ▸ **~та́ть**) (*верёвку*) to untwine, untwist; (*косу*) to undo.
распле|сти́сь, тётся, *past* **~̈лся, ~ла́сь** *pf.* (*of* ▸ **~та́ться**) (*о верёвке*) to untwine, untwist; (*о косе*) to come undone.
расплета́|ть(ся), ю, ет(ся) *impf. of* ▸ **расплести́(сь)**
расплыва́|ться, ется *impf. of* ▸ **расплы́ться**
расплы́вчат|ый (~, ~а) *adj.* (*рисунок*) blurred; (*ответ*) vague.
расплы́|ться, вётся, *past* **~лся, ~ла́сь** *pf.* (*of* ▸ **~ва́ться**)
1 (*о жидкости*) to run; **черни́ла ~лись** the ink has run; (*о фигурах*) to become blurred; (*о массе*) to disperse; (*уплыть*) to swim off.
2 (*coll.*) (*потолстеть*) to spread; to run to fat; **р. в улы́бку** to break into a smile.
расплю́щива|ть(ся), ю, ет(ся) *impf. of* ▸ **расплю́щить(ся)**
расплю́щ|ить, у, ишь *pf.* (*of* ▸ **~ивать**) to flatten, crush.
расплю́щ|иться, ится *pf.* (*of* ▸ **~иваться**) to become flat.
распозна|ва́ть, ю́, ёшь *impf. of* ▸ **~́ть**
распозна́|ть, ю, ешь *pf.* (*of* ▸ **~ва́ть**) to recognize, identify; **р. боле́знь** to diagnose an illness.
располага́|ть[1], ю *impf.* (+ *i.*) to have at one's disposal, have available; **р. вре́менем** to have time available.
располага́|ть[2], ю *impf. of* ▸ **расположи́ть**
располага́|ться, юсь *impf. of* ▸ **расположи́ться**
располага́|ющий
1 *pres. part. act. of* ▸ **~ть[1]**.
2 *pres. part. act. of* ▸ **~ть[2]** *and adj.* pleasant, prepossessing.
располз|а́ться, а́юсь *impf. of* ▸ **~ти́сь**
располз|ти́сь, у́сь, ёшься, *past* **~́ся, ~ла́сь** *pf.* (*of* ▸ **~а́ться**)
1 to crawl (away).
2 (*coll.*) (*об одежде*) to come unravelled; to tear, give at the seams.
расположе́ни|е, я *nt.*
1 (*предметов*) disposition, arrangement; **р. по кварти́рам** (*mil.*) billeting.
2 (*местоположение*) situation, location.
3 (*симпатия*) favour (*Br.*), favor (*US*); sympathies; **по́льзоваться чьим-н. ~ем** to enjoy s.o.'s favour (*Br.*), favor (*US*), to be liked by s.o.
4 : **р. (ду́ха)** disposition, mood, humour (*Br.*), humor (*US*); **быть в плохо́м ~и ду́ха** to be in a bad mood.
располо́жен|ный (~, ~а) *p.p.p. of* ▸ **расположи́ть** *and pred. adj.*
1 (**к** + *d.*) (*питающий чувство симпатии*) well disposed (to, towards).
2 (**к** + *d. or* + *inf.*) (*склонный*) disposed (to), inclined (to); in the mood (for); **я не о́чень ~ сего́дня рабо́тать** I don't feel much like working today.
располож|и́ть, у́, ~́ишь *pf.* (*of* ▸ **располага́ть[2]**)
1 (*разместить*) to dispose, arrange, set out.
2 (*вызвать симпатию в ком-н.*) to win over, gain; **р. кого́-н. к себе́, в свою́ по́льзу** to gain s.o.'s favour (*Br.*), favor (*US*).
располож|и́ться, у́сь, ~́ишься *pf.* (*of* ▸ **располага́ться**) (*разместиться*) to take up position; to settle *or* compose o.s.; to make o.s. comfortable.
распор|о́ть, ю́, ~́ешь *pf.* (*of* ▸ **распа́рывать**) to unstitch, unpick.
распоря|ди́ться, жу́сь, ди́шься *pf.* (*of* ▸ **~жа́ться 1**)
1 (**о** + *p. or* + *inf.*) to order; to see (that); **я ~жу́сь, что́бы вам возмести́ли расхо́ды** I will see that you are reimbursed for the expenses.
2 (+ *i.*) to manage; to deal (with).
распоря́д|ок, ка *m.* order; routine; **пра́вила вну́треннего ~ка** (*в учреждении, на фабрике и т. д.*) (office, factory, *etc.*) regulations.

распоряжа|ться, юсь *impf.*
1 *impf. of* ▸ **распоряди́ться.**
2 (*impf. only*) to give orders, be in charge.

распоряже́ни|е, я *nt.*
1 (*приказ*) order; instruction, direction; **до осо́бого ~я** until further notice.
2 : **име́ть в своём ~и** to have at one's disposal.

распоя́|саться, шусь, шешься *pf.* (*of* ▸ **~сываться**)
1 to take off one's belt; to ungird o.s.
2 (*fig., coll., pej.*) (*стать распущенным*) to throw aside all restraint; to let o.s. go.

распоя́сыва|ться, юсь *impf. of* ▸ **распоя́саться**

распра́в|а, ы *f.* harsh punishment; reprisal; **крова́вая р.** massacre.

распра́в|ить, лю, ишь *pf.* (*of* ▸ **~ля́ть**)
1 (*выпрямить*) to straighten; to smooth out.
2 (*вытянуть*) to spread, stretch; **р. кры́лья** to spread one's wings (*also fig.*).

распра́в|иться[1], ится *pf.* (*of* ▸ **~ля́ться**) (*выпрямиться*) to get smoothed out.

распра́в|иться[2], люсь, ишься *pf.* (*of* ▸ **~ля́ться**) (**с** + *i.*) (*произвести расправу*) to deal (with); **р. без суда́** to take the law into one's own hands; (*распорядиться*) to deal with, dispose of.

расправля́|ть(ся), ю(сь) *impf. of* ▸ **распра́вить(ся)**

распределе́ни|е, я *nt.* distribution; allocation, assignment; **р. нало́гов** assessment of taxes.

распредели́тел|ь, я *m.*
1 (*устройство*) regulator; **р. зажига́ния** distributor.
2 (*учреждение*) distribution centre (*Br.*), center (*US*).

распредели́тельн|ый *adj.* distributive, distributing; **~ая доска́, р. щит** (*tech.*) switchboard; **р. щит(о́к) (с предохрани́телями/про́бками)** (*elec.*) fuse box; **р. вал** (*tech.*) camshaft.

распредел|и́ть, ю́, и́шь *pf.* (*of* ▸ **~я́ть**) to distribute; to allocate, assign; **р. своё вре́мя** to allocate one's time.

распредел|я́ть, я́ю *impf. of* ▸ **~и́ть**

распрода|ва́ть, ю́, ёшь *impf. of* ▸ **~́ть**

распрода́ж|а, и *f.* sale; clearance sale.

распрода́|ть, м, шь, ст, ди́м, ди́те, ду́т, *past* **распро́дал, ~ла́, распро́дало** *pf.* (*of* ▸ **~ва́ть**) (*землю, вещи*) to sell off; (*билеты*) to sell out of; **биле́ты распро́даны** all the tickets are sold.

распро|сти́ться, щу́сь, сти́шься *pf.* (**с** + *i.*) to say goodbye to; **р. с мечто́й** to bid farewell to one's dream(s).

распростране́ни|е, я *nt.* (*слухов, заразы*) spreading; (*знания, идей*) dissemination; (*владений*) expansion; (*оружия*) proliferation; (*товаров*) distribution; **име́ть большо́е р.** to be widely practised (*Br.*), practiced (*US*).

распростран|ённый *p.p.p. of* ▸ **~и́ть** *and adj.* (*мнение*) widespread, prevalent; (*растения*) common.

распространи́тел|ь, я *m.* (*слухов, знаний*) spreader, disseminator; (*книг, газет*) distributor.

распространи́тель|ница, ницы *f. of* ▸ **~**

распростран|и́ть, ю́, и́шь *pf.* (*of* ▸ **~я́ть**)
1 (*слухи, заразу*) to spread; (*знания, информацию*) to disseminate; (*товары, книги*) to distribute; (*письмо, меморандум*) to circulate; (*владения*) to increase.
2 (*расширить*) to extend; **р. де́йствие зако́на на всех** to extend the application of a law to all.
3 (*запах*) to give off.

распростран|и́ться, и́тся *pf.* (*of* ▸ **~я́ться**) (*огонь, слухи, запах*) to spread; (*стать больше*) to extend; (*о законе*) to apply.

распростран|я́ть(ся), я́ю, я́ет(ся) *impf. of* ▸ **~и́ть(ся)**

распроща́|ться, юсь *pf.* (**с** + *i.*; *coll.*) = **распрости́ться**

распряга́|ть, ю *impf. of* ▸ **распря́чь**

распрям|и́ть, лю́, и́шь *pf.* (*of* ▸ **~ля́ть**) (*проволоку*) to straighten, unbend; (*спину*) to straighten.

распрям|и́ться, лю́сь, и́шься *pf.* (*of* ▸ **~ля́ться**) to straighten o.s. up.

распрямля́|ть(ся), ю(сь) *impf. of* ▸ **распрями́ть(ся)**

распря́|чь, гу́, жёшь, гу́т, *past* **~г, ~гла́** *pf.* (*of* ▸ **~га́ть**) to unharness.

распуг|а́ть, а́ю *pf.* (*of* ▸ **~́ивать**) (*coll.*) to scare away, frighten away.

распу́гива|ть, ю *impf. of* ▸ **распуга́ть**

распуска́|ть(ся), ю(сь) *impf. of* ▸ **распусти́ть(ся)**

распу|сти́ть, щу́, ~́стишь *pf.* (*of* ▸ **~ска́ть**)
1 (*учеников*) to dismiss; (*расформировать*) to disband; **р. парла́мент** to dissolve parliament.
2 (*ремень, узел галстука*) to loosen, let out; **р. во́лосы** to let one's hair down; **р. паруса́** to set sail.
3 (*fig., coll.*) (*избаловать*) to allow to get out of hand; to spoil.
4 (*coll.*) (*слухи*) to spread, put out.

распу|сти́ться, щу́сь, ~́стишься *pf.* (*of* ▸ **~ска́ться**)
1 (*bot.*) to open, come out.
2 (*fig., coll.*) (*о детях*) to become undisciplined, get out of hand.

распу́т|ать, аю *pf.* (*of* ▸ **~ывать**)
1 (*узел*) to untangle; to unravel.
2 (*животное*) to untie.
3 (*fig.*) (*сложный вопрос*) to disentangle; to puzzle out.

распу́т|аться, аюсь *pf.* (*of* ▸ **~ываться**)
1 to get disentangled; come undone.
2 (*fig., coll.*) to get disentangled, be cleared up.

распу́т|ный (~ен, ~на) *adj.* dissolute, dissipated, debauched.

распу́тыва|ть(ся), ю(сь) *impf. of* ▸ **распу́тать(ся)**

распух|а́ть, а́ю *impf. of* ▸ **~́нуть**

распу́х|нуть, ну, нешь, *past* **~, ~ла** *pf.* (*of* ▸ **~а́ть**) to swell up.

распу́|щенный *p.p.p. of* ▸ **~сти́ть** *and adj.*

1 (*недисциплинированный*) undisciplined; **р. ребёнок** spoiled child.
2 (*безнравственный*) dissolute, dissipated.

распыли́тел|ь, я *m.* spray(er).

распыл|и́ть, ю́, и́шь *pf.* (*of* ▸ **~я́ть**)
1 (*краску*) to spray.
2 (*fig.*) to scatter; **р. си́лы** to scatter one's forces.

распыл|и́ться, и́тся *pf.* (*of* ▸ **~я́ться**) to disperse, to get scattered.

распыл|я́ть(ся), я́ю, ет(ся) *impf. of* ▸ **~и́ть(ся)**

распя́ти|е, я *nt.* cross, crucifix.

расса́д|а, ы *no pl., f.* seedlings.

расса|ди́ть, жу́, ~́дишь *pf.* (*of* ▸ **~́живать**)
1 (*гостей*) to seat, offer seats.
2 (*посадить порознь*) to separate, seat separately.
3 (*растения*) to plant out.

расса́жива|ть, ю *impf. of* ▸ **рассади́ть**

расса́жива|ться, юсь *impf. of* ▸ **рассе́сться**

расса́сыва|ться, ется *impf. of* ▸ **рассоса́ться**

рассве|сти́, тёт, *past* **~ло́** *pf.* (*of* ▸ **~та́ть**) to dawn; **уже́ ~ло́** it was already light.

рассве́т, а *m.* dawn, daybreak; (*fig.*) (*начало*) dawn.

рассвета́|ть, ет *impf. of* ▸ **рассвести́; ~ет** day is breaking.

рассе́ива|ть(ся), ю, ет(ся) *impf. of* ▸ **рассе́ять(ся)**

рассека́|ть, ю *impf. of* ▸ **рассе́чь**

рассекре́|тить, чу, тишь *pf.* (*of* ▸ **~чивать**) to declassify.

рассекре́чива|ть, ю *impf. of* ▸ **рассекре́тить**

расселе́ни|е, я *nt.*
1 settling (*in a new place*).
2 (*порознь*) separation; settling apart.

рассел|и́ть, ю́, и́шь *pf.* (*of* ▸ **~я́ть**)
1 to settle (*in a new place*).
2 (*порознь*) to separate; to settle apart.

рассел|и́ться, ю́сь, и́шься *pf.* (*of* ▸ **~я́ться**)
1 to settle (*in a new place*).
2 (*порознь*) to separate, settle separately.

рассел|я́ть(ся), я́ю(сь) *impf. of* ▸ **~и́ть(ся)**

рассер|ди́ть, жу́, ~́дишь *pf. of* ▸ **серди́ть**

рассер|ди́ться, жу́сь, ~́дишься *pf.* (*of* ▸ **серди́ться**) (**на** + *a.*) to get, become angry (with, at, about).

рас|се́сться, ся́дусь, ся́дешься, *past* **~се́лся** *pf.* (*of* ▸ **~са́живаться**)
1 to take one's seat.
2 (*coll.*) (*развалиться*) to sprawl.

рассе́|чь, ку́, чёшь, ку́т, *past* **~̈к, ~кла́** *pf.* (*of* ▸ **~ка́ть**)
1 (*разрубить*) to cut through; (*волну, небо*) to cleave.
2 (*поранить*) to cut (badly); **я ~̈к себе́ па́лец** I have cut my finger (badly).

рассе́янно *adv.* absent-mindedly; (*смотреть*) vacantly.

рассе́янност|ь, и *f.* (*невнимательность*) absent-mindedness.

рассе́я|нный *p.p.p. of* ▸ **~ть** *and adj.*
1 (*свет*) diffused.
2 (*население*) scattered, dispersed.
3 (*невнимательный*) absent-minded; **р. взгляд** vacant look.

рассе́|ять, ю, ешь *pf.* (*of* ▸ **~ивать**)
1 (*население, толпу*) to scatter, disperse.
2 (*сомнения*) to dispel.

рассе́|яться, ется *pf.* (*of* ▸ **~иваться**) to disperse; (*в беспорядке*) to scatter; (*о неприятном чувстве*) to pass; **толпа́ ~ялась** the crowd dispersed; **тума́н ~ялся** the fog cleared.

расси|де́ться, жу́сь, ди́шься *pf.* (*of* ▸ **~́живаться**) (*coll.*) to sit for a long time; to sit around.

расси́жива|ться, юсь *impf. of* ▸ **рассиде́ться**

расска́з, а *m.*
1 story.
2 (*очевидца*) account.

расска|за́ть, жу́, ~́жешь *pf.* (*of* ▸ **~́зывать**)
1 (+ *a. and d.*) to tell, relate (*sth. to s.o.*).
2 (**о** + *p.*) to tell of; **р. о де́тстве** to tell of one's childhood.
3 : **р., как всё произошло́** to tell how it all happened.

расска́зчик, а *m.* storyteller, narrator.

расска́зчи|ца, цы *f. of* ▸ **~к**

расска́зыва|ть, ю *impf. of* ▸ **рассказа́ть**

рассла́б|ить, лю, ишь *pf.* (*of* ▸ **~ля́ть**)
1 (*пояс, воротничок*) to loosen.
2 (*мышцы*) to relax.

рассла́б|иться, люсь, ишься *pf.* (*of* ▸ **~ля́ться**) to relax.

расслабля́|ть(ся), ю(сь) *impf. of* ▸ **рассла́бить(ся)**

рассла́ива|ться, ется *impf. of* ▸ **расслои́ться**

рассле́довани|е, я *nt.* investigation; (*leg.*) inquiry; **провести́ р.** (+ *g.*) to hold an inquiry (into).

рассле́д|овать, ую *impf. and pf.* to investigate.

рассло|и́ться, и́тся *pf.* (*of* ▸ **рассла́иваться**) to become stratified (*also fig.*); (*отслоиться*) to flake off.

расслы́ш|ать, у, ишь *pf.* to catch; **я не ~ал вас** I didn't catch what you said.

рассма́трива|ть, ю *impf.*
1 *impf. of* ▸ **рассмотре́ть.**
2 (*impf. only*) (*считать*) to regard (as), consider.
3 (*impf. only*) (*внимательно смотреть*) to scrutinize, examine.

рассмеш|и́ть, у́, и́шь *pf.* to make laugh.

рассме|я́ться, ю́сь, ёшься *pf.* to burst out laughing.

рассмотр|е́ть, ю́, ~́ишь *pf.* (*of* ▸ **рассма́тривать 1**)
1 (*различить*) to discern, make out; **мы с трудо́м ~е́ли на́дпись на па́мятнике** we had difficulty in making out the inscription on the monument.

2 (*обсудить*) to examine, consider; **р. заявле́ние** to consider an application.
расс|ова́ть, у́ю, уёшь *pf.* (*of* ▶ **~о́вывать**) (*coll.*) to shove, stuff; **р. свои́ ве́щи по чемода́нам** to stuff one's things into suitcases.
рассо́выва|ть, ю *impf. of* ▶ **рассова́ть**
рассо́л, а *m.* brine.
рассо́р|иться, юсь, ишься *pf.* (**с** + *i.*) to fall out (with).
рассортир|ова́ть, у́ю *pf.* (*of* ▶ **~о́вывать**) to sort out; (*по ассортименту*) to classify; (*по качеству*) to grade, sort.
рассортиро́выва|ть, ю *impf. of* ▶ **рассортирова́ть**
рассос|а́ться, ётся *pf.* (*of* ▶ **расса́сываться**) (*об опухоли*) to go down; (*coll.*) (*о толпе*) to disperse.
рассо́х|нуться, нется, *past* **~ся, ~лась** *pf.* (*of* ▶ **рассыха́ться**) to crack.
расспра́шива|ть, ю *impf. of* ▶ **расспроси́ть**
расспро|си́ть, шу́, ~сишь *pf.* (*of* ▶ **расспра́шивать**) to question; (**о** + *p.*) (*узнать, спрашивая*) to find out.
рассро́чк|а, и *f.* instalment system; **в ~у** by, in instalments.
расстава́ни|е, я *nt.* parting; **при ~и** on parting.
расста|ва́ться, ю́сь, ёшься *impf. of* ▶ **расста́ться**
расста́в|ить, лю, ишь *pf.* (*of* ▶ **~ля́ть**)
1 (*разместить*) (*книги, мебель*) to place, arrange; (*кадры, работников*) to place, position; **р. часовы́х** to post sentries; (*запятые*) to put, add.
2 (*раздвинуть*) to move apart; **р. но́ги** to stand with one's legs apart.
расставля́|ть, ю *impf. of* ▶ **расста́вить**
расстано́вк|а, и *f.* placing, arrangement.
расста́|ться, нусь, нешься *pf.* (*of* ▶ **~ва́ться**) (**с** + *i.*)
1 to part (with); **я ~лся с ней** I parted with her; **~немся друзья́ми** let us part friends.
2 (*с мечтой, с мыслью*) to give up.
расстёгива|ть(ся), ю(сь) *impf. of* ▶ **расстегну́ть(ся)**
расстег|ну́ть, ну́, нёшь *pf.* (*of* ▶ **~ивать**) to undo, unfasten.
расстег|ну́ться, ну́сь, нёшься *pf.* (*of* ▶ **~иваться**)
1 (*об одежде, о предмете*) to come undone.
2 (*о человеке*) to undo one's coat, shirt, *etc.*; to undo one's buttons.
расстел|и́ть, ю́, ~ешь *pf.* (*of* ▶ **расстила́ть**) to spread (out), to lay (out).
расстел|и́ться, ~ется *pf.* (*of* ▶ **расстила́ться**) to spread.
расстила́|ть(ся), ю, ет(ся) *impf. of* ▶ **расстели́ть(ся)** *and* ▶ **разостла́ть(ся)**
расстоя́ни|е, я *nt.* distance; **на ~и** (*видеть*) at a distance; (*управлять*) from a distance; **на бли́зком ~и** (**от** + *g.*) at a short distance (from); **они́ живу́т на ~и двух миль от ближа́йшего го́рода** they live two miles from the nearest town.
расстра́ива|ть(ся), ю(сь) *impf. of* ▶ **расстро́ить(ся)**
расстре́л, а *m.*
1 (*казнь*) execution (*by firing squad*); **приговори́ть к ~у** to sentence to be shot.
2 (*обстрел*) (+ *g.*) shooting at; firing at, on.
расстре́лива|ть, ю *impf. of* ▶ **расстреля́ть**
расстрел|я́ть, я́ю *pf.* (*of* ▶ **~ивать**)
1 (*убить*) to shoot, execute by shooting.
2 (*танки*) to shoot at; (*демонстрацию*) to open fire on.
3 (*снаряды*) to use up (*in firing*).
расстро́|енный *p.p.p. of* ▶ **~ить** *and adj.* (*здоровье*) damaged, weak; (*нервы*) shattered; (*человек, вид*) upset; (*рояль*) out of tune.
расстро́|ить, ю, ишь *pf.* (*of* ▶ **расстра́ивать**)
1 (*здоровье, хозяйство*) to damage; (*планы*) to upset.
2 (*человека*) to upset.
расстро́|иться, юсь, ишься *pf.* (*of* ▶ **расстра́иваться**)
1 (*о здоровье, хозяйстве*) to be damaged; (*о планах*) to fall through.
2 (**из-за** + *g.*) (*о человеке*) to be upset (over, about).
3 (*mus.*) to become out of tune.
расстро́йств|о, а *nt.* disorder; confusion; **р. желу́дка** stomach upset; **р. пищеваре́ния** indigestion; **не́рвное р.** nervous breakdown; **р. ре́чи** speech defect; **дела́ пришли́ в р.** things are in disarray.
расступ|а́ться, а́ется *impf. of* ▶ **~и́ться**
расступ|и́ться, ~ится *pf.* (*of* ▶ **~а́ться**) to part, make way; **толпа́ ~и́лась** the crowd parted.
рассуди́тел|ьный (~ен, ~ьна) *adj.* reasonable; sensible.
рассу|ди́ть, жу́, ~дишь *pf.*
1 (*людей*) to judge (between), arbitrate (between); **~ди́те нас** be our judge; settle our dispute.
2 (*решить*) to decide.
рассу́д|ок, ка *m.*
1 (*способность*) reason; intellect; **лиши́ться ~ка** to lose one's reason.
2 (*здравый смысл*) good sense.
рассужда́|ть, ю *impf.*
1 (*мыслить*) to reason.
2 (**о** + *p.*, **на** + *a.*) (*обсуждать*) to debate; to argue (about); **р. на каку́ю-н. те́му** to discuss a topic.
рассужде́ни|е, я *nt.*
1 (*процесс*) reasoning.
2 (*usu. pl.*) (*обсуждение*) debate; argument; **без ~й** without argument.
рассчи́т|анный *p.p.p. of* ▶ **~а́ть** *and adj.*
1 calculated, deliberate.
2 (**на** + *a.*) intended (for), designed (for); **кни́га, ~анная на широ́кого чита́теля** a book intended for the general public.
рассчит|а́ть, а́ю *pf.* (*of* ▶ **~ывать 1**) (*стоимость, расходы*) to calculate; **он не ~а́л свои́х сил** he miscalculated his strength.
рассчит|а́ться, а́юсь *pf.* (*of* ▶ **~ываться**) (**с** + *i.*) to settle accounts (with); (*fig.*) to settle scores (with).
рассчи́тыва|ть, ю *impf.*
1 *impf. of* ▶ **рассчита́ть.**

Р

2 (*impf. only*) (**на** + *a.*) (*предполагать*) to count (on, upon), reckon (on, upon); (+ *inf.*) to expect (to), hope (to); **мы ~ли зако́нчить рабо́ту в э́том году́** we were hoping to finish the work this year.
3 (*impf. only*) (**на** + *a.*) (*полагаться*) to count (on, upon), rely (on, upon), depend (upon).

рассчи́тыва|ться, юсь *impf. of* ▸ **рассчита́ться**

рассыла́|ть, ю *impf. of* ▸ **разосла́ть**

рассы́лк|а, и *f.* distribution, dispatch; (*по электронной почте*) mailing.

рассы́п|ать, лю, лешь *pf.* (*of* ▸ **~а́ть**) (*невольно*) to spill; (*разбросать*) to strew, scatter.

рассып|а́ть(ся), а́ю(сь) *impf. of* ▸ **~́ать(ся)**

рассы́п|аться, люсь, лешься *pf.* (*of* ▸ **~а́ться**)
1 (*о муке*) to spill; **моне́ты ~ались по́ полу** the coins spilt onto the floor; (*о толпе*) to scatter; (*о домах*) to be scattered.
2 (*о стене, о хлебе*) to crumble; to disintegrate (*also fig.*).
3 (*coll.*) (**в** + *p.*) to be profuse (in); **р. в похвала́х** (+ *d.*) to shower praises (upon).

рассыха́|ться, ется *impf. of* ▸ **рассо́хнуться**

раста́лкива|ть, ю *impf. of* ▸ **растолка́ть**

раста́плива|ть, ю *impf. of* ▸ **растопи́ть**[1,2]

раста́птыва|ть, ю *impf. of* ▸ **растопта́ть**

растаск|а́ть, а́ю *pf.* (*of* ▸ **~́ивать**) (*coll.*)
1 (*унести по частям*) to take away, remove (*little by little, bit by bit*).
2 (*украсть*) to pilfer, filch.

раста́скива|ть, ю *impf. of* ▸ **растаска́ть** *and* ▸ **растащи́ть**

растащ|и́ть, у́, ~́ишь *pf.* (*of* ▸ **раста́скивать**)
1 (*дерущихся*) to part, separate, drag apart.
2 = **растаска́ть**

раста́|ять, ю, ешь *pf. of* ▸ **та́ять**

раство́р, а *m.*
1 (*chem.*) solution.
2 (*tech.*) (*строительный*) mortar.

раствори́м|ый (~, ~а) *adj.* soluble; **р. ко́фе** instant coffee.

раствори́тел|ь, я *m.* solvent.

раствор|и́ть[1]**, ю́, ~́ишь** *pf.* (*of* ▸ **~я́ть**) (*окно*) to open.

раствор|и́ть[2]**, ю́, и́шь** *pf.* (*of* ▸ **~я́ть**) (*соль*) to dissolve.

раствор|и́ться[1]**, ~́ится** *pf.* (*of* ▸ **~я́ться**) (*об окне*) to open.

раствор|и́ться[2]**, и́тся** *pf.* (*of* ▸ **~я́ться**) (*о соли*) to dissolve; (*fig.*) (*исчезнуть*) to vanish.

раствор|я́ть(ся), я́ю, я́ет(ся) *impf. of* ▸ **~и́ть(ся)**

растека́|ться, юсь *impf. of* ▸ **расте́чься**

расте́ни|е, я *nt.* plant.

растере́ть, разотру́, разотрёшь, *past* **растёр, растёрла** *pf.* (*of* ▸ **растира́ть**)
1 to grind; **р. в порошо́к** to grind to powder.
2 (**по** + *d.*) (*мазь*) to rub (over), spread (over).
3 (*тело*) to rub, massage.

растере́ться, разотру́сь, разотрёшься, *past* **растёрся, растёрлась** *pf.* (*of* ▸ **растира́ться**)
1 (*о зёрнах*) to become powdered, turn into powder.
2 (+ *i.*) (*обтереть себя*) to rub o.s. briskly (with).

растерз|а́ть, а́ю *pf.* (*of* ▸ **~́ывать**)
1 (*умертвить*) to tear to pieces.
2 (*fig., poet.*) (*измучить*) to lacerate; to harrow.

растёрзыва|ть, ю *impf. of* ▸ **растерза́ть**

растёрянност|ь, и *f.* confusion, bewilderment.

растёр|янный *p.p.p. of* ▸ **~я́ть** *and adj.* confused, bewildered.

растер|я́ть, я́ю *pf.* to lose (*little by little*).

растер|я́ться, я́юсь *pf.* (*утратить самообладание*) to lose one's head, nerve; **он не ~я́лся пе́ред лицо́м опа́сности** he kept his head in the face of danger.

расте́|чься, чётся, ку́тся, *past* **~̈кся, ~кла́сь** *pf.* (*of* ▸ **~ка́ться**) (*о воде*) to spill; (*о краске*) to run.

раст|и́, у́, ёшь, *past* **рос, росла́** *impf.* (*of* ▸ **вы́~**)
1 (*biol.*) to grow; (*о детях*) to grow up; **он рос на Украи́не** he grew up in Ukraine.
2 (*увеличиваться*) to grow, increase.
3 (*совершенствоваться*) to advance, develop.

растира́|ть(ся), ю(сь) *impf. of* ▸ **растере́ть(ся)**

расти́тельност|ь, и *f.*
1 (*растения*) vegetation.
2 (*волосы*) hair (*on face or body*).

расти́тельн|ый *adj.* vegetable; **~ое ма́сло** vegetable oil.

ра|сти́ть, щу́, сти́шь *impf.*
1 (*детей*) to raise, bring up; (*кадры*) to nurture.
2 (*цветы*) to grow, cultivate; (*животных*) to rear; **р. бо́роду** to grow a beard.

растлева́|ть, ю *impf. of* ▸ **растли́ть**

растл|и́ть, ю́, и́шь *pf.* (*of* ▸ **~ева́ть**)
1 (*малолетних*) to defile (*minors*).
2 (*морально*) to corrupt, deprave.

растолка́|ть, ю *pf.* (*of* ▸ **раста́лкивать**) (*coll.*)
1 (*толпу*) to push asunder, apart.
2 (*спящего*) to shake (*in order to awaken*).

растолсте́|ть, ю *pf.* to put on weight.

растоп|и́ть[1]**, лю́, ~́ишь** *pf.* (*of* ▸ **раста́пливать**) (*печь*) to light.

растоп|и́ть[2]**, лю́, ~́ишь** *pf.* (*of* ▸ **раста́пливать**) (*сало, лёд*) to melt.

растоп|та́ть, чу́, ~́чешь *pf.* (*of* ▸ **раста́птывать**) to trample, stamp (on), crush (*also fig.*).

растопы́рива|ть, ю *impf. of* ▸ **растопы́рить**

растопы́р|ить, ю, ишь *pf.* (*of* ▸ **~ивать**) (*coll.*) to spread wide, open wide.

расторг|а́ть, а́ю *impf. of* ▸ **~́нуть**

расто́рг|нуть, ну, нешь, *past* **~, ~ла** *pf.* (*of* ▸ **~а́ть**) (*контракт, договор*) to dissolve, annul; **р. брак** to dissolve a marriage.

расточи́тел|ьный (~ен, ~ьна) *adj.*

extravagant, wasteful.

растра́т|а, ы *f.*
1 (*денег, времени*) waste, squandering.
2 (*незаконная*) embezzlement.

растра́|тить, чу, тишь *pf.* (*of* ▸ **~чивать**)
1 to waste, squander.
2 (*незаконно*) to embezzle.

растра́чива|ть, ю *impf. of* ▸ **растра́тить**

растр|ёпанный *p.p.p. of* ▸ **~епа́ть** *and adj.* (*волосы*) dishevelled; (*книга*) tattered.

растреп|а́ть, лю́, ~́лешь *pf.*
1 (*волосы*) to mess up, tousle.
2 (*книгу*) to reduce to tatters, tear.

растреп|а́ться, ~́лется *pf.*
1 (*о волосах*) to get messed up, get dishevelled.
2 (*о книге*) to get tattered, get torn.

растро́га|ть, ю *pf.* to move, touch; **р. кого́-н. до слёз** to move s.o. to tears.

растя́гива|ть(ся), ю(сь) *impf. of* ▸ **растяну́ть(ся)**

растяже́ни|е, я *nt.* (*med.*) strain, sprain.

растя|ну́ть, ну́, ~́нешь *pf.* (*of* ▸ **~́гивать**)
1 (*ковёр, скатерть*) to stretch, spread (out); (*лишить упругости*) to stretch; (*платежи*) to spread.
2 (*med.*) to strain, sprain.
3 (*сделать слишком длинным*) to stretch out; (*fig.*) to protract, drag out.

растя|ну́ться, ну́сь, ~́нешься *pf.* (*of* ▸ **~́гиваться**)
1 to stretch (out); (*стать менее упругим*) to be stretched.
2 (*стать слишком длинным*) to stretch too far; (*fig.*) (*работа, собрание*) to drag on; **обсужде́ние его́ докла́да ~ну́лось на полтора́ часа́** discussion of his lecture dragged on for an hour and a half.

растя́п|а, ы *c.g.* (*coll.*) bungler.

расхва́лива|ть, ю *impf. of* ▸ **расхвали́ть**

расхвал|и́ть, ю́, ~́ишь *pf.* (*of* ▸ **~́ивать**) to lavish, shower praise (on, upon).

расхи́|тить, щу, тишь *pf.* (*of* ▸ **~ща́ть**) to embezzle, misappropriate.

расхища́|ть, ю *impf. of* ▸ **расхи́тить**

расхо́д, а *m.*
1 (*затрата*) expense; (*pl.*) expenses, outlay, cost; **доро́жные ~ы** travel expenses; **накладны́е ~ы** overheads; **де́ньги на карма́нные ~ы** pocket money.
2 (*энергии*) consumption; **р. горю́чего** fuel consumption.
3 (*в бухгалтерии*) expenditure, outlay; **прихо́д и р.** income and expenditure.

расхо|ди́ться, жу́сь, ~́дишься *impf. of* ▸ **разойти́сь**

расхо́д|овать, ую *impf.* (*of* ▸ **из~**)
1 (*деньги, время*) to spend, expend.
2 (*ресурсы*) to use (up), consume; **маши́на ~ует мно́го бензи́на** the car uses a lot of petrol (*Br.*), gas (*US*).

расхожде́ни|е, я *nt.* (*лучей, дорог*) divergence; (*идейное*) difference; **р. во мне́ниях** difference of opinion; (*в тексте*) discrepancy.

расхо|те́ть, чу́, ~́чешь, ти́м, ти́те, тя́т *pf.* (+ *g. or a. or inf.*; *coll.*) to no longer want; **я ~те́л спать** I am no longer sleepy.

расхо|те́ться, ~́чется *pf.* (*impers.* + *d.*; *coll.*) to no longer want; **мне ~те́лось есть** I no longer want to eat.

расхохо|та́ться, чу́сь, ~́чешься *pf.* to burst out laughing.

расцве|сти́, ту́, тёшь, *past* **~̈л, ~ла́** *pf.* (*of* ▸ **~та́ть**) (*цветок, девушка*) to blossom; (*наука, искусство*) to flourish; (*повеселеть*) to become radiant.

расцве́т, а *m.* blossoming; (*науки*) flourishing; flowering; **в ~е сил** in one's prime.

расцвета́|ть, ю *impf. of* ▸ **расцвести́**

расцве́тк|а, и *f.* colour (*Br.*), color (*US*) scheme; colours (*Br.*), colors (*US*).

расцел|ова́ть, у́ю *pf.* to smother with kisses.

расце́нива|ть, ю *impf. of* ▸ **расцени́ть**

расце́нива|ться, ется *impf.* to be regarded.

расцен|и́ть, ю́, ~́ишь *pf.* (*of* ▸ **~́ивать**) (*поступок, слова*) to regard; **его́ речь ~и́ли как провока́цию** his speech was regarded as provocation.

расце́нк|а, и *f.* (*usu. pl.*) (*цена*) tariff, rates.

расчер|ти́ть, чу́, ~́тишь *pf.* (*of* ▸ **~́чивать**) to rule, line.

расче́рчива|ть, ю *impf. of* ▸ **расчерти́ть**

расче|са́ть, шу́, ~́шешь *pf.* (*of* ▸ **~̈сывать**)
1 (*волосы*) to comb; (*лён, шерсть*) to card.
2 (*руку*) to scratch.

расче|са́ться, шу́сь, ~́шешься *pf.* (*of* ▸ **~̈сываться**) (*coll.*) (*расчесать волосы*) to comb one's hair.

расчёск|а, и *f.* comb.

расчёсыва|ть(ся), ю(сь) *impf. of* ▸ **расчеса́ть(ся)**

расчёт[1], а *m.*
1 (*стоимости*) calculation; (*смета*) statement; (*приблизительный*) estimate, reckoning; **из ~а** on the basis (of), at a rate (of); **приня́ть в р.** to take into account, consideration; **по мои́м ~ам** by my reckoning; **в ~е на** (+ *a.*) hoping for, reckoning on.
2 (**с** + *i.*) settling (with); (*оплата*) payment; **нали́чный р.** cash payment; **быть в ~е** (**с** + *i.*) to be quits (with), be even (with); **производи́ть ~ы** (**с** + *i.*) to settle accounts (with).

расчёт[2], а *m.* (*mil.*) crew; **оруди́йный р.** gun crew.

расчётлив|ый (~, ~а) *adj.* thrifty.

расчётн|ый *adj.*
1 calculation; **~ая табли́ца** calculation table.
2 pay, accounts; **р. день** pay day.
3 (*tech.*) rated; **~ая мо́щность** rated capacity.

расчи́|стить, щу, стишь *pf.* (*of* ▸ **~ща́ть**) to clear; **р. путь, доро́гу** (*fig.*) to pave the way.

расчи́|ститься, стится *pf.* (*of* ▸ **~ща́ться**) (*о небе*) to clear.

расчища́|ть(ся), ю, ет(ся) *impf. of* ▸ **расчи́стить(ся)**
расчлен|и́ть, ю́, и́шь *pf.* (*of* ▸ **~я́ть**) to break up, divide.
расчлен|я́ть, я́ю *impf. of* ▸ **~и́ть**
расшат|а́ть, а́ю *pf.* (*of* ▸ **~́ывать**)
1 to shake loose; to make rickety.
2 (*fig.*) (*дисциплину*) to undermine, impair; (*хозяйство*) to cripple; (*нервы, здоровье*) to damage.
расшат|а́ться, а́юсь *pf.* (*of* ▸ **~́ываться**)
1 to get loose; to become rickety.
2 (*fig.*) (*дисциплина*) to be undermined; (*хозяйство*) to be crippled; (*нервы, здоровье*) to go to pieces, crack up.
расша́тыва|ть(ся), ю(сь) *impf. of* ▸ **расшата́ть(ся)**
расшеве́лива|ть, ю *impf. of* ▸ **расшевели́ть**
расшевел|и́ть, ю́, и́шь *pf.* (*of* ▸ **~́ивать**) to stir, shake; (*fig.*) (*стимулировать*) to stir, rouse.
расшиб|а́ть(ся), а́ю(сь) *impf. of* ▸ **расшиби́ть(ся)**
расшиб|и́ть, у́, ёшь, *past* **~́, ~́ла** *pf.* (*of* ▸ **~а́ть**)
1 (*ушибить*) to hurt; to knock, stub.
2 (*coll.*) (*разбить*) to break up, smash to pieces.
расшиб|и́ться, у́сь, ёшься, *past* **~́ся, ~́лась** *pf.* (*of* ▸ **~а́ться**) to hurt o.s., knock o.s.
расшива́|ть, ю *impf. of* ▸ **расши́ть**
расшире́ни|е, я *nt.*
1 (*отверстия*) widening; (*кругозора, знаний*) broadening.
2 (*производства*) expansion.
3 (*med.*) dilation, dilatation.
4 (*comput.*) (*файла*) extension; **пла́та ~я** expansion card (*graphics card, sound card, etc.*).
расши́р|енный *p.p.p. of* ▸ **~ить** *and adj.* (*отверстие*) widened; (*программа*) broadened, more extensive; (*заседание*) expanded; (*зрачки*) dilated.
расши́р|ить, ю, ишь *pf.* (*of* ▸ **~я́ть**) (*отверстие*) to widen; (*производство*) to expand; (*кругозор, знания*) to broaden; (*сферу влияния*) to extend.
расши́р|иться, ится *pf.* (*of* ▸ **~я́ться**) (*об отверстии*) to widen; (*о производстве, о знаниях*) to expand; (*о кругозоре*) to broaden; (*о зрачках*) to dilate.
расшир|я́ть(ся), я́ю, я́ет(ся) *impf. of* ▸ **~́ить(ся)**
расши́ть, разошью́, разошьёшь *pf.* (*of* ▸ **расшива́ть**) to embroider.
расшифр|ова́ть, у́ю *pf.* (*of* ▸ **~о́вывать**) to decipher, decode; (*fig.*) (*угадать смысл*) to figure out.
расшифро́вк|а, и *f.* deciphering, decoding; (*fig.*) interpretation.
расшифро́выва|ть, ю *impf. of* ▸ **расшифрова́ть**
расшнур|ова́ть, у́ю *pf.* (*of* ▸ **~о́вывать**) to unlace.
расшнур|ова́ться, у́юсь *pf.* (*of* ▸ **~о́вываться**) to come unlaced, come undone.
расшнуро́выва|ть(ся), ю(сь) *impf. of* ▸ **расшнурова́ть(ся)**
расшум|е́ться, лю́сь, и́шься *pf.* (*coll.*) to get noisy, kick up a din.
расще́лин|а, ы *f.* cleft, crevice.
ратифика́ци|я, и *f.* ratification.
ратифици́р|овать, ую *impf. and pf.* to ratify.
ра́унд, а *m.* (*sport*) round; (*переговоров*) series, round.
ра́ут, а *m.* reception.
рафини́рован|ный (~, ~а) *adj.* refined.
рацио́н, а *m.* ration.
рационализа́ци|я, и *f.* rationalization, improvement.
рационализи́р|овать, ую *impf. and pf.* to rationalize, improve.
рационали́зм, а *m.* (*phil.*) rationalism.
рациона́льно *adv.* (*мыслить, поступать*) rationally; (*вести хозяйство*) efficiently; **р. испо́льзовать** to make efficient use (of).
рациона́л|ьный (~ен, ~ьна) *adj.* (*поступок*) rational; (*использование средств*) efficient; **~ьное пита́ние** sound nutrition.
ра́ци|я, и *f.* (*на корабле, в здании*) radio set; (*небольшая переносная*) walkie-talkie.
рван|у́ть, у́, ёшь *pf.*
1 (*дёрнуть резко*) to jerk; to tug (at); **р. кого́-н. за рука́в** to tug s.o. by the sleeve.
2 (*машина*) to start (with a jerk).
3 (*coll.*) (*помчаться*) to dash off, shoot off.
4 (*coll.*) (*взорвать*) to explode, blow up; **в сосе́днем до́ме ~у́ло** there was an explosion in the next house.
рван|у́ться, у́сь, ёшься *pf.* to rush, dash.
рва́н|ый *adj.* torn; lacerated; **~ые башмаки́** broken shoes; **~ая ра́на** (*med.*) laceration.
рвать[1]**, рву, рвёшь,** *past* **рвал, рвала́, рва́ло** *impf.*
1 (*одежду*) to tear (up); to rip; **р. на ча́сти** (*предмет*) to tear to pieces; (*человека*) to overburden; **р. письмо́** to tear up a letter; **р. на себе́ во́лосы** to tear one's hair.
2 (*выдёргивать*) to pull out, tear out; **р. зу́бы** to pull out teeth; **р. с ко́рнем** to uproot.
3 (*брать*) to pick, pluck; **р. цветы́** to pick flowers.
рвать[2]**, рвёт,** *past* **рва́ло** *impf.* (*of* ▸ **вы́рвать**[2]) (*impers.; coll.*) to vomit, throw up, be sick.
рва́|ться[1]**, рвётся,** *past* **~лся, ~ла́сь, ~́ло́сь** *impf.*
1 (*об одежде*) to break; to tear; (*об отношениях*) to break up, be severed.
2 (*взрываться*) to burst, explode.
рва́|ться[2]**, рвусь, рвёшься,** *past* **~лся, ~ла́сь, ~́ло́сь** *impf.* (*стремиться*) to strain (to, at); to be bursting (to); **р. в бой/дра́ку** to be spoiling for a fight; **р. к вла́сти** to be hungry for power.
рве́ни|е, я *nt.* zeal, enthusiasm.
рво́т|а, ы *f.*
1 (*действие*) vomiting.
2 (*масса*) vomit.

ре *nt. indecl.* (*mus.*) D.
реабилита́ци|я, и *f.* rehabilitation.
реабилити́р|овать, ую *impf. and pf.* to rehabilitate.
реабилити́р|оваться, уюсь *impf. and pf.*
1 to vindicate o.s.
2 *pass. of* ▸ **~овать**
реаги́р|овать, ую *impf.* (**на** + *a.*)
1 (*на свет*) to react (to).
2 (*pf.* **от~, про~**) (*на критику*) to react (to), respond (to).
реакти́вный *adj.*
1 (*chem., phys.*) reactive.
2 (*tech., aeron.*) jet(-propelled); **р. двигатель** jet engine; **р. самолёт** jet-propelled aircraft, jet.
реа́ктор, а *m.* (*tech.*) reactor.
реакцио́н|ный (~ен, ~на) *adj.* (*pol.*) reactionary.
реа́кци|я, и *f.* reaction.
реализа́ци|я, и *f.* (*планов*) realization; (*договора*) implementation; (*товаров*) sale, disposal.
реали́зм, а *m.* (*in var. senses*) realism.
реализ|ова́ть, у́ю *impf. and pf.* (*pf. also* ▸ **~о́вывать**) (*планы*) to realize; (*договор*) to implement; (*товар*) to sell, dispose of; **р. це́нные бума́ги** to realize securities.
реализо́выва|ть, ю *impf. of* ▸ **реализова́ть**
реали́ст, а *m.* realist.
реалисти́ческий *adj.*
1 (*искусство*) realist.
2 (*взгляд*) realistic.
реалисти́ч|ный (~ен, ~на) *adj.* = **~еский 2**
реа́льност|ь, и *f.*
1 (*действительность*) reality.
2 (*осуществимость*) practicability, feasibility.
реа́л|ьный (~ен, ~ьна) *adj.*
1 (*действительный*) real; **~ьная действи́тельность** reality.
2 (*осуществимый*) practicable, feasible, workable; **р. план** workable plan.
3 (*практический*) realistic; practical.
реанимацио́нн|ый *adj.*: **~ое отделе́ние** intensive care unit.
реанима́ци|я, и *f.* resuscitation; **отделе́ние ~и** intensive care unit.
реаними́р|овать, ую *impf. and pf.*
1 (*человека*) to resuscitate.
2 (*fig.*) to revive.
ребён|ок, ка (*as pl.* **де́ти, дете́й**) *m.* child; (*младенец*) infant; **грудно́й р.** baby.
ребр|о́, а́, *pl.* **~̈а, рёбер, ~̈ам** *nt.*
1 (*anat., tech.*) rib.
2 (*край*) edge; **поста́вить ~о́м** to place edgeways, place on its side.
ребя́та, ребя́т (*coll.*) (*парни*) boys, lads.
рёв, а *m.*
1 roar; bellow, howl; **р. ве́тра** the howling of the wind.
2 (*coll.*) (*плач*) howl (*of a child, etc.*); **подня́ть р.** to raise a howl.
рева́нш, а *m.* revenge; (*sport*) return match.
реве́н|ь, я́ *m.* rhubarb.
рevera
реvera
ревера́нс, а *m.* curtsy.
рев|е́ть, у́, ёшь *impf.*
1 to roar; to bellow, howl.
2 (*coll.*) (*плакать*) to howl.
реви́зи|я, и *f.*
1 (*учреждения*) inspection; (*бухгалтерская*) audit.
2 (*взглядов*) revision.
ревизо́р, а *m.* inspector; (*финансов*) auditor.
ревмати́зм, а *m.* rheumatism.
ревни́в|ый (~, ~а) *adj.* jealous.
ревн|ова́ть, у́ю *impf.* to be jealous; **р. кого́-н.** (**к** + *d.*) to be jealous because of s.o.'s attachment (to), begrudge s.o.'s attachment (to); **она́ ~ова́ла му́жа к его́ рабо́те** she was jealous of her husband's work.
ре́вност|ный (~ен, ~на) *adj.* zealous, fervent.
ре́вност|ь, и *f.* jealousy.
револьве́р, а *m.* revolver.
революционе́р, а *m.* revolutionary.
революционе́р|ка, ки *f. of* ▸ **~**
революцио́н|ный (~ен, ~на) *adj.* revolutionary.
револю́ци|я, и *f.* (*pol. and fig.*) revolution.
рега́т|а, ы *f.* regatta.
ре́гби *nt. indecl.* Rugby (football), rugger.
регби́ст, а *m.* rugby player.
ре́гги *m. indecl.* reggae.
ре́гент, а *m.*
1 regent.
2 (*mus.*) precentor.
регио́н, а *m.* region, area.
региона́льный *adj.* regional.
реги́стр, а *m.* register.
регистра́тор, а *m.* registrar; (*в поликлинике, гостинице*) receptionist.
регистрату́р|а, ы *f.* records office, registry; (*в поликлинике*) reception desk.
регистра́ци|я, и *f.* registration; (*в гостинице*) reception desk.
регистри́р|овать, ую *impf. and pf.* (*pf. also* **за~**) to register, record.
регистри́р|оваться, уюсь *impf. and pf.* (*pf. also* **за~**)
1 to register (o.s.).
2 (*пожениться*) to register one's marriage.
3 *pass. of* ▸ **~овать**
регла́мент, а *m.*
1 (*правила*) regulations; standing orders.
2 (*время для речи*) time limit.
регули́р|овать, ую *impf.*
1 (*движение, цены*) to regulate; to control.
2 (*pf.* **у~**) (*отношения*) to normalize.
3 (*pf.* **от~**) to adjust; **р. мото́р** to tune an engine.
регуля́р|ный (~ен, ~на) *adj.* regular; **~ные войска́** regular troops.
регуля́тор, а *m.* (*tech.*) regulator; (*pl.*) controls (*on TV, etc.*).
редакти́р|овать, ую *impf.*
1 (*pf.* **от~**) (*рукопись*) to edit.
2 (*impf. only*) (*журнал*) to be editor of; to edit.
реда́ктор, а *m.*
1 editor; **гла́вный р.** editor-in-chief, chief editor.
2 : (*comput.*) **те́кстовый р.** (*программа*)

Р

word processor.

редакцио́нн|ый *adj.* editorial, editing; **~ая колле́гия** editorial board; **~ая статья́** editorial.

реда́кци|я, и *f.*
1 (*работники*) editorial staff.
2 (*учреждение*) editorial office.
3 (*действие*) editing; **под ~ей** (+ *g.*) edited (by).
4 (*формулировка*) wording.
5 (*вариант текста*) edition.

реде́|ть, ю *impf.* (*of* ▸ **по~**) to thin, thin out; **~ющие во́лосы** thinning hair.

реди́с, а *no pl., m.* (*collect.*) radish(es).

реди́ск|а, и *f.* (single) radish; (*collect.*) radishes.

ре́дк|ий (~ок, ~ка́, ~ко) *adj.*
1 (*негустой*) thin, sparse; **~кие во́лосы** thin hair; **р. лес** sparse wood.
2 (*необычный*) rare; uncommon, unusual; **~кая кни́га** rare book; **~кая красота́** rare beauty.
3 (*гость, письмо*) occasional.

ре́дко *adv.*
1 (*не густо*) sparsely; far apart.
2 (*не часто*) rarely, seldom.

редколле́ги|я, и *f.* editorial board.

ре́дкост|ь, и *f.*
1 (*населения*) sparseness.
2 (*книги*) rarity; **на р.** uncommonly; **на р. проница́тельный челове́к** a person of rare discernment.
3 (*редкая вещь*) rarity.

рее́стр, а *m.* list, roll, register.

ре́|же *comp. of* ▸ **~дкий** *and* ▸ **~дко**

режи́м, а *m.*
1 (*pol.*) regime.
2 (*распорядок*) routine; procedure; (*med.*) regimen; (*станка*) mode of operation; **р. пита́ния** diet; **р. рабо́ты** mode of operation.
3 (*условия*) conditions; (*tech.*) operating conditions.

режиссёр, а *m.* (*в театре*) producer; (*в кино*) director.

режиссёр|ский *adj. of* ▸ **~**

ре́|зать, жу, жешь *impf.*
1 (*impf. only*) to cut **э́ти но́жницы бо́льше не ~жут** these scissors do not cut any longer.
2 (*impf. only*) (*хлеб*) to cut; to slice.
3 (*pf.* **за~**) (*убивать*) to kill; to slaughter.
4 (*impf. only*) (**по** + *d.*) (*делать изображения*) to carve (on), engrave (on).
5 (*impf. only*) (*причинять боль*) to cut (into); to cause sharp pain; **реме́нь ~зал ему́ плечо́** the strap was cutting into his shoulder; **р. слух** to grate upon the ears.

резв|и́ться, лю́сь, и́шься *impf.* to gambol, romp.

ре́зв|ый (~, ~а́, ~о) *adj.*
1 playful, frisky.
2 (*лошадь*) fast.

резе́рв, а *m.* (*mil., etc.*) reserve(s).

резерва́ци|я, и *f.* reservation.

резерви́р|овать, ую *impf. and pf.* (*pf. also* **за~**) to reserve, book.

резе́рвн|ый *adj.* (*mil. and fin.*) reserve; (*comput.*) backup; **~ая ко́пия** backup copy.

резервуа́р, а *m.* reservoir, tank.

резиде́нци|я, и *f.* residence.

рези́н|а, ы *f.* (India) rubber.

рези́нк|а, и *f.*
1 (*ластик*) rubber (*Br.*), eraser (*US*).
2 (*тесёмка*) (piece of) elastic.
3 (*жвачка*) chewing gum.

рези́нов|ый *adj.* rubber; **~ая тесьма́, ле́нта** rubber band, elastic band.

ре́з|кий (~ок, ~ка́, ~ко) *adj.* (*ветер, слова, увеличение, движение, черты лица*) sharp; (*голос, свет, критика*) harsh; (*изменение, манера*) abrupt; **р. за́пах** strong smell.

резно́й *adj.* carved.

резн|я́, и́ *f.* slaughter.

резолю́ци|я, и *f.*
1 (*решение*) resolution; **вы́нести, приня́ть ~ю** to pass, carry a resolution.
2 (*на документе*) instructions; **наложи́ть ~ю** to append instructions.

резона́нс, а *m.*
1 (*phys.*) resonance.
2 (*fig.*) response.

резонёрств|овать, ую *impf.* to moralize.

резо́н|ный (~ен, ~на) *adj.* reasonable.

результа́т, а *m.* result; outcome; **дать ~ы** to yield results; **в ~е** (*в итоге*) in the end; (+ *g.*) (*вследствие*) as a result (of).

ре́з|че *comp. of* ▸ **~кий**

ре́зчик, а *m.* engraver, carver.

резьб|а́, ы́ *f.* carving.

резюме́ *nt. indecl.* summary, résumé.

рейд, а *m.* raid.

рейс, а *m.* (*автобуса*) trip, run; (*парохода*) voyage, passage; (*самолёта*) flight; **но́мер ~а** flight number.

ре́йтинг, а *m.* rating.

рейту́з|ы, ~ *no sg.* leggings.

рек|а́, и́, *a.* **~́у,** *pl.* **~́и** *f.* river (*also fig.*).

ре́квием, а *m.* (*eccl. and mus.*) requiem.

реквизи́р|овать, ую *impf. and pf.* to requisition.

реквизи́т, а *m.* (*theatr.*) props.

рекла́м|а, ы *f.*
1 (*товара, события*) advertising, publicity.
2 (*объявление*) advertisement.

реклами́р|овать, ую *impf. and pf.* to advertise, publicize.

рекла́мный *adj.* (*агентство, кампания*) advertising; (*оповещательный*) publicity.

рекламода́тел|ь, я *m.* advertiser.

рекоменда́тельн|ый *adj.* recommendatory; **~ое письмо́** letter of recommendation.

рекоменда́ци|я, и *f.* recommendation.

рекоменд|ова́ть, у́ю *impf. and pf.* (*pf. also* ▸ **по~**)
1 (*предложить принять*) to recommend.
2 (+ *d.* + *inf.*) (*советовать*) to recommend, advise; **я вам ~у́ю сходи́ть к врачу́** I recommend you to see a doctor.

реконструи́р|овать, ую *impf. and pf.* to reconstruct.

реконстру́кци|я, и *f.* reconstruction.

реко́рд, а *m.* record; **поби́ть р.** to break a record; **установи́ть р.** to set up, establish a record.

реко́рдный *adj.* record, record-breaking.
рекордсме́н, а *m.* record holder; record breaker; **р. ми́ра** world record holder.
рекордсме́н|ка, ки *f. of* ▸ ~
ре́ктор, а *m.* principal.
реле́ *nt. indecl.* (*tech.*) relay.
религио́з|ный (~ен, ~на) *adj.* religious.
рели́ги|я, и *f.* religion.
рели́кви|я, и *f.* relic; (*семейная*) heirloom.
релье́ф, а *m.* (*art and geol.*) relief.
релье́ф|ный (~ен, ~на) *adj.* relief, raised; (*ткань, обои*) embossed; **~ная ка́рта** relief map; (*fig.*) (*отчётливый*) clear-cut.
рельс, а *m.* rail; **сойти́ с ~ов** to be derailed, go off the rails.
рем|е́нь, ня́ *m.* (*пояс*) belt; (*для багажа*) strap; **р. безопа́сности** seat belt.
реме́сленник, а *m.* artisan, craftsman.
ремес|ло́, ла́, *pl.* **~́ла, ~́ел** *nt.* trade.
реми́сси|я, и *f.* (*med., comm.*) remission.
ремо́нт, а *m.* repair(s); maintenance; (*здания*) refurbishment; (*мелкий*) redecoration; **капита́льный р.** overhaul, refit, major refurbishment, repairs; **в ~е** under repair; **р. о́буви** shoe repair.
ремонти́р|овать, ую *impf. and pf.* (*pf. also* **от~**) (*чинить*) to repair; (*квартиру*) to refurbish, redecorate.
ремо́нт|ный *adj. of* ▸ ~; **~ная мастерска́я** repair shop; **~ные рабо́ты** repair/maintenance work.
Ренесса́нс, а *m.* renaissance.
ре́нт|а, ы *f.*
1 rent; **земе́льная р.** ground rent.
2 (*проценты*) income (*from investments, etc.*); **ежего́дная р.** annuity.
рента́бел|ьный (~ен, ~ьна) *adj.* profitable.
рентге́н, а *m.* X-ray treatment, X-rays.
рентгено́лог, а *m.* radiologist.
рентгеноло́ги|я, и *f.* radiology.
реорганиза́ци|я, и *f.* reorganization.
реорганиз|ова́ть, у́ю *impf. and pf.* to reorganize.
ре́п|а, ы *f.* turnip.
репатриа́нт, а *m.* repatriate.
репатриа́нт|ка, ки *f. of* ▸ ~
репатриа́ци|я, и *f.* repatriation.
репатрии́р|овать, ую *impf. and pf.* to repatriate.
репертуа́р, а *m.* (*theatr. and fig.*) repertoire; **он в своём ~е** he is in his element.
репети́р|овать, ую *impf.* (*pf.* **от~**) (*theatr.*) to rehearse.
репети́тор, а *m.* tutor, coach.
репети́ци|я, и *f.* rehearsal; **генера́льная р.** dress rehearsal.
ре́плик|а, и *f.*
1 (*возражение*) retort; (*ответ*) reply; (*враждебная*) heckling comment.
2 (*theatr.*) cue; **пода́ть ~у** to give the cue.
репорта́ж, а *m.* (*деятельность*) reporting; (*сообщение*) report.
репортёр, а *m.* reporter.
репресси́р|овать, ую *impf. and pf.* to subject to repression.
репре́сси|я, и *f.* (*usu. pl.*) punitive measure.
репроду́ктор, а *m.* loudspeaker.
репроду́кци|я, и *f.* reproduction (*of a picture, etc.*).
репти́ли|я, и *f.* reptile.
репута́ци|я, и *f.* reputation.
ре́пчатый *adj.*: **р. лук** (common) onion.
ресни́ц|а, ы *f.* eyelash.
респекта́бел|ьный (~ен, ~ьна) *adj.* respectable.
респира́тор, а *m.* respirator.
респу́блик|а, и *f.* republic.
республика́н|ец, ца *m.* republican.
республика́н|ка, ки *f. of* ▸ **~ец**
республика́нский *adj.* republican.
рессо́р|а, ы *f.* spring (*of vehicle*).
реставра́тор, а *m.* restorer.
реставра́ци|я, и *f.* restoration.
реставри́р|овать, ую *impf. and pf.* (*pf. also* ▸ **от~**) to restore.
рестора́н, а *m.* restaurant; **р. бы́строго обслу́живания** fast-food restaurant.
ресу́рс, а *m.* (*usu. pl.*) resource; **де́нежные ~ы** financial resources; **после́дний р.** the last resort; **приро́дные ~ы** natural resources.
рефера́т, а *m.*
1 (*книги, статьи*) synopsis, abstract.
2 (*доклад*) paper, essay.
рефере́ндум, а *m.* referendum.
ре́фери *m. indecl.* referee.
рефле́кс, а *m.* reflex.
рефле́кси|я, и *f.* reflection; introspection.
рефлексоло́ги|я, и *f.* reflexology.
рефо́рм|а, ы *f.* reform; **проводи́ть ~ы** to implement reforms.
реформа́тор, а *m.* reformer.
Реформа́ци|я, и *f.* (*hist.*) Reformation.
реформи́р|овать, ую *impf. and pf.* to reform.
рефрижера́тор, а *m.* (*грузовик*) refrigerated lorry (*Br.*), truck (*US*); (*судно*) refrigerated ship.
рецензе́нт, а *m.* reviewer.
реце́нзи|я, и *f.* review; **р. на кни́гу** book review.
реце́пт, а *m.*
1 (*med.*) prescription; **вы́писать р.** to write a prescription.
2 (*cul.*) recipe.
рециди́в, а *m.* (*med., etc.*) recurrence; relapse.
ре́чк|а, и *f.* small river; rivulet.
речн|о́й *adj.* river; **~ы́е пути́ сообще́ния** inland waterways; **~о́е судохо́дство** river navigation.
реч|ь, и *f.*
1 (*способность*) speech.
2 (*произношение*) way of speaking; **отчётливая р.** distinct enunciation.
3 (*стиль языка*) language; **делова́я р.** business language.
4 (*разговор*) conversation, talk; **о чём шла́ р.?** what were they/you talking about?, what was it all about?; **р. идёт о том, где/как/**

когдá *etc.* the question is where/how/when *etc.*; **об э́том не мóжет быть и ~и** that is out of the question.
5 (*выступление*) speech; address; **вы́ступить с ~ью** to make a speech.
6 (*gram.*) speech; **прямáя р.** direct speech; **кóсвенная р.** indirect speech; **чáсти ~и** parts of speech.

реш|áть(ся), áю(сь) *impf. of* ▸ **~и́ть(ся)**

решá|ющий *pres. part. act. of* ▸ **~ть** *and adj.* decisive, deciding; **р. гóлос** casting vote; **р. фáктор** decisive factor.

решéни|е, я *nt.*
1 decision; **прийти́ к ~ю** to come to a decision; **приня́ть р.** to take a decision, make up one's mind.
2 (*суда, дирекции*) judg(e)ment; decision, verdict; **вы́нести р.** to deliver a judg(e)ment; to pass a resolution.
3 (*задачи*) solving; (*к задаче*) solution; answer; (*проблемы*) solution.

решётк|а, и *f.*
1 grating; (*оконная*) grille; (*ограда*) railings; (*садовая*) trellis; (*перед камином*) fireguard; (*радиатора*) grille; **за ~ой** (*fig., coll.*) behind bars (= *in prison*); **посади́ть за ~у** to put behind bars.
2 (*в камине*) (fire) grate.
3 (*в духовке*) shelf.

решет|ó, á, *pl.* **~a** *nt.* sieve.

реши́мост|ь, и *f.* resolution, resoluteness.

реши́тельно *adv.*
1 (*твёрдо*) resolutely.
2 (*категорически*) decidedly, definitely; **р. отказáться** to refuse flatly.

реши́тел|ьный (~ен, ~ьна) *adj.* resolute, determined; **~ьные мéры** drastic measures.

реш|и́ть, ý, и́шь *pf.* (*of* ▸ **~áть**)
1 (+ *inf. or* + *a.*) to decide; **он ~и́л уéхать** he decided to go away.
2 (*найти ответ*) to solve; to settle; **р. задáчу** to solve a problem; to accomplish a task.

реш|и́ться, ýсь, и́шься *pf.* (*of* ▸ **~áться**)
1 (**на** + *a. or* + *inf.*) to make up one's mind (to), decide (to).
2 (*получить решение*) to be resolved.

рé|ять, ет *impf.*
1 (*о птице*) to soar, hover.
2 (*о флаге*) to flutter.

ржавé|ть, ет *impf.* (*of* ▸ **за~**) to rust.

ржáвчин|а, ы *f.* rust.

ржáвый *adj.* rusty.

ржанóй *adj.* rye.

рж|ать, у, ёшь *impf.* to neigh; (*coll.*) laugh loudly.

Ри́г|а, и *f.* Riga.

рикошéт, а *m.* ricochet, rebound; **~ом** on the rebound (*also fig.*).

Рим, а *m.* Rome.

ри́млян|ин, ина, *pl.* **~е, ~** *m.* Roman.

ри́млян|ка, ки *f. of* ▸ **~ин**

ри́мск|ий *adj.* Roman; **Пáпа Р.** the Pope; **~ие ци́фры** Roman numerals.

ринг, а *m.* (*sport*) ring.

ри́н|уться, усь, ешься *pf.* to dash, dart.

Ри́о-де-Жанéйро *m. indecl.* Rio de Janeiro.

рис, а *m.* rice.

риск, а *m.* risk; **на свой (страх и) р.** at one's own risk, at one's peril; **с ~ом (для** + *g.*) at the risk (of); **пойти́ на р.** to run risks, take chances.

рискн|ýть, ý, ёшь *pf.* (+ *inf.*) to take the risk (of), venture (to).

рискóван|ный (~, ~на) *adj.*
1 risky; **~ное предприя́тие** risky venture.
2 (*шутка, тема*) risqué.

риск|овáть, ýю *impf.*
1 to run risks, take chances.
2 (+ *i.*) to risk; (+ *inf.*) to risk, take the risk (of); **ничéм не р.** to run no risk; **р. опоздáть на пóезд** to risk missing the train.

рисовáни|е, я *nt.* (*карандашом*) drawing; (*красками*) painting.

рис|овáть, ýю *impf.* (*of* ▸ **на~**)
1 (*карандашом*) to draw; (*красками*) to paint; **р. с натýры** to draw, paint from life.
2 (*fig.*) (*описывать*) to depict, paint, portray.

ри́сов|ый *adj.* rice; **~ая кáша** rice pudding.

рисýн|ок, ка *m.* (*изображение*) drawing; (*в книге*) illustration; (*в научной статье*) figure; (*на ткани*) pattern, design; (*контур*) outline; **акварéльный р.** watercolour (*Br.*), watercolor (*US*).

ритм, а *m.* (*музыки, сердца*) rhythm; (*работы, жизни*) pace.

ритми́ческ|ий *adj.* rhythmic; **~ая гимнáстика** aerobics.

ритми́ч|ный (~ен, ~на) *adj.* rhythmic; **~ная рабóта** smooth functioning.

ритóрик|а, и *f.* rhetoric.

ритори́ческий *adj.* rhetorical.

ритуáл, а *m.* ritual.

ритуáльный *adj.* ritual.

риф, а *m.* reef; **корáлловый р.** coral reef.

ри́фм|а, ы *f.* rhyme.

рифм|овáть, ýю *impf.* (*слова*) to make rhyme.

рифм|овáться, ýюсь *impf.* to rhyme.

рóб|а, ы *f.* working clothes, overalls.

рóб|кий (~ок, ~кá, ~ко) *adj.* timid, shy.

рóбост|ь, и *f.* timidity, shyness.

рóбот, а *m.* robot.

ров, рва, о рве, во рву *m.* ditch; **крепостнóй р.** moat.

ровéсник, а *m.* person of the same age; peer; **мы с ним ~и** we are of the same age.

ровéсни|ца, цы *f. of* ▸ **~к**

рóвно *adv.*
1 (*равномерно*) regularly, evenly.
2 (*точно*) exactly; **р. пять рублéй** five roubles exactly; (*о времени*) sharp; **р. в час** at one o'clock sharp.

рóв|ный (~ен, ~нá, ~но) *adj.*
1 (*дорога, поверхность*) flat, even, level; (*линия*) straight.
2 (*пульс*) regular; (*шаг, голос*) even; (*характер*) stable.
3 (*одинаковый*) equal; **для ~ного счёта** to make it even; to bring to a round figure; **~ным счётом** exactly.

ровня́|ть, ю *impf.* (*of* ▶ **с~**) to even, level.
рог, а, *pl.* **~а́, ~о́в** *m.*
1 horn; (*олений*) antler.
2 (*музыкальный инструмент*) bugle, horn; **охо́тничий р.** hunting horn.
рога́лик, а *m.* crescent-shaped roll, croissant.
рога́тк|а, и *f.* catapult (*Br.*), slingshot (*US*).
рога́т|ый (~, ~а) *adj.* horned; **кру́пный р. скот** cattle.
рого́ж|а, и *f.* bast, matting.
род, а, о ~е, в ~у́ *m.*
1 (*pl.* **~ы́, ~о́в**) family, kin, clan; **челове́ческий р.** mankind, human race.
2 (*pl.* **~ы́, ~о́в**) (*происхождение*) birth, origin, stock; (*поколение*) generation; **он ~ом из Ирла́ндии** he is an Irishman by birth.
3 (*pl.* **~ы, ~о́в**) (*biol.*) genus.
4 (*pl.* **~а́, ~о́в**) (*mun*) sort, kind; **р. войск** arm of the service; **вся́кого ~а** of all kinds; **тако́го ~а** of such a kind, such; **в не́котором ~е** to some extent; **в своём ~е** in one's own way.
5 (*pl.* **~ы, ~о́в**) (*gram.*) gender; **же́нский р.** feminine (gender).
роддо́м, а *m.* (*abbr. of* **роди́льный дом**) maternity hospital.
роде́о *nt. indecl.* rodeo.
роди́льн|ый *adj.*: **р. дом** maternity hospital; **~ое отделе́ние** maternity unit.
ро́дин|а, ы *f.* native land; home, homeland; **верну́ться на ~у** to return home; **тоска́ по ~е** homesickness.
ро́динк|а, и *f.* birthmark.
роди́тел|и, ей *no sg.* parents.
роди́тельн|ый *adj.* (*gram.*) genitive; **в ~ом падеже́** in the genitive (case).
роди́тельский *adj.* parental, parents'; paternal; **р. комите́т** parents' committee.
ро|ди́ть, жу́, ди́шь, *past* **~ди́л,** (*impf.*) **~ди́ла,** (*pf.*) **~дила́, ~ди́ло** *impf. and pf.*
1 (*impf. also* **рожа́ть**) to bear, give birth (to).
2 (*impf. also* **рожда́ть**) (*fig.*) to give birth, rise (to); (*о почве*) to yield.
ро|ди́ться, жу́сь, ди́шься, *past* **~ди́лся́, ~ди́ла́сь, ~ди́ло́сь** *impf. and pf.* (*impf. also* **рожда́ться**)
1 to be born; **р. преподава́телем** to be a born teacher; (**у** + *g.*): **от пе́рвой жены́ у него́ ~ди́лся сын** he had a son by his first wife.
2 (*fig.*) (*мысль, план, город*) to arise, come into being.
родни́к, а́ *m.* spring.
родн|о́й *adj.*
1 (*мать, брат, дядя*) related by blood; natural; **р. брат** one's brother (*opp. cousin, etc.*); *as n.* **~ы́е, ~ы́х** relations, relatives.
2 (*отечественный*) native; home; **р. язы́к** mother tongue.
родн|я́, и́ *f.* (*collect.*) (*родственники*) relatives.
родов|о́й[1] *adj.*
1 (*ethnol.*) clan.
2 (*наследственный*) ancestral.
3 (*biol.*) generic.
родов|о́й[2] *adj.* birth, labour; **~ы́е схва́тки** contractions.
родонача́льник, а *m.* ancestor, forefather; (*fig.*) (*литературы*) father.
ро́дственник, а *m.* relation, relative; **ближа́йший р.** next of kin.
ро́дственни|ца, цы *f. of* ▶ **~к**
ро́дствен|ный (~ and ~ен, ~на) *adj.*
1 kindred, related; **~ные свя́зи** kinship ties.
2 (*близкий*) related, allied.
3 (*свойственный родственникам*) familiar, intimate.
родств|о́, а́ *nt.* relationship, kinship (*also fig.*); **быть в ~е́ (с** + *i.*) to be related (to).
ро́д|ы, ов *no sg.* birth; childbirth; **в ~ах** in labour (*Br.*), labor (*US*).
ро́ж|а, и *f.* (*coll.*) mug (= *face*); **ко́рчить, стро́ить ~и** to make faces.
рожа́|ть, ю *impf. of* ▶ **роди́ть 1**
рожда́емост|ь, и *f.* birth rate.
рожда́|ть(ся), ю(сь) *impf. of* ▶ **роди́ть(ся)**
рожде́ни|е, я *nt.* birth; **день ~я** birthday; **ме́сто ~я** birthplace; **глухо́й от ~я** deaf from birth.
рождённый *p.p.p. of* ▶ **роди́ть;** (+ *inf.*) born (to), destined (to).
рожде́ственск|ий *adj.* Christmas; **~ая ёлка** Christmas tree; **~ая пе́сня** carol; **р. соче́льник** Christmas Eve.
Рождеств|о́, а́ *nt.* (*праздник*) Christmas; **на Р.** at Christmas (time); **под Р.** on Christmas Eve; (*само рождение*) Nativity.
рож|о́к, ка́ *m.* (*mus.*) horn; bugle; **англи́йский р.** cor anglais.
рожь, ржи *f.* rye.
ро́з|а, ы *f.* (*цветок*) rose; (*растение*) rose tree, rose bush.
розе́тк|а, и *f.*
1 (*украшение*) rosette.
2 (*elec.*) socket; electric outlet.
3 (*для варенья*) jam dish.
розмари́н, а *m.* (*bot.*) rosemary.
ро́зниц|а, ы *f.* retail; **торгова́ть в ~у** to engage in retail trade; to retail.
ро́зничн|ый *adj.* retail; **р. торго́вец** retailer; **~ая цена́** retail price.
ро́зов|ый (~, ~а) *adj.*
1 *adj. of* ▶ **ро́за; ~ое де́рево** rosewood; **р. куст** rose bush.
2 (*цвет*) pink, rose-coloured (*Br.*), -colored (*US*).
3 (*fig.*) rosy.
ро́зыгрыш, а *m.*
1 (*лотереи*) drawing.
2 (*шутка*) practical joke.
ро́зыск, а *m.*
1 (*разыскивание*) search.
2 (*leg.*) (*дознание*) inquiry; **Уголо́вный р.** Criminal Investigation Department (*Br.*), Federal Bureau of Investigation (*US*).
рой, ро́я, *pl.* **рои́** *m.* (*пчёл, комаров*) swarm.
рок[1]**, а** *m.* (*судьба*) fate.
рок[2]**, а** *m.* (*mus.*) rock; **тяжёлый р.** hard rock.
рок-гру́пп|а, ы *f.* rock band.
рок-му́зык|а, и *f.* rock music.
рок-музыка́нт, а *m.* rock musician.

рок-н-ро́лл, а *m.* rock 'n' roll.

роков|о́й *adj.*
1 fateful; fated; **~а́я же́нщина** femme fatale.
2 (*имеющий тяжёлые последствия*) fatal.

ро́кот, а *m.* roar, rumble.

ро́лик, а *m.*
1 roller, castor.
2 *pl.* (*коньки*) roller skates.
3 : **рекла́мный р.** (*cin.*) advertisement; (*фильма*) trailer.
4 (*бумаги, плёнки*) roll.

ро́лик|овый *adj. of* ▸ **~**; **~овые коньки́** roller skates.

рол|ь, и, *pl.* **~и, ~е́й** *f.* (*theatr.*) role (*also fig.*); (*текст*) part; **в ~и** (+ *g.*) in the role (of); **игра́ть р.** (+ *g.*) to take the part (of), play, act; (*fig.*) to matter, count, be of importance; **э́то не игра́ет ~и** it is of no importance, it does not count.

ром, а *m.* rum.

рома́н, а *m.*
1 novel.
2 (*coll.*) (*любовная связь*) love affair; romance.

рома́нс, а *m.* (*mus.*) romance.

рома́нский *adj.* Romance; (*archit.*) Romanesque.

романти́зм, а *m.* romanticism.

рома́нтик, а *m.* romantic.

рома́нтик|а, и *f.* romance.

романти́ческий *adj.* romantic.

романти́ч|ный (~ен, ~на) *adj.* = **~еский**

рома́шк|а, и *f.* chamomile.

ромб, а *m.* (*math.*) rhombus.

роня́|ть, ю *impf.* (*of* ▸ **урони́ть**)
1 (*из рук*) to drop; (*голову, руки*) to let fall; (*книгу с полки*) to knock off; **р. слёзы** to shed tears.
2 (*impf. only*) (*лишаться*) to shed.
3 (*fig.*) (*унижать*) to discredit; **р. себя́ в чьих-н. глаза́х** to discredit o.s. in s.o.'s eyes; (*авторитет*) to lose.

ро́пот, а *m.* murmur, grumble.

рос, ~ла́ *see* ▸ **расти́**

рос|а́, ы́, *pl.* **~ы** *f.* dew.

роско́ш|ный (~ен, ~на) *adj.* luxurious.

ро́скош|ь, и *f.*
1 (*излишества*) luxury; **жить в ~и** to live in luxury.
2 (*великолепие*) splendour (*Br.*), splendor (*US*).

ро́слый *adj.* tall, strapping.

ро́спис|ь, и *f.* painting; **р. стен** wall painting(s), mural(s).

росси́йский *adj.* Russian.

Росси́|я, и *f.* Russia.

россия́н|ин, а, *pl.* **~е, ~** *m.* (*русский*) Russian; (*житель России*) Russian citizen.

россия́н|ка, ки *f. of* ▸ **~ин**

рост, а *m.*
1 (*растений, городов, индустрии*) growth; (*fig.*) (*цен, преступности*) increase, rise.
2 (*вышина*) height, stature; **~ом** in height; **он ~ом с вас** he is (of) your height; **высо́кого ~а** tall; **во весь р.** full length; (*fig.*) in all its magnitude; **встать во весь р.** to stand upright, stand up straight.
3 (*одежды*) length.

ростовщи́к, а́ *m.* usurer, moneylender.

рост|о́к, ка́ *m.* shoot; **пусти́ть ~ки́** to sprout; (*pl.*, + *g.*) beginnings (of).

рот, рта, о рте́, во рту́ *m.* mouth; **не брать в р.** (+ *g.*) not to touch; **зажа́ть, заткну́ть кому́-н. р.** (*coll.*) to shut s.o. up.

ро́т|а, ы *f.* (*mil.*) company.

рота́ци|я, и *f.* rotation.

ротве́йлер, а *m.* Rottweiler.

ро́щ|а, и *f.* small wood, grove.

роя́л|ь, я *m.* piano; grand piano; **игра́ть на ~е** to play the piano.

рту́т|ь, и *f.* mercury.

руба́н|ок, ка *m.* (*tech.*) plane.

руба́шк|а, и *f.*
1 shirt; **ночна́я р.** nightdress.
2 (*игральной карты*) back.

рубе́ж, а́ *m.* boundary, border(line); **жить за ~о́м** to live abroad.

руб|е́ц, ца́ *m.*
1 (*от ран*) scar.
2 (*шов*) hem, seam.

руби́н, а *m.* ruby.

руби́новый *adj.* ruby.

руб|и́ть, лю́, ~ишь *impf.*
1 (*дерево*) to fell.
2 (*дрова*) to chop.
3 (*cul.*) to mince, chop up.

рубл|ь, я́ *m.* rouble; **биле́т сто́ит два ~я́** a ticket costs two roubles.

ру́брик|а, и *f.*
1 (*заголовок*) rubric, heading.
2 (*раздел*) column.

ру́ган|ь, и *f.* (*непристойная*) bad language, swearing, abuse.

руга́тельств|о, а *nt.* abuse; (*непристойное*) swear word.

руга́|ть, ю *impf.*
1 (*pf.* **от~** *or* **вы~**) (*отчитывать*) to scold, tell off.
2 (*pf.* **об~** *or* **от~**) (*оскорблять*) to curse, swear (at), abuse.
3 (*pf.* **об~**) (*критиковать*) to tear to pieces.

руга́|ться, юсь *impf.*
1 to curse, swear, use bad language.
2 (**с** + *i.*) (*ссориться*) to quarrel (with), have a row (with).

руд|а́, ы́, *pl.* **~ы** *f.* ore; **желе́зная р.** iron ore.

рудиме́нт, а *m.* rudiment.

рудни́к, а́ *m.* mine, pit.

руж|ьё, ья́, *pl.* **~ья, ~ей, ~ьям** *nt.* (hand)gun, rifle.

руи́н|а, ы *f.* ruin (*usu. pl.*).

рук|а́, и́, *a.* **~у,** *pl.* **~и, ~, ~а́м** *f.*
■ I.
1 (*кисть*) hand; (*от кисти до плеча*) arm; **пожа́ть ~у** (+ *d.*) to shake hands (with); **вести́ за́ ~у** to lead by the hand; **держа́ть на ~а́х** to hold in one's arms; **р. о́б ~у** hand in hand; **написа́ть от ~и́** to write out by hand; **взять кого́-н. по́д ~у** to take s.o.'s arm.
2 (*почерк*) hand, handwriting.
3 (*сторона*) side; **по пра́вую ~у** on the

right, to the right.
[4] *pl.* (*владение*) hands (*fig.* = *power, possession*); **взять (себя́) в ~и** to take (o.s.) in hand; **держа́ть в свои́х ~а́х** to have in one's clutches; **попа́сться в ~и кому́-н.** to fall into s.o.'s hands.
■ **II.** (*fig.*; *in var. senses*) hand; **э́то бу́дет им на́ ~у** that will serve their purpose; it will be playing into their hands; **на ско́рую ~у** offhand; **под ~о́й** at hand, to hand; **махну́ть ~о́й** (**на** + *a.*) to give up as lost; **наложи́ть на себя́ ~и** to lay hands on o.s.

рука́в, а́, *pl.* **~а́** *m.*
[1] (*одежды*) sleeve.
[2] (*tech.*) (*шланг*) hose.

рукави́ц|а, ы *f.* (*меховая*) mitten; (*рабочая*) gauntlet.

руководи́тел|ь, я *m.*
[1] (*учреждения, отдела*) head, manager; (*делегации, похода, восстания*) leader; **р. прое́кта** project manager; **кла́ссный р.** (*в школе*) class teacher.
[2] (*воспитатель*) instructor; guide; **нау́чный р.** supervisor of studies.

руководи́тель|ница, ницы *coll. f. of* ▶ **~**

руково|ди́ть, жу́, ди́шь *impf.* (+ *i.*) (*учреждением, отделом*) to be in charge of; to manage; (*походом, восстанием*) to lead; (*кружком, клубом*) to run; (*аспирантами*) to supervise; (*побуждать*) to govern.

руково́дств|о, а *nt.*
[1] (*действие*) leadership; guidance; management.
[2] (*то, чему следуют*) guiding principle, guide; **р. к де́йствию** guide to action.
[3] (*книга*) handbook, guide, manual; **р. по эксплуата́ции** instructions for use; user guide.
[4] (*collect.*) (*руководители*) (the) leadership, leaders; governing body.

руково́дств|оваться, уюсь *impf.* (+ *i.*) to follow; to be guided (by).

рукоде́ли|е, я *nt.* needlework.

рукопи́сный *adj.* (*текст*) handwritten; (*фонд*) manuscript.

ру́копис|ь, и *f.* manuscript.

рукопожа́ти|е, я *nt.* handshake.

рукоя́тк|а, и *f.* handle.

рулев|о́й *adj. of* ▶ **руль; ~о́е колесо́** steering wheel; *as n.* **р., ~о́го** *m.*
[1] (*на судне*) helmsman.
[2] (*sport*) cox(swain).

руле́т, а *m.* (*cul.*)
[1] (*пирог*) roll; **мясно́й р.** meat loaf.
[2] (*окорок без кости*) boned gammon.

руле́тк|а, и *f.*
[1] (*для измерения*) tape measure.
[2] (*игра*) roulette.

рул|и́ть, ю́, и́шь *impf.* (*в машине, в лодке*) to steer.

руло́н, а *m.* roll.

рул|ь, я́ *m.* (*судна*) rudder; helm (*also fig.*); (*автомобиля*) (steering) wheel; (*велосипеда*) handlebars; **стоя́ть у ~я́** (*fig.*) to be at the helm.

румы́н, а *m.* Romanian.

Румы́ни|я, и *f.* Romania.

румы́н|ка, ки *f. of* ▶ **~**

румы́нский *adj.* Romanian.

румя́н|а, ~ *no sg.* rouge; blusher.

румя́н|ец, ца *m.* (high) colour; flush; blush.

румя́н|ый (~, ~а) *adj.* rosy, ruddy.

ру́н|а, ы *f.* (*philol.*) rune.

ру́пор, а *m.* megaphone; loud hailer; (*fig.*) (*партии*) mouthpiece.

руса́лк|а, и *f.* mermaid.

ру́сл|о, а, *g. pl.* **ру́сел** *and* **~** *nt.*
[1] (river) bed, channel; **измени́ть р. реки́** to change the course of a river.
[2] (*fig.*) (*направление*) channel, course; **войти́ в обы́чное р.** to resume the normal course.

ру́сск|ая, ой *f. of* ▶ **~ий** *as n.*

ру́сск|ий *adj.* Russian (*also as n.* **р., ~ого** *m.*).

ру́с|ый (~, ~а) *adj.* light brown.

рути́н|а, ы *f.* (*pej.*) routine; rut.

ру́хляд|ь, и *f.* (*collect.*; *coll.*) junk.

ру́хн|уть, у, ешь *pf.* to crash down, tumble down, collapse; (*fig.*) (*планы, мечты*) to collapse, fall through.

руча́|ться, юсь *impf.* (*of* ▶ **поручи́ться**) (**за** + *a.*) to guarantee; to answer (for), vouch (for); **р. голово́й** (**за** + *a.*) to stake one's life (on).

руч|е́й, ья́ *m.* brook, stream.

ру́чк|а, и *f.*
[1] *dim. of* ▶ **рука́.**
[2] (*двери, чайника*) handle; (*кресла, дивана*) arm; **р. две́ри** door handle, doorknob.
[3] (*для письма*) pen; **ша́риковая р.** ballpoint pen.

ручн|о́й *adj.*
[1] hand; (*управление*) manual; **~а́я кладь** hand luggage; **~а́я рабо́та** handwork; **~о́й рабо́ты** handmade; **р. труд** manual labour.
[2] (*зверь, птица*) tame.

ру́ш|ить, у, ишь *impf.* (*здание*) to pull down; (*семью*) to wreck.

ру́ш|иться, ится *impf. and pf.* to fall down, collapse; (*fig.*) (*планы, надежды*) to collapse.

РФ *f. indecl.* (*abbr. of* **Росси́йская Федера́ция**) Russian Federation.

ры́б|а, ы *f.* fish; (*pl., astron.*) Pisces; **ни р. ни мя́со** neither fish nor fowl; **чу́вствовать себя́ как р. в воде́** to feel in one's element.

рыба́к, а́ *m.* fisherman.

рыба́лк|а, и *f.* fishing; fishing trip; **идти́ на ~у** to go fishing.

ры́бн|ый *adj.* fish; **~ые консе́рвы** tinned fish; **~ая ло́вля** fishing; **р. магази́н** fish shop, fishmonger's.

рыболо́в, а *m.* fisherman; angler.

рыболо́вн|ый *adj.* fishing; **~ые принадле́жности, ~ая снасть** fishing tackle.

рыв|о́к, ка́ *m.*
[1] (*резкое движение*) jerk.
[2] (*бегуна*) dash, spurt; (*в тяжёлой атлетике*) snatch.
[3] (*в работе*) push, spurt.

рыг|а́ть, а́ю *impf.* (*of* ▶ **~ну́ть**) to belch.

рыг|ну́ть, ну́, нёшь *inst. pf. of* ▶ **~а́ть**

рыда́ни|е, я *nt.* sobbing.

рыда́|ть, ю *impf.* to sob.

Р

рыж|ий (~, ~á, ~е) *adj.* (*волосы*) red, ginger; (*человек*) red-haired, ginger-haired; (*лошадь*) chestnut.

рыл|о, а *nt.* snout (*of pig, etc.*).

рын|ок, ка *m.*
1 market(place).
2 (*econ.*) market; **внéшний р.** foreign market; **внýтренний р.** domestic, internal market; **на ~ке** on the market.

рыно|чный *adj. of* ▸ **~к; ~чная эконóмика** market economy; **по ~чной ценé** at the market price.

рысáк, á *m.* trotter (*horse*).

ры|скать, щу, щешь *impf.*
1 (**по** + *d.*) (*в поисках*) to scour, ransack; **р. по кармáнам** to ransack one's pockets.
2 (*блуждать*) to rove, roam; **р. глазáми** to let one's eyes roam.

рыс|ь[1], и, о ~и, на ~и́ *f.* (*бег*) trot.

рыс|ь[2], и *f.* (*животное*) lynx.

рытвин|а, ы *f.* rut, groove.

рыть, рóю, рóешь *impf.*
1 (*яму, окопы*) to dig; (*картошку*) to dig up.
2 (*в поисках*) to rummage, root about (in).

рыться, рóюсь, рóешься *impf.* (**в** + *p.*) (*в земле*) to dig (in); (*fig.*) (*в мусоре, в чемодане*) to rummage (in); (*в книгах*) to root about (in).

рыхл|ый (~, ~á, ~о) *adj.* (*почва, камень*) friable, crumbly; (*снег*) loose.

рыцар|ский *adj.*
1 *adj. of* ▸ **~ь; р. поединóк** joust; **р. ромáн** tale of chivalry.
2 (*fig.*) chivalrous.

рыцар|ь, я *m.* knight.

рычáг, á *m.* lever.

рычáни|е, я *nt.* growl, snarl.

рыч|áть, ý, и́шь *impf.* to growl, snarl.

рьян|ый (~, ~а) *adj.* zealous.

рэ́кет, а *m.* racket.

рэкети́р, а *m.* racketeer.

рэп, а *m.* rap (music).

рюкзáк, á *m.* rucksack; backpack.

рю́мк|а, и *f.* (small) glass.

ряби́н|а, ы *f.*
1 (*дерево*) rowan tree, mountain ash.
2 (*ягода*) rowan berry.

ряб|и́ть, и́т *impf.*
1 to ripple.
2 (*impers.*): **у меня ~и́т в глазáх** I am dazzled.

ряб|óй (~, ~á, ~о, ~ы) *adj.*
1 (*лицо*) pockmarked.
2 (*курица*) speckled.

ря́бчик, а *m.* (*zool.*) hazel grouse.

ряб|ь, и *f.*
1 (*на воде*) ripple(s).
2 (*в глазах*) stars.

ря́вк|ать, аю *impf.* (*of* ▸ **~нуть**) (**на** + *a.*; *coll.*) to bellow (at), bark (at).

ря́вк|нуть, ну, нешь *pf. of* ▸ **~ать**

ряд, а, в ~е *and* **в ~ý**, *pl.* **~ы́, ~óв** *m.*
1 (*предметов, лиц*) row; **пéрвый р., послéдний р.** (*theatr.*) front row, back row; **стоя́ть в однóм ~ý (с** + *i.*) to rank (with).
2 (*в армии, в партии*) file, rank; **в пéрвых ~áх** in the first ranks; (*fig.*) in the forefront.
3 (*серия*) series (*also math.*); (*совокупность*) number; **в цéлом ~е слýчаев** in a number of cases.
4 (*торговых палаток*) stalls (*set out in a row*).

рядов|óй *adj.*
1 (*член, работник, случай*) ordinary, common.
2 (*mil.*): **р. состáв** rank and file; men, other ranks; *as n.* **р., ~óго** *m.* private (soldier).

ря́дом *adv.*
1 alongside; (*о двух людях*) side by side; (**с** + *i.*) (*около*) next to; (*в сравнении с*) compared with; **он сиди́т р. с премьéр-мини́стром** he is sitting next to the Prime Minister.
2 (*поблизости*) near, close by, next door; **э́то совсéм р.** it is quite near, close.

ря́с|а, ы *f.* cassock.

Сс

с *prep.*
■ **I.** + *g.*
1 from; off; **с ю́го-востóка** from the south-east; **перевóд с рýсского** translation from Russian; **вернýться с рабóты** to return from work.
2 (*по причине*) for, from, with; **со стыдá** for shame, with shame.
3 on, from; **с однóй, с другóй стороны́** on the one, on the other hand.
4 (*на основании*) with; **с вáшего соглáсия** with your consent.
5 (*посредством*) by, with; **писáть с большóй бýквы** to write with a capital letter.
6 (*о времени*) from, since; as from; **с девяти́ (часóв) до пяти́** from nine (o'clock) till five; **с дéтства** from childhood; **мы с ней не ви́делись с январá** I have not seen her since January.
■ **II.** + *a.* (*приблизительно*): **с пятиэтáжный дом** the size of a five-storey house; **нáша дóчка рóстом с вáшу** our daughter is about the same height as yours.
■ **III.** + *i.*
1 with; and; **с удовóльствием** with pleasure; **мы с вáми** you and I.
2 (*указывает на наличие чего-л.*): **хлеб**

с ма́слом bread and butter; **челове́к со стра́нностями** peculiar person.
[3] (*посредством*) by, on; **получи́ть с пе́рвой по́чтой** to receive by first post.
[4] (*при наступлении чего-л.*) with; **с года́ми** with the years; **с ка́ждым днём** every day.
[5] (*относительно*) with (*or not translated*); **как у вас дела́ с рабо́той?** how is the work going?; **что с ва́ми?** what is the matter with you?; what's up?

с... (*also* **со...** *and* **съ...**) *vbl. pref. indicating*
[1] *unification, movement from various sides to a point, as* **свари́ть** (*металл*) to weld.
[2] *movement or action made in a downward direction, as* **спусти́ться** to descend.
[3] *removal of sth. from somewhere, as* **сорва́ть** to tear off.

са́б|ля, ли, *g. pl.* **~ель** *f.* sabre (*Br.*), saber (*US*).

сабота́ж, а *m.* sabotage.

сабота́жник, а *m.* saboteur.

са́ван, а *m.* shroud, cerement; **сне́жный с.** blanket of snow.

сава́нн|а, ы *f.* (*geog.*) savannah.

са́г|а, и *f.* saga.

сад, а, о ~е, в ~у́, *pl.* **~ы́** *m.* garden; **фрукто́вый с.** orchard; **де́тский с.** kindergarten.

сади́зм, а *m.* sadism.

сади́ст, а *m.* sadist.

сади́ст|ка, ки *f. of* ▸**~**

сади́стский *adj.* sadistic.

са|ди́ться, жу́сь, ди́шься *impf.* (*of* ▸**сесть**); **~ди́(те)сь!** (*polite request*) take a seat!

садо́вник, а *m.* gardener.

садово́дств|о, а *nt.* (*хобби*) gardening; (*наука*) horticulture.

сад|о́вый *adj.*
[1] *adj. of* ▸**~**.
[2] (*культурный*) garden, cultivated.

сад|о́к, ка́ *m.* place for keeping live creatures; **кро́личий с.** rabbit hutch; **ры́бный с.** fish pond.

са́ж|а, и *f.* soot.

сажа́|ть, ю *impf.* (*of* ▸**посади́ть**)
[1] (*цветы*) to plant.
[2] (*гостя*) to seat; (*помещать*) to set, put; (*предлагать сесть*) to offer a seat; **с. в тюрьму́** to put into prison, imprison, jail; **с. под аре́ст** to put under arrest.

са́жен|ец, ца *m.* seedling; sapling.

саза́н, а *m.* wild carp (*Cyprinus carpio*).

сайт, а *m.* (*comput.*) (web)site.

саквоя́ж, а *m.* travelling bag (*Br.*), traveling bag (*US*).

сакрамента́л|ьный (~ен, ~ьна) *adj.* sacramental.

саксофо́н, а *m.* saxophone.

саксофони́ст, а *m.* saxophonist.

саксофони́ст|ка, ки *f. of* ▸**~**

салама́ндр|а, ы *f.* salamander.

сала́т, а *m.*
[1] (*растение*) lettuce.
[2] (*кушанье*) salad.

сала́тниц|а, ы *f.* salad dish, salad bowl.

сала́т|ный *adj. of* ▸**~**; **~ного цве́та** light green.

са́л|ки, ок *pl.* (*sg.* **~ка, ~ки** *f.*) (*игра*) tag, touch.

са́л|о, а *nt.* fat; lard.

сало́н, а *m.*
[1] (*для выставок; магазин*) salon; **автомоби́льный с.** motor car showroom.
[2] (*самолёта, автобуса*) passenger section.
[3] (*в отеле*) lounge; (*на пароходе*) saloon.

салфе́тк|а, и *f.* napkin.

Сальвадо́р, а *m.* El Salvador.

сальвадо́р|ец, ца *m.* Salvadorean.

сальвадо́р|ка, ки *f. of* ▸**~ец**

сальвадо́рский *adj.* Salvadorean.

са́л|ьный (~ен, ~ьна) *adj.* greasy.

са́льто *nt. indecl.* somersault.

салю́т, а *m.* salute.

саля́ми *f. indecl.* salami.

сам, самого́ *m.*; **сама́, само́й,** *a.* **саму́** (*and* **самоё**) *f.*; **~о́, самого́** *nt.*; *pl.* **са́ми, сами́х** *refl. pron.* (*я*) myself, (*ты, вы*) yourself, (*он*) himself, *etc.*; **с. по себе́** in itself, per se; (*без помощи*) by o.s., unassisted; **с. собо́й** of itself, of its own accord.

са́мб|а, ы *f.* samba.

сам|е́ц, ца́ *m.* male (*of species*).

са́мк|а, и *f.* female (*of species*).

са́ммит, а *m.* (*pol.*) summit (meeting).

само... *comb. form* self-, auto-.

самобичева́ни|е, я *nt.* self-reproach.

самобы́т|ный (~ен, ~на) *adj.* original.

самова́р, а *m.* samovar.

самовлюблённый *adj.* narcissistic.

самовнуше́ни|е, я *nt.* auto-suggestion.

самово́лк|а, и *f.* (*coll.*) absence without leave.

самово́л|ьный (~ен, ~ьна) *adj.*
[1] (*человек*) wilful, self-willed.
[2] (*отсутствие*) unauthorized; **~ьная отлу́чка** (*mil.*) absence without leave.

самого́н, а *m.* home-made vodka, hooch, moonshine (*US*).

самоде́льный *adj.* home-made.

самодержа́ви|е, я *nt.* autocracy.

самоде́ятельност|ь, и *f.*
[1] (*художественная с.*) amateur activities (*theatricals, music, etc.*).
[2] initiative, self-motivation.

самоде́ятел|ьный (~ен, ~ьна) *adj.*
[1] (*не профессиональный*) amateur.
[2] self-motivated.

самодово́л|ьный (~ен, ~ьна) *adj.* self-satisfied, smug, complacent.

самодоста́точ|ный (~ен, ~на) *adj.* self-sufficient.

самозабве́н|ный (~ен, ~на) *adj.* selfless.

самозащи́т|а, ы *f.* self-defence (*Br.*), self-defense (*US*).

самозва́н|ец, ца *m.* impostor, pretender.

самока́т, а *m.* (*child's*) scooter.

самоконтро́л|ь, я *m.* self-control.

самокри́тик|а, и *f.* self-criticism.

самокру́тк|а, и *f.* (*coll.*) roll-up (*Br.*), roll-your-own.

самолёт, а *m.* (aero)plane (*Br.*), (air)plane (*US*); aircraft.

самолюби́в|ый (~, ~а) *adj.* proud, haughty.

самолю́би|е, я *nt.* pride, self-esteem; **ло́жное с.** false pride.

самомне́ни|е, я *nt.* conceit, self-importance.

самонаде́ян|ный (~, ~на) *adj.* conceited, arrogant.

самооблада́ни|е, я *nt.* self-control, self-possession, composure.

самообма́н, а *m.* self-deception.

самооборо́н|а, ы *f.* self-defence (*Br.*), self-defense (*US*).

самообслу́живани|е, я *nt.* self-service.

самоопределе́ни|е, я *nt.* self-determination.

самоотве́ржен|ный (~, ~на) *adj.* selfless, self-sacrificing.

самооце́нк|а, и *f.* self-appraisal.

самопи́с|ец, ца *m.*: **бортово́й с.** (*aeron.*) flight recorder.

самопоже́ртвовани|е, я *nt.* self-sacrifice.

самопроизво́л|ьный (~ен, ~ьна) *adj.* spontaneous.

саморо́д|ок, ка *m.* (*min.*) nugget.

самосва́л, а *m.* dump truck.

самосохране́ни|е, я *nt.* self-preservation.

самостоя́тельно *adv.* independently; on one's own.

самостоя́тельност|ь, и *f.* independence.

самостоя́тел|ьный (~ен, ~ьна) *adj.* independent.

самосу́д, а *m.* lynch law, mob law.

самоуби́йственный *adj.* suicidal (*also fig.*).

самоуби́йств|о, а *nt.* suicide; **поко́нчить жизнь ~ом** to commit suicide.

самоуби́йц|а, ы *c.g.* suicide (*victim*).

самоуваже́ни|е, я *nt.* self-esteem.

самоуве́рен|ный (~, ~на) *adj.* self-confident, self-assured.

самоуправле́ни|е, я *nt.* self-government; **ме́стное с.** local government.

самоупра́вств|о, а *nt.* arbitrariness.

самоучи́тел|ь, я *m.* manual for self-tuition; **с. англи́йского языка́** teach-yourself English book.

самоу́чк|а, и *c.g.* self-taught person.

самоцве́т, а *m.* semi-precious stone, gem.

самоце́л|ь, и *f.* end in itself.

самочу́встви|е, я *nt.* general state; **у него́ плохо́е с.** he feels bad; **как ва́ше с.?** how are you (keeping)?

самура́|й, я *m.* samurai.

самши́т, а *m.* box (tree).

са́м|ый *pron.*
[1] (*in conjunction with nn., esp. denoting points of time or place, and with* **тот** *and* **э́тот**) the very, right; **с ~ого нача́ла** from the very outset, right from the start; **с ~ого утра́** ever since the morning, since first thing; **в ~ом углу́** right in the corner; **до ~ого Владивосто́ка** right to, all the way to Vladivostok; **в ~ом де́ле?** indeed?, really?; **на ~ом де́ле** actually, in (actual) fact; **тот с. челове́к, кото́рый...** the very man who ... .
[2]: **тот же с. (, кото́рый/что)** the same (as); **э́тот же с.** the same.
[3] *forms superl. of adjs.; also expr. superl. in conjunction with certain nn. denoting degree of quantity or quality*; **с. глу́пый** the stupidest, the most stupid.

сан, а *m.* rank; office; **высо́кий с.** high office; **духо́вный с.** holy orders, the cloth.

санато́ри|й, я *m.* sanatorium.

санда́л, а *m.* (*bot.*) sandalwood tree.

санда́ли|я, и *f.* sandal.

са́н|и, е́й *no sg.* sledge (*Br.*), sled (*US*); sleigh.

санита́р, а *m.* hospital orderly; (*mil.*) medical orderly.

санита́р|ка, ки *f. of* ▸ **~**

санита́рн|ый *adj.*
[1] (*связанный с медицинской службой*) medical; hospital; **~ая слу́жба** health service, medical service.
[2] (*связанный с санитарией*) sanitary; sanitation; **с. врач** sanitary inspector; **~ые пра́вила** sanitary regulations.

са́н|ки, ок *no sg.*
[1] = **~и.**
[2] (*детские*) toboggan.

Санкт-Петербу́рг, а *m.* St Petersburg.

санкт-петербу́ргский *adj.* St Petersburg.

санкциони́р|овать, ую *impf. and pf.* to sanction.

са́нкци|я, и *f.*
[1] sanction, approval.
[2] *pl.* (*pol., econ.*) sanctions.

санскри́т, а *m.* Sanskrit.

Са́нта-Кла́ус, Са́нта-Кла́уса *m.* Santa Claus.

санта́л, а *m.* = **санда́л**

санте́хник, а *m.* plumber.

санте́хник|а, и *f.* plumbing equipment.

сантиме́тр, а *m.*
[1] centimetre (*Br.*), centimeter (*US*).
[2] (*coll.*) (*лента*) tape measure.

Сан-Франци́ско *m. indecl.* San Francisco.

сапёр, а *m.* (*mil.*) sapper.

сапо́г, а́, *g. pl.* **сапо́г** *m.* boot.

сапо́жник, а *m.* shoemaker, cobbler.

сапо́жный *adj.* boot, shoe; **с. крем** shoe polish.

сапфи́р, а *m.* sapphire.

сара́|й, я *m.* (*для дров, животных*) shed; (*для сена*) barn.

сарафа́н, а *m.* (*платье*) pinafore dress (*Br.*), jumper (*US*).

сарде́льк|а, и *f.* (*fat*) sausage (*of frankfurter type*).

сарди́н|а, ы *f.* sardine, pilchard.

сарка́зм, а *m.* sarcasm.

саркасти́ческий *adj.* sarcastic.

сатан|а́, ы́ *m.* Satan.

сатани́нский *adj.* satanic.

сати́р|а, ы *f.* satire.

сати́рик, а *m.* satirist.

сатири́ческий *adj.* satirical.

сау́дов|ец, ца *m.* Saudi.

саўдов|ка, ки *f. of* ▸ **~ец**
Саўдовск|ая Ара́ви|я, ~ой ~и *f.* Saudi Arabia.
саўдовский *adj.* Saudi.
са́ун|а, ы *f.* sauna.
саундтре́к, а *m.* soundtrack.
сафа́ри *nt. indecl.* safari; **с.-па́рк** safari park.
са́хар, а (у) *m.* sugar.
Саха́р|а, ы *f.* the Sahara (*desert*).
сахари́н, а *m.* saccharin.
са́хар|ить, ю, ишь *impf.* (*of* ▸ **по~**) to sugar, sweeten.
са́харниц|а, ы *f.* sugar bowl.
са́хар|ный *adj. of* ▸ **~**; (*fig.*) sugary; **с. песо́к** granulated sugar.
сач|о́к, ка́ *m.* net; **с. для ба́бочек** butterfly net.
сба́в|ить, лю, ишь *pf.* (*of* ▸ **~ля́ть**) (**с** + *g.*) to reduce.
сбавля́|ть, ю *impf. of* ▸ **сба́вить**
сбаланси́рован|ный (~, ~а) *adj.* well balanced, emotionally stable.
сбе́га|ть, ю *pf.* (**за** + *i.*; *coll.*) to run (for), run to fetch; **~й за до́ктором!** run for a doctor!
сбега́|ть(ся), ю, ет(ся) *impf. of* ▸ **сбежа́ть(ся)**
сбе|жа́ть, гу́, жи́шь, гу́т *pf.* (*of* ▸ **~га́ть**)
1 (**с** + *g.*) (*спуститься*) to run down (from); **с. с ле́стницы** to run downstairs.
2 (*убежать*) to run away.
сбе|жа́ться, жи́тся, гу́тся *pf.* (*of* ▸ **~га́ться**) to come running; to gather, collect.
сберба́нк, а *m.* (*coll.*) = **сберега́тельный банк**
сберега́тельн|ый *adj.*: **~ый банк** savings bank; **~ая кни́жка** passbook, bank book.
сберега́|ть, ю *impf. of* ▸ **сбере́чь**
сбереже́ни|е, я *nt.* (*pl.*) (*деньги*) savings.
сбере́|чь, гу́, жёшь, гу́т, *past* **~г, ~гла́** *pf.* (*of* ▸ **~га́ть**) (*время*) to save; (*семью*) to protect, look after; (*здоровье*) to preserve.
сберка́сс|а, ы *f.* (*coll., hist.*) savings bank.
сберкни́жк|а, и *f.* (*coll.*) savings book.
сбива́|ть, ю *impf. of* ▸ **сбить**
сбива́|ться, юсь *impf.*
1 *impf. of* ▸ **сби́ться.**
2 (*impf. only*) (**на** + *a.*) to resemble; to remind one (of).
сби́вчив|ый (~, ~а) *adj.* inconsistent, contradictory.
сбить, собью́, собьёшь *pf.* (*of* ▸ **сбива́ть**)
1 (*ударом*) to bring down, knock down; (*с чего-л.*) to knock off, dislodge; (*птицу, самолёт*) to bring down, shoot down; (*цену, температуру*) to bring down.
2 (*запутать*) to distract; to deflect; **с. кого́-н. с то́лку** to confuse s.o.
3 (*каблуки, туфли*) to wear down.
4 (*составить*) to knock together; **с. я́щик из досо́к** to knock together a box out of planks.
сби́ться, собью́сь, собьёшься *pf.* (*of* ▸ **сбива́ться 1**)
1 (*сдвинуться с места*) to be dislodged; to slip; **у тебя́ шля́па сби́лась на́бок** your hat is crooked, skew-whiff.
2 (*ошибиться*) to go wrong; **с. с доро́ги, с. с пути́** to lose one's way; to go astray (*also fig.*); **с. со счёта** to lose count.
сближа́|ть(ся), ю(сь) *impf. of* ▸ **сбли́зить(ся)**
сближе́ние, я *nt.*
1 (*pol.*) rapprochement.
2 (*дружба*) intimacy.
сбли́|зить, жу, зишь *pf.* (*of* ▸ **~жа́ть**) to bring together, draw together.
сбли́|зиться, жусь, зишься *pf.* (*of* ▸ **~жа́ться**)
1 (*об интересах*) to converge.
2 (**с** + *i.*) (*о людях*) to become close friends (with).
сбо|й, я *m.* interruption; malfunction.
сбо́ку *adv.* from one side; on one side; **вид с.** side view; **смотре́ть на кого́-н. с.** to look sideways at s.o.
сболтн|у́ть, у́, ёшь *pf.* (*coll.*) to blurt out, let out.
сбор, а *m.*
1 (*действие*) collection; **с. урожа́я** harvest; **с. нало́гов** tax collection.
2 (*деньги*) dues; duty; (*выручка*) takings, returns; **тамо́женный с.** customs duty; **де́лать хоро́шие ~ы** (*theatr.*) to play to full houses, get good box-office returns.
3 (*встреча*) assembly, gathering; **быть в ~е** to be assembled, be in session.
4 *pl.* (*приготовления*) preparations.
сбо́рк|а, и *f.* assembling, assembly, erection.
сбо́рник, а *m.* collection; (*литературных произведений*) anthology.
сбо́рный *adj.*
1 (*дом*) prefabricated; (*мебель*) in kit form.
2 (*из разнородных частей*) mixed, combined; *as n.* national team.
3 (*mil.*) assembly; **с. пункт** assembly point.
сбра́сыва|ть, ю *impf. of* ▸ **сбро́сить**
сбрива́|ть, ю *impf. of* ▸ **сбрить**
сбрить, сбре́ю, сбре́ешь *pf.* (*of* ▸ **сбрива́ть**) to shave off.
сброд, а *no pl., m.* (*collect.*) riff-raff, rabble.
сбро́|сить, шу, сишь *pf.* (*of* ▸ **сбра́сывать**)
1 (*бросить вниз*) to throw down; to drop; **с. бо́мбы** to drop bombs.
2 (*скинуть*) to throw off (*also fig.*); (*кожу, листья*) to shed; **с. (с себя́) одея́ло** to throw off a blanket; (*свергнуть*) to overthrow.
3 (*сбавить*) to reduce.
сбру́|я, и *f.* (*collect.*) harness.
сбыва́|ться, юсь *impf. of* ▸ **сбы́ться**
сбыт, а *no pl., m.* (*econ., comm.*) sale; **ры́нок ~а** (seller's) market.
сбы́ться, сбу́дется, *past* **сбы́лся, сбыла́сь** *pf.* (*of* ▸ **сбыва́ться**) to come true, be realized.
св. (*abbr. of* **свято́й**) St, Saint.
сва́дебный *adj.* wedding; **с. пода́рок** wedding present.
сва́д|ьба, ьбы, *g. pl.* **~еб** *f.* wedding; **справля́ть ~ьбу** to celebrate a wedding.

сва́лива|ть(ся), ю(сь) *impf. of* **свали́ть(ся)**

свал|и́ть, ю́, ~́ишь *pf.* (*of* ▸ **вали́ть**[1] *and* ▸ **~́ивать**)
1 (*ударом*) to throw down, bring down; (*coll.*) (*о болезни*) to lay low.
2 (*дрова, уголь*) to heap up, pile up; **с. вину́** (**на** + *a.*) to lump the blame (on).

свал|и́ться, ю́сь, ~́ишься *pf.* (*of* ▸ **вали́ться** *and* ▸ **~́иваться**) to fall (down), collapse; **с. как снег на́ голову** to come like a bolt from the blue.

сва́лк|а, и *f.* dump; scrap heap.

сваля́|ться, ется *pf.* to get tangled.

сва́рива|ть, ю *impf. of* ▸ **свари́ть**

свар|и́ть, ю́, ~́ишь *pf.*
1 *pf. of* ▸ **вари́ть.**
2 (*impf.* **~́ивать**) (*tech.*) to weld.

свар|и́ться, ~́ится *pf. of* ▸ **вари́ться**

сва́рк|а, и *f.* (*tech.*) welding.

сварли́в|ый (~, ~а) *adj.* quarrelsome, shrewish.

сва́рщик, а *m.* welder.

сва́стик|а, и *f.* swastika.

сва́|я, и *f.* pile.

све́дени|е, я *nt.*
1 (*известие*) piece of information; (*pl.*) information, intelligence.
2 (*знание*) knowledge; attention, consideration, notice; **приня́ть к ~ю** to take into consideration.

све́дущ|ий (~, ~а) *adj.* (**в** + *p.*) knowledgeable (about); (well) versed (in).

све́жест|ь, и *f.* freshness; (*прохлада*) coolness.

све́ж|ий (~, ~а́, ~о́, ~́и́) *adj.* fresh; **~ее бельё** clean underclothes; **с. ве́тер** fresh breeze; **на ~ем во́здухе** in the fresh air; **~ие но́вости** recent news.

свёкл|а, ы *f.* beet, beetroot (*Br.*).

свёк|ор, ра *m.* father-in-law (*husband's father*).

свекро́в|ь, и *f.* mother-in-law (*husband's mother*).

сверг|а́ть, а́ю *impf. of* ▸ **~́нуть**

све́рг|нуть, ну, нешь, *past* **~** *and* **~нул, ~ла** *pf.* (*of* ▸ **~а́ть**) to throw down, overthrow; **с. с престо́ла** to dethrone.

све́р|ить, ю, ишь *pf.* (*of* ▸ **~я́ть**) (+ *a.* **с** + *i.*) to check (sth. against).

све́рк|а, и *f.* collation.

сверка́|ть, ю *impf.* to sparkle; to glitter; to gleam; (*о молнии*) to flash.

сверкн|у́ть, у́, ёшь *inst. pf.* to flash (*also fig.*).

сверл|и́ть, ю́, и́шь *impf.* (*of* ▸ **про~**)
1 (*tech.*) to bore, drill; **с. зуб** to drill a tooth.
2 (*о насекомых*) to bore through.

сверл|о́, а́, *pl.* **~̈а, ~̈** *nt.* (*tech.*) (*инструмент*) drill; (*наконечник*) drill bit.

сверн|у́ть, у́, ёшь *pf.* (*of* ▸ **свора́чивать**)
1 to roll (up); **с. ковёр** to roll up the carpet; **с. ше́ю кому́-н.** to wring s.o.'s neck.
2 (*fig.*) (*сократить*) to reduce, contract, cut down.
3 (*повернуть*) to turn; **с. нале́во** to turn to the left; **с. с доро́ги** to turn off the road.

сверн|у́ться, у́сь, ёшься *pf.* (*of* ▸ **свора́чиваться**)
1 to roll up, curl up; to coil up; **с. клубко́м** to roll o.s. up into a ball.
2 (*о молоке*) to curdle; (*о крови*) to coagulate, clot.
3 (*fig.*) (*сократиться*) to contract.

све́рстник, а *m.* person of the same age; contemporary, peer; **они́ ~и** they are the same age.

све́рстни|ца, цы *f. of* ▸ **~к**

сверх *prep.* + *g.* (*нормы*) above, beyond; over and above; in excess of; **с. пла́на** in excess of the plan; **с. (вся́кого) ожида́ния** beyond (all) expectation.

сверх... *comb. form* super-, supra-, extra-, over-, preter-.

сверхдержа́в|а, ы *f.* superpower.

сверхзвуково́й *adj.* (*phys., aeron.*) supersonic.

сверхпла́новый *adj.* over and above the plan.

све́рху *adv.*
1 from above (*also fig.*); from the top; **с. до́низу** from top to bottom; **смотре́ть на кого́-н. с. вниз** (*fig.*) to look down on s.o.
2 (*на поверхности*) on the surface; on the top.

сверхуро́чн|ый *adj.* overtime; **~ая рабо́та** overtime; *as n.* **~ые, ~ых** (*payment for*) overtime.

сверхчелове́к, а *m.* superman.

сверхъесте́ствен|ный (~, ~на) *adj.* supernatural.

сверч|о́к, ка́ *m.* (*zool.*) cricket.

свер|я́ть, я́ю *impf. of* ▸ **~́ить**

све́|сить, шу, сишь *pf.* (*of* ▸ **~шивать**) to let down, lower; **сиде́ть, ~сив но́ги** to sit with one's legs dangling.

све́|ситься, шусь, сишься *pf.* (*of* ▸ **~шиваться**) to lean over; to hang over; (*о ветвях*) to overhang; **с. че́рез пери́ла** to lean over the banisters.

све|сти́, ду́, дёшь, *past* **~̈л, ~ла́** *pf.* (*of* ▸ **своди́ть**[1])
1 (**с** + *g.*) (*спустить сверху вниз*) to take down (from, off); **с. с ума́** to drive mad.
2 (*соединить; собрать*) to bring together; to put together; to unite; **судьба́ ~ла́ их** fate threw them together; **с. концы́ с конца́ми** to make (both) ends meet.
3 (**к** + *d. or* **на** + *a.*) (*довести*) to reduce (to), bring (to); **с. на нет** to bring to naught.
4 (*о судороге*) to cramp, convulse; **у меня́ ~ло́ но́гу** I have cramp in my foot.

све|сти́сь, дётся, *past* **~̈лся, ~ла́сь** *pf.* (*of* ▸ **своди́ться**) (**к** + *d.*) to come (to), reduce (to).

свет[1], **а** *m.* light (*also fig.*); **лу́нный с.** moonlight; **зажéчь с.** to turn the light on; **в ~́е** (+ *g.*) in the light (of); **на ~у́** in the light; **при ~́е** (+ *g.*) by the light (of).

свет[2], **а** *m.*
1 (*мир*) world (*also fig.*); **Ста́рый, Но́вый с.** the Old, the New World; **тот с.** the next world; **коне́ц ~́а** doomsday, the end of the world; **появи́ться на с.** to come into the

world; **ни за что на ∼е** not for the world.
[2] (*высшее общество*) society; **высший с.** high society.

светá|ть, ет *impf.* (*impers.*): **∼ет** it is dawning, it is getting light, day is breaking.

светúл|о, а *nt.* luminary (*also fig.*); **небéсные ∼а** heavenly bodies.

светúльник, а *m.* lamp.

све|тúть, чý, ∼тишь *impf.*
[1] (*излучать свет*) to shine.
[2] (+ *d.*) to light the way (for); to shine a light (for).

све|тúться, чýсь, ∼тишься *impf.* to shine, gleam.

свéтло-... *comb. form* (*with names of colours*) light-; **свéтло-зелёный** light green.

светловолóс|ый (∼, ∼а) *adj.* light-haired.

свéт|лый (∼ел, ∼лá, ∼ло, ∼лы *and* (*in pred. use*) **∼лó, ∼лы́)** *adj.*
[1] (*комната, волосы, краски*) light; (*день*) bright; **на ýлице ∼лó** it is daylight.
[2] (*fig.*) (*радостный*) bright, radiant, joyous; pure, unclouded; **∼лое бýдущее** bright future.
[3] (*fig.*) (*проницательный*) lucid, clear; **он — ∼лая головá** he has a lucid mind.

светопреставлéни|е, я *nt.*
[1] the end of the world, doomsday.
[2] (*fig., coll.*) chaos.

светофúльтр, а *m.* light filter.

светофóр, а *m.* traffic lights.

свéтск|ий *adj.*
[1] society, fashionable; **∼ая жизнь** high life; **с. человéк** man of the world.
[2] (*манеры*) refined.
[3] (*не церковный*) temporal, lay, secular; worldly.

свет|я́щийся *pres. part. of* ▶ **∼úться** *and adj.* luminous, luminescent.

свеч|á, и, *i.* **∼óй,** *pl.* **∼и, ∼éй, ∼áм** *f.*
[1] candle.
[2]: **с. зажигáния** spark plug.
[3] (*med.*) suppository.

свечéни|е, я *nt.* luminescence, fluorescence; phosphorescence.

свéшива|ть(ся), ю(сь) *impf. of* ▶ **свéсить(ся)**

свидáни|е, я *nt.* meeting; (*деловое*) appointment; (*влюблённых*) date; **назнáчить с.** (**на** + *a.*) to arrange a meeting (for), make an appointment (for), make a date (for); **до ∼я!** goodbye!

свидéтел|ь, я *m.* witness; **с. обвинéния, защúты** witness for the prosecution, for the defence (*Br.*), defense (*US*).

свидéтель|ница, ницы *f. of* ▶ **∼**

свидéтельств|о, а *nt.*
[1] evidence.
[2] (*документ*) certificate; **с. о брáке** marriage certificate.

свидéтельств|овать, ую *impf.*
[1] (**о** + *p. or* + *a. or* + **что**) (*leg.*) to give evidence (concerning); to testify.
[2] (**о** + *p.*) (*подтверждать, доказывать*) to show, attest to, be evidence (of); **э́то письмó ∼ует о егó бестáктности** this letter is evidence of his tactlessness.

свинáрник, а *m.* pigsty.

свин|éц, цá *m.* lead.

свинúн|а, ы *f.* pork.

свúн|ка[1], ки *f. dim. of* ▶ **∼ья́; морскáя с.** guinea pig.

свúнк|а[2], и *f.* (*med.*) mumps.

свин|óй *adj. of* ▶ **∼ья́; ∼áя кóжа** pigskin; **∼áя котлéта** pork chop; **∼óе сáло** lard.

свúнский *adj.* (*coll.*) (*подлый*) swinish; (*грязный*) filthy.

свúнств|о, а *nt.* (*coll.*) (*подлость*) swinishness; (*поступок*) swinish trick; (*грязь*) filth.

свин|тúть, чý, тúшь *pf.* (*of* ▶ **∼чивать**)
[1] (*соединить*) to screw together.
[2] (*гайку*) to unscrew.

свúнчива|ть, ю *impf. of* ▶ **свинтúть**

свин|ья́, ьи́, *pl.* **∼ьи, ∼éй, ∼ьям** *f.*
[1] pig; (*самка*) sow.
[2] (*fig., pej.*) (*человек*) swine; **подложúть ∼ью́** (+ *d.*; *coll.*) to play a dirty trick (on).

свирéл|ь, и *f.* (reed) pipe.

свирéп|ый (∼, ∼а) *adj.* fierce, ferocious.

свис|áть, áю *impf.* to hang down.

свист, а *m.* whistle; whistling.

сви|стéть, щý, стúшь *impf.* to whistle.

свúстн|уть, у, ешь *pf.*
[1] to give a whistle.
[2] (*coll.*) (*украсть*) to steal, snatch.

свист|óк, кá *m.* whistle.

свúтер, а *m.* sweater.

свúт|ок, ка *m.* roll, scroll.

свить, совью́, совьёшь, *past* **свил, свилá, свúло** *pf.* (*of* ▶ **вить**) to twist, wind.

свúться, совьётся, *past* **свúлся, свилáсь** *pf.* (*of* ▶ **вúться**) to roll up, curl up, coil.

свихн|ýться, ýсь, ёшься *pf.* (*coll.*) to go off one's head.

свобóд|а, ы *f.* freedom, liberty; **с. вóли** free will; **с. слóва** freedom of speech; **на ∼е** at large.

свобóдно *adv.*
[1] (*без принуждения*) freely; (*с лёгкостью*) with ease; **онá с. говорúт на пятú языкáх** she speaks five languages fluently.
[2] (*просторно*) loose, loosely.

свобóд|ный (∼ен, ∼на) *adj.*
[1] free.
[2] (*без помех*) free; easy; **с. дóступ** easy access.
[3] (*не занятый*) free; (*номер*) vacant; (*место*) spare; **∼ное врéмя** free time; **∼ное мéсто** vacant seat, spare seat; **вы ∼ны сегóдня вéчером?** are you free this evening?
[4] (*поведение*) free (and easy).
[5] (*одежда*) loose, loose-fitting; flowing.

свободолюбúв|ый (∼, ∼а) *adj.* freedom-loving.

свод[1], а *m.* code; (*документов*) collection; **с. закóнов** code of laws.

свод[2], а *m.* (*перекрытие*) arch, vault; **небéсный с.** the firmament.

сво|дúть[1], жý, ∼дишь *impf. of* ▶ **свестú**

сво|дúть[2], жý, ∼дишь *pf.* (*отвести и привести обратно*) to take (*and bring back*); **мы ∼дúли детéй в кинó** we took the

С

children to the cinema.

сво|ди́ться, ~́дится *impf. of* ▸ **свести́сь**

сво́дк|а, и *f.* summary; report; **с. пого́ды** weather forecast, weather report.

сво́дн|ый *adj.*
1 combined; collated; **~ая табли́ца** summary table, index.
2 step-; **с. брат** stepbrother.

сво́дчатый *adj.* arched, vaulted.

своево́л|ьный (~ен, ~ьна) *adj.* self-willed, wilful.

своевре́мен|ный (~ and ~ен, ~на) *adj.* timely, opportune.

своенра́в|ный (~ен, ~на) *adj.* wilful, capricious.

своеобра́з|ный (~ен, ~на) *adj.* original; peculiar, distinctive.

сво|зи́ть, жу́, ~́зишь *pf.* (*отвезти и привезти обратно*) to take (*and bring back*); **мы ~зи́ли дете́й в цирк** we took the children to the circus.

свой *possessive adj.* one's (my, your, his, *etc., in accordance with subject of sentence or clause*), one's own; **у них с. дом** they have a house of their own; **умере́ть свое́й сме́ртью** to die a natural death; **в своё вре́мя** (*i*) at one time, in my, his, *etc.*, time, (*ii*) (*своевременно*) in due time, in due course; **он не в своём уме́** he is not right in the head; *as n.* **свои́** one's (own) people; **своё** one's own; **доби́ться своего́** to get one's own way.

сво́йствен|ный (~ and ~ен, ~на) *adj.* (+ *d.*) characteristic (of).

сво́йств|о, а *nt.* characteristic.

сво́лоч|ь, и, *g. pl.* **~е́й** *f.* (*coll.*) scum, swine.

свора́чива|ть(ся), ю(сь) *impf. of* ▸ **сверну́ть(ся)**

свор|ова́ть, у́ю *coll. pf. of* ▸ **ворова́ть**

своя́к, а́ *m.* brother-in-law (*husband of wife's sister*).

свояче́ниц|а, ы *f.* sister-in-law (*wife's sister*).

свык|а́ться, а́юсь *impf. of* ▸ **~́нуться**

свы́к|нуться, нусь, нешься, *past* **~ся, ~лась** *pf.* (*of* ▸ **~а́ться**) (**с** + *i.*) to get used (to).

свысока́ *adv.* condescendingly; **обраща́ться с кем-н. с.** to talk down to, patronize s.o.

свы́ше
1 *adv.* from above; (*relig.*) from on high.
2 *prep.* + *g.* (*более*) over, more than; (*вне*) beyond; **с. ты́сячи самолётов уча́ствовало в налёте** over a thousand planes took part in the raid.

свя|за́ть, жу́, ~́жешь *pf.* (*of* ▸ **вяза́ть 1, 2** *and* ▸ **~́зывать**)
1 to tie; to bind (*also fig.*); **с. свою́ судьбу́** (**с** + *i.*) to throw in one's lot (with).
2 (*fig.*) (*соединить*) to connect, link; **быть (те́сно) ~́занным** (**с** + *i.*) to be (closely) connected (with), be bound up (with).
3: **быть ~́занным** (**с** + *i.*; *fig.*) (*повлечь*) to involve, entail; **э́то предприя́тие бу́дет ~́зано с огро́мными расхо́дами** this undertaking will involve huge expense.
4 (*установить связь*) to link, associate; **не́которые ~за́ли эпиде́мию с плохи́м водоснабже́нием** some connected the epidemic with the bad water supply.

свя|за́ться, жу́сь, ~́жешься *pf.* (*of* ▸ **~́зываться 1**) (**с** + *i.*)
1 to get in touch (with), communicate (with).
2 (*coll., pej.*) to get involved (with), get mixed up (with).

свя́зк|а, и *f.*
1 (*ключей*) bunch; (*книг, бумаг*) bundle.
2 (*anat.*) cord; ligament; **голосовы́е ~и** vocal cords.

свя́з|ный (~ен, ~на) *adj.* connected, coherent.

свя́зыва|ть, ю *impf. of* ▸ **связа́ть**

свя́зыва|ться, юсь *impf.*
1 *impf. of* ▸ **связа́ться.**
2 (*impf. only*) (**с** + *i.*) to have to do (with); **не ~йся с ни́ми** don't have anything to do with them.

связ|ь, и, о ~́и, в ~и́ *f.*
1 (*отношение*) connection; **в свя́зи с** (+ *i.*) (*вследствие*) due to; owing to; (*по поводу*) in connection with; **в свя́зи с э́тим** in this connection.
2 (*тесное общение*) link, tie, bond; **дру́жеские ~́и** friendly relations, ties of friendship.
3 (*любовная*) liaison, relationship.
4 (*pl.*) (*близкое знакомство*) connections, contacts; **у него́ мно́го ~́ей в Москве́** he has many influential connections in Moscow.
5 (*сообщение*) communication; **с. по ра́дио** radio communication.
6 (*sg. only*) (*почта, телефон*) (post and tele)communications; **отделе́ние ~́и** (branch) post office.

свят|о́й (~, ~а́, ~о) *adj.*
1 (*священный*) holy; sacred (*also fig.*); **~а́я вода́** holy water; **С. Дух** the Holy Ghost, the Holy Spirit.
2 (*человек*) saintly.
3 *preceding name, or as n.* **с., ~о́го** *m.*, **~а́я, ~о́й** *f.* saint; **причи́слить к ли́ку ~ы́х** (*eccl.*) to canonize.

свя́тост|ь, и *f.* holiness; sanctity.

святота́тств|о, а *nt.* sacrilege.

святы́н|я, и *f.*
1 (*eccl.*) (*предмет*) object of worship; (*место*) sacred place.
2 (*fig.*) (*предмет*) sacred object.

свяще́нник, а *m.* (*православный*) priest (*of Orthodox Church*); clergyman.

свяще́н|ный (~ен, ~на) *adj.* holy; sacred (*also fig.*); **С~ное Писа́ние** Holy Writ, Scripture.

сгиб, а *m.*
1 bend.
2 (*anat.*) flexion.

сгиба́|ть(ся), ю(сь) *impf. of* ▸ **согну́ть(ся)**

сги́н|уть, у, ешь *pf.* (*coll.*) to disappear, vanish.

сгла́|дить, жу, дишь *pf.* (*of* ▸ **~живать**)
1 (*выровнять*) to smooth out.
2 (*fig.*) (*смягчить*) to smooth over, soften.

сгла́|диться, дится *pf.* (*of* ▸ **~живаться**)

1 (*выровняться*) to become smooth.
2 (*fig.*) (*смягчиться*) to be smoothed over, be softened.

сгла́жива|ть(ся), ю, ет(ся) *impf. of* ▸ **сгла́дить(ся)**

сглаз, а *m.* (*coll.*) the evil eye.

сгла́|зить, жу, зишь *pf.* to put the evil eye (on, upon); (*fig., coll.*) to jinx.

сгни|ть, ю́, ёшь *pf.* (*of* ▸ **гнить**) to rot, decay.

сгова́рива|ться, юсь *impf. of* ▸ **сговори́ться**

сговор|и́ться, ю́сь, и́шься *pf.* (*of* ▸ **сгова́риваться**) (**с** + *i.*) to arrange (with).

сгово́рчив|ый (~, ~а) *adj.* compliant, tractable.

сгора́ни|е, я *nt.* combustion; **дви́гатель вну́треннего ~я** internal-combustion engine.

сгор|а́ть, а́ю *impf.*
1 *impf. of* ▸ **~е́ть.**
2 (**от** + *g.*; *fig.*) to be dying (of); **с. от стыда́, любопы́тства** to be dying of shame, curiosity.

сго́рб|иться, люсь, ишься *pf. of* ▸ **го́рбиться**

сго́рблен|ный (~, ~а) *adj.* crooked, bent; hunchbacked.

сгор|е́ть, ю́, и́шь *pf.* (*of* ▸ **~а́ть 1**)
1 to burn down; to be burnt out, down; **наш дом ~е́л** our house was burnt down.
2 (*о топливе*) to be consumed, be used up.

сгоряча́ *adv.* in the heat of the moment; in a fit of temper.

сгреба́|ть, ю *impf. of* ▸ **сгрести́**

сгре|сти́, бу́, бёшь, *past* **~̈б, ~бла́** *pf.* (*of* ▸ **~ба́ть**) (*собрать*) to rake up, rake together.

сгруд|и́ться, и́тся *pf.* (*coll.*) to crowd, mill, bunch.

сгруппир|ова́ть, у́ю *pf. of* ▸ **группирова́ть**

сгуб|и́ть, лю́, ~̂ишь *pf.* (*coll.*) to ruin.

сгу|сти́ть, щу́, сти́шь *pf.* (*of* ▸ **~ща́ть**) to thicken; (*конденсировать*) to condense; **с. кра́ски** (*fig.*) to lay it on thick.

сгу|сти́ться, сти́тся *pf.* (*of* ▸ **~ща́ться**) to thicken; (*конденсироваться*) to condense; (*о крови*) to clot.

сгу́ст|ок, ка *m.* clot.

сгуща́|ть(ся), ю, ет(ся) *impf. of* ▸ **сгусти́ть(ся)**

сда|ва́ть, ю́, ёшь *impf. of* ▸ **сдать; с. экза́мен** to take, sit an examination.

сда|ва́ться, ю́сь, ёшься *impf. of* ▸ **~̂ться**

сдав|и́ть, лю́, ~̂ишь *pf.* (*of* ▸ **~̂ливать**) to squeeze.

сда́влива|ть, ю *impf. of* ▸ **сдави́ть**

сдать, сдам, сдашь, сдаст, сдади́м, сдади́те, сдаду́т, *past* **сдал, сдала́, сда́ло** *pf.* (*of* ▸ **сдава́ть**)
1 (*передать*) to hand over, pass; **с. бага́ж на хране́ние** to deposit one's luggage.
2 (*отдать внаём*) to let, let out, hire out; **с. в аре́нду** to lease.
3 (*возвратить*) to give change.
4 (*уступить*) to surrender, yield, give up.
5 (*экзамен*) to pass (*an examination, a subject, etc.*); **он сдал то́лько латы́нь** he only passed in Latin.
6 (*карты*) to deal (*cards*).
7 (*coll.*) (*о моторе, сердце*) to give out; (*о старике, здоровье*) to become weaker.

сда́|ться, мся, шься, стся, ди́мся, ди́тесь, ду́тся, *past* **~лся, ~ла́сь** *pf.* (*of* ▸ **~ва́ться**) to surrender, yield; (*chess*) to resign.

сда́ч|а, и *f.*
1 (*квартиры*) letting out, hiring out; **с. в аре́нду** leasing.
2 (*города*) surrender.
3 (*деньги*) change; **три рубля́ ~и** three roubles change; **с. с рубля́** change from one rouble; **дать ~и** (+ *d.*; *fig., coll.*) to give as good as one got.

сдвиг, а *m.*
1 displacement; (*geol.*) fault.
2 (*fig.*) (*улучшение*) change (for the better), improvement.

сдвига́|ть(ся), ю(сь) *impf. of* ▸ **сдви́нуть(ся)**

сдви́|нуть, ну, нешь *pf.* (*of* ▸ **~га́ть**)
1 to shift, move, displace; **с. с ме́ста** (*fig.*) to get moving, set in motion.
2 (*соединить*) to move together, bring together.

сдви́|нуться, нусь, нешься *pf.* (*of* ▸ **~га́ться**) to move, budge; **с. с ме́ста** (*fig.*) to progress; **де́ло не ~нулось с ме́ста** no headway has been made.

сде́ла|ть(ся), ю(сь) *pf. of* ▸ **де́лать(ся)**

сде́лк|а, и *f.* transaction, deal, bargain.

сде́льн|ый *adj.* piecework; **~ая опла́та** payment by the piece, by the job; **~ая рабо́та** piecework.

сде́ржан|ный *p.p.p. of* ▸ **сдержа́ть** *and* **(~, ~на)** *adj.* restrained, reserved.

сдерж|а́ть, у́, ~̂ишь *pf.* (*of* ▸ **~̂ивать**)
1 to hold (back); (*неприятеля*) to hold in check, contain.
2 (*fig.*) (*чувства*) to keep back, restrain; **с. слёзы** to suppress tears.
3 (*обещание*) to keep; **с. сло́во** to keep one's word.

сдерж|а́ться, у́сь, ~̂ишься *pf.* (*of* ▸ **~̂иваться**) to restrain o.s., contain o.s.; to check o.s.

сде́ржива|ть(ся), ю(сь) *impf. of* ▸ **сдержа́ть(ся)**

сдира́|ть, ю *impf. of* ▸ **содра́ть**

сдо́хн|уть, у, ешь *pf.* (*of* ▸ **сдыха́ть, до́хнуть**)
1 (*coll.*) (*о животных*) to die.
2 (*vulg. sl., pej.*) (*о людях*) to peg out, kick the bucket.

сдруж|и́ться, у́сь, ~̂ишься *pf.* (**с** + *i.*) to become friends (with).

сдува́|ть, ю *impf. of* ▸ **сдуть**

сду|ть, ~̂ю, ~̂ешь *pf.* (*of* ▸ **~ва́ть**) to blow away, blow off.

сдыха́|ть, ю *impf. of* ▸ **сдо́хнуть**

сеа́нс, а *m.*
1 (*представление*) performance, show.
2 (*массажа, гипноза*) session.
3 (*портретиста*) sitting.

4 (*спиритический*) seance.

себе́[1] *see* ▶ **себя**

себе́[2] *particle (coll.) modifying v. or pron. and usu. containing hint of reproach*; **ничего́ с.** not bad; **так с.** so-so.

себесто́имост|ь, и *f. (econ.)* cost (*of manufacture*); cost price; **прода́ть по ~и** to sell at cost price.

себя́, себе́, собо́й (собо́ю), о себе́ *refl. pron.* oneself; (*я*) myself, (*ты, вы*) yourself, (*он*) himself, *etc.*; **прийти́ в с.** (**от** + *g.*) to get over; to come to one's senses; **не в себе́** not o.s.; **от с.** (*i*) away from o.s., outwards, (*ii*) (*лично, от своего имени*) for o.s., on one's own behalf; **чита́ть про с.** to read to o.s.; **у с.** at home, at one's (own) place.

себялюби́в|ый (~, ~а) *adj.* egoistical, selfish.

се́вер, а *m.* north.

се́верн|ый *adj.* north, northern; (*направление, ветер*) northerly; **с. оле́нь** reindeer; **С. по́люс** North Pole; **~ое сия́ние** northern lights, aurora borealis.

Се́верн|ый Ледови́т|ый океа́н, ~ого ~ого ~а *m.* the Arctic Ocean.

Се́верн|ый поля́рн|ый круг, ~ого ~ого ~а *m.* the Arctic Circle.

североамерика́нский *adj.* North American.

се́веро-восто́к, а *m.* north-east.

се́веро-восто́чный *adj.* north-east, north-eastern.

се́веро-за́пад, а *m.* north-west.

се́веро-за́падный *adj.* north-west, north-western.

североирла́ндский *adj.* Northern Irish.

северя́н|ин, ина, *pl.* **~е, ~** *m.* northerner.

севрю́г|а, и *f.* stellate sturgeon (*Acipenser stellatus*).

сегме́нт, а *m.* segment.

сего́дня *adv.* today; **с. ве́чером** this evening, tonight.

сего́дня|шний *adj. of* ▶ **~; с. день** today; **~шняя газе́та** today's paper.

седе́|ть, ю *impf.* (*of* ▶ **по~**) to go grey (*Br.*), gray (*US*).

седин|а́, ы́, *pl.* **~ы, ~** *f.* grey (*Br.*), gray (*US*) hair(s).

сед|ло́, ла́, *pl.* **~ла, ~ел** *nt.* saddle.

сед|о́й (~, ~а́, ~о, ~ы) *adj.* (*волосы*) grey (*Br.*), gray (*US*); (*человек*) grey-haired (*Br.*), gray-haired (*US*).

седьм|о́й *adj.* seventh; **быть на ~о́м не́бе** to be in the seventh heaven.

сезо́н, а *m.* season.

сезо́нн|ый *adj.* seasonal; **с. биле́т** season ticket; **~ые рабо́ты** seasonal work.

сей *m.*, **сия́** *f.*, **сие́** *nt.*, *pl.* **сии́** *pron.* this; **сию́ мину́ту** this (very) minute; at once, instantly; **до сих пор** up to now, till now, hitherto; **на с. раз** this time, for this once; **по с. день** to this day.

сейсми́ческий *adj.* seismic.

сейсмоопа́с|ный (~ен, ~на) *adj.* earthquake-prone.

сейсмосто́|йкий (~ек, ~йка) *adj.* earthquake-proof.

сейф, а *m.* safe.

сейча́с *adv.*

1 (*теперь*) (right) now, at present, at the (present) moment.

2 (*очень скоро*) presently, soon; **с. же** at once, immediately; **с.!** in a minute!; half a minute!

секи́р|а, ы *f.* axe (*Br.*), ax (*US*).

секре́т, а *m.* secret; **по ~у** confidentially, in confidence.

секрета́р|ша, ши *f. (coll.) f. of* ▶ **~ь**

секрета́р|ь, я́ *m.* secretary; **ли́чный с.** private secretary, personal secretary; **генера́льный с.** secretary general.

секре́тно *adv.* secretly, in secret; (*надпись*) 'secret', 'confidential'; **соверше́нно с.** 'top secret'.

секре́тност|ь, и *f.* secrecy.

секре́т|ный (~ен, ~на) *adj.* secret; confidential.

секре́ци|я, и *f. (physiol.)* secretion.

секс, а *m.* sex.

сексо́лог, а *m.* sexologist.

сексоло́ги|я, и *f.* sexology.

сексуа́льност|ь, и *f.* sexuality.

сексуа́л|ьный (~ен, ~ьна) *adj.* sexual; (*эротичный*) sexy; **~ьное домога́тельство** sexual harassment.

се́кт|а, ы *f.* sect.

секта́нт, а *m.* sectarian; member of a sect.

се́ктор, а, *pl.* **~ы, ~ов** *and* **~а́, ~о́в** *m.*

1 (*math., mil.*) sector; **с. Га́за** the Gaza Strip.

2 (*отдел*) section, department; (*econ.*) sector.

секу́нд|а, ы *f.* second; **одну́ ~у!** just a moment!

секундоме́р, а *m.* stopwatch.

се́кци|я, и *f.* section.

селёдк|а, и *f.* herring.

селезёнк|а, и *f. (physiol.)* spleen.

се́лез|ень, ня *m.* drake.

селекционе́р, а *m.*

1 (*agric.*) breeder.

2 (*sport*) scout.

селе́кци|я, и *f.*

1 (*agric.*) selective breeding.

2 (*sport*) selection.

селе́ни|е, я *nt.* settlement.

сели́тр|а, ы *f. (chem.)* saltpetre (*Br.*), saltpeter (*US*).

сел|и́ть, ю́, и́шь *impf.* (*of* ▶ **по~**) to settle.

сел|и́ться, ю́сь, и́шься *impf.* (*of* ▶ **по~**) to settle.

сел|о́, а́, *pl.* **~а** *nt.* village.

сел|ь, я *m.* (seasonal) mountain torrent.

сельдере́|й, я *m.* celery.

сельд|ь, и, *pl.* **~и, ~е́й** *f.* herring.

се́льск|ий *adj.*

1 (*не городской*) country, rural; **~ая ме́стность** rural area; countryside; **~ое хозя́йство** agriculture, farming.

2 (*школа, улица*) village.

сельскохозя́йственный *adj.* agricultural, farming.

сема́нтик|а, и *f.*

1 (*наука*) semantics.

2 (*значение слова*) meanings.

семафо́р, а *m.* semaphore.
сёмг|а, и *f.* salmon.
семе́йн|ый *adj.*
1 family; domestic; **по ~ым обстоя́тельствам** for domestic reasons.
2 (*имеющий семью*) having a family; **с. челове́к** family man.
семе́йств|о, а *nt.* family.
семена́ *see* ▸ **се́мя**
семёрк|а, и *f.*
1 (*цифра, игральная карта*) seven.
2 (*coll.*) (*автобус, трамвай*) No. 7 (*bus, tram, etc.*).
3 (*группа из семерых*) (group of) seven; **Больша́я с.** the seven economically most developed nations.
се́мер|о, ы́х *num.* (*collect.*) seven.
семе́стр, а *m.* term (*Br.*), semester (*US*).
се́меч|ко, ка, *pl.* **~ки, ~ек** *nt.*
1 *dim. of* ▸ **се́мя.**
2 *pl.* (*подсолнечника*) sunflower seeds; (*тыквенные*) pumpkin seeds.
семидеся́т|ый *adj.* seventieth; **~ые го́ды** the seventies.
семиле́тний *adj.*
1 (*срок*) seven-year.
2 (*ребёнок*) seven-year-old.
семина́р, а *m.* seminar.
семина́ри|я, и *f.* seminary, training college; **духо́вная с.** theological college.
семисо́тый *adj.* seven-hundredth.
семи́т, а *m.* Semite.
семна́дцатый *adj.* seventeenth.
семна́дцат|ь, и *num.* seventeen.
сем|ь, и́, *i.* **~ью́** *num.* seven.
се́мьдесят, семи́десяти, *i.* **семью́десятью** *num.* seventy.
семьсо́т, семисо́т, семиста́м, семьюста́ми, о семиста́х *num.* seven hundred.
се́мью *adv.* seven times.
сем|ья́, ьи́, *pl.* **~́ьи, ~е́й, ~́ьям** *f.* family.
се́м|я, ени, *pl.* **~ена́, ~я́н, ~ена́м** *nt.*
1 (*bot. and fig.*) seed.
2 (*сперма*) semen, sperm.
сена́т, а *m.* senate.
сена́тор, а *m.* senator.
сенберна́р, а *m.* St Bernard (*dog*).
Сенега́л, а *m.* Senegal.
сенега́л|ец, ьца *m.* Senegalese.
сенега́л|ка, ки *f. of* ▸ **~ец**
сенега́льский *adj.* Senegalese.
сенн|о́й *adj.* hay; **~а́я лихора́дка** hay fever.
се́н|о, а *nt.* hay.
сеноко́с, а *m.* haymaking; hayfield.
сенсацио́н|ный (~ен, ~на) *adj.* sensational.
сенса́ци|я, и *f.* sensation.
сентимента́л|ьный (~ен, ~ьна) *adj.* sentimental.
сентя́бр|ь, я́ *m.* September.
сентя́бр|ьский *adj. of* ▸ **~**
сепарати́зм, а *m.* (*pol.*) separatism.
сепарати́ст, а *m.* (*pol.*) separatist.
се́р|а, ы *f.*
1 (*chem.*) sulphur (*Br.*), sulfur (*US*).
2 (*в ушах*) earwax.
серб, а *m.* Serb, Serbian.
Се́рби|я, и *f.* Serbia.
се́рб|ка, ки *f. of* ▸ **~**
се́рбский *adj.* Serb, Serbian.
серва́нт, а *m.* sideboard.
се́рвер, а *m.* (*comput.*) server.
серви́з, а *m.* service, set; **столо́вый с.** dinner service.
серви́р|ова́ть, у́ю *impf. and pf.*: **с. стол** to lay a table.
се́рвис, а *m.* (consumer) service.
серде́чно-сосу́дистый *adj.* cardiovascular.
серде́ч|ный (~ен, ~на) *adj.*
1 of the heart (*also fig.*); (*anat.*) cardiac; **с. при́ступ** heart attack.
2 (*приём*) cordial; (*благодарность*) heartfelt, sincere.
3 (*человек*) warm, warm-hearted.
серди́т|ый (~, ~а) *adj.* (**на** + *a.*) angry (with, at, about), cross (with, about); irate.
сер|ди́ть, жу́, ~́дишь *impf.* (*of* ▸ **рас~**) to anger, make angry.
сер|ди́ться, жу́сь, ~́дишься *impf.* (*of* ▸ **рас~**) (**на** + *a.*) to be angry (with, at, about), be cross (with, about).
се́рд|це, ца, *pl.* **~ца́, ~е́ц** *nt.* heart; **приня́ть (бли́зко) к ~цу** to take to heart; **от всего́ ~ца** from the bottom of one's heart, wholeheartedly.
сердцебие́ни|е, я *nt.* palpitation; (*med.*) tachycardia.
сердцеви́н|а, ы *f.* (*плода, стебля*) core.
серебри́ст|ый (~, ~а) *adj.* silvery.
серебр|о́, а́ *nt.*
1 silver.
2 (*collect.*) silver; **столо́вое с.** silver, plate.
серё́бряный *adj.* silver.
середи́н|а, ы *f.* middle, midst; **золота́я с.** the golden mean.
серёжк|а, и *f.*
1 earring.
2 (*bot.*) catkin.
сержа́нт, а *m.* sergeant.
сериа́л, а *m.* (TV/radio) serial.
сери́йный *adj.* serial; **сери́йный но́мер** serial number; **сери́йный уби́йца** serial killer.
се́ри|я, и *f.* series; (*часть фильма*) part.
се́рн|а, ы *f.* (*zool.*) chamois.
се́рный *adj.* sulphuric (*Br.*), sulfuric (*US*); **~ая кислота́** sulphuric acid.
сероводоро́д, а *m.* (*chem.*) hydrogen sulphide (*Br.*), sulfide (*US*).
серп, а́ *m.* sickle.
серпанти́н, а *m.*
1 (*бумажная лента*) paper streamer.
2 (*дорога*) winding mountain road.
сертифика́т, а *m.* certificate.
сёрфинг, а *m.* surfing.
сёрфинги́ст, а *m.* surfer.
сёрфинги́ст|ка, ки *f. of* ▸ **~**
се́р|ый (~, ~а́, ~о) *adj.*
1 grey (*Br.*), gray (*US*).

С

2 (*fig.*) (*бесцветный*) grey (*Br.*), gray (*US*); dull; drab; **с. день** grey day.
3 (*fig., coll.*) (*необразованный*) dull, dim.

серьг|а́, и́, *pl.* **~и, серёг, ~а́м** *f.* earring.

серьёзно *adv.* seriously; **с.?** seriously?; really?

серьёз|ный (~ен, ~на) *adj.* serious.

се́сси|я, и *f.* session, sitting.

сестр|а́, ы́, *pl.* **~ы, сестёр, ~ам** *f.*
1 sister; **двоюродная с.** (first) cousin.
2 : **медици́нская с.** nurse.

сесть[1]**, ся́ду, ся́дешь,** *past* **сел, се́ла** *pf.* (*of* ▸ **сади́ться**)
1 to sit down; **с. за стол** to sit down to table; **с. рабо́тать** to get down to work.
2 (**в, на** + *a.*) to board, take; **с. на по́езд** to board a train; **с. на ло́шадь** to mount a horse.
3 (*о птице*) to alight, settle, perch; (*о самолёте*) to land.
4 (*о солнце*) to set.
5 : **с. в тюрьму́** to go to prison, jail.

сесть[2]**, ся́дет,** *past* **сел** *pf.* (*of* ▸ **сади́ться**) (*о ткани*) to shrink.

сетево́й *adj.* net, netting, mesh; (*comput.*) network; Internet.

се́тк|а, и *f.* net; (*для багажа*) (luggage) rack.

сет|ь, и, о ~и, в ~и *and* **~и́,** *pl.* **~и, ~е́й** *f.*
1 net (*also fig.*).
2 (*система*) network; system; **лока́льная с.** (*comput.*) local area network, LAN.
3 (**Сеть**) the Net (*Internet*).

Сеу́л, а *m.* Seoul.

сече́ни|е, я *nt.* section; **ке́сарево с.** Caesarean (*Br.*), Cesarean (*US*) (section); **попере́чное с.** cross section.

се́|ять, ю, ешь *impf.* (*of* ▸ **по~**) to sow (*also fig.*); **с. семена́ раздо́ра** to sow the seeds of dissension.

сжа́т|ый *p.p.p. of* ▸ **~ь** *and adj.*
1 compressed (*air, gas*).
2 (*fig.*) condensed, concise.

сжать[1]**, сожму́, сожмёшь** *pf.* (*of* ▸ **сжима́ть**) to squeeze; (*жидкость, газ; изложение*) to compress (*also fig.*); (*чью-н. руку*) to grip; **с. зу́бы** to grit one's teeth; **с. кулаки́** to clench one's fists.

сжать[2]**, сожну́, сожнёшь** *pf. of* ▸ **жать**[2]

сжа́|ться, сожму́сь, сожмёшься *pf.* (*of* ▸ **сжима́ться**)
1 (*о пальцах, зубах*) to tighten, clench.
2 (*о теле*) to contract.

сжечь, сожгу́, сожжёшь, сожгу́т, *past* **сжёг, сожгла́** *pf.* (*of* ▸ **жечь 1** *and* ▸ **сжига́ть**) to burn (up, down); (*в крематории*) to cremate.

сжива́|ться, юсь *impf. of* ▸ **сжи́ться**

сжига́|ть, ю *impf. of* ▸ **сжечь**

сжима́|ть(ся), ю(сь) *impf. of* ▸ **сжа́ть**[1]**(ся)**

сжи́|ться, ву́сь, вёшься, *past* **~лся, ~ла́сь** *pf.* (*of* ▸ **~ва́ться**) (*coll.*) (**с** + *i.*) to get used (to), get accustomed (to).

сза́ди *adv. and prep.* + *g.*
1 *adv.* from behind; behind; from the end; from the rear; **вид с.** rear view; **тре́тий ваго́н с.** the third coach from the rear.
2 *prep.* + *g.* behind.

си *nt. indecl.* (*mus.*) B.

сиби́рск|ий *adj.* Siberian; **~ая я́зва** (*med.*) anthrax.

Сиби́р|ь, и *f.* Siberia.

сига́р|а, ы *f.* cigar.

сигаре́т|а, ы *f.* cigarette.

сигна́л, а *m.* signal; **с. бе́дствия** distress signal.

сигнализа́ци|я, и *f.*
1 (*действие*) signalling (*Br.*), signaling (*US*).
2 (*устройство*) alarm system.
3 (*система*) signalling (*Br.*), signaling (*US*) system.

сигнализи́р|овать, ую *impf. and pf.*
1 to signal.
2 (+ *a. or* **о** + *p.*; *fig.*) to give warning (of).

сиде́лк|а, и *f.* (sick-)nurse.

сиде́нь|е, я *nt.* seat.

си|де́ть, жу́, ди́шь *impf.*
1 to sit; **с. на ко́рточках** to squat.
2 (*находиться*) to be; **с. (в тюрьме́)** to be in prison.
3 (**на** + *p.*) (*об одежде*) to fit, sit (on).

сид|е́ться, и́тся *impf.* (*impers.* + *d.*): **ему́,** *etc.*, **не ~и́тся до́ма** he, *etc.*, can't bear staying at home; **ей не ~и́тся на ме́сте** she can't keep still.

Си́дне|й, я *m.* Sydney.

си́з|ый (~, ~а́, ~о) *adj.* blue-grey (*Br.*), blue-gray (*US*).

си́квел, а *m.* (+ *g. or* **к** + *d.*) sequel (to).

сикх, а *m.* Sikh.

си́кхский *adj.* Sikh.

си́л|а, ы *f.*
1 strength, force; **в ~у** (+ *g.*) by virtue (of), because (of); **быть в ~ах** (+ *inf.*) to be able to, have the strength (to); **изо все́х ~, что есть ~ы** with all one's might; **че́рез ~у** with the greatest of effort; **~ой** by force; **свои́ми ~ами** unaided; **с. во́ли** willpower.
2 (*phys., tech.*) force, power; **лошади́ная с.** horsepower; **с. тя́жести, с. притяже́ния** force of gravity.
3 (*leg. and fig.*) force; **име́ющий ~у** valid; **войти́, вступи́ть в ~у** to come into force, take effect.
4 (*pl.*; *mil.*) forces; **вооружённые ~ы** armed forces.

сила́ч, а́ *m.* strong man.

силико́н, а *m.* silicone.

си́л|иться, юсь, ишься *impf.* to try very hard, make efforts.

силов|о́й *adj.* power; **~а́я устано́вка** power plant; **~ы́е структу́ры** law enforcement agencies.

си́лой *adv.* (*coll.*) by force.

сил|о́к, ка́ *m.* snare.

силуэ́т, а *m.* silhouette.

си́льно *adv.*
1 strongly; violently.
2 (*очень*) very much, greatly; badly.

си́л|ьный (~ён, ~ьна́, ~ьно, ~ьны́) *adj.* strong; powerful; **с. дождь** heavy rain; **~ьное жела́ние** intense desire; **с. за́пах** strong smell.

симбио́з, а *m.* (*biol.*) symbiosis.

си́мвол, а *m.* symbol; **с. ве́ры** (*relig.*) creed.

символизи́р|овать, ую *impf.* to symbolize.

символи́зм, а *m.* symbolism.

символи́ческий *adj.* symbolic(al).

сим-ка́рт|а, ы *f.* SIM (card).

симметри́ч|ный (~ен, ~на) *adj.* symmetrical.

симме́три|я, и *f.* symmetry.

симпатизи́р|овать, ую *impf.* (+ *d.*) to like, be fond of.

симпати́ч|ный (~ен, ~на) *adj.* (*человек*) nice, pleasant; (*лицо, голос, город*) attractive, pleasant.

симпа́ти|я, и *f.* (**к** + *d.*) liking, fondness (for); **чу́вствовать ~ю к кому́-н.** to take a liking to s.o., be drawn to s.o.

симпо́зиум, а *m.* symposium.

симпто́м, а *m.* symptom.

симули́р|овать, ую *impf. and pf.* to simulate, fake, sham.

симфони́ческий *adj.* symphonic; **с. орке́стр** symphony orchestra.

симфо́ни|я, и *f.* symphony.

синаго́г|а, и *f.* synagogue.

Сингапу́р, а *m.* Singapore.

сингапу́р|ец, ца *m.* Singaporean.

сингапу́р|ка, ки *f. of* ▸ **~ец**

сингапу́рский *adj.* Singaporean.

синдика́т, а *m.* (*econ.*) syndicate.

синдро́м, а *m.* (*med.*) syndrome.

синев|а́, ы́ *f.* blue.

синегла́з|ый (~, ~а) *adj.* blue-eyed.

си́н|ий (~ь, ~я́, ~е) *adj.* (dark) blue.

сини́ц|а, ы *f.* tit (*bird*).

сино́ним, а *m.* synonym.

сино́птик, а *m.* weather forecaster.

си́нтаксис, а *m.* syntax.

си́нтез, а *m.* synthesis.

синтеза́тор, а *m.* synthesizer.

синтези́р|овать, ую *impf. and pf.* to synthesize.

синте́тик|а, и *f.* (*collect.*) synthetic, synthetics.

синтети́ческий *adj.* synthetic.

синхро́нный *adj.* synchronous; (*перевод*) simultaneous.

синя́к, а́ *m.* bruise; **с. под гла́зом** black eye.

сиони́зм, а *m.* Zionism.

сиони́ст, а *m.* Zionist.

сиони́ст|ка, ки *f. of* ▸ **~**

си́пл|ый (~, ~а) *adj.* hoarse, husky.

сире́н|а, ы *f.* siren.

сире́невый *adj.* lilac; lilac-coloured.

сире́н|ь, и *f.* lilac.

сири́|ец, йца *m.* Syrian.

сири́|йка, йки *f. of* ▸ **~ец**

сири́йский *adj.* Syrian.

Си́ри|я, и *f.* Syria.

сиро́п, а *m.* syrup.

сирот|а́, ы́, *pl.* **~́ы** *c.g.* orphan.

сиротли́в|ый (~, ~а) *adj.* lonely.

систе́м|а, ы *f.*
1 system.
2 (*тип*) type.

систематизи́р|овать, ую *impf. and pf.* to systematize, order.

системати́ческий *adj.*
1 systematic; methodical.
2 (*регулярный*) regular.

систе́м|ный *adj. of* ▸ **~а; с. ана́лиз/анали́тик** systems analysis/analyst; **с. диск** system disk.

си́с|ька, ьки, *g. pl.* **~ек** *f.* (*coll.*) (*сосок*) nipple, tit; (*грудь*) tit.

си́т|ец, ца *m.* cotton (print); chintz.

си́т|о, а *nt.* sieve.

ситуа́ци|я, и *f.* situation.

си́филис, а *m.* (*med.*) syphilis.

сифо́н, а *m.* siphon.

сия́ни|е, я *nt.* radiance.

сия́|ть, ю *impf.* (*о солнце*) to shine; (*о человеке, от радости*) to beam; (*о лице*) to be radiant.

сказа́ни|е, я *nt.* story, tale, legend.

ска|за́ть, жу́, ~́жешь *pf. of* ▸ **говори́ть 2; как с.!** it depends; **точне́е с.** or rather.

ска|за́ться, ~́жется *pf.* (*of* ▸ **~́зываться**) (**на** + *p.*) to take its toll (on).

ска́зк|а, и *f.*
1 fairy tale.
2 (*coll.*) (*ложь*) (tall) story, fib.

ска́зочник, а *m.* storyteller.

ска́зочн|ый *adj.* fairy-tale; (*необычайный*) fabulous, fantastic; **~ое бога́тство** fabulous wealth.

сказу́ем|ое, ого *nt.* (*gram.*) predicate.

ска́зыва|ться, ется *impf. of* ▸ **сказа́ться**

скака́лк|а, и *f.* skipping rope (*Br.*), jump rope (*US*).

ска|ка́ть, чу́, ~́чешь *impf.*
1 (*pf.* **по~**) to skip, jump; **с. на одно́й ноге́** to hop.
2 (*pf.* **по~**) (*о лошади, о всаднике*) to gallop.
3 (*coll.*) (*резко изменяться*) to fluctuate.

скаков|о́й *adj.* race, racing; **с. круг, ~а́я доро́жка** racecourse; **~а́я ло́шадь** racehorse.

скаку́н, а́ *m.* racehorse.

скал|а́, ы́, *pl.* **~́ы** *f.* rock face, crag; **(отве́сная) с.** cliff.

скали́ст|ый (~, ~а) *adj.* rocky.

ска́лк|а, и *f.* (*cul.*) rolling pin.

скалола́з, а *m.* rock climber.

скальп, а *m.* scalp.

ска́льпел|ь, я *m.* scalpel.

скаме́йк|а, и *f.* bench.

скам|ья́, ьи́, *pl.* **~ьи́, ~е́й** *f.* bench; **с. подсуди́мых** (*leg.*) the dock.

сканда́л, а *m.*
1 scandal.
2 (*ссора*) row, (rowdy) scene.

сканда́л|ьный (~ен, ~ьна) *adj.*
1 (*поведение*) scandalous.
2 (*coll.*) (*человек*) rowdy, quarrelsome.
3 scandal; **~ьная хро́ника** scandal column, page (*of newspaper*).

скандина́в, а *m.* Scandinavian.

Скандина́ви|я, и *f.* Scandinavia.

С

скандина́в|ка, ки *f. of* ▸ **~**
скандина́вский *adj.* Scandinavian.
ска́нер, а *m.* (*comput., med.*) scanner.
скани́р|овать, ую *impf. and pf.* (*med., comput.*) to scan.
ска́плива|ть(ся), ю, ет(ся) *impf. of* ▸ **скопи́ть(ся)**
скарлати́н|а, ы *f.* (*med.*) scarlet fever.
ска́рмлива|ть, ю *impf. of* ▸ **скорми́ть**
скат, а *m.* (*zool.*) ray, skate.
скат|а́ть, а́ю *pf.* (*of* ▸ **~́ывать** *and* ▸ **ката́ть 3**) to roll (up).
ска́терт|ь, и, *pl.* **~и, ~е́й** *f.* tablecloth.
ска|ти́ть, чу́, ~́тишь *pf.* (*of* ▸ **~́тывать**) to roll down.
ска|ти́ться, чу́сь, ~́тишься *pf.* (*of* ▸ **~́тываться**) to roll down.
ска́тыва|ть, ю *impf. of* ▸ **ската́ть** *and* ▸ **скати́ть**
ска́тыва|ться, юсь *impf. of* ▸ **скати́ться**
скафа́ндр, а *m.* protective suit; (*водолаза*) diving suit; (*космонавта*) spacesuit.
ска́чк|а, и *f.*
1 gallop, galloping.
2 *pl.* (*состязание*) horse race; race meeting, the races; **~и с препя́тствиями** steeplechase.
скач|о́к, ка́ *m.*
1 jump, leap, bound; **~ка́ми** by leaps.
2 (*fig.*) (*цен, температуры*) leap.
сква́жин|а, ы *f.* slit, chink; **замо́чная с.** keyhole; **нефтяна́я с.** oil well.
сквер, а *m.* (*small*) public garden.
скве́р|ный (~ен, ~на́, ~но) *adj.* (*человек, поступок*) nasty; (*погода, настроение*) foul, awful.
сквозн|о́й *adj.*
1 through; **~о́е движе́ние** through traffic.
2 (*рана, отверстие*) going right through.
3 (*просвечивающий*) transparent.
сквозня́к, а́ *m.* draught (*Br.*), draft (*US*).
сквозь *prep.* + *a.* through.
скворе́|ц, ца́ *m.* starling.
сквош, а *m.* (*sport*) squash.
скейтбо́рд, а *m.* skateboard.
скейтбо́рдинг, а *m.* skateboarding.
скеле́т, а *m.* skeleton.
ске́птик, а *m.* sceptic (*Br.*), skeptic (*US*).
скепти́ческий *adj.* sceptical (*Br.*), skeptical (*US*).
ски́дк|а, и *f.*
1 reduction, discount; **со ~ой (в** + *a.*) with a reduction (of), at a discount (of).
2 (**на** + *a.*; *fig.*) allowance(s) (for); **сде́лать ~у на во́зраст** to make allowances for age.
ски́дыва|ть, ю *impf. of* ▸ **ски́нуть**
ски́|нуть, ну, нешь *pf.* (*of* ▸ **~́дывать**) (*coll.*)
1 (*одежду*) to throw off, cast off; (*снег с крыши*) to throw down.
2 (*с цены*) to knock off (*from price*).
скинхе́д, а *m.* skinhead.
ски́петр, а *m.* sceptre (*Br.*), scepter (*US*).
скипида́р, а *m.* turpentine.
скис|а́ть, а́ю *impf. of* ▸ **~́нуть**
ски́с|нуть, ну, нешь, *past* **~, ~ла** *pf.* (*of* ▸ **~а́ть**) to go sour, turn sour; (*fig.*) to lose heart.
склад[1], а *m.*
1 (*место*) storehouse; (*mil.*) depot; **това́рный с.** warehouse.
2 (*запас*) store; **с. боеприпа́сов** (*mil.*) ammunition dump.
склад[2], а *m.* (*образ*) way; **с. ума́** cast of mind, mentality.
скла́дк|а, и *f.*
1 pleat, tuck; crease; **ю́бка в ~у** pleated skirt; **с. на брю́ках** trouser crease.
2 (*на коже*) wrinkle.
складн|о́й *adj.* folding, collapsible; **~а́я крова́ть** camp bed (*Br.*), cot (*US*); **с. нож** penknife.
скла́дыва|ть(ся), ю(сь) *impf. of* ▸ **сложи́ть(ся)**
скле́ива|ть(ся), ю, ет(ся) *impf. of* ▸ **скле́ить(ся)**
скле́|ить, ю, ишь *pf.* (*of* ▸ **~ивать** *and* ▸ **кле́ить**) to stick together; to glue together.
скле́|иться, ится *pf.* (*of* ▸ **~иваться**) to stick together (*intrans.*).
склеп, а *m.* burial vault, crypt.
склеро́з, а *m.* (*med.*) sclerosis; **рассе́янный с.** multiple sclerosis.
скло́к|а, и *f.* squabble; row.
склон, а *m.* slope.
склоне́ни|е, я *nt.* (*gram.*) declension.
склон|и́ть, ю́, ~́ишь *pf.* (*of* ▸ **~я́ть**)
1 to incline, bend, bow; **с. го́лову (пе́ред** + *i.*) (*fig.*) to bow one's head (to, before).
2 (*fig.*) (*убедить*) to talk (*s.o.*) over; to win over.
склон|и́ться, ю́сь, ~́ишься *pf.* (*of* ▸ **~я́ться**)
1 to bend, bow.
2 (**к** + *d.*; *fig.*) to give in (to), yield (to).
скло́нност|ь, и *f.* (**к** + *d.*) (*к музыке, живописи*) aptitude (for); (*к полноте, меланхолии*) susceptibility (to), tendency (towards); (*к театру, к пиву*) liking, penchant (for).
скло́н|ный (~ен, ~на) *adj.* (**к** + *d.*) (*к болезни*) prone, susceptible (to); (+ *inf.*) inclined (to).
склон|я́ть, я́ю *impf. of* ▸ **~и́ть**
склон|я́ться, я́юсь *impf. of* ▸ **~и́ться**
скоб|а́, ы́, *pl.* **~́ы, ~, ~а́м** *f.* (*зажим*) clamp; (*изогнутая железная полоса*) staple.
ско́бк|а, и *f.*
1 *dim. of* ▸ **скоба́.**
2 (*знак*) bracket; *pl.* brackets, parentheses; **в ~ах** in brackets; (*fig.*) in parenthesis, by the way, incidentally.
скобл|и́ть, ю́, и́шь *impf.* to scrape; (*доску*) to plane.
ско́в|анный
1 *p.p.p. of* ▸ **~а́ть; с. льда́ми** ice-bound.
2 *adj.* (*движения, мысль*) constrained.
скова́ть, скую́, скуёшь *pf.* (*of* ▸ **ско́вывать**)
1 (*соединить*) to weld together.
2 (*заковать*) to chain; to fetter (*also fig.*).
сковород|а́, ы́, *pl.* **ско́вороды, сковоро́д, ~а́м** *f.* frying pan.
сковоро́дк|а, и *f.* (*coll.*) frying pan.
ско́выва|ть, ю *impf. of* ▸ **скова́ть**

сколáчива|ть, ю *impf. of* ▸ **сколоти́ть**

сколо|ти́ть, чу́, ~́тишь *pf.* (*of* ▸ **сколáчивать**)
1 (*соединить*) to knock together; (*изготовить*) to knock up.
2 (*fig., coll.*) (*набрать*) to get together; to scrape together.

сколь *adv.* how.

сколь|зи́ть, жу́, зи́шь *impf.* (*плавно двигаться*) to slide; to glide; (*терять устойчивость*) to slip.

ско́льз|кий (~ок, ~́кá, ~ко) *adj.* slippery (*also fig.*); (*fig.*) tricky; sensitive, delicate, treacherous.

ско́лько *interrog. and rel. adv.*
1 (*денег, хлеба*) how much; (*книг, людей*) how many; **с. сто́ит?** how much does it cost?; **с. вам лет?** how old are you?; **с. вре́мени?** what time is it?
2 = **наско́лько**

ско́лько-нибудь *adv.* any; **у вас при себе́ е́сть с.-н. де́нег?** have you any money on you?

скомáнд|овать, ую *pf. of* ▸ **комáндовать 1**

скомбини́р|овать, ую *pf. of* ▸ **комбини́ровать**

ско́мка|ть, ю *pf. of* ▸ **ко́мкать**

скомпромети́р|овать, ую *pf. of* ▸ **компромети́ровать**

сконструи́р|овать, ую *pf. of* ▸ **конструи́ровать**

сконцентри́р|овать(ся), ую(сь) *pf. of* ▸ **концентри́ровать(ся)**

скончá|ться, юсь *pf.* to pass away (= *to die*).

скопи́р|овать, ую *pf. of* ▸ **копи́ровать**

скоп|и́ть, лю́, ~́ишь *pf.* (*of* ▸ **скáпливать**) (+ *a. or g.*) (*накопить*) to save (up); to amass, pile up.

скоп|и́ться, ~́ится *pf.* (*of* ▸ **скáпливаться**)
1 to accumulate, pile up.
2 (*о людях*) to gather, collect.

скопле́ни|е, я *nt.* (*народа*) crowd; (*предметов*) accumulation, mass.

скорб|е́ть, лю́, и́шь *impf.* (**о** + *p.*) to grieve (for, over), mourn (for, over), lament.

скорб|ь, и, *pl.* **~́и, ~е́й** *f.* sorrow, grief.

скор|е́е (and **~е́й)**
1 *comp. of* ▸ **~ый** *and* ▸ **~́о; как мо́жно с.** as soon as possible.
2 *adv.* rather, sooner; **с. всего́** most likely, most probably.

скорлуп|á, ы́, *pl.* **~́ы** *f.* shell; **с. opе́ха** nutshell; **яи́чная с.** eggshell.

скорм|и́ть, лю́, ~́ишь *pf.* (*of* ▸ **скáрмливать**) (+ *d.*) to feed (to).

ско́ро *adv.*
1 (*быстро*) quickly, fast.
2 (*вскоре*) soon.

скороговóрк|а, и *f.*
1 (*быстрая речь*) rapid speech, patter.
2 (*придуманная фраза*) tongue-twister.

скоростно́й *adj.* high-speed.

ско́рост|ь, и, *pl.* **~и, ~е́й** *f.*
1 speed; velocity; rate; **со ~ью тридцать миль в час** at thirty miles per hour.
2 : **перейти́ на другу́ю с.** to change gear.

скоросшивáтел|ь, я *m.* binder, file; (*на кольцах*) ring binder.

скорпио́н, а *m.* scorpion; **С.** Scorpio (*sign of zodiac*).

скорректи́ровать *pf. of* ▸ **корректи́ровать**

скорректи́р|овать, ую *pf. of* ▸ **корректи́ровать**

ско́р|ый (~, ~á, ~о) *adj.*
1 (*быстрый*) quick, fast; rapid; **~ая по́мощь** ambulance (service); **на ~ую ру́ку** in rough-and-ready fashion.
2 (*близкий по времени*) near, forthcoming, impending; **в ~ом бу́дущем** in the near future.

скос, а *m.*
1 (*горы, берега*) slope.
2 (*предмета*) slant, bevel.

ско|си́ть[1], шу́, ~́сишь *pf. of* ▸ **коси́ть[1]**

ско|си́ть[2], шу́, си́шь *pf. of* ▸ **коси́ть[2] 1, 2**

скот, á *m.* (*collect.*) cattle; livestock.

скоти́н|а, ы *f.*
1 (*collect.*) cattle; livestock.
2 (*also m.*) (*fig., coll.*) (*грубый человек*) swine, beast.

скотобо́|йня, йни, *g. pl.* **~ен** *f.* slaughterhouse.

скотово́дств|о, а *nt.* cattle breeding, cattle raising.

ско́тский *adj.* (*coll.*) brutal, brutish, bestial.

скотч, а *m.* (*coll.*) adhesive tape; Sellotape (*Br., propr.*); Scotch tape (*US, propr.*).

скрá|сить, шу, сишь *pf.* (*of* ▸ **~шивать**) (*fig.*) to relieve; **он мно́го читáл, что́бы с. своё одино́чество** he read a lot to relieve his loneliness.

скрáшива|ть, ю *impf. of* ▸ **скрáсить**

скреб|о́к, кá *m.* scraper.

скре́жет, а *m.* (*металла*) grating, scraping; (*зубов*) gnashing.

скреп|и́ть, лю́, и́шь *pf.* (*of* ▸ **~ля́ть**)
1 (*соединить*) to fasten (together); (*tech.*) to clamp, brace; (*дружбу*) to cement.
2 (*удостоверить*) to countersign, ratify.

скре́пк|а, и *f.* paper clip.

скрепля́|ть, ю *impf. of* ▸ **скрепи́ть**

скре|сти́, бу́, бёшь, *past* **~̈б, ~блá** *impf.* (*о кошке, ногтями*) to scratch, claw; (*дерево*) to sand; (*кастрюлю*) to scour.

скре|сти́сь, бу́сь, бёшься, *past* **~̈бся, ~блáсь** *impf.* to scratch, make a scratching noise.

скре|сти́ть, щу́, сти́шь *pf.* (*of* ▸ **~́щивать**)
1 to cross; **с. мечи́, с. шпáги** (**с** + *i.*) to cross swords (with) (*also fig.*).
2 (*biol.*) to cross, interbreed.

скрест|и́ться, и́тся *pf.* (*of* ▸ **скре́щиваться**)
1 to cross; (*fig.*) to clash.
2 (*biol.*) to cross, interbreed.

скре́щива|ть(ся), ю, ет(ся) *impf. of* ▸ **скрести́ть(ся)**

скрип, а *m.* (*двери*) squeak, creak; (*снега*) crunch.

скрипа́ч, а́ *m.* violinist.
скрипа́ч|ка, ки *f. of* ▸ ~
скрип|е́ть, лю́, и́шь *impf.* (*of* ▸ **скри́пнуть**) (*о двери*) to squeak, creak; (*о снеге*) to crunch.
скри́пк|а, и *f.* violin; **пе́рвая с.** first violin; (*fig., coll.*) first fiddle.
скри́пн|уть, у, ешь *inst. pf. of* ▸ **скрипе́ть**
скро|и́ть, ю́, и́шь *pf. of* ▸ **крои́ть**
скро́мност|ь, и *f.* modesty.
скро́м|ный (~ен, ~на́, ~но) *adj.* modest.
скрупулёз|ный (~ен, ~на) *adj.* scrupulous.
скру|ти́ть, чу́, ~́тишь *pf.* (*of* ▸ **крути́ть 1** *and* ▸ **~́чивать**)
1 (*верёвки*) to twist (together); (*папиросу*) to roll.
2 (*руки*) to bind, tie up.
скру́чива|ть, ю *impf. of* ▸ **скрути́ть**
скрыва́|ть, ю *impf. of* ▸ **скрыть**
скрыва́|ться, юсь *impf.*
1 *impf. of* ▸ **скры́ться.**
2 (*impf. only*) to lie in hiding; to lie low.
скры́т|ный (~ен, ~на) *adj.* secretive.
скры́т|ый *p.p.p. of* ▸ **~ь** *and adj.* secret, concealed; **с. смысл** hidden meaning.
скр|ыть, о́ю, о́ешь *pf.* (*of* ▸ **~ыва́ть**) (**от** + *g.*) to hide (from), conceal (from).
скр|ы́ться, о́юсь, о́ешься *pf.* (*of* ▸ **~ыва́ться 1**) (**от** + *g.*)
1 (*спрятаться*) to hide (o.s.) (from); (*о преступнике*) to go into hiding.
2 (*удалиться*) to steal away (from), escape, give the slip.
3 (*исчезнуть*) to disappear, vanish.
ску́д|ный (~ен, ~на́, ~но) *adj.* (*средства, обед*) meagre (*Br.*), meager (*US*); (*урожай*) poor; (*знания, сведения*) scanty; (*растительность*) sparse.
скудоу́м|ный (~ен, ~на) *adj.* feeble-minded.
ску́к|а, и *f.* boredom, tedium; **кака́я с.!** what a bore!
скул|а́, ы́, *pl.* **~́ы** *f.* cheekbone.
скул|и́ть, ю́, и́шь *impf.* to whine, whimper (*also fig.*).
ску́льптор, а *m.* sculptor.
скульпту́р|а, ы *f.* sculpture.
ску́мбри|я, и *f.* mackerel.
скунс, а *m.* skunk.
скуп|а́ть, а́ю *impf. of* ▸ **~и́ть**
скуп|и́ть, лю́, ~́ишь *pf.* (*of* ▸ **~а́ть**) to buy up.
скуп|о́й (~, ~а́, ~о, ~́ы) *adj.*
1 stingy, miserly; **с. на слова́** sparing of words.
2 (*fig.*) (*недостаточный*) inadequate.
ску́пост|ь, и *f.* stinginess, miserliness.
ску́тер, а *m.* (*катер*) outboard motor boat; (*мотороллер*) scooter.
скуча́|ть, ю *impf.*
1 to be bored.
2 (**по** + *d.*) to miss, yearn (for).
ску́ч|ный (~ен, ~на́, ~но) *adj.*
1 (*книга*) boring, tedious, dull.
2 (*человек, взгляд*) bored; *as pred.* **мне,** *etc.*, **~но** I, *etc.*, am bored.
ску́ша|ть, ю *pf. of* ▸ **ку́шать**
слабе́|ть, ю *impf. of* ▸ **о~**
слаби́тельн|ый *adj.* (*med.*) laxative; *as n.* **~ое, ~ого** *nt.* laxative.
слабоалкого́льный *adj.* low-alcohol.
слабоне́рв|ный (~ен, ~на) *adj.* having weak nerves; nervous.
сла́бост|ь, и *f.*
1 weakness, feebleness.
2 (**к** + *d.*) (*наклонность*) weakness (for).
слабоу́ми|е, я *nt.* mental handicap; **ста́рческое с.** senile dementia.
слабоу́м|ный (~ен, ~на) *adj.* mentally handicapped.
сла́б|ый (~, ~а́, ~о) *adj.* (*человек, характер, зрение, воля*) weak; (*голос*) feeble; (*верёвка*) slack, loose; (*ветер, боль, надежда*) slight; (*ученик, знания*) weak, poor; (*ребёнок, здоровье*) delicate; **~ое ме́сто** weak point; **с. пол** the weaker sex.
сла́в|а, ы *f.*
1 glory; fame; **во ~у** (+ *g.*) to the glory (of); **на ~у** (*coll.*) wonderfully well, excellently; (*as int.*, + *d.*) hurrah (for)!; **с. бо́гу** thank God, thank goodness.
2 (*репутация*) name, reputation; **до́брая с.** good name; **дурна́я с.** infamy.
3 (*coll.*) (*слухи*) rumour (*Br.*), rumor (*US*).
сла́в|иться, люсь, ишься *impf.* (+ *i.*) to be famous (for), be renowned (for); to have a reputation (for).
сла́в|ный (~ен, ~на́, ~но) *adj.*
1 glorious; famous, renowned.
2 (*coll.*) splendid; lovely; **с. ма́лый** nice chap.
славян|и́н, и́на, *pl.* **~́е, ~́** *m.* Slav.
славя́н|ка, ки *f. of* ▸ **~и́н**
славянофи́л, а *m.* Slavophil(e).
славя́нский *adj.* Slavonic; Slavic; Slav.
слага́|ть, ю *impf. of* ▸ **сложи́ть² 2**
сла́д|кий (~ок, ~ка́, ~ко) *adj.* sweet (*also fig.*); *as n.* **~кое, ~кого** *nt.* dessert.
сладкоёжк|а, и *c.g.* (*coll.*) (person with a) sweet tooth.
сладостра́ст|ный (~ен, ~на) *adj.* sensual, voluptuous.
сла́дост|ь, и *f.*
1 sweetness.
2 *pl.* (*кондитерские изделия*) sweets, sweetmeats.
сла́|зить, жу, зишь *pf.* (*coll.*) to go, climb; **с. в подва́л за дрова́ми** to go down to the cellar for logs.
слайд, а *m.* slide, transparency.
сла́лом, а *m.* (*sport*) slalom.
сла́н|ец, ца *m.* (*min.*) slate.
сласт|ь, и, *pl.* **~́и, ~е́й** *f.* sweets, sweetmeats.
слать, шлю, шлёшь *impf.* to send.
сла́ще *comp. of* ▸ **сла́дкий**
сле́ва *adv.* (**от** + *g.*) on the left (of), to the left (of); **с. напра́во** from left to right.
слегка́ *adv.* lightly, gently; (*немного*) slightly; **с. суту́литься** to stoop slightly.
след, а, *pl.* **~ы́** *m.*
1 (*отпечаток*) track; (*ноги*) footprint,

footstep; **идти́ по чьим-н. ~а́м** (*fig.*) to follow in s.o.'s footsteps; **напа́сть на чей-н. с.** to get on s.o.'s trail.
2 (*fig.*) (*признак*) trace, sign, vestige.

сле|ди́ть, жу́, ди́шь *impf.* (**за** + *i.*)
1 (*смотреть*) to watch; to follow; **с. (глаза́ми) за полётом мяча́** to follow (with one's eyes) the flight of a ball.
2 (*fig.*) to follow; to keep up (with); **с. за междунаро́дными собы́тиями** to keep up with international affairs.
3 (*заботиться*) to look after; to keep an eye (on); **с. за детьми́** to look after children; **с. за поря́дком** to keep order; **с. за тем, что́бы** to see to it that.

сле́дователь|ь, я *m.* investigator.

сле́довательно *conj.* consequently, therefore, hence.

сле́д|овать[1], ую *impf.* (*of* ▸ **по~**)
1 (**за** + *i.*) to follow, go after.
2 (+ *d.*) (*поступать подобно кому-н.*) to follow; (*поступать согласно чему-н.*) to follow; to comply (with); **с. пра́вилам** to conform to the rules.
3 (*impf. only*) (**до** + *g.*, **в** + *a.*) (*отправляться*) to be bound (for); **э́тот по́езд ~ует в Варша́ву** this train is (bound) for Warsaw.
4 (*impf. only*) (*быть следствием*) to follow; to result; **из э́того ~ует, что мы оши́блись** it follows from this that we were mistaken.

сле́д|овать[2], ует *impf.* (*impers.*) (+ *d. and inf.*) (*нужно, должно*) ought, should; **вам ~ует обрати́ться к ре́ктору** you should approach the rector; **как и ~овало ожида́ть** as was to be expected; **как ~ует** as it should be, properly, well and truly.

сле́дом *adv.* (**за** + *i.*) immediately (after, behind); **идти́ с. за кем-н.** to follow s.o. close(ly).

следопы́т, а *m.* pathfinder, tracker.

сле́дстви|е[1], я *nt.* (*результат*) consequence, result; **причи́на и с.** cause and effect.

сле́дстви|е[2], я *nt.* (*leg.*) (*расследование*) investigation.

сле́д|ующий *pres. part. act. of* ▸ **~овать** *and adj.* following, next; **на с. день** next day; **на ~ующей неде́ле** next week.

сле́жк|а, и *f.* surveillance; shadowing.

слез|а́, ы́, *pl.* **~̈ы, ~̈, ~а́м** *f.* tear; **довести́ до ~̈** to reduce to tears.

слеза́|ть, ю *impf. of* ▸ **слезть**

слез|и́ться, и́тся *impf.* to water; **её глаза́ ~и́лись** her eyes were watering.

слез|ть, у, ешь, *past* **~, ~́ла** *pf.* (*of* ▸ **~а́ть**) (**с** + *g.*)
1 (*с дерева*) to come down (from), get down (from); (*с лошади, велосипеда*) to get off; to dismount (from).
2 (*coll.*) (*с автобуса, трамвая*) to get off.
3 (*coll.*) (*о краске, коже*) to come off, peel.

сленг, а *m.* slang.

слеп|е́нь, ня́ *m.* gadfly, horsefly.

слеп|е́ц, ца́ *m.* blind man.

слеп|и́ть[1], лю́, и́шь *impf.* to blind; to dazzle.

слеп|и́ть[2], лю́, ~́ишь *pf. of* ▸ **лепи́ть 1**

сле́п|нуть, ну, нешь, *past* **~, ~ла** *impf.* (*of* ▸ **осле́пнуть**) to go blind.

слеп|о́й (~, ~а́, ~́о) *adj.* blind (*also fig.*); **с. на оди́н глаз** blind in one eye; *as n.* **с., ~о́го** *m.*; **~а́я, ~о́й** *f.* blind person; (*pl., collect.*) the blind.

слепот|а́, ы́ *f.* blindness (*also fig.*).

сле́сар|ь, я *m.* metal worker; (*специалист по замкам*) locksmith; (*специалист по починке*) repair man.

слета́|ть[1], ю *pf.* to fly (*there and back*).

слета́|ть[2], ю *impf. of* ▸ **слете́ть**

слет|а́ться, а́юсь *impf. of* ▸ **~е́ться**

сле|те́ть, чу́, ти́шь *pf.* (*of* ▸ **~та́ть[2]**) (**с** + *g.*).
1 (*вниз*) to fly down (from).
2 (*coll.*) (*упасть*) to fall down, fall off; **с. с ло́шади** to fall from a horse.
3 (*улететь*) to fly away.

слет|е́ться, и́тся *pf.* (*of* ▸ **~а́ться**) to fly together; (*о птицах*) to congregate.

слечь, сля́гу, сля́жешь, *past* **слёг, слегла́** *pf.* to take to one's bed.

сли́в|а, ы *f.*
1 (*плод*) plum.
2 (*дерево*) plum tree.

слива́|ть(ся), ю(сь) *impf. of* ▸ **сли́ть(ся)**

сли́в|ки, ок *no sg.* cream (*also fig.*).

сли́вочн|ый *adj.* cream; creamy; **~ое ма́сло** butter.

сли|за́ть, жу́, ~́жешь *pf.* (*of* ▸ **~́зывать**) to lick off.

сли́зист|ый (~, ~а) *adj.*
1 slimy.
2 (*anat.*) mucous.

слизня́к, а́ *m.* slug.

сли́зыва|ть, ю *impf. of* ▸ **слиза́ть**

сли́з|ь, и *f.*
1 slime.
2 (*anat.*) mucus.

слип|а́ться, а́ется *impf. of* ▸ **~́нуться**

сли́п|нуться, нется, *past* **~ся, ~лась** *pf.* (*of* ▸ **~а́ться**) to stick together.

сли́тный *adj.* united, continuous.

сли́т|ок, ка *m.* ingot, bar; **зо́лото в ~ках** gold bullion.

слить, солью́, сольёшь, *past* **слил, слила́, сли́ло** *pf.* (*of* ▸ **слива́ть**)
1 (*вылить*) to pour out; (*отлить*) to pour off.
2 (*вместе*) to pour together; (*fig.*) to merge, amalgamate.

сли́ться, солью́сь, сольёшься, *past* **сли́лся, слила́сь** *pf.* (*of* ▸ **слива́ться**)
1 (*о ручьях*) to flow together.
2 (*fig.*) (*о голосах*) to blend, mingle; (*о концернах*) to merge, amalgamate.

слич|а́ть, а́ю *impf. of* ▸ **~и́ть**

слич|и́ть, у́, и́шь *pf.* (*of* ▸ **~а́ть**) (**с** + *i.*) to check (with, against).

сли́шком *adv.* too; (*перед глаголами*) too much; **э́то с.!** this is too much!

слия́ни|е, я *nt.*
1 (*рек*) confluence.
2 (*fig.*) (*голосов*) blending; merging; (*концернов*) amalgamation, merger.

слова́к, а *m.* Slovak.

Слова́ки|я, и *f.* Slovakia.

слова́р|ь, я́ *m.*
1 (*книга*) dictionary; (*глоссарий*) glossary,

С

vocabulary (*to particular text*).
2 (*collect.*) (*запас слов*) vocabulary.
слова́цкий *adj.* Slovak, Slovakian.
слова́|чка, чки *f. of* ▸ **~к**
слове́н|ец, ца *m.* Slovene.
Слове́ни|я, и *f.* Slovenia.
слове́н|ка, ки *f. of* ▸ **~ец**
слове́нский *adj.* Slovene, Slovenian.
слове́сный *adj.* verbal, oral.
сло́вно *conj.*
1 (*как будто*) as if.
2 (*как*) like, as.
сло́в|о, а, *pl.* **~а́** *nt.*
1 word; **другими ~а́ми** in other words; **одни́м ~ом** in a word; **на ~а́х** (*i*) (*устно*) by word of mouth, (*ii*) (*только в разговоре*) empty words; **сдержа́ть с.** to keep one's word.
2 (*речь*) speech, speaking; **свобо́да ~а** freedom of speech.
3 (*выступление*) speech, address; **дать, предоста́вить с.** (+ *d.*) to give the floor, to call upon to speak.
словоблу́ди|е, я *nt.* (mere) verbiage, phrase-mongering.
сло́вом *adv.* in a word, in short.
словоохо́тлив|ый (~, ~а) *adj.* talkative, loquacious.
словосочета́ни|е, я *nt.* combination of words.
слог, а, *pl.* **~и, ~о́в** *m.* syllable.
сло́ган, а *m.* slogan.
слоён|ый *adj.*: **~ое те́сто** puff pastry.
сложе́ни|е, я *nt.* (*чисел*) adding; (*math.*) addition.
слож|и́ть[1]**, у́, ~ишь** *pf.* (*of* ▸ **скла́дывать**)
1 (*положить вместе*) to put (together); (*в кучу*) to pile, stack; **с. свои́ ве́щи в чемода́н** to pack one's things in a suitcase.
2 (*числа*) to add (up).
3 (*лист, платье*) to fold (up).
4 *pf. of* ▸ **класть 2**
слож|и́ть[2]**, у́, ~ишь** *pf.*
1 (*impf.* **скла́дывать**) (*сняв, положить*) to take off, put down, set down.
2 (*impf.* **слага́ть**) (**с** + *g.*; *fig.*) to relieve o.s. (of); **с. ору́жие** to lay down one's arms; **с. с себя́ обя́занности** to resign.
слож|и́ться[1]**, у́сь, ~ишься** *pf.* (*of* ▸ **скла́дываться**) (**с** + *i.*) to club together (with); to pool one's resources.
слож|и́ться[2]**, ~ится** *pf.* (*of* ▸ **скла́дываться**) (*о характере; об убеждении*) to form; (*об обстоятельствах*) to turn out; (*о ситуации*) to arise.
сло́жност|ь, и *f.* complication; complexity.
сло́ж|ный (~ен, ~на́, ~но, ~ны́) *adj.*
1 (*составной*) compound; complex.
2 (*трудный*) complicated, complex; (*узор, композиция*) intricate.
сло|й, я, *pl.* **~и́** *m.* layer; stratum (*also fig.*); **все ~и́ населе́ния** all sections of the population.
сло́йк|а, и *f.* (*булочка*) puff.
слома́|ть(ся), ю(сь) *pf. of* ▸ **лома́ть(ся)**
слом|и́ть, лю́, ~ишь *pf.* to break, smash; (*fig.*) to overcome; **~я го́лову** (*coll.*) like mad, at breakneck speed.
слон, а́ *m.*
1 elephant.
2 (*в шахматах*) bishop (*chess*).
слоня́|ться, юсь *impf.* (*coll.*) to loiter about, mooch about (*Br.*).
слуг|а́, и́, *pl.* **~и, ~** *m.* servant.
служа́нк|а, и *f.* maid.
слу́жащ|ий, его *m.* office worker, white-collar worker.
слу́жб|а, ы *f.*
1 service; (*работа*) work; employment; **быть на ~е у кого́-н.** to work for s.o.
2 (*специальная область работы*) (special) service.
3 (*eccl.*) (*богослужение*) church service.
служе́бн|ый *adj.*
1 *adj. of* ▸ **слу́жба;** office; official; work; **с. автомоби́ль** company car; **~ое вре́мя** office hours; **~ая пое́здка** business trip.
2 (*вспомогательный*) auxiliary; secondary.
служ|и́ть, у́, ~ишь *impf.* (*of* ▸ **по~**)
1 (+ *d.*) to serve, devote o.s. (to).
2 (*no pf.*) (+ *i.*) (*работать*) to serve (as); to work (as), be employed (as), be; **с. в а́рмии** to serve in the Army.
3 (+ *i. or* **для** + *g.*) (*функционировать*) to serve (for), do (for), be used (for); **гости́ная ~ит нам и спа́льней** our sitting room serves also as a bedroom; **с. доказа́тельством** (+ *g.*) to serve as evidence (of).
4 (*быть полезным*) to be in use, do duty, serve; **мой ста́рый плащ ещё ~ит** my old mac(k)intosh is still in use.
5 (*pf.* **от~**) (*eccl.*) to celebrate; to conduct, officiate (at); **с. обе́дню** to celebrate mass.
слух, а *m.*
1 hearing; (*mus.*) ear; **игра́ть на с., по ~у** to play by ear.
2 (*известие*) rumour (*Br.*), rumor (*US*); **прошёл с., что** it was rumoured (*Br.*), rumored (*US*) that.
слухово́й *adj.* auditory, aural; **с. аппара́т** hearing aid.
слу́ча|й, я *m.*
1 case; **во вся́ком ~е** in any case, anyhow, anyway; **ни в ко́ем ~е** in no circumstances; **в лу́чшем, ху́дшем ~е** at best, at worst; **в проти́вном ~е** otherwise; **в тако́м ~е** in that case; **на вся́кий с.** to be on the safe side, just in case; **по ~ю** (+ *g.*) by reason (of), on account (of), on the occasion (of).
2 (*происшествие*) event, incident, occurrence; **несча́стный с.** accident.
3 (*возможность*) opportunity, occasion, chance; **упусти́ть удо́бный с.** to miss an opportunity; **при ~е** when an opportunity presents itself.
4 (*случайность*) chance.
случа́йно *adv.*
1 by chance, by accident, accidentally; **я с. подслу́шал их разгово́р** I happened to overhear their conversation.
2 (*как вводное слово*) by any chance; **вы, с., не ви́дели моего́ зо́нтика?** have you by any chance seen my umbrella?
случа́йност|ь, и *f.* chance; **по**

С

счастли́вой ~и by a lucky chance, by sheer luck.

случа́|йный (~ен, ~йна) *adj.*
1 (*ошибка*) accidental; (*встреча, разговор*) chance; (*гость, удача*) unexpected.
2 (*расходы, поручения*) incidental; **с. за́работок** casual earnings.

случ|а́ться, а́ется *impf. of* ▸ **~и́ться**

случ|и́ться, и́тся *pf.* (*of* ▸ **~а́ться**) to happen, come about; **что бы ни ~и́лось** whatever happens, come what may.

слу́шани|е, я *nt.* (*leg.*) hearing.

слу́шател|ь, я *m.*
1 listener; (*pl.*; *collect.*) audience.
2 (*студент*) student.

слуша́тель|ница, ницы *f. of* ▸ **~**

слу́ша|ть, ю *impf.* (*of* ▸ **по~** *and* ▸ **про~ 1**)
1 (*музыку, радио*) to listen (to); **с. ле́кцию** to attend a lecture; **~й(те)!** (*coll.*) listen!, look here!; **~ю!** at your service!; very good!; (*по телефону*) hello!
2 (*изучать*) to attend lectures (on), go to lectures (on).
3 (*слушаться*) to listen (to), obey.
4 (*leg.*) to hear.

слу́ша|ться, юсь *impf.* (*of* ▸ **по~**) to listen (to), obey; **~юсь!** (*mil.*) yes, sir! (*indicating readiness to carry out order*).

слы́ш|ать, у, ишь *impf.* (*of* ▸ **у~**)
1 to hear; **~ишь, ~ите** (*coll.*) do you hear? (*emph. command or direction*).
2 (*impf. only*) (*обладать слухом*) to have the sense of hearing; **не с.** to be hard of hearing.

слы́ш|аться, ится *impf.* (*of* ▸ **по~**) to be heard; to be audible.

слы́шно *as pred., impers.*
1 one can hear; **бы́ло с., как она́ рыда́ла** one could hear her sobbing.
2 (*coll.*): **что с.?** what news?, any news?; **о них ничего́ не с.** nothing has been heard of them.

слы́ш|ный (~ен, ~на́, ~но, ~́ны) *adj.* audible.

слюд|а́, ы́ *f.* mica.

слюн|а́, ы́ *f.* saliva.

сля́кот|ь, и *f.* slush.

см (*abbr. of* **сантиме́тр**) cm, centimetre(s) (*Br.*), centimeter(s) (*US*).

см. (*abbr. of* **смотри́**) see, *vide*.

сма́|зать, жу, жешь *pf.* (*of* ▸ **~зывать**)
1 to lubricate; to grease; **с. йо́дом** to paint with iodine.
2 (*размазать*) to smudge; (*стереть*) to rub off.
3 (*fig., coll.*) (*лишить чёткости*) to slur (over).

сма́зк|а, и *f.*
1 (*действие*) lubrication; greasing.
2 (*вещество*) lubricant; grease.

сма́зыва|ть, ю *impf. of* ▸ **сма́зать**

смак|ова́ть, у́ю *impf.* (*coll.*) to savour (*Br.*), savor (*US*); to relish (*also fig.*).

сманеври́р|овать, ую *pf. of* ▸ **маневри́ровать**

сма́тыва|ть, ю *impf. of* ▸ **смота́ть**

сма́тыва|ться, юсь *impf. of* ▸ **смота́ться**

сма́хива|ть[1], ю *impf. of* ▸ **смахну́ть**

сма́хива|ть[2], ю *impf.* (**на** + *a.*; *coll.*) to look like, resemble.

смах|ну́ть, ну́, нёшь *pf.* (*of* ▸ **~́ивать[1]**) to brush (away, off), flick (away, off); **с. пыль** (**с** + *g.*) to dust.

сма́чива|ть, ю *impf. of* ▸ **смочи́ть**

сме́ж|ный (~ен, ~на) *adj.* (*комнаты, участки*) adjacent, adjoining; (*профессии, понятия*) related.

смека́лк|а, и *f.* (*coll.*) native wit; nous; sharpness.

смек|а́ть, а́ю *impf.* (*of* ▸ **~ну́ть**) (*coll.*) to see the point (of), grasp.

смек|ну́ть, ну́, нёшь *pf. of* ▸ **~а́ть**

сме́ло *adv.*
1 boldly.
2 (*с полной уверенностью*) confidently; **я могу́ с. сказа́ть** I can safely say.

сме́лост|ь, и *f.* boldness, audacity; **взять на себя́ с.** (+ *inf.*) to take the liberty (of), make bold (to).

сме́л|ый (~, ~а́, ~о, ~́ы) *adj.* bold, audacious, daring.

сме́н|а, ы *f.*
1 (*действие*) changing, change; (*замена*) replacement; **с. карау́ла** changing of the guard.
2 (*collect.*) replacements; successors; (*mil.*) relief.
3 (*на заводе*) shift; **у́тренняя, дневна́я, вече́рняя с.** morning, day, night shift.
4 (*белья*) change.

смен|и́ть, ю́, ~́ишь *pf.* (*of* ▸ **~я́ть**)
1 to change; (*работника*) to replace; (*mil.*) to relieve; **с. бельё** to change linen.
2 (*заместить*) to replace, relieve, succeed (s.o.).

смен|и́ться, ю́сь, ~́ишься *pf.* (*of* ▸ **~я́ться**)
1 to hand over; (*mil.*) to be relieved; **с. с дежу́рства** to go off duty.
2 (+ *i.*) to give way (to); **дневно́й зно́й ~и́лся прохла́дой ве́чера** the day's heat gave way to the coolness of evening.

сме́нн|ый *adj.* shift; **~ая рабо́та** shift work.

смен|я́ть, я́ю *impf. of* ▸ **~и́ть**

смен|я́ться, я́юсь *impf. of* ▸ **смени́ться**

сме́р|ить, ю, ишь *pf. of* ▸ **ме́рить 1**

смерк|а́ться, а́ется *impf.* (*of* ▸ **~́нуться**) to get dark; **~а́лось** it was getting dark, twilight was falling.

сме́рк|нуться, нется *pf. of* ▸ **~а́ться**

смерте́льно *adv.*
1 mortally; **с. ра́ненный** mortally wounded.
2 (*coll.*) (*очень*) extremely, terribly.

смерте́л|ьный (~ен, ~ьна) *adj.*
1 (*борьба, враг*) mortal, deadly.
2 (*coll., fig.*) (*сильный, крайний*) deadly, extreme.

сме́ртност|ь, и *f.* mortality, death rate.

сме́рт|ный (~ен, ~на) *adj.*
1 mortal; *as n.* **с., ~ного** *m.* mortal; **просто́й с.** ordinary mortal.
2 deadly, death; **~ная казнь** capital punishment, death penalty; **с. пригово́р** death sentence.

смертоно́с|ный (~ен, ~на) *adj.* mortal, fatal, lethal.
смерт|ь, и, *pl.* **~и, ~е́й** *f.* death; **умере́ть свое́й ~ью** to die a natural death; **до́ ~и** (*fig., coll.*) to death; **быть при́ ~и** to be dying.
смерч, а *m.* tornado, whirlwind.
смеси́тел|ь, я *m.* mixer; (*кран*) mixer tap (*Br.*), mixing faucet (*US*).
сме|сти́, ту́, тёшь, *past* **~л, ~ла́** *pf.* (*of* ▸ **~та́ть**)
1 to sweep off, sweep away; **с. кро́шки со стола́** to sweep crumbs off the table.
2 (*метя, собрать*) to sweep into, together.
сме|сти́ть, щу́, сти́шь *pf.* (*of* ▸ **~ща́ть**)
1 to displace, remove; to shift, move.
2 (*fig.*) (*уволить*) to remove, dismiss.
сме|сти́ться, щу́сь, сти́шься *pf.* (*of* ▸ **~ща́ться**) to change position, become displaced.
смес|ь, и *f.* mixture; (*продукт*) blend.
смета́н|а, ы *f.* sour cream.
смета́|ть, ю *pf. of* ▸ **смести́**
сме|ть, ю *impf.* (*of* ▸ **по~**) to dare; to make bold; **не ~й(те)!** don't you dare!
смех, а (у) *m.* laughter; laugh.
смехотво́р|ный (~ен, ~на) *adj.* laughable, ludicrous.
смеш|а́ть, а́ю *pf.* (*of* ▸ **меша́ть² 2, 3** *and* ▸ **~ивать**)
1 (**с** + *i.*) (*соединить*) to mix (with), blend (with).
2 (*перепутать, путать*) to mix up.
смеш|а́ться, а́юсь *pf.* (*of* ▸ **~иваться**)
1 (*о красках*) to mix, blend; to mingle; **с. с толпо́й** to mingle in the crowd.
2 (*прийти в беспорядок; перепутаться*) to become confused, get mixed up.
сме́шива|ть(ся), ю(сь) *impf. of* ▸ **смеша́ть(ся)**
смеш|и́ть, у́, и́шь *impf.* (*of* ▸ **на~**) to make (s.o.) laugh.
смеш|но́й (~о́н, ~на́) *adj.*
1 funny; *as pred.*: **~но́** it is funny; **вам ~но́?** do you find it funny?
2 (*нелепый*) absurd, ridiculous, ludicrous.
смеш|о́к, ка́ *m.* (*coll.*) chuckle; giggle.
смеща́|ть(ся), ю(сь) *impf. of* ▸ **смести́ть(ся)**
смеще́ни|е, я *nt.*
1 displacement; shift, removal.
2 (*увольнение*) dismissal.
сме|я́ться, ю́сь, ёшься *impf.*
1 to laugh; **с. шу́тке** to laugh at a joke.
2 (**над** + *i.*) to laugh (at), mock, make fun (of).
3 (*coll.*) (*говорить в шутку*) to joke, say in jest.
СМИ *pl. indecl.* (*abbr. of* **сре́дства ма́ссовой информа́ции**) mass media.
смире́ни|е, я *nt.* humbleness, humility, meekness.
смир|и́ться, ю́сь, и́шься *pf.* (*of* ▸ **~я́ться**) to submit; to resign o.s.
сми́р|ный (~ен, ~на́, ~но) *adj.* quiet; submissive.
смир|я́ться, я́юсь *impf. of* ▸ **~и́ться**
смо́кинг, а *m.* dinner jacket.
смол|а́, ы́, *pl.* **~ы** *f.* resin; (*дёготь*) pitch, tar.
смоли́ст|ый (~, ~а) *adj.* resinous.
смолк|а́ть, а́ю *impf. of* ▸ **~нуть**
смо́лк|нуть, ну, нешь, *past* **~, ~ла** *pf.* (*of* ▸ **~а́ть**) (*о голосе, о человеке*) to fall silent; (*о шуме*) to cease.
смоло́ть, смелю́, сме́лешь *pf. of* ▸ **моло́ть**
смолч|а́ть, у́, и́шь *pf.* to hold one's tongue.
смонти́р|овать, ую *pf. of* ▸ **монти́ровать**
сморка́|ть, ю *impf.* (*of* ▸ **вы́~**): **с. нос** to blow one's nose.
сморка́|ться, юсь *impf.* (*of* ▸ **вы́~**) to blow one's nose.
сморо́дин|а, ы *no pl., f.*
1 (*кустарник*) currant bush.
2 (*collect.*) (*ягоды*) currants; **бе́лая, кра́сная, чёрная с.** white currants, redcurrants, blackcurrants.
смо́рщен|ный (~, ~а) *adj.* wrinkled.
смо́рщ|иться, усь, ишься *pf. of* ▸ **мо́рщиться**
смота́|ть, ю *pf.* (*of* ▸ **сма́тывать**) to wind, reel; (*coll.*): **с. у́дочки** to take to one's heels, make off.
смота́|ться, юсь *pf.* (*of* ▸ **сма́тываться**) (*coll.*)
1 (*сходить*) to dash (there and back).
2 (*убраться*) to take to one's heels, make off.
смотр|е́ть, ю́, ~ишь *impf.* (*of* ▸ **по~**)
1 (**на** + *a.*, **в** + *a.*) to look (at); **с. в окно́** to look out of the window; **с. в глаза́, в лицо́** (+ *d.*) to look in the face.
2 (*фильм, пьесу*) to see; (*фильм, телевидение*) to watch; (*книгу, журнал*) to look through.
3 (**за** + *i.*) to look (after); to be in charge (of), supervise; **с. за поря́дком** to keep order.
4 : **~я́ (где, как, *etc.*)** it depends (where, how, *etc.*); **~я́ (по** + *d.*) depending (on), in accordance (with).
смотр|е́ться, ю́сь, ~ишься *impf.* (*of* ▸ **по~**)
1 to look at o.s.; **с. в зе́ркало** to look at o.s. in the mirror.
2 (*no pf.*) (*coll.*) (*хорошо выглядеть*) to look good.
смоч|и́ть, у́, ~ишь *pf.* (*of* ▸ **сма́чивать**) to damp, wet, moisten.
смо|чь, гу́, ~жешь, *past* **~г, ~гла́** *pf. of* ▸ **мочь**
смоше́нничa|ть, ю *pf. of* ▸ **моше́нничать**
смрад, а *m.* stink, stench.
сму́гл|ый (~, ~а́, ~о, ~ы) *adj.* swarthy.
сму|ти́ть, щу́, ти́шь *pf.* (*of* ▸ **~ща́ть**) to embarrass, confuse.
сму|ти́ться, щу́сь, ти́шься *pf.* (*of* ▸ **~ща́ться**) to be embarrassed, be confused.
сму́т|ный (~ен, ~на́, ~но) *adj.* vague; confused; **~ные воспомина́ния** dim recollections.
смуща́|ть(ся), ю(сь) *impf. of* ▸ **смути́ть(ся)**
смуще́ни|е, я *nt.* embarrassment, confusion.
смыва́|ть(ся), ю(сь) *impf. of* ▸ **смы́ть(ся)**

смыка́|ть(ся), ю, ет(ся) *impf. of* ▸**сомкну́ть(ся)**

смысл, а *m.*
1 sense, meaning; **прямо́й, перено́сный с.** literal, metaphorical sense; **в изве́стном ~е** in a sense; **в ~е** (+ *g.*) as regards.
2 (*цель, разумное основание*) sense, point; **име́ть с.** to make sense; **нет никако́го ~а** (+ *inf.*) there is no sense (in), there is no point (in).
3 (*разум*) (good) sense; **здра́вый с.** common sense.

смыслов|о́й *adj. of* ▸**смысл; ~ые отте́нки** shades of meaning.

смыть, смо́ю, смо́ешь *pf.* (*of* ▸**смыва́ть**)
1 (*удалить*) to wash off; (*fig.*) (*позор*) to clear, wipe out.
2 (*снести*) to wash away.

смы́ться, смо́юсь, смо́ешься *pf.* (*of* ▸**смыва́ться**)
1 to wash off, come off.
2 (*fig., coll.*) (*уйти*) to slip away.

смыч|о́к, ка́ *m.* (*mus.*) bow.

смягч|а́ть(ся), а́ю(сь) *impf. of* ▸**~и́ть(ся)**

смягч|и́ть, у́, и́шь *pf.* (*of* ▸**~а́ть**)
1 (*кожу, тон*) to soften.
2 (*боль*) to ease, alleviate; (*наказание*) to mitigate.

смягч|и́ться, у́сь, и́шься *pf.* (*of* ▸**~а́ться**)
1 (*о коже, тоне, взгляде*) to soften, become softer.
2 (*о человеке*) to be mollified; (*о боли, ветре, холоде, ситуации*) to ease (off).

смяте́ни|е, я *nt.* confusion, disarray; commotion.

смять, сомну́, сомнёшь *pf.* (*of* ▸**мять 2**) to crumple; to rumple; **с. пла́тье** to crush a dress.

смя́ться, сомнётся *pf.* (*of* ▸**мя́ться**) to get creased; to get crumpled.

снаб|ди́ть, жу́, ди́шь *pf.* (*of* ▸**~жа́ть**) (+ *i.*) to supply (with), furnish (with), provide (with).

снабжа́|ть, ю *impf. of* ▸**снабди́ть**

снабже́ни|е, я *nt.* supply, supplying, provision.

сна́йпер, а *m.* sniper.

снару́жи *adv.* on the outside; from (the) outside.

снаря́д, а *m.*
1 (*mil.*) projectile, missile; shell.
2 (*прибор*) contrivance, machine, gadget; **гимнасти́ческие ~ы** gymnastic apparatus.

снаря|ди́ть, жу́, ди́шь *pf.* (*of* ▸**~жа́ть**) to equip, fit out.

снаря|ди́ться, жу́сь, ди́шься *pf.* (*of* ▸**~жа́ться**) to equip o.s., get ready.

снаряжа́|ть(ся), ю(сь) *impf. of* ▸**снаряди́ть(ся)**

снаряже́ни|е, я *nt.* equipment, outfit; **ко́нское с.** harness.

снаст|ь, и, *pl.* **~и, ~е́й** *f.*
1 (*collect.*) tackle, gear.
2 (*usu. pl.*) (*на судне*) rigging.

снача́ла *adv.*
1 (*прежде*) at first, at the beginning.
2 (*снова*) all over again.

сна́шива|ть, ю *impf. of* ▸**сноси́ть**[1]

СНГ *nt. indecl.* (*abbr. of* **Содру́жество Незави́симых Госуда́рств**) CIS (*Commonwealth of Independent States*).

снег, а, о ~е, в/на ~у́, *pl.* **~а́** *m.* snow; **идёт с.** it's snowing; **мо́крый с.** sleet.

снеги́р|ь, я́ *m.* bullfinch.

снегоочисти́тельн|ый *adj.*: **~ая маши́на** snowplough (*Br.*), snowplow (*US*).

снегопа́д, а *m.* snowfall.

снегохо́д, а *m.* snowmobile.

снежи́нк|а, и *f.* snowflake.

сне́жн|ый *adj.* snow; snowy; **~ая ба́ба** snow man; **с. зано́с, с. сугро́б** snowdrift; **~ая зима́** snowy winter.

снеж|о́к, ка́ *m.*
1 light snow.
2 (*комок*) snowball; **игра́ть в ~ки́** to have a snowball fight.

снес|ти́[1]**, у́, ёшь,** *past* **~, ~ла́** *pf.* (*of* ▸**сноси́ть**[3])
1 (*вниз*) to fetch down, bring down.
2 (*usu. impers.*) (*о воде*) to carry away; (*о ветре*) to blow off, take off.
3 (*разрушить*) to demolish, pull down.
4 (*срезать*) to cut off, chop off; **с. го́лову кому́-н.** to chop s.o.'s head off.

снес|ти́[2]**, у́, ёшь** *pf.* (*of* ▸**нести́**[2]) to lay (eggs).

снижа́|ть(ся), ю(сь) *impf. of* ▸**сни́зить(ся)**

сниже́ни|е, я *nt.*
1 lowering, reduction; **с. зарпла́ты** wage cut.
2 (*aeron.*) descent.

сни́|зить, жу, зишь *pf.* (*of* ▸**~жа́ть**)
1 (*спустить ниже*) to bring down, lower.
2 (*цены*) to bring down, lower, reduce.

сни́|зиться, жусь, зишься *pf.* (*of* ▸**~жа́ться**)
1 (*спуститься ниже*) to descend, come down.
2 (*температура*) to fall, sink, come down.

сни́зу *adv.* from below (*pol.*; *also fig.*); from the bottom; **с. вверх** upwards; **с. до́верху** from top to bottom; (*внизу*) at, on the bottom.

снима́|ть(ся), ю(сь) *impf. of* ▸**снять(ся)**

сни́м|ок, ка *m.* photograph, photo.

снисходи́тел|ьный (~ен, ~ьна) *adj.* (*не строгий*) indulgent, tolerant, lenient.

сни́|ться, снюсь, сни́шься *impf.* (*of* ▸**при~**) (+ *d.*) to dream; **ей ~лось, что** she dreamed that; **мне ~лся лев** I dreamed about a lion.

сноб, а *m.* snob.

снобизм, а *m.* snobbery.

сно́ва *adv.* again, anew, afresh.

сновиде́ни|е, я *nt.* dream.

сноро́вк|а, и *f.* skill, knack.

снос, а *m.* demolition, pulling down; **дом предназна́чен на с.** the house is to be pulled down.

сно|си́ть[1]**, шу́, ~сишь** *pf.* (*of* ▸**сна́шивать**) to wear out.

сно|си́ть², **шу́**, **~сишь** *pf.* (*coll.*) (*снести и принести*) to take (*and bring back*).

сно|си́ть³, **шу́**, **~сишь** *impf. of* ▸ **снести́¹**

сно́ск|а, **и** *f.* footnote.

сно́с|ный (~ен, ~на) *adj.* (*coll.*) tolerable; fair, reasonable.

снотво́р|ный *adj.* soporific (*also fig.*); **~ное сре́дство** soporific; *as n.* **~ное**, **~ного** *nt.* sleeping pill.

сноубо́рд, **а** *m.* snowboard.

сноубо́рдинг, **а** *m.* snowboarding.

снох|а́, **и́**, *pl.* **~и** *f.* daughter-in-law.

сноше́ни|е, **я** *nt.* (*usu. pl.*) relations, dealings; (*половой акт*) (sexual) intercourse.

сня|ть, **сниму́**, **сни́мешь**, *past* **~л**, **~ла́**, **~ло** *pf.* (*of* ▸ **снима́ть**)
1 (*одежду, крышку*) to take off; (*вниз*) to take down; **с. карти́ну** to take down a picture; **с. оса́ду** to raise a siege; **с. с себя́ отве́тственность** to decline responsibility.
2 (*устранить, отменить*) to remove; to withdraw, cancel; **с. запре́т** to lift a ban; **с. с рабо́ты** to discharge, sack.
3 (*изготовить*) to take, make; to photograph, make a photograph (of); **с. ко́пию (с** + *g.*) to copy, make a copy (of); **с. фильм** to shoot a film.
4 (*взять внаём*) to take, rent (*a house, etc.*).
5 (*sl.*) (*девушку*) to pick up, pull.

сня́|ться, **сниму́сь**, **сни́мешься**, *past* **~лся**, **~ла́сь** *pf.* (*of* ▸ **снима́ться**)
1 (*отделиться*) to come off.
2 (*отправиться*) to move off; **с. с я́коря** to weigh anchor; to get under way (*also fig.*).
3 (*фотографироваться*) to have one's photograph taken.
4 (*сыграть роль в фильме*) to play a part in a film.

со *prep.* = **с**

со... *vbl. pref.* = **с...**

соа́втор, **а** *m.* co-author.

соба́к|а, **и** *f.*
1 dog; **охо́тничья с.** gun dog, hound; **с.-поводы́рь** guide dog; **служе́бная с.** guard dog; **уста́ть как с.** (*coll.*) to be dog-tired.
2 (*comput.*) @ sign (*as used in email addresses*) (*читается* 'at').

соба́|чий *adj. of* ▸ **~ка**; canine; **~чья жизнь** dog's life; **с. хо́лод** intense cold.

собесе́дник, **а** *m.* interlocutor; **он — заба́вный с.** he is amusing company.

собесе́дни|ца, **цы** *f. of* ▸ **~к**

собесе́довани|е, **я** *nt.* conversation, discussion.

собира́|ть, **ю** *impf. of* ▸ **собра́ть**

собира́|ться, **юсь** *impf.*
1 *impf. of* ▸ **собра́ться.**
2 (+ *inf.*) to intend (to), be about (to), be going (to).

собла́зн, **а** *m.* temptation.

соблазни́тел|ьный (~ен, ~ьна) *adj.* tempting; alluring; (*женщина*) seductive.

соблазн|и́ть, **ю́**, **и́шь** *pf.* (*of* ▸ **~я́ть**)
1 (*прельстить*) to tempt.
2 (*обольстить*) to seduce.

соблазн|я́ть, **я́ю** *impf. of* ▸ **~и́ть**

соблюда́|ть, **ю** *impf. of* ▸ **соблюсти́**

соблю|сти́, **ду́**, **дёшь**, *past* **~л**, **~ла́** *pf.* (*of* ▸ **~да́ть**) (*диету*) to keep (to), stick to; (*порядок*) to maintain; to observe; **с. зако́н** to observe a law; **с. сро́ки** to keep to schedule.

собо́й *see* ▸ **себя́**

соболе́знովани|е, **я** *nt.* sympathy; (*pl.*) condolences.

соболе́зн|овать, **ую** *impf.* (+ *d.*) to sympathize (with), commiserate (with).

со́бол|ь, **я**, *pl.* (*furs*) **~я́**, **~е́й** *and* (*animals*) **~и**, **~ей** *m.* sable.

собо́р, **а** *m.*
1 (*hist. or eccl.*) (*съезд*) council, synod, assembly; **вселе́нский с.** ecumenical council.
2 (*церковь*) cathedral.

собо́ю = **собо́й**, *see* ▸ **себя́**

собра́ни|е, **я** *nt.*
1 (*заседание*) meeting, gathering; **о́бщее с.** general meeting.
2 (*государственный орган*) assembly; **учреди́тельное с.** constituent assembly.
3 (*коллекция*) collection; **с. сочине́ний** collected works.

со́бр|анный *p.p.p. of* ▸ **~а́ть** *and adj.*; **с. челове́к** self-disciplined person.

собр|а́ть, **соберу́**, **соберёшь**, *past* **~а́л**, **~ла́**, **~а́ло** *pf.* (*of* ▸ **собира́ть**)
1 (*сведения*) to gather; (*книги, деньги*) to collect; (*цветы*) to pick.
2 (*людей*) to assemble, muster; to convene; **с. после́дние си́лы** to make a last effort.
3 (*tech.*) (*радиоприёмник*) to assemble.

собр|а́ться, **соберу́сь**, **соберёшься**, *past* **~а́лся**, **~ала́сь**, **~а́ло́сь** *pf.* (*of* ▸ **собира́ться**)
1 (*сойтись*) to gather, assemble.
2 (**в** + *a.*) (*приготовиться*) to prepare (for); **с. в го́сти** to get ready to go away (*to visit s.o.*).
3 (+ *inf.*) (*решить*) to intend (to), be about (to), be going (to).
4 (**с** + *i.*, *fig.*) (*сосредоточиться*) to collect; **с. с си́лами** to summon up one's strength.

со́бственник, **а** *m.* owner, proprietor; **зе́мельный с.** landowner.

со́бственни|ца, **цы** *f. of* ▸ **~к**

со́бственно *adv.* actually; **с. говоря́** strictly speaking, as a matter of fact.

собственнору́чно *adv.* with one's own hand.

со́бственност|ь, **и** *f.*
1 (*имущество*) property.
2 (*владение*) possession, ownership; **приобрести́ в с.** to become the owner (of).

со́бственн|ый *adj.* (one's) own; **~ыми глаза́ми** with one's own eyes; **чу́вство ~ого досто́инства** self-respect; **~ой персо́ной** in person; **и́мя ~ое** (*gram.*) proper noun.

собы́ти|е, **я** *nt.* event; **теку́щие ~я** current affairs.

сов|а́, **ы́**, *pl.* **~ы** *f.* owl; (*fig.*) night owl.

сова́ть, **сую́**, **суёшь** *impf.* (*of* ▸ **су́нуть**) to shove, thrust, poke; **с. ру́ки в карма́ны** to stick one's hands in one's pockets; **с. нос (в** + *a.*) (*coll.*) to poke one's nose (into), pry (into).

сова́ться, **сую́сь**, **суёшься** *impf.* (*of* ▸ **су́нуться**) (*coll.*)

1 to push, strain.
2 (**в** + *a.*; *fig.*) (*в чужие дела*) to butt (in); (*с советами*) to poke one's nose (into).

соверш|áть(ся), áю, áет(ся) *impf. of* ▸ **~и́ть(ся)**

совершéнно *adv.*
1 (*превосходно*) perfectly.
2 (*совсем*) absolutely, utterly, completely; **с. вéрно!** quite right!; perfectly true!

совершеннолéти|е, я *nt.* majority; **дости́гнуть ~я** to come of age, attain one's majority.

совершеннолéтний *adj.* of age.

совершéн|ный (~ен, ~на) *adj.*
1 (*превосходный*) perfect.
2 (*coll.*) (*полный*) absolute, complete.

совершéнств|о, а *nt.* perfection; **в ~е** perfectly, to perfection.

совершéнств|овать, ую *impf.* (*of* ▸ **у~**) to perfect; to develop, improve.

совершéнств|оваться, уюсь *impf.* (*of* ▸ **у~**) (**в** + *p.*) to perfect o.s. (in); to improve.

соверш|и́ть, ý, и́шь *pf.* (*of* ▸ **~áть**)
1 (*подвиг*) to accomplish, carry out; to perform; (*преступление*) to commit.
2 (*заключить*) to complete, conclude; **с. сдéлку** to complete a transaction, make a deal.

соверш|и́ться, и́тся *pf.* (*of* ▸ **~áться**) (*liter.*)
1 (*о событии*) to happen.
2 (*о подвиге*) to be accomplished; (*о сделке*) to be completed.

сóвестлив|ый (~, ~а) *adj.* conscientious.

сóвест|ь, и *f.* conscience; **чи́стая, нечи́стая с.** clear, guilty conscience; **на ~и** on one's conscience; **со спокóйной ~ью** with a clear conscience.

совéт, а *m.*
1 advice; **проси́ть ~а** to ask for advice.
2 (*совместное обсуждение*) discussion; **воéнный с.** council of war.
3 (*hist.*) (*орган управления в СССР*) soviet.
4 (*административный орган*) council; **С. безопáсности** Security Council.

совéтник, а *m.* adviser, counsellor.

совéт|овать, ую *impf.* (*of* ▸ **по~**) (+ *d.*) to advise.

совéт|оваться, уюсь *impf.* (*of* ▸ **по~**) (**с** + *i.*) to consult, ask advice (of), seek advice (from).

совéтск|ий *adj.* (*hist.*) Soviet; **~ая влáсть** Soviet rule *or* power; **с. нарóд** the Soviet people.

Совéтск|ий Сою́з, ~ого ~а *m.* (*hist.*) the Soviet Union.

совещáни|е, я *nt.* conference, meeting.

совещá|ться, юсь *impf.*
1 (**о** + *p.*) to deliberate (on, about).
2 (**с** + *i.*) to confer (with), consult.

совладá|ть, ю *pf.* (**с** + *i.*; *coll.*) to control; **с. с собóй** to control o.s.

совладéл|ец, ьца *m.* joint owner.

совладéл|ица, ицы *f. of* ▸ **~ец**

совмести́м|ый (~, ~а) *adj.* compatible.

совме|сти́ть, щý, сти́шь *pf.* (*of* ▸ **~щáть**) to combine.

совмéстно *adv.* in common, jointly.

совмéстн|ый *adj.* joint, combined; **~ые дéйствия** concerted action; **~ое предприя́тие** joint venture.

совмещá|ть, ю *impf. of* ▸ **совмести́ть**

сов|óк, кá *m.* shovel, scoop; **с. для мýсора** dustpan.

совокуплéни|е, я *nt.* copulation.

совокýпност|ь, и *f.* aggregate, sum total; totality; **в ~и** in the aggregate.

совпадá|ть, ю *impf. of* ▸ **совпáсть**

совпадéни|е, я *nt.* coincidence.

совпá|сть, дý, дёшь, *past* **~л** *pf.* (*of* ▸ **~дáть**)
1 (**с** + *i.*) (*произойти одновременно*) to coincide (with); **части́чно с.** to overlap.
2 (*оказаться общим*) to agree, tally; **их показáния не ~дáли** their evidence did not tally.

совра|ти́ть, щý, ти́шь *pf.* (*of* ▸ **~щáть**) (*соблазнить*) to lead astray; (*женщину*) to seduce; (*ребёнка*) to (sexually) abuse.

совр|áть, ý, ёшь, *past* **~áл, ~алá, ~áло** *pf. of* ▸ **врать**

совращá|ть, ю *impf. of* ▸ **соврати́ть**

совращéни|е, я *nt.* corrupting; (*женщины*) seducing, seduction; (*ребёнка*) (sexual) abuse; **с. малолéтних** child (sexual) abuse.

совремéнник, а *m.* contemporary.

совремéнни|ца, цы *f. of* ▸ **~к**

совремéнност|ь, и *f.*
1 (*актуальность*) contemporaneity.
2 (*современная эпоха*) the present (time).

совремéн|ный (~ен, ~на) *adj.* (*относящийся к настоящему времени*) contemporary, present-day; (*человек*) modern; (*техника*) up-to-date, state-of-the-art; **~ная англи́йская литератýра** modern English literature.

совсéм *adv.* quite, entirely, completely; **с. не** not at all, not in the least; **с. не то** nothing of the kind.

соглáси|е, я *nt.*
1 (*разрешение*) consent; **с вáшего ~я** with your consent.
2 (*единомыслие*) agreement; **в ~и** (**с** + *i.*) in accordance (with); **прийти́ к ~ю** to come to an agreement.
3 (*единодушие*) harmony.

согла|си́ться, шýсь, си́шься *pf.* (*of* ▸ **~шáться**)
1 (**на** + *a. or* + *inf.*) to consent (to), agree (to).
2 (**с** + *i.*) to agree (with).

соглáсно *prep.* (+ *d. or* **с** + *i.*) in accordance (with); according (to); **с. договорý** in accordance with the treaty.
■ *adv.* (*жить, петь*) in harmony.

соглáс|ный[1] (~ен, ~на) *adj.*
1 (**на** + *a.*) agreeable (to); **они́ нé были ~ны на нáши услóвия** they would not agree to our conditions.
2 (**с** + *i.*) in agreement (with); **быть ~ным** to agree (with); **~ен, ~на, ~ны?** do you agree?

соглáсн|ый[2] *adj.* (*gram.*) consonant(al); *as n.* **с., ~ого** *m.* consonant.

соглас|овáть, ýю *pf.* (*of* ▸ **~óвывать**) (**с** + *i.*)

С

1 to coordinate (with).
2 : **с. что-н. с кем-н.** to agree sth. with s.o., to come to an agreement with s.o. about sth.

согласо́выва|ть, ю *impf. of* ▸ **согласова́ть**

соглаша́|ться, юсь *impf. of* ▸ **согласи́ться**

соглаше́ни|е, я *nt.* agreement; **заключи́ть с.** to conclude an agreement.

согн|у́ть, у́, ёшь *pf.* (*of* ▸ **гнуть** *and* ▸ **сгиба́ть**) to bend, curve, crook.

согн|у́ться, у́сь, ёшься *pf.* (*of* ▸ **гну́ться** *and* ▸ **сгиба́ться**) to bend, bow (down).

согрева́|ть(ся), ю(сь) *impf. of* ▸ **согре́ть(ся)**

согре́|ть, ю *pf.* (*of* ▸ **~ва́ть**) to warm, heat.

согре́|ться, юсь *pf.* (*of* ▸ **~ва́ться**) to get warm; to warm o.s.

согреш|и́ть, у́, и́шь *pf.* (*of* ▸ **греши́ть 1**) (**про́тив** + *g.*) to sin (against), trespass (against).

со́д|а, ы *f.* soda, sodium carbonate; **питьева́я с.** baking soda.

соде́йстви|е, я *nt.* assistance, help.

соде́йств|овать, ую *impf. and pf.* (+ *d.*) to assist; to further; to contribute (to).

содержа́ни|е, я *nt.*
1 (*семьи*) maintenance, upkeep; **(де́нежное) с.** allowance, financial support; **с. под аре́стом** custody.
2 (*зарплата*) pay.
3 (*содержимое*) content; **с больши́м ~ем** (+ *g.*) rich (in).
4 (*сущность*) substance; content; **фо́рма и с.** form and content.
5 (*книги*) content(s); (*романа*) plot.
6 (*оглавление*) table of contents.

содержа́тел|ьный (~ен, ~ьна) *adj.* rich in content.

содерж|а́ть, у́, ~̃ишь *impf.*
1 (*семью*) to keep, maintain, support.
2 (*магазин*) to keep, have.
3 (**в** + *p.*) to keep (*in a given state*); **с. в поря́дке** to keep in order.
4 (*иметь в себе*) to contain.

содерж|а́ться, у́сь, ~̃ишься *impf.*
1 (*обеспечиваться*) to be kept, be maintained.
2 (*находиться*) to be kept, be.
3 (**в** + *p.*) (*заключаться*) to be contained (by); **в э́той руде́ ~̃ится ура́н** this ore contains uranium.

содержи́м|ое, ого *nt.* contents.

со́дов|ый *adj.* soda; **~ая (вода́)** soda (water).

содра́|ть, сдеру́, сдерёшь, *past* **~л, ~ла́, ~ло** *pf.* (*of* ▸ **сдира́ть** *and* ▸ **драть 2**) to tear off, strip off; **с. ко́жу (с** + *g.*) to skin, flay.

содрог|а́ться, а́юсь *impf. of* ▸ **~ну́ться**

содрог|ну́ться, ну́сь, нёшься *pf.* (*of* ▸ **~а́ться**) to shudder, shake, quake.

содру́жеств|о, а *nt.* community, commonwealth; **Брита́нское С. на́ций** the British Commonwealth.

соедине́ни|е, я *nt.*
1 joining, combination.
2 (*tech.*) joint.
3 (*chem.*) compound.
4 (*mil.*) formation.

Соединённ|ое Короле́вств|о (Великобрита́нии и Се́верной Ирла́ндии), ~ого ~а (В. и С. И.) *nt.* United Kingdom (of Great Britain and Northern Ireland).

Соединённ|ые Шта́т|ы (Аме́рики), ~ых ~ов (А.) *no sg.* United States (of America).

соедин|ённый *p.p.p. of* ▸ **~и́ть** *and adj.* united, joint.

соедин|и́ть, ю́, и́шь *pf.* (*of* ▸ **~я́ть**)
1 (*объединить*) to join, unite.
2 (*присоединить*) to connect, link; **с. (по телефо́ну)** to put through.

соедин|и́ться, ю́сь, и́шься *pf.* (*of* ▸ **~я́ться**)
1 to join, unite.
2 (*chem.*) to combine.
3 *pass. of* ▸ **~и́ть**

соедин|я́ть(ся), я́ю(сь) *impf. of* ▸ **~и́ть(ся)**

сожале́ни|е, я *nt.*
1 (**о** + *p.*) regret (for); **к ~ю** unfortunately.
2 (**к** + *d.*) pity (for).

сожале́|ть, ю *impf.* (**о** + *p. or* + **что**) to regret, deplore.

сожи́тел|ь, я *m.*
1 (*по квартире*) flatmate (*Br.*), room-mate (*US*).
2 (*любовник*) lover.

сожи́тель|ница, ницы *f. of* ▸ **~**

сожр|а́ть, у́, ёшь, *past* **~а́л, ~ала́, ~а́ло** *pf. of* ▸ **жрать**

созва́нива|ться, юсь *impf. of* ▸ **созвони́ться**

созва́|ть, созову́, созовёшь, *past* **~л, ~ла́, ~ло** *pf.* (*of* **созыва́ть**)
1 (*гостей*) to gather; to invite.
2 (*людей на совет*) to call (together), summon; (*митинг, парламент*) to convoke, convene.

созве́зди|е, я *nt.* constellation.

созвон|и́ться, ю́сь, и́шься *pf.* (*of* ▸ **созва́ниваться**) (**с** + *i.*; *coll.*) to speak on the telephone (to).

созву́ч|ный (~ен, ~на) *adj.* (+ *d.*) consonant (with), in keeping (with).

созда|ва́ть(ся), ю́, ёт(ся) *impf. of* ▸ **~̃ть(ся)**

созда́ни|е, я *nt.*
1 (*действие*) creation, making.
2 (*произведение*) creation, work.
3 (*существо*) creature.

созда́тел|ь, я *m.*
1 creator; (*организации*) founder; (*теории*) originator.
2 : **С.** (*Бог*) the Creator.

созда́тель|ница, ницы *f. of* ▸ **~ 1**

созда́|ть, м, шь, ст, ди́м, ди́те, ду́т, *past* **со́зда́л, ~ла́, со́зда́ло** *pf.* (*of* ▸ **~ва́ть**) to create; (*организацию*) to found; (*теорию*) to originate; **с. впечатле́ние** to give the impression; **с. иллю́зию** to create an illusion.

созда́|ться, стся, ду́тся, *past* **~лся, ~ла́сь, ~ло́сь** *and* **~̃лось** *pf.* (*of* ▸ **~ва́ться**) to be created; to arise; **у нас**

создало́сь впечатле́ние, что we gained the impression that.

созерца́|ть, ю *impf.* to contemplate.

созида́тел|ьный (~ен, ~ьна) *adj.* creative, constructive.

созна|ва́ть, ю́, ёшь *impf.*
1 *impf. of* ▸ **~́ть.**
2 to be conscious (of), realize; **я́сно с.** to be alive (to).

созна|ва́ться, ю́сь, ёшься *impf. of* ▸ **~́ться**

созна́ни|е, я *nt.*
1 consciousness; **потеря́ть с.** to lose consciousness; **прийти́ в с.** to regain, recover consciousness.
2 (*ошибки, вины*) recognition, acknowledgement.

созна́тел|ьный (~ен, ~ьна) *adj.*
1 conscious.
2 (*отношение*) intelligent.
3 (*намеренный*) deliberate.

созна́|ть, ю *pf.* (*of* ▸ **~ва́ть 1**) to recognize, acknowledge.

созна́|ться, юсь *pf.* (*of* ▸ **~ва́ться**) (**в** + *p.*) (*в ошибке*) to admit (to); (*в преступлении*) to confess (to); (*leg.*) to plead guilty.

созрева́|ть, ю *impf. of* ▸ **созре́ть**

созре́|ть, ю *pf.* (*of* ▸ **зреть** *and* ▸ **~ва́ть**) (*о плоде*) to ripen; (*о человеке*) to mature; (*о плане*) to develop, mature.

созыва́|ть, ю *impf. of* ▸ **созва́ть**

со|йти́, йду́, йдёшь, *past* **~шёл, ~шла́** *pf.* (*of* ▸ **сходи́ть**[1])
1 (*с лестницы, горы*) to go down, come down; (*с автобуса, поезда*) to get off; **с. на не́т** to come to naught.
2 (*покинуть, уйти*) to leave; **с. с доро́ги** to get out of the way, step aside; **с. с ре́льсов** to come off the rails; **с. с ума́** to go mad, go off one's head.
3 (*о краске, о коже*) to come off.

со|йти́сь, йду́сь, йдёшься, *past* **~шёлся, ~шла́сь** *pf.* (*of* ▸ **сходи́ться**)
1 (*встретиться*) to meet; to come together, gather.
2 (**с** + *i.*) (*подружиться*) to meet, take up (with), become friends (with); (*вступить в сожительство*) to become (*sexually*) intimate (with).
3 (+ *i.*, **в** + *p. or* **на** + *p.*) (*договориться*) to agree (about); **они́ не ~шли́сь хара́ктерами** they could not get on.
4 (*совпасть*) to agree, tally; **счета́ не ~шли́сь** the figures did not tally.

сок, а (у), о ~́е, в ~́е *and* **~у́** *m.* juice.

соковыжима́лк|а, и *f.* juicer.

со́кол, а *m.* falcon.

сокра|ти́ть, щу́, ти́шь *pf.* (*of* ▸ **~ща́ть**)
1 (*статью, путь, рабочий день*) to shorten.
2 (*расходы, штаты*) to reduce, cut down.
3 (*уволить*) to dismiss, discharge, lay off.

сокра|ти́ться, ти́тся *pf.* (*of* ▸ **~ща́ться**)
1 (*о днях*) to grow shorter.
2 (*о расходах*) to decrease.
3 (*coll.*) (*о мышцах*) to contract.

сокраща́|ть(ся), ю, ет(ся) *impf. of* ▸ **сократи́ть(ся)**

сокраще́ни|е, я *nt.*
1 (*рабочего дня*) shortening.
2 (*статьи*) abridgement; **с ~ями** abridged.
3 (*слова*) abbreviation.
4 (*штатов, вооружений*) reduction, cutting down.

сокра|щённый *p.p.p. of* ▸ **~ти́ть** *and adj.* brief; **~щённое сло́во** abbreviation, contraction.

сокрове́н|ный (~, ~на) *adj.* secret, concealed; **~ные мы́сли** innermost thoughts.

сокро́вищ|е, а *nt.* treasure.

сокруши́тел|ьный (~ен, ~ьна) *adj.* shattering; **нанести́ с. уда́р** (+ *d.*) to deal a crippling blow.

со|лга́ть, лгу́, лжёшь, лгу́т, *past* **~лга́л, ~лгала́, ~лга́ло** *pf. of* ▸ **лгать**

солда́т, а, *g. pl.* **~** *m.* soldier.

солда́тик, а *m.*
1 *dim. of* ▸ **солда́т.**
2 (*игрушка*) toy soldier; **игра́ть в ~и** to play soldiers.

солда́т|ский *adj. of* ▸ **~**

солён|ый *adj.*
1 salt; **~ое о́зеро** salt lake.
2 (**со́лон, солона́, со́лоно**) (*cyn*) salty.
3 (*консервированный*) salted; pickled; **с. огуре́ц** pickled cucumber; *as n.* **~ое, ~ого** *nt.* salty food.

соле́нь|е, я *nt.* (*usu. pl.*) salted food(s); pickles.

солида́рност|ь, и *f.* solidarity; **из ~и** (**с** + *i.*) in sympathy (with).

солида́р|ный (~ен, ~на) *adj.* (**с** + *i.*) at one (with), in sympathy (with).

соли́д|ный (~ен, ~на) *adj.*
1 (*прочный*) solid, strong, sound; **~ные зна́ния** sound knowledge.
2 (*серьёзный*) solid, sound; (*надёжный*) reliable, respectable; **с. челове́к** a solid man; **с. журна́л** respectable magazine.
3 (*coll.*) (*значительный*) respectable, sizeable; **~ная су́мма** tidy sum.

соли́ст, а *m.* soloist.

соли́ст|ка, ки *f. of* ▸ **~**

сол|и́ть, ю́, ~́ишь *impf.* (*of* ▸ **по~**)
1 (*cyn*) to salt.
2 (*огурцы*) to pickle; **с. мя́со** to corn meat.

со́лнечн|ый *adj.*
1 sun; solar; **~ое затме́ние** solar eclipse; **с. луч** sunbeam; **с. свет** sunlight, sunshine; **С~ая систе́ма** solar system; **с. уда́р** (*med.*) sunstroke.
2 (*день, погода*) sunny.

со́лнц|е, а *nt.* sun; **на с.** in the sun.

солнцезащи́тн|ый *adj.*: **с. крем** suncream; **~ые очки́** sunglasses.

со́ло
1 *adv.* solo.
2 *n.*; *nt. indecl.* solo.

солов|е́й, ья́ *m.* nightingale.

со́лод, а *m.* malt.

соло́м|а, ы *f.* straw; (*для крыши*) thatch.

соло́менн|ый *adj.* straw; **~ая кры́ша** thatch, thatched roof; **~ая шля́па** straw hat.

соло́минк|а, и *f.* straw; **хвата́ться за ~у** to clutch at straws.

солони́н|а, ы *f.* salted beef, corned beef.

соло́нк|а, и *f.* salt cellar.

сол|ь[1], **и,** *pl.* **∼́и, ∼éй** *f.* salt.
соль[2] *nt. indecl.* (*mus.*) G; **с.-диéз** G sharp; **ключ с.** treble clef.
сóл|ьный *adj. of* ▸ **∼о; с. нóмер** solo; **∼ьная пáртия** solo part.
солянк|а, ∼и *f.* solyanka (*a sharp-tasting Russian soup of vegetables and meat or fish*).
Сомали́ *nt. indecl.* Somalia.
сомали́ *m. indecl.* Somali (*language*).
сомали́|ец, йца *m.* Somali (*person*).
сомали́|йка, йки *f. of* ▸ **∼ец**
сомали́йский *adj.* Somali.
сомати́ческий *adj.* somatic.
сомкн|у́ть, у́, ёшь *pf.* (*of* ▸ **смыкáть**) to close; **с. глазá** to close one's eyes.
сомкн|у́ться, ётся *pf.* (*of* ▸ **смыкáться**) to close (up).
сомневá|ться, юсь *impf.*
1 (**в** + *p.*) to doubt; to question; **я не ∼юсь в егó чéстности** I do not question his integrity.
2 to worry; **мóжете не с.** you need not worry.
сомнéни|е, я *nt.* doubt; uncertainty; **без ∼я, вне (вся́кого) ∼я** without (any) doubt, beyond doubt.
сомни́тел|ьный (∼ен, ∼ьна) *adj.*
1 (*непроверенный*) doubtful, questionable; **∼ьно** it is doubtful, it is open to question.
2 (*подозрительный*) dubious.
сон, сна *m.*
1 sleep; **во сне, сквозь с.** in one's sleep; **со сна** half awake.
2 (*сновидение*) dream; **ви́деть во сне** to dream, have a dream (about).
сонáт|а, ы *f.* (*mus.*) sonata.
сонéт, а *m.* sonnet.
сóнный *adj.* sleepy, drowsy (*also fig.*).
сóн|я, и *f. and c.g.*
1 *f.* (*грызун*) dormouse.
2 *c.g.* (*coll.*) (*человек*) sleepyhead.
соображá|ть, ю *impf.*
1 *impf. of* ▸ **сообрази́ть.**
2 (*impf. only*) **хорошó, плóхо с.** to be quick, slow on the uptake.
соображéни|е, я *nt.* (*причина*) consideration, reason; (*мысль*) notion, idea; **по финáнсовым ∼ям** for financial reasons; **вы́сказать своё ∼я** to express one's views.
сообрази́тел|ьный (∼ен, ∼ьна) *adj.* quick-witted, sharp, bright.
сообра|зи́ть, жу́, зи́шь *pf.* (*of* ▸ **∼жáть 1**)
1 (*взвесить*) to consider, ponder; to weigh (the pros and cons of).
2 (*понять*) to understand, grasp.
сообрáзно *adv.* (**с** + *i.*) in conformity (with).
сообщá *adv.* together, jointly.
сообщ|áть(ся), áю, áет(ся) *impf. of* ▸ **∼и́ть(ся)**
сообщéни|е, я *nt.*
1 (*известие*) communication, report; **срóчное** *or* **э́кстренное с.** news flash.
2 (*связь*) communication; **прямóе с.** through connection; **пути́ ∼я** communications (*rail, road, canal, etc.*).
сообществ|о, а *nt.* (*международное, мировое*) community.
сообщ|и́ть, у́, и́шь *pf.* (*of* ▸ **∼áть**) (+ *a. or* **о** + *p.*) (*уведомить*) to communicate, report, inform, announce; **с. послéдние извéстия** to report the latest news.
сообщ|и́ться, и́тся *pf.* (*of* ▸ **∼áться**) to be communicated.
сообщник, а *m.* accomplice; partner (*in crime*); (*leg.*) accessory.
сообщни|ца, цы *f. of* ▸ **∼к**
соору|ди́ть, жу́, ди́шь *pf.* (*of* ▸ **∼жáть**) to build, erect.
сооружá|ть, ю *impf. of* ▸ **соорудить**
сооружéни|е, я *nt.*
1 (*действие*) building, erection.
2 (*постройка*) building, structure.
соотвéтственно *adv.* accordingly.
соотвéтстви|е, я *nt.* accordance, conformity, correspondence; **в ∼и (с** + *i.*) in accordance (with).
соотвéтств|овать, ую *impf.* (+ *d.*) to correspond (to, with), conform (to); **с. действи́тельности** to correspond to the facts; **с. трéбованиям** to meet the requirements.
соотвéтств|ующий *pres. part. act. of* ▸ **∼овать** *and adj.*
1 (+ *d.*) corresponding (to).
2 (*подходящий*) proper, appropriate; **поступáть ∼ующим óбразом** to act accordingly.
соотéчественник, а *m.* compatriot, fellow countryman.
соотéчественни|ца, цы *f. of* ▸ **∼к**
соотношéни|е, я *nt.* correlation, ratio; **с. сил** correlation of forces, alignment of forces.
сопéрник, а *m.* rival.
сопéрни|ца, цы *f. of* ▸ **∼к**
сопéрнича|ть, ю *impf.* to be rivals; (**с** + *i.*) to compete (with).
соп|éть, лю́, и́шь *impf.* to breathe heavily and noisily through the nose.
сопли́в|ый (∼, ∼а) *adj.* (*coll.*) snotty.
соп|лó, лá, *pl.* **∼́ла, ∼́ел** *and* **∼л** *nt.* nozzle.
сопля́к, á *m.* (*coll., pej.*) milksop.
сопостáв|ить, лю, ишь *pf.* (*of* ▸ **∼ля́ть**) (**с** + *i.*) to compare (with).
сопоставля́|ть, ю *impf. of* ▸ **сопостáвить**
сопрáно *nt. indecl.* (*voice*) & *f. indecl.* (*singer*) (*mus.*) mezzo-soprano.
сопредéл|ьный (∼ен, ∼ьна) *adj.* neighbouring (*Br.*), neighboring (*US*); contiguous.
соприкасá|ться, юсь *impf.* (*of* ▸ **соприкосну́ться**) (**с** + *i.*) to adjoin, be contiguous (to).
соприкосн|у́ться, у́сь, ёшься *pf. of* ▸ **соприкасáться**
сопрово|ди́ть, жу́, ди́шь *pf. of* ▸ **∼ждáть**
сопровождá|ть, ю *impf.* (*of* ▸ **сопроводи́ть**) to accompany.
сопровождá|ться, ется *impf.* (+ *i.*) to be accompanied (by).
сопровождéни|е, я *nt.*
1 (*действие*) accompanying, escort; **в ∼и** (+ *g.*) accompanied (by); escorted (by).

2 (*mus.*) accompaniment; **звуково́е с.** soundtrack.

сопротивле́ни|е, я *nt.* resistance, opposition; (*phys., tech.*) strength; (*elec.*) resistance, impedance; **оказа́ть с.** to put up resistance.

сопротивля́|ться, юсь *impf.* (+ *d.*) to resist, oppose.

сопу́тств|овать, ую *impf.* (+ *d.*) to accompany; **~ующие обстоя́тельства** attendant circumstances, concomitants.

сор, а *m.* litter, rubbish.

сора́тник, а *m.* comrade-in-arms.

сорван|е́ц, ца́ *m.* (*coll.*) (*ребёнок*) a terror; (*девочка*) tomboy.

сорв|а́ть, у́, ёшь, *past* **~а́л, ~ала́, ~а́ло** *pf.* (*of* ▸ **срыва́ть**)
1 (*отделить*) to tear off, break off, tear away, tear down; (*цветок*) to pick, pluck; **с. ве́тку** to break off a branch.
2 (**на** + *p.*) (*выместить*) to vent (upon); **с. гнев на ком-н.** to vent one's anger upon s.o.
3 (*нарушить*) to wreck, ruin, spoil; **с. забасто́вку** to break a strike.

сорв|а́ться, у́сь, ёшься, *past* **~а́лся, ~ала́сь, ~а́ло́сь** *pf.* (*of* ▸ **срыва́ться**)
1 (*освободиться*) to break away, break loose; **с. с пе́тель** to come off its hinges.
2 (*упасть*) to fall, come down; **с. с колоко́льни** to fall from the belfry.
3 (*coll.*) (*не удаться*) to fall through.

соревнова́ни|е, я *nt.*
1 (*sport*) competition, contest; event.
2 (*действие*) competition.

соревн|ова́ться, у́юсь *impf.* (**с** + *i.*) to compete (with, against).

сориенти́р|овать(ся), у́ю(сь) *pf. of* ▸ **ориенти́ровать(ся)**

сор|и́ть, ю́, и́шь *impf.* (*of* ▸ **на~**) (+ *a.* or *i.*) to drop litter; to make a mess; **с. деньга́ми** to throw one's money about.

сорня́к, а́ *m.* weed.

со́рок, *all other cases* **а́** *num.* forty.

соро́к|а, и *f.* magpie.

сороков|о́й *adj.* fortieth; **~ы́е го́ды** the forties.

сороконо́жк|а, и *f.* centipede.

соро́чк|а, и *f.* shirt; blouse; (*нижняя*) camisole; **ночна́я с.** (*мужская*) nightshirt; (*женская*) nightdress.

сорт, а, *pl.* **~а́** *m.*
1 (*качество*) grade, quality; **вы́сший с.** best quality; **пе́рвого ~а** first grade, first-rate.
2 (*разновидность*) sort, kind, variety.

сортир|ова́ть, у́ю *impf.* (*товар, уголь*) to sort, grade; (*корреспонденцию*) to sort; (*comput.*) to sort.

сортиро́вк|а, и *f.* sorting, grading.

сос|а́ть, у́, ёшь *impf.* to suck.

сосе́д, а, *pl.* **~и, ~ей** *m.* neighbour (*Br.*), neighbor (*US*).

сосе́д|ка, ки *f. of* ▸ **~**

сосе́дн|ий *adj.* neighbouring (*Br.*), neighboring (*US*); adjacent, next; **с. дом** the house next door; **~яя ко́мната** the next room.

соси́ск|а, и *f.* sausage; (*варёная*) frankfurter.

со́ск|а, и *f.*
1 (*пустышка*) dummy.
2 (*на бутылке*) treat.

соска́блива|ть, ю *impf. of* ▸ **соскобли́ть**

соска́кива|ть, ю *impf. of* ▸ **соскочи́ть**

соска́льзыва|ть, ю *impf. of* ▸ **соскользну́ть**

соскобл|и́ть, ю́, и́шь *pf.* (*of* ▸ **соска́бливать**) to scrape off.

соскользн|у́ть, у́, ёшь *pf.* (*of* ▸ **соска́льзывать**) (*упасть*) to slip off, slide off; (*с горы*) to slide down.

соскоч|и́ть, у́, ~ишь *pf.* (*of* ▸ **соска́кивать**)
1 (*с трамвая, коня*) to jump off, leap off; (*с дерева*) to jump down, leap down; **с. с крова́ти** to jump out of bed.
2 (*упасть*) to come off; **с. с пе́тель** to come off its hinges.

соскреба́|ть, ю *impf. of* ▸ **соскрести́**

соскре|сти́, бу́, бёшь, *past* **~б, ~бла́** *pf.* (*of* ▸ **~ба́ть**) to scrape away, off.

соску́ч|иться, усь, ишься *pf.*
1 (*почувствовать скуку*) to become bored.
2 (**по** + *d.*) to miss, yearn (for); **с. по друзья́м** to miss one's friends; (*по родине, городу*) be homesick (for).

сослага́тельный *adj.* (*gram.*) subjunctive.

со|сла́ть, шлю́, шлёшь *pf.* (*of* ▸ **ссыла́ть**) to exile, banish.

со|сла́ться, шлю́сь, шлёшься *pf.* (*of* ▸ **ссыла́ться**) (**на** + *a.*)
1 (*указать*) to refer (to), allude (to); (*процитировать*) to cite, quote.
2 (*оправдаться*) to plead; **с. на недомога́ние** to plead indisposition.

сосло́ви|е, я *nt.* (social) class; **дворя́нское с.** the nobility; **духо́вное с.** the clergy.

сослужи́в|ец, ца *m.* colleague, fellow employee.

сослужи́в|ица, ицы *f. of* ▸ **~ец**

сосн|а́, ы́, *pl.* **~ы, со́сен** *f.* pine (tree).

сос|о́к, ка́ *m.* nipple.

сосредото́ченност|ь, и *f.* (degree of) concentration.

сосредото́ч|енный *p.p.p. of* ▸ **~ить** *and adj.* concentrated; **с. взгляд** fixed stare.

сосредото́чива|ть(ся), ю(сь) *impf. of* ▸ **сосредото́чить(ся)**

сосредото́ч|ить, у, ишь *pf.* (*of* ▸ **~ивать**) to concentrate; to focus; **с. внима́ние** (**на** + *p.*) to concentrate one's attention (on, upon).

сосредото́ч|иться, усь, ишься *pf.* (*of* ▸ **~иваться**)
1 (**на** + *p.*) to concentrate (on, upon).
2 *pass. of* ▸ **~ить**

соста́в, а *m.*
1 (*вещества*) composition, make-up; structure; **входи́ть в с.** (+ *g.*) to form part (of).
2 (*коллектив людей*) staff, personnel; **ли́чный с.** personnel; **в по́лном ~е** at full strength; **в ~е** (+ *g.*) numbering, consisting (of); **делега́ция в ~е тридцати́ челове́к** a delegation of thirty (persons); **входи́ть в с.** (+ *g.*) to be a member (of).

соста́в|ить[1], лю, ишь *pf.* (*of* ▸ **~ля́ть**)

1 (*собрать, соединить*) to put together; **с. посу́ду** to stack crockery.
2 (*список, проект*) to make, draw up; to compile; to form, construct; **с. мне́ние** to form an opinion; **с. предложе́ние** to construct a sentence; **с. слова́рь** to compile a dictionary.
3 (*являться*) to be, constitute, make; **э́то не ~ит большо́го труда́** this will not constitute a lot of work.
4 (*образовать*) to form, make, amount to, total; **с. в сре́днем** to average; **расхо́ды ~или пятьсо́т фу́нтов** expenditure amounted to five hundred pounds.

соста́в|ить[2], **лю, ишь** *pf.* (*of* ▸ **~ля́ть**) (*сверху вниз*) to take down, put down; **с. я́щики на́ пол** to put the drawers down on the floor.

соста́в|иться, ится *pf.* (*of* ▸ **~ля́ться**) to form, be formed, come into being.

составля́|ть(ся), ю, ет(ся) *impf. of* ▸ **соста́вить(ся)**

составн|о́й *adj.*
1 (*составленный из некоторых частей*) compound, composite.
2 (*входящий в состав чего-н.*) component; **~а́я часть** component, constituent.

соста́р|ить(ся), ю(сь) *pf. of* ▸ **ста́рить(ся)**

состоя́ни|е, я *nt.*
1 state, condition; position; **в хоро́шем, плохо́м ~и** in good, bad condition; **быть в ~и** (+ *inf.*) to be able (to), be in a position (to).
2 (*имущество*) fortune; **нажи́ть с.** to make a fortune.

состоя́тел|ьный[1] **(~ен, ~ьна)** *adj.* (*богатый*) well off.

состоя́тел|ьный[2] **(~ен, ~ьна)** *adj.* (*обоснованный*) well grounded.

состо|я́ть, ю́, и́шь *impf.*
1 (**из** + *g.*) to consist (of), comprise, be made up (of); **кварти́ра ~и́т из трёх ко́мнат** the flat consists of three rooms.
2 (**в** + *p.*) to consist (in), lie (in), be; **ра́зница ~и́т в том, что...** the difference is that ....
3 (*быть*) to be; **с. в па́ртии** to be a member of a party.

состо|я́ться, и́тся *pf.* to take place; **визи́т не ~я́лся** the visit did not take place.

сострада́ни|е, я *nt.* compassion, sympathy.

состр|и́ть, ю́, и́шь *pf. of* ▸ **остри́ть**

состяза́ни|е, я *nt.* competition, contest; match; **с. по фехтова́нию** fencing match.

состяза́|ться, юсь *impf.* (**с** + *i.*) to compete (with).

сосу́д, а *m.* vessel.

сосу́льк|а, и *f.* icicle.

сосчита́|ть, ю *pf. of* ▸ **счита́ть 1**

сотвор|и́ть, ю́, и́шь *pf. of* ▸ **твори́ть**

со́тк|а, и *f.* (*coll.*) 100 square metres (*0.01 hectare*).

сотк|а́ть, у́, ёшь, *past* **~а́л, ~ала́, ~а́ло** *pf. of* ▸ **ткать**

со́т|ня, ни, *g. pl.* **~ен** *f.* (*сто*) a hundred (*esp. a hundred roubles*).

со́товый *adj.* cellular; **с. телефо́н** cellphone, mobile phone (*Br.*).

сотру́дник, а *m.*
1 (*коллега*) colleague.
2 (*служащий*) employee, worker; **нау́чный с.** research assistant; **с. посо́льства** embassy official.
3 (*газеты, журнала*) contributor.

сотру́дни|ца, цы *f. of* ▸ **~к**

сотру́днича|ть, ю *impf.*
1 (**с** + *i.*) to work (with).
2 (**в** + *p.*) to contribute (to); **с. в газе́те** to contribute to a newspaper; to work on a newspaper.

сотру́дничеств|о, а *nt.* collaboration, cooperation.

сотрясе́ни|е, я *nt.* shaking; **с. мо́зга** (*med.*) concussion.

со́т|ы, ~ *and* **~ов** *no sg.* honeycombs.

со́т|ый *adj.* hundredth; **с. год** the year one hundred; *as n.* **~ая, ~ой** *f.* (a) hundredth.

со́ул, а *m.*: **(му́зыка) с.** soul music.

со́ус, а *m.* sauce; (*мясной*) gravy; (*к салату*) dressing.

со́усник, а *m.* sauce boat, gravy boat.

соуча́стник, а *m.* accomplice; **с. преступле́ния** (*leg.*) accessory to a crime.

соуча́стни|ца, цы *f. of* ▸ **~к**

соф|а́, ы́, *pl.* **~́ы** *f.* sofa.

софи́зм, а *m.* sophism, sophistry.

Софи́|я, и *f.* Sofia.

со́х|нуть, ну, нёшь, *past* **~, ~ла** *impf.*
1 (*о белье*) to dry, get dry; (*о губах*) to become parched.
2 (*вянуть*) to wither; (*fig., coll.*) (*от любви*) to pine.

сохране́ни|е, я *nt.*
1 preservation; conservation; (*попечение*) care, custody.
2 (*права*) retention.

сохран|и́ть, ю́, и́шь *pf.* (*of* ▸ **~я́ть**)
1 (*беречь*) to preserve, keep; to keep safe; **с. ве́рность** (+ *d.*) to remain faithful, loyal (to); **с. на па́мять** to keep as a souvenir.
2 (*не терять*) to keep, retain, reserve; **с. хладнокро́вие** to keep cool; **с. за собо́й пра́во** to reserve the right; (*comput.*) to save.

сохран|и́ться, ю́сь, и́шься *pf.* (*of* ▸ **~я́ться**)
1 to remain (intact); to last out, hold out; **он хорошо́ ~и́лся** he is well preserved.
2 *pass. of* ▸ **~и́ть**

сохра́ннsocт|ь, и *f.* safety, undamaged state; **в ~и** safe, intact.

сохран|я́ть(ся), я́ю(сь) *impf. of* ▸ **~и́ть(ся)**

социа́л-демокра́т, а *m.* social democrat.

социа́л-демократи́ческий *adj.* social democratic.

социали́зм, а *m.* socialism.

социали́ст, а *m.* socialist.

социалисти́ческий *adj.* socialist.

социали́ст|ка, ки *f. of* ▸ **~**

социа́льн|ый *adj.* social; **~ое обеспе́чение** social security; **~ое положе́ние** social status.

социо́лог, а *m.* sociologist.

социологи́ческий *adj.* sociological.

социоло́ги|я, и *f.* sociology.

сочета́ни|е, я *nt.* combination.

сочета́|ть, ю *impf. and pf.* (**с** + *i.*) to combine (with).

сочета́|ться, ется *impf. and pf.*
1 to combine; **в ней ~лся ум с красото́й** she combined intelligence and good looks.
2 (**с** + *i.*) (*гармонировать*) to harmonize (with), go (with); to match.

сочине́ни|е, я *nt.*
1 (*действие*) composing.
2 (*произведение*) work.
3 (*школьное*) composition, essay.

сочин|и́ть, ю́, и́шь *pf.* (*of* ▸ **~я́ть**)
1 (*создать*) to compose (*a liter. or mus. work*); to write.
2 (*выдумать*) to make up, fabricate.

сочин|я́ть, я́ю *impf. of* ▸ **~и́ть**

соч|и́ться, и́тся *impf.* to ooze (out), exude; **с. кро́вью** to bleed.

со́ч|ный (~ен, ~на́, ~но) *adj.*
1 juicy (*also fig.*); succulent.
2 (*fig.*) (*краски*) rich; (*зелень*) lush.

сочу́встви|е, я *nt.* sympathy; **вы́звать с.** to gain sympathy.

сочу́вств|овать, ую *impf.* (+ *d.*) to sympathize (with), feel (for).

сочу́вств|ующий *pres. part. act. of* ▸ **~овать** *and adj.* sympathetic; *as n.* **с., ~ующего** *m.* sympathizer.

сою́з[1], а *m.*
1 (*соглашение*) alliance, union; (*единение*) agreement; **заключи́ть с.** (**с** + *i.*) to conclude an alliance (with).
2 (*организация*) union; league; **профессиона́льный с.** trade union.

сою́з[2], а *m.* (*gram.*) conjunction.

сою́зник, а *m.* ally.

сою́зни|ца, цы *f. of* ▸ **~к**

сою́зн|ый *adj.* allied; **~ые держа́вы** allied powers; (*hist.*) the Allies.

со́|я, и *f.* soya bean.

спаге́тти *nt. and pl. indecl.* spaghetti.

спад, а *m.* (*econ.*) slump, recession.

спада́|ть, ет *impf. of* ▸ **спасть**

спазм, а *m.* spasm.

спа́ива|ть, ю *impf. of* ▸ **спои́ть**

спа́льн|ый *adj.* sleeping; **с. ваго́н** sleeping car; **~ое ме́сто** berth, bunk; **с. мешо́к** sleeping bag.

спа́л|ьня, ьни, *g. pl.* **~ен** *f.*
1 (*комната*) bedroom.
2 (*мебель*) bedroom suite.

спа́рж|а, и *f.* asparagus.

спа́рива|ться, ется *impf. of* ▸ **спа́риться**

спа́р|иться, ится *pf.* (*of* ▸ **~иваться**) (*о животных*) to mate.

спа́рыва|ть, ю *impf. of* ▸ **споро́ть**

спаса́тел|ь, я *m.* lifeguard; rescuer; (*pl.*) rescue party *or* team.

спаса́тельн|ый *adj.* rescue, life-saving; **с. круг, с. по́яс** lifebelt; **~ая ло́дка** lifeboat.

спаса́|ть(ся), ю(сь) *impf. of* ▸ **спасти́(сь)**

спасе́ни|е, я *nt.*
1 (*действие*) rescuing, saving.
2 (*возможность спастись*) rescue, escape; (*relig.*) salvation.

спаси́бо *particle* thanks; thank you; *as n.* thanks; **большо́е вам с.** thank you very much, many thanks.

спаси́тел|ь, я *m.*
1 rescuer.
2 : **С.** (*relig.*) the Saviour (*Br.*), Savior (*US*).

спас|ти́, у́, ёшь, *past* **~, ~ла́** *pf.* (*of* ▸ **~а́ть**) to save; to rescue; **с. положе́ние** to save the situation.

спас|ти́сь, у́сь, ёшься, *past* **~́ся, ~ла́сь** *pf.* (*of* ▸ **~а́ться**)
1 to save o.s., escape.
2 (*relig.*) to be saved, save one's soul.

спа|сть, дёт, *past* **~л** *pf.* (*of* ▸ **~да́ть**)
1 (**с** + *i.*) (*упасть вниз*) to fall down (from).
2 (*о ветре, шуме, жаре*) to abate; (*о температуре*) fall.

спа|ть, сплю, спишь, *past* **~л, ~ла́, ~́ло** *impf.* to sleep, be asleep; **лечь с.** to go to bed; **пора́ с.** it is bedtime; **с. с** (+ *i.*) to sleep with (*euph.*).

спа|я́ть, я́ю *pf.* to solder (together).

СПб (*abbr. of* **Санкт-Петербу́рг**) St Petersburg.

спекта́кл|ь, я *m.* (*theatr.*) performance; show.

спектр, а *m.* spectrum.

спекули́р|овать, ую *impf.*
1 (+ *i. or* **на** + *p.*) to speculate (in); to profiteer (in).
2 (**на** + *p.*; *fig.*) to exploit; to profit (by).

спекуля́нт, а *m.* speculator, profiteer.

спекуляти́вный *adj.* speculative.

спекуля́ци|я, и *f.*
1 (+ *i.*, *or* **на** + *p.*) speculation (in); profiteering.
2 (**на** + *p.*; *fig.*) exploitation (of).

спелеоло́ги|я, и *f.* speleology; potholing.

спе́л|ый (~, ~а́, ~о) *adj.* ripe.

сперва́ *adv.* (*coll.*) at first; first.

спе́реди *adv. and prep.* + *g.* in front (of); at the front, from the front.

спе́рм|а, ы *f.* sperm.

сперматозо́ид, а *m.* (*biol.*) spermatozoon.

спеси́в|ый (~, ~а) *adj.* arrogant, conceited, haughty.

спе|ть[1], ет *impf.* to ripen.

спеть[2], спою́, споёшь *pf. of* ▸ **петь**

специализа́ци|я, и *f.* specialization.

специализи́р|оваться, уюсь *impf. and pf.* (**в** + *p. or* **по** + *d.*) to specialize (in).

специали́ст, а *m.* (**в** + *p. or* **по** + *d.*) specialist (in), expert (in).

специали́ст|ка, ки *f. of* ▸ **~**

специа́льно *adv.* specially, especially.

специа́льност|ь, и *f.*
1 speciality, special interest.
2 (*профессия*) profession.

специа́л|ьный *adj.*
1 special; **с. корреспонде́нт** special correspondent.
2 **(~ен, ~ьна)** specialist; **~ьное образова́ние** specialist education.

специ́фик|а, и *f.* specific character.

специфи́ческий *adj.* specific.

спе́ци|я, и *f.* (*usu. pl.*) spice.

спецна́з, а *m.* (*abbr. of* **отря́д**

специа́льного назначе́ния) special unit.

спецоде́жд|а, ы *f.* working clothes, overalls.

спецслу́жб|а, ы *f.* (*usu. in pl.*) special force.

спецэффе́кт, а *m.* special effect.

спеш|и́ть, у́, и́шь *impf.* (*of* ▸ **по~**)
1 to hurry, be in a hurry; to make haste; (**с** + *i.*) to hurry up (with); **с. домо́й** to be in a hurry to get home; **де́лать не ~а́** to do in leisurely style, take one's time over.
2 (*no pf.*) (*о часах*) to be fast.

спе́шк|а, и *f.* (*coll.*) hurry, rush.

СПИД, а *m.* (*abbr. of* **синдро́м приобретённого иммунодефици́та**) (*med.*) Aids (*acquired immune deficiency syndrome*).

спидо́метр, а *m.* speedometer.

спи́кер, а *m.* (*parl.*) speaker.

спи́лива|ть, ю *impf. of* ▸ **спили́ть**

спил|и́ть, ю́, ~ишь *pf.* (*of* ▸ **~ивать**) (*дерево*) to saw down; (*сук, верхушку*) to saw off.

спин|а́, ы́, *a.* **~у,** *pl.* **~ы** *f.* back; **за ~о́й у кого́-н.** (*fig.*) behind s.o.'s back.

спи́нк|а, и *f.*
1 *dim. of* ▸ **спина́.**
2 back (*of article of furniture or clothing*).

спинно́й *adj.* spinal; **с. мозг** spinal cord.

спира́л|ь, и *f.* spiral.

спирити́зм, а *m.* spiritualism.

спирт, а *m.* alcohol, spirit(s).

спиртн|о́й *adj.* alcoholic, spirituous; **~ы́е напи́тки** alcoholic drinks, spirits; *as n.* **~о́е, ~о́го** *nt.* = **~ы́е напи́тки**.

спи|са́ть, шу́, ~шешь *pf.* (*of* ▸ **~сывать**)
1 (**с** + *i.*) to copy from.
2 (**у** + *g.*) to copy (off), crib (off).
3 (*оборудование*) to write off.

спи́с|ок, ка *m.*
1 (*рукописная копия*) manuscript copy.
2 (*письменный перечень*) list; roll.
3 : **послужно́й с.** service record.

спи́сыва|ть, ю *impf. of* ▸ **списа́ть**

спи́хива|ть, ю *impf. of* ▸ **спихну́ть**

спих|ну́ть, ну́, нёшь *pf.* (*of* ▸ **~ивать**) to push aside, shove aside; (*вниз*) to push down.

спи́ц|а, ы *f.*
1 (*для вязания*) knitting needle.
2 (*колеса*) spoke.

спи́чк|а, и *f.* match.

сплав, а *m.* (*tech.*) alloy.

спла́чива|ть(ся), ю, ет(ся) *impf. of* ▸ **сплоти́ть(ся)**

сплёвыва|ть, ю *impf. of* ▸ **сплю́нуть**

спле|сти́, ту́, тёшь, *past* **~л, ~ла́** *pf.* (*of* ▸ **плести́ 1**) to weave, plait, interlace.

спле́тник, а *m.* gossip, scandalmonger.

спле́тниц|а, ы *f. of* ▸ **спле́тник**

спле́тнича|ть, ю *impf.* to gossip.

спле́т|ня, ни, *g. pl.* **~ен** *f.* gossip; piece of scandal.

спло|ти́ть, чу́, ти́шь *pf.* (*of* ▸ **спла́чивать**)
1 to join.
2 (*fig.*) to unite, rally; **с. ряды́** to close the ranks.

спло|ти́ться, ти́тся *pf.* (*of* ▸ **спла́чиваться**) to unite, rally; to close the ranks.

сплошн|о́й *adj.*
1 unbroken, continuous; **~а́я ма́сса** solid mass.
2 (*всеобщий*) complete.

сплошь *adv.*
1 (*по всей поверхности*) all over.
2 (*coll.*) (*целиком*) completely, entirely; (*без исключения*) without exception; (*исключительно*) only, exclusively.

сплю́н|уть, у, ешь *pf.* (*of* ▸ **сплёвывать**)
1 (*плюнуть*) to spit.
2 (*coll.*) (*косточку*) to spit out.

сплю́щива|ть(ся), ю, ет(ся) *impf. of* ▸ **сплю́щить(ся)**

сплю́щ|ить, у, ишь *pf.* (*of* ▸ **~ивать**) to flatten.

сплю́щ|иться, ится *pf.* (*of* ▸ **~иваться**) to become flat.

спля|са́ть, шу́, ~шешь *pf. of* ▸ **пляса́ть**

спо|и́ть, ю́, и́шь *pf.* (*of* ▸ **спа́ивать**) (*coll.*) to get drunk; to make a drunkard (of).

споко́|йный (~ен, ~йна) *adj.*
1 quiet; calm, tranquil; **~йное мо́ре** calm sea; **~йной но́чи!** good night!
2 (*человек*) quiet, composed.

споко́йстви|е, я *nt.*
1 (*покой*) quiet, tranquillity; calm.
2 (*порядок*) order; **наруше́ние обще́ственного ~я** breach of the peace.
3 (*душевное*) composure, serenity; **с. ду́ха** peace of mind.

спола́скива|ть, ю *impf. of* ▸ **сполосну́ть**

сполз|а́ть, а́ю *impf. of* ▸ **~ти́**

спол|зти́, у́, ёшь, *past* **~, ~ла́** *pf.* (*of* ▸ **~а́ть**)
1 (**с** + *g.*) to climb down (from).
2 (*о шапке*) to slip down.

сполосн|у́ть, у́, ёшь *pf.* (*of* ▸ **спола́скивать**) to rinse (out).

спонси́р|овать, ую *impf. and pf.* to sponsor.

спо́нсор, а *m.* sponsor, backer.

спо́нсорств|о, а *nt.* sponsorship.

спонта́н|ный (~ен, ~на) *adj.* spontaneous.

спор, а *m.*
1 argument; controversy; debate.
2 (*leg.*) dispute.

спо́р|ить, ю, ишь *impf.* (*of* ▸ **по~ 1**) (**о** + *p.*)
1 to argue (about); to dispute (about), debate.
2 (*leg.*) (**о** + *p.*, **за** + *a.*) to dispute; **с. о насле́дстве** to dispute a legacy.
3 (*держать пари*) to bet (on), have a bet (on).

спо́р|ный (~ен, ~на) *adj.* debatable, questionable; disputed, at issue; **с. вопро́с** moot point.

спор|о́ть, ю́, ~ешь *pf.* (*of* ▸ **спа́рывать**) to unstitch, take off (*by cutting stitches*).

спорт, а *m.* sport; **ко́нный с.** equestrianism.

спортза́л, а *m.* sports hall.

спорти́вн|ый *adj.* (*инвентарь, комментатор*) sports; (*человек, фигура*) sporty; (*одежда*) casual; **с. зал** gymnasium; **~ая площа́дка** sports ground, playing field.

спортсме́н, а *m.* sportsman.

спортсме́нк|а, и *f.* sportswoman.

спо́рщик, а *m.* debater, wrangler.

спо́рщи|ца, цы *f. of* ▶ **~к**

спо́соб, а *m.* way, method; means; **таки́м ~ом** in this way.

спосо́бност|ь, и *f.*
1 (*usu. pl.*; **к** + *d.*) (*талант*) ability (for), talent (for), aptitude (for); **челове́к с больши́ми ~ями** person of great abilities; **с. к языка́м** talent for languages, linguistic ability.
2 (*возможность*) capacity; **покупа́тельная с.** purchasing power; **пропускна́я с.** capacity.

спосо́б|ный (~ен, ~на) *adj.*
1 (*талантливый*) able, talented, clever; **с. к матема́тике** good at mathematics.
2 (**на** + *a. or* + *inf.*) capable (of), able (to); **они́ ~ны на всё** they are capable of anything.

спосо́бств|овать, ую *impf.* (+ *d.*)
1 (*помогать*) to assist.
2 (*делать возможным*) to be conducive (to), further, promote.

спотКн|у́ться, у́сь, ёшься *pf.* (*of* ▶ **спотыка́ться**)
1 (**о** + *a.*) to stumble (against, over).
2 (**на** + *p. or* **о** + *a.*; *fig., coll.*) to get stuck (on).
3 (*coll.*) (*оступиться*) to slip up.

спотыка́|ться, юсь *impf. of* ▶ **споткну́ться**

спохва|ти́ться, чу́сь, ~́тишься *pf.* (*of* ▶ **~́тываться**) (*coll.*) to remember suddenly, think suddenly.

спохва́тыва|ться, юсь *impf. of* ▶ **спохвати́ться**

спра́ва *adv.* (**от** + *g.*) on the right (of), to the right (of).

справедли́вост|ь, и *f.*
1 justice; fairness; **поступа́ть по ~и** to act fairly.
2 (*правильность*) truth, correctness.

справедли́в|ый (~, ~а) *adj.*
1 just; fair; **с. судья́** impartial judge.
2 (*правильный*) justified, true, correct; **на́ши подозре́ния оказа́лись ~ыми** our suspicions proved to be justified.

спра́в|ить, лю, ишь *pf.* (*of* ▶ **~ля́ть**) (*coll.*) (*свадьбу, день рождения*) to celebrate.

спра́в|иться[1], люсь, ишься *pf.* (*of* ▶ **~ля́ться**) (**с** + *i.*)
1 (*с работой, детьми*) to cope (with), manage.
2 (*с противником*) to deal (with), get the better (of); **я с ним ~люсь!** I'll deal with him!
3 (*с волнением, со страхом*) to control.

спра́в|иться[2], люсь, ишься *pf.* (*of* ▶ **~ля́ться**) (**о** + *p.*) to ask (about), inquire (about); **с. в словаре́** to consult a dictionary.

спра́вк|а, и *f.*
1 (*сведение*) information; **навести́ ~и** (**о** + *p.*) to inquire (about).
2 (*документ*) certificate; **с. с ме́ста рабо́ты** document confirming that one works at a place.

справля́|ть(ся), ю(сь) *impf. of* ▶ **спра́вить(ся)**

спра́вочник, а *m.* reference book, handbook, guide; **телефо́нный с.** telephone directory.

спра́вочн|ый *adj.* inquiry, information; **~ая** directory enquiries (*Br.*), directory assistance (*US*); **~ое бюро́, с. стол** inquiries/information office.

спра́шива|ть, ю *impf. of* ▶ **спроси́ть**

спресс|ова́ть, у́ю *pf. of* ▶ **прессова́ть**

спринт, а *m.* (*sport*) sprint.

спри́нтер, а *m.* (*sport*) sprinter.

спровоци́р|овать, ую *pf. of* ▶ **провоци́ровать**

спроекти́р|овать, ую *pf. of* ▶ **проекти́ровать**

спрос, а *m.* (*econ.*) demand; (**на** + *a.*) demand (for); **с. и предложе́ние** supply and demand; **по́льзоваться больши́м ~ом** to be much in demand.

спро|си́ть, шу́, ~́сишь *pf.* (*of* ▶ **спра́шивать**)
1 (**о** + *p.*) (*осведомиться*) to ask (about), inquire (about); **с. доро́гу** to ask the way.
2 (+ *a. or g.*) (*попросить*) to ask (for); (*пожелать видеть*) to ask to see, desire to speak (to); **~си́те хозя́йку** ask to see the landlady.
3 (**с** + *g.*) (*призвать к ответу*) to make answer (for), make responsible (for).

спрут, а *m.* octopus.

спры́гива|ть, ю *impf. of* ▶ **спры́гнуть**

спры́г|нуть, ну, нешь *pf.* (*of* ▶ **~ивать**) (**с** + *g.*) to jump off; to jump down (from).

спряга́|ть, ю *impf.* (*of* ▶ **про~**) (*gram.*) to conjugate.

спряже́ни|е, я *nt.* (*gram.*) conjugation.

спря|сть, ду́, дёшь, *past* **~л, ~́ла́, ~́ло** *pf. of* ▶ **прясть**

спря́|тать(ся), чу(сь), чешь(ся) *pf. of* ▶ **пря́тать(ся)**

спу́гива|ть, ю *impf. of* ▶ **спугну́ть**

спуг|ну́ть, ну́, нёшь *pf.* (*of* ▶ **~́ивать**) to frighten off, scare off.

спуск, а *m.*
1 (*флага*) lowering; **с. корабля́** launch(ing).
2 (*с высоты*) descent, descending.
3 (*воды*) release; draining.
4 (*откос*) slope, descent.

спуска́|ть, ю *impf. of* ▶ **спусти́ть**

спуска́|ться, юсь *impf. of* ▶ **спусти́ться**

спу|сти́ть, щу́, ~́стишь *pf.* (*of* ▶ **~ска́ть**)
1 (*флаг, занавеску*) to let down, lower; **с. кора́бль (на́ воду)** to launch a ship.
2 (*освободить*) to let go, let loose, release; **с. куро́к** to pull, release the trigger; **с. соба́ку с при́вязи** to unleash a dog.
3 (*воду, воздух*) to let out; **с. во́ду в туале́те** to flush a lavatory.
4 (*о шине*) to go down.
5 (*coll.*) (*деньги*) to throw away, squander.

спу|сти́ться, щу́сь, ~́стишься *pf.* (*of* ▶ **~ска́ться**) to descend; to come down, go down; (*вниз по течению*) to go downstream; (*о мраке*) to fall; **с. с ле́стницы** to come downstairs.

спустя́ *prep.* + *a.* after; later; **с. год** after a year, a year later.

спу́та|ть(ся), ю(сь) *pf. of* ▸ **пу́тать(ся)**

спу́тник, а *m.*
1 (*человек*) (travelling (*Br.*), traveling (*US*)) companion; **с. жи́зни** husband.
2 (*обстоятельство*) concomitant.
3 (*astron.*) satellite; **с. свя́зи** communications satellite.

спу́тников|ый *adj.*: **~ая связь** satellite link; **~ое телеви́дение** satellite television.

спу́тни|ца, цы *f. of* ▸ **~к 1; с. жи́зни** wife.

спя́|тить, чу, тишь *pf.* (*coll.*) to go nuts, go off one's rocker.

спя́чк|а, и *f.* hibernation.

сраба́тыва|ть, ю *impf. of* ▸ **срабо́тать**

срабо́та|ть, ю *pf.* (*of* ▸ **сраба́тывать**) (*машина, сигнализация*) to work.

сравне́ни|е, я *nt.* comparison; **по ~ю, в ~и (с** + *i.*) by, in comparison (with), compared (with).

сра́внива|ть, ю *impf. of* ▸ **сравни́ть** *and* ▸ **сравня́ть**

сравни́тельно *adv.*
1 (**с** + *i.*) by, in comparison (with).
2: **с. недорого́й/хоро́ший** comparatively cheap/good.

сравни́тельн|ый *adj.* comparative; **~ая сте́пень** (*gram.*) comparative (degree).

сравн|и́ть, ю́, и́шь *pf.* (*of* ▸ **~ивать**) (**с** + *i.*) to compare (to, with).

сравн|и́ться, ю́сь, и́шься *pf.* (**с** + *i.*) to compare (with).

сравн|я́ть, я́ю *pf.* (*of* ▸ **~ивать**) to make even; **с. счёт** (*sport*) to equalize, bring the score level.

сравня́|ться, юсь *pf.* (**с** + *i.*) to become equal (with).

сража́|ть, ю *impf. of* ▸ **срази́ть**

сража́|ться, юсь *impf.* (*of* ▸ **срази́ться**) (**с** + *i.*) to fight; to join battle (with).

сраже́ни|е, я *nt.* battle, engagement.

сра|зи́ть, жу́, зи́шь *pf.* (*of* ▸ **~жа́ть**)
1 (*убить*) to slay.
2 (*fig.*) to overwhelm, crush; **весть о катастро́фе ~зи́ла её** she was crushed by the news of the disaster.

сра|зи́ться, жу́сь, зи́шься *pf. of* ▸ **~жа́ться**

сра́зу *adv.*
1 (*в один приём*) (all) at once.
2 (*немедленно*) straight away, immediately.
3 (*рядом*) right, just; **с. за до́мом** right behind the house.

сраст|а́ться, а́ется *impf. of* ▸ **~и́сь**

сраст|и́сь, ётся, *past* **сро́сся, сросла́сь** *pf.* (*of* ▸ **~а́ться**)
1 (*о корнях*) to grow together; (*о костях*) to knit.
2 (*fig.*) (**с** + *i.*) (*соединиться*) to merge (with).

ср|ать, у, ёшь *impf.* (*of* ▸ **насра́ть**) (*vulg.*) to shit.

сред|а́[1]**, ы́,** *a.* **~у́,** *pl.* **~ы** *f.*
1 (*природная*) environment, surroundings; **окружа́ющая с.** the environment; (*социальная*) environment, milieu; (*biol.*) habitat; **в ~е́** (+ *g.*) among.
2 (*phys., chem.*) medium.

сред|а́[2]**, ы́,** *a.* **~у,** *pl.* **~ы,** *d.* **~а́м** *f.* (*день недели*) Wednesday; **в ~у** on Wednesday.

среди́ *prep.* + *g.*
1 (*в числе*) among; amidst; **с. них** among them, in their midst.
2 (*посредине*) in the middle (of).

Средизе́мн|ое мо́р|е, ~ого ~я *nt.* the Mediterranean (Sea).

средиземномо́рский *adj.* Mediterranean.

среднеазиа́тский *adj.* central Asian.

средневеко́вый *adj.* medieval.

Средневеко́вь|е, я *nt.* the Middle Ages.

сре́дн|ий *adj.*
1 (*комната, ряд*) middle; (*рост*) medium; **С~ие века́** the Middle Ages; **~их лет** middle-aged; **~его ро́ста** of medium height.
2 (*в среднем*) mean, average; **с. за́работок** average earnings; *as n.* **~ее, ~его** *nt.* mean, average; **в ~ем** on average.
3 (*посредственный*) middling, average; **ни́же ~его** below average.
4 (*школа, образование*) secondary.
5: **с. род** (*gram.*) neuter (gender).

средото́чи|е, я *nt.* focus, centre (*Br.*), center (*US*) point.

сре́дств|о, а *nt.*
1 means; facilities; **~а ма́ссовой информа́ции** mass media; **~а передвиже́ния** means of conveyance; **~а к существова́нию** livelihood.
2 (**от** + *g.*) remedy (for); **с. от ка́шля** cough medicine, sth. for a cough.
3 (*pl.*) (*деньги, капитал*) resources; funds.
4 (*pl.*) (*состояние*) means; **жить не по ~ам** to live beyond one's means.

срез, а *m.*
1 (*место*) cut.
2 (*слой*) section.

сре́|зать, жу, жешь *pf.* (*of* ▸ **~за́ть**) (*ветку*) to cut off; **с. у́гол** (*fig.*) to cut off a corner.

среза́|ть, ю *impf. of* ▸ **сре́зать**

срис|ова́ть, у́ю *pf.* (*of* ▸ **~о́вывать**) to copy.

срисо́выва|ть, ю *impf. of* ▸ **срисова́ть**

сровня́|ть, ю *pf. of* ▸ **ровня́ть; с. с землёй** to raze to the ground.

срок, а (у) *m.*
1 (*промежуток времени*) time, period; term; **ме́сячный с.** period of one month; **с. де́йствия** period of validity; **с. полномо́чий** term of office; **~ом на** (+ *a.*) for a period of.
2 (*дата*) date; **кра́йний с.** closing date; **с. хране́ния** shelf life; **в с., к ~у** in time, to time.

сро́чно *adv.* urgently; quickly.

сро́чност|ь, и *f.* urgency.

сро́ч|ный (~ен, ~на) *adj.*
1 (*сообщение, заказ*) urgent.
2 (*ссуда, вклад*) fixed-term; for a fixed period.

сруб|а́ть, а́ю *impf. of* ▸ **~и́ть**

сруб|и́ть, лю́, ~ишь *pf.* (*of* ▸ **~а́ть**) to fell, cut down.

срыв, а *m.*

1 (*плана, работы*) disruption; **с. работы** stoppage.
2 (*неудача*) failure.
срыва́|ть, ю *impf. of* ▶**сорвать**
срыва́|ться, юсь *impf. of* ▶**сорваться**
сса́дин|а, ы *f.* scratch, abrasion.
сса|ди́ть, жу́, ~́дишь *pf.* (*of* ▶**~живать**)
1 (*помочь сойти*) to help down; **с. кого́-н. с ло́шади** to help s.o. down from a horse.
2 (*заставить выйти*) to put off, make get off (*from public transport*).
сса́жива|ть, ю *impf. of* ▶**ссадить**
ссо́р|а, ы *f.* quarrel; **она́ в ~е с сестро́й** she's fallen out with her sister.
ссо́р|ить, ю, ишь *impf.* (*of* ▶**по~**) to cause to quarrel, cause to fall out.
ссо́р|иться, юсь, ишься *impf.* (*of* ▶**по~**) (**с** + *i.*) to quarrel (with), fall out (with).
СССР *m. indecl.* (*abbr. of* **Сою́з Сове́тских Социалисти́ческих Респу́блик**) (*hist.*) USSR (*Union of Soviet Socialist Republics*).
ссу́д|а, ы *f.* loan; **ба́нковская с.** bank loan.
ссуту́л|иться, юсь, ишься *pf. of* ▶**сутулиться**
ссыла́|ть(ся), ю(сь) *impf. of* ▶**сосла́ть(ся)**
ссы́лк|а¹, и *f.* exile, banishment.
ссы́лк|а², и *f.* (**на** + *a.*) (*указание*) reference (to); (*comput.*) link.
ссы́п|ать, лю, лешь *pf.* (*of* ▶**~а́ть**) to pour.
ссып|а́ть, а́ю *impf. of* ▶**~́ать**
стабилизи́р|овать, ую *impf. and pf.* to stabilize.
стабилизи́р|оваться, уется *impf. and pf.* to become stable.
стаби́льност|ь, и *f.* stability.
стаби́л|ьный (~ен, ~ьна) *adj.* stable, firm.
ста́в|ень, ня, *g. pl.* **~ней** *m.* shutter (*on window*).
ста́в|ить, лю, ишь *impf.* (*of* ▶**по~¹**)
1 (*помещать*) to put, place, set; (*что-н. вертикальное*) to stand; **с. цветы́ в ва́зу** to put flowers in a vase; **с. диа́гноз** to diagnose; **с. реко́рд** to set up, create a record; **с. то́чку** to put a full stop; **с. кого́-н. в нело́вкое положе́ние** to put s.o. in an awkward position.
2 (*сооружать*) to put up, erect; (*устанавливать*) to install; **с. па́мятник** to erect a monument.
3 (*назначать*) to put in, install; **с. но́вого гла́вного инжене́ра** to put in a new chief engineer.
4 (*накладывать*) to apply, put on; **с. кому́-н. гра́дусник** to take s.o.'s temperature.
5 (*вопрос, проблему*) to put, present; (*пьесу*) to put on, stage.
6 (**на** + *a.*) (*в игре*) to place, stake (*money on*); **с. на ло́шадь** to back a horse.
ста́вк|а, и *f.*
1 (*fin.*) rate; **проце́нтная с.** interest rate.
2 (*в играх*) stake; **де́лать ~у** (**на** + *a.*) to stake (on); (*fig.*) to count (on), gamble (on).

ста́вленник, а *m.* protégé.
ста́в|ня, ни, *g. pl.* **~ен** *f.* = **ста́вень**
стадио́н, а *m.* stadium.
ста́ди|я, и *f.* stage.
ста́дный *adj.* (*животное*) gregarious; **с. инсти́нкт** herd instinct.
ста́д|о, а, *pl.* **~а́** *nt.* herd; flock.
стаж, а *m.* length of service.
стажёр, а *m.*
1 (*проходящий испытательный срок*) probationer.
2 (*студент*) student (*on special course not leading to degree*); exchange student.
стака́н, а *m.* glass, tumbler.
сталева́р, а *m.* steel founder.
ста́лкива|ть(ся), ю(сь) *impf. of* ▶**столкну́ть(ся)**
стал|ь, и *f.* steel; **нержаве́ющая с.** stainless steel.
стальн|о́й *adj.* steel; **~а́я во́ля** iron will; **~ы́е не́рвы** nerves of steel.
Стамбу́л, а *m.* Istanbul.
стаме́ск|а, и *f.* (*tech.*) chisel.
станда́рт, а *m.*
1 standard.
2 (*fig.*) (*шаблон*) cliché, stereotype.
станда́рт|ный (~ен, ~на) *adj.* standard.
станов|и́ться, лю́сь, ~́ишься *impf. of* ▶**стать**
становле́ни|е, я *nt.* (*идей, характера, государства*) formation; **в проце́ссе ~я** in the making.
стан|о́к, ка́ *m.* (*tech.*) machine tool, machine; **печа́тный с.** printing press; **тка́цкий с.** loom; **тока́рный с.** lathe.
ста́нци|я, и *f.* station; **авто́бусная с.** bus station; **железнодоро́жная с.** railway (*Br.*), railroad (*US*) station.
ста́птыва|ть, ю *impf. of* ▶**стопта́ть**
стара́тел|ьный (~ен, ~ьна) *adj.* assiduous, diligent.
стара́|ться, юсь *impf.* (*of* ▶**по~**)
1 (*усердствовать*) to try; to apply o.s.; **с. изо всех сил** to do one's utmost.
2 (+ *inf.*) (*стремиться*) to try, endeavour; **я ~юсь помо́чь ему́** I'm trying to help him.
стар|е́е *comp. of* ▶**~ый**
старе́ни|е, я *nt.* ageing.
старе́|ть, ю *impf.*
1 (*pf.* **по~**) (*человек*) to grow old, age.
2 (*pf.* **у~**) (*идея, машина*) to become obsolete.
стари́к, а́ *m.* old man; **глубо́кий с.** very old man; **~и́** old people.
старин|а́, ы́ *f.* antiquity, olden times; **в ~у́** in olden days.
стари́нный *adj.* (*книга, обычай*) ancient, old; (*мебель*) antique.
ста́р|ить, ю, ишь *impf.* (*of* ▶**со~**) to age.
ста́р|иться, юсь, ишься *impf.* (*of* ▶**со~**) to age; to grow old.
старомо́д|ный (~ен, ~на) *adj.* old-fashioned; out-of-date.
ста́рост|а, ы *m.* head; **с. кла́сса** (*in school*) class prefect, monitor.
ста́рост|ь, и *f.* old age.
старт, а *m.* (*sport, fig.*) start; **на с.!** on your

marks!
старт|ова́ть, у́ю *impf. and pf.*
1 (*sport*) to start.
2 (*aeron.*) to take off.
3 (*отправляться*) to start out; to depart.
4 (*начинаться*) to begin, commence.
стару́х|а, и *f.* old woman, old lady.
ста́рческий *adj.* old person's; **с. во́зраст** old age; **с. мара́зм** senility.
ста́рше *comp. of* ▸ **ста́рый;** (*взрослее*): **она́ с. меня́ на три го́да** she is three years older than me; (*по служебному положению*): **он ста́рше меня́ по зва́нию** he is senior to me in rank.
старшекла́ссник, а *m.* senior (pupil).
старшекла́ссни|ца, цы *f. of* ▸ **~к**
ста́рш|ий *adj.*
1 (*более старый*) elder, older; **с. брат** older brother; *as n.* **~ие, ~их** (one's) elders, grown-ups.
2 (*самый старый*) oldest, eldest.
3 (*по служебному положению*) senior, superior; (*в названиях*) chief, head; **~ая медсестра́** senior nurse, sister (*Br.*); *as n.* **с., ~его** *m.* chief; (*mil.*) man in charge.
4 (*высший*) senior, upper, higher; **с. класс** (*in school*) higher form (*Br.*), senior grade (*US*).
старшинств|о́, а́ *nt.* seniority; **по ~у́** by seniority.
ста́р|ый (~, ~а́, ~́о) *adj.* old; **с. стиль** the Old Style (*of the Julian calendar*).
ста́скива|ть, ю *impf. of* ▸ **стащи́ть 1**
стати́стик|а, и *f.* statistics.
статисти́ческий *adj.* statistical.
стати́ческий *adj.* static.
ста́тус, а *m.* status.
ста́тус-кво́ *m. & nt. indecl.* status quo.
ста́ту|я, и *f.* statue.
стать[1], ста́ну, ста́нешь *pf.* (*of* ▸ **станови́ться**)
1 (*встать*) to stand; **с. на коле́ни** to kneel; (*поддержать*) to stand up for; **с. на чью-н. сто́рону** to take s.o.'s side, stand up for s.o.
2 (*расположиться*) to take up position; **с. на я́корь** to anchor.
3 (*остановиться*) to stop, come to a halt; **мои́ часы́ ста́ли** my watch has stopped.
стать[2], ста́ну, ста́нешь *pf.* (*of* ▸ **станови́ться**)
1 (+ *inf.*) (*начать*) to begin (to), start; **она́ ста́ла говори́ть** she began talking.
2 (+ *i.*) (*сделаться*) to become, get, grow; **ста́ло темно́** it got dark; **ей ста́ло лу́чше** she was better; she had got better.
3 (**с** + *i.*) (*случиться*) to become (of), happen (to); **что с ни́ми ста́ло?** what has become of them?
4 : **не с.** (*impers.* + *g.*) (*умереть*) to die; (*исчезнуть*) to disappear, go.
стат|ья́, ьи́, *g. pl.* **~е́й** *f.*
1 (*газетная, научная*) article.
2 (*закона, договора*) clause; (*финансового документа*) item; (*в словаре*) entry; **расхо́дная с.** debit item.
стациона́рн|ый *adj.*
1 (*не изменяющийся*) stationary; **с. объе́кт** (*mil.*) stationary target.
2 (*постоянный*) permanent, fixed.
3 (*больничный*) hospital; **с. больно́й** in-patient; **~ое лече́ние** hospitalization.
ста́чива|ть, ю *impf. of* ▸ **сточи́ть**
ста́чк|а, и *f.* (*забастовка*) strike.
стащ|и́ть, у́, ~́ишь *pf.* (*of* ▸ **ста́скивать**)
1 (*сапоги*) to drag off, pull off.
2 (*no impf.*) (*coll.*) (*украсть*) to nick (*Br.*), pinch, swipe.
ста́|я, и *f.* (*птиц*) flock; (*рыб*) school, shoal; (*волков*) pack.
ствол, а́ *m.*
1 (*дерева*) trunk.
2 (*оружия*) barrel; (*coll.*) (*само оружие*) gun.
ствол|ово́й *adj. of* ▸ **~; ~ова́я кле́тка** (*biol.*) stem cell.
ство́рк|а, и *f.* (*двери, зеркала*) leaf, fold; (*ворот, ставней*) half, side.
сте́б|ель, ля, *pl.* **~ли, ~ле́й** *m.* stem, stalk.
стёган|ый *adj.* quilted; **~ое одея́ло** quilt.
стеж|о́к, ка́ *m.* stitch.
стека́|ть, ет *impf. of* ▸ **сте́чь**
стекл|и́ть, ю́, и́шь *impf.* (*of* **за~**) to glaze.
стек|ло́, ла́, *pl.* **~́ла, ~́ол** *nt.* glass; (*collect.*) glassware.
стекловолокн|о́, а́ *nt.* fibreglass (*Br.*), fiberglass (*US*).
стеклоочисти́тел|ь, я *m.* windscreen (*Br.*), windshield (*US*) wiper.
стекля́нн|ый *adj.*
1 glass; **~ые изде́лия** glassware; (*окно, дверь*) glazed.
2 (*fig.*) (*взгляд, глаза*) glassy.
стеко́льщик, а *m.* glazier.
сте́л|а, ы *f.* obelisk.
стел|и́ть, ю́, ~́ешь *impf.* (*of* ▸ **по~**) to spread; **с. посте́ль** to make a bed; **с. ска́терть** to lay a tablecloth.
стелла́ж, а́ *m.* shelves.
сте́льк|а, и *f.* insole.
стемне́|ть, ет *pf. of* ▸ **темне́ть 2**
стен|а́, ы́, *a.* **~́у,** *pl.* **~́ы,** *d.* **~́ам** *f.* wall (*also fig.*); **в ~а́х** (+ *g.*) inside, within the precincts (of).
стенд, а *m.*
1 (*на выставке*) stand (*Br.*), booth (*US*).
2 (*для испытаний*) test bed.
3 (*для стрельбы*) rifle range.
сте́нк|а, и *f.*
1 (*стена*) wall; **гимнасти́ческая с.** wall bars.
2 (*ящика, кастрюли*) side; (*желудка*) wall.
3 (*мебель*) wall unit.
стеногра́фи|я, и *f.* shorthand.
стенокарди́|я, и *f.* angina (pectoris).
степе́н|ный (~ен, ~на) *adj.* staid.
сте́пен|ь, и, *g. pl.* **~е́й** *f.*
1 degree, extent; **до изве́стной ~и, до не́которой ~и** to some extent, to a certain extent.
2 (*math.*) power; **возвести́ в тре́тью с.** to raise to the third power.
3 (*звание*) (academic) degree; (*разряд*) class; **с. бакала́вра** bachelor's degree; **учёная с. до́ктора нау́к** doctorate.
сте́плер, а *m.* stapler.
степ|ь, и, о ~́и, в ~и́, *pl.* **~́и, ~е́й** *f.*

steppe.

стéрв|а, ы *f.* (*sl.*; *as term of abuse*) bastard; (*о женщине*) bitch.

стервя́тник, а *m.* (*zool.*) carrion crow.

стéреосистем|а, ы *f.* stereo (system).

стереоти́п, а *m.* stereotype.

стер|éть, сотрý, сотрёшь, *past* **~̈, ~̈ла** *pf.* (*of* ▸ **стирáть¹**)
1 (*рисунок*) to rub out, erase; (*кассету, перезаписываемый диск*) to erase; (*comput.*) to delete; (*пыль, пот*) to wipe off; **с. с лицá земли́** to wipe off the face of the earth.
2 (*ногу*) to rub sore.
3 (*в порошок*) to grind (down).

стер|éться, сотрётся, *past* **~̈ся, ~̈лась** *pf.* (*of* ▸ **стирáться¹**)
1 (*о надписи, краске*) to rub off; (*fig.*) (*забыться*) to fade.
2 (*о подошвах, пальцах*) to become worn down.

стерé|чь, гý, жёшь, гýт, *past* **~̈г, ~глá** *impf.* (*вещи, стадо*) to guard, watch (over).

стéрж|ень, ня *m.*
1 (*tech.*) pivot; shank, rod; **поршневóй с.** piston rod.
2 (*fig.*) (*основа*) core.

стерилизáци|я, и *f.* sterilization.

стерилиз|овáть, ýю *impf. and pf.* to sterilize.

стери́л|ьный (~ен, ~ьна) *adj.* sterile.

стéрлинг, а *m.* (*fin.*) sterling; **фунт ~ов** pound sterling.

стéрляд|ь, и *f.* (*zool.*) sterlet.

стерóид, а *m.* steroid.

стерп|éть, лю́, ~́ишь *pf.* to bear, suffer, endure.

ст|ёртый *p.p.p. of* ▸ **~ерéть** *and adj.* (*надпись, монета*) worn, faded; (*fig.*) (*очертание*) faint.

стеснéни|е, я *nt.* (*ограничение*) constraint; (*смущение*) shyness, timidness.

стесни́тел|ьный (~ен, ~ьна) *adj.* shy; awkward.

стесня́|ться, юсь *impf.* (*of* ▸ **по~**) (+ *inf.*) to feel too shy (to), be ashamed (to); (+ *g.*) to feel shy (before, of); **не ~йтесь!** don't be shy!; **не с. в срéдствах** to use any means possible.

сте|чь, чёт, кýт, *past* **~̈к, ~клá** *pf.* (*of* ▸ **~кáть**) to flow down.

стилиз|овáть, ýю *impf. and pf.* to stylize.

стили́ст, а *m.*
1 (*мастер стиля*) stylist.
2 (*гримёр*) make-up artist.

стилисти́ческий *adj.* stylistic.

стил|ь, я *m.* style.

сти́л|ьный (~ен, ~ьна) *adj.* stylish.

сти́мул, а *m.* incentive, stimulus.

стимули́р|овать, ую *impf. and pf.* to stimulate, encourage.

стимуля́ци|я, и *f.* stimulation; **с. рóдов** (*med.*) induction.

стипéнди|я, и *f.* grant, scholarship.

стирáльн|ый *adj.* washing; **~ая маши́на** washing machine; **с. порошóк** washing powder.

стирá|ть¹, ю *impf. of* ▸ **стерéть**

стирá|ть², ю *impf.* (*of* ▸ **вы́~**) to wash, launder.

стирá|ться¹, ется *impf. of* ▸ **стерéться**

стирá|ться², ется *impf.* to wash; **хорошó с.** to wash well.

сти́рк|а, и *f.* washing, laundering; **отдáть в ~у** to send to the wash, send to the laundry.

сти́с|нуть, ну, нешь *pf.* to squeeze; **с. зýбы** to clench one's teeth.

стих¹, á *m.* verse; (*pl.*) verses; poetry.

стих² *see* ▸ **~́нуть**

стих|áть, áю *impf. of* ▸ **~́нуть**

стихи́|йный (~ен, ~йна) *adj.*
1 elemental; **~йное бéдствие** natural disaster.
2 (*fig.*) (*протест*) spontaneous, uncontrolled.

стихи́|я, и *f.* element.

сти́х|нуть, ну, нешь, *past* **~, ~ла** *pf.* (*of* ▸ **~áть**) (*шум, ветер, дождь*) to abate, subside, die down; (*человек*) to calm down.

стихотворéни|е, я *nt.* poem.

стлать, стелю́, стéлешь *impf.* (*of* ▸ **по~̈**) = **стели́ть**

сто, ста, *pl.* (*no nom. or a.*) **сот, стам, стáми, стах** *num.* hundred; **нéсколько сот рублéй** several hundred roubles; **я сто раз тебé говори́л** (*coll.*) I've told you a hundred times.

стог, а, в (на) ~ý *and* **в (на) ~́е,** *pl.* **~á** *m.* (*agric.*) stack, rick.

стóимост|ь, и *f.*
1 (*цена*) cost; **с. проéзда** fare; **с. жи́зни** cost of living; **óбщей ~ью в** (+ *a.*) to a total value of.
2 (*econ.*) (*ценность*) value; **номинáльная с.** face/nominal value.

стó|ить, ю, ишь *impf.*
1 to cost (*also fig.*); **скóлько ~ит э́то плáтье?** how much is this dress?; **дóрого с.** to cost dear.
2 (+ *g.*) (*заслуживать*) to be worth; to deserve; **он её не ~ит** he doesn't deserve her; **чегó ~ят егó обещáния?** his promises are worth nothing; (*impers.*): **~ит** it is worth while; **об э́том ~ит подýмать** it's worth thinking about.
3 : **~ит тóлько** (*impers.* + *inf.*) one has only (to).

стóйк|а, и *f.*
1 (*sport*) stand, stance; **с. на рукáх** handstand.
2 (*tech.*) support, prop; (*ворот*) bar.
3 (*прилавок*) bar, counter.

стó|йкий (~ек, ~́йкá, ~йко) *adj.*
1 firm, stable; (*запах*) persistent.
2 (*fig.*) (*характер*) stable; steadfast, staunch.

стóйл|о, а *nt.* stall.

сток, а *m.*
1 (*действие*) flow; drainage, outflow.
2 (*место, устройство*) drain, gutter; sewer.

Стокгóльм, а *m.* Stockholm.

стóл, á *m.*
1 (*предмет мебели*) table; **пи́сьменный с.** desk; **сесть за с.** to sit down to table; **за ~óм** at table.
2 (*питание*) board; (*кухня*) cooking, cuisine; **ры́бный с.** fish diet; **«швéдский» с.** smorgasbord.
3 (*отделение*) department; office; **с.**

нахо́док lost property office.
столб, а́ *m.* post, pole, pillar, column; **телегра́фный с.** telegraph pole.
столб|е́ц, ца́ *m.* (*в газете, словаре*) column.
столбня́к, а́ *m.*
1 (*med.*) tetanus.
2 (*coll.*) stupor; **на неё нашёл с.** she was in a stupor.
столе́ти|е, я *nt.*
1 (*век*) century.
2 (*годовщина*) centenary.
столе́тн|ий *adj.*
1 hundred-year; **С~яя война́** the Hundred Years' War.
2 (*дуб, старец*) hundred-year-old; **~яя годовщи́на** centenary.
столи́ц|а, ы *f.* capital; metropolis.
столи́|чный *adj. of* ▸ **~ца; с. го́род** capital (city).
столкнове́ни|е, я *nt.* (*автомобилей*) collision; (*mil. and fig.*) clash; **вооружённое с.** armed conflict, hostilities; **с. интере́сов** clash of interests.
столкн|у́ть, у́, ёшь *pf.* (*of* ▸ **ста́лкивать**)
1 (*сбросить, сдвинуть*) to push off; **с. ло́дку в во́ду** to push a boat off (into the water).
2 (*сблизить*) to cause to collide; to knock together.
3 (*о случае, обстоятельствах*) to bring together.
столкн|у́ться, у́сь, ёшься *pf.* (*of* ▸ **ста́лкиваться**) (**с** + *i.*)
1 to collide (with) (*also fig.*); (*вступить в конфликт*) to clash (with), conflict (with).
2 (*fig.*) (*встретиться*) to run (into), bump (into); (*с трудностями, равнодушием*) to encounter.
столо́в|ая, ой *f.* (*в доме*) dining room; (*в армии*) mess; (*на работе*) canteen, cafeteria; (*общественная*) cafeteria.
столо́в|ый *adj.* table; **~ое вино́** table wine; **с. прибо́р** cover.
столп|и́ться, и́тся *pf.* to crowd.
сто́лько *adv.* (*с неисчисляемыми*) so much; (*с исчисляемыми*) so many; **с. любви́/де́нег** so much love/money; **нельзя́ с. рабо́тать** you should not work so much; **с. ..., ско́лько** as much ... as; **не с. ..., ско́лько** not so much ... as.
столя́р, а́ *m.* joiner (*Br.*), cabinetmaker.
стомато́лог, а *m.* dental surgeon.
стоматологи́ческий *adj.* dental.
стоматоло́ги|я, и *f.* dentistry.
стон, а *m.* moan, groan.
стон|а́ть, у́, ~́ешь *impf.* to moan, groan (*also fig.*).
стоп *int.* stop!
стоп|а́, ы́, *pl.* **~ы** *f.* (*ноги*) foot (*also fig.*).
сто́пк|а, и *f.* (*куча*) pile, heap.
стоп-ка́др, а *m.* (*пауза*) freeze-frame; (*снимок*) still (picture/image), snapshot.
стоп-кра́н, а *m.* emergency cord (*on train*).
стопроце́нтный *adj.* hundred per cent.
стоп|та́ть, чу́, ~́чешь *pf.* (*of* ▸ **ста́птывать**) (*обувь*) to wear down.
сторг|ова́ться, у́юсь *pf. of* ▸ **торгова́ться 1**

сто́рож, а, *pl.* **~а́, ~е́й** *m.* watchman, guard.
сторожев|о́й *adj.* watch; **~а́я соба́ка** watchdog.
сторож|и́ть, у́, и́шь *impf.* (*дом, стадо*) to guard, watch, keep watch (over).
сторо́жк|а, и *f.* lodge.
сторон|а́, ы́, *a.* **сто́рону,** *pl.* **сто́роны, сторо́н, ~а́м** *f.*
1 side; (*направление*) direction; **в сто́рону** (+ *g.*) in the direction of; **со ~ы́** (+ *g.*) from the direction of; **в сто́рону, в ~е́** aside; **держа́ться в ~е́** to keep aloof; **по ту сто́рону** (+ *g.*) across, on the other side (of); **пра́вая/ле́вая с.** right/left hand side; **с пра́вой, с ле́вой ~ы́** on the right, left side; **с мое́й ~ы́** for my part; **э́то о́чень любе́зно с ва́шей ~ы́** it is very kind of you; **наблюда́ть со ~ы́** to observe from the outside; **со ~ы́** (+ *g.*) (*indicating line of descent*) on the side of; **дед со ~ы́ ма́тери** maternal grandfather; **с одно́й ~ы́..., с друго́й ~ы́** on the one hand ..., on the other hand.
2 (*в споре*) side, party; **вы на чьей ~е́?** whose side are you on?; **тре́тья с.** third party.
3 (*элемент, свойство*) aspect, side.
сторо́нник, а *m.* supporter, advocate; **с. ми́ра** peace campaigner.
сторо́нни|ца, цы *f. of* ▸ **~к**
сточ|и́ть, у́, ~́ишь *pf.* (*of* ▸ **ста́чивать**) to grind off.
сто́чн|ый *adj.* sewage, drainage; **~ые во́ды** sewage.
стошн|и́ть, и́т *pf.* (*impers.*) to be sick, vomit; **меня́ ~и́ло** I was sick.
сто́я *adv.* standing up.
стоя́нк|а, и *f.*
1 (*остановка*) stop; (*автомобилей*) parking; **«с. запрещена́!»** 'no parking!'
2 (*место остановки*) stopping place; (*автомобилей*) parking area; (*судов*) moorage; **автомоби́льная с.** car park (*Br.*), parking lot (*US*).
сто|я́ть, ю́, и́шь *impf.*
1 to stand; **с. в о́череди** to stand in a queue; **с. на коле́нях** to kneel.
2 (*находиться*) to be, be situated, lie; **кни́ги ~я́т на по́лке** the books are on the shelf; **ча́йник ~и́т на плите́** the kettle is on the stove.
3 (*быть*) to be; to continue; **~я́ла хоро́шая пого́да** the weather continued fine.
4 (*жить*) to stay, put up; (*mil.*) to be stationed; **с. ла́герем** to be encamped.
5 (**за** + *a.*) (*защищать*) to stand up (for); (**на** + *p.*) (*настаивать*) to insist (on); **с. на своём** to refuse to give in.
6 (*не двигаться*) to have stopped; to have come to a halt/standstill; **мои́ часы́ ~я́т** my watch has stopped; **~й(те)!** stop!; halt!
сто́|ящий *pres. part. act. of* ▸ **~ить** *and adj.* (*человек*) deserving, worthy; (*дело, предложение*) worthwhile.
стр. *abbr. of*
1 **страни́ца** p, page.
2 **страни́цы** pp., pages.
страда́ни|е, я *nt.* suffering.
страда́тельный *adj.* (*gram.*) passive; **с.**

зало́г passive voice.

страда́|ть, ю *impf.*
1 (*impf. only*) (+ *i.*) to suffer (from); to be subject (to); **с. бессо́нницей** to suffer from insomnia.
2 (*impf. only*) (**от** + *g.*) to suffer (from), be in pain (with); **с. от зубно́й бо́ли** to have (a) toothache.
3 (*pf.* **по~**) (**за** + *a.*) to suffer (for, as a result of).

стра́ж|а, и *f.* guard, watch; **под ~ей** under arrest, in custody; **взять, заключи́ть под ~у** to take into custody.

стран|а́, ы́, *pl.* **~ы** *f.* country; land.

страни́ц|а, ы *f.* page (*also comput., fig., rhet.*).

стра́нно *adv.*
1 strangely, in a strange way.
2 *as pred.* (*необычно*) it is strange; (*непонятно*) funny, odd, queer; **как э́то ни с.** strangely enough; **(мне) с., что** I find it strange that.

стра́нност|ь, и *f.*
1 strangeness.
2 (*странная манера*) oddity, eccentricity; **за ним води́лись ~и** he was an odd person.

стра́н|ный (~ен, ~на́, ~но) *adj.* (*необычный*) strange; (*непонятный*) funny, odd.

стра́нств|овать, ую *impf.* to wander, travel; **с. по све́ту** to wander the earth; to travel the world.

Стра́сбург, а *m.* Strasbourg.

страстн|о́й *adj.* of Holy Week; **С~а́я пя́тница** Good Friday.

стра́ст|ный (~ен, ~на) *adj.* (*речь, поцелуй, человек*) passionate; (*сторонник, поклонник*) ardent.

страст|ь, и, *g. pl.* **~е́й** *f.* (**к** + *d.*) passion (for); **со ~ью** with passion, fervour (*Br.*), fervor (*US*).

стратеги́ческий *adj.* strategic.

страте́ги|я, и *f.* strategy.

стратосфе́р|а, ы *f.* stratosphere.

стра́ус, а *m.* (*африканский*) ostrich.

страх, а *m.* fear; (*сильный*) terror; **со ~у** from fear; **под ~ом сме́рти** on pain of death.

страхова́ни|е, я *nt.* insurance; **с. жи́зни** life insurance.

страх|ова́ть, у́ю *impf.* (*of* **за~**) (**от** + *g.*) to insure (against); **с. себя́** (**от** + *g., fig.*) to insure (against), safeguard o.s. (against).

страх|ова́ться, у́юсь *impf.* (*of* ▸ **за~**) (**от** + *g.*) to insure o.s. (against) (*also fig.*).

страхо́вк|а, и *f.* insurance.

страхово́й *adj.* insurance; **с. по́лис** insurance policy.

страш|и́ть, у́, и́шь *impf.* to frighten, scare.

страш|и́ться, у́сь, и́шься *impf.* (+ *g.*) to be afraid (of), fear.

стра́шно *adv.*
1 terribly, awfully; **с. испуга́ться** to get a terrible fright; **с. обра́доваться** to be awfully glad.
2 *as pred.* it is terrible; it is terrifying; **мне с.** I am terrified; **мне с.** (+ *inf.*) I am terrified to do sth.

стра́ш|ный (~ен, ~на́, ~но) *adj.* (*очень плохой*) terrible, awful, dreadful; (*вызывающий страх*) terrifying, frightening; **с. расска́з** terrifying story; **с. сон** bad dream; **с. шум** (*coll.*) awful din; **С. суд** the Day of Judgement, Doomsday; **ничего́ ~ного** it doesn't matter.

стрекоз|а́, ы́, *pl.* **~ы** *f.* dragonfly.

стреко|та́ть, чу́, ~чешь *impf.* (*о кузнечиках*) to chirr; (*о сороках*) to chatter; (*fig., coll.*) (*болтать*) to rattle, chatter.

стрел|а́, ы́, *pl.* **~ы** *f.* arrow (*also fig.*).

Стрел|е́ц, ьца́ *m.* Sagittarius.

стре́лк|а, и *f.*
1 pointer, indicator; (*часов*) hand; (*компаса*) needle.
2 (*знак*) arrow (*on diagram, etc.*).
3 (*rail.*) point(s) (*Br.*), switch (*US*); **перевести́ ~у** to change the points; (*fig., sl.*) **перевести́ ~и на** (+ *a.*) to lump the blame on.

стрел|о́к, ка́ *m.*
1 shot; **отли́чный с.** good shot.
2 (*mil.*) rifleman; (*в самолёте, в танке*) gunner.

стрельб|а́, ы́, *pl.* **~ы** *f.* shooting, firing.

стрельн|у́ть, у́, ёшь *inst. pf.*
1 to fire a shot.
2 (*impers.*): **у меня́ ~у́ло в у́хе** I had a stab of pain in my ear.
3 (*coll.*) (*сигарету*) to cadge (*Br.*), bum (*US*).

стреля́|ть, ю *impf.*
1 (**в** + *a.* or **по** + *d.*) to shoot (at), fire (at); **с. из револьве́ра, из ружья́** to fire a revolver, a gun; **с. в цель** to shoot at a target; **с. по самолёту** to fire at an aeroplane (*Br.*), airplane (*US*).
2 (*убивать*) to shoot; **с. куропа́ток** to go partridge shooting.
3 (*coll.*) (*сигареты*) to cadge (*Br.*), bum (*US*).
4 (*impers.*) (*о боли*) to have a shooting pain.

стреля́|ться, юсь *impf.*
1 (*самоубийца*) to shoot o.s.
2 (**с** + *i.*) (*на дуэли*) to fight a duel (with firearms) (with).

стремгла́в *adv.* headlong.

стреми́тел|ьный (~ен, ~ьна) *adj.* (*полёт, бег*) swift, headlong; (*рост, развитие*) rapid; (*ручей*) fast-flowing.

стрем|и́ться, лю́сь, и́шься *impf.*
1 (*устремиться*) to rush.
2 (**к** + *d.*) (*добиваться*) to strive (for), seek, aspire (to); (+ *inf.*) to strive (to), try (to); **с. к соверше́нству** to strive for perfection.
3 (**в, на** + *a.*) (*желать попасть*) to want to go (to).

стремле́ни|е, я *nt.* (**к** + *d.*) striving (for), aspiration (to).

стре́м|я, я, *g., d. and p.* **~ени,** *i.* **~енем,** *pl.* **~ена́, ~я́н, ~ена́м** *nt.* stirrup.

стремя́нк|а, и *f.* stepladder, steps.

стресс, а *m.* (*psych.*) stress.

стре́ссовый *adj.* (*положение*) stressful; (*состояние*) stressed.

стриж, а́ *m.* (*zool.*) swift.

стри́жк|а, и *f.*
1 (*действие*) hair cutting; shearing; clipping.
2 (*причёска*) haircut, hairstyle.

стрипти́з, а *m.* striptease.
стриптизёр, а *m.* (*male*) stripper.
стриптизёр|ка, ки *and* **~ша, ~ши** *f.* (*female*) stripper.
стри|чь, гу́, жёшь, гу́т, *past* **~г, ~гла** *impf.*
1 (*pf.* ▸ **о~** *and* ▸ **по~**) (*волосы, ногти, кусты*) to cut, clip.
2 (*pf.* ▸ **о~** *and* ▸ **по~**) (*овец*) to shear; (*пуделя*) to clip.
3 (*pf.* ▸ **по~**) (*человека*): **с. кого́-н.** to cut s.o.'s hair; to give s.o. a haircut.
стри́|чься, гу́сь, жёшься, гу́тся, *past* **~гся, ~глась** *impf.*
1 (*pf.* ▸ **по~**) to cut one's hair; to have one's hair cut.
2 (*no pf.*) (*носить короткие волосы*) to wear one's hair short.
строга́|ть, ю *impf.* (*tech.*) to plane.
стро́г|ий (~, ~а́, ~о) *adj.* (*начальник, правила, диета*) strict; (*наказание, причёска*) severe; **~ие ме́ры** strong measures; **с. пригово́р** severe sentence.
стро́го *adv.* strictly; severely; **с. говоря́** strictly speaking.
стро́гост|ь, и *f.* strictness; severity.
строев|о́й *adj.* (*mil.*)
1 combatant, line; **~а́я слу́жба** (front-)line service, combatant service.
2 drill; **~а́я подгото́вка** drill; **с. шаг** goose-step.
строе́ни|е, я *nt.*
1 (*здание*) building, structure.
2 (*структура*) structure, composition.
строжа́йший *superl. of* ▸ **стро́гий**
стро́же *comp. of* ▸ **стро́гий** *and* ▸ **стро́го**
строи́тел|ь, я *m.* builder, constructor; (*fig.*) creator.
строи́тельн|ый *adj.* building, construction; **~ая площа́дка** building site; **с. раство́р** mortar.
строи́тельств|о, а *nt.* building, construction (*also fig.*); **доро́жное с.** road-building; **жили́щное с.** house-building.
стро́|ить, ю, ишь *impf.* (*of* ▸ **по~**)
1 (*здание, дорогу, мост, плотину*) to build, construct; (*корабль, танк*) to build.
2 (*новую жизнь, общество, счастье*) to create, build.
3 (*фигуры, фразы, мысли*) to construct; to formulate; **с. фра́зу** to construct a sentence.
4 (**на** + *p.*) (*обосновывать*) to base (on); **с. расчёт на** (+ *p.*) to base one's calculations on; **с. отноше́ния на дове́рии** to base relations on trust.
5 (*планы, догадки*) to make; **с. гипоте́зу** to advance a hypothesis.
6 (*ставить строй*) to draw up, form (up).
стро́|иться, юсь, ишься *impf.* (*of* ▸ **по~**)
1 (*строить себе дом*) to build (*a house, etc.*) for o.s.
2 (*mil.*) to draw up, form up; **~йся!** (*mil.*) fall in!
3 *pass. of* ▸ **~ить**
стро|й[1]**, я, о ~е, в ~е,** *pl.* **~и, ~ев** *m.* system, order; structure; **обще́ственный с.** social system.

стро|й[2]**, я, о ~е, в ~ю,** (*pl.* **~и́, ~ёв**) *m.*
1 (*mil., naut., aeron.*) (*порядок*) formation; **со́мкнутый с.** close order.
2 (*mil.*) (*шеренга, часть*) unit in formation; **пе́ред ~ем** in front of the ranks.
3 (*mil. and fig.*) (*действующий состав*) service, commission; **вы́вести из ~я** to disable; to put out of action; **вступи́ть в с.** to come into service, come into operation; **вы́йти из ~я** to be disabled; to become unserviceable; (*машина*) to break down.
стро́йк|а, и *f.*
1 (*действие*) building, construction.
2 (*место*) building site.
строймateриа́л|ы, ов *no sg.* building materials.
стро́|йный (~ен, ~йна́, ~йно, ~йны) *adj.*
1 (*фигура*) well-proportioned; shapely.
2 (*пение*) harmonious; (*ряды*) orderly; (*фраза, доклад*) well-constructed.
строк|а́, и́, *pl.* **~и, ~, ~а́м** *f.* line; (*comput.*) string; **нача́ть с кра́сной/но́вой ~и́** to begin a new paragraph; **чита́ть ме́жду ~** to read between the lines.
стропи́л|о, а *nt.* rafter, beam.
строптив|ый (~, ~а) *adj.* obstinate.
строф|а́, ы́, *pl.* **~ы, ~, ~а́м** *f.* (*liter.*) stanza, verse.
стро́чк|а, и *f.* = **строка́**
стру|и́ться, и́тся *impf.* to stream, flow.
структу́р|а, ы *f.* structure.
структурали́зм, а *m.* structuralism.
структу́рный *adj.* structural.
струн|а́, ы́, *pl.* **~ы** *f.* string.
стру́нный *adj.* (*mus.*): **с. инструме́нт** stringed instrument; **с. кварте́т** string quartet.
струп, а, *pl.* **~ья, ~ьев** *m.* scab.
стру́|сить, шу, сишь *pf. of* ▸ **тру́сить**
струч|о́к, ка́ *m.* pod.
стру|я́, и́, *pl.* **~и** *f.*
1 (*воды*) jet, spurt, stream; (*света, воздуха*) stream; **бить ~ёй** to spurt.
2 (*fig.*) spirit; impetus.
стряс|ти́сь, ётся, *past* **~ся, ~ла́сь** *pf.* (**с** + *i.*; *coll.*) to befall; **беда́ ~ла́сь с на́ми** a disaster befell us; **что с тобо́й ~ло́сь?** what's the matter with you?
стря́хива|ть, ю *impf. of* ▸ **стряхну́ть**
стрях|ну́ть, ну́, нёшь *pf.* (*of* ▸ **~ивать**) to shake off.
студе́нт, а *m.* student, undergraduate; **с.-ме́дик** medical student.
студе́нт|ка, ки *f. of* ▸ **~**
студе́нческий *adj. of* ▸ **студе́нт; с. биле́т** student card.
сту́д|ень, ня *m.* galantine; aspic.
сту́ди|я, и *f.*
1 (*живописца; телестудия*) studio; **с. звукоза́писи** recording studio.
2 (*школа*) (*art, drama, music, etc.*) school.
сту́ж|а, и *f.* severe cold, hard frost.
стук, а *m.* (*в дверь*) knock; (*сердца*) thump; (*пишущей машинки*) clatter; (*падающего предмета*) thud; **с. в дверь** knock at the door; **с. колёс** rumble of wheels.

сту́к|ать(ся), аю(сь) *impf. of* ▸ **~нуть(ся)**
стука́ч, а́ *m.* (*sl.*) police informer.
сту́к|нуть, ну, нешь *pf.* (*of* ▸ **~ать**)
1 (**в** + *a. or* **по** + *d.*) to knock; to bang; **с. в дверь** to knock, bang at (on) the door.
2 (*ударить*) to bang, hit, strike; **с. кого́-н. по спине́** to bang s.o. on the back.
сту́к|нуться, нусь, нешься *pf.* (*of* ▸ **~аться**) (**о** + *a.*) to bang o.s. (against), bump o.s. (against).
стул, а, *pl.* **~ья, ~ьев** *m.* chair.
сту́п|а, ы *f.* mortar.
ступ|а́ть, а́ю *impf. of* ▸ **~и́ть**
ступ|е́нь, е́ни *f.*
1 (*g. pl.* **~е́ней**) (*лестницы*) step; (*стремянки*) rung.
2 (*g. pl.* **~ене́й**) (*этап*) stage; (*разряд*) grade; (*уровень*) level.
ступе́нь|ка, ки *f.* = **~ 1**
ступ|и́ть, лю́, ~ишь *pf.* (*of* ▸ **~а́ть**) to step; to tread.
ступн|я́, и́, *pl.* **~и́, ~е́й** *f.*
1 (*стопа*) foot.
2 (*подошва*) sole.
сту́пор, а *m.* stupor.
стуч|а́ть, у́, и́шь *impf.*
1 (*pf.* **по~**) to knock; to bang; to rap; (*о зубах*) to chatter.
2 (*no pf.*) (*о сердце*) to thump, pound.
3 (*pf.* **на~**) (*sl.*) (**на** + *a.*) (*доносить*) to report (*s.o.*).
стуч|а́ться, у́сь, и́шься *impf.* (*of* ▸ **по~**) (**в** + *a.*) to knock (at); **с. к сосе́ду** to knock at a neighbour's (*Br.*), neighbor's (*US*) door.
стыд, а́ *m.* shame; **к на́шему ~у́** to our shame.
сты|ди́ть, жу́, ди́шь *impf.* (*of* ▸ **при~**) to shame, put to shame.
сты|ди́ться, жу́сь, ди́шься *impf.* (*of* ▸ **по~**) (+ *g.*) to be ashamed (of).
стыдли́в|ый (~, ~а) *adj.* bashful.
сты́дно *as pred.* it is a shame; **ему́,** *etc.*, **с.** he, *etc.*, is ashamed.
стыко́вк|а, и *f.* docking.
стю́ард, а *m.* steward.
стюарде́сс|а, ы *f.* stewardess.
стя́гива|ть, ю *impf. of* ▸ **стяну́ть 1**
стя́гива|ться, юсь *impf. of* ▸ **стяну́ться**
стя|ну́ть, ну́, ~нешь *pf.* (*of* ▸ **~гивать**)
1 (*сапоги*) to pull off.
2 (*pf. only*) (*coll.*) (*украсть*) to pinch (*Br.*), steal.
стя|ну́ться, ну́сь, ~нешься *pf.* (*of* ▸ **~гиваться**)
1 to tighten (*intrans.*).
2 (*coll.*) (*туго подпоясаться*) to gird o.s. tightly.
3 (*войска, демонстранты*) to gather, assemble (*intrans.*).
суахи́ли *m. indecl.* Swahili (*language, people*).
суббо́т|а, ы *f.* Saturday.
субмари́н|а, ы *f.* submarine.
субподря́д, а *m.* subcontract.
субподря́дчик, а *m.* subcontractor.
субсиди́р|овать, ую *impf. and pf.* to subsidize.
субси́ди|я, и *f.* subsidy.
субста́нци|я, и *f.* substance.
субти́тр, а *m.* (*usu. pl.*) subtitle (*in film*).
субтро́пик|и, ов *no sg.* subtropics.
субтропи́ческий *adj.* subtropical.
субъе́кт, а *m.*
1 (*phil., gram., med., leg.*) subject.
2 (*coll.*) (*человек*) fellow, character, type.
субъекти́в|ный (~ен, ~на) *adj.* subjective.
сувени́р, а *m.* souvenir.
суверените́т, а *m.* (*pol., leg.*) sovereignty.
сувере́нный *adj.* (*pol., leg.*) sovereign.
сугро́б, а *m.* snowdrift.
суд, а́ *m.*
1 court, law court; **зал ~а́** courtroom; **заседа́ние ~а́** sitting of the court.
2 (*разбирательство*) trial, legal proceedings; **пода́ть в с. на кого́-н.** to bring an action against s.o.; **отда́ть под с., преда́ть ~у́** to prosecute; **с. присяжных** jury.
3 (*collect.*) (*судьи*) the judges; the bench.
4 (*мнение*) judgement, verdict; **с. исто́рии** verdict of history.
суда́к, а́ *m.* pikeperch (*fish*).
Суда́н, а *m.* (the) Sudan.
суда́н|ец, ца *m.* Sudanese.
суда́н|ка, ки *f. of* ▸ **~ец**
суда́нский *adj.* Sudanese.
суде́бн|ый *adj.* judicial; legal; (*медицина, психиатрия*) forensic; **с. исполни́тель** bailiff, officer of the court; **~ая оши́бка** miscarriage of justice; **~ое разбира́тельство** legal proceedings, hearing of a case; **~ое реше́ние** court decision, court order.
су|ди́ть, жу́, ~дишь *impf.*
1 (**о** + *p.*) (*составлять мнение*) to judge; to form an opinion (about, on); **наско́лько мы могли́ с.** as far as we could judge; **~дя** (**по** + *d.*) judging (by), to judge (from); **~дя по всему́** to all appearances.
2 (*leg.*) (**за** + *a.*) (*преступника*) to try (for).
3 (*осуждать*) to judge, pass judgement (upon); **не ~ди́те их стро́го** don't be hard on them.
4 (*sport*) to referee; (*в крикете, теннисе*) to umpire.
су|ди́ться, жу́сь, ~дишься *impf.* (**с** + *i.*) to sue.
су́д|но, на, *pl.* **~а́, ~о́в** *nt.* vessel.
судове́рф|ь, и *f.* shipyard.
судовладе́л|ец, ьца *m.* shipowner.
судопроизво́дств|о, а *nt.* legal proceedings.
су́дорог|а, и *f.* cramp, convulsion, spasm.
судострое́ни|е, я *nt.* shipbuilding.
судохо́д|ный (~ен, ~на) *adj.*
1 navigable; **с. кана́л** shipping canal.
2: **~ная компа́ния** shipping company.
судохо́дств|о, а *nt.* navigation, shipping.
суд|ьба́, ьбы́, *pl.* **~ьбы, ~еб, ~ьбам** *f.* fate, fortune; (*будущее*) destiny; (*история существования*) story; **благодари́ть ~ьбу́** to thank one's lucky stars; **искуша́ть ~ьбу́** to tempt fate.
суд|ья́, ьи́, *pl.* **~ьи, ~е́й, ~ьям** *m.* (*also f., coll., of woman*)

1 judge; **я вам не с.** who am I to judge you?
2 (*sport*) referee; (*в крикете, теннисе*) umpire; **с. на ли́нии** linesman.

су́д|я *see* ▸ **~и́ть**

суеве́ри|е, я *nt.* superstition.

суеве́р|ный (~ен, ~на) *adj.* superstitious.

сует|а́, ы *f.*
1 (*тщетность*) vanity.
2 (*хлопоты*) bustle, fuss.

суе|ти́ться, чу́сь, ти́шься *impf.* to bustle, fuss.

суетли́в|ый (~, ~а) *adj.* fussy, bustling.

сужде́ни|е, я *nt.* (*мнение*) opinion; (*в логике*) judgement.

су́жива|ться, ется *impf. of* ▸ **су́зиться**

су́|зиться, зится *pf.* (*of* ▸ **~живаться**) to narrow (*intrans.*), get narrow; to taper.

суици́д, а *m.* suicide.

сук, а́, о ~е́, на ~у́, *pl.* **су́чья, су́чьев** *m.* bough.

су́к|а, и *f.* bitch (*also as term of abuse*).

сук|но́, на́, *pl.* **~́на, ~́он** *nt.* (heavy, coarse) cloth.

сумасбро́д|ный (~ен, ~на) *adj.* wild, extravagant.

сумасше́дш|ий *adj.*
1 mad; *as n.* **с., ~его** *m.* madman, lunatic; **~ая, ~ей** *f.* madwoman, lunatic.
2 : **с. дом** (*coll.*) madhouse.
3 (*fig.*) mad, lunatic; **~ая ско́рость** lunatic speed; **э́то бу́дет сто́ить ~их де́нег** it will cost the earth.

сумасше́стви|е, я *nt.* madness, lunacy.

сумато́х|а, и *f.* confusion, chaos.

сумбу́р|ный (~ен, ~на) *adj.* confused, chaotic.

суме́|ть, ю *pf.* (+ *inf.*) to be able (to), manage (to).

су́мк|а, и *f.*
1 bag; **хозя́йственная с.** shopping bag.
2 (*biol.*) pouch.

су́мм|а, ы *f.* sum; **о́бщая/по́лная с.** sum total; (*количество*) amount.

сумма́р|ный (~ен, ~на) *adj.*
1 (*количество*) total.
2 (*обзор*) summary.

сумми́р|овать, ую *impf., pf.*
1 (*складывать*) to add up.
2 (*обобщить*) to summarize; to sum up.

су́мочк|а, и *f.* (*дамская*) handbag.

су́мрак, а *m.* dusk, twilight.

су́мрач|ный (~ен, ~на) *adj.* gloomy (*also fig.*).

сунду́к, а́ *m.* trunk, box, chest.

сунни́т, а *m.* Sunni (Muslim).

су́н|уть(ся), у(сь), ешь(ся) *pf. of* ▸ **сова́ть(ся)**

суп, а, *pl.* **~ы́** *m.* soup.

суперзвезд|а́, ы́, *pl.* **~̈ы, ~̈, ~̈ам** *f.* superstar.

суперма́ркет, а *m.* supermarket.

супермоде́л|ь, и *f.* supermodel.

суперобло́жк|а, и *f.* dust jacket.

су́пниц|а, ы *f.* soup tureen.

супру́г, а *m.*
1 husband, spouse.
2 *pl.* (*муж и жена*) husband and wife, married couple.

супру́г|а, и *f.* wife, spouse.

супру́жеский *adj.* (*чета, жизнь*) married; (*верность, счастье*) marital.

супру́жеств|о, а *nt.* matrimony, wedlock.

суро́в|ый (~, ~а) *adj.*
1 (*взгляд, критика*) severe, stern; (*зима, жизнь, приговор*) harsh; (*красота, воспитание*) austere.
2 (*ткань*) coarse.

сур|о́к, ка́ *m.* marmot; **спать как с.** to sleep like a log.

суррога́т, а *m.* surrogate, substitute.

суррога́тн|ый *adj.* surrogate, substitute; **~ая мать** surrogate mother.

су́слик, а *m.* (*zool.*) ground squirrel, gopher (*US*).

суста́в, а *m.* (*anat.*) joint.

сута́н|а, ы *f.* soutane.

сутенёр, а *m.* pimp.

су́т|ки, ок *no sg.* twenty-four hours; twenty-four-hour period; **це́лые с.** for days and nights.

суту́л|иться, юсь, ишься *impf.* (*of* ▸ **с~**) to stoop.

суту́л|ый (~, ~а) *adj.* round-shouldered, stooping.

сут|ь, и *f.* essence; **с. де́ла** the heart, crux of the matter; **по ~́и де́ла** as a matter of fact.

су́ффикс, а *m.* (*gram.*) suffix.

суха́р|ь, я́ *m.* (*хлебный*) rusk.

су́хо *adv.*
1 coldly; **нас при́няли с.** we were received coldly.
2 *as pred.* it is dry; **на у́лице с.** it is dry out of doors.

сухогру́з, а *m.* bulk carrier.

сухожи́ли|е, я *nt.* (*anat.*) tendon, sinew.

сух|о́й (~, ~а́, ~́о) *adj.*
1 dry; **~и́е дрова́** dry firewood; **~о́е ру́сло реки́** dried-up river bed.
2 (*хлеб*) dry; (*фрукты*) dried; **~о́е молоко́** dried milk.
3 (*кожа*) dried-up; (*рука*) withered; (*худощавый*) lean.
4 (*без влаги, жидкости*) dry; **с. ка́шель** dry cough.
5 (*fig.*) (*холодный*) chilly, cold; **с. приём** chilly reception.

сухопу́тн|ый *adj.* land (*opp. marine, air*); **~ые си́лы** (*mil.*) ground forces.

сухофру́кт|ы, ов *no sg.* dried fruits.

суч|о́к, ка́ *m.* twig.

су́ш|а, и *f.* (dry) land (*opp. sea*); **по ~е** by land.

су́ше *comp. of* ▸ **сухо́й** *and* ▸ **су́хо**

сушёный *adj.* dried.

суши́лк|а, и *f.*
1 (*устройство*) drying apparatus, dryer; **напо́льная с.** clothes horse.
2 (*помещение*) drying room.

суш|и́ть, у́, ~́ишь *impf.* (*of* ▸ **вы́~**) to dry (out).

суш|и́ться, у́сь, ~́ишься *impf.* (*of* ▸ **вы́~**) to dry (out); (*человек*) to get dry.

су́шк|а, и *f.*
1 drying.
2 (*cul.*) dry (*ring-shaped*) cracker.
суще́ствен|ный (~, ~на) *adj.* (*черта, разница*) essential; (*роль, значение*) vital; (*крупный*) substantial; (*вопрос*) important.
существи́тельн|ое *adj.*: **имя с.** (*or as n.* **с., ~ого** *nt.*) noun; **с. мужско́го/же́нского/сре́днего ро́да** masculine/feminine/neuter noun.
существ|о́, а́ *nt.*
1 (*сущность*) essence; **по ~у́** (*говоря*) in essence, essentially; **говори́ть по ~у́** to speak to the point; **не по ~у́** off the point, beside the point.
2 (*живая особь*) being, creature; **люби́мое с.** loved one.
существова́ни|е, я *nt.* existence; **борьба́ за с.** struggle for survival.
существ|ова́ть, у́ю *impf.* to exist.
су́щ|ий *adj.* (*coll.*) (*правда*) absolute; utter; **с. ад** absolute hell; **~ая ерунда́** utter rubbish; **э́то/он ~ее наказа́ние** it/he is the bane of my life.
су́щност|ь, и *f.* essence; **в ~и (говоря́)** in essence, essentially.
сфабрик|ова́ть, у́ю *pf. of* ▸ **фабрикова́ть**
сфе́р|а, ы *f.* sphere; **с. влия́ния** (*pol.*) sphere of influence; **вы́сшие ~ы** highest circles.
сфери́ческий *adj.* spherical.
сфокуси́р|овать(ся), ую(сь) *pf. of* ▸ **фокуси́ровать(ся)**
сформир|ова́ть(ся), у́ю(сь) *pf. of* ▸ **формирова́ть(ся)**
сформули́р|овать, ую *pf. of* ▸ **формули́ровать**
сфотографи́р|овать(ся), ую(сь) *pf. of* ▸ **фотографи́ровать(ся)**
схва|ти́ть, чу́, ~́тишь *pf.*
1 *pf. of* ▸ **хвата́ть[1] 1.**
2 (*pf. only*) (*coll.*) (*простуду*) to catch.
3 (*impf.* **~́тывать**) (*coll.*) (*мысль*) to grasp, comprehend; **с. смысл** to grasp the meaning, catch on.
схва|ти́ться, чу́сь, ~́тишься *pf.*
1 *pf. of* ▸ **хвата́ться.**
2 (*impf.* **~́тываться**) (**с** + *i.*) to grapple (with) (*also fig.*).
схва́тк|а, и *f.* skirmish, fight; (*в спорте*) fight; (*в споре*) clash; **рукопа́шная с.** hand-to-hand fight.
схва́т|ки, ок *no sg.* contractions (*of muscles*); spasms; **родовы́е с.** labour (*Br.*), labor (*US*).
схва́тыва|ть(ся), ю(сь) *impf. of* ▸ **схвати́ть(ся)**
схе́м|а, ы *f.*
1 (*чертёж*) diagram, chart; **с. метро́** metro map.
2 (*сочинения*) sketch, outline, plan.
3 (*elec., radio*) circuit.
схемати́ч|ный (~ен, ~на) *adj.* sketchy, (over)simplified.
схитр|и́ть, ю́, и́шь *pf. of* ▸ **хитри́ть**
схлы́н|уть, у, ешь *pf.*
1 (*о волнах*) to break and flow back.
2 (*о толпе*) to break up; to dwindle.
3 (*о чувствах*) to subside.
схо|ди́ть[1], жу́, ~́дишь *impf. of* ▸ **сойти́**
схо|ди́ть[2], жу́, ~́дишь *pf.* to go (*and come back*); (**за** + *i.*) to go to fetch; **с. посмотре́ть** to go to see; **~ди́ за врачо́м!** go and fetch a doctor!
схо|ди́ться, жу́сь, ~́дишься *impf. of* ▸ **сойти́сь**
схо́дк|а, и *f.* gathering, assembly.
схо́дн|и, ей *pl.* (*sg.* **~я, ~и** *f.*) gangway, gangplank.
схо́д|ный (~ен, ~на) *adj.* (**с** + *i.*) similar (to).
схо́дств|о, а *nt.* likeness, similarity, resemblance; **вне́шнее с.** similarity in appearance.
схо́ж|ий (~, ~а) *adj.* (*coll.*) (**с** + *i.*) similar (to).
сца́па|ть, ю *pf.* (*coll.*) to grab, catch hold (of).
сце|ди́ть, жу́, ~́дишь *pf.* (*of* ▸ **~́живать**) to pour off, decant; (*через сито, марлю*) to strain off.
сце́жива|ть, ю *impf. of* ▸ **сцеди́ть**
сце́н|а, ы *f.*
1 (*подмостки*) stage (*also fig.*).
2 (*эпизод, происшествие*) scene.
3 (*coll.*) scene; **устро́ить ~у** to make a scene.
сцена́ри|й, я *m.*
1 (*фильма, передачи*) scenario, script.
2 (*детальный план*) plan, programme (*Br.*), program (*US*).
3 (*fig.*) (*вариант*) scenario.
сценари́ст, а *m.* scriptwriter.
сценари́ст|ка, ки *f. of* ▸ **~**
сцеп|и́ть, лю́, ~́ишь *pf.* (*of* ▸ **~ля́ть**)
1 (*вагоны, кузова*) to couple.
2 (*пальцы*) to clasp.
сцеп|и́ться, лю́сь, ~́ишься *pf.* (*of* ▸ **~ля́ться**)
1 (*вагоны, детали*) to be coupled; (*ветки*) to be intertwined; to intertwine; (*частицы*) to stick together.
2 (**с** + *i.*; *coll.*) (*начать драться*) to grapple (with).
сцепле́ни|е, я *nt.*
1 (*действие*) coupling.
2 (*tech.*) clutch; (*клеток, вещества*) cohesion; **выключе́ние ~я** clutch release.
сцепля́|ть(ся), ю(сь) *impf. of* ▸ **сцепи́ть(ся)**
сча́стливо *adv.* (*жить, улыбаться*) happily; **с. отде́латься** (**от** + *g.*) to have a lucky escape (from); **счастли́во (остава́ться)!** good luck!
счаст|ли́вый (~́лив, ~́лива) *adj.*
1 (*лицо, детство, человек*) happy; **с. коне́ц** happy end.
2 (*игрок, случай, день*) lucky.
3 : **~ли́вого пути́!** bon voyage!
сча́сть|е, я *nt.*
1 (*чувство*) happiness; **жела́ю вам с.** I wish you happiness.
2 (*удача*) luck, good fortune; **к ~ю** luckily, fortunately; **на на́ше с.** luckily for us; **како́е с., что...** how fortunate that ... .
сче́сть, сочту́, сочтёшь, *past* **счёл, сочла́** *pf. of* ▸ **счита́ть 2, 3**
счёт, а (у), *pl.* **~ы** *and* **~а́** *m.*

С

1 *sg. only* (*действие*) counting, calculation, reckoning; **вести́ с.** (+ *d.*) to keep count (of); **в два ~а** in a jiffy, in a trice.
2 *sg. only* (*sport*) score; **со ~ом 2:1** with a score of 2–1.
3 (*pl.* **~á**) (*в ресторане, за газ, за телефон*) bill; (*накладная*) invoice; **уплати́ть по ~у** to pay the bill.
4 (*pl.* **~á**) (*в банке*) account; **откры́ть с.** to open an account; **за с.** (+ *g.*) at the expense (of).
5 (*fig.*) account, expense; **в с.** (+ *g.*) on the strength (of); **в коне́чном ~е** in the end; **за с.** (+ *g.*) at the expense (of); owing (to); **приня́ть на свой с.** to take (sth.) personally; **на э́тот с.** in this respect.
6 (**~ы**) (*no sg.*; *fig.*) (*претензии*) accounts, score(s); **ста́рые ~ы** old scores; **свести́ ~ы (с** + *i.*) to settle a score (with), get even (with).
7 *see* ▸ **~ы**[1]

счётчик, а *m.* meter; counter; **га́зовый с.** gas meter.

счёт|ы[1]**, ов** *no sg.* abacus.

счёт|ы[2] *see* ▸ **~ 6**

счи́|стить, щу, стишь *pf.* (*of* ▸ **~щáть**) to clean off.

счи́тан|ый *adj.* a few; **остаю́тся ~ые дни (до** + *g.*) one can count the days (until); there are only a few days left (until); **~ое коли́чество** (*денег*) very little; (*предметов*) very few.

счита́|ть, ю *impf.* (*of* ▸ **по~**)
1 (*pf. also* **со~**) to count; **с. дни, мину́ты** to count the days, minutes; **не ~я** not counting.
2 (*pf. also* **счесть**) (+ *i. or* **за** + *a.*) to count, consider, think; to regard (as); **я ~ю его́ надёжным челове́ком** I consider him a reliable person; **с. необходи́мым/ну́жным** to consider it necessary.
3 (*pf. also* **счесть**) **(что)** to consider (that), hold (that).

счита́|ться, юсь *impf.* (*no pf.*)
1 (+ *i.*) to be considered, be thought, be reputed; to be regarded (as); **он ~ется первокла́ссным специали́стом** he is considered a first-rate specialist; **~ется, что...** it is considered that ... .
2 (**с** + *i.*) (*принимать в расчёт*) to consider, take into consideration; to take into account, reckon (with); **он всегда́ ~лся с мои́м мне́нием** he always took my opinion into consideration; **он ни с кем не ~ется** he has no consideration for anyone.

счища́|ть, ю *impf. of* ▸ **счи́стить**

США *no sg., indecl.* (*abbr. of* **Соединённые Шта́ты Аме́рики**) USA (*United States of America*).

сшиб|áть, áю *impf. of* ▸ **~и́ть**

сшиб|и́ть, ý, ёшь, *past* **~,** **~́ла** *pf.* (*of* ▸ **~áть**) (*coll.*) to knock off; **с. с ног** to knock down, knock over.

сшива́|ть, ю *impf. of* ▸ **сшить 2**

сшить, сошью́, сошьёшь *pf.*
1 *pf. of* ▸ **шить.**
2 (*impf.* **сшивáть**) to sew together; (*med.*) to suture.

съ... *vbl. pref.* = **с...**

съеда́|ть, ю *impf.* (*of* ▸ **съесть**) to eat (up).

съедо́б|ный (~ен, ~на) *adj.* edible.

съёжива|ться, юсь *impf. of* ▸ **съёжиться**

съёж|иться, усь, ишься *pf.* (*of* ▸ **~иваться**) (*в комо(че)к; от холода*) to huddle up; (*о листьях, лице*) to shrivel up; (*о ткани*) to shrink.

съезд[1]**, а** *m.* (*собрание*) congress; conference, convention.

съезд[2]**, а** *m.* (*спуск*) descent.

съе́з|дить, жу, дишь *pf.* to go (*and come back*); **как (ты) ~дила?** how was your trip?

съезжа́|ть(ся), ю(сь) *impf. of* ▸ **съе́хать(ся)**

съел *see* ▸ **съесть**

съёмк|а, и *f.*
1 (*местности*) survey, surveying; plotting.
2 (*usu. pl.*) (*фильма*) shooting.

съёмный *adj.* detachable, removable.

съёмщик, а *m.* tenant.

съёмщиц|а, ы *f. of* ▸ **съёмщик**

съестн|о́й *adj.* food; **~ы́е припа́сы** food supplies, provisions; *as n.* **~óе, ~óго** *nt.* food.

съе|сть, м, шь, ст, ди́м, ди́те, дя́т, *past* **~л, ~́ла** *pf. of* ▸ **есть**[1] *and* ▸ **~да́ть**

съе́|хать, ду, дешь *pf.* (*of* ▸ **~зжа́ть**)
1 (*спуститься*) to go down, come down.
2 (*с квартиры*) to move out.
3 (*fig., coll.*) (*двинуться с места*) to come down, slip; **у тебя́ га́лстук ~хал на́бок** your tie is on one side.

съе́|хаться, дусь, дешься *pf.* (*of* ▸ **~зжа́ться**)
1 (*встретиться*) to meet.
2 (*собраться*) to arrive, gather, assemble.

сы́воротк|а, и *f.* serum.

сыгра́|ть, ю *pf. of* ▸ **игра́ть; с. шу́тку (с** + *i.*) to play a practical joke (on).

сымити́р|овать, ую *pf. of* ▸ **имити́ровать**

сымпровизи́р|овать, ую *pf. of* ▸ **импровизи́ровать**

сын, а, *pl.* **~овья́, ~ове́й** *m.* son.

сы́п|ать, лю, лешь *impf.* to pour.

сы́п|аться, лется *impf.*
1 (*о чём-н. мелком*) to fall; (*о сыпучем*) to pour out; (*разбегаться*) to scatter; **мука́ ~алась из мешка́** flour poured out of the bag.
2 (*coll.*) (*о звуках*) to pour forth (*intrans.*), rain down; **уда́ры ~ались гра́дом** blows were raining down, falling thick and fast.
3 (*о штукатурке*) to flake off.

сып|ь, и *f.* (*med.*) rash, eruption.

сыр, а, *pl.* **~ы́** *m.* cheese.

сыре́|ть, ю *impf.* (*of* ▸ **от~**) to become damp.

сы́ро *as pred.* it is damp.

сыроéжк|а, и *f.* russula (*mushroom*).

сыр|о́й (~, ~á, ~́о) *adj.*
1 (*влажный*) damp; (*лето, день*) wet.
2 (*овощи, тесто*) raw, uncooked; **~áя вода́** unboiled water; **~óе мя́со** raw meat.
3 (*незрелый*) green, unripe.
4 (*необработанный*) raw; (*рассказ, план*) unfinished, unrefined.

сыр|о́к, ка́ *m.* (*творожный*) curd cheese; **пла́вленый с.** processed cheese.
сы́рост|ь, и *f.* dampness, humidity.
сырь|ё, я́ *no pl.*, *nt.* raw material(s).
сырьев|о́й *adj. of* **сырьё; ~а́я ба́за** raw material supply.
сыск, а *m.* investigation, detection (*of criminals*).
сы́т|ный (~ен, ~на́, ~но) *adj.* (*обед*) substantial, copious; (*пирог*) filling, rich; (*питательный*) nourishing.
сы́т|ый (~, ~а́, ~о) *adj.*
1 satisfied, full; **спаси́бо, я ~** thank you, I am full.
2 (*откормленный*) well-fed.
3 (*fig.*) (+ *i.*) (*пресыщенный*) fed up with; **я ~ по го́рло** I'm fed up to the back teeth (with).
сы́щик, а *m.* detective.
сэконо́м|ить, лю, ишь *pf. of* ▸ **эконо́мить**
сэр, а *m.* sir.
сюда́ *adv.* here, hither.
сюже́т, а *m.* (*картины, симфонии*) subject; (*романа*) plot.
сюи́т|а, ы *f.* (*mus.*) suite.
сюрпри́з, а *m.* surprise.
сюрту́к, а́ *m.* frock coat.
сюсю́ка|ть, ю *impf.* (*coll.*) to lisp.
сюрреали́зм, а *m.* surrealism.
сюрреали́ст, а *m.* surrealist.
сюрреалисти́ческий *adj.* surrealist.

Тт

т (*abbr. of* **то́нна**) t, ton(s), tonne(s).
таба́к, а́ (у́) *m.* tobacco.
табаке́рк|а, и *f.* snuffbox.
та́бел|ь, я *m.*
1 (*график*) table, chart.
2 (*на заводе*) time board (*for tracking attendance*).
та́бельщик, а *m.* timekeeper.
табле́тк|а, и *f.* tablet, pill; **т. аспири́на** aspirin.
табли́ц|а, ы *f.* table; **электро́нная т.** (*comput.*) spreadsheet.
табло́ *nt. indecl.* (*на вокзале*) information board; (*sport*) scoreboard.
табло́ид, а *m.* tabloid (newspaper).
та́бор, а *m.*
1 (*лагерь*) camp.
2 (*группа цыган*) band of gypsies.
табу́ *nt. indecl.* taboo.
табу́н, а́ *m.* herd (*usu. of horses*).
табуре́т, а *m.* = **~ка**
табуре́т|ка, ки *f.* stool.
тавр|о́, а́, *pl.* **~а, ~, ~а́м** *nt.* brand (*on cattle, etc.*).
тавтоло́ги|я, и *f.* tautology.
таган́, а́ *m.* trivet.
таджи́к, а *m.* Tajik.
Таджикиста́н, а *m.* Tajikistan.
таджи́кский *adj.* Tajik.
таджи́|чка, чки *f. of* ▸ **~к**
таз[1]**, а, в ~у́,** *pl.* **~ы́** *m.* bowl.
таз[2]**, а, в ~е** *and* **в ~у́,** *pl.* **~ы́** *m.* (*anat.*) pelvis.
тазобе́дренный *adj.* (*anat.*) hip; **т. суста́в** hip joint.
Таила́нд, а *m.* Thailand.
таила́нд|ец, ца *m.* Thai.
таила́нд|ка, ки *f. of* ▸ **~ец**
таила́ндский *adj.* Thai.
таи́нствен|ный (~ *and* **~ен, ~на)** *adj.*
1 (*место, шорох, взгляд*) mysterious; (*человек*) enigmatic.
2 (*цель*) secret.
3 (*вид*) secretive.
та́инств|о, а *nt.* (*relig.*) sacrament.
Таи́ти *m. indecl.* Tahiti.
та|и́ть, ю́, и́шь *impf.* (*горе*) to hide, conceal; (*злобу*) to harbour (*Br.*), harbor (*US*); **т. зло́бу (про́тив)** to harbour a grudge (against); **не́чего/что греха́ т.** it must be admitted, we must admit.
та|и́ться, ю́сь, и́шься *impf.*
1 (*coll.*) (*скрываться*) to be (in) hiding, lurk.
2 (*fig.*) (*иметься*) to lurk, be lurking; **что за э́тим ~и́тся?** what lies behind this?
Тайва́н|ь, я *m.* Taiwan.
тайг|а́, и́ *f.* (*geog.*) taiga.
тайко́м *adv.* in secret, surreptitiously; on the quiet.
тайм-а́ут, а *m.* (*перерыв в чём-л.*) time off, time out (*US*); (*sport*) timeout.
та́йн|а, ы *f.*
1 (*то, что непонятно*) mystery.
2 (*секрет*) secret; **храни́ть ~у** to keep a secret.
тайни́к, а́ *m.* hiding place (*for a thing*).
та́йн|ый *adj.* secret; clandestine; **т. аге́нт** undercover agent; **~ое голосова́ние** secret ballot.
та́йский *adj.* Thai.
тайфу́н, а *m.* typhoon.
тайцзицюа́нь *f. indecl.* t'ai chi (chu'an).
так
1 *adv.* (*таким образом*) so; thus, in this way, like this; in such a way; **т. мно́го** so many; **мы сде́лали т.** this is what we did, we did as follows; **т. вот** (*выражает продолжение повествования после отступления*) and so, so then; **т. же** in the same way; **т. и́ли ина́че** whatever happens, one way or another; **т. себе́** so-so, middling; **т. сказа́ть** so to speak;

и т. да́лее (*usu. spelt* **и т. д.**) and so on, and so forth; **(не) т. ли?** isn't it so?
2 *adv.* (*как следует*) as it should be; **не т.** amiss, wrong; **не совсе́м т.** not quite right.
3 *adv.* (*без специальных средств; без последствий*) just like that; **ему́ э́то т. не пройдёт** he won't get away with it like that.
4 *adv.*: **т. (то́лько), про́сто т.** for no special reason, for no reason in particular; just for fun.
5 : **т. как** *conj.* as, since.
6 : **т. что** so; **т. что́бы** so that.

такела́ж, а *m.* rigging.
та́кже *adv.* also, too, as well; (*after neg.*) or, nor.
-таки *particle* (*coll.*) however, though; **опя́ть-т.** again.
тако́в *m.*, **~а́** *f.*, **~о́** *nt.*, *pl.* **~ы́** *pron.* such; **~ы́ тре́бования зако́на** such/these are the legal requirements; **и был т.** (*coll.*) and that was the last we saw of him.
так|о́й *pron.*
1 such; so; **т. же** the same; **он т. до́брый!** he is such a kind man; **~и́м о́бразом** thus, in this way; **в ~о́м слу́чае** in that case.
2 : **кто он т.?** who is he?; **что э́то ~о́е?** what is this?
тако́й-то *pron.* so-and-so; such-and-such.
такси́ *nt. indecl.* taxi.
такси́ст, а *m.* taxi driver.
таксофо́н, а *m.* payphone.
такт[1], а *m.*
1 (*mus., etc.*) (*ритм*) time; **отбива́ть т.** to beat time; (*в нотах*) bar.
2 (*tech.*) stroke (*of engine*).
такт[2], а *m.* (*тактичность*) tact.
та́ктик|а, и *f.* tactics.
такти́ческий *adj.* tactical.
такти́ч|ный (~ен, ~на) *adj.* tactful.
тала́нт, а *m.*
1 (*дар*) talent, gift(s).
2 (*человек*) gifted person.
тала́нтлив|ый (~, ~а) *adj.* talented, gifted.
талисма́н, а *m.* talisman, charm, mascot.
та́ли|я, и *f.* waist.
Та́ллин, а *m.* Tallinn.
тало́н, а *m.* (*на бензин*) coupon; **поса́дочный т.** boarding pass.
тальк, а *m.* talcum powder.
там *adv.* there; **т. же** in the same place; (*при ссылках*) ibid.
та́мбур, а *m.* (*железнодорожного вагона*) platform (*of railway carriage*).
тамбури́н, а *m.* tambourine.
тами́л, а *m.* Tamil.
тами́л|ка, ки *f. of* ▸ **~**
тами́льский *adj.* Tamil.
тамо́женник, а *m.* customs official.
тамо́женный *adj.* customs.
тамо́жн|я, и *f.* customs.
тампо́н, а *m.* tampon.
та́н|ец, ца *m.*
1 (*искусство*) dance; dancing; **уро́ки ~цев** dancing lessons.
2 *pl.* (*вечер*) a dance, dancing; **пойти́ на ~цы** to go to a dance, go dancing.
танзани́|ец, йца *m.* Tanzanian.
танзани́|йка, йки *f. of* ▸ **~ец**
танзани́йский *adj.* Tanzanian.
Танза́ни|я, и *f.* Tanzania.
танк, а *m.* (*mil.*) tank.
та́нкер, а *m.* (*naut.*) tanker.
танки́ст, а *m.* member of tank crew.
танц|ева́ть, у́ю *impf.* to dance.
танцо́вщик, а *m.* (professional) dancer.
танцо́вщиц|а, ы *f. of* ▸ **танцо́вщик**
танцо́р, а *m.* (professional) dancer.
та́почк|а, и *f.* slipper; **спорти́вная т.** sports shoe, sneaker (*US*).
та́р|а, ы *f.* packing, packaging.
тарака́н, а *m.* cockroach.
тара́н, а *m.* (*mil.*)
1 ram; ramming.
2 (*hist.*) battering ram.
тара́нтул, а *m.* tarantula.
тарато́р|ить, ю, ишь *impf.* (*coll.*) to jabber; to gabble.
тарах|те́ть, чу́, ти́шь *impf.* (*coll.*) to rattle, rumble.
таре́лк|а, и *f.*
1 plate; **глубо́кая т.** soup plate.
2 (*tech.*) plate, disc; (*coll.*) (*спутниковая*) (satellite) dish.
3 *pl.* (*mus.*) cymbals.
тари́ф, а *m.* tariff, rate.
таска́|ть(ся), ю(сь) *impf.* (*indet. of* ▸ **тащи́ть(ся)**)
тас|ова́ть, у́ю *impf.* (*of* ▸ **пере~**) to shuffle (*cards*).
тата́р|ин, ина, *pl.* **~ы, ~** *m.* Tatar.
тата́р|ка, ки *f. of* ▸ **~ин**
татаромонго́л, а *n.* Tartar (*hist.*).
татаромонго́льский *adj.* Tartar (*hist.*).
тата́рский *adj.* Tatar.
тату́ир|овать, ую *impf. and pf.* to tattoo.
татуиро́вк|а, и *f.* tattoo.
тахт|а́, ы́ *f.* ottoman.
та́чк|а, и *f.* wheelbarrow; (*coll.*) (*автомобиль*) car.
Ташке́нт, а *m.* Tashkent.
тащ|и́ть, у́, ~ишь *impf.* (*det. of* ▸ **таска́ть**)
1 (*тянуть*) to pull; (*что-н. тяжёлое*) to drag, lug; (*нести*) to carry.
2 (*coll.*) (*вести*) to take; (*fig.*) (*заставлять пойти куда-н.*) to drag off.
3 (*извлекать*) to pull out.
тащ|и́ться, у́сь, ~ишься *impf.* (*det. of* ▸ **таска́ться**)
1 (*идти с трудом*) to drag o.s. along; (*медленно ехать*) to trundle along; (*за кем-н.*) to trail along.
2 (*о подоле*) to drag, trail.
3 **(от** + *g.*) (*sl.*) to be crazy about.
та́яни|е, я *nt.* thaw, thawing.
та́|ять, ю, ешь *impf.* (*of* ▸ **рас~**)
1 to melt; to thaw; **~ет** it is thawing.
2 (*fig.*) (*исчезать*) to melt away, dwindle, wane; **его́ си́лы ~яли** his strength was ebbing.
3 **(от** + *g., fig.*) (*от любви*) to melt (with), languish (with).

Тбили́си *m. indecl.* Tbilisi.
ТВ (*abbr. of* **телеви́дение**) TV (television).
твар|ь, и *f.* creature; (*collect.*) creatures; all creation (*also pej.*); (*pej.*) (*подлый человек*) swine.
тверде́|ть, ет *impf.* to harden, become hard.
твер|ди́ть, жу́, ди́шь *impf.* (+ *a. or* **о** + *p.*) to repeat, say over and over again.
твёрдо *adv.* firmly; (*знать, выучить*) thoroughly.
твердоло́б|ый (~, ~а) *adj.* diehard.
твёрдост|ь, и *f.* hardness; (*fig.*) firmness.
твёрд|ый (~, ~а́, ~о, ~ы) *adj.*
1 (*не мягкий*) hard.
2 (*крепкий*) firm; (*не жидкий*) solid; **т. переплёт** stiff binding; **~ое те́ло** (*phys., chem.*) solid.
3 (*fig.*) (*непоколебимый*) firm; (*установленный*) stable; (*стойкий*) steadfast; **~ое реше́ние** firm decision; **~ые це́ны** stable, fixed prices.
4 (*ling.*) hard; **т. знак** hard sign (*name of Russian letter* «ъ»).
тверды́н|я, и *f.* stronghold (*also fig.*).
тво|й, его́ *m.*, **~я́, ~е́й** *f.*, **~ё, ~его́** *nt.*, *pl.* **~и́, ~и́х** *possessive pron.* (*при существительном*) your; (*без существительного*) yours.
творе́ни|е, я *nt.*
1 (*произведение*) creation; work.
2 (*существо*) creature, being.
твор|е́ц, ца́ *m.* creator; (*Бог*) **Т.** the Creator.
твори́тельный *adj.*: **т. паде́ж** (*gram.*) instrumental case.
твор|и́ть, ю́, и́шь *impf.* (*of* ▸ **со~**)
1 (*создавать*) to create.
2 (*делать*) to do; to make; **т. чудеса́** to work wonders.
твор|и́ться, и́тся *impf.* (*coll.*) to happen, go on.
творо́г, а́ *and* **тво́рог, а** *m.* curd cheese.
тво́рческий *adj.* creative; **т. путь Толсто́го** Tolstoy's career as a writer.
тво́рчеств|о, а *nt.*
1 creation; creative work.
2 (*collect.*) works.
т. е. (*abbr. of* **то есть**) i.e., that is, viz.
теа́тр, а *m.* theatre (*Br.*), theater (*US*); **т. и кино́** stage and screen; **т. вое́нных де́йствий** (*mil.*) theatre of operations.
театра́л, а *m.* theatregoer (*Br.*), theatergoer (*US*).
театра́л|ьный (~ен, ~ьна) *adj.*
1 theatre (*Br.*), theater (*US*); theatrical; **~ьная ка́сса** box office; **~ьная шко́ла** drama school.
2 (*fig.*) (*жест, поза*) theatrical.
Тегера́н, а *m.* Teh(e)ran.
теза́урус, а *m.* thesaurus.
те́зис, а *m.* thesis, proposition.
тёзк|а, и *c.g.* namesake.
текст, а *m.*
1 text.
2 (*песни*) words; (*оперы*) libretto.
тексти́льный *adj.* textile.
тексти́льщик, а *m.* textile worker.
тексти́льщи|ца, цы *f. of* ▸ **~к**
те́кст|овый *adj. of* ▸ **~**; **т. реда́ктор** (*comput.*) word processor.
теку́ч|ий (~, ~а) *adj.*
1 (*phys.*) fluid.
2 (*непостоянный*) fluctuating, unstable.
теку́щ|ий *pres. part. act. of* ▸ **течь**[2] *and adj.*
1 current; of the present moment; **~ие собы́тия** current events, current affairs; **т. счёт** current account (*Br.*), checking account (*US*).
2 (*повседневный*) routine, ordinary; **т. ремо́нт** routine repairs.
тел. (*abbr. of* **телефо́н**) tel., telephone.
теле... *comb. form* tele-.
телевеща́ни|е, я *nt.* television broadcasting.
телеви́дени|е, я *nt.* television, TV.
телевизио́нный *adj.* television.
телеви́зор, а *m.* television set.
теле́г|а, и *f.* cart, wagon.
телегра́мм|а, ы *f.* telegram.
телегра́ф, а *m.*
1 (*система*) telegraph.
2 (*учреждение*) telegraph office.
телеграфи́р|овать, ую *impf. and pf.* to telegraph, wire.
телеграфи́ст, а *m.* telegraphist.
телеграфи́ст|ка, ки *f. of* ▸ **~**
телегра́фн|ый *adj.* telegraph; telegraphic; **~ое аге́нство** news agency; **т. столб** telegraph pole (*Br.*), telephone pole (*US*).
теле́жк|а, и *f.*
1 *dim. of* ▸ **теле́га.**
2 (*багажная; в супермаркете*) trolley (*Br.*), cart (*US*).
телезри́тел|ь, я *m.* (television) viewer.
телеигр|а́, ы́ *f.* game show.
телека́мер|а, ы *f.* television camera.
телекана́л, а *m.* TV channel.
телекоммуника́ци|и, й *f. pl.* telecommunications.
телекомпа́ни|я, и *f.* TV company.
телеконфере́нци|я, и *f.* teleconference, conference call.
те́лекс, а *m.* telex.
телеметри́|я, и *f.* telemetry.
телемо́ст, ~а́, *pl.* **~ы** *m.* satellite (TV) link-up.
тел|ёнок, ёнка, *pl.* **~я́та, ~я́т** *m.* calf.
телеопера́тор, а *m.* TV cameraman.
телепа́т, а *m.* telepathic person.
телепа́ти|я, и *f.* telepathy.
телепереда́ч|а, и *f.* TV programme (*Br.*), program (*US*).
телеско́п, а *m.* telescope.
телескопи́ческий *adj.* telescopic.
теле́сн|ый *adj.* bodily; corporal; physical; **~ое наказа́ние** corporal punishment; **~ого цве́та** flesh-coloured (*Br.*), flesh-colored (*US*).
телесту́ди|я, и *f.* television studio.
телесуфлёр, а *m.* teleprompter, Autocue (*propr.*).
телете́кст, а *m.* teletext.
телефа́кс, а *m.* (tele)fax (machine).
телефо́н, а *m.*

Т

[1] telephone; **позвонить по ~у** (+ *d.*) to telephone, phone, ring up (*Br.*); **т.-автомат** public telephone, call box (*Br.*).
[2] (*coll.*) (*номер*) telephone number.

телефонист, а *m.* telephone operator, telephonist.

телефонист|ка, ки *f. of* ▶ ~

телефон|ный *adj. of* ▶ ~; **~ная книга** telephone directory.

Тел|éц, ьцá *m.* Taurus.

тéлик, а *m.* (*coll.*) (the) telly (*Br.*), (the) TV.

тéл|о, а, *pl.* **~á, ~, ~áм** *nt.* body.

телогрéйк|а, и *f.* body warmer.

телосложéни|е, я *nt.* build, frame.

телохранител|ь, я *m.* bodyguard.

Тель-Авив, а *m.* Tel Aviv.

телятин|а, ы *f.* veal.

теляч|ий *adj. adj. of* ▶ **телёнок; ~ья кóжа** calf(skin); (*cul.*) veal.

тем
[1] *i. sg. m. and nt., d. pl. of* ▶ **тот.**
[2] *conj.* (so much) the; **чем выше, т. лýчше** the taller, the better; **т. лýчше** so much the better; **т. бóлее, что** especially as; **т. не мéнее** nonetheless, nevertheless; **т. сáмым** thus, thereby.

тéм|а, ы *f.*
[1] subject, topic, theme; **перейти к другóй ~е** to change the subject.
[2] (*mus.*) theme.

темáтик|а, и *f.* (*collect.*) subject matter.

тембр, а *m.* timbre.

Тéмз|а, ы *f.* the Thames (*river*).

тéми *i. pl. of* ▶ **тот**

темнé|ть, ю *impf.*
[1] (*pf.* **по~**) to grow *or* become dark; to darken.
[2] (*pf.* **с~**): **~ет** (*impers.*) it gets dark; it is getting dark.
[3] (*impf. only*) (*виднеться*) to show up darkly.

темн|ить, ю, ишь *impf.* (*coll.*) to be deliberately obscure.

темниц|а, ы *f.* dungeon.

темнó *as pred.* it is dark.

тёмно-... *comb. form* (*with names of colours*) dark; **тёмно-синий** dark blue, navy blue.

темноволóс|ый (~, ~а) *adj.* dark-haired.

темнокóж|ий (~, ~а) *adj.* dark-skinned, swarthy.

темнот|á, ы́ *f.* dark, darkness; **в ~é** in the dark; **до ~ы́** before dark.

тём|ный (~ен, ~нá) *adj.*
[1] dark; **~ное пятнó** (*fig.*) (*что-л. позорящее*) dark stain, blemish.
[2] (*неясный*) obscure, vague; **~ное пятнó** obscure place.
[3] (*мрачный*) gloomy, sombre (*Br.*), somber (*US*).
[4] (*подозрительный*) shady, suspicious; **~ное дéло** shady business.
[5] (*невежественный*) ignorant.

темп, а *m.*
[1] (*mus.*) tempo.
[2] (*fig.*) tempo; rate, speed, pace; **в ~е** (*coll.*) quickly.

темперáмент, а *m.* temperament.

темперáмент|ный (~ен, ~на) *adj.* energetic; spirited.

температýр|а, ы *f.*
[1] temperature; **мéрить комý-н. ~у** to take s.o.'s temperature.
[2] (*coll.*) (heightened) temperature; **у негó т.** he's got a temperature.

тéм|я, ени *no pl., nt.* crown, top of the head.

тенденциóз|ный (~ен, ~на) *adj.* (*pej.*) tendentious, biased.

тендéнци|я, и *f.* (**к** + *d.*) tendency (to, towards).

тéндер, а *m.*
[1] (*rail.*) (*вагон*) tender.
[2] (*naut.*) (*корабль*) cutter.
[3] (*comm.*) tender, bid.

тенев|óй *adj.* shady (*also fig.*); **~áя сторонá** shady side; (*fig.*) bad side, seamy side; **~áя экономика** shadow economy.

тéннис, а *m.* tennis.

теннисист, а *m.* tennis player.

теннисист|ка, ки *f. of* ▶ ~

тéнниск|а, и *f.* (*coll.*) tennis shirt, polo shirt.

тéннисн|ый *adj.* tennis; **т. корт, ~ая площáдка** tennis court.

тéнор, а, *pl.* **~á, ~óв** *m.* (*mus.*) tenor.

тент, а *m.* awning.

тен|ь, и, в ~и́, *pl.* **~и, ~éй** *f.*
[1] (*тенистое место*) shade; **сидéть в ~и́** to sit in the shade; **держáться в ~и́** (*fig.*) to keep in the background.
[2] (*тёмное отражение*) shadow; **давáть т.** to cast a shadow.
[3] (*призрак*) shadow, ghost.
[4] (*fig.*) (*малейшая доля*) shadow, atom; **нет ни ~и сомнéния** there is not a shadow of doubt.
[5] (*подозрение*) suspicion; **брóсить т. на когó-н.** to cast suspicion on s.o.

теодолит, а *m.* (*инструмент*) theodolite.

теокрáти|я, и *f.* theocracy.

теологический *adj.* theological.

теолóги|я, и *f.* theology.

теорéм|а, ы *f.* theorem.

теорéтик, а *m.* theorist.

теоретический *adj.* theoretical.

теóри|я, и *f.* theory.

тепéрь *adv.* now; nowadays, today.

теплé|ть, ет *impf.* (*of* ▶ **по~**) to get warm.

теплиц|а, ы *f.* greenhouse, hothouse.

теплó[1] *adv.*
[1] warmly.
[2] *as pred.* it is warm.

тепл|ó[2], á *nt.* heat; warmth; **дéсять грáдусов ~á** ten degrees (*Celsius*) above zero.

тепловóз, а *m.* diesel locomotive.

теплов|óй *adj.* heat; thermal; **т. удáр** (*med.*) heat stroke; **~áя энéргия** thermal energy.

теплот|á, ы́ *f.*
[1] (*phys.*) heat; **единица ~ы́** thermal unit.
[2] warmth (*also fig.*); **душéвная т.** warm-heartedness.

теплохóд, а *m.* motor ship.

тёп|лый (~ел, ~лá) *adj.*
[1] (*одежда, цвета*) warm; **~лое местéчко** (*coll.*) cushy job.

2 (*дача*) warmed, heated.
3 (*приём*) warm, cordial.
4 (*слова*) heartfelt.

терабайт, а *m.* (*comput.*) terabyte.

теракт, а *m.* act of terrorism, terrorist act.

терапевт, а *m.* therapist.

терапевтический *adj.* therapeutic.

терапи|я, и *f.* therapy; **интенсивная т.** intensive care.

тереб|ить, лю, ишь *impf.*
1 (*дёргать*) to pull (at), tug (at).
2 (*fig., coll.*) (*вопросами*) to pester, bother.

тереть, тру, трёшь, *past* **тёр, тёрла** *impf.*
1 (*глаза; грязное место*) to rub.
2 (*сыр*) to grate.
3 (*ногу, об обуви*) to rub, chafe.

тереться, трусь, трёшься, *past* **тёрся, тёрлась** *impf.* to rub o.s.; (**о, об(о)** + *a.*) to rub (against).

тёрк|а, и *f.* (*cul.*) grater.

термин, а *m.* term.

терминал, а *m.* (*at airport; where oil/gas are stored; comput.*) terminal.

терминологи|я, и *f.* terminology.

термит, а *m.* (*zool.*) termite.

термометр, а *m.* thermometer.

термос, а *m.* Thermos (flask) (*propr.*).

термостат, а *m.* thermostat.

тернист|ый (~, ~а) *adj.* (*obs.*) thorny, prickly; **т. путь** (*fig.*) difficult path.

терновник, а *m.* (*bot.*) blackthorn.

терпелив|ый (~, ~а) *adj.* patient.

терпени|е, я *nt.* patience; **вывести из ~я** to exasperate.

терп|еть, лю, ~ишь *impf.*
1 (*pf.* **по~**) (*испытывать*) to suffer, undergo; **т. поражение** to suffer a defeat.
2 (*стойко переносить*) to bear, endure, stand.
3 (*запастись терпением*) to have patience.
4 (*допускать*) to tolerate, suffer, put up (with); **т. не могу** I can't stand it; I hate it; **дело не ~ит отлагательства** the matter won't wait.

терп|еться, ~ится *impf.* (*impers.*): **ему,** *etc.*, **не ~ится** (+ *inf.*) he, *etc.*, is impatient (to).

терпимост|ь, и *f.* tolerance; indulgence.

терпим|ый (~, ~а) *adj.*
1 (*человек, характер*) tolerant; indulgent, forbearing.
2 (*условия, боль, жара*) tolerable, bearable.

терп|кий (~ок, ~ка, ~ко) *adj.* (*вкус, запах*) astringent, sharp; (*яблоко, виноград*) tart, sharp; (*вино*) sharp, rough.

терракот|а, ы *f.* (*глина; изделие*) terracotta.

террас|а, ы *f.* terrace.

территориальный *adj.* territorial.

территори|я, и *f.* territory, confines; area.

террор, а *m.* terror.

терроризир|овать, ую *impf. and pf.* to terrorize.

терроризм, а *m.* terrorism.

террорист, а *m.* terrorist.

террористический *adj.* terrorist.

террорист|ка, ки *f. of* ▸ **~**

терьер, а *m.* terrier (*dog*).

теря|ть, ю *impf.* (*of* ▸ **по~**) to lose; **т. надежду** to lose hope; **т. силу** to become invalid; **т. время на что-н.** to waste time on sth.; **т. в весе** to lose weight; **не т. из виду/вида** to keep in sight; **нам нечего т.** we have nothing to lose.

теря|ться, юсь *impf.* (*of* ▸ **по~**)
1 to be lost; to get lost; (*исчезать*) to disappear.
2 (*становиться слабее*) to fail, decline, weaken.
3 (*лишаться самообладания*) to become flustered.
4 : **т. в догадках** to be lost in conjecture.

те|сать, шу, ~шешь *impf.* to cut, hew.

тесно *adv.*
1 closely (*also fig.*); tightly; narrowly; **быть т. связанным (с** + *i.*) to be closely linked (with).
2 *as pred.* it is crowded; it is (too) tight; **в трамвае было очень т.** the tram was very crowded.

теснот|а, ы *f.*
1 (*свойство*) crowded state; narrowness; tightness; closeness.
2 (*недостаток места*) crush, squash; **жить в ~е** to live cooped up.

тес|ный (~ен, ~на, ~но, ~ны) *adj.*
1 (*непросторный*) crowded, cramped; **мир ~ен!** it's a small world.
2 (*узкий*) narrow.
3 (*пиджак*) (too) tight.
4 (*fig.*) (*близкий*) close, tight; **т. круг друзей** close circle of friends.

тест, а *m.* test.

тестир|овать, ую *impf. and pf.* to test.

тест|о, а *nt.* dough; pastry.

тест|ь, я *m.* father-in-law (*wife's father*).

тесьм|а, ы *f.* tape, ribbon.

тетерев, а, *pl.* **~а, ~ов** *m.* (*zool.*) black grouse.

тетив|а, ы *f.* bowstring.

тётк|а, и *f.*
1 aunt.
2 (*coll., pej.*) (*о немолодой женщине*) woman.

тетрад|ь, и *f.* exercise book (*Br.*), notebook; **т. для рисования** drawing book; sketchbook.

тёт|я, и, *g. pl.* **~ей** *f.*
1 aunt.
2 (*знакомая немолодая женщина; в сочетании с именем собственным*) auntie.
3 (*coll.*) (*женщина*) lady.

тефтел|и, ей (*sg. coll.* **~я, ~и** *f.*) (*cul.*) meatballs.

тех *g., a., p. pl. of* ▸ **тот**

техник, а *m.* technician.

техник|а, и *f.*
1 technology; **наука и т.** science and technology.
2 (*приёмы исполнения*) technique, art.
3 (*collect.*) (*машины*) machinery; technical devices.

техникум, а *m.* technical college.

техническ|ий *adj.* technical; **~ие науки** engineering sciences; **т. термин** technical term; **~ое обслуживание** maintenance.

технолог, а *m.* technologist.

технологический *adj.* technological.

техноло́ги|я, и *f.* technology.
тече́ни|е, я *nt.*
1 (*поток*) flow.
2 (*fig.*) course; **с ~ем вре́мени** in the course of time, in time.
3 (*ток, струя*) current, stream (*also fig.*); **по ~ю, про́тив ~я** with the stream, against the stream (*also fig.*).
4 (*fig.*) (*направление*) trend, tendency.
5 : **в т.** (+ *g.*) during, in the course (of).
теч|ь[1]**, и** *f.* leak; **дать т.** to spring a leak; **заде́лать т.** to stop a leak.
течь[2]**, течёт, теку́т,** *past* **тёк, текла́** *impf.*
1 to flow (*also fig.*); to stream; (*fig.*) (*о времени*) to pass; **у тебя́ кровь течёт из но́са** your nose is bleeding.
2 (*иметь течь*) to leak, be leaky.
тёщ|а, и *f.* mother-in-law (*wife's mother*).
Тибе́т, а *m.* Tibet.
тибе́т|ец, ца *m.* Tibetan.
тибе́т|ка, ки *f. of* ▸ **~ец**
тибе́тский *adj.* Tibetan.
тигр, а *m.* tiger.
ти́кань|е, я *nt.* tick, ticking (*of a clock*).
ти́ка|ть, ет *impf.* to tick.
ти́н|а, ы *no pl., f.* slime; mire.
тине́йджер, а *m.* teenager.
тип, а *m.*
1 type; model.
2 (*coll.*) (*человек*) fellow, character; **стра́нный т.** odd character.
типи́ч|ный (~ен, ~на) *adj.* typical.
типогра́фи|я, и *f.* printing house, press.
типогра́фск|ий *adj.* typographical; **~ое де́ло** typography.
тир, а *m.* shooting range; shooting gallery.
тира́ж, а́ *m.*
1 drawing (*of loan or lottery*); **вы́йти в т.** to be drawn.
2 (*количество экземпляров*) circulation; edition; print run.
тира́н, а *m.* tyrant.
тирани́|я, и *f.* tyranny.
тире́ *nt. indecl.* dash.
тис, а *m.* yew (tree).
ти́ска|ть, ю *impf.* (*of* ▸ **ти́снуть**) (*coll.*) to press, squeeze.
тиск|и́, о́в *no sg.* (*tech.*) vice (*Br.*), vise (*US*); **в ~а́х** (+ *g.*) in the grip (of).
ти́снуть *pf. of* ▸ **ти́скать**
тита́н[1]**, а** *m.* (*myth. and fig.*) titan.
тита́н[2]**, а** *m.* (*chem.*) titanium.
титани́ческий *adj.* titanic.
титр, а *m.* (*usu. pl.*) (*cin.*) title, credit.
ти́тул, а *m.* title.
ти́тул|ьный *adj. of* ▸ **~; т. лист** title page.
тиф, а *m.* typhus; **брюшно́й т.** typhoid (fever).
ти́х|ий (~, ~а́, ~о) *adj.*
1 quiet; (*звук*) low, soft; (*мягкий*) gentle; (*слабый*) faint; **т. го́лос** low voice.
2 (*бесшумный*) silent, noiseless; still; **~ая ночь** still night.
3 (*fig.*) (*спокойный*) quiet, calm; gentle; still; **~ая жизнь** quiet life.
4 (*медленный*) slow, slow-moving; **т. ход** slow speed, slow pace.
Ти́х|ий океа́н, ~ого ~а *m.* the Pacific (Ocean).
ти́хо[1] *adv.*
1 (*негромко*) quietly; softly, gently; **т. постуча́ть** to knock gently.
2 (*бесшумно*) silently, noiselessly.
3 (*fig.*) (*спокойно*) quietly, calmly; still; **сиде́ть т.** to sit still; **т.** gently!, careful!
4 (*медленно*) slowly.
ти́хо[2] *as pred.* it is quiet, there is not a sound; **ста́ло т.** it became quiet.
тихо́нько *adv.* (*coll.*) quietly; softly, gently.
тихоокеа́нский *adj.* Pacific.
ти́ше
1 *comp. of* ▸ **ти́хий** *and* ▸ **ти́хо.**
2 : **т.!** (*i*) (*молчать!*) (be) quiet!, silence!, (*ii*) (*осторожнее!*) gently!; careful!
тишин|а́, ы́ *f.* quiet, silence; stillness; **нару́шить ~у́** to break the silence; **соблюда́ть ~у́** to keep quiet.
т. к. (*abbr. of* **так как**) as, since.
тка́ный *adj.* woven.
ткан|ь, и *f.*
1 fabric, cloth; **льняны́е ~и** linen(s); **шёлковые ~и** silks.
2 (*anat.*) tissue.
ткать, тку, ткёшь, *past* **ткал, ткала́, тка́ло** *impf.* (*of* ▸ **со~**) to weave; **т. паути́ну** to spin a web.
тка́цкий *adj.* weaver's, weaving; **т. стано́к** loom.
ткач, а́ *m.* weaver.
ткачи́х|а, и *f. of* ▸ **ткач**
ткн|уть, у́, ёшь *pf. of* ▸ **ты́кать**
тле́|ть, ет *impf.*
1 (*гнить*) to rot, decay, decompose.
2 (*гореть*) to smoulder (*Br.*), smolder (*US*) (*also fig.*).
тл|я, и, *g. pl.* **~ей** *f.* aphid.
тмин, а *m.* caraway.
то[1] *pron.* (*nom. and a. sg. nt. of* ▸ **тот**) that; **то, что...** the fact that ...; **то́ есть** that is (to say); **а то** *see* ▸ **а; (да) и то** and that, at that.
то[2] *conj.*
1 (*in main clause of conditional sentence*) then (*or not translated*).
2 : **то..., то...** now ..., now ...; **то тут, то там** now here, now there.
3 : **не то..., не то...** either ... or ...; whether ... or ...; half ..., half ...; **не то по глу́пости, не то по зло́бе** either through stupidity or through malice.
4 : **не то, что́бы..., но...** it is not, it was not that ... (but) ... .
-то[1] *emph. particle* (*in coll. Russian oft. merely adds familiar tone*) just, precisely, exactly (*or not translated*); **в то́м-то и де́ло** that's just it; **ва́м-то чего́ боя́ться?** what have *you* to be afraid of?
-то[2] *particle forming indef. prons and advs.* (**кто́-то, како́й-то, когда́-то,** *etc.*).
тобо́й *i. of* ▸ **ты**
това́р, а *m.* (*collect. or in pl.*) goods; wares; (*sg.*) article; product, commodity; **~ы широ́кого потребле́ния** consumer goods.
това́рищ, а *m.*
1 comrade; (*друг*) friend; (*коллега*) colleague; **т. по несча́стью** fellow sufferer, companion

in distress; **т. по рабо́те** colleague; workmate; **т. по шко́ле** school friend.
2 (*официальное обращение к гражданину*) comrade.

това́рищеск|ий *adj.*
1 comradely; friendly.
2 (*sport*) friendly, unofficial; **~ое состяза́ние, ~ая встре́ча** friendly (match) (*Br.*).

това́рный *adj.*
1 goods (*Br.*), freight; **т. знак** trademark; **т. склад** warehouse.
2 (*rail.*) goods (*Br.*), freight; **т. соста́в** goods train (*Br.*), freight train.
3 (*econ.*) (*цены, продукция*) commodity; (*вид*) marketable.

тогда́
1 *adv.* (*в то время; в таком случае*) then (= at that time; in that case).
2 : **когда́..., т. ...** (*conj.*) when; **когда́ решу́сь, т. напишу́ тебе́** I will write to you when I have decided.
3 : **т. как** (*conj.*) whereas, while.

того́ *g. sg. m. and nt. of* ▸ **тот**

тожде́ствен|ный (~, ~на) *adj.* identical.

то́же *adv.* also, as well, too.

ток, а *m.* (*elec.*) current.

тока́рный *adj.* (*tech.*) turning; **т. стано́к** lathe.

то́кар|ь, я *m.* turner, lathe operator.

То́кио *m. indecl.* Tokyo.

токсикома́н, а *m.* glue-sniffer, solvent abuser.

токсикома́ни|я, и *f.* glue-sniffing, solvent abuse.

токси́н, а *m.* (*med.*) toxin.

токси́ческий *adj.* toxic.

ток-шо́у *nt. indecl.* talk show.

толера́нтност|ь, и *f.* tolerance.

толк, а (у) *m.*
1 (*смысл*) sense; understanding; **бе́з ~у** senselessly.
2 (*coll.*) (*польза*) use, profit; **знать т. (в** + *p.*) to know what one is talking about (in).

толк|а́ть, а́ю *impf.* (*of* ▸ **~ну́ть**)
1 to push, shove; (*нечаянно*) to jog; **т. ло́ктем** to nudge.
2 (*sport*): **т. шта́нгу** to lift weights.
3 (**на** + *a.*) (*побуждать*) to push (into), incite (to).

толк|а́ться, а́юсь (*impf. only*) (*толкать друг друга*) to push (one another).

толк|ну́ть, ну́, нёшь *pf. of* ▸ **~а́ть**

толкова́ни|е, я *nt.* interpretation.

толк|ова́ть, у́ю *impf.* to interpret; **оши́бочно, неве́рно т. чьи-н. слова́** to misinterpret, misconstrue s.o.'s words.

толко́в|ый (~, ~а) *adj.*
1 (*человек*) intelligent, sensible.
2 (*объяснение*) intelligible, clear.
3 : **т. слова́рь** defining dictionary.

то́лком *adv.* (*coll.*) plainly, clearly.

толп|а́, ы́, *pl.* **~́ы** *f.* crowd; throng; multitude.

толп|и́ться, и́тся *impf.* to crowd; to throng.

толсте́|ть, ю *impf.* (*of* ▸ **по~**) to grow fat; to put on weight.

толсто́вк|а, и *f.* (*coll.*) sweatshirt.

толстоко́ж|ий (~, ~а) *adj.* thick-skinned (*also fig.*).

то́лст|ый (~, ~а́, ~о, ~́ы) *adj.*
1 (*человек*) fat.
2 (*книга, бумага, слой*) thick.

толстя́к, а́ *m.* (*мужчина*) fat man; (*мальчик*) fat boy.

толч|о́к, ка́ *m.*
1 (*толкающий удар*) push, shove.
2 (*при езде*) jolt, bump; (*при землетрясении*) (earthquake) shock, tremor.
3 (*fig.*) (*побуждение*) push, shove; stimulus; **дать т. эконо́мике** to kick-start the economy.

то́лщ|а, и *f.* thickness; **т. сне́га** depth of snow.

то́лще *comp. of* ▸ **то́лстый**

толщин|а́, ы́ *f.*
1 (*человека*) fatness, corpulence.
2 (*бревна, слоя*) thickness.

то́лько
1 *adv.* only; solely; alone; just; **не т. ..., но и** not only ..., but also; **поду́май(те) т.!** just think!; **т. и всего́, да и т.** (*coll.*) that's all.
2 : **т. что** (*adv. and conj.*) just, only just; **он т. что позвони́л** he has just rung up.
3 *conj.* (+ **как, лишь**) as soon as; one has only to ... .
4 *conj.* only, but; **с удово́льствием, т. не сего́дня** with pleasure, only not today.
5 : **т. бы** (+ *inf.*) (*particle*) if only.

том, а, *pl.* **~а́, ~о́в** *m.* volume.

тома́т, а *m.* tomato.

тома́тный *adj.* tomato; **т. сок** tomato juice.

томи́тел|ьный (~ен, ~ьна) *adj.* (*скучный*) tedious; wearing; (*утомительный*) tiring, exhausting; (*гнетущий*) oppressive; (*мучительный*) agonizing, painful.

том|и́ться, лю́сь, и́шься *impf.* (*голодом, ожиданием*) to be tormented (by); **т. в тюрьме́** to languish in prison.

то́м|ный (~ен, ~́на́, ~но) *adj.* languid, languorous.

тон, а, *pl.* **~́ы** *and* **~а́** *m.*
1 (*pl.* **~́ы**) (*mus. and fig.*) tone; **~́ом вы́ше, ни́же** a tone higher, lower; **хоро́ший, дурно́й т.** good, bad form.
2 (*pl.* **~а́**) (*краски, цвета*) tone, tint.

тона́льност|ь, и *f.* (*mus.*) key.

то́нер, а *m.* toner.

тонзилли́т, а *m.* tonsillitis.

то́ник, а *m.* tonic (water).

то́н|кий (~ок, ~ка́, ~ко, ~́ки́) *adj.*
1 (*слой*) thin; (*фигура*) slim; **т. ло́мтик** thin slice.
2 (*изысканный*) fine; delicate; refined; **~кое бельё** fine linen; (*не грубый*) subtle, fine; **~кое разли́чие** subtle, fine distinction.
3 (*звук*) high, squeaky.
4 (*fig.*) (*проницательный, умный*) shrewd, subtle, penetrating; **т. знато́к** connoisseur.
5 (*зрение, слух*) keen.

то́нко *adv.*
1 (*резать*) thinly.
2 (*чувствовать*) subtly, delicately, finely.

то́нкост|ь, и *f.*
1 thinness; (*фигуры*) slimness.

[2] (*ткани, работы*) fineness.
[3] (*ума*) subtlety.
[4] (*мелкая подробность*) nice point, subtle point; **до ~ей** to a nicety.

то́нн|а, ы *f.* metric ton, tonne.

тонне́л|ь, я *m.* tunnel; (*пешеходный*) subway.

то́нус, а *m.* (*physiol., med.*) tone; **жизненный т.** vitality.

тон|у́ть, у́, ~ешь *impf.*
[1] (*pf.* **за~**) (*о судне*) to sink, go down.
[2] (*pf.* **у~**) (*о человеке*) to drown.
[3] (*pf.* **у~**) (**в** + *p.*) to sink (in); to be lost (in); to be hidden (in, by); **т. в дела́х** to be up to one's eyes in work.

то́ньше *comp. of* ▶**то́нкий** *and* ▶**то́нко**

топ, а *m.* (*одежда*) crop top.

то́п|ать, аю *impf.* (*of* **~нуть**) to stamp; **т. нога́ми** to stamp one's feet.

топ|и́ть[1], лю́, ~ишь *impf.*
[1] (*камин*) to stoke (*a boiler, stove, etc.*).
[2] (*помещение*) to heat.

топ|и́ть[2], лю́, ~ишь *impf.*
[1] (*воск*) to melt (down), render.
[2] : **т. молоко́** to bake milk.

топ|и́ть[3], лю́, ~ишь *impf.*
[1] (*pf.* **по~**) (*корабль*) to sink.
[2] (*pf.* **у~**) (*человека*) to drown; (*fig., coll.*) to wreck, ruin.

топ|и́ться[1], ~ится *impf.* (*о камине*) to burn, be alight.

топ|и́ться[2], ~ится *impf.*
[1] (*о воске*) to melt.
[2] *pass of* ▶**~и́ть[2]**

топ|и́ться[3], лю́сь, ~ишься *impf.* (*of* ▶**у~**) (*о человеке*) to drown o.s.

то́пк|а, и *f.*
[1] (*камина*) stoking.
[2] (*помещения*) heating.
[3] (*часть печи*) furnace; (*rail.*) firebox.

то́плив|о, а *nt.* fuel; **жидкое т.** fuel oil; **твёрдое т.** solid fuel.

топ-моде́л|ь, и *f.* top model.

то́п|нуть, ну, нешь *pf. of* ▶**~ать**

топографи́ческий *adj.* topographical.

то́пол|ь, я, *pl.* **~я́** *m.* poplar.

топо́р, а́ *m.* axe (*Br.*), ax (*US*).

топо́рщ|иться, ится *impf.* (*coll.*)
[1] (*о волосах*) to stand on end, bristle.
[2] (*о еже*) to bristle; (*о птице*) to puff up its feathers.
[3] (*об одежде*) to stick out, pucker.

то́пот, а *m.* tramp; **ко́нский т.** clatter of horses' hoofs.

топ|та́ть, чу́, ~чешь *impf.*
[1] (*траву*) to trample (down).
[2] (*пол*) to make dirty (*with one's feet*).

топ|та́ться, чу́сь, ~чешься *impf.* to shift from one foot to the other; **т. на ме́сте** to mark time (*also fig.*).

топча́н, а́ *m.* trestle bed.

топ|ь, и *f.* bog, marsh, swamp.

То́р|а, ы *f.* (*relig.*) Torah.

торг, а, о ~е, на ~у́, *pl.* **~и́** *m.*
[1] (*действие*) trading.
[2] *pl.* (*аукцион*) auction; **прода́ть с ~о́в** to sell by auction.

торг|ова́ть, у́ю *impf.* (+ *i.*) to trade (in), deal (in), sell.

торг|ова́ться, у́юсь *impf.*
[1] (*pf.* **с~**) (**с** + *i.*) to bargain (with), haggle (with).
[2] (*coll.*) (*спорить*) to argue.

торго́в|ец, ца *m.* merchant; dealer; tradesman; **т. нарко́тиками** drug trafficker/pusher.

торго́вк|а, и *f.* (*coll.*) (female) stallholder; (woman) street trader.

торго́вл|я, и *f.* trade, commerce.

торго́в|ый *adj.* trade, commercial; **т. дом** firm; **~ая то́чка** shop.

тореадо́р, а *m.* toreador.

тор|е́ц, ца́ *m.* butt end, short side, face; (*здания*) gable end.

торже́ствен|ный (~, ~на) *adj.*
[1] ceremonial; (*праздничный*) festive; gala; **т. день** red-letter day.
[2] (*серьёзный*) solemn.

торжеств|о́, а́ *nt.*
[1] celebration; (*pl.*) (*празднество*) festivities, rejoicings.
[2] (*победа*) triumph (= *victory*).
[3] (*радость*) triumph, exultation.

торжеств|ова́ть, у́ю *impf.*
[1] to celebrate; (*fig.*) (*радоваться*) to rejoice.
[2] (**над** + *i.*) to triumph (over); to exult (over).

то́ри *m. indecl.* (*pol.*) Tory.

то́рмоз, а *m.* (*pl.* **~а́**) brake.

тормо|зи́ть, жу́, зи́шь *impf.* (*of* ▶**за~**)
[1] (*tech.*) to brake, apply the brake (to).
[2] (*fig.*) (*замедлить*) to hamper, impede.
[3] (*psych.*) to inhibit.

тормош|и́ть, у́, и́шь *impf.* (*coll.*)
[1] (*дёргать*) to pull (at), tug (at).
[2] (*fig.*) (*вопросами*) to pester, plague.

тороп|и́ть, лю́, ~ишь *impf.* (*of* ▶**по~**)
[1] to hurry, hasten; to press; **меня́ ~ят с оконча́нием рабо́ты** I am being pressed to finish my work.
[2] (*события*) to precipitate.

тороп|и́ться, лю́сь, ~ишься *impf.* (*of* ▶**по~**) to hurry, be in a hurry, hasten.

торопли́в|ый (~, ~а) *adj.* hurried, hasty.

торо́с, а *m.* ice hummock.

торпе́д|а, ы *f.* torpedo.

торс, а *m.* trunk; torso.

торт, а *m.* cake.

торф, а *m.* peat.

торч|а́ть, у́, и́шь *impf.*
[1] (*вверх*) to stick up; (*в сторону*) to stick out; (*о волосах*) to stand on end.
[2] (*coll.*) (*в каком-л. месте*) to hang about.
[3] (*sl.*) (*получать удовольствие*) to feel euphoric (from), get a kick (out of); (*от наркотиков*) to get high (on).

торше́р, а *m.* standard lamp.

тоск|а́, и́ *f.*
[1] (*уныние*) melancholy; (*тревога*) anguish.
[2] (*скука*) boredom, ennui; **одна́ т., сплошна́я т.** a frightful bore.
[3] (**по** + *d.*) longing (for); yearning (for), nostalgia (for); **т. по ро́дине** homesickness.

тоскли́в|ый (~, ~а) *adj.*
[1] (*настроение*) melancholy; depressed, miserable.

2 (*погода, город*) dull, dreary, depressing.

тоск|ова́ть, у́ю *impf.*
1 to be melancholy, be depressed, be miserable.
2 (**по** + *d.*) to long (for), yearn (for), pine (for), miss.

тост[1]**, а** *m.* toast; **провозгласи́ть, предложи́ть т.** (**за** + *a.*) to toast, drink (to); to propose a toast (to).

тост[2]**, а** *m.* (*ломтик хлеба*) piece of toast.

то́стер, а *m.* toaster.

тот *m.*, **та** *f.*, **то** *nt.*, *pl.* **те** *pron.*
1 (*opp.* **э́тот**) that; (*pl.*) those; **в то вре́мя** then, at that time, in those days.
2 (*opp.* **э́тот**) the former; (*replacing 3rd pers. sg. pron.*) he; she; it.
3 (*opp.* **э́тот**) (*другой*) the other; the opposite; **на той стороне́** on the other side.
4 (*opp.* **друго́й, ино́й**) the one; **и тот, и друго́й** both; **ни тот, ни друго́й** neither.
5 : **тот…, (кото́рый)** the … (which); **тот, (кто)** the one (who), the person (who); **тот факт, что** the fact that (*see also* ▸ **то**[1]).
6 : **тот (же), тот (же) са́мый** the same; **одно́ и то же** one and the same thing, the same thing over again; **в то же са́мое вре́мя** at the same time, on the other hand.
7 (*такой, какой нужен*) the right; **не тот** the wrong; **э́то не та дверь** that's the wrong door.
8 + *preps. forms the following conjs.*: **для того́, что́бы** in order that, in order to; **ме́жду тем, как** whereas; **несмотря́ на то, что** in spite of the fact that; **пе́ред тем, как** before; **по́сле того́, как** after; **с тем, что́бы** in order to, with a view to.
9 *forms part of var. adv. phrr. and particles* (*see also* ▸ **то**[1]): **вме́сте с тем** at the same time; **к тому́ же** moreover; **кро́ме того́** besides; **ме́жду тем, тем вре́менем** meanwhile; **тем са́мым** hereby; **тому́ наза́д** ago.

тотализа́тор, а *m.* tote, totalizator.

тоталита́рный *adj.* (*pol.*) totalitarian.

тоте́м, а *m.* totem.

то́тчас *adv.* at once; immediately (*also of spatial relations*).

точёный *adj.* finely moulded (*Br.*), finely molded (*US*); (*о чертах лица*) chiselled (*Br.*), chiseled (*US*).

точи́лк|а, и *f.* (*coll.*) (*для ножей*) steel, knife sharpener; (*для карандашей*) pencil sharpener.

точ|и́ть, у́, ~́ишь *impf.*
1 (*pf.* **на~**) (*нож, карандаш*) to sharpen; **т. зу́бы на кого́-н.** to have a grudge against s.o.
2 (*impf. only*) (*на токарном станке*) to turn.

то́чк|а, и *f.*
1 spot, dot; **ста́вить ~и над «и»** to dot one's 'i's' (and cross one's 't's').
2 (*gram.*) full stop; **т. с запято́й** semicolon.
3 (*math., phys., tech.*) point; **т. замерза́ния, кипе́ния** freezing, boiling point; **т. опо́ры** fulcrum, point of support; (*fig.*) rallying point.
4 (*fig.*) point; **т. зре́ния** point of view; **горя́чая т.** trouble spot.

то́чно[1] *adv.*
1 exactly, precisely; (*пунктуально*) punctually.
2 : **т. так** just so, exactly, precisely; **т. тако́й (же)** just the same.
3 (*действительно*) indeed.

то́чно[2] *conj.* as though, as if; like.

то́чност|ь, и *f.* exactness; precision; accuracy; punctuality; **в ~и** exactly, precisely.

то́ч|ный (~ен, ~на́, ~но, ~́ны) *adj.* exact, precise; accurate; (*пунктуальный*) punctual; **~ные нау́ки** exact sciences; **т. перево́д** accurate translation; **т. прибо́р** precision instrument.

тошн|и́ть, и́т *impf.* (*impers.*): **меня́,** *etc.*, **~и́т** I, *etc.*, feel sick; **меня́ от э́того ~и́т** (*fig.*) it makes me sick, it sickens me.

тошнот|а́, ы́ *f.* sickness, nausea (*also fig.*).

тошнотво́р|ный (~ен, ~на) *adj.* sickening, nauseating (*also fig.*).

то́щ|ий (~, ~а́, ~е) *adj.* gaunt, emaciated; skinny.

трав|а́, ы́, *pl.* **~́ы** *f.* grass; (*специя, лекарственная*) herb; **со́рная т.** weed.

трави́нк|а, и *f.* blade of grass.

трав|и́ть, лю́, ~́ишь *impf.* (*of* ▸ **вы~**) (*тараканов, крыс*) to exterminate, destroy (*by poisoning*).

тра́вл|я, и *f.* hunting; (*fig.*) persecution, tormenting.

тра́вм|а, ы *f.* (*med.*) (*психическая*) trauma; (*физическая*) injury.

травмати́ческий *adj.* (*med., psych.*) traumatic.

травматологи́ческ|ий *adj.*: **~ое отделе́ние** casualty department; **т. пункт** first-aid room.

травоя́дный *adj.* herbivorous.

травян|о́й *adj.*
1 grass; herbaceous; **т. покро́в** grass.
2 : **~а́я насто́йка** herb tea.

траге́ди|я, и *f.* tragedy.

траги́ческ|ий *adj.* tragic; **т. актёр** tragic actor; **~ое зре́лище** tragic sight.

традицио́н|ный (~ен, ~на) *adj.* traditional.

тради́ци|я, и *f.* tradition.

траекто́ри|я, и *f.* trajectory.

тракта́т, а *m.* (*сочинение*) treatise.

тракт|ова́ть, у́ю *impf.*
1 (*вопрос*) to treat, discuss.
2 (*роль*) to interpret (*a part in a play, etc.*).

тракто́вк|а, и *f.* treatment; interpretation.

тра́ктор, а *m.* tractor; **гу́сеничный т., т. на гу́сеничном ходу́** caterpillar tractor.

трактори́ст, а *m.* tractor driver.

трактори́ст|ка, ки *f. of* ▸ **~**

трамб|ова́ть, у́ю *impf.* to ram, tamp.

трамва́|й, я *m.* tram (*Br.*), streetcar (*US*); **речно́й т.** river bus.

трампли́н, а *m.* (*sport and fig.*) springboard; (*лыжный*) ski jump.

транзи́стор, а *m.* transistor.

транзи́т, а *m.* transit.

транзи́т|ный *adj. of* ▸ **~**; **~ная ви́за** transit visa.

транквилиза́тор, а *m.* tranquillizer (*Br.*), tranquilizer (*US*).

транс, а *m.* trance.

трансатланти́ческий *adj.* transatlantic.

транскри́пци|я, и *f.* transcription.

Т

транслúр|овать, ую *impf. and pf.* to broadcast; to relay.

транслитерáци|я, и *f.* transliteration.

трансля́ци|я, и *f.* (*действие*) transmission, broadcasting; (*передача*) broadcast.

трансмúсси|я, и *f.* (*tech.*) transmission.

транснационáльный *adj.* transnational.

транспарáнт, а *m.* banner.

трансплантáци|я, и *f.* (*med.*) transplantation.

трáнспорт, а *m.*
1 (*система перевозки*) transport; **общéственный т.** public transport.
2 (*перевозка*) transportation, conveyance.
3 (*mil.*) train, transport.
4 (*naut.*) supply ship; troopship.

транспортúр|овать, ую *impf. and pf.* to transport.

транспортирóвк|а, и *f.* transport, transportation.

транссексуáл, а *m.* transsexual.

транссибúрск|ий *adj.* Trans-Siberian; **~ая магистрáль** the Trans-Siberian Railway.

трансформáтор, а *m.* (*elec.*) transformer.

трансформáци|я, и *f.* transformation.

трансформúр|овать, ую *impf. and pf.* to transform.

траншé|я, и *f.* (*mil.*) trench.

трап, а *m.* (*naut.*, *aeron.*) gangway.

трáпез|а, ы *f.*
1 (*общий стол*) dining table (*esp. in a monastery*).
2 (*еда*) meal; **делúть ~у (с** + *i.*) to share a meal (with).

трапéци|я, и *f.*
1 (*math.*) trapezium.
2 (*цирковая*) trapeze.

трáсс|а, ы *f.*
1 (*трубопровода, метро*) route, course; **воздýшная т.** airway.
2 (*дорога*) main road, highway (*US*).

трáт|а, ы *f.* expenditure; **пустáя т. врéмени** waste of time.

трá|тить, чу, тишь *impf.* (*of* ▸**ис~** *and* ▸**по~**) to spend, expend, use up; (*понапрасну*) to waste.

трáулер, а *m.* trawler.

трáур, а *m.* mourning.

трáурн|ый *adj.*
1 mourning; funeral; **т. марш** funeral march; **~ое шéствие** funeral procession.
2 (*скорбный*) mournful, sorrowful; funereal.

трафарéт, а *m.* stencil.

трáфик, а (*comput.*) traffic.

трáх|ать, аю *impf. of* ▸**~нуть**

трáх|аться, аюсь *impf. of* ▸**~нуться**

трáх|нуть, ну, нешь *pf.* (*of* ▸**~ать**)
1 (*coll.*) (*стукнуть*) to bang, crash.
2 (*sl.*) (*совершить половой акт*) to screw, hump.

трáх|нуться, нусь, нешься *pf.* (*of* ▸**~аться**)
1 (*coll.*) (*стукнуться*) to bang, crash.
2 (*sl.*) (*совершить половой акт*) to screw, hump.

трéбовани|е, я *nt.*
1 (*действие*) demand, request; **по ~ю** on demand, by request; **останóвка по ~ю** request stop.
2 (*настоятельная просьба*) demand; (*притязание*) claim; **согласúться на чьи-н. ~я** to agree to s.o.'s demands; **вы́двинуть т.** to put in a claim.
3 (*usu. pl.*) (*условие*) requirement, condition; **отвечáть, соотвéтствовать ~ям** to meet requirements.
4 *pl.* (*запросы*) aspirations; needs.

трéбовател|ьный (~ен, ~ьна) *adj.* demanding.

трéб|овать, ую *impf.* (*of* ▸**по~**)
1 (+ *g. or a. or* + **чтóбы**) to demand, require; **онú ~уют, чтóбы мы извинúлись** they demand that we apologize.
2 (*impf. only*) (+ *g.* **от** + *g.*) to expect (from), ask (of); **вы ~уете слúшком мнóго от вáших ученикóв** you expect too much from your pupils.
3 (+ *g.*) (*нуждаться*) to require, need, call (for).

трéб|оваться, уется *impf.* (*of* ▸**по~**) to be needed, be required; **на э́то ~уется мнóго врéмени** it takes a lot of time; **фúрме ~уется бухгáлтер** the company seeks an accountant.

требух|á, ú *no pl.*, *f.* entrails; (*cul.*) offal, tripe.

тревóг|а, и *f.*
1 (*беспокойство*) alarm, anxiety.
2 (*сигнал*) alarm; **бить ~у** to sound the alarm (*also fig.*); **поднять ~у** to raise the alarm.

тревóж|ить, у, ишь *impf.* (*of* **по~**) (*мешать*) to disturb, interrupt.

тревóж|иться, усь, ишься *impf.* (*of* **по~**) to trouble o.s., put o.s. out; **не ~ьтесь!** don't bother (yourself)!

тревóж|ный (~ен, ~на) *adj.*
1 (*полный тревоги*) anxious, uneasy, troubled.
2 (*вызывающий тревогу*) alarming, disturbing.

трезвé|ть, ю *impf.* (*of* ▸**про~**) to sober (up), become sober.

трéзвост|ь, и *f.*
1 sobriety (*also fig.*); **т. умá** cool-headedness.
2 (*воздержание от спиртного*) abstinence; temperance.

трéзв|ый (~, ~á, ~о, ~ы́) *adj.*
1 sober (*also fig.*).
2 (*не пьющий*) teetotal, abstinent.

трезýб|ец, ца *m.* trident.

трéйдер, а *m.* trader (*in stocks and shares*).

трéйлер, а *m.* (*передвижной дом-прицеп*) caravan (*Br.*), trailer (*US*).

трек, а *m.* (*sport*) track.

трелья́ж, а *m.*
1 (*зеркало*) three-leaved mirror.
2 (*для растений*) trellis.

тренажёр, а *m.* training apparatus; **лётный т.** flight simulator; (*sport*) piece of gym equipment.

тренажёрный *adj.*: **т. зал** gym.

трéнер, а *m.* (*sport*) trainer, coach.

трéни|е, я *nt.*
1 friction, rubbing.
2 (*pl.*) (*fig.*) friction.

трéнинг, а *m.* training.

тренир|ова́ть, у́ю *impf.* to train, coach; (*память*) to train.

тренир|ова́ться, у́юсь *impf.* to train o.s., coach o.s.; to be in training.

трениро́вк|а, и *f.* training, coaching.

трено́г|а, и *f.* tripod.

тре́нька|ть, ю *impf.* (*coll.*) (*на гитаре*) to strum.

треп|а́ть, лю́, ~́лешь *impf.* (*of* ▸**по~**)
1 to pull about; (*о ветре*) to blow about; **т. языко́м** (*coll.*) to prattle; **т. чьи-н. не́рвы** to get on s.o.'s nerves.
2 (*одежду*) to wear out.
3 (*по плечу*) to pat.

треп|а́ться, лю́сь, ~́лешься *impf.*
1 (*pf.* **по~**) (*об одежде*) to wear out.
2 (*impf. only*) (*о флагах*) to flutter; (*о волосах*) to blow about.
3 (*pf.* **по~**) (*coll.*) = **трепа́ть языко́м**

тре́пет, а *m.* (*дрожь*) trembling, quivering; (*сердца*) palpitation; (*страх*) trepidation, terror; (*волнение*) agitation; (*уважительность*) awe.

трепе|та́ть, щу́, ~́щешь *impf.*
1 (*дрожать*) to tremble, quiver.
2 (*fig.*) (*испытывать волнение*) to tremble; to thrill; **т. от восто́рга** to thrill with joy; **т. при мы́сли** (**о** + *p.*) to tremble at the thought (of).
3 (**пе́ред** + *i.*) (*fig.*) (*испытывать страх*) to tremble (before).

треск, а *m.* crack; crackle, crackling; **т. огня́** crackling of a fire; **с ~́ом провали́ться** (*fig., coll.*) to be a flop.

треск|а́, и́ *f.* cod.

тре́ска|ться, ется *impf.* (*of* ▸**по~**) to crack; to chap.

тре́сн|уть, у, ешь *pf.*
1 (*о ветке*) to snap.
2 (*о стакане, коже*) to crack; (*лопнуть*) to burst.
3 (+ *i.* **по** + *d.* or + *a.* **по** + *d.*; *coll.*) to bring down with a crash (on); to hit, bang.

трест, а *m.* (*econ.*) trust; (*строительный*) company.

тре́т|ий, ья, ье *adj.*
1 third; **т. но́мер** number three; **полови́на ~ьего** half past two; **стра́ны ~ьего ми́ра** Third World countries.
2 *as n.* **~ье, ~ьего** *nt.* sweet, dessert.

трет|ь, и, *pl.* **~́и, ~е́й** *f.* third.

третьесо́ртный *adj.* third-rate.

треуго́льник, а *m.* triangle.

тре́ф|ы, ~ *pl.* (*sg.* **~а, ~ы** *f.*) (*cards*) clubs; **да́ма ~** queen of clubs.

трёх... *comb. form* three-, tri-.

трёхзна́чный *adj.* three-digit.

трёхколёсный *adj.* three-wheeled; **т. велосипе́д** tricycle.

трёхле́тний *adj.*
1 (*срок*) three-year.
2 (*ребёнок*) three-year-old.

трёхме́рный *adj.* three-dimensional.

трёхме́стный *adj.* three-seater.

трёхсо́тый *adj.* three-hundredth.

трёхцве́тный *adj.* three-coloured (*Br.*), three-colored (*US*); tricolour(ed) (*Br.*), tricolor(ed) (*US*).

трёхчасово́й *adj.*
1 (*экзамен*) three-hour.
2 (*поезд*) three o'clock.

трёхэта́жный *adj.* three-storey (*Br.*), three-story (*US*).

трещ|а́ть, у́, и́шь *impf.*
1 (*о льде*) to crack; **у меня́ голова́ ~и́т** I have a splitting headache; **т. по всем швам** (*fig.*) to go to pieces.
2 (*о дровах*) to crackle; (*о мебели*) to creak; (*о кузнечиках*) to chirr.

тре́щин|а, ы *f.* crack, split (*also fig.*); **дать ~у** to crack, split; (*fig.*) to show signs of cracking.

три, трёх, трём, тремя́, о трёх *num.* three.

трибу́н|а, ы *f.*
1 platform, rostrum.
2 (*на стадионах*) stand.

трибуна́л, а *m.* tribunal.

тривиа́л|ьный (~ен, ~ьна) *adj.* trivial, banal; (*пошлый*) trite.

тригономе́три|я, и *f.* trigonometry.

тридца́т|ый *adj.* thirtieth; **~ые го́ды** the thirties.

три́дцат|ь, и́, *i.* **~ью́** *num.* thirty.

три́жды *adv.* three times, thrice.

трико́ *nt. indecl.* (*колготки*) tights; (*костюм*) leotard.

трикота́ж, а *m.*
1 (*из шерсти*) jersey; (*из хлопка*) cotton jersey.
2 (*collect.*) (*изделия*) knitwear.

трикота́жн|ый *adj.* (*шерстяной*) jersey; (*из хлопка*) knitted; **~ые изде́лия** knitwear.

три́ллер, а *m.* thriller.

триллио́н, а *m.* trillion.

трило́ги|я, и *f.* trilogy.

трина́дцатый *adj.* thirteenth.

трина́дцат|ь, и *num.* thirteen.

три́о *nt. indecl.* (*mus.*) trio.

три́ста, трёхсо́т, трёмста́м, тремяста́ми, трёхста́х *num.* three hundred.

триу́мф, а *m.* triumph; **с ~ом** triumphantly, in triumph.

триумфа́льн|ый *adj.* triumphal; **~ая а́рка** triumphal arch.

тро́гател|ьный (~ен, ~ьна) *adj.* touching; moving, affecting.

тро́га|ть, ю *impf.* (*of* ▸**тро́нуть**)
1 (*прикасаться*) to touch.
2 (*беспокоить*) to disturb, trouble; **не ~й его́!** don't disturb him!; leave him alone!
3 (*волновать*) to touch, move, affect; **т. до слёз** to move to tears.

тро́га|ться[1], юсь *impf.* (*of* ▸**тро́нуться[1]** 1) to be touched, be moved, be affected.

тро́га|ться[2], юсь *impf. of* ▸**тро́нуться[2]**

тро́е, трои́х *num.* (*preceding m. nn. denoting living beings and pluralia tantum*) three; **т. су́ток** seventy-two hours, three days and three nights; **т. друзе́й** three friends.

троебо́рь|е, я *nt.* (*sport*) triathlon.

троекра́тный *adj.* (*вызов*) thrice-repeated; (*чемпион*) three-times; (*штраф*) trebled.

тро́ечник, а *m.* mediocre student.

Тро́иц|а, ы *f.* (*theol.*) Trinity; (*праздник*) Whitsun.

Тро́ицын *adj.*: **Т. день** Whit Sunday.

тро́йк|а, и *f.*
1 (*цифра, игральная карта*) three.
2 (*отметка*) three (*out of five*).
3 (*coll.*) (*автобус, трамвай*) No. 3 (*bus, tram, etc.*).
4 (*группа из троих*) (group of) three; (*три человека*) threesome.
5 (*упряжка*) troika.
6 (*костюм*) three-piece suit.

тройни́к, а́ *m.* (*elec.*) three-way adaptor.

тройн|о́й *adj.* triple, threefold, treble; **т. кана́т** three-ply rope; **т. прыжо́к** triple jump; **в ~о́м разме́ре** threefold, treble.

тролле́йбус, а *m.* trolleybus.

тромб, а *m.* (*med.*) blood clot.

тромбо́з, а *m.* (*med.*) thrombosis.

тромбо́н, а *m.* trombone.

тромбони́ст, а *m.* trombonist.

трон, а *m.* throne.

тро́|нуть, ну, нешь *pf. of* ▶ **~гать**

тро́|нуться[1]**, нусь, нешься** *pf.*
1 *pf. of* ▶ **~гаться**[1].
2 (*pf. only*) (*fig., coll.*) to be touched (= *to lose one's mind*); **он немно́го ~нулся** he is a bit touched, he is a bit cracked.

тро́|нуться[2]**, нусь, нешься** *pf.* (*of* ▶ **~гаться**[2]) (*двинуться с места*) to start, set out; **т. с ме́ста** to make a move, get going; **по́езд ~нулся** the train started.

троп|а́, ы́, *pl.* **~́ы, ~, ~́ам** *f.* path.

тро́пик, а *m.* (*geog.*)
1 tropic; **т. Ра́ка** tropic of Cancer; **т. Козеро́га** tropic of Capricorn.
2 (*pl.*) the tropics.

тропи́нк|а, и *f.* path.

тропи́ческ|ий *adj.* tropical; **~ая лихора́дка** jungle fever.

трос, а *m.* rope, cable, hawser.

тростни́к, а́ *m.* reed; **са́харный т.** sugar cane.

трост|ь, и, *pl.* **~́и, ~е́й** *f.* cane, walking stick.

тротуа́р, а *m.* pavement.

трофе́|й, я *m.* trophy.

троюро́дн|ый *adj.*: **т. брат, ~ая сестра́** second cousin; **т. племя́нник** second cousin once removed (*son of second cousin*).

труб|а́, ы́, *pl.* **~́ы** *f.*
1 pipe; **водопрово́дная т.** water pipe; **водосто́чная т.** drainpipe; **канализацио́нная т.** sewage pipe; **подзо́рная т.** telescope.
2 (*дымовая, заводская*) chimney; (*парохода*) funnel, smokestack.
3 (*mus.*) trumpet; **игра́ть на ~е́** to play the trumpet.
4 (*anat.*) tube; duct.

трубаду́р, а *m.* troubadour.

труба́ч, а́ *m.* trumpeter, trumpet player.

труб|и́ть, лю́, и́шь *impf.*
1 (**в** + *a.*; *mus.*) to blow.
2 (*о трубах*) to sound; to blare.
3 (*давать сигнал*) to sound (*by blast of trumpet, etc.*); **т. сбор** (*mil.*) to sound assembly.
4 (**о** + *p.*; *coll.*) (*разглашать*) to trumpet, proclaim from the housetops.

тру́бк|а, и *f.*
1 tube; pipe; (*свёрток*) roll; **сверну́ть ~ой** to roll up.
2 (*курительная*) (tobacco) pipe; **наби́ть ~у** to fill a pipe.
3 (*телефона*) receiver; **взять, подня́ть ~у** to answer the phone.

трубопрово́д, а *m.* pipeline.

трубочи́ст, а *m.* chimney sweep.

труд, а́ *m.*
1 (*работа*) labour (*Br.*), labor (*US*), work.
2 (*трудность*) difficulty, trouble; **взять на себя́ т.** (+ *inf.*) to take the trouble (to); **с ~о́м** with difficulty; **без ~а́** without difficulty.
3 (*произведение*) (scholarly) work; (*pl.*) (*издание*) transactions.

тру|ди́ться, жу́сь, ~́дишься *impf.* (**над** + *i.*) to toil (over), labour (*Br.*), labor (*US*) (over), work (on).

тру́дно *as pred.* it is hard, it is difficult; **т. сказа́ть** it is hard to say; **мне т.** I find it difficult; **ему́ т. прихо́дится** he has a hard time.

труднодосту́п|ный (~ен, ~на) *adj.* difficult to gain access to.

тру́дност|ь, и *f.* difficulty; (*препятствие*) obstacle.

тру́д|ный (~ен, ~на́, ~но, ~́ны́) *adj.*
1 difficult, hard; (*изнурительный*) arduous; **в ~ную мину́ту** in a time of need.
2 (*человек*) difficult, awkward.
3 (*случай*) serious, grave.

трудов|о́й *adj.*
1 labour (*Br.*), labor (*US*), work; **~о́е законода́тельство** labour (*Br.*), labor (*US*) legislation; **~а́я кни́жка** work record book; **т. стаж** length of service.
2 (*полученный трудом*) earned; hard-earned.

трудого́лик, а *m.* (*coll.*) workaholic.

трудоём|кий (~ок, ~ка) *adj.* labour-intensive (*Br.*), labor-intensive (*US*).

трудолюби́в|ый (~, ~а) *adj.* hard-working, industrious.

трудоспосо́б|ный (~ен, ~на) *adj.* able-bodied; capable of working.

трудоустро́йств|о, а *nt.* placement in a job.

труд|я́щийся *pres. part. of* ▶ **~и́ться** *and adj.* working; *as pl. n.* **~я́щиеся, ~я́щихся** working people, the workers.

тру́женик, а *m.* (*много работающий*) toiler; (+ *g.*) worker, employee.

тру́жени|ца, цы *f. of* ▶ **~к**

труп, а *m.* dead body, corpse; (*животного*) carcass; **то́лько че́рез мой т.** over my dead body.

тру́пп|а, ы *f.* company.

трус, а *m.* coward.

тру́сик|и, ов *no sg.*
1 (*шорты*) shorts.
2 (*плавки*) swimming trunks.
3 (*бельё*) (under)pants; (*женские*) knickers (*Br.*), panties.

тру́|сить, шу, сишь *impf.* (*of* ▶ **с~**)
1 to be a coward; to get cold feet.
2 (**пе́ред** + *i.*) to be afraid (of), be frightened (of).

трусли́в|ый (~, ~а) *adj.* cowardly.
тру́сост|ь, и *f.* cowardice.
трусц|á, ы́ *f.* (*coll.*): **бег ~óй** (*sport*) jogging.
трус|ы́, óв *no sg.* = **~́ики**
трут, а *m.* tinder.
тру́т|ень, ня *m.* (*zool.*) drone; (*fig.*) parasite.
трух|á, и́ *f.* dust (*of rotted wood*); (*fig.*) (*о чём-н. никчёмном*) rubbish.
трущо́б|а, ы *f.* (*often pl.*) (*жильё, район*) slum.
трюк, а *m.*
1 (*акробатический*) feat; (*каскадёра*) stunt; **рекла́мный т.** advertising gimmick.
2 (*fig., pej.*) (*проделка*) trick.
трюм, а *m.* (*naut.*) hold.
трю́фел|ь, я *m.* (*гриб, конфета*) truffle.
тря́пк|а, и *f.*
1 rag; (*для пыли*) duster.
2 (*pl., coll.*) (*одежда*) finery, clothes.
3 (*coll., pej.*) (*человек*) drip.
тряси́н|а, ы *f.* quagmire.
тряс|ти́, у́, ёшь, *past* **~, ~ла́** *impf.*
1 to shake.
2 (*ковёр; крошки*) to shake out.
3 (*о дрожи*) to cause to shake, cause to shiver (*usu. impers.*); **её ~ло́ от стра́ха** she was trembling with fear.
4 (+ *i.*) (*головой, кулаком*) to shake; **т. гри́вой** to toss its mane.
5 (*о вагоне*) to jolt, be jolty; (*impers.*): **в авто́бусе ~ёт** the bus is jolting.
тряс|ти́сь, у́сь, ёшься, *past* **~́ся, ~ла́сь** *impf.*
1 to shake; to tremble, shiver; **т. от хо́лода** to shiver with cold.
2 (**за** + *a.*) (*опасаться*) to worry about.
3 (**пе́ред** + *i.*) (*бояться*) to tremble before, dread.
тряхн|у́ть, у́, ёшь *pf.* to shake; (*в машине*) to give a jolt.
туале́т, а *m.*
1 (*уборная*) lavatory, toilet.
2 (*наряд*) dress; attire.
туале́т|ный *adj. of* ▸ **~; ~ная бума́га** toilet paper; **~ная вода́** toilet water; **~ные принадле́жности** toiletries; **т. сто́лик** dressing table.
ту́б|а¹, ы *f.* (*mus.*) tuba.
ту́б|а², ы *f.* (*большой тюбик*) tube.
туберкулёз, а *m.* tuberculosis.
ту́го *adv.*
1 tight(ly), taut; **т. наби́ть чемода́н** to pack a suitcase tight.
2 (*с трудом*) with difficulty.
туг|о́й (~, ~á, ~́о, ~и́) *adj.*
1 (*узел, воротничок*) tight; (*струна, пружина*) taut.
2 (*плотно набитый*) tightly filled; **т. кошелёк** tightly stuffed purse.
туда́ *adv.* there; (*в ту сторону*) that way; (*куда нужно*) to the right place; **биле́т т. и обра́тно** return ticket; **не т.!** not that way!; **вы не т. попа́ли** (*по телефону*) you have got the wrong number.
ту́же *comp. of* ▸ **туго́й** *and* ▸ **ту́го**
тужу́рк|а, и *f.* double-breasted jacket (*man's*).
туз, á *m.* (*cards*) ace; **ходи́ть ~о́м** to play an ace.
тузе́м|ец, ца *m.* native.
тузе́м|ка, ки *f. of* ▸ **~ец**
тузе́мный *adj.* native, indigenous.
ту́ловищ|е, а *nt.* trunk; torso.
тулу́п, а *m.* sheepskin coat.
тума́к, á *m.* (*coll.*) cuff, punch.
тума́н, а *m.* fog; mist, haze; (*в голове*) fog, haze; **как в ~е** in a daze.
тума́нност|ь, и *f.*
1 (*astron.*) nebula.
2 (*изложения, мысли*) haziness, obscurity.
тума́н|ный (~ен, ~на) *adj.*
1 foggy; misty; hazy.
2 (*fig.*) (*тусклый*) dull, lacklustre (*Br.*), lackluster (*US*).
3 (*fig.*) (*неясный*) hazy, obscure, vague.
ту́мб|а, ы *f.*
1 (*столб*) bollard.
2 (*подставка*) pedestal.
3 (*афишная*) advertisement hoarding (*of cylindrical shape*).
ту́мблер, а *m.* toggle (switch).
ту́мбочк|а, и *f.* bedside table, night table (*US*).
ту́ндр|а, ы *f.* (*geog.*) tundra.
тун|е́ц, цá *m.* tuna (fish).
тунея́д|ец, ца *m.* parasite, sponger.
тунея́д|ка, ки *f. of* ▸ **~ец**
Туни́с, а *m.* (*страна*) Tunisia.
туни́с|ец, ца *m.* Tunisian.
туни́с|ка, ки *f. of* ▸ **~ец**
туни́сский *adj.* Tunisian.
тунне́л|ь, я *m.* = **тонне́ль**
тупи́к, á *m.*
1 blind alley, cul-de-sac.
2 (*rail.*) siding.
3 (*fig.*) (*безвыходное положение*) impasse, deadlock; **зайти́ в т.** to reach a deadlock.
4 : **поста́вить в т.** to stump, nonplus.
туп|и́ть, лю́, ~́ишь *impf.* to blunt.
тупи́ц|а, ы *c.g.* (*coll.*) dimwit.
туп|о́й (~, ~á, ~́о, ~́ы) *adj.*
1 (*нож*) blunt.
2 : **т. у́гол** (*math.*) obtuse angle.
3 (*fig.*) (*боль, чувство*) dull.
4 (*fig.*) (*взгляд, улыбка*) vacant, stupid.
5 (*fig.*) (*человек; ум*) dim; dull.
ту́пост|ь, и *f.*
1 (*ножа*) bluntness.
2 (*fig.*) (*взгляда*) vacancy.
3 (*fig.*) (*ума*) dullness, slowness.
тупоу́м|ный (~ен, ~на) *adj.* dull, obtuse.
тур, а *m.*
1 (*турнира, выборов*) round.
2 (*артиста*) tour.
тураге́нт, а *m.* travel agent.
тураге́нтств|о, а *nt.* travel agency.
турба́з|а, ы *f.* tourist centre (*Br.*), center (*US*).
турби́н|а, ы *f.* (*tech.*) turbine.
туре́цкий *adj.* Turkish.
тури́зм, а *m.* (*путешествия*) tourism; (*спорт*) hiking; **во́дный т.** boating.
тури́ст, а *m.* tourist; (*в походах*) hiker.
туристи́ческ|ий *adj.* tourist; **~ое аге́нтство** travel agency; **т. похо́д** hiking

tour.
тури́ст|ка, ки *f. of* ▶~
туркме́н, а, *g. pl.* **т.** *m.* Turkmen.
Туркмениста́н, а *m.* Turkmenistan.
туркме́н|ка, ки *f. of* ▶~
туркме́нский *adj.* Turkmen.
турне́ *nt. indecl.* tour (*esp. of artistes or sportsmen*).
турни́к, а́ *m.* (*sport*) horizontal bar.
турнике́т, а *m.* turnstile.
турни́р, а *m.* tournament.
ту́р|ок, ка, *g. pl.* **т.** *m.* Turk.
Ту́рци|я, и *f.* Turkey.
тур|ча́нка, ча́нки *f. of* ▶~́ок
ту́скл|ый (~, ~а́, ~о, ~́ы) adj.
1 (*свет*) dim, dull; (*стекло*) opaque; (*металл*) tarnished; (*краска, лак*) matt.
2 (*fig.*) (*взгляд, глаза; стиль*) dull, lacklustre (*Br.*), lackluster (*US*).
тускне́|ть, ет *impf.* (*of* ▶**по~**) (*о свете*) to grow dim; (*о красках, таланте*) to fade; (*о металле, зеркале*) to tarnish.
тус|ова́ться, у́юсь *impf.* (*coll.*) to get together, meet, hang out.
тусо́вк|а, и *f.* (*coll.*) get-together; (*место*) meeting place, hang-out.
тут *adv.*
1 here; **кто т.?** who's there?
2 (*о времени*) now; **т. же** there and then.
ту́ф|ля, ли, *g. pl.* **~ель** *f.* shoe.
ту́хл|ый (~, ~а́, ~о) *adj.* rotten, bad.
ту́х|нуть[1], нет, *past* **~, ~ла** *impf.* (*of* ▶**по~**) (*огонь*) to go out; (*взгляд, глаза*) to become dull.
ту́х|нуть[2], нет, *past* **~, ~ла** *impf.* (*загнивать*) to go bad, become rotten.
ту́ч|а, и *f.*
1 (rain) cloud; storm cloud (*also fig.*); **~и собрали́сь, нави́сли (над** + *i.*) (*fig.*) the clouds are gathering (over).
2 (*пыли*) cloud; (*мух*) swarm.
ту́ч|ный (~ен, ~на́, ~но) *adj.*
1 (*человек*) stout, obese, corpulent.
2 (*почва*) rich, fertile.
ту́ш|а, и *f.* carcass.
тушёнк|а, и *f.* (*coll.*) tinned meat (*Br.*), canned meat (*US*).
тушёный *adj.* (*cul.*) braised, stewed.
туш|и́ть[1], у́, ~́ишь *impf.* (*of* ▶**по~[1]**) (*огонь, пожар*) to extinguish, put out.
туш|и́ть[2], у́, ~́ишь *impf.* (*cul.*) to braise, stew.
тушка́нчик, а *m.* jerboa.
туш|ь, и *f.* Indian ink; **т. (для ресни́ц)** mascara.
тща́тел|ьный (~ен, ~ьна) *adj.* thorough, careful; painstaking.
тщеду́ш|ный (~ен, ~на) *adj.* feeble, frail, weak.
тщесла́ви|е, я *nt.* vanity, vainglory.
тщесла́в|ный (~ен, ~на) *adj.* vain, vainglorious.
тще́тно *adv.* vainly, in vain.
тще́т|ный (~ен, ~на) *adj.* vain, futile.
ты, тебя́, тебе́, тобо́й, о тебе́ *2nd pers. sg. pers. pron.* you; **быть на «ты» (с** + *i*), **говори́ть «ты»** (+ *d.*) to be on familiar terms (with); (*для обобщения*) one, you.
ты|кать, чу, чешь *impf.* (*of* ▶**ткнуть**) (+ *i.* **в** + *a. or* + *a.* **в** + *a.*) to stick (into) (*also fig.*); to poke (into); to prod; to jab (into); **т. па́лкой** to prod with a stick.
тыкв|а, ы *f.* pumpkin, gourd.
тыл, а, о ~́е, в ~у́, *pl.* **~ы́** *m.*
1 back, rear.
2 (*mil.*) rear; (*вся страна*) home front.
3 (*pl.; mil.*) (*вспомогательные части*) rear services.
ты́льн|ый *adj.* back, rear; **~ая пове́рхность руки́** back of the hand.
ты́сяч|а, и, *i.* **~ей** *and* **~ью** *num. and n., f.* thousand; **в ~у раз** a thousand times (*also fig.*); **~и люде́й** thousands of people.
тысячеле́ти|е, я *nt.*
1 (*срок*) a thousand years; millennium.
2 (*годовщина*) thousandth anniversary.
тысячеле́тний *adj.*
1 (*период, годовщина*) thousand-year; millennial.
2 (*здание*) thousand-year-old.
ты́сячн|ый *adj.*
1 thousandth; *as n.* **~ая, ~ой** *f.* thousandth.
2 (*толпа, стадо*) of many thousands.
тьм|а, ы *no pl., f.* (*мрак*) darkness.
тю́бик, а *m.* tube (*of toothpaste, etc.*).
тюк, а́ *m.* bale, package.
тюле́н|ь, я *m.* (*zool.*) seal.
тюл|ь, я *m.* (*text.*) tulle.
тюльпа́н, а *m.* tulip.
тюрба́н, а *m.* turban.
тюр|е́мный *adj. of* ▶**~ьма́; ~е́мное заключе́ние** imprisonment.
тюр|ьма́, ьмы́, *pl.* **~́ьмы, ~́ем** *f.* prison; jail; **заключи́ть, посади́ть в ~ьму́** to put into prison, jail; **сиде́ть в ~ьме́** to be in prison.
тюфя́к, а́ *m.* mattress (*filled with straw, hay, etc.*).
тя́вк|ать, аю *impf.* (*of* ▶**~нуть**) to yap, yelp.
тя́вк|нуть, ну, нешь *inst. pf. of* ▶**~ать**
тя́г|а, и *f.*
1 (*действие*) pulling; (*наземного транспорта*) traction; **на ко́нной ~е** horse-drawn.
2 (*от воздушного транспорта*) thrust; (*стержень рычага*) rod.
3 (*в печи*) draught (*Br.*), draft (*US*).
4 (**к** + *d.*; *fig.*) (*влечение*) pull (towards), attraction (towards); (*стремление*) thirst (for), craving (for); (*склонность*) inclination (to, for); **т. к зна́ниям** thirst for knowledge.
тяга́ч, а́ *m.* tractor (*for pulling train of trailers*).
тя́гост|ный (~ен, ~на) *adj.* painful, distressing; **~ное зре́лище** painful spectacle.
тяго|ти́ть, щу́, ти́шь *impf.* (*обременять*) to burden, be a burden (on, to); (*мысли, обязанности*) to lie heavy (on), oppress.
тяго|ти́ться, щу́сь, ти́шься *impf.* (+ *i.*) to be weighed down, oppressed (by).
тягча́йший *superl. of* ▶**тя́жкий**
тя́жб|а, ы *f.* (civil) suit, lawsuit; litigation.
тяжел|е́е *comp. of* ▶**~̈ый** *and* ▶**~о́**

тяжеле́|ть, ю *impf.*
1 (*становиться тяжелее*) to become heavier; (*толстеть*) to put on weight.
2 (*о глазах*) to become heavy with sleep.

тяжело́[1] *adv.*
1 heavily.
2 (*серьёзно*) seriously, gravely. **т. больно́й** seriously ill.
3 (*с трудом*) with difficulty.

тяжело́[2] *as pred.*
1 (*при поднятии*) it is heavy; (*трудно*) it is hard; **мне т. ходи́ть пешко́м** it's hard for me to walk; (*мучительно*) it is painful, it is distressing.
2 : **ему́,** *etc.*, **т.** (*о настроении*) he, *etc.*, feels miserable, wretched.

тяжелоатле́т, а *m.* (*штангист*) weightlifter.

тяжёл|ый (~, ~а́) *adj.*
1 heavy; **т. чемода́н** heavy suitcase; **~ая атле́тика** (*sport*) weightlifting; **~ое дыха́ние** heavy breathing; **~ая промы́шленность** heavy industry.
2 (*доставляющий беспокойство, неприятность*): **т. за́пах** oppressive, strong smell; **~ая пи́ща** heavy, indigestible food.
3 (*трудный*) hard, difficult; **~ая зада́ча** hard task.
4 (*суровый*) heavy, severe; **~ые поте́ри** heavy casualties; **т. уда́р** severe blow.
5 (*серьёзный*) serious, grave, bad; **~ое ране́ние** serious injury.
6 (*горестный*) hard, painful; **~ые времена́** hard times; **т. день** bad, hard day.
7 (*характер*) difficult.
8 (*стиль*) heavy, ponderous, unwieldy.

тя́жест|ь, и *f.*
1 (*phys.*) gravity; **центр ~и** centre of gravity (*also fig.*).
2 (*тяжёлый предмет*) weight, heavy object.
3 (*вес*) weight, heaviness.
4 (*трудность*) difficulty.

тя́ж|кий (~ек, ~ка́, ~ко) *adj.*
1 (*суровый*) severe; (*серьёзный*) serious, grave; **~кое преступле́ние** grave crime, felony.
2 (*судьба*) hard, difficult.

тян|у́ть, у́, ~́ешь *impf.*
1 (*невод*) to pull, draw; to haul; to drag; **т. на букси́ре** to tow; (*руку, шею*) to stretch out; **т. ру́ку к** (+ *d.*) to reach out for, towards.
2 (*tech.*) (*проволоку*) to draw.
3 (*прокладывать*) to lay; **т. телефо́нную ли́нию** to lay a telephone cable.
4 : **т. жре́бий** to draw lots.
5 (*fig.*) (*влечь*) to draw, attract; **меня́,** *etc.* **~́ет** I, *etc.* long/want; **его́ ~́ет домо́й** he wants to go home.
6 (*произносить*) to drawl, drag out; **т. но́ту** to sustain a note.
7 (*медлить*) to drag out, protract, delay; **т. с отве́том** to delay one's answer.
8 (*всасывать*) to draw up; to take in, suck in; **т. че́рез соло́минку** to suck through a straw.
9 (**из, с** + *g.*) to extract (from); to extort (from).
10 (*убеждать идти*) to drag; **никто́ тебя́ си́лой не ~у́л** nobody forced you to go.

тян|у́ться, у́сь, ~́ешься *impf.*
1 (*о резине*) to stretch.
2 (*о равнине*) to stretch, extend; **тайга́ ~́ется на со́тни киломе́тров** the taiga stretches for hundreds of kilometres (*Br.*), kilometers (*US*).
3 (*о времени*) to drag on; to hang heavy.
4 (**к** + *d.*) (*к матери*) to reach (for), reach out (for); (*к славе*) to strive (after).
5 (**за** + *i.*; *fig., coll.*) (*стремиться сравняться*) to try to keep up (with), try to equal.
6 (*двигаться один за другим*) to move one after the other.

тяну́чк|а, и *f.* (*coll.*) toffee, caramel.

тя́пк|а, и *f.* hoe.

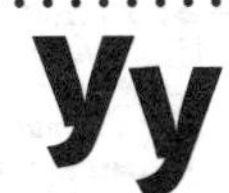

у *prep.* + *g.*
1 (*возле*) by; at; **у окна́** by the window; **у воро́т** at the gate; **у руля́** at the wheel; **у мо́ря** by the sea; **у вла́сти** in power.
2 (*обозначает место действия*) at; with (*oft.* = *French* '*chez*'); **у нас** (*в доме*) at our place, with us, (*в стране*) in our country; **у себя́** at one's (own) place, at home; **я был у парикма́хера** I was at the hairdresser's.
3 (*обозначает принадлежность*): **у меня́ боли́т зуб** my tooth aches; **у неё больна́ мать** her mother is ill.
4 (*указывает на источник*) from, of; **я за́нял де́сять рубле́й у сосе́да** I borrowed ten roubles from a neighbour (*Br.*), neighbor (*US*).
5 (*обозначает владельца*): **у меня́,** *etc.*, I, *etc.*, have; **у вас есть радиоприёмник?** do you have a radio?; **у меня́ к вам ма́ленькая про́сьба** I have a small favour (*Br.*), favor (*US*) to ask of you.

у... *vbl. pref. indicating*
1 *movement away from a place, as* **улете́ть** to fly away.
2 *insertion in sth., as* **умести́ть** to put in.
3 *covering of sth. all over, as* **усе́ять** to strew.
4 *reduction, curtailment, etc., as* **уба́вить** to reduce.
5 *achievement of aim sought, as* **уговори́ть** to persuade; *with adj. roots forms vv. expr. comp. degree, as* **уско́рить** to accelerate.

уба́в|ить, лю, ишь *pf.* (*of* ▸ **~ля́ть**)
1 (+ *a. or g.*) (*жалованье, цену*) to reduce, lower; **у. ход** to reduce speed.

[2]: **у. в вéсе** to lose weight.

убáв|иться, ится *pf.* (*of* **~ля́ться**) to diminish, decrease; **воды́ ~илось** the water (level) has fallen.

убавля́|ть(ся), ю, ет(ся) *impf. of* ▸ **убáвить(ся)**

убаю́к|ать, аю *pf.* (*of* ▸ **~ивать**) to lull (*also fig.*).

убаю́кива|ть, ю *impf. of* ▸ **убаю́кать**

убегá|ть, ю *impf. of* ▸ **убежáть**

убеди́тел|ьный (~ен, ~ьна) *adj.*
[1] (*доказательный*) convincing, persuasive; **быть ~ьным** to be convincing, carry conviction.
[2] (*настойчивый*) pressing; earnest; **~ьная про́сьба** pressing request, earnest entreaty.

убе|ди́ть, *1st pers. sg. not used,* **ди́шь** *pf.* (*of* ▸ **~ждáть**)
[1] (**в** + *p.*) to convince (of).
[2] (+ *inf.*) (*уговорить*) to persuade (to), prevail on (to).

убе|ди́ться, *1st pers. sg. not used,* **ди́шься** *pf.* (*of* ▸ **~ждáться**) (**в** + *p.*) to satisfy o.s. (of); to be convinced (of); **мы ~ди́лись в необходи́мости рефо́рм** we are convinced of the need for reform; **он ~ди́лся, что э́то тру́дно** he is convinced that it is difficult.

убе|жáть, гу́, жи́шь, гу́т *pf.* (*of* ▸ **~гáть**)
[1] (*удалиться бегом*) to run away, run off.
[2] (*спастись бегством*) to escape, flee.

убеждá|ть(ся), ю(сь) *impf. of* ▸ **убеди́ть(ся)**

убеждéни|е, я *nt.*
[1] (*действие*) persuasion.
[2] (*мнение*) conviction, belief.

убеждённо *adv.* with conviction.

убеждённост|ь, и *f.* conviction.

убеждён|ный *p.p.p. of* ▸ **убеди́ть** *and adj.*
[1] (*p.p.p.*) (**~, ~á**) (**в** + *p.*) convinced (of).
[2] (*adj.*) (**~, ~на**) (*тон*) assured.
[3] (*adj.*) (*no short form*) (*непоколебимый*) convinced; staunch; **у. сторо́нник** staunch supporter.

убе́жищ|е, а *nt.*
[1] (*защита*) refuge, asylum; **полити́ческое ~е** political asylum.
[2] (*укрытие*) shelter.

уберегá|ть(ся), ю(сь) *impf. of* ▸ **убере́чь(ся)**

убере́|чь, гу́, жёшь, гу́т, *past* **~г, ~глá** *pf.* (*of* ▸ **~гáть**) (**от** + *g.*) to protect (against), guard (against), keep safe (from), preserve (from).

убере́|чься, гу́сь, жёшься, гу́тся, *past* **~гся, ~глáсь** *pf.* (*of* ▸ **~гáться**) (**от** + *g.*) to protect o.s. (against), guard (*intrans.*) (against).

убивá|ть, ю *impf. of* ▸ **уби́ть**

убийствен|ный (~, ~на) *adj.* (*жара, голод*) unbearable, killing, murderous; (*известие, результат, взгляд, критика*) devastating.

уби́йств|о, а *nt.* killing; (*с заранее обдуманным злым умыслом*) murder; (*политическое*) assassination; **заказно́е у.** contract killing.

уби́йц|а, ы *c.g.* killer; murderer; assassin.

убирá|ть(ся), ю(сь) *impf. of* ▸ **убрáть(ся)**; **~йся!** clear off!, beat it!, hop it!

уби́т|ый (~, ~а) *p.p.p. of* ▸ **~ь** *and adj.*
[1] (*лишённый жизни*) **неприя́тель потеря́л две ты́сячи ~ыми** the enemy lost two thousand killed; *as n.* **у., ~ого** *m.* dead man; (*жертва преступления*) murdered man; (*при аварии*) fatality; **спать как у.** to sleep like a log.
[2] (*fig.*) (*подавленный*) crushed, broken.

уб|и́ть, ью́, ьёшь *pf.* (*of* ▸ **~ивáть**)
[1] to kill; (*предумышленно*) to murder; (*по политическим мотивам*) to assassinate.
[2] (*fig.*) (*уничтожить*) to kill, destroy; **её откáз ~и́л его́** her refusal destroyed him.
[3] (*coll.*) (*потратить*) to waste; **у. врéмя** to kill time.

убо́г|ий (~, ~а) *adj.* (*нищенский*) poverty-stricken (*also fig.*); (*жилище*) wretched; (*мысль, работа*) pathetic, dismal.

убо́р, а *m.*: **головно́й у./головны́е ~ы** headgear.

убо́рист|ый (~, ~а) *adj.* close, small (*of handwriting, etc.*).

убо́рк|а, и *f.*
[1] (*урожая*) harvesting; (*хлопка, ягод*) picking.
[2] (*помещения*) clearing up, tidying up.

убо́рн|ая, ой *f.* (*туалет*) lavatory; toilet.

убо́рщик, а *m.* cleaner.

убо́рщи|ца, цы *f. of* ▸ **~к**

убрá|ть, уберу́, уберёшь, *past* **~л, ~лá, ~ло** *pf.* (*of* ▸ **убирáть**)
[1] (*унести*) to remove, take away; **у. со столá** to clear the table.
[2] (*привести в порядок*) to clear up, tidy up; **у. посте́ль** to make the bed.
[3] (*спрятать куда-н.*) to put away; to store.
[4] (*урожай*) to harvest.
[5] (*fig., coll.*) (*выгнать*) to kick out; (*убить*) to kill, take out.

убрá|ться, уберу́сь, уберёшься, *past* **~лся, ~лáсь, ~ло́сь** *pf.* (*of* ▸ **убирáться**) (*coll.*)
[1] (*навести порядок*) to clear up, tidy up.
[2] (*уйти*) to clear off.

убывá|ть, ю *impf. of* ▸ **убы́ть**

убы́т|ок, ка *m.*
[1] loss; **терпе́ть, нести́ ~ки** to incur losses.
[2] *pl.* (*возмещение*) damages; **взыскáть ~ки** to claim damages.

убы́точ|ный (~ен, ~на) *adj.* unprofitable.

убы́ть, убу́ду, убу́дешь, *past* **у́был, убылá, у́было** *pf.* (*of* ▸ **убывáть**) to decrease; (*о воде*) to subside, go down; (*о луне*) to wane (*also fig.*).

уважá|емый *pres. part. pass. of* ▸ **~ть** *and adj.* respected; (*в письме*) dear.

уважá|ть, ю *impf.* to respect, esteem.

уважéни|е, я *nt.* (**к** + *d.*) respect, esteem (for); **внушáть у.** to command respect; **из ~я** (**к** + *d.*) out of respect (for); **с ~ем** (*в письме*) yours sincerely.

уважи́тел|ьный (~ен, ~ьна) *adj.*
[1] (*достаточный для оправдания*) valid; **~ьная причи́на** valid cause, good reason.
[2] (*почтительный*) respectful, deferential.

ýвал|ень, ьня *m.* (*coll.*) clumsy oaf, clodhopper.

увéдом|ить, лю, ишь *pf.* (*of* ▸ **~лять**) to inform, notify.

уведомлéни|е, я *nt.* notification; (*документ*) letter of advice.

уведомля́|ть, ю *impf. of* ▸ **увéдомить**

увез|ти́, ý, ёшь, *past* **~̀, ~лá** *pf.* (*of* ▸ **увози́ть**) to take (away); (*с собой*) to take with one.

увековéчива|ть, ю *impf. of* ▸ **увековéчить**

увековéч|ить, у, ишь *pf.* (*of* ▸ **~ивать**)
1 (*героев*) to immortalize.
2 (*порядок, систему*) to perpetuate.

увеличéни|е, я *nt.*
1 (*зарплаты*) increase; (*температуры*) rise.
2 (*изображения*) magnification; (*phot.*) (*снимка*) enlargement.

увели́чива|ть(ся), ю, ет(ся) *impf. of* ▸ **увели́чить(ся)**

увеличи́тельн|ый *adj.* magnifying; **~ое стеклó** magnifying glass.

увели́ч|ить, у, ишь *pf.* (*of* ▸ **~ивать**)
1 (*в количестве, в объёме*) to increase.
2 (*изображение*) to magnify; (*phot.*) to enlarge.

увели́ч|иться, ится *pf.* (*of* ▸ **~иваться**) to increase, grow, rise.

увенч|áть, áю *pf.* (*of* ▸ **венчáть 1, 2** *and* ▸ **~̀ивать**) to crown.

увенч|áться, áется *pf.* (*of* ▸ **~̀иваться**) (+ *i.*; *fig.*) to be crowned (with); **у. успéхом** to be crowned with success.

увéнчива|ть(ся), ю, ет(ся) *impf. of* ▸ **увенчáть(ся)**

увéренно *adv.* confidently, with confidence.

увéренност|ь, и *f.*
1 (*шага, голоса*) confidence; **у. в себé** self-confidence.
2 (*убеждённость*) (**в** + *p.*) confidence (in), certainty (of); **мóжно с ~ью сказáть** one can say with confidence, it is safe to say.

увéрен|ный (~, ~на) *adj.*
1 (*твёрдый*) confident, sure; **~ная рукá** sure hand.
2 *as pred.* **(~, ~а)** (*убеждённый*) (**в** + *p.*) confident (in), sure (of), certain (of); **быть ~ным** to be sure, be certain; **он ~ в себé** he is self-confident; **я ~а в нём** I have confidence in him.

увéр|ить, ю, ишь *pf.* (*of* ▸ **~ять**) to assure; (*убедить*) to convince, persuade.

увéр|иться, юсь, ишься *pf.* (*of* ▸ **~яться**) to assure o.s., satisfy o.s.

увер|нýться, нýсь, нёшься *pf.* (*of* ▸ **увoрáчиваться**) (**от** + *g.*) to dodge; (*also fig.*); **у. от прямóго отвéта** to avoid giving a direct answer.

увéр|овать, ую *pf.* (**в** + *a.*) to come to believe (in).

увер|я́ть(ся), я́ю(сь) *impf. of* ▸ **~̀ить(ся)**

увесели́тельн|ый *adj.* pleasure, entertainment; **~ая поéздка** pleasure trip, jaunt.

увéсист|ый (~, ~а) *adj.* (*том*) weighty; **у. удáр** (*coll.*) heavy blow.

уве|сти́, дý, дёшь, *past* **~̀л, ~лá** *pf.* (*of* ▸ **уводи́ть**) to take (away); (*с собой*) to take with one.

увéч|ить, у, ишь *impf.* to maim, mutilate.

увéчь|е, я *nt.* (*повреждение*) (serious) injury; **нанести́ у. комý-н.** to maim, injure s.o.

увéш|ать, аю *pf.* (*of* ▸ **~ивать**) to cover (*with objects suspended*); **у. стéну карти́нами** to cover a wall with pictures.

увéшива|ть, ю *impf. of* ▸ **увéшать**

уви́|деть, жу, дишь *pf.*
1 *pf. of* ▸ **ви́деть; ~дим** we'll see.
2 to catch sight of.

уви́лива|ть, ю *impf.* (**от** + *g.*)
1 *impf. of* ▸ **увильнýть.**
2 (*impf. only*) to try to get out (of).

увильн|ýть, ý, ёшь *pf.* (*of* ▸ **уви́ливать 1**) (**от** + *g.*; *coll.*)
1 to dodge.
2 (*fig.*) (*от ответственности, от налогов*) to evade; to get out (of); **у. от отвéта** to get out of replying.

увлажн|и́ть, ю́, и́шь *pf.* (*of* ▸ **~ять**) to moisten, damp, wet.

увлажн|и́ться, и́тся *pf.* (*of* ▸ **~яться**) to become moist, damp, wet.

увлажн|я́ть(ся), я́ю, я́ет(ся) *impf. of* ▸ **~и́ть(ся)**

увлекáтел|ьный (~ен, ~ьна) *adj.* fascinating; absorbing.

увлекá|ть(ся), ю(сь) *impf. of* ▸ **увлéчь(ся)**

увлечéни|е, я *nt.*
1 (*воодушевление*) animation.
2 (+ *i.*) (*большой интерес*) passion (for); enthusiasm (for); (*влюблённость*) crush (on).
3 (*предмет любви*) (object of) passion.

увлé|чь, кý, чёшь, кýт, *past* **~̀к, ~клá** *pf.* (*of* ▸ **~кáть**)
1 (*увести*) to carry along.
2 (*fig.*) (*о работе*) to carry away, distract.
3 (*восхитить*) to captivate, fascinate.

увлé|чься, кýсь, чёшься, кýтся, *past* **~̀кся, ~клáсь** *pf.* (*of* ▸ **~кáться**) (+ *i.*)
1 (*забыться*) to be carried away (by); (*заинтересоваться*) to become keen (on); **орáтор ~̀кся** the speaker got carried away.
2 (*влюбиться*) fall (for).

уво|ди́ть, жý, ~̀дишь *impf. of* ▸ **увести́**

уво|зи́ть, жý, ~̀зишь *pf. of* ▸ **увезти́**

увóл|ить, ю, ишь *pf.* (*of* ▸ **~ьня́ть**) (*с работы*) to dismiss; to sack; (*mil.*) to discharge.

увóл|иться, юсь, ишься *pf.* (*of* ▸ **~ьня́ться**) (*уйти*) to resign; (*mil.*) to get one's discharge; **у. в отстáвку** to retire.

увольнéни|е, я *nt.* dismissal; (*mil.*) discharge; (*на пенсию*) retiring, pensioning off.

увольня́|ть(ся), ю(сь) *impf. of* ▸ **увóлить(ся)**

уворáчива|ться, юсь *pf. of* ▸ **увернýться**

увы́ *int.* alas!

увядá|ть, ю *impf. of* ▸ **увя́нуть**

увя|зáть[1], жý, ~̀жешь *pf.* (*of* ▸ **~̀зывать**) to coordinate.

увяз|áть[2], áю *impf. of* ▸ **~̀нуть**

увя|зáться, жýсь, ~̀жешься *pf.* (*of* ▸ **~̀зываться**) (*coll.*) (**за** + *i.*) to tag along (behind), follow closely.

увя́з|нуть, ну, нешь, *past* **~, ~ла** *pf.* (*of* ▸ **~а́ть**[2]) (**в** + *p.*) to get stuck (in); to get bogged down (in) (*also fig.*).

увя́зыва|ть, ю *impf. of* ▸ **увяза́ть**[1]

увя́зыва|ться, юсь *impf. of* ▸ **увяза́ться**

увя́|нуть, ну, нешь *pf.* (*of* ▸ **~да́ть**) to fade, wither (*also fig.*).

угад|а́ть, а́ю *pf.* (*of* ▸ **~́ывать**) to guess (right), divine; (*желания*) to anticipate.

уга́дыва|ть, ю *impf. of* ▸ **угада́ть**

Уга́нд|а, ы *f.* Uganda.

угандı́|ец, йца *m.* Ugandan.

угандı́|йка, йки *f. of* ▸ **~ец**

уганди́йский *adj.* Ugandan.

уга́рный *adj.*: **у. газ** carbon monoxide.

угас|а́ть, а́ет *impf.*
1 *impf. of* ▸ **~́нуть.**
2 (*impf. only*) (*огонь*) to die down; **си́лы у него́ ~а́ли** his strength was fading, ebbing.

уга́с|нуть, нет, *past* **~, ~ла** *pf.* (*of* ▸ **~а́ть 1**) (*пламя, свеча*) to go out; (*звук*) to die away; (*чувство*) to be extinguished; (*человек*) to die.

углево́д, а *m.* carbohydrate.

углеки́слый *adj.*: **у. газ** carbon dioxide.

углеро́д, а *m.* carbon.

углова́т|ый (~, ~а) *adj.* (*coll.*) awkward.

углов|о́й *adj.*
1 angle; angular.
2 (*на углу*) corner; **у. дом** corner house; **у. уда́р** (*sport*) corner; *as n.* **у., ~о́го** *m.* (*sport*) corner.

углуб|и́ть, лю́, и́шь *pf.* (*of* ▸ **~ля́ть**)
1 (*яму*) to deepen, make deeper.
2 (*поместить глубоко, глубже*) to drive in deep, sink deeper.
3 (*fig.*) to deepen, extend.

углуб|и́ться, лю́сь, и́шься *pf.* (*of* ▸ **~ля́ться**)
1 (*яма*) to deepen, become deeper.
2 (*fig.*) (*о знаниях*) to deepen, become deeper; (*о противоречиях*) to become intensified.
3 (**в** + *a.*) (*в лес*) to go deep (into); (*в воспоминания*) to become absorbed in, lose o.s. in.
4 (**в** + *a.*; *fig.*) (*в чтение*) to become absorbed (in).

углубле́ни|е, я *nt.*
1 deepening.
2 (*fig.*) deepening, extending; intensification.
3 (*geog.*) hollow, depression, dip.

углубл|ённый (~ён, ~ена́) *adj.* intensive; (*интерес*) profound.

углубля́|ть(ся), ю(сь) *impf. of* ▸ **углуби́ть(ся)**

угна́|ть, угоню́, уго́нишь, *past* **~л, ~ла́, ~ло** *pf.* (*of* ▸ **угоня́ть**) (*украсть*) to steal; (*самолёт*) to hijack.

угнета́|ть, ю *impf.*
1 (*жестоко притеснять*) to oppress.
2 (*удручать*) to depress, dispirit.

угнете́ни|е, я *nt.* oppression.

угнетённ|ый *adj.*
1 (*притесняемый*) oppressed.
2 (*удручённый*) depressed; **быть в ~ом состоя́нии** to be depressed, be in low spirits.

угова́рива|ть, ю *impf.*
1 *impf. of* ▸ **уговори́ть.**
2 (*impf. only*) to try to persuade, urge.

угова́рива|ться, юсь *impf. of* ▸ **уговори́ться**

уговор|и́ть, ю́, и́шь *pf.* (*of* ▸ **угова́ривать 1**) (+ *inf.*) to persuade (to); to talk (into).

уговор|и́ться, ю́сь, и́шься *pf.* (*of* ▸ **угова́риваться**) (*coll.*) (+ *inf.*) to arrange (to), agree (to).

уго|ди́ть[1]**, жу́, ди́шь** *pf.* (*of* ▸ **~жда́ть**) (+ *d.*) (*удовлетворить*) to please, oblige.

уго|ди́ть[2]**, жу́, ди́шь** *pf.* (*coll.*) (**в** + *a.*) (*попасть*) to fall (into), get (into); (*при падении*) to bang (against); **у. в западню́** to fall into a trap; **у. в тюрьму́** to land up in prison.

уго́длив|ый (~, ~а) *adj.* obsequious.

уго́дно
1 *as pred.* (+ *d.*): **там есть всё что у.** there is everything there one could wish for; **как вам у.** as you like; please yourself.
2 *particle forming indef. prons. and advs.*: **кто у.** anyone (you like), whoever you like; **что у.** anything (you like); whatever you like; **ско́лько у.** as much as you like; any amount; **когда́ у.** any time.

угожда́|ть, ю *impf. of* ▸ **угоди́ть**[1]

у́г|ол, ла́, об ~ле́, в ~лу́ *m.*
1 (**в ~ле́**) (*math., phys.*) angle; **под ~ло́м** (**в** + *a.*) at an angle (of); **под прямы́м ~ло́м** at right angles; **у. зре́ния** (*fig.*) point of view.
2 (*улицы, стола, комнаты*) corner; **в ~лу́** in the corner; **на ~лу́** at the corner; **за ~ло́м** round the corner; **из-за ~ла́** (from) round the corner; (*fig.*) on the sly, behind s.o.'s back; **сре́зать у.** to cut off a corner.

уголо́вник, а *m.* (*coll.*) criminal.

уголо́вн|ый *adj.* criminal; **~ое де́ло** criminal case; **у. ко́декс** criminal code; **~ое пра́во** criminal law; **~ое преступле́ние** crime, felony.

у́голь, угля́ *m.*
1 (*pl.* **у́гли, у́глей**) coal; **ка́менный у.** coal; **древе́сный у.** charcoal.
2 (*pl.* **у́гли, у́гле́й**) (*кусок обгоревшего дерева*) a (piece of) coal.
3 (*pl.* **у́гли, угле́й**) (*art*) charcoal.

угомон|и́ть, ю́, и́шь *pf.* (*coll.*) to calm.

угомон|и́ться, ю́сь, и́шься *pf.* (*coll.*) to calm down.

уго́н, а *m.* (*велосипеда*) stealing; (*самолёта*) hijacking; **у. маши́ны** car theft.

уго́нщик, а *m.* thief; (*самолёта*) hijacker; **у. маши́ны** car thief.

угоня́|ть, ю *impf. of* ▸ **угна́ть**

у́г|орь[1]**, ря́** *m.* (*рыба*) eel.

у́г|орь[2]**, ря́** *m.* (*oft. pl.*) (*на коже*) blackhead.

уго|сти́ть, щу́, сти́шь *pf.* (*of* ▸ **~ща́ть**) (+ *i.*) to entertain (to), treat (to); **у. кого́-н. обе́дом** to treat s.o. to dinner.

угоща́|ть, ю *impf. of* ▸ **угости́ть**

угоще́ни|е, я *nt.*
1 (+ *i.*) entertaining (to, with), treating (to).
2 (*то, чем угощают*) refreshments; fare.

угро́б|ить, лю, ишь *pf.* (*coll.*)
1 (*убить*) to do in.

2 (*fig.*) (*загубить*) to ruin, wreck; **у. чью-н. репутáцию** to ruin s.o.'s reputation.

угрожá|ть, ю *impf.* (*кому чем*) to threaten (with); **он ~л емý тюрьмóй** he threatened him with prison; **емý ~ет разорéние** he is in danger of bankruptcy; **емý ~ет опáсность** he is in danger.

угрожá|ющий *pres. part. act. of* ▸ **~ть** *and adj.* threatening, menacing; **~ющее положéние** perilous situation.

угрó́з|а, ы *f.* threat.

угрызéни|е, я *nt.*: **~я сóвести** pangs of conscience.

угрю́м|ый (~, ~а) *adj.* gloomy.

уда|вáться, ётся *impf. of* ▸ **~́ться**

удал|ённый

1 *p.p.p. of* ▸ **~и́ть**

2 *adj.* (*район, доступ к компьютеру*) remote.

удал|и́ть, ю́, и́шь *pf.* (*of* ▸ **~я́ть**)

1 (*отдалить*) to take away, move away.

2 (*убрать, устранить*) to remove; **у. зуб** to extract a tooth.

3 (*заставить уйти*) to remove, send away; (*от дел, обязанностей*) to remove; **у. с пóля** (*sport*) to send off (the field).

удал|и́ться, ю́сь, и́шься *pf.* (*of* ▸ **~я́ться**)

1 (*отдалиться*) to move off, move away.

2 (*уйти*) to leave, withdraw, retire; **у. на покóй** to retire to a quiet life.

удал|óй (удáл, ~á, удáло, удáлы́) *adj.* daring, bold.

удал|я́ть(ся), я́ю(сь) *impf. of* ▸ **~и́ть(ся)**

удáр, а *m.*

1 (*рукой, палкой, топором*) blow; (*ногой*) kick; (*ножом*) stab; **одни́м ~ом** at one stroke; **нанести́ у. комý-н.** to strike s.o. a blow; **у. в спи́ну** (*fig.*) stab in the back; **у. грóма** thunderclap; (*неприятность*) blow; **у. судьбы́** a stroke of bad luck.

2 (*колокола*) stroke.

3 (*mil.*) blow; attack; thrust; **под ~ом** exposed (to attack).

4 (*med.*) (*кровоизлияние в мозг*) stroke; (*сердца, пульса*) beat; **сóлнечный у.** sunstroke.

ударéни|е, я *nt.*

1 (*ling.*) stress, accent; (*fig.*) stress, emphasis.

2 (*знак*) stress (mark).

удáр|ить, ю, ишь *pf.* (*of* ▸ **~я́ть**)

1 (+ *a.* **по** + *d. or* **в** + *a.*) (*нанести удар*) to strike; to hit; **у. когó-н. по лицý** to slap s.o.'s face; **у. кулакóм пó столу** to bang on the table with one's fist.

2 (**в** + *a.*) (*дать сигнал*) to strike; to sound; to beat; **у. в барабáн** to beat a drum.

3 (*раздаться*) to sound; **~ил гром** there was a clap of thunder; (*фонтан, пар*) to gush; (*подействовать резко*): **я́ркий свет ~ил в глазá** a bright light struck his eyes.

4 (**по** + *d.*) (*mil.*) to attack.

5 (**по** + *d.*) to strike (at); to combat; **у. по кармáну** (*coll.*) to hit one's pocket, set one back.

удáр|иться, юсь, ишься *pf.* (*of* ▸ **~я́ться**)

1 (**о** + *a. or* **в** + *a.*) to strike (against), hit.

2 (**в** + *a. or* + *inf.*) to break (into).

удáрник, а *m.* (*mus.*) percussionist.

удáрн|ый *adj.*

1 (*tech. and mil.*) percussive; percussion; **~ая си́ла** striking power, force of impact.

2 (*mus.*) percussion.

3 (*mil.*) striking, shock; **~ые чáсти** shock troops.

4 (*гласный*) stressed.

удар|я́ть(ся), я́ю(сь) *impf. of* ▸ **~́ить(ся)**

удá|ться, стся, дýтся, *past* **~лся, ~лáсь** *pf.* (*of* ▸ **~вáться**)

1 (*получиться*) to be successful, work (well), succeed; **оперáция ~лáсь** the operation was a success; **емý всё ~ётся** he succeeds in everything he does.

2 (*impers.* + *d. and inf.*) to succeed, manage; **мне не ~лóсь написáть статью́ вóвремя** I did not manage to write the article on time.

удáч|а, и *f.* success; (*везение*) good luck, good fortune.

удáчлив|ый (~, ~а) *adj.* successful, lucky.

удáч|ный (~ен, ~на) *adj.*

1 (*успешный*) successful.

2 (*хороший*) good.

удвáива|ть, ю *impf. of* ▸ **удвóить**

удвó|ить, ю, ишь *pf.* (*of* ▸ **удвáивать**) (*увеличить вдвое*) to double; (*усилия*) to redouble.

удéл, а *m.* lot, destiny.

удел|и́ть, ю́, и́шь *pf.* (*of* ▸ **~я́ть**) to give, spare, devote; **у. врéмя чемý-н.** to spare the time for sth.

удел|я́ть, я́ю *impf. of* ▸ **~и́ть**

удерж|áть, ý, ~́ишь *pf.* (*of* ▸ **~́ивать**)

1 (*не выпустить*) to hold, hold on to, not let go.

2 (*сохранить*) to keep, retain; **у. в пáмяти** to retain in one's memory.

3 (*не отпустить; не дать сделать*) to hold back, restrain.

4 (*вычесть*) to deduct, keep back.

удерж|áться, ýсь, ~́ишься *pf.* (*of* ▸ **~́иваться**)

1 (*не отступить*) to hold one's ground, hold out; to stand firm; **у. на ногáх** to remain on one's feet.

2 (**от** + *g.*) to keep o.s. (from), refrain (from); **у. от соблáзна** to resist a temptation; **мы не могли́ у. от смéха** we couldn't help laughing.

удéржива|ть(ся), ю(сь) *impf. of* ▸ **удержáть(ся)**

удешев|и́ть, лю́, и́шь *pf.* (*of* ▸ **~ля́ть**) to reduce the price (of).

удешев|и́ться, и́тся *pf.* (*of* ▸ **~ля́ться**) to become cheaper.

удешевля́|ть(ся), ю, ет(ся) *impf. of* ▸ **удешеви́ть(ся)**

удиви́тельно *adv.*

1 amazingly, surprisingly.

2 (*чудесно*) wonderfully, marvellously (*Br.*), marvelously (*US*).

3 (*очень*) very, extremely.

4 (*as pred.*) it is amazing, it is surprising; (*странно*) it is funny.

удиви́тел|ьный (~ен, ~ьна) *adj.*
1 amazing, surprising.
2 (*чудесный*) wonderful, marvellous (*Br.*), marvelous (*US*).
удив|и́ть, лю́, и́шь *pf.* (*of* ▸ **~ля́ть**) to amaze, surprise.
удив|и́ться, лю́сь, и́шься *pf.* (*of* ▸ **~ля́ться**) (+ *d.*) to be amazed (at), be surprised (at); to marvel (at).
удивле́ни|е, я *nt.* surprise, amazement; **к моему́ вели́кому ~ю** to my great surprise.
удивля́|ть(ся), ю(сь) *impf. of* ▸ **удиви́ть(ся)**
удира́|ть, ю *impf. of* ▸ **удра́ть**
уди́ть, ужу́, у́дишь *impf.*: **у. (ры́бу)** to fish, angle.
удлини́тел|ь, я *m.* extension lead.
удлин|и́ть, ю́, и́шь *pf.* (*of* ▸ **~я́ть**) to lengthen; (*срок*) to extend, prolong.
удлин|и́ться, и́тся *pf.* (*of* ▸ **~я́ться**) (*о тенях*) to become longer; (*о сроке*) to be extended, be prolonged.
удлин|я́ть(ся), я́ю, я́ет(ся) *impf. of* ▸ **~и́ть(ся)**
удму́рт, а *m.* Udmurt.
удму́рт|ка, ки *f. of* ▸ **~**
удму́ртский *adj.* Udmurt.
удо́бно[1] *adv.*
1 (*сидеть*) comfortably.
2 (*расположить*) conveniently.
удо́бно[2] *as pred.* (+ *d.*)
1 (*хорошо*) to feel, be comfortable; to be at one's ease; **нам здесь вполне́ у.** we are very comfortable here.
2 (*подходит*) it is convenient (for), it suits; **у. ли вам прие́хать сра́зу?** is it convenient for you to come at once?
удо́б|ный (~ен, ~на) *adj.*
1 (*кресло, туфли*) comfortable; (*уютный*) cosy (*Br.*), cozy (*US*).
2 (*подходящий*) convenient, suitable; **в ~ное для вас вре́мя** at your convenience; **по́льзоваться ~ным слу́чаем** (+ *inf.*) to take an opportunity (to do sth.).
удобре́ни|е, я *nt.* (*agric.*) fertilizer; (*навоз*) manure.
удо́бр|ить, ю, ишь *pf.* (*of* ▸ **~я́ть**) to fertilize.
удобр|я́ть, я́ю *impf. of* ▸ **~ить**
удо́бств|о, а *nt.* (*употребления*) convenience; **кварти́ра со все́ми ~ами** flat with all (modern) conveniences.
удовлетворе́ни|е, я *nt.* satisfaction, gratification.
удовлетвори́тельно
1 *adv.* satisfactorily.
2 *n.*; *nt. indecl.* (*отметка*) 'satisfactory', 'fair' (*as school or university mark*).
удовлетвори́тел|ьный (~ен, ~ьна) *adj.* satisfactory.
удовлетвор|и́ть, ю́, и́шь *pf.* (*of* ▸ **~я́ть**)
1 to satisfy; to comply (with); **у. запро́сы** to satisfy requirements; **у. про́сьбу** to comply with a request.
2 (+ *d.*) to answer, meet; **у. тре́бованиям** to answer requirements.
удовлетвор|и́ться, ю́сь, и́шься *pf.* (*of* ▸ **~я́ться**) (+ *i.*) to content o.s. (with), be satisfied (with).
удовлетвор|я́ть(ся), я́ю(сь) *impf. of* ▸ **~и́ть(ся)**
удово́льстви|е, я *nt.*
1 (*sg. only*) pleasure; **доста́вить у.** (+ *d.*) to give pleasure; **с ~ем!** with pleasure!
2 (*забава*) amusement; **жить в своё у.** to live a life of leisure.
удорож|а́ть, а́ю *impf. of* ▸ **~и́ть**
удорож|и́ть, у́, и́шь *pf.* (*of* ▸ **~а́ть**) to raise the price (of).
удоста́ива|ть(ся), ю(сь) *impf. of* ▸ **удосто́ить(ся)**
удостовере́ни|е, я *nt.* (*документ*) certificate; **у. ли́чности** identity card, ID.
удостове́р|ить, ю, ишь *pf.* (*of* ▸ **~я́ть**) to certify, attest, witness; **у. по́дпись** to witness a signature.
удостове́р|иться, юсь, ишься *pf.* (*of* ▸ **~я́ться**) (**в** + *p.*) to make sure (of); to assure o.s. (of).
удостовер|я́ть(ся), я́ю(сь) *impf. of* ▸ **~́ить(ся)**
удосто́|ить, ю, ишь *pf.* (*of* ▸ **удоста́ивать**)
1 (+ *a. and g.*) (*звания, степени*) to award (to), confer (on); **у. кого́-н. Но́белевской пре́мии** to award s.o. a Nobel prize.
2 (+ *i.*; *usu. iron.*) (*вниманием*) to favour (*Br.*), favor (*US*) (with); to deign to give; **он не ~ил нас отве́том** he did not deign to give us an answer.
удосто́|иться, юсь, ишься *pf.* (*of* ▸ **удоста́иваться**) (+ *g.*)
1 (*награды*) to receive, be awarded.
2 (*usu. iron.*) (*улыбки*) to be favoured (*Br.*), favored (*US*) (with).
удосу́жива|ться, юсь *impf. of* ▸ **удосу́житься**
удосу́ж|иться, усь, ишься *pf.* (*of* ▸ **~иваться**) (+ *inf.*; *coll.*) to find time (to); to manage.
удочере́ни|е, я *nt.* adoption (*of daughter*).
удочер|и́ть, ю́, и́шь *pf.* (*of* ▸ **~я́ть**) to adopt (*as a daughter*).
удочер|я́ть, я́ю *impf. of* ▸ **~и́ть**
у́дочк|а, и *f.* (fishing) rod (*also in fig., coll. phrr.*); **заки́нуть ~у** to cast a line; to put a line out (= *to try to discover sth.*); **попа́сться на ~у** to swallow the bait.
удра́|ть, удеру́, удерёшь, *past* **~л, ~ла́, ~ло** *pf.* (*of* ▸ **удира́ть**) (*coll.*) to make off; to do a bunk (*Br.*).
удруж|и́ть, у́, и́шь *pf.* (+ *d.*; *coll.*) to do a good turn (*also iron.* = *to do a bad turn*).
удруч|а́ть, а́ю *impf. of* ▸ **~и́ть**
удруч|и́ть, у́, и́шь *pf.* (*of* ▸ **~а́ть**) to depress, dispirit.
уду́шлив|ый (~, ~а) *adj.* suffocating; **~ая жара́** stifling heat.
уду́ш|е, я *nt.* breathlessness; suffocation.
уедине́ни|е, я *nt.* solitude; seclusion.
уединён|ный (~, ~на) *adj.* solitary, secluded.
уедин|и́ться, ю́сь, и́шься *pf.* (*of* ▸ **~я́ться**) (**от** + *g.*) to retire (from), withdraw (from); to go off (by o.s.); **у. в свое́й ко́мнате** to retire to one's room.

уедин|я́ться, я́юсь *impf. of* ▸ **~и́ться**
уезжа́|ть, ю *impf. of* ▸ **уе́хать**
УЕФА́ *m. & f. indecl.* UEFA (*Union of European Football Associations*).
уе́хать, уе́ду, уе́дешь, *imper.* **уезжа́й(те)** *pf.* (*of* ▸ **уезжа́ть**) to go away, leave, depart.
уж[1], а́ *m.* grass snake.
уж[2]
1 *adv.* = **уже́.**
2 *emph. particle* (*coll.*) (*безусловно*) to be sure, indeed, certainly; **уж он узна́ет** he is sure to find out; (*очень*) very; **э́то не так уж сло́жно** it's not so very complicated.
ужа́л|ить, ю, ишь *pf. of* ▸ **жа́лить**
у́жас, а *m.*
1 (*чувство страха*) horror, terror; **прийти́ в у.** to be horrified; **привести́ в у.** to horrify.
2 (*usu. pl.*) (*предмет страха*) horror; **~ы го́лода** the horrors of famine; **фильм ~ов** horror film/movie.
3 *as pred.* (*coll.*) it is awful, it is terrible; **ти́хий у.** horror of horrors; **како́й у.!** how awful!
ужас|а́ть(ся), а́ю(сь) *impf. of* ▸ **~ну́ть(ся)**
ужаса́ющий *adj.* awful, terrible.
ужа́сно[1] *adv.*
1 horribly, terribly; **у. себя́ чу́вствовать** to feel awful.
2 (*coll.*) (*чрезвычайно*) awfully, terribly; **он у. пло́хо игра́ет** he plays terribly badly.
ужа́сно[2] *as pred.* (*coll.*) it is awful, it is terrible.
ужас|ну́ть, ну́, нёшь *pf.* (*of* ▸ **~а́ть**) to horrify, terrify.
ужас|ну́ться, ну́сь, нёшься *pf.* (*of* ▸ **~а́ться**) to be horrified, be terrified.
ужа́с|ный (~ен, ~на) *adj.* awful, terrible.
у́же *comp. of* ▸ **у́зкий, у́зко**
уже́
1 *adv.* already; now; by now; **у. не** no longer; **они́ у. прие́хали** they are here already; **она́ у. не ребёнок** she is no longer a child.
2 *emph. particle* = **уж**
ужесточа́|ть, ю *impf. of* ▸ **ужесточи́ть**
ужесточ|и́ть, у́, и́шь *pf.* (*of* ▸ **~а́ть**) to make more severe.
ужива́|ться, юсь *impf. of* ▸ **ужи́ться**
у́жин, а *m.* supper.
у́жина|ть, ю *impf.* (*of* ▸ **по~**) to have supper.
ужи́|ться, ву́сь, вёшься, *past* **~лся, ~ла́сь** *pf.* (*of* ▸ **~ва́ться**) (**с** + *i.*) to get on (with); **мы с ней так и не ~ли́сь** she and I simply couldn't get on.
узако́нивани|е, я *nt.* legalization.
узако́нива|ть, ю *impf. of* ▸ **узако́нить**
узако́н|ить, ю, ишь *pf.* (*of* ▸ **~ивать**) (*придать законную силу*) to legalize.
узбе́к, а *m.* Uzbek.
Узбекиста́н, а *m.* Uzbekistan.
узбе́кский *adj.* Uzbek.
узбе́|чка, чки *f. of* ▸ **~к**
узде́чк|а, и *f.* bridle.
у́з|ел, ла́ *m.*
1 (*на верёвке*) knot (*also fig.*); (*мера скорости*) knot; **завяза́ть у.** to tie a knot.
2 (*место пересечения*) junction; (*центр*) centre (*Br.*), center (*US*); **телефо́нный у.** telephone exchange.
узел|о́к, ка́ *m.*
1 small knot.
2 (*свёрток*) small bundle.
у́з|кий (~ок, ~ка́, ~ко, ~́ки́) *adj.*
1 narrow; **~кое ме́сто** (*fig.*) bottleneck.
2 (*об одежде*) tight.
3 (*fig.*) (*ограниченный*) narrow, limited; **у. круг друзе́й** narrow circle of friends.
узколо́б|ый (~, ~а) *adj.* (*fig.*) narrow-minded.
узна|ва́ть, ю́, ёшь *impf. of* ▸ **~́ть**
узна́|ть, ю *pf.* (*of* ▸ **~ва́ть**)
1 (*старого друга, свою машину*) to recognize.
2 (*новости*) to learn, hear; (*обнаружить, выяснить*) to find out.
3 (*нужду, любовь*) to get to know; to become familiar with.
у́зник, а *m.* (*rhet.*) prisoner.
у́зниц|а, ы *f. of* ▸ **у́зник**
узо́р, а *m.* pattern, design.
у́зост|ь, и *f.* narrowness (*also fig.*); (*одежды*) tightness.
уике́нд, а *m.* weekend.
уик-э́нд, а *m.* = **уике́нд**
уй|ду́, дёшь *see* ▸ **~ти́**
у́йм|а, ы *f.* (+ *g.*) (*coll.*) lots (of), masses (of).
уйм|у́, ёшь *see* ▸ **уня́ть**
уй|ти́, ду́, дёшь, *past* **ушёл, ушла́** *pf.* (*of* ▸ **уходи́ть 1**)
1 (*покинуть место*) to go away, go off, leave; (**из, от, с** + *g.*) to leave; **у. из ко́мнаты** to leave the room; **у. домо́й** to go (off) home; **мне на́до у.** I must leave.
2 (**от, из** + *g.*) (*спастись, избавиться*) to escape (from), get away (from); to evade.
3 (**от, из, с** + *g.*) (*перестать заниматься чем-н.*) to retire (from), give up; **она́ ушла́ с рабо́ты** she left her job; **у. из поли́тики** to retire from politics; **у. (из жи́зни)** to pass away (= *to die*).
4 (**в** + *a.*) (*погрузиться*) to sink (into); (*fig.*) to bury o.s. (in); **у. в себя́** to retire into one's shell.
5 (**на** + *a.*) (*израсходоваться*) to be spent; **на кни́гу ушёл год** a year was spent on the book.
6 (*о времени, об эпохе*) to pass away, slip away.
ука́з, а *m.* decree.
указа́ни|е, я *nt.* (*инструкция*) instructions, directions.
указа́тел|ь, я *m.*
1 (*прибор, стрелка*) indicator; (*надпись*) sign; (*comput.*) cursor; **доро́жный у.** road sign; **у. у́ровня воды́** water gauge.
2 (*справочный список*) index; **у. имён со́бственных** index of proper names.
3 (*справочная книга*) guide, directory.
указа́тельн|ый *adj.* indicating; **~ая стре́лка** pointer; **у. па́лец** index finger; **у. знак** road sign.
ука|за́ть, жу́, ~́жешь *pf.* (*of* ▸ **~́зывать 1**)
1 (*дорогу*) to show; (*адрес, день*) to indicate.

2 (**на** + *a.*) (*жестом*) to point (at, to); (*fig.*) (*на ошибку, недостаток*) to point out.

укáзк|а, и *f.* pointer.

укáзыва|ть, ю
1 *impf. of* ▶ **указáть.**
2 *no pf.* (*свидетельствовать*) (**на** + *a.*) to indicate.

укат|áть, áю *pf.* (*of* ▶ **∼́ывать**[1])
1 to roll (out); **у. дорóгу** (*катком*) to roll a road; (*ездой*) to make a road smooth.
2 (*coll.*) (*утомить*) to wear out, tire out.

укат|áться, áется *pf.* (*of* ▶ **∼́ываться**[1]) (*o дороге*) to become smooth.

ука|тúть, чý, ∼́тишь *pf.* (*of* ▶ **∼́тывать**[2])
1 (*бочку*) to roll away; (*велосипед*) to wheel away.
2 (*coll.*) (*уехать*) to go off.

ука|тúться, ∼́тится *pf.* (*of* ▶ **∼́тываться**[2]) to roll away (*intrans.*).

укáтыва|ть(ся)[1]**, ю, ет(ся)** *impf. of* ▶ **укатáть(ся)**

укáтыва|ть(ся)[2]**, ю, ет(ся)** *impf. of* ▶ **укатúть(ся)**

укач|áть, áю *pf.* (*of* ▶ **∼́ивать**)
1 (*до сна*) to rock to sleep.
2 (*о море, о езде*) to make sick; (*impers.*): **меня́ ∼áло на парохóде** I was (sea)sick on the boat; **в машине её укáчивает** she gets travel-sick in cars.

укáчива|ть, ю *impf. of* ▶ **укачáть**

уклáд, а *m.* structure; **у. жúзни** style of life; **общéственно-экономúческий у.** social and economic structure.

уклáдыва|ть, ю *impf. of* ▶ **уложúть**

уклáдыва|ться[1]**, юсь** *impf. of* ▶ **уложúться; э́то не ∼ется в головé** it is hard to take it in.

уклáдыва|ться[2]**, юсь** *impf. of* ▶ **улéчься 1, 2**

уклóн, а *m.*
1 slope; (*градиент*) gradient; **под у.** downhill.
2 (*fig.*) (*направленность*) bias; **шкóла с математúческим ∼ом** school with a mathematical bias.

уклон|úться, ю́сь, úшься *pf.* (*of* ▶ **∼я́ться**) (**от** + *g.*) (*избежать*) to avoid; to evade; **у. от ответственности** to evade responsibility; **у. от удáра** to dodge a blow; **у. от прямóго отвéта** to avoid giving a direct answer.

уклóнчив|ый (∼, ∼а) *adj.* evasive.

уклон|я́ться, я́юсь *impf. of* ▶ **∼úться**

укóл, а *m.*
1 (*булавкой*) prick.
2 (*med.*) injection, 'jab'.
3 (*fig.*) (*замечание*) jibe.

укол|óть, ю́, ∼́ешь *pf. of* ▶ **колóть**[2] **1**

укол|óться, ю́сь, ∼́ешься *pf.*
1 (*булавкой*) to prick o.s.
2 (*impf.* **колóться**[2] **2**) (*coll.*) (*о наркомане*) to inject o.s.

укорáчива|ть, ю *impf. of* ▶ **укоротúть**

укорен|úться, úтся *pf.* (*of* ▶ **∼я́ться**) to take, strike root (*also fig.*).

укорен|я́ться, я́ется *impf. of* ▶ **∼úться**

укоро|тúть, чý, тúшь *pf.* (*of* ▶ **укорáчивать**) to shorten.

укрáдкой *adv.* stealthily, furtively.

Украúн|а, ы *f.* (the) Ukraine.

украúн|ец, ца *m.* Ukrainian.

украúн|ка, ки *f. of* ▶ **∼ец**

украúнский *adj.* Ukrainian.

укрá|сить, шу, сишь *pf.* (*of* ▶ **∼шáть**) (*дом, комнату*) to decorate; (*ёлку*) to decorate (*Br.*), trim (*US*); (*речь, стиль*) to embellish; (*жизнь*) to enrich.

укрá|сть, дý, дёшь, *past* **∼л** *pf.* (*of* ▶ **красть**) to steal.

украшá|ть, ю *impf. of* ▶ **укрáсить**

украшéни|е, я *nt.*
1 (*действие*) decorating, decoration.
2 (*предмет*) decoration, ornament; (*ювелирное*) jewellery.
3 (*гордость*) pride; (*выставки*) centrepiece (*Br.*), centerpiece (*US*).

укреп|úть, лю́, úшь *pf.* (*of* ▶ **∼ля́ть**)
1 (*стены, ограду, мускулы*) to strengthen.
2 (*mil.*) to fortify.
3 (*fig.*) (*убеждение, любовь, власть, положение, семью*) to strengthen; **у. дисциплúну** to tighten up discipline.

укреп|úться, лю́сь, úшься *pf.* (*of* ▶ **∼ля́ться**)
1 to become stronger.
2 (*mil.*) to fortify one's position.
3 (*fig.*) (*дисциплина, власть*) to become firmly established; **у. в убеждéнии** to be confirmed in one's belief.

укреплéни|е, я *nt.*
1 strengthening.
2 (*mil.*) fortification.

укрепля́|ть(ся), ю(сь) *impf. of* ▶ **укрепúть(ся)**

укрóм|ный (∼ен, ∼на) *adj.* secluded; sheltered.

укрóп, а *m.* (*bot.*) dill.

укро|тúть, щý, тúшь *pf.* (*of* ▶ **∼щáть**)
1 (*зверя*) to tame.
2 (*чувство*) to curb.

укрощá|ть, ю *impf. of* ▶ **укротúть**

укрывá|ть(ся), ю(сь) *impf. of* ▶ **укры́ть(ся)**

укры́ти|е, я *nt.* (*mil., etc.*) cover, concealment; shelter.

укр|ы́ть, óю, óешь *pf.* (*of* ▶ **∼ывáть**)
1 (*ноги, поля*) to cover (up).
2 (*преступника*) to conceal, harbour (*Br.*), harbor (*US*); (*беженца*) to (give) shelter.

укр|ы́ться, óюсь, óешься *pf.* (*of* ▶ **∼ывáться**)
1 (*одеялом*) to cover o.s. (up).
2 (*от дождя*) to take cover; to seek shelter.
3 (*остаться незаметным*) to escape (s.o.'s) notice.

ýксус, а (у) *m.* vinegar.

укýс, а *m.* bite; (*насекомого*) sting.

уку|сúть, шý, ∼́сишь *pf.* to bite; (*о насекомом*) to sting.

укýт|ать, аю *pf.* (*of* ▶ **∼ывать**) (+ *i. or* **в** + *a.*) to wrap up (in).

укýт|аться, аюсь *pf.* (*of* ▶ **∼ываться**) (*i. or* **в** + *a.*) to wrap o.s. up (in).

укýтыва|ть(ся), ю(сь) *impf. of* ▶ **укýтать(ся)**

ул. (*abbr. of* **ýлица**) St., Street; Rd, Road.

ула́влива|ть, ю *impf. of* ▶ **улови́ть**
ула́|дить, жу, дишь *pf.* (*of* ▶ **~живать**) (*спорный вопрос, дело, недоразумение*) to settle, resolve.
ула́|диться, дится *pf.* (*of* ▶ **~живаться**) to be settled, resolved.
ула́жива|ть(ся), ю, ет(ся) *impf. of* ▶ **ула́дить(ся)**
ула́мыва|ть, ю *impf. of* ▶ **улома́ть**
Ула́н-Ба́тор, а *m.* Ulan Bator.
у́л|ей, ья *m.* (bee)hive.
улет|а́ть, а́ю *impf. of* ▶ **~е́ть**
уле|те́ть, чу́, ти́шь *pf.* (*of* ▶ **~та́ть**) (*о птице*) to fly (away); (*о самолёте, о человеке*) to leave (*by air*).
ул|е́чься, я́гусь, я́жешься, я́гутся, *past* **~ёгся, ~егла́сь** *pf.*
1 (*impf.* **укла́дываться**[2]) (*лечь*) to lie down.
2 (*impf.* **укла́дываться**[2]) (*уместиться*) to find room (*to lie down*).
3 (*о пыли*) to settle.
улизн|у́ть, у́, ёшь *pf.* (*coll.*) to slip away, steal away.
ули́к|а, и *f.* (piece of) evidence; **ко́свенная у.** circumstantial evidence.
ули́тк|а, и *f.* (*zool.*) snail.
у́лиц|а, ы *f.* street; **на ~е** in the street, (*вне дома*) out (of doors), outside.
улич|а́ть, а́ю *impf. of* ▶ **~и́ть**
улич|и́ть, у́, и́шь *pf.* (*of* ▶ **~а́ть**) (+ *a. and* **в** + *p.*) to expose (as); **его́ ~и́ли в кра́же/моше́нничестве** he was exposed as a thief/fraud.
у́личный *adj.* street.
уло́в, а *m.* catch (*of fish*).
улов|и́ть, лю́, ~ишь *pf.* (*of* ▶ **ула́вливать**) (*заметить*) to detect, perceive; (*смысл, связь*) to grasp, understand.
уло́вк|а, и *f.* trick, ruse.
улож|и́ть, у́, ~ишь *pf.* (*of* ▶ **укла́дывать**)
1 (*положить*) to lay; (*положить спать*) to put to bed; **у. в посте́ль** to put to bed.
2 (*чемодан, вещи*) to pack; (*в груду*) to pile, stack.
3 (+ *i.*) (*покрыть*) to cover (with), lay (with).
4 (*рельсы*) to lay.
5 (*волосы*) to style.
улож|и́ться, у́сь, ~ишься *pf.* (*of* ▶ **укла́дываться**[1])
1 (*упаковать вещи*) to pack (up).
2 (**в** + *a.*) (*уместиться*) to go (in), fit (in).
3 (**в** + *a.*) (*в пределы*) to keep (within), confine o.s. (to); **у. в полчаса́** to confine o.s. to half an hour.
4 : **у. в голове́, в созна́ии** to sink in, go in.
улома́|ть, ю *pf.* (*of* ▶ **ула́мывать**) (*coll.*) to talk round; (+ *inf.*) to talk into, prevail upon (to).
улучш|а́ть(ся), а́ю, ет(ся) *impf. of* ▶ **~ить(ся)**
улучше́ни|е, я *nt.* improvement.
улу́чш|ить, у, ишь *pf.* (*of* ▶ **~а́ть**) to improve.
улу́чш|иться, ится *pf.* (*of* ▶ **~а́ться**) to improve.
улыб|а́ться, а́юсь *impf.* (*of* ▶ **~ну́ться**)
1 (+ *d.*) to smile (at); **она́ мне ~ну́лась** she smiled at me.
2 (+ *d.*; *fig.*) (*о жизни, о судьбе*) to smile (upon).
улы́бк|а, и *f.* smile.
улыб|ну́ться, ну́сь, нёшься *pf. of* ▶ **~а́ться**
улы́бчив|ый (~, ~а) *adj.* (*coll.*) smiling; happy.
ультима́тум, а *m.* ultimatum.
ультразву́к, а *m.* ultrasound.
ультразвуково́й *adj.* (*phys.*) ultrasonic.
ультрамари́н, а *m.* ultramarine.
ультрафиоле́товый *adj.* ultraviolet.
ум, а́ *m.* mind, intellect; wits; **склад ~а́** mentality; **быть без ~а́ (от** + *g.*) to be out of one's mind (about), be crazy (about); (**счита́ть,** *etc.*) **в ~е́** (to count, *etc.*) in one's head; **прийти́ на ум** (+ *d.*) to occur to one, cross one's mind; **быть на ~е́** (*coll.*) to be on one's mind; **свести́ с ~а́** to drive mad; (*fig.*) (*очаровать*) to send wild; **сойти́ с ~а́** to go mad.
умал|и́ть, ю́, и́шь *pf.* (*of* ▶ **~я́ть**) to belittle, disparage.
умалишённ|ый *adj.* mad, mentally ill; *as n.* **у., ~ого** *m.*; **~ая, ~ой** *f.* madman; madwoman; **дом ~ых** mental hospital.
ума́лчива|ть, ю *impf. of* ▶ **умолча́ть**
умал|я́ть, я́ю *impf. of* ▶ **~и́ть**
уме́лый *adj.* able, skilful (*Br.*), skillful (*US*).
уме́ни|е, я *nt.* ability, skill.
уменьш|а́ть(ся), а́ю(сь) *impf. of* ▶ **~́ить(ся)**
уменьше́ни|е, я *nt.* reduction, diminution, decrease.
уменьши́тельн|ый *adj.* (*gram.*) diminutive; **~ое и́мя** pet name (*as* Kolya *for* Nikolai).
уме́ньш|ить, ~у, ~ишь *pf.* (*of* ▶ **~а́ть**) to reduce, decrease.
уме́ньш|иться, ~усь, ~ишься *pf.* (*of* ▶ **~а́ться**) to diminish, decrease; to abate.
уме́р|енный *adj.*
1 **(~ен, ~енна)** moderate (*pol.*; *also fig.*); **~енная поли́тика** moderate policy.
2 (*geog.*, *meteor.*) temperate; moderate.
умер|е́ть, умру́, умрёшь, *past* **у́мер, ~ла́, у́мерло** *pf.* (*of* ▶ **умира́ть 1**) to die; **у. есте́ственной, наси́льственной сме́ртью** to die a natural, violent death.
уме́р|ить, ю, ишь *pf.* (*of* ▶ **~я́ть**) (*требования*) to moderate, (*гнев*) to restrain.
умер|тви́ть, щвлю́, тви́шь *pf.* (*of* ▶ **~щвля́ть**) to kill, destroy (*also fig.*).
умерщвля́|ть, ю *impf. of* ▶ **умертви́ть**
умер|я́ть, я́ю *impf. of* ▶ **~́ить**
уме|сти́ть, щу́, сти́шь *pf.* (*of* ▶ **~ща́ть**) to fit, find room (for).
уме|сти́ться, щу́сь, сти́шься *pf.* (*of* ▶ **~ща́ться**) to go in, fit in, find room.
уме́ст|ный (~ен, ~на) *adj.* appropriate; pertinent; (*сделанный вовремя*) opportune, timely; **ва́ше предложе́ние вполне́ ~но** your suggestion is quite in order.
уме́|ть, ю *impf.* (+ *inf.*) to be able (to), know how (to); **она́ ~ет ката́ться на конька́х**

she can skate; **она́ не ~ет притворя́ться** she is incapable of pretending.
умеща́|ть(ся), ю(сь) *impf. of* ▸ **уමести́ть(ся)**
умил|и́ть, ю́, и́шь *pf.* (*of* ▸ **~я́ть**) to move, touch.
умил|и́ться, ю́сь, и́шься *pf.* (*of* ▸ **~я́ться**) to be moved, be touched.
умил|я́ть(ся), я́ю(сь) *impf. of* ▸ **~и́ть(ся)**
умира́|ть, ю *impf.*
1 *impf. of* ▸ **умере́ть.**
2 (*fig.*) (*очень хотеть*) to be dying to; **~ю, как хочу́ спать** I'm dying to have a sleep; (**от** + *g.*) to be dying of; **у. от ску́ки** to be dying of boredom; to be bored to death.
умиротворён|ный (~, ~на) *adj.* tranquil; contented.
умн|е́е *comp. of* ▸ **~́ый** *and* ▸ **~о́**
умне́|ть, ю *impf.* (*of* ▸ **по~**) to grow wiser.
у́мник, а *m.* (*coll.*) (*iron.*) know-all, smart alec.
у́мниц|а, ы *c.g.* (*coll.*)
1 (*о девочке*) good girl; (*о мальчике*) good boy.
2 (*о человеке*) clever person.
умнож|а́ть, а́ю *impf. of* ▸ **~́ить**
умноже́ни|е, я *nt.*
1 increase, rise.
2 (*math.*) multiplication.
умно́ж|ить, у, ишь *pf.* (*of* ▸ **мно́жить** *and* ▸ **~а́ть**)
1 to increase.
2 (*math.*) to multiply.
у́м|ный (~ён, ~на́) *adj.* (*человек*) clever, wise, intelligent; (*лицо, глаза, книга*) intelligent; (*разумный*) sensible.
умозри́тел|ьный (~ен, ~ьна) *adj.* (*phil.*) speculative; (*отвлечённый*) abstract.
умол|и́ть, ю́, ~́ишь *pf.* (*of* ▸ **~я́ть 1**) to prevail upon.
умолк|а́ть, а́ю *impf. of* ▸ **~́нуть**
умо́лк|нуть, ну, нешь, *past* **~, ~ла** *pf.* (*of* ▸ **~а́ть**) (*о человеке*) to fall silent; (*о звуках*) to cease, stop; (*о славе*) to fade.
умолча́ни|е, я *nt.* (*comput.*): **по ~ю** (by) default; **шрифт/настро́йки по ~ю** default font/settings.
умолча́|ть, ю *pf.* (*of* ▸ **ума́лчивать**) (**о** + *p.*) to pass over in silence, fail to mention, suppress, hush up; **нельзя́ у. о** (+ *p.*) one must mention.
умол|я́ть, я́ю *impf.*
1 *impf. of* ▸ **~и́ть.**
2 to entreat, implore.
умопомрачи́тел|ьный (~ен, ~ьна) *adj.* stupendous, tremendous, terrific.
умори́тел|ьный (~ен, ~ьна) *adj.* (*coll.*) hilarious.
у́мственн|о *adv. of* ▸ **~ый; у. отста́лый** retarded, backward.
у́мственный *adj.* mental, intellectual.
умч|а́ться, у́сь, и́шься *pf.*
1 to whirl, hurtle away (*intrans.*).
2 (*fig.*) (*время, детство*) to fly past.
умыва́льник, а *m.* washbasin.
умыва́|ть(ся), ю(сь) *impf. of* ▸ **умы́ть(ся)**

у́мыс|ел, ла *m.* design, intent(ion).
ум|ы́ть, о́ю, о́ешь *pf.* (*of* ▸ **~ыва́ть**) to wash; **у. ру́ки** to wash one's hands (*also fig.*).
ум|ы́ться, о́юсь, о́ешься *pf.* (*of* ▸ **~ыва́ться**) to wash (o.s.).
умы́шленно *adv.* purposely, intentionally.
умы́шленный *adj.* intentional, deliberate; (*убийство*) premeditated.
унасле́д|овать, ую *pf. of* ▸ **насле́довать 1**
унес|ти́, у́, ёшь, *past* **~̈, ~ла́** *pf.* (*of* ▸ **уноси́ть**)
1 (*уходя, взять с собой*) to take away.
2 (*о воде, ветре*) to carry away, remove; (*impers.*): **ло́дку ~ло́ тече́нием** the boat was carried away by the current.
3 (*fig.*) (*о мыслях, мечтах*) to carry (*in thought*).
4 (*fig.*) (*жизнь, здоровье*) to claim; **война́ ~ла́ мно́го жи́зней** the war claimed many lives.
унес|ти́сь, у́сь, ёшься, *past* **~̈ся, ~ла́сь** *pf.* (*of* ▸ **уноси́ться**)
1 (*поезд, машина*) to speed away; (*тучи*) to be whisked away.
2 (*fig.*) (*миновать*) to fly away, fly by.
3 (*fig.*) (*в мыслях, мечтах*) to be carried away.
универма́г, а *m.* (*abbr. of* **универса́льный магази́н**) department store.
универса́л, а *m.* (*coll.*) (*машина*) estate car (*Br.*), station wagon (*US*).
универса́л|ьный (~ен, ~ьна) *adj.*
1 (*проблема, язык*) universal.
2 (*разносторонний*) many-sided; versatile; **~ьные зна́ния** encyclopedic knowledge; **~ьное образова́ние** all-round education.
3 (*инструмент*) multi-purpose, all-purpose; **у. магази́н** department store; **у. си́мвол** (*comput.*) wild card.
универса́м, а *m.* (*abbr. of* **универса́льный магази́н самообслу́живания**) supermarket.
университе́т, а *m.* university; **поступи́ть в у.** to enter, start university; **око́нчить у.** to graduate (from a university).
университе́т|ский *adj. of* ▸ **~**
унижа́|ть(ся), ю(сь) *impf. of* ▸ **уни́зить(ся)**
униже́ни|е, я *nt.* humiliation, degradation, abasement.
унизи́тел|ьный (~ен, ~ьна) *adj.* humiliating, degrading.
уни́|зить, жу, зишь *pf.* (*of* ▸ **~жа́ть**) to humiliate; to degrade.
уни́|зиться, жусь, зишься *pf.* (*of* ▸ **~жа́ться**) to demean o.s.; **у. до лжи/про́сьбы/шантажа́** to stoop to lying/asking/blackmail.
уника́л|ьный (~ен, ~ьна) *adj.* unique.
унима́|ть(ся), ю(сь) *impf. of* ▸ **уня́ть(ся)**
унита́з, а *m.* toilet (bowl).
унифо́рм|а, ы *f.* uniform.
уничтож|а́ть, а́ю *impf. of* ▸ **~́ить**
уничтоже́ни|е, я *nt.*
1 destruction, annihilation.
2 (*упразднение*) abolition, elimination.

уничто́ж|ить, у, ишь *pf.* (*of* ▸ **~а́ть**)
1 to destroy; (*врага*) to annihilate; (*насекомых*) to exterminate.
2 (*упразднить*) to abolish; to do away with.
3 (*fig.*) (*унизить*) to crush.

уно|си́ть(ся), шу́(сь), ~́сишь(ся) *impf. of* ▸ **унести́(сь)**

у́нци|я, и *f.* ounce (*measure*).

уны́л|ый (~, ~а) *adj.*
1 (*человек*) despondent.
2 (*мысль, взгляд*) melancholy, cheerless.

уны́ни|е, я *nt.* despondency, depression.

уня́|ть, уйму́, уймёшь, *past* **~л, ~ла́, ~ло** *pf.* (*of* ▸ **унима́ть**)
1 (*успокоить*) to calm, soothe, pacify.
2 (*боль, кровотечение, слёзы*) to stop; **у. пожа́р** to stop a fire.
3 (*чувства*) to suppress.

уня́|ться, уйму́сь, уймёшься, *past* **~лся, ~ла́сь** *pf.* (*of* ▸ **унима́ться**)
1 (*успокоиться*) to calm down.
2 (*ветер, буря*) to abate, die down; (*боль, обида*) to die down.

упа́д|ок, ка *m.* decline; **у. ду́ха** depression; **у. сил** breakdown.

упа́дочный (~ен, ~на) *adj.*
1 (*искусство*) decadent.
2 depressive; **~ное настрое́ние** depression.

упак|ова́ть, у́ю *pf.* (*of* ▸ **пакова́ть** *and* ▸ **~о́вывать**) to pack (up).

упако́вк|а, и *f.*
1 (*действие*) packing, packaging.
2 (*материал*) packaging; (*пакет*) package.

упако́выва|ть, ю *impf. of* ▸ **упакова́ть**

упа́|сть, ду́, дёшь, *past* **~л** *pf.* (*of* ▸ **па́дать 1**) to fall.

упер|е́ть, упру́, упрёшь, *past* **~̈, ~̈ла** *pf.* (*of* ▸ **упира́ть 1**) (*a.* **в** + *a.*) to rest (against), prop (against), lean (against); **у. ле́стницу в сте́ну** to rest a ladder against the wall.

упер|е́ться, упру́сь, упрёшься, *past* **~̈ся, ~̈лась** *pf.* (*of* ▸ **упира́ться 1**)
1 (+ *i.* **в** + *a.*) to rest (against), lean (against); **у. нога́ми в зе́млю** to dig one's heels in the ground.
2 (*coll., fig.*) (*не согласиться*) to dig one's heels in.

упира́|ть, ю *impf.*
1 *impf. of* ▸ **упере́ть.**
2 (*impf. only*) (**на** + *a.*; *coll.*) to stress, insist (on).

упира́|ться, юсь *impf.*
1 *impf. of* ▸ **упере́ться.**
2 (*impf. only*) (**в** + *a.*) (*сопротивляться*) to come up (against), be held up (by).

упи́тан|ный (~, ~на) *adj.* well fed; (*толстый*) plump.

упла|ти́ть, чу́, ~́тишь *pf.* (*of* ▸ **~́чивать**) to pay; **у. по счёту** to pay a bill, settle an account.

упла́чива|ть, ю *impf. of* ▸ **уплати́ть**

уплыва́|ть, ю *impf. of* ▸ **уплы́ть**

уплы́|ть, ву́, вёшь, *past* **~л, ~ла́, ~ло** *pf.* (*of* ▸ **~ва́ть**) (*вплавь*) to swim away; (*о кораблях*) to sail away; (*о вещах*) to float away.

уподо́б|ить, лю, ишь *pf.* (*of* ▸ **~ля́ть**) to liken.

уподо́б|иться, люсь, ишься *pf.* (*of* ▸ **~ля́ться**) (+ *d.*) to become like.

уподобля́|ть(ся), ю(сь) *impf. of* ▸ **уподо́бить(ся)**

упои́тел|ьный (~ен, ~ьна) *adj.* intoxicating, ravishing.

уполз|а́ть, а́ю *impf. of* ▸ **~ти́**

уполз|ти́, у́, ёшь, *past* **~, ~ла́** *pf.* (*of* ▸ **~а́ть**) to creep, crawl away.

уполномо́ч|енный *p.p.p. of* ▸ **~ить;** *as n.* **у., ~енного** *m.* representative, person authorized; **у. по права́м челове́ка** ombudsman.

уполномо́чива|ть, ю *impf. of* ▸ **уполномо́чить**

уполномо́ч|ить, у, ишь *pf.* (*of* ▸ **~ивать**) (**на** + *a.*) to authorize.

упомина́ни|е, я *nt.* mentioning; (**о** + *p.*) mention (of).

упомина́|ть, ю *impf. of* ▸ **упомяну́ть**

упомян|у́ть, у́, ~́ешь *pf.* (*of* ▸ **упомина́ть**) (+ *a. or* **о** + *p.*) to mention, refer (to).

упо́р, а *m.*
1 rest, support; (*tech.*) brace.
2: **в у.** (*mil.*) point-blank (*also fig.*); **сказа́ть кому́-н. в у.** to tell s.o. point-blank.
3: **сде́лать у.** (**на** + *a. or p.*) to lay stress (on).

упо́р|ный (~ен, ~на) *adj.* (*упрямый*) stubborn; (*настойчивый*) persistent.

упо́рств|о, а *nt.* (*упрямство*) stubbornness; (*настойчивость*) persistence.

упорхн|у́ть, у́, ёшь *pf.* to fly, flit away.

упоря́дочива|ть, ю *impf. of* ▸ **упоря́дочить**

упоря́доч|ить, у, ишь *pf.* (*of* ▸ **~ивать**) to regulate, put in (good) order.

употреби́тел|ьный (~ен, ~ьна) *adj.* (widely-)used; common, usual.

употреб|и́ть, лю́, и́шь *pf.* (*of* ▸ **~ля́ть**) to use; to make use (of).

употребле́ни|е, я *nt.* use; (*применение*) application; **вы́йти из ~я** to fall into disuse.

употребля́|ть, ю *impf. of* ▸ **употреби́ть**

упра́в|иться, люсь, ишься *pf.* (*of* ▸ **~ля́ться**) (**с** + *i.*; *coll.*)
1 (*с работой*) to cope (with), manage.
2 (*с противником*) to deal (with) (= *to get the better of*).

управле́ни|е, я *nt.*
1 management, administration; direction; **орке́стр под ~ем Спивако́ва** orchestra conducted by Spivakov.
2 (*tech.*) control; (*автомобилем*) driving; (*самолётом*) piloting; (*кораблём*) steering; **дистанционное у.** remote control.
3 (*деятельность органов власти*) government.
4 (*учреждение*) office.
5 (*tech.*) (*совокупность приборов*) controls.

управля́|ть, ю *impf.* (+ *i.*)
1 (*учреждением*) to manage, run; (*оркестром, хором*) to conduct; (*страной*) to govern.
2 (*tech.*) (*машиной*) to control, operate; (*автомобилем*) to drive; (*самолётом*) to pilot;

У

(*кораблём, яхтой*) to steer, navigate.

управля́|ться, юсь *impf. of* ▸**упра́виться**

управля́ющ|ий, ∼его *n.* (*в учреждении*) manager; (*в имении*) steward.

упражне́ни|е, я *nt.* (*гимнастическое, музыкальное*) exercise; (*мышц*) exercising; (*голоса, на рояле*) practising (*Br.*), practicing (*US*); **у. па́мяти** memory training.

упражня́|ть, ю *impf.* to exercise, train.

упражня́|ться, юсь *impf.* (**в** + *p.*, **на** + *p.*, **с** + *i.*) to practise (*Br.*), practice (*US*), train (at).

упраздн|и́ть, ю́, и́шь *pf.* (*of* ▸**∼я́ть**) to abolish.

упраздн|я́ть, я́ю *impf. of* ▸**∼и́ть**

упра́шива|ть, ю *impf. of* ▸**упроси́ть 1**

упре|ди́ть, жу́, ди́шь *pf.* (*of* ▸**∼жда́ть**) to forestall, anticipate.

упрежда́|ть, ю *impf. of* ▸**упреди́ть**

упрёк, а *m.* reproach; **бро́сить у. кому́-н.** to reproach s.o.; **ста́вить кому́-н. что-н. в у.** to hold sth. against s.o.

упрек|а́ть, а́ю *impf.* (*of* ▸**∼ну́ть**) (**в** + *p.*) to reproach (for).

упрек|ну́ть, ну́, нёшь *inst. pf. of* ▸**∼а́ть**

упро|си́ть, шу́, ∼́сишь *pf.* (*of* ▸**упра́шивать**)
[1] (*настойчиво просить*) to beg, entreat.
[2] (*pf. only*) (*убедить сделать что-н.*) to prevail upon.

упро|сти́ть, щу́, сти́шь *pf.* (*of* ▸**∼ща́ть**) to simplify; (**до** + *g.*) to reduce (to).

упро|сти́ться, сти́тся *pf.* (*of* ▸**∼ща́ться**) to become simpler, be simplified.

упро́чива|ть(ся), ю(сь) *impf. of* ▸**упро́чить(ся)**

упро́ч|ить, у, ишь *pf.* (*of* ▸**∼ивать**) to strengthen, consolidate; to establish firmly.

упро́ч|иться, усь, ишься *pf.* (*of* ▸**∼иваться**)
[1] to be strengthened, consolidated; to be firmly established; **на́ше положе́ние ∼илось** our position is firmly established.
[2] (*упрочить своё положение*) to establish o.s. (firmly), settle o.s.

упроща́|ть(ся), ю, ет(ся) *impf. of* ▸**упрости́ть(ся)**

упроще́ни|е, я *nt.* simplification.

упру́г|ий (∼, ∼а) *adj.* elastic, resilient; **∼ая похо́дка** springy gait.

упру́гост|ь, и *f.* elasticity, resilience; (*походки*) spring.

у́пряж|ь, и *f.* harness, gear.

упря́м|ец, ца *m.* obstinate person.

упря́м|иться, люсь, ишься *impf.* to be obstinate; (**в** + *p.*) to persist (in).

упря́мств|о, а *nt.* obstinacy, stubbornness.

упря́м|ый (∼, ∼а) *adj.*
[1] (*неуступчивый*) obstinate, stubborn.
[2] (*настойчивый*) persistent.

упря́|тать, чу, чешь *pf.* (*of* ▸**∼тывать**)
[1] (*спрятать*) to hide, conceal.
[2] (*fig., coll.*) (*убрать*) to put away; (*услать*) to banish; **у. в тюрьму́** to lock up.

упря́тыва|ть, ю *impf. of* ▸**упря́тать**

упуска́|ть, ю *impf. of* ▸**упусти́ть**

упу|сти́ть, щу́, ∼́стишь *pf.* (*of* ▸**∼ска́ть**)
[1] (*из рук*) to let go, let slip, let fall; (*отпустить*) to let go; (*не заметить*) to miss.
[2] (*fig.*) (*пропустить*) to let go, let slip; to miss; to lose; **у. возмо́жность, слу́чай** to miss an opportunity.

ура́ *int.* hurrah!; hurray!

уравне́ни|е, я *nt.*
[1] (*в правах*) equalization.
[2] (*math.*) equation.

уравнове́|сить, шу, сишь *pf.* (*of* ▸**∼шивать**)
[1] to balance.
[2] (*fig.*) to counterbalance, offset.

уравнове́|шенный *p.p.p. of* ▸**∼сить** *and adj.* (*fig.*) balanced, steady.

уравнове́шива|ть, ю *impf. of* ▸**уравнове́сить**

урага́н, а *m.* hurricane; (*fig.*) (*событий*) storm.

Ура́л, а *m.* (*горы*) the Urals.

ура́н, а *m.*
[1] (*chem.*) uranium.
[2] (*astron.*): **У.** Uranus.

урв|а́ть, у́, ёшь, *past* **∼а́л, ∼ала́, ∼а́ло** *pf.* (*of* ▸**урыва́ть**) (*coll.*) to snatch (*also fig.*), grab; **у. мину́ту-две для бесе́ды** to snatch a minute or two for a chat.

урегули́р|овать, ую *pf.* (*of* ▸**регули́ровать 2**) (*отношения*) to normalize; (*вопрос, спор*) to settle.

урез|а́ть, а́ю *impf. of* ▸**∼́ать**

уре́|зать, жу, жешь *pf.* (*of* ▸**∼за́ть**)
[1] (*coll.*) (*края*) to cut off; to shorten.
[2] (*бюджет*) to cut down, reduce; (*права*) to reduce; **у. шта́ты** to cut down the staff.

уретри́т, а *m.* (*med.*) urethritis.

у́рн|а, ы *f.*
[1] (*для праха*) urn.
[2] : **избира́тельная у.** ballot box.
[3] (*для мусора*) refuse bin (*Br.*), garbage can (*US*).

у́ров|ень, ня *m.* level; (*fig.*) standard; **у. мо́ря** sea level; **высота́ над ∼нем мо́ря** altitude above sea level; **у. жи́зни** standard of living.

уро́д, а *m.*
[1] freak, monster.
[2] (*некрасивый человек*) ugly person.
[3] (*оскорбление*) bastard (*as a term of abuse, usu. of a man*).

уро́длив|ый (∼, ∼а) *adj.*
[1] (*с уродством*) deformed, misshapen.
[2] (*некрасивый*) ugly.
[3] (*fig.*) (*плохой, ненормальный*) bad; abnormal; faulty; distorted.

уро́д|овать, ую *impf.* (*of* ▸**из∼**)
[1] (*калечить*) to deform, disfigure, mutilate.
[2] (*делать некрасивым*) to make ugly.
[3] (*fig.*) (*искажать*) to distort.

уро́дств|о, а *nt.*
[1] (*физический недостаток*) deformity; disfigurement.
[2] (*некрасивость*) ugliness.
[3] (*fig.*) (*ненормальность*) abnormality.

урожа́|й, я *m.*
[1] harvest; crop; **собра́ть у.** to gather in the harvest.
[2] (*хороший сбор*) bumper crop, abundance

(*also fig., coll.*).

уроже́н|ец, ца *m.* (+*g.*) native (of).

уроже́н|ка, ки *f. of* ▸ **~ец**

уро́к, а *m.*
1 lesson (*also fig.*); **брать ~и** (+ *g.*) to have, take lessons (in); **дава́ть ~и** (+ *g.*) to give lessons (in).
2 (*задание*) homework; **зада́ть у.** to set homework; **сде́лать ~и** to do one's homework.

уро́н, а *no pl., m.* (*материальный*) damages, losses; (*о людях*) casulaties; **нанести́ у.** (*урожаю*) to inflict damage (on); (*врагу*) to inflict casualties (on).

урон|и́ть, ю́, ~́ишь *pf. of* ▸ **роня́ть 1, 3**

уругва́|ец, йца *m.* Uruguayan.

Уругва́|й, я *m.* Uruguay.

уругва́|йка, йки *f. of* ▸ **~ец**

уругва́йский *adj.* Uruguayan.

урч|а́ть, у́, и́шь *impf.* to rumble; (*о собаке*) to growl.

урыва́|ть, ю *impf. of* ▸ **урва́ть**

ус, а *m.*
1 (*see also* ▸ **~ы́**) (*человека*) moustache hair (*Br.*), mustache hair (*US*).
2 (*животного*) whisker.

уса|ди́ть, жу́, ~́дишь *pf.* (*of* ▸ **~́живать**)
1 (*помочь усесться*) to seat, help sit down; (*заставить усесться*) to make sit down.
2 (**за** + *a. or* + *inf.*) to sit (*s.o.*) down; **у. за уро́ки** to sit (*s.o.*) down to his/her lessons.

уса́дьб|а, ы, *g. pl.* **уса́деб** *f.*
1 (*hist.*) (*помещика*) country estate.
2 (*ферма*) farmstead.

уса́жива|ть, ю *impf. of* ▸ **усади́ть**

уса́жива|ться, юсь *impf. of* ▸ **усе́сться**

уса́т|ый (~, ~а) *adj.*
1 (*человек*) with a moustache (*Br.*), mustache (*US*).
2 (*животное*) whiskered.

усва́ива|ть, ю *impf. of* ▸ **усво́ить**

усво́|ить, ю, ишь *pf.* (*of* ▸ **усва́ивать**)
1 (*привычку*) to adopt, acquire; to imitate.
2 (*урок*) to master; to assimilate.
3 (*пищу*) to assimilate.

усе́ива|ть, ю *impf. of* ▸ **усе́ять**

усе́рд|ный (~ен, ~на) *adj.* diligent, painstaking.

усе́|сться, уся́дусь, уся́дешься, *past* **~лся, ~лась** *pf.* (*of* ▸ **уса́живаться**)
1 to take a seat; to settle (down).
2 (**за** + *a. or* + *inf.*) to set (to), settle down (to).

усе́|ять, ю, ешь *pf.* (*of* ▸ **~ивать**) (+ *i.*)
1 (*засеять*) to sow (with).
2 (*покрыть*) to cover (with), dot (with), stud (with), strew (with); **лицо́, ~янное весну́шками** face covered with freckles.

уси|де́ть, жу́, ди́шь *pf.*
1 (*остаться сидеть*) to keep one's place, remain sitting; **он так волнова́лся, что е́ле ~де́л** he was so excited that he could hardly sit still.
2 (*coll.*) (*удержаться на каком-н. месте*) to stay around in a place.

у́сик, а *m.* (*zool.*) antenna, feeler.

усиле́ни|е, я *nt.*
1 (*контроля*) strengthening; (*охраны, прочности*) reinforcement.
2 (*работы*) intensification; (*проблем*) aggravation; (*radio*) amplification.

уси́л|енный *p.p.p. of* ▸ **~ить** *and adj.*
1 (*охрана*) reinforced; **~енное пита́ние** high-calorie diet.
2 (*внимание, скорость*) intensified, increased.

уси́лива|ть(ся), ю, ет(ся) *impf. of* ▸ **уси́лить(ся)**

уси́ли|е, я *nt.* effort; exertion; **приложи́ть все ~я** to make every effort, spare no effort.

усили́тел|ь, я *m.* amplifier.

уси́л|ить, ю, ишь *pf.* (*of* ▸ **~ивать**)
1 (*войска, конструкцию*) to strengthen, reinforce.
2 (*наблюдение, волнение*) to intensify, increase; (*звук*) to amplify.

уси́л|иться, ится *pf.* (*of* ▸ **~иваться**) (*ветер, чувство*) to become stronger; (*дождь, боль*) to intensify, increase (*intrans.*); (*звук*) to grow louder.

уска|ка́ть, чу́, ~́чешь *pf.*
1 (*о зайце*) to bound away; (*coll.*) (*о человеке*) to run off.
2 (*о лошади; на лошади*) to gallop off.

ускольз|а́ть, а́ю *impf. of* ▸ **~нуть**

ускольз|ну́ть, ну́, нёшь *pf.* (*of* ▸ **~а́ть**)
1 (*из рук*) to slip out; (*из-под ног*) to slip away.
2 (*fig., coll.*) (*о человеке*) to slip off.
3 (*fig.*) (**от** + *g.*) to escape; **у. от чьего́-л. внима́ния** to escape one's notice.

ускоре́ни|е, я *nt.* acceleration; speeding up.

уско́р|ить, ю, ишь *pf.* (*of* ▸ **~я́ть**)
1 (*убыстрить*) to quicken; to speed up, accelerate; **у. шаг** to quicken one's pace.
2 (*приблизить*) to hasten; (*смерть, что-н. плохое*) to precipitate.

уско́р|иться, ится *pf.* (*of* ▸ **~я́ться**)
1 (*шаги*) to quicken; (*ход механизма*) to accelerate.
2 (*выздоровление, отъезд*) to be speeded up.

ускор|я́ть(ся), я́ю, я́ет(ся) *impf. of* ▸ **~́ить(ся)**

усле|ди́ть, жу́, ди́шь *pf.* (**за** + *i.*)
1 (*за ребёнком*) to keep an eye (on), mind.
2 (*за ходом разговора*) to follow.

усло́ви|е, я *nt.*
1 (*требование*) condition; stipulation, proviso; **поста́вить ~ем** to make it a condition, stipulate; **при ~и, что; с ~ем, что** on condition that, provided that, providing.
2 *pl.* (*правила, обстоятельства*) conditions; **пого́дные ~я** weather conditions.

усло́в|ный *adj.*
1 (*принятый*) conventional; (*знак, жест*) agreed, prearranged.
2 **(~ен, ~на)** (*с условием*) conditional; **у. пригово́р** (*leg.*) suspended sentence.
3 **(~ен, ~на)** (*относительный*) relative.
4 **(~ен, ~на)** (*воображаемый*) imaginary.
5 (*gram.*) conditional.

усложне́ни|е, я *nt.* complication.

усложн|и́ть, ю́, и́шь *pf.* (*of* ▸ **~я́ть**) to complicate.

усложн|и́ться, и́тся *pf.* (*of* ▸ **~я́ться**) to become complicated.

усложн|я́ть(ся), я́ю, я́ет(ся) *impf. of* ▸ **~и́ть(ся)**

услу́г|а, и *f.*
[1] service; favour (*Br.*), favor (*US*), good turn; **оказа́ть ~у кому́-н.** to do s.o. a service; **к ва́шим ~ам** at your service.
[2] (*pl.*) service(s); **коммуна́льные ~и** public utilities.

услу́жлив|ый (~, ~а) *adj.* obliging.

услы́ш|ать, у, ишь *pf. of* ▸ **слы́шать 1**

усмех|а́ться, а́юсь *impf. of* ▸ **~ну́ться**

усмех|ну́ться, ну́сь, нёшься *pf.* (*of* ▸ **~а́ться**) to smirk; to grin.

усмир|и́ть, ю́, и́шь *pf.* (*of* ▸ **~я́ть**)
[1] (*успокоить*) to pacify; to calm, quieten; (*укротить*) to tame (*also fig.*).
[2] (*мятеж*) to suppress, put down.

усмир|я́ть, я́ю *impf. of* ▸ **~и́ть**

усн|у́ть, у́, ёшь *pf.* to go to sleep, fall asleep (*also fig.*).

усоверше́нств|овать(ся), ую(сь) *pf. of* ▸ **соверше́нствовать(ся)**

усомн|и́ться, ю́сь, и́шься *pf.* (**в** + *p.*) to doubt.

усо́х|нуть, ну, нешь, *past* **~, ~ла** *pf.* (*of* ▸ **усыха́ть**) to dry up, dry out; (*о человеке*) to wither.

успева́|ть, ю *impf.*
[1] *impf. of* ▸ **успе́ть.**
[2] (*impf. only*) (**в** + *p. or* **по** + *d.*) to make progress (in), get on well (in, at) (*studies*).

успе́|ть, ю *pf.* (*of* ▸ **~ва́ть 1**) to have time; to manage; **у. написа́ть** to have time to write; **у. к по́езду** to manage to catch the train; **не ~л я вы́йти из до́ма, как пошёл дождь** no sooner had I left the house than it started to rain.

успе́х, а *m.*
[1] success; **име́ть большо́й у.** to be a great success; **по́льзоваться ~ом** to be a success; **по́льзоваться ~ом у кого́-н.** to be successful with s.o.; **с тем же ~ом** equally well, with the same result; **с ~ом** successfully.
[2] *pl.* success, progress; **де́лать ~и** (**в** + *p.*) to make progress (in).

успе́шно *adv.* successfully.

успе́ш|ный (~ен, ~на) *adj.* successful.

успока́ива|ть(ся), ю(сь) *impf. of* ▸ **успоко́ить(ся)**

успокои́тел|ьный (~ен, ~ьна) *adj.* calming, soothing; reassuring; *as n.* **~ьное, ~ьного** *nt.* sedative.

успоко́|ить, ю, ишь *pf.* (*of* ▸ **успока́ивать**)
[1] to calm (down); (*убедить не тревожиться*) to reassure.
[2] (*боль*) to assuage, deaden.

успоко́|иться, юсь, ишься *pf.* (*of* ▸ **успока́иваться**)
[1] (*о человеке*) to calm down; to compose o.s.
[2] (*быть довольным*) to be satisfied; **у. на дости́гнутом** to be content with what has been achieved.
[3] (*о боли*) to abate; (*о море*) to become still; (*о ветре*) to drop.

уста́в, а *m.* regulations, rules, statutes; (*mil.*) service regulations; (*в монастыре*) rule; **у. университе́та** university statutes; **У. ООН** UN Charter.

уста|ва́ть, ю́, ёшь *impf. of* ▸ **~́ть**

уста́лост|ь, и *f.* fatigue, tiredness.

уста́лый *adj.* tired, weary.

устана́влива|ть(ся), ю, ет(ся) *impf. of* ▸ **установи́ть(ся)**

установ|и́ть, лю́, ~́ишь *pf.* (*of* ▸ **устана́вливать**)
[1] (*поставить, поместить*) to place, put, set up; (*оборудование, механизм*) to install, rig up; (*памятник*) to put up; (*comput.*) (*программу*) to install.
[2] (*показание*) to adjust, regulate, set (to, by); **у. часы́ по ра́дио** to set one's watch by the radio.
[3] (*власть, контакт*) to establish; **у. связь** (**с** + *i.*; *mil.*) to establish communication (with).
[4] (*назначить*) to fix, establish; **у. гра́фик** to fix the schedule.
[5] (*обнаружить, выяснить*) to establish, determine; to ascertain; **у. причи́ну ава́рии** to establish the cause of a crash.

установ|и́ться, ~́ится *pf.* (*of* ▸ **устана́вливаться**) to be established; to set in; **~и́лся обы́чай** it has become a custom.

устано́вк|а, и *f.*
[1] (*действие*) placing, setting up, arrangement; (*оборудования*) installation; (*величины*) setting.
[2] (*часов*) adjustment, setting.
[3] (*tech.*) (*механизм, приспособление*) installation; (*comput.*) set-up.
[4] (*цель*) aim, purpose.
[5] (*директива*) directive.

устано́в|ленный *p.p.p. of* ▸ **~и́ть** *and adj.* established, fixed, prescribed, regulation; **в ~ленном поря́дке** in prescribed manner.

устарева́|ть, ю *impf. of* ▸ **устаре́ть**

устаре́|вший *past. part. act. of* ▸ **~ть** *and adj.* obsolete.

устаре́|ть, ю *pf.* (*of* ▸ **~ва́ть** *and* ▸ **старе́ть 2**) to become obsolete; to become antiquated, out of date.

уста́|ть, ну, нешь *pf.* (*of* ▸ **~ва́ть**) to become tired; **я ~л** I am tired; **у. от** + *g.* get tired of (s.o., sth.); **мы ~ли с доро́ги** we're tired from the journey.

устила́|ть, ю *impf. of* ▸ **устла́ть**

устла́ть, устелю́, усте́лешь *pf.* (*of* ▸ **устила́ть**) (+ *i.*) to cover (with); (*плитами, камнями*) to pave (with).

у́стн|ый *adj.* verbal, oral; **~ая речь** spoken language; **у. экза́мен** oral (examination).

усто́йчивост|ь, и *f.* (*опоры*) stability, steadiness; (*веры*) firmness.

усто́йчив|ый (~, ~а) *adj.* (*опора, плот*) stable, steady; (*вера, принцип*) firm; **~ая пого́да** settled weather.

усто|я́ть, ю́, и́шь *pf.*
[1] (*не упасть*) to keep one's balance, remain standing; **у. на нога́х** to keep one's balance.
[2] (*fig.*) (*в споре*) to stand one's ground.
[3] (*не поддаться*) to resist, hold out; **у. пе́ред собла́зном** to resist a temptation.

усто|я́ться, и́тся *pf.* (*о взглядах*) to become fixed, become permanent.

устра́ива|ть(ся), ю(сь) *impf. of* ▸ **устро́ить(ся)**

устран|и́ть, ю́, и́шь *pf.* (*of* ▸ **~я́ть**)
1 (*убрать в сторону*) to remove; **у. прегра́ды** to remove obstacles; (*уничтожить*) to eliminate.
2 (*уволить*) to remove (*from office*), dismiss.

устран|я́ть, я́ю *impf. of* ▸ **~и́ть**

устраша́ющий *adj.* frightening, appalling.

устрем|и́ться, лю́сь, и́шься *pf.* (*of* ▸ **~ля́ться**)
1 (**на** + *a.*) (*направиться*) to rush (upon, at); to head (for).
2 (**на** + *a.*; **к** + *d.*) (*сосредоточиться*) to be directed (at, towards), be fixed (upon), be concentrated (on); (*о человеке*) to concentrate (on).

устремля́|ться, юсь *impf. of* ▸ **устреми́ться**

у́стриц|а, ы *f.* oyster.

устро́|ить, ю, ишь *pf.* (*of* ▸ **устра́ивать**)
1 (*изготовить, соорудить*) to make, construct.
2 (*концерт*) to arrange, organize.
3 (*вызвать*) to make, cause, create; **у. сканда́л** to make a scene.
4 (*наладить*) to settle, put in (good) order; **у. свои́ дела́** to put one's affairs in order.
5 (*поместить*) to place, fix up; **у. кого́-н. на рабо́ту** to fix s.o. up with work.
6 (*impers.*; *coll.*) (*оказаться удобным*) to suit, be convenient (to, for).

устро́|иться, юсь, ишься *pf.* (*of* ▸ **устра́иваться**)
1 (*прийти в порядок*) to work out (well).
2 (*наладить свои дела*) to manage, get by.
3 (*расположиться*) to settle down, get settled.
4 (*на работу*) to get (*a job*); **он ~ился на желе́зную доро́гу проводнико́м** he has got a job on the railway as a conductor.

устро́йств|о, а *nt.*
1 (*расположение, конструкция*) construction; layout; (*tech.*) working principle(s).
2 (*прибор*) apparatus, device.
3 (*порядок, строй*) structure, system; **обще́ственное у.** social structure.

усту́п, а *m.* (*в стене, скале*) shelf, ledge; (*agric.*) terrace.

уступ|а́ть, а́ю *impf. of* ▸ **~и́ть**

уступ|и́ть, лю́, ~́ишь *pf.* (*of* ▸ **~а́ть**) (+ *d.*)
1 (*в пользу другого*) to let have, give up (to); **у. кому́-н. ме́сто** to give up one's place to s.o.; **у. доро́гу** (+ *d.*) to make way (for), let pass.
2 (*покориться*) to yield (to), give in (to); **у. кому́-н. в спо́ре** to give in to s.o.'s argument.
3 (*быть хуже кого-н., чего-н.*) to be inferior (to); **как расска́зчик он никому́ не ~́ит** as a storyteller he is second to none.

усту́пк|а, и *f.*
1 concession, compromise.
2 (*в цене*) reduction, discount.

усту́пчив|ый (~, ~а) *adj.* pliant, pliable; compliant.

у́сть|е, я, *g. pl.* **~ев** *nt.* (*реки*) mouth, estuary.

усугуб|и́ть, ~лю́, ~и́шь *pf.* (*of* ▸ **~ля́ть**) to increase; to intensify; to aggravate.

усугубля́|ть, ю *impf. of* ▸ **усугуби́ть**

ус|ы́, о́в *pl.* (*sg.* **ус, а** *m.*) (*человека*) moustache (*Br.*), mustache (*US*) (*see also* ▸ **ус**).

усынов|и́ть, лю́, и́шь *pf.* (*of* ▸ **~ля́ть**) to adopt (*as a son*).

усыновле́ни|е, я *nt.* adoption (*of son*).

усыновля́|ть, ю *impf. of* ▸ **усынови́ть**

усып|а́ть, а́ю *impf. of* ▸ **~́ать**

усы́п|ать, лю, лешь *pf.* (*of* ▸ **~а́ть**) (+ *i.*) to strew (with), scatter (with); (*покрыть*) to cover (with).

усып|и́ть, лю́, и́шь *pf.* (*of* ▸ **~ля́ть**)
1 (*перед операцией*) to put to sleep; (*пением, чтением*) to lull to sleep.
2 (*fig.*) (*подозрения*) to lull; (*внимание*) to weaken, undermine.
3 (*больную собаку*) to put to sleep.

усыпля́|ть, ю *impf. of* ▸ **усыпи́ть**

усыха́|ть, ю *impf. of* ▸ **усо́хнуть**

ута́ива|ть, ю *impf. of* ▸ **утаи́ть**

ута|и́ть, ю́, и́шь *pf.* (*of* ▸ **~́ивать**)
1 (*скрыть*) to conceal; (*умолчать*) to keep to o.s., keep secret.
2 (*присвоить*) to appropriate.

ута́птыва|ть, ю *impf. of* ▸ **утопта́ть**

утащ|и́ть, у́, ~́ишь *pf.*
1 to drag away, off (*also fig.*).
2 (*coll.*) (*украсть*) to steal, pinch (*Br.*).

у́твар|ь, и *no pl., f.* (*collect.*) utensils, equipment.

утвер|ди́ть, жу́, ди́шь *pf.* (*of* ▸ **~жда́ть 1**)
1 (*диктатуру, правила*) to establish (*securely, firmly*).
2 (*санкционировать*) to approve; to confirm; (*договор*) to ratify; **у. пове́стку дня** to approve an agenda; **у. в до́лжности** to confirm in a job.

утвер|ди́ться, жу́сь, ди́шься *pf.* (*of* ▸ **~жда́ться**)
1 (*укрепиться*) to gain a foothold, gain a firm hold (*also fig.*); (*порядок, режим*) to become firmly established.
2 (**в** + *p.*) (*поверить*) to be confirmed in (*one's resolve, etc.*); **у. в мы́сли** to become firmly convinced.
3 (**за** + *i.*) (*о репутации*): **за ним ~ди́лась репута́ция хоро́шего инжене́ра** he gained a reputation for being a good engineer.

утвержда́|ть, ю *impf.*
1 *impf. of* ▸ **утверди́ть.**
2 (*impf. only*) to assert, maintain; (*без доказательства*) to claim, allege.

утвержда́|ться, юсь *impf. of* ▸ **утверди́ться**

утвержде́ни|е, я *nt.*
1 (*высказывание*) claim, allegation.
2 (*санкционирование*) approval; confirmation; (*договора*) ratification; (*leg.*) (*завещания*) probate.
3 (*диктатуры, порядка*) establishment.

утека́|ть, ю *impf. of* ▸ **уте́чь**

ут|ёнок, ёнка, *pl.* **~я́та, ~я́т** *m.* duckling.

утепли́тел|ь, я *m.* (*tech.*) insulating material.

утепл|и́ть, ю́, и́шь *pf.* (*of* ▸ **~я́ть**) to insulate.

утепл|я́ть, я́ю *impf. of* ▸ **~и́ть**

У

утер|е́ть, утру́, утрёшь, *past* **~, ~ла** *pf.* (*of* ▸ **утира́ть**) to wipe (off); to wipe dry; **у. пот со лба** to wipe the sweat off one's brow.

утер|е́ться, утру́сь, утрёшься, *past* **~ся, ~лась** *pf.* (*of* ▸ **утира́ться**) to wipe o.s.; to dry o.s.

утерп|е́ть, лю́, ~ишь *pf.* to restrain o.s.

утёс, а *m.* cliff, crag.

уте́чк|а, и *f.* (*жидкости, информации*) leak, leakage; (*убыль*) loss, wastage, dissipation; **у. га́за** gas escape; «**у. мозго́в**» brain drain.

уте́|чь, ку́, чёшь, ку́т, *past* **~к, ~кла́** *pf.* (*of* ▸ **~ка́ть**)
1 to flow away; to leak; (*о газе*) to escape.
2 (*о времени*) to pass, go by.

утеш|а́ть(ся), а́ю(сь) *impf. of* ▸ **~ить(ся)**

утеше́ни|е, я *nt.* comfort, consolation.

уте́ш|ить, у, ишь *pf.* (*of* ▸ **~а́ть**) to comfort, console.

уте́ш|иться, усь, ишься *pf.* (*of* ▸ **~а́ться**)
1 to console o.s.
2 (+ *i.*) (*мыслью, событием*) to take comfort (in).

утилиза́ци|я, и *f.* recycling.

ути́л|ь, я *no pl., m.* (*collect.*) scrap, recyclable waste.

утира́|ть(ся), ю(сь) *impf. of* ▸ **утере́ть(ся)**

утих|а́ть, а́ю *impf. of* ▸ **~нуть**

ути́х|нуть, ну, нешь, *past* **~, ~ла** *pf.* (*of* ▸ **~а́ть**)
1 (*о месте*) to become quiet, still; (*о звуках*) to cease, die away.
2 (*о буре, о боли*) to abate, subside; (*о ветре*) to drop; (*о споре*) to die down.
3 (*о человеке*) to become calm, calm down.

утихоми́рива|ть(ся), ю(сь) *impf. of* ▸ **утихоми́рить(ся)**

утихоми́р|ить, ю, ишь *pf.* (*of* ▸ **~ивать**) to calm down; to pacify, placate.

утихоми́р|иться, юсь, ишься *pf.* (*of* ▸ **~иваться**) to calm down; to abate, subside.

у́тк|а, и *f.* duck.

уткн|у́ть, у́, ёшь *pf.* (*coll.*) to bury; to fix; **у. нос в кни́гу** to bury o.s. in a book.

уткн|у́ться, у́сь, ёшься *pf.* (**в** + *a.*; *coll.*)
1 to bury o.s. (in), one's head (in); **у. в газе́ту** to bury one's head in a newspaper.
2 (*натолкнуться*) to bump (into); **ло́дка ~у́лась в бе́рег** the boat bumped into the bank.

утол|и́ть, ю́, и́шь *pf.* (*of* ▸ **~я́ть**)
1 (*жажду*) to quench, slake; (*голод, любопытство*) to satisfy.
2 (*боль*) to relieve, alleviate.

утол|я́ть, я́ю *impf. of* ▸ **~и́ть**

утоми́тел|ьный (~ен, ~ьна) *adj.*
1 (*утомляющий*) wearisome, tiring.
2 (*скучный*) tiresome; tedious.

утом|и́ть, лю́, и́шь *pf.* (*of* ▸ **~ля́ть**) to tire, weary, fatigue.

утом|и́ться, лю́сь, и́шься *pf.* (*of* ▸ **~ля́ться**) to get tired.

утомле́ни|е, я *nt.* tiredness, weariness, fatigue.

утом|лённый *p.p.p. of* ▸ **~и́ть** *and adj.* tired, weary, fatigued.

утомля́|ть(ся), ю(сь) *impf. of* ▸ **утоми́ть(ся)**

утон|у́ть, у́, ~ешь *pf.* (*of* ▸ **тону́ть 2, 3** *and* ▸ **утопа́ть 1**)
1 (*погибнуть*) to drown, be drowned; (*оказаться под водой*) to sink.
2 (**в** + *p.*; *fig.*) to be lost (in).

утончённый *adj.* refined; exquisite, subtle.

утопа́|ть, ю *impf.*
1 *impf. of* ▸ **утону́ть.**
2 (*impf. only*) (**в** + *p.*; *fig.*) (*в зелени*) to be covered (in); (*в роскоши, богатстве*) to wallow (in).

утопа́ющ|ий *pres. part. act. of* ▸ **утопа́ть;** *as n.* **~ий, ~его** drowning person.

утоп|и́ть, лю́, ~ишь *pf.* (*of* ▸ **топи́ть**[3] **2**)
1 (*человека, животное*) to drown.
2 (*fig., coll.*) (*погубить*) to ruin.
3 (*сделать едва видным*) to bury, embed.

утоп|и́ться, лю́сь, ~ишься *pf.* (*of* ▸ **топи́ться**[3]) to drown o.s.

утопи́ческий *adj.* Utopian.

уто́пи|я, и *f.* Utopia.

уто́пленник, а *m.* drowned man.

уто́пленни|ца, цы *f. of* ▸ **~к**

утоп|та́ть, чу́, ~чешь *pf.* (*of* ▸ **ута́птывать**) to trample down, pound.

уточне́ни|е, я *nt.* clarification, elaboration; **внести́ ~е/~я во что-н.** to elaborate on sth.

уточн|и́ть, ю́, и́шь *pf.* (*of* ▸ **~я́ть**) to make more precise, clarify; to elaborate.

уточн|я́ть, я́ю *impf. of* ▸ **~и́ть**

утра́ива|ть(ся), ю, ет(ся) *impf. of* ▸ **утро́ить**

утрамб|ова́ть, у́ю *pf.* (*of* ▸ **~о́вывать**) to ram, tamp (*road material, etc.*).

утрамбо́выва|ть, ю *impf. of* ▸ **утрамбова́ть**

утра́|тить, чу, тишь *pf.* (*of* ▸ **~чивать**) to lose.

утра́чива|ть, ю *impf. of* ▸ **утра́тить**

у́тренний *adj.* morning, early.

утри́р|овать, ую *impf. and pf.* to exaggerate.

у́тр|о, а (до ~а́, с ~а́), *d.* **~у (к ~у́),** *pl.* **~а, ~, ~ам** (*in sense* '*in the mornings*': *d.* **по ~а́м,** *i.* **утра́ми)** *nt.* morning; **в семь часо́в ~а́** at 7 a.m.; **на сле́дующее у.** the next morning; **с ~а́** early in the morning; **с ~а́ до ве́чера** from morning till night; **до́брое у.!** good morning!

утро́б|а, ы *f.* womb.

утро́|ить(ся), ю, ит(ся) *pf.* (*of* ▸ **утра́ивать(ся)**) to treble.

у́тром *adv.* in the morning; **сего́дня у.** this morning.

утружда́|ть, ю *impf.* to trouble; **у. кого́-н. про́сьбами** to trouble s.o. with requests.

утряс|а́ть(ся), а́ю, а́ет(ся) *impf. of* ▸ **~ти́(сь)**

утряс|ти́, у́, ёшь *pf.* (*of* ▸ **~а́ть**) (*coll.*) to settle.

утряс|ти́сь, ётся, у́тся *pf.* (*of* ▸ **~а́ться**) (*coll.*) (*дело, проблема*) to sort itself out; **всё ~ётся** everything will be sorted out.

уты́к|ать, аю *pf.* (*of* ▸ **~а́ть** *and*

▸ ~ивать) (*coll.*)
1 (*воткнуть*) to stick (in) all over.
2 (*забить*) to stop up, caulk.

утык|а́ть, а́ю *impf. of* ▸ **~а́ть**

уты́кива|ть, ю *impf.* = **утыка́ть**

утю́г, а́ *m.* (*flat*) iron.

уфоло́ги|я, и *f.* ufology.

ух|а́, и́ *f.* ukha (*fish soup*).

уха́б, а *m.* pothole (*in road*).

уха́жива|ть, ю *impf.* (**за** + *i.*)
1 (*за больным*) to nurse, tend; (*за животными, растениями*) to look after.
2 (*за женщиной*) to court; to pay court (to), make advances (to).

ухва|ти́ть, чу́, ~́тишь *pf.*
1 (*схватить*) to lay hold (of); (*захватить для себя*) to seize, grab.
2 (*fig., coll.*) (*понять*) to grasp.

ухва|ти́ться, чу́сь, ~́тишься *pf.* (**за** + *a.*)
1 to grasp, lay hold (of); **у. за ве́тку** to grasp a branch.
2 (*fig., coll.*) (*за возможность*) to seize; to jump (at); **у. за предложе́ние** to jump at an offer; (*за мысль, за человека*) to latch on to.

ухитр|и́ться, ю́сь, и́шься *pf.* (*of* ▸ **~я́ться**) (+ *inf.*) to manage (to), contrive (to).

ухитр|я́ться, я́юсь *impf. of* ▸ **~и́ться**

ухло́п|ать, аю *pf.* (*of* ▸ **~ывать**) (*coll.*)
1 (*убить*) to kill.
2 (*истратить*) to squander.

ухло́пыва|ть, ю *impf. of* ▸ **ухло́пать**

ухмыльн|у́ться, у́сь, ёшься *pf.* (*of* ▸ **ухмыля́ться**) (*coll.*) to smirk, grin.

ухмыл|я́ться, я́юсь *impf. of* ▸ **~ьну́ться**

у́х|о, а, *pl.* **у́ши, уше́й** *nt.* ear; **кра́ем ~а слу́шать** to listen with half an ear; **говори́ть кому́-н. на́ у.** to have a word in s.o.'s ear, have a private word with s.o.

ухо́д[1], а *m.* (*из комнаты; с работы*) leaving; (*с должности*) resignation; (*на пенсию*) retirement; (*поезда*) departure; (*с собрания; в монастырь*) withdrawal.

ухо́д[2], а *m.* (**за** + *i.*) (*за больным, за садом*) looking after; care (of); (*за машиной*) maintenance; (*за зданием*) upkeep.

ухо|ди́ть, жу́, ~́дишь *impf.*
1 *impf. of* ▸ **уйти́.**
2 (*impf. only*) (*простираться*) to stretch, extend.

ухо́жен|ный (~, ~на) *adj.* well looked after, well cared for.

ухудш|а́ть(ся), а́ю, а́ет(ся) *impf. of* ▸ **~́ить(ся)**

ухудше́ни|е, я *nt.* worsening, deterioration.

уху́дш|ить, у, ишь *pf.* (*of* ▸ **~а́ть**) to make worse, worsen.

уху́дш|иться, ится *pf.* (*of* ▸ **~а́ться**) to become worse, worsen, deteriorate (*intrans.*).

уцеле́|ть, ю *pf.* (*остаться целым*) to remain intact, escape destruction; (*остаться живым*) to remain alive, survive.

уцеп|и́ться, лю́сь, ~́ишься *pf.* (**за** + *a.*)
1 to catch hold (of), seize.
2 (*fig., coll.*) (*за предложение*) to jump (at).

уча́ств|овать, ую *impf.* (**в** + *p.*)
1 to take part (in).
2 (*иметь долю*) to have a share (in).

уча́сти|е, я *nt.*
1 participation; **у. в при́былях** profit-sharing; **при ~и, с ~ем** (+ *g.*) with the participation (of), featuring; **принима́ть у.** (**в** + *p.*) to take part (in).
2 (*сочувствие*) sympathy, concern.

участ|и́ться, и́тся *pf.* (*of* ▸ **учаща́ться**) (*удары грома*) to become more frequent; (*шаг, пульс*) to quicken.

уча́стник, а *m.* (+ *g.*) participant (in), member (of); **~и перегово́ров** negotiating parties; **~и соглаше́ния** parties to the agreement; **у. состяза́ния** competitor.

уча́ст|ок, ка *m.*
1 (*земли*) plot; parcel.
2 (*площади, стены, дороги*) part, section.
3 (*в административном делении*) district, area; **избира́тельный у.** (*подразделение*) electoral district, ward, (*здание*) polling station.

у́част|ь, и *f.* lot, fate.

учаща́|ться, ется *impf. of* ▸ **участи́ться**

уча|щённый *p.p.p. of* ▸ **~сти́ть** *and adj.* quickened; faster; **у. пульс** quickened pulse.

уча́щ|ийся *pres. part. of* ▸ **учи́ться;** *as n.* **у., ~егося** *m.*, **~аяся, ~ейся** *f.* student; (*школы*) pupil.

учёб|а, ы *f.*
1 studies; studying, learning; **за ~ой** at one's studies.
2 (*подготовка*) training.

уче́бник, а *m.* textbook.

уче́бн|ый *adj.*
1 educational; school; **у. год** academic year, school year; **~ое заведе́ние** educational institution; **у. план** curriculum.
2 (*mil.*) training, practice; **~ая стрельба́** practice shoot.

уче́ни|е, я *nt.*
1 (*mil.*) exercise; (*pl.*) training.
2 (*система взглядов*) teaching, doctrine.

учени́к, а́ *m.*
1 (*школы*) pupil.
2 (*в ремесле*) apprentice.
3 (*последователь*) disciple, follower.

учени́ц|а, ы *f. of* ▸ **учени́к**

учён|ый (~, ~а) *adj.*
1 (*человек*) learned, erudite; (*coll.*) educated.
2 (*научный*) scholarly; academic; **~ая сте́пень** higher (university) degree (*PhD or higher*).
3 *in titles of certain academic posts and institutions*: **у. сове́т** academic council.
4 *as n.* **у., ~ого** *m.* scholar; (*в университете*) academic; (*в области естественных наук*) scientist.

уч|е́сть, учту́, учтёшь, *past* **~ёл, ~ла́** *pf.* (*of* ▸ **~и́тывать**)
1 (*обстоятельства*) to take into account, consideration.
2 (*товары*) to take stock (of), make an inventory (of).

учёт, а *m.*
1 (*действие*) accounting; **бухга́лтерский у.** accounting, bookkeeping; (*товаров*) stocktaking, inventory-making; (*определение*) calculation.

[2] (*обстоятельств*) taking into account; **без ~а** (+ *g.*) disregarding.
[3] (*регистрация*) registration; **взять на у.** to register.

учи́лищ|е, а *nt.* school, college (*providing specialist instruction at secondary level*); **вое́нное у.** military school.

учи́тел|ь, я *m.*
[1] (*pl.* **~я́**) teacher.
[2] (*pl.* **~и**) (*fig.*) teacher, master (= *authority*).

учи́тельниц|а, ы *f. of* ▸ **учи́тель**

учи́тельск|ая, ой *f.* staff (common) room.

учи́тыва|ть, ю *impf. of* ▸ **уче́сть**

уч|и́ть, у́, ~́ишь *impf.*
[1] (*pf.* **вы́~, на~** *and* **об~**) (+ *a. and d. or* + *inf.*) (*преподавать*) to teach; **у. кого́-н. неме́цкому языку́** to teach s.o. German; **у. игра́ть на скри́пке** to teach to play the violin.
[2] *no pf.* (*быть учителем*) to be a teacher.
[3] **(что)** (*о теории*) to teach (that), say (that).
[4] (*pf.* **вы́~**) (+ *a.*) (*усваивать, запоминать*) to learn; to memorize.

уч|и́ться, у́сь, ~́ишься *impf.*
[1] (*pf.* **вы́~, на~** *and* **об~**) (+ *d. or* + *inf.*) to learn, study.
[2] (*быть студентом*) to be a student; **у. в шко́ле** to go to, be at school.
[3] (*pf.* **вы́~**) (**на кого́-н.;** *coll.*) to study (to be, to become), learn (to be).

учреди́тел|ь, я *m.* founder.

учре|ди́ть, жу́, ди́шь *pf.* (*of* ▸ **~жда́ть**) (*основать*) to found, establish, set up; (*ввести*) to introduce, institute.

учрежда́|ть, ю *impf. of* ▸ **учреди́ть**

учрежде́ни|е, я *nt.*
[1] (*школы, организации*) founding, establishment, setting up; (*ордена*) introduction.
[2] (*заведение*) establishment, institution.

учти́в|ый (~, ~а) *adj.* civil, courteous.

уша́нк|а, и *f.* (*coll.*) cap with ear flaps.

у́ши *see* ▸ **у́хо**

ушиб, а *m.* bruise.

ушиб|и́ть, у́, ёшь, *past* **~́, ~́ла** *pf.* to injure (*by knocking*); (*до синяка*) to bruise.

ушиб|и́ться, у́сь, ёшься, *past* **~́ся, ~́лась** *pf.* to hurt o.s.; to bruise o.s.

ушива́|ть, ю *impf. of* ▸ **уши́ть**

уш|и́ть, ью́, ьёшь *pf.* (*of* ▸ **~ива́ть**) (*dressmaking*) to take in.

ушк|о́, а́, *pl.* **~и́, ~о́в** *nt.* (*у иголки*) eye.

уще́л|ье, ья, *g. pl.* **~ий** *nt.* ravine, gorge.

ущем|и́ть, лю́, и́шь *pf.* (*of* ▸ **~ля́ть**)
[1] (*стеснить*) to limit.
[2] (*оскорбить*) to wound, hurt; **у. чьё-н. самолю́бие** to hurt s.o.'s pride.

ущемле́ни|е, я *nt.* (*fig.*)
[1] (*прав*) limitation.
[2] (*самолюбия*) wounding, hurting.

ущемля́|ть, ю *impf. of* ▸ **ущеми́ть**

уще́рб, а *m.* (*убыток*) detriment; loss; (*вред*) damage, injury; **без ~а (для** + *g.*) without prejudice (to); **в у.** (+ *d.*) to the detriment (of).

ущипн|у́ть, у́, ёшь *pf. of* ▸ **щипа́ть 1**

Уэ́льс, а *m.* Wales.

уэ́льс|ец, ца *m.* Welshman.

уэ́льский *adj.* Welsh.

ую́т, а *m.* cosiness (*Br.*), coziness (*US*).

ую́т|ный (~ен, ~на) *adj.* cosy (*Br.*), cozy (*US*).

уязви́м|ый (~, ~а) *adj.* vulnerable (*also fig.*); **~ое ме́сто** (*fig.*) weak spot.

уязв|и́ть, лю́, и́шь *pf.* (*of* ▸ **~ля́ть**) to wound, hurt.

уязвля́|ть, ю *impf. of* ▸ **уязви́ть**

уясн|и́ть, ю́, и́шь *pf.* (*of* ▸ **~я́ть**) **(себе́, для себя́)** to comprehend.

уясн|я́ть, я́ю *impf. of* ▸ **~и́ть**

Фф

фа *nt. indecl.* (*mus.*) F.

фа́брик|а, и *f.* factory; (*бумажная*) mill.

фабрика́нт, а *m.* manufacturer, factory owner, mill owner.

фабрик|ова́ть, у́ю *impf.* (*of* **с~**) (*fig.*) to fabricate.

фабри́чн|ый *adj.*
[1] factory; manufacturing; **~ое произво́дство** manufacturing.
[2] (*произведённый на фабрике*) factory-made.

фа́бул|а, ы *f.* (*liter.*) plot, story.

фавори́т, а *m.* favourite (*Br.*), favorite (*US*) (*also sport*).

фавори́т|ка, ки *f. of* ▸ **~**

фаго́т, а *m.* (*mus.*) bassoon.

фаготи́ст, а *m.* bassoon player.

фаготи́ст|ка, ки *f. of* ▸ **~**

фа́з|а, ы *f.* phase; stage.

фаза́н, а *m.* pheasant.

файл, а *m.* (*comput.*) file.

фа́кел, а *m.* torch, flare.

факи́р, а *m.* fakir.

факс, а *m.* fax; **посла́ть по ~у** to fax.

факси́миле *nt. indecl.* facsimile.

факт, а *m.* fact.

факти́чески *adv.* in fact, actually.

факти́ческ|ий *adj.* actual; real; virtual; **~ие да́нные** the facts.

фа́ктор, а *m.* factor.

факту́р|а, ы *f.*
[1] (*строение материала*) texture.
[2] (*comm.*) (*usu.* **счёт-ф.**) invoice, bill.

факультати́в|ный (~ен, ~на) *adj.* optional.

факультéт, а *m.* faculty, department.

фала́нг|а, и *f.* (*anat.*; *mil.*, *also hist.*) phalanx.

фа́ллос, а *m.* phallus.

фальсифика́ци|я, и *f.*
1 (*подделывание*) falsification.
2 (*поддельный предмет*) forgery, fake, counterfeit.

фальсифици́р|овать, ую *impf. and pf.*
1 (*историю*) to falsify.
2 (*вино*) to adulterate.

фальцéт, а *m.* (*mus.*) falsetto.

фальшивомонéтчик, а *m.* counterfeiter.

фальши́в|ый (~, ~а) *adj.*
1 (*зубы, волосы*) false; (*документ*) forged, fake; (*жемчуг*) artificial, imitation.
2 (*неискренний*) false; insincere; **ф. комплимéнт** insincere compliment.
3 (*mus.*) out of tune.

фами́ли|я, и *f.*
1 surname.
2 (*род*) family, kin.

фами́льный *adj.* family.

фамилья́р|ный (~ен, ~на) *adj.* overfamiliar; unceremonious.

фана́т, а *m.* (*coll.*) fan.

фанати́зм, а *m.* fanaticism.

фана́тик, а *m.* fanatic.

фанати́ч|ный (~ен, ~на) *adj.* fanatical.

фана́тк|а, и *f. of* ▸ **фана́т;** (*сопровождающая популярных музыкантов*) groupie.

фанéр|а, ы *f.*
1 (*для облицовки*) veneer.
2 (*древесный материал*) plywood.

фантазёр, а *m.* dreamer, visionary.

фантази́р|овать, ую *impf.*
1 (*мечтать*) to dream, indulge in fantasies.
2 (*выдумывать*) to make up, dream up.

фанта́зи|я, и *f.*
1 (*воображение*) fantasy; imagination; **бога́тая ф.** fertile imagination.
2 (*мечта*) fantasy, fancy; **предава́ться ~ям** to indulge in fantasies.
3 (*выдумка*) fabrication.

фанта́ст, а *m.* fantasy writer; science fiction writer.

фанта́стик|а, и *f.* (*collect.*, *liter.*) fantasy; **нау́чная ф.** science fiction; sci-fi.

фантасти́ческий *adj.*
1 (*пейзаж, освещение*) fantastic, fabulous, unreal; (*новость, нахал*) fantastic, incredible.
2 (*литература*) fantasy.

фа́нтик, а *m.* (*coll.*) sweet wrapper.

фанто́м, а *m.* phantom.

фанфа́р|а, ы *f.* (*mus.*)
1 (*инструмент*) bugle.
2 (*торжественная фраза*) fanfare.

фа́р|а, ы *f.* headlight.

Фаренгéйт, а *m.* Fahrenheit; **32 гра́дуса/212 гра́дусов по ~у** (= *0°C/100°C*) 32/212 degrees Fahrenheit.

фаринги́т, а *m.* (*med.*) pharyngitis.

фарисé|й, я *m.* Pharisee (*also fig.*).

фармаколо́ги|я, и *f.* pharmacology.

фармацéвт, а *m.* pharmacist.

фармацевти́ческий *adj.* pharmaceutical.

фарс, а *m.* (*theatr.*) farce (*also fig.*).

фа́ртук, а *m.* apron.

фарфо́р, а *m.*
1 (*материал*) porcelain, china.
2 (*collect.*) (*посуда*) china.

фарш, а *m.* (*начинка*) stuffing; (*мясо*) minced meat.

фарши́р|ова́ть, у́ю *impf.* (*of* ▸ **за~**) (*cul.*) to stuff.

фас, а *m.* front.

фаса́д, а *m.* facade, front.

фасо́л|ь, и *f.* (*растение*) bean plant; (*collect.*) (*плод*) beans.

фасо́н, а *m.* cut; style.

фаталисти́ческий *adj.* fatalistic.

фата́л|ьный (~ен, ~ьна) *adj.* (*совпадение*) fateful; (*последствия*) fatal.

фа́ун|а, ы *f.* fauna.

фаши́зм, а *m.* Fascism.

фаши́ст, а *m.* Fascist.

фаши́ст|ка, ки *f. of* ▸ **~**

фаши́стский *adj.* Fascist.

ФБР *nt. indecl.* (*abbr. of* **Федера́льное бюро́ рассле́дований**) FBI (*Federal Bureau of Investigation*).

февра́л|ь, я́ *m.* February.

федера́льный *adj.* federal.

федерати́вный *adj.* federative, federal.

федера́ци|я, и *f.* federation.

фейервéрк, а *m.* firework(s); (*событие*) firework display.

фека́л|ии, ий *pl.* (*sg.* **~ия, ~ии** *f.*) faeces (*Br.*), feces (*US*).

фе́льдшер, а, *pl.* **~а́** *and* **~ы** *m.* medical assistant.

фельето́н, а *m.* satirical article.

фемини́зм, а *m.* feminism.

фемини́ст, а *m.* feminist.

фемини́ст|ка, ки *f. of* ▸ **~**

фен, а *m.* hairdryer.

фено́мен, а *m.* (*явление*) phenomenon; (*событие, человек*) marvel.

феномена́л|ьный (~ен, ~ьна) *adj.* phenomenal.

феодали́зм, а *m.* feudalism.

феода́льный *adj.* feudal.

ферз|ь, я́, *pl.* **~и́, ~е́й** *m.* (*chess*) queen.

фе́рм|а, ы *f.* farm.

фермéнт, а *m.* enzyme.

фе́рмер, а *m.* farmer.

фестива́л|ь, я *m.* festival.

фети́ш, а *m.* fetish.

фетр, а *m.* felt.

фехтова́ни|е, я *nt.* fencing.

фешенéбел|ьный (~ен, ~ьна) *adj.* fashionable.

фé|я, и *f.* fairy.

фиа́лк|а, и *f.* violet.

фиа́ско *nt. indecl.* fiasco, failure.

фибро́м|а, ы *f.* (*med.*) fibroma.

фи́г|а, и *f.* (*coll.*) fig (*gesture of derision or contempt, consisting of thumb placed between* *index and middle fingers*); **показа́ть кому́-н. ~у** *to make this gesture* (*cf.* to cock a snook, give the V-sign); **получи́ть ~у** to get nothing.

фигн|я́, и́ *f.* (*sl.*) rubbish.

фигу́р|а, ы *f.*
1 figure.
2 (*в шахматах*) piece, chessman (*excluding pawns*).

фигура́л|ьный (~ен, ~ьна) *adj.* figurative, metaphorical.

фигури́ст, а *m.* figure skater.

фигури́ст|ка, ки *f. of* ▸ **~**

фигу́рн|ый *adj.*
1 figured; ornamented.
2 : **~ое ката́ние (на конька́х)** figure skating.

Фи́джи *indecl.* Fiji.

фи́зик, а *m.* physicist.

фи́зик|а, и *f.* physics.

физио́лог, а *m.* physiologist.

физиологи́ческий *adj.* physiological.

физиоло́ги|я, и *f.* physiology.

физионо́ми|я, и *f.* (*coll.*) face; physiognomy (*also joc.*).

физиотерапе́вт, а *m.* physiotherapist.

физиотерапи́|я, и *f.* physiotherapy.

физи́ческ|ий *adj.*
1 physical; **~ая культу́ра** physical training, gymnastics; **ф. труд** manual labour (*Br.*), labor (*US*).
2 *adj. of* ▸ **фи́зика; ф. кабине́т** physics laboratory.

физкульту́р|а, ы *f.* physical training (*abbr.* PT); physical education (*abbr.* PE); **уро́к ~ы** PE lesson; **лече́бная ф.** exercise therapy.

физкульту́рный *adj.* gymnastic; athletic, sports; **ф. зал** gymnasium.

фикси́р|овать, ую *impf. and pf.* (*pf. also* **за~**)
1 (*регистрировать*) to record (*in writing, etc.*).
2 (*внимание, взгляд*) to fix, direct.

фикти́в|ный (~ен, ~на) *adj.* fictitious; **ф. брак** marriage of convenience.

фи́кус, а *m.* (*bot.*) ficus; rubber plant.

филантро́п, а *m.* philanthropist.

филармо́ни|я, и *f.* philharmonic society; (*зал*) concert hall.

филе́ *nt. indecl.* (*cul.*)
1 (*мясо высшего сорта*) fillet.
2 (*кусок мяса или рыбы без костей*) fillet.

филиа́л, а *m.* branch (*of an organization*).

филиппи́н|ец, ца *m.* Filipino.

филиппи́н|ка, ки *f. of* ▸ **~ец**

филиппи́нский *adj.* Philippine; (*язык*) Filipino.

Филиппи́н|ы, ~ *no sg.* the Philippines.

фило́лог, а *m.* philologist.

филологи́ческий *adj.* philological.

филоло́ги|я, и *f.* philology.

фило́соф, а *m.* philosopher.

филосо́фи|я, и *f.* philosophy.

филосо́фский *adj.* philosophic(al).

филосо́фств|овать, ую *impf.* to philosophize.

фильм, а *m.* (*cin.*) film, movie.

фильтр, а *m.* filter.

фильтр|ова́ть, у́ю *impf.* (*of* ▸ **про~** *and* ▸ **от~**) to filter.

фина́л, а *m.*
1 (*спектакля*) finale.
2 (*sport*) final.

финали́ст, а *m.* finalist.

финали́ст|ка, ки *f. of* ▸ **~**

фина́льный *adj.* final; **ф. акко́рд** (*mus.*) final chord; **ф. матч** (*sport*) final.

финанси́р|овать, ую *impf. and pf.* to finance.

финанси́ст, а *m.*
1 (*предприниматель*) financier.
2 (*специалист по финансовым наукам*) financial expert.

фина́нсовый *adj.* financial; **ф. год** fiscal year; **ф. отде́л** finance department.

фина́нс|ы, ов *no sg.* finance(s).

фи́ник, а *m.* date (*fruit*).

фи́ниш, а *m.* (*sport*) finish.

фи́нк|а, и *f. of* ▸ **финн**

Финля́нди|я, и *f.* Finland.

финн, а *m.* Finn.

фи́нский *adj.* Finnish; **Ф. зали́в** Gulf of Finland.

фиоле́товый *adj.* violet.

фи́рм|а, ы *f.* (*econ.*) firm.

фи́рм|енный *adj. of* ▸ **~а;** (*хорошего качества*) high-quality; **~енная этике́тка** proprietary label; **ф. бланк** letterhead; **~енное блю́до** speciality dish.

фисгармо́ни|я, и *f.* (*mus.*) harmonium.

фиска́льный *adj.* (*fin.*) fiscal.

фити́л|ь, я́ *m.* (*лампы, свечи*) wick; (*для воспламенения зарядов*) fuse.

фи́шинг, а *m.* (*comput.*) phishing (*practice of sending out emails in the name of reputable companies in order to induce people to reveal personal information*).

флаг, а *m.* flag.

флагшто́к, а *m.* flagstaff.

флако́н, а *m.* (scent) bottle.

фламе́нко *nt. indecl.* flamenco.

флами́нго *m. indecl.* flamingo.

фланг, а *m.* (*mil.*) flank.

флане́л|ь, и *f.* flannel.

флегма́тик, а *m.* phlegmatic person.

флегмати́ч|ный (~ен, ~на) *adj.* phlegmatic.

фле́йт|а, ы *f.* flute.

флейти́ст, а *m.* flautist.

флейти́ст|ка, ки *f. of* ▸ **~**

фли́гел|ь, я, *pl.* **~я́, ~е́й** *m.*
1 (*пристройка*) wing (*of building*).
2 (*отдельное здание*) outbuilding.

флирт|ова́ть, у́ю *impf.* (**с** + *i.*) to flirt (with).

флома́стер, а *m.* felt-tip pen, marker.

фло́р|а, ы *f.* flora.

Флори́д|а, ы *f.* Florida.

флот, а *m.*
1 fleet; **вое́нно-морско́й ф.** navy.
2 : **возду́шный ф.** (air) fleet.

флю́гер, а, *pl.* **~а́** *m.* weathervane.

фля́г|а, и *f.*

ф

1 flask; (*mil.*) water bottle.
2 (*для молока*) churn.

фо́би|я, и *f.* phobia.

фойе́ *nt. indecl.* foyer.

фокстерье́р, а *m.* fox terrier.

фо́кус[1], **а** *m.* (*phys.*) focus (*also fig.*).

фо́кус[2], **а** *m.* (*трюк*) (conjuring) trick; **пока́зывать ~ы** to do conjuring tricks.

фо́кус-гру́пп|а, ы *f.* focus group.

фокуси́р|овать, ую *impf.* (*of* ▶ **с~**) (*phys.*) to focus; (*fig.*) (**на** + *p.*) to focus (on).

фокуси́р|оваться, уюсь *impf.* (*of* ▶ **с~**) (**на** + *p.*) to focus (on), be focussed (on).

фо́кусник, а *m.* conjuror, juggler.

фольг|а́, и́ *f.* foil.

фолькло́р, а *m.* folklore.

фон, а *m.*
1 background (*also fig.*).
2 (*помехи*) background noise.

фона́рик, а *m.* small lamp; torch (*Br.*), flashlight (*US*).

фона́р|ный *adj. of* ▶ **~ь; ф. столб** lamp post.

фона́р|ь, я́ *m.* (*с ручкой*) lantern; (*уличный*) lamp; light.

фонд, а *m.*
1 (*fin.*) fund; stock, reserves, resources; **валю́тный ф.** currency reserves; **золото́й ф.** gold reserves; **о́бщий ф.** pool.
2 (*pl.*) (*fin.*) (*ценные бумаги*) stocks; (*fig., obs.*) stock.
3 (*организация*) fund, foundation.
4 (*архив*) archive.

фо́нд|овый *adj. of* ▶ **~; ~овая би́ржа** stock exchange.

фоне́тик|а, и *f.* phonetics.

фонта́н, а *m.* fountain; (*fig.*) stream; **нефтяно́й ф.** oil gusher; **бить ~ом** to gush forth.

форе́л|ь, и *f.* trout.

фо́рм|а, ы *f.*
1 form; **по ~е, ... по содержа́нию** in form, ... in content.
2 (*для выпечки*) cake tin; shape.
3 (*tech.*) (*внешнее очертание*) mould (*Br.*), mold (*US*), cast; **отли́ть в ~у** to mould (*Br.*), mold (*US*), cast.
4 (*одежда*) uniform.
5 : **быть в ~е** (*coll.*) to be in (good) form.

форма́льност|ь, и *f.* formality.

форма́л|ьный (~ен, ~ьна) *adj.* formal.

форма́т, а *m.* format.

формати́р|овать, ую *impf.* (*of* ▶ **от~**) (*comput.*) to format.

фо́рменный *adj.*
1 (*платье, фуражка*) uniform.
2 (*coll.*) (*настоящий*) proper, regular, positive.

формир|ова́ть, у́ю *impf.* (*of* ▶ **с~**) to form; to organize; **ф. хара́ктер** to form character; **ф. батальо́н** to raise a battalion.

формир|ова́ться, у́юсь *impf.* (*of* ▶ **с~**)
1 to form, develop (*intrans.*).
2 *pass. of* ▶ **~ова́ть**

фо́рмул|а, ы *f.* formula; formulation.

формули́р|овать, ую *impf. and pf.* (*pf. also* **с~**) to formulate.

формулиро́вк|а, и *f.*
1 formulation.
2 (*сформулированная мысль*) wording.

форпо́ст, а *m.* (*mil.*) advanced post; outpost (*also fig.*).

форс-мажо́р, а *m.* (*also* **~ные обстоя́тельства**) force majeure.

форт, а, о ~́е, в ~у́, *pl.* **~ы́** *m.* (*mil.*) fort.

форте|пиа́но *and* **~пья́но** *nt. indecl.* piano.

фо́рточк|а, и *f.* little window (*small hinged pane for ventilation in windows of Russian houses*).

фо́рум, а *m.* forum.

фосфа́т, а *m.* (*chem.*) phosphate.

фо́сфор, а *m.* phosphorus.

фо́то *nt. indecl.* (*coll.*) photo.

фото... *comb. form* photo-.

фотоальбо́м, а *m.* photograph album.

фотоаппара́т, а *m.* camera.

фотогени́ч|ный (~ен, ~на) *adj.* photogenic.

фото́граф, а *m.* photographer.

фотографи́р|овать, ую *impf.* (*of* ▶ **с~**) to photograph.

фотографи́р|оваться, уюсь *impf.* (*of* ▶ **с~**) to be photographed, have one's photo taken.

фотографи́ческий *adj.* photographic.

фотогра́фи|я, и *f.*
1 (*получение изображений*) photography.
2 (*снимок*) photograph.

фотокопирова́льный *adj.*: **ф. аппара́т** photocopier.

фотоко́пи|я, и *f.* photocopy.

фоторо́бот, а *m.* identikit (*propr.*) (picture).

фотоси́нтез, а *m.* (*bot.*) photosynthesis.

фотоэлеме́нт, а *m.* (*elec.*) photoelectric cell.

фрагме́нт, а *m.* fragment; detail (*of painting, etc.*); **ф. фи́льма** film clip.

фра́з|а, ы *f.*
1 (*предложение*) sentence.
2 (*выражение*) phrase.

фразеологи́ческий *adj.* phraseological; **ф. оборо́т** idiom; **ф. слова́рь** dictionary of idioms.

фрак, а *m.* tailcoat, tails.

фра́кци|я, и *f.* (*pol.*) fraction; faction, group.

фраму́г|а, и *f.* transom.

франкоязы́чный *adj.* francophone.

франт, а *m.* dandy.

Фра́нци|я, и *f.* France.

францу́женк|а, и *f.* Frenchwoman.

францу́з, а *m.* Frenchman.

францу́зский *adj.* French.

фрахт, а *m.* freight.

фрахт|ова́ть, у́ю *impf.* (*of* ▶ **за~**) to charter.

фрега́т, а *m.*
1 (*naut.*) frigate.
2 (*zool.*) frigate bird.

фре́зерный *adj.* (*tech.*) milling; **ф. стано́к** milling machine.

фрео́н|ы, ов *m. pl.* (*sg.* **~, ~а**) CFCs (*abbr.*

Ф

of chlorofluorocarbons).

фре́ск|а, и *f.* fresco.

фриво́л|ьный (~ен, ~ьна) *adj.* frivolous.

фриги́д|ный (~ен, ~на) *adj.* (*med.*) frigid.

фрикаде́льк|а, и *f.* (*мясная*) meatball; (*рыбная*) fishball (*in soup*).

фронт, а, *pl.* **~ы́** *m.* (*mil., meteor.; fig.*) front; **на два ~́а** on two fronts.

фрукт, а *m.* fruit; (*pl.*) fruit (*collect.*).

фрукто́вый *adj.* fruit; **ф. сад** orchard.

ФСБ *f. indecl.* (*abbr. of* **Федера́льная слу́жба безопа́сности**) Federal Security Service.

фтори́д, а *m.* fluoride.

фу́г|а, и *f.* (*mus.*) fugue.

фуга́с, а *m.* (*mil.*) landmine.

фуже́р, а *m.* tall wineglass.

фунда́мент, а *m.* foundation, base (*also fig.*).

фундаментали́зм, а *m.* fundamentalism.

фундаментали́ст, а *m.* fundamentalist.

фундамента́л|ьный (~ен, ~ьна) *adj.*
1 (*прочный*) solid, sound; (*основательный*) thorough(going).
2 (*основной, главный*) main, basic.

фуникулёр, а *m.* funicular (railway).

фу́нкци|я, и *f.* function.

фунт¹, а *m.* (*английская мера*) pound (*equivalent to 453.6 grams*).

фунт², а *m.* (*fin.*): **ф. (сте́рлингов)** pound (sterling).

фунциони́р|овать, ую *impf.* to function.

фу́р|а, ы *f.* (*фургон*) van; (*прицеп*) (truck) trailer.

фура́жк|а, и *f.* peak cap; (*mil.*) service cap.

фурго́н, а *m.* van.

фурниту́р|а, ы *f.* accessories.

фуро́р, а *m.* furore.

фут, а *m.* foot (*measure of length, = 30.48 cm*).

футбо́л, а *m.* football (*Br.*), soccer.

футболи́ст, а *m.* football player (*Br.*), soccer player.

футбо́лк|а, и *f.* T-shirt.

футбо́л|ьный *adj. of* ▸**~**; **~ьные бу́тсы** football boots; **ф. мяч** football.

футля́р, а *m.* case; **ф. для очко́в** spectacle case; **ф. для скри́пки** violin case.

футури́зм, а *m.* futurism.

футури́ст, а *m.* futurist.

фы́рк|ать, аю *impf.* (*of* ▸**~нуть**)
1 (*о животном; о машине*) to snort.
2 (*fig., coll.*) (*брюзжать*) to grouse.

фы́рк|нуть, ну, нешь *inst. pf. of* ▸**~ать**

фэн-шу́й *m. & nt. indecl.* feng shui.

фюзеля́ж, а *m.* fuselage.

ха́кер, а *m.* (*comput.*) hacker.

ха́ки *indecl.*
1 *adj.* khaki.
2 *n.*; *nt.* khaki.

хала́т, а *m.*
1 (*домашний*) dressing gown; (*купальный*) bathrobe.
2 (*рабочий*) overall; **до́кторский х.** doctor's smock.
3 (*восточный*) robe.

хала́т|ный (~ен, ~на) *adj.* careless, negligent.

халту́р|а, ы *f.* (*coll.*)
1 (*небрежная работа*) poor-quality work.
2 (*работа на стороне*) work done on the side; (*деньги*) money earned on the side.

халя́в|а, ы *f.*: **на ~у** (*sl.*) free of charge; for free.

хам, а *m.* (*coll.*) boor, lout.

хамелео́н, а *m.* chameleon (*also fig.*).

хам|и́ть, лю́, и́шь *impf.* (*of* **на~**) (+ *d.*) to be rude (to).

ха́мств|о, а *nt.* (*coll.*) boorishness, loutishness.

хандр|а́, ы́ *f.* depression.

ханж|а́, и́, *g. pl.* **~е́й** *c.g.* sanctimonious person; hypocrite.

ха́нжеский *adj.* sanctimonious; hypocritical.

Хано́|й, я *m.* Hanoi.

ха́ос, а *m.* chaos.

хаоти́ческий *adj.* chaotic.

хаоти́ч|ный (~ен, ~на) *adj.* = **~еский**

хара́ктер, а *m.*
1 (*человека*) character, personality; **они́ не сошли́сь ~ами** they could not get on (together).
2 (*твёрдый характер*) (strong) character; **челове́к с ~ом** determined person, strong character.
3 (*свойство*) character, type; **х. рабо́ты** type of work.

характери́стик|а, и *f.*
1 (*описание*) description.
2 (*отзыв*) reference.

характе́рно *as pred.* it is characteristic; it is typical.

характе́р|ный (~ен, ~на) *adj.*
1 (*свойственный*) characteristic; typical; **э́то для него́ ~но** it is typical of him.
2 (*своеобразный*) distinctive.

хари́зм|а, ы *f.* charisma.

харизмати́ческий *adj.* charismatic.

ха́рк|ать, аю *impf.* (*of* ▸**~нуть**) (*coll.*) to

spit, expectorate; **х. кро́вью** to spit blood.
ха́рк|нуть, ну, нешь *pf. of* ▶ **~ать**
ха́рти|я, и *f.* charter.
харчо́ *nt. indecl.* kharcho (*Caucasian highly seasoned mutton soup*).
ха́р|я, и *f.* (*sl.*) mug (= *face*).
ха́т|а, ы *f.*
1 peasant house (*in Southern Russia, Ukraine, and Byelorussia*); **моя́ х. с кра́ю** it's no concern of mine; that's your, their, *etc.*, funeral.
2 (*sl.*) home, 'pad'.
хвале́б|ный (~ен, ~на) *adj.* laudatory, eulogistic.
хвал|и́ть, ю́, ~́ишь *impf.* (*of* ▶ **по~**) to praise.
хва́ста|ться, юсь *impf.* (*of* ▶ **по~**) (+ *i.*) to boast (of).
хвастли́в|ый (~, ~а) *adj.* boastful.
хвастовств|о́, а́ *nt.* boasting.
хват|а́ть[1], а́ю *impf.* (*of* ▶ **схвати́ть 1**)
1 to snatch, seize, catch hold (of); to grab, grasp.
2 (*impf. only*) (*coll.*) (*вора*) to pick up.
хват|а́ть[2], а́ет *impf.* (*of* ▶ **~и́ть**) *impers.* (+ *g.*) (*быть достаточным*) to suffice, be enough; to last out; **у меня́,** *etc.*, **не ~а́ет** I, *etc.*, am short (of); **у нас не ~а́ет де́нег** we have not enough money; **э́того ещё не ~а́ло!** that's all we, *etc.* need!
хват|а́ться, а́юсь *impf.* (*of* ▶ **схвати́ться 1**) (**за** + *a.*)
1 to snatch (at), catch (at); **х. за соло́минку** to clutch at straws.
2 (*приниматься за дело*) to start doing, take up.
хват|и́ть, ~́ит *pf.* (*of* ▶ **~а́ть[2]**); **~́ит!** that will do!; that's enough!; **с меня́ ~́ит!** I've had enough!
хва|ти́ться, чу́сь, ~́тишься *pf.* (+ *g.*; *coll.*) to miss, notice the absence (of); **по́здно ~ти́лись!** you thought of it too late!
хва́тк|а, и *f.* grasp, grip.
хво́йн|ый *adj.*
1 *adj. of* ▶ **хво́я.**
2 (*дерево*) coniferous; *as n.* **~ые, ~ых** (*bot.*) conifers.
хвора́|ть, ю *impf.* (*coll.*) to be ill (*Br.*), sick (*US*).
хво́рост, а *m.* (*collect.*)
1 (*ветки*) brushwood.
2 (*cul.*) (pastry) straws, twiglets.
хвост, а́ *m.*
1 tail (*also fig.*); **маха́ть ~о́м** to wag one's tail.
2 (*fig.*) (*задняя часть*) tail, rear, tail end; **быть, плести́сь в ~е́** to get behind, lag behind.
хвоста́т|ый (~, ~а) *adj.*
1 (*имеющий хвост*) having a tail; caudate.
2 (*с большим хвостом*) having a large tail.
хво́стик, а *m. dim. of* ▶ **хвост;** (*причёска*) ponytail.
хво́|я, и *f.*
1 needle(s) (*of conifer*).
2 (*collect.*) (*ветви*) branches (*of conifer*).
Хе́льсинки *m. indecl.* Helsinki.
хеппи-э́нд, а *m.* happy ending.
хер, ~́а́, ~́у *m.* (*sl.*) *euph. of* ▶ **хуй**
хе́рес, а *m.* sherry.
хи́жин|а, ы *f.* shack, hut.
хи́л|ый (~, ~́а́, ~о) *adj.* weak, sickly; puny.
химе́р|а, ы *f.* chimera.
хи́мик, а *m.* chemist.
химика́т|ы, ов *pl.* (*sg.* **~, ~а** *m.*) chemicals.
химиотерапи́|я, и *f.* chemotherapy.
хими́ческ|ий *adj.*
1 chemical; **~ие препара́ты** chemicals; **~ая чи́стка (оде́жды)** dry-cleaning; **х. элеме́нт** chemical element.
2 chemistry; **х. кабине́т** chemistry laboratory.
хи́ми|я, и *f.* chemistry.
химчи́стк|а, и *f.* dry-cleaner's.
хи́нди *m. indecl.* Hindi (*language*).
хи́ппи *c.g. indecl.* hippy.
хирома́нти|я, и *f.* palmistry.
хиру́рг, а *m.* surgeon.
хирурги́ческий *adj.* surgical.
хирурги́|я, и *f.* surgery.
хит, а́ *m.* (*coll.*) (*mus. etc.*) hit.
хит-пара́д, а *m.* (*mus.*) the charts.
хитре́ц, а́ *m.* cunning person; (*coll.*) slyboots.
хитр|и́ть, ю́, и́шь *impf.* (*of* ▶ **с~**) to use cunning, guile; to dissemble.
хи́трост|ь, и *f.*
1 (*свойство*) cunning, slyness.
2 (*уловка*) ruse, stratagem.
хитроу́м|ный (~ен, ~на) *adj.*
1 (*изобретательный*) cunning; resourceful.
2 (*сложный*) intricate, complicated.
хи́т|рый (~ёр, ~ра́, ~́ро́) *adj.*
1 (*лукавый*) cunning, sly.
2 (*coll.*) (*изобретательный*) cunning, resourceful.
3 (*coll.*) (*замысловатый*) intricate.
хихи́к|ать, аю *impf.* (*of* ▶ **~нуть**) to giggle, snigger.
хихи́к|нуть, ну, нешь *inst. pf. of* ▶ **~ать**
хище́ни|е, я *nt.* theft; embezzlement, misappropriation.
хи́щник, а *m.* predator; (*животное*) beast of prey; (*птица*) bird of prey.
хи́щ|ный (~ен, ~на) *adj.*
1 predatory; **~ные зве́ри, пти́цы** beasts of prey, birds of prey.
2 (*fig.*) rapacious, grasping.
хладнокро́ви|е, я *nt.* composure, sangfroid.
хладнокро́в|ный (~ен, ~на) *adj.* cool, composed; (*жестокий*) cold-blooded.
хлам, а *m.* (*collect.*) rubbish, trash.
хлеб, а, *pl.* **~́ы** *and* **~а́** *m.*
1 (*sg. only*) bread (*also fig.*).
2 (*pl.* **~́ы**) (*буханка*) loaf.
3 (*pl.* **~а́**) (*семена злаков*) bread grain; (*usu. pl.*) (*злаки*) corn, crops; cereals.
хле́б|ец, ца *m.* rusk, dry toast.
хле́бниц|а, ы *f.* bread basket.
хлебн|у́ть, у́, ёшь *pf.* (*coll.*)
1 (*выпить*) to drink down.
2 (+ *g.*) (*перенести*) to go through, endure, experience.
хле́бн|ый *adj.*

1 *adj. of* ▸ **хлеб 1; ~ые дро́жжи** baker's yeast; **х. магази́н** baker's shop.
2 *adj. of* ▸ **хлеб 3; х. амба́р** granary.
3 (*урожайный*) rich (*in grain*); abundant; grain-producing.

хлебозаво́д, а *m.* bread-baking plant, bakery.

хлеборо́б, а *m.* peasant (engaged in arable farming).

хлев, а, в ~е *or* **в ~у́,** *pl.* **~а́** *m.* cowshed; (*fig., coll.*) pigsty.

хле|ста́ть, щу́, ~щешь *impf.* (*of* ▸ **~стну́ть**)
1 (+ *a. or* **по** + *d.*) to lash; to whip.
2 (*о дожде*) to lash (down), beat (down), pour; to stream, gush.

хлест|ну́ть, ну́, нёшь *inst. pf. of* ▸ **~а́ть**

хли́п|кий (~ок, ~ка́, ~ко) *adj.* (*coll.*)
1 (*стол, мост*) rickety.
2 (*fig.*) (*человек, здоровье*) weak, fragile.

хло́па|ть, ю *impf.* (*of* ▸ **хло́пнуть**)
1 (+ *i. or* **по** + *d.*) to bang; to slap; **х. кали́ткой** to bang the gate; **х. кого́-н. по спине́** to slap s.o. on the back.
2: **х. (в ладо́ши)** (+ *d.*) to clap, applaud.

хлопкоро́б, а *m.* cotton grower.

хло́п|нуть, ну, нешь *inst. pf. of* ▸ **~ать**

хло́п|ок, ка *m.* cotton; **х.-сыре́ц** raw cotton.

хлоп|о́к, ка́ *m.* (*в ладоши*) clap; (*выстрела*) bang.

хло́пот|ы, хлопо́т, ~ам *no sg.*
1 (*занятия по дому, по работе*) jobs, chores; (*заботы*) trouble.
2 (**о** + *p.*) (*старания добиться чего-н.*) efforts (on behalf of, for); pains.

хлопу́шк|а, и *f.* (Christmas) cracker.

хлопчатобума́жный *adj.* cotton.

хло́пь|я, ев *no sg.* flakes (*of snow, etc., also of certain cereal foods*); **кукуру́зные х., пшени́чные х.** corn flakes.

хлор, а *m.* (*chem.*) chlorine.

хлы́н|уть, у, ешь *pf.*
1 (*о крови, дожде*) to gush, pour.
2 (*fig.*) to pour, rush, surge; **толпа́ ~ула на пло́щадь** a crowd poured into the square.

хлыст, а́ *m.* (*прут*) whip, switch.

хлю́па|ть, ю *impf.* (*coll.*)
1 (*грязи*) to squelch; **х. по гря́зи** to squelch through the mud.
2 (*плача, всхлипывать*) to snivel; **х. но́сом** to sniff.

хля́стик, а *m.* half belt (*on back of coat*).

хмел|ь, я *m.* (*bot.*) (*семена*) hops; (*растение*) hop plant.

хму́р|ить, ю, ишь *impf.* (*of* ▸ **на~**): **х. бро́ви** to knit one's brows.

хму́р|иться, юсь, ишься *impf.* (*of* ▸ **на~**)
1 (*хмурить брови*) to frown.
2 (*о погоде, о дне*) to become gloomy; (*о небе*) to be overcast, cloudy.

хму́р|ый (~, ~а́, ~о) *adj.*
1 (*человек*) gloomy, sullen.
2 (*небо, день*) overcast, cloudy; **х. день** dull day.

хмы́ка|ть, ю *impf.* (*coll.*) to hem (*expr. surprise, annoyance, doubt, etc.*).

хо́бби *nt. indecl.* hobby.

хо́бот, а *m.* (*zool.*) trunk, proboscis.

ход, а (у), о ~е, в (на) ~е *and* **~у́** *m.*
1 **(в ~е, на ~у́)** motion, movement, travel, going; speed, pace; **три часа́ ~у** three hours' walk; **за́дний х.** backing, reversing; **дать х.** (+ *d.*) to set in motion, set going; **пойти́ в х.** to come to be widely used; **пусти́ть в х.** to start, set in motion, set going (*also fig.*), put into service.
2 **(в, на ~е)** (*fig.*) (*развитие*) course, progress; **х. мы́слей** train of thought; **х. собы́тий** course of events.
3 **(в ~е, на ~у́)** (*tech.*) work, operation, running; **на холосто́м ~у́** idling.
4 **(на ~е;** *pl.* **~ы́)** (*в шахматах*) move; (*в картах*) lead; **х. бе́лых** white's move.
5 **(в ~е;** *pl.* **~ы́)** (*fig.*) move, gambit; **ло́вкий х.** shrewd move.
6 **(в, на ~е** *and* **~у́;** *pl.* **~ы́)** (*путь*) passage(way), thoroughfare.

хода́тайств|о, а *nt.*
1 (*действие*) petitioning; entreaty, pleading.
2 (*просьба*) petition; application.

хо|ди́ть, жу́, ~дишь *impf.*
1 (*передвигаться, шагая*) to (be able to) walk.
2 (*indet. of* ▸ **идти́**) to go (*on foot*); **х. в кино́** to go to the cinema; **х. под па́русом** to go sailing.
3 (*о поездах*) to run.
4 (*о слухах, новостях*) to pass, go round.
5 (*в картах*) to lead, play; (*в шахматах*) to move; **х. ферзём** to move one's queen.
6 (**в** + *p.*) (*носить*) to wear.

ходу́л|и, ей/ь *pl.* (*sg.* **~я, ~и** *f.*) stilts.

ходьб|а́, ы́ *f.* walking; **це́рковь нахо́дится в пяти́ мину́тах ~ы́ отсю́да** the church is five minutes' walk from here.

ходя́ч|ий *adj.* walking; able to walk; **~ая энциклопе́дия** walking encyclopedia.

хозя́|ин, ина, *pl.* **~ева, ~ев** *m.*
1 (*владелец*) owner, proprietor.
2 (*своей судьбы; в доме*) master; (*предприятия*) boss.
3 (*по отношению к жильцу*) landlord.
4 (*по отношению к гостям*) host.

хозя́йк|а, и, *g. pl.* **хозя́ек** *f.*
1 (*владелица*) owner, proprietress.
2 (*своей судьбы; в доме*) mistress.
3 (*по отношению к жильцу*) landlady.
4 (*по отношению к гостям*) hostess.

хозя́йствен|ный (~, ~на) *adj.*
1 economic, of the economy; **~ная жизнь страны́** the country's economy.
2 (*товары, инвентарь*) household; home management.
3 (*экономный*) economical, thrifty.

хозя́йств|о, а *nt.*
1 (*экономика*) economy; **се́льское х.** agriculture; **дома́шнее х.** housekeeping; **вести́ х.** to manage, carry on management.
2 (*agric.*) farm, holding.
3 (*работы по дому*) housekeeping; **хлопота́ть по ~у** to be busy about the house.

хокке́ист, а *m.* hockey player.

хокке́ист|ка, ки *f. of* ▸ **~**

хокке́|й, я *m.* hockey; **х. с мячо́м, ру́сский х.** bandy; **х. с ша́йбой** ice hockey; **х. на траве́** hockey (*Br.*), field hockey (*US*).

холе́р|а, ы *f.* (*med.*) cholera.
холестери́н, а *m.* cholesterol.
холл, а *m.* hall, vestibule, foyer.
холм, а́ *m.* hill.
холми́ст|ый (~, ~а) *adj.* hilly.
хо́лод, а (у), *pl.* **~а́, ~о́в** *m.*
1 cold; coldness (*also fig.*); **ди́кий х.** bitter cold.
2 *pl.* cold (spell of) weather.
холода́|ть, ет *impf.* (*of* **по~;** *impers.*) (*становиться холоднее*) to turn cold.
холоде́|ть, ю *impf.* (*of* ▸ **по~**) (*руки*) to get cold.
холод|е́ц, ца́ *m.* (*cul.*) meat in jelly.
холоди́льник, а *m.* refrigerator; **ваго́н-х.** refrigerator van.
хо́лодно[1] *adv.* (*fig.*) coldly.
хо́лодно[2] *as pred.* it is cold; **мне,** *etc.*, **х.** I, *etc.*, am cold, feel cold.
холо́д|ный (хо́лоден, ~на́, хо́лодно, хо́лодны́) *adj.*
1 cold; **х. отве́т** cold reply; **х. по́яс** (*geog.*) frigid zone; **~ная война́** cold war; **~ное ору́жие** side arms, cold steel.
2 (*одежда*) light, thin.
холост|о́й (хо́лост, ~а́, хо́лосто) *adj.*
1 unmarried, single; bachelor.
2 (*tech.*) idle, free-running; **на ~о́м ходу́** idling.
3 (*mil.*) blank, dummy; **х. патро́н** blank cartridge.
холостя́к, а́ *m.* bachelor.
холст, а́ *m.*
1 (*ткань*) coarse linen, canvas, burlap.
2 (*art*) canvas.
холу́|й, я *m.* (*coll. obs. and fig., pej.*) lackey.
хому́т, а́ *m.*
1 (*на лошади*) collar.
2 (*tech.*) clamp, ring.
хомя́к, а́ *m.* hamster.
хор, а, *pl.* **~ы́** *m.*
1 choir.
2 (*mus. and fig.*) chorus; **~́ом** all together.
хора́л, а *m.* chorale.
хорва́т, а *m.* Croat.
Хорва́ти|я, и *f.* Croatia.
хорва́т|ка, ки *f. of* ▸ **~**
хорва́тский *adj.* Croatian, Croat.
хор|ёк, ька́ *m.* ferret.
хорео́граф, а *m.* choreographer.
хореогра́фи|я, и *f.* choreography.
хорово́д, а *m.* round dance (*traditional Slavonic folk dance*).
хорон|и́ть, ю́, ~́ишь *impf.* (*of* ▸ **по~** *and* ▸ **за~**) to bury (*also fig.*).
хоро́шенький *adj.* pretty, nice (*also iron.*).
хороше́нько *adv.* (*coll.*) properly, thoroughly, well and truly.
хоро́ш|ий (~, ~а́) *adj.*
1 good.
2 (*приятный*) nice.
3 (*short forms*) (*красивый*) pretty, good-looking.
хорошо́[1]
1 *adv.* well; nicely.
2 *particle* (*выражает согласие*) all right!; OK!
3 *n.*; *nt. indecl.* (*отметка*) good (*mark*).
хорошо́[2] *as pred.* it is good; it is nice; **х., что вы успе́ли прие́хать** it is good that you managed to come.
хо́спис, а *m.* hospice.
хот-до́г, а *m.* hot dog.
хоте́|ть, хочу́, хо́чешь, хо́чет, хоти́м, хоти́те, хотя́т *impf.* (*of* ▸ **за~**) (+ *g.*, *inf. or* **чтóбы**) to want, desire; **я ~л бы** I would like; **х. пить** to be thirsty; **х. сказа́ть** to mean; **е́сли хоти́те** if you like (*also = perhaps*).
хоте́|ться, хо́чется (*no pl. form*) *impf.* (*of* ▸ **за~**) (*impers.* + *d.*) to want; **мне хо́чется** I want; **мне ~лось бы** I would like.
хоть *conj. and particle*
1 *conj.* (*хотя*) although.
2 *conj.* (*даже если*) even if (*esp. in set phrr.*).
3 *particle* (*also* **х. бы**) (*по крайней мере*) at least, if only.
4 : **х. бы** if only.
хотя́ *conj.*
1 although, though.
2 : **х. бы** even if.
3 *as particle*: **х. бы** if only; **э́то я́вствует х. бы из заключи́тельной фра́зы его́ ре́чи** this is evident if only from the final sentence of his speech.
хо́хм|а, ы *f.* (*coll.*) joke, quip, gag.
хо́хот, а *m.* guffaw, loud laugh.
хохо|та́ть, чу́, ~́чешь *impf.* to guffaw, laugh loudly.
храбре́ц, а́ *m.* brave person.
хра́брост|ь, и *f.* bravery, courage.
хра́бр|ый (~, ~а́, ~о, ~́ы́) *adj.* brave, courageous.
храм, а *m.* temple, church, place of worship.
хране́ни|е, я *nt.* keeping, custody; storage, conservation; **ка́мера ~я** left luggage office (*Br.*), baggage room (*US*).
храни́лищ|е, а *nt.* storehouse, depository.
храни́тел|ь, я *m.*
1 keeper, custodian; (*fig.*) repository.
2 (*музея*) curator.
хран|и́ть, ю́, и́шь *impf.* (*старые письма, деньги в банке*) to keep; (*традиции, доброе имя*) to preserve; (*молчание, гордый вид*) to maintain; **х. в та́йне** to keep secret.

храни́т|ься, ~ся *impf.*
1 (*находиться*) to be, be kept.
2 (*быть в сохранности*) to be preserved.
храп|е́ть, лю́, и́шь *impf.*
1 to snore.
2 (*о лошади*) to snort.
хреб|е́т, та́ *m.*
1 (*anat.*) spine, spinal column; (*fig., coll.*) (*спина*) back.
2 (*горная цепь*) (mountain) range; ridge; (*fig.*) crest, peak.
хрен, а (у) *m.* horseradish; **х. с** (+ *i.*) (*coll.*) to hell (with); **ни ~а́** (*coll.*) bugger all.
хрен|о́вый *adj. of* ▸ **~;** (*coll.*) rotten, lousy.
хризанте́м|а, ы *f.* chrysanthemum.
хрип, а *m.* wheeze, wheezing sound.
хрип|е́ть, лю́, и́шь *impf.* to wheeze.
хри́пл|ый (~, ~́а́, ~о) *adj.* hoarse;

wheezy.
хрип|нуть, ну, нешь, *past* **~, ~ла** *impf.* (*of* ▶ **о~**) to become hoarse, lose one's voice.
христи|анин, анина, *pl.* **~áне, ~áн** *m.* Christian.
христиáн|ка, ки *f. of* ▶ **~ин**
христиáнский *adj.* Christian.
христиáнств|о, а *nt.* Christianity.
Христ|óс, á *m.* Christ.
хром, а *m.* (*chem.*) chromium, chrome.
хромá|ть, ю *impf.* to limp, be lame.
хром|óй (~, ~á, ~о) *adj.*
1 lame, limping; **х. на лéвую нóгу** lame in the left leg; *as n.* **х., ~óго** *m.*; **~áя, ~óй** *f.* lame man, woman.
2 (*coll.*) (*нога*) lame.
хромосóм|а, ы *f.* (*biol.*) chromosome.
хрóник|а, и *f.*
1 (*летопись*) chronicle.
2 (*в газете*) news items.
3 (*cin.*) newsreel.
хрони́ческий *adj.* chronic.
хронологи́ческий *adj.* chronological.
хронолóги|я, и *f.* chronology.
хронóметр, а *m.* chronometer.
хрýп|кий (~ок, ~кá, ~ко) *adj.*
1 (*стекло*) fragile, brittle.
2 (*fig.*) (*здоровье, ребёнок*) fragile, frail; delicate.
хруст, а *m.* crunch; crunching sound.
хрустáл|ь, я́ *m.* cut glass, crystal; **гóрный х.** rock crystal.
хрустáльный *adj.*
1 cut glass, crystal.
2 (*fig.*) crystal clear.
хру|стéть, щý, сти́шь *impf.* (*of* ▶ **~стнуть**) to crunch.
хрýст|нуть, ну, нешь *inst. pf. of* ▶ **~éть**
хруст|я́щий *pres. part. of* ▶ **~éть** *and adj.*; **х. картóфель** potato crisps (*Br.*), chips (*US*).
хрюк|ать, аю *impf.* (*of* ▶ **~нуть**) to grunt.
хрюк|нуть, ну, нешь *inst. pf.* (*of* ▶ **~ать**) to give a grunt.
хряк, á *m.* hog.
хрящ, á *m.* (*anat.*) cartilage, gristle.
худ|éе *comp. of* ▶ **~óй¹**
худé|ть, ю *impf.* (*of* ▶ **по~**) to grow thin, lose weight.
худóжествен|ный (~, ~на) *adj.*
1 of art, of the arts; **~ная литератýра** fiction; **х. фильм** feature film; **~ная шкóла** art school.
2 (*красивый*) artistic; tasteful.
худóжник, а *m.* artist; **х. по костю́мам/свéту** costume/lighting designer.
худóжни|ца, цы *f. of* ▶ **~к**
худ|óй¹ (~, ~á, ~о, ~ы́) *adj.* (*не толстый*) thin, lean.
худ|óй² (~, ~á, ~о) *adj.* (*плохой*) bad; **на х. конéц** if the worst comes to the worst.
худощáв|ый (~, ~а) *adj.* thin, lean.
хýд|ший *superl. of* ▶ **~óй²** *and* ▶ **плохóй;** (the) worst.
хуёвый *adj.* (*vulg.*) shitty, crap(py).
хý|же *comp. of* ▶ **~дóй², плохóй,** *and* **плóхо;** worse.
хуй, хýя, *pl.* **хуи́, хуёв** *m.* (*vulg.*) prick, cock (= *penis*); **ни хуя́** fuck all; **пошёл/иди́ нá х.!** fuck off!
хуйн|я́, и́ *f.* (*vulg.*) (*бессмыслица*) (a load of) bollocks, crap; (*что-л. некачественное, ненужное*) crap.
хулигáн, а *m.* hooligan.
хулигáнств|о, а *nt.* hooliganism.
хýнт|а, ы *f.* (*pol.*) junta.
хурм|á, ы́ *f.* persimmon, sharon fruit (*Diospyros*).

Цц

цáп|ать, аю *impf.* (*of* ▶ **~нуть**) (*coll.*) to snatch, grab.
цáп|ля, ли, *g. pl.* **~ель** *f.* heron.
цáп|нуть, ну, нешь *pf. of* ▶ **~ать**
царáп|ать, аю *impf.* (*of* **о~**) to scratch.
царáпа|ться, юсь *impf.* to scratch (*intrans.*); (*друг друга*) to scratch one another.
царáпин|а, ы *f.* scratch.
цар|и́ть, ю́, и́шь *impf.*
1 (*первенствовать*) to hold sway, reign supreme.
2 (*fig.*) (*господствовать*) to reign, prevail; **~и́ла тишинá** silence reigned.
цари́ц|а, ы *f.*
1 (*жена царя*) tsarina.
2 (*fig.*) queen.
цáрск|ий *adj.*
1 tsar's, of the tsar; royal.
2 (*pol.*) tsarist.
3 (*fig.*) regal, kingly; **~ая рóскошь** regal splendour.
цáрств|о, а *nt.*
1 (*государство*) kingdom, realm.
2 (*царствование*) reign.
3 (*fig.*) (*область деятельности*) realm, domain; **живóтное ц.** animal kingdom.
цáрствовани|е, я *nt.* reign; **в ц.** (+ *g.*) during the reign (of).
цáрств|овать, ую *impf.* to reign (*also fig.*).
цар|ь, я́ *m.*
1 tsar.
2 (*fig.*) king, ruler.
цве|сти́, тý, тёшь, *past* **~л, ~лá** *impf.*
1 to flower, bloom, blossom (*also fig.*); **ц. здорóвьем** to be radiant with health.
2 (*fig.*) to prosper, flourish.

цвет[1], **а,** *pl.* **~а́** *m.* (*окраска*) colour (*Br.*), color (*US*); **ц. лица́** complexion.

цвет[2], **а** *m.*
1 (*fig.*) (*лучшая часть*) flower, cream, pick.
2 (*расцвет*) blossoming; (*fig.*) prime; **в ~у́** in blossom.
3 (*collect.*) (*цветы на растении*) blossom.

цвете́ни|е, я *nt.* (*bot.*) flowering, blossoming.

цветни́к, а́ *m.* flower bed.

цветн|о́й *adj.*
1 coloured (*Br.*), colored (*US*); colour (*Br.*), color (*US*); **~о́е стекло́** stained glass; **~а́я капу́ста** cauliflower; **~о́е телеви́дение** colour (*Br.*), color (*US*) television; *as n.* **ц., ~о́го** *m.* (*offens.*) coloured (*Br.*), colored (*US*) person.
2 (*о металлах*) non-ferrous.

цветов|о́й *adj. of* ▶ **цвет**[1]; **~а́я га́мма** colour (*Br.*), color (*US*) spectrum.

цвет|о́к, ка́, *pl.* **~ы́, ~о́в** *m.* flower; (*pl. also* **~ки́, ~ко́в**) (*орган размножения*) flower.

цвето́чн|ый *adj. of* ▶ **цвето́к; ~ая клу́мба** flower bed; **ц. магази́н** flower shop, florist's.

цвету́щий *pres. part. act. of* ▶ **цвести́** *and adj.*
1 (*растение*) flowering, blossoming, blooming; (*здоровье, юноша*) blooming.
2 (*fig.*) (*страна*) flourishing.

це|ди́ть, жу́, ~́дишь *impf.*
1 (*через сито*) to strain, filter.
2 (*coll.*) (*говорить*) to say (through clenched teeth).

целе́б|ный (~ен, ~на) *adj.* healing, medicinal.

цел|ево́й *adj.*
1 *adj. of* ▶ **~ь.**
2 having a special purpose; **~евы́е сбо́ры** funds earmarked for a special purpose.
3 (*постройка*) special.

целенапра́влен|ный (~, ~на) *adj.* purposeful, single-minded.

целесообра́з|ный (~ен, ~на) *adj.* expedient.

целеустремлён|ный (~, ~на) *adj.* purposeful.

целико́м *adv.*
1 (*в целом виде*) whole; **проглоти́ть ц.** to swallow whole.
2 (*полностью*) wholly, entirely; **ц. и по́лностью** utterly and completely.

целин|а́, ы́ *f.* virgin lands.

цели́тел|ь, я *m.* healer.

це́л|ить, ю, ишь *impf.* (*of* ▶ **на~ 1**) to take aim; (**в** + *a.*) to aim (at).

це́л|иться, юсь, ишься *impf.* = **~ить**

целлофа́н, а *m.* cellophane.

целлофа́н|овый *adj. of* ▶ **~**

целлюло́з|а, ы *f.* cellulose.

цел|ова́ть, у́ю *impf.* (*of* ▶ **по~**) to kiss.

цел|ова́ться, у́юсь *impf.* (*of* ▶ **по~**) to kiss (one another).

це́л|ое, ого *nt.*
1 whole.
2 (*math.*) integer.

целому́дрен|ный (~, ~на) *adj.* chaste.

целому́дри|е, я *nt.* chastity.

це́лост|ный (~ен, ~на) *adj.* integrated; complete.

це́л|ый *adj.*
1 (*полный*) whole, entire; **~ое число́** whole number, integer; **в ~ом** as a whole.
2 **(~, ~а́, ~о)** (*неповреждённый*) safe, intact; **~ и невреди́м** safe and sound.

цел|ь, и *f.*
1 (*мишень*) target; **бить в ц., попа́сть в ц.** to hit the target; **бить ми́мо ~́и** to miss.
2 (*предмет стремления*) aim, object, goal, end, purpose; **с ~́ью** (+ *inf.*) with the object (of), in order (to); **пресле́довать ц.** to pursue a goal.

це́л|ьный *adj.*
1 (*из одного куска*) of one piece, solid.
2 **(~ен, ~ьна́, ~ьно)** (*целостный*) entire, integral; single.

Це́льси|й, я *m.* Celsius, centigrade **10° по ~ю** 10° Celsius.

цеме́нт, а *m.* cement.

цен|а́, ы́, *a.* **~́у,** *pl.* **~́ы** *f.*
1 price, cost; **~о́й** (+ *g.*) at the price (of), at the cost (of); **любо́й ~о́й** at any cost; **э́тому ~ы́ нет** it is invaluable.
2 (*fig.*) (*значение*) worth, value; **знать ~́у** (+ *d.*) to know the worth (of); **знать себе́ ~́у** to be self-assured, self-possessed, to know one's own value.

цензу́р|а, ы *f.* censorship.

цени́тел|ь, я *m.* judge, connoisseur, expert.

цени́тель|ница, ницы *f. of* ▶ **~**

цен|и́ть, ю́, ~́ишь *impf.* to value, appreciate; **высоко́ ц.** to rate highly.

це́нник, а *m.* price tag.

це́нност|ь, и *f.*
1 (*цена, стоимость*) price, value.
2 (*fig.*) (*значение*) value, importance.
3 *pl.* (*предметы*) valuables; (*духовные*) values.

це́н|ный (~ен, ~на) *adj.*
1 (*с обозначенной ценой*) containing valuables; representing a stated value; **~ные бума́ги** (*fin.*) securities.
2 (*дорогой*) valuable, costly; **~ная вещь** valuable object.
3 (*fig.*) (*важный*) valuable; precious; important.

цент, а *m.* cent (*unit of currency*).

це́нтнер, а *m.* quintal (= *100 kilograms*).

центр, а *m.* centre (*Br.*), center (*US*).

централиза́ци|я, и *f.* centralization.

центра́льн|ый *adj.* central; **~ые газе́ты** national newspapers; **~ое отопле́ние** central heating.

центри́зм, а *m.* centrism.

центри́ст, а *m.* centrist.

центрифу́г|а, и *f.* (*tech.*) centrifuge.

це́п|кий (~ок, ~́ка́, ~ко) *adj.*
1 (*руки, когти*) tenacious, strong (*also fig.*).
2 (*coll.*) (*упорный*) obstinate, persistent, strong-willed.

цепля́|ть, ю *impf.*
1 **(за** + *a.*; *coll.*) to hang on to, cling to.
2 (*задевать чем-н. загнутым*) to hook.
3 (*coll.*) (*прицеплять*) to hook on (to); to attach (to).

цепля́|ться, юсь *impf.*

1 (**за** + *a.*) (*зацепляться*) to hang on to, cling to.
2 (**за** + *a.*; *coll.*) (*стремиться удержать, сохранить что-н.*) to cling (to); to stick (to).
3 (**к** + *d.*, **за** + *a.*; *coll.*) (*придираться*) to pick (on) (= *to carp at, complain of*).

цепо́чк|а, и *f.*
1 (small) chain.
2 (*ряд*) file, series; **идти́ ~ой** to walk in file.

цеп|ь, и, о ~и, на/в ~и́, *pl.* **~и, ~е́й** *f.*
1 chain; (*pl.*) chains (= *fetters*; *also fig.*); **посади́ть на ц.** to chain (up), shackle.
2 (*гор, островов*) chain.
3 (*mil.*) line, file.
4 (*fig.*) (*ряд*) series, succession; **ц. катастро́ф** succession of disasters.
5 (*elec.*) circuit.

церемо́ни|я, и *f.* ceremony.
церемо́н|ный (~ен, ~на) *adj.* ceremonious.
церко́вник, а *m.* churchman, clergyman.
церко́вный *adj.* church; **ц. ста́роста** churchwarden; **ц. сто́рож** sexton.
це́рк|овь, ви, *i.* **~овью,** *pl.* **~ви, ~ве́й, ~ва́м** *and* **~вя́м** *f.* church.
цех, а, в ~е *and* **в ~у́** *m.*
1 (*pl.* **~á**) (*на заводе*) shop, section.
2 (*pl.* **~и**) (*hist.*) guild.

цивилиза́ци|я, и *f.* civilization.
цивилизо́ван|ный (~, ~на) *adj.* civilized.
цика́д|а, ы *f.* cicada.
цикл, а *m.* cycle; (*лекций, концертов*) series.
цикли́ческий *adj.* cyclic(al).
цикло́н, а *m.* (*meteor.*) cyclone.
цили́ндр, а *m.*
1 cylinder.
2 (*шляпа*) top hat.

цилиндри́ческий *adj.* cylindrical.
цини́зм, а *m.* cynicism.
ци́ник, а *m.* cynic.
цини́ч|ный (~ен, ~на) *adj.* cynical.
цинк, а *m.* (*chem.*) zinc.
ци́нковый *adj.* zinc.
цирк, а *m.* circus.
цирка́ч, а́ *m.* (*coll.*) circus artiste.
цирка́ч|ка, ки *f. of* ▸ **~**
цирк|ово́й *adj. of* ▸ **~**
циркули́р|овать, ую *impf.*
1 (*о жидкостях*) to circulate; **~овали слу́хи** (*coll.*) rumours (*Br.*), rumors (*US*) were circulating.
2 (*coll.*) (*ходить*) to pass, go to and fro.

ци́ркул|ь, я *m.* (pair of) compasses; dividers.
циркуля́р, а *m.* circular (*official*).
циркуля́ци|я, и *f.* circulation.
** цирро́з, а** *m.* (*med.*) cirrhosis.
цисте́рн|а, ы *f.* (*резервуар*) cistern, tank; (*вагон*) tank car; (*автомобиль*) tanker.
цитаде́л|ь, и *f.* citadel; (*fig.*) bulwark, stronghold.
цита́т|а, ы *f.* quotation.
цити́р|овать, ую *impf.* (*of* ▸ **про~**) to quote.
ци́трус|овый *adj.*: *as n.* **~овые, ~овых** citrus plants.
циферблáт, а *m.* dial; (*часов*) face.
ци́фр|а, ы *f.*
1 figure; digit, number, numeral.
2 (*pl.*) (*данные*) figures.

цифров|о́й *adj.*
1 numerical.
2 (*electronics, comput.*) digital; **~а́я за́пись** digital recording.

цо́кол|ь, я *m.*
1 (*archit.*) socle, plinth, pedestal.
2 (*elec.*) cap (*metal extremity of light bulb which is fitted into socket*).

ЦРУ *nt. indecl.* (*abbr. of* **Центра́льное разве́дывательное управле́ние**) CIA (*Central Intelligence Agency*).
цуна́ми *nt. indecl.* tsunami.
цыга́н, а, *pl.* **~е, ~** *m.* Gypsy.
цыга́н|ка, ки *f. of* ▸ **~**
цыга́нский *adj.* Gypsy.
цы́к|ать, аю *impf.* (*of* ▸ **~нуть**) (**на кого́-н.;** *coll.*) to shout at; to silence.
цы́к|нуть, ну *pf. of* ▸ **~ать**
цыпл|ёнок, ёнка, *pl.* **~я́та, ~я́т** *m.* chick(en).
цы́почк|и *n. pl*: **на ц., на ~ах** on tiptoe.

Чч

ч *abbr. of* **час** hour; o'clock.
ч. *abbr. of* **часть** part.
чабре́ц, а́ *m.* (*bot., cul.*) thyme.
ча́вк|ать, аю *impf.* to champ; to munch noisily.
чадр|а́, ы́ *f.* chador (*worn by Muslim women*).
чаев|ы́е, ы́х *no sg.* tip, gratuity.
чаепи́ти|е, я *nt.* tea-drinking.
ча|й, я (ю), *pl.* **~и́, ~ёв** *m.*
1 tea.
2 (*чаепитие*) tea(-drinking); **за ~ем, за ча́шкой ~я** over (a cup of) tea.
3: **дать** (+ *d.*) **на ч.** to tip.

ча́йк|а, и, *g. pl.* **ча́ек** *f.* (sea)gull.
ча́йн|ая, ой *f.* tea room, tea shop.
ча́йник, а *m.* (*для заварки*) teapot; (*для кипячения воды*) kettle.
ча́йн|ый *adj.* tea; **ч. куст** tea plant; **~ая ло́жка** teaspoon; **~ая ча́шка** teacup.
чалм|а́, ы́ *f.* turban.

чан, а, в ~е *and* **в ~у́,** *pl.* **~ы́** *m.* vat, tub, tank.
чароде́|й, я *m.* sorcerer, magician (*also fig.*).
ча́ртер, а *m.* charter.
ча́р|ы, ~ *no sg.* (*coll.*) magic, charms (*also fig.*).
час, а, о ~е, в ~у́ *and* **в ~е,** *pl.* **~ы́** *m.*
1 hour (*also fig.*); **че́тверть ~а́** a quarter of an hour.
2 (*время по часам*): (*g. sg.* **~а́** *after numerals 2, 3, 4*) o'clock; **час** one o'clock; **два ~а́** two o'clock; **во второ́м ~у́** between one and two (o'clock); **кото́рый ч.?** what is the time?
3 (*usu. pl.*) (*время*) hours, time, period; **ч. пик, ~ы́ пик** rush hour.
часа́ми *adv.* for hours.
часо́в|ня, ни, *g. pl.* **~ен** *f.* chapel.
часов|о́й[1]**, о́го** *m.* sentry, guard.
часов|о́й[2] *adj.* (*of* ▶ **час**)
1 (*продолжающийся один час*) of one hour's duration; **ч. переры́в** one hour's interval.
2 (*по часам*) (measured) by the hour; **ч. по́яс** time zone.
часов|о́й[3] *adj. of* ▶ **часы́; ч. магази́н** watch shop, watchmaker's, watch repair shop; **ч. механи́зм** clockwork; **~а́я стре́лка** clock hand, hour hand; **по ~о́й стре́лке** clockwise.
часовщи́к, а́ *m.* watchmaker.
части́ц|а, ы *f.*
1 small part, element.
2 (*phys.*) particle.
3 (*gram.*) particle.
части́чно *adv.* partly, partially.
части́ч|ный (~ен, ~на) *adj.* partial.
ча́стност|ь, и *f.* detail; **в ~и** in particular.
ча́стн|ый *adj.*
1 (*личный*) private, personal; **~ым о́бразом** privately.
2 (*econ.*) private, privately-owned; **~ая со́бственность** private property.
3 (*отдельный, особый*) particular, individual; *as n.* **~ое, ~ого** *nt.* the particular.
ча́сто *adv.* often, frequently.
частот|а́, ы́, *pl.* **~ы** *f.* frequency.
ча́ст|ый (~, ~а́, ~о) *adj.*
1 frequent; **он у нас ч. гость** he is a frequent visitor at our house.
2 (*густой*) close (together); dense, thick; **ч. дождь** steady rain.
3 (*быстрый*) quick, rapid; **ч. ого́нь** (*mil.*) rapid fire.
част|ь, и, *pl.* **~и, ~е́й** *f.*
1 part; portion; **бо́льшей ~ью, по бо́льшей ~и** for the most part, mostly.
2 (*отдел*) section, department.
3 (*coll.*) (*область*) sphere, field; **э́то не по мое́й ~и** this is not my province; **по ~и** (+ *g.*) in connection (with).
4 (*mil.*) unit.
ча́стью *adv.* partly, in part.
час|ы́, о́в *no sg.* clock, watch.
чат, а *m.* (*comput.*) IRC (*abbr. of Internet Relay Chat*).
ча́хл|ый (~, ~а) *adj.* stunted; poor.
ча́х|нуть, ну, нешь, *past* **~, ~ла** *impf.* (*of* ▶ **за~**)
1 (*о растительности*) to wither away.
2 (*о человеке*) to fade away.
чахо́тк|а, и *f.* (*coll.*) consumption.
ча́ш|а, и *f.* cup, bowl (*also fig.*); (*eccl.*) chalice; **ч. весо́в** scale pan.
ча́шк|а, и *f.* (*для питья*) cup.
ча́щ|а, и *f.* thicket.
ча́ще *comp. of* ▶ **ча́стый** *and* ▶ **ча́сто** more often; **ч. всего́** most often, mostly.
чебуре́к, а *m.* cheburek (*kind of lamb pasty originally from Crimea and Caucasus*).
чего́[1] *interrog. adv.* (*coll.*) why? what for?
чего́[2] *g. of* ▶ **что**[1]
чей, чья, чьё, *pl.* **чьи** *interrog. and rel. pron.* whose.
че́й-либо *pron.* = **че́й-нибудь**
че́й-нибудь *pron.* (*в утверждениях*) someone's, somebody's; (*в вопросах*) anyone's, anybody's.
че́й-то *pron.* someone's, somebody's.
чек, а *m.*
1 (*банковский*) cheque (*Br.*), check (*US*); **вы́писать ч.** to write a cheque.
2 (*с указанием суммы, которую следует уплатить*) chit; (*удостоверяющий, что товар оплачен*) receipt.
чеки́ст, а *m.* (*hist.*) agent of the Cheka (*state security organ 1918–22*).
че́к|овый *adj. of* ▶ **~; ~овая кни́жка** chequebook (*Br.*), checkbook (*US*).
чёлк|а, и *f.* fringe (*Br.*), bangs (*US*); (*лошади*) forelock.
челно́к, а́ *m.*
1 (*лодка*) dugout (canoe).
2 (*sl.*) small trader (*travelling to buy things to resell at home*).
челове́к, а, *pl.* **лю́ди** (*g. pl., etc.,* **челове́к, ~ам, ~ами, о ~ах** *only in comb. with nums.*) *m.* man, person, human being.
человеконенави́стнический *adj.* misanthropic.
человекообра́з|ный (~ен, ~на) *adj.* anthropomorphous; (*zool.*) anthropoid.
челове́ческий *adj.*
1 (*относящийся к человеку*) human.
2 (*гуманный*) humane.
челове́честв|о, а *nt.* humanity, mankind.
челове́чност|ь, и *f.* humaneness, humanity.
челове́ч|ный (~ен, ~на) *adj.* humane.
че́люст|ь, и *f.*
1 jaw.
2 (*зубной протез*) dentures.
чем *conj.*
1 than.
2 (+ *comp.*) **ч. ..., тем...** the more ..., the more ...; **ч. скоре́е, тем лу́чше** the sooner, the better.
чемода́н, а *m.* suitcase.
чемпио́н, а *m.* champion.
чемпиона́т, а *m.* championship.
чемпио́н|ка, ки *f. of* ▶ **~**
чепух|а́, и́ *f.* (*coll.*)
1 (*вздор*) nonsense, rubbish.
2 (*незначительное дело*) a trifle, trifling matter; (*пустяки*) trivialities.
3 (*незначительное количество*) trifling

amount.
че́рв|и[1], **е́й**, *pl.* (*sg.* **~а, ~ы** *f.*) (*в картах*) hearts; **коро́ль ~е́й** king of hearts.
че́рв|и[2] *pl. of* ▸ **~ь**
черв|о́вый *adj. of* ▸ **~́и**[1]
черв|ь, я́, *pl.* **~́и, ~е́й** *m.* worm; maggot.
червя́к, а́ *m.*
1 = **червь.**
2 (*tech.*) worm.
черда́к, а́ *m.* attic, loft.
чередова́ни|е, я *nt.* alternation, interchange, rotation.
черед|ова́ть, у́ю *impf.* (**с** + *i.*) to alternate (with).
черед|ова́ться, у́юсь *impf.* to alternate; to take turns.
че́рез *prep.* + *a.*
1 (*улицу, забор*) across; over; (*лес, окно*) through.
2 (*о пунктах следования*) via.
3 (*посредством*) through; **ч. перево́дчика** through an interpreter.
4 (*по прошествии*) in; **ч. полчаса́** in half an hour's time; **я верну́сь ч. год** I shall be back in a year's time.
5 (*минуя какое-н. пространство*) after; (further) on; **ч. три киломе́тра** three kilometres (further) on.
6 (*повторяя в регулярные промежутки*): **ч. ка́ждые три страни́цы** every three pages; **дежу́рить ч. день** to be on duty every other day, on alternate days.
черен|о́к, ка́ *m.*
1 (*рукоятка*) handle.
2 (*hort.*) cutting.
че́реп, а, *pl.* **~а́** *m.* skull, cranium.
черепа́х|а, и *f.*
1 tortoise; (*морская*) turtle; **ползти́ как ч.** to go at a snail's pace.
2 (*панцирь в качестве материала*) tortoiseshell.
черепи́ц|а, ы *f.* tile; (*collect.*) tiles.
черепи́чный *adj.* tile; tiled.
черепн|о́й *adj. of* ▸ **че́реп; ~а́я коро́бка** cranium.
череп|о́к, ка́ *m.* broken piece of pottery.
чересчу́р *adv.* too; (*перед глаголом*) too much.
чере́шн|я, и *f.* cherry (tree) (*Cerasus avium*).
черке́с, а *m.* Circassian.
черке́сский *adj.* Circassian.
черке́шенк|а, и *f. of* ▸ **черке́с**
черне́|ть, ю *impf.*
1 (*pf.* **по~**) (*становиться чёрным*) to turn black, grow black.
2 (*виднеться*) to show up black.
черни́к|а, и *f.* bilberry.
черни́л|а, ~ *no sg.* ink.
черни́льниц|а, ы *f.* inkpot, inkwell.
чернобу́рк|а, и *f.* (*coll.*) silver fox (fur).
чернови́к, а́ *m.* rough copy, draft.
чернов|о́й *adj.*
1 rough, draft; preparatory.
2 : **~а́я рабо́та** (*coll.*) heavy, rough, dirty work.
черноволо́с|ый (~, ~а) *adj.* black-haired.
черногла́з|ый (~, ~а) *adj.* black-eyed.
черногор|ец, ца *m.* Montenegrin.
Черного́ри|я, и *f.* Montenegro.
черного́р|ка, ки *f. of* ▸ **~ец**
черного́рский *adj.* Montenegrin.
чернoко́ж|ий (~, ~а) *adj.* black; *as n.* **ч., ~его** *m.* black (man).
чернорабо́ч|ий, его *m.* unskilled labourer (*Br.*), laborer (*US*).
черносли́в, а *m.* (*collect.*) prunes.
черносо́тен|ец, ца *m.* (*hist.*) member of 'Black Hundred' (*name of armed monarchist anti-Semitic groups in Russia, active 1905–7*); (*fig.*) extreme reactionary, chauvinist.
чернот|а́, ы́ *f.* blackness (*also fig.*); darkness.
чёр|ный (~ен, ~на́) *adj.*
1 black; **ч. ры́нок** black market; **(отложи́ть на) ч. день** (to put by for) a rainy day; **~ное де́рево** ebony; **~ная сморо́дина** blackcurrant; (*чернокожий*) black; *as n.* **ч., ~ного** *m.* (*offens., esp. when referring to person of Caucasian or Central Asian origin*) black (man).
2 (*задний*) back; **ч. ход** back entrance, back door.
3 (*fig.*) (*мысли, дни*) gloomy, melancholy.
черпа́к, а́ *m.* scoop.
че́рп|ать, аю *impf.* (*of* ▸ **~ну́ть**)
1 to draw (up); to scoop; to ladle.
2 (*fig.*) (*извлекать*) to extract, derive.
черп|ну́ть, ну́, нёшь *inst. pf. of* ▸ **~́ать**
чёрств|ый (~, ~а́, ~о) *adj.*
1 stale.
2 (*fig.*) (*бездушный*) hard, callous.
чёрт, а, *pl.* **че́рти, ~е́й** *m.* devil; **ч. возьми́/побери́!** (*coll.*) damn!; **до ~а** (*coll.*) hellishly; **како́го ~а?** (*coll.*) why the hell?
черт|а́, ы́ *f.*
1 (*линия*) line; **провести́ ~у́** to draw a line.
2 (*граница*) boundary.
3 (*свойство*) trait, characteristic; **~ы́ лица́** features; **в о́бщих ~а́х** in general outline.
чертёж, а́ *m.* draft, drawing, sketch.
чертёжник, а *m.* draughtsman.
чер|ти́ть, чу́, ~́тишь *impf.* (*of* ▸ **на~**) (*карту*) to draw; (*план*) to draw up.
чертополо́х, а *m.* thistle.
черче́ни|е, я *nt.* drawing; sketching.
че|са́ть, шу́, ~́шешь *impf.* (*of* ▸ **по~**) to scratch.
че|са́ться, шу́сь, ~́шешься *impf.* (*of* ▸ **по~**)
1 to scratch o.s.
2 (*impf. only*) (*об ощущении зуда*) to itch; **ру́ки у него́**, *etc.*, **~́шутся** (+ *inf.*) he is, *etc.*, itching to … .
чесно́к, а́ (у́) *m.* garlic.
чесо́тк|а, и *f.* (*med.*) scabies.
че́ствова|ть, ую *impf.* to honour (*Br.*), honor (*US*); to pay tribute to.
че́стност|ь, и *f.* honesty, integrity.
че́ст|ный (~ен, ~на́, ~но, ~́ны) *adj.* honest; (*справедливый*) fair; **~ное сло́во!** honestly, truly!
честолюби́в|ый (~, ~а) *adj.* ambitious.
честолю́би|е, я *nt.* ambition.

чест|ь, и *f.* honour (*Br.*), honor (*US*); **в ч.** (+ *g.*) in honour (*Br.*), honor (*US*) (of).
чет|á, ы *f.* pair, couple; **не ч. комý-н.** no match for s.o.
четвéрг, á *m.* Thursday.
четверéньк|и (*coll.*): **на ч., на ~ах** on all fours, on one's hands and knees; **стать на ч.** to go down on all fours.
четвёрк|а, и *f.*
1 (*цифра, игральная карта*) four.
2 (*отметка*) four (*out of five*).
3 (*coll.*) (*автобус, трамвай*) No. 4 (*bus, tram, etc.*).
4 (*группа из четверых*) (group of) four; (*четыре человека*) foursome.
чéтвер|о, ых *num.* four; **нас бы́ло ч.** there were four of us.
четвероно́г|ий *adj.* four-legged; *as n.* **~ое, ~ого** *nt.* quadruped.
четверости́ши|е, я *nt.* (*liter.*) quatrain.
четвёртый *adj.* fourth.
чéтверт|ь, и, *g. pl.* **~éй** *f.*
1 (*четвёртая часть целого*) quarter.
2 (*четверть часа*) quarter (of an hour); **без ~и час** a quarter to one; **ч. деся́того** a quarter past nine.
3 (*учебного года*) term.
4 (*mus.*) crotchet (*Br.*), quarter note (*US*).
четвертьфинáл, а *m.* (*sport*) quarter-final.
чёт|ки, ок *no sg.* (*eccl.*) rosary.
чёт|кий (~ок, ~ка *and* **четкá, ~ко)** *adj.*
1 (*отчётливый*) precise; clear-cut.
2 (*изложение*) clear, well-defined; (*почерк*) legible; (*звук*) plain, distinct; (*речь*) articulate.
чёткост|ь, и *f.*
1 (*движения*) precision, preciseness.
2 (*изложения*) clarity, clearness.
чётный *adj.* even (*of numbers*).
четы́р|е, ёх, ём, ьмя́, о ~ёх *num.* four.
четы́режды *adv.* four times.
четы́р|еста, ёхсо́т, ёмстáм, ьмястáми, о ~ёхстáх *num.* four hundred.
четырёхлéтний *adj.*
1 (*срок*) four-year.
2 (*ребёнок*) four-year-old.
четырёхсо́тый *adj.* four-hundredth.
четырёхуго́льник, а *m.* quadrangle.
четырёхуго́льный *adj.* quadrangular.
четы́рнадцатый *adj.* fourteenth.
четы́рнадцат|ь, и *num.* fourteen.
чех, а *m.* Czech.
чехард|á, ы *f.* (*игра*) leapfrog; (*fig.*) reshuffle.
Чéхи|я, и *f.* Czech Republic.
чех|о́л, лá *m.* (*подушки, кресла*) cover; (*контрабаса*) case.
чечеви́ц|а, ы *f.* lentil; (*collect.*) lentils.
чечéн|ец, ца *m.* Chechen.
чечéн|ка, ки *f. of* ▶ **~ец**
чечéнский *adj.* Chechen.
Чечн|я́, и́ *f.* Chechnya.
чéшк|а, и *f. of* ▶ **чех**
чéшский *adj.* Czech.
чешу|я́, и́ *no pl., f.* (*zool.*) scales.
Чи́ли *f. indecl.* Chile.
чили́|ец, йца *m.* Chilean.
чили́|йка, йки *f. of* ▶ **~ец**
чили́йский *adj.* Chilean.
чин, а, *pl.* **~ы́** *m.*
1 (*разряд*) rank; **в ~е/~áх** high-ranking.
2 (*чиновник*) official.
чин|и́ть, ю́, ~ишь *impf.* (*of* ▶ **по~**) (*обувь, велосипед*) to repair, mend.
чи́н|ный (~ен, ~нá, ~но) *adj.* decorous, proper, orderly.
чино́вник, а *m.* official, functionary.
чип, а *m.* (micro)chip.
чи́пс|ы, ов *no sg.* (potato) crisps (*Br.*), chips (*US*).
чири́ка|ть, ю *impf.* to chirp, twitter.
чири́кн|уть, у, ешь *inst. pf.* to give a chirp.
чи́рк|ать, аю *impf.* (*of* ▶ **~нуть**) (+ *i.*) (**по** + *d.*) to strike sharply (against, on); **ч. спи́чкой** to strike a match.
чи́рк|нуть, ну, нешь *inst. pf. of* ▶ **~ать**
чи́сленност|ь, и *f.* numbers; **ч. населе́ния** population size; (*mil.*) strength.
чи́сленный *adj.* numerical.
числи́тельн|ое, ого *nt.* (*gram.*) numeral.
чи́сл|иться, юсь, ишься *impf.*
1 to be (*in context of calculation or official records*); **в нáшей дерéвне ~ится три́ста жи́телей** there are three hundred inhabitants in our village.
2 (+ *i.*) to be officially, be on paper; **он ещё ~ился завéдующим отдéлом, а все обя́занности исполня́ли егó замести́тели** he was still head of the department on paper, but all the duties were being performed by his deputies.
3 (**за** + *i.*) to be attributed (to), have; **за ним ~ится мнóго недостáтков** he has many failings.
чис|ло́, лá, *pl.* **~ла, ~ел** *nt.*
1 number; **~ло́м** in number; **без ~лá** without number, in great numbers; **в том ~лé** including.
2 (*дата*) date, day (*of month*); **какóе сегóдня ч.?** what is the date today?
3 (*gram.*) number; **еди́нственное, мнóжественное ч.** singular, plural.
числово́й *adj.* numerical.
чисти́лищ|е, а *nt.* (*relig.*) purgatory.
чи́стильщик, а *m.* cleaner.
чи́|стить, щу, стишь *impf.*
1 (*pf.* **по~, вы́~**) to clean; **(щёткой)** to brush.
2 (*pf.* **по~, вы́~**) (*дорожки*) to clear; (*канал*) to dredge.
3 (*pf.* **о~,** *coll. also* **по~**) (*овощи, фрукты*) to peel; (*орехи*) to shell; (*рыбу*) to clean.
чи́стк|а, и *f.*
1 cleaning; **отдáть в ~у** to have cleaned, send to be cleaned.
2 (*pol.*) purge; **этни́ческая ч.** ethnic cleansing.
чи́сто[1] *as pred.* it is clean.
чи́ст|о[2] *adv.*
1 *adv. of* ▶ **~ый; ч.-нáчисто** spotlessly

clean.
2 *as conj.* (*coll.*) just like, just as if.

чистово́й *adj.* fair, clean; **ч. экземпля́р** fair copy.

чистокро́в|ный (~ен, ~на) *adj.* thoroughbred.

чистописа́ни|е, я *nt.* calligraphy.

чистопло́т|ный (~ен, ~на) *adj.* clean; neat, tidy.

чистот|а́, ы́ *f.*
1 cleanliness; (*опрятность*) neatness, tidiness.
2 (*безупречность; отсутствие примесей*) purity.

чи́ст|ый (~, ~а́, ~о, ~ы́) *adj.*
1 clean; (*опрятный*) neat, tidy; (*голос, речь*) clear; **экологи́чески ч.** eco-friendly.
2 (*fig.*) (*безупречный*) pure.
3 (*без примесей*) pure.
4 (*открытый*) clear; open; **ч. лист** blank sheet.
5 (*fin., etc.*) net, clear; **~ая при́быль** clear profit.
6 (*coll.*) (*сущий*) pure, utter; sheer; complete; **~ая случа́йность** pure chance.

чита́льный *adj.*: **ч. зал** reading room.

чита́тел|ь, я *m.* reader.

чита́тель|ница, ницы *f. of* ▸ **~**

чита́|ть, ю *impf.* (*of* ▸ **про~, проче́сть**)
1 to read.
2 : **ч. ле́кцию** to give a lecture; **ч. стихи́** to recite poetry.

чих|а́ть, а́ю *impf.* (*of* ▸ **~ну́ть**) to sneeze.

чих|ну́ть, ну́, нёшь *inst. pf. of* ▸ **~а́ть**

чи́ще *comp. of* ▸ **чи́стый, чи́сто**

член, а *m.*
1 member; (*академик*) Fellow; **ч.-корреспонде́нт** corresponding member (*of an Academy*).
2 (*math.*) term; (*gram.*) part (*of sentence*).
3 (*конечность*) limb; (*половой*) penis.

членоразде́л|ьный (~ен, ~ьна) *adj.* articulate.

чле́нств|о, а *nt.* membership.

чмо́к|ать, аю *impf.* (*of* ▸ **~нуть**) (*coll.*)
1 to smack one's lips.
2 (*целовать*) to give a smacking kiss.
3 (*о грязи*) to squelch.

чмо́к|нуть, ну, нешь *pf. of* ▸ **~ать**

чо́к|аться, аюсь *impf.* (*of* ▸ **~нуться**) to clink glasses (*when drinking toasts*).

чо́кнутый *adj.* (*crazy*) odd, crazy.

чо́к|нуться, нусь, нешься *pf. of* ▸ **~аться**

чо́пор|ный (~ен, ~на) *adj.* prim; stuck-up; standoffish.

ЧП *nt. indecl.* (*abbr. of* **чрезвыча́йное происше́ствие**) incident, emergency; (*катастрофа*) disaster.

чрева́т|ый (~, ~а) *adj.* (+ *i.*) fraught (with).

чрезвыча́йно *adv.* extremely, extraordinarily.

чрезвыча́|йный (~ен, ~йна) *adj.*
1 extraordinary.
2 (*экстренный*) special, emergency; **~йные ме́ры** emergency measures; **~йное положе́ние** state of emergency.

чрезме́р|ный (~ен, ~на) *adj.* excessive, inordinate.

чте́ни|е, я *nt.* reading.

чти́в|о, а *nt.* (*coll., pej.*) reading matter.

чтить, чту, чтишь, чтят (*and* **чтут**) *impf.* to honour (*Br.*), honor (*US*).

что[1], **чего́, чему́, чем, о чём** *interrog. pron.*
1 what?; **что с тобо́й?** what's the matter (with you)?; **что де́лать, что поде́лаешь?** it can't be helped; **для чего́?** why?, what ... for?; **что ты (вы)!** (*expr. surprise, fear, etc.*) you don't mean to say so!
2 (*почему*) why?; **что вы не еди́те?** why aren't you eating?

что[2] (*sometimes printed* **что́**) *rel. pron.* which, that; (*coll.*) (*который*) who; **я зна́ю, что вы име́ете в виду́** I know what you mean; **па́рень, что стоя́л ря́дом со мной** the fellow (who was) standing next to me; **он всё молча́л, что для него́ не характе́рно** he said nothing the whole time, which is unlike him.

что[3] as far as; **что до, что каса́ется** (+ *g.*) as for, with regard (to), as far as ... is concerned.

что[4] *conj.* that; **то, что...** the fact that ... .

чтоб = **что́бы**

что́бы *conj.*
1 (*выражает цель*) in order to, in order that; **ч. ... не** lest.
2 (that); **он хо́чет, ч. она́ пришла́ в шесть часо́в** he wants her to come at 6 o'clock.
3 (*as particle*) (*выражает требование, пожелание*): **ч. я тебя́ бо́льше не ви́дел!** may I never see your face again!

что за (*coll.*)
1 (*interrog.*) what? what sort of ... ?; **что э́то за пти́ца?** what sort of bird is that?
2 (*int.*): **что за день!** what a (marvellous) day!

что́-либо, чего́-либо *indef. pron.* anything.

что́-нибудь, чего́-нибудь *indef. pron.* anything.

что́-то[1], **чего́-то** *indef. pron.* something.

что́-то[2] *adv.* (*coll.*)
1 (*несколько*) somewhat, slightly.
2 (*почему-то*) somehow, for no obvious reason; **что́-то мне не хо́чется идти́** I don't feel like going for some reason.

чуб, а, *pl.* **~ы́** *m.* forelock.

чува́к, а́ *m.* (*sl.*) guy, fellow (*both coll.*).

чува́ш, а́, *pl.* **~и́, ~е́й** *m.* Chuvash.

чува́ш|ка, ки *f. of* ▸ **~**

чува́шский *adj.* Chuvash.

чуви́х|а, и *f.* (*sl.*) chick (*coll.*) (*girl*).

чу́вствен|ный *adj.*
1 **(~, ~на)** sensual.
2 (*phil.*) perceptible; **~ное восприя́тие** perception.

чувстви́тельност|ь, и *f.*
1 (*кожи, прибора, человека*) sensitivity, sensitiveness.

Ч

[2] (*сентиментальность*) sentimentality.

чувстви́тел|ьный (~ен, ~ьна) *adj.*
[1] (*прибор, человек*) sensitive.
[2] (*сентиментальный*) sentimental.
[3] (*толчок, урон*) perceptible.

чу́вств|о, а *nt.*
[1] (*physiol.*) sense; **ч. вку́са** sense of taste; **о́рганы ~** senses, organs of sense.
[2] (*sg. or pl.*) (*сознание*) senses; **лиши́ться ~, упа́сть без ~** to faint, lose consciousness; **прийти́ в ч.** to come round, regain consciousness, come to one's senses.
[3] (*ощущение*) feeling; sense; **ч. ю́мора** sense of humour (*Br.*), humor (*US*); **пита́ть к кому́-н. не́жные ~а** to have a soft spot for s.o.

чу́вств|овать, ую *impf.* (*of* ▸ **по~**)
[1] to feel, sense; **ч. себя́** to feel (*intrans.*); **как вы себя́ ~уете?** how do you feel?
[2] (*уметь воспринимать*) to appreciate, have a feeling (for) (*music, etc.*).

чу́вств|оваться, уется *impf.*
[1] to be perceptible; to make itself felt.
[2] *pass. of* ▸ **~овать**

чугу́н, а́ *m.* cast iron.

чугу́нный *adj.* cast-iron (*also fig.*).

чуда́к, а́ *m.* eccentric, crank.

чуде́с|ный (~ен, ~на) *adj.*
[1] (*сверхъестественный*) miraculous; **~ное исцеле́ние** miraculous healing.
[2] (*чудный*) marvellous (*Br.*), marvelous (*US*), wonderful.

чуд|но́й (~ён, ~на́, ~но́) *adj.* (*странный*) strange, odd.

чу́д|ный (~ен, ~на) *adj.* marvellous (*Br.*), marvelous (*US*), wonderful, lovely.

чу́д|о, а, *pl.* **~еса́, ~е́с** *nt.*
[1] (*сверхъестественное явление*) miracle.
[2] (*нечто поразительное*) wonder, marvel.

чудо́вищ|е, а *nt.* monster.

чудо́вищ|ный (~ен, ~на) *adj.*
[1] monstrous (*also fig., pej.*).
[2] (*огромный*) enormous.

чу́дом *adv.* miraculously; **ч. спасти́сь** to be saved by a miracle.

чудотво́р|ец, ца *m.* miracle-worker.

чужда́|ться, юсь *impf.* (+ *g.*) (*друзей*) to shun, avoid; (*славы*) to stand aloof (from), remain unaffected (by).

чу́жд|ый (~, ~а́, ~о) *adj.*
[1] (+ *d.*) (*идеология, взгляды*) alien (to); extraneous.
[2] (+ *g.*) (*лишенный*) free (from), devoid (of); **он ~ зло́бы** he is devoid of malice.

чуж|о́й *adj.*
[1] (*не свой*) s.o. else's, another's, others'; **на ч. счёт** at s.o. else's expense; *as n.* **~о́е, ~о́го** *nt.* s.o. else's belongings.
[2] (*посторонний*) strange, alien; foreign; *as n.* **ч., ~о́го** *m.* stranger.

чула́н, а *m.* (*для вещей*) storeroom, lumber room; (*для продуктов*) larder.

чул|о́к, ка́, *g. pl.* **ч.** *m.* stocking.

чум|а́, ы́ *f.* plague.

чума́з|ый (~, ~а) *adj.* (*coll.*) grubby, dirty.

чурба́н, а *m.*
[1] block, log.
[2] (*coll.*) (*тупой человек*) blockhead.

чу́рк|а, и *f.* block, lump.

чу́т|кий (~ок, ~ка́, ~ко) *adj.*
[1] keen, sharp; **ч. нюх** keen sense of smell; **ч. сон** light sleep.
[2] (*fig.*) (*отзывчивый*) sensitive; sympathetic; tactful.

чуть
[1] *adv.* (*едва*) hardly, scarcely; just; **ч. (бы́ло) не, ч. ли не** almost, nearly.
[2] *adv.* (*немного*) (just) a little, very slightly.
[3] *conj.* (*как только*) as soon as; **ч. что** at the slightest provocation.

чуть|ё, я́ *nt.*
[1] (*у животных*) scent.
[2] (к + *d. or* на + *a.*) (*fig.*) (*способность*) flair, feeling (for).

чуть-чу́ть *adv.* (*coll.*) a tiny bit; **ч.-ч. не** = **чуть не**

чу́чел|о, а *nt.*
[1] (*животное*) stuffed animal.
[2] (*пугало*) scarecrow (*also fig.*).

чуш|ь, и *f.* (*coll.*) nonsense.

чу́|ять, ю, ешь *impf.* to scent, smell; (*fig.*) to sense, feel.

шабло́н, а *m.*
[1] (*tech.*) template, pattern; (*форма*) mould (*Br.*), mold (*US*).
[2] (*fig., pej.*) cliché; routine.

шаг, а (у) (*after numerals 2, 3, 4* **~а́**) **о ~е, в (на) ~у́/~е,** *pl.* **~и́, ~о́в** *m.* step (*also fig.*); (*походка*) pace; (*большой*) stride; **ш. на ме́сте** marking time; **идти́ бы́стрыми ~а́ми** make rapid strides; **заме́длить ш.** to slow down; **в двух ~а́х, в не́скольких ~а́х** a stone's throw away; **на ка́ждом ~у́** everywhere, at every turn, continually.

шаг|а́ть, а́ю *impf.* (*of* ▸ **~ну́ть**)
[1] (*ступать*) to step; (*ходить*) to walk; (*большими шагами*) to stride; (*мерными шагами*) to pace.
[2] (*coll.*) (*идти*) to go, come.

шаг|ну́ть, ну́, нёшь *inst. pf.* (*of* ▸ **~а́ть**) to take a step; (*fig.*) to make progress.

ша́гом *adv.* at a walk, at a walking pace; slowly; **ш. марш!** (*mil. word of command*) quick march!

ша́йб|а, ы *f.*
[1] (*tech.*) washer.

[2] (*sport*) puck; **хоккей с ~ой** ice hockey.
шайк|а, и, *g. pl.* **шаек** *f.* gang, band.
шакал, а *m.* jackal.
шалаш, а *m.* (*hunter's or fisherman's*) cabin (*made of branches and straw, etc.*).
шал|ить, ю, ишь *impf.* to be naughty; to play up, play tricks (*also of inanimate objects*).
шалост|ь, и *f.* prank; (*pl.*) mischief.
шалун, а *m.* naughty child.
шалун|ья, ьи *f. of* ▸ ~
шалфе|й, я *m.* (*bot.*) sage.
шал|ь, и *f.* shawl.
шальн|ой *adj.* mad, crazy; wild; **~ые деньги** easy money; **~ая пуля** stray bullet.
шаман, а *m.* (*relig.*) shaman.
шампанск|ое, ого *nt.* champagne.
шампиньон, а *m.* field mushroom.
шампун|ь, я *m.* shampoo.
шампур, а *m.* skewer.
шанс, а *m.* chance; **иметь много ~ов, большие ~ы (на** + *a.*) to have a good chance (of).
шансон, а *m.* ballad.
шансонье *m. indecl.* balladeer; singer-songwriter.
шантаж, а *m.* blackmail.
шантажир|овать, ую *impf.* to blackmail.
шантажист, а *m.* blackmailer.
шантажист|ка, ки *f. of* ▸ ~
шапк|а, и *f.*
[1] hat, cap.
[2] (*заголовок*) banner headline(s).
шар, а (*after numerals 2, 3, 4* **~а**), *pl.* **~ы** *m.*
[1] (*math.*) sphere; **земной ш.** the Earth, globe.
[2] (*шаровидный предмет*) spherical object, ball; **воздушный ш.** balloon.
шарах|аться, аюсь *impf.* (*of* ▸ **~нуться**) (*coll.*) (*о лошади*) to shy; (*о толпе*) to start (up); (*бросаться*) to rush, dash.
шарах|нуться, нусь, нешься *pf. of* ▸ **~аться**
шарж, а *m.* caricature, cartoon.
шариат, а *m.* sharia (*Islamic canonical law*).
шариков|ый *adj.*: **~ая ручка** biro (*propr.*), ballpoint (pen).
шар|ить, ю, ишь *impf.* (**в** + *p. or* **по** + *d.*) (*искать ощупью*) to grope about, feel, fumble (in, through); (*о прожекторе*) to sweep (*in order to locate a target*).
шарк|ать, аю *impf.* (+ *i.*) to shuffle.
шарлатан, а *m.* charlatan, fraud; quack.
шарлатан|ка, ки *f. of* ▸ ~
шарм, а *m.* charm.
шарманк|а, и *f.* barrel organ, street organ.
шарманщик, а *m.* organ-grinder.
шарнир, а *m.* (*tech.*) hinge, joint.
шарф, а *m.* scarf.
шасси *nt. indecl.*
[1] (*автомобиля*) chassis.
[2] (*aeron.*) undercarriage.
шаста|ть, ю *impf.* (*coll.*) to roam, hang about.
шата|ть, ю *impf.* to rock, shake.
шата|ться, юсь *impf.*
[1] (*intrans.*) (*о человеке, о вагоне*) to rock, sway, reel.
[2] (*о гвозде*) to be, come loose; (*о стуле, заборе*) to wobble, be unsteady.
[3] (*coll.*) (*бродить*) to roam; to loaf, lounge about.
шатен, а *m.* man/boy with auburn/brown/chestnut hair.
шатен|ка, ки woman/girl with auburn/brown/chestnut hair.
шат|ёр, ра *m.* tent, marquee.
шат|кий (~ок, ~ка, ~ко) *adj.*
[1] (*стол*) unsteady; shaky; (*гайка*) loose.
[2] (*fig.*) unstable, insecure, shaky.
шафер, а, *pl.* **~а** *m.* best man (*at wedding*).
шафран, а *m.* (*bot.*) saffron.
шах[1], а *m.* (*монарх*) Shah.
шах[2], а *m.* (*chess*) check; **ш. и мат** checkmate; **вам ш.** you're in check.
шахматист, а *m.* chess player.
шахматист|ка, ки *f. of* ▸ ~
шахматн|ый *adj.*
[1] chess; **~ая доска** chessboard; **~ая партия** game of chess.
[2] (*с квадратами клеток*) check(ed); chequered (*Br.*), checkered (*US*); **в ~ом порядке** staggered.
шахмат|ы, ~ *no sg.*
[1] (*игра*) chess.
[2] (*фигуры*) chessmen.
шахт|а, ы *f.*
[1] (*горная выработка*) mine, pit.
[2] (*tech.*) (*лифта, вентиляционная*) shaft.
шахтёр, а *m.* miner.
шашк|а[1], и *f.* (*взрывчатка*) charge (*of explosive*).
шашк|а[2], и *f.*
[1] (*в игре*) draught, draughtsman (*Br.*), checker (*US*) (*piece in game of draughts*).
[2] *pl.* (*игра*) draughts (*Br.*), checkers (*US*).
шашлык, а *m.* (*cul.*) kebab, shashlik.
шва *g. sg. of* ▸ **шов**
швабр|а, ы *f.* mop, swab.
шварт|овать, ую *impf.* (*of* ▸ **при~**) (*naut.*) to moor.
шварт|оваться, уюсь *impf.* (*of* ▸ **при~**) (*naut.*) to moor.
швед, а *m.* Swede.
швед|ка, ки *f. of* ▸ ~
шведский *adj.* Swedish.
швейн|ый *adj.* sewing; **~ая машина** sewing machine.
швейцар, а *m.* porter, doorman.
швейцар|ец, ца *m.* Swiss.
Швейцари|я, и *f.* Switzerland.
швейцар|ка, ки *f. of* ▸ **~ец**
швейцарский *adj.* Swiss.
Швеци|я, и *f.* Sweden.
шве|я, и *f.* seamstress.
швыр|нуть, ну, нёшь *inst. pf. of* ▸ **~ять**
швыр|ять, яю *impf.* (*of* ▸ **~нуть**) (+ *a. or i.*) to throw, fling, chuck, hurl.
швыря|ться, юсь *impf.* (*coll.*) (+ *i.*)
[1] (*камнями*) to throw, fling, hurl (at one another).
[2] (*деньгами, друзьями*) to make light (of), trifle (with).
шевел|ить, ю, ишь *impf.* (*of* ▸ **~ьнуть** *and* ▸ **по~**)

1 (*переворачивать*) to turn over.
2 (+ *i.*) (*слегка сдвигать*) to move, stir; **ш. мозгами** (*coll., joc.*) to use one's brains.

шевел|иться, юсь, ишься *impf.* (*of* ▶ **~ьнуться** *and* ▶ **по~**)
1 (*слегка сдвигаться*) to move, stir.
2 (*fig.*) (*о надежде, сомнениях*) to stir.

шевел|ьнуть, ьну, ьнёшь *inst. pf.* (*of* ▶ **~ить**); **пальцем не ш.** not to lift a finger.

шевел|ьнуться, ьнусь, ьнёшься *inst. pf. of* ▶ **~иться**

шевелюр|а, ы *f.* (head of) hair.

шедевр, а *m.* masterpiece.

шезлонг, а *m.* deckchair; lounger.

шейк|а, и, *g. pl.* **шеек** *f.*
1 *dim. of* ▶ **шея.**
2 (*anat.*): **ш. матки** cervix.

шейный *adj. of* ▶ **шея;** (*anat.*) cervical.

шейх, а *m.* sheikh.

шёл *see* ▶ **идти**

шелест, а *m.* rustle, rustling.

шелест|еть, *1st pers. not used,* **ишь** *impf.* to rustle.

шёлк, а (у), о ~е, на (в) ~у/~е, *pl.* **~а** *m.* silk.

шёлковый *adj.* silk.

шелохн|уться, усь, ёшься *pf.* to stir, move.

шелух|а, и *f.* (*плодов, овощей*) skin; peel; (*гороха*) pod.

шелуш|иться, ится *impf.* to peel (off).

шепеляв|ить, лю, ишь *impf.* to lisp.

шеп|нуть, ну, нёшь *inst. pf. of* ▶ **~тать**

шёпот, а *m.* whisper (*also fig.*).

шёпотом *adv.* in a whisper.

шеп|тать, чу, ~чешь *impf.* (*of* ▶ **~нуть** *and* ▶ **про~**) to whisper.

шеп|таться, чусь, ~чешься *impf.* to whisper, converse in whispers.

шеренг|а, и *f.*
1 (*mil.*) rank; file, column.
2 (*fig.*) line, row.

шериф, а *m.* sheriff.

шероховат|ый (~, ~а) *adj.* rough (*also fig.*); (*неровный*) uneven.

шерст|ь, и *f.*
1 (*на животных*) hair.
2 (*волокно*) wool.

шерстяной *adj.* wool, woollen (*Br.*), woolen (*US*).

шершав|ый (~, ~а) *adj.* rough.

шест, а *m.* pole.

шестви|е, я *nt.* procession.

шестерёнк|а, и *f.* (*tech.*) gear (wheel), cogwheel, pinion.

шестёрк|а, и *f.*
1 (*цифра, игральная карта*) six.
2 (*coll.*) (*автобус, трамвай*) number six (*bus, tram, etc.*).
3 (*группа из шестерых*) (group of) six.
4 (*sl.*) (*подчинённый*) slave, dogsbody (*Br.*), gofer.

шестер|о, ых *collect. num.* six.

шестидесятый *adj.* sixtieth.

шестисотый *adj.* six-hundredth.

шестиугольник, а *m.* (*math.*) hexagon.

шестнадцат|ый *adj.* sixteenth; **~ая нота** (*mus.*) semiquaver (*Br.*), sixteenth note (*US*).

шестнадцат|ь, и *num.* sixteen.

шест|ой *adj.* sixth; **одна ~ая** one sixth.

шест|ь, и, *i.* **~ью** *num.* six.

шестьдесят, шестидесяти, *i.* **шестьюдесятью, о шестидесяти** *num.* sixty.

шест|ьсот, исот, истам, ьюстами, о ~истах *num.* six hundred.

шеф, а *m.*
1 (*coll.*) (*начальник*) boss, chief.
2 (*покровитель*) patron, sponsor.

шеф-повар, а, *pl.* **~а, ~ов** *m.* chef.

ше|я, и *f.* neck; **сидеть на ~е у кого-н.** (*coll.*) to live off s.o.

шиворот, а *m.* (*coll.*): **за ш.** by the collar, by the scruff of the neck.

шизофреник, а *m.* (*med.*) schizophrenic; (*coll., offens.*) crazy person.

шизофрени|я, и *f.* (*med.*) schizophrenia.

шиит, а *m.* Shiite (Muslim).

шик, а (у) *m.* stylishness; style.

шикар|ный (~ен, ~на) *adj.* (*coll.*) (*роскошный*) chic, smart, stylish; (*отличный*) gorgeous.

шик|ать, аю *impf.* (*of* ▶ **~нуть**) (*coll.*) (**на** + *a.*) to hush (*by crying 'sh'*); (*в знак неодобрения*) to hiss (at), boo, catcall.

шик|нуть, ну, нешь *pf. of* ▶ **~ать**

шимпанзе *m. indecl.* chimpanzee.

шин|а, ы *f.*
1 tyre (*Br.*), tire (*US*).
2 (*med.*) splint.

шинел|ь, и *f.* greatcoat.

шинк|овать, ую *impf.* (*of* ▶ **на~**) (*cul.*) to shred.

шиншилл|а, ы *f.* chinchilla.

шип, а *m.*
1 (*bot.*) thorn.
2 (*на спортивной обуви*) spike; (*на ботинках альпиниста*) crampon.

шипени|е, я *nt.* hissing; sizzling; sputtering.

шип|еть, лю, ишь *impf.*
1 (*о змее*) to hiss; (*при жарке*) to sizzle; (*о напитке*) to fizz.
2 (*от злости*) to hiss.

шипучий *adj.* (*вино*) sparkling; (*напиток, пиво, вода*) fizzy.

шир|е *comp. of* ▶ **~окий** *and* ▶ **~око**

ширин|а, ы *f.* width, breadth; (*колеи*) gauge (*of railway track*).

ширинк|а, и *f.* fly (*of trousers*).

ширм|а, ы *f.* screen (*also fig.*).

широк|ий (~, ~а, ~о, *pl.* **~и)** *adj.*
1 wide, broad (*also fig.*); **в ~ом смысле** in a broad sense.
2 (*fig.*) big, extensive, general; **товары ~ого потребления** (*econ.*) consumer goods; **ш. круг читателей** the average reader, the general reading public; **жить на ~ую ногу** to live in grand style.

широко *adv.*
1 wide, widely, broadly (*also fig.*); **ш. раскрыть глаза** to open one's eyes wide; **ш. толковать** to interpret loosely.
2 (*в широком масштабе*) extensively, on a

large scale.
широкопле́ч|ий (~, ~а) *adj.* broad-shouldered.
широт|а́, ы́, *pl.* **~ы, ~** *f.*
1 width, breadth.
2 (*geog.*) latitude.
широча́йший *superl. of* ▸ **широ́кий**
ширпотре́б, а *m.* (*collect.*) mass-market goods.
шить, шью, шьёшь *impf.* (*of* ▸ **с~ 1**)
1 to sew.
2 (*изготовлять*) to make (*by sewing*); **ш. себе́ что-н.** to have sth. made.
ши́фер, а *m.* slate.
шифр, а *m.*
1 cipher; code.
2 (*библиотечный*) shelf mark (*Br.*), call number (*US*).
шифр|ова́ть, у́ю *impf.* (*of* ▸ **за~**) to encipher.
ши́шк|а, и *f.*
1 (*bot.*) cone.
2 (*бугорок*) bump; lump.
шишкова́т|ый (~, ~а) *adj.* knobbly; bumpy.
шкал|а́, ы́, *pl.* **~ы** *f.* (*зарплаты, термометра*) scale; (*приёмника*) dial.
шкату́лк|а, и *f.* box, casket, case.
шкаф, а, о ~е, в (на) ~у́, *pl.* **~ы́** *m.* cupboard; (*платяной*) wardrobe; (*кухонный*) dresser; **кни́жный ш.** bookcase (*with doors*); **несгора́емый ш.** safe.
шквал, а *nt.* squall; (*fig.*) (*огня, возмущения*) burst.
шко́л|а, ы *f.*
1 (*учреждение*) school; **ходи́ть в ~у** to go to school; **око́нчить ~у** to leave school; **ш.-интерна́т** boarding school.
2 (*выучка*) schooling, training.
шко́льник, а *m.* schoolboy.
шко́льниц|а, ы *f.* schoolgirl.
шко́льный *adj.* school; **ш. во́зраст** school age.
шку́р|а, ы *f.* skin (*also fig.*), hide, pelt; **быть в чьей-н. ~е** to be in s.o.'s shoes.
шку́рк|а, и *f.*
1 (*шкура*) skin.
2 (*coll.*) (*плода*) rind.
3 (*бумага*) emery paper, sandpaper.
шла *see* ▸ **идти́**
шлагба́ум, а *m.* barrier (*of swing beam type, at road or rail crossing*).
шлак, а *m.* slag; clinker.
шланг, а *m.* hose.
шлем, а *m.* helmet; **защи́тный ш.** (*on building site, etc.*) hard hat.
шлёпан|цы, цев *pl.* (*sg.* **~ец, ~ца** *m.*) slippers.
шлёп|ать, аю *impf.* (*of* ▸ **от~** *and* ▸ **~нуть**) to smack, slap, spank.
шлёп|аться, аюсь *impf.* (*of* ▸ **~нуться**) (*coll.*) to fall with a plop, thud.
шлёп|нуть(ся), ну(сь), нешь(ся) *inst. pf. of* ▸ **~ать(ся)**
шлёшь, шлёт, *etc. see* ▸ **слать**
шли[1] *see* ▸ **идти́**
шли[2] *see* ▸ **слать**
шлиф|ова́ть, у́ю *impf. of* ▸ **от~**
шло *see* ▸ **идти́**
шлю, шлют *see* ▸ **слать**
шлюз, а *m.* lock, sluice, floodgate.
шлю́пк|а, и *f.* launch, boat; **спаса́тельная ш.** lifeboat.
шлю́х|а, и *f.* (*vulg.*) tart.
шля́п|а, ы *f.* hat; **де́ло в ~е** (*coll.*) it's in the bag.
шля́пк|а, и *f.*
1 (*woman's*) hat.
2 (*гвоздя*) head (*of nail, etc.*).
шля́|ться, юсь *impf.* (*coll.*) to loaf about.
шмел|ь, я́ *m.* bumblebee.
шмо́т|ки, ок *no sg.* (*coll.*) clothes.
шмы́г|ать, аю *impf.* (*of* ▸ **~ну́ть 1**) (*coll.*)
1 (+ *i.*) (*ногами, туфлями*) to scrape; (*щеткой*) to brush; **ш. но́сом** to sniff.
2 (*быстро двигаться*) to rush around; to scurry.
шмыг|ну́ть, ну́, нёшь *pf.* (*coll.*)
1 *inst. pf. of* ▸ **~ать.**
2 (*быстро убежать*) to dart, nip, sneak (*in order to escape notice*).
шни́цел|ь, я *m.* (*cul.*) schnitzel.
шнур, а́ *m.*
1 (*верёвка*) cord; lace.
2 (*elec.*) flex, cable.
шнур|ова́ть, у́ю *impf.* (*of* **за~**) (*ботинки*) to lace up.
шнур|о́к, ка́ *m.* lace.
шныр|я́ть, я́ю *impf.* (*coll.*) to dart about.
шов, шва *m.*
1 (*швейный*) seam; **без шва** seamless.
2 (*в вышивании*) stitch.
3 (*хирургический*) stitch, suture; **наложи́ть, снять швы** to put in, remove stitches.
4 (*tech.*) (*место соединения*) joint, seam, junction.
шовини́зм, а *m.* chauvinism.
шовини́ст, а *m.* chauvinist.
шовинисти́ческий *adj.* chauvinistic.
шок, а *m.* (*med., fig.*) shock.
шоки́р|овать, ую *impf.* to shock.
шокола́д, а *m.* chocolate.
шокола́дк|а, и *f.* (*coll.*) (*плитка шоколада*) bar of chocolate; (*конфета*) a chocolate (sweet).
шокола́д|ный *adj. of* ▸ **~**
шо́рох, а *m.* rustle.
шо́рт|ы, ~ *and* **~ов** *no sg.* shorts.
шоссе́ *nt. indecl.* highway; surfaced road.
шотла́нд|ец, ца *m.* Scotsman, Scot.
Шотла́нди|я, и *f.* Scotland; **Но́вая Ш.** (*провинция Канады*) Nova Scotia.
шотла́нд|ка[1], ки *f. of* ▸ **~ец**
шотла́нд|ка[2], ки *f.* (*text.*) tartan, plaid.
шотла́ндский *adj.* Scottish, Scots.
шо́у *nt. indecl.* show.
шо́у-би́знес, а *m.* show business.
шофёр, а *m.* driver; (*персональный*) chauffeur.
шпа́г|а, и *f.* sword; (*sport*) épée; **скрести́ть ~и** to cross swords (*also fig.*).
шпага́т, а *m.*
1 string, cord; (*agric.*) binder twine.

Ш

2 (*в гимнастике*) the splits.
шпаклёвк|а, и *f.*
1 (*действие*) filling, puttying.
2 (*вещество*) putty, filler.
шпа́л|а, ы *f.* (*rail.*) sleeper (*Br.*), cross tie (*US*).
шпан|а́, ы́ *f.* (*coll.*) hooligan; (*also collect.*) rabble.
шпарга́лк|а, и *f.* (*coll.*) crib (sheet) (*in school, university*).
шпа́р|ить, ю, ишь *impf.* (*coll.*)
1 (*pf.* **о~**) (*обливать кипятком*) to scald, pour boiling water on.
2 (*делать, говорить быстро, энергично*) to do, say, *etc.*, in a rush, energetically.
шпа́тел|ь, я *m.* (*tech.*, *art*) palette knife.
шпик, а *m.* (*cul.*) lard.
шпил|ь, я *m.* spire, steeple.
шпи́льк|а, и *f.*
1 (*для волос*) hairpin.
2 (*каблук*) stiletto.
шпина́т, а *m.* spinach.
шпио́н, а *m.* spy.
шпиона́ж, а *m.* espionage.
шпио́н|ить, ю, ишь *impf.* (**за** + *i.*) to spy (on).
шпио́н|ка, ки *f. of* ▸ **~**
шпио́н|ский *adj. of* ▸ **~**
шпо́р|а, ы *f.* spur.
шприц, а *m.* (*med.*) syringe.
шпро́т|ы, ~ *pl.* (*sg.* **~а, ~ы** *f. and* **~, ~а** *m.*) sprats.
шрам, а *m.* scar.
шрапне́л|ь, и *f.* shrapnel.
Шри-Ланк|а́, и́ *f.* Sri Lanka.
шрифт, а, *pl.* **~ы́** *m.* type, type face; (*comput.*) font.
штаб, а, *pl.* **~ы́** *m.* (*mil.*) (*лица*) staff; (*место*) headquarters.
шта́бел|ь, я, *pl.* **~я́, ~е́й** *m.* stack, pile.
штаб-кварти́р|а, ы *f.* (*mil.*) headquarters.
штамп, а *m.*
1 (*tech.*) (*форма*) die, punch.
2 (*печать*) stamp.
3 (*fig.*, *pej.*) (*банальность*) cliché, stock phrase.
штамп|ова́ть, у́ю *impf.*
1 (*tech.*) (*детали*) to punch, press.
2 (*документы*) to stamp.
3 (*fig.*) (*стихи*) to churn out; (*решения*) to rubber-stamp.
шта́нг|а, и *f.*
1 (*sport*) (*стержень с тяжестями*) weight.
2 (*sport*) (*ворот*) goalpost.
штангенци́ркул|ь, я *m.* (*tech.*) sliding callipers, slide gauge.
штанги́ст, а *m.* (*sport*) weightlifter.
штан|ы́, о́в *no sg.* trousers.
штат[1], а *m.* state; **Соединённые Ш~ы Аме́рики** United States of America.
штат[2], а *m.* (*sg. or pl.*) (*сотрудники*) staff.
штати́в, а *m.* tripod, base, support, stand.
шта́тск|ий *adj.* civilian; *as n.* **ш., ~ого** *m.* civilian.
ште́мпел|ь, я, *pl.* **~я́** *m.* stamp; **почто́вый ш.** postmark.
ште́псел|ь, я, *pl.* **~я́** *m.* (*elec.*) (*вилка*) plug.
шти́л|ь, я *m.* (*naut.*) calm.
што́па|ть, ю *impf.* (*of* ▸ **за~**) to darn.
што́пор, а *m.* corkscrew.
што́р|а, ы *f.* blind.
шторм, а *m.* (*naut.*) strong gale (*wind force 9*); (*coll.*) gale.
штормо́вк|а, и *f.* (*coll.*) anorak; parka.
штраф, а *m.* fine; **наложи́ть ш.** to impose a fine.
штраф|но́й *adj.*
1 *adj. of* ▸ **~.**
2 penal, penalty; **~на́я площа́дка** (*sport*) penalty area; **ш. уда́р** (*sport*) penalty kick.
штраф|ова́ть, у́ю *impf.* (*of* ▸ **о~**) to fine.
штрейкбре́хер, а *m.* strike-breaker, blackleg.
штрих, а́ *m.*
1 (*черта*) stroke (*in drawing*).
2 (*fig.*) (*частность*) feature, trait.
штрихко́д, а *m.* bar code.
шту́к|а, и *f.*
1 (*отдельный предмет*) item, one of a kind (*oft. not translated*); **по рублю́ ш.** one rouble each; **я возьму́ шесть ~** I'll have six (*of item in question*).
2 (*coll.*) (*вещь*) thing.
штукату́р, а *m.* plasterer.
штукату́р|ить, ю, ишь *impf.* (*of* ▸ **о~**) to plaster.
штукату́рк|а, и *f.*
1 (*действие*) plastering.
2 (*раствор, слой раствора*) plaster.
штурва́л, а *m.* steering wheel; controls; **стоя́ть за ~ом** to be at the wheel, helm, controls.
штурм, а *m.* (*mil.*) storm, assault.
шту́рман, а *m.* (*naut.*, *aeron.*) navigator.
штурм|ова́ть, у́ю *impf.* to storm, assault.
штык, а́ *m.* bayonet; **встре́тить, приня́ть в ~и́** (*fig.*) to give a hostile reception (to), oppose adamantly.
шты́р|ь, я́ *m.* (*tech.*) pin, dowel.
шу́б|а, ы *f.* fur coat.
шу́лер, а, *pl.* **~а́** *m.* card sharper, cheat.
шум, а (у) *m.*
1 (*звуки*) noise.
2 (*coll.*) (*брань, скандал*) din, uproar, racket; **подня́ть ш.** to kick up a racket.
3 (*fig.*) (*оживлённое обсуждение*) sensation, stir.
шум|е́ть, лю́, и́шь *impf.*
1 (*издавать шум*) to make a noise.
2 (*coll.*) (*браниться, кричать*) to row.
3 (*fig.*) (*оживлённо обсуждать*) to create a stir, fuss, sensation.
шу́м|ный (~ен, ~на́, ~но, ~ны́) *adj.*
1 noisy; loud.
2 (*fig.*) sensational.
шумо́вк|а, и *f.* (*cul.*) perforated spoon, straining ladle.
шу́рин, а *m.* brother-in-law (*wife's brother*).
шуру́п, а *m.* (*tech.*) screw.
шурш|а́ть, у́, и́шь *impf.* to rustle (*also* + *i.*, *trans.*).
шу́ст|рый (~(ё)р, ~ра́, ~ро, ~ры́) *adj.* (*coll.*) smart, bright, sharp.
шут, а́ *m.*
1 (*hist.*) (*при дворе*) fool, jester.
2 (*fig.*, *coll.*) (*паяц*) fool, buffoon, clown.

шу|ти́ть, чу́, ~тишь *impf.* (*of* ▸ **по~**)
1 to joke, jest; **я же не ~чу́** but I'm not joking.
2 (**с** + *i.*) (*несерьёзно относиться*) to play (with), trifle (with); **ш. с огнём** to play with fire.
3 (**над** + *i.*) (*смеяться*) to laugh (at), make fun (of).

шу́тк|а, и *f.* joke, jest; **не ш.** it's no joke; **с ней ~и пло́хи** she is not to be trifled with; **без шу́ток** joking apart; **сказа́ть в ~у** to say as a joke; **не на ~у** in earnest.

шутли́в|ый (~, ~а) *adj.*
1 (*человек, характер*) jokey.
2 (*тон, замечание*) joking, light-hearted; (*рассказ, песня*) humorous.

шутни́к, а́ *m.* joker.

шушу́ка|ться, юсь *impf.* (*coll.*) to whisper; (*fig.*) to gossip.

шху́н|а, ы *f.* schooner.

Щщ

ща|ди́ть, жу́, ди́шь *impf.* (*of* ▸ **по~**) to spare.

щё́б|ень, ня *m.* crushed stone, ballast (*as road surfacing*).

щебе|та́ть, чу́, ~чешь *impf.* to twitter, chirp.

щегольн|у́ть, у́, ёшь *inst. pf. of* ▸ **щеголя́ть 2**

щегол|я́ть, я́ю *impf.* (*coll.*)
1 (**в** + *p.*) (*в новом платье*) to strut around in; to sport.
2 (*pf.* **~ьну́ть**) (+ *i.*) (*своими знаниями*) to show off, parade, flaunt.

ще́дрост|ь, и *f.* generosity.

ще́др|ый (~, ~а́, ~о, ~ы) *adj.* generous; (**на** + *a.*) generous/lavish with.

щек|а́, и́, *a.* **~у/~у́,** *pl.* **~и, ~, ~а́м** *f.* cheek; **уда́рить кого́-н. по ~е́** to slap s.o.'s face.

щеко́лд|а, ы *f.* latch; catch.

щеко|та́ть, чу́, ~чешь *impf.* (*of* ▸ **по~**)
1 to tickle (*also fig.*).
2 (*impers.*): **у меня́ в го́рле,** *etc.*, **~чет** I have a tickle in my throat, *etc.*

щеко́тк|а, и *f.* tickling; **боя́ться ~и** to be ticklish.

щекотли́в|ый (~, ~а) *adj.* delicate, sensitive; **~ая те́ма** delicate subject.

щеко́тно *as pred.* (*impers.* + *d.*) it tickles.

щёлк|ать, аю *impf.* (*of* ▸ **~нуть**)
1 (*человека, по лбу и т. п.*) to flick.
2 (+ *i.*) (*производить звук*) to click, snap, crack; (*comput.*) to click; **два́жды щ.** to double-click.
3 (*impf. only*) (*орехи*) to crack.

щёлк|нуть, ну, нешь *inst. pf. of* ▸ **~ать 1, 2**

щелочно́й *adj.* (*chem.*) alkaline.

щёлоч|ь, и, *pl.* **~и, ~е́й** *f.* (*chem.*) alkali.

щелч|о́к, ка́ *m.* flick (of the fingers); (*comput.*) (*мышью*) click; **двойно́й щ.** double click.

щел|ь, и, *pl.* **~и, ~е́й** *f.* crack; chink; slit; (*в игровом, торговом автомате*) slot.

щен|о́к, ка́ *m.* puppy, pup (*also fig.*); whelp, cub.

щепети́л|ьный (~ен, ~ьна) *adj.*
1 (*человек*) punctilious; (over)scrupulous.
2 (*вопрос*) delicate.

ще́пк|а, и *f.* (*wood*) splinter, chip; (*collect.*) kindling.

щепо́т|ка, ки *f.* pinch (*of salt, snuff, etc.*).

щети́н|а, ы *f.* bristle; (*coll.*) (*борода*) stubble.

щети́н|иться, юсь, ишься *impf. of* ▸ **о~**

щётк|а, и *f.* brush; **зубна́я щ.** toothbrush; **щ. для воло́с** hairbrush.

щи, щей, щам, ща́ми, о щах *no sg.* shchi (*cabbage soup*).

щи́колотк|а, и *f.* ankle.

щип|а́ть, лю́, ~лешь *impf.*
1 (*pf.* **ущипну́ть**) (*защемлять до боли*) to pinch, nip, tweak.
2 (*impf. only*) (*о морозе*) to sting, bite; (*о горчице*) to burn.
3 (*pf.* **о~**) (*птицу*) to pluck.

щипц|ы́, о́в *no sg.* (*каминные*) tongs; (*tech.*) pincers; (*плоскогубцы*) pliers; (*хирургические*) forceps.

щи́пчик|и, ов *no sg.* tweezers.

щит, а́ *m.*
1 shield; **живо́й щ.** human shield.
2 (*ограждение*) shield, screen.
3 (*рекламный*) (display) board.
4 (*tech.*) (*пульт*) panel; *see also* ▸ **распредели́тельный**

щитови́дн|ый *adj.* (*anat.*): **~ая железа́** thyroid gland.

щит|о́к, ка́ *m.*
1 *dim. of* ▸ **~ 2–4;** (*у машины*) dashboard.
2 (*sport*) shin pad.
3 (*elec.*) *see* ▸ **распредели́тельный**

щу́к|а, и *f.* pike (*fish*).

щу́пальц|е, а, *g. pl.* **щу́палец** *nt.* (*zool.*) tentacle; antenna.

щу́па|ть, ю *impf.* (*of* ▸ **по~**) to feel (for), touch; (*fig.*; *coll.*) to size up, suss out; **щ. пульс** (*med.*) to feel the pulse.

щу́пл|ый (~, ~а́, ~о) *adj.* weak, puny, frail.

щу́р|иться, юсь, ишься *impf.* to screw up one's eyes, squint.

Ээ

эвакуа́ци|я, и *f.* evacuation.
эвакуи́р|овать, ую *impf. and pf.* to evacuate (*trans.*).
эвакуи́р|оваться, уюсь *impf. and pf.* to be evacuated.
Эвере́ст, а *m.* (Mt) Everest.
эвкали́пт, а *m.* (*bot.*) eucalyptus.
ЭВМ *f. indecl.* (*abbr. of* **электро́нно-вычисли́тельная маши́на**) computer.
эволю́ци|я, и *f.* evolution.
эвтана́зи|я, и *f.* euthanasia.
эвфеми́зм, а *m.* euphemism.
эги́д|а, ы *f.* aegis; **под ~ой** (+ *g.*) under the aegis (of).
эгои́зм, а *m.* egoism, selfishness.
эгои́ст, а *m.* egoist.
эгоисти́ческий *adj.* egoistic, selfish.
эгоисти́ч|ный (~ен, ~на) *adj.* = **~еский**
эгои́ст|ка, ки *f. of* ▸ **~**
эгоцентри́ч|ный (~ен, ~на) *adj.* egocentric.
Э́динбу́рг, а *m.* Edinburgh.
эй *int.* hey!
эйфори́|я, и *f.* euphoria.
Эквадо́р, а *m.* Ecuador.
эквадо́р|ец, ца *m.* Ecuadorean.
эквадо́р|ка, ки *f. of* ▸ **~ец**
эквадо́рский *adj.* Ecuadorean.
эква́тор, а *m.* equator.
эквивале́нт, а *m.* equivalent.
эквивале́нт|ный (~ен, ~на) *adj.* equivalent.
экза́мен, а *m.* examination; **сдава́ть э.** to take, sit an examination; **сдать э.** to pass an examination; **провали́ться на ~е** to fail an examination; **э. на води́тельские права́** driving test.
экзамена́тор, а *m.* examiner.
экзаменацио́нн|ый *adj. of* ▸ **экза́мен; э. биле́т** examination paper; **~ая се́ссия** examination period, exams.
экзамен|ова́ть, у́ю *impf.* (*of* ▸ **про~**) to examine.
экзе́м|а, ы *f.* (*med.*) eczema.
экземпля́р, а *m.*
1 copy; **переписа́ть в двух ~ах** to make two copies.
2 (*живо́тного, расте́ния*) specimen, example.
экзистенциали́зм, а *m.* existentialism.
экзистенциа́льный *adj.* existential.
экзо́тик|а, и *f.* exotica, exotic objects.
экзоти́ческий *adj.* exotic.
экипа́ж[1]**, а** *m.* (*пово́зка*) carriage.
экипа́ж[2]**, а** *m.* (*кома́нда*) crew (*of ship, aircraft, tank*).
экипиро́вк|а, и *f.*
1 (*де́йствие*) equipping.
2 (*снаряже́ние*) equipment.
эклекти́ч|ный (~ен, ~на) *adj.* eclectic.
эко́лог, а *m.* ecologist.
экологи́ческий *adj.* ecological.
эколо́ги|я, и *f.* ecology.
эконо́мик|а, и *f.*
1 (*нау́ка*) economics.
2 (*страны́*) economy; **ры́ночная э.** market economy.
экономи́ст, а *m.* economist.
эконо́м|ить, лю, ишь *impf.* (*of* ▸ **с~**)
1 (*де́ньги, си́лы*) to use sparingly; to save.
2 (**на** + *p.*) to economize (on), save (on).
экономи́ческий *adj.* economic.
экономи́ч|ный (~ен, ~на) *adj.* economical.
эконо́ми|я, и *f.*
1 economy, saving.
2 : **полити́ческая э.** political economy.
эконо́м|ный (~ен, ~на) *adj.* economical; careful, thrifty.
экосисте́м|а, ы *f.* ecosystem.
экра́н, а *m.*
1 (*cin., TV, comput.*) screen.
2 (*fig.*) (*киноиску́сство*) screen.
3 (*phys., tech.*) screen, shield, shade.
экраниза́ци|я, и *f.* (*cin.*) filming, screening; (*рома́на*) film adaptation.
экс-... *pref.* ex-.
экскава́тор, а *m.* (*tech.*) excavator, mechanical digger.
эксклюзи́в|ный (~ен, ~на) *adj.* exclusive.
экскреме́нт|ы, ов *no sg.* excrement.
экску́рси|я, и *f.* excursion, (conducted) tour, trip.
экскурсово́д, а *m.* guide.
экспанси́в|ный (~ен, ~на) *adj.* effusive.
экспа́нси|я, и *f.* (*pol.*) expansion.
экспатриа́нт, а *m.* expatriate.
экспатриа́нт|ка, ки *f. of* ▸ **~**
экспеди́тор, а *m.* forwarding agent, shipping clerk.
экспеди́ци|я, и *f.*
1 (*де́йствие*) dispatch, forwarding.
2 (*пое́здка; уча́стники э́той пое́здки*) expedition.
экспериме́нт, а *m.* experiment.
эксперимента́льный *adj.* experimental.
эксперимента́тор, а *m.* experimenter.
эксперименти́р|овать, ую *impf.* (**над, с** + *i.*) to experiment (on, with).
экспе́рт, а *m.* expert.
эксперти́з|а, ы *f.* (*leg., med.*) (*expert*) examination, expert opinion; **произвести́ ~у** to make an examination.
экспе́рт|ный *adj. of* ▸ **~; ~ная коми́ссия** commission of experts.

эксплуатáци|я, и *f.*
1 (*pol.*; *pej.*) exploitation.
2 (*природных богатств*) exploitation; (*средств производства*) utilization; (*машин*) operation, running; **сдать в ~ю** to commission, put into operation.

эксплуати́р|овать, ую *impf.*
1 (*pol.*; *pej.*) to exploit.
2 (*природные богатства*) to exploit; (*машины*) to operate, run, work.

экспози́ци|я, и *f.*
1 (*музейная*) display.
2 (*liter.*, *mus.*) exposition.
3 (*phot.*) exposure.

экспонáт, а *m.* exhibit.

экспони́р|овать, ую *impf. and pf.* (*для обозрения*) to exhibit.

э́кспорт, а *m.* export.

экспортёр, а *m.* exporter.

экспорти́р|овать, ую *impf. and pf.* to export.

э́кспорт|ный *adj. of* ▸ ~

экспрéсс, а *m.* express (*train, motor coach, etc.*).

экспресси́в|ный (~ен, ~на) *adj.* expressive.

экспрессиони́зм, а *m.* expressionism.

экспрессиони́ст, а *m.* expressionist.

экспрéсси|я, и *f.* expression.

экспро́мт, а *m.* improvisation; (*mus.*) impromptu.

экстáз, а *m.* ecstasy.

э́кстези *m. indecl.* (*sl.*) ecstasy (*the drug*).

экстенси́в|ный (~ен, ~на) *adj.* extensive.

экстéрн, а *m.* external student; **око́нчить университéт ~ом** to take an external degree.

экстерьéр, а *m.* outward appearance, form (*of an animal*).

экстравагáнт|ный (~ен, ~на) *adj.* eccentric, bizarre.

экстравéрт, а *m.* extrovert.

экстради́ци|я, и *f.* (*leg.*) extradition.

экстраординáр|ный (~ен, ~на) *adj.* extraordinary.

экстрасéнс, а *m.* psychic.

экстремáл|ьный (~ен, ~ьна) *adj.* extreme.

экстреми́зм, а *m.* extremism.

экстреми́ст, а *m.* extremist.

экстреми́стский *adj.* extremist.

э́кстрен|ный (~, ~на) *adj.*
1 (*срочный*) urgent; emergency; **э. вы́зов** urgent summons; **в ~ном слу́чае** in case of emergency.
2 (*чрезвычайный*) extra, special; **~ное заседáние** extraordinary session.

эксцентри́ч|ный (~ен, ~на) *adj.* eccentric.

эласти́ч|ный (~ен, ~на) *adj.* elastic (*also fig.*); **~ные брю́ки** stretch pants.

элевáтор, а *m.*
1 (*agric.*) grain store (*Br.*), elevator (*US*).
2 (*tech.*) hoist.

элегáнт|ный (~ен, ~на) *adj.* elegant, smart.

электорáт, а *m.* electorate.

элéктрик, а *m.* electrician.

электри́ческий *adj.* electric(al).

электри́честв|о, а *nt.*
1 electricity.
2 (*освещение*) electric light; **зажéчь э.** to turn on the light.

электри́чк|а, и *f.* (*coll.*) (suburban) electric train.

электрово́з, а *m.* electric locomotive.

электрогитáр|а, ы *f.* electric guitar.

электродви́гател|ь, я *m.* electric motor.

электромонтёр, а *m.* electrician.

электро́н, а *m.* (*phys.*) electron.

электро́ник|а, и *f.* electronics.

электро́н|ный *adj.*
1 *adj. of* ▸ **~; э. микроско́п** electron microscope.
2 electronic; **~ная по́чта** electronic mail, email (*the system*); **~ное письмо́** email (letter); **э. áдрес** email address; **~ная табли́ца** spreadsheet.

электропо́езд, а *m.* electric train.

электроприбо́р, а *m.* electrical appliance.

электропрово́дк|а, и *f.* electric wiring.

электростáнци|я, и *f.* power station.

электротéхник, а *m.* electrical engineer.

электроэнéрги|я, и *f.* electric power.

элемéнт, а *m.*
1 (*компонент, доля*) element; **э. изображéния** (*comput.*) pixel.
2 (*chem.*) element.

элементáр|ный (~ен, ~на) *adj.* elementary.

эли́т|а, ы *f.* elite.

элитáр|ный (~ен, ~на) *adj.* elite; (*pej.*) elitist.

эли́тный *adj.* best-quality.

эльф, а *m.* elf.

эмалиро́ванн|ый *adj.* enamelled (*Br.*), enameled (*US*); **~ая посу́да** enamel ware.

эмáл|ь, и *f.* enamel.

эмансипáци|я, и *f.* (*also leg.*) emancipation.

эмбáрго *nt. indecl.* (*econ.*) embargo.

эмблéм|а, ы *f.* emblem; (*mil.*) insignia.

эмbrио́н, а *m.* (*biol.*) embryo.

эмигрáнт, а *m.* émigré, emigrant.

эмигрáнт|ка, ки *f. of* ▸ ~

эмигрáци|я, и *f.*
1 emigration.
2 (*collect.*) emigration, émigrés.

эмигри́р|овать, ую *impf. and pf.* to emigrate.

эмоционáл|ьный (~ен, ~ьна) *adj.* emotional.

эмо́ци|я, и *f.* emotion.

эмпири́ческий *adj.* empirical.

эму́льси|я, и *f.* emulsion.

энергéтик, а *m.* energy specialist.

энергéтик|а, и *f.* energy sector (of the economy), power industry.

энергет|и́ческий *adj. of* ▸ **~и́ка**

энерги́ч|ный (~ен, ~на) *adj.* energetic,

vigorous, forceful.
энéрги|я, и *f.*
[1] (*phys.*) energy; power; **затрáта ~и** energy consumption.
[2] (*fig.*) energy; vigour (*Br.*), vigor (*US*), effort.
энергосистéм|а, ы *f.* power (supply) system.
энтомóлог, а *m.* entomologist.
энтомолóги|я, и *f.* entomology.
энтузиáзм, а *m.* enthusiasm.
энтузиáст, а *m.* (+ *g.*) enthusiast (about, for), devotee (of).
энциклопéди|я, и *f.* encyclopedia.
эпидéми|я, и *f.* epidemic.
эпизóд, а *m.* episode.
эпизоди́ческий *adj.* episodic; occasional, sporadic.
эпилéпси|я, и *f.* epilepsy.
эпилéптик, а *m.* epileptic.
эпилепти́ческий *adj.* epileptic.
эпилóг, а *m.* epilogue (*Br.*), epilog (*US*).
эпитáфи|я, и *f.* epitaph.
эпи́тет, а *m.* epithet.
эпопéя, и *f.* epic.
э́пос, а *m.* epic literature.
эпóх|а, и *f.* epoch, age, era.
э́р|а, ы *f.* era; **до нáшей ~ы** BC (*before Christ*); **нáшей ~ы** AD (*Anno Domini*).
эргономи́ч|ный (~ен, ~на) *adj.* ergonomic.
эрéкци|я, и *f.* (*physiol.*) erection.
эрзáц, а *m.* ersatz, substitute.
Эритрé|я, и *f.* Eritrea.
эритроци́т, а *m.* (*physiol.*) erythrocyte, red corpuscle.
эрóзи|я, и *f.* erosion.
эрóтик|а, и *f.*
[1] (*чувственность*) sensuality.
[2] (*collect.*) (*искусство*) erotica.
эроти́ческий *adj.* erotic, sensual.
Эр-Ри́яд, а *m.* Riyadh.
эруди́рован|ный (~, ~на) *adj.* erudite.
эруди́ци|я, и *f.* erudition.
эскадри́л|ья, ьи, *g. pl.* **~ий** *f.* (*aeron.*) squadron.
эскадрóн, а *m.* (*mil.*) (*cavalry*) squadron, troop.
эскалáтор, а *m.* escalator.
эскалóп, а *m.* (*cul.*) escalope.
эски́з, а *m.* (*к картине*) sketch, study; (*чертёж*) draft, outline.
эскимóс, а *m.* Eskimo, Inuit.
эскимóс|ка, ки *f. of* ▸ **~**
эскимóсский *adj.* Eskimo, Inuit.
эскóрт, а *m.* (*mil.*) escort.
эссé *nt. indecl.* essay.
эссéнци|я, и *f.* essence.
эстакáд|а, ы *f.*
[1] (*на железной дороге*) viaduct.
[2] (*на шоссе*) flyover (*Br.*), overpass.
эстафéт|а, ы *f.*
[1] (*sport*) relay race.
[2] (*палочка*) baton (*in relay race*)
эстéт, а *m.* aesthete.
эстéтик|а, и *f.*
[1] aesthetics.
[2] (*художественность*) design.
эстети́ческий *adj.* aesthetic.
эстети́ч|ный (~ен, ~на) *adj.* aesthetic.
эстóн|ец, ца *m.* Estonian.
Эстóни|я, и *f.* Estonia.
эстóн|ка, ки *f. of* ▸ **~ец**
эстóнский *adj.* Estonian.
эстрáд|а, ы *f.*
[1] stage, platform; **вы́йти на ~у** to come on stage.
[2] (*представление*) variety; **арти́ст ~ы** variety performer, artiste.
эстрáд|ный *adj. of* ▸ **~а; э. концéрт** variety show; **~ная му́зыка** popular music.
этáж, á *m.* storey (*Br.*), story (*US*), floor; **пéрвый, вторóй,** *etc.*, **э.** ground floor, first floor, *etc.* (*Br.*), first floor, second floor, *etc.* (*US*).
эталóн, а *m.* standard (*of weights and measures*); (*fig.*) (*мерило*) benchmark.
этáп, а *m.* stage, phase.
э́тик|а, и *f.* ethics.
этикéт, а *m.* etiquette.
этикéтк|а, и *f.* label.
этимолóги|я, и *f.* etymology.
эти́ч|ный (~ен, ~на) *adj.* ethical.
этни́ческий *adj.* ethnic.
этнографи́ческий *adj.* ethnographic(al).
этногрáфи|я, и *f.* ethnography, social anthropology.
э́то[1] *see* ▸ **э́тот**
э́то[2] *emph. particle* (*coll.*); **кудá э. он дéлся?** wherever has he got to?; **э.** ***вы*** **спрáшивали?** was it *you* who was asking?
э́то[3] *pron.* (*as n.*) this (is), that (is); **э. наш дом** this is our house; **э. вéрно** that is true; **не в ~м дéло** that's not the point.
э́тот, э́та, э́то, *pl.* **э́ти** *pron.* this (these); *as n.* (*i*) this one, (*ii*) (*последнее из названных лиц*) the latter.
этю́д, а *m.*
[1] (*art, liter.*) study, sketch.
[2] (*mus.*) (*произведение*) étude.
[3] (*mus.*) (*упражнение*) exercise.
эфéс, а *m.* hilt, handle (*of sword, sabre, etc.*).
эфиóп, а *m.* Ethiopian.
Эфиóпи|я, и *f.* Ethiopia.
эфиóп|ка, ки *f. of* ▸ **~**
эфиóпский *adj.* Ethiopian.
эфи́р, а *m.*
[1] ether; (*fig.*) air; **прямóй э.** live broadcast.
[2] (*chem.*) ether.
эффéкт, а *m.*
[1] effect, impact; **произвести́ э. (на** + *a.*) to have an effect (on), make an impression (on).
[2] (*econ.*) result, consequences.
[3] *pl.* (*theatr.*) effects; **шумовы́е ~ы** sound effects.
эффекти́в|ный (~ен, ~на) *adj.* effective.
эффéкт|ный (~ен, ~на) *adj.* effective, striking; eye-catching.
э́х|о, а *nt.* echo.
эшелóн, а *m.*
[1] (*mil.*) echelon.
[2] (*поезд*) special train.
эякуля́ци|я, и *f.* (*physiol.*) ejaculation.

Юю

юа́н|ь, я *m.* yuan (*Chinese currency unit*).

ЮАР *f. indecl.* (*abbr. of* **Ю́жно-Африка́нская Респу́блика**) RSA (Republic of South Africa).

юбиле́|й, я *m.*
1 (*годовщина*) anniversary; jubilee.
2 (*празднование*) anniversary celebrations.

ю́бк|а, и *f.* skirt; **шотла́ндская ю.** kilt; **ю.-брю́ки** culottes; **держа́ться за чью-н. ~у** to cling to s.o.'s apron strings.

ювели́р, а *m.* jeweller (*Br.*), jeweler (*US*).

ювели́р|ный *adj.*
1 *adj. of* ▸ **~**; **~ные изде́лия** gold and silver ware, jewellery (*Br.*), jewelry (*US*); **ю. магази́н** jeweller's (*Br.*), jeweler's (*US*).
2 (*fig.*) (*тщательный*) fine, intricate.

юг, а *m.* south; the South (*of Russia, etc.*); **на ю́ге** in the south; **к ю́гу от** to the south of.

ю́го-восто́к, а *m.* south-east.

ю́го-восто́чный *adj.* south-east(ern).

ю́го-за́пад, а *m.* south-west.

ю́го-за́падный *adj.* south-west(ern).

Югосла́ви|я, и *f.* (*hist.*) Yugoslavia.

югосла́вский *adj.* (*hist.*) Yugoslav(ian).

южа́н|ин, ина, *pl.* **~е, ~** *m.* southerner.

южа́н|ка, ки *f. of* ▸ **~ин**

южн|е́е, *comp. of* ▸ **~ы́й; ю. Ло́ндона** (to the) south of London.

южноамерика́н|ец, ца *m.* South American.

южноамерика́н|ка, ки *f. of* ▸ **~ец**

южноамерика́нский *adj.* South American.

южноафрика́н|ец, ца *m.* South African.

южноафрика́н|ка, ки *f. of* ▸ **~ец**

южноафрика́нский *adj.* South African.

ю́жный *adj.* south, southern; **Ю́жная Аме́рика** South America; **Ю́жная А́фрика** (*государство*) South Africa; **Ю. по́люс** South Pole.

юл|а́, ы́ top (*child's toy*).

юл|и́ть, ю́, и́шь *impf.* (*coll.*)
1 (*суетиться*) to fuss, fidget.
2 (**пе́ред** + *i.*) (*лебезить*) to play up (to).

ю́мор, а *m.* humour (*Br.*), humor (*US*); **чу́вство ~а** a sense of humour (*Br.*), humor (*US*).

юмори́ст, а *m.* humorist.

юмористи́ческий *adj.* humorous, comic, funny.

юмори́ст|ка, ки *f. of* ▸ **~**

ю́нг|а, и *m.* cabin boy; sea cadet.

ЮНЕ́СКО *f. indecl.* UNESCO (*abbr. of* United Nations Educational, Scientific and Cultural Organization — *Организа́ция Объединённых На́ций по вопро́сам образова́ния, нау́ки и культу́ры*).

юн|е́ц, ца́ *m.* (*coll.*) youth.

юнио́р, а *m.* (*sport*) junior.

юнио́р|ка, ки *f. of* ▸ **~**

ю́ност|ь, и *f.* youth (*age*).

ю́нош|а, и *m.* youth (*person*).

ю́ношеский *adj.* youthful.

ю́н|ый (~, ~а́, ~о) *adj.*
1 young.
2 (*свойственный молодости*) youthful.

юпи́тер, а *m.* (*осветительный прибор*) floodlight.

юриди́ческ|ий *adj.* legal; **~ое лицо́** corporation.

юрисди́кци|я, и *f.* jurisdiction.

юриспруде́нци|я, и *f.* jurisprudence, law (*as academic discipline*).

юри́ст, а *m.* legal expert, lawyer.

ю́р|кий (~ок, ~ка́, ~ко) *adj.* quick-moving, brisk.

ю́ркн|уть, у, ешь *pf.* to scamper away, dart away, plunge.

юро́див|ый *adj.*
1 crazy, simple, touched.
2 *as n.* **ю., ~ого** *m.* holy fool (*idiot believed to possess divine gift of prophecy*).

ю́рт|а, ы *f.* yurt (*nomad's tent in Central Asia*).

юсти́ци|я, и *f.* justice.

ю|ти́ться, чу́сь, ти́шься *impf.* to huddle (together); (*иметь пристанище*) to take shelter.

Яя

я, меня́, мне, мной (мно́ю), обо мне
1 *pers. pron.* I (me).
2 *n.*; *nt. indecl.* the self, the ego; **второ́е я** alter ego.

я́бед|а, ы *f. and c.g.*
1 *f.* (*obs.*) (*клевета*) slander.
2 *c.g.* (*coll.*) informer, telltale (*Br.*).

я́блок|о, а, *pl.* **~и, ~** *nt.* apple; **глазно́е я.** eyeball.

я́блон|я, и *f.* apple tree.

я́блочк|о, а *nt.*

[1] *dim. of* ▸ **я́блоко.**
[2] (*на мишени*) bull's eye.
я́бло|чный *adj. of* ▸ **~ко**
яв|и́ться, лю́сь, ~́ишься *pf.* (*of* ▸ **~ля́ться 1**)
[1] (*прийти по вызову*) to appear, present o.s.; to report; **я. в суд** to appear before the court; **я. на слу́жбу** to report for duty.
[2] (*прибыть*) to turn up, arrive, show up.
явле́ни|е, я *nt.*
[1] phenomenon; (*событие*) occurrence; **приро́дное я.** natural phenomenon.
[2] (*theatr.*) scene.
явля́|ться, юсь *impf.*
[1] *impf. of* ▸ **яви́ться.**
[2] (*impf. only*) (+ *i.*) (*быть*) to be; to represent.
я́вно[1] *adv.* manifestly, patently; obviously.
я́вно[2] *as pred.* it is manifest, patent; it is obvious.
я́в|ный (~ен, ~на) *adj.*
[1] (*открытый*) manifest, patent; overt.
[2] (*очевидный*) obvious.
я́вор, а *m.* sycamore (*tree*).
я́вствен|ный (~, ~на) *adj.* clear, distinct.
ягн|ёнок, ёнка, *pl.* **~я́та, ~я́т** *m.* lamb.
я́год|а, ы *f.* berry; (*collect.*) soft fruit; **пойти́ по ~ы** to go berry picking.
я́годиц|а, ы *f.* buttock.
ягуа́р, а *m.* jaguar.
яд, а (у) *m.* poison; venom (*also fig.*).
я́дерный *adj.* (*phys.*) nuclear; **я. реа́ктор** nuclear reactor.
ядови́т|ый (~, ~а) *adj.*
[1] poisonous; toxic; **я. газ** poison gas; **~ая змея́** poisonous snake.
[2] (*fig.*) (*человек, замечание*) venomous.
ядр|о́, а́, *pl.* **~́а, я́дер, ~́ам** *nt.*
[1] (*ореха*) kernel; (*Земли*) core.
[2] (*phys., biol.*) nucleus.
[3] (*основная группа*) main body (*of a unit, group*).
[4] (*hist., mil.*) ball, shot.
[5] (*sport*) shot; **толка́ние ~а́** putting the shot.
я́зв|а, ы *f.*
[1] ulcer, sore; **я. желу́дка** stomach ulcer.
[2] (*fig.*) (*вред*) plague, curse.
язви́тел|ьный (~ен, ~ьна) *adj.* caustic, biting, sarcastic.
язы́к[1]**, а́,** *pl.* **~и́** *m.*
[1] (*anat.*) tongue; **держа́ть я. за зуба́ми, придержа́ть я.** to hold one's tongue.
[2] (*cul.*) tongue; **копчёный я.** smoked tongue.
язы́к[2]**, а́,** *pl.* **~и́,** *m.* (*речь*) language (*also fig.*); **владе́ть мно́гими ~а́ми** to know many languages.
языкове́д, а *m.* linguist.
языково́й *adj.* linguistic.
языкозна́ни|е, я *nt.* linguistics.
язы́ческий *adj.* heathen, pagan.
язы́чник, а *m.* heathen, pagan.
язы́чни|ца, цы *f. of* ▸ **~к**
яи́чк|о, а, *pl.* **~и** *nt.* (*anat.*) testicle.
яи́чник, а *m.* (*anat.*) ovary.
яи́чниц|а, ы *f.* (*cul.*) fried eggs (*also* **я.-глазу́нья**); **я.-болту́нья** scrambled eggs.
яи́чный *adj. of* ▸ **яйцо́; я. бело́к** white of eggs; **я. желто́к** yolk of egg.
яйцекле́тк|а, и *f.* (*biol.*) ovule.
яйц|о́, а́, *pl.* **~́а, яи́ц, ~́ам** *nt.*
[1] egg; (*biol.*) ovum; **нести́ ~́а** to lay eggs; **я. вкруту́ю** hard-boiled egg.
[2] (*pl., coll.*) (*у мужчины*) balls, nuts (= *testicles*).
я́кобы
[1] *conj.* (*expr. doubt about validity of another's statement*) (*что*) that; **говоря́т, я. он у́мер** they say (= *they claim*) that he has died.
[2] *particle* (*мнимо*) supposedly, allegedly; **мы посмотре́ли э́ту я. стра́шную карти́ну** we have seen this supposedly terrifying film.
я́кор|ь, я, *pl.* **~я́, ~е́й** *m.* (*naut.*) anchor; **стать на я.** to anchor; **бро́сить я.** to cast, drop anchor.
яку́т, а *m.* Yakut.
яку́т|ка, ки *f. of* ▸ **~**
яку́тский *adj.* Yakut.
якша́|ться, юсь *impf.* (**с** + *i.*; *coll.*) to consort (with), hobnob (with).
я́лик, а *m.* skiff, dinghy; yawl.
я́м|а, ы *f.*
[1] pit, hole; **выгребна́я я.** cesspit; **оркестро́вая я.** orchestra pit.
[2] (*coll.*) (*впадина*) hollow.
яма́|ец, йца *m.* Jamaican.
Яма́йк|а, и *f.* Jamaica; (**я.**) Jamaican woman.
яма́йский *adj.* Jamaican; **я. ром** Jamaica rum.
я́мк|а, и *f. dim. of* ▸ **я́ма; я. на щека́х** dimple.
ямщи́к, а́ *m.* coachman.
янва́р|ский *adj. of* ▸ **~ь**
янва́р|ь, я́ *m.* January.
я́нки *m. indecl.* Yank.
янта́р|ь, я́ *m.* amber.
япо́н|ец, ца *m.* Japanese.
Япо́ни|я, и *f.* Japan.
япо́н|ка, ки *f. of* ▸ **~ец**
япо́нский *adj.* Japanese; **я. лак** japan.
ярд, а *m.* yard (*measure, = 0.9144 metre*).
я́р|кий (~ок, ~ка́, ~ко) *adj.*
[1] bright (*of light, colours, etc.*).
[2] (*fig.*) (*впечатляющий*) colourful (*Br.*), colorful (*US*), striking; (*живой*) vivid, graphic; **я. приме́р** striking example.
[3] (*fig.*) (*блестящий*) brilliant, outstanding; impressive; **~кая речь** brilliant speech.
я́ркост|ь, и *f.*
[1] brightness.
[2] (*fig.*) (*живость*) vividness.
[3] (*блеск*) brilliance.
ярлы́к, а́ *m.* label, tag.
я́рмарк|а, и *f.* (trade) fair.
ярм|о́, а́, *pl.* **~́а** *nt.* yoke (*also fig.*); **сбро́сить с себя́ я.** (*fig.*) to cast off the yoke.
я́рост|ный (~ен, ~на) *adj.* furious, fierce, savage.
я́рост|ь, и *f.* fury, rage.
я́рус, а *m.*
[1] (*theatr.*) circle.
[2] (*ряд*) tier.
ярча́йший *superl. of* ▸ **я́ркий**

я́р|че *comp. of* ▶ **~кий**

я́р|ый (~, ~а) *adj.*
1 furious, raging; violent.
2 (*рьяный*) passionate, fervent; **я. сторо́нник/приве́рженец** strong/staunch supporter, stalwart.

я́сен|ь, я *m.* ash tree.

я́сл|и, ей *no sg.* (*детские*) crèche (*Br.*), day nursery.

я́сн|о¹ *adv. of* ▶ **~ый**

я́сно² *as pred.*
1 (*о погоде*) it is fine.
2 (*fig.*) it is clear.
3 (*as affirmative particle*) (*да; понял*) yes, of course.

ясновидящ|ий *adj.* (*also as n.*: **я., ~ая**) clairvoyant.

я́сност|ь, и *f.* (*ночи, неба*) clearness; (*солнца, погоды*) brightness; (*звука*) distinctness; (*fig.*) (*вопроса*) clarity; (*речи, ума*) lucidity, preciseness; **внести́ я. во что-н.** to clarify sth.

я́с|ный (~ен, ~на́, ~но, ~́ны) *adj.*
1 (*ночь, небо*) clear; (*солнце, месяц*) bright; (*погода*) fine.
2 (*звук, дальний берег*) distinct.
3 (*глаза, счастье*) serene.
4 (*fig.*) (*вопрос, намерение*) clear, plain; **~ное де́ло** of course.
5 (*ум, изложение*) lucid; precise, logical.

я́стреб, а, *pl.* **~а́** *and* **~ы** *m.* hawk.

ятага́н, а *m.* yataghan, scimitar.

я́хт|а, ы *f.* yacht.

яхтсме́н, а *m.* yachtsman.

яхтсме́нк|а, и *f.* yachtswoman.

яче́йк|а, и, *g. pl.* **яче́ек** *f.* (*biol., pol.*) cell.

ячме́н|ь¹, я́ *m.* (*злак*) barley.

ячме́н|ь², я́ *m.* (*на глазу*) sty (*in the eye*).

я́шм|а, ы *f.* (*min.*) jasper.

я́щериц|а, ы *f.* lizard.

я́щик, а *m.*
1 box; (*большой*) chest.
2 (*выдвижной*) drawer.

я́щур, а *m.* (*заболевание скота*) foot-and-mouth disease.

Contents

Russian life and culture **412**

Британские и американские культурные реалии **418**

Correspondence and CVs **432**

Заказ номера в гостинице 432
Booking a hotel room 433

Уведомление об отмене заказа 434
Cancelling a reservation 435

Запрос вакансии 436
Enquiry to an employer about jobs 437

Ответ на объявление о наличии вакансии 438
Reply to a job advertisement 439

Просьба о рекомендательном письме 440
Asking for a reference 441

Письмо в отдел кадров 442
Accepting a job 443

Отказ от предложенной работы 444
Declining a job 445

Резюме 446
Curriculum vitae 447

Russian life and culture

автоно́мная о́бласть — autonomous oblast (region) One of the six types of administrative unit into which **Росси́йская Федера́ция** is divided. Of the 88 units, only one is *автоно́мная о́бласть* (the *Jewish Autonomous Oblast*). Like **автоно́мный о́круг, го́род федера́льного значе́ния, край,** and **о́бласть**, this type of unit is not allowed to have its own constitution (Russian *конститу́ция*), unlike the 21 republics. Instead, it has its own charter (Russian *уста́в*). In common with Russia's 87 other constituent units, the single *автоно́мная о́бласть* has its own legislature. Formerly, there were four more autonomous oblasts on the territory of the modern Russian Federation. In 1991 they all changed their status to that of republic (**респу́блика**).

автоно́мный о́круг — autonomous okrug (district) One of the six types of administrative unit into which **Росси́йская Федера́ция** is divided. Of the 88 units, nine are autonomous okrugs (districts). The autonomous okrugs are all located in sparsely populated areas of Siberia and Russia's Far East, where indigenous peoples (except for in *Agin-Buryat Autonomous Okrug*) form a small part of the entire population and Russians usually make up 60–70% of the population.

For more details ▶ **автоно́мная о́бласть**

аттеста́т об основно́м о́бщем образова́нии — basic study course school-leaving certificate A document awarded to students who successfully finish a 9-year course of study at school (without low marks such as *2* (*дво́йка*)) and pass all their final examinations. With this, students can enter any educational institution below the level of a **вуз**.

аттеста́т о сре́днем (по́лном) о́бщем образова́нии — full study course school-leaving certificate A document awarded to students who successfully finish an 11-year course of study at school (without low marks such as *2* (*дво́йка*)) and pass all their final examinations. With this, students can enter a **вуз**.

Бе́лый дом — the White House (*in Moscow*) The generally accepted unofficial name of the seat of the Russian government. *Бе́лый дом* is situated near the centre of Moscow on the left bank of the Moskva River and together with the buildings of the US and UK embassies it forms an equilateral triangle within which the town hall is located.

бли́жнее зарубе́жье (literally 'close foreign countries') — the

former Soviet republics The collective unofficial name for all the former Soviet republics, used especially by telephone operators. Outside Russia it is sometimes considered offensive, mainly because translations of the term in European languages are not quite accurate in register.

Вели́кая Оте́чественная война́ (1941–1945) (literally 'the Great Patriotic War') The Soviet name for the Second World War in the context of the Soviet Union's involvement in it.

Восьмо́е ма́рта, 8-е Ма́рта — 8 March Women's day in Russia (men's day is **23-е Февраля́** or **День защи́тника Оте́чества**). It is still sometimes referred to as *Междунаро́дный же́нский день* (since Communist times) but this is much disputed. Men and boys give flowers (especially blossoming branches of mimosa) and other presents to their female relatives and friends of any age.

вуз — institution of higher education Any type of institution of higher education forming part of the Russian educational system, including *университе́т* (university), *акаде́мия* (academy), and *институ́т* (institute/college). The word *вуз* is an abbreviation of *вы́сшее учёбное заведе́ние*.

Геро́й Росси́йской Федера́ции — Hero of the Russian Federation The highest honorary title in Russia, awarded for heroic deeds. Holders of this title receive a medal *Золота́я звезда́ Геро́я Росси́йской Федера́ции* (Gold Star of the Hero of the Russian Federation), the highest government award of the Russian Federation.

го́род федера́льного значе́ния — city with federal status One of the six types of administrative unit into which **Росси́йская Федера́ция** is divided. Of the 88 units, two are cities with federal status, *Moscow* and *St Petersburg*.

For more details ▶ **автоно́мная о́бласть**

Госуда́рственная ду́ма — the State Duma The lower house of **Федера́льное Собра́ние Росси́йской Федера́ции** (the bicameral parliament of the Russian Federation). *Госуда́рственная ду́ма* has 450 members serving four-year terms.

Два́дцать тре́тье февраля́, 23-е Февраля́ ▶ **День защи́тника Оте́чества**

День защи́тника Оте́чества, 23-е Февраля́ — Day of the Defender of the Fatherland, 23 February Men's day in Russia, similar to **Восьмо́е ма́рта** for women. It is a national holiday for everyone although, nominally, it is a holiday for military men only. Women and girls give presents to their male relatives or friends of any age, whether they serve or have served in the Soviet/Russian forces or not.

День Побéды — Victory Day (*in the Second World War*) VE Day as celebrated in Russia and some other former Soviet republics on 9 May. It is a national holiday in Russia. The date of 9 May (one day later than in western Europe) results from difference in time zones between Russia and western Europe. *День Побéды* is undoubtedly the most respected date in Russian history.

дипло́м о вы́сшем образова́нии — college/university degree certificate A document verifying that a student has graduated from a university or college. In order to qualify for this, students must pass their final exams (*госуда́рственные экза́мены*) and complete and defend a dissertation (*дипло́мная рабо́та*).

край — krai (territory) One of the six types of administrative unit into which **Росси́йская Федера́ция** is divided. Of the 88 units, seven are krais (territories). They were originally (and now they are once more) border areas of Russia (Russian *окра́ины* (sg. *окра́ина*) and *край* having the same stem).

For more details ▶ **автоно́мная о́бласть**

мат — foul language This includes all the numerous derivatives of the words *еба́ть*, *хуй*, *пизда́*, and *блядь* (see the main Dictionary text). In informal situations, these taboo words are very common among people with a low social status, whereas cultured, well-educated, and well-brought-up people (almost) never use them. Traditionally, it is considered unacceptable to utter any of the four words of *мат* in front of women or children, and using *мат* in public is a violation of the law. Violators are liable to a fine (of £10 to £30 approximately, in 2005) or, in exceptional cases, they can even be prosecuted.

национа́льность — (ethnic) nationality In the countries of the former Soviet Union, this traditionally means a person's ethnicity rather than their legal or political status. So if a Russian native speaker refers to someone as *ру́сский по национа́льности*, they usually mean that the person is Russian by language, culture, ethnicity, and even religion (e.g. Russian Orthodox), but the person could be a citizen of any country (the US, Ukraine, Germany, etc.).

нача́льная шко́ла — elementary school The first three or, now usually, four years of schooling that Russian children undergo. Separate institutions of such a kind are now rare in Russia and children usually continue at the same school after their first four years.

Но́вый год — New Year's Day This is the favourite holiday in Russia and some other former Soviet republics, celebrated on 1 January as elsewhere in Europe. New Year's Day and 2 January are traditionally national holidays and since 2005 January 3 and 4 have also been declared holidays.

о́бласть — oblast (region) One of the six types of administrative unit into which **Росси́йская Федера́ция** is divided. Of the 88 units, 48 are oblasts (regions).

For more details ▶ **автоно́мная о́бласть**

Парла́мент Росси́йской Федера́ции ▶ **Федера́льное Собра́ние Росси́йской Федера́ции**

Председа́тель Прави́тельства Росси́йской Федера́ции — Prime Minister of the Russian Federation The official (and only correct) title of the Prime Minister of the Russian Federation. *Председа́тель Прави́тельства Росси́йской Федера́ции* is appointed by **Президе́нт Росси́йской Федера́ции** with the consent of **Госуда́рственная ду́ма** (the lower house of Russia's national parliament).

Президе́нт Росси́йской Федера́ции — President of the Russian Federation Under the current Russian Constitution of 1993, *Президе́нт Росси́йской Федера́ции* is head of the state and has very extensive powers. He or she is directly elected by the citizens of Russia for a term of four years and cannot serve more than two consecutive terms. *Президе́нт Росси́йской Федера́ции* is also Supreme Commander-in-Chief of the Armed Forces of the Russian Federation.

респу́блика — republic One of the six types of administrative unit into which **Росси́йская Федера́ция** is divided. Of the 88 units, 21 are republics. Unlike **автоно́мная о́бласть**, **автоно́мный о́круг**, **го́род федера́льного значе́ния**, **край**, and **о́бласть**, each of the 21 republics has its own constitution (other constituent units have only charters (Russian *уста́в*)), and is entitled to introduce its own official language(s) (*госуда́рственный язы́к*) in addition to Russian.

For more details ▶ **автоно́мная о́бласть**

Рождество́ — Christmas Members of the Orthodox Church celebrate this festival on 7 January and it is a national holiday in Russia. The Russian Orthodox Church still uses the Julian calendar in which 7 January corresponds to 25 December in the Gregorian calendar.

Росси́йская Федера́ция, Росси́я — the Russian Federation, Russia Russia is a federal state consisting of 88 political (constituent) units (Russian *субъе́кты Федера́ции*). They are (January 2006):

— 21 republics (Russian **респу́блика**) ((*the Republic of*) *Adygea, the Republic of Altai, the Republic of Bashkortostan, the Republic of Buryatia, the Chechen Republic, the Chuvash Republic* (also *Chuvashia*), *the Republic of Dagestan, the Ingush Republic, the Kabarda-Balkar Republic, the*

Republic of Kalmykia, the Karachay-Cherkess Republic, the Republic of Karelia, the Republic of Khakassia, the Republic of Komi, the Republic of Mari El, the Republic of Mordovia, the Republic of North Ossetia Alania, the Republic of Sakha (also *Yakutia*), *the Republic of Tatarstan* (also *Tatarstan*), *the Republic of Tuva* (Russian *Tyva*), and *the Udmurt Republic*;

— 7 (6 until 1 December 2005) krais (Russian **край**) (*Altai Krai, Khabarovsk Krai, Krasnodar Krai, Krasnoyarsk Krai, Perm Krai* (since 1 December 2005, formed by the unification of *Perm Oblast* and *Komi-Permyak Autonomous Okrug*), *Primorskiy Krai*, and *Stavropol Krai*);

— 48 (49 until 1 December 2005) oblasts (Russian **о́бласть**) (*Amur Oblast, Arkhangelsk Oblast, Astrakhan Oblast, Belgorod Oblast, Bryansk Oblast, Chelyabinsk Oblast, Chita Oblast, Irkutsk Oblast, Ivanovo Oblast, Kaliningrad Oblast, Kaluga Oblast, Kamchatka Oblast, Kemerovo Oblast, Kirov Oblast, Kostroma Oblast, Kurgan Oblast, Kursk Oblast, Leningrad Oblast, Lipetsk Oblast, Magadan Oblast, Moscow Oblast, Murmansk Oblast, Nizhniy Novgorod Oblast, Novgorod Oblast, Novosibirsk Oblast, Omsk Oblast, Orel Oblast, Orenburg Oblast, Penza Oblast, Perm Oblast* (until 1 December 2005), *Pskov Oblast, Rostov Oblast, Ryazan Oblast, Sakhalin Oblast, Samara Oblast, Saratov Oblast, Sverdlovsk Oblast, Smolensk Oblast, Tambov Oblast, Tver Oblast, Tomsk Oblast, Tula Oblast, Tyumen Oblast, Ulyanovsk Oblast, Vladimir Oblast, Volgograd Oblast, Vologda Oblast, Voronezh Oblast*, and *Yaroslavl Oblast*);

— 2 cities with federal status (Russian **го́род федера́льного значе́ния**) (*Moscow* and *St Petersburg*);

— 1 autonomous oblast (Russian **автоно́мная о́бласть**) (*Jewish Autonomous Oblast*);

— 9 (10 until 1 December 2005) autonomous okrugs (Russian **автоно́мный о́круг**) (*Agin-Buryat Autonomous Okrug, Chukot Autonomous Okrug, Evenki Autonomous Okrug, Knanty-Mansi Yugra Autonomous Okrug, Komi-Permyak Autonomous Okrug* (until 1 December 2005), *Koryak Autonomous Okrug, Nenets Autonomous Okrug, Taymyr* (*Dolgano-Nenets*) *Autonomous Okrug, Ust-Ordyn-Buryat Autonomous Okrug*, and *Yamalo-Nenets Autonomous Okrug*).

Under the current Russian Constitution of 1993, both names — *Росси́я* and *Росси́йская Федера́ция* — can be used as an official name of the country.

Росси́я ▶ Росси́йская Федера́ция

СНГ ▶ Содру́жество Незави́симых Госуда́рств

Сове́т Федера́ции — the Council of the Federation The upper house of **Федера́льное Собра́ние Росси́йской Федера́ции** (the bicameral parliament of the Russian Federation). Each of the 88 constituent units of **Росси́йская Федера́ция** has two representatives in *Сове́т Федера́ции*.

Сово́к, сово́к (*often written in inverted commas*) The former Soviet Union in a pejorative or ironical sense. The term *сово́к* can also mean **1.** a typical Soviet citizen; **2.** the Soviet system as a whole; **3.** the Soviet ideology, lifestyle, etc.; **4.** a person of antiquated ideas living in modern Russia or any of the former Soviet republics.

Содру́жество Незави́симых Госуда́рств, СНГ — the Commonwealth of Independent States, CIS The political alliance of 12 former Soviet republics (Armenia, Azerbaijan, Belarus, Georgia, Kazakhstan, Kyrgyzstan, Moldova, Russia, Tajikistan, Turkmenistan, Ukraine, and Uzbekistan).

сре́дняя общеобразова́тельная шко́ла — secondary school Russian children go to this school until they are 15 so as to get *основно́е о́бщее образова́ние* and **аттеста́т об основно́м о́бщем образова́нии** or until they are 17 so as to get *сре́днее (по́лное) о́бщее образова́ние* and **аттеста́т о сре́днем (по́лном) о́бщем образова́нии.**

суббо́тник — subbotnik A Soviet invention, consisting of a day of unpaid work, originally on Saturdays (its name derives from *суббо́та 'Saturday'*). The first one took place on 12 April 1919 in the locomotive depot of a Moscow railway station called Moskva-Sortirovochnaya, while the first mass *суббо́тник* was held on 10 May 1919 on the Moscow–Kazan railway. They were a quasi-voluntary show of socially useful work. Nowadays the word is still used to denote some kinds of unpaid work such as cleaning areas of communal use, both indoors and outdoors. When performed on Sundays it is also called *воскре́сник.*

триколо́р, росси́йский триколо́р — the Russian tricolour Popular unofficial name of the national flag of the Russian Federation. It has three horizontal bands of red (lower band), blue, and white (upper band). The surest way to memorize order of colours of the Russian tricolour is to remember the name of the Soviet security police *Комите́т госуда́рственной безопа́сности*, usually abbreviated to *КГБ* (*кра́сный* (red), *голубо́й* (blue), *бе́лый* (white)).

Федера́льное Собра́ние Росси́йской Федера́ции — the Federal Assembly of the Russian Federation The official name of the bicameral national legislature of the Russian Federation. The upper house is called **Сове́т Федера́ции** (the Council of the Federation), while the lower house is called **Госуда́рственная ду́ма** (the State Duma).

Британские и американские культурные реалии

ACT — American College Test Экзамен, который сдают школьники в большинстве американских штатов после окончания средней школы. Он включает ряд предметов, в том числе английский язык и математику. Успешная сдача экзамена даёт право на поступление в университет.

African American — афроамериканец В Америке так называют американцев африканского происхождения. Данный термин является более нейтральным, чем слово «чёрный», которое подразумевает цвет кожи.

Afro-Caribbean — афрокариб В Великобритании и Америке так называют людей африканского происхождения, которые живут или ранее проживали на Карибских островах (к последним относятся Большие и Малые Антильские острова, а также Багамы).

A level — advanced level Выпускной экзамен, который сдают школьники в возрасте 18 лет в Англии и Уэльсе. Ученики, планирующие поступать в университет, должны сдать такой экзамен по трём или четырём предметам. За каждый экзамен ставится отдельная оценка. Университеты и другие вузы отбирают студентов на основе оценок, полученных ими за эти экзамены. Предпочтение отдаётся предметам, которые являются профилирующими для избранного абитуриентом факультета.

American dream — американская мечта Основополагающий принцип американской жизни. В соответствии с ним каждый может добиться успеха, особенно материального, если он будет много трудиться. Для иммигрантов американская мечта предполагает также надежду на свободу и равенство.

Asian-American В Америке так принято называть американцев, которые происходят из стран азиатского региона.

AS level — advanced subsidiary level Экзамен, занимающий промежуточное положение между **GCSE** и **A level**. Приёмные комиссии университетов приравнивают его к половине экзамена на **A level**. После окончания средней школы многие учащиеся сдают экзамены и на **AS level**, и на **A level**.

bed and breakfast Весьма распространённая в Великобритании разновидность гостиничного бизнеса. *Bed and breakfasts* функционируют на базе частных домов и маленьких гостиниц. В них можно переночевать и позавтракать за умеренную цену.

The Big Issue Журнал, освещающий серьёзные общественно-политические темы и отличающийся высоким уровнем журналистики. Его можно купить на улицах британских городов. Журнал распространяют бездомные люди, которые покупают его у издательства за установленную цену. Впоследствии они продают журнал с небольшой наценкой. Вырученные средства позволяют им жить, не прося подаяния.

Britannia Так древние римляне называли Великобританию. В наше время это обозначение стало частью национальной символики. Другим важным элементом этой символики является эмблема, на которой Великобритания изображена в виде женщины в шлеме, держащей в руках щит и трезубец. Данная эмблема воспроизводится на монетах достоинством в 50 пенсов. *Rule, Britannia!* («Правь, Британия!») — патриотическая песня, исполняемая обычно на заключительном вечере променадных концертов (**Proms**).

the British Isles — Британские острова В число этих островов входит 2 крупных острова — Великобритания (государство Великобритания) и Ирландия (Ирландская Республика и Северная Ирландия) — и более мелкие острова, располагающиеся вокруг, — Оркнейские, Гебридские, Шетлендские, Нормандские, острова Мэн и Силли.

broadsheet — широкополосная газета В Великобритании газеты, печатающиеся на широких полосах, противопоставляются таблоидам. Различие проводится не только и не столько по формату газеты, сколько по значимости освещаемого материала и по качеству журналистики. Широкополосные газеты, как правило, обсуждают серьёзные общественно-политические вопросы и демонстрируют высокий уровень журналистики.

Cabinet — Кабинет министров Данный правительственный орган Великобритании включает 20 министров, назначаемых премьер-министром. На заседаниях кабинета обсуждаются политика правительства и административные вопросы. Каждый из министров отвечает за одну определенную сферу государственной жизни. Кабинет в целом принимает решения, касающиеся общей политики правительства. Лидер главной оппозиционной партии назначает свой кабинет, называемый теневым кабинетом (**Shadow Cabinet**).

the Capitol — Капитолий Здание конгресса США. Оно находится на Капитолийском холме в Вашингтоне.

the City — Сити Финансовый и торговый центр Лондона. Он располагается в пределах исторического ядра города. В Сити сосредоточены головные офисы многих банков, страховых компаний, брокерских фирм и других финансовых организаций. В Сити работает около 500 тысяч человек.

city technology college (CTC) Школы, дающие специальное среднее образование. Они явились результатом сотрудничества между правительством и различными компаниями. Учебная программа предполагает углублённое изучение точных наук. Такого рода школы часто находятся в центре города.

cockney — кокни Диалект, на котором говорят уроженцы нескольких восточных районов Лондона. Основная черта данного диалекта — так называемый рифмованный сленг (**rhyming slang**). Кокни означает также носителей этого диалекта.

college of further education (CFE) Учебное заведение аналогичное профессионально-техническому училищу в России. В него можно поступить по достижении 16 лет. Такие училища дают как специальное, так и общее среднее образование. Учащиеся имеют возможность подготовиться к сдаче **GCSE** или **A Levels** или получить профессиональную квалификацию. Учебная программа предполагает как полные, так и сокращенные учебные дни.

colleges — колледжи В Америке слово *college* применяется как к средним специальным, так и к высшим учебным заведениям. Учебные заведения, где можно получить среднее специальное образование, проводят обучение на базе двухгодичной программы. Для получения высшего образования и степени бакалавра необходимо пройти 4-годичный курс в университете или в так называемом 4-годичном колледже. Приём в колледжи всех категорий производится на основе результатов выпускных экзаменов и текущих оценок, полученных в средней школе.

the Commonwealth — Британское Содружество Объединение в составе Великобритании и 52 стран — в основном её бывших колоний. По состоянию на ноябрь 2005 года членами Содружества являлись: Австралия, Антигуа и Барбуда, Багамские Острова, Бангладеш, Барбадос, Белиз, Ботсвана, Бруней, Вануату, Великобритания, Гайана, Гамбия, Гана, Гренада, Доминика, Замбия, Индия, Камерун, Канада, Кения, Кипр, Кирибати, Лесото, Маврикий, Малави, Малайзия, Мальдивские Острова, Мальта, Мозамбик, Намибия, Науру, Нигерия,

Новая Зеландия, Пакистан, Папуа – Новая Гвинея, Самоа, Свазиленд, Сейшельские Острова, Сент-Винсент и Гренадины, Сент-Китс и Невис, Сент-Люсия, Сингапур, Соломоновы Острова, Сьерра-Леоне, Танзания, Тонга, Тринидад и Тобаго, Тувалу, Уганда, Фиджи, Шри-Ланка, Южно-Африканская Республика, Ямайка.

Премьер-министры стран Содружества собираются каждые 2 года на конференцию для обсуждения вопросов экономического и культурного сотрудничества и взаимопомощи. Каждые 4 года проводятся спортивные Игры стран Содружества.

Термин *содружество* является также частью официального названия некоторых американских штатов, например, Кентукки, Вирджинии (Виргинии), Пенсильвании, Массачусетса.

community college Разновидность американских университетов. Учебная программа таких университетов нацелена на получение специального образования, в наибольшей степени удовлетворяющего нуждам местной экономики. Данный термин иногда используется в Англии в названиях средних школ.

comprehensive school — средняя общеобразовательная школа В Великобритании дети учатся в такой школе с 11 и до 18 лет.

Congress — конгресс Законодательный орган США. Он состоит из двух палат: палаты представителей и сената. В палату представителей входит 435 членов, избираемых на 2 года. В сенат входит 100 сенаторов (по два от каждого штата), избираемых на 6 лет. Одна треть сенаторов переизбирается или замещается каждые два года. Чтобы провести закон, иначе называемый актом, его проект (билль) должен быть рассмотрен и одобрен обеими палатами, а затем ратифицирован президентом. Конгресс заседает в Вашингтоне в Капитолии на Капитолийском холме. Слова **The Capitol** (Капитолий) и *The Hill* (холм) также относятся к конгрессу.

council tax — местный налог Налог, взимаемый районным советом с местных жителей. Размер налогового взноса зависит от стоимости дома, находящегося во владении налогоплательщика, и количества людей, проживающих в нём.

Downing Street — Даунинг-стрит Улица в центре Лондона, в районе Вестминстер. Дом номер 10 по этой улице является официальной резиденцией премьер-министра Великобритании, дом номер 11 — резиденцией канцлера казначейства (министра финансов). Выражения *Downing Street* и *Number 10* часто означают офис премьер-министра.

elementary school Начальная школа в США. Дети учатся в таких школах с 6 до 12 лет. Иногда их также называют *grade school*.

football pool — футбольный тотализатор Популярная в Великобритании азартная игра. Игроки пытаются предугадать результаты футбольных матчей, ставят определенные суммы на свои прогнозы и заносят предполагаемые результаты на специальные бланки. Выигрыши выплачиваются тем игрокам, чьи прогнозы оказались наиболее точными. Размер выигрыша прямо пропорционален ставке игрока.

further education В Великобритании данный термин применяется ко всем видам образования (кроме университетского) для учащихся от 16 лет и старше. Обязательное школьное образование ограничено возрастом 16 лет. Если учащиеся решили не поступать в университет, то они могут продолжать обучение в системе профессионально-технического и среднего специального образования. В Америке, однако, термин *further education* применяется и к университетскому образованию.

GCSE — General Certificate of Secondary Education Школьный экзамен в Англии и Уэльсе. Все учащиеся сдают эти экзамены после 5 лет обучения в средней школе независимо от их способностей. Большинство сдают экзамены по нескольким предметам. Экзаменационная оценка ставится за каждый предмет в отдельности.

Учащиеся, намеревающиеся продолжать обучение на последней ступени средней школы и сдавать экзамены на **A Level**, должны успешно сдать определённое количество *GCSE*. Школьники могут сочетать *GCSE* с **GNVQ**.

GNVQ — General National Vocational Qualification Школьный экзамен, альтернативный GCSE. Эти экзамены были введены в 1992 году. Предметы, по которым они сдаются, имеют профессионально-техническую направленность. Цель такого обучения — дать учащимся определённые профессиональные знания, сориентировав их таким образом на рынке труда. Многие школьники сочетают *GNVQ* с **GCSE**.

God Save the Queen/King — Боже, храни королеву/короля Государственный гимн Великобритании. Песня, сочинённая неизвестным автором и впервые исполненная в 1745 году в Лондоне. В качестве государственного гимна принята в начале 19 века.

GP (General Practitioner) — врач общей практики/семейный врач Эквивалент участкового врача в России. Такие врачи обслуживают жителей определённого района, зарегистрированных в местной поликлинике. Консультация для пациентов Национальной службы здравоохранения (**National Health Service**) бесплатная. В случае необходимости врач общей практики направляет их на консультацию к врачу-специалисту.

grade school = elementary school

graduate school — аспирантура Этот термин применяется в американском варианте английского языка. Студенты могут поступить в аспирантуру после 3 или 4 лет обучения в университете.

grammar school Тип средней школы в Великобритании, эквивалентный гимназиям в России. В них могут поступать одарённые дети по достижении 11—12 лет при условии успешной сдачи конкурсных экзаменов. На данный момент таких школ осталось очень мало, так как с 1965 года их стали заменять общеобразовательными школами, в которые детей принимают независимо от способностей.

green card — грин-карта, зелёная карта Документ, разрешающий жить и работать в Америке людям, не имеющим американского гражданства. Этот документ обязателен для тех, кто хочет жить и работать в Америке постоянно.

Greyhound Bus Название автобусов самой большой в Америке автобусной компании. Сеть обслуживания данной компании охватывает большинство городов Америки. Наибольшей популярностью этот вид транспорта пользуется у молодёжи и туристов.

high school Средняя школа в Америке. Такие школы имеют две ступени. Первая ступень — так называемая младшая школа (**junior high school**) для детей от 12 до 14 лет. Вторая ступень — так называемая старшая школа (**senior high school**) для детей от 15 до 18 лет. После окончания средней школы учащиеся сдают выпускные экзамены (**ACT**, **SAT**), по результатам которых они могут поступить в университет.

Данный термин иногда используется и в Великобритании.

the House of Commons — палата общин Нижняя палата британского парламента. Члены парламента, заседающие в этой палате, избираются на всеобщих выборах. В палате общин обсуждают вопросы внутренней и внешней политики и принимают новые законы.

the House of Lords — палата лордов Верхняя палата британского парламента. Члены этой палаты не избираются на выборах, а назначаются от главных политических партий страны. Кроме того, часть мест в палате передается по наследству членам аристократических фамилий. В 1999 году количество таких мест было ограничено 92. В функции палаты входит обсуждение и ратификация законов, ранее одобренных палатой общин. Одновременно палата лордов является высшим апелляционным судом страны.

the House of Representatives — палата представителей Нижняя палата конгресса США. В нее входит 435 представителей от американских штатов, которые избираются каждые два года. Число представителей от штатов зависит от численности их населения. Палата представителей принимает новые законы. Все принимаемые законы должны быть одобрены этим органом.

the Houses of Parliament — Британский парламент Двухпалатный орган, состоящий из палаты общин и палаты лордов. Обе палаты заседают в Вестминстерском дворце. Этот дворец представляет собой комплекс зданий в центре Лондона.

independent school — независимая/частная школа В Великобритании так называют школы, которые финансируются не государством, а родителями учеников, вносящими ежегодную плату за их обучение. В эту категорию входят **public school** и **preparatory school**.

infant school Первая ступень начальной школы в Великобритании. Эти школы получили распространение главным образом в Англии. Дети учатся в них три года. Они могут быть самостоятельными или являться частью полной начальной школы, в которой дети учатся до 11 лет.

the Ivy League Это общее название применяется к восьми старейшим и самым престижным университетам США. Все они находятся на восточном побережье страны. В их число входят Гарвардский, Йельский, Колумбийский, Корнеллский, Дартмутский, Браунский, Принстонский и Пенсильванский университеты. Название, принятое для этих университетов — буквально «Лига плюща» — основано на представлении о том, что старые здания этих университетов со временем заросли плющом. Обучение в этих университетах очень дорогое, но некоторые, одарённые студенты получают стипендии.

jobcentre — биржа труда Государственная служба, содействующая людям, ищущим работу. В число услуг, предоставляемых биржами труда, входит реклама вакансий, организация собеседований с работодателями. Биржи труда есть почти во всех городах Великобритании.

junior high school Младшая средняя школа. В Америке так называют первую ступень средней школы. Дети учатся в таких школах после окончания начальной школы (**elementary school**).

Medicaid Тип медицинского страхования, предоставляемого

правительством США малоимущим людям моложе 65 лет.

Medicare Тип медицинского страхования, предоставляемого правительством США людям старше 65 лет.

Middle England — средняя Англия Это выражение часто применяется к среднему классу Великобритании. Так как эта группа населения составляет самую большую часть электората, политические партии стремятся получить на выборах их голоса. Выражение *middle income Britain* имеет аналогичное употребление.

MP (Member of Parliament) — член парламента Это выражение применяется только к членам палаты общин. Они представляют 659 избирательных округов Англии, Уэльса, Шотландии и Северной Ирландии.

the National Health Service (NHS) — Национальная служба здравоохранения В Великобритании система здравоохранения финансируется государством и медицинская помощь в основном бесплатная. Однако пациенты должны платить за зубоврачебные услуги и лекарства. Исключение составляют дети до 18 лет, пенсионеры и беременные женщины. Им эти услуги предоставляются бесплатно.

National Insurance (NI) — национальное страхование Взносы по этому страхованию обязательны для работающей части населения и для работодателей. Они отчисляются из заработной платы и идут в фонд оплаты различных социальных услуг — медицинского обслуживания, пособий по безработице, пенсий и т. д.

the National Lottery — национальная лотерея В Великобритании доходы, получаемые от розыгрышей лотереи, идут на финансирование культурных и спортивных проектов, на охрану памятников и на разного рода благотворительные цели.

the National Trust Добровольная общественная организация по охране архитектурных, исторических и природных памятников Великобритании. Она функционирует за счёт взносов членов организации и доходов, получаемых от её владений. За годы своего существования эта организация выкупила или получила в дар огромные земельные угодья, целые деревни и большое количество зданий, представляющих архитектурную или историческую ценность. Несколько месяцев в году дома-музеи и другие владения организации открыты для посещения.

Native American — коренной американец В настоящее время в Америке так принято называть коренных жителей Северной и Южной

Америки, а также Карибских островов. Этому термину отдаётся предпочтение в официальных контекстах, так как он считается более точным, чем слово «индеец», которое появилось в результате ошибки, сделанной Х. Колумбом. Уверенный в том, что он достиг Индии, он назвал местных жителей индейцами. Тем не менее, слово *индеец* имеет широкое распространение, и коренные жители обеих Америк не считают его оскорбительным.

NBC — National Broadcasting Company Национальная вещательная компания. Первая вещательная компания США. Она была основана в 1926 году. Первый телевизионный канал *NBC* начал свою работу в 1940 году.

the Open University Заочный университет в Великобритании. Обучение на всех факультетах проводится на заочной основе. В этом университете учатся студенты всех возрастов. Они работают самостоятельно и отсылают письменные работы своим преподавателям. Степень, полученная в этом университете, равноценна степени любого другого университета.

Oxbridge Сращение, образованное от названий *Oxford* и *Cambridge*. Оно относится к университетам Оксфорда и Кембриджа и подчеркивает их престиж и особое положение среди других университетов.

Parliament — парламент Британский парламент — высший законодательный орган страны. Он состоит из двух палат: палаты общин и палаты лордов. Парламент собирается в Вестминстерском дворце. Выборы в парламент проходят каждые 5 лет. Все члены палаты общин должны переизбираться. Царствующий монарх открывает новые сессии парламента и подписывает законы.

the Pledge of Allegiance — клятва верности В американских школах каждый учебный день начинается с переклички и с клятвы американскому флагу. Ученики произносят клятву верности и преданности Америке: «Я клянусь в верности флагу Соединенных Штатов Америки и республике, которую он представляет, её народу, единому перед Богом, свободе и справедливости для всех».

Иммигранты, принимающие американское гражданство приносят такую же клятву.

politically correct, PC — политически корректный, политкорректный Идея политической корректности появилась в 80-х годах двадцатого века. Суть её заключается в выработке и повсеместном закреплении языковых и поведенческих норм, лишенных любых предрассудков: будь то предрассудки расовые, половые, национальные или иные. В процессе замены старых выражений новыми — политически корректными — в языке наметилась тенденция к избавлению от многих спорных терминов. Очевидно, что слова *афроамериканец* и *коренной американец* в большей мере соответствуют исторической правде, нежели употребляемые в тех же значениях, соответственно, *чёрный* (или *негр*) и *индеец*. Однако некоторые эвфемизмы, возникшие на этой почве, грешат неопределённостью. Таким, например, является выражение *involuntarily leisured* (дословно «на вынужденном отдыхе»), используемое вместо слова *unemployed* (безработный).

Poppy Day — День маков В Великобритании так называют день, в который страна отмечает годовщину окончания Первой мировой войны. В этот день, называемый также *Remembrance Sunday* (Памятное воскресенье) или *Armistice Day* (День перемирия), поминают жертв обеих мировых войн. Многие люди вдевают в петлицы красные бумажные маки. Маки символизируют цветочные поля Франции и Бельгии, на которых похоронены солдаты, павшие в Первой и Второй мировых войнах. Бумажные маки продаются благотворительными организациями. Средства, вырученные от их продажи, идут на помощь ветеранам войны.

prep/preparatory school В Великобритании так называют частные начальные школы. Дети учатся в них с 7 и до 13 лет. Некоторые из этих школ являются интернатами. Обучение в них, как правило, раздельное для мальчиков и девочек. Ученики, окончившие такие школы, обычно поступают в частные средние школы.

В Америке данное выражение относится к очень престижным частным средним школам, которые готовят учащихся к поступлению в лучшие университеты страны.

primaries — праймериз В США так называют выборы делегатов, направляемых на партийные съезды, во время которых выдвигаются кандидаты в президенты и в вице-президенты.

prom В Америке так называют школьный бал в конце учебного года.

the Proms — promenade concerts — променадные концерты Ежегодный фестиваль классической музыки, проходящий в королевском Альберт-холле в Лондоне. Заключительный вечер променадных концертов являет собой шумное зрелище. Зрители поют под аккомпанемент оркестра традиционные песни *Land of Hope and Glory* и *Rule Britannia!* Слово *Proms* является сокращением от выражения *promenade concert* — променадные концерты, которые называются так, потому что значительная часть зрителей слушает концерты стоя.

public school — частная школа Несмотря на свое название, эти школы являются частными. Обычно в них учатся дети из привилегированных и богатых семей. Это связано с тем, что плата за обучение в таких школах чрезвычайно высокая. В особенности это относится к наиболее престижным из них: Итону (*Eton*), Хэрроу (Харроу) (*Harrow*), Винчестеру (*Winchester*), Рагби (*Rugby*). Все эти школы предоставляют стипендии одарённым детям из малоимущих семей. Большинство этих школ является интернатами. Кроме того, обучение в них раздельно для мальчиков и девочек.

В Америке выражение *public school* относится к государственным школам.

the Queen's Speech — речь королевы Эта речь готовится для королевы британским правительством. Она произносит её в палате лордов на ежегодной церемонии официального открытия парламента. Речь королевы — важное событие в политическом календаре, так как в ней освещаются планы правительства на ближайший год.

received pronunciation (RP) — нормативное произношение Произношение английского языка, принятое за норму в Великобритании. Это произношение свободно от влияния каких-либо региональных диалектов и часто ассоциируется с речью людей из привилегированных слоёв. Произношение, принятое на радио и телевидении, часто ориентируется на эту норму, хотя в последние годы произносительный диапазон дикторов стал включать и региональные варианты.

rhyming slang — рифмованный сленг Особенность диалекта кокни, которая делает его совершенно непонятным для непосвященных. Суть его состоит в том, что отдельные слова заменяются выражениями, которые с ними рифмуются. Например, вместо слова *believe* употребляется сочетание *Adam and Eve*, вместо слова *head* употребляется сочетание *loaf of bread*.

Трудность понимания такой речи усугубляется тем обстоятельством, что носители кокни часто сокращают эти сочетания до отдельных слов. Например, выражение *Use your loaf* означает на самом деле *Use your head*.

SAT 1. Scholastic Aptitude Test. Тест, успешная сдача которого необходима для поступления в американские университеты. Обычно его сдают при окончании средней школы. **2. Standard Assessment Test.** Экзамен, который сдают все школьники Англии и Уэльса в возрасте 7, 11 и 14 лет.

the Scottish Parliament — парламент Шотландии Он открылся в 1999 году после всеобщих шотландских выборов. Парламент уполномочен решать многие вопросы экономической, социальной и культурной политики самостоятельно, без вмешательства парламента Великобритании. Члены шотландского парламента заседают в Эдинбурге, в Холирудхаус (*Holyrood House*).

secondary schools — средние школы В Великобритании существует ряд учебных заведений, дающих среднее образование:

общеобразовательные школы (*comprehensive schools*) — бесплатные школы для мальчиков и девочек, в которых дети учатся независимо от способностей. Эти школы составляют 85% всех средних учебных заведений;

гимназии (*grammar schools*) — школы для более одарённых детей. Они могут быть как частными, так и государственными. Обучение в них обычно раздельное для мальчиков и девочек. Для поступления в такие школы необходимо сдавать вступительный экзамен;

частные школы (*public schools*) — в большинстве случаев это школы-интернаты. Обучение в таких школах очень дорогое.

the Senate — сенат Верхняя палата американского конгресса. В нём заседает 100 сенаторов — по два от каждого штата. Они избираются на 6 лет. Все новые законы должны быть утверждены как сенатом, так и палатой представителей.

Однако сенат отвечает за внешнюю политику и уполномочен «оценивать и одобрять» назначения, сделанные президентом.

senior high school В Америке так называют вторую ступень средней школы. Дети учатся в ней по завершении младшей средней школы (**junior high school**).

Shadow Cabinet ▸ Cabinet

Silicon Valley — Силиконовая долина Так называют долину Санта-Клара в Калифорнии, в которой располагается большое количество компьютерных компаний. Данное название связано с тем, что силикон (кремний) широко используется в электронной промышленности.

the Stars and Stripes Флаг США.

the Star-Spangled Banner **1.** Гимн США. **2.** Одно из названий американского флага.

tabloid — таблоид Малоформатная (бульварная) газета. Такие газеты противопоставляются широкоформатным (широкополосным) газетам (**broadsheet**), которые печатаются на больших листах. Таблоиды ассоциируются с жёлтой прессой, в особенности такие, как *The Sun*, the *Daily Mirror*. В последнее время таблоидный формат печати, как более удобный, стал использоваться и некоторыми серьёзными газетами, например, *The Independent*, *The Times*.

Thanksgiving — День благодарения Зима 1620 года в Новом Свете обернулась катастрофой для английских колонистов. Половина колонии, основанной *отцами-пилигримами*, — первыми поселенцами Северной Америки — погибла в результате болезней. Однако осень 1621 года была урожайной, и это позволило оставшимся колонистам выжить. Они решили отпраздновать это событие обедом. На обед были приглашены индейцы, научившие их охотиться и выращивать кукурузу. В наши дни День благодарения отмечается ежегодно в четвёртый четверг ноября. На обед готовится индейка со сладким картофелем и клюквенным соусом. На десерт подаётся тыквенный пирог. В Канаде День благодарения отмечается во второй понедельник октября.

the three Rs Так называются главные предметы в начальной школе: чтение, письмо, арифметика. В английском произношении этих слов — *Reading*, *wRiting*, *aRithmetic* — первым звуком является *R*.

TOEFL — Test of English as a Foreign Language Экзамен по английскому языку, который должны сдавать иностранцы, поступающие в американские университеты.

Union Jack Так называется флаг Соединенного Королевства Великобритании и Северной Ирландии. На полотнище флага крест св. Георгия, символизирующего Англию, крест св. Андрея, символизирующего Шотландию, и крест св. Патрика, символизирующего Северную Ирландию, объединены в одном изображении.

Wall Street — Уолл-стрит Улица в Нью-Йорке, являющаяся финансовым и торговым центром США. Здесь находится фондовая биржа, головные офисы многих банков и страховых компаний и других финансовых учреждений.

Washington DC — Вашингтон Столица США, названная так в честь первого президента страны Джорджа Вашингтона.
В административно-территориальном отношении этот город полностью совпадает с федеральным округом Колумбия. В Вашингтоне находятся Белый дом, конгресс, Верховный суд, национальные музеи.

welfare Система социальной защиты в США. Эта программа оказывает поддержку людям с низким доходом. Основными элементами программы являются **Medicaid** (оказание бесплатной медицинской помощи), *food stamps* (талоны на продукты питания) и *Head Start* (финансовая поддержка, оказываемая школьникам из бедных семей).

welfare state — государство всеобщего благосостояния В Великобритании данное понятие включает в себя систему социального обеспечения, нацеленную на поддержание высокого уровня жизни всех граждан. Основными элементами данной системы являются бесплатная медицинская помощь (**the National Health Service**), государственное страхование (**National Insurance**) и социальная защита безработных (*Social Security*).

the Welsh Assembly — Ассамблея Уэльса Так называется парламент Уэльса, учреждённый в 1999 году. Он заседает в столице Уэльса Кардиффе. Парламент даёт Уэльсу значительную автономию от британского правительства.

Westminster — Вестминстер Район в центре Лондона. Здесь находятся правительственные учреждения, в том числе британский парламент (**Houses of Parliament**), резиденция премьер-министра (**Downing Street**), Букингемский дворец (*Buckingham Palace*) (резиденция правящего монарха), дворец св. Джеймса (*St James's Palace*) (резиденция принца Уэльского) и др. Слово *Westminster* также означает британский парламент.

Whitehall — Уайтхолл Улица в центре Лондона, на которой расположены многие правительственные учреждения. В средствах массовой информации словом *Whitehall* часто называют британское правительство.

Correspondence and CVs

1. Заказ номера в гостинице

Администратору гостиницы «Дюна»
от главного бухгалтера ОАО «Титан»
Сургучёва Виктора Петровича

Уважаемый администратор!

Прошу Вас забронировать одноместный номер в Вашей гостинице на срок с 15 по 18 апреля 2006 г. на имя Семёновой Анны Петровны. Оплата будет произведена по безналичному расчёту сразу же после подтверждения Вами наличия номера. Ответ прошу направить в Командировочный отдел нашего предприятия по адресу: ОАО «Титан», ул. Московская, д. 21, г. Екатеринбург, 602905.

24.01.2006 Сургучёв В. П.

1. Booking a hotel room

125 Upper Tooting Road
London SW17 7TJ

22/1/05

The Manager
The White Lion Inn
4 Market Street
Kirkby Stephen
CUMBRIA
CA17 4QS

Dear Sir or Madam

We would like to book a double and a twin room at your pub for three nights from 14 to 17 April 2005. Preferably, the rooms should be adjacent and the double should have an en suite bathroom if possible.

Please let us know as soon as possible if you have rooms available for this period, and what your rates are. Do you require a deposit? It would also be extremely helpful if you could send us a hotel brochure describing any other facilities in the rooms such as TV and tea and coffee making facilities.

Thank you for your help. We look forward to hearing from you.

Yours faithfully

Mrs Maureen O'Connell

2. Уведомление об отмене заказа

Издательство «Круг»
ул. Добрынинская, д. 3
117049, г. Москва
телефон (095) 836-31-84

Главному администратору
гостиницы «Москва»
Петрову Александру Григорьевичу
ул. Садовая, д. 12
г. Санкт-Петербург, 190224

Уважаемый администратор!

Я вынужден просить Вас отменить заказ одноместного номера в Вашей гостинице на имя Иванова С. И. на период с 5 по 10 февраля. Моя поездка в Санкт-Петербург откладывается по независящим от меня обстоятельствам по крайней мере на две недели.

Поскольку речь об отмене командировки не идёт, я прошу Вас использовать внесённый мною задаток в счёт оплаты номера, который я закажу, когда определится точная дата моей поездки. Надеюсь, что моя просьба выполнима и что этим отказом я не поставил Вас в неудобное положение.

С уважением,
Иванов С. И.
13.01.2006

2. Cancelling a reservation

20 Millers Lane
Stanway
Colchester
Essex CO3 5PS

27/3/05

Hill View Guest House
St Mary's Mount
Hebden Bridge
North Yorkshire
HX7 5JL

Dear Mrs White

I am writing to inform you that I am afraid I have to cancel our reservation at your bed and breakfast for May 2nd–4th. Unfortunately my husband has been unexpectedly asked to go abroad on business that week and so we are having to postpone our holiday. It is such a disappointment as we were looking forward very much to getting some fresh air away from the city.

We hope now to be able to take a holiday in late June and as soon as we have an idea of the exact dates we'll be in touch again to see if you can accommodate us.

We apologize for any inconvenience. Please retain our deposit for the time being in the hope that we shall see you in June.

Yours sincerely

Margaret Sullivan

3. Запрос вакансии

Начальнику Отдела кадров
Медицинского училища № 2
г. Санкт-Петербурга
Иванову Петру Трофимовичу
от Григорьевой Ольги Николаевны,
проживающей по адресу:
Московский проспект, д. 147, кв. 3
телефон (812) 824-73-54

Уважаемый Пётр Трофимович!

Прошу Вас сообщить о наличии вакансии преподавателя биологии в Вашем училище. В настоящий момент я преподаю биологию и химию в средней школе № 396 Кировского района Санкт-Петербурга. В связи с переменой места жительства я ищу работу преподавателя в новом районе. После окончания Педагогического института им. Герцена в 1987 году я преподавала химию и биологию в средней школе. При наличии вакансии преподавателя в Вашем училище прошу Вас назначить мне собеседование в удобное для Вас время.

С уважением, Григорьева О. Н.
14.01.2006

3. Enquiry to an employer about jobs

73 Brighton Road
Eastbourne
East Sussex
BN21 3YR

4 April 2006

Manager
Rose and Crown Hotel
Eastbourne
East Sussex
BN22 7AP

Dear Mr Davis

I am writing to enquire whether you have any vacancies for bar or restaurant staff over the summer.

I have worked at other hotels in the town in my school holidays over the past few years and have quite a lot of experience at serving behind a bar and waiting at table.

My university term ends on 19 June and I shall then be available until the middle of September when I plan to take two weeks' holiday before returning to Leeds in October.

I would prefer work in the bar or restaurant but would also consider any other jobs you can offer.

I enclose references from two previous employers and a character reference from my university tutor. I look forward to hearing from you.

Yours sincerely

Giles Goodall

4. Ответ на объявление о наличии вакансии

Директору фирмы «Заря»
Логинову Борису Аркадьевичу
от Каца Алексея Владиславовича,
проживающего по адресу:
ул. Сергея Потапова, д. 12/4, кв. 264
г. Калуга, 248921
телефон (0842) 93-14-55

Уважаемый господин директор!

В ответ на объявление в газете «Курьер» от 15 января этого года направляю Вам свое резюме, копию свидетельства об окончании курсов повышения квалификации и справку с настоящего места работы. Меня интересует должность инженера по наладке электронной аппаратуры. В случае если моё предложение заинтересует Вас, я бы хотел узнать подробнее об условиях работы.

С уважением, Кац А. В.
01.02.2006

4. Reply to a job advertisement

23 Church Road
Blundesdon
LOWESTOFT
Norfolk
NR32 3LS

19.6.05

Personnel Manager
The Norfolk Echo
5 High Street
NORWICH
Norfolk
NR3 2HF

Dear Mr Williams

I am writing in response to the advertisement that appeared last week in *The Guardian* for an Assistant Features Editor on the *Norfolk Echo*.

As you will see from my CV, I successfully completed a Media Studies degree at Lancaster University the year before last, since when I have worked in a freelance capacity for my local radio station and my local paper. I am now keen to move on to more permanent employment and believe that the experience I have gained will be relevant to the job advertised.

Apart from my CV, I enclose some examples of my work in the form of articles I have written and a tape of some interviews that I have conducted with people of local interest.

I am available for interview at any time and could take up the post immediately, should I be appointed. Thank you for considering my application.

Yours sincerely

Louise Ashby

5. Просьба о рекомендательном письме

Уважаемый Николай Константинович!

У меня к Вам большая просьба. Не могли бы Вы написать рекомендательное письмо для меня? С тех пор как меня перевели в *СУ-13, я продолжал работать в должности прораба и заочно учился в Петербургском политехническом институте. В июне я наконец получил диплом, а недавно нашёл место инженера на соседнем предприятии. Для поступления на работу в Отделе кадров у меня попросили кроме обычных документов рекомендательное письмо с предыдущего места работы. Поскольку я проработал под Вашим руководством последние шесть лет, я бы хотел попросить написать такое письмо именно Вас. Пожалуйста, направьте письмо на имя начальника Отдела кадров завода «Оптика» Малинина Георгия Сергеевича по адресу: завод «Оптика», ул. Генерала Петрова, д. 1, г. Самара, 443003.

Заранее Вам благодарен,

12.03.2006 Андреев Николай Захарович

*СУ = строительное управление 'construction company'

5. Asking for a reference

6 Highworth Cottages
Inhurst
Tadley
Hants RG26 5JP

1 February 2006

Dear Fiona

I'm sorry I haven't been in touch lately. How are you, and how's life at Basingstoke Comprehensive?

The reason I'm writing is that I was wondering if you would be willing to act as a referee with regard to several jobs I'm applying for at the moment.

After spending the past ten years in industry, I've decided to return to teaching, preferably this time in higher education. As you were my most recent Head of Department I thought that you would be the most suitable person to ask for a reference.

I'm hoping that my practical experience in the food industry will make me better qualified now than I was when I left Basingstoke. So far I have applied for posts at the Oxford College of Further Education and Kingston University, both involving teaching the catering part of the HND leisure industry course.

Please get in touch if you would like further information about what I have been doing or about the requirements for these jobs.

Best wishes

Debbie Brooks

6. Письмо в отдел кадров

Начальнику Отдела кадров
ООО «Огни»
Фокиной Марии Ивановне

Благодарю Вас за письмо от 15 марта с уведомлением о зачислении меня в фирму «Огни» на должность главного механика по наладке оборудования. К сожалению, мои попытки немедленно уволиться с настоящего места работы не привели к успеху, и я вынужден ждать положенные по закону две недели после подачи заявления об увольнении. Таким образом, я смогу приступить к исполнению своих обязанностей на Вашем предприятии не ранее 1 апреля 2005 г. Сожалею о задержке и надеюсь, что это обстоятельство не повлияет на Ваше решение о предоставлении мне рабочего места.

С уважением,
16.03.2005 Григорьев И. П.

6. Accepting a job

19 Ryden Lane
Clevelode
MALVERN
Worcestershire
WR13 8PD

22/3/05

Personnel Department
Worcester College of Higher Education
Victoria Street
WORCESTER
WR2 7JT

Dear Ms Elliott

I was extremely pleased to receive your letter offering me the job of Admissions Secretary at Worcester College, and am glad to inform you that I accept the offer.

As discussed at my interview, I need to give a month's notice at my present job and would therefore like to start work at the beginning of May. This will give me a few days for the move and allow me to get settled into my new flat before starting.

I would be grateful if you could let me know who I should report to or where I should go when I first arrive. Please could you also send me a copy of the Terms and Conditions of Employment that you mentioned at the interview, and details of the pension scheme.

I look forward to seeing you in the near future.

Yours sincerely

Amanda Walker

7. Отказ от предложенной работы

Уважаемый Артур Фёдорович!

Большое Вам спасибо за приглашение на факультет в качестве старшего преподавателя. Скажу сразу, что предложение Ваше очень для меня заманчиво, и будь оно сделано хотя бы на два месяца раньше, я бы безо всякого сомнения сразу же его принял.

Но, к сожалению, в январе моя позиция в корне изменилась. Я получил приглашение из Принстонского университета в Америке принять участие в одном из их проектов. Все формальности с визой, разрешением на работу и даже устройством семьи на время разработки проекта Принстон берёт на себя. Как видите, с моей стороны было бы непростительным не воспользоваться такой уникальной возможностью. Тем не менее, я Вам очень признателен за то, что Вы вспомнили о моей просьбе, хоть и прошёл год. Насколько я знаю, наш общий знакомый Миша Самсонов в настоящий момент рассматривает варианты перехода на другую работу. Его опыт, квалификация и положение во многом сходны с моими, так что, если вакансия ещё открыта, я бы посоветовал Вам связаться с ним. Ещё раз большое спасибо за предложение. Всего Вам хорошего!

Искренне Ваш, Сергей Проничев
03.04.2005

7. Declining a job

145 Meadowcroft Lane
Aylesbury
Bucks HP19 3EW

18 February 2004

Personnel Department
Research Machines plc
St James' House
113 Broadway
LONDON W13 9BE

Dear Mr Carpenter

Thank you for your letter of 11 February in which you offered me the post of Sales Manager at Research Machines.

Unfortunately I am unable to accept the post as I have decided to remain with my present employer, having been offered a substantial salary increase and promotion to Marketing Director since tendering my resignation.

I am very grateful to you for considering my application and would like to say how impressed I was with your company. I hope you will soon find someone suitable to fill the post, and apologize for the inconvenience that I have caused.

Yours sincerely

Michael Green

РЕЗЮМЕ

Ф.И.О.	Михайлова Марина Александровна
Дата рождения, возраст	05.04.1980, 25 лет
Адрес	пр. Байрона, д. 66, кв. 6 г. Петрозаводск, 185000, Республика Карелия
Телефон	(домашний) (8242) 82-32-22, (сотовый) +79217003522
E-mail	mariners@mail.ru
Семейное положение, дети	не замужем, детей нет
Претендую на должность	переводчик (полная занятость)
Заработная плата	от 30 000 рублей
Образование	
2000—2005	Петрозаводский государственный университет, филологический факультет, специальность «Английский язык и литература» (диплом с отличием)
январь-август 2003	Университет штата Канзас, практика для студентов, обучающихся по обмену, специальность «Английский язык» (почётный лист со средним баллом 3,65 из 4)
июнь-август 2002	Летняя школа Университета Осло, специальность «Норвежский язык»
1990—2000	Средняя школа №17 г. Петрозаводска с углублённым изучением английского и финского языков (серебряная медаль)
Иностранные языки	свободное владение английским языком (навыки синхронного перевода), разговорный финский, базовые знания норвежского (чтение и перевод неспециальных текстов)
Опыт работы	
июль-сентябрь 2005	переводчик делегации ЮНЕСКО в Республике Карелия
июнь-август 2004	преподаватель русского языка как иностранного в Летней школе Петрозаводского государственного университета
Дополнительные навыки	компьютер на уровне уверенного пользователя, водительские права категории «В»

CURRICULUM VITAE

Name:	John Phillip Hunt
Address:	24 Mulberry Rd Brixton LONDON SW14 5HU
Telephone:	0181-592284; mobile 07905339242
Email:	jp_hunt@compuserve.com
Nationality:	British
Date of birth:	22/5/83
Marital Status:	Single

Education/Qualifications:

2005–2006	University of Bristol: MSc in Management
2001–2005	King's College, London: BA (hons.) Russian and German, class 2:1
1994–2001	Burford Community College, Oxford Rd, Burford, Oxon. 9 GCSEs (English, Mathematics, Physics, History, Technology, German, Russian, French, Music) 4 A levels: German (A), Russian (B), History (B), English (C)

Work Experience:

September 2003–June 2004	10 months working in Personnel Department of the Max-Plank-Institut für Informatik in Saarbrücken, Germany
July–August 2002	6 weeks teaching English to foreign students at Swan School of English, Oxford
March 2000	1 week's 'shadowing' experience to Assistant Marketing Manager, EAA Technology (Environmental Energy), Didcot
June 1998	2 weeks' work experience at Marks and Spencer, Oxford
Skills:	Computer literate; clean driving licence
Referees:	Dr Michael Edwards (Arts Faculty) King's College London EC12 4HR Dr Elaine Grigson (Management Research Centre) University of Bristol Bristol BS8 1TH

Aa

A¹ /eɪ/ *letter*: **from ~ to Z** от нача́ла до конца́; **~ road** магистра́льная доро́га, (авто)магистра́ль.

A² /eɪ/ *n.*
1 (*mus.*) ля (*nt. indecl.*)
2 (*acad. mark*) «отли́чно», пятёрка.

a /ə, eɪ/, **an** /æn, ən/ *indef. art.*
1 *not usu. translated*: **it's an elephant** э́то слон.
2 (*~ certain*): **in ~ sense** в како́м-то смы́сле; **an old friend of mine** оди́н мой ста́рый знако́мый.
3 (*distributive, in each*) в + *a.*; **twice ~ week** два ра́за в неде́лю; **10 miles an hour** де́сять миль в час; (*for each*) за + *a.*; **10p ~ pound** 10 пе́нсов за фунт; (*from each*) с + *g.*; **they charged £1 ~ head** они́ взя́ли по фу́нту с челове́ка.

A & E (*abbr. of* ***Accident and Emergency***) *n.* (*Br.*) отделе́ние неотло́жной по́мощи (*в больнице*).

aback /ə'bæk/ *adv.*: **we were taken ~ by the news** но́вость нас порази́ла.

abacus /'æbəkəs/ *n.* (*pl.* **~es**) счёт|ы (*pl., g.* -ов).

abandon /ə'bænd(ə)n/ *v.t.*
1 (*forsake, desert*) пок|ида́ть, -и́нуть; ост|авля́ть, -а́вить; **~ ship!** поки́нуть кора́бль!
2 (*renounce*) отка́з|ываться, -а́ться от + *g.*; **we must ~ the idea** мы должны́ отказа́ться от э́той иде́и; **they had ~ed all hope** они́ оста́вили вся́кую наде́жду.
3 (*discontinue*) прекра|ща́ть, -ти́ть; **the search was ~ed** по́иски бы́ли прекращены́.

abandoned /ə'bænd(ə)nd/ *adj.* оста́вленный, поки́нутый.

abandonment /ə'bændənmənt/ *n.*
1 (*desertion*) оставле́ние.
2 (*of a belief, lawsuit, right*) отка́з (от + *g.*).
3 (*neglect*) забро́шенность.
4 (*of a project*) прекраще́ние.
5 : **~ of a ship** оставле́ние (*or* ухо́д с) корабля́.

abase /ə'beɪs/ *v.t.* ун|ижа́ть, -и́зить.

abash /ə'bæʃ/ *v.t.* сму|ща́ть, -ти́ть; **she felt ~ed** она́ была́ смущена́.

abate /ə'beɪt/ *v.i.* (*of storm, feelings, pain*) ут|иха́ть, -и́хнуть; (*of noise*) ум|еньша́ться, -е́ньшиться.

abattoir /'æbətwɑ:(r)/ *n.* скотобо́йня.

abbey /'æbɪ/ *n.* (*pl.* **~s**) абба́тство.

abbot /'æbət/ *n.* абба́т.

abbreviate /ə'bri:vɪeɪt/ *v.t.* сокра|ща́ть, -ти́ть.

abbreviation /əbri:vɪ'eɪʃ(ə)n/ *n.* сокраще́ние, аббревиату́ра.

abdicate /'æbdɪkeɪt/ *v.t.* отка́з|ываться, -а́ться от + *g.*

abdication /æbdɪ'keɪʃ(ə)n/ *n.* отка́з (*от чего*); отрече́ние (от престо́ла).

abdomen /'æbdəmən/ *n.* брюшна́я по́лость; живо́т.

abdominal /æb'dɒmɪn(ə)l/ *adj.* брюшно́й; **~ pain** боль в животе́; **~ wound** ране́ние в живо́т.

abduct /əb'dʌkt/ *v.t.* пох|ища́ть, -и́тить.

abduction /əb'dʌkʃ(ə)n/ *n.* похище́ние.

aberration /æbə'reɪʃ(ə)n/ *n.*
1 (*error of judgement or conduct*) заблужде́ние; **mental ~** помраче́ние рассу́дка, психи́ческое расстро́йство.
2 (*deviation*) отклоне́ние от но́рмы, аберра́ция.

abeyance /ə'beɪəns/ *n.*: **in ~** приостано́вленный; **the matter is in ~** де́ло вре́менно приостано́влено.

abhor /əb'hɔ:(r)/ *v.t.* (**abhorred, abhorring**) испы́т|ывать, -а́ть отвраще́ние к + *d.*

abhorrent /əb'hɒrənt/ *adj.* омерзи́тельный, отврати́тельный; **the very idea is ~ to me** мне проти́вно да́же ду́мать об э́том.

abide /ə'baɪd/ *v.i.* : **~ by** (*comply with*) соблю|да́ть, -сти́; приде́рживаться (*impf.*) + *g.*

abiding /ə'baɪdɪŋ/ *adj.* постоя́нный, неизме́нный.

ability /ə'bɪlɪtɪ/ *n.*
1 (*capacity in general*) спосо́бность; **to the best of one's ~** по ме́ре спосо́бностей.
2 (*pl., gifts*) спосо́бности (*f. pl.*).

abject /'æbdʒekt/ *adj.* (*humble*) уни́женный; **an ~ apology** уни́женная мольба́ о проще́нии; (*craven*): **~ fear** малоду́шный страх; (*despicable*) презре́нный; (*pitiful, wretched*) жа́лкий; **in ~ poverty** в кра́йней нищете́.

ablaze /ə'bleɪz/ *pred. adj.*: **to be ~** пыла́ть, полыха́ть (*both impf.*); **the buildings were ~** зда́ния полыха́ли *or* пыла́ли в огне́.

able /'eɪb(ə)l/ *adj.* (**abler, ablest**)
1 : **be ~ to** мочь, с-; быть в состоя́нии; (*have the strength or power to*): **he was not ~ to walk any farther** он был не в си́лах (*or* не в состоя́нии) идти́ да́льше; (*know how to*) уме́ть (*impf.*); **he is ~ to swim** он уме́ет пла́вать.
2 (*skilful*) уме́лый; (*capable*) спосо́бный.
■ *cpd.* **~-bodied** *adj.* здоро́вый, кре́пкий.

ablution /ə'blu:ʃ(ə)n/ *n.* (*usu. pl., act of washing o.s.*) (*also iron.*) омове́ние; **perform one's ~s** соверш|а́ть, -и́ть омове́ние.

abnormal /æb'nɔ:m(ə)l/ *adj.* ненорма́льный.

abnormality /æbnɔ:'mælɪtɪ/ *n.* ненорма́льность.

aboard /ə'bɔ:d/ *adv.*
1 (*on a ship or aircraft*) на борту́; (*on a train*) в по́езде.
2 (*on to a ship or aircraft*) на́ борт; (*on to a train*) в по́езд.
■ *prep.*: **~ ship** на борт(у́) корабля́.

abode /ə'bəʊd/ *n.* жили́ще; **of no fixed ~** без постоя́нного местожи́тельства.

a

abolish /ə'bɒlɪʃ/ *v.t.* отмен|я́ть, -и́ть.

abolition /æbə'lɪʃ(ə)n/ *n.* отме́на; **the ~ of capital punishment** отме́на сме́ртной ка́зни.

abominable /ə'bɒmɪnəb(ə)l/ *adj.* отврати́тельный, ме́рзкий.

abomination /əbɒmɪ'neɪʃ(ə)n/ *n.* (*detestation*) отвраще́ние, омерзе́ние; (*detestable thing*) ме́рзость; **this hotel is an ~** э́та гости́ница — ме́рзость.

aboriginal /æbə'rɪdʒɪn(ə)l/ *n.* = **aborigine** ■ *adj.* тузе́мный, коренно́й.

aborigine /æbə'rɪdʒɪnɪ/ *n.* тузе́м|ец (*fem.* -ка); абориге́н; коренно́й жи́тель.

abort /ə'bɔ:t/ *v.t.* (*fig., terminate or cancel prematurely*) приостан|а́вливать, -ови́ть.

abortion /ə'bɔ:ʃ(ə)n/ *n.* (*miscarriage*) або́рт; **have an ~** де́лать, с- або́рт.

abortive /ə'bɔ:tɪv/ *adj.* (*fig.*) неуда́вшийся.

abound /ə'baʊnd/ *v.i.* (*exist in large numbers or quantities*) быть в изоби́лии; изоби́ловать (*impf.*).

about /ə'baʊt/ *adv.*
1 (*in the vicinity; in circulation*) вокру́г, круго́м; **is he anywhere ~?** он где́-то здесь?; **up and ~** на нога́х.
2 (*almost*) почти́; **it's ~ time we went** нам пора́ идти́; **and ~ time too!** давно́ пора́!
3 (*approximately*) о́коло + *g.*; приблизи́тельно; **~ 3 o'clock** о́коло трёх часо́в; **he is ~ your height** он приблизи́тельно ва́шего ро́ста; **in ~ half an hour** приме́рно че́рез полчаса́.
4 **~ to** (*ready to, just going to*): **he was ~ to leave when I arrived** он собира́лся уходи́ть, когда́ я пришёл.
■ *prep.* 1 (*at or to var. places, in*) по + *d.*; **walk ~ the room** ходи́ть (*indet.*) по ко́мнате.
2 (*concerning*) о + *p.*; насчёт + *g.*; относи́тельно + *g.*; **what are you talking ~?** о чём вы говори́те?; **how ~ a game of cards?** не сыгра́ть ли нам в ка́рты?; **he has called ~ the rent** он зашёл насчёт квартпла́ты; **she is mad ~ him** она́ без ума́ от него́; **there is no doubt ~ it** в э́том нет сомне́ния.
■ *cpds.* **~-face, ~-turn** *nn.* (*lit.*) поворо́т круго́м; (*fig.*) ре́зкий поворо́т.

above /ə'bʌv/ *prep.*
1 (*over; higher than*) над + *i.*
2 (*more than*) свы́ше + *g.*; **~ 30 tons** свы́ше 30 тонн.
3 (*fig.*): **he is getting ~ himself** он начина́ет зазнава́ться; **~ all** пре́жде всего́; са́мое гла́вное; **over and ~** вдоба́вок к + *d.*
■ *adv.* 1 (*overhead; upstairs*) наверху́; **we live in the flat ~** мы живём в кварти́ре этажо́м вы́ше; (*expr. motion*) наве́рх; **from ~** све́рху.
2 (*in text, speech etc.*) вы́ше; ра́нее.
■ *n.*: **the ~** вышеска́занное; вышеупомя́нутое.
■ *adj.* (*~-mentioned*) вышеупомя́нутый; (*foregoing*) предыду́щий.
■ *cpds.* **~-board** *adj.* (*honourable*) че́стный; (*open, frank*) откры́тый; **~-mentioned** *adj.* вышеупомя́нутый.

abracadabra /æbrəkə'dæbrə/ *n.* абракада́бра.

abrasion /ə'breɪʒ(ə)n/ *n.* сса́дина.

abrasive /ə'breɪsɪv/ *adj.* абрази́вный; (*fig.*) ре́зкий, колю́чий.

abreast /ə'brest/ *adv.* в ряд, на одно́й ли́нии; **three ~** по́ трое/три в ряд; (*fig.*): **~ of events** в ку́рсе собы́тий.

abridge /ə'brɪdʒ/ *v.t.* сокра|ща́ть, -ти́ть.

abroad /ə'brɔ:d/ *adv.* за грани́цей, за рубежо́м; (*motion*) за грани́цу, за рубе́ж; **from ~** из-за грани́цы, из-за рубежа́.

abrupt /ə'brʌpt/ *adj.*
1 (*brusque*) ре́зкий.
2 (*sudden*) внеза́пный.

abscess /'æbsɪs/ *n.* абсце́сс.

abscond /əb'skɒnd/ *v.i.* скр|ыва́ться, -ы́ться; **he ~ed with the takings** он скры́лся с вы́ручкой.

abseil /'æbseɪl/ (*Br.*) *n.* спуск на верёвке. ■ *v.i.* спус|ка́ться, -ти́ться на верёвке.

absence /'æbs(ə)ns/ *n.* отсу́тствие; **in his ~** в его́ отсу́тствие.

absent /'æbs(ə)nt/ *adj.* отсу́тствующий; **he was ~ from school** он отсу́тствовал в шко́ле.
■ *cpd.* **~-minded** *adj.* рассе́янный.

absentee /æbsən'ti:/ *n.* отсу́тствующий.

absenteeism /æbsən'ti:ɪz(ə)m/ *n.* (*from work, school*) (системати́ческие) прогу́лы (*m. pl.*); (*from voting*) абсентеи́зм.

absolute /'æbsəlu:t/ *adj.* соверше́нный; абсолю́тный.

absolutely /'æbsəlu:tlɪ/ *adv.* (*completely*) абсолю́тно; соверше́нно; (*unquestionably*) безусло́вно.

absolutism /'æbsəlu:tɪz(ə)m/ *n.* абсолюти́зм.

absolve /əb'zɒlv/ *v.t.* (*of blame*) призн|ава́ть, -а́ть невино́вным; **he was ~d of all blame** он был при́знан по́лностью невино́вным; (*of sins*) отпус|ка́ть, -ти́ть грехи́ + *d.*; **his sins were ~d** он получи́л отпуще́ние грехо́в; (*of obligation*) освобо|жда́ть, -ди́ть.

absorb /əb'zɔ:b/ *v.t.*
1 (*soak up*) впи́т|ывать, -а́ть.
2 (*engross*) погло|ща́ть, -ти́ть.

absorbent /əb'zɔ:bənt/ *adj.* вса́сывающий, поглоща́ющий.

absorption /əb'zɔ:pʃ(ə)n/ *n.* (*engrossment*): **his ~ in his studies** его́ погружённость в заня́тия.

abstain /əb'steɪn/ *v.i.* возде́рж|иваться, -а́ться; **he ~ed (from drinking) on principle** он возде́рживался (от спиртно́го) из при́нципа; **the Opposition decided to ~ (from voting)** оппози́ция реши́ла воздержа́ться (от голосова́ния).

abstainer /əb'steɪnə(r)/ *n.* (*from drinking*) тре́звенник, непью́щий; (*from voting*) воздержа́вшийся.

abstemious /æb'sti:mɪəs/ *adj.* возде́ржанный.

abstention /əb'stenʃ(ə)n/ *n.* воздержа́ние (от + *g.*); **the resolution was passed with three ~s** резолю́ция была́ принята́ при трёх воздержа́вшихся.

abstinence /'æbstɪnəns/ *n.* воздержа́ние (от + *g.*); (*moderation*) уме́ренность.

abstract /'æbstrækt/ *n.*: **in the ~** абстра́ктно, отвлечённо.

■ *adj.* абстра́ктный, отвлечённый; ~ **art** абстра́ктное иску́сство.

absurd /əb'sɜ:d/ *adj.* неле́пый, абсу́рдный.

absurdity /əb'sɜ:dɪtɪ/ *n.* неле́пость, абсу́рд, абсу́рдность; **reduce to** ~ дов|оди́ть, -ести́ до абсу́рда.

abundance /ə'bʌnd(ə)ns/ *n.* (*plenty*) изоби́лие.

abundant /ə'bʌnd(ə)nt/ *adj.* (*plentiful*) оби́льный; ~ **in** бога́тый, изоби́лующий (*чем*).

abuse[1] /ə'bju:s/ *n.*
[1] (*misuse*) злоупотребле́ние; **drug** ~ злоупотребле́ние нарко́тиками; **sexual** ~ сексуа́льное наси́лие; **child** ~ (*sexual*) совраще́ние малоле́тних; (*physical*) жесто́кое обраще́ние с детьми́; **human rights** ~ наруше́ние прав челове́ка.
[2] (*reviling*) брань; издева́тельство; **term of** ~ оскорбле́ние.

abuse[2] /ə'bju:z/ *v.t.*
[1] (*misuse*) злоупотреб|ля́ть, -и́ть + *i.*
[2] (*revile*) руга́ть (*impf.*); оскорб|ля́ть, -и́ть.

abusive /ə'bju:sɪv/ *adj.* бра́нный, руга́тельный.

abut /ə'bʌt/ *v.i.* (**abutted, abutting**): ~ **on** (*border on*) прилега́ть (*impf.*) к + *d.*; примыка́ть (*impf.*) к + *d.*; (*lean against*) уп|ира́ться, -ере́ться в + *a.*

abysmal /ə'bɪzm(ə)l/ *adj.* ужа́сный.

abyss /ə'bɪs/ *n.* бе́здна, про́пасть.

AC (*abbr. of* ***alternating current***) переме́нный ток.

a/c /ə'kaʊnt/ *n.* (*abbr. of* **account**) счёт.

academic /ækə'demɪk/ *n.* учёный, нау́чный рабо́тник.
■ *adj.* академи́ческий, нау́чный; (*unpractical*) академи́чный; теорети́ческий; нереа́льный.

academician /əkædə'mɪʃ(ə)n/ *n.* акаде́мик.

academy /ə'kædəmɪ/ *n.* акаде́мия; (*police, military, etc.*) учи́лище.

accede /æk'si:d/ *v.i.*
[1] (*agree, assent*) согла|ша́ться, -си́ться (с + *i.*).
[2]: ~ **to** (*grant*): ~ **to a request** удовлетвор|я́ть, -и́ть про́сьбу; (*take up, enter upon*) вступ|а́ть, -и́ть в + *a.*; ~ **to the throne** всходи́ть, взойти́ на престо́л.

accelerate /ək'seləreɪt/ *v.t. & i.* уск|оря́ть(ся), -о́рить(ся); (*motoring*) наб|ира́ть, -ра́ть ско́рость.

acceleration /əkselə'reɪʃ(ə)n/ *n.* ускоре́ние.

accelerator /ək'seləreɪtə(r)/ *n.* (*of car*) педа́ль га́за; акселера́тор.

accent /'æks(ə)nt/ *n.*
[1] (*orthographical sign; emphasis*) ударе́ние; акце́нт.
[2] (*mode of speech*) акце́нт; **he speaks with a slight** ~ он говори́т с лёгким акце́нтом.

accentuate /æk'sentjʊeɪt/ *v.t.* (*fig.*) акценти́ровать (*impf.*); подч|ёркивать, -еркну́ть.

accept /ək'sept/ *v.t.*
[1] (*agree to receive*) прин|има́ть, -я́ть.
[2] (*recognize, admit*) призн|ава́ть, -а́ть; **you must** ~ **this fact** вы должны́ смири́ться с э́тим фа́ктом.

acceptable /ək'septəb(ə)l/ *adj.* прие́млемый.

acceptance /ək'sept(ə)ns/ *n.* (*willing receipt*) приня́тие; (*approval*) одобре́ние.

access /'ækses/ *n.* (*to person or thing*) до́ступ (к + *d.*); ~ **road** подъездно́й путь.
■ *v.t.* (*comput.*): ~ **data** получ|а́ть, -и́ть до́ступ к да́нным.

accessible /ək'sesɪb(ə)l/ *adj.* досту́пный.

accession /ək'seʃ(ə)n/ *n.* вступле́ние.

accessory /ək'sesərɪ/ *n.*
[1] (*leg.*) соуча́стник.
[2] (*pl., ancillary parts*) принадле́жности (*f. pl.*); (*of clothing*) аксессуа́ры (*m. pl.*).

accident /'æksɪd(ə)nt/ *n.*
[1] (*chance*) слу́чай, случа́йность; **by** ~ случа́йно.
[2] (*unintentional action*): **I'm sorry, it was an** ~ прости́те, я неча́янно.
[3] (*mishap*) несча́стный слу́чай; (*rail.*) круше́ние, ава́рия; **car** ~ автомоби́льная катастро́фа, автокатастро́фа, ава́рия; **he had an** ~ он попа́л в ава́рию.

accidental /æksɪ'dent(ə)l/ *adj.*
[1] (*chance*) случа́йный; ~ **death** смерть в результа́те несча́стного слу́чая.
[2] (*incidental*) побо́чный.

acclaim /ə'kleɪm/ *n.* (*public recognition*) призна́ние.

acclamation /æklə'meɪʃ(ə)n/ *n.* (*public recognition*) призна́ние; (*loud approval*) шу́мное одобре́ние; (*enthusiasm*) энтузиа́зм; (*pl., shouts of welcome or applause*) приве́тственные во́згласы (*m. pl.*); **his books won the** ~ **of critics** его́ кни́ги вы́звали шу́мное одобре́ние кри́тиков.

acclimate /ə'klaɪmət/ (*US*) = **acclimatize**

acclimatize /ə'klaɪmətaɪz/ *v.t. & i.* акклиматизи́ровать(ся) (*impf., pf.*).

accolade /'ækəleɪd/ *n.* (*praise*) похвала́; (*reward*) награ́да.

accommodat|e /ə'kɒmədeɪt/ *v.t.*
[1] (*house*) разме|ща́ть, -сти́ть; (*single person*) поме|ща́ть, -сти́ть; предост|авля́ть, -а́вить жильё + *d.*
[2] (*hold, seat*) вме|ща́ть, -сти́ть; **the car will** ~**e 6 persons** маши́на вмеща́ет шесть челове́к; **a hall** ~**ing 500** зал на пятьсо́т челове́к.

accommodating /ə'kɒmədeɪtɪŋ/ *adj.* сгово́рчивый, услу́жливый.

accommodation /əkɒmə'deɪʃ(ə)n/ *n.* жильё; **can you provide a night's** ~**?** мо́жно останови́ться у вас на́ ночь?

accompaniment /ə'kʌmpənɪmənt/ *n.*
[1] (*accompanying*) сопровожде́ние.
[2] (*mus.*) аккомпанеме́нт.

accompanist /ə'kʌmpənɪst/ *n.* (*mus.*) аккомпаниа́тор.

accompany /ə'kʌmpənɪ/ *v.t.*
[1] (*lit., go or be with; fig., occur with*) сопровожда́ть (*impf.*).
[2] (*mus.*) аккомпани́ровать (*impf.*) + *d.*

accomplice /ə'kʌmplɪs/ *n.* соуча́стни|к (*fem.* -ца); соо́бщни|к (*fem.* -ца).

accomplish /ə'kʌmplɪʃ/ *v.t.* (*complete*) заверш|а́ть, -и́ть; (*fulfil, perform*) выполня́ть, вы́полнить; соверш|а́ть, -и́ть.

accomplished /ə'kʌmplɪʃt/ *adj.* соверше́нный, иску́сный.

a

accomplishment /ə'kʌmplɪʃmənt/ *n.* завершéние; выполнéние; (*achievement*) достижéние.

accord /ə'kɔ:d/ *n.*
1 (*agreement*) соглáсие, соглашéние; **with one ~** единодýшно.
2 (*volition*): **of one's own ~** по сóбственному желáнию, по сóбственной вóле.

accordance /ə'kɔ:d(ə)ns/ *n.* соответ́ствие; **in ~ with** в соответ́ствии с + *i.*, соглáсно + *d.*

according /ə'kɔ:dɪŋ/ *adv.*: **~ to** (*in keeping or conformity with*) соглáсно + *d.*; **~ to the law(s)** в соответ́ствии с законодáтельством; по закóну; (*on the authority or information of*) по + *d.*, соглáсно + *d.*; по мнéнию/словáм/сообщéнию + *g.*

accordingly /ə'kɔ:dɪŋlɪ/ *adv.*
1 (*appropriately*) соответ́ственно.
2 (*therefore*) поэ́тому; таки́м óбразом.

accordion /ə'kɔ:dɪən/ *n.* аккордеóн.

accost /ə'kɒst/ *v.t.* прист|авáть, -áть к + *d.* (с разговóрами).

account /ə'kaʊnt/ *n.*
1 (*comm.*) счёт (*pl.* -á); **current ~** текýщий счёт; **deposit ~** депози́тный счёт; **joint ~** óбщий счёт; **do the ~s** пров|оди́ть, -ести́ счетá; **balance ~s** св|оди́ть, -ести́ балáнс.
2 (*statement, report*) отчёт; (*description*) описáние; **by all ~s** сýдя по всемý.
3 (*estimation, consideration*) расчёт; **take into ~, take ~ of** уч|и́тывать, -éсть; прин|имáть, -я́ть во внимáние.
4 (*reason, cause*): **on ~ of** (*because of*) из-за + *g.*; (*in consequence of*) по причи́не + *g.*; (*as a result of*) вслéдствие + *g.*; **on no ~** ни в кóем слýчае.
■ *v.i.* **~ for:** (*lit., fig., give a reckoning of*) отчи́т|ываться, -áться в + *p.*; да|вáть, -ть отчёт в + *p.*; (*fig., answer for*) отв|ечáть, -éтить за + *a.*; **is everyone ~ed for?** никогó не забы́ли?; (*explain*) объясн|я́ть, -и́ть; (*be reason for*) явля́ться (*impf.*) причи́ной + *g.*

accountable /ə'kaʊntəb(ə)l/ *adj.* ответ́ственный; **he is ~ to me** он отчи́тывается пéредо мной.

accountancy /ə'kaʊntənsɪ/ *n.* (*profession*) бухгáлтерское дéло.

accountant /ə'kaʊnt(ə)nt/ *n.* бухгáлтер, счетовóд.

accounting /ə'kaʊntɪŋ/ *n.* бухгалтéрия, счетовóдство.

accrue /ə'kru:/ *v.i.* (**accrues, accrued, accruing**)
1 (*accumulate*) нараст|áть, -и́; **~d interest** нарóсшие процéнты (*m. pl.*).
2 (*come about*): **certain advantages will ~ from this** э́то даст определённые преимýщества.
3 : **~ to** (*fall to the lot of*) дост|авáться, -áться + *d.*

accumulate /ə'kju:mjʊleɪt/ *v.t.* нак|áпливать, -опи́ть; соб|ирáть, -рáть.
■ *v.i.* нак|áпливаться, -опи́ться; ск|áпливаться, -опи́ться.

accumulation /əkju:mjʊ'leɪʃ(ə)n/ *n.* накоплéние.

accuracy /'ækjʊrəsɪ/ *n.* тóчность; (*of aim or shot*) мéткость.

accurate /'ækjʊrət/ *adj.* (*of persons, statements, instruments etc.*) тóчный; (*of aim or shot*) мéткий.

accusation /ækju:'zeɪʃ(ə)n/ *n.* обвинéние.

accusative /ə'kyu:zətɪv/ *adj.* & *n.* вини́тельный (падéж).

accuse /ə'kju:z/ *v.t.* обвин|я́ть, -и́ть; **he was ~d of stealing** егó обвини́ли в крáже.

accused /ə'kju:zd/ *n.*: **the ~** обвиня́емый, подсуди́мый.

accuser /ə'kju:zə(r)/ *n.* обвини́тель (*m.*).

accustom /ə'kʌstəm/ *v.t.* приуч|áть, -и́ть (**to:** к + *d.*): **become ~ed** прив|ыкáть, -ы́кнуть (**to:** к + *d.*).

accustomed /ə'kʌstəmd/ *adj.* (*usual*) обы́чный, привы́чный.

ace /eɪs/ *n.* туз.

acerbic /ə'sə:bɪk/ *adj.* (*astringent*) тéрпкий; (*of speech, manner etc.*) язви́тельный.

acetate /'æsɪteɪt/ *n.* ацетáт; уксуснокúслая соль.

ache /eɪk/ *n.* боль.
■ *v.i.* болéть (*impf.*); ныть (*impf.*); **my head ~s** у меня́ боли́т головá.

achievable /ə'tʃi:vəb(ə)l/ *adj.* достижи́мый.

achieve /ə'tʃi:v/ *v.t.*
1 (*attain*) дост|игáть, -и́чь + *g.*; доб|ивáться, -и́ться + *g.*
2 (*carry out*) выполня́ть, вы́полнить.

achievement /ə'tʃi:vmənt/ *n.* (*attainment*) достижéние; (*carrying out*) выполнéние; (*success*) достижéние, завоевáние.

acid /'æsɪd/ *n.* кислотá; **~ rain** кислóтный дождь; **~ test** (*fig.*) прóбный кáмень.
■ *adj.* ки́слый.

acidic /ə'sɪdɪk/ *adj.* ки́слый.

acidity /ə'sɪdɪtɪ/ *n.* кислóтность.

acknowledge /ək'nɒlɪdʒ/ *v.t.*
1 (*recognize; admit*) призн|авáть, -áть.
2 (*confirm receipt of; reply to*): **~ a letter** подтвер|ждáть, -ди́ть получéние письмá.
3 (*indicate recognition of*): **he did not even ~ me as we passed** он прошёл ми́мо и дáже не поздорóвался.

acknowledg(e)ment /ək'nɒlɪdʒmənt/ *n.*
1 (*recognition, admission*) признáние.
2 (*confirmation*) подтверждéние.

acme /'ækmɪ/ *n.* верх, верши́на.

acne /'æknɪ/ *n.* угри́ (*m. pl.*).

acorn /'eɪkɔ:n/ *n.* жёлудь (*m.*).

acoustic /ə'ku:stɪk/ *adj.* акусти́ческий; звуковóй; **an ~ guitar** класси́ческая гитáра.

acoustics /ə'ku:stɪks/ *n.* (*science; acoustic properties*) акýстика.

acquaint /ə'kweɪnt/ *v.t.* знакóмить, по-; **I ~ed him with the facts** я ознакóмил егó с фáктами; **he soon got ~ed with the situation** он бы́стро ознакóмился с положéнием дел; **be ~ed with s.o.** быть знакóмым с кем-н.

acquaintance /ə'kweɪnt(ə)ns/ *n.* знакóмство; **make the ~ of** знакóмиться, по- с + *i.*; (*person*) знакóмый; **an ~ of mine** оди́н мой знакóмый.

acquiescence /ækwɪ'esəns/ *n.* (*agreement*) соглáсие; (*tractability*) устýпчивость.

acquiescent /ækwɪ'esənt/ *adj.* устýпчивый.

acquire /ə'kwaɪə(r)/ *v.t.* приобре|та́ть, -сти́; **asparagus is an ~d taste** к спа́рже на́до привы́кнуть.

acquisition /ækwɪ'zɪʃ(ə)n/ *n.* приобрете́ние; **the library's new ~s** но́вые библиоте́чные поступле́ния.

acquisitive /ə'kwɪzɪtɪv/ *adj.* стяжа́тельский; жа́дный.

acquisitiveness /ə'kwɪzɪtɪvnɪs/ *n.* стяжа́тельство; жа́дность.

acquit /ə'kwɪt/ *v.t.* (**acquitted, acquitting**) (*declare not guilty*) опра́вд|ывать, -а́ть; **he was ~ted of murder** с него́ сня́ли обвине́ние в убийстве.

acquittal /ə'kwɪt(ə)l/ *n.* (*in court of law*) оправда́ние.

acre /'eɪkə(r)/ *n.* акр.

acreage /'eɪkərɪdʒ/ *n.* пло́щадь земли́ в а́крах.

acrid /'ækrɪd/ *adj.* е́дкий.

acrimonious /ækrɪ'məʊnɪəs/ *adj.* ожесточённый, го́рький.

acrobat /'ækrəbæt/ *n.* акроба́т.

acrobatic /ækrə'bætɪk/ *adj.* акробати́ческий.

acrobatics /ækrə'bætɪks/ *n.* акроба́тика.

across /ə'krɒs/ *adv.*
1 (*crosswise*) поперёк; (*in crosswords*) по горизонта́ли.
2 (*on the other side*) на той стороне́.
3 (*to the other side*) на ту сто́рону.
4 (*in width*): **the river here is more than six miles ~** ширина́ реки́ здесь бо́льше шести́ миль.
■ *prep.* 1 (*from one side of to the other*) че́рез + *a.*, *sometimes omitted with vv. compounded with* пере…; **he went ~ the street** он перешёл у́лицу.
2 (*over the surface of*) по + *d.*; **he hit me ~ the face** он уда́рил меня́ по лицу́.
3 (*athwart*) поперёк + *g.*; **she lay ~ the bed** она́ лежа́ла поперёк крова́ти.
4 (*on the other side of*) на той стороне́ + *g.*, по ту сто́рону + *g.*

acrylic /ə'krɪlɪk/ *n.* акри́л.
■ *adj.* акри́ловый.

act /ækt/ *n.*
1 (*action*) посту́пок; (*feat*) по́двиг; **catch in the ~** пойма́ть (*pf.*) на ме́сте преступле́ния; **an ~ of kindness** до́брое де́ло.
2 (*law*) акт, зако́н.
3 (*of drama*) де́йствие.
4 (*performance*) но́мер; (*fig., coll.*): **put on an ~** притвор|я́ться, -и́ться.
■ *v.t.* игра́ть (*impf.*); **~ a part** (*lit., fig.*) игра́ть роль; **~ the fool** валя́ть (*impf.*) дурака́.
■ *v.i.* 1 (*behave*) поступ|а́ть, -и́ть; вести́ (*det.*) себя́; (*take action, intervene*) прин|има́ть, -я́ть ме́ры.
2 (*serve, function*) де́йствовать (*impf.*); **~ for s.o.** де́йствовать от и́мени кого́-л.; **he is ~ing as interpreter** он выступа́ет в ро́ли перево́дчика.
3 (*have effect*) де́йствовать, по- (**on:** на + *a.*)
4 (*theatr.*) игра́ть.
■ *with advs.*: **~ out** *v.t.* разы́гр|ывать, -а́ть; **~ up** *v.i.* (*coll., misbehave*) шали́ть (*impf.*); (*give trouble*): **my car has been ~ing up** моя́ маши́на барахли́т.

acting /'æktɪŋ/ *n.* (*theatr.*) игра́; (*as skill*) актёрское мастерство́.
■ *adj.* (*doing duty temporarily*): **~ manager** исполня́ющий обя́занности (*abbr.* и. о.) заве́дующего.

action /'ækʃ(ə)n/ *n.*
1 (*acting; activity; effect*) де́йствие; **in ~** в де́йствии; **come into ~** вступ|а́ть, -и́ть в де́йствие; **put out of ~** выводи́ть, вы́вести из стро́я; **out of ~** него́дный к употребле́нию; **take ~** прин|има́ть, -я́ть ме́ры.
2 (*deed*) посту́пок; **~s speak louder than words** дела́ говоря́т са́ми за себя́.
3 (*physical movement*) движе́ние.
4 (*theatr.*): **the ~ takes place in London** де́йствие происхо́дит в Ло́ндоне.
5 (*leg.*) иск, суде́бное де́ло; **bring an ~ against** предъяв|ля́ть, -и́ть иск к + *d.*
6 (*mil.*) бой, де́йствие; **killed in ~** па́вший, поги́бший в бою́.

activate /'æktɪveɪt/ *v.t.* (*make operative*) прив|оди́ть, -ести́ в де́йствие; активизи́ровать (*impf., pf.*).

active /'æktɪv/ *adj.*
1 (*lively; energetic; displaying activity*) акти́вный, де́ятельный; **an ~ volcano** де́йствующий вулка́н.
2 (*gram.*) действи́тельный.
3 (*mil.*): **on ~ service** на действи́тельной слу́жбе.

activism /'æktɪvɪz(ə)m/ *n.* полити́ческая акти́вность.

activist /'æktɪvɪst/ *n.* активи́ст (*fem.* -ка).

activity /æk'tɪvɪtɪ/ *n.*
1 (*being active; exertion of energy*) акти́вность.
2 (*usu. pl., pursuit, sphere of action; doings*) де́ятельность.

actor /'æktə(r)/ *n.* актёр.

actress /'æktrɪs/ *n.* актри́са.

actual /'æktʃʊəl/ *adj.* (*real*) действи́тельный; факти́ческий; **in ~ fact** в действи́тельности; **those were his ~ words** э́то его́ по́длинные слова́.

actually /'æktʃʊəlɪ/ *adv.* (*really; in fact*) действи́тельно; на (са́мом) де́ле; (*in sense 'to tell the truth'*) со́бственно (говоря́).

actuary /'æktʃʊərɪ/ *n.* актуа́рий (*сотрудник компании, производящий страховые расчёты на основе статистического анализа*).

acumen /'ækjʊmən/ *n.* (*judgement*) сообрази́тельность; (*penetration*) проница́тельность; **business ~** делова́я хва́тка.

acupuncture /'ækju:pʌŋktʃə(r)/ *n.* акупункту́ра, иглоука́лывание.

acupuncturist /'ækju:pʌŋktʃərɪst/ *n.* иглотерапе́вт.

acute /ə'kju:t/ *adj.* (**acuter, acutest**) (*in var. senses*) о́стрый; **~ angle** о́стрый у́гол; **~ shortage** о́страя нехва́тка; **~ sense of smell** то́нкое обоня́ние; **~ accent** аку́т.

AD (*abbr. of* ***Anno Domini***) н. э. (на́шей э́ры).

ad /æd/ (*coll.*) = **advertisement**

adage /'ædɪdʒ/ *n.* погово́рка, посло́вица; наро́дная му́дрость; **as the old ~ goes: money talks** как гласи́т дре́вняя му́дрость:

a

де́ньги реша́ют всё.

adagio /əˈdɑːʒɪəʊ/ *n., adj. & adv.* (*pl.* **~s**) (*mus.*) ада́жио (*nt. indecl.*).

adamant /ˈædəmənt/ *adj.* (*fig.*) непрекло́нный.

adapt /əˈdæpt/ *v.t.*
1 приспос|а́бливать, -о́бить.
2 (*text, book*) адапти́ровать (*impf., pf.*); **~ for the stage** инсцени́ровать (*impf., pf.*).
■ *v.i.* приспос|а́бливаться, -о́биться; адапти́роваться (*impf., pf.*).

adaptable /əˈdæptəb(ə)l/ *adj.* приспособля́емый; (*of person*) легко́ приспоса́бливающийся.

adaptation /ædæpˈteɪʃ(ə)n/ *n.* приспособле́ние; (*of book etc.*) адапта́ция; (*for stage*) инсцениро́вка.

adapt|er, -or /əˈdæptə(r)/ *n.* (*tech.*) ада́птер.

add /æd/ *v.t.*
1 (*make an addition of*) приб|авля́ть, -а́вить; **you must ~ water** на́до доба́вить воды́; **~ed to this is the fact that ...** к э́тому ну́жно приба́вить/доба́вить тот факт, что... .
2 (*say in addition*) доб|авля́ть, -а́вить; **I have nothing to ~** мне не́чего доба́вить.
3 (*math.*) скла́дывать, сложи́ть; **~ two and (*or* to) three!** сложи́те два и три!
■ *v.i.* 1 **~ to** (*increase, enlarge*) увели́чи|вать, -ть; уси́ли|вать, -ть; (*knowledge etc.*) углуб|ля́ть, -и́ть.
2 (*perform addition*) *see* ▶ **~ up** *v.i.*
■ *with advs.*: **~ on** *v.t.* приб|авля́ть, -а́вить; доб|авля́ть, -а́вить; **the tip was ~ed on to the bill** чаевы́е бы́ли включены́ в счёт; **~ together** *v.t.* скла́дывать, сложи́ть; **~ up** *v.t.* (*find sum of*) подсч|и́тывать, -ита́ть; подыто́жи|вать, -ть; *v.i.* (*perform addition*): **you can't ~ up!** вы не уме́ете счита́ть!; (*total*): **it ~s up to 50** э́то в су́мме составля́ет 50.
■ *cpds.* **~-ons** *n. pl.* (*comput.*) дополни́тельный встро́енный/встра́иваемый мо́дуль.

addend|um /əˈdendəm/ *n.* (*pl.* **~a**) приложе́ние, дополне́ние.

adder /ˈædə(r)/ *n.* (*snake*) гадю́ка.

addict[1] /ˈædɪkt/ *n.* **(drug ~)** наркома́н (*fem.* -ка).

addict[2] /əˈdɪkt/ *v.t.*: **be, become ~ed to** пристрасти́ться (*pf.*) к + *d.*

addiction /əˈdɪkʃ(ə)n/ *n.* пристра́стие (**to:** к + *d.*); **~ to drugs** наркома́ния.

addictive /əˈdɪktɪv/ *adj.* вызыва́ющий привыка́ние.

addition /əˈdɪʃ(ə)n/ *n.*
1 (*act of adding; thing added*) прибавле́ние; добавле́ние; **in ~ to** в дополне́ние к + *d.*; **in ~** (*as well*) вдоба́вок; (*moreover*) к тому́ же.
2 (*math.*) сложе́ние.

additional /əˈdɪʃən(ə)l/ *adj.* доба́вочный, дополни́тельный.

additive /ˈædɪtɪv/ *n.* доба́вка, добавле́ние.

address /əˈdres/ *n.* а́дрес; **~ book** (*also comput.*) записна́я кни́жка.
■ *v.t.* 1 (*a letter*) адресова́ть (*impf., pf.*).
2 (*speak to*) обра|ща́ться, -ти́ться к + *d.*

addressee /ædreˈsiː/ *n.* адреса́т.

adenoids /ˈædɪnɔɪdz/ *n.* адено́иды (*m. pl.*).

adept /ˈædept/ *adj.* уме́лый; **he is ~ at finding excuses** он ма́стер находи́ть оправда́ния (*or* опра́вдываться).

adequate /ˈædɪkwət/ *adj.*
1 (*sufficient*) доста́точный.
2 (*suitable*) адеква́тный.

adhere /ədˈhɪə(r)/ *v.i.* прил|ипа́ть, -и́пнуть (к + *d.*).

adherence /ədˈhɪərəns/ *n.* (*lit.*) прилипа́ние; (*fig.*) приве́рженность.

adherent /ədˈhɪərənt/ *n.* приве́рженец.

adhesive /ədˈhiːsɪv/ *n.* кле́й; кле́йкое вещество́.
■ *adj.* ли́пкий; (*sticky*) кле́йкий; **~ tape** кле́йкая ле́нта, скотч.

ad hoc /æd ˈhɒk/ *adv.* для да́нного слу́чая; (*attr.*) специа́льный; **~ committee** вре́менный комите́т.

ad infinitum /æd ɪnfɪˈnaɪtəm/ *adv.* до бесконе́чности.

adjacent /əˈdʒeɪs(ə)nt/ *adj.* (*neighbouring*) сосе́дний; сме́жный; **~ to** примыка́ющий к + *d.*; (*geom.*): **~ angles** сме́жные углы́.

adjectival /ædʒɪkˈtaɪv(ə)l/ *adj.* (*gram.*) адъекти́вный.

adjective /ˈædʒɪktɪv/ *n.* (и́мя) прилага́тельное.

adjourn /əˈdʒəːn/ *v.t.* (*postpone*) от|кла́дывать, -ложи́ть; **the meeting was ~ed till Monday** заседа́ние бы́ло отло́жено до понеде́льника.

adjournment /əˈdʒəːnmənt/ *n.* (*postponement*) отсро́чка; (*break in proceedings*) переры́в.

adjudicate /əˈdʒuːdɪkeɪt/ *v.t.* (*a claim*) рассм|а́тривать, -отре́ть.

adjudication /ədʒuːdɪˈkeɪʃ(ə)n/ *n.* (*judgement*) суде́бное/арбитра́жное реше́ние.

adjudicator /əˈdʒuːdɪkeɪtə(r)/ *n.* арби́тр; (*judge*) судья́ (*m.*).

adjunct /ˈædʒʌŋkt/ *n.* (*appendage*) приложе́ние; (*addition*) дополне́ние; (*gram.*) обстоя́тельство.

adjust /əˈdʒʌst/ *v.t.*
1 (*arrange; put right or straight*) прив|оди́ть, -ести́ в поря́док; попр|авля́ть, -а́вить; **he ~ed his tie** он попра́вил га́лстук; (*mechanism*) регули́ровать, от-; нала́|живать, -дить.
2 (*fit, adapt*) приг|оня́ть, -на́ть; под|гоня́ть, -огна́ть; **well-~ed** (*of person*) уравнове́шенный.

adjustable /əˈdʒʌstəb(ə)l/ *adj.* регули́руемый; подвижно́й.

adjustment /əˈdʒʌstmənt/ *n.* (*regulation*) регул|и́рование, -иро́вка; (*correction*) исправле́ние, попра́вка; (*fitting*) подго́нка; (*adaptation*) приспособле́ние.

ad-lib /æd ˈlɪb/ (*coll.*) *n.* экспро́мт; **his speech was full of ~s** в свое́й ре́чи он мно́го импровизи́ровал.
■ *v.i.* (**ad-libbed, ad-libbing**) говори́ть (*impf.*) экспро́мтом.

administer /ədˈmɪnɪstə(r)/ *v.t.* (*manage, govern*) управля́ть (*impf.*) + *i.*; заве́довать (*impf.*) + *i.*

administration /ədmɪnɪˈstreɪʃ(ə)n/ *n.*
1 (*management*) управле́ние.

[2] (*of public affairs*) администрáция; **the A~** администрáция, правúтельство.

administrative /əd'mɪnɪstrətɪv/ *adj.* административный, организациóнный.

administrator /əd'mɪnɪstreɪtə(r)/ *n.* администрáтор.

admirabl|e /'ædmərəb(ə)l/ *adj.* замечáтельный, прекрáсный.

admiral /'ædmər(ə)l/ *n.* адмирáл.

admiration /ædmɪ'reɪʃ(ə)n/ *n.* восхищéние, востóрг.

admire /əd'maɪə(r)/ *v.t.* (*view with pleasure*) любовáться (*impf.*) + *i.* (*or* на + *a.*); (*respect*) восхи|щáться, -тúться + *i.*; восторгáться (*impf.*) + *i.*

admirer /əd'maɪərə(r)/ *n.* поклóнни|к (*fem.* -ца).

admissible /əd'mɪsɪb(ə)l/ *adj.* приéмлемый, допустúмый.

admission /əd'mɪʃ(ə)n/ *n.*
[1] (*permitted entry or access*) вход; дóступ.
[2] (*acknowledgement*) признáние.

admit /əd'mɪt/ *v.t.* & *i.* (**admitted, admitting**)
[1] (*allow, accept*) допус|кáть, -тúть; призн|авáть, -áть; **you must ~ he is right** вы должны́ признáть, что он прав (*or* егó правотý).
[2] (*let in*) впус|кáть, -тúть; (*to organization*) прин|имáть, -ять; **the public are not ~ted to the gardens** э́тот парк закры́т для посещéния; **this ticket ~s one (person)** э́то билéт на однó лицó.
[3] (*confess*) призн|авáть, -áть; **he ~s his guilt** он признаёт свою винý; **~ to feeling ashamed** призн|авáться, -áться, что сты́дно.

admittance /əd'mɪt(ə)ns/ *n.* (*entry*) вход; **no ~!** вход воспрещён!

admittedly /əd'mɪtɪdlɪ/ *adv.* прáвда; признáться.

admixture /əd'mɪkstʃə(r)/ *n.* (*mixing*) смéшивание; (*addition*) при́месь.

admonish /əd'mɒnɪʃ/ *v.t.*
[1] (*reprimand*) дéлать, с- внушéние/ замечáние + *d.*; **the boys were ~ed for being late** мáльчикам сдéлали замечáние за опоздáние.
[2] (*advise, urge*) настоя́тельно совéтовать, по-; убедúтельно просúть, по-.

ad nauseam /æd 'nɔːzɪæm/ *adv.* до тошноты́.

ado /ə'duː/ *n.* (*fuss*) сует́а; **without further ~** без дальнéйших церемóний.

adolescence /ædə'les(ə)ns/ *n.* подросткóвый вóзраст.

adolescent /ædə'les(ə)nt/ *n.* подрóсток.
■ *adj.* подросткóвый.

adopt /ə'dɒpt/ *v.t.*
[1] (*a son*) усынов|ля́ть, -úть; (*a daughter*) удочер|я́ть, -úть.
[2] (*accept*) прин|имáть, -я́ть; (*take over*) перен|имáть, -я́ть; **his methods should be ~ed** слéдует воспóльзоваться егó метóдикой.

adoption /ə'dɒpʃ(ə)n/ *n.*
[1] (*of a son*) усыновлéние; (*of a daughter*) удочерéние.
[2] (*acceptance*) принятие.

adoptive /ə'dɒptɪv/ *adj.* приёмный; **~ parent** усыновúтель (*fem.* -ница).

adorable /ə'dɔːrəb(ə)l/ *adj.* прелéстный, восхитúтельный.

adoration /ædɔː'reɪʃ(ə)n/ *n.* обожáние.

ador|e /ə'dɔː(r)/ *v.t.* (*worship*) обожáть (*impf.*); поклоня́ться (*impf.*) + *d.*; **her ~ing husband** её лю́бящий муж.

adorn /ə'dɔːn/ *v.t.* укр|ашáть, -áсить.

adornment /ə'dɔːnmənt/ *n.* украшéние.

adrenalin /ə'drenəlɪn/ *n.* адреналúн.

adrift /ə'drɪft/ *pred. adj.* & *adv.*: **be ~** дрейфовáть (*impf.*).

adroit /ə'drɔɪt/ *adj.* лóвкий.

adulation /ædjʊ'leɪʃ(ə)n/ *n.* низкопоклóнство, лесть.

adult /'ædʌlt/ *n.* & *adj.*
[1] взрóслый; **~ education** обучéние взрóслых.
[2] (*mature*) зрéлый.

adulterate /ə'dʌltəreɪt/ *v.t.* (*debase*) пóртить, ис-; (*dilute*) разб|авля́ть, -áвить.

adulterous /ə'dʌltərəs/ *adj.* невéрный.

adultery /ə'dʌltərɪ/ *n.* адюльтéр, супрýжеская измéна.

adulthood /'ædʌlthʊd/ *n.* зрéлость; (*of men*) возмужáлость.

advance /əd'vɑːns/ *n.*
[1] (*forward move*) продвижéние; (*mil., also*) наступлéние; (*pl., overtures to a person*): **make ~s to** заúгрывать (*impf.*) с + *i.*
[2] (*progress*) прогрéсс; (*in rank, social position etc.*) продвижéние.
[3] (*increase*) повышéние; **an ~ on his original offer** надбáвка к первоначáльному предложéнию.
[4] (*loan*) ссýда; (*payment beforehand*) авáнс; **an ~ on salary** авáнс под зарплáту.
[5] : **in ~** (*in front*) вперёд; (*beforehand*) зарáнее; **in ~ of** впередú + *g.*
[6] (*attr.*): **~ booking** предварúтельный закáз.
■ *v.t.* [1] (*move forward*) продв|игáть, -úнуть.
[2] (*fig., put forward*): **~ an opinion** выскáзывать, вы́сказать мнéние.
[3] (*fig., further*): **~ s.o.'s interests** отстáивать (*impf.*) чьи-н. интерéсы; служúть, по- чьим-н. интерéсам.
[4] (*of payment*) платúть, за- авáнсом; (*lend*) ссу|жáть, -дúть.
■ *v.i.* [1] (*move forward*) продв|игáться, -úнуться; **~ on** наступáть (*impf.*) на + *a.*
[2] (*progress*) разв|ивáться, -úться; дéлать, с- успéхи.

advanced /əd'vɑːnst/ *adj.*
[1] (*far on*): **~ age, years** преклóнный вóзраст.
[2] (*opp. elementary*): **an ~ course** курс для продвúнутого этáпа (обучéния).
[3] (*progressive*) передовóй.

advancement /əd'vɑːnsmənt/ *n.* (*moving forward*) продвижéние; (*promotion*) продвижéние по слýжбе; (*progress*) прогрéсс.

advantage /əd'vɑːntɪdʒ/ *n.*
[1] (*superiority; more favourable position*) преимýщество, достóинство.
[2] (*profit, benefit*) вы́года, пóльза; **take ~ of sth.** воспóльзоваться (*pf.*) чем-н.; (*abuse*) злоупотреб|ля́ть, -úть чем-н.; **take ~ of s.o.** эксплуатúровать (*impf.*); **you may learn**

a

sth. to your ~ вы мо́жете узна́ть/почерпну́ть для себя́ что́-то поле́зное.
3 (*tennis*): **~ Henman** бо́льше у Хэ́нмена.

advantageous /ædvən'teɪdʒəs/ *adj.* (*favourable*) благоприя́тный; (*profitable*) вы́годный.

advent /'ædvent/ *n.*
1 (*appearance; occurrence*) появле́ние.
2 (**A~:** *eccl.*) Рожде́ственский пост.

adventure /əd'ventʃə(r)/ *n.* приключе́ние; **~ story** приключе́нческий рома́н.

adventurous /əd'ventʃərəs/ *adj.*
1 (*of person*) сме́лый; (*enterprising*) предприи́мчивый.
2 (*of actions*) риско́ванный, авантю́рный.

adverb /'ædvə:b/ *n.* наре́чие.

adverbial /əd'və:bɪəl/ *adj.* (*gram.*) наре́чный, адвербиа́льный.

adversary /'ædvəsərɪ/ *n.* проти́вник.

adverse /'ædvə:s/ *adj.* неблагоприя́тный.

adversity /əd'və:sɪtɪ/ *n.* беда́, несча́стье; **show courage in, under ~** прояв|ля́ть, -и́ть му́жество в беде́; **companions in ~** това́рищи по несча́стью.

advert /'ædvə:t/ (*Br., coll.*) = **advertisement**

advertise /'ædvətaɪz/ *v.t.* (*publicize*) реклами́ровать (*impf., pf.*); (*in newspaper*) да|ва́ть, -ть (*or* поме|ща́ть, -сти́ть) объявле́ние о + *p.*
■ *v.i.*: **she ~d for a secretary** она́ дала́ объявле́ние о вака́нсии секретаря́.

advertisement /əd'və:tɪsmənt, -tɪzmənt/ *n.* рекла́ма; (*classified advertisement*) объявле́ние.

advertising /'ædvətaɪzɪŋ/ *n.* реклами́рование; рекла́мный би́знес; **~ agent** рекла́мный аге́нт.

advice /əd'vaɪs/ *n.* (*also* **piece of ~**) сове́т; **give s.o. a piece of ~** сове́товать, по- кому́-н.

advisable /əd'vaɪzəb(ə)l/ *adj.* целесообра́зный; **it may be ~ to wait** сто́ит, наве́рное, подожда́ть.

advise /əd'vaɪz/ *v.t.*
1 (*counsel*) сове́товать, по- + *d.*; рекомендова́ть (*impf., pf.*) + *d.*; **what do you ~ (me to do)?** что вы посове́туете мне предприня́ть?; **the doctor ~d complete rest** врач рекомендова́л по́лный поко́й; **I ~d him against going** я посове́товал ему́ не ходи́ть туда́; (*give professional advice to*) консульти́ровать, про-.
2 (*comm.: notify*) изве|ща́ть, -сти́ть (*кого о чём*); **please ~ me of receipt** уве́домите меня́ о получе́нии.

advis|er, -or /əd'vaɪzə(r)/ *nn.* (*professional*) консульта́нт; (*to president etc.*) сове́тник (**to:** + *g.*); **legal ~** юриско́нсульт; **medical ~** врач.

advisory /əd'vaɪzərɪ/ *adj.* совеща́тельный, консультати́вный.

advocate[1] /'ædvəkət/ *n.*
1 (*defender*) защи́тник; (*supporter*) сторо́нни|к (*fem.* -ца).
2 (*lawyer*) адвока́т; **devil's ~** (*fig.*) «адвока́т дья́вола».

advocate[2] /'ædvəkeɪt/ *v.t.* (*speak in favour of*) выступа́ть, вы́ступить за + *a.*; (*advise, recommend*) сове́товать, по-; рекомендова́ть (*impf., pf.*).

aegis /'i:dʒɪs/ *n.*: **under the ~ of** под эги́дой + *g.*

aeration /eə'reɪʃ(ə)n/ *n.* прове́тривание; (*of the soil*) аэра́ция.

aerial /'eərɪəl/ *n.* анте́нна.
■ *adj.* (*lit., fig.*) возду́шный; **~ photography** аэрофотосъёмка.

aerobatics /eərə'bætɪks/ *n.* вы́сший пилота́ж; фигу́ры вы́сшего пилота́жа.

aerobic /eə'rəʊbɪk/ *adj.* аэро́бный.

aerobics /eə'rəʊbɪks/ *n.* аэро́бика.

aerodrome /'eərədrəʊm/ *n.* (*Br.*) аэродро́м.

aerodynamic /eərəʊdaɪ'næmɪk/ *adj.* аэродинами́ческий.

aerodynamics /eərəʊdaɪ'næmɪks/ *n.* аэродина́мика.

aeronautics /eərəʊ'nɔ:tɪks/ *n.* аэрона́втика; воздухопла́вание.

aeroplane /'eərəpleɪn/ *n.* (*Br.*) самолёт, аэропла́н.

aerosol /'eərəsɒl/ *n.* аэрозо́ль (*m.*).

aerospace /'eərəʊspeɪs/ *n.* возду́шно-косми́ческое простра́нство.

aesthetic /i:s'θetɪk/ (*US also* **esthetic**) *adj.* эстети́ческий.

aesthetics /i:s'θetɪks/ (*US also* **esthetics**) *n.* эсте́тика.

afar /ə'fɑ:(r)/ *adv.* вдалеке́; **from ~** и́здали, издалека́.

affable /'æfəb(ə)l/ *adj.* приве́тливый; любе́зный.

affair /ə'feə(r)/ *n.*
1 (*business, matter*) де́ло; **that's my ~** э́то моё де́ло; **~s of state** госуда́рственные дела́; **Ministry of Foreign A~s** министе́рство иностра́нных дел.
2 (*also* **love ~**) любо́вная связь; рома́н; **they are having an ~** у них рома́н.

affect /ə'fekt/ *v.t.*
1 (*act on*) де́йствовать, по- на + *a.*; влия́ть, по- на + *a.*; **the climate ~ed his health** кли́мат повлия́л на его́ здоро́вье.
2 (*concern*) каса́ться, косну́ться + *g.*; затр|а́гивать, -о́нуть.
3 (*touch emotionally*) тро́|гать, -нуть; волнова́ть, вз-.
4 (*of disease*): **the lung is ~ed** лёгкое пораженó.

affectation /æfek'teɪʃ(ə)n/ *n.*
1 (*pretence*) вне́шнее (*притворное*) проявле́ние, попы́тка изобрази́ть *что.*
2 (*unnatural behaviour*) притво́рство.
3 (*of language or style*) иску́сственность.

affected /ə'fektɪd/ *adj.* жема́нный, неесте́ственный.

affection /ə'fekʃ(ə)n/ *n.* привя́занность (**for:** к + *d.*); любо́вь (**for:** к + *d.*)

affectionate /ə'fekʃənət/ *adj.* не́жный.

affidavit /æfɪ'deɪvɪt/ *n.* (*leg.*) пи́сьменное показа́ние под прися́гой, аффиде́вит; **make, swear an ~** да|ва́ть, -ть показа́ние под прися́гой.

affiliate /ə'fɪlɪeɪt/ *v.t.*
1 (*join, attach*) присоедин|я́ть, -и́ть (**to:** к + *d.*); **~d company** доче́рняя компа́ния.
2 (*adopt as member*) прин|има́ть, -я́ть в чле́ны.

■ *v.i.* присоедин|я́ться, -и́ться (**with:** к + *d.*).

affiliation /əfɪlɪ'eɪʃ(ə)n/ *n.*
1 присоедине́ние.
2 приня́тие в чле́ны.
3 (*connection*) связь.

affinity /ə'fɪnɪtɪ/ *n.*
1 (*resemblance*) схо́дство; (*relationship*) родство́; (*connection*) связь; (*closeness*) бли́зость.
2 (*liking, attraction*) влече́ние, скло́нность.

affirm /ə'fə:m/ *v.t.* (*assert*) утвер|жда́ть, -ди́ть.

affirmation /æfə'meɪʃ(ə)n/ *n.* утвержде́ние.

affirmative /ə'fə:mətɪv/ *n.*: **he answered in the ~** он отве́тил утверди́тельно.
■ *adj.* утверди́тельный.

afflict /ə'flɪkt/ *v.t.*
1 (*distress: of misfortune etc.*) пост|ига́ть, -и́чь (*or* -и́гнуть); **he was ~ed by a great misfortune** его́ пости́гло большо́е несча́стье.
2 (*pass.: suffer from*): **be ~ed with** страда́ть (*impf.*) + *i.*; **he is ~ed with rheumatism** он страда́ет ревмати́змом; **the ~ed** стра́ждущие (*pl.*).

affliction /ə'flɪkʃ(ə)n/ *n.* (*grief*) го́ре; (*misfortune*) несча́стье; бе́дствие; (*illness*) боле́знь.

affluence /'æfluəns/ *n.* (*wealth*) бога́тство; (*plenty*) изоби́лие.

affluent /'æfluənt/ *adj.* бога́тый.

afford /ə'fɔ:d/ *v.t.* (*with* **can**, *expr. possibility*): **I can't ~ all these books** все э́ти кни́ги мне не по карма́ну; **they can ~ a new car** они́ мо́гут позво́лить себе́ но́вую маши́ну; **I can't ~ the time** мне не́когда.

affront /ə'frʌnt/ *v.t.* оскорб|ля́ть, -и́ть.

Afghan /'æfgæn/ *n.* афга́н|ец (*fem.* -ка); (**~ hound**) афга́нская борза́я.
■ *adj.* афга́нский.

Afghanistan /æf'gænɪstɑ:n/ *n.* Афганиста́н.

aficionado /əfɪsjə'nɑ:dəʊ/ *n.* (*pl.* **~s**) покло́нни|к (*fem.* -ца).

afield /ə'fi:ld/ *adv.*: **far ~** вдалеке́, вдали́; (*expr. motion*) вдаль.

afloat /ə'fləʊt/ *pred. adj.* & *adv.* (*floating on water*) на воде́.

afoot /ə'fʊt/ *pred. adj.* & *adv.*: **there is a plan ~** гото́вится план; **there is sth. ~** что́-то затева́ется.

afore|- /ə'fɔ:(r)/ *comb. form*: **~mentioned** *adj.* вышеупомя́нутый; **~said** *adj.* вышеска́занный.

afraid /ə'freɪd/ *pred. adj.* испу́ганный; **be ~ of** боя́ться (*impf.*) + *g.*; **don't be ~** не бо́йтесь!; **I'm ~ he will die** бою́сь, что он умрёт; **I'm ~ he is out** к сожале́нию, его́ нет.

afresh /ə'freʃ/ *adv.* за́ново.

Africa /'æfrɪkə/ *n.* А́фрика.

African /'æfrɪkən/ *n.* африка́н|ец (*fem.* -ка).
■ *adj.* африка́нский.
■ *cpds.* **~ American** *n.* афроамерика́н|ец (*fem.* -ка); *adj.* афроамерика́нский.

Afrikaans /æfrɪ'kɑ:ns/ *n.* (язы́к) африкаа́нс.

Afrikaner /æfrɪ'kɑ:nə(r)/ *n.* африка́нер, жи́тель Ю́жно-Африка́нской Респу́блики голла́ндского происхожде́ния.

Afro-Caribbean /æfrəʊkærɪ'bi:ən/ *adj.* афрокари́бский.
■ *n.* афрокари́б (*fem.* -ка;) урожён|ец (*fem.* -ка) Кари́бских острово́в африка́нского происхожде́ния.

after /'ɑ:ftə(r)/ *adv.*
1 (*subsequently; then*) пото́м, зате́м; **soon ~** вскоре по́сле э́того.
2 (*later*) поздне́е, по́зже; **3 days ~** спустя́ три дня.
■ *prep.* 1 (*in expressions of time*) по́сле + *g.*; за + *i.*; че́рез + *a.*; спустя́ + *a.*; **~ dinner** по́сле обе́да; **~ you!** то́лько по́сле вас!; **~ that** пото́м, зате́м; **the day ~ tomorrow** послеза́втра; (*in adv. sense*) че́рез две неде́ли; **they met ~ 10 years** они́ встре́тились че́рез де́сять лет; **~ passing his exams, he ...** сдав экза́мены, он...; по́сле того́, как он сдал экза́мены, он...; **it's ~ 6 (o'clock)** уже́ седьмо́й час; (*in sequence*) **day ~ day** день за днём; **one ~ another** оди́н за други́м; **~ all** (*in the end*) в коне́чном счёте; в конце́ концо́в; (*nevertheless*) всё-таки.
2 (*in expressions of place*) за + *i.*; **run ~ s.o.** бежа́ть за кем-н.
3 (*in search of; trying to get*): **the police are ~ him** его́ разы́скивает поли́ция; **what is he ~?** куда́ он ме́тит?; что он замышля́ет?
4 (*in accordance with*) по + *d.*, согла́сно + *d.*; **named ~** на́званный по + *d.* (*or* в честь + *g.*); **he takes ~ his father** он похо́ж на отца́.
■ *conj.* по́сле того́ как; **I arrived ~ he had left** я пришёл по́сле того́, как он ушёл.
■ *cpds.* **~-effect** *n.* после́дствие; **~math** *n.* после́дствия (*nt. pl.*); **~noon** *n.* послеполу́денное вре́мя; **in the ~noon** днём; по́сле обе́да; во второ́й полови́не дня; **at 3 in the ~noon** в три часа́ дня; **good ~noon!** (*in greeting*) до́брый день!; (*in leave-taking*) до свида́ния; **~shave** *n.* лосьо́н по́сле бритья́; **~shock** *n.* повто́рные толчки́; **~taste** *n.* при́вкус; **~thought** *n.* запозда́лая мысль.

afterward /'ɑ:ftəwəd/ *adv.* (*US*) = **afterwards**

afterwards /'ɑ:ftəwədz/ *adv.* (*then*) пото́м; (*subsequently*) впосле́дствии; (*later*) по́зже.

again /ə'gen/ *adv.*
1 (*expr. repetition*) опя́ть, сно́ва; (*afresh, anew*) вновь; (*once more*) ещё раз; (*with certain vv.*) *by use of pref.* пере...; **read ~** перечи́т|ывать, -а́ть; **say ~** повтор|я́ть, -и́ть; **start ~** нач|ина́ть, -а́ть сно́ва; **~ and ~** сно́ва и сно́ва; **now and ~** вре́мя от вре́мени; **once ~** ещё раз.
2 (*with neg.: any more*) бо́льше; **never ~** никогда́ бо́льше; **don't do it ~!** бо́льше э́того не де́лай!
3 (*expr. return to original state or position*): **back ~** обра́тно; **you'll soon be well ~** вы ско́ро попра́витесь.

against /ə'genst/ *prep.*
1 (*in opposition to*) про́тив + *g.*; **I have nothing ~ it** я не име́ю ничего́ про́тив; **I acted ~ my will** я де́йствовал про́тив свое́й во́ли; **~ the rules** не по пра́вилам.
2 (*to oppose or combat*) на + *a.*; **march ~ the enemy** наступа́ть (*impf.*) на врага́.
3 (*compared with*): **3 deaths this year ~ 20 last year** три сме́рти в э́том году́ про́тив двадцати́ в про́шлом.

a

4 (*in contrast with*): **it shows up ~ a dark background** э́то выделя́ется на тёмном фо́не.
5 (*in collision with*) о + *a.*; **knock ~ sth.** ударя́ться, уда́риться о что-н.

age /eɪdʒ/ *n.*
1 (*time of life*) во́зраст; **he is 40 years of ~** ему́ со́рок лет; **when I was your ~** когда́ я был в ва́шем во́зрасте; **she doesn't look her ~** она́ вы́глядит моло́же свои́х лет; **~ of consent** бра́чный во́зраст; (*of inanimate objects*): **what is the ~ of this house?** ско́лько лет э́тому до́му?
2 (*majority*): **he is under ~** он несовершенноле́тний.
3 (*old ~*) ста́рость.
4 (*period*) пери́од; (*century*) век; **Ice A~** леднико́вый пери́од; **Stone A~** ка́менный век; **the Middle A~s** Сре́дние века́; (*coll., often pl., long time*): **the bus left ~s ago** авто́бус ушёл давны́м-давно́; **we have not seen each other for ~s** мы не ви́делись сто лет (*or* це́лую ве́чность).
■ *v.t.* (*pres. part.* **ageing, aging**) ста́рить, со-.
■ *v.i.* (*pres. part.* **ageing, aging**) (*of person*) старе́ть, по-; ста́риться, со-; (*of thing*) старе́ть, у-.
■ *cpds.* **~ group** *n.* возрастна́я гру́ппа; **~ limit** *n.* преде́льный во́зраст.

aged[1] /eɪdʒd/ *adj.* (*of the age of*): **~ six** шести́ лет.

aged[2] /'eɪdʒɪd/ *adj.* (*very old*) престаре́лый.
■ *n.*: **the ~** пожилы́е лю́ди, престаре́лые.

ageism /'eɪdʒɪz(ə)m/ *n.* дискримина́ция по во́зрасту.

ageist /'eɪdʒɪst/ *adj.* дискримини́рующий по во́зрасту.

agency /'eɪdʒənsɪ/ *n.* аге́нтство; **employment ~** аге́нтство по на́йму; **news ~** информацио́нное аге́нтство; **travel ~** туристи́ческое аге́нтство, тураге́нтство.

agenda /ə'dʒendə/ *n.* пове́стка дня.

agent /'eɪdʒ(ə)nt/ *n.* (*person acting for others*) аге́нт; (*representative*) представи́тель (*m.*).

agent provocateur /ɑ:ʒɑ̃ prəvɒkə'tə:(r)/ *n.* (*pl.* **agents provocateurs** *pronunc. same*) провока́тор.

aggravate /'ægrəveɪt/ *v.t.*
1 (*make worse*) усугуб|ля́ть, -и́ть.
2 (*coll., exasperate*) раздраж|а́ть, -и́ть.

aggravation /ægrə'veɪʃ(ə)n/ *n.*
1 (*of an illness, situation*) усугубле́ние.
2 (*exasperation*) раздраже́ние.

aggregate[1] /'ægrɪgət/ *n.*
1 (*total, mass*) совоку́пность; **in the ~** в совоку́пности.
2 (*phys.*) скопле́ние.
3 (*ingredient of concrete*) заполни́тель (*m.*) (бето́на).
■ *adj.* (*total*) совоку́пный; **~ membership** о́бщее число́ чле́нов.

aggregate[2] /'ægrɪgeɪt/ *v.t.* (*collect into a mass*) соб|ира́ть, -ра́ть в це́лое.

aggression /ə'greʃ(ə)n/ *n.* агре́ссия.

aggressive /ə'gresɪv/ *adj.* агресси́вный.

aggressor /ə'gresə(r)/ *n.* агре́ссор.

aggrieve /ə'gri:v/ *v.t.*: **be ~d; feel ~d** быть огорчённым.

aghast /ə'gɑ:st/ *pred. adj.* (*amazed*) потрясённый.

agile /'ædʒaɪl/ *adj.* прово́рный; **an ~ mind** живо́й ум.

agility /ə'dʒɪlɪtɪ/ *n.* прово́рство; **~ of mind** жи́вость ума́.

agitate /'ædʒɪteɪt/ *v.t.* (*excite*) волнова́ть, вз-; **be ~d about sth.** волнова́ться (*impf.*) из-за чего́-н.

agitator /'ædʒɪteɪtə(r)/ *n.*
1 (*pol.*) агита́тор.
2 (*apparatus*) смеси́тель (*m.*); меша́лка (*coll.*).

AGM (*abbr. of* ***Annual General Meeting***) (*Br.*) ежего́дное о́бщее собра́ние.

agnostic /æg'nɒstɪk/ *n.* агно́стик.
■ *adj.* агности́ческий.

ago /ə'gəʊ/ *adv.* тому́ наза́д; **long ~** давно́; **not long ~** неда́вно.

agonize /'ægənaɪz/ *v.i.* (*fig.*): **he ~d over his speech** он му́чился над свое́й ре́чью.

agony /'ægənɪ/ *n.* (*torment*) муче́ние, страда́ние; **I was in ~** я испы́тывал си́льные страда́ния; я му́чился от бо́ли.

agoraphobia /ægərə'fəʊbɪə/ *n.* агорафо́бия, боя́знь откры́того простра́нства.

agoraphobic /ægərə'fəʊbɪk/ *adj.* страда́ющий агорафо́бией.

agree /ə'gri:/ *v.t.* (**agrees, agreed, agreeing**) (*Br.*) согласо́в|ывать, -а́ть (*что с кем*).
■ *v.i.* (**agrees, agreed, agreeing**)
1 (*concur; be of like opinion*) согла|ша́ться, -си́ться (*с кем*) (*used mainly for past and future*); **I quite ~ with you** я соверше́нно с ва́ми согла́сен.
2 (*reach agreement; make common decision*): **we ~d to go together** мы договори́лись е́хать вме́сте; **~ on a price** догов|а́риваться, -ори́ться о цене́.
3 (*consent*) согла|ша́ться, -си́ться (*на что*) (*used mainly for past and future*).
4 (*accept*): **I ~ that it was wrong** согла́сен, что э́то бы́ло непра́вильно; **~ with** (*accept as correct or right*): **I don't ~ with his policy** я не согла́сен с его́ поли́тикой.
5 : **~ with** (*suit*) под|ходи́ть, -ойти́ + *d.*; годи́ться (*impf.*) + *d.*; **fish doesn't ~ with me** от ры́бы мне быва́ет пло́хо.
6 (*conform; tally*): **the adjective ~s with the noun** прилага́тельное согласу́ется с существи́тельным; **his story ~s with mine** его́ расска́з схо́дится с мои́м.

agreeable /ə'gri:əb(ə)l/ *adj.* прия́тный.

agreement /ə'gri:mənt/ *n.*
1 (*consent*) согла́сие; **be in ~ with** согла|ша́ться, -си́ться с + *i.*
2 (*treaty*) соглаше́ние, догово́р; **come to an ~** при|ходи́ть, -йти́ к соглаше́нию.
3 (*gram.*) согласова́ние.

agricultural /ægrɪ'kʌltʃər(ə)l/ *adj.* сельскохозя́йственный.

agriculture /'ægrɪkʌltʃə(r)/ *n.* се́льское хозя́йство.

aground /ə'graʊnd/ *adv.*: **run ~** (*v.i.*) сади́ться, сесть на мель.

ahead /ə'hed/ *adv.* впереди́; (*expr. motion*) вперёд; **be, get ~ of** опере|жа́ть, -ди́ть; **go ~!** (ну) дава́й(те)!

ahoy /ə'hɔɪ/ *int.*: **~ there!, ship ~!** эй, на корабле́/су́дне!; **land ~!** земля́!

aid /eɪd/ *n.*
1 (*help, assistance*) по́мощь; (*support*) подде́ржка; **first ~** пе́рвая по́мощь; **~ agency** организа́ция по оказа́нию по́мощи; **~ worker** рабо́тн|ик (*fem.* -ица) организа́ции по оказа́нию по́мощи; **with the ~ of** при по́мощи + *g.*; **in ~ of** в по́мощь + *d.*
2 (*appliance*) посо́бие; **visual ~s** нагля́дные посо́бия.
■ *v.t.* (*help*) пом|ога́ть, -о́чь + *d.*; (*promote*) спосо́бствовать (*impf.*) + *d.*

aide /eɪd/ *n.* помо́щни|к (*fem.* -ца).

Aids, AIDS /eɪdz/ *n.* (*abbr. of* ***acquired immune deficiency syndrome***) СПИД (синдро́м приобретённого иммунодефици́та).

ailing /'eɪlɪŋ/ *adj.* больно́й; **an ~ economy** больна́я эконо́мика.

ailment /'eɪlmənt/ *n.* неду́г, хворь.

aim /eɪm/ *n.*
1 (*purpose*) цель; **with the ~ of** с це́лью + *g.*
2 (*of a gun, etc.*) прице́л; **take ~ at** прице́л|иваться, -иться в + *a.*
■ *v.t.* нав|оди́ть, -ести́; **~ a blow at** зама́х|иваться, -ну́ться на + *a.*; (*fig.*): **~ one's remarks at** предназн|ача́ть, -а́чить свои́ замеча́ния + *d.*
■ *v.i.* це́лить (*impf.*); **~ at** (*with rifle*) прице́л|иваться, -иться в + *a.*; (*fig.*): **~ at** (*aspire to*) це́литься, на- на + *a.*; стреми́ться (*impf.*) к + *d.*; **~ for** напр|авля́ться, -а́виться в/на + *a.*

aimless /'eɪmlɪs/ *adj.* бесце́льный.

air /eə(r)/ *n.*
1 (*lit.*) во́здух; **get some fresh ~** подыша́ть (*pf.*) све́жим во́здухом; **in the open ~** на откры́том во́здухе; **travel by ~** лета́ть (*impf.*) (самолётом).
2 (*in fig. phrr.*): **clear the ~** разря|жа́ть, -ди́ть атмосфе́ру; **he vanished into thin ~** его́ и след просты́л; **he was walking on ~** он ног под собо́й не чу́вствовал.
3 (*appearance, manner*) (*of person*) вид; (*of place*) дух; **~s and graces** мане́рность; **put on** (*or* **give o.s.**) **~s** задава́ться, ва́жничать (*both impf.*).
4 (*radio, TV*): **go on the ~** выходи́ть, вы́йти в эфи́р; **go off the ~** (*of station*) зак|а́нчивать, -о́нчить переда́чу.
5 (*attr., pert. to aviation*) возду́шный; авиацио́нный, авиа...; (*mil.*) вое́нно-возду́шный; **~ force** вое́нно-возду́шные си́лы; **~ hostess** (*Br.*) бортпроводни́ца, стюарде́сса; **~ terminal** аэровокза́л.
■ *v.t.* 1 (*ventilate*) прове́три|вать, -ть; (*Br., dry*) суши́ть, вы-.
2 (*fig.*) (*opinions, feelings*) выска́зывать, вы́сказать.
■ *v.i.* про|су́шивать, -суши́ть.
■ *cpds.* **~ bag** *n.* авари́йная поду́шка безопа́сности; **~ bed** *n.* (*Br.*) надувно́й матра́ц; **~-conditioned** *adj.* с кондициони́рованным во́здухом; **~ conditioning** *n.* кондициони́рование во́здуха; **~craft** *n.* самолёт, (*collect.*) самолёты, авиа́ция; **~craft-carrier** *n.* авиано́сец; **~crew** *n.* экипа́ж; **~field** *n.* лётное по́ле; **~ gun** *n.* духово́е ружьё; **~ letter** *n.* авиаписьмо́; **~lift** *n.* возду́шная перебро́ска; *v.t.* перебр|а́сывать, -о́сить (*or* перев|ози́ть, -езти́) по во́здуху; **~line** *n.* (*company*) авиакомпа́ния; **~mail** *n.* авиапо́чта; **~plane** *n.* (*US*) = **aeroplane; ~port** *n.* аэропо́рт; **~ raid** *n.* возду́шный налёт; **~-raid warning** возду́шная трево́га; **~-raid shelter** бомбоубе́жище; **~-raid warden** ≈ нача́льник шта́ба гражда́нской оборо́ны; **~ rifle** *n.* пневмати́ческая винто́вка; **~ship** *n.* возду́шный кора́бль; дирижа́бль (*m.*); **~sick** *adj.*: **I was ~sick** меня́ укача́ло в самолёте; **~strip** *n.* взлётно-поса́дочная полоса́; **~tight** *adj.* гермети́ческий; **~ traffic control** *n.* авиадиспе́тчерская слу́жба; **~ traffic controller** *n.* авиадиспе́тчер; **~waves** *n.* радиово́лны.

airing /'eərɪŋ/ *n.* прове́тривание; **~ cupboard** (*Br.*) суши́льный шкаф.

airless /'eəlɪs/ *adj.* (*stuffy*) ду́шный; (*still*) безве́тренный.

airy /'eərɪ/ *adj.* (**airier, airiest**)
1 (*well-ventilated*) све́жий; (*spacious*) просто́рный.
2 (*superficial; light-hearted*) ве́треный, беспе́чный.

aisle /aɪl/ *n.* прохо́д (*ме́жду ряда́ми*).

ajar /ə'dʒɑ:(r)/ *pred. adj.* приоткры́тый.

aka (*abbr. of* ***also known as***) изве́стный та́кже под и́менем.

akin /ə'kɪn/ *pred. adj. & adv.* (*related*) ро́дственный; **~ to** сродни́ + *d.*

alarm /ə'lɑ:m/ *n.*
1 (*warning; warning signal*) трево́га; **false ~** ло́жная трево́га; **fire ~** пожа́рная трево́га.
2 (**~** *clock*) буди́льник.
3 (*fright*): **he ran away in ~** он убежа́л в испу́ге.
■ *v.t.* трево́жить; **to be ~ed** трево́житься, вс-.

alarmist /ə'lɑ:mɪst/ *n.* паникёр (*fem.* -ша).

alas /ə'læs/ *int.* увы́!

Albania /æl'beɪnɪə/ *n.* Алба́ния.

Albanian /æl'beɪnɪən/ *n.*
1 (*person*) алба́н|ец (*fem.* -ка).
2 (*language*) алба́нский язы́к.
■ *adj.* алба́нский.

albeit /ɔ:l'bi:ɪt/ *conj.* пусть (и), хотя́ и.

album /'ælbəm/ *n.* (*book; recordings*) альбо́м.

alchemist /'ælkəmɪst/ *n.* алхи́мик.

alchemy /'ælkəmɪ/ *n.* алхи́мия.

alcohol /'ælkəhɒl/ *n.* (*chem.*) алкого́ль (*m.*); (*spirit*) спирт.
■ *cpd.* **~-free** *adj.* безалкого́льный.

alcoholic /ælkə'hɒlɪk/ *n.* алкого́лик.
■ *adj.* алкого́льный; **~ beverages** спиртно́е; спиртны́е напи́тки (*m. pl.*).

alcoholism /'ælkəhɒlɪz(ə)m/ *n.* алкоголи́зм.

alcove /'ælkəʊv/ *n.* алько́в, ни́ша.

ale /eɪl/ *n.* эль (*m.*); (*beer*) пи́во.

alert /ə'lə:t/ *adj.* (*vigilant*) чу́ткий; (*lively*) живо́й.
■ *v.t.* прив|оди́ть, -ести́ в состоя́ние гото́вности; **~ s.o. to a situation** предупре|жда́ть, -ди́ть кого́-н. о созда́вшейся ситуа́ции.

a

A level /'eɪ levəl/ *n.* (*Br.*) выпускной экзамен в средней школе по профилирующим предметам (с повышенным уровнем сложности).
algebra /'ældʒɪbrə/ *n.* алгебра.
Algeria /æl'dʒɪərɪə/ *n.* Алжир.
Algerian /æl'dʒɪərɪən/ *n.* алжир|ец (*fem.* -ка).
■ *adj.* алжирский.
alias /'eɪlɪəs/ *n.* кличка, прозвище; вымышленное имя.
alibi /'ælɪbaɪ/ *n.* (*pl.* **~s**)
1 (*plea or proof of being elsewhere*) алиби (*nt. indecl.*); **establish an ~** устан|авливать, -овить алиби; **produce an ~** предст|авлять, -авить алиби.
2 (*coll., excuse*) отговорка.
alien /'eɪlɪən/ *n.* иностран|ец (*fem.* -ка); (*extraterrestrial*) инопланетян|ин (*fem.* -ка), пришелец (*из космоса*).
■ *adj.* 1 (*foreign*) иностранный; (*extraterrestrial*) инопланетный.
2 : **~ to** чуждый + *d.*
alienate /'eɪlɪəneɪt/ *v.t.* (*estrange, antagonize*) отвра|щать, -тить; отчуждать (*impf.*).
alight[1] /ə'laɪt/ *pred. adj.* & *adv.* (*on fire*) горящий, в огне; **set ~** заж|игать, -ечь.
alight[2] /ə'laɪt/ *v.i.* (**alighted**)
1 (*Br., dismount*) сходить, сойти (с + *g.*).
2 (*come to earth*) садиться, сесть.
align /ə'laɪn/ *v.t.* выравнивать, выровнять.
alignment /ə'laɪnmənt/ *n.* выравнивание; **out of ~** неровно, не в ряд.
alike /ə'laɪk/ *pred. adj.* (*similar*) (*people*) похожий (на + *a.*); (*objects*) схожий (с + *i.*).
■ *adv.* одинаково; **treat everyone ~** обращаться (*impf.*) со всеми одинаково; **winter and summer ~** как зимой, так и летом.
alimony /'ælɪmənɪ/ *n.* (*leg.*) алимент|ы (*pl., g.* -ов).
alive /ə'laɪv/ *pred. adj.* & *adv.*
1 (*living*) живой; в живых; **buried ~** похороненный заживо; **~ and kicking** жив-здоров (*coll.*);
2 (*alert*): **look ~!** живее!
3 (*infested*): **the bed was ~ with fleas** кровать кишела блохами.
alkali /'ælkəlaɪ/ *n.* (*pl.* **~s**) щёлочь; (*attr.*) щелочной.
alkaline /'ælkəlaɪn/ *adj.* щелочной.
all /ɔ:l/ *pron.* (*everybody*) все; (*everything*) всё; **~ of us** мы все; **the score is 2 ~** счёт 2:2; **~ but** (*almost*) почти, чуть не; **~ in ~** (*in general*) в общем и целом; **above ~** прежде всего; **after ~** в конце концов; в конечном счёте; **he came after ~** он всё же пришёл; **not at ~** совсем/вовсе не; нисколько, ничуть; **'Thank you.' — 'Not at ~!'** «Спасибо». — «Не за что!»; **he has no money at ~** у него совсем нет денег; **once and for ~** раз и навсегда.
■ *adj.* весь; (*every*) всякий; **~ his life** всю свою жизнь; **~ day long** весь день; **~ the time** всё время; **at ~ times** в любое время; всегда; **for ~ that** всё-таки.
■ *adv.* (*quite*) совсем, совершенно; целиком; **~ dressed up** нарядившись; разрядившись в пух и прах; **I got ~ excited** я разволновался; **I knew it ~ along** я всегда это знал; **she lived ~ by herself** она жила совсем одна; **she did it ~ by herself** она сделала это сама; **I am ~ ears** я весь (*m.*)/вся (*f.*) внимание; **~ in** (*exhausted*) выбившийся из сил; (*inclusive of everything*) включая всё; **~ over again** (всё) снова; **~ right!** ладно!, хорошо!; **how are you? — ~ right!;** как дела? — нормально!; **the film was ~ right** фильм был неплохой; **are you ~ right?** с вами всё в порядке?; **~ the same** (*however*) всё-таки; **he's not ~ there** у него не все дома.
■ *cpds.* **~-clear** *n.* отбой (тревоги); **~-important** *adj.* чрезвычайно важный; **~-night** *adj.*: **~-night session** заседание, продолжающееся всю ночь; **~-out** *adj.*: **an ~-out effort** максимальное усилие; **~-star** *adj.*: **with an ~-star cast** с участием звёзд; **~-time** *adj.*: **at an ~-time low** на небывало низком уровне; **~-time record** непревзойдённый рекорд; **~-weather** *adj.* всепогодный.
Allah /'ælə/ *n.* Аллах.
allay /ə'leɪ/ *v.t.* (*doubts, suspicions*) рассе|ивать, -ять; (*fears*) разве|ивать, -ять; **~ pain** ун|имать, -ять боль; **~ thirst/hunger** утол|ять, -ить жажду/голод.
allegation /ælɪ'geɪʃ(ə)n/ *n.* заявление, утверждение.
allege /ə'ledʒ/ *v.t.* утверждать (*impf.*); **an ~d murderer** подозреваемый в убийстве.
allegedly /ə'ledʒɪdlɪ/ *adv.* будто бы, якобы.
allegiance /ə'li:dʒ(ə)ns/ *n.* (*loyalty*) верность; (*devotion*) преданность.
allegorical /ælɪ'gɒrɪk(ə)l/ *adj.* аллегорический.
allegory /'ælɪgərɪ/ *n.* аллегория.
allegro /ə'legrəʊ/ *n., adj.* & *adv.* (*pl.* **~s**) аллегро (*nt. indecl.*).
alleluia /ælɪ'lu:jə/ *n.* & *int.* аллилуйя.
allergic /ə'lə:dʒɪk/ *adj.* аллергический; **I'm ~ to strawberries** у меня аллергия на клубнику.
allergy /'ælədʒɪ/ *n.* аллергия.
alleviate /ə'li:vɪeɪt/ *v.t.* (*relieve, lighten*) облегч|ать, -ить; (*mitigate, soften*) смягч|ать, -ить.
alley /'ælɪ/ *n.* (*pl.* **~s**) переулок; **blind ~** тупик.
alliance /ə'laɪəns/ *n.* союз; (*pol.*) альянс.
allied /'ælaɪd/ *adj.* союзный.
allocate /'æləkeɪt/ *v.t.* (*money*) ассигновать (*impf., pf.*); (*distribute*) разме|щать, -стить; (*assign*) назн|ачать, -ачить.
allocation /ælə'keɪʃ(ə)n/ *n.* (*allocating*) выделение; ассигнование; размещение; назначение; (*sum allocated*) ассигнование.
allot /ə'lɒt/ *v.t.* (**allotted, allotting**) (*distribute*) распредел|ять, -ить; (*assign*) назн|ачать, -ачить; **~ a task** да|вать, -ть задание.
allotment /ə'lɒtmənt/ *n.* (*Br., plot of land*) (земельный) участок.
allow /ə'laʊ/ *v.t.*
1 (*permit*) позв|олять, -олить; разреш|ать, -ить; **~ me!** разрешите!; **he was ~ed to smoke** ему позволили курить; **smoking is not ~ed** курить воспрещается; **no dogs**

~ed вход с собáками воспрещён.
2 (*grant, provide*) да|вáть, -ть; предост|авля́ть, -áвить; допус|кáть, -ти́ть.
■ *v.i.*: **~ for** (*take into account*) уч|и́тывать, -éсть; **not ~ing for expenses** не принимáя в расчёт издéржек; **~ £50 for emergencies** выделя́ть, вы́делить 50 фу́нтов на непредви́денный слу́чай.

allowance /ə'laʊəns/ *n.*
1 (*amount provided*): **monthly ~** мéсячное посóбие; **make s.o. an ~** назначáть, назнáчить содержáние комý-н.; (*mil.*) довóльствие.
2 (*concession*): **we will make an ~ in your case** мы сдéлаем для вас исключéние; **make ~(s) for** уч|и́тывать, -éсть; прин|имáть, -я́ть во внимáние.

alloy /'ælɔɪ/ *n.* сплав.

allud|e /ə'lu:d/ *v.i.*: **~e to** ссылáться, сослáться на + *a.*; упом|инáть, -янýть; (*mean*): **what are you ~ing to?** на что вы намекáете?

allure /ə'ljʊə(r)/ *n.* привлекáтельность, прéлесть.
■ *v.t.* (*entice, attract*) замáн|ивать, -и́ть; (*charm*) завл|екáть, -éчь; очарóв|ывать, -áть.

allusion /ə'lu:ʒ(ə)n/ *n.* намёк; ссы́лка.

ally[1] /'ælaɪ/ *n.* сою́зник.

ally[2] /ə'laɪ/ *v.t.* (*connect*) соедин|я́ть, -и́ть; **~ o.s. with** вступ|áть, -и́ть в сою́з с + *i.*

almanac /'ɔ:lmənæk/ *n.* альманáх.

almighty /ɔ:l'maɪtɪ/ *n.* **the A~** Всемогýщий, Всевы́шний.

almond /'ɑ:mənd/ *n.* миндáль (*m.*).

almost /'ɔ:lməʊst/ *adv.* почти́; (*with vv.*) почти́, чуть не, едвá не.

alone /ə'ləʊn/ *adj.*
1 (*by o.s., itself*) оди́н; еди́нственный.
2 (*... and no other(s)*): **in the month of June ~** тóлько в ию́не мéсяце; **she and I are ~ (together)** мы с ней вдвоём/одни́.
3 **let, leave ~**: **his parents left him ~ all day** роди́тели остáвили егó на цéлый день одногó.

along /ə'lɒŋ/ *adv.*
1 (*on; forward*): **move ~** продв|игáться, -и́нуться; **come ~!** пошли́!; **a few doors ~ from the station** в нéскольких шагáх от вокзáла.
2 (*denoting accompaniment*): **he brought a book ~** он принёс с собóй кни́гу.
3 (*over there; over here*): **he'll be ~ in 10 minutes** он бýдет чéрез дéсять минýт.
4 : **all ~** (*the whole time*) всё врéмя.
■ *prep.* вдоль + *g.*; по + *d.*; **she was walking ~ the river** онá шла вдоль реки́.

alongside /əlɒŋ'saɪd/ *adv.* ря́дом, сбóку; **we stopped and the police car drew up ~** мы останови́лись, и подъéхавшая полицéйская маши́на вствла ря́дом.
■ *prep.* (*also* **~ of**) ря́дом с + *i.*; у + *g.*

aloof /ə'lu:f/ *adj.* сдéржанный, отчуждённый.

aloofness /ə'lu:fnɪs/ *n.* сдéржанность, отчуждённость.

aloud /ə'laʊd/ *adv.* вслух; **read ~** читáть вслух.

alp /ælp/ *n.*: **the A~s** Áльп|ы (*pl., g.* —).

alphabet /'ælfəbet/ *n.* алфави́т, áзбука.

alphabetical /ælfə'betɪk(ə)l/ *adj.* алфави́тный; **in ~ order** в алфави́тном поря́дке.

alpine /'ælpaɪn/ *adj.* альпи́йский.

already /ɔ:l'redɪ/ *adv.* ужé.

Alsatian /æl'seɪʃ(ə)n/ *n.* (*Br.*) немéцкая овчáрка.

also /'ɔ:lsəʊ/ *adv.* тóже; тáкже; (*moreover*) к томý же.

altar /'ɔ:ltə(r)/ *n.* престóл, алтáрь.

alter /'ɔ:ltə(r)/ *v.t.* & *i.* меня́ть(ся) (*impf.*); измен|я́ть(ся), -и́ть(ся); (*remake*) передéл|ывать, -ать; **the dress needs ~ing** э́то плáтье нáдо передéлать.

alteration /ɔ:ltə'reɪʃ(ə)n/ *n.* (*change*) изменéние; (*remaking, e.g. of clothes*) передéлка.

altercation /ɔ:ltə'keɪʃ(ə)n/ *n.* ссóра, перебрáнка.

alternate[1] /ɔ:l'tɜ:nət/ *adj.*
1 (*taking turns*) чередýющийся; **on ~ Saturdays** кáждую вторýю суббóту.
2 (*US, alternative*) альтернати́вный.

alternate[2] /'ɔ:ltəneɪt/ *v.t.* & *i.* чередовáть(ся) (*impf.*); перемежáть(ся) (*impf.*).

alternative /ɔ:l'tɜ:nətɪv/ *n.* альтернати́ва; **there is no ~** другóго вы́бора нет.
■ *adj.* альтернати́вный; **~ medicine** нетрадициóнная медици́на; **~ technology** технолóгия безотхóдного произвóдства.

alternatively /ɔ:l'tɜ:nətɪvlɪ/ *adv.* (*indicating choice*): **a £5,000 fine, ~ one month's imprisonment** штраф 5000 фýнтов и́ли оди́н мéсяц тюрéмного заключéния.

alternator /'ɔ:ltəneɪtə(r)/ *n.* (*elec.*) генерáтор перемéнного тóка.

although /ɔ:l'ðəʊ/ *conj.* хотя́; (*despite the fact that*) несмотря́ на то, что.

altitude /'æltɪtju:d/ *n.* (*of flight*) высотá; (*of a place*) высотá над ýровнем мóря.

alto /'æltəʊ/ *n.* (*pl.* **altos**) альт; (*attr.*) альтóвый.

altogether /ɔ:ltə'geðə(r)/ *adv.*
1 (*entirely*) вполнé; совершéнно; (*completely*) совсéм.
2 (*in all, in general; as a whole*) в цéлом, в óбщем; всегó; **how much is that ~?** скóлько всегó?

altruism /'æltru:ɪz(ə)m/ *n.* альтруи́зм.

altruistic /æltru:'ɪstɪk/ *adj.* альтруисти́ческий.

alumin|ium (*US* **-um**) /æljʊ'mɪnɪəm; ə'lu:mɪnəm/ *n.* алюми́ний.

always /'ɔ:lweɪz/ *adv.* всегдá; (*constantly*) постоя́нно, всё врéмя; **he is ~ after money** он всегдá/постоя́нно дýмает о деньгáх.

Alzheimer's (disease) /'æltshaɪməz/ *n.* болéзнь Альцгéймера.

am /æm/ *1st pers. sing. pres. of* ▶ **be**

a.m. (*abbr. of* ***ante meridiem***) утрá; (*in the morning*) ýтром; **6 ~** шесть часóв утрá.

amalgam /ə'mælgəm/ *n.* амальгáма; (*fig.*) смесь.

amalgamate /ə'mælgəmeɪt/ *v.t.* & *i.* (*companies*) сливáть(ся), сли́ть(ся).

amass /ə'mæs/ *v.t.* накоп|ля́ть, -и́ть.

a

amateur /ˈæmətə(r)/ *n.* люби́тель (*m.*); (*attr.*) люби́тельский.
amateurish /ˈæmətərɪʃ/ *adj.* дилета́нтский; непрофессиона́льный.
amaz|e /əˈmeɪz/ *v.t.* изум|ля́ть, -и́ть; **be ~ed at** изум|ля́ться, -и́ться + *d.*; **~ing** изуми́тельный, удиви́тельный.
amazement /əˈmeɪzmənt/ *n.* изумле́ние.
Amazon /ˈæməz(ə)n/ *n.* (*myth., fig.*) амазо́нка; (*river*) Амазо́нка.
ambassador /æmˈbæsədə(r)/ *n.* посо́л; (*representative*) представи́тель (*m.*).
amber /ˈæmbə(r)/ *n.*
1 (*resin*) янта́рь (*m.*).
2 (*colour*) янта́рный цвет, цвет янтаря́.
ambidextrous /æmbɪˈdekstrəs/ *adj.* одина́ково владе́ющий обе́ими рука́ми.
ambience /ˈæmbɪəns/ *n.* среда́; атмосфе́ра.
ambient /ˈæmbɪənt/ *adj.* окружа́ющий; **~ temperature** температу́ра окружа́ющего во́здуха.
ambiguity /æmbɪˈgju:ɪtɪ/ *n.* двусмы́сленность; нея́сность.
ambiguous /æmˈbɪgjʊəs/ *adj.* двусмы́сленный; нея́сный.
ambition /æmˈbɪʃ(ə)n/ *n.* (*desire for distinction*) честолю́бие, амби́ция; (*aspiration*) стремле́ние.
ambitious /æmˈbɪʃəs/ *adj.* честолюби́вый; амбицио́зный; **an ~ plan** грандио́зный план.
ambivalence /æmˈbɪvələns/ *n.* двойственность.
ambivalent /æmˈbɪvələnt/ *adj.* двойственный.
amble /ˈæmb(ə)l/ *n. v.i.* идти́ (*det.*) лёгкой похо́дкой; прогу́ливаться (*impf.*).
ambulance /ˈæmbjʊləns/ *n.* маши́на ско́рой по́мощи.
ambush /ˈæmbʊʃ/ *n.* заса́да.
■ *v.t.* нап|ада́ть, -а́сть на (*кого*) из заса́ды.
ameba /əˈmi:bə/ (*US*) = **amoeba**
ameliorate /əˈmi:lɪəreɪt/ *v.t.* & *i.* ул|учша́ть(ся), -у́чшить(ся).
amen /ɑ:ˈmen/ *int.* ами́нь.
amend /əˈmend/ *v.t.*
1 (*correct*) испр|авля́ть, -а́вить.
2 (*make changes to*) вн|оси́ть, -ести́ попра́вки/измене́ния в + *a.*
amendment /əˈmendmənt/ *n.*
1 (*reform*) исправле́ние.
2 (*of document etc.*) попра́вка.
amends /əˈmendz/ *n.* возмеще́ние; исправле́ние; **make ~ to s.o.** загла́|живать, -дить вину́ пе́ред + *i.* (*за что*); **he made ~ for his rudeness** он загла́дил свою́ гру́бость.
amenit|y /əˈmi:nɪtɪ/ *n.* (*usu. in pl.*) (*comforts*) удо́бства (*nt. pl.*).
America /əˈmerɪkə/ *n.* Аме́рика.
American /əˈmerɪkən/ *n.* америка́н|ец (*fem.* -ка).
■ *adj.* америка́нский; **~ English** америка́нский вариа́нт англи́йского языка́; **~ Indian** америка́нск|ий инде́ец (*fem.* -ая индиа́нка).
Americanism /əˈmerɪkənɪz(ə)m/ *n.* американи́зм.
amethyst /ˈæmɪθɪst/ *n.* амети́ст; (*attr.*) амети́стовый.
amiable /ˈeɪmɪəb(ə)l/ *adj.* приве́тливый; доброду́шный.
amicable /ˈæmɪkəb(ə)l/ *adj.* дружелю́бный; (*agreement, separation*) дру́жеский; (*divorce*) ми́рный.
amid(st) /əˈmɪd(st)/ *prep.* среди́ + *g.*
■ *cpd.* **~ships** *adv.* посереди́не корабля́; **the torpedo hit us ~** торпе́да попа́ла в са́мый центр на́шего корабля́.
amino acid /əˈmi:nəʊ/ *n.* аминокислота́.
amiss /əˈmɪs/ *pred. adj.* непра́вильный; **something is ~** что́-то нела́дно.
ammeter /ˈæmɪtə(r)/ *n.* ампермéтр.
ammonia /əˈməʊnɪə/ *n.* (*gas*) аммиа́к; (*attr.*) аммиа́чный.
ammunition /æmjʊˈnɪʃ(ə)n/ *n.* боевы́е припа́сы, боеприпа́сы (*m. pl.*).
amnesia /æmˈni:zɪə/ *n.* амнези́я.
amnesty /ˈæmnɪstɪ/ *n.* амни́стия.
amniocentesis /æmnɪəʊsenˈti:sɪs/ *n.* (*med.*) амниоценте́з (*пункция плодного пузыря*).
amoeba /əˈmi:bə/ (*US also* **ameba**) *n.* (*pl.* **amoebas** *or* **amoebae** /-bi:/) амёба.
amok /əˈmɒk/ *adv.*: **run ~** бу́йствовать (*impf.*); беси́ться (*impf.*).
among /əˈmʌŋ/ *prep.*
1 (*between*) ме́жду + *i.*; **conversation ~ friends** разгово́р ме́жду друзья́ми.
2 (*in the midst of*) среди́ + *g.*; ме́жду + *g.*; **~ the trees** среди́ дере́вьев.
3 (*expr. one of a number*) из + *g.*
amongst /əˈmʌŋst/ (*Br.*) = **among**
amoral /eɪˈmɒr(ə)l/ *adj.* амора́льный.
amorphous /əˈmɔ:fəs/ *adj.* (*shapeless*) бесфо́рменный.
amortize /əˈmɔ:taɪz/ *v.t.* амортизи́ровать (*impf., pf.*).
amount /əˈmaʊnt/ *n.*
1 (*sum*) су́мма.
2 (*quantity*) коли́чество; **he spent any ~ of money** он истра́тил ку́чу де́нег.
■ *v.i.*: **~ to** (*add up to*) сост|авля́ть, -а́вить + *g.*; дост|ига́ть, -и́чь + *g.*; **the expenses ~ to £600** расхо́ды составля́ют шестьсо́т фу́нтов; (*be equivalent to*) быть ра́вным/равноси́льным + *d.*; **it ~s to the same thing** э́то сво́дится всё к тому́ же.
amp /æmp/ *n.* (*abbr. of* **ampere**) А (ампе́р).
ampere /ˈæmpeə(r)/ *n.* ампе́р.
ampersand /ˈæmpəsænd/ *n.* амперса́нд (*знак* «&»).
amphetamine /æmˈfetəmɪn/ *n.* амфетами́н.
amphibian /æmˈfɪbɪən/ *n.* земново́дное; амфи́бия.
amphitheatre /ˈæmfɪθɪətə(r)/ (*US* **amphitheater**) *n.* амфитеа́тр.
ample /ˈæmp(ə)l/ *adj.* (**ampler, amplest**) (*sufficient*) доста́точный; (*abundant*) оби́льный.
amplifier /ˈæmplɪfaɪə(r)/ *n.* усили́тель (*m.*).
amplify /ˈæmplɪfaɪ/ *v.t.* уси́ли|вать, -ть.
ampoule /ˈæmpu:l/ *n.* а́мпула.
amputate /ˈæmpjʊteɪt/ *v.t.* ампути́ровать

(*impf.*, *pf.*); отн|имáть, -я́ть.

amulet /'æmjʊlɪt/ *n.* амулéт.

amuse /ə'mju:z/ *v.t.* (*entertain, divert*) развл|екáть, -éчь; (*make laugh*) смеши́ть (*impf.*); позабáвить (*pf.*).

amusement /ə'mju:zmənt/ *n.* 1 (*diversion*) развлечéние, забáва; **~ park** парк с аттракциóнами; лу́на-пáрк. 2 (*tendency to laughter*): **to everyone's ~ the clown fell over** ко всеóбщему удовóльствию клóун упáл.

amusing /ə'mju:zɪŋ/ *adj.* забáвный; (*funny*) смешнóй.

anachronism /ə'nækrənɪz(ə)m/ *n.* анахрони́зм.

anaemia /ə'ni:mɪə/ (*US* **anemia**) *n.* малокрóвие, анеми́я.

anaesthesia /ænɪs'θi:zɪə/ (*US* **anesthesia**) *n.* анестези́я, обезбóливание.

anaesthetic /ænɪs'θetɪk/ (*US* **anesthetic**) *n.* анестези́рующее срéдство; анестéтик; **general/local ~** óбщий/мéстный наркóз; **under ~** под наркóзом.

anaesthetist /ə'ni:sθətɪst/ (*US* **anesthetist**) *n.* анестезиóлог.

anaesthetize /ə'ni:sθətaɪz/ (*US* **anesthetize**) *v.t.* анестези́ровать (*impf.*, *pf.*); обезбóли|вать, -ть.

anal /'eɪn(ə)l/ *adj.* заднепрохóдный, анáльный.

analgesic /ænæl'dʒi:sɪk/ *adj.* болеутоля́ющий.

analogous /ə'næləgəs/ *adj.* аналоги́чный.

analogy /ə'nælədʒɪ/ *n.* аналóгия; схóдство.

analyse /'ænəlaɪz/ (*US* **analyze**) *v.t.* анализи́ровать (*impf.*, *pf.*) (*pf. also* про-).

analysis /ə'nælɪsɪs/ *n.* (*pl.* **analyses** /-si:z/) анáлиз; (*psycho~*) психоанáлиз.

analyst /'ænəlɪst/ *n.* анали́тик; (*political*) комментáтор; (*psych.*) психоанали́тик.

analytic(al) /ænə'lɪtɪk, ænə'lɪtɪk(ə)l/ *adj.* аналити́ческий.

analyze /'ænəlaɪz/ (*US*) = **analyse**

anarchic(al) /ə'nɑ:kɪk, ə'nɑ:kɪk(ə)l/ *adj.* анархи́ческий.

anarchist /'ænəkɪst/ *n.* анархи́ст (*fem.* -ка).

anarchy /'ænəkɪ/ *n.* анáрхия.

anathema /ə'næθəmə/ *n.* (*pl.* **~s**) (*hated thing*): **it's ~ to me** я непримири́мый/я́рый проти́вник э́того; я органи́чески не приéмлю э́того.

anatomical /ænə'tɒmɪk(ə)l/ *adj.* анатоми́ческий.

anatomy /ə'nætəmɪ/ *n.* анатóмия.

ancestor /'ænsestə(r)/ *n.* прéдок.

ancestral /æn'sestr(ə)l/ *adj.* родовóй; **~ home** родовóе имéние.

ancestry /'ænsestrɪ/ *n.* (*lineage*) родослóвная, происхождéние; **he comes of distinguished ~** он благорóдного происхождéния.

anchor /'æŋkə(r)/ *n.* я́корь (*m.*).

anchovy /'æntʃəvɪ/ *n.* анчóус.

ancient /'eɪnʃ(ə)nt/ *adj.* дрéвний; анти́чный; (*very old*) стари́нный; векóвóй; **~ history** дрéвняя истóрия; **~ monument** (*Br.*) пáмятник старины́.

and /ænd/ *conj.* 1 (*connecting words or clauses*) и; (*in addition*) и, да; (*with certain closely linked pairs, esp. of persons*) с + *i.*; **bread ~ butter** хлеб с мáслом; **you ~ I** мы с вáми; (*with nums. denoting addition*) и; плюс; **2 ~ 2 are 4** два и/плюс два — четы́ре; (*to form cpd. num.*) *omitted*: **260** двéсти шестьдеся́т; (*with following fraction*) с + *i.* 2 (*intensive*): **he ran ~ ran** он всё бежáл и бежáл; **they talked for hours ~ hours** они́ разговáривали часáми. 3 (*in order to*) *omitted before inf.*: **try ~ find out** постарáйтесь узнáть; **wait ~ see!** погоди́те — ещё уви́дите!

andante /æn'dæntɪ/ *n., adj. and adv.* (*mus.*) андáнте (*nt. indecl.*).

androgynous /æn'drɒdʒɪnəs/ *adj.* двупóлый; (*bot.*) обоепóлый.

anecdotal /ænɪk'dəʊt(ə)l/ *adj.* анекдоти́ческий.

anecdote /'ænɪkdəʊt/ *n.* истóрия; (*joke*) анекдóт.

anemia /ə'ni:mɪə/ (*US*) = **anaemia**

anemone /ə'nemənɪ/ *n.* анемóн; (*wood ~*) вéтреница; **sea ~** морскóй анемóн; акти́ния.

anesthesia /ænɪs'θi:zɪə/ (*US*) = **anaesthesia**

anesthetic /ænɪs'θetɪk/ (*US*) = **anaesthetic**

anesthetist /ə'ni:sθətɪst/ (*US*) = **anaesthetist**

anesthetize /ə'ni:sθətaɪz/ (*US*) = **anaesthetize**

anew /ə'nju:/ *adj.* (*again*) снóва; (*in a different way*) зáново, по-нóвому.

angel /'eɪndʒ(ə)l/ *n.* (*lit.*, *fig.*) áнгел.

angelic /æn'dʒelɪk/ *adj.* áнгельский.

anger /'æŋgə(r)/ *n.* гнев.
■ *v.t.* серди́ть, рас-; разгнéвать (*pf.*).

angina /æn'dʒaɪnə/ *n.* (*also* **~ pectoris** /'pektərɪs/) стенокарди́я, груднáя жáба.

angle[1] /'æŋg(ə)l/ *n.* у́гол; **right ~** прямóй у́гол; **at right ~s** под прямы́м углóм; (*fig., viewpoint*) тóчка зрéния, подхóд.
■ *v.t.* стáвить, по- под углóм; (*fig.*): **the news was ~d** нóвости бы́ли пóданы тенденциóзно.

angle[2] /'æŋg(ə)l/ *v.i.* (*fish*) уди́ть (*impf.*) ры́бу; (*fig.*): **~ for compliments** напрáшиваться (*impf.*) на комплимéнты.

angler /'æŋglə(r)/ *n.* рыболóв.

Anglican /'æŋglɪkən/ *n.* англикáн|ец (*fem.* -ка).
■ *adj.* англикáнский.

Anglo-Saxon /æŋgləʊ'sæks(ə)n/ *n.* англосаксóнский/древнеангли́йский язы́к.
■ *adj.* англосаксóнский, древнеангли́йский.

Angola /æŋ'gəʊlə/ *n.* Ангóла.

Angolan /æŋ'gəʊlən/ *n.* ангóл|ец (*fem.* -ка).
■ *adj.* ангóльский.

angora /æŋ'gɔ:rə/ *n.* (*cloth*) ангóрская шерсть.
■ *adj.* ангóрский.

angry /'æŋgrɪ/ *adj.* (**angrier, angriest**) серди́тый; **be ~ with** серди́ться (*impf.*) на + *a.* (**over, about sth.** за что-н.); **get ~ with** рассерди́ться (*pf.*) на + *a.*

a

anguish /'æŋgwɪʃ/ *n.* муче́ние; му́ка.
angular /'æŋgjʊlə(r)/ *adj.* углова́тый.
animal /'ænɪm(ə)l/ *n.* живо́тное.
■ *adj.* живо́тный.
■ *cpd.* ~ **rights** *n.* права́ (*nt. pl.*) живо́тных.
animate /'ænɪmeɪt/ *v.t.* ожив|ля́ть, -и́ть; **become ~d** ожив|ля́ться, -и́ться.
animation /ænɪ'meɪʃ(ə)n/ *n.* (*enthusiasm*) воодушевле́ние; (*cin.*) мультиплика́ция, анима́ция.
animosity /ænɪ'mɒsɪtɪ/ *n.* (*hostility*) вражде́бность; **feel ~ against** пита́ть (*impf.*) вражду́ к + *d.*
aniseed /'ænɪsi:d/ *n.* ани́с, ани́совое се́мя.
ankle /'æŋk(ə)l/ *n.* лоды́жка, щи́колотка.
■ *cpd.* ~ **socks** *n. pl.* носки́ (*m. pl.*).
annex[1] /'æneks/ *n.* (*to a building*) пристро́йка, фли́гель (*m.*).
annex[2] /æ'neks/ *v.t.* присоедин|я́ть, -и́ть; (*territory etc.*) аннекси́ровать (*impf., pf.*).
annexation /ænek'seɪʃ(ə)n/ *n.* присоедине́ние; анне́ксия, аннекси́рование.
annexe /'æneks/ (*Br.*) = **annex**[1]
annihilate /ə'naɪəleɪt/ *v.t.* (*destroy*) уничт|ожа́ть, -о́жить.
anniversary /ænɪ'vɜ:sərɪ/ *n.* годовщи́на.
annotate /'ænəteɪt/ *v.t.* снаб|жа́ть, -ди́ть коммента́риями *or* примеча́ниями; **~d text** текст с коммента́риями *or* примеча́ниями.
annotation /ænə'teɪʃ(ə)n/ *n.* (*annotating*) комменти́рование; (*added note*) коммента́рий, примеча́ние.
announce /ə'naʊns/ *v.t.* (*state; declare*) объяв|ля́ть, -и́ть (*что or о чём*); заяв|ля́ть, -и́ть (*что or о чём or relative clause*); (*notify, tell*) сообщ|а́ть, -и́ть (*о чём кому*); **he ~d the results of his researches** он огласи́л результа́ты свои́х иссле́дований.
announcement /ə'naʊnsmənt/ *n.* объявле́ние, заявле́ние; **put an ~ in the newspaper** поме|ща́ть, -сти́ть объявле́ние в газе́те; (*written notification*) извеще́ние; (*on radio etc.*) сообще́ние.
announcer /ə'naʊnsə(r)/ *n.* ди́ктор.
annoy /ə'nɔɪ/ *v.t.* (*vex*) доса|жда́ть, -ди́ть + *d.*; (*irritate*) раздража́ть (*impf.*); де́йствовать (*impf.*) на не́рвы + *d.*; (*pester*) докуча́ть (*impf.*) + *d.*; **I was ~ed with him** я был серди́т на него́.
annoyance /ə'nɔɪəns/ *n.* раздраже́ние.
annoying /ə'nɔɪɪŋ/ *adj.* доса́дный; **how ~!** кака́я доса́да!, вот доса́да!
annual /'ænjʊəl/ *n.*
1 (*publication*) ежего́дник.
2 (*plant*) одноле́тнее расте́ние.
■ *adj.* 1 (*happening once a year*) ежего́дный.
2 (*pert. to whole year*) годово́й; **~ income** годово́й дохо́д.
annually /'ænjʊəlɪ/ *adv.* ежего́дно.
annul /ə'nʌl/ *v.t.* (**annulled, annulling**) аннули́ровать (*impf., pf.*); отмен|я́ть, -и́ть; **the marriage was ~led** брак был при́знан недействи́тельным.
annulment /ə'nʌlmənt/ *n.* аннули́рование, отме́на.
anodyne /'ænədaɪn/ *adj.* безоби́дный.
anomaly /ə'nɒməlɪ/ *n.* анома́лия.
anonymous /ə'nɒnɪməs/ *adj.* анони́мный; безымя́нный.
anorak /'ænəræk/ *n.* аля́ска, ку́ртка с капюшо́ном.
anorexia /ænə'reksɪə/ *n.* аноре́ксия.
anorexic /ænə'reksɪk/ *adj.* страда́ющий аноре́ксией.
another /ə'nʌðə(r)/ *pron. & adj.*
1 (*additional*) ещё; **~ cup of tea?** ещё ча́шку ча́я?; **have ~ go!** попыта́йтесь ещё раз!; **in ~ 10 years** ещё че́рез де́сять лет; **and ~ thing** и вот ещё что.
2 (*similar*): **~ Tolstoy** второ́й Толсто́й.
3 (*different*) друго́й; **~ time** в друго́й раз.
answer /'ɑ:nsə(r)/ *n.*
1 (*reply*) отве́т; **what was his ~?** что он отве́тил?; **in ~ to your letter** в отве́т на Ва́ше письмо́; (*retort*) возраже́ние.
2 (*solution*) отве́т; реше́ние.
■ *v.t.* 1 (*reply to*) отв|еча́ть, -е́тить (*кому, на что*); **~ the door** откр|ыва́ть, -ы́ть дверь; **~ the telephone** под|ходи́ть, -ойти́ к телефо́ну; отв|еча́ть, -е́тить на телефо́нные звонки́.
2 (*correspond to*): **he ~s the description exactly** он то́чно соотве́тствует описа́нию.
3 (*satisfy, grant*): **our prayers were ~ed** на́ши моли́твы бы́ли услы́шаны.
■ *v.i.* 1 (*reply*) отв|еча́ть, -е́тить.
2 :**~ for** руча́ться, поручи́ться за + *a.*; **I will ~ for his honesty** я руча́юсь за его́ че́стность.
3 (*give an account*): **I ~ to no one** я никому́ не обя́зан отчи́тываться.
4 :**~ back** дерзи́ть, на-.
■ *cpd.* **~phone** *n.* (*Br.*) автоотве́тчик.
answerable /'ɑ:nsərəb(ə)l/ *adj.* (*responsible*) отве́тственный (*перед кем за что*).
answering /'ɑ:nsərɪŋ/ *adj.*: **~ machine** автоотве́тчик.
ant /ænt/ *n.* мураве́й.
antagonism /æn'tægənɪz(ə)m/ *n.* антагони́зм.
antagonistic /æntægə'nɪstɪk/ *adj.* антагонисти́ческий.
antagonize /æn'tægənaɪz/ *v.t.* вызыва́ть, вы́звать чьё-н. отчужде́ние; отчужда́ть (*impf.*).
Antarctic /æn'tɑ:ktɪk/ *n.*: **the ~** Анта́рктика.
■ *adj.* антаркти́ческий.
Antarctica /ænt'ɑ:ktɪkə/ *n.* Антаркти́да.
antelope /'æntɪləʊp/ *n.* (*pl.* ~ *or* **~s**) антило́па.
antenatal /æntɪ'neɪt(ə)l/ *adj.* (*Br.*) (*care*) дородово́й; **~ clinic** же́нская консульта́ция.
antenna /æn'tenə/ *n.* (*pl.* **antennae** /-ni:/) (*radio*) анте́нна; (*of insect*) у́сик.
anteroom /'æntɪru:m/ *n.* пере́дняя, прихо́жая.
anthem /'ænθəm/ *n.* гимн; **national ~** госуда́рственный гимн.
anthology /æn'θɒlədʒɪ/ *n.* антоло́гия.
anthrax /'ænθræks/ *n.* сиби́рская я́зва.
anthropological /ænθrəpə'lɒdʒɪk(ə)l/ *adj.* антропологи́ческий.
anthropologist /ænθrə'pɒlədʒɪst/ *n.* (*biological*) антропо́лог; **social ~** этно́граф.

anthropology /ænθrəˈpɒlədʒɪ/ *n.* (*biological*) антрополо́гия; **social** (*or* **cultural** ~) социа́льная антрополо́гия.

anti- /ˈæntɪ/ *pref.* анти..., противо... .

antibiotic /æntɪbaɪˈɒtɪk/ *n.* антибио́тик.

antibody /ˈæntɪbɒdɪ/ *n.* антите́ло.

anticipate /ænˈtɪsɪpeɪt/ *v.t.* (*foresee*) предви́деть (*impf.*); предчу́вствовать (*impf.*); (*expect*) ожида́ть (*impf.*); (*with pleasure*) предвку|ша́ть, -си́ть.

anticipation /æntɪsɪˈpeɪʃ(ə)n/ *n.*
1 (*looking forward to*) ожида́ние.
2 (*foreseeing*) предви́дение, предвосхище́ние; **in ~ of a cold winter** предви́дя холо́дную зи́му.
3 (*foretasting*) предвкуше́ние.

anticlimax /æntɪˈklaɪmæks/ *n.* (ре́зкий) спад (интере́са *и т. п.*); разочарова́ние.

anticlockwise /æntɪˈklɒkwaɪz/ *adj.* & *adv.* (*Br.*) про́тив часово́й стре́лки.

antics /ˈæntɪks/ *n. pl.* проде́лки (*f. pl.*).

antidepressant /æntɪdɪˈpres(ə)nt/ *n.* антидепресса́нт.

antidote /ˈæntɪdəʊt/ *n.* противоя́дие, антидо́т.

antifreeze /ˈæntɪfriːz/ *n.* антифри́з.

antiglobalization /æntɪgləʊbəlaɪˈzeɪʃ(ə)n/ *n.* антиглобализа́ция.

antihistamine /æntɪˈhɪstəmiːn/ *n.* антигистами́н; (*attr.*) антигистами́нный.

antipathy /ænˈtɪpəθɪ/ *n.* антипа́тия; **have, feel an ~ to, against, for** испы́тывать (*impf.*) антипа́тию к + *d.*

Antipodean /æntɪpəˈdiːən/ *adj.* (*geog.*) относя́щийся к Австра́лии и Но́вой Зела́ндии.
■ *n.* антипо́д, жи́тель Австра́лии или Но́вой Зела́ндии.

Antipodes /ænˈtɪpədiːz/ *n.* регио́н Австра́лии и Но́вой Зела́ндии.

antiquated /ˈæntɪkweɪtɪd/ *adj.* (*obsolete*) устаре́лый; (*old-fashioned*) старомо́дный.

antique /ænˈtiːk/ *n.* антиква́рная вещь; **~ dealer** антиква́р; **~ shop** антиква́рный магази́н.
■ *adj.* (*vase, table*) антиква́рный.

antiquity /ænˈtɪkwɪtɪ/ *n.* (*great age*; *olden times*) дре́вность; (*classical times*) анти́чность; (*pl., ancient objects*) антиквариа́т.

anti-Semitic /æntɪsɪˈmɪtɪk/ *adj.* антисеми́тский.

anti-Semitism /æntɪˈsemɪtɪz(ə)m/ *n.* антисемити́зм.

antiseptic /æntɪˈseptɪk/ *n.* антисе́птик.
■ *adj.* антисепти́ческий.

antisocial /æntɪˈsəʊʃ(ə)l/ *adj.* антиобще́ственный.

antithesis /ænˈtɪθɪsɪs/ *n.* (*pl.* **antitheses** /-siːz/) (*contrast of opposite ideas*) антите́за; (*contrast*) контра́ст; (*opposite*) противополо́жность; **he is the ~ of his brother** он по́лная противополо́жность своему́ бра́ту.

anti-war /æntɪˈwɔː(r)/ *adj.* антивое́нный.

antlers /ˈæntləz/ *n. pl.* оле́ньи/лоси́ные рога́.

anus /ˈeɪnəs/ *n.* за́дний прохо́д, а́нус.

anxiety /æŋˈzaɪətɪ/ *n.*
1 (*uneasiness*) беспоко́йство.
2 (*desire*; *keenness*) жела́ние/стремле́ние + *inf.*
3 (*pl., cares, worries*) забо́ты (*f. pl.*).

anxious /ˈæŋkʃəs/ *adj.*
1 (*worried, uneasy*) озабо́ченный; **be ~ about, over** трево́житься (*impf.*) за + *a.*; беспоко́иться (*impf.*) о + *p.*
2 (*causing anxiety*) трево́жный, беспоко́йный.
3 (*keen, desirous*): **I am ~ to see him** мне о́чень хо́чется повида́ться с ним.

any /ˈenɪ/ *pron.*
1 (*in interrog. or conditional sentences*) (*animates*) кто́-нибудь; (*inanimates*) что́-нибудь; **if ~ of them should see him** е́сли кто́-нибудь из них уви́дит его́.
2 (*in neg. sentences*) (*with animates*) никто́; (*with inanimates*) ничто́; ни оди́н; **I don't like ~ of these actors** никто́/ни оди́н из э́тих арти́стов мне не нра́вится; **he never spoke to ~ of our friends** ни с кем из на́ших друзе́й он (никогда́) не говори́л.
3 (*in affirmative sentences*) любо́й; **take ~ of these books** возьми́те любу́ю/любы́е из э́тих книг.
4 : **he has little money, if ~** де́нег у него́ ма́ло, е́сли (они́) вообще́ есть.
■ *adj.* 1 (*in interrog. or conditional sentences*) *untranslated*: **have you ~ children?** у вас есть де́ти?; **have you ~ matches?** (*request*) у вас не бу́дет спи́чек?; (*no matter what*) любо́й, како́й уго́дно.
2 (*in neg. sentences*): **we haven't ~ milk** у нас нет молока́; **haven't you ~ cigarettes?** ра́зве у вас нет сигаре́т?; (*not ~ at all*) никако́й, ни оди́н; **there isn't ~ man who would ...** нет тако́го челове́ка, кото́рый бы ...; (*with* **hardly,** *vv. of prevention etc.*): **there is hardly ~ doubt** нет почти́ никако́го сомне́ния; **without ~ doubt** без/бе́зо вся́кого сомне́ния; **they stopped us from scoring ~ goals** они́ не́ дали нам заби́ть ни одного́ гола́.
3 (*no matter which*) любо́й; **at ~ time** в любо́е вре́мя; (*every*) любо́й, вся́кий; **in ~ case** во вся́ком слу́чае.
■ *adv.* 1 (*in interrog. or conditional sentences*) *untranslated or* ско́лько-нибудь; **do you want ~ more tea?** хоти́те ещё ча́ю?; **if you stay here ~ longer** е́сли вы ещё хоть немно́го заде́ржитесь здесь.
2 (*in neg. sentences*) *untranslated or* ниско́лько; ничу́ть; **I can't go ~ farther** я не могу́ идти́ да́льше; **he doesn't live here ~ more** он здесь бо́льше не живёт.

anybody /ˈenɪbɒdɪ/, **anyone** /ˈenɪwʌn/ *n.* & *pron.*
1 (*in interrog. or conditional sentences*) кто́-нибудь; кто́-либо; **did you meet ~?** вы кого́-нибудь встре́тили?; **if ~ rings, don't answer** е́сли кто позвони́т, не отвеча́йте; **is this ~'s seat?** э́то ме́сто за́нято?
2 (*in neg. sentences*) никто́; **I didn't speak to ~** я ни с кем не говори́л.
3 (*~ at all*; *no matter who*) вся́кий, любо́й; **~ will tell you** любо́й/вся́кий вам ска́жет; **~ who says that is a liar** кто бы э́то ни сказа́л, он лжёц; **~ else** кто́-нибудь ещё; **there was hardly ~ there** там почти́ никого́ не́ было.

anyhow /ˈenɪhaʊ/ *adv.*
1 (*haphazardly*; *carelessly*) ко́е-ка́к; ка́к-нибудь; **the work was done ~** рабо́та была́ сде́лана ко́е-ка́к.
2 (*anyway, in any case*) во вся́ком слу́чае; так и́ли ина́че; (*nevertheless*) всё равно́, всё же; **I shall go ~** я всё равно́ пойду́.

anyone /ˈenɪwʌn/ = **anybody**

anything /ˈenɪθɪŋ/ *n.* & *pron.*
1 (*in interrog. or conditional sentences*) что́-нибудь; что́-либо; что; **is there ~ I can get for you?** вам что́-нибудь принести́?; **have you ~ to say?** у вас (*or* вам) есть, что сказа́ть?
2 (*in neg. sentences*) ничто́; **I haven't ~ to say to that** мне не́чего сказа́ть на э́то.
3 (*everything*) всё; **I'd give ~ to see him again** я о́тдал бы всё, что́бы опя́ть уви́деть его́; **more, better than ~** бо́льше всего́.
4 (**~** *at all*) что уго́дно.
5 (*whatever*): **I will do ~ you suggest** я сде́лаю всё, что вы ска́жете.

anyway /ˈenɪweɪ/ = **anyhow 2**

anywhere /ˈenɪweə(r)/ *adv.*
1 (*in interrog. and conditional sentences*) где́-нибудь; где́-либо; (*of motion*) куда́-нибудь; куда́-либо; **is there a chemist's ~?** здесь есть апте́ка где́-нибудь?; **have you ~ to stay?** у вас есть где останови́ться?
2 (*in neg. sentences*) нигде́; (*of motion*) никуда́; **we haven't been ~ for ages** мы уже́ сто лет нигде́ не́ были.
3 (*in any place at all*; *everywhere*) где уго́дно; везде́; (по)всю́ду; **it is miles from ~** э́то чёрт-те где (нахо́дится).

AOB (*abbr. of* ***any other business***) (*Br.*) ра́зное.

apart /əˈpɑːt/ *adv.*
1 (*position*) в стороне́; (*motion*) в сто́рону; **joking ~** шу́тки в сто́рону; **~ from** (*with the exception of*) за исключе́нием + *g.*; кро́ме + *g.*; (*other than*; *besides*) кро́ме/поми́мо + *g.*
2 (*separate(ly)*; *asunder*) отде́льно; **they lived ~ for 2 years** два го́да они́ жи́ли по́рознь; **I could not tell them ~** я не мог их различи́ть/отличи́ть.
3 (*distant*): **the houses are a mile ~** дома́ нахо́дятся в ми́ле друг от дру́га.

apartheid /əˈpɑːteɪt/ *n.* апарте́йд.

apartment /əˈpɑːtmənt/ *n.*(*US*) кварти́ра; **~ block/house** многокварти́рный дом.

apathetic /æpəˈθetɪk/ *adj.* равноду́шный, апати́чный.

apathy /ˈæpəθɪ/ *n.* апа́тия.

ape /eɪp/ *n.* обезья́на.

aperitif /əperɪˈtiːf/ *n.* аперити́в.

apex /ˈeɪpeks/ *n.* (*pl.* **apexes** *or* **apices**) (*lit.*, *fig.*) верши́на, верх.

aphid /ˈeɪfɪd/ *n.* тля.

aphorism /ˈæfərɪz(ə)m/ *n.* афори́зм.

aphrodisiac /æfrəˈdɪzɪæk/ *n.* сре́дство, уси́ливающее полово́е влече́ние; афродизиа́к.
■ *adj.* уси́ливающий полово́е влече́ние.

apiary /ˈeɪpɪərɪ/ *n.* па́сека, пче́льник.

apocalypse /əˈpɒkəlɪps/ *n.* апока́липсис.

apocalyptic /əpɒkəˈlɪptɪk/ *adj.* апокалипти́ческий.

apocryphal /əˈpɒkrɪf(ə)l/ *adj.*
1 (*bibl.*) апокрифи́ческий.
2 (*of doubtful authenticity*) недостове́рный.

apologetic /əpɒləˈdʒetɪk/ *adj.* извиня́ющийся; **he was very ~** он о́чень извиня́лся; **an ~ smile** винова́тая улы́бка.

apologize /əˈpɒlədʒaɪz/ *v.i.* извин|я́ться, -и́ться (*перед кем за что*).

apolog|y /əˈpɒlədʒɪ/ *n.* извине́ние; **make an ~y to s.o. for sth.** прин|оси́ть, -ести́ извине́ния кому́-н. за что-н.; **please accept my ~ies** прими́те мои́ извине́ния.

apostle /əˈpɒs(ə)l/ *n.* апо́стол.

apostrophe /əˈpɒstrəfɪ/ *n.* (*gram.*) апостро́ф.

appal /əˈpɔːl/ *v.t.* (*US also* **appall; appalled, appalling**) ужас|а́ть, -ну́ть; устраш|а́ть, -и́ть; **I was ~led at the cost** цена́ меня́ ужасну́ла.

appall /əˈpɔːl/ (*US*) = **appal**

appalling /əˈpɔːlɪŋ/ *adj.* ужа́сный, жу́ткий.

apparatus /æpəˈreɪtəs/ *n.*
1 (*instrument*; *appliance*) прибо́р, инструме́нт.
2 (*in laboratory*) аппарату́ра; обору́дование.
3 (*gymnastic*) снаря́ды (*m. pl.*).

apparel /əˈpær(ə)l/ *n.* одея́ние, наря́д.

apparent /əˈpærənt/ *adj.*
1 (*plain, obvious*) очеви́дный; я́вный.
2 (*seeming*) ка́жущийся, мни́мый.

apparently /əˈpærəntlɪ/ *adv.* (*seemingly*) по-ви́димому; вероя́тно; (как) бу́дто.

apparition /æpəˈrɪʃ(ə)n/ *n.* виде́ние, при́зрак.

appeal /əˈpiːl/ *n.*
1 (*earnest request, plea*) обраще́ние (с про́сьбой); (*official*) воззва́ние; **an ~ on behalf of the Red Cross** обраще́ние от и́мени Кра́сного Креста́; **an ~ for support** про́сьба о по́мощи.
2 (*reference to higher authority*) апелля́ция, обжа́лование; **Court of A~** (*in England and Wales*), **court of ~s** (*US*) апелляцио́нный суд.
3 (*attraction*) привлека́тельность; **this life has little ~ for me** э́та жизнь меня́ ма́ло привлека́ет.
■ *v.i.* 1 (*make earnest request*) обра|ща́ться, -ти́ться (**to:** к + *d.*; **for:** за + *i.*) **he ~ed to us for help** он обрати́лся к нам за по́мощью; (*address o.s. to*) апелли́ровать (*impf.*, *pf.*) (**to:** к + *d.*).
2 (*leg.*) апелли́ровать (*impf.*, *pf.*); под|ава́ть, -а́ть апелля́цию; обжа́ловать (*pf.*) пригово́р.
3 : **~ to** (*attract*) привлека́ть (*impf.*); нра́виться (*impf.*) + *d.*

appealing /əˈpiːlɪŋ/ *adj.* (*imploring*) умоля́ющий; (*attractive*) привлека́тельный.

appear /əˈpɪə(r)/ *v.i.*
1 (*become visible*; *arrive*) появ|ля́ться, -и́ться.
2 (*present o.s.*) выступа́ть, вы́ступить; **~ in court** предст|ава́ть, -а́ть пе́ред судо́м; (*of actor*) игра́ть (*impf.*) на сце́не; снима́ться, сня́ться в кино́; (*of book*) выходи́ть, вы́йти (в свет); быть и́зданным.
3 (*seem*) каза́ться, по-; **he ~s to have left** он, ка́жется, уе́хал.
4 (*turn out*) ока́з|ываться, -а́ться; **it ~s his wife is a Swede** ока́зывается, его́ жена́ шве́дка.

appearance /əˈpɪərəns/ *n.*

[1] (*act of appearing*) появле́ние; (*in public*) выступле́ние; ~ **in court** я́вка в суд.
[2] (*look, aspect*) (*of thing*) вид; (*of person*) нару́жность, вне́шность; **judge by ~(s)** суди́ть (*impf.*) по вне́шнему ви́ду; **to, by all ~s** по всем при́знакам; су́дя по всему́.

appease /ə'pi:z/ *v.t.* (*one's conscience*) успок|а́ивать, -о́ить; (*person*) умиротвор|я́ть, -и́ть; (*appetites, passions*) утол|я́ть, -и́ть.

appeasement /ə'pi:zmənt/ *n.*
[1] успокое́ние; умиротворе́ние.
[2] (*of hunger, desire etc.*) утоле́ние.

appendage /ə'pendɪdʒ/ *n.* (*anat.*) отро́сток, прида́ток; (*fig.*) прида́ток.

appendectomy /æpen'dektəmɪ/ *n.* удале́ние аппе́ндикса.

appendices /ə'pendɪsi:z/ *pl. of* ▶ **appendix**

appendicitis /əpendɪ'saɪtɪs/ *n.* аппендици́т.

appendi|x /ə'pendɪks/ *n.* (*pl.* **~ces** *or* **~xes**)
[1] (*anat.*) аппе́ндикс.
[2] (*of a book etc.*) приложе́ние.

appetite /'æpɪtaɪt/ *n.* аппети́т.

appetizer /'æpɪtaɪzə(r)/ *n.* (*hors d'oeuvre*) заку́ска.

appetizing /'æpɪtaɪzɪŋ/ *adj.* аппети́тный.

applaud /ə'plɔ:d/ *v.t.* (*also v.i., clap*) аплоди́ровать (*impf.*) + *d.*

applause /ə'plɔ:z/ *n.* аплодисме́нты (*m. pl.*); рукоплеска́ния (*nt. pl.*).

apple /'æp(ə)l/ *n.* я́блоко.
■ *cpds.* ~ **sauce** *n.* я́блочное пюре́ (*indecl.*); ~ **tree** *n.* я́блоня.

appliance /ə'plaɪəns/ *n.*(*instrument*) прибо́р, приспособле́ние; **domestic ~** бытово́й прибо́р.

applicant /'æplɪkənt/ *n.* кандида́т, претенде́нт; ~ **for a job** кандида́т, претенде́нт на до́лжность.

application /æplɪ'keɪʃ(ə)n/ *n.*
[1] (*applying*) прикла́дывание; наложе́ние.
[2] (*employment*; *use*) примене́ние; приложе́ние.
[3] (*diligence*) прилежа́ние; (*concentration*) сосредото́ченность.
[4] (*request*) (*for work*) заявле́ние; (*for a grant*) зая́вка; (*for permission*) проше́ние; ~ **form** бланк заявле́ния.
[5] (*comput.*) (*also* **application program**) прикладна́я програ́мма; приложе́ние.

apply /ə'plaɪ/ *v.t.*
[1] (*lay, put on*) при|кла́дывать, -ложи́ть; (*dressing, plaster*) накла́дывать, наложи́ть; (*paint, cream*) наноси́ть, нанести́.
[2] (*bring into action*) прил|ага́ть, -ожи́ть; ~ **the brakes** тормози́ть, за-.
[3] (*make use of*) примен|я́ть, -и́ть.
■ *v.i.*: ~ **for** (*a job, grant, pass*) под|ава́ть, -а́ть заявле́ние на + *a.*; ~ **to** (*concern*; *relate to*) относи́ться (*impf.*) к + *d.*

appoint /ə'pɔɪnt/ *v.t.* (*nominate*) назн|ача́ть, -а́чить; **he was ~ed ambassador** он был назна́чен по́слом.

appointment /ə'pɔɪntmənt/ *n.*
[1] (*act of appointing*) назначе́ние.
[2] (*office*) до́лжность.
[3] (*at doctor's etc.*): **to make an ~ with** запи́|сываться, -са́ться на приём к + *d.*; полу|ча́ть, -чи́ть назначе́ние к + *d.*; (*business*) встре́ча.

apportion /ə'pɔ:ʃ(ə)n/ *v.t.* распредел|я́ть, -и́ть; раздел|я́ть, -и́ть.

apposite /'æpəzɪt/ *adj.* (*suitable*) подходя́щий; (*to the point*) уме́стный; уда́чный.

appraisal /ə'preɪz(ə)l/ *n.* оце́нка; (*of performance, of a worker*) аттеста́ция.

appreciable /ə'pri:ʃ(ɪ)əb(ə)l/ *adj.* (*perceptible*) заме́тный; (*considerable*) значи́тельный.

appreciate /ə'pri:ʃɪeɪt/ *v.t.*
[1] (*value*) оц|е́нивать, -ени́ть; цени́ть (*impf.*); **we ~ your help** мы це́ним ва́шу по́мощь.
[2] (*understand*) пон|има́ть, -я́ть.
[3] (*enjoy*): **he has learnt to ~ music** он научи́лся понима́ть и цени́ть му́зыку.
■ *v.i.* (*rise in value*) пов|ыша́ться, -ы́ситься.

appreciation /əpri:ʃɪ'eɪʃ(ə)n/ *n.*
[1] (*estimation, judgement*) оце́нка.
[2] (*understanding*) понима́ние, призна́ние досто́инств.
[3] (*rise in value*) повыше́ние в цене́/сто́имости.
[4] (*gratitude*) призна́тельность.

appreciative /ə'pri:ʃ(ɪ)ətɪv/ *adj.*
[1] (*perceptive of merit*): **an ~ audience** понима́ющая аудито́рия.
[2] (*grateful*) благода́рный, призна́тельный (за + *a.*).

apprehend /æprɪ'hend/ *v.t.*
[1] (*understand*) уясн|я́ть, -и́ть.
[2] (*arrest*) аресто́в|ывать, -а́ть; заде́рж|ивать, -а́ть.

apprehension /æprɪ'henʃ(ə)n/ *n.*
[1] (*fear*) опасе́ние.
[2] (*arrest*) аре́ст, задержа́ние.
[3] (*understanding*) уясне́ние.

apprehensive /æprɪ'hensɪv/ *adj.* озабо́ченный; беспоко́йный; по́лный трево́ги.

apprentice /ə'prentɪs/ *n.* подмасте́рье (*m.*).

apprenticeship /ə'prentɪsʃɪp/ *n.* уче́ние, учени́чество.

approach /ə'prəʊtʃ/ *n.*
[1] (*drawing near*; *advance*) приближе́ние; наступле́ние.
[2] (*fig.*) подхо́д; **his ~ to the subject** его́ подхо́д к предме́ту.
[3] (*access*) по́дступ.
[4] (*fig., overture*) предложе́ние; **they made unofficial ~es** они́ де́лали неофициа́льные предложе́ния.
■ *v.t.* [1] (*come near to*) прибл|ижа́ться, -и́зиться к + *d.*
[2] (*make overtures to*) обра|ща́ться, -ти́ться к + *d.*
■ *v.i.* прибл|ижа́ться, -и́зиться; под|ходи́ть, -ойти́; подъ|езжа́ть, -е́хать.

approachable /ə'prəʊtʃəb(ə)l/ *adj.* досту́пный.

approbation /æprə'beɪʃ(ə)n/ *n.* одобре́ние.

appropriate¹ /ə'prəʊprɪət/ *adj.* соотве́тствующий; (*suitable*) подходя́щий.

appropriate² /ə'prəʊprɪeɪt/ *v.t.*
[1] (*funds*) ассигнова́ть (*impf., pf.*).
[2] (*take possession of*) присв|а́ивать, -о́ить.

approval /ə'pru:v(ə)l/ *n.* одобре́ние; (*confirmation*) утвержде́ние; (*consent*) согла́сие; (*sanction*) апроба́ция; **on ~** на пробу.

approv|e /ə'pru:v/ *v.t.* од|обря́ть, -о́брить; (*confirm*) утвер|жда́ть, -ди́ть.
■ *v.i.* **~e of** од|обря́ть, -о́брить; **an ~ing glance** одобри́тельный взгля́д.

approximate /ə'prɒksɪmət/ *adj.* приблизи́тельный.

approximation /əprɒksɪ'meɪʃ(ə)n/ *n.* приближе́ние; **this is an ~ to the truth** э́то бли́зко к и́стине.

apricot /'eɪprɪkɒt/ *n.* абрико́с.

April /'eɪprɪl/ *n.* апре́ль (*m.*); **~ Fool!** пе́рвое апре́ля — нікому́ не ве́рю! **~ Fool's Day** пе́рвое апре́ля.

apron /'eɪprən/ *n.* (*garment*) пере́дник; фа́ртук.

apt /æpt/ *adj.*
1 (*suitable*) подходя́щий.
2 : **~ to** скло́нный к + *d.*

aptitude /'æptɪtju:d/ *n.* (*capacity*) спосо́бность; **~ test** прове́рка спосо́бностей.

aquaria /ə'kweərɪə/ *pl. of* ▸ **aquarium**

aquari|um /ə'kweərɪəm/ *n.* (*pl.* **~a** *or* **~ums**) аква́риум.

Aquarius /ə'kweərɪəs/ *n.* Водоле́й; **she's (an) Aquarius** она́ — Водоле́й.

aquatic /ə'kwætɪk/ *adj.* водяно́й.

aqueduct /'ækwɪdʌkt/ *n.* акведу́к.

Arab /'ærəb/ *n.* (*person*) ара́б (*fem.* -ка).
■ *adj.* ара́бский.

Arabian /ə'reɪbɪən/ *adj.* арави́йский.

Arabic /'ærəbɪk/ *n.* ара́бский язы́к.
■ *adj.* ара́бский.

arable /'ærəb(ə)l/ *adj.* па́хотный; **~ farming** земледе́лие.

arbitrary /'ɑ:bɪtrərɪ/ *adj.* произво́льный.

arbitrate /'ɑ:bɪtreɪt/ *v.i.* (*act as arbiter*) быть арби́тром; быть трете́йским судьёй.

arbitration /ɑ:bɪ'treɪʃ(ə)n/ *n.* арбитра́ж; трете́йский суд.

arbor /'ɑ:bə(r)/ (*US*) = **arbour**

arboret|um /ɑ:bə'ri:təm/ *n.* (*pl.* **~ums** *or* **~a**) дендра́рий.

arbour /'ɑ:bə(r)/ (*US* **arbor**) *n.* бесе́дка.

arc /ɑ:k/ *n.* дуга́.

arcade /ɑ:'keɪd/ *n.* (*covered passage*) арка́да; (*with shops*) пасса́ж.

arcane /ɑ:'keɪn/ *adj.* таи́нственный, та́йный.

arch /ɑ:tʃ/ *n.* (*curved shape*) а́рка; (*~ed roof; vault*) свод.
■ *v.t.* (*part of the body*) выгиба́ть, вы́гнуть; **the cat ~ed its back** ко́шка вы́гнула спи́ну.

arch- /ɑ:tʃ/ *comb. form* архи...; гла́вный.

archaeological /ɑ:kɪə'lɒdʒɪk(ə)l/ (*US also* **archeological**) *adj.* археологи́ческий.

archaeologist /ɑ:kɪ'ɒlədʒɪst/ (*US also* **archeologist**) *n.* архео́лог.

archaeology /ɑ:kɪ'ɒlədʒɪ/ (*US also* **archeology**) *n.* археоло́гия.

archaic /ɑ:'keɪɪk/ *adj.* архаи́чный; устаре́вший.

archangel /'ɑ:keɪndʒ(ə)l/ *n.* арха́нгел.

archbishop /ɑ:tʃ'bɪʃəp/ *n.* архиепи́скоп.

arch-enemy /ɑ:tʃ'enəmɪ/ *n.* закля́тый враг.

archeological /ɑ:kɪə'lɒdʒɪk(ə)l/ (*US*) = **archaeological**

archeologist /ɑ:kɪ'ɒlədʒɪst/ (*US*) = **archaeologist**

archeology /ɑ:kɪ'ɒlədʒɪ/ (*US*) = **archaeology**

archery /'ɑ:tʃərɪ/ *n.* стрельба́ из лу́ка.

archetypal /ɑ:kɪ'taɪp(ə)l/ *adj.* (*typical*) типи́чный.

archipelago /ɑ:kɪ'peləgəʊ/ *n.* (*pl.* **~s** *or* **~es**) архипела́г.

architect /'ɑ:kɪtekt/ *n.* архите́ктор.

architectural /ɑ:kɪ'tektʃər(ə)l/ *adj.* архитекту́рный; строи́тельный.

architecture /'ɑ:kɪtektʃə(r)/ *n.* архитекту́ра.

architrave /'ɑ:kɪtreɪv/ *n.* (*archit.*) архитра́в.

archive /'ɑ:kaɪv/ *n.* (*also pl.; also comput.*) архи́в.
■ *v.t.* поме|ща́ть, -сти́ть в архи́в; архиви́ровать (*impf., pf.*).

archivist /'ɑ:kɪvɪst/ *n.* архива́риус.

arctic /'ɑ:ktɪk/ *n.*: **the A~** А́рктика.
■ *adj.* аркти́ческий; **A~ Ocean** Се́верный Ледови́тый океа́н.

ardent /'ɑ:d(ə)nt/ *adj.* (*fervent*) горя́чий, пы́лкий; (*passionate*) стра́стный.

ardour /'ɑ:də(r)/ (*US* **ardor**) *n.* жар, пыл, рве́ние.

arduous /'ɑ:djʊəs/ *adj.* тяжёлый.

are /ɑ:/ *2nd pers. sing. pres. and pl. pres. of* ▸ **be**

area /'eərɪə/ *n.*
1 (*measurement*) пло́щадь; **a room 12 square metres in ~** ко́мната пло́щадью в 12 м² (= 12 квадра́тных ме́тров).
2 (*defined or designated space*) пло́щадь; (*expanse*) простра́нство; **vast ~s of forest** обши́рные лесны́е простра́нства.
3 (*region*) райо́н, край, зо́на; **residential ~** жило́й райо́н; **wheat-growing ~** пло́щадь под пшени́цей.
4 (*sphere*) о́бласть, сфе́ра; **in the ~ of research** в о́бласти иссле́дования.

arena /ə'ri:nə/ *n.* (*lit., fig.*) аре́на.

aren't /ɑ:nt/ *neg. of* ▸ **are**

Argentina /ɑ:dʒən'ti:nə/ *n.* (*also* **the Argentine**) Аргенти́на.

Argentine /'ɑ:dʒəntaɪn/, **Argentinian** /ɑ:dʒən'tɪnɪən/ *n.* аргенти́н|ец (*fem.* -ка).
■ *adj.* аргенти́нский.

argue /'ɑ:gju:/ *v.t.* (**argues, argued, arguing**)
1 (*discuss*) обсу|жда́ть, -ди́ть; (*debate*) дебати́ровать (*impf.*); спо́рить (*impf.*) о + *p.*
2 (*contend*) дока́зывать (*impf.*).
■ *v.i.* 1 (*debate; disagree; quarrel*) спо́рить (*impf.*); препира́ться (*impf.*); (*object*) возража́ть (*impf.*); **they ~d over who should drive** они́ спо́рили, кому́ вести́ маши́ну.
2 (*give reasons*) прив|оди́ть, -ести́ до́воды, выступа́ть, вы́ступить (**against:** про́тив + *g.*; **for, in favour of:** в защи́ту + *g.*, за + *a.*).

argument /'ɑ:gjʊmənt/ *n.*
1 (*reason*) аргуме́нт; до́вод; **it's an ~ for staying at home** э́то до́вод в по́льзу того́, что́бы оста́ться до́ма.
2 (*discussion, debate*) спор; **have an ~ over, about** спо́рить (*impf.*) о + *p.*

argumentative /ɑːgjʊˈmentətɪv/ *adj.* сварли́вый.

aria /ˈɑːrɪə/ *n.* а́рия.

arid /ˈærɪd/ *adj.* (*of soil etc.*) сухо́й, пересо́хший; (*of climate*; *lit.*, *fig.*) (*dry*) сухо́й.

Aries /ˈeəriːz/ *n.* (*pl.* ~) Ове́н; **she's (an) Aries** она́ — Ове́н.

arise /əˈraɪz/ *v.i.* (*past* **arose;** *p.p.* **arisen** /əˈrɪz(ə)n/) (*fig.*, *come into being*) возн|ика́ть, -и́кнуть; **if the need should** ~ е́сли возни́кнет необходи́мость; **the question arose** возни́к вопро́с.

aristocracy /ærɪˈstɒkrəsɪ/ *n.* аристокра́тия.

aristocrat /ˈærɪstəkræt/ *n.* аристокра́т.

aristocratic /ærɪstəˈkrætɪk/ *adj.* аристократи́ческий.

arithmetic /əˈrɪθmətɪk/ *n.* арифме́тика.

arithmetical /ærɪθˈmetɪk(ə)l/ *adj.* арифмети́ческий.

arm¹ /ɑːm/ *n.*
1 (*of person*) рука́; **he broke his** ~ он слома́л ру́ку; ~ **in** ~ по́д руку.
2 (*of garment*) рука́в; (*of chair*) ру́чка.
■ *cpds.* ~**band** *n.* нарука́вная повя́зка; ~**chair** *n.* кре́сло; ~**pit** *n.* подмы́шка.

arm² /ɑːm/ *n.* (*pl.*, *weapons*) ору́жие; ~**s race** го́нка вооруже́ний.
■ *v.t.* вооруж|а́ть, -и́ть; (*equip*) снаб|жа́ть, -ди́ть; ~**ed forces** вооружённые си́лы.

armament /ˈɑːməmənt/ *n.* (*also pl.*, *weapons*; *military equipment*) вооруже́ние.

Armenia /ɑːˈmiːnɪə/ *n.* Арме́ния.

Armenian /ɑːˈmiːnɪən/ *n.*
1 (*person*) арм|яни́н (*fem.* -я́нка).
2 (*language*) армя́нский язы́к.
■ *adj.* армя́нский.

armistice /ˈɑːmɪstɪs/ *n.* переми́рие.

armor /ˈɑːmə(r)/ (*US*) = **armour**

armored /ˈɑːməd/ (*US*) = **armoured**

armory /ˈɑːmərɪ/ (*US*) = **armoury**

armour /ˈɑːmə(r)/ (*US* **armor**) *n.* (*for body*) доспе́хи (*m. pl.*).
■ *cpd.* ~**-plated** *adj.* брониро́ванный.

armoured /ˈɑːməd/ (*US* **armored**) *adj.* брониро́ванный, бронено́сный.

armoury /ˈɑːmərɪ/ (*US* **armory**) *n.* арсена́л.

army /ˈɑːmɪ/ *n.* а́рмия; **join the** ~ идти́, пойти́ в а́рмию; (*attr.*) арме́йский.

aroma /əˈrəʊmə/ *n.* арома́т.

aromatherapist /ərəʊməˈθerəpɪst/ *n.* ароматерапе́вт.

aromatherapy /ərəʊməˈθerəpɪ/ *n.* ароматерапи́я.

aromatic /ærəˈmætɪk/ *adj.* (*smell*) арома́тный; (*substance*) ароматиче́ский.

arose /əˈrəʊz/ *past of* ▶ **arise**

around /əˈraʊnd/ (*see also* ▶ **round**) *adv.* вокру́г; круго́м; **all** ~ повсю́ду; **for miles** ~ на ми́ли вокру́г; **they were standing** ~ они́ стоя́ли побли́зости; **this singer has been** ~ **for 30 years** э́тот певе́ц уже́ 30 лет поёт.
■ *prep.* 1 (*encircling*) вокру́г + *g.*; круго́м + *g.*; **they stood** ~ **the table** они́ стоя́ли вокру́г стола́; **the path goes** ~ **the garden** доро́жка огиба́ет сад.
2 (*over*): **he looked** ~ **the house** он осмотре́л дом.
3 (*in the vicinity of*) о́коло + *g.*
4 (*approximately*) о́коло + *g.*; приблизи́тельно.

arouse /əˈraʊz/ *v.t.* (*awaken from sleep*) буди́ть, раз-; (*fig.*) пробу|жда́ть, -ди́ть; (*also sexually*) возбу|жда́ть, -ди́ть.

arrang|e /əˈreɪndʒ/ *v.t.*
1 (*put in order*) прив|оди́ть, -ести́ в поря́док; **she was** ~**ing flowers** она расставля́ла цветы́.
2 (*put in a certain order*; *group*) распол|ага́ть, -ожи́ть; расст|авля́ть, -а́вить.
3 (*settle*) ула́|живать, -дить.
4 (*organize*) устр|а́ивать, -о́ить; организо́в|ывать, -а́ть; (*prepare*; *plan in advance*) подгот|а́вливать, -о́вить; организо́в|ывать, -а́ть; нала́|живать, -дить.
■ *v.i.* догов|а́риваться, -ори́ться; усл|а́вливаться, -о́виться; **I have** ~**ed for somebody to meet him at the station** я распоряди́лся, что́бы его́ встре́тили на ста́нции.

arrangement /əˈreɪndʒmənt/ *n.*
1 (*setting in order*) приведе́ние в поря́док.
2 (*specific order*) расположе́ние.
3 (*pl.*, *planning*, *preparation*) ме́ры (*f. pl.*), приготовле́ния (*nt. pl.*); **make** ~**s for** организо́в|ывать, -а́ть; устр|а́ивать, -о́ить.
4 (*agreement*, *understanding*) соглаше́ние, договорённость.

array /əˈreɪ/ *n.*
1 (*order*): **in battle** ~ в боево́м поря́дке.
2 (*display*) мно́жество.
3 (*dress*, *apparel*) облаче́ние, одея́ние.
■ *v.t.* 1 (*place in order or line*) выстра́ивать, вы́строить; **the troops were** ~**ed for battle** войска́ бы́ли вы́строены в боево́м поря́дке.
2 (*set out*, *display*) выставля́ть, вы́ставить.
3 (*adorn*) укр|аша́ть, -а́сить; **she was** ~**ed in all her finery** она́ облачи́лась в са́мое лу́чшее; (*deck out*, *dress*) над|ева́ть, -е́ть.

arrears /əˈrɪəz/ *n.* (*of payment*) задо́лженность; просро́чка.

arrest /əˈrest/ *n.* аре́ст; **be under** ~ сиде́ть (*impf.*) под аре́стом.
■ *v.t.* аресто́в|ывать, -а́ть.

arrival /əˈraɪv(ə)l/ *n.* прибы́тие; **on his** ~ по его́ прибы́тии; (*of person etc. on foot*) прихо́д; (*of person by vehicle*) прие́зд; (*by air*) прилёт.

arrive /əˈraɪv/ *v.i.*
1 (*reach destination*) приб|ыва́ть, -ы́ть; (*of persons on foot*; *also fig.*) при|ходи́ть, -йти́.
2 : ~ **at a decision/conclusion** приходи́ть, прийти́ к реше́нию/заключе́нию.

arrogance /ˈærəgəns/ *n.* высокоме́рие.

arrogant /ˈærəgənt/ *adj.* высокоме́рный.

arrow /ˈærəʊ/ *n.* стрела́; (*as symbol or indicator*) стре́лка.

arse /ɑːs/ (*US* **ass**) *n.* (*vulg.*) жо́па (*vulg.*).

arsenal /ˈɑːsən(ə)l/ *n.* (*lit.*, *fig.*) арсена́л.

arsenic /ˈɑːsənɪk/ *n.* мышья́к.

arson /ˈɑːs(ə)n/ *n.* поджо́г.

art /ɑːt/ *n.*
1 (*skill*, *craft*) иску́сство; **a work of** ~ произведе́ние иску́сства.
2 (*decorative*) иску́сство; **fine** ~**s** изя́щные/изобрази́тельные иску́сства; ~ **school**

a

художественное училище; **~ gallery** картинная галерея; **~ critic** искусствовед.

artefact, artifact /ˈɑːtɪfækt/ *nn.* художественное изделие; (*sth. small or of little historical/cultural interest*) поделка.

arterial /ɑːˈtɪərɪəl/ *adj.*
1 (*anat.*) артериальный.
2 : **~ road** магистральная дорога; магистраль.

artery /ˈɑːtərɪ/ *n.* (*anat.*) артерия.

artful /ˈɑːtfʊl/ *adj.* хитрый.

arthritic /ɑːˈθrɪtɪk/ *n.* больн|ой (*fem.* -ая) артритом.
■ *adj.* (*of pain*) артритный; (*of person*) страдающ|ий (*fem.* -ая) артритом.

arthritis /ɑːˈθraɪtɪs/ *n.* артрит.

artichoke /ˈɑːtɪtʃəʊk/ *n.* артишок.

article /ˈɑːtɪk(ə)l/ *n.*
1 (*item*) предмет; (*manufactured*) изделие; **~ of clothing** предмет одежды.
2 (*piece of writing*) статья.
3 (*gram.*): **(in)definite ~** (не)определённый артикль.

articulate[1] /ɑːˈtɪkjʊlət/ *adj.* (*of speech*) членораздельный; (*of thoughts*) отчётливый; (*of person*) чётко выражающий свои мысли.

articulate[2] /ɑːˈtɪkjʊleɪt/ *v.t.* (*ideas*) ясно выражать, выразить; (*words*) отчётливо произн|осить, -ести.

articulated /ɑːˈtɪkjʊleɪtɪd/ *adj.*: **~ lorry** (*Br.*) грузовик с прицепом; автопоезд.

artifact /ˈɑːtɪfækt/ = **artefact**

artifice /ˈɑːtɪfɪs/ *n.* хитрость.

artificial /ɑːtɪˈfɪʃ(ə)l/ *adj.* (*not natural*) искусственный; **~ respiration** искусственное дыхание; (*feigned*) притворный.

artillery /ɑːˈtɪlərɪ/ *n.* артиллерия.

artisan /ɑːtɪˈzæn/ *n.* ремесленн|ик (*fem.* -ица).

artist /ˈɑːtɪst/ *n.* художн|ик (*fem.* -ица).

artiste /ɑːˈtiːst/ *n.* артист (*fem.* -ка); профессиональный музыкант, танцор *и т. п.*

artistic /ɑːˈtɪstɪk/ *adj.* (*person*) художественный; (*work*) артистический, артистичный.

artless /ˈɑːtlɪs/ *adj.* (*unskilled*) неискусный; (*ingenuous*) простодушный; (*natural*) безыскусственный.

arty /ˈɑːtɪ/ *adj.* (**artier, artiest**) (*coll.*) вычурный; претенциозно-богемный.
■ *cpd.* **~-farty** /ˈfɑːtɪ/ *adj.* претенциозный.

as /æz/ *adv.* & *conj.*
1 (*expr. comparison or conformity*) как; **~ I was saying** как я говорил; **do ~ follows** делайте следующее; **do it ~ follows** делайте это так/вот как/следующим образом; **such countries ~ Spain** такие страны, как Испания; **the same ~ ...** то же самое, что...; **~ heavy ~ lead** тяжёлый, как свинец; **I am ~ tall ~ he** мы с ним одного роста; **walk ~ fast ~ you can** идите как можно быстрее; **~ quickly ~ possible** как можно скорее; **just ~** так же, как; **~ usual** как всегда; **he pictured the room ~ it would be** он представлял себе, какой будет комната; **so ~ to** (*expr. purpose*) чтобы; (*expr. manner*) так, чтобы.
2 (*expr. capacity or category*) как; **I regard him ~ a fool** я считаю его дураком; **his appointment ~ colonel** присвоение ему звания полковника; **~ your guardian, I ...** как ваш опекун, я...; **~ a rule** как правило; **I said it ~ a joke** я сказал это в шутку.
3 (*concessive*): **young** (*US* **~ young**) **~ I am** хоть я и молод; **much ~ I should like to** как бы мне ни хотелось.
4 (*temporal*) когда; пока, в то время как; **(just) ~ I reached the door** когда я подошёл к двери.
5 (*causative*) так как, поскольку; **~ you are ready, let us begin** поскольку вы уже готовы, давайте начнём.
6 (*var.*): **~ far ~ I know** насколько мне известно; **~ if** будто (бы); как будто (бы); **it is not ~ if I was poor** не то, чтобы я был беден; **~ much ~ ...** столько, сколько...; **I thought ~ much!** так я и думал!; **no one so much ~ looked at us** на нас никто даже не посмотрел; **~ soon ~** как только; **I would just ~ soon go** я предпочёл бы пойти; **~ though** будто (бы); как будто (бы); **~ well** (*in addition*) также, тоже; **he came ~ well ~ John** и он, и Джон пришли; **you might ~ well help me** вы могли бы мне помочь; **it is just ~ well you came** хорошо, что вы пришли.

a.s.a.p. (*abbr. of* ***as soon as possible***) как можно скорее.

asbestos /æzˈbestɒs/ *n.* асбест.

ascend /əˈsend/ *v.t.* подн|иматься, -яться по + *d.* (*or* на + *a.*).

ascend|ancy /əˈsend(ə)nsɪ/ *n.* власть, господство; **gain, obtain ~ over** доб|иваться, -иться власти/господства над + *i.*

ascent /əˈsent/ *n.* восхождение, подъём; **~ of a mountain** восхождение на гору.

ascertain /æsəˈteɪn/ *v.t.* устан|авливать, -овить; выяснять, выяснить.

ascertainable /æsəˈteɪnəb(ə)l/ *adj.*: **it is ~** это можно установить.

ascribe /əˈskraɪb/ *v.t.* припис|ывать, -ать (**to:** + *d.*).

asexual /eɪˈseksjʊəl/ *adj.* бесполый.

ash[1] /æʃ/ *n.* (*bot.*) ясень (*m.*).

ash[2] /æʃ/ *n.*
1 (*also pl.*) зола; пепел.
2 (*pl., human remains*) прах.
■ *cpd.* **~tray** *n.* пепельница.

ashamed /əˈʃeɪmd/ *adj.* пристыженный; **I am, feel ~** мне стыдно; **be ~ of** стыдиться (*impf.*) + *g.*

ashen /ˈæʃ(ə)n/ *adj.* (*pale*) мертвенно-бледный.

ashore /əˈʃɔː(r)/ *adv.* (*position*) на берегу; (*motion*) на берег; **go ~** сходить, сойти на берег.

Asia /ˈeɪʃə/ *n.* Азия; **~ Minor** (*peninsula*) Малая Азия.

Asian /ˈeɪʃ(ə)n/ *n.* азиат (*fem.* -ка).
■ *adj.* азиатский.

aside /əˈsaɪd/ *adv.* (*place*) в стороне; (*motion*) в сторону; (*in reserve*) отдельно, в резерве; **take s.o. ~** отв|одить, -ести кого-н. в сторону; **set, put ~** (*reserve*) от|кладывать, -ложить.

asinine /ˈæsɪnaɪn/ *adj.* (*lit., fig.*) ослиный.

ask /ɑːsk/ *v.t.*
1 (*enquire*) спр|áшивать, -осúть (*что у кого or кого о чём*); **he ~ed me the time** он спросúл меня́, котóрый час.
2 (*pose*): **~ a question** зад|авáть, -áть вопрóс.
3 (*request permission*): **he ~ed to leave the room** он попросúл разрешéния вы́йти из кóмнаты.
4 (*request*) просúть, по- (*что у кого or кого о чём*); **I ~ed him to do it** я попросúл егó сдéлать э́то.
5 (*charge*) просúть, за-; **~ing price** запрáшиваемая ценá.
6 (*invite*) звать, по-; пригла|шáть, -сúть; **~ a girl out** пригла|шáть, -сúть дéвушку на свидáние.
■ *v.i.* 1 (*make enquiries*) спр|áшивать, -осúть (о + *p.*); спр|авля́ться, -áвиться (о + *p.*); **she ~ed after your health** онá справля́лась о вáшем здорóвье.
2 (*make a request*) просúть, по-; **~ for help** просúть, по- о пóмощи; **he ~ed him for a pencil** он попросúл у негó карандáш; **he ~ed for advice** он попросúл совéта.

askance /əˈskæns/ *adv.* кóсо, и́скоса; **he looked at me ~** он посмотрéл на меня́ и́скоса.

askew /əˈskjuː/ *adv.* крúво, кóсо.

asleep /əˈsliːp/ *pred. adj.* спя́щий; **he was sound, fast ~** он спал крéпким сном; **fall ~** зас|ыпáть, -нýть.

AS level *n.* (*Br.*) экзáмен в срéдней шкóле, по ýровню мéжду *GCSE* и *A level.*

asparagus /əˈspærəgəs/ *n.* спáржа.

aspect /ˈæspekt/ *n.*
1 (*look, appearance; expression*) вид, выражéние.
2 (*fig., facet*) аспéкт, сторонá; (*point of view*) тóчка зрéния.
3 (*outlook*) вид.

Asperger's syndrome /ˈæspəːdʒəz/ *n.* (*med.*) синдрóм Аспéргера (*форма аутизма*).

aspersion /əˈspəːʃ(ə)n/ *n.* (*slur*) клеветá; **cast ~s** возв|одúть, -естú клеветý на + *a.*; клеветáть (*impf.*) на + *a.*

asphalt /ˈæsfælt/ *n.* асфáльт.

asphyxiation /æsfɪksɪˈeɪʃ(ə)n/ *n.* удýшье.

aspic /ˈæspɪk/ *n.* заливнóе; **veal in ~** заливнáя теля́тина.

aspiration /æspɪˈreɪʃ(ə)n/ *n.* стремлéние.

aspire /əˈspaɪə(r)/ *v.i.* стремúться (*impf.*).

aspirin /ˈæsprɪn/ *n.* (*pl.* **~** *or* **~s**) аспирúн; (*tablet*) таблéтка аспирúна.

ass[1] /æs/ осёл.

ass[2] /æs/ (*US vulg.*) = **arse**

assail /əˈseɪl/ *v.t.* (*lit., fig.*) нап|адáть, -áсть на + *a.*; атаковáть (*impf., pf.*); **I was ~ed by doubts** меня́ одолевáли сомнéния; **~ with criticism** обрýши|ваться, -ться с крúтикой на + *a.*; **~ with questions** зас|ыпáть, -ы́пать вопрóсами.

assailant /əˈseɪlənt/ *n.* нападáющ|ий (*fem.* -ая).

assassin /əˈsæsɪn/ *n.* убúйца (*c.g.*).

assassinate /əˈsæsɪneɪt/ *v.t.* уб|ивáть, -úть (по политúческим мотúвам).

assassination /əsæsɪˈneɪʃ(ə)n/ *n.* политúческое убúйство.

assault /əˈsɒlt/ *n.* (*in general*) нападéние; (*mil.*) атáка, штурм, прúступ; (*leg.*): **indecent ~** оскорблéние дéйствием на сексуáльной пóчве.
■ *v.t.* нап|адáть, -áсть на + *a.*; (*mil.*) атаковáть (*impf., pf.*); (*leg.*) оскорб|ля́ть, -úть дéйствием.

assemble /əˈsemb(ə)l/ *v.t.* (*gather together*) соб|ирáть, -рáть; (*tech., fit together*) монтúровать, с-.
■ *v.i.* соб|ирáться, -рáться.

assembly /əˈsemblɪ/ *n.*
1 (*assembling*) собирáние, сбор.
2 (*company of persons*) собрáние; (*school*) **~ hall** áктовый зал.
3 (*of machine parts*) сбóрка; **~ line** сбóрочный конвéйер.

assent /əˈsent/ *v.i.* согла|шáться, -сúться (*с чем or на что*).

assert /əˈsəːt/ *v.t.*
1 (*declare; affirm*) утвер|ждáть, -дúть; заяв|ля́ть, -úть.
2 (*stand up for*) отст|áивать, -оя́ть; **~ o.s.** самоутвер|ждáться, -дúться.

assertion /əˈsəːʃ(ə)n/ *n.* утверждéние.

assertive /əˈsəːtɪv/ *adj.* (*self-assured*) самоувéренный.

assess /əˈses/ *v.t.*
1 (*estimate value of; appraise; also fig.*) оцéн|ивать, -úть.
2 (*determine amount of*) определ|я́ть, -úть сýмму/размéр + *g.*

assessment /əˈsesmənt/ *n.* (*valuation*) оцéнка; (*for taxation*) определéние.

asset /ˈæset/ *n.*
1 (*advantage; useful quality*) цéнность.
2 (*pl., fin.*) актúвы.

assiduous /əˈsɪdjʊəs/ *adj.* прилéжный; усéрдный.

assign /əˈsaɪn/ *v.t.*
1 (*task*) возл|агáть, -ожúть; пору|чáть, -чúть; (*person*) назн|ачáть, -áчить; (*resources*) предназн|ачáть, -áчить.
2 (*ascribe*) припúс|ывать, -áть.
3 (*leg., transfer*) перед|авáть, -áть.

assignation /æsɪgˈneɪʃ(ə)n/ *n.*
1 (*of person*) назначéние; (*of resources*) предназначéние; (*of task*) поручéние.
2 (*illicit meeting*) тáйное свидáние.
3 (*leg., transfer*) передáча.

assignment /əˈsaɪnmənt/ *n.* (*task, duty*) поручéние; задáние; (*schoolwork*) задáние.

assimilate /əˈsɪmɪleɪt/ *v.t.* (*absorb by digestion etc., and fig.*) ассимилúровать (*impf., pf.*).
■ *v.i.* ассимилúроваться (*impf., pf.*).

assist /əˈsɪst/ *v.t.* (*help*) пом|огáть, -óчь + *d.*; (*cooperate with*) содéйствовать (*impf., pf.*) + *d.*
■ *v.i.* (*take part*) прин|имáть, -я́ть учáстие.

assistance /əˈsɪst(ə)ns/ *n.* пóмощь; содéйствие.

assistant /əˈsɪst(ə)nt/ *n.* помóщни|к (*fem.* -ца); ассистéнт (*fem.* -ка); **~ manager** заместúтель завéдующего; (*Br., in shop*) продав|éц (*fem.* -щúца).

associate[1] /əˈsəʊʃɪət/ *n.*
1 (*colleague*) коллéга (*c.g.*), товáрищ; (*in business*) партнёр.

a

2 (*of a society*) член общества.

associate[2] /ə'səʊʃɪeɪt/ *v.t.* соедин|я́ть, -и́ть; свя́з|ывать, -а́ть; (*esp. psych.*) ассоции́ровать (*impf., pf.*); **his name was ~d with the cause of reform** его́ и́мя ассоции́ровалось с реформа́торской де́ятельностью.

association /əsəʊsɪ'eɪʃ(ə)n/ *n.*
1 (*uniting; joining*) объедине́ние; соедине́ние.
2 (*connection*) связь; ассоциа́ция.
3 (*group*) ассоциа́ция, о́бщество.

assorted /ə'sɔːtɪd/ *adj.* (*varied*) разнообра́зный.

assortment /ə'sɔːtmənt/ *n.* ассортиме́нт.

assuage /ə'sweɪdʒ/ *v.t.* (*soothe*) успок|а́ивать, -о́ить; (*alleviate*) смягч|а́ть, -и́ть; (*appetite etc.*) утол|я́ть, -и́ть.

assum|e /ə'sjuːm/ *v.t.*
1 (*take on*) прин|има́ть, -я́ть; **~e control of** брать, взять на себя́ управле́ние/руково́дство + *i.*
2 (*feign*) напус|ка́ть, -ти́ть на себя́; **he went under an ~ed name** он был изве́стен под вы́мышленным и́менем.
3 (*suppose*) предпол|ага́ть, -ожи́ть; допус|ка́ть, -ти́ть; **~ing that ...** при усло́вии, что... .

assumption /ə'sʌmpʃ(ə)n/ *n.* предположе́ние; допуще́ние.

assurance /ə'ʃʊərəns/ *n.* завере́ние, уве́рение.

assure /ə'ʃʊə(r)/ *v.t.*
1 (*ensure*) обеспе́чи|вать, -ть.
2 (*assert confidently*) ув|еря́ть, -е́рить; **I can ~ you of this** (я) могу́ вас в э́том уве́рить.

asterisk /'æstərɪsk/ *n.* (*typ.*) звёздочка.

asteroid /'æstərɔɪd/ *n.* астеро́ид.

asthma /'æsmə/ *n.* а́стма.

asthmatic /æs'mætɪk/ *adj.* (*pertaining to asthma*) астмати́ческий; (*suffering from asthma*) страда́ющий а́стмой.

astigmatism /ə'stɪgmətɪz(ə)m/ *n.* астигмати́зм.

astonish /ə'stɒnɪʃ/ *v.t.* пора|жа́ть, -зи́ть; изум|ля́ть, -и́ть; **be ~ed at** пора|жа́ться, -зи́ться + *d.*; изум|ля́ться, -и́ться + *d.*; **his success was ~ing** он име́л порази́тельный успе́х.

astonishment /ə'stɒnɪʃmənt/ *n.* изумле́ние.

astound /ə'staʊnd/ *v.t.* изум|ля́ть, -и́ть; пора|жа́ть, -зи́ть.

astray /ə'streɪ/ *pred. adj. & adv.*: **go ~** (*lit., miss one's way*) заблуди́ться (*pf.*); (*fig.*) сб|ива́ться, -и́ться с пути́; **lead ~** (*fig.*) сб|ива́ть, -ить с пути́ (и́стинного).

astride /ə'straɪd/ *adv.* верхо́м.
■ *prep.*: **~ a horse** верхо́м на ло́шади.

astrologer /ə'strɒlədʒə(r)/ *n.* астро́лог.

astrological /æstrə'lɒdʒɪk(ə)l/ *adj.* астрологи́ческий.

astrology /ə'strɒlədʒɪ/ *n.* астроло́гия.

astronaut /'æstrənɔːt/ *n.* астрона́вт, космона́вт.

astronomer /ə'strɒnəmə(r)/ *n.* астроно́м.

astronomical /æstrə'nɒmɪk(ə)l/ *adj.* (*lit., fig.*) астрономи́ческий.

astronomy /ə'strɒnəmɪ/ *n.* астроно́мия.

astrophysicist /æstrəʊ'fɪzɪsɪst/ *n.* астрофи́зик.

astrophysics /æstrəʊ'fɪzɪks/ *n.* астрофи́зика.

astute /ə'stjuːt/ *adj.* проница́тельный.

asylum /ə'saɪləm/ *n.* прию́т; **political ~** полити́ческое убе́жище.
■ *cpd.* **~ seeker** *n.* претенде́нт (*fem.* -ка) на получе́ние (полити́ческого) убе́жища.

asymmetrical /eɪsɪ'metrɪk(ə)l/ *adj.* асимметри́чный, асимметри́ческий.

at /æt/ *prep.*
1 (*denoting place*) в/на + *p.*; (*near, by*) у + *g.*, при + *p.*; **~ home** до́ма; **~ school** в шко́ле; **~ the station** на вокза́ле/ста́нции; **~ the concert** на конце́рте; **~ my aunt's** у мое́й тёти.
2 (*denoting motion or direction; lit., fig.*): **he sat down ~ the table** он сел за стол; **he arrived ~ Moscow** он при́был в Москву́.
3 (*denoting time or order*): **~ night** но́чью; **~ 2 o'clock** в два часа́; **~ Easter** на Па́сху; **~ the beginning** в нача́ле; **~ first** снача́ла.
4 (*of activity, state, manner, rate etc.*): **~ work** на рабо́те; за рабо́той; **good ~ languages** спосо́бный к языка́м; **~ war** в состоя́нии войны́; **~ 60 mph** со ско́ростью шестьдеся́т миль в час; **~ best** в лу́чшем слу́чае; **~ least** по кра́йней ме́ре; **~ most** са́мое бо́льшее; **~ all** вообще́; (*with neg.*) совсе́м.

ate /et, eɪt/ *past of* ▸ **eat**

atheism /'eɪθɪɪz(ə)m/ *n.* атеи́зм.

atheist /'eɪθɪɪst/ *n.* атеи́ст (*fem.* -ка).

athlete /'æθliːt/ *n.* спортсме́н (*fem.* -ка); **~'s foot** грибко́вое заболева́ние ног.

athletic /æθ'letɪk/ *adj.* атлети́ческий.

athletics /æθ'letɪks/ *n.* атле́тика.

Atlantic /ət'læntɪk/ *n.*: **the ~** Атланти́ческий океа́н.
■ *adj.* атланти́ческий.

atlas /'ætləs/ *n.* а́тлас.

ATM (*abbr. of* ***Automated Teller Machine***) *n.* банкома́т.

atmosphere /'ætməsfɪə(r)/ *n.* атмосфе́ра.

atmospheric /ætməs'ferɪk/ *adj.* атмосфе́рный.

atom /'ætəm/ *n.* а́том; **~ bomb** а́томная бо́мба.

atomic /ə'tɒmɪk/ *adj.* а́томный.

atonal /eɪ'təʊn(ə)l/ *adj.* (*mus.*) атона́льный.

atone /ə'təʊn/ *v.i.*: **~ for** искуп|а́ть, -и́ть.

atrocious /ə'trəʊʃəs/ *adj.* ужа́сный.

atrocity /ə'trɒsɪtɪ/ *n.* зве́рство.

attach /ə'tætʃ/ *v.t.*
1 (*fasten*) прикреп|ля́ть, -и́ть; **the ~ed document** прилага́емый докуме́нт.
2 : **~ o.s. to** присоедин|я́ться, -и́ться к + *d.*
3 (*assign*) прид|ава́ть, -а́ть.
4 (*of affection*): **she is very ~ed to her brother** она́ о́чень привя́зана к своему́ бра́ту.

attaché /ə'tæʃeɪ/ *n.* атташе́ (*m. indecl.*); **~ case** диплома́т.

attachment /ə'tætʃmənt/ *n.*
1 (*comput.*) (*file*) приложе́ние, вло́женный файл.
2 (*affection*) привя́занность.

attack /ə'tæk/ *n.*
1 нападе́ние; (*mil.*) ата́ка, нападе́ние; **our troops were under ~** на́ши войска́ бы́ли

атакóваны.
2 (*fig., criticism*) напáд|ки (*pl., g.* -ок).
3 (*of illness*) при́ступ; припáдок; **he had a heart ~** с ним случи́лся сердéчный при́ступ.
■ *v.t.* 1 (*lit., fig.*) нап|адáть, -áсть на + *a.*; атаковáть (*impf., pf.*); обрýши|ваться, -ться на + *a.*
2 (*a task etc.*) набр|áсываться, -óситься на + *a.*

attacker /ə'tækə(r)/ *n.* нападáющий.

attain /ə'teɪn/ *v.t.* дост|игáть, -и́гнуть (*or* -и́чь) + *g.*; доби|вáться, -и́ться + *g.*

attainment /ə'teɪnmənt/ *n.* достижéние.

attempt /ə'tempt/ *n.*
1 (*endeavour*) попы́тка; **they made no ~ to escape** они́ не предпри́няли попы́тки убежáть.
2 : **~ at**: **her ~ at producing a meal** плод её тщéтных кулинáрных старáний.
3 (*assault*): **an ~ was made on his life** на егó жизнь покушáлись.
■ *v.t.* (*try; try to do*) пытáться, по-; **he was charged with ~ed murder** егó обвини́ли в покушéнии на уби́йство.

attend /ə'tend/ *v.t.* присýтствовать (*impf.*) на + *p.*; **the concert was well ~ed** концéрт собрáл большóе коли́чество зри́телей; **~ school** посещáть (*impf.*) шкóлу.
■ *v.i.* 1 (*be present*) присýтствовать (*impf.*).
2 : **~ to** (*take care of, look after*) следи́ть (*impf.*) за + *i.*; забóтиться, по- о + *p.*; (*deal with*) зан|имáться, -я́ться + *i.*; **are you being ~ed to?** (*in shop*) вас (ужé) обслýживают?

attendance /ə'tend(ə)ns/ *n.*
1 (*presence*) присýтствие.
2 : **in ~** (*present*) присýтствующий.

attendant /ə'tend(ə)nt/ *n.* (*in museum, car park*) служи́тель (*m.*).

attention /ə'tenʃ(ə)n/ *n.*
1 (*heed*) внимáние; **pay ~ to** обра|щáть, -ти́ть внимáние на + *a.*; **draw ~ to** привл|екáть, -éчь внимáние к + *d.*
2 (*mil. command*) сми́рно!; (*posture*) **stand to ~** стоя́ть (*impf.*) сми́рно.
■ *cpd.* **~ deficit disorder** *n.* синдрóм нарушéния внимáния.

attentive /ə'tentɪv/ *adj.*
1 (*heedful*) внимáтельный.
2 (*solicitous*) забóтливый.

attest /ə'test/ *v.t.* (*certify*) удостов|еря́ть, -éрить; (*bear witness to*) свидéтельствовать, за-; (*confirm*) подтвер|ждáть, -ди́ть.
■ *v.i.*: **~ to** свидéтельствовать (*impf.*) о + *p.*

attic /'ætɪk/ *n.* мансáрда, чердáк.

attire /ə'taɪə(r)/ *n.* облачéние, одея́ние; **in night ~** в ночнóм облачéнии.
■ *v.t.* (*dress*) облач|áть, -и́ть; над|евáть, -éть; **she was ~d in white** онá былá вся в бéлом.

attitude /'ætɪtju:d/ *n.* отношéние.

attorney /ə'tə:nɪ/ *n.* (*pl.* **~s**) (*US, lawyer*) адвокáт.

attract /ə'trækt/ *v.t.*
1 (*of physical forces*) притя́|гивать, -нýть; (*fig.*) привл|екáть, -éчь (к себé).
2 (*captivate*) влечь (*impf.*), притя́гивать (*impf.*); **he found himself ~ed to her** он почýвствовал, что увлечён éю.

attraction /ə'trækʃ(ə)n/ *n.*
1 (*phys.*) притяжéние, тяготéние.
2 (*charm*) привлекáтельность.
3 (*thing of interest*) достопримечáтельность; (*amusement*) аттракциóн.

attractive /ə'træktɪv/ *adj.* привлекáтельный; притягáтельный.

attribute[1] /'ætrɪbju:t/ *n.* свóйство.

attribute[2] /ə'trɪbju:t/ *v.t.*: **~ sth. to** (*work of art, quality*) припи́с|ывать, -áть что-н. + *d.*; (*event, result*) отн|оси́ть, -ести́ что-н. к + *d.*

attributive /ə'trɪbjʊtɪv/ *adj.* определи́тельный; атрибути́вный.

attrition /ə'trɪʃ(ə)n/ *n.* трéние; истирáние; (*fig.*) истощéние; измóр; **war of ~** войнá на истощéние.

atypical /eɪ'tɪpɪk(ə)l/ *adj.* нетипи́чный.

aubergine /'əʊbəʒi:n/ *n.* (*Br.*) баклажáн.

auburn /'ɔ:bən/ *adj.* тёмно-ры́жий.

auction /'ɔ:kʃ(ə)n/ *n.* аукциóн; **~ room** аукциóнный зал.
■ *v.t.* (*also* **~ off**) прод|авáть, -áть с аукциóна.

auctioneer /ɔ:kʃə'nɪə(r)/ *n.* аукциони́ст.

audacious /ɔ:'deɪʃəs/ *adj.* (*bold*) смéлый; (*daring*) отвáжный; (*impudent*) дéрзкий.

audacity /ɔ:'dæsɪtɪ/ *n.* смéлость; отвáга; дéрзость.

audible /'ɔ:dɪb(ə)l/ *adj.* слы́шимый, слы́шный.

audience /'ɔ:dɪəns/ *n.* (*listeners*) аудитóрия; слýшатели (*m. pl.*); (*spectators*) зри́тели (*m. pl.*); пýблика.

audiobook /'ɔ:dɪəʊbʊk/ *n.* аудиокни́га.

audio-visual /ɔ:dɪəʊ'vɪʒjʊəl/ *adj.* аудиовизуáльный.

audit /'ɔ:dɪt/ *n.* ревúзия, ауди́т.
■ *v.t.* (**audited, auditing**) пров|еря́ть, -éрить отчётность + *g.*; ревизовáть (*impf., pf.*).

audition /ɔ:'dɪʃ(ə)n/ *n.* прослýшивание, прóба.
■ *v.t.* прослýш|ивать, -ать.

auditor /'ɔ:dɪtə(r)/ *n.* ауди́тор.

auditori|um /ɔ:dɪ'tɔ:rɪəm/ *n.* (*pl.* **~ums** *or* **~a** /-rɪə/) (*where audience sits*) зри́тельный зал.

augment /ɔ:g'ment/ *v.t.* приумн|ожáть, -óжить; увели́чи|вать, -ть.

augur /'ɔ:gə(r)/ *n.* (*hist.*) авгýр (*жрец, толковавший волю богов*).
■ *v.t.* (*portend*) предвещáть (*impf.*).
■ *v.i.* (*of things*) служи́ть (*impf.*) предзнаменовáнием (+ *g.*); **the exam results ~ well for his future** результáты егó экзáменов — хорóшая заявка на бýдущее.

August /'ɔ:gəst/ *n.* áвгуст.

aunt /ɑ:nt/ *n.* тётя, тётка.

aunt|ie, -y /'ɑ:ntɪ/ *nn.* тётушка, тётенька.

au pair /əʊ 'peə(r)/ *n.* ≈ ня́ня-инострáнка.

aural /'ɔ:r(ə)l/ *adj.* слуховóй.

auspices /'ɔ:spɪsɪz/ *n.*
1 (*omens*) предзнаменовáния (*nt. pl.*); **under favourable ~** при благоприя́тных услóвиях.
2 (*patronage*) покрови́тельство; эги́да; **under UN ~** под эги́дой ООН.

auspicious /ɔ:'spɪʃəs/ *adj.* благоприя́тный;

a

on this ~ day в э́тот знамена́тельный день.

austere /ɒ'stɪə(r)/ *adj.* (**austerer, austerest**) стро́гий, суро́вый.

austerity /ɒ'sterɪtɪ/ *n.* стро́гость, суро́вость.

Australia /ɒ'streɪlɪə/ *n.* Австра́лия.

Australian /ɒ'streɪlɪən/ *n.* австрали́|ец (*fem.* -йка).
■ *adj.* австрали́йский.

Austria /'ɒstrɪə/ *n.* А́встрия.

Austrian /'ɒstrɪən/ *n.* австри́|ец (*fem.* -йка).
■ *adj.* австри́йский.

authentic /ɔː'θentɪk/ *adj.* по́длинный.

authenticate /ɔː'θentɪkeɪt/ *v.t.* удостов|еря́ть, -е́рить по́длинность + *g.*

authenticity /ɔːθen'tɪsɪtɪ/ *n.* по́длинность.

author /'ɔːθə(r)/ *n.* (*of specific work*) а́втор; (*writer in general*) писа́тель (*m.*) (*fem.* -ница).

authoritarian /ɔːθɒrɪ'teərɪən/ *adj.* авторита́рный.

authoritative /ɔː'θɒrɪtətɪv/ *adj.* авторите́тный.

authority /ɔː'θɒrɪtɪ/ *n.*
1 (*power; right*) власть; (*legal*) полномо́чие; **who is in ~ here?** кто здесь ста́рший/нача́льник?; **who gave you ~ over me?** кто вам дал пра́во мне прика́зывать?
2 (*usu. pl.: public bodies*) вла́сти (*f. pl.*); о́рганы (*m. pl.*) вла́сти.

authorization /ɔːθəraɪ'zeɪʃ(ə)n/ *n.* (*authorizing*) уполномо́чивание; санкциони́рование; (*sanction*) разреше́ние; са́нкция.

authorize /'ɔːθəraɪz/ *v.t.*
1 (*give authority to*) уполномо́чи|вать, -ть.
2 (*sanction*) разреш|а́ть, -и́ть; дозв|оля́ть, -о́лить; санкциони́ровать (*impf., pf.*).

autism /'ɔːtɪz(ə)m/ *n.* аути́зм.

autistic /ɔː'tɪstɪk/ *adj.* аутисти́ческий; страда́ющий аути́змом.

auto /'ɔːtəʊ/ *n.* (*pl.* **~s**) (*US coll.*) авто́.

autobiographical /ɔːtəʊbaɪə'græfɪk(ə)l/ *adj.* автобиографи́ческий.

autobiography /ɔːtəʊbaɪ'ɒgrəfɪ/ *n.* автобиогра́фия.

autocracy /ɔː'tɒkrəsɪ/ *n.* самодержа́вие, автокра́тия.

autocrat /'ɔːtəkræt/ *n.* самоде́ржец, автокра́т.

autocratic /ɔːtə'krætɪk/ *adj.* самодержа́вный, автократи́ческий; (*dictatorial*) деспоти́ческий.

autocue /'ɔːtəʊkjuː/ *n.* (*Br., propr.*) автосуфлёр.

autograph /'ɔːtəgrɑːf/ *n.* авто́граф.
■ *v.t.* надпи́с|ывать, -а́ть.

automated /'ɔːtəmeɪtɪd/ *adj.* автоматизи́рованный.

automatic /ɔːtə'mætɪk/ *n.* (*firearm*) автомати́ческое ору́жие.
■ *adj.* автомати́ческий.

automation /ɔːtə'meɪʃ(ə)n/ *n.* автоматиза́ция.

automat|on /ɔː'tɒmət(ə)n/ *n.* (*pl.* **~a** *or* **~ons**) автома́т (*робот; человек*).

automobile /'ɔːtəməbiːl/ *n.* автомоби́ль (*m.*).

autonomous /ɔː'tɒnəməs/ *adj.* автоно́мный.

autonomy /ɔː'tɒnəmɪ/ *n.* автоно́мия.

autopilot /'ɔːtəʊpaɪlət/ *n.* автопило́т.

autopsy /'ɔːtɒpsɪ/ *n.* вскры́тие тру́па, аутопси́я.

autumn /'ɔːtəm/ *n.* о́сень; (*attr.*) осе́нний.

autumnal /ɔː'tʌmn(ə)l/ *adj.* осе́нний.

auxiliary /ɔːg'zɪljərɪ/ *n.* (*assistant*) помо́щник; (*gram.*, **~ verb**) вспомога́тельный глаго́л.
■ *adj.* доба́вочный.

avail /ə'veɪl/ *n.* (*use*) по́льза; **his entreaties were of no ~** его́ мольбы́ бы́ли безуспе́шны; **his intervention was of little ~** от его́ вмеша́тельства бы́ло ма́ло по́льзы; **to no ~** напра́сно.
■ *v.t.* 1 (*benefit*) быть поле́зным/вы́годным + *d.*; **our efforts ~ed us nothing** на́ши уси́лия ни к чему́ не привели́.
2 : **~ o.s. of** воспо́льзоваться (*pf.*) + *i.*

availability /əveɪlə'bɪlɪtɪ/ *n.* (*presence*) нали́чие; (*accessibility*) досту́пность.

available /ə'veɪləb(ə)l/ *adj.* (*product*) име́ющийся в прода́же, досту́пный; **it is not ~ in your size** ва́шего разме́ра нет; (*information*): **the information was not ~** информа́ция была́ недосту́пна; (*person*) свобо́дный; **she's not ~** она́ занята́.

avalanche /'ævəlɑːntʃ/ *n.* лави́на.

avarice /'ævərɪs/ *n.* жа́дность.

avaricious /ævə'rɪʃəs/ *adj.* жа́дный.

avenge /ə'vendʒ/ *v.t.* мстить, ото- за + *a.* **she ~d her friend** она́ отомсти́ла за дру́га.

avenue /'ævənjuː/ *n.* (*tree-lined road*) алле́я; (*wide street*) проспе́кт.

average /'ævərɪdʒ/ *n.* (*mean*) сре́днее число́; (*norm*) сре́днее; **above/below ~** вы́ше/ни́же сре́днего; **on ~** в сре́днем.
■ *adj.* сре́дний.
■ *v.t. & i.*: **my expenses ~ £10 a day** мои́ расхо́ды составля́ют в сре́днем де́сять фу́нтов в день; (*do on ~*): **he ~s 6 hours' work a day** он рабо́тает в сре́днем шесть часо́в в день.

averse /ə'vɜːs/ *pred. adj.*: **~ to** не располо́женный к + *d.*; **I am not ~ to a good dinner** я не про́чь хорошо́ пообе́дать.

aversion /ə'vɜːʃ(ə)n/ *n.* отвраще́ние, антипа́тия.

avert /ə'vɜːt/ *v.t.*: **~ one's gaze, eyes** отв|оди́ть, -ести́ взгляд.

aviary /'eɪvɪərɪ/ *n.* пти́чник; волье́р(а) для птиц.

aviation /eɪvɪ'eɪʃ(ə)n/ *n.* авиа́ция.

avid /'ævɪd/ *adj.* жа́дный, а́лчный.

avocado /ævə'kɑːdəʊ/ *n.* (*pl.* **~s**) (**~** *pear*) авока́до (*nt. indecl.*).

avoid /ə'vɔɪd/ *v.t.* (*drive round*) объезжа́ть, объе́хать; (*escape, evade*) избе|га́ть, -жа́ть + *g.*; **I could not ~ meeting him** я не мог избежа́ть встре́чи с ним.

avoidable /ə'vɔɪdəb(ə)l/ *adj.*: **delays are ~** заде́ржек мо́жно избежа́ть; **without ~ delay** без нену́жных/изли́шних заде́ржек.

avuncular /ə'vʌŋkjʊlə(r)/ *adj.* (*manner, tone*) оте́ческий; (*person*) дружелю́бный.

await /ə'weɪt/ *v.t.* ожида́ть (*impf.*) + *g.*

awake /ə'weɪk/ *pred. adj.*: **are you ~ or asleep?** вы спи́те и́ли нет?; **is he ~ yet?** он просну́лся?; **the baby was wide ~** у

ребёнка сна не́ было ни в одно́м глазу́.
■ *v.t.* (*past* **awoke;** *p.p.* **awoken**) буди́ть, раз-.
■ *v.i.* (*past* **awoke;** *p.p.* **awoken**) прос|ыпа́ться, -ну́ться.

awaken /ə'weɪkən/ *v.t.* пробу|жда́ть, -ди́ть.

award /ə'wɔ:d/ *n.* награ́да, приз.
■ *v.t.* прису|жда́ть, -ди́ть (*что кому*).

aware /ə'weə(r)/ *pred. adj.*: **be ~ of** сознава́ть (*impf.*); (*realize*) осозн|ава́ть, -а́ть; **you are probably ~ that ...** вам, вероя́тно, изве́стно, что... .

awareness /ə'weənɪs/ *n.* созна́ние.

away /ə'weɪ/ *adv.*
1 (*at a distance*): **the shops are ten minutes' walk ~** магази́ны нахо́дятся в десяти́ мину́тах ходьбы́ отсю́да.
2 (*not present or near*): **he is ~** он в отъе́зде; **our team are playing ~ (from home)** на́ша кома́нда игра́ет на вы́езде *or* на чужо́м по́ле *or* в гостя́х.
3 (*fig., of time or degree*): **the wedding is three weeks ~** до сва́дьбы (оста́лось) три неде́ли.

awe /ɔ:/ *n.* благогове́ние, тре́пет.
■ *cpd.* **~-inspiring** *adj.* внуша́ющий благогове́ние.

awesome /'ɔ:səm/ *adj.* (*impressive*) впечатля́ющий; (*US coll., fantastic*) потряса́ющий.

awful /'ɔ:fʊl/ *adj.* ужа́сный, стра́шный.

awfully /'ɔ:fəlɪ/ *adv.* ужа́сно; **~ nice** ужа́сно ми́лый.

awkward /'ɔ:kwəd/ *adj.*
1 (*clumsy*) неуклю́жий.
2 (*inconvenient, uncomfortable*) неудо́бный.
3 (*difficult*): **an ~ problem** каверзная пробле́ма.
4 (*embarrassing*): **an ~ silence** нело́вкое молча́ние.
5 (*Br., of person, hard to manage*) тру́дный; **he's being ~ (about it)** он чини́т препя́тствия.

awning /'ɔ:nɪŋ/ *n.* наве́с; тент.

awoke /ə'wəʊk/ *past of* ▸**awake**

awoken /ə'wəʊk(ə)n/ *p.p. of* ▸**awake**

AWOL /'eɪwɒl/ *pred. adj.* (*abbr. of* ***absent without leave***) в самово́льной отлу́чке.

awry /ə'raɪ/ *pred. adj.* криво́й; (*distorted*) искажённый.
■ *adv.* ко́со; (*fig.*): **things went ~** дела́ пошли́ скве́рно.

axe (*US also* **ax**) /æks/ *n.* топо́р.
■ *v.t.* (**axing**) (*fig.*) (*staff, budgets*) уреза́ть, уре́зать; (*a project*) заруб|а́ть, -и́ть.

axes /'æksi:z/ *pl. of* ▸**axis**

axis /'æksɪs/ *n.* (*pl.* **axes**) ось, вал.

axle /'æks(ə)l/ *n.* ось.

azalea /ə'zeɪlɪə/ *n.* аза́лия.

Azerbaijan /æzəbaɪ'dʒɑ:n/ *n.* Азербайджа́н.

Azerbaijani /æzəbaɪ'dʒɑ:nɪ/ *n.* (*pl.* **~s**) (*person*) азербайджа́н|ец (*fem.* -ка); (*language*) азербайджа́нский язы́к.
■ *adj.* азербайджа́нский.

Azov /'æzɒf/ *n.*: **Sea of ~** Азо́вское мо́ре.

Aztec /'æztek/ *n.* ацте́к.
■ *adj.* ацте́кский.

azure /'æʒə(r)/ *n.* лазу́рь.
■ *adj.* лазу́рный, голубо́й.

Bb

B /bi:/ *n.*
1 (*mus.*) си (*nt. indecl.*).
2 (*acad. mark*) «хорошо́», четвёрка.

BA (*abbr. of* ***Bachelor of Arts***) бакала́вр гуманита́рных нау́к.

babble /'bæb(ə)l/ *v.t.* & *i.* болта́ть (*impf.*); лепета́ть (*impf.*); **babbling brook** журча́щий ручей.

babe /beɪb/ *n.* (*sl.*) де́вушка.

baboon /bə'bu:n/ *n.* бабуи́н, павиа́н.

baby /'beɪbɪ/ *n.*
1 младе́нец; (*of animals etc.*) детёныш.
2 (*attr.*): **~ elephant** слонёнок.
■ *cpds.* **~sit** *v.i.* присма́тривать (*impf.*) за детьми́ в отсу́тствие роди́телей; **~sitter** *n.* приходя́щая ня́ня; **~sitting** *n.* присмо́тр за детьми́.

babyish /'beɪbɪɪʃ/ *adj.* де́тский.

baccalaureate /bækə'lɔ:rɪət/ *n.* сте́пень бакала́вра.

bachelor /'bætʃələ(r)/ *n.*
1 холостя́к.
2 (*acad.*) бакала́вр.

back /bæk/ *n.*
1 (*part of body*) спина́; **~ to ~** спино́й к спине́; **as soon as my ~ was turned** не успе́л я отверну́ться.
2 (*fig.*): **behind my ~** за мое́й спино́й.
3 (*of chair*) спи́нка.
4 (*other side, rear*): **~ of an envelope** обра́тная сторона́ конве́рта; **at the ~ of one's mind** подсозна́тельно; в глубине́ души́.
5 (*sport*): **full ~** защи́тник.
6 (*attr.*): **~ door** чёрный ход; **~ seat** за́днее сиде́нье; **~ street** глуха́я у́лица.
■ *adv.* 1 (*to or at the rear*) наза́д, сза́ди.
2 (*returning to former position etc.*) обра́тно; **he is ~ again** он сно́ва здесь; **we shall be ~ before dark** мы вернёмся за́светло; **get one's own ~** отплати́ть (*pf.*) (*кому*).
■ *v.t.* 1 (*move backwards*) дви́|гать, -нуть наза́д (*or* в обра́тном направле́нии); **she ~ed the car into the garage** она́ въе́хала за́дним хо́дом в гара́ж.
2 (*support; also* **~ up**) подде́рж|ивать, -а́ть;
3 (*finance*) финанси́ровать (*impf., pf.*).

4 : ~ **up** (*comput.*) резерви́ровать (*impf.*, *pf.*).
■ *v.i.* 1 (*of motor car*) идти́ (*det.*) за́дним хо́дом.
2 ~ **down (from)** отступ|а́ться, -и́ться (*от чего*); ~ **out (of)** уклон|я́ться, -и́ться (*от чего*).

backache /ˈbækeɪk/ *n.* боль в спине́/поясни́це.

backbencher /ˈbækˈbentʃə(r)/ *n.* (*Br.*) рядово́й член парла́мента; заднескаме́ечник.

backbiting /ˈbækbaɪtɪŋ/ *n.* злосло́вие.

backbone /ˈbækbəʊn/ *n.* позвоно́чник.

backchat /ˈbæktʃæt/ *n.* (*Br.*) де́рзкий отве́т, де́рзость.

back|cloth /ˈbækklɒθ/ (*Br.*), **-drop** *nn.* за́дник.

backdate /bækˈdeɪt/ *v.t.* (*letter*) пом|еча́ть, -е́тить за́дним число́м; (*pay*) пров|оди́ть, -ести́ за́дним число́м.

backdrop /ˈbækdrɒp/ *n.*
1 : **against the ~ of crisis** на фо́не кри́зиса.
2 = **backcloth**

backer /ˈbækə(r)/ *n.* ока́зывающий подде́ржку; субсиди́рующий.

backfire /ˈbækfaɪə(r)/ *v.t.* (*of a car, engine*) издa|ва́ть, -ть обра́тную вспы́шку; (*fig.*) прив|оди́ть, -ести́ к обра́тным результа́там.

background /ˈbækgraʊnd/ *n.*
1 за́дний план, фон; (*attr.*) фо́новый; **in the ~ of the picture** на за́днем пла́не карти́ны; **on a dark ~** на тёмном фо́не; **keep in the ~** (*fig.*) держа́ть(ся) (*impf.*) в тени́.
2 (*of person*) (*parentage*) происхожде́ние; (*education*) образова́ние; (*experience*) о́пыт.
3 (*to a situation*) предысто́рия.
4 : ~ **music** музыка́льное сопровожде́ние/оформле́ние.

backhand /ˈbækhænd/ *n.* уда́р сле́ва.

backhanded /bækˈhændɪd/ *adj.* (*fig.*) сомни́тельный, двусмы́сленный.

backhander /ˈbækhændə(r)/ *n.* (*Br., bribe*) взя́тка.

backing /ˈbækɪŋ/ *n.*
1 (*assistance*) подде́ржка; (*subsidy*) субсиди́рование.
2 (*of cloth*) подкла́дка.

backlash /ˈbæklæʃ/ *n.* (*fig.*) реа́кция.

backlog /ˈbæklɒg/ *n.* го́ры (*f. pl.*) накопи́вшейся рабо́ты.

backpack /ˈbækpæk/ *n.* рюкза́к.

backpacker /ˈbækpækə(r)/ *n.* челове́к, путеше́ствующий с рюкзако́м.

back-pedal /ˈbækped(ə)l/ *v.i.* (*fig.*) идти́ (*det.*), пойти́ на попя́тную.

backside /bækˈsaɪd, ˈbæk-/ *n.* зад, за́дница.

backslash /ˈbækslæʃ/ *n.* обра́тная кося́ черта́.

backslide /ˈbækslaɪd/ *v.t.* вновь подда́ться (*pf.*) искуше́нию; верну́ться (*pf.*) к дурны́м привы́чкам.

backstage /ˈbæksteɪdʒ/ *adv.* за кули́сами.

backstreet /ˈbækstriːt/ *adj.* (*illicit*) подпо́льный.

backstroke /ˈbækstrəʊk/ *n.* пла́вание на спине́.

backtrack /ˈbæktræk/ *v.i.* (*fig.*) идти́ (*det.*), пойти́ на попя́тную.

back-up /ˈbækʌp/ *n.* (*comput.*) резе́рвная ко́пия; бэ́кап.
■ *adj.* (*comput.*) резе́рвный.

backward /ˈbækwəd/ *adj.*
1 (*towards the back*) обра́тный; **a ~ glance** взгляд наза́д.
2 (*lagging*) отста́лый.

backwardness /ˈbækwədnɪs/ *n.* отста́лость; (*disinclination*) неохо́та.

backward(s) /ˈbækwədz/ *adv.* (*in backward direction*) наза́д; (*in reverse order*) в обра́тном поря́дке; **walk ~** пя́титься, по-; **~ and forwards** взад и вперёд; туда́ и обра́тно.

backwater /ˈbækwɔːtə(r)/ *n.* боло́то, ти́хая за́водь.

backyard /bækˈjɑːd/ *n.*
1 (*Br.*) за́дний двор.
2 (*US*) са́д(ик) за до́мом.

bacon /ˈbeɪkən/ *n.* бeко́н; **~ and eggs** яи́чница с бeко́ном.

bacteria /bækˈtɪərɪə/ *pl. of* ▶ **bacterium**

bacterial /bækˈtɪərɪəl/ *adj.* бактериа́льный.

bacteriology /bæktɪərɪˈɒlədʒɪ/ *n.* бактериоло́гия.

bacteri|um /bækˈtɪərɪəm/ *n.* (*pl.* **~a**) бакте́рия.

bad /bæd/ *n.* (*evil*) дурно́е, плохо́е; ху́до.
■ *adj.* (**worse, worst**)
1 плохо́й, дурно́й, скве́рный; **not ~!** непло́хо!; **too ~!** о́чень жаль!
2 (*morally bad*) плохо́й, дурно́й; **a ~ name** дурна́я репута́ция.
3 (*spoilt*) испо́рченный; **go ~** по́ртиться, ис-.
4 (*severe*) си́льный; **I caught a ~ cold** я си́льно простуди́лся.
5 (*harmful*) вре́дный; **smoking is ~ for one** куре́ние вре́дно для здоро́вья.
■ *cpds.* **~-mannered** *adj.* невоспи́танный; **~-tempered** *adj.* раздражи́тельный.

badge /bædʒ/ *n.* значо́к; (*fig.*) си́мвол.

badger /ˈbædʒə(r)/ *n.* барсу́к.

badly /ˈbædlɪ/ *adv.* (**worse, worst**)
1 (*not well*) пло́хо.
2 (*very much*) о́чень; си́льно.
3 : **~ off** в нужде́.

badminton /ˈbædmɪnt(ə)n/ *n.* бадминто́н.

baffle /ˈbæf(ə)l/ *v.t.* (*perplex*) сби|ва́ть, -ть с то́лку; озада́чи|вать, -ть.

bag /bæg/ *n.*
1 су́мка; (*small ~, hand~*) су́мочка; (*paper ~, plastic ~*) паке́т.
2 (*large ~, sack*) мешо́к.
3 (*luggage*) чемода́н; **pack one's ~s** собра́ть (*pf.*) ве́щи пе́ред отъе́здом.
4 (*var.*): **~s under the eyes** мешки́ под глаза́ми.
■ *cpd.* **~pipe(s)** *n.* волы́нка.

baggage /ˈbægɪdʒ/ *n.* бага́ж.
■ *cpds.* **~ handler** *n.* опера́тор на приёме/вы́даче багажа́; **~ reclaim** *n.* пункт вы́дачи багажа́.

baggy /ˈbægɪ/ *adj.* (**baggier, baggiest**) мешкова́тый.

Baghdad /bægˈdæd/ *n.* Багда́д.

Bahamas /bəˈhɑːməz/ *n.*: **the ~** Бага́мские острова́ (*m. pl.*).

bail[1] /beɪl/ *n.* (*pledge*) зало́г; поручи́тельство; **release on ~** отпус|ка́ть, -ти́ть на пору́ки.

■ *v.t.*: **~ s.o. out** брать, взять кого-н. на пору́ки.

bail², bale /beɪl/ *vv.t.* (*also* **~ out**) вычёрпывать, вы́черпать (*воду из лодки*).
■ *v.i.*: **~ out** (*aeron.*) катапульти́роваться (*impf., pf.*).

bailiff /'beɪlɪf/ *n.* (*leg.*) суде́бный при́став; бе́йлиф.

bait /beɪt/ *n.* (*hunting*) прима́нка; (*fishing*) наса́дка;

bake /beɪk/ *v.t.* печь, ис-.
■ *v.i.* пе́чься, ис-.

baker /'beɪkə(r)/ *n.* пе́карь (*m.*).

bakery /'beɪkərɪ/ *n.* пека́рня; (*shop*) бу́лочная.

Baku *n.* Баку́ (*m. indecl.*).

balalaika /bælə'laɪkə/ *n.* балала́йка.

balance /'bæləns/ *n.*
1 (*machine*) вес|ы́ (*pl., g.* -о́в).
2 (*equilibrium*) равнове́сие; **lose one's ~** (*fig.*) теря́ть, по- душе́вное равнове́сие; **hang in the ~** висе́ть (*impf.*) на волоске́.
3 (*bookkeeping*) бала́нс; са́льдо (*indecl.*); **~ of payments** платёжный бала́нс; **~ of trade** торго́вый бала́нс.
■ *v.t.* 1 (*lit.*): **he ~d a pole on his chin** он баланси́ровал шест на подборо́дке.
2 (*make equal*) уравнове́|шивать, -сить.
3 (*weigh one thing against another*) взве́|шивать, -сить; сопост|авля́ть, -а́вить (*что с чем*).
■ *v.i.* (*of accounts*) сходи́ться (*impf.*); (*be in equilibrium*) баланси́ровать (*impf.*).

balanced /'bælənsd/ *adj.* (*of person*) уравнове́шенный; **~ judgement** проду́манное сужде́ние; **~ diet** сбаланси́рованная/рациона́льная дие́та.

balcony /'bælkənɪ/ *n.* балко́н.

bald /bɔ:ld/ *adj.* лы́сый.

bale /beɪl/ *v.i.*: (*Br.*) = **bail²**

Balkan /'bɔ:lkən/ *n.*: **the ~s** Балка́н|ы (*pl., g.* —); Балка́нский полуо́стров.
■ *adj.* балка́нский.

ball¹ /bɔ:l/ *n.* (*dance*) бал.
■ *cpd.* **~room** *n.* танцева́льный зал.

ball² /bɔ:l/ *n.*
1 (*sphere*) шар.
2 (*in football, rugby, tennis*) мяч; (*in golf, table tennis*) мя́чик.
3 (*of wool*) клубо́к.
4 (*pl., vulg.*) (*testicles*) я́йца (*nt. pl.*); (*Br., nonsense*) чепуха́.
■ *cpds.* **~park** *adj.*: **a ~park figure** приме́рная ци́фра; **~point (pen)** *n.* ша́риковая ру́чка.

ballad /'bæləd/ *n.* балла́да.

ballast /'bæləst/ *n.* балла́ст.
■ *v.t.* грузи́ть, на- балла́стом.

ballerina /bælə'ri:nə/ *n.* балери́на.

ballet /'bæleɪ/ *n.* бале́т.
■ *cpd.* **~-dancer** *n.* арти́ст (*fem.* -ка) бале́та.

ballistic /bə'lɪstɪk/ *adj.* баллисти́ческий.

ballistics /bə'lɪstɪks/ *n.* балли́стика.

balloon /bə'lu:n/ *n.* аэроста́т; (*also child's*) возду́шный шар.
■ *v.i.* (*fly in ~*) лета́ть (*indet.*) на возду́шном ша́ре.

ballot /'bælət/ *n.* (*~ paper*) избира́тельный бюллете́нь; (*vote*) голосова́ние.
■ *v.t.* (**balloted, balloting**) пров|оди́ть, -ести́ голосова́ние ме́жду + *i.*
■ *cpd.* **~ box** *n.* избира́тельная у́рна.

Baltic /'bɔ:ltɪk/ *n.*: **the ~ (Sea)** Балти́йское мо́ре, Ба́лтика.
■ *adj.* балти́йский; прибалти́йский; **~ States** (при)балти́йские госуда́рства, Приба́лтика.

balustrade /bælə'streɪd/ *n.* балюстра́да.

bamboo /bæm'bu:/ *n.* бамбу́к.

bamboozle /bæm'bu:z(ə)l/ *v.t.* (*coll.*) одура́чи|вать, -ть; над|ува́ть, -у́ть.

ban /bæn/ *n.* (*prohibition*) запреще́ние, запре́т.
■ *v.t.* (**banned, banning**) запре|ща́ть, -ти́ть.

banal /bə'nɑ:l/ *adj.* бана́льный.

banana /bə'nɑ:nə/ *n.* бана́н.

band¹ /bænd/ *n.*
1 (*braid*) тесьма́; **rubber ~** рези́нка.
2 (*strip*) полоса́.
3 (*radio*): **frequency ~** диапазо́н часто́т.

band² /bænd/ *n.* (*gang*) ба́нда, ша́йка; (*mus.*) орке́стр; **jazz ~** джаз-ба́нд, джаз-орке́стр.
■ *v.t. & i.* **~ together** объедин|я́ться, -и́ться.

bandage /'bændɪdʒ/ *n.* бинт.
■ *v.t.* бинтова́ть, за-; перевя́з|ывать, -а́ть.

bandan(n)a /bæn'dænə/ *n.* цветно́й плато́к, банда́на.

bandit /'bændɪt/ *n.* разбо́йник, банди́т.

bane /beɪn/ *n.* прокля́тие; **it is the ~ of my life** э́то отравля́ет мне жизнь.

bang /bæŋ/ *n.*
1 (*blow*) уда́р.
2 (*crash*) гро́хот; стук.
3 (*explosion*) взрыв.
■ *v.t.* (*strike, thump*) уд|аря́ть, -а́рить; **~ one's fist on the table** сту́кнуть (*pf.*) кулако́м по́ столу; **~ the door** хло́пнуть (*pf.*) две́рью.
■ *v.i.* (*of door, window etc.*) захло́пнуться (*pf.*); **the door is ~ing** дверь хло́пает.
■ *adv.* (*suddenly*) вдруг; (*Br., just, exactly*) пря́мо; как раз.

banger /'bæŋə(r)/ *n.* (*Br., coll.*) (*sausage*) соси́ска; (*car*) драндуле́т.

Bangkok /bæŋ'kɒk/ *n.* Бангко́к.

Bangladesh /bæŋglə'deʃ/ *n.* Бангладе́ш.

Bangladeshi /bæŋglə'deʃɪ/ *n.* (*pl.* **~** *or* **~s**) бангладе́ш|ец (*fem.* -ка).
■ *adj.* бангладе́шский.

bangle /'bæŋg(ə)l/ *n.* брасле́т.

banish /'bænɪʃ/ *v.t.* (*exile*) высыла́ть, вы́слать; (*from one's mind*) от|гоня́ть, -огна́ть.

banisters /'bænɪstəz/ *n.* пери́л|а (*pl., g.* —).

banjo /'bændʒəʊ/ *n.* (*pl.* **~s** *or* **~es**) ба́нджо (*nt. indecl.*).

bank¹ /bæŋk/ *n.* (*of river*) бе́рег.

bank² /bæŋk/ *n.*
1 (*fin.*) банк; **~ account** ба́нковский счёт.
2 (*attr.*) ба́нковский; **~ card** ба́нковская креди́тная ка́рта; **~ clerk** ба́нковский слу́жащий; **~ holiday** ≈ официа́льный нерабо́чий день.
■ *v.t.* (*put into ~*) класть, положи́ть в банк.
■ *v.i.* (*keep money in ~*) держа́ть (*impf.*) де́ньги в ба́нке; **~ on** (*fig., rely on*) пол|ага́ться, -ожи́ться на + *a.*; де́лать, с- ста́вку на + *a.*

■ *cpd.* **~note** *n.* банкно́та.

banker /ˈbæŋkə(r)/ *n.* банки́р.

banking /ˈbæŋkɪŋ/ *n.* (*fin.*) ба́нковское де́ло.

bankroll /ˈbæŋkrəʊl/ *v.t.* финанси́ровать (*impf., pf.*).

bankrupt /ˈbæŋkrʌpt/ *adj.* (*also fig.*) обанкро́тившийся; несостоя́тельный; **go ~** обанкро́титься (*pf.*).

bankruptcy /ˈbæŋkrʌptsɪ/ *n.* банкро́тство, несостоя́тельность.

banner /ˈbænə(r)/ *n.* (*lit., fig.*) зна́мя (*nt. pl.*); (*with slogan*) плака́т.

banns /bænz/ *n.* оглаше́ние (предстоя́щего бра́ка); **ask, call, read the ~** огла|ша́ть, -си́ть имена́ жениха́ и неве́сты.

banquet /ˈbæŋkwɪt/ *n.* пир; (*formal*) банке́т.

banter /ˈbæntə(r)/ *n.* подшу́чивание, подтру́нивание.

■ *v.i.* шути́ть, по-.

baptism /ˈbæptɪz(ə)m/ *n.* креще́ние.

Baptist /ˈbæptɪst/ *n.*

1 : **St John the B~** Иоа́нн Крести́тель (*m.*).

2 (*member of sect*) бапти́ст (*fem.* -ка).

baptize /bæpˈtaɪz/ *v.t.* крести́ть, о-; нар|ека́ть, -е́чь.

bar¹ /bɑː(r)/ *n.*

1 (*rod*) прут; (*of chocolate*) пли́тка; (*of soap*) кусо́к; (*strip, flat piece*) полоса́.

2 (*usu. pl.*) решётка; **behind ~s** за решёткой.

3 (*mus.*) такт.

■ *v.t.* (**barred, barring**) (*bolt*) зап|ира́ть, -ере́ть на засо́в; (*obstruct*) прегра|жда́ть, -ди́ть; (*exclude*) исключ|а́ть, -и́ть; **soldiers ~red the way** солда́ты блоки́ровали доро́гу.

■ *cpd.* **~ code** *n.* штрихко́д.

bar² /bɑː(r)/ *n.* (*legal profession*) адвокату́ра.

bar³ /bɑː(r)/ *n.* (*room*) бар, буфе́т; (*counter*) прила́вок.

■ *cpds.* **~maid** *n.* буфе́тчица, ба́рмен; **~man, ~tender** *nn.* буфе́тчик, ба́рмен.

bar⁴ /bɑː(r)/ *prep.* (*Br. coll., excluding*) исключа́я, не счита́я; **~ none** без исключе́ния.

barbarian /bɑːˈbeərɪən/ *n.* ва́рвар.

■ *adj.* ва́рварский.

barbaric /bɑːˈbærɪk/ *adj.* ва́рварский.

barbarism /ˈbɑːbərɪz(ə)m/ *n.* ва́рварство; (*ling.*) варвари́зм.

barbarity /bɑːˈbærɪtɪ/ *n.* ва́рварство.

barbarous /ˈbɑːbərəs/ *adj.* ва́рварский; (*cruel*) бесчелове́чный.

barbecue /ˈbɑːbɪkjuː/ *n.* (*party*) барбекю́; пикни́к, где подаю́т мя́со, зажа́ренное на ве́ртеле/жаро́вне.

barbed /bɑːbd/ *adj.*: **~ wire** колю́чая про́волока.

barber /ˈbɑːbə(r)/ *n.* парикма́хер (*мужской*); **~'s (shop)** парикма́херская (*мужская*).

barbiturate /bɑːˈbɪtjʊrət/ *n.* барбитура́т.

bare /beə(r)/ *adj.*

1 (*naked, not covered*) го́лый, наго́й; обнажённый; **with one's ~ hands** го́лыми рука́ми; **~ feet** босы́е но́ги.

2 (*empty*) пусто́й.

■ *v.t.*: **~ one's teeth** ска́лить, о- зу́бы.

■ *cpds.* **~back** *adv.* без седла́; **~foot** *adj.* бoсо́й; *adv.* босико́м.

barely /ˈbeəlɪ/ *adv.* едва́.

Barents Sea /ˈbærənts/ *n.* Ба́ренцево мо́ре.

bargain /ˈbɑːgɪn/ *n.*

1 (*deal*) сде́лка, соглаше́ние; **make a ~** заключ|а́ть, -и́ть сде́лку; **it's a ~!** по рука́м!

2 (*thing cheaply acquired*) вы́годная поку́пка.

■ *v.i.* торгова́ться, с-; **~ for** (*expect*) ожида́ть (*impf.*); **it was more than I ~ed for** на э́то я не рассчи́тывал.

barge /bɑːdʒ/ *n.* ба́ржа.

■ *v.i.* (*coll.*): **~ in** (*intrude*) вва́л|иваться, -и́ться.

baritone /ˈbærɪtəʊn/ *n.* (*voice, singer*) барито́н.

barium /ˈbeərɪəm/ *n.* ба́рий.

bark¹ /bɑːk/ *n.* (*of tree etc.*) кора́.

bark² /bɑːk/ *n.* (*of dog*) лай.

■ *v.i.* (*of dog etc.*) ла́ять (*impf.*) (**at:** на + *a.*).

barley /ˈbɑːlɪ/ *n.* ячме́нь (*m.*) (*злак*).

bar mitzvah /bɑː ˈmɪtzvə/ *n.* бар-ми́цва (*m.*) (*в иудаизме: церемония посвящения мальчика, достигшего 13 лет; мальчик, прошедший эту церемонию*).

barmy /ˈbɑːmɪ/ *adj.* (**barmier, barmiest**) (*Br. coll., silly*) чо́кнутый, тро́нутый; **go ~** тро́нуться (*pf.*); спя́тить (*pf.*) (*both coll.*)

barn /bɑːn/ *n.* амба́р, сара́й.

barometer /bəˈrɒmɪtə(r)/ *n.* баро́метр.

baron /ˈbærən/ *n.* баро́н.

baroness /ˈbærənɪs/ *n.* бароне́сса.

baroque /bəˈrɒk/ *n.* баро́кко (*nt. indecl.*).

■ *adj.* баро́чный.

barrack /ˈbærək/ *n.* (*usu. pl.*) каза́рма.

barrage /ˈbærɑːʒ/ *n.* (*mil.*) загражде́ние; (*fig.*): **a ~ of questions** град/шквал вопро́сов.

barrel /ˈbær(ə)l/ *n.*

1 бо́чка.

2 (*of firearm*) ствол.

barren /ˈbærən/ *adj.* (**barrener, barrenest**) беспло́дный.

barricade /bærɪˈkeɪd/ *n.* баррика́да.

barrier /ˈbærɪə(r)/ *n.* барье́р; (*obstacle*) поме́ха, прегра́да.

barring /ˈbɑːrɪŋ/ *prep.* за исключе́нием + *g.*

barrister /ˈbærɪstə(r)/ *n.* (*Br.*) адвока́т.

barrow /ˈbærəʊ/ *n.* (*Br.*) (*handcart*) ручна́я теле́жка; (*wheel~*) та́чка.

■ *cpd.* **~ boy** *n.* у́личный торго́вец (*с тележкой*).

barter /ˈbɑːtə(r)/ *v.i.* обме́н|иваться, -я́ться + *i.*; меня́ться (*impf.*) + *i.*

base¹ /beɪs/ *n.*

1 (*of structure*) фунда́мент, пьедеста́л, основа́ние, ба́зис.

2 (*mil. etc.*) ба́за; **~ camp** ба́за.

■ *v.t.* осно́в|ывать, -а́ть; **the legend is ~d on fact** в осно́ве э́той леге́нды лежа́т действи́тельные собы́тия.

■ *cpd.* **~ball** *n.* бейсбо́л.

base² /beɪs/ *adj.* ни́зкий.

basement /ˈbeɪsmənt/ *n.* подва́л.

bases /ˈbeɪsiːz/ *pl. of* ▸ **basis**

bash /bæʃ/ (*coll.*) *n.* (*Br., attempt*) попы́тка; **have a ~** попыта́ться; (*bang*): **give s.o. a ~ on the head** дава́ть, дать кому́-н. по башке́

(*coll.*).
■ *v.t.* сильно ударя́ть, уда́рить.

bashful /ˈbæʃfʊl/ *adj.* застéнчивый.

basic /ˈbeɪsɪk/ *adj.* основно́й.

basically /ˈbeɪsɪkəlɪ/ *adv.* в основно́м.

basil /ˈbæz(ə)l/ *n.* базили́к.

basin /ˈbeɪs(ə)n/ *n.* (*for food*) ми́ска; (*washbasin*) умыва́льник, ра́ковина.

basis /ˈbeɪsɪs/ *n.* (*pl.* **bases**) осно́ва, ба́зис; **lay the ~ for** заложи́ть (*pf.*) осно́ву + *g.*

bask /bɑːsk/ *v.i.*: **~ in the sun** гре́ться (*impf.*) на со́лнце; (*fig.*): **~ in glory** купа́ться (*impf.*) в луча́х сла́вы.

basket /ˈbɑːskɪt/ *n.* корзи́на, корзи́нка.
■ *cpd.* **~ball** *n.* баскетбо́л.

Basque /bæsk/ *n.* баск (*fem.* -о́нка).
■ *adj.* ба́скский.

bass /beɪs/ *n.* (*voice, singer*) бас; (*~ guitar*) бас-гита́ра; (*double ~*) контраба́с.

bassoon /bəˈsuːn/ *n.* фаго́т.

bassoonist /bəˈsuːnɪst/ *n.* фаготи́ст (*fem.* -ка).

bastard /ˈbɑːstəd/ *n.*
1 (*child*) внебра́чный ребёнок.
2 (*as term of abuse*) уро́д.

bastion /ˈbæstɪən/ *n.* бастио́н.

bat[1] /bæt/ *n.* (*zool.*) лету́чая мышь.

bat[2] /bæt/ *n.* (*sport*) би́та, лапта́.
■ *v.t.* (**batted, batting**) бить (*impf.*) (*or* уд|аря́ть, -а́рить) би́той/лапто́й.

batch /bætʃ/ *n.*
1 (*of bread*) вы́печка.
2 (*consignment*) ку́чка, па́чка; гру́ппа.

bated /ˈbeɪtɪd/: **with ~ breath** затаи́в дыха́ние.

bath /bɑːθ/ *n.* ва́нна; **take, have a ~** прин|има́ть, -я́ть ва́нну; купа́ться, ис-.
■ *v.t.* & *i.* купа́ть(ся), ис-.
■ *cpds.* **~robe** *n.* купа́льный хала́т; **~room** *n.* ва́нная (ко́мната); **~tub** *n.* ва́нна.

bathe /beɪð/*v.t.*
1 (*one's face etc.*) мыть, по-; обм|ыва́ть, -ы́ть; **~ one's eyes, a wound** пром|ыва́ть, -ы́ть глаза́/ра́ну.
2 : **he was ~d in sweat** он облива́лся по́том.
■ *v.i.* купа́ться, ис-.

bather /ˈbeɪðə(r)/ *n.* купа́льщи|к (*fem.* -ца).

bathing /ˈbeɪðɪŋ/ *n.* купа́ние.

baton /ˈbæt(ə)n/ *n.*
1 (*mus.*) дирижёрская па́лочка.
2 (*sport*) эстафе́тная па́лочка.
3 (*Br., policeman's*) дуби́нка.

batsman /ˈbætsmən/ *n.* игро́к с би́той; отбива́ющий мяч.

battalion /bəˈtælɪən/ *n.* батальо́н.

batten /ˈbæt(ə)n/ *n.* ре́йка, пла́нка.
■ *v.t.*: **~ down** (*naut.*) задра́и|вать, -ть.

batter[1] /ˈbætə(r)/ *n.* (*cul.*) взби́тое те́сто.

batter[2] /ˈbætə(r)/ *v.t.* & *i.*
1 (*beat*) колоти́ть, по-; дуба́сить, от-; громи́ть, раз-.
2 (*knock about*): **a ~ed old car/hat** потрёпанная ста́рая маши́на/шля́па.

battery /ˈbætərɪ/ *n.* (*elec.*) (*in car*) батаре́я; (*in torch*) батаре́йка.

battle /ˈbæt(ə)l/ *n.* би́тва, сраже́ние, бой; (*struggle*) борьба́.
■ *v.i.* боро́ться (*impf.*); сража́ться (*impf.*).
■ *cpds.* **~field, ~ground** *nn.* по́ле сраже́ния/бо́я; **~ship** *n.* лине́йный кора́бль, линко́р.

batty /ˈbætɪ/ *adj.* (**battier, battiest**) чо́кнутый, тро́нутый (*coll.*).

bauble /ˈbɔːb(ə)l/ *n.* (*on Christmas tree*) ёлочный шар; (*trinket*) безделу́шка.

bawdy /ˈbɔːdɪ/ *adj.* (**bawdier, bawdiest**) непристо́йный, похабный.

bawl /bɔːl/ *v.t.* & *i.* ора́ть (*impf.*); выкри́кивать, вы́крикнуть; **~ at s.o.** ора́ть на кого́-н.; **~ s.o. out** (*coll.*) наора́ть (*pf.*) на кого́-н.

bay[1] /beɪ/ *n.* (*bot.*) лавр.
■ *cpd.* **~ leaf** *n.* лавро́вый лист.

bay[2] /beɪ/ *n.* (*geog.*) зали́в, бу́хта.

bay[3] /beɪ/ *n.* (*fig. uses*): **keep s.o. at ~** держа́ть (*impf.*) кого́-н. на расстоя́нии.
■ *v.t.* & *i.* ла́ять (*impf.*); залива́ться (*impf.*) ла́ем; выть (*impf.*).

bayonet /ˈbeɪənet/ *n.* штык.

bazaar /bəˈzɑː(r)/ *n.* база́р.

BC (*abbr. of* ***before Christ***) до н. э. (до на́шей э́ры), до рождества́ Христо́ва.

be /biː/ *v.i.* (*sg. pres.* **am, are, is;** *pl. pres.* **are;** *1st and 3rd pers. sg. past* **was;** *2nd pers. sg. past and pl. past* **were;** *pres. subjunctive* **be;** *past subjunctive* **were;** *pres. part.* **being;** *p.p.* **been**)
1 быть (*impf.*); (*exist*) существова́ть (*impf.*); (*as copula in the pres. tense, usu. omitted or expr. by dash*): **the world is round** земля́ кру́глая; **that is a dog** э́то соба́ка.
2 (*more emphatic uses*): **an order is an order** прика́з есть прика́з; **there is a God** Бог есть.
3 (*expr. frequency*) быва́ть (*impf.*); **he is in London every Tuesday** он быва́ет в Ло́ндоне по вто́рникам.
4 (*more formally, with complement*) явля́ться (*impf.*) + *i.*; представля́ть (*impf.*) собо́й.
5 (*expr. present continuous*): **she is crying** она́ пла́чет.
6 (*of place, time, cost etc.*): **it is a mile away** э́то в ми́ле отсю́да; **where is the office?** где нахо́дится о́фис?; **he is 21 today** ему́ сего́дня исполня́ется два́дцать оди́н год; **it is 25 pence a yard** э́то сто́ит два́дцать пять пе́нсов за ярд; (*of person or obj. in a certain position*) стоя́ть, лежа́ть, сиде́ть (*acc. to sense; all impf.*); **the books are on the floor** кни́ги лежа́т на полу́; **Paris is on the Seine** Пари́ж стои́т на Се́не; **he is in hospital** он лежи́т в больни́це; **I was at home all day** я сиде́л до́ма весь день; (*of continuing states*): **the heat was unbearable** жара́ стоя́ла невыноси́мая.
7 (*expr. motion*): **has the postman been?** по́чта уже́ была́?
8 (*become*): **what are you going to ~ when you grow up?** кем ты ста́нешь/бу́дешь, когда́ вы́растешь?
9 (*expr. pass.*): **the house is ~ing built** дом стро́ится; **I am told** мне сказа́ли.
10 (*behave, act a part*): **you are ~ing silly** вы ведёте себя́ глу́по; **am I ~ing a bore?** я вам надое́л?

11 (*uses of pres. part. and gerund*): **~ing a doctor, he knew what to do** бу́дучи врачо́м, он знал, что де́лать; **for the time ~ing** пока́ что, на вре́мя.
12 (*with* **to**): **I am to inform you** я до́лжен сообщи́ть вам; **he is to ~ married today** он сего́дня же́нится; **his wife to ~** его́ бу́дущая жена́.
13 (*var.*): **how are you?** как пожива́ете? **~ that as it may** как бы то ни́ было.

beach /bi:tʃ/ *n.* пляж.

beacon /ˈbi:kən/ *n.* (*signal light, fire*) сигна́льный ого́нь.

bead /bi:d/ *n.*
1 бу́син(к)а; **string of ~s** бу́с|ы (*pl. g.* —).
2 (*drop*) ка́пля.

beady /ˈbi:dɪ/ *adj.* (**beadier, beadiest**): **~ eyes** глаза́-бу́синки.

beak /bi:k/ *n.* клюв.

beaker /ˈbi:k(ə)r/ *n.* (*Br., for drinking*) пластма́ссовый стака́н (с но́сиком); (*in laboratory*) мензу́рка.

beam¹ /bi:m/ *n.* (*of timber etc.*) брус, ба́лка.

beam² /bi:m/ *n.* (*ray*) луч.
■ *v.i.* (*shine*) свети́ть (*impf.*), сия́ть (*impf.*).

bean /bi:n/ *n.* боб; **French ~s** фасо́ль; **string ~s** зелёная фасо́ль.

bear¹ /beə(r)/ *n.* медве́дь (*m.*).

bear² /beə(r)/ *v.t.* (*past* **bore;** *p.p.* **borne, born**)
1 (*carry*) носи́ть (*indet.*), нести́, по- (*det.*); **~ in mind** име́ть (*impf.*) в виду́.
2 (*sustain, support*): **the ice will ~ his weight** лёд вы́держит его́.
3 (*endure, tolerate*) терпе́ть, с-; выноси́ть, вы́нести; сн|оси́ть, -ести́; **I cannot ~ him** я его́ не выношу́.
4 (*be capable of*): **~ comparison** выде́рживать (*impf.*) сравне́ние.
5 (*give birth to*): **be born** роди́ться (*impf., pf.*).
6 (*yield*): **trees/efforts ~ fruit** дере́вья/уси́лия прино́сят плоды́.
■ *v.i.* 1 (*of direction*): **the road ~s to the right** доро́га идёт впра́во.
2 (*exert pressure, affect*): **bring one's energy to ~ on** напра́вить (*pf.*) эне́ргию на + *a.*; **~ with** терпе́ть (*impf.*), переноси́ть (*impf.*).
■ *with advs.*: **~ out** *v.t.* (*confirm*) подтвер|жда́ть, -ди́ть; **~ up** *v.i.* (*endure*) держа́ться (*impf.*).

bearable /ˈbeərəb(ə)l/ *adj.* терпи́мый, сно́сный.

beard /bɪəd/ *n.* борода́.

bearer /ˈbeərə(r)/ *n.* (*one who carries*) несу́щий, нося́щий; **~ of good news** до́брый ве́стник; (*of a cheque*) предъяви́тель (*m.*).

bearing /ˈbeərɪŋ/ *n.*
1 (*deportment*) мане́ра держа́ться.
2 (*relevance*) отноше́ние (к + *d.*).
3 (*direction*): **get one's ~s** определ|я́ть, -и́ть своё местонахожде́ние; ориенти́роваться (*impf., pf.*).

beast /bi:st/ *n.*
1 (*animal*) живо́тное; (*wild animal*) зверь (*m.*).
2 (*nasty person*) скот (*c.g.*).

beastly /ˈbi:stlɪ/ *adj.* (**beastlier, beastliest**) (*unpleasant*) отврати́тельный; **~ weather** ужа́сная пого́да; **a ~ headache** ме́рзкая/гну́сная головна́я боль.

beat /bi:t/ *n.*
1 (*of drum*) бой; (*of heart*) бие́ние; (*rhythm*) ритм; (*mus.*) такт.
2 (*policeman's*) райо́н обхо́да.
■ *v.t.* (*past* **beat;** *p.p.* **beaten**)
1 (*strike*) бить, по-; **~ eggs** взби|ва́ть, -ть я́йца; **~ time** отбива́ть (*impf.*) такт.
2 (*defeat, surpass*) поб|ива́ть, -и́ть; побе|жда́ть, -ди́ть; **he ~ me at chess** он обыгра́л меня́ в ша́хматы; **he ~ the record** он поби́л реко́рд.
■ *v.i.* (*past* **beat;** *p.p.* **beaten**): **his heart is ~ing** его́ се́рдце бьётся; **he heard drums ~ing** он слы́шал бараба́нный бой; **the rain ~ against the windows** дождь стуча́л в о́кна;
■ *with advs.*: **~ back** *v.t.* отб|ива́ть, -и́ть; **~ down** *v.i.*: **the sun ~ down on us** со́лнце нещა́дно пали́ло нас; **~ off** *v.t.*: **~ off an attack** отб|ива́ть, -и́ть ата́ку; **~ up** *v.t.*: **~ s.o. up** изб|ива́ть, -и́ть кого́-н.

beating /ˈbi:tɪŋ/ *n.*
1 (*of heart*) бие́ние.
2 (*thrashing*) по́рка.

beautician /bju:ˈtɪʃ(ə)n/ *n.* космето́лог.

beautiful /ˈbju:tɪfʊl/ *adj.* краси́вый; (*excellent*) прекра́сный.

beauty /ˈbju:tɪ/ *n.* (*quality*) красота́; **~ parlour** космети́ческий кабине́т; **~ spot** (*Br., place*) живопи́сная ме́стность.

beaver /ˈbi:və(r)/ *n.* (*pl.* **~** *or* **~s**) (*zool.*) бобр.

becalm /bɪˈkɑ:m/ *v.t.*: **be ~ed** (*naut.*) штилева́ть (*impf.*); заштил|ева́ть, -е́ть; **a ~ed ship** кора́бль, попа́вший в штиль.

became /bɪˈkeɪm/ *past of* ▸ **become**

because /bɪˈkɒz/ *conj.* потому́ что; **~ of** из-за + *g.*, (*thanks to*) благодаря́ + *d.*

beckon /ˈbekən/ *v.t.* & *i.* мани́ть, по-; заз|ыва́ть, -ва́ть; **I ~ed (to) him to approach** я помани́л его́ к себе́.

become /bɪˈkʌm/ *v.i.* (*past* **became;** *p.p.* **become**) (*come to be*) ста|нови́ться, -ть + *i.*; *often expr. by v. in* …еть; **~ smaller** уме́ньшиться (*pf.*); **what became of him?** что с ним ста́лось?; **he became a waiter** он стал официа́нтом.

bed /bed/ *n.*
1 (*esp. bedstead*) крова́ть; (*esp. bedding*) посте́ль; **go to ~** ложи́ться, лечь спать; (*in sexual sense*) переспа́ть (*pf.*) (**with:** с + *i.*); **get into ~** ложи́ться, лечь в посте́ль/крова́ть; **get out of ~** вста|ва́ть, -ть с посте́ли/крова́ти; **make a ~** уб|ира́ть, -ра́ть посте́ль.
2 (*of the sea*) дно; (*of a river*) ру́сло.
3 : **~ of flowers** клу́мба.
■ *cpds.* **~ and breakfast** (*guest house*) ма́ленькая гости́ница; **~ridden** *adj.* прико́ванный к посте́ли; **~room** *n.* спа́льня; **~side** *n.*: **keep books at one's ~side** держа́ть (*impf.*) кни́ги на ночно́м сто́лике; **~sit** *n.* (*Br.*) одноко́мнатная кварти́ра; **~spread** *n.* покрыва́ло; **~time** *n.* вре́мя ложи́ться/идти́ спать.

bedevil /bɪˈdev(ə)l/ *v.t.* (**bedevilled, bedevilling;** *US* **bedeviled, bedeviling**) (*confuse*) спу́т|ывать, -ать; вн|оси́ть, -ести́

неразбериху в + *a.*
bedlam /ˈbedləm/ *n.* (*fig.*) бедлам, полная неразбериха.
bedraggled /bɪˈdræg(ə)ld/ *adj.* забрызганный.
bee /biː/ *n.* пчела.
■ *cpd.* **~hive** *n.* улей.
beech /biːtʃ/ *n.* бук.
beef /biːf/ *n.* говядина.
■ *cpd.* **~burger** *n.* рубленый бифштекс.
beefy /ˈbiːfɪ/ *adj.* (**beefier, beefiest**) мускулистый.
been /biːn/ *p.p. of* ▶ **be**
beep /biːp/ *n.* гудок.
■ *v.i.* гудеть, про-.
beer /bɪə(r)/ *n.* пиво.
beet /biːt/ *n.* свёкла.
■ *cpd.* **~root** *n.* (*Br.*) свёкла.
beetle /ˈbiːt(ə)l/ *n.* (*zool.*) жук.
befall /bɪˈfɔːl/ *v.t.* & *i.* (*past* **befell** /bɪˈfel/; *p.p.* **befallen** /bɪˈfɔːlən/) (*liter.*) приключ|аться, -иться (с + *i.*); пост|игать, -игнуть (*кого/что*); **what has ~en him?** что с ним стало?
befit /bɪˈfɪt/ *v.t.* (**befitted, befitting**) под|ходить, -ойти + *d.*
before /bɪˈfɔː(r)/ *adv.* раньше; **six weeks ~** шестью неделями раньше; **18 years ~** 18 лет назад.
■ *prep.* [1] (*of time*) перед + *i.*; **~ leaving** перед отъездом; (*earlier than*) до + *g.*; **~ the war** до войны; **the week ~ last** позапрошлая неделя; **don't come ~ I call you** не приходите, пока я вас не позову.
[2] (*of place*) перед + *i.*; впереди + *g.*; **~ my eyes** на моих глазах.
■ *conj.* (*earlier than*) раньше чем; (*immediately* ~) прежде/перед тем, как; (*at a previous time*) до того как; **do it ~ you forget** сделайте это, пока не забыли; **it will be years ~ we meet** пройдут годы, пока мы встретимся; **just ~ you arrived** перед самым вашим приходом.
■ *cpd.* **~hand** *adv.* заранее.
befriend /bɪˈfrend/ *v.t.* дружески отн|оситься, -естись к + *d.*; помогать (*impf.*) + *d.*
befuddle /bɪˈfʌd(ə)l/ *v.t.* одурмани|вать, -ть.
beg /beg/ *v.t.* (**begged, begging**) просить, по-; умолять (*impf.*); **~ s.o. to do sth.** умолять (*impf.*) кого-н. сделать что-н.
■ *v.i.* (**begged, begging**)
[1] (*ask for charity*) просить милостыню, нищенствовать, (*coll.*) побираться (*all impf.*).
[2] : **~ for sth.** умол|ять, -ить о + *p.*; выпрашивать, выпросить что-н.
began /bɪˈgæn/ *past of* ▶ **begin**
beggar /ˈbegə(r)/ *n.* нищий.
begin /bɪˈgɪn/ *v.t.* (**beginning;** *past* **began;** *p.p.* **begun**) нач|инать, -ать; **he began the meeting** он открыл собрание; (*often translated by* за-): **~ to sing** запеть (*pf.*); **he began to cry** он заплакал.
■ *v.i.* нач|инать(ся), -ать(ся); **the meeting began** собрание началось; **he began as a reporter** он начинал репортёром; **to ~ with** во-первых.
beginner /bɪˈgɪnə(r)/ *n.* начинающий.
beginning /bɪˈgɪnɪŋ/ *n.* начало; **at the ~ of April** в начале (*or* в первых числах) апреля.
begonia /bɪˈgəʊnɪə/ *n.* бегония.
begrudge /bɪˈgrʌdʒ/ *v.t.* (*envy s.o. for having sth.*) завидовать, по- (*чему*); **I ~ him his success** я завидую его успехам; (*give resentfully*): **I ~ the time** мне жаль времени.
beguile /bɪˈgaɪl/ *v.t.* (*charm*) очаров|ывать, -ать.
begun /bɪˈgʌn/ *p.p. of* ▶ **begin**
behalf /bɪˈhɑːf/ *n.*: **on/in (*US*) my ~** (*as my representative*) от моего имени/лица; (*for my benefit*) в моих интересах, в мою пользу.
behave /bɪˈheɪv/ *v.i.* вести (*det.*) себя, держаться (*impf.*); **~ well, ~ o.s.** вести себя хорошо; **~ badly** плохо поступ|ать, -ить.
behaviour /bɪˈheɪvjə(r)/ (*US* **behavior**) *n.* поведение; отношение (*к кому*), обращение (*с кем*).
behead /bɪˈhed/ *v.t.* обезглав|ливать, -ить.
behind /bɪˈhaɪnd/ *n.* (*coll.*) зад, задница.
■ *adv.* сзади, позади; **he is ~ in his studies** он отстал в учёбе; **he is ~ with his payments** он запаздывает с уплатой.
■ *prep.* (*expr. place*) за + *i.*; (*expr. motion*) за + *a.*; (*more emphatic*) сзади, позади + *g.*; (*after*) после + *g.*; **he walked (just) ~ me** он шёл следом за мной.
behold /bɪˈhəʊld/ *v.t.* (*past and p.p.* **beheld**) (*arch.*) узреть (*pf.*); **lo and ~!** о чудо!
beige /beɪʒ/ *adj.* беж (*indecl.*).
Beijing /beɪˈdʒɪŋ/ *n.* Пекин.
being /ˈbiːɪŋ/ *n.*
[1] (*existence*) бытие, существование; **come into ~** возн|икать, -икнуть.
[2] (*creature, person*) существо; **human ~** человек.
Beirut /beɪˈruːt/ *n.* Бейрут.
Belarus /beləˈrʌs/ *n.* Беларусь.
belated /bɪˈleɪtɪd/ *adj.* запоздалый.
belch /beltʃ/ *n.* отрыжка.
■ *v.t.* (*smoke etc.*; *also* **~ forth, out**) выбрасывать, выбросить.
■ *v.i.* рыг|ать, -нуть.
beleaguer /bɪˈliːgə(r)/ *v.t.* оса|ждать, -дить.
belfry /ˈbelfrɪ/ *n.* колокольня.
Belgian /ˈbeldʒ(ə)n/ *n.* бельги|ец (*fem.* -йка).
■ *adj.* бельгийский.
Belgium /ˈbeldʒəm/ *n.* Бельгия.
Belgrade /belˈgreɪd/ *n.* Белград.
belief /bɪˈliːf/ *n.*
[1] (*trust*) вера (в + *a.*); доверие (к + *d.*).
[2] (*acceptance as true*; *thing believed*) вера, верование; **the ~s of the Christian church** догмы (*nt. pl.*) христианской церкви.
believe /bɪˈliːv/ *v.t.* верить, по- (*кому, во что*); думать (*impf.*); **I ~ so** думаю, что это так.
■ *v.i.* верить (*impf.*); (*esp. relig.*) веровать (*impf.*); **~ in God** верить (*impf.*) в Бога; **I ~ in taking exercise** я верю в пользу зарядки.
believer /bɪˈliːvə(r)/ *n.*
[1] (*relig.*) верующий.
[2] (*advocate*) сторонни|к (*fem.* -ца) + *g.*
belittle /bɪˈlɪt(ə)l/ *v.t.* преум|еньшать, -еньшить; умал|ять, -ить; **~ o.s.** уничижаться (*impf.*).
bell /bel/ *n.* колокол; (*smaller*) колокольчик; (*of door, telephone, bicycle etc.*) звонок; **ring the ~** звонить (*impf.*) в звонок/колокол; **that**

rings a ~ (*fig., coll.*) да, я что́-то припомина́ю.

bellicose /ˈbelɪkəʊz/ *adj.* вои́нственный.

belligerent /bɪˈlɪdʒərənt/ *adj.* (*aggressive*) вои́нственный.

bellow /ˈbeləʊ/ *v.i.*
1 (*of animal*) мыча́ть, про-; реве́ть (*impf.*).
2 (*shout*) ора́ть (*impf.*).

bellows /ˈbeləʊz/ *n.* мехи́ (*m. pl.*).

belly /ˈbelɪ/ *n.* живо́т, (*coll.*) брю́хо.
■ *cpd.* **~ button** *n.* (*coll.*) пупо́к.

belong /bɪˈlɒŋ/ *v.i.*
1 : **~ to** (*be the property of*) принадле́жать (*impf.*) + *d.*; (*be a member of*) состоя́ть (*impf.*) в + *p.*
2 (*of place*): **these books ~ here** э́ти кни́ги стоя́т здесь; э́ти кни́ги отсю́да.

belongings /bɪˈlɒŋɪŋz/ *n.* ве́щи (*f. pl.*) пожи́тк|и (*pl., g.* -ов).

Belorussia /beləʊˈrʌʃə/, **-n** /beləʊˈrʌʃ(ə)n/ = **Byelorussia, -n**

beloved /bɪˈlʌvɪd/ *n.* возлю́бленн|ый (*fem.* -ая).
■ *adj.* возлю́бленный, люби́мый.

below /bɪˈləʊ/ *adv.* (*of place*) внизу́; (*of motion*) вниз; (*in text etc.*) ни́же; **from ~** снизу.
■ *prep.* (*of place*) под + *i.*; (*of motion*) под + *a.*; (*lower, downstream*) ни́же + *g.*; **he is ~ average height** он ни́же сре́днего ро́ста.

belt /belt/ *n.*
1 (*of leather etc.*) реме́нь (*m.*); (*of cloth*) по́яс (*pl.* -á).
2 (*zone*) по́яс, полоса́; **green ~** зелёный по́яс, зелёная зо́на.
3 (*tech.*) (приводно́й) реме́нь.
■ *v.t.* 1 (*coll., thrash*) поро́ть, вы́-.
2 : **~ out a song** горла́нить (*impf.*) пе́сню.

bemuse /bɪˈmjuːz/ *v.t.* ошелом|ля́ть, -и́ть.

bench /bentʃ/ *n.*
1 (*seat*) скамья́, ла́вка.
2 (*work table*) верста́к, стано́к.
3 (*judges*) су́дьи (*m. pl.*), суде́йская колле́гия.
■ *cpd.* **~mark** *n.* этало́н, станда́рт; **~mark test** этало́нный тест.

bend /bend/ *n.* (*curve*) изги́б; (*in road*) поворо́т; (*in river*) излу́чина.
■ *v.t.* (*past and p.p.* **bent**) (*twist, incline*): **~ an iron bar** из|гиба́ть, -огну́ть желе́зный брус; **the axle is bent** ось погну́лась; **~ one's head over a book** склон|я́ться, -и́ться над кни́гой.
■ *v.i.*: **the trees bent in the wind** дере́вья гну́лись на ветру́; **~ at the knees** сгиба́ться, согну́ться в коле́нях; **~ forward** наклон|я́ться, -и́ться (вперёд).
■ *with advs.*: **~ down** *v.t.* наг|иба́ть, -ну́ть; сгиба́ть, согну́ть; преклон|я́ть, -и́ть; *v.i.* (*also* **~ over**) наг|иба́ться, -ну́ться; перег|иба́ться, -ну́ться.

beneath /bɪˈniːθ/ *adv.* внизу́.
■ *prep.* (*of place*) под + *i.*; (*of motion*) под + *a.*; (*lower than*) ни́же + *g.*; **it is ~ you to complain** жа́ловаться — недосто́йно вас.

benefactor /ˈbenɪfæktə(r)/ *n.* благотвори́тель (*m.*) (*fem.* -ница).

beneficial /benɪˈfɪʃ(ə)l/ *adj.* благотво́рный, поле́зный, вы́годный.

beneficiary /benɪˈfɪʃərɪ/ *n.* (*leg.*) бенефициа́р(ий) (*получатель денег/доходов от чего-л./кого-л.*).

benefit /ˈbenɪfɪt/ *n.*
1 (*advantage*) по́льза, вы́года, преиму́щество; **give s.o. the ~ of one's advice** помо́чь (*pf.*) кому́-н. сове́том; **I gave him the ~ of the doubt** я ему́ пове́рил (на э́тот раз).
2 (*grant*) посо́бие; **unemployment ~** посо́бие по безрабо́тице.
■ *v.t.* (**benefited, benefiting;** *US* **benefitted, benefitting**) прин|оси́ть, -ести́ по́льзу + *d.*, идти́ (*det.*) на по́льзу + *d.*
■ *v.i.* (**benefited, benefiting;** *US* **benefitted, benefitting**) извл|ека́ть, -е́чь по́льзу (из + *g.*).

benevolent /bəˈnevələnt/ *adj.* благожела́тельный.

benign /bɪˈnaɪn/ *adj.* (*of person*) добросерде́чный; (*med.*) доброка́чественный.

bent /bent/ *past and p.p. of* ▸ **bend**

bequest /bɪˈkwest/ *n.* (*object*) вещь, оста́вленная в насле́дство; (*as part of museum collection*) фонд, посме́ртный дар; (*act*) завеща́тельный отка́з иму́щества; **make a ~ of** завеща́ть (*impf., pf.*).

berate /bɪˈreɪt/ *v.t.* брани́ть (*impf.*).

bereave /bɪˈriːv/ *v.t.*: **a ~d husband** неда́вно овдове́вший муж; **the ~d** (*pl.*) ро́дственники поко́йного.

bereavement /bɪˈriːvmənt/ *n.* тяжёлая утра́та/поте́ря.

beret /ˈbereɪ/ *n.* бере́т.

Bering Sea /ˈberɪŋ/ *n.* Бе́рингово мо́ре.

Berlin /bəːˈlɪn/ *n.* Берли́н.

Bermuda /bəˈmjuːdə/ *n.*: (*also* **the ~s**) Берму́дские острова́ (*m. pl.*); **~ shorts** шо́рты-берму́ды.

berry /ˈberɪ/ *n.* я́года.

berserk /bəˈzəːk/ *n.*: **go ~** разъяри́ться (*pf.*), обезу́меть (*pf.*).

berth /bəːθ/ *n.*
1 (*place at wharf*) при́стань, прича́л.
2 : **give s.o. a wide ~** (*fig.*) обходи́ть (*impf.*) кого́-н. стороно́й (*or* за версту́).
3 (*sleeping-place on ship*) ко́йка; (*on train*) спа́льное ме́сто.
■ *v.t.* ста́вить (*impf.*) к прича́лу.
■ *v.i.* прича́ли|вать, -ть.

beseech /bɪˈsiːtʃ/ *v.t.* (*past and p.p.* **besought** /bɪˈsɔːt/ *or* **beseeched**) умол|я́ть, -и́ть; моли́ть (*impf.*).

beset /bɪˈset/ *v.t.* (**besetting;** *past and p.p.* **beset**) окруж|а́ть, -и́ть; оса|жда́ть, -ди́ть.

beside /bɪˈsaɪd/ *prep.*
1 (*alongside*) ря́дом с + *i.*; (*near*) о́коло + *g.*, у + *g.*
2 (*compared with*) по сравне́нию с + *i.*; пе́ред + *i.*; **~ him all novelists are insignificant** по сравне́нию с ним все романи́сты ничего́ не сто́ят.
3 : **~ o.s.** вне себя́.

besides /bɪˈsaɪdz/ *adv.* сверх того́; кро́ме того́.
■ *prep.* кро́ме + *g.*

besiege /bɪˈsiːdʒ/ *v.t.* оса|жда́ть, -ди́ть.

besotted /bɪˈsɒtɪd/ *adj.* одурма́ненный; во власти́ (**with:** + *g.*).

best /best/ *adj.* лу́чший; **we are the ~ of friends** мы бли́зкие друзья́; **at ~** в лу́чшем слу́чае; **do one's ~** сде́лать (*pf.*) всё возмо́жное; **all the ~!** всего́ наилу́чшего!; **hope for the ~** наде́яться (*impf.*) на лу́чшее; **~ man** (*at wedding*) ша́фер.
■ *adv.* лу́чше всего́; **I work ~ in the evening** мне лу́чше всего́ рабо́тается по вечера́м; **you know ~** вам лу́чше знать; **which town did you like ~?** како́й го́род вам бо́льше всего́ понра́вился?
■ *v.t.* брать, взять верх над + *i.*
■ *cpds.* **~-seller** *n.* (*book*) бестсе́ллер; (*Br., author*) а́втор бестсе́ллера; **~-selling** *adj.* ходово́й.

bestow /bɪ'stəʊ/ *v.t.*: **~ a title on s.o.** присв|а́ивать, -о́ить кому́-н. ти́тул.

bet /bet/ *n.* пари́ (*nt. indecl.*), ста́вка.
■ *v.t.* & *i.* (**betting;** *past and p.p.* **bet** *or* **betted**) держа́ть (*impf.*) пари́; **he ~ £5 on a horse** он поста́вил 5 фу́нтов на ло́шадь; **he ~ me £10 I wouldn't do it** он поспо́рил со мной на 10 фу́нтов, что я не сде́лаю э́того.

betray /bɪ'treɪ/ *v.t.* измен|я́ть, -и́ть + *d.*; пред|ава́ть, -а́ть.

betrayal /bɪ'treɪəl/ *n.* преда́тельство, изме́на.

better /'betə(r)/ *adj.* лу́чший, лу́чше; **all the ~** тем лу́чше; **get ~** ул|учша́ться, -у́чшиться; (*in health*) попр|авля́ться, -а́виться; **things are getting ~** дела́ иду́т лу́чше; **get the ~ of s.o.** взять (*pf.*) верх над кем-н.; превзойти́ (*pf.*) кого́-н.
■ *adv.* лу́чше; (*more*) бо́льше; **you had ~ stay here** вам бы лу́чше оста́ться здесь; **I thought ~ of it** я разду́мал/переду́мал; **~ off** бо́лее состоя́тельный.
■ *v.t.* (*improve on*) превзойти́ (*pf.*).

betting /'betɪŋ/ *adj.*: **~ shop** (*Br.*) букме́керскаяконто́ра.

between /bɪ'twi:n/ *adv.*: **I attended the two lectures and had lunch in ~** я посети́л две ле́кции и пообе́дал в переры́ве.
■ *prep.* ме́жду + *i.*; **~ you and me** ме́жду на́ми; **~ two and three months** от двух до трёх ме́сяцев; **choose ~ the two** выбира́ть, вы́брать одно́ из двух; **we bought a car ~ us** мы сообща́ купи́ли маши́ну.

beverage /'bevərɪdʒ/ *n.* напи́ток.

bevy /'bevɪ/ *n.* (*of people*) гру́ппа; (*of birds*) ста́я.

beware /bɪ'weə(r)/ *v.t.* & *i.* остер|ега́ться, -е́чься (*impf.*) + *g.*; **~ of the dog** осторо́жно, зла́я соба́ка.

bewilder /bɪ'wɪldə(r)/ *v.t.* сби|ва́ть, -ть с то́лку; прив|оди́ть, -ести́ в замеша́тельство; **~ed** смущённый, озада́ченный.

bewilderment /bɪ'wɪldəmənt/ *n.* замеша́тельство, озада́ченность.

bewitch /bɪ'wɪtʃ/ *v.t.* околдо́в|ывать, -а́ть.

beyond /bɪ'jɒnd/ *n.*: **he lives at the back of ~** он живёт на краю́ све́та.
■ *adv.* вдали́; вдаль.
■ *prep.* (*of place*) за + *i.*; (*of motion*) за + *a.*; (*later than*) по́сле + *g.*; **~ dispute** бесспо́рно; **~ belief** невероя́тно; **live ~ one's income** жить (*impf.*) не по сре́дствам.

biannual /baɪ'ænjʊəl/ *adj.* выходя́щий два́жды в год; полугодово́й.

bias /'baɪəs/ *n.* предрассу́док, предвзя́тое отноше́ние (*к чему*).
■ *v.t.* (**biased, biasing; biassed, biassing**) (*influence*) склон|я́ть, -и́ть; (*prejudice*) предубе|жда́ть, -ди́ть; **a ~(s)ed opinion** предвзя́тое мне́ние.

bib /bɪb/ *n.* (де́тский) нагру́дник.

Bible /'baɪb(ə)l/ *n.* Би́блия; (*fig.*) би́блия.

biblical /'bɪblɪk(ə)l/ *adj.* библе́йский.

bibliographer /bɪblɪ'ɒgrəfə(r)/ *n.* библио́граф.

bibliographic(al) /bɪblɪə'græfɪk, bɪblɪə'græfɪk(ə)l/ *adj.* библиографи́ческий.

bibliography /bɪblɪ'ɒgrəfɪ/ *n.* библиогра́фия.

bicentenary /baɪsen'ti:nərɪ/ *n.* двухсотле́тие.

bicentennial /baɪsen'tenɪəl/ *n.* двухсотле́тие.

biceps /'baɪseps/ *n.* (*pl.* **~**) би́цепс.

bicker /'bɪkə(r)/ *v.t.* (*squabble*) перебра́ниваться (*impf.*), препира́ться (*impf.*).

bicycle /'baɪsɪk(ə)l/ *n.* велосипе́д.

bid /bɪd/ *n.*
1 (*at auction*) зая́вка; предложе́ние цены́.
2 (*tender*) зая́вка.
3 (*attempt*) ста́вка; попы́тка; **make a ~ for power** сде́лать (*pf.*) ста́вку на захва́т вла́сти.
■ *v.t.* & *i.* (**bidding;** *past* **bid;** *p.p.* **bid**)
1 (*at auction*) предл|ага́ть, -ожи́ть це́ну (*за что*); **~ against s.o.** наб|авля́ть, -а́вить це́ну про́тив кого́-н.
2 (*tender*): **~ for a contract** де́лать, с- зая́вку на контра́кт.

bidder /'bɪdə(r)/ *n.* (*at auction*) аукционе́р; **the highest ~** предложи́вший наивы́сшую це́ну.

bide /baɪd/ *v.t.*: **~ one's time** ждать (*impf.*) благоприя́тного слу́чая.

bidet /'bi:deɪ/ *n.* биде́ (*nt. indecl.*).

biennial /baɪ'enɪəl/ *n.* (*bot.*) двуле́тник.
■ *adj.* двухле́тний.

bifocal /baɪ'fəʊk(ə)l/ *adj.*: **~ spectacles** (*also* **~s**) бифока́льные очки́.

big /bɪg/ *adj.* (**bigger, biggest**) (*in size*) большо́й, кру́пный; (*great*) кру́пный, вели́кий; (*magnanimous*) великоду́шный; (*important*) ва́жный; **a ~ man** (*in stature*) кру́пный мужчи́на; (*in importance*) кру́пная фигу́ра; **as ~ as** величино́й в + *a.*; **think ~** мы́слить (*impf.*) сме́ло/де́рзко; **a ~ noise** (*person*) ши́шка (*coll.*); **my ~ brother** мой ста́рший брат; **a ~ name** (*celebrity*) знамени́тость.
■ *cpd.* **~-headed** *adj.* (*conceited*) зазна́вшийся; возомни́вший о себе́.

bigamy /'bɪgəmɪ/ *n.* бига́мия; (*of man*) двоежёнство; (*of woman*) двоему́жие.

bigoted /'bɪgətɪd/ *adj.* фанати́ческий, фанати́чный.

bike /baɪk/ *n.*
1 (*coll.*) = **bicycle.**
2 (*motorcycle*) мотоци́кл.
■ *v.i.* е́здить (*indet.*) на мотоци́кле.

biker /'baɪkə(r)/ *n.* мотоцикли́ст (*fem.* -ка); (*member of a gang*) ба́йкер.

bikini /bɪ'ki:nɪ/ *n.* бики́ни (*nt. indecl.*).

bilateral /baɪ'lætər(ə)l/ *adj.* двусторо́нний.

bilberry /'bɪlbərɪ/ *n.* черни́ка (*collect.*); (*single*

berry) я́года черни́ки.
bilingual /baɪ'lɪŋgw(ə)l/ *adj.* двуязы́чный.
bill¹ /bɪl/ *n.* (*beak*) клюв.
bill² /bɪl/ *n.*
1 (*comm.*) счёт (*pl.* -á).
2 (*parl.*) законопрое́кт, билль (*m.*).
3 (*advertisement*): **theatre ~** театра́льная афи́ша.
4 (*US, banknote*) банкно́та; **dollar ~** до́лларовая банкно́та.
■ *cpd.* **~board** *n.* доска́ объявле́ний.
billet /'bɪlɪt/ *v.t.* (**billeted, billeting**) (*assign to* **~**) расквартиро́в|ывать, -а́ть; назн|ача́ть, -а́чить (*or* ста́вить, по-) на посто́й (**on s.o.:** к кому́-н.).
billiards /'bɪljədz/ *n.* билья́рд.
billion /'bɪljən/ *n.* (*pl.* **~s** *or* (*with numeral or qualifying word*) **~**) (*thousand million*) миллиа́рд.
billionaire /bɪljə'neə(r)/ *n.* миллиарде́р.
billow /'bɪləʊ/ *v.i.* (*of smoke*) вздыма́ться (*impf.*); (*of fabric*) над|ува́ться, -у́ться.
bin /bɪn/ *n.* (*Br.*) му́сорное ведро́.
binary /'baɪnərɪ/ *adj.* (*math.*) двои́чный.
bind /baɪnd/ *v.t.* (*past and p.p.* **bound**)
1 (*tie, fasten*) свя́з|ывать, -а́ть; **~ together** свя́з|ывать, -а́ть.
2 (*books etc.*) перепле|та́ть, -сти́.
3 (*oblige, exact promise*) обя́з|ывать, -а́ть; **I am bound to say** я до́лжен сказа́ть.
binder /'baɪndə(r)/ *n.* па́пка.
binding /'baɪndɪŋ/ *n.* переплёт.
■ *adj.* обя́зывающий; име́ющий обяза́тельную си́лу.
binge /bɪndʒ/ *n.* (*coll.*) пья́нка; **go on the ~** закути́ть, запи́ть (*both pf.*).
■ *cpd.* **~ drinking** *n.* попо́йка, пья́нка.
bingo /'bɪŋgəʊ/ *n.* лото́ (*indecl.*).
binoculars /bɪ'nɒkjʊləz/ *n.* бино́кль (*m.*).
biochemist /baɪəʊ'kemɪst/ *n.* биохи́мик.
biochemistry /baɪəʊ'kemɪstrɪ/ *n.* биохи́мия.
biodegradable /baɪəʊdɪ'greɪdəb(ə)l/ *adj.* подве́рженный биологи́ческому разложе́нию.
biodiversity /baɪəʊdaɪ'və:sɪtɪ/ *n.* биологи́ческое разнообра́зие.
bioengineering /baɪəʊendʒɪ'nɪərɪŋ/ *n.* биоинжене́рия.
biographer /baɪ'ɒgrəfə(r)/ *n.* био́граф.
biographical /baɪə'græfɪk(ə)l/ *adj.* биографи́ческий.
biography /baɪ'ɒgrəfɪ/ *n.* биогра́фия.
biological /baɪə'lɒdʒɪk(ə)l/ *adj.* биологи́ческий; **~ clock** биологи́ческие часы́; **~ warfare** бактериологи́ческая война́.
biologist /baɪ'ɒlədʒɪst/ *n.* био́лог.
biology /baɪ'ɒlədʒɪ/ *n.* биоло́гия.
biopsy /'baɪɒpsɪ/ *n.* биопси́я.
biotechnology /baɪəʊtek'nɒlədʒɪ/ *n.* биотехноло́гия.
bioterrorism /baɪəʊ'terərɪz(ə)m/ *n.* биотерroríзм.
bioweapon /'baɪəʊwep(ə)n/ *n.* биологи́ческое ору́жие.
bipartisan /baɪpɑ:tɪ'zæn/ *adj.* двухпарти́йный.
bipartite /baɪ'pɑ:taɪt/ *adj.* (*divided into two parts*) состоя́щий из двух часте́й; (*shared by two parties*) двусторо́нний.
birch /bə:tʃ/ *n.* берёза.
bird /bə:d/ *n.* пти́ца; **~ of prey** хи́щная пти́ца; **~'s-eye view** вид с высоты́ пти́чьего полёта; о́бщая перспекти́ва.
■ *cpds.* **~ flu** *n.* пти́чий грипп; **~watcher** *n.* орнито́лог-люби́тель (*m.*).
biro /'baɪərəʊ/ *n.* (*pl.* **~s**) (*Br. propr.*) ша́риковая ру́чка.
birth /bə:θ/ *n.*
1 (*being born*) рожде́ние; (*giving birth*) ро́ды (*pl.*); **~ certificate** свиде́тельство о рожде́нии; **~ control** регули́рование рожда́емости; (*contraception*) противозача́точные ме́ры (*f. pl.*).
2 (*descent*): **an Englishman by ~** англича́нин по происхожде́нию.
■ *cpds.* **~day** *n.* день рожде́ния; рожде́ние; **~mark** *n.* роди́мое пятно́; **~place** *n.* ме́сто рожде́ния; ро́дина; **~ rate** *n.* рожда́емость.
biscuit /'bɪskɪt/ *n.* (*Br.*) пече́нье; (*US*) ≈ бу́лочка.
bisect /baɪ'sekt/ *v.t.* дели́ть, раз- попола́м.
bisexual /baɪ'seksjʊəl/ *adj.* бисексуа́льный.
bishop /'bɪʃəp/ *n.* (*eccl.*) епи́скоп; (*chess*) слон.
bison /'baɪs(ə)n/ *n.* (*pl.* **~**) бизо́н.
bistro /'bi:strəʊ/ *n.* (*pl.* **~s**) бистро́ (*nt. indecl.*).
bit¹ /bɪt/ *n.*
1 кусо́к, кусо́чек; **a ~ of paper** листо́к бума́ги.
2 (*abstr. uses*): **a ~ of news** но́вость; **a ~ of advice** сове́т; **I am a ~ late** я немно́го опозда́л; **~ by ~** ма́ло-пома́лу; **a ~ of a coward** трусова́тый.
bit² /bɪt/ *n.* (*comput.*) бит.
bit³ /bɪt/ *n.* (*of bridle*) уд|ила́ (*pl., g.* -и́л).
bit⁴ /bɪt/ *past of* ▶ **bite**
bitch /bɪtʃ/ *n.*
1 (*of dog*) су́ка.
2 (*coll., spiteful woman*) су́ка (*vulg.*); стерва (*sl.*).
bitchy /'bɪtʃɪ/ *adj.* (**bitchier, bitchiest**) (*coll.*) стервóзный.
bite /baɪt/ *n.*
1 (*act of biting*) куса́ние.
2 (*mouthful*): **I haven't had a ~ to eat** у меня́ куска́ во рту́ не́ было.
3 (*wound caused by biting*) уку́с.
■ *v.t.* (*past* **bit;** *p.p.* **bitten**)
1 куса́ть, укуси́ть.
2 (*fig.*): **~ s.o.'s head off** откуси́ть (*pf.*) кому́-н. го́лову.
■ *v.i.* (*past* **bit;** *p.p.* **bitten**): **does your dog ~?** ва́ша соба́ка куса́ется?; **the fish won't ~** ры́ба не клюёт.
biting /'baɪtɪŋ/ *adj.* (*of wind*) ре́зкий; (*of satire*) е́дкий, язви́тельный.
bitten /'bɪt(ə)n/ *p.p. of* ▶ **bite**
bitter /'bɪtə(r)/ *adj.* (*lit., fig.*) го́рький; **a ~ wind** ре́зкий ве́тер; **~ enemy** зле́йший/закля́тый враг; **to the ~ end** до са́мого конца́.
bivouac /'bɪvʊæk/ *n.* откры́тый ла́герь (*без пала́ток и те́нтов*), бива́к.
■ *v.i.* (**bivouacked, bivouacking**) распол|ага́ться, -ожи́ться откры́тым ла́герем,

бива́ком.

bizarre /bɪ'zɑ:(r)/ *adj.* чудно́й; (*behaviour*) чудакова́тый.

black /blæk/ *n.*
1 (*colour*) чернота́, чёрное; **be in the ~** не име́ть долго́в.
2 (*person*) чернoко́жий.
■ *adj.* 1 (*colour*) чёрный; **a ~ eye** подби́тый глаз.
2 (*person*) чернoко́жий.
3 (*var.*): **~ and white** чёрно-бе́лый; **in ~ and white** (*in writing*) чёрным по бе́лому; **~ ice** гололе́дица; **~ market** чёрный ры́нок; **B~ Sea** Чёрное мо́ре.
■ *v.i.*: **~ out** (*lose consciousness*) теря́ть, по- созна́ние.
■ *cpds.* **~berry** *n.* ежеви́ка (*collect*); я́года ежеви́ки; **~bird** *n.* чёрный дрозд; **~board** *n.* кла́ссная доска́; **~currant** *n.* чёрная сморо́дина; **~head** *n.* у́горь (*m.*); **~mail** *n.* шанта́ж, вымога́тельство; *v.t.* шантажи́ровать (*impf.*); **~mailer** *n.* шантажи́ст, вымога́тель (*m.*); **~out** *n.* (*in wartime*) затемне́ние; (*electricity failure*) авари́йное отключе́ние электроэне́ргии; (*loss of consciousness*) поте́ря созна́ния; **~smith** *n.* кузне́ц; **~ tie** *n.* (*bow tie*) чёрный га́лстук-ба́бочка; (*evening dress*) стро́гий вече́рний костю́м.

blacken /'blækən/ *v.t.* (*reputation*) черни́ть, о-.

bladder /'blædə(r)/ *n.* пузы́рь (*m.*).

blade /bleɪd/ *n.*
1 (*of knife etc.*) ле́звие.
2 (*of oar etc.*) ло́пасть, лопа́тка.
3 (*of grass etc.*) были́нка, стебелёк.

blame /bleɪm/ *n.* (*censure*) порица́ние; осужде́ние; (*fault*) вина́.
■ *v.t.* порица́ть (*impf.*); вини́ть (*impf.*); осу|жда́ть, -ди́ть (*кого за что*); **he was ~d for the mistake** вину́ за оши́бку возложи́ли на него́; **he is entirely to ~** э́то по́лностью его́ вина́; **~ sth. on s.o.** взва́л|ивать, -и́ть вину́ за что-н. на кого́-н.

blameless /'bleɪmlɪs/ *adj.* безупре́чный; неви́нный.

bland /blænd/ *adj.* (*mild*) мя́гкий; (*insipid*) пре́сный.

blank /blæŋk/ *n.* про́пуск; **my mind is a ~ on this subject** у меня́ э́то вы́летело из головы́.
■ *adj.* 1 (*empty*): **a ~ sheet of paper** чи́стый лист бума́ги; **a ~ cheque** незапо́лненный чек; (*fig.*) карт-бла́нш.
2 (*fig.*): **look ~** (*of person*) вы́глядеть (*impf.*) расте́рянным.

blanket /'blæŋkɪt/ *n.* одея́ло; (*horse-cloth*) попо́на; **the hills lay under a ~ of snow** холмы́ бы́ли покры́ты сло́ем сне́га.

blankly /'blæŋklɪ/ *adv.* бессмы́сленно, ту́по.

blare /bleə(r)/ *v.t.*: **~ out** труби́ть, про-.
■ *v.i.* труби́ть, про-; реве́ть (*impf.*).

blaspheme /blæs'fi:m/ *v.t.* (*revile*) поноси́ть (*impf.*), хули́ть (*impf.*).
■ *v.i.* богоху́льствовать (*impf.*), богоху́льничать (*impf.*).

blasphemous /'blæsfiməs/ *adj.* богоху́льный.

blasphemy /'blæsfəmɪ/ *n.* богоху́льство.

blast /blɑ:st/ *n.*
1 : **~ of wind** поры́в ве́тра.
2 (*from explosion*) взрыв.
3 : **at full ~** (*fig.*) в по́лном разга́ре; по́лным хо́дом.
■ *v.t.* взр|ыва́ть, -орва́ть.
■ *v.i.*: **~ off** (*rocketry*) взлет|а́ть, -е́ть; стартова́ть (*impf., pf.*).
■ *cpd.* **~-off** *n.* взлёт; моме́нт ста́рта.

blatant /'bleɪt(ə)nt/ *adj.* (*flagrant*) я́вный, вопию́щий.

blaz|e[1] /bleɪz/ *n.*
1 (*of fire*) пла́мя (*nt.*).
2 (*fig.*): **~e of publicity** шу́мная рекла́ма.
■ *v.i.*: **a fire was ~ing in the hearth** в ками́не пыла́л ого́нь; **the building was ~ing** зда́ние полыха́ло.
■ *with advs.*: **~e up** *v.i.* (*lit., fig.*) всп|ы́хивать, -ы́хнуть.

blaze[2] /bleɪz/ *v.t.*: **~ a trail** про|кла́дывать, -ложи́ть путь.

blazer /'bleɪzə(r)/ *n.* ≈ ку́ртка, (клу́бный/шко́льный) пиджа́к, бле́йзер.

bleach /bli:tʃ/ *n.* отбе́ливатель (*m.*).
■ *v.t.* бели́ть (*impf.*); отбе́л|ивать, -и́ть; (*hair*) обесцве́|чивать, -тить.
■ *v.i.* беле́ть (*impf.*).

bleak /bli:k/ *adj.* уны́лый, безра́достный; (*gloomy*) мра́чный.

bleary-eyed /blɪə(r)/ *adj.* с затума́ненными/му́тными глаза́ми.

bleat /bli:t/ *v.t.* & *i.* мыча́ть (*impf.*), бле́ять (*impf.*).

bleed /bli:d/ *v.t.* (*past and p.p.* **bled** /bled/): **~ s.o.** (*for money*) об|ира́ть, -обра́ть кого́-н.
■ *v.i.* (*past and p.p.* **bled** /bled/) (*of person*) ист|ека́ть, -е́чь кро́вью; (*of wound*) кровоточи́ть (*impf.*); **his nose is ~ing** у него́ но́сом идёт кровь.

bleep /bli:p/ *n.* сигна́л.
■ *v.i.* сигна́лить, про-.
■ *v.t.* (*summon*) вызыва́ть, вы́звать сигна́лом.

bleeper /'bli:pə(r)/ *n.* (*Br.*) пе́йджер.

blemish /'blemɪʃ/ *n.* недоста́ток, изъя́н.

blend /blend/ *n.* смесь.
■ *v.t.* сме́ш|ивать, -а́ть; (*colours, ideas*) сочета́ть (*impf.*).
■ *v.i.* сме́ш|иваться, -а́ться; (*of colours, ideas*) сочета́ться (*impf.*); гармони́ровать (*impf.*).

blender /'blendə(r)/ *n.* (*cul.*) смеси́тель (*m.*), ми́ксер, бле́ндер.

bless /bles/ *v.t.* (*past and p.p.* **blessed**)
1 (*relig.*) благослов|ля́ть, -и́ть; **~ you!** дай вам Бог здоро́вья; (*after sneeze*) бу́дьте здоро́вы!
2 (*prosper, favour*): **he was ~ed with good health** Бог награди́л его́ здоро́вьем.

blessing /'blesɪŋ/ *n.*
1 благослове́ние.
2 : **it is a ~ in disguise** ≈ не́ было бы сча́стья, да несча́стье помогло́!

blew /blu:/ *past of* ▶ **blow**[1]

blight /blaɪt/ *n.* головня́.
■ *v.t.*: **~ s.o.'s hopes** разр|уша́ть, -у́шить чьи-н. наде́жды.

blind /blaɪnd/ *n.* што́ра, ста́вень (*m.*); **Venetian ~** жалюзи́ (*nt. indecl.*).
■ *adj.* 1 слепо́й; **the ~** (*as n.*) слепы́е,

слепцы́ (*m. pl.*); **go ~** сле́пнуть, о-; **a ~ spot** слепо́е пятно́; (*fig.*) пробе́л; **turn a ~ eye to sth.** закр|ыва́ть, -ы́ть глаза́ на что-н.
2 (*concealed*): **a ~ corner** непросма́тривающийся, закры́тый поворо́т; **a blind spot** (*on the road*) мёртвая зо́на; **a ~ date** (*coll.*) свида́ние с незнако́мым/незнако́мой.
3 (*closed up*): **a ~ alley** (*lit., fig.*) тупи́к.
■ *v.t.* ослеп|ля́ть, -и́ть (*also fig.*); (*temporarily*) слепи́ть (*impf.*).
■ *cpd.* **~fold** *adv.* с завя́занными глаза́ми; *v.t.* завя́з|ывать, -а́ть глаза́ + *d.*

blindly /'blaɪndlɪ/ *adv.* (*gropingly*) на о́щупь; (*recklessly*) сле́по.

blindness /'blaɪndnɪs/ *n.* слепота́; (*fig.*) слепота́, ослепле́ние.

bling(-bling) /blɪŋ('blɪŋ)/ *n.* (*coll.*) (*clothing*) гламу́рная оде́жда; (*jewellery*) ца́цки (*f. pl.*) (*sl.*), побряку́шки (*f. pl.*) (*coll.*); ((*containing*) *diamonds*) брю́лики (*m. pl.*) (*coll.*).

blink /blɪŋk/ *n.* морга́ние, мига́ние.
■ *v.t.* & *i.* (*of person*) миг|а́ть, -ну́ть; морг|а́ть, -ну́ть; (*of light*) мерца́ть (*impf.*).

blinkers /'blɪŋkəz/ *n.* (*Br.*) шо́р|ы (*pl., g.* —); нагла́зники (*m. pl.*).

blip /blɪp/ *n.* (*on screen*) отражённый и́мпульс.

bliss /blɪs/ *n.* блаже́нство.

blissful /'blɪsfʊl/ *adj.* блаже́нный.

blister /'blɪstə(r)/ *n.* волды́рь (*m.*).
■ *v.i.* покр|ыва́ться, -ы́ться волдыря́ми/пузыря́ми.

blithe(some) /'blaɪð(səm)/ *adj.* жизнера́достный, беспе́чный.

blitz /blɪts/ *n.* бомбёжка.
■ *v.t.* разбомби́ть (*pf.*).

blizzard /'blɪzəd/ *n.* бура́н, вью́га.

bloated /'bləʊtɪd/ *adj.* разду́тый, разду́вшийся.

blob /blɒb/ *n.* (*small mass*) ка́пля; ша́рик; (*spot of colour*) кля́кса.

block /blɒk/ *n.*
1 (*of wood*) чурба́н, коло́да; (*of stone, marble*) глы́ба.
2 (*for execution*) пла́ха.
3 (*of houses*) кварта́л; **~ of flats** (*Br.*) многокварти́рный дом.
4 (*typ.*): **~ capitals** печа́тные бу́квы.
■ *v.t.* (*obstruct physically*): **roads ~ed by snow** доро́ги, занесённые сне́гом; **the sink is ~ed** ра́ковина засори́лась.
■ *cpd.* **~buster** *n.* (*coll.*) блокба́стер, ка́ссовый фильм.

blockade /blɒ'keɪd/ *n.* блока́да.
■ *v.t.* блоки́ровать (*impf., pf.*).

blog /blɒg/ *n.* = **weblog**

blogger /'blɒgə(r)/ *n.* = **weblogger**

bloke /bləʊk/ *n.* (*Br. coll.*) тип; па́рень (*m.*).

blond(e) /blɒnd/ *n.* блонди́н (*fem.* -ка).
■ *adj.* белоку́рый, све́тлый.

blood /blʌd/ *n.*
1 кровь.
2 (*attr.*): **~ bank** до́норский пункт; **~ donor** до́нор; **~ group** гру́ппа кро́ви; **~ test** ана́лиз кро́ви; (*for paternity*) иссле́дование кро́ви.
3 (*var. fig. uses*): **in cold ~** хладнокро́вно; **we need new ~** нам нужны́ но́вые си́лы.
■ *cpds.* **~ pressure** *n.* кровяно́е давле́ние; **~shed** *n.* кровопроли́тие; **~shot** *adj.* на́литый кро́вью; **~stained** *adj.* запа́чканный кро́вью; **~stream** *n.* ток кро́ви; **~thirsty** *adj.* кровожа́дный.

bloody /'blʌdɪ/ *adj.* (**bloodier, bloodiest**)
1 крова́вый.
2 (*Br., expletive*): **a ~ liar** отча́янный лгун.
■ *adv.* (*sl.*): **~ awful** черто́вский; скве́рный, дрянно́й.

bloom /blu:m/ *n.* (*single flower*) цвето́к; **in ~** в цвету́.
■ *v.i.* цвести́ (*impf.*); (*come into ~*) расцве|та́ть, -сти́.

blossom /'blɒsəm/ *n.* цвет, цвете́ние.
■ *v.i.* цвести́ (*impf.*).

blot /blɒt/ *n.* (*on paper*) кля́кса; (*blemish*) пятно́.
■ *v.t.* & *i.* (**blotted, blotting**) (*smudge*) па́чкать, за-; ста́вить, по- кля́ксу.
■ *with adv.*: **~ out** *v.t.* (*from one's memory*) изгла́|живать, -дить (*or* ст|ира́ть, -ере́ть) из па́мяти.

blotchy /'blɒtʃɪ/ *adj.* (**blotchier, blotchiest**) в пя́тнах.

blouse /blaʊz/ *n.* ко́фточка, блу́зка.

blow[1] /bləʊ/ *v.t.* (*past* **blew;** *p.p.* **blown**)
1 дуть, ду́нуть; **~ a whistle** свисте́ть, за- в свисто́к; дава́ть, дать свисто́к; **~ one's nose** сморка́ться, вы́-.
2 (*of wind*): **the wind blew the papers out of my hand** ве́тер вы́рвал бума́ги у меня́ из рук.
3 (*elec.*): **~ a fuse** переж|ига́ть, -е́чь про́бку.
■ *v.i.* (*past* **blew;** *p.p.* **blown**)
1 (*of wind or person*) дуть, по-, ду́нуть.
2 (*of thing*): **the door blew open** дверь распахну́лась; **the fuse blew** про́бка перегоре́ла.
■ *with advs.*: **~ away** *v.t.* & *i.* ун|оси́ть(ся), -ести́(сь); **~ down** *v.t.* вали́ть, по-; *v.i.*: **the tree blew down** бу́ря повали́ла де́рево; **~ out** *v.t.*: **he blew the candle out** он заду́л свечу́; **~ over** *v.i.*: **the storm blew over** бу́ря ути́хла; **~ up** *v.t.*: **~ up a bridge** взрыва́ть, взорва́ть мост; **~ up a tyre** нака́ч|ивать, -а́ть ши́ну/колесо́; **~ up a photograph** увели́чи|вать, -ть фотогра́фию; *v.i.*: **the mine blew up** ми́на взорвала́сь.
■ *cpds.* **~out** *n.* (*of tyre*) разры́в; (*coll., feast*) оби́льное засто́лье, кутёж; **~torch** *n.* пая́льная ла́мпа.

blow[2] /bləʊ/ *n.* уда́р.

blub /blʌb/ *v.i.* (**blubbed, blubbing**) (*coll.*) реве́ть (*impf.*).

blubber[1] /'blʌbə(r)/ *n.* (*whale fat*) во́рвань.

blubber[2] /'blʌbə(r)/ *v.t.* & *i.* реве́ть (*impf.*), рыда́ть (*impf.*).

bludgeon /'blʌdʒ(ə)n/ *v.t.* бить (*impf.*) дуби́нкой; (*fig.*) принужда́ть (*impf.*).

blue /blu:/ *n.*
1 (*colour*) синева́, голубизна́.
2 (*sky*): **out of the ~** (*fig.*) ни с того́ ни с сего́; **he arrived out of the ~** он нагря́нул неожи́данно.
3 : **the ~s** (*coll.*) тоска́, уны́ние, хандра́.
4 : **~s** (*mus.*) блюз.
■ *adj.* (**bluer, bluest**)
1 (*colour*) (*dark*) си́ний; (*light*) голубо́й.

2 (*coll., sad*): **feel ~** хандри́ть (*impf.*).
3 (*coll., obscene*) неприли́чный, непристо́йный.
■ *cpds.* **~bell** *n.* ди́кий/лесно́й гиаци́нт; **~-collar worker** *n.* произво́дственный рабо́чий; **~print** *n.* (*phot.*) светоко́пия, си́нька; (*fig.*) план.

Bluetooth /ˈbluːtuːθ/ *n.* (*propr.*) Bluetooth, блюту́с (*устройство для передачи информации на небольшое расстояние без проводов*).

bluff /blʌf/ *n.* **call s.o.'s ~** заст|авля́ть, -а́вить кого́-н. раскры́ть ка́рты.
■ *v.t. & i.* блефова́ть (*impf.*); втира́ть (*impf.*) очки́ + *d.*

bluish /ˈbluːɪʃ/ *adj.* (*dark*) синева́тый; (*light*) голубова́тый.

blunder /ˈblʌndə(r)/ *n.* оши́бка, оплошность.
■ *v.i.* блужда́ть (*impf.*); (*grope*) пробира́ться/ дви́гаться (*impf.*) о́щупью; **~ into a table** нат|ыка́ться, -кну́ться на стол.

blunt /blʌnt/ *adj.* (*not sharp*) тупо́й; (*plain-spoken*) прямо́й.
■ *v.t.* тупи́ть (*impf.*).

blur /blɜː(r)/ *n.* ды́мка.
■ *v.t.* (**blurred, blurring**) сма́з|ывать, -ать.

blurb /blɜːb/ *n.* (*coll.*) (изда́тельская) аннота́ция.

blurt /blɜːt/ *v.t.*: **~ out** выпа́ливать, вы́палить.

blush /blʌʃ/ *v.i.* красне́ть, по-.

blusher /ˈblʌʃə(r)/ *n.* (*cosmetic*) румя́на.

bluster /ˈblʌstə(r)/ *n.* (*of storm*) рёв; (*of person*) гро́мкие слова́, угро́зы (*f. pl.*).
■ *v.i.* (*of storm*) реве́ть (*impf.*); (*of person*) расшуме́ться (*pf.*), разбушева́ться (*pf.*).

BO (*abbr. of* ***body odour***) за́пах по́та.

boar /bɔː(r)/ *n.* каба́н.

board /bɔːd/ *n.*
1 (*piece of wood*) доска́ (*also for chess etc.*); **~ game** насто́льная игра́.
2 (*food*) стол; **~ and lodging, bed and ~** пита́ние и прожива́ние; ночле́г и пита́ние.
3 (*table*): **above ~** (*fig.*) в откры́тую, че́стно.
4 (*council*) правле́ние; **~ of directors** правле́ние директоро́в.
5 (*naut. etc.*): **on ~** на борту́.
■ *v.t.* 1 (*cover with ~s; also* **~ up**) обш|ива́ть, -и́ть (*or* покр|ыва́ть, -ы́ть) доска́ми.
2 : **~ a ship** (*go on ~*) сади́ться, сесть на кора́бль.
■ *cpd.* **~room** *n.* зал заседа́ний сове́та директоро́в.

boarder /ˈbɔːdə(r)/ *n.* (*lodger*) жиле́ц, постоя́лец; (*at school*) учени́|к (*fem.* -ца), живу́щ|ий (*fem.* -ая) в шко́ле-интерна́те.

boarding /ˈbɔːdɪŋ/ *n.* (*naut.*) аборда́ж; (*aeron.*) поса́дка.
■ *cpds.* **~ card, ~ pass** *nn.* поса́дочный биле́т; **~ school** *n.* шко́ла-интерна́т.

boast /bəʊst/ *n.* хвастовство́.
■ *v.t. & i.* (**~** *of*) хва́стать(ся), по- + *i.*; хвали́ться, по- + *i.*

boastful /ˈbəʊstfʊl/ *adj.* хвастли́вый.

boat /bəʊt/ *n.* (*small, rowing* **~**) ло́дка, шлю́пка; (*vessel*) су́дно; (*large* **~**) кора́бль (*m.*), парохо́д; **in the same ~** (*fig.*) в одина́ковом положе́нии.
■ *v.i.* (*go* **~***ing*) ката́ться (*indet.*) на ло́дке.
■ *cpd.* **~house** *n.* сара́й для ло́док.

boater /ˈbəʊtə(r)/ *n.* соло́менная шля́па.

bob¹ /bɒb/ *n.* (*hair-style*) коро́ткая стри́жка.

bob² /bɒb/*v.i.* (**bobbed, bobbing**) (*move up and down*) подпры́г|ивать, -нуть; подск|а́кивать, -очи́ть.

bobsled /ˈbɒbsled/ (*US*), **bobsleigh** /ˈbɒbsleɪ/ (*Br.*) *nn.* бобсле́й.

bode /bəʊd/ *v.t. & i.*: **~ ill/well** предвеща́ть/ сули́ть (*impf.*) недо́брое/хоро́шее.

bodice /ˈbɒdɪs/ *n.* корса́ж, лиф.

bodily /ˈbɒdɪlɪ/ *adj.* теле́сный, физи́ческий.

body /ˈbɒdɪ/ *n.*
1 (*of person or animal*) те́ло.
2 (*dead person*) мёртвое те́ло; уби́т|ый (*fem.* -ая).
3 (*of ship*) ко́рпус; (*of car*) ку́зов; (*of aircraft*) фюзеля́ж.
4 (*quantity*) ма́сса, гру́ппа; **~ of evidence** совоку́пность доказа́тельств.
5 (*group*): **public ~** обще́ственная организа́ция.
6 (*strength, consistency*) консисте́нция, вя́зкость.
■ *cpds.* **~builder** *n.* (*person*) культури́ст; (*apparatus*) эспа́ндер; **~building** *n.* культури́зм, бодиби́лдинг; **~guard** *n.* (*group*) ли́чная охра́на; (*individual*) телохрани́тель (*m.*); **~ piercing** *n.* пи́рсинг; **~work** *n.* (*of vehicle*) ку́зов.

bog /bɒg/ *n.* боло́то, трясина.
■ *v.t.* (**bogged, bogging**): **get ~ged down** (*fig.*) вя́знуть, за-, у-.

boggle /ˈbɒg(ə)l/ *v.i.*: **the mind ~s** уму́ непостижи́мо.

boggy /ˈbɒgɪ/ *adj.* (**boggier, boggiest**) боло́тистый.

bogus /ˈbəʊgəs/ *adj.* фикти́вный, притво́рный.

bohemian /bəʊˈhiːmɪən/ *n.* представи́тель (*fem.* -ница) боге́мы.

boil¹ /bɔɪl/ *n.* (*swelling*) гно́йный нары́в, фуру́нкул.

boil² /bɔɪl/ *n.* (*state of* **~***ing*) кипе́ние; **bring to the ~** довести́ (*pf.*) до кипе́ния; вскипяти́ть (*pf.*).
■ *v.t.*: **~ water** кипяти́ть, вс- во́ду; **~ fish/ an egg** вари́ть, с- ры́бу/яйцо́.
■ *v.i.*: **the water is ~ing** вода́ кипи́т; **the egg has ~ed** яйцо́ свари́лось.
■ *with advs.*: **~ down** *v.i.*: **it ~s down to this, that ...** э́то сво́дится к тому́, что...; **~ over** *v.i.* (*lit.*) уходи́ть, уйти́ (*or* убе|га́ть, -жа́ть) че́рез край.

boiler /ˈbɔɪlə(r)/ *n.* отопи́тельный котёл; бо́йлер.
■ *cpd.* **~ suit** *n.* (*Br.*) комбинезо́н.

boiling /ˈbɔɪlɪŋ/ *adj.* кипя́щий; **~ hot** горя́чий, как кипято́к.
■ *cpd.* **~ point** *n.* то́чка кипе́ния.

boisterous /ˈbɔɪstərəs/ *adj.* бу́йный, шумли́вый, шу́мный.

bold /bəʊld/ *n.* (*typ.*) жи́рный шрифт.
■ *adj.* 1 сме́лый, отва́жный; (*impudent*) наха́льный.
2 : **~ strokes** (*in painting*) широ́кие мазки́.

Bolivia /bəlˈɪvɪə/ *n.* Боли́вия.

b

Bolivian /bəlˈɪvɪən/ *n.* боливи́|ец (*fem.* -йка).
■ *adj.* боливи́йский.
bollard /ˈbɒlɑːd/ *n.* (*Br.*) ту́мба.
Bolshevi|k /ˈbɒlʃəvɪk/, **-st** /ˈbɒlʃəvɪst/ *nn.* большеви́|к (*fem.* -чка).
■ *adj.* большеви́стский.
Bolshevism /ˈbɒlʃəvɪz(ə)m/ *n.* большеви́зм.
bolster /ˈbəʊlstə(r)/ *n.* ва́лик.
■ *v.t.* подп|ира́ть, -ере́ть.
bolt[1] /bəʊlt/ *n.*
1 (*on door etc.*) засо́в.
2 (*screw*) болт.
■ *adv.*: **~ upright** пря́мо; вы́тянувшись.
■ *v.t.*: **~ the door** зап|ира́ть, -ере́ть дверь на засо́в.
bolt[2] /bəʊlt/ *v.t.* (*gulp down*) глота́ть, проглоти́ть.
■ *v.i.* (*of horse*) понести́ (*pf.*); (*of person*) ри́нуться (*pf.*), помча́ться (*pf.*), удра́ть (*pf.*).
bomb /bɒm/ *n.* бо́мба; **~ disposal** обезвре́живание неразорва́вшихся бомб.
■ *v.t. & i.* бомби́ть, раз-.
■ *cpds.* **~shell** *n.* артиллери́йский снаря́д; **the news came as a ~shell to them** весть их как гро́мом порази́ла; **~site** *n.* райо́н разру́шенный бомбардиро́вк|ой/-ами.
bombard /bɒmˈbɑːd/ *v.t.*
1 бомби́ть, раз-; бомбардирова́ть (*impf.*); обстре́л|ивать, -я́ть.
2 (*fig.*): **~ s.o. with questions** бомбардирова́ть (*impf.*) кого́-н. вопро́сами.
bombardment /bɒmˈbɑːdmənt/ *n.* бомбардиро́вка, бомбёжка; (*with shells*) артиллери́йский обстре́л.
bombastic /bɒmˈbæstɪk/ *adj.* высокопа́рный, напы́щенный.
bomber /ˈbɒmə(r)/ *n.* (*aircraft*) бомбардиро́вщик; (*person*) террори́ст.
bombing /ˈbɒmɪŋ/ *n.* бомбомета́ние, бомбардиро́вка.
bona fide /bəʊnə ˈfaɪdɪ/ *adj.* добросо́вестный, че́стный.
bond /bɒnd/ *n.*
1 (*link*) связь.
2 (*fin.*) облига́ция; (*pl.*) бо́ны (*f. pl.*).
■ *v.i.* (*form a relationship*) устан|а́вливать, -ови́ть кре́пкие отноше́ния (с + *i.*).
bone /bəʊn/ *n.*
1 кость; **I have a ~ to pick with you** у меня́ к вам прете́нзия.
2 (*substance*) кость; **~ china** твёрдый англи́йский фарфо́р.
■ *v.t.*: **~ fish/meat** отдел|я́ть, -и́ть ры́бу/мя́со от косте́й.
■ *cpds.* **~ dry** *adj.* соверше́нно сухо́й; **~ idle** *adj.* ужа́сно лени́вый.
bonfire /ˈbɒnfaɪə(r)/ *n.* костёр.
bonk /bɒnk/ *v.i.* (*Br. vulg.*) тра́х|аться, -нуться.
bonnet /ˈbɒnɪt/ *n.*
1 (*woman's hat*) ка́пор; чепе́ц, че́пчик.
2 (*Br., of car*) капо́т.
bonny /ˈbɒnɪ/ *adj.* (**bonnier, bonniest**) (*Sc.*) (*comely*) хоро́шенький; (*healthy*): **a ~ baby** кре́пкий ребёнок.
bonus /ˈbəʊnəs/ *n.* пре́мия, премиа́льные (*pl.*); (*fig.*) дополни́тельное преиму́щество, бо́нус.
bony /ˈbəʊnɪ/ *adj.* (**bonier, boniest**) костяно́й, кости́стый.
boo /buː/ *n.* гул/свист неодобре́ния.
■ *v.t.* (**boos, booed**) осви́ст|ывать, -а́ть; **~ an actor off the stage** гу́лом/сви́стом неодобре́ния прогна́ть (*pf.*) актёра со сце́ны.
■ *v.i.* (**boos, booed**) улюлю́кать (*impf.*).
■ *int.* фу!
boob[1] /buːb/ *n.*
1 (*Br. coll., mistake*) прома́шка.
2 (*US coll., simpleton*) простофи́ля (*c.g.*), дурале́й.
■ *v.i.* (*Br. coll.*) оплоша́ть (*pf.*); дать (*pf.*) прома́шку.
boob[2] /buːb/ *n.* (*usu. pl., sl., breasts*) буфера́ (*m. pl., sl.*).
booby /ˈbuːbɪ/ *cpd.* **~-trap** *n.* (*mil.*) ми́на-лову́шка; *v.t.* устан|а́вливать, -ови́ть ми́ны-лову́шки в/на + *p.*
book /bʊk/ *n.*
1 кни́га; (*small*) кни́жка.
2 (*set*): **~ of matches/stamps** кни́жечка спи́чек/ма́рок.
3 (*account*): **keep the ~s** вести́ (*det.*) бухга́лтерские/счётные кни́ги; **in s.o.'s good/bad ~s** на хоро́шем/плохо́м счету́ у кого́-н.
■ *v.t.* (*ticket, table, taxi*) зака́з|ывать, -а́ть; (*hotel room, seat*) брони́ровать, за-; **~ s.o. in at a hotel** брони́ровать, за- для кого́-н. но́мер в гости́нице.
■ *cpds.* **~case** *n.* кни́жный шкаф; (*open-fronted*) кни́жные по́лки (*f. pl.*); **~ club** *n.* клуб книголю́бов; **~keeping** *n.* бухгалте́рия, счетово́дство; **~maker** *n.* букме́кер; **~mark** *n.* (*also comput.*) закла́дка; **~seller** *n.* книготорго́вец; **~shelf** *n.* кни́жная по́лка; **~shop, ~store** (*US*) *nn.* кни́жный магази́н.
bookie /ˈbʊkɪ/ (*coll.*) = **bookmaker**
booking /ˈbʊkɪŋ/ *n.* зака́з.
■ *cpd.* **~ office** *n.* (*Br.*) биле́тная ка́сса.
booklet /ˈbʊklɪt/ *n.* брошю́ра, букле́т.
boom[1] /buːm/ *n.* (*of gun, thunder*) гул, ро́кот; (*of voice*) гул.
■ *v.t. & i.* (*of gun*) бу́хать (*impf.*), грохота́ть (*impf.*); (*of thunder*) глу́хо грохота́ть (*impf.*).
boom[2] /buːm/ *n.* (*comm.*) бум, оживле́ние.
■ *v.i.*: **business is ~ing** де́ло процвета́ет.
boomerang /ˈbuːməræŋ/ *n.* бумера́нг.
boorish /ˈbʊərɪʃ/ *adj.* ха́мский, мужи́цкий.
boost /buːst/ *n.* (*increase*) увеличе́ние; (*stimulus*) толчо́к, сти́мул; **give a ~ to the economy** стимули́ровать (*impf., pf.*) эконо́мику.
■ *v.t.* (*increase*) увели́чи|вать, -ть.
booster /ˈbuːstə(r)/ *n.*: **~ injection** (*med.*) повто́рная приви́вка.
boot /buːt/ *n.*
1 (*footwear*) боти́нок, башма́к; (*knee-length*) сапо́г; **football ~s** бу́тсы (*f. pl.*).
2 (*Br., of a car*) бага́жник.
■ *v.t.*: (*comput.*) загру|жа́ть, -зи́ть.
■ *cpds.* **~leg** *adj.* (*fig.*): **~leg whisky** контраба́ндное ви́ски; **~legger** *n.* самого́нщик.
booth /buːð/ *n.* (*for telephoning*) бу́дка; (*polling ~*) каби́на для голосова́ния.
booty /ˈbuːtɪ/ *n.* добы́ча.
booze /buːz/ *n.* вы́пивка; попо́йка.

■ *v.i.* пья́нствовать (*impf.*), выпива́ть (*impf.*).
bop /bɒp/ (*Br., coll.*) *n.* та́нец под популя́рную му́зыку; (*party*) та́нцы (*m. pl.*) под популя́рную му́зыку.
■ *v.i.* танцева́ть, с- под популя́рную му́зыку.
border /'bɔːdə(r)/ *n.*
1 (*side, edging*): **~ of a lake** бе́рег о́зера; **herbaceous ~** бордю́р из многоле́тних цвето́в.
2 (*frontier*) грани́ца; (*fig.*) грань.
■ *v.t.*: **our garden ~s his field** наш сад грани́чит с его́ по́лем.
■ *v.i.*: **these countries ~ on one another** э́ти стра́ны грани́чат друг с дру́гом; **this ~s on fanaticism** э́то грани́чит с фанати́змом.
■ *cpd.* **~line** *n.* грани́ца; (*fig.*) грань; (*demarcation line*) демаркацио́нная ли́ния; **a ~line case** промежу́точный слу́чай.
bore[1] /bɔː(r)/ *n.* кали́бр, кана́л ствола́.
■ *v.t.* сверли́ть, про-; бури́ть, про-.
bore[2] /bɔː(r)/ *n.* (*person*) ску́чный челове́к; зану́да (*c.g.*); (*thing*): **it's such a bore cooking every day** така́я тоска́ ка́ждый день гото́вить.
■ *v.t.* надо|еда́ть, -е́сть + *d.*; **~ s.o. to death, tears** надо|еда́ть, -е́сть кому́-н. до́ смерти.
bore[3] /bɔː(r)/ *past of* ▸ **bear**[2]
bored /'bɔːd/ *adj.* скуча́ющий; **I am ~** мне ску́чно; **in a ~ voice** ску́чным/скуча́ющим го́лосом; **I am ~ with him** он мне надое́л.
boredom /'bɔːdəm/ *n.* ску́ка, тоска́.
boring /'bɔːrɪŋ/ *adj.* ску́чный, надое́дливый.
born /bɔːn/ *adj. and p.p. of* ▸ **bear**[2]
1: **a ~ poet** прирождённый поэ́т.
2: **be ~** роди́ться (*pf.*).
borne /bɔːn/ *p.p. of* ▸ **bear**[2]
Borneo /'bɔːnɪəʊ/ *n.* Борне́о (*nt. indecl.*).
borough /'bʌrə/ *n.* райо́н.
borrow /'bɒrəʊ/ *v.t. & i.* (*take for a time*) брать, взять на вре́мя; заи́мствовать, по-; зан|има́ть, -я́ть; (*money*) брать, взять взаймы́.
bor(t)sch /bɔːʃ/ *n.* борщ.
Bosnia /'bɒznɪə/ *n.* Бо́сния.
Bosnia–Herzegovina /'bɒznɪə hɜːtsɪgə'viːnə/ *n.* (*also* **Bosnia and Herzegovina**) Бо́сния и Герцегови́на.
bosom /'bʊz(ə)m/ *n.*
1 (*breast*) грудь.
2 (*fig.*) се́рдце, душа́; **~ friend** закады́чный друг.
Bosporus /'bɒspərəs/ *n.* Босфо́р.
boss /bɒs/ *n.* (*master*) босс, хозя́ин, нача́льник.
■ *v.t.*: **~ s.o. about** кома́ндовать (*impf.*) кем-н.
bossy /'bɒsɪ/ *adj.* (**bossier, bossiest**) (*voice, tone*) команди́рский; **your husband is really ~** твой муж привы́к ве́чно кома́ндовать.
botanical /bə'tænɪk(ə)l/ *adj.* ботани́ческий.
botanist /'bɒtənɪst/ *n.* бота́ник.
botany /'bɒtənɪ/ *n.* бота́ника.
botch /bɒtʃ/ *v.t.* зава́л|ивать, -и́ть.
both /bəʊθ/ *pron. & adj.* о́ба (*m., nt.*), о́бе (*f.*); и тот и друго́й; **~ sledges** о́бе па́ры сане́й; **~ of us** мы о́ба.
■ *adv.*: **~ ... and ...** и... и...; **my sister and I ~ helped him** мы о́ба помогли́ ему́, и я, и сестра́.
bother /'bɒðə(r)/ *n.* беспоко́йство; хло́п|оты (*pl., g.* -о́т); возня́; **I had no ~ finding the book** я нашёл кни́гу без труда́.
■ *v.t.* (*disturb*) беспоко́ить, по-; трево́жить, по-; (*pester*): **he is always ~ing me to lend him money** он ве́чно пристаёт ко мне с про́сьбой одолжи́ть ему́ де́нег; **~ (it)!** (*Br.*) чёрт возьми́!; **I can't be ~ed** мне лень, мне недосу́г.
■ *v.i.* беспоко́иться, по-; **don't ~ to make tea** не вози́тесь с ча́ем.
Botox /'bəʊtɒks/ *n.* (*propr.*) (*med.*) бо́токс (*медицинский/косметический препарат*).
bottle /'bɒt(ə)l/ *n.* буты́лка; (*Br., for infants*) буты́лочка, рожо́к.
■ *v.t.* (*put in ~s*) разл|ива́ть, -и́ть по буты́лкам; **~ up** (*conceal*) скры|ва́ть, -ть.
■ *cpds.* **~-fed** *adj.* иску́сственно вско́рмленный; **~neck** *n.* (*fig.*) зато́р; про́бка; у́зкое ме́сто; **~-opener** *n.* открыва́лка (*coll.*); **~-top** *n.* колпачо́к на буты́лку.
bottled /'bɒt(ə)ld/ *adj.*: **~ beer** буты́лочное пи́во.
bottom /'bɒtəm/ *n.*
1 (*lowest part*) дно; (*of mountain*) подно́жие, подо́шва; (*of page*) низ, коне́ц; (*of stairs*) низ, основа́ние; **~ shelf** ни́жняя по́лка; **at the ~ of the class** отстаю́щий в кла́ссе.
2 (*further end*): **~ of the garden/street** коне́ц са́да/у́лицы.
3 (*Br., anat.*) зад; за́дняя часть.
4 (*fig.*): **~ line** (*crux of the matter*) суть де́ла; **get to the ~ of sth.** доб|ира́ться, -ра́ться до су́ти чего́-н.; **he came ~ in algebra** он был са́мым неуспева́ющим по а́лгебре.
boudoir /'buːdwɑː(r)/ *n.* будуа́р.
bougainvill(a)ea /buːgən'vɪlɪə/ *n.* (*bot.*) бугенвилле́я (*scientific name*), (*also known as*) бугенви́ллия.
bough /baʊ/ *n.* сук.
bought /bɔːt/ *past and p.p. of* ▸ **buy**
boulder /'bəʊldə(r)/ *n.* валу́н.
boulevard /'buːləvɑːd/ *n.* бульва́р.
bounce /baʊns/ *n.* подпры́гивание, отско́к.
■ *v.t.* **~ a ball** бить (*impf.*) мячо́м о́б пол (о зе́млю, об сте́нку *и т. п.*).
■ *v.i.* (*of ball etc.*) отск|а́кивать, -очи́ть; подпры́г|ивать, -нуть; (*coll., of cheque*) верну́ться (*pf.*); **~ back** (*fig.*) бы́стро опра́виться.
bouncer /'baʊnsə(r)/ *n.* вышиба́ла (*m.*).
bound[1] /baʊnd/ *n.* (*usu. pl., limit*) грани́ца, преде́л; **the town is out of ~s to troops** вход в го́род солда́там воспрещён.
bound[2] /baʊnd/ *v.i.* пры́г|ать, -нуть; скак|а́ть, -ну́ть; **he ~ed off to fetch the book** он подпры́гнул, что́бы доста́ть кни́гу.
bound[3] /baʊnd/ *adj.*
1 (*certain*): **he is ~ to win** он непреме́нно вы́играет.
2 (*obliged*): **you are not ~ to go** вам не обяза́тельно идти́.
3 (*en route*): **the ship is ~ for New York** парохо́д направля́ется в Нью-Йо́рк.
boundary /'baʊndrɪ/ *n.* (*of a field etc.*) грани́ца, рубе́ж; (*fig.*) преде́л; (*attr.*)

b

пограни́чный.

boundless /'baʊndlɪs/ *adj.* безграни́чный, беспреде́льный.

bountiful /'baʊntɪfʊl/ *adj.* ще́дрый; оби́льный.

bouquet /bu:'keɪ/ *n.* (*of flowers, wine*) буке́т.

bourbon /'bɜ:bən/ *n.* (*whisky*) бурбо́н.

bourgeois /'bʊəʒwɑ:/ *adj.* буржуа́зный.

bourgeoisie /bʊəʒwɑ:'zi:/ *n.* буржуази́я.

bout /baʊt/ *n.*
1 (*at games*) бой, встре́ча, схва́тка.
2 (*of illness*) при́ступ.

boutique /bu:'ti:k/ *n.* (небольшо́й) мо́дный магази́н; бути́к.

bow[1] /bəʊ/ *n.*
1 (*weapon*) лук.
2 (*of violin etc.*) смычо́к.
3 (*knot*) бант.
■ *cpds.* **~-legged** *adj.* кривоно́гий; **~ tie** *n.* (га́лстук-)ба́бочка.

bow[2] /baʊ/ *n.* (*salutation*) покло́н.
■ *v.t.* (*bend*): **~ one's head** склон|я́ть, -и́ть го́лову; **the wind ~ed the trees** ве́тер гнул/клони́л дере́вья.
■ *v.i.* 1 (*salute*) кла́няться, поклони́ться.
2 (*defer*) склон|я́ться, -и́ться (**to, before:** перед + *i.*).

bow[3] /baʊ/ *n.* (*naut.*) нос.

bowel /'baʊəl/ *n.*
1 кишка́.
2 : **~s of the earth** не́др|а (*pl., g.* —) земли́.

bowl[1] /bəʊl/ *n.* ча́ша, ва́за, ми́ска.

bowl[2] /bəʊl/ *n.* **play ~s** игра́ть (*impf.*) в бо́улинг/ке́гли/шары́.
■ *v.t.*: **~ over** (*lit.*) сшиб|а́ть, -и́ть; (*fig.*); **he was ~ed over by her** она́ срази́ла его́.
■ *v.i.* 1 (*cricket*) под|ава́ть, -а́ть мяч.
2 (*play bowls*) игра́ть (*impf.*) в бо́улинг/ке́гли/шары́; **~ing alley** зал для игры́ в бо́улинг; кегельба́н; **~ing green** лужа́йка для игры́ в бо́улинг/шары́.

bowler[1] /'bəʊlə(r)/ *n.* (*at games*) подаю́щий/броса́ющий мяч.

bowler[2] /'bəʊlə(r)/ *n.* (**~** *hat*) котело́к.

box[1] /bɒks/ *n.*
1 (*receptacle*) коро́бка, я́щик; **~ number** но́мер абоне́нтского я́щика.
2 (*theatr.*) ло́жа.
3 (*typ.*) ра́мка.
■ *v.t.* класть, положи́ть в коро́бку/я́щик.
■ *cpd.* **~ office** *n.* (театра́льная) ка́сса.

box[2] /bɒks/ *v.t.*: **~ s.o.'s ears** да|ва́ть, -ть кому́-н. оплеу́ху (*or* по́ уху).
■ *v.i.* (*sport*) бокси́ровать (*impf.*).

boxer /'bɒksə(r)/ *n.* (*sportsman; dog*) боксёр; **~ shorts** боксёрские трусы́.

boxing /'bɒksɪŋ/ *n.* (*sport*) бокс.

Boxing Day /'bɒksɪŋ/ *n.* (*Br.*) второ́й день Рождества́.

boy /bɔɪ/ *n.*
1 (*child*) ма́льчик; **B~ Scout** бойска́ут.
2 (*son*) сын.
■ *cpd.* **~friend** *n.* ≈ па́рень (*m.*), молодо́й челове́к, бойфре́нд.

boycott /'bɔɪkɒt/ *n.* бойко́т.
■ *v.t.* бойкоти́ровать (*impf., pf.*).

boyish /'bɔɪɪʃ/ *adj.* мальчи́шеский.

bra /brɑ:/ *n.* (*pl.* **bras**) (*coll.*) ли́фчик, бюстга́льтер.

brace /breɪs/ *n.*
1 (*support*) подпо́рка, распо́рка.
2 : **~s** (*Br., for trousers*) подтя́ж|ки (*pl., g.* -ек).
3 (*dentistry etc.*) ши́на.
■ *v.t.* 1 (*support*) подп|ира́ть, -ере́ть; **he ~d himself against the wall** он опёрся о сте́ну.
2 (*of nerves*): **he ~d himself to do it** он собра́лся с ду́хом что́бы сде́лать э́то.

bracelet /'breɪslɪt/ *n.* брасле́т.

bracing /'breɪsɪŋ/ *adj.* бодря́щий, укрепля́ющий.

bracken /'brækən/ *n.* па́поротник-орля́к.

bracket /'brækɪt/ *n.*
1 (*support*) кронште́йн.
2 (*typ.*) ско́бка.
3 (*fig.*): **the higher income ~s** гру́ппа населе́ния с бо́лее высо́кими дохо́дами.
■ *v.t.* (**bracketed, bracketing**)
1 (*enclose in ~s*) заключ|а́ть, -и́ть в ско́бки.
2 (*fig.*): **do not ~ me with him** не равня́йте меня́ с ним.

brag /bræg/ *v.i.* (**bragged, bragging**) хва́стать(ся), по- (*чем*).

braid /breɪd/ *n.* (*of hair*) коса́; (*decorative*) галу́н.

Braille /breɪl/ *n.* шрифт Бра́йля; а́збука Бра́йля.

brain /breɪn/ *n.* (*anat.*) мозг; (*pl., cul.*) мозги́.
■ *cpds.* **~child** *n.* плод ра́зума/воображе́ния; **~ drain** *n.* «уте́чка мозго́в»; **~storming session** *n.* коллекти́вное обсужде́ние пробле́м; **~wash** *v.t.* пром|ыва́ть, -ы́ть мозги́ + *d.*; **~washing** *n.* промыва́ние мозго́в; **~wave** *n.*: **he had a ~wave** ему́ пришла́ счастли́вая мысль; его́ осени́ла иде́я.

brainy /'breɪnɪ/ *adj.* (**brainier, brainiest**) (*coll.*) башкови́тый, мозгови́тый.

braise /breɪz/ *v.t.* туши́ть (*impf.*).

brake /breɪk/ *n.* (*on vehicle*) то́рмоз (*pl.* -а́).
■ *v.t. & i.* тормози́ть, за-.

bramble /'bræmb(ə)l/ *n.* ежеви́ка.

bran /bræn/ *n.* о́труб|и (*pl., g.* -е́й).

branch /brɑ:ntʃ/ *n.* (*of tree*) ветвь; ве́тка; (*of family, genus*) ли́ния, ветвь; (*of railway line*) ве́тка; (*comm.*) филиа́л, отделе́ние; (*of knowledge, subject, industry*) о́трасль.
■ *v.i.* (*of organization*): **~ out** разветв|ля́ться, -и́ться; (*of road or rail., also* **~ off**) разветв|ля́ться, -и́ться; ответв|ля́ться, -и́ться.

brand /brænd/ *n.* сорт, ма́рка, бренд; **~ name** фи́рменное назва́ние.
■ *v.t.* 1 (*cattle etc.*) клейми́ть, за-.
2 (*stigmatize*) клейми́ть, за-.
3 (*comm.*): **~ed goods** това́ры с фабри́чным клеймо́м.
■ *cpd.* **~ new** *adj.* соверше́нно но́вый, с иго́лочки.

branding /'brændɪŋ/ *n.* (*comm.*) бре́ндинг (*создание и продвижение на рынке торговых марок*).

brandish /'brændɪʃ/ *v.t.* разма́хивать (*impf.*) + *i.*

brandy /'brændɪ/ *n.* конья́к; бре́нди (*nt. indecl.*).

brash /bræʃ/ *adj.* наха́льный, нагలова́тый,

дёрзкий.

brass /brɑːs/ *n.*

1 (*metal*) латýнь, жёлтая медь.

2 (*mus.*): **the ~** духовы́е инструмéнты (*m. pl.*); медь; **~ band** духовóй оркéстр.

brat /bræt/ *n.* невоспи́танный ребёнок.

bravado /brəˈvɑːdəʊ/ *n.* бравáда.

brave /breɪv/ *n. adj.* хрáбрый, смéлый.

■ *v.t.* бр|осáть, -óсить вы́зов + *d.*

bravery /ˈbreɪvərɪ/ *n.* хрáбрость, смéлость.

bravo /brɑːˈvəʊ/ *int.* брáво!

brawl /brɔːl/ *n.* скандáл.

■ *v.i.* скандáлить (*impf.*).

brawny /ˈbrɔːnɪ/ *adj.* (**brawnier, brawniest**) мускули́стый.

brazen /ˈbreɪz(ə)n/ *adj.* нáглый, бессты́дный.

■ *v.t.*: **~ sth. out** нáгло выкрýчиваться, вы́крутиться из чегó-н.

brazier /ˈbreɪzɪə(r)/ *n.* (*worker*) мéдник; (*pan*) жарóвня.

Brazil /brəˈzɪl/ *n.* Брази́лия.

Brazilian /brəˈzɪljən/ *n.* брази́л|ец (*fem.* -ья́нка).

■ *adj.* брази́льский.

breach /briːtʃ/ *n.*

1 (*violation, interruption*) нарушéние; **~ of trust** злоупотреблéние довéрием.

2 (*gap*) пролóм, брешь.

■ *v.t.* прор|ывáть, -вáть.

bread /bred/ *n.* хлеб; **~ and butter** (*fig.*) хлеб с мáслом.

■ *cpds.* **~-and-butter** *adj.* насýщный; **~bin** *n.* (*Br.*) хлéбница; **~board** *n.* хлéбная доскá; **~crumb** *n.* крóшка; (*pl., cul.*) толчёные сухари́ (*m. pl.*); **~line** *n.*: **on the ~line** (*Br.*) в тяжёлом материáльном положéнии; **~winner** *n.* корми́лец.

breadth /bredθ/ *n.*

1 (*width*) ширинá.

2 (*fig.*): **~ of mind** широтá умá.

break /breɪk/ *n.*

1 (*broken place, gap*) трéщина, разры́в.

2 (*interval*) переры́в, пáуза; (*rest*) переды́шка.

3 (*change*) перемéна.

4 (*coll., opportunity*) возмóжность; **lucky ~** счастли́вый слýчай.

■ *v.t.* (*past* **broke,** *p.p.* **broken**)

1 (*fracture, destroy*) ломáть, с-; (*glass, china*) бить (*or* разбивáть), раз-; **he broke his leg** он сломáл нóгу.

2 (*fig.*): **~ a record** поби́ть (*pf.*) рекóрд.

3 (*convey*): **~ the news** сообщ|áть, -и́ть (неприя́тные) нóвости.

4 (*weaken*): **~ a fall** осл|абля́ть, -áбить си́лу падéния.

5 (*violate*) нар|ушáть, -ýшить; **~ a secret** разгл|ашáть, -аси́ть тáйну.

6 (*interrupt, put an end to*): **~ one's journey** прер|ывáть, -вáть путешéствие.

■ *v.i.* (*past* **broke** *or arch.* **brake;** *p.p.* **broken** *or arch.* **broke**)

1 (*fracture, disperse*) ломáться, с-; обл|áмываться, -омáться; (*of glass, china*) би́ться (*or* разбивáться), раз-; **~ in two** ломáться, с- пополáм.

2 (*fig.*): **~ing point** предéл.

3 (*burst, dawn*): **the storm broke** разрази́лась грозá; **the news broke at 5 o'clock** об э́том стáло извéстно в 5 часóв.

4 (*change*): **his voice broke** (*at puberty*) у негó сломáлся гóлос; **the weather broke** погóда испóртилась.

5 (*var.*): **~ even** ост|авáться, -áться при свои́х.

■ *with preps.*: **burglars broke into the house** граби́тели ворвали́сь в дом; **the house was broken into** в дóме произошлá крáжа со взлóмом.

■ *with advs.*: **~ away** *v.i.*: **~ away from one's jailers** вырывáться, вы́рваться из рук тюрéмщиков; **~ away from a group** отк|áлываться, -олóться от грýппы; **~ down** *v.t.*: **~ down a door** вылáмывать, вы́ломать дверь; **~ down resistance** сломи́ть (*pf.*) сопротивлéние; **~ down expenditure** разб|ивáть, -и́ть расхóды по статья́м; *v.i.*: **the car broke down** маши́на сломáлась; **he broke down** он не вы́держал; **~ in** *v.t.*: **~ in a horse** выезжáть, вы́ездить лóшадь; **~ in a new pair of shoes** разн|áшивать, -оси́ть нóвые тýфли; *v.i.*: **~ in on a conversation** вмéш|иваться, -áться в разговóр; **~ off** *v.t.*: **~ off a twig** отл|áмывать, -оми́ть вéточку; **~ off relations** пор|ывáть, -вáть отношéния (с + *i.*); **~ off an engagement** раст|оргáть, -óргнуть помóлвку; *v.i.*: **he broke off** (*speaking*) он замолчáл; **~ out** *v.i.*: **the prisoner broke out** заключённый сбежáл; **war broke out** разрази́лась/вспы́хнула войнá; **his face broke out in pimples** на егó лицé вы́сыпали пры́щи; **~ up** *v.t.*: **~ up a meeting** прекра|щáть, -ти́ть собрáние; **~ up a family** (*separate*) разб|ивáть, -и́ть семью́; *v.i.* **school ~s up tomorrow** (*Br.*) учáщихся зáвтра распускáют на кани́кулы; **she broke up with her boyfriend** онá разошлáсь с дрýгом.

■ *cpds.* **~away** *n.*: **a ~away faction** отколóвшаяся фрáкция; (*sport*) отры́в; **~down** *n.* (*mechanical*) полóмка; (*of health*) расстрóйство; (*of negotiations*) срыв; (*analysis*) подразделéние, разби́вка; **~-in** *n.* взлом; **~neck** *adj.*: **~neck speed** головокружи́тельная скóрость; **~through** *n.* (*mil.*) проры́в; (*fig.*) скачóк, перелóм, проры́в; **~-up** *n.* развáл, распáд; (*of friendship*) разры́в; **~water** *n.* волнорéз.

breakfast /ˈbrekfəst/ *n.* зáвтрак.

■ *v.i.* зáвтракать, по-.

breast /brest/ *n.*

1 грудь.

2 (*cul.*): **~ of lamb** барáнья груди́нка.

■ *cpds.* **~fed** *adj.* вскóрмленный грýдью; **~feeding** *n.* кормлéние грýдью; **~stroke** *n.* брасс.

breath /breθ/ *n.* дыхáние; (*single ~*) вздох; **out of ~** задыхáясь; **bad ~** дурнóй зáпах изо рта; **catch, hold one's ~** затá|ивать, -и́ть дыхáние; **take s.o.'s ~ away** захвáт|ывать, -и́ть дух у когó-н.

■ *cpd.* **~taking** *adj.* захвáтывающий.

breathalyse /ˈbreθəlaɪz/ (*US* **breathalyze**) *v.t.* пров|еря́ть, -éрить на алкогóль.

breathalyser /ˈbreθəlaɪzə(r)/ (*US propr.* **Breathalyzer**) *n.* алкóметр, алкогóльно-респирáторная трýбка.

breathe /bri:ð/ *v.t.*
[1]: **~ fresh air** дыша́ть (*impf.*) све́жим во́здухом.
[2] (*utter softly*): **~ a sigh** изд|ава́ть, -а́ть вздох; **don't ~ a word!** ни сло́ва бо́льше!
■ *v.i.* дыша́ть (*impf.*).

breather /ˈbri:ðə(r)/ *n.* переды́шка.

breathing /ˈbri:ðɪŋ/ *n.* дыха́ние.
■ *cpd.* **~ space** *n.* переды́шка.

breathless /ˈbreθlɪs/ *adj.* задыха́ющийся, запыха́вшийся.

bred /bred/ *past and p.p. of* ▸ **breed**

breed /bri:d/ *n.* поро́да.
■ *v.t.* (*past and p.p.* **bred**)
[1] (*cause*) поро|жда́ть, -ди́ть.
[2] (*animals*) раз|води́ть, -вести́.
■ *v.i.* (*past and p.p.* **bred**) размн|ожа́ться, -о́житься; плоди́ться, рас-.

breeder /ˈbri:də(r)/ *n.* животново́д, скотово́д.

breeding /ˈbri:dɪŋ/ *n.*
[1] (*by stockbreeders*) разведе́ние.
[2] (*manners etc.*) воспи́танность.
■ *cpd.* **~ ground** *n.* (*fig.*) расса́дник, оча́г.

breeze /bri:z/ *n.* ветеро́к; бриз.
■ *v.i.*: **~ in/out** (*coll.*) влете́ть/вы́лететь (*pf.*).

breezy /ˈbri:zɪ/ *adj.* (**breezier, breeziest**) (*of weather*) све́жий; (*fig., of person*) живо́й, беззабо́тный.

brevity /ˈbrevɪtɪ/ *n.* кра́ткость.

brew /bru:/ *v.t.* (*beer*) вари́ть, с-; (*tea*) зава́р|ивать, -и́ть.
■ *v.i.* [1] (*of tea etc.*) зава́р|иваться, -и́ться.
[2]: **a storm is ~ing** (*lit. and fig.*) гроза́ надвига́ется; **there's trouble ~ing** быть беде́.

brewer /ˈbru:ə(r)/ *n.* пивова́р.

brewery /ˈbru:ərɪ/ *n.* пивова́ренный заво́д.

bribe /braɪb/ *n.* взя́тка, по́дкуп.
■ *v.t.* да|ва́ть, -ть взя́тку + *d.*; **~ s.o. to do sth.** по́дкупом доб|ива́ться, -и́ться чего́-н. от кого́-н.

bribery /ˈbraɪbərɪ/ *n.* взя́точничество.

brick /brɪk/ *n.* кирпи́ч; **~s** (*collect.*) кирпи́ч; (*attr.*) кирпи́чный.
■ *v.t.*: **~ up** за|кла́дывать, -ложи́ть кирпичо́м.
■ *cpd.* **~layer** *n.* ка́менщик.

bridal /ˈbraɪd(ə)l/ *adj.* сва́дебный.

bride /braɪd/ *n.* неве́ста.
■ *cpds.* **~groom** *n.* жени́х; **~smaid** *n.* подру́жка неве́сты.

bridge[1] /brɪdʒ/ *n.*
[1] мост (*also in dentistry*).
[2] (*naut.*) капита́нский мо́стик.
[3] (*of nose*) перено́сица.
[4] (*of violin*) подста́вка.
■ *v.t.*: **~ a river** нав|оди́ть, -ести́ мост че́рез ре́ку; (*join by bridging*) соедин|я́ть, -и́ть мосто́м; (*fig.*): **~ a gap** восп|олня́ть, -о́лнить пробе́л.

bridge[2] /brɪdʒ/ *n.* (*game*) бридж.

bridle /ˈbraɪd(ə)l/ *n.* узда́, узде́чка.
■ *v.t.* (*a horse*) взну́зд|ывать, -а́ть; (*fig.*) обу́зд|ывать, -а́ть.
■ *v.i.* (*fig.*) зад|ира́ть, -ра́ть нос.
■ *cpds.* **~ path** (*Br.*) *n.* верхова́я тропа́.

brief /bri:f/ *n.*
[1] (*lawyer's*) изложе́ние де́ла.
[2] (*Br.*) (*instructions*) инстру́кция.
[3] (*pl., coll., underpants*) трус|ы́ (*pl., g.* -о́в).
■ *adj.* коро́ткий, недо́лгий; **in ~** вкра́тце.
■ *v.t.* [1]: **~ a lawyer** (*Br.*) поруч|а́ть, -и́ть адвока́ту веде́ние де́ла.
[2] (*mil. etc.*) инструкти́ровать (*impf., pf.*).
■ *cpd.* **~case** *n.* портфе́ль (*m.*).

briefing /ˈbri:fɪŋ/ *n.* инструкта́ж; (*press*) бри́финг.

briefly /ˈbri:flɪ/ *adv.* кра́тко, сжа́то.

brigade /brɪˈgeɪd/ *n.* брига́да.

brigadier /brɪgəˈdɪə(r)/ *n.* (*also* **~ general**) брига́дный генера́л.

brigand /ˈbrɪgənd/ *n.* разбо́йник.

bright /braɪt/ *adj.*
[1] (*clear, shining*) я́ркий, све́тлый; **a ~ day** я́сный день; **~ red** я́рко-кра́сный; **a ~ room** све́тлая ко́мната.
[2] (*cheerful*): **look on the ~ side** смотре́ть (*impf.*) на ве́щи оптимисти́чески.
[3] (*clever*): **a ~ girl** толко́вая де́вочка; **a ~ idea** блестя́щая мысль.

brighten /ˈbraɪt(ə)n/ *v.t.* (*also* **~ up**): ожив|ля́ть, -и́ть.
■ *v.i.* (*also* **~ up**): **the weather ~ed** пого́да проясни́лась.

brightness /ˈbraɪtnɪs/ *n.* (*lustre*) я́ркость; (*cleverness*) блеск, смышлёность.

brilliance /ˈbrɪlɪəns/ *n.* (*brightness*) я́ркость; (*intelligence*) блеск (ума́).

brilliant /ˈbrɪljənt/ *adj.* (*lit., fig.*) сверка́ющий, блестя́щий; (*Br. coll., excellent*) замеча́тельный.

brim /brɪm/ *n.* край; (*of hat*) поля́ (*nt. pl.*).

brine /braɪn/ *n.* рассо́л.

bring /brɪŋ/ *v.t.* (*past and p.p.* **brought**) (*cause to come, deliver*): (*a thing*) прин|оси́ть, -ести́; (*a person*) прив|оди́ть, -ести́; **it brought tears to my eyes** э́то вы́звало у меня́ слёзы.
■ *with advs.*: **~ about** *v.t.* (*cause*) вызыва́ть, вы́звать; произв|оди́ть, -ести́; **~ back** *v.t.* прин|оси́ть, -ести́ (*or* прив|оди́ть, -ести́) наза́д; **~ down** *v.t.* (*an aircraft*) сби|ва́ть, -ть; **~ prices down** сн|ижа́ть, -и́зить це́ны; **~ forward** *v.t.* (*advance date of*) перен|оси́ть, -ести́ на бо́лее ра́нний срок; **~ in** *v.t.* вн|оси́ть, -ести́; вв|оди́ть, -ести́; **~ in a verdict** выноси́ть, вы́нести верди́кт; **~ off** *v.t.*: **~ off a manoeuvre** (*Br.*), **maneuver** (*US*) успе́шно заверш|а́ть, -и́ть опера́цию; **~ on** *v.t.*: **this brought on a bad cold** э́то вы́звало си́льный на́сморк; **~ out** *v.t.* выноси́ть, вы́нести; выводи́ть, вы́вести; (*make evident*) выявля́ть, вы́явить; (*publish*) выпуска́ть, вы́пустить; **the curtains ~ out the green in the carpet** занаве́ски оттеня́ют зе́лень ковра́; **~ round** *v.t.* (*restore to consciousness*) прив|оди́ть, -ести́ в себя́; (*persuade*) убе|жда́ть, -ди́ть; **~ up** *v.t.* (*educate*) воспи́т|ывать, -а́ть; (*vomit*): **he brought up his dinner** его́ вы́рвало по́сле обе́да; **~ up a subject** подн|има́ть, -я́ть вопро́с; зав|оди́ть, -ести́ разгово́р о чём-н.

brink /brɪŋk/ *n.* край (*also fig.*).

brisk /brɪsk/ *adj.* (*of movement*) ско́рый; (*of air, wind*) све́жий.

bristle /ˈbrɪs(ə)l/ *n.* щети́на.
■ *v.i.* (*of hair*) стоя́ть (*impf.*) ды́бом; встать (*pf.*) ды́бом; (*of animal, also fig., of person*) ощети́ни|ваться, -ться.

Britain /ˈbrɪt(ə)n/ *n.* А́нглия, Брита́ния.
British /ˈbrɪtɪʃ/ *n.*: **the ~** брита́нцы (*both m. pl.*).
■ *adj.* брита́нский; **~ Isles** Брита́нские острова́.
Briton /ˈbrɪt(ə)n/ *n.* брита́н|ец (*fem.* -ка); англича́н|ин (*fem.* -ка).
brittle /ˈbrɪt(ə)l/ *adj.* ло́мкий, хру́пкий.
broach /brəʊtʃ/ *v.t.*: **~ a subject** подн|има́ть, -я́ть вопро́с.
broad /brɔːd/ *adj.*
1 (*wide*) широ́кий.
2: **in ~ daylight** средь бе́ла дня.
3 (*decided*): **a ~ hint** то́лстый намёк; **a ~ accent** си́льный акце́нт.
4 (*approximate*): **in ~ outline** в о́бщих черта́х.
■ *cpds.* **~band** *n.* (*comput.*) широкополо́сная переда́ча да́нных; **~ bean** *n.* фасо́ль; **~cast** *n.* трансля́ция; *v.t.* трансли́ровать (*impf.*, *pf.*); *v.i.* вести́ (*det.*) радиопереда́чу, телепереда́чу; **~caster** *n.* (*radio*) радиожурнали́ст, (*TV*) тележурнали́ст; **~casting** *n.* (*radio*) радиовеща́ние, (*TV*) телевеща́ние; трансля́ция; **~-minded** *adj.* широ́ких взгля́дов; **~sheet** *n.* газе́та большо́го форма́та.
broaden /ˈbrɔːd(ə)n/ *v.t.* & *i.* расш|иря́ть(ся), -и́рить(ся).
broadly /ˈbrɔːdlɪ/ *adv.* (*in the main*) в основно́м; **~ speaking** вообще́ говоря́.
broccoli /ˈbrɒkəlɪ/ *n.* бро́кколи (*nt. indecl.*).
brochure /ˈbrəʊʃə(r)/ *n.* брошю́ра.
broil /brɔɪl/ *v.t.* (*US, cul.*) жа́рить, за- на откры́том огне́.
broke /brəʊk/ *adj.* (*coll.*) разори́вшийся, безде́нежный.
broken /ˈbrəʊkən/ *adj.*
1: **a ~ leg** сло́манная нога́; **~ English** ло́маный англи́йский язы́к.
2 (*~-down*): **a ~ marriage** расстро́енный брак; **a ~ home** разби́тая семья́.
3 (*crushed*): **a ~ man** сло́мленный челове́к.
■ *cpds.* **~-down** *adj.* (*of machine*) сло́манный; **~-hearted** *adj.* с разби́тым се́рдцем.
broker /ˈbrəʊkə(r)/ *n.* ма́клер, бро́кер.
brolly /ˈbrɒlɪ/ (*Br. coll.*) = **umbrella** *n.*
bronchitis /brɒŋˈkaɪtɪs/ *n.* бронхи́т.
bronze /brɒnz/ *n.* бро́нза; (*attr.*) бро́нзовый.
brooch /brəʊtʃ/ *n.* брошь.
brood /bruːd/ *n.* пото́мство.
■ *v.i.* 1 (*of bird*) сиде́ть (*impf.*) на я́йцах.
2: **~ over an insult** копи́ть (*impf.*) в себе́ оби́ду.
broody /ˈbruːdɪ/ *adj.* (**broodier, broodiest**)
1 (*thoughtful*) заду́мчивый; (*morose*) угрю́мый.
2: **a ~ hen** (хоро́шая) насе́дка.
3 (*of a woman*): **she's feeling ~** в ней просну́лся матери́нский инсти́нкт.
brook /brʊk/ *n.* (*stream*) руче́й.
broom /bruːm/ *n.* метла́.
■ *cpd.* **~stick** *n.* (*witch's*) помело́.
brothel /ˈbrɒθ(ə)l/ *n.* борде́ль (*m.*), публи́чный дом.
brother /ˈbrʌðə(r)/ *n.* брат.
■ *cpd.* **~-in-law** *n.* (*sister's husband, husband's sister's husband*) зять (*m.*); (*wife's ~*) шу́рин; (*husband's ~*) де́верь (*m.*); (*wife's sister's husband*) свoя́к.
brotherly /ˈbrʌðəlɪ/ *adj.* бра́тский.
brought /brɔːt/ *past and p.p. of* ▶ **bring**
brow /braʊ/ *n.* (*forehead*) лоб, чело́; (*of hill*) гре́бень (*m.*).
brown /braʊn/ *n.* кори́чневый цвет.
■ *adj.* 1 кори́чневый; (*grey-~*) бу́рый; **~ bread** се́рый хлеб; **~ paper** обёрточная бума́га.
2 (*tanned*) загоре́лый.
■ *v.t.* поджа́ри|вать, -ть.
brownish /ˈbraʊnɪʃ/ *adj.* коричнева́тый.
browse /braʊz/ *v.i.* щипа́ть (*impf.*) траву́.
browser /ˈbraʊzə(r)/ *n.* (*comput.*) бра́узер.
bruise /bruːz/ *n.* синя́к, кровоподтёк; (*on fruit*) вмя́тина.
■ *v.t.* ста́вить, по- синя́к + *d.*; (*fruit*) помя́ть, поби́ть (*both pf.*); **I ~d my shoulder** я ушиб плечо́.
brunette /bruːˈnet/ *n.* брюне́тка.
brunt /brʌnt/ *n.* гла́вный уда́р; **bear the ~ of the work** выноси́ть, вы́нести всю тя́жесть рабо́ты.
brush /brʌʃ/ *n.* (*for sweeping*) щётка; (*painter's*) кисть.
■ *v.t.* (*clean*) чи́стить, по-; (*touch slightly*): **the branches ~ed my cheek** ве́тви слегка́ косну́лись мое́й щеки́.
■ *v.i.*: **~ against sth.** слегка́ каса́ться, косну́ться чего́-н.; **~ past s.o.** прон|оси́ться, -ести́сь ми́мо кого́-н.
■ *with advs.*: **~ aside** *v.t.*: **~ aside difficulties** отме|та́ть, -сти́ тру́дности; **~ up** *v.t.*: **~ up one's French** освеж|а́ть, -и́ть в па́мяти францу́зский; *v.i.*: **~ up on a subject** освеж|а́ть, -и́ть зна́ния по како́му-н. предме́ту.
■ *cpd.* **~wood** *n.* хво́рост, валёжник.
brusque /brʊsk/ *adj.* ре́зкий.
Brussels /ˈbrʌs(ə)lz/ *n.* Брюссе́ль (*m.*); **~ sprouts** брюссе́льская капу́ста.
brutal /ˈbruːt(ə)l/ *adj.* жесто́кий.
brutality /bruːˈtælɪtɪ/ *n.* жесто́кость.
brutalize /ˈbruːtəlaɪz/ *v.t.* ожесточ|а́ть, -и́ть; огруб|ля́ть, -и́ть.
brute /bruːt/ *n.* (*animal*) живо́тное, зверь (*m.*); (*person*) скоти́на (*c.g.*).
■ *adj.*: **~ force** гру́бая, физи́ческая си́ла.
B.Sc. (*abbr. of* ***Bachelor of Science***) бакала́вр (есте́ственных) нау́к.
BSE (*abbr. of* ***bovine spongiform encephalopathy***) бы́чья губкови́дная энцефалопати́я.
bubble /ˈbʌb(ə)l/ *n.* пузы́рь (*m.*); (*of air, gas*) пузырёк; **~ bath** пе́на для ва́нны.
■ *v.i.* (*of water*) пузы́риться (*impf.*), кипе́ть (*impf.*).
Bucharest /buːkəˈrest/ *n.* Бухаре́ст.
buck[1] /bʌk/ *n.*
1 (*male animal*) саме́ц.
2 (*coll., dollar*) до́ллар.
3: **pass the ~** (*coll.*) снима́ть, снять с себя́ отве́тственность.
buck[2] /bʌk/ *v.i.* (*of horse*) брыка́ться (*impf.*).
bucket /ˈbʌkɪt/ *n.* ведро́.
■ *v.i.* (**bucketed, bucketing**) (*Br., rain*): **it's**

~ing down льёт как из ведра́.

buckle /ˈbʌk(ə)l/ *n.* пря́жка.
■ *v.t.* 1 (*coat, shoe*) застёг|ивать, -ну́ть.
2 (*wheel*) гнуть, по-; деформи́ровать (*impf., pf.*).
■ *v.i.* 1 (*of coat, shoe*) застёг|иваться, -ну́ться.
2 (*of wheel*) гну́ться, по-; деформи́роваться (*impf., pf.*).
3 (*of knees*) под|гиба́ться, -огну́ться.

buckwheat /ˈbʌkwiːt/ *n.* гречи́ха; (*attr.*) гре́чневый.

bud /bʌd/ *n.* по́чка; (*flower not fully opened*) буто́н.
■ *v.i.* (**budded, budding**) (*of plant*) покр|ыва́ться, -ы́ться по́чками; (*fig.*) распус|ка́ться, -ти́ться.

Budapest /buːdəˈpest/ *n.* Будапе́шт.

Buddhism /ˈbʊdɪz(ə)m/ *n.* будди́зм.

Buddhist /ˈbʊdɪst/ *n.* будди́ст.
■ *adj.* будди́йский, будди́стский.

buddleia /ˈbʌdlɪə/ *n.* (*bot.*) буд(д)ле́я.

buddy /ˈbʌdɪ/ *n.* (*US coll.*) дружи́ще (*m.*), прия́тель (*m.*).

budge /bʌdʒ/ *v.t.*: **I cannot ~ this rock** я не могу́ сдви́нуть э́тот ка́мень.
■ *v.i.*: **the bookcase won't ~ an inch** кни́жный шкаф невозмо́жно сдви́нуть с ме́ста.

budgerigar /ˈbʌdʒərɪɡɑː(r)/ *n.* волни́стый попуга́йчик.

budget /ˈbʌdʒɪt/ *n.* бюдже́т.
■ *v.t. & i.* (**budgeted, budgeting**): **~ (funds) for a project** ассигнова́ть (*impf., pf.*) определённую су́мму на прое́кт.

budgie /ˈbʌdʒɪ/ (*coll.*) = **budgerigar**

Buenos Aires /bweɪnɒs ˈaɪrɪz/ *n.* Буэ́нос-А́йрес.

buff /bʌf/ *n.* (*colour*) тёмно-жёлтый цвет.

buffalo /ˈbʌfələʊ/ *n.* (*pl.* **~** *or* **~es**) (*wild ox*) бу́йвол.

buffer /ˈbʌfə(r)/ *n.* (*rail., comput., fig.*) бу́фер.

buffet¹ /bʌfɪt/ *v.t.* (**buffeted, buffeting**) уд|аря́ть, -а́рить в + *a.*

buffet² /ˈbʊfeɪ/ *n.* (*refreshment bar*) буфе́т; (*meal*) а-ля фурше́т.

bug /bʌɡ/ *n.* (*small insect*) бука́шка, жучо́к; (*coll., germ*) зара́за; (*microphone*) жучо́к.
■ *v.t.* (**bugged, bugging**): **the room was ~ged** (*coll.*) в ко́мнате бы́ли устано́влены подслу́шивающие устро́йства; (*coll., annoy*) раздраж|а́ть, -и́ть.

bugger /ˈbʌɡə(r)/ (*Br. vulg.*) *n.* (*as term of abuse*) сво́лочь; **poor ~** несча́стный.
■ *v.t.*: **~ all** ни хрена́; **~ (it)!** чёрт возьми́! **~ them!** да хрен с ни́ми!
■ *v.i.*: **~ off!** прова́ливай!; убира́йся!

buggy /ˈbʌɡɪ/ *n.* (**baby ~**) лёгкая де́тская коля́ска.

bugle /ˈbjuːɡ(ə)l/ *n.* горн.

build /bɪld/ *n.* телосложе́ние.
■ *v.t.* (*past and p.p.* **built**)
1 стро́ить, по-; выстра́ивать, вы́строить; **~ a nest** вить, с- гнездо́.
2: **a well-built man** хорошо́ сложённый челове́к.
3 (*fig.*): **~ a new world** созд|ава́ть, -а́ть но́вый мир.
■ *with advs.*: **~ up** *v.t.*: **~ s.o. up** (*in health*) укреп|ля́ть, -и́ть кому́-н. здоро́вье; (*in prestige*) популяризи́ровать (*impf., pf.*) кого́-н.; **~ up a business** созд|ава́ть, -а́ть де́ло; *v.i.*: **work has built up over the past year** за после́дний год накопи́лось мно́го рабо́ты.
■ *cpd.* **~-up** *n.* (*accumulation*) скопле́ние; рост, разви́тие, развёртывание; (*coll., boosting*) популяриза́ция, созда́ние и́мени.

builder /ˈbɪldə(r)/ *n.* строи́тель (*m.*).

building /ˈbɪldɪŋ/ *n.*
1 (*structure*) зда́ние, постро́йка, строе́ние; (*premises*) помеще́ние.
2 (*activity*) (по)стро́йка; (*esp. large-scale*) строи́тельство; **~ site** стро́йка; **~ society** (*Br.*) (жили́щно-)строи́тельное о́бщество; ≈ ипоте́чный банк.

built /bɪlt/ *past and p.p. of* ▶ **build**

built-in /bɪlt/ *adj.*: **a ~ cupboard** встро́енный/стенно́й шкаф.

built-up /bɪlt/ *adj.*: **~ area** застро́енный райо́н.

bulb /bʌlb/ *n.* (*bot., anat.*) лу́ковица; (*of lamp*) ла́мпочка.

Bulgaria /bʌlˈɡeərɪə/ *n.* Болга́рия.

Bulgarian /bʌlˈɡeərɪən/ *n.* (*person*) болга́р|ин (*fem.* -ка); (*language*) болга́рский язы́к.
■ *adj.* болга́рский.

bulge /bʌldʒ/ *n.* вы́пуклость.
■ *v.i.* (*swell*) выпя́чиваться, вы́пятиться; (*of bag etc.*) над|ува́ться, -у́ться.

bulimia /bʊˈlɪmɪə/ *n.* булими́я.

bulimic /bʊˈlɪmɪk/ *adj.* страда́ющий булими́ей.

bulk /bʌlk/ *n.*
1 (*size*) величина́, ма́сса, объём.
2 (*in large quantities*): **~ buying** опто́вые заку́пки.
3 (*greater part*) основна́я ма́сса/часть.

bulky /ˈbʌlkɪ/ *adj.* (**bulkier, bulkiest**) громо́здкий.

bull /bʊl/ *n.* (*ox*) бык; (*elephant, whale etc.*) саме́ц.
■ *cpds.* **~dog** *n.* бульдо́г; **~dozer** *n.* бульдо́зер; **~fight** *n.* бой быко́в; **~fighter** *n.* тореадо́р; **~ring** *n.* аре́на для бо́я быко́в; **~seye** *n.* (*of target*) я́блочко.

bullet /ˈbʊlɪt/ *n.* пу́ля.
■ *cpd.* **~proof** *adj.* пуленепробива́емый; **~proof vest** бронежиле́т.

bulletin /ˈbʊlɪtɪn/ *n.* (*official statement*) бюллете́нь (*m.*); (*news report*) сво́дка (новосте́й), вы́пуск, сообще́ние.

bullock /ˈbʊlək/ *n.* вол.

bully /ˈbʊlɪ/ *n.* громи́ла (*m.*), задира (*c.g.*).
■ *v.t.* запу́г|ивать, -а́ть.

bum /bʌm/ *n.* (*coll.*)
1 (*Br., buttocks*) зад, за́дница.
2 (*US, vagrant*) бродя́га (*m.*).

bumblebee /ˈbʌmb(ə)lbiː/ *n.* шмель (*m.*).

bump /bʌmp/ *n.*
1 (*thump*) глухо́й уда́р; (*collision*) толчо́к.
2 (*swelling, protuberance*) ши́шка.
■ *v.t.* уд|аря́ть, -а́рить; ушиб|а́ть, -и́ть; **I ~ed my knee as I fell** я ушиб коле́но при паде́нии.
■ *v.i.*: **his car ~ed into ours** его́ маши́на вре́залась в на́шу; **I ~ed into him in London** я наткну́лся на него́ в Ло́ндоне.

bumper /ˈbʌmpə(r)/ *n.*
1 (*of car*) бáмпер.
2: **~ crop** небывáлый/невидáнный урожáй.

bumpkin /ˈbʌmpkɪn/ *n.* мужлáн.

bumptious /ˈbʌmpʃəs/ *adj.* самоувéренный, зазнáвшийся.

bumpy /ˈbʌmpɪ/ *adj.* (**bumpier, bumpiest**) (*of road*) ухáбистый, трýский; **a ~ flight** ≈ болтáнка.

bumsters /ˈbʌmstəz/ *n.* бáмстер|ы (*pl.*, *g.* -ов) (*брюки, сидящие низко на бедрах*).

bun /bʌn/ *n.*
1 (*cul.*) бýлочка, плю́шка.
2 (*of hair*) пучóк.

bunch /bʌntʃ/ *n.*
1 (*of flowers*) букéт; (*of grapes*) кисть, гроздь; (*of bananas*) гроздь; **~ of keys** свя́зка ключéй.
2 (*coll.*, *group*) компáния, грýппа.

bundle /ˈbʌnd(ə)l/ *n.*
1 (*of clothes etc.*) ýзел; (*of sticks*) вязáнка; (*of hay*) охáпка.
2: **she is a ~ of nerves** онá комóк нéрвов.
■ *v.t.* 1 **~ up** свя́з|ывать, -áть в ýзел/вязáнку.
2 (*shove*) запи́х|ивать, -áть.

bung /bʌŋ/ *n.* зáтычка, втýлка.
■ *v.t.* 1 (*cask etc.*) зат|ыкáть, -кнýть; закупóри|вать, -ть; **the sink is ~ed up** рáковина засори́лась; **my nose is ~ed up** у меня́ залóжен нос.
2 (*Br. sl.*, *throw*) швыр|я́ть, -нýть.

bungalow /ˈbʌŋgələʊ/ *n.* бýнгало (*indecl.*).

bungle /ˈbʌŋg(ə)l/ *v.t.* пóртить, на-; пýтать, с-.

bunk[1] /bʌŋk/ *n.* (*sleeping berth*) кóйка; **~ bed** двухъя́русная кровáть.

bunk[2] /bʌŋk/ (*Br.*) *v.i.* см|ывáться, -ы́ться; **~ off** (*coll.*): **to ~ off lessons/school** прог|ýливать, -уля́ть урóки, сачковáть (*impf.*).

bunker /ˈbʌŋkə(r)/ *n.* (*underground shelter*) бýнкер, блиндáж; (*golf*) я́ма.

buoy /bɔɪ/ *n.* буй, бáкен; (*life~*) спасáтельный буй/круг.
■ *v.t.*: **~ up** (*fig.*, *support*) поддéрж|ивать, -áть; (*cheer up*) подбáдривать, -одри́ть.

buoyant /ˈbɔɪənt/ *adj.* плавýчий; (*of person*) жизнерáдостный; (*of hopes, market*) оживлённый; (*of prices*) имéющий тендéнцию к повышéнию.

burden /ˈbə:d(ə)n/ *n.* (*load*) нóша, груз; (*fig.*) брéмя (*nt.*); обýза.
■ *v.t.* (*load*) нагру|жáть, -зи́ть; (*fig.*) обремен|я́ть, -и́ть.

bureau /ˈbjʊərəʊ/ *n.* (*pl.* **~x** *or* **~s**) (*Br.*, *desk*) бюрó (*indecl.*), контóрка; (*US*, *chest*) комóд; (*office*) бюрó; **~ de change** обмéнный пункт.

bureaucracy /bjʊəˈrɒkrəsɪ/ *n.* бюрокрáтия.

bureaucrat /ˈbjʊərəkræt/ *n.* бюрокрáт, чинóвник.

bureaucratic /bjʊərəˈkrætɪk/ *adj.* бюрократи́ческий.

bureaux /ˈbjʊərəʊz/ *pl. of* ▶ **bureau**

burgeon /ˈbə:dʒ(ə)n/ *v.i.* да|вáть, -ть пóчки; распус|кáться, -ти́ться.

burger /ˈbə:gə(r)/ *n.* котлéта; **~ bar** гáмбургерная, котлéтная.

burglar /ˈbə:glə(r)/ *n.* квартúрный вор, взлóмщик.

burglarize /ˈbə:gləraɪz/ (*US*) = **burgle** *v.t.*

burglary /ˈbə:glərɪ/ *n.* ограблéние (дóма/óфиса), крáжа с взлóмом.

burgle /ˈbə:g(ə)l/ *v.t.* грáбить, о-.

burial /ˈberɪəl/ *n.* погребéние, захоронéние.

burly /ˈbə:lɪ/ *adj.* (**burlier, burliest**) здоровéнный, дю́жий.

Burma /ˈbə:mə/ *n.* (*hist.*) Би́рма.

burn /bə:n/ *n.* ожóг.
■ *v.t.* (*past and p.p.* **burnt** *or* **burned**) (*destroy by fire*) сж|игáть, -ечь; **~ o.s.** обж|игáться, -éчься; **the meat is ~t** мя́со сгорéло/подгорéло.
■ *v.i.* (*past and p.p.* **burnt** *or* **burned**) горéть (*impf.*).
■ *with advs.*: **~ down** *v.t.* сж|игáть, -ечь; *v.i.*: **the house ~t down** дом сгорéл дотлá; **~ out** *v.t.*: **the fire ~t itself out** пожáр вы́жег всё дотлá и стих/костёр догорéл (до углéй) и потýх; **~ o.s. out** (*fig.*) сгорéть (*pf.*).

burner /ˈbə:nə(r)/ *n.*
1 (*of stove etc.*) горéлка, конфóрка; **to put on the back burner** отодв|игáть, -и́нуть на зáдний план.
2 (*for CDs/DVDs*) (CD/DVD-)резáк (*sl.*) (*устройство для записи информации на компакт-диск*).

burning /ˈbə:nɪŋ/ *n.* горéние.
■ *adj.* (*of fever*) сжигáющий; (*of shame*) жгýчий; (*of zeal*) нейстóвый.

burnt /bə:nt/ *past and p.p. of* ▶ **burn**

burp /bə:p/ (*coll.*) *n.* отры́жка, рыгáние.
■ *v.i.* рыг|áть, -нýть.

burrow /ˈbʌrəʊ/ *n.* норá.
■ *v.i.* рыть, вы́- нору́/рыть, про- ходы́.

bursary /ˈbə:sərɪ/ *n.* (*Br.*) (*grant*) стипéндия.

burst /bə:st/ *n.* взрыв; **a ~ of energy** вспы́шка/взрыв энéргии; **~ of applause** взрыв аплодисмéнтов; **~ of machine-gun fire** пулемётная óчередь.
■ *v.t.* (*past and p.p.* **burst**) раз|рывáть, -орвáть; **the river ~ its banks** рекá вы́шла из берегóв.
■ *v.i.* (*past and p.p.* **burst**): **the balloon ~** воздýшный шар лóпнул; **he is ~ing with health** он пы́шет здорóвьем; **he was ~ing with pride** егó распирáло от гóрдости; **the door ~ open** дверь распахнýлась.
■ *with preps.*: **~ into tears** разрыдáться (*pf.*); **~ into a room** врывáться, ворвáться в кóмнату; **~ into flame(s)** вспы́х|ивать, -нуть.
■ *with advs.*: **~ out** *v.i.* (*exclaim*) вы́палить (*pf.*); **~ out laughing** расхохотáться (*pf.*).

bury /ˈberɪ/ *v.t.*
1 (*inter*) хорони́ть, по-.
2 (*hide in earth*) зар|ывáть, -ы́ть.

bus /bʌs/ *n.* (*pl.* **buses** *or US* **busses**) автóбус.
■ *cpds.* **~ conductor** *n.* кондýктор автóбуса; **~ driver** *n.* води́тель (*m.*) автóбуса; **~ station** *n.* автóбусная стáнция; **~ stop** *n.* автóбусная остановка.

bush /bʊʃ/ *n.* (*shrub*) куст; (*wild land*) некультиви́рованная земля́.

bushy /ˈbʊʃɪ/ *adj.* (**bushier, bushiest**) (*of beard etc.*) густóй; (*of plant*) кусти́стый; (*of tail*) пуши́стый.

business /ˈbɪznɪs/ *n.*
1 (*affair*) дéло; **it is none of your ~** э́то не

ва́ше де́ло; э́то вас не каса́ется; **mind your own ~** не вме́шивайтесь/су́йтесь не в своё де́ло.
2 (*work*): **get down to ~** бра́ться, взя́ться за де́ло.
3 (*comm. etc.*): **~ hours, hours of ~** (*of an office*) часы́ приёма/заня́тий/рабо́ты; **~ card** визи́тка, визи́тная ка́рточка; **he is in the wool ~** он занима́ется торго́влей ше́рстью; **go into ~** заня́ться (*pf.*) комме́рцией; **on ~** по де́лу.
4 (*establishment*) фи́рма, предприя́тие.
■ *cpds.* **~like** *adj.* делово́й, практи́чный; **~man** *n.* коммерса́нт, бизнесме́н, деле́ц; **~woman** *n.* би́знес-ле́ди, бизнесву́мен (*both f. indecl.*), делова́я же́нщина.

busker /ˈbʌskə(r)/ *n.* у́личный музыка́нт.

busses /ˈbʌsɪz/ *US pl. of* ▸ **bus**

bust¹ /bʌst/ *n.* (*sculpture; bosom*) бюст.

bust² /bʌst/ (*coll.*) *v.i.* (*past and p.p.* **busted** *or* **bust**) (*also* **go ~**) лома́ться, с-; **the business went ~** де́ло ло́пнуло.

bustle /ˈbʌs(ə)l/ *n.* сумато́ха, суета́.
■ *v.i.* (*also* **~ about**) суети́ться, тормоши́ться (*both impf.*).

bustling /ˈbʌslɪŋ/ *adj.* суетли́вый; **a ~ city** оживлённый го́род.

busy /ˈbɪzɪ/ *adj.* (**busier, busiest**)
1 (*occupied*) за́нятый; **I had a ~ day** я весь день был(а́) в дела́х; **he was ~ packing** он был за́нят упако́вкой; **the line is ~** (*US*) но́мер за́нят.
2 : **a ~ street** шу́мная/оживлённая у́лица.
■ *v.t.*: **~ o.s.** зан|има́ться, -я́ться.

but /bʌt/ *adv.* **we can ~ try** попы́тка — не пы́тка.
■ *prep. & conj.* (*except*): **no one ~ me** никто́, кро́ме меня́; **she is anything ~ beautiful** она́ далеко́ не краса́вица; **the last ~ one** предпосле́дний; **next door ~ one** че́рез одну́ дверь; **~ for me he would have stayed** е́сли бы не я, он бы оста́лся; **I cannot help ~ think ...** я не могу́ не ду́мать, что... .
■ *conj.* но.

butcher /ˈbʊtʃə(r)/ *n.* мясни́к; **~'s (shop)** мясна́я ла́вка, мясно́й павильо́н.
■ *v.t.* (*cattle*) забива́ть (*impf.*); (*people*) истреб|ля́ть, -и́ть.

butchery /ˈbʊtʃərɪ/ *n.* (*trade*) торго́вля мя́сом; (*massacre*) резня́.

butler /ˈbʌtlə(r)/ *n.* дворе́цкий.

butt¹ /bʌt/ (*fig., target*): **a ~ for ridicule** мише́нь для насме́шек.

butt² /bʌt/ *n.* (*of rifle*) прикла́д; (*of cigarette*) оку́рок; (*US coll., buttocks*) зад, за́дница.

butt³ /bʌt/ *v.i.*: **~ in** (*interrupt*) встр|ева́ть, -ять.

butter /ˈbʌtə(r)/ *n.* ма́сло.
■ *v.t.* нама́з|ывать, -ать ма́слом; **~ up** (*fig.*) льсти́ть, по- + *d.*
■ *cpds.* **~cup** *n.* лю́тик; **~fingers** *n.* растя́па (*c.g.*).

butterfly /ˈbʌtəflaɪ/ *n.*
1 ба́бочка; **I have butterflies in my stomach** у меня́ се́рдце ёкает.
2 : **~ stroke** (*swimming*) баттерфля́й.

buttock /ˈbʌtək/ *n.* я́годица.

button /ˈbʌt(ə)n/ *n.*
1 пу́говица.
2 (*knob*) кно́пка; **press a ~** наж|има́ть, -а́ть кно́пку.
3 (*US, badge*) значо́к.
■ *v.t.* (*also* **~ up**) застёг|ивать, -ну́ть.
■ *cpd.* **~hole** *n.* петля́, петли́ца; (*Br., flower*) цвето́к в петли́це; *v.t.* (*fig.*) задер́ж|ивать, -а́ть разгово́ром.

buttress /ˈbʌtrɪs/ *n.* (*archit.*) подпо́р(к)а; (*fig.*) опо́ра.

buy /baɪ/ *n.*: **a good ~** вы́годная поку́пка.
■ *v.t.* (**buys, buying;** *past and p.p.* **bought**) покупа́ть, купи́ть; **~ s.o. a drink** ста́вить, по- кому́-н. вы́пивку.
■ *with advs.*: **~ off** *v.t.* откуп|а́ться, -и́ться (*от кого*); **~ out** *v.t.*: **~ s.o. out** выкупа́ть, вы́купить чью-н. до́лю; **~ up** *v.t.* скуп|а́ть, -и́ть.
■ *cpd.* **~out** *n.* (*comm.*) вы́куп.

buyer /ˈbaɪə(r)/ *n.* покупа́тель (*m.*).

buzz /bʌz/ *n.* жужжа́ние; (*of talk*) гул, жужжа́ние.
■ *v.t.* (*summon with buzzer*) звони́ть, по-; вызыва́ть, вы́звать сигна́лом.
■ *v.i.* (*of insect, projectile*) жужжа́ть (*impf.*).

buzzard /ˈbʌzəd/ *n.* сары́ч, каню́к; (*US, turkey vulture*) гриф-инде́йка.

buzzer /ˈbʌzə(r)/ *n.* (*elec.*) зу́ммер.

by /baɪ/ *adv.* (*near*) побли́зости; (*alongside*) ря́дом; (*past*) ми́мо; **the days went ~** дни шли оди́н за други́м.
■ *prep.* 1 (*near*): **sit ~ the fire** сиде́ть (*impf.*) у ками́на; **I was going ~ the house** я шёл ми́мо до́ма; **~ o.s.** (*alone*) (соверше́нно) оди́н/одна́; (*unaided*) сам/сама́, самостоя́тельно; **a path ~ the river** доро́жка у/вдоль реки́; **~ the way** кста́ти.
2 (*along, via*): **~ land and sea** по су́ше и по мо́рю; **~ the nearest road** ближа́йшей доро́гой.
3 (*of time limit*): **~ Thursday** к четвергу́; **~ now** тепе́рь; **he should know ~ now** пора́ бы уж ему́ знать; **~ then** к тому́ вре́мени.
4 (*means*) *often expr. by i. case*; (**~** *means of*) при по́мощи + *g.*; **a book ~ Tolstoy** кни́га Толсто́го; **~ my watch** по мои́м часа́м; **~ rail** по желе́зной доро́ге; **~ taxi** на/в такси́; **~ law** по зако́ну; **a letter written ~ hand** письмо́, напи́санное от руки́.
5 (*of rate or measurement*): **little ~ little** ма́ло-пома́лу; **bread came down in price ~1 rouble** хлеб подешеве́л на оди́н рубль; **sell sth. ~ the yard** прод|ава́ть, -а́ть что-н. на я́рды; **one ~ one** оди́н за други́м; по одному́, поодино́чке; **day ~ day** день за днём; **we divide thirty ~ five** де́лим 30 на́ 5; **a room 13 feet ~ 12** ко́мната трина́дцать фу́тов на двена́дцать.

bye-bye /ˈbaɪbaɪ, bəˈbaɪ/ *int.* пока́!; всего́ хоро́шего!

by-election /ˈbaɪɪlekʃ(ə)n/ *n.* (*Br.*) дополни́тельные вы́боры (*m. pl.*).

Byelorussia /bjeləʊˈrʌʃə/ *n.* Белору́ссия.

Byelorussian /bjeləʊˈrʌʃ(ə)n/ *n.* (*person*) белору́с (*fem.* -ка); (*language*) белору́сский язы́к.
■ *adj.* белору́сский.

bygone /ˈbaɪgɒn/ *n.* (*usu. pl.*): **let ~s be ~s** что бы́ло, то прошло́.

■ *adj.* проше́дший, мину́вший.
bypass /'baɪpɑːs/ *n.* объе́зд, обхо́д; (*med.*) шунт; **heart ~** корона́рное шунти́рование.
■ *v.t.* об|ходи́ть, -ойти́ (*also fig.*).
by-product /'baɪprɒdʌkt/ *n.* побо́чный проду́кт.
bystander /'baɪstændə(r)/ *n.* зри́тель (*m.*).
byte /baɪt/ *n.* (*comput.*) байт.
Byzantine /baɪ'zæntaɪn/ *adj.* (*lit., fig.*) византи́йский; **~ Empire** Византи́я, Византи́йская импе́рия.
Byzantium /bɪ'zæntɪəm/ *n.* (*city*) Виза́нтий.

Cc

C[1] /siː/ *n.*
1 (*mus.*) до (*nt. indecl.*).
2 (*acad. mark*) «удовлетвори́тельно», тро́йка.
C[2] (*abbr. of* ***Celsius*** /'selsɪəs/ *or* ***centigrade*** /'sentɪgreɪd/) C (= *гра́дусов по Це́льсию or по шкале́ Це́льсия*).
c. *abbr. of*
1 ***century*** в. (век); столе́тие.
2 ***circa*** ок. (о́коло).
3 ***cent(s)*** це́нт(ы).
cab /kæb/ *n.*
1 (*taxi*) такси́ (*nt. indecl.*); кеб.
2 (*of lorry etc.*) каби́на води́теля.
■ *cpd.* **~ driver** *nn.* шофёр такси́.
cabaret /'kæbəreɪ/ *n.* кабаре́ (*nt. indecl.*), эстра́дное представле́ние.
cabbage /'kæbɪdʒ/ *n.* капу́ста.
cabby /'kæbɪ/ *n.* (*coll.*) такси́ст.
cabin /'kæbɪn/ *n.* каби́на; (*in ship etc.*) каю́та.
cabinet /'kæbɪnɪt/ *n.*
1 (*piece of furniture*) го́рка, (застеклённый) шка́ф(чик).
2 (*pol.*) кабине́т (мини́стров).
cable /'keɪb(ə)l/ *n.* (*elec.*) ка́бель (*m.*); **~ TV** ка́бельное телеви́дение.
cackle /'kæk(ə)l/ *v.t.* & *i.* гогота́ть.
cactus /'kæktəs/ *n.* (*pl.* **cacti** /-taɪ/ *or* **cactuses**) ка́ктус.
CAD (*abbr. of* ***computer-aided design***) автоматизи́рованное проекти́рование.
caddy /'kædɪ/ *n.* ча́йница.
cadet /kə'det/ *n.* (*mil.*) каде́т, курса́нт.
cadge /kædʒ/ *v.t.* & *i.* выкля́нчивать, вы́клянчить; (*coll.*) стрел|я́ть, -ьну́ть (*что у кого*).
Caesarean /sɪ'zeərɪən/ (*US also* **Cesarean**) *adj.*: **~ birth, operation, section** ке́сарево сече́ние.
cafe /'kæfeɪ/ *n.* кафе́ (*nt. indecl.*).
cafeteria /kæfɪ'tɪərɪə/ *n.* кафете́рий.
caffeine /'kæfiːn/ *n.* кофеи́н.
cage /keɪdʒ/ *n.* кле́тка.
Cairo /'kaɪrəʊ/ *n.* Каи́р.
cajole /kə'dʒəʊl/ *v.t.* обха́живать (*impf.*).
cake /keɪk/ *n.*
1 (*sponge ~*) кекс; (*with cream*) торт.
2 (*fig.*): **a piece of ~** (*coll.*) пустяко́вое де́ло.
calamity /kə'læmɪtɪ/ *n.* бе́дствие.
calcium /'kælsɪəm/ *n.* ка́льций.
calculat|e /'kælkjʊleɪt/ *v.t.*
1 (*compute*) вычисля́ть, вы́числить.
2 (*estimate*) рассчи́т|ывать, -а́ть.
3 (*plan*): **a ~ed risk** обду́манный риск.
calculating /'kælkjʊleɪtɪŋ/ *adj.* расчётливый, себе́ на уме́.
calculation /kælkjʊ'leɪʃ(ə)n/ *n.* вычисле́ние.
calculator /'kælkjʊleɪtə(r)/ *n.* калькуля́тор.
Calcutta /kæl'kʌtə/ *n.* Кальку́тта.
calendar /'kælɪndə(r)/ *n.* календа́рь.
calf[1] /kɑːf/ *n.* (*pl.* **calves**) (*of cattle*) телёнок.
■ *cpd.* **~skin** *n.* опо́ек.
calf[2] /kɑːf/ *n.* (*pl.* **calves**) (*of leg*) икра́.
calibrate /'kælɪbreɪt/ *v.t.* калиброва́ть (*impf., pf.*), градуи́ровать (*impf., pf.*).
calibre /'kælɪbə(r)/ (*US* **caliber**) *n.* кали́бр.
California /kælɪ'fɔːnɪə/ *n.* Калифо́рния.
call /kɔːl/ *n.*
1 (*cry*) зов, о́клик.
2 (*of bird*) крик.
3 (*teleph.*): **telephone ~** звоно́к по телефо́ну.
4 (*visit*): **pay a ~** нан|оси́ть, -ести́ визи́т.
5 (*summons, demand*) зов, клич, призы́в; **the doctor is on ~** врач на вы́зове.
6 (*need*): **there is no ~ for him to worry** ему́ не́чего волнова́ться.
■ *v.t.* 1 (*name*) наз|ыва́ть, -ва́ть; **he is ~ed John** его́ зову́т Джо́н(ом); **~ a strike** приз|ыва́ть, -ва́ть к забасто́вке.
2 (*summon*): **~ a doctor/taxi!** вы́зовите врача́/такси́!
3 (*announce*): **~ a meeting** соз|ыва́ть, -ва́ть собра́ние.
■ *v.i.* 1 (*cry*) звать, по-; окл|ика́ть, -и́кнуть.
2 (*visit*) за|ходи́ть, -йти́; **I ~ed on him** я зашёл к нему́; **the train ~s at every station** по́езд остана́вливается на ка́ждой ста́нции.
3 **~ for** (*pick up*): **I ~ed for him at 6** я зашёл за ним в 6 часо́в; (*demand*): **the situation ~s for courage** обстоя́тельства тре́буют му́жества.
4 **~ on**: **the president ~ed on the world community for help** президе́нт призва́л на по́мощь мирово́е соо́бщество.
■ *with advs.*: **~ back** *v.t.* & *i.* (*on telephone*) позвони́ть (*pf.*) сно́ва (+ *d.*); **~ in** *v.t.* (*a specialist*) вызыва́ть, вы́звать; **~ off** *v.t.* (*cancel*) отмен|я́ть, -и́ть; **~ out** *v.t.* (*summon away*) от|зыва́ть, -озва́ть; (*doctor*) вызыва́ть, вы́звать; *v.i.* выклика́ть, вы́кликнуть; **~ up**

v.t. (*telephone*) звони́ть, по- (*кому*) по телефо́ну; (*evoke*) вызыва́ть, вы́звать; (*for mil. service*) призы|ва́ть, -ва́ть.
■ *cpds.* **~ box** *n.* (*Br.*) телефо́нная бу́дка; **~ centre** *n.* колл-це́нтр, информацио́нно-спра́вочная слу́жба.

C

caller /ˈkɔːlə(r)/ *n.* (*visitor*) посети́тель (*fem.* -ница); (*telephone*) позвони́вший (по телефо́ну).

calligraphy /kəˈlɪgrəfɪ/ *n.* каллигра́фия.

callous /ˈkæləs/ *adj.* чёрствый.

calm /kɑːm/ *n.* споко́йствие, тишина́.
■ *adj.* споко́йный.
■ *v.t.* & *i.* (*also* **~ down**) успок|а́ивать(ся), -о́ить(ся).

calorie /ˈkælərɪ/ *n.* кало́рия.

calves /kɑːvz/ *pl. of* ▸**calf**[1], **calf**[2]

camaraderie /kæməˈrɑːdərɪ/ *n.* това́рищеские отноше́ния.

Cambodia /kæmˈbəʊdɪə/ *n.* Камбо́джа.

Cambodian /kæmˈbəʊdɪən/ *n.* (*person*) камбоджи́|ец (*fem.* -йка).
■ *adj.* камбоджи́йский.

camcorder /ˈkæmkɔːdə(r)/ *n.* портати́вная видеока́мера.

came /keɪm/ *past of* ▸**come**

camel /ˈkæm(ə)l/ *n.* верблю́д.

camellia /kəˈmiːlɪə/ *n.* каме́лия.

camera /ˈkæmrə/ *n.* фотоаппара́т.
■ *cpds.* **~man** *n.* опера́тор; **~ phone** *n.* камерофо́н, моби́льный телефо́н с фото-/видео|ка́мерой.

camomile /ˈkæməmaɪl/ *n.* рома́шка.

camouflage /ˈkæməflɑːʒ/ *n.* маскиро́вка.
■ *v.t.* маскирова́ть, за-.

camp[1] /kæmp/ *n.* ла́герь.
■ *v.i.* (*pitch camp*) разб|ива́ть, -и́ть ла́герь; **go ~ing** жить (*impf.*) в пала́тках; **~(ing) site** ке́мпинг, турба́за.
■ *cpds.* **~ bed** *n.* (*Br.*) раскладу́шка; **~fire** *n.* похо́дный костёр.

camp[2] /kæmp/ *adj.* женоподо́бный.

campaign /kæmˈpeɪn/ *n.* кампа́ния.
■ *v.i.* уча́ствовать (*impf.*) в похо́де; (*fig.*) вести́ (*det.*) кампа́нию.

campaigner /kæmˈpeɪnə(r)/ *n.* уча́стник кампа́нии.

camper /ˈkæmpə(r)/ *n.* (*person*) ночу́ющий на откры́том во́здухе; (*vehicle*) (*Br., also* **~ van**) автодо́м (*автомобиль, не прицеп*); (*US*) жило́й/тури́стский автоприце́п.

camping /ˈkæmpɪŋ/ *n.* ке́мпинг.

campus /ˈkæmpəs/ *n.* (*pl.* **~es**) университе́тский городо́к.

can[1] /kæn/ *n.*
1 (*for liquids*) бидо́н.
2 (*for food*) (консе́рвная) ба́нка.
■ *v.t.* (**canned, canning**) консерви́ровать (*impf., pf.*).
■ *cpd.* **~-opener** *n.* консе́рвный нож.

can[2] /kæn/ *v.i.* (*3rd pers. sg. pres.* **can;** *past* **could;** *neg.* **cannot, can't**) (*expr. ability or permission*) мочь (*impf.*); (*expr. capability*) уме́ть (*impf.*); **he can't clean his teeth yet** он ещё не уме́ет чи́стить зу́бы; **I ~ see him** я ви́жу его́; **I ~ understand that** я понима́ю (*or* могу́ поня́ть) э́то; **as soon as you ~** как то́лько смо́жете; как мо́жно скоре́е.

Canada /ˈkænədə/ *n.* Кана́да.

Canadian /kəˈneɪdɪən/ *n.* (*person*) кана́д|ец (*fem.* -ка).
■ *adj.* кана́дский.

canal /kəˈnæl/ *n.* кана́л.

canary /kəˈneərɪ/ *n.* канаре́йка; **C~ Islands** Кана́рские острова́.

Canberra /ˈkænbərə/ *n.* Канбе́рра.

cancel /ˈkæns(ə)l/ *v.t.* (**cancelled, cancelling;** *US also* **canceled, canceling**) отмен|я́ть, -и́ть. (*impf.*).

cancellation /kænsəˈleɪʃ(ə)n/ *n.* отме́на, аннули́рование.

cancer /ˈkænsə(r)/ *n.*
1 (*astron.*) Рак.
2 (*med.*) рак.

candid /ˈkændɪd/ *adj.* и́скренний.

candidate /ˈkændɪdət/ *n.* кандида́т.

candle /ˈkænd(ə)l/ *n.* свеча́.
■ *cpds.* **~light** *n.* свет свечи́/свече́й; **~stick** *n.* подсве́чник.

candour /ˈkændə(r)/ (*US* **candor**) *n.* открове́нность, и́скренность; беспристра́стность.

candy /ˈkændɪ/ *n.* (*US*) конфе́ты, сла́сти (*f. pl.*).

cane /keɪn/ *n.*
1 (*bot.*) камы́ш, тростни́к; **~ chair** плетёное кре́сло.
2 (*for punishment*) ро́зга.

canine /ˈkeɪnaɪn/ *adj.* соба́чий; **~ tooth** клык.

cannabis /ˈkænəbɪs/ *n.* (*resin*) гаши́ш; (*dried leaves*) анаша́, марихуа́на.

cannibal /ˈkænɪb(ə)l/ *n.* каннiба́л.

cannibalism /ˈkænɪbəlɪz(ə)m/ *n.* каннибали́зм, людое́дство.

cannon /ˈkænən/ *n.* пу́шка, ору́дие.
■ *v.i.* (*Br.*) (*collide*) ст|а́лкиваться, -олкну́ться.
■ *cpd.* **~ball** *n.* пу́шечное ядро́.

cannot /ˈkænɒt, kəˈnɒt/ *neg. of* ▸**can**[2]

canoe /kəˈnuː/ *n.* кано́э (*nt. indecl.*).
■ *v.i.* (**canoes, canoed, canoeing**) плыть (*det.*) в челноке́ (*or* на кано́э).

canopy /ˈkænəpɪ/ *n.*
1 (*covering over bed etc.*) балдахи́н, по́лог.
2 (*of parachute*) ку́пол.
3 (*fig.*) по́лог, покро́в.

can't /kɑːnt/ *neg. of* ▸**can**[2]

cantankerous /kænˈtæŋkərəs/ *adj.* сварли́вый.

canteen /kænˈtiːn/ *n.*
1 (*eating place*) столо́вая.
2 (*water container*) фля́га.

canter /ˈkæntə(r)/ *v.i.* е́хать (*impf.*) лёгким гало́пом.

canvas /ˈkænvəs/ *n.* холст.

canvass /ˈkænvəs/ *v.t.* & *i.*: **~ a constituency** вести́ (*det.*) предвы́борную агита́цию в избира́тельном о́круге; **~ opinions** соб|ира́ть, -ра́ть мне́ния.

canvasser /ˈkænvəsə(r)/ *n.* агита́тор.

canyon /ˈkænjən/ *n.* каньо́н.

cap /kæp/ *n.*
1 (*of uniform*) фура́жка; (*baseball* **~**) ке́пка.
2 (*of bottle*) кры́шка; (*of pen*) колпачо́к.

■ *v.t.* (**capped, capping**) (*excel*) прев|осходи́ть, -зойти́; **to ~ it all** в доверше́ние ко всему́.
capability /keɪpəˈbɪlɪtɪ/ *n.* спосо́бность.
capable /ˈkeɪpəb(ə)l/ *adj.*
1 (*gifted*) спосо́бный.
2 (*~ of*) спосо́бный на + *a.*
capacious /kəˈpeɪʃəs/ *adj.* просто́рный.
capacity /kəˈpæsɪtɪ/ *n.*
1 (*ability to hold*) вмести́мость; **the hall's seating ~ is 500** вмести́мость за́ла — пятьсо́т мест; **the room was filled to ~** ко́мната была́ запо́лнена до отка́за.
2 (*of engine*) (наибо́льшая) мо́щность.
3 (*position*): **in my ~ as critic** как кри́тик.
cape[1] /keɪp/ *n.* (*garment*) наки́дка, плащ.
cape[2] /keɪp/ (*geog.*) мыс.
capers /ˈkeɪpəz/ *n. pl.* (*cul.*) ка́персы (*m. pl.*).
capillary /kəˈpɪlərɪ/ *adj.* капилля́рный; **~ action** капилля́рное притяже́ние, капилля́рность.
capital /ˈkæpɪt(ə)l/ *n.*
1 (*principal city*) столи́ца.
2 (*upper-case letter*) прописна́я/загла́вная бу́ква.
3 (*wealth*) капита́л.
■ *adj.* 1 (*involving death penalty*): **~ punishment** сме́ртная казнь.
2 (*econ.*): **~ expenditure** капита́льные затра́ты.
3 (*upper-case*) прописно́й.
capitalism /ˈkæpɪtəlɪz(ə)m/ *n.* капитали́зм.
capitalist /ˈkæpɪtəlɪst/ *n.* капитали́ст.
capitalize /ˈkæpɪtəlaɪz/ *v.t. & i.*: **~ on s.o.'s misfortune** наж|ива́ться, -и́ться на чьём-н. несча́стье.
capitulate /kəˈpɪtjʊleɪt/ *v.t.* капитули́ровать (*impf., pf.*).
cappuccino /kæpʊˈtʃiːnəʊ/ *n.* (*pl.* **~s**) капуч(ч)и́но (*m. & nt. indecl.*).
capricious /kəˈprɪʃəs/ *adj.* прихотли́вый, капри́зный.
Capricorn /ˈkæprɪkɔːn/ *n.* Козеро́г.
capsize /kæpˈsaɪz/ *v.t. & i.* опроки́|дывать(ся), -нуть(ся).
capsule /ˈkæpsjuːl/ *n.* (*med.*) ка́псула.
captain /ˈkæptɪn/ *n.*
1 (*head of team*) капита́н кома́нды.
2 (*army rank*) капита́н.
3 (*naval rank*) капита́н пе́рвого ра́нга.
caption /ˈkæpʃ(ə)n/ *n.* (*title*) по́дпись к карти́нке.
captivating /ˈkæptɪveɪtɪŋ/ *adj.* плени́тельный.
captive /ˈkæptɪv/ *n.* пле́нник, пле́нный.
captivity /kæpˈtɪvɪtɪ/ *n.* плен, плене́ние.
capture /ˈkæptʃə(r)/ *n.* по́имка, захва́т.
■ *v.t.* брать, взять в плен; **~ s.o.'s attention** прико́в|ывать, -а́ть чьё-н. внима́ние.
car /kɑː(r)/ *n.* (легково́й) автомоби́ль, маши́на; **~ boot sale** (*Br.*) прода́жа (пря́мо) из бага́жника.
■ *cpds.* **~ ferry** *n.* автопаро́м; **~ hire** *n.* прока́т автомоби́лей; **~ park** *n.* (*Br.*) па́ркинг, автостоя́нка; **~sick** *adj.*: **do you get ~sick?** вас ука́чивает в маши́не?
carafe /kəˈræf/ *n.* графи́н.
caramel /ˈkærəmel/ *n.* караме́ль.
carat /ˈkærət/ (*US also* **karat**) *n.* кара́т.
caravan /ˈkærəvæn/ *n.* (*horse-drawn*) фурго́н, кры́тая теле́га; (*Br., trailer*) жило́й/тури́стский автоприце́п, тре́йлер.
■ *v.i.* (**caravanned, caravanning**) (*Br.*): **go ~ning** путеше́ствовать (*impf.*) в тре́йлере.
caraway /ˈkærəweɪ/ *n.* тмин; **~ seed** тми́нное се́мя.
carbohydrate /kɑːbəˈhaɪdreɪt/ *n.* углево́д.
carbon /ˈkɑːbən/ *n.*
1 (*element*) углеро́д; **~ monoxide** уга́рный газ; **~ dioxide** углеки́слый газ.
2 : **~ copy** (*fig.*) (то́чная) ко́пия.
carburettor /kɑːbəˈretə(r)/ (*US* **carburetor**) *n.* карбюра́тор.
carcass /ˈkɑːkəs/ *n.*
1 (*of animal*) ту́ша; **~ meat** (*Br.*) парно́е мя́со.
2 (*of building, ship etc.*) карка́с, о́стов, ко́рпус.
carcinogenic /kɑːsɪnəˈdʒenɪk/ *adj.* канцероге́нный.
carcinoma /kɑːsɪˈnəʊmə/ *n.* (*pl.* **~s** *or* **~ta**) карцино́ма, ра́ковое новообразова́ние.
card /kɑːd/ *n.*
1 (*material*) карто́н; (*piece*) ка́рточка; (*postcard*) откры́тка.
2 (*playing ~*) игра́льная ка́рта; **play ~s** игра́ть, сыгра́ть в ка́рты.
cardboard /ˈkɑːdbɔːd/ *n.* карто́н; **~ box** карто́нная коро́бка.
cardiac /ˈkɑːdɪæk/ *adj.* серде́чный; **~ arrest** остано́вка се́рдца.
cardigan /ˈkɑːdɪgən/ *n.* шерстяна́я ко́фта, кардига́н; (*man's*) вя́заная ку́ртка.
cardinal /ˈkɑːdɪn(ə)l/ *n.* (*eccl.*) кардина́л.
■ *adj.* (*principal*) кардина́льный; **~ number** коли́чественное числи́тельное; **a matter of ~ importance** де́ло чрезвыча́йной ва́жности.
cardiologist /kɑːdɪˈɒlədʒɪst/ *n.* кардио́лог.
cardiology /kɑːdɪˈɒlədʒɪ/ *n.* кардиоло́гия.
care /keə(r)/ *n.*
1 (*serious attention*) осторо́жность; **handle this with ~** обраща́йтесь с э́тим осторо́жно; **take ~ you don't fall** смотри́те, не упади́те.
2 (*charge*) забо́та, попече́ние; **take a child into ~** (*Br.*) взять (*pf.*) ребёнка под опе́ку госуда́рства.
3 (*anxiety*): **free from ~** свобо́дный от забо́т.
■ *v.i.* 1 (*feel anxiety*): **I don't ~ what they say** мне всё равно́, что они́ ска́жут; **who ~s?** не всё ли равно́?; **I couldn't ~ less** (*coll.*) мне-то что?; мне наплева́ть.
2 (*feel inclination*): **would you ~ for a walk?** не хоти́те ли пойти́ погуля́ть?
3 (*look after*): **he is well ~d for** за ним хоро́ший ухо́д.
■ *cpds.* **~free** *adj.* беззабо́тный; **~taker** *n.* сто́рож, смотри́тель (*m.*) зда́ния.
career /kəˈrɪə(r)/ *n.* карье́ра, профе́ссия.
■ *v.i.* мча́ться (*impf.*).
careful /ˈkeəfʊl/ *adj.*
1 (*attentive*) осторо́жный; **be ~ not to fall** бу́дьте осторо́жны, не упади́те; **he is ~ with his money** он не тра́тит де́нег зря.
2 (*of work*) тща́тельный.

C

careless /ˈkeəlɪs/ *adj.* (*thoughtless*) неосторо́жный; **a ~ mistake** оши́бка по невнима́тельности; (*negligent*) небре́жный.

carer /ˈkeərə(r)/ *n.* (*Br.*) челове́к, уха́живающий за ребёнком, больны́м, инвали́дом *и т. д.*

caress /kəˈres/ *v.t.* ласка́ть (*impf.*).

cargo /ˈkɑːgəʊ/ *n.* (*pl.* **~es** *or* **~s**) груз; **~ ship** торго́вое су́дно.

Caribbean /kærɪˈbiːən, kəˈrɪbɪən/ *adj.* кари́бский; (*as n.*) **the ~ (sea)** Кари́бское мо́ре.

caricature /ˈkærɪkətjʊə(r)/ *n.* карикату́ра.

caring /ˈkeərɪŋ/ *adj.* забо́тливый.

carnage /ˈkɑːnɪdʒ/ *n.* бо́йня.

carnation /kɑːˈneɪʃ(ə)n/ *n.* гвозди́ка (*декоративное растение*).

carnival /ˈkɑːnɪv(ə)l/ *n.* (*annual merrymaking*) ежего́дный карнава́л; (*Shrovetide*) Ма́сленица.

carnivore /ˈkɑːnɪvɔː(r)/ *n.* плотоя́дное/хи́щное живо́тное.

carnivorous /kɑːˈnɪvərəs/ *adj.* плотоя́дный.

carol /ˈkær(ə)l/ *n.* ≈коля́дка; рожде́ственская пе́сня.
■ *cpd.* **~-singing** *n.* рожде́ственские песнопе́ния; ≈коля́дки.

carousel /kærəˈsel/ *n.* карусе́ль.

carpenter /ˈkɑːpɪntə(r)/ *n.* пло́тник.

carpentry /ˈkɑːpɪntrɪ/ *n.* (*occupation*) пло́тничество, пло́тницкое де́ло.

carpet /ˈkɑːpɪt/ *n.* ковёр.
■ *v.t.* **(carpeted, carpeting)** уст|ила́ть, -ла́ть ковра́ми.

carriage /ˈkærɪdʒ/ *n.*
1 (*road vehicle*) экипа́ж.
2 (*Br., rail car*) пассажи́рский ваго́н.
3 (*Br., transport of goods*) перево́зка, доста́вка.
4 (*of typewriter*) каре́тка.
■ *cpd.* **~way** *n.* (*Br.*) прое́зжая часть (доро́ги).

carrier /ˈkærɪə(r)/ *n.*
1 (*transport agent*) транспортёр.
2 (*receptacle*): **~ bag** (*Br.*) су́мка для поку́пок.
3 (*of disease*) перено́счик (боле́зни).

carrot /ˈkærət/ *n.* морко́вь.

carry /ˈkærɪ/ *v.t.*
1 (*transport*) носи́ть (*indet.*), нести́ (*det.*); (*of or by vehicle*) вози́ть (*indet.*), везти́ (*det.*); **pipes ~ water** вода́ идёт по тру́бам; **wires ~ sound** звук передаётся по провода́м; **what weight will the bridge ~?** на како́й вес рассчи́тан э́тот мост?
2 (*have*): **I always ~ an umbrella (money) with me** у меня́ всегда́ с собо́й зо́нтик (всегда́ при себе́ есть де́ньги); **this crime carries a heavy penalty** э́то преступле́ние влечёт за собо́й тяжёлое наказа́ние.
■ *v.i.*: **the shot carried 200 yards** снаря́д пролете́л 200 я́рдов.
■ *with advs.*: **~ away** *v.t.* (*fig.*): **he was carried away by his feelings** он оказа́лся во вла́сти чувств; он увлёкся; **~ forward, over** *vv.t.* (*transfer*) перен|оси́ть, -ести́; **~ off** *v.t.* (*remove*) ун|оси́ть, -ести́; **he carried the situation off well** он уда́чно вы́шел из положе́ния; **~ on** *v.t.* (*conduct, perform*): **~ on a conversation/business** вести́ (*det.*) разгово́р/де́ло; *v.i.* (*continue*) прод|олжа́ть, -о́лжить; **~ on with your work** продолжа́йте рабо́ту; (*talk, behave excitedly*) волнова́ться (*impf.*); **~ out** *v.t.* (*execute*) выполня́ть, вы́полнить.
■ *cpd.* **~cot** *n.* (*Br.*) переносна́я де́тская крова́тка.

cart /kɑːt/ *n.* теле́жка.
■ *cpd.* **~wheel** *n.* колесо́ теле́ги; **turn ~wheels** кувырк|а́ться, -ну́ться колесо́м.

carte blanche /kɑːt ˈblɑ̃ʃ/ *n.* карт-бла́нш (*m. indecl.*).

cartel /kɑːˈtel/ *n.* (*comm.*) карте́ль (*m.*).

cartilage /ˈkɑːtɪlɪdʒ/ *n.* хря́щ.

cartographer /kɑːˈtɒgrəfə(r)/ *n.* карто́граф.

cartography /kɑːˈtɒgrəfɪ/ *n.* картогра́фия.

carton /ˈkɑːt(ə)n/ *n.* (*large box*) карто́нка; (*for milk etc.*) паке́т.

cartoon /kɑːˈtuːn/ *n.* (*in newspaper*) карикату́ра; (*film*) мультфи́льм.

cartoonist /kɑːˈtuːnɪst/ *n.* карикатури́ст.

cartridge /ˈkɑːtrɪdʒ/ *n.* (*mil.*) патро́н; (*for printer*) ка́ртридж; (*for camera*) кассе́та.

carve /kɑːv/ *v.t.* (*cut*) ре́зать (*impf.*); (*shape by cutting*): **~ a statue out of wood** выреза́ть, вы́резать ста́тую из де́рева; **he ~d out a career for himself** он сде́лал карье́ру; **~ meat** ре́зать, на- мя́со.
■ *with adv.*: **~ up** *v.t.* (*fig.*) раздел|я́ть, -и́ть.

carving /ˈkɑːvɪŋ/ *n.* (*object*) резна́я рабо́та, резьба́.

cascade /kæsˈkeɪd/ *n.* каска́д; водопа́д.
■ *v.i.* па́дать/ниспада́ть (*both impf.*) каска́дом.

case[1] /keɪs/ *n.*
1 (*instance*) слу́чай, обстоя́тельство, де́ло; **in that ~** в тако́м/э́том слу́чае; **in any ~** во вся́ком слу́чае; **in ~ of fire** в слу́чае пожа́ра.
2 (*med.*) слу́чай, заболева́ние; **~ history** исто́рия боле́зни.
3 (*hypothesis*): **take an umbrella in ~ it rains (***or* **in ~ of rain)** возьми́те зо́нтик на слу́чай дождя́; **just in ~** на вся́кий слу́чай.
4 (*leg.*) суде́бное де́ло.
5 (*gram.*) паде́ж.

case[2] /keɪs/ *n.* (*container*) я́щик, ларе́ц, коро́бка; (*for spectacles etc.*) футля́р; (*Br., suitcase*) чемода́н; **glass ~** витри́на.

cash /kæʃ/ *n.* нали́чные (де́н|ьги, *pl.*, *g.* -ег); **~ on delivery** нало́женным платежо́м; **~ desk** (*Br.*) ка́сса; **~ machine** банкома́т, де́нежный автома́т; **~ register** ка́ссовый аппара́т, ка́сса.
■ *v.t.*: **~ a cheque** получ|а́ть, -и́ть де́ньги по че́ку; **~ in** получ|а́ть, -и́ть де́ньги по + *d.*
■ *v.i.*: **~ in on** (*fig.*) воспо́льзоваться (*pf.*) + *i.*

cashback /ˈkæʃbæk/ *n.* кешбэ́к (*получение наличных денег с дебетовой карточки в предприятии розничной торговли при оплате покупки; компенсационная скидка с цены покупки*).

cashcard /ˈkæʃkɑːd/ *n.* (*Br.*) ка́рточка для банкома́та.

cashew /ˈkæʃuː/ *n.* (оре́х) ке́шью.

cashier /kæˈʃɪə(r)/ *n.* касси́р.

cashmere /ˈkæʃmɪə(r)/ *n.* кашеми́р.

cashpoint /ˈkæʃpɔɪnt/ *n.* (*Br.*) банкома́т.

casino /kə'si:nəʊ/ *n.* (*pl.* **~s**) казинó (*nt. indecl.*).
casket /'kɑ:skɪt/ *n.* шкатýлка; (*US, coffin*) гроб.
Caspian /'kæspɪən/ *n.* (**the ~ Sea**) Каспи́йское мóре.
casserole /'kæsərəʊl/ *n.* (*container*) кастрю́ля для тушéния; (*food*) рагý (*nt. indecl.*).
cassette /kə'set/ *n.* кассéта; **~ player** плéер; **~ recorder** кассéтный магнитофóн.
cassock /'kæsək/ *n.* ря́са.
cast /kɑ:st/ *n.*
1 (*mould*) фóрма для отли́вки; (*object*): **plaster ~** ги́псовый слéпок.
2 (*theatr., cin.*) состáв актёров.
■ *v.t.* (*past and p.p.* **~**)
1 (*throw*) бр|осáть, -óсить.
2 (*fig.*): **~ a vote** проголосовáть (*pf.*); отдáть (*pf.*) гóлос; **~ doubt on** подв|ергáть, -éргнуть сомнéнию; **~ a spell (up)on** околд|óвывать, -овáть.
3 (*pour*) отл|ивáть, -и́ть; **~ iron** чугýн.
4 (*theatr.*): **~ a play** распредел|я́ть, -и́ть рóли в пьéсе.
■ *cpds.* **~away** *n.* & *adj.* потерпéвший кораблекрушéние; **~-iron** *adj.* чугýнный; (*fig.*) стальнóй, желéзный; **~-off** *n.* & *adj.*: **~-off clothing** обнóск|и (*pl., g.* -ов), старьё.
castanets /kæstə'nets/ *n.* кастаньéты (*f. pl.*) (*ударный музыкальный инструмент в виде скреплённых пластин, надеваемых на пальцы рук*).
caste /kɑ:st/ *n.* кáста.
caster /'kɑ:stə(r)/ *n.*: **~ sugar** (*Br.*) сáхарный песóк.
castigate /'kæstɪgeɪt/ *v.t.* бичевáть (*impf.*).
casting /'kɑ:stɪŋ/ *n.* (*theatr., cin.*) распределéние ролéй.
castle /'kɑ:s(ə)l/ *n.* зáмок; (*at chess*) ладья́.
castrate /kæ'streɪt/ *v.t.* кастри́ровать (*impf., pf.*).
casual /'kæʒʊəl/ *adj.*
1 (*chance*) случáйный.
2 (*careless*) небрéжный, беспéчный; (*familiar*) развя́зный; **clothes for ~ wear** простáя/повседнéвная одéжда.
casualty /'kæʒʊəltɪ/ *n.* (*person*) пострадáвший от несчáстного слýчая; (*mil.*) уби́тый; **~ department** (*Br.*) травматологи́ческое отделéние.
cat /kæt/ *n.*
1 кóшка.
2 (*idioms*): **let the ~ out of the bag** проб|áлтываться, -олтáться; выбáлтывать, вы́болтать секрéт; **it's raining ~s and dogs** дождь льёт как из ведрá.
■ *cpds.* **~nap** *v.i.* вздремнýть (*pf.*); **~walk** *n.* рабóчие мостк|и́ (*pl., g.* -óв); (*in fashion house*) пóдиум.
catalogue /'kætəlɒg/ (*US* **catalog**) *n.* каталóг.
■ *v.t.* (**catalogues, catalogued, cataloguing;** *US* **catalogs, cataloged, cataloging**) каталогизи́ровать (*impf., pf.*).
catalyst /'kætəlɪst/ *n.* катализáтор.
catalytic /kætə'lɪtɪk/ *adj.*: **~ converter** каталити́ческий нейтрализáтор (выхлопны́х гáзов).
catapult /'kætəpʌlt/ *n.* (*Br., toy*) рогáтка.
cataract /'kætərækt/ *n.* (*med.*) катарáкта.
catarrh /kə'tɑ:(r)/ *n.* катáр.
catastrophe /kə'tæstrəfɪ/ *n.* катастрóфа.
catastrophic /kætə'strɒfɪk/ *adj.* катастрофи́ческий.
catch /kætʃ/ *n.*
1 (*act of catching*) пóимка, захвáт.
2 (*amount caught*) улóв, добы́ча.
3 (*trap*) улóвка, ловýшка; **there must be a ~ in it** здесь есть какóй-то подвóх.
4 (*fastener*) щекóлда, защёлка, шпингалéт.
■ *v.t.* & *i.* (*past and p.p.* **caught**)
1 (*seize*) лови́ть, поймáть; **he caught the ball** он поймáл мяч; **~ a fish** поймáть (*pf.*) ры́бу; **~ a fugitive** поймáть (*pf.*) беглецá.
2 (*of entanglement, fastening etc.*): **her dress caught on a nail** онá зацепи́лась плáтьем за гвоздь; **he caught his foot** у негó застря́ла ногá.
3 (*intercept, detect*): **I caught him stealing** я застáл егó, за воровствóм; **we were caught in the storm** нас засти́гла бýря.
4 (*be in time for*): **~ a train** успéть (*pf.*) на пóезд.
5 (*fig.*): **I didn't ~ what you said** я прослýшал, что вы сказáли; **~ s.o.'s eye** привлéчь (*pf.*) чьё-н. внимáние; **~ fire** загорéться (*pf.*); **~ a glimpse of** уви́деть (*pf.*) мéльком; **~ hold of** схвати́ть, улови́ть (*both pf.*).
6 (*be infected by*) схвати́ть, получи́ть (*both pf.*); **~ cold** простуди́ться (*pf.*).
■ *with advs.*: **~ on** *v.i.*: **the fashion did not ~ on** э́та мóда не привилáсь; **~ out** *v.t.* (*Br.*): **he was caught out in a mistake** егó поймáли/подлови́ли на оши́бке; **~ up** *v.t.* & *i.*: **he caught the others up; he caught up with the others** он догнáл остальны́х; **I must ~ up on my work** я запусти́л рабóту — тепéрь нáдо нагоня́ть.
■ *cpds.* **~phrase** *n.* мóдное выражéние, словéчко; **~-22 situation** *n.* безвы́ходное положéние; парадоксáльная ситуáция.
catching /'kætʃɪŋ/ *adj.* зарáзный.
catchy /'kætʃɪ/ (**catchier, catchiest**) *adj.* легкó запоминáющийся, прили́пчивый.
categorical /kætɪ'gɒrɪk(ə)l/ *adj.* категори́ческий.
categorize /'kætɪgəraɪz/ *v.t.* распредел|я́ть, -и́ть по категóриям.
category /'kætɪgərɪ/ *n.* категóрия.
cater /'keɪtə(r)/ *v.i.*: **~ for** (*Br.*) пост|авля́ть, -áвить прови́зию для + *g.*; (*fig.*) обслýж|ивать, -и́ть.
caterer /'keɪtərə(r)/ *n.* (*oft. pl., company*) фи́рма, обслýживающая банкéты, свáдьбы *и т. п.*
caterpillar /'kætəpɪlə(r)/ *n.* гýсеница.
catharsis /kə'θɑ:sɪs/ *n.* (*pl.* **catharses** /-si:z/) кáтарсис.
cathartic /kə'θɑ:tɪk/ *adj.* очищáющий.
cathedral /kə'θi:dr(ə)l/ *n.* (кафедрáльный) собóр.
Catholic /'kæθəlɪk/ *n.* катóл|ик (*fem.* -и́чка).
■ *adj.* (*relig.*) католи́ческий; **Roman ~** ри́мско-католи́ческий.
Catholicism /kə'θɒlɪsɪz(ə)m/ *n.* католици́зм,

католи́чество.
cattle /ˈkæt(ə)l/ *n.* скот, скоти́на.
catty /ˈkætɪ/ *adj.* (**cattier, cattiest**) ехи́дный.
Caucasus /ˈkɔːkəsəs/ *n.* Кавка́з.
caught /kɔːt/ *past and p.p. of* ▶ **catch**
cauldron /ˈkɔːldrən/ *n.* котёл.
cauliflower /ˈkɒlɪflaʊə(r)/ *n.* цветна́я капу́ста.
cause /kɔːz/ *n.*
1 (*reason*) причи́на, по́вод.
2 (*need*) причи́на, основа́ние; **there is no ~ for alarm** нет основа́ний/причи́н для беспоко́йства.
3 (*purpose*): **the ~ of peace** де́ло ми́ра; **a good ~** пра́вое де́ло.
■ *v.t.* вызыва́ть, вы́звать; **~ s.o. trouble** (*or* **a loss)** причин|я́ть, -и́ть кому́-н. беспоко́йство/убы́тки; **what ~d the accident?** что послужи́ло причи́ной несча́стного слу́чая?
caution /ˈkɔːʃ(ə)n/ *n.*
1 (*prudence*) осторо́жность.
2 (*Br., warning*) предостереже́ние, предосторо́жность.
■ *v.t.* предостер|ега́ть, -е́чь.
cautious /ˈkɔːʃəs/ *adj.* осторо́жный, осмотри́тельный.
cavalier /kævəˈlɪə(r)/ *n.* (*gallant; royalist*) кавале́р.
■ *adj.* бесцеремо́нный, надме́нный.
cavalry /ˈkævəlrɪ/ *n.* кавале́рия, ко́нница.
cave[1] /keɪv/ *n.* пеще́ра.
■ *cpd.* **~man** *n.* пеще́рный челове́к, троглоди́т.
cave[2] /keɪv/ *v.i.*: **~ in** (*lit.*) прова́л|иваться, -и́ться; (*fig.*) сд|ава́ться, -а́ться.
cavernous /ˈkæv(ə)nəs/ *adj.* пеще́ристый.
caviar /ˈkævɪɑː(r)/ *n.* икра́.
cavity /ˈkævɪtɪ/ *n.* по́лость; (*in tooth*) дупло́.
cavort /kəˈvɔːt/ *v.i.* скака́ть (*impf.*).
caw /kɔː/ *v.t.* & *i.* ка́рк|ать, -нуть.
cayenne /keɪˈen/ *n.*: **~ pepper** кайе́нский пе́рец.
CCTV (*abbr. of* ***closed-circuit TV***) систе́ма видеонаблюде́ния, видеонаблюде́ние.
CD (*abbr. of* ***compact disc***) компа́кт-ди́ск; **~ player** проигрыватель (*m.*) компа́кт-ди́сков, CD-пле́ер.
CD-ROM (*abbr. of* ***compact disc — read-only memory***) компа́кт-ди́ск (*штампо́ванный*); **~ drive** при́вод компа́кт-ди́сков.
cease /siːs/ *v.t.* прекра|ща́ть, -ти́ть.
■ *v.i.* прекра|ща́ться, -ти́ться.
■ *cpd.* **~fire** *n.* прекраще́ние огня́.
ceaseless /ˈsiːslɪs/ *adj.* непреста́нный, непреры́вный.
cedar /ˈsiːdə(r)/ *n.* кедр.
cede /siːd/ *v.t.* сда|ва́ть, -ть.
ceilidh /ˈkeɪlɪ/ *n.* вечери́нка с шотла́ндской или ирла́ндской наро́дной му́зыкой и та́нцами.
ceiling /ˈsiːlɪŋ/ *n.* потоло́к.
celebrate /ˈselɪbreɪt/ *v.t.* & *i.*
1 (*mark an occasion*) пра́здновать, от-.
2 : **~ a marriage** соверш|а́ть, -и́ть обря́д бракосочета́ния.
celebrated /ˈselɪbreɪtɪd/ *adj.* знамени́тый.
celebration /selɪˈbreɪʃ(ə)n/ *n.* пра́зднование, торжества́ (*nt. pl.*), прославле́ние; **~of marriage** соверше́ние обря́да бракосочета́ния.
celebrity /sɪˈlebrɪtɪ/ *n.* (*fame*) знамени́тость; (*person*) знамени́тость.
■ *cpd.* **~ culture** *n.* культ знамени́тостей; культу́ра, сформиро́ванная ку́льтом знамени́тостей.
celery /ˈselərɪ/ *n.* (листово́й) сельдере́й.
celestial /sɪˈlestɪəl/ *adj.* (*astron., fig.*) небе́сный; **~ globe** гло́бус звёздного не́ба.
celibate /ˈselɪbət/ *adj.* безбра́чный, да́вший обе́т безбра́чия.
cell /sel/ *n.*
1 (*in prison*) ка́мера.
2 (*biol.*) кле́тка.
■ *cpd.* **~phone** *n.* со́товый телефо́н.
cellar /ˈselə(r)/ *n.* по́греб, подва́л.
cellist /ˈtʃelɪst/ *n.* виолончели́ст (*fem.* -ка).
cello /ˈtʃeləʊ/ *n.* (*pl.* **~s**) виолонче́ль.
cellophane /ˈseləfeɪn/ *n.* целлофа́н; (*attr.*) целлофа́новый.
Celt /kelt/ *n.* кельт.
Celtic /ˈkeltɪk/ *adj.* ке́льтский.
cement /sɪˈment/ *n.* цеме́нт.
■ *cpd.* **~ mixer** *n.* бетономеша́лка.
cemetery /ˈsemɪtərɪ/ *n.* кла́дбище.
censor /ˈsensə(r)/ *n.* це́нзор.
■ *v.t.* подв|ерга́ть, -е́ргнуть цензу́ре.
censorious /senˈsɔːrɪəs/ *adj.* сверхкрити́чный, приди́рчивый.
censorship /ˈsensəʃɪp/ *n.* цензу́ра.
censure /ˈsensjə(r)/ *n.* кри́тика.
■ *v.t.* критикова́ть (*impf.*).
census /ˈsensəs/ *n.* (*pl.* **~es**) пе́репись (населе́ния).
cent /sent/ *n.* цент.
centen|ary /senˈtiːnərɪ/ (*Br.*), **-nial** /senˈtenɪəl/ (*US*) *n.* столе́тие.
center /ˈsentə(r)/ (*US*) = **centre**
centigrade /ˈsentɪgreɪd/ *adj.*: **20° ~** 20 гра́дусов Це́льсия (*or* по Це́льсию).
centilitre /ˈsentɪliːtə(r)/ (*US* **centiliter**) *n.* сантили́тр.
centimetre /ˈsentɪmiːtə(r)/ (*US* **centimeter**) *n.* сантиме́тр.
centipede /ˈsentɪpiːd/ *n.* многоно́жка.
central /ˈsentr(ə)l/ *adj.*
1 (*pert. to a centre*) центра́льный; **C~ America** Центра́льная Аме́рика; **C~ Asia** Сре́дняя А́зия; **the house is very ~** дом нахо́дится в са́мом це́нтре го́рода.
2 (*principal*) центра́льный, гла́вный.
centralize /ˈsentrəlaɪz/ *v.t.* централизова́ть (*impf., pf.*).
centre /ˈsentə(r)/ (*US* **center**) *n.*
1 (*middle*) центр; **~ of gravity** центр тя́жести.
2 (*fig.*): **shopping ~** торго́вый центр.
3 (*pol.*) центр.
■ *v.t.* поме|ща́ть, -сти́ть в це́нтре.
■ *v.i.* сосредото́чи|ваться, -ться; **the discussion ~d round this point** диску́ссия сосредото́чилась вокру́г э́того

вопро́са.
■ *cpds.* ~ **forward** *n.* (*sport*) центра́льный напада́ющий; ~**piece** *n.* орнамента́льная ва́за в середи́не стола́; (*fig.*) гла́вное украше́ние.

century /'sentʃərɪ/ *n.* столе́тие, век.

CEO (*abbr. of* ***chief executive officer***) гла́вный исполни́тельный дире́ктор.

ceramic /sɪ'ræmɪk/ *adj.* керами́ческий.

ceramics /sɪ'ræmɪks/ *n.* кера́мика.

cereal /'sɪərɪəl/ *n.* хле́бный злак; **(breakfast)** ~ хло́пья (к за́втраку) (*корнфлекс и т. п.*).

cerebral /'serɪbr(ə)l/ *adj.* мозгово́й, церебра́льный.

ceremonial /serɪ'məʊnɪəl/ *adj.* церемониа́льный, обря́довый.

ceremonious /serɪ'məʊnɪəs/ *adj.* церемо́нный.

ceremony /'serɪmənɪ/ *n.* (*rite*) обря́д, церемо́ния; (*formal behaviour*) церемо́нность; **stand (up)on** ~ церемо́ниться (*impf.*).

certain /'sə:t(ə)n/ *adj.*
1 (*undoubted*) несомне́нный; **I cannot say for** ~ я не могу́ сказа́ть наверняка́; **make** ~ **of** (*ascertain*) удостов|еря́ться, -е́риться в чём-н.; **he is** ~ **to succeed** наверняка́ он добьётся успе́ха.
2 (*confident*) уве́ренный; **I am** ~ **he will come** я уве́рен, что он придёт.
3 (*unspecified*) изве́стный, не́который; **a** ~ **person** не́кто, не́кое лицо́; **under** ~ **conditions** при изве́стных усло́виях; **a** ~ (*some*) **pleasure** не́которое удово́льствие.

certainly /'sə:tənlɪ/ *adv.* (*without doubt*) несомне́нно, наверняка́, наве́рно(е); (*expr. obedience or consent*) коне́чно, безусло́вно.

certainty /'sə:təntɪ/ *n.*
1 (*being certainly true*) несомне́нность.
2 (*certain fact*) несомне́нный факт.

certificate /sə'tɪfɪkət/ *n.* удостовере́ние, свиде́тельство, сертифика́т.

certify /'sə:tɪfaɪ/ *v.t.* удостов|еря́ть, -е́рить.

cervical /sə:'vaɪk(ə)l/ *adj.* ше́йный; ~ **smear** (*Br.*) мазо́к с ше́йки ма́тки.

cervix /'sə:vɪks/ *n.* (*pl.* **cervices** /-si:z/) ше́я; (*of womb*) ше́йка (ма́тки).

Cesarean /sɪ'zeərɪən/ (*US*) = **Caesarean**

cessation /se'seɪʃ(ə)n/ *n.* прекраще́ние, остано́вка; ~ **of hostilities** прекраще́ние вое́нных де́йствий.

cf. (*abbr. of Latin* ***confer*** = ***compare with***) ср., сравни́.

CFCs (*abbr. of* ***chlorofluorocarbons***) фрео́ны (*m. pl.*).

chafe /tʃeɪf/ *v.i.* нат|ира́ться, -ере́ться.

chaffinch /'tʃæfɪntʃ/ *n.* зя́блик.

chain /tʃeɪn/ *n.* цепь; (*pl., fetters*) це́пи (*f. pl.*), око́в|ы (*pl., g.* —); (*fig.*): ~ **of events, consequences** цепь собы́тий/после́дствий; ~ **reaction** цепна́я реа́кция.
■ *v.t.* прико́в|ывать, -а́ть це́пью.
■ *cpds.* ~**-smoke** *v.t.* кури́ть (*impf.*) одну́ сигаре́ту за друго́й; ~**-smoker** *n.* заядлый кури́льщик; ~ **store** *n.* оди́н из се́ти фи́рменных магази́нов.

chair /tʃeə(r)/ *n.*
1 стул.
2 (~*man*) председа́тель (*m.*).
■ *v.t.* (*preside over*) председа́тельствовать (*impf.*) на + *p.*
■ *cpds.* ~**lift** *n.* подвесно́й подъёмник; ~**man,** ~**person** *nn.* = **chair 2**

chaise longue /ʃeɪz 'lɒŋ(g)/ *n.* (*pl.* **chaise longues** *or* **chaises longues** *pronunc. same*) шезло́нг.

chalet /'ʃæleɪ/ *n.* шале́ (*nt. indecl.*).

chalk /tʃɔ:k/ *n.* мел.

challenge /'tʃælɪndʒ/ *n.* вы́зов.
■ *v.t.* вызыва́ть, вы́звать; (*dispute*) оспа́ривать (*impf.*); ~ **s.o. to a race** вызыва́ть, вы́звать кого́-н. на состяза́ние.

challenger /'tʃælɪndʒə(r)/ *n.* претенде́нт (*fem.* -ка).

challenging /'tʃælɪndʒɪŋ/ *adj.* тру́дный, но интере́сный.

chamber /'tʃeɪmbə(r)/ *n.*
1 (*room*) ко́мната; (*pl., apartment*) кварти́ра; ~ **music** ка́мерная му́зыка.
2 (*hall, e.g. of parliament*) зал, за́ла.
3 (*official body*) пала́та; **C~ of Commerce** торго́вая пала́та.
■ *cpd.* ~**maid** *n.* го́рничная.

chameleon /kə'mi:lɪən/ *n.* хамелео́н.

champagne /ʃæm'peɪn/ *n.* шампа́нское.

champion /'tʃæmpɪən/ *n.*
1 (*defender*) побо́рни|к, защи́тни|к (*fem.* -ца).
2 (*prizewinner*) чемпио́н (*fem., coll.* -ка).

championship /'tʃæmpɪənʃɪp/ *n.* (*advocacy*) защи́та; (*sport*) чемпио́нство; чемпиона́т, пе́рвенство.

chance /tʃɑ:ns/ *n.*
1 (*casual occurrence*) слу́чай, случа́йность; **by** ~ случа́йно; **game of** ~ аза́ртная игра́.
2 (*possibility, opportunity*) шанс, возмо́жность; **the** ~**s are that he will come** все ша́нсы за то, что он придёт; **I had no** ~ **of winning** у меня́ не́ было никаки́х ша́нсов на успе́х.

chancellor /'tʃɑ:nsələ(r)/ *n.* ка́нцлер; (*Br., of university*) ре́ктор; **C~ of the Exchequer** ка́нцлер казначе́йства, мини́стр фина́нсов.

chancy /'tʃɑ:nsɪ/ *adj.* (**chancier, chanciest**) (*coll.*) риско́ванный.

chandelier /ʃændɪ'lɪə(r)/ *n.* лю́стра.

change /tʃeɪndʒ/ *n.*
1 (*alteration*) измене́ние; (*substitution*) переме́на; ~ **of air, scene** переме́на обстано́вки; **for a** ~ для разнообра́зия.
2 (*spare set*) сме́на; **he took a** ~ **of underwear with him** он взял с собо́й сме́ну белья́.
3 (*money*) ме́лкие де́н|ьги (*pl., g.* -ег); (*returned as balance*) сда́ча; **have you** ~ **for a pound?** вы не разменя́ете оди́н фунт (ме́лочью)?
4 (*of trains etc.*) переса́дка.
■ *v.t.* 1 (*alter, replace*) меня́ть, по-; ~ **(one's) clothes** переод|ева́ться, -е́ться; ~ **one's mind** разду́м|ывать, -ать; переду́м|ывать, -ать; ~ **the subject** смени́ть/перемени́ть (*both pf.*) те́му разгово́ра; ~ **trains** перес|а́живаться, -е́сть на друго́й по́езд.
2 (*reclothe etc.*): ~ **a baby** перепел|ёнывать, -ена́ть; ~ **a bed** меня́ть, по- посте́льное бельё.
3 (*money*): ~ **a five pound note** разменя́ть

(*pf.*) пятифу́нтовую бума́жку; **~ euros into pounds** обменя́ть (*pf.*) е́вро на фу́нты (сте́рлингов).
4 (*exchange*): **~ places with s.o.** (*lit.*) поменя́ться (*pf.*) места́ми с кем-н.
■ *v.i.* 1: **he has ~d a lot** он си́льно измени́лся/перемени́лся; **caterpillars ~ into butterflies** гу́сеницы превраща́ются в ба́бочек.
2 (*rail.*) перес|а́живаться, -е́сть.
■ *cpd.* **~over** *n.* (*of leader etc.*) сме́на.

changeable /ˈtʃeɪndʒəb(ə)l/ *adj.*: **~ weather** изме́нчивая пого́да; (*of person*) изме́нчивый, непостоя́нный.

changing room /ˈtʃeɪndʒɪŋ/ *n.* (*sport*) раздева́лка; (*Br., in shop*) приме́рочная.

channel /ˈtʃæn(ə)l/ *n.*
1 (*strait*) проли́в, кана́л; **the English C~** Ла-Ма́нш; **the C~ Islands** Норма́ндские острова́; **C~ Tunnel** тонне́ль под Ла-Ма́ншем.
2 (*fig.*): **through the usual ~s** обы́чным путём.
3 (*television*) кана́л.
■ *v.t.* (**channelled, channelling;** *US* **channeled, channeling**) (*fig.*): **his energies are ~led into sport** вся его́ эне́ргия ухо́дит на спорт.

channel-hop /ˈtʃæn(ə)lhɒp/ *v.i.* (*coll.*)
1 (*TV*) (ча́сто) переключа́ть (*impf.*) телевизио́нные кана́лы.
2 (*Br.*) (ча́сто) пересека́ть (*impf.*) Ла-Ма́нш.

chant /tʃɑːnt/ *n.* песнь; (*eccl.*) пе́ние.
■ *v.t.* восп|ева́ть, -е́ть.
■ *v.i.* петь (*impf.*).

chaos /ˈkeɪɒs/ *n.* ха́ос.

chaotic /keɪˈɒtɪk/ *adj.* хаоти́ческий, хаоти́чный.

chap¹ /tʃæp/ *v.t.* (**chapped, chapping**): **~ped hands** потре́скавшиеся ру́ки.

chap² /tʃæp/ *n.* (*Br. coll.*) па́рень (*m.*), ма́лый.

chapel /ˈtʃæp(ə)l/ *n.* часо́вня, моле́льня.

chaperon(e) /ˈʃæpərəʊn/ *n.* компаньо́нка.
■ *v.t.* сопрово|жда́ть, -ди́ть.

chaplain /ˈtʃæplɪn/ *n.* капелла́н, свяще́нник.

chapter /ˈtʃæptə(r)/ *n.* глава́.

char /tʃɑː(r)/ *v.t.* (**charred, charring**) обу́гли|вать, -ть.

character /ˈkærɪktə(r)/ *n.*
1 (*nature*) сво́йство, ка́чество.
2 (*personal qualities*) хара́ктер.
3 (*distinctive person*): **she is quite a ~** она́ оригина́льная ли́чность.
4 (*fictional*) персона́ж.
5 (*letter, symbol*) бу́ква, ли́тера, знак; **Chinese ~s** кита́йские иеро́глифы (*m. pl.*).

characteristic /kærɪktəˈrɪstɪk/ *n.* характе́рная черта́.
■ *adj.* характе́рный, типи́чный.

characterization /kærɪktəraɪˈzeɪʃ(ə)n/ *n.*
1 (*description*) характери́стика.
2 (*by author or actor*) созда́ние о́браза; тракто́вка.

characterize /ˈkærɪktəraɪz/ *v.t.*
1 (*describe*) характеризова́ть (*impf., pf.*).
2 (*distinguish*) отлича́|ть, -и́ть.

characterless /ˈkærɪktəlɪs/ *adj.* (*undistinguished*) бесхара́ктерный, зауря́дный.

charade /ʃəˈrɑːd/ *n.* шара́да.

charcoal /ˈtʃɑːkəʊl/ *n.* древе́сный у́голь.
■ *cpd.* **~-grey** *n.* & *adj.* тёмно-се́рый, пе́пельный (цвет).

charge /tʃɑːdʒ/ *n.*
1 (*for gun*) заря́д.
2 (*elec.*) заря́д.
3 (*expense*) цена́, расхо́ды (*m. pl.*); **what is the ~?** ско́лько э́то сто́ит?; **a ~ account** счёт в магази́не; **~ card** креди́тная ка́рточка; **free of ~** беспла́тно.
4 (*duty, care*): **she's in ~ of the hospital** она́ возглавля́ет больни́цу; **take ~ of a business** взять (*pf.*) на себя́ руково́дство де́лом.
5 (*person entrusted*): **the nurse took her ~s for a walk** ня́ня повела́ свои́х пито́мцев на прогу́лку.
6 (*accusation*) обвине́ние; **bring a ~ against s.o.** выдвига́ть, вы́двинуть обвине́ние про́тив кого́-н.
7 (*attack*) нападе́ние, ата́ка.
■ *v.t.* 1 (*accuse*) обвин|я́ть, -и́ть; **he is ~d with murder** его́ обвиня́ют в уби́йстве.
2 (*debit*): **~ the amount/goods to me** запиши́те су́мму/това́ры на мой счёт.
3 (*ask price*): **he ~d £5 for the book** он запроси́л 5 фу́нтов за э́ту кни́гу.
4 (*also v.i.; attack*): **the troops ~d the enemy** войска́ атакова́ли непри́ятеля.

chariot /ˈtʃærɪət/ *n.* колесни́ца.

charisma /kəˈrɪzmə/ *n.* хари́зма, обая́ние.

charismatic /kærɪzˈmætɪk/ *adj.* харизмати́ческий.

charitable /ˈtʃærɪtəb(ə)l/ *adj.* ми́лостивый, снисходи́тельный.

charity /ˈtʃærɪtɪ/ *n.*
1 (*kindness*) любо́вь к бли́жнему.
2 (*institution*) благотвори́тельная организа́ция; **~ concert** благотвори́тельный конце́рт.
■ *cpd.* **~ shop** *n.* благотвори́тельный магази́н поде́ржанных веще́й.

charlatan /ˈʃɑːlət(ə)n/ *n.* шарлата́н.

charm /tʃɑːm/ *n.*
1 (*attraction*) обая́ние, очарова́ние.
2 (*talisman*) амуле́т.
■ *v.t.* очаро́в|ывать, -а́ть.

charming /ˈtʃɑːmɪŋ/ *adj.* очарова́тельный.

chart /tʃɑːt/ *n.*
1 (*record*) табли́ца, гра́фик.
2 (*pl., hit parade*) хит-пара́д.
■ *v.t.* черти́ть, на- ка́рту + *g.*; **~ s.o.'s progress** де́лать, с- диагра́мму чьего́-н. продвиже́ния.

charter /ˈtʃɑːtə(r)/ *n.*
1 (*grant of rights*) ха́ртия, гра́мота.
2 (*hire*) фрахто́вка, наём; **~ flight** ча́ртерный рейс.
■ *v.t.* 1 (*grant diploma to*): **~ed accountant** (*Br.*) бухга́лтер-экспе́рт, ауди́тор.
2 (*hire*) фрахтова́ть, за-.

chase /tʃeɪs/ *n.* пого́ня.
■ *v.t.* гоня́ться (*indet.*), гна́ться (*det.*), погна́ться (*pf.*) за + *i.*; **~ away** отгоня́ть, отогна́ть; **he owes us a reply — please ~ him up** (*coll.*) мы ждём его́ отве́та — поторопи́те-ка его́!
■ *v.i.*: **~ after** гна́ться, по- за + *i.*; охо́титься

(*impf.*) за + *i.*
chasm /'kæz(ə)m/ *n.* бездна, пропасть (*also fig.*).
chassis /'ʃæsɪ/ *n.* (*pl.* ~ /-sɪz/) шасси (*nt. indecl.*).
chaste /tʃeɪst/ *adj.* целому́дренный.
chasten /'tʃeɪs(ə)n/ *v.t.* (*punish, subdue*) смир|я́ть, -и́ть; **the rebuke had a ~ing effect** упрёк подействовал отрезвляюще.
chastise /tʃæs'taɪz/ *v.t.* нака́з|ывать, -а́ть; кара́ть, по-.
chastity /'tʃæstɪtɪ/ *n.* целому́дрие.
chat /tʃæt/ *n.* болтовня́, бесе́да.
■ *v.t.* (**chatted, chatting**): **~ s.o. up** (*Br. coll.*) заи́грывать (*impf.*) с кем-н.
■ *v.i.* (**chatted, chatting**) болта́ть, по-.
■ *cpds.* **~line** *n.* кана́л многосторо́нней свя́зи (*для общения по телефону или в Интернете*); **~ room** *n.* (*comput.*) разде́л ча́та; **~ show** *n.* (*Br.*) бесе́да/интервью́ (*nt. indecl.*) со знамени́тостями.
chatter /'tʃætə(r)/ *n.* болтовня́, трескотня́.
■ *v.i.* 1 болта́ть, тарато́рить (*both impf.*).
2: **his teeth are ~ing** у него́ зу́бы стуча́т (от хо́лода/испу́га).
chatty /'tʃætɪ/ *adj.* (**chattier, chattiest**) болтли́вый, говорли́вый; (*style*) разгово́рный.
chauffeur /'ʃəʊfə(r)/ *n.* (персона́льный) шофёр.
chauvinism /'ʃəʊvɪnɪz(ə)m/ *n.* шовини́зм.
chauvinist /'ʃəʊvɪnɪst/ *n.* шовини́ст (*fem.* -ка); **male ~** сторо́нник дискримина́ции же́нщин; мужско́й шовини́ст.
chauvinistic /ʃəʊvɪ'nɪstɪk/ *adj.* шовинисти́ческий.
chav /tʃæv/ *n.* (*Br., sl.*) го́пни|к (*fem.* -ца) (*особенно по внешним атрибутам*) (*sl.*), (*collect. also*) гопота́ (*sl.*); па́рень (*m.*)/де́вушка из рабо́чего райо́на (*по интересам*).
cheap /tʃi:p/ *adj.* дешёвый.
cheapen /'tʃi:pən/ *v.t.* (*degrade*) ун|ижа́ть, -и́зить; **~ o.s.** (*fig.*) роня́ть (*impf.*) себя́.
cheat /tʃi:t/ *n.* (*person*) обма́нщик, плут, жу́лик.
■ *v.t.* & *i.* обм|а́нывать, -ану́ть.
Chechen /'tʃetʃen/ *n.* чече́н|ец (*fem.* -ка).
■ *adj.* чече́нский.
Chechnya /'tʃetʃnjə/ *n.* Чечня́.
check¹ /tʃek/ *n.*
1 (*restraint*) заде́ржка.
2 (*verification*) контро́ль (*m.*).
3 (*at chess*) шах.
4 (*US, used for paying*) чек.
5 (*US, bill in restaurant*) счёт (*pl.* -а́).
6 (*US, for hat, luggage etc.*) номеро́к; квита́нция.
7 (*US, tick*) га́лочка.
■ *v.t.* 1 (*restrain*) сде́рж|ивать, -а́ть.
2 (*verify*) контроли́ровать, про-.
3 (*US, tick*) отм|еча́ть, -е́тить га́лочкой.
■ *with advs.*: **~ in** *v.i.* (*at hotel*) регистри́роваться, за-; *v.t.* (*baggage*) сд|ава́ть, -ать; **~ out** *v.i.* (*from hotel*) выпи́сываться, вы́писаться; **~ up** *v.i.*: **~ up on sth.** пров|еря́ть, -е́рить что-н.
■ *cpds.* **~list** *n.* контро́льный спи́сок, пе́речень (*m.*); **~out** *n.* ка́сса; **~point** *n.* контро́льный пункт; **~-up** *n.* прове́рка.
■ *int.* **~!** (*at chess*) шах!
check² /tʃek/ *n.* (*pattern*) клётка; (*attr., also* **~ed**) клётчатый.
checker /'tʃekə(r)/ (*US*) = **chequer**
checkers /'tʃekəz/ *n.* (*US*) ша́шк|и (*pl., g.* -ек).
checkmate /'tʃekmeɪt/ *n.* шах и мат.
cheek /tʃi:k/ *n.*
1 (*part of face*) щека́.
2 (*impudence*) на́глость.
■ *cpd.* **~bone** *n.* скула́.
cheeky /'tʃi:kɪ/ *adj.* (**cheekier, cheekiest**) наха́льный.
cheer /'tʃɪə(r)/ *n.*
1 (*shout*): **three ~s for our visitors!** троекра́тное ура́ на́шим гостя́м!; **~s!** (*as toast*) (за) ва́ше здоро́вье!
2 (*pl., as int.*) (*Br. coll.*) спаси́бо.
■ *v.t.* приве́тствовать (*impf.*).
■ *v.i.* (*utter ~s*) изд|ава́ть, -а́ть восто́рженные кри́ки.
■ *with adv.*: **~ up** *v.t.* & *i.* ободр|я́ть(ся), -и́ть(ся); *v.i.* повеселе́ть (*pf.*); **~ up!** не уныва́йте!
■ *cpd.* **~leader** *n.* де́вушка из гру́ппы подде́ржки (спорти́вной кома́нды), чирли́дер.
cheerful /'tʃɪəfʊl/ *adj.* весёлый, ра́достный.
cheese /tʃi:z/ *n.* сыр.
■ *cpds.* **~burger** *n.* чи́збургер; **~cake** *n.* ватру́шка.
cheetah /'tʃi:tə/ *n.* гепа́рд.
chef /ʃef/ *n.* шеф-по́вар.
chemical /'kemɪk(ə)l/ *n.* хими́ческий проду́кт; (*pl.*) химика́ты (*m. pl.*).
■ *adj.* хими́ческий.
chemist /'kemɪst/ *n.*
1 (*scientist*) хи́мик.
2 (*Br., pharmacist*) апте́карь (*m.*); **~'s shop** (*Br.*) апте́ка.
chemistry /'kemɪstrɪ/ *n.* хи́мия.
chemotherapy /ki:mə'θerəpɪ/ *n.* химиотерапи́я.
cheque /tʃek/ (*US* **check**) *n.* чек; **he made the ~ out to me** он вы́писал чек на моё и́мя.
■ *cpd.* **~book** *n.* че́ковая кни́жка; **~book journalism** *n.* заказна́я журнали́стика.
chequer /'tʃekə(r)/ (*US* **checker**) *v.t.*: **~ed flag** клётчатый, ша́хматный флажо́к; **~ed career** (*fig.*) бу́рная жизнь.
cherish /'tʃerɪʃ/ *v.t.*
1 (*love*) не́жно люби́ть (*impf.*).
2 (*of hopes etc.*) леле́ять (*impf.*).
cherry /'tʃerɪ/ *n.*
1 (*sour*) (*fruit*) ви́шня; (*tree*) ви́шня, вишнёвое де́рево.
2 (*sweet*) (*fruit*) чере́шня; (*tree*) чере́шня, чере́шневое де́рево.
■ *cpd.* **~-pick** *v.t.* & *i.* от|бира́ть, -обра́ть (*things*) лу́чшее/(*people, animals*) лу́чших.
cherub /'tʃerəb/ *n.* (*pl.* **~im** /-ɪm/) херуви́м.
chess /tʃes/ *n.* ша́хмат|ы (*pl., g.* —).
■ *cpds.* **~board** *n.* ша́хматная доска́; **~ player** *n.* шахмати́ст (*fem.* -ка).
chest /tʃest/ *n.*
1 (*furniture*) сунду́к; **~ of drawers** шкаф с выдвижны́ми я́щиками.

C

2 (*anat.*) грудна́я кле́тка; **get sth. off one's ~** облегчи́ть (*pf.*) ду́шу.
chestnut /'tʃesnʌt/ *n.* (*tree, fruit*) кашта́н.
chew /tʃu:/ *v.t.* & *i.* жева́ть (*impf.*); **~ upon, ~ over** (*fig.*) пережёвывать (*impf.*); **~ing gum** жева́тельная рези́нка.
chewy /'tʃu:ɪ/ *adj.* (**chewier, chewiest**) (*coll.*) тягу́чий.
chic /ʃi:k/ *adj.* (**chicer, chicest**) элега́нтный, шика́рный.
chick /tʃɪk/ *n.* птене́ц.
■ *cpd.* **~peas** *n. pl.* (*bot.*) нут (обыкнове́нный/культу́рный), туре́цкий/бара́ний горо́х.
chicken /'tʃɪkɪn/ *n.* цыплёнок; (*as food*) куря́тина, цыплёнок, ку́рица.
■ *cpd.* **~pox** *n.* ветряна́я о́спа, ветря́нка (*coll.*).
chicory /'tʃɪkərɪ/ *n.* (*bot.*) цико́рий (корнево́й).
chief /tʃi:f/ *n.*
1 (*leader*) вождь (*m.*), глава́ (*m.*).
2 (*senior official*) шеф, нача́льник; **~ of staff** нача́льник шта́ба.
■ *adj.* 1 (*most important*) гла́вный, основно́й, важне́йший.
2 (*senior*) гла́вный, ста́рший.
chiefly /'tʃi:flɪ/ *adv.* гла́вным о́бразом.
chiffon /'ʃɪfɒn/ *n.* шифо́н.
chilblain /'tʃɪlbleɪn/ *n.* обморо́женное ме́сто.
child /tʃaɪld/ *n.* (*pl.* **children**) дитя́ (*nt.*), ребёнок.
■ *cpds.* **~ benefit** *n.* посо́бие на ребёнка; **~birth** *n.* ро́д|ы (*pl.*, *g.* -ов); **~care** *n.* ухо́д за детьми́ (*особенно в детских садах и яслях*).
childhood /'tʃaɪldhʊd/ *n.* де́тство.
childish /'tʃaɪldɪʃ/ *adj.* де́тский, ребя́ческий.
childless /'tʃaɪldlɪs/ *adj.* безде́тный.
childlike /'tʃaɪldlaɪk/ *adj.* де́тский.
children /'tʃɪldr(ə)n/ *pl. of* ▸ **child**
Chile /'tʃɪlɪ/ *n.* Чи́ли (*f. indecl.*).
Chilean /'tʃɪlɪən/ *n.* чили́|ец (*fem.* -йка).
■ *adj.* чили́йский.
chill /tʃɪl/ *n.*
1 (*physical*; *fig.*) хо́лод.
2 (*med.*) просту́да; **catch a ~** просту|жа́ться, -ди́ться.
■ *adj.* холо́дный.
■ *v.t.* (*lit.*) охла|жда́ть, -ди́ть; (*fig.*) осту|жа́ть, -ди́ть.
■ *v.i.*: **~ out** (*coll.*) рассл|абля́ться, -а́биться.
chilli /'tʃɪlɪ/ *n.* (*US* **chili**) (*pl.* **-es**) кра́сный стручко́вый пе́рец.
chilly /'tʃɪlɪ/ *adj.* (**chillier, chilliest**) холо́дный.
chime /tʃaɪm/ *n.* перезво́н.
■ *v.t.*: **the clock ~d midnight** часы́ проби́ли по́лночь.
chimney /'tʃɪmnɪ/ *n.* труба́, дымохо́д.
chimpanzee /tʃɪmpæn'zi:/ *n.* шимпанзе́ (*m. indecl.*).
chin /tʃɪn/ *n.* подборо́док.
China[1] /'tʃaɪnə/ *n.* Кита́й.
china[2] /'tʃaɪnə/ *n.* фарфо́р.
Chinese /tʃaɪ'ni:z/ *n.* (*pl.* **~**) (*person*) кита́|ец (*fem.* -я́нка); (*language*) кита́йский язы́к.
■ *adj.* кита́йский.
chink[1] /tʃɪŋk/ *n.* (*crevice*) щель.
chink[2] /tʃɪŋk/ *n.* (*sound*) звя́канье.
chintz /tʃɪnts/ *n.* си́тец; (*attr.*) си́тцевый.
chip /tʃɪp/ *n.*
1 (*of wood*) ще́пка; стру́жка; (*of china*) оско́лок.
2 (*fig.*): **he has a ~ on his shoulder** он де́ржится вызыва́юще.
3 : **the cup has a ~** у ча́шки отко́лот кусо́к.
4 (*pl.*, *food*) (*Br.*) карто́фель (*m.*) соло́мкой/фри; (*US*) чи́псы (*m. pl.*).
5 (*at games*) фи́шка, ма́рка.
6 (*in microelectronics*) чип, микросхе́ма.
■ *v.t.* (**chipped, chipping**) струга́ть, вы́стругать; отк|а́лывать, -оло́ть; отб|ива́ть, -и́ть; обб|ива́ть, -и́ть.
■ *v.i.* (**chipped, chipping**) : **~ in** (*coll.*) вме́ш|иваться, -а́ться; влез|а́ть, -ть (в разгово́р).
■ *cpd.* **~board** *n.* фиброли́т; (*attr.*) фиброли́товый.
chipmunk /'tʃɪpmʌŋk/ *n.* бурунду́к.
chiropodist /kɪ'rɒpədɪst/ *n.* специали́ст (*fem.* -ка) по лече́нию заболева́ний стопы́.
chiropody /kɪ'rɒpədɪ/ *n.* лече́ние заболева́ний стопы́.
chiropractor /'kaɪərəʊpræktə(r)/ *n.* хиропра́ктик.
chirp /tʃə:p/ *v.t.* & *i.* чири́кать (*impf.*); щебета́ть (*impf.*).
chirpy /'tʃəpɪ/ *adj.* (**chirpier, chirpiest**) (*coll.*) бо́дрый.
chisel /'tʃɪz(ə)l/ *n.* долото́, стаме́ска.
■ *v.t.* (**chiselled, chiselling; *US* chiseled, chiseling**) вая́ть, из-.
chit-chat /'tʃɪttʃæt/ *n.* болтовня́, пересу́д|ы (*pl.*, *g.* -ов).
chivalrous /'ʃɪvəlrəs/ *adj.* ры́царский.
chivalry /'ʃɪvəlrɪ/ *n.* ры́царство.
chive /tʃaɪv/ *n.* лук-ре́занец.
chivvy /'tʃɪvɪ/ *v.t.* (*Br. coll.*) гоня́ть (*impf.*).
chloride /'klɔ:raɪd/ *n.* хлори́д.
chlorine /'klɔ:ri:n/ *n.* хлор.
chock /tʃɒk/:
■ *cpds.* **~-a-block** *adj.* загромождённый; **~-full** *adj.* битко́м наби́тый.
chocolate /'tʃɒkələt/ *n.* шокола́д (*also drink*); (*~-coated sweet*) шокола́дная конфе́та; **~ bar** пли́тка шокола́да; **~ biscuit** шокола́дное пече́нье.
choice /tʃɔɪs/ *n.*
1 (*choosing*) вы́бор, отбо́р.
2 (*thing chosen*) вы́бор.
3 (*variety*) вы́бор.
choir /'kwaɪə(r)/ *n.* хор.
■ *cpd.* **~boy** *n.* пе́вчий.
choke /tʃəʊk/ *n.* (*in car*) возду́шная засло́нка; дро́ссель (*m.*).
■ *v.t.* 1 (*throttle*) души́ть, за-.
2 (*block*) заку́пор|ивать, -ить; **the garden is ~d with weeds** сорняки́ заглуши́ли сад.
■ *v.i.* зад|ыха́ться, -охну́ться.
choker /'tʃəʊkə(r)/ *n.* коро́ткое ожере́лье, колье́ (*nt. indecl.*).
cholera /'kɒlərə/ *n.* холе́ра.
cholesterol /kə'lestərɒl/ *n.* холестери́н.
choose /tʃu:z/ *v.t.* (*past* **chose;** *p.p.* **chosen**) выбира́ть, вы́брать; **there are five to ~ from** мо́жно выбира́ть из пяти́; **I chose to**

remain я предпочёл оста́ться.

choosy /'tʃu:zɪ/ *adj.* (**choosier, choosiest**) разбо́рчивый.

chop /tʃɒp/ *n.*
1 (*cut*) ру́бящий уда́р.
2 (*of meat*) отбивна́я котле́та.
■ *v.t.* (**chopped, chopping**) руби́ть (*impf.*); (*cut*) нар|еза́ть, -е́зать; кроши́ть (*impf.*); ~ **up** нар|еза́ть, -е́зать; ~ **a tree down** руби́ть, с- де́рево.

choppy /'tʃɒpɪ/ *adj.* (**choppier, choppiest**) (*of sea*) неспоко́йный.

chopstick /'tʃɒpstɪk/ *n.* па́лочка для еды́.

choral /'kɔ:r(ə)l/ *adj.* хорово́й.

chord /kɔ:d/ *n.* (*mus.*) акко́рд.

chore /tʃɔ:(r)/ *n.* (*odd job*) случа́йная рабо́та.

choreographer /kɒrɪ'ɒgrəfə(r)/ *n.* балетме́йстер, хорео́граф.

choreography /kɒrɪ'ɒgrəfɪ/ *n.* хореогра́фия.

chorister /'kɒrɪstə(r)/ *n.* хори́ст (*fem.* -ка).

chortle /'tʃɔ:t(ə)l/ *v.i.* фы́ркать (*impf.*); дави́ться (*impf.*) от сме́ха.

chorus /'kɔ:rəs/ *n.* (*pl.* ~**es**)
1 (*singers*) хор.
2 (*refrain*) припе́в, рефре́н.

chose /tʃəʊz/ *past of* ▸ **choose**

chosen /'tʃəʊz(ə)n/ *p.p. of* ▸ **choose**

Christ /kraɪst/ *n.* Христо́с.

christen /'krɪs(ə)n/ *v.t.* крести́ть (*impf.*, *pf.*); **he was ~ed John** при креще́нии ему́ да́ли и́мя Джон.

christening /'krɪs(ə)nɪŋ/ *n.* креще́ние.

Christian /'krɪstɪən/ *n.* христи|ани́н (*fem.* -а́нка).
■ *adj.* христиа́нский; ~ **name** и́мя (*nt.*) (*в противополо́жность фами́лии*).

Christianity /krɪstɪ'ænɪtɪ/ *n.* христиа́нство.

Christmas /'krɪsməs/ *n.* (*pl.* ~**es**) Рождество́; ~ **card** рожде́ственская откры́тка; ~ **Day** пе́рвый день Рождества́; ~ **Eve** кану́н Рождества́; ~ **tree** рожде́ственская, нового́дняя ёлка.

chromatic /krə'mætɪk/ *adj.*
1 (*pert. to colour*) цветно́й.
2 (*mus.*) хромати́ческий.

chrome /krəʊm/ *n.* хром.

chromosome /'krəʊməsəʊm/ *n.* хромосо́ма.

chronic /'krɒnɪk/ *adj.*
1 (*med.*) хрони́ческий.
2 (*fig.*, *incessant*) хрони́ческий, постоя́нный.

chronicle /'krɒnɪk(ə)l/ *n.* хро́ника, ле́топись.
■ *v.t.* вести́ (*det.*) хро́нику + *g.*

chronological /krɒnə'lɒdʒɪk(ə)l/ *adj.* хронологи́ческий.

chrysanthemum /krɪ'sænθəməm/ *n.* хризанте́ма.

château /'ʃætəʊ/ *n.* (*pl.* ~**x** *pronunc. same or* /-təʊz/) за́мок.

chubby /'tʃʌbɪ/ *adj.* (**chubbier, chubbiest**) то́лстенький, пу́хленький.

chuck /tʃʌk/ *v.t.* (*coll.*, *throw*) швыр|я́ть, -ну́ть.
■ *with advs.*: (*coll.*): ~ **away** *v.t.* (*lit.*) выбра́сывать, вы́бросить; ~ **out** *v.t.* (*thing or person*) вы́кинуть (*pf.*); вы́швырнуть (*pf.*).

chuckle /'tʃʌk(ə)l/ *n.* сда́вленный смешо́к, смех.
■ *v.i.* фы́ркать (*impf.*) от сме́ха, посме́иваться (*impf.*).

chuffed /tʃʌft/ *adj.* (*Br. coll.*) дово́льный.

chum /tʃʌm/ *n.* прия́тель (*m.*), дружо́к.

chunk /tʃʌŋk/ *n.* то́лстый кусо́к/ломо́ть (*m.*).

chunky /'tʃʌŋkɪ/ *adj.* (**chunkier, chunkiest**) (*person*) корена́стый; (*jumper*) то́лстый.

church /tʃə:tʃ/ *n.* це́рковь; (*building*) це́рковь (*esp. Orthodox*), храм.
■ *cpds.* ~**goer** *n.*: **he is a regular ~goer** он регуля́рно хо́дит в це́рковь; ~**yard** *n.* пого́ст, кла́дбище при це́ркви.

churlish /'tʃə:lɪʃ/ *adj.* ха́мский, гру́бый.

churn /tʃə:n/ *n.* (*tub*) маслобо́йка; (*Br.*, *can*) бидо́н.
■ *v.t.*: ~ **butter** сби|ва́ть, -ть ма́сло; (*fig.*): **he ~s out novels** он печёт рома́ны (как блины́); **the propeller ~ed up the waves** винт взвихри́л во́лны.

chute /ʃu:t/ *n.* (*slide, slope*) жёлоб, спуск; (*for amusement*) гора́, го́рка; (*for rubbish*) мусоропрово́д.

chutney /'tʃʌtnɪ/ *n.* ча́тни (*nt. indecl.*) (*индийская приправа из фруктов* (*реже овощей*) *с добавлением уксуса, острых специй и сахара; подаётся к мясу или сыру*).

CIA (*abbr. of* ***Central Intelligence Agency***) ЦРУ (Центра́льное разве́дывательное управле́ние).

cicada /sɪ'kɑ:də/ *n.* (*zool.*) цика́да.

cider /'saɪdə(r)/ *n.* (*Br*, *alcoholic drink*) сидр; (*US*, *non-alcoholic drink*) я́блочный напи́ток.

cigar /sɪ'gɑ:(r)/ *n.* сига́ра.

cigarette /sɪgə'ret/ *n.* сигаре́та; (*of Russian type*) папиро́са.
■ *cpd.* ~**-lighter** *n.* зажига́лка.

cinder /'sɪndə(r)/ *n.*: (*pl.*) шлак, зола́, пе́пел.

cinecamera /'sɪnɪkæmrə/ *n.* кинока́мера, киноаппара́т.

cinema /'sɪnɪmə/ *n.* кино́.

cinematography /sɪnɪmə'tɒgrəfɪ/ *n.* кинематогра́фия.

cinnamon /'sɪnəmən/ *n.* кори́ца.

circa /'sə:kə/ *prep.* приблизи́тельно; о́коло + *g.*

circle /'sə:k(ə)l/ *n.*
1 (*math.*, *fig.*) круг, окру́жность; **a ~ of trees** кольцо́ дере́вьев; **go round in a ~** (*fig.*, *e.g. argument*) возвраща́ться (*impf.*) к исхо́дной то́чке.
2 (*theatr.*): **dress ~** бельэта́ж; **upper ~** балко́н.
■ *v.t.*: **the earth ~s the sun** земля́ враща́ется вокру́г со́лнца.
■ *v.i.*: **the hawk ~d** я́стреб кружи́л в не́бе (*or* опи́сывал круги́).

circuit /'sə:kɪt/ *n.*
1 (*distance, journey round*): **he made a ~ of the camp** он обошёл ла́герь.
2 (*elec.*) цепь; ~**-breaker** автомати́ческий выключа́тель.

circuitous /sə:'kju:ɪtəs/ *adj.* кру́жный, око́льный.

circular /'sə:kjʊlə(r)/ *n.* циркуля́р.
■ *adj.* кругово́й.

circulate /'sə:kjʊleɪt/ *v.i.* циркули́ровать (*impf.*, *pf.*); **she ~d among the guests** она́

обходи́ла госте́й.
circulation /sə:kjʊ'leɪʃ(ə)n/ *n.* (*of blood*) кровообраще́ние; (*of air*) циркуля́ция.
circumcise /'sə:kəmsaɪz/ *v.t.* соверш|а́ть, -и́ть обреза́ние + *d.*
circumcision /sə:kəm'sɪʒ(ə)n/ *n.* обреза́ние.
circumference /sə'kʌmfərəns/ *n.* окру́жность.
circumnavigate /sə:kəm'nævɪgeɪt/ *v.t.* пла́вать (*indet.*) вокру́г + *g.*; **Drake ~d the globe** Дрейк соверши́л кругосве́тное пла́вание.
circumspect /'sə:kəmspekt/ *adj.* осмотри́тельный.
circumstance /'sə:kəmst(ə)ns/ *n.*
1 (*fact, detail*) обстоя́тельство, усло́вие; **in, under the ~s** в да́нных усло́виях/обстоя́тельствах; **under no ~s** ни при каки́х усло́виях/обстоя́тельствах.
2 (*condition of life*) материа́льное положе́ние.
circumstantial /sə:kəm'stænʃ(ə)l/ *adj.*: **~ evidence** ко́свенные ули́ки (*f. pl.*).
circumvent /sə:kəm'vent/ *v.t.* об|ходи́ть, -ойти́; (*outwit, cheat*) перехитри́ть (*pf.*).
circus /'sə:kəs/ *n.* (*pl.* **~es**) цирк; (*fig.*) балага́н.
cirrhosis /sɪ'rəʊsɪs/ *n.* цирро́з.
CIS (*abbr. of* ***Commonwealth of Independent States***) СНГ (Содру́жество Незави́симых Госуда́рств); (*attr., coll.*) эсэнгэ́шный.
cistern /'sɪst(ə)n/ *n.* цисте́рна, бак.
citadel /'sɪtədel/ *n.* (*lit., fig.*) цитаде́ль.
cite /saɪt/ *v.t.* (*quote*) цити́ровать, про-.
citizen /'sɪtɪz(ə)n/ *n.* гражд|ани́н (*fem.* -а́нка); (*of city*) жи́тель (*fem.* -ница).
citizenship /'sɪtɪzənʃɪp/ *n.* гражда́нство, по́дданство.
citrus /'sɪtrəs/ *n.*: **~ fruit** ци́трусовые (*nt. pl.*).
city /'sɪtɪ/ *n.* го́род; (*of London*) Си́ти (*m. indecl.*); **~ centre** (*Br.*), **center** (*US*) центр го́рода.
civic /'sɪvɪk/ *adj.* гражда́нский.
civil /'sɪv(ə)l/ *adj.*
1 (*pert. to a community*): **~ war** гражда́нская война́; **~ rights** гражда́нские права́; **~ servant** госуда́рственный слу́жащий, чино́вник; **~ service** госуда́рственная слу́жба.
2 (*polite*) ве́жливый.
civilian /sɪ'vɪlɪən/ *n.* & *adj.* шта́тский.
civilization /sɪvɪlaɪ'zeɪʃ(ə)n/ *n.* цивилиза́ция.
civilize /'sɪvɪlaɪz/ *v.t.* цивилизова́ть (*impf., pf.*).
claim /kleɪm/ *n.*
1 (*assertion of right*) притяза́ние.
2 (*assertion*) утвержде́ние, заявле́ние.
3 (*demand*) тре́бование.
■ *v.t.* 1 (*demand*) тре́бовать, по- + *g.*
2 (*assert as fact*) утвер|жда́ть, -ди́ть; **he ~s to own the land** он заявля́ет, что э́та земля́ принадлежи́т ему́.
claimant /'kleɪmənt/ *n.* претенде́нт (*fem.* -ка) (*на что*).
clairvoyant /kleə'vɔɪənt/ *n.* & *adj.* ясновидя́щ|ий (*fem.* -ая).
clam /klæm/ *n.* двуство́рчатый морско́й моллю́ск.
■ *v.i.* (**clammed, clamming**): **~ up** (*coll.*) уходи́ть, уйти́ в себя́.
clamber /'klæmbə(r)/ *v.i.* кара́бкаться, вс- (*на что*).
clammy /'klæmɪ/ *adj.* (**clammier, clammiest**) холо́дный и ли́пкий.
clamour /'klæmə(r)/ (*US* **clamor**) *n.* шум (*m. pl.*).
■ *v.i.* шуме́ть (*impf.*).
clamp /klæmp/ *n.* (*implement*) зажи́м.
■ *v.t.* заж|има́ть, -а́ть.
■ *v.i.*: **~ down on** (*fig.*) заж|има́ть, -а́ть.
■ *cpd.* **~down** *n.* стро́гий запре́т, стро́гие ме́ры (*против чего*).
clan /klæn/ *n.* клан.
clandestine /klæn'destɪn/ *adj.* та́йный.
clang /'klæŋ/ *n.* лязг.
■ *v.t.* & *i.* ля́зг|ать, -нуть; звене́ть (*impf.*).
clap /klæp/ *n.* (*of thunder*) уда́р; (*of applause*) хлопо́к, хло́панье; **let's give him a ~!** похло́паем ему́!
■ *v.t.* (**clapped, clapping**) (*strike, slap*): **~ one's hands** хло́п|ать, -нуть в ладо́ши.
■ *v.i.* (**clapped, clapping**) хло́пать (*impf.*).
clarification /klærɪfɪ'keɪʃ(ə)n/ *n.* проясне́ние.
clarify /'klærɪfaɪ/ *v.t.* вн|оси́ть, -ести́ я́сность в + *a.*
clarinet /klærɪ'net/ *n.* кларне́т.
clarinettist /klærɪ'netɪst/ *n.* кларнети́ст (*fem.* -ка).
clarity /'klærɪtɪ/ *n.* я́сность.
clash /klæʃ/ *n.*
1 (*sound*) гул.
2 (*conflict*): **~ of views** расхожде́ние во взгля́дах.
■ *v.t.*: **he ~ed the cymbals** он уда́рил в цимба́лы.
■ *v.i.* 1 (*sound*): **the cymbals ~ed** зазвене́ли цимба́лы.
2 (*conflict*): **the armies ~ed** а́рмии столкну́лись; (*coincide inconveniently*): **the two concerts ~** о́ба конце́рта совпада́ют по вре́мени; **the colours ~** э́ти цвета́ не гармони́руют друг с дру́гом.
clasp /klɑ:sp/ *n.* пря́жка.
■ *v.t.*: **~ s.o. by the hand** сж|има́ть, -ать кому́-н. ру́ку.
class /klɑ:s/ *n.*
1 (*group*) класс, разря́д; (*railway etc.*): **he went first ~** он е́хал пе́рвым кла́ссом.
2 (*social*) класс.
3 (*scholastic*) класс; (*period of instruction*): **a mathematics ~** уро́к матема́тики; **he attended ~es in French** он посеща́л заня́тия по францу́зскому (языку́); (*US*): **the ~ of 1955** вы́пуск 1955 го́да.
4 (*distinction*) класс, шик.
■ *v.t.* классифици́ровать (*impf., pf.*).
■ *cpds.* **~-conscious** *adj.* кла́ссово-созна́тельный; **~mate** *nn.* одноκла́ссни|к (*fem.* -ца); **~room** *n.* кла́ссная ко́мната, класс.
classic /'klæsɪk/ *n.*
1 кла́ссик.
2 (*pl., studies*): **he studied ~s** он изуча́л

классическую филологию.
■ *adj.* классический.
classical /'klæsɪk(ə)l/ *adj.* классический.
classifiable /'klæsɪfaɪəb(ə)l/ *adj.* поддающийся классификации.
classification /klæsɪfɪ'keɪʃ(ə)n/ *n.* классификация.
classif|y /'klæsɪfaɪ/ *v.t.* классифицировать (*impf., pf.*); **~ied** (*secret*) засекреченный; **~ied ad** тематическое объявление.
classy /'klɑːsɪ/ *adj.* (**classier, classiest**) стильный (*coll.*).
clatter /'klætə(r)/ *n.* (*of metal*) грохот; (*of hoofs, plates, cutlery etc.*) стук, звон, звяканье.
■ *v.i.* греметь; грохотать (*both impf.*).
clause /klɔːz/ *n.*
1 (*gram.*) предложение.
2 (*leg.*) статья.
claustrophobia /klɔːstrə'fəʊbɪə/ *n.* клаустрофобия.
claustrophobic /klɔːstrə'fəʊbɪk/ *adj.*: **I'm ~** я страдаю клаустрофобией.
claw /klɔː/ *n.* (*of animal, bird*) коготь (*m.*); (*of crustacean*) клешня; (*of machinery*) кулак, лапа, клещ|и (*pl., g.* -ей).
clay /kleɪ/ *n.* глина.
clean /kliːn/ *adj.*
1 (*not dirty*) чистый; **keep a room ~** содержать (*impf.*) комнату в чистоте.
2 (*fresh*): **a ~ sheet of paper** чистый лист бумаги.
3 (*pure, unblemished*) чистый, незапятнанный.
4 (*neat, smooth*): **~ lines** чёткие очертания; чистые линии.
■ *v.t.* чистить (*impf.*); **~ one's teeth** чистить, по- зубы; **~ a car** мыть, вы- машину; **~ a window** прот|ирать, -ереть окно; **he had his suit ~ed** он отдал костюм в чистку.
■ *with advs.*: **~ out** *v.t.*: **~ out a room** убрать (*pf.*) комнату; **~ up** *v.t.*: **~ o.s. up** прив|одить, -ести себя в порядок; **~ up a city** (*fig.*) очистить (*pf.*) город.
■ *cpds.* **~-cut** *adj.* резко очерченный; **~-shaven** *adj.* чисто выбритый.
cleaner /'kliːnə(r)/ *n.* (*person*) уборщи|к (*fem.* -ца); **he sent the suit to the ~'s** он отдал костюм в чистку; (*substance*) моющее средство; очиститель (*m.*).
cleanliness /'klenlɪnɪs/ *n.* чистота.
cleanse /klenz/ *v.t.* оч|ищать, -истить.
cleanser /'klenzə(r)/ *n.* средство для очищения кожи.
clear /klɪə(r)/ *adj.*
1 (*easy to see*) ясный, отчётливый; (*evident*) явный, очевидный.
2 (*bright*) яркий, ясный; **on a ~ day** в погожий день.
3 (*transparent*) прозрачный.
4 (*of sound*) чистый.
5 (*intelligible, certain*): **make sth. ~ to s.o.** объясн|ять, -ить что-н. кому-н.; **make o.s. ~** объясн|яться, -иться; **I am not ~ what he wants** мне неясно, чего он хочет.
6 (*safe, free*) свободный; **~ of debt** свободный от долгов; **~ of suspicion** вне подозрений; **my conscience is ~** моя совесть чиста; **keep a ~ head** сохранять (*impf.*) ясный ум.
■ *adv.*: **stand ~ of the gates** стоять (*impf.*) в стороне от ворот; **keep ~ of** держаться (*impf.*) в стороне от + *g.*
■ *v.t.* 1 (*make ~*) оч|ищать, -истить; **the streets were ~ed of snow** улицы очистили от снега; **~ land** расч|ищать, -истить землю; **she ~ed the table** она убрала со стола; **he was ~ed for security** его засекретили; **he ~ed his throat** он откашлялся; **he ~ed the things out of the drawer** он освободил ящик.
2 (*jump over; get past*): **the horse ~ed the hedge** лошадь взяла барьер.
3 (*make profit of*): **we ~ed £50** мы получили 50 фунтов прибыли.
4 : **~ a debt** погасить (*pf.*) долг.
■ *v.i.*: *see* ▶ **~ up.**
■ *with advs.*: **~ away** *v.t.* уб|ирать, -рать; *v.i.* (*disperse*) рассе|иваться, -яться; **~ off** *v.i.* (*coll., go away*) уб|ираться, -раться; **~ out** *v.t.*: **she ~ed out the cupboard** она очистила шкаф; *v.i.* (*coll., go away*) убраться (*pf.*); **~ up** *v.t.* (*tidy, remove*) уб|ирать, -рать; **~ up a mystery** разгадать (*pf.*) тайну; *v.i.*: **the weather ~ed up** погода прояснилась.
■ *cpds.* **~-cut** *adj.* (*fig.*) чёткий; **~-headed** *adj.* толковый.
clearance /'klɪərəns/ *n.*
1 (*removal of obstruction etc.*) очистка, расчистка; **~ sale** распродажа.
2 : **security ~** допуск к секретной работе.
clearing /'klɪərɪŋ/ *n.* просека, поляна.
clearly /'klɪəlɪ/ *adv.* (*distinctly*) ясно; (*evidently*) очевидно, конечно.
cleavage /'kliːvɪdʒ/ *n.* «ручеёк», ложбинка бюста.
cleaver /'kliːvə(r)/ *n.* нож мясника.
clef /klef/ *n.* ключ; **treble ~** скрипичный ключ.
clematis /'klemətɪs/ *n.* клематис, ломонос.
clench /klentʃ/ *v.t.*: **~ one's teeth** стиснуть (*pf.*) зубы; **~ one's fist** сж|имать, -ать кулаки.
clergy /'klɜːdʒɪ/ *n.* духовенство, клир.
■ *cpd.* **~man** *n.* духовное лицо; (*Protestant*) пастор.
cleric /'klerɪk/ *n.* церковник, духовное лицо.
clerical /'klerɪk(ə)l/ *adj.*
1 (*of clergy*) клерикальный.
2 (*of clerks*) канцелярский, конторский; **~ error** канцелярская ошибка.
clerk /klɑːk/ *n.*
1 (*in office*) секретарь (*m.*), делопроизводитель (*m.*); **bank ~** банковский служащий.
2 (*official*) служащий; (*of court*) регистратор.
3 (*US, shop assistant*) продавец; (*US, hotel receptionist*) (дежурный) администратор.
clever /'klevə(r)/ *adj.* (**cleverer, cleverest**) умный; (*skilful*) ловкий; **he is ~ with his fingers** у него умелые руки.
cliché /'kliːʃeɪ/ *n.* (*fig.*) клише (*nt. indecl.*).
click /klɪk/ *n.* щёлканье, щелчок.
■ *v.t.* щёлк|ать, -нуть + *i.*
■ *v.i.* щёлк|ать, -нуть; (*comput.*): **~ on an icon** щёлк|ать, -нуть (мышкой) на иконке.
client /'klaɪənt/ *n.* клиент (*fem.* -ка).
clientele /kliːɒn'tel/ *n.* клиентура.

C

cliff /klɪf/ *n.* утёс, скала́.

climactic /klaɪˈmæktɪk/ *adj.* кульминацио́нный.

climate /ˈklaɪmɪt/ *n.* кли́мат; (*fig.*) атмосфе́ра; ~ **change** измене́ние кли́мата.

climatic /klaɪˈmætɪk/ *adj.* климати́ческий.

climax /ˈklaɪmæks/ *n.* кульмина́ция.
■ *v.i.* (*culminate*) дост|ига́ть, -и́чь кульмина́ции, апоге́я.

climb /klaɪm/ *n.* подъём, восхожде́ние.
■ *v.t.* вл|еза́ть, -езть на + *a.*
■ *v.i.* ла́зить (*indet.*), лезть (*det.*); ~ **up a tree** влез|а́ть, -ть на де́рево; ~ **over a wall** перел|еза́ть, -е́зть че́рез сте́ну; ~ **down a ladder** слез|а́ть, -ть с ле́стницы; ~ **on to a table** зал|еза́ть, -е́зть на стол.
■ *cpd.* ~**down** *n.* (*fig.*) отступле́ние, усту́пка.

climber /ˈklaɪmə(r)/ *n.* альпини́ст (*fem.* -ка); (*plant*) вью́щееся расте́ние.

climbing /ˈklaɪmɪŋ/ *n.* альпини́зм.

clime /klaɪm/ *n.* (*poet.*, *region*) край, сторона́.

clinch /klɪntʃ/ *v.t.*: ~ **a bargain** заключи́ть (*pf.*) сде́лку (*окончательно согласовав все условия*).

cling /klɪŋ/ *v.i.* (*past and p.p.* **clung**) (*adhere*) цепля́ться (*impf.*) (**to:** за + *a.*); (*fig.*): **they clung together** они́ держа́лись вме́сте; **a** ~**ing dress** облега́ющее пла́тье.

clinic /ˈklɪnɪk/ *n.* кли́ника.

clinical /ˈklɪnɪk(ə)l/ *adj.*
1 клини́ческий.
2 (*fig.*) бесстра́стный.

clink /klɪŋk/ *v.t.* звене́ть (*impf.*) + *i.*
■ *v.i.* звене́ть (*impf.*); чо́к|аться, -нуться.

clip¹ /klɪp/ *n.* (*for hair*) зако́лка.
■ *v.t.* (**clipped, clipping**) заж|има́ть, -а́ть.
■ *cpds.* ~**board** *n.* доска́ с зажи́мом для бума́ги; ~**-on** *adj.* пристёгивающийся.

clip² /klɪp/ *n.* (*cin.*) отры́вок (из фи́льма).
■ *v.t.* (**clipped, clipping**) : ~ **a hedge** подстр|ига́ть, -и́чь живу́ю и́згородь; ~ **s.o.'s wings** (*fig.*) подре́зать (*pf.*) кому́-н. кры́лышки.

clipper /ˈklɪpə(r)/ *n.* (*pl.*, *for nails*) куса́ч|ки (*pl.*, *g.* -ек).

clipping /ˈklɪpɪŋ/ *n.* (*from newspaper*) газе́тная вы́резка.

cloak /kləʊk/ *n.* плащ, ма́нтия.
■ *v.t.* (*fig.*) прикр|ыва́ть, -ы́ть.
■ *cpd.* ~**room** *n.* (*for clothes*) гардеро́б, раздева́лка; (*Br.*, *lavatory*) убо́рная.

clock /klɒk/ *n.* час|ы́ (*pl.*, *g.* -о́в); **he works round the** ~ он рабо́тает кру́глые су́тки; **put the** ~ **forward** ста́вить, по- часы́ вперёд; **put the** ~ **back** (*lit.*) перев|оди́ть, -ести́ часы́ наза́д; (*fig.*) поверну́ть (*pf.*) вре́мя вспять.
■ *v.i.*: ~ **in, on** (*Br.*) отм|еча́ться, -е́титься по прихо́де на рабо́ту; ~ **out, off** (*Br.*) отм|еча́ться, -е́титься при ухо́де с рабо́ты.
■ *cpd.* ~**work** *n.* часово́й механи́зм; **the ceremony went like** ~**work** церемо́ния прошла́ без сучка́, без задо́ринки.

clockwise /ˈklɒkwaɪz/ *adj.* & *adv.* (дви́жущийся) по часово́й стре́лке.

clog /klɒg/ *n.* (*shoe*) башма́к на деревя́нной подо́шве; сабо́ (*nt. indecl.*).

cloister /ˈklɔɪstə(r)/ *n.* арка́да.

clone /kləʊn/ *n.* клон.
■ *v.t.* размн|ожа́ть, -о́жить вегетати́вным путём; клони́ровать (*impf.*, *pf.*).

cloning /ˈkləʊnɪŋ/ *n.* клони́рование.

close¹ /kləʊs/ *adj.*
1 (*near*) бли́зкий; **he had a** ~ **shave, call** он был на волосо́к от ги́бели; ~ **resemblance** большо́е схо́дство.
2 (*intimate*) бли́зкий; **a** ~ **friend** бли́зкий друг.
3 (*compact*): ~ **texture** пло́тная ткань.
4 (*attentive*): **keep a** ~ **watch on s.o.** тща́тельно следи́ть (*impf.*) за кем-н.; ~ **examination** тща́тельное обсле́дование; ~ **attention** при́стальное внима́ние.
5 (*of games etc.*): **a** ~ **contest** упо́рная борьба́.
6 (*stuffy*): ду́шный.
■ *adv.*: **he lives** ~ **to, by the church** он живёт побли́зости от це́ркви; **follow** ~ **behind s.o.** сле́довать (*impf.*) непосре́дственно за кем-н.
■ *cpds.* ~**-fitting** *adj.* облега́ющий; ~**-up** *n.* (*cin.*) кру́пный план.

close² /kləʊz/ *n.* (*end*) коне́ц; **bring to a** ~ заверш|а́ть, -и́ть, зак|а́нчивать, -о́нчить; **the meeting drew to a** ~ собра́ние подошло́ к концу́.
■ *v.t.* 1 (*shut*) закр|ыва́ть, -ы́ть; **the museum is** ~**d** музе́й не рабо́тает.
2 (*end, complete*): ~ **a meeting** закр|ыва́ть, -ы́ть собра́ние; ~ **a deal** заключ|а́ть, -и́ть сде́лку; **the closing scene of the play** заключи́тельная сце́на пье́сы; **the closing date is December 1** после́дний срок — пе́рвое декабря́.
■ *v.i.* 1 (*shut*) закр|ыва́ться, -ы́ться; **the door** ~**d** дверь закры́лась.
2 (*cease*): **he** ~**d with this remark** он зако́нчил э́тим замеча́нием.
3 (*come closer*) сбл|ижа́ться, -и́зиться; **the soldiers** ~**d up** солда́ты сомкну́ли ряды́.
■ *with advs.*: ~ **down** *v.t.* закр|ыва́ть, -ы́ть; *v.i.* (*e.g. of a factory*) закр|ыва́ться, -ы́ться; ~ **up** *v.t.* & *i.* закр|ыва́ть(ся), -ы́ть(ся).

closely /ˈkləʊslɪ/ *adv.*: **it** ~ **resembles pork** э́то о́чень напомина́ет свини́ну; (*attentively*) внима́тельно; **watch** ~ при́стально следи́ть (*impf.*) за + *i.*; ~ **connected** те́сно/про́чно свя́занный.

closet /ˈklɒzɪt/ *n.* (*US*) (стенно́й) шкаф.

closure /ˈkləʊʒə(r)/ *n.* закры́тие.

clot /klɒt/ *n.* сгу́сток, комо́к.
■ *v.i.* (**clotted, clotting**) свёртываться, сверну́ться.

cloth /klɒθ/ *n.*
1 (*material*) ткань, мате́рия.
2 (*piece of* ~) тря́пка.

clothes /kləʊðz/ *n.* пла́тье, оде́жда.
■ *cpds.* ~ **brush** *n.* платяна́я щётка; ~ **line** *n.* верёвка для белья́; ~ **peg** (*Br.*), ~**pin** (*US*) *nn.* прище́пка.

clothing /ˈkləʊðɪŋ/ *n.* оде́жда.

cloud /klaʊd/ *n.*
1 (*in the sky*) о́блако; ту́ча.
2 (*of unhappiness etc.*): **this cast a** ~ **over our meeting** э́то омрачи́ло на́шу встре́чу.
■ *v.t.* покр|ыва́ть, -ы́ть облака́ми; (*fig.*)

омрач|áть, -и́ть; **eyes ~ed with tears** глаза́, помутне́вшие от слёз.
■ *v.i.*: **the sky ~ed over, up** (*US*) не́бо затяну́ло облака́ми/ту́чами.

cloudy /ˈklaʊdɪ/ *adj.* (**cloudier, cloudiest**) о́блачный; (*of liquid*) му́тный.

clout /klaʊt/ *n.* (*coll., blow*) затре́щина; (*coll., influence*) влия́ние.

clove[1] /kləʊv/ *n.*: **a ~ of garlic** зу́бчик чеснока́.

clove[2] /kləʊv/ *n.* (*aromatic*) гвозди́ка (*пряность*).

clover /ˈkləʊvə(r)/ *n.* кле́вер.

clown /klaʊn/ *n.* кло́ун.
■ *v.i.* стро́ить (*impf.*) из себя́ шута́.

club[1] /klʌb/ *n.* (*weapon*) дуби́нка; (*at golf*) клю́шка; (*pl., at cards*) тре́фы (*f. pl.*).

club[2] /klʌb/ *n.* (*society*) клуб.
■ *v.i.* (**clubbed, clubbing**) **they ~bed together to pay the fine** они́ сложи́лись и уплати́ли штраф; **they're always going out ~bing** (*coll.*) они́ — постоя́нные посети́тели ночны́х клу́бов.

cluck /klʌk/ *v.i.* куда́хтать, клохта́ть (*both impf.*).

clue /kluː/ *n.* ключ, нить; (*for crossword*) определе́ние; **the police found a ~** поли́ция нашла́ ули́ку; **I haven't a ~** (*coll.*) поня́тия не име́ю.

clueless /ˈkluːlɪs/ *adj.* (*coll.*) бестолко́вый; не в ку́рсе.

clump /klʌmp/ *n.* (*cluster*) гру́ппа.

clumsy /ˈklʌmzɪ/ *adj.* (**clumsier, clumsiest**) неуклю́жий, нело́вкий.

clung /klʌŋ/ *past and p.p. of* ▶ **cling**

cluster /ˈklʌstə(r)/ *n.* скопле́ние.
■ *v.i.* соб|ира́ться, -ра́ться гру́ппами; **the children ~ed round the teacher** де́ти столпи́лись вокру́г учи́теля.

clutch /klʌtʃ/ *n.*
1 (*pl., grasp*) ла́пы (*f. pl.*), ко́гти (*m. pl.*).
2 (*of car*) сцепле́ние; **~ pedal** педа́ль сцепле́ния.
■ *v.t. & i.* хвата́ться, схвати́ться (за + *a.*); **he ~ed (at) the rope** он ухвати́лся за верёвку.

clutter /ˈklʌtə(r)/ *n.* сумато́ха, суета́.
■ *v.t.* (*also* **~ up**) загромо|жда́ть, -зди́ть.

cm /ˈsentɪmiːtə(r)(z)/ *n.* (*abbr. of* ***centimetre(s)***) см (сантиме́тр(ы)).

Co. /kəʊ/ *n.* (*abbr. of* ***company***) К° (компа́ния).

c/o (*abbr. of* ***care of***) че́рез; **John Smith c/o David Green** Дэ́виду Гри́ну для переда́чи Джо́ну Сми́ту.

coach[1] /kəʊtʃ/ *n.*
1 (*horse-drawn*) каре́та, экипа́ж.
2 (*railway*) пассажи́рский ваго́н.
3 (*Br., bus*) (тури́стский, междугоро́дный) авто́бус.
■ *cpd.* **~ tour** *n.* авто́бусная экску́рсия.

coach[2] /kəʊtʃ/ *n.* (*trainer*) тре́нер.
■ *v.t.* репети́ровать (*impf.*); (*train*) тренирова́ть, на-.

coagulate /kəʊˈægjʊleɪt/ *v.t.* сгу|ща́ть, -сти́ть; (*phys., chem.*) коагули́ровать (*impf., pf.*); (*med., of blood*) свёртывать, сверну́ть.
■ *v.i.* сгу|ща́ться, -сти́ться; (*phys., chem.*) коагули́роваться (*impf., pf.*); (*med., of blood*) свёртываться, сверну́ться.

coal /kəʊl/ *n.* (*mineral*) ка́менный у́голь; (*Br., piece of* ~) у́голь (*m.*); (*fig.*): **haul s.o. over the ~s** да|ва́ть, -ть нагоня́й кому́-н.
■ *cpds.* **~field** *n.* каменноу́гольный бассе́йн; **~ mine** *nn.* у́гольная ша́хта; **~ miner** *n.* шахтёр.

coalition /kəʊəˈlɪʃ(ə)n/ *n.* (*pol.*) коали́ция.

coarse /kɔːs/ *adj.* (*of material*) гру́бый; (*of sand, sugar*) кру́пный; **~ manners** гру́бые/вульга́рные мане́ры.

coast /kəʊst/ *n.* морско́й бе́рег.
■ *v.i.* (*bicycle downhill*) кати́ться (*impf.*) на велосипе́де с горы́.
■ *cpds.* **~guard** *n.* (*officer*) сотру́дник (тамо́женной) берегово́й охра́ны; (*collect.*) берегова́я охра́на; **~line** *n.* берегова́я ли́ния.

coastal /ˈkəʊstəl/ *adj.* берегово́й, прибре́жный.

coaster /ˈkəʊstə(r)/ *n.* подно́с, подста́вка.

coat /kəʊt/ *n.*
1 (*overcoat*) пальто́ (*nt. indecl.*); **~ of arms** герб.
2 (*of animal*) шерсть, мех.
3 (*of paint etc.*) слой.
■ *v.t.* покр|ыва́ть, -ы́ть; **the pill is ~ed with sugar** пилю́ля в са́харной оболо́чке.
■ *cpd.* **~ hanger** *n.* ве́шалка.

coating /ˈkəʊtɪŋ/ *n.* (*layer*) слой.

co-author /kəʊˈɔːθə(r)/ *n.* соа́втор.

coax /kəʊks/ *v.t.* угов|а́ривать, -ори́ть.

cobble /ˈkɒb(ə)l/ *n.* (*also* **~stone(s)**) булы́жник.

cobbled /ˈkɒb(ə)ld/ *adj.*: **~ street** булы́жная мостова́я.

cobra /ˈkəʊbrə/ *n.* ко́бра; очко́вая змея́.

cobweb /ˈkɒbweb/ *n.* паути́на.

cocaine /kəˈkeɪn/ *n.* кокаи́н.

cock[1] /kɒk/ *n.*
1 (*male domestic fowl*) пету́х.
2 (*male bird*) пету́х, саме́ц.
■ *cpds.* **~ and bull** *adj.*: **~ and bull story** вздор, небыли́ца; **~pit** *n.* (*aeron.*) каби́на; **~roach** *n.* тарака́н; **~tail** *n.* (*drink*) кокте́йль (*m.*).

cock[2] /kɒk/ *v.t.*
1 (*stick up etc.*): **the horse ~ed (up) its ears** ло́шадь навостри́ла у́ши.
2 (*of gun*) взв|оди́ть, -ести́ куро́к + *g.*

cockerel /ˈkɒkər(ə)l/ *n.* петушо́к.

cockle /ˈkɒk(ə)l/ *n.* сердцеви́дка, съедо́бный моллю́ск.

cockney /ˈkɒknɪ/ *n. & adj.* ко́кни ((*person*) *c.g. indecl.*; (*language*) *m. indecl.*); **~ accent** акце́нт ко́кни.

cocky /ˈkɒkɪ/ *adj.* (**cockier, cockiest**) наха́льный.

cocoa /ˈkəʊkəʊ/ *n.* кака́о (*nt. indecl.*).

coconut /ˈkəʊkənʌt/ *n.* коко́с, коко́совый оре́х.

cocoon /kəˈkuːn/ *n.* ко́кон.

COD (*abbr. of* ***cash on delivery***) упла́та при доста́вке.

cod /kɒd/ *n.* (*pl.* ~) треска́.

coda /ˈkəʊdə/ *n.* (*mus.*) ко́да.

code /kəʊd/ *n.* (*of laws, conduct*) ко́декс; (*set of symbols*) код.

■ *v.t.* (*encode*) кодировать (*impf., pf.*).
codeine /'kəʊdi:n/ *n.* кодеин.
co-educational /kəʊedju:'keɪʃ(ə)nəl/ *adj.* совме́стного обуче́ния.
coerce /kəʊ'ə:s/ *v.t.* прин|ужда́ть, -у́дить.
coercion /kəʊ'ə:ʃ(ə)n/ *n.* принужде́ние; **he paid under ~** он заплати́л под давле́нием; его́ прину́дили заплати́ть.
coercive /kəʊ'ə:sɪv/ *adj.* принуди́тельный.
coexist /kəʊɪg'zɪst/ *v.i.* сосуществова́ть (*impf.*).
coexistence /kəʊɪg'zɪst(ə)ns/ *n.* сосуществова́ние.
C. of E. (*abbr. of* ***Church of England***) Англика́нская це́рковь.
coffee /'kɒfɪ/ *n.* ко́фе (*m. indecl.*); **two ~s** два ко́фе; **black ~** чёрный ко́фе; **white ~** ко́фе с молоко́м.
■ *cpds.* **~ bar** *n.* буфе́т; **~ bean** *n.* (*on tree*) кофе́йный боб; (*as product*) кофе́йное зерно́; (*pl.*) ко́фе в зёрнах; **~ break** *n.* переры́в на ко́фе; **~ pot** *n.* кофе́йник; **~ table** *n.* кофе́йный/журна́льный сто́лик.
coffer /'kɒfə(r)/ *n.* (*chest*) сунду́к; (*pl., fig., funds*) казна́.
coffin /'kɒfɪn/ *n.* гроб.
cog /kɒg/ *n.* зуб (*pl.* -ья); зубе́ц.
cogent /'kəʊdʒ(ə)nt/ *adj.* убеди́тельный.
cogitate /'kɒdʒɪteɪt/ *v.i.* размышля́ть (*impf.*) (*о чём or над чем*).
cognac /'kɒnjæk/ *n.* конья́к.
cognizant /'kɒgnɪz(ə)nt/ *adj.* зна́ющий, осведомлённый.
cohabit /kəʊ'hæbɪt/ *v.i.* (**cohabited, cohabiting**) сожи́тельствовать (*impf.*).
coherent /kəʊ'hɪərənt/ *adj.* свя́зный, после́довательный.
cohesion /kəʊ'hi:ʒ(ə)n/ *n.* сцепле́ние; сплочённость.
cohort /'kəʊhɔ:t/ *n.* кого́рта.
coil /kɔɪl/ *n.* вито́к; кольцо́.
■ *v.t. & i.* (*also* **~ up**) свёртывать(ся), сверну́ть(ся) кольцо́м (*or* в кольцо́).
coin /kɔɪn/ *n.* моне́та.
■ *v.t.* **~ a phrase** созд|ава́ть, -а́ть выраже́ние.
■ *cpds.* **~ box** *n.* (*Br., telephone*) телефо́н-автома́т; **~-operated** *adj.* моне́тный.
coincide /kəʊɪn'saɪd/ *v.i.* совп|ада́ть, -а́сть.
coincidence /kəʊ'ɪnsɪd(ə)ns/ *n.* совпаде́ние.
coincidental /kəʊɪnsɪ'dent(ə)l/ *adj.* случа́йный.
coke[1] /kəʊk/ *n.* кокс.
coke[2] /kəʊk/ *n.* (*sl., cocaine*) кокаи́н.
colander /'kʌləndə(r)/ *n.* дуршла́г.
cold /kəʊld/ *n.*
[1] хо́лод.
[2] (*illness*) просту́да; **catch (a) ~** просту|жа́ться, -ди́ться.
■ *adj.* [1] (*at low temperature*) холо́дный; **I am, feel ~** мне хо́лодно.
[2] (*fig.*): **in ~ blood** хладнокро́вно; **get ~ feet** (*coll.*) тру́сить, с-.
[3] (*unfeeling*): **a ~ person** холо́дный челове́к.
■ *cpds.* **~-blooded** *adj.* (*of reptile, fish*) холоднокро́вный; (*fig.*) бесчу́вственный, безжа́лостный; **~-shoulder** *v.t.* ока́з|ывать, -а́ть кому́-н. холо́дный приём.
coleslaw /'kəʊlslɔ:/ *n.* капу́стный сала́т (*свежие капуста, морковь, лук под майонезом*).
colic /'kɒlɪk/ *n.* ко́лик|и (*pl., g.* —).
collaborate /kə'læbəreɪt/ *v.i.* сотру́дничать (*impf.*).
collaboration /kəlæbə'reɪʃ(ə)n/ *n.* сотру́дничество.
collapse /kə'læps/ *n.* (*of a building; of prices, market, etc.*) обва́л; (*of negotiations etc.*) прова́л; (*of hopes etc.*) круше́ние; (*of resistance etc.*) разва́л; (*med.*) колла́пс.
■ *v.i.* (*of a building etc.*) обва́л|иваться, -и́ться; (*of person*) вали́ться, с-.
collapsible /kə'læpsɪb(ə)l/ *adj.* складно́й.
collar /'kɒlə(r)/ *n.*
[1] (*of garment*) воротни́к; **hot under the ~** (*fig., excited, vexed*) рассе́рженный.
[2] (*of dog*) оше́йник.
■ *cpd.* **~bone** *n.* (*anat.*) ключи́ца.
collate /kə'leɪt/ *v.t.* слич|а́ть, -и́ть.
collateral /kə'lætər(ə)l/ *adj.* побо́чный, дополни́тельный; **~ security** (*fin.*) дополни́тельное обеспе́чение (*кредита*).
colleague /'kɒli:g/ *n.* колле́га (*c.g.*).
collect /kə'lekt/ *v.t.*
[1] (*gather together*) соб|ира́ть, -ра́ть; **~ed works** (по́лное) собра́ние сочине́ний.
[2] (*of debts, taxes*) соб|ира́ть, -ра́ть.
[3] (*of stamps etc.*) коллекциони́ровать (*impf.*).
[4] (*fetch*) заб|ира́ть, -ра́ть.
■ *v.i.* соб|ира́ться, -ра́ться.
collected /kə'lektɪd/ *adj.* (*calm*) со́бранный.
collection /kə'lekʃ(ə)n/ *n.* (*of valuables etc.*) колле́кция; (*accumulation*) скопле́ние; (*church etc.*) сбор; (*of mail*) вы́емка.
collective /kə'lektɪv/ *n.* (*cooperative unit*) коллекти́в.
■ *adj.* коллекти́вный; **~ farm** колхо́з.
collector /kə'lektə(r)/ *n.* (*of stamps etc.*) коллекционе́р; **a ~'s piece** ре́дкий/уника́льный экземпля́р; (*of taxes, debts*) сбо́рщик.
college /'kɒlɪdʒ/ *n.*
[1] (*school*) ко́лледж.
[2] (*university*) университе́т; институ́т.
[3] (*within university*) университе́тский ко́лледж.
collide /kə'laɪd/ *v.i.* ст|а́лкиваться, -олкну́ться.
colliery /'kɒlɪərɪ/ *n.* каменноу́гольная ша́хта.
collision /kə'lɪʒ(ə)n/ *n.* столкнове́ние.
colloquial /kə'ləʊkwɪəl/ *adj.* разгово́рный.
colloquialism /kə'ləʊkwɪəlɪz(ə)m/ *n.* разгово́рное выраже́ние/сло́во.
collusion /kə'lu:ʒ(ə)n/ *n.* сго́вор; **act in ~** де́йствовать (*impf.*) по сго́вору.
Colombia /kə'lɒmbɪə/ *n.* Колу́мбия.
Colombian /kə'lɒmbɪən/ *n.* колумби́|ец (*fem.* -йка).
■ *adj.* колумби́йский.
colon[1] /'kəʊlɒn/ *n.* (*anat.*) то́лстая/ободо́чная кишка́.
colon[2] /'kəʊlɒn/ *n.* (*gram.*) двоето́чие.
colonel /'kə:n(ə)l/ *n.* полко́вник.

colonial /kəˈləʊnɪəl/ *adj.* колониа́льный.
colonialism /kəˈləʊnɪəlɪz(ə)m/ *n.* колониали́зм.
colonist /ˈkɒlənɪst/ *n.* колони́ст (*fem.* -ка).
colonization /ˌkɒlənaɪˈzeɪʃ(ə)n/ *n.* колониза́ция.
colonize /ˈkɒlənaɪz/ *v.t.* колонизова́ть, колонизи́ровать (*both impf., pf.*).
colonizer /ˈkɒlənaɪzə(r)/ *n.* колониза́тор.
colony /ˈkɒlənɪ/ *n.* коло́ния.
colossal /kəˈlɒs(ə)l/ *adj.* колосса́льный, грома́дный.
colour /ˈkʌlə(r)/ (*US* **color**) *n.*
1 (*lit.*) цвет; **change ~** (*lit.*) меня́ть, по- цвет; (*fig.*) бледне́ть, по-/красне́ть, по-; **the film is in ~** э́то цветно́й фильм; **~ film** цветна́я плёнка; **~ scheme** цветова́я га́мма; **~ television** цветно́е телеви́дение.
2 (*of face*) цвет лица́.
3 (*pl., paints*) кра́ски.
4 (*of race*): **a person of ~** представи́тель (*fem.* -ница) небе́лой ра́сы.
■ *v.t.* 1 (*paint*) кра́сить, по-.
2 (*imbue*): **his action was ~ed by envy** его́ посту́пок был отча́сти продикто́ван за́вистью.
■ *v.i.* (*blush*) красне́ть, по-.
■ *cpds.* **~-blind** *adj.* страда́ющий дальтони́змом; **~ fast** *adj.* цветосто́йкий.
coloured /ˈkʌləd/ (*US* **colored**) *adj.* цветно́й.
colourful /ˈkʌləfʊl/ (*US* **colorful**) *adj.* кра́сочный, я́ркий; **a ~ personality** я́ркая/колори́тная ли́чность.
colouring /ˈkʌlərɪŋ/ (*US* **coloring**) *n.* окра́ска; (*complexion*) цвет лица́.
colourless /ˈkʌləlɪs/ (*US* **colorless**) *adj.* (*lit., fig.*) бесцве́тный.
colt /kəʊlt/ *n.* (*young horse*) жеребёнок.
column /ˈkɒləm/ *n.*
1 (*pillar*) коло́нна.
2 (*in book etc.*) столбе́ц.
3 (*regular feature in newspaper*): **weekly ~** еженеде́льная коло́нка/ру́брика.
4 (*mil. etc.*) коло́нна.
columnist /ˈkɒləmnɪst/ *n.* обозрева́тель (*m.*).
coma /ˈkəʊmə/ *n.* (*pl.* **~s**) ко́ма.
comb /kəʊm/ *n.* расчёска.
■ *v.t.* расчёс|ывать, -а́ть; причёс|ывать, -а́ть.
combat /ˈkɒmbæt/ *n.* бой.
■ *v.t.* (**combated, combating**) боро́ться (*impf.*) с + *i.* (*or* про́тив + *g.*).
combatant /ˈkɒmbət(ə)nt/ *n.* бое́ц; вою́ющая сторона́.
combination /ˌkɒmbɪˈneɪʃ(ə)n/ *n.* сочета́ние.
combine[1] /ˈkɒmbaɪn/ *n.*
1 (*group of persons*) объедине́ние.
2 (**~ harvester**) комба́йн.
combine[2] /kəmˈbaɪn/ *v.t.* сочета́ть (*impf.*); **~ forces** объедин|я́ть, -и́ть (*or* соедин|я́ть, -и́ть) си́лы.
combustion /kəmˈbʌstʃ(ə)n/ *n.* воспламене́ние; сгора́ние; **spontaneous ~** самовоспламене́ние; **internal ~ engine** дви́гатель вну́треннего сгора́ния.
come /kʌm/ *v.i.* (*past* **came;** *p.p.* **come**)
1 (*move near, arrive*) при|ходи́ть, -йти́; **he has ~ a hundred miles** он прие́хал за сто миль; **~ along!** пойдёмте!; **~ into the house!** заходи́те/зайди́те в дом!
2 (*of inanimate things; lit., fig.*): **the dress ~s to her knees** пла́тье дохо́дит ей до коле́н; **the feeling ~s and goes** э́то чу́вство то появля́ется, то исчеза́ет; **it came as a shock to me** э́то бы́ло для меня́ уда́ром.
3 (*fig. uses with 'into'*): **he has ~ into a fortune** он получи́л большо́е насле́дство; **the party came into power** па́ртия пришла́ к вла́сти.
4 (*happen*) случа́ться, быва́ть (*both impf.*); **Christmas ~s once a year** Рождество́ быва́ет раз в году́; **how ~ he was late?** как получи́лось, что он опозда́л?; **in years to ~** в после́дующие го́ды; в бу́дущем; **~ what may** будь, что бу́дет; **how ~?** (*coll.*) э́то почему́ же?; как так?
5 (*amount*): **the bill ~s to £5** счёт равня́ется пяти́ фу́нтам; **his plans came to nothing** из его́ пла́нов ничего́ не вы́шло.
6 (*become, prove to be*): **his dreams came true** его́ мечты́ осуществи́лись/сбыли́сь; **his shoelace came undone** у него́ шнуро́к развяза́лся.
7 (*fig., find o.s. in a position*): **I have ~ to see that he is right** я убеди́лся, что он прав.
8 (*of person, originate*) прои|сходи́ть, -зойти́; **he ~s from Scotland** он уроже́нец Шотла́ндии.
■ *with preps.*: **~ across** (*encounter*) нат|а́лкиваться, -олкну́ться на + *a.*; **~ from**: **wine ~s from grapes** вино́ получа́ется из виногра́да; **~ into**: **he came into a large estate** ему́ доста́лось большо́е име́ние; **~ off** (*become detached from*): **a button came off my coat** от моего́ пальто́ оторвала́сь пу́говица; **~ over** (*fig.*): **what came over you?** что на вас нашло́?; **~ under**: **what heading does this ~ under?** к како́й ру́брике э́то отно́сится?
■ *with advs.*: **~ across (as)** показа́ться (*pf.*) (+ *i.*); **~ apart** *v.i.* (*unfastened*) ра|сходи́ться, -зойти́сь; **~ away** *v.i.* (*become detached*) отл|а́мываться, -ома́ться *or* -оми́ться (**from:** от + *g.*); **~ back** *v.i.* (*return*) возвра|ща́ться, -ти́ться; верну́ться (*pf.*); **~ down** *v.i.*: **her hair ~s down to her waist** её во́лосы дохо́дят до по́яса; (*of prices*) па́дать, упа́сть; (*fig.*): **he came down with influenza** он слёг с гри́ппом; **~ forward** *v.i.* (*offer one's services*) предл|ага́ть, -ожи́ть свои́ услу́ги; **~ in** *v.i.* (*lit.*) входи́ть, войти́; **the tide came in** наступи́л прили́в; **it came in handy** э́то пригоди́лось; **~ off** *v.i.* (*become detached*) отва́л|иваться, -и́ться; (*happen, succeed*): **the experiment came off** о́пыт уда́лся; (**~ *off duty***): **he ~s off at 10** он ухо́дит со слу́жбы в 10; **~ on** *v.i.* (*follow*) сле́довать (*impf.*); (*progress*) де́лать (*impf.*) успе́хи; (*start, set in*): **I have a cold coming on** у меня́ начина́ется просту́да; (*of actor; appear*) появ|ля́ться, -и́ться; **~ out** *v.i.* (*lit.*) выходи́ть, вы́йти; **the sun came out** появи́лось/вы́глянуло со́лнце; (*become known, appear*): **the book came out** кни́га вы́шла; (*disappear*): **the stains came out** пя́тна сошли́; (*declare o.s.*): **he came out against the plan** он вы́ступил про́тив пла́на;

(*publicly acknowledge one's homosexuality*) откры́то призн|ава́ть, -а́ть свою́ гомосексуа́льность; (*Br., go on strike*) забастова́ть (*pf.*); **she came out in a rash** (*Br.*) она́ покры́лась сы́пью; **~ over** *v.i.*: **they came over to England** они́ прие́хали в А́нглию; **~ round** *v.i.* (*change mind*): **he came round to my view** он пришёл-таки к моей то́чке зре́ния; (*yield*): **she'll ~ round** (*Br.*) она́ усту́пит/согласи́тся; (*recover consciousness*) при|ходи́ть, -йти́ в себя́; очну́ться (*pf.*); **~ through** *v.i.* (*survive experience*) пережи́ть (*pf.*); **~ to** *v.i.* (*recover one's senses*) при|ходи́ть, -йти́ в себя́; **~ up** *v.i.*: **the sun came up** со́лнце взошло́; **the seeds came up** семена́ взошли́; **the water came up to my waist** вода́ доходи́ла мне до по́яса; **the question came up** встал вопро́с; **the case ~s up tomorrow** э́то де́ло разбира́ется за́втра; **he came up against a difficulty** он столкну́лся с тру́дностями; **he came up with a suggestion** он внёс предложе́ние.
■ *cpds.* **~back** *n.* (*return*) возвраще́ние; **~uppance** /kʌm'ʌpəns/ *n.* (*coll.*): **he got his ~uppance** он получи́л по заслу́гам.

comedian /kə'mi:dɪən/ *n.* ко́мик.

comedy /'kɒmɪdɪ/ *n.* коме́дия.

comet /'kɒmɪt/ *n.* коме́та.

comfort /'kʌmfət/ *n.*
1 (*physical ease*) комфо́рт.
2 (*relief of suffering*) утеше́ние, отра́да.
3 (*thing that brings ~*) утеше́ние, успокое́ние.
■ *v.t.* ут|еша́ть, -е́шить.

comfortabl|e /'kʌmftəb(ə)l/ *adj.* удо́бный, ую́тный, комфорта́бельный, комфо́ртный; **the car holds six people ~y** э́та маши́на свобо́дно вмеща́ет шесть челове́к; **he is ~y off** он живёт в доста́тке.

comforter /'kʌmfətə(r)/ *n.* (*US, quilt*) стёганое одея́ло.

comforting /'kʌmfətɪŋ/ *adj.* утеши́тельный, успокои́тельный.

comfy /'kʌmfɪ/ *adj.* (*coll.*) удо́бный, ую́тный.

comic /'kɒmɪk/ *n.*
1 (*coll., comedian*) ко́мик, юмори́ст.
2 (*magazine*) ко́микс.
■ *adj.* коми́ческий, юмористи́ческий; **~ strip** ко́микс.

comical /'kɒmɪk(ə)l/ *adj.* коми́чный, смешно́й.

coming /'kʌmɪŋ/ *n.* прие́зд, прихо́д; **~ and going** движе́ние взад-вперёд.
■ *adj.* бу́дущий, наступа́ющий.

comma /'kɒmə/ *n.* запята́я.

command /kə'mɑ:nd/ *n.*
1 (*order; also comput.*) кома́нда.
2 (*authority*) кома́ндование; **he is in ~ of the army** он кома́ндует а́рмией.
3 (*control*) контро́ль (*m.*).
4 (*knowledge*): **she has a good ~ of French** она́ непло́хо владе́ет францу́зским (языко́м).
5 (*mil.*) кома́ндование; **~ post** кома́ндный пункт, КП.
■ *v.t.* & *i.*
1 (*give orders to*) прика́з|ывать, -а́ть + *d.*
2 (*have authority over*) кома́ндовать (*impf.*) + *i.*
3 (*be able to use or enjoy*) располага́ть (*impf.*) + *i.*; **he ~s respect** он заслу́живает уваже́ния.

commandant /kɒmən'dænt/ *n.* коменда́нт.

commandeer /kɒmən'dɪə(r)/ *v.t.* реквизи́ровать (*impf.*, *pf.*).

commander /kə'mɑ:ndə(r)/ *n.* команди́р, кома́ндующий.

commanding /kə'mɑ:ndɪŋ/ *adj.* **~ officer** команди́р; **a ~ presence** внуши́тельная оса́нка.

commando /kə'mɑ:ndəʊ/ *n.* (*pl.* **~s**) деса́нтник-диверса́нт, диверса́нт-разве́дчик; (*pl.*) кома́ндос (*indecl.*, *pl.*).

commemorate /kə'meməreɪt/ *v.t.* (*celebrate memory of*) отм|еча́ть, -е́тить (*годовщину, событие*).

commemorative /kə'memərətɪv/ *adj.* па́мятный, мемориа́льный.

commence /kə'mens/ *v.t.* & *i.* нач|ина́ть(ся), -а́ть(ся).

commend /kə'mend/ *v.t.*
1 (*entrust*) вв|еря́ть, -е́рить; поруч|а́ть, -и́ть; **he ~ed his soul to God** он посвяти́л себя́ Бо́гу.
2 (*praise*) хвали́ть, по-.

commendable /kə'mendəb(ə)l/ *adj.* похва́льный.

commensurate /kə'menʃərət/ *adj.* разме́рный.

comment /'kɒment/ *n.* замеча́ние, коммента́рий.
■ *v.t.* & *i.* комменти́ровать (*impf.*, *pf.*); толкова́ть (*impf.*).

commentary /'kɒməntərɪ/ *n.* коммента́рий.

commentator /'kɒmənteɪtə(r)/ *n.* коммента́тор (*m.*).

commerce /'kɒmə:s/ *n.* комме́рция.

commercial /kə'mə:ʃ(ə)l/ *n.* рекла́ма, рекла́мная переда́ча.
■ *adj.* комме́рческий, торго́вый.

commercialize /kə'mə:ʃəlaɪz/ *n.* ста́вить, по- на комме́рческую осно́ву; вн|оси́ть, -ести́ комме́рческий дух в + *a.*

commiserate /kə'mɪzəreɪt/ *v.i.* выража́ть, вы́разить соболе́знование (**with:** *кому*).

commissar /'kɒmɪsɑ:(r)/ *n.* комисса́р.

commission /kə'mɪʃ(ə)n/ *n.*
1 (*authorization*) полномо́чие.
2 (*comm.*) комиссио́нн|ые (*pl.*, *g.* -ых).
3 (*committee*) коми́ссия.
■ *v.t.* поруч|а́ть, -и́ть (*что кому*); **he ~ed me to buy this** он поручи́л мне купи́ть э́то; **he ~ed a portrait from the artist** он заказа́л худо́жнику портре́т; **a ~ed officer** офице́р.

commissioner /kə'mɪʃənə(r)/ *n.* член коми́ссии.

commit /kə'mɪt/ *v.t.* (**committed, committing**)
1 (*perform*) соверш|а́ть, -и́ть.
2 (*engage*): **he ~ted himself to helping her** он взя́лся помо́чь ей.
3 : **a ~ted writer** иде́йный писа́тель.

commitment /kə'mɪtmənt/ *n.* обяза́тельство.

committee /kə'mɪtɪ/ *n.* комите́т, коми́ссия.

commodity /kə'mɒdɪtɪ/ *n.* това́р, предме́т

потребле́ния.

commodore /ˈkɒmədɔ:(r)/ *n.* (*in navy or merchant marine*) коммодо́р, капита́н пе́рвого ра́нга; (*of yacht club*) командо́р.

common /ˈkɒmən/ *n.*
1 (*land*) пусты́рь (*m.*), вы́гон.
2 (*sth. usual or shared*): **you have a lot in ~ with her** у вас с ней мно́го о́бщего.
■ *adj.* (**commoner, commonest**)
1 (*belonging to more than one, general*) о́бщий; **it is ~ knowledge that ...** общеизве́стно, что... .
2 (*belonging to the public*): **~ land** обще́ственная земля́.
3 (*ordinary, usual*) обы́чный, обы́денный, обыкнове́нный; **the ~ people** (просто́й) наро́д; **~ sense** здра́вый смысл.
4 (*vulgar*) вульга́рный, по́шлый.
■ *cpds.* **~-law** *adj.*: **~-law marriage** незарегистри́рованный брак; **~-law wife** сожи́тельница; **~place** *n.* бана́льность; *adj.* бана́льный; **~ room** *n.* (*Br.*) (*senior*) учи́тельская, преподава́тельская; (*junior*) студе́нческая ко́мната о́тдыха.

commonly /ˈkɒmənlɪ/ *adv.* (*usually*) обы́чно, обыкнове́нно.

commonwealth /ˈkɒmənwelθ/ *n.*: **the British C~** Брита́нское Содру́жество (на́ций); **C~ of Independent States** Содру́жество Незави́симых Госуда́рств.

commotion /kəˈməʊʃ(ə)n/ *n.* волне́ние, возня́.

communal /ˈkɒmjʊn(ə)l/ *adj.* обще́ственный, коммуна́льный.

commune /ˈkɒmju:n/ *n.* (*administrative unit*) общи́на, комму́на; (*Russian hist., peasant ~*) мир.

communicate /kəˈmju:nɪkeɪt/ *v.t.* сообщ|а́ть, -и́ть.
■ *v.i.* свя́з|ываться, -а́ться; сообщ|а́ть, -и́ть (*кому о чём*); **~ with s.o.** обща́ться (*impf.*) с кем-н.

communication /kəmju:nɪˈkeɪʃ(ə)n/ *n.* обще́ние; связь, сообще́ние, коммуника́ция.

communicative /kəˈmju:nɪkətɪv/ *adj.* общи́тельный, разгово́рчивый.

communion /kəˈmju:nɪən/ *n.* прича́стие.

communism /ˈkɒmjʊnɪz(ə)m/ *n.* коммуни́зм.

communist /ˈkɒmjʊnɪst/ *n.* коммуни́ст (*fem.* -ка).
■ *adj.* коммунисти́ческий.

community /kəˈmju:nɪtɪ/ *n.* общи́на, гру́ппа населе́ния.

commute /kəˈmju:t/ *v.i.* (*to work*) е́здить (*indet.*) ка́ждый день на значи́тельное расстоя́ние на рабо́ту.

commuter /kəˈmju:tə(r)/ *n.* (*traveller*) жи́тель (*fem.* -ница) при́города, (регуля́рно) е́здящ|ий (*fem.* -ая) на рабо́ту в го́род (на авто́бусе, по́езде и т. п.).

compact /kəmˈpækt/ *adj.* (*concise*) сжа́тый, компа́ктный; **~ disc** /ˈkɒmpækt/ компа́кт-ди́ск; **~ disc player** прои́грыватель (*m.*) компа́кт-ди́сков.

companion /kəmˈpænjən/ *n.* спу́тни|к (*fem.* -ца).

companionship /kəmˈpænjənʃɪp/ *n.* дру́жеское обще́ние; дру́жеские отноше́ния.

company /ˈkʌmpənɪ/ *n.*
1 (*companionship*): **I was glad of his ~** я был рад его́ о́бществу; **keep s.o. ~** сост|авля́ть, -а́вить кому́-н. компа́нию.
2 (*associates, guests*): **we have ~ this evening** у нас сего́дня бу́дут го́сти.
3 (*commercial firm*) това́рищество, компа́ния; **~ car** служе́бная маши́на.
4 (*theatr.*) тру́ппа.
5 (*mil.*) ро́та.

comparable /ˈkɒmpərəb(ə)l/ *adj.* сравни́мый.

comparative /kəmˈpærətɪv/ *adj.*
1 сравни́тельный.
2 (*relative*) относи́тельный.

compare /kəmˈpeə(r)/ *v.t.* сра́вн|ивать, -и́ть.
■ *v.i.* сра́вн|иваться, -и́ться.

comparison /kəmˈpærɪs(ə)n/ *n.* сравне́ние; **in, by ~ with** по сравне́нию с + *i.*

compartment /kəmˈpɑ:tmənt/ *n.* купе́ (*nt. indecl.*).

compass /ˈkʌmpəs/ *n.*
1 (*mariner's*) ко́мпас; **points of the ~** стра́ны све́та.
2 (*geom., also* **pair of ~es**) ци́ркуль (*m.*).

compassion /kəmˈpæʃ(ə)n/ *n.* сострада́ние.

compassionate /kəmˈpæʃənət/ *adj.* сострада́тельный.

compatible /kəmˈpætəb(ə)l/ *adj.* совмести́мый.

compatriot /kəmˈpætrɪət/ *n.* сооте́чественник.

compel /kəmˈpel/ *v.t.* (**compelled, compelling**) заст|авля́ть, -а́вить.

compelling /kəmˈpelɪŋ/ *adj.* непреодоли́мый, неотрази́мый.

compensate /ˈkɒmpenseɪt/ *v.t.*: **~ s.o. for sth.** компенси́ровать (*impf., pf.*) (*кому что*); **they expressed a willingness to ~ fans for their expenditure** они́ вы́разили гото́вность компенси́ровать боле́льщикам затра́ты; **he was ~d for his injuries** он получи́л компенса́цию за свои́ уве́чья.
■ *v.i.*: **~ for** возме|ща́ть, -сти́ть; компенси́ровать (*impf., pf.*); **his personality ~s for his appearance** его́ ли́чные ка́чества компенси́руют его́ вне́шность.

compensation /kɒmpenˈseɪʃ(ə)n/ *n.* компенса́ция; **pay ~** выпла́чивать, вы́платить компенса́цию.

compete /kəmˈpi:t/ *v.i.* (*vie*) конкури́ровать (*impf.*); **~ with, against s.o. for sth.** конкури́ровать (*impf.*) с кем-н. из-за чего́-н.; (*in sport*) состяза́ться (*impf.*).

competenc|e /ˈkɒmpɪt(ə)ns/, **-y** /ˈkɒmpɪtənsɪ/ *nn.* уме́ние, компете́нтность.

competent /ˈkɒmpɪt(ə)nt/ *adj.* компете́нтный.

competition /kɒmpəˈtɪʃ(ə)n/ *n.*
1 (*rivalry*) сопе́рничество.
2 (*contest*) состяза́ние.

competitive /kəmˈpetɪtɪv/ *adj.* (*person*) честолюби́вый; **~ prices** конкурентоспосо́бные це́ны.

competitor /kəmˈpetɪtə(r)/ *n.* конкуре́нт.

compilation /kɒmpɪˈleɪʃ(ə)n/ *n.* (*act*) собира́ние; (*result*) сбо́рник.

compile /kəmˈpaɪl/ *v.t.* соб|ира́ть, -ра́ть.

complacent /kəmˈpleɪs(ə)nt/ *adj.* самодово́льный.

complain /kəmˈpleɪn/ *v.i.* жа́ловаться, по- (на + *a.*); **he ~s of frequent headaches** он жа́луется на ча́стые головны́е бо́ли.

complaint /kəmˈpleɪnt/ *n.* жа́лоба.

complement /ˈkɒmplɪmənt/ *v.t.* доп|олня́ть, -о́лнить.

complementary /kɒmplɪˈmentərɪ/ *adj.* дополни́тельный; **~ medicine** (*Br.*) альтернати́вная, нетрадицио́нная медици́на.

complete /kəmˈpliːt/ *adj.*
1 (*whole*) по́лный.
2 (*finished*) зако́нченный, завершённый; **when will the work be ~?** когда́ бу́дет завершён э́тот труд?
3 (*thorough*) соверше́нный.
■ *v.t.* зак|а́нчивать, -о́нчить; (*fill in*) зап|олня́ть, -о́лнить.

completely /kəmˈpliːtlɪ/ *adv.* соверше́нно, по́лностью.

completion /kəmˈpliːʃ(ə)n/ *n.* заверше́ние.

complex /ˈkɒmpleks/ *n.* ко́мплекс.
■ *adj.* сло́жный, ко́мплексный.

complexion /kəmˈplekʃ(ə)n/ *n.* цвет лица́.

complexity /kəmˈpleksɪtɪ/ *n.* сло́жность.

compliance /kəmˈplaɪəns/ *n.* усту́пчивость.

compliant /kəmˈplaɪənt/ *adj.* усту́пчивый.

complicate /ˈkɒmplɪkeɪt/ *v.t.* осложн|я́ть, -и́ть.

complicated /ˈkɒmplɪkeɪtɪd/ *adj.* сло́жный.

complication /kɒmplɪˈkeɪʃ(ə)n/ *n.* (*complicating circumstance*) осложне́ние; (*med.*): **~s set in** после́довали осложне́ния.

complicity /kəmˈplɪsɪtɪ/ *n.* соуча́стие.

compliment /ˈkɒmplɪmənt/ *n.* комплиме́нт; похвала́.
■ *v.t.* говори́ть (*impf.*) комплиме́нты + *d.* (*по поводу чего*).

complimentary /kɒmplɪˈmentərɪ/ *adj.*
1 (*laudatory*) похва́льный, ле́стный.
2 : **~ ticket** контрама́рка, пригласи́тельный биле́т.

comply /kəmˈplaɪ/ *v.i.*: **~ with** уступ|а́ть, -и́ть (+ *d.*).

component /kəmˈpəʊnənt/ *n.* компоне́нт.
■ *adj.* составно́й.

compose /kəmˈpəʊz/ *v.t.* & *i.*
1 (*make up*) сост|авля́ть, -а́вить; **the party was ~d of teachers** гру́ппа состоя́ла из учителе́й.
2 (*liter., mus.*) сочин|я́ть, -и́ть.
3 (*control, assuage*): **~ o.s.** успок|а́иваться, -о́иться; **a ~d manner** сде́ржанная мане́ра.

composer /kəmˈpəʊzə(r)/ *n.* (*mus.*) компози́тор.

composite /ˈkɒmpəzɪt/ *adj.* составно́й.

composition /kɒmpəˈzɪʃ(ə)n/ *n.*
1 (*act of composing*) сочине́ние, составле́ние.
2 (*liter. or mus. work*) произведе́ние, сочине́ние.
3 (*school exercise*) сочине́ние.
4 (*make-up*) соста́в; **~ of the soil** соста́в по́чвы.

compost /ˈkɒmpɒst/ *n.* компо́ст.

composure /kəmˈpəʊʒə(r)/ *n.* споко́йствие.

compound¹ /ˈkɒmpaʊnd/ *n.* (*enclosure*) огоро́женное ме́сто.

compound² /ˈkɒmpaʊnd/ *n.* (*mixture*) смесь; (*gram.*) сло́жное сло́во; (*chem.*) соедине́ние.
■ *adj.* составно́й, сло́жный; **~ fracture** осложнённый перело́м.

comprehend /kɒmprɪˈhend/ *v.t.* пон|има́ть, -я́ть.

comprehensible /kɒmprɪˈhensɪb(ə)l/ *adj.* поня́тный, постижи́мый.

comprehension /kɒmprɪˈhenʃ(ə)n/ *n.* понима́ние, постиже́ние.

comprehensive /kɒmprɪˈhensɪv/ *adj.* (*of wide scope*) всеобъе́млющий, исче́рпывающий; **~ school** (*Br.*) общеобразова́тельная шко́ла со ста́ршими кла́ссами.

compress¹ /ˈkɒmpres/ *n.* (*to relieve inflammation*) компре́сс.

compress² /kəmˈpres/ *v.t.* (*physically*) сж|има́ть, -ать.

comprise /kəmˈpraɪz/ *v.t.* включ|а́ть, -и́ть в себя́.

compromise /ˈkɒmprəmaɪz/ *n.* компроми́сс.
■ *v.t.* компромети́ровать, с-.
■ *v.i.* при|ходи́ть, -йти́ к компроми́ссу.

compulsion /kəmˈpʌlʃ(ə)n/ *n.* принужде́ние; **on, under ~** по принужде́нию.

compulsive /kəmˈpʌlsɪv/ *adj.* (*irresistible*) непреодоли́мый; (*inveterate*) заядлый.

compulsory /kəmˈpʌlsərɪ/ *adj.* обяза́тельный.

computer /kəmˈpjuːtə(r)/ *n.* компью́тер; **~ dating** подбо́р супру́гов с по́мощью компью́тера; **~ game** компью́терная игра́; **~ graphics** компью́терная гра́фика; **~-literate** со зна́нием компью́тера; **~ programmer** программи́ст (*fem.* -ка); **~ programming** программи́рование; **~ science** вычисли́тельная те́хника.
■ *cpds.* **~-aided design** *n.* автоматизи́рованное проекти́рование; **~-aided learning** *n.* маши́нное обуче́ние.

computerize /kəmˈpjuːtəraɪz/ *v.t.* компьютеризи́ровать (*impf.*, *pf.*).

comrade /ˈkɒmreɪd/ *n.* това́рищ.

comradeship /ˈkɒmreɪdʃɪp/ *n.* това́рищество.

con /kɒn/ *v.t.* (**conned, conning**) над|ува́ть, -у́ть.

conceal /kənˈsiːl/ *v.t.* ута́|ивать, -и́ть.

concede /kənˈsiːd/ *v.t.* уступ|а́ть, -и́ть.

conceit /kənˈsiːt/ *n.* самомне́ние, самонаде́янность.

conceited /kənˈsiːtɪd/ *adj.* самонаде́янный.

conceivabl|e /kənˈsiːvəb(ə)l/ *adj.* мы́слимый, постижи́мый; **he may ~y be right** не исключено́, что он пра́в.

conceive /kənˈsiːv/ *v.t.* (*imagine*) заду́м|ывать, -ать.
■ *v.i.* зач|ина́ть, -а́ть, забере́менеть (*pf.*).

concentrate /ˈkɒnsəntreɪt/ *v.t.* сосредото́чи|вать, -ть.
■ *v.i.* сосредото́чи|ваться, -ться; **he ~d on his work** он сосредото́чился на свое́й рабо́те.

concentration /kɒnsənˈtreɪʃ(ə)n/ *n.*

1 (*of troops etc.*): **~ camp** концентрацио́нный ла́герь, концла́герь (*m.*).
2 (*of attention etc.*) сосредото́ченность.

concept /'kɒnsept/ *n.* поня́тие.

conception /kən'sepʃ(ə)n/ *n.*
1 (*notion*) конце́пция.
2 (*physiol.*) зача́тие.

conceptual /kən'septjʊəl/ *adj.* концептуа́льный.

concern /kən'sə:n/ *n.*
1 (*affair*) отноше́ние.
2 (*business*) конце́рн; **a going ~** де́йствующее предприя́тие.
3 (*anxiety*) беспоко́йство.
■ *v.t.* 1 (*have to do with*) каса́ться (*impf.*) + *g.*; **~ed** (*involved*) заинтересо́ванный; **the parties ~ed** заинтересо́ванные сто́роны; **as far as that is ~ed** что каса́ется э́того.
2 (*cause anxiety to*) беспоко́ить (*impf.*); **~ed** (*anxious*) озабо́ченный; **I am ~ed about the future** меня́ беспоко́ит бу́дущее.

concerning /kən'sə:nɪŋ/ *prep.* относи́тельно + *g.*

concert /'kɒnsət/ *n.* конце́рт.
■ *cpd.* **~ hall** *n.* конце́ртный зал.

concerted /kən'sə:tɪd/ *adj.*: **a ~ effort to eradicate poverty** совме́стные уси́лия, напра́вленные на искорене́ние бе́дности.

concertina /kɒnsə'ti:nə/ *n.* концерти́но (*nt. indecl.*), гармо́ника.

concerto /kən'tʃeətəʊ/ *n.* (*pl.* **~s**) конце́рт.

concession /kən'seʃ(ə)n/ *n.*
1 (*yielding; thing yielded*) усту́пка; **as a special ~** идя́ навстре́чу.
2 (*preferential rate*) льго́та; (*reduction*) ски́дка.

conciliatory /kən'sɪlɪətərɪ/ *adj.* примири́тельный.

concise /kən'saɪs/ *adj.* кра́ткий, сжа́тый.

conclave /'kɒnkleɪv/ *n.* конкла́в; (*fig.*) та́йное совеща́ние.

conclud|e /kən'klu:d/ *v.t.*
1 (*terminate*) зак|а́нчивать, -о́нчить; **~ing** заключи́тельный, заверша́ющий; (*session etc.*) закр|ыва́ть, -ы́ть.
2 (*infer*) де́лать, с- вы́вод, что… .
■ *v.i.* (*end*) зак|а́нчиваться, -о́нчиться.

conclusion /kən'klu:ʒ(ə)n/ *n.* оконча́ние.

conclusive /kən'klu:sɪv/ *adj.* реша́ющий.

concoct /kən'kɒkt/ *v.t.* (*a drink etc.*) стря́пать, со-; (*a story etc.*) стря́пать, со-.

concoction /kən'kɒkʃ(ə)n/ *n.* (*drink etc.*) смесь; (*invention of story*) сочине́ние, приду́мывание; (*story invented*) вы́думка.

concrete /'kɒŋkri:t/ *n.* бето́н.

concur /kən'kə:(r)/ *v.i.* (**concurred, concurring**)
1 (*of circumstance etc.*) совп|ада́ть, -а́сть; сходи́ться, сойти́сь.
2 (*agree, consent*) согла|ша́ться, -си́ться (с + *i.*).

concurrent /kən'kʌrənt/ *adj.* (*simultaneous, agreeing*) совпада́ющий; (*math.*) сходя́щийся, встреча́ющийся; **~ly** одновре́менно.

concuss /kən'kʌs/ *v.t.* (*med.*) вызыва́ть, вы́звать сотрясе́ние мо́зга у + *g.*

concussion /kən'kʌʃ(ə)n/ *n.* (*med.*) сотрясе́ние мо́зга.

condemn /kən'dem/ *v.t.* осу|жда́ть, -ди́ть; (*blame*) порица́ть (*impf.*); **~ed cell** (*Br.*) ка́мера сме́ртника; (*declare unfit for use*) призн|ава́ть, -а́ть неприго́дным.

condemnation /kɒndem'neɪʃ(ə)n/ *n.* осужде́ние; порица́ние; (*of building*) призна́ние него́дным.

condensation /kɒnden'seɪʃ(ə)n/ *n.* (*phys.*) конденса́ция, сгуще́ние, уплотне́ние.

condense /kən'dens/ *v.t.* конденси́ровать (*impf., pf.*); **~d milk** сгущённое молоко́.
■ *v.i.* (*phys.*) конденси́роваться (*impf., pf.*).

condescend /kɒndɪ'send/ *v.i.* сни|сходи́ть, -зойти́.

condescending /kɒndɪ'sendɪŋ/ *adj.* снисходи́тельный.

condescension /kɒndɪ'senʃ(ə)n/ *n.* снисхожде́ние, снисходи́тельность.

condition /kən'dɪʃ(ə)n/ *n.*
1 (*state*) состоя́ние, положе́ние.
2 (*fitness*): **the athlete is out of ~** спортсме́н не в фо́рме.
3 (*pl., circumstances*) усло́вия (*nt. pl.*).
4 (*requisite, stipulation*) усло́вие; **on ~ that …** при усло́вии, что… .

conditional /kən'dɪʃən(ə)l/ *adj.*: **the ~ (mood)** (*gram.*) усло́вное наклоне́ние.

conditioner /kən'dɪʃənə(r)/ *n.* бальза́м для воло́с.

condolence /kən'dəʊləns/ *n.* (*also pl.*) соболе́знование.

condom /'kɒndɒm/ *n.* презервати́в.

condominium /kɒndə'mɪnɪəm/ *n.* (*US*) кондоми́ниум.

condone /kən'dəʊn/ *v.t.* про|ща́ть, -сти́ть.

conducive /kən'dju:sɪv/ *adj.* спосо́бствующий.

conduct[1] /'kɒndʌkt/ *n.* поведе́ние.

conduct[2] /kən'dʌkt/ *v.t.*
1 (*lead, guide*) води́ть (*indet.*), вести́ (*det.*).
2 (*manage*) вести́ (*det.*); **~ an experiment** ста́вить, по- о́пыт.
3 (*mus., also v.i.*) дирижи́ровать (*impf.*) (+ *i.*).
4 (*phys.*) проводи́ть (*impf.*).

conductive /kən'dʌktɪv/ *adj.* (*tech.*) проводя́щий.

conductor /kən'dʌktə(r)/ *n.*
1 (*mus.*) дирижёр.
2 (*of bus, tram*) конду́ктор; (*US, of train*) проводни́к.
3 (*phys.*) проводни́к.

cone /kəʊn/ *n.*
1 (*geom.*) ко́нус.
2 (*for ice cream*) ва́фельная тру́бочка.

confectioner /kən'fekʃ(ə)nə(r)/ *n.* конди́тер.

confectionery /kən'fekʃ(ə)n(ə)rɪ/ *n.* (*wares*) конди́терские изде́лия.

confederation /kənfedə'reɪʃ(ə)n/ *n.* сою́з; федера́ция; конфедера́ция.

confer[1] /kən'fə:(r)/ *v.t.* (**conferred, conferring**) (*grant*) (**on s.o.** + *d.*) присв|а́ивать, -о́ить.

confer[2] /kən'fə:(r)/ *v.i.* (**conferred, conferring**) (*consult*) совеща́ться (*impf.*) (с + *i.*).

conference /'kɒnfərəns/ *n.* конфере́нция, совеща́ние.
■ *cpd.* **~ call** *n.* телеконфере́нция,

C

селе́кторное совеща́ние.
confess /kən'fes/ *v.t. & i.*
1 призн|ава́ть, -а́ть; **he ~ed to the crime** он созна́лся в преступле́нии.
2 (*eccl.*) (*~ one's sins*) испове́д|оваться, -аться.
confession /kən'feʃ(ə)n/ *n.*
1 (*avowal*) призна́ние, созна́ние.
2 (*to a priest*) и́споведь.
confetti /kən'fetı/ *n.* конфетти́ (*nt. indecl.*).
confide /kən'faɪd/ *v.i.*: **~ in s.o.** (*impart secrets to*) дели́ться, по- (*своими планами и т. п.*) с + *i.*
confidence /'kɒnfɪd(ə)ns/ *n.*
1 (*confiding of secrets*) дове́рие; **I tell you this in ~** я говорю́ вам э́то конфиденциа́льно (*or* по секре́ту).
2 (*secret*) та́йна; конфиденциа́льное сообще́ние.
3 (*trust*): **I have ~ in him** я уве́рен в нём; я ве́рю в него́.
4 (*certainty, assurance*) уве́ренность.
5 : **~ trick** моше́нничество.
confident /'kɒnfɪd(ə)nt/ *adj.* уве́ренный; (*self-confident*) самоуве́ренный.
confidential /kɒnfɪ'denʃ(ə)l/ *adj.* конфиденциа́льный.
confidentiality /kɒnfɪdenʃɪ'ælɪtɪ/ *n.* конфиденциа́льность.
configuration /kənfɪgə'reɪʃ(ə)n/ *n.* конфигура́ция.
confine[1] /'kɒnfaɪn/ *n.* (*usu. pl.*) грани́цы (*f. pl.*).
confine[2] /kən'faɪn/ *v.t.* ограни́чи|вать, -ть.
confinement /kən'faɪnmənt/ *n.* (*imprisonment*) заключе́ние; **solitary ~** одино́чное заключе́ние.
confirm /kən'fɜ:m/ *v.t.*
1 (*establish as certain*) утвер|жда́ть, -ди́ть; подтвер|жда́ть, -ди́ть; **his appointment was ~ed** его́ назначе́ние бы́ло утверждено́.
2 (*of person*): **a ~ed drunkard** го́рький пья́ница; **a ~ed bachelor** убеждённый холостя́к.
3 (*relig.*): **be ~ed** про|ходи́ть, -йти́ обря́д конфирма́ции.
confirmation /kɒnfə'meɪʃ(ə)n/ *n.*
1 (*of report etc.*) подтвержде́ние.
2 (*relig.*) конфирма́ция.
confiscate /'kɒnfɪskeɪt/ *v.t.* конфискова́ть (*impf., pf.*).
conflict[1] /'kɒnflɪkt/ *n.* конфли́кт.
conflict[2] /kən'flɪkt/ *v.t.* быть в конфли́кте (с + *i.*).
conform /kən'fɔ:m/ *v.i.* подчин|я́ться, -и́ться (+ *d.*).
conformist /kən'fɔ:mɪst/ *n.* конформи́ст.
conformity /kən'fɔ:mɪtɪ/ *n.* (*correspondence, accordance*) соотве́тствие; (*compliance*) подчине́ние; (*conformism*) конформи́зм.
confound /kən'faʊnd/ *v.t.*
1 (*amaze*) пора|жа́ть, -зи́ть; потряс|а́ть, -ти́.
2 (*confuse*) сме́ш|ивать, -а́ть; спу́т|ывать, -ать.
3 (*as expletive*): **~ it!** чёрт возьми́!; **he is a ~ed nuisance** он ужа́сно доку́члив.
confront /kən'frʌnt/ *v.t.* смотре́ть (*impf.*) в лицо́ + *d.*; встр|еча́ть, -е́тить.
confrontation /kɒnfrʌn'teɪʃ(ə)n/ *n.* конфронта́ция.
confuse /kən'fju:z/ *v.t.*
1 (*throw into confusion*) сму|ща́ть, -ти́ть; **his question ~d me** его́ вопро́с смути́л меня́.
2 (*mistake*) спу́т|ывать, -ать; **he ~d Austria with Australia** он спу́тал А́встрию с Австра́лией.
confusion /kən'fju:ʒ(ə)n/ *n.* смуще́ние; (*mix-up*) пу́таница.
congeal /kən'dʒi:l/ *v.i.* свёр|тываться, -ну́ться.
congenial /kən'dʒi:nɪəl/ *adj.* бли́зкий по ду́ху.
congenital /kən'dʒenɪt(ə)l/ *adj.*: **~ defect** врождённый дефе́кт.
congested /kən'dʒestɪd/ *adj.* (*roads*) перегру́женный.
congestion /kən'dʒestʃ(ə)n/ *n.* перегру́женность.
■ *cpd.* **congestion charge** *n.* пла́та за въезд в центр го́рода.
conglomerate /kən'glɒmərət/ *n.* конгломера́т.
conglomeration /kənglɒmə'reɪʃ(ə)n/ *n.* конгломера́т.
Congo /'kɒngəʊ/ *n.* (*country*) Ко́нго (*nt. indecl.*); **Democratic Republic of the Congo** (*formerly Zaire*) Демократи́ческая Респу́блика Ко́нго.
Congolese /kɒŋgə'li:z/ *n.* (*native of Congo or Democratic Republic of the Congo*) конголе́з|ец (*fem.* -ка).
■ *adj.* конголе́зский.
congratulate /kən'grætjʊleɪt/ *v.t.* поздр|авля́ть, -а́вить (*кого с чем*).
congratulation /kəngrætjʊ'leɪʃ(ə)n/ *n.* поздравле́ние; **~s!** поздравля́ю!
congratulatory /kən'grætjʊlətərɪ/ *adj.* поздрави́тельный.
congregate /'kɒŋgrɪgeɪt/ *v.i.* соб|ира́ться, -ра́ться; сходи́ться, сойти́сь.
congregation /kɒŋgrɪ'geɪʃ(ə)n/ *n.* прихожа́не (*m. pl.*).
congress /'kɒŋgres/ *n.*
1 (*organized meeting*) конгре́сс, съезд.
2 (*pol., hist.*) конгре́сс; **C~** (*US*) конгре́сс США.
■ *cpds.* **~man** *n.* член конгре́сса, конгрессме́н; **~woman** *n.* же́нщина-член конгре́сса.
conifer /'kɒnɪfə(r)/ *n.* хво́йное де́рево.
conjecture /kən'dʒektʃə(r)/ *n.* предположе́ние, дога́дка.
■ *v.t. & i.* предпол|ага́ть, -ожи́ть; гада́ть (*impf.*).
conjugal /'kɒndʒʊg(ə)l/ *adj.* супру́жеский, бра́чный.
conjugate /'kɒndʒʊgeɪt/ *v.t.* спряга́ть, про-.
conjugation /kɒndʒʊ'geɪʃ(ə)n/ *n.* спряже́ние.
conjunction /kən'dʒʌŋkʃ(ə)n/ *n.* (*gram.*) сою́з.
conjunctivitis /kəndʒʌŋktɪ'vaɪtɪs/ *n.* конъюнктиви́т.
conjure /'kʌndʒə(r)/ *v.t. & i.*
1 (*fig.*): **~ up** вызыва́ть, вы́звать в воображе́нии.
2 (*perform tricks*) пока́з|ывать, -а́ть фо́кусы.
conjur|er, -or /'kʌndʒərə(r)/ *nn.* фо́кусник.

connect /kə'nekt/ *v.t.* (*join*) соедин|я́ть, -и́ть; **the towns are ~ed by railway** э́ти города́ соединены́ желе́зной доро́гой; (*associate*) свя́з|ывать, -а́ть.
■ *v.i.* соедин|я́ться, -и́ться; **the train ~s with the one from London** э́тот по́езд согласо́ван по расписа́нию с ло́ндонским (по́ездом).

connection /kə'nekʃ(ə)n/ *n.*
1 (*joining up*) соедине́ние, связь.
2 (*fig., link*) связь.
3 (*of transport*) согласо́ванность расписа́ния; **I missed my ~** я не успе́л сде́лать переса́дку.
4 (*association*) связь.
5 (*teleph.*): **the ~ was bad** телефо́н пло́хо рабо́тал.

connive /kə'naɪv/ *v.i.*: **~ at** потво́рствовать (*impf.*) + *d.*

connoisseur /kɒnə'sə:(r)/ *n.* знато́к, цени́тель (*m.*).

connotation /kɒnə'teɪʃ(ə)n/ *n.* побо́чное значе́ние.

conquer /'kɒŋkə(r)/ *v.t.* & *i.* (*overcome*; *obtain by conquest*) завоёв|ывать, -а́ть.

conqueror /'kɒŋkərə(r)/ *n.* завоева́тель (*m.*).

conquest /'kɒŋkwest/ *n.* завоева́ние.

conscience /'kɒnʃ(ə)ns/ *n.* со́весть; **clear ~** чи́стая со́весть; **guilty ~** нечи́стая со́весть.

conscientious /kɒnʃɪ'enʃəs/ *adj.* сознáтельный; **~ objector** отка́зывающийся от вое́нной слу́жбы по убежде́нию.

conscious /'kɒnʃəs/ *adj.*
1 (*physically aware*) сознаю́щий, ощуща́ющий.
2 (*mentally aware*) сознаю́щий, понима́ющий; **I was ~ of having offended him** я сознава́л, что оскорби́л его́.
3 (*realized*) сознаю́щий, созна́тельный; **a ~ effort** созна́тельное уси́лие.

consciousness /'kɒnʃəsnɪs/ *n.*
1 (*physical*) созна́ние; **he lost ~** он потеря́л созна́ние; **she regained ~** она́ пришла́ в себя́/созна́ние.
2 (*mental*) созна́тельность.

conscript /'kɒnskrɪpt/ *n.* новобра́нец, призывни́к.

conscription /kən'skrɪpʃ(ə)n/ *n.* во́инская пови́нность.

consecrate /'kɒnsɪkreɪt/ *v.t.* освя|ща́ть, -ти́ть.

consecutive /kən'sekjʊtɪv/ *adj.* после́довательный.

consensus /kən'sensəs/ *n.* согла́сие, единоду́шие; (*pol.*) консе́нсус.

consent /kən'sent/ *n.* согла́сие.
■ *v.i.* согла|ша́ться, -си́ться.

consequence /'kɒnsɪkwəns/ *n.*
1 (*result*) сле́дствие, после́дствие.
2 (*importance*) ва́жность, значе́ние.

consequential /kɒnsɪ'kwenʃ(ə)l/ *adj.*
1 (*consequent*) сле́дующий/вытека́ющий (*из чего*).
2 (*important*) ва́жный, значи́тельный.

consequently /'kɒnsɪkwentlɪ/ *adv.* сле́довательно, зна́чит, (*coll.*) ста́ло быть.

conservation /kɒnsə'veɪʃ(ə)n/ *n.* сохране́ние, охра́на; **~ area** запове́дник.

conservationist /kɒnsə'veɪʃənɪst/ *n.* боре́ц за охра́ну приро́ды.

conservative /kən'sə:vətɪv/ *n.* консерва́тор.
■ *adj.* консервати́вный.

conservatory /kən'sə:vətərɪ/ *n.*
1 (*Br., room*) застеклённая вера́нда.
2 (*mus.*) консервато́рия.

conserve /kən'sə:v; *n. only also* 'kɒnsə:v/ *n.* (*preserved fruit*) варе́нье.
■ *v.t.* (*fruit*) консерви́ровать, за-; (*protect*) сохран|я́ть, -и́ть; **~ one's strength** бере́чь (*impf.*) свои́ си́лы.

consider /kən'sɪdə(r)/ *v.t.* & *i.* рассм|а́тривать, -отре́ть; **we are ~ing going to Canada** мы поду́мываем о пое́здке в Кана́ду; **~ yourself under arrest** счита́йте, что вы аресто́ваны; **he is ~ed clever** его́ счита́ют у́мным; он счита́ется у́мным; (*make allowance for*) счита́ться (*impf.*) с + *i.*; **we must ~ his feelings** мы должны́ счита́ться с его́ чу́вствами.

considerable /kən'sɪdərəb(ə)l/ *adj.* значи́тельный.

considerate /kən'sɪdərət/ *adj.* внима́тельный, забо́тливый.

consideration /kənsɪdə'reɪʃ(ə)n/ *n.*
1 (*reflection*) рассмотре́ние; **take into ~** прин|има́ть, -я́ть во внима́ние.
2 (*making allowance*): **he showed ~ for my feelings** он счита́лся с мои́ми чу́вствами; он щади́л мои́ чу́вства.
3 (*reason, factor*) соображе́ние.

considering /kən'sɪdərɪŋ/ *adv.* & *prep.* учи́тывая.

consign /kən'saɪn/ *v.t.* (*send*) пос|ыла́ть, -ла́ть.

consignment /kən'saɪnmənt/ *n.* (*consigning*) отпра́вка; (*goods*) груз, па́ртия това́ра.

consist /kən'sɪst/ *v.i.*: **~ of** состоя́ть (*impf.*) из + *g.*; **~ in**: **his task ~s in defining work norms** его́ рабо́та заключа́ется/состои́т в определе́нии норм вы́работки.

consistency /kən'sɪstənsɪ/ *n.*
1 (*of mixture etc.*) консисте́нция.
2 (*adherence to logic*) после́довательность.

consistent /kən'sɪst(ə)nt/ *adj.* (*of argument etc.*) после́довательный; (*of person*) после́довательный.

consolation /kɒnsə'leɪʃ(ə)n/ *n.* утеше́ние, отра́да.

console[1] /'kɒnsəʊl/ *n.* (*panel*) пульт управле́ния.

console[2] /kən'səʊl/ *v.t.* ут|еша́ть, -е́шить.

consolidate /kən'sɒlɪdeɪt/ *v.t.* укреп|ля́ть, -и́ть.

consonant /'kɒnsənənt/ *n.* (*phon.*) согла́сный (звук).

consorti|um /kən'sɔ:tɪəm/ *n.* (*pl.* **~a** *or* **~ums**) консо́рциум.

conspicuous /kən'spɪkjʊəs/ *adj.* заме́тный.

conspiracy /kən'spɪrəsɪ/ *n.* за́говор; конспира́ция.

conspirator /kən'spɪrətə(r)/ *n.* загово́рщик.

conspiratorial /kənspɪrə'tɔ:rɪəl/ *adj.* загово́рщический, конспира́торский.

conspire /kən'spaɪə(r)/ *v.t.* & *i.* устр|а́ивать, -о́ить за́говор.

constable /'kɒnstəb(ə)l/ *n.* (*Br.*) полице́йский.
constant /'kɒnst(ə)nt/ *adj.* постоя́нный.
constantly /'kɒnst(ə)ntlɪ/ *adj.* постоя́нно.
constellation /kɒnstə'leɪʃ(ə)n/ *n.* созве́здие.
consternation /kɒnstə'neɪʃ(ə)n/ *n.* смяте́ние, у́жас.
constipate /'kɒnstɪpeɪt/ *v.t.*: **he is ~d** у него́ запо́р.
constipation /kɒnstɪ'peɪʃ(ə)n/ *n.* запо́р.
constituency /kən'stɪtjʊənsɪ/ *n.* избира́тельный о́круг.
constituent /kən'stɪtjʊənt/ *n.* (*elector*) избира́тель (*fem.* -ница); (*element*) составна́я часть.
constitute /'kɒnstɪtju:t/ *v.t.* сост|авля́ть, -а́вить.
constitution /kɒnstɪ'tju:ʃ(ə)n/ *n.*
1 (*make-up*) строе́ние, структу́ра.
2 (*pol.*) конститу́ция.
constitutional /kɒnstɪ'tju:ʃən(ə)l/ *adj.* конституцио́нный.
constrain /kən'streɪn/ *v.t.* (*force*) прин|ужда́ть, -у́дить; заст|авля́ть, -а́вить; вынужда́ть, вы́нудить; (*restrict*) ограни́чи|вать, -ть; **~ed** (*embarrassed*) стеснённый.
constraint /kən'streɪnt/ *n.* ограниче́ние.
constrict /kən'strɪkt/ *v.t.* сж|има́ть, -ать.
constriction /kən'strɪkʃ(ə)n/ *n.* сжа́тие, суже́ние.
construct /kən'strʌkt/ *v.t.* стро́ить, по-.
construction /kən'strʌkʃ(ə)n/ *n.* построе́ние, строи́тельство, стро́йка; (*thing constructed*) постро́йка, сооруже́ние; **the road is under ~** доро́га стро́ится.
constructive /kən'strʌktɪv/ *adj.* (*pert. to construction*; *helpful*) конструкти́вный.
construe /kən'stru:/ *v.t.* (**construes, construed, construing**) (*interpret*) истолко́в|ывать, -а́ть.
consul /'kɒns(ə)l/ *n.* ко́нсул.
consulate /'kɒnsjʊlət/ *n.* ко́нсульство.
consult /kən'sʌlt/ *v.t.* : **~ a book** спр|авля́ться, -а́виться в кни́ге; **~ a lawyer** сове́товаться, по- с юри́стом.
■ *v.i.* сове́товаться, по- (с + *i.*); **~ with s.o.** консульти́роваться (*impf.*, *pf.*) с кем-н.; **~ing room** кабине́т (врача́).
consultancy /kən'sʌltənsɪ/ *n.* (*company*) консульти́рующая фи́рма; (*job*) до́лжность консульта́нта.
consultant /kən'sʌlt(ə)nt/ *n.* консульта́нт.
consultation /kɒnsəl'teɪʃ(ə)n/ *n.* консульта́ция.
consultative /kən'səltətɪv/ *adj.* консультати́вный, совеща́тельный.
consume /kən'sju:m/ *v.t.*
1 (*eat or drink*) съ|еда́ть, -есть.
2 (*use up*) потреб|ля́ть, -и́ть.
3 (*destroy*) истреб|ля́ть, -и́ть; **the fire ~d the huts** пожа́р уничто́жил лачу́ги.
4 : **he was ~d with envy/curiosity** его́ снеда́ла за́висть; его́ снеда́ло любопы́тство.
consumer /kən'sju:mə(r)/ *n.* потреби́тель (*m.*); **~ goods** потреби́тельские това́ры; **~ society** о́бщество потребле́ния.
consummate /'kɒnsjʊmeɪt/ *v.t.* (*marriage*) осуществ|ля́ть, -и́ть (*бра́чные отноше́ния*).
consumption /kən'sʌmpʃ(ə)n/ *n.* потребле́ние, поглоще́ние.
contact /'kɒntækt/ *n.*
1 (*lit., fig.*) конта́кт, соприкоснове́ние; **bring, come into ~ with** установи́ть (*pf.*) конта́кт с + *i.* **~ lenses** конта́ктные ли́нзы.
2 (*of person*): **he made useful ~s** он завяза́л поле́зные знако́мства.
■ *v.t.* связа́ться (*pf.*) с + *i.*
contagious /kən'teɪdʒəs/ *adj.* зара́зный.
contain /kən'teɪn/ *v.t.*
1 (*hold within itself*) содержа́ть (*impf.*) в себе́.
2 (*be capable of holding*) вмеща́ть (*impf.*); **how much does this bottle ~?** ско́лько вмеща́ет э́та буты́лка?
3 (*control*) сде́рж|ивать, -а́ть; **he could not ~ his enthusiasm** он не мог сдержа́ть своего́ восто́рга.
container /kən'teɪnə(r)/ *n.*
1 (*receptacle*) сосу́д.
2 (*for transport*) конте́йнер; **~ ship/truck** контейнерово́з.
contaminate /kən'tæmɪneɪt/ *v.t.* зара|жа́ть, -зи́ть.
contamination /kəntæmɪ'neɪʃ(ə)n/ *v.t.* зараже́ние.
contemplate /'kɒntəmpleɪt/ *v.t.*
1 (*gaze at*) созерца́ть (*impf.*).
2 (*envisage, plan*) обду́м|ывать, -ать.
contemplation /kɒntəm'pleɪʃ(ə)n/ *n.* созерца́ние, размышле́ние, обду́мывание.
contemplative /kən'templətɪv/ *adj.* созерца́тельный.
contemporary /kən'tempərərɪ/ *n.* совреме́нни|к, све́рстни|к (*fem.* -ца).
■ *adj.* совреме́нный.
contempt /kən'tempt/ *n.* презре́ние; **~ of court** оскорбле́ние суда́, неуваже́ние к суду́.
contemptible /kən'temptɪb(ə)l/ *adj.* презре́нный.
contemptuous /kən'temptjʊəs/ *adj.* презри́тельный.
contend /kən'tend/ *v.t.* утвержда́ть (*impf.*).
■ *v.i.* (*compete*) состяза́ться (*impf.*); сопе́рничать (*impf.*).
content[1] /'kɒntent/ *n.* (*lit., fig.*) содержа́ние; (*pl.*) содержи́мое; **(table of) ~s** оглавле́ние, содержа́ние.
content[2] /kən'tent/ *adj.* дово́льный.
■ *v.t.* удовлетвор|я́ть, -и́ть; **a ~ed look** дово́льный вид.
contention /kən'tenʃ(ə)n/ *n.* (*strife*) спор.
contentious /kən'tenʃəs/ *adj.* вздо́рный, зади́ристый.
contentment /kən'tentmənt/ *n.* удовлетворённость.
contest *n.* /'kɒntest/ ко́нкурс, состяза́ние.
■ *v.t.* & *i.* /kən'test/
1 (*dispute*) осп|а́ривать, -о́рить.
2 (*contend for*) отст|а́ивать, -оя́ть; боро́ться (*impf.*) за + *a.*
contestant /kən'test(ə)nt/ *n.* конкуре́нт (*fem.* -ка).
context /'kɒntekst/ *n.* конте́кст; **in the ~ of today's America** в усло́виях совреме́нной Аме́рики.

continent /ˈkɒntɪnənt/ *n.* контине́нт.
continental /kɒntɪˈnent(ə)l/ *adj.* континента́льный; ~ **quilt** (*Br.*) стёганое одея́ло; ~ **breakfast** лёгкий у́тренний за́втрак.
contingency /kənˈtɪndʒənsɪ/ *n.* возмо́жное обстоя́тельство; ~ **plan** вариа́нт пла́на; альтернати́вный план.
contingent /kənˈtɪndʒ(ə)nt/ *n.* (*mil.*) континге́нт.
continual /kənˈtɪnjʊəl/ *adj.* постоя́нный.
continuation /kəntɪnjʊˈeɪʃ(ə)n/ *n.* продолже́ние.
continue /kənˈtɪnju:/ *v.t.* (**continues, continued, continuing**) прод|олжа́ть, -о́лжить; **'to be ~d'** (*of story etc.*) продолже́ние сле́дует.
■ *v.i.* (**continues, continued, continuing**) прод|олжа́ться, -о́лжиться; **the wet weather ~s** сыра́я пого́да де́ржится.
continuity /kɒntɪˈnju:ɪtɪ/ *n.* непреры́вность.
continuous /kənˈtɪnjʊəs/ *adj.* непреры́вный; (*gram.*) дли́тельный.
continu|um /kənˈtɪnjʊəm/ *n.* (*pl.* **~a**) конти́нуум.
contort /kənˈtɔ:t/ *v.t.* иска|жа́ть, -зи́ть.
contortion /kənˈtɔ:ʃ(ə)n/ *n.* искаже́ние; искривле́ние.
contour /ˈkɒntʊə(r)/ *n.* ко́нтур; ~ **line** горизонта́ль.
contraband /ˈkɒntrəbænd/ *n.* контраба́нда.
contraception /kɒntrəˈsepʃ(ə)n/ *n.* предупрежде́ние бере́менности.
contraceptive /kɒntrəˈseptɪv/ *n.* противозача́точное сре́дство.
■ *adj.* противозача́точный.
contract[1] /ˈkɒntrækt/ *n.* (*agreement*) контра́кт, догово́р; ~ **killer** ки́ллер, наёмный уби́йца; ~ **killing** заказно́е уби́йство.
contract[2] /kənˈtrækt/ *v.t.* (*conclude*) заключ|а́ть, -и́ть (*договор/контракт*).
■ *v.i.* (*agree*) прин|има́ть, -я́ть на себя́ обяза́тельство; **he ~ed to build a bridge** он подряди́лся постро́ить мост.
contract[3] /kənˈtrækt/ *v.t.* (*shorten*) сокра|ща́ть, -ти́ть; (*tighten*) сж|има́ть, -ать.
■ *v.i.* (*shorten*) сокра|ща́ться, -ти́ться; **metal ~s** мета́лл сжима́ется; (*tighten*) сж|има́ться, -а́ться.
contraction /kənˈtrækʃ(ə)n/ *n.* (*of metal*) сжа́тие; (*med.*) родова́я схва́тка.
contractor /kənˈtræktə(r)/ *n.* (*person*) подря́дчик.
contradict /kɒntrəˈdɪkt/ *v.t.* противоре́чить (*impf.*) + *d.*
contradiction /kɒntrəˈdɪkʃ(ə)n/ *n.* противоре́чие.
contradictory /kɒntrəˈdɪktərɪ/ *adj.* противоречи́вый.
contralto /kənˈtræltəʊ/ *n.* (*pl.* **~s**) (*singer*) контра́льто (*f. indecl.*).
contraption /kənˈtræpʃ(ə)n/ *n.* (*coll.*) приспособле́ние.
contrary /ˈkɒntrərɪ/ *n.* противополо́жность; **on the ~** (как раз) наоборо́т; **there is no evidence to the ~** нет доказа́тельств проти́вного/обра́тного.
■ *adj.* противополо́жный, проти́вный, обра́тный.
■ *adv.*: ~ **to my expectations** вопреки́ мои́м ожида́ниям.
contrast *n.* /ˈkɒntrɑ:st/ контра́ст; **in ~ to** в противополо́жность + *d.*; **by ~ with** по сравне́нию с + *i.*
■ *v.t.* /kənˈtrɑ:st/ противопост|авля́ть, -а́вить.
■ *v.i.* /kənˈtrɑ:st/ контрасти́ровать (*impf.*, *pf.*).
contravene /kɒntrəˈvi:n/ *v.t.* противоре́чить (*impf.*) + *d.*; **he ~d the law** он нару́шил зако́н.
contravention /kɒntrəˈvenʃ(ə)n/ *n.* наруше́ние; **in ~ of** в наруше́ние + *g.*
contribute /kənˈtrɪbju:t/ *v.t.* (*money etc.*) же́ртвовать, по-; **he ~d £5** он внёс 5 фу́нтов.
■ *v.i.* соде́йствовать (*impf.*) + *d.*; **he ~s to our magazine** он пи́шет для на́шего журна́ла.
contribution /kɒntrɪˈbju:ʃ(ə)n/ *n.*: **a ~ of £5** поже́ртвование/взнос в пять фу́нтов; **his ~ to our success** его́ вклад в наш успе́х.
contributor /kənˈtrɪbjʊtə(r)/ *n.* (*writer*) (постоя́нный) сотру́дник; (*of funds*) же́ртвователь (*m.*).
contributory /kənˈtrɪbjʊtərɪ/ *adj.* соде́йствующий, спосо́бствующий; ~ **factor** спосо́бствующий фа́ктор; ~ **negligence** встре́чная вина́, вина́ потерпе́вшего; **a ~ pension scheme** (*Br.*) пенсио́нная систе́ма, осно́ванная на отчисле́ниях из за́работка рабо́тающих.
contrite /kənˈtraɪt/ *adj.* сокруша́ющийся, ка́ющийся.
contrition /kənˈtrɪʃ(ə)n/ *n.* сокруше́ние, раска́яние, пока́яние.
contrive /kənˈtraɪv/ *v.t.* (*devise*) заду́м|ывать, -ать; (*succeed*): **he ~d to offend everybody** он умудри́лся оби́деть всех; **~d** (*artificial*) иску́сственный.
control /kənˈtrəʊl/ *n.*
1 (*power to direct etc.*) управле́ние, регули́рование; **he lost ~ of the car** он потеря́л управле́ние автомоби́лем; **he is in ~ of the situation** он хозя́ин положе́ния; **the situation is under ~** ситуа́ция нормализова́лась/нахо́дится под контро́лем; **the children are out of ~** де́ти не слу́шаются.
2 (*means of regulating*) контро́ль (*m.*).
3 (*pl., of a machine etc.*) рычаги́ (*m. pl.*) управле́ния.
4 : ~ **panel** прибо́рная доска́; пульт управле́ния; ~ **room** пункт управле́ния; ~ **tower** (*aeron.*) контро́льно-диспе́тчерский пункт.
■ *v.t.* (**controlled, controlling**) контроли́ровать, про-; регули́ровать (*impf.*, *pf.*); ~ **one's temper** владе́ть (*impf.*) собо́й; ~ **prices** регули́ровать це́ны.
controversial /kɒntrəˈvɜ:ʃ(ə)l/ *adj.* спо́рный.
controversy /ˈkɒntrəvɜ:sɪ/ *n.* поле́мика, спор.
convalesce /kɒnvəˈles/ *v.i.* выздора́вливать, поправля́ться (*both impf.*).
convalescent /kɒnvəˈles(ə)nt/ *adj.* выздора́вливающий, поправля́ющийся.
convene /kənˈvi:n/ *v.t.* (*people*) соб|ира́ть, -ра́ть; (*meeting*) соз|ыва́ть, -ва́ть.
■ *v.i.* соб|ира́ться, -ра́ться.

convenience /kən'vi:niəns/ *n.* удо́бство; **at your ~** когда́ вам бу́дет удо́бно; **~ foods** пищевы́е полуфабрика́ты; **marriage of ~** фикти́вный брак.
■ *cpd.* **~ store** *n.* магази́н ша́говой досту́пности, (круглосу́точный) магази́н това́ров повседне́вного спро́са.

convenient /kən'vi:niənt/ *adj.* удо́бный, подходя́щий; **if it is ~ for you** е́сли вам удо́бно.

convent /'kɒnv(ə)nt/ *n.* (же́нский) монасты́рь.

convention /kən'venʃ(ə)n/ *n.*
1 (*congress*) съезд.
2 (*treaty*) конве́нция.
3 (*custom*) обы́чай.

conventional /kən'venʃən(ə)l/ *adj.* обы́чный; **a ~ person** челове́к, кото́рый приде́рживается усло́вностей.

converge /kən'vɜ:dʒ/ *v.i.* сходи́ться, сойти́сь.

conversant /kən'vɜ:s(ə)nt/ *adj.* знако́мый (**with:** с + *i.*), осведомлённый (**with:** в + *p.*).

conversation /kɒnvə'seiʃ(ə)n/ *n.* разгово́р, бесе́да, речь.

converse /kən'vɜ:s/ *v.i.* бесе́довать (*impf.*).

conversion /kən'vɜ:ʃ(ə)n/ *n.*
1 (*transformation*) превраще́ние, перехо́д.
2 (*relig. etc.*) обраще́ние (в + *a.*).
3 (*comm.*): **~ of pounds into dollars** перево́д фу́нтов в до́ллары.

convert[1] /'kɒnvɜ:t/ *n.* (ново)обращённый.

convert[2] /kən'vɜ:t/ *v.t.*
1 (*change*) превра|ща́ть, -ти́ть; **the house was ~ed into flats** дом был разби́т на кварти́ры.
2 (*relig. etc.*) обра|ща́ть, -ти́ть.
3 (*comm.*): **~ pounds into euros** перевести́ (*pf.*) фу́нты (сте́рлингов) в е́вро.
■ *v.i.*: **he ~ed to Buddhism** он обрати́лся в будди́зм.

convertible /kən'vɜ:tib(ə)l/ *n.* (*car*) автомоби́ль (*m.*) с откидны́м/открыва́ющимся ве́рхом.

convex /'kɒnveks/ *adj.* вы́пуклый.

convey /kən'vei/ *v.t.*
1 (*carry, transmit*) перев|ози́ть, -езти́.
2 (*impart*) перед|ава́ть, -а́ть.

conveyancing /kən'veiənsiŋ/ *n.* (*leg.*) составле́ние нотариа́льных а́ктов о переда́че иму́щества.

conveyor /kən'veiə(r)/ *n.*: **~ belt** конве́йерная ле́нта.

convict[1] /'kɒnvikt/ *n.* осуждённый.

convict[2] /kən'vikt/ *v.t.* (*leg.*) осу|жда́ть, -ди́ть (**for:** за + *a.*).

conviction /kən'vikʃ(ə)n/ *n.*
1 (*leg.*) осужде́ние.
2 (*settled opinion*) убежде́ние, убеждённость.
3 (*persuasive force*) убежде́ние.

convince /kən'vins/ *v.t.* убе|жда́ть, -ди́ть.

convincing /kən'vinsiŋ/ *adj.* убеди́тельный.

convivial /kən'viviəl/ *adj.* (*of person*) компане́йский, весёлый; (*of evening etc.*) весёлый.

convoy /'kɒnvɔi/ *n.* конво́й; тра́нспортная коло́нна с конво́ем.

convulsion /kən'vʌlʃ(ə)n/ *n.* (*pl., med.*) конву́льсия, су́дорога.

coo /ku:/ *v.t.* & *i.* (**coos, cooed**) воркова́ть (*impf.*).

cook /kʊk/ *n.* (*male*) по́вар; (*fem.*) куха́рка.
■ *v.t.* гото́вить, при-.
■ *v.i.* (*food*) гото́виться, при-; (*person*) гото́вить (*impf.*).
■ *cpd.* **~book** (*US*) *n.* пова́ренная кни́га.

cooker /'kʊkə(r)/ *n.* (*Br.*) (*stove*) плита́.

cookery /'kʊkəri/ *n.* кулинари́я, стряпня́.
■ *cpd.* **~ book** (*Br.*) *n.* пова́ренная кни́га.

cookie /'kʊki/ *n.* (*US, small cake*) пече́нье.

cooking /'kʊkiŋ/ *n.* (*cuisine*) ку́хня.
■ *adj.*: **~ apple** я́блоко для запека́ния.

cool /ku:l/ *n.*
1 прохла́да.
2 : **lose one's ~** (*coll.*) вы́йти (*pf.*) из себя́, потеря́ть (*pf.*) самооблада́ние.
■ *adj.* 1 (*lit.*) прохла́дный, све́жий.
2 (*unexcited*) хладнокро́вный.
3 (*unenthusiastic*) прохла́дный.
4 (*coll., splendid*) клёвый, кла́ссный; **~!** класс!
■ *v.t.* охла|жда́ть, -ди́ть.
■ *v.i.* охла|жда́ться, -ди́ться; **~ down, off** ост|ыва́ть, -ы́ть; **~ing-off period** пери́од обду́мывания и перегово́ров.

coop /ku:p/ *n.* куря́тник.
■ *v.t.* сажа́ть, посади́ть в кле́тку; **~ up** (*fig.*) держа́ть (*impf.*) взаперти́.

cooperate /kəʊ'ɒpəreit/ *v.i.* сотру́дничать (*impf.*).

cooperation /kəʊɒpə'reiʃ(ə)n/ *n.* сотру́дничество.

cooperative /kəʊ'ɒpərətiv/ *n.* кооперати́в.
■ *adj.* кооперати́вный.

co-opt /kəʊ'ɒpt/ *v.t.* коопти́ровать (*impf., pf.*).

coordinate /kəʊ'ɔ:dinət; *v. only* kəʊ'ɔ:dineit/ *n.* (*math., geog.*) координа́та; (*pl.*) о́си (*f. pl.*) координа́т.
■ *v.t.* координи́ровать (*impf., pf.*).

coordination /kəʊɔ:di'neiʃ(ə)n/ *n.* координа́ция.

cop /kɒp/ *n.* (*sl., policeman*) полице́йский, коп.

cope /kəʊp/ *v.i.* спр|авля́ться, -а́виться (с + *i.*).

Copenhagen /kəʊpən'heigən/ *n.* Копенга́ген.

copious /'kəʊpiəs/ *adj.* оби́льный.

copper /'kɒpə(r)/ *n.* медь.

copulate /'kɒpjʊleit/ *v.i.* совокуп|ля́ться, -и́ться.

copy /'kɒpi/ *n.*
1 (*version*) ко́пия, ру́копись.
2 (*of book etc.*) экземпля́р.
■ *v.t.* & *i.* перепи́с|ывать, -а́ть; (*imitate*) подража́ть (*impf.*) + *d.*; **~ out a letter** переписа́ть (*pf.*) письмо́; **he copied in the examination** он спи́сывал на экза́мене.
■ *cpd.* **~right** *n.* а́вторское пра́во.

cord /kɔ:d/ *n.* (*rope, string*) верёвка; (*flex*) шнур.

cordial /'kɔ:diəl/ *n.* (*Br.*) подслащённый напи́ток.
■ *adj.* серде́чный, раду́шный.

cordless /'kɔ:dlis/ *adj.* беспроводно́й; **~ (tele)phone** радиотелефо́н.

cordon /'kɔ:d(ə)n/ *n.* (*of police etc.*) оцепле́ние, кордо́н.
■ *v.t.* (*also* **~ off**) оцеп|ля́ть, -и́ть.

corduroy /'kɔ:dərɔɪ/ *n.* вельвéт.

core /kɔ:(r)/ *n.* (*of fruit*) сердцевѝна; (*fig.*) центр, ядрó, суть; **~ of a problem** суть проблéмы.

Corfu /kɔ:'fu:/ *n.* Кóрфу (*m. indecl.*).

coriander /kɒrɪ'ændə(r)/ *n.* кориáндр; (*of fresh leaves, usu.*) кинзá.

cork /kɔ:k/ *n.* прóбка; (*attr.*) прóбковый.
■ *cpd.* **~screw** *n.* штóпор.

corn[1] /kɔ:n/ *n.*
1 (*Br., grain, seed*) зернó.
2 (*Br., wheat*) пшенѝца.
3 (*US, maize*) кукурýза.
■ *cpds.* **~flakes** *n. pl.* корнфлéкс; **~flour** *n.* (*Br.*) кукурýзная/рѝсовая мукá; **~ on the cob** *n.* кукурýза в почáтках.

corn[2] /kɔ:n/ *n.* (*on foot*) мозóль.

cornea /'kɔ:nɪə/ *n.* роговѝца; роговáя оболóчка.

corner /'kɔ:nə(r)/ *n.*
1 (*place where lines etc. meet*) ýгол; **at, on the ~** на углý; **round the ~** (*lit.*) за углóм; (*fig., near*) ря́дом; **in a tight ~** в затруднéнии; **he looked out of the ~ of his eye** он следѝл крáешком глáза.
2 (*football*) угловóй удáр, кóрнер.
■ *v.t.* заг|оня́ть, -нáть в ýгол; **the fugitive was ~ed** беглецá загнáли в ýгол; **he ~ed the market** он завладéл ры́нком, скупѝв весь товáр.
■ *cpd.* **~stone** *n.* (*fig.*) краеугóльный кáмень.

cornet /'kɔ:nɪt/ *n.*
1 (*mus. instrument*) корнéт; корнéт-а-пистóн.
2 (*Br., for ice cream*) вáфельный рожóк.

cornettist /kɔ:'netɪst/ *n.* корнетѝст.

cornice /'kɔ:nɪs/ *n.* карнѝз.

corny /'kɔ:nɪ/ *adj.* (**cornier, corniest**) (*coll.*) плóский, избѝтый.

coronary /'kɒrənərɪ/ *n.* коронаротромбóз.

coronation /kɒrə'neɪʃ(ə)n/ *n.* коронáция.

coroner /'kɒrənə(r)/ *n.* слéдователь (*m.*) (*по делам о насильственной или скоропостижной смерти*).

corporal[1] /'kɔ:pr(ə)l/ *n.* (*officer*) капрáл.

corporal[2] /'kɔ:pr(ə)l/ *adj.*: **~ punishment** телéсное наказáние.

corporate /'kɔ:pərət/ *adj.*
1 (*collective*) óбщий.
2 (*of, forming a corporation*) корпоратѝвный.

corporation /kɔ:pə'reɪʃ(ə)n/ *n.* (*company*) акционéрное óбщество.
■ *cpd.* **~ tax** *n.* налóг с дохóдов компáний.

corps /kɔ:(r)/ *n.* (*pl.* **~** /kɔ:z/) (*mil., dipl.*) кóрпус.

corpse /kɔ:ps/ *n.* труп.

corpuscle /'kɔ:pʌs(ə)l/ *n.* корпýскула, тéльце, частѝца.

correct /kə'rekt/ *adj.*
1 (*right, true*) прáвильный, вéрный, тóчный.
2 (*of behaviour*) коррéктный.
■ *v.t.* испр|авля́ть, -áвить.

correction /kə'rekʃ(ə)n/ *n.* исправлéние.
■ *cpd.* **~ fluid** *n.* корректѝрующая жѝдкость.

correspond /kɒrɪ'spɒnd/ *v.i.*
1 (*match, harmonize*) соотвéтствовать (*impf.*) (+ *d.*).
2 (*exchange letters*) перепѝсываться (*impf.*) (с + *i.*).

correspondence /kɒrɪ'spɒnd(ə)ns/ *n.* корреспондéнция, перепѝска; **~ course** курс заóчного обучéния.

correspondent /kɒrɪ'spɒnd(ə)nt/ *n.* корреспондéнт.

corresponding /kɒrɪ'spɒndɪŋ/ *adj.* соотвéтственный, соотвéтствующий.

corridor /'kɒrɪdɔ:(r)/ *n.* коридóр.

corroborate /kə'rɒbəreɪt/ *v.t.* подтвер|ждáть, -дѝть.

corrode /kə'rəʊd/ *v.t.* разъ|едáть, -éсть.
■ *v.i.* ржавéть, за-.

corrosion /kə'rəʊʒ(ə)n/ *n.* коррóзия, ржáвчина.

corrosive /kə'rəʊsɪv/ *adj.* коррозѝйный, разъедáющий, éдкий; (*fig.*) разъедáющий.

corrugate /'kɒrʊgeɪt/ *v.t.*: **~d iron** волнѝстое/рифлёное желéзо.

corrupt /kə'rʌpt/ *adj.*
1 (*depraved*) развращённый.
2 (*dishonest*) продáжный.
3 (*comput.*) повреждённый.
■ *v.t.* 1 (*deprave*) развра|щáть, -тѝть.
2 (*comput.*) иска|жáть, -зѝть.

corruption /kə'rʌpʃ(ə)n/ *n.* разложéние; развращéние.

corset /'kɔ:sɪt/ *n.* корсéт.

Corsica /'kɔ:sɪkə/ *n.* Кóрсика.

cortisone /'kɔ:tɪzəʊn/ *n.* (*med.*) кортизóн.

cosh /kɒʃ/ *n.* (*Br.*) дубѝнка.

cosmetic /kɒz'metɪk/ *n.* космéтика.
■ *adj.* косметѝческий.

cosmic /'kɒzmɪk/ *adj.* космѝческий.

cosmology /kɒz'mɒlədʒɪ/ *n.* космолóгия.

cosmonaut /'kɒzmənɔ:t/ *n.* космонáвт.

cosmopolitan /kɒzmə'pɒlɪt(ə)n/ *n.* космополѝт.
■ *adj.* космополитѝческий.

cosmos /'kɒzmɒs/ *n.* кóсмос.

Cossack /'kɒsæk/ *n.* казá|к (*fem.* -чка); (*attr.*) казáцкий, казáчий.

cosset /'kɒsɪt/ *v.t.* (**cosseted, cosseting**) баловáть (*impf.*); нéжить (*impf.*).

cost /kɒst/ *n.*
1 (*monetary*) ценá, стóимость; **~ price** себестóимость; **~ of living** прожѝточный мѝнимум.
2 (*expense, loss*) ценá; **at all ~s** любóй ценóй.
■ *v.t. & i.*
1 (*past and p.p.* **~**) (*involve expense*) стóить (*impf.*); **this ~ me £5** э́то стóило мне 5 фýнтов; э́то обошлóсь мне в 5 фýнтов.
2 (*past and p.p.* **~ed**) (*assess ~ of*) оцéн|ивать, -ѝть издéржки (*предприятия и т. п.*).
■ *cpd.* **~-effective** *adj.* рентáбельный.

co-star /'kəʊstɑ:(r)/ *n.* партнёр (*fem.* -ша) (в другóй глáвной рóли).
■ *v.t.*: **a picture ~ring X and Y** фильм с учáстием двух звёзд — X и У.
■ *v.i.*: **they ~red in that picture** онѝ снимáлись в э́том фѝльме в глáвных роля́х.

costly /'kɒstlɪ/ *adj.* (**costlier, costliest**) дорогóй.

costume /'kɒstju:m/ *n.* костю́м; (*attr.*): ~

jewellery бижутéрия.

cosy /ˈkəʊzɪ/ (*US* **cozy**) *adj.* (**cosier, cosiest**) уютный.

cot /kɒt/ *n.* (*Br., child's bed*) дéтская кровáтка; (*US, camp bed*) раскладýшка; ~ **death** (*Br.*) внезáпная смéрть (ребёнка грудного вóзраста).

cottage /ˈkɒtɪdʒ/ *n.* коттéдж; дáча; ~ **cheese** (прессóванный) творóг.

cotton /ˈkɒt(ə)n/ *n.*
1 (*plant*) хлóпок, хлопчáтник.
2 (*fabric*) хлóпок.
3 (*thread*) нúтки (*f. pl.*).
4 (*attr.*) хлопчатобумáжный.
■ *cpd.* ~ **wool** *n.* (*Br.*) вáта.

couch /kaʊtʃ/ *n.* (*sofa*) кушéтка, дивáн; (*bed*) кровáть.

couchette /kuːˈʃet/ *n.* спáльное мéсто.

cough /kɒf/ *n.* кáшель (*m.*).
■ *v.t.* & *i.* кáшлять (*impf.*).
■ *cpds.* ~ **medicine,** ~ **mixture** (*Br.*) *nn.* микстýра от кáшля.

could /kʊd/ *v. aux., see* ▸ **can²**

couldn't /ˈkʊd(ə)nt/ *neg. of* ▸ **could**

council /ˈkaʊns(ə)l/ *n.* совéт; **town** ~ городскóй совéт; муниципалитéт.
■ *cpd.* ~ **house** *n.* (*Br., dwelling*) муниципáльный дом; жилóй дом, принадлежáщий муниципáльному совéту.

councillor /ˈkaʊnsələ(r)/ (*US also* **councilor**) *n.* член совéта.

counsel /ˈkaʊns(ə)l/ *n.* (*barrister(s)*) адвокáт.
■ *v.t.* (**counselled, counselling;** *US* **counseled, counseling**) совéтовать, по- (+ *d.*).

counsellor /ˈkaʊnsələ(r)/ (*US* **counselor**) *n.* совéтник.

counsellorship /ˈkaʊnsələ(r)ʃɪp/ *n.* дóлжность совéтника.

count¹ /kaʊnt/ *n.* (*nobleman*) граф (*не британский*).

count² /kaʊnt/ *n.*
1 (*reckoning*) счёт, подсчёт; **keep** ~ вестú (*det.*) счёт.
2 (*total*) итóг; **the** ~ **was 200** итóг равнялся 200 (двумстáм).
3 (*leg.*) пункт обвинúтельного заключéния.
■ *v.t.* (*number, reckon*) считáть, со-; ~ **your change!** провéрьте сдáчу!; **50 people, not ~ing the children** 50 человéк, не считáя детéй.
■ *v.i.* 1 (*reckon, number*) считáть (*impf.*); ~ **up to 10!** считáйте до десятú!
2 (*be reckoned*) считáться (*impf.*); **that doesn't** ~ э́то не в счёт (*or* не считáется).
3 (*rely*) рассчúтывать (*impf.*) (на + *a.*); **I** ~ **(up)on you to help** я рассчúтываю на вáшу пóмощь.
■ *cpd.* **~down** *n.* (обрáтный) отсчёт врéмени.

countenance /ˈkaʊntɪnəns/ *n.* (*face*) лицó, óблик; выражéние лицá.
■ *v.t.* поддéрж|ивать, -áть.

counter¹ /ˈkaʊntə(r)/ *n.*
1 (*at games*) фúшка, мáрка.
2 (*in shop*) прилáвок; **under the** ~ (*fig.*) из-под полы́/прилáвка.

counter² /ˈkaʊntə(r)/ *v.t.* & *i.* (*oppose, parry*) противодéйствовать (*impf.*) + *d.*

counteract /kaʊntəˈrækt/ *v.t.* противодéйствовать (*impf.*) + *d.*

counter-attack /ˈkaʊntərətæk/ *n.* контратáка.

counterclockwise /kaʊntəˈklɒkwaɪz/ *adj.* & *adv.* (*US*) (движущийся) прóтив часовóй стрéлки.

counter-espionage /kaʊntərˈespɪənɑːʒ, -ɪdʒ/ *n.* контрразвéдка.

counterfeit /ˈkaʊntəfɪt, -fiːt/ *adj.* поддéльный, подлóжный.
■ *v.t.* & *i.* поддéл|ывать, -ать; (*fig., simulate*) подражáть (*impf.*) + *d.*

counterfoil /ˈkaʊntəfɔɪl/ *n.* (*Br.*) корешóк (чéка, квитáнции *и т. п.*).

counterpart /ˈkaʊntəpɑːt/ *n.* пáра (*к чему*), дополнéние; (*person*) коллéга (*c.g.*).

counterproductive /kaʊntəprəˈdʌktɪv/ *adj.* нецелесообрáзный.

countersign /ˈkaʊntəsaɪn/ *v.t.* стáвить, по- вторýю пóдпись на + *p.*

countess /ˈkaʊntɪs/ *n.* графúня.

countless /ˈkaʊntlɪs/ *adj.* бесчúсленный.

country /ˈkʌntrɪ/ *n.*
1 (*geog., pol.*) странá.
2 (*opp. town*) дерéвня; **in the** ~ зá городом, на дáче; (**~side**) прирóда; ~ **house, seat** помéстье; ~ **club** загорóдный клуб.
3 (*terrain*) мéстность; **difficult** ~ труднопроходúмая мéстность.
■ *cpd.* **~side** *n.* сéльская мéстность; ландшáфт.

county /ˈkaʊntɪ/ *n.* грáфство.

coup /kuː/ *n.* (*pl.* **coups** /kuːz/) удáчный ход.
■ *cpd.* ~ **d'état** *n.* госудáрственный переворóт.

coupé /ˈkuːpeɪ/ *n.* закры́тый двухдвéрный автомобúль.

couple /ˈkʌp(ə)l/ *n.* (*objects or people*) пáра.

coupon /ˈkuːpɒn/ *n.* купóн, талóн.

courage /ˈkʌrɪdʒ/ *n.* хрáбрость, смéлость, мýжество; **take, pluck up** ~ мужáться (*impf.*); соб|ирáться, -рáться с дýхом;

courageous /kəˈreɪdʒəs/ *adj.* хрáбрый.

courgette /kʊəˈʒet/ *n.* (*Br.*) кабачóк.

courier /ˈkʊrɪə(r)/ *n.* (*messenger*) курьéр; (*travel guide*) экскурсовóд.

course /kɔːs/ *n.*
1 (*movement, process*) ход, течéние; ~ **of events** ход собы́тий; **in due** ~ в дóлжное/своё врéмя; **of** ~ конéчно.
2 (*direction*) курс, направлéние; **we are on** ~ мы идём по кýрсу.
3 (*race~*) скаковóй круг.
4 (*series*) курс; **a** ~ **of lectures** курс лéкций; **a** ~ **of treatment** курс лечéния.
5 (*cul.*) блю́до; **main** ~ вторóе блю́до.

court /kɔːt/ *n.*
1 (*yard*) двор.
2 (*space for playing games*) площáдка для игр; (*tennis*) корт.
3 (*sovereign's etc.*) двор.
4 (*leg.*) суд; ~ **of law, justice** суд.
■ *v.t.* (*a woman*) ухáживать (*impf.*) за + *i.*
■ *cpds.* **~house** *n.* здáние судá; ~ **martial** *n.* воéнный суд; **~-martial** *v.t.* (**-martialled, -martialling;** (*US*)

-martialed, -martialing) суди́ть (*impf.*) вое́нным судо́м; **~room** *n.* зал суда́; **~yard** *n.* двор.

courteous /ˈkəːtɪəs/ *adj.* ве́жливый, учти́вый.

courtesan /kɔːtɪˈzæn/ *n.* куртиза́нка.

courtesy /ˈkəːtɪsɪ/ *n.* ве́жливость, учти́вость.
■ *cpd.* **~ bus** *n.* беспла́тный авто́бус.

courtier /ˈkɔːtɪə(r)/ *n.* придво́рный.

courtship /ˈkɔːtʃɪp/ *n.* уха́живание.

cousin /ˈkʌz(ə)n/ *n.* (*male*) двою́родный брат; (*fem.*) двою́родная сестра́; **second ~** трою́родный брат (*fem.* трою́родная сестра́).

cove /kəʊv/ *n.* бу́хточка.

covenant /ˈkʌvənənt/ *n.* соглаше́ние, догово́р; **C~ of the League of Nations** Уста́в Ли́ги На́ций; (*relig.*) заве́т.
■ *v.t.* & *i.* заключ|а́ть, -и́ть соглаше́ние; догов|а́риваться, -ори́ться (*с кем о чём*).

cover /ˈkʌvə(r)/ *n.*
1 (*lid*) кры́шка.
2 (*loose ~ing of chair etc.*) чехо́л; (*pl., bedclothes*) посте́ль.
3 (*of book etc.*) переплёт, обло́жка.
4 (*shelter, protection*) укры́тие, прикры́тие; **take ~** укр|ыва́ться, -ы́ться.
5 (*at table*): **~ charge** пла́та за дополни́тельное обслу́живание (*музыку в ресторане и т. п.*).
6 (*Br., insurance*) страхова́ние.
■ *v.t.* 1 (*overspread etc.; also* **~ up, ~ over**) покр|ыва́ть, -ы́ть; **~ a chair** об|ива́ть, -и́ть стул; **she ~ed her face in, with her hands** она́ закры́ла лицо́ рука́ми; **the roads are ~ed with snow** доро́ги занесены́ сне́гом.
2 (*fig.*) покр|ыва́ть, -ы́ть.
3 (*protect*) закр|ыва́ть, -ы́ть; **are you ~ed against theft?** вы застрахо́ваны от кра́жи?
4 (*aim weapon at*) це́литься (*impf.*) в + *a.*
5 (*meet, satisfy*) покр|ыва́ть, -ы́ть.
6 (*deal with*): **the lectures ~ a wide field** ле́кции охва́тывают широ́кий круг вопро́сов.
7 (*of correspondence*): **~ing letter** сопроводи́тельное письмо́.
■ *cpd.* **~-up** *n.* сокры́тие; **~ version** *n.* (*mus.*) ка́вер-ве́рсия (*песни*).

coverage /ˈkʌvərɪdʒ/ *n.* охва́т.

covert /ˈkəʊvəːt/ *adj.* скры́тый.

covet /ˈkʌvɪt/ *v.t.* (**coveted, coveting**) жа́ждать (*impf.*) + *g.*; (*coll.*) за́риться (*impf.*) на + *a.*

cow /kaʊ/ *n.* коро́ва.
■ *cpd.* **~boy** *n.* ковбо́й.

coward /ˈkaʊəd/ *n.* трус (*fem.* -и́ха).

cowardice /ˈkaʊədɪs/ *n.* тру́сость.

cowardly /ˈkaʊədlɪ/ *adj.* трусли́вый.

cower /ˈkaʊə(r)/ *v.i.* съёжи|ваться, -ться.

cowslip /ˈkaʊslɪp/ *n.* первоцве́т.

coy /kɔɪ/ *adj.* (**coyer, coyest**) стыдли́вый.

cozy /ˈkəʊzɪ/ (*US*) = **cosy**

crab /kræb/ *n.* краб; (*astron.*): **the C~** Рак.

crack /kræk/ *n.*
1 (*in a cup, ice etc.*) тре́щина; (*in wall, floor etc.*) щель.
2 (*sudden noise*) треск, щёлканье.
3 (*coll., attempt*) попы́тка; **have a ~ at sth.** попыта́ть (*pf.*) свои́ си́лы в чём-н.
4: **at ~ of dawn** с (пе́рвой) заре́й.
5: **a ~ shot** первокла́ссный стрело́к.
6 (*drug*) крэк.
■ *v.t.* 1 (*a plate, a bone*) раск|а́лывать, -оло́ть; **~ a nut** расколо́ть (*pf.*) оре́х; **~ a code** разгада́ть (*pf.*) шифр.
2: **~ a whip** щёлк|ать, -нуть кнуто́м; **~ a joke** отпусти́ть (*pf.*) шу́тку.
■ *v.i.* 1 (*get broken or fissured*) да|ва́ть, -ть тре́щину; **the glass ~ed** стекло́ тре́снуло; (*fig., give way*): **he did not ~ under torture** пы́тки не сломи́ли его́.
2 (*of sound*) щёлк|ать, -нуть.
■ *with advs.*: **~ down** *v.i.*: **~ down on** прин|има́ть, -я́ть круты́е ме́ры про́тив + *g.*; **~ up** *v.i.* (*of person: suffer collapse*) надломи́ться (*pf.*); разва́л|иваться, -и́ться.

cracker /ˈkrækə(r)/ *n.*
1 (*biscuit*) кре́кер.
2 (*Christmas ~*) хлопу́шка.

crackle /ˈkræk(ə)l/ *n.* (*sound*) треск, потре́скивание.
■ *v.i.* (*of sound*) потре́скивать (*impf.*).

cradle /ˈkreɪd(ə)l/ *n.* (*lit., fig.*) колыбе́ль.
■ *v.t.*: **~ a child in one's arms** держа́ть (*impf.*) ребёнка на рука́х.

craft /krɑːft/ *n.*
1 (*skill*) ло́вкость, уме́ние.
2 (*occupation*) ремесло́; **arts and ~s** иску́сства и ремёсла (*nt. pl.*).
3 (*pl.* **~**) (*boat*) су́дно.
■ *cpd.* **~sman** *n.* реме́сленник, ма́стер.

crafty /ˈkrɑːftɪ/ *adj.* (**craftier, craftiest**) хи́трый.

crag /kræg/ *n.* скала́, утёс.

cram /kræm/ *v.t.* (**crammed, cramming**)
1 (*insert forcefully*) запи́х|ивать, -а́ть/-ну́ть; (*fill*): **the shelves are ~med with books** по́лки ло́мятся от книг.
2 (*v.t.* & *i.*) (*study intensively*) уси́ленно занима́ться (пе́ред экза́меном) (*impf.*).

cramp /kræmp/ *n.* су́дорога.
■ *v.t.* стесн|я́ть, -и́ть.

cranberry /ˈkrænbərɪ/ *n.* клю́ква (*collect.*).

crane /kreɪn/ *n.* (*bird*) жура́вль (*m.*); (*machine*) (грузо)подъёмный кран.

crank[1] /kræŋk/ *n.* (*handle*) кривоши́п.

crank[2] /kræŋk/ *n.* (*person*) чуда́|к (*fem.* -чка).

cranny /ˈkrænɪ/ *n.* тре́щина.

crap /kræp/ (*vulg.*) *n.* говно́ (*о низком качестве*) (*vulg.*); (*nonsense*) вздо́р, чепуха́.

crash /kræʃ/ *n.*
1 (*noise*) гро́хот.
2 (*smash*) ава́рия, круше́ние; **he was killed in a car/plane ~** он поги́б в автомоби́льной/авиацио́нной катастро́фе; (*comput.*) фата́льный сбой.
3: **a ~** (*intensive*) **course** ускоре́нный курс.
■ *v.t.* разб|ива́ть, -и́ть; гро́хнуть (*pf.*); **he ~ed the aircraft** он разби́л самолёт.
■ *v.i.* 1: **the plane ~ed** самолёт потерпе́л ава́рию (*or* разби́лся).
2 (*comput.*) зав|иса́ть, -и́снуть.
■ *cpds.* **~ helmet** *n.* шлем автого́нщика/мотоцикли́ста; мотошле́м; **~-land** *v.t.* & *i.* соверш|а́ть, -и́ть авари́йную поса́дку; **~-landing** *n.* авари́йная поса́дка.

crass /kræs/ *adj.* глу́пый; **~ stupidity** непроходи́мая ту́пость, полне́йшая глу́пость.

crate /kreɪt/ *n.* я́щик.
crater /ˈkreɪtə(r)/ *n.* кра́тер; (*bomb* ~) воро́нка.
cravat /krəˈvæt/ *n.* широ́кий га́лстук; ше́йный плато́к.
crave /kreɪv/ *v.t.* & *i.* (*desire*) жа́ждать (*impf.*) + *g.*
craving /ˈkreɪvɪŋ/ *n.* стра́стное жела́ние.
crawfish *see* ▸ **crayfish**
crawl /krɔːl/ *n.*
1 (*~ing motion*) по́лзание; **traffic was reduced to a ~** тра́нспорт тащи́лся е́ле-е́ле.
2 (*swimming stroke*) кроль (*m.*).
■ *v.i.* 1 по́лзать (*indet.*), ползти́ (*det.*); **he ~ed on his hands and knees** он полз на четвере́ньках.
2 (*kowtow*) пресмыка́ться (*impf.*) (**to:** пе́ред + *i.*).
3 : **the ground is ~ing with ants** земля́ кишмя́ киши́т муравья́ми.
crayfish /ˈkreɪfɪʃ/, **crawfish** /ˈkrɔːfɪʃ/ *nn.* (*freshwater*) речно́й рак; (*marine*) лангу́ст.
crayon /ˈkreɪən/ *n.* цветно́й каранда́ш; цветно́й мело́к; пасте́ль.
craze /kreɪz/ *n.* ма́ния, помеша́тельство.
crazy /ˈkreɪzɪ/ *adj.* (**crazier, craziest**) безу́мный, сумасше́дший; **~ about sth.** поме́шанный на чём-н.; **he is ~ about her** он без ума́ от неё.
creak /kriːk/ *v.i.* скрипе́ть (*impf.*).
cream /kriːm/ *n.*
1 (*top part of milk*) сли́в|ки (*pl.*, *g.* -ок).
2 (*dish or sweet*) крем; **~ cake** торт с кре́мом; кре́мовое пиро́жное.
3 (*polish, cosmetic etc.*) крем, мазь; **face ~** крем для лица́.
4 (*attr.*, *~-coloured*) кре́мового цве́та.
■ *v.t.* (*apply ~ to*) на|кла́дывать, -ложи́ть крем на + *a*; **~ off** от|бира́ть, -обра́ть.
creamy /ˈkriːmɪ/ *adj.* (**creamier, creamiest**) жи́рный.
crease /kriːs/ *n.* скла́дка.
■ *v.t.* (*newspaper, trousers*) мять, с-/из-.
■ *v.i.* (*form ~s*) мя́ться, с-/из-.
create /kriːˈeɪt/ *v.t.* созд|ава́ть, -а́ть.
creation /kriːˈeɪʃ(ə)n/ *n.*
1 (*act, process*) созда́ние, созида́ние.
2 (*product of imagination*) творе́ние.
creative /kriːˈeɪtɪv/ *adj.* тво́рческий.
creativity /kriːeɪˈtɪvɪtɪ/ *n.* тво́рческий дар.
creator /kriːˈeɪtə(r)/ *n.* созда́тель (*m.*).
creature /ˈkriːtʃə(r)/ *n.* созда́ние, тварь, существо́.
crèche /kreʃ/ *n.* (*Br.*) (де́тские) я́сл|и (*pl.*, *g.* -ей).
credential /krɪˈdenʃ(ə)l/ *n.* (*usu. pl.*) квалифика́ция.
credibility /kredɪˈbɪlɪtɪ/ *n.* убеди́тельность.
credible /ˈkredɪb(ə)l/ *adj.* (*of person*) заслу́живающий дове́рия.
credit /ˈkredɪt/ *n.*
1 (*belief, trust, confidence*) ве́ра, дове́рие.
2 (*honour*): **the work does you ~** э́та рабо́та де́лает вам честь.
3 (*fin.*) креди́т; **buy on ~** покупа́ть (*pf.*) в креди́т; **~ card** креди́тная ка́рточка.
■ *v.t.* (**credited, crediting**)
1 (*believe sth.*) ве́рить, по- + *d.*
2 : **I ~ed him with more sense** я счита́л его́ бо́лее благоразу́мным.
■ *cpd.* **~worthy** *adj.* кредитоспосо́бный.
creditable /ˈkredɪtəb(ə)l/ *adj.* (*praiseworthy*) де́лающий честь (+ *d.*); (*believable*) правдоподо́бный, вероя́тный.
creditor /ˈkredɪtə(r)/ *n.* кредито́р.
credulous /ˈkredjʊləs/ *adj.* легкове́рный, дове́рчивый.
creed /kriːd/ *n.* вероуче́ние; (*fig.*) убежде́ния (*nt. pl.*).
creek /kriːk/ *n.* (*inlet*) зали́в, бу́хта; (*small river*) ре́чка.
creep /kriːp/ *n.* (*coll.*) несно́сный/отврати́тельный тип.
■ *v.i.* (*past and p.p.* **crept**) по́лзать (*indet.*), ползти́ (*det.*); **old age ~s up on one unnoticed** ста́рость подкра́дывается незаме́тно.
creeper /ˈkriːpə(r)/ *n.* (*plant*) ползу́чее/вью́щееся расте́ние.
creepy /ˈkriːpɪ/ *adj.* (**creepier, creepiest**)
1 жу́ткий.
2 (*of flesh*) в мура́шках.
■ *cpd.* **~-crawly** *n.* бука́шка.
cremate /krɪˈmeɪt/ *v.t.* креми́ровать (*impf.*, *pf.*).
cremation /krɪˈmeɪʃ(ə)n/ *n.* крема́ция.
cremator|ium /kreməˈtɔːrɪəm/ *n.* (*pl.* **~a** *or* **~ums**) кремато́рий.
creosote /ˈkriːəsəʊt/ *n.* креозо́т.
crept /krept/ *past and p.p. of* ▸ **creep**
crescent /ˈkrez(ə)nt/ *n.*
1 (*moon*) лу́нный серп.
2 (*symbol of Islam*) полуме́сяц.
cress /kres/ *n.* кресс-сала́т.
crest /krest/ *n.*
1 (*tuft of feathers; top of a wave, hill*) гре́бень (*m.*).
2 (*her. device*) герб.
crevasse /krəˈvæs/ *n.* рассе́лина в леднике́.
crevice /ˈkrevɪs/ *n.* щель, расще́лина.
crew /kruː/ *n.*
1 (*of vessel*) кома́нда, экипа́ж; (*of aircraft*) экипа́ж.
2 (*team*) брига́да, арте́ль.
3 : **~ cut** стри́жка ёжиком.
crib /krɪb/ *n.* де́тская крова́тка с се́ткой.
cricket[1] /ˈkrɪkɪt/ *n.* (*insect*) сверчо́к.
cricket[2] /ˈkrɪkɪt/ *n.* (*game*) кри́кет.
crime /kraɪm/ *n.* (*offence*) преступле́ние; (*collect.*) престу́пность.
Crimea /kraɪˈmɪə/ *n.* Крым.
Crimean /kraɪˈmɪən/ *adj.* кры́мский.
criminal /ˈkrɪmɪn(ə)l/ *n.* престу́пни|к (*fem.* -ца).
■ *adj.* 1 (*guilty*) престу́пный; **he has a ~ history** у него́ престу́пное про́шлое.
2 (*pert. to crime*) уголо́вный, кримина́льный.
criminologist /krɪmɪˈnɒlədʒɪst/ *n.* кримино́лог.
criminology /krɪmɪˈnɒlədʒɪ/ *n.* криминоло́гия.
crimson /ˈkrɪmz(ə)n/ *n.* мали́новый цвет.
■ *adj.* мали́новый.
cringe /krɪndʒ/ *v.i.* (**cringing**) раболе́пствовать (*impf.*).
crippl|e /ˈkrɪp(ə)l/ *n.* кале́ка (*c.g.*).

■ *v.t.* калéчить, ис-; (*fig.*); **strikes are ~ing industry** забастóвки расшáтывают промы́шленность.

crisis /ˈkraɪsɪs/ *n.* (*pl.* **crises** /-siːz/) кри́зис.

crisp /krɪsp/ *n.* (*Br.*) (*pl.*) хрустя́щий картóфель, чи́пс|ы (*pl.*, *g.* -ов).

■ *adj.* (*of substance*) хрустя́щий; **a ~ biscuit** рассы́пчатое печéнье; **a ~ lettuce** свéжий салáт; (*of style, orders etc.*) чекáнный.

■ *cpd.* **~bread** *n.* сухари́ (*m. pl.*); хрустя́щие хлéбцы (*m. pl.*).

criss-cross /ˈkrɪskrɒs/ *adj.* перекрéщивающийся.

■ *v.t.* расчéр|чивать, -ти́ть крест-нáкрест.

criteri|on /kraɪˈtɪərɪən/ *n.* (*pl.* **~a**) критéрий.

critic /ˈkrɪtɪk/ *n.* кри́тик.

critical /ˈkrɪtɪk(ə)l/ *adj.*

1 (*decisive*) крити́ческий; **the patient's condition is ~** больнóй в крити́ческом состоя́нии.

2 (*fault-finding*) крити́ческий, крити́чный.

criticism /ˈkrɪtɪsɪz(ə)m/ *n.* кри́тика; **I have only one ~ to make** у меня́ тóлько однó замечáние.

criticize /ˈkrɪtɪsaɪz/ *v.t.* (*adversely*) критиковáть (*impf*).

critique /krɪˈtiːk/ *n.* кри́тика; (*review*) рецéнзия, крити́ческая статья́.

croak /krəʊk/ *v.t.* & *i.* квáкать (*impf.*).

Croat /ˈkrəʊæt/ *n.* хорвáт (*fem.* -ка).

Croatia /krəʊˈeɪʃə/ *n.* Хорвáтия.

Croatian /krəʊˈeɪʃ(ə)n/ *adj.* хорвáтский.

crochet /ˈkrəʊʃeɪ, -ʃɪ/ *n.* вя́зка крючкóм.

■ *v.t.* & *i.* (**crocheted** /-ʃeɪd/, **crocheting** /-ʃeɪɪŋ/) вязáть (*impf.*) крючкóм.

crockery /ˈkrɒkərɪ/ *n.* гли́няная/фая́нсовая посу́да.

crocodile /ˈkrɒkədaɪl/ *n.* крокоди́л.

crocus /ˈkrəʊkəs/ *n.* (*pl.* **crocuses** *or* **croci** /-kaɪ/) крóкус, шафрáн; **autumn ~** осéнний крóкус.

croissant /ˈkrwʌsɑ̃/ *n.* круассáн, францу́зский рогáлик.

crony /ˈkrəʊnɪ/ *n.* дружóк, закады́чный друг.

crook /krʊk/ *n.* мошéнник, жу́лик.

crooked /ˈkrʊkɪd/ *adj.* (**crookeder, crookedest**)

1 (*bent*) сóгнутый, изóгнутый.

2 (*coll., dishonest*) бесчéстный.

crop /krɒp/ *n.* урожáй, жáтва.

■ *v.i.* (**cropped, cropping**) (*fig.*): **difficulties ~ped up** появи́лись/возни́кли тру́дности.

■ *cpd.* **~ top** *n.* (*fashion*) топ.

croquet /ˈkrəʊkeɪ/ *n.* крокéт.

cross /krɒs/ *n.*

1 крест.

2 (*mixing of breeds*) пóмесь, гибри́д.

■ *adj.* 1 (*transverse*) поперéчный, перекрёстный.

2 (*angry*) серди́тый; злой (**with:** на + *a.*).

■ *v.t.* 1 (*go across, traverse; also* **~ over**): **~ a road/bridge** пере|ходи́ть, -йти́ чéрез дорóгу/мост; **~ the Channel** перепл|ывáть, -ы́ть Ла-Мáнш; **the idea never ~ed my mind** э́та мысль никогдá не приходи́ла мне в гóлову.

2 (*draw lines across*): **~ a cheque** (*Br.*) перечёрк|ивать, -ну́ть чек.

3 (*place across*) скрé|щивать, -сти́ть; **~ one's legs** скрести́ть (*pf.*) нóги.

4: **~ o.s.** крести́ться, пере-.

■ *v.i.*: **he ~ed to where I was sitting** он перешёл к томý мéсту, где я сидéл; **he ~ed from Dover to Calais** он переправился из Ду́вра в Калé.

■ *with advs.*: **~ off, out** *vv.t.* вычёркивать, вы́черкнуть.

■ *cpds.* **~-check** *n.* свéрка; *v.t.* & *i.* св|еря́ть(ся), -éрить(ся); **~-country** *adj.*: **a ~-country race** бег по пересечённой мéстности, кросс; **~-country runner** кроссмéн; **~-examine** *v.t.* подв|ергáть, -éргнуть перекрёстному допрóсу; (*fig.*) допр|áшивать, -оси́ть; **~-eyed** *adj.* косоглáзый, косóй; **~fire** *n.* (*mil.*) перекрёстный огóнь; **~-legged** *adj.* (сидя́щий) положи́в нóгу нá ногу; **~ purposes** *n. pl.* недоразумéние; **~-question** *v.t.* допр|áшивать, -оси́ть; **~-reference** *n.* перекрёстная ссы́лка; **~road** *n.* перекрёсток; пересекáющая дорóга; **at the ~ roads** (*fig.*) на распу́тье; **~ section** *n.* поперéчное сечéние; **~word** *n.* кроссвóрд.

crossing /ˈkrɒsɪŋ/ *n.* перехóд.

crotch /krɒtʃ/ *n.* промéжность.

crotchet /ˈkrɒtʃɪt/ *n.* (*Br., mus.*) четвертнáя нóта.

crouch /kraʊtʃ/ *v.i.* сгибáться, согну́ться.

croupier /ˈkruːpɪeɪ/ *n.* (*at gambling*) крупьé (*m. indecl.*).

crouton /ˈkruːtɒn/ *n.* (*cul.*) грéнка.

crow[1] /krəʊ/ *n.* ворóна; **~'s-nest** (*naut.*) наблюдáтельный пост на мáчте, «ворóнье гнездó».

crow[2] /krəʊ/ *n.* (*of cock*) кукарéканье.

■ *v.t.* кукарéкать (*impf.*).

crowbar /ˈkrəʊbɑː(r)/ лом.

crowd /kraʊd/ *n.* толпá.

■ *v.t.* зап|олня́ть, -óлнить; **~ed street** многолю́дная у́лица; **the room was ~ed with furniture** кóмната былá загромождена́ мéбелью.

■ *v.i.* (*assemble in a ~*) толпи́ться, с-; **they ~ed into the room** они́ наби́лись в кóмнату.

crown /kraʊn/ *n.*

1 корóна, венéц.

2 (*dental work*) корóнка.

3 (*attr.*): **C~ jewels** королéвские/цáрские регáлии (*f. pl.*).

■ *v.t.* 1: **he was ~ed king** егó короновáли (на цáрство).

2: **~ a tooth** стáвить, по- корóнку на зуб.

crucial /ˈkruːʃ(ə)l/ *adj.* (*decisive*) решáющий.

crucible /ˈkruːsɪb(ə)l/ *n.* ти́гель (*m.*); (*fig.*) горни́ло (*rhet.*).

crucifix /ˈkruːsɪfɪks/ *n.* распя́тие, крест.

crucifixion /kruːsɪˈfɪkʃ(ə)n/ *n.* распя́тие (на крестé).

crucify /ˈkruːsɪfaɪ/ *v.t.* расп|инáть, -я́ть.

crude /kruːd/ *adj.*

1 (*of materials*): **~ oil** сырáя нефть.

2 (*graceless*) гру́бый, неотёсанный.

3 (*ill-made*): **~ paintings** аляповáтые карти́ны.

cruel /ˈkruːəl/ *adj.* (**crueller, cruellest** *or*

crueler, cruelest) жесто́кий.
cruelty /ˈkru:əltɪ/ *n.* жесто́кость.
cruise /kru:z/ *n.* (*pleasure voyage*) морско́е путеше́ствие, круи́з; **~ missile** крыла́тая раке́та.
■ *v.i.* (*sail or drive about*) курси́ровать (*impf.*); (*go on a cruise, cruises*) соверша́ть (*impf.*) круи́з(ы).
cruiser /ˈkru:zə(r)/ *n.* (*warship*) кре́йсер; **cabin ~** прогу́лочный ка́тер с каю́той.
crumb /krʌm/ *n.* кро́шка.
crumble /ˈkrʌmb(ə)l/ *v.t.* (*bread etc.*) кроши́ть, рас-.
■ *v.i.* кроши́ться (*impf.*); (*of a wall*) обва́л|иваться, -и́ться; (*fig., of hopes etc.*) ру́шиться (*impf., pf.*).
crumpet /ˈkrʌmpɪt/ *n.* ≈ сдо́бная лепёшка.
crumple /ˈkrʌmp(ə)l/ *v.t.* мять, с-/из-; **~ up a sheet of paper** ско́мкать (*pf.*) лист бума́ги.
crunch /krʌntʃ/ *v.t.* & *i.* грызть (*impf.*) с хру́стом.
crusade /kru:ˈseɪd/ *n.* (*lit., fig.*) кресто́вый похо́д.
crusader /kru:ˈseɪdə(r)/ *n.* кресторо́сец (*fig.*); боре́ц.
crush /krʌʃ/ *n.*
1 (*crowd*) да́вка.
2 (*infatuation*): **she has a ~ on him** она́ без ума́ от него́.
■ *v.t.* 1 (*squash*) разда́в|ливать, -и́ть.
2 (*crumple*) мять, из-/с-.
3 (*defeat*) сокруш|а́ть, -и́ть; **our hopes were ~ed** на́ши наде́жды ру́хнули; **a ~ing defeat** по́лное пораже́ние, разгро́м.
crust /krʌst/ *n.* (*of bread*) ко́рка; (*of pastry*) ко́рочка; **the earth's ~** земна́я кора́.
crustacean /krʌˈsteɪʃ(ə)n/ *n.* ракообра́зное.
crutch /krʌtʃ/ *n.* косты́ль (*m.*).
crux /krʌks/ *n.* (*pl.* **~es** *or* **cruces**) суть.
cry /kraɪ/ *n.* крик.
■ *v.t.* крича́ть (*impf.*).
■ *v.i.* 1 (*weep*) пла́кать (*impf.*).
2 (*shout*) крича́ть (*impf.*).
■ *with advs.*: **~ off** *v.t.* & *i.* (*an engagement*) отмен|я́ть, -и́ть (свида́ние); **~ out** *v.i.* (*in pain or distress*) вскри́к|ивать, -нуть; **he cried out in pain** он вскри́кнул от бо́ли.
crypt /krɪpt/ *n.* склеп.
cryptic /ˈkrɪptɪk/ *adj.* таи́нственный, зага́дочный.
crystal /ˈkrɪst(ə)l/ *n.*
1 (*substance*) го́рный хруста́ль.
2 (*glassware*) хруста́ль (*m.*); **~ ball** маги́ческий криста́лл.
■ *cpd.* **~ clear** *adj.* (*fig.*) я́сный как бо́жий день.
crystallize /ˈkrɪstəlaɪz/ *v.t.*
1 (*form into crystals*) кристаллизова́ть (*impf., pf.*), за- (*pf.*).
2 (*clarify*) вопло|ща́ть, -ти́ть в определённую фо́рму.
3: **~d fruit** заса́харенные фру́кты.
■ *v.i.* 1 (*form into crystals*) кристаллизова́ться (*impf., pf.*); вы́- (*pf.*).
2: **his plans ~d** его́ пла́ны определи́лись.
cub /kʌb/ *n.* детёныш.
Cuba /ˈkju:bə/ *n.* Ку́ба; **in ~** на Ку́бе.
Cuban /ˈkju:bən/ *n.* куби́н|ец (*fem.* -ка).
■ *adj.* куби́нский.
cube /kju:b/ *n.*
1 (*math.*) куб.
2 (*solid*) ку́бик.
■ *v.t.* (*cut into* **~s**) нар|еза́ть, -е́зать ку́биками.
cubic /ˈkju:bɪk/ *adj.* куби́ческий.
cubicle /ˈkju:bɪk(ə)l/ *n.* (*at a swimming pool; in a toilet*) каби́нка; (*in a shop*) приме́рочная.
cubism /ˈkju:bɪz(ə)m/ *n.* куби́зм.
cubist /ˈkju:bɪst/ *n.* куби́ст (*fem.* -ка).
cuckoo /ˈkʊku:/ *n.* куку́шка.
cucumber /ˈkju:kʌmbə(r)/ *n.* огуре́ц.
cuddle /ˈkʌd(ə)l/ *v.t.* (& *i.*) обнима́ть(ся).
cue[1] /kju:/ *n.* (*theatr.*) ре́плика.
cue[2] /kju:/ *n.* (*sport*) кий.
cuff /kʌf/ *n.*
1 (*part of sleeve*) манже́та; **off the ~** (*fig.*) экспро́мтом.
2 (*US, trouser turnup*) отворо́т.
■ *cpd.* **~links** *n. pl.* за́понки (*f. pl.*).
cuisine /kwɪˈzi:n/ *n.* (*национальная*) ку́хня.
cul-de-sac /ˈkʌldəsæk/ *n.* (*also fig.*) тупи́к.
culinary /ˈkʌlɪnərɪ/ *adj.* кулина́рный.
cull /kʌl/ *n.* (*of seals*) отбо́р, брако́вка.
■ *v.t.* 1 (*select*) от|бира́ть, -обра́ть; под|бира́ть, -обра́ть; (*flowers etc.*) соб|ира́ть, -ра́ть.
2 (*slaughter*) бить (*impf.*).
culminate /ˈkʌlmɪneɪt/ *v.i.*: **~ in** заверш|а́ться, -и́ться + *i.*
culpable /ˈkʌlpəb(ə)l/ *adj.* вино́вный.
culprit /ˈkʌlprɪt/ *n.* престу́пник.
cult /kʌlt/ *n.* культ.
cultivate /ˈkʌltɪveɪt/ *v.t.* (*land*) возде́л|ывать, -ать; (*crops*) культиви́ровать (*impf.*).
cultivator /ˈkʌltɪveɪtə(r)/ *n.* (*person*) земледе́лец; (*implement*) культива́тор.
cultural /ˈkʌltʃər(ə)l/ *adj.* культу́рный.
culture /ˈkʌltʃə(r)/ *n.* (*civilization*) культу́ра, быт.
cultured /ˈkʌltʃəd/ *adj.* (*of person*) интеллиге́нтный, культу́рный.
cumbersome /ˈkʌmbəsəm/ *adj.* громо́здкий, обремени́тельный.
cumin /ˈkʌmɪn/ *n.* тмин.
cumulative /ˈkju:mjʊlətɪv/ *adj.* кумуляти́вный.
cunning /ˈkʌnɪŋ/ *n.* хи́трость.
■ *adj.* (**cunninger, cunningest**) хи́трый.
cunt /kʌnt/ *n.* (*vulg.*) (*genitals*) пизда́ (*vulg.*); (*as term of abuse*) су́ка.
cup /kʌp/ *n.* ча́шка, (*liter.*) ча́ша.
■ *v.t.* (**cupped, cupping**): **~ one's hand** держа́ть (*impf.*) ру́ку го́рстью.
cupboard /ˈkʌbəd/ *n.* шкаф, буфе́т.
cupola /ˈkju:pələ/ *n.* ку́пол.
curable /ˈkjʊərəb(ə)l/ *adj.* излечи́мый.
curate /ˈkjʊərət/ *n.* вика́рий.
curator /kjʊəˈreɪtə(r)/ *n.* (*of museum etc.*) храни́тель (*m.*).
curb /kə:b/ *n.*
1 узда́.
2 = **kerb**
■ *v.t.* (*fig.*) обузд|ывать, -а́ть.
curd /kə:d/ *n.* творо́г; **~ cheese** (*Br.*) творо́г.
curdle /ˈkə:d(ə)l/ *v.i.* свёр|тываться, -ну́ться.
cure /ˈkjʊə(r)/ *n.* лека́рство, сре́дство.

■ *v.t.* 1 (*make healthy*) выле́чивать, вы́лечить; **he was ~d of asthma** он вы́лечился от а́стмы.
2 (*remedy*): (*disease*) выле́чивать, вы́лечить.
3 (*meat*) соли́ть, по-; вя́лить, про-.

curfew /'kɜ:fju:/ *n.* коменда́нтский час.

curiosity /kjʊərɪ'ɒsɪtɪ/ *n.* любопы́тство, любозна́тельность.

curious /'kjʊərɪəs/ *adj.*
1 (*inquisitive*) любопы́тный, любозна́тельный.
2 (*odd*) стра́нный; **~ly enough** как ни стра́нно.

curl /kɜ:l/ *n.* (*of hair*) ло́кон, завито́к.
■ *v.t.*: **~ one's hair** зав|ива́ть, -и́ть во́лосы.
■ *v.i.*: **her hair ~s naturally** у неё во́лосы вью́тся от приро́ды; **the dog ~ed up by the fire** соба́ка сверну́лась клубко́м у ками́на.

curlers /'kɜ:ləz/ *n.* бигуди́ (*pl., indecl.*).

curly /'kɜ:lɪ/ *adj.* (**curlier, curliest**) кудря́вый.

currant /'kʌrənt/ *n.* изю́м, кори́нка.

currency /'kʌrənsɪ/ *n.* валю́та; де́н|ьги (*pl., g.* -ег).

current /'kʌrənt/ *n.*
1 (*of air, water*) струя́, пото́к.
2 (*elec.*) ток.
■ *adj.* 1 (*of present time*) теку́щий; **~ affairs, events** теку́щие собы́тия; **the ~ issue of a magazine** теку́щий/очередно́й но́мер журна́ла.
2 : **~ account** (*Br., comm.*) теку́щий счёт.

currently /'kʌrəntlɪ/ *adv.* тепе́рь, в настоя́щее вре́мя.

curricul|um /kə'rɪkjʊləm/ *n.* (*pl.* **~a**) курс обуче́ния; **~ vitae** (кра́ткая) биогра́фия.

curry[1] /'kʌrɪ/ *n.* (*cul.*) ка́рри (*nt. indecl.*).

curry[2] /'kʌrɪ/ *v.t.*: **~ favour with s.o.** подли́з|ываться, -а́ться к кому́-н.

curse /kɜ:s/ *n.*
1 (*execration*) прокля́тие.
2 (*bane*) прокля́тие, бич.
3 (*oath*) богоху́льство.
■ *v.t.* 1 (*pronounce ~ on*) прокл|ина́ть, -я́сть.
2 (*abuse, scold*) руга́ть (*impf.*).
3 : **he is ~d with a violent temper** Госпо́дь награди́л его́ необу́зданным нра́вом.
■ *v.i.* (*swear, utter ~s*) руга́ться (*impf.*).

cursor /'kɜ:sə(r)/ *n.* (*comput.*) курсо́р.

cursory /'kɜ:sərɪ/ *adj.* бе́глый, пове́рхностный.

curt /kɜ:t/ *adj.* отры́вистый, ре́зкий.

curtail /kɜ:'teɪl/ *v.t.* сокра|ща́ть, -ти́ть.

curtain /'kɜ:t(ə)n/ *n.* занаве́ска, што́ра.

curts(e)y /'kɜ:tsɪ/ *n.*ревера́нс, приседа́ние.
■ *v.i.* прис|еда́ть, -е́сть.

curve /kɜ:v/ *n.* (*line*) крива́я; (*bend in road*) изги́б.
■ *v.t.* сгиба́ть, согну́ть.
■ *v.i.* из|гиба́ться, -огну́ться; **the road ~s** доро́га извива́ется.

cushion /'kʊʃ(ə)n/ *n.* (дива́нная) поду́шка.
■ *v.t.*: **~ a blow** смягч|а́ть, -и́ть уда́р.

cushy /'kʊʃɪ/ *adj.* (**cushier, cushiest**) (*coll.*): **~ job** непы́льная рабо́та.

cusp /kʌsp/ *n.* (*of moon*) рог; (*of leaf*) о́стрый коне́ц; (*of tooth*) ко́нчик.

custard /'kʌstəd/ *n.* сла́дкий крем/со́ус из яи́ц и молока́.

custodian /kʌ'stəʊdɪən/ *n.* (*of property etc.*) администра́тор; (*of museum etc.*) храни́тель (*m.*).

custody /'kʌstədɪ/ *n.*
1 (*guardianship*) опе́ка, попече́ние.
2 (*arrest*): **take, give into ~** брать, взять под стра́жу.

custom /'kʌstəm/ *n.*
1 (*habit*) обы́чай.
2 (*Br., clientele*) клиенту́ра.
3 (*pl., establishment*) тамо́жня; (*pl., duties*) тамо́женные по́шлины (*f. pl.*); **~s officer** тамо́женник.
■ *cpd.* **~-made** *adj.* сде́ланный/изгото́вленный на зака́з.

customary /'kʌstəmərɪ/ *adj.* обы́чный, привы́чный.

customer /'kʌstəmə(r)/ *n.* (*purchaser*) покупа́тель (*m.*).

customize /'kʌstəmaɪz/ *v.t.* под|гоня́ть, -огна́ть в соотве́тствии с тре́бованиями зака́зчика; изгот|а́вливать, -о́вить по индивидуа́льному зака́зу.

cut /kʌt/ *n.*
1 (*act of ~ting*) ре́зка; (*in finger*) поре́з; (*slit*) разре́з.
2 (*reduction*) сниже́ние.
3 (*omission*) купю́ра.
■ *v.t.* (**cutting;** *past and p.p.* **~**)
1 (*divide, separate, wound, extract by ~ting*) ре́зать (*impf.*); разр|еза́ть, -е́зать; отр|еза́ть, -е́зать; **he ~ himself on the tin** он поре́зался/пора́нился о консе́рвную ба́нку; **~ sth. in two** разр|еза́ть, -е́зать что-н. попола́м.
2 (*make by ~ting*): **~ me a piece of cake** отре́жьте мне кусо́к то́рта; **~ a key** выта́чивать, вы́точить ключ; **~ a jewel** грани́ть, о- драгоце́нный ка́мень; **~ glass** гранёное стекло́; хруста́ль (*m.*).
3 (*trim*) подстр|ига́ть, -и́чь; **~ one's nails** подстр|ига́ть, -и́чь но́гти; **have one's hair ~** стри́чься, по-.
4 (*reduce*) сн|ижа́ть, -и́зить.
5 : **the baby ~ a tooth** у ребёнка проре́зался зуб.
■ *v.i.* (**cutting;** *past and p.p.* **~**)
1 (*make incision*) ре́зать (*impf.*); **this knife doesn't ~** э́тот нож не ре́жет.
2 (*in pass. sense*) ре́заться (*impf.*); **sandstone ~s easily** песча́ник легко́ ре́жется.
3 (*run, take short ~*): **we ~ across the fields** мы прошли́ кратча́йшим путём, напряму́ю че́рез поля́.
■ *with advs.*: **~ back** *v.t.* (*prune*) подр|еза́ть, -е́зать; (*fig, reduce, limit*) сокра|ща́ть, -ти́ть; **~ down** *v.t.* (*e.g. a tree*) руби́ть, с-; **~ down expenses** сокра|ща́ть, -ти́ть расхо́ды; **~ off** *v.t.*: **he ~ the chicken's head off** он отруби́л цыплёнку го́лову; **I was ~ off while talking** меня́ разъедини́ли/прерва́ли во вре́мя разгово́ра; **they ~ off our electricity** у нас отключи́ли/вы́ключили электри́чество; **we were ~ off by the tide** прили́в отре́зал нас от су́ши; **he ~ himself off from the world** он отгороди́лся от ми́ра; **~ out** *v.t.*: **he ~ out a picture from the paper** он вы́резал карти́нку из газе́ты;

~ **out smoking** бро́сить (*pf.*) кури́ть; ~ **up** *v.t.*: **he ~ up his meat** он наре́зал мя́со.
■ *cpds.* ~ **and paste** *v.t.* (*comput.*) вы́резать и вста́вить; **~back** *n.* (*reduction*) сокраще́ние; **~-price** *adj.* продава́емый по сни́женной цене́; **~-rate** (*US*) = **cut-price; ~-throat** *n.* головоре́з; **~-throat competition** ожесточённая/беспоща́дная конкуре́нция.

cute /kjuːt/ *adj.* симпати́чный, ми́лый.

cutlery /ˈkʌtlərɪ/ *n.* столо́вые прибо́ры.

cutlet /ˈkʌtlɪt/ *n.* отбивна́я котле́та.

cutting /ˈkʌtɪŋ/ *n.*
1 (*Br., press* ~) вы́резка.
2 (*of plant*) отро́сток.
■ *adj.*: **a ~ retort** язви́тельный/ре́зкий отве́т; **the ~ edge of technology** са́мая совреме́нная те́хника.

C.V. (*abbr. of* ***curriculum vitae***) (кра́ткая) автобиогра́фия.

cyanide /ˈsaɪənaɪd/ *n.* циани́д.

cybercafe /ˈsaɪbəkæfeɪ/ *n.* интерне́т-кафе́.

cybercrime /ˈsaɪbəkraɪm/ *n.* (*comput.*)
1 (*offence*) киберпреступле́ние.
2 (*collect.*) киберпресту́пность.

cybernetics /saɪbəˈnetɪks/ *n.* киберне́тика.

cyberspace /ˈsaɪbəspeɪs/ *n.* киберпростра́нство.

cyclamen /ˈsɪkləmən/ *n.* (*pl.* ~ *or* **~s**) циклaméн.

cycle /ˈsaɪk(ə)l/ *n.*
1 (*series, rotation*) цикл, круг.
2 (*bicycle*) велосипе́д.
■ *v.i.* е́здить (*indet.*) на велосипе́де.
■ *cpd.* ~ **lane** *n.* (*Br.*) велосипе́дная доро́жка.

cyclic(al) /ˈsɪklɪk, ˈsɪklɪk(ə)l/ *adj.* цикли́ческий.

cycling /ˈsaɪklɪŋ/ *n.* езда́ на велосипе́де.

cyclist /ˈsaɪklɪst/ *n.* велосипеди́ст.

cyclone /ˈsaɪkləʊn/ *n.* цикло́н.

cygnet /ˈsɪɡnɪt/ *n.* молодо́й ле́бедь.

cylinder /ˈsɪlɪndə(r)/ *n.* цили́ндр.

cylindrical /sɪˈlɪndrɪk(ə)l/ *adj.* цилиндри́ческий.

cymbal /ˈsɪmb(ə)l/ *n.* таре́лка (*музыкальный инструмент*).

cynic /ˈsɪnɪk/ *n.* ци́ник.

cynical /ˈsɪnɪk(ə)l/ *adj.* цини́чный.

cynicism /ˈsɪnɪsɪz(ə)m/ *n.* цини́зм.

cypress /ˈsaɪprəs/ *n.* кипари́с.

Cypriot /ˈsɪprɪət/ *n.* киприо́т (*fem.* -ка).
■ *adj.* ки́прский.

Cyprus /ˈsɑɪprəs/ *n.* Кипр.

Cyrillic /sɪˈrɪlɪk/ *adj.* кирилли́ческий; ~ **alphabet** кири́ллица.

cyst /sɪst/ *n.* киста́.

cystitis /sɪˈstaɪtɪs/ *n.* цисти́т.

cytology /saɪˈtɒlədʒɪ/ *n.* цитоло́гия.

czar /zɑː(r)/ = **tsar, tzar**

Czech /tʃek/ *n.* чех (*fem.* че́шка); (*language*) че́шский язы́к.
■ *adj.* че́шский; ~ **Republic** Че́хия.

Dd

D /diː/ *n.*
1 (*mus.*) ре (*nt. indecl.*).
2 (*acad. mark*) «неудовлетвори́тельно», дво́йка.
■ *cpd.* **~-Day** *n.* день (*m.*) нача́ла вое́нной опера́ции, день «Д».

dab /dæb/ *n.* (*small quantity*) мазо́к.
■ *v.t. & i.* (**dabbed, dabbing**) при|кла́дывать, -ложи́ть; **she ~bed (at) her eyes with a handkerchief** она́ прикла́дывала к глаза́м плато́к.

dabble /ˈdæb(ə)l/ *v.i.*: **he ~s in politics** он игра́ет в поли́тику.

dacha /ˈdætʃə/ *n.* да́ча.

dachshund /ˈdækshʊnd/ *n.* та́кса (*порода собак*).

dad /dæd/, **-dy** /ˈdædɪ/ *nn.* (*coll.*) па́па (*m.*), па́почка (*m.*).

daddy /ˈdædɪ/ = **dad**

daffodil /ˈdæfədɪl/ *n.* нарци́сс жёлтый.

daft /dɑːft/ *adj.* (*Br.*) (*person*) тро́нутый (*coll.*); (*action*) бестолко́вый, глу́пый.

Dagestan /dæɡɪˈstɑːn/ *n.* Дагеста́н.

Dagestani /dæɡɪˈstɑːnɪ/ *n.* (*pl.* **~s**) дагеста́н|ец (*fem.* -ка).
■ *adj.* дагеста́нский.

dagger /ˈdæɡə(r)/ *n.* кинжа́л; **she looked ~s at him** она́ пронзи́ла его́ взгля́дом.

dahlia /ˈdeɪlɪə/ *n.* георги́н.

daily /ˈdeɪlɪ/ *n.* (*newspaper*) ежедне́вная газе́та.
■ *adj.* ежедне́вный.
■ *adv.* ежедне́вно, ка́ждый день.

dainty /ˈdeɪntɪ/ *n.* ла́комство, деликате́с.
■ *adj.* (**daintier, daintiest**) (*refined, delicate*) изя́щный, изы́сканный.

dairy /ˈdeərɪ/ *n.*
1 (*room or building*) маслоде́льня.
2 (*shop*) моло́чный магази́н; (*attr.*) моло́чный.

daisy /ˈdeɪzɪ/ *n.* маргари́тка.

dally /ˈdælɪ/ *v.i.*
1 (*play, toy*) балова́ться (*impf.*) (**with:** + *i.*).
2 (*flirt*) флиртова́ть (*impf.*).
3 (*waste time*) тра́тить (*impf.*) вре́мя по́пусту.

Dalmatian /dælˈmeɪʃ(ə)n/ *n.* (*dog*) далма́тский дог, далмати́н.

dam /dæm/ *n.* да́мба, плоти́на, запру́да.

damage /ˈdæmɪdʒ/ *n.*
1 (*harm, injury*) вред, повреждéние.
2 (*pl., leg.*) убы́тк|и (*pl., g.* -ов).
■ *v.t.* (*physically*) повре|ждáть, -ди́ть + *d.*; (*morally*) вреди́ть, на-, причин|я́ть, -и́ть вред + *d.*

dame /deɪm/ *n.*
1 (*fem. eqv. of knight*) дейм, кавалéрственная дáма.
2 (*US coll., woman*) бабёнка (*coll.*).

damn /dæm/ *n.* (*negligible amount*): **I don't care a ~** мне наплевáть.
■ *v.t.* 1 (*doom to hell*) прокл|инáть, -я́сть.
2 (*as expletive*): **~ (it all)!** чёрт возьми́!

damned /dæmd/ *n., adj. & adv.*: **a ~ fool** пóлный дурáк; **it's a ~ nuisance** (э́то) чертóвски досáдно.

damp /dæmp/ *n.* влáжность, сы́рость.
■ *adj.* влáжный, сырóй.
■ *v.t.* (*also* **dampen**)
1 (*lit.*) см|áчивать, -очи́ть; увлажн|я́ть, -и́ть.
2 (*fig.*): **~ s.o.'s ardour** осту|жáть, -ди́ть чей-н. пыл.

dance /dɑːns/ *n.*
1 тáнец.
2 (*party*) танцевáльный вéчер; тáнцы (*m. pl.*).
■ *v.t.* танцевáть, с-.
■ *v.i.* танцевáть, с-; плясáть, с-.

dancer /ˈdɑːnsə(r)/ *n.* (*professional*) танцóр, танцóвщи|к (*fem.* -ца); (*non-professional*): **she's a good ~** онá хорошó танцýет.

dancing /ˈdɑːnsɪŋ/ *n.* тáнцы (*m. pl.*).

dandelion /ˈdændɪlaɪən/ *n.* одувáнчик.

dandruff /ˈdændrʌf/ *n.* пéрхоть.

dandy /ˈdændɪ/ *n.* дéнди (*m. indecl.*), щёголь (*m.*), франт.
■ *adj.* (**dandier, dandiest**) (*US coll.*) превосхóдный; пéрвый класс (*pred.*).

Dane /deɪn/ *n.* датчáн|ин (*fem.* -ка).

danger /ˈdeɪndʒə(r)/ *n.* опáсность; **in ~** в опáсности; **he is in ~ of falling** он рискýет упáсть.

dangerous /ˈdeɪndʒərəs/ *adj.* опáсный, рискóванный.

dangle /ˈdæŋg(ə)l/ *v.t.* болтáть (*impf.*) + *i.*
■ *v.i.* болтáться (*impf.*).

Danish /ˈdeɪnɪʃ/ *n.* (*language*) дáтский язы́к.
■ *adj.* дáтский.

dank /dæŋk/ влáжный, сырóй.

dapper /ˈdæpə(r)/ *adj.* щеголевáтый.

dare /deə(r)/ *n.* вы́зов.
■ *v.t.* бр|осáть, -óсить вы́зов + *d.*; **I ~ you to jump over the wall!** а ну, перепры́гни чéрез э́ту стéну!
■ *v.i.* 1 (*have courage*) осмéли|ваться, -ться.
2 (*have impudence*) сметь, по-.
3: **I ~ say (that) ...** нáдо ду́мать (*or* полагáю), что... .
■ *cpd.* **~devil** *adj.* отчáянный, бесшабáшный.

daring /ˈdeərɪŋ/ *adj.* отвáжный, дéрзкий.

dark /dɑːk/ *n.* темнотá, тьма; **before/after ~** до/пóсле наступлéния темноты́; (*ignorance*): **I am in the ~ as to his plans** я в невéдении относи́тельно егó плáнов.
■ *adj.* 1 (*lacking light*) тёмный; **~ glasses** (*spectacles*) тёмные/сóлнечные очки́.
2 (*in colour*) тёмный; тёмного цвéта; **~-haired** темноволóсый; **~-skinned** темнокóжий; (*with names of colours*) тёмно-; **~ blue** тёмно-си́ний; **~ green** тёмно-зелёный.
3 (*of complexion*) сму́глый.
4 (*fig.*) тёмный, покры́тый мрáком.

darken /ˈdɑːkən/ *v.t.* затемн|я́ть, -и́ть.
■ *v.i.* темнéть, по-.

darkness /ˈdɑːknɪs/ *n.* темнотá.

darling /ˈdɑːlɪŋ/ *n.* дорогóй, ми́лый, роднóй, люби́мый; **she's a ~** онá прéлесть.

darn /dɑːn/ *v.t. & i.* (*mend*) штóпать, за-.

dart /dɑːt/ *n.* стрелá, дрóтик.
■ *cpd.* **~board** *n.* мишéнь для стрел.

dash /dæʃ/ *n.*
1 (*sudden rush, race*) рывóк, бросóк; **let's make a ~ for it** давáй(те) побежи́м тудá.
2 (*admixture*): **a ~ of pepper** щепóтка пéрца.
3 (*written stroke*) тирé (*indecl.*).
■ *v.t.* 1 (*throw violently*) швыр|я́ть, -нýть; **the ship was ~ed against the rocks** сýдно вы́бросило на скáлы.
2 (*perform rapidly*): **he ~ed off a sketch** он сдéлал набрóсок.
3 (*fig., disappoint*) разр|ушáть, -ýшить; **his hopes were ~ed** егó надéжды ру́хнули.
■ *v.i.* мчáться (*impf.*); **she ~ed into the shop** онá ворвалáсь в магази́н; **he ~ed off to town** он умчáлся в гóрод.

dashboard /ˈdæʃbɔːd/ *n.* прибóрная панéль/доскá.

dashing /ˈdæʃɪŋ/ *adj.* сти́льный.

data /ˈdeɪtə/ *n.* (*sg. or pl.*) дáнные (*nt. pl.*); **~ capture** сбор дáнных; **~ processing** обрабóтка информáции.

database /ˈdeɪtəbeɪs/ *n.* бáза дáнных.

date[1] /deɪt/ *n.* (*fruit*) фи́ник.

date[2] /deɪt/ *n.*
1 (*indication of time*) дáта, числó; **what's the ~ today?** какóе сегóдня числó?
2 (*period*) перúод; **at an early ~** (*soon*) в ближáйшем бýдущем; **out of ~** устарéлый; **up to ~** новéйший, совремéнный.
3 (*appointment*) свидáние.
■ *v.t.* 1 (*indicate ~ on*) дати́ровать (*impf., pf.*).
2 (*US, go out with*) встречáться (*impf.*) с + *i.*; **dating agency** агéнтство знакóмств.
■ *v.i.*: **this church ~s from the 14th century** э́та цéрковь относи́тся к XIV вéку.

dated /ˈdeɪtɪd/ *adj.* (*out of date*) устарéвший, устарéлый.

dative /ˈdeɪtɪv/ *adj. & n.* дáтельный (падéж).

daughter /ˈdɔːtə(r)/ *n.* дочь.
■ *cpd.* **~-in-law** *n.* невéстка, снохá.

daunt /dɔːnt/ *v.t.* устраш|áть, -и́ть; обескурáжи|вать, -ть.

dawdle /ˈdɔːd(ə)l/ *v.i.* мéшкать (*impf.*).

dawn /dɔːn/ *n.* рассвéт, заря́; **at ~** на рассвéте; на зарé.
■ *v.i.* 1 (*of daybreak*) светáть (*impf.*).
2 (*fig.*): **it ~ed on me that...** меня́ осени́ло, что... .

day /deɪ/ *n.*
1 (*time of daylight*) день (*m.*); (*attr.*) дневнóй; **twice a ~** два рáза в день.
2 (*24 hours*) день (*m.*), сýт|ки (*pl., g.* -ок); **a ~**

and a half полтора́ дня.
3 (*as point of time*): **what ~ (of the week) is it?** како́й сего́дня день (неде́ли)?; **one ~** (*past*) одна́жды; (*future*) когда́-нибудь; **every other ~** че́рез день; **some ~** когда́-нибу́дь;**~ in, ~ out; ~ after ~** изо дня в день; **(on) the ~ I met you** в день на́шей встре́чи; **(on) the ~ before** накану́не (*чего*); **I took a ~ off** я взял выходно́й; **we had a ~ out** (*Br.*) мы провели́ день вне до́ма.
4 (*as work period*): **he works a 5-hour ~** у него́ пятичасово́й рабо́чий день.
5 (*period*) пора́, вре́мя (*nt.*); **these ~s** (*nowadays*) тепе́рь, в на́ши дни; **in those ~s** в те дни; в то вре́мя.
6 (*denoting contest*): **his arrival saved the ~** его́ прие́зд спас положе́ние.
■ *cpds.* **~break** *n.* рассве́т; **~care** *adj.*: **~-care facilities** (*for children*) детса́д; (*for babies, toddlers*) я́сл|и (*pl., g.* -ей); **~dream** *n.* грёза, мечта́; *v.i.* мечта́ть (*impf.*); **~light** *n.* (*period*): **in broad ~light** средь бе́ла дня; **~ nursery** *n.* (*crèche*) де́тские я́сл|и (*pl., g.* -ей); **~time** *n.* день (*m.*); **in the ~time** днём; *adj.* дневно́й; **~-to-~** *adj.* повседне́вный.

daze /deɪz/ *n.*: **he was in a ~** он был поражён/как в тума́не.
■ *v.t.* пора|жа́ть, -зи́ть.

dazzle /'dæz(ə)l/ *v.t.*
1 (*lit.*) ослеп|ля́ть, -и́ть.
2 (*fig.*) пора|жа́ть, -зи́ть.

dB (*abbr. of* ***decibel(s)***) дБ (децибе́л).

DC (*abbr. of* ***direct current***) постоя́нный ток.

deacon /'di:kən/ *n.* дья́кон.

dead /ded/ *n.*: **at ~ of night** глубо́кой но́чью.
■ *adj.* 1 (*no longer living*) мёртвый, уме́рший; (*in accident etc.*) поги́бший, уби́тый; (*of animal*) до́хлый; **~ body** труп, мёртвое те́ло; **~ flowers/leaves** увя́дшие цветы́/ли́стья; **he is ~** он у́мер; (*killed*) он уби́т; (*as n.*: **the ~**) уме́ршие, поко́йные.
2 (*inert*) **~ end** (*lit., fig.*) тупи́к; **a ~-end job** бесперспекти́вная рабо́та.
3 (*spent, uncharged*): **the telephone went ~** телефо́н отключи́лся.
4 (*abrupt, exact, complete*) внеза́пный; **~ loss** (*fig., failure*) по́лный прова́л; **he's a ~ loss** он неуда́чник, от него́ то́лку не бу́дет; **a ~ certainty** по́лная уве́ренность.
■ *adv.*: **he stopped ~** он останови́лся как вко́панный; **~ on time** мину́та в мину́ту; **~ tired** смерте́льно уста́лый; **he is ~ set on going to London** он реши́л пое́хать в Ло́ндон во что бы то ни ста́ло.
■ *cpds.* **~line** *n.* преде́льный/кра́йний срок; **~lock** *n.* мёртвая то́чка; тупи́к; **~pan** *adj.* (*coll.*) невырази́тельный.

deaden /'ded(ə)n/ *v.t.* осл|абля́ть, -а́бить; **the drug ~s pain** лека́рство притупля́ет боль.

deadly /'dedlɪ/ *adj.* (**deadlier, deadliest**) смерте́льный; **~ enemy** смерте́льный враг.

deaf /def/ *adj.*
1 глухо́й; **~ mute** глухонемо́й; (*as n.*: **the ~**) глухи́е.
2 (*fig.*): **turn a ~ ear to** не слу́шать (*impf.*); не обраща́ть (*impf.*) внима́ния на + *a.*
■ *cpd.* **~ aid** *n.* (*Br.*) слухово́й аппара́т.

deafening /'defənɪŋ/ *adj.* оглуши́тельный.

deal /di:l/ *n.*
1 (*amount*) коли́чество; **a great, good ~ (of)** мно́го + *g.*
2 (*business agreement*) сде́лка; **it's a ~!** договори́лись!; по рука́м!
■ *v.t.* (*past and p.p.* **dealt**) (*cards*) сда|ва́ть, -ть.
■ *v.i.* (*past and p.p.* **dealt**)
1 (*do business*) торгова́ть (*impf.*); **he ~s in furs** он торгу́ет меха́ми.
2 : **~ with** (*treat*) обраща́ться с + *i.*; (*impf.*); (*cope with*) справля́ться, спра́виться с + *i.*; **he ~t with the problem skilfully** он уме́ло подошёл к э́тому вопро́су.
3 : **~ with** (*discuss a subject etc.*) (*of person*) зан|има́ться, -я́ться (*impf.*) + *i.*; (*of book*) рассм|а́тривать, -отре́ть.

dealer /'di:lə(r)/ *n.* торго́вец, ди́лер.

dealing /'di:lɪŋ/ *n.*
1 (*trade*): **~ in real estate** торго́вля недви́жимостью.
2 (*pl., association*) торго́вые дела́; сде́лки (*f. pl.*).

dealt /delt/ *past and p.p of* ▸ **deal**

dean /di:n/ *n.* (*eccl.*) дека́н, настоя́тель (*m.*); (*acad.*) дека́н.

dear /dɪə(r)/ *n.* ми́лый, дорого́й.
■ *adj.* 1 (*beloved*) люби́мый, дорого́й.
2 (*lovable*) сла́вный, ми́лый.
3 (*in informal letters*) дорого́й; (*in formal letters*) уважа́емый.
4 (*costly*) дорого́й.
■ *int.*: **oh ~!; ~ me!** о, го́споди!; бо́же ты мой!

dearly /'dɪəlɪ/ *adv.* (*fondly*) не́жно; (*at a high price*) до́рого.

dearth /də:θ/ *n.* нехва́тка, недоста́ток.

death /deθ/ *n.*
1 (*act or fact of dying*) смерть; **~ penalty** сме́ртная казнь; **drink o.s. to ~** ум|ира́ть, -ере́ть от пья́нства; **work o.s. to ~** рабо́тать (*impf.*) на изно́с; **at ~'s door** на поро́ге сме́рти.
2 (*instance of dying*) ги́бель.
3 (*utmost limit*): **he was bored to ~** ему́ бы́ло до́ смерти ску́чно; **I'm sick to ~ of it** мне э́то надое́ло до́ смерти.
■ *cpds.* **~bed** *n.* сме́ртное ло́же; **~ toll** *n.* число́ поги́бших; **~ trap** *n.*: **this theatre is a ~ trap in case of fire** в слу́чае пожа́ра э́тот теа́тр су́щая западня́.

deathly /'deθlɪ/ *adj. & adv.* (**deathlier, deathliest**) смерте́льный; **~ pale** смерте́льно бле́дный; **~ silence** мёртвая тишина́.

debar /dɪ'bɑ:(r)/ *v.t.* (**debarred, debarring**) препя́тствовать, вос- + *d.*

debarkation /di:bɑ:'keɪʃ(ə)n/ *n.* = **disembarkation**

debatable /dɪ'beɪtəb(ə)l/ *adj.* спо́рный.

debate /dɪ'beɪt/ *n.* диску́ссия; (*in parliament*) деба́т|ы (*pl., g.* -ов).

debauch /dɪ'bɔ:tʃ/ *v.t.*
1 (*pervert morally*) развра|ща́ть, -ти́ть.
2 (*seduce*) совра|ща́ть, -ти́ть; обол|ьща́ть, -сти́ть.

debauchery /dɪ'bɔ:tʃərɪ/ *n.* развра́т, распу́щенность.

debit /'debɪt/ *n.* де́бет.

■ *v.t.* (**debited, debiting**) дебетова́ть (*impf., pf.*).
debonair /debə'neə(r)/ *adj.* обходи́тельный, учти́вый.
debrief /di:'bri:f/ *v.t.* расспр|а́шивать, -оси́ть; **~ s.o.** заслу́ш|ивать, -ать чей-н. отчёт.
debris /'debri:/ *n.* оско́лки (*m. pl.*); обло́мки (*m. pl.*).
debt /det/ *n.* долг; **get into ~** входи́ть, войти́ в долги́.
debtor /'detə(r)/ *n.* должни́к.
debugger *n.* /di:'bʌgə(r)/ (*comput.*) програ́мма отла́дки, отла́дчик.
debunk /di:'bʌŋk/ *v.t.* (*coll.*) разве́нч|ивать, -а́ть.
debut /'deɪbju:/ *n.* дебю́т.
debutante /'debju:tɑ:nt/ *n.* (*making first appearance in fashionable society*) де́вушка, впервы́е выезжа́ющая в свет; (*theatr., sport*) дебюта́нтка.
decade /'dekeɪd/ *n.* десятиле́тие.
decadence /'dekəd(ə)ns/ *n.* упа́док, декаде́нтство.
decadent /'dekəd(ə)nt/ *adj.* упа́дочный, декаде́нтский.
decaffeinated /di:'kæfɪneɪtɪd/ *adj.* без кофеи́на.
decant /dɪ'kænt/ *v.t.* (*pour wine*) сце́|живать, -ди́ть; перел|ива́ть, -и́ть (*из бутылки в графин*).
decanter /dɪ'kæntə(r)/ *n.* графи́н.
decapitate /dɪ'kæpɪteɪt/ *v.t.* обезгла́в|ливать, -ить.
decay /dɪ'keɪ/ *n.* разложе́ние; **tooth ~** разруше́ние зубо́в.
■ *v.i.* разл|ага́ться, -ожи́ться.
deceased /dɪ'si:st/ *adj.* поко́йный; *as n.*: **the ~** поко́йник.
deceit /dɪ'si:t/ *n.* обма́н, ложь.
deceitful /dɪ'si:tfʊl/ *adj.* обма́нчивый, лжи́вый.
deceive /dɪ'si:v/ *v.t.* & *i.* обма́н|ывать, -у́ть; **~ o.s.** обма́н|ываться, -у́ться.
December /dɪ'sembə(r)/ *n.* дека́брь (*m.*).
decency /'di:sənsɪ/ *n.* прили́чие.
decent /'di:s(ə)nt/ *adj.*
1 (*not obscene*) прили́чный, присто́йный.
2 (*proper, adequate*) прили́чный, подходя́щий.
3 (*Br. coll., kind, well-conducted*) поря́дочный.
decentralize /di:'sentrəlaɪz/ *v.t.* децентрализова́ть (*impf., pf.*).
deception /dɪ'sepʃ(ə)n/ *n.* обма́н.
deceptive /dɪ'septɪv/ *adj.* обма́нчивый.
decibel /'desɪbel/ *n.* децибе́л.
decide /dɪ'saɪd/ *v.t.* реш|а́ть, -и́ть; **~ a question** реш|а́ть, -и́ть вопро́с.
■ *v.i.* реш|а́ться, -и́ться; **~ between alternatives** де́лать, с- вы́бор; **~ on going** реши́ть (*pf.*) пое́хать; **~ against going** реши́ть (*pf.*) не е́хать.
deciduous /dɪ'sɪdjʊəs/ *adj.* ли́ственный, листопа́дный.
decimal /'desɪm(ə)l/ *adj.* десяти́чный; **~ point** запята́я, отделя́ющая це́лое от дро́би (*в странах английского языка в числах с десятичными дробями вместо запятой используется точка: 7,1 пишут как 7.1*).
decipher /dɪ'saɪfə(r)/ *v.t.* (*fig., make out*) раз|бира́ть, -обра́ть.
decision /dɪ'sɪʒ(ə)n/ *n.* реше́ние; **make, take, come to a ~** прин|има́ть, -я́ть реше́ние.
decisive /dɪ'saɪsɪv/ *adj.* реши́тельный.
decisiveness /dɪ'saɪsɪvnɪs/ *n.* реши́тельность.
deck /dek/ *n.*
1 (*of ship*) па́луба.
2 (*US, of cards*) коло́да.
■ *cpd.* **~chair** *n.* шезло́нг.
declaim /dɪ'kleɪm/ *v.t.* & *i.* деклами́ровать (*impf.*).
declaration /deklə'reɪʃ(ə)n/ *n.* деклара́ция.
declare /dɪ'kleə(r)/ *v.t.* & *i.*
1 (*say solemnly*) заяв|ля́ть, -и́ть; **he ~d that he was innocent** он заяви́л о свое́й невино́вности.
2 (*pronounce*) объяв|ля́ть, -и́ть; **I ~ the meeting open** объявля́ю собра́ние откры́тым.
3 (*at customs*) деклари́ровать (*impf., pf.*).
declassify /di:'klæsɪfaɪ/ *v.t.* рассекре́|чивать, -тить (*документы*).
declension /dɪ'klenʃ(ə)n/ *n.* (*gram.*) склоне́ние.
decline /dɪ'klaɪn/ *n.*
1 (*fall*) паде́ние.
2 (*decay*) упа́док, зака́т.
■ *v.t.* 1 отклон|я́ть, -и́ть; **he ~d the invitation** он отклони́л приглаше́ние.
2 (*gram.*) склоня́ть, про-.
■ *v.i.* 1 (*sink*) па́дать, упа́сть; при|ходи́ть, -йти́ в упа́док.
2 (*refuse*) отка́з|ываться, -а́ться.
decode /di:'kəʊd/ *v.t.* расшифро́в|ывать, -а́ть.
decompose /di:kəm'pəʊz/ *v.i.* (*decay*) разл|ага́ться, -ожи́ться.
decontaminate /di:kən'tæmɪneɪt/ *v.t.* обеззара́|живать, -зить; (*remove radioactivity from*) дезактиви́ровать (*impf., pf.*).
decor /'deɪkɔ:(r)/ *n.* (*of room*) убра́нство; (*of stage*) декора́ции (*f. pl.*).
decorate /'dekəreɪt/ *v.t.*
1 (*adorn*) укр|аша́ть, -а́сить (*impf.*).
2 (*paint, furnish etc.*) отде́л|ывать, -ать.
decoration /dekə'reɪʃ(ə)n/ *n.* украше́ние, убра́нство.
decorative /'dekərətɪv/ *adj.* декорати́вный.
decorator /'dekəreɪtə(r)/ *n.* (*painter*) маля́р, (*paperer*) окле́йщик обо́ев.
decorum /dɪ'kɔ:rəm/ *n.* вне́шнее прили́чие; этике́т, деко́рум.
decoy /'di:kɔɪ/ *v.t.* прима́н|ивать, -и́ть.
decrease *n.* /'di:kri:s/ уменьше́ние, убыва́ние.
■ *v.i.* /dɪ'kri:s/ ум|еньша́ться, -е́ньшиться; уб|ыва́ть, -ы́ть.
decree /dɪ'kri:/ *n.*
1 (*pol.*) ука́з.
2 (*leg.*) суде́бное реше́ние.
decrepit /dɪ'krepɪt/ *adj.* дря́хлый, ве́тхий.
dedicate /'dedɪkeɪt/ *v.t.* (*devote*) посвя|ща́ть, -ти́ть (*что-н. кому-н.*); (*assign*) предназн|ача́ть, -а́чить (*что-н. кому-н.*).
dedicated /'dedɪkeɪtɪd/ *adj.* пре́данный, беззаве́тный.
dedication /dedɪ'keɪʃ(ə)n/ *n.* (*devotion*) пре́данность, самоотве́рженность;

(*inscription*) посвящéние.
deduce /dɪ'dju:s/ *v.t.* выводи́ть, вы́вести; заключ|áть, -и́ть.
deduct /dɪ'dʌkt/ *v.t.* вычитáть, вы́честь.
deduction /dɪ'dʌkʃ(ə)n/ *n.* (*subtraction*) вы́чет; (*inference*) вы́вод, заключéние.
deed /di:d/ *n.*
1 (*sth. done*) дéйствие, постýпок.
2 (*leg.*) акт, докумéнт.
deem /di:m/ *v.t.* полагáть (*impf.*), считáть, счесть.
deep /di:p/ *adj.*
1 глубóкий.
2 (*with measurement*): **a hole 6 feet ~** я́ма глубинóй в 6 фýтов.
3 (*submerged, lit., fig.*): **~ in thought** задýмавшийся; погружённый в раздýмья.
4 (*extreme*) глубóкий.
5 (*of colour*) тёмный, насы́щенный.
6 (*low-pitched*) ни́зкий.
■ *adv.* глубокó.
■ *cpds.* **~-freeze** *n.* морози́льник; **~-fry** *v.t.* зажáри|вать, -ть; **~-rooted** *adj.*: **~-rooted belief** глубокó укорени́вшееся мнéние; **~-sea** *adj.*: **~-sea fishing** глубоковóдный лов; **~-vein thrombosis** *n.* (*med.*) тромбóз глубóких вен.
deepen /'di:pən/ *v.t.* & *i.*
1 (*make, become deeper*) углуб|ля́ть(ся), -и́ть(ся).
2 (*intensify*) уси́ли|вать(ся), -ть(ся).
3 (*make, become lower in pitch*) пон|ижáть(ся), -и́зить(ся).
deeply /'di:plɪ/ *adv.* глубокó; **he is ~ in debt** он влез в долги́ пó уши.
deer /dɪə(r)/ *n.* (*pl.* **~**) олéнь (*m.*).
deface /dɪ'feɪs/ *v.t.* искa|жáть, -зи́ть.
defamatory /dɪ'fæmətərɪ/ *adj.* клеветни́ческий.
default /dɪ'fɔ:lt/ *n.*
1 (*neglect*): **he won the match by ~** он вы́играл матч из-за нея́вки проти́вника.
2 (*comput.*) значéние по умолчáнию.
3 (*fin.*) дефóлт.
■ *v.i.* не выполня́ть, вы́полнить обя́зательства.
defeat /dɪ'fi:t/ *n.* поражéние.
■ *v.t.* нан|оси́ть, -ести́ поражéние + *d.*; **they were ~ed** они́ потерпéли поражéние.
defeatism /dɪ'fi:tɪz(ə)m/ *n.* поражéнчество.
defeatist /dɪ'fi:tɪst/ *n.* поражéнец; (*fig.*) пессими́ст.
■ *adj.* поражéнческий, пессимисти́ческий.
defecate /'defɪkeɪt/ *v.i.* испражн|я́ться, -и́ться.
defect[1] /'di:fekt/ *n.* дефéкт; порóк.
defect[2] /dɪ'fekt/ *v.i.* перебе|гáть, -жáть (**from:** от + *g.*; **to:** к + *d.*, на + *a.*).
defection /dɪ'fekʃ(ə)n/ *n.* дезерти́рство; **there were several ~s from the party** нéсколько человéк вы́шло/вы́шли из пáртии.
defective /dɪ'fektɪv/ *adj.* несовершéнный.
defector /dɪ'fektə(r)/ *n.* перебéжчи|к (*fem.* -ца).
defence /dɪ'fens/ (*US* **defense**) *n.* оборóна, защи́та; **in ~ of** в защи́ту + *g.*
defenceless /dɪ'fenslɪs/ (*US* **defenseless**) *adj.* беззащи́тный.
defend /dɪ'fend/ *v.t.* обороня́ть (*impf.*).
defendant /dɪ'fend(ə)nt/ *n.* ответчик.
defender /dɪ'fendə(r)/ *n.* защи́тник.
defense /dɪ'fens/ (*US*) = **defence**
defenseless /dɪ'fenslɪs/ (*US*) = **defenceless**
defensive /dɪ'fensɪv/ *adj.* оборони́тельный; **he has a ~ manner** он как бýдто оправдывается.
defer[1] /dɪ'fɜ:(r)/ *v.t.* (**deferred, deferring**) (*postpone*) отсрóчи|вать, -ть.
defer[2] /dɪ'fɜ:(r)/ *v.i.* (**deferred, deferring**): **~ to** считáться (*impf.*) с + *i.*
deference /'defərəns/ *n.* уважéние, почти́тельность.
deferential /defə'renʃ(ə)l/ *adj.* почти́тельный.
defiance /dɪ'faɪəns/ *n.* вы́зов; **in ~ of** вопреки́ + *d.*
defiant /dɪ'faɪənt/ *adj.* вызывáющий.
deficiency /dɪ'fɪʃənsɪ/ *n.*
1 (*lack*) нехвáтка, отсýтствие.
2 (*pl., shortcomings*) недостáтки (*m. pl.*).
deficient /dɪ'fɪʃ(ə)nt/ *adj.* недостáточный, непóлный.
deficit /'defɪsɪt/ *n.* дефици́т, недочёт.
defile /dɪ'faɪl/ *v.t.* оскверн|я́ть, -и́ть.
define /dɪ'faɪn/ *v.t.* определ|я́ть, -и́ть.
definite /'defɪnɪt/ *adj.*
1 (*specific*) определённый; **~ article** (*gram.*) определённый арти́кль.
2 (*clear, exact*) тóчный, чёткий.
definitely /'defɪnɪtlɪ/ *adv.* определённо, тóчно; **he is ~ coming** он непремéнно/тóчно придёт.
definition /defɪ'nɪʃ(ə)n/ *n.* (*clearness of outline*) я́сность, чёткость; (*statement of meaning*) определéние.
definitive /dɪ'fɪnɪtɪv/ *adj.* окончáтельный.
deflect /dɪ'flekt/ *v.t.* & *i.* отклон|я́ть(ся), -и́ть(ся).
deflection /dɪ'flekʃ(ə)n/ *n.* отклонéние.
deforestation /di:fɒrɪ'steɪʃ(ə)n/ *n.* обезлéсение.
deform /dɪ'fɔ:m/ *v.t.* урóдовать, из-.
defraud /dɪ'frɔ:d/ *v.t.* обмáн|ывать, -ýть.
defrost /di:'frɒst/ *v.t.* (*food, refrigerator*) размор|áживать, -óзить.
deft /deft/ *adj.* лóвкий, искýсный.
defunct /dɪ'fʌŋkt/ *adj.* несуществýющий, исчéзнувший.
defuse /di:'fju:z/ *v.t.* сн|имáть, -ять взрывáтель + *g.*; (*fig.*) разря|жáть, -ди́ть.
defy /dɪ'faɪ/ *v.t.*
1 (*challenge*) вызывáть, вы́звать.
2 (*fig.*): **the problem defies solution** проблéма неразреши́ма.
degenerate *adj.* /dɪ'dʒenərət/ вы́родившийся, дегенерати́вный.
■ *v.i.* /dɪ'dʒenəreɪt/ вырождáться, вы́родиться (*impf.*).
degradation /degrə'deɪʃ(ə)n/ *n.* (*moral*) упáдок, деградáция.
degrade /dɪ'greɪd/ *v.t.* прин|ижáть, -и́зить.
degrading /dɪ'greɪdɪŋ/ *adj.* унизи́тельный.
degree /dɪ'gri:/ *n.*
1 (*unit of measurement*) грáдус.

2 (*step, stage*) сте́пень; у́ровень (*m.*); **by ~s** постепе́нно; **to a ~** до изве́стной сте́пени.
3 (*acad.*) (учёная) сте́пень.

dehumanize /di:'hju:mənaɪz/ *v.t.* дегуманизи́ровать (*impf.*, *pf.*).

dehydrate /di:haɪ'dreɪt/ *v.t.* обезво́|живать, -дить.

de-icer /dɪ:'aɪsə(r)/ *n.* антиобледени́тель (*m.*).

deify /'deɪɪfaɪ/ *v.t.* обожеств|ля́ть, -и́ть; боготвори́ть, о-.

deign /deɪn/ *v.t.*: **he did not ~ to answer us** он не соизво́лил отве́тить нам.

deity /'deɪɪtɪ/ *n.* божество́.

dejected /dɪ'dʒektɪd/ *adj.* удручённый, пода́вленный.

delay /dɪ'leɪ/ *n.* заде́ржка, отсро́чка, промедле́ние; **without ~** неме́дленно.
■ *v.t.* от|кла́дывать, -ложи́ть.

delegate *n.* /'delɪgət/ делега́т, представи́тель (*m.*).
■ *v.t.* /'delɪgeɪt/: **~ s.o.** делеги́ровать (*impf.*, *pf.*) кого́-н.; **~ a task** поруч|а́ть, -и́ть рабо́ту (*кому*).

delegation /delɪ'geɪʃ(ə)n/ *n.* делега́ция.

delete /dɪ'li:t/ *v.t.* вычёркивать, вы́черкнуть; (*comput.*) удал|я́ть, -и́ть.

Delhi /'delɪ/ *n.* Де́ли (*m. indecl.*).

deliberate /dɪ'lɪbərət/ *adj.* (*intentional*) наме́ренный; (*slow*) осмотри́тельный.

deliberately /dɪ'lɪbərətlɪ/ *adv.* наме́ренно.

deliberation /dɪlɪbə'reɪʃ(ə)n/ *n.* (*pondering*) обду́мывание; (*pl.*) диску́ссия; (*slowness*) медли́тельность, неторопли́вость.

delicacy /'delɪkəsɪ/ *n.* (*exquisiteness*) утончённость, то́нкость; (*proneness to injury*) хру́пкость; (*critical nature*) щекотли́вость, делика́тность.

delicate /'delɪkət/ *adj.*
1 (*fine, exquisite*) то́нкий.
2 (*easily injured*) хру́пкий.

delicatessen /delɪkə'tes(ə)n/ *n.* гастроно́м.

delicious /dɪ'lɪʃəs/ *adj.* о́чень вку́сный.

delight /dɪ'laɪt/ *n.* удово́льствие, наслажде́ние; **take ~ in sth.** на|ходи́ть, -йти́ удово́льствие в чём-н.
■ *v.t.* дост|авля́ть, -а́вить наслажде́ние + *d.*; **I am ~ed to accept the invitation** я с ра́достью принима́ю приглаше́ние.

delightful /dɪ'laɪtfʊl/ *adj.* восхити́тельный, очарова́тельный.

delineate /dɪ'lɪnɪeɪt/ *v.t.* (*e.g. a frontier*) очéр|чивать, -ти́ть; (*e.g. character*) изобра|жа́ть, -зи́ть.

delinquency /dɪ'lɪŋkwənsɪ/ *n.* престу́пность.

delinquent /dɪ'lɪŋkwənt/ *n.* правонаруши́тель (*fem.* -ница).

delirious /dɪ'lɪrɪəs/ *adj.* в бреду́ (*pred.*)

delirium /dɪ'lɪrɪəm/ *n.* бред; **~ tremens** бе́лая горя́чка.

deliver /dɪ'lɪvə(r)/ *v.t.*
1 (*of birth*): **she delivered a child** (*assisted at birth*) она́ приняла́ ребёнка.
2 (*give, present*): **~ judgment** выноси́ть, вы́нести реше́ние; **~ a speech** произн|оси́ть, -ести́ речь.
3 (*send out, convey*) дост|авля́ть, -а́вить.

delivery /dɪ'lɪvərɪ/ *n.*
1 (*childbirth*) ро́д|ы (*pl.*, *g.* -ов).
2 (*distribution*) доста́вка; **charges payable on ~** опла́та при доста́вке.

delphinium /del'fɪnɪəm/ *n.* (*pl.* **~s**) (*bot.*) дельфи́ниум.

delta /'deltə/ *n.* де́льта.

delude /dɪ'lu:d/ *v.t.* вв|оди́ть, -ести́ в заблужде́ние; **he ~d himself into believing that ...** он уве́рил себя́ в то́м, что... .

deluge /'delju:dʒ/ *n.*
1 (*lit.*) пото́п.
2 (*fig.*) пото́к.

delusion /dɪ'lu:ʒ(ə)n/ *n.* заблужде́ние.

de luxe /də 'lʌks/ *adj.* роско́шный; **a ~ cabin** каю́та люкс.

delve /delv/ *v.i.*: **~ in(to) one's pockets** ры́ться (*impf.*) в карма́нах.

demand /dɪ'mɑ:nd/ *n.*
1 (*claim*) тре́бование; **there are many ~s on my time** у меня́ мно́го дел.
2 (*desire to obtain*) потре́бность, спро́с; **there is no ~ for this article** на э́тот това́р нет спро́са.
■ *v.t.* тре́бовать, по- + *g. or a.*

demanding /dɪ'mɑ:ndɪŋ/ *adj.* тре́бовательный.

demean /dɪ'mi:n/ *v.t.*: **~ o.s.** роня́ть, урони́ть своё досто́инство.

demented /dɪ'mentɪd/ *adj.* сумасше́дший.

dementia /dɪ'menʃə/ *n.* слабоу́мие.

demilitarize /di:'mɪlɪtəraɪz/ *v.t.* демилитаризова́ть (*impf.*, *pf.*).

demise /dɪ'maɪz/ *n.* конч́ина.

demo /'deməʊ/ *n.* (*pl.* **~s**) (*coll.*) = **demonstration**

demobilize /di:'məʊbɪlaɪz/ *v.t.* демобилизова́ть (*impf.*, *pf.*).

democracy /dɪ'mɒkrəsɪ/ *n.* демокра́тия.

democrat /'deməkræt/ *n.* демокра́т.

democratic /demə'krætɪk/ *adj.* демократи́ческий.

demographic /demə'græfɪk/ *adj.* демографи́ческий.

demography /dɪ'mɒgrəfɪ/ *n.* демогра́фия.

demolish /dɪ'mɒlɪʃ/ *v.t.* сн|оси́ть, -ести́.

demolition /demə'lɪʃ(ə)n/ *n.* разруше́ние, снос.

demon /'di:mən/ *n.* де́мон.

demonic /dɪ'mɒnɪk/ *adj.* дья́вольский.

demonstrable /'demɒnstrəb(ə)l/ *adj.* доказу́емый.

demonstrate /'demənstreɪt/ *v.t.*
1 (*prove*) дока́з|ывать, -а́ть.
2 (*show in operation*) демонстри́ровать, про-.
■ *v.i.* уча́ствовать (*impf.*) в демонстра́ции.

demonstration /demən'streɪʃ(ə)n/ *n.* (*proof*) доказа́тельство; (*public manifestation*) демонстра́ция.

demonstrative /dɪ'mɒnstrətɪv/ *adj.* экспанси́вный.

demonstrator /'demənstreɪtə(r)/ *n.* демонстра́нт.

demoralize /dɪ'mɒrəlaɪz/ *v.t.* деморализова́ть (*impf.*, *pf.*).

demote /dɪ'məʊt/ *v.t.* пон|ижа́ть, -и́зить (в

до́лжности).
demure /dɪˈmjʊə(r)/ *adj.* (**demurer, demurest**) скро́мный.
den /den/ *n.*
1 (*animal's lair*) берло́га.
2 (*of thieves*) прито́н.
3 (*study*) каби́нет.
denationalization /diːnæʃənəlaɪˈzeɪʃ(ə)n/ *n.* денационализа́ция.

d

denationalize /diːˈnæʃənəlaɪz/ *v.t.* денационализи́ровать (*impf., pf.*).
denial /dɪˈnaɪəl/ *n.* отрица́ние; ~ **of justice** отка́з в правосу́дии.
denim /ˈdenɪm/ *n.* джинсо́вая ткань.
■ *adj.* джинсо́вый.
Denmark /ˈdenmɑːk/ *n.* Да́ния.
denomination /dɪnɒmɪˈneɪʃ(ə)n/ *n.*
1 (*name, nomenclature*) наименова́ние.
2 (*relig.*) вероисповеда́ние.
3 : **money of small ~s** де́нежные зна́ки (*m. pl.*) ма́лого досто́инства.
denote /dɪˈnəʊt/ *v.t.* обозн|ача́ть, -а́чить.
denounce /dɪˈnaʊns/ *v.t.*
1 (*speak against*) осу|жда́ть, -ди́ть.
2 (*inform against*) дон|оси́ть, -ести́ на + *a.*
dense /dens/ *adj.* густо́й.
density /ˈdensɪtɪ/ *n.* густота́.
dent /dent/ *n.* (*mark*) вмя́тина, (*hollow*) вы́боина.
■ *v.t.* ост|авля́ть, -а́вить вмя́тину в/на + *p.*
dental /ˈdent(ə)l/ *adj.* (*of teeth*) зубно́й; ~ **floss** зубна́я нить; ~ **surgeon** = **dentist**
dentist /ˈdentɪst/ *n.* зубно́й врач, данти́ст, стомато́лог.
dentistry /ˈdentɪstrɪ/ *n.* стоматоло́гия.
dentures /ˈdentʃəz/ *n. pl.* зубно́й проте́з.
deny /dɪˈnaɪ/ *v.t.*
1 (*contest truth of*) отрица́ть (*impf.*).
2 (*repudiate*) отр|ека́ться, -е́чься от + *g.*
3 (*refuse*) отка́з|ывать, -а́ть (*кому в чём*).
deodorant /diːˈəʊdərənt/ *n.* дезодора́нт.
depart /dɪˈpɑːt/ *v.i.*
1 (*go away*) отпр|авля́ться, -а́виться.
2 : ~ **from** (*custom, plan etc.*) отступ|а́ть, -и́ть от + *g.*
department /dɪˈpɑːtmənt/ *n.*
1 отде́л; ~ **store** универма́г.
2 (*of government*) департа́мент, ве́домство.
3 (*of univ.*) ка́федра.
departmental /diːpɑːtˈment(ə)l/ *adj.* ве́домственный.
departure /dɪˈpɑːtʃə(r)/ *n.* (*going away*) отъе́зд; (*of train*) отправле́ние.
depend /dɪˈpend/ *v.i.*
1 (*be conditional*) зави́сеть (*impf.*) (**on:** от + *g.*); **that ~s; it all ~s** как сказа́ть.
2 (*rely*) пол|ага́ться, -ожи́ться (**on:** на + *a.*).
dependable /dɪˈpendəb(ə)l/ *adj.* надёжный.
dependant /dɪˈpend(ə)nt/ (*US* **dependent**) *n.* иждиве́н|ец (*fem.* -ка).
dependence /dɪˈpend(ə)ns/ *n.* зави́симость (от + *g.*); (*reliance*) дове́рие (к + *d.*).
dependency /dɪˈpendənsɪ/ *n.* (*pol.*) коло́ния.
dependent /dɪˈpend(ə)nt/ *adj.* зави́симый.
depict /dɪˈpɪkt/ *v.t.* изобра|жа́ть, -зи́ть.
depiction /dɪˈpɪkʃ(ə)n/ *n.* описа́ние, изображе́ние.
deplete /dɪˈpliːt/ *v.t.* истощ|а́ть, -и́ть.
deplorable /dɪˈplɔːrəb(ə)l/ *adj.* плаче́вный.
deplore /dɪˈplɔː(r)/ *v.t.* сожале́ть (*impf.*) о + *p.*
deploy /dɪˈplɔɪ/ *v.t.* развёр|тывать, -ну́ть.
deployment /dɪˈplɔɪmənt/ *n.* развёртывание; размеще́ние.
depopulate /diːˈpɒpjʊleɪt/ *v.t.* истреб|ля́ть, -и́ть/уничт|ожа́ть, -о́жить/ум|еньша́ть, -е́ньшить населе́ние + *g.*
depopulation /diːpɒpjʊˈleɪʃ(ə)n/ *n.* сокраще́ние населе́ния.
deport /dɪˈpɔːt/ *v.t.* депорти́ровать (*impf., pf.*).
deportation /diːpɔːˈteɪʃ(ə)n/ *n.* депорта́ция, вы́сылка.
depose /dɪˈpəʊz/ *v.t.* св|ерга́ть, -е́ргнуть (с престо́ла).
deposit /dɪˈpɒzɪt/ *n.*
1 (*sum in bank*) вклад; ~ **account** (*Br.*) депози́тный счёт.
2 (*advance payment*) зада́ток; (*layer*) отложе́ние.
3 (*of ore etc.*) за́лежь; (*of precious metals and stones*) ро́ссыпь.
■ *v.t.* (**deposited, depositing**) класть, положи́ть; (*place in bank*) депони́ровать (*impf., pf.*).
depot /ˈdepəʊ/ *n.* (*place of storage*) склад; (*US, train or bus station*) ста́нция.
deprave /dɪˈpreɪv/ *v.t.* развра|ща́ть, -ти́ть.
depravity /dɪˈprævɪtɪ/ *n.* развра́т, развращённость.
depreciate /dɪˈpriːʃɪeɪt/ *v.i.* обесце́ни|ваться, -ться.
depreciation /dɪpriːʃɪˈeɪʃ(ə)n, -sɪˈeɪʃ(ə)n/ *n.* обесце́нивание, обесце́нение.
depress /dɪˈpres/ *v.t.*
1 (*push down*) наж|има́ть, -а́ть на + *a.*
2 (*fig.*): **~ed area** райо́н, пострада́вший от экономи́ческой депре́ссии.
3 (*make sad*) удруч|а́ть, -и́ть.
depressing /dɪˈpresɪŋ/ *adj.* удруча́ющий.
depression /dɪˈpreʃ(ə)n/ *n.* депре́ссия, тоска́.
deprivation /deprɪˈveɪʃ(ə)n/ *n.* лише́ние.
deprive /dɪˈpraɪv/ *v.t.* лиш|а́ть, -и́ть (*кого чего*); **~d** (*underprivileged*) обездо́ленный.
depth /depθ/ *n.*
1 (*deepness*) глубина́; **6 feet in ~** глубино́й в шесть фу́тов; **be out of one's ~** не достава́ть (*impf.*) нога́ми до дна; (*fig.*): **I am out of my ~ in this job** э́та рабо́та мне не по плечу́.
2 (*extremity*): **~ of despair** глубо́кое отча́яние; **~ of winter** глубо́кая зима́.
deputize /ˈdepjʊtaɪz/ *v.i.*: **~ for s.o.** заме|ща́ть (*impf.*) кого́-н.
deputy /ˈdepjʊtɪ/ *n.*
1 (*substitute*) замести́тель (*m.*); **~ chairman** замести́тель (*m.*) председа́теля.
2 (*member of parliament*) депута́т.
derail /diːˈreɪl/ *v.t.*: **be derailed** (*of train*) сходи́ть, сойти́ с ре́льсов.
derailment /dɪˈreɪlmənt, diː-/ *n.* сход с ре́льсов.
derange /dɪˈreɪndʒ/ *v.t.* св|оди́ть, -ести́ с ума́.
deregulate /diːˈregjʊleɪt/ *v.t.* отмен|я́ть, -и́ть (госуда́рственное) регули́рование (*чего*).

deregulation /diːregjʊˈleɪʃ(ə)n/ *n.* отмéна (госудáрственного) регулúрования.
derelict /ˈderəlɪkt/ *adj.* забрóшенный.
dereliction /derɪˈlɪkʃ(ə)n/ *n.* забрóшенность, запýщенность; **~ of duty** нарушéние (служéбного) дóлга.
deride /dɪˈraɪd/ *v.t.* высмéивать, вы́смеять; осмé|ивать, -я́ть.
derision /dɪˈrɪʒ(ə)n/ *n.* осмея́ние, высмéивание.
derisive /dɪˈraɪsɪv/ *adj.* (*scornful*) насмéшливый.
derisory /dɪˈraɪsərɪ/ *adj.* (*ludicrous*) смешнóй, ничтóжный.
derive /dɪˈraɪv/ *v.t.* извл|екáть, -éчь; **~ pleasure from** получ|áть, -и́ть удовóльствие от + *g.*
dermatitis /dəːməˈtaɪtɪs/ *n.* дерматúт.
dermatologist /dəːməˈtɒlədʒɪst/ *n.* дерматóлог.
derogatory /dɪˈrɒgətərɪ/ *adj.* пренебрежúтельный.
descend /dɪˈsend/ *v.t.* сходúть, сойтú с + *g.*
■ *v.i.* 1 (*go down*) спус|кáться, -тúться.
2 (*originate*) происходúть (*impf.*); **he is ~ed from a ducal family** он происхóдит из гéрцогского рóда.
3 (*attack*) набр|áсываться, -óситься.
descendant /dɪˈsend(ə)nt/ *n.* потóмок.
descent /dɪˈsent/ *n.*
1 (*act of descending*) спуск.
2 (*ancestry*) происхождéние.
describe /dɪˈskraɪb/ *v.t.* опúс|ывать, -áть; **~ s.o. as** наз|ывáть, -вáть когó-н. (кем-н./какúм-н.).
description /dɪˈskrɪpʃ(ə)n/ *n.* описáние.
descriptive /dɪˈskrɪptɪv/ *adj.* описáтельный.
desecrate /ˈdesɪkreɪt/ *v.t.* осквер|я́ть, -úть.
desegregate /diːˈsegrɪgeɪt/ *v.t.* & *i.* десегрегúровать (*impf., pf.*) (*отменять сегрегацию*).
desert[1] /dɪˈzəːt/ *n.*: **get one's ~s** получ|áть, -úть по заслýгам.
desert[2] /ˈdezət/ *n.* (*waste land*) пусты́ня.
■ *adj.* пусты́нный; **~ island** необитáемый óстров.
desert[3] /dɪˈzəːt/ *v.t.*
1 (*go away from*) ост|авля́ть, -áвить; **the streets were ~ed** на ýлицах нé было ни душú.
2 (*abandon*) пок|идáть, -úнуть.
■ *v.i.* дезертúровать (*impf., pf.*).
deserter /dɪˈzəːtə(r)/ *n.* дезертúр.
desertion /dɪˈzəːʃ(ə)n/ *n.* дезертúрство.
deserve /dɪˈzəːv/ *v.t.* & *i.* заслýж|ивать, -úть.
deserving /dɪˈzəːvɪŋ/ *adj.* похвáльный.
desiccate /ˈdesɪkeɪt/ *v.t.* высýшивать, вы́сушить; **~d coconut** сушёный кокóс.
design /dɪˈzaɪn/ *n.*
1 (*drawing, plan*) план, проéкт.
2 (*art of drawing*) рисовáние.
3 (*tech.: layout, system*) конструкция, проéкт; **~ of a car** констрýкция автомобúля; **~ of a building** проéкт здáния.
4 (*pattern*) узóр, рисýнок.
5 (*version of product*) модéль.
■ *v.t.* сост|авля́ть, -áвить план + *g.*
designate /ˈdezɪgneɪt/ *v.t.* (*specify* (*a time*) *etc.*) обозн|ачáть, -áчить; (*appoint to a post*) назн|ачáть, -áчить.
designer /dɪˈzaɪnə(r)/ *n.* (*of dresses, decorations*) модельéр; (*tech.*) констрýктор; (*industrial*) дизáйнер.
■ *cpd.* **~ baby** *n.* ребёнок, рождённый из эмбриóна, вы́бранного из нéскольких эмбриóнов, котóрые бы́ли получены мéтодом экстракорпорáльного оплодотворéния.
desirable /dɪˈzaɪərəb(ə)l/ *adj.* желáтельный; (*attractive*) привлекáтельный.
desire /dɪˈzaɪə(r)/ *n.* желáние, стремлéние.
■ *v.t.* желáть, по-; **it leaves much to be ~ed** э́то оставля́ет желáть лýчшего *or* мнóгого.
desk /desk/ *n.* пúсьменный стол; (*with sloping top*) контóрка; (*information centre*) спрáвочный стол.
desktop /ˈdesktɒp/ *adj.* настóльный; **~ publishing** настóльная полиграфúя; **~ publishing system** настóльная издáтельская систéма.
■ *n.* (*also comput.*) рабóчий стол.
desolate /ˈdesələt/ *adj.* забрóшенный.
despair /dɪˈspeə(r)/ *n.* отчáяние.
■ *v.i.* отчá|иваться, -яться; **I ~ of him** я утрáтил вéру в негó.
despatch /dɪˈspætʃ/ (*Br.*) = **dispatch**
desperate /ˈdespərət/ *adj.*
1 (*wretched*) отчáянный.
2 (*in extreme need*): **he is ~ for money** он испы́тывает крáйнюю нуждý в деньгáх.
desperation /despəˈreɪʃ(ə)n/ *n.* отчáяние.
despicable /dɪˈspɪkəb(ə)l/ *adj.* презрéнный.
despise /dɪˈspaɪz/ *v.t.* презирáть (*impf.*).
despite /dɪˈspaɪt/ *prep.* несмотря́ на + *a.*
despondency /dɪˈspɒndənsɪ/ *n.* уны́ние.
despondent /dɪˈspɒnd(ə)nt/ *adj.* уны́лый.
despot /ˈdespɒt/ *n.* дéспот.
despotic /deˈspɒtɪk/ *adj.* (*system, rule*) деспотúческий; (*person, style*) деспотúчный.
despotism /ˈdespətɪz(ə)m/ *n.* деспотúзм.
dessert /dɪˈzəːt/ *n.* десéрт.
■ *cpd.* **~spoon** *n.* десéртная лóжка.
destabilize /diːˈsteɪbɪlaɪz/ *v.t.* дестабилизúровать (*impf., pf.*).
destination /destɪˈneɪʃ(ə)n/ *n.* мéсто назначéния.
destine /ˈdestɪn/ *v.t.* предназн|ачáть, -áчить; **the plan was ~ed to fail** э́тот план был обречён на провáл.
destiny /ˈdestɪnɪ/ *n.* судьбá.
destitute /ˈdestɪtjuːt/ *adj.* нуждáющийся.
destroy /dɪˈstrɔɪ/ *v.t.* (*building*) разр|ушáть, -ýшить; (*friendship, hope*) разб|ивáть, -úть; (*kill*) истреб|ля́ть, -úть.
destroyer /dɪˈstrɔɪə(r)/ *n.*
1 (*one who destroys*) разрушúтель (*m.*).
2 (*nav.*) эсмúнец; эскáдренный миноносец.
destruction /dɪˈstrʌkʃ(ə)n/ *n.* уничтожéние, разрушéние.
destructive /dɪˈstrʌktɪv/ *adj.* разрушúтельный.
desultory /ˈdezəltərɪ/ *adj.* отры́вочный; **~ reading** бессистéмное чтéние.

d

detach /dɪ'tætʃ/ *v.t.* отдел|я́ть, -и́ть.
detachable /dɪ'tætʃəb(ə)l/ *adj.* съёмный, отделя́емый.
detached /dɪ'tætʃt/ *adj.* (*unemotional*) равноду́шный, отчуждённый; **a ~ house** отде́льный дом.
detail¹ /'di:teɪl/ *n.* дета́ль; **go into ~(s)** входи́ть, вдава́ться (*both impf.*) в подро́бности; **in ~** подро́бно, дета́льно.
detail² /'di:teɪl/ *v.t.* входи́ть (*impf.*) в подро́бности + *g.*
detain /dɪ'teɪn/ *v.t.* заде́рж|ивать, -а́ть; **he was ~ed by the police** он был заде́ржан поли́цией.
detainee /di:teɪ'ni:/ *n.* заде́ржанный.
detect /dɪ'tekt/ *v.t.* (*discover*) обнару́жи|вать, -ть; (*discern*) ул|а́вливать, -ови́ть.
detection /dɪ'tekʃ(ə)n/ *n.* (*of crime*) рассле́дование, раскры́тие.
detective /dɪ'tektɪv/ *n.* сы́щик, детекти́в; **~ novel** детекти́в, детекти́вный рома́н.
detector /dɪ'tektə(r)/ *n.* (*radio*) дете́ктор.
detention /dɪ'tenʃ(ə)n/ *n.* (*at school*) оставле́ние по́сле уро́ков; (*confinement*) заключе́ние (под стра́жу).
■ *cpd.* **~ centre** (*for asylum seekers*) *n.* приёмник-распредели́тель (*для* (*нелегальных*) *мигрантов*).
deter /dɪ'tə:(r)/ *v.t.* (**deterred, deterring**) уде́рж|ивать, -а́ть.
detergent /dɪ'tə:dʒ(ə)nt/ *n.* мо́ющее сре́дство; (*washing powder*) стира́льный порошо́к.
deteriorate /dɪ'tɪərɪəreɪt/ *v.t.* & *i.* ух|удша́ть(ся), -у́дшить(ся).
determination /dɪtə:mɪ'neɪʃ(ə)n/ *n.*
1 (*deciding upon*) реше́ние.
2 (*resoluteness*) реши́мость.
determine /dɪ'tə:mɪn/ *v.t.* реш|а́ть, -и́ть; **he is ~d to go (***or* **on going)** он твёрдо реши́л е́хать.
determined /dɪ'tə:mɪnd/ *adj.* реши́тельный.
deterrent /dɪ'terənt/ *n.* сре́дство устраше́ния/сде́рживания.
detest /dɪ'test/ *v.t.* ненави́деть (*impf.*).
detestable /dɪ'testəb(ə)l/ *adj.* отврати́тельный.
detonate /'detəneɪt/ *v.t.* детони́ровать (*impf.*, *pf.*).
detour /'di:tʊə(r)/ *n.* (*on foot*) обхо́д; (*by transport*) объе́зд.
detract /dɪ'trækt/ *v.i.*: **~ from** умал|я́ть, -и́ть.
detriment /'detrɪmənt/ *n.*: **he works long hours to the ~ of his health** он рабо́тает сверх но́рмы в уще́рб своему́ здоро́вью.
detrimental /detrɪ'ment(ə)l/ *adj.* вре́дный.
deuce /dju:s/ *n.* (*tennis*) ра́вный счёт.
devaluation /di:vælju:'eɪʃ(ə)n/ *n.* обесце́нение; (*fin.*) девальва́ция.
devalue /di:'vælju:/ *v.t.* (**devalues, devalued, devaluing**) обесце́ни|вать, -ть; (*fin.*) девальви́ровать (*impf.*, *pf.*).
■ *v.i.* (**devalues, devalued, devaluing**) пров|оди́ть, -ести́ девальва́цию.
devastat|e /'devəsteɪt/ *v.t.* (*fig.*) убива́ть, уби́ть; **a ~ing remark** уничтожа́ющее/убийственное замеча́ние.
devastation /devə'steɪʃ(ə)n/ *n.* опустоше́ние, разоре́ние.
develop /dɪ'veləp/ *v.t.* (**developed, developing**)
1 (*cause to unfold*) разв|ива́ть, -и́ть; (*work up, polish*) обраб|а́тывать, -о́тать.
2 (*phot.*) прояв|ля́ть, -и́ть.
3 (*contract*): **he ~ed a cough** у него́ появи́лся ка́шель.
4 (*open up for residence etc.*) разв|ива́ть, -и́ть.
■ *v.i.* (**developed, developing**) разв|ива́ться, -и́ться; **~ into** превра|ща́ться, -ти́ться в + *a.*
developer /dɪ'veləpə(r)/ *n.* (*builder*) застро́йщик.
development /dɪ'veləpmənt/ *n.*
1 (*unfolding*) разви́тие, рост.
2 (*event*) собы́тие, обстоя́тельство.
3 (*of land etc.*) разви́тие (райо́на); (*building*) застро́йка.
deviate /'di:vɪeɪt/ *v.i.* отклон|я́ться, -и́ться (**from:** от + *g.*).
deviation /di:vɪ'eɪʃ(ə)n/ *n.* отклоне́ние, отхо́д.
device /dɪ'vaɪs/ *n.*
1 (*method*) приём; **he was left to his own ~s** он был предоста́влен самому́ себе́.
2 (*instrument*) приспособле́ние, прибо́р.
devil /'dev(ə)l/ *n.* чёрт, дья́вол.
devious /'di:vɪəs/ *adj.* (*road*) изви́листый, око́льный; (*fig.*) лука́вый, нейскренний.
devise /dɪ'vaɪz/ *v.t.* (*think out*) приду́м|ывать, -ать.
devoid /dɪ'vɔɪd/ *adj.* лишённый; **~ of fear** бесстра́шный.
devolution /di:və'lu:ʃ(ə)n/ *n.* переда́ча/делеги́рование вла́сти.
devolve /dɪ'vɒlv/ *v.t.* (*delegate*) перед|ава́ть, -а́ть.
■ *v.i.* пере|ходи́ть, -йти́; **the work ~d on/to me** рабо́ту пе́редали мне; **the estate ~d on/to a distant cousin** име́ние перешло́ к да́льнему ро́дственнику.
devote /dɪ'vəʊt/ *v.t.* посвя|ща́ть, -ти́ть; **he ~s his time to study** он посвяща́ет всё своё вре́мя учёбе; **she is ~d to her children** она́ пре́дана свои́м де́тям; **a ~d friend** пре́данный друг.
devotee /devə'ti:/ *n.* приве́рженец.
devotion /dɪ'vəʊʃ(ə)n/ *n.*
1 (*being devoted*) пре́данность.
2 (*love*) пре́данность.
devour /dɪ'vaʊə(r)/ *v.t.* пож|ира́ть, -ра́ть.
devout /dɪ'vaʊt/ *adj.* благочести́вый.
dew /dju:/ *n.* роса́.
dexterity /dek'sterɪtɪ/ *n.* ло́вкость, прово́рство.
dext(e)rous /'dekstrəs/ *adj.* ло́вкий, прово́рный.
diabetes /daɪə'bi:ti:z/ *n.* диабе́т.
diabetic /daɪə'betɪk/ *n.* диабе́тик.
■ *adj.* диабети́ческий.
diabolic(al) /daɪə'bɒlɪk, daɪə'bɒlɪk(ə)l/ *adj.* дья́вольский.
diagnose /'daɪəgnəʊz/ *v.t.* диагности́ровать (*impf.*, *pf.*).
diagnosis /daɪəg'nəʊsɪs/ *n.* (*pl.* **diagnoses**

/-si:z/) диа́гноз.
diagnostic /daɪəg'nɒstɪk/ *adj.* диагности́ческий.
diagonal /daɪ'ægən(ə)l/ *n.* диагона́ль.
■ *adj.* диагона́льный; **~ly** по диагона́ли.
diagram /'daɪəgræm/ *n.* диагра́мма.
dial /'daɪ(ə)l/ *n.*
1 (*of clock*) цифербла́т.
2 (*of radio etc.*) шкала́.
■ *v.t. & i.* (**dialled, dialling;** *US* **dialed, dialing**): **~ a number** наб|ира́ть, -ра́ть но́мер; **~ the police station** звони́ть, по- в поли́цию; **~ling tone** дли́нный гудо́к; сигна́л «ли́ния свобо́дна».
dialect /'daɪəlekt/ *n.* диале́кт, го́вор.
dialogue /'daɪəlɒg/ (*US also* **dialog**) *n.* диало́г.
dialysis /daɪ'ælɪsɪs/ *n.* диа́лиз.
diameter /daɪ'æmɪtə(r)/ *n.* диа́метр.
diametric(al) /daɪə'metrɪk, daɪə'metrɪk(ə)l/ *adj.* диаметра́льный.
diamond /'daɪəmənd/ *n.*
1 (*precious stone*) алма́з.
2 (*geom.*) ромб.
3 (*at cards*) бу́б|ны (*pl., g.* -ен).
diaper /'daɪəpə(r)/ *n.* (*US*) подгу́зник.
diaphragm /'daɪəfræm/ *n.* диафра́гма.
diarrhoea /daɪə'rɪə/ (*US* **diarrhea**) *n.* поно́с.
diary /'daɪərɪ/ *n.* (*journal*) дневни́к; (*engagement book*) календа́рь (*m.*).
diaspora /daɪə'æspərə/ *n.* диа́спора.
dice /daɪs/ *n.* (*cube*) игра́льные ко́сти (*f. pl.*); (*game of* ~) игра́ в ко́сти.
■ *v.t. & i.* нар|еза́ть, -е́зать ку́биками.
dichotomy /daɪ'kɒtəmɪ/ *n.* дихотоми́я; (*contrast*) противопоставле́ние.
Dictaphone /'dɪktəfəʊn/ *n.* (*propr.*) диктофо́н.
dictate /dɪk'teɪt/ *v.t. & i.* (*specify, command*) диктова́ть, про-; **I won't be ~d to** я не позво́лю ста́вить мне усло́вия.
dictation /dɪk'teɪʃ(ə)n/ *n.* (*to class*) дикта́нт; (*to secretary*) дикто́вка.
dictator /dɪk'teɪtə(r)/ *n.* дикта́тор.
dictatorial /dɪktə'tɔ:rɪəl/ *adj.* дикта́торский.
dictatorship /dɪk'teɪtəʃɪp/ *n.* диктату́ра.
dictionary /'dɪkʃənrɪ/ *n.* слова́рь (*m.*).
did /dɪd/ *past of* ▶ **do**
didactic /daɪ'dæktɪk/ *adj.* поучи́тельный, дидакти́ческий.
didn't /'dɪdn(ə)nt/ *neg. of* ▶ **did**
die /daɪ/ *v.i.* (**dies, died, dying**)
1 (*of person*) ум|ира́ть, -ере́ть (*pf.*); (*in accident, in war*) ги́бнуть, по-; (*of animals*) под|ыха́ть, -о́хнуть; (*of plants*) ув|яда́ть, -я́нуть; пог|иба́ть, -и́бнуть.
2 (*fig.*): **I'm dying to see him** я до́ смерти хочу́ его́ ви́деть.
■ *with advs.*: **~ down** (*of fire*) уг|аса́ть, -а́снуть; (*of noise*) ут|иха́ть, -и́хнуть; **the wind ~d down** ве́тер ути́х; (*of feeling*) ум|ира́ть, -ере́ть; **~ out** вымира́ть, вы́мереть.
diesel /'di:z(ə)l/ *n.* (**~ engine, motor**) ди́зель (*m.*); **~ oil** ди́зельное то́пливо.
diet /'daɪət/ *n.*
1 (*customary food*) пи́ща, пита́ние.
2 (*medical régime*) дие́та; **go on a ~** сади́ться, сесть на дие́ту; **he is on a ~** он (сиди́т) на дие́те.
dietitian /daɪə'tɪʃ(ə)n/ *n.* (врач-)дието́лог.
differ /'dɪfə(r)/ *v.i.*
1 (*be different*) отлича́ться (*impf.*); **they ~ in size** они́ различа́ются разме́ром, по разме́ру.
2 (*disagree*) ра|сходи́ться, -зойти́сь во мне́ниях; **we agreed to ~** мы реши́ли прекрати́ть бесполе́зный спор.
difference /'dɪfrəns/ *n.*
1 (*state of being unlike*) отли́чие, разли́чие, ра́зница; **it makes no ~ whether you go or not** соверше́нно безразли́чно, идёте вы и́ли нет.
2 (*dispute*) разногла́сие, спор.
different /'dɪfrənt/ *adj.* друго́й, ра́зный, разли́чный; **they live in ~ houses** они́ живу́т в ра́зных дома́х; **she wears a ~ hat each day** на ней ка́ждый день друга́я шля́па; **of ~ kinds** ра́зного ро́да; **he became a ~ person** он стал други́м челове́ком; **~ from** непохо́жий на + *a.*; отли́чный от + *g.*
differentiate /dɪfə'renʃɪeɪt/ *v.t.* различ|а́ть, -и́ть.
differently /'dɪfrəntlɪ/ *adv.* по-ино́му; по-друго́му.
difficult /'dɪfɪkəlt/ *adj.* тру́дный (*also of person*).
difficulty /'dɪfɪkəltɪ/ *n.* тру́дность, затрудне́ние; **I have ~ in understanding him** я с трудо́м его́ понима́ю.
diffident /'dɪfɪd(ə)nt/ *adj.* неуве́ренный в себе́; засте́нчивый, стесни́тельный.
diffuse[1] /dɪ'fju:s/ *adj.* (*of light etc.*) рассе́янный; (*of style*) расплы́вчатый.
diffuse[2] /dɪ'fju:z/ *v.t.* (*light, heat etc.*) рассе́|ивать, -ять; (*learning etc.*) распростран|я́ть, -и́ть.
dig /dɪg/ *n.*
1 (*poke*) толчо́к.
2 (*fig.*) насме́шка.
3 (*archaeol.*) (*expedition*) раско́пки (*f. pl.*).
■ *v.t. & i.* (**digging;** *past and p.p.* **dug**) копа́ть, вы́-; **he dug a hole** он вы́рыл я́му; **they are ~ging for gold** они́ и́щут зо́лото.
■ *with advs.*: **~ out** *v.t.* выка́пывать, вы́копать; **~ up** *v.t.* отк|а́пывать, -опа́ть.
digest /daɪ'dʒest, dɪ-/ *v.t.* (*food*) перева́р|ивать, -и́ть; (*information etc.*) усв|а́ивать, -о́ить.
■ *v.i.* перева́р|иваться, -и́ться.
digestion /daɪ'dʒestʃ(ə)n/ *n.* перева́ривание.
digger /'dɪgə(r)/ *n.* (*machine*) экскава́тор.
digit /'dɪdʒɪt/ *n.* (*finger or toe*) па́лец; (*numeral*) ци́фра.
digital /'dɪdʒɪt(ə)l/ *adj.* цифрово́й; **~ camera** цифрова́я (фото)ка́мера; **~ clock** цифровы́е/электро́нные час|ы́ (*pl., g.* -о́в).
digitize /'dɪdʒɪtaɪz/ *v.t.* оцифр|о́вывать, -ова́ть; преобраз|о́вывать, -ова́ть в цифрову́ю фо́рму.
dignified /'dɪgnɪfaɪd/ *adj.* по́лный досто́инства.
dignitary /'dɪgnɪtərɪ/ *n.* сано́вник; высокопоста́вленное лицо́.

dignity /ˈdɪɡnɪtɪ/ *n.* досто́инство.
digress /daɪˈɡres/ *v.i.* отклон|я́ться, -и́ться (от те́мы).
digression /daɪˈɡreʃ(ə)n/ *n.* отклоне́ние.
dilapidated /dɪˈlæpɪdeɪtɪd/ *adj.* ве́тхий.
dilate /daɪˈleɪt/ *v.t.* расш|иря́ть, -и́рить.
■ *v.i.* расш|иря́ться, -и́риться.
dilemma /daɪˈlemə/ *n.* диле́мма.
diligent /ˈdɪlɪdʒ(ə)nt/ *adj.* приле́жный.
dill /dɪl/ *n.* укро́п; **~ pickle** марино́ванный огуре́ц.
dilute /daɪˈljuːt/ *v.t.* разв|оди́ть, -ести́.
dim /dɪm/ *adj.* (**dimmer, dimmest**) (*of light etc.*) ту́склый; (*of memory etc.*) сму́тный.
■ *v.t.* (**dimmed, dimming**) затума́ни|вать, -ть; **~ one's headlights** пере|ходи́ть, -йти́ на бли́жний свет.
dime /daɪm/ *n.* десятице́нтовик.
dimension /daɪˈmenʃ(ə)n/ *n.*
1 (*extent*) разме́р.
2 (*direction of measurement*) измере́ние.
diminish /dɪˈmɪnɪʃ/ *v.t.* ум|еньша́ть, -е́ньшить.
diminutive /dɪˈmɪnjʊtɪv/ *n.* (*gram.*) уменьши́тельное сло́во.
■ *adj.* (*small*) миниатю́рный.
dimple /ˈdɪmp(ə)l/ *n.* я́мочка; (*ripple*) рябь.
din /dɪn/ *n.* гам.
din|e /daɪn/ *v.i.* у́жинать, по-; **~ing car** ваго́н-рестора́н; **~ing room** столо́вая (ко́мната).
diner /ˈdaɪnə(r)/ *n.* (*person*) у́жинающий.
dinghy /ˈdɪŋɡɪ/ *n.* ма́ленькая шлю́пка, я́лик; (*inflatable*) надувна́я ло́дка.
dingy /ˈdɪndʒɪ/ *adj.* (**dingier, dingiest**) тёмный, мра́чный.
dinner /ˈdɪnə(r)/ *n.* у́жин; **have ~** обе́дать, по-/у́жинать, по-.
■ *cpds.* **~ hour** *n.* час обе́да/у́жина; **~ jacket** *n.* смо́кинг; **~ party** *n.* зва́ный обе́д; **~ time** *n.* вре́мя у́жина.
dinosaur /ˈdaɪnəsɔː(r)/ *n.* диноза́вр.
dip /dɪp/ *n.*
1 (*immersion*) погруже́ние.
2 (*bathe*) ныря́ние.
3 (*slope*) спуск, укло́н.
4 (*cul.*) со́ус.
■ *v.t.* (**dipped, dipping**)
1 (*immerse*) окун|а́ть, -у́ть; мак|а́ть, -ну́ть; погру|жа́ть, -зи́ть.
2 (*lower briefly*) приспус|ка́ть, -ти́ть; **~ headlights** (*Br.*) переключ|а́ть, -и́ть фа́ры на (*or* включ|а́ть, -и́ть) бли́жний свет.
■ *v.i.* (**dipped, dipping**)
1 (*go below surface*) окун|а́ться, -у́ться.
2 (*fig.*): **~ into one's purse** раскоше́ли|ваться, -ться.
3 (*slope away*): **the (plot of) land ~s to the south** уча́сток име́ет накло́н к ю́гу.
4 (*fall slightly*) пон|ижа́ться, -и́зиться.
■ *cpd.* **~stick** *n.* уровнеме́р, щуп.
diphtheria /dɪfˈθɪərɪə/ *n.* дифтери́я, дифтери́т.
diphthong /ˈdɪfθɒŋ/ *n.* дифто́нг.
diploma /dɪˈpləʊmə/ *n.* дипло́м.
diplomacy /dɪpˈləʊməsɪ/ *n.* диплома́тия; (*tact*) дипломати́чность.
diplomat /ˈdɪpləmæt/ *n.* (*lit., fig.*) диплома́т.
diplomatic /dɪpləˈmætɪk/ *adj.* (*lit., fig.*) дипломати́ческий.
dire /ˈdaɪə(r)/ *adj.* ужа́сный; **he is in ~ need of help** он кра́йне нужда́ется в по́мощи.
direct /daɪˈrekt/ *adj.* (*straight*) прямо́й; (*straightforward*) прямо́й; **he has a ~ way of speaking** он говори́т всё пря́мо в лицо́; **~ flight** прямо́й/беспереса́дочный полёт/рейс.
■ *adv.* пря́мо.
■ *v.t.* 1 (*indicate the way*): **can you ~ me to the station?** вы не ска́жете, как пройти́ на вокза́л?
2 (*address*) адресова́ть (*impf., pf.*); напр|авля́ть, -а́вить; **my remarks were ~ed to him** мои́ замеча́ния бы́ли адресо́ваны ему́.
3 (*manage, control*) руководи́ть (*impf.*) + *i.*; **he ~ed the play** он поста́вил пье́су.
direction /daɪˈrekʃ(ə)n, dɪ-/ *n.*
1 (*course*) направле́ние; **they dispersed in all ~s** они́ разошли́сь в ра́зные сто́роны.
2 (*pl., instructions*) указа́ния (*nt. pl.*).
directive /daɪˈrektɪv/ *n.* директи́ва, указа́ние.
directly /daɪˈrektlɪ, dɪ-/ *adv.*
1 (*in var. senses of direct*) пря́мо.
2 (*at once*) неме́дленно, то́тчас.
director /daɪˈrektə(r), dɪ-/ *n.*
1 (*of company etc.*) дире́ктор.
2 (*theatr.*) режиссёр.
directory /daɪˈrektərɪ/ *n.* (*reference work*) спра́вочник, указа́тель (*m.*); **~ assistance** (*US*), **~ enquiries** (*Br.*) спра́вочная.
dirge /dəːdʒ/ *n.* погреба́льное пе́ние.
dirt /dəːt/ *n.*
1 (*unclean matter*) грязь.
2 (*earth*) грунт, земля́; **~ track** мотоцикле́тный трек.
dirty /ˈdəːtɪ/ *adj.* (**dirtier, dirtiest**)
1 (*not clean*) гря́зный.
2 (*obscene*) поха́бный.
3 (*nasty*) гря́зный, га́дкий; **he played a ~ trick on me** он подложи́л мне свинью́; **he gave me a ~ look** (*coll.*) он посмотре́л на меня́ серди́то.
■ *v.t. & i.* грязни́ть(ся), за-; па́чкать(ся), за-.
disability /dɪsəˈbɪlɪtɪ/ *n.* (*inability to work*) нетрудоспосо́бность; (*physical defect*) инвали́дность.
disable /dɪsˈeɪb(ə)l/ *v.t.* (*physically*) кале́чить, ис-; **~d person** инвали́д.
disadvantage /dɪsədˈvɑːntɪdʒ/ *n.* невы́годное положе́ние; **be at a ~** ока́з|ываться, -а́ться в невы́годном положе́нии.
■ *v.t.* де́йствовать (*impf.*) в уще́рб + *d.*; **~d** (*underprivileged*) обездо́ленный.
disaffected /dɪsəˈfektɪd/ *adj.* недово́льный.
disagree /dɪsəˈɡriː/ *v.i.* (**disagrees, disagreed, disagreeing**)
1 (*differ*) не соотве́тствовать (*impf.*) (**with:** + *d.*).
2 (*in opinion*) не согла|ша́ться, -си́ться; **I ~ with you** я с ва́ми не согла́сен.
3 (*have adverse effect*): **oysters ~ with me** я пло́хо переношу́ у́стриц.
disagreeable /dɪsəˈɡriːəb(ə)l/ *adj.* (*unpleasant*) неприя́тный; (*of person*)

неприве́тливый.

disagreement /dɪsə'gri:mənt/ *n.* разногла́сие.

disallow /dɪsə'laʊ/ *v.t.* (*reject*) отклон|я́ть, -и́ть; (*goal*) не засч|и́тывать, -ита́ть.

disappear /dɪsə'pɪə(r)/ *v.i.* исч|еза́ть, -е́знуть.

disappearance /dɪsə'pɪərəns/ *n.* исчезнове́ние.

disappoint /dɪsə'pɔɪnt/ *v.t.* разочаро́в|ывать, -а́ть.

disappointing /dɪsə'pɔɪntɪŋ/ *adj.* разочаро́вывающий.

disappointment /dɪsə'pɔɪntmənt/ *n.* разочарова́ние; **to my ~** к моему́ огорче́нию.

disapproval /dɪsə'pru:v(ə)l/ *n.* неодобре́ние.

disapprove /dɪsə'pru:v/ *v.i.* **~ of:** не одобря́ть (*impf.*).

disapproving /dɪsə'pru:vɪŋ/ *adj.* неодобри́тельный.

disarm /dɪs'ɑ:m/ *v.t.* разоруж|а́ть, -и́ть.

disarmament /dɪs'ɑ:məmənt/ *n.* разоруже́ние.

disarray /dɪsə'reɪ/ *n.* смяте́ние, расстро́йство.

disassociate /dɪsə'səʊsɪeɪt/ = **dissociate**

disaster /dɪ'zɑ:stə(r)/ *n.* бе́дствие.

disastrous /dɪ'zɑ:strəs/ *adj.* ги́бельный.

disband /dɪs'bænd/ *v.t.* распус|ка́ть, -ти́ть; расформиро́в|ывать, -а́ть.
■ *v.i.* расп|ада́ться, -а́сться; **the (theatre) company ~ed** тру́ппа распа́лась.

disbelief /dɪsbɪ'li:f/ *n.* неве́рие.

disbelieve /dɪsbɪ'li:v/ *v.t.* (*person*) не ве́рить (*impf.*) + *d.*; (*account, evidence*) не ве́рить (*impf.*) + *d.* (*or* в + *a.*).

disc /dɪsk/ (*US and comput.* **disk**) *n.*
1 диск.
2 (*comput.*): **floppy ~** ги́бкий диск; **~ drive** дисково́д.
■ *cpd.* **~ jockey** *n.* диск-жоке́й, дидже́й.

discard /dɪ'skɑ:d/ *v.t.* выбра́сывать, вы́бросить.

discernible /dɪsə:n'ɪb(ə)l/ *adj.* различи́мый.

discerning /dɪ'sə:nɪŋ/ *adj.* проница́тельный.

discernment /dɪ'sə:nmənt/ *n.* проница́тельность.

discharge *n.* /'dɪstʃɑ:dʒ/
1 (*of fluid*) слив, (*of gas*) вы́брос.
2 (*med.*) выделе́ния (*pl.*).
3 (*performance, e.g. of duty*) исполне́ние; (*of a debt*) упла́та.
4 (*release, dismissal*) увольне́ние, освобожде́ние.
■ *v.t.* /dɪs'tʃɑ:dʒ/
1 (*emit liquid*) слива́ть, слить.
2 (*med.*) выделя́ть, вы́делить.
3 (*from hospital*) выпи́сывать, вы́писать.

disciple /dɪ'saɪp(ə)l/ *n.* (*relig.*) апо́стол.

disciplinarian /dɪsɪplɪ'neərɪən/ *n.* сторо́нник дисципли́ны; **he is a good ~** он уме́ет подде́рживать дисципли́ну.

disciplinary /dɪsɪ'plɪnərɪ/ *adj.* дисциплина́рный; **take ~ action** прин|има́ть, -я́ть дисциплина́рные ме́ры.

discipline /'dɪsɪplɪn/ *n.* дисципли́на.

disclaim /dɪs'kleɪm/ *v.t.* отр|ека́ться, -е́чься от + *g.*

disclose /dɪs'kləʊz/ *v.t.* разоблач|а́ть, -и́ть.

disco /'dɪskəʊ/ *n.* (*pl.* **~s**) (*coll.*) = **discotheque**

discolor (*US*) = **discolour**

discolour /dɪs'kʌlə(r)/ (*US* **discolor**) *v.i.* (*lose colour*) обесцве́|чиваться, -титься.
■ *v.t.* (*make change colour*) меня́ть, по- цвет + *g.*; **rain ~ed the water** дождь поменя́л цвет воды́; **smoking had ~ed his teeth** его́ зу́бы пожелте́ли от куре́ния; (*make lose colour*) обесцве́|чивать, -тить.

discomfort /dɪs'kʌmfət/ *n.* неудо́бство.

disconcert /dɪskən'sə:t/ *v.t.* волнова́ть, вз-.

disconnect /dɪskə'nekt/ *v.t.* (*gas etc.*) отключ|а́ть, -и́ть; **we were ~ed** (*telephone*) нас разъедини́ли/прерва́ли.

disconnection /dɪskə'nekʃ(ə)n/ *n.* разъедине́ние, отключе́ние.

discontent /dɪskən'tent/ *n.* недово́льство.

discontented /dɪskən'tentɪd/ *adj.* недово́льный.

discontinue /dɪskən'tɪnju:/ *v.t.* (**discontinues, discontinued, discontinuing**) прекра|ща́ть, -ти́ть.

discord /'dɪskɔ:d/ *n.* (*disagreement*) разногла́сие; (*disharmony*) разла́д, раздо́р; (*mus.*) диссона́нс.

discotheque /'dɪskətek/ *n.* дискоте́ка.

discount *n.* /'dɪskaʊnt/ ски́дка.
■ *v.t.* /dɪs'kaʊnt/ снижа́ть, сни́зить це́ну на + *a.*

discourage /dɪ'skʌrɪdʒ/ *v.t.* обескура́жи|вать, -ть.

discourteous /dɪs'kə:tɪəs/ *adj.* неве́жливый.

discover /dɪ'skʌvə(r)/ *v.t.* (*place, fact*) откр|ыва́ть, -ы́ть; (*find out*) узн|ава́ть, -а́ть.

discovery /dɪ'skʌvərɪ/ *n.* откры́тие; обнаруже́ние.

discredit /dɪs'kredɪt/ *n.* (*loss of repute*) дискредита́ция; **bring s.o. into ~** (*or* **bring ~ upon s.o.**) компромети́ровать, с- кого́-н.; дискредити́ровать (*impf., pf.*) кого́-н.; **he is a ~ to the school** он дискредити́рует шко́лу.
■ *v.t.* (**discredited, discrediting**) дискредити́ровать (*impf., pf.*).

discreditable /dɪs'kredɪtəb(ə)l/ *adj.* (*shameful*) позо́рный.

discreet /dɪ'skri:t/ *adj.* (**discreeter, discreetest**) такти́чный.

discrepancy /dɪs'krepənsɪ/ *n.* расхожде́ние.

discrete /dɪ'skri:t/ *adj.* обосо́бленный.

discretion /dɪ'skreʃ(ə)n/ *n.*
1 (*prudence, good judgment*) осмотри́тельность.
2 (*freedom to judge*) усмотре́ние; **I leave this to your ~** я оставля́ю э́то на ва́ше усмотре́ние.

discretionary /dɪ'skreʃənərɪ/ *adj.* дискрецио́нный (*позволяющий распоряжаться по своему усмотрению*).

discriminate /dɪ'skrɪmɪneɪt/ *v.i.*: **~ against** дискримини́ровать (*impf., pf.*).

discriminating /dɪ'skrɪmɪneɪtɪŋ/ *adj.* разбо́рчивый.

discrimination /dɪskrɪmɪ'neɪʃ(ə)n/ *n.* дискримина́ция.
discriminatory /dɪ'skrɪmɪnətərɪ/ *adj.* пристра́стный.
discus /'dɪskəs/ *n.* (*pl.* **~es**) (*sport*) диск.
discuss /dɪ'skʌs/ *v.t.* дискути́ровать (*impf.*).
discussion /dɪ'skʌʃ(ə)n/ *n.* обсужде́ние, диску́ссия.

d

disdain /dɪs'deɪn/ *n.* презре́ние.
■ *v.t.* през|ира́ть, -ре́ть; пренебр|ега́ть, -е́чь + *i.*; **he ~ed to reply** он не соизво́лил отве́тить.
disdainful /dɪs'deɪnfʊl/ *adj.* презри́тельный.
disease /dɪ'zi:z/ *n.* боле́знь.
diseased /dɪ'zi:zd/ *adj.* (*lit.*, *fig.*) больно́й.
disembark /dɪsɪm'bɑ:k/ *v.t.* & *i.* выса́живать(ся), вы́садить(ся).
disembarkation /dɪsɪmbɑ:'keɪʃ(ə)n/ *n.* вы́садка, вы́грузка.
disembod|y /dɪsɪm'bɒdɪ/ *v.t.* (*set free from the body*) освобо|жда́ть, -ди́ть от теле́сной оболо́чки; **a ~ied spirit** освобождённая душа́.
disenchant /dɪsɪn'tʃɑ:nt/ *v.t.* разочаро́в|ывать, -а́ть.
disentangle /dɪsɪn'tæŋg(ə)l/ *v.t.* & *i.* распу́т|ывать(ся), -ать(ся); выпу́тывать(ся), вы́путать(ся).
disfigure /dɪs'fɪgə(r)/ *v.t.* уро́довать, из-; обезобра́|живать, -зить.
disfigurement /dɪs'fɪgərmənt/ *n.* (*act*) обезобра́живание; (*result*) уро́дство.
disgrace /dɪs'greɪs/ *n.*
1 (*loss of respect*) бесче́стье, позо́р.
2 (*disfavour*) неми́лость, опа́ла; **he is in ~** он в неми́лости.
3 (*cause of shame*) позо́р.
■ *v.t.* позо́рить, о-; (*bring shame upon*): **he ~d the family name** он покры́л позо́ром свою́ семью́.
disgraceful /dɪs'greɪsfʊl/ *adj.* позо́рный, недосто́йный.
disgruntled /dɪs'grʌnt(ə)ld/ *adj.* недово́льный; раздражённый.
disguise /dɪs'gaɪz/ *n.* маскиро́вка.
■ *v.t.* (*weapons, objects, intentions*) маскирова́ть, за-; (*with clothing*) переод|ева́ть, -е́ть; (*emotions*) скры|ва́ть, -ть.
disgust /dɪs'gʌst/ *n.* отвраще́ние.
■ *v.t.* внуш|а́ть, -и́ть отвраще́ние + *d.*
disgusting /dɪs'gʌstɪŋ/ *adj.* отврати́тельный.
dish /dɪʃ/ *n.*
1 (*vessel, contents*) блю́до; **wash, do the ~es** мыть, вы- посу́ду.
2 (*coll., TV satellite ~*) таре́лка.
■ *v.t.*: **~ out** (*food*) ра|скла́дывать, -зложи́ть по таре́лкам (*edy*).
■ *cpds.* **~cloth** *n.* ку́хонная/посу́дная тря́пка; **~ towel** (*US*) *n.* ку́хонное/посу́дное полоте́нце; **~washer** *n.* посудомо́ечная маши́на.
dishearten /dɪs'hɑ:t(ə)n/ *v.t.* прив|оди́ть, -ести́ в уны́ние; **I was ~ed** я упа́л ду́хом.
dishevelled /dɪ'ʃev(ə)ld/ (*US* **disheveled**) *adj.* взъеро́шенный.
dishonest /dɪs'ɒnɪst/ *adj.* нече́стный, бесче́стный.
dishonesty /dɪs'ɒnɪstɪ/ *n.* нече́стность, бесче́стность.
dishonour /dɪs'ɒnə(r)/ (*US* **dishonor**) *n.* бесче́стье, позо́р.
dishonourable /dɪs'ɒnərəb(ə)l/ (*US* **dishonorable**) *adj.* бесче́стный.
dishy /'dɪʃɪ/ *adj.* (**dishier, dishiest**) (*Br. coll.*) аппети́тный, привлека́тельный.
disillusion /dɪsɪ'lu:ʒ(ə)n/ *v.t.* разочаро́в|ывать, -а́ть.
disillusionment /dɪsɪ'lu:ʒənmənt/ *n.* разочарова́ние.
disincentive /dɪsɪn'sentɪv/ *n.* сде́рживающее обстоя́тельство.
disinfect /dɪsɪn'fekt/ *v.t.* дезинфици́ровать (*impf.*, *pf.*).
disinfectant /dɪsɪn'fekt(ə)nt/ *n.* дезинфици́рующее сре́дство.
disingenuous /dɪsɪn'dʒenjʊəs/ *adj.* нейскренний.
disinherit /dɪsɪn'herɪt/ *v.t.* (**disinherited, disinheriting**) лиш|а́ть, -и́ть насле́дства.
disintegrate /dɪs'ɪntɪgreɪt/ *v.i.* расп|ада́ться, -а́сться.
disinterested /dɪs'ɪntrɪstɪd/ *adj.* бескоры́стный.
disjointed /dɪs'dʒɔɪntɪd/ *adj.* (*fig.*) бессвя́зный.
disk /dɪsk/ (*US, comput.*) = **disc**
diskette /dɪ'sket/ *n.* (*comput.*) диске́та.
dislike /dɪs'laɪk/ *n.* (*feeling*) неприя́знь; (*often pl.*; *disliked thing*) антипа́тия; **I took a ~ to him** я невзлюби́л его́.
■ *v.t.* не люби́ть (*impf.*) + *g.*
dislocate /'dɪsləkeɪt/ *v.t.* вы́вихнуть (*pf.*).
dislodge /dɪs'lɒdʒ/ *v.t.* сме|ща́ть, -сти́ть.
disloyal /dɪs'lɔɪəl/ *adj.* нелоя́льный.
disloyalty /dɪs'lɔɪəltɪ/ *n.* нелоя́льность, неве́рность.
dismal /'dɪzm(ə)l/ *adj.* мра́чный, уны́лый, гнету́щий.
dismantle /dɪs'mænt(ə)l/ *v.t.* раз|бира́ть, -обра́ть.
dismay /dɪs'meɪ/ *n.* смяте́ние.
dismiss /dɪs'mɪs/ *v.t.*
1 (*send away*) распус|ка́ть, -ти́ть.
2 (*discharge from service*) ув|ольня́ть, -о́лить.
3 (*reject*): **I ~ed the idea** я оста́вил э́ту мысль.
4 (*leg.*): (*a case*) прекра|ща́ть, -ти́ть.
dismissal /dɪs'mɪsəl/ *n.* увольне́ние.
dismissive /dɪs'mɪsɪv/ *adj.* презри́тельный.
dismount /dɪs'maʊnt/ *v.i.* (*from horse*) спе́ши|ваться, -ться; (*from bicycle*) слез|а́ть, -ть.
disobedient /dɪsə'bi:dɪənt/ *adj.* непослу́шный.
disobey /dɪsə'beɪ/ *v.t.* не слу́шаться, по- + *g.*; не повинова́ться (*impf.*, *pf.*) + *d.*
disorder /dɪs'ɔ:də(r)/ *n.* (*untidiness*) беспоря́док; (*riot*) беспоря́дки (*m. pl.*); (*med.*) расстро́йство.
disorderly /dɪs'ɔ:dəlɪ/ *adj.* (*untidy*) беспоря́дочный; (*unruly*) бу́йный; **~ conduct** хулига́нство.
disorganize /dɪs'ɔ:gənaɪz/ *v.t.* дезорганизова́ть (*impf.*, *pf.*).

disorient /dɪsˈɔːrɪənt/ *v.t.* дезориенти́ровать (*impf., pf.*).

disorientate /dɪsˈɔːrɪənteɪt/ (*Br.*) = **disorient**

disown /dɪsˈəʊn/ *v.t.* отка́з|ываться, -а́ться от + *g.*

disparage /dɪˈspærɪdʒ/ *v.t.* (*belittle*) преум|еньша́ть, -е́ньшить; говори́ть (*impf.*) с пренебреже́нием о + *p.*

disparate /ˈdɪspərət/ *adj.* несхо́жий.

disparity /dɪˈspærɪtɪ/ *n.* расхожде́ние; (*incongruity*) несоотве́тствие.

dispassionate /dɪˈspæʃənət/ *adj.* бесстра́стный.

dispatch /dɪˈspætʃ/ *n.* сообще́ние.
■ *v.t.* 1 (*send off*) отпр|авля́ть, -а́вить.
2 (*deal with*) спр|авля́ться, -а́виться с + *i.*

dispel /dɪˈspel/ *v.t.* (**dispelled, dispelling**) рассе́|ивать, -ять.

dispensable /dɪˈspensəb(ə)l/ *adj.* необяза́тельный.

dispensary /dɪˈspensərɪ/ *n.* апте́ка; (*in hospital*) пункт разда́чи лека́рств.

dispensation /dɪspenˈseɪʃ(ə)n/ *n.*
1 (*dealing out*) разда́ча.
2 (*order*) зако́н; **under the Mosaic ~** по Моисе́еву зако́ну.
3 (*exemption*) освобожде́ние, исключе́ние; (*permission*) разреше́ние.

dispense /dɪˈspens/ *v.t.*
1 (*deal out*) разд|ава́ть, -а́ть.
2 (*of prescription*) пригот|овля́ть, -о́вить.
■ *v.i.*: **~ with** (*do without*) об|ходи́ться, -ойти́сь без + *g.*

dispenser /dɪˈspensə(r)/ *n.*
1 (*of medicines*) фармаце́вт.
2 (*machine*) торго́вый автома́т.

disperse /dɪˈspəːs/ *v.t.* рассе́|ивать, -ять; **the policeman ~d the crowd** полице́йский разогна́л толпу́.
■ *v.i.* рассе́|иваться, -яться.

displace /dɪsˈpleɪs/ *v.t.* сме|ща́ть, -сти́ть; **~d persons** перемещённые ли́ца.

display /dɪˈspleɪ/ *n.*
1 (*manifestation*) пока́з, проявле́ние.
2 (*of goods etc.*) вы́ставка.
3 (*of computer*) диспле́й.
■ *v.t.* (*quality, emotion*) прояв|ля́ть, -и́ть; обнару́жи|вать, -ть; (*on screen, in a picture*) демонстри́ровать, про-; (*goods etc.*) выставля́ть, вы́ставить.

displease /dɪsˈpliːz/ *v.t.*: **I am ~d with you** я недово́лен ва́ми.

displeasure /dɪsˈpleʒə(r)/ *n.* недово́льство, неудово́льствие; **incur s.o.'s ~** навл|ека́ть, -е́чь на себя́ (*or* вызыва́ть, вы́звать) чьё-н. недово́льство.

disposable /dɪˈspəʊzəb(ə)l/ *adj.* ра́зовый, однора́зовый.

disposal /dɪˈspəʊz(ə)l/ *n.*
1 (*getting rid of*) удале́ние, устране́ние.
2 (*control*) распоряже́ние.

dispose /dɪˈspəʊz/ *v.t.*: **he is well ~d towards me** он хорошо́ ко мне отно́сится.
■ *v.i.* (*with prep.* **of**) изб|авля́ться, -а́виться от + *g.*

disposition /dɪspəˈzɪʃ(ə)n/ *n.*
1 (*arrangement*) расположе́ние.
2 (*character*) нрав, хара́ктер; **he has a cheerful ~** у него́ весёлый нрав.

dispossess /dɪspəˈzes/ *v.t.* лиш|а́ть, -и́ть (*кого чего*); от|бира́ть, -обра́ть (*что у кого*).

disproportionate /dɪsprəˈpɔːʃənət/ *adj.* непропорциона́льный.

disprove /dɪsˈpruːv/ *v.t.* опров|ерга́ть, -е́ргнуть.

disputable /dɪˈspjuːtəb(ə)l/ *adj.* спо́рный.

dispute /dɪˈspjuːt/ *n.*
1 (*argument*) ди́спут; (*disagreement*) спор.
2 (*quarrel*) ссо́ра, разногла́сие.
■ *v.t.* (*call in question, oppose*) осп|а́ривать, -о́рить.

disqualify /dɪsˈkwɒlɪfaɪ/ *v.t.* дисквалифици́ровать (*impf., pf.*).

disquiet /dɪsˈkwaɪət/ *n.* беспоко́йство, трево́га.
■ *v.t.* беспоко́ить, о-, трево́жить, вс-.

disregard /dɪsrɪˈgɑːd/ *n.* пренебреже́ние + *i.*; **he showed ~ for his teachers** он проявля́л неуваже́ние к учителя́м.
■ *v.t.* игнори́ровать (*impf., pf.*).

disrepair /dɪsrɪˈpeə(r)/ *n.* неиспра́вность; **fall into ~** при|ходи́ть, -йти́ в упа́док/запусте́ние.

disreputable /dɪsˈrepjʊtəb(ə)l/ *adj.* (*behaviour*) позо́рный; (*company, person*) по́льзующийся дурно́й сла́вой.

disrepute /dɪsrɪˈpjuːt/ *n.* дурна́я сла́ва; **fall into ~** приобре|та́ть, -сти́ дурну́ю сла́ву.

disrespect /dɪsrɪˈspekt/ *n.* неуваже́ние (**for, to:** к + *d.*).

disrespectful /dɪsrɪˈspektfʊl/ *adj.* непочти́тельный.

disrupt /dɪsˈrʌpt/ *v.t.* (*event*) срыва́ть, сорва́ть; (*process, system*) прер|ыва́ть, -ва́ть.

disruption /dɪsˈrʌpʃ(ə)n/ *n.* срыв.

disruptive /dɪsˈrʌptɪv/ *adj.* разруши́тельный, подрывно́й.

dissatisfaction /dɪsætɪsˈfækʃ(ə)n/ *n.* неудовлетворённость.

dissatisf|y /dɪˈsætɪsfaɪ/ *v.t.* не удовлетвор|я́ть, -и́ть; **he is ~ied with his job** он недово́лен свое́й рабо́той.

dissect /dɪˈsekt/ *v.t.* вскр|ыва́ть, -ы́ть.

disseminate /dɪˈsemɪneɪt/ *v.t.* распростран|я́ть, -и́ть.

dissent /dɪˈsent/ *n.* несогла́сие.

dissertation /dɪsəˈteɪʃ(ə)n/ *n.* диссерта́ция.

disservice /dɪsˈsəːvɪs/ *n.* плоха́я услу́га; уще́рб; **he did me a ~** он нанёс мне уще́рб; он навреди́л мне; **his words did great ~ to the cause** его́ слова́ нанесли́ большо́й уще́рб де́лу.

dissident /ˈdɪsɪd(ə)nt/ *n.* (*pol.*) диссиде́нт.
■ *adj.* несогла́сный.

dissimilar /dɪˈsɪmɪlə(r)/ *adj.* несхо́дный.

dissipated /ˈdɪsɪpeɪtɪd/ *adj.* беспу́тный; (*life style*) разгу́льный.

dissociate /dɪˈsəʊʃɪeɪt/ *v.t.*: **~ o.s.** отмеж|ёвываться, -ева́ться (от + *g.*); **I ~ myself from what has been said** я отмежёвываюсь от того́, что бы́ло ска́зано.

dissolute /ˈdɪsəluːt/ *adj.* распу́щенный, беспу́тный, распу́тный.

dissolve /dɪˈzɒlv/ *v.t.*

1 (*phys.*) раствор|я́ть, -и́ть.
2 : **the queen ~d parliament** короле́ва распусти́ла парла́мент.
■ *v.i.* (*phys.*) раствор|я́ться, -и́ться.

dissuade /dɪ'sweɪd/ *v.t.* отгов|а́ривать, -ори́ть (*кого от чего*).

distance /'dɪst(ə)ns/ *n.*
1 (*measure of space*) диста́нция, расстоя́ние; **he lives within walking ~ of the office** от его́ до́ма до рабо́ты мо́жно дойти́ пешко́м; **in the ~** вдалеке́; **from a ~** и́здали, издалека́.
2 (*fig.*): **keep one's ~** держа́ться (*impf.*) в стороне́ (от + *g.*).

distant /'dɪst(ə)nt/ *adj.*
1 (*in space*) далёкий, да́льний.
2 (*fig., remote*): **a ~ cousin** да́льний ро́дственник.
3 (*reserved*) сде́ржанный, холо́дный.

distaste /dɪs'teɪst/ *n.* отвраще́ние (**for:** к + *d.*).

distasteful /dɪs'teɪstfʊl/ *adj.* отврати́тельный, неприя́тный.

distillery /dɪ'stɪlərɪ/ *n.* ликёрово́дочный заво́д.

distinct /dɪ'stɪŋkt/ *adj.*
1 (*sound*) вня́тный; (*picture*) отчётливый; (*advantage, possibility*) очеви́дный.
2 (*different*) отли́чный (от + *g.*).

distinction /dɪ'stɪŋkʃ(ə)n/ *n.*
1 (*difference*) отли́чие.
2 (*discrimination*) разли́чие.
3 (*special quality*) отличи́тельная осо́бенность; **a writer of ~** выдаю́щийся писа́тель.
4 (*mark of honour*) отли́чие.

distinctive /dɪ'stɪŋktɪv/ *adj.* отличи́тельный.

distinguish /dɪ'stɪŋgwɪʃ/ *v.t.* различ|а́ть, -и́ть.

distinguished /dɪ'stɪŋgwɪʃt/ *adj.* выдаю́щийся, ви́дный.

distort /dɪ'stɔːt/ *v.t.* искрив|ля́ть, -и́ть; **~ facts** извра|ща́ть, -ти́ть фа́кты.

distract /dɪ'strækt/ *v.t.* отвл|ека́ть, -е́чь; **it ~s me from my work** э́то отвлека́ет меня́ от рабо́ты.

distraction /dɪ'strækʃ(ə)n/ *n.* поме́ха.

distraught /dɪ'strɔːt/ *adj.* обезу́мевший.

distress /dɪ'stres/ *n.*
1 (*physical suffering*) изнуре́ние, изнеможе́ние.
2 (*mental suffering*) трево́га, депре́ссия.
3 (*danger*) бе́дствие; **a ship in ~** су́дно, те́рпящее бе́дствие.
■ *v.t.* огорч|а́ть, -и́ть.

distressing /dɪ'stresɪŋ/ *adj.* огорчи́тельный.

distribute /dɪ'strɪbjuːt/ *v.t.*
1 (*deal out*) распредел|я́ть, -и́ть; (*goods*) распростран|я́ть, -и́ть.
2 (*spread*) распредел|я́ть, -и́ть.

distribution /dɪstrɪ'bjuːʃ(ə)n/ *n.* распределе́ние; (*of goods*) распростране́ние.

distributor /dɪ'strɪbjʊtə(r)/ *n.* (*comm.*) дистрибью́тор.

district /'dɪstrɪkt/ *n.* райо́н, о́круг; (*attr.*) райо́нный, окружно́й; **~ attorney** (*US*) окружно́й прокуро́р.

distrust /dɪs'trʌst/ *v.t.* не доверя́ть (*impf.*) + *d.*

distrustful /dɪs'trʌstfʊl/ *adj.* недове́рчивый.

disturb /dɪ'stəːb/ *v.t.* беспоко́ить, о-; (*peace*) нар|уша́ть, -у́шить; **he was ~ed by the news** он был обеспоко́ен но́востью.

disturbance /dɪ'stəːbəns/ *n.* (*act of troubling*) наруше́ние; (*riot*) волне́ния (*nt. pl.*).

disturbing /dɪ'stəːbɪŋ/ *adj.* трево́жный.

disuse /dɪs'juːs/ *n.*: **fall into ~** выходи́ть, вы́йти из употребле́ния.

disused /dɪs'juːsd/ *adj.*: **a ~ well** забро́шенный коло́дец.

ditch /dɪtʃ/ *n.* кана́ва; ров.
■ *v.t.* (*coll.*): **~ one's plans** забр|а́сывать, -о́сить свои́ пла́ны; **~ s.o.** бр|оса́ть, -о́сить кого́-н.

dither /'dɪðə(r)/ *v.i.* (*coll.*) колеба́ться, по-.

ditto /'dɪtəʊ/ *n.* (*pl.* **~s**) то же.

diva /'diːvə/ *n.* (*pl.* **~s**) примадо́нна, ди́ва.

divan /dɪ'væn/ *n.* тахта́, дива́н; **~ bed** дива́н-крова́ть.

dive /daɪv/ *n.* ныро́к, ныря́ние; (*of aircraft*) пики́рование.
■ *v.i.* (*past and p.p.* **dived** *or US also* **dove**) (*plunge into water*) ныр|я́ть, -ну́ть; (*in diving suit*) погру|жа́ться, -зи́ться.

diver /'daɪvə(r)/ *n.* ныря́льщик; водола́з.

diverge /daɪ'vəːdʒ/ *v.i.* ра|сходи́ться, -зойти́сь.

diverse /daɪ'vəːs/ *adj.* разнообра́зный.

diversify /daɪ'vəːsɪfaɪ/ *v.t.* разнообра́зить (*impf.*).

diversion /daɪ'vəːʃ(ə)n, dɪ-/ *n.*
1 (*turning aside*) отклоне́ние; **traffic ~** (*Br.*) объе́зд.
2 (*amusement*) развлече́ние, заба́ва.
3 : **create a ~** отвл|ека́ть, -е́чь внима́ние.

diversity /daɪ'vəːsɪtɪ, dɪ-/ *n.* разнообра́зие.

divert /daɪ'vəːt, dɪ-/ *v.t.* (*deflect*) отклон|я́ть, -и́ть; (*entertain*) развл|ека́ть, -е́чь.

divest /daɪ'vest/ *v.t.*: **~ s.o. of sth.** лиш|а́ть, -и́ть *кого* + *g.*; **~ o.s. of responsibilities** сложи́ть (*pf.*) с себя́ обя́занности.

divide /dɪ'vaɪd/ *n.* расхожде́ние.
■ *v.t.* 1 (*share*) дели́ть, по-, раз-; **they ~d the money equally** они́ раздели́ли де́ньги по́ровну.
2 (*math.*) дели́ть, раз-; **~ 27 by 3** 27 дели́ть, раз- на́ 3.
3 (*separate*) раздел|я́ть, -и́ть; **dividing line** разграничи́тельная ли́ния.
4 (*cause disagreement*) разъедин|я́ть, -и́ть.
■ *v.i.* дели́ться, раз-; **the road ~s** доро́га разветвля́ется.

dividend /'dɪvɪdend/ *n.* (*fin.*) дивиде́нд.

divine /dɪ'vaɪn/ *adj.* (**diviner, divinest**) боже́ственный.

diving /'daɪvɪŋ/ *n.* ныря́ние.
■ *cpds.* **~ board** *n.* трампли́н, вы́шка (для прыжко́в в во́ду); **~ suit** *n.* скафа́ндр.

divisible /dɪ'vɪzɪb(ə)l/ *adj.* (раз)дели́мый.

division /dɪ'vɪʒ(ə)n/ *n.*
1 (*math.*) деле́ние.
2 (*dividing*) разделе́ние, разде́л.
3 (*mil.*) диви́зия.
4 (*department*) отде́л.

divisive /dɪ'vaɪsɪv/ *adj.* вызыва́ющий разногла́сия.

divorce /dɪ'vɔːs/ *n.* (*leg.*) разво́д.

■ *v.t.* (*leg.*) разв|оди́ть, -ести́; **he ~d his wife** он развёлся с жено́й; **she is ~d** она́ разведена́.
■ *v.i.* разв|оди́ться, -ести́сь.

divorcee /dɪvɔː'siː/ (*US* **divorcé** (*m.*), **divorcée** (*f.*)) *n.* разведённый (муж), разведённая (жена́).

divulge /daɪ'vʌldʒ/ *v.t.* разгла|ша́ть, -си́ть.

DIY (*abbr. of* ***do it yourself***) (*Br.*): **~ store** магази́н «Уме́лые ру́ки».

dizzy /'dɪzɪ/ *adj.* (**dizzier, dizziest**) испы́тывающий головокруже́ние; **I feel ~** у меня́ кру́жится голова́.

DJ (*abbr. of* ***disc jockey***) дидже́й.

DNA (*abbr. of* ***deoxyribonucleic acid***) ДНК (дезоксирибонуклеи́новая кислота́).

do /duː/ *v.t.* & *aux.* (*3rd pers. sing. pres.* **does;** *past* **did;** *p.p.* **done**)
1 (*as aux. or substitute for v. already used: not translated unless emph.*): **I ~ not smoke** я не курю́; **did you not see me?** ра́зве вы меня́ не ви́дели?; **I ~ want to go** я о́чень хочу́ пойти́; **~ tell me** пожа́луйста, расскажи́те мне; **they promised to help, and they did** они́ обеща́ли помо́чь и помогли́; **so ~ I** я то́же.
2 (*perform, carry out*): **what can I ~ for you?** чем могу́ служи́ть?; **what ~es he ~ (for a living)?** чем он занима́ется?; **the team did well** кома́нда вы́ступила успе́шно; **easier said than ~ne** легко́ сказа́ть; **well ~ne!** молоде́ц!
3 (*render*): **it ~es him credit** э́то де́лает ему́ честь; **it won't ~ any good** э́то бесполе́зно, э́то ничего́ не даст.
4 (*solve*): **~ a sum** реш|а́ть, -и́ть арифмети́ческую зада́чу.
5 (*attend to*): **he ~es book reviews** он рецензи́рует кни́ги; **we did geography today** сего́дня мы занима́лись геогра́фией.
6 (*arrange, clean, tidy*): **~ one's hair** прич|ёсываться, -еса́ться; **~ the dishes** мыть, по- посу́ду.
7 (*cook*): **well ~ne** хорошо́ прожа́ренный; **the potatoes are ~ne** карто́шка свари́лась/гото́ва.
8 (*coll., swindle*) над|ува́ть, -у́ть.
9 : **~ne!** (*agreed*) по рука́м!
■ *v.i.* (*3rd pers. sing. pres.* **does;** *past* **did;** *p.p.* **done**)
1 (*act, behave*): **~ as I tell you** де́лай, что тебе́ говоря́т.
2 (*be satisfactory, fitting or advisable*): **the scraps will ~ for the dog** объе́дки пойду́т соба́ке; **this will never ~** э́то никуда́ не годи́тся; так не пойдёт; **that will ~!** (*is enough*) хва́тит!; дово́льно!; **tomorrow will ~** мо́жно и за́втра.
3 (*fare, succeed*): **how-~-you-~?** здра́вствуйте!; как пожива́ете?; **how did he ~ in his exams?** как он сдал экза́мены?; **my roses are ~ing well** мои́ ро́зы хорошо́ расту́т; **the patient is ~ing well** больно́й поправля́ется.
■ *with preps.*: **what shall we ~ about lunch?** как насчёт обе́да?; **~ s.o. out of sth.** (*cheat, deprive of*) выма́нивать, вы́манить что-н. у кого́-н.; **what have you ~ne with the keys?** куда́ вы де́ли ключи́?; **I could ~ with a drink** я охо́тно (*or* с удово́льствием) вы́пил бы; **that coat could ~ with a clean** не помеша́ло бы вы́чистить э́то пальто́; **he ~esn't know what to ~ with himself** он не зна́ет, чем заня́ться; **it is nothing to ~ with you** э́то вас не каса́ется; **these books are ~ne with** э́ти кни́ги бо́льше не нужны́; **we must ~ without luxuries** мы должны́ обойти́сь без ро́скоши; **I can ~ without his silly jokes** мне надое́ли его́ дура́цкие шу́тки.
■ *with advs.*: **~ away** *v.i.*: **~ away with** конча́ть, ко́нчить с + *i.*; **~ in** *v.t.* (*sl., kill*) уб|ира́ть, -ра́ть; (*coll., exhaust*): **I am ~ne in** я измо́тан; **~ out** *v.t.* (*Br., clean, e.g. a room*) уб|ира́ть, -ра́ть; (*Br., clear, e.g. a cupboard*) вычища́ть, вы́чистить; **~ up** *v.t.* (*repair, refurnish*): **~ up a room** отде́л|ывать, -ать ко́мнату; (*fasten*): **~ up a parcel** завя́з|ывать, -а́ть паке́т; **~ up a dress** застёг|ивать, -ну́ть пла́тье.
■ *cpd.* **~-it-yourself** *adj.* самоде́льный.

Dobermann (pinscher) /'dəʊbəmən ('pɪnʃə(r))/ (*US* **Doberman**) *n.* доберма́н(-пи́нчер).

docile /'dəʊsaɪl/ *adj.* послу́шный, поко́рный.

dock[1] /dɒk/ *n.* (*in court*) скамья́ подсуди́мых.

dock[2] /dɒk/ *n.*
1 (*naut.*) док.
2 (*pl., port facilities*) верфь.
3 (*wharf*) при́стань.
■ *v.i.* (*go into ~*) входи́ть, войти́ в док; (*of space vehicles*) стыкова́ться, со-.
■ *cpd.* **~yard** *n.* верфь.

docker /'dɒkə(r)/ *n.* до́кер; порто́вый рабо́чий.

doctor /'dɒktə(r)/ *n.*
1 (*of medicine*) врач, до́ктор.
2 (*acad.*) до́ктор.
■ *v.t.* (*falsify*) подде́л|ывать, -ать.

doctoral /'dɒktər(ə)l/ *adj.* до́кторский.

doctorate /'dɒktərət/ *n.* сте́пень до́ктора.

doctrine /'dɒktrɪn/ *n.* доктри́на.

document /'dɒkjʊmənt/ *n.* (*also comput.*) докуме́нт.

documentary /dɒkjʊ'mentərɪ/ *n.* документа́льный фильм.

documentation /dɒkjʊmen'teɪʃ(ə)n/ *n.* документа́ция.

doddery /'dɒdərɪ/ *adj.* трясу́щийся от ста́рости; дря́хлый.

dodge /dɒdʒ/ *n.* увёртка.
■ *v.t.* увил|ивать, -ьну́ть от + *g.*; **~ a blow** увора́чиваться, уверну́ться от уда́ра.
■ *v.i.* уклон|я́ться, -и́ться (от + *g.*).

dodgy /'dɒdʒɪ/ *adj.* (**dodgier, dodgiest**) (*Br. coll.*) (*suspicious*) подозри́тельный; (*risky*) риско́ванный.

does /dʌz/ *3rd pers. sing. pres. of* ▸ **do**

doesn't /'dʌz(ə)nt/ *neg. of* ▸ **does**

doff /dɒf/ *v.t.* сн|има́ть, -ять (*шля́пу*).

dog /dɒg/ *n.*
1 соба́ка, пёс (*also fig., pej.*).
2 (*male*) кобе́ль (*m.*).
3 (*fig.*): **go to the ~s** разори́ться (*pf.*), пойти́ (*pf.*) пра́хом.
■ *cpds.* **~ collar** *n.* оше́йник; (*coll., clergyman's*) кру́глый сто́ячий воротни́к; **~-eared** *adj.* потрёпанный; **~house** *n.*

(*US*) конурá; **in the ~house** (*coll.*) в немúлости; **~-paddle** *v.i.* плáвать (*indet.*) по-собáчьи; **~sbody** *n.* (*Br.*) ишáк, работя́га (*c.g.*).

dogged /ˈdɒgɪd/ *adj.* упóрный, насты́рный (*coll.*).

dogma /ˈdɒgmə/ *n.* дóгма; (*specific*) дóгмат.

dogmatic /dɒgˈmætɪk/ *adj.* (*views*) догматúческий; (*person*) догматúчный.

dogmatism /ˈdɒgmətɪz(ə)m/ *n.* догматúзм.

doing /ˈduːɪŋ/ *n.*: **this was his ~** э́то егó рук дéло; **it will take some ~** придётся постарáться; э́то не тáк прóсто.

doldrums /ˈdɒldrəmz/ *n.* (*geog.*) экваториáльная штилевáя полосá; (*fig.*) уны́ние, хандрá; **be in the ~** быть в уны́нии, хандрúть (*impf.*).

dole /dəʊl/ *n.* (*Br.*) (*benefit*) пособие по безрабóтице; **he is on the ~** он получáет пособие по безрабóтице.
■ *v.t.*: **~ out** разд|авáть, -áть.

doleful /ˈdəʊlfʊl/ *adj.* скóрбный.

doll /ˈdɒl/ *n.* кýкла.

dollar /ˈdɒlə(r)/ *n.* дóллар.

dollop /ˈdɒləp/ *n.* (*coll.*) солúдная пóрция.

dolphin /ˈdɒlfɪn/ *n.* дельфúн.

domain /dəˈmeɪn/ *n.* (*fig.*) óбласть; (*comput.*) домéн.

dome /dəʊm/ *n.* кýпол.

domed /dəʊmd/ *adj.* куполообрáзный; **~ forehead** вы́пуклый лоб.

domestic /dəˈmestɪk/ *adj.*
1 (*of the home*; *of animals*) домáшний.
2 (*not foreign*) отéчественный, внýтренний.

domesticate /dəˈmestɪkeɪt/ *v.t.* (*tame*) приручи|áть, -úть.

domesticity /dɒməˈstɪsɪtɪ/ *n.* семéйная/ домáшняя жизнь.

domicile /ˈdɒmɪsaɪl/ *n.* (*dwelling*) мéсто жúтельства.
■ *v.t.*: **~d in England** имéющий постоя́нное местожúтельство в Áнглии.

dominance /ˈdɒmɪnəns/ *n.* преоблáдание, господство.

dominant /ˈdɒmɪnənt/ *adj.* доминúрующий.

dominate /ˈdɒmɪneɪt/ *v.t.* & *i.*
1 (*prevail*) доминúровать (*impf.*) (над + *i.*).
2 (*influence*) подавля́ть (*impf.*); **she ~s her daughter** онá подавля́ет дочь.

domination /dɒmɪˈneɪʃ(ə)n/ *n.* госпóдство.

domineering /dɒmɪˈnɪərɪŋ/ *adj.* влáстный.

Dominican /dəˈmɪnɪkən/ *adj.*: **the ~ Republic** Доминикáнская Респýблика.

domino /ˈdɒmɪnəʊ/ *n.* (*pl.* **~es**) кость доминó; (*pl.*, *game*) доминó (*nt. indecl.*).

don /dɒn/ *n.*
1 (*Spanish title*) дон; **D~ Juan** (*fig.*) донжуáн.
2 (*univ.*) преподавáтель (*m.*).

donate /dəʊˈneɪt/ *v.t.* дарúть, по-.

donation /dəʊˈneɪʃ(ə)n/ *n.* дар.

done /dʌn/ *p.p. of* ▸ **do**

donkey /ˈdɒŋkɪ/ *n.* осёл (*also fig.*).

donor /ˈdəʊnə(r)/ *n.* дарúтель (*fem.* -ница); (*of blood, transplant*) дóнор.

don't /dəʊnt/ *neg. of* ▸ **do**

doodle /ˈduːd(ə)l/ *v.t.* & *i.* чúркать (*impf.*).

doom /duːm/ *n.* (*ruin*) гúбель.
■ *v.t.* обр|екáть, -éчь на + *a.*

door /dɔː(r)/ *n.*
1 (*of room etc.*) дверь; (*of cupboard etc.*) двéрца; **behind closed ~s** (*in secret*) за закры́тыми дверя́ми.
2 (*fig.*): **a ~ to success** путь к успéху.
■ *cpds.* **~bell** *n.* дверной звонóк; **~-handle** *n.* дверная рýчка; **~keeper** *n.* приврáтник; швейцáр; **~knob** *n.* крýглая дверная рýчка; **~man** *n.* = **~keeper**; **~mat** *n.* половúк; **~step** *n.* порóг; **~-to-~** *adj.*: **~ salesman** коммивояжёр; **~-to-~** *adj.*: **~ salesman** коммивояжёр; **~way** *n.* дверной проём.

dope /dəʊp/ *n.*
1 (*drug*) дурмáн, наркóтик.
2 (*sl.*, *fool*) дýрень (*m.*).
■ *v.t.* 1 (*make unconscious*) дурмáнить, о-.
2 (*put narcotic in*) накáч|ивать, -áть наркóтиками.

dopey /ˈdəʊpɪ/ *adj.* (**dopier, dopiest**) (*bemused by drug or sleep*) одурмáненный; (*coll.*, *foolish*) чóкнутый.

dormant /ˈdɔːmənt/ *adj.* (*of animals*) в спя́чке; **~ volcano** спя́щий вулкáн.

dormitory /ˈdɔːmɪtərɪ/ *n.* óбщая спáльня.

dormouse /ˈdɔːmaʊs/ *n.* (*pl.* **dormice**) сóня.

DOS /dɒs/ (*abbr. of* ***disk operating system***) ДОС (дúсковая операциóнная систéма).

dose /dəʊs/ *n.* дóза.
■ *v.t.* лечúть (*impf.*) дóзами лекáрства.

doss /dɒs/ *v.i.* (*Br. coll.*; *also* **~ down**) ночевáть, пере-; (*also* **~ around**) бездéльничать (*impf.*).
■ *cpd.* **~house** *n.* ночлéжка.

dossier /ˈdɒsɪə(r)/ *n.* досьé (*nt. indecl.*), дéло.

dot /dɒt/ *n.* тóчка; **on the ~** тóчно.
■ *v.t.* (**dotted, dotting**): **~ted line** пунктúр; пунктúрная лúния.

dotage /ˈdəʊtɪdʒ/ *n.* стáрческое слабоýмие, марáзм; **he is in his ~** он впал в дéтство/ марáзм.

dot-com company /dɒtˈkɒm/ *n.* интернéт-компáния.

dote /dəʊt/ *v.i.*: **~ on** (*child, friend*) обожáть (*impf.*).

double /ˈdʌb(ə)l/ *n.*
1 (*two shots of vodka etc.*) двойнáя мéра.
2 (*person resembling another*) двойнúк.
3 (*running pace*): **at the ~** (*Br.*), **on the ~** (*US*) бéглым шáгом.
4 (*tennis*) пáрная игрá; **mixed ~s** смéшанные пáры (*f. pl.*).
■ *adj.* 1 (*in two parts*; *twice as much*) двойнóй; **~ bed** дву(х)спáльная кровáть; **~ room** (*in hotel*) двухмéстный нóмер; **'Anna' is spelt with a ~ 'n'** «Áнна» пúшется с двумя́ «н».
2 (*mus.*): **~ bass** контрабáс.
■ *adv.* вдвóе; **bend ~** сгибáть(ся), согнýть(ся) вдвóе; **pay ~** платúть, за- вдвойнé; **he sees ~** у негó двóится в глазáх.
■ *v.t.* удв|áивать, -óить.
■ *v.i.* 1 (*become twice as great*) удв|áиваться, -óиться.
2 (*turn sharply*): **he ~d back on his tracks** он пошёл обрáтно по своемý слéду.
3 (*bend*) кóрчиться, с-; **he ~d up with the pain** он скóрчился от бóли.
4 (*combine roles*): **I ~d for him** я дублúровал

его́; **the porter ~s as waiter** носи́льщик рабо́тает официа́нтом по совмести́тельству.
■ *cpds.* **~-barrelled** (*US* **barreled**) *adj.* **~-barrelled name** (*Br.*) двойна́я фами́лия; **~-breasted** *adj.* двубо́ртный; **~-check** *v.t.* перепров|еря́ть, -е́рить; **~-click** *v.i.* (*comput.*) два́жды щёлк|ать, -нуть; **~-cross** *n.* вероло́мство; *v.t.* обма́н|ывать, -у́ть; **~-decker** *n.* (*bus*) двухэта́жный авто́бус; **~ Dutch** *n.* (*Br.*) тараба́рщина, кита́йская гра́мота; **~-park** *v.t.* & *i.* ста́вить, по- (маши́ну) во второ́й ряд; **~ take** *n.* (*fig.*) заме́дленная реа́кция.

doubt /daʊt/ *n.* сомне́ние; **there is no ~ that ...** нет сомне́ния в том, что...; **the question is in ~** э́тот вопро́с ещё не я́сен; **without ~** вне сомне́ния; несомне́нно; **no ~** несомне́нно, безусло́вно.
■ *v.t.* & *i.* сомнева́ться (*impf.*) (в + *p.*); **I ~ that, whether he will come** (я) сомнева́юсь, что он придёт.

doubtful /ˈdaʊtfʊl/ *adj.*
1 (*feeling doubt*) сомнева́ющийся.
2 (*causing doubt*) сомни́тельный.

dough /dəʊ/ *n.* те́сто.
■ *cpd.* **~nut** *n.* по́нчик.

dour /dʊə(r)/ *adj.* суро́вый.

douse /daʊs/ *v.t.* (*drench*) зал|ива́ть, -и́ть; (*extinguish*) гаси́ть, по-.

dove /dʌv/ *n.* го́лубь (*m.*).

dowdy /ˈdaʊdɪ/ *adj.* (**dowdier, dowdiest**) неэлега́нтный.

down¹ /daʊn/ *n.* (*hair, fluff*) пух, пушо́к.

down² /daʊn/ *n.* невзго́да; **ups and ~s** взлёты (*m. pl.*) и паде́ния (*nt. pl.*).
■ *adj.* напра́вленный вниз/кни́зу.
■ *adv.* 1 (*expr. motion/place*) вниз/внизу́; **the blinds are ~** што́ры спу́щены; **prices are ~** це́ны упа́ли; (*fig.*): **he is £15 ~** он в убы́тке на 15 фу́нтов.
2 (*expr. movement to lower level*): **climb ~** слез|а́ть, -ть; **come ~** спус|ка́ться, -ти́ться.
3 (*expr. change of position*): **sit ~** сади́ться, сесть; **lie ~** ложи́ться, лечь; **fall ~** па́дать, упа́сть; **knock s.o. ~** сби|ва́ть, -ть; **he bent ~** он нагну́лся.
4 (*reduction*): **the wind died ~** ве́тер ути́х; **the house burnt ~** дом сгоре́л дотла́.
5 : **~ with the government!** доло́й прави́тельство!
■ *prep.* 1 (*expr. downward direction*): **we walked ~ the hill** мы шли́ с горы́ (*or* под гору); **tears ran ~ her face** слёзы текли́/кати́лись у неё по лицу́.
2 (*at, to a lower or further part of*): **further ~ the river** да́льше вниз по реке́; **we sailed ~ the Volga** мы плы́ли вниз по Во́лге; **he lives ~ the street** он живёт да́льше по э́той у́лице.
3 (*along*): **he walked ~ the street** он шёл по у́лице.

down-and-out /daʊnəˈnaʊt/ *n.* бродя́га (*m.*); бездо́мный.

downcast /ˈdaʊnkɑːst/ *adj.* (*dejected*) удручённый; пода́вленный.

downfall /ˈdaʊnfɔːl/ *n.* паде́ние.

downgrade /ˈdaʊngreɪd/ *v.t.* пон|ижа́ть, -и́зить в чи́не.

downhearted /daʊnˈhɑːtɪd/ *adj.* пода́вленный.

downhill /ˈdaʊnhɪl/ *adv.* по́д гору; вниз; **go ~** (*fig.*) кати́ться (*det.*) по накло́нной пло́скости.

download /daʊnˈləʊd/ *v.t.* (*comput.*) загру|жа́ть, -зи́ть.

downmarket /ˈdaʊnˈmɑːkɪt/ *adj.* (*Br.*) дешёвый.

downpour /ˈdaʊnpɔː(r)/ *n.* ли́вень (*m.*).

downright /ˈdaʊnraɪt/ *adj.* (*straightforward, blunt*) прямо́й; (*absolute*) соверше́нный; я́вный.

downshift /ˈdaʊnʃɪft/ *v.i.*
1 (*US, motoring*) переключ|а́ть, -и́ть на ни́жнюю ско́рость.
2 (*at work*) пере|ходи́ть, -йти́ на ме́нее напряжённую, хотя́ и нижеопла́чиваемую рабо́ту.

downsize /ˈdaʊnsaɪz/*v.t.* & *i.* (*comm.*) ум|еньша́ть, -е́ньшить разме́ры (компа́нии) за счёт увольне́ния рабо́тников.

Down's syndrome /daʊnz/ *n.* боле́знь/синдро́м Да́уна.

downstairs /ˈdaʊnsteəz/ *adj.*: **~ rooms** ко́мнаты пе́рвого этажа́.
■ *adv.* (*expr. place*) внизу́; (*expr. motion*) вниз.

downstream /ˈdaʊnstriːm/ *adv.* вниз по тече́нию.

down-to-earth /ˈdaʊntəəːθ/ *adj.* практи́чный.

downtown /ˈdaʊntaʊn/ *adj.* (*US*) располо́женный в делово́й ча́сти го́рода.

downtrodden /ˈdaʊntrɒd(ə)n/ *adj.* угнетённый.

downturn /ˈdaʊntəːn/ *n.* (*fall, reduction*) паде́ние, спад.

downward /ˈdaʊnwəd/ *adj.* спуска́ющийся.

downwards /ˈdaʊnwədz/ *adv.* вниз.

doze /dəʊz/ *v.i.* дрема́ть (*impf.*); **~ off** задрема́ть (*pf.*).

dozen /ˈdʌz(ə)n/ *n.*
1 (*pl.* **~**) дю́жина.
2 : **~s of** мно́жество, ма́сса + *g.*

dozy /ˈdəʊzɪ/ *adj.* (**dozier, doziest**) сонли́вый; (*Br., not alert*) рассе́янный.

drab /dræb/ *adj.* (**drabber, drabbest**) се́рый.

draft /drɑːft/ *n. see also* ▸ **draught**
1 (*outline, rough copy*) набро́сок, чернови́к.
2 (*order for payment*) чек, тра́тта.
3 (*US, conscription*) призы́в; **~ dodger** лицо́, уклоня́ющееся от вое́нной слу́жбы.
■ *v.t.* 1 (*detach for duty*) наря|жа́ть, -ди́ть.
2 (*conscript*) приз|ыва́ть, -ва́ть.
3 (*prepare ~ of*) набр|а́сывать, -оса́ть чернови́к + *g.*

draftsman /ˈdrɑːftsmən/ *n.* (*of contracts etc.*) состави́тель (*m.*) (*законопроекта и т. п.*); (*US, one who draws*) чертёжник.

drafty /ˈdrɑːftɪ/ (*US*) = **draughty**

drag /dræg/ *n.* (*coll.*) (*person*) зану́да; (*thing*) тоска́ зелёная.
■ *v.t.* (**dragged, dragging**) (*pull*) тяну́ть, волочи́ть, тащи́ть (*all impf.*); **I had to ~ him to the party** мне пришло́сь тащи́ть его́ на вечери́нку; **~ one's feet** (*fig.*) тяну́ть, ме́длить (*both impf.*).
■ *v.i.* (**dragged, dragging**)

1 (*trail*) волочи́ться (*impf.*).
2 (*be slow or tedious*) тяну́ться (*impf.*).
■ *with adv.*: ~ **on** *v.i.*: **the performance ~ged on till 11** представле́ние затяну́лось до оди́ннадцати часо́в.

dragon /ˈdrægən/ *n.* (*fabulous beast*) драко́н.
■ *cpd.* **~fly** *n.* стрекоза́.

dragoon /drəˈguːn/ *v.t.* прин|ужда́ть, -у́дить; **he was ~ed into obeying** его́ заста́вили подчини́ться.

drain /dreɪn/ *n.*
1 (*channel carrying off sewage etc.*) водосто́к; (*pl., system of ~s*) канализа́ция.
2 (*cause of exhaustion*) истоще́ние; **it is a ~ on my energy** э́то истоща́ет мою́ эне́ргию.
■ *v.t.* 1 (*water etc.*) отв|оди́ть, -ести́.
2 (*land etc.*) осуш|а́ть, -и́ть (*impf.*); **~ing board** (*Br.*), **drainboard** (*US*) суши́лка.
■ *v.i.* 1 (*flow away*) ут|ека́ть, -е́чь.
2 (*lose moisture*) высыха́ть, вы́сохнуть.
■ *cpd.* **~pipe** *n.* дрена́жная труба́.

drainage /ˈdreɪnɪdʒ/ *n.*
1 (*draining or being drained*) дрена́ж, осуше́ние.
2 (*system of drains*) канализа́ция.

drake /dreɪk/ *n.* се́лезень (*m.*).

drama /ˈdrɑːmə/ *n.* дра́ма.

dramatic /drəˈmætɪk/ *adj.* (*pert. to drama*) драмати́ческий; (*exciting*) драмати́чный.

dramatics /drəˈmætɪks/ *n.* (*staging of plays*) драмати́ческое иску́сство; теа́тр; **amateur ~** люби́тельский/самоде́ятельный теа́тр.

dramatist /ˈdræmətɪst/ *n.* драмату́рг.

dramatize /ˈdræmətaɪz/ *v.t.* (*turn into a play*) инсцени́ровать (*impf., pf.*); (*exaggerate*) драматизи́ровать (*impf., pf.*).

drank /dræŋk/ *past of* ▸ **drink**

drape /dreɪp/ *n.* (*usu. pl.*) за́навес, портье́ра.
■ *v.t.* драпирова́ть, за-.

drastic /ˈdræstɪk/ *adj.* реши́тельный, круто́й.

draught /drɑːft/ (*US* **draft**) *n.*
1 (*current of air*) тя́га; **there is a ~ in here** здесь сквози́т.
2 (*of liquor*): **~ beer, beer on ~** пи́во из бо́чки.
3 (*pl., Br., game*) ша́шки (*f. pl.*).

draughtsman /ˈdrɑːftsmən/ *n.* чертёжник.

draughty /ˈdrɑːftɪ/ (*US* **drafty**) *adj.* (**draughtier, draughtiest**): **this is a ~ room** в э́той ко́мнате постоя́нный сквозня́к.

draw /drɔː/ *n.* (*in lottery*) ро́зыгрыш; (**~n** *game*) ничья́.
■ *v.t.* (*past* **drew;** *p.p.* **drawn**)
1 (*pull, move*) тяну́ть (*impf.*); таска́ть (*indet.*), тащи́ть, по-; **~ the curtains** (*close*) задв|ига́ть, -и́нуть занаве́ски; (*open*) раздв|ига́ть, -и́нуть занаве́ски.
2 (*extract*) выта́скивать, вы́тащить; **~ a knife** выхва́тывать, выхватить нож; **~ blood** ра́нить (*impf., pf.*) кого́-н. до кро́ви; **~ lots** тяну́ть, вы- жре́бий.
3 (*obtain from a source*): **~ money out of the bank** снима́ть, снять де́ньги в ба́нке; **~ on one's savings** тра́тить, по- свои́ сбереже́ния.
4 (*attract*) привл|ека́ть, -е́чь; **I drew him into the conversation** я втяну́л *or* вовлёк его́ в разгово́р.
5 (*trace, depict*) рисова́ть, на-; черти́ть, на-.
6 (*of mental operations*): **~ a distinction/comparison** пров|оди́ть, -ести́ разли́чие/сравне́ние; **~ conclusions** при|ходи́ть, -йти́ к вы́водам.
7 (*of contest*): **the match was ~n** матч зако́нчился вничью́.
■ *v.i.* (*past* **drew;** *p.p.* **drawn**) (*move, come*) придв|ига́ться, -и́нуться; **the day drew to a close** день бли́зился к концу́.
■ *with advs.*: **~ in** *v.i.*: **the train drew in** по́езд подошёл к перро́ну; (*shorten*): **the days are ~ing in** дни стано́вятся коро́че; **~ out** *v.t.* (*extract*) выта́скивать, вы́тащить; вытя́гивать, вы́тянуть; (*prolong*) затя́|гивать, -ну́ть; (*encourage to speak*): **~ s.o. out** вызыва́ть, вы́звать кого́-н. на разгово́р; *v.i.*: **the train drew out** по́езд отошёл; **~ up** *v.t.*: (*plan, contract etc.*) сост|авля́ть, -а́вить.
■ *cpd.* **~back** *n.* (*disadvantage*) недоста́ток.

drawer /drɔː(r)/ *n.* (*in table etc.*) (выдвижно́й) я́щик.

drawing /ˈdrɔːɪŋ/ *n.*
1 (*technique*) рисова́ние.
2 (*piece of ~*) рису́нок.
■ *cpds.* **~ board** *n.* чертёжная доска́; **~ pin** *n.* (*Br.*) кно́пка; **~ room** *n.* гости́ная.

drawl /drɔːl/ *n.* протя́жное произноше́ние.

drawn /drɔːn/ *p.p. of* ▸ **draw**

dread /dred/ *v.t.* боя́ться (*impf.*) + *g.*; **I ~ to think what may happen** мне стра́шно поду́мать, что мо́жет случи́ться.

dreadful /ˈdredfʊl/ *adj.* ужа́сный.

dream /driːm/ *n.*
1 (*appearance in sleep*) сон, сновиде́ние.
2 (*fantasy*) мечта́, мечта́ние.
■ *v.t. & i.* (*past and p.p.* **dreamed** /dremt, driːmd/ *or* **dreamt** /dremt/)
1 (*in sleep*) ви́деть (*impf.*) сон; **I ~t of you** вы мне сни́лись; я ви́дел вас во сне.
2 (*imagine*) пом|ышля́ть, -ы́слить о + *p.*; **I never ~t of doing so** у меня́ и в мы́слях не́ было де́лать э́того; **he ~t up a plan** (*coll.*) он сочини́л план.

dreamer /ˈdriːmə(r)/ *n.* (*dreamy person*) мечта́тель (*m.*); (*visionary*) фантазёр.

dreamt /dremt/ *past and p.p. of* ▸ **dream**

dreamy /ˈdriːmɪ/ *adj.* (**dreamier, dreamiest**) мечта́тельный; (*coll., lovely*) восхити́тельный.

dreary /ˈdrɪərɪ/ *adj.* (**drearier, dreariest**) (*gloomy*) тоскли́вый; (*dull*) се́рый.

dregs /dregz/ *n. pl.* отсто́й, оса́док.

drench /drentʃ/ *v.t.* пром|а́чивать, -очи́ть.

dress /dres/ *n.*
1 (*clothing, costume*) оде́жда, наря́д, туале́т; **~ circle** бельэта́ж; **~ rehearsal** генера́льная репети́ция.
2 (*woman's garment*) пла́тье.
■ *v.t.* 1 (*clothe*) од|ева́ть, -е́ть (*кого во что*).
2 (*prepare*) припр|авля́ть, -а́вить; **~ a salad** запр|авля́ть, -а́вить сала́т.
3 (*of a wound*) перевя́з|ывать, -а́ть.
■ *v.i.* 1 (*put on one's clothes*) од|ева́ться, -е́ться; **~ up** (**~** *elaborately*) наря|жа́ться, -ди́ться; **they ~ed up as pirates** они́ наряди́лись пира́тами.
2 (*choose clothes*) од|ева́ться, -е́ться; **he ~es well** он хорошо́ одева́ется.
■ *cpd.* **~ code** *n.* дресс-ко́д (*правила-*

ограничения в отношении допустимой одежды); **~maker** портниха.

dresser[1] /'dresə(r)/ *n.*: **she is a good ~** она́ хорошо́ одева́ется.

dresser[2] /'dresə(r)/ *n.* (*sideboard*) буфе́т; (*US, chest of drawers*) шкаф с выдвижны́ми я́щиками.

dressing /'dresɪŋ/ *n.*
1 (*med.*) повя́зка.
2 (*US, stuffing*) начи́нка.
3 (*of salad etc.*) запра́вка.
■ *cpds.* **~ gown** *n.* хала́т; **~ room** *n.* (*theatr.*) артисти́ческая убо́рная; **~ table** *n.* туале́тный сто́лик.

dressy /'dresɪ/ *adj.* (**dressier, dressiest**) шика́рный, наря́дный.

drew /dru:/ *past of* ▸ **draw**

dribble /'drɪb(ə)l/ *n.* (*trickle*) стру́йка.
■ *v.t.*: **~ a ball** вести́ (*det.*) мяч.
■ *v.i.* (*of baby*) пус|ка́ть, -ти́ть слю́ни.

drier = **dryer**

drift /drɪft/ *n.*
1 (*of tide etc.*) тече́ние.
2 (*heap of snow, leaves etc.*) нано́с, ку́ча.
3 (*meaning*) смысл; **I get his ~** я понима́ю, куда́ он кло́нит.
■ *v.i.* дрейфова́ть (*impf.*); **the boat ~ed out to sea** ло́дку отнесло́ в мо́ре; **they were friends but ~ed apart** они́ бы́ли друзья́ми, но их пути́ постепе́нно разошли́сь.

drill[1] /drɪl/ *n.* (*instrument*) (*small*) дрель; (*large*) бур, бура́в; (*dentist's*) бормаши́на.
■ *v.t.* сверли́ть, про-; working бури́ть, про-; **~ a hole** сверли́ть, про- отве́рстие.
■ *v.i.* бури́ть (*impf.*); **~ for oil** бури́ть (*impf.*) нефтяну́ю сква́жину.

drill[2] /drɪl/ *n.* (*mil.*) строева́я подгото́вка.
■ *v.t.* (*troops*) обуч|а́ть, -и́ть строево́й подгото́вке.

drink /drɪŋk/ *n.*
1 (*liquid*) напи́ток, питьё.
2 (*quantity*) глото́к.
3 (*alcoholic*) вы́пивка, спиртно́й напи́ток.
■ *v.t.* (*past* **drank;** *p.p.* **drunk**)
1 (*consume liquid*) пить, вы́-; **~ing water** питьева́я вода́.
2 (*of alcoholic liquor*) пить (*or* выпива́ть), вы́-.
■ *v.i.* (*past* **drank;** *p.p.* **drunk**) (*consume liquid*) пить (*impf.*).
■ *cpd.* **~-driving** *n.* (*Br.*) вожде́ние в нетре́звом состоя́нии.

drinkable /'drɪŋkəb(ə)l/ *adj.* (*capable of being drunk*) питьево́й, го́дный для питья́; (*palatable*) вку́сный.

drip /drɪp/ *n.* (*action*) ка́панье; (*drop*) ка́пля; (*weak person*) тря́пка.
■ *v.i.* (**dripped, dripping**) ка́пать (*impf.*).

dripping /'drɪpɪŋ/ *n.* (*pl., US, liquid*) ка́пли (*f. pl.*); (*Br., cul.*) топлёный жир.

drive /draɪv/ *n.*
1 (*ride in vehicle*) езда́; **go for a ~** прокати́ться, поката́ться (*both pf.*) (на маши́не); **the station is an hour's ~ away** до ста́нции час езды́.
2 (*private road*) подъездна́я доро́га.
3 (*hit, stroke, at tennis etc.*) драйв, си́льный уда́р.
4 (*energy*) напо́ристость, напо́р.
5 (*organized effort*) кампа́ния; **a ~ for new members** кампа́ния по привлече́нию но́вых чле́нов.
6 (*driving gear*) переда́ча, при́вод.
7 (*comput.*) при́вод; **disk ~** дисково́д; **hard ~** жёсткий диск.
■ *v.t.* (*past* **drove;** *p.p.* **driven**)
1 (*force to move*) гоня́ть (*indet.*), гнать (*det.*); выбива́ть, вы́бить.
2 (*operate*) управля́ть (*impf.*) + *i.*; **~ a car** води́ть (*indet.*) маши́ну.
3 (*impel, of objects*): **he drove a nail into the plank** он вбил гвоздь в до́ску.
4 (*impel, fig.*): **~ s.o. mad** св|оди́ть, -ести́ кого́-н. с ума́.
■ *v.i.* (*past* **drove;** *p.p.* **driven**)
1 (*operate vehicle*) води́ть (*indet.*), вести́ (*det.*) маши́ну.
2 (*be impelled*): **driving rain** проливно́й дождь.

driven /'drɪv(ə)n/ *p.p. of* ▸ **drive**

driver /'draɪvə(r)/ *n.*
1 (*of vehicle*) води́тель (*m.*), шофёр; **~'s license** (*US*) води́тельские права́.
2 (*comput.*) дра́йвер.

driving /'draɪvɪŋ/ *n.* езда́; **~ instructor** преподава́тель (*m.*) автошко́лы.
■ *cpds.* **~ licence** (*Br.*) *n.* води́тельские права́; **~ school** *n.* автошко́ла; **~ test** *n.* экза́мен на вожде́ние.

drizzle /'drɪz(ə)l/ *n.* и́зморось.
■ *v.i.* мороси́ть (*impf.*).

dromedary /'drɒmɪdərɪ/ *n.* дромаде́р, дромеда́р, одного́рбый верблю́д.

drone /drəʊn/ *n.*
1 (*bee*) тру́тень (*m.*).
2 (*of engine*) гуде́ние; (*of voice*) жужжа́ние.

drool /dru:l/ *v.i.* пус|ка́ть, -ти́ть слю́ни.

droop /dru:p/ *v.i.* (*of flowers, head*) ни́кнуть, по-.

drop /drɒp/ *n.*
1 (*small quantity of liquid*) ка́пля; (*fig.*): **a ~ in the bucket, ocean** ка́пля в мо́ре.
2 (*fall*) паде́ние; **~ in prices/temperature** паде́ние цен; пониже́ние температу́ры; **there is a ~ of 30 feet behind this wall** за э́той стено́й 30-фу́товый обры́в.
■ *v.t.* (**dropped, dropping**)
1 (*allow, cause to fall*) роня́ть, урони́ть; **~ a parcel at s.o.'s house** ост|авля́ть, -а́вить паке́т у чьего́-н. до́ма.
2 (*impel, force down*) сра|жа́ть, -зи́ть.
3 (*lower*): **~ one's voice** пон|ижа́ть, -и́зить го́лос.
4 (*send, utter casually*): **~ s.o. a line** черкну́ть (*pf.*) кому́-н. па́ру строк; **~ a hint** оброни́ть (*pf.*) намёк.
5 (*allow to descend, disembark*) выса́живать, вы́садить; **please ~ me at the station** пожа́луйста, вы́садите меня́ у ста́нции.
■ *v.i.* (**dropped, dropping**)
1 (*fall, descend*) па́дать, упа́сть.
2 (*become weaker or lower*) па́дать, упа́сть; **the wind ~ped** ве́тер стих/утих.
3 (*sink, collapse*) па́дать, упа́сть; **he ~ped (on) to his knees** он упа́л/опусти́лся на коле́ни.
■ *with advs.*: **~ in** *v.i.* (*coll.*): **he ~ped in on**

me он заглянул ко мне; **~ off** *v.i.* (*become fewer or less*) ум|еньшаться, -еньшиться; (*coll., doze off*) заснуть (*pf.*); **~ out** *v.i.*: **five runners ~ped out** пять бегунов выбыли из соревнования; **he ~ped out of school** он бросил школу.
■ *cpd.* **~out** *n.* человек, поставивший себя вне общества.

droppings /'drɒpɪŋz/ *n. pl.* (*of animals and birds*) помёт.

dross /drɒs/ *n.* шлак, окалина, дросс; (*fig.*) отбросы (*m. pl.*).

drought /draʊt/ *n.* засуха.

drove /drəʊv/ *past of* ▸ **drive**

drown /draʊn/ *v.t.*
1 (*kill by immersion*) топить, у-.
2 (*of sound*) приглуш|ать, -ить.
■ *v.i.* тонуть, у-.

drowsy /'draʊzɪ/ *adj.* (**drowsier, drowsiest**) (*feeling sleepy*) сонный.

drudgery /'drʌdʒərɪ/ *n.* изнурительная работа.

drug /drʌg/ *n.*
1 (*medicinal substance*) медикамент, лекарство.
2 (*narcotic or stimulant*) наркотик; **~ addict** наркоман; **~ addiction** наркомания; **~ trafficker** *or* **pusher** наркоделец.
■ *v.t.* (**drugged, drugging**) (*food etc.*) подмеш|ивать, -ать наркотики в + *a.*; (*person*) да|вать, -ть наркотики + *d.*
■ *cpds.* **~ abuse** *adj.* употребление наркотиков; **~store** *n.* (*US*) ≈ аптека.

drum /drʌm/ *n.*
1 (*instrument*) барабан.
2 (*container for oil etc.*) металлическая бочка.
■ *v.t.* (**drummed, drumming**) барабанить (*impf.*); **~ up support** соз|ывать, -вать подмогу; **~ sth. into s.o.'s head** вд|албливать, -олбить что-н. кому-н. в голову.
■ *v.i.* (**drummed, drumming**) барабанить (*impf.*).
■ *cpd.* **~stick** *n.* барабанная палочка; (*of fowl*) ножка.

drummer /'drʌmə(r)/ *n.* барабанщ|ик (*fem.* -ица).

drunk[1] /drʌŋk/ *n.* пьяный.
■ *adj.* пьяный.

drunk[2] /drʌŋk/ *p.p. of* ▸ **drink**

drunkard /'drʌŋkəd/ *n.* пьяница (*c.g.*), алкоголик.

drunken /'drʌŋkən/ *adj.* пьяный.

dry /draɪ/ *adj.* (**drier** /'draɪə(r)/, **driest** /'draɪɪst/)
1 (*free from moisture*) сухой.
2: **~ run** (*trial*) пробный забег.
3 (*of humour*) сухой; (*of remark etc.*) иронический.
■ *v.t.* сушить (*or* высушивать), вы-; **~ o.s.** вытираться, вытереться; **~ the dishes** вытирать, вытереть посуду; **~ one's hands** вытирать, вытереть руки; **dried fruit(s)** сушёные фрукты.
■ *v.i.* сохнуть, вы-; сушиться (*or* высушиваться), вы-.
■ *cpd.* **~-clean** *v.t.* подв|ергать, -ергнуть химической чистке.

dryer /'draɪə(r)/ *n.* сушилка, сушильный автомат.

DSL (*abbr. of* ***digital subscriber line***) (*teleph., comput.*) (цифровая) выделенная линия.

DTD (*abbr. of* ***Document Type Definition***) *n.* (*comput.*) описание шаблона документа.

dual /'dju:əl/ *adj.* двойственный, двойной; **~ carriageway** (*Br.*) дорога с двусторонним движением и разделительным барьером; **~ nationality** двойное гражданство.

dub /dʌb/ *v.t.* (**dubbed, dubbing**) (*film*) дублировать (*impf.*).

dubious /'dju:bɪəs/ *adj.* (*feeling doubt*) сомневающийся; (*inspiring mistrust*) сомнительный.

Dublin /'dʌblɪn/ *n.* Дублин.

duchess /'dʌtʃɪs/ *n.* герцогиня.

duchy /'dʌtʃɪ/ *n.* герцогство, княжество.

duck[1] /dʌk/ *n.* (*pl.* **~** *or* **~s**) (*bird*) утка; (*as food*) утиное мясо.

duck[2] /dʌk/ *v.t.* погру|жать, -зить; **~ one's head** быстро наг|ибать, -нуть голову; (*evade*): **~ a question** уклон|яться, -иться от ответа.
■ *v.i.* окун|аться, -уться.

duckling /'dʌklɪŋ/ *n.* утёнок.

duct /'dʌkt/ *n.* (*anat.*) канал, проток.

dud /dʌd/ *adj.* (*useless*) непригодный; (*counterfeit*) поддельный.

dude /dju:d, du:d/ *n.* пижон (*coll.*).

due /dju:/ *n.* должное.
■ *adj.* 1 (*payable*) причитающийся; **when is the rent ~?** когда надо платить за квартиру?
2 (*proper*) должный, надлежащий; **in ~ time** в своё время; **in ~ course** в свою очередь, своим чередом; **I am ~ for a haircut** мне пора постричься.
3 (*expected*): **he is ~ to speak twice** он должен выступить дважды.
4: **~ to** (*coll., owing to*) благодаря + *d.*; (*because of*) из-за + *g.*
■ *adv.* точно, прямо; **the village lies ~ south** деревня лежит прямо на юг отсюда.

duel /'dju:əl/ *n.* дуэль.

duet /dju:'et/ *n.* дуэт.

duff|el, -le /'dʌf(ə)l/ *n.*
1 (*text.*): **~ coat** пальто из шерстяной байки с капюшоном.
2: **~ bag** вещевой мешок.

dug /dʌg/ *past and p.p. of* ▸ **dig**

duke /dju:k/ *n.* герцог.

dull /dʌl/ *adj.*
1 (*not clear or bright*) тусклый; **~ weather** пасмурная погода.
2 (*uninteresting*) скучный.
■ *v.t.* притуп|лять, -ить.

duly /'dju:lɪ/ *adv.* (*in due manner*) должным образом; (*at the right time*) в должное время, своевременно.

dumb /dʌm/ *adj.*
1 (*unable to speak*) немой.
2 (*US coll., stupid*) глупый.
■ *v.t.*: **~ down** (*coll.*) популяризировать (*impf., pf.*).
■ *cpd.* **~-bell** *n.* гантель.

dum(b)found /dʌm'faʊnd/ *v.t.*

ошара́ш|ивать, -ить.

dummy /ˈdʌmɪ/ *n.* ку́кла; **tailor's ~** манеке́н; **baby's ~** (*Br.*) со́ска.
■ *adj.* (*imitation*) подставно́й; **~ run** про́бный забе́г.

dump /dʌmp/ *n.*
1 (*place for tipping refuse*) (му́сорная) сва́лка.
2 (*ammunition store*) вре́менный полево́й скла́д.
3 (*seedy place*) дыра́ (*coll.*).
■ *v.t.* 1 (*throw away*) выбра́сывать, вы́бросить.
2 (*deposit carelessly*) сва́л|ивать, -и́ть.
3 (*coll., abandon*) броса́ть, бро́сить.

dumpy /ˈdʌmpɪ/ *adj.* (**dumpier, dumpiest**) призе́мистый.

dune /dju:n/ *n.* дю́на.

dung /dʌŋ/ *n.* (*manure*) наво́з.

dungarees /dʌngəˈri:z/ *n.* комбинезо́н.

dungeon /ˈdʌndʒ(ə)n/ *n.* темни́ца.

duo /ˈdju:əʊ/ *n.* (*pl.* **~s**) дуэ́т.

dupe /dju:p/ *n. v.t.* ост|авля́ть, -а́вить в дурака́х; над|ува́ть, -у́ть.

duplicate[1] /ˈdju:plɪkət/ *n.* дублика́т; (то́чная) ко́пия.
■ *adj.* запасно́й.

duplicate[2] /ˈdju:plɪkeɪt/ *v.t.* удв|а́ивать, -о́ить.

duplicity /dju:ˈplɪsɪtɪ/ *n.* двули́чность.

durable /ˈdjʊərəb(ə)l/ *adj.* про́чный; долгове́чный.

duration /djʊəˈreɪʃ(ə)n/ *n.* продолжи́тельность.

duress /djʊəˈres/ *n.*: **under ~** под нажи́мом/давле́нием.

during /ˈdjʊərɪŋ/ *prep.* (*throughout*) в тече́ние + *g.*; (*at some point in*) во вре́мя + *g.*

dusk /dʌsk/ *n.* су́мер|ки (*pl., g.* -ек).

dust /dʌst/ *n.* пыль.
■ *v.t.* 1 (*remove ~ from*) ст|ира́ть, -ере́ть пыль с + *g.*
2 (*sprinkle*) пос|ыпа́ть, -ы́пать.
■ *cpds.* **~bin** *n.* (*Br.*) му́сорный я́щик; **~ cover** *n.* (*for chair etc.*) чехо́л; (*of book*) суперобло́жка; **~cart** *n.* (*Br.*) мусорово́з; **~man** *n.* (*Br.*) му́сорщик; **~pan** *n.* сово́к для му́сора.

duster /ˈdʌstə(r)/ *n.* (*Br., cloth*) тря́пка для пы́ли.

dusty /ˈdʌstɪ/ *adj.* (**dustier, dustiest**) пы́льный.

Dutch /dʌtʃ/ *n.*
1 (*language*) голла́ндский/нидерла́ндский язы́к.
2 (*pl., people*) голла́ндцы (*m. pl.*).

dutiful /ˈdju:tɪfʊl/ *adj.* пре́данный; (*obedient*) послу́шный.

duty /ˈdju:tɪ/ *n.*
1 (*moral obligation*) долг, обя́занность.
2 (*official employment*) служе́бные обя́занности; дежу́рство; **on ~** на дежу́рстве; **off ~** свобо́дный; вне слу́жбы; в свобо́дное/неслуже́бное вре́мя.
3 (*fin.*) по́шлина, сбор; **customs ~** тамо́женная по́шлина.
■ *cpd.* **~-free** *adj.* беспо́шлинный.

duvet /ˈdu:veɪ/ *n.* (*Br.*) стёганое одея́ло.

DVD *abbr.* (*of* ***digital versatile disk***) DVD, Ди-ви-ди́ (*m. indecl.*); **~ player** DVD-плéер.

dwarf /dwɔ:f/ *n.* (*pl.* **dwarfs** *or* **dwarves**) ка́рлик.

dwell /dwel/ *v.i.* (*past and p.p.* **dwelt** *or* **dwelled**) : **~ (up)on** (*expatiate on*) распространя́ться (*impf.*) о + *p.*

dwelling /ˈdwelɪŋ/ *n.* жильё, жили́ще.
■ *cpds.* **~ house** *n.* жило́й дом; **~ place** *n.* местожи́тельство.

dwelt /dwelt/ *past and p.p. of* ▶ **dwell**

dwindle /ˈdwɪnd(ə)l/ *v.i.* сокра|ща́ться, -ти́ться.

dye /daɪ/ *n.* кра́ска.
■ *v.t.* (**dyeing**) кра́сить, по-.
■ *v.i.* (**dyeing**) кра́ситься, по-.

dying /ˈdaɪɪŋ/ *adj.* умира́ющий, предсме́ртный.

dynamic /daɪˈnæmɪk/ *n.* (*force*) дви́жущая си́ла; (*pl., science*) дина́мика.
■ *adj.* (*pertaining to force*) динами́ческий; (*energetic*) динами́чный.

dynamism /ˈdaɪnəmɪz(ə)m/ *n.* динами́зм.

dynamite /ˈdaɪnəmaɪt/ *n.* динами́т (*also fig.*).

dynamo /ˈdaɪnəməʊ/ *n.* (*pl.* **~s**) дина́мо (*nt. indecl.*); дина́мо-маши́на.

dynasty /ˈdɪnəstɪ/ *n.* дина́стия.

dysentery /ˈdɪsəntrɪ/ *n.* дизентери́я.

dyslexia /dɪsˈleksɪə/ *n.* (*med.*) дисле́ксия (*неспособность к чтению*).

dyslexic /dɪsˈleksɪk/ *adj.*: **he is ~** он дисле́ктик.

Ee

E /i:/ *n.*
1 (*mus.*) ми (*nt. indecl.*).
2 (*acad. mark*) «кол», едини́ца.

e|- *prefix* (*comput.*) электро́нный; **~-banking** ба́нковские услу́ги че́рез Интерне́т, интерне́т-ба́нкинг; **~-book** электро́нная кни́га; **~-commerce** электро́нная коммéрция; **~-learning** электро́нное обуче́ние.

each /i:tʃ/ *pron. & adj.* ка́ждый; **he gave ~ (one) of us a book** он ка́ждому из нас дал по кни́ге; **he sat with a child on ~ side of him** он сиде́л ме́жду двумя́ детьми́; **the apples cost 20 pence ~** я́блоки сто́ят два́дцать пе́нсов шту́ка (*or* за шту́ку); **~ other** друг дру́га; **2 ~** по́ два/двое; **500 ~** по пятьсо́т.

eager /ˈiːgə(r)/ *adj.* стремя́щийся (**for:** к + *d.*); **he is ~ to go** он рвётся идти́.

eagerness /ˈiːgənɪs/ *n.* рве́ние, стремле́ние.

eagle /ˈiːg(ə)l/ *n.* орёл.

ear[1] /ɪə(r)/ *n.*
1 (*anat.*) у́хо.
2 : **~ for music** музыка́льный слух; **she plays by ~** она́ игра́ет на слух; **play it by ~** (*fig.*) пол|ага́ться, -ожи́ться на чутьё.
■ *cpds.* **~ache** *n.* боль в у́хе; **~drum** *n.* бараба́нная перепо́нка; **~mark** *v.t.* (*fig.*) предназн|ача́ть, -а́чить; ассигнова́ть (*impf.*, *pf.*); **~phone, ~piece** *nn.* нау́шник; ра́ковина телефо́нной тру́бки; **~ring** *n.* серьга́.

ear[2] /ɪə(r)/ *n.* (*bot.*) ко́лос.

earl /əːl/ *n.* (*британский*) граф.

earl|y /ˈəːlɪ/ *adj.* (**earlier, earliest**) ра́нний; **in one's ~y days, life** в ю́ности/мо́лодости; **in the ~y part of this century** в нача́ле э́того столе́тия; **we are ~y** мы пришли́ ра́но; **on Tuesday at (the) ~iest** не ра́ньше вто́рника.
■ *adv.* ра́но; **come as ~y as possible** приходи́те как мо́жно ра́ньше; **two hours ~ier** на два часа́ ра́ньше.

earn /əːn/ *v.t.* & *i.* зараб|а́тывать, -о́тать; (*deserve*) заслу́ж|ивать, -и́ть; **~ one's living** зараба́тывать (*impf.*) на жизнь.

earnest /ˈəːnɪst/ *n.*: **in ~** серьёзно, всерьёз.
■ *adj.* серьёзный.

earnings /ˈəːnɪŋz/ *n.* за́работок.

earth /əːθ/ *n.*
1 (*planet, world*) земля́; **why on ~?** с како́й ста́ти?; заче́м то́лько?; **who on ~?** кто то́лько?; кто же?; **like nothing on ~** ни на что не похо́жий.
2 (*dry land*) земля́.
3 (*soil*) земля́, по́чва.
4 (*Br., elec.*) земля́, заземле́ние.

earthenware /ˈəːθ(ə)nweə(r)/ *n.* гонча́рные изде́лия; гли́няная посу́да.

earthly /ˈəːθlɪ/ *adj.* земно́й; **there is no ~ reason why ...** нет ни мале́йшей причи́ны, что́бы…; **he hasn't an ~** (*Br. coll.*) у него́ нет ни мале́йшего ша́нса.

earthquake /ˈəːθkweɪk/ *n.* землетрясе́ние.

earthy /ˈəːθɪ/ *adj.* (**earthier, earthiest**) (*smell etc.*) землян́ой; (*fig.*) приземлённый, грубова́тый.

ease /iːz/ *n.*
1 (*facility*) лёгкость.
2 (*comfort*) поко́й, о́тдых, досу́г; **be, feel at ~** чу́вствовать (*impf.*) себя́ непринуждённо; **put s.o. at his ~** приободри́ть (*pf.*) кого́-н.
■ *v.t.*: **~ tension** осл|абля́ть, -а́бить напряжённость; **~ congestion** разгру|жа́ть, -зи́ть движе́ние; **~ s.o.'s anxiety** успок|а́ивать, -о́ить кого́-н.
■ *v.i.*: **~ off on drinking** (*coll.*) пить (*impf.*) ме́ньше; **the pressure of work ~d (up)** напряжённость рабо́ты спа́ла.

easel /ˈiːz(ə)l/ *n.* мольбе́рт.

easily /ˈiːzɪlɪ/ *adv.* легко́, без труда́; **he is ~ the best** он безусло́вно са́мый лу́чший; **he may ~ be late** он вполне́ мо́жет опозда́ть.

east /iːst/ *n.* восто́к; **to the ~ of London** к восто́ку от Ло́ндона.
■ *adv.* на восто́к; к восто́ку; **travel ~** дви́гаться (*impf.*) на восто́к; **~ of Moscow** к восто́ку от Москвы́.
■ *adj.* восто́чный; **~ wind** восто́чный ве́тер.

Easter /ˈiːstə(r)/ *n.* Па́сха; **at ~** на Па́сху; **~ Day, Sunday** Све́тлое/Христо́во воскресе́нье, Па́сха; **~ Monday** Све́тлый понеде́льник; **~ egg** пасха́льное яйцо́.

easterly /ˈiːstəlɪ/ *n.* (*wind*) восто́чный ве́тер.
■ *adj.* восто́чный.

eastern /ˈiːst(ə)n/ *adj.* восто́чный.

eastward /iːsθwəd/ *adj.* восто́чный.
■ *adv.* (*also* **~s**) на восто́к; к восто́ку, в восто́чном направле́нии.

easy /ˈiːzɪ/ *adj.* (**easier, easiest**)
1 (*not difficult*) лёгкий; **the book is ~ to read** кни́га легко́ чита́ется; **he is ~ to get on with** у него́ лёгкий хара́ктер.
2 (*comfortable*) споко́йный, лёгкий; **he leads an ~ life** у него́ лёгкая жизнь; **I am ~** (*coll., have no preference*) мне всё равно́.
■ *adv.*: **take it ~!** (*don't exert yourself*) рассла́бьтесь!; (*don't worry*) не волну́йтесь!; (*don't hurry*) не спеши́те!
■ *cpd.* **~-going** *adj.* благоду́шный.

eat /iːt/ *v.t.* & *i.* (*past* **ate;** *p.p.* **eaten**) есть, съ-; (*politely, of others*) ку́шать, по-/с-; **~ one's dinner** пообе́дать/поу́жинать (*pf.*).
■ *with advs.*: **~ out** *v.i.* есть (*impf.*) вне до́ма; **~ up** *v.t.* до|еда́ть, -е́сть; (*fig.*): **he is ~en up with curiosity** его́ съеда́ет любопы́тство.

eaten /ˈiːt(ə)n/ *p.p. of* ▸ **eat**

eavesdrop /ˈiːvzdrɒp/ *v.i.* подслу́ш|ивать, -ать.

ebb /eb/ *n.* отли́в.
■ *v.i.* (*of tide*) уб|ыва́ть, -ы́ть; (*fig.*) ослаб|ева́ть, -е́ть.

ebony /ˈebənɪ/ *n.* эбе́новое/чёрное де́рево; (*fig., black*) чёрный как смоль.

ebullient /ɪˈbʌlɪənt/ *adj.* кипу́чий, по́лный энтузиа́зма.

EC (*abbr. of* ***European Community***) ЕС (Европе́йское соо́бщество).

eccentric /ɪkˈsentrɪk/ *n.* чуда́к; оригина́л.
■ *adj.* эксцентри́чный.

eccentricity /eksenˈtrɪsɪtɪ/ *n.* (*quality*) чуда́чество, эксцентри́чность; (*eccentric habit*) стра́нность.

ecclesiastical /ɪkliːzɪˈæstɪk(ə)l/ *adj.* духо́вный, церко́вный.

ECG (*abbr. of* ***electrocardiogram***) ЭКГ (электрокардиогра́мма).

echelon /ˈeʃəlɒn/ *n.*
1 (*level, rank*) чин, ранг.
2 (*mil. formation*) эшело́н; **in ~** эшело́нами.

echo /ˈekəʊ/ *n.* (*pl.* **echoes**) э́хо.
■ *v.t.* (**echoes, echoed**) вто́рить (*impf.*) + *d.*; **~ s.o.'s words** вто́рить чьим-н. слова́м.
■ *v.i.* (**echoes, echoed**) отд|ава́ться, -а́ться э́хом.

eclair /ɪˈkleə(r)/ *n.* экле́р.

eclectic /ɪˈklektɪk/ *adj.* эклекти́ческий; эклекти́чный.

eclipse /ɪˈklɪps/ *n.* (*astron.*) затме́ние.
■ *v.t.* (*lit., fig.*) затм|ева́ть, -и́ть.

eco-friendly /ˈiːkəʊfrendlɪ/ *adj.*

экологи́чески безвре́дный.
ecological /i:kə'lɒdʒɪk(ə)l/ *adj.* экологи́ческий.
ecologist /ɪ'kɒlədʒɪst/ *n.* эко́лог.
ecology /ɪ'kɒlədʒɪ/ *n.* эколо́гия.
economic /i:kə'nɒmɪk/ *adj.* [1] экономи́ческий, хозя́йственный. [2] (*paying*) рента́бельный. ■ *cpd.* **~ migrant** *n.* экономи́ческий мигра́нт.
economical /i:kə'nɒmik(ə)l/ *adj.* эконо́мный, бережли́вый.
economics /i:kə'nɒmɪks, ek-/ *n.* эконо́мика.
economist /ɪ'kɒnəmɪst/ *n.* экономи́ст.
economize /ɪ'kɒnəmaɪz/ *v.i.* эконо́мить, с-; **~ on fuel** эконо́мить, с- то́пливо.
economy /ɪ'kɒnəmɪ/ *n.* [1] (*thrift*) эконо́мия, хозя́йственность, бережли́вость; **~ class** эконо́м-класс. [2] (*economic system*) эконо́мика, хозя́йство.
ecosystem /'i:kəʊsɪstəm/ *n.* экосисте́ма.
ecotourism /i:kəʊ'tʊərɪz(ə)m/ *n.* экотури́зм.
ecstasy /'ekstəsɪ/ *n.* [1] (*strong emotion*) экста́з. [2] (*the drug*) э́кстези (*m. indecl.*).
ecstatic /ɪk'stætɪk/ *adj.* экстати́ческий, в экста́зе.
Ecuador /'ekwədɔ:(r)/ *n.* Эквадо́р.
Ecuadorean /ekwə'dɔ:rɪən/ *n.* эквадо́р|ец (*fem.* -ка). ■ *adj.* эквадо́рский.
eczema /'eksɪmə/ *n.* экзе́ма.
edge /edʒ/ *n.* [1] (*sharpened side*) остриё, ле́звие. [2] (*fig.*): **be on ~** быть в не́рвном состоя́нии. [3] (*border*) грань; край. ■ *v.t. & i.* [1] (*border*) окайм|ля́ть, -и́ть; **~ a path with plants** обса́|живать, -ди́ть доро́жку цвета́ми. [2] (*move obliquely*): **~ one's way through a crowd** проб|ира́ться, -ра́ться че́рез толпу́; **he ~d closer to me** он пододви́нулся ко мне.
edge|ways /'edʒweɪz/, **-wise** /'edʒwaɪz/ *advs.* бо́ком; **I could not get a word in ~** я не мог сло́ва вста́вить.
edible /'edɪb(ə)l/ *adj.* съедо́бный.
edifice /'edɪfɪs/ *n.* зда́ние; (*fig.*) структу́ра, систе́ма.
edifying /'edɪfaɪɪŋ/ *adj.* назида́тельный, поучи́тельный.
Edinburgh /'edɪnbərə/ *n.* Э́динбу́рг.
edit /'edɪt/ *v.t.* (**edited, editing**) (*a text, newspaper*) редакти́ровать, от-; (*film etc.*) монти́ровать, с-.
edition /ɪ'dɪʃ(ə)n/ *n.* изда́ние; (*e.g. of newspaper*) вы́пуск.
editor /'edɪtə(r)/ *n.* реда́ктор.
editorial /edɪ'tɔ:rɪəl/ *n.* передови́ца, передова́я статья́. ■ *adj.* редакцио́нный; реда́кторский; **~ office** реда́кция.
educate /'edjʊkeɪt/ *v.t.* да|ва́ть, -ть образова́ние + *d.*; **~d speech** культу́рная речь.
education /edjʊ'keɪʃ(ə)n/ *n.* образова́ние, культу́ра; (*upbringing*) воспита́ние.
educational /edjʊ'keɪʃən(ə)l/ *adj.* (*pert. to education*) образова́тельный; (*instructive*) воспита́тельный, уче́бный.
EEC (*abbr. of* ***European Economic Community***) ЕЭС (Европе́йское экономи́ческое соо́бщество).
eel /i:l/ *n.* у́горь (*m.*).
eer|ie (*US* **-y**) /'ɪərɪ/ *adj.* (**eerier, eeriest**) жу́ткий.
effect /ɪ'fekt/ *n.* [1] (*result*) результа́т; **punishment had no ~ on him** наказа́ние на него́ не поде́йствовало; **to no ~** безрезульта́тно; **take ~** (*e.g. medicine*) де́йствовать, по-. [2] (*validity*) де́йствие; **come into ~** вступ|а́ть, -и́ть в си́лу. [3] (*sensual etc. impression*) впечатле́ние, эффе́кт. ■ *v.t.*: осуществ|ля́ть, -и́ть; выполня́ть, вы́полнить.
effective /ɪ'fektɪv/ *adj.* [1] (*efficacious*) эффекти́вный. [2] (*operative*) име́ющий си́лу; де́йствующий.
effeminate /ɪ'femɪnət/ *adj.* женоподо́бный.
effervesce /efə'ves/ *v.i.* пузыри́ться (*impf.*); (*fig.*) искри́ться (*impf.*).
effervescence /efə'ves(ə)ns/ *n.* шипе́ние; (*fig.*) весёлое оживле́ние, кипе́ние.
effervescent /efə'ves(ə)nt/ *adj.* пузыря́щийся, шипу́чий; (*fig.*) искря́щийся, кипу́чий.
effete /ɪ'fi:t/ *adj.* сла́бый, упа́дочный; (*degenerate*) вы́родившийся.
efficacious /efɪ'keɪʃəs/ *adj.* эффекти́вный, де́йственный.
efficacy /'efɪkəsɪ/ *n.* эффекти́вность, де́йственность.
efficiency /ɪ'fɪʃənsɪ/ *n.* делови́тость; эффекти́вность, производи́тельность.
efficient /ɪ'fɪʃ(ə)nt/ *adj.* делови́тый, исполни́тельный; эффекти́вный, производи́тельный.
effigy /'efɪdʒɪ/ *n.* изображе́ние; **burn s.o. in ~** сжечь (*pf.*) чьё-н. изображе́ние/чу́чело.
effort /'efət/ *n.* уси́лие, попы́тка; (*pl.*) рабо́та; **make an ~** приложи́ть (*pf.*) уси́лие.
effortless /'efətlɪs/ *adj.* непринуждённый; не тре́бующий уси́лий; **with ~ skill** с непринуждённой ло́вкостью.
effrontery /ɪ'frʌntərɪ/ *n.* на́глость, наха́льство.
effusive /ɪ'fju:sɪv/ *adj.* экспанси́вный; **he was ~ in his gratitude** он рассыпа́лся в благода́рностях.
e.g. (*abbr. of* ***exempli gratia***) напр. (наприме́р).
egalitarian /ɪgælɪ'teərɪən/ *adj.* эгалита́рный.
egalitarianism /ɪgælɪ'teərɪənɪz(ə)m/ *n.* эгалитари́зм.
egg[1] /eg/ *n.* яйцо́. ■ *cpds.* **~ cup** *n.* рю́мка для яйца́; **~plant** *n.* (*US*) баклажа́н.
egg[2] /eg/ *v.t.*: **~ on** подстрек|а́ть, -ну́ть.
ego /'i:gəʊ/ *n.* (*pl.* **egos**) (*self-esteem*) самолю́бие.
egocentric /i:gəʊ'sentrɪk/ *adj.* эгоцентри́ческий, эгоцентри́чный.
egoism /'i:gəʊɪz(ə)m/ *n.* эгои́зм.

egoist /ˈi:gəʊɪst/ *n.* эгоист (*fem.* -ка).
egotist /ˈi:gətɪst/ *n.* эгоцентрист (*fem.* -ка).
egotistic(al) /i:gəˈtɪstɪk, i:gəˈtɪstɪk(ə)l/ *adj.* эгоцентрический.
Egypt /ˈi:dʒɪpt/ *n.* Египет.
Egyptian /ɪˈdʒɪpʃ(ə)n/ *n.* египтян|ин (*fem.* -ка).
■ *adj.* египетский.
eiderdown /ˈaɪdədaʊn/ *n.* (*Br.*, *quilt*) пуховое одеяло.
eight /eɪt/ *n.* (число/номер) восемь; (*figure; thing numbered 8; group of* ~) восьмёрка.
■ *adj.* восемь + *g. pl.*
eighteen /eɪˈti:n/ *n.* восемнадцать.
■ *adj.* восемнадцать + *g. pl.*
eighteenth /eɪˈti:nθ/ *n.* (*date*) восемнадцатое число; (*fraction*) одна восемнадцатая.
■ *adj.* восемнадцатый.
eighth /eɪtθ/ *n.* (*date*) восьмое (число); (*fraction*) одна восьмая.
■ *adj.* восьмой.
eightieth /ˈeɪtɪɪθ/ *n.* одна восьмидесятая.
■ *adj.* восьмидесятый.
eight|y /ˈeɪtɪ/ *n.* восемьдесят; **he is in his ~ies** ему за восемьдесят.
either /ˈaɪðə(r)/ *pron.* & *adj.* (*one or other*) любой, каждый; тот или другой; **do ~ of these roads lead to town?** какая-нибудь из этих дорог ведёт к городу?; **~ book will do** любая из этих книг годится; **I do not like ~ (one)** мне не нравится ни тот, ни другой; **on ~ side of the window** по обеим сторонам окна.
■ *adv.* & *conj.*: **I do not like Smith, or Jones ~** я не люблю ни Смита, ни Джонса; (*intensive*): **it was not long ago ~** это было не так уж давно; **~ ... or** или... или; либо... либо; то ли... то ли; не то... не то.
ejaculate /ɪˈdʒækjʊleɪt/ *v.t.* (*utter suddenly*) воскл|ицать, -икнуть.
■ *v.i.* (*physiol.*) эякулировать (*impf.*, *pf.*), изв|ергать, -ергнуть семя.
ejaculation /ɪdʒækjʊˈleɪʃ(ə)n/ *n.* (*physiol.*) эякуляция.
eject /ɪˈdʒekt/ *v.t.* (*lit.*, *fig.*) выбрасывать, выбросить.
■ *v.i.* (*aeron.*): **the pilot ~ed** лётчик катапультировался.
eke /i:k/ *v.t.*: **~ out** (*supplement*) восп|олнять, -олнить; **~ out a livelihood** кое-как перебиваться (*impf.*).
elaborate[1] /ɪˈlæbərət/ *adj.* искусно сделанный.
elaborate[2] /ɪˈlæbəreɪt/ *v.t.* разраб|атывать, -отать; **~ on** (*develop*) разв|ивать, -ить; (*make more precise*) уточн|ять, -ить.
elapse /ɪˈlæps/ *v.i.* про|ходить, -йти.
elastic /ɪˈlæstɪk/ *n.* резинка.
■ *adj.* (*lit.*) эластичный; упругий; **~ band** (*Br.*) резинка.
elate /ɪˈleɪt/ *v.t.*: **he was ~d at the news** новость окрылила его.
elation /ɪˈleɪʃ(ə)n/ *n.* ликование, восторг.
elbow /ˈelbəʊ/ *n.* локоть (*m.*).
■ *cpd.* **~ grease** *n.* (*joc.*) усиленная полировка.
elder[1] /ˈeldə(r)/ *adj.* старший.
elder[2] /ˈeldə(r)/ *n.* (*bot.*) бузина (*красная, чёрная*).
■ *cpd.* **~berry** *n.* ягода бузины.
elderly /ˈeldəlɪ/ *adj.* пожилой.
eldest /ˈeldɪst/ *adj.* самый старший.
elect /ɪˈlekt/ *adj.* избранный; **president-~** избранный президент.
■ *v.t.* изб|ирать, -рать; выбирать, выбрать; **they ~ed him king** они избрали его королём; **he ~ed to go** он предпочёл пойти.
election /ɪˈlekʃ(ə)n/ *n.* выборы (*m. pl.*); **~ campaign** предвыборная/избирательная кампания.
electoral /ɪˈlektər(ə)l/ *adj.* избирательный.
electorate /ɪˈlektərət/ *n.* (*body of voters*) избиратели (*m. pl.*).
electric /ɪˈlektrɪk/ *adj.* электрический; **~ blanket** одеяло-грелка; **~ shock** удар электрическим током.
electrical /ɪˈlektrɪk(ə)l/ *adj.* электрический; **~ engineering** электротехника.
electrician /ɪlekˈtrɪʃ(ə)n/ *n.* электрик (*coll.*), (электро)монтёр.
electricity /ɪlekˈtrɪsɪtɪ/ *n.* электричество.
electrify /ɪˈlektrɪfaɪ/ *v.t.* (*charge with electricity; also fig.*) электризовать, на-.
electrocardiogram /ɪlektrəʊˈkɑ:dɪəgræm/ *n.* электрокардиограмма.
electrocute /ɪˈlektrəkju:t/ *v.t.* (*execute*) казнить (*impf.*, *pf.*) на электрическом стуле; **he was ~d** (*by accident*) его убило током.
electrode /ɪˈlektrəʊd/ *n.* электрод.
electromagnetic /ɪlektrəʊmægˈnetɪk/ *adj.* электромагнитный.
electron /ɪˈlektrɒn/ *n.* электрон; **~ microscope** электронный микроскоп.
electronic /ɪlekˈtrɒnɪk/ *adj.* электронный; **~ tagging** электронная слежка.
electronics /ɪlekˈtrɒnɪks/ *n.* электроника.
elegance /ˈelɪgəns/ *n.* элегантность, изящество.
elegant /ˈelɪgənt/ *adj.* элегантный, изящный.
element /ˈelɪmənt/ *n.*
1 (*earth, air etc.*) стихия; (*fig.*): **in one's ~** в своей стихии.
2 (*chem.*) элемент.
3 (*feature, constituent*) элемент; составная часть.
4 (*elec.*) элемент.
elementary /elɪˈmentərɪ/ *adj.* элементарный; **~ school** начальная школа.
elephant /ˈelɪfənt/ *n.* (*pl.* **~** *or* **~s**) слон.
elevate /ˈelɪveɪt/ *v.t.* (*lit.*) подн|имать, -ять; **~d railway** надземная железная дорога.
elevated /ˈelɪveɪtɪd/ *adj.* (*lofty*) высокий, возвышенный.
elevator /ˈelɪveɪtə(r)/ *n.*
1 (*machine*) грузоподъёмник, элеватор.
2 (*US, lift*) лифт.
eleven /ɪˈlev(ə)n/ *n.* одиннадцать.
elevenses /ɪˈlevənzɪz/ *n.* (*Br. coll.*) лёгкий завтрак около одиннадцати часов утра.
eleventh /ɪˈlevənθ/ *n.* (*date*) одиннадцатое (число); (*fraction*) одна одиннадцатая.
■ *adj.* одиннадцатый.
elf /elf/ *n.* (*pl.* **elves**) эльф.
elicit /ɪˈlɪsɪt/ *v.t.* (**elicited, eliciting**) извл|екать, -ечь; допыт|ываться, -аться; **~ a**

fact выявля́ть, вы́явить факт; **~ a reply** доби́ться (*pf.*) отве́та.

eligibility /elɪdʒɪ'bɪlɪtɪ/ *n.* пра́во на избра́ние.

eligible /'elɪdʒɪb(ə)l/ *adj.* могу́щий быть и́збранным; **to be ~ for** име́ть пра́во на + *a.*

eliminate /ɪ'lɪmɪneɪt/ *v.t.*
1 (*rule out*) исключ|а́ть, -и́ть.
2 (*sport*): **he was ~d on the first round** он вы́был в пе́рвом ту́ре.

elimination /ɪlɪmɪ'neɪʃ(ə)n/ *n.* устране́ние.

elite /eɪ'li:t/ *n.* эли́та; **an ~ regiment** отбо́рный полк.

elitist /ɪ'li:tɪst/ *adj.* элита́рный.

elixir /ɪ'lɪksɪə(r)/ *n.* эликси́р.

Elizabethan /ɪlɪzə'bi:θ(ə)n/ *n.* совреме́нник эпо́хи (короле́вы) Елизаве́ты.
■ *adj.* елизаве́тинский, относя́щийся к эпо́хе короле́вы Елизаве́ты.

elk /elk/ *n.* (*pl.* **~** *or* **~s**) лось (*m.*).

ellipse /ɪ'lɪps/ *n.* э́ллипс, ова́л.

elliptical /ɪ'lɪptɪkəl/ *adj.* (*math., gram.*) эллипти́ческий.

elm /elm/ *n.* (*tree; wood*) вяз.

elongate /'i:lɒŋgeɪt/ (*usu. as* **elongated** *adj.*) *v.t.* удлин|я́ть, -и́ть.

elongation /i:lɒŋ'geɪʃ(ə)n/ *n.* удлине́ние.

elope /ɪ'ləʊp/ *v.i.* (та́йно) бежа́ть (*det.*) (с возлю́бленным).

eloquent /'eləkwənt/ *adj.* красноречи́вый.

El Salvador /el 'sælvədɔ:(r)/ *n.* Сальвадо́р.

else /els/ *adj.* & *adv.* друго́й; **no one ~** никто́ друго́й; бо́льше никто́; **everyone ~** все остальны́е; **nowhere ~** ни в како́м друго́м ме́сте; **everywhere ~** везде́, то́лько не здесь/там; **what ~ could I say?** что ещё я мог сказа́ть?; **do you want anything ~** (*more*)**?** вы хоти́те ещё что-нибу́дь?; **or ~** и́ли же.
■ *cpd.* **~where** *adv.* (*in another place*) где́-нибудь ещё, в друго́м ме́сте; (*to another place*) куда́-нибудь ещё, в друго́е ме́сто.

elude /ɪ'lu:d/ *v.t.* изб|ега́ть, -ежа́ть, -е́гнуть + *g.*; ускольз|а́ть, -ну́ть от + *g.*

elusive /ɪ'lu:sɪv, ɪ'lju:sɪv/ *adj.* неулови́мый.

elves /elvz/ *pl. of* ▶ **elf**

emaciate /ɪ'meɪsɪeɪt/ *v.t.* изнур|я́ть, -и́ть, истощ|а́ть, -и́ть.

email /'i:meɪl/ (*also* **e-mail**) *n.* (*system, letters*) электро́нная по́чта; (*letter*) электро́нное письмо́; **~ address** электро́нный а́дрес.
■ *v.t.* (*a person*) пос|ыла́ть, -ла́ть электро́нное письмо́ (*кому-н.*); (*information, a document*) пос|ыла́ть, -ла́ть электро́нной по́чтой.

emanate /'eməneɪt/ *v.i.* излуча́ться (*impf.*); истека́ть (*impf.*).

emancipate /ɪ'mænsɪpeɪt/ *v.t.* эмансипи́ровать (*impf., pf.*).

emancipation /ɪmænsɪ'peɪʃ(ə)n/ *n.* эмансипа́ция.

embalm /ɪm'bɑ:m/ *v.t.* бальзами́ровать (*impf., pf.*) (*pf. also* за-, на-).

embankment /ɪm'bæŋkmənt/ *n.* (*wall etc.*) на́сыпь, гать; (*roadway*) на́бережная.

embargo /em'bɑ:gəʊ/ *n.* (*pl.* **~es**) эмба́рго (*nt. indecl.*); **lift, raise an ~** снима́ть, снять эмба́рго (с + *g.*).

embark /ɪm'bɑ:k/ *v.i.* (*go on board*) грузи́ться, по-; сади́ться, сесть на кора́бль; (*fig.*) пус|ка́ться, -ти́ться (в + *a.*); **~ on an undertaking** предприн|има́ть, -я́ть де́ло.

embarkation /embɑ:'keɪʃ(ə)n/ *n.* (*of goods*) погру́зка; (*of people*) поса́дка.

embarrass /ɪm'bærəs/ *v.t.* сму|ща́ть, -ти́ть.

embarrassing /ɪm'bærəsɪŋ/ *adj.* щекотли́вый, вызыва́ющий смуще́ние.

embarrassment /ɪm'bærəsmənt/ *n.* смуще́ние, замеша́тельство.

embassy /'embəsɪ/ *n.* посо́льство.

embattled /ɪm'bæt(ə)ld/ *adj.* (*ready for war*) приведённый в боеву́ю гото́вность; (*in difficulties*) в тру́дном положе́нии.

embed /ɪm'bed/ *v.t.* (**embedded, embedding**): **stones ~ded in rock** ка́мни, вмуро́ванные в скалу́; **facts ~ded in one's memory** фа́кты, вре́завшиеся в па́мять.

embellish /ɪm'belɪʃ/ *v.t.* укр|аша́ть, -а́сить; (*a tale etc.*) приукра́|шивать, -сить.

embellishment /ɪm'belɪʃmənt/ *n.* приукра́шивание.

embers /'embəz/ *n. pl.* (*coals etc.*) тле́ющие уголькѝ (*m. pl.*).

embezzle /ɪm'bez(ə)l/ *v.t.* растра́|чивать, -тить.

embezzlement /ɪm'bezəlmənt/ *n.* растра́та.

emblem /'embləm/ *n.* эмбле́ма; (*national*) герб.

embodiment /ɪm'bɒdɪmənt/ *n.* воплоще́ние, олицетворе́ние.

embody /ɪm'bɒdɪ/ *v.t.* вопло|ща́ть, -ти́ть.

embrace /ɪm'breɪs/ *n.* объя́тие.
■ *v.t.* 1 (*clasp in one's arms*) обн|има́ть, -я́ть.
2 (*include*) включ|а́ть, -и́ть.
■ *v.i.* обн|има́ться, -я́ться.

embroider /ɪm'brɔɪdə(r)/ *v.t.* вышива́ть, вы́шить; (*a story etc.*) приукра́|шивать, -сить.

embroidery /ɪm'brɔɪdərɪ/ *n.* вышива́ние, вы́шивка.

embroil /ɪm'brɔɪl/ *v.t.* впу́т|ывать, -ать; вовл|ека́ть, -е́чь.

embryo /'embrɪəʊ/ *n.* (*pl.* **~s**) эмбрио́н.

embryology /embrɪ'ɒlədʒɪ/ *n.* эмбриоло́гия.

embryonic /embrɪ'ɒnɪk/ *adj.* эмбриона́льный; (*fig.*) недора́звитый; в заро́дыше.

emerald /'emər(ə)ld/ *n.* изумру́д; **~ green** изумру́дно-зелёный.

emerge /ɪ'mə:dʒ/ *v.i.* всплы|ва́ть, -ть; появ|ля́ться, -и́ться; (*fig.*) возн|ика́ть, -и́кнуть.

emergence /ɪ'mə:dʒəns/ *n.* появле́ние, возникнове́ние.

emergency /ɪ'mə:dʒənsɪ/ *n.* кра́йняя необходи́мость; ава́рия; (*for use in ~*) запасно́й, запа́сный, вре́менный; **~ exit** запа́сный вы́ход; **~ landing** вы́нужденная поса́дка.

emigrant /'emɪgrənt/ *n.* эмигра́нт (*fem.* -ка).

emigrate /'emɪgreɪt/ *v.i.* эмигри́ровать (*impf., pf.*).

emigration /emɪ'greɪʃ(ə)n/ *n.* эмигра́ция.

émigré /'emɪgreɪ/ *n.* эмигра́нт (*особенно политический*) (*fem.* -ка).

eminence /'emɪnəns/ *n.*
1 (*high ground*) высота́; возвыше́ние.
2 (*celebrity*) знамени́тость; **reach, win,**

attain ~ добиться (*pf.*) славы/известности.
3 (*title*): **His E~** Его Высокопреосвященство.

eminent /'emɪnənt/ *adj.* (*of person*) выдающийся, знаменитый.

emission /ɪ'mɪʃ(ə)n/ *n.* (*of gas, heat*) выделение; (*of light*) излучение; (*pl.*) выбросы.

emit /ɪ'mɪt/ *v.t.* (**emitted, emitting**) (*smoke, smell*) испус|кать, -тить; (*light*) излуч|ать, -ить; (*gas, heat*) выделять, выделить; (*sound*) изд|авать, -ать.

emotion /ɪ'məʊʃ(ə)n/ *n.* (*feeling*) эмоция; (*agitation*) волнение.

emotional /ɪ'məʊʃən(ə)l/ *adj.* эмоциональный.

emotive /ɪ'məʊtɪv/ *adj.* эмоционально волнующий.

empathy /'empəθɪ/ *n.* сопереживание.

emperor /'empərə(r)/ *n.* император.

emphasis /'emfəsɪs/ *n.* (*pl.* **emphases** /-si:z/) ударение, выразительность; **lay ~ on** подчёрк|ивать, -нуть.

emphasize /'emfəsaɪz/ *v.t.* подчёрк|ивать, -нуть.

emphatic /ɪm'fætɪk/ *adj.* эмфатический, выразительный.

emphysema /emfɪ'si:mə/ *n.* (*med.*) эмфизема.

empire /'empaɪə(r)/ *n.* империя.

empirical /ɪm'pɪrɪk(ə)l/ *adj.* эмпирический.

empiricism /ɪm'pɪrɪsɪz(ə)m/ *n.* эмпиризм.

employ /ɪm'plɔɪ/ *v.t.*
1 (*engage to work*) нан|имать, -ять; давать, дать работу + *d.*; **be ~ed** работать (*impf.*), служить (*impf.*).
2 (*use*) примен|ять, -ить.

employee /emplɔɪ'i:, -'plɔɪi:/ *n.* служащий.

employer /ɪm'plɔɪə(r)/ *n.* работодатель (*m.*).

employment /ɪm'plɔɪmənt/ *n.*
1 (*service for pay*) работа, служба; **~ agency** кадровое агентство; бюро по трудоустройству.
2 (*occupation*) занятие.
3 (*use*) применение, использование.

empower /ɪm'paʊə(r)/ *v.t.* уполномочи|вать, -ть.

empress /'emprɪs/ *n.* императрица.

emptiness /'emptɪnɪs/ *n.* (*lit., fig.*) пустота.

empt|y /'emptɪ/ *adj.* (**emptier, emptiest**) пустой; порожний; (*fig.*): **~y words** пустые слова.
■ *v.t.* опорожн|ять, -ить; **~y water out of a jug** вылить (*pf.*) воду из кувшина.
■ *v.i.* опорожн|яться, -иться; **the streets ~ied** улицы опустели.
■ *cpd.* **~y-handed** *adj.* с пустыми руками.

EMS *abbr. of* 1 ***European Monetary System***) ЕВС (Европейская валютная система).
2 **Enhanced Message/Messaging Service: ~ message** EMS-сообщение.

emu /'i:mju:/ *n.* эму (*m. indecl.*).

emulate /'emjʊleɪt/ *v.t.* подражать (*impf.*) + *d.*

emulsion /ɪ'mʌlʃ(ə)n/ *n.* эмульсия.

enable /ɪ'neɪb(ə)l/ *v.t.* (*make able*) да|вать, -ть возможность + *d.*; (*make possible*) делать, с- возможным.

enact /ɪ'nækt/ *v.t.* (*make law*) вв|одить, -ести в действие; утвер|ждать, -дить; (*act*) играть, сыграть (*роль*); разыгр|ывать, -ать; (*carry out*) соверш|ать, -ить.

enactment /ɪ'næktmənt/ *n.* введение закона в силу; утверждение (закона *и т. п.*); (*of s.o.'s fantasies*) игра.

enamel /ɪ'næm(ə)l/ *n.* эмаль.

encampment /ɪn'kæmpmənt/ *n.* расположение лагерем; (*camp*) лагерь (*m.*).

encapsulate /ɪn'kæpsjʊleɪt/ *v.t.* (*fig.*) заключ|ать, -ить в себе; **an ~d dream** сон во сне.

enchant /ɪn'tʃɑ:nt/ *v.t.* обвор|аживать, -ожить; очаров|ывать, -ать.

enchanting /ɪn'tʃɑ:ntɪŋ/ *adj.* чарующий, обворожительный.

encircle /ɪn'sə:k(ə)l/ *v.t.* окруж|ать, -ить.

enclave /'enkleɪv/ *n.* анклав.

enclos|e /ɪn'kləʊz/ *v.t.*
1 (*surround, fence*) окруж|ать, -ить; **~e a garden with a wall** обн|осить, -ести сад стеной.
2 (*in letter etc.*) при|кладывать, -ложить; **a letter ~ing an invoice** письмо с приложением счёта.

enclosure /ɪn'kləʊʒə(r)/ *n.* (*fence*) ограждение, ограда; (*in letter*) приложение.

encode /ɪn'kəʊd/ *v.t.* кодировать (*impf., pf.*) (*pf. also* за-); шифровать, за-.

encompass /ɪn'kʌmpəs/ *v.t.* (*surround*) окруж|ать, -ить; (*contain, comprise*) заключ|ать, -ить; (*cope with, accomplish*) осуществ|лять, -ить; (*envelop*) окут|ывать, -ать.

encore /'ɒŋkɔ:(r)/ *n.* & *int.* бис.

encounter /ɪn'kaʊntə(r)/ *n.* встреча.
■ *v.t.* встр|ечаться, -етиться с + *i.*

encourage /ɪn'kʌrɪdʒ/ *v.t.* ободр|ять, -ить; **I ~d him to go** я уговаривал его идти.

encouragement /ɪn'kʌrɪdʒmənt/ *n.* ободрение, поощрение, поддержка.

encouraging /ɪn'kʌrɪdʒɪŋ/ *adj.* ободряющий.

encroach /ɪn'krəʊtʃ/ *v.i.* поку|шаться, -ситься (на + *a.*); **~ on s.o.'s rights** посяг|ать, -нуть на чьи-н. права.

encrypt /en'krɪpt/ *v.t.* шифровать, за-.

encumber /ɪn'kʌmbə(r)/ *v.t.* (*burden*) обремен|ять, -ить; **~ o.s. with luggage** взвал|ивать, -ить на себя багаж.

encumbrance /ɪn'kʌmbrəns/ *n.* обуза, препятствие.

encyclopedia /ensaɪklə'pi:dɪə, ɪn-/ *n.* энциклопедия.

encyclopedic /ɪnsaɪklə'pi:dɪk/ *adj.* энциклопедический.

end /end/ *n.*
1 (*extremity; lit., fig.*) конец; **two hours on ~** (*in succession*) два часа подряд; **third from the ~** третий с краю; **at the ~ of August** в конце (*or* в последних числах) августа.
2 (*of elongated object*) конец, край; **he stood the box on (its) ~** он поставил ящик стоймя (*coll.*).
3 (*remnant, small part*): **candle ~** огарок; **cigarette ~** окурок.
4 (*conclusion*) окончание; **in the ~** в конце концов; в конечном счёте; **come to an ~**

ок|а́нчиваться, -о́нчиться; конча́ться, ко́нчиться; **put an ~ to** класть, положи́ть коне́ц + *d.*; **he stayed till the bitter ~** он остава́лся на ме́сте до са́мого конца́; **~ product** коне́чный проду́кт.
5 (*purpose*) цель; **to this ~** с э́той це́лью; **any means to an ~** все сре́дства хороши́.
■ *v.t.* конча́ть, ко́нчить; **~ a quarrel** прекра|ща́ть, -ти́ть ссо́ру; **~ one's days** рассчита́ться с жи́знью.
■ *v.i.* конча́ться, ко́нчиться; **the road ~s here** доро́га конча́ется здесь; **the story ~s happily** э́то расска́з со счастли́вым концо́м.
■ *with adv.*: **~ up** *v.i.*: **he ~ed up in jail** он ко́нчил тюрьмо́й; **he ~ed up at the opera** в конце́ концо́в он попа́л-таки в о́перу.

endanger /ɪnˈdeɪndʒə(r)/ *v.t.* подв|ерга́ть, -е́ргнуть опа́сности; ста́вить (*impf.*) под угро́зу; **~ed species** вымира́ющий вид.

endear /ɪnˈdɪə(r)/ *v.t.*: **this speech ~ed him to me** э́та речь расположи́ла меня́ к нему́; **an ~ing smile** покоря́ющая/подкупа́ющая улы́бка.

endearment /ɪnˈdɪəmənt/ *n.* ла́ска; **term of ~** ла́сковое обраще́ние.

endeavour /ɪnˈdevə(r)/ (*US* **endeavor**) *n.* стара́ние, стремле́ние.
■ *v.i.* стара́ться, по-.

ending /ˈendɪŋ/ *n.* (*action*) оконча́ние (*also gram.*); (*of book, play*) коне́ц.

endive /ˈendaɪv/ *n.* сала́т энди́вий; (*US, chicory crown*) цико́рий (*верхняя наземная часть*).

endless /ˈendlɪs/ *adj.* бесконе́чный.

endorse /ɪnˈdɔːs/ *v.t.*
1 (*sign*) индосси́ровать (*impf., pf.*); **~ a cheque** распи́с|ываться, -а́ться на че́ке.
2 (*support*) подвер|жда́ть, -ди́ть.

endorsement /ɪnˈdɔːsmənt/ *n.*
1 переда́точная на́дпись; индоссаме́нт; резолю́ция (*начальника на документе*).
2 (*support*) подтвержде́ние.

endow /ɪnˈdaʊ/ *v.t.* одар|я́ть, -и́ть.

endowment /ɪnˈdaʊmənt/ *n.*
1 (*act of endowing*) поже́ртвование.
2 (*funds*) вклад, поже́ртвование.
3 (*talent*) одарённость.

endurable /ɪnˈdjʊərəb(ə)l/ *adj.* прие́млемый, сно́сный.

endurance /ɪnˈdjʊərəns/ *n.* (*physical*) про́чность; (*mental*) выно́сливость.

endure /ɪnˈdjʊə(r)/ *v.t.* выноси́ть, вы́нести.
■ *v.i.* (*last*) прод|олжа́ться, -о́лжиться.

enema /ˈenɪmə/ *n.* (*med.*) кли́зма.

enemy /ˈenəmɪ/ *n.* враг, не́друг.

energetic /enəˈdʒetɪk/ *adj.* энерги́чный.

energy /ˈenədʒɪ/ *n.* (*phys. or mental*) эне́ргия.

enforce /ɪnˈfɔːs/ *v.t.*: **~ a judg(e)ment** (*leg.*) прив|оди́ть, -ести́ в исполне́ние суде́бное реше́ние; **~ a law** следи́ть (*impf.*) за соблюде́нием зако́на.

enforceable /ɪnˈfɔːsəb(ə)l/ *adj.* осуществи́мый, обеспе́ченный правово́й са́нкцией.

enforcement /ɪnˈfɔːsmənt/ *n.* осуществле́ние; **law ~** наблюде́ние за соблюде́нием зако́нов.

engage /ɪnˈgeɪdʒ/ *v.t.*
1 (*occupy*) зан|има́ть, -я́ть; **he is ~d in reading** он за́нят чте́нием; **he ~d me in conversation** он вовлёк меня́ в разгово́р; **the line is ~d** (*teleph.*) но́мер за́нят; **~d signal, tone** (*Br.*) коро́ткие гудки́; сигна́л «за́нято»; **the lavatory is ~d** убо́рная занята́.
2 (*pledge to marry*): **Tom and Mary are ~d** Том и Мэ́ри помо́лвлены; **they got ~d** они́ обручи́лись.
3 (*tech.*) зацеп|ля́ть, -и́ть; включ|а́ть, -и́ть.
■ *v.i.* 1 (*undertake*) бра́ться, взя́ться.
2 (*embark, busy o.s.*) зан|има́ться, -я́ться чем-н.; **he ~d in this venture** он взя́лся за э́то предприя́тие.

engagement /ɪnˈgeɪdʒmənt/ *n.*
1 (*to marry*) помо́лвка; **~ ring** обруча́льное кольцо́.
2 (*appointment to meet etc.*) свида́ние, встре́ча.

engender /ɪnˈdʒendə(r)/ *v.t.* (*fig.*) поро|жда́ть, -ди́ть.

engine /ˈendʒɪn/ *n.* дви́гатель (*m.*); мото́р.
■ *cpd.* **~ driver** *n.* (*Br.*) машини́ст.

engineer /endʒɪˈnɪə(r)/ *n.* инжене́р, меха́ник.
■ *v.t.* (*tech.*) проекти́ровать, с-; (*fig.*) зат|ева́ть, -е́ять.

engineering /endʒɪˈnɪərɪŋ/ *n.* машинострое́ние; **civil ~** гражда́нское строи́тельство.

England /ˈɪŋglənd/ *n.* А́нглия.

English /ˈɪŋglɪʃ/ *n.*
1 (*language*) англи́йский язы́к.
2: **the ~** (*people*) англича́не.
■ *adj.* англи́йский.
■ *cpds.* **~man** *n.* англича́нин; **~woman** *n.* англича́нка.

engrave /ɪnˈgreɪv/ *v.t.* гравирова́ть, вы́-.

engraving /ɪnˈgreɪvɪŋ/ *n.* гравю́ра.

engross /ɪnˈgrəʊs/ *v.t.*: **he was ~ed in his work** он был поглощён рабо́той.

engulf /ɪnˈgʌlf/ *v.t.* погло|ща́ть, -ти́ть.

enhance /ɪnˈhɑːns/ *v.t.* уси́ли|вать, -ть.

enhancement /ɪnˈhɑːnsmənt/ *n.* усиле́ние, повыше́ние.

enigma /ɪˈnɪgmə/ *n.* зага́дка.

enigmatic /enɪgˈmætɪk/ *adj.* зага́дочный.

enjoy /ɪnˈdʒɔɪ/ *v.t.*
1 (*get pleasure from*) насла|жда́ться, -ди́ться + *i.*; **I ~ed talking to him** мне доставля́ло удово́льствие говори́ть с ним; **we ~ed our holiday** мы хорошо́ провели́ о́тпуск; **~ o.s.** весели́ться (*impf.*); наслажда́ться (*impf.*); хорошо́ пров|оди́ть, -ести́ вре́мя.
2 (*possess*) располага́ть (*impf.*) + *i.*; **~ good/bad health** облада́ть хоро́шим/плохи́м здоро́вьем.

enjoyable /ɪnˈdʒɔɪəb(ə)l/ *adj.* прия́тный.

enjoyment /ɪnˈdʒɔɪmənt/ *n.* наслажде́ние, удово́льствие.

enlarge /ɪnˈlɑːdʒ/ *v.t.* увели́чи|вать, -ть.
■ *v.i.* расш|иря́ться, -и́риться; **he ~d on the point** он подро́бнее останови́лся на э́том.

enlargement /ɪnˈlɑːdʒmənt/ *n.* увеличе́ние; расшире́ние.

enlighten /ɪnˈlaɪt(ə)n/ *v.t.* просве|ща́ть, -ти́ть.

enlightening /ɪnˈlaɪt(ə)nɪŋ/ *adj.*

e

поучи́тельный.
enlightenment /ɪnˈlaɪtənmənt/ *n.* просвещённость; **the E~** (*hist.*) Просвеще́ние.
enlist /ɪnˈlɪst/ *v.t.* вербова́ть, за-; **~ s.o.'s support** заруч|а́ться, -и́ться чьей-н. подде́ржкой.
■ *v.i.* поступ|а́ть, -и́ть на вое́нную слу́жбу.
enlistment /ɪnˈlɪstmənt/ *n.*
1 (*of workers*) вербо́вка.
2 (*mil.*) поступле́ние на вое́нную слу́жбу.
enliven /ɪnˈlaɪv(ə)n/ *v.t.* ожив|ля́ть, -и́ть.
en masse /ɑ̃ ˈmæs/ *adv.* в ма́ссе.
enmity /ˈenmɪtɪ/ *n.* вражда́.
enormity /ɪˈnɔːmɪtɪ/ *n.* чудо́вищность.
enormous /ɪˈnɔːməs/ *adj.* грома́дный, огро́мный; **~ly** чрезвыча́йно.
enough /ɪˈnʌf/ *n.* доста́точное коли́чество; дово́льно, доста́точно; **£5 is ~** пяти́ фу́нтов доста́точно; **(that's) ~!** доста́точно!; дово́льно!; **there is ~ to go round** хва́тит на всех; **I have had ~ of your lies** надое́ла мне ва́ша ложь.
■ *adj.* доста́точный; **I have just ~ money** де́нег у меня́ в обре́з (на + *a.*).
■ *adv.* доста́точно; **are you warm ~?** вы не замёрзли?; вам тепло́?; **curiously ~** как ни стра́нно.
enquire /ɪnˈkwaɪə(r), ɪŋ-/ *v.t.* спр|а́шивать, -оси́ть.
■ *v.i.* осв|едомля́ться, -е́домиться; **~ into a matter** рассле́довать (*pf.*) де́ло; **~ after s.o.** спр|а́шивать, -оси́ть о ком-н.
enquiring /ɪnˈkwaɪərɪŋ, ɪŋ-/ *adj.*: **an ~ look** вопроси́тельный взгляд; **an ~ mind** пытли́вый ум.
enquir|y /ɪnˈkwaɪərɪ, ɪŋ-/ *n.* расспро́сы (*m. pl.*); **make ~ies** нав|оди́ть, -ести́ спра́вки.
enrage /ɪnˈreɪdʒ/ *v.t.* беси́ть, вз-.
enrich /ɪnˈrɪtʃ/ *v.t.* обога|ща́ть, -ти́ть.
enrol /ɪnˈrəʊl/ *v t. & i.* (**enrolled, enrolling**) зач|исля́ть(ся), -и́слить(ся).
enrolment /ɪnˈrəʊlmənt/ *n.* зачисле́ние, приём.
ensconce /ɪnˈskɒns/ *v.t.*: **~ o.s.** устр|а́иваться, -о́иться, укр|ыва́ться, -ы́ться.
ensemble /ɒnˈsɒmb(ə)l/ *n.* анса́мбль (*m.*).
enshrine /ɪnˈʃraɪn/ *v.t.* поме|ща́ть, -сти́ть в ра́ку; (*fig.*) храни́ть (*impf.*).
ensign /ˈensaɪn/ *n.*
1 (*flag*) (кормово́й) флаг.
2 (*hist., standard-bearer*) пра́порщик.
3 (*US nav.*) мла́дший лейтена́нт.
enslave /ɪnˈsleɪv/ *v.t.* порабо|ща́ть, -ти́ть.
ensu|e /ɪnˈsjuː/ *v.i.* (**ensues, ensued, ensuing**) сле́довать (*impf.*) (*from* из + *g.*); **in ~ing years** в после́дующие го́ды.
ensure /ɪnˈʃʊə(r)/ *v.t.* (*make certain; secure*) обеспе́чи|вать, -ть.
entail /ɪnˈteɪl/ *v.t.* влечь (*impf.*) за собо́й.
entangle /ɪnˈtæŋg(ə)l/ *v.t.* (*lit.*) запу́т|ывать, -ать; (*fig.*) впу́т|ывать, -ать; **he ~d himself with women** он запу́тался в отноше́ниях с же́нщинами.
enter /ˈentə(r)/ *v.t. & i.*
1 (*go into*) входи́ть, войти́ в + *a.*; **~ the army** вступ|а́ть, -и́ть в а́рмию; **the idea never ~ed my head** э́та мысль никогда́ не приходи́ла мне в го́лову.
2 (*include in record*) запи́с|ывать, -а́ть; (*comput.*) вводи́ть, ввести́; **~ a horse for a race** заяв|ля́ть, -и́ть ло́шадь для ска́чек; **~ (o.s.) for an examination** под|ава́ть, -а́ть докуме́нты на уча́стие в экза́мене.
■ *with prep.*: **~ into conversation** вступ|а́ть, -и́ть в разгово́р; **he ~ed into the spirit of the game** он прони́кся ду́хом игры́.
enterprise /ˈentəpraɪz/ *n.*
1 (*undertaking*) предприя́тие.
2 (*initiative*) предприи́мчивость.
3 (*econ.*): **free ~** свобо́дное предпринима́тельство.
enterprising /ˈentəpraɪzɪŋ/ *adj.* предприи́мчивый.
entertain /entəˈteɪn/ *v.t.* развл|ека́ть, -е́чь; прин|има́ть, -я́ть; **~ friends** уго|ща́ть, -сти́ть друзе́й; (*amuse*) развл|ека́ть, -е́чь.
entertainer /entəˈteɪnə(r)/ *n.* арти́ст эстра́ды.
entertaining /entəˈteɪnɪŋ/ *adj.* интере́сный, занима́тельный.
entertainment /entəˈteɪnmənt/ *n.*
1 (*social*) приём госте́й.
2 (*amusement*) развлече́ние.
3 (*spectacle*) представле́ние.
enthral /ɪnˈθrɔːl/ (*US* **enthrall**) *v.t.* (**enthralled, enthralling**) (*fascinate*) увл|ека́ть, -е́чь; **an ~ling play** захва́тывающая пье́са.
enthuse /ɪnˈθjuːz/ *v.i.* (*coll.*) восторга́ться (*impf.*) (*чем*).
enthusiasm /ɪnˈθjuːzɪæz(ə)m/ *n.* восто́рг, энтузиа́зм.
enthusiast /ɪnˈθjuːzɪæst/ *n.* энтузиа́ст (*fem.* -ка).
enthusiastic /ɪnθjuːzɪˈæstɪk/ *adj.* восто́рженный; по́лный энтузиа́зма.
entice /ɪnˈtaɪs/ *v.t.* соблазн|я́ть, -и́ть.
enticement /ɪnˈtaɪsmənt/ *n.* (*action*) зама́нивание; (*lure*) прима́нка, собла́зн.
entire /ɪnˈtaɪə(r)/ *adj.* це́лый, по́лный, це́льный; **~ly** целико́м, соверше́нно.
entirety /ɪnˈtaɪərətɪ/ *n.* полнота́, це́льность.
entitle /ɪnˈtaɪt(ə)l/ *v.t.*
1 (*authorize*) да|ва́ть, -ть пра́во на + *a.*; **you are ~d to two books a month** вам полага́ется две кни́ги в ме́сяц.
2: **a book ~d 'Progress'** кни́га под загла́вием «Прогре́сс».
entitlement /ɪnˈtaɪt(ə)lmənt/ *n.* (*right*) пра́во.
entity /ˈentɪtɪ/ *n.* существо́.
entomologist /entəˈmɒlədʒɪst/ *n.* энтомо́лог.
entomology /entəˈmɒlədʒɪ/ *n.* энтомоло́гия.
entourage /ɒntʊəˈrɑːʒ/ *n.* антура́ж, окруже́ние.
entrance[1] /ˈentrəns/ *n.* вход; **~ examination** вступи́тельный экза́мен; **~ fee** вступи́тельный взнос; **~ hall** прихо́жая, вестибю́ль (*m.*).
entrance[2] /ɪnˈtrɑːns/ *v.t.* восторга́ть (*impf.*).
entrant /ˈentrənt/ *n.* (*person entering school, profession etc.*) поступа́ющий; (*competitor*) уча́стник.

entreat /ɪn'tri:t/ *v.t.* умол|я́ть, -и́ть.

entreaty /ɪn'tri:tɪ/ *n.* мольба́.

entrench /ɪn'trentʃ/ *v.t.* окруж|а́ть, -и́ть око́пами; **the enemy were ~ed nearby** враг окопа́лся вблизи́; **~ o.s.** ок|а́пываться, -опа́ться; (*fig.*) **customs ~ed by tradition** обы́чаи, закреплённые тради́цией.

entrepreneur /ɒntrəprə'nə:(r)/ *n.* предпринима́тель (*m.*).

entrepreneurial /ɒntrəprə'nə:rɪəl/ *adj.* предпринима́тельский.

entrust /ɪn'trʌst/ *v.t.* вв|еря́ть, -е́рить; **I ~ed the task to him (***or* **~ed him with the task)** я дал ему́ поруче́ние.

entry /'entrɪ/ *n.*
1 (*going in*) вход.
2 (*access*) до́ступ; **he gained ~ to the house** он пробра́лся в дом.
3 (*item*) за́пись; **dictionary ~** слова́рная статья́; **~ in a diary** за́пись в дневнике́.
4 (*inscription*; *competitor*): **~ form** вступи́тельная анке́та; **there was a large ~ for the race** на ска́чки записа́лось мно́го уча́стников.

entryphone /'entrɪfəʊn/ *n.* (*Br.*, *propr.*) домофо́н.

enunciate /ɪ'nʌnsɪeɪt/ *v.t.* (*express*) формули́ровать, с-; (*pronounce*) произн|оси́ть, -ести́.

envelop /ɪn'veləp/ *v.t.* (**enveloped, enveloping**) обёр|тывать, -ну́ть; оку́т|ывать, -ать; **hills ~ed in mist** холмы́, оку́танные тума́ном; **a baby ~ed in a shawl** младе́нец, завёрнутый в шаль; **~ed in mystery** покры́тый та́йной.

envelope /'ɒnvələʊp/ *n.* конве́рт.

enviable /'envɪəb(ə)l/ *adj.* зави́дный.

envious /'envɪəs/ *adj.* зави́стливый.

environment /ɪn'vaɪərənmənt/ *n.* окруже́ние, среда́; **the ~** окружа́ющая среда́.
■ *cpd.* **~-friendly** *adj.* экологи́чески безвре́дный.

environmental /ɪnvaɪərən'ment(ə)l/ *adj.* окружа́ющий; **~ studies** изуче́ние окружа́ющей среды́.

environmentalism /ɪnvaɪərən'mentəlɪz(ə)m/ *n.* защи́та окружа́ющей среды́.

environmentalist /ɪnvaɪərən'mentəlɪst/ *n.* сторо́нник защи́ты окружа́ющей среды́.

environs /ɪn'vaɪərənz/ *n.* окре́стности (*f. pl.*).

envisage /ɪn'vɪzɪdʒ/ *v.t.* (*consider*) рассм|а́тривать, -отре́ть; (*visualize*) предви́деть (*impf.*).

envoy /'envɔɪ/ *n.* диплома́т.

envy /'envɪ/ *n.* за́висть.
■ *v.t.* зави́довать, по- + *d.*; **I ~ him** я ему́ зави́дую; **I ~ his patience** я зави́дую его́ терпе́нию.

enzyme /'enzaɪm/ *n.* энзи́м.

epaulette /'epəlet/ *n.* эполе́т.

ephemeral /ɪ'femər(ə)l/ *adj.* эфеме́рный.

epic /'epɪk/ *n.* эпи́ческая поэ́ма, эпопе́я.
■ *adj.* эпи́ческий; (*on a grand scale*) грандио́зный.

epicentre /'epɪsentə(r)/ (*US* **epicenter**) *n.* эпице́нтр.

epidemic /epɪ'demɪk/ *n.* эпиде́мия.

epidural /epɪ'djʊər(ə)l/ *n.* эпидура́льная инъе́кция.

epilepsy /'epɪlepsɪ/ *n.* эпиле́псия.

epileptic /epɪ'leptɪk/ *n.* эпиле́птик.
■ *adj.* эпилепти́ческий.

episode /'epɪsəʊd/ *n.* (*occurrence*) эпизо́д; (*instalment*) часть.

episodic /epɪ'sɒdɪk/ *adj.* (*composed of episodes*) состоя́щий из отде́льных эпизо́дов; (*incidental, occasional*) эпизоди́ческий.

epitaph /'epɪtɑ:f/ *n.* эпита́фия, надгро́бная на́дпись.

epitome /ɪ'pɪtəmɪ/ *n.* воплоще́ние.

epitomize /ɪ'pɪtəmaɪz/ *v.t.* вопло|ща́ть, -ти́ть.

epoch /'i:pɒk/ *n.* эпо́ха.

eponymous /ɪ'pɒnɪməs/ *adj.* и́менем кото́рого на́зван (*fem.* -а, *nt.* -о) + *nom.*; (*hero*) загла́вный (*роль, герой*).

equal /'i:kw(ə)l/ *n.* ро́вня; **our boss treats us all as ~s** наш нача́льник обраща́ется со все́ми на́ми на ра́вных.
■ *adj.* 1 (*same, equivalent*) ра́вный, одина́ковый.
2 (*adequate*) спосо́бный; **he is ~ to the task** он вполне́ мо́жет спра́виться с э́той зада́чей.
■ *v.t.* & *i.* (**equalled, equalling;** *US* **equaled, equaling**)
1 (*math.*) равня́ться (*impf.*) (*чему*).
2: **he ~s me in strength** мы с ним равны́ по си́ле.

equality /ɪ'kwɒlɪtɪ/ *n.* ра́венство, равнопра́вие.

equalize /'i:kwəlaɪz/ *v.t.* & *i.* ура́вн|ивать, -я́ть.

equalizer /'i:kwəlaɪzə(r)/ *n.* (*sport*) гол, сра́внивающий счёт.

equally /'i:kwəlɪ/ *adv.*
1 (*to an equal extent*) одина́ково.
2 (*also, likewise*) ра́вным о́бразом; наравне́.
3 (*evenly*): **he divided the money ~** он раздели́л де́ньги по́ровну.

equanimity /ekwə'nɪmɪtɪ/ *n.* душе́вное равнове́сие; споко́йствие; **with ~** споко́йно.

equate /ɪ'kweɪt/ *v.t.* отождеств|ля́ть, -и́ть; **he ~s wealth with happiness** он отождествля́ет бога́тство со сча́стьем.

equation /ɪ'kweɪʒ(ə)n/ *n.* уравне́ние.

equator /ɪ'kweɪtə(r)/ *n.* эква́тор.

equidistant /i:kwɪ'dɪst(ə)nt/ *adj.* равноотстоя́щий; **these towns are ~ from London** э́ти города́ располо́жены на одина́ковом расстоя́нии от Ло́ндона.

equilibri|um /i:kwɪ'lɪbrɪəm/ *n.* (*lit., fig.*) равнове́сие.

equinox /'ekwɪnɒks/ *n.* равноде́нствие.

equip /ɪ'kwɪp/ *v.t.* (**equipped, equipping**) снаря|жа́ть, -ди́ть.

equipment /ɪ'kwɪpmənt/ *n.* снаряже́ние, экипиро́вка.

equitable /'ekwɪtəb(ə)l/ *adj.* справедли́вый.

equity /'ekwɪtɪ/ *n.*
1 (*fairness*) справедли́вость.
2 (*pl., fin.*) обыкнове́нные а́кции (*f. pl.*).

equivalent /ɪ'kwɪvələnt/ *n.* эквивале́нт.
■ *adj.* эквивале́нтный.

equivocal /ɪ'kwɪvək(ə)l/ *adj.* двусмы́сленный, сомни́тельный.

era /ˈɪərə/ *n.* э́ра.
eradicate /ɪˈrædɪkeɪt/ *v.t.* искорен|я́ть, -и́ть.
erase /ɪˈreɪz/ *v.t.* ст|ира́ть, -ере́ть.
eraser /ɪˈreɪzə(r)/ *n.* рези́нка.
erect /ɪˈrekt/ *adj.* прямо́й.
■ *v.t.* (*build, set up*) воздв|ига́ть, -и́гнуть; соору|жа́ть, -ди́ть.
erection /ɪˈrekʃ(ə)n/ *n.* (*setting up*) сооруже́ние; (*building*) зда́ние; (*physiol.*) эре́кция.
ergonomic /ɜːɡəˈnɒmɪk/ *adj.* эргономи́чный.
Eritrea /erɪˈtreɪə/ *n.* Эритре́я.
ERM (*abbr. of* ***exchange-rate mechanism***) МВК (механи́зм валю́тных ку́рсов).
ermine /ˈɜːmɪn/ *n.* (*pl.* **~** *or* **~s**) (*animal, fur*) горноста́й.
erode /ɪˈrəʊd/ *v.t.* разъ|еда́ть, -е́сть; (*fig.*) подт|а́чивать, -очи́ть.
erosion /ɪˈrəʊʒ(ə)n/ *n.* разъеда́ние, эро́зия; (*fig.*): **the ~ of his hopes** постепе́нное разруше́ние его́ наде́жд.
erotic /ɪˈrɒtɪk/ *adj.* эроти́ческий.
eroticism /ɪˈrɒtɪsɪz(ə)m/ *n.* эроти́зм.
err /ɜː(r)/ *v.i.* ошиб|а́ться, -и́ться; заблужда́ться (*impf.*).
errand /ˈerənd/ *n.* поруче́ние.
errant /ˈerənt/ *adj.*
[1] (*misbehaving*) заблу́дший.
[2] (*stray, wandering*) стра́нствующий; **knight ~** стра́нствующий ры́царь.
erratic /ɪˈrætɪk/ *adj.* неусто́йчивый; (*of person*) беспоря́дочный; **~ally** нерегуля́рно.
erroneous /ɪˈrəʊnɪəs/ *adj.* оши́бочный.
error /ˈerə(r)/ *n.* оши́бка, заблужде́ние; **the letter was sent in ~** письмо́ бы́ло отпра́влено по оши́бке.
erstwhile /ˈɜːstwaɪl/ *adj.* да́вний, давни́шний; **an ~ friend** да́вний/стари́нный друг.
erudite /ˈeruːdaɪt/ *adj.* эруди́рованный, учёный.
erudition /eruːˈdɪʃ(ə)n/ *n.* эруди́ция.
erupt /ɪˈrʌpt/ *v.i.* (*of volcano*) изверга́ться (*impf.*).
eruption /ɪˈrʌpʃ(ə)n/ *n.*
[1] (*of volcano etc.*) изверже́ние.
[2] (*fig.*) взрыв.
escalate /ˈeskəleɪt/ *v.i.* разраста́ться (*impf.*).
escalation /eskəˈleɪʃ(ə)n/ *n.* эскала́ция.
escalator /ˈeskəleɪtə(r)/ *n.* эскала́тор.
escapade /ˈeskəpeɪd/ *n.* (экстравага́нтная) вы́ходка.
escape /ɪˈskeɪp/ *n.*
[1] (*becoming free*) побе́г, бе́гство.
[2] (*avoidance*) спасе́ние, избавле́ние; **he had a narrow ~ from shipwreck** он едва́ спа́сся при кораблекруше́нии.
■ *v.t.* избе|га́ть, -жа́ть + *g.*; **he ~d death** он оста́лся в живы́х; **nothing ~s you!** всё(-то) вы замеча́ете!
■ *v.i.* бежа́ть (*det.*); уходи́ть, уйти́; соверши́ть (*pf.*) побе́г; **an ~d prisoner** бе́глыйароста́нт.
escapism /ɪˈskeɪpɪz(ə)m/ *n.* бе́гство от действи́тельности; эскапи́зм.
escort[1] /ˈeskɔːt/ *n.* (*mil.*) конво́й, эско́рт; **police ~** (*of criminal*) конво́й; **her ~ to the ball** её кавале́р на балу́.
escort[2] /ɪˈskɔːt/ *v.t.* сопрово|жда́ть, -ди́ть; (*mil.*) эскорти́ровать (*impf., pf.*); **I ~ed him to his seat** я провёл его́ на ме́сто.
Eskimo /ˈeskɪməʊ/ *n.* (*pl.* **~** *or* **~s**) эскимо́с (*fem.* -ка).
■ *adj.* эскимо́сский.
esophagus /iːˈsɒfəɡəs/ (*US*) = **oesophagus**
esoteric /iːsəʊˈterɪk/ *adj.* эзотери́ческий.
especially /ɪˈspeʃ(ə)lɪ/ *adj.* осо́бенно.
espionage /ˈespɪənɑːʒ/ *n.* шпиона́ж.
espouse /ɪˈspaʊz/ *v.t.*: **~ a cause** (целико́м) отд|ава́ться, -а́ться де́лу.
espresso /eˈspresəʊ/ *n.* (*pl.* **~s**) (*coffee*) ко́фе «эспре́ссо».
essay /ˈeseɪ/ *n.* (*attempt*) попы́тка, про́ба; (*literary composition*) о́черк, эссе́ (*nt. indecl.*); (*in school*) сочине́ние.
essence /ˈes(ə)ns/ *n.*
[1] (*philos.*) су́щность, существо́.
[2] (*extract*) эссе́нция.
essential /ɪˈsenʃ(ə)l/ *n.* су́щность.
■ *adj.* [1] (*necessary*) необходи́мый; **it is ~ that I should know** о́чень ва́жно, что́бы я знал.
[2] (*fundamental*) суще́ственный; **~ly** суще́ственно; по существу́; в су́щности.
[3] : **~ oils** эфи́рные масла́.
establish /ɪˈstæblɪʃ/ *v.t.*
[1] (*found, set up*) учре|жда́ть, -ди́ть; устан|а́вливать, -ови́ть.
[2] (*prove, gain acceptance for*) утвер|жда́ть, -ди́ть; **~ one's reputation** созд|ава́ть, -а́ть себе́ репута́цию; **E~ed Church** госуда́рственная це́рковь.
establishment /ɪˈstæblɪʃmənt/ *n.*
[1] (*setting up*) учрежде́ние, установле́ние.
[2] (*of a fact etc.*) установле́ние.
[3] (*institution*) учрежде́ние, заведе́ние; **educational ~** уче́бное заведе́ние.
[4] (*business concern*) заведе́ние, де́ло.
[5] (*set of institutions or key persons*): **the E~** «исте́блишмент».
estate /ɪˈsteɪt/ *n.*
[1] (*landed property*) поме́стье, име́ние; **~ agent** (*Br.*) аге́нт по прода́же недви́жимости; **~ car** (*Br.*) автомоби́ль (*m.*) с ку́зовом «универса́л»; универса́л (*coll.*); **housing ~** (*Br.*) жило́й масси́в.
[2] (*property*) иму́щество; **real ~** недви́жимость.
esteem /ɪˈstiːm/ *n.* уваже́ние.
estimate[1] /ˈestɪmət/ *n.*
[1] (*assessment*) оце́нка.
[2] (*comm.*) сме́та.
estimate[2] /ˈestɪmeɪt/ *v.t.* оце́н|ивать, -и́ть.
estimation /estɪˈmeɪʃ(ə)n/ *n.* (*judgment*) оце́нка, сужде́ние.
Estonia /ɪˈstəʊnɪə/ *n.* Эсто́ния.
Estonian /ɪˈstəʊnɪən/ *n.* эсто́н|ец (*fem.* -ка).
■ *adj.* эсто́нский.
estrange /ɪˈstreɪndʒ/ *v.t.* отдал|я́ть, -и́ть; **his ~d wife** жена́, с кото́рой он живёт разде́льно.
estrogen /ˈiːstrədʒ(ə)n/ (*US*) = **oestrogen**
estuary /ˈestjʊərɪ/ *n.* эстуа́рий, у́стье.
etc. /et ˈsetərə/ *adv.* (*abbr. of* ***et cetera***) и т. д., и т. п. (и так да́лее; и тому́ подо́бное).

etch /etʃ/ *v.t.* & *i.* травить, вы́-; гравировать, вы́-; (*fig.*): **it is ∼ed on my memory** это запечатлелось у меня в памяти.
etching /'etʃɪŋ/ *n.* офорт, гравюра.
eternal /ɪ'tə:n(ə)l/ *adj.* вечный (*also fig.*).
eternity /ɪ'tə:nɪtɪ/ *n.* вечность.
ether /'i:θə(r)/ *n.* (*phys., chem.*) эфир.
ethereal /ɪ'θɪərɪəl/ *adj.* эфирный, неземной; **∼ beauty** неземная красота.
ethical /'eθɪk(ə)l/ *adj.* этичный.
ethics /'eθɪk/ *n. pl.* этика; мораль.
Ethiopia /i:θɪ'əʊpɪə/ *n.* Эфиопия.
Ethiopian /i:θɪ'əʊpɪən/ *n.* эфиоп (*fem.* -ка).
■ *adj.* эфиопский.
ethnic /'eθnɪk(ə)l/ *adj.* этнический; **∼ cleansing** этническая чистка.
ethos /'i:θɒs/ *n.* дух, характер.
etiquette /'etɪket/ *n.* этикет.
etymological /etɪmə'lɒdʒɪk(ə)l/ *adj.* этимологический.
etymology /etɪ'mɒlədʒɪ/ *n.* этимология.
EU (*abbr. of* ***European Union***) ЕС (Европейский союз).
eucalyp|tus /ju:kə'lɪptəs/ *n.* (*pl.* **∼tuses** *or* **∼ti** /-taɪ/) эвкалипт.
Eucharist /'ju:kərɪst/ *n.* евхаристия, святое причастие.
eulogy /'ju:lədʒɪ/ *n.* хвалебная речь, панегирик; (*at funeral*) надгробная речь.
euphemism /'ju:fɪmɪz(ə)m/ *n.* эвфемизм.
euphemistic /ju:fɪ'mɪstɪk/ *adj.* эвфемистический.
euphoria /ju:'fɔ:rɪə/ *adj.* эйфория.
euphoric /ju:'fɒrɪk/ *adj.* в приподнятом настроении.
eureka /jʊə'ri:kə/ *int.* эврика.
euro /'jʊərəʊ/ *n.* (*pl.* **∼s**) евро (*m. indecl.*).
Euro|- /'jʊərəʊ/ *comb. form* евро...; **∼-MP** депутат Европарламента; **∼sceptic** евроскептик; **e∼zone** Еврозона.
Europe /'jʊərəp/ *n.* Европа.
European /jʊərə'pɪən/ *n.* европе|ец (*fem.* -йка).
■ *adj.* европейский.
euthanasia /ju:θə'neɪzɪə/ *n.* эвтаназия, умерщвление из милосердия.
evacuate /ɪ'vækjʊeɪt/ *v.t.* эвакуировать (*impf., pf.*).
evacuation /ɪvækjʊ'eɪʃ(ə)n/ *n.* (*removal*) эвакуация; (*physiol.*) очищение кишечника, испражнение.
evacuee /ɪvækju:'i:/ *n.* эвакуированный.
evade /ɪ'veɪd/ *v.t.* избе|гать, -жать + *g.*; **∼ a blow/question** уклон|яться, -иться от удара/ответа.
evaluate /ɪ'væljʊeɪt/ *v.t.* оцен|ивать, -ить.
evaluation /ɪvæljʊ'eɪʃ(ə)n/ *n.* оценка.
evangelical /i:væn'dʒelɪk(ə)l/ *adj.* евангелический.
evangelism /ɪ'vændʒəlɪz(ə)m/ *n.* проповедь Евангелия; (*fig.*) проповедничество.
evangelist /ɪ'vændʒəlɪst/ *n.* (*author of gospel*) евангелист; (*preacher*) проповедник Евангелия.
evaporate /ɪ'væpəreɪt/ *v.t.* & *i.* испар|ять(ся), -ить(ся) (*also fig.*).
evaporation /ɪvæpə'reɪʃ(ə)n/ *n.* испарение.
evasion /ɪ'veɪʒ(ə)n/ *n.* (*avoidance*) уклонение; (*prevarication*) увёртка.
evasive /ɪ'veɪsɪv/ *adj.* (*of answer*) уклончивый; (*of person*) увёртливый.
eve /i:v/ *n.* (*day or evening before*) канун (*also fig.*); **on the ∼ of** накануне + *g.*
even /'i:v(ə)n/ *adj.* (**evener, evenest**)
1 (*level, smooth*) ровный.
2 (*equal*) равный; **the score is ∼** счёт равный; **get ∼ with s.o.** расквитаться (*pf.*) с кем-н.
3 (*divisible by 2*) чётный.
■ *adv.* даже; и; хотя бы; **he won't ∼ notice** он и не заметит; **not ∼** даже не; **this applies ∼ more to French** это ещё в большей степени относится к французскому языку.
■ *v.t.* (*make even or equal*) выравнивать, выровнять.
evening /'i:vnɪŋ/ *n.* вечер; **in the ∼** вечером; **one ∼** однажды вечером; **this ∼** сегодня вечером; **tomorrow ∼** завтра вечером; **∼ dress, clothes** (*of either sex*) вечерний туалет; **∼ dress, gown** (*woman's*) вечернее платье.
evenness /'i:vənnɪs/ *n.* (*physical smoothness*) гладкость; (*uniformity*) равномерность; (*of temper, tone etc.*) ровность, уравновешенность; (*of odds, contest etc.*) равенство.
event /ɪ'vent/ *n.*
1 (*occurrence*) событие.
2 (*hypothesis*) случай; **in the ∼ of his coming** в случае его прихода; **in any ∼** в любом случае.
3 (*sports race*) забег, заезд; (*type of sport*) вид спорта.
eventful /ɪ'ventfʊl/ *adj.* насыщенный событиями.
eventual /ɪ'ventjʊəl/ *adj.* конечный.
eventuality /ɪventjʊ'ælɪtɪ/ *n.* возможность, случай.
eventually /ɪ'ventjʊəlɪ/ *adv.* со временем; в конце концов.
ever /'evə(r)/ *adv.*
1 (*always*) всегда; **for ∼** навсегда, навечно; **∼ after, since** с тех (самых) пор; **∼ since** (*conj.*) с тех пор, как... .
2 (*at any time*): **do you ∼ see him?** вы его хоть иногда видите?; **scarcely, hardly ∼** почти никогда; очень редко; **as good as ∼** не хуже, чем раньше; **better than ∼** лучше, чем когда-либо.
3 (*intensive*): **why ∼ did you do it?** зачем же вы это сделали?; **∼ so rich** (*Br.*) невероятно богатый; (*coll.*); **thank you ∼ so much** (*Br.*) я вам чрезвычайно благодарен.
■ *cpds.* **∼green** *n.* (*bot.*) вечнозелёное растение; *adj.* вечнозелёный; **∼lasting** *adj.* вечный.
every /'evrɪ/ *adj.* каждый, всякий; **I have ∼ confidence in him** я в нём совершенно уверен; **∼ ten minutes** каждые десять минут; **∼ other car** каждый второй автомобиль; **∼ other day** через день; **∼ now and again; ∼ so often; ∼ once in a while** время от времени; по временам; иногда.
■ *cpds.* **∼body, ∼one** *prons.* каждый;

вся́кий; все (*pl.*); **~body else** все остальны́е; **~day** *adj.* повседне́вный; обыкнове́нный, бытово́й; **~one** *pron.* = **~body; ~thing** *pron.* всё; **~where** *adv.* везде́, повсю́ду.

evict /ɪ'vɪkt/ *v.t.* выселя́ть, вы́селить.

eviction /ɪ'vɪkʃ(ə)n/ *n.* выселе́ние.

evidence /'evɪd(ə)ns/ *n.*
1 (*indication*) доказа́тельство, свиде́тельство.
2 (*leg.*) свиде́тельские показа́ния (*nt. pl.*); ули́ка; да́нные (*nt. pl.*); **give ~** да|ва́ть, -ть свиде́тельские показа́ния.
■ *v.t.* служи́ть, по- доказа́тельством, ули́кой (*чего*).

evident /'evɪd(ə)nt/ *adj.* очеви́дный, я́сный; **it was ~ from his behaviour that ...** бы́ло ви́дно по его́ поведе́нию, что... .

evil /'i:vɪl/ *n.* зло.
■ *adj.* злой, дурно́й.

evocation /evə'keɪʃ(ə)n/ *n.* вызыва́ние; воскреше́ние в па́мяти.

evocative /ɪ'vɒkətɪv/ *adj.* навева́ющий воспомина́ния.

evoke /ɪ'vəʊk/ *v.t.* вызыва́ть, вы́звать; пробу|жда́ть, -ди́ть; нап|omина́ть, -о́мнить.

evolution /i:və'lu:ʃ(ə)n/ *n.* эволю́ция.

evolutionary /i:və'lu:ʃənərɪ/ *adj.* эволюцио́нный.

evolve /ɪ'vɒlv/ *v.i.* разв|ива́ться, -и́ться.

ewe /ju:/ *n.* овца́.

ex /eks/ *n.* (*coll.*) бы́вший муж, бы́вшая жена́.

ex- /eks/ *pref.* (*former*) экс-..., бы́вший.

exacerbate /ek'sæsəbeɪt/ *v.t.* (*pain etc.*) обостр|я́ть, -и́ть.

exact /ɪg'zækt/ *adj.* то́чный.

exactly /ɪg'zæktlɪ/ *adv.* то́чно; (*of numbers, quantities*) ро́вно.

exaggerate /ɪg'zædʒəreɪt/ *v.t.* преувели́чи|вать, -ть.

exaggeration /ɪgzædʒə'reɪʃ(ə)n/ *n.* преувеличе́ние.

exalt /ɪg'zɔ:lt/ *v.t.* (*make higher in rank etc.*) пов|ыша́ть, -ы́сить; (*praise*) превозн|оси́ть, -ести́.

exaltation /egzɔ:l'teɪʃ(ə)n/ *n.*
1 (*raising in rank etc.*) повыше́ние.
2 (*worship*) возвели́чение, возвели́чивание.
3 (*mental or emotional transport*) экзальта́ция.

exam /ɪg'zæm/ = **examination**

examination /ɪgzæmɪ'neɪʃ(ə)n/ *n.* экза́мен; **~ paper** (*written by examinee*) экзаменацио́нная рабо́та; (*questions set*) вопро́сы (*m. pl.*) (для экзаменацио́нной рабо́ты); **take an ~** сдава́ть (*impf.*) экза́мен; **pass an ~** сдать (*pf.*) экза́мен.

examine /ɪg'zæmɪn/ *v.t.*
1 (*inspect*) осм|а́тривать, -отре́ть; **~ passports** пров|еря́ть, -е́рить паспорта́; **~ a patient** осм|а́тривать, -отре́ть больно́го.
2 (*acad.*) экзаменова́ть, про-.

examiner /ɪg'zæmɪnə(r)/ *n.* (*acad.*) экзамена́тор.

example /ɪg'zɑ:mp(ə)l/ *n.*
1 (*illustration, model*) приме́р; **for ~** наприме́р.
2 (*warning*) уро́к; **let this be an ~ to you** пусть э́то послу́жит вам уро́ком.

exasperate /ɪg'zɑ:spəreɪt/ *v.t.* изв|оди́ть, -ести́.

exasperation /ɪgzɑ:spə'reɪʃ(ə)n/ *n.* раздраже́ние.

excavate /'ekskəveɪt/ *v.t.* копа́ть (*impf.*); выка́пывать, вы́копать; раск|а́пывать, -опа́ть.

excavation /ekskə'veɪʃ(ə)n/ *n.* (*site*) раско́пки (*f. pl.*); (*action*) выка́пывание.

excavator /'ekskəveɪtə(r)/ *n.* (*person*) землеко́п; (*machine*) экскава́тор.

exceed /ɪk'si:d/ *v.t.* прев|ыша́ть, -ы́сить.

exceedingly /ɪk'si:dɪŋlɪ/ *adv.* весьма́, чрезвыча́йно.

excel /ɪk'sel/ *v.i.* (**excelled, excelling**) выделя́ться (*impf.*); **he ~s in sport** он превосхо́дный спортсме́н.

excellency /'eksələnsɪ/ *n.*: **His E~** его́ превосходи́тельство.

excellent /'eksələnt/ *adj.* отли́чный.

except /ɪk'sept/ *prep.* (*also* **~ing**) исключа́я + *a.*; кро́ме + *g.*; за исключе́нием + *g.*; ра́зве лишь/то́лько; **the essay is good ~ for the spelling mistakes** сочине́ние хоро́шее, е́сли не счита́ть орфографи́ческих оши́бок.

exception /ɪk'sepʃ(ə)n/ *n.*
1 исключе́ние; **with the ~ of** за исключе́нием + *g.*
2: **take ~ to** об|ижа́ться, -и́деться на + *a.*

exceptional /ɪk'sepʃən(ə)l/ *adj.* исключи́тельный.

excerpt /'eksə:pt/ *n.* вы́держка, цита́та.

excess /ɪk'ses/ *n.* изли́шек, избы́ток; **in ~ of £20** свы́ше двадцати́ фу́нтов; /'ekses/: **~ baggage** изли́шек багажа́.

excessive /ɪk'sesɪv/ *adj.* изли́шний; (*extreme*) чрезме́рный.

exchange /ɪks'tʃeɪndʒ/ *n.*
1 (*act of exchanging*) обме́н + *g./i.*; **in ~ for** в обме́н на + *a.*
2 (*fin.*) разме́н, обме́н; **~ rate/control** валю́тный курс/контро́ль.
3 (*teleph.*) (центра́льная) телефо́нная ста́нция.
■ *v.t.* меня́ть, об-/по- (*что на что*); (*reciprocally*) меня́ться, об-/по- + *i.*; **we ~d places** мы поменя́лись места́ми.

exchequer /ɪks'tʃekə(r)/ *n.* казначе́йство, казна́.

excise[1] /'eksaɪz/ *n.* акци́з; **~ officer** акци́зный чино́вник.

excise[2] /ɪk'saɪz/ *v.t.* выреза́ть, вы́резать; отр|еза́ть, -е́зать.

excision /ɪk'sɪʒ(ə)n/ *n.* выреза́ние, отреза́ние; (*med.*) иссече́ние, удале́ние.

excitable /ɪk'saɪtəb(ə)l/ *adj.* легко́ возбуди́мый.

excite /ɪk'saɪt/ *v.t.* волнова́ть, вз-; **don't ~ yourself** (*or* **get ~d**) не волну́йтесь.

excitement /ɪk'saɪtmənt/ *n.* возбужде́ние, волне́ние.

exciting /ɪk'saɪtɪŋ/ *adj.* захва́тывающий.

exclaim /ɪk'skleɪm/ *v.t. & i.* воскл|ица́ть, -и́кнуть.

exclamation /eksklə'meɪʃ(ə)n/ *n.* восклица́ние; **~ mark** восклица́тельный знак.

exclude /ɪk'sklu:d/ *v.t.* исключ|а́ть, -и́ть.

exclusion /ɪk'sklu:ʒ(ə)n/ *n.* исключéние.

exclusive /ɪk'sklu:sɪv/ *adj.*
1 (*sole*) исключи́тельный, еди́нственный.
2 : **~ of** (*not counting*) без + *g.*, не счита́я + *g.*
3 (*high-class*) эксклюзи́вный; **an ~ club** клуб для и́збранных.

exclusivity /eksklu:'sɪvɪtɪ/ *n.* эксклюзи́вность.

excommunicate /ekskə'mju:nɪkeɪt/ *v.t.* отлуч|а́ть, -и́ть от це́ркви.

excrement /'ekskrɪmənt/ *n.* экскреме́нты (*m. pl.*).

excrete /ɪk'skri:t/ *v.t.* выделя́ть, вы́делить.

excruciating /ɪk'skru:ʃɪeɪtɪŋ/ *adj.* мучи́тельный.

excursion /ɪk'skə:ʃ(ə)n/ *n.* (*trip*) экску́рсия.

excuse[1] /ɪk'skju:s/ *n.* извине́ние, оправда́ние, отгово́рка; **a poor ~** сла́бая отгово́рка; **please make my ~s to the hostess** пожа́луйста, переда́йте мои́ извине́ния хозя́йке.

excuse[2] /ɪk'skju:z/ *v.t.*
1 (*forgive*) извин|я́ть, -и́ть; про|ща́ть, -сти́ть; **please ~ my coming late (*or* me for coming late)** извини́те, что я пришёл по́здно; **~ me, what time is it?** прости́те, кото́рый час?
2 (*release*): **I ~d him from attending** я позво́лил ему́ не прису́тствовать.

ex-directory /eksdaɪ'rektərɪ/ *adj.* (*Br.*) не внесённый в телефо́нную кни́гу; **he's ~** его́ но́мера нет в телефо́нной кни́ге.

execute /'eksɪkju:t/ *v.t.*
1 (*carry out*) выполня́ть, вы́полнить; исп|олня́ть, -о́лнить.
2 (*put to death*) казни́ть (*impf.*, *pf.*).

execution /eksɪ'kju:ʃ(ə)n/ *n.*
1 (*carrying out*) исполне́ние, выполне́ние.
2 (*capital punishment*) казнь.

executioner /eksɪ'kju:ʃənə(r)/ *n.* пала́ч.

executive /ɪg'zekjʊtɪv/ *n.* (руководя́щий) рабо́тник.
■ *adj.* 1 (*executing laws etc.*) исполни́тельный.
2 (*managing*) руководя́щий.

executor /ɪg'zekjʊtə(r)/ *n.* (*of a will*) исполни́тель завеща́ния, душеприка́зчик.

exemplary /ɪg'zemplərɪ/ *adj.* приме́рный, образцо́вый.

exemplify /ɪg'zemplɪfaɪ/ *v.t.* служи́ть, по- приме́ром + *g.*

exempt /ɪg'zempt/ *adj.* освобождённый, свобо́дный (*от чего*).
■ *v.t.* освобо|жда́ть, -ди́ть.

exemption /ɪg'zempʃ(ə)n/ *n.* освобожде́ние (*от чего*).

exercise /'eksəsaɪz/ *n.*
1 (*physical activity*) заря́дка, упражне́ние; **you should take more ~** вам ну́жно бо́льше вре́мени уделя́ть физи́ческим упражне́ниям.
2 (*trial of skill*): **military ~s** вое́нные уче́ния; (*in lesson*) упражне́ние; (*fig.*): **the object of the ~** цель э́того предприя́тия.
■ *v.t.* 1 (*exert, use*) выка́зывать, вы́казать; проявл|я́ть, -и́ть; **~ authority** примен|я́ть, -и́ть власть.
2 (*physically*) упражня́ть (*impf.*).
■ *v.i.* упражня́ться (*impf.*).
■ *cpd.* **~ book** *n.* (*Br.*) (учени́ческая) тетра́дь.

exert /ɪg'zə:t/ *v.t.* осуществ|ля́ть, -и́ть; **~ o.s.** постара́ться (*pf.*).

exertion /ɪg'zə:ʃ(ə)n/ *n.* напряже́ние, уси́лие.

exhale /eks'heɪl/ *v.i.* выдыха́ть, вы́дохнуть.

exhaust /ɪg'zɔ:st/ *n.* (*apparatus*) вы́хлоп, вы́пуск; (*expelled gas*) отрабо́танный газ.
■ *v.t.* истощ|а́ть, -и́ть; изнур|я́ть, -и́ть; **I feel ~ed** я соверше́нно без сил.

exhausting /ɪg'zɔ:stɪŋ/ *adj.* изнури́тельный, утоми́тельный.

exhaustion /ɪg'zɔ:stʃ(ə)n/ *n.* переутомле́ние, изнеможе́ние.

exhaustive /ɪg'zɔ:stɪv/ *adj.* исче́рпывающий, всесторо́нний.

exhibit /ɪg'zɪbɪt/ *n.* (*in museum etc.*) экспона́т.
■ *v.t.* (**exhibited, exhibiting**)
1 (*e.g. painting*) экспони́ровать (*impf.*, *pf.*).
2 (*fig., display*) прояв|ля́ть, -и́ть.

exhibition /eksɪ'bɪʃ(ə)n/ *n.* (*public show*) вы́ставка; **he made an ~ of himself** он сде́лал себя́ посме́шищем.

exhibitionist /eksɪ'bɪʃənɪst/ *n.* хвасту́н (*coll.*); (*suffering from psychosexual disorder*) эксгибициони́ст.

exhilarat|e /ɪg'zɪləreɪt/ *v.t.* весели́ть, раз-; **~ing news** ра́достное изве́стие.

exhilaration /ɪgzɪlə'reɪʃ(ə)n/ *n.* весе́лье; прия́тное возбужде́ние.

exhort /ɪg'zɔ:t/ *v.t.* приз|ыва́ть, -ва́ть (*кого к чему*); увещева́ть (*impf.*).

exhortation /egzɔ:'teɪʃ(ə)n/ *n.* призы́в, увещева́ние.

exhume /eks'hju:m/ *v.t.* эксгуми́ровать (*impf.*, *pf.*); (*fig.*) раск|а́пывать, -опа́ть; выка́пывать, вы́копать.

exile /'eksaɪl/ *n.*
1 (*banishment*) изгна́ние.
2 (*person*) изгна́нник.
■ *v.t.* изг|оня́ть, -на́ть; ссыла́ть, сосла́ть.

exist /ɪg'zɪst/ *v.i.* существова́ть (*impf.*).

existence /ɪg'zɪst(ə)ns/ *n.* существова́ние.

existential /egzɪ'stenʃ(ə)l/ *adj.* экзистенциа́льный.

existentialism /egzɪ'stenʃəlɪz(ə)m/ *n.* экзистенциали́зм.

exit /'eksɪt, 'egzɪt/ *n.* (*also comput.*) вы́ход.
■ *v.i.* (**exited, exiting**) уходи́ть, уйти́; (*comput.*) выходи́ть, вы́йти.

exonerate /ɪg'zɒnəreɪt/ *v.t.* опра́вд|ывать, -а́ть; сн|има́ть, -ять обвине́ние с + *g.* (*в чём*).

exorbitant /ɪg'zɔ:bɪt(ə)nt/ *adj.* непоме́рный, чрезме́рный.

exorcism /'eksɔ:sɪz(ə)m/ *n.* экзорци́зм, изгна́ние злых ду́хов.

exorcize /'eksɔ:saɪz/ *v.t.* изг|оня́ть, -на́ть злых ду́хов из + *g.*

exotic /ɪg'zɒtɪk/ *adj.* экзоти́ческий.

expand /ɪk'spænd/ *v.t.* (*lit., fig.*) расш|иря́ть, -и́рить; **heat ~s metals** при нагрева́нии мета́ллы расширя́ются.
■ *v.i.* расш|иря́ться, -и́риться; увели́чи|ваться, -ться в объёме.

expanse /ɪk'spæns/ *n.* протяже́ние.

expansion /ɪk'spænʃ(ə)n/ *n.* расшире́ние;

(*pol.*) экспа́нсия; (*increase*) подъём.
expatriate /eks'pætrɪət/ *n.* & *adj.* экспатриа́нт (*fem.* -ка).
expect /ɪk'spekt/ *v.t.*
1 (*of future or probable event*) ждать (*impf.*), ожида́ть (*impf.*) + *g.*; **I ~ to see him** я рассчи́тываю встре́титься с ним.
2 (*require*) ожида́ть (*impf.*) + *g.*; **I ~ you to be punctual** я наде́юсь/рассчи́тываю, что вы бу́дете пунктуа́льны.
3 (*suppose*) полага́ть (*impf.*); **I ~ you are hungry** я полага́ю, вы голодны́.
4: **she is ~ing** (*coll.*, *pregnant*) она́ ожида́ет ребёнка.
expectancy /ɪk'spektənsɪ/ *n.* ожида́ние; предвкуше́ние.
expectant /ɪk'spekt(ə)nt/ *adj.* выжида́ющий; **an ~ mother** бу́дущая мать.
expectation /ekspek'teɪʃ(ə)n/ *n.* ожида́ние; **contrary to ~** вопреки́ ожида́ниям; **come up to ~s** оправда́ть (*pf.*) ожида́ния.
expectorant /ek'spektərənt/ *n.* (*med.*) отха́ркивающее сре́дство.
expediency /ɪk'spi:dɪənsɪ/ *n.* вы́года.
expedient /ɪk'spi:dɪənt/ *n.* приём, спо́соб.
■ *adj.* целесообра́зный; (*advantageous*) вы́годный.
expedition /ekspə'dɪʃ(ə)n/ *n.* экспеди́ция.
expeditionary /ekspɪ'dɪʃənərɪ/ *adj.* экспедицио́нный; **~ force** экспедицио́нные войска́.
expel /ɪk'spel/ *v.t.* (**expelled, expelling**) (*compel to leave*) исключ|а́ть, -и́ть; выгоня́ть, вы́гнать.
expend /ɪk'spend/ *v.t.* (*capital*) расхо́довать, из-; тра́тить, ис-; (*ammunition*) расхо́довать, из-; (*time, efforts*) тра́тить, ис-/по-.
expenditure /ɪk'spendɪtʃə(r)/ *n.* расхо́д, тра́та.
expense /ɪk'spens/ *n.*
1 (*monetary cost*) расхо́д; **at my ~** (*lit.*) за мой счёт; **go to ~** нести́ (*det.*) расхо́ды; **spare no ~** не жале́ть (*impf.*) средств; **~ account** ава́нсовый отчёт.
2 (*detriment*): **a joke at my ~** шу́тка на мой счёт.
expensive /ɪk'spensɪv/ *adj.* дорого́й, дорогосто́ящий.
experience /ɪk'spɪərɪəns/ *n.*
1 (*process of gaining knowledge etc.*) о́пыт.
2 (*event*) слу́чай; **an unpleasant ~** неприя́тный слу́чай.
■ *v.t.* испы́т|ывать, -а́ть.
experienced /ɪk'spɪərɪənst/ *adj.* о́пытный.
experiment /ɪk'sperɪmənt/ *n.* экспериме́нт, о́пыт.
■ *v.i.* эксперименти́ровать (*impf.*).
experimental /ɪksperɪ'ment(ə)l/ *adj.* эксперимента́льный, про́бный.
experimentation /ɪksperɪmen'teɪʃ(ə)n/ *n.* эксперименти́рование.
expert /'ekspə:t/ *n.* экспе́рт, знато́к, специали́ст (*по чему*).
■ *adj.* квалифици́рованный; уме́лый; **an ~ driver** о́пытный шофёр; **~ advice** сове́т специали́ста; **he is ~ at persuading people** он ма́стер угова́ривать.
expertise /ekspə:'ti:z/ *n.* (*skill, knowledge*) компете́нтность.
expire /ɪk'spaɪə(r)/ *v.i.* (*of period, licence etc.*) ист|ека́ть, -е́чь.
expiry /ɪk'spaɪərɪ/ *n.* истече́ние (сро́ка).
explain /ɪk'spleɪn/ *v.t.* объясн|я́ть, -и́ть; изъясн|я́ть, -и́ть.
explanation /eksplə'neɪʃ(ə)n/ *n.* объясне́ние.
explanatory /ɪk'splænətərɪ/ *adj.* объясни́тельный.
expletive /ɪk'spli:tɪv/ *n.* (*oath*) бра́нное выраже́ние; (*gram.*) вставно́е сло́во.
explicable /ɪk'splɪkəb(ə)l/ *adj.* объясни́мый.
explicit /ɪk'splɪsɪt/ *adj.* я́сный, чёткий, то́чный.
explode /ɪk'spləʊd/ *v.t.* вз|рыва́ть, -орва́ть.
■ *v.i.* вз|рыва́ться, -орва́ться.
exploit[1] /'eksplɔɪt/ *n.* по́двиг.
exploit[2] /ɪk'splɔɪt/ *v.t.*
1 (*use or develop economically; misuse*) эксплуати́ровать (*impf.*).
2 (*an advantage etc.*) испо́льзовать (*impf.*, *pf.*).
exploitation /eksplɔɪ'teɪʃ(ə)n/ *n.* эксплуата́ция (*also of person*).
exploitative /ɪk'splɔɪtətɪv/ *adj.* эксплуата́торский, эксплуатацио́нный.
exploration /eksplə'reɪʃ(ə)n/ *n.* (*geog.*) иссле́дование; (*of possibilities etc.*) изуче́ние.
exploratory /ɪk'splɒrətərɪ/ *adj.* иссле́довательский; **~ talks** предвари́тельные перегово́ры.
explore /ɪk'splɔ:(r)/ *v.t.*
1 (*geog.*) иссле́довать (*impf.*, *pf.*).
2 (*possibilities etc.*) изуч|а́ть, -и́ть.
explorer /ɪk'splɔ:rə(r)/ *n.* иссле́дователь (*m.*) (*fem.* -ница).
explosion /ɪk'spləʊʒ(ə)n/ *n.* (*of bomb etc.*) взрыв; (*of rage etc.*) вспы́шка; **population ~** демографи́ческий взрыв.
explosive /ɪk'spləʊsɪv/ *n.* взры́вчатое вещество́.
■ *adj.* взры́вчатый, взрывно́й; (*situation*) взрывоопа́сный.
exponent /ɪk'spəʊnənt/ *n.* (*advocate*) сторо́нник; представи́тель (*m.*).
exponential /ekspə'nenʃ(ə)l/ *adj.* (*math.*) экспоненциа́льный, показа́тельный.
export[1] /'ekspɔ:t/ *n.* э́кспорт, вы́воз.
export[2] /ek'spɔ:t/ *v.t.* экспорти́ровать (*impf.*, *pf.*); вывози́ть, вы́везти.
exportation /ekspɔ:'teɪʃ(ə)n/ *n.* экспорти́рование.
exporter /ek'spɔ:tə(r)/ *n.* экспортёр.
expose /ɪk'spəʊz/ *v.t.*
1 (*physically*) выставля́ть, вы́ставить; **~ o.s.** (*indecently*) обнаж|а́ться, -и́ться.
2 (*unmask*) разоблач|а́ть, -и́ть.
exposition /ekspə'zɪʃ(ə)n/ *n.* (*setting forth facts etc.*) изложе́ние; (*exhibition*) экспози́ция, вы́ставка.
exposure /ɪk'spəʊʒə(r)/ *n.*
1 (*physical*): **~ to light** выставле́ние на свет; **he died of ~** он поги́б от хо́лода.
2 (*unmasking*) разоблаче́ние.
3 (*phot.*) экспози́ция.
expound /ɪk'spaʊnd/ *v.t.* (*a theory*) изл|ага́ть, -ожи́ть; (*a text*) толкова́ть (*impf.*).

express[1] /ɪk'spres/ *n.* (~ *train*) экспре́сс; курье́рский по́езд.
■ *adj.* (*urgent, high-speed*) сро́чный; **~ letter** сро́чное письмо́; **~ mail** э́кстренная по́чта.
■ *adv.* сро́чно, спе́шно; **the goods were sent ~** (*urgently*) това́р был отпра́влен экспре́ссом.

express[2] /ɪk'spres/ *v.t.* (*show in words etc.*) выража́ть, вы́разить; **~ o.s.** выража́ться, вы́разиться; выска́зывать, вы́сказать.

expression /ɪk'spreʃ(ə)n/ *n.*
1 (*act of expressing*) выраже́ние.
2 (*word, term*) выраже́ние (*also math.*).

expressionism /ɪk'spreʃənɪz(ə)m/ *n.* экспрессиони́зм.

expressionist /ɪkspreʃə'nɪst/ *n.* экспрессиони́ст.

expressive /ɪk'spresɪv/ *adj.* вырази́тельный.

expulsion /ɪk'spʌlʃ(ə)n/ *n.* изгна́ние; исключе́ние.

expurgate /'ekspəgeɪt/ *v.t.*: **~ a book** исключ|а́ть, -и́ть (*or* изыма́ть, изъя́ть) нежела́тельные места́ из кни́ги.

exquisite /ek'skwɪzɪt/ *adj.* (*perfected*) утончённый.

exquisiteness /eks'kwɪzɪtnɪs/ *n.* утончённость; (*of pain*) острота́.

extemporize /ɪk'stempəraɪz/ *v.t.* & *i.* и|мпровизи́ровать, сы-; **he ~d a speech** он произнёс импровизи́рованную речь.

extend /ɪk'stend/ *v.t.*
1 (*stretch out*) протя́|гивать, -ну́ть.
2 (*make longer, wider or larger*) удлин|я́ть, -и́ть; расш|иря́ть, -и́рить; **~ a railway** продли́ть (*pf.*) железнодоро́жную ли́нию; **~ one's premises** расш|иря́ть, -и́рить помеще́ние.
3 (*prolong*) продл|ева́ть, -и́ть; **~ one's leave/passport** продл|ева́ть, -и́ть о́тпуск/па́спорт; **an ~ed** (*lengthy*) **visit** дли́тельный визи́т.
■ *v.i.* простира́ться (*impf.*); **the garden ~s to the river** сад простира́ется до реки́.

extension /ɪk'stenʃ(ə)n/ *n.*
1 (*stretching out*) вытя́гивание, удлине́ние.
2 (*enlarging in space or time*) расшире́ние, увеличе́ние; **~ of leave** продле́ние о́тпуска; **~ lead** (*elec.*) удлини́тель (*m.*).
3 (*additional part of building etc.*) пристро́йка (**to:** к + *d.*).
4 (*teleph.*) (*telephone*) паралле́льный телефо́н; (*number*) доба́вочный (но́мер); **my number is 5652, ~ 10** мой но́мер 5652, доба́вочный 10.

extensive /ɪk'stensɪv/ *adj.* (*wide, far-reaching*) простра́нный.

extent /ɪk'stent/ *n.*
1 (*phys. size, length etc.*) протяже́ние.
2 (*fig., range*) разме́р; круг; диапазо́н.
3 (*degree*) сте́пень; **to some** (*or* **a certain**) **~** до не́которой/изве́стной сте́пени.

extenuat|e /ɪk'stenjʊeɪt/ *v.t.* преум|еньша́ть, -е́ньшить; **~ing circumstances** смягча́ющие обстоя́тельства.

exterior /ɪk'stɪərɪə(r)/ *n.* (*of object*) вне́шняя сторона́; (*archit.*) экстерье́р.
■ *adj.* вне́шний.

exterminate /ɪk'stə:mɪneɪt/ *v.t.* истреб|ля́ть, -и́ть.

extermination /ɪkstə:mɪ'neɪʃ(ə)n/ *n.* истребле́ние.

external /ɪk'stə:n(ə)l/ *n.* вне́шность.
■ *adj.* вне́шний; **for ~ use only** то́лько для нару́жного употребле́ния.

extinct /ɪk'stɪŋkt/ *adj.* (*of volcano*) поту́хший; (*of species, custom*) вы́мерший.

extinction /ɪk'stɪŋkʃ(ə)n/ *n.* угаса́ние; (*of species etc.*) вымира́ние.

extinguish /ɪk'stɪŋgwɪʃ/ *v.t.* (*light, fire*) гаси́ть, по-; (*hopes etc.*) уб|ива́ть, -и́ть.

extinguisher /ɪk'stɪŋgwɪʃə(r)/ *n.* огнетуши́тель (*m.*).

extol /ɪk'stəʊl/ *v.t.* (**extolled, extolling**) превозн|оси́ть, -ести́.

extort /ɪk'stɔ:t/ *v.t.* вымога́ть (*impf.*).

extortion /ɪk'stɔ:ʃ(ə)n/ *n.* вымога́тельство.

extortionate /ɪk'stɔ:ʃənət/ *adj.* вымога́тельский.

extortionist /ɪk'stɔ:ʃənə(r)/ *n.* вымога́тель (*m.*).

extra /'ekstrə/ *n.*
1 (*additional item*) что-н. дополни́тельное.
2 (*minor performer*) стати́ст (*fem.* -ка), актёр (*fem.* актри́са) массо́вки.
■ *adj.* (*additional*) доба́вочный, дополни́тельный; **~ time** (*sport*) дополни́тельное вре́мя; **it costs £1, postage ~** э́то сто́ит 1 фунт без пересы́лки.
■ *adv.* сверх-, осо́бо; **~ strong** (*e.g. drink*) осо́бой кре́пости.

extract[1] /'ekstrækt/ *n.* вы́держка.

extract[2] /ɪk'strækt/ *v.t.* (*cork*) вытаскивать, вы́тащить; (*tooth*) удал|я́ть, -и́ть.

extra-curricular /ekstrəkə'rɪkjʊlə(r)/ *adj.* проводи́мый сверх уче́бного пла́на.

extradite /'ekstrədaɪt/ *v.t.* (*hand over*) выдава́ть, вы́дать (*обвиняемого преступника*); экстради́ровать (*impf., pf.*).

extradition /ekstrə'dɪʃ(ə)n/ *n.* вы́дача (престу́пника); экстради́ция.

extramarital /ekstrə'mærɪt(ə)l/ *adj.*: **~ affair** внебра́чная связь.

extramural /ekstrə'mjʊər(ə)l/ *adj.* (*outside city*) за́городный; (*Br., acad.*): **~ student** ≈ заочни|к, вече́рни|к (*fem.* -ца) (*both coll.*).

extraneous /ɪk'streɪnɪəs/ *adj.* посторо́нний, чужо́й.

extraordinary /ɪk'strɔ:dɪnərɪ/ *adj.* (*unusual*) необы́чный; (*impressive*) необыча́йный; (*specially convened*) чрезвыча́йный.

extrapolate /ɪk'stræpəleɪt/ *v.t.* & *i.* (*math., fig.*) экстраполи́ровать (*impf., pf.*).

extraterrestrial /ekstrətɪ'restrɪəl/ *adj.* внеземно́й.
■ *n.* инопланетя́н|ин (*fem.* -ка).

extravagance /ɪk'strævəgəns/ *n.* (*lack of thrift*) расточи́тельность; (*luxury*) изли́шество; (*unusualness*) экстравага́нтность.

extravagant /ɪk'strævəgənt/ *adj.* расточи́тельный; **he was ~ with water** он расхо́довал сли́шком мно́го воды́.

extravaganza /ɪkstrævə'gænzə/ *n.* фе́ерия.

extreme /ɪk'stri:m/ *n.*
1 (*high degree*) кра́йность.
2 (*of conduct etc.*) кра́йность; **he went to**

~s to satisfy them он пошёл на крáйние мéры, чтóбы угодúть им.
■ *adj.* крáйний, предéльный; **the ~ edge of the city** сáмая окрáина гóрода.
extremely /ɪk'stri:mlɪ/ *adv.* крáйне.
extremism /ɪk'stri:mɪz(ə)m/ *n.* экстремúзм.
extremist /ɪk'stri:mɪst/ *n.* экстремúст.
■ *adj.* экстремúстский.
extremity /ɪk'stremɪtɪ/ *n.*
1 (*end, extreme point*) край.
2 (*pl., hands and feet*) конéчности (*f. pl.*).
3 (*extreme quality*) крáйность; **the ~ of his grief** безмéрность егó гóря.
4 (*hardship*) крáйность; **reduced to ~** доведённый до крáйности.
5 (*pl., extreme measures*) крáйние мéры (*f. pl.*).
extricate /'ekstrɪkeɪt/ *v.t.* высвобождáть, вы́свободить; **~ o.s. from a difficulty** вы́путаться (*pf.*) из затруднéния.
extrovert /'ekstrəvə:t/ *n.* экстравéрт.
exuberance /ɪg'zju:bərəns/ *n.* (*profusion*) изобúлие; (*of character*) экспансúвность.
exuberant /ɪg'zju:bərənt/ *adj.* (*of imagination etc.*) богáтый, бýйный; (*of spirits etc.*) экспансúвный.
exude /ɪg'zju:d/ *v.i.* проступ|áть, -úть; выделя́ть, вы́делить; **he ~d cheerfulness** он излучáл весéлье.
exult /ɪg'zʌlt/ *v.i.* торжествовáть, ликовáть (*both impf.*).
exultant /ɪg'zʌltənt/ *adj.* торжествýющий, ликýющий.
exultation /ɪgzʌl'teɪʃ(ə)n/ *n.* торжествó, ликовáние.
eye /aɪ/ *n.*
1 (*organ of vision*) глаз.
2 (*var. idioms*): **make ~s at s.o.** (*coll.*) стрóить (*impf.*) глáзки комý-н.; **keep an ~ on** (*e.g. a saucepan, children, the time*) следúть (*impf.*) за + *i.*; **an ~ for an ~** óко за óко; **before s.o.'s very ~s** на глазáх у когó-н.; **he has an ~ for colour** он чýвствует цвет; **I caught her ~** я поймáл её взгляд; **see ~ to ~ with** сходúться (*impf.*) во взгля́дах с + *i.*
3 (*special sense*): **~ of a needle** игóльное ушкó.
■ *v.t.* (**eyes, eyed, eyeing** *or* **eying**) разгля́д|ывать, -éть; наблюдáть (*impf.*).
■ *cpds.* **~ball** *n.* глазнóе я́блоко; **~brow** *n.* бровь; **~brow pencil** карандáш для бровéй; **~-catching** *adj.* эффéктный; **~ drops** глазны́е кáпли; **~ hospital** *n.* глазнáя больнúца; **~lash** *n.* реснúца; **~lid** *n.* вéко; **without batting an ~lid** (*coll.*) глáзом не моргнýв; **~liner** *n.* карандáш для подведéния глаз; **~shadow** *n.* тéни (*f. pl.*) для век; **~sight** *n.* зрéние; **he has good ~sight** у негó хорóшее зрéние; **~sore** *n.* урóдство; **~witness** *n.* очевúдец.
-eyed /aɪd/ *comb. form*: **blue~** голубоглáзый.

Ff

F¹ /ef/ *n.* (*mus.*) фа (*nt. indecl.*).
F² /'færənhaɪt/ (*abbr. of* **Fahrenheit**) F (= *грáдусов по Фаренгéйту or по шкалé Фаренгéйта*).
fable /'feɪb(ə)l/ *n.* бáсня.
fabric /'fæbrɪk/ *n.* (*text.*) ткань, матéрия; (*of a building etc., fig.*) структýра.
fabricate /'fæbrɪkeɪt/ *v.t.* (*invent*) сочин|я́ть, -úть; (*falsify*) фабриковáть, с-.
fabrication /fæbrɪ'keɪʃ(ə)n/ *n.* (*story etc.*) вы́думка; **complete ~** сплошнáя вы́думка; (*falsification*) поддéлка, фальсификáция (*вещь; процесс*).
fabulous /'fæbjʊləs/ *adj.* роскóшный, баснослóвный.
façade /fə'sɑ:d/ *n.* (*archit.*) фасáд.
face /feɪs/ *n.*
1 (*front part of head*) лицó; **look s.o. in the ~** (*lit.*) посмотрéть (*pf.*) комý-н. в глазá; **I came ~ to ~ with him** я столкнýлся с ним лицóм к лицý; **I told him so to his ~** я сказáл емý э́то в лицó; **she laughed in my ~** онá рассмея́лась мне в лицó; **he shut the door in my ~** он захлóпнул дверь пéред моúм нóсом; **in the ~ of danger** пéред лицóм опáсности.
2 (*facial expression*) лицó; выражéние лицá; **he made/pulled a ~** он скóрчил/сострóил рóжу; **his ~ fell** он изменúлся в лицé; у негó вы́тянулось лицó.
3 (*composure*): **he saved his ~** он спас свою репутáцию.
4 (*physical surface*) лицó; (*of clock*) циферблáт; **he laid the card ~ down** он положúл кáрту лицóм вниз (*or* рубáшкой вверх); **~ value** (*of currency*) номинáльная стóимость; **I took his words at ~ value** я при́нял егó словá за чúстую монéту.
■ *v.t.* 1 (*physically*) стоя́ть (*impf.*) лицóм к + *d.*; **the man facing us** человéк, сидя́щий *и т. п.* прóтив нас.
2 (*confront*) смотрéть (*impf.*) в лицó *чему*; **we must ~ facts** нáдо смотрéть фáктам в лицó; **let's ~ it!** (*coll.*) нáдо глядéть прáвде в глазá!
■ *v.i.*: **the house ~s south** дом обращён фасáдом на юг; **their house ~s ours** их дом напрóтив нáшего; **he ~d up to the difficulties** он не испугáлся трýдностей.
■ *cpd.* **~lift** *n.* подтя́жка кóжи на лицé; (*fig.*) внéшнее обновлéние, косметúческий ремóнт.
faceless /'feɪslɪs/ *adj.* (*anonymous*) безлúчный, безлúкий.
facet /'fæsɪt/ *n.* грань; (*fig.*) аспéкт.
facetious /fə'si:ʃəs/ *adj.* шутлúвый,

шу́точный.

facetiousness /fəˈsiːʃəsnɪs/ *n.* (неуме́стная) шутли́вость.

facial /ˈfeɪʃ(ə)l/ *n.* масса́ж лица́.
■ *adj.* лицево́й.

facile /ˈfæsaɪl/ *adj.* (*easy, fluent*) лёгкий, свобо́дный; (*superficial*) пове́рхностный.

facilitate /fəˈsɪlɪteɪt/ *v.t.* спосо́бствовать (*impf.*) + *d.*

facilit|y /fəˈsɪlɪtɪ/ *n.* (*ease*) лёгкость; (*appliance, installation*) сооруже́ние; **~ies for study** усло́вия (*nt. pl.*) для учёбы; **sports ~ies** спорти́вное обору́дование; помеще́ния (*nt. pl.*) для заня́тия спо́ртом.

facsimile /fækˈsɪmɪlɪ/ *n.* (*exact copy*) факси́миле (*nt. indecl.*); (*fax*) факс.

fact /fækt/ *n.* факт; **as a matter of ~** факти́чески; на са́мом де́ле; **the ~ is that ...** де́ло в том, что...; **in ~** (*actually*) факти́чески; в/на са́мом де́ле; (*intensifying*): **I think so, in ~ I'm quite sure** я так ду́маю, бо́лее того́, я уве́рен в э́том.
■ *cpd.* **~-finding** *adj.* занима́ющийся установле́нием фа́ктов, рассле́дованием обстоя́тельств.

faction /ˈfækʃ(ə)n/ *n.* фра́кция, группиро́вка.

factional /ˈfækʃənəl/ *adj.* фракцио́нный.

factor /ˈfæktə(r)/ *n.* фа́ктор.

factory /ˈfæktərɪ/ *n.* фа́брика, заво́д.

factual /ˈfæktjʊəl/ *adj.* факти́ческий.

faculty /ˈfækəltɪ/ *n.*
1 (*power, aptitude*) спосо́бность.
2 (*Br., part of university*) факульте́т.
3 (*US, body of teachers*) профе́ссорско-преподава́тельский соста́в.

fad /fæd/ *n.* (*craze*) увлече́ние; (*whim*) при́хоть.

fade /feɪd/ *v.t.*
1 (*cause to lose colour*) обесцве́|чивать, -тить.
2 (*cin., radio*): **~ out** постепе́нно ум|еньша́ть, -е́ньшить си́лу звука; **~ in** постепе́нно увели́чи|вать, -ть си́лу зву́ка.
■ *v.i.* 1 (*lose colour*) обесцве́|чиваться, -титься.
2 (*fig.*): **his hopes ~d** его́ наде́жды раста́яли.

faeces /ˈfiːsiːz/ (*US* **feces**) *n.* фека́лии (*f. pl.*); испражне́ния (*nt. pl.*).

fag¹ /fæg/ *n.* (*Br.*) (*coll., tiring task*) изнури́тельная рабо́та.
■ *v.t.* (**fagged, fagging**) (*tire*) утом|ля́ть, -и́ть; выма́тывать, вы́мотать; **I am ~ged out** я вконе́ц вы́мотался.

fag² /fæg/ *n.* (*Br. coll., cigarette*) сигаре́та, папиро́ска.
■ *cpd.* **~ end** *n.* (*Br., butt*) оку́рок, (*fig.*) коне́ц (*чего*); оста́ток (*чего*).

Fahrenheit /ˈfærənhaɪt/ *n.* (*abbr.* **F**) Фаренге́йт.

fail /feɪl/ *n.*: **without ~** обяза́тельно, непреме́нно.
■ *v.t.* 1 (*exam*) не сда|ва́ть, -ть; (*drugs test; of sportsman/addict*) не про|ходи́ть, -йти́ (тест на до́пинг/нарко́тики).
2 (*disappoint, desert*) подв|оди́ть, -ести́; **words ~ me** я не нахожу́ слов.
■ *v.i.* 1 (*fall short, decline*) ух|удша́ться, -у́дшиться; недостава́ть (*impf.*); **the crops ~ed** хлеб не уроди́лся; **his eyesight is ~ing** его́ зре́ние слабе́ет; **he is in ~ing health** его́ здоро́вье ухудша́ется.
2 (*not succeed*): **he ~ed in the exam** он провали́лся на экза́мене; **he ~ed to convince her** ему́ не удало́сь (*or* он не суме́л) убеди́ть её.
3 (*omit*) упус|ка́ть, -ти́ть; **he never ~s to write** он никогда́ не забыва́ет писа́ть.

failing /ˈfeɪlɪŋ/ *n.* (*defect*) недоста́ток.
■ *prep.* за неиме́нием + *g.*

failure /ˈfeɪljə(r)/ *n.*
1 (*unsuccess*) неуда́ча, неуспе́х, прова́л.
2 (*person*) неуда́чник.
3 (*non-functioning*) ава́рия; **heart ~** остано́вка се́рдца.
4 (*omission*): **his ~ to answer is a nuisance** о́чень доса́дно, что он не отвеча́ет.

faint /feɪnt/ *n.* (*med.*) о́бморок; **in a dead ~** в глубо́ком о́бмороке.
■ *adj.* 1 (*weak, indistinct*) сла́бый, неотчётливый; **I haven't the ~est idea** я не име́ю ни мале́йшего поня́тия.
2 (*giddy*): **I feel ~** мне ду́рно.
■ *v.i.* (*lose consciousness*) па́дать, упа́сть в о́бморок; (*grow weak*) слабе́ть (*impf.*).
■ *cpd.* **~-hearted** *adj.* трусли́вый, малоду́шный.

fair¹ /feə(r)/ *n.* (*trade fair*) (вы́ставка-)я́рмарка; (*fun fair*) я́рмарка; аттракцио́ны (*m.pl.*).
■ *cpd.* **~ground** *n.* я́рмарочная пло́щадь.

fair² /feə(r)/ *adj.*
1 (*beautiful*) прекра́сный, краси́вый; **the ~ sex** прекра́сный пол.
2 (*of weather*) я́сный.
3 (*abundant*): **a ~ amount** (*a lot*) значи́тельное/изря́дное коли́чество.
4 (*average*) сно́сный; **he has a ~ chance of success** у него́ неплохи́е ша́нсы на успе́х; **his performance was only ~** его́ выступле́ние бы́ло та́к себе.
5 (*equitable*): **~ share** зако́нная до́ля; **~ play** че́стная игра́; справедли́вость; **it is ~ to say that ...** со всей справедли́востью мо́жно сказа́ть, что... .
6 (*of hair*) све́тлый, (*blond*) белоку́рый; **a ~ complexion** све́тлый цвет лица́.
■ *cpds.* **~-haired** *adj.* белоку́рый; **~-minded** *adj.* справедли́вый.

fairly /ˈfeəlɪ/ *adv.*
1 (*moderately*) дово́льно, сно́сно, терпи́мо.
2 (*justly*) че́стно, справедли́во.

fairness /ˈfeərnɪs/ *n.* (*equity*) справедли́вость, че́стность; **in all ~** со всей справедли́востью.

fairy /ˈfeərɪ/ *n.* фе́я.
■ *cpds.* **~ story, ~ tale** *nn.* ска́зка; (*fig.*) ска́зка, небыли́ца.

fait accompli /feɪt əˈkɒmplɪ/ *n.* (*pl.* **faits accomplis** *pronunc. same*) сверши́вшийся факт.

faith /feɪθ/ *n.*
1 (*trust*) ве́ра, дове́рие; **I have no ~ in doctors** я не ве́рю доктора́м.
2 (*relig.*) ве́ра.
3 (*sincerity*): **in good ~** че́стно,

добросо́вестно.

faithful /ˈfeɪθfʊl/ *adj.* то́чный, достове́рный; (*as n.*) **the ~** (*believers*) правове́рные.

faithfully /ˈfeɪθfʊlɪ/ *adv.* то́чно, ве́рно; **yours ~** (*Br., formal letter ending*) с уваже́нием; и́скренне ваш.

faithless /ˈfeɪθlɪs/ *adj.* вероло́мный.

fake /feɪk/ *n.* (*sham*) подде́лка; (*attr.*) подде́льный.
■ *v.t.* подде́л|ывать, -ать.

falcon /ˈfɔːlkən/ *n.* со́кол.

fall /fɔːl/ *n.*
1 (*physical drop*) паде́ние.
2 (*moral*) паде́ние; **~ from grace** нра́вственное паде́ние.
3 (*diminution*) пониже́ние; **~ in prices** паде́ние цен.
4 (*pl., waterfall*) водопа́д.
5 (*US, autumn*) о́сень.
■ *v.i.* (*past* **fell;** *p.p.* **fallen**)
1 па́дать, упа́сть; **he fell over a chair** он упа́л, споткну́вшись о стул; **he fell off his horse** он упа́л с ло́шади.
2 (*drop, sink*) па́дать, упа́сть; **prices fell** це́ны сни́зились/упа́ли; **the temperature fell** температу́ра упа́ла; **my spirits fell ~** я упа́л/пал ду́хом.
3 (*of defeat etc.*) па́|дать, -сть; **the government fell** прави́тельство па́ло.
4 (*pass into a state*): **he fell ill** он заболе́л; **he fell in love with her** он влюби́лся в неё.
5 (*come*): **darkness fell** наступи́ла темнота́.
■ *with prep.*: **~ for** (~ *in love with*) увл|ека́ться, -е́чься + *i.*; (*be taken in by*): **he fell for her story** он пове́рил её слова́м.
■ *with advs.*: **~ apart** расп|ада́ться, -а́сться; **~ back** (*mil.*) отступ|а́ть, -и́ть; **~ back on sth.** приб|ега́ть, -е́гнуть к чему́-н.; **~ behind** (*e.g. in walking*) отст|ава́ть, -а́ть; (*with rent*) зап|а́здывать, -озда́ть с упла́той за кварти́ру; **~ down** (*lit.*) па́дать, упа́сть; **~ in** впасть (*во что*); **the roof fell in** кры́ша ру́хнула/обвали́лась; **the soldiers fell in** солда́ты постро́ились; **~ off** па́дать, упа́сть (*с чего*); **attendance is ~ing off** посеща́емость па́дает; **~ out** выпада́ть, вы́пасть; **his hair fell out** у него́ вы́пали во́лосы; (*quarrel*) поссо́риться (*pf.*); **~ over** па́дать, упа́сть; **~ through** прова́л|иваться, -и́ться.
■ *cpd.* **~out** *n.* (*nuclear*) радиоакти́вные оса́дки (*m. pl.*).

fallacious /fəˈleɪʃəs/ *adj.* оши́бочный, ло́жный.

fallacy /ˈfæləsɪ/ *n.* (*false belief*) заблужде́ние.

fallen /ˈfɔːl(ə)n/ *p.p. of* ▸ **fall**

fallible /ˈfælɪb(ə)l/ *adj.* подве́рженный оши́бкам.

Fallopian tube /fəˈləʊpɪən/ *n.* фалло́пиева труба́.

fallow /ˈfæləʊ/ *adj.* (*agric.*) вспа́ханный под пар; **~ land** пар (*земля*); **lie ~** ост|ава́ться, -а́ться под па́ром.

false /fɔːls/ *adj.*
1 (*wrong*) ло́жный, оши́бочный, фальши́вый; **~ start** фальста́рт (*races*); срыв в са́мом нача́ле; **~ alarm** ло́жная трево́га.
2 (*deceitful*) лжи́вый, вероло́мный; **~ pretences** обма́н, притво́рство.
3 (*sham*) фальши́вый; **~ teeth** иску́сственные зу́бы; **~ bottom** двойно́е дно.

falsehood /ˈfɔːlshʊd/ *n.* ложь, непра́вда; **he told a ~** он сказа́л непра́вду.

falsify /ˈfɔːlsɪfaɪ/ *v.t.* подде́л|ывать, -ать.

falsity /ˈfɔːlsɪtɪ/ *n.* (*falsehood, inaccuracy*) ло́жность, оши́бочность.

falter /ˈfɔːltə(r)/ *v.i.* (*move or act hesitatingly*) спот|ыка́ться, -кну́ться; (*in speaking*) зап|ина́ться, -ну́ться.

fame /feɪm/ *n.* сла́ва; репута́ция.

familiar /fəˈmɪlɪə(r)/ *adj.*
1 (*common, usual*) обы́чный, привы́чный.
2 (*of acquaintance*) знако́мый; **I am ~ with the subject** я знако́м с э́тим предме́том.

familiarity /fəmɪlɪˈærɪtɪ/ *n.*
1 (*close acquaintance*) бли́зкое знако́мство (с + *i.*).
2 (*of manner*) фамилья́рность.

familiarize /fəˈmɪlɪəraɪz/ *v.t.* ознак|омля́ть, -о́мить (*кого с чем*); **~ o.s. with sth.** ознако́миться (*pf.*) с чем-н.

family /ˈfæmɪlɪ/ *n.*
1 (*parents and children*) семья́.
2 (*attr.*) семе́йный; **~ name** (*surname*) фами́лия; **~ tree** родосло́вное де́рево; **~ planning** контро́ль (*m.*) над рожда́емостью.

famine /ˈfæmɪn/ *n.* го́лод.

famished /ˈfæmɪʃt/ *adj.* (*coll.*): **I'm ~** я си́льно проголода́лся; я умира́ю с го́лоду.

famous /ˈfeɪməs/ *adj.* знамени́тый, просла́вленный.

fan¹ /fæn/ *n.* ве́ер; (*ventilator*) вентиля́тор.
■ *v.t.* (**fanned, fanning**): **~ o.s.** обма́хиваться (*impf.*) ве́ером.
■ *v.i.* (**fanned, fanning**): **~ out** (*e.g. roads*) расходи́ться (*impf.*) ве́ером; (*e.g. soldiers*) разв|ора́чиваться, -ерну́ться ве́ером.

fan² /fæn/ *n.* (*coll., devotee*) боле́льщи|к (*fem.* -ца), фана́т (*fem.* -ка), люби́тель (*m.*) (*fem.* -ница).
■ *cpd.* **~ mail** *n.* пи́сьма (*nt. pl.*) от покло́нников.

fanatic /fəˈnætɪk/ *n.* фана́тик.

fanatical /fəˈnætɪk(ə)l/ *adj.* фанати́чный.

fanaticism /fəˈnætɪsɪz(ə)m/ *n.* фанати́зм.

fanciful /ˈfænsɪfʊl/ *adj.* капри́зный; причу́дливый.

fancy /ˈfænsɪ/ *n.*
1 (*imagination*) фанта́зия.
2 (*thing imagined*) фанта́зия.
3 (*liking*) скло́нность; **he took a ~ to her** он е́ю увлёкся.
4 (*as adj.*) (**fancier, fanciest**): **~ dress** маскара́дный костю́м; **~-dress ball** костюми́рованный бал; **this dress is too ~ to wear to work** для рабо́ты ну́жно пла́тье поскромне́е.
■ *v.t.* 1 (*imagine*): **~ (that)!** вообрази́(те)!
2 (*Br., like*) хоте́ть (*impf.*) + *g.*; жела́ть (*impf.*); **she fancies him** (*coll.*) он ей нра́вится; **what do you ~ for dinner?** чего́ бы вам хоте́лось на у́жин?

fanfare /ˈfænfeə(r)/ *n.* фанфа́ра.

fang /fæŋ/ *n.* (*of wolf etc.*) клык; (*of snake*) ядови́тый зуб.

fantasize /ˈfæntəsaɪz/ *v.i.* фантази́ровать (*impf.*).

fantastic /fænˈtæstɪk/ *adj.* (*wild, strange*) фантасти́ческий, фантасти́чный; (*coll., marvellous*) потряса́ющий, изуми́тельный.

fantasy /ˈfæntəsɪ/ *n.* фанта́зия; (*genre*) фанта́стика.

FAQ (*abbr. of* ***frequently asked questions***) (*comput.*) ча́сто задава́емые вопро́сы.

far /fɑː(r)/ *adj.* (**further, furthest** *or* **farther, farthest**) да́льний, далёкий, отдалённый; **the F~ East** Да́льний Восто́к; **at the ~ end of the street** на друго́м конце́ у́лицы.
■ *adv.* (**further, furthest** *or* **farther, farthest**) далеко́; **~ away, off** о́чень далеко́; **they came from ~ and wide** они́ съе́хались отовсю́ду (*or* со всех концо́в); **~ better** (на)мно́го/гора́здо лу́чше; **it is ~ from true** э́то совсе́м не так; **so ~** (*until now*) до сих пор; пока́ (что); **as, so ~ as** (*of distance*) до (*чего*); (*of extent*) наско́лько; поско́льку; **as ~ as I know** наско́лько мне изве́стно; **as ~ as I am concerned** что каса́ется меня́; **he went so ~ as to say ...** он да́же сказа́л...; **how ~** (*of distance*) как далеко́; (*of extent*) наско́лько; **he will go ~** (*succeed*) он далеко́ пойдёт; **he has gone too ~ this time** на э́тот раз он зашёл сли́шком далеко́.
■ *cpds.* **~away** *adj.* (*distant*) далёкий, отдалённый; **~-fetched** *adj.* с натя́жкой; притя́нутый за́ волосы/у́ши; **~-off** *adj.* отдалённый; **~-reaching** *adj.* далеко́ иду́щий; **~-sighted** *adj.* (*prudent etc.*) дальнови́дный, предусмотри́тельный; (*long-sighted*) дальнозо́ркий.

farce /fɑːs/ *n.* (*theatr., fig.*) фарс.

farcical /ˈfɑːsɪk(ə)l/ *adj.* смехотво́рный.

fare /feə(r)/ *n.* (*cost*) пла́та за прое́зд.

farewell /feəˈwel/ *n.* проща́ние.

farm /fɑːm/ *n.* фе́рма.
■ *v.t. & i.*
1 (*agric.*) занима́ться (*impf.*) се́льским хозя́йством.
2 : **~ out work** отд|ава́ть, -а́ть рабо́ту.
■ *cpds.* **~house** *n.* фе́рмерский дом; **~yard** *n.* двор фе́рмы.

farmer /ˈfɑːmə(r)/ *n.* фе́рмер.
■ *cpd.* **~s' market** *n.* ры́нок сельскохозя́йственной проду́кции.

farming /ˈfɑːmɪŋ/ *n.* се́льское хозя́йство, фе́рмерство.

farther /ˈfɑːðə(r)/ (*see also* ▸ **further**) *adj.* бо́лее отдалённый; дальне́йший.
■ *adv.* да́льше, да́лее.

farthest /ˈfɑːðɪst/ (*see also* ▸ **furthest**) *adj.* са́мый да́льний.
■ *adv.* да́льше всего́.

fascinate /ˈfæsɪneɪt/ *v.t.* очаро́в|ывать, -а́ть.

fascinating /ˈfæsɪneɪtɪŋ/ *adj.* очарова́тельный.

fascination /fæsɪˈneɪʃ(ə)n/ *n.* очарова́ние.

Fascism /ˈfæʃɪz(ə)m/ *n.* фаши́зм.

Fascist /ˈfæʃɪst/ *n.* фаши́ст (*fem.* -ка).
■ *adj.* фаши́стский.

fashion /ˈfæʃ(ə)n/ *n.*
1 (*way*) о́браз, мане́ра; **after a ~** (*indifferently*) до не́которой сте́пени.
2 (*prevailing style*) мо́да; **in ~** в мо́де; **out of ~** вы́шедший из мо́ды; **~ designer** моделье́р; **~ house** дом моде́лей; **~ show** пока́з мод.
■ *v.t.* (*e.g. an object*) прид|ава́ть, -а́ть фо́рму + *d.*

fashionable /ˈfæʃnəb(ə)l/ *adj.* мо́дный.

fast[1] /fɑːst/ *n.* (*relig.*) пост.
■ *v.i.* пости́ться (*impf.*).

fast[2] /fɑːst/ *adv.* (*firmly*) про́чно, кре́пко; **she was ~ asleep** она́ кре́пко спала́; **the car stuck ~** маши́на застря́ла/завя́зла.

fast[3] /fɑːst/ *adj.* (*rapid*) ско́рый, бы́стрый; **~ lane** (*on road*) скоростно́й ряд; **~-food restaurant** рестора́н бы́строго обслу́живания; **my watch is ~** мои́ часы́ спеша́т.

fasten /ˈfɑːs(ə)n/ *v.t.* (*coat*) застёг|ивать, -ну́ть; (*laces*) завя́з|ывать, -а́ть; (*seat-belt*) пристёг|ивать, -ну́ть.
■ *v.i.* зап|ира́ться, -ере́ться; **the dress ~s down the back** пла́тье застёгивается на спине́.

fasten|er /ˈfɑːs(ə)nə(r)/, **-ing** /ˈfɑːsnɪŋ/ *nn.* запо́р, задви́жка.

fastidious /fæˈstɪdɪəs/ *adj.* привере́дливый, щепети́льный; разбо́рчивый.

fat /fæt/ *n.* жир.
■ *adj.* (**fatter, fattest**)
1 (*of person etc.*) то́лстый, жи́рный, ту́чный; **get ~** толсте́ть, по-.
2 (*rich*): **a ~ profit** больша́я при́быль.

fatal /ˈfeɪt(ə)l/ *adj.*
1 (*causing death*) смерте́льный; **a ~ accident** несча́стный слу́чай со смерте́льным исхо́дом.
2 (*disastrous*) рокову́й, фата́льный.

fatalism /ˈfeɪtəlɪz(ə)m/ *n.* фатали́зм.

fatalistic /feɪtəˈlɪstɪk/ *adj.* фаталисти́ческий.

fatality /fəˈtælətɪ/ *n.* (*natural calamity*) стихи́йное бе́дствие; (*fatal accident*) смерть от несча́стного слу́чая.

fate /feɪt/ *n.* судьба́, у́часть, уде́л, до́ля.

fateful /ˈfeɪtfʊl/ *adj.* рокова́й.

father /ˈfɑːðə(r)/ *n.*
1 (*male parent, also fig.*) оте́ц, роди́тель (*m.*).
2 : **F~ Christmas** Дед Моро́з.
3 (*priest*) оте́ц, ба́тюшка.
■ *v.t.* поро|жда́ть, -ди́ть.
■ *cpds.* **~-in-law** *n.* (*husband's ~*) свёкор; (*wife's ~*) тесть (*m.*); **~land** *n.* оте́чество.

fatherhood /ˈfɑːðəhʊd/ *n.* отцо́вство.

fatherly /ˈfɑːðəlɪ/ *adj.* оте́ческий.

fathom /ˈfæð(ə)m/ *n.* морска́я саже́нь.
■ *v.t.* (*fig.*) пост|ига́ть, -и́гнуть.

fatigue /fəˈtiːg/ *n.* уста́лость (*also, tech.,* **metal ~**); (*mil.*) (*pl., menial tasks*) хозя́йственная рабо́та.

fatten /ˈfæt(ə)n/ *v.t.* (*animal*) отк|а́рмливать, -орми́ть на убо́й.

fattening /ˈfæt(ə)nɪŋ/ *adj.* калори́йный.

fatty /ˈfætɪ/ *adj.* (**fattier, fattiest**) жи́рный, жирово́й.

fatuous /ˈfætjʊəs/ *adj.* самодово́льно-глу́пый; бессмы́сленный.

faucet /ˈfɔːsɪt/ *n.* (*US, tap*) кран.

fault /fɔːlt/ *n.*
1 (*imperfection*) недоста́ток, дефе́кт; **find ~ with s.o.** на|ходи́ть, -йти́ недоста́тки у кого́-н.
2 (*in mechanism*) дефе́кт.
3 (*error*) оши́бка.
4 (*blame*) вина́; **it's (all) your ~** э́то ва́ша вина́; э́то всё из-за вас.
5 (*at tennis etc.*) непра́вильная пода́ча; **double ~** двойна́я оши́бка.
6 (*geol.*) разло́м, сдвиг.
■ *v.t.* на|ходи́ть, -йти́ недоста́тки в + *p.*; **I could not ~ his argument** я не мог придра́ться к его́ аргумента́ции.

faultless /ˈfɔːltlɪs/ *adj.*: **~ precision** безупре́чная то́чность.

faulty /ˈfɔːltɪ/ *adv.* (**faultier, faultiest**) повреждённый.

fauna /ˈfɔːnə/ *n.* (*pl.* **~s**) фа́уна.

faux pas /fəʊ ˈpɑː/ *n.* (*pl.* **~**) беста́ктность.

favour /ˈfeɪvə(r)/ (*US* **favor**) *n.*
1 (*goodwill*) благоскло́нность; **find ~ in s.o.'s eyes** сниска́ть (*pf.*) чьё-н. расположе́ние; **I am in ~ of the plan** я — за э́тот план.
2 (*kindly act*) одолже́ние, любе́зность, услу́га; **he did me a ~** он оказа́л мне любе́зность.
3 (*advantage*) по́льза; **this is in his ~** э́то говори́т в его́ по́льзу; **the exchange rate is in our ~** курс обме́на валю́ты вы́годен для нас.
■ *v.t.* 1 (*support*) благоприя́тствовать (*impf.*) + *d.*
2 (*treat with partiality*) ока́з|ывать, -а́ть предпочте́ние + *d.*

favourable /ˈfeɪvərəb(ə)l/ (*US* **favorable**) *adj.* благоприя́тный, благоскло́нный; **a ~ report** положи́тельный отчёт.

favourite /ˈfeɪvərɪt/ (*US* **favorite**) *n.* (*preferred person*) люби́мец, фавори́т; (*horse*) фавори́т.
■ *adj.* люби́мый, излю́бленный.

favouritism /ˈfeɪvərɪtɪz(ə)m/ (*US* **favoritism**) *n.*: **a teacher shouldn't show ~** у учи́теля не должно́ быть люби́мчиков.

fawn[1] /fɔːn/ *n.* (*deer*) оленёнок.

fawn[2] /fɔːn/ *v.i.* (*of person*): **~ on s.o.** подли́з|ываться, -а́ться к кому́-н.

fax /fæks/ *n.* факс; **~ machine** факс, факси́мильный аппара́т.
■ *v.t.* пос|ыла́ть, -ла́ть фа́ксом.

faze /feɪz/ *v.t.* сму|ща́ть, -ти́ть.

FBI (*abbr. of* ***Federal Bureau of Investigation***) ФБР (Федера́льное бюро́ рассле́дований).

FC (*abbr. of* ***football club***) футбо́льный клуб, ФК.

fear /fɪə(r)/ *n.*
1 (*terror*) страх, боя́знь, опасе́ние; **your ~s are groundless** ва́ши опасе́ния напра́сны.
2 (*likelihood*): **I was silent for ~ of offending him** я молча́л, боя́сь оби́деть его́; **there is no ~ of my losing the money** не бо́йтесь, де́ньги я не потеря́ю.
■ *v.t. & i.* боя́ться (*impf.*) + *g.*; опаса́ться (*impf.*) + *g.*; **he ~s death** он бои́тся сме́рти; **I ~ the worst** я опаса́юсь ху́дшего; **I ~ for his life** я опаса́юсь за его́ жизнь.

fearful /ˈfɪəfʊl/ *adj.* (*terrible*) ужа́сный; (*timid*) боязли́вый; **I was ~ of waking him** я боя́лся разбуди́ть его́.

fearless /ˈfɪəlɪs/ *adj.* бесстра́шный.

fearsome /ˈfɪəsəm/ *adj.* устраша́ющий, гро́зный.

feasible /ˈfiːzɪb(ə)l/ *adj.* осуществи́мый.

feast /fiːst/ *n.*
1 (*relig.*) (церко́вный) пра́здник.
2 (*meal*) пир.
■ *v.t. & i.* пирова́ть (*impf.*); пра́здновать (*impf.*); **he ~ed his eyes on the scene** он любова́лся э́тим зре́лищем.

feat /fiːt/ *n.* по́двиг; **~ of engineering** выдаю́щееся достиже́ние инжене́рного иску́сства.

feather /ˈfeðə(r)/ *n.* перо́.

feature /ˈfiːtʃə(r)/ *n.*
1 (*part of face*) черта́.
2 (*aspect*) черта́, осо́бенность.
3 (*main item*): **this journal makes a ~ of sport** э́тот журна́л широко́ освеща́ет спорти́вные собы́тия; **~ (film)** худо́жественный фильм.
■ *v.t.* (*give prominence to*) поме|ща́ть, -сти́ть на ви́дном ме́сте.
■ *v.i.* (*figure prominently*) быть/явля́ться (*impf.*) характе́рной черто́й.

February /ˈfebrʊərɪ/ *n.* февра́ль (*m.*).

feckless /ˈfeklɪs/ *adj.* безала́берный.

fed /fed/ *past and p.p. of* ▸ **feed**

federal /ˈfedər(ə)l/ *adj.* федера́льный.

federalism /ˈfedərəlɪz(ə)m/ *n.* федерали́зм.

federation /fedəˈreɪʃ(ə)n/ *n.* федера́ция.

fee /fiː/ *n.* (*professional charge*) гонора́р; **school ~s** пла́та за обуче́ние.

feeble /ˈfiːb(ə)l/ *adj.* (**feebler, feeblest**) хи́лый, сла́бый.

feed /fiːd/ *n.* (*animal's*) корм; (*baby's*) кормле́ние.
■ *v.t.* (*past and p.p.* **fed**)
1 (*give food to*) корми́ть, на-; (*fig.*): **I am fed up** (*coll.*) я сыт по го́рло; мне надое́ло.
2 (*fig.*): **he fed information into the computer** он ввёл да́нные в компью́тер.
■ *cpd.* **~back** *n.* (*elec.*) обра́тная связь; (*fig.*) о́тклик, о́тзыв(ы); реа́кция.

feel /fiːl/ *n.* (*sensation*) ощуще́ние; (*contact*) осяза́ние; **he has a ~ for language** у него́ есть чу́вство языка́.
■ *v.t.* (*past and p.p.* **felt**)
1 (*explore by touch*) щу́пать, по-; **~ the edge of a knife** тро́гать, по- ле́звие ножа́; **~ the weight of this box!** чу́вствуете, ско́лько ве́сит э́тот я́щик!
2 (*grope*) пробира́ться (*impf.*) о́щупью; **he felt his way in the dark** он пробира́лся о́щупью в темноте́.
3 (*be aware of*) чу́вствовать, по-; **did you ~ the earthquake?** вы почу́вствовали землетрясе́ние?
4 (*be affected by*) чу́вствовать, по-; **he ~s (*or* is ~ing) the heat** жара́ пло́хо де́йствует на него́; он пло́хо перено́сит жару́.
5 (*be of opinion*): счита́ть (*impf.*); **I ~ you should go** по-мо́ему, вам сле́дует пойти́/сходи́ть.
■ *v.i.* (*past and p.p.* **felt**)

1 (*experience sensation*): **I ~ cold** мне хо́лодно; **I ~ hungry** я го́лоден; **I ~ sure** я уве́рен; **I ~ bad about not inviting him** мне со́вестно, что я не пригласи́л его́; **I ~ like (going for) a walk** мне хо́чется прогуля́ться; **I don't ~ up to going** я не в состоя́нии идти́; **it ~s like rain** похо́же, бу́дет дождь; **I ~ for you** я вам сочу́вствую.
2 (*produce sensation*) да|ва́ть, -ть ощуще́ние (*чего*); **your hands ~ cold** у вас холо́дные ру́ки; **how does it ~ to be home?** каково́ оказа́ться до́ма?
3 (*grope*): **he felt in his pocket for a coin** он поша́рил в карма́не, ища́ моне́ту; **he felt along the wall for the door** он пыта́лся нащу́пать дверь в стене́.

feeler /'fiːlə(r)/ *n.* (*zool.*) щу́пальце, у́сик; (*fig.*): **he put out ~s** он прозонди́ровал по́чву; он заки́нул у́дочку.

feeling /'fiːlɪŋ/ *n.*
1 (*power of sensation*) ощуще́ние, чу́вство.
2 (*sense*) созна́ние, чу́вство.
3 (*opinion*): **I have a ~ he won't come** у меня́ предчу́вствие, что он не придёт.
4 (*emotion*) чу́вство, страсть; **he spoke with ~** он говори́л с чу́вством.
5 (*sensitivity*) чувстви́тельность; **you hurt his ~s** вы его́ оби́дели.

feet /fiːt/ *pl. of* ▸ **foot**

feign /feɪn/ *v.t.* (*simulate*) симули́ровать (*impf.*, *pf.*); **~ madness** симули́ровать безу́мие.

feisty /'faɪstɪ/ *adj.* (**feistier, feistiest**) (*person*) хра́брый, сме́лый; (*dog*) сме́лый, бесстра́шный; (*action*) сме́лый, реши́тельный; (*spirit*) реши́тельный.

feline /'fiːlaɪn/ *n.* живо́тное из семе́йства коша́чьих.
■ *adj.* коша́чий.

fell[1] /fel/ *v.t.* (*person*) сби|ва́ть, -ть с ног; (*tree*) руби́ть, с-; вали́ть, с-/по-.

fell[2] /fel/ *past of* ▸ **fall**

fellow /'feləʊ/ *n.*
1 (*chap*) па́рень (*m.*).
2 (*acad. & professional*) колле́га; сотру́дник; (*Br.*, *of a college*) член сове́та ко́лледжа.
■ *cpds.* **~ countryman** *n.* соотече́ственник; **~ countrywoman** *n.* соотече́ственница.

fellowship /'feləʊʃɪp/ *n.* (*companionship*) това́рищество, бра́тство; (*association*) корпора́ция; колле́гия (*адвокатов и т. п.*).

felony /'felənɪ/ *n.* (тя́жкое) уголо́вное преступле́ние.

felt[1] /felt/ *n.* (*material*) во́йлок, фетр.
■ *cpd.* **~-tip pen** *n.* флома́стер.

felt[2] /felt/ *past and p.p. of* ▸ **feel**

female /'fiːmeɪl/ *n.* (*woman or girl*) же́нщина; (*animal*) са́мка, ма́тка.
■ *adj.* же́нский.

feminine /'femɪnɪn/ *adj.* же́нский.

femininity /femɪ'nɪnɪtɪ/ *n.* же́нственность.

feminism /'femɪnɪz(ə)m/ *n.* фемини́зм.

feminist /'femɪnɪst/ *n.* фемини́ст (*fem.* -ка).

femme fatale /fæm fə'tɑːl/ *n.* (*pl.* **femmes fatales** *pronunc. same*) рокова́я же́нщина.

femur /'fiːmə(r)/ *n.* бедро́.

fen /fen/ *n.* топь, боло́то.

fence /fens/ *n.* забо́р, и́згородь, огра́да; **sit on the ~** занима́ть (*impf.*) нейтра́льную/ выжида́тельную пози́цию.
■ *v.t.* (*also* **~ in, off, round**) огор|а́живать, -оди́ть.

fencer /'fensə(r)/ *n.* фехтова́льщик.

fencing /'fensɪŋ/ *n.* фехтова́ние.

fend /fend/ *v.i.*: **~ for o.s.** полага́ться (*impf.*) на себя́.

fender /'fendə(r)/ *n.*
1 (*in front of fire*) ≈ ками́нная решётка.
2 (*US*, *of car*) крыло́.

feng shui /feŋ 'ʃuːɪ/ *n.* фэн-шу́й (*m.* & *nt. indecl.*).

fennel /'fen(ə)l/ *n.* фе́нхель (*m.*), сла́дкий укро́п.

fern /fəːn/ *n.* (*pl.* **~** *or* **~s**) па́поротник.

ferocious /fə'rəʊʃəs/ *adj.* свире́пый, лю́тый.

ferocity /fə'rɒsɪtɪ/ *n.* свире́пость, лю́тость.

ferret /'ferɪt/ *n.* (*zool.*) хорёк.
■ *v.t.* (**ferreted, ferreting**): **~ out** (*fig.*) выи́скивать, вы́искать.
■ *v.i.* (**ferreted, ferreting**): **~ about** (*fig.*) ры́скать (*impf.*).

Ferris wheel /'ferɪs/ *n.* чёртово колесо́.

ferry /'ferɪ/ *n.* (*boat*) паро́м.
■ *v.t.* (*convey to and fro*) перев|ози́ть, -езти́ (*or* перепр|авля́ть, -а́вить) на паро́ме; отв|ози́ть, -езти́.

fertile /'fəːtaɪl/ *adj.*
1 (*of soil*) плодоро́дный; (*of humans, animals*) плодови́тый.
2 (*fig.*): **a ~ imagination** бога́тое воображе́ние.

fertility /fəː'tɪlɪtɪ/ *n.* плодоро́дие; плодови́тость; **~ drug** препара́т от беспло́дия.

fertilize /'fəːtɪlaɪz/ *v.t.* (*biol.*) оплодотвор|я́ть, -и́ть; (*of soil*) удоб|ря́ть, -о́брить.

fertilizer /'fəːtɪlaɪzə(r)/ *n.* (*of soil*) удобре́ние.

fervent /'fəːv(ə)nt/ *adj.* (*fig.*) горя́чий, пы́лкий.

fervid /'fəːvɪd/ *adj.* пы́лкий, пла́менный.

fervour /'fəːvə(r)/ (*US* **fervor**) *n.* жар, пыл, страсть.

fester /'festə(r)/ *v.i.* гнои́ться, за-/на-; нагн|а́иваться, -ои́ться.

festival /'festɪv(ə)l/ *n.* фестива́ль (*m.*).

festive /'festɪv/ *adj.* пра́здничный.

festivity /fe'stɪvɪtɪ/ *n.* пра́зднество, торжество́.

festoon /fe'stuːn/ *n.* гирля́нда.
■ *v.t.* укр|аша́ть, -а́сить гирля́ндами.

fetal /'fiːt(ə)l/ *adj.* заро́дышевый, эмбриона́льный; **~ position** положе́ние эмбрио́на (в ма́тке).

fetch /fetʃ/ *v.t.*
1 (*go and get*) прин|оси́ть, -ести́; (*children from school, dry-cleaning*) заб|ира́ть, -ра́ть; **they ~ed the doctor** они́ вы́звали врача́.
2 (*of price*): **his house ~ed £150,000** он вы́ручил 150 000 фу́нтов за свой дом.

fetching /'fetʃɪŋ/ *adj.* привлека́тельный.

fête /feɪt/ *n.* пра́зднество, пра́здник.

fetid /'fetɪd/ *adj.* воню́чий, зловóнный.

fetish /'fetɪʃ/ *n.* (*lit.*, *fig.*) фети́ш.

fetter /'fetə(r)/ *n.* (*pl.*) ножны́е кандал|ы́ (*pl.*,

g. -óв); (*fig.*) окóв|ы (*pl.*, *g.* —).
■ *v.t.* закóв|ывать, -áть в кандалы́; (*fig.*) скóв|ывать, -áть.

fettle /ˈfet(ə)l/ *n.*: **in fine ~** в хорóшем состоя́нии (*condition*)/настроéнии (*mood*).

fetus /ˈfi:təs/ (*pl.* **~es**) плод, зарóдыш.

feud /fju:d/ *n.* враждá.
■ *v.i.* враждовáть (*с кем*) (*impf.*).

feudal /ˈfju:d(ə)l/ *adj.* феодáльный.

fever /ˈfi:və(r)/ *n.* жар; **he has a high ~** у негó жар.

feverish /ˈfi:vərɪʃ/ *adj.* лихорáдочный.

few /fju:/ *n.* & *adj.* немнóгие (*pl.*); немнóго (+ *g.*); мáло + *g.*; **~ (people) know the truth** немнóгие знáют прáвду; **a ~ (people)** немнóгие (лю́ди); нéсколько человéк; **a good ~** (*Br.*), **quite a ~** довóльно мнóго + *g.*; **~ and far between** рéдкие; **every ~ minutes** кáждые нéсколько минýт.

fewer /ˈfju:ə(r)/ *n.* & *adj.* мéнее, мéньше; **he wrote no ~ than 60 books** он написáл ни мнóго ни мáло 60 книг.

fiancé /fɪˈɒnseɪ/ *n.* жени́х.

fiancée /fɪˈɒnseɪ/ *n.* невéста.

fiasco /fɪˈæskəʊ/ *n.* (*pl.* **~s**) фиáско (*nt. indecl.*), провáл.

fib /fɪb/ *n.* вы́думка, непрáвда.
■ *v.i.* (**fibbed, fibbing**) прив|ирáть, -рáть (*coll.*).

fibre /ˈfaɪbə(r)/ (*US* **fiber**) *n.*
1 (*filament*) волокнó.
2 (*in diet*) клетчáтка.
■ *cpds.* **~glass** *n.* стекловолокнó; стеклоплáстик; **~-optic** *adj.* волокóнно-опти́ческий.

fickle /ˈfɪk(ə)l/ *adj.* перемéнчивый, непостоя́нный.

fiction /ˈfɪkʃ(ə)n/ *n.*
1 (*invention, pretence*) вы́мысел, вы́думка, фи́кция.
2 (*novels etc.*) беллетри́стика; **work of ~** худóжественное произведéние.

fictional /ˈfɪkʃənəl/ *adj.* вы́мышленный; беллетристи́ческий.

fictitious /fɪkˈtɪʃəs/ *adj.* подлóжный, фикти́вный; **a ~ name** вы́мышленное и́мя.

fiddle /ˈfɪd(ə)l/ *v.t.* (*Br.*, *falsify*) поддéл|ывать, -ать.
■ *v.i.* (*fidget, tamper*) вертéться (*impf.*); крути́ться (*impf.*); вози́ться (*impf.*); **he ~d with his tie** он тереби́л свой гáлстук; **don't ~ with my papers!** не трóгайте мои́ бумáги!

fidelity /fɪˈdelɪtɪ/ *n.* (*loyalty*) вéрность.

fidget /ˈfɪdʒɪt/ *v.i.* (**fidgeted, fidgeting**) ёрзать (*impf.*).

fidgety /ˈfɪdʒɪtɪ/ *adj.* суетли́вый, непосéдливый.

field /fi:ld/ *n.*
1 (*piece of ground*) пóле; **~ events** лёгкая атлéтика.
2 (*physical range, area*) пóле.
3 (*area of activity or study*) óбласть; пóле/сфéра дéятельности.
■ *cpds.* **~ day** *n.* (*fig.*, *day of successful exploits*) знаменáтельный/пáмятный день; **~work** *n.* (*research*) исслéдования (*nt. pl.*) в естéственных услóвиях.

fiend /fi:nd/ *n.* (*devil*) дья́вол; (*evil person*) злодéй, и́зверг; (*fig.*): **dope ~** наркомáн; **fresh air ~** (заядлый) люби́тель свéжего вóздуха.

fiendish /ˈfi:ndɪʃ/ *adj.* дья́вольский, злодéйский.

fierce /fɪəs/ *adj.* (**fiercer, fiercest**) свирéпый, лю́тый; **~ competition** жестóкая конкурéнция.

fiery /ˈfaɪərɪ/ *adj.* (**fierier, fieriest**) óгненный, плáменный; **a ~ temper** вспы́льчивый/горя́чий харáктер; **a ~ horse** горя́чая лóшадь.

fifteen /fɪfˈti:n/ *n.* пятнáдцать; **she is ~** ей пятнáдцать лет.
■ *adj.* пятнáдцать + *g. pl.*

fifteenth /fɪfˈti:nθ/ *n.* (*date*) пятнáдцатое (числó); (*fraction*) однá пятнáдцатая.
■ *adj.* пятнáдцатый.

fifth /fɪfθ/ *n.* (*date*) пя́тое (числó); (*fraction*) однá пя́тая.
■ *adj.* пя́тый.

fiftieth /ˈfɪftɪɪθ/ *n.* (*fraction*) однá пятидеся́тая.
■ *adj.* пятидеся́тый.

fift|y /ˈfɪftɪ/ *n.* пятьдеся́т, полсóтни; **the ~ies** (*decade*) пятидеся́тые гóды; **he is in his ~ies** емý за пятьдеся́т (лет); емý пошёл шестóй деся́ток; **we shared expenses ~y-~y** мы раздели́ли расхóды поплáм.
■ *adj.* пятьдеся́т + *g. pl.*

fig /fɪg/ *n.* (*fruit*) инжи́р; **~ tree** *n.* инжи́р, фи́говое дéрево.

fight /faɪt/ *n.* бой, схвáтка, дрáка.
■ *v.t.* & *i.* (*past and p.p.* **fought**) дрáться, по-; сра|жáться, -зи́ться; (*wage war*) воевáть (*impf.*); **the boys/dogs are ~ing** мáльчики/собáки дерýтся; **~ a battle** вести́ (*det.*) бой; **~ an election** вести́ (*det.*) предвы́борную борьбý; **~ a lawsuit** суди́ться (*impf.*); **he fought his way forward** он пробивáлся/протáлкивался вперёд; **he fought off a cold** он (бы́стро) спрáвился с простýдой; **they fought off the enemy** они́ отби́ли врагá; **~ back** *v.i.* отб|ивáться, -и́ться.

fighter /ˈfaɪtə(r)/ *n.*
1 (*one who fights*) боéц; (*fig.*) борéц.
2 (*~ aircraft*) истреби́тель (*m.*).

fighting /ˈfaɪtɪŋ/ *n.* бой, сражéние.
■ *adj.* боевóй; **we have a ~ chance** стóит попытáться.

figment /ˈfɪgmənt/ *n.* вы́мысел; **a ~ of the imagination** плод воображéния.

figurative /ˈfɪgərətɪv/ *adj.* перенóсный.

figure /ˈfɪgə(r)/ *n.*
1 (*numerical sign*) ци́фра; **double ~s** двузнáчные чи́сла; **a six-~ number** шестизнáчное числó.
2 (*diagram, illustration*) рисýнок.
3 (*human form*) фигýра; **I saw a ~ approaching** я уви́дел приближáвшуюся ко мне фигýру; **she has a good ~** у неё хорóшая фигýра.
4 (*person of importance*) фигýра, выдаю́щаяся ли́чность.
■ *v.t.*: **~ out** (*calculate*) вычисля́ть, вы́числить; (*understand*) пон|имáть, -я́ть; **I can't ~ him out** я не могý егó поня́ть.
■ *v.i.* 1 (*appear*) фигури́ровать (*impf.*); **this**

did not ~ in my plans это не входи́ло в мои́ пла́ны.
[2] (*US coll.*): **it ~s** (*makes sense, is plausible*) э́то похо́же на пра́вду; **I ~ they'll be late** я ду́маю, что они́ опозда́ют.
■ *cpds.* **~head** *n.* носово́е украше́ние, фигу́ра на носу́ корабля́; (*fig.*) номина́льный руководи́тель; **~ skating** *n.* фигу́рное ката́ние.

figurine /fɪgjʊ'ri:n/ *n.* фигу́рка, статуэ́тка.

Fiji /'fi:dʒi:/ *n.* Фи́джи (*indecl.*).

filament /'fɪləmənt/ *n.* (*thread*) волокно́, нить; (*elec.*) нить нака́ла.

file¹ /faɪl/ *n.* (*tool*) напи́льник.
■ *v.t.* подпи́л|ивать, -и́ть; **~ one's nails** подпи́л|ивать, -и́ть но́гти.

file² /faɪl/ *n.*
[1] (*for papers*) па́пка, скоросшива́тель (*m.*).
[2] (*set of papers etc.*) де́ло, досье́ (*nt. indecl.*).
[3] (*comput.*) файл.
■ *v.t.* [1] (*documents*) подш|ива́ть, -и́ть.
[2]: **~** (*lodge*) **a complaint** под|ава́ть, -а́ть жа́лобу; **~ suit against s.o.** возбу|жда́ть, -ди́ть суде́бное де́ло про́тив кого́-н.

file³ /faɪl/ *n.* (*row*) ряд, шере́нга; коло́нна; **in single ~** гусько́м; по одному́.
■ *v.i.* идти́ (*det.*) гусько́м/коло́нной; **the prisoners ~d out** заключённые выходи́ли гусько́м друг за дру́гом.

filing /'faɪlɪŋ/ *n.* (*of papers*) регистра́ция бума́г.
■ *cpd.* **~ cabinet** *n.* шкаф, сейф.

Filipino /fɪlɪ'pi:nəʊ/ *n.* (*pl.* **~s**) филиппи́н|ец (*fem.* -ка).
■ *adj.* филиппи́нский.

fill /fɪl/*v.t.*
[1] (*make full*) нап|олня́ть, -о́лнить; зап|олня́ть, -о́лнить; **he ~ed the hole with sand** он запо́лнил я́му песко́м; **I was ~ed with admiration** я был по́лон восхище́ния.
[2]: **~ a tooth** пломбирова́ть, за-.
[3] (*fig., of office etc.*) зан|има́ть, -я́ть; **~ a vacancy** зап|олня́ть, -о́лнить вака́нтную до́лжность.
[4]: **~ a need** удовлетвор|я́ть, -и́ть потре́бность.
■ *v.i.* (*become full*) нап|олня́ться, -о́лниться.
■ *with advs.*: **~ in** *v.t.* (*Br., complete*) зап|олня́ть, -о́лнить; **he ~ed in the form** (*Br.*) он запо́лнил бланк/анке́ту; (*coll., inform*): **I ~ed him in** я ввёл его́ в курс де́ла; **~ out** *v.t.* (*US, a form*) зап|олня́ть, -о́лнить; *v.i.* расш|иря́ться, -и́риться; **~ up** *v.t.* (*make full*) нап|олня́ть, -о́лнить; *v.i.* (*become full*) нап|олня́ться, -о́лниться.

fillet /'fɪlɪt/ *n.* филе́ (*nt. indecl.*).
■ *v.t.* (**filleted, filleting**) (*of fish, take off bone*) отдел|я́ть, -и́ть мя́со от косте́й.

filling /'fɪlɪŋ/ *n.* (*in tooth*) пло́мба; (*in pie*) начи́нка.
■ *adj.* (*of food*) сы́тный.
■ *cpd.* **~ station** *n.* автозапра́вочная *or* бензозапра́вочная ста́нция; (бензо)запра́вка.

film /fɪlm/ *n.*
[1] (*thin coating*) плёнка.
[2] (*material for producing pictures*) (*phot.*) фотоплёнка; (*cin.*) киноплёнка.
[3] (*motion picture*) фильм; **~ crew** съёмочная гру́ппа; **~ star** кинозвезда́; **~ studies** кинове́дение; **~ studio** киносту́дия.
■ *v.t. & i.* сн|има́ть, -ять.

filter /'fɪltə(r)/ *n.* (*for liquid*) фильтр; (*for light*) светофи́льтр.
■ *v.t.* (*purify*) фильтрова́ть, от-/про-.

filth /fɪlθ/ *n.* грязь.

filthy /'fɪlθɪ/ *adj.* (**filthier, filthiest**) гря́зный.

fin /fɪn/ *n.* плавни́к.

final /'faɪn(ə)l/ *n.*
[1] (*Br., pl., exam at end of degree course*) выпускно́й экза́мен; (*US, exam at end of term, year, class*) ито́говый экза́мен.
[2] (*match*) фина́л.
■ *adj.* [1] (*last in order*) после́дний.
[2] (*decisive*) оконча́тельный, реша́ющий.

finale /fɪ'nɑ:lɪ/ *n.* (*mus., fig.*) фина́л.

finalist /'faɪnəlɪst/ *n.* финали́ст (*fem.* -ка).

finalize /'faɪnəlaɪz/ *v.t.* (*give final form to*) заверш|а́ть, -и́ть; (*settle, e.g. arrangements*) (оконча́тельно) ула́|живать, -дить.

finally *adv.* (*after a long time*) в конце́ концо́в; (*once and for all*) оконча́тельно; (*lastly*) наконе́ц.

finance /'faɪnæns/ *n.* фина́нсы (*m. pl.*); дохо́ды (*m. pl.*).
■ *v.t.* финанси́ровать (*impf., pf.*).

financial /faɪ'nænʃ(ə)l/ *adj.* фина́нсовый.

financier /faɪ'nænsɪə(r)/ *n.* финанси́ст.

finch /fɪntʃ/ *n.* зя́блик.

find /faɪnd/ *n.* (*discovery, esp. valuable*) нахо́дка.
■ *v.t.* (*past and p.p.* **found**)
[1] (*discover, encounter*) на|ходи́ть, -йти́; (*by search*) раз|ыска́ть, от- (*both pf.*); **pine trees are found in several countries** сосна́ растёт/встреча́ется во мно́гих стра́нах; **I ~ it hard to understand him** мне тру́дно поня́ть его́.
[2] (*judge*): **the jury found him guilty** прися́жные призна́ли его́ вино́вным.
[3] (*obtain*) получ|а́ть, -и́ть; **he found time to read** он находи́л вре́мя для чте́ния.
[4]: **~ out** (*detect*) узн|ава́ть, -а́ть; (*ascertain*) выясня́ть, вы́яснить; **have you found out (about) the trains?** вы узна́ли расписа́ние поездо́в?

finding /'faɪndɪŋ/ *n.* (*conclusion; also pl.*) вы́вод(ы).

fine¹ /faɪn/ *n.* (*punishment*) штраф, пе́ня.
■ *v.t.* штрафова́ть, о-; **he was ~d £5** его́ оштрафова́ли на 5 фу́нтов.

fine² /faɪn/ *adj.*
[1] (*of weather*) я́сный, хоро́ший.
[2] (*handsome, excellent*) прекра́сный, замеча́тельный; **a ~ view** прекра́сный вид.
[3] (*exquisite*) то́нкий; **~ workmanship** то́нкая рабо́та.
[4] (*of small particles*) ме́лкий; **~ dust** ме́лкая пыль.
[5] (*thin*) то́нкий, о́стрый; **a pencil with a ~ point** о́стро отто́ченный каранда́ш.
[6] (*subtle*) утончённый, то́нкий; **a ~ distinction** то́нкое разли́чие; **the ~ arts** изобрази́тельные/изя́щные иску́сства.
■ *adv.*: **he cut it ~** (*of time*) он оста́вил себе́ вре́мени в обре́з; **that suits me ~** (*coll.*) э́то меня́ вполне́ устра́ивает.

fineness /'faɪnnɪs/ *n.* (*delicacy*) то́нкость,

утончённость, изя́щество.
finery /'faɪnərɪ/ *n.* пы́шный наря́д.
finesse /fɪ'nes/ *n.* (*delicacy*) делика́тность, то́нкость.
finger /'fɪŋgə(r)/ *n.* па́лец (*also of glove*).
■ *v.t.* тро́гать, по-.
■ *cpds.* **~nail** *n.* но́готь (*m.*); **~print** *n.* отпеча́ток па́льца; *v.t.* (*take s.o.'s ~prints*) сн|има́ть, -ять отпеча́тки па́льцев у + *g.*; **~tip** *n.* ко́нчик па́льца.
finicky /'fɪnɪkɪ/ *adjs.* (чересчу́р) разбо́рчивый, привере́дливый.
finish /'fɪnɪʃ/ *n.*
1 (*conclusion*) оконча́ние, коне́ц.
2 (*polish*) отде́лка.
■ *v.t.* 1 (*end*) зак|а́нчивать, -о́нчить; конча́ть, ко́нчить; **I ~ed the book** я (за)ко́нчил кни́гу; **he ~ed (off, up) the pie** он дое́л весь пиро́г; **we will ~ the job** мы зако́нчим рабо́ту.
2 (*perfect*) соверше́нствовать (*impf.*); **~ing touch** после́дний штрих.
3 (*coll., exhaust, kill*) изнур|я́ть, -и́ть; **the fever ~ed him off** лихора́дка доконáла/прико́нчила его́.
■ *v.i.* конча́ться, ко́нчиться; зак|а́нчиваться, -о́нчиться; **have you ~ed with that book?** вам бо́льше не нужна́ э́та кни́га?; **~ing post** фи́ниш.
finite /'faɪnaɪt/ *adj.* коне́чный; име́ющий преде́л.
Finland /'fɪnlənd/ *n.* Финля́ндия.
Finn /fɪn/ *n.* фин|н (*fem.* -ка).
Finnish /'fɪnɪʃ/ *n.* (*language*) фи́нский язы́к.
■ *adj.* фи́нский.
fiord /fjɔ:d/ = **fjord**
fir /fə:(r)/ *n.* (*also* **~ tree**) ель.
fire /'faɪə(r)/ *n.*
1 (*phenomenon of combustion*) ого́нь (*m.*); **the house is on ~** дом загоре́лся/гори́т; **set ~ to** подж|ига́ть, -е́чь; **catch ~** загор|а́ться, -е́ться.
2 (*burning fuel*) ого́нь (*m.*); **light a ~** разж|ига́ть, -е́чь ками́н; топи́ть, за- печь.
3 (*conflagration*) пожа́р; **~!** пожа́р!
4 (*of ~arms*) ого́нь (*m.*), стрельба́; **open ~** откр|ыва́ть, -ы́ть ого́нь.
■ *v.t.* 1 (*set fire to*) подж|ига́ть, -е́чь.
2 (*of ~arms*) стреля́ть (*impf.*) из + *g.*; **~ a rifle** стреля́ть (*impf.*) из ружья́; **~ a shot** вы́стрелить (*pf.*).
■ *v.i.* (*of ~arms*) стреля́ть (*impf.*); **the troops ~d at the enemy** войска́ стреля́ли по врагу́.
■ *cpds.* **~ alarm** *n.* (*alert*) пожа́рная трево́га; (*device*) автомати́ческий пожа́рный сигна́л; **~arm** *n.* огнестре́льное ору́жие; **~ bomb** *n.* зажига́тельная бо́мба; **~ brigade** *n.* (*Br.*) пожа́рная кома́нда; **~ engine** *n.* пожа́рная маши́на; **~ escape** *n.* пожа́рная ле́стница; **~ extinguisher** *n.* огнетуши́тель (*m.*); **~fighter** *n.* пожа́рный; пожа́рник (*coll.*); **~guard** *n.* ками́нная решётка; **~lighter** *n.* (*Br.*) расто́пка; **~man** *n.* пожа́рный; пожа́рник (*coll.*); **~place** *n.* ками́н, оча́г; **~proof** *adj.* огнеупо́рный; *v.t.* прид|ава́ть, -а́ть огнесто́йкость + *d.*; **~side** *n.* ме́сто о́коло ками́на; (*fig.*) дома́шний оча́г; **~ station** *n.* пожа́рное депо́ (*nt. indecl.*); **~wood** *n.* дров|а́ (*pl., g.* —); **~work(s)** *n.* фейерве́рк (*also fig.*).
firing /'faɪərɪŋ/ *n.* (*shooting*) стрельба́; **~ line** ли́ния огня́.
firm¹ /fə:m/ *n.* фи́рма.
firm² /fə:m/ *adj.*
1 (*physically*) кре́пкий, твёрдый.
2 (*fig.*) усто́йчивый, сто́йкий, непоколеби́мый; **you must be ~ with him** вы должны́ быть с ним стро́же; **a ~ offer** твёрдое предложе́ние.
■ *adv.* твёрдо, усто́йчиво; **stand ~** стоя́ть (*impf.*) твёрдо.
firmament /'fə:məmənt/ *n.* небе́сный свод.
firmware /'fə:mweə(r)/ *n.* (*comput.*) микропрогра́мма, встро́енная програ́мма; проши́вка (*sl.*).
first /fə:st/ *n.*
1 (*beginning*): **at ~** снача́ла, сперва́.
2 (*date*) пе́рвое (число́); **on the ~ of May** пе́рвого ма́я.
3 (*Br., acad.*) вы́сшая оце́нка/отме́тка.
■ *adj.* 1 (*in time or place*) пе́рвый; **on the ~ floor** (*Br.*) на второ́м этаже́; (*US*) на пе́рвом этаже́; **at ~ glance** на пе́рвый взгляд; **hear sth. at ~ hand** узн|ава́ть, -а́ть что-н. из пе́рвых рук; **~ name** и́мя; **~ night** (*theatr.*) премье́ра; **in the ~ place** во-пе́рвых, в пе́рвую о́чередь; **I will go there ~ thing tomorrow** за́втра я пе́рвым де́лом зайду́ туда́; **the ~ time I saw him** когда́ я в пе́рвый раз уви́дел его́.
2 (*in rank or importance*) пе́рвый; **~ cousin** двою́родный брат, двою́родная сестра́.
■ *adv.* 1 (*before all; also* **~ and foremost, ~ of all**) пре́жде всего́; в пе́рвую о́чередь.
2 (*initially*) сперва́, снача́ла; (*in the ~ place*) во-пе́рвых; (*for the ~ time*) впервы́е; **I ~ met him last year** я познако́мился с ним в про́шлом году́.
■ *cpds.* **~ aid** *n.* пе́рвая по́мощь; **~-aid kit** санита́рная су́мка; апте́чка; **~-class** *adj.* (*excellent*) первокла́ссный; *adv.* (*of travel*) пе́рвым кла́ссом; **~-night** *adj.*: **~-night nerves** волне́ние пе́ред премье́рой; **~-rate** *adj.* первокла́ссный.
firstly /'fə:stlɪ/ *adv.* во-пе́рвых.
fiscal /'fɪsk(ə)l/ *adj.* фиска́льный, фина́нсовый.
fish /fɪʃ/ *n.* (*pl.* **~** *or* **~es**) ры́ба.
■ *v.t. & i.* лови́ть/уди́ть (*impf.*) ры́бу; (*fig.*): **~ for compliments** напра́шиваться (*impf.*) на комплиме́нты; **~ for information** выу́живать, вы́удить све́дения.
■ *cpds.* **~monger** *n.* торго́вец ры́бой; **~net** *n.*: **~net stockings** ажу́рные чулки́.
fisherman /'fɪʃəmən/ *n.* рыба́к; (*angler for pleasure*) рыболо́в.
fishery /'fɪʃərɪ/ *n.* (*fish farm*) рыбово́дческое хозя́йство.
fishing /'fɪʃɪŋ/ *n.* ры́бная ло́вля; **the boys have gone ~** ма́льчики ушли́ на рыба́лку.
■ *cpds.* **~ line** *n.* ле́ска; **~ net** *n.* рыболо́вная сеть; **~ rod** *n.* уди́лище.
fishy /'fɪʃɪ/ *adj.* (**fishier, fishiest**) ры́бий, ры́бный; (*coll., suspect*) нечи́стый, подозри́тельный.
fissure /'fɪʃə(r)/ *n.* тре́щина, расще́лина.
■ *v.i.* тре́скаться, по-; тре́снуть (*pf.*).
fist /fɪst/ *n.* кула́к.

fit[1] /fɪt/ *n.*
1 (*attack of illness*) при́ступ, припа́док.
2 (*outburst*): **~ of coughing** при́ступ ка́шля; **his jokes had us in ~s** от его́ шу́ток мы пока́тывались со́ смеху.
3: **in ~s and starts** уры́вками.

fit[2] /fɪt/ *n.* (*of a garment etc.*): **this jacket is a tight ~** э́тот пиджа́к узкова́т.
■ *adj.* (**fitter, fittest**)
1 (*suitable*) го́дный, приго́дный, подходя́щий; **see, think ~** счита́ть, сче́сть ну́жным; **a meal ~ for a king** ца́рская тра́пеза; **you are not ~ to be seen** вам нельзя́ пока́зываться в тако́м ви́де.
2 (*in good health*) здоро́вый; **keep (o.s.) ~** подде́рживать (*impf.*) хоро́шую (спорти́вную) фо́рму.
■ *v.t.* (**fitted, fitting**)
1 (*equip*: *also* **~ out; ~ up**) снаря|жа́ть, -ди́ть; снаб|жа́ть, -ди́ть; экипирова́ть (*impf.*, *pf.*); обору́довать (*impf.*, *pf.*).
2 (*install*): **~ted carpet** (*Br.*) ковёр во всю ко́мнату; **~ted kitchen** (*Br.*) встро́енная ку́хня; **he ~ted a new lock on the door** он вста́вил но́вый замо́к в дверь; (*fig.*, *accommodate*): **I can ~ you in next week** я могу́ назна́чить вам встре́чу на сле́дующей неде́ле.
3 (*make suitable, adapt*) приспос|а́бливать, -о́бить; (*correspond to in dimensions*: *also v.i.*) под|ходи́ть, -ойти́ + *d.*; **the dress ~s you** э́то пла́тье хорошо́ на вас сиди́т; **that ~s in with my plans** э́то вполне́ совпада́ет с мои́ми пла́нами.
4 (*insert*: *also v.i.*): **tubes that ~ into one another** тру́бки, вставля́ющиеся одна́ в другу́ю.

fitful /ˈfɪtfʊl/ *adj.* неро́вный, преры́вистый.

fitness /ˈfɪtnɪs/ *n.* хоро́шее здоро́вье.

fitter /ˈfɪtə(r)/ *n.* (*of machinery*) монтёр, сбо́рщик.

fitting /ˈfɪtɪŋ/ *n.*
1 (*of clothes*) приме́рка.
2 (*fixture in building*) обору́дование.
■ *adj.* подходя́щий, го́дный.
■ *cpd.* **~ room** *n.* приме́рочная.

five /faɪv/ *n.* (число́/но́мер) пять; (**~** *people*) пя́теро; пять челове́к; **in ~s, ~ at a time** по пяти́, пятёрками; (*figure, thing numbered 5, group of* **~**) пятёрка; **~ (o'clock)** пять (часо́в); **he is ~** ему́ пять лет; **~ to 4 (o'clock)** без пяти́ четы́ре; **~ past 6** пять мину́т седьмо́го.
■ *adj.* пять + *g. pl.*; **~ sixes are thirty** пя́тью шесть — три́дцать.

fiver /ˈfaɪvə(r)/ *n.* (*Br.*) пятёрка (*coll.*) (*пятифунтовая банкнота*).

fix /fɪks/ *n.* (*dilemma*) затрудни́тельное положе́ние; (*coll., injection of drug*) уко́л.
■ *v.t.* 1 (*make firm*) укреп|ля́ть, -и́ть; (*fig.*): **~ the blame on s.o.** взва́л|ивать, -и́ть вину́ на кого́-н.
2 (*direct steadily*) напр|авля́ть, -а́вить; **~ed gaze** при́стальный/неподви́жный взгляд.
3 (*determine, settle*: *also v.i.*) **let us ~ (on) a date** дава́йте договори́мся о да́те.
4 (*provide*: *also* **~ up**): **can you ~ (up) a room for me?** (*or* **~ me up with a room?**) мо́жете ли вы найти́/подыска́ть для меня́ ко́мнату?
5 (*coll., repair*): **he ~ed the radio in no time** он в два счёта почини́л радиоприёмник; (*US, prepare*): **I will ~ the drinks** я приготóвлю напи́тки.

fixation /fɪkˈseɪʃ(ə)n/ *n.* (*psych.*) викса́ция.

fixed /ˈfɪksd/ *adj.* неподви́жный, закреплённый, постоя́нный; **~ idea** навя́зчивая иде́я, иде́я фикс; **~ rate** фикси́рованная ста́вка.

fixer /ˈfɪksə(r)/ *n.* (*phot.*) фикса́ж; (*sl., organizer*) посре́дник.

fixture /ˈfɪkstʃə(r)/ *n.*
1 (*fitting in building*) приспособле́ние.
2 (*Br., sporting event*) предстоя́щее спорти́вное состяза́ние/мероприя́тие.

fizzle /ˈfɪz(ə)l/ *v.i.*: **~ out** око́нчиться (*pf.*) ниче́м.

fizzy /ˈfɪzɪ/ *adj.* (**fizzier, fizziest**) шипу́чий.

fjord, fiord /fjɔːd/ *n.* фьорд, фио́рд.

flabby /ˈflæbɪ/ *adj.* (**flabbier, flabbiest**) вя́лый, дря́блый.

flag[1] /flæg/ *n.* (*emblem*) флаг, зна́мя (*nt.*).
■ *v.t.* (**flagged, flagging**)
1 (*mark*) ме́тить, по-.
2 (*signal*: *also v.i.*) (*fig.*): **~ (down) a passing car** остан|а́вливать, -ови́ть проезжа́ющую маши́ну.
■ *cpd.* **~pole** *n.* флагшто́к.

flag[2] /flæg/ *v.i.* (**flagged, flagging**) (*grow weary*) ослаб|ева́ть, -е́ть; (*fig.*): **the conversation was ~ging** разгово́р не кле́ился.

flagon /ˈflægən/ *n.* графи́н/кувши́н для вина́.

flagrant /ˈfleɪgrənt/ *adj.* вопию́щий, возмути́тельный.

flail /fleɪl/ *v.t.* & *i.* (*fig.*) маха́ть (*impf.*) (+ *i.*); **he charged with his hands ~ing** он наступа́л, разма́хивая рука́ми.

flair /ˈfleə(r)/ *n.* нюх, чутьё; **a ~ for languages** спосо́бности (*f. pl.*) к языка́м.

flake /fleɪk/ *n.* (*pl.*) хло́пь|я (*pl.*, *g.* -ев); **~s of snow** снежи́нки (*f. pl.*).
■ *v.i.* (*peel*) шелуши́ться (*impf.*); слои́ться (*impf.*); **the rust ~d off** ржа́вчина отслои́лась.

flamboyance /flæmˈbɔɪəns/ *n.* цвети́стость; я́ркость.

flamboyant /flæmˈbɔɪənt/ *adj.* (*person, behaviour*) колори́тный; (*clothing*) бро́ский, я́ркий; (*style*) цвети́стый.

flame /fleɪm/ *n.* ого́нь (*m.*), пла́мя (*nt.*); **burst into ~(s)** вспы́х|ивать, -нуть; **the house was in ~s** дом был охва́чен пла́менем.

flaming /ˈfleɪmɪŋ/ *adj.*
1 (*ablaze*) пыла́ющий, горя́щий.
2 (*fig., violent*): **they had a ~ row** у них произошёл стра́шный сканда́л.

flamingo /fləˈmɪŋgəʊ/ *n.* (*pl.* **~s** *or* **~es**) флами́нго (*m. indecl.*).

flammable /ˈflæməb(ə)l/ *adj.* горю́чий; легко́ воспламеня́ющийся.

flan /flæn/ *n.* откры́тый пиро́г.

flank /flæŋk/ *n.* (*mil.*) фланг.
■ *v.t.*: **he was ~ed by guards** по обе́ сто́роны от него́ шла/стоя́ла стра́жа.

flannel /ˈflæn(ə)l/ *n.*
1 (*kind of cloth*) флане́ль.
2: **face ~** (*Br.*) махро́вая салфе́тка для

лицá.

flap /flæp/ *n.*
[1] (*hinged piece etc.*): **the table has two ~s** у столá две откидны́е доски́; (*of pocket, envelope*) клáпан.
[2] (*waving motion*) взмах.
■ *v.t. & i.* (**flapped, flapping**) взмáх|ивать, -нýть + *i.*; **the bird ~ped its wings** пти́ца взмахнýла кры́льями.

flare¹ /fleə(r)/ *n.* (*effect of flame*) сверкáние; (*illuminating device*) сигнáльная ракéта; осветѝтельный патрóн.
■ *v.i.* сверк|áть, -нýть; горéть (*impf.*) неро́вным плáменем; (*fig.*): **she ~s up at the least thing** онá взрывáется из-за кáждого пустякá.

flare² /fleə(r)/ *n.*: **~s** (*trousers*) брю́ки клёш.
■ *v.t. & i.* расш|иря́ться, -и́риться; **~d skirt** ю́бка клёш.

flash /flæʃ/ *n.*
[1] (*burst of light*) вспы́шка, прóблеск; **a ~ of lightning** вспы́шка мóлнии; **he had a ~ of inspiration** на негó нашлó вдохновéние.
[2] (*instant*) мгновéние, миг; **he answered in a ~** он мгновéнно отвéтил.
■ *v.t.*: **he ~ed the light in my face** он напрáвил свет мне в лицó; (*fig.*): **he ~ed a glance at her** он метнýл на неё взгляд.
■ *v.i.* сверк|áть, -нýть; вспы́х|ивать, -нуть; мельк|áть, -нýть; **the light ~ed on and off** свет то вспы́хивал, то гас; **cars ~ed by** маши́ны мчáлись ми́мо.
■ *cpds.* **~back** *n.* (*cin.*) ретроспекти́ва, обрáтный кадр; **~bulb** *n.* (*phot.*) лáмпа-вспы́шка; **~ flood** *n.* ли́вневый пáводок; **~light** *n.* (*US*) кармáнный/электри́ческий фонáрь.

flashy /ˈflæʃɪ/ *adj.* (**flashier, flashiest**) крич́áщий, показнóй, эффéктный.

flask /flɑːsk/ *n.* фля́га, фля́жка.

flat /flæt/ *n.*
[1] (*Br., apartment*) кварти́ра; **~mate** (*Br.*) сосéд (*fem.* -ка) по кварти́ре.
[2] (*mus.*) бемóль (*m.*).
[3] (*level object or area*) плóскость; **the ~ of the hand** ладóнь.
■ *adj. & adv.* (**flatter, flattest**)
[1] (*level*) плóский, рóвный; **~ tyre** (*Br.*), **tire** (*US*) спýщенная ши́на; **the battery is ~** (*Br.*) батарéя сéла; **he fell ~ on his back** он упáл нáвзничь.
[2] (*uniform*) однообрáзный; **~ rate** еди́ная стáвка.
[3] (*unqualified*) прямóй, категори́ческий; **~ out** (*sl., exhausted*) вы́дохшийся; **drive ~ out** (*coll., at top speed*) гнать (*impf.*) на всю катýшку; **in ten seconds ~** рóвно за дéсять секýнд.
[4] (*dull, insipid*) скýчный, вя́лый, бесцвéтный.
[5] (*mus.*): **she sings ~ on the high notes** онá фальши́вит на высóких нóтах.
■ *cpd.* **~bed** *adj.* (*comput.*) планшéтный; **~bed scanner** планшéтный скáнер.

flatly /ˈflætlɪ/ *adv.* (*refuse*) категори́чески.

flatten /ˈflæt(ə)n/ *v.t.*
[1] (*make smooth*) вырáвнивать, вы́ровнять.
[2] (*reduce thickness of*) расплю́щи|вать, -ть; **he ~ed himself against the wall** он прижáлся к стенé.
[3] (*lay low*) **the gale ~ed the corn** бýрей примя́ло хлебá.

flatter /ˈflætə(r)/ *v.t.* льсти́ть, по- + *d.*

flattering /ˈflætərɪŋ/ *adj.* лéстный, льсти́вый; (*of person*) льсти́вый.

flattery /ˈflætərɪ/ *n.* лесть.

flatulence /ˈflætjʊləns/ *n.* скоплéние гáзов; (*fig.*) напы́щенность, высокопáрность.

flaunt /flɔːnt/ *v.t.* афиши́ровать (*impf.*); щегол|я́ть, -ьнýть + *i.*

flautist /ˈflɔːtɪst/ *n.* флейти́ст (*fem.* -ка).

flavour /ˈfleɪvə(r)/ (*US* **flavor**) *n.* аромáт, вкус.
■ *v.t.* припр|авля́ть, -áвить.

flavouring /ˈfleɪvərɪŋ/ (*US* **flavoring**) *n.* припрáва; спéции (*f. pl.*).

flaw /flɔː/ *n.* (*defect*) изъя́н, недостáток.

flawed /flɔːd/ *adj.* имéющий недостáтки.

flawless /ˈflɔːlɪs/ *adj.* безупрéчный.

flax /flæks/ *n.* (*plant*) лён; (*fibre*) кудéль (*волокно льна*).

flea /fliː/ *n.* блохá.

fleck /flek/ *n.* крáпинка, пятнó; (*of dust*) пыли́нка.
■ *v.t.* покр|ывáть, -ы́ть пя́тнами/крáпинками.

fled /fled/ *past and p.p. of* ▸ **flee**

fledg(e)ling /ˈfledʒlɪŋ/ *n.* тóлько что опери́вшийся птенéц.

flee /fliː/ *v.t.* (*past and p.p.* **fled**) избе|гáть, -жáть.
■ *v.i.* (*past and p.p.* **fled**) бежáть, с-.

fleece /fliːs/ *n.* рунó, овéчья шерсть.

fleecy /ˈfliːsɪ/ *adj.* (**fleecier, fleeciest**) шерсти́стый.

fleet /fliːt/ *n.*
[1] (*collection of vessels*) флоти́лия, флот.
[2] (*of vehicles*) парк.

fleeting /ˈfliːtɪŋ/ *adj.* бéглый, мимолётный; **a ~ glimpse** бéглый взгляд.

Flemish /ˈflemɪʃ/ *n.* (*language*) фламáндский язы́к; **the ~** (*people*) фламáндцы (*m. pl.*).
■ *adj.* фламáндский.

flesh /fleʃ/ *n.*
[1] (*bodily tissue*) плоть, тéло.
[2] (*fig.*): **my own ~ and blood** (*children*) моя́ плоть и кровь; (*relatives*) моя́ родня́.
[3] (*of fruit*) мя́коть.

fleshy /ˈfleʃɪ/ *adj.* (**fleshier, fleshiest**) (*of persons*) тóлстый, тýчный.

flew /fluː/ *past of* ▸ **fly³**

flex¹ /fleks/ *n.* (*Br.*) (ги́бкий) шнур.

flex² /fleks/ *v.t.* сгибáть, согнýть; **~ one's muscles** напр|ягáть, -я́чь мýскулы.

flexibility /fleksɪˈbɪlɪtɪ/ *n.* эласти́чность; (*fig.*) ги́бкость.

flexible /ˈfleksɪb(ə)l/ *adj.* эласти́чный, ги́бкий; (*fig.*) ги́бкий.

flexitime /ˈfleksɪtaɪm/ *n.* ненорми́рованный рабóчий день.

flick /flɪk/ *n. jerk*) толчóк; (*light touch*): **a ~ of the whip** лёгкий удáр хлыстóм.
■ *v.t.* (*shake with a jerk*) встр|я́хивать, -яхнýть; (*propel with finger end*) щёлк|ать, -нуть; (*touch*) стегнýть (*pf.*).
■ *v.i.*: **~ through** просм|áтривать, -отрéть.

flicker /ˈflɪkə(r)/ *n.* (*of light*) мерцáние; (*fig.*): **a ~ of hope** прóблеск надéжды.

■ *v.i.* (*flutter*) трепета́ть (*impf.*); (*burn or shine fitfully*) мерца́ть (*impf.*).

flight[1] /flaɪt/ *n.*
1 полёт; (*journey by air*): **a non-stop ~** беспоса́дочный полёт; (*a particular ~*) рейс; **the next ~ from London to Paris** сле́дующий рейс по маршру́ту Ло́ндон — Пари́ж; **~ path** курс полёта; **~ recorder** бортово́й самопи́сец.
2 (*fig.*): **~ of fancy** полёт фанта́зии.
3 : **~ of stairs** ле́стничный марш.
■ *cpds.* **~ attendant** *n.* стю́ард; (*fem.* -е́сса); **~ engineer** *n.* бортмеха́ник.

flight[2] /flaɪt/ *n.* бе́гство, побе́г; **take ~** обра|ща́ться, -ти́ться в бе́гство.

flighty /ˈflaɪtɪ/ *adj.* (**flightier, flightiest**) ве́треный, капри́зный.

flimsy /ˈflɪmzɪ/ *adj.* (**flimsier, flimsiest**) то́нкий, непро́чный; **a ~ structure** непро́чная постро́йка; **a ~ excuse** сла́бое оправда́ние.

flinch /flɪntʃ/ *v.i.* вздр|а́гивать, -о́гнуть.

fling /flɪŋ/ *n.*
1 (*sexual*) коро́ткий рома́н, интри́жка.
2 : **he had his ~** он повесели́лся/нагуля́лся вво́лю.
■ *v.t.* (*past and p.p.* **flung**): **~ o.s. into a chair** бр|оса́ться, -о́ситься в кре́сло; **she flung her arms around me** она́ обняла́ меня́.
■ *with adv.*: **~ open the window** распа́х|ивать, -ну́ть окно́.

flint /flɪnt/ *n.* креме́нь (*m.*).

flip /flɪp/ *n.* щелчо́к.
■ *adj.* (*flippant*) де́рзкий.
■ *v.t.* (**flipped, flipping**) (*a coin*) подбр|а́сывать, -о́сить.
■ *v.i.* (*coll., go crazy*) сходи́ть, сойти́ с ума́.

flip-flop /ˈflɪpflɒp/ *n.* (*usu. in pl.*) (*footwear*) вьетна́мка (*обувь*).

flippancy /ˈflɪpənsɪ/ *n.* легкомы́слие, ве́треность.

flippant /ˈflɪpənt/ *adj.* легкомы́сленный, ве́треный.

flipper /ˈflɪpə(r)/ *n.* плавни́к, ласт; (*diver's appendage*) ласт.

flirt /flɜːt/ *n.* коке́тка; люби́тель (*m.*) поуха́живать.
■ *v.i.* коке́тничать (*impf.*) (с + *i.*); (*fig.*): **~ with** (*an idea etc.*) поду́мывать о + *p.*

flirtation /flɜːˈteɪʃ(ə)n/ *n.* флирт; коке́тство; (*fig.*) игра́.

flirtatious /flɜːˈteɪʃəs/ *adj.* коке́тливый.

flit /flɪt/ *v.i.* (**flitted, flitting**) порх|а́ть, -ну́ть.

float /fləʊt/ *n.*
1 (*for line or net*) поплаво́к, буй; (*for learning to swim*) пла́вательная доска́.
2 (*Br., cart*) платфо́рма на колёсах.
■ *v.t.* спус|ка́ть, -ти́ть на́ воду; (*comm.*): **~ a company** учре|жда́ть, -ди́ть акционе́рное о́бщество.
■ *v.i.* 1 пла́вать (*indet.*), плыть (*det.*); **the boat ~ed downriver** ло́дку несло́ тече́нием вниз по реке́.
2 (*in air*) плыть (*det.*).

floating /ˈfləʊtɪŋ/ *adj.* пла́вающий, плаву́чий; **~ voter** колеблю́щийся избира́тель.

flock /flɒk/ *n.* (*of birds*) ста́я; (*of sheep or goats*) ста́до.
■ *v.i.* стека́ться (*impf.*).

flog /flɒg/ *v.t.* (**flogged, flogging**) стега́ть, от-.

flood /flʌd/ *n.*
1 (*inundation*) наводне́ние, полово́дье, разли́в.
2 (*fig.*): **she burst into ~s of tears** она́ разрыда́лась.
■ *v.t.* затоп|ля́ть, -и́ть; **the basement was ~ed** подва́л затопи́ло.
■ *v.i.* разл|ива́ться, -и́ться.
■ *cpds.* **~gate** *n.* шлюз; **open the ~gates (to)** (*fig.*) да|ва́ть, -ть во́лю (*чему*); **~light** *n.* проже́ктор; *v.t.* осве|ща́ть, -ти́ть проже́кторами.

floor /flɔː(r)/ *n.*
1 пол; **~ lamp** (*US*) торше́р.
2 : **take the ~** (*in public assembly*) брать, взять сло́во; (*in dance hall*) пойти́ (*pf.*) танцева́ть.
3 (*storey*) эта́ж.
■ *v.t.* (*coll., knock down*) сби|ва́ть, -ть с ног; (*fig., nonplus*) сра|жа́ть, -зи́ть; **the question ~ed him** вопро́с срази́л его́.
■ *cpds.* **~board** *n.* полови́ца; **~cloth** *n.* (*Br.*) полова́я тря́пка; **~ show** *n.* представле́ние в кабаре́.

flooring /ˈflɔːrɪŋ/ *n.* насти́л, пол.

flop /flɒp/ *n.* (*failure*) прова́л.
■ *v.i.* (**flopped, flopping**)
1 (*move limply*): **~ down in a chair** плю́х|аться, -нуться в кре́сло.
2 (*coll., fail*) прова́л|иваться, -и́ться.

floppy /ˈflɒpɪ/ *adj.* (**floppier, floppiest**) болта́ющийся, свиса́ющий; **~ disk** (*comput.*) дискéта, ги́бкий диск.

flora /ˈflɔːrə/ *n.* (*pl.* **floras** *or* **florae** /-riː/) фло́ра.

floral /ˈflɔːr(ə)l, ˈflɒ-/ *adj.* цвето́чный.

florid /ˈflɒrɪd/ *adj.* (*ornate*) цвети́стый, витиева́тый; (*ruddy*) кра́сный, багро́вый.

florist /ˈflɒrɪst/ *n.* продаве́ц цвето́в; (*fem.*) цвето́чница.

floss /flɒs/ *n.*: **dental ~** зубна́я нить.

flotation /fləʊˈteɪʃ(ə)n/ *n.* распрода́жа а́кций компа́нии.

flotilla /fləˈtɪlə/ *n.* флоти́лия (ме́лких судо́в).

flotsam /ˈflɒtsəm/ *n.* (вы́брошенный и) пла́вающий на пове́рхности груз, му́сор.

flounce[1] /flaʊns/ *v.i.* бр|оса́ться, -о́ситься; **~ out (of a room)** вылета́ть, вы́лететь из ко́мнаты.

flounce[2] /flaʊns/ *n.* (*trimming*) обо́рка.

flounder /ˈflaʊndə(r)/ *v.i.* бара́хтаться (*impf.*); (*fig.*) пу́таться в слова́х.

flour /ˈflaʊə(r)/ *n.* мука́.

flourish /ˈflʌrɪʃ/ *n.*
1 (*wave of hand etc.*) широ́кий жест.
2 (*literary embellishment*) цвети́стость.
■ *v.t.* разма́хивать (*impf.*) + *i.*
■ *v.i.* процвета́ть (*impf.*).

flourishing /ˈflʌrɪʃɪŋ/ *adj.* процвета́ющий, преуспева́ющий.

flout /flaʊt/ *v.t.* поп|ира́ть, -ра́ть.

flow /fləʊ/ *n.* тече́ние, пото́к; **in full ~** в разга́ре.
■ *v.i.* 1 течь, ли́ться (*both impf.*); **the Oka**

~s into the Volga Ока́ впада́ет в Во́лгу.
2 (*fig., move freely*) ли́ться, течь (*both impf.*).
■ *cpd.* **~ chart/diagram** *n.* блок-схе́ма.

flower /ˈflaʊə(r)/ *n.* цвето́к; цветко́вое расте́ние; **in ~** в цвету́; **~ arrangement** цвето́чная компози́ция.
■ *v.i.* (*blossom; flourish*) цвести́ (*impf.*).
■ *cpds.* **~ bed** *n.* клу́мба; **~pot** *n.* цвето́чный горшо́к.

flowery /ˈflaʊərɪ/ *adj.* покры́тый цвета́ми; (*fig.*) цвети́стый.

flown /fləʊn/ *p.p. of* ▸ **fly**[3]

flu /fluː/ *n.* (*coll.*) грипп.

fluctuate /ˈflʌktjʊeɪt/ *v.i.* колеба́ться (*impf.*).

fluctuation /flʌktjʊˈeɪʃ(ə)n/ *n.* колеба́ние.

flue /fluː/ *n.* дымохо́д.
■ *cpd.* **~ pipe** *n.* (*tech.*) жарова́я труба́.

fluency /ˈfluːənsɪ/ *n.* пла́вность, бе́глость.

fluent /ˈfluːənt/ *adj.* пла́вный, бе́глый; **he speaks Russian ~ly** он свобо́дно говори́т по-ру́сски.

fluff /flʌf/ *n.* пух, пушо́к.
■ *v.t.* 1 (*make fluffy*) взби|ва́ть, -ть.
2 (*coll., bungle*) пу́тать, с-; **~ one's lines** заб|ыва́ть, -ы́ть свои́ слова́.

fluffy /ˈflʌfɪ/ *adj.* (**fluffier, fluffiest**) пуши́стый.

fluid /ˈfluːɪd/ *n.* жи́дкость.
■ *adj.* жи́дкий, теку́чий; (*fig.*) неопределённый, переме́нчивый; **~ ounce** жи́дкая у́нция.

fluidity /fluːˈɪdɪtɪ/ *n.* теку́честь; (*fig.*) переме́нчивость, неопределённость.

fluke /fluːk/ *n.* (*lucky stroke*) (неожи́данная) уда́ча, случа́йность.

flung /flʌŋ/ *past and p.p. of* ▸ **fling**

fluorescent /flʊəˈres(ə)nt/ *adj.* флюоресци́рующий.

fluoride /ˈflʊəraɪd/ *n.* фтори́д.

flurry /ˈflʌrɪ/ *n.* (*gust*) шквал; (*agitation*) волне́ние, сумато́ха.

flush /flʌʃ/ *n.* (*flow of water*) внеза́пный прили́в; (*blush*) прили́в кро́ви.
■ *v.t.* 1 (*swill clean*) пром|ыва́ть, -ы́ть; **~ the lavatory** спус|ка́ть, -ти́ть во́ду в убо́рной.
2 (*make red*) зал|ива́ть, -и́ть кра́ской.
■ *v.i.* красне́ть, по-.

fluster /ˈflʌstə(r)/ *v.t.* волнова́ть, вз-; будора́жить, вз-.

flute /fluːt/ *n.* (*instrument*) фле́йта.

flutter /ˈflʌtə(r)/ *n.* трепета́ние, дрожь.
■ *v.t.* мах|а́ть, -ну́ть + *i.*
■ *v.i.* трепета́ть (*impf.*); (*of birds*) переп|а́рхивать, -орхну́ть.

flux /flʌks/ *n.* постоя́нная сме́на; **everything was in a state of ~** всё находи́лось в состоя́нии непреры́вного измене́ния.

fly[1] /flaɪ/ *n.* му́ха.
■ *cpd.* **~ spray** *n.* (*fluid*) жи́дкость от мух; (*instrument*) аэрозо́ль (*m.*) от мух.

fly[2] /flaɪ/ *n.* (*on trousers*) ши́ринка.

fly[3] /flaɪ/ *v.t.* (*past* **flew;** *p.p.* **flown**): **~ an aircraft** управля́ть (*impf.*) самолётом; **~ home the wounded** дост|авля́ть, -а́вить ра́неных в тыл самолётом.
■ *v.i.* (*past* **flew;** *p.p.* **flown**)
1 (*move through the air*) лета́ть (*indet.*), лете́ть (*det.*), по-; **he has never flown** он никогда́ не лета́л.
2 (*move swiftly*): **I must ~!** ну, я побежа́л!; **he flew downstairs** он ку́барем скати́лся с ле́стницы; **~ into a passion** вспыли́ть (*pf.*); **~ off the handle** (*coll.*) сорва́ться (*pf.*); **send ~ing** швыр|я́ть, -ну́ть; (*of person*) сби|ва́ть, -ть с ног; **time flies** вре́мя лети́т.
■ *with advs.*: **leaves were ~ing about** повсю́ду кружи́лись ли́стья; **~ away** улет|а́ть, -е́ть; **the plane flew in to refuel and flew off again** самолёт прилете́л на запра́вку и вновь/сно́ва улете́л.
■ *cpds.* **~-by-night** *n.* ненадёжный челове́к; **~over** *n.* (*Br., bridge, overpass*) эстака́да; путепрово́д.

flyer /ˈflaɪə(r)/ *n.* (*handbill*) рекла́мный листо́к.

flying /ˈflaɪɪŋ/ *n.* полёт; **he likes ~** он лю́бит лета́ть; **~ visit** блицвизи́т; кра́ткое посеще́ние.
■ *adj.*: **pass with ~ colours** пройти́, сдать (*both pf.*) с бле́ском; **~ saucer** лета́ющая таре́лка; **get off to a ~ start** сра́зу пойти́ (*pf.*) хорошо́ (*or* в го́ру).

foal /fəʊl/ *n.* жеребёнок.

foam /fəʊm/ *n.* пе́на; **~ rubber** по́ристая рези́на.
■ *v.i.* пе́ниться (*impf.*); **he was ~ing at the mouth** (*fig, coll.*) он весь кипе́л от зло́сти.

fob /fɒb/ *v.t.* (**fobbed, fobbing**): **~ s.o. off with promises** корми́ть (*impf.*) кого́-н. обеща́ниями.

focal /ˈfəʊk(ə)l/ *adj.*: **~ point** фока́льная то́чка; (*fig.*): **the ~ point in his argument** гла́вный пункт его́ доказа́тельств.

foci /ˈfəʊsaɪ/ *pl. of* ▸ **focus**

focus /ˈfəʊkəs/ *n.* (*pl.* **focuses** *or* **foci** /-saɪ/) (*math., phys., phot.*) фо́кус; **out of ~** не в фо́кусе; (*fig.*) центр, средото́чие; **he became the ~ of interest** он оказа́лся в це́нтре внима́ния.
■ *v.t.* (**focused, focusing** *or* **focussed, focussing**) (*binoculars, camera*) настр|а́ивать, -о́ить; (*rays*) фокуси́ровать, с-; (*attention*) сосредо|та́чивать, -то́чить.
■ *cpd.* **~ group** *n.* фо́кус-гру́ппа.

fodder /ˈfɒdə(r)/ *n.* корм для скота́.

foe /fəʊ/ *n.* враг, не́друг.

foet|al /ˈfiːt(ə)l/, **-us** /ˈfiːt(ə)s/ (*Br.*) = **fet|al, -us**

fog /fɒg/ *n.* тума́н.
■ *v.t.* (**fogged, fogging**) (*fig.*): **the windows are ~ged up** о́кна запоте́ли.
■ *cpds.* **~horn** *n.* тума́нный горн, тума́нная сире́на; **~ lamp/light** *n.* противотума́нная фа́ра.

fog(e)y /ˈfəʊgɪ/ *n.* (*pl.* **fogeys** *or* **fogies**) старомо́дный/отста́лый челове́к.

fogg|y /ˈfɒgɪ/ *adj.* (**foggier, foggiest**) тума́нный.

foible /ˈfɔɪb(ə)l/ *n.* сла́бость; сла́бая стру́нка.

foil[1] /fɔɪl/ *n.* (*thin metal*) фольга́, стани́оль (*m.*).

foil[2] /fɔɪl/ *v.t.* сби|ва́ть, -ть со сле́да.

foist /fɔɪst/ *v.t.* навя́з|ывать, -а́ть (*что кому*).

fold[1] /fəʊld/ *n.* скла́дка; **the ~s of a dress** скла́дки пла́тья.
■ *v.t.* скла́дывать, сложи́ть; св|ёртывать (*or*

-ора́чивать), -ерну́ть; **~ one's arms** скре́|щивать, -сти́ть ру́ки на груди́.
■ *v.i.* скла́дываться, сложи́ться; (*fig.*): **the play ~ed after a week** пье́са сошла́ со сце́ны че́рез неде́лю; **their business ~ed** они́ сверну́ли де́ло.

fold² /fəʊld/ *n.* (*for sheep*) заго́н; **return to the ~** (*fig.*) верну́ться (*pf.*) в ло́но (*церкви и т. п.*).

folder /ˈfəʊldə(r)/ *n.* (*container for papers*) скоросшива́тель (*m.*); (*also comput.*) па́пка.

folding /ˈfəʊldɪŋ/ *adj.* складно́й.

foliage /ˈfəʊlɪɪdʒ/ *n.* листва́.

folk /fəʊk/ *n.* (*pl.* **folk** *or* **folks**) наро́д, лю́д|и (*pl.*, *g.* -е́й).

folklore /ˈfəʊklɔ:(r)/ *n.* фолькло́р.

follow /ˈfɒləʊ/ *v.t.* & *i.*
1 (*proceed or happen after*) сле́довать, по- за + *i.*; **he ~ed (in) his father's footsteps** он пошёл по стопа́м отца́; **as ~s** сле́дующим о́бразом; как сле́дует ни́же; **his plan was as ~s** его́ план был тако́в.
2 (*as inference*) сле́довать (*impf.*) из + *g.*; **it does not ~ that ...** э́то во́все не зна́чит, что... .
3 (*pursue*) следи́ть (*impf.*) за + *i.*; **don't look now, we're being ~ed** не огля́дывайтесь, за на́ми следя́т.
4 (*keep to*) приде́рживаться (*impf.*) + *g.*; (*fig.*, *be guided by*): **~ s.o.'s advice/example** сле́довать, по- чьему́-н. сове́ту/приме́ру.
5 (*fig.*, *keep track of*): **I don't ~ you** я вас не понима́ю; **~ the news in the papers** следи́ть (*impf.*) за новостя́ми в газе́тах.
■ *with advs.*: **~ through** *v.t.* & *i.* сле́довать (*impf.*) (за + *i.*) до конца́; **~ up** *v.t.* (*look into*) раз|бира́ть, -обра́ть; **~ up a suggestion** уч|и́тывать, -е́сть чьё-н. предложе́ние.
■ *cpd.* **~-up** *n.* продолже́ние; (*med.*) контро́ль (*m.*).

follower /ˈfɒləʊwə(r)/ *n.* после́дователь (*m.*) (*fem.* -ница); сторо́нни|к (*fem.* -ца).

following /ˈfɒləʊwɪŋ/ *n.* после́дователи (*m. pl.*); приве́рженцы (*m. pl.*).
■ *adj.* (*ensuing*) сле́дующий; **(on) the ~ day** на сле́дующий день; (*about to be specified*): **we shall need the ~** нам потре́буется сле́дующее.

folly /ˈfɒlɪ/ *n.* глу́пость.

foment /fəˈment/ *v.t.* (*hatred etc.*) подстрек|а́ть, -ну́ть.

fond /fɒnd/ *adj.*
1 (*pred.*, *with* **of**): **he became ~ of her** он привяза́лся к ней; **are you ~ of music?** вы лю́бите му́зыку?
2 (*loving*) не́жный, лю́бящий; **~ memories** прия́тные/до́брые воспомина́ния.

fondle /ˈfɒnd(ə)l/ *v.t.* ласка́ть (*impf.*).

font /fɒnt/ *n.* (*eccl.*) купе́ль.

food /fu:d/ *n.* пи́ща, пита́ние; еда́; (*fig.*): **~ for thought** пи́ща для размышле́ний.
■ *cpds.* **~ poisoning** *n.* пищево́е отравле́ние; **~ processor** *n.* ку́хонный комба́йн; **~stuff** *n.* пищево́й проду́кт.

fool /fu:l/ *n.* (*simpleton*) дура́к, глупе́ц; (*jester*) шут; **play the ~** дура́читься (*impf.*); валя́ть (*impf.*) дурака́; **make a ~ (out) of s.o.** дура́чить, о- кого́-н.
■ *v.t.* (*deceive*) одура́чи|вать, -ть.
■ *v.i.*: **~ about, around** валя́ть (*impf.*) дурака́.
■ *cpd.* **~proof** *adj.* (*reliable*) безотка́зный, ве́рный.

foolhardy /ˈfu:lhɑ:dɪ/ *adj.* (**foolhardier, foolhardiest**) безрассу́дно хра́брый.

foolish /ˈfu:lɪʃ/ *adj.* глу́пый; дура́цкий.

foolishness /ˈfu:lɪʃnɪs/ *n.* глу́пость.

foot /fʊt/ *n.* (*pl.* **feet**)
1 (*extremity of leg*) ступня́, нога́; стопа́ ноги́; (*lowest part, bottom*): **at the ~ of the hill** у подно́жия холма́; **at the ~ of the page** в конце́ страни́цы; **at the ~ of the stairs** внизу́ ле́стницы; **at the ~ of the bed** в нога́х крова́ти.
2 (*unit of length*) фут; **six ~ (or feet) tall** шести́ фу́тов ро́стом.
■ *phrr.*: **we came here on ~** мы пришли́ сюда́ пешко́м; **put one's ~ down** (*fig.*) зан|има́ть, -я́ть твёрдую/реши́тельную пози́цию; **put one's ~ in it** (*fig.*) дать (*pf.*) ма́ху; **stand on one's own (two) feet** стоя́ть (*impf.*) на нога́х; быть самостоя́тельным.
■ *v.t.*: **~ the bill** опла́|чивать, -ти́ть счёт.
■ *cpds.* **~-and-mouth disease** *n.* я́щур; **~ball** *n.* (*Br.*) футбо́л; (*US*) америка́нский футбо́л; **~bridge** *n.* пешехо́дный мо́стик; **~hold** *n.* то́чка опо́ры; **~lights** *n. pl.* ра́мпа (*sg.*); **~note** *n.* сно́ска; **~path** *n.* тропа́, тропи́нка; **~print** *n.* след ноги́; **~step** *n.* шаг, по́ступь; **~stool** *n.* скаме́ечка для ног; **~wear** *n.* о́бувь.

footage /ˈfʊtɪdʒ/ *n.* киноматериа́л.

footer /ˈfʊtə(r)/ *n.* (*line of text*) ни́жний колонти́тул.

footing /ˈfʊtɪŋ/ *n.* (*foothold*) опо́ра для ног(и́); **lose one's ~** оступи́ться (*pf.*); (*fig.*) потеря́ть (*pf.*) по́чву под нога́ми; **on an equal ~** на ра́вной ноге́.

for /fɔ:(r)/ *prep.*
1 (*with the object or purpose of*) для + *g.*; ра́ди + *g.*; **~ example** наприме́р; **they have gone ~ a walk** они́ пошли́ гуля́ть; (*destination*) на + *a.*; к + *d.*; **the train ~ Moscow** по́езд на Москву́; (*aspiration*): **prospecting ~ oil** разве́дка нефтяны́х месторожде́ний.
2 (*denoting reason; on account of*) ра́ди + *g.*, для + *g.*; **he is known ~ his generosity** он изве́стен свое́й ще́дростью; (*accorded to*): **the penalty ~ treason is death** наказа́ние за госуда́рственную изме́ну — сме́ртная казнь; (*on the occasion of*): **I gave him a book ~ his birthday** я подари́л ему́ кни́гу на день рожде́ния; **he went abroad ~ his holidays** в о́тпуск он пое́хал за грани́цу.
3 (*representative of*): **A ~ Anna** «А» как в сло́ве «А́нна»; (*in support; in favour of*): **a vote ~ freedom** го́лос за свобо́ду; (*denoting purpose*): **they need premises ~ a school** им ну́жно помеще́ние под шко́лу; **ready ~ departure** гото́в(ый) к отъе́зду; (*on behalf of*) за + *a.*, от + *g.*; **speak ~ yourself!** говори́те за себя́!
4 (*denoting intended recipient*): **there is a letter ~ you** вам письмо́.
5 (*denoting duration or extent*): **~ a long time** на до́лгое вре́мя; в тече́ние до́лгого вре́мени; **I haven't seen him ~ (some)**

days я не ви́дел его́ не́сколько дней; **there is no house ~ miles** на мно́го киломе́тров вокру́г нет ни еди́ного до́ма; (*intended duration*): **~ ever and ever** навсегда́, на ве́ки ве́чные; **they are going away ~ a few days** они́ уезжа́ют на не́сколько дней.
6 (*denoting relationship*; *in respect of*): **as ~ me, myself** что каса́ется меня́; **luckily ~ her** на её сча́стье, к сча́стью для неё; (*in relation to what is normal or suitable*): **warm ~ the time of year** тепло́ для э́того вре́мени го́да; **it's cold enough ~ snow** хо́лодно — того́ и гляди́ пойдёт снег; **not bad ~ a beginner** непло́хо для новичка́.
7 (*in return ~*, *instead of*): **get something ~ nothing** получ|а́ть, -и́ть что-н. да́ром; **once (and) ~ all** раз и навсегда́.
8 (*despite*): **~ all that, I still love him** но несмотря́ на всё, я его́ люблю́.
9 (*with certain expressions of time*): **~ the first time** в пе́рвый раз; **the wedding is arranged ~ June the 1st** сва́дьба назна́чена на пе́рвое ию́ня.

forage /ˈfɒrɪdʒ/ *n.* фура́ж, корм.
■ *v.i.* (*search*) разы́скивать (*impf.*).
■ *cpd.* **~ cap** *n.* фура́жка.

foray /ˈfɒreɪ/ *n.* набе́г.

forbade /fəˈbæd, fəˈbeɪd/, **forbad** /fəˈbæd/ *past of* ▸ **forbid**

forbearance /fɔːˈbeərəns/ *n.* возде́ржанность, терпели́вость, терпе́ние.

forbid /fəˈbɪd/ *v.t.* (**forbidding;** *past* **forbade** *or* **forbad;** *p.p.* **forbidden**) запре|ща́ть, -ти́ть (*кому что*).

forbidden /fəˈbɪd(ə)n/ *adj.* запрещённый, запре́тный.

forbidding /fəˈbɪdɪŋ/ *adj.* (*unfriendly*) неприя́зненный; (*threatening*) гро́зный.

force /fɔːs/ *n.*
1 (*strength*: *lit.*, *fig.*) си́ла; **use ~** приб|ега́ть, -е́гнуть к си́ле; **in full ~** в по́лном соста́ве; **by ~** си́лой, наси́льно.
2 (*body of men, usu. armed*) вооружённый отря́д; **(Police) F~** поли́ция; (*pl.*): **the (Armed) F~s** а́рмия, вооружённые си́лы.
3 (*binding power, validity*) де́йственность; **in ~** (*of law etc.*) в си́ле.
4 (*phys.*) си́ла.
■ *v.t.* 1 (*compel, constrain*) заст|авля́ть, -а́вить; **he was ~ed to sell the house** он был вы́нужден прода́ть дом; **~d** (*laugh etc.*) принуждённый.
2 (*apply ~ to*): **~ (open) the door** выла́мывать, вы́ломать дверь.
■ *cpd.* **~-feed** *v.t.* корми́ть (*impf.*) наси́льно.

forceful /ˈfɔːsfʊl/ *adj.* си́льный, убеди́тельный.

forceps /ˈfɔːseps/ *n.* (*pl.* ~) хирурги́ческие щипц|ы́ (*pl.*, *g.* -о́в).

forcible /ˈfɔːsɪb(ə)l/ *adj.* наси́льственный; (*forceful*) убеди́тельный; **~ entry** наси́льственное вторже́ние.

ford /fɔːd/ *n.* брод.
■ *v.t.* пере|ходи́ть, -йти́ вброд.

fore /fɔː(r)/ *n.*: **come to the ~** выдвига́ться, вы́двинуться.
■ *adj.* (*as pref.*) пред... .

forearm /ˈfɔːrɑːm/ *n.* предпле́чье.

foreboding /fɔːˈbəʊdɪŋ/ *n.* дурно́е предчу́вствие.

forecast /ˈfɔːkɑːst/ *n.* предсказа́ние; (*also* **weather ~**) прогно́з пого́ды.
■ *v.t.* (*past and p.p.* **~** *or* **~ed**) предска́з|ывать, -а́ть.

forecaster /ˈfɔːkɑːstə(r)/ *n.*: **weather ~** сино́птик.

forecourt /ˈfɔːkɔːt/ *n.* пере́дний двор.

forefather /ˈfɔːfɑːðə(r)/ *n.* пре́док, пра́отец.

forefinger /ˈfɔːfɪŋgə(r)/ *n.* указа́тельный па́лец.

forefront /ˈfɔːfrʌnt/ *n.* аванга́рд; **in the ~ of the battle** на передово́й (ли́нии).

forego /fɔːˈgəʊ/ *v.i.*: **a ~ne conclusion** предрешённый исхо́д.

foreground /ˈfɔːgraʊnd/ *n.* (*lit.*, *fig.*) пере́дний план.

forehand /ˈfɔːhænd/ *adj.* (*tennis*): **~ stroke** уда́р спра́ва.

forehead /ˈfɒrɪd, ˈfɔːhed/ *n.* лоб.

foreign /ˈfɒrən/ *adj.*
1 (*of or pertaining to another country or countries*) иностра́нный, заграни́чный; **~ affairs** междунаро́дные отноше́ния; **F~ Secretary** (*Br.*) мини́стр иностра́нных дел; **~ trade** вне́шняя торго́вля.
2 (*alien*) чужо́й, чу́ждый.

foreigner /ˈfɒrənə(r)/ *n.* иностра́н|ец (*fem.* -ка).

foreleg /ˈfɔːleg/ *n.* пере́дняя ла́па/нога́.

foreman /ˈfɔːmən/ *n.* ма́стер, деся́тник; **~ of the jury** старшина́ (*m.*) присяжных.

foremost /ˈfɔːməʊst/ *adj.* са́мый пере́дний.
■ *adv.*: **first and ~** пре́жде всего́; в пе́рвую о́чередь.

forename /ˈfɔːneɪm/ *n.* и́мя (*nt.*) (*в отличие от фамилии*).

forensic /fəˈrensɪk/ *adj.* суде́бный; **~ expert, scientist** суде́бно-медици́нский экспе́рт.

foreplay /ˈfɔːpleɪ/ *n.* предвари́тельные ла́ски, прелю́дия (*перед половым актом*).

forerunner /ˈfɔːrʌnə(r)/ *n.* предше́ственни|к (*fem.* -ца).

foresee /fɔːˈsiː/ *v.t.* предви́деть (*impf.*).

foreseeable /fɔːˈsiːəb(ə)l/ *adj.*: **in the ~ future** в обозри́мом бу́дущем.

foreshadow /fɔːˈʃædəʊ/ *v.t.* предвеща́ть (*impf.*).

foreshore /ˈfɔːʃɔː(r)/ *n.* берегова́я полоса́, затопля́емая прили́вом.

foresight /ˈfɔːsaɪt/ *n.* предусмотри́тельность.

foreskin /ˈfɔːskɪn/ *n.* кра́йняя плоть.

forest /ˈfɒrɪst/ *n.* лес.

forestall /fɔːˈstɔːl/ *v.t.* предвосх|ища́ть, -и́тить; опере|жа́ть, -ди́ть; предупре|жда́ть, -ди́ть.

forester /ˈfɒrɪstə(r)/ *n.* лесни́к.

forestry /ˈfɒrɪstrɪ/ *n.* лесово́дство.

foretaste /ˈfɔːteɪst/ *n.* предвкуше́ние.

foretell /fɔːˈtel/ *v.t.* предска́з|ывать, -а́ть.

forethought /ˈfɔːθɔːt/ *n.* предусмотри́тельность.

forever /fəˈrevə(r)/ *adv.* навсегда́, наве́чно; (*continually*) постоя́нно, ве́чно.

forewarn /fɔːˈwɔːn/ *v.t.* предупре|жда́ть, -ди́ть.

foreword /ˈfɔːwəːd/ *n.* предисло́вие.

forfeit /ˈfɔːfɪt/ *n.* (*penalty*) штраф, конфиска́ция.
■ *v.t.* (**forfeited, forfeiting**) теря́ть, по- (пра́во на) + *a.*

forgave /fəˈgeɪv/ *past of* ▸ **forgive**

forge /fɔːdʒ/ *n.* (*workshop*) ку́зница.
■ *v.t. & i.*
1 (*shape metal*) кова́ть (*impf.*).
2 (*fabricate*) изобре|та́ть, -сти́; (*counterfeit*) подде́л|ывать, -ать.
3 : **~ ahead** вырыва́ться, вы́рваться вперёд.

forger /ˈfɔːdʒə(r)/ *n.* подде́лыватель (*m.*); фальсифика́тор; (*of money*) фальшивомоне́тчик.

forgery /ˈfɔːdʒərɪ/ *n.* подде́лка.

forget /fəˈget/ *v.t. & i.* (**forgetting;** *past* **forgot;** *p.p.* **forgotten** *or esp. US* **forgot**) заб|ыва́ть, -ы́ть; **I forgot all about the lecture** я соверше́нно забы́л о ле́кции.
■ *cpd.* **~-me-not** *n.* (*bot.*) незабу́дка.

forgetful /fəˈgetfʊl/ *adj.* забы́вчивый.

forgivable /fəˈgɪvəb(ə)l/ *adj.* прости́тельный.

forgive /fəˈgɪv/ *v.t. & i.* (*past* **forgave;** *p.p.* **forgiven**) про|ща́ть, -сти́ть; **I ~ you for everything** я вам всё проща́ю.

forgiveness /fəˈgɪvnɪs/ *n.* проще́ние.

forgo /fɔːˈgəʊ/ *v.t.* (**forgoes** /-ˈgəʊz/; *past* **forwent;** *p.p.* **forgone** /-ˈgɒn/) отка́з|ываться, -а́ться от + *g.*

forgot /fəˈgɒt/ *past and esp. US p.p. of* ▸ **forget**

forgotten /fəˈgɒt(ə)n/ *p.p. of* ▸ **forget**

fork /fɔːk/ *n.*
1 (*for cul. use*) ви́лка.
2 (*agric.*) ви́лы (*f. pl.*).
3 (*bifurcation*) разви́лка.
■ *v.i.* (*bifurcate*) раздв|а́иваться, -ои́ться; **~ out** (*sl., provide money*) отва́л|ивать, -и́ть; раскоше́ли|ваться, -ться (**for:** на + *a.*).
■ *cpd.* **~lift** *n.* (*in full* **~lift truck**) автопогру́зчик.

forked /fɔːkt/ *adj.*: **~ lightning** зигзагообра́зная мо́лния.

forlorn /fɔːˈlɔːn/ *adj.* забро́шенный.

form /fɔːm/ *n.*
1 (*shape*) фо́рма, вид; (*figure*) фигу́ра.
2 (*kind, variant*) вид, фо́рма.
3 (*of health*) состоя́ние; **in good ~** в хоро́шей фо́рме; (*of spirits*): **he appeared in great ~** он был в отли́чной фо́рме.
4 (*document*) бланк, анке́та.
5 (*Br., class in school*) класс.
■ *v.t.* 1 (*fashion*) формирова́ть, с-; **he ~ed the clay into a vase** гли́на под его́ рука́ми преврати́лась в ва́зу; (*by discipline, training etc.*) тренирова́ть, на-; **his character was ~ed at school** его́ хара́ктер сформирова́лся в шко́ле.
2 (*organize, create*) организ|о́вывать, -ова́ть; **they ~ed an alliance** они́ со́здали/образова́ли сою́з; **he was unable to ~ a government** он не смог сформирова́ть прави́тельство.
3 (*conceive*): **they ~ed a plan** они́ вы́работали план.
4 (*mil. etc.*) стро́ить, по-; **~ a queue** (*Br.*), **line** (*US*) образ|о́вывать, -ова́ть о́чередь.
5 (*constitute*) сост|авля́ть, -а́вить; **this ~s the basis of our discussion** э́то составля́ет осно́ву на́шей диску́ссии.
■ *v.i.* (*take shape, appear*): **ice ~ed on the window** на окне́ образова́лся/возни́к моро́зный узо́р; **an idea ~ed in his mind** в его́ мозгу́ возни́кла иде́я.

formal /ˈfɔːm(ə)l/ *adj.* официа́льный.

formality /fɔːˈmælɪtɪ/ *n.* форма́льность.

formalize /ˈfɔːməlaɪz/ *v.t.* оф|ормля́ть, -о́рмить.

format /ˈfɔːmæt/ *n.* (*also comput.*) форма́т.
■ *v.t.* (*comput.*) формати́ровать, от-.

formation /fɔːˈmeɪʃ(ə)n/ *n.* образова́ние, формирова́ние.

formative /ˈfɔːmətɪv/ *adj.* формиру́ющий, образу́ющий; **he spent his ~ years in France** го́ды, когда́ скла́дывался/формирова́лся его́ хара́ктер, он провёл во Фра́нции.

former /ˈfɔːmə(r)/ *adj.*
1 (*earlier*) предше́ствующий; **my ~ husband** мой бы́вший муж.
2 (*first mentioned of two*) пе́рвый.

formerly /ˈfɔːməlɪ/ *adv.* пре́жде, ра́ньше.

formidable /ˈfɔːmɪdəb(ə)l/ *adj.* (*frightening*) устраша́ющий, гро́зный; (*huge*) огро́мный.

formless /ˈfɔːmlɪs/ *adj.* бесфо́рменный.

formula /ˈfɔːmjʊlə/ *n.* (*pl.* **formulas** *or* **formulae** /-liː/) (*math., chem.*) фо́рмула.

formulate /ˈfɔːmjʊleɪt/ *v.t.* формули́ровать, с-.

fornicate /ˈfɔːnɪkeɪt/ *v.i.* развра́тничать (*impf.*); вести́ (*det.*) распу́тную жизнь.

forsake /fɔːˈseɪk/ *v.t.* (*past* **forsook** /-ˈsʊk/; *p.p.* **forsaken** /-ˈseɪk(ə)n/) пок|ида́ть, -и́нуть; ост|авля́ть, -а́вить; бр|оса́ть, -о́сить.

fort /fɔːt/ *n.* форт.

forte /ˈfɔːteɪ/ *n.* (*strong point*) си́льная сторона́.

forth /fɔːθ/ *adv.* вперёд, да́льше; **and so ~** и так да́лее; **from this day ~** с э́того дня; впредь.

forthcoming /fɔːθˈkʌmɪŋ/ *adj.* предстоя́щий; **the clerk was not very ~ with information** чино́вник не о́чень охо́тно дава́л све́дения.

forthright /ˈfɔːθraɪt/ *adj.* прямо́й, прямолине́йный.

fortieth /ˈfɔːtɪɪθ/ *n.* (*fraction*) одна́ сорокова́я.
■ *adj.* сороково́й.

fortification /fɔːtɪfɪˈkeɪʃ(ə)n/ *n.* укрепле́ние.

fortif|y /ˈfɔːtɪfaɪ/ *v.t.* укреп|ля́ть, -и́ть; **~ied wines** креплёные ви́на.

fortitude /ˈfɔːtɪtjuːd/ *n.* сто́йкость; си́ла ду́ха.

fortnight /ˈfɔːtnaɪt/ (*Br.*) *n.* две неде́ли.

fortnightly /ˈfɔːtnaɪtlɪ/ *adj.* двухнеде́льный.
■ *adv.* раз в две неде́ли.

fortress /ˈfɔːtrɪs/ *n.* кре́пость.

fortuitous /fɔːˈtjuːɪtəs/ *adj.* случа́йный.

fortunate /ˈfɔːtʃənət/ *adj.* счастли́вый, уда́чный; **~ly** к сча́стью.

fortune /ˈfɔːtʃuːn/ *n.*
1 (*chance*) уда́ча, сча́стье, форту́на; **by good ~** по сча́стью.
2 (*fate*) судьба́; **the Gypsy (woman) told**

my ~ цыга́нка (по/на)гада́ла мне.
[3] (*large sum*) состоя́ние, бога́тство; **make a ~** разбогате́ть (*pf.*).
■ *cpd.* **~-teller** *n.* гада́лка, ворожея́.
fort|y /'fɔːtɪ/ *n.* со́рок; **the ~ies** (*decade*) сороковы́е го́ды (*m. pl.*); **they are both in their ~ies** (*age*) им обо́им за со́рок.
■ *adj.* сорок + *g. pl.*
forward /'fɔːwəd/ *n.* (*sport*) напада́ющий.
■ *adj.* (*situated to the fore*) пере́дний; (*progressive*) прогресси́вный; (*pert*) нагловáтый, развя́зный.
■ *adv.* (*onward; towards one*) вперёд; **please come ~** пожа́луйста, вы́йдите вперёд; **the meeting has been brought ~ a day** собра́ние перенесли́ на́ день ра́ньше; (*towards the future*): **I look ~ to meeting her** я с нетерпе́нием жду встре́чи с ней.
■ *v.t.* (*send*) пос|ыла́ть, -ла́ть; отпр|авля́ть, -а́вить; (*send on*) перес|ыла́ть, -ла́ть.
■ *cpd.* **~ slash** *n.* коса́я черта́, слеш.
forwards /'fɔːwədz/ *adv.* вперёд.
forwent /fɔː'went/ *past of* ▸ **forgo**
fossil /'fɒs(ə)l/ *n.* окамене́лость.
foster /'fɒstə(r)/ *v.t.* (*Br., assign to someone else to rear*) отд|ава́ть, -а́ть на воспита́ние; (*fig.*) (*hope*) пита́ть (*impf.*); (*hatred*) се́ять, по-.
■ *cpds.* **~-child** *n.* приёмный ребёнок, воспи́танник; **~-father** *n.* приёмный оте́ц; **~-mother** *n.* приёмная мать.
fought /fɔːt/ *past and p.p. of* ▸ **fight**
foul /faʊl/ *n.* (*sport*) наруше́ние (пра́вил игры́).
■ *adj.* гря́зный, отврати́тельный; **a ~ smell** злово́ние; **~ language** скверносло́вие, ру́гань; **~ weather** отврати́тельная пого́да; непого́да; **~ play** (*sport*) гру́бая игра́; (*violence*) нечи́стое де́ло.
■ *v.t.* (*defile*) загрязн|я́ть, -и́ть; па́чкать, за-; засор|я́ть, -и́ть; (*obstruct*) образо́в|ывать, -а́ть зато́р в + *p.*
■ *cpds.* **~-mouthed** *adj.* сквернoсло́вящий.
found[1] /faʊnd/ *v.t.* осно́в|ывать, -а́ть; за|кла́дывать, -ложи́ть; (*base*) осно́в|ывать, -а́ть.
found[2] /faʊnd/ *past and p.p. of* ▸ **find**
foundation /faʊn'deɪʃ(ə)n/ *n.*
[1] (*establishing*) основа́ние, учрежде́ние.
[2] (*base of building etc.*) фунда́мент; (*fig.*) осно́ва.
[3] : **~ cream** крем под пу́дру.
founder /'faʊndə(r)/ *n.* основа́тель (*m.*) (*fem.* -ница).
foundry /'faʊndrɪ/ *n.* лите́йная.
fountain /'faʊntɪn/ *n.* фонта́н.
■ *cpd.* **~ pen** *n.* автору́чка.
four /fɔː(r)/ *n.* (число́/но́мер) четы́ре; (**~** *people*) че́тверо; (*figure; thing numbered 4; group of* **~**) четвёрка; **he got down on all ~s** он опусти́лся на четвере́ньки.
■ *adj.* четы́ре + *g. sg.*
■ *cpds.* **~-letter** *adj.*: **~-letter word** (*fig.*) руга́тельство; непристо́йное сло́во; **~-wheel** *adj.*: **~-wheel drive** (*attr.*) с при́водом на четы́ре колеса́; (*n.*) внедоро́жник, вездехо́д.
fourteen /fɔː'tiːn/ *n.* & *adj.* четы́рнадцать (+ *g. pl.*).
fourteenth /fɔː'tiːnθ/ *n.* (*date*) четы́рнадцатое (число́); (*fraction*) одна́ четы́рнадцатая.
■ *adj.* четы́рнадцатый.
fourth /fɔːθ/ *n.*
[1] (*date*) четвёртое (число́).
[2] (*fraction*) одна́ четвёртая.
■ *adj.* четвёртый.
fowl /faʊl/ *n.* (*pl.* **~** *or* **~s**) (*domestic*) дома́шняя пти́ца.
fox /fɒks/ *n.* лиса́, лиси́ца.
■ *cpds.* **~hound** *n.* го́нчая; **~-hunting** *n.* (верхова́я) охо́та на лис.
foyer /'fɔɪeɪ/ *n.* фойе́ (*nt. indecl.*).
fraction /'frækʃ(ə)n/ *n.* дробь.
fractious /'frækʃəs/ *adj.* капри́зный.
fracture /'fræktʃə(r)/ *n.* (*of a bone*) перело́м.
■ *v.t.* & *i.* лома́ть(ся), с-.
fragile /'frædʒaɪl/ *adj.* хру́пкий.
fragility /frə'dʒɪlɪtɪ/ *n.* ло́мкость, хру́пкость.
fragment /'frægmənt/ *n.* обло́мок, оско́лок; (*of writing*) фрагме́нт.
fragmentary /'frægməntərɪ/ *adj.* отры́вочный, фрагмента́рный.
fragmentation /frægmən'teɪʃ(ə)n/ *n.* разры́в на ме́лкие ча́сти; **~ bomb** оско́лочная бо́мба.
fragrance /'freɪgrəns/ *n.* арома́т.
fragrant /'freɪgrənt/ *adj.* арома́тный.
frail /freɪl/ *adj.* хру́пкий.
frame /freɪm/ *n.*
[1] (*structural skeleton*) скеле́т, костя́к.
[2] (*wood or metal surround*) ра́ма, ра́мка.
[3] : **~ of mind** настрое́ние; расположе́ние ду́ха.
[4] (*cin.*) кадр.
■ *v.t.* [1] (*compose*) сост|авля́ть, -а́вить; созд|ава́ть, -а́ть.
[2] (*surround*): **~ a picture** вст|авля́ть, -а́вить карти́ну в ра́м(к)у.
■ *cpd.* **~work** *n.* карка́с, о́стов; (*fig.*): **within the ~work of the constitution** в ра́мках конститу́ции.
franc /fræŋk/ *n.* франк.
France /frɑːns/ *n.* Фра́нция.
franchise /'fræntʃaɪz/ *n.* (*right of voting*) пра́во го́лоса; (*comm.*) привиле́гия, франши́за.
frank /fræŋk/ *adj.* открове́нный, и́скренний.
frankfurter /'fræŋkfəːtə(r)/ *n.* соси́ска (*копчёная*).
frantic /'fræntɪk/ *adj.* неи́стовый, безу́мный; **she became ~ with grief** она́ обезу́мела от го́ря.
fraternal /frə'təːn(ə)l/ *adj.* бра́тский.
fraternity /frə'təːnɪtɪ/ *n.* бра́тство.
fraternize /'frætənaɪz/ *v.i.* брата́ться (*impf.*).
fraud /frɔːd/ *n.* (*fraudulent act*) обма́н, моше́нничество; (*impostor*) обма́нщик, моше́нник.
fraudulent /'frɔːdjʊlənt/ *adj.* обма́нный, фальши́вый, моше́ннический.
fraught /frɔːt/ *adj.* по́лный; **the expedition is ~ with danger** экспеди́ция чрева́та опа́сностями; (*tense*) напряжённый.
fray /freɪ/ *v.t.* & *i.* прот|ира́ть(ся), -ере́ть(ся).
frazzle /'fræz(ə)l/ *n.*: **worn to a ~** доведённый до изнеможе́ния.
freak /friːk/ *n.* (*unusual occurrence*): **~ weather conditions** необы́чные пого́дные

усло́вия; (*abnormal person or thing*) уро́д, вы́родок; **~ of nature** оши́бка приро́ды; (*enthusiast*) фана́т; **health ~** поме́шанный на здоро́вье.
■ *v.i.*: **~ (out)** (*coll.*) при|ходи́ть, -йти́ в возбужде́ние.

freakish /'fri:kɪʃ/ *adj.* причу́дливый, чудно́й.

freckle /'frek(ə)l/ *n.* весну́шка.

free /fri:/ *adj.* (**freer** /'fri:ə(r)/, **freest** /'fri:ɪst/)
1 свобо́дный, во́льный; **you are ~ to leave** вы мо́жете уйти́; **they gave us a ~ hand** они́ предоста́вили нам по́лную свобо́ду де́йствий; **set ~** освобо|жда́ть, -ди́ть; **~ fall** свобо́дное паде́ние; **~ speech** свобо́да сло́ва; **~ will** свобо́да во́ли; **he left of his own ~ will** он ушёл доброво́льно/сам (*or* по свое́й во́ле).
2 (*without constraint*) непринуждённый, раско́ванный.
3 (*without payment*) беспла́тный; **~ of charge** беспла́тный; **~ gift** полу́ченное да́ром.
4 (*unoccupied*) свобо́дный, неза́нятый.
5 (*liberal*) ще́дрый; **~ with one's money** ще́дрый, расточи́тельный.
■ *v.t.* (*release, e.g. a rope*) высвобожда́ть; (*liberate*) освобо|жда́ть, -ди́ть.
■ *cpds.* **~-for-all** *n.* (*competition*) откры́тый (для всех) ко́нкурс; **~lance(r)** *n.* лицо́ свобо́дной профе́ссии; внешта́тный сотру́дник; **F~mason** *n.* масо́н; **F~masonry** *n.* масо́нство; **F~phone** *n.* (*Br.*) беспла́тный телефо́н; **~-range** *adj.*: **~-range eggs** я́йца от кур на свобо́дном вы́гуле; **~way** *n.* (*US*) скоростна́я автостра́да.

freedom /'fri:dəm/ *n.* свобо́да; **~ of speech** свобо́да сло́ва.

freesia /'fri:ʒə/ *n.* (*bot.*) фре́зия.

freez|e /fri:z/ *n.* (*period of frost*) замора́живание; **wage ~e** замора́живание за́работной пла́ты.
■ *v.t.* (*past* **froze;** *p.p.* **frozen**) замор|а́живать, -о́зить; **frozen food** моро́женые проду́кты; **~e assets/prices** замор|а́живать, -о́зить фо́нды/це́ны.
■ *v.i.* (*past* **froze;** *p.p.* **frozen**)
1 (*impers.*) моро́зить (*impf.*); **it's ~ing outside** на дворе́ стра́шный моро́з.
2 (*congeal with cold*): **the roads are frozen** доро́ги покры́лись льдом; **the pipes are frozen (up)** тру́бы промёрзли; **~ing point** то́чка замерза́ния.
3 (*fig., become rigid*) заст|ыва́ть, -ы́ть; (*as command*) **~e!** стоя́ть!, ни с ме́ста!
4 (*become chilled*) зам|ерза́ть, -ёрзнуть; **I'm ~ing** я замёрз.

freezer /'fri:zə(r)/ *n.* (*domestic appliance*) морози́льник; **~ compartment** морози́лка.

freight /freɪt/ *n.* фрахт.

freighter /'freɪtə(r)/ *n.* (*vessel*) грузово́е су́дно; (*aircraft*) грузово́й самолёт.

French /frentʃ/ *n.* (*language*) францу́зский язы́к; **the ~** (*people*) францу́зы (*m. pl.*).
■ *adj.* францу́зский; **French Canadian** франкокана́д|ец (*fem.* -ка); **~ fries** карто́фель (*m.*) соло́мкой/фри; **~ Riviera** Лазу́рный Бе́рег; **~ window** двуство́рчатое окно́ до по́ла; (*pl.*) две́ри в сад.
■ *cpds.* **~man** *n.* францу́з; **~woman** *n.* францу́женка.

frenetic /frə'netɪk/ *adj.* неи́стовый.

frenzied /'frenzɪd/ *adj.* неи́стовый, взбешённый.

frenzy /'frenzɪ/ *n.* неи́стовство, бе́шенство.

frequency /'fri:kwənsɪ/ *n.* частота́.

frequent /'fri:kwənt/ *adj.* ча́стый.

frequently /'fri:kwəntlɪ/ *adv.* ча́сто.

fresco /'freskəʊ/ *n.* (*pl.* **~s** *or* **~es**) фре́ска.

fresh /freʃ/ *adj.*
1 (*new*) све́жий, но́вый.
2 (*recent in origin*): **~ bread** све́жий хлеб; **it is still ~ in my memory** э́то ещё свежо́ в мое́й па́мяти.
3 (*as opposed to salt*) пре́сный.
4 (*cool, refreshing*) све́жий, прохла́дный.
5 (*unspoilt, unsullied*) све́жий, незапя́тнанный; **~ air** све́жий во́здух.
6 (*lively*) бо́дрый, живо́й.
7 (*impudent*) развя́зный, де́рзкий.
■ *cpd.* **~water** *adj.* пресново́дный.

freshen /'freʃ(ə)n/ *v.i.*: **she's gone to ~ up** она́ пошла́ привести́ себя́ в поря́док.

freshly /'freʃlɪ/ *adv.* (*recently*) неда́вно; то́лько что.

fret /fret/ *v.i.* (**fretted, fretting**) волнова́ться; му́читься (*both impf.*).

fretful /'fretfʊl/ *adj.* раздражи́тельный, капри́зный.

Freudian /'frɔɪdɪən/ *adj.*: **~ slip** огово́рка по Фре́йду.

friction /'frɪkʃ(ə)n/ *n.* тре́ние; (*fig.*) тре́ния (*nt. pl.*).

Friday /'fraɪdeɪ/ *n.* пя́тница.

fridge /frɪdʒ/ *n.* холоди́льник.
■ *cpd.* **~-freezer** *n.* (*Br.*) двухка́мерный холоди́льник.

friend /frend/ *n.* (*male*) друг, прия́тель; (*female*) подру́га, прия́тельница; **be ~s** дружи́ть (*impf.*) (*с кем*); **make ~s** подружи́ться (*pf.*) (*с кем*).

friendly /'frendlɪ/ *adj.* (**friendlier, friendliest**) дру́жеский, това́рищеский.

friendship /'frendʃɪp/ *n.* дру́жба.

frieze /fri:z/ *n.* (*decorative band*) бордю́р, фриз.

frigate /'frɪgət/ *n.* (*hist.*) фрега́т; (*small destroyer*) эска́дренный мино́носец; сторожево́й кора́бль.

fright /fraɪt/ *n.* страх, испу́г; **give s.o. a ~** испуга́ть (*pf.*) кого́-н.; напуга́ть (*pf.*) кого́-н.; **I got the ~ of my life** я жу́тко испуга́лся.

frighten /'fraɪt(ə)n/ *v.t.* пуга́ть, на-/ис-; **she is ~ed of the dark** она́ бои́тся темноты́.

frightening /'fraɪtnɪŋ/ *adj.* стра́шный.

frightful /'fraɪtfʊl/ *adj.* (*terrible*) ужа́сный, стра́шный; (*coll., hideous*) безобра́зный.

frigid /'frɪdʒɪd/ *adj.*
1 (*cold*) холо́дный; **~ zone** аркти́ческий по́яс.
2 (*unfeeling*) холо́дный, безразли́чный; (*sexually*) холо́дный, фриги́дный.

frill /frɪl/ *n.* обо́рочка.

frilly /'frɪlɪ/ *adj.* (**frillier, frilliest**) с

оборками.

fringe /frɪndʒ/ *n.*
[1] (*ornamental border*) бахрома́.
[2] (*Br., of hair*) чёлка.
[3] (*fig., edge, margin*) край, кайма́; ~ **benefits** дополни́тельные льго́ты (*f. pl.*).

frisk /frɪsk/ *v.t.* (*search*) обы́ск|ивать, -а́ть.

frisky /ˈfrɪskɪ/ *adj.* (**friskier, friskiest**) ре́звый, игри́вый.

frisson /ˈfriːsɔ̃/ *n.* дрожь (*от предвкушаемого удовольствия*).

fritter /ˈfrɪtə(r)/ *v.t.*: ~ **away** транжи́рить, рас-.

frivolity /frɪˈvɒlɪtɪ/ *n.* легкомы́слие.

frivolous /ˈfrɪvələs/ *adj.* легкомы́сленный, пусто́й.

frizzy /ˈfrɪzɪ/ *adj.* (**frizzier, frizziest**) вью́щийся, курча́вый.

frock /frɒk/ *n.* пла́тье; **party** ~ вече́рнее пла́тье.
■ *cpd.* ~ **coat** *n.* сюрту́к.

frog /frɒg/ *n.* лягу́шка; **I've got a ~ in my throat** (*fig.*) я охри́п.
■ *cpd.* ~**man** *n.* ныря́льщик с аквала́нгом.

frolic /ˈfrɒlɪk/ *v.i.* (**frolicked, frolicking**) шали́ть (*impf.*); резви́ться (*impf.*).

from /frɒm/ *prep.*
[1] (*denoting origin of movement, measurement or distance*): **the train ~ London to Paris** по́езд из Ло́ндона в Пари́ж; **guests ~ Ukraine** го́сти с Украи́ны; **10 miles ~ here** в десяти́ ми́лях отсю́да; ~ **the beginning of the book** с нача́ла кни́ги; ~ **end to end** от одного́ конца́ до друго́го; **far ~ it!** отню́дь!; во́все нет!
[2] (*expr. separation*): **I took the key ~ him** я взял у него́ ключ; **released ~ prison** вы́пущенный из тюрьмы́.
[3] (*denoting personal origin*): **a letter ~ my son** письмо́ от моего́ сы́на.
[4] (*expr. material origin*): **wine is made ~ grapes** вино́ де́лается из виногра́да.
[5] (*expr. origin in time*): ~ **the very beginning** с са́мого нача́ла; ~ **beginning to end** с нача́ла до конца́; ~ **now on** с э́того моме́нта; ~ **February to October** с февраля́ по октя́брь; ~ **time to time** вре́мя от вре́мени.
[6] (*expr. source or model*): **he quoted ~ memory** он цити́ровал по па́мяти; **he spoke ~ the heart** он говори́л от души́.
[7] (*expr. cause*) от/с + *g.*; **suffer ~ arthritis** страда́ть (*impf.*) артри́том.
[8] (*expr. difference*): **I can't tell him ~ his brother** я не могу́ отличи́ть его́ от его́ бра́та.
[9] (*expr. change*): **things went ~ bad to worse** дела́ шли всё ху́же и ху́же.
[10] (*with numbers*): ~ **1 to 10** от одного́ до десяти́; **it will last ~ 10 to 15 days** э́то продли́тся 10—15 дней; **they cost ~ £5 (upwards)** они́ сто́ят от 5 фу́нтов и вы́ше.
[11] (*with advs.*): ~ **above** све́рху; ~ **below** сни́зу; ~ **inside** изнутри́; ~ **outside** снару́жи; ~ **afar** издалека́; ~ **under the table** из-под стола́.

frond /frɒnd/ *n.* ветвь с ли́стьями; лист (па́поротника).

front /frʌnt/ *n.*
[1] (*foremost side or part*) перёд; пере́дняя сторона́; **he walked in ~ of the procession** он шёл впереди́ проце́ссии; **in ~ of the house** пе́ред до́мом; **in ~ of the children** при де́тях; **back to ~** за́дом наперёд.
[2] (*archit.*) фаса́д.
[3] (*fighting line*) фронт; **he was sent to the ~** его́ посла́ли на фронт; **in the ~ line** на передово́й ли́нии.
[4] (*Br., road bordering sea*) на́бережная.
[5] (*meteor.*) фронт.
[6] (*attr.*): ~ **benches** (*pol.*) скамьи́ для мини́стров и ли́деров оппози́ции в парла́менте; ~ **door** пара́дная дверь; ~ **page** пе́рвая страни́ца/полоса́; ~ **page news** основны́е но́вости в газе́те.

frontier /ˈfrʌntɪə(r)/ *n.* грани́ца.

frost /frɒst/ *n.* моро́з.
■ *v.t.*: **the windows were ~ed over** о́кна замёрзли; ~**ed glass** ма́товое стекло́.
■ *cpd.* ~**bite** *n.* обмороже́ние, отмороже́ние.

frosting /ˈfrɒstɪŋ/ *n.* (*US, cul.*) глазу́рь.

frosty /ˈfrɒstɪ/ *adj.* (**frostier, frostiest**) моро́зный; (*fig., unfriendly*) холо́дный, ледяно́й.

froth /frɒθ/ *n.* пе́на.

frothy /ˈfrɒθɪ/ *adj.* (**frothier, frothiest**) пе́нистый; (*fig.*) пусто́й.

frown /fraʊn/ *v.i.* хму́риться, на-; **the authorities ~ on gambling** вла́сти неодобри́тельно отно́сятся к аза́ртным и́грам.

froze /frəʊz/ *past of* ▸ **freeze**

frozen /ˈfrəʊz(ə)n/ *adj.* замёрзший, засты́вший; (*icebound*) ско́ванный льдом.

frugal /ˈfruːg(ə)l/ *adj.* бережли́вый.

fruit /fruːt/ *n.* фрукт.
■ *cpds.* ~ **cake** *n.* фрукто́вый кекс; ~ **juice** *n.* фрукто́вый сок; ~ **machine** *n.* (*Br.*) игрово́й автома́т; ~ **salad** *n.* фрукто́вый сала́т.

fruitful /ˈfruːtfʊl/ *adj.* плодотво́рный.

fruition /fruːˈɪʃ(ə)n/ *n.*: **come to ~** осуществ|ля́ться, -и́ться.

fruitless /ˈfruːtlɪs/ *adj.* (*lit., fig.*) беспло́дный.

fruity /ˈfruːtɪ/ *adj.* (**fruitier, fruitiest**) фрукто́вый.

frustrate /frʌˈstreɪt/ *v.t.* разочаро́в|ывать, -а́ть; **I feel ~d** я обескура́жен.

frustration /frʌˈstreɪʃ(ə)n/ *n.*
[1] (*thwarting*) круше́ние (*планов/надежд*).
[2] (*disappointment*) разочарова́ние.

fr|y /fraɪ/ *v.t.* жа́рить, за-/из-/по-; ~**ied egg(s)** яи́чница; ~**ied potato** жа́реная карто́шка; ~**ing pan** сковорода́.
■ *v.i.* жа́риться (*impf.*).

ft (*abbr. of* **foot, feet**) фу́т(ы).

fuchsia /ˈfjuːʃə/ *n.* фу́ксия.

fuck /fʌk/ (*vulg.*) *n.*: **he doesn't give a ~** ему́ по́ хую (*or* по́ хуй) (*euph.*: по́ фигу *or* по́ фиг).
■ *v.t.* еба́ть, вы- (*euph.*: тра́х|ать, -нуть); ~ **it!** чёрт возьми́/побери́! (*euph.*); блядь! (*euph.*: блин!).
■ *v.i.* еба́ться, по- (*euph.*: тра́х|аться, -нуться).
■ *with advs.*: ~ **about/around** занима́ться, страда́ть (*both impf.*) хуйнёй (*euph.*: хернёй); ~ **off!** отъеби́сь (от меня́)!; пошёл/иди́ на́

хуй! (*euph.*: на́ фиг!); **~ up** *v.t.* (*sth.*) зап|а́рывать, -оро́ть (*no vulg. equ.*); (*a game, contest etc.*) прос|ира́ть, -ра́ть; про|ёбывать, -еба́ть; (*s.o.*) док|а́нывать, -она́ть (*no vulg. equ.*); *v.i.* лажа́ть (*impf.*), облажа́ться (*pf.*) (*no vulg. equs.*); порта́чить, на- (*no vulg. equ.*).
■ *cpd.* **~ all** (*Br.*) ни хуя́ (*euph.*: ни хрена́); **to do ~ all** ни хуя́ не де́лать.

fucking /ˈfʌkɪŋ/ *adj.* (*vulg. expletive*) ёбаный (*euph.*: до́лбаный).

fudge /fʌdʒ/ *n.* (*sweetmeat*) сли́вочная пома́дка.
■ *v.t.* & *i.* (*an issue, question*) уклон|я́ться, -и́ться от + *g.*; (*facts, figures*) подтасо́в|ывать, -а́ть; **~ accounts** подде́л|ывать, -ать счета́.

fuel /ˈfju:əl/ *n.* то́пливо, горю́чее.
■ *v.t.* (**fuelled, fuelling; *US* fueled, fueling**) снаб|жа́ть, -ди́ть (*or* запр|авля́ть, -а́вить) то́пливом.

fugitive /ˈfju:dʒɪtɪv/ *n.* бегл|е́ц (*fem.* -я́нка).

fugue /fju:g/ *n.* (*mus.*) фу́га.

fulcr|um /ˈfʊlkrəm/ *n.* (*pl.* **~a** *or* **~ums**) то́чка опо́ры; то́чка приложе́ния си́лы.

fulfil /fʊlˈfɪl/ (*US* **fulfill**) *v.t.* (**fulfilled, fulfilling**) выполня́ть, вы́полнить.

fulfilment /fʊlˈfɪl mənt/ (*US* **fulfillment**) *n.* (*accomplishment*) выполне́ние, исполне́ние; (*satisfaction*) удовлетворе́ние.

full /fʊl/ *adj.*
1 (*filled to capacity*) по́лный; **the hotel is ~ (up)** все ко́мнаты в гости́нице за́няты; (*having plenty*): **~ of ideas** по́лон иде́й/за́мыслов; **~ of life** жизнера́достный; по́лон жи́зни.
2 (*complete*): **we waited a ~ hour** мы жда́ли це́лый час; **~ moon** полнолу́ние; **~ stop** то́чка.
■ *adv.* 1 (*very*): **you know ~ well** вы са́ми прекра́сно зна́ете.
2 (*completely*): **she turned the radio on ~** она́ включи́ла ра́дио на по́лную мо́щность/гро́мкость.
■ *cpds.* **~back** *n.* защи́тник; **~-grown** *adj.* взро́слый; **~-length** *adj.* во всю длину́; **~-length dress** пла́тье до пят; **~-scale** *adj.* в по́лном объёме; **~-time** *adj.* (*of job*) занима́ющий всё (рабо́чее) вре́мя.

fully /ˈfʊlɪ/ *adv.* вполне́, по́лностью, соверше́нно, до конца́.

fulsome /ˈfʊlsəm/ *adj.* чрезме́рный, тошнотво́рный.

fumble /ˈfʌmb(ə)l/ *v.t.* теребить (*impf.*) в рука́х; **~ a ball** упусти́ть (*pf.*) мяч.
■ *v.i.* ры́ться (*impf.*); **he ~d in his pockets for a key** он ры́лся в карма́нах, ища́ ключ.

fume /fju:m/ *n.* дым, ко́поть.
■ *v.i.* (*fig.*): **fuming with rage** кипя́щий от гне́ва.

fumigate /ˈfju:mɪgeɪt/ *v.t.* оку́р|ивать, -и́ть.

fun /fʌn/ *n.* ве́селье, заба́ва; **make ~ of, poke ~ at** насмеха́ться (*impf.*) над + *i.*; **he is ~ to be with** с ним не соску́чишься; **we had ~ at the party** в гостя́х бы́ло ве́село.
■ *cpd.* **~fair** *n.* (*Br.*) увесели́тельный парк.

function /ˈfʌŋkʃ(ə)n/ *n.*
1 (*purpose*) фу́нкция, назначе́ние.
2 (*social gathering*) ве́чер.
3 : **~ key** (*comput.*) функциона́льная кла́виша.
■ *v.i.* функциони́ровать, де́йствовать (*both impf.*).

functional /ˈfʌŋkʃən(ə)l/ *adj.* функциона́льный.

functionary /ˈfʌŋkʃənərɪ/ *n.* функционе́р, должностно́е лицо́.

fund /fʌnd/ *n.* фонд, запа́с, резе́рв; (*pl., resources*) фо́нды (*m. pl.*); **he is in ~s** (*Br.*) он при деньга́х.
■ *v.t.* финанси́ровать (*impf., pf.*); (*fin.*) консолиди́ровать (*impf., pf.*).
■ *cpd.* **~-raising** *n.* сбор средств; **a ~-raising dinner** (*for charity*) благотвори́тельный банке́т.

fundamental /fʌndəˈment(ə)l/ *adj.* основно́й, суще́ственный.

fundamentalism /fʌndəˈmentəlɪz(ə)m/ *n.* фундаментали́зм.

fundamentalist /fʌndəˈmentəlɪst/ *n.* фундаментали́ст.

funeral /ˈfju:nər(ə)l/ *n.* по́хор|оны (*pl., g.* -о́н); **~ parlour, home** (*US*) похоро́нное бюро́.

funereal /fju:ˈnɪərɪəl/ *adj.* мра́чный; тра́урный.

fungi /ˈfʌŋgaɪ, ˈfʌndʒaɪ/ *pl. of* ▸ **fungus**

fungicide /ˈfʌndʒɪsaɪd/ *n.* фунгици́д; (*med.*) противогрибко́вое сре́дство, противогрибко́вый препара́т.

fungus /ˈfʌŋgəs/ *n.* (*pl.* **fungi** *or* **funguses**) грибо́к; (ни́зший) гриб.

funnel /ˈfʌn(ə)l/ *n.* воро́нка; (*of ship*) дымова́я труба́.

funny /ˈfʌnɪ/ *adj.* (**funnier, funniest**)
1 (*amusing*) смешно́й, заба́вный.
2 (*strange*) стра́нный; **I have a ~ feeling you're right!** я подозрева́ю, что вы пра́вы.

fur /fə:(r)/ *n.*
1 (*animal hair*) шерсть.
2 (*as worn*) мех (*pl.* -а́).

furious /ˈfjʊərɪəs/ *adj.*
1 (*violent*) бу́йный, неи́стовый.
2 (*enraged*) взбешённый; **she was ~ with him** она́ разозли́лась на него́ не на шу́тку.

furnace /ˈfə:nɪs/ *n.* горн, оча́г, печь, то́пка.

furnish /ˈfə:nɪʃ/ *v.t.* обст|авля́ть, -а́вить.

furnishings /ˈfə:nɪʃɪŋz/ *n.* обстано́вка.

furniture /ˈfə:nɪtʃə(r)/ *n.* ме́бель.

furore /fjʊəˈrɔ:rɪ/ *n.* фуро́р.

furrier /ˈfʌrɪə(r)/ *n.* мехови́к, скорня́к.

furrow /ˈfʌrəʊ/ *n.*
1 (*in the earth etc.*) борозда́, жёлоб; **plough a lonely ~** (*fig.*) де́йствовать (*impf.*) в одино́чку.
2 (*wrinkle*) глубо́кая морщи́на.
■ *v.t.* (*fig.*): **~ed brow** намо́рщенный лоб.

furry /ˈfə:rɪ/ *adj.* (**furrier, furriest**) покры́тый ме́хом; пушно́й.

further /ˈfə:ðə(r)/ *adj.* (*see also* ▸ **farther**)
1 дальне́йший; (*additional*) доба́вочный, дополни́тельный; **~ education** (*Br.*) дальне́йшее образова́ние (*после школы, не высшее*) **until ~ notice** впредь до дальне́йшего уведомле́ния.
2 (*more distant*) да́льний.
■ *adv.* да́лее, да́льше; **I can go no ~** я не могу́ да́льше идти́.
■ *v.t.* продв|ига́ть, -и́нуть; соде́йствовать (*impf.*) + *d.*; спосо́бствовать (*impf.*) + *d.*

furtherance /ˈfəːðərəns/ *n.* продвиже́ние; **in ~ of this plan** для осуществле́ния э́того пла́на.
furthermore /fəːðəˈmɔː(r)/ *adv.* к тому́ же; кро́ме того́.
furthest /ˈfəːðɪst/ *adj.* са́мый да́льний.
■ *adv.* да́льше всего́.
furtive /ˈfəːtɪv/ *adj.* скры́тный.
fury /ˈfjʊərɪ/ *n.* я́рость.
fuse[1] /fjuːz/ *n.* (*elec.*) предохрани́тель (*m.*), про́бка.
■ *v.t.* & *i.* (*Br.*, *elec.*): **he ~d the lights** он пережёг про́бки; **the lights ~d** про́бки перегоре́ли.
■ *cpds.* **~ box** *n.* распредели́тельный щит(о́к) (с предохрани́телями/про́бками); **~ wire** *n.* про́волока для предохрани́теля.
fuse[2], **fuze** /fjuːz/ *n.* (*igniting device*) запа́л, фити́ль (*m.*).
fuselage /ˈfjuːzəlɑːʒ/ *n.* фюзеля́ж.
fusion /ˈfjuːʒ(ə)n/ *n.* (*blending*, *coalition*) сплав, слия́ние.
fuss /fʌs/ *n.* суета́, шум (из-за пустяко́в); **make a ~ about, over sth.** суети́ться (*impf.*) вокру́г чего́-н.; **make a ~ of s.o.** (*Br.*) суетли́во опека́ть (*impf.*) кого́-н.
■ *v.i.* суети́ться (*impf.*); **she ~es over her children** она́ ве́чно во́зится со свои́ми детьми́.
fussy /ˈfʌsɪ/ *adj.* (**fussier, fussiest**) разбо́рчивый; **I'm not ~ (about) what I eat** я не привере́длив в еде́.
futile /ˈfjuːtaɪl/ *adj.* напра́сный, тще́тный.
futility /fjuːˈtɪlɪtɪ/ *n.* тще́тность, бесполе́зность.
futon /ˈfuːtɒn/ *n.* япо́нский матра́с (*в складной деревянной раме; расстилается на полу в качестве кровати или кресла*).
future /ˈfjuːtʃə(r)/ *n.*
1 бу́дущее; **in (the) ~** в бу́дущем.
2 (*gram.*) бу́дущее вре́мя.
■ *adj.* бу́дущий; **belief in a ~ life** ве́ра в загро́бную жизнь.
futuristic /fjuːtʃəˈrɪstɪk/ *adj.* футуристи́ческий.
fuze /fjuːz/ = **fuse**[2]
fuzzy /ˈfʌzɪ/ *adj.* (**fuzzier, fuzziest**) (*fluffy*) пуши́стый; (*blurred*) расплы́вчатый.

Gg

G /dʒiː/ *n.* (*mus.*) соль (*nt. indecl.*).
gab /gæb/ (*coll.*) *n.*: **he has the gift of the ~** у него́ хорошо́ подве́шен язы́к .
gabble /ˈgæb(ə)l/ *n.* бормота́ние; (*sl.*) трёп, болтовня́.
■ *v.t.* & *i.* бормота́ть, про-.
gaberdine /gæbəˈdiːn/ *n.* (*material*) габарди́н; (*attr.*) габарди́новый.
gadget /ˈgædʒɪt/ *n.* (*coll.*) штуко́вина, хитроу́мное приспособле́ние; (*comput.*, *mobile teleph.*) га́джет.
gaffe /gæf/ *n.* ло́жный шаг, оплo̓шность.
gag /gæg/ *n.*
1 (*to prevent speech etc.*) кляп.
2 (*joke*) шу́тка, хо́хма.
■ *v.t.* (**gagged, gagging**) вст|авля́ть, -а́вить кляп + *d.*; (*fig.*) зат|ыка́ть, -кну́ть рот + *d.*
■ *v.i.* (**gagged, gagging**) (*retch*) дави́ться (*impf.*).
gaga /ˈgɑːgɑː/ *adj.* (*sl.*) чо́кнутый, слабоу́мный; **go ~** впа|да́ть, -сть в мара́зм; выжива́ть, вы́жить из ума́.
gage /geɪdʒ/ (*US*) = **gauge**
gaiety /ˈgeɪətɪ/ (*US* **gayety**) *n.* весёлость, весе́лье.
gain /geɪn/ *n.*
1 (*profit*) при́быль.
2 (*increase*) увеличе́ние.
■ *v.t.* овлад|ева́ть, -е́ть; доб|ива́ться, -и́ться + *g.*; доб|ыва́ть, -ы́ть; приобре|та́ть, -сти́; **he ~ed 5 pounds in weight** он попра́вился на 5 фу́нтов; **the patient is ~ing strength** пацие́нт набира́ется сил.
■ *v.i.* 1 (*reap profit, benefit, advantage*) извл|ека́ть, -е́чь по́льзу/вы́году; **how do I stand to ~ from it?** кака́я мне от э́того по́льза/вы́года?
2 (*move ahead*): **my watch ~s (three minutes a day)** мои́ часы́ спеша́т (на три мину́ты в день); **he ~ed on his rival** он нагоня́л сопе́рника.
gainful /ˈgeɪnfʊl/ *adj.* при́быльный; дохо́дный; **~ employment** хорошо́ опла́чиваемая рабо́та.
galaxy /ˈgæləksɪ/ *n.* гала́ктика; (**the G~**) Гала́ктика.
gale /geɪl/ *n.* бу́ря.
gallant /ˈgælənt/ *adj.*
1 (*attentive to ladies*) гала́нтный.
2 (*brave*) до́блестный.
gallery /ˈgælərɪ/ *n.*
1 (*walk, passage*) галере́я.
2 (*picture ~*) карти́нная галере́я.
3 (*theatr.*) балко́н.
galley /ˈgælɪ/ *n.* (*pl.* **~s**)
1 (*ship*) гале́ра.
2 (*ship's kitchen*) ка́мбуз; (*in aircraft*) ку́хня на борту́ самолёта.
3 (*typ.*) (**~ *proof***) гра́нка.
■ *cpd.* **~ slave** *n.* раб на гале́рах.
Gallic /ˈgælɪk/ *adj.* (*Gaulish*) га́лльский; (*French*) францу́зский.
galling /ˈgɔːlɪŋ/ *adj.* (*fig.*) раздража́ющий.
gallivant /ˈgælɪvænt/ *v.i.* (*coll.*) шля́ться (*impf.*); слоня́ться (*impf.*).
gallon /ˈgælən/ *n.* галло́н.
gallop /ˈgæləp/ *n.* гало́п.
■ *v.i.*: скака́ть (*impf.*) (гало́пом); (*fig.*): **we**

~ed through our work мы в спешке закончили (нашу/свою) работу.

gallows /ˈgæləʊz/ *n.* виселица; **send s.o. to the ~** отправить (*pf.*) кого-н. на виселицу.
■ *cpd.* **~ humour** (*US* **humor**) *n.* юмор висельника.

galore /gəˈlɔː(r)/ *adv.* (*coll.*) в изобилии, сколько угодно.

galvanize /ˈgælvənaɪz/ *v.t.* оцинков|ывать, -ать; (*fig.*) побу|ждать, -дить.

Gambia /ˈgæmbɪə/ *n.* Гамбия.

gamble /ˈgæmb(ə)l/ *n.* азартная игра; (*risky undertaking*) рискованное предприятие.
■ *v.t.* & *i.* играть (*impf.*) в азартные игры; **~ away a fortune** проиграть (*pf.*) состояние.

gambler /ˈgæmblə(r)/ *n.* игрок; картёжник.

gambling /ˈgæmblɪŋ/ *n.* азартные игры (*f. pl.*).

game /geɪm/ *n.*
1 игра; **we had a ~ of golf** мы сыграли партию в гольф.
2 (*plan, trick*) игра; **he gave the ~ away** он раскрыл свои карты.
3 (*hunted animal*) дичь; зверь (*m.*).
■ *cpds.* **~keeper** *n.* охраняющий дичь егерь; **~ plan** *n.* стратегия; **~ reserve** *n.* охотничий заказник/заповедник; **~s console** *n.* игровая консоль, игровая приставка; **~ show** *n.* телеигра, игровое шоу (*indecl.*).

gammon /ˈgæmən/ *n.* (*Br.*) окорок.

gamut /ˈgæmət/ *n.* (*mus.*) гамма; (*fig.*) диапазон, гамма; **she ran the ~ of the emotions** она передала всю гамму чувств.

gang /gæŋ/ *n.* (*of workmen*) бригада; (*of prisoners*) партия (заключённых); (*of criminals*) шайка, банда.
■ *v.i.*: **they ~ed up on me** они ополчились против/на меня.
■ *cpds.* **~land** *n.* преступный мир; **~master** *n.* (*Br.*) бригадир; **~way** *n.* (*from ship to shore or aircraft to ground*) трап.

gangrene /ˈgæŋgriːn/ *n.* гангрена.

gangster /ˈgæŋstə(r)/ *n.* бандит.

gannet /ˈgænɪt/ *n.* (*bird*) олуша; (*Br., fig., glutton*) обжора.

gantry /ˈgæntrɪ/ *n.* помост; **~ crane** эстакадный кран.

gap /gæp/ *n.* (*in a wall etc.*) брешь, пролом; (*in conversation*) пауза; (*of 5 years etc.*) перерыв; (*between rich and poor, theory and practice*) разрыв; (*in application form, s.o.'s knowledge*) пробел.
■ *cpd.* **~ year** *n.* (*Br.*) год перед поступлением в университет (*который выпускник школы проводит работая или путешествуя*).

gap|e /geɪp/ *v.i.* (*stare*) зевать (*impf.*) (по сторонам); **a ~ing wound** зияющая рана; **the chasm ~ed before him** перед ним зияла пропасть.

garage /ˈgærɑːdʒ/ *n.* (*for keeping a car*) гараж; (*where petrol is sold*) бензозаправочная станция; (*for repairing cars*) автосервис.

garbage /ˈgɑːbɪdʒ/ *n.* (*US, rubbish*) мусор (*also fig.*); хлам; (*nonsense*) чепуха, вздор.
■ *cpds.* **~ can** *n.* (*US*) (*outside*) мусорный бак; (*in kitchen*) мусорное ведро; **~ dump** *n.* свалка; **~ truck** *n.* (*US*) мусоровоз.

garble /ˈgɑːb(ə)l/ *v.t.* (*distort*) иска|жать, -зить.

garden /ˈgɑːd(ə)n/ *n.*
1 (*plot of ground*) сад; **vegetable ~** огород.
2 (*attr.*) садовый; **~ centre** (*US* **center**) садовый центр; **~ party** светский приём на открытом воздухе.
■ *v.i.* заниматься (*impf.*) садоводством.

gardener /ˈgɑːdnə(r)/ *n.* садовник.

gargle /ˈgɑːg(ə)l/ *v.i.* полоскать, про- горло.

garish /ˈgeərɪʃ/ *adj.* пёстрый.

garland /ˈgɑːlənd/ *n.* гирлянда.

garlic /ˈgɑːlɪk/ *n.* чеснок.

garment /ˈgɑːmənt/ *n.* предмет одежды.

garnet /ˈgɑːnɪt/ *n.* (*min.*) гранат.

garnish /ˈgɑːnɪʃ/ *n.* (*cul.*) гарнир.
■ *v.t.* (*cul.*) под|авать, ать (*что с чем*).

garret /ˈgærɪt/ *n.* мансарда; чердак.

garrison /ˈgærɪs(ə)n/ *n.* гарнизон.

garter /ˈgɑːtə(r)/ *n.* подвязка; **~ belt** (*US*) пояс с подвязками.

gas /gæs/ *n.* (*pl.* **~es**)
1 (*aeriform fluid*) газ.
2 (*attr.*) газовый; **~ cooker** (*Br.*) газовая плита; **~ fire** (*Br.*) газовый камин; **~ mask** противогаз; **~ oven** (*domestic*) газовая духовка.
3 (*US, petrol*) бензин, горючее; **~ station** (*US*) бензозаправочная станция.
■ *v.t.* (**gases, gassed, gassing**) умер|щвлять, -твить газом.

gash /gæʃ/ *n.* разрез.
■ *v.t.* разр|езать, -езать.

gasol|ine, -ene /ˈgæsəliːn/ *n.* газолин; (*US, petrol*) бензин.

gasp /gɑːsp/ *n.* глоток воздуха; **at one's last ~** при последнем издыхании.
■ *v.t.* & *i.* зад|ыхаться, -охнуться; **he was ~ing for breath** он задыхался; **he ~ed with astonishment** он открыл рот от удивления.

gastric /ˈgæstrɪk/ *adj.* желудочный; **~ juice** желудочный сок; **~ ulcer** язва желудка.

gastroenteritis /gæstrəʊentəˈraɪtɪs/ *n.* гастроэнтерит.

gastronomic /gæstrəˈnɒmɪk/ *adj.* гастрономический.

gastronomy /gæˈstrɒnəmɪ/ *n.* гастрономия.

gate /geɪt/ *n.* вор|ота (*pl., g.* -от); (*city ~*) городские ворота; (*at airport*) выход.
■ *cpds.* **~crash** *v.t.* & *i.* при|ходить, -йти без приглашения; **~crasher** *n.* незваный гость.

gateau /ˈgætəʊ/ *n.* (*pl.* **~s** *or* **~x** /-əʊz/) (*Br.*) торт.

gather /ˈgæðə(r)/ *n.* (*in cloth*) сборки (*f. pl.*).
■ *v.t.* 1 (*pick, e.g. flowers, harvest; also* **~ in**) соб|ирать, -рать.
2 (*collect, also* **~ up**) соб|ирать, -рать.
3 (*understand*) заключ|ать, -ить; **I ~ he's abroad** он как будто за границей.
4 (*pull together*): **~ one's thoughts, wits** соб|ираться, -раться с мыслями.
5 (*sewing*) соб|ирать, -рать в складки.
■ *v.i.* соб|ираться, -раться; **a crowd ~ed** собралась толпа.

gathering /ˈgæðərɪŋ/ *n.* собрание.

g

gaudy /'gɔːdɪ/ *adj.* (**gaudier, gaudiest**) крича́щий.

gauge /geɪdʒ/ (*US* **gage**) *n.*
1 (*thickness, diameter etc.*) разме́р; (*rail.*): **standard ~** станда́ртная колея́.
2 (*instrument*) шабло́н.
■ *v.t.* 1 (*measure*) изм|еря́ть, -е́рить.
2 (*fig., estimate*) оце́н|ивать, -и́ть.

gaunt /gɔːnt/ *adj.* (*person*) исхуда́лый.

gauntlet /'gɔːntlɪt/ *n.* рукави́ца; (*armoured glove*) ла́тная рукави́ца; **throw down the ~** (*fig.*) бро́сить (*pf.*) перча́тку/вы́зов; **pick up the ~** приня́ть (*pf.*) вы́зов.

gauze /gɔːz/ *n.* ма́рля, газ.

gave /geɪv/ *past of* ▸ **give**

gawk /gɔːk/ *v.i.* = **gawp**

gawp /gɔːp/ *v.i.* (*Br.*) глазе́ть (*impf.*); пя́лить (*impf.*) глаза́ (на + *a.*).

gay /geɪ/ *adj.* (**gayer, gayest**) весёлый; (*coll., homosexual*) гомосексуа́льный, голубо́й; (*as n.*) гей, гомосексуали́ст.

gayety /'geɪətɪ/ (*US*) = **gaiety**

gaze /geɪz/ *n.* при́стальный взгляд.
■ *v.i.* при́стально гляде́ть.

gazebo /gə'ziːbəʊ/ *n.* (*pl.* **~s** *or* **~es**) бельведе́р.

gazelle /gə'zel/ *n.* газе́ль.

GB (*abbr. of* ***Great Britain***) Великобрита́ния.

GBH (*abbr. of* ***grievous bodily harm***) (*Br., leg.*) тяжёлые теле́сные поврежде́ния.

GCSE (*abbr. of* ***General Certificate of Secondary Education***) (*Br.*) ≈ аттеста́т о непо́лном сре́днем образова́нии.

GDP (*abbr. of* ***gross domestic product***) ВВП (валово́й вну́тренний проду́кт).

gear /gɪə(r)/ *n.*
1 (*equipment, clothing*) принадле́жности (*f. pl.*), аксессуа́ры (*m. pl.*); оде́жда; **hunting ~** охо́тничье снаряже́ние.
2 (*of car etc.*) зубча́тая переда́ча; **change ~** переключ|а́ть, -и́ть переда́чу; **the car is in ~** маши́на на переда́че.
■ *v.t.*: **~ up** гото́вить (*impf.*); пригот|а́вливать, -о́вить.
■ *cpds.* **~box** *n.* коро́бка переда́ч; **~ lever** *n.* (*Br.*) рыча́г переключе́ния переда́ч/скоросте́й; **~ shift** *n.* (*US*) = **~ lever**

geese /giːs/ *pl. of* ▸ **goose**

gel /dʒel/ *n.* гель (*m.*).

gelatin(e) /'dʒelətɪn, 'dʒelətiːn/ *n.* желати́н.

gem /dʒem/ *n.* драгоце́нный ка́мень.

Gemini /'dʒemɪnaɪ/ *n.* Близнецы́ (*m. pl.*).

gender /'dʒendə(r)/ *n.* род.

gene /dʒiːn/ *n.* ген; **~ therapy** ге́нная терапи́я.

genealogical /dʒiːnɪə'lɒdʒɪk(ə)l/ *adj.* родосло́вный; генеалоги́ческий.

genealogist /dʒiːnɪ'ælədʒɪst/ *n.* специали́ст по генеало́гии.

genealogy /dʒiːnɪ'ælədʒɪ/ *n.* генеало́гия.

genera /'dʒenərə/ *pl. of* ▸ **genus**

general /'dʒenər(ə)l/ *n.* генера́л.
■ *adj.* 1 (*universal or nearly so*) о́бщий; генера́льный; **~ election** всео́бщие вы́боры; **~ strike** всео́бщая забасто́вка; **~ knowledge** о́бщие зна́ния; **~ practitioner** участко́вый врач; терапе́вт.
2 (*usual*) обы́чный; **~ opinion** о́бщее мне́ние; **in ~** вообще́.

generalization /dʒenərəlaɪ'zeɪʃ(ə)n/ *n.* обобще́ние.

generalize /'dʒenərəlaɪz/ *v.t.* & *i.* обобщ|а́ть, -и́ть.

generally /'dʒenərəlɪ/ *adv.*
1 (*usually*) обы́чно.
2 (*widely*) широко́.
3 (*approximately*) вообще́; **~ speaking** вообще́ говоря́.

generate /'dʒenəreɪt/ *v.t.* поро|жда́ть, -ди́ть; **~ heat** выделя́ть (*impf.*) тепло́; **~ hatred** вызыва́ть (*impf.*) не́нависть.

generation /dʒenə'reɪʃ(ə)n/ *n.*
1 (*of heat etc.*) генера́ция.
2 (*geneal.*) поколе́ние; **the ~ gap** пробле́ма отцо́в и дете́й.

generator /'dʒenəreɪtə(r)/ *n.* генера́тор.

generic /dʒɪ'nerɪk/ *adj.* (*of a class*) родово́й; (*general*) о́бщий; (*of drug*) непатенто́ванный, о́бщего ти́па.

generosity /dʒenə'rɒsɪtɪ/ *n.* великоду́шие.

generous /'dʒenərəs/ *adj.*
1 (*liberal*) ще́дрый.
2 (*plentiful*) оби́льный.

genesis /'dʒenɪsɪs/ *n.* ге́незис; возникнове́ние; **(Book of) G ~** кни́га Бытия́.

genetic /dʒɪ'netɪk/ *adj.* генети́ческий; **~ engineering** ге́нная инжене́рия; **~ fingerprinting** ге́нная дактилоскопи́я; **~ modification** генети́ческая модифика́ция; **~ally modified** генети́чески модифици́рованный; **~ profiling** генети́ческое профили́рование; **~ screening** генети́ческий скри́нинг.

geneticist /dʒɪ'netɪsɪst/ *n.* гене́тик.

genetics /dʒɪ'netɪks/ *n.* гене́тика.

genial /'dʒiːnɪəl/ *adj.* серде́чный.

geniality /dʒiːnɪ'ælɪtɪ/ *n.* раду́шие; доброду́шие.

genie /'dʒiːnɪ/ *n.* джинн, дух.

genital /'dʒenɪt(ə)l/ *adj.* полово́й; (*pl.*) половы́е о́рганы (*m. pl.*), генита́лии (*f. pl.*).

genitive /'dʒenɪtɪv/ *n.* & *adj.* роди́тельный (паде́ж).

genius /'dʒiːnɪəs/ *n.* ге́ний.

genocide /'dʒenəsaɪd/ *n.* геноци́д.

genome /'dʒiːnəʊm/ *n.* гено́м.

genre /'ʒɑ̃rə/ *n.* жанр.

genteel /dʒen'tiːl/ *adj.* благовоспи́танный; «благоро́дный»; с аристократи́ческими зама́шками.

Gentile /'dʒentaɪl/ *n.* нееврей́.
■ *adj.* неевре́йский.

gentle /'dʒent(ə)l/ *adj.* (**gentler, gentlest**) мя́гкий, ти́хий, делика́тный; **a ~ slope** поло́гий скло́н; **a ~ breeze** лёгкий ветеро́к; **a ~ hint** то́нкий намёк.

gentleman /'dʒent(ə)lmən/ *n.* джентльме́н.

gently /'dʒentlɪ/ *adv.* мя́гко; делика́тно.

gentry /'dʒentrɪ/ *n.* нетитуло́ванное дворя́нство.

Gents /dʒent/ *n.* (**the ~**) (*sg., Br.*) (*lavatory*) мужско́й туале́т.

genuine /'dʒenjʊɪn/ *adj.* настоя́щий; по́длинный; **~ sorrow** и́скренняя печа́ль; **a**

~ **person** прямóй/и́скренний человéк.
genus /'dʒi:nəs/ *n.* (*pl.* **genera**) род.
geographer /dʒɪ'ɒgrəfə(r)/ *n.* геóграф.
geographic(al) /dʒi:ə'græfɪk(ə)l/ *adj.* географи́ческий.
geography /dʒɪ'ɒgrəfɪ/ *n.* геогрáфия.
geological /dʒi:ə'lɒdʒɪk(ə)l/ *adj.* геологи́ческий.
geologist /dʒɪ'ɒlədʒɪst/ *n.* геóлог.
geology /dʒɪ'ɒlədʒɪ/ *n.* геолóгия.
geometric(al) /dʒɪə'metrɪkəl/ *adj.* геометри́ческий.
geometry /dʒɪ'ɒmɪtrɪ/ *n.* геомéтрия.
geopolitical /dʒi:əʊpə'lɪtɪk(ə)l/ *adj.* геополити́ческий.
Georgia /'dʒɔ:dʒɪə/ *n.* (*in Caucasus*) Грýзия.
Georgian /'dʒɔ:dʒ(ə)n/ *n.* грузи́н (*fem.* -ка). ■ *adj.* грузи́нский.
geranium /dʒə'reɪnɪəm/ *n.* герáнь.
geriatric /dʒerɪ'ætrɪk/ *adj.* гериатри́ческий.
geriatrics /dʒerɪ'ætrɪks/ *n.* гериатри́я.
germ /dʒə:m/ *n.* микрóб, бактéрия; ~ **warfare** бактериологи́ческая войнá; (*fig.*) зачáток.
German /'dʒə:mən/ *n.*
1 (*person*) нéм|ец (*fem.* -ка).
2 (*language*) немéцкий язы́к.
■ *adj.* немéцкий; (*esp. pol.*) гермáнский; ~ **measles** краснýха; ~ **shepherd (dog)** немéцкая овчáрка.
germane /dʒə:'meɪn/ *adj.* умéстный; подходя́щий.
Germanic /dʒə:'mænɪk/ *adj.* гермáнский.
Germany /'dʒə:mənɪ/ *n.* Гермáния.
germinate /'dʒə:mɪneɪt/ *v.i.* прораст|áть, -и́.
germination /dʒə:mɪ'neɪʃ(ə)n/ *n.* прорастáние; (*fig.*) зарождéние; разви́тие.
gerontology /dʒerən'tɒlədʒɪ/ *n.* геронтолóгия.
gerund /'dʒerənd/ *n.* герýндий.
gestation /dʒe'steɪʃ(ə)n/ *n.* берéменность; (*fig.*) созревáние.
gesticulate /dʒe'stɪkjʊleɪt/ *v.i.* жестикули́ровать (*impf.*).
gesture /'dʒestʃə(r)/ *n.* жест.
■ *v.i.* жестикули́ровать (*impf.*).
get /get/ *v.t.* (**getting;** *past* **got** *p.p.* **got** *or US* **gotten**)
1 (*obtain, receive*) получ|áть, -и́ть; **I've got it!** (*answer to problem etc.*) э́врика!; **I ~ you** (*coll., understand*) пóнял!; **this room ~s a lot of sun** э́та кóмната óчень сóлнечная; **I got** (*bought*) **a new suit** я приобрёл/купи́л нóвый костю́м.
2 (*of suffering etc.*): **he got 2 years** (*sentence*) он получи́л 2 гóда (тюрьмы́); **he got the measles** он заболéл кóрью; **he got a blow on the head** он получи́л удáр по головé; **she got her feet wet** онá промочи́ла нóги.
3 (*fetch, lay hands on*) дост|авáть, -áть; доб|ывáть, -ы́ть; **I got him a chair** я принёс емý стул; ~ **me the manager!** позови́те мне завéдующего!
4 (*bring into a position or state*): **we got him home** мы достáвили егó домóй; **we got the piano through the door** мы пронесли́ пиани́но чéрез дверь.
5 (*p.p., expr. possession*): **he has got a book** у негó есть кни́га.
6 (*p.p., expr. obligation*): **I have got to go** я дóлжен идти́.
7 (*persuade*) заст|авля́ть, -áвить; **I got him to tell me everything** я застáвил егó рассказáть мне всё; **I got the fire to burn** мне удалóсь разжéчь огóнь.
8 (*factitive*): **I got my hair cut** я постри́гся.
9 (*denoting progress or achievement*): **I got to know him** я познакóмился с ним бли́же; **I got to like travelling** я полюби́л путешéствия; **he got to be manager** он стал дирéктором.
■ *v.i.* (**getting;** *past* **got;** *p.p.* **got** *or US* **gotten**)
1 (*become, be*) ста|нови́ться, -ть; **he got red in the face** он покраснéл; **he got angry** он разозли́лся; **he got drunk** он напи́лся; **he got married** он жени́лся; **he got ready** он приготóвился; **he got killed** егó уби́ли; он поги́б; **we got talking** мы разговори́лись.
2 (*arrive*) приб|ывáть, -ы́ть; **when did you ~ here?** когдá вы сюдá при́были?; **where has my book got to?** кудá дéлась/девáлась моя́ кни́га?
■ *with preps.*: **the officer got his troops across the river** офицéр перепрáвил свои́ войскá чéрез рéку; **I cannot ~ at the books** я не могý добрáться до э́тих книг; **we must ~ at the truth** мы должны́ добрáться до и́стины; **what is he ~ting at?** (*trying to say*) что он хóчет сказáть?; кудá он клóнит?; **she is always ~ting at me** (*Br., criticizing*) онá всегдá ко мне придирáется; **he got in(to) the taxi** он сел в такси́; **I cannot ~ into these shoes** я не могý влезть в э́ти тýфли; **he got into the club** егó при́няли в клуб; **he got off his horse** он соскочи́л с коня́; **he got on his bicycle** он сел на велосипéд; **the lion got out of its cage** лев вы́скочил из клéтки; **I got out of going to the party** я отвертéлся/уклони́лся от вечери́нки; **I got £6 out of him** я вы́жал из негó 6 фýнтов; **we got over the wall** мы перелéзли чéрез стéну; **I cannot ~ over his rudeness** я не могý прийти́ в себя́ от егó грýбости; **we got round the difficulty** мы спрáвились с э́той проблéмой; **she got round him** ей удалóсь егó уговори́ть/провести́; **I got through the work** я продéлал всю рабóту; **he got through his exam** он сдал экзáмен; **we got to Paris by noon** мы добрали́сь до Пари́жа к полýдню; **the children got up to mischief** (*Br.*) дéти расшали́лись; **we got up to chapter 5** мы дошли́ до 5-й (пя́той) главы́.
■ *with advs.*: ~ **about,** ~ **around** *v.i.*: **he ~s about a great deal** он постоя́нно в разъéздах; **a car makes it easier to ~ about** с маши́ной лéгче поспевáть всю́ду; ~ **across** *v.t.*: **the speaker got his point across** выступáющий чётко изложи́л свою́ тóчку зрéния; ~ **along** *v.i.*: **they ~ along** (*agree*) **very well** они́ отли́чно лáдят; ~ **around** *v.i.* = ~ **about** *or* ~ **round;** ~ **away** *v.i.*: **the prisoner got away** заключённый бежáл; **he got away with cheating** емý удалóсь сжýльничать; ~

back *v.t.*: **he got his books back** он получи́л обра́тно/наза́д свои́ кни́ги; *v.i.*: **he got back from the country** он верну́лся из дере́вни; **~ by** *v.i.*: **please let me ~ by** (*pass*) разреши́те мне пройти́, пожа́луйста; **~ down** *v.t.*: **he got a book down from the shelf** он снял кни́гу с по́лки; **this weather ~s me down** э́та пого́да де́йствует на меня́ удруча́юще; *v.i.*: **he got down from his horse** он соскочи́л/слез с коня́; **he got down to his work** он засе́л за рабо́ту; **~ in** *v.i.*: **the burglar got in through the window** вор прони́к в дом че́рез окно́; **the train got in early** по́езд пришёл ра́но; **we didn't ~ in to the concert** мы не попа́ли на конце́рт; **he got in** (*was elected*) **for Chester** он прошёл на вы́борах в Че́стере; **~ off** *v.t.* (*remove*) сн|има́ть, -ять; **his lawyer got him off** (*acquitted*) адвока́т доби́лся его́ оправда́ния; *v.i.*: **he got off at the next station** он сошёл (с по́езда) на сле́дующей ста́нции; **I got off (to sleep) early** я ра́но засну́л; **we got off** (*started*) **at 9 a.m.** мы вы́шли/вы́ехали/отпра́вились в 9 часо́в; **he got off with a fine** он отде́лался штра́фом; **~ on** *v.t.*: **~ your clothes on!** оде́ньтесь!; *v.i.*: **how are you ~ting on?** как дела́?; **she is ~ting on** (*Br., making progress*) она́ де́лает успе́хи; (*growing old*) она́ старе́ет; **~ting on for** (*nearly*) почти́; **~ on with your work!** займи́тесь свое́й рабо́той!; **they ~ on (well) together** (*Br.*) они́ ла́дят ме́жду собо́й; **~ out** *v.t.*: **they got the book out** (*published*) они́ изда́ли/вы́пустили кни́гу; *v.i.*: **~ out!** убира́йтесь!; **the secret got out** секре́т стал изве́стен; **~ (a)round** *v.i.*: **I haven't got (a)round to writing to him** я ника́к не соберу́сь написа́ть ему́; **~ through** *v.t.* (*an exam*) выде́рживать, вы́держать экза́мен; **~ together** *v.t.*: **he got an army together** он собра́л а́рмию; *v.i.*: **we must ~ together and have a talk** мы должны́ встре́титься и поговори́ть; **~ up** *v.t.*: **they got me up at 7** они́ по́дняли меня́ в 7 часо́в; *v.i.* (*from bed, chair etc.*) вста|ва́ть, -ть; **the wind/sea is ~ting up** поднима́ется ве́тер; мо́ре начина́ет волнова́ться.

■ *cpd.* **~-together** *n.* (*meeting, gathering*) встре́ча, сбо́рище.

Ghana /ˈgɑːnə/ *n.* Га́на.

Ghanaian /gɑːˈneɪən/ *n.* га́н|ец (*fem.* -ка).
■ *adj.* га́нский.

ghastly /ˈgɑːstlɪ/ *adj.* (**ghastlier, ghastliest**) ужа́сный.

gherkin /ˈgəːkɪn/ *n.* корнишо́н.

ghetto /ˈgetəʊ/ *n.* (*pl.* **~s** *or* **~es**) ге́тто (*nt. indecl.*); **~ blaster** (*coll.*) перено́сно́й магнитофо́н, магнито́ла.

ghost /gəʊst/ *n.* привиде́ние; дух.

ghostly /ˈgəʊstlɪ/ *adj.* (**ghostlier, ghostliest**) похо́жий на привиде́ние.

GI (*abbr. of* ***government issue***; = *American soldier*) (*pl.* **GIs**) «джи-а́й» (*indecl.*); (америка́нский) солда́т.

giant /ˈdʒaɪənt/ *n.* гига́нт.

gibber /ˈdʒɪbə(r)/ *v.i.* тарато́рить (*impf.*); говори́ть (*impf.*) невня́тно; лопота́ть (*impf.*) (*coll.*).

gibberish /ˈdʒɪbərɪʃ/ *n.* тараба́рщина.

gibbon /ˈgɪbən/ *n.* гиббо́н.

giblets /ˈdʒɪblɪts/ *n.* потрох|а́ (*pl., g.* -о́в).

Gibraltar /dʒɪˈbrɔːltə/ *n.* Гибралта́р.

giddy /ˈgɪdɪ/ *adj.* (**giddier, giddiest**) головокружи́тельный; **I feel ~** у меня́ кру́жится голова́.

gift /gɪft/ *n.*
1 (*thing given*) пода́рок; **~ shop** магази́н пода́рков; **~ voucher** (*Br.*)/**token** (*Br.*)/**certificate** (*US*) пода́рочный тало́н/купо́н.
2 (*talent*) дарова́ние; дар; **he has a ~ for languages** у него́ спосо́бности (*f. pl.*)/тала́нт к языка́м.

gifted /ˈgɪftɪd/ *adj.* одарённый.

gig[1] /gɪg/ *n.* (*coll.*) (*performance*) выступле́ние, конце́рт.

gig[2] /gɪg/ *n.* (*comput., coll.*) гиг (*coll. abbr. of* гигаба́йт).

giga- /ˈgɪgə/ *comb. form* гига…; **~byte** гигаба́йт; **~watt** гигава́тт.

gigantic /dʒaɪˈgæntɪk/ *adj.* гига́нтский.

giggle /ˈgɪg(ə)l/ *n.* хихи́канье.
■ *v.i.* хихи́к|ать, -нуть.

gilt /gɪlt/ *n.* позоло́та.

gimmick /ˈgɪmɪk/ *n.* трюк.

gin /dʒɪn/ *n.* джин.

ginger /ˈdʒɪndʒə(r)/ *n.* (*bot., cul.*) имби́рь (*m.*); (*attr.*) имби́рный.

gingerly /ˈdʒɪndʒəlɪ/ *adj.* (кра́йне) осторо́жный.
■ *adv.* осторо́жно.

Gipsy, Gypsy /ˈdʒɪpsɪ/ *n.* цыга́н (*fem.* -ка).
■ *adj.* цыга́нский.

giraffe /dʒɪˈrɑːf/ *n.* (*pl.* **~** *or* **~s**) жира́ф.

girder /ˈgəːdə(r)/ *n.* (*beam*) ба́лка.

girdle /ˈgəːd(ə)l/ *n.*
1 (*belt etc.*) по́яс; куша́к.
2 (*corset*) корсе́т.

girl /gəːl/ *n.* (*child*) де́вочка; (*young woman*) де́вушка; (*pej.*) девчо́нка; **G~ Guide, Scout** де́вочка-ска́ут, гёрлска́ут.
■ *cpd.* **~friend** *n.* (*female friend*) подру́га; (*female sexual partner*) де́вушка.

girlish /ˈgəːlɪʃ/ *adj.* деви́ческий; (*of a boy*) изне́женный, (*coll.*) как девчо́нка.

girth /gəːθ/ *n.* (*of horse*) подпру́га; (*of tree, person etc.*) обхва́т; разме́р.

gist /dʒɪst/ *n.* суть.

give /gɪv/ *n.*
1 (*elasticity*) пода́тливость, эласти́чность.
2 : **~ and take** взаи́мные усту́пки (*f. pl.*).
■ *v.t.* (*past* **gave**; *p.p.* **given** /ˈgɪv(ə)n/)
1 да|ва́ть, -ть; **I gave the porter my luggage ~** я о́тдал свой бага́ж носи́льщику; **two years, ~ or take a month or so** о́коло двух лет — ме́сяцем бо́льше и́ли ме́ньше.
2 (*as a present*) дари́ть, по-; **he was ~n a book** ему́ подари́ли кни́гу.
3 (*~ in exchange*): **I gave a good price for it** я за э́то хорошо́ заплати́л; **he gave as good as he got** он отплати́л той же моне́той.
4 (*provide, inflict*): **he ~s me a lot of trouble** он доставля́ет мне мно́го хлопо́т; **he**

has ~n me his cold я заразился от него насморком; **he gave** (*cited*) **an example** он привёл пример; **~ him my regards** передайте ему привет от меня; **~ pleasure** дост|авлять, -авить удовольствие.
5 (*devote*) удел|ять, -ить; посвя|щать, -тить; **he gave a lot of time to the work** он уделил этой работе много времени; **he gave his life for her** он отдал за неё жизнь.
6 (*allow*): **I ~ you an hour to get ready** я даю вам час на сборы/приготовления.
7 (*organize*) устр|аивать, -оить; **they gave a dance** они устроили танцевальный вечер.
8 (*special uses of* **~n**): **at a ~n** (*specified, agreed, particular*) **time** в определённое время; **~n name** (*forename*) имя (*nt.*); **he is ~n to boasting** он склонен к хвастовству; **~ that ...** при том, что... .
■ *v.i.* (*past* **gave;** *p.p.* **given** /'gɪv(ə)n/) (*yield*) подд|аваться, -аться; под|аваться, -аться.
■ *with advs.*: **~ away** *v.t.* дарить, по-; **he gave away the secret** он выдал секрет; **he gave the game away** (*revealed a secret*) он проболтался; он выдал секрет; **~ back** *v.t.* (*restore*) возвра|щать, -тить; **~ in** *v.t.*: **he gave in his** (*exam*) **paper** (*Br.*) он сдал свою экзаменационную работу; *v.i.* (*yield*) подд|аваться, -аться; уступ|ать, -ить; **he gave in to my persuasion** он поддался моим уговорам; **~ off** *v.t.* (*emit*) испус|кать, -тить; изд|авать, -ать; **~ out** *v.t.* (*distribute*) распредел|ять, -ить; *v.i.* кончаться, кончиться; **his strength gave out** его силы иссякли; **~ up** *v.t.* ост|авлять, -авить; (*resign, surrender*) отказ|ываться, -аться + *g.*; **he gave up his seat to her** он уступил ей место; **the murderer gave himself up** убийца сдался; (*desist from*) бр|осать, -осить; **he gave up smoking** он бросил курить; (*abandon hope of*): **we gave it up as a bad job** мы махнули рукой на это дело; *v.i.* **I ~ up!** сдаюсь!
■ *cpd.* **~away** *n.* (*coll.*) (*betrayal of secret etc.*): **her tears were a ~away** слёзы выдавали её.

glacier /'glæsɪə(r)/ *n.* ледник.

glad /glæd/ *adj.* (**gladder, gladdest**) довольный; **I am ~ to meet you** рад с вами познакомиться.

gladden /'glæd(ə)n/ *v.t.* радовать, об-; **flowers ~ the scene** цветы оживляют вид; **wine ~s the heart** вино веселит душу.

gladiator /'glædɪeɪtə(r)/ *n.* гладиатор.

gladio|lus /glædɪ'əʊləs/ *n.* (*pl.* **~li** /-laɪ/ *or* **~luses**) гладиолус.

gladly /'glædlɪ/ *adv.* охотно.

glamor /'glæmə(r)/ (*US*) = **glamour**

glamorous /'glæmərəs/ *adj.* обольстительный; (*of job etc.*) заманчивый.

glamour /'glæmə(r)/ (*US* **glamor**) *n.* волшебство.

glamo(u)rize /'glæməraɪz/ *v.t.* приукра|шивать, -сить.

glanc|e /glɑ:ns/ *n.* взгляд.
■ *v.t.* & *i.*
1 (*look*) взглянуть (*pf.*); **he ~ed at the clock** он взглянул на часы; **he ~ed round the room** он оглядел комнату.
2 (*bounce*) отск|акивать, -очить; **a ~ing blow** скользящий удар.

gland /glænd/ *n.* железа.

glandular /'glændjʊlə(r)/ *adj.*: **~ fever** воспаление гланд.

glare /gleə(r)/ *n.* (*fierce light*) ослепительный свет/блеск; (*angry look*) свирепый взгляд.
■ *v.t.* & *i.*: **~ at s.o.** испепел|ять, -ить кого-н. взглядом.

glaring /'gleərɪŋ/ *adj.* (*e.g. headlights*) слепящий; (*of mistake etc.*) грубый.

glass /glɑ:s/ *n.*
1 (*substance*) стекло.
2 (*for drinking*) (*tumbler*) стакан; (*wine ~*) рюмка, бокал.
3 (*~ware*) стеклянная посуда.
4 (*Br., mirror*) зеркало.
5 (*pl., spectacles*) очк|и (*pl.*, *g.* -ов).

glassy /'glɑ:sɪ/ *adj.* (**glassier, glassiest**): **a ~ stare** тусклый/застывший взгляд.

glaucoma /glɔ:'kəʊmə/ *n.* глаукома.

glaze /gleɪz/ *n.* глазурь.
■ *v.t.* (*pottery*) покр|ывать, -ыть глазурью.

gleam /gli:m/ *n.* проблеск.
■ *v.i.* поблёскивать (*impf.*).

glean /gli:n/ *v.t.* (*information*) соб|ирать, -рать.

glee /gli:/ *n.* (*delight*) веселье; ликование.

gleeful /'gli:fʊl/ *adj.* ликующий.

glen /glen/ *n.* лощина.

glib /glɪb/ *adj.* (**glibber, glibbest**) бойкий на язык; **a ~ excuse** благовидный предлог.

glide /glaɪd/ *v.i.* скольз|ить, -нуть; (*in aircraft*) планировать, с-.

glider /'glaɪdə(r)/ *n.* планер.

gliding /'glaɪdɪŋ/ *n.* (*sport*) планеризм.

glimmer /'glɪmə(r)/ *n.*: **a ~ of hope** проблеск/луч надежды.

glimpse /glɪmps/ *n.* проблеск; **I caught a ~ of him** он промелькнул у меня перед глазами.
■ *v.t.* увидеть (*pf.*) мельком.

glint /glɪnt/ *n.* блеск; (*reflection*) отблеск.
■ *v.i.* блестеть (*impf.*); (*flash*) вспых|ивать, -нуть.

glisten /'glɪs(ə)n/ *v.i.* сверк|ать, -нуть.

glitch /glɪtʃ/ *n.* небольшое затруднение.

glitter /'glɪtə(r)/ *n.* блеск, сверкание.
■ *v.i.* блестеть (*impf.*); сверкать (*impf.*).

glitz /glɪts/ *n.* (показной) блеск, лоск, шик.

glitzy /'glɪtsɪ/ *adj.* (**glitzier, glitziest**) впечатляющий внешне (*or* своим видом), (*disapproving only*) показушный; (*party*) гламурный.

gloat /gləʊt/ *v.i.* злорадствовать (*impf.*).

global /'gləʊb(ə)l/ *adj.* (*total*) всеобщий; (*worldwide*) глобальный; **~ warming** глобальное потепление.

globalization /gləʊbəlaɪ'zeɪʃ(ə)n/ *n.* глобализация.

globe /gləʊb/ *n.* шар.
■ *cpd.* **~trotter** *n.* заядлый турист.

globule /'glɒbju:l/ *n.* шарик; капелька.

gloom /glu:m/ *n.* (*dark*) тьма; (*despondency*) мрачность.

gloomy /'glu:mɪ/ *adj.* (**gloomier, gloomiest**) (*dark*) мрачный; (*depressing*) гнетущий; (*depressed*) хмурый; унылый.

glorify /ˈglɔːrɪfaɪ/ *v.t.* просл|авля́ть, -а́вить.

glorious /ˈglɔːrɪəs/ *adj.* сла́вный, великоле́пный; **a ~ day** (*weather*) изуми́тельный день.

glory /ˈglɔːrɪ/ *n.*
1 (*renown, honour*) сла́ва.
2 (*splendour*) великоле́пие.
■ *v.i.* упива́ться (*impf.*) + *i.*; **~ in one's strength** упива́ться свое́й си́лой.

gloss /glɒs/ *n.* (*lit., fig.*) лоск; **~ paint** блестя́щий лак.
■ *v.t.*: **~ over faults** обойти́ (*pf.*) оши́бки молча́нием.

glossary /ˈglɒsərɪ/ *n.* глосса́рий.

glossy /ˈglɒsɪ/ *adj.* (**glossier, glossiest**) гля́нцевый; лощёный; **a ~ photograph** гля́нцевая фотогра́фия; **~ magazines** гля́нцевые журна́лы.

glove /glʌv/ *n.* перча́тка; **~ compartment** (*in car*) бардачо́к.

glow /gləʊ/ *n.* (*of fire, sunset etc.*) за́рево; (*of feelings*) пыл.
■ *v.i.* (*incandesce*) накал|я́ться, -и́ться; (*shine*) свети́ться (*impf.*); **he ~ed with pride** его́ распира́ла го́рдость; **he described the trip in ~ing colours** он опи́сывал путеше́ствие в ра́дужных тона́х.

glower /ˈglaʊə(r)/ *v.i.* серди́то смотре́ть (*impf.*) (**at:** на + *a.*).

glucose /ˈgluːkəʊs/ *n.* глюко́за.

glue /gluː/ *n.* клей.
■ *v.t.* (**glues, glued, gluing** *or* **glueing**) прикле́и|вать, -ть.
■ *cpds.* **~-sniffer** *n.* токсикома́н; **~-sniffing** *n.* токсикома́ния.

glum /glʌm/ *adj.* (**glummer, glummest**) угрю́мый.

glut /glʌt/ *n.* избы́ток.

gluten /ˈgluːt(ə)n/ *n.* клейкови́на.

glutton /ˈglʌt(ə)n/ *n.* обжо́ра (*c.g.*); **a ~ for work** жа́дный к рабо́те.

gluttonous /ˈglʌtənəs/ *adj.* прожо́рливый.

gluttony /ˈglʌtənɪ/ *n.* обжо́рство.

glycerine /ˈglɪsəriːn/ (*US* **glycerin**) *n.* глицери́н.

GM (*abbr. of* ***genetically modified***): **~ foods** генети́чески модифици́рованные проду́кты.

GMT = **Greenwich (mean) time**

gnarl|ed /nɑːld/, **-y** /ˈnɑːlɪ/ *adjs.* шишкова́тый; сучкова́тый.

gnash /næʃ/ *v.t.*: **~ one's teeth** скрежета́ть (*impf.*) зуба́ми.

gnat /næt/ *n.* кома́р, мо́шка.

gnaw /nɔː/ *v.t.* & *i.* грызть (*impf.*).

gnome /nəʊm/ *n.* (*goblin etc.*) гном.

GNP (*abbr. of* ***Gross National Product***) ВНП (валово́й национа́льный проду́кт).

GNVQ (*abbr. of* ***General National Vocational Qualification***) *n.* (*Br.*) Общенациона́льное свиде́тельство о профессиона́льной квалифика́ции.

go /gəʊ/ *n.* (*pl.* **~es**)
1 (*movement, animation*): **she's on the ~ from morning to night** она́ с утра́ до ве́чера на нога́х.
2 (*turn, attempt*) попы́тка; **now it's my ~** тепе́рь моя́ о́чередь.
■ *v.i.* (*3rd pers. sing. pres.* **goes;** *past* **went;** *p.p.* **gone**) (*see also* ▸ **gone**).
1 (*on foot*) ходи́ть (*indet.*), идти́ (*det.*), пойти́ (*pf.*); (*ride etc.*) е́здить (*indet.*), е́хать (*det.*), пое́хать (*pf.*); (*by train*) е́хать по́ездом; (*by plane*) лета́ть (*indet.*), лете́ть (*det.*), полете́ть (*pf.*) (самолётом); **this train ~es to London** э́тот по́езд идёт в Ло́ндон.
2 (*fig., with general idea of motion or direction*): **this road ~es to York** э́та доро́га ведёт в Йорк; **he ~es to school** (*is a schoolboy*) он хо́дит в шко́лу; **let me ~!** отпусти́те меня́!; **there is still an hour to ~** ещё час в запа́се; **his plans went wrong** его́ пла́ны сорвали́сь.
3 (*with cognate etc. object*): **he went a long way** он пошёл/ушёл далеко́; **they went halves** они́ раздели́ли всё попола́м; **the balloon went 'pop'** шар ло́пнул.
4 (*idea of progress or outcome*): **how's it ~ing?** (*health, affairs*) как дела́?; как пожива́ете?; **everything is ~ing well** всё (идёт) хорошо́; **the party/play went well** вечери́нка/пье́са прошла́ хорошо́.
5 (*expr. tenor or tendency*): **the story ~es that ...** расска́зывают, что... .
6 (*set out, depart*): **the post ~es at 5 p.m.** по́чта ухо́дит в 5 часо́в дня.
7 (*pass, disappear*): **our holiday went in a flash** на́ши кани́кулы пролете́ли мгнове́нно; **it's ~ne 4** (*o'clock*) уже́ бо́льше четырёх; пошёл пя́тый час; **I wish this pain would ~** хоть бы прошла́ э́та боль!; **all my money is ~ne** все мои́ де́ньги уплы́ли.
8 (*become*): **the milk went sour** молоко́ прокисло; **she went red in the face** она́ покрасне́ла.
9 (*function*): **I can't get my watch to ~** у меня́ не заво́дятся часы́.
10 (*sound*): **come in when the bell ~es** входи́те, когда́ зазвони́т звоно́к.
11 (*be known, accepted, usual*): **what he says ~es** его сло́во — зако́н; **anything ~es** всё сойдёт; **it ~es without saying** э́то само́ собо́й разуме́ется.
12 (*expr. impending or predicted action*): **I'm ~ing to sneeze** я сейча́с чихну́; **it's ~ing to rain** собира́ется дождь.
13 (*expr. intention*): **I am ~ing to ask him** я реши́л спроси́ть его́.
14 (*be sold*): **the picture went for a song** карти́ну про́дали за бесце́нок; **these cakes are ~ing cheap** э́ти пиро́жные сто́ят дёшево (*or* иду́т по дешёвке).
■ *with preps.*: **how shall I ~ about this?** как мне за э́то взя́ться?; **he went about his business** он заня́лся свои́ми дела́ми; **the dog went after the hare** соба́ка погнала́сь за за́йцем; **the decision went against them** реше́ние бы́ло не в их по́льзу; **he went** (*passed*) **by the window** он прошёл ми́мо окна́; **I went for a drink** я отпра́вился вы́пить; **the dog went for his legs** соба́ка хвата́ла его́ за́ ноги; **he will always ~ for the best** он всегда́ бу́дет стреми́ться к лу́чшему; **he went into the house** он вошёл в дом; **he had to ~ into hospital** ему́ пришло́сь лечь в больни́цу; **it won't ~ into the box** (*is too big*) э́то не войдёт в коро́бку; **I've ~ne off prawns** (*Br. coll.*) я разлюби́л креве́тки; **I am ~ing on a**

course я поступа́ю на ку́рсы; **all his money went on food** все его́ де́ньги пошли́/уходи́ли на еду́; **we have no evidence to ~ on** для э́того у нас нет никаки́х основа́ний; **I went over his work with him** вме́сте с ним я прошёлся по его́ рабо́те; **we have ~ne over** (*discussed*) **that** мы э́то обсужда́ли; **we went round the gallery** мы обошли́ галере́ю; **~ through the main gate!** проходи́те че́рез гла́вные воро́та!; **she went through his pockets** она́ обша́рила у него́ все карма́ны; **he has ~ne through a lot** ему́ довело́сь мно́гое испыта́ть; **I'll ~ through the main points again** я хочу́ повтори́ть гла́вные пу́нкты; **he went through the money in a week** он растра́тил де́ньги за неде́лю; **the estate went to her nephew** иму́щество перешло́ её племя́ннику; **the prize went to him** он вы́играл приз; **the money will ~ towards a new car** де́ньги пойду́т на поку́пку но́вой маши́ны; **he went up the stairs** он стал поднима́ться (*or* пошёл вверх) по ле́стнице; **this tie ~es with your suit** э́тот га́лстук подхо́дит к ва́шему костю́му; **he has been ~ing with her for months** он встреча́ется с ней уже́ не́сколько ме́сяцев; **we went without a holiday** мы обошли́сь без о́тпуска.

■ *with advs.*: **~ ahead!** вперёд!; **~ along** *v.i.*: **I cannot ~ along with that** я не могу́ с э́тим согласи́ться; **~ around** *v.i.*: **he is ~ing around with my sister** он встреча́ется с мое́й сестро́й; (*US*) = **~ round** *v.i.*; **~ away** *v.i.* уходи́ть, уйти́; **~ away!** уходи́те!; **~ back** *v.i.* идти́ (*det.*) наза́д; возвра|ща́ться, -ти́ться; **he went back on his word** он не сдержа́л своего́ сло́ва; **this custom ~es back to the 15th century** э́тот обы́чай восхо́дит к пятна́дцатому ве́ку; **~ by** *v.i.*: **as the years ~ by** с года́ми; **~ down** *v.i.*: спус|ка́ться, -ти́ться; **he went down on his knees** он опусти́лся на коле́ни; **the sun went down** со́лнце се́ло; **she went down with flu** (*Br.*) она́ слегла́ с гри́ппом; **prices are ~ing down** це́ны па́дают; **his story went down well** его́ расска́з был хорошо́ при́нят; **~ in** *v.i.* (*enter*) входи́ть, войти́; **the sun went in** со́лнце зашло́; **he went in for the competition** он при́нял уча́стие в ко́нкурсе; **~ off** *v.i.*: **he went off without a word** он ушёл без еди́ного сло́ва; **the alarm clock went off** буди́льник зазвене́л; **the light has ~ne off** свет пога́с; **the fruit has ~ne off** (*Br.*) фру́кты погни́ли; **his work has ~ne off lately** в после́днее вре́мя он стал рабо́тать ху́же; **the party went off well** вечери́нка прошла́ хорошо́; **~ on** *v.i.*: **the lights went on** загоре́лся свет; **I can't ~ on any longer** я так бо́льше не могу́; **shall we ~ on to the next item?** дава́йте перейдём к сле́дующему пу́нкту?; **~ on playing!** продолжа́йте игра́ть; **what is ~ing on here?** что тут происхо́дит?; **~ on at** (*nag*) пили́ть (*impf.*); набра́сываться (*impf.*) на + *a.*; **he went on** (*stage*) **after the interval** он вы́шел на сце́ну по́сле антра́кта; **as time ~es on** со вре́менем; **~ out** *v.i.* (*exit*) выходи́ть, вы́йти; **the light went out** свет пога́с; **the tide was ~ing out** шёл отли́в; **~ over** *v.i.*: **he went over to France** он перепра́вился во Фра́нцию; **the country went over to decimal coinage** страна́ перешла́ на десяти́чную моне́тную систе́му; **~ round** *v.i.*: **I went round to see him** (*Br.*) я пошёл его́ навести́ть; **we had to ~ round by the park** (*Br.*) нам пришло́сь идти́ в обхо́д че́рез парк; **he ~es round collecting money** (*Br.*) он обхо́дит всех и собира́ет де́ньги; **is there enough food to ~ round?** (*Br.*) хва́тит ли еды́ на всех?; **~ through** *v.i.*: **I cannot ~ through with the plan** я не могу́ осуществи́ть э́тот план; **the deal went through** сде́лка состоя́лась; **has their divorce ~ne through?** они́ уже́ развели́сь?; **~ together** *v.i.*: **they were ~ing together** (*keeping company*) **for years** они́ встреча́лись мно́гие го́ды; **these colours ~ together** э́ти цвета́ гармони́руют; **~ under** *v.i.*: **his business went under** его́ де́ло ло́пнуло; **~ up** *v.i.* подн|има́ться, -я́ться; **he went up to bed** он пошёл спать; **prices have ~ne up** це́ны повы́сились.

■ *cpds.* **~-ahead** *n.* разреше́ние, «добро́», «зелёная у́лица»; **~-between** *n.* посре́дник; **~-cart** *n.* (*also* **~-kart**) карт; **~-slow** *n.* (*Br.*) части́чная забасто́вка.

goad /gəʊd/ *n.* *v.t.* погоня́ть (*impf.*); (*prod*) пришпо́ри|вать, -ть; (*tease, torment*) раздража́ть (*impf.*).

goal /gəʊl/ *n.*
1 (*objective*) цель.
2 (*sport*) воро́т|а (*pl., g.* —).
■ *cpds.* **~keeper** *n.* врата́рь (*m.*); **~post** *n.* шта́нга.

goalie /ˈgəʊlɪ/ *n.* (*coll.*) врата́рь (*m.*).

goat /gəʊt/ *n.* коза́; (*male*) козёл.

gobble[1] /ˈgɒb(ə)l/ *v.t.* жрать, по-/со-.

gobble[2] /ˈgɒb(ə)l/ *v.i.* (*of a turkey*) кулды́кать (*impf.*).

gobbledygook /ˈgɒb(ə)ldɪgu:k/ *n.* (*sl.*) болтоло́гия, (пусто́й) набо́р слов; (*in speech of politicians also*) витиева́тая демаго́гия; (*in documents*) бюрократи́ческий жарго́н, канцеляри́т.

goblin /ˈgɒblɪn/ *n.* домово́й, го́блин.

god /gɒd/ *n.* (*deity*) бог; (**G~:** *supreme being*) Бог; божество́; **my G~!** Бо́же мой!; Го́споди!
■ *cpds.* **~child** *n.* кре́стни|к (*fem.* -ца); **~-daughter** *n.* кре́стница; **~father** *n.* кре́стный (оте́ц); **~-forsaken place** медве́жий у́гол; **~mother** *n.* крёстная (мать); **~parent** *n.* крёстный (оте́ц); крёстная (мать); **~send** *n.* нахо́дка; ≈ сам Бог посла́л; **~son** *n.* кре́стник.

goddess /ˈgɒdɪs/ *n.* боги́ня.

goes /gəʊz/ *3rd pers. sing. pres. of* ▶ **go**

goggles /ˈgɒg(ə)lz/ *n.* тёмные/защи́тные очк|и́ (*pl., g.* -о́в).

going /ˈgəʊɪŋ/ *n.*
1 (*departure*) отъе́зд, ухо́д.
2 (*progress, speed*) ско́рость; **fifty miles an hour is good ~** 50 миль в час — хоро́шая ско́рость; **this book is heavy ~** э́та кни́га тру́дно чита́ется; **the conversation was heavy ~** разгово́р не кле́ился.
■ *adj.* 1 (*working*): **a ~ concern** де́йствующее предприя́тие.

2 (*Br., to be had*): **one of the best newspapers ~** одна́ из лу́чших ны́нешних газе́т.
■ *cpd.* **~s-on** *n. pl.* (*coll.*) поведе́ние; посту́пки (*m. pl.*); дела́ (*nt. pl.*); «дели́шки» (*nt. pl.*).

gold /gəʊld/ *n.* & *adj.* (*metal*) зо́лото; **~ medal** золота́я меда́ль; **he's as good as ~** (*of child*) он зо́лото, а не ребёнок.
■ *cpds.* **~ dust** *n.* золото́й песо́к; **~fish** *n.* золота́я ры́бка; **~ mine** *n.* золото́й рудни́к; (*fig.*): **the shop is a ~ mine** э́тот магази́н — золото́е дно; **~ rush** *n.* золота́я лихора́дка.

golden /'gəʊld(ə)n/ *adj.* (*lit., fig.*) золото́й; (*of colour*) золоти́стый; **the ~ age** золото́й век; **receive a ~ handshake on retirement** получи́ть (*pf.*) вознагражде́ние при ухо́де на пе́нсию; **miss a ~ opportunity** упусти́ть (*pf.*) редча́йшую возмо́жность.

golf /gɒlf/ *n.* гольф.
■ *cpds.* **~ club** *n.* (*association*) клуб люби́телей игры́ в гольф; (*implement*) клю́шка; **~ course** *n.* площа́дка/по́ле для игры́ в гольф.

golfer /'gɒlfə(r)/ *n.* игро́к в гольф.

gondola /'gɒndələ/ *n.* (*boat; airship car*) гондо́ла.

gone /gɒn/ *adj.* (*see also* ▸ **go**).
1 (*departed, past*) уе́хавший.
2 (*dead*) уме́рший, усо́пший.

gong /gɒŋ/ *n.* (*instrument*) гонг.

gonorrhoea /gɒnə'rɪə/ (*US* **gonorrhea**) *n.* гоноре́я.

good /gʊd/ *n.*
1 (*~ness, ~ action*) добро́, бла́го; **he is up to no ~** он заду́мал что́-то недо́брое.
2 (*benefit*) по́льза; **drink it! it will do you ~** вы́пейте э́то — вам поле́зно; **it's no ~ complaining** что то́лку жа́ловаться?
3 : **for ~** (*permanently*) навсегда́.
4 (*pl., property*) добро́.
5 (*pl., merchandise*) това́р(ы); **~s train** това́рный по́езд.
■ *adj.* (**better, best**)
1 (*in most senses*) хоро́ший; до́брый; (*of food*) вку́сный; **~ idea!** прекра́сная мысль!; **a ~ player** си́льный игро́к; **G~ Friday** Страстна́я пя́тница; **~ heavens!** бо́же мой!
2 (*of health, condition etc.*) хоро́ший; здоро́вый; **I don't feel so ~ today** (*coll.*) я себя́ нева́жно чу́вствую сего́дня; **apples are ~ for you** я́блоки поле́зны для здоро́вья.
3 (*favourable, fortunate*): **~ luck!** жела́ю успе́ха; **it's a ~ thing we stayed at home** хорошо́, что мы оста́лись до́ма.
4 (*kind*) любе́зный, до́брый; **that's very ~ of you** э́то о́чень ми́ло с ва́шей стороны́.
5 (*of skill*): **~ at** спосо́бный к + *d.*; си́льный в + *p.*; **she's ~ at maths** она́ спосо́бна к матема́тике; **he is no ~ at his job** он взя́лся не за своё де́ло.
6 (*suitable*) подходя́щий.
7 (*well-behaved*) воспи́танный; послу́шный; **be ~!** веди́ себя́ прили́чно!
8 (*var.*): **~ morning!** до́брое у́тро!; **it's ~ to see you** прия́тно вас ви́деть; **a ~ while ago** давны́м-давно́; **he was as ~ as his word** он сдержа́л своё сло́во; **he as ~ as refused to go** он факти́чески отказа́лся идти́.
■ *cpds.* **~-for-nothing** *n.* безде́льник, никчёмный челове́к; **~-humoured** (*US* **-humored**) *adj.* доброду́шный; **~-looking** *adj.* краси́вый; хоро́ш/хороша́ собо́й; **~-natured** *adj.* доброду́шный; **~night** *int.* споко́йной но́чи!; **~will** *n.* (*friendship*) доброжела́тельность; (*of business*) репута́ция.

goodbye /gʊd'baɪ/ *n.* проща́ние.
■ *int.* до свида́ния!; проща́йте.

goodness /'gʊdnɪs/ *n.*
1 (*virtue*) доброта́.
2 (*kindness*) любе́зность.
3 (*nourishment*): **these apples are full of ~** э́ти я́блоки о́чень поле́зны/пита́тельны.
4 (*euph., God*): **G~ me!** вот те на́!; **thank ~!** сла́ва бо́гу!

gooey /'gu:ɪ/ *adj.* (**gooier, gooiest**) (*coll.*) кле́йкий; ли́пкий.

google /'gu:g(ə)l/ *v.t.* & *i.* иска́ть (*impf.*) в Интерне́те (*в поисковой системе Google* (*propr.*))

goose /gu:s/ *n.* (*pl.* **geese**)
1 гусь (*m.*); (*fem. also*) гусы́ня.
2 (*simpleton*) простофи́ля (*c.g.*).
■ *cpds.* **~berry** *n.* крыжо́вник (*collect.*); я́года крыжо́вника; **play ~berry** (*Br., coll.*) ока́з|ываться, -а́ться тре́тьим ли́шним; **~flesh** *n.* гуся́тина; **it gives me ~flesh** у меня́ от э́того мура́шки по те́лу бе́гают; **~-step** *n.* (*mil.*) гуси́ный шаг.

gorge /gɔ:dʒ/ *n.* уще́лье.
■ *v.t.* & *i.* объ|еда́ться, -е́сться; **the lion ~ed (itself) on its prey** лев жа́дно поглоща́л свою́ добы́чу.

gorgeous /'gɔ:dʒəs/ *adj.* (*magnificent*) великоле́пный; (*richly coloured*) кра́сочный.

gorilla /gə'rɪlə/ *n.* гори́лла.

gormless /'gɔ:mlɪs/ *adj.* (*Br. dial. and coll.*) безду́мный; дура́шливый.

gorse /gɔ:s/ *n.* (*bot.*) утёсник обыкнове́нный.

gory /'gɔ:rɪ/ *adj.* (**gorier, goriest**) кровопроли́тный; **~ details** крова́вые подро́бности.

gosh /gɒʃ/ *int.* (*coll.*) бо́же мой!

gosling /'gɒzlɪŋ/ *n.* гусёнок.

gospel /'gɒsp(ə)l/ *n.* Ева́нгелие.

gossip /'gɒsɪp/ *n.*
1 (*talk*) сплётня.
2 (*person*) сплётни|к (*fem.* -ца).
3 (*attr.*): **~ column** коло́нка све́тской хро́ники.
■ *v.i.* (**gossiped, gossiping**) сплётничать, на-.

got /gɒt/ *past and p.p. of* ▸ **get**

Gothic /'gɒθɪk/ *n.* го́тика, готи́ческий стиль.
■ *adj.* готи́ческий.

gotten /'gɒt(ə)n/ *US p.p. of* ▸ **get**

gouache /gʊ'ɑ:ʃ/ *n.* гуа́шь.

goulash /'gu:læʃ/ *n.* гуля́ш.

gourmet /'gʊəmeɪ/ *n.* гурма́н.

gout /gaʊt/ *n.* пода́гра.

govern /'gʌv(ə)n/ *v.t.*
1 (*rule; also v.i.*) пра́вить (*impf.*) + *i.*; (*control, influence*) руководи́ть (*impf.*) + *i.*; **~ing body** (*of hospital, school, etc.*) дире́кция, правле́ние.
2 (*apply to*): **the same principle ~s both cases** оди́н и тот же при́нцип примени́м в обо́их слу́чаях.

governess /'gʌvənɪs/ *n.* гуверна́нтка.

government /ˈɡʌvənmənt/ *n.* (*rule*) правле́ние; (*system*) фо́рма правле́ния.

governmental /ɡʌvənˈment(ə)l/ *adj.* прави́тельственный.

governor /ˈɡʌvənə(r)/ *n.*
1 (*ruling official*) губерна́тор.
2 (*member of governing body*) член правле́ния.

gown /ɡaʊn/ *n.* (*woman's*) пла́тье; (*academic or official*) ма́нтия.

GP (*abbr. of* ***general practitioner***) врач о́бщей пра́ктики; уча́стко́вый врач.

GPS (*abbr. of* ***Global Positioning System***) *n.* глоба́льная спу́тниковая навигацио́нная систе́ма.

grab /ɡræb/ *v.t.* & *i.* (**grabbed, grabbing**) схва́т|ывать, -и́ть; **he ~bed me by the lapels** он схвати́л меня́ за ла́цканы.

grace /ɡreɪs/ *n.*
1 (*elegance*) гра́ция, изя́щество; **airs and ~s** (*iron.*) жема́нство.
2 (*dispensation*) отсро́чка; **the law allows 3 days' ~** по зако́ну полага́ется 3 дня отсро́чки (*or* льго́тных дня); (*prayer before meal*) моли́тва; **say ~** моли́ться (*impf.*) пе́ред едо́й.

graceful /ˈɡreɪsfʊl/ *adj.* грацио́зный; изя́щный.

gracious /ˈɡreɪʃəs/ *adj.* ми́лостивый; любе́зный; **~ living** краси́вая жизнь.
■ *int.* **good(ness) ~ (me)!** ба́тюшки!; бо́же мой!

grade /ɡreɪd/ *n.*
1 (*assessed category*) сте́пень; (*of quality*) сорт; (*of rank*) сте́пень; класс; (*US, class in school*) класс; **~ school** (*US*) нача́льная шко́ла.
2 (*school rating*) отме́тка; оце́нка.
3 (*US*): **~ crossing** (железнодоро́жный) перее́зд.
■ *v.t.* сортирова́ть, рас-.

gradient /ˈɡreɪdɪənt/ *n.* градие́нт.

gradual /ˈɡrædjʊəl/ *adj.* постепе́нный.

gradually /ˈɡrædjʊəlɪ/ *adv.* постепе́нно.

graduate[1] /ˈɡrædjʊət/ *n.* (*of university, school etc.*) выпускни́|к (*fem.* -ца).

graduate[2] /ˈɡrædjʊeɪt/ *v.i.* (*from university*) ок|а́нчивать, -о́нчить университе́т/вуз; (*US, from school*) шко́лу.

graduation /ɡrædjʊˈeɪʃ(ə)n/ *n.* (*receiving degree*) получе́ние дипло́ма/сте́пени; (*US*) оконча́ние шко́лы.

graffiti /ɡrəˈfiːtɪ/ *n.* (*sing.* **graffito** /-təʊ/) гра́ффити (*indecl., pl.*), на́дписи (*f. pl.*) (на стена́х/забо́рах).

graft /ɡrɑːft/ *n.* (*tissue*) переса́женная ткань.
■ *v.t.* (*surg.*) переса́|живать, -ди́ть; (*hort., also fig.*) прив|ива́ть, -и́ть.

grain /ɡreɪn/ *n.*
1 (*collect., seed of cereal plants*) зерно́; (*single seed*) зерно́.
2 (*small particle*) зёрнышко; **~ of sand** песчи́нка; **there is not a ~ of truth in it** в э́том нет ни крупи́цы/гра́на/ка́пли пра́вды.
3 (*of wood*) волокно́.
4: **it goes against the ~ with me** (*fig.*) э́то мне не по душе́/нутру́.

gram /ɡræm/ = **gram(me)**

grammar /ˈɡræmə(r)/ *n.* грамма́тика.
■ *cpd.* **~ school** *n.* (*Br.*) сре́дняя шко́ла с гуманита́рным укло́ном.

grammatical /ɡrəˈmætɪk(ə)l/ *adj.* граммати́ческий.

gram(me) /ɡræm/ *n.* грамм.

gramophone /ˈɡræməfəʊn/ *n.* граммофо́н; **~ record** грампласти́нка.

gran /ɡræn/ (*Br.*) = **granny**

granary /ˈɡrænərɪ/ *n.* амба́р.

grand /ɡrænd/ *adj.*
1 (*great, important*) вели́кий; грандио́зный; **~ piano** роя́ль (*m.*).
2 (*elevated, imposing*) вели́чественный.
3 (*all embracing*): **~ total** о́бщая су́мма.
■ *cpds.* **~child** *n.* внук (*fem.* вну́чка); **~ad** *n.* (*coll.*) де́душка (*m.*); **~daughter** *n.* вну́чка; **~father** *n.* де́душка (*m.*); **~father clock** высо́кие напо́льные часы́; **~ma** *n.* (*coll.*) ба́бушка; **~mother** *n.* ба́бушка; **~pa** *n.* (*coll.*) де́душка (*m.*); **~parent** *n.* де́душка (*fem.* ба́бушка); **~son** *n.* внук; **~stand** *n.* трибу́на.

grandeur /ˈɡrændʒə(r)/ *n.* вели́чие; великоле́пие.

grandiose /ˈɡrændɪəʊs/ *adj.* грандио́зный.

granite /ˈɡrænɪt/ *n.* грани́т.

granny /ˈɡrænɪ/ *n.* (*coll.*) ба́бушка.

grant /ɡrɑːnt/ *n.* (*sum etc. conferred*) дота́ция; (*to student*) стипе́ндия.
■ *v.t.* 1 (*bestow*) дарова́ть (*impf., pf.*); жа́ловать, по-.
2 (*concede*) призн|ава́ть, -а́ть; **~ed, he has done all he could** согла́сен: он сде́лал всё, что мог.
3: **he takes my help for ~ed** он принима́ет мою́ по́мощь как до́лжное.

granulate /ˈɡrænjʊleɪt/ *v.t.* & *i.*: **~d sugar** са́харный песо́к.

granule /ˈɡrænjuːl/ *n.* зерно́, гра́нула.

grape /ɡreɪp/ *n.*: **a ~** виногра́дина; **bunch of ~s** гроздь виногра́да.
■ *cpds.* **~fruit** *n.* грейпфру́т; **~vine** *n.* виногра́дная лоза́; (*fig.*): **I heard on the ~vine that ...** до меня́ дошли́ слу́хи (о том), что... .

graph /ɡrɑːf/ *n.* гра́фик.
■ *cpd.* **~ paper** *n.* бума́га в клё́тку, миллиметро́вка (*coll.*).

graphic /ˈɡræfɪk/ *adj.*
1 (*pertaining to drawing etc.*) изобрази́тельный.
2 (*vivid*) кра́сочный.

graphics /ˈɡræfɪks/ *n.* гра́фика.
■ *cpd.* **~ card** *n.* (*comput.*) видеока́рта, графи́ческая пла́та.

graphologist /ɡrəˈfɒlədʒɪst/ *n.* графо́лог.

graphology /ɡrəˈfɒlədʒɪ/ *n.* графоло́гия.

grapple /ˈɡræp(ə)l/ *v.i.*: **~ with a problem** бра́ться, взя́ться за пробле́му.

grasp /ɡrɑːsp/ *n.*
1 (*grip*) хва́тка.
2 (*comprehension*) понима́ние.
■ *v.t.* (*seize*) схва́т|ывать, -и́ть; (*comprehend*) схва́т|ывать, -и́ть смысл + *g.*
■ *v.i.*: **~ at, for** (*lit., fig.*) ухвати́ться (*pf.*) за + *a.*

grass /ɡrɑːs/ *n.*

1 травá.
2 (*lawn*) газóн.
3 (*sl., marijuana*) марихуáна, «трáвка».
■ *cpds.* **~hopper** *n.* кузнéчик; **~-roots** *adj.* (*coll.*) низовóй, из низóв; **~-roots opinion is against the plan** рядовы́е грáждане настрóены прóтив э́того плáна; **~ snake** *n.* уж.

grassy /'grɑːsɪ/ *adj.* (**grassier, grassiest**) травянóй; травяни́стый.

grate¹ /greɪt/ *n.* (*fireplace*)ками́нная решётка; ками́н.

grate² /greɪt/ *v.t.* терéть (*impf.*); **~d cheese** тёртый сыр.
■ *v.i.* 1: **~ on** (*fig.*) раздражáть (*impf.*).
2 (*make harsh sound*) скр|ипéть, -и́пнуть.

grateful /'greɪtfʊl/ *adj.* благодáрный; признáтельный.

grater /'greɪtə(r)/ *n.* тёрка.

gratify /'grætɪfaɪ/ *v.t.* дост|авля́ть, -áвить удовóльствие + *d.*

grating /'greɪtɪŋ/ *n.* решётка.

gratis /'grɑːtɪs/ *adj.* бесплáтный.
■ *adv.* бесплáтно.

gratitude /'grætɪtjuːd/ *n.* благодáрность.

gratuitous /grə'tjuːɪtəs/ *adj.*
1 (*unwarranted*) беспричи́нный; **a ~ insult** незаслу́женное оскорблéние.
2 (*free*) даровóй; безвозмéздный; **~ advice** бесплáтный совéт.

gratuity /grə'tjuːɪtɪ/ *n.* (*tip*) чаевы́|е (*pl.*, *g.* -х).

grave¹ /greɪv/ *n.* моги́ла.
■ *cpds.* **~stone** *n.* надгрóбная плитá; **~yard** *n.* клáдбище.

grave² /greɪv/ *adj.* серьёзный.

gravel /'græv(ə)l/ *n.* грáвий.

gravitate /'grævɪteɪt/ *v.i.* (*fig.*) тяготéть (*impf.*) (**to(wards):** к + *d.*).

gravity /'grævɪtɪ/ *n.*
1 (*force*) си́ла притяжéния.
2 (*weight*) тя́жесть; **centre of ~** центр тя́жести; **law of ~** закóн всеми́рного тяготéния.
3 (*seriousness*) серьёзность; тя́жесть.

gravy /'greɪvɪ/ *n.* подли́вка.

gray /greɪ/ (*US*) = **grey**

graze¹ /greɪz/ *n.* (*abrasion*) цaрáпина; ссáдина.
■ *v.t.* зад|евáть, -éть; **he fell and ~d his knee** он упáл и оцарáпал колéно.

graze² /greɪz/ *v.i.*: **he has 40 sheep out to ~** у негó (в стáде/отáре) пасётся 40 овéц.

grease /griːs/ *n.* (*fat*) жир; (*lubricant*) смáзка.
■ *v.t.* смáз|ывать, -ать.
■ *cpd.* **~paint** *n.* грим.

greasy /'griːsɪ, -zɪ/ *adj.* (**greasier, greasiest**) жи́рный.

great /greɪt/ *adj.*
1 большóй, вели́кий; (*famous*) знамени́тый; **they are ~ friends** они́ больши́е друзья́; **a ~ many people** мáсса нарóду; **a ~ deal of courage** незауря́дная хрáбрость.
2 (*coll., splendid*) замечáтельный; **we had a ~ time** мы замечáтельно провели́ врéмя.
3 (*eminent, distinguished*) вели́кий; **a ~ occasion** торжéственное собы́тие.
4: **G~ Britain** Великобритáния.
■ *cpds.* **~-aunt** *n.* двою́родная бáбушка; **~-granddaughter** *n.* прáвнучка; **~-grandfather** *n.* прáдед; **~-grandmother** *n.* прабáбушка; **~-grandson** *n.* прáвнук; **~-nephew** *n.* внучáтый племя́нник; **~-niece** *n.* внучáтая племя́нница; **~-uncle** *n.* двою́родный дед.

greatly /'greɪtlɪ/ *adv.* óчень, си́льно, значи́тельно; **I was ~ amused** э́то меня́ си́льно позабáвило.

Greece /griːs/ *n.* Грéция.

greed /griːd/ *n.* жáдность; (*for food*) прожóрливость.

greedy /'griːdɪ/ *adj.* (**greedier, greediest**) (*for money etc.*) жáдный; (*for food*) прожóрливый.

Greek /griːk/ *n.*
1 (*person*) гре|к (*fem.* -чáнка).
2 (*language*) грéческий язы́к; **Ancient ~** древнегрéческий язы́к; **it's (all) ~ to me** э́то для меня́ китáйская грáмота.
■ *adj.* грéческий.

green /griːn/ *n.*
1 (*colour*) зелёный цвет; зелёное; **dressed in ~** одéтый в зелёное.
2 (*pl., vegetables*) зéлень.
3 (*grassy area*) лужáйка; (*on golf course*) площáдка вокру́г лу́нки.
■ *adj.* зелёный; (*unripe*) незрéлый; (*fig., inexperienced*) «зелёный».
■ *cpds.* **~grocer** *n.* (*Br.*) продав|éц (*fem.* -щи́ца) зéлени; **~house** *n.* тепли́ца; **~house effect** парникóвый *or* тепли́чный эффéкт.

greenery /'griːnərɪ/ *n.* зéлень.

greenish /'griːnɪʃ/ *adj.* зеленовáтый.

Greenland /'griːnlənd/ *n.* Гренлáндия.
■ *adj.* гренлáндский.

Greenwich (mean) time /'grenɪtʃ/ *n.* врéмя по Гри́нвичу.

greet /griːt/ *v.t.* (*socially*) здорóваться, по- с + *i.*; (*welcome*) приветствовать (*impf.*).

greeting /'griːtɪŋ/ *n.* (*on meeting*) привéтствие; **~s!** привéт!; (*on a special occasion*): **birthday ~s** поздравлéние с днём рождéния; **~s card** поздрави́тельная откры́тка.

gregarious /grɪ'geərɪəs/ *adj.* стáдный; (*fig., also*) общи́тельный.

grenade /grɪ'neɪd/ *n.* гранáта.

grew /gruː/ *past of* ▶ **grow**

grey /greɪ/ (*US* **gray**) *n.* сéрый цвет; сéрое.
■ *adj.* сéрый; **~ area** (*fig.*) óбласть неопределённости; **he has gone quite ~** он си́льно поседéл; **his face turned ~** он побледнéл.
■ *cpds.* **~-haired, ~-headed** *adjs.* седóй, седовлáсый; **~hound** *n.* англи́йская борзáя.

greyish /'greɪɪʃ/ (*US* **grayish**) *adj.* серовáтый.

grid /grɪd/ *n.*
1 (*grating*) решётка.
2 (*map reference squares*) координáтная сéтка.
3 (*power supply system*) энергосистéма.

griddle /'grɪd(ə)l/ *n.* сковорóдка.

gridlock /'grɪdlɒk/ *n.* затóр.

grief /griːf/ *n.* (*sorrow*) гóре, печáль;

(*disaster*): **he will come to ~** он пло́хо ко́нчит.

grievance /ˈgri:v(ə)ns/ *n.* прете́нзия; недово́льство.

grieve /gri:v/ *v.t.* огорч|а́ть, -и́ть.
■ *v.i.* горева́ть (*impf.*); **she ~d for her husband** она́ горева́ла о му́же.

grievous /ˈgri:vəs/ *adj.* го́рестный; **~ bodily harm** (*leg.*) тяжёлые теле́сные поврежде́ния (*nt. pl.*).

grill /grɪl/ *n.* (*Br., on cooker*) гриль (*m.*).
■ *v.t.* (*Br., cook*) жа́рить, за- на гри́ле; (*coll., interrogate*) учин|я́ть, -и́ть допро́с + *d.*

grille /grɪl/ *n.* решётка.

grim /grɪm/ *adj.* (**grimmer, grimmest**) суро́вый, мра́чный, гро́зный.

grimace /ˈgrɪməs/ *n.* грима́са.
■ *v.i.* грима́сничать (*impf.*).

grime /graɪm/ *n.* са́жа; грязь.

grimy /ˈgraɪmɪ/ *adj.* (**grimier, grimiest**) чума́зый; гря́зный.

grin /grɪn/ *n.* усме́шка; ухмы́лка.
■ *v.i.* (**grinned, grinning**) усмех|а́ться, -ну́ться; ухмыл|я́ться, -ьну́ться.

grind /graɪnd/ *n.* (*coll.*) изнури́тельный труд.
■ *v.t.* (*past and p.p.* **ground**)
[1] (*crush*) моло́ть, с-; **ground almonds** мо́лотый минда́ль.
[2] (*wear down*) изн|а́шивать, -оси́ть.
[3]: **~ one's teeth** скрежета́ть/скрипе́ть (*both impf.*) зуба́ми.
■ *v.i.* (*past and p.p.* **ground**)
[1] (*rub, grate*) раст|ира́ть, -ере́ть.
[2]: **~ to a halt** остан|а́вливаться, -ови́ться (с ля́згом).
■ *cpd.* **~stone** *n.* точи́ло; **he kept his nose to the ~stone** он труди́лся без о́тдыха.

grip /grɪp/ *n.* схва́тывание; (*fig.*) понима́ние; **come to ~s with a problem** вплотну́ю заня́ться (*pf.*) пробле́мой; **take a ~ of yourself!** возьми́те себя́ в ру́ки!; **he is losing his ~** хва́тка у него́ уже́ не та.
■ *v.t.* (**gripped, gripping**) (*hold tightly*) схва́т|ывать, -и́ть; (*hold the attention of*) захва́т|ывать, -и́ть; **a ~ping story** захва́тывающий расска́з.

gripe /graɪp/ (*coll.*) *n.*
[1] (*pl., colic pains*) ко́лик|и (*pl., g.* —).
[2] (*grumble, complaint*) ворча́ние.
■ *v.i.* (*complain*) ворча́ть (*impf.*).

grisly /ˈgrɪzlɪ/ *adj.* (**grislier, grisliest**) ужаса́ющий.

grist /grɪst/ *n.* (*fig.*): **it will bring ~ to the mill** э́то принесёт дохо́д; **all is ~ to his mill** он из всего́ извлека́ет вы́году.

gristle /ˈgrɪs(ə)l/ *n.* хрящ.

grit /grɪt/ *n.* гра́вий.
■ *v.t.* (**gritted, gritting**)
[1] (*spread ~ on*): **the streets were ~ted at the first sign of frost** при пе́рвых при́знаках моро́за у́лицы посы́пали песко́м.
[2]: **~ one's teeth** (*fig.*) сти́снуть (*pf.*) зу́бы.

gritty /ˈgrɪtɪ/ *adj.* (**grittier, grittiest**) песча́ный; (*fig., of style*) шерохова́тый.

grizzle /ˈgrɪz(ə)l/ *v.i.* (*Br. coll., fret*) капри́зничать (*impf.*); хны́кать (*impf.*).

groan /grəʊn/ *n.* стон.
■ *v.i.* стона́ть, за-.

grocer /ˈgrəʊsə(r)/ *n.* бакале́йщик; **~'s shop** бакале́я.

grocery /ˈgrəʊsərɪ/ *n.* (*pl., goods*) бакале́я.

groggy /ˈgrɒgɪ/ *adj.* (**groggier, groggiest**) нетвёрдо стоя́щий на нога́х.

groin /grɔɪn/ *n.* (*anat.*) пах.

groom /gru:m/ *n.* (*for horses*) ко́нюх; (*bride~*) жени́х.
■ *v.t.* [1]: **~ a horse** ходи́ть (*impf.*) за ло́шадью.
[2] (*prepare, coach*) гото́вить; **he is being ~ed for President** его́ про́чат в президе́нты.

groove /gru:v/ *n.* желобо́к.

grope /grəʊp/ *v.t. & i.* идти́ (*det.*) о́щупью; ощу́п|ывать, -ать; **he ~d his way towards the door** он о́щупью добра́лся до две́ри.

gross /grəʊs/ *n.* (*pl.* **~**) (*number*) гросс (*12 дюжин*).
■ *adj.* [1] (*coarse*) гру́бый.
[2] (*obese*) ту́чный.
[3] (*opp. net*) валово́й; **~ domestic product** валово́й вну́тренний проду́кт; **~ national product** валово́й национа́льный проду́кт; **~ weight** вес бру́тто.
■ *v.t.*: **we ~ed £1,000** мы получи́ли о́бщую при́быль в 1000 фу́нтов.

grotesque /grəʊˈtesk/ *adj.* гроте́скный.

grotto /ˈgrɒtəʊ/ *n.* (*pl.* **~es** *or* **~s**) грот.

grouchy /ˈgraʊtʃɪ/ *adj.* (**grouchier, grouchiest**) (*coll.*) ворчли́вый; брюзгли́вый.

ground[1] /graʊnd/ *n.*
[1] (*surface of earth*) земля́; грунт; **it suits me down to the ~** э́то меня́ вполне́ устра́ивает; **~ floor** пе́рвый эта́ж; **~ forces** сухопу́тные войска́.
[2] (*soil, also fig.*) по́чва.
[3] (*position*) положе́ние; **this opinion is gaining ~** э́та то́чка зре́ния получа́ет всё бо́льшее распростране́ние; **they held their ~ well** они́ сто́йко держа́лись.
[4] (*area, distance*) расстоя́ние; **we covered a lot of ~** (*distance*) мы покры́ли большо́е расстоя́ние; (*fig., work*) мы заме́тно продви́нулись вперёд.
[5] (*defined area of activity*) площа́дка; **football ~** футбо́льная площа́дка; **sports ~** спорти́вная площа́дка.
[6] (*pl., estate*) сад, парк, зе́мли (*f. pl.*).
[7] (*pl., dregs*) гу́ща.
[8] (*reason*) основа́ние; **I have no ~s for complaint** у меня́ нет основа́ний жа́ловаться.
■ *v.t.* [1] (*run aground*) сажа́ть, посади́ть на мель.
[2] (*prevent from flying*) запре|ща́ть, -ти́ть полёты + *g.*
■ *cpds.* **~nut** *n.* земляно́й оре́х; **~work** *n.* фунда́мент, осно́вы (*f. pl.*).

ground[2] /graʊnd/ *past and p.p. of* ▸ **grind**

grounding /ˈgraʊndɪŋ/ *n.* (*basic instruction*) подгото́вка.

groundless /ˈgraʊndlɪs/ *adj.* беспричи́нный, беспо́чвенный, необосно́ванный.

group /gru:p/ *n.*
[1] (*assemblage*) гру́ппа; коллекти́в; (*political etc. unit*) группиро́вка; фра́кция.
[2] (*attr.*) группово́й; **~ therapy** группова́я

психотерапи́я.
■ *v.t. & i.* группирова́ть(ся), с-.

grouse /graʊs/ *n.* (*pl.* **~**) (*bird*) шотла́ндская куропа́тка.

grout /graʊt/ *n.* (*mortar*) цеме́нтный раство́р.
■ *v.t.* зал|ива́ть, -и́ть цеме́нтом.

grove /grəʊv/ *n.* ро́ща.

grovel /'grɒv(ə)l/ *v.i.* (**grovelled, grovelling;** *US* **groveled, groveling**) лежа́ть (*impf.*) ниц/распростёршись; (*fig.*) пресмыка́ться (*impf.*) (**to:** пе́ред + *i.*).

grow /grəʊ/ *v.t.* (*past* **grew;** *p.p.* **grown**) расти́ть, вы́-; выра́щивать (*impf.*); разводи́ть (*impf.*); **he is ~ing a beard** он отра́щивает бо́роду.
■ *v.i.* (*past* **grew;** *p.p.* **grown**)
1 (*of habitat*) расти́, вы́расти; **ivy ~s on walls** плющ растёт на сте́нах.
2 (*of development*): **he grew (by) 5 inches** он вы́рос на 5 дю́ймов; **she has ~n into a young lady** она́ преврати́лась в молоду́ю же́нщину; **she is letting her hair ~** она́ отра́щивает во́лосы; **he looks quite ~n up** он вы́глядит совсе́м взро́слым; **~n-ups** взро́слые (*pl.*); **I grew to like him** со вре́менем он стал мне нра́виться; **it's a habit I've never ~n out of** э́то привы́чка, от кото́рой я никогда́ не мог изба́виться; **he grew out of his clothes** он вы́рос из оде́жды; **the tune ~s on one** э́тот моти́в начина́ет нра́виться со вре́менем; (*increase*) увели́чи|ваться, -ться; уси́ли|ваться, -ться; **he listened with ~ing impatience** он слу́шал с расту́щим нетерпе́нием.
3 (*become*) ста|нови́ться, -ть; **as he grew older, he ...** с во́зрастом он...; **she grew pale** она́ побледне́ла.

grower /'grəʊə(r)/ *n.* (*cultivator*) садово́д.

growl /graʊl/ *n.* рыча́ние.
■ *v.i.* рыча́ть (*impf.*).

grown /grəʊn/ *p.p. of* ▶ **grow**

growth /grəʊθ/ *n.* (*development*) рост; (*increase*) приро́ст; (*path.*) наро́ст.

grubby /'grʌbɪ/ *adj.* (**grubbier, grubbiest**) гря́зный, запа́чканный.

grudg|e /grʌdʒ/ *n.* прете́нзия, недоброжела́тельность; **I bear him no ~e** я на него́ не в оби́де.
■ *v.t.* зави́довать, по- (*чему*); **I do not ~e him his success** я не зави́дую его́ успе́ху; **I ~e paying so much** мне жаль сто́лько плати́ть; **he obeyed ~ingly** он неохо́тно вы́полнил приказа́ние.

gruel /'gru:əl/ *n.* жи́дкая (овся́ная) ка́ша, каши́ца.

gruelling /'gru:əlɪŋ/ (*US* **grueling**) *adj.* изма́тывающий.

gruesome /'gru:səm/ *adj.* жу́ткий.

gruff /grʌf/ *adj. of voice*) хри́плый.

grumble /'grʌmb(ə)l/ *v.i.* (*complain*) ворча́ть (*impf.*); (*rumble*) грохота́ть (*impf.*).

grumpy /'grʌmpɪ/ *adj.* (**grumpier, grumpiest**) сварли́вый.

grunt /grʌnt/ *n.* (*animal*) хрю́канье; (*human*) ворча́ние.
■ *v.i.* (*of animals*) хрю́к|ать, -нуть; (*of humans*) ворча́ть, про-.

guarantee /gærən'ti:/ *n.* гара́нтия.
■ *v.t.* (**guarantees, guaranteed**) страхова́ть, за-; **it is ~d to last 10 years** срок го́дности/гара́нтии — 10 лет; **~d against rust** гаранти́рованный от корро́зии.

guard /gɑ:d/ *n.*
1 (*state of alertness*) настороже́нность; **he was caught off his ~** его́ заста́ли врасплох́; (*mil.*): **on ~ duty** на часа́х; в карау́ле.
2 (*man appointed to keep ~*) охра́нник, карау́льный; (*collect.*) охра́на, стра́жа.
3 (*Br., of a train*) проводни́к.
4 (*protective device*) защи́тное устро́йство.
■ *v.t.* охраня́ть (*impf.*); бере́чь (*impf.*).
■ *v.i.* бере́чься (*impf.*), остерега́ться (*impf.*) (**against:** + *g.*); **everything was done to ~ against infection** бы́ли при́няты все ме́ры про́тив инфе́кции.
■ *cpds.* **~ dog** *n.* сторожева́я соба́ка; **~sman** *n.* гварде́ец.

guarded /'gɑ:dɪd/ *adj.* сде́ржанный; осторо́жный.

guardian /'gɑ:dɪən/ *n.*
1 (*protector*) опеку́н; **~ angel** а́нгел-храни́тель (*m.*).
2 (*leg.*) опеку́н.

Guatemala /gwɑ:tə'mɑ:lə/ *n.* Гватема́ла.

Guatemalan /gwɑ:tə'mɑ:lən/ *n.* гватема́л|ец (*fem.* -ка).
■ *adj.* гватема́льский.

guerrilla /gə'rɪlə/ *n.* партиза́н; **~ warfare** партиза́нская война́.

guess /ges/ *n.* дога́дка; **at a rough ~** гру́бо/ориентиро́вочно.
■ *v.t.* 1 (*estimate*) прики́|дывать, -нуть; **I would ~ his age at 40** я бы дал ему́ лет 40.
2 (*conjecture*) дога́д|ываться, -а́ться (*о чём*).
3 (*coll., expect, suppose*) полага́ть (*impf.*); **I ~ you are right** вероя́тно, вы пра́вы.
■ *v.i.* гада́ть (*impf.*); **she likes to keep him ~ing** ей нра́вится держа́ть его́ в неве́дении.
■ *cpd.* **~work** *n.* дога́дки (*f. pl.*).

guest /gest/ *n.*
1 (*one privately entertained*) гость (*m.*).
2 (*at a hotel etc.*) постоя́лец.
■ *cpds.* **~ house** *n.* пансио́н; **~ room** *n.* ко́мната для госте́й.

guffaw /gʌ'fɔ:/ *n.* го́гот (*смех*).
■ *v.i.* гогота́ть (*impf.*) (*смеяться*).

guidance /'gaɪd(ə)ns/ *n.* руково́дство.

guide /gaɪd/ *n.*
1 (*leader*) руководи́тель (*m.*); (*for travellers, tourists etc.*) гид, экскурсово́д.
2 (*directing principle*) руково́дство.
3 (*manual*) уче́бник; **~ to fishing** руково́дство по ры́бной ло́вле.
4 : **(Girl) G~** де́вочка-скау́т.
■ *v.t.* води́ть (*indet.*), вести́ (*det.*), по-; руководи́ть (*impf.*) + *i.*; **be ~d by principles** руково́дствоваться (*impf.*) при́нципами.
■ *cpds.* **~book** *n.* путеводи́тель (*m.*); **~ dog** *n.* соба́ка-поводы́рь; **~line** *n.* директи́ва.

guild /gɪld/ *n.*
1 (*hist.*) ги́льдия.
2 ассоциа́ция, сою́з.

guillotine /'gɪləti:n/ *n.*
1 гильоти́на.

2 (*for paper, metal, etc.*) ре́зальная маши́на.

guilt /gɪlt/ *n.* вина́.

guilty /ˈgɪltɪ/ *adj.* (**guiltier, guiltiest**) вино́вный; **he pleaded ~ to the crime** он призна́л себя́ вино́вным в преступле́нии; **~ conscience** нечи́стая со́весть; **a verdict of ~/not ~** обвини́тельный/оправда́тельный пригово́р.

guinea pig /ˈgɪnɪ pɪg/ *n.* морска́я сви́нка; (*fig.*) «подо́пытный кро́лик».

guise /gaɪz/ *n.* (*dress*) наря́д; (*pretence*) предло́г; **under the ~ of friendship** под ви́дом дру́жбы.

guitar /gɪˈtɑː(r)/ *n.* гита́ра.

guitarist /gɪˈtɑːrɪst/ *n.* гитари́ст (*fem.* -ка).

gulf /gʌlf/ *n.*
1 (*deep bay*) зали́в; бу́хта; **the G~ Stream** Гольфстри́м.
2 (*abyss*) бе́здна.
3 (*fig.*) про́пасть.

gull /gʌl/ *n.* (*bird*) ча́йка.

gullet /ˈgʌlɪt/ *n.* пищево́д; **it sticks in my ~** (*fig.*) э́то стои́т у меня́ поперёк го́рла.

gullible /ˈgʌlɪb(ə)l/ *adj.* легкове́рный.

gully /ˈgʌlɪ/ *n.* лощи́на.

gulp /gʌlp/ *n.* большо́й глото́к; **he took a ~ of tea** он глотну́л ча́ю.
■ *v.t.* глот|а́ть, -ну́ть.

gum¹ /gʌm/ *n.* (*anat.*) десна́.

gum² /gʌm/ *n.* (*adhesive*) клей; (*resin*) каме́дь; (*chewing ~*) жева́тельная рези́нка.

gumption /ˈgʌmpʃ(ə)n/ *n.* (*coll.*) смышлённость; нахо́дчивость.

gun /gʌn/ *n.* (*cannon*) пу́шка, ору́дие; (*pistol*) пистоле́т; (*rifle*) ружьё; **he stuck to his ~s** (*fig.*) он не сдал пози́ций; **jump the ~** (*fig.*) сова́ться, су́нуться ра́ньше вре́мени.
■ *v.t.* (**gunned, gunning**) стреля́ть (*impf.*); **the refugees were ~ned down** бе́женцев расстреля́ли.
■ *cpds.* **~fire** *n.* оруди́йный ого́нь; **~man** *n.* банди́т; террори́ст; **~point** *n.*: **at ~point** угрожа́я ору́жием; под ду́лом пистоле́та; **~powder** *n.* по́рох; **~shot** *n.* руже́йный вы́стрел.

gunner /ˈgʌnə(r)/ *n.* канони́р; артиллери́ст.

gurgle /ˈgɜːg(ə)l/ *n.* бу́льканье.
■ *v.i.* бу́лькать (*impf.*).

guru /ˈgʊruː, ˈguːruː/ *n.* гуру́ (*m. indecl.*).

gush /gʌʃ/ *v.i.* хлы́нуть (*pf.*).

gust /gʌst/ *n.* поры́в ве́тра.

gusto /ˈgʌstəʊ/ *n.* (*relish*) смак; (*zeal*) жар.

gusty /ˈgʌstɪ/ *adj.* (**gustier, gustiest**) бу́рный; поры́вистый; **a ~ day** ве́треный день.

gut /gʌt/ *n.*
1 (*intestine*) кишка́.
2 (*pl.*) (*intestines, stomach*) кишки́ (*f. pl.*); (*fig., courage and determination*) вы́держка; **he hadn't the ~s to tackle the burglar** у него́ не хвати́ло му́жества задержа́ть граби́теля; **~ reaction** инстинкти́вная реа́кция.
■ *v.t.* (**gutted, gutting**)
1 (*eviscerate*) потроши́ть, вы́-.
2 (*destroy contents of*) опустош|а́ть, -и́ть.

gutsy /ˈgʌtsɪ/ *adj.* (**gutsier, gutsiest**) упо́рный, де́рзкий.

gutter /ˈgʌtə(r)/ *n.* (*under eaves*) водосто́чный жёлоб; (*at roadside*) сто́чная кана́ва.

guttural /ˈgʌtər(ə)l/ *adj.* горта́нный; горлово́й; (*phon.*) веля́рный, задненёбный.

guy /gaɪ/ *n.* ма́лый; **wise ~** у́мник.

guzzle /ˈgʌz(ə)l/ *v.t.* (*eat*) есть, съ- с жа́дностью; (*drink*) пить, вы́- с жа́дностью; (*fig., consume*) про|еда́ть, -е́сть.

gym /dʒɪm/ *n.* (*coll.*) (*gymnasium*) гимнасти́ческий зал; (*gymnastics*) гимна́стика.
■ *cpd.* **~ shoe** *n.* спорти́вная та́почка.

gymkhana /dʒɪmˈkɑːnə/ *n.* конноспорти́вные состяза́ния (*nt. pl.*).

gymnasi|um /dʒɪmˈneɪzɪəm/ *n.* (*pl.* **~ums** *or* **~a**) гимнасти́ческий зал.

gymnast /ˈdʒɪmnæst/ *n.* гимна́ст (*fem.* -ка).

gymnastic /dʒɪmˈnæstɪk/ *adj.* гимнасти́ческий.

gymnastics /dʒɪmˈnæstɪks/ *n.* гимна́стика.

gynaecological /gaɪnəkəˈlɒdʒɪk(ə)l/ (*US* **gynecological**) *adj.* гинекологи́ческий.

gynaecologist /gaɪnəˈkɒlədʒɪst/ (*US* **gynecologist**) *n.* гинеко́лог.

gynaecology /gaɪnəˈkɒlədʒɪ/ (*US* **gynecology**) *n.* гинеколо́гия.

Gypsy /ˈdʒɪpsɪ/ = **Gipsy**

gyrate /dʒaɪəˈreɪt/ *v.i.* враща́ться (*impf.*).

Hh

haberdashery /ˈhæbədæʃərɪ/ *n.* (*Br.*) (*shop*) галантере́йный магази́н; (*wares*) галантере́я.

habit /ˈhæbɪt/ *n.*
1 (*settled practice*) привы́чка; **get into/out of the ~ (of ...ing)** прив|ыка́ть, -ы́кнуть (+ *inf.*)/отв|ыка́ть, -ы́кнуть (+ *inf. or* от + *g.*).
2 (*nun's/monk's dress*) ря́са.

habitable /ˈhæbɪtəb(ə)l/ *adj.* приго́дный для жилья́.

habitat /ˈhæbɪtæt/ *n.* есте́ственная среда́ (*растения, животного*).

habitual /həˈbɪtjʊəl/ *adj.* привы́чный; обы́чный; **a ~ liar** неисправи́мый лгун.

hack /hæk/ *v.t.* разруб|а́ть, -и́ть; руби́ть (*impf.*).
■ *v.i.*: **~ into** (*comput.*) прон|ика́ть, -и́кнуть в + *a.*; взл|а́мывать, -ома́ть.

hacker /ˈhækə(r)/ *n.* (*comput.*) ха́кер.

hackneyed /ˈhæknɪd/ *adj.* изби́тый.
had /hæd/ *past and p.p. of* ▶ **have**
haddock /ˈhædək/ *n.* (*pl.* ~) пи́кша.
hadn't /ˈhæd(ə)nt/ *neg. of* ▶ **had**
haematologist /hiːməˈtɒlədʒɪst/ (*US* **hematologist**) *n.* гемато́лог.
haematology /hiːməˈtɒlədʒɪ/ (*US* **hematology**) *n.* гематоло́гия.
haemoglobin /hiːməˈgləʊbɪn/ (*US* **hemoglobin**) *n.* гемоглоби́н.
haemophilia /hiːməˈfɪlɪə/ (*US* **hemophilia**) *n.* гемофили́я.
haemophiliac /hiːməˈfɪlɪæk/ (*US* **hemophiliac**) *n.* гемофи́лик.
haemorrhage /ˈhemərɪdʒ/ (*US* **hemorrhage**) *n.* кровоизлия́ние.
haemorrhoids /ˈhemərɔɪdz/ (*US* **hemorrhoids**) *n. pl.* геморро́й.
hag /hæg/ *n.* карга́, ве́дьма (*usu. fig.*).
haggard /ˈhægəd/ *adj.* измождённый.
haggle /ˈhæg(ə)l/ *v.i.* торгова́ться (*impf.*).
hail[1] /heɪl/ *n.* (*frozen rain*) град.
■ *v.i.*: **it is ~ing** идёт град.
■ *cpds.* **~stone** *n.* гра́дина; **~storm** *n.* гроза́ с гра́дом.
hail[2] /heɪl/ *v.t.*
1 (*acclaim*) провозгла|ша́ть, -си́ть; (*praise*) превозноси́ть (*impf.*).
2 (*summon*) под|зыва́ть, -озва́ть; **he ~ed a taxi** он подозва́л такси́.
hair /heə(r)/ *n.*
1 (*single strand*) во́лос, воло́сок.
2 (*head of* ~) во́лосы (*m. pl.*).
3 (*of animals*) шерсть, щети́на.
■ *cpds.* **~brush** *n.* щётка для воло́с; **~cut** *n.* стри́жка; **have a ~cut** стри́чься, по-; **~do** *n.* (*coll.*) причёска; **~dresser** *n.* парикма́хер; **~dresser's** *n.* (*shop, salon*) парикма́херская; **~dryer** *n.* фен; **~grip** *n.* (*Br.*) зако́лка; **~pin** *n.* шпи́лька; **~pin bend** (*Br.*), **turn** (*US*) круто́й поворо́т; **~-raising** *adj.* жу́ткий; **~spray** *n.* лак для воло́с; **~style** *n.* причёска.
hairy /ˈheərɪ/ *adj.* (**hairier, hairiest**) волоса́тый.
Haiti /ˈheɪtɪ/ *n.* Гаи́ти (*m. indecl.*).
hake /heɪk/ *n.* хек.
halcyon /ˈhælsɪən/ *adj.* (*fig.*) ти́хий, безмяте́жный.
hale /heɪl/ *adj.* кре́пкий; **~ and hearty** кре́пкий и бо́дрый.
half /hɑːf/ *n.* (*pl.* **halves**)
1 (*one of two equal parts*) полови́на; **one and a ~** полтора́; **he cut the loaf in ~** он разре́зал хлеб попола́м; **~ an hour** полчаса́; **~ past two** полови́на тре́тьего; **they agreed to go halves** они́ согласи́лись подели́ть попола́м.
2 (*of a game*) пери́од, тайм.
■ *adv.*: **~ asleep** со́нный; **~ dead** полуживо́й; **~ as much** вдво́е ме́ньше; **~ as much again** в полтора́ ра́за бо́льше; **I ~ expected it** я почти́ ждал э́того.
■ *cpds.* **~back** *n.* полузащи́тник; **~-brother** *n.* (*having same father*) единокро́вный брат; (*having same mother*) единоутро́бный брат; **~-hearted** *adj.* нереши́тельный; без энтузиа́зма; **~-hour** *n.*, *also* **~ an hour** полчаса́; **every ~-hour** ка́ждые полчаса́; **~ mast** *n.*: **at ~ mast** приспу́щенный (*флаг*); **~-moon** *n.* полуме́сяц; **~-pound** *n.*, *also* **~ a pound** полфу́нта; **~-price** *adj.* полцены́; **at ~-price** за полцены́; **~-sister** *n.* (*having same father*) единокро́вная сестра́; (*having same mother*) единоутро́бная сестра́; **~-term** *n.*: **~-term (holiday)** (*Br.*) кани́кул|ы (*pl.*, *g.* —) в середи́не триме́стра; **~-time** *n.* коне́ц та́йма; **the teams changed ends at ~-time** кома́нды поменя́лись места́ми по́сле пе́рвого та́йма; **~way** *adj.* лежа́щий на полпути́; **~way house** (*fig.*) компроми́сс; полуме́ра; *adv.* на полпути́; **we met ~way from the station** мы встре́тились на полпути́ от вокза́ла.
halibut /ˈhælɪbət/ *n.* (*pl.* ~) па́лтус.
halitosis /hælɪˈtəʊsɪs/ *n.* дурно́й за́пах изо рта́.
hall /hɔːl/ *n.*
1 (*place of assembly*) зал.
2 (*lobby*; *also* **~way**) пере́дняя, холл; **~ of residence** (*Br.*) общежи́тие.
■ *cpd.* **~mark** *n.* проби́рное клеймо́; (*fig.*) отличи́тельный при́знак; *v.t.* ста́вить, по- про́бу на + *p.*
hallelujah /hælɪˈluːjə/ *n.* & *int.* аллилу́йя.
hallo *see* ▶ **hello**
Halloween /hæləʊˈiːn/ *n.* кану́н Дня Всех Святы́х (*31 октября*).
hallucination /həluːsɪˈneɪʃ(ə)n/ *n.* галлюцина́ция.
halo /ˈheɪləʊ/ *n.* (*pl.* **~es** *or* **~s**) (*round saint's head*) нимб; (*fig.*) орео́л.
halt /hɒlt/ *n.* остано́вка; **come to a ~** останА́вливаться, -ови́ться; **call a ~** де́лать, с- прива́л; (*fig.*) да|ва́ть, -ть отбо́й.
■ *v.t.* остан|а́вливать, -ови́ть.
■ *v.i.* (*stop*) остан|а́вливаться, -ови́ться; **~! who goes there?** стой! кто идёт?
halter /ˈhɒltə(r)/ *n.* (*for a horse*) по́вод.
halve /hɑːv/ *v.t.* (*divide in two*) дели́ть, раз- попола́м; (*reduce by half*) ум|еньша́ть, -е́ньшить (*or* сокра|ща́ть, -ти́ть) наполови́ну.
halves /hɑːvz/ *pl. of* ▶ **half**
ham /hæm/ *n.* ветчина́.
hamburger /ˈhæmbəːgə(r)/ *n.*
1 га́мбургер.
2 (*US*) (*minced beef*) говя́жий фарш.
hamlet /ˈhæmlɪt/ *n.* дереву́шка.
hammer /ˈhæmə(r)/ *n.* молото́к.
■ *v.t.* (*beat*) уд|аря́ть, -а́рить; (*defeat*) бить, по-; **~ in** вби|ва́ть, -ть; **we ~ed out a plan** мы разрабо́тали план.
■ *v.i.* стуча́ть (*impf.*); колоти́ть (*impf.*); **someone was ~ing on the door** кто́-то колоти́л в дверь.
hammock /ˈhæmək/ *n.* гама́к.
hamper[1] /ˈhæmpə(r)/ *n.* корзи́на с кры́шкой.
hamper[2] /ˈhæmpə(r)/ *v.t.* меша́ть, по- + *d.*; стесня́ть (*impf.*).
hamster /ˈhæmstə(r)/ *n.* хомя́к.
hand /hænd/ *n.*
1 (*lit., fig.*) рука́, кисть; **~ luggage** (*Br.*), **baggage** (*US*) ручна́я кладь; **I shall have my ~s full next week** на сле́дующей неде́ле я бу́ду о́чень за́нят; **~ in ~** (*lit., fig.*)

рука́ о́б руку; (*lit. only*) **walk ~in ~** ходи́ть (*impf.*) (держа́сь) за́ руку.
2 (*vbl. phrr.*): **let me give, lend you a ~!** дава́йте я вам помогу́!; **she had a ~ in his downfall** в его́ паде́нии она́ сыгра́ла не после́днюю роль; **they were holding ~s** они́ держа́лись за́ руки; **try one's ~ at sth.** про́бовать, по- себя́ в чём-н.
3 (*prepositional phrr.*): **you should take that child in ~** вы должны́ взять э́того ребёнка на́ руки; **on ~** в нали́чии; в распоряже́нии; **he has a sick father on his ~s** у него́ на рука́х больно́й оте́ц; **things are getting out of ~** собы́тия выхо́дят из-под контро́ля.
4 (*member of crew or team*): **all ~s on deck!** все наве́рх; **farm ~** рабо́тник на фе́рме.
5 (*side*): **on the one ~ ..., on the other ~** (*fig.*) с одно́й стороны́..., с друго́й стороны́.
6 (*of a clock*) стре́лка.
7 (*set of cards*) ка́рты (*f. pl.*); **show one's ~** (*fig.*) раскр|ыва́ть, -ы́ть ка́рты.
■ *v.t.* перед|ава́ть, -а́ть; **~ me the paper, please** переда́йте мне газе́ту, пожа́луйста.
■ *with advs.*: **he ~ed back the money** он верну́л де́ньги; **the custom was ~ed down** э́тот обы́чай передава́лся из поколе́ния в поколе́ние; **will you ~ in your resignation?** вы пода́дите заявле́ние об ухо́де?; **the teacher ~ed out books** учи́тель разда́л кни́ги; **the king ~ed over his authority to parliament** коро́ль пе́редал власть парла́менту.
■ *cpds.* **~bag** *n.* (*Br.*) су́мочка, да́мская су́мка; **~ball** *n.* (*game*) ручно́й мяч, гандбо́л; **~book** *n.* посо́бие; руково́дство; **~brake** *n.* ручно́й то́рмоз; **~cuff** *n.* нару́чник; *v.t.* над|ева́ть, -е́ть нару́чники + *d.* or на + *a.*; **~ grenade** *n.* ручна́я грана́та; **~made** *adj.* сде́ланный вручну́ю; ручно́й рабо́ты; **~out** *n.* (*gift*) подая́ние; ми́лостыня; (*for publicity*) рекла́мный листо́к; **~-picked** *adj.* тща́тельно отобра́нный; **~set** *n.* (*telephone*) тру́бка; **~s-free** (*device etc.*) *adj.* оставля́ющий ру́ки свобо́дными (*прибор и т. п.*); **~shake** *n.* рукопожа́тие; **~s-on** *adj.* практи́ческий, свя́занный с жи́знью; **~s-on experience** практи́ческий о́пыт; **~stand** *n.* сто́йка на рука́х; **~writing** *n.* по́черк; **~written** *adj.* напи́санный от руки́.

handful /'hændfʊl/ *n.* горсть; (*coll.*): **this child is a ~** с э́тим ребёнком хлопо́т не оберёшься.

handicap /'hændɪkæp/ *n.* поме́ха, препя́тствие.
■ *v.t.* (**handicapped, handicapping**) чини́ть (*impf.*) препя́тствия (*кому*); **~ped person** (*physically*) инвали́д; челове́к с ограни́ченными возмо́жностями; (*mentally*) у́мственно отста́лый челове́к.

handicraft /'hændɪkrɑːft/ *n.* ремесло́, ручна́я рабо́та.

handiwork /'hændɪwəːk/ *n.* ручна́я рабо́та.

handkerchie|f /'hæŋkətʃiːf/ *n.* (*pl.* **~fs** or **~ves**) носово́й плато́к.

handle /'hænd(ə)l/ *n.* (*of door, cup*) ру́чка; (*of sword, tool*) рукоя́ть, рукоя́тка.
■ *v.t.* 1 (*take or hold in the hands*) тро́гать (*impf.*).
2 (*manage, deal with, treat*) обраща́ться (*impf.*) с + *i.*; обходи́ться (*impf.*) с + *i.*; спр|авля́ться, -а́виться с + *i.*; **he ~d the affair very well** он прекра́сно спра́вился с э́тим де́лом; **the officer ~d his men well** офице́р уме́ло кома́ндовал свои́ми солда́тами.
■ *cpd.* **~bars** *n. pl.* (*of a bicycle*) руль (*m.*).

handsome /'hænsəm/ *adj.* (**handsomer, handsomest**) краси́вый.

handy /'hændɪ/ *adj.* (**handier, handiest**)
1 (*to hand, available*) (име́ющийся) под руко́й.
2 (*convenient*) удо́бный, (*coll.*) сподру́чный; **it may come in ~** э́то мо́жет пригоди́ться.
■ *cpd.* **~man** *n.* разнорабо́чий.

hang /hæŋ/ *n.*: **I can't get the ~ of this machine (or of his argument)** я не могу́ разобра́ться в э́той маши́не (*or* в его́ до́водах).
■ *v.t.* (*past and p.p.* **hung,** *except in sense 3*: *past and p.p.* **hanged**)
1 (*suspend*) ве́шать, пове́сить.
2 (*decorate*) разве́|шивать, -сить.
3 (*execute by ~ing*) ве́шать, пове́сить; **Judas ~ed himself** Иу́да пове́сился.
■ *v.i.* (*past and p.p.* **hung,** *except in sense 3*: *past and p.p.* **hanged**)
1 (*be suspended*) висе́ть (*impf.*); (*fig.*): **the threat of dismissal hung over him** над ним нави́сла угро́за увольне́ния.
2 (*lean*) све́|шиваться, -ситься; **don't ~ out of the window** не высо́вывайтесь из окна́.
3 (*be executed*): **he will ~ for it** он попадёт за э́то на ви́селицу.
4 (*loiter, stay close*): **he hung round the door** он задержа́лся у две́ри.
■ *with advs.*: **~ about** (*Br.*), **~ around** *v.i.* болта́ться (*impf.*); шата́ться (*impf.*); **~ back** *v.i.* отст|ава́ть, -а́ть; **~ on** *v.i.* (*cling*) держа́ться (*impf.*) (**to:** за + *a.*); (*persist*) упо́рствовать (*impf.*); **~ on!** (*coll.*) погоди́те!; **~ out** *v.t.* выве́шивать, вы́весить; **she hung out the washing** она́ вы́весила бельё; *v.i.* (*protrude*): **his shirt was ~ing out** руба́шка вы́лезла у него́ из брюк; (*coll., relax*) тусова́ться (*impf.*); **~ together** *v.i.* (*make sense*): **the story doesn't ~ together** ≈ концы́ с конца́ми не схо́дятся; **~ up** *v.t.* (*fasten on nail etc.*) веша́ть, пове́сить; *v.i.* (*end telephone conversation*) веша́ть, пове́сить тру́бку.
■ *cpds.* **~-glider** *n.* (*craft*) дельтапла́н; **~-gliding** *n.* дельтапланери́зм; **~over** *n.* (*from drink*) похме́лье, перепо́й; **~-up** *n.* (*coll.*) ко́мплекс.

hangar /'hæŋə(r)/ *n.* анга́р.

hanger /'hæŋə(r)/ *n.* (*for clothes*) ве́шалка.
■ *cpd.* **~-on** *n.* приспе́шник.

hanging /'hæŋɪŋ/ *n.*
1 висе́ние; (*execution*) пове́шение.
2 (*pl., tapestry etc.*) портье́ры (*f. pl.*).

hanker /'hæŋkə(r)/ *v.i.*: **~ after/for** жа́ждать + *g.*

hanky /'hæŋkɪ/ (*coll.*) = **handkerchief**

Hanoi /hæ'nɔɪ/ *n.* Хано́й.

haphazard /hæp'hæzəd/ *adj.* случа́йный.

hapless /'hæplɪs/ *adj.* несча́стный; злополу́чный.

happen /'hæp(ə)n/ *v.i.*

1 (*occur*) случ|а́ться, -и́ться; прои|сходи́ть, -зойти́; получ|а́ться, -и́ться; **I hope nothing has ~ed to him** наде́юсь, с ним ничего́ не случи́лось.
2 (*chance*): **as it ~s I can help you** в да́нном слу́чае я могу́ вам помо́чь; **we ~ed to meet** мы неожи́данно/случа́йно встре́тились.

happily /ˈhæpɪlɪ/ *adv.*
1 (*contentedly*) сча́стливо.
2 (*fortunately*) к сча́стью.
3 (*gladly*) с удово́льствием.

happiness /ˈhæpɪnɪs/ *n.* сча́стье.

happy /ˈhæpɪ/ *adj.* (**happier, happiest**)
1 (*contented*) счастли́вый.
2 (*fortunate*) счастли́вый, уда́чливый; **~ medium** золота́я середи́на; **~ birthday!** с днём рожде́ния!; **~ Christmas!** с Рождество́м (Христо́вым)!
3 (*pleased*) дово́льный (*чем*); **we shall be ~ to come** мы с удово́льствием придём.
■ *cpd.* **~-go-lucky** *adj.* беззабо́тный; беспе́чный.

harangue /həˈræŋ/ *v.t.* увещева́ть (*impf.*).

harass /ˈhærəs/ *v.t.* изв|оди́ть, -ести́.

harassment /ˈhærəsmənt/ *n.* тра́вля; изма́тывание; **sexual ~** сексуа́льное домога́тельство.

harbinger /ˈhɑːbɪndʒə(r)/ *n.* предве́стник.

harbour /ˈhɑːbə(r)/ (*US* **harbor**) *n.* га́вань, порт.
■ *v.t.* да|ва́ть, -ть убе́жище + *d.*; **~ing a criminal** укрыва́тельство престу́пника; (*fig.*): **I ~ no grudge against him** я не держу́ на него́ зла.

hard /hɑːd/ *adj.*
1 (*firm, solid*) твёрдый; про́чный; **~ core** (*fig., nucleus of resistance etc.*) ядро́; **~ and fast rules** жёсткие пра́вила; **~ copy** (*comput.*) распеча́тка; **~ disk** (*comput.*) жёсткий диск; **~ hat** защи́тный шлем.
2 (*difficult*) тру́дный; **bargains are ~ to come by** достава́ть ве́щи по невысо́ким це́нам непро́сто.
3 (*unsentimental, relentless*): **don't be too ~ on her!** не бу́дьте к ней сли́шком стро́ги.
4 (*vigorous, harsh*): **~ times** тяжёлые времена́; **it's a ~ life** жизнь трудна́; тру́дно живётся; **~ liquor** кре́пкие напи́тки; **~ drugs** сильноде́йствующие нарко́тики; **~ water** жёсткая вода́.
5 (*intensive*): **~ work** тяжёлая/тру́дная рабо́та; **~ labour** исправи́тельно-трудовы́е рабо́ты; (*fig.*) ка́торга.
6 (*coll., unfortunate*): **~ luck** (*Br.*)**!** не везёт!; **his parents are ~ up** его́ роди́тели — лю́ди небога́тые.
7 : **~ of hearing** глухова́тый; туго́й на́ ухо.
8 (*of money*): **~ cash** нали́чность; нали́чные (де́ньги); **~ currency** твёрдая валю́та.
■ *adv.* 1 (*solid*): **the ground froze ~** земля́ промёрзла.
2 (*with force*): **it is raining ~** идёт си́льный дождь.
3 (*persistently*): **work** (*study*) **~** усе́рдно занима́ться (*impf.*); **I tried ~ to make him understand** я изо всех сил стара́лся разъясни́ть ему́ (*что*).
■ *cpds.* **~back** *n.* (*book*) кни́га в жёстком переплёте *or* в твёрдой обло́жке; **~board** *n.* древе́сно-волокни́стая плита́, ДВП; **~-boiled** *adj.*: **a ~-boiled egg** яйцо́ вкрутую́; **~-core** *adj.* (*criminal*) закорене́лый; (*pornography*) открове́нный; жёсткий; **~-earned** *adj.* зарабо́танный тяжёлым трудо́м; **~-headed** *adj.* тре́звый; практи́чный; **~-hearted** *adj.* бессерде́чный; неумоли́мый; **~-hitting** *adj.* (*e.g. speech*) жёсткий; бескомпроми́ссный; **~liner** *n.* сторо́нник жёсткой ли́нии; **~-nosed** *adj.* упря́мый, непримири́мый; **~-pressed** *adj.* находя́щийся в тру́дном положе́нии; **~ware** *n.* скобяны́е изде́лия/това́ры; (*mil., coll.*) те́хника; (*comput.*) аппарату́ра; **~-wearing** *adj.* но́ский; **~-working** *adj.* работя́щий; (*at studies*) усе́рдный.

harden /ˈhɑːd(ə)n/ *v.t.* (*make hard*) де́лать, с- твёрдым; (*fig.*) ожесточ|а́ть, -и́ть; **he ~ed his heart** его́ се́рдце ожесточи́лось; **a ~ed criminal** закорене́лый престу́пник; рецидиви́ст.
■ *v.i.* тверде́ть, за-; (*fig.*): **opinion ~ed** мне́ние укорени́лось.

hardly /ˈhɑːdlɪ/ *adv.*
1 (*with difficulty*) с трудо́м.
2 (*only just*) едва́; **I had ~ sat down when the phone rang** едва́ я сел, как зазвони́л телефо́н.
3 (*not reasonably*) вряд ли; **you can ~ expect her to agree** вы едва́ (*or* вряд) ли мо́жете рассчи́тывать на её согла́сие.
4 (*almost not*): **~ ever** почти́ никогда́; **I ~ know him** я его́ почти́ не зна́ю; **there's ~ any money left** де́нег почти́ не оста́лось.

hardship /ˈhɑːdʃɪp/ *n.* невзго́ды (*f. pl.*).

hardy /ˈhɑːdɪ/ *adj.* (**hardier, hardiest**) закалённый; (*of plants*) морозосто́йкий.

hare /heə(r)/ *n.* за́яц.

harem /ˈhɑːriːm/ *n.* гаре́м.

haricot /ˈhærɪkəʊ/ *n.* (**~ bean**) фасо́ль (обыкнове́нная) (*collect.*).

harm /hɑːm/ *n.* вред, уще́рб; **there's no ~ (in) trying** попы́тка не пы́тка.
■ *v.t.* вреди́ть, по- + *d.*; причин|я́ть, -и́ть (*or* нан|оси́ть, -ести́) вред + *d.*

harmful /ˈhɑːmfʊl/ *adj.* вре́дный.

harmless /ˈhɑːmlɪs/ *adj.* (*not injurious*) безвре́дный; (*innocent*) безоби́дный.

harmonic /hɑːˈmɒnɪk/ *adj.* гармони́ческий.

harmonica /hɑːˈmɒnɪkə/ *n.* губна́я гармо́ника.

harmonious /hɑːˈməʊnɪəs/ *adj.* (*lit., fig.*) гармони́чный.

harmonize /ˈhɑːmənaɪz/ *v.t.* (*mus.*) гармонизи́ровать (*impf., pf.*).

harmony /ˈhɑːmənɪ/ *n.* гармо́ния.

harness /ˈhɑːnɪs/ *n.* у́пряжь.
■ *v.t.* запр|яга́ть, -я́чь; (*fig.*) (*of natural forces*) обузд|ывать, -а́ть; (*of energies etc.*) мобилизова́ть (*impf., pf.*).

harp /hɑːp/ *n.* а́рфа.
■ *v.i.* (*fig.*): **~ on sth.** тверди́ть (*impf.*) о чём-н.

harpist /ˈhɑːpɪst/ *n.* арфи́ст (*fem.* -ка).

harpoon /hɑːˈpuːn/ *n.* гарпу́н.

harpsichord /ˈhɑːpsɪkɔːd/ *n.* клавеси́н.

harrow /ˈhærəʊ/ *v.t.*: **a ~ing tale**

душераздира́ющая исто́рия.

harsh /hɑ:ʃ/ *adj.*
1 (*rough*) гру́бый, ре́зкий.
2 (*severe*) суро́вый.

hart /hɑ:t/ *n.* саме́ц оле́ня.

harvest /'hɑ:vɪst/ *n.* (*yield*) урожа́й; (~*ing*) жа́тва, сбор урожа́я; ~ **festival** пра́здник урожа́я.
■ *v.t.* соб|ира́ть, -ра́ть; жать, с-.

has /hæz/ *3rd pers. sg. pres. of* ▶ **have**

hashish /'hæʃi:ʃ/ *n.* гаши́ш.

hasn't /'hæz(ə)nt/ *neg. of* ▶ **has**

hassle /'hæs(ə)l/ *n.* (*coll.*) канитéль.

hassock /'hæsək/ *n.*
1 (*Br.*) поду́шечка для коленопреклоне́ния.
2 (*US*) пуф.

haste /heɪst/ *n.* спе́шка.

hasten /'heɪs(ə)n/ *v.t.* (*hurry*) торопи́ть, по-.
■ *v.i.* торопи́ться, по-, спеши́ть (*impf.*); **I ~ to add that ...** спешу́ доба́вить, что... .

hasty /'heɪstɪ/ *adj.* (**hastier, hastiest**) (*hurried*) поспе́шный; (*rash, ill-considered*) поспе́шный.

hat /hæt/ *n.* шля́па; (*fur, knitted*) ша́пка.
■ *cpd.* **~-trick** *n.*: **he scored a ~-trick** (*fig., of footballer etc.*) он сде́лал хет-три́к.

hatch[1] /hætʃ/ *n.* (*opening*) люк; (*cover*) кры́шка.
■ *cpd.* **~back** *n.* хетчбэ́к.

hatch[2] /hætʃ/ *v.t.* (*egg*) выси́живать, вы́сидеть; (*fig., plot*) вына́шивать, вы́носить; зам|ышля́ть, -ы́слить.
■ *v.i.* (*also* **~ out**) (*bird*) вылупля́ться, вы́лупиться.

hatchet /'hætʃɪt/ *n.* топо́р, топо́рик.

hate /heɪt/ *n.* не́нависть.
■ *v.t.* ненави́деть (*impf.*); (*dislike strongly*) ненави́деть (*impf.*); **I ~ getting up early** я ненави́жу ра́но встава́ть.

hateful /'heɪtfʊl/ *adj.* ненави́стный.

hatred /'heɪtrɪd/ *n.* не́нависть (**for:** к + *d.*).

haughty /'hɔ:tɪ/ *adj.* (**haughtier, haughtiest**) высокоме́рный.

haul /hɔ:l/ *n.*
1: **a long ~** (*fig.*) до́лгое де́ло.
2: **a ~ of fish** уло́в; (*fig., booty*) добы́ча, уло́в.
■ *v.t. & i.* тяну́ть (*impf.*); тащи́ть (*impf.*).

haulage /'hɔ:lɪdʒ/ *n.* транспортиро́вка.

haulier /'hɔ:lɪə(r)/ *n.* (*Br.*) перево́зчик.

haunch /hɔ:ntʃ/ *n.* бедро́.

haunt /hɔ:nt/ *n.* излю́бленное ме́сто.
■ *v.t. & i.* неотсту́пно пресле́довать (*impf.*); **a ~ed house** дом с привиде́ниями; **a ~ing melody** навя́зчивая мело́дия.

have /hæv/ *n.*: **the ~s and the ~-nots** иму́щие и неиму́щие.
■ *v.t.* (*3rd pers. sg. pres.* **has;** *past and p.p.* **had**)
1 име́ть; (*possess*) облада́ть + *i.*; *often expr. by* у + *g.*; **she has blue eyes** у неё голубы́е глаза́; **I ~ no doubt** у меня́ нет сомне́ний; **he had the courage to refuse** у него́ хвати́ло му́жества отказа́ться; **I ~ no idea** поня́тия не име́ю.
2 (*contain*): **June has 30 days** в ию́не 30 дней.
3 (*experience*): **~ a good time!** жела́ю вам хорошо́ провести́ вре́мя; (*suffer from*): **he has a cold** у него́ на́сморк.
4 (*bear*) роди́ть (*impf., pf.*); **she is having a baby in May** в ма́е у неё роди́тся ребёнок.
5 (*receive, obtain*): **we had news of him yesterday** вчера́ мы получи́ли изве́стие о нём; (*tolerate*): **I won't ~ it!** э́того я не потерплю́!
6 (*show, exercise*): **~ pity on me** сжа́льтесь надо мно́й; **he had no mercy** он был безжа́лостен.
7 (*undertake, perform*): **~ a game of tennis** сыгра́ть (*pf.*) в те́ннис; **~ a go** (*coll.*) пыта́ться, по-.
8 (*partake of, enjoy*): **~ dinner** у́жинать (*impf.*).
9 (*coll., swindle*): **you've been had** вас провели́/наду́ли.
10 (*with inf., be obliged to*) (*need to*): **I ~ to finish by tomorrow** я до́лжен зако́нчить к за́втрашнему дню; **I ~ to sit down** мне на́до сесть; (*be obliged*) быть обя́занным; **you don't ~ to go** вы не обя́заны идти́; (*having no choice*) быть вы́нужденным; **I ~ to accept the invitation** я был вы́нужден приня́ть приглаше́ние.
11 (*phrr. with it*): **let him ~ it!** (*sl., attack him*) дай ему́ хороше́нько!; покажи́ ему́!; **he has it in for me** (*coll.*) у него́ зуб на меня́; **~ it out with s.o.** объясн|я́ться, -и́ться с кем-н.
■ *with advs.*: **can I ~ my watch back?** могу́ я получи́ть свои́ часы́ обра́тно?; **he had his coat off** он был без пальто́; **she had a red dress on** на ней бы́ло кра́сное пла́тье; **~ s.o. on** (*Br.*) разы́гр|ывать, -а́ть кого́-н.; **he was had up for speeding** (*Br. coll.*) его́ задержа́ли за превыше́ние ско́рости.
■ *miscellaneous phrr.*: **you had better, best give the book back** вам не меша́ло бы верну́ть кни́гу; **it has nothing to do with you** к вам э́то (нико́им о́бразом) не отно́сится; вас э́то соверше́нно не каса́ется; **I'll ~ nothing to do with it** я не жела́ю име́ть никако́го отноше́ния к э́тому.

haven /'heɪv(ə)n/ *n.* га́вань; (*fig.*) прию́т.

haven't /'hæv(ə)nt/ *neg. of* ▶ **have**

haversack /'hævəsæk/ *n.* рюкза́к.

havoc /'hævək/ *n.* (*destruction*) разгро́м; (*fig.*) **play ~ with** вн|оси́ть, -ести́ беспоря́док/ха́ос в + *a.*

Hawaii /hə'waɪɪ/ *n.* Гава́йи (*m. pl.*).

hawk /hɔ:k/ *n.* я́стреб (*also fig., pol.*).

hawthorn /'hɔ:θɔ:n/ *n.* боя́рышник.

hay /heɪ/ *n.* се́но; **~ fever** поллино́з, аллерги́я на пыльцу́ расте́ний.
■ *cpds.* **~stack** *n.* стог се́на; **~wire** *n.* (*sl.*): **everything went ~wire** всё пошло́ наперекося́к.

hazard /'hæzəd/ *n.* опа́сность.
■ *v.t.* отва́ж|иваться, -иться + *inf. or* на + *a.*; **he ~ed a remark** он отва́жился вы́сказать замеча́ние.
■ *cpd.* **~ lights** *n. pl.* авари́йные фа́ры (*f. pl.*).

hazardous /'hæzədəs/ *adj.* риско́ванный.
■ *cpd.* **~ waste** *n.* вре́дные отхо́ды (*m. pl*).

haze /heɪz/ *n.* ды́мка.

hazel /'heɪz(ə)l/ *n.* (*tree*) лесно́й оре́х; (*colour*) оре́ховый цвет; **~ eyes** ка́рие глаза́.
■ *cpd.* **~nut** *n.* лесно́й оре́х.

hazy /ˈheɪzɪ/ *adj.* (**hazier, haziest**) подёрнутый ды́мкой; (*fig.*) сму́тный, тума́нный.

HDTV (*abbr. of* ***high-definition television***) ТВЧ (телеви́дение высо́кой чёткости).

he /hi:/ *pron.* (*obj.* **him**) он; тот.

head /hed/ *n.*

1 голова́; **~ first** голово́й вперёд; **from ~ to foot, toe** с головы́ до ног; **I cannot make ~ or tail of it** я не могу́ в э́том разобра́ться; **this is all completely over my ~** всё э́то вы́ше моего́ понима́ния; **shake one's ~** кача́ть, по- голово́й; **a ~ cold** на́сморк.

2 (*mind, brain*): **he has a good ~ for figures** он хорошо́ счита́ет; **he's off his ~** он спя́тил (*coll.*); (*faculties*): **the wine went to his ~** вино́ уда́рило ему́ в го́лову; **success went to his ~** успе́х вскружи́л ему́ го́лову; (*balance, composure*): **he lost/kept his ~** он потеря́л го́лову / он не теря́л головы́.

3 (*on a coin*): **~s or tails?** орёл и́ли ре́шка?

4 (*unit*): **£5 a ~** пять фу́нтов с ка́ждого.

5 (*upper or principal end*): **at the ~ of the table** во главе́ стола́.

6 (*principal member*) глава́ (*c.g.*), ста́рший; **~ of state** глава́ госуда́рства; **~ of the family** глава́ семьи́; (*attr., principal*): **~ office** гла́вная конто́ра, центр.

7 (*culmination*): **to come to a ~** назр|ева́ть, -е́ть.

■ *v.t.* 1 (*direct*): **he is ~ed for home** он направля́ется домо́й.

2 (*strike with head*): **he ~ed the ball into the net** он заби́л мяч в се́тку голово́й.

3 (*be in charge of*) возгл|авля́ть, -а́вить; **he ~ed the team** он возглавля́л кома́нду.

■ *v.i.* (*move, steer*) напр|авля́ться, -а́виться; (*fig.*): **he is ~ing for disaster** он пло́хо ко́нчит.

■ *cpds.* **~ache** *n.* головна́я боль; **I have a ~ache** у меня́ боли́т голова́; **~band** *n.* головна́я повя́зка; **~dress** *n.* (замыслова́тый/экзоти́ческий) головно́й убо́р; **~hunter** *n.* (*fig.*) челове́к, перема́нивающий специали́стов из други́х организа́ций; **~lamp, ~light** *nn.* фа́ра; **~line** *n.* заголо́вок; (*pl.*) (гла́вные) но́вости дня; **he hit the ~lines** его́ и́мя не сходи́ло с пе́рвых поло́с газе́т; **~long** *adv.* голово́й вперёд; (*in a rush*) стремгла́в; **~master, ~mistress** *nn.* (*Br.*) дире́ктор шко́лы; **~-on** *adj.* лобово́й, встре́чный; **a ~-on collision** лобово́е столкнове́ние; **~phone** *n.* нау́шник; **~quarters** *n.* штаб-кварти́ра; (*mil.*) штаб, ста́вка; **~rest** *n.* подголо́вник; **~scarf** *n.* косы́нка; **~set** *n.* (*pair of ~phones*) нау́шники (*m. pl.*); **~stone** *n.* (*tombstone*) надгро́бный ка́мень; **~strong** *adj.* своево́льный, упря́мый; **~ teacher** *n.* дире́ктор шко́лы; **~way** *n.* продвиже́ние вперёд; (*fig.*): **we are not making much ~way** мы продвига́емся сли́шком ме́дленно.

headed /ˈhedɪd/ *adj.*: **~ notepaper** (*of organization*) ге́рбовая бума́га; (*of person*) имення́я бума́га.

header /ˈhedə(r)/ *n.*

1 (*in soccer*) уда́р голово́й.

2 (*line of text*) колонти́тул.

heading /ˈhedɪŋ/ *n.* (*title*) заголо́вок, загла́вие; (*section*) ру́брика.

heady /ˈhedɪ/ *adj.* (**headier, headiest**) хмельно́й; (*also fig.*) пьяня́щий.

heal /hi:l/ *v.t.* (*person*) исцел|я́ть, -и́ть; (*wound*) зале́ч|ивать, -и́ть.

■ *v.i.* заж|ива́ть, -и́ть.

healer /ˈhi:lə(r)/ *n.* ле́карь (*m.*).

healing /ˈhi:lɪŋ/ *n.* лече́ние.

health /helθ/ *n.* здоро́вье; **in good ~** здоро́вый; **~ centre** поликли́ника; **~ food** натура́льная пи́ща; **~ insurance** медици́нская страхо́вка; **~ service** слу́жба здравоохране́ния, здравоохране́ние.

healthy /ˈhelθɪ/ *adj.* (**healthier, healthiest**) здоро́вый.

heap /hi:p/ *n.*

1 (*pile*) ку́ча, гру́да.

2 (*pl., coll., large quantity*) ма́сса, ку́ча, у́йма; **he has ~s of money** у него́ у́йма/ку́ча де́нег.

■ *v.t.*: **a ~ed** (*Br.*), **heaping** (*US*) **spoonful** ло́жка с ве́рхом; **they ~ed honours** (*US* **honors**) **on him** его́ осы́пали по́честями.

hear /hɪə(r)/ *v.t.* & *i.* (*past and p.p.* **heard** /hə:d/)

1 (*perceive with ear*) слы́шать, у-; **I can't ~ a word** я не слы́шу ни сло́ва; **I ~d him shout** я услы́шал, как он закрича́л; **I ~ someone coming** я слы́шу, что кто-то идёт *or* (чьи́-то) шаги́.

2 (*listen to*): **~ evidence** слу́шать, за- показа́ния свиде́телей; **his prayer was ~d** его́ моли́твы бы́ли услы́шаны; **I won't ~ of it!** я и слы́шать об э́том не хочу́!

3 (*learn*) слы́шать, у-; **have you ~d the news?** вы слы́шали но́вости?; **have you ~d from your brother?** что слы́шно от ва́шего бра́та?; **I've never ~d of him** я о нём никогда́ не слы́шал.

4 : **~!, ~!** пра́вильно!; ве́рно ска́зано!

■ *cpd.* **~say** *n.* слу́хи (*m. pl.*).

hearing /ˈhɪərɪŋ/ *n.*

1 (*perception*) слух; **~ aid** слухово́й аппара́т.

2 (*leg.*) слу́шание.

hearse /hə:s/ *n.* катафа́лк.

heart /hɑ:t/ *n.*

1 (*organ*) се́рдце; **~ attack** серде́чный при́ступ; инфа́ркт; **~ disease** боле́знь се́рдца; **~ failure** разры́в се́рдца; **~ transplant** переса́дка се́рдца.

2 (*soul; seat of emotions*) се́рдце, душа́; **he had set his ~ on winning** он стра́стно жела́л вы́играть; **don't take it to ~** не принима́йте э́то бли́зко к се́рдцу; (*enthusiasm*): **his ~ is not in his work** у него́ душа́ не лежи́т к рабо́те; (*courage*): **he lost ~** он пал ду́хом; **take ~!** не па́дайте ду́хом!; (*memory*): **I learnt it by ~** я вы́учил э́то наизу́сть.

3 (*centre*) середи́на, сердцеви́на; **this book gets to the ~ of the matter** э́та кни́га затра́гивает са́мую суть де́ла.

4 (*pl., cards*) чѐрв|и (*pl., g.* -е́й).

■ *cpds.* **~ache** *n.* серде́чная боль; **~beat** *n.* сердцебие́ние; **~breaking** *adj.* душераздира́ющий; **~broken** *adj.* с разби́тым се́рдцем; **~burn** *n.* изжо́га; **~felt** *adj.* душе́вный, глубоко́ прочу́вствованный; **~-throb** *n.* (*coll.*) люби́мец; **~-to-~** *adj.*: **a ~-to-~ talk** разгово́р по душа́м.

hearten /ˈhɑːt(ə)n/ *v.t.* ободр|я́ть, -и́ть.

hearth /hɑːθ/ *n.* оча́г.

heartless /ˈhɑːtlɪs/ *adj.* бессерде́чный.

hearty /ˈhɑːtɪ/ *adj.* (**heartier, heartiest**)
1 (*cordial*) серде́чный.
2 (*healthy*): **a ~ appetite** прекра́сный аппети́т.
3 (*cheerful*) весёлый.

heat /hiːt/ *n.*
1 (*hotness*) жара́; (*warmth*) тепло́.
2 (*warmth of feeling*) теплота́; (*passion*) горя́чность; **in the ~ of the moment** сгоряча́.
3 (*in running*) забе́г; (*in horse racing*) зае́зд; (*in swimming*) заплы́в.
4 (*of animals*) те́чка; **our dog in on ~** у на́шей соба́ки те́чка.
■ *v.t.* 1 (*raise temperature of*) нагр|ева́ть, -е́ть; **the potatoes were ~ed up** карто́шку разогре́ли; **~ed swimming pool** бассе́йн с подогре́вом.
2 : **a ~ed argument** жа́ркий спор.
■ *cpds.* **~stroke** *n.* теплово́й уда́р; **~wave** *n.* полоса́/пери́од си́льной жары́.

heater /ˈhiːtə(r)/ *n.* обогрева́тель (*m.*).

heath /hiːθ/ *n.*
1 (*Br., waste land*) пу́стошь.
2 (*shrub*) ве́реск.

heathen /ˈhiːð(ə)n/ *n.* язы́чник.
■ *adj.* язы́ческий.

heather /ˈheðə(r)/ *n.* ве́реск.

heating /ˈhiːtɪŋ/ *n.* обогрева́ние, отопле́ние.

heave /hiːv/ *v.t.* (*past and p.p.* **heaved**) (*lift*) подн|има́ть, -я́ть; (*throw*) бр|оса́ть, -о́сить; **~ a sigh** (тяжело́) взд|ыха́ть, -охну́ть.
■ *v.i.* (*past and p.p.* **heaved** *or esp. naut.* **hove**)
1 (*pull*): **they ~d on the rope** они́ вы́брали кана́т.
2 (*retch*) ту́житься (*impf.*) (при рво́те).
3 (*rise and fall*) вздыма́ться (*impf.*).

heaven /ˈhev(ə)n/ *n.*
1 (*sky, firmament*) не́бо, небе́сный свод.
2 (*paradise*) рай, ца́рство небе́сное.
3 (*God*): **thank ~ for that** сла́ва бо́гу; **for ~'s sake** ра́ди бо́га; **(good) ~s!** го́споди!; бо́же мой!

heavenly /ˈhevənlɪ/ *adj.*
1 (*in or of heaven*) небе́сный.
2 (*coll., wonderful*) изуми́тельный; ди́вный.

heavily /ˈhevɪ/ *adv.* значи́тельно, си́льно; **he fell ~** он тяжело́ ру́хнул; **they were ~ defeated** они́ потерпе́ли тяжёлое пораже́ние.

heavy /ˈhevɪ/ *adj.* (**heavier, heaviest**) тяжёлый; **a ~ blow** (*lit., fig.*) тяжёлый уда́р; **a ~ cold** си́льный на́сморк; **he is a ~ drinker** он си́льно пьёт; **with a ~ heart** с тяжёлым се́рдцем; **~ metal** (*coll., mus.*) хе́ви-ме́тал; **~ rain** си́льный/проливно́й дождь; **he is a ~ sleeper** у него́ кре́пкий сон; **a ~ sky** хму́рое не́бо; **~ traffic** интенси́вное движе́ние.
■ *cpds.* **~-handed** *adj.* неуклю́жий; **~weight** *n.* (*sport, fig.*) тяжелове́с.

Hebrew /ˈhiːbruː/ *n.* (*language*) древнеевре́йский язы́к; (*modern*) иври́т.
■ *adj.* древнеевре́йский; (*modern*) иври́тский.

heckle /ˈhek(ə)l/ *v.t.* (*fig.*) переб|ива́ть, -и́ть.
■ *v.i.* переб|ива́ть, -и́ть ора́тора.

heckler /ˈheklə(r)/ *n.* челове́к, кото́рый пыта́ется переби́ть ора́тора; крику́н.

hectare /ˈhekteə(r)/ *n.* (*10,000 square metres*) гекта́р.

hectic /ˈhektɪk/ *adj.* (*busy*) лихора́дочный, бу́рный.

hector /ˈhektə(r)/ *v.t.* запу́г|ивать, -а́ть.

hedge /hedʒ/ *n.* жива́я и́згородь.
■ *v.t.*: **~ one's bets** (*fig.*) перестрах|о́вываться, -ова́ться.
■ *v.i.* (*prevaricate*) увил|ивать, -ьну́ть.
■ *cpds.* **~hog** *n.* ёж; **~row** *n.* шпале́ра, жива́я и́згородь.

hedonism /ˈheːdənɪz(ə)m/ *n.* гедони́зм.

hedonist /ˈhedənɪst/ *n.* гедони́ст.

hedonistic /hedəˈnɪstɪk/ *adj.* гедонисти́ческий.

heed /hiːd/ *n.* внима́ние.
■ *v.t.* уч|и́тывать, -е́сть; внима́ть, внять + *d.*

heedless /ˈhiːdlɪs/ *adj.* беззабо́тный, беспе́чный; **she continued, ~ of danger** она́ продолжа́ла, невзира́я на опа́сность.

heel /hiːl/ *n.* пя́тка; **he fell head over ~s** он полете́л вверх торма́шками; **he took to his ~s** он бро́сился наутёк.

hefty /ˈheftɪ/ *adj.* (**heftier, heftiest**) (*person*) здорове́нный; (*blow*) здоро́вый.

heifer /ˈhefə(r)/ *n.* тёлка, не́тель.

height /haɪt/ *n.*
1 высота́; (*of person*) рост.
2 (*high ground*) верши́на, верху́шка.
3 (*utmost degree*) вы́сшая сте́пень; **the ~ of fashion** после́дний крик мо́ды; **the gale was at its ~** шторм был в разга́ре.

heighten /ˈhaɪt(ə)n/ *v.t.* уси́ли|вать, -ть.
■ *v.i.* (*fig.*) уси́ли|ваться, -ться.

heinous /ˈheɪnəs/ *adj.* гну́сный, омерзи́тельный.

heir /eə(r)/ *n.* насле́дник.

heiress /ˈeərɪs/ *n.* насле́дница.

heirloom /ˈeəluːm/ *n.* фами́льная рели́квия.

held /held/ *past and p.p. of* ▶ **hold**

helicopter /ˈhelɪkɒptə(r)/ *n.* вертолёт.

heliport /ˈhelɪpɔːt/ *n.* вертолётный аэродро́м; (*small or at the top of building*) вертолётная площа́дка.

helium /ˈhiːlɪəm/ *n.* ге́лий.

hell /hel/ *n.*
1 (*place or state*) ад; **he went through ~** он перенёс му́ки а́да.
2 (*coll. or sl., expr. vexation or emphasis*) **oh ~!** чёрт возьми́!; **go to ~!** иди́ к чёрту; **what the ~ do you want?** что вам ну́жно, чёрт возьми́/побери́?; **they made the ~ of a noise** они́ ужа́сно шуме́ли; **we had a ~ of a time** мы черто́вски хорошо́ повесели́лись; **just for the ~ of it** за здоро́во живёшь, про́сто так.

hellish /ˈhelɪʃ/ *adj.* а́дский.

hello (*also* **hallo**) /həˈləʊ/ *int.* (*greeting*) здра́вствуй(те)!; (*coll.*) приве́т!; (*on telephone*) алло́!

helm /helm/ *n.* (*tiller*) руль, ру́мпель (*both*

m.); **take the ~** (*lit., fig.*) вста|ва́ть, -ть у штурва́ла/руля́.

helmet /ˈhelmɪt/ *n.* шлем; (*modern soldier's or fireman's*) ка́ска.

help /help/ *n.* по́мощь; **he walks with the ~ of a stick** он хо́дит с па́лкой; **your advice was a great ~ to us** ваш сове́т нам о́чень помо́г.
■ *v.t.* 1 (*assist*) пом|ога́ть, -о́чь + *d.*; **please ~ me up** помоги́те мне, пожа́луйста, подня́ться.
2 (*serve with food etc.*) уго|ща́ть, -сти́ть; **may I ~ you to (some more) salad?** могу́ я положи́ть вам (ещё) немно́го сала́та?; **~ yourself!** угоща́йтесь!; бери́те, пожа́луйста!
3 (*prevent; also v.i.*): **I can't ~ it** я не могу́ ничего́ поде́лать; **I can't ~ laughing** я не могу́ удержа́ться от сме́ха; я не могу́ не смея́ться; **it can't be ~ed** ничего́ не поде́лаешь.
■ *v.i.* (*avail, be of use*) быть поле́зным; **crying won't ~** слеза́ми го́рю не помо́жешь.
■ *cpd.* **~line** *n.* слу́жба/телефо́н дове́рия.

helper /ˈhelpə(r)/ *n.* помо́щник; (*of a craftsman*) подру́чный.

helpful /ˈhelpfʊl/ *adj.* поле́зный; (*obliging*) услу́жливый.

helping /ˈhelpɪŋ/ *n.* по́рция.

helpless /ˈhelplɪs/ *adj.* беспо́мощный.

Helsinki /ˈhelsɪŋkɪ, helˈsɪŋkɪ/ *n.* Хе́льсинки (*m. indecl.*).

hem /hem/ *n.* край, подо́л.
■ *v.t.* (**hemmed, hemming**)
1 (*sew the edge of*) подш|ива́ть, -и́ть.
2: **~ in, ~ about, ~ round** окруж|а́ть, -и́ть.

hema- /ˈhiːmə/ (*US*) = **haema-**

hemisphere /ˈhemɪsfɪə(r)/ *n.* полуша́рие.

hemo- (*US*) = **haemo-**

hemp /hemp/ *n.* (*plant*) конопля́; (*fibre*) пенька́; **Indian ~** (*plant*) конопля́ инди́йская; (*drug*) (*dried leaves and flowers*) марихуа́на, анаша́; (*resin*) гаши́ш.

hen /hen/ *n.* (*domestic fowl*) ку́рица; (*female of bird species*) са́мка пти́цы.
■ *cpds.* **~ party** *n.* (*coll.*) деви́чник; **~pecked** *adj.*: **he is ~pecked** жена́ де́ржит его́ под каблуко́м.

hence /hens/ *adv.* (*from here*) отсю́да; (*from now*): **3 years ~** че́рез три го́да; (*consequently*) отсю́да, сле́довательно.

henchman /ˈhentʃmən/ *n.* приспе́шник.

hepatitis /hepəˈtaɪtɪs/ *n.* гепати́т.

her /hɜː(r)/ *obj. of* **she; he loves ~** он лю́бит её; **he looks at ~** он смо́трит на неё; *poss. adj.* её; **~ husband** её муж; (*referring to subj. of sentence*) свой; **she loves ~ husband** она́ лю́бит своего́ му́жа.

herald /ˈher(ə)ld/ *v.t.* возве|ща́ть, -сти́ть.

heraldic /heˈrældɪk/ *adj.* геральди́ческий.

heraldry /ˈherəldrɪ/ *n.* гера́льдика.

herb /hɜːb/ *n.* трава́; **~ tea** (*camomile etc.*) травяно́й чай; (*blackcurrant etc.*) фрукто́вый чай.

herbaceous /hɜːˈbeɪʃəs/ *adj.* травяно́й; **~ border** цвето́чный бордю́р.

herbal /ˈhɜːb(ə)l/ *n.* травни́к; **~ medicine** траволече́ние.
■ *adj.* травяно́й; **~ tea** = **herb tea**

herbalist /ˈhɜːbəlɪst/ *n.* специали́ст по лека́рственным расте́ниям.

herbivore /ˈhɜːbɪvɔː(r)/ *n.* травоя́дное живо́тное.

Herculean /hɜːkjʊˈliːən/ *adj.* геркуле́сов; (*fig.*): **~ efforts** титани́ческие уси́лия.

herd /hɜːd/ *n.* ста́до.
■ *v.t.* сгоня́ть, согна́ть (вме́сте).

here /hɪə(r)/ *n.*: **from ~ to there** отсю́да — туда́; **my house is near ~** мой дом ря́дом.
■ *adv.* 1 (*in this place*) здесь, тут.
2 (*to this place, in this direction*) сюда́; **come ~!** иди́те сюда́!
3 (*demonstrative*) вот; **~ I am!** вот и я!; я тут!; **~ he comes!** вот и он!; **~ we are at last!** наконе́ц-то (мы) пришли́/прие́хали/при́были; **~'s to our victory!** за на́шу побе́ду!
4 (*with offers*): **~ you are!** пожа́луйста.
5 (*phr.*): **he looked ~ and there** он поиска́л там и сям (*coll.*).

hereabouts /hɪərəˈbaʊts/ *adv.* побли́зости.

hereafter /hɪərˈɑːftə(r)/ *n.*: **the ~** загро́бная жизнь.

hereby /hɪəˈbaɪ/ *adv.* сим (*arch.*); э́тим; настоя́щим.

hereditary /hɪˈredɪtərɪ/ *adj.* насле́дственный.

heredity /hɪˈredɪtɪ/ *n.* насле́дственность.

heresy /ˈherəsɪ/ *n.* е́ресь.

heretic /ˈherətɪk/ *n.* ерети́|к (*fem.* -чка).

heretical /hɪˈretɪk(ə)l/ *adj.* ерети́ческий.

heritage /ˈherɪtɪdʒ/ *n.* насле́дство; (*fig.*) насле́дие.

hermaphrodite /hɜːˈmæfrədaɪt/ *n.* гермафроди́т.

hermetic /hɜːˈmetɪk/ *adj.* гермети́ческий; **~ally sealed** гермети́чески закры́тый.

hermit /ˈhɜːmɪt/ *n.* отше́льник.

hernia /ˈhɜːnɪə/ *n.* гры́жа.

hero /ˈhɪərəʊ/ *n.* (*pl.* **~es**) геро́й.
■ *cpd.* **~ worship** *n.* преклоне́ние пе́ред геро́ями.

heroic /hɪˈrəʊɪk/ *adj.* (*person, attempt*) герои́ческий.

heroin /ˈherəʊɪn/ *n.* герои́н.

heroine /ˈherəʊɪn/ *n.* герои́ня.

heroism /ˈherəʊɪz(ə)m/ *n.* герои́зм.

heron /ˈherən/ *n.* ца́пля.

herpes /ˈhɜːpiːz/ *n.* лиша́й.

herring /ˈherɪŋ/ *n.* сельдь; (*as food*) селёдка.

hers /hɜːz/ *pron.* её; **is this handkerchief ~?** э́то её плато́к?; **friends of ~** её друзья́.

herself /həˈself/ *pron.*
1 (*refl.*) себя́, -сь (*suff.*); **she looked at ~ in the mirror** она́ посмотре́ла на себя́ в зе́ркало; **she fell down and hurt ~** она́ упа́ла и ушибла́сь.
2 (*emph.*) сама́; **she said so ~** она́ сама́ э́то сказа́ла.
3 (*after preps.*) одна́; сама́; **she lives by ~** она́ живёт одна́.
4 (*her normal state*): **she is not ~ today** сего́дня она́ сама́ не своя́.

hertz /hɜːts/ *n.* (*pl.* **~**) герц.

hesitant /ˈhezɪt(ə)nt/ *adj.* колеблю́щийся.

hesitate /'hezɪteɪt/ *v.i.* колеба́ться (*impf.*); **don't ~ to ask** непреме́нно спроси́те.
hesitation /hezɪ'teɪʃ(ə)n/ *n.* колеба́ние.
hessian /'hesɪən/ *n.* (*cloth*) мешкови́на.
heterogeneous /hetərəʊ'dʒi:nɪəs/ *adj.* неоднoро́дный, разнохара́ктерный.
heterosexual /hetərəʊ'seksjʊəl/ *n.* гетеросексуа́л(ьный челове́к).
■ *adj.* гетеросексуа́льный.
hexagon /'heksəgən/ *n.* шестиуго́льник.
hexagonal /hek'sægən(ə)l/ *adj.* шестиуго́льный.
hey /heɪ/ *int.* эй!
heyday /'heɪdeɪ/ *n.* расцве́т, зени́т.
HGV (*abbr. of* ***heavy goods vehicle***) (*Br.*) большегру́зный автомоби́ль.
hi /haɪ/ *int.* приве́т!
hiatus /haɪ'eɪtəs/ *n.* (*pl.* **~es**)
1 (*gap*) про́пуск, пробе́л.
2 (*between vowels*) зия́ние.
hibernate /'haɪbəneɪt/ *v.i.* впада́ть (*impf.*) в зи́мнюю спя́чку.
hibiscus /hɪ'bɪskəs/ *n.* (*pl.* **~es**) (*bot.*) гиби́скус.
hicc|up, -ough /'hɪkʌp/ *n.* ико́та; (*slight delay*) зами́нка.
■ *v.i.* (**hiccuped, hiccuping**) ик|а́ть, -ну́ть.
hid /hɪd/ *past of* ▶ **hide²**
hidden /'hɪd(ə)n/ *p.p. of* ▶ **hide²**
hide¹ /haɪd/ *n.* (*skin*) шку́ра; (*leather*) ко́жа.
hide² /haɪd/ *v.t.* (*past* **hid;** *p.p.* **hidden**) пря́тать, с-; скры|ва́ть, -ть.
■ *v.i.* (*past* **hid;** *p.p.* **hidden**) пря́таться, с-; скр|ыва́ться, -ы́ться.
■ *cpds.* **~-and-seek** *n.* пря́т|ки (*pl.*, *g.* -ок); **~away, ~out** *nn.* укры́тие.
hideous /'hɪdɪəs/ *adj.* уро́дливый, безобра́зный; (*unpleasant*) ме́рзкий.
hiding¹ /'haɪdɪŋ/ *n.* (*coll.*, *thrashing*): **she gave him a good ~** она́ его́ вы́порола как сле́дует.
hiding² /'haɪdɪŋ/ *n.* (*concealment*) укры́тие; **he went into ~** он скры́лся.
■ *cpd.* **~ place** *n.* укры́тие.
hierarchical /haɪə'rɑ:kɪk(ə)l/ *adj.* иерархи́ческий.
hierarchy /'haɪərɑ:kɪ/ *n.* иера́рхия.
hieroglyph /'haɪərəglɪf/ *n.* иеро́глиф.
hieroglyphic /haɪərə'glɪfɪk/ *adj.* иероглифи́ческий.
hieroglyphics /haɪərə'glɪfɪks/ *n.* иеро́глифы, иероглифи́ческое письмо́.
hi-fi /'haɪfaɪ/ (*abbr. of* ***high fidelity***) *n.* (*pl.* **~s**) (*coll.*) (высокока́чественная) стереосисте́ма.
higgledy-piggledy /hɪgəldɪ'pɪgəldɪ/ *adj.* беспоря́дочный; сумбу́рный.
■ *adv.* впереме́шку; беспоря́дочно.
high /haɪ/ *n.*: **prices reached a new ~** це́ны дости́гли небыва́ло высо́кого у́ровня.
■ *adj.* 1 (*tall, elevated*) высо́кий (*also mus.*); **ten feet ~** высото́й в 10 фу́тов; **~ jump** прыжо́к в высоту́; **~ tide** больша́я вода́, прили́в.
2 (*chief, important*): **~ command** вы́сшее кома́ндование; **in ~ places** (*fig.*) в верха́х, в вы́сших сфе́рах; **~ street** (*Br.*) гла́вная у́лица.
3 (*greater than average; extreme*): **~ blood pressure** высо́кое (кровяно́е) давле́ние; **in ~ spirits** в отли́чном/припо́днятом настрое́нии.
4 (*at its peak*): **~ noon** по́лдень; **~ summer** середи́на/разга́р ле́та; **it is ~ time** давно́ пора́; **it is ~ time I was gone** мне уже́ давно́ пора́ идти́.
5 (*on drugs*) под кайфом; **to be ~ on cocaine** быть под кокаи́ном.
■ *adv.*: **~ up** высоко́; (*of direction*) ввысь.
■ *cpds.* **~brow** *n.* интеллектуа́л; *adj.* интеллектуа́льный, серьёзный; **~-class** *adj.* первокла́ссный, высо́кого кла́сса; **~-flyer** *n.* (*person likely to succeed*) подаю́щий больши́е наде́жды (*or* многообеща́ющий) челове́к; **~-handed** *adj.* вла́стный, своево́льный; **~-heeled** *adj.* на высо́ком каблуке́; **~ heels** *n. pl.* ту́фли на высо́ком каблуке́; **the H~lands** *n. pl.* се́вер и се́веро-за́пад Шотла́ндии; **~light** *n.* (*pl.*, *in hair*) цветны́е пря́ди (*f. pl.*); (*fig.*) кульминацио́нный моме́нт; *v.t.* (*fig.*, *emphasize*) выделя́ть, вы́делить (*also comput.*); заостр|я́ть, -и́ть внима́ние на + *p.*; **~lighter** *n.* флома́стер; **~-pitched** *adj.* высо́кий; **~-ranking** *adj.* высокопоста́вленный; **~-rise** *adj.*: **~-rise apartment blocks** высо́тные многокварти́рные дома́; **~ road** *n.* шоссе́ (*nt. indecl.*); **~-speed** *adj.* скоростно́й; **~-tech** *adj.* высокотехнологи́чный; **~-tech company** (*using latest technology*) компа́ния, испо́льзующая передову́ю те́хнику и передовы́е техноло́гии; (*producing ~-tech goods*) компа́ния, производя́щая изде́лия высо́кой сло́жности; **~way** *n.* шоссе́ (*nt. indecl.*); **H~way Code** пра́вила доро́жного движе́ния.
highly /'haɪlɪ/ *adv.* весьма́, о́чень; **~ paid** высокоопла́чиваемый; **he speaks ~ of you** он о вас о́чень хорошо́ отзыва́ется; **~ strung** (*Br.*) взви́нченный, нерво́зный; **she is ~ thought of** её о́чень це́нят.
Highness /'haɪnɪs/ *n.*: **His Royal H~** Его́ Короле́вское Высо́чество.
hijack /'haɪdʒæk/ *v.t.* уг|оня́ть, -на́ть; пох|ища́ть, -и́тить.
hijacker /'haɪdʒækə(r)/ *n.* уго́нщик, похити́тель (*m.*).
hike¹ /haɪk/ *n.* (*walk*) турпохо́д.
hike² /haɪk/ (*coll.*) *n.* (*rise*) подъём.
■ *v.t.* (*raise*) подн|има́ть, -я́ть.
hiker /'haɪkə(r)/ *n.* пе́ший тури́ст.
hiking /'haɪkɪŋ/ *n.* пе́ший тури́зм.
hilarious /hɪ'leərɪəs/ *adj.* весёлый.
hilarity /hɪ'lærɪtɪ/ *n.* весе́лье, поте́ха.
hill /hɪl/ *n.* холм.
■ *cpds.* **~side** *n.* склон холма́; **~top** *n.* верши́на холма́.
hillock /'hɪlək/ *n.* хо́лмик, буго́р.
hilly /'hɪlɪ/ *adj.* (**hilier, hilliest**) холми́стый.
him /hɪm/ *obj. of* ▶ **he**
Himalayas /hɪmə'leɪəz/ *n.* Гимала́|и (*pl.*, *g.* -ев).
himself /hɪm'self/ *pron.*
1 (*refl.*) себя́, -ся (*suff.*); **I hope he behaves ~** наде́юсь, что он бу́дет вести́ себя́ прили́чно; **he hurt ~** он уши́бся.

2 (*emph.*) сам; **he did the job ~** он сам сде́лал э́ту рабо́ту.
3 (*after preps.*) оди́н; сам; **he did it by ~** он сде́лал э́то сам; **he lives by ~** он живёт оди́н.
4 (*in his normal state*): **he is not ~ today** он сего́дня сам не свой.

hind /haɪnd/ *adj.*: **the dog stood on its ~ legs** соба́ка вста́ла на за́дние ла́пы.
■ *cpd.* **~sight** *n.*: **he spoke with ~sight** он говори́л, зна́я, чем ко́нчилось де́ло.

hinder /ˈhɪndə(r)/ *v.t.* меша́ть, по- + *d.*

Hindi /ˈhɪndɪ/ *n.* (*language*) хи́нди (*m. indecl.*).

hindrance /ˈhɪndrəns/ *n.* поме́ха, препя́тствие.

Hindu /ˈhɪnduː/ *n.* (*pl.* **~s**) инду́с (*fem.* -ка).
■ *adj.* инду́сский.

Hinduism /ˈhɪnduːɪz(ə)m/ *n.* индуи́зм.

Hindustani /hɪndʊˈstɑːnɪ/ *n.* (*language*) хиндуста́ни (*m. indecl.*).

hinge /hɪndʒ/ *n.* шарни́р; (*on door*) петля́.
■ *v.i.* (**hingeing** *or* **hinging**): **it all ~d on this event** всё бы́ло свя́зано с э́тим собы́тием.

hint /hɪnt/ *n.* (*suggestion*) намёк; **he is always dropping ~s** он всегда́ говори́т намёками; **there was a ~ of frost** начина́ло подмора́живать; (*written advice*) сове́т.
■ *v.t.* & *i.* намек|а́ть, -ну́ть на + *a.*; **I ~ed that I needed a holiday** я намекну́л, что мне ну́жен о́тпуск; **what are you ~ing (at)?** на что вы намека́ете?

hip¹ /hɪp/ *n.* бедро́.

hip² /hɪp/ *int.*: **~, ~, hooray!** гип-гип, ура́!

hip³ /hɪp/ *adj.* (**hipper, hippest**) (*coll.*) мо́дный, круто́й (*sl.*).

hipp|ie, -y /ˈhɪpɪ/ *n.* (*coll.*) хи́ппи (*c.g., indecl.*).

hippo /ˈhɪpəʊ/ *n.* (*pl.* **~s**) (*coll.*) гиппопота́м, бегемо́т.

hippopotamus /hɪpəˈpɒtəməs/ *n.* бегемо́т.

hire /ˈhaɪə(r)/ *n.* (*engagement of person*) наём; (*of thing*) наём, прока́т; **cars for ~** маши́ны напрока́т.
■ *v.t.* (*Br., a place*) сн|има́ть, -ять; (*Br., equipment, a car*) брать, взять напрока́т; (*a worker*) нан|има́ть, -я́ть.
■ *cpd.* **~ purchase** *n.* (*Br.*) поку́пка в рассро́чку.

his /hɪz/ *pron.* его́; **is this book ~?** э́то его́ кни́га?; **friends of ~** его́ друзья́.
■ *poss. adj.* его́; **this is ~ book** э́то его́ кни́га; (*referring to subj. of sentence*) свой; **he loves ~ children** он лю́бит свои́х дете́й.

Hispanic /hɪˈspænɪk/ *adj.* испа́нский; латиноамерика́нский.

hiss /hɪs/ *n.* шипе́ние.
■ *v.i.* (*of snake*) шипе́ть, за-; (*of audience*) свисте́ть (*impf.*).

historian /hɪˈstɔːrɪən/ *n.* исто́рик.

historic /hɪˈstɒrɪk/ *adj.* истори́ческий.

historical /hɪˈstɒrɪk(ə)l/ *adj.* истори́ческий.

history /ˈhɪstərɪ/ *n.* исто́рия.

histrionic /hɪstrɪˈɒnɪk/ *adj.* (*theatrical*) театра́льный, мелодрамати́ческий.

hit /hɪt/ *n.* (*blow*) уда́р, толчо́к; **~ man** наёмный/профессиона́льный уби́йца, ки́ллер; (*coll., success*) успе́х; (*popular song*) хит; шля́гер.
■ *v.t.* (**hitting;** *past and p.p.* **~**)
1 (*strike*) уд|аря́ть, -а́рить; **he fell and ~ his head on a stone** он упа́л и уда́рился голово́й о ка́мень; **the bullet ~ him in the shoulder** пу́ля попа́ла ему́ в плечо́; **the car ~ a tree** маши́на вре́залась в де́рево; **to ~ the target/mark** поп|ада́ть, -а́сть в цель.
2 (*fig. uses*): **the idea suddenly ~ me** меня́ вдруг осени́ло.
3 (*encounter*): **he ~ a bad patch** (*coll.*) у него́ начала́сь полоса́ неуда́ч.
■ *with advs.*: **~ back** *v.t.*: **if he ~s you, ~ him back** е́сли он вас уда́рит, уда́рьте его́ то́же; (*fig., at critics etc.*) да|ва́ть, -ть отпо́р (+ *d.*); **~ off** *v.t.*: **~ it off** ла́дить (*impf.*).

hitch /hɪtʃ/ *n.* заде́ржка.
■ *v.t.* 1 (*fasten*) привя́з|ывать, -а́ть; прицеп|ля́ть, -и́ть.
2 (*coll.*): **~ a lift** подъ|езжа́ть, -е́хать на попу́тной маши́не.
■ *v.i.* (*coll.; also* **~-hike**) е́здить автосто́пом.
■ *cpds.* **~-hiker** *n.* (*coll.*) путеше́ствующий автосто́пом; **~-hiking** *n.* «голосова́ние», езда́ автосто́пом (*or* на попу́тных маши́нах).

hither /ˈhɪðə(r)/ *adv.* сюда́.
■ *cpd.* **~to** *adv.* до сих пор.

HIV (*med., abbr. of* ***human immunodeficiency virus***) ВИЧ (ви́рус иммунодефици́та челове́ка); **~-positive** ВИЧ-инфици́рованный.

hive /haɪv/ *n.* у́лей; (*fig.*): **the office is a ~ of industry** рабо́та в о́фисе кипи́т.

HND (*abbr. of* ***Higher National Diploma***) (*Br.*) дипло́м о вы́сшем техни́ческом образова́нии.

hoar /hɔː(r)/ *adj.* седо́й.
■ *cpd.* **~ frost** *n.* и́ней, и́зморозь.

hoard /hɔːd/ *n.* (та́йный) запа́с, склад.
■ *v.t.* припря́т|ывать, -ать.

hoarding /ˈhɔːdɪŋ/ *n.*
1 (*Br., for poster display*) рекла́мный щит.
2 (*Br., fence round building site*) забо́р/огра́да вокру́г стройплоща́дки.

hoarse /hɔːs/ *adj.* хри́плый.

hoax /həʊks/ *n.* надува́тельство.

hob /hɒb/ *n.* (*Br.*) пове́рхность ку́хонной плиты́.

hobble /ˈhɒb(ə)l/ *v.i.* ковыля́ть (*impf.*).

hobby /ˈhɒbɪ/ *n.* хо́бби (*nt. indecl.*).

hobnob /ˈhɒbnɒb/ *v.i.* (**hobnobbed, hobnobbing**) води́ться (*impf.*), зна́ться (*impf.*) (*с кем*).

hockey /ˈhɒkɪ/ *n.* (*on field*) хокке́й на траве́; **ice ~** хокке́й (с ша́йбой/на льду).
■ *cpd.* **~ stick** *n.* клю́шка.

hoe /həʊ/ *n.* моты́га, тя́пка.
■ *v.t.* & *i.* (**hoes, hoed, hoeing**) разрыхля́ть (*impf.*) моты́гой.

hog /hɒg/ *n.* бо́ров; (*US, also fig.*) свинья́; **go the whole ~** дов|оди́ть, -ести́ де́ло до конца́; идти́, пойти́ на всё.
■ *v.t.* (**hogged, hogging**) (*monopolize*): **he ~ged the conversation** он не дава́л никому́ сло́ва вста́вить.

Hogmanay /ˈhɒgmənei/ *n.* (*Sc.*) кану́н Но́вого го́да.

hoist /hɔɪst/ *v.t.* подн|има́ть, -я́ть.

hold /həʊld/ *n.*
[1] (*grasp, grip*) удéрживание, захвáт; **he caught ~ of the rope** он ухватился за канáт; **he kept ~ of the reins** он не выпускáл повóдья из рук; **he seized, took ~ of my arm** он схватил/взял меня́ зá руку; **I got ~ of a plumber** я нашёл/отыскáл водопровóдчика; **where did you get ~ of those tickets?** где вы достáли э́ти билéты; **it's difficult to get ~ of her** её трýдно застáть.
[2] (*means of pressure*): **she has a ~ on, over him** онá имéет над ним власть.
[3] (*ship's*) трюм.
■ *v.t.* (*past and p.p.* **held**)
[1] (*clasp, grip*) держáть (*impf.*); **they sat ~ing hands** они́ сидéли держáсь зá руки.
[2] (*maintain, keep in a certain position*): **~ it!** (*coll.*) (*don't move*) не дви́гайтесь!; не шевели́тесь!; (*fig., keep*): **they were held to a draw** их принýдили к ничьéй; **~ the line!** (*teleph.*) не клади́те трýбку!
[3] (*detain*) зад|éрживать, -ержáть; **he was held prisoner** егó держáли в пленý.
[4] (*contain*) вме|щáть, -сти́ть; **the hall ~s a thousand** зал вмещáет ты́сячу человéк.
[5] (*consider*) полагáть (*impf.*), считáть (*impf.*); **the court held that ...** суд признáл, что...; **he was held responsible** емý пришлóсь держáть отвéт; **I don't ~ it against him** я не стáвлю емý э́то в винý.
[6] (*restrain*): **she held her breath** онá затаи́ла дыхáние.
[7] (*have, own*) владéть (*impf.*) + *i.*; **~ the record** быть рекордсмéном; **we ~ the same views** мы придéрживаемся одинáковых взгля́дов.
[8] (*occupy, remain in possession of*): **he held his ground** он не уступáл; он не сдавáлся; **I can ~ my own against anyone** я могý потягáться с кем угóдно.
[9] (*carry on, conduct*) пров|оди́ть, -ести́; **the meeting was held at noon** собрáние состоя́лось (*or* провели́) в пóлдень.
■ *v.i.* (*past and p.p.* **held**)
[1] (*grasp*): **~ tight!** держи́тесь крéпче/крéпко.
[2] (*remain*): **~ still!** не дви́гайтесь!
[3] (*remain unbroken, unchanged, intact*): **will the rope ~?** вы́держит ли верёвка?; **how long will the weather ~?** дóлго ли продéржится/простои́т такáя погóда?
■ *with advs.*: **~ back** *v.t.* (*restrain*) удéрж|ивать, -áть; **I couldn't ~ him back** я не мог егó удержáть; (*withhold*) удéрж|ивать, -áть; *v.i.* (*refrain*) воздéрж|иваться, -áться (*от чего*); **~ down** *v.t.* (*fig.*): **do you think you can ~ the job down?** сумéете ли вы удержáться на э́той дóлжности?; **we will try to ~ prices down** мы постарáемся сдержáть рóст цен; **they held off the attack** они́ отби́ли атáку; *v.i.* (*stay away*): **the rain held off all morning** дождя́ так и нé было всё ýтро; **~ on** *v.t.* (*keep in position*) прикреп|ля́ть, -и́ть; *v.i.* (*cling*) держáться (**to:** за + *a.*); (*fig.*): **you should ~ on to those shares** вам нáдо держáться за э́ти áкции; (*coll., wait*): **~ on a minute till I'm ready** подождите: я бýду готóв чéрез минýту; (*on the telephone*): **~ on, please!** не вéшайте трýбку!; **~ out** *v.t.* (*extend*) прот|я́гивать, -янýть; **I can't ~ out any hope** я не могý вас ничéм обнадёжить; *v.i.* (*endure, refuse to yield*) держáться, про-; **the men are ~ing out for more money** рабóчие настáивают на повышéнии зарплáты; **~ up** *v.t.* (*lift, hold erect*) подн|имáть, -я́ть; **the boy held up his hand** мáльчик пóднял рýку; (*delay*) задéрж|ивать, -áть; **traffic was held up by fog** движéние останови́лось из-за тумáна; (*waylay*): **the robbers held them up at pistol point** банди́ты огрáбили их, угрожáя пистолéтом.
■ *cpds.* **~all** *n.* (*Br.*) вещевóй мешóк; **~-up** *n.* (*delay*) задéржка; (*robbery*) вооружённый грабёж.

holder /ˈhəʊldə(r)/ *n.*
[1] (*possessor*) владéлец; обладáтель (*m.*).
[2] (*fin.; container*) держáтель (*m.*).

hole /həʊl/ *n.*
[1] (*cavity*) дырá.
[2] (*opening*) отвéрстие.
[3] (*burrow*) норá.
[4] (*phrr.*): **the purchase made a ~ in his savings** покýпка остáвила брешь в егó сбережéниях; **~ in the wall** (*Br. coll.*) банкомáт.

holiday /ˈhɒlɪdeɪ/ *n.* (*Br.*)
[1] (*day off*) выходнóй (день); **bank ~** официáльный нерабóчий день.
[2] (*annual leave*) óтпуск, óтдых; (*school, university vacation*) кани́кул|ы (*pl., g.* —); (*leisure time*) óтдых; **he is on ~** он в óтпуске/отпускý; у негó кани́кулы; **~ camp** (лéтний) лáгерь.
■ *cpd.* **~maker** *n.* отдыхáющий; тури́ст (*fem.* -ка).

holistic /hɒˈlɪstɪk/ *adj.* цéлостный.

Holland /ˈhɒlənd/ *n.* (*country or province*) Голлáндия.

hollow /ˈhɒləʊ/ *n.* вы́емка.
■ *adj.* [1] (*not solid*) пустóй, пóлый.
[2] (*of sounds*) глухóй.
[3] (*fig., false, insincere*) фальши́вый, лжи́вый; **~ laughter** неестéственный смех.
[4] (*sunken*) ввали́вшийся, впáлый; **~ cheeks** ввали́вшиеся щёки.

holly /ˈhɒlɪ/ *n.* остроли́ст.

hollyhock /ˈhɒlɪhɒk/ *n.* алтéй рóзовый.

holocaust /ˈhɒləkɔːst/ *n.* мáссовое уничтожéние; **the H~** холокóст.

holster /ˈhəʊlstə(r)/ n. кобурá.

holy /ˈhəʊlɪ/ *adj.* (**holier, holiest**) свящéнный, святóй; **the H~ Ghost, Spirit** Святóй Дух; **the H~ Land** Святáя земля́ (*об Израиле и Палестине*).

homage /ˈhɒmɪdʒ/ *n.* почтéние, преклонéние; **we pay ~ to his genius** мы преклоня́емся пéред егó гéнием.

home /həʊm/ *n.*
[1] (*place where one resides or belongs*) дом; (*attr.*) домáшний; **~ economics** домоводство; **~ help** (*Br.*) приходя́щая домрабóтница; **she left ~** онá поки́нула (роди́тельский) дом; **at home** (*in one's house*) дóма; (*on one's ~ ground*) у себя́; (*e.g. football*) на своём пóле; **make yourself at ~** бýдьте как дóма; **I feel at ~ here** я чýвствую себя́ здесь как дóма.
[2] (*institution*): **a ~ for the disabled** дом инвали́дов; **he put his parents into a ~** он

поместил своих родителей в дом престарелых.
3 (*attr., opp. foreign; native, local*): **~ affairs** внутренние дела; **H~ Office** (*Br.*) Министерство внутренних дел; **H~ Secretary** (*Br.*) министр внутренних дел; **~ team** команда хозяев поля; **~ town** родной город.
■ *adv.* 1 (*at or to one's own house*): **he was on his way ~** он шёл/ехал домой; **is he ~ yet?** он (уже) дома?
2 (*in or to one's own country*): **he came ~ from abroad** он вернулся из-за границы.
3 (*to the point aimed at*): **bring sth. ~ to s.o.** дов|одить, -ести что-н. до чьего-н. сознания; **his remarks struck ~** его замечания попали в цель.
■ *cpds.* **~ entertainment system** *n.* домашний развлекательный центр; **~-grown** *adj.* (*vegetables*) домашний, с огорода; (*not foreign*) отечественный; **~land** *n.* родина, родная страна; **~-made** *adj.* домашний; **~ page** *n.* (*comput.*) стартовая страница в Интернете; **~sick** *adj.* скучающий/тоскующий по дому/родине; **~work** *n.* домашнее задание.

homeless /ˈhəʊmlɪs/ *adj.* бездомный.

homely /ˈhəʊmlɪ/ *adj.* (**homelier, homeliest**)
1 (*Br., cosy*) домашний, уютный.
2 (*Br., unpretentious*): **a ~ meal** неприхотливая еда.
3 (*US, unattractive*) некрасивый.

homeopath /ˈhəʊmɪəʊpæθ, ˈhɒmɪ-/ *n.* гомеопат.

homeopathic /həʊmɪəʊˈpæθɪk, ˈhɒmɪ-/ *adj.* гомеопатический.

homeopathy /həʊmɪˈɒpəθɪ, hɒmɪ-/ *n.* гомеопатия.

homeward /ˈhəʊmwəd/ *adv.* (*also* **~s**) домой.

homicidal /hɒmɪˈsaɪd(ə)l/ *adj.* замышляющий убийство.

homicide /ˈhɒmɪsaɪd/ *n.* (*crime*) убийство.

homogeneous /hɒməˈdʒiːnɪəs/ *adj.* однородный.

homophobia /həʊməˈfəʊbɪə/ *n.* ненависть к гомосексуалистам, гомофобия.

homosexual /hɒməˈseksjʊəl/ *n.* гомосексуалист.
■ *adj.* гомосексуальный.

homosexuality /hɒməseksjʊˈælɪtɪ/ *n.* гомосексуализм.

Honduran /hɒnˈdjʊərən/ *n.* гондурас|ец (*fem.* -ка).
■ *adj.* гондурасский.

Honduras /hɒnˈdjʊərəs/ *n.* Гондурас.

hone /həʊn/ *v.t.* (*sharpen*) точить, за-; (*fig.*) отт|ачивать, -очить.

honest /ˈɒnɪst/ *adj.* (*fair*) честный; (*candid*): **to be ~ (with you)** честно говоря.

honestly /ˈɒnɪstlɪ/ *adv.*
1 (*straightforwardly*) честно.
2 (*candidly*) прямо, чистосердечно; **~!** честное слово!

honesty /ˈɒnɪstɪ/ *n.*
1 (*integrity*) честность.
2 (*candour*) прямота, искренность.

honey /ˈhʌnɪ/ *n.* мёд; (*US coll., darling*) дорогой, милый.
■ *cpd.* **~moon** *n.* медовый месяц; *v.i.* пров|одить, -ести медовый месяц.

Hong Kong /hɒŋˈkɒŋ/ *n.* Гонконг.

honk /hɒŋk/ *v.i.* гудеть (*impf.*).

honor /ˈɒnə(r)/ (*US*) = **honour**

honorable /ˈɒnərəb(ə)l/ (*US*) = **honourable**

honorari|um /ɒnəˈreərɪəm/ *n.* (*pl.* **~ums** *or* **~a**) гонорар.

honorary /ˈɒnərərɪ/ *adj.* почётный.

honour /ˈɒnə(r)/ (*US* **honor**) *n.*
1 (*good character, reputation*) честь.
2 (*dignity, credit*) честь; **the reception was held in his ~** приём был устроен в его честь.
3 (*as title*) **Your H~** ваша честь.
4 (*pl., academic distinction*): **~s degree** ≈степень балакавра.
■ *v.t.* 1 (*respect, do ~ to*) оказ|ывать, -ать честь + *d.*
2 (*fulfil obligation*) выполнять, выполнить; **he failed to ~ the agreement** он не выполнил соглашения; **will the cheque be ~ed?** будет ли уплачено по этому чеку?

honourable /ˈɒnərəb(ə)l/ (*US* **honorable**) *adj.* честный, достойный.

hood /hʊd/ *n.*
1 (*headgear*) капюшон.
2 (*Br., of car*) складной верх.
3 (*US, of car engine*) капот.

hoodie /ˈhʊdɪ/ *n.* (*coll.*) толстовка с капюшоном.

hoodwink /ˈhʊdwɪŋk/ *v.t.* одурачи|вать, -ть; пров|одить, -ести (*coll.*).

hoof /huːf/ *n.* (*pl.* **hoofs** *or* **hooves**) копыто.

hook /hʊk/ *n.*
1 (*curved device*) крючок (*also for fishing and as fastening*), крюк; **the receiver was off the ~** трубка была снята; **get off the ~** (*coll.*) вызволять, вызволить; **let off the ~** (*coll.*) выручать, выручить.
2 (*boxing blow*) хук, боковой удар.
■ *v.t.* (*usu. with advs., fasten*): **she ~ed up her dress** она застегнула платье (на крючки).

hooligan /ˈhuːlɪgən/ *n.* хулиган.

hooliganism /ˈhuːlɪgənɪz(ə)m/ *n.* хулиганство.

hoop /huːp/ *n.*
1 (*plaything*) обруч.
2 (*Br., croquet*) ворот|а (*pl., g.* —).

hooray! /hʊˈreɪ/ *int.* ура.

hoot /huːt/ *n.* (*owl's cry*) уханье; (*warning note*) гудок, сигнал.
■ *v.i.* (*of a car etc.*) гудеть, про-; (*of an owl*) ух|ать, -нуть; (*of a person*): **we ~ed with laughter** мы покатывались со смеху.

hooter /ˈhuːtə(r)/ *n.*
1 (*Br., of car, factory*) гудок.
2 (*sl.*) (*nose*) рубильник (*нос*).

Hoover /ˈhuːvə(r)/ (*Br.*) *n.* (*propr.*) пылесос.
■ *v.t.* (**h~**) пылесосить, про-.

hooves /huːvz/ *pl. of* ▸ **hoof**

hop[1] /hɒp/ *n.* подскок, скачок (на одной ноге).
■ *v.i.* (**hopped, hopping**) прыгать, скакать (*both impf.*).

hop² /hɒp/ *n.* (*bot.*) хмель (*m.*).
hope /həʊp/ *n.* надéжда; **don't raise my ~s in vain** не обнадёживайте меня́ понапрáсну.
■ *v.t.* & *i.* надéяться (*impf.*); **I ~ to see you soon** надéюсь, скóро вас уви́деть; **let's ~ so!** бу́дем надéяться!; **I ~ not** надéюсь, что нет.
hopeful /ˈhəʊpfʊl/ *adj.*
1 (*having hope*): **I am ~ of success** я надéюсь/рассчи́тываю на успéх.
2 (*inspiring hope*) обнадёживающий; **a ~ sign** обнадёживающий знак.
hopefully /ˈhəʊpfʊlɪ/ *adv.*: **~ he will arrive soon** нáдо надéяться, он скóро приéдет.
hopeless /ˈhəʊplɪs/ *adj.*
1 (*affording no hope*) безнадёжный; **a ~ situation** безнадёжное положéние.
2 (*coll., incapable*): **he's quite ~ at science** тóчные нау́ки емý совершéнно не даю́тся.
horde /hɔːd/ *n.* (*fig.*) пóлчище.
horizon /həˈraɪz(ə)n/ *n.* (*lit., fig.*) горизóнт.
horizontal /hɒrɪˈzɒnt(ə)l/ *adj.* горизонтáльный.
hormonal /hɔːˈməʊnəl/ *adj.* гормонáльный.
hormone /ˈhɔːməʊn/ *n.* гормóн; **~ replacement therapy** гормонáльная терапи́я.
horn /hɔːn/ *n.*
1 (*of cattle*) рог.
2 (*mus.*) (*French horn*) валтóрна; (*hunting horn*) рог.
3 (*of car*) гудóк.
hornet /ˈhɔːnɪt/ *n.* шéршень (*m.*); **his words stirred up a ~'s nest** (*fig.*) егó словá потревóжили оси́ное гнездó.
hornist /ˈhɔːnɪst/ *n.* валторни́ст (*fem.* -ка).
horoscope /ˈhɒrəskəʊp/ *n.* гороскóп.
horrendous /həˈrendəs/ *adj.* ужáсный.
horri|ble /ˈhɒrɪb(ə)l/, **-d** /ˈhɒrɪd/ *adjs.* ужáсный.
horrific /həˈrɪfɪk/ *adj.* ужасáющий.
horrify /ˈhɒrɪfaɪ/ *v.t.* потряс|áть, -ти́.
horror /ˈhɒrə(r)/ *n.* ýжас; **~ film** фильм ýжасов; (*extreme dislike*): **I have a ~ of cats** я терпéть не могý кóшек.
horse /hɔːs/ *n.* лóшадь, конь (*m.*); **I had it straight from the ~'s mouth** я узнáл э́то из пéрвых рук.
■ *cpds.* **~back** *n.*: **on ~back** верхóм; **~back riding** (*US*) = **~ riding; ~ chestnut** *n.* каштáн кóнский; **~power** *n.* лошади́ная си́ла; **20 ~power** 20 лошади́ных сил; **~ race, ~ racing** *nn.* скáчки (*f. pl.*), бегá (*m. pl.*); **~radish** *n.* хрен; **~ riding** *n.* верховáя ездá; **~shoe** *n.* подкóва.
horticultural /hɔːtɪˈkʌltʃər(ə)l/ *adj.* садовóдческий.
horticultur(al)ist /hɔːtɪˈkʌltʃər(əl)ɪst/ *n.* садовóд.
horticulture /ˈhɔːtɪkʌltʃə(r)/ *n.* садовóдство.
hose /həʊz/ *n.* (*also* **~pipe**) шланг.
hosiery /ˈhəʊzɪərɪ/ *n.* чулóчно-носóчные издéлия (*nt. pl.*).
hospice /ˈhɒspɪs/ *n.* хóспис.
hospitable /hɒˈspɪtəb(ə)l/ *adj.* гостеприи́мный.
hospital /ˈhɒspɪt(ə)l/ *n.* больни́ца; **he is in ~** он (лежи́т) в больни́це.
■ *cpd.* **~ trust** *n.* (*Br.*) больни́чный трест (*больница Национальной службы здравоохранения, управляемая на правах доверительной собственности*).
hospitality /hɒspɪˈtælɪtɪ/ *n.* гостеприи́мство.
hospitalize /ˈhɒspɪtəlaɪz/ *v.t.* госпитализи́ровать (*impf., pf.*).
host¹ /həʊst/ *n.* хозя́ин.
■ *v.t.* организовáть (*impf., pf.*).
host² /həʊst/ *n.* (*multitude*) мнóжество, мáсса.
hostage /ˈhɒstɪdʒ/ *n.* залóжник.
hostel /ˈhɒst(ə)l/ *n.* общежи́тие.
hostelry /ˈhɒstəlrɪ/ *n.* (*arch. or joc.*) постоя́лый двор.
hostess /ˈhəʊstɪs/ *n.* хозя́йка.
hostile /ˈhɒstaɪl/ *adj.* враждéбный.
hostility /hɒˈstɪlɪtɪ/ *n.* враждéбность.
hot /hɒt/ *adj.* (**hotter, hottest**)
1 (*water, object*) горя́чий; (*weather*) жáркий; **I am ~** мне жáрко; **a ~ flush** прили́в крóви; **in the ~ seat** (*coll.*) на отвéтственной дóлжности.
2 (*spicy*) óстрый.
3: **~ on the scent, trail** по горя́чему слéду.
■ *cpds.* **~bed** *n.* парни́к; (*fig.*) рассáдник, очáг; **~-blooded** *adj.* пы́лкий, стрáстный; **~ dog** *n.* хот-дóг; **~-headed** *adj.* вспы́льчивый, горя́чий; **~line** *n.* (*for enquiries*) горя́чая ли́ния; (*between governments*) прямáя телефóнная связь; **~plate** *n.* пли́тка; **~-tempered** *adj.* вспы́льчивый; **~-water bottle** *n.* грéлка.
hotel /həʊˈtel/ *n.* гости́ница, отéль (*m.*).
hotelier /həʊˈtelɪə(r)/ *n.* хозя́ин гости́ницы.
hound /haʊnd/ *n.* охóтничья собáка.
■ *v.t.*: **~ out** выживáть, вы́жить.
hour /aʊə(r)/ *n.*
1 (*period*) час; **boats for hire by the ~** прокáт лóдок с почасовóй оплáтой.
2 (*of clock time*): **every ~ on the ~** в начáле кáждого чáса.
3 (*specific period of time*): **in office ~s** в рабóчее врéмя; **out of ~s** в нерабóчее врéмя.
hourly /ˈaʊəlɪ/ *adj.*
1 (*occurring once an hour*) ежечáсный.
2: **an ~ wage** почасовáя оплáта.
■ *adv.* ежечáсно; (*at any time*) с чáсу на час.
house¹ /haʊs/ *n.*
1 (*habitation*) дом, здáние; (*parl.*): **H~ of Commons** палáта óбщин; **H~ of Lords** палáта лóрдов; **H~ of Representatives** палáта представи́телей.
2 (*audience*) зал, аудитóрия; **they played to a full ~** на их выступлéнии зал был пóлон; (*Br., performance*) (*theatr.*) представлéние.
■ *cpds.* **~boat** *n.* плаву́чий дом; **~bound** *adj.*: **he is ~bound** он не выхóдит из дóма; **~hold** *n.* дом; домáшний круг; (*attr.*): **~hold appliances** бытовы́е прибóры; **her name is a ~hold word; she is a ~hold name** её все знáют; **~holder** *n.* домовладéлец; **~ husband** *n.* муж, веду́щий домáшнее хозя́йство; **~keeper** *n.* экономка; **~keeping** *n.* домáшнее хозя́йство; **~-proud** *adj.* лю́бящий занимáться благоустрóйством и украшéнием дóма; **~-to-~** *adj.*: **a ~-to-~ search** óбыск

всех домо́в подря́д; пова́льный о́быск; **~-trained** *adj.* (*Br.*) приу́ченный жить (*or* не па́чкать) в до́ме (*о собаке, кошке*); **~-warming** *n.* новосе́лье; **~wife** *n.* домохозя́йка; **~work** *n.* дома́шние дела́.

house² /haʊz/
1 (*provide house(s) for*) сели́ть, по-.
2 (*accommodate*) вме|ща́ть, -сти́ть; **this building ~s the city council** в э́том зда́нии размеща́ется муниципалите́т.
3 (*store*) храни́ть (*impf.*).

housing /ˈhaʊzɪŋ/ *n.* жильё; **~ association** жили́щно-строи́тельная ассоциа́ция; **~ benefit** (*Br.*) посо́бие на вы́плату квартпла́ты; **~ development, ~ estate** (*Br.*), **~ project** (*US*) жило́й микрорайо́н.

hovel /ˈhɒv(ə)l/ *n.* лачу́га.

hover /ˈhɒvə(r)/ *v.i.* пари́ть (*impf.*); (*fig.*): **to ~ around s.o.** ви́ться (*impf.*) вокру́г + *g.*
■ *cpd.* **~craft** *n.* ховеркра́фт; су́дно на возду́шной поду́шке.

how /haʊ/ *adv.*
1 (*in direct and indirect questions*) как; каки́м о́бразом?; **~ come?** (*coll.*) как э́то?; **~ come you are late?** почему́ э́то вы опа́здываете?; **~ are you?** как пожива́ете?; **~ do you know that?** отку́да вы э́то зна́ете?; **~ about a drink?** не хоти́те ли вы́пить?
2 (*with adjs. and advs.*): **~ far is it?** как далеко́ э́то нахо́дится?; **~ many, much?** ско́лько?; **~ old is she?** ско́лько ей лет?
3 (*in indirect statements or questions*): **I told him ~ I'd been abroad** я рассказа́л ему́, как я съе́здил за грани́цу.
4 (*in exclamations*): **~ I wish I were there!** как бы мне хоте́лось сейча́с быть там!

however /haʊˈevə(r)/ *adv.* (*with adj.*) како́й бы ни; как ни; **~ strong he is** како́й бы он ни был си́льный; (*with adv.*) как бы ни; **~ hard he tried** как он ни стара́лся; (*in questions*) как же; **~ did you find out that?** как же вы узна́ли э́то?; (*nevertheless*) одна́ко, и всё же; **~, he forgot** одна́ко он забы́л.

howl /haʊl/ *n.* вой.
■ *v.t.* & *i.* выть (*impf.*); **listen to the wolves ~ing!** послу́шайте, как во́ют во́лки.

howler /ˈhaʊlə(r)/ *n.* (*coll.*, *solecism*) грубе́йшая оши́бка, ля́псус.

HQ (*abbr. of* ***headquarters***) штаб-кварти́ра; (*mil.*) штаб, ста́вка.

HRH (*abbr. of* ***Her*|*His Royal Highness***) (*Br.*) Её/Его́ Короле́вское Высо́чество.

HRT (*abbr. of* ***hormone replacement therapy***) гормона́льная терапи́я.

hub /hʌb/ *n.* ступи́ца; (*fig.*) центр.
■ *cpd.* **~cap** *n.* колпа́к.

hubbub /ˈhʌbʌb/ *n.* шум, го́вор, го́мон, гвалт.

huddle /ˈhʌd(ə)l/ *v.i.* толпи́ться, с-; **they ~d together for warmth** они́ прижа́лись друг к дру́гу, что́бы согре́ться.

hue¹ /hjuː/ *n.* (*colour*) отте́нок, тон (*pl.* -á).

hue² /hjuː/ *n.*: **~ and cry** крик; (*outcry*) возмуще́ние.

huff /hʌf/ *n.*: **he walked off in a ~** он ушёл вконе́ц разоби́женный.

huffy /ˈhʌfɪ/ *adj.* (**huffier, huffiest**) оби́женный.

hug /hʌg/ *n.* объя́тие.
■ *v.t.* (**hugged, hugging**) обн|има́ть, -я́ть.

huge /hjuːdʒ/ *adj.* огро́мный, грома́дный; (*event*) грандио́зный.

hull /hʌl/ *n.* (*of ship*) ко́рпус; (*of aircraft*) фюзеля́ж.

hum /hʌm/ *n.* (*of insects*) жужжа́ние; (*of machines*) гуде́ние, гул.
■ *v.t.* & *i.* (**hummed, humming**)
1 (*make murmuring sound*) (*of insects*) жужжа́ть (*impf.*); (*of cars*) гуде́ть (*impf.*).
2 (*sing with closed lips*) напева́ть (*impf.*).

human /ˈhjuːmən/ *n.* челове́к.
■ *adj.* челове́ческий; **~ being** челове́к; **~ nature** челове́ческая приро́да; **~ resources department** отде́л ка́дров; **~ rights** права́ челове́ка; **human shield** живо́й щит.

humane /hjuːˈmeɪn/ *adj.* гума́нный, челове́чный.

humanism /ˈhjuːmənɪz(ə)m/ *n.* гумани́зм.

humanist /ˈhjuːmənɪst/ *n.* гумани́ст.

humanitarian /hjuːmænɪˈteərɪən/ *adj.* гуманита́рный; гума́нный.

humanit|y /hjuːˈmænɪtɪ/ *n.*
1 (*the human race*) челове́чество.
2 (*humaneness*) гума́нность.
3 : **the ~ies** гуманита́рные нау́ки (*f. pl.*).

humble /ˈhʌmb(ə)l/ *adj.* (**humbler, humblest**) скро́мный, поко́рный, смире́нный.

humbug /ˈhʌmbʌg/ *n.* (*deceit, hypocrisy*) надува́тельство; (*hypocrite, fraud*) обма́нщик, очковтира́тель (*m.*); (*nonsense*) чушь, вздо́р; (*Br., boiled sweet*) ледене́ц.

humdrum /ˈhʌmdrʌm/ *adj.* однообра́зный, ну́дный.

humid /ˈhjuːmɪd/ *adj.* вла́жный.

humidifier /hjuːˈmɪdɪfaɪ(ə)r/ *n.* увлажни́тель (*m.*) во́здуха.

humidity /hjuːˈmɪdɪtɪ/ *n.* вла́жность.

humiliate /hjuːˈmɪlɪeɪt/ *v.t.* ун|ижа́ть, -и́зить.

humiliation /hjuːmɪlɪˈeɪʃ(ə)n/ *n.* униже́ние.

humility /hjuːˈmɪlɪtɪ/ *n.* смире́ние; скро́мность.

hummock /ˈhʌmək/ *n.* буго́р, приго́рок.

humor /ˈhjuːmə(r)/ (*US*) = **humour**

humorist /ˈhjuːmərɪst/ *n.* (*facetious person*) остря́к, весельча́к; (*humorous writer etc.*) юмори́ст.

humorless /ˈhjuːməlɪs/ (*US*) = **humourless**

humorous /ˈhjuːmərəs/ *adj.* юмористи́ческий.

humour /ˈhjuːmə(r)/ (*US* **humor**) *n.*
1 (*disposition*) нрав, душе́вный склад.
2 (*amusement*) ю́мор; **he has little sense of ~** у него́ сла́бое чу́вство ю́мора.
■ *v.t.* потака́ть (*impf.*) + *d.*

humourless /ˈhjuːməlɪs/ (*US* **humorless**) *adj.* лишённый чу́вства ю́мора; ску́чный.

hump /hʌmp/ *n.* горб.

hunch /hʌntʃ/ *n.* чутьё, интуи́ция.
■ *v.t.*: **he ~ed (up) his shoulders** он ссуту́лился/сго́рбился.

hundred /ˈhʌndrəd/ *n.* (*pl.* **~s** *or* (*with numeral or qualifying word*) **~**) (числó, но́мер) сто; (*collect*) со́тня; **a ~ and fifty** сто

пятьдеся́т, полтора́ста; **~s of people** со́тни людей; **I'm one ~ per cent behind you** я стопроцентно на ва́шей стороне́; **in the nineteen ~s** в девятисо́тые го́ды.
■ *adj.* сто + *g. pl.*; **a ~ miles away** (*fig.*) за ты́сячу вёрст.
■ *cpd.* **~weight** *n.* (*Imperial — approx. 50.8 kilograms*) англи́йский це́нтнер; (*US — approx. 45.4 kilograms*) америка́нский це́нтнер.

hundredth /ˈhʌndrədθ/ *n.* (*fraction*) одна́ со́тая.
■ *adj.* со́тый.

hung /hʌŋ/ *past and p.p. of* ▶ **hang**

Hungarian /hʌŋˈgeərɪən/ *n.* (*person*) венгр (*fem.* венге́рка); (*language*) венге́рский язы́к.
■ *adj.* венге́рский.

Hungary /ˈhʌŋgərɪ/ *n.* Ве́нгрия.

hunger /ˈhʌŋgə(r)/ *n.* го́лод.
■ *cpd.* **~ strike** *n.* голодо́вка.

hungry /ˈhʌŋgrɪ/ *adj.* (**hungrier, hungriest**) голо́дный.

hunk /hʌŋk/ *n.* большо́й кусо́к; (*of bread*) ломо́ть (*m.*) хле́ба.

hunt /hʌnt/ *n.*
1 (*~ing expedition*) охо́та.
2 (*search*) охо́та (**for:** на + *a.*); по́иск|и (*pl.*, *g.* -ов) (**for:** + *g.*).
■ *v.t. & i.* (*e.g. animals*) охо́титься (*impf.*) (на + *a.*); (*persons or things*) охо́титься (*impf.*) за + *i.*; вести́ (*det.*) по́иски + *g.*

hunter /ˈhʌntə(r)/ *n.* охо́тник.

hunting /ˈhʌntɪŋ/ *n.* охо́та.

hurdle /ˈhɜːd(ə)l/ *n.* (*in athletics & fig.*) барье́р, препя́тствие.

hurl /hɜːl/ *v.t.* бр|оса́ть, -о́сить; **he ~ed abuse at me** он осы́пал меня́ оскорбле́ниями.

hurr|ah /hʊˈrɑː/, **-ay** /hʊˈreɪ/ *n. & int.* ура́!

hurricane /ˈhʌrɪkən/ *n.* урага́н.

hurr|y /ˈhʌrɪ/ *n.* спе́шка, поспе́шность; **he was in no ~y to go** он не спеши́л уходи́ть; **in his ~y, he forgot his briefcase** в спе́шке он забы́л взять портфе́ль.
■ *v.t.* 1 (*cause to move hastily*) торопи́ть, по-.
2 (*perform hastily*): **don't ~y the job** рабо́тайте не спеша́.
■ *v.i.* (*move hastily*) спеши́ть, по-; торопи́ться, по-; **he ~ied home** он спеши́л домо́й; **they ~ied to finish the work** они́ спеши́ли зако́нчить рабо́ту.
■ *with advs.*: **~y along there, please!** потора́пливайтесь, пожа́луйста!; **~y up!** потора́пливайтесь!

hurt /hɜːt/ *n.* (*offence*) оби́да.
■ *v.t.* (*past and p.p.* **~**) (*inflict pain on*) ушиб|а́ть, -и́ть; причин|я́ть, -и́ть боль + *d.*; **I won't ~ you** я не причиню́ вам бо́ли (*or* не сде́лаю вам бо́льно); **these shoes ~ (me)** э́ти ту́фли мне жмут; (*injure*) ушиб|а́ть, -и́ть; **he fell and ~ his back** он упа́л и ушиб спи́ну; **~ o.s.** ушиб|а́ться, -и́ться, ударя́ться, уда́риться; (*damage*) вреди́ть, по-; (*offend, pain*) об|ижа́ть, -и́деть; зад|ева́ть, -е́ть; **now you've ~ his feelings** ну вот, вы его́ и оби́дели.
■ *v.i.* (*past and p.p.* **~**) (*be sore*) боле́ть (*impf.*): **my arm ~s** у меня́ боли́т/но́ет рука́; (*do damage*): **it won't ~ to wait** не меша́ло бы подожда́ть.

hurtful /ˈhɜːtfʊl/ *adj.* оби́дный.

hurtle /ˈhɜːt(ə)l/ *v.t. & i.* нести́сь (*impf.*), мча́ться (*impf.*).

husband /ˈhʌzbənd/ *n.* муж (*pl.* -ья́).

hush /hʌʃ/ *v.t.*: **she ~ed the baby to sleep** она́ убаю́кала ребёнка; **the scandal was ~ed up** сканда́л замя́ли.
■ *v.i.*: **~!** (*as int.*) ти́ше!; молчи́те!
■ *cpd.* **~-~** *adj.* (*coll.*) та́йный, засекре́ченный.

husk /hʌsk/ *n.* шелуха́, (*of nuts*) скорлупа́.
■ *v.t.* очища́ть, очи́стить; лущи́ть, об-.

husky[1] /ˈhʌskɪ/ *n.* (*Eskimo dog*) эскимо́сская ла́йка, ха́ски (*f. indecl.*).

husky[2] /ˈhʌskɪ/ *adj.* (**huskier, huskiest**) (*hoarse*) сухо́й, хри́плый.

hustle /ˈhʌs(ə)l/ *n.* су́толока, да́вка.
■ *v.t.*: **the police ~d him away** его́ уволокли́ полице́йские.

hut /hʌt/ *n.* (*small building*) хи́жина; (*barrack*) бара́к.

hutch /hʌtʃ/ *n.* (*for pets*) кле́тка.

hyacinth /ˈhaɪəsɪnθ/ *n.* гиаци́нт.

hybrid /ˈhaɪbrɪd/ *n.* гибри́д.

hybridize /ˈhaɪbrɪdaɪz/ *v.t.* скре́|щивать, -сти́ть; гибридизи́ровать (*impf.*).

hydrangea /haɪˈdreɪndʒə/ *n.* горте́нзия.

hydraulic /haɪˈdrɒlɪk/ *adj.* гидравли́ческий.

hydrochloric /haɪdrəˈklɒrɪk/ *adj.*: **~ acid** соля́ная кислота́.

hydroelectric /haɪdrəʊɪˈlektrɪk/ *adj.* гидроэлектри́ческий.

hydrofoil /ˈhaɪdrəfɔɪl/ *n.* су́дно на подво́дных кры́льях; раке́та.

hydrogen /ˈhaɪdrədʒ(ə)n/ *n.* водоро́д.

hyena /haɪˈiːnə/ *n.* гие́на.

hygiene /ˈhaɪdʒiːn/ *n.* гигие́на.

hygienic /haɪˈdʒiːnɪk/ *adj.* гигиени́ческий.

hygieniest /ˈhaɪdʒiːnɪst/ *n.* ассисте́нт зубно́го врача́ (*специалист по гигиене полости рта*).

hymn /hɪm/ *n.* (церко́вный) гимн.

hype /haɪp/ *n.* (*coll.*) крикли́вая рекла́ма.
■ *adj.*: **~d-up** ду́тый, ли́повый.

hyperactive /haɪpəˈræktɪv/ *adj.* чрезме́рно акти́вный.

hyperbole /haɪˈpɜːbəlɪ/ *n.* гипе́рбола, преувеличе́ние.

hyperlink /ˈhaɪpəlɪŋk/ *n.* (*comput.*) гиперссы́лка, гиперте́кстовая ссы́лка.

hypermarket /ˈhaɪpəmɑːkɪt/ *n.* (*Br.*) гиперма́ркет.

hypertension /haɪpəˈtenʃ(ə)n/ *n.* (*med.*) высо́кое кровяно́е давле́ние.

hypertext /ˈhaɪpətekst/ *n.* (*comput.*) гиперте́кст.

hyphen /ˈhaɪf(ə)n/ *n.* дефи́с, чёрточка (*coll.*).

hypnosis /hɪpˈnəʊsɪs/ *n.* гипно́з.

hypnotic /hɪpˈnɒtɪk/ *adj.* гипноти́ческий.

hypnotism /ˈhɪpnətɪz(ə)m/ *n.* гипноти́зм.

hypnotist /ˈhɪpnətɪst/ *n.* гипнотизёр.

hypnotize /ˈhɪpnətaɪz/ *v.t.* гипнотизи́ровать, за-.

hypochondriac /haɪpəˈkɒndrɪæk/ *n.*

ипохо́ндрик.

hypocrisy /hɪ'pɒkrɪsɪ/ *n.* лицеме́рие.

hypocrite /'hɪpəkrɪt/ *n.* лицеме́р.

hypocritical /hɪpə'krɪtɪk(ə)l/ *adj.* лицеме́рный, неи́скренний.

hypodermic /haɪpə'də:mɪk/ *adj.*: ~ **syringe/needle** шприц/игла́ для подко́жных инъе́кций.

hypothermia /haɪpəʊ'θə:mɪə/ *n.* гипотерми́я.

hypothesis /haɪ'pɒθɪsɪs/ *n.* (*pl.* **hypotheses** /-si:z/) гипо́теза.

hypothetical /haɪpə'θetɪk(ə)l/ *adj.* гипотети́ческий.

hysterectomy /hɪstə'rektəmɪ/ *n.* удале́ние ма́тки.

hysteria /hɪ'stɪərɪə/ *n.* истери́я.

hysterical /hɪ'sterɪk(ə)l/ *adj.* истери́чный.

hysterics /hɪ'sterɪks/ *n.* исте́рика.

Hz (*abbr. of* ***hertz***) Гц (герц).

I /aɪ/ *pron.* (*obj.* **me**) я; **he and ~ were there** мы с ним бы́ли там; **he is older than ~** он ста́рше меня́.

Iberian /aɪ'bɪərɪən/ *n.* (*hist.*) ибе́р (*fem.* -ка). ■ *adj.* ибери́йский.

ibex /'aɪbeks/ *n.* (*pl.* **~es**) ка́менный козёл, козеро́г.

ice /aɪs/ *n.* лёд.
■ *v.t.* [1] (*cover with* ~): **the pond was soon ~d over** пруд вско́ре затяну́ло/скова́ло льдом.
[2] (*cul.*) глазирова́ть (*impf., pf.*).
■ *cpds.* **~-cold** *adj.* ледяно́й; **~ cream** *n.* моро́женое; **~ cube** *n.* ку́бик льда; **~ hockey** *n.* хокке́й (на льду); **~ lolly** *n.* (*Br. coll.*) моро́женое на па́лочке; **~ rink** *n.* като́к; **~ skate** *n.* конёк; *v.i.* ката́ться (*impf.*) на конька́х.

iceberg /'aɪsbə:g/ *n.* а́йсберг.

Iceland /'aɪslənd/ *n.* Исла́ндия.

Icelandic /aɪs'lændɪk/ *n.* исла́ндский язы́к. ■ *adj.* исла́ндский.

ichthyologist /ɪkθɪ'ɒlədʒɪst/ *n.* ихтио́лог.

ichthyology /ɪkθɪ'ɒlədʒɪ/ *n.* ихтиоло́гия.

icicle /'aɪsɪk(ə)l/ *n.* сосу́лька.

icing /'aɪsɪŋ/ *n.* (*on cake*) са́харная глазу́рь.

icon /'aɪkɒn/ *n.* ико́на; (*comput.*) ико́н(к)а, пиктогра́мма.

iconoclastic /aɪkɒnə'klæstɪk/ *adj.* (*fig.*) иконобо́рческий.

icy /'aɪsɪ/ *adj.* (**icier, iciest**) (*cold, lit., fig.*) ледяно́й; (*covered with ice*) покры́тый льдом.

ID (*abbr. of* ***identification***) удостовере́ние ли́чности.

idea /aɪ'dɪə/ *n.*
[1] (*mental concept; suggestion, plan*) иде́я; **a good ~** хоро́шая иде́я.
[2] (*thought*) мысль; **I can't bear the ~ of it** (одна́) мысль об э́том мне проти́вна.
[3] (*notion; impression*) поня́тие, представле́ние; **I've no ~** (я) поня́тия не име́ю.
[4] (*aim, intention*) иде́я, за́мысел, наме́рение.
[5] (*opinion, belief*) мне́ние, взгляд.

ideal /aɪ'di:əl/ *n.* идеа́л. ■ *adj.* идеа́льный.

idealism /aɪ'dɪəlɪz(ə)m/ *n.* идеали́зм.

idealist /aɪ'dɪəlɪst/ *n.* идеали́ст.

idealistic /aɪdɪə'lɪstɪk/ *adj.* идеалисти́ческий.

ideally /aɪ'dɪəlɪ/ *adv.* идеа́льно; (*as sentence adverb*) в идеа́ле.

identical /aɪ'dentɪk(ə)l/ *adj.* тожде́ственный, иденти́чный; **~ twins** однояйцо́вые близнецы́.

identification /aɪdentɪfɪ'keɪʃ(ə)n/ *n.*: **~ of a body** опозна́ние тру́па; (*attr.*) опознава́тельный.

identif|y /aɪ'dentɪfaɪ/ *v.t.*
[1] (*establish identity of*) опозн|ава́ть, -а́ть; идентифици́ровать (*impf., pf.*).
[2] (*associate*), *also v.i.* (*coll.*): **he ~ied (himself) with the movement** он стал убеждённым сторо́нником э́того движе́ния.

identikit /aɪ'dentɪkɪt/ *n.* (*propr.*): **an ~ (picture)** фоторо́бот.

identity /aɪ'dentɪtɪ/ *n.* ли́чность; **~ card** удостовере́ние ли́чности; **~ theft** кра́жа ли́чной информа́ции (*с целью получить доступ к банковскому счёту и т. п.*)

ideological /aɪdɪə'lɒdʒɪk(ə)l/ *adj.* идеологи́ческий, иде́йный.

ideology /aɪdɪ'ɒlədʒɪ/ *n.* идеоло́гия.

idiocy /'ɪdɪəsɪ/ *n.* (*mental condition*) идиоти́зм; (*med.*) слабоу́мие; (*stupidity; stupid behaviour*) идио́тство.

idiom /'ɪdɪəm/ *n.* (*expression*) идио́ма; (*language; way of speaking*) наре́чие, го́вор, язы́к.

idiomatic /ɪdɪə'mætɪk/ *adj.* идиомати́ческий; **he speaks ~ Russian** он свобо́дно владе́ет ру́сским языко́м; он говори́т по-ру́сски как ру́сский.

idiosyncrasy /ɪdɪəʊ'sɪŋkrəsɪ/ *n.* своеобра́зие.

idiosyncratic /ɪdɪəʊsɪŋ'krætɪk/ *adj.* своеобра́зный.

idiot /'ɪdɪət/ *n.* идио́т (*fem.* -ка).

idiotic /ɪdɪ'ɒtɪk/ *adj.* идио́тский.

idle /'aɪd(ə)l/ *adj.* (**idler, idlest**)
[1] (*not working*) нерабо́тающий; (*unemployed*) безрабо́тный; (*of factories etc.*) безде́йствующий; (*of machinery*) простаи́вающий.

2 (*lazy*) пра́здный, лени́вый.
3 (*purposeless*) пусто́й; **out of ~ curiosity** из пра́здного/пусто́го любопы́тства; **~ talk** пуста́я болтовня́.
■ *v.t.*: **he ~d away his life** он растра́тил свою́ жизнь впусту́ю.
■ *v.i.* 1 (*be ~*) безде́льничать (*impf.*).
2 (*of an engine*): **the motor ~s well** мото́р хорошо́ рабо́тает на холосто́м ходу́.

idol /ˈaɪd(ə)l/ *n.* и́дол, куми́р.

idolatry /aɪˈdɒlətrɪ/ *n.* идолопокло́нство; (*fig.*) обожа́ние.

idolize /ˈaɪdəlaɪz/ *v.t.* (*fig.*) боготвори́ть (*impf.*).

idyll /ˈɪdɪl/ *n.* иди́ллия.

idyllic /ɪˈdɪlɪk/ *adj.* идиллли́ческий.

i.e. (*abbr. of* ***id est***) т. е. (то есть).

if /ɪf/ *conj.*
1 (*condition or supposition*) е́сли, е́сли бы; **~ he comes** е́сли он придёт; **~ I were you** на ва́шем ме́сте; **he talks as ~ he were the boss** он говори́т, как бу́дто он нача́льник.
2 (*though*) хотя́, пусть; **a pleasant, ~ chilly, day** прия́тный, хотя́ и прохла́дный день.
3 (*whether*): **do you know ~ he is at home?** вы не зна́ете, он до́ма?; **see ~ the door is locked** посмотри́те, заперта́ ли дверь.

igloo /ˈɪgluː/ *n.* и́глу (*nt. indecl.*).

ignite /ɪgˈnaɪt/ *v.t.* заж|ига́ть, -е́чь.
■ *v.i.* заж|ига́ться, -е́чься.

ignition /ɪgˈnɪʃ(ə)n/ *n.* (*~ system in engine*) зажига́ние; **~ key** ключ зажига́ния.

ignoble /ɪgˈnəʊb(ə)l/ *adj.* (**ignobler, ignoblest**) (*base*) по́длый, ни́зкий, посты́дный; (*of lowly birth*) ни́зкого происхожде́ния.

ignominious /ɪgnəˈmɪnɪəs/ *adj.* позо́рный, посты́дный; **an ~ death** бесcла́вная смерть.

ignominy /ˈɪgnəmɪnɪ/ *n.* (*dishonour*) позо́р, бесче́стье.

ignoramus /ɪgnəˈreɪməs/ *n.* (*pl.* **~es**) неве́жда.

ignorance /ˈɪgnərəns/ *n.* (*in general*) неве́жество; (*of certain facts*) незна́ние, неве́дение.

ignorant /ˈɪgnərənt/ *adj.* неве́жественный; **I was ~ of his intentions** я не знал о его́ наме́рениях.

ignore /ɪgˈnɔː(r)/ *v.t.* игнори́ровать (*impf., pf.*).

iguana /ɪgˈwɑːnə/ *n.* игуа́на.

ilk /ɪlk/ *n.*: **and others of his ~** (*coll.*) и други́е того́ же ро́да; и ему́ подо́бные.

ill /ɪl/ *n.* зло; **I meant him no ~** я не жела́л ему́ зла.
■ *adj.* 1 (*unwell*) больно́й, нездоро́вый; **he looks ~** он вы́глядит больны́м; **he was taken (*or* fell) ~ with a fever** он заболе́л лихора́дкой; **I feel ~** мне нехорошо́; я пло́хо себя́ чу́вствую.
2 (*bad*) дурно́й; **~ effects** па́губные после́дствия; **~ health** нездоро́вье, недомога́ние; **~ humour** (*US* **humor**), **temper** (*mood*) дурно́е настрое́ние; **~-treatment** дурно́е обраще́ние; **~ will** зла́я во́ля, зло́ба; **I bear you no ~ will** я не жела́ю вам зла.
■ *adv.* пло́хо, ду́рно; **~ at ease** не по себе́; **to feel ~ at ease** чу́вствова́ть, по- себя́ нело́вко; **I can ~ afford it** я с трудо́м могу́ себе́ э́то позво́лить; **I have never spoken ~ of him** я никогда́ не отзыва́лся о нём пло́хо.
■ *cpds.* **~-informed** *adj.* пло́хо осведомлённый; **~-mannered** *adj.* невоспи́танный, пло́хо воспи́танный; **~-treat, ~-use** *vv.t.* пло́хо об|ходи́ться, -ойти́сь с + *i*.

illegal /ɪˈliːg(ə)l/ *adj.* незако́нный, нелега́льный.

illegible /ɪˈledʒɪb(ə)l/ *adj.* неразбо́рчивый.

illegitimate /ɪlɪˈdʒɪtɪmət/ *adj.* незаконнорождённый.

illicit /ɪˈlɪsɪt/ *adj.* незако́нный, недозво́ленный.

illiterate /ɪˈlɪtərət/ *adj.* негра́мотный.

illness /ˈɪlnɪs/ *n.* боле́знь.

illogical /ɪˈlɒdʒɪk(ə)l/ *adj.* нелоги́чный.

illuminate /ɪˈluːmɪneɪt/ *v.t.* осве|ща́ть, -ти́ть; **an ~d sign** светя́щаяся рекла́ма.

illumination /ɪluːmɪˈneɪʃ(ə)n/ *n.* освеще́ние.

illusion /ɪˈluːʒ(ə)n/ *n.* иллю́зия, обма́н; **I was under an ~** я был во вла́сти иллю́зии; **I have no ~s about him** относи́тельно него́ у меня́ нет никаки́х иллю́зий.

illusionist /ɪˈluːʒənɪst/ *n.* иллюзиони́ст, фо́кусник.

illus|ive /ɪˈluːsɪv/, **-ory** /ɪˈluːsərɪ/ *adjs.* иллюзо́рный, при́зрачный.

illustrate /ˈɪləstreɪt/ *v.t.* иллюстри́ровать (*impf., pf.*).

illustration /ɪləˈstreɪʃ(ə)n/ *n.* иллюстра́ция.

illustrative /ˈɪləstrətɪv/ *adj.* иллюстрати́вный, поясни́тельный; **a work ~ of his genius** произведе́ние, пока́зывающее его́ гениа́льность/тала́нт.

illustrator /ˈɪləstreɪtə(r)/ *n.* иллюстра́тор.

illustrious /ɪˈlʌstrɪəs/ *adj.* просла́вленный, знамени́тый.

image /ˈɪmɪdʒ/ *n.*
1 (*representation*) изображе́ние.
2 (*likeness*) ко́пия, портре́т; **he was the ~ of his father** он был то́чной ко́пией (*or* живы́м портре́том) своего́ отца́.
3 (*impression made on others*) и́мидж, репута́ция.
■ *cpd.* **~ consultant** *n.* консульта́нт по и́миджу.

imagery /ˈɪmɪdʒərɪ/ *n.* (*in writing*) о́бразность.

imaginable /ɪˈmædʒɪnəb(ə)l/ *adj.* вообрази́мый; **we had the greatest trouble ~** у нас бы́ли невообрази́мые хло́поты.

imaginary /ɪˈmædʒɪnərɪ/ *adj.* вообража́емый.

imagination /ɪmædʒɪˈneɪʃ(ə)n/ *n.* воображе́ние.

imaginative /ɪˈmædʒɪnətɪv/ *adj.* (*person*) одарённый/облада́ющий (больши́м/бога́тым) воображе́нием; (*literature*) худо́жественный.

imagine /ɪˈmædʒɪn/ *v.t.*
1 (*form mental picture of*) вообра|жа́ть, -зи́ть.
2 (*conceive*) предст|авля́ть, -а́вить себе́; **I cannot ~ how it happened** я не могу́ предста́вить себе́, как э́то случи́лось.

3 (*suppose*) предпол|ага́ть, -ожи́ть.
4 (*guess*) дога́д|ываться, -а́ться; пон|има́ть, -я́ть.

imam /ɪˈmɑːm/ *n.* има́м.

imbalance /ɪmˈbæləns/ *n.* отсу́тствие равнове́сия, неусто́йчивость; несоотве́тствие.

imbecile /ˈɪmbəsiːl/ *n.* глупе́ц, дура́к (*fem.* ду́ра) (*coll.*).
■ *adj.* глу́пый.

imbibe /ɪmˈbaɪb/ *v.t.* (*drink*) погло|ща́ть, -ти́ть; пить, вы́-; (*fig., assimilate*) усв|а́ивать, -о́ить; впи́т|ывать, -а́ть; **he ~d new ideas** он впита́л но́вые иде́и.

imbue /ɪmˈbjuː/ *v.t.* (**imbues, imbued, imbuing**)
1 (*lit., saturate*) пропи́т|ывать, -а́ть; (*dye*) окра́|шивать, -сить.
2 (*fig., inspire*) всел|я́ть, -и́ть (*что в кого*); (*fill*): **~d with hatred** прони́кнутый не́навистью.

IMF (*abbr. of* ***International Monetary Fund***) МВФ (Междунаро́дный валю́тный фонд).

imitate /ˈɪmɪteɪt/ *v.t.* копи́ровать (*impf.*); и|мити́ровать, сы-.

imitation /ɪmɪˈteɪʃ(ə)n/ *n.* имита́ция, подде́лка; **~ leather** иску́сственная ко́жа.

immaculate /ɪˈmækjʊlət/ *adj.* безупре́чный.

immaterial /ɪməˈtɪərɪəl/ *adj.* (*unimportant*) несуще́ственный.

immature /ɪməˈtjʊə(r)/ *adj.* незре́лый.

immeasurable /ɪˈmeʒərəb(ə)l/ *adj.* неизмери́мый.

immediate /ɪˈmiːdɪət/ *adj.*
1 (*direct, closest possible*) непосре́дственный; (*next in order*) очередно́й; **in the ~ neighbourhood** в непосре́дственной бли́зости; **my ~ neighbours** мои́ ближа́йшие сосе́ди; **on his ~ left** сра́зу нале́во от него́; **in the ~ future** в ближа́йшем бу́дущем.
2 (*without delay*) неме́дленный, мгнове́нный.
3 (*urgent*) безотлага́тельный.

immediately /ɪˈmiːdɪətlɪ/ *adv.* неме́дленно, то́тчас (же), сра́зу, мгнове́нно.

immemorial /ɪmɪˈmɔːrɪəl/ *adj.* незапа́мятный; **from time ~** с незапа́мятных времён.

immense /ɪˈmens/ *adj.* огро́мный, грома́дный.

immensity /ɪˈmensɪtɪ/ *n.* безме́рность, необъя́тность.

immerse /ɪˈməːs/ *v.t.* погр|ужа́ть, -зи́ть.

immersion /ɪˈməːʃ(ə)n/ *n.* (*lit., fig.*) погруже́ние; **~ heater** водонагрева́тель (погружа́емого ти́па).

immigrant /ˈɪmɪgrənt/ *n.* иммигра́нт (*fem.* -ка).

immigration /ɪmɪˈgreɪʃ(ə)n/ *n.* иммигра́ция.

imminent /ˈɪmɪnənt/ *adj.* надвига́ющийся.

immobile /ɪˈməʊbaɪl/ *adj.* неподви́жный.

immobilize /ɪˈməʊbɪlaɪz/ *v.t.* лиш|а́ть, -и́ть подви́жности; **I was ~d by a broken leg** я не мог дви́гаться из-за сло́манной ноги́.

immoderate /ɪˈmɒdərət/ *adj.* неуме́ренный.

immoral /ɪˈmɒr(ə)l/ *adj.* безнра́вственный.

immorality /ɪməˈrælɪtɪ/ *n.* безнра́вственность.

immortal /ɪˈmɔːt(ə)l/ *n.* & *adj.* бессме́ртный.

immortality /ɪmɔːˈtælɪtɪ/ *n.* бессме́ртие.

immortalize /ɪˈmɔːtəlaɪz/ *v.t.* увекове́чи|вать, -ть.

immovable *adj.* недви́жимый.

immune /ɪˈmjuːn/ *adj.*: **~ system** иммýнная систе́ма; **~ to disease** невосприи́мчивый к боле́зни; **~ to criticism** неподвла́стный кри́тике.

immunity /ɪˈmjuːnɪtɪ/ *n.* иммуните́т (**to/against** (*med.*)**:** к + *d.*/про́тив + *g.*; **from** (*leg.*)**:** от/про́тив + *g.*); **diplomatic ~** дипломати́ческий иммуните́т.

immunization /ɪmjuːnaɪˈzeɪʃ(ə)n/ *n.* иммуниза́ция.

immunize /ˈɪmjuːnaɪz/ *v.t.* вакцини́ровать (*impf., pf.*) (**against:** от + *g.*); де́лать, с- невосприи́мчивым (**against:** к + *d.*).

immunology /ɪmjuːˈnɒlədʒɪ/ *n.* иммуноло́гия.

immutable /ɪˈmjuːtəb(ə)l/ *adj.* неизме́нный, непрело́жный.

imp /ɪmp/ *n.* (*lit.; fig., mischievous child*) дьяволёнок, чертёнок, бесёнок; (*fig. only*) постре́л.

impact /ˈɪmpækt/ *n.* (*collision*) столкнове́ние; (*striking force*) уда́р, толчо́к; (*fig., effect, influence*) возде́йствие, влия́ние.

impair /ɪmˈpeə(r)/ *v.t.* (*damage*) повре|жда́ть, -ди́ть; (*spoil*) по́ртить, ис-.

impairment /ɪmˈpeəmənt/ *n.* поврежде́ние; по́рча; подры́в; ослабле́ние; ухудше́ние.

impale /ɪmˈpeɪl/ *v.t.* прок|а́лывать, -оло́ть; пронз|а́ть, -и́ть; прот|ыка́ть, -кну́ть; **he ~d himself on his sword** он пронзи́л себя́ мечо́м; **he fell and was ~d on the railings** он свали́лся на огра́ду и проткну́л себе́ живо́т.

impart /ɪmˈpɑːt/ *v.t.* перед|ава́ть, -а́ть.

impartial /ɪmˈpɑːʃ(ə)l/ *adj.* беспристра́стный.

impartiality /ɪmpɑːʃɪˈælɪtɪ/ *n.* беспристра́стность.

impassable /ɪmˈpɑːsəb(ə)l/ *adj.* (*on foot*) непроходи́мый; (*for vehicles*) непрое́зжий.

impasse /ˈæmpɑːs/ *n.* тупи́к; **things reached an ~** дела́ зашли́ в тупи́к.

impassioned /ɪmˈpɑːʃ(ə)nd/ *adj.* стра́стный, пы́лкий.

impassive /ɪmˈpæsɪv/ *adj.* безмяте́жный.

impatience /ɪmˈpeɪʃəns/ *n.* нетерпе́ние; (*irritation*) раздраже́ние.

impatient /ɪmˈpeɪʃ(ə)nt/ *adj.* нетерпели́вый; (*irritable*) раздражи́тельный, раздражённый; **he was getting ~** он теря́л терпе́ние, он раздража́лся; **he is ~ to begin** ему́ не те́рпится нача́ть.

impeach /ɪmˈpiːtʃ/ *v.t.* (*pol.*) обвин|я́ть, -и́ть (*кого в чём*).

impeachment /ɪmˈpiːtʃmənt/ (*pol.*) *n.* импи́чмент.

impeccable /ɪmˈpekəb(ə)l/ *adj.* безупре́чный.

impecunious /ɪmpɪˈkjuːnɪəs/ *adj.* безде́нежный, малообеспе́ченный.

impedance /ɪmˈpiːd(ə)ns/ *n.* (*elec.*) по́лное сопротивле́ние, импеда́нс.

impede /ɪmˈpiːd/ *v.t.* (*obstruct*)

препя́тствовать (*impf.*) + *d.*; (*hinder*) меша́ть, по- (*кому/чему*).

impediment /ɪm'pedɪmənt/ *n.*
1 (*obstruction*) препя́тствие; **an ~ to progress** препя́тствие на пути́ прогре́сса.
2 (*speech defect*) дефе́кт ре́чи.

impel /ɪm'pel/ *v.t.* (**impelled, impelling**) (*drive; force*) прин|ужда́ть, -у́дить; заст|авля́ть, -а́вить; побу|жда́ть, -ди́ть; **conscience ~led him to speak the truth** со́весть прину́дила его́ говори́ть пра́вду; **I feel ~led to say** я вы́нужден сказа́ть.

impending /ɪm'pendɪŋ/ *adj.* предстоя́щий.

impenetrable /ɪm'penɪtrəb(ə)l/ *adj.* непроница́емый.

imperative /ɪm'perətɪv/ *n.* (*gram.*) повели́тельное наклоне́ние, императи́в.
■ *adj.* (*essential*): **it is ~ that you come at once** вам необходи́мо то́тчас яви́ться.

imperceptible /ɪmpə'septɪb(ə)l/ *adj.* незначи́тельный.

imperfect /ɪm'pə:fɪkt/ *n.* (*gram.*) проше́дшее несоверше́нное вре́мя, имперфе́кт.
■ *adj.* несоверше́нный, дефе́ктный.

imperfection /ɪmpə'fekʃ(ə)n/ *n.* (*incompleteness, faultiness*) несоверше́нство, неполнота́; (*fault*) дефе́кт, изъя́н; недоста́ток.

imperfective /ɪmpə'fektɪv/ *n.* & *adj.* (*gram.*) несоверше́нный (вид).

imperial /ɪm'pɪərɪəl/ *adj.* импе́рский.

imperialism /ɪm'pɪərɪəlɪz(ə)m/ *n.* империали́зм.

imperialist /ɪm'pɪərɪəlɪst/ *n.* империали́ст.

imperialist(ic) /ɪmpɪərɪə'lɪst(ɪk)/ *adj.* империалисти́ческий.

impermeable /ɪm'pə:mɪəb(ə)l/ *adj.* непроница́емый.

impersonal /ɪm'pə:sən(ə)l/ *adj.* безли́чный.

impersonate /ɪm'pə:səneɪt/ *v.t.* (*act the part of*) игра́ть (*impf.*) роль + *g.*; (*pretend to be*) выдава́ть (*impf.*) себя́ за + *a.*

impersonator /ɪm'pə:səneɪtə(r)/ *n.* пароди́ст, имита́тор.

impertinence /ɪm'pə:tɪnəns/ *n.* де́рзость, на́глость, наха́льство.

impertinent /ɪm'pə:tɪnənt/ *adj.* де́рзкий, на́глый, наха́льный.

imperturbable /ɪmpə'tə:bəb(ə)l/ *adj.* невозмути́мый.

impervious /ɪm'pə:vɪəs/ *adj.* непроница́емый; (*fig.*): **~ to criticism** глухо́й к кри́тике.

impetuous /ɪm'petjʊəs/ *adj.* (*impulsive*) импульси́вный; (*unpremeditated*) необду́манный.

impetus /'ɪmpɪtəs/ *n.* толчо́к; и́мпульс; (*fig.*) толчо́к, сти́мул.

impinge /ɪm'pɪndʒ/ *v.i.* (**impinging**): **~ on** посяг|а́ть, -ну́ть на + *a.*

implacable /ɪm'plækəb(ə)l/ *adj.* неумоли́мый.

implant *v.t.* /ɪm'plɑ:nt/ (*med.*) вв|оди́ть, -ести́; (*fig., instil*) внедр|я́ть, -и́ть.
■ *n.* /'ɪmplɑ:nt/ (*med.*) импланта́т.

implausible /ɪm'plɔ:zɪb(ə)l/ *adj.* неправдоподо́бный.

implement¹ /'ɪmplɪmənt/ *n.* ору́дие, инструме́нт; **farm ~s** сельскохозя́йственные ору́дия.

implement² /'ɪmplɪment/ *v.t.* выполня́ть, вы́полнить.

implementation /ɪmplɪmen'teɪʃ(ə)n/ *n.* выполне́ние, осуществле́ние.

implicate /'ɪmplɪkeɪt/ *v.t.* вовл|ека́ть, -е́чь; **the evidence ~d him** ули́ки пока́зывали на его́ прича́стность.

implication /ɪmplɪ'keɪʃ(ə)n/ *n.* (*implying; thing implied*) скры́тый смысл; (*significance*) значе́ние.

implicit /ɪm'plɪsɪt/ *adj.*
1 (*implied*) подразумева́емый, недоска́занный.
2 (*unquestioning*) безогово́рочный.

implore /ɪm'plɔ:(r)/ *v.t.* умол|я́ть, -и́ть; **he ~d my forgiveness** он моли́л меня́ о проще́нии.

impl|y /ɪm'plaɪ/ *v.t.*
1 (*hint*) намека́ть (*impf.*) на + *a.*; **he ~ied that I was wrong** он намека́л на то (*or* дал поня́ть), что я не прав.
2 (*mean*) подразумева́ть (*impf.*); **what do his words ~y?** что означа́ют его́ слова́?

impolite /ɪmpə'laɪt/ *adj.* неве́жливый.

imponderable /ɪm'pɒndərəb(ə)l/ *adj.* (*fig.*) неулови́мый.

import¹ /'ɪmpɔ:t/ *n.* (*bringing from abroad*) и́мпорт, ввоз; (*pl., goods introduced*) и́мпортные/ввози́мые това́ры (*m. pl.*).

import² /ɪm'pɔ:t, 'ɪm-/ *v.t.* импорти́ровать (*impf., pf.*); вв|ози́ть, -езти́.

importance /ɪm'pɔ:t(ə)ns/ *n.* значе́ние, ва́жность; **it is of no ~** э́то не име́ет значе́ния.

important /ɪm'pɔ:t(ə)nt/ *adj.* ва́жный; **it is ~ for you to realize it** ва́жно, что́бы вы по́няли э́то.

importer /ɪm'pɔ:tə(r)/ *n.* импортёр.

impose /ɪm'pəʊz/ *v.t.* (*tax, penalty etc.*) нал|ага́ть, -ожи́ть (*что на кого*); **the government ~d a tax on wealth** госуда́рство обложи́ло бога́тых нало́гом; **he ~s his views on everyone** он всем навя́зывает свои́ взгля́ды.
■ *v.i.*: **~ on** (*take advantage of*): **he ~s on his friends** он испо́льзует свои́х друзе́й.

imposing /ɪm'pəʊzɪŋ/ *adj.* внуши́тельный.

imposition /ɪmpə'zɪʃ(ə)n/ *n.*
1 (*imposing of obligation, burden etc.*) возложе́ние, наложе́ние.
2 (*of tax etc.*) обложе́ние.
3 (*unreasonable demand*) чрезме́рное тре́бование.

impossibility /ɪmpɒsɪ'bɪlɪtɪ/ *n.* невозмо́жность.

impossible /ɪm'pɒsɪb(ə)l/ *adj.* невозмо́жный; **don't ask me to do the ~** не тре́буйте от меня́ невозмо́жного.

impostor /ɪm'pɒstə(r)/ *n.* обма́нщи|к (*fem.* -ца).

impotence /'ɪmpət(ə)ns/ *n.* беcси́лие; (*sexual*) импоте́нция.

impotent /'ɪmpət(ə)nt/ *adj.* беcси́льный.

impound /ɪm'paʊnd/ *v.t.* конфискова́ть (*impf., pf.*).

impoverished /ɪm'pɒvərɪʃt/ *adj.* бе́дный, обедне́вший.

impracticable /ɪm'præktɪkəb(ə)l/ *adj.* нереа́льный, неосуществи́мый.

impractical /ɪm'præktɪk(ə)l/ *adj.* непракти́чный.

imprecise /ɪmprɪ'saɪs/ *adj.* нето́чный.

impregnable /ɪm'pregnəb(ə)l/ *adj.* непристу́пный.

impregnate /'ɪmpregneɪt/ *v.t.* (*fertilize*) оплодотвор|я́ть, -и́ть; (*saturate*) пропи́т|ывать, -а́ть; **~d wood** импрегни́рованная (*пропитанная*) древеси́на.

impresario /ɪmprɪ'sɑːrɪəʊ/ *n.* (*pl.* **~s**) импреса́рио (*m. indecl.*), антрепенёр.

impress /ɪm'pres/ *v.t.*
[1] (*on the mind*) запечатл|ева́ть, -е́ть; **we ~ed on them the need for caution** мы внуши́ли им необходи́мость соблюда́ть осторо́жность.
[2] (*have a strong effect on*) произв|оди́ть, -ести́ впечатле́ние на + *a.*; **he did not ~ me at all** он не произвёл на меня́ никако́го впечатле́ния.
■ *v.i.* произв|оди́ть, -ести́ впечатле́ние.

impression /ɪm'preʃ(ə)n/ *n.*
[1] (*imprint*) отпеча́ток, о́ттиск.
[2] (*effect*) эффе́кт, результа́т; впечатле́ние; **make, create an ~** произв|оди́ть, -ести́ впечатле́ние.
[3] (*notion*) впечатле́ние, представле́ние; **I was under the ~ that ...** я полага́л, что...; **I have a strong ~ that ...** я почти́ уве́рен, что... .

impressionable /ɪm'preʃənəb(ə)l/ *adj.* впечатли́тельный.

Impressionism /ɪm'preʃənɪz(ə)m/ *n.* импрессиони́зм.

Impressionist /ɪm'preʃənɪst/ *n.*
[1] (*art*) импрессиони́ст.
[2] (*mimic*) пароди́ст, имита́тор.

impressive /ɪm'presɪv/ *adj.* внуши́тельный, впечатля́ющий, си́льный.

imprint[1] /'ɪmprɪnt/ *n.* (*lit., fig.*) отпеча́ток; (*fig.*) печа́ть.

imprint[2] /ɪm'prɪnt/ *v.t.* отпеча́т|ывать, -ать; (*fig.*) запечатл|ева́ть, -е́ть.

imprison /ɪm'prɪz(ə)n/ *v.t.* заключ|а́ть, -и́ть в тюрьму́; заточ|а́ть, -и́ть.

imprisonment /ɪm'prɪzənmənt/ *n.* тюре́мное заключе́ние.

improbability /ɪmprɒbə'bɪlɪtɪ/ *n.* неправдоподо́бие, невероя́тность.

improbable /ɪm'prɒbəb(ə)l/ *adj.* неправдоподо́бный, невероя́тный.

impromptu /ɪm'prɒmptjuː/ *adj.* импровизи́рованный.

improper /ɪm'prɒpə(r)/ *adj.*
[1] (*unsuitable*) неподходя́щий, несоотве́тствующий; неуме́стный.
[2] (*incorrect*) непра́вильный.
[3] (*unseemly*) неприли́чный, непристо́йный.

impropriety /ɪmprə'praɪətɪ/ *n.* неуме́стность; непра́вильность; непристо́йность, неприли́чие.

improv|e /ɪm'pruːv/ *v.t.* (*make better*) ул|учша́ть, -у́чшить; **he has ~ed his French** он де́лает успе́хи во францу́зском (языке́).
■ *v.i.* [1] (*become better*) ул|учша́ться, -у́чшиться; **wine ~es with age** с года́ми вино́ стано́вится лу́чше; **his health is ~ing** он (*or* его́ здоро́вье) поправля́ется.
[2]: **~e on** (*produce sth. better than*): **I can ~e on that** я могу́ предложи́ть не́что лу́чшее.

improvement /ɪm'pruːvmənt/ *n.* улучше́ние; **there has been an ~ in the weather** пого́да улу́чшилась; (*rebuilding etc.*) перестро́йка; перестано́вка.

improvidence /ɪm'prɒvɪd(ə)ns/ *n.* непредусмотри́тельность; расточи́тельность, небережли́вость.

improvident /ɪm'prɒvɪd(ə)nt/ *adj.* (*heedless of the future*) непредусмотри́тельный; (*wasteful*) расточи́тельный, небережли́вый.

improvisation /ɪmprəvaɪ'zeɪʃ(ə)n/ *n.* импровиза́ция.

improvise /'ɪmprəvaɪz/ *v.t.* & *i.* (*music, speech etc.*) импровизи́ровать (*impf.*); (*arrange as makeshift*) мастери́ть, с-; **an ~d dinner** импровизи́рованный у́жин.

imprudent /ɪm'pruːd(ə)nt/ *adj.* опроме́тчивый, неблагоразу́мный, неосторо́жный.

impudence /'ɪmpjʊd(ə)nt/ *n.* де́рзость; бессты́дство; наха́льство; на́глость.

impudent /'ɪmpjʊd(ə)nt/ *adj.* наха́льный, на́глый.

impulse /'ɪmpʌls/ *n.* толчо́к.

impulsive /ɪm'pʌlsɪv/ *adj.* импульси́вный.

impunity /ɪm'pjuːnɪtɪ/ *n.*: **with ~** безнака́занно.

impure /ɪm'pjʊə(r)/ *adj.* нечи́стый, гря́зный.

impurity /ɪm'pjʊərɪtɪ/ *n.* нечистота́, грязь; (*pl., foreign substances*) при́меси (*f. pl.*).

in /ɪn/ *adj.* (*coll., fashionable*) популя́рный, мо́дный; **he knows all the '~' people** он зна́ет всех ну́жных люде́й.
■ *adv.* [1] (*at home*) до́ма; **tell them I'm not ~** скажи́те, что меня́ нет до́ма; (**~** *one's office etc.*): **the boss is not ~ yet** нача́льника ещё нет (*у себя в кабинете*).
[2] (*arrived at station, port etc.*): **the train has been ~ (for) 10 minutes** по́езд пришёл 10 мину́т тому́ наза́д.
[3] (**~** *fashion*): **short skirts are ~ again** коро́ткие ю́бки опя́ть в мо́де.
[4] (**~** *power*): **which party was ~ then?** кака́я па́ртия была́ тогда́ у вла́сти?
■ *prep.* [1] (*position*) в/на + *p.*; (*inhabited places*): **~ Moscow** в Москве́; (*countries and territories*): **~ France** во Фра́нции; **~ the Crimea** в Крыму́; (*open spaces and flat areas*): **~ the street** на у́лице; **in the country(side)** в дере́вне; **~ the garden** в саду́; (*buildings*): **~ the school** в шко́ле; (*activities*): **~ the lesson** на уро́ке; **~ the war** на войне́; во вре́мя войны́; (*groups*): **~ the crowd** в толпе́; (*points of compass*): **~ the (Far) East** на (Да́льнем) Восто́ке; (*vehicles*): **let's go ~ the car** пое́дем на маши́не; (*natural phenomena*): **~ the fresh air** на све́жем во́здухе; **~ darkness** в темноте́; **~ the rain** под дождём; (*books*): **~ the Bible** в Би́блии.
[2] (*motion*) в (*rarely* на) + *a.*: **they arrived ~**

the city они́ при́были в го́род; **look ~ the mirror** посмотри́те в зе́ркало.
3 (*time*) (*specific centuries, years and decades*): **~ the 20th century** в двадца́том ве́ке; **~ 1975** в ты́сяча девятьсо́т се́мьдесят пя́том году́; **~ May** в ма́е; **~ (the) future** в бу́дущем; (*ages of history, events, periods*): **~ the Middle Ages** в Сре́дние века́; **3 times ~ one day** три ра́за в/за оди́н день; (*seasons*): **~ spring** весно́й; (*times of day*): **~ the morning** у́тром; **~ the mornings** по утра́м; (*at the end of*): **I shall finish this book ~ 3 days' time** я зако́нчу/дочита́ю э́ту кни́гу че́рез три дня; (*in the course of*): **he completed it ~ 6 weeks** он зако́нчил э́то в тече́ние шести́ неде́ль.
4 (*condition, situation*): **~ his absence** в его́ отсу́тствие; **~ these circumstances** при/в э́тих усло́виях; **~ power** у вла́сти.
5 (*manner*): **~ a whisper** шёпотом; **~ detail** подро́бно; **~ secret** под секре́том, по секре́ту; **~ turn** по о́череди.
6 (*language*): **~ Russian** по-ру́сски.
7 (*material*): **a statue ~ marble** ста́туя из мра́мора.
8 (*ratio: out of*): **only 1 ~ every 10 survived** из ка́ждых десяти́ вы́жил то́лько оди́н.

inability /ɪnə'bɪlɪtɪ/ *n.* неспосо́бность.

in absentia /ɪn æb'sentɪə/ *adv.* зао́чно.

inaccessible /ɪnæk'sesɪb(ə)l/ *adj.* недосту́пный, непристу́пный.

inaccuracy /ɪn'ækjʊrəsɪ/ *n.* нето́чность.

inaccurate /ɪn'ækjʊrət/ *adj.* нето́чный.

inaction /ɪn'ækʃ(ə)n/ *n.* безде́йствие.

inactive /ɪn'æktɪv/ *adj.* безде́йственный, безде́йствующий.

inactivity /ɪnæk'tɪvɪtɪ/ *n.* безде́йствие.

inadequacy /ɪn'ædɪkwəsɪ/ *n.* недоста́точность, неполноце́нность; (*personal*) неспосо́бность, неполноце́нность.

inadequate /ɪn'ædɪkwət/ *adj.* недоста́точный.

inadvertent /ɪnəd'vɜ:t(ə)nt/ *adj.* неумы́шленный, нечая́нный, нево́льный.

inadvisable /ɪnəd'vaɪzəb(ə)l/ *adj.* нецелесообра́зный, нежела́тельный.

inane /ɪ'neɪn/ *adj.* глу́пый, пусто́й, неле́пый.

inanimate /ɪn'ænɪmət/ *adj.* неодушевлённый.

inanity /ɪn'ænɪtɪ/ *n.* глу́пость; неле́пость.

inapplicable /ɪn'æplɪkəb(ə)l, ɪnə'plɪk-/ *adj.* неприме́нимый.

inappropriate /ɪnə'prəʊprɪət/ *adj.* неуме́стный, неподходя́щий.

inarticulate /ɪnɑ:'tɪkjʊlət/ *adj.* косноязы́чный.

inasmuch /ɪnəz'mʌtʃ/ *adv.*: **~ as** так как; ввиду́ того́, что; поско́льку.

inasmuch as /ɪnəz'mʌtʃ/ *adj.* так как; ввиду́ того́, что.

inattentive /ɪnə'tentɪv/ *adj.* невнима́тельный.

inaudible /ɪn'ɔ:dɪb(ə)l/ *adj.* неслы́шный.

inaugural /ɪ'nɔ:gjʊr(ə)l/ *n.* торже́ственная речь при вступле́нии в до́лжность.
■ *adj.* вступи́тельный, инаугурацио́нный.

inaugurate /ɪ'nɔ:gjʊreɪt/ *v.t.*
1 (*install with ceremony*) (торже́ственно) вв|оди́ть, -ести́ в до́лжность; **the President was ~d** президе́нт вступи́л в до́лжность.
2 (*launch; officiate at opening of*) откр|ыва́ть, -ы́ть; (*fig.*): **they ~d many reforms** они́ провели́ мно́го рефо́рм; **he ~d a new policy** он положи́л нача́ло но́вой поли́тике; **a new era was ~d** начала́сь но́вая э́ра.

inauguration /ɪnɔ:gjʊ'reɪʃ(ə)n/ *n.* (*of official*) вступле́ние в до́лжность.

inauspicious /ɪnɔ:'spɪʃəs/ *adj.* злове́щий.

in-basket /'ɪnbɑ:skɪt/ *n.* (*US*) корзи́на для входя́щей корреспонде́нции.

inbox /'ɪnbɒks/ *n.* (*comput.*) входя́щие (сообще́ния).

inbuilt /ɪn'bɪlt/ *adj.* врождённый.

incalculable /ɪn'kælkjʊləb(ə)l/ *adj.* неисчисли́мый.

incandescent /ɪnkæn'des(ə)nt/ *adj.* накалённый, раскалённый; (*of light*) светя́щийся от нагре́ва; (*fig.*) пы́лкий.

incantation /ɪnkæn'teɪʃ(ə)n/ *n.* заклина́ние, закля́тие.

incapable /ɪn'keɪpəb(ə)l/ *adj.* неспосо́бный; **he is ~ of understanding** он неспосо́бен поня́ть (*что*); **~ of lying** неспосо́бный на ложь.

incapacitate /ɪnkə'pæsɪteɪt/ *v.t.*: **he was ~d for 3 weeks** он вы́был из стро́я на три неде́ли.

incapacity /ɪnkə'pæsɪtɪ/ *n.* неспосо́бность.

incarcerate /ɪn'kɑ:səreɪt/ *v.t.* заточ|а́ть, -и́ть (в тюрьму́).

incarceration /ɪnkɑ:sə'reɪʃ(ə)n/ *n.* заточе́ние (в тюрьму́).

incarnation /ɪnkɑ:'neɪʃ(ə)n/ *n.* воплоще́ние, олицетворе́ние.

incendiary /ɪn'sendɪərɪ/ *n.* **(~ bomb)** зажига́тельная бо́мба.

incense¹ /'ɪnsens/ *n.* ла́дан, фимиа́м.

incense² /'ɪnsens/ *v.t.* разгне́вать (*pf.*); **she was ~d at, by his behaviour** его́ поведе́ние привело́ её в я́рость.

incentive /ɪn'sentɪv/ *n.* побужде́ние, сти́мул; **~ bonus** поощри́тельная пре́мия.

inception /ɪn'sepʃ(ə)n/ *n.* нача́ло, начина́ние.

incessant /ɪn'ses(ə)nt/ *adj.* непреста́нный, непреры́вный.

incest /'ɪnsest/ *n.* кровосмеше́ние.

incestuous /ɪn'sestjʊəs/ *adj.* кровосмеси́тельный.

inch /ɪntʃ/ *n.* дюйм.

incidence /'ɪnsɪd(ə)ns/ *n.*
1 (*range or scope of effect*) охва́т, сфе́ра де́йствия; **the ~ of a disease** число́ заболе́вших (*or* слу́чаев заболева́ния).
2 (*phys., falling; contact*) паде́ние, накло́н; **angle of ~** у́гол паде́ния.

incident /'ɪnsɪd(ə)nt/ *n.* слу́чай, собы́тие; происше́ствие, инциде́нт.

incidental /ɪnsɪ'dent(ə)l/ *adj.* (*casual*) случа́йный; (*secondary*) побо́чный; **~ music** музыка́льное сопровожде́ние.

incidentally /ɪnsɪ'dentəlɪ/ *adv.* (*in passing*) попу́тно.

incinerate /ɪn'sɪnəreɪt/ *v.t.* испепел|я́ть,

-и́ть.
incinerator /ɪnˈsɪnəreɪtə(r)/ *n.* мусоросжига́тельная печь.
incision /ɪnˈsɪʒ(ə)n/ *n.* надре́з.
incisive /ɪnˈsaɪsɪv/ *adj.* ре́жущий; (*fig.*): **an ~ tone** ре́зкий тон; **an ~ mind** о́стрый/проница́тельный ум.
incite /ɪnˈsaɪt/ *v.t.* (*stir up*) возбу|жда́ть, -ди́ть; (*urge*) побу|жда́ть, -ди́ть; **he ~d them to revolt** он подстрека́л их к мятежу́.
incitement /ɪnˈsaɪtmənt/ *n.* (*inciting*) подстрека́тельство; (*spur, stimulus*) побужде́ние, сти́мул.
inclination /ɪnklɪˈneɪʃ(ə)n/ *n.*
1 (*tendency*) накло́нность.
2 (*desire*) охо́та, жела́ние; **he has lost all ~ to work** он потеря́л вся́кое жела́ние рабо́тать.
incline /ɪnˈklaɪn/ *v.t.*
1 (*bend forward or down*) склон|я́ть, -и́ть.
2 (*fig., dispose*) склон|я́ть, -и́ть; **I am ~d to agree with you** я скло́нен согласи́ться с ва́ми; **if you feel ~d (to do so)** е́сли вы располо́жены э́то сде́лать.
■ *v.i.* 1 (*lean, slope*) наклон|я́ться, -и́ться.
2 (*tend*) склон|я́ться, -и́ться; **he ~s to(wards) leniency** он скло́нен проявля́ть снисходи́тельность.
includ|e /ɪnˈkluːd/ *v.t.* включ|а́ть, -и́ть; **5 members, ~ing the President** пять чле́нов, включа́я президе́нта; **service ~ed** включа́я услу́ги.
inclusion /ɪnˈkluːʒ(ə)n/ *n.* включе́ние.
inclusive /ɪnˈkluːsɪv/ *adj.* & *adv.*
1: **~ of** (*including*) включа́я; включа́ющий в себя́; содержа́щий в себе́.
2: **from February 2nd to 20th ~** со второ́го февраля́ по двадца́тое включи́тельно.
incognito /ɪnkɒɡˈniːtəʊ/ *adv.* инко́гнито.
incoherent /ɪnkəʊˈhɪərənt/ *adj.* бессвя́зный.
income /ˈɪŋkʌm/ *n.* дохо́д.
■ *cpd.* **~ tax** *n.* подохо́дный нало́г.
incoming /ˈɪnkʌmɪŋ/ *adj.* входя́щий, поступа́ющий, прибыва́ющий; **the ~ tide** прили́в; **~ calls** поступа́ющие/входя́щие звонки́; **~ mail** входя́щая по́чта.
incom(m)unicado /ɪnkəmjuːnɪˈkɑːdəʊ/ *adj.* & *adv.* лишённый пра́ва перепи́ски и сообще́ния; в изоля́ции.
incomparable /ɪnˈkɒmpərəb(ə)l/ *adj.* несравне́нный, бесподо́бный.
incompatible /ɪnkəmˈpætɪb(ə)l/ *adj.* несовмести́мый.
incompetence /ɪnˈkɒmpɪt(ə)ns/ *n.* неспосо́бность, некомпете́нтность; неуме́ние.
incompetent /ɪnˈkɒmpɪt(ə)nt/ *adj.* (*person*) неспосо́бный, некомпете́нтный; (*work*) неуме́лый.
incomplete /ɪnkəmˈpliːt/ *adj.* (*not full*) непо́лный; (*unfinished*) незавершённый, незако́нченный.
incomprehensible /ɪnkɒmprɪˈhensɪb(ə)l/ *adj.* непоня́тный, непостижи́мый.
inconceivable /ɪnkənˈsiːvəb(ə)l/ *adj.* невообрази́мый.
inconclusive /ɪnkənˈkluːsɪv/ *adj.* (*of argument etc.*) неубеди́тельный; **the vote was ~** голосова́ние не́ дало определённых результа́тов.
incongruity /ˈɪnkɒŋˈɡruːɪtɪ/ *n.* несоотве́тствие; неуме́стность.
incongruous /ɪnˈkɒŋɡrʊəs/ *adj.* (*out of keeping*) несоотве́тствующий, неподходя́щий; (*out of place*) неуме́стный.
inconsequential /ɪnkɒnsɪˈkwenʃ(ə)l/ *adj.* (*insignificant*) незначи́тельный; (*irrelevant, immaterial*) несуще́ственный.
inconsiderate /ɪnkənˈsɪdərət/ *adj.* невнима́тельный (к други́м), нечу́ткий.
inconsistency /ɪnkənˈsɪst(ə)nsɪ/ *n.* непосле́довательность; противоречи́вость.
inconsistent /ɪnkənˈsɪst(ə)nt/ *adj.* (*of a person*) непосле́довательный; (*of an account*) противоречи́вый.
inconsolable /ɪnkənˈsəʊləb(ə)l/ *adj.* неуте́шный, безуте́шный.
inconspicuous /ɪnkənˈspɪkjʊəs/ *adj.* незаме́тный.
incontestable /ɪnkənˈtestəb(ə)l/ *adj.* неоспори́мый.
incontinent /ɪnˈkɒntɪnənt/ *adj.* (*unrestrained*) несде́ржанный; (*med.*): **he was ~** он страда́л недержа́нием (мочи́/ка́ла).
incontrovertible /ɪnkɒntrəˈvɜːtɪb(ə)l/ *adj.* неоспори́мый.
inconvenience /ɪnkənˈviːnɪəns/ *n.* неудо́бство, беспоко́йство.
■ *v.t.* причин|я́ть, -и́ть неудо́бство + *d.*
inconvenient /ɪnkənˈviːnɪənt/ *adj.* неудо́бный.
incorporate /ɪnˈkɔːpəreɪt/ *v.t.*
1 (*combine*) объедин|я́ть, -и́ть.
2 (*include*) включ|а́ть, -и́ть.
incorrect /ɪnkəˈrekt/ *adj.* (*inaccurate*) непра́вильный; (*untrue*) неве́рный.
incorrigible /ɪnˈkɒrɪdʒɪb(ə)l/ *adj.* неисправи́мый.
increase[1] /ˈɪnkriːs/ *n.* рост, возраста́ние; увеличе́ние; **unemployment is on the ~** безрабо́тица растёт/увели́чивается; (*amount of ~*) приро́ст; **my shares show an ~ of 5** мои́ а́кции подняли́сь на пять проце́нтов.
increase[2] /ɪnˈkriːs/ *v.t.* увели́чи|вать, -ть; (*extend*): **~ one's influence** расш|иря́ть, -и́рить своё влия́ние; (*raise*): **~ prices** пов|ыша́ть, -ы́сить це́ны; (*intensify*): **this merely ~d his determination** э́то то́лько укрепи́ло его́ реши́мость.
■ *v.i.* увели́чи|ваться, -ться; (*grow*) расти́ (*impf.*); (*intensify*) уси́ли|ваться, -ться; (*expand*) расш|иря́ться, -и́риться; (*rise*): **sugar ~d in price** са́хар повы́сился в цене́ (*or* подорожа́л).
increasingly /ɪnˈkriːsɪŋlɪ/ *adv.* всё бо́лее; **it becomes ~ difficult** стано́вится всё трудне́е.
incredibl|e /ɪnˈkredɪb(ə)l/ *adj.* невероя́тный; **he was ~y stupid** он был невероя́тно глуп.
incredulous /ɪnˈkredjʊləs/ *adj.* недове́рчивый.
increment /ˈɪnkrɪmənt/ *n.* (*regular salary increase*) приба́вка.
incriminating /ɪnˈkrɪmɪneɪtɪŋ/ *adj.* изоблича́ющий.
incubate /ˈɪŋkjʊbeɪt/ *v.t.* (*of a bird*) сиде́ть

(*impf.*) на (яйцах); (*hatch by artificial heat*) инкубировать (*impf., pf.*).
■ *v.i.* (*of a disease*) находиться (*impf.*) в инкубационном периоде.

incubator /ˈɪŋkjʊbeɪtə(r)/ *n.* инкубатор.

inculcate /ˈɪnkʌlkeɪt/ *v.t.* внедр|ять, -ить; внуш|ать, -ить.

incumbent /ɪnˈkʌmbənt/ *n.*
1 (*eccl.*) приходский священник.
2 (*holder of a post*) занимающий (*какую-н.*) должность.
■ *adj.* (*holding office*) занимающий пост, должность; **the ~ president** нынешний президент; (*necessary as a duty*): **~ upon** возлежащий на + *p.*; возложенный на + *a.*; **it is ~ upon you to warn them** вы обязаны предупредить их.

incur /ɪnˈkɜː(r)/ *v.t.* (**incurred, incurring**) навл|екать, -ечь на себя; **he ~red heavy expenses** он понёс большие расходы.

incurable /ɪnˈkjʊərəb(ə)l/ *adj.* (*of sick person*) безнадёжный; (*fig.*): **an ~ optimist** неисправимый оптимист; (*of disease*) неизлечимый.

incursion /ɪnˈkɜːʃ(ə)n/ *n.* вторжение, налёт, набег.

indebted /ɪnˈdetɪd/ *adj.* (*owing money*) в долгу, должный; (*owing gratitude*) обязанный.

indecency /ɪnˈdiːs(ə)nsɪ/ *n.* неприличие, непристойность; **an act of gross ~** непристойное действие.

indecent /ɪnˈdiːs(ə)nt/ *adj.* неприличный, непристойный; **~ exposure** непристойное обнажение тела.

indecipherable /ɪndɪˈsaɪfərəb(ə)l/ *adj.* не поддающийся расшифровке; (*of handwriting etc.*) неразборчивый.

indecision /ɪndɪˈsɪʒ(ə)n/ *n.* нерешительность.

indecisive /ɪndɪˈsaɪsɪv/ *adj.* (*irresolute*) нерешительный; (*not producing a result*) не решающий.

indeclinable /ɪndɪˈklaɪnəb(ə)l/ *adj.* несклоняемый.

indeed /ɪnˈdiːd/ *adv.*
1 (*really, actually*) действительно; в самом деле; вот именно.
2 (*expr. emphasis*): **thanks very much ~** премного вам благодарен; **"Will you come?" — "I will ~"** «Вы придёте?» — «Непременно/обязательно».
3 (*expr. intensification*) к тому же; мало/более того; даже.

indefatigable /ɪndɪˈfætɪgəb(ə)l/ *adj.* неутомимый.

indefensible /ɪndɪˈfensɪb(ə)l/ *adj.* (*mil.*) непригодный для обороны; (*unjustified*) не имеющий оправдания, непростительный; **an ~ statement** неприемлемое утверждение.

indefinable /ɪndɪˈfaɪnəb(ə)l/ *adj.* неопределимый.

indefinite /ɪnˈdefɪnɪt/ *adj.*
1 (*not clearly defined*) неопределённый.
2 (*unlimited*) неограниченный.
3 (*gram.*): **~ article** неопределённый артикль.

indefinitely /ɪnˈdefɪnɪtlɪ/ *adv.* на неопределённое время.

indelible /ɪnˈdelɪb(ə)l/ *adj.* (*lit., fig.*) несмываемый.

indentation /ɪndenˈteɪʃ(ə)n/ *n.* (*notch, cut*) зубец, вырез, зазубрина; (*in coastline etc.*) извилина.

independence /ɪndɪˈpend(ə)ns/ *n.* независимость (**from:** от + *g.*).

independent /ɪndɪˈpend(ə)nt/ *adj.* независимый, самостоятельный; не зависящий (от + *g.*); (*in adv. sense*): **~ of** независимо от + *g.*; помимо + *g.*

in-depth /ɪnˈdepθ/ *adj.* обстоятельный.

indescribable /ɪndɪˈskraɪbəb(ə)l/ *adj.* неописуемый.

indestructible /ɪndɪˈstrʌktɪb(ə)l/ *adj.* неразрушимый.

indeterminate /ɪndɪˈtɜːmɪnət/ *adj.* (*not fixed; indefinite*) неопределённый; **an ~ sentence** неопределённый приговор; (*not settled; undecided*) нерешённый; неокончательный; **an ~ result** неокончательный результат; (*vague; indefinable*) неясный, смутный.

index /ˈɪndeks/ *n.*
1 (*indicative figure*) индекс; **retail price ~** индекс розничных цен.
2 (*alphabetical*) указатель (*m.*); **card ~** картотека; **~ card** (картотечная) карточка.
3 : **~ finger** указательный палец.
■ *v.t.* (*econ., also* **~-link** (*Br.*)) индексировать (*impf., pf.*).

India /ˈɪndɪə/ *n.* Индия.

Indian /ˈɪndɪən/ *n.*
1 (*native of India*) инди|ец (*fem.* -анка).
2 **(American ~)** инд|еец (*fem.* -ианка).
■ *adj.* 1 (*of India*) индийский; **~ Ocean** Индийский океан.
2 (*North American*) индейский; **~ summer** бабье лето.

indicate /ˈɪndɪkeɪt/ *v.t.* (*point to*) указ|ывать, -ать; (*be a sign of*) свидетельствовать (*impf.*) о + *p.*

indication /ɪndɪˈkeɪʃ(ə)n/ *n.* (*sign*) знак, указатель (*m.*); (*hint*) признак, намёк; **he gave no ~ of his feelings** он ничем не выдал своих чувств.

indicative /ɪnˈdɪkətɪv/ *n.* (*gram.*) изъявительное наклонение.
■ *adj.*: **~ of** (*suggesting, showing*) указывающий на + *a.*

indicator /ˈɪndɪkeɪtə(r)/ *n.*
1 (*pointer of instrument*) стрелка; указатель (*m.*).
2 (*Br., on vehicle*) указатель (*m.*) поворота.

indict /ɪnˈdaɪt/ *v.t.* предъяв|лять, -ить обвинение + *d.*

indictment /ɪnˈdaɪtmənt/ *n.* (*charge*) обвинительный акт; (*fig.*): **these figures are an ~ of government policy** эти цифры служат обвинительным документом против политики правительства.

indifference /ɪnˈdɪfrəns/ *n.* безразличие; равнодушие.

indifferent /ɪnˈdɪfrənt/ *adj.* (*without interest*) безразличный; (*mediocre*) посредственный.

indigenous /ɪnˈdɪdʒɪnəs/ *adj.* туземный.

indigestible /ɪndɪˈdʒestɪb(ə)l/ *adj.*

неудобовари́мый.
indigestion /ɪndɪ'dʒestʃ(ə)n/ *n.* несваре́ние желу́дка.
indignant /ɪn'dɪgnənt/ *adj.* возмущённый; **I was ~ at his remark** его́ замеча́ние возмути́ло меня́.
indignation /ɪndɪg'neɪʃ(ə)n/ *n.* возмуще́ние.
indignit|y /ɪn'dɪgnɪtɪ/ *n.* униже́ние, оскорбле́ние; **we were subjected to various ~ies** мы подве́рглись вся́ческим униже́ниям.
indirect /ɪndaɪ'rekt/ *adj.* непрямо́й, ко́свенный.
indiscreet /ɪndɪ'skri:t/ *adj.* беста́ктный.
indiscretion /ɪndɪ'skreʃ(ə)n/ *n.* нескро́мность; (*indiscreet act*) неосторо́жный посту́пок.
indiscriminate /ɪndɪ'skrɪmɪnət/ *adj.* 1 (*undiscriminating*) неразбо́рчивый. 2 (*random*) де́йствующий без разбо́ра.
indispensable /ɪndɪ'spensəb(ə)l/ *adj.* необходи́мый.
indisposed /ɪndɪ'spəʊzd/ *adj.* (*unwell*) (немно́го) нездоро́вый; **the Queen is ~** короле́ве нездоро́вится.
indisposition /ɪndɪspə'zɪʃ(ə)n/ *n.* (*disinclination*) нерасположе́ние, нежела́ние; (*feeling unwell*) недомога́ние.
indisputable /ɪndɪ'spju:təb(ə)l/ *adj.* неоспори́мый.
indistinct /ɪndɪ'stɪŋkt/ *adj.* (*of things seen or heard*) нея́сный; невня́тный; (*vague*) сму́тный, расплы́вчатый.
indistinguishable /ɪndɪ'stɪŋgwɪʃəb(ə)l/ *adj.* (*not recognizably different*) неразличи́мый, неотличи́мый; **he is ~ from his brother** его́ невозмо́жно отличи́ть от бра́та; **the two are ~** э́ти дво́е неразличи́мы.
individual /ɪndɪ'vɪdjʊəl/ *n.* 1 (*single being*) ли́чность, индиви́дуум, едини́ца, о́собь. 2 (*type of person*) челове́к, тип. ■ *adj.* 1 (*single, particular*) отде́льный. 2 (*of or for one person*) ли́чный, ча́стный; **the teacher gave each pupil ~ attention** учи́тель уделя́л внима́ние ка́ждому ученику́. 3 (*distinctive*) характе́рный, осо́бенный.
individualism /ɪndɪ'vɪdjʊəlɪz(ə)m/ *n.* индивидуали́зм.
individuality /ɪndɪvɪdjʊ'ælɪtɪ/ *n.* индивидуа́льность.
indoctrinate /ɪn'dɒktrɪneɪt/ *v.t.* внуш|а́ть, -и́ть при́нципы + *d.*
indolent /'ɪndələnt/ *adj.* лени́вый, вя́лый.
indomitable /ɪn'dɒmɪtəb(ə)l/ *adj.* неукроти́мый.
Indonesia /ɪndə'ni:zɪə/ *n.* Индоне́зия.
Indonesian /ɪndə'ni:zjən/ *n.* (*person*) индонези́|ец (*fem.* -йка); (*language*) индонези́йский язы́к. ■ *adj.* индонези́йский.
indoor /'ɪndɔ:(r)/ *adj.* ко́мнатный; **~ games** ко́мнатные и́гры; **~ swimming pool** закры́тый бассе́йн.
indoors /ɪn'dɔ:z/ *adv.* (*expr. position*) в до́ме; взаперти́; (*expr. motion*) в дом, внутрь.
induce /ɪn'dju:s/ *v.t.* 1 (*persuade, prevail on*) убе|жда́ть, -ди́ть; **nothing will ~ him to change his mind** ничто́ не заста́вит его́ измени́ть реше́ние. 2 (*bring about*) вызыва́ть, вы́звать; **illness ~d by fatigue** боле́знь, вы́званная переутомле́нием.
inducement /ɪn'dju:smənt/ *n.* (*motive, incentive*) сти́мул; **there is no ~ for me to stay here** ничто́ не уде́рживает меня́ здесь; (*bribe*) по́дкуп.
induction /ɪn'dʌkʃ(ə)n/ *n.* введе́ние, вступле́ние.
indulge /ɪn'dʌldʒ/ *v.t.* (*gratify, give way to*) потво́рствовать (*impf.*) + *d.*; (*spoil*) по́ртить, ис-; балова́ть, из-. ■ *v.i.* (*allow o.s. pleasure*) увлека́ться (*impf.*) (*чем*); **he ~s in a cigar** он позволя́ет себе́ вы́курить сига́ру.
indulgence /ɪn'dʌldʒ(ə)ns/ *n.* 1 (*gratification*) потво́рство. 2 (*pleasure indulged in*) удово́льствие; **smoking is his only ~** куре́ние — его́ еди́нственная сла́бость.
indulgent /ɪn'dʌldʒ(ə)nt/ *adj.* потво́рствующий; **~ parents** не сли́шком стро́гие роди́тели.
industrial /ɪn'dʌstrɪəl/ *adj.* промы́шленный, индустриа́льный; **~ accident** несча́стный слу́чай на произво́дстве; **~ action** (*Br.*) забасто́вочные де́йствия; **~ estate** (*Br.*) промы́шленная зо́на; **~ relations** произво́дственные отноше́ния (ме́жду работода́телями и (их) рабо́тниками).
industrialist /ɪn'dʌstrɪəlɪst/ *n.* промы́шленник; фабрика́нт.
industrialization /ɪndʌstrɪəlaɪ'zeɪʃ(ə)n/ *n.* индустриализа́ция.
industrialize /ɪn'dʌstrɪəlaɪz/ *v.t.* индустриализи́ровать (*impf., pf.*).
industrious /ɪn'dʌstrɪəs/ *adj.* трудолюби́вый.
industry /'ɪndəstrɪ/ *n.* 1 (*branch of manufacture*) о́трасль. 2 (*the world of manufacture*) индустри́я; промы́шленность; **he intends to go into ~** он хо́чет заня́ться произво́дством. 3 (*diligence*) трудолю́бие.
inebriated /ɪ'ni:brɪeɪtɪd/ *adj.* пья́ный.
inedible /ɪn'edɪb(ə)l/ *adj.* несъедо́бный.
ineffective /ɪnɪ'fektɪv/ *adj.* неэффекти́вный.
ineffectual /ɪnɪ'fektʃʊəl/ *adj.* безрезульта́тный.
inefficiency /ɪnɪ'fɪʃ(ə)nsɪ/ *n.* неэффекти́вность, неспосо́бность.
inefficient /ɪnɪ'fɪʃ(ə)nt/ *adj.* (*of persons*) неуме́лый, неспосо́бный; (*of organizations, etc.*) неэффекти́вный; (*of machines*) непроизводи́тельный.
ineligible /ɪn'elɪdʒɪb(ə)l/ *adj.* (*for office*) неподходя́щий; (*for a benefit*) не име́ющий пра́ва (**for:** на + *a.*).
inept /ɪ'nept/ *adj.* неуме́лый.
ineptitude /ɪ'neptɪtju:d/ *n.* неуме́ние; (*act*) глу́пая вы́ходка.
inequality /ɪnɪ'kwɒlɪtɪ/ *n.* нера́венство.
inequity /ɪn'ekwɪtɪ/ *n.* несправедли́вость.
inert /ɪ'nə:t/ *adj.* (*fig.*) вя́лый, безде́ятельный.
inertia /ɪ'nə:ʃə/ *n.* ине́ртность; (*phys.*) ине́рция.

inescapable /ɪnɪ'skeɪpəb(ə)l/ *adj.* неизбе́жный.

inevitability /ɪnevɪtə'bɪlɪtɪ/ *n.* неизбе́жность.

inevitable /ɪn'evɪtəb(ə)l/ *adj.* неизбе́жный, немину́емый.

inexcusable /ɪnɪk'skju:zəb(ə)l/ *adj.* непрости́тельный.

inexhaustible /ɪnɪg'zɔ:stɪb(ə)l/ *adj.* (*unfailing*) неистощи́мый, неисчерпа́емый.

inexpensive /ɪnɪk'spensɪv/ *adj.* недорого́й.

inexperienced /ɪnɪk'spɪərɪənsd/ *adj.* нео́пытный.

inexplicable /ɪnɪk'splɪkəb(ə)l/ *adj.* необъясни́мый.

in extremis /ɪn ek'stri:mɪs/ *adv.* в кра́йнем слу́чае.

infallible /ɪn'fælɪb(ə)l/ *adj.* надёжный.

infamous /'ɪnfəməs/ *adj.* (*person*) бесcла́вный; (*behaviour*) позо́рный.

infancy /'ɪnfənsɪ/ *n.* младе́нчество.

infant /'ɪnf(ə)nt/ *n.* младе́нец; ~ **school** (*Br.*) шко́ла для малыше́й, мла́дшие кла́ссы нача́льной шко́лы.

infantile /'ɪnfəntaɪl/ *adj.*
1 де́тский, младе́нческий; ~ **paralysis** де́тский парали́ч.
2 (*childish*) инфанти́льный.

infantry /'ɪnfəntrɪ/ *n.* пехо́та.
■ *cpd.* **~man** *n.* пехоти́нец.

infatuate /ɪn'fætjʊeɪt/ *v.t.*: **he is ~d with her** она́ покори́ла/плени́ла его́.

infatuation /ɪnfætjʊ'eɪʃ(ə)n/ *n.* влюблённость, увлече́ние.

infect /ɪn'fekt/ *v.t.* (*lit., fig.*) зара|жа́ть, -зи́ть; **the wound became ~ed** ра́на загнои́лась.

infection /ɪn'fekʃ(ə)n/ *n.* инфе́кция; **he caught the ~ from his brother** он зарази́лся от бра́та.

infectious /ɪn'fekʃəs/ *adj.* (*disease*) зара́зный, инфекцио́нный; (*person*) зара́зный; (*fig.*) зарази́тельный.

infer /ɪn'fə:(r)/ *v.t.* (**inferred, inferring**) заключ|а́ть, -и́ть; предпол|ага́ть, -ожи́ть.

inferior /ɪn'fɪərɪə(r)/ *n.* подчинённый.
■ *adj.* 1 (*lower in position, rank etc.*) ни́зший.
2 (*poorer in quality*) ху́дший.
3 (*of less importance*) неполноце́нный; **he makes me feel ~** в его́ прису́тствии у меня́ появля́ется ко́мплекс неполноце́нности.

inferiority /ɪnfɪərɪ'ɒrɪtɪ/ *n.* (*of position*) бо́лее ни́зкое положе́ние; (*of quality*) низкосо́ртность; ~ **complex** ко́мплекс неполноце́нности.

infernal /ɪn'fə:n(ə)l/ *adj.*
1 (*of hell*) а́дский.
2 (*devilish, abominable*) а́дский, дья́вольский; **an ~ machine** а́дская маши́на.
3 (*coll., confounded*) черто́вский; **an ~ nuisance** прокля́тие.

inferno /ɪn'fə:nəʊ/ *n.* (*pl.* **~s**) (*lit., fig.*) ад.

infertile /ɪn'fə:taɪl/ *adj.* (*soil*) неплодоро́дный; (*woman, man*) беспло́дный.

infertility /ɪnfə:'tɪlɪtɪ/ *n.* неплодоро́дность, беспло́дность.

infest /ɪn'fest/ *v.t.* наводн|я́ть, -и́ть; **the house is ~ed with rats** дом наводнён кры́сами.

infidel /'ɪnfɪd(ə)l/ *n.* & *adj.* (*rel.*) неве́рный.

infidelity /ɪnfɪ'delɪtɪ/ *n.* неве́рность, изме́на (*супру́жеская*).

in-fighting /'ɪnfaɪtɪŋ/ *n.* (*fig.*) междоусо́бица, вну́тренняя борьба́.

infiltrate /'ɪnfɪltreɪt/ *v.t.* прон|ика́ть, -и́кнуть.

infinite /'ɪnfɪnɪt/ *adj.* бесконе́чный, беспреде́льный.

infinitesimal /ɪnfɪnɪ'tesɪm(ə)l/ *adj.* бесконе́чно ма́лый.

infinitive /ɪn'fɪnɪtɪv/ *n.* инфинити́в, неопределённая фо́рма глаго́ла.

infinity /ɪn'fɪnɪtɪ/ *n.* бесконе́чность.

infirm /ɪn'fə:m/ *adj.* (*physically*) не́мощный, дря́хлый.

infirmary /ɪn'fə:mərɪ/ *n.* больни́ца.

inflame /ɪn'fleɪm/ *v.t.*: **the wound became ~d** ра́на воспали́лась.

inflammable /ɪn'flæməb(ə)l/ *adj.* легко́ воспламеня́ющийся, горю́чий.

inflammation /ɪnflə'meɪʃ(ə)n/ *n.* воспале́ние.

inflammatory /ɪn'flæmətərɪ/ *adj.* (*fig.*) зажига́тельный; подстрека́тельский.

inflatable /ɪn'fleɪtəb(ə)l/ *adj.* надувно́й.

inflate /ɪn'fleɪt/ *v.t.* над|ува́ть, -у́ть.

inflation /ɪn'fleɪʃ(ə)n/ *n.* (*econ.*) инфля́ция.

inflection /ɪn'flekʃ(ə)n/ *n.* (*gram.*) фле́ксия.

inflexible /ɪn'fleksɪb(ə)l/ *adj.* неги́бкий, жёсткий; (*fig.*) непрекло́нный, непоколеби́мый.

inflict /ɪn'flɪkt/ *v.t.* (*a blow*) нан|оси́ть, -ести́; (*pain*) причин|я́ть, -и́ть.

influence /'ɪnflʊəns/ *n.* (*power to affect or change*) влия́ние, возде́йствие; **she is a good ~ on him** она́ на него́ хорошо́ влия́ет; **under the ~ (of drink)** под возде́йствием (алкого́ля).
■ *v.t.* влия́ть, по- на + *a.*; ока́з|ывать, -а́ть влия́ние на + *a.*; **he was ~d by what he saw** уви́денное повлия́ло на него́.

influential /ɪnflʊ'enʃ(ə)l/ *adj.* влия́тельный.

influenza /ɪnflʊ'enzə/ *n.* грипп.

influx /'ɪnflʌks/ *n.* (*fig.*) наплы́в.

inform /ɪn'fɔ:m/ *v.t.* сообщ|а́ть, -и́ть + *d.*; информи́ровать (*impf., pf.*); осв|едомля́ть, -е́домить; ста́вить, по- в изве́стность; **I was not ~ed of the facts** мне не сообщи́ли о фа́ктах; **keep me ~ed** держи́те меня́ в ку́рсе дел.
■ *v.i.* дон|оси́ть, -ести́; **he ~ed against, on his comrades** он донёс на свои́х това́рищей.

informal /ɪn'fɔ:m(ə)l/ *adj.* неофициа́льный; непринуждённый; **it will be an ~ party** ве́чер бу́дет дру́жеский; ~ **dress** повседне́вная оде́жда.

information /ɪnfə'meɪʃ(ə)n/ *n.* информа́ция; све́дения (*nt. pl.*); спра́вка; да́нные (*nt. pl.*); **a useful piece of ~** поле́зная информа́ция; ~ **desk** спра́вочный стол; ~ **technology** информа́тика.

informative /ɪn'fɔ:mətɪv/ *adj.* информати́вный.

informer /ɪn'fɔ:mə(r)/ *n.* (*police ~*) осведоми́тель (*fem.* -ница); (*against s.o.*) доно́счи|к (*fem.* -ца).

infra-red /ɪnfrə'red/ *adj.* инфракра́сный.

infrastructure /'ɪnfrəstrʌktʃə(r)/ *n.* инфраструкту́ра.

infrequent /ɪn'fri:kwənt/ *adj.* ре́дкий.

infringe /ɪn'frɪndʒ/ *v.t. & i.* нар|уша́ть, -у́шить; **this does not ~ on your rights** э́то не ущемля́ет ва́ших прав.

infringement /ɪn'frɪndʒmənt/ *n.* наруше́ние.

infuriat|e /ɪn'fjʊərɪeɪt/ *v.t.* прив|оди́ть, -ести́ в я́рость/бе́шенство; разъяр|я́ть, -и́ть; **an ~ing delay** возмути́тельная заде́ржка.

ingenious /ɪn'dʒi:nɪəs/ *adj.* изобрета́тельный; остроу́мный.

ingenuity /ɪndʒɪ'nju:ɪtɪ/ *n.* изобрета́тельность; оригина́льность.

ingenuous /ɪn'dʒenjʊəs/ *adj.* простоду́шный, наи́вный.

ingot /'ɪŋgət/ *n.* сли́ток.

ingrained /ɪn'greɪnd/ *adj.*
1: **~ dirt** въе́вшаяся грязь.
2 (*fig.*) закорене́лый, врождённый.

ingratitude /ɪn'grætɪtju:d/ *n.* неблагода́рность.

ingredient /ɪn'gri:dɪənt/ *n.* (*of mixture*) компоне́нт; ингредие́нт; **hard work is an important ~ of success** упо́рный труд — ва́жная составля́ющая успе́ха.

inhabit /ɪn'hæbɪt/ *v.t.* (**inhabited, inhabiting**) жить (*impf.*) в + *p.*; обита́ть (*impf.*) в + *p.*; **is the island ~ed?** э́тот о́стров обита́ем?

inhabitant /ɪn'hæbɪt(ə)nt/ *n.* жи́тель (*fem.* -ница); жиле́ц.

inhale /ɪn'heɪl/ *v.t.* вд|ыха́ть, -охну́ть.
■ *v.i.* затя́гиваться (*сигаретой и т. п.*).

inhaler /ɪn'heɪlə(r)/ *n.* (*device*) ингаля́тор.

inherent /ɪn'herənt/ *adj.* сво́йственный, прису́щий.

inherit /ɪn'herɪt/ *v.t.* (**inherited, inheriting**) насле́довать (*impf., pf.; pf. also* у-).
■ *v.i.* (**inherited, inheriting**) получ|а́ть, -и́ть насле́дство.

inheritance /ɪn'herɪt(ə)ns/ *n.* (*inheriting*) насле́дование; (*sth. inherited*) насле́дство.

inhibit /ɪn'hɪbɪt/ *v.t.* (**inhibited, inhibiting**) (*restrain*) угнета́ть (*impf.*); ско́в|ывать, -а́ть; **an ~ed person** ско́ванный челове́к.

inhibition /ɪnhɪ'bɪʃ(ə)n/ *n.* торможе́ние.

inhospitable /ɪnhɒ'spɪtəb(ə)l/ *adj.* негостеприи́мный.

inhuman /ɪn'hju:mən/ *adj.* бесчелове́чный.

inhumane /ɪnhju:'meɪn/ *adj.* негума́нный.

inhumanity /ɪnhju:'mænɪtɪ/ *n.* бесчелове́чность, жесто́кость.

initial /ɪ'nɪʃ(ə)l/ *n.* нача́льная бу́ква; (*pl., as signature*) инициа́лы (*m. pl.*).
■ *adj.* нача́льный.
■ *v.t.* (**initialled, initialling;** *US* **initialed, initialing**): **~ a document** ста́вить, по- инициа́лы под докуме́нтом.

initially /ɪ'nɪʃəlɪ/ *adv.* внача́ле, снача́ла.

initiate[1] /ɪ'nɪʃɪət/ *n.* посвящённый.

initiate[2] /ɪ'nɪʃɪeɪt/ *v.t.*
1 (*set in motion*) нач|ина́ть, -а́ть.
2 (*introduce*) приобщ|а́ть, -и́ть (к + *d.*); **he was ~d into the mysteries of science** его́ посвяти́ли в та́йны нау́ки.

initiative /ɪ'nɪʃətɪv/ *n.* инициати́ва; **he took the ~** он взял инициати́ву на себя́.

inject /ɪn'dʒekt/ *v.t.* вв|оди́ть, -ести́; впры́с|кивать, -нуть; **the drug was ~ed into the bloodstream** лека́рство ввели́ в ве́ну; **he learned to ~ himself with insulin** он научи́лся де́лать себе́ уко́лы/инъе́кции инсули́на.

injection /ɪn'dʒekʃ(ə)n/ *n.* впры́скивание; инъе́кция.

injunction /ɪn'dʒʌŋkʃ(ə)n/ *n.* (*leg.*) суде́бный запре́т.

injure /'ɪndʒə(r)/ *v.t.* (*physically*) ушиб|а́ть, -и́ть; повре|жда́ть, -ди́ть; ра́нить (*impf., pf.*); (*fig.*): **he will ~ his own reputation** он сам испо́ртит себе́ репута́цию.

injured /'ɪndʒəd/ *adj.* (*suffering injury*) ра́неный; (*as n.*): **the dead and ~** уби́тые и ра́неные; (*offended*) оби́женный.

injury /'ɪndʒərɪ/ *n.* ра́на, ране́ние, ушиб, тра́вма.

injustice /ɪn'dʒʌstɪs/ *n.* несправедли́вость.

ink /ɪŋk/ *n.* черни́л|а (*pl., g.* —).
■ *cpd.* **~jet** *adj.*: **~jet printer** (*comput.*) стру́йный при́нтер.

inkling /'ɪŋklɪŋ/ *n.* (*hint*) намёк; (*suspicion*) подозре́ние.

inland /'ɪnlənd/ *adj.* располо́женный внутри́ страны́; **I~ Revenue** (*Br.*) Госуда́рственная нало́говая слу́жба.
■ *adv.* (*motion*) внутрь/вглубь страны́; (*place*) внутри́ страны́.

in-law /'ɪnlɔ:/ *n.*: **~s** ро́дственники (*m. pl.*) со стороны́ му́жа/жёны, свояки́ (*coll.*) (*m. pl.*).

inla|y /ɪn'leɪ/ *n.* инкруста́ция.
■ *v.t.* инкрусти́ровать (*impf., pf.*); **an ~id floor** парке́тный пол с инкруста́цией.

in loco parentis /ɪn 'ləʊkəʊ pə'rentɪs/ *adv.* в ка́честве роди́телей.

inmate /'ɪnmeɪt/ *n.* (*of hospital, home etc.*) больно́й, пацие́нт; (*of prison*) заключённый.

inn /ɪn/ *n.* тракти́р.

innate /ɪ'neɪt/ *adj.* врождённый.

inner /'ɪnə(r)/ *adj.* вну́тренний.

innocence /'ɪnəs(ə)ns/ *n.* невино́вность.

innocent /'ɪnəs(ə)nt/ *adj.*
1 (*leg.*) невино́вный.
2 (*harmless*) неви́нный.
3 (*without sin*) неви́нный, безгре́шный.

innocuous /ɪ'nɒkjʊəs/ *adj.* безвре́дный, безоби́дный.

innovation /ɪnə'veɪʃ(ə)n/ *n.* нововведе́ние.

innovative /'ɪnəveɪtɪv/ *adj.* нова́торский.

innovator /'ɪnəveɪtə(r)/ *n.* нова́тор.

innuendo /ɪnjʊ'endəʊ/ *n.* (*pl.* **~es** *or* **~s**) инсинуа́ция; (*hint*) намёк.

inoculate /ɪ'nɒkjʊleɪt/ *v.t.* де́лать, с- приви́вку; прив|ива́ть, -и́ть; **he was ~d against smallpox** ему́ сде́лали приви́вку от о́спы/ему́ привили́ о́спу.

inoculation /ɪnɒkjʊ'leɪʃ(ə)n/ *n.* приви́вка.

inoffensive /ɪnə'fensɪv/ *adj.* необи́дный.

inoperable /ɪn'ɒpərəb(ə)l/ *adj.* (*untreatable by surgery*) неопера́бельный; (*unworkable*) непримени́мый; **the plan proved to be ~** план оказа́лся невыполни́мым.

inordinate /ɪn'ɔ:dɪnət/ *adj.* непоме́рный,

чрезме́рный, неуме́ренный.

inorganic /ɪnɔːˈgænɪk/ *adj.* неоргани́ческий.

inpatient /ˈɪnpeɪʃ(ə)nt/ *n.* стациона́рный/ко́ечный больно́й.

input /ˈɪnpʊt/ *n.* (*investment, resources*) вложе́ние; (*contribution*) вклад; (*comput., of data*) ввод.
■ *v.t.* (*comput.*) вв|оди́ть, -ести́ (в + *a.*).

inquest /ˈɪŋkwest/ *n.* (*in criminal case*) сле́дствие; (*investigation*) рассле́дование.

inquire /ɪnˈkwaɪə(r)/ (*see also* ▸ **enquire**) *v.i.* спр|авля́ться, -а́виться; нав|оди́ть, -ести́ спра́вки.

inquiry /ɪnˈkwaɪərɪ/ (*see also* ▸ **enquiry**) *n.* (*investigation*) рассле́дование; (*in criminal case*) сле́дствие; **court of ~** сле́дственная коми́ссия.

inquisition /ɪnkwɪˈzɪʃ(ə)n/ *n.* (*questioning*) допро́с; **he was subjected to an ~** он был под сле́дствием; (*hist.*) инквизи́ция.

inquisitive /ɪnˈkwɪzɪtɪv/ *adj.* любопы́тный.

inroad /ˈɪnrəʊd/ *n.* (*encroachment*) посяга́тельство; **the holiday will make a large ~ into/on my savings** кани́кулы поглотя́т бо́льшую часть мои́х сбереже́ний.

insane /ɪnˈseɪn/ *adj.* безу́мный, сумасше́дший; (*leg.*) невменя́емый.

insanitary /ɪnˈsænɪtərɪ/ *adj.* антисанита́рный, негигиени́чный.

insanity /ɪnˈsænɪtɪ/ *n.* (*madness*) сумасше́ствие; безу́мие; (*leg.*) невменя́емость.

insatiable /ɪnˈseɪʃəb(ə)l/ *adj.* ненасы́тный.

inscribe /ɪnˈskraɪb/ *v.t.*
1 (*engrave*) высека́ть, вы́сечь; выреза́ть, вы́резать; начерта́ть (*pf.*); **the stone was ~d with their names** их имена́ бы́ли вы́сечены на ка́мне; **a verse is ~d on his tomb** на его́ надгро́бном ка́мне вы́сечена стихотво́рная эпита́фия.
2 (*autograph*) надпи́с|ывать, -а́ть; **please ~ your name in the book** пожа́луйста, распиши́тесь в кни́ге.

inscription /ɪnˈskrɪpʃ(ə)n/ *n.* на́дпись.

inscrutable /ɪnˈskruːtəb(ə)l/ *adj.* (*smile*) зага́дочный; (*face*) непроница́емый.

insect /ˈɪnsekt/ *n.* насеко́мое; **~ bite** уку́с насеко́мого.

insecticide /ɪnˈsektɪsaɪd/ *n.* инсектици́д.

insecure /ɪnsɪˈkjʊə(r)/ *adj.*
1 (*unsafe; unreliable*) ненадёжный, небезопа́сный; **his position in the firm is ~** его́ положе́ние в фи́рме ша́ткое.
2 (*lacking confidence*) неуве́ренный (в себе́).

insecurity /ɪnsɪˈkjʊərɪtɪ/ *n.* ненадёжность, небезопа́сность; неуве́ренность.

insemination /ɪnsemɪˈneɪʃ(ə)n/ *n.* оплодотворе́ние; **artificial ~** иску́сственное оплодотворе́ние.

insensible /ɪnˈsensɪb(ə)l/ *adj.* (*numb*) нечувстви́тельный; **his hands were ~ with cold** от хо́лода его́ ру́ки потеря́ли чувстви́тельность; (*unconscious*) бесчу́вственный; (*unaware*) не сознаю́щий; **he was ~ of the danger** он не сознава́л опа́сности.

insensitive /ɪnˈsensɪtɪv/ *adj.* нечувстви́тельный; невосприи́мчивый, равноду́шный.

inseparable /ɪnˈsepərəb(ə)l/ *adj.* неразде́льный, неразры́вный.

insert /ɪnˈsəːt/ *v.t.* вст|авля́ть, -а́вить; поме|ща́ть, -сти́ть; **he ~ed the key in the lock** он вста́вил ключ в замо́к.

insertion /ɪnˈsəːʃ(ə)n/ *n.* (*inserting*) вкла́дывание, помеще́ние, введе́ние; (*sth. inserted*) вста́вка.

inside /ɪnˈsaɪd/ *n.*
1 (*interior*) вну́треннее простра́нство; вну́тренняя часть; **~ out** наизна́нку; **the thieves turned everything ~ out** во́ры переверну́ли всё вверх дном; **he knows the subject ~ out** он зна́ет предме́т вдоль и поперёк.
2 (*of road*): **it is forbidden to pass on the ~** обго́н спра́ва/сле́ва (*when driving on the right/left*) запрещён.
■ *adj.* вну́тренний; **~ pocket** вну́тренний карма́н; **he received ~ information** он получи́л информа́цию из вну́тренних исто́чников.
■ *adv.* 1 (*in the interior*) внутри́; **I opened the box and there was nothing ~** я откры́л коро́бку — внутри́ бы́ло пу́сто.
2 (*indoors*) внутри́, в помеще́нии, до́ма.
■ *prep.* 1 (*of place*) (*motion*) в + *a.*, внутрь + *g.*; **dogs are not allowed ~ the shop** с соба́ками вход в магази́н запрещён; (*position*) в + *p.*, внутри́ + *g.*; **have you seen ~ the house?** вы ви́дели дом изнутри́?
2 (*of time*) в преде́лах + *g.*, в тече́ние + *g.*; **I shall be back ~ (of) a week** я верну́сь не поздне́е, чем че́рез неде́лю.

insider /ɪnˈsaɪdə(r)/ *n.* (*comm.*): **~ trading** (незако́нное) уча́стие в биржевы́х сде́лках с испо́льзованием информа́ции из вну́тренних исто́чников.

insight /ˈɪnsaɪt/ *n.* проница́тельность; понима́ние; **gain an ~ into sth.** пости́|гнуть, -чь что-н.

insignificant /ɪnsɪgˈnɪfɪkənt/ *adj.* малова́жный, ничто́жный.

insincere /ɪnsɪnˈsɪə(r)/ *adj.* нeiскренний.

insinuate /ɪnˈsɪnjʊeɪt/ *v.t.* (*hint*) намек|а́ть, -ну́ть на + *a.*

insinuation /ɪnsɪnjʊˈeɪʃ(ə)n/ *n.* (*hint*) намёк; инсинуа́ция.

insipid /ɪnˈsɪpɪd/ *adj.* ску́чный, вя́лый.

insist /ɪnˈsɪst/ *v.t.* & *i.* наст|а́ивать, -оя́ть на + *p.*; тре́бовать, по- + *g.*; **he ~ed on his rights** он наста́ивал на свои́х права́х; **he ~ed on my accompanying him** он настоя́л на том, что́бы я его́ сопровожда́л.

insistence /ɪnˈsɪst(ə)ns/ *n.* (*quality*) насто́йчивость; (*act*) настоя́ние, насто́йчивое тре́бование.

insistent /ɪnˈsɪst(ə)nt/ *adj.* насто́йчивый; **he was ~ that I should go** он наста́ивал на том, что́бы я пошёл.

insofar as /ɪnsəʊˈfɑː(r)/ *conj.* (посто́льку) поско́льку.

insole /ˈɪnsəʊl/ *n.* сте́лька.

insolence /ˈɪnsələns/ *n.* наха́льство.

insolent /ˈɪnsələnt/ *adj.* наха́льный.

insolvent /ɪnˈsɒlv(ə)nt/ *adj.* неплатёжеспосо́бный; несостоя́тельный.

insomnia /ɪnˈsɒmnɪə/ *n.* бессо́нница.

insomniac /ɪn'sɒmnɪæk/ *n.* страдáющий бессóнницей.
insouciance /ɪn'su:sɪəns/ *n.* небрéжность.
insouciant /ɪn'su:sɪənt/ *adj.* небрéжный.
inspect /ɪn'spekt/ *v.t.* осм|áтривать, -отрéть.
inspection /ɪn'spekʃ(ə)n/ *n.* осмóтр, инспéкция.
inspector /ɪn'spektə(r)/ *n.* (*inspecting official*) инспéктор; (*police officer*) инспéктор (полиции).
inspiration /ɪnspɪ'reɪʃ(ə)n/ *n.* вдохновéние.
inspire /ɪn'spaɪə(r)/ *v.t.*
1 (*influence creatively*) вдохнов|лять, -ить; **he is an ~d musician** он вдохновéнный музыкáнт.
2 (*instil*) всел|ять, -ить; **his work does not ~ me with confidence** егó рабóта не вызывáет у меня довéрия.
instability /ɪnstə'bɪlɪtɪ/ *n.* нестабильность, неустóйчивость; (*of character*) неуравновéшенность.
install /ɪn'stɔ:l/ *v.t.* (**installed, installing**)
1 (*a person in office*) вв|одить, -ести в дóлжность.
2 (*machine; also comput.*) устан|áвливать, -овить.
installation /ɪnstə'leɪʃ(ə)n/ *n.* (*of thing*) установка; (*art*) инсталляция; (*comput.*) инсталляция, установка.
instalment /ɪn'stɔ:lmənt/ *n.* (*US also* **installment**)
1 (*partial payment*) взнос; **we are paying for our carpet by ~s (*or* on the ~ plan)** мы плáтим за ковёр в рассрóчку.
2 (*of published work*) отрывок, выпуск.
instance /'ɪnst(ə)ns/ *n.*
1 (*example*) примéр; **for ~** напримéр.
2 (*particular case*) слýчай; **in this ~** в э́том/ дáнном слýчае.
instant /'ɪnst(ə)nt/ *n.* мгновéние; **come here this ~!** иди сюдá сию же минýту!
■ *adj.* 1 (*immediate*) мгновéнный; немéдленный.
2 (*of food preparation*): **~ coffee** растворимый кóфе.
instantaneous /ɪnstən'teɪnɪəs/ *adj.* мгновéнный.
instead /ɪn'sted/ *adv.* взамéн (+ *g.*); **~ of** вмéсто + *g.*; **let me go ~ (of you)** давáйте я пойдý вмéсто вас; **if the steak is off I'll have chicken ~** éсли бифштéксов нет, я возьмý кýрицу.
instep /'ɪnstep/ *n.* подъём (ноги́).
instigate /'ɪnstɪgeɪt/ *v.t.* подстрекáть (*impf.*), провоцировать, с-.
instil /ɪn'stɪl/ *v.t.* (**instilled, instilling**) (*lit.*) вл|ивáть, -ить; (*fig.*) внуш|áть, -ить; прив|ивáть, -ить.
instinct /'ɪnstɪŋkt/ *n.* инстинкт.
instinctive /ɪn'stɪŋktɪv/ *adj.* инстинктивный, безотчётный.
institute /'ɪnstɪtju:t/ *n.* институ́т.
■ *v.t.* устан|áвливать, -овить; учре|ждáть, -дить.
institution /ɪnstɪ'tju:ʃ(ə)n/ *n.* учреждéние, организáция, заведéние, институ́т; **charitable ~** благотвори́тельное учреждéние; **mental ~** психиатрическая лечéбница.
institutional /ɪnstɪ'tju:ʃən(ə)l/ *adj.* институциóнный; **she is in need of ~ care** её слéдует госпитализировать; **~ reform** рефóрма учреждéний.
instruct /ɪn'strʌkt/ *v.t.*
1 (*teach*) учить, на- (*когó чемý*).
2 (*order*) инструктировать (*impf., pf.; pf. also* про-); **I was ~ed to call on you** мне бы́ло прикáзано зайти к вам.
instruction /ɪn'strʌkʃ(ə)n/ *n.* (*direction*) указáние; руковóдство; **follow the ~s on the packet** слéдуйте указáниям на пакéте; (*order*) распоряжéние, прикáз.
■ *cpd.* **~ book** *n.* руковóдство.
instructive /ɪn'strʌktɪv/ *adj.* поучи́тельный.
instructor /ɪn'strʌktə(r)/ *nn.* (*sport*) инстрýктор; (*teacher*) учи́тель (*fem.* -ница).
instrument /'ɪnstrəmənt/ *n.*
1 (*implement*) инструмéнт; **~ panel** пульт управлéния.
2 (*musical ~*) (музыкáльный) инструмéнт.
instrumental /ɪnstrə'ment(ə)l/ *n.* (*gram.*) твори́тельный падéж.
■ *adj.* 1 (*serving as means*): **~ to our purpose** полéзный для нáшей цéли.
2 (*mus.*) инструментáльный.
3 (*gram.*) твори́тельный.
instrumentalist /ɪnstrə'mentəlɪst/ *n.* инструменталист.
insubordinate /ɪnsə'bɔ:dɪnət/ *adj.* непокóрный.
insubordination /ɪnsəbɔ:dɪ'neɪʃ(ə)n/ *n.* неподчинéние; непокóрность.
insubstantial /ɪnsəb'stænʃ(ə)l/ *adj.* (*not real, imaginary*) нереáльный, иллюзóрный; (*building, structure*) непрóчный; (*evidence*) слáбый, неубеди́тельный; (*meal*) несы́тный.
insufferable /ɪn'sʌfərəb(ə)l/ *adj.* невыноси́мый.
insufficient /ɪnsə'fɪʃ(ə)nt/ *adj.* недостáточный.
insular /'ɪnsjʊlə(r)/ *adj.* островнóй; (*fig.*) ограни́ченный, ýзкий.
insulate /'ɪnsjʊleɪt/ *v.t.* (*protect from escape of electricity*) изоли́ровать (*impf., pf.*); (*protect from escape of heat*) утепл|ять, -ить, теплоизоли́ровать (*impf., pf.*).
insulation /ɪnsjʊ'leɪʃ(ə)n/ *n.* (*against escape of electricity*) изоляция; (*against escape of heat*) теплоизоляция.
insulin /'ɪnsjʊlɪn/ *n.* инсули́н.
insult[1] /'ɪnsʌlt/ *n.* оскорблéние; оби́да.
insult[2] /ɪn'sʌlt/ *v.t.* оскорб|лять, -и́ть; **~ing language** оскорби́тельные выражéния.
insuperable /ɪn'su:pərəb(ə)l, ɪn'sju:-/ *adj.* непреодоли́мый.
insupportable /ɪnsə'pɔ:təb(ə)l/ *adj.* нестерпи́мый, невыноси́мый, неснóсный.
insurance /ɪn'ʃʊərəns/ *n.* страховáние, страхóвка; **~ company** страховáя компáния; **~ policy** страховóй пóлис; **National I~** (*Br.*) госудáрственное страховáние; **take out ~** страховáться, за-.
insure /ɪn'ʃʊə(r)/ *v.t.* страховáть, за-.
insurgent /ɪn'sə:dʒ(ə)nt/ *n.* повстáнец.
insurmountable /ɪnsə'maʊntəb(ə)l/ *adj.* непреодоли́мый.

insurrection /ɪnsə'rekʃ(ə)n/ *n.* восста́ние.

intact /ɪn'tækt/ *adj.* нетро́нутый, це́лый.

intake /'ɪnteɪk/ *n.* (*Br., of recruits, students, etc.*) набо́р; (*amount taken into body*) потребле́ние; **~ of breath** вздох.

intangible /ɪn'tændʒɪb(ə)l/ *adj.*
1 (*non-material*) неосяза́емый, неулови́мый.
2 (*vague, obscure*): **~ ideas** сму́тные/нея́сные представле́ния.

integral /'ɪntɪgr(ə)l/ *adj.* неотъе́млемый, суще́ственный.

integrate /'ɪntɪgreɪt/ *v.t.* интегри́ровать (*impf., pf.*).
■ *v.i.* объедин|я́ться, -и́ться.

integration /ɪntɪ'greɪʃ(ə)n/ *n.* интегра́ция.

integrity /ɪn'tegrɪtɪ/ *n.* че́стность, це́льность.

intellect /'ɪntəlekt/ *n.* интелле́кт, ум, рассу́док; **the great ~s of the age** вели́кие умы́ эпо́хи.

intellectual /ɪntɪ'lektjʊəl/ *n.* интеллиге́нт (*fem.* -ка), интеллектуа́л (*fem.* -ка).
■ *adj.* интеллектуа́льный, у́мственный.

intelligence /ɪn'telɪdʒ(ə)ns/ *n.*
1 (*mental power*) ум, интелле́кт; **I had the ~ to refuse his offer** у меня́ хвати́ло ума́ не приня́ть его́ предложе́ния.
2 (*mil.*) разве́дка.

intelligent /ɪn'telɪdʒ(ə)nt/ *adj.* у́мный, смышлёный, сообрази́тельный.

intelligentsia /ɪntelɪ'dʒentsɪə/ *n.* интеллиге́нция.

intelligible /ɪn'telɪdʒɪb(ə)l/ *adj.* поня́тный, вня́тный.

intend /ɪn'tend/ *v.t.*
1 (*have in mind*) намерева́ться, хоте́ть, собира́ться (*all impf.*).
2 (*mean*) предназн|ача́ть, -а́чить; **a book ~ed for advanced students** кни́га, рассчи́танная на продви́нутый эта́п обуче́ния.

intense /ɪn'tens/ *adj.* (**intenser, intensest**)
1 (*extreme*) си́льный, интенси́вный.
2 (*ardent*) напряжённый.

intensify /ɪn'tensɪfaɪ/ *v.t.* уси́ли|вать, -ть; увели́чи|вать, -ть.

intensity /ɪn'tensɪtɪ/ *n.* си́ла, интенси́вность.

intensive /ɪn'tensɪv/ *adj.* интенси́вный; **~ care unit** отделе́ние реанима́ции.

intent¹ /ɪn'tent/ *n.*: **to all ~s and purposes** факти́чески, на са́мом де́ле.

intent² /ɪn'tent/ *adj.*
1 (*earnest, eager*) увлечённый, ре́вностный; (*expression*) сосредото́ченный.
2 (*resolved*): **he was ~ on getting a first** он был по́лон реши́мости получи́ть дипло́м с отли́чием.

intention /ɪn'tenʃ(ə)n/ *n.* наме́рение; у́мысел; **I have no ~ of going to the party** у меня́ нет наме́рения идти́ на вечери́нку.

intentional /ɪn'tenʃən(ə)l/ *adj.* умы́шленный, наме́ренный; **he ignored me ~ly** он наме́ренно не заме́тил меня́.

interact /ɪntər'ækt/ *v.i.* взаимоде́йствовать (*impf.*).

interaction /ɪntər'ækʃ(ə)n/ *n.* взаимоде́йствие.

interactive /ɪntər'æktɪv/ *adj.* (*comput.*) интеракти́вный, диало́говый.

intercept /ɪntə'sept/ *v.t.* перехва́т|ывать, -и́ть.

interchange /'ɪntətʃeɪndʒ/ *n.* обме́н; **~ of views** обме́н мне́ниями.
■ *v.t.* обме́н|ивать, -я́ть; обме́н|иваться, -я́ться + *i.*

interchangeable /ɪntə'tʃeɪndʒəb(ə)l/ *adj.* взаимозаменя́емый.

intercity /ɪntə'sɪtɪ/ *adj.* междугоро́дный.

intercom /'ɪntəkɒm/ *n.* (*in an office, plane*) селе́ктор; (*to get into a house*) домофо́н.

interconnect /ɪntəkə'nekt/ *v.i.* соедин|я́ться, -и́ться.

intercontinental /ɪntəkɒntɪ'nent(ə)l/ *adj.* межконтинента́льный; **~ ballistic missile** межконтинента́льная баллисти́ческая раке́та.

intercourse /'ɪntəkɔːs/ *n.* (*sexual*) (полово́е) сноше́ние.

interdependent /ɪntədɪ'pend(ə)nt/ *adj.* взаимозави́симый.

interest /'ɪntrest/ *n.*
1 (*attention, curiosity*) интере́с; **show, take a great, keen ~ in sth.** проя́в|ля́ть, -и́ть большо́й интере́с к чему́-н.
2 (*quality arousing ~*) занима́тельность; **his books lack ~ for me** меня́ его́ кни́ги не занима́ют.
3 (*pursuit*) интере́с; **a man of wide ~s** челове́к с широ́ким кру́гом интере́сов.
4 (*oft. pl., advantage*) интере́сы (*m. pl.*), по́льза, вы́года; **it is in your ~ to listen to his advice** в ва́ших же интере́сах прислу́шаться к его́ сове́там.
5 (*charge on loan*) (*paid*) ссу́дный проце́нт; проце́нты (*m. pl.*); (*received*) проце́нтный дохо́д; **rate of ~, ~ rate** проце́нтная ста́вка; (*fig.*): **my kindness was repaid with ~** меня́ ще́дро вознагради́ли за мою́ доброту́.
■ *v.t.* интересова́ть (*impf.*); (*cause a person to take interest*) заинтересова́ть (*pf.*).
■ *cpd.* **~-free** *adj.* беспроце́нтный.

interested /'ɪntrestɪd/ *adj.*
1 (*having interest*) интересу́ющийся; **are you ~ in football?** вы интересу́етесь футбо́лом?
2 (*not impartial*) заинтересо́ванный; **an ~ party** заинтересо́ванная сторона́.

interesting /'ɪntrestɪŋ/ *adj.* интере́сный.

interface /'ɪntəfeɪs/ *n.* (*comput.*) интерфе́йс; (*fig.*) взаимосвя́зь, взаимоде́йствие.

interfer|e /ɪntə'fɪə(r)/ *v.i.* вме́ш|иваться, -а́ться; **don't ~e in my affairs** не вме́шивайтесь в мои́ дела́; **she is an ~ing old lady** она́ назо́йливая стару́ха.

interference /ɪntə'fɪərəns/ *n.* вмеша́тельство, поме́ха; (*radio, TV*) поме́хи (*f. pl.*).

intergalactic /ɪntəgə'læktɪk/ *adj.* межгалакти́ческий.

intergovernmental /ɪntəgʌvən'ment(ə)l/ *adj.* межправи́тельственный.

interim /'ɪntərɪm/ *n.* промежу́ток вре́мени; **in the ~** тем вре́менем.
■ *adj.* (*temporary*) вре́менный; (*provisional*) промежу́точный.

interior /ɪn'tɪərɪə(r)/ *n.*

1 (*inside*) внýтренняя часть, прострáнство внутрú.
2 (*of building*) интерьéр; **~ decorator** худóжник по интерьéру.
3 (*home affairs*): **Minister of the I~** минúстр внýтренних дел.
■ *adj.* внýтренний.

interject /ɪntə'dʒekt/ *v.t.* вст|авля́ть, -áвить; (*coll.*) вверну́ть (*pf.*); **'It's not true,' he ~ed** «Э́то непрáвда», — встáвил он.

interjection /ɪntə'dʒekʃ(ə)n/ *n.* восклицáние; (*gram.*) междомéтие.

interlock /ɪntə'lɒk/ *v.t.* & *i.* соедин|я́ть(ся), -úть(ся), сцеп|ля́ть(ся), -úть(ся).

interloper /'ɪntələʊpə(r)/ *n.* незвáный гость.

interlude /'ɪntəlu:d/ *n.* переры́в; (*theatr.*) антрáкт.

intermarry /ɪntə'mærɪ/ *v.i.* смéш|иваться, -áться; роднúться, по- путём брáка.

intermediary /ɪntə'mi:dɪərɪ/ *n.* посрéдни|к (*fem.* -ца).
■ *adj.* посрéднический.

intermediate /ɪntə'mi:dɪət/ *adj.* промежу́точный.

interminable /ɪn'tɜ:mɪnəb(ə)l/ *adj.* бесконéчный, нескончáемый, вéчный.

intermission /ɪntə'mɪʃ(ə)n/ *n.* антрáкт.

intermittent /ɪntə'mɪt(ə)nt/ *adj.* преры́вистый.

intern[1] /'ɪntɜ:n/ *n.* (*US*) (*medical student*) молодóй врач, интéрн; (*trainee*) стажёр, практикáнт.

intern[2] /ɪn'tɜ:n/ *v.t.* интернúровать (*impf.*, *pf.*).

internal /ɪn'tɜ:n(ə)l/ *adj.* внýтренний; **I~ Revenue Service** (*US*) *see* ▸ **IRS**

international /ɪntə'næʃən(ə)l/ *n.* (*Br.*, *sporting event*) междунарóдные соревновáния (*nt. pl.*).
■ *adj.* междунарóдный, интернационáльный; **I~ Monetary Fund** Междунарóдный валю́тный фонд.

internee /ɪntɜ:'ni:/ *n.* интернúрованный.

Internet *n.* (**the ~**) Интернéт; **on the ~** в Интернéте; **~ service provider** провáйдер.

internment /ɪn'tɜ:nmənt/ *n.* интернúрование; **~ camp** лáгерь (*m.*) для интернúрованных (лиц).

interplay /'ɪntəpleɪ/ *n.* взаимодéйствие, взаимосвя́зь.

interpolate /ɪn'tɜ:pəleɪt/ *v.t.* интерполúровать (*impf.*, *pf.*); вст|авля́ть, -áвить.

interpret /ɪn'tɜ:prɪt/ *v.t.* (**interpreted, interpreting**)
1 (*explain*) толковáть (*impf.*); истолк|óвывать, -овáть; **how do you ~ this dream?** как вы объясня́ете э́тот сон?
2 (*understand*) истолкóв|ывать, -áть.
■ *v.i.* перев|одúть, -естú (у́стно).

interpretation /ɪntɜ:prɪ'teɪʃ(ə)n/ *n.* интерпретáция, толковáние.

interpreter /ɪn'tɜ:prɪtə(r)/ *n.* (у́стный) переводчи|к (*fem.* -ца).

interracial /ɪntə'reɪʃ(ə)l/ *adj.* межрáсовый.

interregn|um /ɪntə'regnəm/ *n.* (*pl.* **~ums** *or* **~a**) междуцáрствие; междувлáстие.

interrogate /ɪn'terəgeɪt/ *v.t.* допр|áшивать, -осúть.

interrogation /ɪnterə'geɪʃ(ə)n/ *n.* допрóс.

interrogative /ɪntə'rɒgətɪv/ *adj.* вопросúтельный.

interrupt /ɪntə'rʌpt/ *v.t.* & *v.i.* прер|ывáть, -вáть; переб|ивáть, -úть; **don't ~ when I am speaking** не перебивáйте, когдá я говорю́; **he ~ed me as I was reading** он прервáл моё чтéние.

interruption /ɪntə'rʌpʃ(ə)n/ *n.* помéха; нарушéние; вторжéние.

intersect /ɪntə'sekt/ *v.t.* & *i.* перес|екáть(ся), -éчь(ся).

intersection /ɪntə'sekʃ(ə)n/ *n.* (*crossroads*) перекрёсток.

intersperse /ɪntə'spɜ:s/ *v.t.* разбр|áсывать, -осáть; расс|ыпáть, -ы́пать; **red flowers ~d with yellow ones** крáсные цветы́ вперемéжку с жёлтыми; **his talk was ~d with anecdotes** он пересыпáл/разбавля́л (*coll.*) своё выступлéние анекдóтами.

interstate /'ɪntəsteɪt/ *adj.* (*between regions of country*) межштáтный; (*between countries*) межгосудáрственный.

interval /'ɪntəv(ə)l/ *n.*
1 (*of time*) промежу́ток, отрéзок врéмени; интервáл; **we see each other at ~s** мы ви́димся врéмя от врéмени; **at ~s of an hour** с интервáлами в час.
2 (*of place*) расстоя́ние; **the posts were set at ~s of 10 feet** столбы́ бы́ли расстáвлены на расстоя́нии десятú фу́тов (друг от дру́га).
3 (*Br.*, *theatr.*) антрáкт.

intervene /ɪntə'vi:n/ *v.i.* вмéш|иваться, -áться; **the government ~d in the dispute** в конфлúкт вмешáлось прави́тельство.

intervention /ɪntə'venʃ(ə)n/ *n.* вмешáтельство.

interview /'ɪntəvju:/ *n.* деловáя встрéча; собесéдование; (*with the media*) интервью́ (*nt. indecl.*); **an ~ for a job** собесéдование при приёме на рабóту; **he gave an ~ to the press** он дал интервью́ журналúстам.
■ *v.t.* (*with the media*) интервьюúровать (*impf.*, *pf.*); **only certain candidates were ~ed** собесéдование провелú тóлько с нéсколькими кандидáтами.

interviewee /ɪntəvju:'i:/ *n.* интервьюúруемый, дающий интервью́.

interviewer /'ɪntəvju:ə(r)/ *n.* (*for media*) интервьюéр; (*for job*) проводя́щий собесéдование.

interwar /ɪntə'wɔ:(r)/ *adj.*: **~ period** перúод мéжду двумя́ мировы́ми вóйнами.

intestate /ɪn'testət/ *adj.*: **to die ~** умир|áть, -éть, не остáвив завещáния.

intestine /ɪn'testɪn/ *n.* кишéчник.

intimacy /'ɪntɪməsɪ/ *n.* интúмность, блúзость.

intimate /'ɪntɪmət/ *adj.*
1 (*close*) блúзкий.
2 (*private, personal*) интúмный, лúчный; **the ~ details of his life** подрóбности егó лúчной жúзни.
3 (*detailed*) основáтельный; **he has an ~ knowledge of the subject** он досконáльно

зна́ет предме́т.

intimidate /ɪn'tɪmɪdeɪt/ *v.t.* запу́г|ивать, -а́ть; угрожа́ть (*impf.*) + *d.*

into /'ɪntʊ/ *prep.*

1 (*expr. motion to a point within*) в + *a.*

2 (*expr. extent*) до; **far ~ the night** до по́здней но́чи.

3 (*expr. change or process*) *usu.* в + *a. or* на + *a.*; **the rain turned ~ snow** дождь перешёл в снег; **translate ~ French** перев|оди́ть, -ести́ на францу́зский.

4 (*coll., of a devotee*): **he's ~ jazz** он увлека́ется джа́зом.

intolerable /ɪn'tɒlərəb(ə)l/ *adj.* невыноси́мый.

intolerance /ɪn'tɒlərəns/ *n.* нетерпи́мость.

intolerant /ɪn'tɒlərənt/ *n.* нетерпи́мый; **~ of** (*unable to bear*) не выно́сящий + *g.*

intone /ɪn'təʊn/ *v.t.* (*utter in particular tone*) интони́ровать (*impf.*); (*recite with prolonged sounds*) чита́ть нараспе́в (*impf.*).

intoxicate /ɪn'tɒksɪkeɪt/ *v.t.* (*lit., fig.*) опьян|я́ть, -и́ть.

intoxication /ɪntɒksɪ'keɪʃ(ə)n/ *n.* опьяне́ние.

intractable /ɪn'træktəb(ə)l/ *adj.* (*of person*) упря́мый, непоко́рный, несгово́рчивый; (*of problems, metal*) неподатливый; **~ illness** трудноизлечи́мое заболева́ние; **~ pain** неустрани́мая боль.

intransigent /ɪn'trænsɪdʒ(ə)nt/ *adj.* непреклóнный.

intransitive /ɪn'trænsɪtɪv/ *adj.* неперехо́дный.

intravenous /ɪntrə'viːnəs/ *adj.* внутриве́нный.

in-tray /'ɪntreɪ/ *n.* (*Br.*) насто́льная корзи́на для входя́щей корреспонде́нции.

intrepid /ɪn'trepɪd/ *adj.* неустраши́мый, бесстра́шный.

intricate /'ɪntrɪkət/ *adj.* запу́танный, сло́жный.

intrigu|e *n.* /'ɪntriːg/ интри́га; про́иски (*m. pl.*).

■ *v.t.* /ɪn'triːg/ (**intrigues, intrigued, intriguing**) интригова́ть, за-; интересова́ть, за-; **I was ~ed to learn** мне бы́ло интере́сно узна́ть; **an ~ing prospect** зама́нчивая перспекти́ва.

intrinsic /ɪn'trɪnzɪk/ *adj.* прису́щий, по́длинный; **~ value** по́длинная це́нность.

introduce /ɪntrə'djuːs/ *v.t.*

1 (*bring in*) вв|оди́ть, -ести́; (при)вн|оси́ть, -ести́; **many improvements have been ~d** ввели́ мно́го усоверше́нствований.

2 (*present*) предст|авля́ть, -а́вить; знако́мить, по- (*кого с кем*); **may I ~ my fiancée?** разреши́те предста́вить (вам) мою неве́сту.

introduction /ɪntrə'dʌkʃ(ə)n/ *n.*

1 (*bringing in*) введе́ние, установле́ние.

2 (*sth. brought in*) но́вшество, нововведе́ние.

3 (*presentation*) представле́ние; **letter of ~** рекоменда́тельное письмо́.

4 (*preliminary matter in book, speech etc.*) введе́ние, вступле́ние.

introductory /ɪntrə'dʌktərɪ/ *adj.* вступи́тельный, вво́дный.

introspection /ɪntrə'spekʃ(ə)n/ *n.* интроспе́кция, самоана́лиз.

introvert /'ɪntrəvəːt/ *n.* за́мкнутый челове́к, интрове́рт.

intrud|e /ɪn'truːd/ *v.t.* нав|я́зывать, -яза́ть.

■ *v.i.* вт|орга́ться, -о́ргнуться; **you are ~ing on my time** вы посяга́ете на моё вре́мя.

intruder /ɪn'truːdə(r)/ *n.* граби́тель (*m.*).

intrusion /ɪn'truːʒ(ə)n/ *n.* вторже́ние.

intrusive /ɪn'truːsɪv/ *adj.* назо́йливый.

intuition /ɪntjuː'ɪʃ(ə)n/ *n.* инту́иция; чутьё.

intuitive /ɪn'tjuːɪtɪv/ *adj.* интуити́вный.

inundate /'ɪnəndeɪt/ *v.t.* наводн|я́ть, -и́ть; **I was ~d with letters** меня́ засы́пали пи́сьмами.

invade /ɪn'veɪd/ *v.t.* вторга́ться, вто́ргнуться в + *a.*

invader /ɪn'veɪdə(r)/ *n.* захва́тчик.

invalid[1] /'ɪnvəlɪd/ *n.* больно́й.

invalid[2] /ɪn'valɪd/ *adj.* недействи́тельный, не име́ющий (зако́нной) си́лы.

invalidate /ɪn'vælɪdeɪt/ *v.t.* аннули́ровать (*impf., pf.*).

invaluable /ɪn'væljʊəb(ə)l/ *adj.* неоцени́мый, бесце́нный.

invariable /ɪn'veərɪəb(ə)l/ *adj.* неизме́нный, постоя́нный.

invariably /ɪn'veərɪəblɪ/ *adv.* неизме́нно.

invasion /ɪn'veɪʒ(ə)n/ *n.* вторже́ние, наше́ствие; **~ of privacy** вторже́ние в ли́чную жизнь.

inveigle /ɪn'veɪg(ə)l/ *v.t.* соблазн|я́ть, -и́ть; оболь|ща́ть, -сти́ть; **they ~d him into the conspiracy** они́ вовлекли́ его́ в за́говор; **he was ~d into signing a cheque** его́ обма́ном заста́вили подписа́ть чек.

invent /ɪn'vent/ *v.t.* изобре|та́ть, -сти́; (*think up*) приду́м|ывать, -ать.

invention /ɪn'venʃ(ə)n/ *n.* изобрете́ние.

inventive /ɪn'ventɪv/ *adj.* изобрета́тельный, нахо́дчивый.

inventor /ɪn'ventə(r)/ *n.* изобрета́тель (*m.*).

inventory /'ɪnvəntərɪ/ *n.* инвента́рь (*m.*).

invert /ɪn'vəːt/ *v.t.*: **~ed commas** (*Br.*) кавы́чки (*f. pl.*).

invertebrate /ɪn'vəːtɪbrət/ *n.* беспозвоно́чное (живо́тное).

■ *adj.* беспозвоно́чный.

invest /ɪn'vest/ *v.t.* вкла́дывать, вложи́ть; инвести́ровать (*impf., pf.*).

■ *v.i.* вкла́дывать, вложи́ть де́ньги/капита́л; (*coll., spend money usefully*): **I must ~ in a new hat** мне придётся потра́титься на но́вую шля́пу.

investigate /ɪn'vestɪgeɪt/ *v.t.* (*crime, facts*) рассле́довать (*impf., pf.*); (*study*) иссле́довать (*impf., pf.*).

investigation /ɪnvestɪ'geɪʃ(ə)n/ *n.* (*criminal*) рассле́дование, сле́дствие; (*study*) иссле́дование.

investigative /ɪn'vestɪgətɪv/ *adj.*: **~ journalism** журнали́стика рассле́дований.

investigator /ɪn'vestɪgeɪtə(r)/ *n.* (*in police*) сле́дователь (*m.*); (*researcher*) иссле́дователь (*m.*).

investment /ɪn'vestmənt/ *n.* (*investing*)

инвести́рование; (*sum invested*) инвести́ция; **~ bank** инвестицио́нный банк.

investor /ɪn'vestə(r)/ *n.* вкла́дчик, инве́стор.

inveterate /ɪn'vetərət/ *adj.* закорене́лый, зая́длый.

invidious /ɪn'vɪdɪəs/ *adj.* оскорби́тельный; оби́дный; **an ~ comparison** оби́дное/оскорби́тельное сравне́ние.

invigilate /ɪn'vɪdʒɪleɪt/ *v.i.* (*Br.*) наблюда́ть (*impf.*) за экзамену́ющимися.

invigilator /ɪn'vɪdʒɪleɪtə(r)/ *n.* официа́льный наблюда́тель (*на экзамене*).

invigorating /ɪn'vɪgəreɪtɪŋ/ *adj.* бодря́щий.

invincible /ɪn'vɪnsɪb(ə)l/ *adj.* непобеди́мый.

invisible /ɪn'vɪzɪb(ə)l/ *adj.* неви́димый, незри́мый.

invitation /ɪnvɪ'teɪʃ(ə)n/ *n.* приглаше́ние.

invite /ɪn'vaɪt/ *v.t.*
1 (*request to come*) пригла|ша́ть, -си́ть; **she ~d him into her flat** она́ пригласи́ла его́ к себе́ на кварти́ру; **I am seldom ~d out** меня́ ре́дко куда́-либо приглаша́ют.
2 (*request*) предл|ага́ть, -ожи́ть; **we were ~d to choose** нам был предоста́влен вы́бор.

invoice /'ɪnvɔɪs/ *n.* счёт, счёт-факту́ра.
■ *v.t.* выпи́сывать, вы́писать счёт кому́-н. (на това́ры).

invoke /ɪn'vəʊk/ *v.t.* взыва́ть, воззва́ть; приз|ыва́ть, -ва́ть; **~ the law** взыва́ть, воззва́ть к зако́ну.

involuntary /ɪn'vɒləntərɪ/ *adj.* (*accidental*) нечая́нный; (*uncontrollable*) непроизво́льный.

involve /ɪn'vɒlv/ *v.t.*
1 (*implicate*) вовл|ека́ть, -е́чь; **it will not ~ you in any expense** э́то не потре́бует от вас никаки́х расхо́дов.
2 (*entail*) влечь, по- за собо́й; вызыва́ть, вы́звать; **it would ~ my living in London** в тако́м слу́чае мне бы пришло́сь жить в Ло́ндоне.

involved /ɪn'vɒlvd/ *adj.* сло́жный, запу́танный.

involvement /ɪn'vɒlvmənt/ *n.* (*participation*) прича́стность; (*personal*) связь, вовлечённость.

invulnerable /ɪn'vʌlnərəb(ə)l/ *adj.* неуязви́мый.

inward /'ɪnwəd/ *adj.* (*lit., fig.*) вну́тренний.

inward(s) /'ɪnwəd(z)/ *adv.* (*expr. motion*) внутрь.

in-your-face /ɪnjɔː'feɪs/ *adj.* (*coll.*) жёсткий, провокацио́нный.

iodine /'aɪədiːn/ *n.* йод.

iota /aɪ'əʊtə/ *n.* (*lit., fig.*) йо́та; **we will not yield one ~** мы не отсту́пим ни на йо́ту; **I don't care one ~** мне реши́тельно всё равно́.

IOU /aɪəʊ'juː/ *n.* долгова́я распи́ска.

IQ (*abbr. of* ***intelligence quotient***) коэффицие́нт интелле́кта/у́мственного разви́тия.

IRA
1 (*abbr. of* ***Irish Republican Army***) ИРА́ (Ирла́ндская республика́нская а́рмия).
2 (*abbr. of* ***individual retirement account***) (*US*) индивидуа́льные пенсио́нные вкла́ды (*m. pl.*).

Iran /ɪ'rɑːn/ *n.* Ира́н.

Iranian /ɪ'reɪnɪən/ *n.* ира́н|ец (*fem.* -ка).
■ *adj.* ира́нский.

Iraq /ɪ'rɑːk/ *n.* Ира́к.

Iraqi /ɪ'rɑːkɪ/ *n.* (*pl.* **~s**) ира́кец, жи́тель (*fem.* -ница) Ира́ка.
■ *adj.* ира́кский.

irascible /ɪ'ræsɪb(ə)l/ *adj.* раздражи́тельный, вспы́льчивый.

irate /aɪ'reɪt/ *adj.* серди́тый, гне́вный.

Ireland /'aɪələnd/ *n.* Ирла́ндия.

iridescent /ɪrɪ'des(ə)nt/ *adj.* ра́дужный, перели́вчатый.

iris /'aɪərɪs/ *n.*
1 (*plant*) и́рис.
2 (*of eye*) ра́дужная оболо́чка.

Irish /'aɪərɪʃ/ *n.*
1 (*language*) ирла́ндский язы́к.
2 : **the ~** ирла́ндцы (*m. pl.*).
■ *adj.* ирла́ндский.
■ *cpds.* **~man** *n.* ирла́ндец; **~woman** *n.* ирла́ндка.

iron /'aɪən/ *n.*
1 (*metal*) желе́зо.
2 (*for ironing*) утю́г.
■ *adj.* (*lit., fig.*) желе́зный.
■ *v.t.* (*clothes*) гла́дить, по-/вы́-; **~ out** (*fig.*) сгла́|живать, -дить.
■ *v.i.* гла́дить (*impf.*); **she spent the whole evening ~ing** она́ гла́дила весь ве́чер.
■ *cpds.* **~monger** *n.* (*Br.*) торго́вец скобяны́ми изде́лиями; **~monger's (shop)** (*Br.*) магази́н скобяны́х изде́лий/това́ров.

ironic(al) /aɪ'rɒnɪk(əl)/ *adj.* ирони́ческий.

ironing /'aɪənɪŋ/ *n.*
1 (*action*) гла́женье; **~ board** глади́льная доска́.
2 (*linen*) бельё для гла́женья.

irony /'aɪrənɪ/ *n.* иро́ния.

irrational /ɪ'ræʃən(ə)l/ *adj.* (*not endowed with reason*) неразу́мный; (*illogical; absurd*) иррациона́льный.

irreconcilable /ɪ'rekənsaɪləb(ə)l/ *adj.* непримири́мый.

irrefutable /ɪrɪ'fjuːtəb(ə)l/ *adj.* неопровержи́мый.

irregular /ɪ'regjʊlə(r)/ *adj.*
1 (*contrary to rule*) непра́вильный; (*contrary to custom, norm*) непри́нятый.
2 (*variable in occurrence*) нерегуля́рный; **he keeps ~ hours** у него́ неупоря́доченный режи́м.
3 (*uneven*) неро́вный; **~ teeth** неро́вные зу́бы.
4 (*unequal*) неодина́ковый; **at ~ intervals** с неодина́ковыми интерва́лами.
5 (*gram.*) непра́вильный.

irregularity /ɪregjʊ'lærɪtɪ/ *n.* непра́вильность, нерегуля́рность.

irrelevant /ɪ'relɪv(ə)nt/ *adj.* неуме́стный, неподходя́щий.

irreparable /ɪ'repərəb(ə)l/ *adj.*: **an ~ mistake** непоправи́мая оши́бка; **an ~ loss** безвозвра́тная потеря/утра́та; **my watch suffered ~ damage** мои́ часы́ окончательно сломались.

irreplaceable /ɪrɪ'pleɪsəb(ə)l/ *adj.* незаменимый.

irrepressible /ɪrɪ'presɪb(ə)l/ *adj.* неукротимый, неугомонный, неудержимый.

irreproachable /ɪrɪ'prəʊtʃəb(ə)l/ *adj.* безупречный.

irresistible /ɪrɪ'zɪstɪb(ə)l/ *adj.* неотразимый.

irresolute /ɪ'rezəlu:t/ *adj.* нерешительный.

irrespective /ɪrɪ'spektɪv/ *adj.*: **~ of** невзирая/несмотря на + *a.*

irresponsible /ɪrɪ'spɒnsɪb(ə)l/ *adj.* безответственный.

irreverence /ɪ'revərəns/ *n.* непочтительность, неуважение.

irreverent /ɪ'revərənt/ *adj.* непочтительный.

irreversible /ɪrɪ'vɜ:sɪb(ə)l/ *adj.* (*process*) необратимый; (*decision*) неотменяемый.

irrevocable /ɪ'revəkəb(ə)l/ *adj.* бесповоротный.

irrigate /'ɪrɪgeɪt/ *v.t.* оро|шать, -сить.

irrigation /ɪrɪ'geɪʃ(ə)n/ *n.* орошение, ирригация.

irritability /ɪrɪtə'bɪlɪtɪ/ *n.* раздражительность; (*of skin etc.*) чувствительность.

irritable /'ɪrɪtəb(ə)l/ *adj.*
1 (*easily annoyed*) раздражительный.
2 (*of skin etc.*) чувствительный.

irritant /'ɪrɪt(ə)nt/ *n.* раздражитель (*m.*).

irritate /'ɪrɪteɪt/ *v.t.* раздражать (*impf.*).

irritation /ɪrɪ'teɪʃ(ə)n/ *n.* раздражение.

IRS (*abbr. of* ***Internal Revenue Service***) (*US*) Государственная налоговая служба.

is /ɪz/ *3rd pers. sing. pres. of* ▸ **be**

Islam /'ɪzlɑ:m/ *n.* ислам, мусульманство.

Islamic /ɪz'læmɪk/ *adj.* мусульманский, исламский.

island /'aɪlənd/ *n.* остров; **traffic ~** островок безопасности.

islander /'aɪləndə(r)/ *n.* островитян|ин (*fem.* -ка).

isle /aɪl/ *n.* остров.

isn't /'ɪz(ə)nt/ *neg. of* ▸ **is**

isolate /'aɪsəleɪt/ *v.t.* изолировать (*impf., pf.*) (*also med.*); разобщ|ать, -ить; **an ~d village** отдалённая деревня.

isolation /aɪsə'leɪʃ(ə)n/ *n.* изоляция, разобщение; **a case considered in ~** отдельно взятый случай.

isolationism /aɪsə'leɪʃənɪz(ə)m/ *n.* изоляционизм.

ISP (*abbr. of* ***Internet service provider***) (интернет-)провайдер.

Israel /'ɪzreɪl/ *n.* (*bibl., pol.*) Израиль (*m.*).

Israeli /ɪz'reɪlɪ/ *n.* (*pl.* **~s**) *n.* израильтян|ин (*fem.* -ка).
■ *adj.* израильский.

issue /'ɪʃu:/ *n.*
1 (*publication, production*) выпуск, издание; (*sth. published or produced*) выпуск, издание; **recent ~s of a magazine** последние номера журнала.
2 (*topic*) вопрос; предмет обсуждения; **I don't want to make an ~ of it** я не хочу делать из этого проблему.
■ *v.t.* (**issues, issued, issuing**)
1 (*publish*) выпускать, выпустить; изд|авать, -ать; **a book ~d last year** книга, изданная в прошлом году.
2 (*supply*) выдавать, выдать; снаб|жать, -дить.

Istanbul /ɪstæn'bʊl/ *n.* Стамбул.

isthmus /'ɪsθməs/ *n.* (*pl.* **~es**) перешеек, перемычка.

IT (*abbr. of* ***information technology***) информатика.

it /ɪt/ *pron.*
1 он (она, оно); (*impersonal, often untranslated*) это; **who is ~?** кто это?; **~'s the postman** это почтальон; **I don't speak Russian but I understand ~** я не говорю по-русски, но понимаю.
2 (*impersonal or indefinite*): **~ is cold** холодно; **~ is 6 o'clock** (сейчас) шесть часов; **~ is raining** идёт дождь; **~ is 5 miles to Oxford** до Оксфорда пять миль.
3 (*emph. another word*): **~ was John who laughed** это Джон смеялся.

Italian /ɪ'tæljən/ *n.* (*person*) итальян|ец (*fem.* -ка); (*language*) итальянский язык.
■ *adj.* итальянский.

italics /ɪ'tælɪks/ *n.* курсив; **in ~** курсивом.

Italy /'ɪtəlɪ/ *n.* Италия.

itch /ɪtʃ/ *n.* зуд.
■ *v.i.* чесаться (*impf.*).

itchy /'ɪtʃɪ/ *adj.* (**itchier, itchiest**) (*skin*) зудящий; (*causing itchiness*) вызывающий зуд.

item /'aɪtəm/ *n.* пункт, номер; **news ~** (короткое) сообщение.

itemize /'aɪtəmaɪz/ *v.t.* переч|ислять, -ислить; сост|авлять, -авить перечень + *g.*; **an ~d account** подробный счёт.

itinerary /aɪ'tɪnərərɪ/ *n.* маршрут, план пути (*m.*).

its /ɪts/ *poss. adj.* его, её; (*pert. to subject of sentence*) свой; **the horse broke ~ leg** лошадь сломала ногу.

itself /ɪt'self/ *n.*
1 (*refl.*) себя; -ся/-сь (*suff.*); **the cat was washing ~** кот умывался.
2 (*emph.*) сам; **she is kindness ~** она сама доброта; **by ~** (*alone*) один, одиноко, в отдалении; (*automatically*) самостоятельно.

ITV (*abbr. of* ***Independent Television***) (*Br.*) Независимое (коммерческое) телевидение (*телеканал в Великобритании*).

IVF *n.* (*abbr. of* ***in vitro fertilization***) экстракорпоральное оплодотворение.

ivory /'aɪvərɪ/ *n.*
1 (*substance*) слоновая кость; **the I~ Coast** Кот-д'Ивуар.
2 (*colour*) цвет слоновой кости.

ivy /'aɪvɪ/ *n.* плющ.

jab /dʒæb/ *n.*
1 (*sharp blow*) тычо́к.
2 (*Br. coll., injection*) уко́л.
■ *v.t.* (**jabbed, jabbing**)
1 (*poke*) ты́кать, ткну́ть.
2 (*thrust*) втыка́ть, воткну́ть.

jabber /ˈdʒæbə(r)/ *n.* трескотня́.
■ *v.t.* тарато́рить, про-.
■ *v.i.* треща́ть (*impf.*), тарато́рить (*impf.*).

jack /dʒæk/ *n.*
1 (*name*): **~ of all trades** ма́стер на все ру́ки.
2 (*card*) вале́т.
3 (*lifting device*) домкра́т.
■ *v.t.*: **~ in** (*Br. coll., give up*) бр|оса́ть, -о́сить.
■ *cpds.* **~daw** *n.* га́лка; **~knife** *v.i.*: **the lorry ~knifed** грузови́к занесло́; **~pot** *n.* джекпо́т; **he hit the ~pot** (*fig.*) ему́ кру́пно повезло́.

jackal /ˈdʒæk(ə)l/ *n.* шака́л.

jacket /ˈdʒækɪt/ *n.* (*informal*) ку́ртка; (*part of suit*) пиджа́к.

jade¹ /dʒeɪd/ *n.* (*min.*) нефри́т.

jade² /dʒeɪd/ *v.t.* (*esp. p.p.*): **you look ~d** у вас утомлённый вид.

jagged /ˈdʒægɪd/ *adj.* зубча́тый.

jaguar /ˈdʒægjʊə(r)/ *n.* ягуа́р.

jail /dʒeɪl/ *n.* тюрьма́.
■ *v.t.* заключ|а́ть, -и́ть в тюрьму́.

jailer /ˈdʒeɪlə(r)/ *n.* тюре́мщик.

jam¹ /dʒæm/ *n.* (*Br., preserve*) джем.

jam² /dʒæm/ *n.* (*crush*) да́вка; **traffic ~** про́бка.
■ *v.t.* (**jammed, jamming**)
1 (*cram*) зап|и́хивать, -ихну́ть; **she ~med everything into the cupboard** она́ всё запихну́ла в шкаф; (*force*): **he ~med the brakes on** он ре́зко затормози́л.
2 (*cause to stick or stop*): **the machine got ~med** стано́к засто́порило/закли́нило.
3 (*obstruct*) заб|ива́ть, -и́ть; **the crowds ~med every exit** толпа́ заби́ла все вы́ходы; (*radio*) глуши́ть, за-.
■ *v.i.* (**jammed, jamming**) (*get stuck*) застр|ева́ть, -я́ть.
■ *cpd.* **~-packed** *adj.* наби́тый до отка́за.

Jamaica /dʒəˈmeɪkə/ *n.* Яма́йка.

Jamaican /dʒəˈmeɪkən/ *n.* яма́|ец (*fem.* -йка).
■ *adj.* яма́йский.

jangle /ˈdʒæŋg(ə)l/ *n.* ре́зкий звук.
■ *v.i.* бренча́ть (*impf.*).
■ *v.t.* звя́к|ать, -нуть в + *a.*

janitor /ˈdʒænɪtə(r)/ *n.* вахтёр.

January /ˈdʒænjʊərɪ/ *n.* янва́рь (*m.*).

Japan /dʒəˈpæn/ *n.* Япо́ния.

Japanese /dʒæpəˈniːz/ *n.* (*pl.* **~**) (*person*) япо́н|ец (*fem.* -ка); (*language*) япо́нский язы́к.
■ *adj.* япо́нский.

japonica /dʒəˈpɒnɪkə/ *n.* айва́ япо́нская.

jar¹ /dʒɑː(r)/ *n.* (*vessel*) ба́нка.

jar² /dʒɑː(r)/ *v.t.* (**jarred, jarring**) сотряс|а́ть, -ти́.
■ *v.i.* (**jarred, jarring**)
1 (*sound discordantly*) дисгармони́ровать (*impf.*).
2: **~ on** (*irritate*) раздраж|а́ть, -и́ть.

jargon /ˈdʒɑːgən/ *n.* жарго́н.

jasmine /ˈdʒæzmɪn/ *n.* жасми́н.

jaundice /ˈdʒɔːndɪs/ *n.* желту́ха.
■ *v.t.* (*usu. p.p.*): **he took a ~d view of the affair** он мра́чно смотре́л на э́то де́ло.

jaunt /dʒɔːnt/ *n.* увесели́тельная пое́здка/прогу́лка.

jaunty /ˈdʒɔːntɪ/ *adj.* (**jauntier, jauntiest**) бо́йкий.

javelin /ˈdʒævlɪn/ *n.* (мета́тельное) копьё.

jaw /dʒɔː/ *n.* че́люсть.

jay /dʒeɪ/ *n.* со́йка.
■ *cpds.* **~walk** *v.i.* пере|ходи́ть, -йти́ у́лицу неосторо́жно; **~walker** *n.* неосторо́жный пешехо́д.

jazz /dʒæz/ *n.* джаз.
■ *v.t.*: **~ up** (*fig., enliven*) ожив|ля́ть, -и́ть.
■ *cpd.* **~ band** *n.* джаз-орке́стр, джаз-ба́нд.

jazzy /ˈdʒæzɪ/ *adj.* (**jazzier, jazziest**) бро́ский, я́ркий.

JCB /dʒeɪsiːˈbiː/ *n.* (*Br. propr.*) экскава́тор.

JCR (*abbr. of* ***Junior Common Room***) (*Br.*) студе́нческая ко́мната о́тдыха.

jealous /ˈdʒeləs/ *adj.*
1 (*of affection etc.*) ревни́вый; **she was ~ of her husband's secretary** она́ ревнова́ла му́жа к секрета́рше.
2 (*envious*) зави́стливый; **I am ~ of his success!** я зави́дую его́ успе́ху.

jealousy /ˈdʒeləsɪ/ *n.* ре́вность; (*envy*) за́висть.

jeans /dʒiːnz/ *n. pl.* джи́нс|ы (*pl., g.* -ов).

jeep /dʒiːp/ *n.* (*propr.*) джип.

jeer /dʒɪə(r)/ *v.t. & i.* (*taunt*) глуми́ться (*impf.*) (над + *i.*); (*deride*) насмеха́ться (*impf.*) (над + *i.*).

jelly /ˈdʒelɪ/ *n.*
1 (*Br.*) желе́ (*nt. indecl.*).
2 (*US, jam*) джем.
■ *cpd.* **~fish** *n.* меду́за.

jeopardize /ˈdʒepədaɪz/ *v.t.* (*endanger*) подв|ерга́ть, -е́ргнуть опа́сности; (*put at risk*) рискова́ть (*impf.*) + *i.*

jeopardy /ˈdʒepədɪ/ *n.* опа́сность; **his life was in ~** его́ жизнь была́ в опа́сности.

jerk /dʒɜːk/ *n.*
1 (*pull*) рыво́к; (*jolt*) уда́р.
2 (*twitch*) су́дорожное вздра́гивание.
3 (*US coll., idiot*) ду́рень (*m.*), тупи́ца (*c.g.*).
■ *v.t.* дёр|гать, -нуть.
■ *v.i.*: **the train ~ed to a halt** по́езд ре́зко останови́лся.

jerky /ˈdʒɜːkɪ/ *adj.* (**jerkier, jerkiest**) су́дорожный.

jersey /ˈdʒɜːzɪ/ *n.* (*pl.* **~s**) свитер.
jest /dʒest/ *n.* шутка; **in ~** в шутку.
■ *v.i.* шутить, по-.
jester /ˈdʒestə(r)/ *n.* (*hist.*) шут.
Jesus /ˈdʒiːzəs/ *n.* Иисус; (*as expletive*): **~ (Christ)!** боже!
jet¹ /dʒet/ *n.* (*min.*) гагат.
■ *adj.* (**~-black**) чёрный как смоль.
jet² /dʒet/ *n.*
1 (*stream of water etc.*) струя.
2 (**~ engine**) реактивный двигатель; (**~ aircraft**) реактивный самолёт.
■ *v.i.* (**jetted, jetting**) летать (*indet.*) на реактивном самолёте.
■ *cpds.* **~ lag** *n.* нарушение суточного ритма; **~ set** *n.* международная элита.
jettison /ˈdʒetɪs(ə)n/ *v.t.* (*lit., fig.*) выбрасывать, выбросить (за борт).
jetty /ˈdʒetɪ/ *n.* пристань, мол.
Jew /dʒuː/ *n.* еврей (*fem.* -ка).
jewel /ˈdʒuːəl/ *n.* (*precious stone*) драгоценный камень; (*fig.*) сокровище.
jeweller /ˈdʒuːələ(r)/ (*US* **jeweler**) *n.* ювелир.
jewellery /ˈdʒuːəlrɪ/ (*US also* **jewelry**) *n.* ювелирные изделия; драгоценности (*f. pl.*).
Jewish /ˈdʒuːɪʃ/ *adj.* еврейский.
jib /dʒɪb/ *n.*
1 (*naut.*) кливер.
2 (*of crane*) стрела.
jibe /dʒaɪb/ *n.* (*taunt*) насмешка.
jiffy /ˈdʒɪfɪ/ *n.* (*coll.*) миг; **in a ~** мигом.
jig /dʒɪg/ *n.* (*dance*) джига.
jiggle /ˈdʒɪg(ə)l/ *v.t.* покачивать (*impf.*).
jigsaw /ˈdʒɪgsɔː/ *n.* (*tool*) ажурная пила; (*puzzle*) (составная) картинка-загадка, пазл.
jihad *n.* (*relig.*) джихад.
jilt /dʒɪlt/ *v.t.* бр|осать, -осить.
jingle /ˈdʒɪŋg(ə)l/ *n.* (*ringing sound*) звяканье; (*advertising tune*) рекламная песенка.
■ *v.t. & i.* звяк|ать, -нуть (+ *i.*).
jingoistic /dʒɪŋgəʊˈɪstɪk/ *adj.* шовинистический.
jinx /dʒɪŋks/ *n.* (*coll.*) злые чары (*f. pl.*); **put a ~ on** сглазить (*pf.*).
jitter /ˈdʒɪtə(r)/ *n.* (*coll.*): **have the ~s** нервничать (*impf.*).
jittery /ˈdʒɪtərɪ/ *adj.* (*coll.*) нервный.
jive /dʒaɪv/ *n.* джайв (*танец*).
■ *v.i.* исп|олнять, -олнить (*impf.*) джайв.
job /dʒɒb/ *n.*
1 (*piece of work*) работа; задание; **my ~ is to wash the dishes** моя обязанность — мыть посуду; (*difficult task*): **we had a ~ finding them** мы с трудом их отыскали.
2 (*product of work*): **you've made a good ~ of that** вы сделали это хорошо.
3 (*employment; position*) работа; место; **what is your ~?** какая у вас работа?; **get a ~** на|ходить, -йти работу.
4 (*circumstance, fact*): **it's a good ~ you stayed at home** (*Br.*) хорошо, что вы остались дома.
■ *cpd.* **~-seeker** *n.* лицо, ищущее работу; **~-share** *v.i.* делить (*impf.*) рабочее место и зарплату.
jobcentre /ˈdʒɒbsentə(r)/ *n.* (*Br.*) центр по трудоустройству, биржа труда.
jobless /ˈdʒɒblɪs/ *adj.* безработный.
jockey /ˈdʒɒkɪ/ *n.* (*pl.* **~s**) жокей.
jockstrap /ˈdʒɒkstræp/ *n.* суспензорий.
jocular /ˈdʒɒkjʊlə(r)/ *adj.* весёлый.
jodhpurs /ˈdʒɒdpəz/ *n.* брюк|и (*pl., g.* —) для верховой езды.
jog /dʒɒg/ *n.*
1 (*nudge*) толчок.
2 (*trot*) бег трусцой.
■ *v.t.* (**jogged, jogging**): **~ s.o.'s elbow** толк|ать, -нуть кого-н. под локоть; **~ s.o.'s memory** освеж|ать, -ить чью-н. память.
■ *v.i.* (**jogged, jogging**) бегать (*indet.*) трусцой.
jogger /ˈdʒɒgə(r)/ *n.* любитель (*m.*) оздоровительного бега.
jogging /ˈdʒɒgɪŋ/ *n.* оздоровительный бег; бег трусцой.
join /dʒɔɪn/ *n.* связь, соединение.
■ *v.t.* 1 (*connect*) соедин|ять, -ить; **the towns are ~ed by a railway** эти города соединяет железная дорога.
2 (*enter*) вступ|ать, -ить в + *a.*; **~ a club** вступ|ать, -ить в клуб; **~ the army** идти, пойти в армию.
3 (*enter s.o.'s company*) присоедин|яться, -иться к + *d.*; (*meet*) встр|ечаться, -етиться с + *i.*; **may I ~ you?** разрешите присоединиться к вам?
4 (*flow or lead into*) соедин|яться, -иться с + *i.*; сл|иваться, -иться с + *i.*
■ *v.i.* 1 (*be connected*) соедин|яться, -иться; (*be united*) объедин|яться, -иться; (*come together*) сходиться, сойтись; (*flow together*) сл|иваться, -иться.
2 (*become a member*) стать (*impf.*) членом (*чего*).
■ *with advs.*: **~ in** *v.i.* (*take part*) прин|имать, -ять участие; (*in conversation, discussion etc.*) вступ|ать, -ить в + *a.*; **~ up** *v.t. & i.* соедин|ять(ся), -ить(ся); *v.i.* (*coll., enlist*) идти, пойти в армию.
joiner /ˈdʒɔɪnə(r)/ *n.* столяр.
joinery /ˈdʒɔɪnərɪ/ *n.* столярная работа; **do, practise ~** столярничать (*impf.*).
joint /dʒɔɪnt/ *n.*
1 (*place of juncture; means of joining*) соединение; стык.
2 (*anat.*) сустав, сочленение.
3: **a ~ of meat** (*Br.*) кусок мяса (*к обеду*).
4 (*coll.*) (*place*) притон.
5 (*sl., marijuana cigarette*) косяк.
■ *adj.* 1 (*combined; shared*) совместный; **~ action** совместные действия (*nt. pl.*); (*common*) общий; **~ account** общий/совместный счёт; **~ efforts** общие/совместные усилия; **~ venture** совместное предприятие.
2 (*sharing*): **~ owner** совладелец.
joist /dʒɔɪst/ *n.* балка.
jok|e /dʒəʊk/ *n.* шутка; (*story*) анекдот; (*witticism*) острота; (*laughing stock*) посмешище; **it's no ~e** это не шутка!; **crack, make a ~e** шутить, по-; **play a ~e on s.o.** сыграть (*pf.*) шутку с кем-н.
■ *v.i.* шутить, по-; **I was only ~ing** я всего лишь пошутил.
joker /ˈdʒəʊkə(r)/ *n.* (*one who jokes*) шутник;

J

(*cards*) джо́кер.

jollity /ˈdʒɒlɪtɪ/ *n.* весе́лье, увеселе́ние.

jolly /ˈdʒɒlɪ/ *adj.* (**jollier, jolliest**) (*cheerful*) весёлый; (*entertaining*) ра́достный.
■ *adv.* (*Br. coll., very*) о́чень.

jolt /dʒɒlt/ *n.* толчо́к; (*fig.*) уда́р, потрясе́ние.
■ *v.t.* & *i.* трясти́(сь) (*impf.*).

Jordan /ˈdʒɔːd(ə)n/ *n.* (*country*) Иорда́ния; (*river*) Иорда́н.

Jordanian /dʒɔːˈdeɪnɪən/ *n.* иорда́н|ец (*fem.* -ка).
■ *adj.* иорда́нский.

jostle /ˈdʒɒs(ə)l/ *v.t.* толк|а́ть, -ну́ть.

jot /dʒɒt/ *v.t.* (**jotted, jotting**): **~ down** набр|а́сывать, -оса́ть.

journal /ˈdʒəːn(ə)l/ *n.* журна́л.

journalism /ˈdʒəːnəlɪz(ə)m/ *n.* журнали́стика.

journalist /ˈdʒəːnəlɪst/ *n.* журнали́ст (*fem.* -ка).

journey /ˈdʒəːnɪ/ *n.* (*pl.* **~s**) (*expedition; trip*) (*long*) путеше́ствие; (*shorter*) пое́здка; **be, go on a ~** путеше́ствовать (*impf.*); (*travel; travelling time*) путь.
■ *v.i.* (**journeys, journeyed**) путеше́ствовать (*impf.*).

joust /dʒaʊst/ *n.* (ры́царский) турни́р.
■ *v.i.* состяза́ться (*impf.*) на турни́ре.

jovial /ˈdʒəʊvɪəl/ *adj.* весёлый.

joy /dʒɔɪ/ *n.* (*gladness*) ра́дость.
■ *cpds.* **~ride** *n.* пое́здка ра́ди заба́вы на укра́денной автомаши́не; **~rider** *n.* автово́р-лиха́ч, уго́нщик-лиха́ч.
■ *cpd.* **~rider** *n.* лиха́ч, управля́ющий у́гнанным автомоби́лем; **~riding** *n.* риско́ванная езда́ на у́гнанном автомоби́ле.

joyful /ˈdʒɔɪfʊl/ *adj.* ра́достный.

joyless /ˈdʒɔɪlɪs/ *adj.* безра́достный.

joyous /ˈdʒɔɪəs/ *adj.* ра́достный; (*happy*) весёлый.

jubilant /ˈdʒuːbɪlənt/ *adj.* лику́ющий.

jubilee /ˈdʒuːbɪliː/ *n.* юбиле́й.

Judaism /ˈdʒuːdeɪɪz(ə)m/ *n.* иудаи́зм.

judge /dʒʌdʒ/ *n.*
1 (*legal functionary*) судья́ (*m.*).
2 (*arbiter*) арби́тр, судья́.
3 (*expert*) знато́к, цени́тель (*m.*).
■ *v.t.* 1 (*pass ~ment on*) суди́ть (*impf.*) о + *i.*; (*assess*) оце́н|ивать, -и́ть.
2 (*consider*) счита́ть (*impf.*); **he was ~d to be innocent** его́ сочли́ невино́вным.
■ *v.i.* суди́ть (*impf.*); **to ~ from what you say** су́дя по тому́, что вы сказа́ли.

judg(e)ment /ˈdʒʌdʒmənt/ *n.*
1 (*sentence*) суде́бное реше́ние, пригово́р.
2 (*opinion; estimation*) мне́ние; сужде́ние.

judicial /dʒuːˈdɪʃ(ə)l/ *adj.* суде́бный.

judiciary /dʒuːˈdɪʃɪərɪ/ *n.* су́дьи (*m. pl.*); суде́бная власть.

judicious /dʒuːˈdɪʃəs/ *adj.* рассуди́тельный.

judo /ˈdʒuːdəʊ/ *n.* дзюдо́ (*nt. indecl.*).

jug /dʒʌg/ *n.* кувши́н.

juggernaut /ˈdʒʌgənɔːt/ *n.* (*Br., lorry*) многото́нный грузови́к.

juggle /ˈdʒʌg(ə)l/ *v.i.* (*lit., fig.*) жонгли́ровать (*impf.*).

juggler /ˈdʒʌglə(r)/ *n.* жонглёр.

jugular /ˈdʒʌgjʊlə(r)/ *n.* (**~ vein**) яре́мная ве́на.

juice /dʒuːs/ *n.* (*bot., physiol.*) сок; (*fruit ~*) (фрукто́вый) сок.

juicer /ˈdʒuːsə(r)/ *n.* соковыжима́лка.

juicy /ˈdʒuːsɪ/ *adj.* (**juicier, juiciest**) со́чный; (*coll., scandalous*) сма́чный.

jukebox /ˈdʒuːkbɒks/ *n.* музыка́льный автома́т (*для проигрывания дисков*).

July /dʒuːˈlaɪ/ *n.* ию́ль (*m.*).

jumble /ˈdʒʌmb(ə)l/ *n.* (*untidy heap*) ку́ча; (*muddle*) беспоря́док, пу́таница; (*coll., unwanted articles*) хлам; **~ sale** (*Br.*) дешёвая распрода́жа (*в благотворительных целях*).
■ *v.t.* (*also* **~ up**) переме́ш|ивать, -а́ть.

jumbo /ˈdʒʌmbəʊ/ *n.* (*pl.* **~s**) (*also* **~ jet**) реакти́вный ла́йнер; (*attr., huge*) гига́нтский.

jump /dʒʌmp/ *n.* прыжо́к, скачо́к; (*obstacle*) препя́тствие; (*fig., abrupt rise*) скачо́к; (*fig., start, shock*) вздра́гивание.
■ *v.t.* 1 (*~ over, across*) перепры́г|ивать, -нуть че́рез + *a.*
2 (*var. fig. uses*): **~ the queue** про|ходи́ть, -йти́ без о́череди; **you've ~ed a few lines** вы пропусти́ли (*or* перескочи́ли че́рез) не́сколько строк.
■ *v.i.* 1 пры́г|ать, -нуть; (*on horseback*) вск|а́кивать, -очи́ть.
2 (*fig.*) переска́кивать (*impf.*); **he ~ed from one topic to another** он переска́кивал с одно́й те́мы на другу́ю.
3 (*start*) подск|а́кивать, -очи́ть; **the noise made me ~** звук заста́вил меня́ подскочи́ть.
4 (*make sudden movement*) подск|а́кивать, -очи́ть; **shares ~ed to a new level** а́кции подскочи́ли в цене́.
5 (*fig. uses*): **I would ~ at the chance** я бы ухвати́лся за э́ту возмо́жность; **~ on s.o.** (*attack*) набр|а́сываться, -о́ситься на кого́-н.; (*rebuke*) ре́зко оса|жда́ть, -ди́ть кого́-н.
■ *with advs.*: **he ~ed back in surprise** он отпря́нул в удивле́нии; **she ~ed down from the fence** она́ спры́гнула с забо́ра; **if you want a lift, ~ in!** е́сли хоти́те, что́бы я вас подбро́сил, залеза́йте (в маши́ну)!; **~ up from one's chair** вск|а́кивать, -очи́ть со сту́ла; **~ up and down** пры́гать/подпры́гивать (*impf.*) вверх и вниз.
■ *cpd.* **~ lead** *n.* (*Br.*) электри́ческий ка́бель (для за́пуска дви́гателя автомоби́ля от посторо́ннего исто́чника эне́ргии).

jumper /ˈdʒʌmpə(r)/ *n.* (*Br., sweater*) дже́мпер; (*US, pinafore dress*) сарафа́н.

jumpy /ˈdʒʌmpɪ/ *adj.* (**jumpier, jumpiest**) не́рвный, дёрганый.

junction /ˈdʒʌŋkʃ(ə)n/ *n.* (*meeting point: of railways*) у́зел; (*of roads*) пересече́ние (доро́г); (*of rivers*) слия́ние.

juncture /ˈdʒʌŋktʃə(r)/ *n.* (*joining*) соедине́ние; **at a critical ~** в крити́ческий моме́нт; **at this ~** в да́нный моме́нт.

June /dʒuːn/ *n.* ию́нь (*m.*).

jungle /ˈdʒʌŋg(ə)l/ *n.* джу́нгл|и (*pl., g.* -ей).

junior /ˈdʒuːnɪə(r)/ *n.*: **he is my ~ by 5 years** он на пять лет мла́дше меня́.
■ *adj.* мла́дший; **~ partner** мла́дший партнёр; **~ school** (*Br.*) нача́льная шко́ла (*для детей 7—11 лет*); **~ high school** (*US*)

неполная средняя школа (*7, 8, 9 классы*).

juniper /ˈdʒu:nɪpə(r)/ *n.* можжевельник; (*attr.*) можжевёловый.

junk /dʒʌŋk/ *n.* (*rubbish*) хлам; **~ food** неполноценная пища.
■ *cpds.* **~ mail** *n.* рекламные рассылки; **~ shop** *n.* лавка старьёвщика.

junk|ie, -y /ˈdʒʌŋkɪ/ *n.* (*sl., drug addict*) наркоман.

Jupiter /ˈdʒu:pɪtə(r)/ *n.* (*myth., astron.*) Юпитер.

jurisdiction /dʒʊərɪsˈdɪkʃ(ə)n/ *n.* (*legal authority*) юрисдикция; **have ~ over** иметь (*impf.*) юрисдикцию над + *i.*

jurisprudence /dʒʊərɪsˈpru:d(ə)ns/ *n.* юриспруденция.

juror /ˈdʒʊərə(r)/ *n.* присяжный (заседатель).

jury /ˈdʒʊərɪ/ *n.* присяжные (заседатели) (*m. pl.*).
■ *cpd.* **~ box** *n.* скамья присяжных.

just /dʒʌst/ *adj.* (*equitable*) справедливый; (*deserved*) справедливый, заслуженный.
■ *adv.* 1 точно, как раз, именно; **it was ~ 3 o'clock** было ровно три часа.
2: **~ like, as** (*expr. comparison*) точно так же, как (и); точно, как; **that's ~ like him** (*typical*) это так похоже на него; **he is ~ as lazy as ever** он всё такой же ленивый; **it's ~ as well I warned you** хорошо, что я вас предупредил.
3: **~ about** (*approximately*): **~ about right** почти так/правильно; (*almost*): **I've ~ about finished** я почти (за)кончил.
4 (*expr. time*) только что; (*very recently*): **I saw him ~ now** я только что видел его; **~ as** (*expr. time*) (как) только; **~ as he entered the room** только он вошёл в комнату; (*at this moment*): **I'm ~ off** я ухожу прямо сейчас/как раз сейчас.
5 (*barely*) едва; **I ~ caught the train** я едва успел на поезд; **he had ~ come in when the phone rang** только он вошёл, как зазвонил телефон; **(wait) ~ a minute!** (одну) минут(к)у!
6 (*merely*) только; **~ listen to this!** вы только послушайте!; **I went ~ to hear him** я пошёл только, чтобы послушать его; **~ fancy!** подумать только!; **~ you wait!** ну, погоди!; **~ in case** на всякий случай.
7 (*positively, absolutely*) так и; просто(-напросто); **it's ~ splendid!** это просто великолепно!; **not ~ yet** ещё не/нет.

justice /ˈdʒʌstɪs/ *n.*
1 (*fairness; equity*) справедливость; **to do him ~** отдавая ему должное.
2 (*system of institutions*) правосудие, юстиция; **bring s.o. to ~** отд|авать, -ать кого-н. под суд.
3: **J~ of the Peace** (*Br.*) мировой судья.

justifiable /ˈdʒʌstɪfaɪəb(ə)l/ *adj.* оправданный.

justification /dʒʌstɪfɪˈkeɪʃ(ə)n/ *n.* оправдание; **he objected, and with ~** он возразил и не без оснований.

justif|y /ˈdʒʌstɪfaɪ/ *v.t.* оправд|ывать, -ать; **I was ~ied in suspecting ...** я имел все основания подозревать...; **~y o.s.** оправд|ываться, -аться.

jut /dʒʌt/ *v.i.* (**jutted, jutting**) (*usu.* **~ out**) выступать (*impf.*); выдаваться (*impf.*).

juvenile /ˈdʒu:vənaɪl/ *n.* подросток.
■ *adj.* юный, юношеский; **~ delinquent** несовершеннолетний преступник/правонарушитель; **~ delinquency** преступность среди несовершеннолетних, подростковая преступность.

juxtapose /dʒʌkstəˈpəʊz/ *v.t.* поме|щать, -стить бок о бок; (*for comparison*) сопост|авлять, -авить (*кого с кем or что с чем*).

juxtaposition /dʒʌkstəpəˈzɪʃ(ə)n/ *n.* соседство, близость; (*for comparison*) сопоставление.

Kk

Kabul /ˈkɑ:bʊl/ *n.* Кабул.

kale /keɪl/ *n.* листовая капуста.

kaleidoscope /kəˈlaɪdəskəʊp/ *n.* калейдоскоп.

kangaroo /kæŋgəˈru:/ *n.* кенгуру (*m. indecl.*).

karaoke /kærɪˈəʊkɪ/ *n.* караоке (*nt. indecl.*).

karate /kəˈrɑ:tɪ/ *n.* карате (*nt. indecl.*).

Kashmir /kæʃˈmɪə(r)/ *n.* Кашмир.

kayak /ˈkaɪæk/ *n.* каяк (*эскимосская лодка; лёгкая спортивная одноместная лодка*).

Kazakh /kəˈzæk/ *n.* (*pl.* **~s**) (*person*) каза|х (*fem.* -шка); (*language*) казахский язык.

Kazakhstan /kæzəkˈstɑ:n/ *n.* Казахстан.

kebab /kɪˈbæb/ *n.* шашлык.

keel /ki:l/ *n.* киль (*m.*).
■ *v.i.*: **~ over** опроки|дываться, -нуться.

keen /ki:n/ *adj.* (*lit., fig.: sharp, acute*) острый; **~ eyesight** острое зрение; (*piercing*) пронзительный; (*strong, intense*) сильный; **~ interest** живой интерес; (*eager; energetic*) ревностный; **a ~ pupil** усердный ученик; **~ competition** трудное соревнование; (*enthusiastic*) страстный; **a ~ sportsman** страстный спортсмен; **be ~ on** сильно/страстно увл|екаться, -ечься + *i.*; **I am not ~ on chess** я не особенно увлекаюсь шахматами; **he is ~ on your coming** ему очень хочется, чтобы вы пришли.

keep /ki:p/ *n.*
1 (*sustenance*) пропитание; **earn one's ~** зараб|атывать, -отать себе на пропитание.
2: **for ~s** насовсем (*coll.*).
■ *v.t.* (*past and p.p.* **kept**)

1 (*retain possession of*) держа́ть (*impf.*), не отдава́ть (*impf.*); ост|авля́ть, -а́вить (себе́ *or* при себе́); (*preserve*) храни́ть (*impf.*); сохран|я́ть, -и́ть; (*save, put by*): **I shall ~ this paper to show my mother** я сохраню́ э́ту газе́ту, что́бы показа́ть ма́тери.
2 (*cause to remain*): **the traffic kept me awake** у́личное движе́ние не дава́ло мне спать; **the garden ~s me busy** сад не даёт мне сиде́ть сложа́ ру́ки; **~ the house clean** содержа́ть (*impf.*) дом в чистоте́/поря́дке; **~ it to yourself** пома́лкивайте об э́том (*coll.*); **~ an eye on sth.** пригля́дывать (*impf.*) за чем-н.; **where do you ~ the salt?** где вы храни́те соль?
3 (*cause to continue*): **I don't like to be kept waiting** я не люблю́, когда́ меня́ заставля́ют ждать; **that will ~ you going till lunchtime** тепе́рь вы продéржитесь до обе́да.
4 (*remain in, on*): **~ one's seat** (*remain sitting*) не встава́ть (*impf.*); (*retain, preserve*): **~ one's balance** сохраня́ть/уде́рживать (*both impf.*) равнове́сие.
5 (*have charge of; manage; maintain*) име́ть, держа́ть, содержа́ть (*all impf.*); **the shop was kept by an Italian** владе́льцем ла́вки был италья́нец; **he wants to ~ pigs** он хо́чет держа́ть свине́й.
6 (*accounts, records, diary*) вести́ (*det.*).
7 (*detain*) заде́рж|ивать, -а́ть; **I won't ~ you** я вас не задержу́.
8 (*fulfil, be faithful to*) сде́рж|ивать, -а́ть; соблю|да́ть, -сти́; **~ the law** соблюда́ть зако́н; **~ one's word** держа́ть, с- сло́во; **I can't ~ the appointment** я не могу́ прийти́ на встре́чу.
■ *v.i.* (*past and p.p.* **kept**)
1 (*remain*) держа́ться (*impf.*); остава́ться (*impf.*); **the weather kept fine** стоя́ла хоро́шая пого́да; **I can't ~ warm here** я не могу́ здесь согре́ться; **how are you ~ing?** (*Br.*) как пожива́ете?; как жизнь? (*coll.*); **I exercise to ~ fit** я занима́юсь гимна́стикой/спо́ртом, что́бы быть в фо́рме; **we still ~ in touch** мы всё ещё подде́рживаем отноше́ния/связь.
2 (*continue*) продолжа́ть (*impf.*) + *inf.*; **she ~s giggling** она́ всё хихи́кает.
3 (*remain fresh*): **the food will ~ in the refrigerator** еда́ в холоди́льнике не испо́ртится.
■ *with preps.*: **you must ~ at it till it's finished** не отвлека́йтесь, пока́ не (за)ко́нчите; **what are you trying to ~ from me?** что вы скрыва́ете от меня́?; **'~ off the grass!'** «по газо́нам не ходи́ть»; **~ out of s.o.'s way** (*avoid him*) избега́ть (*impf.*) кого́-н.; **he cannot ~ out of trouble for long** он ве́чно попада́ет в исто́рии; **he ~s himself to himself** он замыка́ется в себе́; **~ to the path** держа́ться (*impf.*) тропи́нки; **~ to the point** не отклоня́ться (*impf.*) от те́мы.
■ *with advs.*: **~ away** *v.t.*: **she kept her daughter away from school** она́ не пуска́ла дочь в шко́лу; *v.i.*: **he tried to ~ away from them** он стара́лся их избега́ть; **~ back** *v.t.* (*restrain*) сде́рж|ивать, -а́ть; (*retain*): **they ~ back £100 from my wages** из мое́й зарпла́ты уде́рживают сто фу́нтов; (*repress*): **she could hardly ~ back her tears** она́ едва́ сде́рживала слёзы; **~ down** *v.t.*: **~ your voice down!** не повыша́йте го́лоса!; (*limit, control*): **they tried to ~ down expenses** они́ стара́лись расхо́довать как мо́жно ме́ньше; (*oppress*) держа́ть (*impf.*) в подчине́нии; (*digest*): **he can't ~ anything down** его́ желу́док ничего́ не принима́ет; **~ off** *v.t.* (*repel*): **my hat will ~ the rain off** моя́ шля́па защити́т меня́ от дождя́; *v.i.* (*stay at a distance*): **I hope the rain ~s off** я наде́юсь, что дождь не начнётся; **~ on** *v.t.* (*continue to employ, educate*): **they won't ~ you on after 60** они́ уво́лят вас, когда́ вам испо́лнится 60 лет; *v.i.* (*with pres. part., continue*): **she kept on glancing out of the window** она́ то и де́ло выгля́дывала из окна́; **he kept on reading** он продолжа́л чита́ть; **~ out** *v.t.* (*exclude*): **we put up a fence to ~ out trespassers** мы постро́или/поста́вили забо́р, что́бы посторо́нние не заходи́ли на террито́рию; *v.i.*: **'Private — ~ out!'** (*notice*) «посторо́нним вход воспрещён!»; **~ up** *v.t.* (*prevent from falling or sinking*): **he could not ~ his trousers up** у него́ всё вре́мя сва́ливались брю́ки; (*fig., sustain, maintain*): **~ one's strength up** подкрепля́ть (*impf.*) си́лы; (*continue*): **~ up the good work!** продолжа́йте в том же ду́хе!; **he could not ~ up the payments** он был не в состоя́нии регуля́рно плати́ть; (*prevent from going to bed*): **the baby kept us up half the night** ребёнок не дава́л нам спать полно́чи; *v.i.* (*stay level*): **we kept up with them the whole way** всю доро́гу мы не отстава́ли от них; (*remain in touch*): **I try to ~ up with the news** я стара́юсь следи́ть за собы́тиями.

keeper /ˈkiːpə(r)/ *n.* (*in zoo*) служи́тель (*m.*) (зоопа́рка); (*Br., museum ~*) смотри́тель (*m.*).

keeping /ˈkiːpɪŋ/ *n.*
1 : **in safe ~** в надёжных рука́х.
2 : **be in ~ with** соотве́тствовать (*impf.*) + *d.*

keg /keg/ *n.* бочо́нок.

kennel /ˈken(ə)l/ *n.* конура́.

Kenya /ˈkenjə/ *n.* Ке́ния.

Kenyan /ˈkenjən/ *n.* кени́|ец (*fem.* -йка).
■ *adj.* кени́йский.

kept /kept/ *past and p.p. of* ▸ **keep**

kerb /kɜːb/ (*US* **curb**) *n.* обо́чина.

kerfuffle /kəˈfʌf(ə)l/ *n.* (*Br.*) (*coll.*) шум, завару́ха.

kernel /ˈkɜːn(ə)l/ *n.* (*of nut or fruit stone*) ядро́.

keros|ene, -ine /ˈkerəsiːn/ *n.* кероси́н; (*attr.*) кероси́новый.

kestrel /ˈkestr(ə)l/ *n.* (*zool.*) пустельга́.

ketchup /ˈketʃʌp/ *n.* ке́тчуп.

kettle /ˈket(ə)l/ *n.* ча́йник.

key /kiː/ *n.* (*pl.* **keys**)
1 ключ.
2 (*fig., sth. providing access or solution*) ключ; **the ~ to understanding the political situation** ключ к понима́нию полити́ческой ситуа́ции.
3 (*attr., important, essential*) ключево́й, важне́йший.

4 (*of piano or computer*) кла́виша; (*pl.*) клавиату́ра.
5 (*mus.*) тона́льность.
■ *v.t.* (**keys, keyed**): ~ **up** взви́н|чивать, -ти́ть.
■ *cpds.* **~board** *n.* (*mus., comput.*) клавиату́ра; **~boarder** *n.* опера́тор компью́тера; **~board(s)** *n.* (*mus. instrument*) кла́вишные (*pl.*); **~hole** *n.* замо́чная сква́жина; **~hole surgery** *n.* (*Br.*) полостна́я опера́ция с минима́льным вскры́тием; ~ **ring** *n.* кольцо́ для ключе́й.

kg /ˈkɪləgræm/ *n.* (*abbr. of* ***kilogram(s)***) кг (килогра́мм).

KGB (*abbr. of Russian; hist.*) КГБ (Комите́т госуда́рственной безопа́сности).

khaki /ˈkɑːkɪ/ *n.* (*pl.* **~s**) ха́ки (*nt. indecl.*).
■ *adj.*: **a ~ shirt** руба́шка цве́та ха́ки.

kick /kɪk/ *n.*
1 уда́р, пино́к.
2 (*recoil*) отда́ча.
3 (*coll., stimulus*): **get a ~ out of sth.** получ|а́ть, -и́ть удово́льствие от чего́-н.
■ *v.t.* уд|аря́ть, -а́рить ного́й; **he ~ed me on the shin** он уда́рил меня́ по го́лени; **he ~ed the ball** он уда́рил по мячу́; **I could have ~ed myself** я рвал на себе́ во́лосы; ~ **the habit** (*coll., give up addiction*) бро́сить (*pf.*) употребля́ть нарко́тики/кури́ть/пить *и т. д.*
■ *v.i.* (*of animals*) ляга́ться (*impf.*); брыка́ться (*impf.*).
■ *with advs.*: ~ **about, around** *vv.t.*: **they were ~ing a ball about** они́ гоня́ли мяч; ~ **off** *v.i.* (*football*) нач|ина́ть, -а́ть игру́; (*coll., begin*) нач|ина́ть, -а́ть; ~ **out** *v.t.* (*eject, expel*) выгоня́ть, вы́гнать; ~ **up** *v.t.* (*coll., create*): ~ **up a row** устр|а́ивать, -о́ить сканда́л.
■ *cpds.* **~-boxing** *n.* кикбо́ксинг; **~-off** *n.* нача́ло (игры́); **~-start** *v.t.* (*lit. and fig.*): **to ~-start the economy** дать толчо́к эконо́мике.

kid[1] /kɪd/ *n.*
1 (*young goat*) козлёнок.
2 (*leather*) ла́йка; ~ **gloves** ла́йковые перча́тки.
3 (*coll., child*) малы́ш; **my ~ brother** мой мла́дший брат.

kid[2] /kɪd/ *v.t.* (**kidded, kidding**)
1 (*coll., deceive*) над|ува́ть, -у́ть; **who are you ~ding?** кого́ вы хоти́те обману́ть?
2 (*tease*) дразни́ть (*impf.*).
■ *v.i.* (**kidded, kidding**) (*tease with untruths*): **you're ~ding!** врёшь!

kidnap /ˈkɪdnæp/ *v.t.* (**kidnapped, kidnapping;** *US* **kidnaped, kidnaping**) пох|ища́ть, -и́тить.

kidnapper /ˈkɪdnæpə(r)/ *n.* похити́тель (*m.*).

kidney /ˈkɪdnɪ/ *n.* (*pl.* **~s**) по́чка.
■ *cpd.* ~ **bean** *n.* фасо́ль (*collect.*).

Kiev /ˈkiːef/ *n.* Ки́ев.

kill /kɪl/ *v.t.*
1 уб|ива́ть, -и́ть; (*rats etc.*) трави́ть (*impf.*); ~ **o.s.** ко́нчить самоуби́йством; (*fig., coll.*): **my feet are ~ing me** я без за́дних ног; ~ **time** уб|ива́ть, -и́ть вре́мя.
2 (*animals for food*) ре́зать, за-.
3 (*destroy*) уничт|ожа́ть, -о́жить; **this drug ~s the pain** э́то лека́рство снима́ет боль.
■ *cpd.* **~joy** *n.* брюзга́ (*c.g.*).

killer /ˈkɪlə(r)/ *n.* (*murderer*) уби́йца (*c.g.*); ~ **whale** каса́тка; (*coll., sth. hilarious*) что-н. умори́тельное.

killing /ˈkɪlɪŋ/ *n.* (*murder*) уби́йство; (*slaughter of animals*) убо́й, забо́й.

kiln /kɪln/ *n.* печь.

kilo /ˈkiːləʊ/ *n.* (*pl.* **kilos**) кило́ (*indecl.*).

kilobyte /ˈkɪləbaɪt/ *n.* килоба́йт.

kilogram /ˈkɪləgræm/ *n.* килогра́мм.

kilohertz /ˈkɪləhɜːts/ *n.* килоге́рц.

kilometre /ˈkɪləmiːtə(r)/ (*US* **kilometer**) *n.* киломе́тр.

kilowatt /ˈkɪləwɒt/ *n.* килова́тт.

kilt /kɪlt/ *n.* (шотла́ндская) ю́бка, килт.

kimono /kɪˈməʊnəʊ/ *n.* (*pl.* **~s**) кимоно́ (*nt. indecl.*).

kin /kɪn/ *n.* (*family*) семья́; (*relations*) родня́ (*collect.*); ро́дственники (*m. pl.*); **kith and ~** родны́е и бли́зкие; **next of ~** ближа́йш|ий ро́дственни|к (*fem.* -ая -ца).

kind /kaɪnd/ *n.*
1 (*sort, variety*) род, сорт, разнови́дность; **all ~s of goods** вся́кие/ра́зные това́ры; **a ~ of** своего́ ро́да; **what ~ of?** что за?; како́й?; **what ~ of a painter is he?** что он за худо́жник?
2: ~ **of** (*coll., to some extent*): **I ~ of expected it** я как бы ожида́л э́того.
3: **in ~** нату́рой; **pay in ~** плати́ть, за- нату́рой.
■ *adj.* до́брый, любе́зный.
■ *cpd.* **~-hearted** *adj.* добросерде́чный.

kindergarten /ˈkɪndəgɑːt(ə)n/ *n.* де́тский сад.

kindle /ˈkɪnd(ə)l/ *v.t.* разж|ига́ть, -е́чь; (*fig., arouse*) возбу|жда́ть, -ди́ть.

kindliness /ˈkaɪndlɪnɪs/ *n.* доброта́.

kindling /ˈkɪndlɪŋ/ *n.* (*firewood*) расто́пка; ще́пки (*f. pl.*).

kindly /ˈkaɪndlɪ/ *adj.* (**kindlier, kindliest**) до́брый, доброду́шный.
■ *adv.* 1 (*in a kind manner*) любе́зно, ми́ло.
2 (*please*): ~ **ring me tomorrow** бу́дьте добры́, позвони́те мне за́втра.
3: **he does not take ~ to criticism** он не лю́бит кри́тики.

kindness /ˈkaɪndnɪs/ *n.*
1 (*benevolence*) доброта́.
2 (*kind act*) любе́зность.

kindred /ˈkɪndrɪd/ *adj.* (*lit., fig.*) ро́дственный; ~ **ideas** ро́дственные иде́и; **a ~ spirit** родна́я душа́.

kinetic /kɪˈnetɪk/ *adj.* кинети́ческий.

king /kɪŋ/ *n.*
1 коро́ль (*m.*).
2 (*chess*) коро́ль; (*draughts, checkers*) да́мка; (*cards*): ~ **of diamonds** бубно́вый коро́ль.
■ *cpd.* **~fisher** *n.* (голубо́й) зиморо́док.

kingdom /ˈkɪŋdəm/ *n.* короле́вство; **the animal ~** живо́тное ца́рство.

kink /kɪŋk/ *n.* (*in rope etc.*) переги́б; (*in metal*) изги́б.

kinky /ˈkɪŋkɪ/ *adj.* (**kinkier, kinkiest**) (*twisted*) кручёный; (*coll., perverted*) извращённый; со стра́нностями.

kinsfolk /ˈkɪnzfəʊk/ *n.* родня́ (*collect.*).

kinsman /ˈkɪnzmən/ *n.* ро́дственник.
kinswoman /ˈkɪnzwʊmən/ *n.* ро́дственница.
kiosk /ˈki:ɒsk/ *n.* кио́ск; **telephone ~** (*Br.*) телефо́нная бу́дка, автома́т.
kip /kɪp/ (*Br.*) *n.* (*coll., sleep*) сон.
■ *v.i.* (**kipped, kipping**)
1 : **~ down for the night** устро́иться (*pf.*) на ночь.
2 (*sleep*) кема́рить, по- (*coll.*).
kipper /ˈkɪpə(r)/ *n.* копчёная селёдка.
Kirghiz /ˈkɜ:gɪz/ *n.* = **Kyrgyz**
Kirghizia /kɪəˈgɪzɪə/ *n.* = **Kyrgyzstan**
kiss /kɪs/ *n.* поцелу́й; **give s.o. a ~ on the cheek** поцелова́ть (*pf.*) кого́-н. в щёку; **~ of life** иску́сственное дыха́ние.
■ *v.t.* целова́ть, по-; **they ~ed each other goodbye** они́ поцелова́лись на проща́ние.
■ *v.i.* целова́ться, по-.
kit /kɪt/ *n.* (*Br., personal equipment, esp. clothing*) снаряже́ние; (*for particular activity*) набо́р/компле́кт (спорти́вных) принадле́жностей; (*set of parts for assembly*) констру́ктор.
■ *v.t. & i.* (**kitted, kitting**) (*Br.*) (*usu.* **~ out**) снаря|жа́ть(ся), -ди́ть(ся).
■ *cpd.* **~bag** *n.* вещмешо́к.
kitchen /ˈkɪtʃɪn/ *n.* ку́хня.
kite /kaɪt/ *n.* (возду́шный/бума́жный) змей; **fly a ~** (*lit.*) запус|ка́ть, -ти́ть змея́.
kitsch /kɪtʃ/ *n.* китч.
kitten /ˈkɪt(ə)n/ *n.* котёнок.
kitty /ˈkɪtɪ/ *n.* (*at cards etc.*) пу́лька, банк.
kiwi /ˈki:wi:/ *n.* (*pl.* **kiwis**) ки́ви (*m. indecl.*); **~ fruit** ки́ви (*m. & nt. indecl.*).
kleptomania /kleptəʊˈmeɪnɪə/ *n.* клептома́ния.
kleptomaniac /kleptəʊˈmeɪnɪæk/ *n.* клептома́н (*fem.* -ка).
km /ˈkɪləmi:tə(r)(z)/*n.* (*abbr. of* ***kilometre(s)***) км (киломе́тр).
knack /næk/ *n.* (*skill, faculty*) сноро́вка, уме́ние; **have the ~** име́ть (*impf.*) сноро́вку (**of/for:** в + *p.*).
knacker /ˈnækə(r)/ *n.* (*Br.*) ску́пщик ста́рых лошаде́й; **~'s yard** живодёрня.
knackered /ˈnækəd/ *adj.* (*Br. coll.*) измо́танный.
knapsack /ˈnæpsæk/ *n.* ра́нец.
knead /ni:d/ *v.t.* меси́ть, за-.
knee /ni:/ *n.* коле́н|о (*pl.* -и); **he was on his ~s** он стоя́л на коле́нях.
■ *v.t.* (**knees, kneed, kneeing**) уд|аря́ть, -а́рить коле́ном.
■ *cpds.* **~cap** *n.* коле́нная ча́шечка; **~-deep** *pred. adj. & adv.*: **he stood ~-deep in water** он стоя́л по коле́но в воде́; **~-length** *adj.* до коле́н.
kneel /ni:l/ *v.i.* (*past and p.p.* **knelt** *or esp. US* **kneeled**)
1 (*also* **~ down:** *go down on one's knees*) ста|нови́ться, -ть на коле́ни.
2 (*be in* **~***ing position*) стоя́ть (*impf.*) на коле́нях.
knelt /nelt/ *past and p.p. of* ▸ **kneel**
knew /nju:/ *past of* ▸ **know**
knickers /ˈnɪkəz/ *n.* (*Br., undergarment*) тру́сик|и (*pl., g.* -ов).
knick-knack /ˈnɪknæk/ *n.* безделу́шка.
knife /naɪf/ *n.* (*pl.* **knives**) нож.
■ *v.t.* (*kill*) зак|а́лывать, -оло́ть ножо́м; (*injure*) ра́нить (*impf.*).
■ *cpds.* **~-edge** *n.*: **on a ~-edge** (*fig.*) вися́щий на волоске́; **~point** *n.*: **at ~point** угрожа́я ножо́м.
knight /naɪt/ *n.*
1 (*hist.*) ры́царь (*m.*).
2 (*member of order*) кавале́р.
3 (*chess*) конь (*m.*).
■ *v.t.* ≈ присв|а́ивать, -о́ить (*кому*) ры́царское (ненасле́дственное дворя́нское) зва́ние.
knighthood /ˈnaɪthʊd/ *n.* ры́царство; ры́царское зва́ние.
knit /nɪt/ *v.t.* (**knitting;** *past and p.p.* **knitted** *or* **knit**) вяза́ть, с-.
■ *v.i.* (**knitting;** *past and p.p.* **knitted** *or* **knit**)
1 (*do* **~***ting*) вяза́ть (*impf.*).
2 (*of bones*) сраст|а́ться, -и́сь.
■ *cpd.* **~wear** *n.* трикота́жные изде́лия.
knitting /ˈnɪtɪŋ/ *n.* (*action*) вяза́ние; (*thing being knitted*) вяза́нье.
■ *cpd.* **~ needle** *n.* вяза́льная спи́ца.
knives /naɪvz/ *pl. of* ▸ **knife**
knob /nɒb/ *n.* (*handle*) ру́чка; (*button*) кно́пка.
knobbly /ˈnɒblɪ/ *adj.* шишкова́тый, бугорча́тый.
knock /nɒk/ *n.*
1 (*rap*) стук.
2 (*blow*) уда́р.
3 (*fig.*): **the pound has taken some ~s lately** в после́днее вре́мя положе́ние фу́нта (сте́рлингов) си́льно пошатну́лось.
■ *v.t.* 1 (*hit*) удар|я́ть, -а́рить; **the blow ~ed him flat** уда́р сбил его́ с ног; **he ~ed the glass off the table** он смахну́л стака́н со стола́; **I ~ed the gun out of his hand** я вы́бил из его́ руки́ пистоле́т.
2 (*fig. uses*): **~ into shape** прив|оди́ть, -ести́ в поря́док; **I'll ~ a pound off the price** я сбро́шу/ски́ну/сба́влю фунт с цены́.
3 (*criticize*) ха́ять (*impf.*) (*coll.*).
■ *v.i.* 1 (*rap*) стуча́ть; **~ at the door** стуча́ть(ся), по- в дверь.
2 : **~ against** (*collide with*) нат|ыка́ться, -кну́ться на + *a.*
3 (*of engine*) стуча́ть (*impf.*).
■ *with advs.*: **~ back** *v.t.* (*Br., disconcert*): **the news ~ed me back** изве́стие привело́ меня́ в замеша́тельство; (*coll., consume*): **he can ~ back 5 pints in as many minutes** он за пять мину́т мо́жет опроки́нуть/вы́лакать пять кру́жек (пи́ва); (*Br. coll., cost*): **that will ~ me back a bit** э́то ста́нет мне в копе́ечку; **~ down** *v.t.* (*strike to ground*) сби|ва́ть, -ть с ног; вали́ть, с-; **he was ~ed down by a car** его́ сби́ла маши́на; (*demolish*) сн|оси́ть, -ести́; **~ off** *v.t.* (*lit.*) сби|ва́ть, -ть; (*coll. uses*): (*deduct from price*) сб|авля́ть, -а́вить; *v.i.* (*stop work*) свора́чиваться, сверну́ться (*sl.*); **~ out** *v.t.* (*make unconscious*) оглуш|а́ть, -и́ть; **the blow on his head ~ed him out** он был оглушён уда́ром по голове́; (*eliminate from contest*): **he was ~ed out in the first round** он вы́был в пе́рвом ту́ре; **~ over** *v.t.* опроки́|дывать, -нуть.
■ *cpds.* **~-down** *adj.*: **at a ~-down price**

по дешёвке (*coll.*); **~out** *n.* (*boxing*) нока́ут; (*Br., competition*) соревнова́ния (*nt. pl.*) по олимпи́йской систе́ме; (*attr.*): **~out blow** сокруши́тельный уда́р.

knocker /ˈnɒkə(r)/ *n.* (*on door*) (дверно́й) молото́к.

knocking /ˈnɒkɪŋ/ *n.* (*noise*) стук.

knot /nɒt/ *n.* (*in rope etc.*; *in wood*; *measure of speed*) у́зел; **tie a ~ in a rope** завя́з|ывать, -а́ть у́зел на верёвке; **tie sth. in a ~** завя́з|ывать, -а́ть что-н. узло́м.
■ *v.t.* & *i.* (**knotted, knotting**) завя́з|ывать(ся), -а́ть(ся).

know /nəʊ/ *n.*: **be in the ~** быть в ку́рсе де́ла.
■ *v.t.* (*past* **knew;** *p.p.* **known**)
1 (*be aware, have knowledge of*) знать (*impf.*): **I ~ nothing about it** я об э́том ничего́ не зна́ю; **for all I ~** кто его́ зна́ет; **who ~s?** как знать?; **I knew it!** (я) так и знал!
2 (*recognize, distinguish*) знать, у-; узн|ава́ть, -а́ть; отлич|а́ть, -и́ть; **I ~ him by sight** я зна́ю его́ в лицо́; **he knew her at once** он сра́зу её узна́л.
3 (*be acquainted, familiar with*) знать (*impf.*); быть знако́мым с + *i.*; **get to ~ s.o.** знако́миться, по- с кем-н.; **I have ~n him since childhood** я знако́м с ним с де́тства.
4 (*be versed in*; *understand*; *have experience in*) зна́ть (*impf.*), понима́ть (*impf.*), разбира́ться (*impf.*) в + *p.*; **he ~s Russian** он зна́ет ру́сский язы́к; он владе́ет ру́сским языко́м; **~ how to** уме́ть, с-.
■ *v.i.* (*past* **knew;** *p.p.* **known**): **let s.o. ~** сообщ|а́ть, -и́ть (*or* да|ва́ть, -ть знать) кому́-н.; **will you let me ~?** вы сообщи́те мне?; **do you ~ of a good restaurant?** вы зна́ете (*or* вы мо́жете порекомендова́ть) хоро́ший рестора́н?; **I don't ~ him, but I ~ of him** ли́чно я с ним незнако́м, но наслы́шан о нём; **did you ~ about the accident?** вы зна́ли об э́том несча́стном слу́чае?
■ *cpds.* **~-all** *n.* (*US* **~-it-all**) всезна́йка (*c.g.*); **~-how** *n.* уме́ние; но́у-ха́у (*nt. indecl.*); о́пыт.

knowing /ˈnəʊɪŋ/ *adj.* (*significant*): **a ~ look** понима́ющий/многозначи́тельный взгляд.

knowledge /ˈnɒlɪdʒ/ *n.* зна́ние; (*understanding*): **our ~ of the subject is as yet limited** на́ши позна́ния в э́той о́бласти пока́ ограни́чены; (*range of information or experience*): **to the best of my ~** наско́лько мне изве́стно.

knowledgeable /ˈnɒlɪdʒəb(ə)l/ *adj.* хорошо́ осведомлённый.

known /nəʊn/ *adj.* изве́стный; *see also* ▸ **know** *v.t.* & *i.*

knuckle /ˈnʌk(ə)l/ *n.* (*anat.*) костя́шка (па́льца).
■ *v.i.*: **~ down to one's work** прин|има́ться, -я́ться за де́ло.

koala /kəʊˈɑːlə/ *n.* **(~ bear)** коа́ла (*m.*), су́мчатый медве́дь.

Kolkata /kɒlˈkɑːtə/ *n.* Кальку́тта.

kopeck /ˈkəʊpek/ *n.* копе́йка.

Koran /kɔːˈrɑːn/ *n.* Кора́н.

Korea /kəˈriːə/ *n.* Коре́я.

Korean /kəˈriːən/ *m.* (*person*) коре́|ец (*fem.* -я́нка); (*language*) коре́йский язы́к.
■ *adj.* коре́йский.

kosher /ˈkəʊʃə(r)/ *adj.* (*relig.*) коше́рный.

Kosovan /ˈkɒsəv(ə)n/ *n.* жи́тель (*fem.* -ница) Ко́сово.
■ *adj.* ко́совский.

Kosovo /ˈkɒsəvə/ *n.* Ко́сово (*nt. decl. and indecl.*).

ko(w)tow /kaʊˈtaʊ/ *n.* ни́зкий покло́н.
■ *v.i.* де́лать, с- ни́зкий покло́н; (*fig.*) раболе́пствовать (*impf.*), пресмыка́ться (*impf.*) (*перед кем*).

kudos /ˈkjuːdɒs/ *n.* сла́ва.

kumquat /ˈkʌmkwɒt/ *n.* кумква́т (*дерево семейства цитрусовых с очень маленькими плодами оранжевого цвета*; *плоды этого дерева*).

kung fu /kʊŋ ˈfuː/ *n.* кун-фу́ (*nt. indecl.*).

Kurd /kəːd/ *n.* курд (*fem.* -я́нка).

Kurdish /ˈkəːdɪʃ/ *n.* ку́рдский язы́к.
■ *adj.* ку́рдский.

Kurdistan /kəːdɪˈstɑːn/ *n.* Курдиста́н.

Kuwait /kʊˈweɪt/ *n.* Куве́йт.

Kuwaiti /kʊˈweɪtɪ/ *n.* куве́йт|ец (*fem.* -ка).
■ *adj.* куве́йтский.

kvass /kvɑːs/ *n.* квас.

Kyrgyz /ˈkəːgɪz/ *n.* (*pl.* **~**) (*person*) кирги́з (*fem.* -ка); (*language*) кирги́зский язы́к.
■ *adj.* кирги́зский.

Kyrgyzstan /ˈkəːgɪˈstɑːn/ *n.* Кыргызста́н.

Ll

L (*abbr. of* ***learner***) (*Br.*): **~-plate** ≈ «У» (*на учебной машине*).

l /ˈliːtə(r)(z)/ *n.* (*abbr. of* ***litre(s)***) л (литр).

lab /læb/ (*coll.*) = **laboratory**

label /ˈleɪb(ə)l/ *n.* ярлы́к, этике́тка.
■ *v.t.* (**labelled, labelling;** *US* **labeled, labeling**) (*stick ~ on*) накле́и|вать, -ть ярлы́к на + *a.*; (*fig.*): **he was ~led a fascist** ему́ прикле́или ярлы́к фаши́ста.

labor /ˈleɪbə(r)/ *etc. see* ▸ **labour** *etc.*; **~ union** (*US*) профсою́з.

laboratory /ləˈbɒrətərɪ/ *n.* лаборато́рия; **~ assistant** лабора́нт (*fem.* -ка).

laborious /ləˈbɔːrɪəs/ *adj.* (*difficult*) тру́дный, тяжёлый; (*toilsome*) трудоёмкий.

labour /ˈleɪbə(r)/ (*US* **labor**) *n.*
1 (*toil, work*) труд, рабо́та.
2 (*workforce*) рабо́чие (*pl.*).

3 : **(L~ Party)** лейбори́стская па́ртия, лейбори́сты (*m. pl.*); **the L~ government** лейбори́стское прави́тельство.
4 (*childbirth*) ро́д|ы (*pl.*, *g.* -ов); **be in ~** рожа́ть (*impf.*).
■ *v.t.*: **~ a point** вдава́ться (*impf.*) в изли́шние подро́бности.
■ *v.i.* 1 (*toil*) труди́ться (*impf.*).
2 (*strive*): **he is ~ing to finish his book** он прилага́ет все уси́лия, что́бы (за)ко́нчить кни́гу.
■ *cpds.* **~-intensive** *adj.* трудоёмкий; **~-saving** *adj.* рационализа́торский.

labourer /ˈleɪbərə(r)/ (*US* **laborer**) *n.* рабо́чий.

Labrador /ˈlæbrədɔ:(r)/ *n.* Лабрадо́р; (*dog*) лабрадо́р.

laburnum /ləˈbə:nəm/ *n.* (*bot.*) бобо́вник, золото́й дождь.

labyrinth /ˈlæbərɪnθ/ *n.* (*lit.*, *fig.*) лабири́нт.

labyrinthine /læbəˈrɪnθaɪn/ *adj.* (*lit.*) лабири́нтный; (*fig.*) запу́танный.

lace /leɪs/ *n.*
1 (*openwork fabric*) кру́жево, кружева́ (*nt. pl.*).
2 (*of shoe etc.*) шнуро́к.
■ *v.t.* (*fasten or tighten with ~*) шнурова́ть, за-; **he ~d up his shoes** он зашнурова́л боти́нки.
■ *cpd.* **~-ups** *n. pl.* (*Br.*) о́бувь на шнуро́вке/шнурка́х.

lacerate /ˈlæsəreɪt/ *v.t.* (*lit.*, *fig.*) терза́ть, рас-/ис-; растерз|ывать, -а́ть; (*wound*) ра́нить (*impf.*, *pf.*).

lack /læk/ *n.* недоста́ток.
■ *v.t.* & *i.*: **he ~s sth.** ему́ чего́-то недостаёт; **he ~s, is ~ing in courage** у него́ не хвата́ет хра́брости.
■ *cpd.* **~lustre** (*US* **luster**) *adj.* ту́склый, без бле́ска.

lackadaisical /lækəˈdeɪzɪk(ə)l/ *adj.* вя́лый, апати́чный.

lackey /ˈlækɪ/ *n.* (*pl.* **~s**) (*lit.*, *fig.*) лаке́й; (*fig.*) подхали́м.

laconic /ləˈkɒnɪk/ *adj.* лакони́чный.

lacquer /ˈlækə(r)/ *n.* политу́ра (*no pl.*); лак.

lad /læd/ *n.* (*boy*) ма́льчик; (*fellow, youth*) па́рень (*m.*).

ladder /ˈlædə(r)/ *n.*
1 ле́стница.
2 (*Br., in stocking*) спусти́вшаяся петля́.
■ *v.t.* & *i.* (*Br.*): **I have ~ed my stocking; my stocking has ~ed** у меня́ спусти́лась петля́ на чулке́.

laden /ˈleɪd(ə)n/ *adj.*: **he returned ~ with books** он верну́лся нагру́женный кни́гами; **the table was ~ with food** стол ломи́лся от еды́; **she was ~ with cares** она́ была́ обременена́ забо́тами.

ladies /ˈleɪdɪs/ *n. see* ▶ **lady 2**

ladle /ˈleɪd(ə)l/ *n.* поло́вник.

lady /ˈleɪdɪ/ *n.*
1 (*woman*) да́ма; (*as title*) ле́ди (*f. indecl.*); **Ladies and Gentlemen** да́мы и господа́.
2 : **the Ladies** (*sg.*), (*US*) **ladies' room** (*lavatory*) же́нский туале́т.
■ *cpds.* **~bird,** (*US*) **~bug** *nn.* бо́жья коро́вка.

lag¹ /læg/ *n.* (*delay*) запа́здывание.
■ *v.i.* (**lagged, lagging**) отст|ава́ть, -а́ть; **the children were ~ging (behind)** де́ти плели́сь позади́.

lag² /læg/ *v.t.* (**lagged, lagging**) (*wrap in felt etc.*) изоли́ровать/покрыва́ть (*impf.*) (во́йлоком).

lager /ˈlɑ:gə(r)/ *n.* све́тлое пи́во.

lagoon /ləˈgu:n/ *n.* лагу́на.

laid /leɪd/ *past and p.p. of* ▶ **lay²**

laid-back /leɪdˈbæk/ *adj.* непринуждённый, споко́йный.

lain /leɪn/ *p.p. of* ▶ **lie²**

lair /leə(r)/ *n.* ло́гово.

laissez-faire /leseɪˈfeə(r)/ *n.* невмеша́тельство; поли́тика невмеша́тельства прави́тельства в эконо́мику.

lake /leɪk/ *n.* о́зеро.

lama /ˈlɑ:mə/ *n.* (*relig.*) ла́ма (*m.*).

lamb /læm/ *n.* ягнёнок, бара́шек; (*meat*) бара́шек; **~ chop** бара́нья котле́та.

lambaste /læmˈbeɪst/ *v.t.* дуба́сить, от- (*coll.*).

lame /leɪm/ *adj.*
1 хромо́й.
2 (*fig., of excuse etc.*) сла́бый.

lament /ləˈment/ *n.* плач.
■ *v.t.* опла́к|ивать, -ать.

lamentable /ˈlæməntəb(ə)l/ *adj.* плаче́вный.

lamentation /læmənˈteɪʃ(ə)n/ *n.* (*lamenting*) се́тование; (*lament*) плач.

laminate /ˈlæmɪneɪt/ *v.t.* (*overlay with protective layer*) ламини́ровать (*impf.*, *pf.*).

lamp /læmp/ *n.* ла́мпа.
■ *cpds.* **~ post** *nn.* фона́рный столб; **~shade** *n.* абажу́р.

lampoon /læmˈpu:n/ *n.* па́сквиль (*m.*).
■ *v.t.* писа́ть, на- па́сквиль на + *a.*

LAN (*abbr. of* ***local area network***) (*comput.*) лока́льная сеть.

lance /lɑ:ns/ *n.* пи́ка.
■ *v.t.* (*med.*) вскры|ва́ть, -ть ланце́том.

land /lænd/ *n.*
1 земля́; (*dry ~*) су́ша; **travel by ~** е́хать (*det.*) су́шей (*or* по су́ше); **reach ~** дост|ига́ть, -и́гнуть бе́рега.
2 (*ground, soil*) грунт, по́чва; **work the ~** обраба́тывать (*impf.*) зе́млю; **a house with some ~** дом с земе́льным уча́стком.
3 (*country*) земля́, страна́; (*state*) госуда́рство.
4 (*property*) земля́, име́ние; **his ~s extend for several miles** его́ владе́ния простира́ются на не́сколько миль.
■ *v.t.* 1 : **~ an aircraft** сажа́ть, посади́ть (*or* приземл|я́ть, -и́ть) самолёт.
2 : **~ a fish** выта́скивать, вы́тащить ры́бу на бе́рег.
3 (*win*) выи́грывать, вы́играть; (*secure*): **he ~ed himself a good job** он пристро́ился на хоро́шую рабо́ту.
4 (*get, involve*): **he ~ed himself with a lot of work** он загрузи́л себя́ рабо́той.
■ *v.i.* 1 (*of passengers*) выса́живаться, вы́садиться.
2 (*of aircraft*) приземл|я́ться, -и́ться; (*spacecraft on moon*) прилун|я́ться, -и́ться.
3 (*of athlete, after jump*) приземл|я́ться, -и́ться.

[4] (*fall, lit. or fig.*): **she ~ed in trouble** онá попáла в бедý; **the ball ~ed on his head** мяч попáл емý в гóлову.
[5]: **~ up** (*coll., arrive*) приб|ывáть, -ы́ть; **I ~ed up in the wrong street** я очути́лся не на той ýлице.
■ *cpds.* **~lady** *n.* (*Br., of pub*) хозя́йка; (*of building*) домовладéлица, хозя́йка; **~line** *n.* назéмная ли́ния свя́зи; **~lord** *n.* (*Br., of pub*) хозя́ин; (*owner of ~*) землевладéлец; (*of building*) домовладéлец, хозя́ин; **~mark** *n.* (*prominent feature*) замéтный объéкт на мéстности, ориенти́р; (*fig.*) вéха; **~mine** *n.* фугáс; **~owner** *n.* землевладéл|ец (*fem.* -ица); **~slide** *n.* óползень (*m.*); (*pol.*): **they won by a ~slide** они́ победи́ли с огрóмным перевéсом (голосóв).

landed /'lændɪd/ *adj.*
[1] (*possessing land*) землевладéльческий; **~ gentry** помéщики (*m. pl.*).
[2] (*consisting of land*): **~ property** земéльные владéния.

landing /'lændɪŋ/ *n.*
[1] (*bringing or coming to earth*) посáдка, приземлéние; (*on the moon*) прилунéние.
[2] (*putting ashore; depositing by air*) вы́садка.
[3] (*mil.*) десáнт.
[4] (*on stairs*) (лéстничная) площáдка.
■ *cpds.* **~ gear** *n.* шасси́ (*nt. indecl.*); **~ strip** *n.* посáдочная полосá.

landscape /lændskeɪp, 'læns-/ *n.* (*picture*) пейзáж; (*scenery*) ландшáфт.
■ *cpd.* **~ gardening** *n.* ландшáфтный дизáйн.

lane /leɪn/ *n.*
[1] (*narrow street*) переýлок; (*country road*) дорóжка.
[2] (*of traffic*) ряд.
[3] (*air route*) трácса.
[4] (*for shipping*) морскóй путь.
[5] (*on racetrack, swimming pool*) дорóжка.

language /'læŋgwɪdʒ/ *n.* язы́к; (*esp. spoken*) речь; **bad ~** сквернословие; **~ laboratory** лингафóнный кабинéт.

languid /'læŋgwɪd/ *adj.* тóмный, вя́лый.

languish /'læŋgwɪʃ/ *v.i.* томи́ться (*impf.*).

languor /'læŋgə(r)/ *n.* тóмность, вя́лость; (*pleasant*) истóма.

languorous /'læŋgərəs/ *adj.* тóмный; пóлный истóмы.

lank /læŋk/ *adj.*: **~ hair** глáдкие/прямы́е вóлосы.

lanky /'læŋkɪ/ *adj.* (**lankier, lankiest**) долговя́зый.

lantern /'lænt(ə)n/ *n.* фонáрь (*m.*).

lap¹ /læp/ *n.*: **the boy sat on his mother's ~** мáльчик сидéл у мáтери на колéнях; **he lives in the ~ of luxury** ≈ он живёт в (обстанóвке) рóскоши.
■ *cpds.* **~ dance** *n.* эроти́ческий тáнец, исполня́емый в непосрéдственной бли́зости к клиéнту, заказáвшему егó; **~top (computer)** *n.* портати́вный компью́тер; лэптóп.

lap² /læp/ *n.* (*circuit of racetrack*) круг.
■

lap³ /læp/ *n.v.t.* (**lapped, lapping**)
[1] (*drink with tongue*) лакáть, вы́-; **the cat ~ped up the milk** кóшка вы́лакала молокó.
[2] (*fig., accept eagerly*) жáдно глотáть (*impf.*); **he ~ped up their compliments** он жáдно лови́л их комплимéнты.

lapel /lə'pel/ *n.* лáцкан, отворóт.

Lapp /læp/ *n.*
[1] (*person*) саáми (*m. & f. indecl.*); лопáр|ь (*fem.* -ка).
[2] (*also* **~ish:** *language*) саáмский/лопáрский язы́к; язы́к саáми.
■ *adj.* [1] (*also* **~ish**) лопáрский, саáмский.
[2] (*of Lapland*) лаплáндский.

lapse /læps/ *n.*
[1] (*slight mistake*) упущéние; (*of memory*) провáл (в) пáмяти.
[2] (*interval*) промежýток.
■ *v.i.* [1] (*decline morally*) пасть (*pf.*); **he ~d into his old ways** он приня́лся за стáрое; **~ into silence** зам|олкáть, -óлкнуть.
[2] (*leg., become void*) теря́ть, по- си́лу.

larch /lɑːtʃ/ *n.* (*tree*) ли́ственница.

lard /lɑːd/ *n.* сáло.

larder /'lɑːdə(r)/ *n.* кладовáя.

large /lɑːdʒ/ *n.*: **at ~** (*free*) на вóле, на свобóде; (*in general*) целикóм; во всём объёме; **the public at ~** ширóкая пýблика.
■ *adj.* большóй, крýпный.
■ *adv.*: **by and ~** вообщé говоря́.
■ *cpd.* **~-scale** *adj.* крупномасштáбный.

largely /'lɑːdʒlɪ/ *adv.* (*to a great extent*) по бóльшей чáсти; в значи́тельной стéпени.

lark¹ /lɑːk/ *n.* (*bird*) жáворонок.

lark² /lɑːk/ *n.* (*coll.*), (*amusement*) забáва; **for a ~** шýтки рáди.

larva /'lɑːvə/ *n.* (*pl.* **larvae** /-viː/) личи́нка.

laryngitis /lærɪn'dʒaɪtɪs/ *n.* ларинги́т.

larynx /'lærɪŋks/ *n.* (*pl.* **larynges**) гортáнь.

lascivious /lə'sɪvɪəs/ *adj.* похотли́вый.

laser /'leɪzə(r)/ *n.* лáзер; (*attr.*) лáзерный.

lash¹ /læʃ/ *n.* **(eye ~)** ресни́ца.

lash² /læʃ/ *n.* (*stroke*) удáр (плéтью).
■ *v.t.* (*with whip, wind, rain*) хлест|áть, -нýть.
■ *v.i.*: **the rain ~ed against the window** дождь хлестáл в окнó.
■ *with advs.*: **~ out** *v.i.* (*with fists*) наки́|дываться, -нуться (*на когó*); (*verbally*) набр|áсываться, -óситься (с кри́тикой) (*на когó*).

lasso /læ'suː/ *n.* (*pl.* **~s** *or* **~es**) аркáн, лассó (*nt. indecl.*).
■ *v.t.* (**lassoes, lassoed**) аркáнить, за-.

last /lɑːst/ *n.* (*final or most recent person or thing*): **he was the ~ of his line** он был послéдним в родý; **our house is the ~ in the road** наш дом послéдний/крáйний на ýлице; **at ~** наконéц; (*as excl.*) наконéц-то!
■ *adj.* [1] (*latest; final; ~ of series*) послéдний; **in the ~ 7 years** в послéдние 7 лет; **at the very ~ moment** в сáмый послéдний момéнт; **~ rites** причащéние пéред смéртью; **~ name** фами́лия; **~ but one** предпослéдний.
[2] (*preceding, of time*) прóшлый; **~ week** на прóшлой недéле; **~ night we got home late** вчерá вéчером мы пóздно вернýлись (домóй).
[3] (*least likely or suitable*): **she is the ~ person to help** от неё мéньше всегó мóжно ожидáть пóмощи; **that's the ~ thing I**

would have expected э́того я ника́к не ожида́л.
■ *adv.* 1 (*in order*) по́сле всех; **he finished ~** он ко́нчил после́дним.
2 (*for the ~ time*) в после́дний раз.
3 (*~ly, in the ~ place*) на после́днем ме́сте.
■ *v.i.* 1 (*go on, continue*) дли́ться, про-; прод|олжа́ться, -о́лжиться; **the rain won't ~ long** дождь ско́ро пройдёт.
2 (*of clothes*): **this suit has ~ed well** э́тот костю́м хорошо́ но́сится.
■ *v.i. & t.* (*be sufficient for*) хват|а́ть, -и́ть на + *a.*; **£100 ~s (me) a week** сто фу́нтов (мне) хвата́ет на неде́лю.
■ *cpds.* **~-ditch** *adj.* отча́янный; **~-minute** *adj.* (сде́ланный) в после́днюю мину́ту.

lasting /ˈlɑːstɪŋ/ *adj.* (*enduring*) про́чный, продолжи́тельный.

lastly /ˈlɑːstlɪ/ *adv.* в заключе́ние; наконе́ц.

latch /lætʃ/ *n.* (*bar*) щеко́лда; (*lock*) защёлка.
■ *v.i.*: **~ on to** смекну́ть (*pf.*) (*coll.*).

late /leɪt/ *adj.*
1 (*far on in time*) по́здний; **it is ~** по́здно; **in ~ May** к концу́/в конце́ ма́я; **the ~ 19th century** коне́ц 19 ве́ка; **he is in his ~ 40s** ему́ почти́/под пятьдеся́т.
2 (*behind time*): **be ~ for the train** оп|а́здывать, -озда́ть на по́езд; **he was an hour ~** он опозда́л на ча́с; **I was ~ in replying** я опозда́л отве́тить (*or* с отве́том).
3 (*recent*) неда́вний; после́дний; **his ~st book** его́ после́дняя кни́га.
4 (*deceased*) поко́йный.
■ *adv.* по́здно; **stay up ~** по́здно ложи́ться (*impf.*); **a year ~r** спустя́ год.

latecomer /ˈleɪtkʌmə(r)/ *n.* опозда́вший.

lately /ˈleɪtlɪ/ *adv.* в после́днее вре́мя.

latent /ˈleɪt(ə)nt/ *adj.* скры́тый.

lateral /ˈlætər(ə)l/ *adj.* боково́й, горизонта́льный; **~ section** попере́чный разре́з.

latest /ˈleɪtɪst/ *adj.* после́дний; са́мый но́вый.

lathe /leɪð/ *n.* тока́рный стано́к.

lather /ˈlɑːðə(r)/ *n.* (мы́льная) пе́на.

Latin /ˈlætɪn/ *n.* латы́нь; лати́нский язы́к.
■ *adj.* лати́нский; **~ America** Лати́нская Аме́рика.
■ *cpd.* **~ American** *adj.* латиноамерика́нский; *n.* латиноамерика́н|ец (*fem.* -ка).

Latino /ləˈtiːnəʊ/ *n.* (*pl.* **~s**) & *adj.* = **Latin American**

latitude /ˈlætɪtjuːd/ *n.* (*geog., fig.*) широта́.

latter /ˈlætə(r)/ *pron.* & *adj.* после́дний, второ́й; **of cream and yogurt, the ~ is healthier** что каса́ется сли́вок и йо́гурта, то после́дний поле́знее.

latterly /ˈlætəlɪ/ *adv.* (*of late*) (в/за) после́днее вре́мя; (*towards the end*) к концу́, под коне́ц.

lattice /ˈlætɪs/ *n.* решётка; (*attr.*; *also* **~d**) решётчатый.

Latvia /ˈlætvɪə/ *n.* Ла́твия.

Latvian /ˈlætvɪən/ *n.* (*person*) латви́|ец (*fem.* -йка); латы́ш (*fem.* -ка); (*language*) латы́шский язы́к.
■ *adj.* латви́йский, латы́шский.

laudable /ˈlɔːdəb(ə)l/ *adj.* похва́льный.

laugh /lɑːf/ *n.* смех; **we had a good ~ over it** мы от души́ посмея́лись над э́тим.
■ *v.t.*: **he was ~ing his head off** он хохота́л как безу́мный.
■ *v.i.* смея́ться (*impf.*) (**at:** над + *i.*); **burst out ~ing** рассмея́ться (*pf.*); расхохота́ться (*pf.*); **he ~s at my jokes** он смеётся, когда́ я шучу́; **it's nothing to ~ at** ничего́ смешно́го; **I couldn't stop ~ing** я смея́лся так, что не мог останови́ться.
■ *with adv.*: **~ off** *v.t.*: **~ sth. off** отде́л|ываться, -аться от чего́-н. шу́ткой.

laughable /ˈlɑːfəb(ə)l/ *adj.* смешно́й, смехотво́рный.

laughing /ˈlɑːfɪŋ/ *n.* смех.
■ *cpd.* **~ stock** *n.* посме́шище.

laughter /ˈlɑːftə(r)/ *n.* смех.

launch[1] /lɔːntʃ/ *n.* (*motor boat*) ка́тер.

launch[2] /lɔːntʃ/ *n.* (*of ship*) спуск (на́ воду); (*of rocket or spacecraft*) за́пуск; (*of product*) вы́пуск.
■ *v.t.* (*set afloat*): **~ a ship** спус|ка́ть, -ти́ть кора́бль на́ воду; (*send into air*): **~ a rocket** запус|ка́ть, -ти́ть раке́ту; (*initiate*): **~ a campaign** нач|ина́ть, -а́ть (*or* откр|ыва́ть, -ы́ть) кампа́нию; **~ an enterprise/product** пус|ка́ть, -ти́ть предприя́тие/проду́кт в прода́жу.
■ *cpd.* **~(ing) pad** *n.* ста́ртовая площа́дка.

launder /ˈlɔːndə(r)/ *v.t.*
1 стира́ть, вы́-.
2 (*fig.*): **~ money** отм|ыва́ть, -ы́ть де́ньги.

laund(e)rette /lɔːnˈdret/ *n.* (*Br.*) пра́чечная самообслу́живания.

laundry /ˈlɔːndrɪ/ *n.*
1 (*establishment*) пра́чечная.
2 (*clothes*) бельё (для сти́рки *or* из сти́рки).

laurel /ˈlɒr(ə)l/ *n.* лавр.

lava /ˈlɑːvə/ *n.* ла́ва.

lavatory /ˈlævətərɪ/ *n.* убо́рная, туале́т.

lavender /ˈlævɪndə(r)/ *n.* лава́нда.

lavish /ˈlævɪʃ/ *adj.* ще́дрый.
■ *v.t.*: **~ money on sth.** пром|а́тывать, -ота́ть де́ньги на что-н.; **~ praise on s.o.** расточа́ть (*impf.*) похвалы́ кому́-н.

law /lɔː/ *n.*
1 (*rule or body of rules for society*) зако́н; **by ~** по зако́ну; **break the ~** нар|уша́ть, -у́шить зако́н.
2 (*as subject of study, profession, system*) пра́во, юсти́ция; **~ and order** правопоря́док; **~ school** юриди́ческий вуз; **read, study ~** изуч|а́ть, -и́ть пра́во.
3 (*phys., math.*): **~ of gravity** зако́н всеми́рного тяготе́ния; **~ of probability** тео́рия вероя́тностей.
■ *cpds.* **~-abiding** *adj.* законопослу́шный; **~ court** *n.* суд; **~-enforcement** *n.* (*attr.*): **~-enforcement agencies** правоохрани́тельные о́рганы; **~giver, ~maker** *nn.* законода́тель (*m.*); **~suit** *n.* суде́бный проце́сс.

lawful /ˈlɔːfʊl/ *adj.* зако́нный.

lawless /ˈlɔːlɪs/ *adj.* (*of country etc.*) ди́кий; (*of person*) непоко́рный.

lawn /lɔːn/ *n.* газо́н.
■ *cpd.* **~mower** *n.* газонокоси́лка.

lawyer /ˈlɔɪə(r)/ *n.* юри́ст; (*advocate, barrister*) адвока́т.

lax /læks/ *adj.* нестро́гий.

laxative /ˈlæksətɪv/ *n.* слаби́тельное (сре́дство).

lay[1] /leɪ/ *past of* ▶ **lie**[2]

lay[2] /leɪ/ *v.t.* (*past and p.p.* **laid**)
1 (*put down, deposit*) класть, положи́ть; ~ **an egg** нести́, с- яйцо́; (*set in position*): ~ **bricks** класть (*impf.*) кирпичи́; ~ **a foundation** (*lit., fig.*) за|кла́дывать, -ложи́ть фунда́мент; ~ **a trap** ста́вить, по- лову́шку.
2 (*prepare*): ~ **a fire** пригото́вить (*pf.*) всё, что́бы развести́ ого́нь; ~ **the table for dinner** накр|ыва́ть, -ы́ть стол к обе́ду.
■ *v.i.* (*past and p.p.* **laid**) (*sc. eggs*) нести́сь (*impf.*).
■ *with advs.*: ~ **down** *v.t.*: ~ **down one's arms** (*surrender*) скла́дывать, сложи́ть ору́жие; (*formulate, prescribe*): ~ **down conditions/rules** устан|а́вливать, -ови́ть (*or* формули́ровать, с-) усло́вия/пра́вила; (*sacrifice*): ~ **down one's life for one's friends** же́ртвовать, по- жи́знью (*or* отд|ава́ть, -а́ть жизнь) за друзе́й; ~ **off** *v.t.* (*suspend from work*) ув|ольня́ть, -о́лить (со слу́жбы); ~ **on** *v.t.* (*Br., provide supply of*) пров|оди́ть, -ести́; (*coll.*): **he promised to ~ on some drinks** он обеща́л поста́вить вы́пивку; (*arrange*) устр|а́ивать, -о́ить; ~ **out** *v.t.* (*arrange for display etc.*) выставля́ть, вы́ставить; (*garden etc.*) разб|ива́ть, -и́ть.
■ *cpds.* **~about** *n.* (*coll.*) лентя́й (*fem.* -ка); **~-by** *n.* (*Br.*) придоро́жная площа́дка для стоя́нки автомоби́лей; **~-off** *n.* (*of workers*) сокраще́ние шта́тов; **~out** *n.* (*arrangement*) расположе́ние; (*of town etc.*) планиро́вка; (*of garden etc.*) разби́вка; (*plan*) чертёж, план.

lay[3] /leɪ/ *adj.*
1 (*opp. clerical*) мирско́й.
2 (*opp. professional*): ~ **opinion** непрофессиона́льное мне́ние.
■ *cpd.* **~man** *n.* (*non-specialist*) непрофессиона́л, неспециали́ст.

layer /ˈleɪə(r)/ *n.* слой, пласт.

laze /leɪz/ *v.t. & i.*: ~ **about** слоня́ться (*impf.*) без де́ла.

laziness /ˈleɪzɪnɪs/ *n.* лень, ле́ность.

lazy /ˈleɪzɪ/ *adj.* (**lazier, laziest**) лени́вый; **be ~** лени́ться (*impf.*); **I was too ~ to write to him** мне бы́ло лень ему́ (на)писа́ть.

lb /paʊnd(z)/ *n.* (*abbr. of* ***libra***) фунт.

LCD (*abbr. of* ***liquid-crystal display***) ЖК-диспле́й (жидкокристалли́ческий диспле́й).

leach /liːtʃ/ *v.t. & i.* выщела́чивать(ся), вы́щелочить(ся) (*о почве, горной породе*).

lead[1] /led/ *n.*
1 (*metal*) свине́ц.
2 (*in pencil*) графи́т, гри́фель (*m.*).
■ *cpd.* **~-free** *adj.* неэтили́рованный.

lead[2] /liːd/ *n.*
1 (*direction, guidance; initiative*) руково́дство; **take the ~** брать, взять на (себя́) руково́дство/инициати́ву.
2 (*first place*): **be in the ~** стоя́ть (*impf.*) во главе́; (*sport*) быть впереди́; вести́ (*det.*); (*fig.*) стоя́ть (*impf.*) во главе́, пе́рвенствовать (*impf.*); **take the ~** (*sport*) выходи́ть, вы́йти вперёд.
3 (*clue*): **the police are looking for a ~** поли́ция пыта́ется напа́сть на след.
4 (*Br., cord, strap*) поводо́к, при́вязь.
5 (*elec.*) про́вод (*pl.* -а́).
■ *v.t.* (*past and p.p.* **led**)
1 (*conduct*) води́ть (*indet.*), вести́ (*det.*), повести́ (*pf.*); **he led his troops into battle** он повёл солда́т в бой.
2 (*fig., bring, incline, induce*): ~ **s.o. to believe** созда́ть (*pf.*) впечатле́ние у кого́-н., что… .
3 (*be in charge of*): ~ **an expedition/orchestra** руководи́ть (*impf.*) экспеди́цией/орке́стром; (*command*) кома́ндовать (*impf.*) + *i.*; (*act as chief or head of*) возгл|авля́ть, -а́вить.
4 (*pass, spend*): ~ **an idle life** вести́ (*det.*) пра́здную жизнь.
■ *v.i.* (*past and p.p.* **led**)
1 (*of a road etc.*) вести́ (*det.*).
2 (*be first or ahead*) быть впереди́.
■ *with advs.*: ~ **away** *v.t.* отв|оди́ть, -ести́; ув|оди́ть, -ести́; ~ **in** *v.t.* вв|оди́ть, -ести́; ~ **up** *v.i.*: ~ **up to** (*lit.*) подв|оди́ть, -ести́ к + *d.*; (*precede, form preparation for*) подгот|овля́ть, -о́вить; **the events that led up to the war** собы́тия, приве́дшие к войне́.

leaded /ˈledɪd/ *adj.* (*petrol*) этили́рованный.

leaden /ˈled(ə)n/ *adj.* (*lit., fig.*) свинцо́вый.

leader /ˈliːdə(r)/ *n.*
1 руководи́тель (*m.*), ли́дер; (*comm.*) ли́дер.
2 (*mil.*) команди́р.
3 (*Br., in newspaper*) передова́я (статья́).

leadership /ˈliːdərʃɪp/ *n.* (*role of leader; group of leaders*) руково́дство; (*qualities of a leader*) ли́дерство.

leading /ˈliːdɪŋ/ *adj.* (*foremost*) веду́щий; (*outstanding*) выдаю́щийся; ~ **lady** исполни́тельница гла́вной ро́ли; ~ **question** наводя́щий вопро́с.

leaf /liːf/ *n.* (*pl.* **leaves**)
1 (*of tree or plant*) лист (*pl.* -ья).
2 (*of book*) лист (*pl.* -ы́); (*fig.*): **turn over a new ~** нач|ина́ть, -а́ть но́вую жизнь, испра́виться (*pf.*).
■ *v.t.*: ~ **through** перели́ст|ывать, -а́ть.

leaflet /ˈliːflɪt/ *n.* листо́вка.

leafy /ˈliːfɪ/ *adj.* (**leafier, leafiest**) густоли́ственный.

league /liːg/ *n.* (*alliance*) ли́га; **in ~ with** в сою́зе с + *i.*; (*pej.*) в сго́воре с + *i.*; **be not in the same ~ as s.o.** быть не того́ кла́сса; **football ~** футбо́льная ли́га; ~ **table** (*Br.*) (*sport*) табли́ца результа́тов; (*fig.*) сравни́тельный гра́фик.

leak /liːk/ *n.* (*hole*) течь; (*escape of fluid*) уте́чка; (*fig., of information*) уте́чка информа́ции.
■ *v.t.* (*fig.*) выдава́ть, вы́дать.
■ *v.i.* (*roof, boat*) течь (*impf.*); **leak out** (*liquid, gas*) прос|а́чиваться, -очи́ться; (*fig.*): **the affair ~ed out** де́ло вы́плыло нару́жу.
■ *cpd.* **~-proof** *adj.* непроница́емый.

leakage /ˈliːkɪdʒ/ *n.* (*lit., fig.*) уте́чка.

leaky /ˈliːkɪ/ *adj.* (**leakier, leakiest**) дыря́вый, име́ющий течь; **a ~ pipe/roof** протека́ющая труба́/кры́ша.

lean[1] /liːn/ *adj.*
1 (*thin*) то́щий; (*fig.*): **~ years** ску́дные го́ды.
2 (*of meat*) нежи́рный.

lean[2] /liːn/ *v.t.* (*past and p.p.* **leaned** /liːnd, lent/ *or esp. Br.* **leant**) прислон|я́ть, -и́ть (*что к чему*); оп|ира́ть, -ере́ть (*что обо что*).
■ *v.i.* (*past and p.p.* **leaned** /liːnd, lent/ *or esp. Br.* **leant**)
1 (*incline from vertical*) наклон|я́ться, -и́ться; **~ out of the window** высо́вываться, вы́сунуться из окна́.
2 (*support o.s.*) прислон|я́ться, -и́ться; оп|ира́ться, -ере́ться; **he was ~ing against a tree** он стоя́л, прислони́вшись к де́реву; (*fig.*): **he ~s** (*depends*) **on his wife for support** он опира́ется на подде́ржку жены́; **I had to ~** (*coll., put pressure*) **on him to get results** мне пришло́сь нажа́ть на него́, что́бы доби́ться результа́тов.

leaning /ˈliːnɪŋ/ *n.* (*inclination*) скло́нность; (*tendency*) пристра́стие.

leant /lent/ *esp. Br. past and p.p. of* ▶ **lean**[2]

leap /liːp/ *n.* прыжо́к, скачо́к.
■ *v.t.* (*past and p.p.* **leaped** /liːpt, lept/ *or* **leapt** /lept/) (**~** *over*) переск|а́кивать, -очи́ть (*or* перепры́г|ивать, -нуть) че́рез + *a.*
■ *v.i.* (*past and p.p.* **leaped** /liːpt, lept/ *or* **leapt** /lept/) пры́г|ать, -нуть; **my heart ~t for joy** у меня́ се́рдце подскочи́ло от ра́дости; **~ to one's feet** вск|а́кивать, -очи́ть; **he ~t** (*fig.*) **at my offer** он ухвати́лся за моё предложе́ние.
■ *cpds.* **~frog** *n.* чехарда́; **~ year** *n.* високо́сный год.

learn /lɜːn/ *v.t.* (*past and p.p.* **learned** /lɜːnt, lɜːnd/ *or esp. Br.* **learnt**) учи́ться, на- + *d. or inf.*; изуч|а́ть, -и́ть; (*study*) занима́ться (*impf.*) + *i.*; **he ~ed (how) to ride** он научи́лся е́здить верхо́м; **he is ~ing to be an interpreter** он у́чится на перево́дчика; **where did you ~ Russian?** где вы изуча́ли ру́сский язы́к?
■ *v.i.* (*past and p.p.* **learned** /lɜːnt, lɜːnd/ *or esp. Br.* **learnt**): **you can ~ from his mistakes** учи́тесь на его́ оши́бках.

learned /ˈlɜːnɪd/ *adj.* учёный.

learner /ˈlɜːnə(r)/ *n.* начина́ющий; (**~** *driver*) начина́ющий води́тель(, не име́ющий води́тельских прав).

learning /ˈlɜːnɪŋ/ *n.* (*process*) уче́ние; изуче́ние; (*body of knowledge*) нау́ка.
■ *cpd.* **~ curve** *n.* гра́фик приобрете́ния на́выка.

learnt /lɜːnt/ *esp. Br. past and p.p. of* ▶ **learn**

lease /liːs/ *n.* аре́нда.
■ *v.t.* (*of lessee*) арендова́ть (*impf., pf.*); брать, взять в аре́нду/внаём; (*of lessor*) сд|ава́ть, -ать в аре́нду.
■ *cpds.* **~hold** *n.* аре́нда; **~holder** *n.* аренда́тор.

leash /liːʃ/ *n.* поводо́к.

least /liːst/ *n.*: **to say the ~** мя́гко говоря́; **the ~ he could do is to pay for the damage** он мог бы по кра́йней ме́ре возмести́ть уще́рб; **at ~** по кра́йней ме́ре; не ме́ньше + *g.*; **at ~ once a year** не ре́же, чем раз в год; **he is at ~ as tall as you** он ва́шего ро́ста, а мо́жет быть и вы́ше; **you should at ~ have warned me** вы бы хоть предупреди́ли меня́; **not in the ~** ничу́ть, ниско́лько; **he is not in the ~ interested** он совсе́м не заинтересо́ван (*pred.*).
■ *adj.* (*smallest*) наиме́ньший; **that's the ~ of my worries** э́то меня́ ме́ньше всего волну́ет; (*slightest*) мале́йший; **he hasn't the ~ idea about it** он не име́ет ни мале́йшего поня́тия об э́том.
■ *adv.* ме́ньше всего́; **it is the ~ successful of his books** э́то наиме́нее уда́чная из его́ книг; **with the ~ possible trouble** с наиме́ньшими хло́потами; с наиме́ньшей затра́той сил.

leather /ˈleðə(r)/ *n.* ко́жа.
■ *adj.* ко́жаный.

leave /liːv/ *n.* о́тпуск; **he is on ~** он в о́тпуске.
■ *v.t.* (*past and p.p.* **left**)
1 (*allow or cause to remain*) ост|авля́ть, -а́вить; **the wound left a scar** от ра́ны оста́лся шрам; **has anyone left a message?** никто́ ничего́ не передава́л?; (*with indication of state or circumstances*): **~ me alone!** оста́вьте меня́ (в поко́е)!; **~ the door open!** оста́вьте дверь откры́той!; (*p.p., remaining*): **I have no money left** у меня́ не оста́лось де́нег.
2 (**~** *behind by accident*) заб|ыва́ть, -ы́ть; **I left my umbrella at home** я забы́л зо́нтик до́ма.
3 (*bequeath*) завеща́ть (*impf., pf.*); **she was left a large inheritance by her uncle** дя́дя оста́вил ей большо́е насле́дство.
4 (*abandon*) бр|оса́ть, -о́сить; пок|ида́ть, -и́нуть; **he left his wife for another woman** он бро́сил свою́ жену́ ра́ди друго́й же́нщины.
5 (*entrust*) предост|авля́ть, -а́вить; **~ it to him** пусть он э́то сде́лает; **~ it to me** я э́тим займу́сь.
6 (*go away from*) выходи́ть, вы́йти из + *g.*; (*by vehicle*) выезжа́ть, вы́ехать из + *g.*; (*by air*) вылета́ть, вы́лететь из + *g.*; **I ~ the house at eight** я выхожу́ и́з дому в во́семь часо́в; (**~** *for good, quit*) бр|оса́ть, -о́сить; пок|ида́ть, -и́нуть; **he left his job** он бро́сил свою́ рабо́ту; **he ~s school this year** он конча́ет шко́лу в э́том году́.
■ *v.i.* (*past and p.p.* **left**)
1 (*of person on foot*) уходи́ть, уйти́; (*by transport*) уезжа́ть, уе́хать; (*by air*) улет|а́ть, -е́ть.
2 (*of train*) от|ходи́ть, -ойти́; (*of boat*) от|ходи́ть, -ойти́; отпл|ыва́ть, -ы́ть; (*of aircraft*) вылета́ть, вы́лететь.
■ *with advs.*: **~ behind** *v.t.* ост|авля́ть, -а́вить по́сле себя́; (*forget to take*): **he left his hat behind** он забы́л свою́ шля́пу; (*abandon*): **he was left behind on the island** он оказа́лся бро́шенным на о́строве; (*outstrip*): **we left him far behind** мы оста́вили его́ далеко́ позади́; **~ on** *v.t.*: **I left the light on** я оста́вил свет включённым; **~ out** *v.t.*: **she left the washing out in the rain** она́ оста́вила бельё под дождём; (*omit*) пропус|ка́ть, -ти́ть; **I felt left out** я почу́вствовал себя́ ли́шним; **~ over** *v.t.* (*pass., remain*): ост|ава́ться, -а́ться; **a lot was left over after dinner** по́сле обе́да оста́лось

ещё много еды́.

leaves /li:vz/ *pl. of* ▶ **leaf**

Lebanese /lebə'ni:z/ *n.* (*pl.* ~) лива́н|ец (*fem.* -ка).
■ *adj.* лива́нский.

Lebanon /'lebənən/ *n.* Лива́н.

lecher /'letʃə(r)/ *n.* развра́тник, распу́тник.

lecherous /'letʃərəs/ *adj.* развра́тный, распу́тный.

lechery /'letʃərɪ/ *n.* развра́т.

lectern /'lektə:n/ *n.* анало́й (*в церкви*); (*in lecture room*) пюпи́тр.

lecture /'lektʃə(r)/ *n.* ле́кция.
■ *v.t.* чита́ть, про- ле́кцию/нота́цию + *d.*
■ *v.i.*: **he ~s in Russian** он чита́ет ле́кции по ру́сскому языку́.
■ *cpds.* **~ hall, ~ room, ~ theatre** *nn.* аудито́рия.

lecturer /'lektʃərə(r)/ *n.* ле́ктор; (*Br., univ.*) преподава́тель (*m.*).

led /led/ *past and p.p. of* ▶ **lead²**

ledge /ledʒ/ *n.* (*shelf*) пла́нка, по́лочка; (*projection*) вы́ступ.

ledger /'ledʒə(r)/ *n.* (*book*) гроссбу́х; (гла́вная) учётная кни́га.

leech /li:tʃ/ *n.* пия́вка.

leek /li:k/ *n.* лук-поре́й.

leer /lɪə(r)/ *n.* ухмы́лка.
■ *v.i.* ухмыл|я́ться, -ьну́ться; **~ at** хи́тро/зло́бно смотре́ть, по- на + *a.*

leeway /'li:weɪ/ *n.* (*fig.*) свобо́да де́йствий.

left¹ /left/ *n.*
1 (*side, direction*): **from the ~** сле́ва; **to the ~** нале́во; **on, to my ~** нале́во от меня́; **on, from my ~** сле́ва от меня́.
2 (*pol.*): **the L~** ле́вые (*pl.*) (па́ртии).
■ *adj.* ле́вый; **~ wing** (*pol.*) ле́вое крыло́.
■ *adv.* нале́во; **turn ~** св|ора́чивать, -ерну́ть нале́во.
■ *cpds.* **~-hand** *adj.* ле́вый; **on the ~-hand side of the street** по ле́вой стороне́ у́лицы; **car with ~-hand drive** маши́на с левосторо́нним управле́нием (*or* с рулём сле́ва); **~-handed** *adj.* де́лающий всё ле́вой руко́й, левору́кий; **~-handed person** левша́ (*c.g.*); **~-wing** *adj.* ле́вый.

left² /left/ *past and p.p. of* ▶ **leave**

leftovers /'leftəʊvəz/ *n. pl.* оста́тк|и (*pl., g.* -ов); (*food*) объе́дк|и (*pl., g.* -ов).

leg /leg/ *n.*
1 нога́; (*dim.*) но́жка; **pull s.o.'s ~** разыгр|ывать, -а́ть кого́-н.
2 (*meat*): **~ of lamb** бара́нья нога́.
3 (*of furniture etc.*) но́жка.
4 (*of garment*): **trouser ~** штани́на.
5 (*stage of journey etc.*) эта́п.

legacy /'legəsɪ/ *n.* насле́дство, насле́дие.

legal /'li:g(ə)l/ *adj.*
1 (*pert. to or based on law*) юриди́ческий, правово́й; **~ aid** (*Br.*) беспла́тная юриди́ческая по́мощь неиму́щим; **take ~ advice** консульти́роваться, про- с юри́стом.
2 (*permitted or ordained by law*) зако́нный, лега́льный; **~ holiday** (*US*) официа́льный нерабо́чий день; **~ tender** зако́нное платёжное сре́дство; **within one's ~ rights (to)** впра́ве (*по закону*) (+ *inf.*).
3 (*involving court proceedings*) суде́бный; **~ action** суде́бный иск; **take ~ action against** возбу|жда́ть, -ди́ть де́ло про́тив + *g.*; предъяв|ля́ть, -и́ть иск (к) + *d.*

legality /lɪ'gælɪtɪ/ *n.* зако́нность, лега́льность.

legalization /li:gəlaɪ'zeɪʃ(ə)n/ *n.* узако́нивание, легализа́ция.

legalize /'li:gəlaɪz/ *v.t.* узако́ни|вать, -ть.

legato /lɪ'gɑ:təʊ/ *n. & adv.* (*pl.* **~s**) (*mus.*) лега́то (*nt. indecl.*).

legend /'ledʒ(ə)nd/ *n.* леге́нда.

legendary /'ledʒəndərɪ/ *adj.* легенда́рный.

leggings /'legɪŋz/ *n.* (*stretch trousers*) ле́гинс|ы (*pl., g.* -ов).

legible /'ledʒɪb(ə)l/ *adj.* разбо́рчивый.

legislate /'ledʒɪsleɪt/ *v.i.* изд|ава́ть, -а́ть зако́ны.

legislation /ledʒɪs'leɪʃ(ə)n/ *n.* законода́тельство.

legislative /'ledʒɪslətɪv/ *adj.* законода́тельный.

legislature /'ledʒɪslətʃə(r)/ *n.* (*assembly*) законода́тельный о́рган; (*institutions*) законода́тельные учрежде́ния.

legitimacy /lɪ'dʒɪtɪməsɪ/ *n.* зако́нность.

legitimate /lɪ'dʒɪtɪmət/ *adj.* (*lawful*) зако́нный; (*justifiable*): **~ demands** справедли́вые тре́бования.

legitimize /lɪ'dʒɪtɪmaɪz/ *v.t.* узако́ни|вать, -ть.

leisure /'leʒə(r)/ *n.* свобо́дное вре́мя; **at one's ~** (*in free time*) в свобо́дное вре́мя; (*unhurriedly*) не спеша́; **~ centre** спорти́вно-развлека́тельный ко́мплекс; **~ time** вре́мя досу́га.

leisured /'leʒəd/ *adj.* досу́жий, пра́здный; **the ~ classes** нерабо́тающие кла́ссы/слой о́бщества.

leisurely /'leʒəlɪ/ *adj.* неспе́шный, неторопли́вый.

leitmoti|f, -v /'laɪtməʊti:f/ *n.* лейтмоти́в.

lemon /'lemən/ *n.* лимо́н; (*attr.*) лимо́нный.

lemonade /lemə'neɪd/ *n.*
1 (*Br., carbonated drink*) лимона́д.
2 (*drink of lemon juice and water*) напи́ток из со́ка лимо́на с водо́й.

lemur /'li:mə(r)/ *n.* лему́р.

lend /lend/ *v.t.* (*past and p.p.* **lent**)
1 да|ва́ть, -ть взаймы́; од|а́лживать,-олжи́ть; ссу|жа́ть, -ди́ть (*кого чем or что кому*); **~ me £5** одолжи́те мне (*or* да́йте мне взаймы́) пять фу́нтов; **~ me the book for a while** да́йте мне кни́гу на вре́мя.
2 (*impart*) прид|ава́ть, -а́ть.
3 (*proffer*): **~ a hand** (*help*) ока́з|ывать, -а́ть по́мощь (*кому*); (*help out in difficulty*) выруча́ть, вы́ручить.

lender /'lendə(r)/ *n.* заимода́вец, кредито́р.

length /leŋkθ/ *n.*
1 (*dimension, measurement*) длина́; **2 metres in ~** 2 ме́тра длино́й.
2 (*racing etc.*): **the horse won by a ~** ло́шадь опереди́ла други́х на ко́рпус.
3 (*of time*) продолжи́тельность, дли́тельность, срок; **the chief fault of this film is its ~** гла́вный недоста́ток э́того фи́льма — его́ растя́нутость; **at ~** (*finally*) наконе́ц; (*in detail*) во всех подро́бностях.

[4] (*extent, degree*): **he went to great ~s not to offend them** он сделал всё возмо́жное, что́бы не оби́деть их.
[5] (*piece of material*) кусо́к; отре́з.

lengthen /ˈleŋkθ(ə)n/ *v.t. & i.* удлин|я́ть(ся), -и́ть(ся).

lengthy /ˈleŋkθɪ/ *adj.* (**lengthier, lengthiest**) дли́нный, затя́нутый; (*in time*) дли́тельный.

leniency /ˈli:nɪənsɪ/ *n.* снисхожде́ние; мя́гкость.

lenient /ˈli:nɪənt/ *adj.* (*of person*) снисходи́тельный; (*of punishment etc.*) мя́гкий.

Leningrad /ˈlenɪngræd/ *n.* (*hist.*) Ленингра́д; (*attr.*) ленингра́дский.

lens /lenz/ *n.* (*anat., opt.*) ли́нза; (*phot.*) объекти́в.

Lent /lent/ *n.* Вели́кий пост.

lent /lent/ *past and p.p. of* ▸ **lend**

lentil /ˈlentɪl/ *n.* чечеви́ца.

Leo /ˈli:əʊ/ *n.* (*pl.* **Leos**) (*astr.*) Лев.

leopard /ˈlepəd/ *n.* леопа́рд.

leotard /ˈli:ətɑ:d/ *n.* трико́ (*indecl.*).

leper /ˈlepə(r)/ *n.* прокажённый.

leprosy /ˈleprəsɪ/ *n.* прока́за.

lesbian /ˈlezbɪən/ *n.* (*homosexual*) лесбия́нка.
■ *adj.* лесби́йский.

lesion /ˈli:ʒ(ə)n/ *n.* поврежде́ние, пораже́ние.

less /les/ *n.* ме́ньшее коли́чество; **you should eat ~** вам сле́дует ме́ньше есть; **~ than £50** ме́нее 50 фу́нтов; **in ~ than an hour** ме́ньше чем за час.
■ *adj.* [1] (*smaller*) ме́ньший.
[2] (*not so much*) ме́ньше; **eat ~ meat!** е́шьте ме́ньше мя́са!
■ *adv.* ме́ньше, ме́нее; не так, не сто́лько; **he is ~ intelligent than his sister** он не так умён, как его́ сестра́; **the ~ you think about it the better** чем ме́ньше об э́том ду́мать, тем лу́чше; **~ and ~** всё ме́ньше и ме́ньше.
■ *prep.* ми́нус; за вы́четом + *g.*; **I paid him his wages, ~ what he owed me** я вы́дал ему́ зарпла́ту за вы́четом су́ммы, кото́рую он мне задолжа́л.

lessen /ˈles(ə)n/ *v.t. & i.* ум|еньша́ть(ся), -е́ньшить(ся).

lesser /ˈlesə(r)/ *adj.* ме́ньший.

lesson /ˈles(ə)n/ *n.* уро́к, заня́тие; **English ~s** уро́ки англи́йского языка́; **teach s.o. a ~** (*rebuke, punish*) дать (*pf.*) уро́к кому́-н.

let[1] /let/ *n.* (*Br., of property*) аре́нда; **take a house on a long ~** снять (*pf.*) дом на дли́тельный срок.
■ *v.t.* (**letting;** *past and p.p.* **let**) (*also* **~ out**) сда|ва́ть, -ть внаём.

let[2] /let/ *v.t.* (**letting;** *past and p.p.* **let**)
[1] (*allow*) позв|оля́ть, -о́лить + *d.*; разреш|а́ть, -и́ть + *d.*; **~ me help you** позво́льте вам помо́чь; **he won't ~ me work** он не даёт мне рабо́тать; **~ go** (*relax grip on*) выпуска́ть, вы́пустить из рук; отпус|ка́ть, -ти́ть; **~ o.s. go** увл|ека́ться, -е́чься; (*set free*) выпуска́ть, вы́пустить; **~ one's hair grow** отпус|ка́ть, -ти́ть во́лосы.
[2] (*cause to*): **~ s.o. know** да|ва́ть, -ть кому́-н. знать; сообщ|а́ть, -и́ть кому́-н.
[3] (*in imper. or hortatory sense*): **~ me see** (*reflect*) погоди́те; да́йте поду́мать; **just ~ him try it!** пусть то́лько попро́бует!
[4] (**~** *come or go*): **shall I ~ you into a secret?** хоти́те я раскро́ю вам та́йну?; **he was ~ out of prison** его́ вы́пустили из тюрьмы́.
■ *with advs.*: **~ alone** *v.t.*: **~ alone** (*not to mention*) не то́лько что, не говоря́ уже́ о + *p.*; **they haven't got a radio, ~ alone television** у них и ра́дио нет, не говоря́ уже́ о телеви́зоре; **~ down** *v.t.* (*disappoint*) разочаро́в|ывать, -а́ть; (*fail to support*) подв|оди́ть, -ести́ (*coll.*); (*Br., deflate*): **~ down tyres** спус|ка́ть, -ти́ть ши́ны; (*lengthen*): **~ down a dress** отпуска́ть, отпусти́ть пла́тье; **~ in** *v.t.* (*admit*) впус|ка́ть, -ти́ть; **the window doesn't ~ in much light** че́рез э́то окно́ проника́ет ма́ло све́та; **my shoes ~ in water** мои́ ту́фли протека́ют/промока́ют; **he ~ himself in** он сам откры́л дверь и вошёл; **what have I ~ myself in for?** во что я ввяза́лся?; **~ off** *v.t.* (*discharge*) разря|жа́ть, -ди́ть; **~ off fireworks** запуска́ть (*impf.*) фейерве́рк; (*not punish*) не нака́зывать (*impf.*); **he was ~ off lightly** он легко́ отде́лался; (*excuse*) про|ща́ть, -сти́ть + *d.*; **they ~ him off his debt** ему́ прости́ли долг; **~ on** *v.t. & i.* (*coll., divulge*) прогов|а́риваться, -ори́ться; **~ out** *v.t.*: **~ out a scream** завизжа́ть (*pf.*); взви́згнуть (*pf.*); **~ out a secret** прогов|а́риваться, -ори́ться; проболта́ться (*pf.*); **~ up** *v.i.* (*weaken, diminish*) ослаб|ева́ть, -е́ть; (*stop for a while*) приостан|а́вливаться, -ови́ться; (*relax*) перед|ыха́ть, -охну́ть.
■ *cpd.* **~-down** *n.* (*disappointment, anticlimax*) разочарова́ние.

lethal /ˈli:θ(ə)l/ *adj.* (*fatal*) смерте́льный; (*designed to kill*) смертоно́сный.

lethargic /lɪˈθɑ:dʒɪk/ *adj.* вя́лый.

letter /ˈletə(r)/ *n.*
[1] (*of alphabet*) бу́ква.
[2] (*written communication*) письмо́.
■ *cpds.* **~ bomb** *n.* бо́мба в конве́рте; **~ box** *n.* (*Br.*) почто́вый я́щик; **~head, ~ heading** *n.* (*paper*) фи́рменный бланк.

lettuce /ˈletɪs/ *n.* сала́т (*расте́ние*).

leukaemia /lu:ˈki:mɪə/ (*US* **leukemia**) *n.* белокро́вие, лейкеми́я.

level /ˈlev(ə)l/ *n.* у́ровень; **on a ~ with** на одно́м у́ровне с + *i.*; **talks at Cabinet ~** перегово́ры на прави́тельственном у́ровне.
■ *adj.* (*even*) ро́вный; (*flat*) пло́ский; (*horizontal*) горизонта́льный; **~ crossing** (*Br.*) (железнодоро́жный) перее́зд; **the water was ~ with the banks** вода́ была́ вро́вень с берега́ми; **draw ~ with** наг|оня́ть, -на́ть.
■ *v.t.* (**levelled, levelling;** *US* **leveled, leveling**)
[1] (*make ~*) ур|а́внивать, -овня́ть; выра́внивать, вы́ровнять.
[2] (*raze to ground*) ср|а́внивать, -овня́ть с земле́й.
[3] (*aim*) нав|оди́ть, -ести́; наце́ли|вать, -ть; **she ~led a gun at his head** она́ прице́лилась ему́ в го́лову; (*criticism, accusation*) напр|авля́ть, -а́вить (**at:** про́тив + *g.*).
■ *with advs.*: **~ off, ~ out** *vv.t.* (*smooth out*) сгла́|живать, -дить; (*make ~, even, identical*)

ур|а́внивать, -овня́ть.
■ *cpd.* **~-headed** *adj.* тре́звый, рассуди́тельный.

lever /'li:və(r)/ *n.* (*lit., fig.*) рыча́г.

leverage /'li:vərɪdʒ/ *n.* (*action*) де́йствие/уси́лие рычага́; **use ~ on s.o.** (*fig.*) повлия́ть (*pf.*) на кого́-н.

levitation /levɪ'teɪʃ(ə)n/ *n.* левита́ция.

levity /'levɪtɪ/ *n.* легкомы́слие.

levy /'levɪ/ *n.* обложе́ние.
■ *v.t.* взима́ть (*impf.*) (**on:** с + *g.*).

lewd /lju:d/ *adj.* (*of person*) развра́тный; (*of joke, suggestion*) непристо́йный, гря́зный.

lexical /'leksɪk(ə)l/ *adj.* лекси́ческий.

lexicon /'leksɪkən/ *n.* (*dictionary*) слова́рь, лексико́н; (*vocabulary of writer etc.*) ле́ксика.

liability /laɪə'bɪlɪtɪ/ *n.*
1 (*responsibility*) отве́тственность.
2 (*pl., debts*) долги́ (*m. pl.*).
3 (*handicap*): **he's nothing but a ~y** он про́сто обу́за.

liable /'laɪəb(ə)l/ *adj.*
1 (*answerable*) отве́тственный (за + *a.*).
2 (*subject*): **he is ~ to a heavy fine** его́ мо́гут подве́ргнуть большо́му штра́фу.
3 (*apt, likely*): **she is ~ to forget it** она́ скло́нна забыва́ть об э́том.

liaise /lɪ'eɪz/ *v.i.* устана́вливать/подде́рживать (*impf.*) связь (с + *i.*).

liaison /lɪ'eɪzɒn/ *n.* связь.

liar /'laɪə(r)/ *n.* лгун (*fem.* -ья).

libel /'laɪb(ə)l/ *n.* клевета́.
■ *v.t.* (**libelled, libelling;** *US* **libeled, libeling**) клевета́ть (*на кого*), о- (*кого*), на- (*на кого*); **they ~led me** они́ оклевета́ли меня́, они́ наклевета́ли на меня́.

libellous /'laɪbələs/ (*US* **libelous**) *adj.* клеветни́ческий.

liberal /'lɪbər(ə)l/ *n.* либера́л.
■ *adj.* 1 (*generous*) ще́дрый; (*abundant*) оби́льный.
2 (*broadminded*): **a man of ~ views** челове́к широ́ких взгля́дов.
3 (*pol.*) либера́льный.
■ *cpd.* **L~ Democrat** *n.* (*pol.*) либера́л-демокра́т.

liberalization /lɪbərəlaɪ'zeɪʃ(ə)n/ *n.* демократиза́ция, либерализа́ция.

liberalize /'lɪbərəlaɪz/ *v.t.* либерализова́ть (*impf., pf.*).

liberate /'lɪbəreɪt/ *v.t.* освобо|жда́ть, -ди́ть.

liberation /lɪbə'reɪʃ(ə)n/ *n.* освобожде́ние.

liberator /'lɪbəreɪtə(r)/ *n.* освободи́тель (*fem.* -ница).

Liberia /laɪ'bɪərɪə/ *n.* Либе́рия.

Liberian /laɪ'bɪərɪən/ *n.* либери́|ец (*fem.* -йка).
■ *adj.* либери́йский.

libertarian /lɪbə'teərɪən/ *n.* (*advocate of freedom*) боре́ц за демократи́ческие свобо́ды.

liberty /'lɪbətɪ/ *n.* свобо́да; **at ~** находя́щийся на свобо́де; **you are at ~ to go** вы во́льны уйти́.

libido /lɪ'bi:dəʊ/ *n.* (*pl.* **~s**) либи́до (*nt. indecl.*).

Libra /'li:brə/ *n.* (*astron.*) Вес|ы́ (*pl., g.* -о́в).

librarian /laɪ'breərɪən/ *n.* библиоте́карь (*m.*).

library /'laɪbrərɪ/ *n.* библиоте́ка.

Libya /'lɪbɪə, 'lɪbjə/ *n.* Ли́вия.

Libyan /'lɪbɪən, 'lɪbjən/ *n.* ливи́|ец (*fem.* -йка).
■ *adj.* ливи́йский.

licence /'laɪs(ə)ns/ (*US also* **license**) *n.*
1 (*permission*) разреше́ние; (*for trade*) лице́нзия.
2 (*permit*) свиде́тельство; **driving ~** води́тельские права́.
3 (*freedom*) во́льность.
■ *cpd.* **~ plate** *n.* (*US*) номерно́й знак.

license /'laɪs(ə)ns/ (*US also* **licence**) *v.t.*
1 (*authorize*) разреш|а́ть, -и́ть *что*; да|ва́ть, -ть разреше́ние на *что*.
2 (*grant permit, permission to*) разреш|а́ть, -и́ть + *d.*; **~d premises** (*inn*) заведе́ние, облада́ющее лице́нзией на прода́жу спиртны́х напи́тков.

licensee /laɪsən'si:/ *n.* облада́тель (*fem.* -ница) разреше́ния/лице́нзии; (*of public house*) хозя́|ин (*fem.* -йка) ба́ра.

licensing /'laɪsənsɪŋ/ *n.* лицензи́рование.

licentious /laɪ'senʃəs/ *adj.* распу́щенный.

lichen /'laɪkən/ *n.* лиша́йник.

lick /lɪk/ *v.t.*
1 лиз|а́ть, -ну́ть; **~ one's lips**/(*coll.*) **chops** обли́з|ывать, -а́ть гу́бы; обли́з|ываться, -а́ться; (*fig.*): **~ one's wounds** зали́з|ывать, -а́ть ра́ны.
2 (*coll., defeat*) поб|ива́ть, -и́ть.

licorice /'lɪkərɪs, -rɪʃ/ = **liquorice**

lid /lɪd/ *n.* кры́шка.

lido /'li:dəʊ, 'laɪ-/ *n.* (*pl.* **lidos**) (обще́ственный) пляж.

lie[1] /laɪ/ *n.* (*falsehood*) ложь; **tell a ~** лгать, со-.
■ *v.i.* (**lies, lied, lying**) лгать, со-; врать, со-/на-; **he ~d to me** он мне солга́л.

lie[2] /laɪ/ *v.i.* (**lying;** *past* **lay;** *p.p.* **lain**)
1 (*repose*) лежа́ть, по-; **~ low** притаи́ться (*pf.*).
2 (*be; be situated*) находи́ться (*impf.*); быть располо́женным.
3 (*fig., reside, rest*): **the choice ~s with you** вы́бор зави́сит от вас; вам выбира́ть; **she knows where her interests ~** она́ своего́ не упу́стит.
4 (**~ down**) ложи́ться, лечь; приле́чь (*pf.*); **he went and lay on the bed** он лёг на крова́ть.
■ *with advs.*: **~ about, ~ around** валя́ться (*impf.*); **~ ahead** предстоя́ть (*impf.*); **~ down** ложи́ться, лечь; **I shall ~ down for an hour** я приля́гу на час/часо́к.
■ *cpds.* **~-down** *n.* (*Br.*): **she had a ~** она́ полежа́ла; **~-in** *n.* (*Br.*): **we had a ~** мы вста́ли по́здно.

lieu /lu:/ *n.*: **in ~ of** вме́сто + *g.*

lieutenant /lef'tenənt/ *n.* лейтена́нт.

life /laɪf/ *n.* (*pl.* **lives**)
1 (*being alive*) жизнь; **save s.o.'s ~** спасти́ (*pf.*) жизнь кому́-н.; **~ insurance** страхова́ние жи́зни; (*existence*): **that's ~!** такова́ жизнь!; (*way or style of ~*) быт; **family ~** дома́шний быт; **country, village ~** дереве́нская жизнь.
2 (*period, span of ~*): **have the time of one's ~** прекра́сно проводи́ть (*impf.*) вре́мя; **he has had a good/quiet ~** он про́жил

хоро́шую/споко́йную жизнь; **~ sentence** пожи́зненное заключе́ние (*как приговор*); (*of inanimate things, durability*) долгове́чность; срок слу́жбы.
3 (*animation*) жи́вость; **the ~ and soul of the party** душа́ о́бщества; **the child is full of ~** ребёнок о́чень живо́й; **the play came to ~ in the third act** к тре́тьему де́йствию пье́са оживи́лась.
4 (*living things*) жизнь; **is there ~ on Mars?** есть ли жизнь на Ма́рсе?; **animal ~** живо́тный мир.
■ *cpds.* **~belt** *n.* (*Br.*) спаса́тельный круг; **~boat** *n.* спаса́тельная ло́дка; **~ coach** *n.* персона́льный наста́вник; **~ expectancy** *n.* вероя́тная продолжи́тельность жи́зни; **~guard, ~saver** *nn.* спаса́тель (*fem.* -ница) (на пля́же); **~ jacket** *n.* спаса́тельный жиле́т; **~like** *adj.* реалисти́чный; **~line** *n.* (*fig.*) еди́нственная наде́жда; спаси́тельное сре́дство; (*of communication line*) связу́ющий мост (**to:** с + *i.*); **~long** *adj.* пожи́зненный; **they were ~long friends** они́ бы́ли друзья́ми всю жизнь; **~-saving** *n.* спасе́ние; **~-size(d)** *adj.* в натура́льную величину́; **~span** *n.* (*of person, animal*) продолжи́тельность жи́зни; (*of machine, tool*) срок эксплуата́ции; **~style** *n.* о́браз жи́зни; **~-support** *adj.*: **~-support system** систе́ма жизнеобеспе́чения; **~time** *n.* жизнь; **in s.o.'s ~time** при жи́зни кого́-н.; **the chance of a ~ time** ре́дкий/исключи́тельный слу́чай; **it's a ~time since I saw her** я не ви́дел её це́лую ве́чность.

lifeless /ˈlaɪflɪs/ *adj.* (*dead*) мёртвый; (*inanimate*) неживо́й; (*inert*) безжи́зненный.

lift /lɪft/ *n.*
1 (*in car etc.*): **give s.o. a ~** подв|ози́ть, -езти́ кого́-н.
2 (*fig., of spirits*): **the news gave her a ~** от э́той но́вости она́ воспря́нула ду́хом.
3 (*Br., apparatus*) лифт.
■ *v.t.* 1 (*raise*) подн|има́ть, -я́ть.
2 (*remove*): **~ a ban** сн|има́ть, -ять запре́т.
■ *v.i.* (*disperse*) рассе́|иваться, -яться; (*cease*) прекра|ща́ться, -ти́ться.
■ *with advs.*: **~ off** *v.t.* сн|има́ть, -ять; *v.i.* (*of rocket*) от|рыва́ться, -орва́ться от земли́; **~ up** *v.t.* подн|има́ть, -я́ть.
■ *cpd.* **~-off** *n.* отры́в от земли́.

ligament /ˈlɪgəmənt/ *n.* свя́зка.

light[1] /laɪt/ *n.*
1 свет; **stand against the ~** стоя́ть (*impf.*) про́тив све́та; **bring to ~** выводи́ть, вы́вести на чи́стую во́ду; **come to ~** обнару́жи|ваться, -ться; выплыва́ть, вы́плыть; **shed, throw ~ on sth.** прол|ива́ть, -и́ть свет на что-н.; (*in a picture*): **effects of ~ and shade** эффе́кты све́та и те́ни; (*lighting*) освеще́ние; (*fig.*): **this book shows him in a bad ~** э́та кни́га пока́зывает его́ в невы́годном све́те; (*point of ~*): **the ~s of the town** огни́ го́рода.
2 (*lamp*) ла́мпа; **~ bulb** ла́мпочка; (*of car*) фа́ра; **traffic ~s** светофо́р.
3 (*flame*) ого́нь (*m.*); **have you a ~?** у вас огонька́ не бу́дет?
■ *adj.* 1 (*opp. dark*) све́тлый; **get ~** рассве|та́ть, -сти́.
2 (*in colour*) све́тлый; све́тлого цве́та; **~-haired** светловоло́сый; **~-skinned** светлоко́жий; (*with names of colours*) све́тло-; **~ green** све́тло-зелёный; **~ blue** све́тло-голубо́й.
■ *v.t.* (*past* **lit;** *p.p.* **lit** *or* (*attr.*) **lighted**) (*also* **~ up**)
1 (*kindle*) заж|ига́ть, -е́чь; **~ a fire** разв|оди́ть, -ести́ ого́нь; **~ (up) a cigarette** заку́р|ивать, -и́ть папиро́су.
2 (*illuminate*) осве|ща́ть, -ти́ть; **~ the way for s.o.** свети́ть, по- кому́-н.; (*fig.*): **a smile lit up his face** улы́бка озари́ла его́ лицо́.
■ *cpds.* **~house** *n.* мая́к; **~weight** *n.* (*sport; fig.*) легкове́с; **~ year** *n.* светово́й год.

light[2] /laɪt/ *adj.* (*opp. heavy*) лёгкий; **our casualties were light** на́ши поте́ри бы́ли незначи́тельны; **~ music** лёгкая му́зыка; **~ reading** лёгкое чте́ние; **a ~ sentence** мя́гкий пригово́р; **I am a ~ sleeper** я чу́тко сплю.
■ *cpds.* **~-headed** *adj.*: **she felt ~-headed** у неё закружи́лась голова́; **~-hearted** *adj.* (*carefree*) беспе́чный; (*of action*) необду́манный; **~weight** *adj.* (*suit*) лёгкий; (*fig.*) несерьёзный, легкове́сный.

lighten[1] /ˈlaɪt(ə)n/ *v.t.* (*make less heavy or easier*) облегч|а́ть, -и́ть.

lighten[2] /ˈlaɪt(ə)n/ *v.i.* (*grow brighter*) светле́ть, по-.

lighter /ˈlaɪtə(r)/ *n.* (*for cigarettes etc.*) зажига́лка.

lighting /ˈlaɪtɪŋ/ *n.* освеще́ние.

lightly /ˈlaɪtlɪ/ *adv.* легко́; **you have got off ~** вы легко́ отде́лались.

lightning /ˈlaɪtnɪŋ/ *n.* мо́лния; **he was struck by ~** в него́ уда́рила мо́лния.
■ *adj.*: **with ~ speed** молниено́сно.

like[1] /laɪk/ *n.* (*sth. equal or similar*) подо́бное; **music, dancing and the ~** му́зыка, та́нцы и тому́ подо́бное; (*person*) подо́бный; **the ~s of me, us** наш брат.
■ *adj.* (**more like, most like**) подо́бный, похо́жий.
■ *prep.* 1 (*similar to, characteristic of*) похо́жий на + *a.*; **she is ~ her mother** она́ похо́жа на мать; **what's she ~?** что она́ за челове́к?; **a house ~ yours** дом вро́де ва́шего; **it sounds ~ thunder** как бу́дто гром греми́т; **it sounds ~ a good idea** э́то, пожа́луй, хоро́шая иде́я; **a person ~ that** тако́й челове́к.
2 (*inclined towards*): **I don't feel ~ it** мне (что́-то) не хо́чется; **I felt ~ crying** мне хоте́лось пла́кать; **I feel ~ an ice cream** я бы не прочь съесть моро́женое.
■ *cpd.* **~-minded** *adj.* приде́рживающийся тех же взгля́дов.

like[2] /laɪk/ *v.t.* (*take pleasure in*) люби́ть (*impf.*), цени́ть (*impf.*); **he ~s living in Paris** ему́ нра́вится жить в Пари́же; **she ~d dancing** она́ люби́ла танцева́ть; **I ~ him** он мне нра́вится; **we ~d the play** пье́са нам понра́вилась; **would you ~ a drink?** хоти́те вы́пить (чего́-нибудь)?; **if you ~** е́сли хоти́те; **I should ~ to meet him** мне хоте́лось бы познако́миться с ним; **he would ~ to come** он хоте́л бы прийти́; **as you ~** как уго́дно.

likeable /ˈlaɪkəb(ə)l/ *adj.* симпати́чный.

likelihood /ˈlaɪklɪhʊd/ *n.* вероя́тность; **in all ~** по всей вероя́тности.

likely /ˈlaɪklɪ/ *adj.* (**likelier, likeliest**)
[1] (*probable*) вероя́тный; (*plausible*) правдоподо́бный.
[2] (*to be expected*): **he is ~ to come** он, вероя́тно, придёт.

liken /ˈlaɪkən/ *v.t.* упод|обля́ть, -о́бить (*кого/что кому/чему*).

likeness /ˈlaɪknɪs/ *n.* схо́дство, подо́бие; **a family ~** фами́льное схо́дство.

likewise /ˈlaɪkwaɪz/ *adv.* подо́бно.

liking /ˈlaɪkɪŋ/ *n.* симпа́тия (*к кому*); **I took a ~ to him** я почу́вствовал к нему́ симпа́тию; **is the meat done to your ~?** э́то мя́со пригото́влено, как вы лю́бите?

lilac /ˈlaɪlək/ *n.* сире́нь.

lilt /lɪlt/ *n.* (*tune*) напе́в; (*rhythm*) ритм.
■ *v.i.*: **a ~ing melody** мелоди́чный напе́в.

lily /ˈlɪlɪ/ *n.* ли́лия; **~ of the valley** ла́ндыш.

limb /lɪm/ *n.*
[1] (*of body; also fig.*) член; коне́чность.
[2] (*branch of tree*) сук, ветвь.

limber /ˈlɪmbə(r)/ *v.i.*: **~ up** разм|ина́ться, -я́ться.

limbo /ˈlɪmbəʊ/ *n.* (*pl.* **~s**)
[1] (*relig.*) лимб.
[2] (*fig.*): **our plans are in ~** на́ши пла́ны повиса́ют в во́здухе.

lime[1] /laɪm/ *n.* (*fruit*) лайм; **~ juice** сок ла́йма.

lime[2] /laɪm/ *n.* (*tree*) ли́па.

lime[3] /laɪm/ *n.* (*calcium oxide*) и́звесть.
■ *cpds.* **~light** *n.* (*lit.*) свет ра́мпы; (*fig.*): **be in the ~light** быть знамени́тостью; **~stone** *n.* известня́к.

limit /ˈlɪmɪt/ *n.*
[1] (*terminal point*) преде́л; **set, fix a ~ to sth.** устан|а́вливать, -ови́ть преде́л чему́-н.; **I am willing to help you, within ~s** я гото́в помо́чь вам в преде́лах возмо́жного.
[2] (*boundary*) грани́ца.
[3] (*time ~*) (преде́льный) срок; **age ~** преде́льный во́зраст.
■ *v.t.* (**limited, limiting**) ограни́чи|вать, -ть (*кого/что чем*); **~ed (liability) company** (*Br.*) компа́ния с ограни́ченной отве́тственностью.

limitation /lɪmɪˈteɪʃ(ə)n/ *n.* (*condition*) огово́рка; (*drawback*) недоста́ток; **he has his ~s** он не лишён недоста́тков; (*limiting, being limited*) ограниче́ние.

limitless /ˈlɪmɪtlɪs/ *adj.* безграни́чный, беспреде́льный; (*of time*) бесконе́чный.

limousine /lɪmʊˈziːn/ *n.* лимузи́н.

limp[1] /lɪmp/ *n.* хромота́; **he has a ~** он хрома́ет/прихра́мывает.
■ *v.i.* хрома́ть (*impf.*).

limp[2] /lɪmp/ *adj.*
[1] (*flexible*) мя́гкий.
[2] (*flabby*) вя́лый.

linchpin, lynchpin /ˈlɪntʃpɪn/ *n.* чека́; (*fig., of person or thing*) тот/то, на ком/чём всё де́ржится.

line[1] /laɪn/ *n.*
[1] (*cord*) верёвка; **hang washing on the ~** разве́сить (*pf.*) бельё на верёвке; (*fishing ~*) ле́ска.
[2] (*wire, cable for communication*) ли́ния (свя́зи); ка́бель (*m.*); про́вод; **he is on the ~** он говори́т по телефо́ну; он у телефо́на.
[3] (*rail.*) ли́ния; (*track*) полотно́; ре́льсы (*m. pl.*).
[4] (*transport system*) ли́ния; **air ~s** возду́шные ли́нии.
[5] (*long narrow mark*) ли́ния, черта́; (*imagined straight ~*): **~ of fire** направле́ние стрельбы́.
[6] (*on face etc.*) скла́дка.
[7] (*drawn, painted etc.*) штрих.
[8] (*boundary*) грани́ца, преде́л, черта́.
[9] (*row*) ряд, ли́ния; **stand in ~** стоя́ть (*impf.*) в ряд; (*US, queue*) стоя́ть (*impf.*); **in ~ with** в одну́ ли́нию (*or* в ряд) с + *i.*; (*fig.*) в согла́сии/соотве́тствии с + *i.*; **bring into ~** (*fig.*) привле́чь (*pf.*) *кого* на свою́ сто́рону; **come, fall into ~** (*fig.*) согласова́ться (*impf., pf.*).
[10] (*mil., entrenched position*): **front ~** ли́ния фро́нта.
[11] (*of print or writing*) строка́; **on ~ 10 there's a mistake** в деся́той строке́ оши́бка; (*pl., actor's part*) роль.
[12] (*lineage*) ли́ния.
[13] (*course, direction, track*) направле́ние, ли́ния; **take a firm, hard, strong ~** зан|има́ть, -я́ть твёрдую пози́цию; стро́го об|ходи́ться, -ойти́сь (*с кем*).
[14] (*province*): **his ~ of business** род его́ заня́тий.
[15] (*class of goods*) сорт, род, моде́ль (това́ра).
■ *v.t.* [1] (*mark with ~s*) линова́ть, раз-; **~d paper** лино́ванная бума́га; **his face was deeply ~d** его́ лицо́ бы́ло изборождено́ морщи́нами.
[2] (*form a ~ along*) стоя́ть (*impf.*); **police ~d the street** полице́йские стоя́ли по обе́им сторона́м у́лицы.
■ *with adv.*: **~ up** *v.t.* (*align*) выстра́ивать, вы́строить в ряд/ли́нию; (*queue up*) ста|нови́ться, -ть в о́чередь.
■ *cpds.* **~sman** *n.* (*sport*) боково́й судья́; **~-up** *n.* (*sport*) соста́в кома́нды; (*mus.*) соста́в анса́мбля/(поп-)гру́ппы; (*TV*) расписа́ние переда́ч.

line[2] /laɪn/ *v.t.*
[1] (*put lining into*) ста́вить, по- на подкла́дку; **her coat is ~d with silk** у неё пальто́ на шёлковой подкла́дке.
[2] (*fig.*) заст|авля́ть, -а́вить; **the wall was ~d with books** стена́ была́ заста́влена кни́гами.

lineage /ˈlɪnɪɪdʒ/ *n.* (*ancestry*) происхожде́ние; (*genealogy*) родосло́вная.

linear /ˈlɪnɪə(r)/ *adj.* лине́йный.

linen /ˈlɪnɪn/ *n.*
[1] (*material: smooth*) лён.
[2] (*~ articles*) бельё; (*bed ~*) посте́льное бельё.
■ *adj.* полотня́ный.

liner /ˈlaɪnə(r)/ *n.* ла́йнер.

linger /ˈlɪŋgə(r)/ *v.i.* (*take one's time*) ме́длить (*impf.*); (*stay on*) заде́рж|иваться, -а́ться; **I have ~ing doubts** мои́ сомне́ния не рассе́ялись.
■ *with adv.*: **~ on** *v.i.* (*of doubt etc.: remain*) ост|ава́ться, -а́ться.

lingerie /ˈlæʒərɪ/ *n.* да́мское бельё.

linguist /ˈlɪŋgwɪst/ *n.* лингви́ст, языкове́д.
linguistic /lɪŋˈgwɪstɪk/ *adj.* лингвисти́ческий.
linguistics /lɪŋˈgwɪstɪks/ *n.* лингви́стика.
lining /ˈlaɪnɪŋ/ *n.* подкла́дка.
link /lɪŋk/ *n.*
1 (*of chain; also fig.*) звено́.
2 (*connection*) связь; (*comput.*) ссы́лка.
■ *v.t.* (*unite*) соедин|я́ть, -и́ть; (*join*) свя́з|ывать, -а́ть; **~ arms with s.o.** идти́ (*det.*) по́д руку с кем-н.
■ *with adv.*: **~ up** *v.t. & i.* соедин|я́ться, -и́ться.
■ *cpd.* **~-up** *n.* связь, соедине́ние.
lino /ˈlaɪnəʊ/ (*pl.* **linos**) (*Br.*) = **linoleum**
linoleum /lɪˈnəʊlɪəm/ *n.* лино́леум.
linseed /ˈlɪnsiːd/ *n.* льняно́е се́мя; **~ oil** льняно́е ма́сло.
lintel /ˈlɪnt(ə)l/ *n.* при́толока (*верхний брус дверной/оконной рамы*).
lion /ˈlaɪən/ *n.* лев.
■ *cpd.* **~ cub** *n.* львёнок.
lioness /ˈlaɪənɪs/ *n.* льви́ца.
lip /lɪp/ *n.*
1 губа́ (*dim.* гу́бка).
2 (*edge of cup, wound etc.*) край.
■ *cpds.* **~-read** *v.t. & i.* чита́ть (*impf.*) с губ; **~salve** *n.* (*Br.*) гигиени́ческая губна́я пома́да; **~ service** *n.*: **pay ~ service to sth.** призн|ава́ть, -а́ть что-н. то́лько на слова́х; **~stick** *n.* (*substance*) губна́я пома́да; (*applicator*) тю́бик губно́й пома́ды.
liqueur /lɪˈkjʊə(r)/ *n.* ликёр.
liquid /ˈlɪkwɪd/ *n.* жи́дкость.
■ *adj.* жи́дкий; **~ assets** (*fin.*) ликви́дные акти́вы.
liquidate /ˈlɪkwɪdeɪt/ *v.t.* (*all senses*) ликвиди́ровать (*impf., pf.*).
liquidation /lɪkwɪˈdeɪʃ(ə)n/ *n.* ликвида́ция.
liquidize /ˈlɪkwɪdaɪz/ *v.t.* (*Br., cul.*) пропус|ка́ть, -ти́ть че́рез смеси́тель/ми́ксер; (*by hand*) прот|ира́ть, -ере́ть сквозь си́то.
liquidizer /ˈlɪkwɪdaɪzə(r)/ *n.* (*Br., cul.*) смеси́тель (*m.*), ми́ксер.
liquor /ˈlɪkə(r)/ *n.* (спиртно́й) напи́ток; **~ store** (*US*) ви́нный магази́н.
liqu|orice, lic- /ˈlɪkərɪs, -rɪʃ/ *n.* (*plant*) соло́дка, лакри́чник; (*substance*) лакри́ца.
lisp /lɪsp/ *n.* шепеля́вость; **he has a ~** он шепеля́вит.
list[1] /lɪst/ *n.* (*inventory, enumeration*) спи́сок, пе́речень (*m.*); **~ price** цена́ по прейскура́нту.
■ *v.t.* (*make a ~ of*) сост|авля́ть, -а́вить спи́сок + *g.*; (*enter on a ~*) вн|оси́ть, -ести́ в спи́сок; **~ed building** зда́ние, находя́щееся под охра́ной госуда́рства.
list[2] /lɪst/ *v.i.* (*of ship*) накреня́ться (*impf.*).
listen /ˈlɪs(ə)n/ *v.i.* слу́шать, по-; **~ to** слу́шать, по- + *a.*; **do you ~ to the radio?** вы слу́шаете ра́дио?; (*pay attention*) прислу́ш|иваться, -аться к + *d.*; **don't ~ to him!** не обраща́йте на него́ внима́ния!; **I was ~ing for the bell** я (напряжённо) ждал звонка́; **he ~ed in on their conversation** он подслу́шал их разгово́р.
listener /ˈlɪsənə(r)/ *n.* слу́шатель (*m.*).
listing /ˈlɪstɪŋ/ *n.* (*list*) спи́сок; (*entry*) упомина́ние.
listless /ˈlɪstlɪs/ *adj.* вя́лый.
lit /lɪt/ *past and p.p. of* ▸ **light[1]**
litany /ˈlɪtənɪ/ *n.* (*Orthodox*) ектенья́; (*Catholic*) лита́ния; (*fig., tedious enumeration*) ску́чное перечисле́ние.
literacy /ˈlɪtərəsɪ/ *n.* гра́мотность.
literal /ˈlɪtər(ə)l/ *adj.* буква́льный.
literary /ˈlɪtərərɪ/ *adj.* литерату́рный.
literate /ˈlɪtərət/ *adj.* гра́мотный.
literature /ˈlɪtərətʃə(r)/ *n.* литерату́ра.
lithe /laɪð/ *adj.* ги́бкий.
lithograph /ˈlɪθəgrɑːf/ *n.* литогра́фия; **~ print** литогра́фский о́ттиск.
Lithuania /lɪθʊˈeɪnɪə/ *n.* Литва́.
Lithuanian /lɪθʊˈeɪnɪən/ *n.* (*person*) лито́в|ец (*fem.* -ка); (*language*) лито́вский язы́к.
■ *adj.* лито́вский.
litigate /ˈlɪtɪgeɪt/ *v.i.* суди́ться (*impf.*).
litigation /lɪtɪˈgeɪʃ(ə)n/ *n.* тя́жба; суде́бный проце́сс.
litigious /lɪˈtɪdʒəs/ *adj.*
1 (*fond of going to law*) сутя́жнический; **a ~ person** сутя́жни|к (*fem.* -ца).
2 (*pert. to litigation*): **~ procedure** процеду́ра суде́бного разбира́тельства.
litmus /ˈlɪtməs/ *n.* ла́кмус; **~ paper** ла́кмусовая бума́га.
litre /ˈliːtə(r)/ (*US* **liter**) *n.* литр.
litter /ˈlɪtə(r)/ *n.*
1 (*refuse*) сор, отбро́с|ы (*pl., g.* -ов).
2 : **cat ~** коша́чья подсти́лка.
3 (*newly-born animals*) помёт.
■ *v.t.* сори́ть, на-; **the table is ~ed with books** стол зава́лен кни́гами.
■ *cpd.* **~ bin** *n.* (*Br.*) му́сорный я́щик.
little /ˈlɪt(ə)l/ *n.* (*not much*) ма́ло, немно́го, немно́жко + *g.*; **I see ~ of him now** я тепе́рь ре́дко ви́жу его́; **~ or nothing** почти́ ничего́; ма́ло что; (*small amount*): **he knows a ~ Japanese** он немно́го зна́ет япо́нский; **~ by ~** ма́ло-пома́лу; постепе́нно.
■ *adj.* (**littler, littlest; less** *or* **lesser; least**)
1 (*small*) ма́ленький, небольшо́й; **~ finger** мизи́нец.
2 (*young*): **~ boy** (ма́ленький) ма́льчик; **~ girl** (ма́ленькая) де́вочка.
3 (*trivial*) ме́лкий; незначи́тельный.
4 (*not tall or long*) невысо́кий; недли́нный; **wait here for a ~ while** подожди́те здесь немно́жко.
5 (*small, of quantity*) ма́ло, немно́го, немно́жко + *g.*; **there is ~ butter left** ма́сла оста́лось ма́ло.
■ *adv.* (**less, least**)
1 (*not much*) ма́ло; **I see him very ~** я ма́ло/ре́дко с ним ви́жусь; **~ more** ненамно́го/немно́гим бо́льше; **he is ~ better than a thief** он про́сто-на́просто вор; (*not at all*): **~ did he know I was following him** он и не подозрева́л, что я иду́ за ним.
2 (**a ~:** *slightly, somewhat*) немно́го, немно́жко; **I am a ~ happier now** тепе́рь я не́сколько успоко́ился; **she is a ~ over 40** ей немно́гим бо́льше сорока́.
liturgy /ˈlɪtədʒɪ/ *n.* (*eccl.*) литурги́я.

live[1] /laɪv/ *adj.*
[1] (*living*) живóй.
[2] (*not spent or exploded*): ~ **ammunition** боевы́е патрóны; **a ~ wire** (*lit.*) прóвод под тóком/напряжéнием; (*fig.*) человéк с изю́минкой.
[3] (*not recorded*): ~ **broadcast** прямáя передáча; живóй эфи́р; ~ **music** живáя мýзыка; **the game was broadcast ~** матч трансли́ровался непосрéдственно со стадиóна (*or* шёл в прямóй трансля́ции).
■ *adv.* (*as or at an actual event*) живьём (*coll.*); **he sang ~** он пел живьём.
■ *cpd.* **~stock** *n.* домáшний скот.

live[2] /lɪv/ *v.i.*
[1] (*be alive*) жить (*impf.*).
[2] (*subsist*): **they ~ on vegetables** они́ питáются овощáми.
[3] (*depend for one's living*) жить (*impf.*); **he ~s off his friends** он живёт за счёт друзéй; **he ~s on his reputation** он живёт за счёт бы́лых заслýг.
[4] (*conduct o.s.*) жить (*impf.*); **he ~d up to my expectations** он не обманýл мои́х ожидáний; (*arrange one's diet, habits etc.*): **he ~s well** он живёт хорошó (*or* на ширóкую нóгу).
[5] (*continue alive*): **the doctors think he won't ~** врачи́ дýмают, что он не вы́живет; **he ~d to regret it** впослéдствии он об э́том жалéл; (*fig., survive*): **his fame will ~ for ever** слáва егó не умрёт.
[6] (*reside*) жить, проживáть (*both impf.*); обитáть (*impf.*); **where do you ~?** где вы живёте; ~ **with** (*fig. tolerate*) мири́ться, при- с + *i.*
■ *with advs.*: ~ **in** *v.i.* (*of student*) жить (*impf.*) в общежи́тии; ~ **on** *v.i.*: **his memory ~s on** пáмять о нём живá; ~ **up** *v.t.*: ~ **it up** (*coll.*) жить (*impf.*) ширóко, вести́ (*impf.*) бýрную жизнь.
■ *cpd.* **~-in** *adj.*: **~-in nanny** ня́ня, живýщая в семьé; **~-in lover** сожи́тель (*fem.* -ница).

livelihood /ˈlaɪvlɪhʊd/ *n.* срéдства (*nt. pl.*) к существовáнию.

lively /ˈlaɪvlɪ/ *adj.* (**livelier, liveliest**) (*lit., fig.*) живóй.

liven /ˈlaɪv(ə)n/ *v.t.* & *i.* (*also* ~ **up**) ожив|ля́ть(ся), -и́ть(ся).

liver /ˈlɪvə(r)/ *n.* (*anat.*) пéчень; (*food*) печёнка.

livery /ˈlɪvərɪ/ *n.* (*of servants*) ливрéя; (*of a guild etc.*) фóрма; (*for horses*) прокóрм; ~ **stable** плáтная конюшня.

lives[1] /laɪvz/ *pl. of* ▸ **life**

lives[2] /lɪvz/ *2nd pers. sg. pres. of* ▸ **live**[2]

livid /ˈlɪvɪd/ *adj.* (*crimson*) багрóвый; (*coll., of temper*): **be ~** чернéть, по-.

living /ˈlɪvɪŋ/ *n.*
[1] (*process, manner of ~*): ~ **conditions** услóвия жи́зни; **cost of ~** стóимость жи́зни; **standard of ~** жи́зненный ýровень.
[2] (*livelihood*) срéдства (*nt. pl.*) к жи́зни; **earn one's ~** зарабáтывать, -óтать себé на жизнь.
■ *adj.* живóй; **within ~ memory** на пáмяти живýщих.
■ *cpd.* ~ **room** *n.* гости́ная.

lizard /ˈlɪzəd/ *n.* я́щерица.

llama /ˈlɑːmə/ *n.* лáма (*живóтное*).

load /ləʊd/ *n.*
[1] (*burden*) нóша; груз, нагрýзка; тя́жесть; (*fig.*) брéмя.
[2] (*amount carried*) груз; **a ~ of bricks** груз кирпичéй.
[3] (*pl., coll., large amount*) ýйма, мáсса.
■ *v.t.* [1] (*cargo etc.*) грузи́ть, по-.
[2] (*ship, vehicle etc.*) грузи́ть, на-.
[3] (*fig., with cares etc.*) обремен|я́ть, -и́ть (*кого чем*).
[4] (*with gifts, praises etc.*) ос|ыпáть, -ы́пать (*кого чем*).
[5] (*firearm, camera etc.*) заря|жáть, -ди́ть.
[6] (*fig.*): **a ~ed question** провокациóнный вопрóс.
[7] (*sl.*): **he's ~ed** (*rich*) он (пóлностью/хорошó) упакóван.
[8] (*comput.*) загру|жáть, -зи́ть.
■ *with advs.*: ~ **down** *v.t.* обремен|я́ть, -и́ть; ~ **up** *v.t.* нагру|жáть, -зи́ть; *v.i.* грузи́ться, на-.

loaf[1] /ləʊf/ *n.* (*pl.* **loaves**) бухáнка.

loaf[2] /ləʊf/ *v.i.* (*coll.*; *also* ~ **about**) лóдырничать (*impf.*).

loafer /ˈləʊfə(r)/ *n.* лóдырь (*m.*).

loam /ləʊm/ *n.* сугли́нок.

loan /ləʊn/ *n.*
[1] (*sum lent*) заём, ссýда.
[2] (*lending or being lent*): **take on ~; have the ~ of** (*of money*) брать, взять взаймы́; (*of objects*) брать, взять на врéмя.
■ *v.t.* одолж|áть, -и́ть.
■ *cpd.* ~ **shark** *n.* (*coll.*) ростовщи́к.

loath /ləʊθ/ *pred. adj.*: **he was ~ to do anything** он ничегó не хотéл дéлать.

loathe /ləʊð/ *v.t.* ненави́деть (*impf.*).

loathing /ˈləʊðɪŋ/ *n.* отвращéние; **feel ~ for** испы́тывать (*impf.*) отвращéние к + *d.*

loathsome /ˈləʊðsəm/ *adj.* отврати́тельный, омерзи́тельный.

loaves /ləʊvz/ *pl. of* ▸ **loaf**[1]

lob /lɒb/ *n.* (*high-pitched ball*) свечá.
■ *v.t.* (**lobbed, lobbing**): ~ **a ball** под|авáть, -áть свечý.

lobby /ˈlɒbɪ/ *n.* вестибю́ль (*m.*); (*theatr.*) фойé (*nt. indecl.*); (*group*) лóбби (*nt. indecl.*).
■ *v.t.* агити́ровать (*impf.*).

lobbying /ˈlɒbɪɪŋ/ *n.* агитáция.

lobe /ləʊb/ *n.* (*of ear*) мóчка.

lobelia /ləˈbiːlɪə/ *n.* (*bot.*) лобéлия.

lobster /ˈlɒbstə(r)/ *n.* омáр.

local /ˈləʊk(ə)l/ *n.* (*inhabitant*) мéстный жи́тель; (*Br., public house*) мéстный паб, мéстная пивнáя.
■ *adj.* мéстный; здéшний; (*of that place*) (*coll.*) тáмошний; ~ **anaesthetic** мéстный наркóз; ~ **authority** (*Br.*) мéстные влáсти; ~ **call** мéстный телефóнный разговóр; ~ **government** мéстное самоуправлéние; **2 o'clock ~ time** два часá по мéстному врéмени.

locale /ləʊˈkɑːl/ *n.* мéсто (дéйствия); мéстность.

locality /ləʊˈkælɪtɪ/ *n.* мéстность; (*neighbourhood*): **there is no cinema in the ~** нигдé поблизости нет кинó.

localize /ˈləʊkəlaɪz/ *v.t.* локализовáть (*impf.,*

pf.).

locally /'ləʊkəlɪ/ *adv.*: **he is well known ~** он извéстен в э́тих края́х; **he works ~** он рабо́тает побли́зости.

locate /ləʊ'keɪt/ *v.t.*
1: **be ~d** (*situated*) находи́ться (*impf.*).
2 (*determine position of*) определ|я́ть, -и́ть ме́сто/местоположе́ние + *g.*; **has the fault been ~d?** нашли́ поврежде́ние?; определи́ли ли ме́сто поврежде́ния?

location /ləʊ'keɪʃ(ə)n/ *n.*
1 (*determining of place*) определе́ние (ме́ста).
2 (*position*) местонахожде́ние.
3: **on ~** (*cin.*) на нату́ре; **shooting on ~** нату́рная съёмка.

locative /'lɒkətɪv/ *n.* & *adj.* (*gram.*) ме́стный (паде́ж).

loch /lɒk/ *n.* о́зеро (*в Шотландии*); **L~ Ness** о́зеро Лох-Не́сс.

lock¹ /lɒk/ *n.* (*of hair*) ло́кон.

lock² /lɒk/ *n.*
1 (*on door or firearm*) замо́к; **under ~ and key** под замко́м; (*on door or gate*) запо́р.
2 (*on canal*) шлюз.
■ *v.t.* 1 (*secure; restrict movement of*) зап|ира́ть, -ере́ть (на замо́к); **I was ~ed out** дверь была́ заперта́, и я не мог войти́.
2 (*cause to stop moving or revolving*) тормози́ть, за-; **he ~ed the steering** он заблоки́ровал руль.
3 (*interlace*) спле|та́ть, -сти́; **his fingers were ~ed together** он сцепи́л ру́ки.
■ *v.i.*: **does this chest ~?** э́тот сунду́к запира́ется?
■ *with advs.*: **~ in** *v.t.* зап|ира́ть, -ере́ть *кого* в ко́мнате/до́ме *и т. п.*; **he ~ed himself in** он за́перся́ на ключ; **~ out** *v.t.* зап|ира́ть, -ере́ть дверь и не впуска́ть; **~ up** *v.t.* зап|ира́ть, -ере́ть на замо́к; (*imprison*) сажа́ть, посади́ть (*в тюрьму*).
■ *cpd.* **~smith** *n.* сле́сарь (*m.*).

locker /'lɒkə(r)/ *n.* (*cupboard*) шка́фчик.
■ *cpd.* **~ room** *n.* раздева́лка.

locket /'lɒkɪt/ *n.* медальо́н.

locomotion /ləʊkə'məʊʃ(ə)n/ *n.* передвиже́ние.

locomotive /ləʊkə'məʊtɪv/ *n.* локомоти́в.

locum /'ləʊkəm/ *n.* (*pl.* **~s**) (*coll.*) = **locum tenens**

locum tenens /'ləʊkəm 'ti:nenz/ *n.* (*pl.* **locum tenentes** /"l3Uk3m tI"nenti:z/) (*doctor or clergyman*) вре́менный замести́тель (*m.*).

locust /'ləʊkəst/ *n.* (*insect*) саранча́ (*also collect.*).

lodge /lɒdʒ/ *n.*
1 (*cottage*) дом приврáтника.
2 (*porter's apartment*) сторо́жка.
■ *v.t.* (*fig., enter*): **~ a complaint/appeal** обра|ща́ться, -ти́ться с жа́лобой/апелля́цией.
■ *v.i.* 1 (*reside*) жить (*impf.*); прожива́ть (*impf.*); **he ~s with us** он наш жиле́ц.
2 (*become stuck*) застр|ева́ть, -я́ть; **a bone ~d in his throat** кость застря́ла у него́ в го́рле.

lodger /'lɒdʒə(r)/ *n.* жиле́ц.

lodging /'lɒdʒɪŋ/ *n.* (*pl.*) меблиро́ванные ко́мнаты (*f. pl.*).

loft /lɒft/ *n.* черда́к.

lofty /'lɒftɪ/ *adj.* (**loftier, loftiest**) (*high*) высо́кий; (*exalted*) возвы́шенный; (*haughty*) высокоме́рный.

log¹ /lɒg/ *n.*
1 (*of wood*) бревно́, чурба́н.
2 (*for fire*) поле́но; **he slept like a ~** он спал как уби́тый; **~ cabin** (бреве́нчатая) хи́жина.

log² /lɒg/ *n.* (**~book**) ва́хтенный журна́л; (*of aircraft*) бортово́й журна́л; (*of car*) формуля́р.
■ *v.t.* (**logged, logging**) (*record*) занос|и́ть, -ести́ в ва́хтенный журна́л; **~ in/on** (*comput.*) входи́ть, войти́ в систе́му; **~ out/off** (*comput.*) выходи́ть, вы́йти из систе́мы.
■ *cpd.* **~book** *n.* = **log²** *n.*

loganberry /'ləʊgənbərɪ/ *n.* лога́нова я́года (*гибрид малины с ежевикой*).

logarithm /'lɒgərɪð(ə)m/ *n.* логари́фм.

loggerhead /'lɒgəhed/ *n.*: **they are at ~s** они́ в ссо́ре (*or* не в лада́х) друг с дру́гом.

logic /'lɒdʒɪk/ *n.* ло́гика.

logical /'lɒdʒɪk(ə)l/ *adj.* (*based on logic, e.g. conclusion, explanation*) логи́ческий; (*reasonable, e.g. action*) логи́чный.

logistic(al) /lə'dʒɪstɪk, lə'dʒɪstɪk(ə)l/ *adj.* организацио́нный.

logistics /lə'dʒɪstɪks/ *n.* организа́ция; (*mil.*) материа́льно-техни́ческое обеспе́чение.

logo /'ləʊgəʊ/ *n.* (*pl.* **logos**) эмбле́ма.

loin /lɔɪn/ *n.* (*meat*) филе́ (*nt. indecl.*) (*мясное*).

loiter /'lɔɪtə(r)/ *v.i.* ме́шкать (*impf.*).

loll /lɒl/ *v.i.*
1 (*sit or stand in lazy attitude*) сиде́ть/стоя́ть (*impf.*) разваля́сь.
2 (*of tongue etc.: hang loose*) выва́ливаться (*impf.*).

lollipop /'lɒlɪpɒp/ *n.* леденéц на па́лочке.

London /'lʌnd(ə)n/ *n.* Ло́ндон.

lone /ləʊn/ *adj.* одино́кий, уединённый.

lonely /'ləʊnlɪ/ *adj.* (**lonelier, loneliest**)
1 (*solitary, alone*) одино́кий; **lead a ~ existence** вести́ (*det.*) одино́кий о́браз жи́зни.
2 (*isolated*) уединённый.

loner /'ləʊnə(r)/ *n.* (*coll.*) одино́чка (*c.g.*).

lonesome /'ləʊnsəm/ *adj.* одино́кий.

long¹ /lɒŋ/ *n.*: **I shan't be away for ~** я уезжа́ю ненадо́лго; я ско́ро верну́сь; **it won't take ~** э́то не займёт мно́го вре́мени.
■ *adj.* 1 (*of space, measurement*) дли́нный; **the table is 2 metres ~** длина́ э́того стола́ — 2 ме́тра; **how ~ is this river?** какова́ длина́ э́той реки́?; **~ jump** прыжо́к в длину́.
2 (*of distance*) да́льний; **a ~ journey** да́льний/до́лгий путь.
3 (*of time*) до́лгий; **my holiday is 2 weeks ~** мой о́тпуск дли́тся две неде́ли; **for a ~ time** до́лго, давно́; надо́лго; **a ~ time ago** мно́го вре́мени тому́ наза́д; давны́м-давно́.
4 (*prolonged*) дли́тельный; **a ~ illness** затяжна́я боле́знь.
■ *adv.* 1 (*a ~ time*): **I shan't be ~** я ско́ро верну́сь; я не задержу́сь; **~ after** (*prep.*) до́лгое вре́мя по́сле + *g.*; **~ before** (*prep.*) задо́лго до + *g.*; **~ ago** (давны́м-)давно́; **before ~** вско́ре, ско́ро.
2 (*for a ~ time*): **how ~ have you been here?** вы здесь давно́?; **~ live the Queen!** да здра́вствует короле́ва!
3 (*throughout*): **all day ~** це́лый день; **all**

night ~ всю ночь напролёт.
4: **as ~ as I live** пока́ я жив; **stay as ~ as you like** остава́йтесь, ско́лько хоти́те; **as ~ as you don't mind** е́сли вам всё равно́; е́сли вы не возража́ете.
5: **so ~!** пока́! (*coll.*).
6: **no ~er** бо́льше не; **I can't wait much ~er** намно́го до́льше ждать я не могу́.
■ *cpds.* **~-awaited** *adj.* долгожда́нный; **~-distance** *adj.*: **~-distance call** междугоро́дный/междунаро́дный вы́зов; **~-distance runner** бегу́н на дли́нные диста́нции; **~-haired** *adj.* длинноволо́сый; **~ johns** *n. pl.* кальсо́н|ы (*pl.*, *g.* —); **~-range** *adj.* (*of gun*) дальнобо́йный; (*of forecast, policy etc.*) долгосро́чный; **~-sighted** *adj.* дальнозо́ркий; **~-standing** *adj.* стари́нный, долголе́тний; **~-term** *adj.* долгосро́чный; (*of plans etc.*) перспекти́вный; **~-winded** *adj.* многосло́вный.

long[2] /lɒŋ/ *v.i.*: **~ for sth.** жа́ждать (*impf.*) чего́-н.; **~ to do sth.** мечта́ть (*impf.*) де́лать что́-то.

longevity /lɒn'dʒevɪtɪ/ *n.* (*of person*) долголе́тие; (*of thing*) долгове́чность.

longing /'lɒŋɪŋ/ *n.* (*eager desire*) жа́жда (**for:** + *g.*); (*melancholy desire*) тоска́ (**for:** по + *d.*).

longitude /'lɒŋgɪtju:d/ *n.* долгота́.

longitudinal /lɒŋgɪ'tju:dɪn(ə)l/ *adj.* (*of longitude*) долго́тный; (*lengthwise*) продо́льный.

loo /lu:/ *n.* (*Br. coll., lavatory*) сорти́р (*coll.*).

look /lʊk/ *n.*
1 (*glance*) взгляд.
2: **have, take a ~ at** (*examine*) осм|а́тривать, -отре́ть; рассм|а́тривать, -отре́ть.
3: **have a ~ for** (*search for*) иска́ть, по-.
4 (*expression*) выраже́ние; **there was a ~ of horror on his face** его́ лицо́ выража́ло у́жас.
5 (*appearance*) вид; **he has given the shop a new ~** он (по́лностью) преобрази́л магази́н; (*pl., personal appearance*) нару́жность, вне́шность.
■ *v.t.* 1 (*inspect, scrutinize*): **~ s.o. in the face, eye** смотре́ть, по- в глаза́ кому́-н.
2 (*have the appearance of*) вы́глядеть (*impf.*) + *i.*: **he made me ~ a fool** он поста́вил меня́ в дура́цкое положе́ние; **he ~s his age** ему́ вполне́ дашь его́ го́ды; **she is thirty, but she does not ~ it** ей три́дцать, но ей сто́лько не дашь.
■ *v.i.* 1 (*use one's eyes; pay attention*) смотре́ть, по-; **he ~ed out of the window to see if she was coming** он посмотре́л в окно́, не идёт ли она́; (*search*) иска́ть, по-.
2 (*face*) выходи́ть (*impf.*); **the windows ~ on to the garden (street)** о́кна выхо́дят в сад (на у́лицу).
3 (*appear*) вы́глядеть (*impf.*) + *i.*; **she is ~ing well** она́ хорошо́ вы́глядит; **everybody ~ed tired** у всех был уста́лый вид; **that ~s tasty** у э́того блю́да аппети́тный вид; **things ~ black** пло́хо де́ло; **that ~s suspicious** э́то подозри́тельно; **~ like** (*resemble*) вы́глядеть (*impf.*) + *i.*; походи́ть (*impf.*) на + *a.*; **he ~s like his father** он похо́ж на отца́; (*give expectation of*): **it ~s like rain** собира́ется (*or* похо́же, (что) бу́дет) дождь.
■ *with preps.*: **~ after** (*care for*) уха́живать (*impf.*) за + *i.*; **she has four children to ~ after** на её попече́нии че́тверо дете́й; (*keep safe*) храни́ть (*impf.*); (*be responsible for*) занима́ться (*impf.*) + *i.*; **~ at** (*direct gaze on*) смотре́ть, по- на + *a.*; **he was ~ing at a book** он смотре́л на кни́гу; (*inspect, examine*) смотре́ть, по- на + *a.*; осм|а́тривать, -отре́ть; **the customs men ~ed at our luggage** тамо́женники осмотре́ли наш бага́ж; **~ for** (*seek*) иска́ть, по-; **he is ~ing for a job** он и́щет ме́сто/рабо́ту; **~ into** (*investigate, examine*) иссле́довать (*impf.*); рассм|а́тривать, -отре́ть; **~ on** (*regard*) счита́ть (*impf.*); **I ~ on him as my son** я счита́ю его́ свои́м сы́ном; **~ round** (*inspect*) осм|а́тривать, -отре́ть; **they ~ed through** (*examined*) **our papers** они́ просмотре́ли на́ши бума́ги; **he quickly ~ed through the newspaper** он бы́стро пробежа́л глаза́ми газе́ту; **~ to** (*turn to*) обра|ща́ться, -ти́ться к + *d.*; **we ~ed to him for help** мы рассчи́тывали на его́ по́мощь.
■ *with advs.*: **~ back** *v.i.*: **~ back on** вспомина́ть (*impf.*); **~ down** *v.i.* (*lower one's gaze*) опус|ка́ть, -ти́ть глаза́; **~ down on** смотре́ть (*impf.*) свысока́ на + *a.*; презира́ть (*impf.*); **~ forward**: **~ forward to** предвкуша́ть (*impf.*); ждать (*impf.*) + *g.* с нетерпе́нием; **I ~ forward to meeting you** жду с нетерпе́нием, когда́ уви́жусь с ва́ми; **~ in** *v.i.*: **~ in** (*call*) **on s.o.** загля́|дывать, -ну́ть (*or* забе|га́ть, -жа́ть) к кому́-н.; **~ on** *v.i.* наблюда́ть, смотре́ть (*both impf.*); **~ out** *v.i.* (*be careful*) быть начеку́/настороже́; **~ out!** осторо́жно!; (*keep one's eyes open*): **she stood at the door ~ing out for the postman** она́ стоя́ла в дверя́х, высма́тривая почтальо́на; **we are ~ing out for a house** мы присма́триваем дом; **~ round, ~ around** *v.i.* (*turn one's head*) огля́|дываться, -ну́ться; (*make an inspection*) осм|а́триваться, -отре́ться; **~ up** *v.t.* (*visit*) наве|ща́ть, -сти́ть; (*~ for, seek information on*) оты́ск|ивать, -а́ть; *v.i.* (*raise one's eyes*) подн|има́ть, -я́ть глаза́ (**at s.o.:** на кого́-н.); (*improve*) ул|учша́ться, -у́чшиться; **things are ~ing up** дела́ иду́т на попра́вку; **~ up to** (*respect*) уважа́ть (*impf.*).
■ *cpds.* **~alike** *n.* двойни́к; **~-in** *n.*: **I didn't get a ~-in** меня́ не подпусти́ли к пирогу́; **~out** *n.* (*post*) наблюда́тельный пункт; (*watch*): **be on the ~out for** (*e.g. a house*) присма́тривать (*impf.*) себе́.

loom[1] /lu:m/ *n.* тка́цкий стано́к.

loom[2] /lu:m/ *v.i.*
1 (*appear indistinctly; also* **~ up**) нея́сно вырисо́вываться (*impf.*).
2 (*impend*) нав|иса́ть, -и́снуть.

loop /lu:p/ *n.* (*also comput.*) петля́.

loophole /'lu:phəʊl/ *n.* (*fig.*) лазе́йка.

loose /lu:s/ *n.*: **on the ~** в загу́ле; на свобо́де; на во́ле.
■ *adj.* 1 (*free, unconfined*) свобо́дный; **break ~** вы́рваться (*pf.*) на свобо́ду; **let ~** (*e.g. a dog*) спус|ка́ть, -ти́ть с цепи́.
2 (*not fastened or held together*): **~ papers** отде́льные листы́.

3 (*not secure or firm*): **at a ~ end** (*fig.*) без де́ла; **I have a ~ tooth** у меня́ зуб шата́ется; **the nut is ~** га́йка разболта́лась; **the button is ~** пу́говица болта́ется.
4 (*slack*) сла́бо натя́нутый; **~ clothes** широ́кая/просто́рная оде́жда.
5 (*not compact or dense*): **~ weave** неплóтная ткань.
6 (*imprecise*): **a ~ translation** приблизи́тельный/во́льный перево́д.
7 (*morally lax*) распу́щенный.

loosen /ˈluːs(ə)n/ *v.t.* (*tongue*) развя́з|ывать, -а́ть; (*screw*) отви́н|чивать, -ти́ть; (*by shaking or pulling*) расшáт|ывать, -а́ть; (*tie, rope, belt etc.*) осл|абля́ть, -а́бить.

loot /luːt/ *n.* добы́ча.
■ *v.t.* гра́бить, раз-.

looter /ˈluːtə(r)/ *n.* мародёр, граби́тель (*m.*).

lopsided /lɒpˈsaɪdɪd/ *adj.* (*grin*) криво́й; (*fig.*) неравноме́рный, односторо́нний.

loquacious /lɒˈkweɪʃəs/ *adj.* словоохо́тливый, болтли́вый.

lord /lɔːd/ *n.*
1 (*Br., nobleman*) лорд.
2 (*ruler; also fig.*) власти́тель (*m.*); **~ of the manor** владе́лец поме́стья.
3 (*God*) Госпо́дь; **Our L~** (*Christ*) Госпо́дь.
■ *v.t.*: **~ it over s.o.** кома́ндовать (*impf.*) кем-н.

lordship /ˈlɔːdʃɪp/ *n.*: **Your L~** ва́ша све́тлость/ми́лость.

lorry /ˈlɒrɪ/ *n.* (*Br.*) грузови́к.

los|e /luːz/ *v.t.* (*past and p.p.* **lost**)
1 теря́ть, по-; **~t property office** (*Br.*), **~t and found department** (*US*) бюро́ нахо́док; **~e patience** выходи́ть, вы́йти из терпе́ния; **~e one's temper** серди́ться, рас-.
2: **be, get ~t** (*~e one's way*) заблуди́ться (*pf.*); **get ~t!** исче́зни!, кати́сь! (*coll.*); (*fig.*): **~t in thought** заду́мавшись.
3 (*in contest, sport, gambling*) проигр|ывать, -а́ть; **he ~t the argument** его́ победи́ли в спо́ре; **they ~t the match** они́ проигра́ли.
4 (*of a clock*) отст|ава́ть, -а́ть на + *a.*
■ *v.i.* 1 проигр|ывать, -а́ть; теря́ть, по-; **~e out** (*coll.*) потерпе́ть (*pf.*) неуда́чу.
2 (*of a clock*): **my watch is ~ing** мои́ часы́ отстаю́т.

loser /ˈluːzə(r)/ *n.* (*at a game*) проигра́вший; (*person who habitually fails*) неуда́чник; **he is a good (bad) ~** он (не) уме́ет досто́йно прои́грывать.

loss /lɒs/ *n.*
1 поте́ря.
2 (*monetary*) убы́ток.
3: **I am at a ~ to answer** я затрудня́юсь отве́тить.

lost /lɒst/ *past and p.p. of* ▸ **lose**

lot /lɒt/ *n.*
1: **draw ~s** тяну́ть (*impf.*) жре́бий; (*fig., destiny*) судьба́, у́часть, до́ля.
2 (*plot of land*) уча́сток.
3 (*in auction*) лот.
4: **the ~** (*Br. coll., everything*) всё; **that's the ~!** вот и всё!
5 (**a ~, ~s:** *a large number, amount*) мно́го; **a ~ of people** мно́го наро́ду; мно́гие; **I don't see a ~ of him nowadays** тепе́рь мы с ним ма́ло/ре́дко ви́димся; **there were ~s of apples left** оста́лась у́йма/ку́ча я́блок; **he plays a ~ of football** он мно́го игра́ет в футбо́л.
■ *adv.* **(a ~)**
1 (*often*) ча́сто; **we went to the theatre a ~** мы ча́сто ходи́ли в теа́тр.
2 (*with comps.: much*) гора́здо, намно́го; **a ~ worse** гора́здо ху́же.

lotion /ˈləʊʃ(ə)n/ *n.* лосьо́н.

lottery /ˈlɒtərɪ/ *n.* лотере́я.

loud /laʊd/ *adj.* шу́мный; (*fig.*): **~ colours** крича́щие кра́ски.
■ *adv.* гро́мко; **out ~** вслух.
■ *cpd.* **~speaker** *n.* громкоговори́тель (*m.*), дина́мик.

lounge /laʊndʒ/ *n.* (*Br., sitting room*) гости́ная; (*at airport*) зал ожида́ния; (*bar*) бар пе́рвого кла́сса.
■ *v.i.*: **~ about** (*idly*) безде́льничать (*impf.*).

lousy /ˈlaʊzɪ/ *adj.* (**lousier, lousiest**) (*coll.*) парши́вый, отврати́тельный.

lout /laʊt/ *n.* хам.

loutish /ˈlaʊtɪʃ/ *adj.* ха́мский; неотёсанный.

lovable /ˈlʌvəb(ə)l/ *adj.* ми́лый.

love /lʌv/ *n.*
1 любо́вь; **he sent you his ~** он проси́л переда́ть вам серде́чный приве́т; **be in ~ (with s.o.)** быть влюблённым в кого́-н.; **fall in ~ with s.o.** влюб|ля́ться, -и́ться в кого́-н.; **make ~** (*have sexual intercourse*) зан|има́ться, -я́ться любо́вью; **~ affair** рома́н; (*pej.*) любо́вная связь; (*Br., in address*): **(my) ~!** (мой) ми́лый!; (моя́) ми́лая!
2 (*zero score*) ноль (*m.*).
■ *v.t.* люби́ть (*impf.*); **I ~ the way he smiles** мне ужа́сно нра́вится, как он улыба́ется; **I ~ walking in the rain** я обожа́ю гуля́ть под дождём.

loveless /ˈlʌvlɪs/ *adj.* нелю́бящий, без любви́; **~ marriage** брак без любви́.

lovely /ˈlʌvlɪ/ *adj.* (**lovelier, loveliest**) (*beautiful*) краси́вый; (*charming*) преле́стный.

lover /ˈlʌvə(r)/ *n.*
1 любо́вни|к (*fem.* -ца); (*pl.*) влюблённые.
2 (*devotee*) люби́тель (*m.*) (*fem.* -ница).

loving /ˈlʌvɪŋ/ *adj.* лю́бящий; (*tender*) не́жный.

low /ləʊ/ *n.*
1 (*meteor.*) цикло́н.
2 (*~ point or level*): **the pound fell to an all-time ~** фунт дости́г небыва́ло ни́зкого у́ровня.
■ *adj.* 1 ни́зкий, невысо́кий; **~ tide, water** ма́лая вода́, отли́в; (*of pitch of sound*) ни́зкий; (*of volume of sound*) негро́мкий, ти́хий; **he spoke in a ~ voice** он говори́л, пони́зив го́лос (*or* ти́хим го́лосом); **keep a ~ profile** вести́ себя́ сде́ржанно.
2 (*base*) ни́зкий, по́длый; **a ~ trick** по́длая уло́вка.
3 (*nearly empty; scanty*): **a ~ attendance** ни́зкая/плоха́я посеща́емость; **we are getting ~ on sugar** у нас остаётся малова́то са́хара.
4 (*poor, depressed*): **I was feeling ~** я чу́вствовал себя́ нева́жно.
■ *adv.* ни́зко.
■ *cpds.* **~-alcohol** *adj.* слабоалкого́льный; **~brow** *adj.* нера́звитый; **~-calorie** *adj.*

малокалорийный; **~-cut** *adj.* с низким/глубоким вырезом; **~-down** *n.* (*information*) подноготная (*coll.*); *adj.* подлый, скверный; **~-fat** *adj.* маложирный; **~-key** *adj.* (*fig.*) сдержанный; **~land** *n.* (*usu. pl.*) низменность; **~-lying** *adj.* низменный; **~-paid** *adj.* малооплачиваемый.

lower /'ləʊə(r)/ *adj.* нижний.
■ *v.t.* 1 (*e.g. boat, flag*) спус|кать, -тить; (*eyes*) опус|кать, -тить; (*price*) сн|ижать, -изить; (*voice*) пон|ижать, -изить.
2 (*decrease*) ум|еньшать, -еньшить.
3 (*debase*) ун|ижать, -изить.

lowly /'ləʊlɪ/ *adj.* (**lowlier, lowliest**) (*humble*) скромный; (*primitive*) низший.

loyal /'lɔɪəl/ *adj.* (*faithful*) верный; (*devoted*) преданный; (*pol.*) лояльный.

loyalist /'lɔɪəlɪst/ *n.* лоялист (*fem.* -ка).

loyalty /'lɔɪəltɪ/ *n.* верность, преданность, лояльность.

lozenge /'lɒzɪndʒ/ *n.* таблетка(-леденец).

LP (*abbr. of* ***long-playing record***) долгоиграющая пластинка.

LSD *abbr. of* (*pharm.*) ***lysergic acid diethylamide*** ЛСД (диэтиламид лизергиновой кислоты).

Ltd /'lɪmɪtɪd/ *adj.* (*Br., comm., abbr. of* ***limited liability company***) ООО (общество с ограниченной ответственностью).

lubricat|e /'lu:brɪkeɪt/ *v.t.* смаз|ывать, -ать.

lubrication /lu:brɪ'keɪʃ(ə)n/ *n.* смазывание.

lucid /'lu:sɪd/ *adj.* ясный.

lucidity /lu:'sɪdɪtɪ/ *n.* ясность.

luck /lʌk/ *n.*: **good/bad ~** счастье/несчастье; **good ~!; the best of ~!** желаю счастья/удачи/успеха!; **bad, hard ~!** не повезло!

luckily /'lʌkɪlɪ/ *adv.* к счастью.

lucky /'lʌkɪ/ *adj.* (**luckier, luckiest**)
1 (*of person*) счастливый, удачливый; (*of things, actions, events*) удачный; **you're ~ to be alive** скажи спасибо, что остался в живых.
2 (*bringing luck*): **a ~ charm** счастливый талисман.

lucrative /'lu:krətɪv/ *adj.* прибыльный.

lucre /'lu:kə(r)/ *n.* прибыль, нажива; **filthy ~** презренный металл.

ludicrous /'lu:dɪkrəs/ *adj.* смехотворный.

lug /lʌg/ *v.t.* (**lugged, lugging**) (*coll.*) тащить (*impf.*).

luggage /'lʌgɪdʒ/ *n.* багаж.
■ *cpd.* **~ rack** *n.* (*in train*) сетка/полка для багажа.

lugubrious /lu:'gu:brɪəs/ *adj.* (*mournful*) скорбный; (*dismal*) мрачный.

lukewarm /lu:k'wɔ:m/ *adj.* тепловатый.

lull /lʌl/ *n.* (*in storm, fighting etc.*) затишье; (*in conversation*) пауза, перерыв.
■ *v.t.* (*~ to sleep*) убаюк|ивать, -ать; **~ s.o. into a false sense of security** усып|лять, -ить чью-н. бдительность.

lullaby /'lʌləbaɪ/ *n.* колыбельная (песня).

lumbar /'lʌmbə(r)/ *adj.* поясничный.

lumber[1] /'lʌmbə(r)/ *n.* (*US, timber*) пиломатериалы (*m. pl.*).
■ *v.t.* (*Br., encumber*) обременять (*impf.*); **I'm ~ed with my mother-in-law** тёща сидит у меня на шее.
■ *cpd.* **~jack** *n.* лесоруб.

lumber[2] /'lʌmbə(r)/ *v.i.* (*also* **~ along**) двигаться (*impf.*) тяжело.

luminary /'lu:mɪnərɪ/ *n.* (*lit., fig.*) светило.

luminous /'lu:mɪnəs/ *adj.* светящийся.

lump /lʌmp/ *n.*
1 (*of earth, dough etc.*) ком; **~ of sugar** кусок сахара; **~ in the throat** комок в горле.
2 (*swelling*) шишка, опухоль.
3 : **~ sum** единовременно выплачиваемая сумма.
■ *v.t.*: **~ together** (*treat alike*) ставить (*impf.*) на одну доску.

lumpectomy /lʌm'pektəmɪ/ *n.* удаление опухоли молочной железы.

lumpy /'lʌmpɪ/ *adj.* (**lumpier, lumpiest**) комковатый.

lunacy /'lu:nəsɪ/ *n.* безумие.

lunar /'lu:nə(r)/ *adj.* лунный.

lunatic /'lu:nətɪk/ *n.* сумасшедший.

lunch /lʌntʃ/ *n.* обед.
■ *v.i.* обедать, по-.
■ *cpds.* **~ break, ~ hour, ~time** *nn.* обеденный перерыв.

lung /lʌŋ/ *n.* лёгкое.

lunge /lʌndʒ/ *v.i.* (**lungeing** *or* **lunging**) броситься (*pf.*), (**forward:** вперёд; **at:** на + *a.*).

lupin /'lu:pɪn/ *n.* люпин.

lurch[1] /lə:tʃ/ *n.*: **leave s.o. in the ~** пок|идать, -инуть кого-н. в беде.

lurch[2] /lə:tʃ/ *v.i.* шататься (*impf.*); **the drunken man ~ed across the street** пьяный, пошатываясь, перешёл улицу.

lure /ljʊə(r)/ *n.* (*decoy*) приманка; (*fig., enticement*) соблазн; **the ~ of foreign travel** заманчивость заграничных путешествий.
■ *v.t.* (*persons*) заман|ивать, -ить; **a rival firm ~d him away** конкурирующая фирма переманила его (к себе).

lurid /'ljʊərɪd/ *adj.* (*gaudy*) кричащий; (*sensational*) сенсационный; **~ details** жуткие подробности.

lurk /lə:k/ *v.i.* прита|иваться, -иться.

luscious /'lʌʃəs/ *adj.* (*succulent*) сочный.

lush /lʌʃ/ *adj.* пышный, роскошный.

lust /lʌst/ *n.*
1 (*sexual passion*) похоть.
2 (*craving*): **~ for power** жажда власти.
■ *v.i.*: **~ for, after s.o.** испыт|ывать, -ать вожделение к кому-н.

luster /'lʌstə(r)/ (*US*) = **lustre**

lustful /'lʌstfʊl/ *adj.* похотливый.

lustre /'lʌstə(r)/ (*US* **luster**) *n.* блеск.

lustrous /'lʌstrəs/ *adj.* (*brilliant*) блестящий; (*glossy*) глянцевитый.

lusty /'lʌstɪ/ *adj.* (**lustier, lustiest**) (*healthy*) здоровый; (*vigorous*) бодрый.

lute /lu:t/ *n.* (*mus.*) лютня.

Luxembourg /'lʌksəmbə:g/ *n.* Люксембург.
■ *adj.* люксембургский.

Luxembourger /'lʌksəmbə:gə(r)/ *n.* люксембурж|ец (*fem.* -(ен)ка).

luxuriance /lʌg'zjʊərɪəns/ *n.* изобилие;

пы́шность.
luxuriant /lʌg'zjʊərɪənt/ *adj.* (*of growth*) бу́йный.
luxuriate /lʌg'zjʊərɪeɪt/ *v.i.* (*enjoy o.s.*): **~ in sth.** наслажда́ться (*impf.*) чем-н.
luxurious /lʌg'zjʊərɪəs/ *adj.* роско́шный.
luxury /'lʌkʃərɪ/ *n.*
1 (*luxuriousness*) ро́скошь.
2 (*object of ~*) предме́т ро́скоши; **~ apartment** роско́шная кварти́ра.
lying /'laɪɪŋ/ *n.* (*telling lies*) ложь.
■ *adj.* лжи́вый.
lymph /lɪmf/ *n.* (*physiol.*) ли́мфа.
■ *cpds.* **~ gland, node** *nn.* лимфати́ческий у́зел.
lynch /lɪntʃ/ *v.t.* линчева́ть (*impf., pf.*).
lynchpin /'lɪntʃpɪn/ = **linchpin**
lyre /'laɪə(r)/ *n.* ли́ра.
■ *cpd.* **~bird** *n.* пти́ца-ли́ра, лирохво́ст.
lyric /'lɪrɪk/ *n.* (*usu. in pl.*; *words of song*) слова́ (*nt. pl.*) / текст пе́сни.
lyrical /'lɪrɪk(ə)l/ *adj.* лири́ческий; **he waxed ~ about, over ...** он расчу́вствовался, говоря́ о... .
lyricist /'lɪrɪsɪst/ *n.* а́втор слов/те́кста (*песни/мюзикла*).

Mm

m /'mi:tə(r)(z)/ *n.* (*abbr. of* ***metre(s)***) м (метр).
m- *pref.* моби́льный; **m-commerce** моби́льная комме́рция.
MA (*abbr. of* ***Master of Arts***) маги́стр гуманита́рных нау́к.
mac /mæk/ (*Br. coll.*) = **mac(k)intosh**
macabre /mə'kɑ:br(ə)/ *adj.* мра́чный.
macaroni /mækə'rəʊnɪ/ *n.* макаро́н|ы (*pl., g.* —).
Macedonia /mæsə'dəʊnɪə/ *n.* Македо́ния.
Macedonian /mæsɪ'dəʊnɪən/ *n.* македо́н|ец (*fem.* -ка).
■ *adj.* македо́нский.
machination /mækɪ'neɪʃ(ə)n/ *n.* (*usu. pl.*) махина́ция; ко́зни (*f. pl.*); интри́га.
machine /mə'ʃi:n/ *n.* маши́на, механи́зм.
■ *cpds.* **~ gun** *n.* пулемёт; **~-readable** *adj.* (*comput.*) машиночита́емый.
machinery /mə'ʃi:nərɪ/ *n.* (*collect., machines*) маши́ны (*f. pl.*); (*fig.*): **the ~ of government** прави́тельственные структу́ры (*f. pl.*).
machinist /mə'ʃi:nɪst/ *n.* машини́ст; (*Br., sewing-machine operator*) шве́йник, (*fem.*) швея́.
macho /'mætʃəʊ/ *adj.* мужско́й, мужи́цкий; му́жественный.
mackerel /'mækr(ə)l/ *n.* (*pl.* **~** *or* **~s**) ску́мбрия.
mac(k)intosh /'mækɪntɒʃ/ *n.* (*Br.*) дождеви́к (*плащ*).
macro /'mækrəʊ/ *n.* (*pl.* **~s**) (*comput.*) макрокома́нда.
macrocosm /'mækrəʊkɒz(ə)m/ *n.* макроко́см(ос).
mad /mæd/ *adj.* (**madder, maddest**)
1 (*insane*) сумасше́дший; **go ~** сходи́ть, сойти́ с ума́; **drive s.o. ~** св|оди́ть, -ести́ кого́-н. с ума́.
2 (*of animals*) бе́шеный; **~ cow disease** коро́вье бе́шенство.
3 (*wildly foolish*) шально́й; **~ly in love** безу́мно влюблённый.
4 (*coll., angry*) серди́тый; **be, get ~** вы́йти (*pf.*) из себя́; **she was ~ with me for breaking the vase** она́ разозли́лась на меня́ за то, что я разби́л ва́зу.
5 : **~ about** (*infatuated with, enthusiastic for*) в восто́рге (*or* без па́мяти) от + *g.*
■ *cpd.* **~man** *n.* сумасше́дший.
Madagascar /mædə'gæskə(r)/ *n.* Мадагаска́р.
madam /'mædəm/ *n.* (*form of address*) мада́м, госпожа́.
maddening /'mædənɪŋ/ *adj.* несно́сный.
made /meɪd/ *past and p.p. of* ▸ **make**
■ *cpd.* **~-to-measure** *adj.* сде́ланный (как) на зака́з.
Madeira /mə'dɪərə/ *n.* Маде́йра; (*wine*) маде́ра.
Madrid /mə'drɪd/ *n.* Мадри́д.
madrigal /'mædrɪg(ə)l/ *n.* мадрига́л.
madness /'mædnɪs/ *n.* (*insanity*) сумасше́ствие; (*folly*) безу́мие.
maestro /'maɪstrəʊ/ *n.* маэ́стро (*m. indecl.*).
Mafia /'mæfɪə/ *n.* ма́фия.
magazine[1] /mægə'zi:n/ *n.* (*cartridge chamber*) магази́н (*автомата*).
magazine[2] /mægə'zi:n/ *n.* (*periodical*) журна́л.
magenta /mə'dʒentə/ *n.* краснова́то-лило́вый/пурпу́рный цвет.
■ *adj.* краснова́то-лило́вый; (*clothes*) мали́новый, пурпу́рный; (*dye, ink*) пурпу́рный.
maggot /'mægət/ *n.* личи́нка.
magic /'mædʒɪk/ *n.* (*lit., fig.*) ма́гия, волшебство́.
■ *adj.* волше́бный, маги́ческий.
magical /'mædʒɪk(ə)l/ *adj.* волше́бный.
magician /mə'dʒɪʃ(ə)n/ *n.* (*sorcerer*) волше́бник; (*conjurer*) фо́кусник.
magisterial /mædʒɪ'stɪərɪəl/ *adj.* (*of a magistrate*) суде́йский; (*authoritative*) авторите́тный.
magistrate /'mædʒɪstrət/ *n.* мирово́й судья́ (*m.*).
magnanimous /mæg'nænɪməs/ *adj.*

великоду́шный.

magnate /'mægneɪt/ *n.* магна́т.

magnesium /mæg'ni:zɪəm/ *n.* ма́гний.

magnet /'mægnɪt/ *n.* (*lit., fig.*) магни́т.

magnetic /mæg'netɪk/ *adj.* магни́тный.

magnetism /'mægnɪtɪz(ə)m/ *n.* магнети́зм.

magnetize /'mægnɪtaɪz/ *v.t.* намагни́|чивать, -тить; (*fig.*) гипнотизи́ровать, за-.

magnification /mægnɪfɪ'keɪʃ(ə)n/ *n.* увеличе́ние; (*of a radio signal*) усиле́ние; (*exaggeration*) преувеличе́ние.

magnificence /mæg'nɪfɪs(ə)ns/ *n.* великоле́пие.

magnificent /mæg'nɪfɪs(ə)nt/ *adj.* великоле́пный.

magnify /'mægnɪfaɪ/ *v.t.* увели́чи|вать, -ть; **~ing glass** увеличи́тельное стекло́, лу́па.

magnitude /'mægnɪtju:d/ *n.* (*size*) величина́; (*importance*) ва́жность.

magnolia /mæg'nəʊlɪə/ *n.* магно́лия.

magpie /'mægpaɪ/ *n.* соро́ка.

mahogany /mə'hɒgənɪ/ *n.* (*wood, tree*) кра́сное де́рево.

maid /meɪd/ *n.* (*domestic servant*) прислу́га; (*in hotel*) го́рничная.
■ *cpd.* **~servant** *n.* прислу́га, служа́нка.

maiden /'meɪd(ə)n/ *n.* де́ва.
■ *adj.* 1 (*of a girl*) де́вичий; **~ name** де́вичья фами́лия.
2 (*first*): **~ speech** пе́рвая речь (новои́збранного чле́на парла́мента); **~ voyage** пе́рвый рейс.

mail /meɪl/ *n.*
1 (*postal system*) по́чта; **~ order** почто́вый зака́з.
2 (*letters*) по́чта, пи́сьма (*nt. pl.*).
■ *v.t.* отпр|авля́ть, -а́вить (по по́чте); **the firm has me on its ~ing list** я состою́ в спи́ске подпи́счиков фи́рмы.
■ *cpds.* **~box** *n.* (*US; also comput.*) почто́вый я́щик; **~man** *n.* (*US*) почтальо́н; **~-order** *adj.* торгу́ющий по почто́вым зака́зам; **~shot** *n.* (*Br.*) рекла́мная рассы́лка.

maim /meɪm/ *v.t.* кале́чить, ис-.

main /meɪn/ *n.* (*sg. and* (*Br.*) *pl., principal supply line*) магистра́ль; (*sewerage*) канализа́ция; (*water*) водопрово́д; водопрово́дная магистра́ль; (*gas*) газопрово́д; (*electricity*) ка́бель (*m.*).
■ *adj.* гла́вный, основно́й; **~ course** (*of meal*) основно́е блю́до; **~ line** (*rail*) железнодоро́жная магистра́ль; **~ road** магистра́ль, гла́вная доро́га; **~ street** гла́вная у́лица.
■ *cpds.* **~land** *n.* (*continent*) матери́к; (*opp. island*): **they live on the ~land** они́ живу́т на большо́й земле́; **~stream** *n.* (*fig.*) госпо́дствующая тенде́нция.

mainframe /'meɪnfreɪm/ *adj.*: **~ computer** больша́я ЭВМ.

mainly /'meɪnlɪ/ *adv.* гла́вным о́бразом.

maintain /meɪn'teɪn/ *v.t.*
1 (*keep up*) подде́рживать (*impf.*); (*preserve*) сохран|я́ть, -и́ть.
2 (*support*) содержа́ть (*impf.*); **he has a wife and child to ~** ему́ прихо́дится содержа́ть жену́ и ребёнка.
3 (*keep in repair*): обслу́живать (*impf.*).
4 (*assert as true*) утвержда́ть (*impf.*); **he ~ed his innocence** он наста́ивал на свое́й невино́вности.

maintenance /'meɪntənəns/ *n.*
1 (*maintaining*) поддержа́ние.
2 (*of dependants*) содержа́ние.
3 (*of machinery etc.*) (техни́ческое) обслу́живание.

maison(n)ette /meɪzə'net/ *n.* двухэта́жная кварти́ра.

maize /meɪz/ *n.* кукуру́за, маи́с.

majestic /mə'dʒestɪk/ *adj.* вели́чественный.

majesty /'mædʒɪstɪ/ *n.* (*stateliness*) вели́чественность; (*title*): **His/Her M~** Его́/Её Вели́чество.

major /'meɪdʒə(r)/ *n.*
1 (*rank*) майо́р.
2 (*mus.*: **~ key**) мажо́р.
3 (*US, main subject of study*) основно́й предме́т (*в колле́дже*).
■ *adj.* 1 (*greater*) бо́льший; (*principal, more important*) гла́вный; **~ road** гла́вная доро́га.
2 (*significant*) кру́пный; **a ~ operation** кру́пная опера́ция.
3 (*mus.*) мажо́рный; **~ key** мажо́рная тона́льность.
■ *v.i.*: **he ~ed in physics** (*US*) он специализи́ровался по фи́зике.

Majorca /mə'jɔ:kə/ *n.* Мальо́рка.

majority /mə'dʒɒrɪtɪ/ *n.* большинство́; бо́льшая часть; (*in elections etc.*): **the government has a ~ of 60** у прави́тельства — большинство́ в 60 голосо́в.

make /meɪk/ *n.* (*brand*): **a good ~ of car** автомоби́ль хоро́шей ма́рки.
■ *v.t.* (*past and p.p.* **made**)
1 (*create, construct*) де́лать, с-; (*build*) стро́ить, по-; **what is this made of?** из чего́ э́то сде́лано?
2 (*sew*) шить, с-; **a suit made to order** костю́м, сши́тый на зака́з.
3 (*manufacture*) изгот|а́вливать, -о́вить; произв|оди́ть, -ести́; **the factory ~s shoes** фа́брика произво́дит о́бувь.
4 (*prepare*) гото́вить, при-; вари́ть, с-; **she made breakfast** она́ пригото́вила за́втрак; **~ a bed** (*prepare it for sleeping*) стели́ть, по- посте́ль; (*tidy it after use*) уб|ира́ть, -ра́ть посте́ль.
5 (*equal*) равня́ться (*impf.*) + *d.*; **four plus two ~s six** четы́ре плюс два равня́ется шести́; (*constitute*) **it ~s sense** э́то разу́мно.
6 (*understand*) пон|има́ть, -я́ть; **what do you ~ of this sentence?** как вы понима́ете э́то предложе́ние?; (*estimate*): **what do you ~ the time?** кото́рый час на ва́ших часа́х?
7 (*reach*) дост|ига́ть, -и́чь + *g.*; **he made it** (*succeeded*) **after three years** он дости́г успе́ха че́рез три го́да; (*earn*) зараб|а́тывать, -о́тать; **he ~s a good living** он хорошо́ зараба́тывает.
8 (*cause to be*) де́лать, с- + *a. and i.*; **the rain ~s the road slippery** от дождя́ доро́га стано́вится ско́льзкой; **~ s.o. angry** серди́ть, рас- кого́-н.; (*appoint, elect*): **they made him chairman** его́ вы́брали председа́телем.
9 (*compel, cause to*) заст|авля́ть, -а́вить; **I'll ~**

you pay for this! вы у меня́ за э́то заплати́те!; **don't ~ me laugh!** не смеши́те меня́!; **~ do with/without sth.** об|ходи́ться, -ойти́сь чем-н./без чего́-н.
■ *v.i.* (*past and p.p.* **made**) (*with certain preps.*: *move, proceed*): **~ after** пус|ка́ться, -ти́ться вслед за + *i.*; **~ for** (*head towards*) напр|авля́ться, -а́виться на + *a. or* к + *d.*
■ *with advs.*: **~ off** *v.i.* (*hurry away*) сбе|га́ть, -жа́ть; **~ out** *v.t.* (*write out*): **~ out a bill/cheque** выпи́сывать, вы́писать счёт/чек; (*assert*) утвержда́ть (*impf.*); **they ~ out he was drunk** они́ утвержда́ют, что он был пьян; (*understand*) раз|бира́ться, -обра́ться в + *p.*; **I can't ~ him out** я не могу́ его́ поня́ть; (*discern, distinguish*) различ|а́ть, -и́ть; **~ up** *v.t.* (*pay; pay the residue of*) допла́|чивать, -ти́ть; **I shall ~ up the difference out of my own pocket** я доплачу́ ра́зницу из своего́ карма́на; (*repay*) возме|ща́ть, -сти́ть; **we must ~ it up to him somehow** мы должны́ ка́к-то возмести́ть ему́ э́то; (*prepare*) гото́вить, при-/из-; **~ up a bed** заст|ила́ть, -ели́ть посте́ль; (*fig.*): **~ up one's mind** реш|а́ть, -и́ть; (*form, compose*) сост|авля́ть, -а́вить; **life is made up of disappointments** жизнь полна́ разочарова́ний; (*invent*) выду́мывать, вы́думать; сочин|я́ть, -и́ть; **the whole story was made up** вся э́та исто́рия была́ вы́думана; (*assemble*) соб|ира́ть, -ра́ть; **~ (it) up** (*be reconciled*) мири́ться, по-; (*with cosmetics*) кра́сить, по-; **she was heavily made up** она́ была́ си́льно накра́шена; **~ up for** (*compensate for*) возме|ща́ть, -сти́ть; **this will ~ up for everything** э́тим всё бу́дет компенси́ровано.
■ *cpds.* **~-believe** *n.*: **he lives in a world of ~-believe** он живёт в ми́ре грёз; **~shift** (*adj.*): **a ~shift shelter** на́скоро сколо́ченное укры́тие; **~-up** *n.* (*composition*): **there is some cowardice in his ~-up** он не́сколько трусова́т; (*cosmetics*) макия́ж, косме́тика; (*theatr., etc.*) грим; **~-up artist** *n.* визажи́ст; **~-up room** *n.* гримёрная.

maker /'meɪkə(r)/ *n.* производи́тель (*m.*).

making /'meɪkɪŋ/ *n.*
1 (*pl., potential qualities*): **he has all the ~s of a general** у него́ есть все зада́тки, что́бы стать генера́лом.
2 (*creation*) созда́ние; **the difficulties were not of my ~** э́ти тру́дности возни́кли не из-за меня́; (*manufacture, production*) изготовле́ние, произво́дство; (*preparation*) приготовле́ние.

malachite /'mælәkaɪt/ *n.* малахи́т; (*attr.*) малахи́товый.

maladjusted /mælә'dʒʌstɪd/ *adj.* (*fig., of person*) пло́хо приспосо́бленный.

malady /'mælәdɪ/ *n.* (*lit., fig.*) неду́г, боле́знь.

malaise /mә'leɪz/ *n.* (*bodily discomfort*) недомога́ние; (*disquiet*) беспоко́йство.

malaria /mә'leәrɪә/ *n.* маляри́я.

Malaya /mә'leɪә/ *n.* Мала́йя.

Malay(an) /mә'leɪ(әn)/ *n.* (*person*) мала́|ец (*fem.* -йка); (*language*) мала́йский язы́к.
■ *adj.* мала́йский.

Malaysia /mә'leɪʒә/ *n.* Мала́йзия.

Malaysian /mә'leɪʒ(ә)n/ *adj.* малайзи́йский.
■ *n.* малайзи́|ец (*fem.* -йка).

malcontent /'mælkәntent/ *n.* & *adj.* недово́льный.

male /meɪl/ *n.* (*person*) мужчи́на (*m.*); (*animal etc.*) саме́ц.
■ *adj.* мужско́й; **~ animal** саме́ц.

malevolence /mә'levәlәns/ *n.* недоброжела́тельность, злора́дство.

malevolent /mә'levәlәnt/ *adj.* недоброжела́тельный, злора́дный.

malformation /mælfɔː'meɪʃ(ә)n/ *n.* непра́вильное образова́ние, поро́к разви́тия; уро́дство.

malformed /mæl'fɔːmd/ *adj.* непра́вильно/пло́хо сформиро́ванный.

malfunction /mæl'fʌŋkʃ(ә)n/ *n.* неспра́вная рабо́та, отка́з.
■ *v.i.* неспра́вно де́йствовать (*impf.*).

malice /'mælɪs/ *n.* зло́ба; **I bear you no ~** я не пита́ю к вам зло́бы.

malicious /mә'lɪʃәs/ *adj.* (*of person*) злой; (*of thought, act etc.*) зло́бный.

malign /mә'laɪn/ *v.t.* клевета́ть, о- (*кого*), на- (*на кого*); **he ~ed me** он оклевета́л меня́, он наклевета́л на меня́.

malignant /mә'lɪgnәnt/ *adj.* злой, зло́бный; (*med.*) злока́чественный.

malinger /mә'lɪŋgә(r)/ *v.i.* симули́ровать (*impf., pf.*) боле́знь.

malingerer /mә'lɪŋgәrә(r)/ *n.* симуля́нт (*fem.* -ка).

mall /mæl/ *n.* торго́вый центр.

mallard /'mælɑːd/ *n.* (*pl.* **~** *or* **~s**) кря́ква.

malleable /'mælɪәb(ә)l/ *adj.* пода́тливый.

mallet /'mælɪt/ *n.* деревя́нный молото́к.

malnutrition /mælnjuː'trɪʃ(ә)n/ *n.* недоеда́ние.

malpractice /mæl'præktɪs/ *n.* (*of doctor*) престу́пная небре́жность (врача́); (*leg., abuse of trust*) злоупотребле́ние дове́рием.

Malta /'mɔːltә/ *n.* Ма́льта.

Maltese /mɔː'tiːz/ *n.* (*pl.* **~**) (*person*) мальти́|ец (*fem.* -йка); (*language*) мальти́йский язы́к.
■ *adj.* мальти́йский.

maltreat /mæl'triːt/ *v.t.* ду́рно обраща́ться (*impf.*) с + *i.*

maltreatment /mæl'triːtmәnt/ *n.* дурно́е обраще́ние (*с кем*).

mammal /'mæm(ә)l/ *n.* млекопита́ющее (живо́тное).

mammogram /'mæmәgræm/ *n.* маммогра́мма.

mammoth /'mæmәθ/ *n.* ма́монт.
■ *adj.* (*huge*) гига́нтский, грома́дный.

man /mæn/ *n.* (*pl.* **men**)
1 (*adult male*) мужчи́на (*m.*); **they talked ~ to ~** они́ говори́ли как мужчи́на с мужчи́ной; **old ~** стари́к.
2 (*mankind*) челове́к, челове́чество.
3 (*person*) челове́к (*pl.* лю́ди).
4 (*husband*) муж.
5 (*piece in chess*) ша́хматная фигу́ра; (*in draughts*) ша́шка.
■ *v.t.* (**manned, manning**)
1 (*a post*) зан|има́ть, -я́ть.
2 (*guns, machines*) обслу́живать (*impf.*).
■ *cpds.* **~hole** *n.* люк; **~-made** *adj.*

искýсственный; (*text.*) синтетический; **~power** *n.* рабóчая сила.

manag|e /'mænɪdʒ/ *v.t.*
[1] (*control, conduct*) управлять, руководить, завéдовать (*all impf.* + *i.*); **they ~ed the business between them** они вдвоём управляли предприятием; **~ing director** дирéктор-распорядитель (*m.*).
[2] (*handle*) владеть (*impf.*) + *i.*; **I can't ~e it** это мне не по силам.
[3] (*be ~er of*): **he has ~ed the team for 10 years** он руководил командой в течéние десяти лет; **the singer was looking for someone to ~e him** певéц подыскивал себé импрессáрио.
[4] (*cope with*) спр|авляться, -áвиться с + *i.*; **I can't ~e this work** я не справлюсь с этой работой.
[5] (*contrive*) сумéть (*pf.*); **I ~ed to convince him** мне удалось убедить его.
■ *v.i.* (*cope*) спр|авляться, -áвиться; (*get by, make do*) об|ходиться, -ойтись.

manageable /'mænɪdʒəb(ə)l/ *adj.* выполнимый.

management /'mænɪdʒmənt/ *n.*
[1] (*control, controlling*) управлéние (*чем*), мéнеджмент.
[2] (*handling person or thing*) обращéние; **staff ~** обращéние с личным состáвом.
[3] (*managers*) администрáция, дирéкция.

manager /'mænɪdʒə(r)/ *n.* (*controller of business etc.*) завéдующий (*чем*); (*sport*) стáрший трéнер; (*of s.o.'s career*) мéнеджер.

manageress /mænɪdʒə'res/ *n.* завéдующая (*чем*).

managerial /mænɪ'dʒɪərɪəl/ *adj.* административный; управлéнческий.

mandarin /'mændərɪn/ *n.* (*orange*) мандарин.

mandate /'mændeɪt/ *n.* (*official order*) мандáт; (*given by voters*) накáз.

mandatory /'mændətərɪ/ *adj.* обязáтельный.

mandolin /mændə'lɪn/ *n.* мандолина.

mane /meɪn/ *n.* грива.

maneuver /mə'nu:və(r)/ (*US*) = **manoeuvre**

manful /'mænfʊl/ *adj.* мýжественный.

manger /'meɪndʒə(r)/ *n.* ясл|и (*pl.*, *g.* -ей).

mangle /'mæŋg(ə)l/ *v.t.* (*mutilate*) урóдовать, из-.

mango /'mæŋgəʊ/ *n.* (*pl.* **~es** *or* **~s**) мáнго (*nt. indecl.*).

mangy /'meɪndʒɪ/ *adj.* (**mangier, mangiest**) паршивый, шелудивый (*coll.*).

manhandle /'mænhænd(ə)l/ *v.t.* (*move by manual effort*) та|скáть (*indet.*), -щить (*det.*) (вручнýю); (*treat roughly*) изб|ивáть, -ить.

mania /'meɪnɪə/ *n.* мáния.

maniac /'meɪnɪæk/ *n.* маньяк.

manic /'mænɪæk/ *n.* безýмный.

manicure /'mænɪkjʊə(r)/ *n.* маникюр.
■ *v.t.* дéлать, с- маникюр + *d.*

manicurist /'mænɪkjʊərɪst/ *n.* (*fem.*) маникюрша.

manifest /'mænɪfest/ *adj.* явный, очевидный.
■ *v.t.* (*show clearly*) ясно покáз|ывать, -áть; (*exhibit*) проявл|ять, -ить.

manifestation /mænɪfe'steɪʃ(ə)n/ *n.* проявлéние.

manifesto /mænɪ'festəʊ/ *n.* (*pl.* **~s**) манифéст.

manifold /'mænɪfəʊld/ *adj.* (*numerous*) многочисленный; (*various*) разнообрáзный.

manikin /'mænɪkɪn/ *n.* (*undersized person*) человéчек; (*dwarf*) кáрлик; (*artist's dummy*) манекéн.

Manila /mə'nɪlə/ *n.* Манила.
■ *adj.* манильский; **~ paper** манильская бумáга.

manipulate /mə'nɪpjʊleɪt/ *v.t.* (*lit.*, *fig.*; *also pej.*) манипулировать (*impf.*) + *i.*

manipulation /mənɪpjʊ'leɪʃ(ə)n/ *n.* манипуляция.

manipulative /mə'nɪpjʊlətɪv/ *adj.* (*person*) жуликовáтый (*coll.*); (*behaviour, practice*) жýльнический (*coll.*).

mankind /mæn'kaɪnd/ *n.* человéчество.

manliness /'mænlɪnɪs/ *n.* мýжественность.

manly /'mænlɪ/ *adj.* (**manlier, manliest**) подобáющий мужчине.

mannequin /'mænɪkɪn/ *n.* (*person*) манекéнщица; (*dummy*) манекéн.

manner /'mænə(r)/ *n.*
[1] (*way, fashion, mode*) óбраз; **in a ~ of speaking** в нéкотором смысле.
[2] (*pl.*, *ways of life*; *customs*) обычаи (*m. pl.*).
[3] (*style of behaviour*) манéра; **he has an awkward ~** он дéржится нелóвко.
[4] (*pl.*, *behaviour*) манéры (*f. pl.*); **good, bad ~s** хорóшие/плохие манéры; (*polite behaviour*): **have you no ~s?** как ты себя ведёшь?

mannered /'mænəd/ *adj.* (*affected*) манéрный.

mannerism /'mænərɪz(ə)m/ *n.* (*affected habitual gesture etc.*) манéра; (*excessive use of these*) манéрность.

manoeuvrable /mə'nu:vrəb(ə)l/ (*US* **maneuverable**) *adj.* манёвренный, подвижнóй.

manoeuvre /mə'nu:və(r)/ (*US* **maneuver**) *n.* манёвр.
■ *v.t.* маневрировать (*impf.*) + *i.*; **I ~d him to his chair** мне удалось подвести его к стýлу.
■ *v.i.* (*lit.*, *fig.*) маневрировать (*impf.*).

manor /'mænə(r)/ *n.* (*estate*) помéстье; (**~** *house*) особняк.

mansion /'mænʃ(ə)n/ *n.* особняк.

manslaughter /'mænslɔ:tə(r)/ *n.* непредумышленное убийство.

mantel(piece) /'mænt(ə)lpi:s/ *n.* каминная пóлка.

mantra /'mæntrə/ *n.* мáнтра.

manual /'mænjʊəl/ *n.* (*handbook*) посóбие.
■ *adj.* (*operated by hand*) ручнóй; (*performed by hand*): **~ labour** физический труд.

manufacture /mænjʊ'fæktʃə(r)/ *n.* изготовлéние; (*on large scale*) произвóдство.
■ *v.t.* изгот|áвливать, -óвить; произв|одить, -ести; **~ed goods** промтовáры (*m. pl.*).

manufacturer /mænjʊ'fæktʃərə(r)/ *n.* изготовитель (*m.*), производитель (*m.*).

manure /mə'njʊə(r)/ *n.* навóз.

manuscript /'mænjʊskrɪpt/ *n.* рýкопись.

many /'menɪ/ *adj.* (**more, most**) мнóгие; **~ times** мнóго раз; **half as ~** вдвóе мéньше; **twice as ~** вдвóе бóльше; **as, so ~ (as)**

сто́лько(, ско́лько); **not as ~ as** не так мно́го, как; **not ~** немно́го, не так уж мно́го.

map /mæp/ *n.* ка́рта; (*e.g. of rail system*) схе́ма; **town ~** план го́рода.
■ *v.t.* (**mapped, mapping**): **~ out** (*make ~ of*): **he ~ped out his route before leaving** он соста́вил маршру́т пе́ред отъе́здом; (*fig., plan*) плани́ровать, рас-; **he ~ped out his plans** он прики́нул, что ему́ ну́жно де́лать.

maple /ˈmeɪp(ə)l/ *n.* клён; (*attr.*) кleно́вый.

marathon /ˈmærəθ(ə)n/ *n.* марафо́н; **~ runner** марафо́нец.

maraud /məˈrɔːd/ *v.i.* мародёрствовать (*impf., pf.*).

marble /ˈmɑːb(ə)l/ *n.*
1 (*substance*) мра́мор.
2 (*in child's game*) стекля́нный ша́рик; **play ~s** игра́ть (*impf.*) в ша́рики.
■ *adj.* (*lit., fig.*) мра́морный.

March /mɑːtʃ/ *n.* март.

march /mɑːtʃ/ *n.* (*mil.*) марш; (*pol.*) марш, демонстра́ция.
■ *v.i.* 1 (*mil.*) марширова́ть, про-; **we watched them ~ past** мы смотре́ли, как они́ прошли́ стро́ем; **quick ~!** ша́гом марш!
2 (*walk determinedly*): **he ~ed into the room** он сме́ло вошёл в ко́мнату.
■ *with adv.*: **~ along** *v.i.*: **they were ~ing along singing** они́ маршировáли с пе́снями.

mare /meə(r)/ *n.* кобы́ла.

margarine /mɑːdʒəˈriːn/ *n.* маргари́н.

margin /ˈmɑːdʒɪn/ *n.*
1 (*edge*) край; (*of page*) по́ле (*usu. pl.*); **in the ~** на поля́х.
2 (*extra amount*) запа́с; **he won by a narrow ~** он победи́л с небольши́м преиму́ществом.

marginal /ˈmɑːdʒɪn(ə)l/ *adj.* (*insignificant*) незначи́тельный; минима́льный.

marguerite /mɑːgəˈriːt/ *n.* нивя́ник (*крупная полевая ромашка*).

marigold /ˈmærɪgəʊld/ *n.* (*also called* **common** *or* **pot ~**, *genus Calendula*) ноготки́ (*m. pl.*); (*also called* **French** *or* **African ~**, *genus Tagetes*) ба́рхатцы (*m. pl.*).

marijuana /mærɪˈ(h)wɑːnə/ *n.* марихуа́на.

marina /məˈriːnə/ *n.* мари́на, при́стань для яхт.

marinade /ˈmærɪneɪd/ *n.* марина́д.
■ *v.t.* (*also* **marinate** /-neɪt/) маринова́ть, за-.

marine /məˈriːn/ *n.*
1 (*fleet*): **mercantile, merchant ~** торго́вый флот.
2 (*naval infantryman*) солда́т морско́й пехо́ты, морско́й пехоти́нец.
■ *adj.* морско́й.

marital /ˈmærɪt(ə)l/ *adj.*: **~ status** семе́йное положе́ние.

maritime /ˈmærɪtaɪm/ *adj.* (*of the sea*): **~ law** морско́е пра́во; (*situated by the sea*) примо́рский.

marjoram /ˈmɑːdʒərəm/ *n.* майора́н садо́вый.

mark /mɑːk/ *n.*
1 (*imperfection; stain, spot, etc.*) пятно́.
2 (*trace*) след; **you have left dirty ~s on the floor** вы наследи́ли на полу́.
3 (*sign, symbol*) знак; **as a ~ of goodwill** в знак расположе́ния.
4 (*reference point*) ме́тка; (*fig., standard*): **his work was not up to the ~** его́ рабо́та была́ не на высоте́.
5 (*starting line*) старт; **on your ~s, get set, go!** на старт, внима́ние, марш!
6 (*assessment of performance*) отме́тка; **he always gets good ~s** он всегда́ получа́ет хоро́шие отме́тки; (*preceded by number*) балл.
■ *v.t.* 1 (*stain, scar, scratch etc.*): **a tablecloth ~ed with coffee stains** ска́терть, забры́зганная ко́фе; **the table was badly ~ed** стол был си́льно запа́чкан.
2 (*indicate*) отм|еча́ть, -е́тить; **is our village ~ed on this map?** на́ша дере́вня нанесена́ на э́ту ка́рту?; **the prices are clearly ~ed** це́ны чётко проста́влены.
3 (*observe and remember*): **a ~ed man** челове́к, взя́тый на заме́тку; (*Br., football etc.: follow closely*) закр|ыва́ть, -ы́ть; (*notice*) зам|еча́ть, -е́тить; **~ my words!** помяни́те моё сло́во!
4 (*assign ~s to*): **~ an exercise** пров|еря́ть, -е́рить упражне́ние.
■ *with advs.*: **~ down** *v.t.* (*reduce price of*): **all the goods were ~ed down for the sale** для распрода́жи це́ны на все това́ры бы́ли сни́жены; **~ off** *v.t.* отм|еча́ть, -е́тить; **~ out** *v.t.*: **a tennis court had been ~ed out** те́ннисный корт был расче́рчен/разме́чен; (*preselect, destine*): **he was ~ed out for promotion** его́ реши́ли повы́сить в до́лжности; **~ up** *v.t.* (*raise price of*): **goods were ~ed up after the budget** це́ны бы́ли повы́шены по́сле объявле́ния фина́нсовой сме́ты.

marked /mɑːkt/ *adj.* (*noticeable*) заме́тный.

markedly /ˈmɑːkɪdlɪ/ *adv.*: **they were ~ different** они́ заме́тно отлича́лись друг от дру́га.

marker /ˈmɑːkə(r)/ *n.* (*indicator*) индика́тор; (*flag*) сигна́льный флажо́к; (*pen*) флома́стер.

market /ˈmɑːkɪt/ *n.*
1 (*gathering; event; place of business*) ры́нок, база́р; (*attr.*) ры́ночный, база́рный.
2 (*trade*) торго́вля; **there is no ~ for these goods** на э́ти това́ры нет спро́са.
3 (*share prices*) це́ны (*f. pl.*); **the ~ is falling** це́ны па́дают; **~ research** изуче́ние конъюнкту́ры/возмо́жностей ры́нка; **~ value** ры́ночная сто́имость.
4 : **on the ~** (*available for purchase*): **he put his house on the ~** он вы́ставил свой дом на прода́жу.
■ *v.t.* (**marketed, marketing**) (*advertise*) реклами́ровать (*impf.*); (*sell*) продава́ть (*impf.*).
■ *cpds.* **~ day** *n.* (*Br.*) база́рный день; **~ economy** *n.* ры́ночная эконо́мика; **~ forces** *n. pl.* ры́ночные си́лы (*f. pl.*); **~ gardener** *n.* (*Br.*) владе́лец огоро́дного хозя́йства; **~ leader** *n.* ли́дер ры́нка; **~place** *n.* база́рная пло́щадь; (*fig.*) ры́нок; **~ research** *n.* иссле́дование ры́нка; **~ share** *n.* до́ля ры́нка; **~ town** *n.* (небольшо́й) го́род с ры́нком.

marketable /ˈmɑːkɪtəb(ə)l/ *adj.* (*produced for sale*) това́рный; (*selling quickly*) хо́дкий.

marketing /ˈmɑːkɪtɪŋ/ *n.* ма́ркетинг; **~ manager** ме́неджер по ма́ркетингу.

marking /'mɑːkɪŋ/ *n.*
[1] (*on animals etc.*) окра́ска.
[2] (*for identification*) знак.

marksman /'mɑːksmən/ *n.* стрело́к.

marmalade /'mɑːməleɪd/ *n.*: **orange ~** апельси́новый джем.

maroon[1] /mə'ruːn/ *n.* & *adj.* (*colour*) тёмно-бордо́вый цвет.

maroon[2] /mə'ruːn/ *v.t.* выса́живать, вы́садить на необита́емый о́стров *и т. п.*; (*fig.*, *pass.*) застр|ева́ть, -я́ть; **we were ~ed in Paris** мы застря́ли в Пари́же.

marquee /mɑː'kiː/ *n.* (*Br.*) (больша́я) пала́тка.

marriage /'mærɪdʒ/ *n.*
[1] (*married state*) брак; **~ of convenience** фикти́вный брак.
[2] (*ceremony*) сва́дьба; бракосочета́ние.
[3] (*attr.*) бра́чный; **~ certificate** свиде́тельство о бра́ке; **~ guidance** (*Br.*) семе́йная консульта́ция.

married /'mærɪd/ *adj.*
[1] (*of man*) жена́тый (**to:** на + *p.*); (*of woman*) заму́жняя, (*pred.*) за́мужем (**to:** за + *i.*); **they are ~** (*to each other*) они́ жена́ты.
[2] (*pert. to marriage*) супру́жеский; **a ~ couple** супру́жеская па́ра.

marrow /'mærəʊ/ *n.*
[1] (*anat.*) (ко́стный) мозг.
[2] **(vegetable ~)** (*Br.*) кабачо́к.

marry /'mærɪ/ *v.t.*
[1] (*of man*) жени́ться (*impf.*, *pf.*) на + *p.*
[2] (*of woman*) выходи́ть, вы́йти за́муж за + *a.*
[3] (*of priest*) венча́ть, об-.
■ *v.i.* (*of man*) жени́ться (*impf.*, *pf.*); (*of woman*) выходи́ть, вы́йти за́муж; (*of couple*) пожени́ться (*pf.*); (*relig.*) венча́ться, об-.

Mars /mɑːz/ *n.* (*myth.*, *astron.*) Марс.

marsh /mɑːʃ/ *n.* боло́то.
■ *cpd.* **~land** *n.* боло́тистая ме́стность.

marshal /'mɑːʃ(ə)l/ *n.*
[1] (*mil.*) ма́ршал.
[2] (*organizer*) распоряди́тель.
[3] (*US, head of police*) нача́льник полице́йского уча́стка.
■ *v.t.* (**marshalled, marshalling;** *US* **marshaled, marshaling**)
[1] (*draw up in order*): **~ troops** выстра́ивать, вы́строить войска́; (*fig.*): **~ one's forces** соб|ира́ть, -ра́ть си́лы.
[2] (*direct*): **~ a crowd** напр|авля́ть, -а́вить толпу́.

marshy /'mɑːʃɪ/ *adj.* (**marshier, marshiest**) боло́тистый.

marsupial /mɑː'suːpɪəl/ *n.* су́мчатое живо́тное.
■ *adj.* су́мчатый.

martial /'mɑːʃ(ə)l/ *adj.* (*military*) вое́нный; **~ arts** спорти́вная борьба́; **~ law** вое́нное положе́ние.

martyr /'mɑːtə(r)/ *n.* му́чени|к (*fem.* -ца).
■ *v.t.* му́чить, за-.

martyrdom /'mɑːtədəm/ *n.* му́ченичество.

marvel /'mɑːv(ə)l/ *n.* чу́до.
■ *v.t.* & *i.* (**marvelled, marvelling;** *US* **marveled, marveling**) (*wonder*) диви́ться (*impf.*) + *d.*; удив|ля́ться, -и́ться + *d.*

marvellous /'mɑːvələs/ (*US* **marvelous**) *adj.* (*astonishing*) изуми́тельный; (*splendid*) чуде́сный.

Marxism /'mɑːksɪz(ə)m/ *n.* маркси́зм.

Marxist /'mɑːksɪst/ *n.* маркси́ст (*fem.* -ка).
■ *adj.* маркси́стский.

marzipan /'mɑːzɪpæn/ *n.* марципа́н (*кондитерское изделие; начинка, глазурь*).

mascara /mæ'skɑːrə/ *n.* тушь для ресни́ц.

mascot /'mæskɒt/ *n.* талисма́н.

masculine /'mæskjʊlɪn/ *adj.* мужско́й.

masculinity /mæskjʊ'lɪnɪtɪ/ *n.* му́жественность.

mash /mæʃ/ *n.* (*Br.*, *potato*) пюре́ (*nt. indecl.*).
■ *v.t.* (*cul.*): **~ed potatoes** карто́фельное пюре́.

mask /mɑːsk/ *n.* ма́ска.
■ *v.t.* над|ева́ть, -е́ть ма́ску на + *a.*; (*fig.*) **she ~ed her feelings** она́ скрыва́ла свои́ чу́вства.

masochism /'mæsəkɪz(ə)m/ *n.* мазохи́зм.

masochist /'mæsə'kɪst/ *n.* мазохи́ст.

masochistic /mæsə'kɪstɪk/ *adj.* мазохи́стский.

mason /'meɪs(ə)n/ *n.* ка́менщик; **(M~, Free~)** масо́н.

masonry /'meɪsənrɪ/ *n.* ка́менная кла́дка.

masquerade /mæskə'reɪd/ *n.* (*lit.*, *fig.*) маскара́д.
■ *v.i.*: **he ~d as a general** он выдава́л себя́ за генера́ла.

Mass /mæs/ *n.* (*relig.*) ме́сса, литурги́я; (*in Orthodox church*) обе́дня.

mass /mæs/ *n.*
[1] (*phys. etc.*) ма́сса.
[2] (*large number*) мно́жество; **~es of people** ма́сса наро́ду; **the ~es** (наро́дные/широ́кие) ма́ссы; (*pl.*, *coll.*, *a large amount*): **there's ~es of food** полно́ еды́.
[3] (*attr.*) ма́ссовый; **~ destruction** ма́ссовое уничтоже́ние; **the ~ media** сре́дства ма́ссовой информа́ции (*abbr.* СМИ); масс(-)ме́диа (*pl. indecl.*); **~ production** ма́ссовое произво́дство.
■ *v.t.* соб|ира́ть, -ра́ть; **~ troops** сосредото́чи|вать, -ть войска́.
■ *v.i.* соб|ира́ться, -ра́ться; **the clouds are ~ing** собира́ются облака́.
■ *cpd.* **~-produce** *v.t.*: **these toys are ~-produced** э́ти игру́шки ма́ссового произво́дства.

massacre /'mæsəkə(r)/ *n.* бо́йня.
■ *v.t.* переб|ива́ть, -и́ть.

massage /'mæsɑːʒ/ *n.* масса́ж.
■ *v.t.* масси́ровать (*impf.*, *pf.*).

masseur /mæ'sɜː(r)/ *n.* массажи́ст.

masseuse /mæ'sɜːz/ *n.* массажи́стка.

massive /'mæsɪv/ *adj.* (*large and heavy*) масси́вный; (*substantial*) огро́мный.

mast /mɑːst/ *n.* ма́чта.

mastectomy /mæs'tektəmɪ/ *n.* мастэктоми́я (*ампутация молочной железы*).

master /'mɑːstə(r)/ *n.*
[1] (*one in control, boss*) хозя́ин; (*owner*) владе́лец; **~ of ceremonies** распоряди́тель (*m.*), конферансье́ (*nt. indecl.*).
[2] (*Br.*, *teacher*) учи́тель (*m.*); (*in university*): **M~ of Arts** маги́стр гуманита́рных нау́к.
[3] (*skilled craftsman, expert*) ма́стер; **~**

builder строитель-подрядчик.
[4] (*original*) подлинник.
[5] (*attr.*): ~ **bedroom** главная спальня; ~ **plan** генеральный план.
■ *v.t.* [1] (*gain control of*) спр|авляться, -авиться с + *i*.
[2] (*acquire knowledge of, skill in*) овлад|евать, -еть + *i*.; **it is a language which can be ~ed in 6 months** этим языком можно овладеть за шесть месяцев.
[3] (*overcome*) овлад|евать, -еть + *i*.; ~ **one's feelings** владеть, о- своими чувствами.
■ *cpds.* ~ **key** *n.* отмычка; ~**mind** *n.* руководитель (*m.*); *v.t.*: **he ~minded the plan** он разработал весь план; ~**piece** *n.* шедевр.
masterful /ˈmɑːstəfʊl/ *adj.* властный.
masterly /ˈmɑːstəlɪ/ *adj.* мастерский.
mastery /ˈmɑːstərɪ/ *n.*
[1] (*authority*) власть.
[2] (*skill*) мастерство.
[3] (*knowledge*) владение.
masturbate /ˈmæstəbeɪt/ *v.i.* мастурбировать (*impf.*).
masturbation /mæstəˈbeɪʃ(ə)n/ *n.* мастурбация.
mat[1] /mæt/ *n.*
[1] (*floor covering*) коврик.
[2] (*to protect table*) подставка.
mat[2] /mæt/ *v.t.* (**matted, matting**): **his hair was ~ted with blood** его волосы слиплись от крови.
matador /ˈmætədɔː(r)/ *n.* матадор.
match[1] /mætʃ/ *n.* (*for producing flame*) спичка.
■ *cpd.* ~**box** *n.* спичечная коробка.
match[2] /mætʃ/ *n.*
[1] (*equal*) пара, ровня; **he's no ~ for her** он ей не пара.
[2] (*thing resembling or suiting another*): **these curtains are a good ~ for the carpet** эти занавески подходят к ковру.
[3] (*game*) соревнование, состязание; матч, игра; **football ~** футбольный матч.
■ *v.t.* (*suit; correspond to*) под|ходить, -ойти к + *d*.; гармонировать (*impf.*) с + *i*.; **her hat doesn't ~ her dress** её шляпа не подходит к платью; (*find a ~ for*): **we try to ~ the jobs with the applicants** мы стараемся подбирать подходящую работу для кандидатов.
■ *v.i.* (*correspond: be identical*): **the handbag and gloves don't ~** сумочка и перчатки не гармонируют друг с другом.
■ *cpd.* ~ **point** *n.* очко, решающее исход матча; матч-пойнт.
mate /meɪt/ *n.*
[1] (*Br., companion*; (*coll.*) *form of address*) брат, друг.
[2] (*one of a pair of animals or birds*) самец; (*fem.*) самка.
[3] (*assistant*) помощник.
[4] (*ship's ~*) помощник капитана.
■ *v.t. & i.* спари|вать(ся), -ть(ся).
material /məˈtɪərɪəl/ *n.*
[1] (*substance*) материал; **raw ~(s)** сырьё; (*fig., of person*): **he is good officer ~** из него выйдет хороший офицер; (*subject matter*): **there is good ~ there for a novel** там есть хороший материал для романа.
[2] (*fabric*) материя.
[3] (*pl.*): **writing ~s** письменные принадлежности.
■ *adj.* материальный.
materialism /məˈtɪərɪəlɪz(ə)m/ *n.* материализм.
materialist /məˈtɪərɪəlɪst/ *n.* материалист.
materialistic /mətɪərɪəˈlɪstɪk/ *adj.* материалистический.
materialize /məˈtɪərɪəlaɪz/ *v.i.* материализоваться (*impf., pf.*).
maternal /məˈtɜːn(ə)l/ *adj.* (*motherly*) материнский.
maternity /məˈtɜːnɪtɪ/ *n.* материнство; (*attr.*): ~ **leave** декретный отпуск.
math /mæθ/ *n.* (*US coll., abbr.*) = **mathematics**
mathematical /mæθəˈmætɪk(ə)l/ *adj.* математический.
mathematician /mæθəməˈtɪʃ(ə)n/ *n.* математик.
mathematics /mæθəˈmætɪks/ *n.* математика.
maths /mæθs/ *n.* (*Br. coll., abbr.*) = **mathematics**
matinée /ˈmætɪneɪ/ *n.* дневное представление.
mating /ˈmeɪtɪŋ/ *n.* спаривание; ~ **season** сезон спаривания.
matriarchal /meɪtrɪˈɑːk(ə)l/ матриархальный.
matriculate /məˈtrɪkjʊleɪt/ *v.i.* быть принятым в высшее учебное заведение.
matriculation /mətrɪkjʊˈleɪʃ(ə)n/ *n.* зачисление в высшее учебное заведение.
matrimonial /mætrɪˈməʊnɪəl/ *adj.* супружеский; брачный.
matrimony /ˈmætrɪmənɪ/ *n.* брак.
matri|x /ˈmeɪtrɪks/ *n.* (*pl.* ~**ces** /-siːz/ *or* ~**xes**) матрица.
matron /ˈmeɪtrən/ *n.*
[1] (*Br., in hospital*) старшая сестра.
[2] (*in school*) экономка.
matt /mæt/ *adj.* матовый; ~ **paint** матовая краска.
matter /ˈmætə(r)/ *n.*
[1] (*phys., phil*) материя; (*substance*) вещество.
[2] (*physiol.*): **grey ~** серое вещество; (*pus*) гной.
[3] (*material for reading*) материалы (*m. pl.*); **printed ~** печатный материал.
[4] (*question; issue*) вопрос; дело; **that's quite another ~** это совсем другое дело; **it is a ~ of course** само собой разумеется; **as a ~ of fact** (*to tell the truth*) по правде сказать; (*in reality*) на самом деле; (*incidentally*) собственно (говоря); **it is a ~ for the police** это дело полиции; **a ~ of life and death** вопрос жизни и смерти; **that's a ~ of opinion** это спорный вопрос; (*pl., affairs*) дела; **to make ~s worse** в довершение ко всем бедам.
[5]: **the ~** (*wrong, amiss*): **what's the ~?** в чём дело?; **is (there) anything the ~?** что-нибудь не ладно?; **what's the ~ with him?** что с ним?; **there's nothing the ~ (with me)** (у меня) всё в порядке.
[6] (*importance*): **no ~ what I do, the result**

will be the same что бы я ни сде́лал, результа́т бу́дет тот же.
■ *v.i.* име́ть (*impf.*) значе́ние; **it doesn't ~ to me** э́то не име́ет для меня́ значе́ния.
■ *cpd.* **~-of-fact** *adj.* приземлённый, лишённый фанта́зии; сухо́й, делово́й.

mattress /'mætrɪs/ *n.* матра́с, матра́ц.

mature /mə'tjʊə(r)/ *adj.* (**maturer, maturest**) зре́лый; **~ student** (*Br.*) студе́нт (*fem.* -ка) зре́лого во́зраста.
■ *v.i.* 1 (*lit., fig., ripen, develop*) созр|ева́ть, -е́ть; **children ~ earlier nowadays** в на́ши дни де́ти развива́ются быстре́е.
2 (*become due for payment*): **the policy ~s next year** в бу́дущем году́ наступа́ет срок вы́платы по страхово́му по́лису.

maturity /mə'tjʊərɪtɪ/ *n.* зре́лость.

maudlin /'mɔ:dlɪn/ *adj.* слюня́во сентимента́льный; плакси́вый во хмелю́.

maul /mɔ:l/ *v.t.* терза́ть, рас-; **he was ~ed to death by a tiger** его́ растерза́л тигр.

Mauritania /mɒrɪ'teɪnɪə/ *n.* Маврита́ния.

mausole|um /mɔ:sə'li:əm/ *n.* мавзоле́й.

mauve /məʊv/ *n.* & *adj.* розова́то-лило́вый (цвет).

maverick /'mævərɪk/ *n.* (*fig., dissenter*) диссиде́нт; (*attr.*) неприка́янный.

mawkish /'mɔ:kɪʃ/ *adj.* при́торный.

maxim /'mæksɪm/ *n.* (*aphorism*) афори́зм.

maximize /'mæksɪmaɪz/ *v.t.* максима́льно увели́чи|вать, -ть.

maximum /'mæksɪməm/ *n.* ма́ксимум.
■ *adj.* максима́льный.

May /meɪ/ *n.* май; **~ Day** Пе́рвое ма́я; пра́здник Пе́рвого ма́я.
■ *cpd.* **~day** *n.* (*distress signal*) сигна́л бе́дствия.

may /meɪ/ *v. aux.* (*3rd pers. sing. pres.* **may;** *past* **might**)
1 (*expr. possibility*) мо́жет быть; пожа́луй; **it ~ be true** возмо́жно, э́то пра́вда; **it ~ not be true** возмо́жно, э́то не так; **he might have lost his way without my help** без моего́ по́мощи он мог бы заблуди́ться; **you ~ well be right** вполне́ возмо́жно, вы и пра́вы.
2 (*expr. permission*): **~ I come and see you?** мо́жно мне (*or* могу́ я) к вам зайти́?; **you ~ go if you wish** е́сли хоти́те, мо́жете идти́.
3 (*expr. reproach*): **you might have asked my permission** мо́жно бы́ло бы спроси́ть моего́ согла́сия.
4 (*in main clause, expr. wish or hope*): **~ the best man win!** да победи́т сильне́йший!
■ *cpd.* **~be** *adv.* мо́жет быть.

mayhem /'meɪhem/ *n.* разгро́м.

mayonnaise /meɪə'neɪz/ *n.* майоне́з.

mayor /meə(r)/ *n.* мэр.

mayoress /'meərɪs/ *n.* (*mayor's wife*) жена́ мэ́ра; (*female mayor*) же́нщина-мэр.

maze /meɪz/ *n.* лабири́нт; (*fig.*) пу́таница.

MBA (*abbr. of* ***Master of Business Administration***) маги́стр ме́неджмента.

MBE (*abbr. of* ***Member of the Order of the British Empire***) кавале́р о́рдена Брита́нской импе́рии 5-й (*низшей*) сте́пени.

MC (*abbr. of* ***Master of Ceremonies***) конферансье́ (*nt. indecl.*), распоряди́тель (*m.*),

MD (*abbr. of* ***Managing Director***) (*Br.*) дире́ктор-распоряди́тель.

ME (*abbr. of* ***myalgic encephalitis***) миалги́ческий энцефали́т, синдро́м хрони́ческой уста́лости.

me /mi:/ *obj. of* ▶ **I**

meadow /'medəʊ/ *n.* луг.

meagre /'mi:gə(r)/ (*US* **meager**) *adj.* ску́дный.

meal /mi:l/ *n.* еда́, тра́пеза; **we have 3 ~s a day** мы еди́м три ра́за в день.

mean[1] /mi:n/ *n.* (*average*) середи́на.
■ *cpds.* **~time** *n.*: **in the ~time** ме́жду тем; **~while** *adv.* ме́жду тем, тем вре́менем.

mean[2] /mi:n/ *adj.*
1 (*niggardly*) скупо́й.
2 (*spiteful*) зло́бный; **don't be ~ to him** не обижа́йте его́.
3 (*inferior*): **he is a man of no ~ abilities** он челове́к незауря́дных спосо́бностей.

mean[3] /mi:n/ *v.t.* (*past and p.p.* **meant**)
1 (*intend*) име́ть (*impf.*) в виду́; намерева́ться (*impf.*); **I ~ to solve this problem** я наме́рен реши́ть э́тот вопро́с; **I ~t no harm** я не жела́л зла; **I ~t it as a joke** я хоте́л пошути́ть; **I didn't ~ to hurt you** я не хоте́л вас оби́деть.
2 (*design, destine*) предназн|ача́ть, -а́чить; **they were ~t for each other** они́ бы́ли со́зданы друг для дру́га.
3 (*of person, intend to convey*) хоте́ть (*impf.*) сказа́ть; **what do you ~?** что вы э́тим хоти́те сказа́ть?
4 (*of words etc., signify*) зна́чить (*impf.*), означа́ть (*impf.*); **this sentence ~s nothing to me** э́то предложе́ние ничего́ мне не говори́т; **does my friendship ~ nothing to you?** неуже́ли моя́ дру́жба ничего́ для вас не зна́чит?; (*entail, involve*): **organizing a fête ~s a lot of hard work** подгото́вка к пра́зднику тре́бует мно́го уси́лий.

meander /mɪ'ændə(r)/ *v.i.* (*of streams, roads etc.*) извива́ться, ви́ться (*both impf.*).

meaning /'mi:nɪŋ/ *n.* значе́ние.

meaningful /'mi:nɪŋfʊl/ *adj.* значи́тельный.

meaningless /'mi:nɪŋlɪs/ *adj.* бессмы́сленный.

meanness /'mi:nnɪs/ *n.* по́длость, ни́зость; ску́пость.

means /mi:nz/ *n.*
1 (*instrument, method*) спо́соб; **a ~ to an end** сре́дство для достиже́ния це́ли; **by ~ of** посре́дством + *g.*; с по́мощью + *g.*; **by all ~** (*US, without fail*) непреме́нно; (*expr. permission*) коне́чно; пожа́луйста; **it was by no ~ easy** э́то бы́ло отню́дь не про́сто.
2 (*facilities*): **~ of communication** (*transport*) сре́дства сообще́ния; (*telecommunication*) сре́дства свя́зи.
3 (*resources*) сре́дства; **a man of ~** челове́к со сре́дствами; **~ test** прове́рка нужда́емости; **live beyond one's ~** жить (*impf.*) не по сре́дствам.

meant /ment/ *past and p.p. of* ▶ **mean**[3]

measles /'mi:z(ə)lz/ *n.* корь.

measly /'mi:zlɪ/ *adj.* (**measlier, measliest**) жа́лкий.

measurable /'meʒərəb(ə)l/ *adj.* измери́мый.

measure /'meʒə(r)/ *n.*
1 (*calculated quantity, size, etc.*; *system of ~ment*) мéра; (*portion, of whisky etc.*) пóрция.
2 (*measuring rod*; *tape measure*) измери́тельная линéйка; рулéтка.
3 (*step*) мéра, мероприя́тие.
■ *v.t.* 1 (*find size etc. of*) мéрить, с-; изм|еря́ть, -éрить; **he was ~d for a suit** с негó сня́ли мéрку для костю́ма.
2 (*amount to when ~d*): **the room ~s 12 ft across** кóмната ширинóй в двена́дцать фу́тов.
■ *with advs.*: **~ off, ~ out** *vv.t.* отм|еря́ть, -éрить; **~ up** *v.i.*: **the team has not ~d up to our expectations** комáнда не оправдáла нáших ожидáний.

measured /'meʒəd/ *adj.*
1 (*steps*) размéренный; **~ tread** мéрная пóступь.
2 (*tone*) умéренный; (*considered*; *careful*) обду́манный, осторóжный.

measurement /'meʒəmənt/ *n.* (*measuring*) измерéние; (*dimension*) размéр; **take s.o.'s ~s** снять (*pf.*) мéрку с когó-н.; **waist ~** объём тáлии.

meat /mi:t/ *n.* мя́со.

meaty /'mi:tɪ/ *adj.* (**meatier, meatiest**) мяси́стый.

Mecca /'mekə/ *n.* Мéкка (*also fig.*).

mechanic /mɪ'kænɪk/ *n.* механик.

mechanical /mɪ'kænɪk(ə)l/ *adj.* механи́ческий; **~ engineering** машинострoéние.

mechanics /mɪ'kænɪks/ *n.* (*lit., fig.*) механика.

mechanism /'mekənɪz(ə)m/ *n.* механи́зм.

mechanization /mekənaɪ'zeɪʃ(ə)n/ *n.* механизáция.

mechanize /'mekənaɪz/ *v.t. & i.* механизи́ровать(ся) (*impf., pf.*).

Med /med/ *n.* (*Br. coll., abbr.*): **the ~** Средизéмное мóре.

medal /'med(ə)l/ *n.* медáль; (*mil. award*) óрден (*pl.* -á).

medallion /mə'dæljən/ *n.* медальóн.

medallist /'medəlɪst/ (*US* **medalist**) *n.* (*recipient*) медали́ст (*fem.* -ка).

meddle /'med(ə)l/ *v.i.*: **~ in** (*interfere in*) вмéш|иваться, -áться в + *a.*; **~ with** (*touch, tamper with*) трó|гать, -нуть.

meddlesome /'medəlsəm/ *adj.* назóйливый; **he is a ~ person** он всё врéмя вмéшивается не в свои́ делá.

media /'mi:dɪə/ *see* ▸ **medium** *n.* **4**

mediate /'mi:dɪeɪt/ *v.i.* выступáть, вы́ступить посрéдником.

mediation /mi:dɪ'eɪʃ(ə)n/ *n.* посрéдничество.

mediator /'mi:dɪeɪtə(r)/ *n.* посрéдник.

medic /'medɪk/ *n.* (*coll.*) (студéнт-)мéдик.

medical /'medɪk(ə)l/ *n.* (*coll.*, *~ examination*): **have a ~** про|ходи́ть, -йти́ медици́нский осмóтр (*abbr.* медосмóтр).
■ *adj.* медици́нский; врачéбный; **~ certificate** спрáвка от врачá.

medicament /mɪ'dɪkəmənt/ *n.* лекáрство, медикамéнт.

medication /medɪ'keɪʃ(ə)n/ *n.* (*medicine*) лекáрство; (*treatment*) лечéние.

medicinal /mə'dɪsɪn(ə)l/ *adj.* (*of medicine*) лекáрственный; (*curative*) целéбный.

medicine /'medsɪn/ *n.*
1 (*science, practice*) медици́на.
2 (*substance*) лекáрство; медикамéнт, миксту́ра.
■ *cpds.* **~ cabinet** *n.* аптéчка; **~ man** *n.* знáхарь (*m.*).

medieval /medɪ'i:v(ə)l/ *adj.* средневекóвый.

mediocre /mi:dɪ'əʊkə(r)/ *adj.* посрéдственный.

mediocrity /mi:dɪ'ɒkrɪtɪ/ *n.* посрéдственность.

meditate /'medɪteɪt/ *v.i.* размышля́ть (*impf.*) (**on:** о + *p.*); (*relig.*) медити́ровать (*impf.*).

meditation /medɪ'teɪʃ(ə)n/ *n.* размышлéние; (*relig.*) медитáция.

meditative /'medɪtətɪv/ *adj.* заду́мчивый.

Mediterranean /medɪtə'reɪnɪən/ *n.* (**~ Sea**) Средизéмное мóре.
■ *adj.* средиземномóрский.

medium /'mi:dɪəm/ *n.* (*pl.* **media** *or* **mediums**)
1 (*middle quality*) середи́на; **he strikes a happy ~** он придéрживается золотóй середи́ны.
2 (*means, agency*) срéдство.
3 (*spiritualist*) мéдиум.
4 : **the media** (*sc. of communication*) срéдства мáссовой информáции.
■ *adj.* (*intermediate*) промежу́точный; (*average*) срéдний.
■ *cpds.* **~ dry** *adj.* полусухóй; **~-sized** *adj.* срéднего размéра.

medley /'medlɪ/ *n.* (*pl.* **medleys**) смесь; (*mus.*) попурри́ (*nt. indecl.*).

meek /mi:k/ *adj.* крóткий.

meet /mi:t/ *n.* (*of sportsmen, etc.*) сбор.
■ *v.t.* (*past and p.p.* **met**)
1 (*encounter*) встр|ечáть, -éтить; (*make acquaintance of*) знакóмиться, по- с + *i.*; **I met your sister in Moscow** я познакóмился с вáшей сестрóй в Москвé.
2 (*face*): **I am ready to ~ your challenge** я готóв приня́ть ваш вы́зов.
3 (*experience, suffer*): **~ one's death** поги́бнуть (*pf.*).
4 (*pay, settle*): **this will barely ~ my expenses** э́то с трудóм покрóет мои́ расхóды.
■ *v.i.* (*past and p.p.* **met**)
1 (*of persons, come together*) встр|ечáться, -éтиться; **our eyes met** нáши глазá встрéтились; (*become acquainted*) знакóмиться, по-; **we met at a dance** мы познакóмились на тáнцах.
2 (*assemble*) соб|ирáться, -рáться; **the council met to discuss the situation** совéт собрáлся, чтóбы обсуди́ть положéние.
3 (*of things, qualities etc.: come into contact*) сходи́ться (*impf.*); **the rivers Oka and Volga ~ at Nizhniy Novgorod** Ни́жний Нóвгород — мéсто слия́ния рек Оки́ и Вóлги; **make (both) ends ~** (*fig.*) св|оди́ть, -ести́ концы́ с концáми.
4 **~ with**: **~ with difficulties** испы́т|ывать, -áть затруднéния; **he met with an accident** с ним произошёл несчáстный слу́чай.

■ *with adv.*: ~ **up** *v.i.* (*coll.*): **we met up** (*or* **I met up with him) in London** мы встре́тились в Ло́ндоне.

meeting /ˈmiːtɪŋ/ *n.*
1 (*encounter*) встре́ча; (*by arrangement*) свида́ние.
2 (*gathering*) собра́ние.
3 (*sports* ~) (спорти́вное) состяза́ние; (*race* ~) ска́чки (*f. pl.*).
■ *cpds.* ~ **place, point** *nn.* ме́сто встре́чи.

meg /meg/ *n.* (*comput.*, *coll.*) мег (*coll. of* мегаба́йт).

megabyte /ˈmegəbaɪt/ *n.* (*comput.*) мегаба́йт.

megalomania /megələˈmeɪnɪə/ *n.* ма́ния вели́чия, мегалома́ния.

megalomaniac /megələˈmeɪnɪæk/ *n.* страда́ющий ма́нией вели́чия.

megaphone /ˈmegəfəʊn/ *n.* мегафо́н.

melancholy /ˈmelənkəlɪ/ *n.* уны́ние.
■ *adj.* (*of person*) уны́лый; (*of things*) гру́стный.

mellow /ˈmeləʊ/ *adj.*
1 (*of voice, sound, colour, light*) со́чный.
2 (*of wine*) вы́держанный.
3 (*of character*) подобре́вший.
■ *v.t.*: **age has ~ed him** го́ды смягчи́ли его́ хара́ктер.
■ *v.i.* (*of person*) смягч|а́ться, -и́ться.

melodic /mɪˈlɒdɪk/ *adj.* мелоди́чный.

melodious /mɪˈləʊdɪəs/ *adj.* мелоди́чный; ~ **voice** певу́чий го́лос.

melodrama /ˈmelədrɑːmə/ *n.* (*lit.*, *fig.*) мелодра́ма.

melodramatic /melədrəˈmætɪk/ *adj.* мелодрамати́ческий.

melody /ˈmelədɪ/ *n.* мело́дия.

melon /ˈmelən/ *n.* ды́ня.

melt /melt/ *v.t.*
1 (*reduce to liquid*) раст|а́пливать, -опи́ть.
2 (*fig., soften*) размягч|а́ть, -и́ть.
■ *v.i.* 1 (*become liquid*) та́ять, рас-.
2 (*fig., soften*) смягч|а́ться, -и́ться; **her heart ~ed at the sight** её се́рдце смягчи́лось при ви́де э́того.
■ *with adv.*: ~ **down** *v.t.* распл|авля́ть, -а́вить.

melting point /ˈmeltɪŋ pɔɪnt/ *n.* температу́ра плавле́ния.

member /ˈmembə(r)/ *n.* член, уча́стни|к (*fem.* -ца) (*о́бщества и т. п.*).

membership /ˈmembəʃɪp/ *n.* (*being a member*) чле́нство; (*collect., members*) чле́ны (*m. pl.*).

membrane /ˈmembreɪn/ *n.* перепо́нка, мембра́на.

memento /məˈmentəʊ/ *n.* (*pl.* **~es** *or* **~s**) сувени́р.

memo /ˈmeməʊ/ *n.* (*pl.* **~s**) = **memorandum**

memoir /ˈmemwɑː(r)/ *n.* (*pl., autobiography*) воспомина́ния (*nt. pl.*), мемуа́р|ы (*pl., g.* -ов).

memorable /ˈmemərəb(ə)l/ *adj.* па́мятный; незабыва́емый.

memorandum /meməˈrændəm/ *n.* запи́ска.

memorial /məˈmɔːrɪəl/ *n.* па́мятник.

memorize /ˈmeməraɪz/ *v.t.* зау́ч|ивать, -и́ть (наизу́сть).

memory /ˈmemərɪ/ *n.*
1 (*faculty; its use*) па́мять; **I have a bad ~ for faces** у меня́ плоха́я па́мять на ли́ца; **in ~ of** в па́мять + *g.*
2 (*recollection*) воспомина́ние.
3 (*comput.*) па́мять.

men /men/ *pl. of* ▸ **man.**
■ *cpd.* **~'s room** *n.* (*US*) мужско́й туале́т.

menace /ˈmenɪs/ *n.* угро́за.
■ *v.t.* угрожа́ть (*impf.*) + *d.*

ménage /meɪˈnɑːʒ/ *n.* хозя́йство; ~ **à trois** брак втроём.

menagerie /mɪˈnædʒərɪ/ *n.* (*lit., fig.*) звери́нец.

mend /mend/ *n.*: **be on the ~** идти́ (*det.*) на попра́вку.
■ *v.t.* 1 (*repair*) чини́ть, по-; заш|ива́ть, -и́ть.
2 (*improve, reform*) испр|авля́ть, -а́вить; ~ **one's ways** испр|авля́ться, -а́виться.
■ *v.i.* (*regain health*) выздора́вливать, вы́здороветь; **his leg is ~ing nicely** его́ нога́ зажива́ет хорошо́.

mendacious /menˈdeɪʃəs/ *adj.* лжи́вый.

menial /ˈmiːnɪəl/ *adj.* лаке́йский; ~ **work** чёрная рабо́та.

meningitis /menɪnˈdʒaɪtɪs/ *n.* менинги́т.

menopause /ˈmenəpɔːz/ *n.* кли́макс.

menstrual /ˈmenstrʊəl/ *adj.* менструа́льный.

menstruate /ˈmenstrʊeɪt/ *v.i.* менструи́ровать (*impf.*).

menstruation /menstrʊˈeɪʃ(ə)n/ *n.* менструа́ция.

menswear /ˈmenzweə(r)/ *n.* мужска́я оде́жда.

mental /ˈment(ə)l/ *adj.*
1 (*of the mind*) у́мственный; **~ly handicapped** у́мственно отста́лый.
2 (*pert. to ~ illness*) психи́ческий; ~ **home, hospital** психиатри́ческая больни́ца.
3 (*carried out in the mind*) мы́сленный.

mentality /menˈtælɪtɪ/ *n.* менталите́т.

mention /ˈmenʃ(ə)n/ *n.* упомина́ние; **there was a ~ of him in the paper** в газе́те упомина́лось его́ и́мя.
■ *v.t.* упом|ина́ть, -яну́ть (*кого/что or о ком/чём*); **I shall ~ it to him** я скажу́ ему́ об э́том; ~ **s.o.'s name** наз|ыва́ть, -ва́ть чьё-н. и́мя; **don't ~ it!** не́ за что!; ничего́; не сто́ит!; **not to ~** (*or* **without ~ing**) не говоря́ уже о + *p.*

mentor /ˈmentɔː(r)/ *n.* наста́вник, ме́нтор.

menu /ˈmenjuː/ *n.* (*also comput.*) меню́ (*nt. indecl.*).

MEP (*abbr. of* ***Member of the European Parliament***) депута́т Европарла́мента.

mercantile /ˈmɜːkəntaɪl/ *adj.* торго́вый; ~ **marine** торго́вый флот.

mercenary /ˈmɜːsɪnərɪ/ *n.* наёмник.
■ *adj.* коры́стный.

merchandise /ˈmɜːtʃəndaɪz/ *n.* това́ры (*m. pl.*).

merchant /ˈmɜːtʃ(ə)nt/ *n.* (*hist.*) купе́ц; (*with qualifying word: dealer*) торго́вец; **wine ~** торго́вец ви́нами; ~ **marine** (*US*), **navy** (*Br.*) торго́вый флот; ~ **bank** (*Br.*) комме́рческий банк.

merciful /ˈmɜːsɪfʊl/ *adj.* милосе́рдный, сострада́тельный; **his death was a ~**

release смерть была́ для него́ бла́гом.
merciless /ˈmɜ:sɪlɪs/ *adj.* беспоща́дный, безжа́лостный.
mercurial /mɜ:ˈkjʊərɪəl/ *adj.*
1 (*of mercury*) рту́тный; **~ poisoning** отравле́ние рту́тью.
2 (*of person, lively*) живо́й; (*volatile*) непостоя́нный, изме́нчивый.
mercury /ˈmɜ:kjʊrɪ/ *n.* ртуть.
mercy /ˈmɜ:sɪ/ *n.*
1 (*compassion, clemency*) милосе́рдие; поща́да; **beg for ~** проси́ть (*impf.*) поща́ды; **show ~ to (or have ~y on)** щади́ть, по-.
2 (*power*): **at the ~ of** во вла́сти + *g.*
mere /mɪə(r)/ *adj.* (**merest**)
1 (*simple; pure*) просто́й; чи́стый; (*nothing but*) не бо́лее чем; всего́ лишь; то́лько; **he is a ~ child** он всего́ лишь ребёнок.
2 (*alone*) оди́н (то́лько); **the ~ sight of him disgusts me** оди́н его́ вид вызыва́ет у меня́ отвраще́ние.
merely /ˈmɪəlɪ/ *adv.* (*simply*) про́сто; (*only*) то́лько.
merge /mɜ:dʒ/ *v.t. & i.* сл|ива́ть(ся), -и́ть(ся).
merger /ˈmɜ:dʒə(r)/ *n.* объедине́ние.
meringue /məˈræŋ/ *n.* безе́ (*nt. indecl.*).
merit /ˈmerɪt/ *n.* (*deserving quality, worth*) досто́инство.
■ *v.t.* (**merited, meriting**) заслу́ж|ивать, -и́ть.
meritocracy /merɪˈtɒkrəsɪ/ *n.* о́бщество, управля́емое людьми́ с наибо́льшими спосо́бностями.
mermaid /ˈmɜ:meɪd/ *n.* руса́лка.
merriment /ˈmerɪmənt/ *n.* весе́лье.
merry /ˈmerɪ/ *adj.* (**merrier, merriest**) (*happy, full of gaiety*) весёлый; **M~ Christmas!** с Рождество́м (Христо́вым)!
■ *cpd.* **~-go-round** *n.* карусе́ль.
mesh /meʃ/ *n.*
1 (*space in net etc.*) яче́йка.
2 (*pl., network*) сеть.
■ *v.i.* (*interlock*) зацеп|ля́ться, -и́ться.
mesmerize /ˈmezməraɪz/ *v.t.* (*lit., fig.*) гипнотизи́ровать, за-.
mess[1] /mes/ *n.*
1 (*disorder*) беспоря́док; **the room was in a complete ~** ко́мната была́ в соверше́нном беспоря́дке; **make a ~ of** (*spoil; bungle*) прова́л|ивать, -и́ть.
2 (*confusion*) пу́таница.
3 (*trouble*) неприя́тность, беда́, го́ре; **get o.s. into a ~** вли́пнуть (*pf.*) (*coll.*).
■ *v.i.*: **~ with** (*interfere with*) вме́шиваться (*impf.*) в + *a.*
■ *with advs.*: **~ about** *v.t.* (*Br., inconvenience*) причиня́ть (*impf.*) неудо́бство + *d.*; *v.i.* (*work half-heartedly or without plan*) ковыря́ться (*impf.*); (*potter, idle about*) кани́телиться (*impf.*); **~ about with** (*fiddle with*) вози́ться (*impf.*) с + *i.*; **~ around** *v.t. & i.* = **~ about**; **~ up** *v.t.* (*make dirty*) па́чкать, пере-; (*bungle*) прова́л|ивать, -и́ть; (*put into confusion*) перепу́т|ывать, -ать.
mess[2] /mes/ *n.* (*eating place*) столо́вая.
message /ˈmesɪdʒ/ *n.* (*formal*) сообще́ние; (*informal*) запи́ска, за́пись.
messenger /ˈmesɪndʒə(r)/ *n.* курье́р, посы́льный.
Messiah /mɪˈsaɪə/ *n.* Месси́я (*m.*).
Messrs /ˈmesəz/ *pl. of* ▸ **Mr**
messy /ˈmesɪ/ *adj.* (**messier, messiest**) (*untidy*) неу́бранный; (*slovenly*) неря́шливый; (*unpleasant*) неприя́тный.
met /met/ *past and p.p. of* ▸ **meet**
metabolic /metəˈbɒlɪk/ *adj.*: **~ disease** наруше́ние обме́на веще́ств.
metabolism /mɪˈtæbəlɪz(ə)m/ *n.* обме́н веще́ств.
metal /ˈmet(ə)l/ *n.* мета́лл.
■ *adj.* металли́ческий.
metallic /məˈtælɪk/ *adj.* металли́ческий.
metallurgist /meˈtælədʒɪst/ *n.* металлу́рг.
metallurgy /mɪˈtælədʒɪ/ *n.* металлурги́я.
metamorphosis /metəˈmɔ:fəsɪs/ *n.* (*pl.* **metamorphoses** /-si:z/) метаморфо́за.
metaphor /ˈmetəfɔ:(r)/ *n.* мета́фора.
metaphorical /metəˈfɒrɪk(ə)l/ *adj.* метафори́ческий; **~ly speaking** о́бразно говоря́.
metaphysical /metəˈfɪzɪk(ə)l/ *adj.* метафизи́ческий.
metaphysics /metəˈfɪzɪks/ *n.* метафи́зика.
mete /mi:t/ *v.t.*: **~ out** определ|я́ть, -и́ть.
meteor /ˈmi:tɪə(r)/ *n.* метео́р.
meteoric /mi:tɪˈɒrɪk/ *adj.* (*fig.*) головокружи́тельный.
meteorite /ˈmi:tɪəraɪt/ *n.* метеори́т.
meteorological /mi:tɪərəˈlɒdʒɪk(ə)l/ *adj.* метеорологи́ческий; **~ office** (*US* **center**) слу́жба пого́ды.
meteorologist /mi:tɪəˈrɒlədʒɪst/ *n.* метеоро́лог.
meteorology /mi:tɪəˈrɒlədʒɪ/ *n.* метеороло́гия.
meter[1] /ˈmi:tə(r)/ *n.* (*apparatus*) счётчик; **gas ~** га́зовый счётчик.
■ *v.t.* изм|еря́ть, -е́рить; зам|еря́ть, -е́рить.
meter[2] /ˈmi:tə(r)/ (*US*) = **metre**
methane /ˈmi:θeɪn/ *n.* мета́н.
method /ˈmeθəd/ *n.* (*way*) ме́тод, спо́соб; (*system*) систе́ма, мето́дика.
methodical /mɪˈθɒdɪk(ə)l/ *adj.* системати́ческий.
Methodist /ˈmeθədɪst/ (*relig.*) *n.* методи́ст (*fem.* -ка); (*attr.*) методи́стский.
methodology /meθəˈdɒlodʒɪ/ *n.* методоло́гия.
meths /meθs/ (*Br. coll.*) = **methylated spirit**
methylated /ˈmeθɪleɪtɪd/ *adj.*: **~ spirit** денатура́т.
meticulous /məˈtɪkjʊləs/ *adj.* тща́тельный.
meticulousness /məˈtɪkjʊləsnɪs/ *n.* тща́тельность, аккура́тность.
metre /ˈmi:tə(r)/ (*US* **meter**) *n.* метр.
metric /ˈmetrɪk/ *adj.* метри́ческий.
metronome /ˈmetrənəʊm/ *n.* метроно́м.
metropolis /mɪˈtrɒpəlɪs/ *n.* столи́ца.
metropolitan /metrəˈpɒlɪt(ə)n/ *adj.* столи́чный.
mettle /ˈmet(ə)l/ *n.* си́ла хара́ктера.

mews /mju:z/ *n.* (*Br.*) коню́шни (*f. pl.*) (переде́ланные в жило́е помеще́ние).
Mexican /'meksɪkən/ *n.* мексика́н|ец (*fem.* -ка).
■ *adj.* мексика́нский.
Mexico /'meksɪkəʊ/ *n.* Ме́ксика; ~ **City** Ме́хико (*m. indecl.*).
mezzanine /'metsəni:n/ *n.* мезони́н, полуэта́ж.
mezzo /'metsəʊ/ *adv.* по́лу-; ~ **forte** дово́льно гро́мко.
■ *cpd.* ~**-soprano** *n.* (*pl.* ~**s**) (*singer*) ме́ццо-сопра́но (*f. indecl.*); (*voice*) ме́ццо-сопра́но (*nt. indecl.*).
miaow /mɪ'aʊ/ *v.i.* мяу́кать (*impf.*).
mice /maɪs/ *pl. of* ▸ **mouse**
microbe /'maɪkrəʊb/ *n.* микро́б.
microbiologist /maɪkrəʊbaɪ'ɒlədʒɪst/ *n.* микробио́лог.
microbiology /maɪkrəʊbaɪ'ɒlədʒɪ/ *n.* микробиоло́гия.
microchip /'maɪkrəʊtʃɪp/ *n.* микросхе́ма, чип.
microclimate /'maɪkrəʊklaɪmət/ *n.* микрокли́мат.
microcosm /'maɪkrəkɒz(ə)m/ *n.* микроко́см.
microfiche /'maɪkrəʊfi:ʃ/ *n.* микрофи́ша (*несколько фотографий на микроплёнке*).
microfilm /'maɪkrəʊfɪlm/ *n.* микрофи́льм, микроплёнка.
microlight /'maɪkrəʊlaɪt/ *n.* (*Br.*) сверхлёгкий персона́льный самолёт.
micro-organism /maɪkrəʊ'ɔ:gənɪz(ə)m/ *n.* микрооргани́зм.
microphone /'maɪkrəfəʊn/ *n.* микрофо́н.
microprocessor /maɪkrəʊ'prəʊsesə(r)/ *n.* микропроце́ссор.
microscope /'maɪkrəskəʊp/ *n.* микроско́п.
microscopic /maɪkrə'skɒpɪk/ *adj.* микроскопи́ческий.
microwave /'maɪkrəʊweɪv/ *n.*: ~ **oven** микроволно́вая печь.
mid /mɪd/ *adj.* & *pref.*: **in ~ air** (высоко́) в во́здухе; **from ~ June to ~ July** с середи́ны ию́ня до середи́ны ию́ля.
■ *cpds.* ~**day** *n.* по́лдень (*m.*); ~**night** *n.* по́лночь; ~**summer** *n.* середи́на ле́та; *adj.* **M~summer Day** Ива́нов день (*24 июня*); ~**way** *adv.* на полпути́; **the M~ west** *n.* Сре́дний За́пад США; ~**winter** *n.* середи́на зимы́.
middle /'mɪd(ə)l/ *n.*
1 середи́на; **in the ~ of** среди́ + *g.*; (*of time*): **in the ~ of the night** посреди́ но́чи; **I was in the ~ of getting ready** в тот моме́нт я как раз собира́лся.
2 (*waist*) та́лия.
■ *adj.* сре́дний; **the M~ Ages** Сре́дние века́; **the ~ classes** сре́дние сло́и о́бщества; сре́дний класс; **M~ East** Бли́жний Восто́к; ~ **school** (*Br.*) сре́дняя шко́ла.
■ *cpds.* ~**-aged** *adj.* сре́дних лет; ~**-class** *adj.* относя́щийся к сре́днему кла́ссу; ~**man** *n.* посре́дник; ~**weight** *n.* & *adj.* (боксёр) сре́днего ве́са.
middling /'mɪdlɪŋ/ *adj.* сре́дний, второсо́ртный; **fair to ~** так себе́.
midge /mɪdʒ/ *n.* кома́р, мо́шка.
midget /'mɪdʒɪt/ *n.* ка́рлик.
midriff /'mɪdrɪf/ *n.* ве́рхняя часть живота́.
midst /mɪdst/ *n.* середи́на; **in the ~ of** среди́, в разга́р + *g.*, ме́жду + *i.*; **a stranger in our ~** чужо́й среди́ нас.
midwife /'mɪdwaɪf/ *n.* акуше́рка.
miff /mɪf/ *v.t.* (*coll.*): **he was ~ed by my remark** моё замеча́ние оби́дело его́.
might[1] /maɪt/ *n.*
1 (*power*) мощь.
2 (*strength*) си́ла; **with (all his) ~ and main** изо всех сил, что бы́ло мо́чи.
might[2] /maɪt/ *v. aux. see* ▸ **may**
mighty /'maɪtɪ/ *adj.* (**mightier, mightiest**) мо́щный.
migraine /'mi:greɪn/ *n.* мигре́нь.
migrant /'maɪgrənt/ *n.* переселе́нец.
■ *adj.* кочу́ющий.
migrate /maɪ'greɪt/ *v.i.* пересел|я́ться, -и́ться; (*of birds*) соверш|а́ть, -и́ть перелёт.
migration /maɪ'greɪʃ(ə)n/ *n.* мигра́ция; перелёт.
migratory /maɪ'greɪtərɪ/ *adj.* перелётный.
mike /maɪk/ (*coll.*) = **microphone**
mild /maɪld/ *adj.* мя́гкий; **a ~ day** тёплый день.
mildew /'mɪldju:/ *n.* пле́сень.
mile /maɪl/ *n.* ми́ля; (*fig.*): **I was ~s away** я замечта́лся; **it sticks out a ~** э́то броса́ется в глаза́.
■ *cpd.* ~**stone** *n.* ка́мень с указа́нием расстоя́ния; (*fig.*) ве́ха.
mileage /'maɪlɪdʒ/ *n.*
1 (*distance in miles*) расстоя́ние в ми́лях; (*of car*) пробе́г автомоби́ля в ми́лях.
2 (*travel expenses*) проездны́е (*pl.*).
milieu /mɪ'ljə:/ *n.* (*pl.* ~**x** *or* ~**s**) окруже́ние, среда́.
militancy /'mɪlɪt(ə)nsɪ/ *n.* вои́нственность.
militant /'mɪlɪt(ə)nt/ *n.* бое́ц, боре́ц.
■ *adj.* вои́нствующий.
militarism /'mɪlɪtərɪz(ə)m/ *n.* милитари́зм.
militaristic /mɪlɪtə'rɪstɪk/ *adj.* милитари́стский, милитаристи́ческий.
military /'mɪlɪtərɪ/ *n.*: **the ~** военнослу́жащие (*m. pl.*), войска́ (*nt. pl.*).
■ *adj.* вое́нный; ~ **service** вое́нная слу́жба; (*as liability*) во́инская пови́нность.
militate /'mɪlɪteɪt/ *v.i.*: ~ **against** препя́тствовать (*impf.*) + *d.*; говори́ть (*impf.*) про́тив + *g.*; **his age ~s against him** ему́ меша́ет во́зраст.
militia /mɪ'lɪʃə/ *n.* мили́ция.
milk /mɪlk/ *n.* молоко́.
■ *v.t.* дои́ть, по-; (*fig.*): **they ~ed him of all his cash** они́ вы́качали из него́ все де́ньги.
■ *cpds.* ~**man** *n.* продаве́ц молока́, моло́чник; ~**shake** *n.* моло́чный кокте́йль.
milky /'mɪlkɪ/ *adj.* (**milkier, milkiest**) моло́чный; **the M~ Way** Мле́чный Путь.
mill /mɪl/ *n.* (*for grinding corn*) ме́льница; (*factory*) фа́брика.
■ *v.t.* моло́ть, пере-.
■ *v.i.* (*coll.*): **a crowd was ~ing around the entrance** лю́ди толпи́лись у вхо́да.

millenni|um /mɪ'lenɪəm/ *n.* (*pl.* **~ums** *or* **~a**) тысячеле́тие.

miller /'mɪlə(r)/ *n.* ме́льник.

milligram(me) /'mɪlɪgræm/ *n.* миллигра́м.

millimetre /'mɪlɪmi:tə(r)/ (*US* **-meter**) *n.* миллиме́тр.

milliner /'mɪlɪnə(r)/ *n.* (*fem.*) ма́стер по изготовле́нию же́нских шляп.

million /'mɪljən/ *n.* & *adj.* (*pl.* **~s** *or* (*with numeral or qualifying word*) **~**) миллио́н (+ *g.*).

millionaire /mɪljə'neə(r)/ *n.* миллионе́р.

millionth /'mɪljənθ/ *n.* миллио́нная часть. ■ *adj.* миллио́нный.

milometer /maɪ'lɒmɪtə(r)/ *n.* (*Br.*) счётчик пробе́га.

mime /maɪm/ *n.* (*performance*; *technique*) пантоми́ма; (*artist*) арти́ст пантоми́мы. ■ *v.t.* (*act by miming*) изобра|жа́ть, -зи́ть пантоми́мой. ■ *v.i.* (*pretend to sing*) петь, с-/про- под фоногра́мму.

mimic /'mɪmɪk/ *n.* имита́тор. ■ *v.t.* (**mimicked, mimicking**) передра́зн|ивать, -и́ть.

mimicry /'mɪmɪkrɪ/ *n.* (*imitation*) имити́рование; подража́ние (+ *d.*).

minaret /mɪnə'ret/ *n.* минаре́т.

minc|e /mɪns/ *n.* (*Br.*) фарш. ■ *v.t.* руби́ть (*impf.*); **~ed beef** говя́жий фарш; **~ing machine** мясору́бка.

mind /maɪnd/ *n.*
1 (*intellect*) ум; **you must be out of your ~** вы с ума́ сошли́.
2 (*remembrance*): **bear in ~** по́мнить (*impf.*); **the tune went clean out of my ~** я на́чисто забы́л э́ту мело́дию.
3 (*opinion*) мне́ние; **he spoke his ~ on the subject** он открове́нно вы́сказался на э́ту те́му; **he doesn't know his own ~** он сам не зна́ет, чего́ он хо́чет; **try to keep an open ~!** постара́йтесь быть объекти́вн|ым (*fem.* -ой).
4 (*intention*) наме́рение; **he changed his ~** он переду́мал; **I have made up my ~ to stay** я реши́л оста́ться.
5 (*thought*) мы́сли (*f. pl.*); **I had something on my ~** меня́ что́-то трево́жило; **I set his ~ at rest** я его́ успоко́ил; **it took her ~ off her troubles** э́то отвлекло́ её от (её) забо́т/невзго́д; **I cannot read his ~** я не могу́ угада́ть/проче́сть его́ мы́сли; **I can see him in my ~'s eye** он стои́т у меня́ пе́ред глаза́ми.
6 (*way of thinking*) настрое́ние; **to my ~** на мой взгляд; мне ка́жется (*or* я счита́ю), что.
7 (*attention*): **keep your ~ on what you are doing** не отвлека́йтесь.
■ *v.t.* 1 (*take care, charge of*) присм|а́тривать, -отре́ть за + *i.*; **~ your own business!** не вме́шивайтесь не в своё де́ло!
2 (*worry about*) забо́титься (*impf.*) о + *p.*; беспоко́иться о + *p.*; **never ~ the expense** не ду́майте о расхо́дах; **~ your head!** осторо́жнее, не ушиби́те го́лову.
3 (*object to*) возра|жа́ть, -зи́ть на + *a.*; име́ть (*impf.*) что-н. про́тив + *g.*; **I don't ~ the cold** я не бою́сь хо́лода; **would you ~ opening the door?** откро́йте, пожа́луйста, дверь; **I wouldn't ~ going for a walk** я не прочь прогуля́ться.
■ *v.i.* 1 (*worry*) беспоко́иться (*impf.*); трево́житься (*impf.*); **we're rather late, but never ~** мы немно́го опа́здываем, ну, ничего́!
2 (*object*) возра|жа́ть, -зи́ть; **do you ~ if I smoke?** вы не про́тив, е́сли я закурю́?
■ *cpd.* **~-boggling** *adj.* порази́тельный.

minder /'maɪndə(r)/ *n.* (*Br., child minder*) ня́ня; (*coll., bodyguard*) телохрани́тель (*m.*).

mindful /'maɪndfʊl/ *adj.* забо́тливый; **we must be ~ of the children** мы должны́ ду́мать о де́тях; **I was ~ of his advice** я по́мнил его́ сове́т; **he was ~ of his duty** он сознава́л свой долг.

mindless /'maɪndlɪs/ *adj.*
1 (*thoughtless*) безду́мный; (*stupid*) глу́пый.
2 (*not requiring intelligence*): **~ drudgery** механи́ческий труд.

mine[1] /maɪn/ *n.*
1 (*excavation*) ша́хта; рудни́к.
2 (*explosive device*) ми́на.
■ *v.t.* 1 (*excavate*): **~ coal/ore** добыва́ть (*impf.*) у́голь/руду́.
2 (*mil.*) мини́ровать, за-.
■ *v.i.* разраб|а́тывать, -о́тать рудни́к.
■ *cpd.* **~field** *n.* ми́нное по́ле.

mine[2] /maɪn/ *pron.*: **that book is ~** э́то моя́ кни́га; **a friend of ~** (оди́н) мой друг/знако́мый.

miner /'maɪnə(r)/ *n.* (*coal* **~**) шахтёр.

mineral /'mɪnər(ə)l/ *n.* минера́л, руда́. ■ *adj.* минера́льный; **~ water** минера́льная вода́.

mineralogical /mɪnərə'lɒdʒɪk(ə)l/ *adj.* минералоги́ческий.

mineralogist /mɪnə'rælədʒɪst/ *n.* минерало́г.

mineralogy /mɪnə'rælədʒɪ/ *n.* минерало́гия.

minestrone /mɪnɪ'strəʊnɪ/ *n.* италья́нский овощно́й суп с ме́лкими макаро́нными изде́лиями.

mingle /'mɪŋg(ə)l/ *v.i.* сме́шиваться (*impf.*); **~ with** (*frequent*) обща́ться (*impf.*) с + *i.*

mini /'mɪnɪ/ *n.* (*pl.* **minis**) (*garment*) ми́ни (*юбка и т. д.*).

miniature /'mɪnɪtʃə(r)/ *n.* миниатю́ра. ■ *adj.* миниатю́рный.

minibus /'mɪnɪbʌs/ *n.* микроавто́бус.

minicab /'mɪnɪkæb/ *n.* (*Br.*) такси́ (*nt. indecl.*).

minidisc /'mɪnɪdɪsk/ *n.* ми́ни-ди́ск.

minim /'mɪnɪm/ *n.* (*Br., mus.*) полови́нная но́та.

minimal /'mɪnɪm(ə)l/ *adj.* минима́льный.

minimalism /'mɪnɪməlɪz(ə)m/ *n.* минимали́зм.

minimalist /'mɪnɪməlɪst/ *n.* минимали́ст. ■ *adj.* минимали́стский.

minimize /'mɪnɪmaɪz/ *v.t.* (*reduce to minimum*) дов|оди́ть, -ести́ до ми́нимума; (*make light of*) преум|еньша́ть, -е́ньшить.

minimum /'mɪnɪməm/ *n.* ми́нимум; (*attr.*) минима́льный.

mining /'maɪnɪŋ/ *n.* го́рное де́ло, го́рная промы́шленность.

minion /'mɪnjən/ *n.* приспе́шник.

miniskirt /'mɪnɪskə:t/ *n.* ми́ни-ю́бка.

minister /ˈmɪnɪstə(r)/ *n.*
1 (*head of government dept.*) министр.
2 (*clergyman*) священник, пастор.
■ *v.i.*: ~ **to** служить (*impf.*) + *d.*; прислуживать (*impf.*) + *d.*

ministerial /mɪnɪˈstɪərɪəl/ *adj.* министерский.

ministry /ˈmɪnɪstrɪ/ *n.* министерство.

mink /mɪŋk/ *n.* норка.

minnow /ˈmɪnəʊ/ *n.* пескарь (*m.*).

minor /ˈmaɪnə(r)/ *n.* (*person under age*) несовершеннолетний.
■ *adj.* 1 (*of lesser importance*) второстепенный; малозначительный, мелкий, небольшой.
2 (*mus.*) минорный.

minority /maɪˈnɒrɪtɪ/ *n.* меньшинство, меньшая часть; (*attr.*): ~ **group** меньшинство.

Minsk *n.* Минск.

minstrel /ˈmɪnstr(ə)l/ *n.* менестрель (*m.*).

mint[1] /mɪnt/ *n.* (*bot.*) мята; (*a sweet*) мятная конфета.

mint[2] /mɪnt/ *n.* (*fin.*) монетный двор.
■ *v.t.* чеканить (*impf.*).

minuet /mɪnjʊˈet/ *n.* менуэт.

minus /ˈmaɪnəs/ *n.* минус.
■ *adj.* отрицательный; ~ **sign** (знак) минус.
■ *prep.* минус; без + *g.*; ~ **1** минус один; **he came back ~ an arm** он вернулся без руки.

minuscule /ˈmɪnəskjuːl/ *adj.* крохотный, очень маленький.

minute[1] /ˈmɪnɪt/ *n.*
1 (*fraction of hour or degree*) минута; **he left it to the last ~** он отложил всё до последней минуты.
2 (*moment*) мгновение, момент, миг; **just a ~** (одну) минутку!; **I'll tell him the ~ he arrives** как только он придёт, я ему скажу.
3 (*usu. pl., record*) протокол.

minute[2] /maɪˈnjuːt/ *adj.* (**minutest,** *no comp.*) (*tiny*) мелкий, крохотный.

minutiae /maɪˈnjuːʃɪaɪ/ *n.* мелочи (*f. pl.*); детали (*f. pl.*).

minx /mɪŋks/ *n.* (*joc.*) озорница; (*coquette*) кокетка.

miracle /ˈmɪrək(ə)l/ *n.* чудо.

miraculous /mɪˈrækjʊləs/ *adj.* чудесный.

mirage /ˈmɪrɑːʒ/ *n.* (*lit., fig.*) мираж.

mire /ˈmaɪə(r)/ *n.* трясина; болото; **his name was dragged through the ~** его смешали с грязью.

mirror /ˈmɪrə(r)/ *n.* зеркало.
■ *v.t.* отра|жать, -зить.

mirth /mɜːθ/ *n.* (*gladness*) веселье; (*laughter*) смех.

misadventure /mɪsədˈventʃə(r)/ *n.* несчастье, несчастный случай; **death by ~** смерть от несчастного случая.

misapprehension /mɪsæprɪˈhenʃ(ə)n/ *n.* превратное понимание; **I was under a ~** я заблуждался.

misappropriate /mɪsəˈprəʊprɪeɪt/ *v.t.* (незаконно) присв|аивать, -оить.

misappropriation /mɪsəprəʊprɪˈeɪʃ(ə)n/ *n.* незаконное присвоение.

misbehave /mɪsbɪˈheɪv/ *v.i.* дурно себя вести (*det.*).

miscalculate /mɪsˈkælkjʊleɪt/ *v.t.* плохо рассчит|ывать, -ать.
■ *v.i.* просчит|ываться, -аться.

miscalculation /mɪskælkjʊˈleɪʃ(ə)n/ *n.* просчёт.

miscarriage /ˈmɪskærɪdʒ, mɪsˈkærɪdʒ/ *n.*
1 (*biol.*) выкидыш; **she had a ~** у неё произошёл выкидыш.
2 : ~ **of justice** ошибка правосудия.

miscarr|y /mɪsˈkærɪ/ *v.i.*
1 (*of a woman*) иметь (*impf.*) выкидыш.
2 (*fail*) терпеть (*impf.*) неудачу; **his plans ~ied** его планы провалились.

miscellaneous /mɪsəˈleɪnɪəs/ *adj.* смешанный; разнообразный.

mischief /ˈmɪstʃɪf/ *n.* озорство; проказы (*f. pl.*); **he is always getting into ~** он всегда проказничает/шалит.

mischievous /ˈmɪstʃɪvəs/ *adj.* озорной, шаловливый.

misconception /mɪskənˈsepʃ(ə)n/ *n.* неправильное представление/понимание.

misconduct /mɪsˈkɒndʌkt/ *n.* дурное поведение; **professional ~** нарушение профессиональной этики; должностное преступление.

misconstrue /mɪskənˈstruː/ *v.t.* неправильно истолков|ывать, -ать.

misdeed /mɪsˈdiːd/ *n.* преступление.

misdemeanour /mɪsdɪˈmiːnə(r)/ (*US* **misdemeanor**) *n.* проступок.

misdiagnose /mɪsdaɪəgˈnəʊz/ *v.t.* (*med.*) ставить, по- неверный диагноз; **her depression was ~d as stress** у неё была депрессия, а ей ошибочно поставили диагноз «стресс».

miser /ˈmaɪzə(r)/ *n.* скряга (*c.g.*), скуп|ой (*fem.* -ая).

miserable /ˈmɪzərəb(ə)l/ *adj.*
1 (*unhappy*) жалкий, несчастный.
2 (*causing wretchedness*) плохой, скверный; **what ~ weather!** какая скверная погода!
3 (*mean*): **a ~ sum (of money)** ничтожная/мизерная сумма.

miserly /ˈmaɪzəlɪ/ *adj.* скупой.

misery /ˈmɪzərɪ/ *n.*
1 (*suffering*) страдание; мучение.
2 (*extreme poverty*) нищета, бедность.
3 (*Br. coll., person who complains*) зануда (*c.g.*), нытик.

misfire /mɪsˈfaɪə(r)/ *v.i.* да|вать, -ть осечку; (*tech., of ignition*) выпадать, выпасть; (*fig.*) не состояться (*impf.*); **his plans ~d** его план сорвался.

misfit /ˈmɪsfɪt/ *n.* неприспособленный человек.

misfortune /mɪsˈfɔːtʃuːn, -tjuːn/ *n.* (*bad luck*) беда, несчастье; **I had the ~ to lose my purse** я имел несчастье потерять кошелёк; (*stroke of bad luck*) несчастье, неудача.

misgiving /mɪsˈgɪvɪŋ/ *n.* опасение; дурное предчувствие.

misguided /mɪsˈgaɪdɪd/ *adj.*: **I was ~ enough to trust him** я имел неосторожность довериться ему; ~ **enthusiasm** энтузиазм, достойный лучшего

применéния.
mishandle /mɪs'hænd(ə)l/ *v.t.* (*ill-treat*) плóхо/дýрно обращáться (*impf.*) с + *i.*; (*manage inefficiently*) плóхо вести́ (*det.*) (дéло).
mishap /'mɪshæp/ *n.* неудáча.
mishear /mɪs'hɪə(r)/ *v.t.* нетóчно расслы́шать (*pf.*).
misinform /mɪsɪn'fɔ:m/ *v.t.* непрáвильно информи́ровать (*impf.*, *pf.*).
misinformation /mɪsɪnfə'meɪʃ(ə)n/ *n.* невéрная информáция; дезинформáция.
misinterpret /mɪsɪn'tə:prɪt/ *v.t.* непрáвильно пон|имáть, -я́ть.
misinterpretation /mɪsɪntə:prɪ'teɪʃ(ə)n/ *n.* непрáвильное понимáние/толковáние.
misjudge /mɪs'dʒʌdʒ/ *v.t.* невéрно оцéн|ивать, -и́ть.
mislay /mɪs'leɪ/ *v.t.* затеря́ть (*pf.*).
mislead /mɪs'li:d/ *v.t.* вв|оди́ть, -ести́ в заблуждéние.
mismanage /mɪs'mænɪdʒ/ *v.t.* плóхо управля́ть (*impf.*) + *i.*
mismanagement /mɪs'mænɪdʒmənt/ *n.* плохóе управлéние/руковóдство; (*inefficiency*) нераспоряди́тельность.
misnomer /mɪs'nəʊmə(r)/ *n.* непрáвильное назвáние/и́мя.
misogynist /mɪ'sɒdʒɪnɪst/ *n.* женоненави́стник.
misogyny /mɪ'sɒdʒɪnɪ/ *n.* женоненави́стничество.
misplaced /mɪs'pleɪst/ *adj.* (*inappropriate*) неумéстный; (*unfounded*) безосновáтельный.
misprint /'mɪsprɪnt/ *n.* опечáтка.
mispronounce /mɪsprə'naʊns/ *v.t.* непрáвильно произн|оси́ть, -ести́.
misquote /mɪs'kwəʊt/ *v.t.* нетóчно цити́ровать, про-; **I have been ~d** мои́ словá искази́ли.
misread /mɪs'ri:d/ *v.t.* (*read incorrectly*) читáть, про- непрáвильно; (*misinterpret*) непрáвильно истолкóв|ывать, -áть.
misrepresent /mɪsreprɪ'zent/ *v.t.* искa|жáть, -зи́ть.
misrepresentation /mɪsreprɪzen'teɪʃ(ə)n/ *n.* искажéние (фáктов).
misrule /mɪs'ru:l/ *n.* (*bad government*) плохóе правлéние; (*lawlessness*) беспоря́док, анáрхия.
miss¹ /mɪs/ *n.* (*failure to hit etc.*) прóмах; **I gave the meeting a ~** (*Br.*) я не пошёл на собрáние.
■ *v.t.* 1 (*fail to hit or catch*): **he ~ed the ball** он пропусти́л мяч; **he ~ed the bus** он опоздáл на автóбус.
2 (*fig.*, *fail to grasp*) не пон|имáть, -я́ть; не улови́ть (*pf.*); **you have ~ed the point** вы не пóняли сýти.
3 (*fail to hear or see*) не услы́шать (*pf.*); пропус|кáть, -ти́ть; **you must not ~ this film** не пропусти́те э́тот фильм.
4 (*fail to meet*): **you've just ~ed him!** вы с ним чуть-чýть разминýлись!
5 (*escape by chance*) избе|гáть, -жáть; **we just ~ed having an accident** мы чуть не попáли в катастрóфу.
6 (*regret absence of*) скучáть (*impf.*) соскýчиться (*pf.*) по + *d.*; **she ~es her husband** онá скучáет по мýжу; **he ~ed Moscow** он соскýчился по Москвé.
■ *v.i.* (*fail to hit target*) промáх|иваться, -нýться; не поп|адáть, -áсть в цель.
■ *with adv.*: **~ out** *v.t.* упус|кáть, -ти́ть; пропус|кáть, -ти́ть; **you have ~ed out the most important thing** вы пропусти́ли/упусти́ли сáмое вáжное; *v.i.* (*coll.*): **he ~ed out on all the fun** он пропусти́л сáмое весёлье; **I felt I was ~ing out** я чýвствовал, что мнóгое упускáю.
miss² /mɪs/ *n.* мисс.
mis-sell /mɪs'sel/ *v.t.* прод|авáть, -áть обмáнным/нечéстным путём.
misshapen /mɪs'ʃeɪpən/ *adj.* урóдливый.
missile /'mɪsaɪl/ *n.*
1 (*object thrown*) метáтельный предмéт.
2 (*weapon thrown or fired*) снаря́д.
3 (*rocket weapon*) ракéта.
missing /'mɪsɪŋ/ *adj.* недостаю́щий; потеря́вшийся; **there is a page ~** не хватáет страни́цы; **he went ~** он пропáл (бéз вести).
mission /'mɪʃ(ə)n/ *n.*
1 (*mil.*) задáние.
2 (*pol.*, *relig.*) ми́ссия.
missionary /'mɪʃənərɪ/ *n.* миссионéр (*fem.* -ка).
missive /'mɪsɪv/ *n.* послáние.
misspell /mɪs'spel/ *v.t.* & *i.* непрáвильно написáть (*pf.*); сдéлать (*pf.*) орфографи́ческую оши́бку.
mist /mɪst/ *n.* (*lit.*, *fig.*) тумáн, ды́мка, мгла.
■ *v.t.* & *i.* затумáни|вать(ся), -ть(ся); **my glasses have ~ed over** у меня́ запотéли очки́.
mistake /mɪ'steɪk/ *n.* оши́бка; заблуждéние; **by ~** по оши́бке; **make no ~ (about it)** бýдьте увéрены.
■ *v.t.* (*misunderstand*) ошиб|áться, -и́ться в + *p.*; (*misrecognize*): **he mistook me for my brother** он при́нял меня́ за моегó брáта.
mistaken /mɪ'steɪkən/ *adj.*
1 (*in error*): **if I am not ~** éсли я не ошибáюсь.
2 (*ill-judged*; *erroneous*) неосмотри́тельный.
mistletoe /'mɪs(ə)ltəʊ/ *n.* омéла.
mistress /'mɪstrɪs/ *n.*
1 (*woman in charge*) хозя́йка.
2 (*lover*) любóвница.
mistrial /mɪs'traɪəl/ *n.* непрáвильное судéбное разбирáтельство.
mistrust /mɪs'trʌst/ *n.* недовéрие.
■ *v.t.* не доверя́ть (*impf.*) + *d.*
misty /'mɪstɪ/ *adj.* (**mistier, mistiest**) тумáнный.
misunder|stand /mɪsʌndə'stænd/ *v.t.* непрáвильно пон|имáть, -я́ть; **she felt ~stood** онá чýвствовала, что её не понимáют.
misunderstanding /mɪsʌndə'stændɪŋ/ *n.* недоразумéние.
misuse¹ /mɪs'ju:s/ *n.* непрáвильное употреблéние; злоупотреблéние (*чем*).
misuse² /mɪs'ju:z/ *v.t.* (*use improperly*) непрáвильно употреб|ля́ть, -и́ть; (*treat badly*) дýрно обращáться (*impf.*) с + *i.*
miter /'maɪtə(r)/ (*US*) = **mitre**
mitigat|e /'mɪtɪgeɪt/ *v.t.* смягч|áть, -и́ть;

~ing circumstances смягча́ющие обстоя́тельства.
mitigation /mɪtɪ'geɪʃ(ə)n/ *n.* смягче́ние, ослабле́ние; **a plea in ~** хода́тайство о смягче́нии пригово́ра.
mitre /'maɪtə(r)/ (*US* **miter**) *n.* (*bishop's headgear*) ми́тра.
mitten /'mɪt(ə)n/ *n.* рукави́ца.
mix /mɪks/ *n.* смесь.
■ *v.t.* [1] (*mingle*) сме́ш|ивать, -а́ть; (*combine*) сочета́ть (*impf.*); **I like to ~ business with pleasure** я люблю́ сочета́ть прия́тное с поле́зным.
[2] (*prepare by ~ing*) сме́ш|ивать, -а́ть; переме́ш|ивать, -а́ть.
■ *v.i.* (*of persons*) обща́ться (*impf., pf.*); **she won't ~ with her neighbours** она́ не хо́чет обща́ться с сосе́дями.
■ *with advs.*: **~ up** *v.t.* (**~** *thoroughly*) (хорошо́) переме́ш|ивать, -а́ть; (*confuse*) перепу́т|ывать, -ать; **I ~ed him up with his father** я перепу́тал его́ с его́ отцо́м; **a ~ed-up child** (*coll.*) тру́дный ребёнок; (*involve*) впу́т|ывать, -ать.
■ *cpd.* **~-up** *n.* недоразуме́ние.
mixed /mɪkst/ *adj.* сме́шанный, переме́шанный; **(place for) ~ bathing** о́бщий пляж; **I have ~ feelings about it** у меня́ на э́тот счёт противоречи́вые чу́вства.
mixer /'mɪksə(r)/ *n.* (*for cement*) меша́лка; (*for food*) ми́ксер.
mixture /'mɪkstʃə(r)/ *n.* смесь.
ml *n. abbr. of*
[1] ***millilitre(s)*** /'mɪlɪli:tə(r)(z)/ мл (миллили́тр).
[2] ***mile(s)*** /maɪl(z)/ ми́ля.
mm /'mɪlɪmi:tə(r)(z)/ *n.* (*abbr. of* ***millimetre(s)***) мм (миллиме́тр).
MMR (*abbr. of* ***measles, mumps, and rubella***) (*med.*) MMR, приви́вка «корь-сви́нка-красну́ха».
MMS (*abbr. of* ***Multimedia Message/ Messaging Service***): **~ message** MMS-сообще́ние.
moan /məʊn/ *n.* стон; (*coll., complaint*) стон, нытьё.
■ *v.t. & i.* стона́ть (*impf.*); (*coll., complain*) ныть (*impf.*).
moat /məʊt/ *n.* ров с водо́й.
mob /mɒb/ *n.* толпа́.
■ *v.t.* (**mobbed, mobbing**) нап|ада́ть, -а́сть на + *a.*
mobile /'məʊbaɪl/ *n.* (*Br.*) моби́льный/ со́товый телефо́н.
■ *adj.* [1] (*easily moved*) передвижно́й, переносно́й; **~ phone** (*Br.*) моби́льный/ со́товый телефо́н; (*troops*) подви́жный.
[2] (*person*) моби́льный.
mobility /mə'bɪlɪtɪ/ *n.* подви́жность, моби́льность.
mobilization /məʊbɪlaɪ'zeɪʃ(ə)n/ *n.* мобилиза́ция.
mobilize /'məʊbɪlaɪz/ *v.t.* мобилизова́ть (*impf., pf.*).
■ *v.i.* мобилизова́ться (*impf., pf.*).
moccasin /'mɒkəsɪn/ *n.* мокаси́н.
mock /mɒk/ *adj.* подде́льный, фальши́вый; **~ examination** (*Br.*) предэкзаменацио́нная прове́рка.
■ *v.t.* насмеха́ться (*impf.*) над + *i.*
mockery /'mɒkərɪ/ *n.* (*ridicule*) издева́тельство; (*parody*) паро́дия.
MOD (*abbr. of* ***Ministry of Defence***) Министе́рство оборо́ны.
mod /mɒd/ *n. adj.*: **~ cons** (*Br.*) совреме́нные удо́бства; **with all ~ cons** (*Br.*) (*in advertisement*) со всеми удо́бствами.
mode /məʊd/ *n.* ме́тод.
model /'mɒd(ə)l/ *n.*
[1] (*representation*) моде́ль, схе́ма.
[2] (*pattern*) образе́ц, станда́рт; **he is a ~ of gallantry** он образе́ц гала́нтности; **a ~ husband** идеа́льный муж.
[3] (*person posing for artist*) нату́рщи|к (*fem.* -ца).
[4] (*woman displaying clothes etc.*) манеке́нщица, моде́ль.
[5] (*design*) моде́ль, тип.
■ *v.t.* (**modelled, modelling;** *US* **modeled, modeling**) де́лать, с- моде́ль + *g.*; **she ~led the dress** (*wore it as a ~*) она́ демонстри́ровала пла́тье; (*fig.*): **he ~s himself upon his father** он сле́дует приме́ру своего́ отца́.
modem /'məʊdem/ *n.* моде́м.
moderate[1] /'mɒdərət/*adj.* уме́ренный; сре́дний; **~ drinker** уме́ренно пью́щий челове́к.
moderate[2] /'mɒdəreɪt/ *v.t.* ум|еря́ть, -е́рить; смягч|а́ть, -и́ть.
■ *v.i.* смягч|а́ться, -и́ться.
moderation /mɒdə'reɪʃ(ə)n/ *n.* уме́ренность; **in ~** уме́ренно.
modern /'mɒd(ə)n/ *adj.* совреме́нный; **~ languages** но́вые языки́.
modernism /'mɒdənɪz(ə)m/ *n.* модерни́зм.
modernization /mɒdənaɪ'zeɪʃ(ə)n/ *n.* модерниза́ция.
modernize /'mɒdənaɪz/ *v.t.* модернизи́ровать (*impf., pf.*).
modest /'mɒdɪst/ *adj.* скро́мный.
modesty /'mɒdɪstɪ/ *n.* скро́мность.
modicum /'mɒdɪkəm/ *n.* чу́точка, толи́ка.
modification /mɒdɪfɪ'keɪʃ(ə)n/ *n.* модифика́ция.
modify /'mɒdɪfaɪ/ *v.t.* модифици́ровать (*impf.*).
modish /'məʊdɪʃ/ *adj.* мо́дный.
modulate /'mɒdjʊleɪt/ *v.t.* (*vary pitch of; also radio*) модули́ровать (*impf.*).
module /'mɒdju:l/ *n.* (*independent unit*) блок, се́кция; (*unit of study*) курс.
mogul /'məʊg(ə)l/ *n.* (*fig., tycoon*) магна́т.
mohair /'məʊheə(r)/ *n.* мохе́р; (*attr.*) мохе́ровый.
moist /mɔɪst/ *adj.* вла́жный, сыро́й.
moisten /'mɔɪs(ə)n/ *v.t.* увлажн|я́ть, -и́ть; см|а́чивать, -очи́ть.
moisture /'mɔɪstʃə(r)/ *n.* вла́жность, вла́га.
moisturize /'mɔɪstʃəraɪz/ *v.t.* увлажн|я́ть, -и́ть.
moisturizer /'mɔɪstʃəraɪzə(r)/ *n.* увлажня́ющий крем.
mold /məʊld/, **-y** /'məʊldɪ/ (*US*) = **mould**[1,2], **mouldy**
Moldova /mɒl'dəʊvə/ *n.* Молдо́ва.
Moldovan /mɒl'dəʊv(ə)n/ *n.* молдава́н|ин (*f.* -ка).

■ *adj.* молда́вский.
mole[1] /məʊl/ *n.* (*on skin*) ро́динка.
mole[2] /məʊl/ *n.* (*zool.*) крот; (*secret agent*) аге́нт, внедри́вшийся в иностра́нную разве́дку.
molecular /mə'lekjʊlə(r)/ *adj.* молекуля́рный.
molecule /'mɒlɪkju:l/ *n.* моле́кула.
molest /mə'lest/ *v.t.* прист|ава́ть, -а́ть к + *d.*
mollify /'mɒlɪfaɪ/ *v.t.* смягч|а́ть, -и́ть; успок|а́ивать, -о́ить.
mollusc /'mɒləsk/ *n.* моллю́ск.
mollycoddle /'mɒlɪkɒd(ə)l/ *v.t.* не́жить (*impf.*).
Molotov cocktail /'mɒlətɒf 'kɒkteɪl/ *n.* буты́лка с зажига́тельной сме́сью.
molt /məʊlt/ (*US*) = **moult**
molten /'məʊlt(ə)n/ *adj.* распла́вленный.
moment /'məʊmənt/ *n.* моме́нт, миг; **he will be here (at) any ~ now** он здесь бу́дет с мину́ты на мину́ту; **I am busy at the ~** я сейча́с за́нят.
momentarily /'məʊməntərɪlɪ/ *adv.* на мгнове́ние; (*US, very soon*) че́рез не́сколько мину́т.
momentary /'məʊməntərɪ/ *adj.* мгнове́нный.
momentous /mə'mentəs/ *adj.* ва́жный.
momentum /mə'mentəm/ *n.* (*pl.* **momenta**) (*phys.*) ине́рция; (*fig., impetus*) дви́жущая си́ла; и́мпульс.
monarch /'mɒnək/ *n.* мона́рх.
monarchist /'mɒnəkɪst/ *n.* монархи́ст (*fem.* -ка).
■ *adj.* монархи́стский.
monarchy /'mɒnəkɪ/ *n.* мона́рхия.
monastery /'mɒnəstrɪ/ *n.* монасты́рь (*m.*).
monastic /mə'næstɪk/ *adj.* (*of monasteries*) монасты́рский; **~ order** мона́шеский о́рден; **~ life** мона́шеская жизнь.
Monday /'mʌndeɪ/ *n.* понеде́льник.
monetarism /'mʌnɪtərɪz(ə)m/ *n.* монетари́зм.
monetarist /'mʌnɪtərɪst/ *n.* монетари́ст.
■ *adj.* монетари́стский.
monetary /'mʌnɪtərɪ/ *adj.* де́нежный.
money /'mʌnɪ/ *n.* (*pl.* **moneys** *or* **monies**) де́н|ьги (*pl. g.* -ег); **I got my ~'s worth** я получи́л сполна́ за свои́ де́ньги; **make ~** (*earn money*) зараб|а́тывать, -о́тать; (*become rich*) разбогате́ть (*pf.*).
■ *cpds.* **~ box** *n.* (*Br.*) копи́лка; **~ laundering** *n.* отмыва́ние денег; **~lender** *n.* ростовщи́к; **~ order** *n.* почто́вый перево́д.
Mongolia /mɒŋ'gəʊlɪə/ *n.* Монго́лия.
Mongolian /mɒŋ'gəʊlɪən/ *n.* (*person*) монго́л (*fem.* -ка); (*language*) монго́льский язы́к.
■ *adj.* монго́льский.
mongrel /'mɒŋgr(ə)l/ *n.* дворня́га.
monitor /'mɒnɪt(ə)r/ *n.* (*TV, comput.*) монито́р.
■ *v.t.* следи́ть (*impf.*) за + *i.*
monk /mʌŋk/ *n.* мона́х.
monkey /'mʌŋkɪ/ *n.* (*pl.* **~s**) обезья́на.
mono /'mɒnəʊ/ *n.* мо́но; **recorded in ~** запи́санный монофони́чески.
monochrome /'mɒnəkrəʊm/ *n.* однокра́сочное изображе́ние.
■ *adj.* одноцве́тный, монохро́мный.
monogamous /mə'nɒgəməs/ *adj.* монога́мный, единобра́чный.
monogamy /mə'nɒgəmɪ/ *n.* монога́мия, единобра́чие.
monogram /'mɒnəgræm/ *n.* моногра́мма.
monograph /'mɒnəgrɑ:f/ *n.* моногра́фия.
monolith /'mɒnəlɪθ/ *n.* моноли́т.
monolithic /mɒnə'lɪθɪk/ *adj.* (*lit., fig.*) моноли́тный.
monologue /'mɒnəlɒg/ *n.* моноло́г.
monopolize /mə'nɒpəlaɪz/ *v.t.*: **he ~s the conversation** он не даёт никому́ вста́вить сло́ва.
monopoly /mə'nɒpəlɪ/ *n.* монопо́лия.
monosodium glutamate /mɒnə'səʊdɪəm 'glu:təmeɪt/ *n.* глутама́т на́трия (*пищевая добавка*).
monosyllabic /mɒnəsɪ'læbɪk/ *adj.* односло́жный.
monotone /'mɒnətəʊn/ *n.*: **in a ~** без вся́кого выраже́ния, моното́нно.
monotonous /mə'nɒtənəs/ *adj.* моното́нный.
monotony /mə'nɒtənɪ/ *n.* моното́нность, однообра́зие.
monsoon /mɒn'su:n/ *n.* сезо́н дожде́й.
monster /'mɒnstə(r)/ *n.* (*misshapen creature*) уро́д; (*imaginary animal*) чудо́вище; (*person of exceptional cruelty etc.*) чудо́вище, и́зверг.
monstrosity /mɒn'strɒsɪtɪ/ *n.* чудо́вище.
monstrous /'mɒnstrəs/ *adj.* (*monsterlike*) ужа́сный; (*huge*) грома́дный, исполи́нский.
Montenegro /mɒntɪ'ni:grəʊ/ *n.* Черного́рия.
month /mʌnθ/ *n.* ме́сяц.
monthly /'mʌnθlɪ/ *n.* (*periodical*) ежеме́сячник.
■ *adj.* ме́сячный.
■ *adv.* ежеме́сячно.
monument /'mɒnjʊmənt/ *n.* па́мятник, монуме́нт.
monumental /mɒnjʊ'ment(ə)l/ *adj.* монумента́льный; (*fig.*) колосса́льный.
moo /mu:/ *v.i.* (**moos, mooed**) мыча́ть, про-.
mooch /mu:tʃ/ *v.i.*
1 (*usu.* **~ about/around**) (*Br. coll., loiter*) слоня́ться (*impf.*) (без де́ла).
2 (*US coll., cadge*) попроша́йничать (*impf.*).
mood /mu:d/ *n.* (*state of mind*) настрое́ние; **I am not in the ~ for conversation** я не располо́жен к разгово́ру.
moody /'mu:dɪ/ *adj.* (**moodier, moodiest**) (*gloomy*) угрю́мый; (*subject to changes of mood*) капри́зный; переме́нчивого настрое́ния.
moon /mu:n/ *n.* луна́; (*astron.*) Луна́; **new ~** молодо́й ме́сяц, новолу́ние.
■ *cpds.* **~light** *n.* лу́нный свет; **by ~light** при луне́; *v.i.* (*coll.*) подхалту́ри|вать, -ть; **~lighting** *n.* (*coll.*) халту́ра; **~lit** *adj.* за́литый лу́нным све́том.
moor[1] /mʊə(r)/ *n.* ме́стность, поро́сшая ве́реском.
■ *cpd.* **~land** *n.* ве́ресковая пу́стошь.
moor[2] /mʊə(r)/ *v.t.* ста́вить, по- на прича́л;

швартова́ть, при-.
■ *v.i.*: **they ~ed in the harbour** они́ пришвартова́лись в га́вани.
mooring /'mʊərɪŋ/ *n.* прича́л.
Moorish /'mʊərɪʃ/ *adj.* маврита́нский.
moose /mu:s/ *n.* (*pl.* ~) америка́нский лось.
moot /mu:t/ *adj.*: **a ~ point** спо́рный пункт.
■ *v.t.*: **the question was ~ed** вопро́с поста́вили на обсужде́ние.
mop /mɒp/ *n.* шва́бра; **~ of hair** копна́ воло́с.
■ *v.t.* (**mopped, mopping**) прот|ира́ть, -ере́ть; вытира́ть, вы́тереть; **she ~ped the floor** она́ протёрла пол; **he ~ped his brow** он вы́тер лоб.
■ *with adv.*: **~ up** *v.t.* (*spilt liquid*) вытира́ть, вы́тереть.
mope /məʊp/ *v.i.* хандри́ть (*impf.*).
moped /'məʊped/ *n.* мопе́д.
moral /'mɒr(ə)l/ *n.*
1 мора́ль.
2 (*pl.*) нра́в|ы (*pl.*, *g.* -ов).
■ *adj.* 1 (*ethical*) мора́льный; нра́вственный.
2 (*virtuous*) нра́вственный.
morale /mə'rɑ:l/ *n.* мора́льное состоя́ние.
moralist /'mɒrəlɪst/ *n.* морали́ст (*fem.* -ка).
morality /mə'rælɪtɪ/ *n.* нра́вственность, э́тика.
moralize /'mɒrəlaɪz/ *v.i.* морализи́ровать (*impf.*).
morass /mə'ræs/ *n.* боло́то; тряси́на.
moratorium /mɒrə'tɔ:rɪəm/ *n.* (*pl.* **moratoriums** *or* **moratoria** /-rɪə/) морато́рий; **impose a ~** объяв|ля́ть, -и́ть морато́рий.
morbid /'mɔ:bɪd/ *adj.* боле́зненный, нездоро́вый.
more /mɔ:(r)/ *n.* & *adj.* (*greater amount or number*) бо́льше, бо́лее; **a little ~** побо́льше; **he received ~ than I did** он получи́л бо́льше меня́; (*additional amount or number*) ещё; бо́льше; **~ tea** ещё ча́ю; **have you any ~ matches?** у вас ещё оста́лись спи́чки?; **there is no ~ soup** су́па бо́льше нет.
■ *adv.* бо́льше, бо́лее; (*rather*) скоре́е; **~ or less** бо́лее и́ли ме́нее; **I like beef ~ than lamb** я предпочита́ю говя́дину бара́нине; **she is ~ beautiful than her sister** она́ краси́вее свое́й сестры́; **~ and ~** всё бо́лее и бо́лее; **the ~ the better** чем бо́льше, тем лу́чше; **~ than once** не раз; **once ~** сно́ва, опя́ть, ещё раз.
moreover /mɔ:'rəʊvə(r)/ *adv.* кро́ме того́; сверх того́.
morgue /mɔ:g/ *n.* морг.
moribund /'mɒrɪbʌnd/ *adj.* умира́ющий, отмира́ющий.
morning /'mɔ:nɪŋ/ *n.*
1 у́тро; **in the ~** у́тром; **it began to rain in the ~** дождь пошёл с утра́; **on Monday ~** в понеде́льник у́тром; **this ~** сего́дня у́тром; **good ~!** до́брое у́тро!
2 (*attr.*) у́тренний.
Moroccan /mə'rɒkən/ *n.* марокка́н|ец (*fem.* -ка).
■ *adj.* марокка́нский.
Morocco /mə'rɒkəʊ/ *n.* Маро́кко (*nt. indecl.*).
moron /'mɔ:rɒn/ *n.* (*coll.*) идио́т (*fem.* -ка).
morose /mə'rəʊs/ *adj.* (*gloomy*) мра́чный; (*unsociable*) необщи́тельный.
morphine /'mɔ:fi:n/ *n.* мо́рфий.
morris dance /'mɒrɪs/ *n.* мо́ррис (*народный английский танец*).
Morse /mɔ:s/ *n.* **(~ code)** а́збука Мо́рзе.
morsel /'mɔ:s(ə)l/ *n.* кусо́чек.
mortal /'mɔ:t(ə)l/ *n.* сме́ртный.
■ *adj.* смерте́льный, смертоно́сный; **a ~ wound** смерте́льная ра́на.
mortality /mɔ:'tælɪtɪ/ *n.* сме́ртность.
mortar /'mɔ:tə(r)/ *n.* (*building material*) известко́вый раство́р.
mortgage /'mɔ:gɪdʒ/ *n.* ссу́да на поку́пку до́ма.
■ *v.t.* за|кла́дывать, -ложи́ть.
mortician /mɔ:'tɪʃ(ə)n/ *n.* (*US*) похоро́нных дел ма́стер.
mortify /'mɔ:tɪfaɪ/ *v.t.* (*shame, humiliate*) об|ижа́ть, -и́деть; ун|ижа́ть, -и́зить; **a ~ing defeat** унизи́тельное пораже́ние.
mortuary /'mɔ:tjʊərɪ/ *n.* морг, поко́йницкая.
mosaic /məʊ'zeɪɪk/ *n.* моза́ика.
■ *adj.* мозаи́чный.
Moscow /'mɒskəʊ/ *n.* Москва́; (*attr.*) моско́вский.
mosque /mɒsk/ *n.* мече́ть.
mosquito /mɒ'ski:təʊ/ *n.* (*pl.* **~es**) кома́р.
moss /mɒs/ *n.* мох.
most /məʊst/ *n.* (*greatest part*) бо́льшая часть; **I was in bed ~ of the time** бо́льшую часть вре́мени я провёл в посте́ли; (*greatest amount*) наибо́льшее коли́чество; **£5 at the ~** ма́ксимум 5 фу́нтов; **you must make the ~ of your chances** вам ну́жно наилу́чшим о́бразом испо́льзовать свои́ возмо́жности.
■ *adj.*: **~ people** большинство́ люде́й; **~ of us** большинство́ из нас; **who has the ~ money?** у кого́ бо́льше всех де́нег?
■ *adv.* 1 (*expr. comparison*): **what I ~ desire** чего́ я бо́льше всего́ хочу́; **the ~ beautiful** са́мый краси́вый.
2 (*very*) о́чень, весьма́.
mostly /'məʊstlɪ/ *adv.* гла́вным о́бразом.
MOT (*abbr. of* ***Ministry of Transport***) (*Br.*) Министе́рство тра́нспорта; **~ (test)** ≈ техосмо́тр.
motel /məʊ'tel/ *n.* моте́ль (*m.*).
moth /mɒθ/ *n.* моты́лёк, ночна́я ба́бочка.
mother /'mʌðə(r)/ *n.*
1 мать.
2 (*attr.*) матери́нский; **~ country** ро́дина; **~ tongue** родно́й язы́к.
■ *v.t.* относи́ться (*impf.*) по-матери́нски к + *d.*
■ *cpds.* **~board** *n.* (*comput.*) матери́нская пла́та; **~-in-law** *n.* (*wife's mother*) тёща; (*husband's mother*) свекро́вь; **~-of-pearl** *n.* перламу́тр; *adj.* перламу́тровый.
motherhood /'mʌðəhʊd/ *n.* матери́нство.
motherly /'mʌðəlɪ/ *adj.* не́жный, забо́тливый.
motif /məʊ'ti:f/ *n.* моти́в.
motion /'məʊʃ(ə)n/ *n.*
1 (*movement*) движе́ние; **the car was in ~** маши́на дви́галась; **he set the plan in ~** он приступи́л к осуществле́нию пла́на.
2 (*proposal*) предложе́ние.

■ *v.t. & i.*: **he ~ed to them to leave** он показа́л же́стом, что́бы они́ ушли́.

motionless /'məʊʃənlɪs/ *adj.* неподви́жный.

motivate /'məʊtɪveɪt/ *v.t.* (*induce*) побу|жда́ть, -ди́ть; **he is highly ~d** у него́ есть мо́щный сти́мул.

motivation /məʊtɪ'veɪʃ(ə)n/ *n.* побужде́ние, сти́мул.

motive /'məʊtɪv/ *n.* по́вод, моти́в, побужде́ние.

motley /'mɒtlɪ/ *adj.*: **a ~ crew** пёстрая толпа́.

motor /'məʊtə(r)/ *n.*
1 (*engine*) дви́гатель (*m.*), мото́р.
2 (*also* **~ car** *Br.*) автомоби́ль (*m.*); **~ show** автосало́н; **the ~ trade** торго́вля автомоби́лями.
■ *cpds.* **~bike** *n.* мотоци́кл; **~ boat** *n.* мото́рная ло́дка; **~cycle** *n.* мотоци́кл; **~cyclist** *n.* мотоцикли́ст; **~ racing** *n.* (*Br.*) автомоби́льные го́нки (*abbr.* автого́нки) (*f. pl.*); **~ scooter** *n.* моторо́ллер; **~way** *n.* (*Br.*) автостра́да, автомагистра́ль.

motorcade /'məʊtəkeɪd/ *n.* автоколо́нна.

motorist /'məʊtərɪst/ *n.* автомобили́ст (*fem.* -ка).

motorize /'məʊtəraɪz/ *v.t.* моторизова́ть (*impf., pf.*).

mottled /'mɒtəld/ *adj.* пятни́стый, кра́пчатый.

motto /'mɒtəʊ/ *n.* (*pl.* **~es** *or* **~s**) деви́з; ло́зунг.

mould[1] /məʊld/ (*US* **mold**) *n.* (*container*) фо́рма.
■ *v.t.* лепи́ть, с-; (*fig.*) формирова́ть, с-.

mould[2] /məʊld/ (*US* **mold**) *n.* (*fungus*) пле́сень.

mouldy /'məʊldɪ/ (*US* **moldy**) *adj.* (**mo(u)ldier, mo(u)ldiest**) запле́сневелый.

moult /məʊlt/ (*US* **molt**) *v.i.* линя́ть (*impf.*).

mound /maʊnd/ *n.* (*for burial or fortification*) на́сыпь; (*heap*) ку́ча.

mount /maʊnt/ *n.*: **M~ Everest** гора́ Эвере́ст.
■ *v.t.* 1 (*ascend, get on to*) вз|бира́ться, -обра́ться на + *a.*; подн|има́ться, -я́ться на + *a.*; **he ~ed his horse** он сел на ло́шадь.
2 (*put, fix on a ~*) вст|авля́ть, -а́вить в опра́ву; опр|авля́ть, -а́вить.
3 (*set up*): **the enemy ~ed an offensive** враг предпри́нял наступле́ние.
■ *v.i.* (*increase*) расти́ (*impf.*); (*also* **~ up**) нак|а́пливаться, -опи́ться.

mountain /'maʊntɪn/ *n.*
1 гора́.
2 (*attr.*) го́рный.

mountaineer /maʊntɪ'nɪə(r)/ *n.* альпини́ст (*fem.* -ка).

mountaineering /maʊntɪ'nɪərɪŋ/ *n.* альпини́зм.

mountainous /'maʊntɪnəs/ *adj.* гори́стый.

mourn /mɔːn/ *v.t.* опла́кивать (*impf.*).
■ *v.i.* скорбе́ть (*impf.*); печа́литься (*impf.*); **she ~ed for her child** она́ опла́кивала смерть своего́ ребёнка.

mourner /'mɔːnə(r)/ *n.* прису́тствующий на похорона́х.

mournful /'mɔːnfʊl/ *adj.* ско́рбный, тра́урный.

mourning /'mɔːnɪŋ/ *n.* скорбь; тра́ур.

mouse /maʊs/ *n.* (*pl.* **mice**) мышь; (*comput., pl. also* **~s**) мышь, мы́шка.
■ *cpds.* **~ mat** (*Br.*), **~ pad** (*US*) *nn.* ко́врик для мы́ши.

mousse /muːs/ *n.* мусс.

moustache /mə'stɑːʃ/ (*US* **mustache**) *n.* ус|ы́ (*pl., g.* -о́в).

mouth[1] /maʊθ/ *n.* рот; (*fig.*): **~ of a cave** вход в пеще́ру; **~ of a river** у́стье реки́.
■ *cpds.* **~ organ** *n.* губна́я гармо́ника; **~wash** *n.* полоска́ние для рта; **~-watering** *adj.* вку́сный, аппети́тный.

mouth[2] /maʊð/ *v.t.*: **the actor ~ed his words** актёр напы́щенно деклами́ровал.

mouthful /'maʊθfʊl/ *n.* кусо́к, глото́к.

move /muːv/ *n.*
1 (*in games*) ход; **it's your ~** ваш ход!; (*fig., action*) посту́пок; ход, шаг.
2 (*initiation of action*) движе́ние; **it's time we made a ~** (*Br.*) нам пора́ дви́гаться; **get a ~ on!** дви́гайтесь!, потора́пливайтесь!
3 (*change of residence*) перее́зд.
■ *v.t.* 1 (*change position of, put in motion*) дви́гать (*impf.*); передв|ига́ть, -и́нуть; **he ~d his chair nearer the fire** он пододви́нул стул к ками́ну.
2 (*affect, provoke*) тро́гать, тро́нуть; волнова́ть, вз-; **the sight ~d him to tears** зре́лище тро́нуло его́ до слёз.
■ *v.i.* 1 (*change position; be in motion*) дви́|гаться, -нуться; **the lever won't ~** рыча́г не сдвига́ется; **don't ~!** не дви́гайтесь!; **a moving staircase** эскала́тор.
2 (*change one's residence*) пере|езжа́ть, -е́хать.
3 (*make progress*) развива́ться (*impf.*).
4 (*stir*) шевели́ться (*impf.*); **nobody ~d to help him** никто́ не пошевели́лся, что́бы ему́ помо́чь.
■ *with advs.*: **~ about, ~ around** *v.i.* пере|езжа́ть, -е́хать; разъезжа́ть (*impf.*); **he ~s about a lot** он мно́го разъезжа́ет; **~ along** *v.i.*: **~ along there, please!** проходи́те, пожа́луйста!; **~ away** *v.t. & i.* удал|я́ть(ся), -и́ть(ся); **they ~d away from here** они́ перее́хали отсю́да; **~ in** *v.i.* (*take up abode*): **they ~d in next door** они́ посели́лись в сосе́днем до́ме; **~ on** *v.i.* продв|ига́ться, -и́нуться; идти́ (*det.*) да́льше; **she stopped and then ~d on** она́ останови́лась, а зате́м опя́ть продо́лжила путь; **he ~d on to a better job** он перешёл на бо́лее подходя́щую рабо́ту; **~ out** *v.i.*: **we have to ~ out tomorrow** мы должны́ съе́хать за́втра; **~ over** *v.i.* (*to make room*) подв|ига́ться, -и́нуться; **~ up** *v.i.* подв|ига́ться, -и́нуться; **~ up and let me sit down!** подви́ньтесь и да́йте мне сесть.

movement /'muːvmənt/ *n.*
1 (*state of moving, motion*) движе́ние, перемеще́ние.
2 (*of the body or part of it*) жест, телодвиже́ние.
3 (*group united by common purpose*) движе́ние.

movie /ˈmuːvɪ/ *n.* (*coll.*) фильм, кинокарти́на; **he's gone to the ~s** он пошёл в кино́.

moving /ˈmuːvɪŋ/ *adj.* волну́ющий, тро́гательный.

mow /məʊ/ *v.t.* & *i.* (*p.p.* **mowed** *or* **mown**) коси́ть, с-; **he ~ed the lawn** он подстри́г траву́/газо́н.

mower /ˈməʊə(r)/ *n.* коси́лка.

Mozambican /məʊzæmˈbiːkən/ *n.* мозамби́кец; жи́тель (*fem.* -ница) Мозамби́ка. ▪ *adj.* мозамби́кский.

Mozambique /məʊzæmˈbiːk/ *n.* Мозамби́к.

MP (*abbr. of* ***Member of Parliament***) член парла́мента.

mpg (*abbr. of* ***miles per gallon***) (*сто́лько-то*) миль на галло́н бензи́на.

mph (*abbr. of* ***miles per hour***) (*сто́лько-то*) миль в час.

MP3 *n.* (*comput.*) MP3, МП3 (*формат сжатия аудиоданных*); **MP3 player** MP3-плеер.

Mr /ˈmɪstə(r)/ *n.* (*abbr. of* ***mister***) (*pl.* **Messrs**) г-н (господ|и́н, *pl.* -а́).

Mrs /ˈmɪsɪz/ *n.* (*abbr. of* ***mistress***) (*pl.* ~) г-жа (госпожа́).

MS *abbr. of* ***multiple sclerosis*** рассе́янный склеро́з.

Ms /mɪz, məz/ *n.* г-жа (госпожа́).

M.Sc. (*abbr. of* ***Master of Science***) магистр (есте́ственных) нау́к.

Mt /maʊnt/ *n.* (*abbr. of* ***Mount***) г. (гора́).

much /mʌtʃ/ *n.* & *adj.* (**more, most**) мно́гое; мно́го + *g.*; **his work is not up to ~** его́ рабо́та не отлича́ется высо́ким ка́чеством; **too ~** сли́шком (мно́го); мно́го; **I don't see ~ of him** я его́ ре́дко ви́жу; **he doesn't read ~** он ма́ло чита́ет; **he is not ~ of an actor** он актёр нева́жный; **how ~** ско́лько + *g.*; **very ~** о́чень (мно́го); о́чень си́льно; **as ~ again** ещё сто́лько же; **I thought as ~** я так и ду́мал; **so ~** сто́лько + *g.*
▪ *adv.* (**more, most**)
[1] (*by far*) гора́здо; **~ better** гора́здо лу́чше; **~ the best** гора́здо лу́чше други́х/остальны́х.
[2] (*greatly*) о́чень; нема́ло; **I am ~ obliged to you** премно́го вам обя́зан; **it doesn't ~ matter** э́то не име́ет большо́го значе́ния; **so ~ the better** тем лу́чше; **how ~ do you love me?** как си́льно ты меня́ лю́бишь?; **~ to my surprise** к моему́ вели́кому удивле́нию; **~ as I should like to go** как бы я ни хоте́л пойти́; **not ~!** (*coll., very ~*) о́чень да́же!; а как же!
[3] (*about*) приме́рно, почти́; **his condition is ~ the same** его́ состоя́ние приме́рно тако́е же.

muck /mʌk/ (*coll.*) *n.* (*dirt*) грязь; (*anything disgusting*) дрянь.
▪ *with advs.*: **~ about** (*Br.*) *v.t.* (*inconvenience*) причин|я́ть, -и́ть неудо́бство + *d.*; *v.i.*: **he was ~ing about with the radio** он вози́лся с ра́дио; **~ in** *v.i.* (*Br.*): **if we all ~ in we shall soon get it done** е́сли мы вме́сте за э́то возьмёмся, то бы́стро э́то сде́лаем.

mud /mʌd/ *n.* грязь; сля́коть.

muddle /ˈmʌd(ə)l/ *n.*
[1] (*mess; disorder*) беспоря́док; неразбери́ха; **things have got into a ~** всё перепу́талось/смеша́лось.
[2] (*confusion of mind*) пу́таница.
▪ *v.t.* [1] (*bring into disorder*) перепу́т|ывать, -ать; вн|оси́ть, -ести́ беспоря́док в + *a.*; **you have ~d (up) my papers** вы смеша́ли мои́ бума́ги.
[2] (*confuse*) пу́тать, на-; сби|ва́ть, -ть с то́лку; **don't ~ me (up)** не сбива́йте меня́ с то́лку.

muddy /ˈmʌdɪ/ *adj.* (**muddier, muddiest**) гря́зный.

muesli /ˈm(j)uːzlɪ/ *n.* мю́сли (*смесь злаков, орехов и сухих фруктов*) (*nt. indecl.*).

muffin /ˈmʌfɪn/ *n.* (*Br.*) ≈ горя́чая бу́лочка; (*US*) сдо́бная бу́лочка.

muffle /ˈmʌf(ə)l/ *v.t.*
[1] (*wrap up*) ку́тать, за-; **he was ~d up in an overcoat** он был заку́тан в пальто́.
[2] (*of sound*) глуши́ть, за-.

mug[1] /mʌg/ *n.* (*vessel*) кру́жка.

mug[2] /mʌg/ *n.* (*Br. coll., simpleton*) балбе́с.

mug[3] /mʌg/ *v.t.* (**mugged, mugging**) (*Br. coll., attack*) нап|ада́ть, -а́сть на + *a.*; (*rob*) гра́бить, о-; **~ging** у́личный грабёж.

mugger /ˈmʌgə(r)/ *n.* у́личный граби́тель.

muggy /ˈmʌgɪ/ *adj.* (**muggier, muggiest**) (*damp and warm*) вла́жный и тёплый; (*close*) ду́шный.

mulberry /ˈmʌlbərɪ/ *n.* (*tree*) ту́товое де́рево, шелкови́ца; (*fruit*) ту́товая я́года, шелкови́ца (*collect.*); (*attr., colour*) багро́вый.

mulch /mʌltʃ/ *n.* му́льча (*защитная подстилка из сухой травы, листьев, навоза и т. п.*).
▪ *v.t.* мульчи́ровать (*impf., pf.*).

mule[1] /mjuːl/ *n.* мул; (*fig., of person*) упря́мый осёл.

mule[2] /mjuːl/ *n.* (*slipper*) шлёпанец.

mull[1] /mʌl/ *v.t.*: **~ wine** вари́ть, с- глинтве́йн.

mull[2] /mʌl/ *v.t.*: **~ over** (*ponder*) размышля́ть (*impf.*) над + *i.*

mullah /ˈmʊlə/ *n.* мулла́ (*m.*).

mullet /ˈmʌlɪt/ *n.* кефа́ль.

multicoloured /ˈmʌltɪkʌləd/ (*US* **multicolored**) *adj.* многоцве́тный, кра́сочный.

multicultural /mʌltɪˈkʌltʃər(ə)l/ *adj.* многокульту́рный, многонациона́льный.

multiculturalism /mʌltɪˈkʌltʃərəlɪz(ə)m/ *n.* мультикультурали́зм.

multifarious /mʌltɪˈfeərɪəs/ *adj.* разнообра́зный.

multilateral /mʌltɪˈlætər(ə)l/ *adj.* многосторо́нний.

multimedia /mʌltɪˈmiːdɪə/ *n.* мультиме́диа (*pl. indecl.*); (*attr.*) мультимеди́йный.

multinational /mʌltɪˈnæʃən(ə)l/ *adj.* многонациона́льный.

multiple /ˈmʌltɪp(ə)l/ *n.* кра́тное число́.
▪ *adj.* многочи́сленный; **~ sclerosis** рассе́янный склеро́з.

multiplication /mʌltɪplɪˈkeɪʃ(ə)n/ *n.* умноже́ние.

multiplicity /mʌltɪˈplɪsɪtɪ/ *n.* многочи́сленность, разнообра́зие.

multiply /ˈmʌltɪplaɪ/ *v.t.* умн|ожа́ть, -о́жить.

■ *v.i.* размн|ожа́ться, -о́житься.
multi-purpose /mʌltɪ'pɜ:pəs/ *adj.* многоцелево́й.
multiracial /mʌltɪ'reɪʃ(ə)l/ *adj.* многонациона́льный, многора́совый.
multi-storey /mʌltɪ'stɔ:rɪ/ *adj.* многоэта́жный.
multitask /'mʌltɪtɑ:sk/ *v.i.*
1 (*comput.*) рабо́тать (*impf.*) в многозада́чном режи́ме.
2 (*fig.*) де́лать, с- мно́го дел одновре́ме́нно.
multitude /'mʌltɪtju:d/ *n.* мно́жество, ма́сса.
mum /mʌm/ *n.* (*Br. coll., mother*) ма́ма.
mumble /'mʌmb(ə)l/ *v.t. & i.* (*mutter*) бормота́ть, про-.
mumbo-jumbo /mʌmbəʊ'dʒʌmbəʊ/ *n.* тараба́рщина.
mummy[1] /'mʌmɪ/ *n.* (*embalmed corpse*) му́мия.
mummy[2] /'mʌmɪ/ *n.* (*Br. coll., mother*) ма́ма, ма́мочка.
mumps /mʌmps/ *n.* сви́нка (*заболевание*).
munch /mʌntʃ/ *v.t. & i.* жева́ть (*impf.*).
mundane /mʌn'deɪn/ *adj.* земно́й, мирско́й.
municipal /mju:'nɪsɪp(ə)l/ *adj.* муниципа́льный, городско́й.
municipality /mju:nɪsɪ'pælɪtɪ/ *n.* муниципалите́т.
munitions /mju:'nɪʃ(ə)ns/ *n. pl.* снаряже́ние, вооруже́ние; (*attr.*): **~ factory** вое́нный заво́д.
mural /'mjʊər(ə)l/ *n.* фре́ска.
murder /'mɜ:də(r)/ *n.* уби́йство.
■ *v.t.* уб|ива́ть, -и́ть.
murderer /'mɜ:dərə(r)/ *n.* уби́йца (*c.g.*).
murderous /'mɜ:dərəs/ *adj.* смертоно́сный.
murky /'mɜ:kɪ/ *adj.* (**murkier, murkiest**) мра́чный, тёмный.
murmur /'mɜ:mə(r)/ *n.* ро́пот.
■ *v.t. & i.* говори́ть (*impf.*) ти́хо; бормота́ть, про-; шепта́ть, про-.
muscle /'mʌs(ə)l/ *n.* мы́шца, му́скул.
■ *v.i.* (*coll.*): **he ~d in on the conversation** он ввяза́лся в разгово́р.
Muscovite /'mʌskəvaɪt/ *n.* москви́ч (*fem.* -ка).
■ *adj.* моско́вский.
muscular /'mʌskjʊlə(r)/ *adj.* (*pert. to muscle*) мы́шечный; (*with strong muscles*) мускули́стый; си́льный.
muse[1] /mju:z/ *n.* (*myth.*) му́за.
muse[2] /mju:z/ *v.i.* размышля́ть (*impf.*); заду́мываться (*impf.*).
museum /mju:'zɪəm/ *n.* музе́й.
mushroom /'mʌʃru:m/ *n.* гриб.
mushy /'mʌʃɪ/ *adj.* (**mushier, mushiest**) мя́гкий; (*fig.*) слаща́вый.
music /'mju:zɪk/ *n.* му́зыка.
musical /'mju:zɪk(ə)l/ *n.* мю́зикл.
■ *adj.* музыка́льный.
musician /mju:'zɪʃ(ə)n/ *n.* музыка́нт.
musicologist /mju:zɪ'kɒlədʒɪst/ *n.* музыкове́д.
musicology /mju:zɪ'kɒlədʒɪ/ *n.* музыкове́дение.
musket /'mʌskɪt/ *n.* мушке́т.
Muslim /'mʊzlɪm, 'mʌ-/ *n.* мусульма́н|ин (*fem.* -ка).
■ *adj.* мусульма́нский.
mussel /'mʌs(ə)l/ *n.* ми́дия.
must /mʌst/ *n.* (*coll., necessary item*): **the Tower of London is a ~ for visitors** тури́сты должны́ непреме́нно посмотре́ть Ло́ндонский Та́уэр.
■ *v. aux.* (*3rd pers. sing. pres.* **must;** *past* **had to** *or in indirect speech* **must**)
1 (*expr. necessity*): **one ~ eat to live** что́бы жить, ну́жно есть; **~ you go so soon?** неуже́ли вам уже́ на́до уходи́ть?; **~ you behave like that?** неуже́ли вы ина́че не мо́жете?; (*expr. obligation*): **we ~ not be late** нам нельзя́ опа́здывать; **I ~ admit** я до́лжен призна́ть.
2 (*with neg., expr. prohibition*): **cars ~ not be parked here** стоя́нка маши́н запрещена́.
3 (*expr. certainty or strong probability*): **you ~ be tired** вы, наве́рно, уста́ли; **you ~ have known that** не мо́жет быть, что́бы вы э́того не зна́ли.
mustache /mə'stɑ:ʃ/ (*US*) = **moustache**
mustard /'mʌstəd/ *n.* (*plant; relish*) горчи́ца.
muster /'mʌstə(r)/ *n.*: **will his work pass ~?** (*fig.*) его́ рабо́та годи́тся?
■ *v.t.* (*summon together*) соб|ира́ть, -ра́ть; (*fig.*): **he ~ed up all his courage** он собра́лся с ду́хом.
■ *v.i.* (*assemble*) соб|ира́ться, -ра́ться.
mustn't /'mʌs(ə)nt/ *neg. of* ▸ **must**
musty /'mʌstɪ/ *adj.* (**mustier, mustiest**) за́тхлый.
mutant /'mju:t(ə)nt/ *n.* (*biol.*) мута́нт.
mutate /mju:'teɪt/ *v.i.* (*biol.*) мути́ровать (*impf., pf.*); (*change*) видоизмен|я́ться, -и́ться.
mutation /mju:'teɪʃ(ə)n/ *n.* (*biol.*) мута́ция; (*change*) измене́ние.
mute /mju:t/ *adj.*
1 (*silent*) безмо́лвный.
2 (*dumb*) немо́й.
■ *v.t.* приглуш|а́ть, -и́ть.
mutilate /'mju:tɪleɪt/ *v.t.* уве́чить, из-.
mutilation /mju:tɪ'leɪʃ(ə)n/ *n.* уве́чье.
mutineer /mju:tɪ'nɪə(r)/ *n.* мятёжник.
mutinous /'mju:tɪnəs/ *adj.* мятёжный.
mutiny /'mju:tɪnɪ/ *n.* мятёж.
■ *v.i.* бунтова́ть, взбунтова́ться.
mutter /'mʌtə(r)/ *v.t. & i.* бормота́ть (*impf.*); говори́ть (*impf.*) невня́тно.
mutton /'mʌt(ə)n/ *n.* бара́нина.
mutual /'mju:tʃʊəl/ *adj.* взаи́мный; **~ aid** взаимопо́мощь.
muzzle /'mʌz(ə)l/ *n.*
1 (*animal's*) мо́рда.
2 (*guard for this*) намо́рдник.
3 (*of firearm*) ду́ло.
■ *v.t.* над|ева́ть, -е́ть намо́рдник на + *a.*; (*fig.*) заст|авля́ть, -а́вить молча́ть.
my /maɪ/ *poss. adj.* мой; (*belonging to speaker*) свой; **I lost ~ pen** я потеря́л свою́ ру́чку.
Myanmar /maɪən'mɑ:(r)/ *n.* Мья́нма.
myopia /maɪ'əʊpɪə/ *n.* миопи́я, близору́кость.
myopic /maɪ'ɒpɪk/ *adj.* близору́кий.

myriad /'mɪrɪəd/ *n.* несметное число́; мириа́д|ы (*pl.*, *g.* —).
■ *adj.* несчётный.

myrrh /mə:(r)/ *n.* (*fragrant resin*) ми́рра.

myself /maɪ'self/ *pron.*
1 (*refl.*) себя́; -ся/-сь (*suff.*); **I said to ~** я сказа́л себе́; **I hurt ~** я уши́бся/уши́блась.
2 (*emph.*) сам; **I did it ~** я сам э́то сде́лал; **I did it by ~** (*without help*) я э́то сде́лал сам; **I am not ~ today** я сего́дня немно́го не в фо́рме (*or* сам не свой).
3 (*after preps.*): **dancing takes me out of ~** та́нцы развлека́ют меня́.

mysterious /mɪ'stɪərɪəs/ *adj.* таи́нственный, зага́дочный.

mystery /'mɪstərɪ/ *n.* та́йна, секре́т, зага́дка.

mystic /'mɪstɪk/ *n.* ми́стик.
■ *adj.* (*also* **~al** /'mɪstɪk(ə)l/) мисти́ческий.

mysticism /'mɪstɪsiz(ə)m/ *n.* ми́стика.

mystify /'mɪstɪfaɪ/ *v.t.* озада́чи|вать, -ть.

mystique /mɪ'sti:k/ *n.* таи́нственность, зага́дочность.

myth /mɪθ/ *n.* (*lit., fig.*) миф.

mythical /'mɪθɪk(ə)l/ *adj.* мифи́ческий.

mythological /mɪθə'lɒdʒɪk(ə)l/ *adj.* мифологи́ческий.

mythology /mɪ'θɒlədʒɪ/ *n.* мифоло́гия.

myxomatosis /mɪksəmə'təʊsɪs/ *n.* миксомато́з (*заболевание кроликов*).

Nn

nab /næb/ *v.t.* (**nabbed, nabbing**) захва́т|ывать, -и́ть; заст|ава́ть, -а́ть.

naff /næf/ *adj.* (*Br.*) безвку́сный.

nag /næg/ *v.t.* (**nagged, nagging**) пили́ть (*impf.*).

nagging /'nægɪŋ/ *adj.* приди́рчивый; **a ~ pain** но́ющая боль.

nail /neɪl/ *n.*
1 (*on finger or toe*) но́готь (*m.*).
2 (*metal spike*) гвоздь (*m.*).
■ *v.t.* 1 приб|ива́ть, -и́ть (*что к чему*); пригво|жда́ть, -зди́ть.
2 (*pin down*): **he tried to evade the issue but I ~ed him down** он пыта́лся уйти́ от пробле́мы, но я прижа́л его́ к сте́нке.
■ *cpds.* **~ brush** *n.* щёт(оч)ка для ногте́й; **~ file** *n.* пи́л(оч)ка (для ногте́й); **~ polish** *n.* лак для ногте́й; **~ varnish** *n.* (*Br.*) лак для ногте́й.

naive /naɪ'i:v/ *adj.* наи́вный, простоду́шный.

naivety, naïvety /naɪ'i:vɪtɪ/ *n.* наи́вность, простоду́шие.

naked /'neɪkɪd/ *adj.* го́лый.

nakedness /'neɪkɪdnɪs/ *n.* нагота́, обнажённость.

name /neɪm/ *n.*
1 (*esp.* **fore~**) и́мя (*nt.*); (*surname*) и́мя, фами́лия; (*of pet*) кли́чка; **what is his ~?** как его́ зову́т/фами́лия?
2 (*of a thing*) назва́ние.
3 (*reputation*) и́мя, репута́ция; **he made a ~ for himself** он со́здал/сде́лал себе́ и́мя.
4 : **call s.o. ~s** руга́ть (*impf.*) кого́-н (нехоро́шими слова́ми).
■ *v.t.* 1 (*give ~ to*) наз|ыва́ть, -ва́ть; да|ва́ть, -ть и́мя + *d.*; **they haven't yet ~d the baby** они́ ещё не́ дали ребёнку и́мя; **he was ~d Andrew after his grandfather** его́ назва́ли Андре́ем в честь де́да.
2 (*recite*) наз|ыва́ть, -ва́ть; **the pupil ~d the chief cities of Europe** учени́к назва́л/перечи́слил гла́вные города́ Евро́пы; (*state*) наз|ыва́ть, -ва́ть; **~ your price!** назна́чьте це́ну!; (*identify*): **how many stars can you ~** (*sc. identify*)**?** ско́лько звёзд вы мо́жете определи́ть?
■ *cpds.* **~-dropping** *n.* (*coll.*) ≈ хвастовство́ свои́ми знако́мствами/свя́зями; **~sake** *n.* (*with same first ~*) тёзка (*c.g.*).

namely /'neɪmlɪ/ *adv.* (а) и́менно; то есть.

Namibia /nə'mɪbɪə/ *n.* Нами́бия.

Namibian /nə'mɪbɪən/ *n.* намиби́|ец (*fem.* -йка).
■ *adj.* намиби́йский.

nanny /'nænɪ/ *n.* (*for child*) ня́ня, ня́нечка.
■ *cpd.* **~ goat** *n.* коза́.

nanotechnology /nænəʊtek'nɒlədʒɪ/ *n.* нанотехноло́гия.

nap /næp/ *n.* (*short sleep*) коро́ткий сон; **have, take a ~** вздремну́ть (*pf.*).

napalm /'neɪpɑ:m/ *n.* напа́лм; (*attr.*) напа́лмовый.

nape /neɪp/ *n.* загри́вок.

napkin /'næpkɪn/ *n.* **(table ~)** салфе́тка.

nappy /'næpɪ/ *n.* (*Br. coll.*) подгу́зник.

narcissistic /nɑ:sɪ'sɪstɪk/ *adj.* самовлюблённый.

narcis|sus /nɑ:'sɪsəs/ *n.* (*pl.* **~si** /-saɪ/) нарци́сс.

narcotic /nɑ:'kɒtɪk/ *n.* нарко́тик.
■ *adj.* наркоти́ческий.

narrate /nə'reɪt/ *v.t.*
1 (*story*) расска́з|ывать, -а́ть.
2 : **~ a film/broadcast** чита́ть (*impf.*) текст от а́втора.

narrative /'nærətɪv/ *n.* (*story*) расска́з.
■ *adj.* повествова́тельный.

narrator /nə'reɪtə(r)/ *n.* расска́зч|ик (*fem.* -ица); (*theatr., cin.*) а́вторский го́лос, ди́ктор.

narrow /'nærəʊ/ *adj.* (**narrower, narrowest**) (*lit., fig.*)
1 у́зкий.
2 (*with little margin*): **a ~ majority** незначи́тельное большинство́; **he had a ~ escape from death** он чу́дом избежа́л сме́рти.
■ *v.t.*: **the choice was ~ed down to two candidates** вы́бор свёлся к двум

кандидату́рам.
■ *v.i.* (*of river, road*) су́|живаться, -зиться.
■ *cpds.* **~-gauge** *adj.* узкоколе́йный; **~-minded** *adj.* узколо́бый, ограни́ченный.

nasal /ˈneɪz(ə)l/ *adj.* (*of, for the nose*) носово́й; (*of the voice*) гнуса́вый.

nasturtium /nəˈstɜːʃəm/ *n.* насту́рция.

nasty /ˈnɑːstɪ/ *adj.* (**nastier, nastiest**)
1 (*offensive, e.g. smell or taste*) неприя́тный, проти́вный.
2 (*morally offensive*) ме́рзкий, га́дкий, гну́сный.
3 (*unkind, unpleasant*) злой; **a ~ remark** зло́е замеча́ние; **a ~ temper** тяжёлый хара́ктер; **he played a ~ trick on me** он сыгра́л со мной злу́ю шу́тку; (*of the elements*): **~ weather** скве́рная пого́да.
4 (*threatening*) опа́сный; **there was a ~ look in his eye** его́ вид не предвеща́л ничего́ до́брого.
5 (*difficult*): **that's a ~ rock to climb** на э́ту скалу́ нелегко́ взобра́ться.

nation /ˈneɪʃ(ə)n/ *n.* (*population*) на́ция; (*people*) наро́д; (*country*) страна́.
■ *cpd.* **~wide** *adj.* общенациона́льный, всенаро́дный; **a ~wide search** ро́зыск/по́иски (*m. pl.*) по всей стране́.

national /ˈnæʃən(ə)l/ *n.* гражд|ани́н (*fem.* -а́нка).
■ *adj.* (*of the state*) госуда́рственный; (*of the country or population as a whole*) наро́дный, всенаро́дный; (*central*; *opp. provincial*) центра́льный; (*pert. to a particular nation or ethnic group*) национа́льный; **~ anthem** госуда́рственный гимн; **N~ Health Service** Национа́льная слу́жба здравоохране́ния; **N~ Insurance** Госуда́рственное страхова́ние; **~ newspapers** центра́льные газе́ты; **~ service** во́инская пови́нность.

nationalism /ˈnæʃənəlɪz(ə)m/ *n.* национали́зм.

nationalist /ˈnæʃənəlɪst/ *n.* национали́ст (*fem.* -ка).

nationalistic /næʃənəˈlɪstɪk/ *adj.* националисти́ческий.

nationality /næʃəˈnælɪtɪ/ *n.* по́дданство; гражда́нство; (*ethnic group, e.g. within Russia*) национа́льность.

nationalization /næʃənəlaɪˈzeɪʃ(ə)n/ *n.* национализа́ция.

nationalize /ˈnæʃənəlaɪz/ *v.t.* национализи́ровать (*impf., pf.*).

native /ˈneɪtɪv/ *n.*
1 (*indigenous inhabitant*) тузе́м|ец (*fem.* -ка).
2 : **a ~ of** урожéн|ец (*fem.* -ка) + *g.*
3 (*of animal, plant*): **the kangaroo/eucalyptus is a ~ of Australia** ро́дина кенгуру́/эвкали́пта — Австра́лия.
■ *adj.* 1 (*of one's birth*) родно́й; **~ language** родно́й язы́к.
2 (*indigenous*) тузе́мный; **N~ American** америка́нск|ий инде́ец (*fem.* -ая индиа́нка); **~ population** тузе́мное/коренно́е/ме́стное населе́ние.

nativity /nəˈtɪvɪtɪ/ *n.* Рождество́ Христо́во.

NATO /ˈneɪtəʊ/ *n.* (*abbr. of* ***North Atlantic Treaty Organization***) НА́ТО (Организа́ция Североатланти́ческого догово́ра).

natter /ˈnætə(r)/ (*Br. coll.*) *n.*: **I came in for a ~** я зашёл поболта́ть.
■ *v.i.* болта́ть (*impf.*).

natural /ˈnætʃər(ə)l/ *adj.*
1 (*found in, pertaining to nature*) есте́ственный, приро́дный; стихи́йный; **~ phenomena** явле́ния приро́ды; **~ resources** приро́дные ресу́рсы/бога́тства.
2 (*normal, not surprising*) есте́ственный, норма́льный; **it is ~ for parents to love their children** для роди́телей есте́ственно люби́ть свои́х дете́й.
3 (*simple, unaffected*) просто́й; простоду́шный.
■ *cpd.* **~-born** *adj.* прирождённый.

naturalism /ˈnætʃərəlɪz(ə)m/ *n.* натурали́зм.

naturalist /ˈnætʃərəlɪst/ *n.* натурали́ст.

naturalistic /nætʃərəˈlɪstɪk/ *adj.* натуралисти́ческий.

naturalization /nætʃərəlaɪˈzeɪʃ(ə)n/ *n.* натурализа́ция; акклиматиза́ция.

naturalize /ˈnætʃərəlaɪz/ *v.t.* (*admit to citizenship*) натурализова́ть (*impf., pf.*); (*of animals, plants: introduce to another country*) акклиматизи́ровать (*impf., pf.*).

naturally /ˈnætʃərəlɪ/ *adv.* есте́ственно.

nature /ˈneɪtʃə(r)/ *n.*
1 (*force, natural phenomena*) приро́да; **~ reserve** запове́дник.
2 (*temperament*) нату́ра, хара́ктер; **human ~** челове́ческая приро́да; **it was his ~ to be proud** он был го́рдым по нату́ре.
3 (*essential quality*) приро́да, хара́ктер; **by, in the (very) ~ of things** по приро́де веще́й.

naturism /ˈneɪtʃərɪz(ə)m/ *n.* (*nudism*) нуди́зм.

naturist /ˈneɪtʃərɪst/ *n.* (*nudist*) нуди́ст (*fem.* -ка).

naughtiness /ˈnɔːtɪnɪs/ *n.* озорство́.

naughty /ˈnɔːtɪ/ *adj.* (**naughtier, naughtiest**)
1 (*e.g. child's behaviour*) непослу́шный, шаловли́вый, озорно́й; **be ~** озорнича́ть (*impf.*); **you were ~ today** ты сего́дня пло́хо себя́ вёл.
2 (*risqué*) риско́ванный.

nausea /ˈnɔːzɪə/ *n.* тошнота́.

nauseat|e /ˈnɔːzɪeɪt/ *v.t.* вызыва́ть, вы́звать тошноту́ у + *g.*; **~ing** тошнотво́рный.

nauseous /ˈnɔːzɪəs/ *adj.* тошнотво́рный; **I feel ~** меня́ тошни́т.

nautical /ˈnɔːtɪk(ə)l/ *adj.* морско́й.

naval /ˈneɪv(ə)l/ *adj.* морско́й; (*of the navy*) вое́нно-морско́й; **~ base** вое́нно-морска́я ба́за; **~ officer** морско́й офице́р.

nave /neɪv/ *n.* (*of church*) неф.

navel /ˈneɪv(ə)l/ *n.* пупо́к (*coll.*).

navigable /ˈnævɪgəb(ə)l/ *adj.* (*of river, sea*) судохо́дный.

navigate /ˈnævɪgeɪt/ *v.t.* (*of person*): **~ a ship/aircraft** управля́ть (*impf.*) кораблём/самолётом; **~ a river/sea** пла́вать (*indet.*), плыть (*det.*) по реке́/мо́рю.
■ *v.i.* (*in ship*) пла́вать (*indet.*), плыть (*det.*); (*in aircraft*) лет|а́ть (*indet.*), -е́ть (*det.*).

navigation /nævɪˈgeɪʃ(ə)n/ *n.* навига́ция.

navigator /ˈnævɪgeɪtə(r)/ *n.* (*naut., aeron.*) шту́рман, навига́тор.

navy /'neɪvɪ/ *n.*
[1] (*naval forces*) вое́нно-морски́е си́лы (*f. pl.*); (*ships of war*) вое́нно-морско́й флот.
[2] (~ *blue*) тёмно-си́ний цвет.
■ *cpd.* **~-blue** *adj.* тёмно-си́ний.

Nazi /'nɑ:tsɪ/ *n.* (*pl.* **Nazis**) наци́ст (*fem.* -ка).
■ *adj.* наци́стский.

Nazism /'nɑ:tsɪz(ə)m/ *n.* наци́зм.

near /nɪə(r)/ *adj.*
[1] (*close at hand, in space or time*) бли́зкий; **the station is quite ~ (to) our house** ста́нция (нахо́дится) совсе́м бли́зко от на́шего до́ма; **in the ~ future** в ближа́йшем бу́дущем.
[2]: **the ~ side** (*of road or vehicle in Britain*) ле́вая сторона́.
[3] (*narrowly achieved*): **a ~ miss** непрямо́е попада́ние; **we won, but it was a ~ thing** мы победи́ли, но с трудо́м.
■ *adv.* [1] (*of place or time*) бли́зко; **come a little ~er** подойди́те побли́же.
[2] (*fig.*): **the bus was nowhere ~ full** авто́бус был далеко́ не по́лный; **she is nowhere ~ as old as her husband** она́ далеко́ не так стара́, как её муж.
■ *v.t.* прибл|ижа́ться, -и́зиться к + *d.*; **he is ~ing his end** он при́ смерти.
■ *prep.* о́коло, во́зле, близ, бли́зко от, у (*all* + *g.*); **~ here** недалеко́ отсю́да; **come ~er the fire!** подвига́йтесь к ками́ну; **we are no ~er a solution** мы ничу́ть не приблизи́лись/бли́же к реше́нию.
■ *cpds.* **~by** *adj., adv.* располо́женный побли́зости; близлежа́щий, сосе́дний; **he was standing ~by** он стоя́л бли́зко/ря́дом; **~sighted** *adj.* близору́кий.

nearly /'nɪəlɪ/ *adv.* (*almost*) почти́; **he ~ fell** он чуть не упа́л; **we are ~ there** мы почти́ прие́хали/пришли́; **there is not ~ enough to eat** еды́ далеко́ не доста́точно.

nearness /'nɪənɪs/ *n.* бли́зость.

neat /ni:t/ *adj.*
[1] (*of appearance*) опря́тный, аккура́тный.
[2] (*clear, precise*) чёткий, изя́щный.
[3] (*of liquor etc., undiluted*) неразба́вленный.
[4] (*US coll., excellent*) отли́чный, кла́ссный.

nebulous /'nebjʊləs/ *adj.* (*fig.*) тума́нный.

necessarily /nesə'serɪlɪ/ *adv.* обяза́тельно; **it is not ~ true** э́то не обяза́тельно так.

necessary /'nesəsərɪ/ *adj.* (*indispensable*) необходи́мый; (*compulsory*) необходи́мый, обяза́тельный; (*inevitable*) неизбе́жный; **it is ~ to eat in order to live** что́бы жить, необходи́мо пита́ться; **it is not ~ to dress for dinner** переодева́ться к обе́ду необяза́тельно; мо́жно не одева́ться к обе́ду.

necessitate /nɪ'sesɪteɪt/ *v.t.* вызыва́ть, вы́звать; обусло́в|ливать, -ить.

necessity /nɪ'sesɪtɪ/ *n.*
[1] (*inevitability*) неизбе́жность.
[2] (*need*) нужда́, необходи́мость; **of ~** по необходи́мости.
[3] (*necessary thing*): **the telephone is a ~** телефо́н не ро́скошь, а предме́т пе́рвой необходи́мости.

neck /nek/ *n.*
[1] ше́я; **stick one's ~ out** (*coll.*) ста́вить, по- себя́ под уда́р; **~ and ~** ноздря́ в ноздрю́; голова́ в го́лову.
[2] (*of var. objects*): **~ of a bottle** го́рлышко буты́лки; **~ of a shirt** во́рот руба́шки.
■ *cpds.* **~lace** *n.* ожере́лье; **~line** *n.* вы́рез (пла́тья); **~tie** *n.* га́лстук.

nectar /'nektə(r)/ *n.* некта́р.

nectarine /'nektərɪn/ *n.* нектари́н, гла́дкий пе́рсик.

née /neɪ/ *adj.* урождённая.

need /ni:d/ *n.* (*want, requirement*) нужда́; **the house is in ~ of repair** дом нужда́ется в ремо́нте; **my ~s are few** у меня́ скро́мные потре́бности; (*necessity*) необходи́мость; **if ~ be** в слу́чае необходи́мости; **there's no ~ to get upset** не́зачем расстра́иваться; **there is no ~ for him to read the whole book** ему́ необяза́тельно/не́зачем чита́ть всю кни́гу.
■ *v.t.* [1] (*require*) нужда́ться (*impf.*) в + *p.*; **the grass ~s cutting** газо́н сле́дует подстри́чь; **he ~s a haircut** ему́ пора́ (по)стри́чься.
[2] (*with inf., be obliged, under necessity*): **~ I come today?** мне ну́жно приходи́ть сего́дня?; **you ~n't do it all tomorrow** вам не обяза́тельно ко́нчить всю рабо́ту за́втра; **you ~ not have bothered** напра́сно вы беспоко́ились; **I ~ not** (*have no reason to*) мне не́зачем; **he ~ not come** он мо́жет не приходи́ть.

needful /'ni:dfʊl/ *adj.* необходи́мый.

needle /'ni:d(ə)l/ *n.* игла́, иго́лка.
■ *v.t.* (*irritate, tease*) подд|ева́ть, -е́ть.
■ *cpd.* **~work** *n.* рукоде́лие.

needless /'ni:dlɪs/ *adj.* (*unnecessary*) нену́жный; (*inappropriate*) неуме́стный; **~ to say** (само́ собо́й) разуме́ется.

needy /'ni:dɪ/ *adj.* (**needier, neediest**) нужда́ющийся.

nefarious /nɪ'feərɪəs/ *adj.* злоде́йский.

negate /nɪ'geɪt/ *v.t.* св|оди́ть, -ести́ на нет.

negation /nɪ'geɪʃ(ə)n/ *n.* опроверже́ние.

negative /'negətɪv/ *n.*
[1] (*statement, reply, word*) отрица́ние.
[2] (*phot.*) негати́в.
■ *adj.* отрица́тельный.

neglect /nɪ'glekt/ *n.*
[1] (*failure to attend to*) пренебреже́ние + *i.*; **~ of one's duties** пренебреже́ние свои́ми обя́занностями.
[2] (*lack of care*) запу́щенность; **~ of one's children** отсу́тствие забо́ты о свои́х де́тях.
[3] (*failure to notice*) невнима́ние (**of:** к + *d.*).
[4] (*uncared-for state*) запу́щенность, забро́шенность; **the house was in a state of ~** дом был запу́щен/забро́шен.
■ *v.t.* [1] (*work*) запус|ка́ть, -ти́ть; забр|а́сывать, -о́сить; (*duty*) пренебр|ега́ть, -е́чь + *i.*
[2] (*leave uncared for*) забр|а́сывать, -о́сить, ост|авля́ть, -а́вить без внима́ния; **he ~s his family** он забро́сил свою́ семью́; **~ed children** безнадзо́рные/забро́шенные де́ти; **a ~ed garden** запу́щенный/забро́шенный сад.
[3] (*with inf., fail*) заб|ыва́ть, -ы́ть; **he ~ed to wind up the clock** он забы́л завести́ часы́.

neglectful /nɪ'glektfʊl/ *adj.* небре́жный, невнима́тельный; **he is ~ of his interests** он не забо́тится о со́бственных интере́сах.

negligence /'neglɪdʒ(ə)ns/ *n.* небре́жность.

negligent /ˈneglɪdʒ(ə)nt/ *adj.* (*careless*) небре́жный; (*inattentive*) невнима́тельный.

negligible /ˈneglɪdʒɪb(ə)l/ *adj.* незначи́тельный.

negotiable /nɪˈgəʊʃəb(ə)l/ *adj.*
[1]: **~ conditions, terms** усло́вия, кото́рые мо́гут служи́ть предме́том перегово́ров.
[2] (*navigable*) проходи́мый; (*of roads*) прое́зжий.

negotiate /nɪˈgəʊʃɪeɪt/ *v.t.*
[1] (*conduct negotiations over*) вести́ (*impf.*) перегово́ры о + *p.*; (*conclude agreement on*) при|ходи́ть, -йти́ к соглаше́нию о + *p.*
[2] (*get over or through*) проб|ира́ться, -ра́ться че́рез + *a.*; **~ a corner** брать, взять поворо́т.
■ *v.i.* догов|а́риваться, -ори́ться.

negotiation /nɪgəʊʃɪˈeɪʃ(ə)n/ *n.* (*process*) обсужде́ние; (*talks*) перегово́ры (*m. pl.*).

negotiator /nɪˈgəʊʃɪeɪtə(r)/ *n.* уча́стник перегово́ров.

Negro /ˈni:grəʊ/ *n.* (*pl.* **Negroes**) негр.
■ *adj.* негритя́нский.

neigh /neɪ/ *v.i.* ржать (*impf.*).

neighbour /ˈneɪbə(r)/ (*US* **neighbor**) *n.* сосе́д (*fem.* -ка).

neighbourhood /ˈneɪbəhʊd/ (*US* **neighborhood**) *n.*
[1] (*locality*) ме́стность, окре́стность; (*district*) райо́н.
[2] (*neighbours*) сосе́ди (*m. pl.*).

neighbouring /ˈneɪbərɪŋ/ (*US* **neighboring**) *adj.* сосе́дний.

neighbourly /ˈneɪbəlɪ/ (*US* **neighborly**) *adj.* добрососе́дский; **in a ~ fashion** по-сосе́дски; **that's not a ~ thing to do** э́то не по-сосе́дски.

neither /ˈnaɪðə(r)/ *pron.* & *adj.* ни тот, ни друго́й; **~ of them knows** ни оди́н (*or* никто́) из них не зна́ет.
■ *adv.* [1]: **~ ... nor** ни... ни; **~ he nor I went** ни он, ни я не пошли́.
[2] (*after neg. clause*): **he didn't go and ~ did I** он не пошёл, и я то́же.

neoclassical /ni:əʊˈklæsɪk(ə)l/ *adj.* неоклассици́ческий.

neon /ˈni:ɒn/ *adj.* нео́новый; **~ light** нео́новый свет; **~ sign** нео́новая рекла́ма.

neo-Nazi /ni:əʊˈnɑ:tsɪ/ *n.* неонаци́ст (*fem.* -ка).

Nepal /nɪˈpɔ:l/ *n.* Непа́л.

Nepal|ese /nepəˈli:z/, **-i** /nɪˈpɔ:lɪ/ *n.* (*pl.* **~ese, ~i** *or* **~is**) непа́л|ец (*fem.* -ка).
■ *adj.* непа́льский.

nephew /ˈnefju:/ *n.* племя́нник.

nepotism /ˈnepətɪz(ə)m/ *n.* семе́йственность, кумовство́.

Neptune /ˈneptju:n/ *n.* Непту́н.

nerd /nə:d/ *n.* зану́да (*c.g.*).

nerve /nə:v/ *n.*
[1] нерв; **he doesn't know what ~s are** он не зна́ет, что тако́е не́рвы; **he gets on my ~s** он де́йствует мне на не́рвы.
[2] (*courage, assurance*) сме́лость; **lose one's ~** робе́ть, о-; (*coll., impudence*) на́глость; **he's got a ~** ну и нагле́ц!
■ *cpd.* **~-racking** *adj.* (*situation*) нерво́зный; (*time*) напряжённый.

nervous /ˈnə:vəs/ *adj.*
[1] (*pert. to nerves*) не́рвный; **he had a ~ breakdown** у него́ бы́ло не́рвное расстро́йство; **he's a ~ wreck** э́то челове́к с подо́рванной не́рвной систе́мой.
[2] (*highly strung*) не́рвный.
[3] (*agitated*) не́рвный, взволно́ванный; **I'm ~** я не́рвничаю.
[4] (*apprehensive*) не́рвный, не́рвничающий.

nervousness /ˈnə:vəsnɪs/ *n.* не́рвность, нерво́зность.

nest /nest/ *n.* гнездо́, **~ of tables** компле́кт сто́ликов (*вставляющихся один в другой*).
■ *v.i.* (*of birds*) гнезди́ться (*impf.*).
■ *cpd.* **~ egg** *n.* (*fig., savings*) сбереже́ния (*nt. pl.*).

nestle /ˈnes(ə)l/ *v.t.* & *i.*: **~ (one's head/face) against s.o./sth.** приж|има́ться, -а́ться (голово́й/лицо́м) к кому́/чему́-н.; **a village (lay) ~d at the foot of the hill** у подно́жия горы́ приюти́лась дере́вня.

net[1] /net/ *n.*
[1] (*fruit ~, mosquito ~ etc.*) се́тка; (*snare for birds, fishing ~ and fig.*) сеть, се́ти (*f. pl.*).
[2] (*fabric*) тюль (*m.*); **~ curtains** тю́левые занаве́ски.
[3]: **the Net** (*comput.*) Сеть, Интерне́т.
■ *v.t.* (**netted, netting**) (*fish etc.*) лови́ть, пойма́ть в сеть/се́ти; **he ~ted the ball** он заки́нул мяч в се́тку; (*at football*) он заби́л гол.
■ *cpds.* **~ball** *n.* нетбо́л (*род баскетбола*); **~work** *n.* сеть; *v.t.* (*Br., TV, radio*) перед|ава́ть, -а́ть по (телевизио́нной/радиотрансляцио́нной) се́ти; (*comput.*) свя́з|ывать, -а́ть в о́бщую сеть; *v.i.* (*fig.*) нала́|живать, -дить конта́кты/свя́зи.

net[2]**, nett** /net/ *adj.* чи́стый; **~ income** чи́стый дохо́д.
■ *v.t.* (**netted, netting**) (*obtain as profit*) получ|а́ть, -и́ть чи́стыми; де́лать, с-.

nether /ˈneðə(r)/ *adj.* ни́жний; **~ regions** преиспо́дняя.
■ *cpd.* **~most** *adj.* са́мый ни́жний.

Netherlands /ˈneðələndz/ *n.* Нидерла́нд|ы (*pl., g.* -ов).

nett /net/ (*Br.*) = **net**[2]

netting /ˈnetɪŋ/ *n.* се́тка.

nettle /ˈnet(ə)l/ *n.* крапи́ва.

neuralgia /njʊəˈrældʒə/ *n.* невралги́я.

neurological /njʊərəˈlɒdʒɪk(ə)l/ *adj.* неврологи́ческий.

neurologist /njʊəˈrɒlədʒɪst/ *n.* невропато́лог, невро́лог.

neurology /njʊəˈrɒlədʒɪ/ *n.* невроло́гия.

neurosis /njʊəˈrəʊsɪs/ *n.* (*pl.* **neuroses** /-si:z/) невро́з.

neurotic /njʊəˈrɒtɪk/ *adj.* невроти́ческий.

neuter /ˈnju:tə(r)/ *n.* сре́дний род.
■ *adj.* (*gram.*) сре́дний; сре́днего ро́да.
■ *v.t.* кастри́ровать (*impf., pf.*).

neutral /ˈnju:tr(ə)l/ *n.* (*of gears*): **in ~** в нейтра́льном положе́нии; на нейтра́льной переда́че; **put the car in(to) ~** поста́вить (*pf.*) маши́ну на нейтра́льную переда́чу.
■ *adj.* нейтра́льный.

neutrality /nju:ˈtrælɪtɪ/ *n.* нейтралите́т.

neutralize /ˈnju:trəlaɪz/ *v.t.* нейтрализова́ть (*impf., pf.*).

neutron /'nju:trɒn/ *n.* нейтро́н.
Neva /'ni:və/ *n.* Нева́.
never /'nevə(r)/ *adv.* никогда́ (... не); (*not once*) ни ра́зу (... не); **you ~ know** как знать?; **~ before** никогда́ ра́ньше; **I believed him once, but ~ again** одна́жды я ему́ пове́рил, но бо́льше никогда́ не пове́рю; (*emphatic for not*) так и не; **he ~ even tried** он да́же не попро́бовал; (*Br., expr. incredulity*) **~!** не мо́жет быть!
■ *cpds.* **~-ending** *adj.* бесконе́чный; **it's a ~-ending job** э́той рабо́те конца́ нет; **~theless** *adv.* одна́ко; *conj.* тем не ме́нее.
new /nju:/ *adj.*
1 но́вый; **N~ Year** Но́вый год; **Happy N~ Year!** с Но́вым го́дом!; **N~ Year's Day** день Но́вого го́да; **N~ Year's Eve** кану́н Но́вого го́да; **as good as ~** совсе́м как но́вый.
2 (*modern, advanced*) нове́йший, после́дний; **the ~est fashions** нове́йшие/после́дние мо́ды.
3 (*fresh*) молодо́й; **~ potatoes** молодо́й карто́фель; **~ moon** молодо́й ме́сяц, новолу́ние.
4 (*unaccustomed*): **I am ~ to this work** я в э́том де́ле новичо́к; (*unfamiliar*) **this work is ~ to me** э́та рабо́та для меня́ непривы́чна.
■ *cpds.* **N~ Age** *n.* филосо́фская систе́ма, бази́рующаяся на ве́ре в альтернати́вный о́браз жи́зни; **~born** *adj.* новорождённый; **~comer** *n.* новичо́к; **~-found** *adj.*: **a ~-found interest** но́вое увлече́ние (+ *i.*)
newel /'nju:əl/ *n.*
1 коло́нна винтово́й ле́стницы.
2 (*also* **~ post**) баля́сина пери́л.
newly /'nju:lɪ/ *adv.*
1 (*recently*) неда́вно, но́во-; **~ arrived** неда́вно прибы́вший, новоприбы́вший.
2 (*anew*) вновь; **a ~ painted gate** свежевы́крашенная кали́тка.
■ *cpd.* **~-wed** *n.*: **the ~-weds** молодожён|ы (*pl., g.* -ов).
newness /'nju:nɪs/ *n.* новизна́.
news /nju:z/ *n.*
1 но́вости (*f. pl.*); (*piece of* ~) но́вость, весть; **have you heard the ~?** вы слы́шали но́вость?
2 (*in press or radio*) но́вости (*f. pl.*), после́дние изве́стия; **~ agency** информацио́нное аге́нтство; **~ bulletin** (*Br.*) вы́пуск новосте́й; **~ conference** пресс-конфере́нция; **~ flash** э́кстренное сообще́ние.
■ *cpds.* **~agent** *n.* (*shop*) газе́тный кио́ск; (*person*) = **~vendor; ~caster** *n.* ди́ктор; **~letter** *n.* информацио́нный бюллете́нь; **~paper** *n.* газе́та; (*attr.*) газе́тный; **~reader** *n.* (*Br.*) ди́ктор (*последних известий*); **~vendor** *n.* (*Br.*) продав|е́ц (*fem.* -щи́ца) газе́т.
newt /nju:t/ *n.* трито́н.
New York /nju:' jɔ:k/ *n.* Нью-Йо́рк.
New Zealand /nju: 'zi:lənd/ *n.* Но́вая Зела́ндия.
New Zealander /nju: 'zi:ləndə(r)/ *n.* новозела́нд|ец (*fem.* -ка).
next /nekst/ *n.* (*in order*): **the week after ~** че́рез неде́лю; **~, please!** сле́дующий!; **~ of kin** ближа́йший ро́дственник.
■ *adj.* 1 (*of place: nearest*) ближа́йший; (*adjacent*) сосе́дний, сме́жный; **he lives ~ door** он живёт ря́дом.
2: **~ to** (*fig., almost*) почти́; **I got it for ~ to nothing** я купи́л э́то за бесце́нок.
3 (*in a series*) очередно́й; (*future*) бу́дущий, сле́дующий; **~ day** на друго́й/сле́дующий день; **~ Friday** в сле́дующую пя́тницу; **~ October** в сле́дующем октябре́; **~ week** на бу́дущей/сле́дующей неде́ле; **~ year** в бу́дущем году́; **~ time we'll go to London** в сле́дующий раз мы пое́дем в Ло́ндон.
■ *adv.*: **what ~?** э́того ещё не хвата́ло!; **what will he do ~?** а тепе́рь что он наду́мает?; **~ to** ря́дом с + *i.*; **he stood ~ to the fire** он стоя́л во́зле ками́на.
■ *cpd.* **~-door** *adj.* сосе́дний; **~-door neighbour** ближа́йший сосе́д.
NHS (*abbr. of* ***National Health Service***) Национа́льная слу́жба здравоохране́ния.
nib /nɪb/ *n.* перо́.
nibble /'nɪb(ə)l/ *v.t.* поку́сывать (*impf.*).
■ *v.i.*: **~ at sth.** грызть (*impf.*) что-н.
Nicaragua /nɪkə'rægjʊə/ *n.* Никара́гуа (*nt. & f. indecl.*).
Nicaraguan /nɪkə'rægjʊən/ *n.* никарагуа́н|ец (*fem.* -ка).
■ *adj.* никарагуа́нский.
nice /naɪs/ *adj.* (*agreeable*) прия́тный, ми́лый; (*good*) хоро́ший; (*of person*) прия́тный, ми́лый, симпати́чный, любе́зный; **that's very ~ of you** э́то о́чень ми́ло с ва́шей стороны́; **this soup tastes ~** э́тот суп вку́сный; **the children were ~ and clean** де́ти бы́ли чи́стенькие.
■ *cpd.* **~-looking** *adj.* ми́лый, симпати́чный.
nicely /'naɪslɪ/ *adv.* (*well, satisfactorily*) хорошо́; (*agreeably*) прия́тно; (*kindly*) ми́ло.
nicety /'naɪsɪtɪ/ *n.*
1 (*usu. in pl.*) (*suble detail or distinction*) то́нкость, ме́лкая подро́бность.
2 (*exactness*) то́чность; (*accuracy*) аккура́тность; **to a ~** то́чно.
niche /ni:ʃ/ *n.* ни́ша.
nick /nɪk/ *n.*
1 (*notch*) зару́бка.
2: **in the ~ of time** в (са́мый) после́дний моме́нт; как раз во́время.
■ *v.t.* 1 (*cut*) де́лать, с- зару́бку на + *p.*; **he ~ed his chin shaving** он поре́зал себе́ подборо́док во вре́мя бритья́.
2 (*Br. sl., arrest*) брать, взять.
3 (*Br., steal*) спере́ть (*pf.*) (*sl.*).
nickel /'nɪk(ə)l/ *n.* (*metal*) ни́кель (*m.*); (*US coin*) пятице́нтовик.
nickname /'nɪkneɪm/ *n.* про́звище, кли́чка.
■ *v.t.* прозва́ть (*pf.*) + *a. and i.*
nicotine /'nɪkəti:n/ *n.* никоти́н.
niece /ni:s/ *n.* племя́нница.
Nigeria /naɪ'dʒɪərɪə/ *n.* Ниге́рия.
Nigerian /naɪ'dʒɪərɪən/ *n.* нигери́|ец (*fem.* -йка).
■ *adj.* нигери́йский.
niggardly /'nɪgədlɪ/ *adj.* скупо́й.
niggle /'nɪg(ə)l/ *v.t.* дёргать, придира́ться (*both impf.*) к + *d.*
niggling /'nɪglɪŋ/ *adj.* приди́рчивый.

nigh /naɪ/ (*arch.*) = **near**
night /naɪt/ *n.*
1 ночь; (*waking hours of darkness*) вечер; **all ~ (long)** всю ночь (напролёт); **last ~** вчера́ ве́чером/но́чью; **at, by ~** но́чью; **on Saturday ~** в суббо́ту ве́чером; **good ~!**; (*coll.*) **~-~!** споко́йной но́чи!
2 (*attr.*) ночно́й; **~ life** ночна́я жизнь (го́рода); **~ shift** ночна́я сме́на.
■ *cpds.* **~club** *n.* ночно́й клуб; **~dress** *n.* ночна́я соро́чка/руба́шка; **~mare** *n.* (*also fig.*) кошма́р; **have a ~mare** ви́деть (*impf.*) кошма́рный сон; **~marish** *adj.* кошма́рный; **~ school** *n.* вече́рняя шко́ла; **~-time** *n.* ночно́е вре́мя; **in the ~-time** но́чью; **~watchman** *n.* ночно́й сто́рож.
nightie /ˈnaɪtɪ/ *n.* ночна́я руба́шка/соро́чка.
nightingale /ˈnaɪtɪŋgeɪl/ *n.* солове́й.
nightly /ˈnaɪtlɪ/ *adj.* (*happening every night*) ежено́щный; ежевече́рний; **~ performances** ежедне́вные вече́рние представле́ния.
■ *adv.* ежено́щно; ка́ждую ночь; ка́ждый ве́чер.
nil /nɪl/ *n.* нуль (*m.*).
Nile /naɪl/ *n.* Нил.
nimble /ˈnɪmb(ə)l/ *adj.* (**nimbler, nimblest**) (*agile*) прово́рный, шу́стрый (*coll.*); (*dextrous*) ло́вкий.
nine /naɪn/ *n.* (число́/но́мер) де́вять; (*figure; thing numbered 9; group of ~*) девя́тка; (*cf. examples under* ▸ **five**).
■ *adj.* де́вять + *g. pl.*
nineteen /naɪnˈtiːn/ *n.* девятна́дцать; **talk ~ to the dozen** тарато́рить (*impf.*).
■ *adj.* девятна́дцать + *g. pl.*
nineteenth /naɪnˈtiːnθ/ *n.* (*date*) девятна́дцатое число́; (*fraction*) одна́ девятна́дцатая.
■ *adj.* девятна́дцатый.
ninetieth /ˈnaɪntɪɪθ/ *n.* одна́ девяно́стая.
■ *adj.* девяно́стый.
ninet|y /ˈnaɪntɪ/ *n.* девяно́сто; **he is in his ~ies** ему́ за девяно́сто; **in the ~ies** (*decade*) в девяно́стых года́х.
■ *adj.* девяно́сто + *g. pl.*
ninth /naɪnθ/ *n.* (*date*) девя́тое число́; (*fraction*) одна́ девя́тая.
■ *adj.* девя́тый.
nip /nɪp/ *n.*
1 (*pinch*) щипо́к.
2 (*small bite*) уку́с.
3 (*of frost*): **there's a ~ in the air today** сего́дня моро́з пощи́пывает.
■ *v.t.* (**nipped, nipping**)
1 (*pinch*) щип|а́ть, -ну́ть.
2 (*bite*) укуси́ть, кусну́ть (*both pf.*).
■ *v.i.* (**nipped, nipping**)
1 (*pinch*) щипа́ться (*impf.*).
2 (*Br., usu. with advs., move smartly*): **I must ~ along to the shop** мне ну́жно сбе́гать в магази́н; **he ~ped out to have a smoke** он вы́скочил покури́ть.
nipple /ˈnɪp(ə)l/ *n.* сосо́к.
nippy /ˈnɪpɪ/ *adj.* (**nippier, nippiest**)
1 (*nimble*) прово́рный.
2 (*chilly*): **the weather is ~** моро́зит.
nirvana /nəːˈvɑːnə/ *n.* нирва́на.
nit /nɪt/ *n.* гни́да.
■ *cpd.* **~-pick** *v.i.* (*sl.*) придира́ться (*impf.*) к мелоча́м.
nitrate /ˈnaɪtreɪt/ *n.* нитра́т.
nitrogen /ˈnaɪtrədʒ(ə)n/ *n.* азо́т.
nitty-gritty /nɪtɪˈgrɪtɪ/ *n.* (*sl.*) суть де́ла; **the ~ of politics** полити́ческая ку́хня.
nitwit /ˈnɪtwɪt/ *n.* о́лух (*coll.*).
no /nəʊ/ *adj.*
1 (*not any*) никако́й; **there's ~ food in the house** в до́ме нет (никако́й) еды́; **it's ~ use complaining** нет (никако́го) смы́сла жа́ловаться; **~ doubt** несомне́нно; **~ one** никто́; **I spoke to ~ one** я ни с кем не говори́л; *see also* ▸ **nobody.**
2 (*not a; quite other than*) не; **he's ~ fool** он (во́все) не дура́к; **in ~ time** (*very quickly*) в коро́ткий срок, в два счёта (*coll.*).
3 (*expr. refusal or prohibition*): **~ smoking** кури́ть воспреща́ется; **~ entry** вход воспрещён; нет вхо́да.
■ *adv.* (*with comps., not at all, in no way*) не; **~ better than before** ничу́ть не лу́чше, чем ра́ньше; **he ~ longer lives there** он там бо́льше не живёт; **there is ~ more bread** хле́ба бо́льше нет; **~ sooner said than done!** ска́зано — сде́лано!; **~ sooner had he said it than ...** не успе́л он сказа́ть, как… .
■ *particle* нет; **~ thank you** нет, спаси́бо; (*after negative statement or question, sometimes*) да; **"You don't like him, do you?" — "No, I don't"** «Ведь он вам не нра́вится?» — «Да, не нра́вится».
■ *cpds.* **~-fly** *adj.*: **~-fly zone** запре́тная возду́шная зо́на; **~-go** *adj.*: **~-go area** (*Br.*) запре́тная о́бласть.
nobble /ˈnɒb(ə)l/ *v.t.* (*Br. sl.*)
1 (*horse*) по́ртить, ис-.
2 (*bribe*) подма́з|ывать, -ать; подкуп|а́ть, -и́ть.
nobility /nəʊˈbɪlɪtɪ/ *n.* (*quality*) благоро́дство; (*titled class*) дворя́нство.
noble /ˈnəʊb(ə)l/ *n.* двор|яни́н (*fem.* -я́нка).
■ *adj.* (**nobler, noblest**)
1 (*of character*) благоро́дный.
2 (*belonging to the nobility*) дворя́нский.
nobody /ˈnəʊbədɪ/ *n.* ничто́жный челове́к, ничто́жество.
■ *pron.* (*also* **no one**) никто́ (… не); **~ knows** никто́ не зна́ет; **there was ~ present** никого́ не́ было; *see also* ▸ **no** *adj.* **1**
nocturnal /nɒkˈtəːn(ə)l/ *adj.* ночно́й.
nod /nɒd/ *n.* киво́к; **give a ~ of the head to s.o.** кив|а́ть, -ну́ть голово́й кому́-н.
■ *v.t.* (**nodded, nodding**): **~ one's head** кив|а́ть, -ну́ть.
■ *v.i.* (**nodded, nodding**) кив|а́ть, -ну́ть.
node /nəʊd/ *n.* (*bot., phys.*) у́зел; (*astron., math.*) то́чка пересече́ния.
nodule /ˈnɒdjuːl/ *n.* (*bot., med.*) узело́к.
noise /nɔɪz/ *n.*
1 (*din*) шум; **make a ~** шуме́ть, за-.
2 (*sound*) звук.
noisy /ˈnɔɪzɪ/ *adj.* (**noisier, noisiest**) (*of thing*) шу́мный; (*of person*) шумли́вый.
nomad /ˈnəʊmæd/ *n.* коче́вник.
nomenclature /nəʊˈmenklətʃə(r)/ *n.* номенклату́ра.
nominal /ˈnɒmɪn(ə)l/ *adj.* номина́льный.

nominate /ˈnɒmɪneɪt/ *v.t.* (*appoint, e.g. person*) назн|ача́ть, -а́чить; (*propose, e.g. candidate*) выставля́ть, вы́ставить кандидату́ру + *g.*; (*for a prize*) номини́ровать (*impf., pf.*).

nomination /nɒmɪˈneɪʃ(ə)n/ *n.* назначе́ние; (*for a prize*) номина́ция.

nominee /nɒmɪˈniː/ *n.* кандида́т; (*for a prize*) номина́нт.

nominative /ˈnɒmɪnətɪv/ *adj.* & *n.* имени́тельный (падёж).

non- /nɒn/ *pref.* неі

non-alcoholic /nɒnælkəˈhɒlɪk/ *adj.* безалкого́льный.

non-aligned /nɒnəˈlaɪnd/ *adj.* (*pol.*) неприсоедини́вшийся (к политі́ческим бло́кам).

non-believer /nɒnbɪˈliːvə(r)/ *n.* неве́рующий.

nonchalance /ˈnɒnʃələns/ *n.* беззабо́тность; безразли́чие.

nonchalant /ˈnɒnʃələnt/ *adj.* беззабо́тный.

non-committal /nɒnkəˈmɪt(ə)l/ *adj.* (*evasive*) укло́нчивый.

non-compliance /nɒnkəmˈplaɪəns/ *n.*: **~ with regulations** несоблюде́ние пра́вил.

nonconformist /nɒnkənˈfɔːmɪst/ *adj.* нонконформи́стский.

non-cooperation /nɒnkəʊɒpəˈreɪʃ(ə)n/ *n.* отка́з от сотру́дничества.

nondescript /ˈnɒndɪskrɪpt/ *adj.* невзра́чный, безли́чный.

none /nʌn/ *pron.* (*person*) никто́; **~ of us is perfect** никто́ из на́с не явля́ется соверше́нством; **~ of the people died** ни оди́н челове́к не у́мер; (*thing*) ничто́; **there is ~ of it left** из э́того ничего́ не оста́лось; **it's ~ of your business** э́то не ва́ше де́ло.
■ *adv.*: **he is ~ the worse for his accident** он ничу́ть не пострада́л по́сле ава́рии.

nonentity /nɒˈnentɪtɪ/ *n.* (*person*) ничто́жество.

non-essential /nɒnɪˈsenʃ(ə)l/ *adj.* несуще́ственный.

non-event /nɒnɪˈvent/ *n.* собы́тие сомни́тельной ва́жности.

non-existence /nɒnɪɡˈzɪst(ə)ns/ *n.* небытие́.

non-existent /nɒnɪɡˈzɪst(ə)nt/ *adj.* несуществу́ющий.

non-fiction /nɒnˈfɪkʃ(ə)n/ *n.* документа́льная про́за/литерату́ра.

non-interference /nɒnɪntəˈfɪərəns/ *n.* невмеша́тельство.

non-intervention /nɒnɪntəˈvenʃ(ə)n/ *n.* невмеша́тельство.

non-member /nɒnˈmembə(r)/ *n.* не член.

no-nonsense /nəʊˈnɒns(ə)ns/ *adj.* *businesslike*) делово́й; (*strict*) стро́гий.

nonplus /nɒnˈplʌs/ *v.t.* (**nonplussed, nonplussing**) прив|оди́ть, -ести́ в замеша́тельство.

non-profit(-making) /nɒnˈprɒfɪt(meɪkɪŋ)/ *adj.* некомме́рческий.

nonsense /ˈnɒns(ə)ns/ *n.*
1 (*sth. without meaning*) бессмы́слица; (*rubbish*) вздор; ерунда́ (*coll.*); **talk ~** говори́ть (*impf.*) вздор/ерунду́.
2 (*foolish conduct*) глу́пость; **let's have no more ~!** хва́тит валя́ть дурака́!

nonsensical /nɒnˈsensɪk(ə)l/ *adj.* бессмы́сленный.

non-smoker /nɒnˈsməʊkə(r)/ *n.* некуря́щий.

non-smoking /nɒnˈsməʊkɪŋ/ *adj.*: **~ compartment** купе́ (*nt. indecl.*) для некуря́щих.

non-starter /nɒnˈstɑːtə(r)/ *n.* (*coll.*) (*of plan, idea*) до́хлый но́мер, до́хлое де́ло.

non-stick /nɒnˈstɪk/ *adj.*: **a ~ saucepan** кастрю́ля с непригора́ющим покры́тием.

non-stop /nɒnˈstɒp/ *adj.*
1 (*of train or coach*) иду́щий/е́дущий без остано́вок; (*of aircraft or flight*) беспоса́дочный.
2 (*continuous*) непреры́вный.
■ *adv.* 1 беспоса́дочно.
2: **he talks ~** он говори́т без у́молку.

noodles /ˈnuːd(ə)lz/ *n. pl.* (*cul.*) лапша́.

nook /nʊk/ *n.* уголо́к; **I searched every ~ and cranny** я обша́рил ка́ждый уголо́к.

noon /nuːn/ *n.* по́лдень (*m.*); **12 ~** двена́дцать часо́в дня.

no one /ˈnəʊwʌn/ *pron. see* ▸ **nobody**

noose /nuːs/ *n.* (*loop*) петля́; (*lasso*) арка́н.

nor /nɔː(r)/ *conj.*: **they had neither arms ~ provisions** у них не́ было ни ору́жия, ни провиа́нта; **you are not well, ~ am I** вам нездоро́вится, и мне то́же.

norm /nɔːm/ *n.* но́рма, пра́вило.

normal /ˈnɔːm(ə)l/ *adj.* (*regular, standard*) норма́льный; (*usual*) обы́чный; **I ~ly use the bus** обы́чно я е́ду авто́бусом; (*sane, well balanced*) норма́льный.

normality /nɔːˈmælɪtɪ/ *n.* норма́льность.

north /nɔːθ/ *n.* се́вер; (*naut.*) норд; **the ~ of England** се́вер А́нглии/се́верная часть А́нглии; **in the ~** на се́вере; **from the ~** с се́вера; **to the ~** на се́вер.
■ *adj.* се́верный; **N~ America** Се́верная Аме́рика; **N~ American** (*n.*) североамерика́н|ец (*fem.* -ка); (*adj.*) североамерика́нский; **N~ Pole** Се́верный по́люс; **N~ Sea** Се́верное мо́ре.
■ *adv.*: **we went ~** мы поéхали на се́вер.
■ *cpds.* **~bound** *adj.* направля́ющийся на се́вер; **~-east** *n.* се́веро-восто́к; *adj.* (*also* **~-easterly, ~-eastern**) се́веро-восто́чный; се́веро-восто́чный; **~-east wind** норд-о́ст; *adv.* к се́веро-восто́ку; **~-west** *n.* се́веро-за́пад; *adj.* (*also* **~-westerly, ~-western**) се́веро-за́падный; **~-west wind** норд-ве́ст; *adv.* к се́веро-за́паду.

northerly /ˈnɔːðəlɪ/ *n.* (*wind*) се́верный ве́тер.
■ *adj.* се́верный.

northern /ˈnɔːð(ə)n/ *adj.* се́верный; **N~ Ireland** Се́верная Ирла́ндия; **N~ Irish** североирла́ндский.

northerner /ˈnɔːðənə(r)/ *n.* северя́н|ин (*fem.* -ка).

northward /ˈnɔːθwəd/ *adj.* се́верный.
■ *adv.* (*also* **~s**) на се́вер; к се́веру, в се́верном направле́нии.

Norway /ˈnɔːweɪ/ *n.* Норве́гия.

Norwegian /nɔːˈwiːdʒ(ə)n/ *n.* (*person*)

норве́ж|ец (*fem.* -ка); (*language*) норве́жский язы́к.
■ *adj.* норве́жский.

nose /nəʊz/ *n.*
1 нос; (*dim.*) но́сик; **blow one's ~** сморка́ться, вы́-; **look down one's ~ at s.o.** смотре́ть, по- свысока́ на кого́-н.; **rub s.o.'s ~ in sth.** ты́кать, ткнуть кого́-н. но́сом во что-н.; **turn up one's ~ at sth.** вороти́ть (*impf.*) нос от чего́-н.
2 (*sense of smell*) нюх, чутьё.
■ *v.t.*: **~ into** (*pry, meddle*) сова́ться, су́нуться (*or* сова́ть, су́нуть нос) в + *a.*
■ *cpds.* **~bleed** *n.*: **he has frequent ~bleeds** у него́ ча́сто идёт но́сом (*or* из но́са) кровь; **~dive** *n.* пики́рование; **prices took a ~dive** це́ны ре́зко упа́ли; *v.i.* пики́ровать (*impf.*, *pf.*).

nosey /ˈnəʊzɪ/ = **nosy**

nostalgia /nɒˈstældʒə/ *n.* ностальги́я.

nostalgic /nɒˈstældʒɪk/ *adj.* (*person*): **be ~ for** тоскова́ть по + *d.*; (*thing*) ностальги́ческий.

nostril /ˈnɒstrɪl/ *n.* ноздря́.

nos|y, -ey /ˈnəʊzɪ/ *adj.* (**nosier, nosiest**) (*coll.*) любопы́тный.

not /nɒt/ *adv.*
1 не; (*as pred.*) нет; **she is ~ here** её здесь нет.
2 (*elliptical phrr.*): **guilty or ~, he is my son** вино́вен он и́ли нет, а он мой сын; **whether or ~** так и́ли ина́че; **I hope ~** наде́юсь, что нет.
3 (**~** *even*): **~ one of them moved** ни оди́н из них не подви́нулся.
4 (**~** *at all*): **'Do you mind if I smoke?' — 'N~ at all!'** «Вы не возража́ете, е́сли я закурю́?» — «Нисколько/ничу́ть»; **'Many thanks!' — 'N~ at all!'** «Большо́е спаси́бо!» — «Не сто́ит! (*or* Пожа́луйста!)».
5 (*var. phrr.*): **~ on your life** ни в ко́ем слу́чае; **~ in the least** ничу́ть; нисколько.

notable /ˈnəʊtəb(ə)l/ *n.* знамени́тость.
■ *adj.* (*perceptible*) заме́тный; (*remarkable*) замеча́тельный; (*well known*) изве́стный.

notably /ˈnəʊtəblɪ/ *adv.* заме́тно.

notary /ˈnəʊtərɪ/ *n.* (*also* **~ public**) нота́риус.

notch /nɒtʃ/ *n.* зару́бка.
■ *v.t.* 1 (*mark with* **~**) де́лать, с- зару́бку на + *p.*
2 : **~ up a point** (*in game*) выи́грывать, вы́играть очко́.

note /nəʊt/ *n.*
1 (*communication*) запи́ска; **he left a ~ for you** он оста́вил вам запи́ску.
2 (*written record*) за́пись; **make a ~ of sth.** запи́с|ывать, -а́ть что-н.
3 (*attention, notice*) внима́ние; **take ~ of** (*observe*) прин|има́ть, -я́ть во внима́ние; (*heed*) прин|има́ть, -я́ть к све́дению.
4 (*mus.*) но́та; (*key of instrument*) кла́виша.
5 (*Br., currency*) банкно́та.
■ *v.t.* 1 (*observe, notice*) зам|еча́ть, -е́тить; (*heed*) обра|ща́ть, -ти́ть внима́ние на + *a.*
2 : **~ down** (*in writing*) запи́с|ывать, -а́ть.
■ *cpds.* **~book** *n.* записна́я кни́жка, **~book computer** *n.* ноутбу́к; **~pad** *n.* блокно́т; **~paper** *n.* пи́счая бума́га; **~worthy** *adj.* досто́йный внима́ния.

noted /ˈnəʊtɪd/ *adj.* изве́стный, знамени́тый; **~ for his courage** изве́стный свои́м му́жеством.

nothing /ˈnʌθɪŋ/ *pron.* ничто́, ничего́ (*coll.*); **she is ~ to me** она́ для меня́ ничто́; **there's ~ to be ashamed of** в э́том нет ничего́ посты́дного; **there's ~ worse than getting wet through** нет ничего́ ху́же, чем промо́кнуть насквозь; **there's ~ like a hot bath** нет ничего́ лу́чше горя́чей ва́нны; **~ much** ма́ло; **there's ~ wrong with that** ничего́ в э́том плохо́го нет; **he did ~ to help** он ниче́м не помо́г; **I have ~ to do** мне не́чего де́лать; **it has ~ to do with me** э́то меня́ не каса́ется; **they had ~ to eat** им не́чего бы́ло есть, у них не́ бы́ло никако́й еды́; **I have ~ but praise for him** я не могу́ им нахвали́ться; **he had ~ on** (*was naked*) он был соверше́нно го́лый; **~ of the kind** ничего́ подо́бного; **he will stop at ~** он ни пе́ред чем не остано́вится; **for ~** (*without cause*) ни за что́, ни про что́; (*to no purpose*) зря, напра́сно, да́ром; (*free of charge*) беспла́тно.
■ *adv.*: **she is ~ like her sister** она́ совсе́м не похо́жа на сестру́; **this exam is ~ like as hard as the last** э́тот экза́мен гора́здо/куда́ ле́гче предыду́щего.

notice /ˈnəʊtɪs/ *n.*
1 (*intimation*) предупрежде́ние.
2 (*time limit*): **I have to give my employer a month's ~** (*of resignation*) я до́лжен предупреди́ть хозя́ина за ме́сяц (об ухо́де с рабо́ты); **at short ~** в после́днюю мину́ту; в сро́чном поря́дке; **till further ~** впредь до дальне́йшего уведомле́ния.
3 (*written announcement*) объявле́ние.
4 (*attention*) внима́ние; **he took no ~ of me** он не обраща́л на меня́ внима́ния.
■ *v.t.* (*observe*) зам|еча́ть, -е́тить.
■ *cpd.* **~ board** *n.* (*Br.*) доска́ объявле́ний.

noticeable /ˈnəʊtɪsəb(ə)l/ *adj.* заме́тный.

notifiable /ˈnəʊtɪfaɪəb(ə)l/ *adj.* (*of disease etc.*) подлежа́щий регистра́ции.

notification /nəʊtɪfɪˈkeɪʃ(ə)n/ *n.* извеще́ние.

notif|y /ˈnəʊtɪfaɪ/ *v.t.*
1 (*inform*) изве|ща́ть, -сти́ть; сообщ|а́ть, -и́ть + *d.*; **I was ~ied of your arrival** меня́ извести́ли/мне сообщи́ли о ва́шем (предстоя́щем) прие́зде; **he ~ied me of his address** он сообщи́л мне свой а́дрес.
2 (*register*) регистри́ровать (*impf.*, *pf.*); **all births must be ~ied** все рожде́ния подлежа́т регистра́ции.

notion /ˈnəʊʃ(ə)n/ *n.* поня́тие, представле́ние.

notional /ˈnəʊʃən(ə)l/ *adj.* (*ostensible, imaginary*) вообража́емый, мни́мый.

notoriety /nəʊtəˈraɪətɪ/ *n.* дурна́я сла́ва, печа́льная изве́стность; **his arrest won him a brief ~** его́ аре́ст со́здал/принёс ему́ на вре́мя печа́льную изве́стность.

notorious /nəʊˈtɔːrɪəs/ *adj.* (*well known*) (обще)изве́стный; (*pej.*) пресло́вутый; печа́льно изве́стный.

notwithstanding /nɒtwɪðˈstændɪŋ/ *adv.* всё-таки.
■ *prep.* несмотря́ на + *a.*

nought /nɔ:t/ *n.*
[1] (*zero*) нуль (*m.*).
[2] (*figure 0*) ноль (*m.*).
noun /naʊn/ *n.* (и́мя) существи́тельное.
nourish /'nʌrɪʃ/ *v.t.* (*lit.*, *fig.*) пита́ть (*impf.*).
nourishment /'nʌrɪʃmənt/ *n.* пита́ние.
nouveau riche /nu:vəʊ 'ri:ʃ/ *n.* (*pl.* **nouveaux riches** *pronunc. same*) нувори́ш.
novel /'nɒv(ə)l/ *n.* рома́н.
■ *adj.* необы́чный.
novelist /'nɒvəlɪst/ *n.* писа́тель (*fem.* -ница); романи́ст (*fem.* -ка).
novelty /'nɒvəltɪ/ *n.* (*newness*) новизна́; (*new thing*) нови́нка; но́вшество.
November /nəʊ'vembə(r)/ *n.* ноя́брь (*m.*).
novice /'nɒvɪs/ *n.*
[1] (*relig.*) послу́шни|к (*fem.* -ца).
[2] (*beginner*) новичо́к.
now /naʊ/ *adv.*
[1] (*at the present time*) тепе́рь, сейча́с, ны́не; в настоя́щее вре́мя; (*opp. previously*): **I'm married ~** я тепе́рь жена́т; **(every) ~ and then** вре́мя от вре́мени; поро́й; (*with preps.*): **before ~** (*hitherto*) до сих пор; (*in the past*) в про́шлом; **by ~** к э́тому вре́мени; **he should be here by ~** он до́лжен уже́ быть здесь; **from ~ on** впредь; отны́не.
[2] (*this time*): **~ you've broken the glass** ну, вот вы и разби́ли стака́н.
[3] (*at once*; *at this moment*) сейча́с; **I must go ~** мне пора́ (уходи́ть); **he was here just ~** он то́лько что был здесь; **only ~** то́лько тепе́рь.
[4] (*emphatic*) ну, так, ита́к; **~ you just listen to me** нет, вы послу́шайте, что я вам скажу́; **~ why didn't I think of that?** как же я об э́том не поду́мал?
■ *conj.* (*also* **~ that**) по́сле того́ как.
nowadays /'naʊədeɪz/ *adv.* в на́ши дни; в на́ше вре́мя; ны́не.
nowhere /'nəʊweə(r)/ *adv.* нигде́; (*motion*) никуда́; **the house was ~ near the park** дом стоя́л о́чень далеко́ от па́рка; **he was ~ near 60** ему́ ещё бы́ло далеко́ до шести́десяти (лет); **this conversation is getting us ~** э́тот разгово́р нас ни к чему́ не приведёт; **there's ~ to sit** не́где сесть.
noxious /'nɒkʃəs/ *adj.* вре́дный, па́губный.
nozzle /'nɒz(ə)l/ *n.* сопло́.
nuance /'nju:ɑ̃s/ *n.* отте́нок, нюа́нс.
nub /nʌb/ *n.* (*fig.*, *point*, *gist*) суть.
nubile /'nju:baɪl/ *adj.* (*mature*) зре́лый, созре́вший; (*alluring*) прельсти́тельный.
nuclear /'nju:klɪə(r)/ *adj.*
[1] (*phys.*) я́дерный; **~ bomb** я́дерная бо́мба; **~ energy** я́дерная эне́ргия; **~ power station** а́томная электроста́нция; **~ reactor** а́томный/я́дерный реа́ктор.
[2]: **~ family** ма́лая/нуклеа́рная семья́.
nucleus /'nju:klɪəs/ *n.* (*pl.* **nuclei**) (*phys.*, *fig.*) ядро́; (*biol.*) заро́дыш.
nude /nju:d/ *n.*
[1] (*art*) обнажённая (фигу́ра).
[2]: **in the ~** в го́лом ви́де, нагишо́м (*coll.*).
■ *adj.* го́лый, обнажённый, наго́й.
nudge /nʌdʒ/ *v.t.* подт|а́лкивать, -олкну́ть.
nudist /'nju:dɪst/ *n.* нуди́ст (*fem.* -ка).
nudity /'nju:dɪtɪ/ *n.* нагота́.
nugget /'nʌgɪt/ *n.* саморо́док (*золота*).
nuisance /'nju:s(ə)ns/ *n.* (*annoyance*) доса́да; (*inconvenience*) неудо́бство; **what a ~!** кака́я доса́да!
null /nʌl/ *adj.*: **become ~ and void** утра́|чивать, -тить (зако́нную) си́лу.
nullify /'nʌlɪfaɪ/ *v.t.* аннули́ровать (*impf.*, *pf.*).
numb /nʌm/ *adj.*
[1] (*of body*) онеме́лый, онеме́вший; (*of extremities*: **~** *with cold*) окочене́лый.
[2] (*of mind, senses*) онеме́вший, оцепене́вший; **go ~** неме́ть, о-, цепене́ть, о-.
■ *v.t.*: **my hand was ~ed with cold** моя́ рука́ окочене́ла от хо́лода.
number /'nʌmbə(r)/ *n.*
[1] (*numeral*) число́, ци́фра.
[2] (*quantity, amount*) число́, коли́чество; **the average ~ in a class is 30** сре́дняя чи́сленность кла́сса — 30 челове́к/ученико́в; **there were a large ~ of people there** там бы́ло мно́го наро́ду/большо́е коли́чество люде́й; **a ~ of professors attended the lecture** ле́кцию слу́шали не́сколько профессоро́в.
[3] (*identifying*) но́мер; **he was ~ 3 on the list** он шёл тре́тьим но́мером в спи́ске; **look after ~ one** (*fig.*) забо́титься (*impf.*) о со́бственной персо́не; **telephone ~** но́мер телефо́на; **you have the wrong ~** вы не туда́ звони́те/попа́ли; (*song or item in stage performance*) но́мер.
■ *v.t.* [1] (*count*) переч|исля́ть, -и́слить; **his days are ~ed** его́ дни сочтены́.
[2] (*give ~ to*) нумерова́ть, про-.
[3] (*amount to*) насчи́тываться (*impf.*).
■ *cpd.* **~ plate** *n.* (*Br.*) номерно́й знак.
numeracy /'nju:mərəsɪ/ *n.* зна́ние арифме́тики.
numeral /'nju:mər(ə)l/ *n.* ци́фра.
numerical /nju:'merɪk(ə)l/ *adj.* чи́сленный, числово́й.
numerous /'nju:mərəs/ *adj.* многочи́сленный.
nun /nʌn/ *n.* мона́хиня, мона́шенка.
nunnery /'nʌnərɪ/ *n.* же́нский монасты́рь.
nuptial /'nʌpʃ(ə)l/ *adj.* сва́дебный.
nurse /nə:s/ *n.*
[1] (**~** *maid*) ня́ня, ня́нька (*coll.*).
[2] (*of the sick*) сиде́лка; (*orderly*) санита́рка; (*senior* **~**) медсестра́; **male ~** (*orderly*) санита́р; (*senior*) медбра́т.
■ *v.t.* [1] (*suckle*) корми́ть (*impf.*) (гру́дью).
[2] (*attend to*) уха́живать (*impf.*) за + *i.*
[3] (*fig.*): **~ hopes** леле́ять (*impf.*) наде́жду.
nursery /'nə:sərɪ/ *n.*
[1] (*room*) де́тская.
[2] (*institution etc. for care of young*): **day ~** (дневны́е) я́сл|и (*pl.*, *g.* -ей).
[3]: **~ nurse** (*Br.*) воспита́тельница я́слей/де́тского са́да; **~ school** де́тский сад, детса́д; **~ rhyme** де́тские стишки́ (*m. pl.*); де́тская пе́сенка.
[4] (*hort.*) пито́мник.
nursing /'nə:sɪŋ/ *n.* (*career*) профе́ссия медсестры́; **~ home** (ча́стная) лече́бница, (ча́стный) санато́рий; (*old people's home*) дом (для) престаре́лых.
nurture /'nə:tʃə(r)/ *v.t.* (*nourish*) пита́ть (*impf.*); (*rear*) воспи́т|ывать, -а́ть.

nut /nʌt/ *n.*
1 орéх.
2 (*for securing bolt*) гáйка.
■ *cpds.* **~crackers** *n. pl.* щипц|ы́ (*pl.*, *g.* -óв) для орéхов; **~shell** *n.* орéховая скорлупá; **in a ~shell** (*fig.*) крáтко; в двух словáх.
nutmeg /ˈnʌtmeg/ *n.* мускáтный орéх.
nutrient /ˈnjuːtrɪənt/ *n.* питáтельное веществó.
nutrition /njuːˈtrɪʃ(ə)n/ *n.* питáние.
nutritional /njuːˈtrɪʃən(ə)l/ *adj.* (*deficiency, value*) питáтельный; (*advice*) диети́ческий.
nutritious /njuːˈtrɪʃəs/ *adj.* питáтельный.
nutty /ˈnʌtɪ/ *adj.* (**nuttier, nuttiest**)
1 (*of taste*) с при́вкусом орéха.
2 (*crazy*) чóкнутый (*coll.*).
nuzzle /ˈnʌz(ə)l/ *v.t.* & *i.*: **~ (against, up to) s.o./sth.** ты́каться (*impf.*) нóсом в когó-н./что-н.
nylon /ˈnaɪlɒn/ *n.* нейлóн.
■ *adj.* нейлóновый.
nymph /nɪmf/ *n.* ни́мфа.
nymphomaniac /nɪmfəˈmeɪnɪæk/ *n.* нимфомáнка.

Oo

O /əʊ/ *n.* (*nought*) нуль (*m.*), ноль (*m.*).
oak /əʊk/ *n.* (*tree*; *wood*) дуб; (*attr.*) дубóвый.
OAP (*abbr. of* ***old-age pensioner***) (*Br.*) пенсионéр (*fem.* -ка) (по стáрости).
oar /ɔː(r)/ *n.* веслó.
oasis /əʊˈeɪsɪs/ *n.* (*pl.* **oases** /-siːz/) оáзис.
oast house /ˈəʊsthaʊs/ *n.* хмелесуши́льня.
oat /əʊt/ *n.* (*in pl.*) овёс; **sow one's wild ~s** (*fig.*) прож|игáть, -éчь мóлодость; перебеси́ться (*pf.*).
■ *cpd.* **~meal** *n.* толокнó; овся́ная крупá.
oath /əʊθ/ *n.*
1 прися́га; **on** (*Br.*), **under ~** под прися́гой.
2 (*profanity*) прокля́тие.
obdurate /ˈɒbdjʊrət/ *adj.* (*stubborn*) упря́мый; (*hard-headed*) ожесточённый.
OBE (*abbr. of* ***Officer of the Order of the British Empire***) кавалéр óрдена Бритáнской импéрии 4-й стéпени.
obedience /əˈbiːdɪəns/ *n.* повиновéние.
obedient /əˈbiːdɪənt/ *adj.* послýшный, покóрный.
obelisk /ˈɒbəlɪsk/ *n.* обели́ск.
obese /əʊˈbiːs/ *adj.* тýчный.
obesity /əʊˈbiːsɪtɪ/ *n.* тýчность.
obey /əˈbeɪ/ *v.t.* (*comply with*): **~ the laws** подчин|я́ться, -и́ться закóнам; (*be obedient to*): **~ one's parents** слýшаться, по- роди́телей.
■ *v.i.* повиновáться (*impf.*, *pf.*).
obfuscate /ˈɒbfʌskeɪt/ *v.t.* (*darken, obscure*) затемн|я́ть, -и́ть; (*confuse*) смущ|áть, -ти́ть.
obfuscation /ɒbfʌsˈkeɪʃ(ə)n/ *n.* затемнéние; смущéние.
obituary /əˈbɪtjʊərɪ/ *n.* некролóг.
object[1] /ˈɒbdʒɪkt/ *n.*
1 (*material thing*) предмéт, вещь.
2 (*focus*) предмéт, объéкт.
3 (*purpose, aim*) цель; **I had no particular ~ in view** никакóй определённой цéли я не преслéдовал.
4 (*gram.*) дополнéние.
object[2] /əbˈdʒekt/ *v.i.* возра|жáть, -зи́ть (прóтив + *g.*); протестовáть (*impf.*) (прóтив + *g.*); выдвигáть, вы́двинуть возражéния (прóтив + *g.*); **I ~ to being treated like this** я протестýю прóтив такóго обращéния; **do you ~ to my smoking?** вам не мешáет, что я курю́?; **I'll open a window if you don't ~** я открóю окнó, éсли вы не возражáете.
objection /əbˈdʒekʃ(ə)n/ *n.* возражéние, протéст; **I have no ~ to your going abroad** я не возражáю (*or* я ничегó не имéю) прóтив вáшей поéздки за грани́цу.
objectionable /əbˈdʒekʃənəb(ə)l/ *adj.* нежелáтельный; неприéмлемый.
objective /əbˈdʒektɪv/ *n.* цель.
■ *adj.* объекти́вный.
objectivity /ɒbdʒekˈtɪvɪtɪ/ *n.* объекти́вность.
objector /əbˈdʒektə(r)/ *n.* возражáющий; **conscientious ~** человéк, откáзывающийся от воéнной слýжбы из принципиáльных соображéний.
obligate /ˈɒblɪgeɪt/ *v.t.* обя́з|ывать, -áть.
obligation /ɒblɪˈgeɪʃ(ə)n/ *n.* (*promise, commitment*) обязáтельство; (*duty, responsibility*) обя́занность; **be under an ~ to s.o.** быть обя́занным комý-н.
obligatory /əˈblɪgətərɪ/ *adj.* обязáтельный.
oblige /əˈblaɪdʒ/ *v.t.*
1 (*compel*) вынуждáть, вы́нудить; **we are ~d to remind you** мы вы́нуждены напóмнить вам.
2 (*do favour to*) обя́з|ывать, -áть; **I am much ~d to you** я вам óчень обя́зан/благодáрен.
obliging /əˈblaɪdʒɪŋ/ *adj.* услýжливый.
oblique /əˈbliːk/ *adj.*
1 (*slanting*) косóй.
2 (*gram. and fig.*) кóсвенный.
obliterate /əˈblɪtəreɪt/ *v.t.* (*lit.*, *fig.*) ст|ирáть, -ерéть (с лицá земли́).
obliteration /əblɪtəˈreɪʃ(ə)n/ *n.* стирáние.
oblivion /əˈblɪvɪən/ *n.* забвéние.
oblivious /əˈblɪvɪəs/ *adj.*: **to be ~ of** не имéть никакóго поня́тия о + *p.*; **he was ~ to her objections** он был глух к её возражéниям.
oblong /ˈɒblɒŋ/ *n.* продолговáтая фигýра.
■ *adj.* продолговáтый.
obnoxious /əbˈnɒkʃəs/ *adj.* проти́вный.

oboe /'əʊbəʊ/ *n.* гобо́й.
oboist /'əʊbəʊist/ *n.* гобои́ст (*fem.* -ка).
obscene /əb'si:n/ *adj.* непристо́йный.
obscenit|y /əb'senɪtɪ/ *n.* непристо́йность.
obscure /əb'skjʊə(r)/ *adj.* 1 (*not easily understood*) нея́сный. 2 (*little known*) малоизве́стный. ■ *v.t.* (*darken; also fig.*) затемн|я́ть, -и́ть; (*conceal from sight*) заслон|я́ть, -и́ть.
obscurity /əb'skjʊərɪtɪ/ *n.* (*lack of clarity*) нея́сность; (*being unknown*) безве́стность.
obsequious /əb'si:kwɪəs/ *adj.* подобостра́стный, раболе́пный.
observable /əb'zə:vəb(ə)l/ *adj.* заме́тный, различи́мый.
observance /əb'zə:v(ə)ns/ *n.* 1 (*of rule, law, custom etc.*) соблюде́ние. 2 (*rite, ceremony*) обря́д; (*ritual*) ритуа́л.
observant /əb'zə:v(ə)nt/ *adj.* наблюда́тельный; внима́тельный.
observation /ɒbzə'veɪʃ(ə)n/ *n.* наблюде́ние; **keep s.o. under ~** держа́ть (*impf.*) кого́-н. под наблюде́нием.
observatory /əb'zə:vətərɪ/ *n.* обсервато́рия.
observe /əb'zə:v/ *v.t.* 1 (*notice*) зам|еча́ть, -е́тить; (*see*) ви́деть, у-. 2 (*watch*) наблюда́ть (*impf.*) за + *i.* 3 (*remark*) зам|еча́ть, -е́тить.
observer /əb'zə:və(r)/ *n.* наблюда́тель (*m.*).
obsess /əb'ses/ *v.t.* завлад|ева́ть, -е́ть (*чьим-н.*) умо́м.
obsession /əb'seʃ(ə)n/ *n.* (*being obsessed*) одержи́мость; (*fixed idea*) навя́зчивая иде́я.
obsessive /əb'sesɪv/ *adj.* навя́зчивый.
obsolescence /ɒbsə'les(ə)ns/ *n.* устарева́ние; **planned, built-in ~** запланиро́ванная устаре́лость (*товара*).
obsolescent /ɒbsə'les(ə)nt/ *adj.* устарева́ющий.
obsolete /'ɒbsəli:t/ *adj.* устаре́лый; **become ~** выходи́ть, вы́йти из употребле́ния; отж|ива́ть, -и́ть.
obstacle /'ɒbstək(ə)l/ *n.* препя́тствие; **~ course** (*sport*) полоса́ препя́тствий; **~ race** бег/ска́чки с препя́тствиями.
obstetric(al) /əb'stetrɪk, əb'stetrɪk(ə)l/ *adj.* акуше́рский, родовспомога́тельный.
obstetrician /ɒbstə'trɪʃ(ə)n/ *n.* акуше́р (*fem.* -ка).
obstetrics /əb'stetrɪks/ *n.* акуше́рство.
obstinate /'ɒbstɪnət/ *adj.* (*stubborn*) упря́мый; (*persistent*) насто́йчивый.
obstruct /əb'strʌkt/ *v.t.* меша́ть (*impf.*) + *d.*, препя́тствовать (*impf.*) + *d.*; **~ the road** загра|жда́ть, -ди́ть доро́гу; **~ the view** заслон|я́ть, -и́ть вид.
obstruction /əb'strʌkʃ(ə)n/ *n.* загражде́ние; (*hindrance*) препя́тствие.
obstructive /əb'strʌktɪv/ *adj.* (*policy*) препя́тствующий; (*object*) загора́живающий; (*parl.*) обструкцио́нный.
obtain /əb'teɪn/ *v.t.* (*procure*) доб|ыва́ть, -ы́ть; (*acquire*) приобре|та́ть, -сти́.
obtainable /əb'teɪnəb(ə)l/ *adj.* достижи́мый, досту́пный; **is this model still ~?** э́ту моде́ль мо́жно ещё приобрести́?
obtrusive /əb'tru:sɪv/ *adj.* навя́зчивый, назо́йливый.
obtuse /əb'tju:s/ *adj.* (*lit., fig.*) тупо́й.
obviate /'ɒbvɪeɪt/ *v.t.* (*evade, circumvent*) избе|га́ть, -жа́ть + *g.*; (*remove*) устран|я́ть, -и́ть.
obvious /'ɒbvɪəs/ *adj.* очеви́дный, я́сный; **~ly** очеви́дно.
occasion /ə'keɪʒ(ə)n/ *n.* слу́чай; **on many ~s** во мно́гих слу́чаях; ча́сто; **on the ~ of his marriage** по слу́чаю его́ бра́ка; **today is a special ~** сего́дня осо́бый день; **rise to the ~** ока́з|ываться, -а́ться на высоте́ положе́ния.
occasional /ə'keɪʒən(ə)l/ *adj.* случа́йный; (*infrequent*) ре́дкий.
occasionally /ə'keɪʒən(ə)lɪ/ *adv.* вре́мя от вре́мени, поро́й, иногда́, и́зредка.
occult /ɒ'kʌlt/ *n.*: **the ~** оккульти́зм.
occupancy /'ɒkjʊpənsɪ/ *n.* заня́тие; (*taking, holding possession*) завладе́ние; (*holding on lease*) аре́нда, владе́ние.
occupant /'ɒkjʊpənt/ *n.* 1 (*tenant*) жиле́ц, аренда́тор, нанима́тель (*m.*). 2 : **the ~s of the car** е́хавшие в маши́не.
occupation /ɒkjʊ'peɪʃ(ə)n/ *n.* 1 (*taking possession*) завладе́ние. 2 (*mil.*) оккупа́ция; **army of ~** оккупацио́нная а́рмия. 3 (*pastime*) заня́тие, время(пре)провожде́ние. 4 (*employment*) заня́тие; профе́ссия.
occupational /ɒkjʊ'peɪʃən(ə)l/ *adj.* профессиона́льный; **~ hazard** риск, свя́занный с хара́ктером рабо́ты; профессиона́льный/произво́дственный риск.
occupier /'ɒkjʊpaɪə(r)/ *n.* (*Br.*) прожива́ющий.
occup|y /'ɒkjʊpaɪ/ *v.t.* 1 (*take over; take possession of*) зан|има́ть, -я́ть; завлад|ева́ть, -е́ть + *i.* 2 (*employ*): **he ~ies his time with crossword puzzles** он посвяща́ет всё своё вре́мя разга́дыванию/реше́нию кроссво́рдов.
occur /ə'kə:(r)/ *v.i.* (**occurred, occurring**) 1 (*take place*) случ|а́ться, -и́ться. 2 (*of thought*) при|ходи́ть, -йти́ в го́лову, на ум; **it ~red to me that ...** мне пришло́ в го́лову, что... .
occurrence /ə'kʌrəns/ *n.* происше́ствие, слу́чай.
ocean /'əʊʃ(ə)n/ *n.* океа́н.
oceanic /əʊʃɪ'ænɪk/ *adj.* океани́ческий, океа́нский.
oceanographer /əʊʃə'nɒgrəfə(r)/ *n.* океано́граф.
oceanography /əʊʃə'nɒgrəfɪ/ *n.* океаногра́фия.
ochre /'əʊkə(r)/ *n.* (*US* **ocher**) о́хра.
o'clock /ə'klɒk/ *adv.*: **two ~** два часа́; **at 10 ~ at night** в де́сять часо́в ве́чера.
octagon /'ɒktəgən/ *n.* восьмиуго́льник.
octagonal /ɒk'tægən(ə)l/ *adj.* восьмиуго́льный.
octave /'ɒktɪv/ *n.* окта́ва.
October /ɒk'təʊbə(r)/ *n.* октя́брь (*m.*).
octopus /'ɒktəpəs/ *n.* (*pl.* **octopuses**) осьмино́г, спрут.
odd /ɒd/ *adj.*

[1] (*not even*): ~ **numbers** нечётные чи́сла.
[2] (*not matching*) непа́рный; **I was wearing ~ socks** я был в ра́зных носка́х.
[3] (*not in a set*) разро́зненный.
[4] (*with some remainder*) с ли́шним; **40 ~** со́рок с ли́шним (*or* с чем-то).
[5] (*occasional*) случа́йный; **~ jobs** случа́йная рабо́та; **he made the ~ mistake** (*coll.*) ему́ случа́лось ошиба́ться.
[6] (*strange*) стра́нный, эксцентри́чный, чудно́й.

oddity /ˈɒdɪtɪ/ *n.* (*person*) чуда́|к (*fem.* -чка); (*thing*) причу́дливая вещь.

oddly /ˈɒdlɪ/ *adv.*: **~ enough** как (э́то) ни стра́нно; предста́вьте себе́.

odds /ɒdz/ *n. pl.*
[1] (*balance of advantage*): **the ~ are in our favour** переве́с на на́шей стороне́; **the ~ were against his winning** у него́ бы́ло ма́ло ша́нсов на вы́игрыш.
[2] (*betting*): **long ~** нера́вные ша́нсы (*m. pl.*); **short ~** почти́ ра́вные ша́нсы.
[3] (*variance*): **be at ~ with s.o.** не ла́дить (*impf.*) с кем-н.
[4] : **~ and ends** (*leftovers*) оста́тки (*m. pl.*); (*sundries*) вся́кая вся́чина.

ode /əʊd/ *n.* о́да.

odious /ˈəʊdɪəs/ *adj.* (*hateful*) ненави́стный, одио́зный; (*foul, vile*) гну́сный; (*repulsive*) отврати́тельный.

odour /ˈəʊdə(r)/ (*US* **odor**) *n.* (*smell*) за́пах.

odyssey /ˈɒdɪsɪ/ *n.* (*pl.* **~s**) одиссе́я, приключе́ния (*nt. pl.*).

oedema /ɪˈdiːmə/ (*US* **edema**) *n.* отёк.

oesopha|gus /iːˈsɒfəgəs/ (*US* **esophagus**) *n.* (*pl.* **~gi** /-dʒaɪ/ *or* **~guses**) пищево́д.

oestrogen /ˈiːstrədʒ(ə)n/ (*US* **estrogen**) *n.* эстроге́н.

O

of /ɒv/ *prep., expr. by g. and/or var. preps.*:
[1] (*origin*): **Lawrence ~ Arabia** Ло́уренс Арави́йский.
[2] (*cause*): **he died ~ fright** он у́мер от испу́га.
[3] (*material*) из + *g.*; **what is it made ~?** из чего́ э́то сде́лано?
[4] (*composition*): **a bunch ~ keys** свя́зка ключе́й; **a family ~ 8** семья́ из восьми́ челове́к.
[5] (*contents*): **a bottle ~ milk** (*full*) буты́лка молока́.
[6] (*qualities*): **a man ~ ability** спосо́бный челове́к.
[7] (*possession*): **the property ~ the state** госуда́рственная со́бственность.
[8] (*partitive*): **some ~ us** не́которые/ко́е-кто из нас; **a quarter ~ an hour** че́тверть ча́са; **most ~ all** осо́бенно; бо́льше всего́/всех; **a friend ~ ours** оди́н из на́ших знако́мых.
[9] (*separation, distance*): **within 10 miles ~ London** в десяти́ ми́лях от Ло́ндона.

off /ɒf/ *adj.*
[1] (*nearer to centre of road*): **on the ~ side** (*in Britain*) на пра́вой стороне́.
[2] (*improbable*): **I went on the ~ chance of finding him in** я пошёл туда́ наудачу — вдруг заста́ну (его́).
[3] (*substandard*): **it was one of my ~ days** в тот день я был не в са́мой лу́чшей фо́рме.
[4] (*inactive*): **the ~ season** мёртвый сезо́н.

■ *adv.* [1] (*away*): **two miles ~** в двух ми́лях отту́да/отсю́да; **the elections are still two years ~** до вы́боров ещё два го́да; **it's time I was ~; I must be ~** мне пора́ (уходи́ть).
[2] (*disconnected*): **the electricity was ~** электри́чество бы́ло отключено́.
[3] (*ended, cancelled*): **their engagement is ~** их помо́лвка расто́ргнута; **the match is ~** матч отменён.
[4] (*not working*): **day ~** выходно́й (день); **he was ~ sick** он отсу́тствовал/не́ был на рабо́те по боле́зни.
[5] (*not fresh*): **the fish is ~** ры́ба испо́ртилась (*or* с душко́м (*coll.*)).
■ *prep.* (*from; away from; up or down from*): **the car went ~ the road** маши́на съе́хала с доро́ги; **~ work** не на рабо́те; **he fell ~ the ladder** он упа́л с ле́стницы; **he took 50p ~ the price** он сни́зил це́ну на пятьдеся́т пе́нсов; он сба́вил с цены́ пятьдеся́т пе́нсов; (*disinclined for*): **he is ~ his food** он потеря́л аппети́т.

offal /ˈɒf(ə)l/ *n.* (*of meat*) потроха́ (*m. pl.*); (*entrails*) требуха́.

offence /əˈfens/ (*US* **offense**) *n.*
[1] (*crime*) правонаруше́ние, преступле́ние.
[2] (*affront*) оби́да; **cause, give ~ to** оскорб|ля́ть, -и́ть.
[3] (*mil.*) наступле́ние.

offend /əˈfend/ *v.t.* об|ижа́ть, -и́деть.
■ *v.i.* греши́ть (*impf.*).

offender /əˈfendə(r)/ *n.* (*against law*) правонаруши́тель (*m.*) (*fem.* -ница).

offense /əˈfens/ (*US*) = **offence**

offensive /əˈfensɪv/ *n.* нападе́ние; (*mil.*) наступле́ние; **go on the ~** пере|ходи́ть, -йти́ в наступле́ние; (*fig.*) зан|има́ть, -я́ть наступа́тельную пози́цию.
■ *adj.* (*causing offence*) оскорби́тельный; (*of person*) отврати́тельный, проти́вный.

offer /ˈɒfə(r)/ *n.*
[1] предложе́ние.
[2] : **be on ~** (*Br., for sale at reduced price*) прод|ава́ться, -а́ться со ски́дкой.
■ *v.t.* предл|ага́ть, -ожи́ть; **he ~ed me a drink** он предложи́л мне вы́пить; **~ an opinion** выража́ть, вы́разить своё мне́ние; **he did not ~ to help** он не предложи́л помо́чь.

offering /ˈɒfərɪŋ/ *n.*
[1] (*sacrifice*) подноше́ние, же́ртва.
[2] (*contribution*) поже́ртвование.

offhand /ɒfˈhænd, ˈɒfhænd/ *adj.* развя́зный, бесцеремо́нный.
■ *adv.* сра́зу, без подгото́вки.

office /ˈɒfɪs/ *n.*
[1] (*position of responsibility*) до́лжность, слу́жба; **the party in ~** па́ртия, находя́щаяся у вла́сти; **he held ~ for 10 years** он занима́л до́лжность/пост де́сять лет.
[2] (*premises*) о́фис, конто́ра, канцеля́рия; **~ block** администрати́вное зда́ние; **~ hours** часы́ рабо́ты; рабо́чее/служе́бное вре́мя.
[3] (*for services*) бюро́ (*nt. indecl.*); **booking ~** биле́тная ка́сса.

officer /ˈɒfɪsə(r)/ *n.*
[1] (*in armed forces*) офице́р.
[2] (*official*) должностно́е лицо́, чино́вник;

customs ~ тамо́женник.

official /əˈfɪʃ(ə)l/ *n.* должностно́е лицо́, чино́вник.
■ *adj.* (*authoritative*) официа́льный; (*relating to office*) служе́бный, должностно́й.

officiate /əˈfɪʃɪeɪt/ *v.i.* (*be in charge*) распоряжа́ться (*impf.*); (*at church service*) соверш|а́ть, -и́ть богослуже́ние; **~ at a wedding** соверш|а́ть, -и́ть обря́д бракосочета́ния; **~ as chairman** председа́тельствовать (*impf.*).

officious /əˈfɪʃəs/ *adj.* навя́зчивый, назо́йливый.

offing /ˈɒfɪŋ/ *n.*: **in the ~** (*fig.*) в перспекти́ве.

off-key /ɒfˈkiː/ *adj.* (*lit., fig.*) фальши́вый.

off-licence /ˈɒflaɪs(ə)ns/ *n.* (*Br.*) ви́нный магази́н.

offline /ɒfˈlaɪn/ *adj.* (*comput.*) автоно́мный, офла́йновый; (*disconnected*) отключённый.

offload /ɒfˈləʊd/ *v.t.* разгру|жа́ть, -зи́ть.

off-peak /ˈɒfpiːk/ *adj.* непи́ковый.

off-putting /ˈɒfpʊtɪŋ/ *adj.* (*coll.*) отта́лкивающий.

off season /ˈɒfsiːz(ə)n/ *n.* межсезо́нье.
■ *adj.* несезо́нный.

offset /ˈɒfset/ *v.t.*
1 (*take into consideration*) засчи́т|ывать, -а́ть; **donations to charity can be ~ against tax** поже́ртвования на благотвори́тельные це́ли мо́гут засчи́тываться при упла́те нало́гов.
2 (*compensate for*) возме|ща́ть, -сти́ть.

offshoot /ˈɒfʃuːt/ *n.* побе́г; (*fig.*) о́трасль.

offshore /ˈɒfʃɔː(r)/ *adj.* (*close to shore*) прибре́жный; (*at a distance*) морско́й; (*foreign*) заграни́чный; (*fin.*) офшо́рный.

offside /ɒfˈsaɪd/ *n.* (*football*) положе́ние вне игры́, офса́йд.

offspring /ˈɒfsprɪŋ/ *n.* (*pl.* **~**) пото́мок, о́тпрыск; (*pl.*) пото́мство.

offstage /ɒfˈsteɪdʒ/ *adj.* реа́льный.

off-the-cuff /ɒfðəˈkʌf/ *adj.* импровизи́рованный.

off-the-record /ɒfðəˈrekɔːd/ *adj.* неофициа́льный.

off-white /ˈɒfwaɪt/ *adj.* гря́зно-бе́лый.

often /ˈɒf(ə)n/ *adv.* (**oftener, oftenest**) ча́сто; **every so ~** вре́мя от вре́мени.

ogle /ˈəʊg(ə)l/ *v.t.* пожира́ть (*impf.*) глаза́ми.

ogre /ˈəʊgə(r)/ *n.* велика́н-людое́д; (*fig.*) стра́шный челове́к.

oh /əʊ/ *int.* о!, ах!; (*expr. surprise, fright, pain*) ой!

ohm /əʊm/ *n.* ом.

oil /ɔɪl/ *n.*
1 ма́сло; **engine ~** маши́нное ма́сло.
2 (*petroleum*) нефть.
■ *v.t.* (*lubricate*) сма́з|ывать, -ать.
■ *cpds.* **~field** *n.* месторожде́ние не́фти; **~ painting** *n.* ма́сло, холст, карти́на; **~ rig** *n.* нефтяна́я вы́шка; **~skin** *n.* непромока́емый костю́м; **~ slick** *n.* плёнка не́фти на воде́; **~ tanker** *n.* (*ship*) та́нкер; (*vehicle*) нефтево́з; **~ well** *n.* нефтяна́я сква́жина.

oily /ˈɔɪlɪ/ *adj.* (**oilier, oiliest**) ма́сляный.

ointment /ˈɔɪntmənt/ *n.* мазь.

OK, okay /əʊˈkeɪ/ *n.* (*pl.* **~s**) (*coll.*) одобре́ние, «добро́».
■ *adj.* (*safe, well*): **she is ~** она́ в поря́дке; (*acceptable*): **are you sure it's ~?** э́то ничего́?; **I'll be back soon, ~?** я ско́ро верну́сь, ла́дно?
■ *adv.*: **the meeting went off ~** собра́ние прошло́ норма́льно; **he is doing ~** у него́ всё хорошо́/норма́льно.
■ *v.t.* (**OK's, OK'd, OK'ing**) од|обря́ть, -о́брить.
■ *int.* ла́дно!, хорошо́!

old /əʊld/ *n.*: **the ~** (*people*) старики́ (*m. pl.*), пожилы́е/престаре́лые (лю́ди).
■ *adj.* (**older, oldest**)
1 ста́рый; (*object, house*) стари́нный; **~ age** ста́рость; **~-age pension** (*Br.*) пе́нсия по ста́рости; **~ man** (*also coll., husband or father*) стари́к; **~ woman** (*also coll., wife*) стару́ха; **~ people's/folk's home** дом престаре́лых; **grow ~** ста́риться, со-.
2 (*expr. age*): **how ~ is he?** ско́лько ему́ лет?; **my son is 4 years ~** моему́ сы́ну четы́ре го́да.
3 (*longstanding*) стари́нный, давни́шний; **they are ~ friends** они́ стари́нные/да́вние друзья́.
4 (*former*) бы́вший, пре́жний.
■ *cpd.* **~-fashioned** *adj.* старомо́дный.

oligarch /ˈɒlɪgɑːk/ *n.* олига́рх.

oligarchic(al) /ɒlɪˈgɑːkɪk, ɒlɪˈgɑːkɪk(ə)l/ *adj.* олигархи́ческий.

oligarchy /ˈɒlɪgɑːkɪ/ *n.* олига́рхия.

olive /ˈɒlɪv/ *n.* масли́на.
■ *adj.* оли́вковый; **~ oil** оли́вковое ма́сло.

Olympic /əˈlɪmpɪk/ *adj.*: **~ Games, ~s** Олимпи́йские и́гры.

ombudsman /ˈɒmbʊdzmən/ *n.* о́мбудсмен; уполномо́ченный по права́м челове́ка.

omelet(te) /ˈɒmlɪt/ *n.* омле́т.

omen /ˈəʊmən/ *n.* знак.

ominous /ˈɒmɪnəs/ *adj.* злове́щий.

omission /əˈmɪʃ(ə)n/ *n.* про́пуск.

omit /əˈmɪt/ *v.t.* (**omitted, omitting**) пропус|ка́ть, -ти́ть.

omnibus /ˈɒmnɪbəs/ *n.*
1 (*obs.*) о́мнибус, авто́бус.
2 (**~** *volume*) сбо́рник, антоло́гия.

omnipotence /ɒmˈnɪpət(ə)ns/ *n.* всемогу́щество.

omnipotent /ɒmˈnɪpət(ə)nt/ *adj.* всемогу́щий.

omnipresent /ɒmnɪˈprez(ə)nt/ *adj.* вездесу́щий.

omniscience /ɒmˈnɪsɪəns/ *n.* всеве́дение.

omniscient /ɒmˈnɪsɪənt/ *adj.* всеве́дущий.

omnivorous /ɒmˈnɪvərəs/ *adj.* всея́дный.

on /ɒn/ *adv.*
1 (*expr. continuation*): **straight ~** пря́мо; **and so ~** и так да́лее; **from now ~** (начина́я) с э́того дня; **he went ~ (and ~) about his dog** он без конца́ говори́л о свое́й соба́ке; (*expr. extension*): **further ~** да́льше; **later ~** по́зже.
2 (*placed, spread etc.* **~** *sth.*): **he had his glasses ~** он был в очка́х; он наде́л очки́.
3 (*arranged, available*): **what's ~ tonight?** (*TV*) что сего́дня по програ́мме?; что сего́дня

O

показывают?; **is the match still ~?** матч не отменили/отменён?
4 (*turned, switched* ~): **the kettle is ~** чайник поставлен/включён; **the light is ~** свет включён; **the radio was ~ full blast** радио было включено на всю мощь.
5 : **it's not ~** (*coll., feasible*) так не пойдёт.
■ *prep.* 1 (*expr. position*) на + *p.*; **~ the table** на столе; (*supported by*): **stand ~ one leg** стоять (*impf.*) на одной ноге; **the look ~ his face** выражение его лица; (*as means of transport*) на + *p.*; **~ horseback** верхом; **~ foot** пешком; **I came ~ the bus** я приехал на автобусе; (~ *one's person*): **I have no money ~ me** у меня нет при себе денег; (*expr. relative position*): **~ my left** слева от меня.
2 (*expr. final position*) на + *a.*; **he sat down ~ the sofa** он сел на диван.
3 (*expr. point of contact*): **he hit me ~ the head** он ударил меня по голове; **he knocked ~ the door** он постучал в дверь; **she dried her hands ~ a towel** она вытерла руки полотенцем.
4 (*of a medium of communication*) по + *d.*; **~ the radio/telephone/television** по радио/телефону/телевизору.
5 (*expr. time*): **~ Tuesday** во вторник; **~ time** вовремя; своевременно; **~ the 8th of May** восьмого мая; **~ Tuesdays** по вторникам.
6 (*immediately after*): **~ his arrival** по его приезде; **~ seeing him she ran off** увидев его, она убежала; (*during*): **~ my way home** по дороге домой.
7 (*concerning*): **an article ~ Pushkin** статья о Пушкине.
8 (*at the expense of*): **drinks are ~ me** я угощаю; **the joke was ~ me** шутка обернулась против меня.
9 (*taking drugs etc.*): **he's ~ drugs** он (регулярно) принимает наркотики.

on-board /ˈɒnbɔːd/ *adj.* бортовой.

once /wʌns/ *adv.*
1 (один) раз; **~ again, more** ещё раз.
2 (*as soon as*): **~ you hesitate you are lost** стоит (только) заколебаться, и ты пропал.
3 (*at one time, formerly*) некогда; одно время; однажды; когда-то; **~ upon a time there was** (давным-давно) жил-был.
4 : **at ~** (*immediately*) сейчас же; (*simultaneously*) в то же время.
■ *cpd.* **~-over** *n.* (*coll.*): **give s.o./sth. the ~-over** бегло осм|атривать, -отреть кого/что-н.

oncologist /ɒŋˈkɒlədʒɪst/ *n.* онколог.

oncology /ɒŋˈkɒlədʒɪ/ *n.* онкология.

oncoming /ˈɒnkʌmɪŋ/ *adj.* приближающийся, наступающий.

one /wʌn/ *n.*
1 (*number*) один; (*in counting*): **~, 2, 3** раз/один, два, три.
2 (*hour*) час; **~ o'clock** (*a.m.*) час ночи; (*p.m.*) час дня.
3 (*age*): **he's only ~** ему всего/только год(ик).
4 (*person*): **little ~s** дети; **our loved ~s** наши близкие; **he is not ~ to refuse** он не из тех, кто отказывается.
5 (*member of a group*) один; **~ of my friends** один из моих друзей; **the ~ with the beard** тот(, который) с бородой; **I for ~ don't believe him** что касается меня, то я не верю ему; **~ of these days** как-нибудь на днях; **~ another** друг друга; **~ after the other; ~ by ~** один за другим; **~ at a time** по одному; по очереди.
6 (*referring to category understood*): **which book do you want, the red or the green ~?** какую книгу вы хотите, красную или зелёную?
■ *pron.*: **~ never knows** никогда не знаешь; **~ gets used to anything** человек ко всему привыкает.
■ *adj.* 1 один; **price ~ rouble** цена (один) рубль; (*with pluralia tantum*) одни; **~ watch** одни часы.
2 (*only*) единственный; **the ~ way to do it** единственный способ сделать это.
3 (*the same*) тот же самый.
4 (*particular but unspecified*): **~ evening** как-то/однажды вечером; **~ day** (*in past*) однажды; (*in future*) когда-нибудь.
■ *cpds.* **~-off** *adj.* (*Br. coll.*) уникальный, единственный; **~-parent family** *n.* семья с одним родителем; **~-sided** *adj.* (*prejudiced*) однобокий, односторонний; **~-time** *adj.* бывший; былой; **~-to-one** *adj.* непосредственный; **~-way** *adj.*: **~-way traffic** одностороннее движение; **~-way street** улица с односторонним движением; **~-way ticket** билет в одну сторону (*or* в одном направлении).

onerous /ˈəʊnərəs/ *adj.* обременительный, тягостный.

oneself /wʌnˈself/ *pron.* (*refl.*) себя, -ся (*suff.*); **talk to ~** говорить (*impf.*) с самим собой.

ongoing /ˈɒngəʊɪŋ/ *adj.* (*continuing*): **~ process** поступательный процесс; (*in progress*) текущий.

onion /ˈʌnjən/ *n.* луковица; (*pl., collect.*) (репчатый) лук.

online /ɒnˈlaɪn/ *adj.* (*comput.*) (*information, program*) онлайновый, диалоговый, интерактивный; (*connected*) подключённый.

onlooker /ˈɒnlʊkə(r)/ *n.* зритель (*m.*).

only /ˈəʊnlɪ/ *adj.* единственный; **she was an ~ child** она была единственным ребёнком; **I was the ~ one there** кроме меня там никого не было.
■ *adv.* только; всего; **~ just** (*recently*) только что; (*barely*) едва; **I have ~ just arrived** я только что прибыл; **he was ~ just in time** он едва успел; **if ~ you knew** если бы вы только знали; **the soup was ~ warm** суп был еле тёплый.
■ *conj.* но; **I would go myself, ~ I'm tired** я пошёл бы сам, но я устал.

onomatopoeia /ɒnəmætəˈpiːə/ *n.* звукоподражание.

on-screen /ɒnˈskriːn/ *adj.* (*comput.*) экранный; **follow the ~ instructions** следуйте инструкциям на экране.

onset /ˈɒnset/ *n.* начало, наступление.

on-site /ˈɒnsaɪt/ *adj.* на местах/месте.

onslaught /ˈɒnslɔːt/ *n.* атака, нападение.

onto /ˈɒntuː/ = **on** *prep.* **2**

onus /ˈəʊnəs/ *n.* (*pl.* **onuses**) бремя,

ответственность.
onward /'ɒnwəd/ *adj.* продвигающийся.
■ *adv.* (*also* **~s**) вперёд, далее; **from now ~** впредь, отныне; **from then ~** с тех пор; (*in future*) с того времени.
oops! /ʊps/ *int.* (*coll.*) ой!
ooze /u:z/ *v.t.* (*emit*): **the wound ~d blood** из раны сочилась кровь; (*fig.*): **he ~d self-confidence** он источал самоуверенность.
■ *v.i.* медленно течь (*impf.*).
opal /'əʊp(ə)l/ *n.* опал.
opaque /əʊ'peɪk/ *adj.* (**opaquer, opaquest**) непрозрачный.
open /'əʊpən/ *n.*
1 (*~ space*; *~ air*) открытое пространство; **in the ~** под открытым небом.
2 (*fig.*): **bring sth. into the ~** выявлять, выявить.
■ *adj.* 1 открытый; **in the ~ air** на открытом воздухе; **~ competition** открытое соревнование; **~ contempt** явное/нескрываемое презрение; **in ~ country** на открытой местности; **~ day** (*Br., at school*) день открытых дверей; **~ market** открытый рынок; **have an ~ mind on sth.** не иметь предвзятого мнения о + *p.*; **on the ~ road** на пустой/свободной дороге; **~ ticket** билет с открытой датой; **the door flew ~** дверь распахнулась.
2 (*accessible, available*) доступный; **the road is ~ to traffic** дорога открыта для движения.
3 (*frank*) открытый, откровенный.
■ *v.t.* 1 откр|ывать, -ыть; (*book, newspaper*) откр|ывать, -ыть; раскр|ывать, -ыть.
2 (*fig.*): **he ~ed an account** он открыл счёт; **a new business has been ~ed** открыли новый бизнес.
■ *v.i.* 1 откр|ываться, -ыться.
2 (*fig., begin*) нач|инаться, -аться; **the play ~s with a long speech** пьеса начинается длинным монологом; **the new play ~s on Saturday** новая пьеса идёт с субботы.
3 (*of door etc.*): **the windows ~ on to a courtyard** окна выходят во двор.
■ *with adv.*: **~ up** *v.t.*: **he ~ed up the boot (of the car)** он открыл багажник; *v.i.*: **he ~ed up about his visit** он откровенно рассказал о своей поездке.
■ *cpds.* **~-air** *adj.*: **~-air life** жизнь на открытом воздухе; **~-heart** *adj.*: **~-heart operation** операция, проводимая на отключённом сердце; **~-minded** *adj.* непредвзятый, непредубеждённый; **~-plan** *adj.* с открытой планировкой.
opener /'əʊpənə(r)/ *n.* консервный нож.
opening /'əʊpənɪŋ/ *n.*
1 (*aperture*) отверстие.
2 (*beginning*) начало; (*of play, speech*) вступление.
3 (*job*) место, вакансия.
■ *adj.* (*initial*) начальный, первый; **~ remarks** вступительные замечания; (*working*): **~ hours** рабочие часы; часы работы.
openly /'əʊpənlɪ/ *adv.* открыто; (*frankly*) откровенно; (*publicly*) публично, открыто.
openness /'əʊpənnɪs/ *n.* (*frankness*) открытость, откровенность; (*pol.*) гласность.
opera /'ɒpərə/ *n.* опера.
■ *cpds.* **~ glass** *n.* театральный бинокль; **~ house** *n.* оперный театр.
operable /'ɒpərəb(ə)l/ *adj.*
1 (*med.*) операбельный.
2 (*workable*) действующий, функционирующий.
operate /'ɒpəreɪt/ *v.t.*
1 (*control work of*) управлять (*impf.*) + *i.*; **the machine is ~d by electricity** эта машина работает на электричестве.
2 (*put into effect*): **we ~ a simple system** мы применяем простую систему.
■ *v.i.* 1 (*work, act*) работать (*impf.*); **the brakes failed to ~** тормоза отказали.
2 : **~ on** (*med.*) оперировать (*impf., pf.*) (**for:** по поводу + *g.*).
operatic /ɒpə'rætɪk/ *adj.* оперный.
operating /'ɒpəreɪtɪŋ/ *adj.*
1 (*med.*): **~ room** (*US*), **theatre** (*Br.*) операционная.
2 (*comput.*): **~ system** операционная система.
operation /ɒpə'reɪʃ(ə)n/ *n.*
1 (*action, effect*) действие; работа; **bring into ~** прив|одить, -ести в действие.
2 (*process*) процесс, операция.
3 (*control*) эксплуатация, управление.
4 (*med.*) операция.
5 (*mil.*) операция, действия (*nt. pl.*).
operational /ɒpə'reɪʃən(ə)l/ *adj.* действующий; **the factory is fully ~** завод полностью готов к эксплуатации.
operative /'ɒpərətɪv/ *n.* (*machine operator*) станочник; квалифицированный рабочий; оператор (*какого-н. устройства*).
■ *adj.* действенный.
operator /'ɒpəreɪtə(r)/ *n.*
1 (*one who works a machine*) оператор.
2 (*telephonist*) телефонист (*fem.* -ка).
operetta /ɒpə'retə/ *n.* оперетта.
ophthalmic /ɒf'θælmɪk/ *adj.* глазной; **~ optician** (*Br.*) окулист.
ophthalmologist /ɒfθæl'mɒlɒdʒɪst/ *n.* офтальмолог.
ophthalmology /ɒfθæl'mɒlədʒɪ/ *n.* офтальмология.
opiate /'əʊpɪət/ *n.* опиат; (*fig.*) опиум.
opinion /ə'pɪnjən/ *n.* (*judgement*) мнение; (*view*) взгляд; **in my ~** по моему мнению, по-моему, на мой взгляд; **~ poll** опрос общественного мнения; (*estimate*): **have a high/low ~ of** быть высокого/невысокого мнения о + *p.*
opinionated /ə'pɪnjəneɪtɪd/ *adj.* догматичный.
opium /'əʊpɪəm/ *n.* опиум.
opponent /ə'pəʊnənt/ *n.* оппонент, противник; (*sport*) противник, соперник.
opportune /'ɒpətju:n/ *adj.* своевременный, уместный.
opportunism /ɒpə'tju:nɪz(ə)m/ *n.* оппортунизм.
opportunist /ɒpə'tju:nɪst/ *n.* оппортунист.
■ *adj.* оппортунистический.
opportunistic /ɒpətju:'nɪstɪk/ *adj.* оппортунистический.
opportunity /ɒpə'tju:nɪtɪ/ *n.* (*favourable circumstance*) удобный случай; (*good chance*)

O

возмóжность; **he took the ~ to ...** он воспóльзовался слýчаем, чтóбы... .

oppos|e /ə'pəʊz/ *v.t.*
1 (*set against*): **as ~ed to** в отли́чие от + *g.*; **I am firmly ~ed to the idea** я реши́тельно прóтив э́той идéи.
2 (*set o.s. against*): **the ~ing side** проти́вная сторонá; (*sport*) комáнда проти́вника; (*show opposition to*) проти́виться (*impf.*) + *d.*

opposite /'ɒpəzɪt/ *n.* противополóжность; **just the ~** как раз наоборóт.
■ *adj.* противополóжный; **his house is ~ ours** егó дом (стои́т) напрóтив нáшего; **in the ~ direction** в обрáтном направлéнии; **~ number** лицó, занимáющее такýю же дóлжность в другóй организáции.
■ *adv.* напрóтив.
■ *prep.* (на)прóтив + *g.*

opposition /ɒpə'zɪʃ(ə)n/ *n.*
1 (*resistance*) сопротивлéние, противодéйствие; **he offered no ~** он не оказáл никакóго сопротивлéния.
2 (*Br., pol.*) оппози́ция.

oppress /ə'pres/ *v.t.* угнетáть (*impf.*).

oppression /ə'preʃ(ə)n/ *n.* (*oppressing*) угнетéние, гнёт, притеснéние, тирани́я; (*being oppressed*) угнетённость.

oppressive /ə'presɪv/ *adj.* угнетáющий, давя́щий; **~ weather** угнетáющая/дýшная погóда.

oppressor /ə'presə(r)/ *n.* угнетáтель (*m.*).

opt /ɒpt/ *v.i.*: **~ for** выбирáть, вы́брать; **~ out of** откáз|ываться, -áться от учáстия в + *p.*
■ *cpd.* **~-out** *n.* откáз от учáстия в чём-н.

optic /'ɒptɪk/ *adj.*: **~ nerve** зри́тельный нерв.

optical /'ɒptɪk(ə)l/ *adj.* опти́ческий; **~ illusion** опти́ческий обмáн.

optician /ɒp'tɪʃ(ə)n/ *n.* окули́ст.

optics /'ɒptɪks/ *n.* óптика.

optimism /'ɒptɪmɪz(ə)m/ *n.* оптими́зм.

optimist /'ɒptɪmɪst/ *n.* оптими́ст (*fem.* -ка).

optimistic /ɒptɪ'mɪstɪk/ *adj.* оптимисти́ческий, оптимисти́чный.

optimize /'ɒptɪmaɪz/ *v.t.* оптимизи́ровать (*impf., pf.*).

optimum /'ɒptɪməm/ *adj.* оптимáльный.

option /'ɒpʃ(ə)n/ *n.* вы́бор; **I have no ~ but to ...** у меня́ нет другóго вы́бора, (крóме) как... .

optional /'ɒpʃən(ə)l/ *adj.* необязáтельный.

optometrist /ɒp'tɒmɪtrɪst/ *n.* (*US*) окули́ст.

opulence /'ɒpjʊləns/ *n.* богáтство, оби́лие, изоби́лие.

opulent /'ɒpjʊlənt/ *adj.* (*wealthy*) богáтый; (*abundant*) оби́льный.

or /ɔ:(r)/ *conj.*
1 и́ли; **two ~ three** два-три.
2 (*~ else*) и́ли, инáче; и́ли же; а (не) то; **we must hurry ~ we'll be late** нýжно поторáпливаться, а то опоздáем.
3 : **there were 20 ~ so people present** там бы́ло человéк 20 (*or* óколо двадцати́ человéк).

oral /'ɔ:r(ə)l/ *n.* ýстный экзáмен.
■ *adj.* (*by word of mouth*) ýстный; (*pert. to mouth*) стоматологи́ческий; (*contraceptive, sex*) орáльный; **~ hygiene** гигиéна пóлости рта.

orange /'ɒrɪndʒ/ *n.*
1 (*fruit*) апельси́н.
2 (*tree*) апельси́новое дéрево.
3 (*colour*) орáнжевый цвет.
■ *adj.* (*colour*) орáнжевый.
■ *cpd.* **~ juice** *n.* апельси́новый сок.

orang-utan /ɔ:ræŋu:'tæn/ *n.* орангутáн(г).

oration /ɔ:'reɪʃ(ə)n/ *n.* речь.

orator /'ɒrətə(r)/ *n.* орáтор.

orbit /'ɔ:bɪt/ *n.* орби́та.
■ *v.i.* (**orbited, orbiting**) (*move in ~*) вращáться (*impf.*) по орби́те.

orchard /'ɔ:tʃəd/ *n.* (фруктóвый) сад.

orchestra /'ɔ:kɪstrə/ *n.* оркéстр.

orchestral /ɔ:'kestr(ə)l/ *adj.* оркестрóвый.

orchestrate /'ɔ:kɪstreɪt/ *v.t.* оркестровáть (*impf., pf.*); (*fig.*) организóв|ывать, -áть.

orchestration /ɔ:kɪ'streɪʃ(ə)n/ *n.* оркестрóвка.

orchid /'ɔ:kɪd/ *n.* орхидéя.

ordain /ɔ:'deɪn/ *v.t.*
1 (*eccl.*) посвя|щáть, -ти́ть в духóвный сан.
2 (*destine*) предпи́с|ывать, -áть.

ordeal /ɔ:'di:l/ *n.* мýка.

order /'ɔ:də(r)/ *n.*
1 (*arrangement*) поря́док; (*sequence, succession*) послéдовательность; **in alphabetical ~** в алфави́тном поря́дке; **in ~ of importance** по стéпени вáжности.
2 (*result of arrangement or control*) поря́док; **everything is in ~** всё в поря́дке; (*settled state*): **restore ~** восстан|áвливать, -ови́ть поря́док; **out of ~** неиспрáвный, в плохóм состоя́нии.
3 (*instruction*) прикáз, распоряжéние, поручéние; **give an, the ~** отд|авáть, -áть прикáз; **under s.o.'s ~s** под комáндой когó-н.
4 (*direction to supply*) закáз (на + *a.*); **on ~** по закáзу.
5 (*pl., eccl.*): **holy ~s** духóвный сан; **take ~s** прин|имáть, -я́ть духóвный сан.
6 : **in ~ to** (для тогó,) чтóбы + *inf.*; **in ~ that** (для тогó,) чтóбы + *past tense.*
■ *v.t.* 1 (*arrange*) прив|оди́ть, -ести́ в поря́док.
2 (*command*) прикáз|ывать, -áть; распоря|жáться, -ди́ться; **he ~ed the soldiers to leave** он приказáл солдáтам разойти́сь.
3 (*reserve; request*) закáз|ывать, -áть.
4 : **~ s.o. about** комáндовать (*impf.*) + *i.*
■ *cpd.* **~ form** *n.* бланк закáза.

orderliness /'ɔ:dəlɪnɪs/ *n.* (*order*) поря́док; (*methodical nature*) аккурáтность.

orderly /'ɔ:dəlɪ/ *n.* санитáр.
■ *adj.* 1 (*organized*) организóванный.
2 (*quiet, well behaved*) ти́хий, послýшный.

ordinal /'ɔ:dɪn(ə)l/ *n.* (*~ number*) поря́дковое числи́тельное.

ordinary /'ɔ:dɪnərɪ/ *n.*: **out of the ~** необы́чный, незауря́дный.
■ *adj.* (*usual*) обы́чный; (*average*) обыкновéнный; (*normal*) нормáльный.

ordination /ɔ:dɪ'neɪʃ(ə)n/ *n.* (*eccl.*) рукоположéние.

ore /ɔ:(r)/ *n.* рудá.

oregano /ɒrɪ'gɑ:nəʊ/ *n.* души́ца

обыкнове́нная, ди́кий майора́н.

organ /'ɔ:gən/ *n.*
1 (*mus.*) орга́н.
2 (*biol., pol. etc.*) о́рган; ~ **donor** до́нор; ~ **transplant** переса́дка о́ргана.

organic /ɔ:'gænɪk/ *adj.* органи́ческий; ~ **food** натура́льные пищевы́е проду́кты.

organism /'ɔ:gənɪz(ə)m/ *n.* органи́зм.

organist /'ɔ:gənɪst/ *n.* органи́ст (*fem* -ка).

organization /ɔ:gənaɪ'zeɪʃ(ə)n/ *n.* организа́ция.

organizational /ɔ:gənaɪ'zeɪʃən(ə)l/ *adj.* организацио́нный.

organize /'ɔ:gənaɪz/ *v.t.* организо́в|ывать, -а́ть; устр|а́ивать, -о́ить; ~**d crime** организо́ванная престу́пность.

organizer /'ɔ:gənaɪzə(r)/ *n.* организа́тор.

orgasm /'ɔ:gæz(ə)m/ *n.* орга́зм.

orgy /'ɔ:dʒɪ/ *n.* о́ргия; (*fig.*) разгу́л.

Orient /'ɔ:rɪənt/ *n.* Восто́к.
■ *v.t.* = **orient(ate)**

oriental /ɔ:rɪ'ent(ə)l/ *adj.* восто́чный.

orient(ate) /'ɒrɪent(eɪt)/ *v.t.* (*determine position of*) ориенти́ровать (*impf., pf.*) (*pf. also* с-); ~ **o.s.** ориенти́роваться (*impf., pf.*) (*pf. also* с-).

orientation /ɒrɪen'teɪʃ(ə)n/ *n.* (*lit., fig.*) ориентиро́вка, ориента́ция.

orienteering /ɔ:rɪen'tɪərɪŋ/ *n.* спорти́вное ориенти́рование, ориенти́рование на ме́стности.

orifice /'ɒrɪfɪs/ *n.* (*aperture*) отве́рстие; (*mouth*) у́стье.

origin /'ɒrɪdʒɪn/ *n.* нача́ло, исто́чник.

original /ə'rɪdʒɪn(ə)l/ *n.* по́длинник, оригина́л.
■ *adj.* 1 (*first, earliest*) первонача́льный; **the ~ inhabitants** иско́нные жи́тели.
2 (*inventive*) оригина́льный, самобы́тный.

originality /ərɪdʒɪ'nælɪtɪ/ *n.* оригина́льность, самобы́тность.

originally /ə'rɪdʒɪnəlɪ/ *adv.* (*in the first place*) первонача́льно, исхо́дно; (*in origin*) по происхожде́нию.

originate /ə'rɪdʒɪneɪt/ *v.i.* брать, взять нача́ло; (*arise*) возн|ика́ть, -и́кнуть.

ornament /'ɔ:nəmənt/ *n.*
1 (*adornment*) украше́ние.
2 (*decorative article*) орна́мент.

ornamental /ɔ:nə'ment(ə)l/ *adj.* декорати́вный.

ornamentation /ɔ:nəmen'teɪʃ(ə)n/ *n.* украше́ние.

ornate /ɔ:'neɪt/ *adj.* бога́то укра́шенный.

ornithological /ɔ:nɪθə'lɒdʒɪk(ə)l/ *adj.* орнитологи́ческий.

ornithologist /ɔ:nɪ'θɒlədʒɪst/ *n.* орнито́лог.

ornithology /ɔ:nɪ'θɒlədʒɪ/ *n.* орнитоло́гия.

orphan /'ɔ:f(ə)n/ *n.* сирота́ (*c.g.*).

orphanage /'ɔ:fənɪdʒ/ *n.* прию́т для сиро́т.

orthodox /'ɔ:θədɒks/ *adj.* ортодокса́льный, правове́рный; **the O~ Church** правосла́вная це́рковь.

orthodoxy /'ɔ:θədɒksɪ/ *n.* (*relig.*) ортодокса́льность, правове́рность; (*fig.*) ортодокса́льность.

orthographic(al) /ɔ:θə'græfɪk, ɔ:θə'græfɪk(ə)l/ *adj.* орфографи́ческий.

orthography /ɔ:'θɒgrəfɪ/ *n.* правописа́ние, орфогра́фия.

orthopaedic /ɔ:θə'pi:dɪk/ (*US* **orthopedic**) *adj.* ортопеди́ческий.

orthopaedics /ɔ:θə'pi:dɪks/ (*US* **orthopedics**) *n.* ортопе́дия.

oscillate /'ɒsɪleɪt/ *v.t.* кача́ть (*impf.*).
■ *v.i.* (*swing*) кача́ться (*impf.*); (*elec., radio; also fig.*) колеба́ться (*impf.*).

oscillation /ɒsɪ'leɪʃ(ə)n/ *n.* колеба́ние; (*elec.*) осцилля́ция.

Oslo /'ɒzləʊ/ *n.* О́сло (*m. indecl.*).

osmosis /ɒz'məʊsɪs/ *n.* (*biol., chem.*) о́смос.

ostensibl|e /ɒ'stensɪb(ə)l/ *adj.* (*for show*) показно́й; (*professed*) мни́мый; **he called ~y to thank me** он пришёл я́кобы для того́, что́бы поблагодари́ть меня́.

ostentation /ɒsten'teɪʃ(ə)n/ *n.* (*display*) показна́я ро́скошь.

ostentatious /ɒsten'teɪʃəs/ *adj.* показно́й, хвастли́вый.

osteopath /'ɒstɪəpæθ/ *n.* остеопа́т.

osteopathy /ɒstɪ'ɒpəθɪ/ *n.* остеопа́тия.

ostracize /'ɒstrəsaɪz/ *v.t.* подв|ерга́ть, -е́ргнуть остраки́зму.

ostrich /'ɒstrɪtʃ/ *n.* стра́ус (*африканский*); (*attr.*) страуси́ный.

other /'ʌðə(r)/ *pron.* друго́й, ино́й; ~**s may disagree with you** други́е/ины́е мо́гут с ва́ми не согласи́ться; **one after the ~** оди́н за други́м; **someone or ~** кто́-нибудь; (*expr. reciprocity*): **they were in love with each ~** они́ бы́ли влюблены́ друг в дру́га; (*pl., additional ones; more*) ещё + *g.*; (*remaining ones*) остальны́е.
■ *adj.* 1 друго́й; **on the ~ side of the road** на друго́й/той стороне́ доро́ги; **some ~ time** в друго́й раз.
2 (*additional*) ещё + *g.*
3 (*remaining*) остально́й; **we shall visit the ~ museums tomorrow** мы посети́м остальны́е музе́и за́втра.
4 : **the ~ day** на днях; **every ~ day** че́рез день.

otherwise /'ʌðəwaɪz/ *adv.*
1 (*in a different way*) ина́че, по-друго́му, други́м спо́собом.
2 (*in other respects*): в други́х отноше́ниях; **the house is cold but ~ comfortable** дом холо́дный, но в остально́м удо́бный.
3 (*if not; or else*) ина́че, а то; **I went, ~ I would have missed them** я пошёл, ина́че я бы их не заста́л.

Ottawa /'ɒtəwə/ *n.* Отта́ва.

otter /'ɒtə(r)/ *n.* вы́дра.

Ottoman /'ɒtəmən/ *n.* (*pl.* ~**s**)
1 (*hist.*) оттома́н.
2 (*sofa*) оттома́нка, тахта́.
■ *adj.* оттома́нский.

ouch /aʊtʃ/ *int.* ой!, ай!

ought /ɔ:t/ *v. aux.*
1 (*expr. duty*) до́лжен; **you ~ to go there** вы должны́ (*or* вам сле́дует) туда́ пойти́; **you ~ to have gone yesterday** вам сле́довало пойти́ туда́ вчера́.
2 (*expr. desirability*) до́лжен; на́до (+ *d.*); **you ~ to have seen his face** на́до бы́ло ви́деть его́ лицо́.

3 (*expr. probability*) должно́ быть, вероя́тно; **he ~ to be there by now** сейча́с он, вероя́тно (*or* должно́ быть), уже́ там.

ounce /aʊns/ *n.* (*weight*) у́нция (= *28,35 г*).

our /ˈaʊə(r)/ *poss. adj.* наш.

ours /ˈaʊəz/ *pron.* & *pred. adj.* наш; **~ is a blue car** на́ша маши́на си́няя; **this tree is ~** э́то де́рево на́ше.

ourselves /aʊəˈselvz/ *pron.*
1 (*refl.*) себя́; -сь (*suff.*); **we washed ~** мы умы́лись; (*after preps.*): **we can only depend on ~** мы мо́жем полага́ться то́лько на себя́ (сами́х).
2 (*emph.*) са́ми; **we ~ were not present** са́ми мы не прису́тствовали.
3 : **by ~** (*alone*) са́ми (по себе́); (*without aid*) са́ми, одни́.

oust /aʊst/ *v.t.* (*force out*; *also fig.*) вытесня́ть, вы́теснить; (*expel*) выгоня́ть, вы́гнать.

out /aʊt/ *pred. adj.* & *adv.*
1 (*away from home, room, usual place etc.*): **he is ~** его́ нет до́ма; (*sport*) вне игры́.
2 (**~** *of doors*) на дворе́; на у́лице; **it is quite warm ~ today** сего́дня на дворе́ тепло́; **he was ~ and about all day** он был на нога́х весь день; **we were ~ in the garden** мы бы́ли в саду́; (*fig., intent*): **they are ~ to get him** они́ (во что бы то ни ста́ло) наме́рены его́ пойма́ть.
3 (*visible*): **the stars are ~** вы́сыпали звёзды; **the sun will be ~ this afternoon** по́сле полу́дня пока́жется/появи́тся со́лнце; (*revealed*): **the secret is, was ~** секре́т раскры́лся (*or* стал всем изве́стен); (*published*): **my book is ~ at last** моя́ кни́га, наконе́ц, вы́шла (из печа́ти).
4 (*at departure*): **he stumbled on the way ~** выходя́, он споткну́лся; (*at a distance*): **the tide is ~** сейча́с отли́в.
5 (*astray, wrong*): **I wasn't far ~** я не намно́го оши́бся.
6 (*coll.*, **~** *of favour, fashion*): **short hair is ~** коро́ткая стри́жка сейча́с не в мо́де.
7 (*over*): **before the week is ~** до оконча́ния неде́ли; (*extinguished*): **the fire is ~** ого́нь поту́х.
8 : **~ of** (*movement*) из + *g.*; **he fell ~ of the window** он вы́пал из окна́; (*material*): **made ~ of silk** (сши́тый) из шёлка, шёлковый; (*from among*): **2 students ~ of 40** два студе́нта из сорока́; (*motive*): **~ of pity/love/respect** из жа́лости/любви́/уваже́ния (*к кому/чему*); **~ of grief/joy** с го́ря/ра́дости; **~ of boredom** от/со ску́ки; (*outside*): **~ of danger** вне опа́сности; **~ of doors** на у́лице, на дворе́, на во́здухе; **feel ~ of it** чу́вствовать (*impf.*) себя́ чужи́м (*or* ни при чём); **~ of control** вне контро́ля; **~ of fashion** не в мо́де; (*without*): **~ of breath** запыха́вшийся; **~ of work** безрабо́тный.
■ *v.t.* (*coll., expose as being homosexual*) изоблич|а́ть, -и́ть в гомосексуали́зме.

out-and-out /aʊtəndˈaʊt/ *adj.* соверше́нный, по́лный, отъя́вленный.

outback /ˈaʊtbæk/ *n.* глушь.

outboard /ˈaʊtbɔːd/ *adj.*: **~ motor** подвесно́й мото́р.

outbox /ˈaʊtbɒks/ *n.* (*comput.*) исходя́щие (сообще́ния).

outbreak /ˈaʊtbreɪk/ *n.* вспы́шка.

outbuilding /ˈaʊtbɪldɪŋ/ *n.* надво́рное строе́ние, надво́рная постро́йка.

outburst /ˈaʊtbəːst/ *n.* вспы́шка, взрыв.

outcast /ˈaʊtkɑːst/ *n.* изгна́нник, отве́рженный.

outcome /ˈaʊtkʌm/ *n.* исхо́д, результа́т.

outcry /ˈaʊtkraɪ/ *n.* проте́ст, (обще́ственное) негодова́ние.

outdo /aʊtˈduː/ *v.t.* прев|осходи́ть, -зойти́.

outdoor /ˈaʊtdɔː(r)/ *adj.*: **~ games** и́гры на откры́том во́здухе, подви́жные и́гры; **~ clothes** ве́рхнее пла́тье.

outdoors /aʊtˈdɔːz/ *adv.* на откры́том во́здухе, на дворе́; (*expr. motion*) на во́здух.

outer /ˈaʊtə(r)/ *adj.* (*external*) вне́шний; (*further away*): **~ space** ко́смос.

outfit /ˈaʊtfɪt/ *n.* компле́кт (оде́жды).

outgoing /ˈaʊtgəʊɪŋ/ *adj.*
1 (*departing*): **the ~ president** президе́нт, уходя́щий с поста́; **~ mail** исходя́щая по́чта.
2 (*sociable*): **an ~ person** общи́тельный/ужи́вчивый челове́к.

outgoings /ˈaʊtgəʊɪŋz/ *n.* (*Br.*) расхо́ды (*m. pl.*).

outgrow /aʊtˈgrəʊ/ *v.t.*
1 (*grow too large for*) вы́раста́ть, вы́расти из + *g.*
2 (*discard with time*) выраста́ть, вы́расти из + *g.*

outhouse /ˈaʊthaʊs/ *n.* надво́рное строе́ние; (*US, lavatory*) убо́рная во дворе́, отхо́жее ме́сто.

outing /ˈaʊtɪŋ/ *n.* прогу́лка, экску́рсия.

outlandish /aʊtˈlændɪʃ/ *adj.* дико́винный, чудно́й.

outlast /aʊtˈlɑːst/ *v.t.* (*outlive*) переж|ива́ть, -и́ть.

outlaw /ˈaʊtlɔː/ *n.* лицо́, объя́вленное вне зако́на.
■ *v.t.* объяв|ля́ть, -и́ть вне зако́на.

outlay /ˈaʊtleɪ/ *n.* изде́ржки (*f. pl.*).

outlet /ˈaʊtlet, -lɪt/ *n.*
1 (*lit.*) выходно́е/выпускно́е отве́рстие.
2 (*shop*) фи́рменный магази́н.
3 (*for energies etc.*) отду́шина, вы́ход.

outline /ˈaʊtlaɪn/ *n.*
1 (*contour*) ко́нтур, очерта́ние (*often in pl.*).
2 (*of speech, article*) конспе́кт.
■ *v.t.* нам|еча́ть, -е́тить в о́бщих черта́х.

outlive /aʊtˈlɪv/ *v.t.* переж|ива́ть, -и́ть.

outlook /ˈaʊtlʊk/ *n.*
1 (*prospect, lit., fig.*) вид, перспекти́ва; (*weather etc.*) прогно́з.
2 (*point of view*) то́чка зре́ния.

outlying /ˈaʊtlaɪɪŋ/ *adj.* отдалённый, удалённый.

outmoded /aʊtˈməʊdɪd/ *adj.* старомо́дный, немо́дный, устаре́лый.

outnumber /aʊtˈnʌmbə(r)/ *v.t.* прев|осходи́ть, -зойти́ *кого/что* чи́сленно.

out-of-court settlement /aʊtəvˈkɔːt/ *n.* (*leg.*) мирова́я сде́лка, урегули́рованная вне суда́.

out-of-date /aʊtəvˈdeɪt/ *adj.* устаре́лый, старомо́дный.

outpatient /ˈaʊtpeɪʃ(ə)nt/ *n.* амбулато́рный

больно́й; ~ **department** поликли́ника, амбулато́рная отделе́ние.

outpost /'aʊtpəʊst/ *n.* отдалённое поселе́ние.

output /'aʊtpʊt/ *n.*
[1] (*production*) вы́пуск, проду́кция, произво́дство.
[2] (*productivity*) производи́тельность.
■ *v.t.* (*comput.*) выводи́ть, вы́вести.

outrage /'aʊtreɪdʒ/ *n.* (*outrageous situation*) безобра́зие; (*outrageous act*) безобра́зный посту́пок; (*anger*) негодова́ние.

outrageous /aʊt'reɪdʒəs/ *adj.* безобра́зный, возмути́тельный.

outrider /'aʊtraɪdə(r)/ *n.* (*usu. pl.*) эско́рт.

outright /'aʊtraɪt/ *adj.* (*direct*) прямо́й, откры́тый; (*absolute*) совершённый.
■ *adv.* (*right out*) пря́мо, откры́то.

outset /'aʊtset/ *n.* нача́ло; **at the** ~ внача́ле; **from the** ~ с са́мого нача́ла.

outside *n.* /aʊt'saɪd/ нару́жная сторона́; **from, on the** ~ снару́жи; **at the (very)** ~ са́мое бо́льшее.
■ *adj.* /'aʊtsaɪd/
[1] (*external, exterior*) нару́жный, вне́шний.
[2] (*extreme*) кра́йний; **he has an** ~ **chance of winning** у него́ есть при́зрачные ша́нсы на вы́игрыш.
■ *adv.* /aʊt'saɪd/ снару́жи; извне́; (*to the* ~) нару́жу.
■ *prep.* /aʊt'saɪd/ вне + *g.*, из + *g.* (*beyond bounds of*) за преде́лами + *g.*; ~ **the door/ window** за две́рью/окно́м.

outsider /aʊt'saɪdə(r)/ *n.* посторо́нний; (*in contest, lit., fig.*) аутса́йдер.

outsize /'aʊtsaɪz/ *adj.* нестанда́ртный.

outskirts /'aʊtskɜ:ts/ *n.* (*of town*) окра́ина.

outsource /aʊt'sɔ:s/ *v.t.* (*econ.*) отд|ава́ть, -а́ть на́ сторону/на субподря́д.

outspoken /aʊt'spəʊkən/ *adj.* прямо́й, открове́нный.

outstanding /aʊt'stændɪŋ/ *adj.* (*prominent, eminent*) выдаю́щийся; (*still to be done*) невы́полненный; (*unpaid*) неопла́ченный.

outstay /aʊt'steɪ/ *v.t.*: ~ **one's welcome** загости́ться (*pf.*).

outstretched /'aʊtstretʃd, aʊt'stretʃd/ *adj.* (*hand*) протя́нутый.

outstrip /aʊt'strɪp/ *v.t.* (*lit., fig.*) опере|жа́ть, -ди́ть.

outward /'aʊtwəd/ *adj.* (*external*) нару́жный, вне́шний.

outwardly /'aʊtwədlɪ/ *adv.* вне́шне, на вид.

outwards /'aʊtwədz/ *adv.* нару́жу.

outweigh /aʊt'weɪ/ *v.t.* переве́|шивать, -сить.

outwit /aʊt'wɪt/ *v.t.* (**outwitted, outwitting**) перехитри́ть (*pf.*).

oval /'əʊv(ə)l/ *n.* ова́л.
■ *adj.* ова́льный.

ovarian /ə'veərɪən/ *adj.* яи́чниковый; ~ **cancer** рак яи́чников.

ovary /'əʊvərɪ/ *n.* яи́чник.

ovation /əʊ'veɪʃ(ə)n/ *n.* ова́ция.

oven /'ʌv(ə)n/ *n.* духо́вка.

over /'əʊvə(r)/ *adv.*
[1] (*across; to, on the other side*): ~ **there** (вон) там; **I asked him** ~ я пригласи́л его́ к себе́.
[2] (*covering surface*): **all** ~ (*everywhere*) повсю́ду; **I felt hot and cold all** ~ меня́ (всего́) броса́ло то в жар, то в хо́лод.
[3] (*at an end*): **the meeting is** ~ собра́ние ко́нчилось.
[4] (*also* ~ **again:** *once more*) опя́ть, сно́ва, ещё раз; ~ **and** ~ **again** ты́сячу раз, сно́ва и сно́ва.
[5] (*in excess*): **sums of £5 and** ~ су́ммы в/от 5 фу́нтов и вы́ше; **I had £3 (left)** ~ у меня́ ещё остава́лось три фу́нта.
■ *prep.* [1] (*above*) над + *i.*; **a roof** ~ **one's head** кры́ша над голово́й; (*expr. division*): **five** ~ **two** (*math.*) пять дробь два.
[2] (*to the far side of*) че́рез + *a.*; **a bridge** ~ **the river** мост че́рез ре́ку; **I threw the ball** ~ **the wall** я переки́нул мяч че́рез сте́ну; **he jumped** ~ **the puddles** он перепры́гнул (че́рез) лу́жи; (*down from*): **he fell** ~ **the cliff** он упа́л со скалы́; (*against*): **he tripped** ~ **a stone** он споткну́лся о ка́мень.
[3] (*on the far side of*): **he lives** ~ **the way** он живёт че́рез у́лицу.
[4] (*resting on*): **he pulled his cap** ~ **his eyes** он надви́нул ша́пку на глаза́; **crossing one leg** ~ **the other** заки́нув но́гу на́ ногу; (*across,* ~ *the surface of*) по + *d.*; **all** ~ **the world** во всём ми́ре; по всему́ све́ту.
[5] (*more than*) бо́льше/свы́ше + *g.*; ~ **a year ago** бо́льше/свы́ше го́да (тому́) наза́д; **children** ~ **5** де́ти ста́рше пяти́ лет; ~ **600** свы́ше шестисо́т.
[6] (*during*): **much has happened** ~ **the past two years** за после́дние два го́да мно́гое случи́лось/произошло́.
[7] (*on the subject of*): **he gets angry** ~ **nothing** он зли́тся из-за пустяко́в; **a quarrel** ~ **money** ссо́ра из-за де́нег.

overall /'əʊvərɔ:l/ *n.* (*Br.*) рабо́чий хала́т; (*pl.*) комбинезо́н.
■ *adj.* (*total*) по́лный; (*general*) (все)о́бщий.
■ *adv.* (*taken as a whole*) в це́лом.

overawe /əʊvər'ɔ:/ *v.t.* внуш|а́ть, -и́ть благогове́йный страх + *d.*

overbalance /əʊvə'bæləns/ (*Br.*) *v.i.* теря́ть, по- равнове́сие.

overbearing /əʊvə'beərɪŋ/ *adj.* вла́стный.

overboard /'əʊvəbɔ:d/ *adv.*: **man** ~**!** челове́к за бо́ртом!

overbook /əʊvə'bʊk/ *v.t.*: **the plane was** ~**ed** биле́тов на самолёт бы́ло про́дано бо́льше, чем име́лось мест.

overcast /'əʊvəkɑ:st/ *adj.* покры́тый облака́ми.

overcharge /əʊvə'tʃɑ:dʒ/ *v.t.* назн|ача́ть, -а́чить завы́шенную це́ну (*кому*) (**for:** за + *a.*).

overcoat /'əʊvəkəʊt/ *n.* пальто́ (*nt. indecl.*).

overcome /əʊvə'kʌm/ *v.t.* (*prevail over*) преодол|ева́ть, -е́ть; (*of emotion*) охва́т|ывать, -и́ть.

over-confident /əʊvə'kɒnfɪd(ə)nt/ *adj.* самонаде́янный.

overcook /əʊvə'kʊk/ *v.t.* (*by roasting, frying*) пережа́р|ивать, -ить; (*by boiling*) перева́р|ивать, -и́ть.

overcrowd /əʊvə'kraʊd/ *v.t.* переп|олня́ть, -о́лнить.

overdo /əʊvə'du:/ *v.t.*: ~ **it** перестара́ться

(*pf.*); переб|áрщивать, -орщи́ть (*coll.*); переусéрдствовать (*pf.*) (*в чём*).

overdose /ˈəʊvədəʊs/ *n.* передозирóвка, чрезмéрная дóза.

overdraft /ˈəʊvədrɑːft/ *n.* (*deficit in bank account*) овердрáфт, перерасхóд; (*agreement*) разрешéние на превышéние креди́та.

overdraw /əʊvəˈdrɔː/ *v.t.*: **I am £100 ~n** я превы́сил креди́т в бáнке на 100 фýнтов.

overdue /əʊvəˈdjuː/ *adj.* запоздáлый; **the baby is 2 weeks ~** ребёнок дóлжен был роди́ться две недéли томý назáд; (*of payment*) просрóченный.

overeat /əʊvərˈiːt/ *v.i.* пере|едáть, -éсть; объ|едáться, -éсться.

overestimate /əʊvərˈestɪmeɪt/ *v.t.* переоцéн|ивать, -и́ть.

over-excited /əʊvərɪkˈsaɪtɪd/ *adj.* крáйне возбуждённый.

overflow /ˈəʊvəfləʊ/ *n. v.t. & i.* перел|ивáться, -и́ться (*через что*); **the river ~s its banks** рекá заливáет берегá (*or* выхóдит из берегóв); **~ing with** (*fig.*) преиспóлненный + *g.*

overground /ˈəʊvəgraʊnd/ *adj.* надзéмный.

overgrow /əʊvəˈgrəʊ/ *v.t.*: **be ~n (with)** зараст|áть, -ú (+ *i.*).

overhaul /ˈəʊvəhɔːl/ *n.* (*of machine*) осмóтр; (*of system*) пересмóтр.
■ *v.t.* осм|áтривать, -отрéть; ремонти́ровать, от-; пересм|áтривать, -отрéть.

overhead /ˈəʊvəhed/ *n.* (*usu. pl.*) накладны́е расхóды (*m. pl.*).
■ *adj.*: **~ projector** диапроéктор; **~ railway** надзéмная желéзная дорóга.
■ *adv.* наверхý, вверхý; (*in the sky*) на нéбе.

overhear /əʊvəˈhɪə(r)/ *v.t.* нечáянно услы́шать (*pf.*).

overheat /əʊvəˈhiːt/ *v.t. & i.* перегр|евáть(ся), -éть(ся).

overindulge /əʊvərɪnˈdʌldʒ/ *v.i.*: **~ in sth.** злоупотреб|ля́ть, -и́ть чем-н.

overjoyed /əʊvəˈdʒɔɪd/ *adj.* вне себя́ от рáдости.

overkill /ˈəʊvəkɪl/ *n.* (*fig.*) вы́ход за предéлы необходи́мости.

overland /ˈəʊvəlænd/ *adj.* сухопýтный.
■ *adv.* по сýше.

overlap /ˈəʊvəlæp/ *v.i.* за|ходи́ть, -йти́ оди́н на другóй; (*coincide*) (части́чно) совп|адáть, -áсть.

overleaf /əʊvəˈliːf/ *adv.* на оборóте (страни́цы).

overload /ˈəʊvələʊd/*v.t.* перегру|жáть, -зи́ть.

overlook /əʊvəˈlʊk/ *v.t.*
1 (*open on to*) выходи́ть (*impf.*) на + *a.*; **our house is not ~ed** наш дом защищён от посторóнних взгля́дов; **a view ~ing the lake** вид на óзеро.
2 (*fail to notice*) просмотрéть (*pf.*), проглядéть (*pf.*), пропус|кáть, -ти́ть; (*disregard*) упус|кáть, -ти́ть.

overly /ˈəʊvəlɪ/ *adv.* сли́шком, чересчýр.

overnight /əʊvəˈnaɪt/ *adj.*: **an ~ stay** ночёвка, ночлéг; **~ bag** дорóжная сýмка, небольшóй чемодáн.
■ *adv.* (*through the night*) всю ночь; (*during the night*) зá ночь; **stay ~** ночевáть, за-.

overpass /ˈəʊvəpɑːs/ *n.* эстакáда.

overpayment /əʊvəˈpeɪmənt/ *n.* переплáта.

overpopulated /əʊvəˈpɒpjʊleɪtɪd/ *adj.* перенаселённый.

overpower /əʊvəˈpaʊə(r)/ *v.t.* одол|евáть, -éть; (*overwhelm*) сокруш|áть, -и́ть; **~ing smell** óчень си́льный зáпах.

overrate /əʊvəˈreɪt/ *v.t.* переоцéн|ивать, -и́ть.

overreach /əʊvəˈriːtʃ/ *v.t.* (*outwit*) перехитри́ть (*pf.*); **~ o.s.** (*defeat one's object*) перестарáться (*pf.*).

overreact /əʊvərɪˈækt/ *v.i.* реаги́ровать, от-/про- чрезмéрно рéзко.

overrid|e /əʊvəˈraɪd/ *v.t.* (*reject*) отв|ергáть, -éргнуть; **~ing** (*aim*) основнóй, первостепéнный; (*consideration*) глáвный, решáющий.

overrule /əʊvəˈruːl/ *v.t.* (*annul*) аннули́ровать (*impf., pf.*); **I was ~d** моё возражéние отвéргли.

overrun /əʊvəˈrʌn/ *v.t.*
1 (*of enemy*) соверш|áть, -и́ть набéг на + *a.*
2 (*infest*): **the garden is ~ with weeds** сад зарóс сорнякáми; **the house is ~ with rats** дом киши́т кры́сами.
■ *v.i.*: **the broadcast is ~ning by 20 minutes** передáча идёт на 20 минýт дóльше полóженного врéмени.

overseas *adj.* /ˈəʊvəsiːz/ (*trip*) загрáничный; (*visitor*) инострáнный.
■ *adv.* /əʊvəˈsiːz/ за грани́цей.

oversee /əʊvəˈsiː/ *v.t.* надзирáть (*impf.*) за + *i.*

overseer /ˈəʊvəsiːə(r)/ *n.* надсмóтрщик, надзирáтель (*m.*).

overshadow /əʊvəˈʃædəʊ/ *v.t.* (*lit., fig.*) заслон|я́ть, -и́ть.

overshoot /əʊvəˈʃuːt/ *v.t.* (*junction, traffic lights*) про|езжáть, -éхать; проск|áкивать, -очи́ть; **~ the mark** (*lit.*) брать, взять вы́ше цéли; (*fig.*) за|ходи́ть, -йти́ сли́шком далекó.
■ *v.i.*: **the plane overshot on landing** (при посáдке) самолёт перелетéл тóчку приземлéния.

oversight /ˈəʊvəsaɪt/ *n.* недосмóтр, упущéние.

oversimplify /əʊvəˈsɪmplɪfaɪ/ *v.t.* сли́шком упро|щáть, -сти́ть.

oversleep /əʊvəˈsliːp/ *v.i.* прос|ыпáть, -пáть.

overspend /əʊvəˈspend/ *v.i.* трáтить, по-сли́шком мнóго.

overstep /əʊvəˈstep/ *v.t.* преступ|áть, -и́ть.

oversubscribe /əʊvəsəbˈskraɪb/ *v.t.*: **the course is ~ed** курс переполнен.

overt /əʊˈvəːt/ *adj.* я́вный, очеви́дный.

overtake /əʊvəˈteɪk/ *v.t.* об|гоня́ть, -огнáть.

over the top /əʊvəðəˈtɒp/ *adj.* чрезмéрный.

overthrow /əʊvəˈθrəʊ/ *v.t.* ниспров|ергáть, -éргнуть.

overtime /ˈəʊvətaɪm/ *n.* сверхурóчная рабóта.
■ *adv.* сверхурóчно.

overtone /ˈəʊvətəʊn/ *n.* оттéнок.

overture /ˈəʊvətjʊə(r)/ *n.* увертю́ра.

overturn /əʊvəˈtəːn/ *v.t. & i.* опроки́|дывать(ся), -нуть(ся).

overview /ˈəʊvəvju:/ *n.* обзо́р.
overweight /ˈəʊvəweɪt/ *adj.* ве́сящий бо́льше но́рмы.
overwhelm /əʊvəˈwelm/ *v.t.* (*in battle*) сокруш|а́ть, -и́ть; (*fig.*): **his kindness ~ed me** я был ошеломлён/потрясён его́ доброто́й; **~ing majority** подавля́ющее большинство́.
overwork /əʊvəˈwɜ:k/ *v.t. & i.* переутом|ля́ть(ся), -и́ть(ся).
overwrought /əʊvəˈrɔ:t/ *adj.* сли́шком возбуждённый, не́рвный; **she is ~** у неё не́рвное истоще́ние.
ovulate /ˈɒvjʊleɪt/ *v.i.* овули́ровать (*impf., pf.*).
ovulation /ɒvjʊˈleɪʃ(ə)n/ *n.* овуля́ция.
owe /əʊ/ *v.t. & i.* быть до́лжным + *d.*; **you ~ us £50** вы должны́ нам 50 фу́нтов; **I ~ you for the ticket** я до́лжен вам за биле́т.
owing /ˈəʊɪŋ/ *adj.*
1 (*yet to be paid*) причита́ющийся.
2 : **~ to** (*attributable to*) по причи́не + *g.*; (*on account of, because of*) из-за + *g.*
owl /aʊl/ *n.* сова́.
own /əʊn/ *pron.*: **get one's ~ back on s.o.** поквита́ться (*pf.*) с кем-н.; **on one's ~** (*alone*) в одино́честве; (*independently*) самостоя́тельно, сам (по себе́).
■ *adj.* со́бственный, свой; **my ~ house** мой со́бственный дом; **this house is not my ~** э́тот дом мне не принадлежи́т; **can I have a room of my ~?** мо́жно получи́ть отде́льную ко́мнату?; **of one's ~ accord** по со́бственному побужде́нию; по со́бственной во́ле; **my ~ father** мой родно́й оте́ц.
■ *v.t.* владе́ть (*impf.*) + *i.*; **who ~s this bag?** чья э́то су́мка?; **the land was ~ed by my father** (э́та) земля́ принадлежа́ла моему́ отцу́ (*or* э́той землёй владе́л мой оте́ц).
■ *v.i.*: **~ up (to sth.)** призн|ава́ться, -а́ться (в чём-н.); **I ~ to having told a lie** я признаю́сь, что солга́л.
owner /ˈəʊnə(r)/ *n.* владе́л|ец (*fem.* -ица).
ownership /ˈəʊnəʃɪp/ *n.* владе́ние (**of:** + *i.*); со́бственность (**of:** на + *a.*).
ox /ɒks/ *n.* (*pl.* **oxen**) бык.
oxide /ˈɒksaɪd/ *n.* о́кись, окси́д.
oxidize /ˈɒksɪdaɪz/ *v.t.* окисл|я́ть, -и́ть.
oxygen /ˈɒksɪdʒ(ə)n/ *n.* кислоро́д.
oyster /ˈɔɪstə(r)/ *n.* у́стрица.
ozone /ˈəʊzəʊn/ *n.* озо́н; **~ layer** озо́нный/озо́новый слой.

Pp

p *n. abbr. of*
1 ***penny*** /ˈpenɪ/ (*pl.* ***pence***) (*Br.*) пе́нни (*nt. indecl.*), пенс.
2 ***page*** /peɪdʒ/ с(тр). (страни́ца).
PA *abbr. of* (*Br.*) ***personal assistant*** ли́чный секрета́рь.
pace /peɪs/ *n.*
1 (*step*) шаг.
2 (*speed*): **keep ~ with** посп|ева́ть, -е́ть за + *i.*
■ *v.i.*: **he ~d up and down** он ходи́л взад и вперёд.
■ *cpd.* **~maker** *n.* (*leader*) ли́дер, задаю́щий темп; (*med.*) (электро)кардиостимуля́тор, электри́ческий стимуля́тор се́рдца.
pacific /pəˈsɪfɪk/ *n.*: **the P~ (Ocean)** Ти́хий океа́н.
pacifism /ˈpæsɪfɪz(ə)m/ *n.* пацифи́зм.
pacifist /ˈpæsɪfɪst/ *n.* пацифи́ст (*fem.* -ка).
pacify /ˈpæsɪfaɪ/ *v.t.* успок|а́ивать, -о́ить.
pack /pæk/ *n.*
1 (*rucksack*) рюкза́к.
2 (*packet*) па́чка, паке́т.
3 (*collection*) набо́р; **it's all a ~ of lies** э́то сплошна́я ложь.
4 (*animals*): **~ of wolves** ста́я волко́в.
5 (*Br., cards*) коло́да.
■ *v.t.* 1 (*put into container*) упако́в|ывать, -а́ть; укла́дывать, уложи́ть; **~ed lunch** бутербро́ды с собо́й.
2 (*put into small space*): **they were ~ed in there like sardines** они́ наби́лись туда́ как се́льди в бо́чке.
3 (*cover for protection*) упако́в|ывать, -а́ть; **the glass is ~ed in cotton wool** стекло́ упако́вано в ва́ту.
4 (*fill*) зап|олня́ть, -о́лнить; **he ~ed his bags and left** он уложи́л чемода́ны и уе́хал; **the hall was ~ed** зал был битко́м наби́т.
■ *v.i.* 1 : **(~ one's clothes)** укла́дываться, уложи́ться.
2 (*crowd together*): **they ~ed into the car** они́ вти́снулись в автомоби́ль.
■ *with advs.*: **~ in** *v.t.*: (*coll., stop, give up*) прекра|ща́ть, -ти́ть; **~ up** *v.t.*: (*coll., stop*): **I ~ed up smoking last year** я бро́сил кури́ть в про́шлом году́; *v.i.*: **we spent the day ~ing up** мы це́лый день укла́дывались; (*coll., stop working*): **the engine ~ed up** (*Br.*) мото́р отказа́л.
package /ˈpækɪdʒ/ *n.* (*parcel*) посы́лка; (*comput.*) паке́т; (*fig.*): **~ deal** ко́мплексная сде́лка.
■ *v.t.* упако́в|ывать, -а́ть; (*fig.*): **a ~ holiday, tour** (*Br.*) организо́ванная туристи́ческая пое́здка; пое́здка по путёвке.
packet /ˈpækɪt/ *n.* (*of cigarettes, biscuits*) па́чка; (*of crisps*) паке́т.
packing /ˈpækɪŋ/ *n.* упако́вка.
pact /pækt/ *n.* соглаше́ние, догово́р.
pad /pæd/ *n.*
1 (*small cushion*) поду́шечка; (*for protection*) прокла́дка.
2 (*block of paper*) блокно́т.
3 (*launching platform*) ста́ртовая площа́дка.
■ *v.t.* (**padded, padding**)

[1] (*cushion*) наб|ива́ть, -и́ть; (*coat*) подб|ива́ть, -и́ть.
[2] (*fig.*, *also* ~ **out**) разб|авля́ть, -а́вить.
■ *v.i.* (**padded, padding**) (*coll.*, *move softly*) бесшу́мно дви́гаться (*impf.*).
padding /ˈpædɪŋ/ *n.* наби́вка.
paddle[1] /ˈpæd(ə)l/ *n.* гребо́к (*весло*).
■ *v.t.* & *i.* грести́ (*impf.*).
paddl|e[2] /ˈpæd(ə)l/ *n.*: **the children have gone for a ~e** де́ти пошли́ поплеска́ться в воде́.
■ *v.i.* (*walk in shallow water*) шлёпать (*impf.*) по воде́; **~ing pool** (*Br.*) де́тский бассе́йн, лягуша́тник (*coll.*).
paddock /ˈpædək/ *n.* (*small field, esp. for horses*) вы́гул; (*at racecourse, track*) па́ддо́к (*техническая зона на ипподроме между конюшнями и беговой дорожкой, где лошадей готовят к забегу; аналогичное место для гоночных машин непосредственно возле трассы*).
padlock /ˈpædlɒk/ *n.* вися́чий замо́к.
■ *v.t.* ве́шать, пове́сить замо́к на + *a.*
paediatric /piːdɪˈætrɪk/ (*US* **pediatric**) *adj.* педиатри́ческий.
paediatrician /piːdɪəˈtrɪʃ(ə)n/ (*US* **pediatrician**) *n.* педиа́тр.
paediatrics /piːdɪˈætrɪks/ (*US* **pediatrics**) *n.* педиатри́я.
paedophile /ˈpiːdəfaɪl/ (*US* **pedophile**) *n.* педофи́л.
paedophilia /piːdəˈfɪlɪə/ (*US* **pedophilia**) *n.* педофили́я.
pagan /ˈpeɪɡən/ *n.* язы́чни|к (*fem.* -ца).
■ *adj.* язы́ческий.
paganism /ˈpeɪɡənɪz(ə)m/ *n.* язы́чество.
page[1] /peɪdʒ/ *n.* (*of a book etc.*) страни́ца.
page[2] /peɪdʒ/ *n.* ма́льчик-слуга́.
■ *v.t.*: **please have Mr. Smith ~d** пожа́луйста, вы́зовите господи́на Сми́та по пе́йджеру.
pageant /ˈpædʒ(ə)nt/ *n.* представле́ние, де́йство.
pageantry /ˈpædʒəntrɪ/ *n.* пы́шность, пара́дность.
pager /ˈpeɪdʒə(r)/ *n.* пе́йджер.
paid /peɪd/ *past and p.p. of* ▸**pay**; **put ~ to** (*coll.*) класть, положи́ть коне́ц + *d.*
pail /peɪl/ *n.* ведро́.
pain /peɪn/ *n.*
[1] (*suffering*) боль; **he is in great ~** его́ му́чают бо́ли; (*localized*): **he had severe stomach ~s** у него́ бы́ли о́стрые бо́ли в желу́дке; **he is a ~ in the neck** (*coll.*) он стои́т всем поперёк го́рла.
[2] (*pl.*, *trouble, effort*) стара́ния (*nt. pl.*), хло́п|оты (*pl.*, *g.* -о́т); **he takes great ~s over every picture** он подо́лгу рабо́тает над ка́ждой карти́ной.
■ *cpd.* **~killer** *n.* болеутоля́ющее (сре́дство).
painful /ˈpeɪnfʊl/ *adj.* (*of part of body*) больно́й; (*causing pain*) боле́зненный, мучи́тельный.
painless /ˈpeɪnlɪs/ *adj.* безболе́зненный.
painstaking /ˈpeɪnzteɪkɪŋ/ *adj.* стара́тельный, усе́рдный.
paint /peɪnt/ *n.* кра́ска.
■ *v.t.* [1] (*portray in colours*) рисова́ть, на-.
[2] (*cover with ~*) кра́сить, по-/вы́-.
■ *v.i.* рисова́ть (*impf.*); писа́ть (*impf.*) кра́сками.
■ *cpds.* **~box** *n.* набо́р кра́сок; **~brush** *n.* кисть.
painter /ˈpeɪntə(r)/ *n.* (*artist*) худо́жник; (*decorator*) маля́р.
painting /ˈpeɪntɪŋ/ *n.*
[1] (*profession*) жи́вопись.
[2] (*work of art*) карти́на.
pair /peə(r)/ *n.* па́ра; **they walked along in ~s** они́ шли па́рами; **~ of scissors** но́жниц|ы (*pl.*, *g.* —); **two ~s of trousers** дво́е (*or* две па́ры) брюк.
■ *with adv.*: **~ off** *v.t.* & *i.* разб|ива́ть(ся), -и́ть(ся) на па́ры; (*coll.*, *marry*) жени́ться (*impf.*, *pf.*), пожени́ться (*pf.*).
pajamas /pɪˈdʒɑːməz/ (*US*) = **pyjamas**
Pakistan /pɑːkɪˈstɑːn/ *n.* Пакиста́н.
Pakistani /pɑːkɪˈstɑːnɪ/ *n.* (*pl.* **~s**) пакиста́н|ец (*fem.* -ка).
■ *adj.* пакиста́нский.
pal /pæl/ (*coll.*) *n.* дружо́к.
palace /ˈpælɪs/ *n.* дворе́ц.
palaeography /pælɪˈɒɡrəfɪ/ (*US* **paleography**) *n.* палеогра́фия.
palatable /ˈpælətəb(ə)l/ *adj.* вку́сный.
palate /ˈpælət/ *n.* нёбо.
palatial /pəˈleɪʃ(ə)l/ *adj.* роско́шный, великоле́пный.
palaver /pəˈlɑːvə(r)/ *n.* (*coll.*) суета́.
pale /peɪl/ *adj.* (*of complexion*) бле́дный; **she turned ~** она́ побледне́ла; (*of colours*) све́тлый; **~ blue** све́тло-голубо́й.
■ *v.i.* бледне́ть, по-; (*fig.*): **the event ~d into insignificance** э́то собы́тие отошло́ на за́дний план.
Palestine /ˈpælɪstaɪn/ *n.* Палести́на.
Palestinian /pælɪˈstɪnɪən/ *n.* палести́н|ец (*fem.* -ка).
■ *adj.* палести́нский.
palette /ˈpælɪt/ *n.* (*lit.*, *fig.*) пали́тра.
pall[1] /pɔːl/ *n.* покро́в; **a ~ of smoke hung over the city** пелена́ ды́ма висе́ла над го́родом.
■ *cpd.* **~-bearer** *n.* несу́щий гроб.
pall[2] /pɔːl/ *v.i.* при|еда́ться, -е́сться/ надо|еда́ть, -е́сть (**on:** + *d.*).
pallet /ˈpælɪt/ *n.* (*for loads*) поддо́н.
palliative /ˈpælɪətɪv/ *n.* паллиати́в, полуме́ра.
■ *adj.* паллиати́вный; смягча́ющий.
pallid /ˈpælɪd/ *adj.* бле́дный.
pallor /ˈpælə(r)/ *n.* бле́дность.
pally /ˈpælɪ/ *adj.* (**pallier, palliest**) (*coll.*) (*friendly*) дружелю́бный; **be ~ with s.o.** быть с кем-н. на коро́ткой ноге́.
palm[1] /pɑːm/ *n.* (*tree*) па́льма; **P~ Sunday** Ве́рбное воскресе́нье.
palm[2] /pɑːm/ *n.* (*of hand*) ладо́нь.
■ *v.t.*: **~ sth. off on s.o.** (*or* **s.o. off with sth.**) подс|о́вывать, -у́нуть что-н. кому́-н.
palmistry /ˈpɑːmɪstrɪ/ *n.* хирома́нтия.
palpable /ˈpælpəb(ə)l/ *adj.* ощути́мый.
palpitate /ˈpælpɪteɪt/ *v.i.* пульси́ровать (*impf.*).
palpitation /pælpɪˈteɪʃ(ə)n/ *n.* сердцеби́ение;

just to watch him gave me ~s оди́н его́ вид приводи́л меня́ в тре́пет.

paltry /'pɔːltrɪ/ *adj.* (**paltrier, paltriest**) (*worthless*) ничто́жный; (*petty, mean*) ме́лкий.

pamper /'pæmpə(r)/ *v.t.* балова́ть, из-.

pamphlet /'pæmflɪt/ *n.* (*printed leaflet*) брошю́ра.

pan[1] /pæn/ *n.* кастрю́ля; **(frying ~)** сковорода́.
■ *v.t.* (**panned, panning**) (*coll., criticize severely*) разн|оси́ть, -ести́.
■ *v.i.* (**panned, panning**) (*fig.*): **everything ~ned out well** (всё) вы́шло как нельзя́ лу́чше.

pan[2] /pæn/ *v.i.* (**panned, panning**) (*of camera*) повора́чиваться (*impf.*).

panacea /pænə'siːə/ *n.* панаце́я.

panache /pə'næʃ/ *n.* (*flamboyance*) рисо́вка, щегольство́.

Panama /'pænəmɑː/ *n.* Пана́ма; **~ Canal** Пана́мский кана́л.

pancake /'pæŋkeɪk/ *n.* блин; ола́дья; **P~ Day** вто́рник на Ма́сленой неде́ле, в кото́рый пеку́т блины́.

pancreatic /pæŋkrɪ'ætɪk/ *adj.* панкреати́ческий.

panda /'pændə/ *n.* па́нда.

pandemonium /pændɪ'məʊnɪəm/ *n.* стра́шный шум (*скандал*), смяте́ние, столпотворе́ние.

pander /'pændə(r)/ *v.i.* (*minister*) потво́рствовать (*impf.*) (**to:** + *d.*).

pane /peɪn/ *n.* око́нное стекло́.

panel /'pæn(ə)l/ *n.*
1 (*of door etc.*) пане́ль.
2 : **~ of judges** жюри́ (*nt. indecl.*), суде́йская гру́ппа; **~ game** (*Br.*) виктори́на.
3 (*for instruments*) пульт; **control ~** пульт управле́ния.

panellist /'pænəlɪst/ (*US* **panelist**) *n.* (*in discussion*) уча́стник диску́ссии/кру́глого стола́; (*judge*) член жюри́.

pang /pæŋ/ *n.*
1 (*sharp pain*) ко́лики (*f. pl.*); **~s of hunger** голо́дные бо́ли.
2 (*mental*) му́ки (*f. pl.*); **a ~ of conscience** угрызе́ния (*nt. pl.*) со́вести.

panic /'pænɪk/ *n.* па́ника.
■ *v.t.* (**panicked, panicking**) (*coll.*): **they were ~ked into surrender** они́ впа́ли в па́нику и сдали́сь.
■ *v.i.* (**panicked, panicking**) паникова́ть (*impf.*).
■ *cpd.* **~-stricken** *adj.* охва́ченный па́никой.

panicky /'pænɪkɪ/ *adj.* (*coll.*) (*action*) пани́ческий; (*person*): **he was ~** он паникова́л.

pannier /'pænɪə(r)/ *n.* корзи́на.

panorama /pænə'rɑːmə/ *n.* (*lit., fig.*) панора́ма.

panoramic /pænə'ræmɪk/ *adj.* панора́мный.

pansy /'pænzɪ/ *n.* аню́тин|ы гла́з|ки (*pl., g.* -ых -ок).

pant /pænt/ *v.i.* тяжело́ дыша́ть (*impf.*).

panther /'pænθə(r)/ *n.* панте́ра; (*US*) пу́ма.

panties /'pæntɪz/ *n.* (*coll.*) тру́сик|и (*pl., g.* -ых -ов).

pantomime /'pæntəmaɪm/ *n.* (*Br., entertainment*) рожде́ственское представле́ние.

pantry /'pæntrɪ/ *n.* кладова́я.

pants /pænts/ *n.* (*Br., underwear*) трус|ы́ (*pl., g.* -о́в); (*coll. or US, trousers*) брю́к|и (*pl., g.* —).

pantyhose /'pæntɪhəʊz/ *n.* (*US*) колго́т|ки (*pl., g.* -ок).

papacy /'peɪpəsɪ/ *n.* па́пство.

papara|zzo /pæpə'rætsəʊ/ *n.* (*pl.* **~zzi** /-tsɪ/) папара́цци (*c.g. indecl.*); фотокорреспонде́нт, рабо́тающий на бульва́рную пре́ссу.

paper /'peɪpə(r)/ *n.*
1 бума́га; (*attr.*): **~ bag** бума́жный паке́т; **~ handkerchief** бума́жная салфе́тка.
2 **(news~)** газе́та; (*attr.*): **~ round** доста́вка газе́т (на́ дом); **~ shop** газе́тный кио́ск.
3 (*pl., documents*) докуме́нты (*m. pl.*), бума́ги (*f. pl.*).
4 **(examination ~)** (*Br.*) экзаменацио́нная рабо́та.
5 (*essay, lecture*) докла́д.
6 **(wall~)** обо́|и (*pl., g.* -ев).
■ *v.t.* (*put wall~ on*) окле́и|вать, -ть обо́ями.
■ *cpds.* **~back** *n.* кни́га в бума́жном/мя́гком переплёте; **~ clip** *n.* канцеля́рская скре́пка; **~work** *n.* канцеля́рская рабо́та.

paprika /'pæprɪkə/ *n.* (*spice*) па́прика.

Papua New Guinea /'pæpjʊə njuː 'gɪnɪ/ *n.* Па́пуа – Но́вая Гвине́я.

Papua New Guinean /'pæpjʊə njuː 'gɪnɪən/ *n.* па́пуа-новогвине́|ец (*fem.* -йка).
■ *adj.* па́пуа-новогвине́йский.

par /pɑː(r)/ *n.*
1 (*equality*) ра́венство; **this is on a ~ with his other work** (э́та) рабо́та на у́ровне его́ други́х.
2 (*face value*) цена́; **above ~** вы́ше номина́льной цены́; **below ~** ни́же номина́льной цены́.
3 (*standard*): **I feel below ~ today** я сего́дня нева́жно себя́ чу́вствую.

parable /'pærəb(ə)l/ *n.* при́тча.

parabola /pə'ræbələ/ *n.* (*pl.* **parabolas** *or* **parabolae** /-liː/) пара́бола.

parabolic /pærə'bɒlɪk/ *adj.* (*geom.*) параболи́ческий.

paracetamol /pærə'siːtəmɒl/ *n.* (*Br.*) парацетамо́л.

parachute /'pærəʃuːt/ *n.* парашю́т; (*attr.*) **~ jump** прыжо́к с парашю́том.
■ *v.i.*: **the pilot ~d out of the aircraft** пило́т вы́бросился из самолёта с парашю́том.

parachutist /'pærəʃuːtɪst/ *n.* парашюти́ст (*fem.* -ка).

parade /pə'reɪd/ *n.*
1 (*public procession*) ше́ствие, пара́д.
2 (*of troops*) пара́д.
■ *v.t.* выставля́ть, вы́ставить напока́з.
■ *v.i.* ше́ствовать (*impf.*).
■ *cpd.* **~ ground** *n.* плац.

paradise /'pærədaɪs/ *n.* рай.

paradox /'pærədɒks/ *n.* парадо́кс.

paradoxical /pærə'dɒksɪk(ə)l/ *adj.* парадокса́льный.

paraffin /'pærəfɪn/ *n.*
1 (*Br.*, **~ oil**) кероси́н.
2 (**~ wax**) парафи́н.

P

paragon /'pærəgən/ *n.* образéц.
paragraph /'pærəgrɑ:f/ *n.* абзáц, парáграф.
Paraguay /'pærəgwaɪ/ *n.* Парагвáй.
parallel /'pærəlel/ *n.*
1 (*line*) параллéльная лѝния; (*of latitude*) параллéль.
2 (*fig.*) параллéль.
■ *adj.* параллéльный; (*similar*) аналогѝчный.
parallelogram /pærə'leləgræm/ *n.* параллелогрáмм.
Paralympics /pærə'lɪmpɪks/ *n.* Параолимпѝйские ѝгры (*f. pl*).
paralyse /'pærəlaɪz/ (*US* **paralyze**) *v.t.* (*lit., fig.*) парализовáть (*impf., pf.*).
paralysis /pə'rælɪsɪs/ *n.* (*pl.* **paralyses** /-si:z/) (*lit., fig.*) паралѝч.
paralytic /pærə'lɪtɪk/ *adj.* (*lit.*) паралитѝческий, парализóванный; (*Br., incapably drunk*) мертвéцки пьяный.
paramedic /pærə'medɪk/ *n.* медрабóтник (*без высшего образования*).
parameter /pə'ræmɪtə(r)/ *n.* (*math., comput.; also fig.*) парáметр.
paramilitary /pærə'mɪlɪtərɪ/ *adj.* военизѝрованный.
paramount /'pærəmaʊnt/ *adj.* первостепéнный.
paranoia /pærə'nɔɪə/ *n.* паранóйя.
paranoid /'pærənɔɪd/ *n.* паранóик.
■ *adj.* паранóидный.
paranormal /pærə'nɔ:m(ə)l/ *adj.* паранормáльный.
parapet /'pærəpɪt/ *n.* (*low wall*) парапéт; (*trench defence*) брýствер.
paraphernalia /pærəfə'neɪlɪə/ *n.* причиндáл|ы (*pl., g.* -ов) (*coll., joc.*).
paraphrase /'pærəfreɪz/ *v.t.* пересказ|ывать, -áть.
paraplegic /pærə'pli:dʒɪk/ *adj.* парализóванный.
parasailing *n.* (*sport*) парасéйлинг (*полёты на парашюте за катером*).
parasite /'pærəsaɪt/ *n.* паразѝт.
parasitic /pærə'sɪtɪk/ *adj.* (*lit., fig.*) паразитѝческий.
parasol /'pærəsɒl/ *n.* зóнтик (от сóлнца).
paratrooper /'pærətru:pə(r)/ *n.* (авиа)десáнтник.
parcel /'pɑ:s(ə)l/ *n.* пакéт, бандерóль, посылка.
■ *v.t.* (**parcelled, parcelling;** *US* **parceled, parceling**) (*pack up; also* ~ **up**) паковáть, у-.
parch /pɑ:tʃ/ *v.t.* иссуш|áть, -ѝть; **the ground was ~ed** землѝ вы́сохла; **my lips are ~ed** у меня́ запеклѝсь гýбы.
parchment /'pɑ:tʃmənt/ *n.* пергáмент.
pardon /'pɑ:d(ə)n/ *n.*
1 извинéние, прощéние.
2 (*leg.*) помѝлование; **they were granted a free ~** их помѝловали.
■ *v.t.* (*forgive*) про|щáть, -стѝть; (*excuse*) извин|я́ть, -ѝть; (*leg.*) мѝловать, по-.
parent /'peərənt/ *n.* (*father or mother*) родѝтель (*fem.* -ница); **~ company** компáния-учредѝтель.
parentage /'peərəntɪdʒ/ *n.* происхождéние; **he is of mixed ~** он происхóдит от смéшанного брáка.
parental /pə'rent(ə)l/ *adj.* родѝтельский.
parenthes|is /pə'renθəsɪs/ *n.* (*pl.* **parentheses** /-si:z/) (*word*) ввóдное слóво; (*sentence*) ввóдное предложéние; (*pl., text mark*) крýглые скóбки (*f. pl.*); **in ~es** в скóбках.
parenthood /'peərənthʊd/ *n.* (*fatherhood*) отцóвство; (*motherhood*) материнство.
parenting /'peərəntɪŋ/ *n.* воспитáние.
Paris /'pærɪs/ *n.* Парѝж.
parish /'pærɪʃ/ *n.* (*eccl.*) прихóд; (*Br., civil*) óкруг.
parishioner /pə'rɪʃənə(r)/ *n.* прихожáн|ин (*fem.* -ка).
parity /'pærɪtɪ/ *n.* (*equality*) рáвенство, паритéт.
park /pɑ:k/ *n.*
1 (*public garden*) парк.
2 (*protected area of countryside*) парк.
3 (*grounds of country mansion*) угóд|ья (*pl., g.* -ий).
■ *v.t.* паркова́ть, при-.
■ *v.i.* паркова́ться, при-.
■ *cpd.* **park-and-ride** *n.* «паркýйся и поезжáй (дáльше)» (*система периферийных автостоянок, где автовладельцы оставляют свои автомобили и пересаживаются на общественный транспорт*).
parking /'pɑ:kɪŋ/ *n.* (авто)стоя́нка; **'no ~!'** «стоя́нка запрещенá!»
■ *cpds.* **~ lot** *n.* (*US*) стоя́нка; мéсто стоя́нки; **~ meter** *n.* счётчик на стоя́нке; **~ place** *n.* мéсто для паркóвки; **~ ticket** *n.* штраф за нарушéние прáвил стоя́нки/паркóвки.
Parkinson's disease /'pɑ:kɪns(ə)nz/ *n.* болéзнь Паркинсóна.
parlance /'pɑ:ləns/ *n.* язы́к; манéра выражéния; **in common ~** в просторéчии.
parliament /'pɑ:ləmənt/ *n.* парлáмент.
parliamentarian /pɑ:ləmen'teərɪən/ *n.* (*member of parliament*) парламентáрий.
parliamentary /pɑ:lə'mentərɪ/ *adj.* парлáментский, парламентáрный.
parlour /'pɑ:lə(r)/ (*US* **parlor**) *n.* (*in house*) гостѝная; **beauty ~** косметѝческий кабинéт/салóн; **funeral ~** похорóнное бюрó (*nt. indecl.*); **ice cream ~** кафé-морóженое.
parochial /pə'rəʊkɪəl/ *adj.* прихóдский; (*fig.*) ограни́ченный, ýзкий.
parochialism /pə'rəʊkɪəlɪz(ə)m/ *n.* ограни́ченность, ýзость.
parody /'pærədɪ/ *n.* парóдия.
■ *v.t.* пародѝровать (*impf., pf.*).
parole /pə'rəʊl/ *n.* чéстное слóво; **he was released on ~** егó освободѝли под чéстное слóво.
paroxysm /'pærəksɪz(ə)m/ *n.* (*med., also fig.*) прѝступ.
parquet /'pɑ:kɪ, -keɪ/ *n.* паркéт; **~ floor** паркéтный пол.
parrot /'pærət/ *n.* (*lit., fig.*) попугáй.
parry /'pærɪ/ *v.t.* (*blow*) отра|жáть, -зѝть; (*question*) парѝровать (*impf., pf.*).
parsimonious /pɑ:sɪ'məʊnɪəs/ *adj.* скупóй.
parsley /'pɑ:slɪ/ *n.* петрýшка.
parsnip /'pɑ:snɪp/ *n.* пастернáк.

parson /ˈpɑːs(ə)n/ *n.* пáстор; **~'s nose** (*of fowl*) «архиерéйский нос», кури́ная гу́зка.
part /pɑːt/ *n.*
1 часть; (*portion*) дóля; **for the most ~** бóльшей чáстью; **in ~** части́чно, отчáсти; (*component*): **spare ~s** запасны́е чáсти; (*gram.*): **~s of speech** чáсти рéчи.
2 (*share*) учáстие; **take ~ in** прин|имáть, -я́ть учáстие в + *p.*
3 (*actor's role or lines*) роль.
4 (*side in dispute etc.*) сторонá; **for my ~** с моéй стороны́, что касáется меня́.
5 (*US, in one's hair*) пробóр.
■ *adv.* части́чно, чáстью, отчáсти; **the wall is ~ brick and ~ stone** стенá слóжена части́чно из кирпичá, части́чно из кáмня.
■ *v.t.* раздел|я́ть, -и́ть; **the policeman ~ed the crowd** полицéйский раздви́нул толпу́; **his hair was ~ed in the middle** егó вóлосы бы́ли расчёсаны на прямóй пробóр.
■ *v.i.* (*of people*) расст|авáться, -áться; **the crowd ~ed** толпá расступи́лась; **she has ~ed from her husband** онá разошлáсь с му́жем; **he hates to ~ with his money** он óчень не лю́бит расставáться с деньгáми.
■ *cpds.* **~ exchange** *n.* (*Br.*) сдéлка, при котóрой стáрая вещь обмéнивается на нóвую с доплáтой; **~-time** *adj., adv.* на полстáвки; **I want a ~-time job** я хочу́ рабóтать на полстáвки; **he works ~-time** он рабóтает на полстáвки.
partial /ˈpɑːʃ(ə)l/ *adj.*
1 (*opp. total*) части́чный.
2 (*biased*) пристрáстный.
3 : **~ to** (*fond of*) неравноду́шный к + *d.*
participant /pɑːˈtɪsɪpənt/ *n.* учáстник.
participate /pɑːˈtɪsɪpeɪt/ *v.i.* учáствовать (*impf.*).
participation /pɑːtɪsɪˈpeɪʃ(ə)n/ *n.* учáстие.
participle /ˈpɑːtɪsɪp(ə)l/ *n.* причáстие.
particle /ˈpɑːtɪk(ə)l/ *n.* (*also gram.*) части́ца.
particular /pəˈtɪkjʊlə(r)/ *n.* чáстность; **in ~** (*specifically*) в чáстности; (*especially*) осóбенно; (*pl.*) дáнные (*pl.*); **let me take down your ~s** разреши́те мне записáть вáши дáнные.
■ *adj.* 1 (*specific*) осóбенный, осóбый; **for no ~ reason** без осóбой причи́ны.
2 (*fastidious*) привередливый; **she is not ~ about her dress** ей всё равнó, что надéть.
particularly /pəˈtɪkjʊləlɪ/ *adv.* осóбенно.
parting /ˈpɑːtɪŋ/ *n.*
1 (*leave-taking*) прощáние.
2 (*Br., of the hair*) пробóр.
partisan /pɑːtɪˈzæn/ *n.* партизáн (*fem.* -ка).
partition /pɑːˈtɪʃ(ə)n/ *n.* (*division*) раздéл; (*dividing structure*) перегорóдка.
■ *v.t.* дели́ть, раз-/по-; **~ off** отгор|áживать, -оди́ть.
partly /ˈpɑːtlɪ/ *adv.* части́чно, отчáсти.
partner /ˈpɑːtnə(r)/ *n.* (*business, sexual, cards, dancing etc.*) партнёр (*fem. coll.* -ша); (*in marriage*) супру́г (*fem.* -а).
partnership /ˈpɑːtnəʃɪp/ *n.* товáрищество; партнёрство; **to go into ~ (with)** входи́ть, войти́ в партнёрство (с + *i.*).
partridge /ˈpɑːtrɪdʒ/ *n.* (*pl.* **~** *or* **~s**) куропáтка.
party /ˈpɑːtɪ/ *n.*
1 (*political group*) пáртия; **~ line** поли́тика (*or* полити́ческий курс) пáртии.
2 (*group*) компáния, гру́ппа.
3 (*social gathering*) вечери́нка.
4 (*participant in contract etc.*) сторонá.
5 (*attr., shared*): **~ line** (*teleph.*) óбщая телефóнная ли́ния (*see also sense* **1**).
■ *cpd.* **~ political** *adj.* парти́йный; **~ political broadcast** (*Br.*) пропаганди́стское выступлéние пáртии по рáдио и́ли телеви́дению.
pass /pɑːs/ *n.*
1 (*qualifying standard in exam*) сдáча экзáмена.
2 (*document*) прóпуск (*pl.* -á).
3 (*transfer of ball in game*) пас, передáча.
4 (*lunge*) вы́пад; (*coll., amorous approach*): **he made a ~ at her** он к ней приставáл (*coll.*).
5 (*mountain defile*) ущéлье, перевáл.
■ *v.t.* 1 (*go by*) про|ходи́ть, -йти́ (ми́мо + *g.*); **I ~ed him in the street** я прошёл ми́мо негó на у́лице.
2 (*go, get through*) про|ходи́ть, -йти́; **will your car ~ the test** пройдёт ли вáша маши́на прове́рку?; **~ an exam** сдать (*pf.*) экзáмен.
3 (*spend*) пров|оди́ть, -ести́.
4 (*accept*) пропус|кáть, -ти́ть; (*approve*) од|обря́ть, -óбрить.
5 (*hand over*) перед|авáть, -áть; **~ (me) the salt, please!** передáйте мне соль, пожáлуйста!
6 (*utter*) произн|оси́ть, -ести́; **the judge ~ed sentence** судья́ вы́нес приговóр.
■ *v.i.* 1 (*proceed, move*) про|ходи́ть, -йти́; перепр|авля́ться, -áвиться; (*get through*): **let me ~!** дáйте мне пройти́!, разреши́те пройти́!
2 (*go by, elapse*) про|ходи́ть, -йти́; **time ~es slowly** врéмя прохóдит мéдленно.
3 (*qualify in exam etc.*) про|ходи́ть, -йти́.
■ *with advs.*: **~ away** *v.i.* (*die*) скончáться (*pf.*); **~ by** *v.t.* & *i.* про|ходи́ть, -йти́ (ми́мо + *g.*); **~ down** *v.t.* перед|авáть, -áть; **~ off** *v.t.* (*dismiss*): **he ~ed off the whole affair as a joke** он обрати́л всё дéло в шу́тку; (*falsely represent*): **he tried to ~ off the picture as genuine** он выдавáл карти́ну за пóдлинник; *v.i.* (*go away*) прекра|щáться, -ти́ться; **~ on** *v.t.* перед|авáть, -áть; *v.i.* про|ходи́ть, -йти́; (*euph., die*) скончáться (*pf.*); **~ out** *v.i.* (*coll., lose consciousness*) отключ|áться, -и́ться.
■ *cpds.* **~ key** *n.* отмы́чка; **P~over** *n.* еврéйская Пáсха; **~word** *n.* (*also comput.*) парóль (*m.*).
passable /ˈpɑːsəb(ə)l/ *adj.* (*affording passage*) проходи́мый; (*tolerable*) снóсный.
passage /ˈpæsɪdʒ/ *n.*
1 (*going by*) прохóд; (*going across, over*) переéзд; перелёт; **a bird of ~** перелётная пти́ца; (*transition, change*) перехóд; (*going through, way through*) прохóд.
2 (*crossing by ship etc.*) рейс.
3 (*corridor*) коридóр.
4 (*literary excerpt*) отры́вок, текст.
■ *cpd.* **~way** *n.* коридóр.
passé /ˈpæseɪ/ *adj.* устарéлый, немóдный.
passenger /ˈpæsɪndʒə(r)/ *n.* пассажи́р; **~ train** пассажи́рский пóезд.
passer-by /pɑːsəˈbaɪ/ *n.* прохóжий.

passing /'pɑːsɪŋ/ *n.*: **I will mention in ~** я замечу между прочим.
■ *adj.* (*transient*): **a ~ fancy** мимолётное увлечение.

passion /'pæʃ(ə)n/ *n.* страсть.

passionate /'pæʃənət/ *adj.* страстный, пылкий.

passive /'pæsɪv/ *n.* (*gram.*) страдательный залог.
■ *adj.* пассивный; **~ smoking** пассивное курение; (*gram.*) пассивный, страдательный.

passivity /pæ'sɪvɪtɪ/ *n.* пассивность.

passport /'pɑːspɔːt/ *n.* паспорт.

past /pɑːst/
1 прошлое.
2 (*gram.*) прошедшее время.
■ *adj.* 1 (*bygone*) минувший, прошлый; (*pred., gone by*) мимо; **the time for that is ~** время (для) этого давно миновало.
2 (*preceding*) прошлый, последний; **for the ~ few days** за последние несколько дней; **during the ~ week** за последнюю/эту неделю.
3 (*gram.*) прошедший; **~ participle** причастие прошедшего времени; **~ tense** прошедшее время.
■ *adv.* мимо; **the soldiers marched ~** солдаты прошли мимо.
■ *prep.* 1 (*after*) после + *g.*; **it is ~ eight (o'clock)** сейчас девятый час; **ten ~ one** десять минут второго.
2 (*by*) мимо + *g.*; **he drove ~ the house** он проехал мимо дома.
3 (*to the far side of*) за + *a.*; (*on the far side of*) за + *i.*; **you've gone ~ the turning** вы проехали поворот.
4 (*beyond*) свыше + *g.*, сверх + *g.*; **he was a fine actor, but he's ~ it now** (*coll.*) когда-то он был хорошим актёром, но это в прошлом; **I wouldn't put it ~ him to steal the money** я думаю, что он способен украсть деньги.

pasta /'pæstə/ *n.* макарон|ы (*pl., g.* —).

paste /peɪst/ *n.* (*adhesive*) клей.
■ *v.t.* 1 (*stick*) накле|ивать, -ить; прикле|ивать, -ить.
2 (*comput.*) вст|авлять, -авить.

pastel /'pæst(ə)l/ *n.* (*crayon*) пастель; **~ shades** пастельные краски.

pasteurize /'pɑːstʃəraɪz/ *v.t.* пастеризовать (*impf., pf.*).

pastiche /pæ'stiːʃ/ *n.* (*literary imitation*) стилизация (**of:** под + *a.*); подделка.

pastime /'pɑːstaɪm/ *n.* время(пре)провождение.

pastor /'pɑːstə(r)/ *n.* пастор.

pastoral /'pɑːstər(ə)l/ *adj.* пасторальный.

pastry /'peɪstrɪ/ *n.* (*dough*) тесто; (*tart*) пирожное.

pasturage /'pɑːstʃərɪdʒ/ *n.* (*grazing land*) пастбище; (*grazing*) выпас.

pasture /'pɑːstjə(r)/ *n.* пастбище.

pat[1] /pæt/ *n.*
1 (*light touch*) хлопок; шлепок.
2 (*of butter*) кусочек.
■ *v.t.* (**patted, patting**) похлоп|ывать, -ать; (*a dog*) гладить, по-.

pat[2] /pæt/ *adj.* готовый; **he had his lesson off** (*US* **down**) **~** он выучил урок назубок.

patch /pætʃ/ *n.*
1 (*covering over hole*) заплата; (*over eye*) повязка; (*comput.*) патч, «заплат(к)а».
2 (*distinctive area*) клочок; **~es of blue sky** клочки голубого неба; **there were ~es of ice on the road** на дороге местами была гололедица.
3 (*piece of ground*) участок.
4 (*scrap*) лоскут.
■ *v.t.* (*mend*) латать, за-.
■ *with adv.*: **~ up** *v.t.* (*lit.*) чинить, по-; (*fig.*) ула|живать, -дить.

patchy /'pætʃɪ/ *adj.* (*fig., of knowledge*) отрывочный; (*fig., of uneven quality*) неровный.

patent /'peɪt(ə)nt/ *n.* патент.
■ *adj.* 1: **~ leather** лакированная кожа.
2 (*obvious*) очевидный.
■ *v.t.* патентовать, за-.

paternal /pə'tɜːn(ə)l/ *adj.* отцовский.

paternalistic /pətɜːnə'lɪstɪk/ *adj.* (*pol.*) патерналистский; (*manner, tone*) покровительственный.

paternity /pə'tɜːnɪtɪ/ *n.* отцовство; **~ leave** отпуск по уходу за ребёнком (для отца).

path /pɑːθ/ *n.* (*track for walking*) тропа, тропинка; дорожка; (*fig.*) путь (*m.*); (*course, trajectory*) траектория; **the ~ of a bullet** траектория полёта пули.

pathetic /pə'θetɪk/ *adj.* жалкий.

pathological /pæθə'lɒdʒɪk(ə)l/ *adj.* патологический.

pathologist /pə'θɒlədʒɪst/ *n.* патолог.

pathology /pə'θɒlədʒɪ/ *n.* патология.

pathos /'peɪθɒs/ *n.* горечь, печаль.

patience /'peɪʃ(ə)ns/ *n.*
1 терпение; **she lost ~ with him** она потеряла с ним всякое терпение.
2 (*Br., card game*) пасьянс.

patient /'peɪʃ(ə)nt/ *n.* пациент, больной.
■ *adj.* терпеливый.

patio /'pætɪəʊ/ *n.* (*pl.* **~s**) дворик.

patriarchal /peɪtrɪ'ɑːk(ə)l/ *adj.* патриархальный.

patriot /'peɪtrɪət/ *n.* патриот (*fem.* -ка).

patriotic /pætrɪ'ɒtɪk/ *adj.* патриотический.

patriotism /'pætrɪətɪz(ə)m/ *n.* патриотизм.

patrol /pə'trəʊl/ *n.*
1 (*action*) патрулирование, дозор; **~ car** (полицейская) патрульная машина; **~ vessel** сторожевой корабль.
2 (*~ling body*) патруль (*m.*).
■ *v.t.* & *i.* (**patrolled, patrolling**) патрулировать (*impf.*).

patron /'peɪtrən/ *n.*
1 (*supporter*) покровитель (*m.*), патрон; **a ~ of the arts** покровитель искусств, меценат; **~ saint** свят|ой заступни|к (*fem.* -ая -ца).
2 (*customer*) (постоянный) клиент.

patronage /'pætrənɪdʒ/ *n.* покровительство, шефство.

patronize /'pætrənaɪz/ *v.t.* (*visit as customer*) постоянно посещать (*impf.*); (*treat condescendingly*) отн|оситься, -естись свысока к + *d.*

patronymic /pætrə'nɪmɪk/ *n.* отчество.

patter[1] /'pætə(r)/ *n.* (*of salesman*)

скороговóрка.

patter² /ˈpætə(r)/ *n.* (*tapping sound*) стук, постýкивание.
■ *v.i.* барабáнить (*impf.*), (*of feet*) топотáть (*impf.*) (*coll.*).

pattern /ˈpæt(ə)n/ *n.*
1 (*decorative design*) узóр.
2 (*example*) образéц.
3 (*model for production*) вы́кройка; **dress ~** вы́кройка плáтья.
4 (*system*) óбраз, манéра; **new ~s of behaviour** (*Br.*), **behavior** (*US*) нóвые нóрмы (*f. pl.*) поведéния.
■ *v.t.*: **a ~ed dress** плáтье с узóрами.

paucity /ˈpɔːsɪtɪ/ *n.* нехвáтка, скýдость.

paunch /pɔːntʃ/ *n.* брюшкó, живóт.

pauper /ˈpɔːpə(r)/ *n.* бедня́к.

pause /pɔːz/ *n.* (*intermission*) переры́в; (*in speaking*) пáуза.
■ *v.i.* остан|áвливаться, -ови́ться.

pave /peɪv/ *v.t.* мости́ть, вы́-; (*fig.*): **his proposal ~d the way to a lasting peace** егó предложéние проложи́ло путь к прóчному ми́ру.

pavement /ˈpeɪvmənt/ *n.*
1 (*Br., footway*) тротуáр.
2 (*US, paved surface*) мостовáя.

pavilion /pəˈvɪljən/ *n.* (*Br., sport*) павильóн.

paving stone /ˈpeɪvɪŋ stəʊn/ *n.* брусчáтка.

paw /pɔː/ *n.* лáпа.

pawn¹ /pɔːn/ *n.* (*chessman, also fig.*) пéшка.

pawn² /pɔːn/ *v.t.* за|клáдывать, -ложи́ть.
■ *cpds.* **~broker** *n.* человéк, даю́щий дéньги под залóг (вещéй); **~shop** *n.* ломбáрд.

pay /peɪ/ *n.* (*wages*) зарплáта; жáлованье.
■ *v.t.* (*past and p.p.* **paid**)
1 (*give in return for sth.*) плати́ть, за-, у-; **she always ~s cash** онá всегдá плáтит нали́чными; (*contribute*): **everyone must ~ his share** кáждый дóлжен внести́ свою́ дóлю.
2 (*remunerate*) плати́ть, за-, оплá|чивать, -ти́ть (**s.o.:** + *d.*); **we are paid on Fridays** нам плáтят по пя́тницам; мы получáем зарплáту по пя́тницам.
3 (*bestow*): **~ attention to me!** послýшайте меня́!; **~ s.o. a compliment** дéлать, с- комý-н. комплимéнт; **~ s.o. a visit** наве|щáть, -сти́ть когó-н.
4 (*benefit, profit*): **it will ~ you to wait** вам стóит подождáть.
■ *v.i.* (*past and p.p.* **paid**)
1 (*give money*) расплá|чиваться, -ти́ться.
2 (*suffer*) плати́ть, за-; плати́ться, по- (за + *a.*); **he paid for his carelessness** он поплати́лся за своё легкомы́слие.
3 (*yield a return*) окуп|áться, -и́ться; давáть, дать при́быль.
■ *with advs.*: **~ back** *v.t.* (*reimburse*): **he paid me back in person** он ли́чно вернýл мне дéньги; (*have revenge on*) отплати́ть (*pf.*) + *d.*; **~ in** *v.t.* вн|оси́ть, -ести́; **~ off** *v.t.* рассчи́т|ываться, -áться с + *i.*; (**~** *wages and discharge*) рассчи́т|ывать, -áть; *v.i.* (*bring profit*) окуп|áться, -и́ться; **~ out** *v.t.* (*expend*) выплáчивать, вы́платить; **~ up** *v.i.* (**~** *amount due*) рассчи́т|ываться, -áться сполнá.
■ *cpds.* **~ day** *n.* платёжный день; **~ packet** (*Br.*) *n.* зáработок, (*coll.*) полýчка; **~phone** *n.* телефóн-автомáт; **~slip** *n.* (*Br.*) квитáнция о вы́даче зарплáты; **~ TV** *n.* плáтное телеви́дение.

payable /ˈpeɪəb(ə)l/ *adj.* оплáчиваемый; подлежáщий уплáте.

PAYE (*abbr. of* ***pay-as-you-earn***) (*Br.*) автомати́ческое отчислéние подохóдного налóга из зарплáты.

payment /ˈpeɪmənt/ *n.* (*paying*) оплáта, платёж; (*sum paid*) плáта; (*of debt etc.*) уплáта.

PC *abbr. of*
1 ***personal computer*** ПК (персонáльный компью́тер).
2 ***politically correct*** полити́чески коррéктный, политкоррéктный.

PDA (*abbr. of* ***Personal Digital Assistant***) *n.* «электрóнный помóщник».

PE (*abbr. of* ***physical education***) физкультýра.

pea /piː/ *n.* горóшина.
■ *cpd.* **~nut** *n.* арáхис, землянóй орéх; **~nut butter** пáста из тёртого арáхиса.

peace /piːs/ *n.*
1 (*freedom from war*) мир; **~ talks** ми́рные переговóры.
2 (*freedom from civil disorder*) спокóйствие, поря́док.
3 (*quiet*) спокóйствие, покóй; **can we have some ~ and quiet?** нельзя́ ли поти́ше?; **~ of mind** спокóйствие дýха.
■ *cpds.* **~keeping** *adj.*: **~keeping force** миротвóрческие войскá (*nt. pl.*)/си́лы (*f. pl.*); **~maker** *n.* миротвóрец; **~time** *n.* ми́рное врéмя.

peaceful /ˈpiːsfʊl/ *adj.* ми́рный.

peach /piːtʃ/ *n.*
1 (*fruit*) пéрсик.
2 (*tree*) пéрсиковое дéрево.

peacock /ˈpiːkɒk/ *n.* павли́н.

peak /piːk/ *n.*
1 (*mountain top*) пик, верши́на.
2 (*of cap*) козырёк.
3 (*fig., highest point*) пик, верши́на; **~ viewing hours** прáйм-тáйм.
■ *v.i.*: **demand ~ed** спрос дости́г вы́сшей тóчки.

peaked /piːkt/ *adj.*
1 остроконéчный; **~ cap** (фóрменная) фурáжка.
2 (*haggard; also* **peaky**) осýнувшийся.

peaky /ˈpiːkɪ/ *adj.* (**peakier, peakiest**) = **peaked 2**

peal /piːl/ *n.* (*of bells*) трезвóн; (*of laughter*) взрыв.

pear /peə(r)/ *n.*
1 (*fruit*) грýша.
2 (*tree*) грýшевое дéрево, грýша.

pearl /pɜːl/ *n.* жемчýжина.

peasant /ˈpez(ə)nt/ *n.* крестья́н|ин (*fem.* -ка).

peat /piːt/ *n.* торф.

pebble /ˈpeb(ə)l/ *n.* гáлька.

pebbly /ˈpeblɪ/ *adj.* покры́тый гáлькой.

pecan /ˈpiːkən/ *n.* орéх пекáн.

peck /pek/ *n.* (*made by beak*) клевóк; (*fig., hasty kiss*): **he gave her a ~ on the cheek** он чмóкнул её в щё(ч)ку.

■ *v.t.* клевáть, клю́нуть; поклевáть (*pf.*).
■ *v.i.* (*fig.*): **she ~ed at her food** онá едвá дотрóнулась до еды́; **~ing order** ≈ неофициáльная иерáрхия.

peckish /ˈpekɪʃ/ *adj.* (*Br. coll.*) голóдный.

pectoral /ˈpektər(ə)l/ *adj.* (*anat.*) груднóй.

peculiar /pɪˈkjuːlɪə(r)/ *adj.*
1 (*exclusive*) осóбенный, своеобрáзный.
2 (*strange*) стрáнный.

peculiarity /pɪkjuːlɪˈærɪtɪ/ *n.* (*characteristic*) свóйство; (*oddity*) стрáнность.

pecuniary /pɪˈkjuːnɪərɪ/ *adj.* дéнежный.

pedagogic(al) /pedəˈgɒgɪk((ə)l)/ *adj.* педагоги́ческий.

pedal /ˈped(ə)l/ *n.* педáль.
■ *v.i.* (**pedalled, pedalling;** *US* **pedaled, pedaling**) éхать (*det.*) на велосипéде.

pedant /ˈped(ə)nt/ *n.* педáнт (*fem. also* -ка).

pedantic /pɪˈdæntɪk/ *adj.* педанти́чный.

pedantry /ˈped(ə)ntrɪ/ *n.* педанти́чность.

peddle /ˈped(ə)l/ *v.t.* торговáть (*impf.*) вразнóс.

peddler /ˈpedlə(r)/ *n.* (*of drugs*) торгóвец наркóтиками.

pedestal /ˈpedɪst(ə)l/ *n.* пьедестáл.

pedestrian /pɪˈdestrɪən/ *n.* пешехóд.
■ *adj.* пешехóдный; **~ crossing** (*Br.*) перехóд; **~ precinct** пешехóдная зóна.

pediatric /piːdɪˈætrɪk/, **-ian** /piːdɪəˈtrɪʃ(ə)n/, **-s** /piːdɪˈætrɪks/ (*US*) = **paediatric** *etc.*

pedicure /ˈpedɪkjʊə(r)/ *n.* (*treatment*) педикю́р; (*person*) педикю́рша.

pedigree /ˈpedɪgriː/ *n.* происхождéние; (*attr.*): **~ cattle** племеннóй скот.

pedophile /ˈpiːdəfaɪl/ (*US*) = **paedophile**

pedophilia /piːdəˈfɪlɪə/ (*US*) = **paedophilia**

pee /piː/ (*coll.*) *n.* (*urination*) пи-пи́ (*nt. indecl.*); (*urine*) мочá.
■ *v.i.* (**pees, peed**) мочи́ться, по-.

peek /piːk/ (*coll.*) *n.* взгляд укрáдкой.

peel /piːl/ *n.* (*thin skin of fruit*) кожурá; (*of vegetables*) шелухá; (*rind of orange etc.*) кóрка.
■ *v.t.* 1 (*remove skin from*) оч|ищáть, -и́стить.
2 (*remove from surface*) сн|имáть, -ять.
■ *v.i.* 1 (*lose skin*) шелуши́ться (*impf.*).
2 (*come away from surface; also* **~ away, ~ off**) слез|áть, -ть; обл|езáть, -éзть; **the paint has begun to ~ (off)** крáска началá облезáть.

peeling /ˈpiːlɪŋ/ *n.* (*of fruit*) кожурá; (*of vegetables*) шелухá.

peep[1] /piːp/ *n.* (*furtive or hasty look*) взгляд укрáдкой; **take, have a ~ at** взгляну́ть (*pf.*) на + *a.*
■ *v.i.* погля́д|ывать, -éть; **he ~ed in at the window** он загляну́л в окнó.
■ *cpd.* **~hole** *n.* глазóк.

peep[2] /piːp/ *v.i.* (*chirp*) пищáть, пи́скнуть; чири́к|ать, -нуть.

peer[1] /pɪə(r)/ *n.*
1 (*equal*) рáвн|ый (*fem.* -ая); (*person of the same age*) ровéсни|к (*fem.* -ца); свéрстни|к (*fem.* -ца); **~ group** ровéсники, свéрстники (*m. pl.*); **~ (group) pressure** давлéние грýппы (свéрстников).
2 (*noble*) пэр.

peer[2] /pɪə(r)/ *v.i.* (*look closely*) всм|áтриваться, -отрéться (в + *a.*).

peerage /ˈpɪərɪdʒ/ *n.* пэ́рство, ти́тул пэ́ра.

peeved /piːvd/ *adj.* (*coll.*) : **he looks ~** у негó недовóльный вид.

peg /peg/ *n.* (*for holding sth. down*) кóлышек; **(clothes ~)** (*Br.*) прищéпка; **(hat ~, coat ~)** вéшалка, крючóк.

pejorative /pɪˈdʒɒrətɪv/ *adj.* уничижи́тельный.

pelican /ˈpelɪkən/ *n.* пеликáн.

pellet /ˈpelɪt/ *n.* шáрик.

pelt /pelt/ *v.t.* (*assail*) забр|áсывать, -осáть; **they ~ed him with stones/insults** они́ забросáли егó камня́ми/оскорблéниями.
■ *v.i.* стучáть, барабáнить (*both impf.*); **the rain was ~ing down** дождь барабáнил вовсю́.

pelvic /ˈpelvɪk/ *adj.* тáзовый; **~ girdle** тáзовый пóяс.

pelvis /ˈpelvɪs/ *n.* (*pl.* **pelvises**) таз.

pen[1] /pen/ *n.* (*writing instrument*) ру́чка.
■ *cpds.* **~friend** *n.* (*Br.*) друг (*fem.* подру́га) по перепи́ске; **~knife** *n.* перочи́нный нóж(ик); **~ pal** (*US*) = **~friend**

pen[2] /pen/ *n.* (*enclosure*) загóн.

penal /ˈpiːn(ə)l/ *adj.*: **~ code** уголóвный кóдекс; **~ colony** исправи́тельная колóния.

penalize /ˈpiːnəlaɪz/ *v.t.* накáз|ывать, -áть.

penalty /ˈpenəltɪ/ *n.* (*punishment*) наказáние; (*fine*) штраф; (*football, also* **~ kick**) пенáльти (*m. indecl.*).

penance /ˈpenəns/ *n.* епитимья́; покая́ние; **he must do ~ for his sins** он дóлжен замоли́ть/искупи́ть свои́ грехи́.

pence /pens/ *n.* see ▸ **penny**

penchant /ˈpɑ̃ʃɑ̃/ *n.* склóнность (**for:** к + *d.*).

pencil /ˈpensɪl/ *n.* карандáш.
■ *v.t.* (**pencilled, pencilling;** *US* **penciled, penciling**): **~ in** (*arrange provisionally*) дéлать, с- предвари́тельную замéтку насчёт + *g.*
■ *cpds.* **~ case** *n.* пенáл; **~ sharpener** *n.* точи́лка.

pendant /ˈpend(ə)nt/ *n.* кулóн.

pending /ˈpendɪŋ/ *adj.* рассмáтриваемый.
■ *prep.* до + *g.*; в ожидáнии + *g.*

pendulous /ˈpendjʊləs/ *adj.* подвеснóй.

pendulum /ˈpendjʊləm/ *n.* мáятник.

penetrate /ˈpenɪtreɪt/ *v.t.* прон|икáть, -и́кнуть в + *a.*

penetrating /ˈpenɪtreɪtɪŋ/ *adj.* си́льный; óстрый; **a ~ voice** пронзи́тельный гóлос.

penguin /ˈpeŋgwɪn/ *n.* пингви́н.

penicillin /penɪˈsɪlɪn/ *n.* пеницилли́н.

peninsula /pəˈnɪnsjʊlə/ *n.* полуóстров.

penis /ˈpiːnɪs/ *n.* (*pl.* **penises**) пéнис, половóй член.

penitence /ˈpenɪt(ə)ns/ *n.* раскáяние.

penitent /ˈpenɪt(ə)nt/ *adj.* раскáивающийся.

penitentiary /penɪˈtenʃərɪ/ *n.* тюрьмá.

pennant /ˈpenənt/ *n.* флажóк, вы́мпел.

penniless /ˈpenɪlɪs/ *adj.* бездéнежный, без грошá (*pred.*).

penny /ˈpenɪ/ *n.* (*pl. for separate coins* **pennies,** *for a sum of money* **pence**) пéнни (*nt. indecl.*), пенс; (*US cent*) цент; **at last the ~ has dropped!** (*Br. coll.*) наконéц-то дошлó.

pension /ˈpenʃ(ə)n/ *n.* пе́нсия; **old-age ~** пе́нсия по ста́рости.

pensionable /ˈpenʃənəb(ə)l/ *adj.*: **~ age** пенсио́нный во́зраст; **his job is ~** его́ рабо́та даёт ему́ пра́во на пе́нсию.

pensioner /ˈpenʃənə(r)/ *n.* пенсионе́р (*fem.* -ка).

pensive /ˈpensɪv/ *adj.* заду́мчивый.

pent /pent/ *adj.*: **~-up feelings** сде́рживаемые чу́вства.

pentagon /ˈpentəgən/ *n.* пятиуго́льник; **the P~** (*US War Department*) Пентаго́н.

pentathlon /penˈtæθlən/ *n.* пятибо́рье.

Pentecost /ˈpentɪkɒst/ *n.* Пятидеся́тница (*христианский праздник*).

penthouse /ˈpenthaʊs/ *n.* (*apartment*) роско́шная кварти́ра на после́днем этаже́; пентха́ус.

penultimate /pɪˈnʌltɪmət/ *adj.* предпосле́дний.

penury /ˈpenjʊrɪ/ *n.* бе́дность, нужда́.

peony /ˈpiːənɪ/ *n.* пио́н.

people /ˈpiːp(ə)l/ *n.*
1 (*persons*) лю́д|и (*pl.*, *g.* -е́й); **few ~** ма́ло люде́й; **most ~ will object** большинство́ (люде́й) бу́дет про́тив.
2 (*nation; proletariat*) наро́д.
3 (*inhabitants*) жи́тели (*m. pl.*); (*citizens*) гра́ждане (*m. pl.*).
4 (*persons grouped by type*): **young ~** молодёжь, молоды́е лю́ди; **old ~** старики́ (*m. pl.*).

pep /pep/ *n.*: **~ talk** нака́чка.
■ *v.t.* (**pepped, pepping**) (*usu.* **~ up**) ожив|ля́ть, -и́ть.

pepper /ˈpepə(r)/ *n.* (*condiment*) пе́рец; (*vegetable*) (*sweet* **~**) (сла́дкий) пе́рец.
■ *cpds.* **~corn** *n.* перчи́нка; **~ mill** *n.* ме́льница для пе́рца; **~mint** *n.* (*sweet*) мя́тный ледене́ц.

peptic /ˈpeptɪk/ *adj.* пепти́ческий, пищевари́тельный; **~ ulcer** язва желу́дка.

per /pɜː(r)/ *prep.* в + *a.*; на + *a.*; с + *g.*; **60 miles ~ hour** 60 миль в час; **they collected 20 pence ~ man** они́ собра́ли по 20 пе́нсов с челове́ка.

per capita /pə ˈkæpɪtə/ *adv.* на ду́шу (населе́ния).

perceive /pəˈsiːv/ *v.t.* (*with mind*) пост|ига́ть, -и́гнуть, -и́чь; (*through senses*) восприн|има́ть, -я́ть.

per cent /pə ˈsent/ (*US* **percent**) *n., adv.* проце́нт.

percentage /pəˈsentɪdʒ/ *n.* (*of people/things*) проце́нт; (*of substance*) проце́нтное содержа́ние.

perceptible /pəˈseptɪb(ə)l/ *adj.* ощути́мый.

perception /pəˈsepʃ(ə)n/ *n.* (*process*) восприя́тие, ощуще́ние; (*discernment*) осозна́ние, понима́ние.

perceptive /pəˈseptɪv/ *adj.* восприи́мчивый; (*observant*) проница́тельный.

perch /pɜːtʃ/ *n.* (*of bird*) насе́ст.
■ *v.t.* & *i.* сади́ться, сесть; **he ~ed on a stool** он присе́л на табуре́т.

percipient /pəˈsɪpɪənt/ *adj.* воспринима́ющий.

percolate /ˈpɜːkəleɪt/ *v.t.* про|ходи́ть, -йти́ че́рез + *a.*
■ *v.i.* прос|а́чиваться, -очи́ться; **water ~s through sand** вода́ проса́чивается/прохо́дит сквозь песо́к; **I'm waiting for the coffee to ~** я жду, пока́ ко́фе профильтру́ется; **~ through** (*fig.*) (*news, idea, fashion*) (постепе́нно) распростран|я́ться, -и́ться, получ|а́ть, -и́ть распростране́ние (*среди людей, в обществе*); (*news also*) (постепе́нно) ста|нови́ться, -ть изве́стным (**to:** + *d.*).

percolator /ˈpɜːkəleɪtə(r)/ *n.* (*cul.*) перколя́тор, кофева́рка.

percussion /pəˈkʌʃ(ə)n/ *n.*: (**~ instruments**) уда́рные инструме́нты (*m. pl.*).

peremptory /pəˈremptərɪ/ *adj.* (*imperious*) повели́тельный; непререка́емый.

perennial /pəˈrenɪəl/ *adj.* (*plant*) многоле́тний; (*enduring*) ве́чный.

perestroika /perɪˈstrɔɪkə/ *n.* перестро́йка.

perfect[1] /ˈpɜːfɪkt/ *adj.*
1 (*complete; absolute*) соверше́нный; по́лный; **I am ~ly sure of it** я соверше́нно/по́лностью уве́рен в э́том.
2 (*faultless*) соверше́нный, безупре́чный; **he speaks ~ English** он в соверше́нстве владе́ет англи́йским (языко́м).
3 (*exact, precise*) абсолю́тный; **~ pitch** (*mus.*) абсолю́тный слух; (*corresponding to requirements*): **the dress is a ~ fit** пла́тье сиди́т безупре́чно.
4 (*gram.*) перфе́ктный, соверше́нный; **~ tense** перфе́кт.

perfect[2] /pəˈfekt/ *v.t.* соверше́нствовать, у-.

perfection /pəˈfekʃ(ə)n/ *n.* соверше́нство; **she dances to ~** она́ безупре́чно танцу́ет.

perfectionist /pəˈfekʃənɪst/ *n.* взыска́тельный челове́к.

perfidious /pəːˈfɪdɪəs/ *adj.* вероло́мный, кова́рный.

perforate /ˈpɜːfəreɪt/ *v.t.* перфори́ровать (*impf.*); **a ~d appendix** прободно́й/перфорати́вный аппендици́т.

perform /pəˈfɔːm/ *v.t.*
1 (*task*) выполня́ть, вы́полнить.
2 (*piece of music*) исп|олня́ть, -о́лнить; (*play*) игра́ть, сыгра́ть.
■ *v.i.* 1 (*in public*) игра́ть, сыгра́ть; выступа́ть, вы́ступить.
2 (*function*) рабо́тать (*impf.*); **my car ~s well on hills** моя́ маши́на хорошо́ идёт в го́ру.

performance /pəˈfɔːməns/ *n.*
1 (*of task*) выполне́ние.
2 (*of a machine, vehicle etc.*) ход, характери́стика.
3 (*public appearance*) выступле́ние.
4 (*of play etc.*) представле́ние.

performer /pəˈfɔːmə(r)/ *n.* исполни́тель (*m.*) (*fem.* -ница).

perfume /ˈpɜːfjuːm/ *n.* дух|и́ (*pl.*, *g.* -о́в), парфю́м.
■ *v.t.* (*impart odour to*) де́лать, с- благоуха́нным.

perfumery /pəˈfjuːmərɪ/ *n.* (*business*) парфюме́рия; (*shop*) парфюме́рный магази́н; **~ department** парфюме́рия.

perfunctory /pəˈfʌŋktərɪ/ *adj.* (*glance,*

P

inspection) повéрхностный; (*kiss, smile*) небрéжный.
pergola /ˈpɜ:gələ/ *n.* садóвая áрка, áрка из вьющихся растéний.
perhaps /pəˈhæps/ *adv.* мóжет быть; возмóжно; пожáлуй.
peril /ˈperɪl/ *n.* опáсность; риск.
perilous /ˈperɪləs/ *adj.* опáсный; рискóванный.
perimeter /pəˈrɪmɪtə(r)/ *n.* перимéтр.
period /ˈpɪərɪəd/ *n.*
1 перúод; **she has ~s of depression** у неё бывáют перúоды депрéссии; **for a long ~** дóлгое врéмя.
2 (*previous age*) эпóха; **~ furniture** старúнная мéбель.
3 (*lesson*) урóк.
4 (*med.*) мéсячные (*pl.*); **~ pains** (*Br.*) мéсячные бóли (*f. pl.*).
5 (*US, full stop*) тóчка.
periodic /pɪərɪˈɒdɪk/ *adj.* периодúческий.
periodical /pɪərɪˈɒdɪk(ə)l/ *n.* периодúческое издáние.
peripatetic /perɪpəˈtetɪk/ *adj.* (*teacher*) приходя́щий; (*itinerant*) бродя́чий.
peripheral /pəˈrɪfər(ə)l/ *n.* (*comput.*) периферúйное устрóйство.
■ *adj.* (*lit.*) периферúйный; (*fig.*) несущéственный; побóчный.
periphery /pəˈrɪfərɪ/ *n.* (*boundary*) гранúца, чертá; (*also fig.*) периферúя.
periscope /ˈperɪskəʊp/ *n.* перискóп.
perish /ˈperɪʃ/ *v.i.*
1 пог|ибáть, -úбнуть.
2: **the rubber has ~ed** резúна пришлá в негóдность.
perishable /ˈperɪʃəb(ə)l/ *adj.* (*pl., as n.*) скоропóртящийся товáр.
perjure /ˈpɜ:dʒə(r)/ *v.t.*: **~ o.s.** да|вáть, -ть лóжное показáние под прися́гой, лжесвидéтельствовать (*impf.*).
perjury /ˈpɜ:dʒərɪ/ *n.* лжесвидéтельство.
perk /pɜ:k/ *v.i. & t.*: **~ up** (*liven up*) ожив|ля́ть(ся), -úть(ся).
perky /ˈpɜ:kɪ/ *adj.* (**perkier, perkiest**) (*coll.*) весёлый, оживлённый.
perm /pɜ:m/ *n.* перманéнтная завúвка, перманéнт.
■ *v.t.*: **she had her hair ~ed** онá сдéлала себé перманéнтную завúвку/перманéнт.
permafrost /ˈpɜ:məfrɒst/ *n.* вéчная мерзлотá.
permanence /ˈpɜ:mənəns/ *n.* неизмéнность.
permanent /ˈpɜ:mənənt/ *adj.* постоя́нный.
permeable /ˈpɜ:mɪəb(ə)l/ *adj.* проницáемый.
permeate /ˈpɜ:mɪeɪt/ *v.t.* пропúт|ывать, -áть; прон|икáть, -úкнуть в + *a.*
permissible /pəˈmɪsɪb(ə)l/ *adj.* допустúмый, позволúтельный.
permission /pəˈmɪʃ(ə)n/ *n.* позволéние, разрешéние.
permissive /pəˈmɪsɪv/ *adj.*: **~ society** óбщество вседозвóленности.
permit[1] /ˈpɜ:mɪt/ *n.* разрешéние, прóпуск (*pl.* -á); **work ~** разрешéние на рабóту.
permit[2] /pəˈmɪt/ *v.t.* (**permitted, permitting**) разреш|áть, -úть, позв|оля́ть, -óлить; **smoking ~ted** курúть разрешáется.
■ *v.i.* (**permitted, permitting**): **if circumstances ~** éсли обстоя́тельства позвóлят.
permutation /pɜ:mjʊˈteɪʃ(ə)n/ *n.* (*math.*) перестанóвка; (*fig.*) вариáнт, модификáция.
pernicious /pəˈnɪʃəs/ *adj.* пáгубный, врéдный; **~ anaemia** злокáчественное малокрóвие.
pernickety /pəˈnɪkɪtɪ/ *adj.* (*coll.*) привередлúвый.
peroxide /pəˈrɒksaɪd/ *n.* пéрекись; **a ~ blonde** крáшеная блондúнка.
perpendicular /pɜ:pənˈdɪkjʊlə(r)/ *adj.* перпендикуля́рный.
perpetrate /ˈpɜ:pɪtreɪt/ *v.t.* соверш|áть, -úть.
perpetrator /ˈpɜ:pɪtreɪtə(r)/ *n.* винóвник (+ *g.*), винóвный (в + *p.*).
perpetual /pəˈpetjʊəl/ *adj.* вéчный.
perpetuate /pəˈpetjʊeɪt/ *v.t.* увековéчи|вать, -ть.
perpetuity /pɜ:pɪˈtju:ɪtɪ/ *n.* вéчность; **in ~** навсегдá, (на)вéчно.
perplex /pəˈpleks/ *v.t.* озадáчи|вать, -ть.
persecute /ˈpɜ:sɪkju:t/ *v.t.* преслéдовать (*impf.*).
persecution /pɜ:sɪˈkju:ʃ(ə)n/ *n.* преслéдование.
persecutor /ˈpɜ:sɪkju:tə(r)/ *n.* преслéдователь (*m.*) (*fem.* -ница).
perseverance /pɜ:sɪˈvɪərəns/ *n.* упóрство, настóйчивость.
persevere /pɜ:sɪˈvɪə(r)/ *v.i.* проявл|я́ть, -úть упóрство/настóйчивость (в + *p.*); **you must ~ in (at, with) your work** вы должны́ проявúть упóрство/настóйчивость в своéй рабóте.
Persian /ˈpɜ:ʃ(ə)n/: **~ Gulf** Персúдский залúв.
persist /pəˈsɪst/ *v.i.* (*continue stubbornly*) упóрно/настóйчиво продолжáть (*impf.*); (*continue*) сохран|я́ться, -úться; **fog will ~ all day** тумáн продéржится весь день.
persistence /pəˈsɪst(ə)ns/ *n.* упóрство, настóйчивость.
persistent /pəˈsɪst(ə)nt/ *adj.* (*stubborn*) упóрный, настóйчивый; (*continuous*) постоя́нный.
person /ˈpɜ:s(ə)n/ *n.*
1 (*individual*) человéк.
2 (*of particular category; also gram.*) лицó; **first ~ singular** пéрвое лицó едúнственного числá.
personable /ˈpɜ:sənəb(ə)l/ *adj.* привлекáтельный.
personal /ˈpɜ:sən(ə)l/ *adj.* лúчный; **~ column** (*of newspaper*) колóнка чáстных объявлéний; **~ computer** персонáльный компью́тер; **~ organizer** органáйзер; **~ stereo** плéер; **don't make ~ remarks!** не переходúте на лúчности!
personality /pɜ:səˈnælɪtɪ/ *n.*
1 (*character*) лúчность.
2 (*famous person*) знаменúтость.
personally /ˈpɜ:sənəlɪ/ *adv.* лúчно.
personification /pəsɒnɪfɪˈkeɪʃ(ə)n/ *n.* олицетворéние, воплощéние; **he is the ~ of selfishness** он явля́ется воплощéнием

эгоизма.

personif|y /pə'sɒnɪfaɪ/ *v.t.* вопло|щать, -тить; **she was kindness ~ied** она была воплощением доброты.

personnel /pɜ:sə'nel/ *n.* персонал; штат; кадры (*m. pl.*); **~ department** отдел кадров.

perspective /pə'spektɪv/ *n.*
1 перспектива.
2 (*fig.*): **you must see, get things in ~** надо видеть вещи в их истинном свете.

perspex /'pɜ:speks/ *n.* (*Br. propr.*) плексиглас, органическое стекло, оргстекло.

perspicacious /pɜ:spɪ'keɪʃəs/ *adj.* проницательный.

perspicacity /pɜ:spɪ'kæsɪtɪ/ *n.* проницательность.

perspicuous /pə'spɪkjʊəs/ *adj.* ясный, понятный.

perspiration /pɜ:spɪ'reɪʃ(ə)n/ *n.* пот.

perspire /pə'spaɪə(r)/ *v.i.* потеть, вс-.

persuade /pə'sweɪd/ *v.t.*
1 (*convince*) убе|ждать, -дить; **I ~d him of my innocence** я убедил его в моей невиновности.
2 (*induce*) угов|аривать, -орить; **he was ~d to sing** его уговорили спеть.

persuasion /pə'sweɪʒ(ə)n/ *n.* (*persuading*) убеждение; (*conviction*) убеждение; (*denomination*) вероисповедание.

persuasive /pə'sweɪsɪv/ *adj.* убедительный; (*of person*) обладающий даром убеждения.

pert /pɜ:t/ *adj.* дерзкий, нахальный.

pertain /pə'teɪn/ *v.i.* (*relate*) относиться (*impf.*) (**to:** к + *d.*).

pertinent /'pɜ:tɪnənt/ *adj.* уместный.

perturb /pə'tɜ:b/ *v.t.* тревожить, вс-.

Peru /pə'ru:/ *n.* Перу (*nt. & f. indecl.*).

peruse /pə'ru:z/ *v.t.* рассм|атривать, -отреть.

Peruvian /pə'ru:vɪən/ *n.* перуан|ец (*fem.* -ка).
■ *adj.* перуанский.

pervade /pə'veɪd/ *v.t.* прониз|ывать, -ать.

pervasive /pə'veɪsɪv/ *adj.* пронизывающий.

perverse /pə'vɜ:s/ *adj.* превратный.

perversion /pə'vɜ:ʃ(ə)n/ *n.* (*distortion; sexual deviation*) извращение.

perversity /pə'vɜ:sɪtɪ/ *n.* превратность.

pervert[1] /'pɜ:vɜ:t/ *n.* (*sexual deviant*) извращенец.

pervert[2] /pə'vɜ:t/ *v.t.* извра|щать, -тить; **~ the course of justice** иска|жать, -зить ход правосудия.

pessimism /'pesɪmɪz(ə)m/ *n.* пессимизм.

pessimist /'pesɪmɪst/ *n.* пессимист (*fem.* -ка).

pessimistic /pesɪ'mɪstɪk/ *adj.* пессимистический; (*person*) пессимистичный.

pest /pest/ *n.* (*harmful creature*) вредитель (*m.*); (*of person*) зануда (*c.g.*).

pester /'pestə(r)/ *v.t.* докучать (*impf.*); **he keeps ~ing me for money** он всё время пристаёт ко мне насчёт денег.

pesticide /'pestɪsaɪd/ *n.* пестицид.

pestilence /'pestɪləns/ *n.* чума.

pet /pet/ *n.*
1 (*animal, bird etc.*) питомец, домашнее животное; **~ food** корм для домашних животных.
2 (*favourite*) любим|ец (*fem.* -ица), баловень (*m.*); **his ~ subject** его излюбленная тема; **~ name** ласкательное/уменьшительное имя.
■ *v.t.* (**petted, petting**) (*fondle*) ласкать, при-.
■ *v.i.* (**petted, petting**) (*coll., fondle each other*) обниматься (*impf.*).

petal /'pet(ə)l/ *n.* лепесток.

peter /'pi:tə(r)/ *v.i.*: **~ out** (*run dry, low*) исс|якать, -якнуть; (*of a path*) постепенно исч|езать, -езнуть.

petite /pə'ti:t/ *adj.* миниатюрный.

petition /pɪ'tɪʃ(ə)n/ *n.* (*signed by many people*) петиция; (*application to court*) исковое заявление.
■ *v.t.* под|авать, -ать прошение *кому or во что.*
■ *v.i.*: **~ for divorce** под|авать, -ать заявление о разводе.

petrif|y /'petrɪfaɪ/ *v.t.* (*fig.*) прив|одить, -ести в оцепенение; **I was ~ied** я оцепенел.

petrochemicals /petrəʊ'kemɪk(ə)ls/ *n. pl.* нефтепродукты (*m. pl.*), нефтехимические продукты (*m. pl.*).

petrol /'petr(ə)l/ *n.* (*Br.*) бензин; **fill up with ~** запр|авляться, -авиться бензином; **~ pump** (*at garage*) бензоколонка; **~ station** бензозаправочная станция, бензоколонка; **~ tank** бензобак.

petroleum /pə'trəʊlɪəm/ *n.* нефть.

petticoat /'petɪkəʊt/ *n.* нижняя юбка.

petty /'petɪ/ *adj.* (**pettier, pettiest**)
1 (*trivial*) мелкий, маловажный.
2 (*small-minded*) мелочный.
3 (*of small amounts*): **~ cash** деньги на мелкие расходы; **~ theft** мелкая кража.

petulance /'petjʊləns/ *n.* раздражительность.

petulant /'petjʊlənt/ *adj.* раздражительный.

petunia /pɪ'tju:nɪə/ *n.* петуния.

pew /pju:/ *n.* (церковная) скамья.

pewter /'pju:tə(r)/ *n.* (*alloy*) сплав олова с медью/со свинцом; (*vessels made of ~*) оловянная посуда.
■ *adj.* оловянный.

phallic /'fælɪk/ *adj.* фаллический; **~ symbol** фаллический символ.

phallus /'fæləs/ *n.* (*pl.* **phalli** /-laɪ, -lɪ/ *or* **phalluses**) фаллос.

phantom /'fæntəm/ *n.* фантом.

Pharaoh /'feərəʊ/ *n.* фараон.

pharmaceutical /fɑ:mə'sju:tɪk(ə)l/ *adj.* фармацевтический.

pharmacist /'fɑ:məsɪst/ *n.* фармацевт.

pharmacology /fɑ:mə'kɒlədʒɪ/ *n.* фармакология.

pharmacy /'fɑ:məsɪ/ *n.* (*dispensary*) аптека; (*science, practice*) аптечное дело.

pharynx /'færɪŋks/ *n.* (*pl.* **pharynges** /fə'rɪndʒi:z/) зев; глотка.

phase /feɪz/ *n.* фаза; (*stage*) стадия.
■ *v.t.*: **a ~d withdrawal** поэтапный вывод; **~ out** (*weapons*) поэтапно сн|имать, -ять с вооружения.

Ph.D. (*abbr. of* ***Doctor of Philosophy***) ≈ степень кандидата наук.

pheasant /ˈfez(ə)nt/ *n.* фаза́н.
phenomena /fɪˈnɒmɪnə/ *pl. of* ▸ **phenomenon**
phenomenal /fɪˈnɒmɪn(ə)l/ *adj.* феномена́льный.
phenomenon /fɪˈnɒmɪnən/ *n.* (*pl.* **phenomena**) фено́мен.
philanderer /fɪˈlændərə(r)/ *n.* волоки́та (*m.*).
philanthropic /fɪlənˈθrɒpɪk/ *adj.* филантропи́ческий.
philanthropist /fɪˈlænθrəpɪst/ *n.* филантро́п (*fem.* -ка).
philanthropy /fɪˈlænθrəpɪ/ *n.* филантро́пия.
philatelist /fɪˈlætəlɪst/ *n.* филатели́ст (*fem.* -ка).
philately /fɪˈlætəlɪ/ *n.* филатели́я.
Philippines /ˈfɪlɪpi:nz/ *n.pl.* (**the ~**) Филиппи́н|ы (*pl., g.* —).
philistine /ˈfɪlɪstaɪn/ *n.* (*fig.*) обыва́тель (*m.*).
philological /fɪləˈlɒdʒɪk(ə)l/ *adj.* языкове́дческий; филологи́ческий.
philologist /fɪˈlɒlədʒɪst/ *n.* языкове́д; фило́лог.
philology /fɪˈlɒlədʒɪ/ *n.* (*language*) языкове́дение; (*language and literature*) филоло́гия.
philosopher /fɪˈlɒsəfə(r)/ *n.* фило́соф.
philosophic(al) /fɪləˈsɒfɪk((ə)l)/ *adj.* филосо́фский.
philosophize /fɪˈlɒsəfaɪz/ *v.i.* филосо́фствовать (*impf.*).
philosophy /fɪˈlɒsəfɪ/ *n.* филосо́фия.
phishing /ˈfɪʃɪŋ/*n.* (*comput.*) фи́шинг (*рассылка электронных сообщений пользователям сети Интернет от имени солидных компаний с целью получения их личных данных*).
phlegm /flem/ *n.* (*secretion*) мокро́та; (*fig.*) флегмати́чность.
phlegmatic /flegˈmætɪk/ *adj.* флегмати́чный.
phobia /ˈfəʊbɪə/ *n.* фо́бия, страх.
phoenix /ˈfi:nɪks/ *n.* (*myth.*) фе́никс.
phone /fəʊn/ (*see also* ▸ **telephone**) *n.* телефо́н.
■ *v.t.* & *i.* звони́ть, по- (*кому*).
■ *with advs.*: **~ back** *v.t.* & *i.* перезвони́ть (*pf.*); **~ up** *v.t.* & *i.* звони́ть, по- (*кому*).
■ *cpds.* **~card** *n.* телефо́нная ка́рточка; **~-in** *n.* програ́мма «Звони́те — отвеча́ем».
phonetic /fəˈnetɪk/ *adj.* фонети́ческий.
phon(e)y /ˈfəʊnɪ/ (*sl.*) *n.* (*pl.* **phoneys** *or* **phonies**) (*person*) шарлата́н; (*thing*) подде́лка.
■ *adj.* (**phonier, phoniest**) подде́льный.
phosphate /ˈfɒsfeɪt/ *n.* фосфа́т.
phosphorus /ˈfɒsfərəs/ *n.* фо́сфор.
photo /ˈfəʊtəʊ/ *n.* (*pl.* **photos**) (*coll.*) фо́то (*nt. indecl.*), сни́мок.
■ *cpds.* **~call** (*Br.*) = **~ opportunity**; **~copier** *n.* фотокопирова́льный аппара́т; **~copy** *n.* фотоко́пия, ксероко́пия; *v.t.* сн|има́ть, -ять фотоко́пию (с) + *g.*; **~ opportunity** сеа́нс фотосъёмки, фотосе́ссия (*для прессы*).
photogenic /fəʊtəʊˈdʒenɪk/ *adj.* фотогени́чный.
photograph /ˈfəʊtəgrɑ:f/ *n.* фотогра́фия.
■ *v.t.* фотографи́ровать, с-.
photographer /fəˈtɒgrəfə(r)/ *n.* фото́граф.
photographic /fəʊtəˈgræfɪk/ *adj.* фотографи́ческий.
photography /fəˈtɒgrəfɪ/ *n.* фотогра́фия, фотосъёмка.
photosynthesis /fəʊtəʊˈsɪnθɪsɪs/ *n.* фотоси́нтез.
phrase /freɪz/ *n.* фра́за.
■ *v.t.* формули́ровать, с-.
■ *cpd.* **~ book** *n.* разгово́рник.
phraseology /freɪzɪˈɒlədʒɪ/ *n.* фразеоло́гия.
physical /ˈfɪzɪk(ə)l/ *adj.* физи́ческий; (*relating to the body*): **~ education/training** физи́ческое воспита́ние/трениро́вка; физкульту́ра; **~ly handicapped** физи́чески неполноце́нный; **have you had your ~ (examination)?** вы прошли́ медици́нский осмо́тр?
physician /fɪˈzɪʃ(ə)n/ *n.* врач.
physicist /ˈfɪzɪsɪst/ *n.* фи́зик.
physics /ˈfɪzɪks/ *n.* фи́зика.
physiognomy /fɪzɪˈɒnəmɪ/ *n.* (*facial features*) физионо́мия; (*general appearance*) о́блик.
physiological /fɪzɪəˈlɒdʒɪk(ə)l/ *adj.* физиологи́ческий.
physiology /fɪzɪˈɒlədʒɪ/ *n.* физиоло́гия.
physiotherapist /fɪzɪəʊˈθerəpɪst/ *n.* физиотерапе́вт.
physiotherapy /fɪzɪəʊˈθerəpɪ/ *n.* физиотерапи́я.
physique /fɪˈzi:k/ *n.* телосложе́ние.
pianist /ˈpɪənɪst/ *n.* piани́ст (*fem.* -ка).
piano /pɪˈænəʊ/ *n.* (*pl.* **pianos**) фортепиа́но, фортепья́но (*nt. indecl.*); (*upright*) пиани́но (*nt. indecl.*).
piccolo /ˈpɪkələʊ/ *n.* (*pl.* **~s**) пи́кколо (*nt. indecl.*).
pick /pɪk/ *n.*
1 (*~axe*) кирка́.
2 (*selection*): **take your ~!** выбира́йте!; **the ~ of the bunch** са́мый лу́чший.
■ *v.t.* 1 (*pluck*) рвать, со-; (*gather*) соб|ира́ть, -ра́ть.
2 (*probe*) ковыря́ть (*impf.*); **stop ~ing your nose!** не ковыря́й в носу́!
3 (*make by ~ing*): **he ~ed a hole in the cloth** он продыря́вил ткань.
4 (*select*) выбира́ть, вы́брать; **she ~ed her way through the mud** она́ осторо́жно ступа́ла по гря́зи; **the captains ~ed sides** капита́ны определи́ли соста́в(ы) кома́нд; **he's trying to ~ a quarrel** он и́щет по́вод(а) для ссо́ры.
■ *v.i.* (*select*) выбира́ть, вы́брать; **~ and choose** быть разбо́рчивым.
■ *with preps.*: **~ at** ковыря́ть, по-; **the child ~ed at** (*trifled with*) **his food** ребёнок поковыря́л еду́ ви́лкой; **~ on** (*find fault with*) прид|ира́ться, -ра́ться к + *d.*
■ *with advs.*: **~ out** *v.t.* (*select*): **he ~ed out the best for himself** са́мое лу́чшее он отобра́л для себя́; (*distinguish*): **I ~ed him out in the crowd** я узна́л его́ в толпе́; **~ up** *v.t.* (*lift*) подн|има́ть, -я́ть; (*acquire, gain*) приобре|та́ть, -сти́; **he has ~ed up an American accent** он приобрёл америка́нский акце́нт; (*provide transport for*)

заб|ира́ть, -ра́ть/под|бира́ть, -обра́ть; **I never ~ up hitch-hikers** я никогда́ не беру́ «голосу́ющих» на доро́ге; (*apprehend*): **the culprit was ~ed up by the police** престу́пник был заде́ржан поли́цией; *v.i.* (*resume*): **he ~ed up where he had left off** он возобнови́л бесе́ду с того́ ме́ста, где останови́лся; *v.i.* (*recover health*) опр|авля́ться, -а́виться/попр|авля́ться, -а́виться; (*improve*) ул|учша́ться, -у́чшиться; **trade is ~ing up** торго́вля оживля́ется.
■ *cpds.* **~axe** (*US also* **~ax**) *n.* кирка́; **~-me-up** *n.* тонизи́рующее сре́дство; **~pocket** *n.* карма́нник, карма́нный вор; **~up** *n.* (*van*) пика́п.

picket /ˈpɪkɪt/ *n.* (*of strikers*) пике́т.
■ *v.t.* (**picketed, picketing**) пикети́ровать (*impf.*); **the workers are ~ing the factory** рабо́чие пикети́руют фа́брику.

picking /ˈpɪkɪŋ/ *n.*
1 (*gathering*) сбор.
2 (*pl., remains*) оста́тки (*m. pl.*); объе́дки (*m. pl.*).

pickle /ˈpɪk(ə)l/ *n.*
1 (*usu. pl., preserved vegetables*) соле́нья (*pl.*).
2 (*coll., predicament*) напа́сть.
■ *v.t.* маринова́ть, за-.

picky /ˈpɪkɪ/ *adj.* (**pickier, pickiest**) (*coll.*) разбо́рчивый.

picnic /ˈpɪknɪk/ *n.* пикни́к.

pictorial /pɪkˈtɔːrɪəl/ *n.* иллюстри́рованное изда́ние.
■ *adj.* изобрази́тельный; (*illustrated*) иллюстри́рованный.

picture /ˈpɪktʃə(r)/ *n.*
1 (*depiction*) карти́на; (*drawing*) рису́нок; (*image on TV screen*) карти́нка, изображе́ние.
2 (*embodiment*) олицетворе́ние; **he looks the ~ of health** он пы́шет здоро́вьем.
3 (*coll., of information*): **he will soon put you in the ~** он вско́ре введёт вас в курс (де́ла).
4 (*film*) (кино)фи́льм, (кино)карти́на; (*pl., cinema show, cinema*) кино́ (*nt. indecl.*).
■ *v.t.*: **~ to yourself** вообрази́те/предста́вьте себе́.
■ *cpd.* **~ book** *n.* кни́жка с карти́нками.

picturesque /pɪktʃəˈresk/ *adj.* живопи́сный.

pie /paɪ/ *n.* пиро́г; (*small one*) пирожо́к.

piece /piːs/ *n.*
1 (*portion, bit*) кусо́к; **a ~ of bread** кусо́к хле́ба; **a ~ of paper** листо́к бума́ги, бума́жка; **to pull, tear to ~s** раз|рыва́ть, -орва́ть на ча́сти/куски́; **to go to ~s** лома́ться, с-.
2 (*example*): **a ~ of news** но́вость; **a ~ of advice** сове́т; **I gave him a ~ of my mind** я его́ отчита́л.
3 (*object of art etc.*) произведе́ние (иску́сства); **~ of furniture** предме́т ме́бели.
4 (*chess*) фигу́ра.
5 (*coin*) моне́та.
■ *with adv.*: **~ together** *v.t.* соедин|я́ть, -и́ть; (*fig.*) свя́з|ывать, -а́ть.
■ *cpd.* **~meal** *adj.* части́чный; *adv.* по частя́м.

pier /pɪə(r)/ *n.* (*structure projecting into sea*) пирс; (*landing stage*) прича́л; (*breakwater*) мол.

pierc|e /pɪəs/ *v.t.* прок|а́лывать, -оло́ть; **she had her ears ~ed** она́ проколо́ла у́ши; **a ~ing cry** пронзи́тельный крик.

piety /ˈpaɪɪtɪ/ *n.* на́божность.

pig /pɪg/ *n.* (*animal*) свинья́; (*greedy person*): **he made a ~ of himself** он нае́лся, как свинья́.
■ *cpds.* **~-headed** *adj.* упря́мый (как осёл); **~sty** *n.* (*lit., fig.*) свина́рник.

pigeon /ˈpɪdʒɪn/ *n.* го́лубь (*m.*).
■ *cpd.* **~hole** *n.* (*compartment*) отделе́ние для бума́г; *v.t.* (*categorize*) классифици́ровать (*impf., pf.*).

piggy /ˈpɪgɪ/: *cpds.* **~back** *adv.* на спине́; **~ bank** *n.* копи́лка.

piglet /ˈpɪglɪt/ *n.* поросёнок.

pigment /ˈpɪgmənt/ *n.* пигме́нт.

pigmentation /pɪgmənˈteɪʃ(ə)n/ *n.* пигмента́ция.

pike /paɪk/ *n.* (*pl.* **~**) (*fish*) щу́ка.

pile /paɪl/ *n.* (*heap*) ку́ча, гру́да; (*coll., large quantity*) ку́ча, ма́сса.
■ *v.t.* 1 (*heap up*) сва́л|ивать, -и́ть в ку́чу.
2 (*load*) нав|а́ливать, -али́ть; заст|авля́ть, -а́вить.
■ *with advs.*: **~ in** *v.i.* (*coll., crowd into*) наб|ива́ться, -и́ться; **~ up** *v.i.* (*accumulate*) (*of objects*) нагромо|жда́ться, -зди́ться; (*of work, debts*) нак|а́пливаться, -опи́ться.
■ *cpd.* **~-up** *n.* (*crash*) столкнове́ние не́скольких маши́н.

piles /paɪlz/ *n. pl.* (*med.*) геморро́й.

pilfer /ˈpɪlfə(r)/ *v.t.* & *i.* ворова́ть (*impf.*).

pilgrim /ˈpɪlgrɪm/ *n.* palo ́мник.

pilgrimage /ˈpɪlgrɪmɪdʒ/ *n.* пало́мничество.

pill /pɪl/ *n.* пилю́ля, табле́тка; **she is on the ~** она́ принима́ет противозача́точные табле́тки.

pillage /ˈpɪlɪdʒ/ *n.* мародёрство, грабёж.
■ *v.t.* гра́бить, раз-.
■ *v.i.* мародёрствовать (*impf.*); гра́бить (*impf.*).

pillar /ˈpɪlə(r)/ *n.* столб, коло́нна.

pillion /ˈpɪljən/ *n.*: **she rode ~** она́ е́хала на за́днем сиде́нье мотоци́кла.

pillow /ˈpɪləʊ/ *n.* поду́шка.
■ *cpd.* **~case** *n.* на́волочка.

pilot /ˈpaɪlət/ *n.*
1 (*of aircraft*) лётчи|к (*fem.* -ца), пило́т.
2 (*attr., fig.*) про́бный, о́пытный; **~ scheme** экспериме́нт.
■ *v.t.* (**piloted, piloting**) (*lit.*) пилоти́ровать (*impf.*).

pimp /pɪmp/ *n.* сутенёр.

pimple /ˈpɪmp(ə)l/ *n.* прыщ, пры́щик.

pimply /ˈpɪmplɪ/ *adj.* прыща́вый.

PIN /pɪn/ *n.* (*abbr. of* ***personal identification number***) персона́льный код.

pin /pɪn/ *n.*
1 була́вка.
2 (*securing peg*) прище́пка.
■ *v.t.* (**pinned, pinning**)
1 (*fasten*) прик|а́лывать, -оло́ть; (*fig.*): **~ accusation, blame on s.o.** сва́л|ивать, -и́ть вину́ на кого́-н.
2 (*immobilize*) приж|има́ть, -а́ть; **the bandits ~ned him against the wall** банди́ты прижа́ли его́ к стене́.
■ *with advs.*: **~ down** *v.t.* (*lit.*) прик|а́лывать,

-олóть; (*fig., commit to an action or opinion*) припир|áть, -ерéть к стéнке; **~ up** *v.t.* прик|áлывать, -олóть; вéшать, повéсить.
■ *cpds.* **~ball** *n.* (*game, machine*) пинбóл; **~point** *n.* (*lit.*) остриё булáвки; *v.t.* (*fig.*) тóчно определ|я́ть, -и́ть; **~stripe** (*suit*) *n.* костю́м в тóнкую свéтлую полóску; **~-up** *n.* фотогрáфия красóтки (в журнáле).

pinafore /ˈpɪnəfɔ:(r)/ *n.* (*Br., apron*) фáртук; **~ dress** плáтье-сарафáн.

pincers /ˈpɪnsəz/ *n. pl.*
1 (*of crab*) клешн|и́ (*pl., g.* -éй).
2 (*tech.*) клéщ|и (*pl., g.* -éй).

pinch /pɪntʃ/ *n.*
1 (*nip*) щипóк.
2 (*small amount*) щепóтка.
■ *v.t.* 1 (*squeeze*) (*objects*) прищем|ля́ть, -и́ть; (*person*) щипáть, ущипну́ть.
2 (*Br., steal*) стащи́ть (*pf.*) (*coll.*).

pine[1] /paɪn/ *n.* соснá.
■ *cpds.* **~apple** *n.* ананáс; **~ cone** *n.* соснóвая ши́шка.

pin|e[2] /paɪn/ *v.i.*
1 (*languish*) чáхнуть, за-; томи́ться (*impf.*); **she is ~ing away** онá чáхнет.
2 (*long*): **~e for** жáждать (*impf.*) + *g.*

ping-pong /ˈpɪŋpɒŋ/ *n.* пинг-пóнг.

pink /pɪŋk/ *n.* (*flower*) гвозди́ка; (*colour*) рóзовый цвет.
■ *adj.* (*of colour*) рóзовый.

pinnacle /ˈpɪnək(ə)l/ *n.* (*fig.*) верши́на.

pint /paɪnt/ *n.* пи́нта.

pioneer /paɪəˈnɪə(r)/ *n.* пионéр, новáтор.
■ *v.t. & i.* быть пионéром (*в чём*).

pious /ˈpaɪəs/ *adj.* набóжный.

pip /pɪp/ *n.* (*Br.*) сéмечко; зёрнышко.

pipe /paɪp/ *n.*
1 (*conduit*) трубá.
2 (*mus. instrument*) ду́дка; (*pl., bagpipes*) волы́нка.
3 (*for smoking*) тру́бка.
■ *v.t.* 1 (*convey by ~s*) пус|кáть, -ти́ть по трубáм.
2 : **~d music** музыкáльная трансля́ция (в общéственном мéсте).
■ *cpds.* **~ dream** *n.* несбы́точная мечтá; **~line** *n.* (*for oil*) нефтепровóд; (*fig.*): **in the ~line** на подхóде (*coll.*).

piper /ˈpaɪpə(r)/ *n.* (*bag ~*) волы́нщи|к (*fem.* -ца); **he who pays the ~ calls the tune** кто плáтит, тот и распоряжáется.

piping /ˈpaɪpɪŋ/ *adv.*: **~ hot** с пы́лу, с жáру.

piquancy /ˈpi:kənsɪ/ *n.* (*lit., fig.*) пикáнтность.

piquant /ˈpi:kɑ:nt/ *adj.* (*lit., fig.*) пикáнтный.

pique /pi:k/ *n.* досáда; **in a fit of ~** в пору́ве раздражéния.

piracy /ˈpaɪrəsɪ/ *n.* пирáтство.

pirate /ˈpaɪərət/ *n.* пирáт; (*infringer of copyright*) наруши́тель (*m.*) áвторского прáва, пирáт.
■ *v.t.* (*video, software*) выпускáть, вы́пустить пирáтскую кóпию + *g.*

pirouette /pɪrʊˈet/ *n.* пиру́эт.

Pisces /ˈpaɪsi:z/ *n.* (*pl.* ~) Ры́бы (*f. pl.*).

piss /pɪs/ *v.i.* (*vulg.*) ссать, по- (*vulg.*); **~ off!** (*Br.*) отцепи́сь!; провáливай!

pissed /pɪst/ *adj.* (*vulg.*) (*Br., drunk*) в жóпу пья́ный (*vulg.*); **~ off** (*US also* ~) обозлённый.

pistachio /pɪˈstɑ:ʃɪəʊ/ *n.* (*pl.* **~s**) фистáшка.

pistol /ˈpɪst(ə)l/ *n.* пистолéт.

piston /ˈpɪst(ə)n/ *n.* пóршень (*m.*).

pit[1] /pɪt/ *n.*
1 (*a large hole*) котловáн; (*for gravel*) карьéр.
2 : **the ~s** (*sl.*) ху́же нéкуда.
■ *v.t.* (**pitted, pitting**): **he ~ted his wits against the law** он пытáлся обойти́ закóн.
■ *cpd.* **~fall** *n.* западня́, капкáн.

pit[2] /pɪt/ *n.* (*US, fruit stone*) кóсточка.

pitch[1] /pɪtʃ/ *n.*
1 (*of voice or instrument*) высотá.
2 (*Br., area for games*) пóле, площáдка.
■ *v.t.* 1 (*set up, erect*): **they ~ed camp for the night** они́ разби́ли нá ночь лáгерь.
2 (*throw*) бр|осáть, -óсить.
3 (*mus.*): **the song is ~ed too high for me** э́та пéсня сли́шком высокá для моегó гóлоса.
■ *v.i.* (*of ship*): **the ship was ~ing** корáбль испы́тывал килеву́ю кáчку; (*of person, fall forwards*) пáдать, упáсть нáвзничь.
■ *with adv.*: **~ in** *v.i.* (*join in with vigour*) горячó/энерги́чно брáться, взя́ться (*за что*).
■ *cpd.* **~fork** *n.* (сенны́е) ви́л|ы (*pl., g.* —).

pitch[2] /pɪtʃ/ *cpds.* **~-black** *adj.* чёрный как смоль; **~-dark** *adj.*: **it is ~-dark here** здесь тьма кромéшная; здесь темны́м-темнó (*coll.*).

pitcher /ˈpɪtʃə(r)/ *n.* (*jug*) кувши́н; (*at baseball*) подаю́щий.

piteous /ˈpɪtɪəs/ *adj.* жáлкий; (*voice, song, words*) жáлобный.

pith /pɪθ/ *n.* (*plant tissue*) сердцеви́на, мя́коть; (*essential part*) суть; (*vigour, force*) энéргия, си́ла.

pithy /ˈpɪθɪ/ *adj.* (**pithier, pithiest**) (*fig.*) сжáтый; содержáтельный.

pitiful /ˈpɪtɪfʊl/ *adj.* жáлкий.

pitiless /ˈpɪtɪlɪs/ *adj.* безжáлостный.

pittance /ˈpɪt(ə)ns/ *n.* жáлкие гроши́ (*m. pl.*).

pituitary /pɪˈtju:ɪtərɪ/ *n.* (*in full* **~ gland**) гипóфиз.

pity /ˈpɪtɪ/ *n.*
1 (*compassion*) жáлость; **have, take ~ on** сжáлиться (*pf.*) над + *i.*
2 (*cause for regret*) жаль; **what a ~!** как жаль/жáлко!
■ *v.t.* жалéть, по-.

pivot /ˈpɪvət/ *v.i.* (**pivoted, pivoting**) вращáться (*impf.*).

pixel /ˈpɪks(ə)l/ *n.* (*comput.*) пи́ксель (*m.*), элемéнт изображéния.

pix|y, -ie /ˈpɪksɪ/ *n.* эльф.

pizza /ˈpi:tsə/ *n.* пи́цца.

placard /ˈplækɑ:d/ *n.* плакáт.

placate /pləˈkeɪt/ *v.t.* умиротвор|я́ть, -и́ть.

place /pleɪs/ *n.*
1 мéсто; **all over the ~** (*everywhere*) повсю́ду; (*in confusion*) повсю́ду, в беспоря́дке; **everything is in ~** всё на мéсте; **your laughter is out of ~** ваш смех неумéстен; **that put him in his ~** э́то постáвило егó на мéсто; **he took his ~ in the queue** (*Br.*), **in (the) line** (*US*) он зáнял

ме́сто в о́череди; (*seat*): **he gave up his ~ to a lady** он уступи́л своё ме́сто да́ме; (*fig., position*): **put yourself in my ~** поста́вьте себя́ на моё ме́сто; (*fig.*): **take ~** состоя́ться (*pf.*); име́ть (*impf.*) ме́сто; **in ~ of** вме́сто + *g.*
2 (*locality*) ме́сто; **in ~s** (*here and there*) места́ми.
3 (*building*) дом; жили́ще; **~ of work** ме́сто рабо́ты; **come round to my ~!** заходи́те ко мне!
4 (*position*) ме́сто; **our team took first ~** на́ша кома́нда заняла́ пе́рвое ме́сто; **in the first ~** во-пе́рвых.
■ *v.t.* 1 (*stand*) ста́вить, по-; (*lay*) класть, положи́ть.
2 (*comm.*): **I ~d an order with them** я помести́л у них зака́з.
3 (*identify*) определ|я́ть, -и́ть; **I know those lines, but I cannot ~ them** мне знако́мы э́ти стро́чки, но я не могу́ вспо́мнить, отку́да они́.
■ *cpds.* **~ mat** *n.* подста́вка/салфе́тка под столо́вый прибо́р; **~ name** *n.* географи́ческое назва́ние.

placebo /plə'si:bəʊ/ *n.* (*pl.* **~s**) (*med.*) плаце́бо (*nt. indecl.*); имита́ция лека́рственного сре́дства.

placen|ta /plə'sentə/ *n.* (*pl.* **~tae** /-ti:/ *or* **~tas**) плаце́нта.

placid /'plæsɪd/ *adj.* споко́йный.

plagiarism /'pleɪdʒərɪz(ə)m/ *n.* плагиа́т.

plagiarize /'pleɪdʒəraɪz/ *v.i.* занима́ться (*impf.*) плагиа́том.
■ *v.t.*: **he ~d my book** его́ рабо́та целико́м спи́сана с мое́й кни́ги.

plague /pleɪg/ *n.*
1 (*pestilence*) чума́.
2 (*infestation*): **a ~ of rats** наше́ствие крыс.
■ *v.t.* (**plagues, plagued, plaguing**) (*pester*) докуча́ть (*impf.*) + *d.*

plaice /pleɪs/ *n.* (*pl.* **~**) ка́мбала.

plaid /plæd/ *n.* (*fabric*) шотла́ндка (*ткань*).

plain /pleɪn/ *n.* равни́на.
■ *adj.* 1 (*clear*) я́сный, я́вный; **her distress was ~ to see** она́ я́вно страда́ла.
2 (*easy to understand*) я́сный, поня́тный.
3 (*not patterned*): **~ blue shirt** одното́нная (*or* гла́дкая) голуба́я руба́шка; **~ paper** нелино́ванная бума́га; (*simple, ordinary*) просто́й; **~ food** проста́я пи́ща.
4 (*unattractive*) некраси́вый.
5 : **~ chocolate** чёрный шокола́д; **~ flour** (*Br.*) мука́ без доба́вок.
■ *cpd.* **~-clothes** *adj.* оде́тый в шта́тское.

plaintiff /'pleɪntɪf/ *n.* ист|е́ц (*fem.* -и́ца).

plaintive /'pleɪntɪv/ *adj.* печа́льный.

plait /plæt/ *n.* (*Br.*) коса́.
■ *v.t.* запле|та́ть, -сти́.

plan /plæn/ *n.* план; (*drawing*) чертёж; (*schedule*): **all went according to ~** всё прошло́ по пла́ну; (*project*) план, прое́кт.
■ *v.t.* (**planned, planning**) плани́ровать, за-; (*design*) проекти́ровать, с-.
■ *v.i.* (**planned, planning**) намерева́ться, плани́ровать (*both impf.*); **we must ~ ahead** на́до ду́мать о бу́дущем.

plane[1] /pleɪn/ *n.* (*tool*) руба́нок, струг.
■ *v.t.* строга́ть, вы́-.

plane[2] /pleɪn/ *n.*
1 (*flat surface*) пло́скость.
2 (*aeroplane*) самолёт.
3 (*fig., level*) у́ровень (*m.*).

planet /'plænɪt/ *n.* плане́та.

plank /plæŋk/ *n.* доска́.

plankton /'plæŋkt(ə)n/ *n.* планкто́н.

planning /'plænɪŋ/ *n.* плани́рование; **~ permission** (*Br.*) разреше́ние на строи́тельство.

plant /plɑ:nt/ *n.*
1 (*vegetable organism*) расте́ние.
2 (*industrial machinery*) обору́дование.
3 (*factory*) заво́д.
■ *v.t.* 1 (*put in ground*) сажа́ть, посади́ть; (*seeds*) се́ять, по-.
2 (*fig.*): **~ evidence** подбр|а́сывать, -о́сить у́лики; подде́л|ывать, -ать доказа́тельства.

plantation /plɑ:n'teɪʃ(ə)n/ *n.* планта́ция.

planter /'plɑ:ntə(r)/ *n.* (*person who plants seeds, bulbs, trees*) сажа́льщик, се́ятель (*of seeds only*); (*plantation owner*) планта́тор; (*agric. machine*) се́ялка; (*container for plants*) декорати́вный горшо́к (для расте́ний).

plaque /plæk/ *n.* (*tablet*) доще́чка; (*on teeth*) зубно́й ка́мень.

plasma /'plæzmə/ *n.* пла́зма; **~ screen** (*TV, comput.*) пла́зменный экра́н.

plaster /'plɑ:stə(r)/ *n.*
1 (*for coating walls etc.*) штукату́рка; **~ cast** ги́псовый сле́пок.
2 (*Br., med.*) пла́стырь (*m.*).
■ *v.t.* 1 (*wall*) штукату́рить, о-.
2 (*cover*) облеп|ля́ть, -и́ть; **his boots were ~ed with mud** его́ боти́нки бы́ли обле́плены гря́зью.

plasterer /'plɑ:stərə(r)/ *n.* штукату́р.

plastic /'plæstɪk/ *n.* пла́стик, пластма́сса; (*coll., credit card*) креди́тная ка́рточка.
■ *adj.* 1 (*made of ~*) пластма́ссовый; пла́стиковый; **~ bag** полиэтиле́новый мешо́к/паке́т.
2 (*art*) пласти́ческий; **~ surgery** (*practice*) пласти́ческая хирурги́я; (*operation*) пласти́ческая опера́ция.

plasticine /'plæstɪsi:n/ *n.* (*propr.*) пластили́н.

plate /pleɪt/ *n.*
1 (*shallow dish*) (ме́лкая) таре́лка.
2 (*sheet of metal, glass etc.*) лист, пласти́н(к)а.
3 (*illustration*) вкладна́я иллюстра́ция, вкле́йка.
4 : (**dental ~**) вставна́я че́люсть.
■ *v.t.*: **silver-~d spoons** посеребрённые ло́жки.
■ *cpd.* **~-glass** *adj.* из зерка́льного стекла́.

plateau /'plætəʊ/ *n.* (*pl.* **~x** /-z/ *or* **~s**) плато́ (*nt. indecl.*).

platform /'plætfɔ:m/ *n.*
1 (*at station*) платфо́рма, перро́н.
2 (*for speakers*) трибу́на; (*fig., pol.*) (полити́ческая) платфо́рма.
3 (*comput.*) платфо́рма.

platinum /'plætɪnəm/ *n.* пла́тина.

platitude /'plætɪtju:d/ *n.* изби́тая фра́за, бана́льность.

platonic /plə'tɒnɪk/ *adj.* платони́ческий.

platoon /plə'tu:n/ *n.* взвод.

platter /'plætə(r)/ *n.* блю́до.

plaudit /ˈplɔːdɪt/ *n.* (*usu. pl.*) (*applause*) аплодисмéнт|ы (*pl.*, *g.* -ов); (*praise*) похвалá (*sg.*).

plausibility /plɔːzɪˈbɪlɪtɪ/ *n.* вероя́тность, правдоподóбие.

plausible /ˈplɔːzɪb(ə)l/ *adj.* (*statement*) правдоподóбный, вероя́тный; (*person*) убеди́тельный.

play /pleɪ/ *n.*
1 (*dramatic work*) пьéса; (*in theatre*) спектáкль (*m.*).
2 (*recreation*) игрá; **~ on words** игрá слов.
3 (*sport*): **the ball was out of ~** мяч был вне игры́.
4 (*fig.*, *action*) дéйствие, дéятельность; **all his strength was brought into ~** он мобилизовáл все свои́ си́лы.
■ *v.t.* 1 (*perform, take part in*) игрáть, сыгрáть в + *a.*; **~ football** игрáть (*impf.*) в футбóл.
2 (*perform on*) игрáть, сыгрáть на + *p.*; **can you ~ the piano?** вы игрáете на роя́ле?
3 (*perform piece of music*) исп|олня́ть, -óлнить; (*CD*) про|и́грывать, -игрáть.
4 (*perpetrate*): **he is always ~ing tricks on me** он всегдá надо мнóй подшу́чивает.
5 (*enact role of*) игрáть, сыгрáть.
6 (*cards*): **he ~ed the ace** он пошёл с тузá.
■ *v.i.* игрáть, сыгрáть; (*have fun*) игрáть, забавля́ться (*both impf.*); (*take part in game*) игрáть (*impf.*); **they ~ed to win** они́ игрáли с азáртом.
■ *with advs.*: **~ down** *v.t.* (*fig.*, *minimize*) преум|еньшáть, -éньшить; **~ up** *v.i.* (*Br.*, *misbehave*) распус|кáться, -ти́ться.
■ *cpds.* **~boy** *n.* плейбóй; **~ground** *n.* площáдка для игр; **~group** *n.* (*Br.*) дошкóльная грýппа; **~house** *n.* теáтр; **~mate** *n.* прия́тель (*fem.* -ница); **~-off** *n.* решáющая встрéча; повтóрная встрéча пóсле ничьéй; **~school** *n.* ≈ дéтский сад; **~thing** *n.* (*lit.*, *fig.*) игрýшка; **~time** *n.* (шкóльная) переме́на; **~wright** *n.* драматýрг.

player /ˈpleɪə(r)/ *n.*
1 (*of game*) игрóк; спортсмéн.
2 (*actor*) актёр.
3 (*musician*) исполни́тель.

playful /ˈpleɪfʊl/ *adj.* игри́вый, шаловли́вый.

playfulness /ˈpleɪfʊlnɪs/ *n.* игри́вость.

playing /ˈpleɪɪŋ/: *cpds.* **~ card** *n.* игрáльная кáрта; **~ field** *n.* спорти́вное пóле.

plaza /ˈplɑːzə/ *n.* плóщадь.

PLC, plc (*abbr. of* ***public limited company***) (*Br.*) откры́тая/публи́чная компáния с ограни́ченной отвéтственностью.

plea /pliː/ *n.*
1 (*leg.*) заявлéние (отвéтчика); **he entered a ~ of guilty** он признáл себя́ винóвным.
2 (*appeal*) прóсьба.

plead /pliːd/ *v.t.*
1 (*case*) вести́ (*impf.*).
2 (*offer as excuse*) ссылáться, сослáться на + *a.*; **the defendant ~ed insanity** подсуди́мый сослáлся на невменя́емость.
3 (*declare o.s.*): **my client ~s (not) guilty** мой клиéнт (не) признаёт себя́ винóвным.
■ *v.i.* приз|ывáть, -вáть; умоля́ть (*impf.*); **he ~ed with me to stay** он умоля́л меня́ остáться.

pleasant /ˈplez(ə)nt/ *adj.* (**pleasanter, pleasantest**) прия́тный.

pleasantry /ˈplezəntrɪ/ *n.* (*amiable remark*) любéзность.

please /pliːz/ *v.t.* нрáвиться, по- + *d.*; рáдовать, по-; дост|авля́ть, -áвить удовóльствие + *d.*; **I was not very ~d at, by, with the results** я был не óчень довóлен результáтами; **I shall be ~d to attend** я бýду рад приня́ть учáстие.
■ *v.i.* 1 (*give pleasure*) уго|ждáть, -ди́ть.
2 (*think fit*) изволить (*impf.*); **do as you ~** дéлайте, как хоти́те.
3 (*polite request*): **~ shut the door** пожáлуйста, закрóйте дверь.

pleasing /ˈpliːzɪŋ/ *adj.* прия́тный.

pleasurable /ˈpleʒərəb(ə)l/ *adj.* прия́тный.

pleasure /ˈpleʒə(r)/ *n.* удовóльствие; **it's a ~!** (*sc. to oblige*) не стóит!

pleat /pliːt/ *n.* склáдка.
■ *v.t.*: **~ed skirt** плиссирóванная юбка.

plectr|um /ˈplektrəm/ *n.* (*pl.* **~ums** *or* **~a**) (*mus.*) (*for guitar etc.*) медиáтор, плектр.

pledge /pledʒ/ *n.* обéт, обещáние.
■ *v.t.* отд|авáть, -áть в залóг.

plenteous /ˈplentɪəs/ *adj.* оби́льный.

plentiful /ˈplentɪfʊl/ *adj.* оби́льный.

plenty /ˈplentɪ/ *n.* (*a lot*) мнóго; мнóжество; **we have ~** у нас мнóго; **we have ~ of time to spare** у нас мнóго врéмени в запáсе; **he has ~ of money** у негó мнóго дéнег; (*sufficient*): **that will be ~** э́того бýдет достáточно.

plethora /ˈpleθərə/ *n.* (*med.*) полнокрóвие; (*fig.*, *over-abundance*) избы́ток.

pleurisy /ˈplʊərɪsɪ/ *n.* (*med.*) плеври́т.

pliable /ˈplaɪəb(ə)l/ *adj.* ги́бкий.

pliers /ˈplaɪəz/ *n.* клéщ|и (*pl.*, *g.* -éй).

plight /plaɪt/ *n.* (незави́дная) ýчасть.

plimsoll /ˈplɪms(ə)l/ *n.* (*Br.*): **~s** паруси́новые тýфли (*f. pl.*).

plinth /plɪnθ/ *n.* цóколь; постамéнт.

plod /plɒd/ *v.t.* & *i.* (**plodded, plodding**) тащи́ться (*impf.*).

plonk /plɒŋk/ *n.* (*Br. sl.*, *cheap wine*) дешёвое винó, бормотýха (*coll.*).
■ *v.t.* (*coll.*, *put down heavily*) грóх|ать, -нуть; бáх|ать, -нуть.

plot /plɒt/ *n.*
1 (*piece of ground*) учáсток (земли́).
2 (*outline of play etc.*) фáбула, сюжéт.
3 (*conspiracy*) зáговор.
■ *v.t.* (**plotted, plotting**)
1 (*conspire to achieve*): **they ~ted his ruin** они́ готóвили емý ги́бель.
2 (*mark on a graph*) нан|оси́ть, -ести́ (*данные*) на кáрту/грáфик.
■ *v.i.* (**plotted, plotting**) (*conspire*) организóвывать, организовáть (*both impf.*) зáговор.

plough /plaʊ/ (*US* **plow**) *n.* плуг.
■ *v.t.* пахáть, вс-.
■ *v.i.* (*fig.*) продв|игáться, -и́нуться; **I ~ed through the book** я с трудóм оси́лил кни́гу.
■ *with advs.*: **~ back** *v.t.*: **profits are ~ed back** при́быль вклáдывается в дéло/реинвести́руется; **~ up** *v.t.* распáх|ивать,

-áть.

ploy /plɔɪ/ *n.* уло́вка.

pluck /plʌk/ *v.t.*
1 (*flowers*) срыва́ть, сорва́ть.
2 (*bird*) ощи́п|ывать, -а́ть.
3 (*eyebrows*) выщи́пывать, вы́щипать.
4 (*mus.*) перебира́ть (*impf.*) стру́ны + *g.*
5 (*twitch, pull at; also v.i.*) дёр|гать, -нуть.
■ *with adv.*: ~ **up** *v.t.*: ~ **up courage** соб|ира́ться, -ра́ться с ду́хом.

plucky /ˈplʌkɪ/ *adj.* (**pluckier, pluckiest**) (*coll.*) сме́лый, отва́жный.

plug /plʌg/ *n.*
1 (*stopper, e.g. of bath*) про́бка, заты́чка.
2 (*elec. connector*) ви́лка; (*socket*) розе́тка.
3 (*spark* ~) свеча́ зажига́ния.
4 (*coll., advertisement*) рекла́ма.
■ *v.t.* (**plugged, plugging**) (*stop up*) зат|ыка́ть, -кну́ть; (*coll., advertise*) реклами́ровать (*impf., pf.*).
■ *with adv.*: ~ **in** *v.t.* включ|а́ть, -и́ть.
■ *cpds.* ~**hole** *n.* (*Br.*) сто́чное отве́рстие; ~**-in** *adj.* вставно́й.

plum /plʌm/ *n.*
1 (*fruit, tree*) сли́ва.
2 (*fig.*): **a ~ job** тёплое месте́чко.

plumage /ˈpluːmɪdʒ/ *n.* опере́ние.

plumb /plʌm/ *adj.* (*vertical*) вертика́льный.
■ *adv.* (*coll.*) (*exactly*) то́чно; (*US, utterly*) соверше́нно, совсе́м.
■ *v.t.* (*sound*) изм|еря́ть, -е́рить ло́том; (*fig.*): **he ~ed the depths of absurdity** он дошёл до по́лного абсу́рда.

plumber /ˈplʌmə(r)/ *n.* водопрово́дчик.

plumbing /ˈplʌmɪŋ/ *n.* канализа́ция, водопрово́дно-канализацио́нная сеть.

plume /pluːm/ *n.*
1 (*feather*) перо́; **a ~ of smoke** шлейф ды́ма.
2 (*in headdress*) султа́н, плюма́ж.
■ *v.t.*: **the bird ~s its feathers** пти́ца охора́шивается (*or* чи́стит пёрышки); (*fig.*): **he ~s himself on his skill** он кичи́тся свои́м мастерство́м.

plummet /ˈplʌmɪt/ *v.i.* (**plummeted, plummeting**) об|рыва́ться, -орва́ться.

plump /plʌmp/ *adj.* пу́хлый.

plunder /ˈplʌndə(r)/ *n.* (*looting*) грабёж; (*loot*) добы́ча.
■ *v.t.* гра́бить, раз-.

plunge /plʌndʒ/ *n.* (*fig.*): **he took the ~** он реши́л: была́ не была́.
■ *v.t.* погру|жа́ть, -зи́ть; **the room was ~d into darkness** ко́мната погрузи́лась во мрак.
■ *v.i.* окун|а́ться, -у́ться.

pluperfect /pluːˈpɜːfɪkt/ *n.* (*gram.*) плюсквамперфе́кт, давнопроше́дшее вре́мя.
■ *adj.* плюсквамперфе́ктный, давнопроше́дший.

plural /ˈplʊər(ə)l/ *n.* мно́жественное число́.
■ *adj.*: ~ **noun** существи́тельное во мно́жественном числе́.

pluralism /ˈplʊərəlɪz(ə)m/*n.* плюрали́зм.

plus /plʌs/ *n.* плюс.
■ *adj.* доба́вочный; ~ **sign** (знак) плюс.
■ *prep.* плюс; **3 ~ 4 is 7** три плюс четы́ре — семь.

plush /plʌʃ/ *n.* плюш.
■ *adj.* (*made of* ~) плю́шевый; (*sl., sumptuous; also* **plushy**) шика́рный.

plutonium /pluːˈtəʊnɪəm/ *n.* плуто́ний.

ply[1] /plaɪ/ *n.* (*layer*) слой; (*strand*) нить; **three-~** (*plywood*) трёхсло́йная фане́ра; **three-~ yarn** трёхни́точная пря́жа.
■ *cpd.* ~**wood** *n.* фане́ра; *adj.* фане́рный.

ply[2] /plaɪ/ *v.t.*
1 (*work at*): **he plies an honest trade** он зараба́тывает на хлеб че́стным трудо́м.
2 (*keep supplied*) корми́ть, на-; **I was plied with food** меня́ хорошо́ накорми́ли.
■ *v.i.* курси́ровать (*impf.*).

PM (*abbr. of* ***Prime Minister***) премье́р-мини́стр.

p.m. (*abbr. of* ***post meridiem***) по́сле полу́дня; **at 3 p.m.** в 3 часа́ дня.

PMT (*abbr. of* ***premenstrual tension***) (*Br.*) предменструа́льное напряже́ние.

pneumatic /njuːˈmætɪk/ *adj.* пневмати́ческий; ~ **drill** пневмати́ческий отбо́йный молото́к.

pneumonia /njuːˈməʊnɪə/ *n.* воспале́ние лёгких, пневмони́я.

PO (*abbr. of* ***Post Office***) по́чта.
■ *cpd.* ~ **box** *n.* абоне́нтский я́щик.

poach[1] /pəʊtʃ/ *v.t.* (*cul.*): ~ **eggs** вари́ть, с- (яйцо́-)пашо́т.

poach[2] /pəʊtʃ/ *v.t. & i.*: ~ **game** занима́ться (*impf.*) браконье́рством; браконье́рствовать (*impf.*).

poacher /ˈpəʊtʃə(r)/ *n.* браконье́р.

pocket /ˈpɒkɪt/ *n.*
1 (*in clothing*) карма́н.
2 (*at billiards*) лу́за.
3 (*attr., miniature*) карма́нный.
■ *v.t.* (**pocketed, pocketing**) класть, положи́ть в карма́н.
■ *cpds.* ~**book** *n.* (*US, handbag*) су́мочка; (*US, wallet*) бума́жник; ~**knife** *n.* карма́нный но́ж(ик); ~ **money** *n.* (*Br.*) карма́нные де́н|ьги (*pl., g.* -ег).

pod /pɒd/ *n.* стручо́к.

podgy /ˈpɒdʒɪ/ *adj.* (**podgier, podgiest**) (*Br.*) то́лстенький, призе́мистый.

podium /ˈpəʊdɪəm/ *n.* возвыше́ние/по́диум.

poem /ˈpəʊɪm/ *n.* стихотворе́ние; (*long narrative*) поэ́ма.

poet /ˈpəʊɪt/ *n.* поэ́т.

poetic /pəʊˈetɪk/ *adj.* поэти́ческий.

poetry /ˈpəʊɪtrɪ/ *n.* (*also fig.*) поэ́зия.

pogrom /ˈpɒgrəm/ *n.* погро́м.

poignant /ˈpɔɪnjənt/ *adj.* о́стрый, го́рький.

point /pɔɪnt/ *n.*
1 (*sharp end*) остриё.
2 (*tip*) ко́нчик.
3 (*promontory*) мыс.
4 (*dot*) то́чка; **decimal ~** (*in Russian usage*) запята́я (*отделяющая десятичную дробь от целого числа*); **two ~ five (2.5)** две це́лых (и) пять деся́тых.
5 (*mark, position*) ме́сто, пункт; ~ **of view** то́чка зре́ния.
6 (*moment*) моме́нт; **at this ~ he turned round** в э́тот моме́нт/тут он поверну́лся; **I was on the ~ of leaving** я уже́ собра́лся уходи́ть.

7 (*unit*) едини́ца; **up to a ~** до изве́стной сте́пени.
8 (*unit of evaluation*) пункт, очко́; **they won on ~s** они́ вы́играли по очка́м.
9 (*chief idea, meaning, purpose*) суть, вопро́с, смысл; **that is beside the ~** не в э́том суть/де́ло; **come to the ~** до|ходи́ть, -йти́ до гла́вного/су́ти (де́ла); **I don't see the ~ of the joke** э́та шу́тка мне непоня́тна; **I made a ~ of seeing him** я счёл необходи́мым повида́ться с ним; **you missed the ~** вы не по́няли су́ти (де́ла); **there was no ~ in staying** не име́ло смы́сла остава́ться; **what's the ~ of it?** како́й в э́том смысл?
10 (*item*) пункт; **we agree on certain ~s** по не́которым пу́нктам мы схо́димся.
11 (*quality*) черта́; **singing is not my strong ~** я не силён в пе́нии.
■ *v.t.* ука́з|ывать, -а́ть; пока́з|ывать, -а́ть; **he ~ed a gun at her** он навёл на неё пистоле́т.
■ *v.i.* ука́з|ывать, -а́ть (**at, to:** на + *a.*); **everything ~s to his guilt** всё ука́зывает на его́ вину́.
■ *with adv.*: **~ out** *v.t.* ука́з|ывать, -а́ть на + *a.*
■ *cpd.* **~-blank** *adj.* (*lit.*) прямо́й; (*fig.*) категори́ческий; *adv.* пря́мо, в упо́р.

pointed /'pɔɪntɪd/ *adj.*
1 (*e.g. a stick*) остроконе́чный.
2 (*significant*) о́стрый, ко́лкий; подчёркнутый.

pointer /'pɔɪntə(r)/ *n.*
1 (*of balance etc.*) стре́лка, указа́тель (*m.*).
2 (*indication*) намёк.

pointing /'pɔɪntɪŋ/ *n.* (*of wall etc.*) расши́вка швов.

pointless /'pɔɪntlɪs/ *adj.* бессмы́сленный.

poise /pɔɪz/ *n.* уравнове́шенность, самооблада́ние.
■ *v.t.*: **he is ~d to attack** он гото́в к нападе́нию.

poison /'pɔɪz(ə)n/ *n.* яд, отра́ва.
■ *v.t.* (*lit., fig.*) отрав|ля́ть, -и́ть; **food ~ing** пищево́е отравле́ние; **he has food ~ing** он отрави́лся.

poisonous /'pɔɪz(ə)nəs/ *adj.* ядови́тый; (*fig.*) вре́дный.

poke /pəʊk/ *n.* толчо́к.
■ *v.t.* 1 (*prod*) ты́кать, ткнуть; **to ~ the fire** меша́ть, по- у́гли в ками́не.
2 (*thrust*) пиха́ть, пихну́ть/сова́ть, су́нуть; **he ~d his tongue out** он вы́сунул язы́к; **he ~s his nose into other people's business** он суёт нос не в своё де́ло.
■ *v.i.*: **he ~d about among the rubbish** он ры́лся в му́соре.

poker /'pəʊkə(r)/ *n.*
1 (*for a fire*) кочерга́.
2 (*game*) по́кер.
■ *cpd.* **~-faced** *adj.* с ка́менным лицо́м.

poky /'pəʊkɪ/ *adj.* (**pokier, pokiest**) (*coll.*) те́сный.

Poland /'pəʊlənd/ *n.* По́льша.

polar /'pəʊlə(r)/ *adj.* поля́рный; **~ bear** бе́лый медве́дь.

Pole /pəʊl/ *n.* (*person*) поля́к (*fem.* по́лька).

pole[1] /pəʊl/ *n.* (*of earth, elec., and fig.*) по́люс.
■ *cpd.* **P~ Star** *n.* Поля́рная звезда́.

pole[2] /pəʊl/ *n.* (*post*) столб, шест.
■ *cpds.* **~ vault** *n.* прыжо́к с шесто́м; **~-vaulter** *n.* прыгу́н (*fem.* -ья) с шесто́м, шесто́вик.

polemic /pə'lemɪk/ *n.* поле́мика, спор.
■ *adj.* (*also* **~al**) полеми́ческий, спо́рный.

police /pə'li:s/ *n.* поли́ция, (*in Russia*) мили́ция; **~ constable** (*Br.*) полице́йский; **~ force** поли́ция.
■ *v.t.* охраня́ть, подде́рживать (*both impf.*) поря́док в + *p.*
■ *cpds.* **~man** *n.* полице́йский; (*in Russia*) милиционе́р; **~ officer** *n.* полице́йский; **~ station** *n.* (полице́йский) уча́сток; (*in Russia*) отделе́ние мили́ции; **~woman** *n.* же́нщина-полице́йский/милиционе́р.

policy /'pɒlɪsɪ/ *n.* (*planned action*) поли́тика; (*insurance*) (страхово́й) по́лис.
■ *cpd.* **~holder** *n.* держа́тель (*m.*) страхово́го по́лиса.

polio(myelitis) /'pəʊlɪəʊ(maɪ'laɪtɪs)/ *n.* полиомиели́т.

Polish /'pəʊlɪʃ/ *n.* (*language*) по́льский язы́к.
■ *adj.* по́льский.

polish /'pɒlɪʃ/ *n.*
1 (*brightness*) полиро́вка.
2 (*substance used for ~ing*) полирова́льная па́ста.
3 (*fig., refinement*) лоск, блеск.
■ *v.t.* полирова́ть, от-; (*metal; also fig.*) шлифова́ть, от-.
■ *with adv.*: **~ off** *v.t.* (*coll., finish*) разде́л|ываться, -аться с + *i.*, поко́нчить (*pf.*) с + *i.*

polite /pə'laɪt/ *adj.* (**politer, politest**) ве́жливый.

politic /'pɒlɪtɪk/ *adj.*
1 (*prudent*) благоразу́мный.
2 : **the body ~** госуда́рство.

political /pə'lɪtɪk(ə)l/ *adj.* полити́ческий; **~ correctness** полит(и́ческая)корре́ктность; **~ly correct** полит(и́чески)корре́ктный; **~ prisoner** полит(и́ческий)заключённый.

politician /pɒlɪ'tɪʃ(ə)n/ *n.* поли́тик.

politicize /pə'lɪtɪsaɪz/ *v.t.* политизи́ровать (*impf., pf.*).

politics /'pɒlɪtɪks/ *n.* поли́тика; (*political views*) полити́ческие взгля́ды (*m. pl.*)/убежде́ния (*nt. pl.*).

poll /pəʊl/ *n.* (*voting process*) голосова́ние; (*opinion canvass*) опро́с.
■ *v.t.* 1 (*receive*) получ|а́ть, -и́ть/наб|ира́ть, -ра́ть.
2 (*take votes of*): **they ~ed the meeting** они́ поста́вили вопро́с на голосова́ние.

pollen /'pɒlən/ *n.* цвето́чная пыльца́.

pollinate /'pɒlɪneɪt/ *v.t.* опыл|я́ть, -и́ть.

polling /'pəʊlɪŋ/ *n.* голосова́ние.
■ *cpds.* **~ booth** *n.* (*Br.*) каби́на для голосова́ния; **~ day** *n.* день вы́боров; **~ station** *n.* избира́тельный уча́сток.

pollutant /pə'lu:tənt/ *n.* загрязни́тель (*m.*).

pollute /pə'lu:t/ *v.t.* загрязн|я́ть, -и́ть.

pollution /pə'lu:ʃ(ə)n/ *n.* загрязне́ние.

polo /'pəʊləʊ/ *n.* по́ло (*nt. indecl.*).
■ *cpd.* **~ neck** *n.* (*Br.*) сви́тер с кру́глым высо́ким воротнико́м.

polyester /pɒlɪ'estə(r)/ *n.* (*fabric*)

полиэфи́рная ткань.

polygamy /pəˈlɪgəmɪ/ *n.* полига́мия.

polygon /ˈpɒlɪgɒn/ *n.* многоуго́льник.

Polynesia /pɒlɪˈniːʒə/ *n.* Полине́зия.

Polynesian /pɒlɪˈniːʒ(ə)n/ *n.* полинези́|ец (*fem.* **~**йка).
■ *adj.* полинези́йский.

polyp /ˈpɒlɪp/ *n.* (*zool., med.*) поли́п.

polystyrene /pɒlɪˈstaɪriːn/ *n.* полистиро́л.

polytechnic /pɒlɪˈteknɪk/ *n.* полите́хникум.
■ *adj.* политехни́ческий институ́т, полите́х (*coll.*).

polythene /ˈpɒlɪθiːn/ *n.* (*Br.*) полиэтиле́н; (*attr.*) полиэтиле́новый.

polyurethane /pɒlɪˈjʊərəθeɪn/ *n.* полиурета́н.

pomegranate /ˈpɒmɪgrænɪt, ˈpɒmgrænɪt/ *n.* грана́т (*дерево, плод*).

pomp /pɒmp/ *n.* пы́шность, по́мпа.

pompom /ˈpɒmpɒm/, **pompon** /ˈpɒmpɒn/ *nn.* (*tuft*) помпо́н.

pomposity /pɒmˈpɒsɪtɪ/ *n.* помпе́зность; (*of person*) напы́щенность.

pompous /ˈpɒmpəs/ *adj.* помпе́зный; (*of person*) напы́щенный.

poncho /ˈpɒntʃəʊ/ *n.* (*pl.* **~s**) по́нчо (*nt. indecl.*).

pond /pɒnd/ *n.* пруд.

ponder /ˈpɒndə(r)/ *v.t.* обду́м|ывать, -ать.
■ *v.i.* размышля́ть (*impf.*).

pong /pɒŋ/ *n.* (*Br. coll.*) вонь, զлово́ние.

pontiff /ˈpɒntɪf/ *n.*: **supreme ~** (*the Pope*) Па́па Ри́мский.

pontificate /pɒnˈtɪfɪkət/ *v.i.* (*fig., lay down the law*) веща́ть (*impf.*) (*говорить важно, напыщенно*).

pony /ˈpəʊnɪ/ *n.* (*horse*) по́ни (*m. indecl.*).
■ *cpd.* **~tail** *n.* хво́стик (*причёска*).

poodle /ˈpuːd(ə)l/ *n.* пу́дель (*m.*).

pool[1] /puːl/ *n.* (*small body of water*) пруд; (*puddle*) лу́жа; **(swimming ~)** (пла́вательный) бассе́йн.

pool[2] /puːl/ *n.*
1 (*total of staked money*) совоку́пность ста́вок; (*in cards*) банк; **football ~s** футбо́льный тотализа́тор.
2 (*common reserve*) о́бщий фонд.
3 (*billiards game*) пул.
■ *v.t.* объедин|я́ть, -и́ть (в о́бщий фонд).

poor /pɔːə(r)/ *n.* (*collect.*: **the ~**) беднота́, бедняки́ (*m. pl.*), бе́дные (*pl.*).
■ *adj.* 1 (*indigent*) бе́дный.
2 (*unfortunate*) бе́дный, несча́стный.
3 (*small*) ску́дный; плохо́й; **a ~ harvest** ни́зкий урожа́й.
4 (*of low quality*) плохо́й; **~ health** плохо́е здоро́вье.

poorly /ˈpɔːəlɪ/ *adj.* (*Br.*) нездоро́вый.
■ *adv.* пло́хо; **this book is ~ written** э́та кни́га пло́хо напи́сана.

pop[1] /pɒp/ *n.* (*explosive sound*) щелчо́к, хлопо́к; (*coll., gaseous drink*) газиро́вка.
■ *adv.*: **the balloon went ~** ша́рик ло́пнул.
■ *v.t.* **(popped, popping)**
1 (*cause to explode*): **~ a balloon** прок|а́лывать, -оло́ть ша́рик.
2 (*put suddenly*) сова́ть, су́нуть.
■ *v.i.* **(popped, popping)** (*make explosive sound*) хло́п|ать, -нуть, щёлк|ать, -нуть.
■ *with advs.* (*coll.*): **they ~ped in for a drink** они́ заскочи́ли/забежа́ли вы́пить; **she kept ~ping out all day** она́ весь день куда́-то выска́кивала; **he ~ped up unexpectedly** он появи́лся неожи́данно.
■ *cpd.* **~corn** *n.* попко́рн, возду́шная кукуру́за; **~-up** *n.* (*comput.*) всплыва́ющее окно́.

pop[2] /pɒp/ *n.* (*coll.*) (*music*) поп-му́зыка.
■ *adj.*: **~ group** поп-гру́ппа; **~ star** поп-звезда́.

pope /pəʊp/ *n.* (*also* **the Pope**) Па́па Ри́мский (*m.*).

poplar /ˈpɒplə(r)/ *n.* то́поль (*m.*).

poppy /ˈpɒpɪ/ *n.* мак.
■ *cpd.* **~ seed** *n.* мак.

populace /ˈpɒpjʊləs/ *n.* (*the masses*) ма́ссы (*f. pl.*).

popular /ˈpɒpjʊlə(r)/ *adj.*
1 (*of the people*) наро́дный.
2 (*suited to the needs, tastes etc. of the people*): **the ~ press** ма́ссовая пре́сса/печа́ть.
3 (*generally liked*) по́льзующийся о́бщей симпа́тией; **he is ~ with the ladies** он име́ет успе́х у же́нщин.

popularity /pɒpjʊˈlærɪtɪ/ *n.* популя́рность; успе́х.

popularize /ˈpɒpjʊləraɪz/ *v.t.* популяризи́ровать (*impf., pf.*).

populate /ˈpɒpjʊleɪt/ *v.t.* насел|я́ть, -и́ть.

population /pɒpjʊˈleɪʃ(ə)n/ *n.* населе́ние; жи́тели (*m. pl.*).

populous /ˈpɒpjʊləs/ *adj.* многолю́дный, густонаселённый.

porcelain /ˈpɔːsəlɪn/ *n.* фарфо́р; (*attr.*) фарфо́ровый.

porch /pɔːtʃ/ *n.* (*covered entrance*) крыльцо́; (*US, veranda*) вера́нда.

porcupine /ˈpɔːkjʊpaɪn/ *n.* дикобра́з.

pore[1] /pɔː(r)/ *n.* по́ра.

pore[2] /pɔː(r)/ *v.i.*: **he likes to ~ over old books** он лю́бит сиде́ть над ста́рыми кни́гами.

pork /pɔːk/ *n.* свини́на.

porn(o) /ˈpɔːn(əʊ)/ *n.* (*coll.*) порногра́фия, по́рно (*nt. indecl.*) (*coll.*), порну́ха (*coll.*).

pornographic /pɔːnəˈgræfɪk/ *adj.* порнографи́ческий.

pornography /pɔːˈnɒgrəfɪ/ *n.* порногра́фия.

porridge /ˈpɒrɪdʒ/ *n.* овся́ная ка́ша.

port[1] /pɔːt/ *n.* (*harbour*) порт, га́вань; **~ of call** порт захо́да.

port[2] /pɔːt/ *n.* (*wine*) портве́йн.

port[3] /pɔːt/ *n.* (*comput.*) порт.

port[4] /pɔːt/ *n.* (*left side*) ле́вый борт.
■ *adj.* ле́вый; **~ side** ле́вый борт; **~ wind** ве́тер с ле́вого бо́рта.

portable /ˈpɔːtəb(ə)l/ *adj.* портати́вный.

portal /ˈpɔːtəb(ə)l/ *n.* (*comput.*) порта́л.

portcullis /pɔːtˈkʌlɪs/ *n.* опускна́я решётка.

portend /pɔːˈtend/ *v.t.* предвеща́ть (*impf.*).

portent /ˈpɔːt(ə)nt/ *n.* (*omen*) предзнаменова́ние; (*marvel*) чу́до.

porter /ˈpɔːtə(r)/ *n.*
1 (*carrier of luggage*) носи́льщик.
2 (*US, sleeping car attendant*) проводни́к.

3 (*Br.*, *doorkeeper*) швейца́р.

portfolio /pɔːtˈfəʊlɪəʊ/ *n.* (*pl.* **~s**)
1 (*case*) портфе́ль (*m.*); (*artist's*) па́пка (*с образцами работ*); (*fashion model's*) портфо́лио (*nt. indecl.*).
2 (*pol.*, *fin.*) портфе́ль (*m.*).

porthole /ˈpɔːthəʊl/ *n.* иллюмина́тор.

portion /ˈpɔːʃ(ə)n/ *n.* (*part*, *share*) часть; до́ля; (*of food*) по́рция.

portly /ˈpɔːtlɪ/ *adj.* (**portlier, portliest**) доро́дный, по́лный, ту́чный.

portrait /ˈpɔːtrɪt/ *n.* портре́т.

portray /pɔːˈtreɪ/ *v.t.* (*depict*, *describe*) рисова́ть, на- портре́т + *g.*; (*act part of*) игра́ть, сыгра́ть.

portrayal /pɔːˈtreɪəl/ *n.* изображе́ние.

Portugal /ˈpɔːtjʊg(ə)l/ *n.* Португа́лия.

Portuguese /pɔːtjʊˈgiːz/ *n.* (*pl.* **~**)
1 (*person*) португа́л|ец (*fem.* -ка).
2 (*language*) португа́льский язы́к.
■ *adj.* португа́льский.

pose /pəʊz/ *n.* по́за.
■ *v.t.* (*put forward*) предл|ага́ть, -ожи́ть; изл|ага́ть, -ожи́ть.
■ *v.i.* 1 (*take up a position*) пози́ровать (*impf.*); **he ~s as an expert** он выдаёт себя́ за знатока́/специали́ста.
2 (*behave in an affected way*) рисова́ться (*impf.*).

poser /ˈpəʊzə(r)/ *n.* (*problem*) головоло́мка; (*person*) позёр.

posh /pɒʃ/ *adj.* (*coll.*) шика́рный; (*people*) све́тский.

position /pəˈzɪʃ(ə)n/ *n.*
1 (*place occupied by s.o. or sth.*) ме́сто, положе́ние.
2 (*situation*) положе́ние; **that puts me in an awkward ~** э́то ста́вит меня́ в неудо́бное/нело́вкое положе́ние; **I am not in a ~ to say** я не в состоя́нии сказа́ть.
3 (*attitude*, *opinion*) пози́ция.
4 (*post*) до́лжность, ме́сто.
■ *v.t.* поме|ща́ть, -сти́ть.

positive /ˈpɒzɪtɪv/ *adj.*
1 (*definite*) несомне́нный, определённый.
2 (*certain*) уве́ренный, убеждённый; **are you ~ you saw him?** вы уве́рены, что ви́дели его́?
3 (*assertive*) самоуве́ренный.
4 (*practical*, *helpful*) позити́вный, конструкти́вный; **~ discrimination** дискримина́ция в по́льзу определённой гру́ппы.
5 (*gram.*, *math.*, *elec.*) положи́тельный.

positively /ˈpɒzɪtɪvlɪ/ *adv.* (*with conviction*) с уве́ренностью; (*definitely*) несомне́нно; (*for emphasis*): **she was ~ rude to me** она́ была́ со мно́й про́сто груба́.

possess /pəˈzes/ *v.t.*
1 (*own*, *have*) владе́ть (*impf.*) + *i.*; (*good qualities*) облада́ть (*impf.*) + *i.*
2 (*influence*) овлад|ева́ть, -е́ть; **whatever ~ed him to do that?** что его́ заста́вило поступи́ть таки́м о́бразом?

possession /pəˈzeʃ(ə)n/ *n.*
1 (*ownership*, *occupation*) владе́ние; **they took ~ of the house** они́ ста́ли владе́льцами до́ма.
2 (*property*) иму́щество, со́бственность.

possessive /pəˈzesɪv/ *n.* (*gram.*) притяжа́тельный паде́ж.
■ *adj.* 1 (*gram.*) притяжа́тельный.
2 (*of person*) собственни́ческий; (*jealous*) ревни́вый.

possibility /pɒsɪˈbɪlɪtɪ/ *n.* возмо́жность; вероя́тность.

possible /ˈpɒsɪb(ə)l/ *adj.* возмо́жный; **as soon as ~** как мо́жно скоре́е; **I have done everything ~ to help** я сде́лал всё возмо́жное, что́бы помо́чь.

possibly /ˈpɒsɪblɪ/ *adv.* возмо́жно; **how can I ~ do that?** как же я могу́ э́то сде́лать?; **I can't ~** я ника́к не смогу́.

post[1] /pəʊst/ *n.* (*of wood*, *metal etc.*) столб.
■ *v.t.* (*display publicly*) выве́шивать, вы́весить; **the results will be ~ed (up) on the board** результа́ты бу́дут вы́вешены на доске́.

post[2] /pəʊst/ *n.* (*Br.*, *mail*) по́чта; **by return of ~** с обра́тной по́чтой; **I must take these letters to the ~** я до́лжен отнести́ э́ти пи́сьма на по́чту; **if you hurry you will catch the ~** е́сли вы поспеши́те, то успе́ете до отпра́вки по́чты; **has the ~ come yet?** по́чта уже́ была́/пришла́?
■ *v.t.* 1 (*Br.*, *dispatch by mail*) отпр|авля́ть, -а́вить по по́чте.
2 (*fig.*) изве|ща́ть, -сти́ть; **keep me ~ed (of events)** держи́те меня́ в ку́рсе (дел).
■ *cpds.* **~box** *n.* почто́вый я́щик; **~card** *n.* откры́тка; **~code** *n.* (*Br.*) почто́вый и́ндекс; **~man** *n.* (*Br.*) почтальо́н; **~mark** *n.* почто́вый ште́мпель; **~ office** *n.* по́чта; **~woman** *n.* (*Br.*) почтальо́н, почтальо́нка (*coll.*).

post[3] /pəʊst/ *n.*
1 (*place of duty*) пост; **at one's ~** на посту́.
2 (*job*) до́лжность, пост.
■ *v.t.* 1 (*assign to place of duty*) назн|ача́ть, -а́чить на до́лжность.
2 (*mil.*, *guard*, *sentry*) выставля́ть, вы́ставить.

postage /ˈpəʊstɪdʒ/ *n.* почто́вые расхо́ды (*m. pl.*); почто́вый сбор.

postal /ˈpəʊst(ə)l/ *adj.* почто́вый; **~ order** (*Br.*) (де́нежный) почто́вый перево́д.

post-date /pəʊstˈdeɪt/ *v.t.*
1 (*give a date later than the actual one*) дати́ровать (*impf.*) бо́лее по́здним число́м.
2 (*occur later than*) сле́довать, по- за + *i.*

poste-haste /pəʊstˈheɪst/ *adv.* о́чень бы́стро, неме́дленно.

poster /ˈpəʊstə(r)/ *n.* (*placard*) афи́ша, плака́т; (*advertising*) по́стер.

posterior /pɒˈstɪərɪə(r)/ *n.* зад.
■ *adj.* (*subsequent*) после́дующий; (*behind*) за́дний.

posterity /pɒˈsterɪtɪ/ *n.* пото́мк|и (*pl.*, *g.* -ов).

postgraduate /pəʊstˈgrædjʊət/ *n.*: **~ student** аспира́нт (*fem.* -ка).
■ *adj.* аспира́нтский.

posthumous /ˈpɒstjʊməs/ *adj.* посме́ртный.

postmodern /pəʊstˈmɒd(ə)n/ *adj.* постмодерни́стский.

postmodernism /pəʊstˈmɒdənɪz(ə)m/ *n.* постмодерни́зм.

post-mortem /pəʊstˈmɔːtəm/ *n.* вскры́тие (тру́па), аутопси́я.

post-natal /pəʊst'neɪt(ə)l/ *adj.* послеродово́й.

postpone /pəʊs'pəʊn/ *v.t.* отсро́чи|вать, -ть; от|кла́дывать, -ложи́ть.

postscript /'pəʊskrɪpt/ *n.* постскри́птум.

postulate /'pɒstjʊleɪt/ *v.t.* постули́ровать (*impf.*, *pf.*).

posture /'pɒstʃə(r)/ *n.* оса́нка.
■ *v.i.* пози́ровать (*impf.*).

post-war /pəʊst'wɔ:(r)/ *adj.* послевое́нный.

posy /'pəʊzɪ/ *n.* буке́т цвето́в.

pot[1] /pɒt/ *n.* горшо́к; **~s and pans** ку́хонная посу́да/у́тварь; **a ~ of tea** ча́йник с зава́ренным ча́ем; **~ plant** (*Br.*) горше́чное расте́ние; **his work is going to ~** (*coll.*) его́ рабо́та идёт насма́рку.
■ *v.t.* (**potted, potting**)
1 (*preserves*) консерви́ровать, за-.
2 (*plants*) сажа́ть, посади́ть в горшо́к.
3 (*fig., abridge*): **~ted history** кра́ткая исто́рия.
4 (*billiards*) заг|оня́ть, -на́ть в лу́зу.
■ *cpds.* **~ belly** *n.* (большо́й) живо́т, пу́зо; **~hole** *n.* (*in road*) вы́боина; **~holing** *n.* (*Br.*) спелеоло́гия.

pot[2] /pɒt/ *n.* (*coll., marijuana*) анаша́.

potash /'pɒtæʃ/ *n.* пота́ш, углеки́слый ка́лий.

potassium /pə'tæsɪəm/ *n.* ка́лий; (*attr.*) ка́лиевый, кали́йный.

potato /pə'teɪtəʊ/ *n.* (*pl.* **~es**) (*collect., and pl.*) карто́фель (*m.*), (*single* **~**) карто́фелина; **~ chips** (*US*), **~ crisps** (*Br.*) хрустя́щий карто́фель.

potent /'pəʊt(ə)nt/ *adj.* (*powerful*) си́льный, могу́щественный; (*of alcoholic drink*) кре́пкий.

potential /pə'tenʃ(ə)l/ *n.* потенциа́л.
■ *adj.* потенциа́льный.

potion /'pəʊʃ(ə)n/ *n.* насто́йка, сна́добье; **love ~** любо́вный напи́ток.

potter[1] /'pɒtə(r)/ *n.* гонча́р.

potter[2] /'pɒtə(r)/ *v.i.* (*e.g. in garden*) копа́ться, ковыря́ться (*both impf.*).

pottery /'pɒtərɪ/ *n.* кера́мика.

potty[1] /'pɒtɪ/ *n.* (*coll., chamber pot*) горшо́к.

potty[2] /'pɒtɪ/ *adj.* (**pottier, pottiest**) (*Br.*) (*crazy*) чо́кнутый (*coll.*).

pouch /paʊtʃ/ *n.* су́мочка, мешо́чек; (*kangaroo's*) су́мка.

pouf(fe) /pu:f/ *n.* (*seat*) пуф.

poultry /'pəʊltrɪ/ *n.* дома́шняя пти́ца (*collect.*).

pounce /paʊns/ *v.i.* набр|а́сываться, -о́ситься; **the cat ~d on the mouse** ко́шка бро́силась на мышь.

pound[1] /paʊnd/ *n.*
1 (*weight*) фунт.
2 (*money*) фунт (сте́рлингов).

pound[2] /paʊnd/ *n.* (*enclosure*) заго́н.

pound[3] /paʊnd/ *v.t.*
1 (*crush*) разб|ива́ть, -и́ть.
2 (*thump*) колоти́ть (*impf.*).
■ *v.i.* 1 (*thump*): **he ~ed at the door** он колоти́л в дверь; **her heart was ~ing with excitement** её се́рдце колоти́лось от волне́ния.
2 (*run heavily*) мча́ться/нести́сь (*both impf.*) с гро́хотом.

pour /pɔ:(r)/ *v.t.* лить (*impf.*); нал|ива́ть, -и́ть; **will you ~ me (out) a cup of tea?** нале́йте мне, пожа́луйста, ча́шку ча́я; (*fig.*): **he ~ed scorn on the idea** он вы́смеял э́ту иде́ю.
■ *v.i.* ли́ться (*impf.*); (*fig.*): **the crowd ~ed out of the theatre** (*Br.*), **theater** (*US*) толпа́ повали́ла из теа́тра (*coll.*); (*of rain*) лить (*impf.*) как из ведра́; **it was ~ing with rain** шёл проливно́й дождь, дождь лил как из ведра́.
■ *with advs.* (*fig.*): **letters ~ed in** посы́пались пи́сьма; **she ~ed out a tale of woe** она́ излила́ своё го́ре.

pout /paʊt/ *v.i.* над|ува́ть, -у́ть гу́бы; ду́ться, на-.

poverty /'pɒvətɪ/ *n.* бе́дность, нищета́; **on the ~ line** на гра́ни нищеты́.
■ *cpd.* **~-stricken** ни́щий.

POW (*abbr. of* ***prisoner of war***) военнопле́нный.

powder /'paʊdə(r)/ *n.* (*chem., med. etc.*) порошо́к; (*cosmetic*) пу́дра.
■ *v.t.* 1 (*reduce to* **~**) превра|ща́ть, -ти́ть в порошо́к; **~ed milk** порошко́вое/сухо́е молоко́.
2 (*apply* **~** *to*) пу́дрить, на-.

powdery /'paʊdərɪ/ *adj.* порошкообра́зный; рассы́пчатый.

power /'paʊə(r)/ *n.*
1 (*ability, capacity*) си́ла, мощь; **purchasing ~** покупа́тельная спосо́бность.
2 (*pl., faculties*): **he was at the height of his ~s** он был в расцве́те сил.
3 (*vigour*) эне́ргия.
4 (*electrical energy*) эне́ргия; **there was a ~ cut** электроэне́ргию вре́менно отключи́ли; (*mechanical energy*) мо́щность.
5 (*control*) власть; **I have him in my ~** он в мое́й вла́сти; **in ~** у вла́сти.
6 (*right*) полномо́чия (*nt. pl.*), пра́во.
7 (*influential person or organization*) си́ла.
8 (*state*) держа́ва.
9 (*supernatural force*) си́ла.
10 (*coll., large amount*) ма́сса, мно́жество; **this medicine has done me a ~ of good** э́то лека́рство принесло́ мне огро́мную по́льзу.
11 (*math.*): **two to the ~ of ten** два в деся́той сте́пени.
■ *v.t.* (*supply with electrical energy*) снаб|жа́ть, -ди́ть эне́ргией; (*supply with mechanical energy*) прив|оди́ть, -ести́ в де́йствие.
■ *cpds.* **~boat** *n.* мото́рный ка́тер; **~ drill** *n.* электри́ческая дрель; **~ line** *n.* ли́ния электропереда́чи; **~-point** *n.* (*Br.*) ште́псельная розе́тка; **~ plant, ~ station** *nn.* электроста́нция.

powerful /'paʊəfʊl/ *adj.* си́льный, мо́щный; **a ~ speech** я́ркая речь.

powerless /'paʊəlɪs/ *adj.* бесси́льный.

pp (*abbr. of* ***per procurationem***): **John Brown pp A. Smith** по дове́ренности Джо́на Бра́уна подписа́л А. Смит.

pp. (*abbr. of* ***pages***) стр./сс. (страни́цы).

PR *abbr. of*
1 ***public relations*** пиа́р.
2 ***proportional representation***

пропорциона́льное представи́тельство.

practicable /'præktɪkəb(ə)l/ *adj.* (*feasible*) осуществи́мый, реа́льный.

practical /'præktɪk(ə)l/ *adj.*
1 (*concerned with practice*) практи́ческий; **a ~ joke** ро́зыгрыш, шу́тка; **he is a ~ man** он практи́чный челове́к.
2 (*workable, feasible*) осуществи́мый, реа́льный.

practicality /præktɪ'kælɪtɪ/ *n.* практи́чность.

practically /'præktɪkəlɪ/ *adv.*
1 (*in a practical manner*) практи́чески; на де́ле.
2 (*almost*) практи́чески, факти́чески.

practice /'præktɪs/ *n.*
1 (*performance*) пра́ктика; **the idea will not work in ~** э́та иде́я на пра́ктике неосуществи́ма.
2 (*habitual performance*) обы́чай, обыкнове́ние.
3 (*repeated exercise*) упражне́ние, трениро́вка, пра́ктика; **I am badly out of ~** я давно́ не упражня́лся/практикова́лся.
4 (*work of doctor, lawyer etc.*) пра́ктика.
■ *v.t.* & *i.*: (*US*) = **practise**

practis|e /'præktɪs/ (*US* **practice**) *v.t.*
1 (*perform habitually*) де́лать, с- по привы́чке; (*for exercise*) упражня́ть (*impf.*), отраб|а́тывать, -о́тать; (*sport game etc.*) упражня́ться (*impf.*) в + *p.*; (*instrument*): **she was ~ing the piano** она́ упражня́лась на роя́ле/фортепиа́но.
2 (*a profession etc.*) практикова́ть (*impf.*); **a ~ing physician** практику́ющий врач.
■ *v.i.* упражня́ться (*impf.*); тренирова́ться (*impf.*).

practitioner /præk'tɪʃənə(r)/ *n.* практику́ющий специали́ст.

pragmatic /præg'mætɪk/ *adj.* прагмати́ческий.

pragmatism /'prægmətɪz(ə)m/ *n.* прагмати́зм.

pragmatist /'prægmətɪst/ *n.* прагма́тик.

Prague /prɑ:g/ *n.* Пра́га.

prairie /'preərɪ/ *n.* пре́рия.

praise /preɪz/ *n.* похвала́.
■ *v.t.* (*voice admiration of*) хвали́ть, по-; (*give glory to*) восхвал|я́ть, -и́ть.
■ *cpd.* **~worthy** *adj.* досто́йный похвалы́, похва́льный.

pram /præm/ *n.* (*Br.*) (де́тская) коля́ска.

prance /prɑ:ns/ *v.i.* (*of horse*) гарцева́ть (*impf.*); (*of person*) ва́жничать (*impf.*).

prank /præŋk/ *n.* вы́ходка, проде́лка.

prankster /'præŋkstə(r)/ *n.* шутни́к, прока́зник.

prat /præt/ *n.* (*Br. coll., idiot*) идио́т (*fem.* -ка).

prattle /'præt(ə)l/ *n.* болтовня́; (*childish*) ле́пет.
■ *v.i.* болта́ть (*impf.*); (*of child*) лепета́ть, про-.

prawn /prɔ:n/ *n.* креве́тка.

pray /preɪ/ *v.i.* моли́ться, по-; **the farmers ~ed for rain** фе́рмеры моли́ли Бо́га, что́бы пошёл дождь; **we will ~ for the Queen** мы бу́дем моли́ться за короле́ву.

prayer /'preə(r)/ *n.* моли́тва; **say one's ~s** моли́ться, по-.

preach /pri:tʃ/ *v.t.* пропове́довать (*impf.*).
■ *v.i.* чита́ть про́поведь.

preacher /'pri:tʃə(r)/ *n.* пропове́дник.

preamble /pri:'æmb(ə)l/ *n.* преа́мбула.

prearrange /pri:ə'reɪndʒ/ *v.t.* организо́в|ывать, -а́ть зара́нее.

precarious /prɪ'keərɪəs/ *adj.*
1 (*uncertain*) ненадёжный; **a ~ foothold** ненадёжная опо́ра.
2 (*dangerous, risky*) опа́сный, риско́ванный.

precaution /prɪ'kɔ:ʃ(ə)n/ *n.* предосторо́жность.

precautionary /prɪ'kɔ:ʃənərɪ/ *adj.* предупреди́тельный.

precede /prɪ'si:d/ *v.t.* предше́ствовать (*impf.*) + *d.*

precedence /'presɪd(ə)ns/ *n.* первоочерёдность; **this question takes ~** э́тот вопро́с до́лжен рассма́триваться в пе́рвую о́чередь.

precedent /'presɪd(ə)nt/ *n.* прецеде́нт; **set a ~** созд|ава́ть, -а́ть прецеде́нт.

precept /'pri:sept/ *n.* (*moral instruction*) наставле́ние; (*rule*) пра́вило.

precinct /'pri:sɪŋkt/ *n.*
1 (*Br., area of restricted access*): **pedestrian ~** пешехо́дная зо́на; **shopping ~** торго́вый центр.
2 (*US, police or electoral district*) уча́сток.

precious /'preʃəs/ *adj.* (*valued*) це́нный; (*stone*) драгоце́нный.

precipice /'presɪpɪs/ *n.* про́пасть, обры́в.

precipitate[1] /prɪ'sɪpɪtət/ *adj.* (*rash*) опроме́тчивый.

precipitate[2] /prɪ'sɪpɪteɪt/ *v.t.*
1 (*fig.*) вв|ерга́ть, -е́ргнуть; **the country was ~d into war** страну́ вве́ргли в войну́.
2 (*bring on rapidly*) уск|оря́ть, -о́рить.

precipitation /prɪsɪpɪ'teɪʃ(ə)n/ *n.* (*rain etc.*) оса́д|ки (*pl., g.* -ов).

precipitous /prɪ'sɪpɪtəs/ *adj.* (*steep*) обры́вистый, круто́й; (*hasty*) поспе́шный.

precise /prɪ'saɪs/ *adj.* то́чный, аккура́тный.

precisely /prɪ'saɪslɪ/ *adv.* то́чно; (*with numbers or quantities*) ро́вно; (*as reply*: '*quite so*') соверше́нно ве́рно; вот и́менно.

precision /prɪ'sɪʒ(ə)n/ *n.* то́чность; аккура́тность.

preclude /prɪ'klu:d/ *v.t.* (*prevent*) предотвра|ща́ть, -ти́ть; (*make impossible*) исключ|а́ть, -и́ть.

precocious /prɪ'kəʊʃəs/ *adj.* ра́но разви́вшийся, ра́нний.

preconceived /pri:kən'si:vd/ *adj.* предвзя́тый.

preconception /pri:kən'sepʃ(ə)n/ *n.* предвзя́тое мне́ние.

precondition /pri:kən'dɪʃ(ə)n/ *n.* предвари́тельное усло́вие.

precursor /pri:'kɜ:sə(r)/ *n.* предше́ственни|к (*fem.* -ца); (*of event*) предве́стник.

pre-date /pri:'deɪt/ *v.t.* предше́ствовать (*impf.*) + *d.*

predator /'predətə(r)/ *n.* хи́щник.

predatory /'predətərɪ/ *adj.* хи́щный.

predecease /pri:dɪ'si:s/ *v.t.*: **he ~d her** он у́мер ра́ньше её.

predecessor /'pri:dɪsesə(r)/ *n.* предше́ственни|к (*fem.* -ца).
predetermine /pri:dɪ'tɜ:mɪn/ *v.t.* предреш|а́ть, -и́ть.
predicament /prɪ'dɪkəmənt/ *n.* тру́дное положе́ние.
predicate /'predɪkət/ *n.* (*gram.*) сказу́емое.
predicative /prɪ'dɪkətɪv/ *adj.* предикати́вный.
predict /prɪ'dɪkt/ *v.t.* предска́з|ывать, -а́ть.
predictable /prɪ'dɪktəb(ə)l/ *adj.* предсказу́емый.
prediction /prɪ'dɪkʃ(ə)n/ *n.* предсказа́ние.
predilection /pri:dɪ'lekʃ(ə)n/ *n.* пристра́стие, скло́нность (**for:** к + *d.*).
predispose /pri:dɪ'spəʊz/ *v.t.* предраспол|ага́ть, -ожи́ть.
predominance /prɪ'dɒmɪnəns/ *n.* (*control; superiority*) госпо́дство; (*preponderance*) преоблада́ние.
predominant /prɪ'dɒmɪnənt/ *adj.* преоблада́ющий.
predominantly /prɪ'dɒmɪnəntlɪ/ *adv.* преиму́щественно.
predominate /prɪ'dɒmɪneɪt/ *v.i.* преоблада́ть (*impf.*).
pre-eminence /pri:'emɪnəns/ *n.* превосхо́дство, преиму́щество.
pre-eminent /pri:'emɪnənt/ *adj.* выдаю́щийся.
pre-empt /pri:'empt/ *v.t.* предупре|жда́ть, -ди́ть.
pre-emptive /pri:'emptɪv/ *adj.*: **~ strike** упрежда́ющий уда́р.
preen /pri:n/ *v.t.* (*of bird*): **~ one's feathers** чи́стить, по- пе́рья; (*of person*): **preen o.s.** прихор|а́шиваться, -оши́ться (*coll.*).
prefabricate /pri:'fæbrɪkeɪt/ *v.t.*: **~d house** (*coll.* **prefab**) сбо́рный дом.
preface /'prefəs/ *n.* предисло́вие.
prefect /'pri:fekt/ *n.* (*Br., at school*) ста́роста (*c.g.*).
prefer /prɪ'fɜ:(r)/ *v.t.* (**preferred, preferring**)
1 (*like better*) предпоч|ита́ть, -е́сть; **I ~ juice to water** я предпочита́ю сок воде́.
2 (*submit*): **~ charges** предъяв|ля́ть, -и́ть обвине́ния.
preferable /'prefərəb(ə)l/ *adj.* предпочти́тельный.
preference /'prefərəns/ *n.* предпочте́ние.
preferential /prefə'renʃ(ə)l/ *adj.* предпочти́тельный; льго́тный.
prefix /'pri:fɪks/ *n.* приста́вка, пре́фикс.
pregnancy /'pregnənsɪ/ *n.* бере́менность.
pregnant /'pregnənt/ *adj.* бере́менная; **become ~** забере́менеть (*pf.*).
preheat /pri:'hi:t/ *v.t.* предвари́тельно подогр|ева́ть, -е́ть.
prehistoric /pri:hɪ'stɒrɪk/ *adj.* доистори́ческий.
prejudge /pri:'dʒʌdʒ/ *v.t.* предреш|а́ть, -и́ть.
prejudice /'predʒʊdɪs/ *n.* предрассу́док, предубежде́ние.
■ *v.t.* 1 (*cause to have a ~*): **you are ~d against him** вы отно́ситесь к нему́ с предубежде́нием.
2 (*harm*) нан|оси́ть, -ести́ уще́рб + *d.*
prejudiced /'predʒʊdɪst/ *adj.* предубеждённый.
preliminary /prɪ'lɪmɪnərɪ/ *adj.* предвари́тельный.
prelude /'prelju:d/ *n.* (*mus., fig.*) прелю́дия.
premarital /pri:'mærɪt(ə)l/ *adj.* добра́чный.
premature /premə'tjʊə(r)/ *adj.* преждевре́менный; **~ baby** недоно́шенный ребёнок.
premeditate /pri:'medɪteɪt/ *v.t.*: **~d murder** преднаме́ренное уби́йство.
premenstrual /pri:'menstrʊəl/ *adj.* предменструа́льный.
premier /'premɪə(r)/ *n.* премье́р(-мини́стр).
■ *adj.* пе́рвый; гла́вный.
premiership /'premɪəʃɪp/ *n.* премье́рство.
première /'premɪeə(r)/ *n.* премье́ра.
premise /'premɪs/ *n.* (*phil.*) посы́лка; предположе́ние.
premises /'premɪsɪz/ *n. pl.* помеще́ние.
premium /'pri:mɪəm/ *n.* (*pl.* **~s**)
1 (*payment for insurance*) (страхова́я) пре́мия.
2 (*additional payment*) припла́та.
3 : **at a ~** вы́ше номина́ла.
premonition /premə'nɪʃ(ə)n/ *n.* предчу́вствие.
prenatal /pri:'neɪt(ə)l/ *adj.* предродово́й.
preoccupation /pri:ɒkjʊ'peɪʃ(ə)n/ *n.* озабо́ченность.
preoccupy /pri:'ɒkjʊpaɪ/ *v.t.* забо́тить, о-.
preparation /prepə'reɪʃ(ə)n/ *n.* подгото́вка, приготовле́ние; **she was packing in ~ for the journey** она́ укла́дывала ве́щи, гото́вясь к пое́здке; (*pl., preparatory measures*) приготовле́ния (*nt. pl.*).
preparatory /prɪ'pærətərɪ/ *adj.* подготови́тельный.
prepare /prɪ'peə(r)/ *v.t.* гото́вить (*impf.*); пригот|а́вливать, -о́вить; подгот|а́вливать, -о́вить; **the tutor ~d him for his exams** учи́тель подгото́вил его́ к экза́менам.
■ *v.i.* подгот|а́вливаться, -о́виться; пригот|а́вливаться, -о́виться.
preponderance /prɪ'pɒndərəns/ *n.* переве́с, преиму́щество.
preposition /prepə'zɪʃ(ə)n/ *n.* (*gram.*) предло́г.
prepositional /prepə'zɪʃənəl/ *n.* & *adj.* (*gram.*) предло́жный (паде́ж).
prepossessing /pri:pə'zesɪŋ/ *adj.* располага́ющий, привлека́тельный.
preposterous /prɪ'pɒstərəs/ *adj.* возмути́тельный.
prerequisite /pri:'rekwɪzɪt/ *n.* предпосы́лка.
prerogative /prɪ'rɒgətɪv/ *n.* (*of ruler, etc.*) прерогати́ва; (*privilege*) привиле́гия.
Presbyterian /prezbɪ'tɪərɪən/ *n.* пресвитериа́н|ин (*fem.* -ка).
■ *adj.* пресвитериа́нский.
preschool /'pri:sku:l/ *adj.* дошко́льный.
prescribe /prɪ'skraɪb/ *v.t.*
1 (*impose*) предпи́с|ывать, -а́ть.
2 (*med.*) пропи́с|ывать, -а́ть.
prescription /prɪ'skrɪpʃ(ə)n/ *n.* (*from*

doctor) реце́пт; (*medicine*) лека́рство.

prescriptive /prɪ'skrɪptɪv/ *adj.*
1 (*giving directions*) предпи́сывающий.
2 (*leg.*): **~ right** пра́во(, осно́ванное на) да́вности.

presence /'prez(ə)ns/ *n.* прису́тствие; **~ of mind** прису́тствие ду́ха.

present[1] /'prez(ə)nt/ *n.*
1 (*time now at hand*) настоя́щее (вре́мя); **at ~** в настоя́щее вре́мя; сейча́с.
2 (*gram.*, **~ tense**) настоя́щее вре́мя.
■ *adj.* 1 (*at hand*) прису́тствующий; **no one else was ~** никого́ бо́льше не́ было.
2 (*in question*) да́нный; **in the ~ case** в да́нном слу́чае.
3 (*existent*) настоя́щий; **at the ~ time** в настоя́щее вре́мя; сейча́с; **under ~ circumstances** в да́нных обстоя́тельствах.
4 (*gram.*) настоя́щего вре́мени; **~ participle** прича́стие настоя́щего вре́мени.
■ *cpd.* **~-day** *adj.* совреме́нный, ны́нешний.

present[2] /'prez(ə)nt/ *n.* (*gift*) пода́рок.

present[3] /prɪ'zent/ *v.t.*
1 (*offer, put forward*) дари́ть, по-; вруч|а́ть, -и́ть; преподн|оси́ть, -ести́; **as soon as an opportunity ~s itself** как то́лько предста́вится слу́чай; **he ~ed his case well** он хорошо́ изложи́л свои́ до́воды; (*give*) предост|авля́ть, -а́вить; **I was ~ed with a choice** мне предоста́вили вы́бор.
2 (*introduce*) предст|авля́ть, -а́вить.

presentable /prɪ'zentəb(ə)l/ *adj.* прили́чный.

presentation /prezən'teɪʃ(ə)n/ *n.*
1 (*making a present*) подноше́ние, вруче́ние.
2 (*production*) предъявле́ние.
3 (*exposition*) изложе́ние, пода́ча.

presenter /prɪ'zentə(r)/ *n.* (*TV, radio*) веду́щ|ий (*fem.* -ая).

presentiment /prɪ'zentɪmənt/ *n.* предчу́вствие; **he had a ~ of danger** он предчу́вствовал опа́сность.

presently /'prezəntlɪ/ *adv.* (*soon*) вско́ре; (*US, at present*) сейча́с, в настоя́щее вре́мя, в да́нный моме́нт.

preservation /prezə'veɪʃ(ə)n/ *n.* (*act of preserving*) сохране́ние; консерви́рование; (*of materials*) консерва́ция; (*of monuments, etc.*) охра́на.

preservative /prɪ'zə:vətɪv/ *n.* (*in food*) консерва́нт.

preserve /prɪ'zə:v/
1 (*jam*) варе́нье.
2 (*area for protection of game, etc.*) запове́дник.
■ *v.t.* 1 (*save; protect*) сохран|я́ть, -и́ть.
2 (*keep from decomposition, etc.*) консерви́ровать, за-.
3 (*maintain*) подде́рж|ивать, -а́ть; храни́ть, со-.

preside /prɪ'zaɪd/ *v.i.* председа́тельствовать (*impf.*).

presidency /'prezɪdənsɪ/ *n.* президе́нтство.

president /'prezɪd(ə)nt/ *n.* (*of State, bank etc.*) президе́нт.

presidential /prezɪ'denʃ(ə)l/ *adj.* президе́нтский.

press /pres/ *n.*
1 (*act of ~ing*): **she gave his trousers a ~** она́ погла́дила ему́ брю́ки.
2 (*machine for ~ing or printing*) пресс.
3 (*newspaper world*) печа́ть, пре́сса; **~ agency** аге́нтство печа́ти; **~ conference** пресс-конфере́нция; (*newspaper reaction*) о́тклик, реце́нзия; **a good ~ helps to sell a book** хоро́шие о́тклики в печа́ти спосо́бствуют сбы́ту кни́ги.
■ *v.t.* 1 (*exert physical pressure on*) наж|има́ть, -а́ть; **~ the button** наж|има́ть, -а́ть (на) кно́пку.
2 (*push*) приж|има́ть, -а́ть; **he ~ed his nose against the window** он прижа́л нос к окну́.
3 (*iron*) гла́дить, по-.
4 (*clasp*) сжима́ть, сжать; **he ~ed her hand** он сжал ей ру́ку.
5 (*fig., sustain vigorously*): **~ charges** выдвига́ть, вы́двинуть обвине́ние.
6 (*urge*): **they ~ed me to stay** они́ угова́ривали меня́ оста́ться.
■ *v.i.*: **if you ~ too hard, the pencil will break** е́сли сли́шком нажима́ть, каранда́ш слома́ется; **~ for** (*reform, enqiury etc.*) добива́ться (*impf.*) + *g.*
■ *with advs.*: **~ forward** *v.i.* прот|а́лкиваться, -олкну́ться (вперёд); **~ on** *v.i.* продолжа́ть (*impf.*).
■ *cpds.* **~ stud** *n.* (*Br.*) кно́пка (*на одежде*); **~-up** *n.* (*Br.*) отжима́ние; **do ~-ups** отж|има́ться, -а́ться (от по́ла).

pressing /'presɪŋ/ *adj.* настоя́тельный, неотло́жный.

pressure /'preʃə(r)/ *n.*
1 давле́ние.
2 (*compulsive influence*) давле́ние, возде́йствие; **put ~ on** ока́з|ывать, -а́ть давле́ние/нажи́м на + *a.*; наж|има́ть, -а́ть на + *a.* (*coll.*); **~ group** ≈ инициати́вная гру́ппа; движе́ние.
■ *cpd.* **~ cooker** *n.* скорова́рка.

pressurize /'preʃəraɪz/ *v.t.*
1 герметизи́ровать (*impf.*).
2 (*fig.*) ока́з|ывать, -а́ть давле́ние на + *a.*; **he was ~d into writing a confession** его́ заста́вили написа́ть призна́ние.

prestige /pre'sti:ʒ/ *n.* прести́ж.

prestigious /pre'stɪdʒəs/ *adj.* прести́жный.

presumably /prɪ'zju:məblɪ/ *adv.* вероя́тно.

presume /prɪ'zju:m/ *v.t.*
1 (*assume*) полага́ть (*impf.*).
2 (*with inf.: venture*) брать, взять на себя́ сме́лость; **I would not ~ to argue with you** я не возьму́ на себя́ сме́лость с ва́ми спо́рить.

presumptuous /prɪ'zʌmptjʊəs/ *adj.* самонаде́янный.

presuppose /pri:sə'pəʊz/ *v.t.* (зара́нее) предпол|ага́ть, -ожи́ть; допус|ка́ть, -ти́ть.

pre-tax /pri:'tæks/ *adj.* до вы́чета нало́гов.

pretence /prɪ'tens/ (*US* **pretense**) *n.*
1 (*pretending*) притво́рство; **he made a ~ of reading the newspaper** он притвори́лся, что чита́ет газе́ту; **by/under/on false ~s** обма́нным путём.
2 (*pretext, excuse*) предло́г; **he called under the ~ of asking advice** он зашёл под предло́гом спроси́ть сове́та.

pretend /prɪ'tend/ *v.t.* & *i.* притворя́ться

(*impf.*); де́лать (*impf.*) вид; **she is ~ing to be asleep** она́ притворя́ется, что спит; **~ to be pirates** игра́ть в пира́тов (*о детях*).
pretense /prɪ'tens/ (*US*) = **pretence**
pretension /prɪ'tenʃ(ə)n/ *n.* претенцио́зность.
pretentious /prɪ'tenʃəs/ *adj.* претенцио́зный; показно́й.
pretext /'pri:tekst/ *n.* предло́г; **on/under the ~ of** под предло́гом + *g.*
pretty /'prɪtɪ/ *adj.* (**prettier, prettiest**) краси́вый, хоро́шенький.
■ *adv.* доста́точно, дово́льно; **~ much** (*nearly*) почти́.
prevail /prɪ'veɪl/ *v.i.*
1 (*win*) торжествова́ть, вос-; (*of idea*) возоблада́ть (*impf.*).
2 (*be widespread*) преоблада́ть (*impf.*); **~ing winds** преоблада́ющие ве́тры.
3 : **~ on** (*persuade*) убе|жда́ть, -ди́ть.
prevalence /'prevələns/ *n.* распростране́ние.
prevalent /'prevələnt/ *adj.* распространённый.
prevaricate /prɪ'værɪkeɪt/ *v.i.* виля́ть (*impf.*).
prevarication /prɪværɪ'keɪʃ(ə)n/ *n.* увиливание.
prevent /prɪ'vent/ *v.t.* (*stop happening*) предотвра|ща́ть, -ти́ть; (*make unable to do*) меша́ть, по- + *d.*; **illness ~ed him from coming** боле́знь помеша́ла ему́ прийти́.
preventable /prɪ'ventəb(ə)l/ *adj.* предотврати́мый.
preventative /prɪ'ventətɪv/ = **preventive**
prevention /prɪ'venʃ(ə)n/ *n.* предотвраще́ние, предупрежде́ние.
preventive /prɪ'ventɪv/ *adj.* предупреди́тельный; **~ medicine** профила́ктика.
preview /'pri:vju:/ *n.* (*of film*) (предвари́тельный) просмо́тр; (*of exhibition*) вернисаж.
previous /'pri:vɪəs/ *adj.* (*earlier, former*) предыду́щий.
previously /'pri:vɪəslɪ/ *adv.* ра́ньше.
pre-war /pri:'wɔ:(r)/ *adj.* довое́нный, предвое́нный.
prey /preɪ/ *n.* добы́ча.
■ *v.i.* охо́титься (*impf.*); **owls ~ on mice** со́вы охо́тятся на мыше́й; (*fig.*): **the crime ~ed upon his mind** (совершённое) преступле́ние мучи́ло его́, не дава́ло ему́ поко́я.
price /praɪs/ *n.*
1 цена́; **they wanted peace at any ~** им ну́жен был мир любо́й ценой.
2 (*value*) це́нность.
■ *v.t.* (*fix ~ of*) оце́н|ивать, -и́ть.
■ *cpds.* **~ list** *n.* прайс-ли́ст, прейскура́нт; **~ tag** *n.* це́нник, ярлы́к (*с указанием цены*).
priceless /'praɪslɪs/ *adj.* (*invaluable*) бесце́нный; (*coll., amusing*) бесподо́бный.
pricey /'praɪsɪ/ *adj.* (**pricier, priciest**) (*coll.*) дорого́й.
prick /prɪk/ *n.* шип; колю́чка.
■ *v.t.* прок|а́лывать, -оло́ть.
■ *with adv.*: **~ up** *v.t.*: **~ up one's ears** навостри́ть (*pf.*) у́ши.
prickle /'prɪk(ə)l/ *n.* (*thorn*) колю́чка, шип; (*of hedgehog etc.*) игла́.
■ *v.t.* & *i.* коло́ть(ся), у-.
prickly /'prɪklɪ/ *adj.* (**pricklier, prickliest**) (*having spines or thorns*) колю́чий; (*causing a prickling sensation*) ко́лкий, ко́лющий(ся); (*fig., easily offended*) оби́дчивый.
pride /praɪd/ *n.* го́рдость; **he takes ~ in his work** он горди́тся свое́й рабо́той.
■ *v.t.*: **~ o.s. on** горди́ться (*impf.*) + *i.*
priest /pri:st/ *n.* свяще́нник.
priesthood /'pri:sthʊd/ *n.* свяще́нство.
prig /prɪg/ *n.* педа́нт; (*hypocrite*) ханжа́ (*c.g.*).
priggish /'prɪgɪʃ/ *adj.* педанти́чный; (*hypocritical*) ха́нжеский.
prim /prɪm/ *adj.* (**primmer, primmest**) (*also* **~ and proper**) чо́порный.
prima /pri:mə/ *adj.*: **~ ballerina** при́ма-балери́на; **~ donna** (*lit.*) примадо́нна, ди́ва; (*fig.*) примадо́нна.
primarily /'praɪmərɪlɪ/ *adv.* (*principally*) в основно́м.
primary /'praɪmərɪ/ *n.* (*US, election*) предвари́тельные вы́бор|ы (*pl., g.* -ов).
■ *adj.* 1 (*original*) первонача́льный; **~ school** (*Br.*) нача́льная шко́ла.
2 (*basic, principal*) основно́й; **~ colours** (*Br.*), **colors** (*US*) основны́е цвета́; **of ~ importance** первостепе́нной ва́жности.
primate /'praɪmeɪt/ *n.* (*archbishop*) прима́с; (*mammal*) прима́т.
prime /praɪm/ *n.*: **in the ~ of life** в расцве́те сил; **he is past his ~** его́ лу́чшие дни/го́ды (оста́лись) позади́.
■ *adj.* 1 (*principal*) гла́вный; **~ minister** премье́р-мини́стр.
2 (*excellent*) первокла́ссный; **~ beef** говя́дина вы́сшего со́рта; **~ time** (*TV, radio*) прайм-та́йм.
3 (*fundamental*): **~ mover** инициа́тор.
■ *v.t.* 1 (*firearm*) заря|жа́ть, -ди́ть; (*engine, pump*) запр|авля́ть, -а́вить.
2 (*supply with facts etc.*) инструкти́ровать (*impf., pf.*).
primeval /praɪ'mi:v(ə)l/ *adj.* первобы́тный.
primitive /'prɪmɪtɪv/ *adj.* примити́вный; (*of earliest man, tribes*) первобы́тный.
primordial /praɪ'mɔ:dɪəl/ *adj.* перви́чный, первобы́тный; (*fundamental*) основно́й.
primrose /'prɪmrəʊz/ *n.* первоцве́т (*лесное растение*).
primula /'prɪmjʊlə/ *n.* при́мула.
prince /prɪns/ *n.* князь (*m.*); (*son of royalty*) принц.
princely /'prɪnslɪ/ *adj.* (**princelier, princeliest**) кня́жеский; (*splendid*) великоле́пный; (*generous*): **~ sum** ца́рская су́мма.
princess /prɪn'ses/ *n.* принце́сса.
principal /'prɪnsɪp(ə)l/ *n.* дире́ктор, ре́ктор.
■ *adj.* гла́вный, основно́й.
principality /prɪnsɪ'pælɪtɪ/ *n.* кня́жество.
principally /'prɪnsɪpəlɪ/ *adv.* гла́вным о́бразом, преиму́щественно.
principle /'prɪnsɪp(ə)l/ *n.* при́нцип, нача́ло; **in ~** в при́нципе; **on ~** из при́нципа.
print /prɪnt/ *n.*
1 (*mark made on surface by pressure*) след;

отпеча́ток.
2 (*letters, etc.*) шрифт; печа́ть; **the book is in ~** кни́га ещё продаётся; **the book is out of ~** кни́га бо́льше не продаётся.
3 (*picture*) гравю́ра, эста́мп; (*by photography*) репроду́кция.
■ *v.t.* 1 (*impress*) печа́тать, на-/от-; (*fig.*) запечатл|ева́ть, -е́ть.
2 (*produce by ~ing process*) печа́тать, на-/от-.
3 (*write in imitation of ~*) писа́ть, на- печа́тными бу́квами.
■ *with adv.*: **~ out** *v.t.* (*comput.*) распеча́т|ывать, -ать.
■ *cpd.* **~out** *n.* (*comput.*) распеча́тка.

printer /'prɪntə(r)/ *n.* (*person*) печа́тник, типо́граф; (*printing house*) типогра́фия; (*comput.*) при́нтер.

prior /'praɪə(r)/ *adj.* (*earlier*) пре́жний; (*more important*) первоочередно́й.
■ *adv.*: **~ to** до + *g.*

prioritize /praɪ'ɒrɪtaɪz/ *v.t.* определ|я́ть, -и́ть приорите́ты в + *p.*

priority /praɪ'ɒrɪtɪ/ *n.* приорите́т.

priory /'praɪərɪ/ *n.* монасты́рь (*m.*).

prise /praɪz/ (*US* **prize**) *v.t.* взл|а́мывать, -ома́ть; **the box was ~d open** я́щик взлома́ли; (*fig.*) разн|има́ть, -я́ть; **they ~d the combatants apart** они́ разня́ли деру́щихся.

prism /'prɪz(ə)m/ *n.* при́зма.

prison /'prɪz(ə)n/ *n.*
1 тюрьма́.
2 (*attr.*) тюре́мный; **~ camp** исправи́тельно-трудово́й ла́герь; **~ sentence** тюре́мный срок.

prisoner /'prɪznə(r)/ *n.*
1 (*detained by civil authorities*) заключённый.
2 (*~ of war*) пле́нный, военнопле́нный.

prissy /'prɪsɪ/ *adj.* (**prissier, prissiest**) чо́порный, жема́нный; (*of style*) вы́чурный.

pristine /'prɪsti:n/ *adj.* чи́стый; нетро́нутый.

privacy /'prɪvəsɪ/ *n.* уедине́ние.

private /'praɪvət, -vɪt/ *n.*
1 (*soldier*) рядово́й.
2: **in ~** (*meet, talk*) с гла́зу на глаз.
■ *adj.* 1 (*personal*) ча́стный, ли́чный; **in ~ life** в ли́чной жи́зни; **~ property** ча́стная со́бственность; **for ~ reasons** по ли́чным причи́нам.
2 (*not open to the general public*) закры́тый.
3 (*secret*) та́йный, секре́тный.
4 (*without official status*) ча́стный; неофициа́льный; **~ eye** (*coll.*) ча́стный сы́щик, детекти́в.

privation /praɪ'veɪʃ(ə)n/ *n.* (*hardship*) лише́ния (*nt. pl.*); нужда́; (*loss*) утра́та; лише́ние.

privatization /praɪvətaɪ'zeɪʃ(ə)n/ *n.* приватиза́ция.

privatize /'praɪvətaɪz/ *v.t.* приватизи́ровать (*impf., pf.*).

privet /'prɪvɪt/ *n.* (*bot.*) бирючи́на.

privilege /'prɪvɪlɪdʒ/ *n.* привиле́гия.

privileged /'prɪvɪlɪdʒd/ *adj.* привилегиро́ванный.

prize[1] /praɪz/ *n.*
1 (*reward for merit in sport etc.*) приз; (*esp. monetary*) пре́мия.
2 (*attr., awarded as prize*) призово́й; **~ money** призовы́е де́н|ьги (*pl., g.* -ег); (*~-winning*) премиро́ванный; (*possession*) бесце́нный.
■ *cpds.* **~-giving** *n.* (*Br.*) церемо́ния вруче́ния награ́д; **~winner** *n.* призёр.

prize[2] /praɪz/ (*US*) = **prise**

pro[1] /prəʊ/ *n.* (*pl.* **pros**) (*point in favour*): **~s and cons** за и про́тив.
■ *prep.* (*coll., in favour of*) за + *a.*

pro[2] /prəʊ/ *n.* (*pl.* **pros**) (*coll., professional*) профессиона́л (*fem.* -ка); про́фи (*c.g. indecl.*) (*coll.*).

proactive /prəʊ'æktɪv/ *adj.* де́йственный.

probability /prɒbə'bɪlɪtɪ/ *n.* вероя́тность; **in all ~** по всей вероя́тности.

probable /'prɒbəb(ə)l/ *adj.* вероя́тный.

probably /'prɒbəblɪ/ *adv.* вероя́тно.

probate /'prəʊbeɪt/ *n.* утвержде́ние завеща́ния.

probation /prə'beɪʃ(ə)n/ *n.*: **be on ~** (*at work*) про|ходи́ть, -йти́ испыта́тельный срок; (*leg.*) быть усло́вно осуждённым; **~ officer** должностно́е лицо́, осуществля́ющее надзо́р за усло́вно осуждёнными.

probationary /prə'beɪʃənərɪ/ *adj.* испыта́тельный.

probationer /prə'beɪʃənə(r)/ *n.* (*trainee*) стажёр; практика́нт; (*offender on probation*) усло́вно осуждённый.

probe /prəʊb/ *n.* (*instrument*) зонд; (*fig., investigation*) рассле́дование.
■ *v.t. & i.* иссле́довать (*impf., pf.*).

problem /'prɒbləm/ *n.* пробле́ма, вопро́с; **~ child** тру́дный ребёнок; (*math. etc.*) зада́ча.

problematic(al) /prɒblə'mætɪk(əl)/ *adj.* проблемати́чный.

procedure /prə'si:djə(r)/ *n.* процеду́ра.

proceed /prə'si:d/ *v.i.*
1 (*go on*) прод|олжа́ть, -о́лжить.
2 (*start*) прин|има́ться, -я́ться (за + *a.*); **she ~ed to lay the table** она́ приняла́сь накрыва́ть на стол.

proceedings /prə'si:dɪŋz/ *n. pl.*
1 (*activity*) де́ятельность.
2 (*legal action*) суде́бное де́ло, иск.

proceeds /'prəʊsi:dz/ *n. pl.* вы́ручка, дохо́д.

process /'prəʊses/ *n.*
1 проце́сс.
2 (*course*) тече́ние, ход; **we're in the ~ of buying a house** сейча́с мы покупа́ем дом.
■ *v.t.* 1 (*treat in special way; also comput.*) обраб|а́тывать, -о́тать.
2 (*subject to routine handling*) оф|ормля́ть, -о́рмить.

procession /prə'seʃ(ə)n/ *n.* проце́ссия, ше́ствие.

processor /'prəʊsesə(r)/ *n.* (*comput.*) проце́ссор.

proclaim /prə'kleɪm/ *v.t.* провозгла|ша́ть, -си́ть.

proclamation /prɒklə'meɪʃ(ə)n/ *n.* провозглаше́ние.

proclivity /prə'klɪvɪtɪ/ *n.* скло́нность, накло́нность.

procrastinate /prəʊ'kræstɪneɪt/ *v.i.* ме́длить (*impf.*).

procreate /'prəʊkrɪeɪt/ *v.t. & i.* произв|оди́ть,

-ести́ (пото́мство).

procure /prəˈkjʊə(r)/ *v.t.* дост|ава́ть, -а́ть.

procurement /prəˈkjʊəmənt/ *n.* приобрете́ние, получе́ние; (*of equipment etc.*) поста́вка.

prod /prɒd/ *n.* тычо́к.
■ *v.t.* (**prodded, prodding**) ты́кать, ткнуть.

prodigal /ˈprɒdɪg(ə)l/ *adj.* (*wasteful*) расточи́тельный; **the P～ Son** блу́дный сын; (*lavish*) ще́дрый.

prodigious /prəˈdɪdʒəs/ *adj.* (*amazing*) потряса́ющий; (*enormous*) огро́мный.

prodigy /ˈprɒdɪdʒɪ/ *n.* вундерки́нд.

produce[1] /ˈprɒdjuːs/ *n.* проду́кты (*m. pl.*) (*пищевые*).

produce[2] /prəˈdjuːs/ *v.t.*
1 (*make, manufacture*) произв|оди́ть, -ести́; выпуска́ть, вы́пустить.
2 (*bring about*) вызыва́ть, вы́звать; прин|оси́ть, -ести́.
3 (*present*) предст|авля́ть, -а́вить; **can you ～ proof of your words?** мо́жете ли вы предста́вить что́-либо в доказа́тельство/подтвержде́ние ва́ших слов?
4 (*show*) предъяв|ля́ть, -и́ть; **you must ～ a ticket** вы должны́ предъяви́ть биле́т.
5 (*yield*) произв|оди́ть, -ести́; **this soil ～s good crops** э́то по́чва даёт хоро́ший урожа́й.
6 (*theatr.*) ста́вить, по-; (*cin.*) выпуска́ть, вы́пустить.

producer /prəˈdjuːsə(r)/ *n.*
1 (*of goods*) производи́тель (*m.*).
2 (*stage, TV*) режиссёр-постано́вщик.
3 (*film*) продю́сер.

product /ˈprɒdʌkt/ *n.* проду́кт, изде́лие; (*pl.*) проду́кция (*collect.*), това́ры (*m. pl.*).

production /prəˈdʌkʃ(ə)n/ *n.*
1 (*manufacture*) произво́дство; **～ line** произво́дственная ли́ния.
2 (*yield*) производи́тельность.
3 (*stage, film*) постано́вка, режиссу́ра.

productive /prəˈdʌktɪv/ *adj.* (*tending to produce*) производи́тельный; (*yielding well*) плодоро́дный.

productivity /prɒdʌkˈtɪvɪtɪ/ *n.* производи́тельность, продукти́вность.

profane /prəˈfeɪn/ *adj.* (*secular*) мирско́й; (*heathen*) язы́ческий; (*irreverent*) богоху́льный.
■ *v.t.* профани́ровать (*impf., pf.*); осквер|ня́ть, -и́ть.

profanit|y /prəˈfænɪtɪ/ *n.* (*irreverence*) богоху́льство; (*swearing*) скверносло́вие; **to utter ～ies** скверносло́вить (*impf.*).

profess /prəˈfes/ *v.t.*
1 (*claim to have or feel*) заяв|ля́ть, -и́ть; **he ～es an interest in architecture** он заявля́ет, что интересу́ется архитекту́рой.
2 (*claim, pretend*) претендова́ть (*impf.*); **I don't ～ to know much about music** я не претенду́ю на больши́е позна́ния в му́зыке; **he ～es to be an expert at chess** он выдаёт себя́ за первокла́ссного шахмати́ста.

profession /prəˈfeʃ(ə)n/ *n.* профе́ссия.

professional /prəˈfeʃən(ə)l/ *n.* профессиона́л.
■ *adj.* профессиона́льный.

professionalism /prəˈfeʃənəlɪz(ə)m/ *n.* профессионали́зм.

professor /prəˈfesə(r)/ *n.* (*holder of university chair*) профе́ссор; (*US, university teacher*) преподава́тель.

proffer /ˈprɒfə(r)/ *n.* предложе́ние.
■ *v.t.* предл|ага́ть, -ожи́ть; **he ～ed his hand** он протяну́л ру́ку.

proficiency /prəˈfɪʃ(ə)nsɪ/ *n.* мастерство́, уме́ние.

proficient /prəˈfɪʃ(ə)nt/ *adj.* уме́лый.

profile /ˈprəʊfaɪl/ *n.* про́филь (*m.*); **he kept a low ～** он стара́лся не выделя́ться.

profit /ˈprɒfɪt/ *n.* при́быль.
■ *v.t.* (**profited, profiting**) прин|оси́ть, -ести́ по́льзу + *d.*
■ *v.i.* (**profited, profiting**) по́льзоваться, вос- (+ *i.*); извл|ека́ть, -е́чь по́льзу (из + *g.*); **he has not ～ed from his experience** он не воспо́льзовался свои́м о́пытом.

profitability /prɒfɪtəˈbɪlɪtɪ/ *n.* дохо́дность, при́быльность, рента́бельность.

profitable /ˈprɒfɪtəb(ə)l/ *adj.* (*advantageous*) поле́зный, вы́годный; (*lucrative*) дохо́дный.

profiteer /prɒfɪˈtɪə(r)/ *n.* спекуля́нт.
■ *v.i.* спекули́ровать (*impf.*).

profligate /ˈprɒflɪgət/ *n.* (*dissolute person*) развра́тник; (*extravagant person*) расточи́тель (*m.*).
■ *adj.* (*dissolute*) распу́тный; (*extravagant*) расточи́тельный.

profound /prəˈfaʊnd/ *adj.* (**profounder, profoundest**) глубо́кий.

profundity /prəˈfʌndɪtɪ/ *n.* глубина́.

profuse /prəˈfjuːs/ *adj.* (*plentiful*) оби́льный; (*lavish*) ще́дрый; **he apologized ～ly** он рассыпа́лся в извине́ниях.

profusion /prəˈfjuːʒ(ə)n/ *n.* изоби́лие.

progesterone /prəʊˈdʒestərəʊn/ *n.* прогестеро́н.

prognosis /prɒgˈnəʊsɪs/ *n.* (*pl.* **prognoses** /-siːz/) прогно́з.

program /ˈprəʊgræm/ *n.* (*comput.*) програ́мма; (*US*) = **programme**
■ *v.t.* (**programmed, programming**) (*comput., also fig.*) программи́ровать, за-; (*US*) = **programme**

programme /ˈprəʊgræm/ *n.* програ́мма; (*radio, TV*) переда́ча; (*plan*) програ́мма, план.
■ *v.t.* (**programmed, programming**) (*schedule*): **the meeting is ～d for today** собра́ние назна́чено на сего́дня.

programmer /ˈprəʊgræmə(r)/ *n.* (*comput.*) программи́ст (*fem.* -ка).

progress[1] /ˈprəʊgres/ *n.*
1 (*forward movement*) движе́ние вперёд.
2 (*advance, development*) прогре́сс; **～ report** докла́д о хо́де рабо́ты; **a meeting is in ～** идёт заседа́ние.

progress[2] /prəˈgres/ *v.i.* прогресси́ровать (*impf.*); продв|ига́ться, -и́нуться (вперёд).

progression /prəˈgreʃ(ə)n/ *n.* продвиже́ние.

progressive /prəˈgresɪv/ *adj.*
1 (*favouring progress*) прогресси́вный, передово́й.
2 (*gradual*) поступа́тельный, постепе́нный.

prohibit /prəˈhɪbɪt/ *v.t.* (**prohibited, prohibiting**) запре|ща́ть, -ти́ть.

prohibition /prəʊhɪ'bɪʃ(ə)n, prəʊɪ'b-/ *n.* запреще́ние.

prohibitive /prə'hɪbɪtɪv/ *adj.* запрети́тельный, запреща́ющий.

project[1] /'prɒdʒekt/ *n.* (*scheme*) прое́кт, план; (*at school*) рабо́та.

project[2] /prə'dʒekt/ *v.t.* (*throw*) выбра́сывать, вы́бросить.
■ *v.i.* (*protrude*) выдава́ться (*impf.*); выступа́ть (*impf.*).

projectile /prə'dʒektaɪl/ *n.* снаря́д.

projection /prə'dʒekʃ(ə)n/ *n.*
1 (*planning*) проекти́рование.
2 (*throwing, propulsion*) отбра́сывание.
3 (*cin.*) прое́кция (изображе́ния); **~ room** (кино)проекцио́нная каби́на.
4 (*psych., geom.*) прое́кция.
5 (*protrusion*) вы́ступ.

projector /prə'dʒektə(r)/ *n.* (*apparatus*) прое́ктор.

proletarian /prəʊlɪ'teərɪən/ *n.* пролета́рий.
■ *adj.* пролета́рский.

proletariat /prəʊlɪ'teərɪət/ *n.* пролетариа́т.

pro-life /prəʊ'laɪf/ *adj.* возража́ющий про́тив або́ртов.

proliferate /prə'lɪfəreɪt/ *v.i.* распростран|я́ться, -и́ться.

proliferation /prəlɪfə'reɪʃ(ə)n/ *n.* (бы́строе) размноже́ние, пролифера́ция; (*fig.*) распростране́ние.

prolific /prə'lɪfɪk/ *adj.* (*lit.*) плодоро́дный; (*fig.*) плодови́тый.

prologue /'prəʊlɒg/ (*US* **prolog**) *n.* проло́г.

prolong /prə'lɒŋ/ *v.t.* продл|ева́ть, -и́ть.

promenade /prɒmə'nɑːd/ *n.* (*Br., place of pedestrian resort*) ме́сто для гуля́ния.

prominence /'prɒmɪnəns/ *n.* (*importance*) ви́дное положе́ние.

prominent /'prɒmɪnənt/ *adj.*
1 (*projecting*) выступа́ющий.
2 (*important*) выдаю́щийся.

promiscuity /prɒmɪ'skjuːɪtɪ/ *n.* распу́щенность.

promiscuous /prə'mɪskjʊəs/ *adj.* распу́щенный.

promise /'prɒmɪs/ *n.*
1 (*assurance*) обеща́ние; **he kept his ~** он сдержа́л своё обеща́ние.
2 (*ground for expectation*) наде́жда; **he shows ~** он подаёт наде́жды.
■ *v.t. & i.* обеща́ть, по-; **he ~d to be here by 7** он обеща́л быть здесь к 7 часа́м; **I ~d myself a quiet evening** я реши́л споко́йно провести́ ве́чер.

promising /'prɒmɪsɪŋ/ *adj.* перспекти́вный; многообеща́ющий, подаю́щий наде́жды.

promontory /'prɒməntərɪ/ *n.* мыс.

promote /prə'məʊt/ *v.t.*
1 (*raise to higher rank*) продв|ига́ть, -и́нуть; пов|ыша́ть, -ы́сить (в чи́не/зва́нии).
2 (*encourage, support*) поощр|я́ть, -и́ть; подде́рж|ивать, -а́ть.
3 (*publicize*) реклами́ровать (*impf.*).

promoter /prə'məʊtə(r)/ *n.* (*of event*) аге́нт, промо́утер; (*of cause*) пропаганди́ст (*fem.* -ка).

promotion /prə'məʊʃ(ə)n/ *n.* продвиже́ние, повыше́ние; (*encouragement, support*) поощре́ние, подде́ржка; (*publicizing*) рекла́ма, промо́ушен.

prompt[1] /prɒmpt/ *v.t. & i.*
1 (*assist memory of*) подска́з|ывать, -а́ть + *d.*; (*theatr.*) суфли́ровать (*impf.*) + *d.*
2 (*impel*) побу|жда́ть, -ди́ть.

prompt[2] /prɒmpt/ *adj.* бы́стрый, неме́дленный; **he arrived ~ly at 9** он прие́хал то́чно в де́вять.

prompter /'prɒmptə(r)/ *n.* суфлёр.

prone /prəʊn/ *adj.*
1 (*face downwards*) лежа́щий ничко́м, лежа́щий вниз лицо́м.
2 : **~ to** (*liable to*) скло́нный к + *d.*

prong /prɒŋ/ *n.* зубе́ц.

pronoun /'prəʊnaʊn/ *n.* местоиме́ние.

pronounce /prə'naʊns/ *v.t.* произн|оси́ть, -ести́.

pronounced /prə'naʊnst/ *adj.* (*decided*) я́вный; **he walks with a ~ limp** он си́льно/заме́тно хрома́ет.

pronouncement /prə'naʊnsmənt/ *n.* заявле́ние; выска́зывание.

pronunciation /prənʌnsɪ'eɪʃ(ə)n/ *n.* произноше́ние.

proof /pruːf/ *n.* доказа́тельство; (*typ.*) корректу́ра.
■ *cpd.* **~reader** *n.* корре́ктор.

prop[1] /prɒp/ *n.* (*support*) сто́йка; подпо́рка; (*fig.*) опо́ра, подде́ржка.
■ *v.t.* (**propped, propping**) (*also* **prop up**)
1 подп|ира́ть, -ере́ть; **~ the ladder against the wall!** приста́вьте ле́стницу к стене́!
2 (*fig.*) подде́рж|ивать, -а́ть.

prop[2] /prɒp/ *n.* (*coll., theatr.*) бутафо́рия, реквизи́т.

propaganda /prɒpə'gændə/ *n.* пропага́нда.

propagate /'prɒpəgeɪt/ *v.t.* (*plants*) разв|оди́ть, -ести́; (*ideas*) распростран|я́ть, -и́ть.

propagation /prɒpə'geɪʃ(ə)n/ *n.* размноже́ние; (*fig.*) распростране́ние.

propagator /'prɒpəgeɪtə(r)/ *n.* (*person*) распространи́тель (*fem.* -ница); (*for plants*) микропарни́к.

propel /prə'pel/ *v.t.* (**propelled, propelling**) прив|оди́ть, -ести́ в движе́ние.

propeller /prə'pelə(r)/ *n.* пропе́ллер.

propensity /prə'pensɪtɪ/ *n.* предрасполо́женность, скло́нность.

proper /'prɒpə(r)/ *adj.*
1 (*suitable*) подходя́щий, ну́жный.
2 (*decent*) (благо)присто́йный, прили́чный.
3 (*correct*) пра́вильный; **in the ~ sense of the word** в прямо́м смы́сле сло́ва.

properly /'prɒpəlɪ/ *adv.* (*correctly*) подоба́юще, как сле́дует; **you must be ~ dressed** вы должны́ оде́ться подоба́юще.

property /'prɒpətɪ/ *n.*
1 (*possession(s)*) со́бственность; иму́щество.
2 (*house*) дом; (*estate*) име́ние; (*real estate*) недви́жимость.
3 (*attribute*) сво́йство.

prophecy /'prɒfɪsɪ/ *n.* проро́чество.

prophesy /'prɒfɪsaɪ/ *v.t. & i.* проро́чить, на-.

prophet /'prɒfɪt/ *n.* проро́к.

prophetic /prə'fetɪk/ *adj.* проро́ческий.

prophylactic /prɒfɪ'læktɪk/ *n.* профилакти́ческое сре́дство.
■ *adj.* профилакти́ческий.

proponent /prə'pəʊnənt/ *n.* пропаганди́ст, побо́рник (*чего*).

proportion /prə'pɔːʃ(ə)n/ *n.*
1 (*part*) часть, до́ля.
2 (*ratio*) пропо́рция, соотноше́ние; **in ~** пропорциона́льно, соразме́рно.
3 (*due relation*) соразме́рность; **his ambitions are out of all ~** его́ честолю́бие выхо́дит за вся́кие ра́мки.
4 (*pl., dimensions*) разме́р, разме́ры (*m. pl.*).

proportional /prə'pɔːʃən(ə)l/ *adj.* пропорциона́льный; **~ representation** пропорциона́льное представи́тельство.

proportionate /prə'pɔːʃənət/ *adj.* соразме́рный; **payment will be ~ to effort** опла́та бу́дет соотве́тствовать затра́ченным уси́лиям.

proposal /prə'pəʊz(ə)l/ *n.* предложе́ние.

propose /prə'pəʊz/ *v.t.*
1 (*suggest*) предл|ага́ть, -ожи́ть; **he ~d (marriage) to her** он сде́лал ей предложе́ние (*стать женой*).
2 (*put forward*) выдвига́ть, вы́двинуть.
3 (*intend*) предпол|ага́ть, -ожи́ть; намерева́ться (*impf.*); **I ~ to leave tomorrow** я намерева́юсь е́хать за́втра.

proposition /prɒpə'zɪʃ(ə)n/ *n.*
1 (*statement*) заявле́ние.
2 (*proposed scheme*) предложе́ние.

propound /prə'paʊnd/ *v.t.* предл|ага́ть, -ожи́ть на обсужде́ние; изл|ага́ть, -ожи́ть.

proprietor /prə'praɪətə(r)/ *n.* владе́лец, хозя́ин.

proprietorial /prəpraɪə'tɔːrɪəl/ *adj.* со́бственнический.

propriety /prə'praɪɪtɪ/ *n.* (*fitness*) уме́стность; (*correctness of behaviour*) пра́вила поведе́ния; пра́вила прили́чия, (благо)присто́йность.

pro rata /prəʊ 'rɑːtə/ *adv.* пропорциона́льно; соотве́ственно.

prosaic /prə'zeɪɪk/ *adj.* прозаи́ческий.

proscribe /prə'skraɪb/ *v.t.* запре|ща́ть, -ти́ть.

prose /prəʊz/ *n.* про́за.

prosecute /'prɒsɪkjuːt/ *v.t.* (*leg.*) возбу|жда́ть, -ди́ть де́ло про́тив + *g.*

prosecution /prɒsɪ'kjuːʃ(ə)n/ *n.*
1 (*carrying on legal proceedings*) обвине́ние; предъявле́ние и́ска.
2 (*prosecuting party*) обвине́ние; **counsel for the ~** обвини́тель (*m.*) (в уголо́вном проце́ссе).

prosecutor /'prɒsɪkjuːtə(r)/ *n.* обвини́тель (*m.*).

prospect /'prɒspekt/ *n.* перспекти́ва; **there is no ~ of success** нет наде́жды на успе́х; **a job without ~s** рабо́та без перспекти́в.

prospective /prə'spektɪv/ *adj.* бу́дущий.

prospector /prə'spektə(r)/ *n.* разве́дчик, стара́тель (*m.*).

prospectus /prə'spektəs/ *n.* (*pl.* **~es**) проспе́кт (*рекламное издание*).

prosper /'prɒspə(r)/ *v.i.* преусп|ева́ть, -е́ть.

prosperity /prɒ'sperɪtɪ/ *n.* процвета́ние.

prosperous /'prɒspərəs/ *adj.* процвета́ющий.

prostate /'prɒsteɪt/ *n.* (*also* **~ gland**) проста́та, предста́тельная железа́.

prosthe|sis /'prɒsθiːsɪs/ *n.* (*pl.* **~ses** /-siːz/) проте́з.

prosthetic /prɒs'θetɪk/ *adj.* проте́зный.

prostitute /'prɒstɪtjuːt/ *n.* проститу́тка; **male ~** мужчи́на-проститу́тка.
■ *v.t.*: **~ o.s.** зан|има́ться, -я́ться проститу́цией; (*fig.*) торгова́ть (*impf.*) собо́й.

prostitution /prɒstɪ'tjuːʃ(ə)n/ *n.* (*lit., fig.*) проститу́ция.

prostrate /'prɒstreɪt/ *adj.*
1 (*lying face down*) распростёртый.
2 (*overcome*): **she was ~ with grief** она́ была́ сло́млена го́рем.

protagonist /prə'tægənɪst/ *n.* гла́вный геро́й.

protect /prə'tekt/ *v.t.* защи|ща́ть, -ти́ть.

protection /prə'tekʃ(ə)n/ *n.*
1 (*defence*) защи́та; **~ racket** рэ́кет.
2 (*care*) попече́ние.

protectionism /prə'tekʃ(ə)nɪz(ə)m/ *n.* протекциони́зм.

protectionist /prə'tekʃ(ə)nɪst/ *n.* протекциони́ст.
■ *adj.* протекциони́стский.

protective /prə'tektɪv/ *adj.* защи́тный.

protégé /'prɒtɪʒeɪ/ *n.* (*fem.* **protégée**) протеже́ (*c.g., indecl.*).

protein /'prəʊtiːn/ *n.* протеи́н, бело́к.

pro tem /prəʊ 'tem/ *adv.* на вре́мя, вре́менно.

protest[1] /'prəʊtest/ *n.* проте́ст; возраже́ние; **~ march** марш проте́ста.

protest[2] /prə'test/ *v.t.*
1 (*affirm*) утвержда́ть (*impf.*); **he continued to ~ his innocence** он продолжа́л наста́ивать на свое́й невино́вности.
2 (*US, object to*) возража́ть/протестова́ть (*impf.*) про́тив + *g.*
■ *v.i.*: **~ against** протестова́ть (*impf.*) про́тив + *g.*; **~ about** выража́ть, вы́разить недово́льство + *i.*

Protestant /'prɒtɪst(ə)nt/ *n.* протеста́нт (*fem.* -ка).
■ *adj.* протеста́нтский.

protestation /prɒtɪ'steɪʃ(ə)n/ *n.* (*affirmation*) (торже́ственное) заявле́ние; **~s of innocence** торже́ственные заявле́ния о невино́вности.

protester /prəʊ'testə(r)/ *n.* протесту́ющ|ий (*fem.* -ая).

protocol /prəʊtə'kɒl/ *n.* протоко́л.

prototype /'prəʊtətaɪp/ *n.* прототи́п.

protract /prə'trækt/ *v.t.* затя́|гивать, -ну́ть; **a ~ed visit** затяну́вшийся визи́т; **a ~ed war** затяжна́я война́.

protractor /prə'træktə(r)/ *n.* (*geom.*) транспорти́р.

protrud|e /prə'truːd/ *v.i.* выдава́ться (*impf.*); **~ing teeth** выпира́ющие зу́бы.

proud /praʊd/ *adj.* го́рдый; **to be ~ (of)** горди́ться (+ *i.*); **this is a ~ day for the school** э́то торже́ственный/ра́достный день для шко́лы; (*arrogant*) надме́нный.

prove /pruːv/ *v.t.* (*p.p.* **proved** *or* **proven** /'pruːv(ə)n/) дока́з|ывать, -а́ть; **he ~d his worth** он показа́л себя́ досто́йным

P

человéком; **he needs to ~ himself to others** емý надо утвердить себя в глазáх других.
■ *v.i.* (*p.p.* **proved** *or* **proven** /'pru:v(ə)n, 'prəʊ-/) (*turn out*) окáз|ываться, -áться; **the alarm ~d (to be) a hoax** тревóга оказáлась лóжной.

provenance /'prɒvɪnəns/ *n.* происхождéние.

proverb /'prɒvə:b/ *n.* послóвица.

proverbial /prə'və:bɪəl/ *adj.*
1 (*pert. to provs.*) вошéдший в поговóрку/послóвицу, как *кто-н.*/*что-н.* из той поговóрки/послóвицы; **~ wisdom** нарóдная мýдрость.
2 (*notorious*) общеизвéстный.

provide /prə'vaɪd/ *v.t.*
1: **~ s.o. with sth.** обеспéчи|вать, -ть когó-н. чем-н.; снабж|áть, -дить когó-н. чем-н.
2 (*prescribe*) предусм|áтривать, -отрéть.
■ *v.i.* (*prepare o.s.*) пригот|áвливаться, -óвиться; **she had three children to ~ for** у неё на содержáнии бы́ло трóе детéй.

provid|ed /prə'vaɪdɪd/, **-ing** /prə'vaɪdɪŋ/ *conjs.* при услóвии, что; éсли.

providence /'prɒvɪd(ə)ns/ *n.*
1 (*foresight*) предусмотрúтельность; (*thrift*) расчётливость.
2 (*divine care*): **he escaped by a special ~** егó спаслó (тóлько) провидéние; (**P~:** *God*) Провидéние, прóмысл Бóжий.

provider /prə'vaɪdə(r)/ *n.* снабжéнец; постáвщи|к (*fem.* -ца); (*breadwinner*): **her husband is a good ~** её муж хорошó обеспéчивает семью́; (*comput.*, *Internet service* ~) провáйдер.

province /'prɒvɪns/ *n.* óбласть; **in the ~s** в провúнции, на перифéрии.

provincial /prə'vɪnʃ(ə)l/ *adj.* (*lit.*, *fig.*) провинциáльный.

provision /prə'vɪʒ(ə)n/ *n.*
1 (*supplying*) снабжéние.
2 (*pl.*, *supplies*, *esp. food*) провúзия.
3 (*preparation*) обеспéчение; **their father had made ~ for them** отéц обеспéчил их на бýдущее.

provisional /prə'vɪʒən(ə)l/ *adj.* врéменный.

proviso /prə'vaɪzəʊ/ *n.* (*pl.* **~s**) услóвие, оговóрка; **with the ~ that …** с услóвием (*or* с оговóркой), что… .

provocation /prɒvə'keɪʃ(ə)n/ *n.* провокáция; **I did it under ~** меня́ спровоцúровали на э́то.

provocative /prə'vɒkətɪv/ *adj.* (*challenging*) вызывáющий; (*alluring*) соблазнúтельный.

provoke /prə'vəʊk/ *v.t.*
1 (*cause*) вызывáть, вы́звать; провоцúровать, с-.
2 (*anger*) сердúть, рас-.

prow /praʊ/ *n.* нос (*cудна*).

prowess /'praʊɪs/ *n.* (*skill*) мастерствó; (*valour*) дóблесть.

prowl /praʊl/ *v.t.* (*a place*) ры́скать (*impf.*) по + *d.*
■ *v.i.* ры́скать (*impf.*).

proximity /prɒk'sɪmɪtɪ/ *n.* блúзость; сосéдство.

proxy /'prɒksɪ/ *n.* (*authorization*) полномóчие, довéренность; **they voted by ~** онú голосовáли по довéренности.

prude /pru:d/ *n.* ханжá (*c.g.*).

prudence /'pru:d(ə)ns/ *n.* благоразýмие.

prudent /'pru:d(ə)nt/ *adj.* благоразýмный.

prudish /'pru:dɪʃ/ *adj.* стыдлúвый; (*pej.*) хáнжеский.

prune[1] /pru:n/ *n.* чернослúв.

prune[2] /pru:n/ *v.t.* (*trim*) обр|езáть, -éзать; подр|езáть, -éзать.

prurient /'prʊərɪənt/ *adj.* похотлúвый.

pry /praɪ/ *v.i.* вмéш|иваться, -áться (в чужúе делá).

PS (*abbr. of* ***postscript***) постскрúптум, припúска.

psalm /sɑ:m/ *n.* псалóм.

pseudonym /'sju:dənɪm/ *n.* псевдонúм.

psych /saɪk/ *v.t.*: **~ o.s. up** настр|áивать, -óить себя́.

psyche /'saɪkɪ/ *n.* душá; дух.

psychedelic /saɪkɪ'delɪk/ *adj.* (*experience*) психоделúческий; (*clothes*, *colours*) чуднóй; (*drug*) галлюциногéнный.

psychiatric /saɪkɪ'ætrɪk/ *adj.* психиатрúческий.

psychiatrist /saɪ'kaɪətrɪst/ *n.* психиáтр.

psychiatry /saɪ'kaɪətrɪ/ *n.* психиатрúя.

psychic /'saɪkɪk/ *n.* экстрасéнс.
■ *adj.* ≈ ясновúдящ|ий (*fem.* -ая).

psychoanalyse /saɪkəʊ'ænəlaɪz/ (*US* **-analyze**) *v.t.* подв|ергáть, -éргнуть психоанáлизу.

psychoanalysis /saɪkəʊə'nælɪsɪs/ *n.* психоанáлиз.

psychoanalyst /saɪkəʊ'ænəlɪst/ *n.* психоаналúтик.

psychological /saɪkə'lɒdʒɪk(ə)l/ *adj.* психологúческий.

psychologist /saɪ'kɒlədʒɪst/ *n.* психóлог.

psychology /saɪ'kɒlədʒɪ/ *n.* психолóгия.

psychopath /'saɪkəpæθ/ *n.* психопáт (*fem.* -ка).

psychopathic /saɪkə'pæθɪk/ *adj.* психопатúческий; **he is ~** он психопáт.

psychosis /saɪ'kəʊsɪs/ *n.* (*pl.* **psychoses** /-si:z/) психóз.

psychosomatic /saɪkəʊsə'mætɪk/ *adj.* психосоматúческий.

psychotherapist /saɪkəʊ'θerəpɪst/ *n.* психотерапéвт.

psychotherapy /saɪkəʊ'θerəpɪ/ *n.* психотерапúя.

psychotic /saɪ'kɒtɪk/ *adj.* психотúческий, душевнобольнóй.

PTA (*abbr. of* ***parent-teacher association***) ассоциáция учителéй и родúтелей, учúтельско-родúтельский комитéт.

PTO (*abbr. of* ***please turn over***) см. на об. (смотрú на оборóте).

pub /pʌb/ *n.* (*Br. coll.*) пивнáя; паб; кабáк.

puberty /'pju:bətɪ/ *n.* половóе созревáние.

pubescent /pju:'bes(ə)nt/ *adj.* достúгший половóй зрéлости, половозрéлый.

pubic /'pju:bɪk/ *adj.* лобкóвый, лóнный; **~ hair** лобкóвые вóлосы.

public /'pʌblɪk/ *n.*
1 (*community*) общéственность; нарóд; **the**

library is open to the ~ вход в библиоте́ку свобо́дный.
[2] (*audience*) пу́блика; **I have never spoken in ~** я никогда́ не выступа́л пе́ред пу́бликой.
■ *adj.* [1] (*pert. to people in general*) obще́ственный; **~ opinion** обще́ственное мне́ние; **~ relations** свя́зи с обще́ственностью; **in the ~ interest** в интере́сах о́бщества/госуда́рства.
[2] (*pert. to politics or the state*) обще́ственный, госуда́рственный; **a ~ figure** обще́ственный де́ятель; **~ prosecutor** прокуро́р; **~ sector** госуда́рственный се́ктор.
[3] (*shared by the community*) публи́чный, обще́ственный; **~ convenience** (*Br.*) обще́ственный туале́т; **~ holiday** устано́вленный зако́ном пра́здник; **~ transport** обще́ственный тра́нспорт.
[4] (*done openly, in view of others*) публи́чный, гла́сный, откры́тый; **~ inquiry** публи́чное/откры́тое рассле́дование.
■ *cpds.* **~ address system** *n.* набо́р звукоусили́тельной аппарату́ры для выступле́ний; **~ house** *n.* (*Br.*) пивна́я, паб; **~ school** *n.* (*Br.*) ча́стная шко́ла; (*US*) госуда́рственная шко́ла.

publican /'pʌblɪkən/ *n.* (*Br.*) содержа́тель (*m.*) ба́ра/па́ба.

publication /pʌblɪ'keɪʃ(ə)n/ *n.* публика́ция, опубликова́ние, изда́ние.

publicity /pʌb'lɪsɪtɪ/ *n.*
[1] (*public notice, dissemination*) гла́сность, огла́ска.
[2] (*advertisement*) реклами́рование, рекла́ма, пабли́сити (*nt. indecl.*); **~ campaign** рекла́мная кампа́ния.

publicize /'pʌblɪsaɪz/ *v.t.* реклами́ровать (*impf.*); огла|ша́ть, -си́ть.

publish /'pʌblɪʃ/ *v.t.*
[1] (*books, newspapers*) изд|ава́ть, -а́ть; выпуска́ть, вы́пустить.
[2] (*letter, article, information, author*) публикова́ть, о-.

publisher /'pʌblɪʃə(r)/ *n.* изда́тель (*m.*).

publishing /'pʌblɪʃɪŋ/ *n.*: **~ house** изда́тельство.

pudding /'pʊdɪŋ/ *n.* пу́динг, запека́нка; (*Br.*, *sweet course*) сла́дкое; **black ~** кровяна́я колбаса́.

puddle /'pʌd(ə)l/ *n.* (*pool*) лу́жа.

puerile /'pjʊəraɪl/ *adj.* де́тский, инфанти́льный.

Puerto Rican /pwɜ:təʊ 'ri:kən/ *n.* пуэрторика́н|ец (*fem.* -ка).
■ *adj.* пуэ́рто-рика́нский.

Puerto Rico /pwɜ:təʊ 'ri:kəʊ/ *n.* Пуэ́рто-Ри́ко (*nt. indecl.*).

puff /pʌf/ *n.*
[1] (*of breath*) вы́дох.
[2] (*of smoke*) дымо́к, клуб.
[3] (*of air or wind*) дунове́ние.
[4]: **~ pastry** слоёное те́сто.
■ *v.t.* [1] (*breathe out*) выдыха́ть, вы́дохнуть; **he ~ed smoke in my face** он вы́дохнул дым мне в лицо́.
[2] (*make out of breath*): **I was ~ed after the climb** по́сле подъёма у меня́ появи́лась оды́шка.
[3]: **~ out** (*smoke*) выпуска́ть, вы́пустить; (*chest*): **he ~ed out his chest with pride** он го́рдо вы́пятил грудь.
[4]: **~ed-up** (*haughty*) наду́тый.
■ *v.i.* [1] (*breathe quickly*): **he was ~ing and panting** он пыхте́л.
[2] (*emit smoke*) дыми́ться (*impf.*).
[3]: **~ up** (*swell*) расп|уха́ть, -у́хнуть.

puffin /'pʌfɪn/ *n.* ту́пик, топо́рик (*птица*).

puffy /'pʌfɪ/ *adj.* (**puffier, puffiest**) (*eyes*) опу́хший; (*face*) отёчный.

pugnacious /pʌg'neɪʃəs/ *adj.* драчли́вый, вои́нственный.

puke /pju:k/ *n.* (*coll.*) рво́та, блевоти́на.
■ *v.i.* блева́ть (*impf.*) (*coll.*); **he ~d** его́ вы́рвало.

pull /pʊl/ *n.* (*traction*) тя́га; (*act*) дёрганье; **he gave a ~ on the rope** он дёрнул (за) верёвку.
■ *v.t.* [1] (*draw towards one, tug, jerk*) тяну́ть, по-; тащи́ть, по-; **he ~ed me by the sleeve** он потяну́л меня́ за рука́в.
[2] (*fig.*): **she ~ed a face at him** она́ скo̍рчила ему́ грима́су.
[3] (*extract*): **he ~ed a gun on me** он вы́хватил пистоле́т и навёл его́ на меня́.
[4] (*strain*) растя́|гивать, -ну́ть.
■ *v.i.* тяну́ть, по-; **they ~ed on the rope** они́ потяну́ли за верёвку.
■ *with advs.*: **~ apart** *v.t.* (*also* **~ to pieces**) раз|рыва́ть, -орва́ть (на куски́); (*fig.*, *criticize severely*) разн|оси́ть, -ести́ в пух и прах; **~ away** *v.i.* (*move off*) от|ходи́ть, -ойти́; от|рыва́ться, -орва́ться; **~ back** *v.t.* отта́|скивать, -щи́ть; оття́|гивать, -ну́ть; *v.i.* отступ|а́ть, -и́ть; **~ down** *v.t.* (*lower by ~ing*) спус|ка́ть, -ти́ть; (*demolish*) сн|оси́ть, -ести́; **~ in** *v.i.* (*drive or move to a standstill*) остан|а́вливаться, -ови́ться; **the train ~ed in** по́езд подошёл к перро́ну; **he ~ed in to the kerb** (*Br.*), **up to the curb** (*US*) он подъе́хал к тротуа́ру; (*drive or move towards near side of road*): **he ~ed in to avoid a collision** он прижа́лся к обо́чине, что́бы избежа́ть столкнове́ния; **~ off** *v.t.* (*remove, detach*) стя́|гивать, -ну́ть; сн|има́ть, -ять; (*coll.*, *achieve*) успе́шно заверш|а́ть, -и́ть; **~ on** *v.t.* натя́|гивать, -ну́ть; **~ out** *v.t.* (*extract*) вытa̍скивать, вы́тащить; (*withdraw*) выводи́ть, вы́вести; **the troops should be ~ed out** войска́ сле́дует вы́вести; *v.i.* (*drive or move away*) от|ходи́ть, -ойти́; (*of driving manoeuvres*) отъ|езжа́ть, -е́хать; **he ~ed out to overtake** он пошёл на обго́н; (*troops*) от|ходи́ть, -ойти́; **~ through** *v.i.* (*recover from illness*) попр|авля́ться, -а́виться; **~ together** *v.t.*: **~ yourself together!** возьми́те себя́ в ру́ки!; *v.i.* (*fig.*) сраб|а́тываться, -о́таться; **if we all ~ together, we shall win** объедини́вшись, мы победи́м; **~ up** *v.t.* (*uproot*) вырыва́ть, вы́рвать; (*raise*) вытя́гивать, вы́тянуть; (*draw nearer*) придв|ига́ть, -и́нуть; **~ up a chair!** придви́ньте стул!; (*bring to a halt*) остан|а́вливать, -ови́ть; (*reprimand*) отчи́т|ывать, -а́ть; *v.i.* (*come to a halt*) остан|а́вливаться, -ови́ться.
■ *cpd.* **~-up** *n.* (*gymnastic exercise*) подтя́гивание.

pulley /'pʊlɪ/ *n.* (*pl.* **pulleys**) шкив.

pullover /'pʊləʊvə(r)/ *n.* пуло́вер, сви́тер.

pulp /pʌlp/ *n.*
1 (*of fruit*) мя́коть.
2 (*fig.*) ме́сиво; бесфо́рменная ма́сса.
pulpit /ˈpʊlpɪt/ *n.* ка́федра (*в церкви*).
pulsate /pʌlˈseɪt/ *v.i.* пульси́ровать (*impf.*).
pulse /pʌls/ *n.* пульс.
pulverize /ˈpʌlvəraɪz/ *v.t.* (*reduce to powder*) размельч|а́ть, -и́ть; (*fig., smash, demolish*) уничт|ожа́ть, -о́жить.
puma /ˈpjuːmə/ *n.* пу́ма.
pummel /ˈpʌm(ə)l/ *v.t.* (**pummelled, pummelling;** *US* **pummeled, pummeling**) колоти́ть, по-, бить, из- (*кулаками*).
pump /pʌmp/ *n.* насо́с, по́мпа.
■ *v.t.* 1 (*transfer by* ~*ing*) кача́ть, на-.
2 (*fig.*): **I ~ed him for information** я выспра́шивал его́; я выве́дывал у него́ све́дения.
3 (*also* ~ **up:** *inflate*) нака́ч|ивать, -а́ть.
pumpkin /ˈpʌmpkɪn/ *n.* ты́ква.
pun /pʌn/ *n.* игра́ слов, каламбу́р.
punch /pʌntʃ/ *n.*
1 (*blow with fist*) уда́р кулако́м.
2 (*fig., energy*) эне́ргия, ого́нь (*m.*).
3 (*tool for perforating, e.g. paper*) дыроко́л.
■ *v.t.* 1 (*hit with fist*) уд|аря́ть, -а́рить кулако́м.
2 (*perforate*) компости́ровать (*impf.*).
■ *cpds.* **~line** *n.* концо́вка, развя́зка (*анекдота и т. п.*); **~-up** *n.* (*Br., coll.*) дра́ка.
punctilious /pʌŋkˈtɪlɪəs/ *adj.* скрупулёзный.
punctual /ˈpʌŋktjʊəl/ *adj.* пунктуа́льный, то́чный.
punctuate /ˈpʌŋktjʊeɪt/ *v.t.* (*insert punctuation marks in*) ста́вить, по- зна́ки препина́ния в + *a.*; (*fig., interrupt, intersperse*) прер|ыва́ть, -ва́ть.
punctuation /pʌŋktjʊˈeɪʃ(ə)n/ *n.* пунктуа́ция; ~ **mark** знак препина́ния.
puncture /ˈpʌŋktʃə(r)/ *n.* проко́л.
■ *v.t.* прок|а́лывать, -оло́ть.
pundit /ˈpʌndɪt/ *n.* знато́к, специали́ст.
pungent /ˈpʌndʒ(ə)nt/ *adj.* о́стрый.
punish /ˈpʌnɪʃ/ *v.t.* нака́з|ывать, -а́ть; кара́ть, по-.
punishment /ˈpʌnɪʃmənt/ *n.* наказа́ние.
punitive /ˈpjuːnɪtɪv/ *adj.* кара́тельный; ~ **taxation** высо́кое налогообложе́ние.
punk /pʌŋk/ *n.*
1 (*admirer of* ~ *rock*) панк; (~ *rock*) панк-ро́к.
2 (*US coll.*) (*worthless person*) дрянь.
■ *adj.* па́нковский.
punnet /ˈpʌnɪt/ *n.* (*Br.*) корзи́н(оч)ка.
punt /pʌnt/ *n.* (*boat*) плоскодо́нка.
punter /ˈpʌntə(r)/ *n.*
1 (*Br.*) (*at cards*) понтёр; (*at races*) игро́к; (*client*) клие́нт (*fem.* -ка).
2 (*in American football and rugby*) игро́к, бью́щий по подбро́шенному мячу́.
puny /ˈpjuːnɪ/ *adj.* (**punier, puniest**) (*undersized, feeble*) тщеду́шный, хи́лый.
pup /pʌp/ *n.* (*young dog*) щено́к.
pupil /ˈpjuːp(ə)l/ *n.*
1 (*one being taught*) учени́|к (*fem.* -ца).
2 (*of eye*) зрачо́к.
puppet /ˈpʌpɪt/ *n.*: **glove** ~ ку́кла; **string** ~ марионе́тка; (*fig.*) марионе́тка.
puppy /ˈpʌpɪ/ *n.* щено́к; ~ **fat/love** де́тская пу́хлость/любо́вь.
purchase /ˈpəːtʃɪs/ *n.* (*buying; thing bought*) поку́пка, приобрете́ние.
■ *v.t.* (*buy*) покупа́ть, купи́ть.
purchaser /ˈpəːtʃɪsə(r)/ *n.* покупа́тель (*fem.* -ница).
pure /pjʊə(r)/ *adj.* чи́стый.
purée /ˈpjʊəreɪ/ *n.* пюре́ (*nt. indecl.*).
purely /ˈpjʊəlɪ/ *adv.* исключи́тельно, соверше́нно, чи́сто.
purgatory /ˈpəːgətərɪ/ *n.* чисти́лище; (*fig.*) ад.
purge /pəːdʒ/ *n.* очище́ние.
■ *v.t.* (*lit., fig.*) оч|ища́ть, -и́стить.
purify /ˈpjʊərɪfaɪ/ *v.t.* оч|ища́ть, -и́стить.
purist /ˈpjʊərɪst/ *n.* пури́ст.
puritan /ˈpjʊərɪt(ə)n/ *n.* (*lit., fig.*) пурита́н|ин (*fem.* -ка).
■ *adj.* пурита́нский.
puritanical /pjʊərɪˈtænɪk(ə)l/ *adj.* пурита́нский.
purity /ˈpjʊərɪtɪ/ *n.* чистота́.
purple /ˈpəːp(ə)l/ *n.* лило́вый/фиоле́товый цвет.
■ *adj.* лило́вый, фиоле́товый.
purport[1] /ˈpəːpɔːt/ *n.* смысл, суть.
purport[2] /pəˈpɔːt/ *v.t.* (*state*) подразумева́ть (*impf.*); (*claim*): **this book is not all it ~s to be** э́та кни́га не совсе́м така́я, како́й она́ претенду́ет быть.
purpose /ˈpəːpəs/ *n.* (*aim*) цель; (*intention*) наме́рение; **on** ~ наро́чно, специа́льно; **she went out with the ~ of buying clothes** она́ вы́шла с це́лью купи́ть оде́жду.
■ *cpd.* **~-built** *adj.* (*Br.*) вы́строенный специа́льно.
purposeful /ˈpəːpəsfʊl/ *adj.* целеустремлённый.
purposely /ˈpəːpəslɪ/ *adv.* наро́чно, (пред)наме́ренно, специа́льно.
purr /pəː(r)/ *v.i.* мурлы́кать (*impf.*).
purse /pəːs/ *n.* (*for money*) кошелёк; (*US, handbag*) су́мочка.
■ *v.t.* мо́рщить, с-; **he ~d (up) his lips** он поджа́л гу́бы.
■ *cpd.* ~ **strings** *n. pl.*: **her husband holds the ~ strings** (*fig.*) её муж распоряжа́ется деньга́ми.
pursue /pəˈsjuː/ *v.t.* (**pursues, pursued, pursuing**)
1 (*chase*) пресле́довать (*impf.*).
2 (*strive after*) добива́ться (*impf.*) + *g.*
3 (*course*) сле́довать (*impf.*) + *d.*; (*interest*) занима́ться (*impf.*) + *i.*; (*activity*) предприн|има́ть, -я́ть; (*policy*) проводи́ть (*impf.*).
pursuer /pəˈsjuːə(r)/ *n.* пресле́дователь (*m.*).
pursuit /pəˈsjuːt/ *n.*
1 (*chase*) пресле́дование; пого́ня; **he escaped, with the police in hot ~** он бежа́л, пресле́дуемый поли́цией по пята́м.
2 (*seeking*) по́иск|и (*pl., g.* -ов); **he will stop at nothing in ~ of his ends** он не остано́вится ни пе́ред чем для достиже́ния свои́х це́лей.
3 (*recreation*) заня́тие.

pus /pʌs/ *n.* гной.

push /pʊʃ/ *n.* толчо́к.

■ *v.t.* 1 (*exert pressure to move*) толк|а́ть, -ну́ть; пих|а́ть, -ну́ть.
2 (*fig., urge*) подт|а́лкивать, -олкну́ть; вынужда́ть, вы́нудить.
3 (*press*) наж|има́ть, -а́ть.
4 (*promote*) реклами́ровать (*impf.*); прот|а́лкивать, -олкну́ть.
■ *v.i.* 1 (*exert force*) толка́ться (*impf.*); **don't ~!** не толка́йтесь!
2 (*force one's way*) прот|а́лкиваться, -олкну́ться; **he ~ed past me** он проле́з вперёд, оттолкну́в меня́.
■ *with advs.*: **~ around** *v.t.* (*fig.*): **I won't be ~ed around** я не позво́лю кома́ндовать (на́до) мно́й; **~ aside/away** *v.t.* отт|а́лкивать, -олкну́ть; **~ in** *v.t.* вт|а́лкивать, -олкну́ть; *v.i.* втира́ться, втере́ться; **don't ~ in!** (*intrude*) не ле́зьте; **~ on** *v.i.* продв|ига́ться, -и́нуться (вперёд); **~ over** *v.t.* опроки́|дывать, -нуть; **~ past** *v.i.* прот|а́лкиваться, -олкну́ться; **~ through** *v.t.* (*lit., fig.*) прот|а́лкивать, -олкну́ть.
■ *cpds.* **~chair** *n.* (*Br.*) (де́тская) прогу́лочная коля́ска; **~-up** *n.* (*US*) отжима́ние; **do ~-ups** отж|има́ться, -а́ться (от по́ла).

pusher /ˈpʊʃə(r)/ *n.* (*coll.*) (*drug ~*) наркоторго́вец.

pushy /ˈpʊʃɪ/ *adj.* (**pushier, pushiest**) напо́ристый.

puss /pʊs/ *n.* (*cat*) ко́шечка, ки́ска.

put /pʊt/ *v.t.* (**putting;** *past and p.p.* **put**)
1 (*move into a certain position*) класть, положи́ть; (*stand*) ста́вить, по-; (*set*) сажа́ть, посади́ть; **~ the money in your pocket!** положи́те де́ньги в карма́н!; **~ yourself in my place!** поста́вьте себя́ на моё ме́сто!; **I ~ the matter into the hands of my lawyer** я поручи́л э́то де́ло своему́ адвока́ту; **she ~ a cloth on the table** она́ накры́ла стол ска́тертью; **she ~ the children to bed** она́ уложи́ла дете́й; **where did I ~ that book** куда́ я дел э́ту кни́гу?
2 (*thrust*) вонз|а́ть, -и́ть; **he ~ his fist through the window** он проби́л окно́ кулако́м.
3 (*bring into a certain state or relationship*): **that ~s me at a disadvantage** э́то ста́вит меня́ в невы́годное положе́ние; **his cold ~ him off his food** из-за просту́ды он потеря́л аппети́т; (*impose, bring in*): **the tax ~s a heavy burden on the rich** нало́г ложи́тся тяжёлым бре́менем на бога́тых; (*set, arrange*): **~ in order** прив|оди́ть, -ести́ в поря́док; (*appoint to a job*) ста́вить, по-; **~ s.o. in charge of** ста́вить, по- кого́-н. во главе́ + *g.*; (*offer*): **they ~ their house on the market** они́ объяви́ли о прода́же до́ма; (*invest*) вкла́дывать, вложи́ть; поме|ща́ть, -сти́ть.
4 (*estimate, consider*): **I would ~ her (age) at about 65** я дал бы ей лет 65; **I wouldn't ~ it past him to be lying** с него́ ста́нется: соврёт и де́нег не возьмёт; **he ~s a high value on courtesy** он высоко́ це́нит ве́жливость.
5 (*submit*) выдвига́ть, вы́двинуть; зад|ава́ть, -а́ть; **may I ~ a suggestion?** мо́жно мне внести́ предложе́ние?
6 (*express*) изл|ага́ть, -ожи́ть; **how can I ~ it?** как бы э́то сказа́ть?; **will you ~ that in writing?** вы мо́жете изложи́ть э́то на бума́ге?
■ *with advs.*: **~ across** *v.t.* (*make clear, communicate*) объясн|я́ть, -и́ть; **~ away** *v.t.* (*tidy*) уб|ира́ть, -ра́ть; (*save*) от|кла́дывать, -ложи́ть; **~ back** *v.t.* (*replace, restore*) класть, положи́ть на ме́сто; (*of clock*) перев|оди́ть, -ести́ наза́д; (*postpone*) от|кла́дывать, -ложи́ть; **~ by** *v.t.* (*save*) от|кла́дывать, -ложи́ть; **~ down** *v.t.* (*place on ground etc.*) класть, положи́ть на зе́млю; **~ your gun down!** бро́сьте ору́жие!; опусти́те ружьё!; (*allow to alight*): **the bus stopped to ~ down passengers** авто́бус останови́лся, что́бы вы́садить пассажи́ров; (*make deposit of*) вн|оси́ть, -ести́ (*задаток*); (*lower*) сн|ижа́ть, -и́зить; (*repress*) подав|ля́ть, -и́ть; **the rebellion was quickly ~ down** восста́ние бы́ло бы́стро пода́влено; (*write down*) запи́с|ывать, -а́ть; (*kill sick animal*) усып|ля́ть, -и́ть; умерщв|ля́ть, -и́ть; **~ forward** *v.t.* (*advance*): **the clocks are ~ forward in spring** весно́й часы́ перево́дят вперёд; (*propose*) выдвига́ть, вы́двинуть; **his name was ~ forward** была́ вы́двинута его́ кандидату́ра; (*bring nearer*) передв|ига́ть, -и́нуть вперёд; **~ in** *v.t.* (*cause to enter; insert*) вст|авля́ть, -а́вить; (*install*) вст|авля́ть, -а́вить; (*contribute*): **I ~ in a word for him** я вста́вил за него́ слове́чко; (*submit, present*) под|ава́ть, -а́ть; **I ~ in an application** я по́дал заявле́ние; (*work*): **I ~ in 6 hours today** я сего́дня отрабо́тал 6 часо́в; *v.i.* (*of boat or crew*) за|ходи́ть, -йти́ в порт; (*apply*): **she ~ in for a job as secretary** она́ подала́ заявле́ние на до́лжность/ме́сто секретаря́; **~ off** *v.t.* (*postpone*) от|кла́дывать, -ложи́ть; отсро́чи|вать, -ть; (*fob off*): **he ~ me off with promises** он отде́лался от меня́ обеща́ниями; (*deter*) отпу́г|ивать, -ну́ть; **we were ~ off by the weather** мы переду́мали из-за пого́ды; (*repel*) отт|а́лкивать, -олкну́ть; **I was ~ off by his tactlessness** меня́ оттолкну́ла его́ беста́ктность; (*distract*): **I can't recite if you keep ~ting me off** я не могу́ деклами́ровать, когда́ вы меня́ отвлека́ете; **~ on** *v.t.* (*clothes etc.*) над|ева́ть, -е́ть; (*place in position*): **when the pot is full, ~ the lid on** когда́ кастрю́ля напо́лнится, накро́йте её кры́шкой; (*assume*): **he ~ on an air of innocence** он напусти́л на себя́ неви́нный вид; (*increase*) увели́чи|вать, -ть; **you're ~ting on weight** вы полне́ете/поправля́етесь; (*light, radio etc.*) включ|а́ть, -и́ть; (*play, concert etc.*) ста́вить, по-; **~ out** *v.t.*: (*place outside door*) выставля́ть, вы́ставить за дверь; (*extend, protrude*): **~ your tongue out!** покажи́те язы́к!; **he ~ out his hand in welcome** он протяну́л ру́ку для приве́тствия; (*arrange so as to be seen*) выставля́ть, вы́ставить; выкла́дывать, вы́ложить; (*hang up outside*) выве́шивать, вы́весить; **she ~ the washing out to dry** она́ вы́весила бельё суши́ться; (*extinguish*) туши́ть, по-; гаси́ть, по-; **~ the lights out!** потуши́те свет!; **~ your cigarette out!** погаси́те сигаре́ту!; (*dislocate*) выви́хивать, вы́вихнуть; (*inconvenience*) нар|уша́ть, -у́шить

пла́ны + *g.*; **would it ~ you out to come at 3?** вас не затрудни́т прийти́ в 3 часа́?; (*vex*) раздраж|а́ть, -и́ть; **~ through** *v.t.* (*accomplish*) осуществ|ля́ть, -и́ть; (*connect by telephone*) соедин|я́ть, -и́ть; **~ together** *v.t.* (*bring close or into contact*) соедин|я́ть, -и́ть; (*assemble*) сост|авля́ть, -а́вить; (*construct from components*) соб|ира́ть, -ра́ть; **~ up** *v.t.* (*raise, hold up*) подн|има́ть, -я́ть; **~ up your hand if you know the answer!** кто зна́ет отве́т, подними́те ру́ку!; (*display*) выставля́ть, вы́ставить; (*erect*) воздв|ига́ть, -и́гнуть; стро́ить, по-; **shall we ~ the curtains up?** бу́дем ве́шать занаве́ски?; (*increase*) пов|ыша́ть, -ы́сить; **~ up prices** (*Br.*) подн|има́ть, -я́ть це́ны; (*offer*) выдвига́ть, вы́двинуть; **he ~ up no resistance** он не оказа́л никако́го сопротивле́ния; (*supply*) вн|оси́ть, -ести́; (*accommodate*): **he ~ me up for the night** я переночева́л у него́; (*coll., introduce*): **I ~ him up to that trick** я его́ научи́л э́тому приёму/трю́ку; *v.i.* (*tolerate*) мири́ться, при- (*с кем/чем*); **I won't ~ up with any nonsense** я не потерплю́ никаки́х глу́постей.
■ *cpd.* **~-down** *n.* (*snub*) ре́зкость.

putrefy /ˈpjuːtrɪfaɪ/ *v.i.* (*go bad*) гнить, с-; (*fester*) разл|ага́ться, -ожи́ться.

putrid /ˈpjuːtrɪd/ *adj.* (*decomposed*) гнило́й; (*coll., unpleasant*) отврати́тельный.

putt /pʌt/ *n.* уда́р, загоня́ющий мяч в лу́нку (*в гольфе*).
■ *v.i.* (**putted, putting**) заг|оня́ть, -на́ть мяч в лу́нку; **~ing green** лужа́йка с лу́нками (*в гольфе*).

putty /ˈpʌtɪ/ *n.* зама́зка, шпаклёвка.

puzzle /ˈpʌz(ə)l/ *n.* зага́дка; (*for entertainment*) головоло́мка, пазл.
■ *v.t.* озада́чи|вать, -ть; прив|оди́ть, -ести́ в недоуме́ние.

PVC (*abbr. of* ***polyvinyl chloride***) ПВХ (поливинилхлори́д).

pygmy /ˈpɪgmɪ/ *n.* пигме́й.

pyjamas /pəˈdʒɑːməz/ (*US* **pajamas**) *n.* пижа́ма; **~ trousers** пижа́мные штаны́.

pylon /ˈpaɪlən/ *n.* (*for electricity*) опо́ра (*линии электропередач*).

pyramid /ˈpɪrəmɪd/ *n.* (*lit., fig.*) пирами́да.

pyre /ˈpaɪə(r)/ *n.* погреба́льный костёр.

Pyrenees /pɪrəˈniːz/ *n.* Пирене́|и (*pl., g.* -ев).

pyrotechnics /paɪərəʊˈteknɪks/ *n.* (*art of making fireworks*) пироте́хника; (*firework display; also fig.*) фейерве́рк.

python /ˈpaɪθ(ə)n/ *n.* пито́н.

Qq

Qatar /kæˈtɑː(r)/ *n.* Ка́тар.

quack /kwæk/ *n.* (*sound*) кря́канье.
■ *v.i.* кря́кать (*impf.*).

quadruple /ˈkwɒdrʊp(ə)l/ *adj.* учетверённый.
■ *v.t.* & *i.* увели́чи|вать(ся), -ть(ся) в четы́ре ра́за.

quagmire /ˈkwɒgmaɪə(r)/ *n.* (*also fig.*) боло́то.

quail /kweɪl/ *v.i.* тру́сить, с-.

quaint /kweɪnt/ *adj.* причу́дливый, чудно́й.

quake /kweɪk/ *v.i.* дрожа́ть (*impf.*); содрог|а́ться, -ну́ться.

qualification /kwɒlɪfɪˈkeɪʃ(ə)n/ *n.*
1 (*skill*) квалифика́ция.
2 (*modification*) ограниче́ние.

qualifier /ˈkwɒlɪfaɪə(r)/ *n.* (*match*) отбо́рочное соревнова́ние, отбо́рочный матч; (*person, team*) челове́к, проше́дший (*or* кома́нда, проше́дшая) отбо́рочные соревнова́ния.

qualif|y /ˈkwɒlɪfaɪ/ *v.t.*
1 (*for job*) гото́вить (*impf.*) **I am not ~ied to advise you** я недоста́точно компете́нтен, что́бы дава́ть вам сове́ты; (*make entitled*) дава́ть, дать пра́во + *inf. or* на + *a.*; **he is a ~ied doctor** он дипломи́рованный врач.
2 (*modify*) огов|а́ривать, -ори́ть; уточн|я́ть, -и́ть; **I must ~y my statement** я до́лжен сде́лать огово́рку.
■ *v.i.* (*be eligible* (*for*)) име́ть (*impf.*) пра́во (на + *a.*); **will you ~y for a pension?** бу́дете ли вы име́ть пра́во на пе́нсию?; (*sport*): **our team failed to ~** на́ша кома́нда не прошла́ отбо́рочные соревнова́ния.

qualitative /ˈkwɒlɪtətɪv/ *adj.* ка́чественный.

quality /ˈkwɒlɪtɪ/ *n.*
1 (*degree of merit*) ка́чество; (*excellence*) высо́кое ка́чество, доброка́чественность.
2 (*characteristic*) ка́чество, сво́йство.
■ *adj.* (высоко)ка́чественный.

qualm /kwɑːm/ *n.* сомне́ние, колеба́ние.

quandary /ˈkwɒndərɪ/ *n.* затрудни́тельное положе́ние.

quango /ˈkwæŋgəʊ/ *n.* (*pl.* **~s**) (*Br. coll.*) полуавтоно́мная организа́ция.

quantifiable /ˈkwɒntɪfaɪəb(ə)l/ *adj.* измери́мый.

quantitative /ˈkwɒntɪtətɪv/ *adj.* коли́чественный.

quantity /ˈkwɒntɪtɪ/ *n.*
1 (*measurable property*) коли́чество; **~ surveyor** (*Br.*) инжене́р-планови́к.
2 (*amount*) коли́чество.

quantum /ˈkwɒntəm/ *n.*: **~ leap** (*fig.*) скачо́к.

quarantine /ˈkwɒrəntiːn/ *n.* каранти́н.
■ *v.t.* содержа́ть (*impf.*) в каранти́не.

quarrel /ˈkwɒr(ə)l/ *n.*
1 (*altercation*) ссо́ра.
2 (*cause for complaint*) по́вод для ссо́ры, прете́нзия; **I have no ~ with him on that**

score у меня́ нет к нему́ прете́нзий по э́тому по́воду.
■ *v.t.* (**quarrelled, quarrelling;** *US* **quarreled, quarreling**) (*dispute*) ссо́риться, по-; (*take issue*): **I cannot ~ with his logic** я не могу́ не согласи́ться с его́ ло́гикой.

quarrelsome /'kwɒrəlsəm/ *adj.* сварли́вый.

quarry¹ /'kwɒrɪ/ *n.* (*prey*) добы́ча.

quarry² /'kwɒrɪ/ *n.* (*for stone etc.*) карье́р.
■ *v.t.* (*extract*) доб|ыва́ть, -ы́ть.

quarter /'kwɔ:tə(r)/ *n.*
1 (*fourth part*) че́тверть; (*of hour*): **a ~ to six** без че́тверти шесть; **a ~ past six** че́тверть седьмо́го; (*of year*) кварта́л.
2 (*US coin*) два́дцать пять це́нтов.
3 (*district*) кварта́л.
4 (*pl., lodgings*) каза́рмы (*f. pl.*); кварти́ры (*f. pl.*).
5 : **at close ~s** в те́сном сосе́дстве, вблизи́.
■ *v.t.* (*divide into four*) дели́ть, раз- на четы́ре ча́сти.
■ *cpds.* **~-final** *n.* четвертьфина́л.

quarterly /'kwɔ:təlɪ/ *adj.* кварта́льный.
■ *adv.* ежекварта́льно; раз в три ме́сяца.

quartet /kwɔ:'tet/ *n.* кварте́т.

quartz /kwɔ:ts/ *n.* кварц.

quash /kwɒʃ/ *v.t.* подав|ля́ть, -и́ть.

quaver /'kweɪvə(r)/ *n.*
1 (*trembling tone*) дрожа́ние.
2 (*Br., mus.*) восьма́я но́та.
■ *v.i.* дрожа́ть (*impf.*).

quay /ki:/ *n.* прича́л.
■ *cpd.* **~side** *n.* при́стань.

queasy /'kwi:zɪ/ *adj.* (**queasier, queasiest**): **I feel a little ~** меня́ немно́го тошни́т.

queen /kwi:n/ *n.*
1 короле́ва.
2 (*fig.*) короле́ва, цари́ца.
3 (*~ bee*) ма́тка.
4 (*at chess*) ферзь (*m.*).
5 (*at cards*) да́ма.
6 : **Q~'s Counsel** адвока́т вы́сшего ра́нга.

queer /kwɪə(r)/ *adj.* стра́нный.

quell /kwel/ *v.t.* подав|ля́ть, -и́ть.

quench /kwentʃ/ *v.t.*: **~ one's thirst** утол|я́ть, -и́ть жа́жду.

querulous /'kwerʊləs/ *adj.* ворчли́вый.

query /'kwɪərɪ/ *n.* вопро́с.
■ *v.t.* выража́ть, вы́разить сомне́ние в + *p.*; усомни́ться (*pf.*) в + *p.*

quest /kwest/ *n.* по́иски (*m. pl.*); **the ~ for happiness** по́иски сча́стья.

question /'kwestʃ(ə)n/ *n.*
1 (*interrogation; problem*) вопро́с; **it is only a ~ of finding the money** де́ло то́лько за тем, что́бы найти́ де́ньги; **a holiday is out of the ~** об о́тпуске не мо́жет быть и ре́чи; **the man in ~** челове́к, о кото́ром идёт речь.
2 (*doubt, objection*) сомне́ние; **his statements were called in ~** его́ заявле́ния бы́ли поста́влены под сомне́ние.
■ *v.t.* 1 (*interrogate*) допр|а́шивать, -оси́ть.
2 (*cast doubt on*) ста́вить, по- под сомне́ние.
■ *cpd.* **~ mark** *n.* вопроси́тельный знак.

questionable /'kwestʃənəb(ə)l/ *adj.* сомни́тельный.

questioner /'kwestʃənə(r)/ *n.* задаю́щий/зада́вший вопро́с(ы).

questionnaire /kwestʃə'neə(r)/ *n.* анке́та.

queue /kju:/ (*Br.*) *n.* о́чередь; **he was trying to jump the ~** он пыта́лся пройти́ без о́череди.
■ *v.i.* (**queues, queued, queuing** *or* **queueing**) (*also* **~ up**) станови́ться, стать в о́чередь.

quibble /'kwɪb(ə)l/ *v.i.* (*argue*) препира́ться (*impf.*).

quiche /ki:ʃ/ *n.* откры́тый пиро́г с сы́ром, беко́ном, о́вощами *и т. п.*

quick /kwɪk/ *n.*: **he bit his nails to the ~** он искуса́л все но́гти; **his words cut me to the ~** его́ слова́ заде́ли меня́ за живо́е.
■ *adj.* 1 (*rapid*) бы́стрый, ско́рый; **he is a ~ worker** он бы́стро рабо́тает.
2 (*lively*) живо́й; (*quick-minded*) сообрази́тельный; **he has a ~ temper** он о́чень вспы́льчив.
■ *adv.* бы́стро; **~, get a doctor!** скоре́е позови́те врача́!
■ *cpds.* **~sand(s)** *n.* зыбу́чий песо́к; зыбу́чие пески́; **~-tempered** *adj.* вспы́льчивый; **~-witted** *adj.* смышлёный, нахо́дчивый.

quicken /'kwɪkən/ *v.t.* (*make quicker*) уск|оря́ть, -о́рить; (*stimulate*) возбу|жда́ть, -ди́ть.
■ *v.i.* (*become quicker*) уск|оря́ться, -о́риться.

quid /kwɪd/ *n.* (*pl.* **~**) (*Br. coll., £1*) фунт (сте́рлингов).

quiet /'kwaɪət/ *n.* (*silence*) тишина́; (*repose*) поко́й.
■ *adj.* (**quieter, quietest**)
1 (*making little or no sound*) ти́хий; бесшу́мный; **can't you keep ~?** ты не мо́жешь помолча́ть?
2 (*undisturbed*) споко́йный, ми́рный; **we had a ~ night** ночь прошла́ споко́йно.
3 (*of gentle disposition*) споко́йный, ти́хий.
4 (*private; concealed*) та́йный; скры́тый; **on the ~** (*coll.*) (*secretly*) тайко́м; втихомо́лку; (*in confidence*) под (больши́м) секре́том.
■ *int.* ти́ше!

quieten /'kwaɪət(ə)n/ *v.t. & i.* (*Br., also* **~ down**) успок|а́ивать(ся), -о́ить(ся).

quietness /'kwaɪətnɪs/ *n.* (*stillness*) тишина́; (*repose*) поко́й; (*of manner*) невозмути́мость, споко́йствие.

quiff /kwɪf/ *n.* (*Br.*) чёлка; (*tuft*) зачёс.

quill /kwɪl/ *n.* перо́; (*of porcupine*) игла́ (*дикобраза*).

quilt /kwɪlt/ *n.* стёганое одея́ло.
■ *v.t.*: **~ed bathrobe, bedcover** стёганый хала́т/стёганое покрыва́ло.

quip /kwɪp/ *n.* остро́та.
■ *v.i.* (**quipped, quipping**) остри́ть, с-.

quirk /kwə:k/ *n.* причу́да.

quirky /'kwə:kɪ/ *adj.* (**quirkier, quirkiest**) причу́дливый.

quit /kwɪt/ *v.t.* (**quitting;** *past and p.p.* **quitted** *or* **quit**)
1 (*leave*) ост|авля́ть, -а́вить.
2 (*coll., stop*) прекра|ща́ть, -ти́ть.
■ *v.i.* (**quitting;** *past and p.p.* **quitted** *or* **quit**)
1 (*leave job etc.*): **the maid was given notice to ~** го́рничную предупреди́ли об

увольнении.
[2] (*leave off*) перест|авáть, -áть.

quite /kwaɪt/ *adv.*
[1] (*entirely*) совсéм, совершéнно, вполнé; **I ~ agree** я вполнé/совершéнно соглáсен; **~ right!** совершéнно вéрно! **have you ~ finished?** ну, вы кóнчили?; **that is ~ another matter** э́то совсéм другóе дéло.
[2] (*to a certain extent*) довóльно; **it is ~ cold here** здéсь довóльно хóлодно; **I ~ like cycling** я не прочь покатáться на велосипéде; **~ a long time** довóльно мнóго врéмени; **~ a few** довóльно мнóго; немáло.

quits /kwɪts/ *pred. adj.*: **now we are ~** тепéрь мы квиты́.

quiver /ˈkwɪvə(r)/ *v.i.* дрожáть, за-.

quiz /kwɪz/ *n.* (*pl.* **quizzes**) (*test of knowledge*) виктори́на; (*US, school test*) контрóльная (рабóта).
■ *v.t.* (**quizzed, quizzing**) выспрáшивать, вы́спросить.

quizzical /ˈkwɪzɪk(ə)l/ *adj.* насмéшливый, ирони́ческий.

quorum /ˈkwɔːrəm/ *n.* квóрум.

quota /ˈkwəʊtə/ *n.* (*pl.* **~s**) квóта, нóрма.

quotation /kwəʊˈteɪʃ(ə)n/ *n.*
[1] (*passage quoted*) цитáта; **~ marks** кавы́ч|ки (*pl., g.* -ек).
[2] (*estimate of cost*) ценá, стóимость.

quote /kwəʊt/ *n.*
[1] (*coll., quotation*) цитáта.
[2] (*pl., coll., quotation marks*) кавы́ч|ки (*pl., g.* -ек).
■ *v.t.* [1] (*repeat words of*) цити́ровать, про-.
[2] (*refer to*) ссылáться, сослáться на + *a*.
[3] : **~ a price** назн|ачáть, -áчить цéну.

Rr

rabbi /ˈræbaɪ/ *n.* (*pl.* **~s**) равви́н.

rabbit /ˈræbɪt/ *n.* крóлик.

rabble /ˈræb(ə)l/ *n.* сброд, чернь.
■ *cpds.* **~-rouser** *n.* демагóг; **~-rousing** *n.* демагóгия.

rabid /ˈræbɪd/ *adj.* (*with rabies; also fig.*) бéшеный.

rabies /ˈreɪbiːz/ *n.* бéшенство.

rac(c)oon /rəˈkuːn/ *n.* енóт.

race¹ /reɪs/ *n.* бег на скóрость, гóнка; забéг; **(horse) ~s** скáчки (*f. pl.*).
■ *v.t.*: **I'll ~ you to the corner** посмóтрим, кто быстрéе добежи́т до углá.
■ *v.i.* [1] (*compete in speed*) состязáться (*impf.*) в скóрости.
[2] (*move at speed*) нести́сь (*impf.*); мчáться, по-.
■ *cpds.* **~horse** *n.* скаковáя лóшадь; **~track** *n.* трéк.

race² /reɪs/ *n.* (*ethnic*) рáса.

racer /ˈreɪsə(r)/ *n.* гóнщик.

racial /ˈreɪʃ(ə)l/ *adj.* рáсовый.

racing /ˈreɪsɪŋ/ *n.* (**horse ~**) скáчки (*f. pl.*); (**motor ~**) автогóнки (*f. pl.*); **~ car** гóночный автомоби́ль; **~ driver** гóнщик.

racism /ˈreɪsɪz(ə)m/ *n.* раси́зм.

racist /ˈreɪsɪst/ *n.* раси́ст (*fem.* -ка).
■ *adj.* раси́стский.

rack¹ /ræk/ *n.* стóйка с пóлками; стеллáж; (*plate ~*) подстáвка для посу́ды; (*luggage ~*) багáжная пóлка/сéтка.

rack² /ræk/ *v.t.* му́чить, из-; **he was ~ed with pain** он кóрчился от бóли; (*fig.*): **I ~ed my brains for an answer** я ломáл гóлову над отвéтом.

rac|ket¹, -quet /ˈrækɪt/ *n.* ракéтка.

racket² /ˈrækɪt/ *n.*
[1] (*din*) шум, гам.
[2] (*coll.*) (*dishonest scheme*) жу́льническое предприя́тие.

racketeer /rækɪˈtɪə(r)/ *n.* рэкети́р.

raconteur /rækɒnˈtɜː(r)/ *n.* хорóший расскáзчик.

racoon /rəˈkuːn/ = **racoon**

racy /ˈreɪsɪ/ *adj.* (**racier, raciest**) (*piquant, lively*) óстрый, пря́ный; **a ~ style** бóйкий/я́ркий стиль.

radar /ˈreɪdɑː(r)/ *n.* радиолокáция; (*apparatus*) радáр; **radar screen** экрáн радáра.

radiance /ˈreɪdɪəns/ *n.* сия́ние, блеск; **the sun's ~** сóлнечное сия́ние.

radiant /ˈreɪdɪənt/ *adj.* сия́ющий; **she was ~ with happiness** онá сия́ла от счáстья.

radiate /ˈreɪdɪeɪt/ *v.t.* & *i.* излуч|áть(ся), -и́ть(ся); (*fig.*): **his face ~d happiness** егó лицó свети́лось рáдостью.

radiation /reɪdɪˈeɪʃ(ə)n/ *n.* радиáция, излучéние.

radiator /ˈreɪdɪeɪtə(r)/ *n.* (*heating device*) батарéя, радиáтор; (*of car*) радиáтор.

radical /ˈrædɪk(ə)l/ *n.* (*pol.*) радикáл.
■ *adj.* (*fundamental*) коренно́й; (*pol.*) радикáльный.

radio /ˈreɪdɪəʊ/ *n.* (*pl.* **radios**) (*means of communication*) рáдио (*nt. indecl.*); (*receiving apparatus*) радиоприёмник; **~-controlled** радиоуправля́емый; **~ station** радиостáнция.
■ *v.t.* (**radioes, radioed**)
[1] (*send by ~*) перед|авáть, -áть (по рáдио).
[2] (*contact by ~*) ради́ровать (*pf.*) + *d*.

radioactive /reɪdɪəʊˈæktɪv/ *adj.* радиоакти́вный.

radioactivity /reɪdɪəʊækˈtɪvɪtɪ/ *n.* радиоакти́вность.

radiographer /reɪdɪˈɒgrəfə(r)/ *n.* рентгенóлог, радиографи́ст.

radiography /reɪdɪˈɒgrəfɪ/ *n.* рентгеногрáфия, радиогрáфия.

radiologist /reɪdɪ'ɒlədʒɪst/ *n.* радио́лог, рентгено́лог.

radiology /reɪdɪ'ɒlədʒɪ/ *n.* рентгеноло́гия, радиоло́гия.

radiotherapy /reɪdɪəʊ'θerəpɪ/ *n.* радиотерапи́я.

radish /'rædɪʃ/ *n.* реди́ска; (*pl., collect.*) реди́с.

radius /'reɪdɪəs/ *n.* ра́диус.

raffle /'ræf(ə)l/ *n.* лотере́я.

raft /rɑːft/ *n.* (сплавно́й) плот.

rafter /'rɑːftə(r)/ *n.* стропи́ло.

rag /ræg/ *n.* (*cloth*) тря́пка, лоску́т; (*pl., torn or tattered clothing*) лохмо́ть|я (*pl., g.* -ев).

rag|e /reɪdʒ/ *n.*
1 (*violent anger*) я́рость, гнев.
2 (*dominant fashion*) после́дний крик мо́ды.
■ *v.i.*: **he ~d at his wife** он наки́нулся на свою́ жену́; **the wind ~d all day** ве́тер бушева́л весь день; **a ~ing thirst** мучи́тельная жа́жда.

ragged /'rægɪd/ *adj.*
1 (*torn*) рва́ный, потрёпанный; (*wearing torn clothes*) обо́рванный.
2 (*rough*): **a ~ beard** косма́тая борода́; **~ clouds** рва́ные облака́.

raid /reɪd/ *n.* (*by police*) обла́ва, рейд; (*by criminals*) налёт; (*mil.*) рейд, налёт.
■ *v.t.*: **our bombers ~ed Hamburg** на́ши бомбардиро́вщики соверши́ли налёт на Га́мбург; **the flat was ~ed in his absence** в его́ отсу́тствие кварти́ру огра́били.

rail /reɪl/ *n.*
1 (*bar for support etc.*) перекла́дина, ре́йка; (*of staircase*) пери́л|а (*pl., g.* —); (*for hanging things on*) ве́шалка.
2 (*of railway track*) рельс; (*railway transport*): **by ~** по́ездом.
■ *cpds.* **~road** *n.* (*US*) желе́зная доро́га; **~way** *n.* желе́зная доро́га; (*attr.*) железнодоро́жный.

railing(s) /'reɪlɪŋ(z)/ *n.* огра́да, решётка.

rain /reɪn/ *n.* дождь (*m.*).
■ *v.i.*: **it is ~ing** идёт дождь; **it was ~ing hard** шёл си́льный дождь.
■ *cpds.* **~bow** *n.* ра́дуга; **~ check** *n.* (*US*) обеща́ние приня́ть приглаше́ние в друго́й раз; **~coat** *n.* плащ; **~drop** *n.* ка́пля дождя́; **~fall** *n.* оса́дк|и (*pl., g.* -ов).

rainforest /'reɪnfɒrɪst/ *n.* тропи́ческий лес.

rainy /'reɪnɪ/ *adj.* (**rainier, rainiest**) дождли́вый; **save, keep for a ~ day** откла́дывать, отложи́ть на чёрный день.

raise /reɪz/ *n.* (*US, rise in salary*) приба́вка.
■ *v.t.* 1 (*lift*) подн|има́ть, -я́ть; (*make higher*) пов|ыша́ть, -ы́сить; **the government ~d the duty on tobacco** прави́тельство повы́сило по́шлину на таба́к; **the news ~d my hopes** изве́стие укрепи́ло мои́ наде́жды; (*make louder*): **don't ~ your voice** не повыша́йте го́лоса.
2 (*bring up*): **may I ~ one question?** мо́жно мне зада́ть вопро́с?; (*evoke*): **you ~d a doubt in my mind** вы зарони́ли мне в ду́шу сомне́ние.
3 (*give voice to*): **she ~d the alarm** она́ подняла́ трево́гу.
4 (*collect*): **she ~d money for charity** она́ собрала́ де́ньги на благотвори́тельные це́ли.
5 (*rear*): **they ~d a family** они́ вы́растили дете́й.

raisin /'reɪz(ə)n/ *n.* изю́минка.

rake /reɪk/ *n.* (*tool*) гра́бл|и (*pl., g.* -ель *or* -лей).
■ *v.t.*: **he ~d the soil level** он разрыхли́л грунт.
■ *with advs.*: **~ in** *v.t.*: **he ~d in the money** (*fig., coll.*) он загреба́л де́ньги лопа́той; **~ up** *v.t.* сгре|ба́ть, -сти́; (*fig.*): **why ~ up an old quarrel?** заче́м вороши́ть ста́рую ссо́ру?

rakish /'reɪkɪʃ/ *adj.* (*of man*) распу́тный, бесшаба́шный; (*of hat*) залихва́тски/ли́хо/небре́жно наде́тый.

rall|y /'rælɪ/ *n.*
1 (*mass gathering*) ми́тинг.
2 (*at tennis etc.*) (затяжно́й) обме́н уда́рами, се́рия.
3 (*motor race*) авторa̋лли (*nt. indecl.*).
■ *v.t.* (*reassemble*) соб|ира́ть, -ра́ть (в строй).
■ *v.i.* 1 (*reassemble*) соб|ира́ться, -ра́ться.
2 (*revive*): **he ~ied from his illness** он опра́вился от боле́зни; **the market ~ied** ры́нок о́жил/ожи́вился.

RAM /ræm/ *n.* (*comput.*) (*abbr. of* ***random-access memory***) операти́вная па́мять, ОЗУ (операти́вное запомина́ющее устро́йство).

ram /ræm/ *n.* бара́н.
■ *v.t.* (**rammed, ramming**)
1 (*drive by force*): **stakes were ~med into the ground** ко́лья бы́ли вби́ты в зе́млю.
2 (*strike with force*): **the ship ~med the bridge** кора́бль наскочи́л на мост.
■ *cpd.* **~ raid** *n.* ограбле́ние с испо́льзованием тяжёлой (строи́тельной) те́хники.

Ramadan /'ræmədæn/ *n.* (*relig.*) Рамаза́н, Рамада́н.

rambl|e /'ræmb(ə)l/ *n.* прогу́лка.
■ *v.i.* 1 (*walk*) прогу́л|иваться, -я́ться.
2 (*fig., of speech*) болта́ть (*impf.*) языко́м; **a ~ing speaker** многосло́вный ора́тор; **a ~ing speech** бессвя́зная речь.

rambler /'ræmblə(r)/ *n.* (*hiker*) люби́тель пешехо́дного тури́зма.

ramification /ræmɪfɪ'keɪʃ(ə)n/ *n.* разветвле́ние; (*consequence*) после́дствие.

ramp /ræmp/ *n.* (*slope*) скат, укло́н.

rampage /'ræmpeɪdʒ/ *v.i.* бу́йствовать, буя́нить (*both impf.*).

rampant /'ræmpənt/ *adj.* свире́пствующий, безу́держный.

rampart /'ræmpɑːt/ *n.* крепостно́й вал.

ramshackle /'ræmʃæk(ə)l/ *adj.* обветша́лый.

ran /ræn/ *past of* ▸ **run**

ranch /rɑːntʃ/ *n.* ра́нчо (*nt. indecl.*), фе́рма.

rancher /'rɑːntʃə(r)/ *n.* владе́лец ра́нчо; скотово́д.

rancid /'rænsɪd/ *adj.* прого́рклый, ту́хлый.

rancour /'ræŋkə(r)/ (*US* **rancor**) *n.* зло́ба.

R & B (*abbr. of* ***rhythm and blues***) ри́тм-энд-блю́з; (*modern style*) ар-эн-би́ (*m. indecl.*) (*usu. written in Roman*).

R & D (*abbr. of* ***research and development***) нау́чно-иссле́довательская рабо́та.

random /'rændəm/ *n.*: **at ~** наобу́м, науга́д,

наудáчу.
■ *adj.* случáйный.

randy /'rændɪ/ *adj.* (**randier, randiest**) (*Br.*) распýтный, похотли́вый.

rang /ræŋ/ *past of* ▸ **ring²**

range /reɪndʒ/ *n.*
1 (*row, series*) цепь, ряд.
2 (*grazing area*) неогорóженное пáстбище; (*hunting ground*) охóтничье угóдье.
3 (*area for firing, bombing etc.*) полигóн; **rifle ~** стрéльбище.
4 (*operating distance*) дáльность, рáдиус; **they fired at close ~** они́ стреля́ли с бли́зкого расстоя́ния.
5 (*extent*) диапазóн.
6 (*selection*) набóр; (*assortment*) ассортимéнт.
7 (*stove*) кýхонная плитá.
■ *v.i.* 1 (*wander*): **tigers ~d through the jungle** ти́гры броди́ли по джýнглям.
2 (*extend*) простирáться (*impf.*); **my research ~s over a wide field** мои́ исслéдования охвáтывают ширóкую óбласть.
3 (*vary between limits*) колебáться (*impf.*).

ranger /'reɪndʒə(r)/ *n.* лесни́к, объéздчик.

rank¹ /ræŋk/ *n.*
1 (*row*) ряд; (*taxi ~*) (*Br.*) стоя́нка такси́.
2 (*line of soldiers*) шерéнга; **the men broke ~(s)** солдáты нарýшили строй; **among the ~s of the unemployed** в рядáх безрабóтных.
3 (*usu. pl., common soldiers*): **~ and file** (*mil. etc.*) рядовы́е.
4 (*in armed forces*) звáние, чин.
5 (*social position*): **people of all ~s of society** представи́тели всех слоёв óбщества.
■ *v.t.* (*class*) классифици́ровать (*impf., pf.*); **he was ~ed among the great poets** егó причисля́ли к вели́ким поэ́там.
■ *v.i.* (*have a place*): **a high-~ing officer** стáрший офицéр.

rank² /ræŋk/ *adj.*
1 (*foul; offensive*): **the skunk gives off a ~ odour** (*Br.*), **odor** (*US*) от скýнса исхóдит зловóние.
2 (*gross*) чрезмéрный; **~ outsider** совершéнно посторóнний человéк.

rankle /'ræŋk(ə)l/ *v.i.* терзáть, мучи́ть (*both impf.*).

ransack /'rænsæk/ *v.t.*
1 (*search*) обшáри|вать, -ть.
2 (*plunder*) грáбить, раз-.

ransom /'rænsəm/ *n.* вы́куп; **he was held to ~** (*lit.*) за негó трéбовали вы́куп; (*fig.*) егó шантажи́ровали.

rant /rænt/ *v.i.* разглагóльствовать (*impf.*).

rap /ræp/ *n.*
1 (*light blow*) лёгкий удáр, стук.
2 (*~ music*) рэп.
■ *v.t.* (**rapped, rapping**) слегкá уд|аря́ть, -áрить по + *d.*
■ *v.i.* (**rapped, rapping**) ст|учáть, -ýкнуть; **he ~ped on the door** он постучáл в дверь.

rapacious /rə'peɪʃəs/ *adj.* жáдный, ненасы́тный.

rape¹ /reɪp/ *n.* изнаси́лование.
■ *v.t.* наси́ловать, из-.

rape² /reɪp/ *n.* (*bot.*) рапс.

rapid /'ræpɪd/ *adj.* (**rapider, rapidest**) бы́стрый, скóрый.

rapidity /rə'pɪdɪtɪ/ *n.* быстротá, скóрость.

rapist /'reɪpɪst/ *n.* наси́льник.

rapport /ræ'pɔː(r)/ *n.* взаимопонимáние, контáкт.

rapture /'ræptʃə(r)/ *n.* востóрг.

rapturous /'ræptʃərəs/ *adj.* востóрженный.

rare¹ /reə(r)/ *adj.* (**rarer, rarest**) (*uncommon*) рéдкий.

rare² /reə(r)/ *adj.* (**rarer, rarest**) (*bloody*): **a ~ steak** бифштéкс с крóвью.

rarefied /'reərɪfaɪd/ *adj.* (*phys.*) разрежённый; (*fig.*) утончённый, изы́сканный.

rarely /'reəlɪ/ *adv.* рéдко, нечáсто, и́зредка.

raring /'reərɪŋ/ *adj.* (*coll.*): **he was ~ to go** емý не терпéлось приступи́ть к дéлу.

rarity /'reərɪtɪ/ *n.* (*uncommonness*) рéдкость; (*thing valued for this*) (большáя) рéдкость.

rascal /'rɑːsk(ə)l/ *n.* мошéнник, плут.

rash¹ /ræʃ/ *n.* сыпь.

rash² /ræʃ/ *adj.* опромéтчивый.

rasher /'ræʃə(r)/ *n.* лóмтик (бекóна).

rasp /rɑːsp/ *n.* (*file*) рáшпиль (*m.*), напи́льник; (*grating sound*) скрéжет.
■ *v.t.* (*scrape*) скрести́, скобли́ть, терéть (*all impf.*).
■ *v.i.* скрежетáть (*impf.*); **a ~ing voice** скрипýчий гóлос.
■ *with advs.*: **~ away, ~ off** *vv.t.* соск|áбливать, -обли́ть; **~ out** *v.t.* (*e.g. an order*) гáркнуть (*pf.*).

raspberry /'rɑːzbərɪ/ *n.* мали́на (*collect.*).

Rastafarian /ræstə'feərɪən/ *n.* (*relig.*) растафáри (*c.g. indecl.*).
■ *adj.* растафариáнский.

rat /ræt/ *n.* кры́са.
■ *cpd.* **~ race** *n.* бéшеная погóня за успéхом/богáтством.

rate /reɪt/ *n.*
1 (*proportion*) нóрма, размéр; **~ of exchange** курс обмéна; **birth ~** рождáемость.
2 (*speed*) скóрость; **we shall never get there at this ~** при таки́х тéмпах мы тудá никогдá не доберёмся.
3 (*price*) расцéнка, тари́ф.
4 (*Br., tax on property etc.*) мéстный налóг.
5 : **at any ~** (*in any case*) во вся́ком слýчае.
■ *v.t.* оцéн|ивать, -и́ть.
■ *cpd.* **~payer** *n.* (*Br.*) плати́льщик мéстных налóгов.

rather /'rɑːðə(r)/ *adv.*
1 (*by preference*): **I would ~ die than consent** я скорéе умрý, чем соглашýсь; **I'd ~ have coffee** я предпочёл бы кóфе; **I'd ~ not say** я лýчше промолчý.
2 (*somewhat*) довóльно, нéсколько; **the result was ~ surprising** результáт был довóльно неожи́данным; **it is ~ a pity** а жаль всё же; **the effect was ~ spoiled** эффéкт был смáзан/подпóрчен.

ratification /rætɪfɪ'keɪʃ(ə)n/ *n.* ратификáция.

ratify /'rætɪfaɪ/ *v.t.* ратифици́ровать (*impf., pf.*).

rating /'reɪtɪŋ/ *n.* рéйтинг.

ratio /'reɪʃɪəʊ/ *n.* (*pl.* **~s**) отношéние, соотношéние.

ration /'ræʃ(ə)n/ *n.* рацио́н, паёк.
■ *v.t.*: **they were ~ed to one loaf a week** их паёк своди́лся к одно́й буха́нке в неде́лю; **meat was severely ~ed** мя́со бы́ло стро́го нормиро́вано.
rational /'ræʃən(ə)l/ *adj.* разу́мный, рациона́льный.
rationale /ræʃə'nɑ:l/ *n.* основна́я причи́на.
rationalism /'ræʃənəlɪz(ə)m/ *n.* рационали́зм.
rationality /ræʃə'nælɪtɪ/ *n.* разу́мность, рациона́льность.
rationalize /'ræʃənəlaɪz/ *v.t.* (*give reasons for*) разу́мно объясн|я́ть, -и́ть; (*make more efficient*) рационализи́ровать (*impf., pf.*).
rattle /'ræt(ə)l/ *n.*
1 (*sound*) треск, гро́хот.
2 (*child's toy*) погрему́шка.
■ *v.t.*: **he ~d the money box** он встряхну́л копи́лку.
■ *v.i.*: **the hail ~d on the roof** град бараба́нил по кры́ше.
■ *cpd.* **~snake** *n.* грему́чая змея́.
ratty /'rætɪ/ *adj.* (**rattier, rattiest**) (*coll.*) (*Br., irritable*) злой, раздражи́тельный.
raucous /'rɔ:kəs/ *adj.* ре́зкий, хри́плый.
raunchy /'rɔ:ntʃɪ/ *adj.* (**raunchier, raunchiest**) распу́тный.
ravage /'rævɪdʒ/ *v.t.* опустош|а́ть, -и́ть.
rave /reɪv/ *n.* (*party*) весёлая вечери́нка.
■ *adj.*: **~ review** восто́рженный о́тзыв.
■ *v.i.* (*in delirium*) бре́дить (*impf.*); (*in delight*): **they ~d about the play** они́ бы́ли в восто́рге от пье́сы.
raven /'reɪv(ə)n/ *n.* во́рон.
■ *cpd.* **~-haired** *adj.* с волоса́ми цве́та во́ронова крыла́ (*or* чёрными как смоль).
ravenous /'rævənəs/ *adj.*: **I am ~** я го́лоден как волк.
ravine /rə'vi:n/ *n.* овра́г, лощи́на.
raving /'reɪvɪŋ/ *adj.* & *adv.* (*insane*): **a ~ lunatic** бу́йно поме́шанный; **you must be ~ mad** ты совсе́м спя́тил.
ravioli /rævɪ'əʊlɪ/ *n.* равио́л|и (*m. pl., g.* -ей).
ravishing /'rævɪʃɪŋ/ *adj.* восхити́тельный.
raw /rɔ:/ *adj.*
1 (*uncooked*) сыро́й.
2 (*unprocessed*) необрабо́танный; **~ data** необрабо́танные да́нные; **~ materials** сырьё.
3 (*inexperienced*) нео́пытный, зелёный.
4 (*of weather*) сыро́й.
5 (*harsh*): **he got a ~ deal** (*coll.*) с ним суро́во обошли́сь.
Rawlplug /'rɔ:lplʌg/ *n.* (*Br., propr.*) волоко́нная/пла́стиковая вста́вка для крепле́ния винто́в в ка́менной/кирпи́чной кла́дке.
ray /reɪ/ *n.* (*lit., fig.*) луч.
raze /reɪz/ *v.t.* разр|уша́ть, -у́шить до основа́ния.
razor /'reɪzə(r)/ *n.* бри́тва; **electric ~** электробри́тва.
■ *cpd.* **~ blade** *n.* ле́звие.
re /ri:/ *prep.* каса́тельно + *g.*
reach /ri:tʃ/ *n.*
1 (*extent of stretch*) разма́х рук, длина́ руки́; (*fig.*): **we are within easy ~ of London** от нас легко́ добра́ться до Ло́ндона; от нас до Ло́ндона руко́й пода́ть.
2 (*stretch of river*): **the upper ~es of the Thames** верхо́вья (*nt. pl.*) Те́мзы.
■ *v.t.* 1 (*fetch*) дотя́|гиваться, -ну́ться до + *g*; **I can just ~ the shelf** я е́ле-е́ле доста́ю (*or* могу́ дотяну́ться) до по́лки.
2 (*arrive at*) дост|ига́ть, -и́гнуть + *g.*; **your letter ~ed me only yesterday** ва́ше письмо́ дошло́ до меня́ то́лько вчера́; **~ agreement** прийти́ (*pf.*) к соглаше́нию.
■ *v.i.* 1 (*stretch out hand*) тяну́ться, по- руко́й; **he ~ed for his rifle** он потяну́лся к винто́вке.
2 (*extend*) простира́ться, тяну́ться (*both impf.*).
■ *with advs.*: **~ down** *v.i.*: **he ~ed down and picked up the coin** он нагну́лся и по́днял моне́ту; **~ up** *v.i.* протяну́ть (*pf.*) ру́ку вверх.
react /rɪ'ækt/ *v.i.* реаги́ровать, от-/про-.
reaction /rɪ'ækʃ(ə)n/ *n.* реа́кция.
reactionary /rɪ'ækʃənərɪ/ *n.* реакционе́р.
■ *adj.* реакцио́нный.
reactor /rɪ'æktə(r)/ *n.* (*tech.*) реа́ктор.
read /ri:d/ *v.t.* (*past and p.p.* **read** /red/)
1 (*peruse*) чита́ть, про- *or* проче́сть; **have you ~ this book?** вы чита́ли э́ту кни́гу?; **can you ~ music?** вы уме́ете игра́ть по но́там?
2 (*discern*): **he ~ my thoughts** он чита́л мои́ мы́сли.
3 (*Br., study*) изуча́ть (*impf.*); **he is ~ing law** он у́чится на юриди́ческом факульте́те.
4 (*examine*): **~ a meter** сн|има́ть, -ять показа́ния счётчика.
■ *v.i.* (*past and p.p.* **read** /red/): **he can neither ~ nor write** он не уме́ет ни чита́ть, ни писа́ть.
■ *with advs.*: **~ out** *v.t.* прочи́т|ывать, -а́ть; огла|ша́ть, -си́ть; **~ through** *v.t.* прочи́т|ывать, -а́ть; **~ up on** *v.i.* мно́го чита́ть (*impf.*); **he ~ up on the subject** он подчита́л ко́е-что по э́тому предме́ту.
readable /'ri:dəb(ə)l/ *adj.*
1 (*legible*) разбо́рчивый.
2 (*enjoyable*) (*coll.*) интере́сный.
reader /'ri:də(r)/ *n.* чита́тель (*fem.* -ница).
readily /'redɪlɪ/ *adv.* (*willingly*) охо́тно; (*without difficulty*) легко́, без труда́.
reading /'ri:dɪŋ/ *n.*
1 (*pursuit*) чте́ние.
2 (*interpretation*) толкова́ние.
3 (*of instrument*) показа́ние.
■ *cpd.* **~ room** *n.* чита́льный зал.
readjust /ri:ə'dʒʌst/ *v.t.* попр|авля́ть, -а́вить.
■ *v.i.*: **after the war he found it hard to ~** по́сле войны́ ему́ бы́ло тру́дно приспосо́биться к ми́рной жи́зни.
ready /'redɪ/ *adj.* (**readier, readiest**) (*prepared*) гото́вый (*к чему*); пригото́вленный, подгото́вленный; **I'm just getting ~** я почти́ гото́в; **she got the children ~ for school** она́ собрала́ дете́й в шко́лу; (*willing*) гото́вый; **I am ~ to admit I was wrong** гото́в призна́ть, что я был непра́в.
■ *adv.*: **they sell meat ~ cooked** там продаётся мясна́я кулинари́я.

r

■ *cpds.* **~-made** *adj.* гото́вый; **~-to-wear** *adj.* гото́вый.

real /ri:l/ *adj.* (*actual*) настоя́щий; реа́льный; **in ~ life** в жи́зни; **~ silver** настоя́щее серебро́.
■ *cpds.* **~ estate** *n.* недви́жимость; **~ time** *adj.* (*comput.*) (рабо́тающий/происходя́щий) в режи́ме реа́льного вре́мени.

realign /ri:ə'laɪn/ *v.t.* перестр|а́ивать, -о́ить.

realism /'ri:əlɪz(ə)m/ *n.* реали́зм.

realist /'rɪəlɪst/ *n.* реали́ст (*fem.* -ка).

realistic /rɪə'lɪstɪk/ *adj.* реалисти́чный, практи́чный.

reality /rɪ'ælɪtɪ/ *n.* реа́льность, действи́тельность.
■ *cpd.* **~ TV** *n.* реа́лити-ТВ (*nt. indecl.*).

realization /rɪəlaɪ'zeɪʃ(ə)n/ *n.* осозна́ние.

realize /'rɪəlaɪz/ *v.t.*
1 (*be aware of*) осозн|ава́ть, -а́ть; (*grasp mentally*) сообра|жа́ть, -зи́ть; **he ~d his mistake at once** он сра́зу же осозна́л свою́ оши́бку; **do you ~ what you have done?** вы понима́ете, что вы сде́лали?; **I didn't ~ you wanted it** до меня́ не дошло́, что э́то вам ну́жно.
2 (*convert into fact*) осуществ|ля́ть, -и́ть; **I will help you to ~ your ambition** я помогу́ вам осуществи́ть ва́ши стремле́ния.

really /'rɪəlɪ/ *adv.* действи́тельно; в/на са́мом де́ле; **do you ~ mean it?** вы серьёзно?; **I am ~ sorry for you** мне вас и́скренне жаль; **~?** (*expr. surprise*) серьёзно?; (*acknowledging information*) да?, пра́вда?; **~!** (*expr. indignation*) ну, зна́ете!; **not ~** не о́чень, не осо́бенно.

realm /relm/ *n.* (*fig.*) сфе́ра, о́бласть, мир.

reap /ri:p/ *v.t.* & *i.* жать, с-.

reappear /ri:ə'pɪə(r)/ *v.i.* сно́ва появ|ля́ться, -и́ться.

reappraise /ri:ə'preɪz/ *v.t.* пересм|а́тривать, -отре́ть.

rear[1] /rɪə(r)/ *n.* за́дняя ча́сть, сторона́.
■ *adj.*: **~ entrance** чёрный ход; **~ wheel** за́днее колесо́.
■ *cpd.* **~-view mirror** *n.* зе́ркало за́днего ви́да.

rear[2] /rɪə(r)/ *v.t.* (*bring up*) расти́ть, вы́-; (*breed*) развод|и́ть, -ести́.
■ *v.i.* (*also* **~ up**) ста|нови́ться, -ть на дыбы́; **the horse ~ed in terror** ло́шадь (в)стала́ на дыбы́ от испу́га.

rearm /ri:'ɑ:m/ *v.t.* & *i.* перевооруж|а́ть(ся), -и́ть(ся).

rearmament /ri:'ɑ:məmənt/ *n.* перевооруже́ние.

rearrange /ri:ə'reɪndʒ/ *v.t.* (*objects*) перест|авля́ть, -а́вить; (*a meeting*) передв|ига́ть, -и́нуть вре́мя + *g.*

rearrangement /ri:ə'reɪndʒmənt/ *n.* перестано́вка.

reason /'ri:z(ə)n/ *n.*
1 (*cause, ground*) причи́на; **with ~** обосно́ванно.
2 (*good sense*) благоразу́мие; **he will not listen to ~** он не прислу́шивается к го́лосу ра́зума.
■ *v.i.*: **it is useless to ~ with him** его́ бесполе́зно убежда́ть; ло́гика на него́ не де́йствует.

reasonable /'ri:zənəb(ə)l/ *adj.*
1 (*sensible*) (благо)разу́мный.
2 (*fairly good*) дово́льно хоро́ший, неплохо́й.

reasoning /'ri:zənɪŋ/ *n.* рассужде́ние.

reassert /ri:ə'sə:t/ *v.t.* сно́ва подтвер|жда́ть, -ди́ть.

reassess /ri:ə'ses/ *v.t.* переоце́н|ивать, -и́ть.

reassessment /ri:ə'sesmənt/ *n.* переоце́нка.

reassurance /ri:ə'ʃʊərəns/ *n.* (повто́рное) завере́ние, подтвержде́ние.

reassur|e /ri:ə'ʃɔ:(r)/ *v.t.* успок|а́ивать, -о́ить; подбодр|я́ть, -и́ть; **his words were most ~ing** его́ слова́ звуча́ли са́мым ободря́ющим о́бразом.

rebate /'ri:beɪt/ *n.* возвра́т перепла́ченной су́ммы.

rebel[1] /'reb(ə)l/ *n.* повста́нец.

rebel[2] /rɪ'bel/ *v.i.* (**rebelled, rebelling**) восст|ава́ть, -а́ть.

rebellion /rɪ'beljən/ *n.* восста́ние, мяте́ж, бунт.

rebellious /rɪ'beljəs/ *adj.* (*in revolt*) восста́вший, мяте́жный; (*disobedient*) непоко́рный.

reboot /ri:'bu:t/ *v.t.* (*comput.*) перезагру|жа́ть, -зи́ть.

rebound[1] /rɪ'baʊnd/ *n.* отско́к; **on the ~** на отско́ке; (*fig.*): **he married her on the ~** он жени́лся на ней по́сле разочарова́ния в любви́ к друго́й.

rebound[2] /rɪ'baʊnd/ *v.i.* отск|а́кивать, -очи́ть.

rebuff /rɪ'bʌf/ *n.* отпо́р, ре́зкий отка́з.
■ *v.t.* дава́ть, дать отпо́р + *d.*; ре́зко отклон|я́ть, -и́ть; (*mil.*): **the enemy's attack was ~ed** ата́ка неприя́теля была́ отражена́.

rebuild /ri:'bɪld/ *v.t.* сно́ва стро́ить, по-.

rebuke /rɪ'bju:k/ *n.* упрёк, уко́р.
■ *v.t.* упрек|а́ть, -ну́ть; укоря́ть (*impf.*).

rebut /rɪ'bʌt/ *v.t.* (**rebutted, rebutting**) опров|ерга́ть, -е́ргнуть.

rebuttal /rɪ'bʌtəl/ *n.* опроверже́ние.

recalcitrant /rɪ'kælsɪtrənt/ *adj.* непоко́рный.

recall[1] /'ri:kɔ:l/ *n.* воспомина́ние.

recall[2] /rɪ'kɔ:l/ *v.t.*
1 (*summon back*) от|зыва́ть, -озва́ть.
2 (*to mind*) нап|омина́ть, -о́мнить.

recant /rɪ'kænt/ *v.t.* & *i.* публи́чно ка́яться, по- (*в чём*); отр|ека́ться, -е́чься (*от чего*).

recap /'ri:kæp/ *n.* повторе́ние.
■ *v.t.* & *i.* (**recapped, recapping**) = **recapitulate**

recapitulate /ri:kə'pɪtjʊleɪt/ *v.t.* повтор|я́ть, -и́ть.

recapture /ri:'kæptʃə(r)/ *v.t.* взять (*pf.*) обра́тно; (*fig.*) восстан|а́вливать, -ови́ть в па́мяти.

recce /'rekɪ/ (*Br., coll.*) = **reconnaissance**

reced|e /rɪ'si:d/ *v.i.*
1 (*move back*) отступ|а́ть, -и́ть; (*move away*) удал|я́ться, -и́ться; **the tide was ~ing** вода́ спада́ла; **~ing hair** реде́ющие во́лосы.
2 (*diminish*) ум|еньша́ться, -е́ньшиться.

receipt /rɪ'si:t/ *n.*

[1] (*receiving*) получе́ние.
[2] (*pl., money received*) де́нежные поступле́ния, прихо́д.
[3] (*written acknowledgement*) распи́ска, квита́нция.

receive /rɪ'si:v/ *v.t.*
[1] (*get, be given*) получ|а́ть, -и́ть; **he ~s stolen goods** (*Br.*) он укрыва́ет кра́деное.
[2] (*admit*) прин|има́ть, -я́ть; (*greet*) прин|има́ть, -я́ть; **how was your speech ~d?** как бы́ло встре́чено ва́ше выступле́ние?

receiver /rɪ'si:və(r)/ *n.*
[1] **(telephone ~)** (телефо́нная) тру́бка.
[2] **(radio ~)** (радио)приёмник.

recent /'ri:s(ə)nt/ *adj.*
[1] (*occurring lately*) неда́вний.
[2] (*modern*) совреме́нный.

recently /'ri:səntlɪ/ *adv.* неда́вно, на дня́х, за после́днее вре́мя; **until quite ~** ещё совсе́м неда́вно.

receptacle /rɪ'septək(ə)l/ *n.* вмести́лище.

reception /rɪ'sepʃ(ə)n/ *n.*
[1] (*of guests etc.*) приём; **~ desk** (*in hotel*) регистра́ция; (*in hospital*) регистрату́ра.
[2] (*greeting*) встре́ча, приём; **he was given a great ~** ему́ устро́или великоле́пный приём.
[3] (*of radio signals*) приём.

receptionist /rɪ'sepʃənɪst/ *n.* (*in hotel, hospital*) регистра́тор, дежу́рный; (*in a business firm*) секрета́рь (*m.*) по приёму посети́телей.

receptive /rɪ'septɪv/ *adj.* восприи́мчивый.

recess /rɪ'ses/ *n.*
[1] (*vacation*) переры́в; (*US, between classes*) переме́на.
[2] (*niche*) ни́ша, алько́в.

recession /rɪ'seʃ(ə)n/ *n.* спад.

recharge /ri:'tʃɑ:dʒ/ *v.t.* перезаря|жа́ть, -ди́ть.

recipe /'resɪpɪ/ *n.* (*lit., fig.*) реце́пт.

recipient /rɪ'sɪpɪənt/ *n.* получа́тель (*fem.* -ница).

reciprocal /rɪ'sɪprək(ə)l/ *adj.* взаи́мный.

reciprocate /rɪ'sɪprəkeɪt/ *v.t.* отв|еча́ть, -е́тить взаи́мностью.
■ *v.i.* отпла́|чивать, -ти́ть.

reciprocity /resɪ'prɒsɪtɪ/ *n.* взаи́мность; взаимоде́йствие; обме́н.

recital /rɪ'saɪt(ə)l/ *n.* изложе́ние.

recite /rɪ'saɪt/ *v.t.* деклами́ровать, про-.

reckless /'reklɪs/ *adj.* безрассу́дный; **he drove ~ly** он неосторо́жно вёл маши́ну.

reckon /'rekən/ *v.t.*
[1] (*calculate*) счита́ть, по-.
[2] (*think*) счита́ть (*impf.*).
■ *v.i.* [1] (*count*) счита́ть (*impf.*); **he is a man to be ~ed with** с таки́м челове́ком, как он, ну́жно счита́ться.
[2] (*rely*) рассчи́тывать (*impf.*) (*на кого/что*); **he ~ed on making a clear profit** он рассчи́тывал на чи́стую при́быль.

reckoning /'rekənɪŋ/ *n.* счёт, вычисле́ние.

reclaim /rɪ'kleɪm/ *v.t.*
[1] (*bring under cultivation*) осв|а́ивать, -о́ить.
[2] (*demand return of*) тре́бовать, по- обра́тно.

reclamation /reklə'meɪʃ(ə)n/ *n.* освое́ние.

recline /rɪ'klaɪn/ *v.i.* (полу)лежа́ть (*impf.*); **reclining nude** лежа́щая обнажённая.

recluse /rɪ'klu:s/ *n.* затво́рник, отше́льник.

recognition /rekəg'nɪʃ(ə)n/ *n.*
[1] (*knowing again*) опознава́ние, узнава́ние; (*comput.*) распознава́ние.
[2] (*acknowledgement*) призна́ние.

recognizable /'rekəgnaɪzəb(ə)l/ *adj.* опознава́емый.

recognize /'rekəgnaɪz/ *v.t.*
[1] (*know again*) узн|ава́ть, -а́ть.
[2] (*acknowledge*) призн|ава́ть, -а́ть; **he was ~d as the lawful heir** он был при́знан зако́нным насле́дником.

recoil /'ri:kɔɪl/ *v.i.* отпря́нуть (*pf.*).

recollect /rekə'lekt/ *v.t.* всп|омина́ть, -о́мнить.

recollection /rekə'lekʃ(ə)n/ *n.* па́мять.

recommend /rekə'mend/ *v.t.*
[1] (*speak well of*) рекомендова́ть (*impf., pf.*), от-/по- (*pf.*).
[2] (*advise*) рекомендова́ть, по- + *d.*

recommendation /rekəmen'deɪʃ(ə)n/ *n.* рекоменда́ция.

recompense /'rekəmpens/ *n.* компенса́ция.

reconcile /'rekənsaɪl/ *v.t.*
[1] (*make friendly*) мири́ть, по-.
[2] (*make compatible*) совме|ща́ть, -сти́ть.
[3] (*resign*): **~ o.s.** смир|я́ться, -и́ться (**to:** с + *i.*).

reconciliation /rekənsɪlɪ'eɪʃ(ə)n/ *n.* примире́ние.

reconnaissance /rɪ'kɒnɪs(ə)ns/ *n.* разве́дка, рекогносциро́вка.

reconnoitre /rekə'nɔɪtə(r)/ (*US* **reconnoiter**) *v.t. & i.* разве́дывать (*impf.*).

reconsider /ri:kən'sɪdə(r)/ *v.t.* пересм|а́тривать, -отре́ть.
■ *v.i.* переду́мать (*pf.*).

reconstitute /ri:'kɒnstɪtju:t/ *v.t.* воспроизв|оди́ть, -ести́.

reconstruct /ri:kən'strʌkt/ *v.t.* восстан|а́вливать, -ови́ть; воссозд|ава́ть, -а́ть; (*fig.*): **the police ~ed the crime** поли́ция воспроизвела́ карти́ну преступле́ния.

reconstruction /ri:kən'strʌkʃ(ə)n/ *n.* восстановле́ние, воссозда́ние; (*of acts etc.*) воспроизведе́ние, воссозда́ние.

record[1] /'rekɔ:d/ *n.*
[1] (*written note, document*) за́пись, учёт; **the teacher keeps a ~ of attendance** учи́тель ведёт учёт посеща́емости; **weather ~s** да́нные наблюде́ний за пого́дными явле́ниями.
[2] (*state of being recorded, esp. as evidence*) за́пись; **this is off the ~** э́то не должно́ быть пре́дано огла́ске.
[3] (*past conduct, achievement*) про́шлое; **this firm has a bad ~ for strikes** э́та фи́рма изве́стна многочи́сленными забасто́вками; **the defendant had a (criminal) ~** у обвиня́емого ра́нее име́лись суди́мости.
[4] (*sound recording*) (грам)пласти́нка.
[5] (*best performance*) реко́рд; **world ~** мирово́й реко́рд; (*attr.*) реко́рдный, небыва́лый; **cars have had ~ sales** про́дано реко́рдное коли́чество маши́н.
■ *cpds.* **~-breaking** *adj.* реко́рдный; **~ holder** *n.* рекордсме́н (*fem.* -ка); **~ player** *n.* прои́грыватель (*m.*).

record² /rɪˈkɔːd/ *v.t.*
[1] (*set down in writing*; *aslo fig.*) запи́с|ывать, -а́ть.
[2] (*on tape, film etc.*) запи́с|ывать, -а́ть (на плёнку).
[3] (*of instrument*: *register*) регистри́ровать, за-.
recorder /rɪˈkɔːdə(r)/ *n.* (*mus.*) (англи́йская) фле́йта.
recording /rɪˈkɔːdɪŋ/ *n.* за́пись.
recount¹ /riːˈkaʊnt/ *n.* (*second count*) пересчёт.
■ *v.t.* пересчи́т|ывать, -а́ть.
recount² /rɪˈkaʊnt/ *v.t.* (*narrate*) расска́з|ывать, -а́ть.
recoup /rɪˈkuːp/ *v.t.* : **~ one's losses** возвраща́ть, верну́ть поте́рянное.
recourse /rɪˈkɔːs/ *n.*: **have ~ to** приб|ега́ть, -е́гнуть к + *d.*
recover /rɪˈkʌvə(r)/ *v.t.* (*regain*) получ|а́ть, -и́ть обра́тно; верну́ть (*pf.*); **he tried to ~ his losses** он пыта́лся верну́ть поте́рянное; (*win back*) отвоё|вывать, -а́ть.
■ *v.i.* попр|авля́ться, -а́виться; **we must help the country to ~** мы должны́ помо́чь стране́ сно́ва встать на́ ноги.
recovery /rɪˈkʌvərɪ/ *n.*
[1] (*regaining possession*) возвра́т; возмеще́ние; **the ~ of your money will take time** пройдёт вре́мя, пре́жде чем вы полу́чите свои́ де́ньги обра́тно.
[2] (*revival*) выздоровле́ние; **he made a rapid ~** он бы́стро popра́вился.
[3] (*rehabilitation*) восстановле́ние; **~ vehicle** авари́йный автомоби́ль.
recreate /riːkrɪˈeɪt/ *v.t.* вновь созд|ава́ть, -а́ть.
recreation /rekrɪˈeɪʃ(ə)n/ *n.* о́тдых; развлече́ние.
recrimination /rɪkrɪmɪˈneɪʃ(ə)n/ *n.* встре́чное обвине́ние.
recruit /rɪˈkruːt/ *n.* (*mil.*) новобра́нец.
■ *v.t.* (*enlist*) вербова́ть, за-; наб|ира́ть, -ра́ть.
recruitment /rɪˈkruːtmənt/ *n.* вербо́вка.
rectangle /ˈrektæŋg(ə)l/ *n.* прямоуго́льник.
rectangular /rekˈtæŋgʊlə(r)/ *adj.* прямоуго́льный.
rectify /ˈrektɪfaɪ/ *v.t.* испр|авля́ть, -а́вить.
rector /ˈrektə(r)/ *n.* (*Br.*) (*clergyman*) ≈ прихо́дский свяще́нник.
rectory /ˈrektərɪ/ *n.* (*Br.*) дом прихо́дского свяще́нника.
rectum /ˈrektəm/ *n.* (*pl.* **rectums** *or* **recta**) пряма́я кишка́.
recuperate /rɪˈkuːpəreɪt/ *v.i.* попр|авля́ться, -а́виться.
recuperation /rɪkuːpəˈreɪʃ(ə)n/ *n.* выздоровле́ние.
recur /rɪˈkɜː(r)/ *v.i.* (**recurred, recurring**) повтор|я́ться, -и́ться; **a ~ring headache** хрони́ческие головны́е бо́ли (*f. pl.*).
recurrence /rɪˈkʌrəns/ *n.* повторе́ние.
recurrent /rɪˈkʌrənt/ *adj.* повторя́ющийся.
recycle /riːˈsaɪk(ə)l/ *v.t.* перераб|а́тывать, -о́тать.
recycling /riːˈsaɪklɪŋ/ *n.* повто́рное испо́льзование, перерабо́тка.
red /red/ *n.*
[1] кра́сный цвет; **~ doesn't suit her** кра́сное ей не идёт; **she was dressed in ~** она́ была́ оде́та в кра́сное.
[2] (*debit side of account*) долг, задо́лженность; **in the ~** в долга́х.
■ *adj.* (**redder, reddest**) кра́сный; а́лый; **she went ~ in the face** она́ покрасне́ла; **R~ Crescent** Кра́сный Полуме́сяц; **R~ Cross** Кра́сный Крест; **~-light district** кварта́л публи́чных домо́в; **~ tape** (*fig.*) (канцеля́рская) волоки́та.
■ *cpds.* **~currant** *n.* кра́сная сморо́дина; **~-handed** *adj.*: **he was caught ~-handed** его́ пойма́ли на ме́сте преступле́ния (*or* с поли́чным); **~head** *n.* ры́жий (*человек*); **~-headed** *adj.* ры́жий; **~-hot** *adj.* раскалённый докрасна́.
redden /ˈred(ə)n/ *v.t.* окра́|шивать, -сить в кра́сный цвет.
■ *v.i.* красне́ть, по-.
reddish /ˈredɪʃ/ *adj.* краснова́тый.
redecorate /riːˈdekəreɪt/ *v.t.* отде́л|ывать, -ать; ремонти́ровать, от-.
redeem /rɪˈdiːm/ *v.t.*
[1] (*get back, recover*) выкупа́ть, вы́купить.
[2] (*relig.*): **Christ came to ~ sinners** Христо́с пришёл искупи́ть грехи́ люде́й.
[3] (*compensate*): **he has one ~ing feature** у него́ есть одно́ положи́тельное ка́чество.
redemption /rɪˈdempʃ(ə)n/ *n.* (*relig.*) искупле́ние; **past ~** без наде́жды на спасе́ние.
redeploy /riːdɪˈplɔɪ/ *v.t.* & *i.* (*mil.*) передислоци́ровать(ся) (*impf.*, *pf.*).
redeployment /riːdɪˈplɔɪmənt/ *n.* передислока́ция; перераспределе́ние.
redevelop /riːdɪˈveləp/ *v.t.* перестр|а́ивать, -о́ить.
redial /riːˈdaɪ(ə)l/ *v.t.* & *i.* повто́рно наб|ира́ть, -ра́ть (но́мер).
rediscover /riːdɪˈskʌvə(r)/ *v.t.* откр|ыва́ть, -ы́ть за́ново.
redo /riːˈduː/ *v.t.* переде́л|ывать, -ать.
redouble /riːˈdʌb(ə)l/ *v.t.* & *i.* удв|а́ивать(ся), -о́ить(ся); **he ~d his efforts** он удво́ил свои́ уси́лия.
redoubtable /rɪˈdaʊtəb(ə)l/ *adj.* гро́зный; устраша́ющий.
redress /rɪˈdres/ *n.* возмеще́ние; **I shall seek ~** я бу́ду добива́ться компенса́ции.
■ *v.t.* возме|ща́ть, -сти́ть; **their victory ~ed the balance of forces** их побе́да восстанови́ла равнове́сие сил.
reduce /rɪˈdjuːs/ *v.t.*
[1] (*make less or smaller*) ум|еньша́ть, -е́ньшить; сокра|ща́ть, -ти́ть; (*lower*) сн|ижа́ть, -и́зить; сб|авля́ть, -а́вить; **all prices are ~d** все це́ны сни́жены.
[2] (*bring, compel*) дов|оди́ть, -ести́ (*до чего*); вынужда́ть, вы́нудить; **the film ~d her to tears** фильм растро́гал её до слёз; **the family was ~d to begging** семья́ была́ обречена́ на нищету́.
reduction /rɪˈdʌkʃ(ə)n/ *n.* сокраще́ние; сниже́ние; **a ~ in numbers** коли́чественное сокраще́ние; **price ~s** сниже́ние цен.
redundancy /rɪˈdʌnd(ə)nsɪ/ *n.* (*Br.*) (*dismissal*) увольне́ние.
redundant /rɪˈdʌnd(ə)nt/ *adj.* (*superfluous*)

излишний; (*at work*): **many workers were made ~** (*Br.*) многих рабочих уволили.

reed /ri:d/ *n.*
1 (*bot.*) тростник, камыш.
2 (*mus.*) язычок.

reef /ri:f/ *n.* риф.

reek /ri:k/ *v.i.* вонять, про-; **his clothes ~ed of tobacco** от его одежды несло табаком.

reel[1] /ri:l/ *n.* (*winding device*) катушка; рулон.
■ *with advs.*: **the fisherman ~ed in the line** рыбак смотал удочку; **the guide ~ed off a lot of dates** гид выпалил целый ряд исторических дат.

reel[2] /ri:l/ *v.i.* кружиться (*impf.*); **he ~ed under the blow** он зашатался от удара.

re-elect /ri:ɪ'lekt/ *v.t.* переизб|ирать, -рать.

re-emerge /ri:ɪ'mə:dʒ/ *v.i.* вновь появ|ляться, -иться.

re-examine /ri:ɪg'zæmɪn/ *v.t.* вновь рассм|атривать, -отреть.

ref /ref/ (*coll.*) = **referee 2**

refectory /rɪ'fektərɪ/ *n.* (*in monastery*) трапезная; (*in school, college*) столовая.

refer /rɪ'fə:(r)/ *v.t.* (**referred, referring**) (*pass on, direct*) от|сылать, -ослать; **the clerk ~red me to the manager** служащий отослал меня к начальнику.
■ *v.i.* (**referred, referring**)
1 (*have recourse*) спр|авляться, -авиться; **he ~red to the dictionary** он справился в словаре; **the speaker ~red to his notes** оратор заглянул в конспект.
2 (*allude*): **~ to** (*mention*) упом|инать, -януть; (*cite*) ссылаться, сослаться на + *a.*

referee /refə'ri:/ *n.*
1 (*arbitrator*) арбитр.
2 (*at games*) судья (*m.*); рефери (*m. indecl.*).
3 (*person supplying testimonial*) поручитель (*m.*).
■ *v.t.* & *i.* (**referees, refereed**): **he agreed to ~ the match** он согласился судить матч.

reference /'refərəns/ *n.*
1 (*referring for decision etc.*) отсылка; **he acted without ~ to his superiors** он действовал без согласования с начальством.
2 (*relation*) отношение; **with ~ to your letter** в связи с вашим письмом.
3 (*allusion*) упоминание, ссылка; **the book contains many ~s to the Queen** в книге часто упоминается королева.
4 (*in text*) ссылка, сноска.
5 (*referring for information*) справка; **~ book** справочник.
6 (*testimonial*) отзыв, рекомендация, характеристика; (*person supplying ~*) поручитель (*m.*).

referend|um /refə'rendəm/ *n.* (*pl.* **~ums** *or* **~a**) референдум.

referral /rɪ'fə:r(ə)l/ *n.* направление.

refill[1] /'ri:fɪl/ *n.* (*for pen etc.*) запасной стержень.

refill[2] /ri:'fɪl/ *v.t.* нап|олнять, -олнить вновь.

refine /rɪ'faɪn/ *v.t.*
1 (*purify*) оч|ищать, -истить.
2 (*make more cultured*) совершенствовать, у-; **~d manners** утончённые/изысканные манеры.

refinement /rɪ'faɪnmənt/ *n.*
1 (*good manners*) благовоспитанность.
2 (*improving change, addition*) улучшение, усовершенствование.

refinery /rɪ'faɪnərɪ/ *n.* (*oil*) нефтеочистительный завод.

refit[1] /'ri:fɪt/ *n.* ремонт, переоборудование.

refit[2] /ri:'fɪt/ *v.t.* чинить, по-; переоборудовать (*impf.*, *pf.*); ремонтировать, от-.

reflect /rɪ'flekt/ *v.t.* отра|жать, -зить.
■ *v.i.* 1 (*produce a reflection*) отра|жаться, -зиться; (*fig., bring discredit*): **your behaviour** (*Br.*), **behavior** (*US*) **~s on us all** ваше поведение ложится пятном на нас всех.
2 (*consider*) задуматься (*pf.*) (над + *i.*); **I ~ed (on/upon) how fortunate I had been** я подумал о том, как мне повезло.

reflection /rɪ'flekʃ(ə)n/ *n.*
1 (*of light, heat etc.*) отражение.
2 (*consideration*) размышление; **on ~, I may have been wrong** поразмыслив я решил, что, возможно, (я) был неправ.

reflex /'ri:fleks/ *n.* (*also* **~ action**) рефлекс.

reflexive /rɪ'fleksɪv/ *adj.* возвратный.

reflexologist /ri:flek'sɒlədʒɪst/ *n.* рефлексотерапевт.

reflexology /ri:flek'sɒlədʒɪ/ *n.* (*med.*) рефлексология.

reform /rɪ'fɔ:m/ *n.* реформа.
■ *v.t.* (*a system*) ул|учшать, -учшить; реформировать (*impf.*, *pf.*); (*a person*) перевоспит|ывать, -ать; испр|авлять, -авить.
■ *v.i.* испр|авляться, -авиться.

reformat /ri:'fɔ:mæt/ *v.t.* (*comput.*) форматировать, от- заново.

Reformation /refə'meɪʃ(ə)n/ *n.* Реформация.

reformer /rɪ'fɔ:mə(r)/ *n.* реформатор.

reformist /rɪ'fɔ:mɪst/ *n.* реформист.

refraction /rɪ'frækʃ(ə)n/ *n.* преломление; рефракция.

refrain[1] /rɪ'freɪn/ *n.* припев.

refrain[2] /rɪ'freɪn/ *v.i.* сдерж|иваться, -аться; **I could hardly ~ from laughing** я еле сдерживался от смеха.

refresh /rɪ'freʃ/ *v.t.* освеж|ать, -ить; **let me ~ your memory** позвольте напомнить вам.

refresher /rɪ'freʃə(r)/ *n.* (*also* **~ course**) курс переподготовки.

refreshing /rɪ'freʃɪŋ/ *adj.* освежающий.

refreshment /rɪ'freʃmənt/ *n.* еда; питьё; **~s are served on the train** в поезде можно перекусить.

refrigerate /rɪ'frɪdʒəreɪt/ *v.t.* замор|аживать, -озить.

refrigeration /rɪfrɪdʒə'reɪʃ(ə)n/ *n.* замораживание.

refrigerator /rɪ'frɪdʒəreɪtə(r)/ *n.* холодильник.

refuel /ri:'fju:əl/ *v.i.* запр|авляться, -авиться.

refuge /'refju:dʒ/ *n.* убежище; пристанище; **the cat took ~ beneath the table** кот спрятался под столом.

refugee /refjʊ'dʒi:/ *n.* беженец (*fem.* -ка); **~ camp** лагерь (*m.*) беженцев.

refund[1] /'ri:fʌnd/ *n.* возмещение убытков.

refund[2] /rɪ'fʌnd/ *v.t.* возме|щать, -стить (*что*

r

кому).

refurbish /ri:ˈfɜ:bɪʃ/ *v.t.* отде́л|ывать, -ать.

refurbishment /ri:ˈfɜ:bɪʃmənt/ *n.* (капита́льный) ремо́нт.

refusal /rɪˈfju:z(ə)l/ *n.* отка́з.

refuse[1] /ˈrefju:s/ *n.* му́сор; **~ collection** убо́рка му́сора.

refuse[2] /rɪˈfju:z/ *v.t.* & *i.* (*decline to give*) отка́з|ывать, -а́ть (*кому в чём*); (*reject*) отв|ерга́ть, -е́ргнуть; (*decline sth. offered*) отка́з|ываться, -а́ться от + *g.*

refute /rɪˈfju:t/ *v.t.* опров|ерга́ть, -е́ргнуть.

regain /rɪˈgeɪn/ *v.t.* получ|а́ть, -и́ть обра́тно; **he never ~ed consciousness** он так и не пришёл в созна́ние.

regal /ˈri:g(ə)l/ *adj.* короле́вский.

regale /rɪˈgeɪl/ *v.t.* уго|ща́ть, -сти́ть; по́тчевать (*impf.*).

regard /rɪˈgɑ:d/ *n.*

1 (*respect*) отноше́ние; **in this ~** в э́том отноше́нии; **in, with ~ to your request** что каса́ется ва́шей про́сьбы.

2 (*consideration*) внима́ние, забо́та; **he paid no ~ to her feelings** он не счита́лся с её чу́вствами.

3 (*esteem*) уваже́ние (к + *d.*); **he holds your opinion in high ~** он о́чень высоко́ це́нит ва́ше мне́ние.

4 (*pl., greetings*) приве́т; **give him my warmest ~s** переда́йте ему́ от меня́ серде́чный приве́т.

■ *v.t.* 1 (*consider*) расце́н|ивать, -и́ть; сч|ита́ть, -есть; **he was ~ed as a hero** его́ счита́ли геро́ем.

2 (*concern*): **as ~s, ~ing** относи́тельно + *g.*; что каса́ется + *g.*; насчёт + *g.*

3 (*look at*) разгля́д|ывать, -е́ть.

regardless /rɪˈgɑ:dlɪs/ *adj.* невнима́тельный (к + *d.*); **~ of expense** не счита́ясь с расхо́дами.

regatta /rɪˈgætə/ *n.* рега́та.

regenerate /rɪˈdʒenəreɪt/ *v.t.* & *i.* возро|жда́ть(ся), -ди́ть(ся).

regent /ˈri:dʒ(ə)nt/ *n.* ре́гент.

reggae /ˈregeɪ/ *n.* ре́гги (*m. indecl.*).

regime /reɪˈʒi:m/ *n.* режи́м, строй; **under the old ~** при ста́ром режи́ме.

regiment /ˈredʒɪmənt/ *n.* полк.

regimental /redʒɪˈment(ə)l/ *adj.* полково́й.

region /ˈri:dʒ(ə)n/ *n.* райо́н, о́бласть; регио́н; **in the ~ of £5,000** приблизи́тельно 5000 фу́нтов.

regional /ˈri:dʒənəl/ *adj.* райо́нный, областно́й; региона́льный.

register /ˈredʒɪstə(r)/ *n.* (*record, list*) рее́стр; за́пись; (*in school*) журна́л.

■ *v.t.* 1 (*enter on official record*) регистри́ровать, за-; оф|ормля́ть, -о́рмить; **~ed letter** заказно́е письмо́.

2 (*of an instrument: record*) пока́з|ывать, -а́ть; отм|еча́ть, -е́тить.

3 (*express*) выража́ть, вы́разить.

■ *v.i.* (*record one's name*) регистри́роваться, за-.

registrar /redʒɪsˈtrɑ:(r)/ *n.* (*keeper of records*) регистра́тор; (*Br., in hospital*) врач, проходя́щий пра́ктику по специа́льности.

registration /redʒɪˈstreɪʃ(ə)n/ *n.* регистра́ция; **~ number of a car** (*Br.*) (регистрацио́нный) но́мер маши́ны.

registry /ˈredʒɪstrɪ/ *n.* регистрату́ра; **~ office** (*Br.*): **they were married at a ~** они расписа́лись в за́гсе; они́ зарегистри́ровались.

regress /rɪˈgres/ *v.i.* дви́гаться (*impf.*) в обра́тном направле́нии, регресси́ровать (*impf.*).

regret /rɪˈgret/ *n.* сожале́ние; **I found to my ~ that I was late** я обнаружи́л, к своему́ сожале́нию, что опозда́л; **I have no ~s** я ни о чём не жале́ю.

■ *v.t.* (**regretted, regretting**) сожале́ть (*impf.*); **I ~ losing my temper** я сожале́ю, что вы́шел из себя́; **I ~ to say ...** к сожале́нию, я до́лжен сказа́ть...; **you will live to ~ this** вы ещё пожале́ете об э́том.

regretful /rɪˈgretfʊl/ *adj.* опеча́ленный; по́лный сожале́ния.

regrettable /rɪˈgretəb(ə)l/ *adj.* приско́рбный.

regular /ˈregjʊlə(r)/ *n.*

1 (**~ soldier**) солда́т регуля́рной а́рмии.

2 (*coll.*, **~ customer**) завсегда́тай; постоя́нный посети́тель.

■ *adj.* 1 (*orderly in appearance, symmetrical*) пра́вильный, регуля́рный.

2 (*steady, unvarying*) регуля́рный, норма́льный; **a ~ pulse** ритми́чный пульс; **he keeps ~ hours** у него́ стро́гий/чёткий режи́м (дня).

3 (*US, ordinary*) регуля́рный, обы́чный.

regularity /regjʊˈlærɪtɪ/ *n.* регуля́рность.

regularly /ˈregjʊləlɪ/ *adv.* регуля́рно.

regulate /ˈregjʊleɪt/ *v.t.* регули́ровать (*impf.*).

regulation /regjʊˈleɪʃ(ə)n/ *n.*

1 (*control*) регули́рование.

2 (*rule*) пра́вило.

regulator /ˈregjʊleɪtə(r)/ *n.* (*person*) отве́тственное лицо́; (*body*) отве́тственная организа́ция; (*device*) регуля́тор, стабилиза́тор.

regulatory /regjʊˈleɪtərɪ/ *adj.* регули́рующий; **~ body** о́рган управле́ния.

regurgitate /rɪˈgɜ:dʒɪteɪt/ *v.t.* отры́г|ивать, -ну́ть.

rehabilitate /ri:həˈbɪlɪteɪt/ *v.t.* перевоспи́т|ывать, -а́ть.

rehabilitation /ri:həbɪlɪˈteɪʃ(ə)n/ *n.* перевоспита́ние; реабилита́ция.

rehearsal /rɪˈhɜ:s(ə)l/ *n.* репети́ция.

rehearse /rɪˈhɜ:s/ *v.t.* репети́ровать, от-.

rehouse /ri:ˈhaʊz/ *v.t.* пересел|я́ть, -и́ть.

reign /reɪn/ *n.* ца́рствование, власть.

■ *v.i.* ца́рствовать (*impf.*); (*fig.*) цари́ть (*impf.*).

reimburse /ri:ɪmˈbɜ:s/ *v.t.* возме|ща́ть, -сти́ть (*что кому*).

reimbursement /ri:ɪmˈbɜ:smənt/ *n.* возмеще́ние, возвраще́ние.

reincarnation /ri:ɪnkɑ:ˈneɪʃ(ə)n/ *n.* перевоплоще́ние.

reindeer /ˈreɪndɪə(r)/ *n.* (*pl.* **~** *or* **~s**) се́верный оле́нь.

reinforce /ri:ɪnˈfɔ:s/ *v.t.* усили|вать, -ть.

reinforcement /ri:ɪnˈfɔ:smənt/ *n.* усиле́ние; (*pl., troops*) подкрепле́ние.

reins /reɪnz/ *n. pl.* во́ж|жи (*pl., g.* -же́й).

reinstate /riːɪn'steɪt/ *v.t.* восстан|áвливать, -ови́ть в правáх/дóлжности/положéнии.
reinstatement /riːɪn'steɪtmənt/ *n.* восстановлéние в правáх/дóлжности/положéнии.
reissue /riː'ɪʃuː/ *n. v.t.* переизд|авáть, -áть.
reiterate /riː'ɪtəreɪt/ *v.t.* повтор|я́ть, -и́ть.
reject[1] /'riːdʒekt/ *n.* (*discarded article*) неподходя́щая вещь; (*comm.*) бракóванное издéлие; (*pl., collect.*) брак.
reject[2] /rɪ'dʒekt/ *v.t.* отклон|я́ть, -и́ть; отв|ергáть, -éргнуть; **my offer was ~ed out of hand** моё предложéние срáзу же отклони́ли.
rejection /rɪ'dʒekʃ(ə)n/ *n.* откáз, отклонéние.
rejoice /rɪ'dʒɔɪs/ *v.i.* рáдоваться, об- (*чему*).
rejuvenate /rɪ'dʒuːvəneɪt/ *v.t.* омол|áживать, -оди́ть.
rekindle /riː'kɪnd(ə)l/ *v.t.* разж|игáть, -éчь вновь.
relapse /rɪ'læps/ *n.* рециди́в.
■ *v.i.* снóва предáться (*pf.*) (*чему*); **he ~d into bad ways** он снóва сби́лся с пути́; **she ~d into silence** онá (снóва) замолчáла.
relate /rɪ'leɪt/ *v.t.*
1 (*narrate*) расскáз|ывать, -áть о + *p.*
2 (*establish relation between*) свя́з|ывать, -áть (*что с чем*).
■ *v.i.* относи́ться (*impf.*) (**to:** к + *d.*).
related /rɪ'leɪtɪd/ *adj.*
1 (*logically connected*) свя́занный (с + *i.*); взаимосвя́занный (друг с дрýгом).
2 (*by blood or marriage*): **he and I are ~** мы с ним рóдственники.
relation /rɪ'leɪʃ(ə)n/ *n.*
1 (*connection*) отношéние; **in, with ~ to** относи́тельно + *g.*
2 (*pl., dealings*) отношéния (*nt. pl.*); **international ~s** междунарóдные отношéния.
3 (*family member*) рóдственни|к (*fem.* -ца).
relationship /rɪ'leɪʃənʃɪp/ *n.* (*relevance*) связь, отношéние; (*between people or groups*) взаимоотношéния (*nt. pl.*), связь; (*kinship*) родствó.
relative /'relətɪv/ *n.* (*family member*) рóдственни|к (*fem.* -ца).
■ *adj.* 1 (*comparative*) относи́тельный, сравни́тельный; **he is a ~ newcomer** он здесь относи́тельно недáвно.
2 (*gram.*): **~ pronoun** относи́тельное местоимéние.
relatively /'relətɪvlɪ/ *adv.* относи́тельно; **~ly speaking** вообщé говоря́.
relativity /relə'tɪvɪtɪ/ *n.* относи́тельность; **theory of ~** теóрия относи́тельности.
relax /rɪ'læks/ *v.i.* (*rest*) рассл|абля́ться, -áбиться; отдыхáть (*impf.*); **I like to ~ in the sun** я люблю́ посидéть на сóлнце; **a ~ed atmosphere** спокóйная атмосфéра; (*slacken*) осл|абевáть, -абéть.
■ *v.t.* (*control, attention*) осл|абля́ть, -áбить; **he ~ed his grip** он разжáл рýку; (*person*) рассл|абля́ть, -áбить.
relaxation /riːlæk'seɪʃ(ə)n/ *n.*
1 (*rest, recreation*) óтдых, развлечéние.
2 (*of control*) ослаблéние.
3 (*of tension*) разря́дка.
relay /'riːleɪ/ *n.*
1 (*fresh team*) смéна.
2 **(~ race)** эстафéтный бег.
■ *v.t.* (*transmit*) трансли́ровать (*impf., pf.*).
release /rɪ'liːs/ *n.*
1 (*liberation*) освобождéние.
2 (*unfastening*) освобождéние.
3 (*device for doing this*) спуск.
4 (*of book, recording, film*) вы́пуск.
■ *v.t.* 1 (*liberate*) освобо|ждáть, -ди́ть.
2 (*unfasten*) отпус|кáть, -ти́ть; выпускáть, вы́пустить; **do not ~ the brake** не отпускáйте тóрмоз.
3 (*book, CD, film*) выпускáть, вы́пустить.
relegate /'relɪgeɪt/ *v.t.* от|сылáть, -ослáть; **the team was ~d to the second division** (*Br.*) комáнду перевели́ во вторóй дивизиóн.
relegation /relɪ'geɪʃ(ə)n/ *n.* понижéние, перевóд (в бóлее ни́зкий класс *и т. п.*).
relent /rɪ'lent/ *v.i.* смягч|áться, -и́ться; подобрéть (*pf.*).
relentless /rɪ'lentlɪs/ *adj.* безжáлостный.
relevance /'relɪv(ə)ns/ *n.* отношéние к дéлу; умéстность.
relevant /'relɪv(ə)nt/ *adj.* относя́щийся к дéлу; умéстный; **~ to** относя́щийся к + *d.*
reliability /rɪlaɪə'bɪlɪtɪ/ *n.* надёжность; достовéрность.
reliable /rɪ'laɪəb(ə)l/ *adj.* надёжный; (*of a statement*) достовéрный.
reliance /rɪ'laɪəns/ *n.* (*trust*) довéрие; **I place great ~ upon him** я емý óчень доверя́ю; (*dependence*) зави́симость; **~ on drugs** зави́симость от наркóтиков.
reliant /rɪ'laɪənt/ *adj.* (*dependent*) зави́симый, завися́щий; **they are completely ~ on their pension** они́ пóлностью зави́сят от своéй пéнсии.
relic /'relɪk/ *n.* рели́квия.
relief /rɪ'liːf/ *n.*
1 (*alleviation*) облегчéние.
2 (*assistance*) пособие; **~ agency** организáция по оказáнию пóмощи; **a ~ fund for flood victims** фонд пóмощи жéртвам наводнéния.
3 (*sculpture etc.*) рельéф; **~ map** рельéфная кáрта.
relieve /rɪ'liːv/ *v.t.*
1 (*alleviate*) облегч|áть, -и́ть; **I was ~d to get your letter** я был рад получи́ть вáше письмó.
2 (*bring assistance to*) при|ходи́ть, -йти́ на пóмощь + *d.*
3 (*unburden*) освобо|ждáть, -ди́ть (*кого от чего*); **this ~s me of the necessity to speak** э́то освобождáет меня́ от необходи́мости говори́ть.
4 (*replace on duty*) смен|я́ть, -и́ть.
religion /rɪ'lɪdʒ(ə)n/ *n.* рели́гия, вéра; вероисповéдание.
religious /rɪ'lɪdʒəs/ *adj.* религиóзный.
relinquish /rɪ'lɪŋkwɪʃ/ *v.t.* (*abandon*) ост|авля́ть, -áвить; (*surrender*) сд|авáть, -ать; **he ~ed his claims** он отказáлся от свои́х трéбований.
relish /'relɪʃ/ *n.*

[1] (*zest*) (большо́е/нескрыва́емое) удово́льствие; **he ate with ~** он ел с аппети́том.
[2] (*sauce*) припра́ва.
■ *v.t.* получ|а́ть, -и́ть удово́льствие от + *g.*; (*coll.*); **I don't ~ the prospect** меня́ не прельща́ет перспекти́ва.

relocate /ri:ləʊ'keɪt/ *v.t. & i.* переме|ща́ть(ся), -сти́ть(ся).

relocation /ri:ləʊ'keɪʃən/ *n.* перемеще́ние.

reluctance /rɪ'lʌkt(ə)ns/ *n.* нежела́ние; неохо́та.

reluctant /rɪ'lʌkt(ə)nt/ *adj.* неохо́тный; **she was ~ to leave home** ей не хоте́лось покида́ть дом.

rely /rɪ'laɪ/ *v.i.* полага́ться (*impf.*); наде́яться (*impf.*) (*both* на + *a.*); **you can ~ on me** вы мо́жете на меня́ положи́ться.

remain /rɪ'meɪn/ *v.i.* ост|ава́ться, -а́ться; (*stay*) пребыва́ть (*impf.*); **he ~ed silent** он храни́л молча́ние.

remainder /rɪ'meɪndə(r)/ *n.* (*rest*) оста́т|ок, -ки (*m. pl.*); (*of people*) остальны́е (*pl.*).

remains /rɪ'meɪnz/ *n.* оста́тки (*m. pl.*), оста́нк|и (*pl., g.* -ов).

remand /rɪ'mɑ:nd/ *n.*: **on ~** под стра́жей; **~ home** (*Br.*) исправи́тельный дом для несовершенноле́тних.
■ *v.t.*: **he was ~ed in custody** он содержа́лся под стра́жей.

remark /rɪ'mɑ:k/ *n.* замеча́ние.
■ *v.t.* зам|еча́ть, -е́тить.

remarkable /rɪ'mɑ:kəb(ə)l/ *adj.* удиви́тельный; замеча́тельный.

remarry /ri:'mærɪ/ *v.i.* вступ|а́ть, -и́ть в но́вый брак.

remedial /rɪ'mi:dɪəl/ *adj.* (*educ.*) корректи́вный.

remedy /'remɪdɪ/ *n.* (*cure*) сре́дство, лека́рство (**for:** от + *g.*).
■ *v.t.* испр|авля́ть, -а́вить.

remember /rɪ'membə(r)/ *v.t.*
[1] (*have in one's memory*) по́мнить (*impf.*); **I ~ you saying it** я по́мню, что вы э́то сказа́ли; **I ~ her as a girl** я по́мню её де́вочкой.
[2] (*recall*) всп|омина́ть, -о́мнить; **he couldn't remember how many meetings he had had in the past days** он не смог вспо́мнить число́ встреч, на кото́рых он побыва́л за после́дние дни.
[3] (*not forget*) не заб|ыва́ть, -ы́ть, име́ть (*impf.*) в виду́; **~ to turn out the light** не забу́дьте погаси́ть свет.

remembrance /rɪ'membrəns/ *n.* па́мять; **in ~ of** в па́мять о + *p.*

remind /rɪ'maɪnd/ *v.t.* нап|омина́ть, -о́мнить (*кому что or о чём or + inf.*); **he ~s me of my father** он напомина́ет мне отца́; **he ~ed me to buy bread** он напо́мнил мне купи́ть хле́ба.

reminder /rɪ'maɪndə(r)/ *n.* напомина́ние.

reminisce /remɪ'nɪs/ *v.i.* пред|ава́ться, -а́ться воспомина́ниям.

reminiscence /remɪ'nɪs(ə)ns/ *n.* воспомина́ние.

reminiscent /remɪ'nɪs(ə)nt/ *adj.*
[1] (*of person, recalling the past*): **he became ~** он преда́лся воспомина́ниям.
[2]: **~ of** (*tending to remind one of sth. or suggest sth.*) напомина́ющий; вызыва́ющий воспомина́ния о + *p.*; **his music is ~ of Brahms** его́ му́зыка напомина́ет Бра́мса.

remiss /rɪ'mɪs/ *adj.* хала́тный; неради́вый; **that was very ~ of me** с моe̗й стороны́ э́то бы́ло недобросо́вестно.

remission /rɪ'mɪʃ(ə)n/ *n.* (*med.*) реми́ссия.

remit /'ri:mɪt/ *n.* зада́чи (*f. pl.*), компете́нция.

remnant /'remnənt/ *n.* (*remains*) оста́ток; (*of cloth*) оста́ток.

remodel /ri:'mɒd(ə)l/ *v.t.* переде́л|ывать, -ать.

remonstrate /'remənstreɪt/ *v.i.* протестова́ть (*impf.*); возра|жа́ть, -зи́ть; (*exhort*): **he ~d with me** он увещева́л меня́.

remorse /rɪ'mɔ:s/ *n.* угрызе́ния (*nt. pl.*) со́вести.

remorseful /rɪ'mɔ:sfʊl/ *adj.* по́лный раска́яния.

remorseless /rɪ'mɔ:slɪs/ *adj.* безжа́лостный.

remortgage /ri:'mɔ:gɪdʒ/ *v.t.* (*fin.*) переза|кла́дывать, -ложи́ть.

remote /rɪ'məʊt/ *adj.* (**remoter, remotest**) отдалённый, глухо́й; **a ~ ancestor** далёкий пре́док; **~ control** (*control*) дистанцио́нное управле́ние; (*device*) пульт ДУ, пульт дистанцио́нного управле́ния; **there is a ~ possibility of its happening** не исключено́, что э́то случи́тся; **I haven't the ~st idea** не име́ю ни мале́йшего поня́тия; **he was not even ~ly interested** он не прояви́л ни мале́йшего интере́са (к + *d.*).
■ *cpd.* **~-controlled** *adj.* с дистанцио́нным управле́нием.

remoteness /rɪ'məʊtnɪs/ *n.* отдалённость.

removal /rɪ'mu:v(ə)l/ *n.* (*taking away*) удале́ние; (*Br., of furniture*) перево́зка.

remove /rɪ'mu:v/ *v.t.*
[1] (*take away, off*) уб|ира́ть, -ра́ть; ун|оси́ть, -ести́; **how can I ~ these stains?** как мо́жно вы́вести э́ти пя́тна?
[2] (*dismiss*): **he was ~d from office** его́ сня́ли с рабо́ты.

remover /rɪ'mu:və(r)/ *n.*: **furniture ~** (*Br.*) перево́зчик ме́бели; **stain ~** пятновыводи́тель (*m.*).

remunerate /rɪ'mju:nəreɪt/ *v.t.* (*person*) вознагра|жда́ть, -ди́ть; (*work*) опла́|чивать, -ти́ть.

remuneration /rɪmju:nə'reɪʃ(ə)n/ *n.* вознагражде́ние.

Renaissance /rɪ'neɪs(ə)ns/ *n.* (*hist.*) Ренесса́нс.

rename /ri:'neɪm/ *v.t.* переимено́в|ывать, -а́ть.

render /'rendə(r)/ *v.t.* (*cause to be*): **he was ~ed speechless** он онеме́л.

rendezvous /'rɒndeɪvu:/ *n.* (*pl.* **~** /-vu:z/) рандеву́ (*nt. indecl.*), свида́ние.
■ *v.i.* (**rendezvouses** /-vu:z/; **rendezvoused** /-vu:d/; **rendezvousing** /-vu:ɪŋ/) встр|еча́ться, -е́титься.

rendition /ren'dɪʃ(ə)n/ *n.* (*performance*) исполне́ние; (*translation*) перево́д.

renegade /'renɪgeɪd/ *n.* ренега́т, отсту́пник.
■ *adj.* ренега́тский, отсту́пнический.

reneg(u)e /rɪ'neɪg/ *v.i.*: **he ~d on his promise** он нарýшил своё обещáние.
renew /rɪ'nju:/ *v.t.* возобнов|лять, -и́ть.
renewable /rɪ'nju:əb(ə)l/ *adj.*: **~ resources** возобновля́емые ресýрсы.
renewal /rɪ'nju:əl/ *n.* возобновлéние.
renounce /rɪ'naʊns/ *v.t.* откáз|ываться, -áться от + *g.*
renouncement /rɪ'naʊnsmənt/ *n.* отречéние, откáз.
renovate /'renəveɪt/ *v.t.* ремонти́ровать, от-; реставри́ровать (*impf., pf.*) (*pf. also* от-).
renovation /renə'veɪʃ(ə)n/ *n.* реставрáция; ремóнт.
renown /rɪ'naʊn/ *n.* слáва; извéстность; **a preacher of ~** проповéдник, пóльзующийся большóй извéстностью; **he won ~ on the battlefield** он завоевáл слáву на пóле бóя.
renowned /rɪ'naʊnd/ *adj.* извéстный.
rent[1] /rent/ *n.* (*tear, split*) дырá.
rent[2] /rent/ *n.* (*for premises*) арéндная плáта; (*for a flat*) квартплáта.
■ *v.t.* [1] (*car, equipment*) брать, взять напрокáт; (*a place*) сн|имáть, -ять.
[2] : **~ (out)** (*car*) давáть, дать напрокáт; (*building*) сд|авáть, -áть.
■ *cpd.* **~ boy** *n.* (*Br., coll.*) мужчи́на-проститýтка.
rental /'rent(ə)l/ *n.* размéр арéндной плáты.
renunciation /rɪnʌnsɪ'eɪʃ(ə)n/ *n.* отречéние, откáз.
reorganization /ri:ɔ:gənaɪ'zeɪʃ(ə)n/ *n.* реорганизáция.
reorganize /ri:'ɔ:gənaɪz/ *v.t.* реорганизóв|ывать, -áть.
rep[1] /rep/ (*coll.*) = **representative** *n.*
rep[2] /rep/ (*coll.*) = **repertory 2**
repair /rɪ'peə(r)/ *n.*
[1] (*restoring*) ремóнт.
[2] (*condition*): **the house is in good ~** дом в хорóшем состоя́нии.
■ *v.t.* (*mend*) ремонти́ровать, от-; чини́ть, по-; (*restore*) восстан|áвливать, -ови́ть.
■ *cpd.* **~man** *n.* мáстер.
reparation /repə'reɪʃ(ə)n/ *n.* компенсáция; возмещéние ущéрба; (*pl., compensation for war damage*) (воéнные) репарáции (*f. pl.*).
repartee /repɑ:'ti:/ *n.* остроýмный разговóр.
repatriate /ri:'pætrɪeɪt/ *v.t.* репатрии́ровать (*impf., pf.*).
repatriation /ri:pætrɪ'eɪʃ(ə)n/ *n.* репатриáция.
repay /ri:'peɪ/ *v.t.* (*debt*) выплáчивать, вы́платить (*кому*).
repayable /ri:'peɪəb(ə)l/ *adj.* подлежáщий уплáте.
repayment /ri:'peɪmənt/ *n.* вы́плата, возмещéние.
repeal /rɪ'pi:l/ *n.* отмéна, аннули́рование.
■ *v.t.* аннули́ровать (*impf., pf.*).
repeat /rɪ'pi:t/ *n.* повторéние.
■ *v.t.* повтор|я́ть, -и́ть; **after ~ed attempts** пóсле неоднокрáтных попы́ток.
repeatedly /rɪ'pi:tɪdlɪ/ *adv.* неоднокрáтно.
repel /rɪ'pel/ *v.t.* (**repelled, repelling**)
[1] (*enemy, attack*) отб|ивáть, -и́ть.
[2] (*be repulsive to*) оттáлкивать (*impf.*).
repellent /rɪ'pelənt/ *n.*: **insect ~** срéдство от насекóмых.
■ *adj.* (*repulsive*) оттáлкивающий.
repent /rɪ'pent/ *v.t.* & *i.* кáяться (*impf.*); раскá|иваться, -яться (*в чём*).
repentance /ri:'pənt(ə)ns/ *n.* раскáяние.
repentant /ri:'pənt(ə)nt/ *adj.* раскáивающийся.
repercussion /ri:pə'kʌʃ(ə)n/ *n.* (*usu. pl.*) послéдствия (*nt. pl.*).
repertoire /'repətwɑ:(r)/ *n.* репертуáр.
repertory /'repətərɪ/ *n.*
[1] (*repertoire*) репертуáр.
[2] (*also* ▸**rep,** *coll.*): **~ company** постоя́нная трýппа с определённым репертуáром; **~ theatre** (*Br.*), **theater** (*US*) репертуáрный теáтр.
[3] (*fig., store*) запáс.
repetition /repɪ'tɪʃ(ə)n/ *n.* повторéние.
repetitious /repɪ'tɪʃəs/ = **repetitive**
repetitive /rɪ'petɪtɪv/ *adj.* повторя́ющийся; скýчный; **~ strain injury** трáвма, вы́званная повторя́ющимся движéнием.
replace /rɪ'pleɪs/ *v.t.*
[1] (*put back*) класть, положи́ть (*or* стáвить, по-) на мéсто; возвра|щáть, -ти́ть.
[2] (*provide substitute for*) замен|я́ть, -и́ть; **the vase cannot be ~d** э́то уникáльная вáза.
[3] (*take the place of*) заме|щáть, -сти́ть; **he ~d me as secretary** он замещáл/смени́л меня́ в дóлжности секретаря́.
replacement /rɪ'pleɪsmənt/ *n.* (*provision of substitute*) замещéние, замéна; (*substitute*) замéна.
replay[1] /'ri:pleɪ/ *n.* (*of a game*) переигрóвка.
replay[2] /ri:'pleɪ/ *v.t.* (*sport*) переи́гр|ывать, -áть.
replenish /rɪ'plenɪʃ/ *v.t.* (*one's wardrobe*) поп|олня́ть, -óлнить; **he ~ed his glass** он снóва напóлнил стакáн.
replete /rɪ'pli:t/ *adj.* напóлненный; сы́тый, богáтый (*чем*); **~ with food** наéвшийся вдóволь.
replica /'replɪkə/ *n.* кóпия.
replicate /'replɪkeɪt/ *v.t.* копи́ровать, с-.
reply /rɪ'plaɪ/ *n.* отвéт.
■ *v.i.* отв|ечáть, -éтить.
report /rɪ'pɔ:t/ *n.* доклáд, отчёт; **newspaper ~** сообщéние, извéстие, репортáж; **school ~** (*Br.*), **~ card** (*US*) отчёт об успевáемости.
■ *v.t.* [1] (*give news or account of*) сообщ|áть, -и́ть; сост|авля́ть, -áвить отчёт о + *p.*; **it has been ~ed that ...** сообщáлось, что... .
[2] (*inform against*) жáловаться, по- на + *a.*; **I shall ~ you for insolence** я пожáлуюсь на вас за вáшу дéрзость.
■ *v.i.* [1] (*give information*) до|клáдывать, -ложи́ть; дéлать, с- доклáд; предст|авля́ть, -áвить отчёт.
[2] (*present o.s.*) яв|ля́ться, -и́ться (*кудá-н.*).
reporter /rɪ'pɔ:tə(r)/ *n.* репортёр.
repository /rɪ'pɒzɪtərɪ/ *n.* (*receptacle*) храни́лище, вмести́лище; (*store*) склад; (*fig.*): **he is a ~ of information** он неиссякáемый истóчник информáции.
repossess /ri:pə'zes/ *v.t.* из|ымáть, -ъя́ть за неплатёж.

reprehensible /reprɪ'hensɪb(ə)l/ *adj.* предосуди́тельный.

represent /reprɪ'zent/ *v.t.*
1 (*speak or act for*) представля́ть (*impf.*).
2 (*constitute, amount to*) представля́ть (*impf.*) собо́й.
3 (*portray*) изобра|жа́ть, -зи́ть; **what does this picture ~?** что изображено́ на э́той карти́не?; (*make out*): **he ~ed himself as an expert** он выдава́л себя́ за знатока́.
4 (*symbolize, correspond to*) символизи́ровать (*impf., pf.*), изобража́ть (*impf.*), обознача́ть (*impf.*).

representation /reprɪzen'teɪʃ(ə)n/ *n.*
1 (*portrayal*) изображе́ние.
2 : (*pl.*) (*statements*): **diplomatic ~s** дипломати́ческие представле́ния (*заявления*).
3 (*being represented*) представи́тельство.

representative /reprɪ'zentətɪv/ *n.* представи́тель (*m.*) (*fem.* -ница).
■ *adj.* показа́тельный, типи́чный.

repress /rɪ'pres/ *v.t.*
1 (*put down*) подав|ля́ть, -и́ть.
2 (*restrain*) сде́рж|ивать, -а́ть.

repression /rɪ'preʃ(ə)n/ *n.* (*of feelings*) подавле́ние; (*of people*) репре́ссия.

repressive /rɪ'presɪv/ *adj.* репресси́вный.

reprieve /rɪ'pri:v/ *n.* (*leg.*) отсро́чка исполне́ния (сме́ртного) пригово́ра.

reprimand /'reprɪmɑ:nd/ *n.* вы́говор, замеча́ние.
■ *v.t.* де́лать, с- вы́говор/замеча́ние + *d.*

reprint[1] /'ri:prɪnt/ *n.* перепеча́тка.

reprint[2] /ri:'prɪnt/ *v.t.* перепеча́т|ывать, -ать.

reprisal /rɪ'praɪz(ə)l/ *n.* отве́тное де́йствие.

reproach /rɪ'prəʊtʃ/ *n.* упрёк, уко́р.
■ *v.t.* упрек|а́ть, -ну́ть; укоря́ть (*impf.*).

reproachful /rɪ'prəʊtʃfʊl/ *adj.* укори́зненный.

reprobate /'reprəbeɪt/ *n.* негодя́й, нечести́вец.
■ *adj.* нечести́вый; безнра́вственный.

reproduce /ri:prə'dju:s/ *v.t.* (*copy*) воспроизв|оди́ть, -ести́.
■ *v.i.* (*of animals*) размн|ожа́ться, -о́житься.

reproduction /ri:prə'dʌkʃ(ə)n/ *n.* (*biol.*) размноже́ние; (*art*) репроду́кция.

reproductive /ri:prə'dʌktɪv/ *adj.* (*biol.*) полово́й.

reproof /rɪ'pru:f/ *n.* порица́ние.

reprove /rɪ'pru:v/ *v.t.* де́лать, с- вы́говор + *d.*

reptile /'reptaɪl/ *n.* пресмыка́ющееся, репти́лия.

republic /rɪ'pʌblɪk/ *n.* респу́блика.

republican /rɪ'pʌblɪkən/ *n.* республика́нец.
■ *adj.* республика́нский.

repudiate /rɪ'pju:dɪeɪt/ *v.t.* отв|ерга́ть, -е́ргнуть.

repugnance /rɪ'pʌgnəns/ *n.* отвраще́ние.

repugnant /rɪ'pʌgnənt/ *adj.* отврати́тельный.

repulse /rɪ'pʌls/ *v.t.* (*drive back*) отб|ива́ть, -и́ть; (*refuse*) отт|а́лкивать, -олкну́ть.

repulsion /rɪ'pʌlʃ(ə)n/ *n.* отвраще́ние.

repulsive /rɪ'pʌlsɪv/ *adj.* отврати́тельный.

reputable /'repjʊtəb(ə)l/ *adj.* почте́нный.

reputation /repjʊ'teɪʃ(ə)n/ *n.* репута́ция.

repute /rɪ'pju:t/ *n.*: **an artist of ~** худо́жник с и́менем.
■ *v.t.*: **he is ~d to be rich** он счита́ется бога́тым; говоря́т, что он бога́т; **the ~d father** предполага́емый оте́ц.

reputedly /rɪ'pju:tɪdlɪ/ *adv.* по о́бщему мне́нию.

request /rɪ'kwest/ *n.* про́сьба; **a programme** (*Br.*), **program** (*US*) **of ~s** конце́рт по зая́вкам.
■ *v.t.* проси́ть, по-.

requiem /'rekwɪəm/ *n.* (*mus.*) ре́квием; (*relig.*) панихи́да.

require /rɪ'kwaɪə(r)/ *v.t.*
1 (*need*) нужда́ться (*impf.*) в + *p.*; **the matter ~s some thought** над э́тим на́до поду́мать.
2 (*demand*) тре́бовать, по- + *g.*; **my attendance is ~d by law** по зако́ну я обя́зан прису́тствовать; **I have done all that is ~d** я сде́лал всё, что тре́буется.

requirement /rɪ'kwaɪəmənt/ *n.*
1 (*need*) потре́бность.
2 (*demand*) тре́бование.

requisite /'rekwɪzɪt/ *adj.* необходи́мый.

requisition /rekwɪ'zɪʃ(ə)n/ *v.t.* реквизи́ровать (*impf., pf.*).

reschedule /ri:'ʃedju:l/ *v.t.* перен|оси́ть, -ести́.

rescue /'reskju:/ *n.* спасе́ние, вы́ручка; **he came to my ~** он пришёл мне на по́мощь/вы́ручку.
■ *v.t.* (**rescues, rescued, rescuing**) спас|а́ть, -ти́.

rescuer /'reskju:ə(r)/ *n.* спаси́тель (*fem.* -ница).

research /rɪ'sə:tʃ/ *n.* изуче́ние, иссле́дование, изыска́ние; **~ and development** нау́чно-иссле́довательская рабо́та.
■ *v.t. & i.* иссле́довать (*impf., pf.*).

researcher /rɪ'sə:tʃə(r)/ *n.* иссле́дователь (*fem.* -ница).

resemblance /rɪ'zembləns/ *n.* схо́дство.

resemble /rɪ'zemb(ə)l/ *v.t.* походи́ть (*impf.*) на + *a.*

resent /rɪ'zent/ *v.t.* возму|ща́ться, -ти́ться + *i.*; **I ~ your interfering in my affairs** мне о́чень не нра́вится, что вы вме́шиваетесь в мои́ дела́.

resentful /rɪ'zentfʊl/ *adj.* возмущённый.

resentment /rɪ'zentmənt/ *n.* возмуще́ние.

reservation /rezə'veɪʃ(ə)n/ *n.*
1 (*booking*) (предвари́тельный) зака́з.
2 (*limitation*) огово́рка.
3 (*for indigenous people*) резерва́ция.

reserve /rɪ'zə:v/ *n.*
1 (*store*) запа́с, резе́рв.
2 (*mil.*) резе́рв.
3 (*~ player*) запасно́й (игро́к).
4 (*area*) запове́дник; **game ~** охо́тничий запове́дник.
5 (*reticence*) сде́ржанность.
■ *v.t.* 1 (*save*) бере́чь, с-; прибер|ега́ть, -е́чь.
2 (*set aside*) резерви́ровать, за-; (*ticket, table*) зака́з|ывать, -а́ть; (*hotel room*) брони́ровать, за-.

reserved /rɪ'zə:vd/ *adj.*

1 (*booked*) зака́занный (зара́нее).
2 (*reticent*) сде́ржанный.

reservist /rɪˈzəːvɪst/ *n.* резерви́ст.

reservoir /ˈrezəvwɑː(r)/ *n.* водохрани́лище, водоём.

reset /riːˈset/ *v.t.* (*clock*) перест|авля́ть, -а́вить; (*trap*) сно́ва ста́вить, по-.

resettle /riːˈset(ə)l/ *v.t.* пересел|я́ть, -и́ть.
■ *v.i.* пересел|я́ться, -и́ться.

resettlement /riːˈsetəlmənt/ *n.* переселе́ние.

reshuffle /riːˈʃʌf(ə)l/ *n.*: **Cabinet ~** перестано́вки в Кабине́те мини́стров.

reside /rɪˈzaɪd/ *v.i.* прожива́ть (*impf.*); жить (*impf.*).

residence /ˈrezɪd(ə)ns/ *n.*
1 (*residing*) прожива́ние.
2 (*home, mansion*) дом, резиде́нция.

resident /ˈrezɪd(ə)nt/ *n.* (*inhabitant*) (постоя́нный) жи́тель; (*Br., in hotel*) постоя́лец.
■ *adj.* постоя́нно прожива́ющий.

residential /rezɪˈdenʃ(ə)l/ *adj.*: **a ~ area** жило́й райо́н.

residual /rɪˈzɪdjʊəl/ *adj.* оста́точный, оста́вшийся.

residue /ˈrezɪdjuː/ *n.* оста́ток.

resign /rɪˈzaɪn/ *v.t.*
1 (*give up*) отка́з|ываться, -а́ться от + *g.*; **he ~ed his post as Chancellor** он по́дал в отста́вку с поста́ ка́нцлера.
2 (*reconcile*): **he ~ed himself to defeat** он смири́лся с пораже́нием.
■ *v.i.* под|ава́ть, -а́ть (*or* уходи́ть, уйти́) в отста́вку; уходи́ть, уйти́ с рабо́ты.

resignation /rezɪgˈneɪʃ(ə)n/ *n.*
1 (*resigning of office*) отста́вка; **he handed in his ~** он по́дал заявле́ние об отста́вке/ухо́де.
2 (*acceptance of fate*) поко́рность.

resigned /rɪˈzaɪnd/ *adj.* поко́рный, смири́вшийся (с + *i.*).

resilience /rɪˈzɪlɪəns/ *n.* эласти́чность, упру́гость; (*fig.*) выно́сливость, живу́честь, жизнеспосо́бность.

resilient /rɪˈzɪlɪənt/ *adj.* эласти́чный; (*fig.*) выно́сливый.

resin /ˈrezɪn/ *n.* смола́.

resist /rɪˈzɪst/ *v.t.*
1 (*oppose*) сопротивля́ться (*impf.*) + *d.*
2 (*refrain from*) возде́рж|иваться, -а́ться от + *g.*; **I could not ~ the temptation to smile** я не мог удержа́ться от улы́бки; **she cannot ~ chocolates** она́ не мо́жет усто́ять пе́ред шокола́дом.

resistance /rɪˈzɪst(ə)ns/ *n.* сопротивле́ние; **(~ movement)** движе́ние сопротивле́ния.

resistant /rɪˈzɪst(ə)nt/ *adj.* сопротивля́ющийся.

resit /riːˈsɪt/ *v.t.* (*Br.*): **~ an examination** передава́ть (*impf.*) экза́мен.

resolute /ˈrezəluːt/ *adj.* реши́тельный.

resolution /rezəˈluːʃ(ə)n, -ˈljuːʃ(ə)n/ *n.*
1 (*firmness of purpose*) реши́мость.
2 (*vow*): **New Year ~** новогодний заро́к.
3 (*expression of intent*) резолю́ция.
4 (*comput., TV, phot., etc.*) (*of screen, camera, etc.*) разреше́ние.

resolve /rɪˈzɒlv/ *n.* (*determination*) реши́тельность, реши́мость.
■ *v.t.* & *i.*
1 (*decide*) реш|а́ть, -и́ть; прин|има́ть, -я́ть реше́ние.
2 (*settle*) (раз)реш|а́ть, -и́ть; **their quarrel was ~d** их спор разреши́лся.

resonance /ˈrezənəns/ *n.* резона́нс, гул.

resonant /ˈrezənənt/ *adj.* звуча́щий.

resonate /ˈrezoneɪt/ *v.i.* резони́ровать, звуча́ть (*both impf.*)

resort /rɪˈzɔːt/ *n.*
1 (*recourse*): **in the last ~** в кра́йнем слу́чае.
2 (*place*): **holiday ~** куро́рт; **seaside ~** морско́й куро́рт.
■ *v.i.* (*have recourse*) приб|ега́ть, -е́гнуть (**to:** к + *d.*).

resound /rɪˈzaʊnd/ *v.i.* звуча́ть (*impf.*); **the hall ~ed with voices** в за́ле раздава́лись голоса́; (*fig.*): **a ~ing success** оглуши́тельный успе́х.

resource /rɪˈsɔːs/ *n.* запа́сы (*m. pl.*); ресу́рсы (*m. pl.*).

resourceful /rɪˈsɔːsfʊl, -ˈzɔːsfʊl/ *adj.* изобрета́тельный.

resourcefulness /rɪˈzɔːsfʊlnɪs/ *n.* изобрета́тельность, нахо́дчивость.

respect /rɪˈspekt/ *n.*
1 (*esteem*) уваже́ние.
2 (*reference*): **with ~ to** что каса́ется + *g.*
3 (*pl., polite greetings*) почте́ние; **he came to pay his ~s** он пришёл засвиде́тельствовать своё почте́ние.
■ *v.t.* уважа́ть (*impf.*); почита́ть (*impf.*).

respectability /rɪspektəˈbɪlɪtɪ/ *n.* респекта́бельность.

respectable /rɪˈspektəb(ə)l/ *adj.* прили́чный.

respectful /rɪˈspektfʊl/ *adj.* почти́тельный.

respective /rɪˈspektɪv/ *adj.* соотве́тственный; **we went off to our ~ rooms** мы разошли́сь по свои́м ко́мнатам; **the boys and girls were taught woodwork and sewing ~ly** ма́льчиков и де́вочек учи́ли соотве́тственно столя́рному де́лу и шитью́.

respiration /respɪˈreɪʃ(ə)n/ *n.* дыха́ние.

respirator /ˈrespɪreɪtə(r)/ *n.* респира́тор.

respiratory /rɪˈspɪrətərɪ/ *adj.* дыха́тельный.

respite /ˈrespaɪt/ *n.* (*rest*) переды́шка.

resplendent /rɪˈsplend(ə)nt/ *adj.* блиста́тельный.

respond /rɪˈspɒnd/ *v.i.*
1 (*reply*) отв|еча́ть, -е́тить (**to:** на + *a.*).
2 (*react*) реаги́ровать, от- (**to:** на + *a.*); **his illness is ~ing to treatment** его́ боле́знь поддаётся лече́нию.

response /rɪˈspɒns/ *n.*
1 (*reply*) отве́т; **in ~ to your enquiry** в отве́т на ваш запро́с.
2 (*reaction*) реа́кция, о́тклик.

responsibility /rɪspɒnsɪˈbɪlɪtɪ/ *n.* отве́тственность; **I take full ~ for my actions** я беру́ на себя́ по́лную отве́тственность за свои́ де́йствия.

responsible /rɪˈspɒnsɪb(ə)l/ *adj.*

1 (*accountable*) отве́тственный; **she is ~ for cleaning my room** убо́рка мое́й ко́мнаты вхо́дит в её обя́занности; (*to blame*): **who was ~ for breaking the window?** кто разби́л окно́?
2 (*trustworthy*) надёжный.
3 (*involving responsibility*) ва́жный.

responsive /rɪ'spɒnsɪv/ *adj.* отзы́вчивый.

rest¹ /rest/ *n.*
1 (*relaxation*) о́тдых; **I'm going (up) to have a ~** (я) пойду́ приля́гу.
2 (*undisturbed state*) поко́й; **I set his mind at ~** я его́ успоко́ил.
3 (*intermission*) передышка; **they took a short ~** они́ сде́лали небольшу́ю переды́шку.
4 (*prop*) опо́ра.
■ *v.t.* 1 (*give ~ to*) да|ва́ть, -ть о́тдых + *d.*
2 (*place for support*) класть, положи́ть (на + *a.*); прислон|я́ть, -и́ть (*что к чему*).
■ *v.i.* 1 (*relax*) лежа́ть (*impf.*); отд|ыха́ть, -охну́ть.
2 (*fig.*, *remain*) ост|ава́ться, -а́ться; **the decision ~s with you** реше́ние зави́сит от вас.
3 (*be supported*) опира́ться (*impf.*) (*на что*).
■ *cpd.* **~room** *n.* (*US, toilet*) туале́т.

rest² /rest/ *n.* (*remainder*) оста́ток; (*remaining things, people*) остальны́е (*pl.*).

restart /ri:'stɑ:t/ *v.t.* (*begin again*) вновь начин|а́ть, -а́ть; (*car*) сно́ва зав|оди́ть, -ести́.

restaurant /'restərɒnt/ *n.* рестора́н; **~ car** ваго́н-рестора́н.

restful /'restfʊl/ *adj.* успока́ивающий.

restive /'restɪv/ *adj.* (*of horse*) норови́стый; (*of person*) стропти́вый; (*restless*) беспоко́йный.

restless /'restlɪs/ *adj.* беспоко́йный.

restock /ri:'stɒk/ *v.i.* поп|олня́ть, -о́лнить запа́сы.

restoration /restə'reɪʃ(ə)n/ *n.* реставра́ция.

restore /rɪ'stɔ:(r)/ *v.t.*
1 (*goods to owner*) возвра|ща́ть, -ти́ть (*or* верну́ть); (*former state or situation*) восстан|а́вливать, -ови́ть; **order was ~d** поря́док был восстано́влен.
2 (*monument, work of art*) реставри́ровать (*impf.*, *pf.*) (*pf. also* от-).

restorer /rɪ'stɔ:rə(r)/ *n.* реставра́тор.

restrain /rɪ'streɪn/ *v.t.* сде́рж|ивать, -а́ть; **his manner was ~ed** он был сде́ржан.

restraint /rɪ'streɪnt/ *n.*
1 (*self-control*) сде́ржанность.
2 (*constraint*) ограниче́ние.

restrict /rɪ'strɪkt/ *v.t.* ограни́чи|вать, -ть.

restriction /rɪ'strɪkʃ(ə)n/ *n.* ограниче́ние.

restrictive /rɪ'strɪktɪv/ *adj.* ограничи́тельный.

result /rɪ'zʌlt/ *n.* результа́т, сле́дствие; **he died as a ~ of his injuries** он у́мер от ран.
■ *v.i.* 1 (*arise*) сле́довать (*impf.*) (*из чего*).
2 (*end*) конча́ться, ко́нчиться (**in:** + *i.*); **the quarrel ~ed in bloodshed** ссо́ра ко́нчилась кровопроли́тием.

resume /rɪ'zju:m/ *v.t.* (*continue*) прод|олжа́ть, -о́лжить; (*take again*): **he ~d command** он сно́ва при́нял кома́ндование (*чем*).
■ *v.i.*: **let us ~ after lunch** продо́лжим по́сле обе́да.

résumé /'rezjʊmeɪ/ *n.* резюме́ (*nt. indecl.*).

resumption /rɪ'zʌmpʃ(ə)n/ *n.* продолже́ние.

resurface /ri:'sɜ:fɪs/ *v.t.* меня́ть, смени́ть покры́тие + *g.*
■ *v.i.* всплы|ва́ть, -ть.

resurgence /rɪ'sɜ:dʒ(ə)ns/ *n.* возрожде́ние.

resurrect /rezə'rekt/ *v.t.* воскре|ша́ть, -си́ть.

resurrection /rezə'rekʃ(ə)n/ *n.* (*of Christ*) воскресе́ние; (*fig.*) воскреше́ние.

resuscitate /rɪ'sʌsɪteɪt/ *v.t.* прив|оди́ть, -ести́ в созна́ние; реаними́ровать (*impf.*, *pf.*).

resuscitation /rɪsʌsɪ'teɪʃ(ə)n/ *n.* реанима́ция (*искусственное дыхание*).

retail /'ri:teɪl/ *n.* ро́зничная прода́жа.
■ *v.i.* продава́ться (*impf.*) в ро́зницу.

retailer /'ri:teɪlə(r)/ *n.* ро́зничный торго́вец.

retain /rɪ'teɪn/ *v.t.* уде́рживать (*impf.*); сохран|я́ть, -и́ть.

retainer /rɪ'teɪnə(r)/ *n.*
1 (*hist.*) васса́л; (*servant*) слуга́ (*m.*).
2 (*fee*) предвари́тельный гонора́р.

retaliate /rɪ'tælɪeɪt/ *v.i.* отпла́|чивать, -ти́ть той же моне́той.

retaliation /rɪtælɪ'eɪʃ(ə)n/ *n.* отпла́та, возме́здие.

retard /rɪ'tɑ:d/ *v.t.*: **a ~ed child** у́мственно отста́лый ребёнок.

retentive /rɪ'tentɪv/ *adj.*: **a ~ memory** це́пкая па́мять; **a soil ~ of moisture** по́чва, сохраня́ющая вла́гу.

rethink /ri:'θɪŋk/ *v.t.* пересм|а́тривать, -отре́ть.

reticent /'retɪs(ə)nt/ *adj.* молчали́вый.

retina /'retɪnə/ *n.* (*pl.* **retinas** *or* **retinae** /-ni:/) сетча́тка.

retinue /'retɪnju:/ *n.* сви́та.

retir|e /rɪ'taɪə(r)/ *v.i.*
1 (*from employment*) уходи́ть, уйти́ в отста́вку.
2 (*withdraw*) удал|я́ться, -и́ться; **he has a ~ing disposition** он застéнчивый челове́к.

retired /rɪ'taɪəd/ *adj.* (находя́щийся) на пе́нсии.

retirement /rɪ'taɪəmənt/ *n.* отста́вка, вы́ход на пе́нсию (*or* в отста́вку); **~ age** пенсио́нный во́зраст.

retort /rɪ'tɔ:t/ *n.* возраже́ние.
■ *v.t.* & *i.* отв|еча́ть, -е́тить ре́зко (*or* тем же).

retrace /ri:'treɪs/ *v.t.*: **~ one's steps** возвраща́ться, верну́ться тем же путём.

retract /rɪ'trækt/ *v.t.* отка́з|ываться, -а́ться от + *g.*
■ *v.i.* втя́|гиваться, -ну́ться.

retrain /ri:'treɪn/ *v.t.* & *i.* переквалифици́ровать(ся) (*impf.*, *pf.*).

retreat /rɪ'tri:t/ *n.* отступле́ние, отхо́д.
■ *v.i.* (*withdraw*) удал|я́ться, -и́ться.

retrench /rɪ'trentʃ/ *v.i.* (*economize*) эконо́мить, с-.

retrial /'ri:traɪəl/ *n.* повто́рное слу́шание де́ла.

retribution /retrɪ'bju:ʃ(ə)n/ *n.* возме́здие, ка́ра.

retrieval /rɪ'tri:v(ə)l/ *n.* (*recovery, getting back*) возвраще́ние.

retrieve /rɪ'tri:v/ *v.t.* брать, взять обра́тно.

retriever /rɪ'tri:və(r)/ *n.* охо́тничья поиско́вая соба́ка; ретри́вер.

retrograde /'retrəgreɪd/ *adj.* (*fig.*) реакцио́нный.

retrogressive /retrə'gresɪv/ *adj.* регресси́рующий.

retrospect /'retrəspekt/ *n.*: **in ~** ретроспекти́вно.

retrospective /retrə'spektɪv/ *adj.* ретроспекти́вный; **a ~ law** зако́н, име́ющий обра́тную си́лу.
■ *n.* (*exhibition*) итого́вая вы́ставка рабо́т худо́жника.

return /rɪ'tə:n/ *n.*
[1] (*coming or going back*) возвраще́ние; **many happy ~s (of the day)!** с днём рожде́ния!; **~ fare** сто́имость обра́тного прое́зда.
[2] **(~ ticket)** (*Br.*) обра́тный биле́т.
[3] (*profit*) дохо́д.
[4] (*giving, sending, putting*) отда́ча, возвра́т.
[5] (*reciprocation*): **in ~ (for)** взаме́н (+ *g.*); (*in response to*) в отве́т (на + *a.*).
[6] (*report*) отчёт, ра́порт; **income tax ~** нало́говая деклара́ция.
[7] (*comput.*) возвра́т.
■ *v.t.* [1] (*give, send, put, back*) возвра|ща́ть, -ти́ть (*or* верну́ть); **he ~ed the ball accurately** он хорошо́ отби́л мяч.
[2] (*declare*) до|кла́дывать, -ложи́ть; **the jury ~ed a verdict of guilty** прися́жные призна́ли обвиня́емого вино́вным.
■ *v.i.* возвра|ща́ться, -ти́ться (*or* верну́ться).

reunion /ri:'ju:njən/ *n.* (*reuniting*) воссоедине́ние; (*meeting of old friends etc.*) встре́ча (ста́рых друзе́й).

reunite /ri:ju:'naɪt/ *v.t.* & *i.* воссоедин|я́ть(ся), -и́ть(ся).

reusable /ri:'ju:zəb(ə)l/ *adj.* многокра́тного по́льзования.

reuse /ri:'ju:z/ *v.t.* сно́ва испо́льзовать (*impf.*, *pf.*).

rev /rev/ *v.t.* & *i.* **(revved, revving)** (*also* **~ up**) увели́чи|вать, -ть оборо́ты (мото́ра).

revamp /ri:'væmp/ *v.t.* (*fig.*) обнов|ля́ть, -и́ть.

reveal /rɪ'vi:l/ *v.t.* обнару́жи|вать, -ть; **this account is very ~ing** э́тот отчёт о́чень показа́телен; **she wore a ~ing dress** она́ была́ в откры́том пла́тье.

revel /'rev(ə)l/ *v.i.* (**revelled, revelling;** *US* **reveled, reveling**) наслажда́ться (*impf.*) (+ *i.*); **she ~s in gossip** она́ обожа́ет спле́тни.

revelation /revə'leɪʃ(ə)n/ *n.* откры́тие, открове́ние.

reveller /'revələ(r)/ (*US* **reveler**) *n.* кути́ла (*m.*), гуля́ка (*c.g.*).

revelry /'revəlrɪ/ *n.* попо́йка, разгу́л.

revenge /rɪ'vendʒ/ *n.* месть; **he took his ~ on me** он мне отомсти́л.
■ *v.t.*: **he ~d himself on his enemies** он отомсти́л свои́м врага́м.

revenue /'revənju:/ *n.* дохо́д.

reverberate /rɪ'və:bəreɪt/ *v.i.* отра|жа́ться, -зи́ться.

revere /rɪ'vɪə(r)/ *v.t.* почита́ть (*impf.*).

reverence /'revərəns/ *n.* почита́ние, почте́ние.

reverend /'revərənd/ *adj.*: **the R~ John Smith** его́ преподо́бие Джон Смит.

reverent(ial) /'revərənt, revə'renʃ(ə)l/ *adj.* почти́тельный.

reverie /'revərɪ/ *n.* мечта́ние.

reversal /rɪ'və:s(ə)l/ *n.* по́лная переме́на.

reverse /rɪ'və:s/ *n.*
[1] (*opposite*) противополо́жность; **the ~ is true** де́ло обстои́т как раз наоборо́т.
[2] (*~ gear*): **he put the car into ~** он включи́л за́дний ход.
■ *adj.* обра́тный, противополо́жный; **in ~ order** в обра́тном поря́дке; **in ~ gear** за́дним хо́дом.
■ *v.t.* [1] (*turn round, invert*) пов|ора́чивать, -ерну́ть обра́тно.
[2] (*drive backwards*): **he ~d (the car) into a wall** он дал за́дний ход и вре́зался в стену́.
■ *v.i.* (*of driver*) да|ва́ть, -ть за́дний ход.

reversible /rɪ'və:sɪb(ə)l/ *adj.* (*process etc.*) обрати́мый; (*garment*) двусторо́нний.

revert /rɪ'və:t/ *v.i.* возвра|ща́ться, -ти́ться; **the fields have ~ed to scrub** поля́ вновь поросли́ куста́рником; **he ~ed to his old ways** он взя́лся за ста́рое; (*of property, rights etc.*) пере|ходи́ть, -йти́ (*к прежнему владельцу*).

review /rɪ'vju:/ *n.*
[1] (*re-examination, retrospect*) пересмо́тр.
[2] (*of mil. forces etc.*) пара́д.
[3] (*of book etc.*) реце́нзия.
[4] (*periodical*) обозре́ние.
■ *v.t.* [1] (*re-examine*) пересм|а́тривать, -отре́ть.
[2] (*inspect*) просм|а́тривать, -отре́ть.
[3] (*write critical account of*) рецензи́ровать, от-.

reviewer /rɪ'vju:ə(r)/ *n.* рецензе́нт.

revise /rɪ'vaɪz/ *v.t.* (*one's views*) пересм|а́тривать, -отре́ть; (*correct a text, an opinion*) испр|авля́ть, -а́вить.
■ *v.i.* (*Br.*): **I must ~ for the exams** я до́лжен повтори́ть материа́л к экза́менам.

revision /rɪ'vɪʒ(ə)n/ *n.* (*of text*) прове́рка, перерабо́тка; (*for exams*) повторе́ние.

revitalize /ri:'vaɪtəlaɪz/ *v.t.* вновь ожив|ля́ть, -и́ть.

revival /rɪ'vaɪv(ə)l/ *n.* (*return to consciousness, health etc.*) возвраще́ние созна́ния; **a ~ of interest** оживле́ние интере́са; (*return to use, popularity*) возрожде́ние.

revive /rɪ'vaɪv/ *v.t.* (*custom, hope*) возро|жда́ть, -ди́ть; (*economy*) ожив|ля́ть, -и́ть.
■ *v.i.* (*flowers, person*) ож|ива́ть, -и́ть; (*custom, hope*) возро|жда́ться, -ди́ться; (*regain consciousness*) при|ходи́ть, -йти́ в себя́.

revoke /rɪ'vəʊk/ *v.t.* отмен|я́ть, -и́ть.

revolt /rɪ'vəʊlt/ *n.* восста́ние.
■ *v.t.* вызыва́ть, вы́звать отвраще́ние у + *g.*; **a ~ing sight** отврати́тельное зре́лище.
■ *v.i.* восст|ава́ть, -а́ть; бунтова́ть (*impf.*); взбунтова́ться (*pf.*).

revolution /revə'lu:ʃ(ə)n/ *n.*
[1] (*one complete rotation*) оборо́т.
[2] (*pol., fig.*) револю́ция.

revolutionary /revə'lu:ʃənərɪ/ *n.* революционе́р (*fem.* -ка).
■ *adj.* революцио́нный.

revolutionize /revə'lu:ʃənaɪz/ *v.t.* революционизи́ровать (*impf.*, *pf.*).

revolv|e /rɪ'vɒlv/ *v.i.* враща́ться (*impf.*); **~ing doors** враща́ющиеся две́ри; (*fig.*): **he thinks**

everything ~es around him он мнит себя́ це́нтром вселе́нной.
revolver /rɪ'vɒlvə(r)/ *n.* револьве́р.
revue /rɪ'vjuː/ *n.* обозре́ние, ревю́ (*nt. indecl.*).
revulsion /rɪ'vʌlʃ(ə)n/ *n.* отвраще́ние.
reward /rɪ'wɔːd/ *n.*
1 (*for achievement*) награ́да (за + *a.*).
2 (*sum offered*) пре́мия.
■ *v.t.* (воз)награ|жда́ть, -ди́ть; **it was a ~ing task** де́ло сто́ило того́.
rewind /riː'waɪnd/ *v.t.* перем|а́тывать, -ота́ть.
rewire /riː'waɪə(r)/ *v.t.*: **~ a house** замен|я́ть, -и́ть прово́дку в до́ме.
reword /riː'wɜːd/ *v.t.* переформули́ровать (*impf., pf.*).
rework /riː'wɜːk/ *v.t.* перераб|а́тывать, -о́тать.
rewrite /riː'raɪt/ *v.t.* (*copy out*) перепи́с|ывать, -а́ть; (*rework*) перераб|а́тывать, -о́тать.
rhapsod|y /'ræpsədɪ/ *n.* (*mus.*) рапсо́дия; (*fig.*): **he went into ~ies over her dress** он пел дифира́мбы её туале́ту/наря́ду.
rhetoric /'retərɪk/ *n.* рито́рика.
rhetorical /rɪ'tɒrɪk(ə)l/ *adj.* ритори́ческий.
rheumatic /ruː'mætɪk/ *n.* (*sufferer from rheumatism*) ревма́тик; (*pl., coll., rheumatism*) ревмати́зм.
■ *adj.* ревмати́ческий; **~ fever** ревмати́зм.
rheumatism /'ruːmətɪz(ə)m/ *n.* ревмати́зм.
rheumatoid /'ruːmətɔɪd/ *adj.* ревмато́идный, ревмати́ческий; **~ arthritis** ревмато́идный артри́т.
rhino /'raɪnəʊ/ *n.* (*pl.* **~s** *or* **~**) = **rhinoceros**
rhinoceros /raɪ'nɒsərəs/ *n.* (*pl.* **~** *or* **~es**) носоро́г.
Rhodes /rəʊdz/ *n.* Ро́дос.
rhododendron /rəʊdə'dendrən/ *n.* рододе́ндрон.
rhubarb /'ruːbɑːb/ *n.* реве́нь (*m.*).
rhyme /raɪm/ *n.* ри́фма; (*poem*) стих.
■ *v.t. & i.* рифмова́ть(ся) (*impf.*).
rhythm /'rɪð(ə)m/ *n.* ритм.
rhythmic /'rɪðmɪk/ *adj.* ритми́чный, ритми́ческий.
rib /rɪb/ *n.* (*anat.*) ребро́; **spare ~s** (*of meat*) рёбрышки (*nt. pl.*).
ribald /'rɪb(ə)ld/ *adj.* непристо́йный, скабрёзный.
ribbon /'rɪbən/ *n.* ле́нта, тесьма́.
rice /raɪs/ *n.* рис.
rich /rɪtʃ/ *n.* (*collect.*, **the ~**) бога́тые (*pl.*).
■ *adj.* 1 (*wealthy*) бога́тый.
2 (*fertile*) плодоро́дный.
3 (*of food*) жи́рный.
riches /'rɪtʃɪz/ *n.* бога́тство.
richness /'rɪtʃnɪs/ *n.* бога́тство; (*of food*) жи́рность.
Richter scale /'rɪktə/ *n.* шкала́ Ри́хтера.
rickety /'rɪkɪtɪ/ *adj.* ша́ткий, неусто́йчивый.
ricochet /'rɪkəʃeɪ/ *n.* рикоше́т; **~ fire** стрельба́ на рикоше́тах.
■ *v.i.* (**ricocheted** /-ʃeɪd/; **ricocheting** /-ʃeɪɪŋ/) рикошети́ровать (*impf., pf.*); бить (*impf.*) рикоше́том.
rid /rɪd/ *v.t.* (**ridding;** *past and p.p.* **rid**) освобо|жда́ть, -ди́ть; изб|авля́ть, -а́вить; **get ~ of** изб|авля́ться, -а́виться от + *g.*; **we were glad to be, get ~ of him** мы бы́ли ра́ды от него́ изба́виться.
riddance /'rɪd(ə)ns/ *n.*: **good ~ to him!** ≈ ска́тертью доро́га!
ridden /'rɪd(ə)n/ *p.p. of* ▸ **ride**
riddle[1] /'rɪd(ə)l/ *n.* зага́дка.
riddle[2] /'rɪd(ə)l/ *v.t.* (*pierce all over*) решети́ть, из-; **he was ~d with bullets** пу́ли изрешети́ли его́ те́ло.
ride /raɪd/ *n.*
1 (*on horseback*) прогу́лка верхо́м; (*by vehicle*) пое́здка, езда́.
2 (*excursion*) прогу́лка.
3 (*fairground attraction*) аттракцио́н.
■ *v.t. & i.* (*past* **rode;** *p.p.* **ridden**)
1 (*on horseback*) е́здить (*indet.*), е́хать (*det.*), по- (верхо́м) (на + *p.*); ката́ться (*impf.*) (верхо́м) (на + *p.*).
2 (*on a vehicle*) е́здить (*indet.*), е́хать (*det.*), по- (на + *p.*); **I ~ a bicycle to work** я е́зжу на рабо́ту на велосипе́де.
■ *with advs.*: **~ out** *v.t.*: **we shall ~ out our present troubles** мы пережи́вём ны́нешние тру́дности; **~ up** *v.i.* (*approach on horseback*) подъ|езжа́ть, -е́хать верхо́м; (*of clothing*) зад|ира́ться, -ра́ться.
rider /'raɪdə(r)/ *n.* (*horseman*) вса́дни|к (*fem.* -ца); (*cyclist*) велосипеди́ст (*fem.* -ка).
ridge /rɪdʒ/ *n.*
1 край; спи́нка.
2 (*of high land*) го́рный хребе́т.
ridicule /'rɪdɪkjuːl/ *n.* насме́шка.
■ *v.t.* подн|има́ть, -я́ть на́ смех.
ridiculous /rɪ'dɪkjʊləs/ *adj.* (*funny*) смехотво́рный; (*stupid, attr.*) смешно́й; (*stupid, pred.*) глу́пый; **don't be ~!** не бу́дь(те) посме́шищем!; **~ly low prices** до смешно́го ни́зкие це́ны.
riding /'raɪdɪŋ/ *n.* верхова́я езда́.
■ *cpd.* **~ school** *n.* шко́ла верхово́й езды́.
rife /raɪf/ *adj.* распространённый.
riff /rɪf/ *n.* (*mus.*) рифф.
riff-raff /'rɪfræf/ *n.* подо́нки (*m. pl.*) о́бщества; сброд.
rifle /'raɪf(ə)l/ *n.* винто́вка.
rift /rɪft/ *n.*
1 тре́щина, щель.
2 (*fig.*) разла́д.
rig /rɪg/ *n.* бурова́я вы́шка.
■ *v.t.* (**rigged, rigging**) (*conduct fraudulently*): **the elections were ~ged** результа́ты вы́боров бы́ли подтасо́ваны.
■ *with adv.*: **~ up** *v.t.* (на́скоро) соору|жа́ть, -ди́ть.
Riga /'riːgə/ *n.* Ри́га.
rigging /'rɪgɪŋ/ *n.* такела́ж.
right /raɪt/ *n.*
1 (*what is morally good*) правота́; справедли́вость; **the child must learn the difference between ~ and wrong** ребёнка сле́дует научи́ть отлича́ть добро́ от зла́.
2 (*entitlement*) пра́во; **by ~s** по справедли́вости; че́стно говоря́; **~ of way** пра́во прохо́да/прое́зда.
3 (*~-hand side etc.*) пра́вая сторона́; **on, to the ~** напра́во; **on, from the ~** спра́ва.
4 (*pol.*): **the R~** пра́вые (*pl.*).

■ *adj.* [1] (*just, morally good*) пра́вый, справедли́вый; **I try to do what is ~** я стара́юсь поступа́ть че́стно; **you were ~ to refuse** вы пра́вильно сде́лали, что отказа́лись.
[2] (*correct, true*) пра́вильный, ве́рный; **what is the ~ time?** вы мо́жете сказа́ть то́чное вре́мя?; **~ side up** в пра́вильном положе́нии; **that's ~!** пра́вильно!; ве́рно!; **I set him ~ on a few points** я ему́ ко́е-что разъясни́л.
[3] (*in order, good health*): **I don't feel ~** я пло́хо себя́ чу́вствую; **this medicine will soon put you ~** от э́того лека́рства вы ско́ро попра́витесь; **are you all ~?** с ва́ми всё в поря́дке?; (*expr. doubt*) вам нехорошо́?; вам пло́хо?; **all ~, I'll come with you!** ла́дно, я пойду́ с ва́ми!; **~!** (*expr. agreement or consent*) ве́рно!; хорошо́!
[4] (*opp. left*) пра́вый.
[5] : **~ angle** прямо́й у́гол.
■ *adv.* [1] (*straight*) пря́мо; **carry ~ on!** всё вре́мя пря́мо!
[2] (*exactly*) то́чно; **~ here/there** пря́мо здесь/там; **~ now** сейча́с; в да́нный моме́нт.
[3] (*immediately*) сра́зу (же); **~ away** сра́зу (же), пря́мо сейча́с, неме́дленно, сию́ мину́ту.
[4] (*all the way*) по́лностью; **he turned ~ round** он поверну́лся круго́м; **I went ~ back to the beginning** я верну́лся к са́мому нача́лу; **he came ~ up to me** он подошёл ко мне вплотну́ю.
[5] (*correctly, properly*) справедли́во; пра́вильно; **he can do nothing ~** у него́ ничего́ не ла́дится; **have I guessed ~?** я угада́л?
[6] (*of direction*) напра́во.
■ *v.t.* (*correct*) испр|авля́ть, -а́вить.
■ *cpds.* **~-hand** *adj.* пра́вый; **~-hand drive** правосторо́ннее управле́ние; **~-hand man** (*fig.*) ве́рный помо́щник, пра́вая рука́; **~-handed** *adj.* де́лающий всё пра́вой руко́й, правору́кий; **~-wing** *adj.* (*pol.*) пра́вых взгля́дов; пра́вый.

righteous /ˈraɪtʃəs/ *adj.* пра́ведный.

rightful /ˈraɪtfʊl/ *adj.* зако́нный.

rightly /ˈraɪtlɪ/ *adv.*
[1] (*correctly*) пра́вильно; **~ or wrongly, I believe he is lying** так э́то и́ли нет, но я ду́маю, он лжёт.
[2] (*justly*) справедли́во.

rigid /ˈrɪdʒɪd/ *adj.* жёсткий; (*fig.*) неги́бкий; **~ discipline** стро́гая дисципли́на.

rigidity /rɪˈdʒɪdɪtɪ/ *n.* жёсткость; (*fig.*) неги́бкость.

rigmarole /ˈrɪgmərəʊl/ *n.* каните́ль.

rigorous /ˈrɪgərəs/ *adj.* стро́гий.

rigour /ˈrɪgə(r)/ (*US* **rigor**) *n.* стро́гость.

rile /raɪl/ *v.t.* (*coll.*) серди́ть, рас-; раздраж|а́ть, -и́ть; **it ~d him to lose the game** его́ зли́ло, что он проигра́л.

rim /rɪm/ *n.* о́бод; край.

rind /raɪnd/ *n.* (*of orange, cheese*) ко́рка; (*of bacon*) кожура́, шку́рка.

ring¹ /rɪŋ/ *n.*
[1] (*ornament*) кольцо́; (*with stone; signet ~*) пе́рстень (*m.*); **engagement ~** кольцо́, пода́ренное при помо́лвке; **wedding ~** обруча́льное кольцо́.
[2] (*circle*) кольцо́, круг; **he had ~s under his eyes** у него́ бы́ли тёмные круги́ под глаза́ми.
[3] (*conspiracy*) ша́йка, ба́нда; **spy ~** шпио́нская организа́ция.
[4] (*of circus, boxing etc.*) аре́на, ринг.
[5] (*of cooker*) конфо́рка.
■ *cpds.* **~ binder** *n.* скоросшива́тель (*m.*); **~leader** *n.* глава́рь (*m.*); **~ road** *n.* (*Br.*) кольцева́я доро́га.

ring² /rɪŋ/ *n.*
[1] (*sound of bell*) звоно́к; **there was a ~ at the door** в дверь позвони́ли.
[2] (*Br., telephone call*) звоно́к; **give me a ~ tomorrow** позвони́те мне за́втра.
■ *v.t.* (*past* **rang;** *p.p.* **rung**)
[1] звони́ть, по- в + *a.*
[2] (*Br., telephone, also* **~ up**) звони́ть, по- + *d.*
■ *v.i.* (*past* **rang;** *p.p.* **rung**)
[1] звони́ть, по-; **the bells are ~ing** звоня́т колокола́; **the telephone rang** зазвони́л телефо́н; (*fig.*): **his words ~ true** его́ слова́ звуча́т правдоподо́бно.
[2] (*Br., telephone*) звони́ть, по-; **we must ~ for the doctor** мы должны́ вы́звать врача́ (по телефо́ну).
[3] (*resound*) огла|ша́ться, -си́ться (*чем*).
■ *with advs.*: **~ off** *v.i.* (*Br.*) повéсить (*pf.*) тру́бку; **~ out** *v.i.*: **a shot rang out** разда́лся вы́стрел.
■ *cpd.* **~tone** *n.* мелóдия звонка́, рингто́н (*в мобильном телефоне*).

ringing /ˈrɪŋɪŋ/ *adj.* зво́нкий.

ringlet /ˈrɪŋlɪt/ *n.* (*curl*) ло́кон.

rink /rɪŋk/ *n.* като́к.

rinse /rɪns/ *n.* полоска́ние.
■ *v.t.* полоска́ть, про-.

Rio (de Janeiro) /ˈriːəʊ (də dʒəˈnɪərəʊ)/ *n.* Ри́о-де-Жане́йро (*m. indecl.*).

riot /ˈraɪət/ *n.*
[1] (*revolt*) мяте́ж, бунт.
[2] (*fig.*): **she allowed her fancy to run ~** она́ дала́ по́лную во́лю воображе́нию; **the weeds are running ~** сорняки́ бу́йно разраста́ются; **the garden was a ~ of colour** сад пестре́л все́ми кра́сками.
■ *v.i.* (*rebel*) бесчи́нствовать (*impf.*).

rioter /ˈraɪətə(r)/ *n.* бунта́рь (*m.*), мяте́жник.

riotous /ˈraɪətəs/ *adj.* (*rebellious*) мяте́жный; (*wildly enthusiastic*) безу́держный, шу́мный.

rip /rɪp/ *v.t.* (**ripped, ripping**) рвать, разо-; **he ~ped his trousers on a nail** он порва́л брю́ки о гвоздь; **he ~ped open the envelope** он разорва́л конве́рт; **~ off** (*coll., steal*) об|дира́ть, -одра́ть; **she ~ped up the letter** она́ разорвала́ письмо́.
■ *v.i.* (**ripped, ripping**) рва́ться, разо-.
■ *cpd.* **~-off** *n.* (*coll.*): **it's a ~-off** э́то обдира́ловка.

ripe /raɪp/ *adj.* спе́лый, зре́лый; **the corn is ~** хлеба́ поспе́ли/созре́ли; **~ cheese** вы́держанный сыр.

ripen /ˈraɪpən/ *v.i.* зреть (*or* созрева́ть), со-.
■ *v.t.*: **the sun ~ed the tomatoes** помидо́ры созре́ли на со́лнце.

ripple /ˈrɪp(ə)l/ *n.* рябь.
■ *v.t.* & *i.* покр|ыва́ть(ся), -ы́ть(ся) ря́бью.

rise /raɪz/ *n.*
[1] (*slope; fig. ascent*) подъём.
[2] (*increase*) повыше́ние, увеличе́ние; **a ~ in**

temperature повышéние температýры; **they asked for a ~** (*Br.*) они попросѝли об увеличéнии зарплáты.
[3] (*origin*): **give ~ to** вызывáть, вы́звать.
■ *v.i.* (*past* **rose;** *p.p.* **risen** /ˈrɪz(ə)n/)
[1] (*get up from bed*) встаǀвáть, -ть (нá ноги); (*from seated or kneeling position*) встаǀвáть, -ть; поднǀимáться, -я́ться; (*into the air*) поднǀимáться, -я́ться; (*from the dead*) воскрǀесáть, -éснуть; (*above the horizon*) восходѝть, взойтѝ; **when the sun ~s** когдá восхóдит сóлнце; **he will always ~ to the occasion** он не растеря́ется в любóй ситуáции.
[2] (*slope upwards*) поднǀимáться, -я́ться; (*tower*): **the cliffs rose sheer above them** над нѝми крýто возвышáлись скáлы.
[3] (*increase in amount*) возрастáть (*impf.*); увелѝчиǀваться, -ться; **rising costs** увелѝчивающиеся расхóды; (*in level*): **the waters are rising** водá поднимáется/прибывáет; **the bread has ~n** хлеб подня́лся (*на дрожжах*); **the temperature is rising** температýра повышáется; (*in price*) повǀышáться, -ы́ситься в ценé; дорожáть, по-; (*in pitch*): **his voice rose in anger** в гнéве он повы́сил гóлос.
risible /ˈrɪzɪb(ə)l/ *adj.* смешнóй, смехотвóрный.
risk /rɪsk/ *n.* риск; **he takes many ~s** он лю́бит рисковáть; **he ran the ~ of defeat** он рисковáл потерпéть поражéние.
■ *v.t.* рисковáть (*impf.*) + *i.*
risky /ˈrɪskɪ/ *adj.* (**riskier, riskiest**) рискóванный, опáсный.
risotto /rɪˈzɒtəʊ/ *n.* (*pl.* **~s**) ризóтто (*nt. indecl.*).
risqué /ˈrɪskeɪ/ *adj.* рискóванный.
rite /raɪt/ *n.* обря́д.
ritual /ˈrɪtjʊəl/ *n.* ритуáл; (*collect.*) обря́дность.
■ *adj.* ритуáльный.
rival /ˈraɪv(ə)l/ *n.* сопéрник; (*in business*) конкурéнт.
■ *adj.* сопéрничающий; **the ~ team** комáнда протѝвника.
■ *v.t.* (**rivalled, rivalling;** *US* **rivaled, rivaling**) сопéрничать (*impf.*) с + *i.*
rivalry /ˈraɪvəlrɪ/ *n.* сопéрничество; (*in business*) конкурéнция.
river /ˈrɪvə(r)/ *n.* рекá; (*attr.*) речнóй; **up/down ~** вверх/вниз по рекé.
■ *cpd.* **~side** *n.* прибрéжная полосá; *adj.* прибрéжный, стоя́щий на берегý рекѝ.
rivet /ˈrɪvɪt/ *n.* заклёпка.
■ *v.t.* (**riveted, riveting**) клепáть (*impf.*); склёпǀывать, -áть.
riveting /ˈrɪvɪtɪŋ/ *adj.* (*coll.*) захвáтывающий.
Riyadh /rɪˈjɑːd/ *n.* Эр-Ря́д.
road /rəʊd/ *n.*
[1] (*thoroughfare*) дорóга; (*attr.*) дорóжный; **~ works** (*Br.*) дорóжно-ремóнтные рабóты.
[2] (*fig.*) путь (*m.*), дорóга; **he is on the ~ to recovery** он на путѝ к выздоровлéнию.
■ *cpds.* **~block** *n.* блокпóст; **~ map** *n.* кáрта (автомобѝльных) дорóг; (*fig.*) путеводная нить; **~ rage** *n.* (*Br.*) прѝступ гнéва/я́рости водѝтеля автомобѝля; **~show** *n.* (*radio, TV*) репортáж с мéста событий; (*pol.*) выезднóе заседáние, встрéча с избирáтелями; **~side** *n.* обóчина дорóги; **~worthy** *adj.* пригóдный для езды́ по дорóгам.
roam /rəʊm/ *v.t.* & *i.* бродѝть, стрáнствовать, скитáться (*all impf.*); **he ~ed the streets** он бродѝл по ýлицам.
roar /rɔː(r)/ *n.* (*of animal, people*) рёв; **~s of laughter** взры́вы хóхота.
■ *v.t.* & *i.* ревéть (*impf.*); **he ~ed with laughter** он хохотáл во всё гóрло.
roast /rəʊst/ *n.* жаркóе.
■ *v.t.* жáрить, за-, из-; **~ beef** жáреная/запечённая говя́дина.
■ *v.i.* грéться (*impf.*).
rob /rɒb/ *v.t.* (**robbed, robbing**) (*person*) обкрáдывать, обокрáсть; грáбить, о-; (*building*) грáбить, о-; **I have been ~bed** меня́ обокрáли/ограбили; **the bank was ~bed** банк ограбили; **they ~bed him of his watch** онѝ укрáли у негó часы́; (*fig., deprive*) лишǀáть, -ѝть (*кого-н. чего-н.*).
robber /ˈrɒbə(r)/ *n.* грабѝтель (*m.*), вор.
robbery /ˈrɒbərɪ/ *n.* (*of person, building*) ограблéние, грабёж; (*when life-threatening*) разбóй.
robe /rəʊb/ *n.* мáнтия; (*US, dressing gown; also* **bath~**) (купáльный) халáт.
robin /ˈrɒbɪn/ *n.* малѝновка.
robot /ˈrəʊbɒt/ *n.* (*lit., fig.*) рóбот.
robust /rəʊˈbʌst/ *adj.* (**robuster, robustest**) крéпкий, сѝльный.
rock[1] /rɒk/ *n.* (*solid part of earth's crust*) гóрная порóда; (*boulder*) валýн; **the firm is on the ~s** (*coll.*) фѝрма прогорéла; (*US, stone, pebble*) кáмень (*m.*); **whisky on the ~s** (*coll.*) вѝски со льдом.
■ *cpds.* **~ bottom** *n.* (*fig.*): **at ~-bottom prices** по сáмым нѝзким цéнам; **~ climber** *n.* скалолáз; **~ climbing** *n.* скалолáзание; **~ face** *n.* скалá; **~fall** *n.* камнепáд; **~ garden** *n.* (*also* **~ery**) альпинáрий, альпѝйская гóрка.
rock[2] /rɒk/ *n.* (*music*) рок; **~ star** рок-звездá.
■ *v.t.* (*sway gently*) качǀáть, -нýть; укáчǀивать, -áть; **she ~ed the baby to sleep** онá укачáла/убаю́кала ребёнка; (*shake*) трястѝ, по-; **the earthquake ~ed the house** дом шатáлся от землетрясéния.
■ *v.i.* (*sway gently*) качáться (*impf.*); **~ing chair** качáлка.
■ *cpd.* **~ 'n' roll** *n.* рок-н-рóлл.
rocket /ˈrɒkɪt/ *n.* ракéта.
■ *v.i.* (**rocketed, rocketing**) (*fig.*): **prices ~ed** цéны рéзко подскочѝли.
rocky /ˈrɒkɪ/ *adj.* (**rockier, rockiest**)
[1] (*of rock; full of rocks*) скалѝстый, каменѝстый; **the R~ Mountains, the Rockies** (*coll.*) Скалѝстые гóры (*f. pl.*).
[2] (*unsteady*) неустóйчивый, шáткий.
rococo /rəˈkəʊkəʊ/ *n.* рококó (*nt. indecl.*).
■ *adj.* в стѝле рококó.
rod /rɒd/ *n.*
[1] (*slender stick*) прут; (*fishing ~*) ýдочка; (*instrument of chastisement*) рóзга.
[2] (*metal bar*) стéржень (*m.*).
rode /rəʊd/ *past of* ▶ **ride**
rodent /ˈrəʊd(ə)nt/ *n.* грызýн.

rogue /rəʊg/ *n.* жу́лик, моше́нник.
■ *cpd.* **~ state** *n.* (*pol.*) госуда́рство-изго́й.

roguish /'rəʊgɪʃ/ *adj.* (*villainous*) жулькова́тый; (*playful*) прока́зливый, озорно́й.

role /rəʊl/ *n.* (*lit., fig.*) роль; **title ~** загла́вная роль.
■ *cpds.* **~ model** *n.* образе́ц для подража́ния; **~-play** *v.i.* разы́гр|ывать, -а́ть ро́ли.

roll /rəʊl/ *n.*
1 (*of cloth, paper, film etc.*) руло́н.
2 (*list*) рее́стр, спи́сок.
3 (*of bread*) бу́лочка.
4 (*rumbling sound*) раска́т; бой бараба́на.
■ *v.t.* 1 (*move by revolving*) ката́ть (*indet.*), кати́ть (*det.*), по-.
2 (*flatten by use of cylinder*) ката́ть, рас-; раска́тывать (*impf.*); **she was ~ing pastry** она́ раска́тывала те́сто; **~ing pin** ска́лка.
3 (*shape into cylinder or sphere*) свёр|тывать, -ну́ть; свора́чивать (*impf.*).
■ *v.i.* 1 (*move by revolving*) кати́ться (*impf.*); ска́тываться (*impf.*); **the car began to ~ downhill** маши́на покати́лась вниз.
2 (*sway*) кача́ться (*impf.*); колыха́ться (*impf.*).
3 (*make deep sound*) греме́ть (*impf.*); грохота́ть (*impf.*).
■ *with advs.*: **~ along** *v.i.*: **we were ~ing along at 30 mph** маши́на кати́лась со ско́ростью 30 миль в час; **~ over** *v.i.*: **he ~ed over and went to sleep again** он переверну́лся на друго́й бок и сно́ва засну́л; **~ up** *v.t.* свёр|тывать, -ну́ть; (*sleeves*) засу́ч|ивать, -и́ть.
■ *cpd.* **~-up** *n.* (*Br., cigarette*) самокру́тка.

roller /'rəʊlə(r)/ *n.* ро́лик; като́к; (*for paint*) ва́лик; (*pl., for hair*) бигуди́ (*nt. pl., indecl.*).
■ *cpds.* **~ coaster** *n.* америка́нские го́рки (*f. pl.*); **~ skate** *v.i.* ката́ться (*indet.*) на ро́ликах; **~ skates, ~blades** (*propr.*) *n. pl.* ро́лики (*m. pl.*), ро́ликовые коньки́ (*m. pl.*).

ROM /rɒm/ *n. comput.* (*abbr. of* ***read only memory***) ПЗУ (постоя́нное запомина́ющее устро́йство).

Roman /'rəʊmən/ *n.* (*also hist.*) ри́млян|ин (*fem.* -ка).
■ *adj.* 1 (*of Rome*) ри́мский; **the ~ alphabet** лати́нский алфави́т.
2 (*relig.*): **~ Catholic** (*n.*) като́л|ик (*fem.* -и́чка); *adj.* католи́ческий.

romance /rəʊ'mæns/ *n.*
1 (*novel, love affair*) рома́н.
2 (*romantic atmosphere*) рома́нтика.
3: **R~ languages** рома́нские языки́.

Romanesque /rəʊmə'nesk/ *n. & adj.* рома́нский (стиль).

Romania /rəʊ'meɪnɪə/ *n.* Румы́ния.

Romanian /rəʊ'meɪnɪən/ *n.* (*person*) румы́н (*fem.* -ка); (*language*) румы́нский язы́к.
■ *adj.* румы́нский.

romantic /rəʊ'mæntɪk/ *n.* рома́нтик.
■ *adj.* романти́ческий, романти́чный.

romanticism /rəʊ'mæntɪsɪz(ə)m/ *n.* романти́зм.

romanticize /rəʊ'mæntɪsaɪz/ *v.i.* романтизи́ровать (*impf., pf.*).

Romany /'rɒmənɪ/ *n.* (*Gypsy*) цыга́н (*fem.* -ка); (*language*) цыга́нский язы́к.
■ *adj.* цыга́нский.

Rome /rəʊm/ *n.* Рим.

romp /rɒmp/ *n.* возня́.
■ *v.i.* резви́ться (*impf.*).

roof /ru:f/ *n.* кры́ша; **~ of the mouth** нёбо.
■ *cpd.* **~ rack** *n.* бага́жник (на кры́ше автомоби́ля).

rook /rʊk/ *n.* (*bird*) грач; (*chess*) ладья́.

room /ru:m/ *n.*
1 ко́мната; **~ service** обслу́живание в но́мере.
2 (*space*) ме́сто, простра́нство; **there's plenty of ~** полно́ ме́ста.
3 (*scope*) возмо́жность.
■ *cpd.* **~-mate** *n.* сосе́д (*fem.* -ка) по ко́мнате.

roomy /'ru:mɪ/ *adj.* (**roomier, roomiest**) просто́рный, вмести́тельный.

rooster /'ru:stə(r)/ *n.* (*US*) пету́х.

root /ru:t/ *n.*
1 (*of plant*) ко́рень (*m.*); **take ~** пус|ка́ть, -ти́ть ко́рни; **the idea took ~ in his mind** э́та мысль засе́ла у него́ в голове́.
2 (*fig., source*) причи́на; **~ cause** основна́я причи́на; **money is the ~ of all evil** де́ньги — ко́рень зла.
■ *v.t.* 1 (*fig.*): **he is a man of deeply ~ed prejudices** он челове́к с укорени́вшимися предрассу́дками.
2 (*transfix*): **he stood ~ed to the ground** он стоя́л как вко́панный.
■ *with advs.*: **~ about** *v.i.* (*lit., fig.*) ры́ться (*impf.*); **~ out** *v.t.* (*lit., fig.*) вырыва́ть, вы́рвать с ко́рнем.

rope /rəʊp/ *n.* (*cord*) верёвка, кана́т; (*fig.*): **he knows the ~s** он зна́ет все ходы́ и вы́ходы; он зна́ет, что к чему́.
■ *v.t.* привя́з|ывать, -а́ть (*что к чему*).
■ *with adv.*: **~ in** *v.t.* (*coll., enlist*) втя́|гивать, -ну́ть; **I was ~d in to help** меня́ запрягли́ в э́то де́ло.

rosary /'rəʊzərɪ/ *n.* чёт|ки (*pl., g.* -ок).

rose[1] /rəʊz/ *n.* ро́за.
■ *cpds.* **~bud** *n.* буто́н ро́зы; **~ bush** *n.* ро́зовый куст; **~-coloured** (*US* **-colored**) *adj.* ро́зовый; **he sees the world through ~-coloured spectacles** (*Br.*), **glasses** (*US*) он смо́трит на мир че́рез ро́зовые очки́.

rose[2] /rəʊz/ *past of* ► **rise**

rosemary /'rəʊzmərɪ/ *n.* розмари́н.

rosette /rəʊ'zet/ *n.* розе́тка (*украшение*).

roster /'rɒstə(r)/ *n.* гра́фик дежу́рств.

rostrum /'rɒstrəm/ *n.* трибу́на.

rosy /'rəʊzɪ/ *adj.* (**rosier, rosiest**) ро́зовый; **~ cheeks** румя́ные щёки.

rot /rɒt/ *n.* гние́ние; гниль.
■ *v.t.* (**rotted, rotting**) по́ртить, ис-.
■ *v.i.* (**rotted, rotting**) гнить, с-; по́ртиться, ис-.

rota /'rəʊtə/ *n.* (*Br.*) гра́фик дежу́рств.

rotary /'rəʊtərɪ/ *adj.* враща́ющийся.

rotate /rəʊ'teɪt/ *v.t. & i.* враща́ть(ся) (*impf.*).

rotation /rəʊ'teɪʃ(ə)n/ *n.* враще́ние; оборо́т.

rote /rəʊt/ *n.*: **he learnt the poem by ~** он вы́учил стихотворе́ние наизу́сть.

rotten /'rɒt(ə)n/ *adj.* (**rottener, rottenest**) (*decayed*) гнило́й; (*corrupt*) разложи́вшийся;

r

испóрченный; (*very unfortunate*) отврати́тельный; **I'm feeling ~** я себя́ погáно чу́вствую.

Rottweiler /ˈrɒtvaɪlə(r)/ *n.* ротвéйлер.

rotund /rəʊˈtʌnd/ *adj.* (*spherical*) округлённый; (*corpulent, plump*) пóлный.

rouble /ˈru:b(ə)l/ *n.* рубль (*m.*).

rouge /ru:ʒ/ *n.* (*cosmetic*) румя́н|а (*pl., g.* —).
■ *v.t. & i.* румя́нить(ся), на-.

rough /rʌf/ *adj.*
[1] (*opp. smooth, even, level*) шероховáтый, нерóвный.
[2] (*opp. calm, gentle*) бу́рный; **a ~ crowd** хамовáтая пу́блика; **the students were ~ly handled by the police** поли́ция гру́бо обращáлась со студéнтами.
[3] (*arduous*) тру́дный; **he had a ~ time** емý пришлóсь ту́го.
[4] (*crude*) гру́бый; **a ~-and-ready meal** едá, приготóвленная на скóрую ру́ку.
[5] (*rudimentary*) черновóй; **a ~ sketch** черновóй набросок.
[6] (*approximate*) приблизи́тельный; **at a ~ guess** по приблизи́тельной оцéнке; **~ly speaking** гру́бо говоря́.
■ *v.t.*: **~ it** (*coll.*) жить (*impf.*) без удóбств.
■ *cpd.* **~shod** *adj.* подкóванный на шипы́; *adv.* (*fig.*): **he rode ~shod over their feelings** он совершéнно не щади́л их чувств.

roughage /ˈrʌfɪdʒ/ *n.* гру́бая пи́ща.

roughen /ˈrʌf(ə)n/ *v.t. & i.* дéлать(ся), с- гру́бым/шероховáтым.

roulette /ru:ˈlet/ *n.* рулéтка.

round /raʊnd/ *n.*
[1] (*circular or ~ed object*) круг, окру́жность; (*Br., slice*) лóмтик.
[2] (*regular cycle*) цикл; обхóд; круговорóт; **the doctor is on his ~s** дóктор дéлает обхóд.
[3] (*stage in contest*) тур, этáп, рáунд.
[4] (*set, series*): **he bought a ~ of drinks** он постáвил по стакáнчику всем прису́тствующим; **a ~ of applause** аплодисмéнты (*m. pl.*).
[5] (*of ammunition*) патрóн.
■ *adj.* [1] (*circular, spherical*) кру́глый; **~ shoulders** суту́лые плéчи.
[2] (*involving circular motion*) кругóвой; **~ trip** поéздка в óба концá.
[3] (*of numbers*) кру́глый; **a ~ dozen** цéлая дю́жина.
■ *adv.* (*Br.*): **all the year ~** кру́глый год; **the tree is six feet ~** э́то дéрево шесть фу́тов в окру́жности; **he went a long way ~** он сдéлал изря́дный крюк; **he was ~ at our house** он зашёл к нам.
■ *v.t.* [1] (*go ~*) огибáть, обогну́ть; об|ходи́ть, -ойти́ кругóм; **we ~ed the corner** мы заверну́ли/сверну́ли зá угол.
[2] (*~ a number up or down*) округл|я́ть, -и́ть.
■ *v.i.* (*turn aggressively*): **he ~ed on me with abuse** он обру́шился на меня́ с брáнью; **he ~ed on his pursuers** он наброśился на свои́х преслéдователей.
■ *with advs.*: **~ off** *v.t.* (*smooth*) вырáвнивать, вы́ровнять; (*bring to a conclusion*) заверш|áть, -и́ть; **~ up** *v.t.* сгоня́ть, согнáть; **the courier ~ed up the party** гид собрáл свою́ гру́ппу.
■ *prep.* (*Br.*)
[1] (*encircling*) вокру́г, кругóм, óколо (*all + g.*); **they sat ~ the table** они́ сидéли вокру́г столá.
[2] (*to or at all points of*): **he looked ~ the room** он осмотрéл (всю) кóмнату; **they went ~ the galleries** они обошли́ карти́нные галерéи.
[3]: **~ the corner** за углóм, (*of motion*) зá угол.
■ *cpds.* **~about** *n.* (*merry-go-round*) карусéль; (*Br., traffic island*) кольцевáя трáнспортная развя́зка; *adj.* окóльный; **~-the-clock** *adj.* круглосу́точный; **~-the-world** *adj.* кругосвéтный; **~-up** *n.* (*of news*) свóдка новостéй; (*of cattle*) загóн скóта; (*raid*) облáва.

rounders /ˈraʊndəz/ *n.* англи́йская лаптá.

rouse /raʊz/ *v.t.*
[1] (*wake*) буди́ть, раз-.
[2] (*stimulate to action, interest etc.*) подстрекáть (*impf.*); побу|ждáть, -ди́ть.

rout /raʊt/ *n.* разгрóм.
■ *v.t.* разби|вáть, -и́ть нáголову.

route /ru:t/ *n.* (*of bus etc.*) маршру́т; (*way*) путь, дорóга.

routine /ru:ˈti:n/ *n.*
[1] (*regular course of action*) заведённый поря́док; (*attr.*) регуля́рный; повседнéвный.
[2] (*theatr.*) нóмер, выступлéние.

rov|e /rəʊv/ *v.i.* скитáться (*impf.*); **he has a ~ing disposition** он лю́бит стрáнствовать; **a ~ing correspondent** разъезднóй корреспондéнт.

row[1] /rəʊ/ *n.* (*line*) ряд.

row[2] /rəʊ/ *v.t.*: **he ~ed the boat in to shore** он привёл лóдку к бéрегу.
■ *v.i.* грести́ (*impf.*); **~boat** (*US*), **~ing boat** (*Br.*) гребнáя шлю́пка.

row[3] /raʊ/ *n.*
[1] (*Br., noise*) шум.
[2] (*Br., argument*) ссóра; спор; (*dispute*) ди́спут, диску́ссия; **I had a ~ with the neighbours** (*Br.*) я поругáлся с сосéдями.
■ *v.i.* (*quarrel*) ссóриться, по-.

rowan /ˈrəʊən/ *n.* ряби́на.

rowdy /ˈraʊdɪ/ *adj.* (**rowdier, rowdiest**) гру́бый, шу́мный.

rowing /ˈrəʊɪŋ/ *n.* (*sport*) грéбля.

rowlock /ˈrɒlək/ *n.* уклю́чина.

royal /ˈrɔɪəl/ *adj.* королéвский, цáрский; **His R~ Highness** Егó Королéвское Высóчество; **~ blue** я́рко-си́ний цвет.

royalist /ˈrɔɪəlɪst/ *n.* роя́ли́ст (*fem.* -ка).
■ *adj.* роялúстский.

royalty /ˈrɔɪəltɪ/ *n.*
[1] (*royal person(s)*) члéн(ы) королéвской семьи́.
[2] (*payment*) áвторский гонорáр.

RSI (*abbr. of* ***repetitive strain injury***) трáвма, вы́званная повторя́ющимся движéнием.

RSVP (*abbr. of* ***répondez, s'il vous plaît***) бу́дьте любéзны отвéтить.

rub /rʌb/ *n. v.t.* (**rubbed, rubbing**) (*part of the body*) терéть (*impf.*); пот|ирáть, -ерéть; (*chafe*) нат|ирáть, -ерéть; (*sth. with a substance*) нат|ирáть, -ерéть + *i.*
■ *v.i.* (**rubbed, rubbing**) терéться (*impf.*).

■ *with advs.*: ~ **in** *v.t.* вт|ирáть, -ерéть; **it was my fault; don't ~ it in!** я виновáт, но скóлько мóжно упрекáть?; ~ **off** *v.t.* ст|ирáть, -ерéть; ~ **out** *v.t.* отт|ирáть, -ерéть; ст|ирáть, -ерéть; ~ **up** *v.t.* нач|ищáть, -йстить; полировáть, от-; **you ~bed him (up) the wrong way** вы к немý не так подошли́.

rubber /ˈrʌbə(r)/ *n.*
1 (*substance*) рези́на; (*attr.*) рези́новый; ~ **band** рези́нка; ~ **gloves** рези́новые перчáтки.
2 (*Br.*, *eraser*) лáстик, рези́нка.
■ *cpd.* **~-stamp** *v.t.* (*coll.*) подпи́с|ывать, -áть не глядя.

rubbish /ˈrʌbɪʃ/ *n.* (*Br.*) (*refuse*) мýсор; хлам (*also fig.*); (*nonsense*) чепухá, вздор.
■ *cpds.* ~ **bin** *n.* мýсорное ведрó; ~ **dump,** ~ **tip** *nn.* свáлка.

rubble /ˈrʌb(ə)l/ *n.* булы́жник, щéбень (*m.*).

rubella /ru:ˈbelə/ *n.* (*med.*) краснýха.

ruble /ˈru:b(ə)l/ = **rouble**

ruby /ˈru:bɪ/ *n.* руби́н.

rucksack /ˈrʌksæk/ *n.* рюкзáк.

rudder /ˈrʌdə(r)/ *n.* руль (*m.*).

ruddy /ˈrʌdɪ/ *adj.* (**ruddier, ruddiest**) румя́ный.

rude /ru:d/ *adj.*
1 (*impolite*) грýбый; невоспи́танный; **don't be ~!** не грубúте!; **he was ~ to the teacher** он нагрубúл учи́телю.
2 (*indecent*) грýбый, непристóйный.

rudiment /ˈru:dɪmənt/ *n.* (*in pl.*) элементáрные знáния.

rudimentary /ru:dɪˈmentərɪ/ *adj.* элементáрный.

rueful /ˈru:fʊl/ *adj.* печáльный, удручённый.

ruffian /ˈrʌfɪən/ *n.* головорéз, бандúт.

ruffle /ˈrʌf(ə)l/ *n.* (*frill*) обóрка.
■ *v.t.*: **a breeze ~d the surface of the lake** от вéтра óзеро покры́лось ря́бью; **she ~d his hair** онá взъерóшила емý вóлосы; **the bird ~d up its feathers** пти́ца взъерóшила пéрья; **he never gets ~d** он всегдá невозмути́м.

rug /rʌg/ *n.* ковёр.

rugby (football) /ˈrʌgbɪ/ *n.* рéгби (*nt. indecl.*).
■ *cpd.* ~ **player** *n.* регби́ст.

rugged /ˈrʌgɪd/ *adj.*
1 (*rough, uneven*) нерóвный; **a ~ coast** скали́стый бéрег.
2 (*irregular*) грýбый; ~ **features** рéзкие черты́.

rugger /ˈrʌgə(r)/ (*Br. coll.*) = **rugby (football)**

ruin /ˈru:ɪn/ *n.*
1 (*downfall*) ги́бель, крушéние.
2 (*collapsed or destroyed state*; *building in this state*) развáлины, руи́ны (*both f. pl.*); **the house fell into ~** дом совершéнно развали́лся; (*fig.*) **their plans lay in ~s** их плáны рýхнули.
■ *v.t.* разр|ушáть, -ýшить; уничт|ожáть, -óжить; губи́ть, по-; **he was ~ed** (*in business*) он разори́лся; **the rain ~ed my suit** дождь испóртил мой костю́м; **a ~ed building** разрýшенное здáние.

rule /ru:l/ *n.*
1 (*regulation*; *principle*) прáвило; **smoking is against the ~s** кури́ть не разрешáется.
2 (*normal practice*) привы́чка, обы́чай; **as a ~** как прáвило.
3 (*government*) правлéние, госпóдство.
4 (*measuring stick*) линéйка.
■ *v.t.* 1 (*govern*) управля́ть (*impf.*) + *i.*; руководи́ть (*impf.*) + *i.*
2 (*decree*) постан|авливать, -ови́ть; **the umpire ~d that the ball was not out** судья́ объяви́л, что мяч нé был в áуте.
3 : **~d paper** линóванная бумáга.
■ *v.i.* (*hold sway*) прáвить (*impf.*); управля́ть (*impf.*); **ruling classes** прáвящие клáссы.
■ *with adv.*: ~ **out** *v.t.* (*exclude*) исключ|áть, -и́ть.

ruler /ˈru:lə(r)/ *n.* (*reigning person*) прави́тель (*m.*); (*measuring stick*) линéйка.

ruling /ˈru:lɪŋ/ *n.* (*decree*) постановлéние; решéние.

rum /rʌm/ *n.* ром.

rumba /ˈrʌmbə/ *n.* рýмба.
■ *v.i.* (**rumbas, rumbaed** /-bəd/ *or* **rumba'd, rumbaing** /-bə(r)ɪŋ/) танцевáть, с- рýмбу.

rumbl|e /ˈrʌmb(ə)l/ *n.* громыхáние, гул.
■ *v.i.* громыхáть (*impf.*); гремéть, за-/про-; **thunder was ~ing in the distance** вдалекé гремéл гром.

ruminant /ˈru:mɪnənt/ *n.* жвáчное живóтное.
■ *adj.* жвáчный.

ruminate /ˈru:mɪneɪt/ *v.i.* (*ponder*) раздýмывать (*impf.*).

rumination /ru:mɪˈneɪʃ(ə)n/ *n.* (*fig.*) размышлéние.

rummage /ˈrʌmɪdʒ/ *v.i.* ры́ться (*impf.*).

rumour /ˈru:mə(r)/ (*US* **rumor**) *n.* слух; тóлк|и (*pl.*, *g.* -ов).
■ *v.t.*: **the ~ed visit** визи́т, о котóром прошёл слух.

rumple /ˈrʌmp(ə)l/ *v.t.* (*clothes*) мять, по-; (*hair*) ерóшить, взъ-.

rumpus /ˈrʌmpəs/ *n.* (*pl.* **rumpuses**) шум; скандáл; **kick up a ~** подн|имáть, -я́ть шум; ~ **room** (*US*) кóмната для игр и развлечéний.

run /rʌn/ *n.*
1 (*action of ~ning*) бег, пробéг; **he went for a ~ before breakfast** он сдéлал пробéжку пéред зáвтраком; **the prisoner made a ~ for it** заключённый бежáл/удрáл; **the prisoner is on the ~** заключённый нахóдится в бегáх.
2 (*trip, journey, route*) поéздка, рейс, маршрýт.
3 (*continuous stretch*) перúод; отрéзок врéмени; **he had a ~ of good luck** у негó былá полосá везéния; **the play had a long ~** пьéса шла дóлго; **in the long ~** в конéчном счёте.
4 (*score at cricket etc.*) очкó.
5 (*for fowls etc.*) загóн.
6 (*US, ladder in stocking*) спусти́вшаяся петля́.
■ *v.t.* (**running;** *past* **ran;** *p.p.* **run**)
1 (*execute*): **he ran a good race** он хорошó пробежáл (дистáнцию).
2 (*cover*) бежáть (*det.*), про-; **he can ~ the mile in under a minute** он мóжет

пробежа́ть ми́лю ме́ньше чем за мину́ту.
3 (*convey in car*) подв|ози́ть, -езти́ (на маши́не); **shall I ~ you home?** хоти́те, я подвезу́ вас домо́й?
4 (*cause to go*): **he ran his fingers over the keys** он пробежа́л па́льцами по кла́вишам; **he ran his eye over the page** он пробежа́л глаза́ми страни́цу; **I shall ~ (water into) the bath** я напущу́ воды́ в ва́нну.
5 (*operate*) управля́ть (*impf.*) + *i.*; **who is ~ning the shop?** кто ве́дает ла́вкой?; **he ~s a small business** у него́ своё небольшо́е де́ло; **she ~s the house single-handed** она́ сама́ ведёт хозя́йство; **he ran the engine for a few minutes** он завёл мото́р на не́сколько мину́т.
■ *v.i.* (**running;** *past* **ran;** *p.p.* **run**)
1 (*move quickly*) бе́гать (*indet.*), бежа́ть (*det.*), побежа́ть (*pf.*); **I had to ~ for the train** мне пришло́сь бежа́ть, что́бы поспе́ть на по́езд; **he ran for his life** он удира́л изо всех сил; **~ for it!** беги́!
2 (*come by chance*) столкну́ться (*pf.*) (с + *i.*); натолкну́ться (*pf.*) (на + *a.*); **I ran into, across an old friend** я случа́йно встре́тил ста́рого това́рища.
3 (*compete*) соревнова́ться (*impf.*); (*fig.*): **he ran for president** он баллоти́ровался в президе́нты.
4 (*of public transport*) ходи́ть (*indet.*); **there are no trains ~ning** поезда́ не хо́дят.
5 (*of machines etc.: function*) де́йствовать (*impf.*); **most cars ~ on petrol** (*Br.*), **gasoline** (*US*) большинство́ маши́н рабо́тает на бензи́не; **leave the engine ~ning!** не выключа́йте мото́р!
6 (*flow*) течь, протека́ть, струи́ться (*all impf.*); **tears/sweat ran down his face** слёзы кати́лись (*or* пот струи́лся) по его́ щека́м; **his nose was ~ning** у него́ текло́ из носу.
7 (*of colour, ink*) линя́ть, по-.
8 (*extend*) тяну́ться (*impf.*); простира́ться (*impf.*); **the gardens ~ down to the river** сады́ тя́нутся до реки́; **his income ~s into five figures** его́ дохо́д измеря́ется пятизна́чной ци́фрой.
9 (*continue*) быть действи́тельным; **the lease has seven years to ~** догово́р о на́йме действи́телен ещё семь лет; **the play has been ~ning for five years** пье́са идёт пять лет; **it ~s in their family** э́то у них насле́дственное.
■ *further phrr. with preps.*: **~ into** (*collide with*) налете́ть (*impf.*) на + *a.*; (*encounter*): **he ran into debt** он зале́з/влез в долги́; **~ over, through** (*review*) повтор|я́ть, -и́ть.
■ *with advs.*: **~ about** *v.i.* бе́гать (*indet.*); **~ away** *v.i.* убе|га́ть, -жа́ть; уд|ира́ть, -ра́ть; **~ back** *v.i.*: **he ran back to apologize** он прибежа́л наза́д, что́бы извини́ться; **~ down** *v.t.*: **don't ~ your battery down** не тра́тьте батаре́ю; **she is always ~ning down her neighbours** она́ ве́чно поно́сит сосе́дей; **you look very ~ down** у вас о́чень утомлённый вид; **~ off** *v.i.* убе|га́ть, -жа́ть; уд|ира́ть, -ра́ть; **he ran off with the jewels** он сбежа́л с драгоце́нностями; **~ out** *v.i.* (*come to an end*) конча́ться, ко́нчиться; **he will soon ~ out of money** у него́ ско́ро ко́нчатся де́ньги; **~ over** *v.t.* задави́ть (*pf.*); **he was ~ over by a car** его́ задави́ла маши́на; **~ up** *v.t.*: **he ran up a bill at the tailor's** он задолжа́л портно́му; *v.i.*: **she ran up to tell me the news** она́ прибежа́ла, что́бы сообщи́ть мне но́вость; **he ran up against a snag** он натолкну́лся на препя́тствие.
■ *cpds.* **~away** *n.* (*fugitive*) бегл|е́ц (*fem.* -я́нка); (*attr.*): **a ~away horse** ло́шадь, кото́рая понесла́; **~-in** *n.* (*fight, squabble*) схва́тка; **~-of-the-mill** *adj.* обы́чный, сре́дний; **~-up** *n.* (*run preparatory to action*) разбе́г; (*fig.*): **the ~-up to the election** (*Br.*) предвы́борная пора́/кампа́ния; **~way** *n.* (*aeron.*) взлётно-поса́дочная полоса́.

rung[1] /rʌŋ/ *n.* (*of ladder*) ступе́нька.

rung[2] /rʌŋ/ *p.p. of* ▸ **ring**[2]

runner /ˈrʌnə(r)/ *n.*
1 (*athlete*) бегу́н.
2 (*horse in race*) рыса́к, (бегова́я) ло́шадь.
3 (*narrow cloth, rug*) доро́жка.
4 (*bot., shoot*) побе́г; **~ bean** (*Br.*) зелёная (стручко́вая) фасо́ль.
■ *cpd.* **~-up** *n.* уча́стник/кандида́т, заня́вший второ́е ме́сто.

running /ˈrʌnɪŋ/ *n.*
1 (*sport*) бег; **I shall take up ~** я займу́сь бе́гом; **~ shoes** кроссо́в|ки (*pl., g.* -ок).
2 (*contest*) состяза́ние; **they are out of the ~ for the Cup** они́ вы́были из соревнова́ний на ку́бок.
3 (*operation*) управле́ние (*чем*).
■ *adj.* 1 (*performed while events proceed*) теку́щий; **~ commentary** репорта́ж (с ме́ста собы́тия).
2 (*continuous*) непреры́вный; **~ costs** (*of business*) теку́щие расхо́ды (*m. pl.*); (*of car*) расхо́ды (*m. pl.*) на содержа́ние маши́ны.
3 (*in succession*) подря́д, кря́ду; **he won three times ~** он вы́играл три ра́за подря́д.
4 : **~ water** водопрово́д.

runny /ˈrʌnɪ/ *adj.* (**runnier, runniest**) теку́чий, жи́дкий; **a ~ nose** мо́крый нос, на́сморк.

rupture /ˈrʌptʃə(r)/ *n.* проры́в; перело́м.
■ *v.t.* (*burst, break*) прор|ыва́ть, -ва́ть
■ *v.i.* раз|рыва́ться, -орва́ться.

rural /ˈrʊər(ə)l/ *adj.* се́льский.

ruse /ruːz/ *n.* уло́вка, ухищре́ние.

rush[1] /rʌʃ/ *n.* (*bot.*) тростни́к.

rush[2] /rʌʃ/ *n.* стреми́тельное движе́ние; **he made a ~ for the goal** он бро́сился к воро́там; (*bustle*) спе́шка; (*increase in activity*): **the Christmas ~** предрожде́ственская суета́; **in the ~ hour** в часы́ пик.
■ *v.t.* 1 (*speed*) торопи́ть, по-; **troops were ~ed to the front** войска́ бы́ли сро́чно перебро́шены на фронт; **the order was ~ed through** зака́з бы́стро проверну́ли; **I refuse to be ~ed into a decision** я отка́зываюсь принима́ть реше́ние в спе́шке.
2 (*charge*) брать, взять шту́рмом.
■ *v.i.* мча́ться, по-; бр|оса́ться, -о́ситься; кида́ться, ки́нуться; **she ~ed off without saying goodbye** она́ убежа́ла, не попроща́вшись; **they ~ed to congratulate her** они́ бро́сились её поздравля́ть.

rusk /rʌsk/ *n.* суха́рь (*m.*).

Russia /ˈrʌʃə/ *n.* Росси́я.

Russian /ˈrʌʃ(ə)n/ *n.*
1 (*person of Russian nationality*) русск|ий (*fem.* -ая); (*person of Russian citizenship*) россиян|ин (*fem.* -ка).
2 (*language*) русский язык; **do you speak ~?** вы говорите по-русски?
■ *adj.* русский; **~ doll** матрёшка.
■ *cpd.* **~-speaking** *adj.* русскоязычный.
rust /rʌst/ *n.* ржавчина.
■ *v.i.* ржаветь, за-.
rustic /ˈrʌstɪk/ *adj.* деревенский, сельский.
rustle /ˈrʌs(ə)l/ *n.* шелест, шорох.
■ *v.t.* шелестеть (*impf.*) + *i.*; шуршать (*impf.*) + *i.*
■ *v.i.* шелестеть (*impf.*); шуршать (*impf.*).
rusty /ˈrʌstɪ/ *adj.* (**rustier, rustiest**) ржавый; (*fig.*) (*out of practice*): **his Russian is ~** он подзабыл русский.
rut /rʌt/ *n.* (*wheel track*) колея, выбоина; (*fig.*) рутина; **it is easy to get into a ~** легко погрязнуть в рутине.
ruthless /ˈruːθlɪs/ *adj.* безжалостный, жестокий.
Rwanda /rʊˈændə/ *n.* Руанда.
rye /raɪ/ *n.* рожь; **~ bread** ржаной хлеб; **(~ whisky)** ржаное виски (*nt. indecl.*).

Ss

sabbath /ˈsæbəθ/ *n.* (*Jewish*) суббота; (*Christian*) воскресенье.
sabbatical /səˈbætɪk(ə)l/ *n.* (*also* **~ leave**) творческий отпуск.
sabotage /ˈsæbətɑːʒ/ *n.* диверсия, саботаж.
■ *v.t.* саботировать (*impf.*, *pf.*).
saboteur /sæbəˈtəː(r)/ *n.* саботажни|к (*fem.* -ца), диверсант (*fem.* -ка).
sabre /ˈseɪbə(r)/ *n.* сабля.
saccharine /ˈsækəriːn/ *adj.* сахарный, сахаристый; (*fig.*) слащавый, приторный.
sachet /ˈsæʃeɪ/ *n.* (*Br.*) пакетик (*шампуня и т. п.*).
sack[1] /sæk/ *n.*
1 (*bag*) мешок.
2 (*coll.*, *dismissal*): **get the ~** быть уволенным; **I got the ~** меня выгнали.
■ *v.t.* (*coll.*, *dismiss*) выгонять, выгнать; ув|ольнять, -олить.
sack[2] /sæk/ *v.t.* (*plunder*) грабить, раз-.
sacrament /ˈsækrəmənt/ *n.* таинство.
sacred /ˈseɪkrɪd/ *adj.* священный, святой.
sacrifice /ˈsækrɪfaɪs/ *n.* (*lit.*, *fig.*) жертва.
■ *v.t.* (*lit.*, *at altar*) прин|осить, -ести (*кого/что*) в жертву; (*give up*) жертвовать, по- + *i.*
sacrificial /sækrɪˈfɪʃ(ə)l/ *adj.* жертвенный.
sacrilege /ˈsækrɪlɪdʒ/ *n.* святотатство.
sacrilegious /sækrɪˈlɪdʒəs/ *adj.* святотатственный, кощунственный.
sacrosanct /ˈsækrəʊsæŋkt/ *adj.* священный.
sad /sæd/ *adj.* (**sadder, saddest**) грустный, печальный; **I feel ~** мне грустно; **a ~ event** печальное событие; (*regrettable*) прискорбный; **it is ~ that you failed the exams** очень жаль, что вы провалились на экзаменах.
sadden /ˈsæd(ə)n/ *v.t.* печалить, о-.
saddle /ˈsæd(ə)l/ *n.* седло.
■ *v.t.* 1 седлать, о-.
2 (*fig.*, *burden with task, guilt etc.*): **~ s.o. with sth.** взвал|ивать, -ить что-н. на кого-н.
sadism /ˈseɪdɪz(ə)m/ *n.* садизм.
sadist /ˈseɪdɪst/ *n.* садист (*fem.* -ка).
sadistic /səˈdɪstɪk/ *adj.* садистский.
sadness /ˈsædnɪs/ *n.* грусть, печаль, тоска.
sae (*abbr. of* ***stamped addressed envelope***) (*Br.*) конверт с маркой и обратным адресом.
safari /səˈfɑːrɪ/ *n.* (*pl.* **~s**) сафари (*nt. indecl.*); **~ park** сафари-парк.
safe[1] /seɪf/ *n.* сейф.
safe[2] /seɪf/ *adj.*
1 (*affording security, not dangerous*) безопасный; (*reliable*) надёжный; **in s.o.'s ~ keeping** у кого-н. на сохранении; **to be on the ~ side** на всякий случай, для (большей) верности.
2 (*free from danger*): **we are ~ from attack** мы можем не опасаться нападения; **~ house** конспиративная квартира; укрытие; **~ sex** безопасный секс; (*unhurt, undamaged*): **we saw them home ~ and sound** мы доставили их домой целыми и невредимыми (*or* в целости и сохранности).
3 (*cautious, moderate*) осторожный; **better ~ than sorry** бережёного Бог бережёт; **I decided to play ~** я решил не рисковать.
4 (*certain*): **it's a ~ bet** можно быть уверенным.
■ *cpds.* **~ conduct** *n.* (*document*) охранная грамота; **~ deposit** *n.* хранилище с сейфами; **~guard** *n.* охрана, страховка, гарантия (от + *g.*); защитная мера, меры безопасности; *v.t.* гарантировать (*impf.*, *pf.*); охран|ять, -ить.
safely /ˈseɪflɪ/ *adv.*
1 (*unharmed*) благополучно, в сохранности; **we returned ~** мы благополучно вернулись; **the parcel arrived ~** посылка пришла в целости и сохранности.
2 (*with confidence*) уверенно, с уверенностью; **I can ~ say that ...** я могу с уверенностью сказать, что... .
3 (*securely*) надёжно.
safety /ˈseɪftɪ/ *n.* безопасность; **road ~** безопасность на дорогах; **~ net** (*fig.*) страховка.
■ *cpds.* **~ belt** *n.* ремень (*m.*) безопасности;

~ **pin** *n.* англи́йская була́вка.
saffron /'sæfrən/ *n.* (*substance*) шафра́н; (*colour*) шафра́нный/шафра́новый цвет (*оранжево-жёлтый*).
■ *adj.* шафра́нный, шафра́новый.
sag /sæg/ *v.i.* (**sagged, sagging**) (*of rope, curtain*) пров|иса́ть, -и́снуть; (*of ceiling*) прог|иба́ться, -ну́ться; (*of cheeks, breasts*) обв|иса́ть, -и́снуть.
saga /'sɑ:gə/ *n.* са́га; (*fig.*): **he told me the ~ of his escape** он пове́дал мне (фантасти́ческую) исто́рию своего́ побе́га.
sagacious /sə'geɪʃ(ə)s/ *adj.*
1 (*of person*) му́дрый; (*of animal*) у́мный.
2 (*perspicacious*) проница́тельный, му́дрый; (*of action: far-sighted*) дальнови́дный, прозорли́вый.
sage[1] /seɪdʒ/ *n.* (*bot.*) шалфе́й.
sage[2] /seɪdʒ/ *n.* (*wise man*) мудре́ц.
Sagittarius /sædʒɪ'teərɪəs/ *n.* Стреле́ц.
Sahara /sə'hɑ:rə/ *n.* Саха́ра.
said /sed/ *past and p.p. of* ▸ **say**
sail /seɪl/ *n.*
1 па́рус; **in full ~** на всех паруса́х; **make, set ~ for** отпл|ыва́ть, -ы́ть в/на + *a.*; отпр|авля́ться, -а́виться в/на + *a.*
2 (*voyage on water*) пла́вание.
■ *v.t.* 1 (*of person or ship*) пла́вать (*indet.*), плыть (*det.*) в + *p.*; (*cover a distance*) пропл|ыва́ть, -ы́ть; **we ~ed 150 miles** мы проплы́ли/прошли́ 150 миль.
2 (*control navigation of*) управля́ть (*impf.*) + *i.*
■ *v.i.* 1 пл|а́вать (*indet.*), -ыть (*det.*), поплы́ть (*pf.*); **the ship ~ed into harbour** (*Br.*), **harbor** (*US*) кора́бль вошёл в га́вань; **we ~ed out to sea** мы вы́шли в мо́ре; **they ~ed up the coast** они́ плы́ли вдоль бе́рега.
2 (*fig., move gracefully*) плыть (*det.*); пла́вно дви́гаться (*impf.*); пропл|ыва́ть, -ы́ть; **he ~ed through** (*made light work of*) **the exams** он с лёгкостью (*or* без труда́) сдал экза́мены.
■ *cpd.* **~boat** *n.* (*US*) па́русная ло́дка.
sailboard /'seɪlbɔ:d/ *n.* виндсёрф(ер).
sailboarder /'seɪlbɔ:də(r)/ *n.* виндсёрфинги́ст.
sailboarding /'seɪlbɔ:dɪŋ/ *n.* виндсёрфинг.
sailing /'seɪlɪŋ/ *n.* (*as sport*) па́русный спорт.
■ *cpds.* **~ boat** *n.* (*Br.*) па́русная ло́дка; **~ ship** *n.* па́русное су́дно, па́русник.
sailor /'seɪlə(r)/ *n.* моря́к, матро́с.
saint /seɪnt/ *n.* свято́й; **S~ Valentine's Day** день свято́го Валенти́на.
sainthood /'seɪnthʊd/ *n.* свя́тость.
saintly /'seɪntlɪ/ *adj.* (**saintlier, saintliest**) свято́й.
sake /seɪk/ *n.*: **for the ~ of** ра́ди + *g.*; **for God's, heaven's, goodness ~** ра́ди бо́га (*or* всего́ свято́го); **for old times' ~** по ста́рой па́мяти.
salable /'seɪləb(ə)l/ (*US*) = **saleable**
salacious /sə'leɪʃəs/ *adj.* (*indecent*) непристо́йный, скабрёзный.
salad /'sæləd/ *n.* сала́т.
■ *cpds.* **~ dressing** *n.* запра́вка для сала́та.
salami /sə'lɑ:mɪ/ *n.* (*pl.* **~s**) копчёная колбаса́, саля́ми (*f. indecl.*).
salary /'sælərɪ/ *n.* зарпла́та.
sale /seɪl/ *n.*
1 прода́жа, сбыт; **be on, for ~** име́ться (*impf.*) в прода́же; **~ (selling) price** прода́жная цена́; **~s assistant, sales clerk** (*US*) продав|е́ц (*fem.* -щи́ца).
2 (*event*): (*clearance* **~**) распрода́жа; **~ (reduced) price** сни́женная цена́, цена́ со ски́дкой.
■ *cpds.* **~sman** *n.* (*in shop*) продаве́ц; (*travelling door-to-door*) коммивояжёр; **~swoman** *n.* (*in shop*) продавщи́ца.
saleable /'seɪləb(ə)l/ (*US also* **salable**) *adj.* ходово́й, хо́дкий (*both coll.*).
salient /'seɪlɪənt/ *n.* (*in fortifications*) вы́ступ; (*in line of attack or defence*) вы́ступ, клин.
■ *adj.* (*jutting out*) выдаю́щийся, выступа́ющий; (*fig.*) выдаю́щийся, я́ркий.
saline /'seɪlaɪn/ *n.* (*solution*) соляно́й раство́р; (*med.*) физиологи́ческий раство́р.
■ *adj.* солёный, соляно́й; **~ spring** солёный исто́чник; **~ solution** соляно́й раство́р.
saliva /sə'laɪvə/ *n.* слюна́.
salivate /'sælɪveɪt/ *v.i.* выделя́ть, вы́делить слюну́.
salmon /'sæmən/ *n.* лосо́сь (*m.*); сёмга.
salmonella /sælmə'nelə/ *n.* сальмоне́лла.
salon /'sælɒn/ *n.* сало́н.
saloon /sə'lu:n/ *n.* (*on ship*) сало́н; **~ (bar)** (*Br.*) бар; **~ (car)** (*Br.*) седа́н.
salt /sɔ:lt/ *n.* соль.
■ *adj.*: **~ water** морска́я вода́.
■ *v.t.* 1 (*cure in brine*) соли́ть, за-.
2 (*sprinkle with* **~**) соли́ть, по-.
■ *cpd.* **~ cellar** *n.* соло́нка.
salty /'sɔ:ltɪ, 'sɒl-/ *adj.* (**saltier, saltiest**) (*lit., fig.*) солёный.
salubrious /sə'lu:brɪəs/ *adj.* (*healthy*) здоро́вый; (*curative*) целе́бный, цели́тельный.
salutary /'sæljʊtərɪ/ *adj.* благотво́рный.
salute /sə'lu:t/ *n.* отда́ние че́сти; во́инское приве́тствие.
■ *v.t. & i.* отд|ава́ть, -а́ть честь (*кому*).
Salvadorean /sælvə'dɔ:rɪən/ *n.* сальвадо́р|ец (*fem.* -ка).
■ *adj.* сальвадо́рский.
salvage /'sælvɪdʒ/ *n.* (*saving ship or property*) спасе́ние (иму́щества); (*what is saved*) спасённое иму́щество; спасённый груз *и т. п.*
■ *v.t.* (*save*) спас|а́ть, -ти́; (*preserve*) сохран|я́ть, -и́ть.
salvation /sæl'veɪʃ(ə)n/ *n.* спасе́ние (души́), избавле́ние; **S~ Army** А́рмия спасе́ния.
salve /sælv/ *n.* (*lit., fig.*) бальза́м.
■ *v.t.* (*fig., soothe*) успок|а́ивать, -о́ить.
Samaritan /sə'mærɪt(ə)n/ *n.*: **good ~** (*bibl.*) до́брый самаритя́нин.
samba /'sæmbə/ *n.* са́мба.
same /seɪm/ *adj.* тот же (са́мый); тако́й же; оди́н (и тот же); (*unvarying*) одина́ковый, неизме́нный, ро́вный; **is that the ~ man we saw yesterday?** э́то тот же челове́к, кото́рого мы ви́дели вчера́?; **we are the ~ age** мы одни́х лет (*or* одного́ во́зраста); **in the ~ way** таки́м же о́бразом; **at the ~ time** в то же вре́мя, одновре́ме́нно; (*however*) в то же вре́мя, ме́жду тем; **the village looks just the ~ as ever (it did)** дере́вня вы́глядит тако́й же, как всегда́; **it's the ~**

everywhere везде́ одина́ково.
■ *pron.* тот же (са́мый); **it's all the ~ to me** мне всё равно́; **~ again, please!** то же са́мое, пожа́луйста!; **... and the ~ to you!** ... и вам та́кже (*or* того́ же)!
■ *adv.*: **I don't feel the ~ towards him** я измени́л своё отноше́ние к нему́; **all the ~** (*nevertheless*) всё-таки; всё равно́; всё же; **just the ~** (*despite that*) тем не ме́нее; **~ here!** я то́же!

samovar /'sæməvɑ:(r)/ *n.* самова́р.

sample /'sɑ:mp(ə)l/ *n.* (*comm., fig.*) образе́ц, обра́зчик, приме́р; (*med.*) про́ба.
■ *v.t.* (*wine, food etc.*) про́бовать, по-; (*try out*) про́бовать, по-.

sanatorium /sænə'tɔ:rɪəm/ (*US* **sanitarium**) *n.* санато́рий.

sanctify /'sæŋktɪfaɪ/ *v.t.* освя|ща́ть (*or* святи́ть), -ти́ть; (*justify*) опра́вд|ывать, -а́ть.

sanctimonious /sæŋktɪ'məʊnɪəs/ *adj.* ха́нжеский.

sanction /'sæŋkʃ(ə)n/ *n.* са́нкция.
■ *v.t.* (*authorize*) санкциони́ровать (*impf., pf.*); (*approve*) од|обря́ть, -обри́ть.

sanctity /'sæŋktɪtɪ/ *n.* свя́тость.

sanctuary /'sæŋktjʊərɪ/ *n.*
[1] (*holy place*) святи́лище.
[2] (*asylum*) убе́жище.
[3] (*for wild life*) запове́дник.

sanctum /'sæŋktəm/ *n.* (*pl.* **~s**) святи́лище; (*fig.*, '*den*') прибе́жище.

sand /sænd/ *n.* песо́к.
■ *v.t.* (*polish; also* **~ down**) шлифова́ть, от-.
■ *cpds.* **~ dune** *n.* дю́на; **~paper** *n.* (шлифова́льная) шку́рка; *v.t.* чи́стить, за- (*or* шлифова́ть, от-) шку́ркой; **~stone** *n.* песча́ник.

sandal /'sænd(ə)l/ *n.* санда́лия.

sandwich /'sænwɪdʒ/ *n.* бутербро́д; **ham ~** бутербро́д с ветчино́й; **~ bar** бутербро́дная.
■ *v.t.*: **his car was ~ed between two lorries** его́ маши́на была́ зажа́та ме́жду двумя́ грузовика́ми.
■ *cpd.* **~ course** *n.* (*Br.*) курс обуче́ния, чередую́щий тео́рию с пра́ктикой.

sandy /'sændɪ/ *adj.* (**sandier, sandiest**)
[1] (*consisting of sand*) песча́ный; (*resembling sand*) песо́чный.
[2] (*hair*) рыжева́тый.

sane /seɪn/ *adj.* (*opp. mad*) норма́льный, психи́чески здоро́вый; (*idea, plan*) здра́вый.

San Francisco /sæn fræn'sɪskəʊ/ *n.* Сан-Франци́ско (*m. indecl.*).

sang /sæŋ/ *past of* ▶ **sing**

sanguine /'sæŋgwɪn/ *adj.* (*optimistic*) оптимисти́чный.

sanitarium /sænɪ'teərɪəm/ (*US*) = **sanatorium**

sanitary /'sænɪtərɪ/ *adj.* санита́рный, гигиени́ческий; **~ towel** (*Br.*), **napkin** (*US*) гигиени́ческая прокла́дка.

sanitation /sænɪ'teɪʃ(ə)n/ *n.* канализацио́нная систе́ма.

sanitize /'sænɪtaɪz/ *v.t.* де́лать, с- бо́лее прие́млемым.

sanity /'sænɪtɪ/ *n.* (*state of being sane*) здра́вый ум.

sank /sæŋk/ *past of* ▶ **sink**

Santa Claus /'sæntə klɔ:z/ *n.* (*in Russia*) ≈ Дед Моро́з; (*in Britain, US, etc.*) Са́нта-Кла́ус.

sap /sæp/ *n.* (*of plants*) сок.
■ *v.t.* (**sapped, sapping**) (*fig.*): **~ s.o.'s strength** истощ|а́ть, -и́ть чьи-н. си́лы.

sapling /'sæplɪŋ/ *n.* (*tree*) молодо́е де́ревце.

sapphire /'sæfaɪə(r)/ *n.* (*stone*) сапфи́р; (*colour*) лазу́рь.

sarcasm /'sɑ:kæz(ə)m/ *n.* сарка́зм.

sarcastic /sɑ:'kæstɪk/ *adj.* саркасти́ческий.

sarcopha|gus /sɑ:'kɒfəgəs/ *n.* (*pl.* **~i** /-gaɪ/) саркофа́г.

sardine /sɑ:'di:n/ *n.* сарди́н(к)а.

sardonic /sɑ:'dɒnɪk/ *adj.* зло́бно-насме́шливый, язви́тельный.

sari /'sɑri:/ *n.* (*pl.* **~s**) са́ри (*nt. indecl.*) (*индийская национальная женская одежда*).

sarong /sə'rɒŋ/ *n.* саро́нг (*малай(зий)ская/индонезийская национальная одежда*).

SARS /sɑ:z/ *n.* (*abbr. of* ***severe acute respiratory syndrome***) атипи́чная пневмони́я, САРС (*тяжёлый о́стрый респирато́рный синдро́м*).

sash /sæʃ/ *n.* (*round waist*) по́яс; (*over shoulder*) (о́рденская) ле́нта.

sat /sæt/ *past and p.p. of* ▶ **sit**

Satan /'seɪt(ə)n/ *n.* Сатана́ (*m.*).

satanic /sə'tænɪk/ *adj.* сатани́нский, а́дский.

satanism /'seɪtənɪz(ə)m/ *n.* сатани́зм.

satchel /'sætʃ(ə)l/ *n.* ра́нец.

satellite /'sætəlaɪt/ *n.* (иску́сственный) спу́тник; **~ dish** спу́тниковая анте́нна; **~ television broadcasting** спу́тниковое телеви́дение.

satiate /'seɪʃɪeɪt/ *v.t.* нас|ыща́ть, -ы́тить.

satin /'sætɪn/ *n.* а́тлас.
■ *adj.* атла́сный.

satire /'sætaɪə(r)/ *n.* сати́ра.

satirical /sə'tɪrɪk(ə)l/ *adj.* сатири́ческий.

satirist /'sætərɪst/ *n.* сати́рик.

satirize /'sætɪraɪz/ *v.t.* высме́ивать, вы́смеять.

satisfaction /sætɪs'fækʃ(ə)n/ *n.* удовлетворе́ние, удовлетворённость.

satisfactory /sætɪs'fæktərɪ/ *adj.* удовлетвори́тельный, хоро́ший.

satisf|y /'sætɪsfaɪ/ *v.t.*
[1] удовлетвор|я́ть, -и́ть; **~y one's hunger** утол|я́ть, -и́ть го́лод; **a ~ied customer** дово́льный клие́нт.
[2] (*convince*) убе|жда́ть, -ди́ть; **I ~ied him of my innocence** я убеди́л его́ в мое́й невино́вности.
[3] (*fulfil*): **~y an obligation** выполня́ть, вы́полнить обяза́тельство.
[4] (*of food*): **a ~ying lunch** сы́тный обе́д.

satphone /'sætfəʊn/ *n.* спу́тниковый телефо́н.

satsuma /sæt'su:mə/ *n.* мандари́н.

saturate /'sætʃəreɪt/ *v.t.* нас|ыща́ть, -ы́тить; **the carpet became ~d with water** ковёр пропита́лся водо́й; **I was ~d** (*wet through*) я весь промо́к.

saturation /sætʃə'reɪʃ(ə)n/ *n.* насыще́ние, насы́щенность.

Saturday /'sætədeɪ/ *n.* суббо́та.

Saturn /'sæt(ə)n/ *n.* (*astron., myth.*) Сату́рн.

S

sauce /sɔːs/ *n.* (*cul.*) со́ус, подли́вка.
■ *cpd.* **~pan** *n.* кастрю́ля.

saucer /ˈsɔːsə(r)/ *n.* блю́дце.

saucy /ˈsɔːsɪ/ *adj.* (**saucier, sauciest**) (*cheeky*) де́рзкий; (*Br., coquettish*) коке́тливый.

Saudi /ˈsaʊdɪ/ *n.* (*pl.* **~s**) сау́дов|ец (*fem.* -ка).
■ *adj.* сау́довский; **~ Arabia** Сау́довская Ара́вия.

sauerkraut /ˈsaʊəkraʊt/ *n.* ки́слая/ква́шеная капу́ста.

sauna /ˈsɔːnə/ *n.* (*also* **~ bath**) са́уна, фи́нская (парна́я) ба́ня.

saunter /ˈsɔːntə(r)/ *v.i.* идти́ (*det.*) не торопя́сь.

sausage /ˈsɒsɪdʒ/ *n.* соси́ска.
■ *cpd.* **~ roll** *n.* соси́ска, запечённая в бу́лочке.

savage /ˈsævɪdʒ/ *n.* дика́р|ь (*fem.* -ка).
■ *adj.* 1 (*of animals: fierce*) свире́пый.
2 (*of attack, blow etc.*) жесто́кий, я́ростный.
■ *v.t.* (жесто́ко) иск|у́сывать, -уса́ть; (*fig.*) раст|ерзывать, -ерза́ть.

sav|e /seɪv/ *n.* (*football etc.*): **the goalkeeper made a brilliant ~e** врата́рь блестя́ще отби́л уда́р.
■ *v.t.* 1 (*rescue*) спас|а́ть, -ти́; изб|авля́ть, -а́вить; **he ~ed my life** он спас мне жизнь; **she was ~ed from drowning** ей не да́ли утону́ть; (*protect*) храни́ть (*impf.*).
2 (*put by*) бере́чь, с-; от|кла́дывать, -ложи́ть; копи́ть, на-; **I ~ed (up) £100 towards a holiday** я скопи́л 100 фу́нтов на о́тпуск; **~e me something to eat!** оста́вьте мне что́-нибудь пое́сть!; (*collect*) соб|ира́ть, -ра́ть; (*avoid using or spending*) эконо́мить, с-; **he took the bus to ~e time** он пое́хал авто́бусом, что́бы сэконо́мить вре́мя; (*obviate need for, expense of etc.*) эконо́мить, с-; **that will ~e me £100** я сэконо́млю на э́том сто фу́нтов; **I ~ed him the trouble of replying** я изба́вил его́ от необходи́мости отвеча́ть; (*comput.*) сохран|я́ть, -и́ть.
■ *v.i.* эконо́мить, с-; копи́ть (*impf.*); **he is ~ing up for a bicycle** он откла́дывает/ко́пит де́ньги (*or* он ко́пит) на велосипе́д.

saver /ˈseɪvə(r)/ *n.* (*investor*) вкла́дчик.

saving /ˈseɪvɪŋ/ *n.*
1 (*salvation*) спасе́ние.
2 (*economy*) эконо́мия.
3 (*pl., money laid by*) сбереже́ния (*nt. pl.*); **~s account** сберега́тельный счёт; **~s bank** сберега́тельная ка́сса, сберега́тельный банк.
■ *adj.*: **~ grace** (*fig.*) положи́тельное/спаси́тельное сво́йство/ка́чество.

saviour /ˈseɪvjə(r)/ (*US* **savior**) *n.* спаси́тель (*m.*).

savour /ˈseɪvə(r)/ (*US* **savor**) *n.* вкус.
■ *v.t.* смакова́ть (*impf.*).

savoury /ˈseɪvərɪ/ (*US* **savory**) *adj.* несла́дкий.

saw[1] /sɔː/ *n.* (*tool*) пила́.
■ *v.t.* (*p.p.* **sawn** /sɔːn/ *or* **sawed**) пили́ть (*impf.*); распи́л|ивать, -и́ть.
■ *v.i.* (*p.p.* **sawn** /sɔːn/ *or* **sawed**) пили́ть (*impf.*).
■ *with adv.*: **~ off** *v.t.* отпи́л|ивать, -и́ть; **~n-off** (*US* **sawed-off**) **shotgun** обре́з.
■ *cpd.* **~dust** *n.* опи́л|ки (*pl., g.* -ок).

saw[2] /sɔː/ *past of* ▸ **see**

sax /sæks/ (*coll.*) = **saxophone**

saxophone /ˈsæksəfəʊn/ *n.* саксофо́н.

saxophonist /sækˈsɒfənɪst/ *n.* саксофони́ст (*fem.* -ка).

say /seɪ/ *n.* (*expression of opinion*): **let s.o. have his ~** да|ва́ть, -ть кому́-н. вы́сказаться; **we had no ~ in the matter** с на́шим мне́нием в э́том де́ле не счита́лись.
■ *v.t.* & *i.* (*3rd pers. sing. pres.* **says** /sez/; *past and p.p.* **said**)
1 говори́ть, сказа́ть; **he ~s I am lazy** он говори́т, что я лени́в; **I must ~** призна́ться; **she is said to be rich** говоря́т, она́ бога́та; **when all is said and done** в конце́ концо́в, в коне́чном счёте; **~ good morning to s.o.** здоро́ваться, по- с кем-н.; **that is to ~** (*in other words; viz.*) то есть; други́ми слова́ми; **it goes without ~ing** (само́ собо́й) разуме́ется; слов нет.
2 (*of inanimate objects: indicate*): **the signpost ~s London** на указа́теле напи́сано «Ло́ндон»; **the clock ~s 5 o'clock** часы́ пока́зывают пять.
3 (*formulate, express*): **~ a prayer** произн|оси́ть, -ести́ моли́тву.

saying /ˈseɪɪŋ/ *n.* поговорка.

scab /skæb/ *n.* струп, ко́рка.

scaffold /ˈskæfəʊld/ *n.*
1 эшафо́т, пла́ха; **die on the ~** умира́ть, умере́ть на эшафо́те.
2 = **~ing**
■ *v.t.* обстр|а́ивать, -о́ить леса́ми.

scaffolding /ˈskæfəʊldɪŋ/ *n.* лес|а́ (*pl., g.* -о́в) (*строи́тельные*).

scald /skɔːld, skɒld/ *v.t.* ошпа́ри|вать, -ть; **~ing water** круто́й кипято́к.

scale[1] /skeɪl/ *n.*
1 (*of fish, reptile etc.*) чешу́йка; (*pl., collect.*) чешуя́.
2 (*on teeth*) (зубно́й) ка́мень (*m.*).

scale[2] /skeɪl/ *n.*
1 (*of balance*) ча́ш(к)а (весо́в).
2 (*pl., weighing machine*) вес|ы́ (*pl., g.* -о́в).

scale[3] /skeɪl/ *n.*
1 (*grading*) шкала́; **~ of charges** шкала́ расце́нок.
2 (*of map, and fig.*) масшта́б; **~ drawing** масшта́бный чертёж.
3 (*size*) разме́р.
4 (*mus.*) га́мма.
■ *v.t.* (*climb*): **~ a wall** влез|а́ть, -ть (*or* зал|еза́ть, -е́зть) на сте́ну; **~ a mountain** вз|бира́ться, -обра́ться на́ гору.
■ *with adv.*: **~ down** *v.t.* пон|ижа́ть, -и́зить; ум|еньша́ть, -е́ньшить; (*fig.*) сокра|ща́ть, -ти́ть.

scales /skeɪlz/ *n. pl.* (*weighing machine*) вес|ы́ (*pl., g.* -о́в).

scalp /skælp/ *n.* скальп.

scalpel /ˈskælp(ə)l/ *n.* ска́льпель (*m.*).

scam /skæm/ *n.* (*sl.*) обма́н, надува́тельство.

scamper /ˈskæmpə(r)/ *v.i.* мча́ться (*impf.*), бе́гать (*indet.*); **the dog ~ed off** соба́ка умча́лась.

scampi /ˈskæmpɪ/ *n.* креве́тки (*f. pl.*) (*кру́пные, пригото́вленные*).

scan /skæn/ *v.t.* (**scanned, scanning**)
1 (*survey*) обв|оди́ть, -ести́ взгля́дом; (*glance through*) пробе|га́ть, -жа́ть (глаза́ми).

2 (*comput.*, *med.*) скани́ровать (*impf.*).

scandal /'skænd(ə)l/ *n.* сканда́л; **it is a ~** э́то безобра́зие.

scandalize /'skændəlaɪz/ *v.t.* шоки́ровать (*impf.*, *pf.*).

scandalous /'skændələs/ *adj.* (*shocking*) сканда́льный; (*disgraceful*) позо́рный, безобра́зный, возмути́тельный.

Scandinavia /skændɪ'neɪvɪə/ *n.* Скандина́вия.

Scandinavian /skændɪ'neɪvɪən/ *n.* скандина́в (*fem.* -ка).
■ *adj.* скандина́вский.

scanner /'skænə(r)/ *n.* (*comput.*, *med.*) ска́нер.

scant /skænt/ *adj.* (*inadequate*) недоста́точный.

scanty /'skæntɪ/ *adj.* (**scantier, scantiest**) ску́дный.

scapegoat /'skeɪpgəʊt/ *n.* козёл отпуще́ния.

scar /skɑ:(r)/ *n.* шрам, рубе́ц; (*fig.*) след, ра́на.
■ *v.t.* (**scarred, scarring**) (*mark with ~*) ост|авля́ть, -а́вить шра́мы на + *p.*

scarce /skeəs/ *adj.* ре́дкий.

scarcely /'skeəslɪ/ *adv.* едва́; почти́ не.

scarcity /'skeəsɪtɪ/ *n.*
1 (*insufficiency*) недоста́ток, нехва́тка, дефици́т; **it was a time of great ~** э́то бы́ло вре́мя больши́х лише́ний.
2 (*rarity*) ре́дкость; **~ value** сто́имость, определя́емая дефици́том.

scare /skeə(r)/ *n.* (*fright*) испу́г; **give s.o. a ~** пуга́ть, ис- кого́-н.; (*alarm*, *panic*) па́ника.
■ *v.t.* пуга́ть, ис-; **I felt ~d** я боя́лся; **they were ~d stiff** они́ до́ смерти перепуга́лись.
■ *with advs.*: **~ away, ~ off** *vv.t.* отпу́г|ивать, -ну́ть; спу́г|ивать, -ну́ть.
■ *cpds.* **~crow** *n.* пу́гало, (огоро́дное) чу́чело; **~monger** *n.* паникёр (*fem.* -ша).

scarf /skɑ:f/ *n.* (*pl.* **scarves** *or* **~s**) шарф.

scarlet /'skɑ:lɪt/ *n.* а́лый цвет.
■ *adj.* а́лый; **~ fever** скарлати́на.

scarves /skɑ:vz/ *pl. of* ▶ **scarf**

scary /'skeərɪ/ *adj.* (**scarier, scariest**) (*coll.*) стра́шный, жу́ткий.

scathing /'skeɪðɪŋ/ *adj.* е́дкий.

scatter /'skætə(r)/ *v.t.*
1 (*throw here and there*) разбр|а́сывать, -оса́ть; (*sprinkle*) расс|ыпа́ть, -ы́пать; пос|ыпа́ть, -ы́пать.
2 (*pass.*): **~ed villages** разбро́санные (там и тут) сёла.
3 (*disperse*) раз|гоня́ть, -огна́ть.
■ *v.i.* (*disperse*) рассе́|иваться, -яться.

scavenge /'skævɪndʒ/ *v.i.* ры́ться/копа́ться (*impf.*) в отбро́сах.

scavenger /'skævɪndʒə(r)/ *n.* (*animal*) живо́тное, пита́ющееся па́далью; (*person*) помо́ечник; челове́к, собира́ющий ве́щи и/и́ли еду́ на помо́йках.

scenario /sɪ'nɑ:rɪəʊ/ *n.* (*pl.* **~s**) *also fig.* сцена́рий.

scene /si:n/ *n.*
1 (*stage*, *of play*) сце́на.
2 (*place*) ме́сто; **change of ~** переме́на обстано́вки.
3 (*set*, *decor*) декора́ция; (*fig.*): **behind the ~s** за кули́сами.
4 (*view*) карти́на.

scenery /'si:nərɪ/ *n.* (*theatr.*) декора́ции (*f. pl.*); (*landscape*) пейза́ж, вид.

scenic /'si:nɪk/ *adj.*
1 (*picturesque*) живопи́сный; **~ beauty** живопи́сность (ландша́фта).
2 (*theatr.*) сцени́ческий; **~ effects** сцени́ческие эффе́кты (*m. pl.*).

scent /sent/ *n.*
1 (*odour*) за́пах, арома́т, благоуха́ние.
2 (*perfume*) дух|и́ (*pl.*, *g.* -о́в).
3 (*trail*, *also fig.*) след.
■ *v.t.*: **~ed candle** аромати́ческая свеча́.

sceptic /'skeptɪk/ (*US* **skeptic**) *n.* ске́птик.

sceptical /'skeptɪk(ə)l/ (*US* **skeptical**) *adj.* скепти́ческий.

scepticism /'skeptɪsɪz(ə)m/ (*US* **skepticism**) *n.* скептици́зм.

sceptre /'septə(r)/ (*US* **scepter**) *n.* ски́петр.

schedule /'ʃedju:l/ *n.*
1 (*list*) спи́сок, пе́речень (*m.*).
2 (*timetable*) план, расписа́ние; **a full ~** больша́я програ́мма; **be behind ~** оп|а́здывать, -озда́ть; **be ahead of ~** опере|жа́ть, -ди́ть гра́фик; **on ~** во́время/то́чно.
■ *v.t.* 1 (*tabulate*) сост|авля́ть, -а́вить спи́сок + *g.*; **a ~d flight** регуля́рный рейс.
2 (*time*; *plan*) рассчи́т|ывать, -а́ть; нам|еча́ть, -е́тить; **we are ~d to finish by May** по пла́ну мы должны́ ко́нчить к ма́ю.

schematic /skɪ'mætɪk/ *adj.* схемати́ческий; (*simplistic*, *formulaic*) схемати́чный.

scheme /ski:m/ *n.*
1 (*plan*) прое́кт, план.
2 (*plot*) про́иск|и (*pl.*, *g.* -ов).
■ *v.i.* интригова́ть (*impf.*).

schism /'ksɪz(ə)m/ *n.* раско́л; (*relig. also*) схи́зма.

schizophrenia /skɪtsə'fri:nɪə/ *n.* шизофрени́я.

schizophrenic /skɪtsə'frenɪk/ *n.* шизофре́н|ик (*fem.* -и́чка).
■ *adj.* шизофрени́ческий.

scholar /'skɒlə(r)/ *n.* учёный.

scholarly /'skɒləlɪ/ *adj.* учёный, академи́ческий.

scholarship /'skɒləʃɪp/ *n.* (*erudition*) учёность; (*grant*) стипе́ндия.

school /sku:l/ *n.*
1 (*for educating children*) шко́ла; **at ~** в шко́ле; **go to ~** ходи́ть (*indet.*) в шко́лу; учи́ться (*impf.*) в шко́ле; **we were at ~ together** мы учи́лись в одно́й шко́ле; **~ fees** пла́та за обуче́ние; **~ report** шко́льный та́бель; **boys'/girls' ~** мужска́я/же́нская шко́ла.
2 (*US*, *university*) университе́т; (*department of university*): **~ of law** юриди́ческий факульте́т.
3 (*for specialist education*) учи́лище; **military ~** вое́нное учи́лище; **~ of art** худо́жественное учи́лище.
■ *cpds.* **~bag** *n.* шко́льная су́мка; **~ book** *n.* уче́бник; **~boy** *n.* шко́льник; **~children** *n.* шко́льники (*m. pl.*); **~girl** *n.* шко́льница; **~-leaver** *n.* (*Br.*) выпускни́|к

(*fem.* -ца); **~-leaving** *adj.*: **~-leaving age** (*Br.*) во́зраст, до кото́рого обуче́ние в шко́ле обяза́тельно; **~ run** *n.* путь, кото́рый ежедне́вно проде́лывают роди́тели, отвозя́щие дете́й в шко́лу на автомоби́ле; **~ teacher** *n.* учи́тель (*fem.* -ница).

schooling /'sku:lɪŋ/ *n.* (об)уче́ние.

schooner /'sku:nə(r)/ *n.* (*naut.*) шху́на; (*Br., for sherry*) фуже́р; (*US, for beer*) большо́й пивно́й бока́л.

science /'saɪəns/ *n.*
1 (*systematic knowledge*) нау́ка.
2 (*natural ~s*) есте́ственные нау́ки; **~ fiction** нау́чная фанта́стика.

scientific /saɪən'tɪfɪk/ *adj.* нау́чный.

scientist /'saɪəntɪst/ *n.* учёный (*в области естественных наук*).

sci-fi /'saɪfaɪ/ *n.* (*coll.*) нау́чная фанта́стика.

scintillating /'sɪntɪleɪtɪŋ/ *adj.* блестя́щий.

scissors /'sɪzəz/ *n.* но́жниц|ы (*pl., g.* —).

scoff[1] /skɒf/ *v.i.* смея́ться (*impf.*); **~ at** издева́ться/глуми́ться/насмеха́ться (*all impf.*) над + *i.*

scoff[2] /skɒf/ (*Br. coll.*) *v.t.* & *i.* жрать, со-.

scold /skəʊld/ *v.t.* руга́ть, об-.

scone /skɒn/ *n.* ≈ небольшо́й кекс.

scoop /sku:p/ *n.*
1 (*for food*) ло́жка.
2 (*journ.*) ≈ сенса́ция.
■ *v.t.* 1 (*lift with ~*) заче́рп|ывать, -ну́ть; (*also* **~ out**) выче́рпывать, вы́черпать.
2 (*win*) выи́грывать, вы́играть.

scooter /'sku:tə(r)/ *n.* (*child's*) самока́т; (*motor ~*) моторо́ллер.

scope /skəʊp/ *n.*
1 (*range*) разма́х, охва́т; **this is beyond the ~ of our enquiry** э́то выхо́дит за преде́лы/ра́мки на́шего рассле́дования.
2 (*outlet*): **the game offers ~ for the children's imagination** э́та игра́ даёт просто́р де́тскому воображе́нию.

scorch /skɔ:tʃ/ *v.t.* (*burn, dry up*) жечь, с-; выжига́ть, вы́жечь; (*clothes etc.*) подпа́л|ивать, -и́ть.

score /skɔ:(r)/ *n.*
1 (*in games*) счёт; **what's the ~?** како́й счёт?; **keep the ~** вести́ (*det.*) счёт.
2 (*mus.*): **(full) ~** партиту́ра.
3 (*twenty*) два́дцать; о́коло двадцати́.
4 : **on that/this ~** на э́тот счёт.
■ *v.t.* 1 (*scratch*) цара́пать, ис-; **~ out, through** вычёркивать, вы́черкнуть.
2 (*win*) выи́грывать, вы́играть; **~ a goal** (*football*) заб|ива́ть, -и́ть гол.
■ *v.i.* выи́грывать, вы́играть очко́; (*football*) заб|ива́ть, -и́ть гол.

scorn /skɔ:n/ *n.* презре́ние.
■ *v.t.* презира́ть (*impf.*); пренебр|ега́ть, -е́чь + *i.*

scornful /'skɔ:nfʊl/ *adj.* (*person*): **he was ~ of the idea** он отнёсся к э́той иде́е с презре́нием; (*glance etc.*) презри́тельный.

Scorpio /'skɔ:pɪəʊ/ *n.* (*pl.* **~s**) Скорпио́н.

Scot /skɒt/ *n.* шотла́нд|ец (*fem.* -ка).

Scotch /skɒtʃ/ *n.* (*whisky*) шотла́ндское ви́ски (*nt. indecl.*), скотч.
■ *adj.* шотла́ндский; **~ tape** (*propr.*) кле́йкая ле́нта, скотч.

scot-free /skɒt'fri:/ *adv.*: **go/get off ~** (*unpunished*) ост|ава́ться, -а́ться безнака́занным.

Scotland /'skɒtlənd/ *n.* Шотла́ндия.

Scots /skɒts/ *n.* (*ling.*) шотла́ндский го́вор.
■ *adj.* шотла́ндский.
■ *cpds.* **~man** *n.* шотла́ндец; **~woman** *n.* шотла́ндка.

Scotsman /'skɒtsmən/ *n.* шотла́ндец.

Scotswoman /'skɒtswʊmən/ *n.* шотла́ндка.

Scottish /'skɒtɪʃ/ *adj.* шотла́ндский.

scoundrel /'skaʊndr(ə)l/ *n.* подле́ц.

scour[1] /'skaʊə(r)/ *v.t.* (*cleanse*) чи́стить, вы́-.

scour[2] /'skaʊə(r)/ *v.t.* (*range in search or pursuit*) обры́скать (*pf.*); **he ~ed the town for his daughter** он обе́гал весь го́род в по́исках до́чери.

scourer /'skaʊrə(r)/ *n.* (*for saucepans etc.*) металли́ческая моча́лка; ёж.

scourge /skə:dʒ/ *n.* бич.

scout /skaʊt/ *n.*
1 (*mil.*) разве́дчик.
2 (*Boy S~*) ска́ут, бойска́ут; (*Girl S~*) де́вочка-ска́ут.
■ *v.i.*: **I have been ~ing about for a present** я обходи́л все магази́ны в по́исках пода́рка.

scowl /skaʊl/ *n.* серди́тый/хму́рый взгляд.
■ *v.i.*: **he ~ed at me** он хму́ро/серди́то посмотре́л на меня́.

Scrabble /'skræb(ə)l/ *n.* (*propr.*) скрэбл (≈ игра «Эруди́т»).

scrabble /'skræb(ə)l/ *v.i.*: **~ about** ша́рить (*impf.*); **~ about for sth.** разы́скивать (*impf.*) что-н.

scramble /'skræmb(ə)l/ *n.*
1 (*climb with hands and feet*) кара́бканье.
2 (*struggle to get sth.*) сва́лка; (*fig.*) борьба́, схва́тка.
■ *v.t.*: **~d eggs** яи́чница-болту́нья.
■ *v.i.* кара́бкаться, вс-; вз|бира́ться, -обра́ться; **the boys ~d over the wall** ма́льчики переле́зли че́рез забо́р.

scrap /skræp/ *n.*
1 (*small piece*) кусо́чек; (*of metal*) обло́мок; (*of cloth*) обре́зок; лоску́т; (*fragment*) обры́вок; **~s of paper** клочки́ (*m. pl.*) бума́ги.
2 (*pl., waste food*) объе́дк|и (*pl., g.* -ов).
3 (*waste material*) ути́ль (*m.*); (**~** *metal*) металлоло́м; (**~** *paper*) макулату́ра.
■ *v.t.* (**scrapped, scrapping**)
1 (*make into ~*) перевра|ща́ть, -ти́ть в лом.
2 (*coll., discard*) (*plan*) отмен|я́ть, -и́ть.
■ *cpds.* **~book** *n.* альбо́м для накле́ивания вы́резок; **~ heap** *n.* сва́лка; **~ iron** *n.* металли́ческий лом; **~yard** *n.* (*Br.*) сва́лка.

scrape /skreɪp/ *n.*: **get into a ~** влипнуть (*pf.*) в исто́рию (*coll.*).
■ *v.t.* 1 (*abrade*) скобли́ть, вы́-; (*graze*) сса́|живать, -ди́ть; (*scratch*): **he ~d his car against a tree** он поцара́пал маши́ну о де́рево.
2 (*clean*) выска́бливать (*or* скобли́ть), вы́скоблить.
■ *v.i.* 1 (*rub*): **my hand ~d against the wall** я ссади́л себе́ ру́ку о сте́ну.
2 (*get through*): **she just ~d into the final** она́ с трудо́м вы́шла в фина́л.
■ *with advs.*: **~ along, ~ by** *vv.i.* (*get by*)

переб|ива́ться, -и́ться; **we can just ~ by** мы ко́е-как перебива́емся; **~ through** *v.i.* проти́с|киваться, -нуться; **she ~d through (her exam)** она́ с трудо́м сдала́ экза́мен; **~ together** *v.t.* (*money etc.*) наскре|ба́ть, -сти́.

scratch /skrætʃ/ *n.*
1 (*mark*) цара́пина.
2 (*noise*) цара́панье.
3 (*wound*) цара́пина, сса́дина.
4 (*fig.*): **come up to ~** де́лать (*impf.*) то, что поло́жено; **start from ~** нач|ина́ть, -а́ть с нача́ла/нуля́.
■ *v.t.* 1 цара́пать, о-; **he ~ed letters on the wall** он нацара́пал бу́квы на стене́.
2 (*to relieve itching*) чеса́ть, по-; **~ one's head** чеса́ть (*impf.*) го́лову.
■ *v.i.* 1 (*of person*, **~ o.s.**) чеса́ться, по-.
2 (*of animal*): **does your cat ~?** ва́ша ко́шка цара́пается?
■ *with advs.*: **~ about, ~ around** *vv.i.*: **the chickens ~ed around for food** ку́ры клева́ли зе́млю в по́исках пи́щи; **~ out** *v.t.*: **~ s.o.'s eyes out** выцара́пывать, вы́царапать глаза́ кому́-н.

scrawl /skrɔːl/ *n.* кара́кул|и (*f. pl.*, *g.* -ей *and* -ь).
■ *v.t.* черк|а́ть, -ну́ть; цара́пать, на-.
■ *v.i.* писа́ть (*impf.*) кара́кулями.

scrawny /ˈskrɔːnɪ/ *adj.* (**scrawnier, scrawniest**) костля́вый, то́щий.

scream /skriːm/ *n.*
1 пронзи́тельный крик; (*shriek*) вопль (*m.*); (*high-pitched* ~) визг.
2 (*coll.*, *funny affair*): **it was a ~!** (э́то была́) умо́ра!
■ *v.t.* выкри́кивать, вы́крикнуть.
■ *v.i.* вопи́ть (*impf.*); (*high-pitched*) визжа́ть (*impf.*); **he was ~ing for help** он взыва́л о по́мощи.

screech /skriːtʃ/ *n.* пронзи́тельный крик, визг; (*of object*) скрип, скре́жет.
■ *v.i.* пронзи́тельно крича́ть, за-; (*of gears, tyres etc.*) скрежета́ть (*impf.*).

screen /skriːn/ *n.*
1 (*partition*) перегоро́дка.
2 (*furniture*) ши́рма.
3 (*shelter*) прикры́тие; **behind a ~ of trees** под прикры́тием дере́вьев.
4 (*cin., TV, comput.*) экра́н.
■ *v.t.* 1 (*protect*) защи|ща́ть, -ти́ть.
2 (*hide*) укр|ыва́ть, -ы́ть.
3 (*separate*) отгор|а́живать, -оди́ть; **we ~ed off the kitchen from the dining room** мы отгороди́ли ку́хню от столо́вой.
4 (*fig., investigate; also med.*): **be ~ed (for)** про|ходи́ть, -йти́ прове́рку на + *a.*
5 (*show on* ~) пока́з|ывать, -а́ть.
■ *cpds.* **~play** *n.* сцена́рий; **~writer** *n.* сценари́ст.

screw /skruː/ *n.* винт, болт, шуру́п.
■ *v.t.* зави́н|чивать, -ти́ть; **the cupboard was ~ed to the wall** шкаф был приви́нчен к стене́.
■ *with advs.*: **~ up** *v.t.* зави́н|чивать, -ти́ть; (*crumple*) ко́мкать, с-; **~ up one's eyes** щу́рить, со- глаза́; **a face ~ed up with pain** лицо́, искажённое от бо́ли; **~ up one's courage** соб|ира́ться, -ра́ться с ду́хом; (*sl.*, *spoil*) напорта́чить (*pf.*); зава́л|ивать, -и́ть.
■ *cpds.* **~ cap, ~ top** *nn.* нави́нчивающаяся кры́шка; **~driver** *n.* отвёртка.

scribble /ˈskrɪb(ə)l/ *v.t. & i.*
1 (*make marks (on)*) черка́ть, ис-; **the children ~ed all over the wall** де́ти исчерка́ли всю сте́ну.
2 (*write hastily*) черка́ть, на-; (*write untidily*) цара́пать, на-.

scribe /skraɪb/ *n.* (*hist.*) пи́сец; (*bibl.*) кни́жник; (*hack*) писа́ка (*c.g.*).

scrimp /skrɪmp/ = **skimp**

script /skrɪpt/ *n.* (*writing system*) письмо́; (*text*) текст, сцена́рий.
■ *cpd.* **~writer** *n.* сценари́ст.

scripture(s) /ˈskrɪptʃə(z)/ *n.* Писа́ние.

scroll /skrəʊl/ *n.* (*of parchment*) сви́ток; (*archit.*) завито́к.
■ *v.i.* (*comput.*) прокр|у́чивать, -ути́ть.
■ *cpd.* **~ bar** *n.* (*comput.*) полоса́ прокру́тки.

scrot|um /ˈskrəʊtəm/ *n.* (*pl.* **~a** *or* **~ums**) мошо́нка.

scrounge /skraʊndʒ/ *v.t.* (*coll.*) (*cadge*) стрел|я́ть, -ьну́ть (*coll.*).
■ *v.i.* (*cadge*) попроша́йничать (*impf.*).

scrounger /ˈskraʊndʒə(r)/ *n.* (*coll.*) попроша́йка (*c.g.*).

scrub[1] /skrʌb/ *n.* (*brushwood*) куста́рник; (*area*) за́росли (*f. pl.*).

scrub[2] /skrʌb/ *n.*: **give sth. a ~** вычища́ть, вы́чистить что-н.
■ *v.t.* (**scrubbed, scrubbing**) скрести́ (*impf.*); тере́ть (*impf.*); (*clean*) чи́стить, по-; дра́ить, на-; **~ the floor** мыть, вы- пол; **~bing brush** жёсткая щётка.

scruff /skrʌf/ *n.*: **take s.o. by the ~ of the neck** хвата́ть, схвати́ть кого́-н. за ши́ворот/загри́вок.

scruffy /ˈskrʌfɪ/ *adj.* (**scruffier, scruffiest**) (*coll.*) неопря́тный.

scrumptious /ˈskrʌmpʃəs/ *adj.* (*coll.*) о́чень вку́сный, сма́чный.

scruple /ˈskruːp(ə)l/ *n.* сомне́ния (*nt. pl.*); **have ~s about doing sth.** со́веститься, по- сде́лать что-н.; **have no ~s about doing sth.** не стесня́ться, по- сде́лать что-н.

scrupulous /ˈskruːpjʊləs/ *adj.* тща́тельный, скрупулёзный, педанти́чный.

scrutinize /ˈskruːtɪnaɪz/ *v.t.* (*examine*) рассм|а́тривать, -отре́ть; (*stare at*) при́стально смотре́ть (*impf.*) на + *a.*

scrutiny /ˈskruːtɪnɪ/ *n.*
1 (*searching gaze*) внима́тельный/испыту́ющий взгляд.
2 (*close investigation*) тща́тельное рассле́дование/рассмотре́ние/иссле́дование.

scuba /ˈskuːbə/ *n.* ску́ба, аквала́нг; **~-diver** аквалангист; **~-diving** подво́дное пла́вание со ску́бой.

scud /skʌd/ *v.i.* (**scudded, scudding**) нести́сь, про-; (*naut.*) идти́ (*det.*) под ве́тром.

scuff /skʌf/ *v.t.*: **~** (*wear away*) **one's shoes** сн|а́шивать, -оси́ть о́бувь.

scuffle /ˈskʌf(ə)l/ *n.* потасо́вка, схва́тка.

scullery /ˈskʌlərɪ/ *n.* судомо́йня.
■ *cpd.* **~ maid** *n.* судомо́йка.

sculpt /skʌlpt/ *v.t.* ва́ять, из-; (*model in clay etc.*) лепи́ть, вы-; (*in stone*) высека́ть, вы́сечь; (*in wood*) ре́зать, вы-.
■ *v.i.* быть/рабо́тать (*impf.*) ску́льптором.

S

sculptor /ˈskʌlptə(r)/ *n.* скýльптор.
sculpture /ˈskʌlptʃə(r)/ *n.* скульптýра.
scum /skʌm/ *n.* пéна; (*fig.*) подóнки (*m. pl.*).
scurry /ˈskʌrɪ/ *n.* суетá, спéшка; **there was a ~ towards the exit** все брóсились к вы́ходу; **the ~ of mice under the floor** возня́ мышéй под пóлом.
■ *v.i.* (*also* **~ about**) суетли́во бéгать (*impf.*); сновáть (*impf.*); **~ through one's work** нáспех продéл|ывать, -ать рабóту.
■ *with advs.*: **~ away, ~ off** *vv.i.* убе|гáть, -жáть; (*disperse*) разбе|гáться, -жáться.
scuttle /ˈskʌt(ə)l/ *v.i.* ю́ркнуть (*pf.*); сновáть (*impf.*).
scythe /saɪð/ *n.* косá.
sea /siː/ *n.* мóре; **at ~** (*lit.*) в мóре; **by ~** мóрем; **by the ~** у мóря, на мóре; (*attr.*): **~ air** морскóй вóздух; **~ journey, voyage, trip** морскóе путешéствие.
■ *cpds.* **~food** *n.* морепродýкты (*m. pl.*); **~front** *n.* примóрский бульвáр, нáбережная; **~gull** *n.* чáйка; **~ horse** *n.* морскóй конёк; **~ level** *n.* ýровень (*m.*) мóря; **~ lion** *n.* морскóй лев; **~man** *n.* моря́к, матрóс; **~plane** *n.* гидросамолёт; **~shell** *n.* морскáя рáковина; **~shore** *n.* морскóй бéрег, взмóрье; **~sick** *adj.*: **I was ~sick** меня́ укачáло (*на корабле*); **~side** *n.* морскóе побере́жье; *adj.* примóрский; **a ~side resort** морскóй курóрт; **~ urchin** *n.* морскóй ёж; **~water** *n.* морскáя водá; **~weed** *n.* морскáя вóдоросль; **~worthy** *adj.* мореxóдный, гóдный к плáванию.
seal¹ /siːl/ *n.* (*zool.*) тюлéнь (*m.*); **(fur ~)** кóтик.
seal² /siːl/ *n.* (*on document etc.*) печáть.
■ *v.t.* 1 (*affix ~ to*) при|клáдывать, -ложи́ть печáть к + *d.*
2 (*confirm*): **~ a bargain** скреп|ля́ть, -и́ть сдéлку.
3 (*close securely*) запечáт|ывать, -ать; плóтно/нáглухо закр|ывáть, -ы́ть; **a ~ed envelope** запечáтанный конвéрт; **the police ~ed off all exits from the square** поли́ция перекры́ла все вы́ходы с плóщади.
4 (*decide*): **his fate is ~ed** егó ýчасть решенá.
seam /siːm/ *n.* шов, рубéц.
seamless /ˈsiːmlɪs/ *adj.* без шва; из одногó кускá.
seamstress /ˈsemstrɪs/ *n.* швея́.
seance /ˈseɪɑ̃s/ *n.* спирити́ческий сеáнс.
search /sɜːtʃ/ *n.*
1 (*quest, also comput.*) пóиск (*usu. pl.*); **make a ~ for s.o./sth.** искáть (*impf.*) когó-н./что-н.; **a man in ~ of a wife** мужчи́на, и́щущий себé женý.
2 (*examination*) óбыск.
■ *v.t.* 1 (*examine*) обы́ск|ивать, -áть; пров|оди́ть, -ести́ осмóтр + *g.*; (*rummage through*) обшáри|вать, -ть.
2 (*peer at*) обв|оди́ть, -ести́ взгля́дом.
3 (*penetrate*): **~ing questions** подрóбные вопрóсы.
■ *v.i.* искáть (*impf.*); (*of police, customs*) пров|оди́ть, -ести́ óбыск; **~ for** искáть (*impf.*), разы́скивать (*impf.*); **~ through** просм|áтривать, -отрéть; **he ~ed through all his papers for the contract** он перерыл/перебрáл все свои́ бумáги в пóисках договóра.
■ *cpds.* **~ engine** *n.* (*comput.*) поискóвая систéма/маши́на; **~light** *n.* прожéктор; **~ party** *n.* поискóвая грýппа; **~ warrant** *n.* óрдер на óбыск.
season /ˈsiːz(ə)n/ *n.*
1 сезóн; (*of year*) врéмя гóда; **strawberries are in ~** сейчáс сезóн клубни́ки; **holiday ~** сезóн отпускóв.
2 (*Br.*) (*also* **~ ticket**) сезóнный/проезднóй билéт; (*for concerts etc.*) абонемéнт.
■ *v.t.* 1 (*mature: of timber, wine etc.*) вы́держивать, вы́держать.
2 (*acclimatize*): **a ~ed traveller** (*Br.*), **traveler** (*US*) óпытный путешéственник.
3 (*spice*) припр|авля́ть, -áвить; **a highly ~ed dish** óстрое блю́до.
seasonable /ˈsiːzənəb(ə)l/ *adj.* (*suited to the season*) соотвéтствующий сезóну; (*opportune*) своеврéменный.
seasonal /ˈsiːzən(ə)l/ *adj.* сезóнный.
seasoning /ˈsiːzənɪŋ/ *n.* (*cul.*) приправа.
seat /siːt/ *n.*
1 (*place to sit*) сидéнье; (*chair*) стул; (*bench*) скамья́, скамéйка.
2 (*place in vehicle, theatre etc.*) мéсто; **take one's ~** зан|имáть, -я́ть мéсто; **he booked a ~** он заказáл билéт.
3 (*of chair*) сидéнье.
4 (*of trousers*) зад (у) брюк.
■ *v.t.* 1 (*make sit*) сажáть, посади́ть.
2 (*provide with ~s*) вме|щáть, -сти́ть; **this table ~s twelve** за э́тот стол мóжно посади́ть двенáдцать человéк.
■ *cpd.* **~ belt** *n.* ремéнь (*m.*) безопáсности.
seating /ˈsiːtɪŋ/ *n.* (*allocation of places*) рассáживание; (*placing at table*) размещéние гостéй за столóм.
secateurs /sekəˈtɜːz/ *n. pl.* (*Br.*) садóвые нóжниц|ы (*pl., g.* —).
secede /sɪˈsiːd/ *v.i.* отдел|я́ться, -и́ться (**from:** от + *g.*); выходи́ть, вы́йти (**from:** из + *g.*).
secession /sɪˈseʃ(ə)n/ *n.* отделéние (**from:** от + *g.*); вы́ход (**from:** из + *g.*).
seclude /sɪˈkluːd/ *v.t.*: **a ~d spot** уединённый/укрóмный уголóк.
seclusion /sɪˈkluːʒ(ə)n/ *n.* уединéние, изоля́ция.
second /ˈsekənd/ *n.*
1 вторóй; **on the ~ of May** вторóго мáя.
2 (*pl., imperfect goods*) второсóртный/бракóванный товáр.
3 (*measure of time*) секýнда; **wait a ~!** однý секýнду!; **~(s) hand** (*of clock*) секýндная стрéлка.
■ *adj.* вторóй; (*other*) другóй; **Charles the S~** Карл Вторóй; **on the ~ (US third) floor** на трéтьем этажé; **the ~ largest city** вторóй по величинé гóрод; (*additional*) добáвочный; **~ helping** добáвка; **~ name** (*Br.*) фами́лия; **have ~ thoughts** передýмать, раздýмать (*both pf.*); **~ cousin** троюродный брат (*fem.* троюродная сестрá).
■ *v.t.* (*support*) поддéрж|ивать, -áть.
■ *cpds.* **~ best** *adj.* не сáмый лýчший; (*inferior*) второсóртный; **~-class** *adj.*: **~-class cabin** каю́та вторóго клáсса; **~-class citizens** грáждане вторóго сóрта;

adv.: **we travel ~-class** мы е́здим вторы́м кла́ссом; **~ hand** *n. see* ▶ **second** *n.* **3**; *adj.* (*previously used*) подéржанный; **~-hand bookshop** букинисти́ческий магази́н; (*indirect*): **~-hand information** информа́ция из вторы́х рук; *adv.*: **I bought the car ~-hand** я купи́л подéржанную маши́ну; **~-rate** *adj.* (*of goods*) второсо́ртный; (*mediocre*) посрéдственный.

secondary /'sekəndərɪ/ *adj.* (*less important*) втори́чный; (*school*) срéдний.

secondly /'sekəndlɪ/ *adv.* во-вторы́х.

secondment /sɪ'kɒndmənt/ *n.* (*Br.*) командиро́вка.

secrecy /'si:krɪsɪ/ *n.* секрéтность.

secret /'si:krɪt/ *n.* секрéт, та́йна; **keep a ~** храни́ть, со- секрéт; **in ~** секрéтно, та́йно.
■ *adj.* секрéтный, та́йный; (*hidden*) потайно́й, секрéтный; (*undisclosed*): **I was ~ly glad to see him** в глубинé души́ я был рад его́ ви́деть.

secretarial /sekrɪ'teərɪəl/ *adj.* секретáрский.

secretary /'sekrɪtərɪ, 'sekrətrɪ/ *n.* секретáр|ь (*fem., coll., typist etc.* -ша); **S~ of State** (*UK*) мини́стр; (*US*) госуда́рственный секретáрь, мини́стр инострáнных дел.

secrete /sɪ'kri:t/ *v.t.*
1 (*physiol. etc.*) выделя́ть, вы́делить.
2 (*conceal*) укр|ывáть, -ы́ть; пря́тать, с-; **~ o.s.** укр|ывáться, -ы́ться; пря́таться, с-.

secretive /'si:krɪtɪv/ *adj.* скры́тный, зáмкнутый.

sect /sekt/ *n.* сéкта.

sectarian /sek'teərɪən/ *adj.* сектáнтский.

section /'sekʃ(ə)n/ *n.*
1 (*separate or distinct part*) сéкция; (*severed portion*) кусо́к; **~ of the population** часть населéния; **~ of a book** раздéл кни́ги; (*department*) отдéл, отделéние.
2 (*geom. etc.*) разрéз; **~ drawing** чертёж в разрéзе; сечéние.

sector /'sektə(r)/ *n.* сéктор.

secular /'sekjʊlə(r)/ *adj.* (*this-worldly*) мирско́й; (*lay*) свéтский.

secure /sɪ'kjʊə(r)/ *adj.*
1 (*free from care*) споко́йный; **feel ~ about sth.** не беспоко́иться (*impf.*) о чём-н.
2 (*safe*) про́чный, надёжный; (*reliable*) надёжный; (*assured*): **a ~ income** гаранти́рованный/вéрный дохо́д.
■ *v.t.* 1 (*make safe*) закреп|ля́ть, -и́ть; застрахо́в|ывать, -áть.
2 (*insure*) страховáть, за-.
3 (*obtain*) дост|авáть, -áть.

security /sɪ'kjʊərɪtɪ/ *n.*
1 (*safety*) безопáсность; **~ guard** охрáнник, секью́рити (*m. indecl.*); **he is a ~ risk** он неблагонадёжен.
2 (*guarantee*) гарáнтия.
3 (*pledge*) зало́г, гарáнтия; **~ for a loan** гарáнтия зáйма; заклáд.
4 (*pl., bonds*) цéнные бумáги (*f. pl.*).

sedate[1] /sɪ'deɪt/ *adj.* степéнный, уравновéшенный.

sedate[2] /sɪ'deɪt/ *v.t.* да|вáть, -ть успоко́ительное + *d.*

sedation /sɪ'deɪʃ(ə)n/ *n.* успокоéние; **under ~** под дéйствием успоко́ительного.

sedative /'sedətɪv/ *n.* успоко́ительное (срéдство).

sedentary /'sedəntərɪ/ *adj.* (*of posture etc.*) сидя́чий; **a ~ way of life** сидя́чий/малоподви́жный о́браз жи́зни; (*of person*) неподви́жный, малоподви́жный.

sediment /'sedɪmənt/ *n.* осáдок, отсто́й.

sedimentary /sedɪ'mentərɪ/ *adj.* осáдочный.

sedition /sɪ'dɪʃ(ə)n/ *n.* подстрекáтельство к мятежу́.

seduce /sɪ'dju:s/ *v.t.* соблазн|я́ть, -и́ть.

seducer /sɪ'dju:sə(r)/ *n.* соблазни́тель (*m.*); обольсти́тель (*m.*).

seduction /sɪ'dʌkʃ(ə)n/ *n.* (*act of ~*) обольщéние; (*temptation*) соблáзн.

seductive /sɪ'dʌktɪv/ *adj.* соблазни́тельный.

see /si:/ *v.t.* (*past* **saw;** *p.p.* **seen**)
1 ви́деть; **I saw her arrive** я ви́дел, как она приéхала; **did you ~ anyone leaving?** вы ви́дели, что́бы кто́-нибудь выходи́л?
2 (*look at, watch*) смотрéть, по- на + *a.*; **~ p 4** см. стр./с. 4; **let me ~ that** дáйте мне на э́то посмотрéть; **the film is worth ~ing** э́тот фильм сто́ит посмотрéть; **~ the sights** осм|áтривать, -отрéть достопримечáтельности.
3 (*imagine*) предст|авля́ть, -áвить себé (*что*).
4 (*find out*) посмотрéть (*pf.*), узн|авáть, -áть; **I'll ~ if I can get tickets** я посмотрю́, смогу́ ли я достáть билéты.
5 (*comprehend*) ви́деть, у-; пон|имáть, -я́ть; **I don't ~ what good that is** я не ви́жу, какáя от э́того по́льза; **as far as I can ~** наско́лько я понимáю.
6 (*consider*) ду́мать, по-; **I'll ~** я поду́маю; посмо́трим.
7 (*meet*) ви́деть, у-; встр|ечáть, -éтить; (*associate*) ви́деться (*impf.*), встречáться (*impf.*) (*с кем*); **they stopped ~ing each other** они́ разошли́сь (*or* перестáли встречáться); (*visit*) посе|щáть, -ти́ть; наве|щáть, -сти́ть; **we went to ~ our friends** мы навести́ли нáших друзéй; **come and ~ me, us sometime** заходи́те кáк-нибудь; **~ you on Tuesday!** до вто́рника!
8 (*consult*): **I went to ~ him about a job** я пошёл к немý поговори́ть о рабо́те; **can I ~ you for a moment?** мо́жно вас на мину́тку?
9 (*escort*) прово|жáть, -ди́ть; **he saw her to the door** он проводи́л её до двéри.
10 (*ensure*) следи́ть, про-; **~ (to it) that the door is locked** проследи́те, что́бы зáперли дверь.
■ *v.i.* 1 ви́деть (*impf.*); **can you ~ from where you are?** вам оттýда ви́дно?; **he cannot ~** (*is blind*) он не ви́дит; он слеп; **we saw through him** мы раскуси́ли его́.
2 (*make provision; take care; give attention; organize*) забо́титься, по- (*о чём*); (*arrange, organize*) забо́титься, по-; **she ~s to the laundry** онá вéдает сти́ркой; **I have to ~ to the children** мне прихо́дится забо́титься о дéтях; **he saw to it that I got the money** он позабо́тился о том, что́бы я получи́л дéньги.
■ *with advs.*: **~ off** *v.t.* (*accompany*) прово|жáть, -ди́ть; **we saw them off at the**

S

station мы проводи́ли их на по́езд; ~ **out** *v.t.* прово|жа́ть, -ди́ть до вы́хода; **I can ~ myself out** ≈ я сам найду́ доро́гу; ~ **through** *v.t.*: **who will ~ the job through?** кто доведёт де́ло до конца́?
■ *cpd.* **~-through** *adj.* прозра́чный.

seed /si:d/ *n.*
1 (*lit.*, *fig.*) се́мя (*nt.*); (*of apple, melon, sunflower*) се́мечко; **go, run to ~** (*lit.*) идти́, пойти́ на семена́; (*fig.*, *of person*) сд|ава́ть, -ать.
2 (*sport*: **~ed player**) посе́янный игро́к.

seedling /ˈsi:dlɪŋ/ *n.* се́янец.

seedy /ˈsi:dɪ/ *adj.* (**seedier, seediest**) (*shabby*) потрёпанный; (*sleazy*) захуда́лый.

seek /si:k/ *v.t.* (*past and p.p.* **sought**) (*look for*) иска́ть (*impf.*) + *a.*/*g. of concrete*/*abstract object*; ~ **out** разыска́ть (*pf.*); отыска́ть (*pf.*); (*enquire into*) иска́ть (*impf.*); (*ask for*): ~ **advice** проси́ть, по- сове́та.

seem /si:m/ *v.i.* каза́ться, по-; предст|авля́ться, -а́виться; **it ~s to me** мне ка́жется; по-мо́ему; **it ~s like only yesterday** как бу́дто э́то бы́ло вчера́; **she ~s young** она́ мо́лодо вы́глядит; **I ~ed to hear a voice** мне показа́лось, что я слы́шал чей-то го́лос.

seen /si:n/ *p.p. of* ▶ **see**

seep /si:p/ *v.i.* (*also* ~ **out, through**) прос|а́чиваться, -очи́ться.

see-saw /ˈsi:sɔ:/ *n.* (доска́-)качёл|и (*pl.*, *g.* -ей).
■ *v.i.* (*fig.*) колеба́ться (*impf.*).

seeth|e /si:ð/ *v.i.* (*of liquids, and fig.*) бурли́ть (*impf.*); **the streets were ~ing with people** у́лицы кише́ли наро́дом/людьми́.

segment /ˈsegmənt/ *n.* сегме́нт; (*of fruit*) до́лька.

segregate /ˈsegrɪgət/ *v.t.* отдел|я́ть, -и́ть; раздел|я́ть, -и́ть.

segregation /segrɪˈgeɪʃ(ə)n/ *n.* (*separation*) отделе́ние, изоля́ция; (*racial*) (ра́совая) сегрега́ция.

seismologist /saɪzˈmɒlədʒɪst/ *n.* сейсмологи́ческий.

seismology /saɪzˈmɒlədʒɪ/ *n.* сейсмоло́гия.

seize /si:z/ *v.t.*
1 (*grasp*; *lay hold of*) хвата́ть, схвати́ть; **he ~d** (*hold of*) **the rope** он схвати́л (*or* ухвати́лся за) верёвку; ~ **an opportunity** ухв|а́тываться, -ати́ться за возмо́жность; по́льзоваться, вос- слу́чаем.
2 (*power, land*) захва́т|ывать, -и́ть; брать, взять.
■ *v.i.* (*jam*; *also* ~ **up**) за|еда́ть, -е́сть; застр|ева́ть, -я́ть.

seizure /ˈsi:ʒə(r)/ *n.* (*capture*) захва́т; (*confiscation*) конфиска́ция; (*attack of illness*) при́ступ, припа́док; (*stroke*) уда́р.

seldom /ˈseldəm/ *adv.* ре́дко.

select /sɪˈlekt/ *adj.* и́збранный, элита́рный.
■ *v.t.* выбира́ть, вы́брать; от|бира́ть, -обра́ть; под|бира́ть, -обра́ть.

selection /sɪˈlekʃ(ə)n/ *n.*
1 (*choice*) вы́бор.
2 (*assortment*) подбо́р, ассортиме́нт.

selective /sɪˈlektɪv/ *adj.* (*choosing carefully*) разбо́рчивый; (*partial*) вы́борочный.

self /self/ *n.* (*pl.* **selves**) (*individuality*) су́щность; (*personality*) ли́чность; **I am not my former ~** я уже́ не тот, что пре́жде.

self-absorbed /selfəbˈzɔ:bd/ *adj.* поглощённый собо́й.

self-addressed /selfəˈdrest/ *adj.*: ~ **envelope** конве́рт с обра́тным а́дресом отправи́теля.

self-adhesive /selfədˈhi:sɪv/ *adj.* самоклея́щийся.

self-assurance /selfəˈʃʊərəns/ *n.* уве́ренность (в себе́).

self-assured /selfəˈʃʊəd/ *adj.* (само)уве́ренный.

self-awareness /selfəˈweənɪs/ *n.* самосозна́ние.

self-catering /selfˈkeɪtərɪŋ/ *n.* (*Br.*): ~ **apartment** жильё с самообслу́живанием; ~ **holiday** путёвка, включа́ющая жильё с самообслу́живанием.

self-centred /selfˈsentəd/ (*US* **-centered**) *adj.* эгоцентри́чный.

self-confessed /selfkənˈfest/ *adj.* открове́нный.

self-confidence /selfˈkɒnfɪd(ə)ns/ *n.* уве́ренность (в себе́).

self-confident /selfˈkɒnfɪd(ə)nt/ *adj.* уве́ренный (в себе́).

self-conscious /selfˈkɒnʃəs/ *adj.* (*awkward*) нело́вкий; (*shy*) засте́нчивый; (*embarrassed*) смущённый.

self-contained /selfkənˈteɪnd/ *adj.* (*person*) самостоя́тельный, незави́симый; (*Br.*, *of accommodation*) отде́льный.

self-control /selfkənˈtrəʊl/ *n.* самооблада́ние.

self-controlled /selfkənˈtrəʊld/ *adj.* вы́держанный.

self-criticism /selfˈkrɪtɪsɪz(ə)m/ *n.* самокри́тика.

self-defence /selfdɪˈfens/ (*US* **-defense**) *n.* самооборо́на, самозащи́та.

self-denial /selfdɪˈnaɪəl/ *n.* самоотрече́ние; **practise ~** отка́зывать (*impf.*) себе́ во всём; ограни́чивать (*impf.*) себя́.

self-destruct /selfdɪˈstrʌkt/ *v.i.* (*tech.*) самоликвиди́роваться (*impf.*, *pf.*).

self-destructive /selfdɪˈstrʌktɪv/ *adj.* самоуби́йственный.

self-determination /selfdɪtə:mɪˈneɪʃ(ə)n/ *n.* самоопределе́ние.

self-discipline /selfˈdɪsɪplɪn/ *n.* вну́тренняя дисципли́на.

self-effacing /selfɪˈfeɪsɪŋ/ *adj.* скро́мный.

self-employed /selfɪmˈplɔɪd/ *adj.* рабо́тающий не по на́йму.

self-esteem /selfɪˈsti:m/ *n.* самоуваже́ние, самолю́бие.

self-evident /selfˈevɪd(ə)nt/ *adj.* очеви́дный.

self-explanatory /selfɪkˈsplænətərɪ/ *adj.* не тре́бующий разъясне́ний.

self-expression /selfɪkˈspreʃ(ə)n/ *n.* самовыраже́ние.

self-fulfilling /selffʊlˈfɪlɪŋ/ *adj.*: ~ **prophecy** предсказа́ние, влия́ющее на результа́т.

self-governing /selfˈgʌvənɪŋ/ *adj.*

самоуправля́ющийся, автоно́мный.
self-government /self'gʌvənmənt/ *n.* самоуправле́ние.
self-help /self'help/ *n.* самопо́мощь.
self-image /self'ɪmɪdʒ/ *n.* самооце́нка, со́бственное представле́ние о себе́.
self-important /selfɪm'pɔ:t(ə)nt/ *adj.* ва́жный, самонаде́янный.
self-indulgent /selfɪn'dʌldʒ(ə)nt/ *adj.* избало́ванный.
self-inflicted /selfɪn'flɪktɪd/ *adj.* нанесённый самому́ себе́.
self-interest /self'ɪntrest/ *n.* со́бственный интере́с; коры́сть.
selfish /'selfɪʃ/ *adj.* эгоисти́чный, эгоисти́ческий, коры́стный.
selfishness /'selfɪʃnɪs/ *n.* эгоисти́чность, эгои́зм.
selfless /'selflɪs/ *adj.* самоотве́рженный, беззаве́тный.
self-made /'selfmeɪd/ *adj.*: **he is a ~ man** он сам себя́ сде́лал; он челове́к, вы́бившийся из низо́в.
self-pity /self'pɪtɪ/ *n.* жа́лость к себе́.
self-portrait /self'pɔ:trɪt/ *n.* автопортре́т.
self-possessed /selfpə'zest/ *adj.* хладнокро́вный, невозмути́мый.
self-possession /selfpə'zeʃ(ə)n/ *n.* хладнокро́вие, невозмути́мость.
self-preservation /selfprezə'veɪʃ(ə)n/ *n.* самосохране́ние.
self-proclaimed /selfprə'kleɪmd/ *adj.* самозва́ный.
self-raising /self'reɪzɪŋ/ (*US* **self-rising**) *adj.*: **~ flour** мука́ с разрыхли́телем.
self-reliant /selfrɪ'laɪənt/ *adj.* самостоя́тельный.
self-respect /selfrɪ'spekt/ *n.* самоуваже́ние.
self-righteous /self'raɪtʃəs/ *adj.* ха́нжеский.
self-rule /self'ru:l/ *n.* самоуправле́ние.
self-sacrifice /self'sækrɪfaɪs/ *n.* самопоже́ртвование.
self-satisfied /self'sætɪsfaɪd/ *adj.* самодово́льный.
self-sealing /self'si:lɪŋ/ *adj.* самозакле́ивающийся.
self-service /self'sə:vɪs/ *n.* самообслу́живание.
self-sufficient /selfsə'fɪʃ(ə)nt/ *adj.* самостоя́тельный; (*econ.*): **Russia is 70% ~ in oil/food production** Росси́я обеспе́чивает свои́ потре́бности в не́фти/продово́льствии на 70% за счёт вну́тренних ресу́рсов.
self-taught /self'tɔ:t/ *adj.*: **a ~ man, woman** самоу́чка (*c.g.*).
self-willed /self'wɪld/ *adj.* своево́льный.
sell /sel/ *v.t.* (*past and p.p.* **sold**)
1 прод|ава́ть, -а́ть; торгова́ть (*impf.*) + *i.*; **I'll ~ you this carpet for £20** я прода́м вам э́тот ковёр за 20 фу́нтов; **~ing price** прода́жная цена́; **this shop ~s stamps** в э́том магази́не продаю́тся почто́вые ма́рки.
2 (*coll., put across*): **he was unable to ~ his idea to the management** ему́ не удало́сь убеди́ть правле́ние приня́ть его́ предложе́ние.
■ *v.i.* (*past and p.p.* **sold**)
1 (*of person*): **you were wise to ~ when you did** вы во́время про́дали свой това́р.
2 (*of goods*): **the house sold for £90,000** за дом вы́ручили 90 000 фу́нтов.
■ *with advs.*: **~ off** *v.t.* распрод|ава́ть, -а́ть; **they sold off the goods at a reduced price** они́ распро́дали това́р по сни́женной цене́; **~ out** *v.i.* **the book sold out** э́та кни́га разошла́сь; **the shop sold out of cigarettes** магази́н распро́дал все сигаре́ты; **they have sold out of tickets** все биле́ты про́даны; **they were accused of ~ing out to the enemy** их обвини́ли в том, что они́ продали́сь врагу́.
■ *cpds.* **~-by date** *n.* (*Br.*) срок го́дности; **~-out** *n.* спекта́кль/конце́рт/спорти́вный матч с по́лным за́лом/стадио́ном *и т. п.*; аншла́г.
seller /'selə(r)/ *n.* продав|е́ц (*fem.* -щи́ца); торго́в|ец (*fem.* -ка).
Sellotape /'seləteɪp/ *n.* (*Br., propr.*) скотч, кле́йкая ле́нта.
selves /selvz/ *pl. of* ▸ **self**
semantic /sɪ'mæntɪk/ *adj.* семанти́ческий, смыслово́й.
semaphore /'seməfɔ:(r)/ *n.* семафо́р.
■ *v.t. & i.* сигнализи́ровать (*impf., pf.*) флажка́ми.
semen /'si:mən/ *n.* се́мя (*nt.*), спе́рма.
semester /sɪ'mestə(r)/ *n.* семе́стр.
semi /'semɪ/ *n.* (*pl.* **~s**) (*Br. coll.*) = **~-detached house.**
■ *pref.* полу… .
■ *cpds.* **~-automatic** *adj.* полуавтомати́ческий; **~breve** *n.* (*Br.*) це́лая но́та; **~circle** *n.* полукру́г; **~circular** *adj.* полукру́глый; **~colon** *n.* то́чка с запято́й; **~conductor** *n.* полупроводни́к; **~-conscious** *adj.* в полубессозна́тельном состоя́нии; **~-detached** *adj.*: **~-detached house** оди́н из двух особняко́в, име́ющих о́бщую сте́ну; **~-final** *n.* полуфина́л; **~-finalist** *n.* полуфинали́ст (*fem.* -ка); **~-skimmed** *adj.* (*Br.*) обезжи́ренный; **~tone** *n.* полуто́н.
seminal /'semɪn(ə)l/ *adj.*
1 семенно́й; **~ fluid** семенна́я жи́дкость.
2 (*fig.*) (*work*) эпоха́льный; (*idea*) плодотво́рный.
seminar /'semɪnɑ:(r)/ *n.* семина́р.
seminary /'semɪnərɪ/ *n.* семина́рия.
Semitic /sɪ'mɪtɪk/ *adj.* семити́ческий, семи́тский; (*language*) семи́тский.
semolina /semə'li:nə/ *n.* ма́нная крупа́, ма́нка (*coll.*).
senate /'senɪt/ *n.* сена́т; (*univ.*) сове́т.
senator /'senətə(r)/ *n.* сена́тор.
send /send/ *v.t.* (*past and p.p.* **sent**) (*dispatch*) пос|ыла́ть, -ла́ть; отпр|авля́ть, -а́вить; **he sent me a book** он присла́л мне кни́гу; **I shall ~ you to bed** я отпра́влю тебя́ спать; **the teacher sent him out of the room** учи́тель вы́ставил/вы́гнал его́ из кла́сса.
■ *v.i.* (*past and p.p.* **sent**): **he sent for a doctor** он вы́звал врача́; он посла́л за врачо́м.
■ *with advs.*: **~ away** *v.i.*: **~ away for sth.** выпи́сывать, вы́писать что-н., зак|а́зывать,

S

-азáть что-н.; ~ **back** *v.t.* (*person*) пос|ылáть, -лáть назáд; (*thing*) от|сылáть, -ослáть; ~ **in** *v.t.*: **he sent in his bill** он послáл счёт; ~ **in a report** предст|авлять, -áвить отчёт; ~ **off** *v.t.* (*dispatch*) отпр|авлять, -áвить; **he was sent off by the referee** судья удалил егó с пóля; ~ **on** *v.t.* (*forward*) перес|ылáть, -лáть; ~ **out** *v.t.* высылáть, вы́слать; (*distribute*) ра|ссылáть, -зослáть; (*emit*): ~ **out heat** выделять, вы́делить теплó; ~ **up** *v.t.*: (*coll.*, *ridicule*) высмéивать, вы́смеять.
■ *cpds.* **~-off** *n.* прóвод|ы (*pl. g.* -ов); **he got a marvellous** (*Br.*), **marvelous** (*US*) **~-off from his friends** друзья устрóили емý замечáтельные прóводы; **~-up** *n.* (*coll.*, *parody, satire*) парóдия, сатира.

sender /'sendə(r)/ *n.* отправитель (*m.*).

Senegal /senɪ'gɔ:l/ *n.* Сенегáл.

senile /'si:naɪl/ *adj.* стáрческий; ~ **dementia** стáрческое слабоýмие; (*of person*) дряхлый.

senility /sɪ'nɪlɪtɪ/ *n.* (*physical*) дряхлость; (*mental*) стáрческое слабоýмие.

senior /'si:nɪə(r)/ *n.*: **he is my ~ by 5 years** он на пять лет стáрше меня.
■ *adj.* (*in age*) стáрший (вóзрастом, годáми); (*in position*) стáрший (по чину/звáнию); ~ **citizen** пожилóй человéк, человéк пенсиóнного вóзраста.

seniority /si:nɪ'ɒrɪtɪ/ *n.* старшинствó.

sensation /sen'seɪʃ(ə)n/ *n.*
1 (*feeling*) ощущéние.
2 (*exciting event*) сенсáция.

sensational /sen'seɪʃən(ə)l/ *adj.* сенсациóнный.

sensationalism /sen'seɪʃənəlɪz(ə)m/ *n.* сенсациóнность.

sense /sens/ *n.*
1 (*faculty*) чýвство; **the five ~s** пять чувств; **a keen ~ of hearing** óстрый слух.
2 (*feeling*; *perception*; *appreciation*) чýвство, ощущéние; **have you no ~ of shame?** у вас стыдá нет!; ~ **of humour** (*Br.*), **humor** (*US*) чýвство юмора.
3 (*pl.*, *sanity*) ум; **take leave of one's ~s** сходить, сойти с умá; **come to one's ~s** брáться, взяться за ум.
4 (*common* ~) здрáвый смысл; **he had the ~ to call the police** у негó хватило умá вы́звать полицию.
5 (*meaning*) смысл, значéние; **in a ~** в извéстном/нéкотором смы́сле; **make ~ of** пон|имáть, -ять; раз|бирáться, -обрáться в + *p.*; **it makes ~** это разýмно.
■ *v.t.* чýвствовать, по-; ощу|щáть, -тить.

senseless /'senslɪs/ *adj.*
1 (*foolish*) бессмы́сленный.
2 (*unconscious*) бесчýвственный; **knock s.o. ~** оглуш|áть, -ить когó-н.

sensible /'sensɪb(ə)l/ *adj.* (благо)разýмный; ~ **shoes** практичная óбувь.

sensitive /'sensɪtɪv/ *adj.* чувствительный, восприимчивый; (*tender*): ~ **skin** нéжная кóжа; (*painful*): ~ **tooth** больнóй зуб; (*potentially embarrassing*): **a ~ topic** щекотливая/деликáтная тéма.

sensitivity /sensɪ'tɪvɪtɪ/ *n.* чувствительность.

sensor /'sensə(r)/ *n.* (*tech.*) дáтчик.

sensual /'sensjʊəl/ *adj.* чýвственный.

sensuous /'sensjʊəs/ *adj.* чýвственный.

sent /sent/ *past and p.p. of* ▶ **send**

sentence /'sent(ə)ns/ *n.*
1 (*gram.*) предложéние.
2 (*leg.*) приговóр.
■ *v.t.* пригов|áривать, -орить.

sentiment /'sentɪmənt/ *n.*
1 (*feeling*) чýвство.
2 (*opinion*) мнéние, тóчка зрéния; **those are my ~s** таковó моё мнéние.

sentimental /sentɪ'ment(ə)l/ *adj.* сентиментáльный.

sentimentality /sentɪmen'tælɪtɪ/ *n.* сентиментáльность.

sentry /'sentrɪ/ *n.* часовóй.

Seoul /səʊl/ *n.* Сеýл.

separate[1] /'sepərət/ *adj.* отдéльный; (*distinct*) осóбый; (*not together*) раздéльный; **two ~ questions** два самостоятельных/рáзных вопрóса; **they are living ~ly** они живýт/проживáют отдéльно/раздéльно.

separate[2] /'sepəreɪt/ *v.t.* (*set apart*) отдел|ять, -ить; (*part*) разлуч|áть, -ить; **he is ~d from his family** он не живёт с семьёй.
■ *v.i.* 1 (*become detached*) отдел|яться, -иться.
2 (*of man and wife*) ра|сходиться, -зойтись (*о супругах*).

separation /sepə'reɪʃ(ə)n/ *n.* отделéние, разделéние; (*of spouses*) раздéльное проживáние (*о супругах*).

separatism /'sepərətɪzm/ *n.* сепаратизм.

separatist /'sepərətɪst/ *n.* сепаратист (*fem.* -ка).

September /sep'tembə(r)/ *n.* сентябрь (*m.*).

septic /'septɪk/ *adj.* септический; **the wound has gone ~** рáна загноилась.

sepulchral /sɪ'pʌlkr(ə)l/ *adj.* (*of a tomb*): ~ **stone** надгрóбный/моги́льный кáмень; (*gloomy*): ~ **voice** замоги́льный гóлос.

sepulchre /'sepəlkə(r)/ (*US* **sepulcher**) *n.* гробница; (*in cave*) склеп.

sequel /'si:kw(ə)l/ *n.* продолжéние (**to:** + *g.*), сиквел (**to:** + *g. or* к + *d.*).

sequence /'si:kwəns/ *n.*
1 (*succession*) послéдовательность; порядок; ~ **of events** ход/послéдовательность событий.
2 (*part of film*) эпизóд.

sequential /sɪ'kwenʃ(ə)l/ *adj.* послéдовательный.

sequester /sɪ'kwestə(r)/ *v.t.*
1 (*isolate, detach*) изоли́ровать (*impf.*, *pf.*); ~ **o.s. from the world** удал|яться, -иться от мира; **a ~ed village** уединённая дерéвня.
2 (*leg. etc.*: *confiscate*; *also* **sequestrate**) (*take temporary possession*) секвестровáть (*impf.*, *pf.*); (*confiscate*) конфисковáть (*impf.*, *pf.*).

sequestrate /'si:kwɪstreɪt/ = **sequester** *v.t.* **2**

sequestration /si:kwɪ'streɪʃ(ə)n/ *n.* секвéстр, арéст имýщества.

sequin /'si:kwɪn/ *n.* (*spangle*) блёстка.

Serb /sɜ:b/ *n.* серб (*fem.* -ка).

Serbia /'sɜ:bɪə/ *n.* Сéрбия.

Serbian /'sɜ:bɪən/ *n.* (*native*) серб (*fem.* -ка); (*language*) сéрбский язы́к.
■ *adj.* сéрбский.

Serbo-Croat(ian) /sɜːbəʊ'krəʊæt, sɜːbəʊkrəʊ'eɪʃ(ə)n/ *n.* серб(ск)охорва́тский язы́к.
■ *adj.* серб(ск)охорва́тский.
serenade /serə'neɪd/ *n.* серена́да.
■ *v.t. & i.* петь, с- серена́ду (*кому*).
serene /sɪ'riːn/ *adj.* (**serener, serenest**) безмяте́жный, споко́йный.
serf /sɜːf/ *n.* крепостно́й; **emancipation of the ~s** раскрепоще́ние крестья́н.
sergeant /'sɑːdʒ(ə)nt/ *n.* сержа́нт.
serial /'sɪərɪəl/ *n.* (*story etc.*) рома́н, выходя́щий отде́льными вы́пусками; (*TV*) многосери́йный телефи́льм; сериа́л.
■ *adj.*: **~ killer** сери́йный уби́йца; **~ number** сери́йный но́мер.
serialize /'sɪərɪəlaɪz/ *v.t.* (*publish in successive parts*) изд|ава́ть, -а́ть вы́пусками; (*screen in successive parts*) выпуска́ть, вы́пустить се́риями.
series /'sɪəriːz/ *n.* (*pl.* ~)
1 (*succession*) се́рия.
2 (*TV*) цикл програ́мм.
serious /'sɪərɪəs/ *adj.*
1 (*thoughtful*) серьёзный; **I am ~ about this** я говорю́ э́то всерьёз; **you can't be ~** вы шу́тите; **take sth. ~ly** отн|оси́ться, -ести́сь серьёзно к + *d.*; (*words*) (вос)прин|има́ть, -я́ть что-н. всерьёз.
2 (*important; not slight*) серьёзный, суще́ственный, ва́жный; **~ crime** тя́жкое/серьёзное преступле́ние; **he is ~ly ill** он серьёзно/тяжело́ бо́лен.
seriousness /'sɪərɪəsnɪs/ *n.* серьёзность; ва́жность; **in all ~** без шу́ток; со всей серьёзностью.
sermon /'sɜːmən/ *n.* про́поведь.
serpent /'sɜːpənt/ *n.* змея́; (*bibl.*) змий.
serrated /se'reɪtɪd/ *adj.* зубча́тый, зазу́бренный.
serum /'sɪərəm/ *n.* сы́воротка.
servant /'sɜːv(ə)nt/ *n.* (*male, also fig.*) слуга́ (*m.*); (*maid* ~) служа́нка, прислу́га.
serve /sɜːv/ *n.* (*at tennis*) пода́ча.
■ *v.t.* 1 (*be servant to; give service to*) служи́ть (*impf.*) + *d.*; **if my memory ~s me correctly/well** е́сли па́мять мне не изменя́ет.
2 (*meet needs of, satisfy*): **~ a purpose** служи́ть (*impf.*) це́ли; **this box has ~d its purpose** э́та коро́бка сослужи́ла свою́ слу́жбу; (*provide service to*) обслу́ж|ивать, -и́ть; **the railway ~s all these villages** желе́зная доро́га обслу́живает все э́ти сёла.
3 (*supply with food, goods etc.*) под|ава́ть, -а́ть + *d.*; **the waiter ~d us with vegetables** официа́нт по́дал (нам) о́вощи; **are you being ~d?** вас кто́-нибудь обслу́живает?
4 (*proffer*) под|ава́ть, -а́ть; **dinner is ~d** обе́д по́дан; **~ a ball** под|ава́ть, -а́ть мяч.
5 (*fulfil, go through*): **~ one's sentence** отб|ыва́ть, -ы́ть срок.
6 (*treat*): **it ~s him right** так ему́ и на́до; подело́м ему́.
■ *v.i.* служи́ть (*impf.*); **he ~d in the army** он служи́л в а́рмии; **~ on a jury** быть прися́жным; **the plank ~d as a bench** доска́ служи́ла ла́вкой/скамьёй.
server /'sɜːvə(r)/ *n.* (*at tennis*) подаю́щий; (*comput.*) се́рвер.
service /'sɜːvɪs/ *n.*
1 (*employment*) слу́жба; **length of ~** стаж.
2 (*branch of public work*) слу́жба; **public, civil ~** госуда́рственная слу́жба; **do one's military ~** отб|ыва́ть, -ы́ть во́инскую пови́нность; **the ~s** вооружённые си́лы (*f. pl.*).
3 (*work done for s.o. or sth.*) услу́га; (*by hotel staff etc.*) обслу́живание, се́рвис; **~ charge** пла́та за обслу́живание.
4 (*system to meet public need*): **postal ~** почто́вая слу́жба; **a frequent train ~ to London** регуля́рное железнодоро́жное сообще́ние с Ло́ндоном.
5 (*attention to*) техобслу́живание; **~ station** (*for petrol*) бензозапра́вочная ста́нция, бензоколо́нка; (*for repairs*) ста́нция техни́ческого обслу́живания.
6 (*eccl.*) слу́жба; обря́д; **marriage/burial ~** венча́ние/отпева́ние.
7 (*in tennis*) пода́ча.
■ *v.t.*: **~ a vehicle** пров|оди́ть, -ести́ осмо́тр и теку́щий ремо́нт маши́ны.
■ *cpds.* **~man** *n.* военнослу́жащий; **~woman** *n.* военнослу́жащая.
serviceable /'sɜːvɪsəb(ə)l/ *adj.* поле́зный, го́дный.
serviette /sɜːvɪ'et/ *n.* (*Br.*) салфе́тка.
servile /'sɜːvaɪl/ *adj.* (*of person or behaviour*) раболе́пный, подобостра́стный.
servility /sɜː'vɪlɪtɪ/ *n.* подобостра́стие.
serving /'sɜːvɪŋ/ *n.* (*of food*) по́рция.
servitude /'sɜːvɪtjuːd/ *n.* ра́бство; **penal ~** ка́торжные рабо́ты (*f. pl.*).
session /'seʃ(ə)n/ *n.* заседа́ние; (*period*) се́ссия.
set /set/ *n.*
1 (*collection; outfit*) набо́р; (*complete set*) компле́кт; (*pictures, coins, books, etc. collected*) колле́кция; **chess ~** ша́хмат|ы (*pl., g.* —); **dinner ~** столо́вый серви́з; **~ of teeth** (*dentures*) зубно́й проте́з.
2 (*receiving apparatus*): **television ~** телеви́зор.
3 (*tennis*) сет, па́ртия.
4 (*theatr.*) декора́ция.
5 (*cin.*): **on the ~** на съёмочной площа́дке.
■ *adj.* 1 (*fixed*): **a ~ smile** засты́вшая улы́бка; **he has ~ opinions** у него́ установи́вшиеся взгля́ды; **he is ~ in his ways** он не изменя́ет свои́м привы́чкам; **~ phrase** клише́ (*indecl.*), шабло́нное выраже́ние; (*prearranged*): **at the ~ time** в устано́вленное вре́мя; **~ menu** ко́мплексное меню́; (*prescribed*): **~ books** обяза́тельная литерату́ра.
2 (*coll., ready*): **all ~?** гото́вы?; **we were all ~ to go** мы совсе́м уже собрали́сь идти́.
3 (*resolved*): **he is ~ on going to the cinema** он настро́ился идти́ в кино́; **he was dead ~ against the idea** он был реши́тельно/категори́чески про́тив э́того предложе́ния.
■ *v.t.* (**setting;** *past and p.p.* ~)
1 (*lay*) класть, положи́ть; (*place*) разме|ща́ть, -сти́ть; распол|ага́ть, -ожи́ть; (*arrange;* ~ *out*) расст|авля́ть, -а́вить.
2 (*adjust, prepare*) ста́вить, по-; **I always ~ my watch by the station clock** я всегда́

ста́влю часы́ по станцио́нным часа́м; **they ~ a trap for him** они́ устро́или ему́ лову́шку; **~ the table** накр|ыва́ть, -ы́ть (на) стол.
[3] (*make straight or firm*): **~ a bone** впр|авля́ть, -а́вить кость; **~ s.o.'s hair** укла́дывать, уложи́ть кому́-н. во́лосы.
[4] (*fig., apply*): **~ one's heart on** стра́стно жела́ть (*impf.*) + *g.*
[5] (*make or put into specified state*) прив|оди́ть, -ести́; **he ~ the boat in motion** он привёл ло́дку в движе́ние; **~ s.o.'s mind at ease, rest** успок|а́ивать, -о́ить кого́-н.; **~ on fire** подж|ига́ть, -е́чь; (*incite*): **he ~ his dog on me** он натрави́л на меня́ свою́ соба́ку.
[6] (*start*) заст|авля́ть, -а́вить (+ *inf.*); **the smoke ~ her coughing** она́ зака́шлялась от ды́ма.
[7] (*present*) зад|ава́ть, -а́ть.
[8] (*establish*): **he is ~ting his children a bad example** он подаёт свои́м де́тям дурно́й приме́р.
[9] (*an exam*) сост|авля́ть, -а́вить.
[10]: **~ sth. to music** класть, положи́ть что-н. на му́зыку.
[11] (*situate*): **he ~ the scene in Paris** ме́стом де́йствия он избра́л Пари́ж.
■ *v.i.* (**setting;** *past and p.p.* **~**)
[1] (*of sun*) сади́ться, сесть.
[2] (*become firm or solid*) затверд|ева́ть, -е́ть; тверде́ть (*impf.*); (*of jelly*) заст|ыва́ть, -ы́ть; (*of cement*) схва́т|ываться, -и́ться.
■ *with preps.*: **~ about (doing) sth.** прин|има́ться, -я́ться за что-н.; **~ (up)on s.o.** нап|ада́ть, -а́сть на кого́-н.
■ *with advs.*: **~ aside** *v.t.* (*allocate*) выделя́ть, вы́делить; (*reserve*) от|кла́дывать, -ложи́ть; **~ back** *v.t.* (*delay, damage*) зам|едля́ть, -е́длить; отбр|а́сывать, -о́сить наза́д; нан|оси́ть, -ести́ уро́н + *d.*; (*coll., cost*): **the trip ~ him back a few pounds** пое́здка влете́ла ему́ в копе́ечку; **~ down** *v.t.* (*make statement or record*): **he ~ down his complaint in writing** он изложи́л свою́ жа́лобу в пи́сьменном ви́де; **she ~ down her impressions in a diary** она́ заноси́ла/запи́сывала свои́ впечатле́ния в дневни́к; **~ forth** *v.t.* (*declare*) изл|ага́ть, -ожи́ть; *v.i.* (*leave*) отпр|авля́ться, -а́виться; **~ in** *v.i.* (*take hold*): **winter is ~ting in** наступа́ет зима́; **the rain ~ in early** дождь начался́ ра́но; **~ off** *v.t.* (*cause to explode*): **they were ~ting off fireworks** они́ устро́или фейерве́рк; (*cause*): **his arrest ~ off a wave of protest** его́ аре́ст вы́звал волну́ проте́стов; (*enhance*): **the ribbon will ~ off your complexion** ле́нта оттени́т/подчеркнёт цвет ва́шего лица́; (*compensate*) возме|ща́ть, -сти́ть; **~ off gains against losses** баланси́ровать, с- при́быль и убы́тки; (*cause to start*): **the story ~ them off laughing** э́тот расска́з рассмеши́л их; *v.i.* (*leave*) (*on foot*) пойти́ (*pf.*), (*by transport*) пое́хать (*pf.*); отпр|авля́ться, -а́виться; **~ out** *v.t.* (*arrange, display*) распол|ага́ть, -ожи́ть; (*expound*) изл|ага́ть, -ожи́ть; *v.i.* (*leave*) пойти́, пое́хать (*both pf.*); отпр|авля́ться, -а́виться; (*attempt*): **he ~ out to conquer Europe** он заду́мал покори́ть Евро́пу; **~ to** *v.i.* (*make a start*) прин|има́ться, -я́ться; (*begin to fight or argue*) сцеп|ля́ться, -и́ться (*coll.*); схв|а́тываться, -ати́ться; **~ up** *v.t.* (*erect*) устан|а́вливать, -ови́ть; (*form*): **we ~ up a committee** мы организова́ли комите́т; (*establish*): **~ up a school** осно́в|ывать, -а́ть шко́лу; (*claim, put forward*): **he ~s himself up to be a scholar** он изобража́ет из себя́ учёного; (*restore to health*): **a holiday will ~ you up** о́тдых вас поста́вит на́ ноги; *v.i.* **she ~ up in business** она́ организова́ла своё де́ло.
■ *cpds.* **~back** *n.* (*delay*) заде́ржка; (*failure*) неуда́ча; (*difficulty*) затрудне́ние; **~-to** *n.* (*coll., fight*) схва́тка; **~-up** *n.* (*coll., arrangement*) поря́дки (*m. pl.*); обстано́вка; (*comput.*) устано́вка.

settee /se'ti:/ *n.* (небольшо́й) дива́н.

setting /'setɪŋ/ *n.*
[1] (*of sun etc.*) захо́д, зака́т.
[2] (*of gems*) опра́ва.
[3] (*background*) обстано́вка, окруже́ние.

settle /'set(ə)l/ *v.t.*
[1] (*place securely*): **~ o.s. in an armchair** ус|а́живаться, -е́сться в кре́сло.
[2] (*install*) поме|ща́ть, -сти́ть; устр|а́ивать, -о́ить.
[3] (*calm*) успок|а́ивать, -о́ить.
[4] (*reconcile*) ула́|живать, -дить; **their differences were soon ~d** их разногла́сия бы́ли ско́ро ула́жены.
[5] (*decide*) реш|а́ть, -и́ть; **that ~s it** тогда́ всё (я́сно).
[6] (*pay*): **~ a bill** плати́ть, за- по счёту; **~ a debt** гаси́ть, по-/упл|а́чивать, -ати́ть долг.
■ *v.i.* [1] (*sink down; come to rest*) ос|еда́ть, -е́сть; **the dust will soon ~** (*fig.*) шуми́ха ско́ро уля́жется; (*alight*) ус|а́живаться, -е́сться.
[2] (*become fixed*) устан|а́вливаться, -ови́ться.
[3] (*become comfortable, accustomed; also* **~ down**): **the dog ~d in its basket** соба́ка улегла́сь в свое́й корзи́не.
[4] (*make one's home*) посел|я́ться, -и́ться.
■ *with advs.*: **~ down** *v.i.* (*in home*) устр|а́иваться, -о́иться; (*in job*) осв|а́иваться, -о́иться; (*adopt sober ways*) остепен|я́ться, -и́ться; (*become quiet*) успок|а́иваться, -о́иться; **he ~d down to write letters** он принялся́/усе́лся писа́ть пи́сьма; **~ in** *v.i.* осв|а́иваться, -о́иться; **~ up** *v.t.* упла́|чивать, -ти́ть; *v.i.* распла́|чиваться, -ти́ться (*с кем*).

settlement /'setəlmənt/ *n.*
[1] (*colony*) поселе́ние; (*settled place*) посёлок.
[2] (*agreement*) соглаше́ние; **reach a ~** дост|ига́ть, -и́чь соглаше́ния.
[3] (*payment*) упла́та, расчёт; **~ of an account** упла́та по счёту.

settler /'setlə(r)/ *n.* поселе́нец.

seven /'sev(ə)n/ *n.* (число́/но́мер) семь; (**~** *people*) се́меро, семь челове́к; (*figure; thing numbered 7; group of* **~**) семёрка.
■ *adj.* семь + *g. pl.*

seventeen /sevən'ti:n/ *n.* & *adj.* семна́дцать + *g. pl.*

seventeenth /sevən'ti:nθ/ *n.* (*date*) семна́дцатое (число́); (*fraction*) одна́ семна́дцатая.
■ *adj.* семна́дцатый.

seventh /'sev(ə)nθ/ *n.* (*date*) седьмо́е (число́); (*fraction*) седьма́я часть.
■ *adj.* седьмо́й.

seventieth /'sevəntɪɪθ/ *n.* одна́ семидеся́тая.

■ *adj.* семидеся́тый.

seventy|y /'sevəntɪ/ *n.* се́мьдесят; **he is in his ~ies** ему́ за се́мьдесят; ему́ (пошёл) восьмо́й деся́ток; **in the ~ies** (*decade*) в семидеся́тых года́х; в семидеся́тые го́ды.
■ *adj.* се́мьдесят + *g. pl.*

sever /'sevə(r)/ *v.t.* отдел|я́ть, -и́ть; **~ a rope** перер|еза́ть, -е́зать верёвку; **~ one's connection with** пор|ыва́ть, -ва́ть связь с + *i.*

several /'sevr(ə)l/ *pron.*: **~ of my friends** не́которые из мои́х друзе́й.
■ *adj.* не́сколько + *g. pl.*; **myself and ~ others** я и не́сколько други́х люде́й.

severance /'sevərəns/ *n.* отделе́ние, разры́в; **~ pay** выходно́е посо́бие; компенса́ция при увольне́нии.

severe /sɪ'vɪə(r)/ *adj.*
1 (*stern, strict*) стро́гий, суро́вый.
2 (*violent*) жесто́кий, си́льный; **~ pain** си́льная/стра́шная боль.

severity /sɪ'verɪtɪ/ *n.* стро́гость, суро́вость; серьёзность.

sew /səʊ/ *v.t. & i.* (*p.p.* **sewn** *or* **sewed**) шить, с-; **~ a button on to a dress** приш|ива́ть, -и́ть пу́говицу к пла́тью.

sewage /'su:ɪdʒ/ *n.* сто́чные во́ды (*f. pl.*).

sewer /'su:ə(r)/ *n.* (*conduit*) сто́чная труба́, канализацио́нная труба́.

sewing /'səʊɪŋ/ *n.* шитьё; (*attr.*) шве́йный.
■ *cpd.* **~ machine** *n.* шве́йная маши́н(к)а.

sewn /səʊn/ *p.p. of* ▸ **sew**

sex /seks/ *n.*
1 пол; (*attr.*) полово́й; **~ change** опера́ция по измене́нию по́ла; **~ education** полово́е воспита́ние.
2 (*sexual activity*) секс; (*sexual intercourse*) полово́е сноше́ние; **have ~ with s.o.** (*coll.*) спать, пере- с кем-н.
■ *with adv.*: **~ up** *v.t.* (*coll.*) ожив|ля́ть, -и́ть (*делать более ярким, выразительным*).

sexiness /'seksɪnɪs/ *n.* сексуа́льность.

sexism /'seksɪz(ə)m/ *n.* секси́зм; (*towards women*) женоненави́стнический.

sexist /'seksɪst/ *adj.* секси́стский.

sextet /sek'stet/ *n.* сексте́т.

sexual /'seksjʊəl/ *adj.* (*organ, disease, reproduction*) полово́й; (*relations*) сексуа́льный.

sexuality /seksjʊ'ælɪtɪ/ *n.* сексуа́льность.

sexy /'seksɪ/ *adj.* (**sexier, sexiest**) (*coll.*) сексуа́льный; (*film, novel*) эроти́ческий.

shabbiness /'ʃæbɪnɪs/ *n.* (*of clothes*) изно́шенность; (*of building, room, area*) убо́гость; (*of behaviour*) по́длость.

shabby /'ʃæbɪ/ *adj.* (**shabbier, shabbiest**) (*clothes, personal appearance*) потрёпанный; (*building, room, area*) убо́гий; (*behaviour*) по́длый.

shack /ʃæk/ *n.* лачу́га.

shackle /'ʃæk(ə)l/ *n.* (*pl., fetters, also fig.*) око́в|ы (*pl., g.* —).
■ *v.t.* (*lit., fetter*) зако́в|ывать, -а́ть в око́вы; (*impede*) ско́в|ывать, -а́ть; стесня́ть (*impf.*).

shade /ʃeɪd/ *n.*
1 (*unilluminated area*) тень; **put in(to) the ~** (*fig.*) затм|ева́ть, -и́ть.
2 (*tint, nuance*) отте́нок, тон.
3 (*of lamp*) абажу́р.
4 (*US, blind*) што́ра.
■ *v.t.* 1 (*screen from light*) затен|я́ть, -и́ть; (*shield from light etc.*) заслон|я́ть, -и́ть.
2 (*restrict light of*) приглуш|а́ть, -и́ть.

shadow /'ʃædəʊ/ *n.* тень; **he has ~s under his eyes** у него́ (чёрные/тёмные) круги́ под глаза́ми; **~ cabinet** (*Br.*) теново́й кабине́т.
■ *v.t.* (*watch and follow secretly*) (та́йно) следи́ть/сле́довать (*impf.*) за + *i.*

shadowy /'ʃædəʊɪ/ *adj.* (*shady*) тени́стый; (*dim*) нея́сный; (*vague*) сму́тный.

shady /'ʃeɪdɪ/ *adj.* (**shadier, shadiest**)
1 (*in shadow*) теново́й.
2 (*coll., suspect*) сомни́тельный, тёмный.

shaft /ʃɑ:ft/ *n.*
1 (*of lance or spear*) дре́вко.
2 (*of light*) луч.
3 (*tech., rod*) вал.
4 (*of mine*) ша́хта, ствол ша́хты.

shag[3] /ʃæg/ (*Br., vulg.*) *v.t.* тра́х|ать, -нуть.
■ *v.i.* тра́х|аться, -нуться.

shaggy /'ʃægɪ/ *adj.* (**shaggier, shaggiest**) лохма́тый.

shake /ʃeɪk/ *n.* встря́ска; **give s.o./sth. a ~** встря́х|ивать, -ну́ть кого́-н./что-н.
■ *v.t.* (*past* **shook;** *p.p.* **shaken** /'ʃeɪk(ə)n/)
1 тряс|ти́, -хну́ть; сотряс|а́ть, -ти́ (*что, чем*); **they shook hands** они́ пожа́ли друг дру́гу ру́ки; **he shook his head** он покача́л голово́й.
2 (*shock*) потряс|а́ть, -ти́; (*morally*) колеба́ть, по-.
■ *v.i.* (*past* **shook;** *p.p.* **shaken** /'ʃeɪk(ə)n/)
1 (*vibrate*) трясти́сь (*impf.*); сотряса́ться (*impf.*).
2 (*tremble*) дрожа́ть, за-; **his hands shook** у него́ дрожа́ли ру́ки; **he was shaking with fever** его́ трясла́ лихора́дка.
■ *with advs.*: **~ off** *v.t.* (*fig., of pursuers, illness, habit etc.*) отде́л|ываться, -аться от + *g.*; изб|авля́ться, -а́виться от + *g.*; **~ up** *v.t.* встря́х|ивать, -ну́ть; (*mix by shaking*): **~ up a medicine** взб|а́лтывать, -олта́ть лека́рство.
■ *cpd.* **~-up** *n.* (*in cabinet etc.*) ка́дровая перестано́вка; (*in a system, in a service*) коренны́е переме́ны (*f. pl.*).

shaky /'ʃeɪkɪ/ *adj.* (**shakier, shakiest**) ша́ткий, нетвёрдый; **his position in the party is ~** его́ положе́ние в па́ртии ша́ткое/непро́чное; **a ~ voice** дрожа́щий го́лос.

shall /ʃæl/ *v. aux.*
1 (*in 1st person*) *usu. translated by future tense*: **I ~ go** я пойду́.
2 (*interrog.*): **~ I wait?** мне подожда́ть?; **~ we have dinner now?** не пообе́дать ли нам сейча́с?; дава́йте пообе́даем.

shallot /ʃə'lɒt/ *n.* (лук-)шало́т.

shallow /'ʃæləʊ/ *adj.* ме́лкий; (*fig.*): **~ mind** пове́рхностный/неглубо́кий ум.

sham /ʃæm/ *n.*
1 (*pretence*) притво́рство; **his illness is only a ~** его́ боле́знь то́лько/одно́ притво́рство; (*hypocrisy*) лицеме́рие.
2 (*counterfeit*) подде́лка.
■ *adj.* 1 (*feigned*) притво́рный.
2 (*counterfeit*) подде́льный.
■ *v.i.* (**shammed, shamming**): **he is ~ming** он притворя́ется.

S

shaman /'ʃæmən/ *n.* шама́н.
shambles /'ʃæmb(ə)lz/ *n.* (*coll., mess*) беспоря́док, ха́ос, барда́к.
shame /ʃeɪm/ *n.*
1 (*sense of guilt*) стыд; **~ on you!** как тебе́ (*or* вам) не сты́дно!
2 (*disgrace*) позо́р, срам; **bring ~ on** позо́рить, о-.
3 (*sth. regrettable*) жа́лость, доса́да; **what a ~!** как жаль!
■ *v.t.* 1 (*cause to feel ashamed*) сму|ща́ть, -ти́ть; стыди́ть, при-.
2 (*disgrace*) позо́рить, о-.
shameful /'ʃeɪmfʊl/ *adj.* позо́рный, посты́дный.
shameless /'ʃeɪmlɪs/ *adj.* бессты́дный; (*unscrupulous*) бессо́вестный.
shampoo /ʃæm'pu:/ *n.* шампу́нь (*m.*).
■ *v.t.* (**shampoos, shampooed**) мыть, вы- шампу́нем.
shandy /'ʃændɪ/ *n.* смесь пи́ва с лимона́дом.
shan't /ʃɑ:nt/ *neg. of* ▸ **shall**
shanty /'ʃæntɪ/ *n.*: **~ town** трущо́бный посёлок.
shape /ʃeɪp/ *n.*
1 (*outward form*) фо́рма; (*outline*) очерта́ние; **take ~** (*become clear*) проясн|я́ться, -и́ться.
2 (*vague figure*) о́браз.
3 (*order*) поря́док; **put** (*coll., knock*) **sth. into ~** прив|оди́ть, -ести́ что-н. в поря́док; (*condition*) фо́рма, состоя́ние; **he is exercising to get into ~** он трениру́ется, что́бы обрести́ (спорти́вную) фо́рму.
■ *v.t.* прид|ава́ть, -а́ть фо́рму + *d.*; (*from wood*) выреза́ть, вы́резать; (*from clay*) лепи́ть, вы́-/с-; (*fig.*): **~ s.o.'s character** формирова́ть, с- чей-н. хара́ктер.
■ *with adv.*: **~ up** *v.i.* (*take ~*) скла́дываться, сложи́ться.
shapeless /'ʃeɪplɪs/ *adj.* бесфо́рменный.
shapely /'ʃeɪplɪ/ *adj.* (**shapelier, shapeliest**) хорошо́ сложённый; стро́йный; **~ legs** стро́йные но́ги.
shard /ʃɑ:d/ *n.* (*broken piece*) черепо́к.
share /ʃeə(r)/ *n.*
1 (*part*) часть; (*portion*) до́ля; **fair ~** причита́ющаяся до́ля (*кому*).
2 (*of capital*) а́кция.
■ *v.t.* дели́ть, раз- (*что с кем*); **he ~s all his secrets with me (*or* I ~ all his secrets)** он де́лится со мной все́ми свои́ми секре́тами; **~ an office with s.o.** рабо́тать (*impf.*) с кем-н. в одно́й ко́мнате; **we must all ~ the blame** мы все несём отве́тственность за э́то.
■ *v.i.*: **I ~ in your grief** я разделя́ю ва́ше го́ре.
■ *with adv.*: **~ out** *v.t.* (*divide*) дели́ть, раз-; (*allocate*) распредел|я́ть, -и́ть.
■ *cpd.* **~holder** *n.* акционе́р.
shark /ʃɑ:k/ *n.* (*also fig.*) аку́ла.
sharp /ʃɑ:p/ *n.* (*mus.*) дие́з.
■ *adj.* 1 (*edged, pointed; also fig., of senses etc.*) о́стрый; ре́зкий; **~ knife** о́стрый нож; **~ pencil** о́стрый каранда́ш; **~ features** ре́зкие черты́ лица́; (*keen*): **~ eyes** о́строе зре́ние; **~ ears** то́нкий слух; **~ wits** о́стрый ум; (*of sounds*): **~ voice** ре́зкий го́лос; (*severe*): **a ~ remark** ко́лкое замеча́ние; **~ tongue** злой/о́стрый язы́к; **~ frost** си́льный моро́з; **~ wind** ре́зкий ве́тер; **~ pain** о́страя/ре́зкая боль; (*sour*) ки́слый.
2 (*abrupt*) круто́й, ре́зкий; **~ turn** круто́й поворо́т; **a ~ drop in the temperature** ре́зкое паде́ние температу́ры; **a ~ rise in prices** ре́зкое повыше́ние.
3 (*artful*) хи́трый.
■ *adv.* 1 (*at a ~ angle*): **turn ~ right** кру́то пов|ора́чивать, -ерну́ть напра́во.
2 (*punctually*): **at four o'clock ~** то́чно/ро́вно в четы́ре (часа́).
3 (*mus.*): **he sings ~** он поёт сли́шком высоко́.
sharpen /'ʃɑ:pən/ *v.t.* (*knife etc.*) точи́ть, на-; зат|а́чивать, -очи́ть; (*pencil*) заостр|я́ть, -и́ть; точи́ть, под-.
sharpener /'ʃɑ:pənə(r)/ *n.* **(pencil ~)** точи́лка.
sharpness /'ʃɑ:pnɪs/ *n.* (*of knife etc.*) острота́; (*of voice etc.*) ре́зкость; (*of outline, photograph etc.*) чёткость; (*astringency*) те́рпкость, е́дкость.
shatter /'ʃætə(r)/ *v.t.* (*breakables, hopes*) разб|ива́ть, -и́ть; (*of health or nerves*) расстр|а́ивать, -о́ить; **I was ~ed** (*Br. coll., exhausted*) я вы́мотался до преде́ла; **I was ~ed by the news** я был потрясён/уби́т э́той но́востью.
■ *v.i.* разб|ива́ться, -и́ться.
shave /ʃeɪv/ *n.*
1 бритьё; **have a ~** побри́ться (*pf.*).
2 (*coll., escape*): **we had a close ~** мы бы́ли на волосо́к от ги́бели.
■ *v.t.* (*p.p.* **shaved** *or* (*as adj.*) **shaven**): **~ one's chin/beard** выбрива́ть, вы́брить подборо́док; брить, по- бо́роду.
■ *v.i.* (*p.p.* **shaved**) бри́ться, по-; **he does not ~ every day** он бре́ется не ка́ждый день.
■ *with adv.*: **~ off** *v.t.* сбри|ва́ть, -ть.
shaver /'ʃeɪvə(r)/ *n.* (*razor*) бри́тва; **electric ~** электробри́тва.
shaving /'ʃeɪvɪŋ/ *n.*
1 (*action*) бритьё.
2 (**~s**, *of wood or metal*) стру́жка.
■ *cpds.* **~ brush** *n.* помазо́к; **~ cream, ~ foam** *nn.* крем, пе́на для бритья́.
shawl /ʃɔ:l/ *n.* шаль.
she /ʃi:/ *pron.* (*obj.* **her**) она́; **~ and I** я и она́; мы с ней.
sheaf /ʃi:f/ *n.* (*pl.* **sheaves**) (*of corn*) сноп; **~ of papers** па́чка/свя́зка бума́г.
shear /ʃɪə(r)/ *n.* (*pl., pair of ~s*) (садо́вые) но́жниц|ы (*pl., g.* —).
■ *v.t.* (*past* **sheared;** *p.p.* **shorn** *or* **sheared**) (*sheep*) стри́чь, о-.
sheath /ʃi:θ/ *n.* (*of weapon*) но́ж|ны (*pl., g.* -ен); (*Br., condom*) презервати́в.
sheaves /ʃi:vz/ *pl. of* ▸ **sheaf**
shed[1] /ʃed/ *n.* сара́й; (*for aircraft*) анга́р.
shed[2] /ʃed/ *v.t.* (**shedding;** *past and p.p.* **~**)
1 (*load, skin*) сбр|а́сывать, -о́сить; **trees ~ their leaves** дере́вья роня́ют ли́стья/листву́.
2 (*blood, tears*) прол|ива́ть, -и́ть.
3 (*diffuse*): **~ light on** (*lit., fig.*) пролива́ть, проли́ть (*or* бр|оса́ть, -о́сить) свет на + *a.*
4 : **~ jobs** сокра|ща́ть, -ти́ть рабо́чие места́.
sheen /ʃi:n/ *n.* (*gloss*) лоск; (*brightness*) блеск, сия́ние.

sheep /ʃi:p/ *n.* (*pl.* **~**) овца́; (*male*) бара́н.
■ *cpd.* **~skin** *n.* овчи́на; ове́чья шку́ра; бара́нья ко́жа.

sheepish /'ʃi:pɪʃ/ *adj.* сконфу́женный.

sheer /ʃɪə(r)/ *adj.*
1 (*absolute*) соверше́нный, су́щий, я́вный.
2 (*precipitous*) отве́сный; перпендикуля́рный; **a ~ drop** круто́й обры́в.
3 (*text., diaphanous*) прозра́чный.

sheet /ʃi:t/ *n.*
1 (*bed linen*) простыня́.
2 (*flat piece*): лист (*pl.* -ы́); **~ of water/ice** слой воды́/льда; **~ music** но́ты (*f. pl.*).

sheik(h) /ʃeɪk/ *n.* шейх.

shelf /ʃelf/ *n.* (*pl.* **shelves**)
1 по́лка; **set of shelves** стелла́ж.
2 (*ledge of rock etc.*) вы́ступ.
■ *cpd.* **~ life** *n.* срок хране́ния.

shell /ʃel/ *n.*
1 (*of mollusc etc.*) ра́ковина, раку́шка; (*of tortoise*) па́нцирь (*m.*); (*of egg, nut*) скорлупа́.
2 (*of building*) нару́жные сте́ны.
3 (*of bomb*) оболо́чка; (*missile*) снаря́д.
■ *v.t.* 1: **~ peas** лущи́ть, об- горо́х; **~ eggs** чи́стить, о- я́йца.
2 (*bombard*) обстре́л|ивать, -я́ть (артиллери́йскими снаря́дами).
■ *with adv.*: **~ out** *v.i.* раскоше́ли|ваться, -ться (*coll.*).
■ *cpd.* **~fish** *n.* (*mollusc*) моллю́ск; (*crustacean*) ракообра́зное.

shelter /'ʃeltə(r)/ *n.*
1 (*protection*) укры́тие, защи́та; **take ~ from** укр|ыва́ться, -ы́ться от + *g.*
2 (*building etc. providing ~*) прию́т, убе́жище; (*for homeless people*) ночле́жка.
■ *v.t.* 1 (*provide refuge for*) приюти́ть (*pf.*); **~ed housing** (*Br.*) дома́, обору́дованные необходи́мыми удо́бствами для престаре́лых/инвали́дов.
2 (*protect*) оберега́ть (*impf.*); защи|ща́ть, -ти́ть.
■ *v.i.* укр|ыва́ться, -ы́ться; пря́таться, с- (**from:** от + *g.*).

shelves /ʃelvz/ *pl. of* ▸ **shelf**

shelving /'ʃelvɪŋ/ *n.* стелла́ж.

shepherd /'ʃepəd/ *n.* пасту́х.

sheriff /'ʃerɪf/ *n.* шери́ф.

sherry /'ʃerɪ/ *n.* хе́рес.

Shetland /'ʃetlənd/ *n.*: **the ~s (*also* the ~ Islands)** Шетле́ндские острова́ (*m. pl.*).

shield /ʃi:ld/ *n.* щит.
■ *v.t.* заслон|я́ть, -и́ть; защи|ща́ть, -ти́ть; (*fig.*) огра|жда́ть, -ди́ть.

shift /ʃɪft/ *n.*
1 (*change of position etc.*) сдвиг, измене́ние, перемеще́ние.
2 (*of workers*) сме́на; **work (in) ~s** рабо́тать (*impf.*) посме́нно; **he is on the night ~** он рабо́тает в ночну́ю сме́ну.
■ *v.t.* (*move*) сме|ща́ть, -сти́ть; дви́|гать, -нуть; (*transfer*) переме|ща́ть, -сти́ть; (*remove*) уб|ира́ть, -ра́ть.
■ *v.i.* переме|ща́ться, -сти́ться.
■ *cpd.* **~ work** *n.* (по)сме́нная рабо́та.

shifty /'ʃɪftɪ/ *adj.* (**shiftier, shiftiest**): **a ~ fellow** ско́льзкий тип; **~ eyes** бе́гающие гла́зки (*m. pl.*).

Shiite /'ʃi:aɪt/ *n.* шии́т.

shilly-shally /'ʃɪlɪʃælɪ/ *v.i.* колеба́ться (*impf.*).

shimmer /'ʃɪmə(r)/ *v.i.* мерца́ть (*impf.*).

shin /ʃɪn/ *n.* го́лень.

shin|e /ʃaɪn/ *n.*
1 (*brightness*) блеск; (*gloss*) гля́нец, лоск.
2 (*coll.*): **take a ~e to s.o.** увл|ека́ться, -е́чься кем-н.
■ *v.t.* (*past and p.p.* **shined**)
1 (*polish*) чи́стить, вы́-/по-; **~e shoes** чи́стить, вы́-/по- ту́фли.
2: **~e a light in s.o.'s face** осве|ща́ть, -ти́ть фонарём чьё-н. лицо́.
■ *v.i.* (*past and p.p.* **shone** *or* **shined**)
1 (*emit light*) свети́ть(ся) (*impf.*); (*brightly*) сия́ть (*impf.*); **the sun ~es** со́лнце сия́ет; (*fig.*): **his face shone with happiness** его́ лицо́ сия́ло от сча́стья; **~ing eyes** сия́ющие глаза́.
2 (*glitter*) блиста́ть (*impf.*); блес|те́ть, -ну́ть.
3 (*fig., excel*) блиста́ть (*impf.*); блесте́ть (*impf.*); **he is a ~ing example of industry** он явля́ет собо́й замеча́тельный приме́р трудолю́бия.

shingle /'ʃɪŋg(ə)l/ *n.* (*pebbles*) га́лька.

shingles /'ʃɪŋg(ə)lz/ *n.* (*med.*) опоя́сывающий лиша́й.

shiny /'ʃaɪnɪ/ *adj.* (**shinier, shiniest**) блестя́щий.

ship /ʃɪp/ *n.* кора́бль (*m.*); су́дно.
■ *v.t.* (**shipped, shipping**) отпр|авля́ть, -а́вить.
■ *cpds.* **~building** *n.* судострое́ние, кораблестрое́ние; **~owner** *n.* судовладе́лец; **~wreck** *n.* кораблекруше́ние; *v.t.*: **be ~wrecked** терпе́ть, по- кораблекруше́ние; **~yard** *n.* верфь; судострои́тельный заво́д.

shipment /'ʃɪpmənt/ *n.*
1 (*dispatch*) отпра́вка, отгру́зка.
2 (*goods shipped*) па́ртия това́ра.

shipping /'ʃɪpɪŋ/ *n.*
1 (*transport*) перево́зка, транспортиро́вка.
2 (*ships*) флот.

shirk /ʃɜ:k/ *v.t.* уклон|я́ться, -и́ться от + *g.*
■ *v.i.* ло́дырничать (*impf.*).

shirt /ʃɜ:t/ *n.* руба́шка; соро́чка.
■ *cpd.* **~sleeve** *n.*: **in ~sleeves** без пиджака́.

shirty /'ʃɜ:tɪ/ *adj.* (**shirtier, shirtiest**) (*Br., coll.*): **get ~** раздраж|а́ться, -и́ться.

shit /ʃɪt/ (*vulg.*) *n.* говно́; (*as expletive*) чёрт!

shitty /'ʃɪtɪ/ *adj.* (**shittier, shittiest**) (*vulg.*) говённый, говня́ный (*euph.*: дерьмо́вый).

shiver /'ʃɪvə(r)/ *n.* дрожь; **it gives me the ~s to think of it** от одно́й мы́сли об э́том меня́ броса́ет в дрожь.
■ *v.i.* дрожа́ть (*impf.*).

shoal /ʃəʊl/ *n.* (*of fish*) кося́к (*рыб*).

shock[1] /ʃɒk/ *n.*
1 (*violent jar or blow*) толчо́к, уда́р; **I got an electric ~** меня́ уда́рило то́ком; **~ wave** взрывна́я волна́.
2 (*disturbing impression*) потрясе́ние, шок; **the news gave him a ~** но́вость потрясла́ его́; (*distressing surprise*) уда́р.
3 (*med.*) шок.
■ *v.t.* 1 (*distress*): **I was ~ed to hear of the disaster** я был потрясён сообще́нием о катастро́фе.

S

[2] (*offend sense of decency*) шоки́ровать (*impf., pf.*).
■ *cpd.* ~ **absorber** *n.* амортиза́тор.

shock² /ʃɒk/ *n.* (*of hair*) копна́ воло́с.

shocking /'ʃɒkɪŋ/ *adj.* (*disturbing*) ужаса́ющий; (*scandalous*) шоки́рующий, сканда́льный.

shod /ʃɒd/ *past and p.p. of* ▶ **shoe**

shoddy /'ʃɒdɪ/ *adj.* (**shoddier, shoddiest**) дрянно́й, некачественный.

shoe /ʃu:/ *n.*
[1] ту́фля.
[2]: (**horse~**) подко́ва.
■ *v.t.* (**shoes, shoeing;** *past and p.p.* **shod**) (*horse*) подко́в|ывать, -а́ть.
■ *cpds.* ~**lace** *n.* шнуро́к; ~ **shop** *n.* обувно́й магази́н.

shone /ʃɒn/ *past and p.p. of* ▶ **shine**

shoo /ʃu:/ *v.t.* (**shoos, shooed**): ~ **away,** ~ **off** отпу́г|ивать, -ну́ть.

shook /ʃʊk/ *past of* ▶ **shake**

shoot /ʃu:t/ *n.*
[1] (*bot.*) росто́к, побе́г.
[2] (~*ing expedition*) охо́та.
■ *v.t.* (*past and p.p.* **shot**)
[1] (*discharge, fire*): **to ~ an arrow** пус|ка́ть, -ти́ть стрелу́; **these guns ~ rubber bullets** э́ти ру́жья стреля́ют рези́новыми пу́лями.
[2] (*kill*) застрели́ть (*pf.*); (*wound*) ра́нить (*impf., pf.*); **he was shot in the head** пу́ля попа́ла ему́ в го́лову.
[3] (*propel*): ~ **a bolt** (*on door*) задв|ига́ть, -и́нуть засо́в.
[4] (*cin., film, scene*) сн|има́ть, -ять, засня́ть (*pf.*) (*фильм, эпизод*).
■ *v.i.* (*past and p.p.* **shot**)
[1] (*fire, of person or weapon*) стреля́ть (*impf.*) (**at:** в + *a.*); **he was shot at twice** в него́ два́жды стреля́ли.
[2] (*dart*) прон|оси́ться, -ести́сь; **he shot out of the doorway** он вы́скочил из подъе́зда; **a ~ing pain** стреля́ющая боль; **a ~ing star** па́дающая звезда́.
[3] (*football etc.*): бить (*impf.*) по мячу́.
■ *with advs.*: ~ **down** *v.t.*: **we shot down five enemy aircraft** мы сби́ли пять самолётов проти́вника; ~ **up** *v.i.* (*of prices etc.*) подск|а́кивать, -очи́ть; (*sl., inject drugs*) ширя́ться, на-.
■ *cpd.* ~**-out** *n.* (*coll.*) перестре́лка.

S

shooting /'ʃu:tɪŋ/ *n.* (*marksmanship; attack*) стрельба́; (*hunting*) охо́та.
■ *cpd.* ~ **range** *n.* тир; (*outdoor*) стре́льбище, полиго́н.

shop /ʃɒp/ *n.*
[1] магази́н; (*small* ~) ла́вка; **talk ~** разгова́ривать/говори́ть (*both impf.*) о (свои́х профессиона́льных) дела́х.
[2] (*work*~) мастерска́я, цех; **on the ~ floor** (*Br.*) в цеху́/це́хе.
■ *v.i.* (**shopped, shopping**) де́лать, с- поку́пки; **she ~ped around** она́ ходи́ла по магази́нам и прице́нивалась.
■ *cpds.* ~ **assistant** *n.* (*Br.*) продав|е́ц (*fem.* -щи́ца); ~**keeper** *n.* владе́л|ец (*fem.* -ица) магази́на; ~**lifter** *n.* магази́нный вор; ~**lifting** *n.* воровство́ в магази́нах; магази́нная кра́жа; ~**-soiled** (*Br.*), ~**worn** (*US*) *adjs.* залежа́вшийся; ~ **window** *n.* витри́на.

shopper /'ʃɒpə(r)/ *n.* покупа́тель (*fem.* -ница).

shopping /'ʃɒpɪŋ/ *n.* поку́пки (*f. pl.*); **do one's ~** де́лать, с- поку́пки; ~ **centre** торго́вый центр.
■ *cpd.* ~**-bag** *n.* хозя́йственная су́мка.

shore¹ /ʃɔ:(r)/ *n.* бе́рег; **on the ~** на берегу́.

shore² /ʃɔ:(r)/ *v.t.*: ~ **up** подп|ира́ть, -ере́ть; крепи́ть (*impf.*).

shorn /ʃɔ:n/ *p.p. of* ▶ **shear**

short /ʃɔ:t/ *n.*
[1] (~ *film*) короткометра́жный фильм.
[2] (*Br.,* ~ *drink*) кре́пкий напи́ток.
■ *adj.* [1] коро́ткий; (*of* ~ *duration*) кра́ткий, недо́лгий; (*of stature*) невысо́кого ро́ста; (*small*) небольшо́й; **this dress is too ~** э́то пла́тье сли́шком ко́ротко; **the days are getting ~er** дни стано́вятся коро́че; **a ~ time ago** неда́вно; ~ **circuit** коро́ткое замыка́ние; ~ **cut** (*route*) кратча́йший путь; **at ~ range** с бли́зкого расстоя́ния; ~ **story** расска́з; **make ~ work of sth.** бы́стро распр|авля́ться, -а́виться с чем-н.; **I want my hair cut ~** я хочу́ ко́ротко постри́чься.
[2] (*brief*): **in ~** коро́че говоря́; (одни́м) сло́вом; **for ~** сокращённо; для кра́ткости.
[3] (*curt, sharp*) ре́зкий.
[4] (*insufficient*): **in ~ supply** дефици́тный; **I am 2 pounds ~** мне не хвата́ет двух фу́нтов.
[5]: **be ~ of sth.** (*lacking*) испы́тывать (*impf.*) недоста́ток в чём-н.; **be ~ of breath** запыха́ться (*impf.*).
[6]: ~ **of** (*except*) кро́ме + *g.*
[7] (*of pastry*) рассы́пчатый, песо́чный.
■ *adv.* [1] (*abruptly*): **he stopped ~** он вдруг останови́лся; (*while speaking*) он вдруг замолча́л.
[2]: ~ **of** (*without reaching*): **fall ~ of a target** не дост|ига́ть, -и́чь це́ли; **we ran ~ of potatoes** у нас ко́нчилась карто́шка.
■ *cpds.* ~**bread,** ~**cake** *nn.* песо́чное пече́нье; ~**-change** *v.t.* (*coll.*) обсчи́т|ывать, -а́ть; ~**-circuit** *v.t.* зам|ыка́ть, -кну́ть на́коротко; ~**coming** *n.* недоста́ток; ~**fall** *n.* недоста́ток, дефици́т; ~**hand** *n.* стеногра́фия; ~**hand typist** (*Br.*) стенографи́стка; ~**list** *n.* шорт-ли́ст, коро́ткий спи́сок кандида́тов, соиска́телей *и т. п.*; *v.t.* зан|оси́ть, -ести́ в шорт-ли́ст, коро́ткий спи́сок; ~**-lived** *adj.* недолгове́чный, мимолётный; ~**-range** *adj.* (*of gun*) с небольшо́й да́льностью стрельбы́; (*of missile*) бли́жнего де́йствия; (*of forecast*) краткосро́чный; ~**-sighted** *adj.* (*lit., fig.*) близору́кий; ~**-sleeved** *adj.* (*shirt*) с коро́ткими рукава́ми; ~**-staffed** *adj.* страда́ющий недоста́тком рабо́тников; ~**-term** *adj.* краткосро́чный; ~**-wave** *adj.* коротковолно́вый.

shortage /'ʃɔ:tɪdʒ/ *n.* недоста́ток, нехва́тка, дефици́т.

shorten /'ʃɔ:t(ə)n/ *v.t.* & *i.* укор|а́чивать(ся), -оти́ть(ся).

shortly /'ʃɔ:tlɪ/ *adv.*
[1] (*soon*) ско́ро; ~ **before** незадо́лго до + *g.*; ~ **after** вско́ре по́сле + *g.*
[2] (*sharply*) ре́зко.

shorts /ʃɔ:ts/ *n.* (*short trousers*) шо́рт|ы (*pl.*, *g.* — *and* -ов); (*US, underpants*) трус|ы́ (*pl.*, *g.* -о́в).

shot¹ /ʃɒt/ *n.*
1 (*discharge of firearm*) вы́стрел; **take a ~ at** вы́стрелить (*pf.*) в + *a.* *or* по + *d.*
2 (*stroke, at games etc.*) уда́р.
3 (*of person*) стрело́к; **he's a good ~** он хоро́ший стрело́к.
4 (*phot.*) сни́мок; (*cin.*) кадр.
5 (*small dose*): **~ of liquor** глото́к спиртно́го; (*injection*) уко́л.
■ *cpds.* **~gun** *n.* дробови́к; **~-put(ting)** *n.* (*sport*) толка́ние ядра́.

shot² /ʃɒt/ *past and p.p. of* ▸ **shoot**

should /ʃʊd/ *v. aux.*
1 (*conditional*): **I ~ say** я бы сказа́л; **I ~ have thought so** на́до полага́ть; каза́лось бы; **~ he die** (в слу́чае) е́сли он умрёт; **I ~n't think so** не ду́маю.
2 (*expr. duty*): **you ~ tell him** вы должны́ ему́ сказа́ть.
3 (*expr. probability or expectation*): **we ~ be there by noon** мы должны́ поспе́ть туда́ к полу́дню; **how ~ I know?** отку́да мне знать?
4 (*expr. purpose*): **he suggested that I ~ go** он предложи́л мне уйти́.

shoulder /ˈʃəʊldə(r)/ *n.* плечо́.
■ *v.t.* (*lit.*): **~ a heavy load** взва́л|ивать, -и́ть на себя́ тяжёлый груз; (*fig.*): **~ responsibility** брать, взять на себя́ отве́тственность.
■ *cpd.* **~ blade** *n.* лопа́тка.

shouldn't /ˈʃʊd(ə)nt/ *neg. of* ▸ **should**

shout /ʃaʊt/ *n.* крик.
■ *v.t.* выкри́кивать, вы́крикнуть.
■ *v.i.* кр|ича́ть, -и́кнуть; **don't ~ at me** не кричи́те на меня́; **~ for help** звать, по- на по́мощь.
■ *with advs.*: **~ down** *v.t.*: **he was ~ed down** его́ слова́ бы́ли заглушены́ кри́ком/кри́ками; **~ out** *v.t.* выкри́кивать, вы́крикнуть; *v.i.* закрича́ть (*pf.*).

shove /ʃʌv/ *n.* толчо́к; **give s.o. a ~** пихну́ть/толкну́ть (*pf.*) кого́-н.
■ *v.t.* толк|а́ть, -ну́ть; **~ sth. into one's pocket** сова́ть, су́нуть что-н. себе́ в карма́н; **he ~d his way forward** он проти́снулся вперёд.
■ *with advs.*: **~ aside, ~ away** *vv.t.* отт|а́лкивать, -олкну́ть.

shovel /ˈʃʌv(ə)l/ *n.* лопа́та; (*mechanical*) экскава́тор.
■ *v.t.* (**shovelled, shovelling;** *US* **shoveled, shoveling**): **~ snow off a path** сгре|ба́ть, -сти́ снег с доро́жки; расч|ища́ть, -и́стить доро́жку от сне́га.

show /ʃəʊ/ *n.*
1 (*manifestation*): **make a ~ of force** демонстри́ровать, про- си́лу; (*semblance*) ви́димость.
2 (*exhibition*) пока́з, вы́ставка; шо́у; **for ~** для ви́ду; напока́з; (*ostentation*) пы́шность, пара́дность.
3 (*entertainment*) представле́ние; шо́у.
■ *v.t.* (*p.p.* **shown** *or* **showed**)
1 (*disclose, reveal, offer for inspection*) пока́з|ывать, -а́ть; **this dress will not ~ the dirt** на э́том пла́тье грязь не бу́дет заме́тна; **he has nothing to ~ for his efforts** он зря стара́лся; **~ o.s.** (*appear*) появ|ля́ться, -и́ться; пока́з|ываться, -а́ться.
2 (*exhibit publicly*) выставля́ть, вы́ставить; (*a film*) пок|а́зывать, -аза́ть.
3 (*display*) проявл|я́ть, -и́ть; демонстри́ровать, про-.
4 (*point out*) ука́з|ывать, -а́ть на + *a.*; (*demonstrate*) пок|а́зывать, -аза́ть; **he ~ed me how to play** он показа́л мне, как игра́ть; (*explain*) объясн|я́ть, -и́ть.
5 (*conduct*) прово|жа́ть, -ди́ть; **he ~ed me to the door** он проводи́л меня́ до две́ри.
■ *v.i.* (*p.p.* **shown** *or* **showed**)
1 (*be visible*) видне́ться (*impf.*); **the stain will not ~** пятно́ не бу́дет заме́тно.
2 (*be exhibited*): **what films are ~ing?** каки́е фи́льмы пока́зывают/иду́т?
■ *with advs.*: **~ in** *v.t.* вв|оди́ть, -ести́/пров|оди́ть, -ести́ в ко́мнату/дом; **~ off** *v.t.* (*display to advantage*) вы́годно подчёркивать (*impf.*); **the frame ~s off the picture** в э́той ра́мке карти́на подчёркнуто хорошо́ смо́трится; (*boastfully*) выставля́ть (*impf.*) напока́з, щеголя́ть (*impf.*) + *i.*; *v.i.* рисова́ться (*impf.*); **~ out** *v.t.* пров|оди́ть, -ести́ к вы́ходу; **~ up** *v.t.* (*make conspicuous*) выделя́ть, вы́делить; *v.i.* (*coll., appear*) появ|ля́ться, -и́ться; (*be conspicuous*): **the flowers ~ed up against the white background** цветы́ выделя́лись на бе́лом фо́не.
■ *cpds.* **~ business** *n.* шо́у-би́знес; **~case** *n.* витри́на; **~down** *n.* про́ба сил; оконча́тельная прове́рка; **~jumping** *n.* конку́р; **~-off** *n.* позёр (*fem.* -ка); хвасту́н (*fem.* -ья) (*coll.*); **~room** *n.* демонстрацио́нный зал.

shower /ˈʃaʊə(r)/ *n.*
1 (*of rain/snow*) кратковре́менный дождь/снег.
2 (**~ bath**) душ; **take a ~** прин|има́ть, -я́ть душ.
■ *v.t.* 1 (*with water etc.*) зал|ива́ть, -и́ть.
2 (*with bullets etc.*) ос|ыпа́ть, -ы́пать гра́дом (*пуль и т. п.*).
■ *v.i.* прин|има́ть, -я́ть душ.

showery /ˈʃaʊərɪ/ *adj.* дождли́вый.

shown /ʃəʊn/ *p.p. of* ▸ **show**

showy /ˈʃəʊɪ/ *adj.* (**showier, showiest**) я́ркий, бро́ский.

shrank /ʃræŋk/ *past of* ▸ **shrink**

shrapnel /ˈʃræpn(ə)l/ *n.* шрапне́ль.

shred /ʃred/ *n.*
1 (*of cloth*) клочо́к; **tear to ~s** раз|рыва́ть, -орва́ть в кло́чья.
2 (*fig., bit*): **not a ~ of evidence** ни мале́йших доказа́тельств; **not a ~ of truth** ни ка́пли пра́вды.
■ *v.t.* (**shredded, shredding**) (*tear*) раз|рыва́ть, -орва́ть; (*cut*) разр|еза́ть, -е́зать.

shredder /ˈʃredə(r)/ *n.* (*for documents*) маши́на для уничтоже́ния бума́ги.

shrew /ʃru:/ *n.* (*zool.*) землеро́йка; (*woman*) сварли́вая же́нщина.

shrewd /ʃru:d/ *adj.* проницáтельный.

shriek /ʃri:k/ *n.* визг; **~s of laughter** визгли́вый смех.
■ *v.i.* визжа́ть (*impf.*); взви́зг|ивать, -нуть.

shrill /ʃrɪl/ *adj.* пронзи́тельный.

shrimp /ʃrɪmp/ *n.* креве́тка.

shrine /ʃraɪn/ *n.* (*tomb*) гробни́ца; (*chapel*) часо́вня; (*lit., fig., hallowed place*) святы́ня, храм.

shrink /ʃrɪŋk/ *v.t.* (*past* **shrank;** *p.p.* **shrunk** *or esp. as adj.* **shrunken**): **hot water will ~ this fabric** от горя́чей воды́ э́тот материа́л ся́дет.
■ *v.i.* (*past* **shrank;** *p.p.* **shrunk**)
1 (*of clothes*) сади́ться, сесть; (*of wood*) сс|ыха́ться, -о́хнуться.
2 (*grow smaller*) сокра|ща́ться, -ти́ться.
3 (*recoil*) отпря́нуть (*pf.*); **he shrank (back) from the fire** он отпря́нул от огня́.

shrivel /ˈʃrɪv(ə)l/ *v.t.* (**shrivelled, shrivelling;** *US* **shriveled, shriveling**) (*dry up*) высу́шивать, вы́сушить; (*wrinkle*) мо́рщить, с-.
■ *v.i.* (**shrivelled, shrivelling;** *US* **shriveled, shriveling**) (*dry up*) высыха́ть, вы́сохнуть; (*wrinkle up*) смо́рщи|ваться, -ться.

shroud /ʃraʊd/ *n.* са́ван.
■ *v.t.* оку́т|ывать, -ать.

Shrove Tuesday /ʃrəʊv/ *n.* вто́рник на Ма́сленой неде́ле.

shrub /ʃrʌb/ *n.* (*bot.*) куст.

shrubbery /ˈʃrʌbərɪ/ *n.* кустa̋рник; уча́сток са́да, заса́женный куста́рником.

shrug /ʃrʌg/ *n.*: **with a ~ (of the shoulders)** пожа́в плеча́ми.
■ *v.t.* & *i.* (**shrugged, shrugging**): **~ (one's shoulders)** пож|има́ть, -а́ть плеча́ми; **~ sth. off** отм|а́хиваться, -ахну́ться от чего́-н.

shrunk(en) /ˈʃrʌŋk((ə)n)/ *p.p. of* ▸ **shrink**

shudder /ˈʃʌdə(r)/ *n.* дрожь.
■ *v.i.* дрожа́ть, за-; содрог|а́ться, -ну́ться.

shuffle /ˈʃʌf(ə)l/ *v.t.*
1: **~ one's feet** ша́ркать (*impf.*) нога́ми.
2: **~ cards** тасова́ть, пере- ка́рты.
■ *v.i.*: **~ along, about** волочи́ть (*impf.*) но́ги.

shun /ʃʌn/ *v.t.* (**shunned, shunning**) избега́ть (*impf.*) + *g.*

shunt /ʃʌnt/ *v.t.* (*rail.*) перев|оди́ть, -ести́ (*поезд, вагон*).
■ *v.i.* маневри́ровать (*impf.*).

shut /ʃʌt/ *v.t.* (**shutting;** *past and p.p.* **~**) закр|ыва́ть, -ы́ть.
■ *v.i.* (**shutting;** *past and p.p.* **~**) закр|ыва́ться, -ы́ться.
■ *with advs.*: **~ down** *v.t.* закр|ыва́ть, -ы́ть; (*comput.*) выключа́ть, вы́ключить; заверш|а́ть, -и́ть рабо́ту; *v.i.* закр|ыва́ться, -ы́ться; **~ off** *v.t.* (*stop supply of*) отключ|а́ть, -и́ть; **~ out** *v.t.* (*exclude*) исключ|а́ть, -и́ть; **~ out light/noise** не пропус|ка́ть, -ти́ть све́та/шу́ма; **~ up** *v.t.* (*close*) зап|ира́ть, -ере́ть; **their house is ~ up for the winter** дом у них заколо́чен на́ зиму; (*confine*): **the boy was ~ up in his room** ма́льчик был за́перт в ко́мнате; (*silence*): **they soon ~ him up** они́ ско́ро заста́вили его́ замолча́ть; *v.i.* (*be, become silent*): **~ up!** замолчи́!, заткни́сь! (*coll.*).
■ *cpd.* **~down** *n.* закры́тие; (*comput.*) выключе́ние, заверше́ние рабо́ты.

shutter /ˈʃʌtə(r)/ *n.*
1 (*on window*) ста́вень (*m.*).
2 (*phot.*) затво́р.

shuttle /ˈʃʌt(ə)l/ *n.*: **~ service** регуля́рное движе́ние/сообще́ние.
■ *v.i.* снова́ть (*impf.*).
■ *cpd.* **~cock** *n.* вола́н.

shy /ʃaɪ/ *adj.* (**shyer, shyest**) (*bashful*) засте́нчивый; (*timid*) ро́бкий.
■ *v.i.* (*of person*): **~ away from sth.** шара́х|аться, -нуться от чего́-н.

Siamese /saɪəˈmiːz/ *n.* (*pl.* **~**) (*also* **~ cat**) сиа́мская ко́шка.
■ *adj.* сиа́мский; **~ twins** сиа́мские близнецы́ (*m. pl.*).

Siberia /saɪˈbɪərɪə/ *n.* Сиби́рь.

Siberian /saɪˈbɪərɪən/ *n.* сибиря́|к (*fem.* -чка).
■ *adj.* сиби́рский.

sibling /ˈsɪblɪŋ/ *n.* (*brother*) родно́й брат; (*sister*) родна́я сестра́.

sick /sɪk/ *adj.*
1 (*unwell*) больно́й.
2 (*nauseated*): **I feel ~** меня́ тошни́т/мути́т; **he was ~** его́ вы́рвало.
3: **~ of: I am ~ to death of her** она́ мне надое́ла до́ смерти.
4 (*morbid*) ме́рзкий, жу́ткий; **~ joke** ме́рзкий анекдо́т.
■ *cpds.* **~bay** *n.* лазаре́т; **~ leave** *n.* о́тпуск по боле́зни; **he is on ~ leave** он на больни́чном (*coll.*); **~ pay** *n.* опла́та по больни́чному листу́.

sicken /ˈsɪkən/ *v.t.* (*fig., disgust*) вызыва́ть, вы́звать отвраще́ние у *кого*; **~ing** отврати́тельный, проти́вный.
■ *v.i.* (*become ill*) забол|ева́ть, -е́ть; **he is ~ing for influenza** (*Br.*) он заболева́ет гри́ппом.

sickle /ˈsɪk(ə)l/ *n.* серп.

sickly /ˈsɪklɪ/ *adj.* (**sicklier, sickliest**) (*unhealthy*) боле́зненный; (*inducing nausea*) тошнотво́рный.

sickness /ˈsɪknɪs/ *n.* (*ill health*) нездоро́вье; (*nausea*) тошнота́.

side /saɪd/ *n.*
1 сторона́; **on the right/left ~** с пра́вой/с ле́вой стороны́; спра́ва/сле́ва; **on the ~** (*coll., additionally, illicitly*) на стороне́.
2 (*edge*) край; **by the ~ of the lake** на берегу́ о́зера; **on the ~ of the mountain** на скло́не горы́.
3 (*of room, table*) коне́ц.
4 (*of the body*) бок; **at my ~** ря́дом со мной; **they were standing ~ by ~** они́ стоя́ли бок о́ бок/ря́дом.
5 (*of a building*) бокова́я стена́; **~ entrance** боково́й вход.
6 (*aspect*) сторона́; **I can see the funny ~ of the affair** мне очеви́дна смешна́я сторона́ (де́ла).
7 (*party*) сторона́; **take ~s with s.o.** прин|има́ть, -я́ть (*or* ста|нови́ться, -ть на) чью-н. сто́рону.
8 (*Br., team*) кома́нда.
9 (*attr.*) боково́й.
■ *v.i.*: **~ with s.o.** ста|нови́ться, -ть на чью-н. сто́рону.
■ *cpds.* **~board** *n.* буфе́т, серва́нт; **~boards** (*Br.*), **~burns** *nn.* (*coll.*) бакенба́рд|ы (*pl., g.* —); **~ effect** *n.* побо́чное де́йствие; **~line** *n.* (*work*) побо́чная рабо́та; (*goods*) неосновно́й това́р; **~long** *adv.* и́скоса; **~ plate** *n.* ма́ленькая таре́лка; **~show** *n.* (*at fair*) аттракцио́н;

~step *v.t.* (*fig.*) уклон|я́ться, -и́ться от + *g.*; **~ street** *n.* переу́лок; **~track** *v.t.* (*distract*): **I meant to finish the job, but I was ~tracked** я собира́лся зако́нчить (э́ту) рабо́ту, но меня́ отвлекли́; **~walk** *n.* (*US*) тротуа́р; **~ways** *adj.* боково́й; *adv.* (*to one* ~) вбок; (*of motion*) бо́ком.

siding /ˈsaɪdɪŋ/ *n.* (*rail.*) запа́сный путь.

sidle /ˈsaɪd(ə)l/ *v.i.*: **~ up to s.o.** под|ходи́ть, -ойти́ к кому́-н. бочко́м.

siege /siːdʒ/ *n.* оса́да, блока́да; **lay ~ to** оса|жда́ть, -ди́ть.

siesta /sɪˈestə/ *n.* сие́ста.

sieve /sɪv/ *n.* си́то.
■ *v.t.* просе́|ивать, -ять.

sift /sɪft/ *v.t.* просе́|ивать, -ять; (*fig.*): **~ the facts** тща́тельно рассм|а́тривать, -отре́ть фа́кты.

sigh /saɪ/ *n.* вздох.
■ *v.i.* взд|ыха́ть, -охну́ть.

sight /saɪt/ *n.*
1 (*faculty*) зре́ние.
2 (*seeing, being seen*) вид; **I can't bear the ~ of him** я его́ ви́деть не могу́; **catch ~ of** зам|еча́ть, -е́тить; **lose ~ of** теря́ть, по- из ви́ду; **at first ~** с пе́рвого взгля́да; на пе́рвый взгляд; (*range of vision*): **come into ~** пока́з|ываться, -а́ться; появ|ля́ться, -и́ться; **in ~** на виду́; **keep out of ~** не пока́з|ывать(ся), -а́ть(ся) (на глаза́); **he would not let her out of his ~** он с неё глаз не спуска́л.
3 (*spectacle*) вид, зре́лище; **a ~ for sore eyes** (*coll.*) прия́тное зре́лище; **see the ~s** осм|а́тривать, -отре́ть достопримеча́тельности.
4 (*aiming device*) прице́л; **he set his ~s on becoming a professor** он ме́тил в профессора́ (*coll.*).
■ *v.t.* (*spot*) зам|еча́ть, -е́тить; ви́деть, у-.
■ *cpds.* **~seeing** *n.* осмо́тр достопримеча́тельностей; **~seer** *n.* тури́ст (*fem.* -ка); экскурса́нт (*fem.* -ка).

sign /saɪn/ *n.*
1 (*mark; gesture*) знак; **~ language** язы́к же́стов; (*symbol*) си́мвол; **plus/minus/equals ~** знак плюс/ми́нус/ра́венства.
2 (*indication*) при́знак; **there's still no ~ of him** его́ всё нет и нет.
3 (**~board**) вы́веска; **road/traffic ~** доро́жный знак.
■ *v.t. & i.* подпи́с|ывать(ся), -а́ть(ся); распи́с|ываться, -а́ться.
■ *with advs.*: **~ on** *v.i.* (*Br., as unemployed*) регистри́роваться, за- в спи́сках безрабо́тных; (*also* **~ up**) (*register*) регистри́роваться, за-; *v.t. & i.* (*for job*) нан|има́ть(ся), -я́ть(ся).
■ *cpd.* **~post** *n.* указа́тель (*m.*).

signal /ˈsɪgn(ə)l/ *n.* (*also as needed for mobile phone to work*) сигна́л.
■ *v.i.* (**signalled, signalling;** *US* **signaled, signaling**) сигнализи́ровать (*impf., pf.*).

signatory /ˈsɪgnətərɪ/ *n.* подписа́вшийся.
■ *adj.*: **~ powers** держа́вы, подписа́вшие догово́р.

signature /ˈsɪgnətʃə(r)/ *n.*
1 по́дпись.
2 (*mus.*): **~ tune** (*Br.*) (музыка́льная) заста́вка.

signet /ˈsɪgnɪt/ *n.* печа́тка; **~ ring** кольцо́ с печа́ткой.

significance /sɪgˈnɪfɪkəns/ *n.* значе́ние.

significant /sɪgˈnɪfɪkənt/ *adj.* значи́тельный; (*important*) ва́жный.

signify /ˈsɪgnɪfaɪ/ *v.t.* означа́ть (*impf.*).

Sikh /siːk, sɪk/ *n.* сикх.
■ *adj.* си́кхский.

Sikhism /ˈsiːkɪz(ə)m/ *n.* сикхи́зм.

silage /ˈsaɪlɪdʒ/ *n.* си́лос.

silence /ˈsaɪləns/ *n.* молча́ние; тишина́; **in ~** в молча́нии/тишине́; мо́лча.
■ *v.t.* заст|авля́ть, -а́вить замолча́ть.

silencer /ˈsaɪlənsə(r)/ *n.* глуши́тель (*m.*).

silent /ˈsaɪlənt/ *adj.* (*saying nothing*) безмо́лвный; **keep ~** молча́ть (*impf.*); (*taciturn*) молчали́вый; **fall, become ~** замолча́ть (*pf.*); умолка́ть, умо́лкнуть; (*mute*): **~ film** немо́й фильм.

silhouette /sɪluːˈet/ *n.* силуэ́т.

silicon /ˈsɪlɪkən/ *n.*: **~ chip** кре́мниевый чип.

silicone /ˈsɪlɪkəʊn/ *n.* силико́н; (*attr.*) силико́новый.

silk /sɪlk/ *n.* шёлк; (*attr.*) шёлковый.

silky /ˈsɪlkɪ/ *adj.* (**silkier, silkiest**) шелкови́стый.

sill /sɪl/ *n.* подоко́нник.

silly /ˈsɪlɪ/ *adj.* (**sillier, silliest**) глу́пый.

silo /ˈsaɪləʊ/ *n.* (*pl.* **~s**) (*tower; pit on farm*) си́лосная ба́шня/я́ма; (*for missile*) ста́ртовая ша́хта (*раке́ты*).

silt /sɪlt/ *n.* ил.

silver /ˈsɪlvə(r)/ *n.*
1 (*metal; silverware*) серебро́.
2 (*colour*) сере́бряный цвет.
■ *adj.* (*made of* ~) сере́бряный; (*resembling* ~) серебри́стый; **~ birch** бе́лая берёза; **~ paper** (*Br.*) фольга́.

silvery /ˈsɪlvərɪ/ *adj.* серебри́стый.

SIM /sɪm/ (*also* **SIM card**) *n.* сим-ка́рта, SIM-ка́рта.

similar /ˈsɪmɪlə(r)/ *adj.*
1 (*alike*) схо́дный, похо́жий.
2: **~ to** похо́жий на + *a.*; подо́бный + *d.*

similarity /sɪmɪˈlærɪtɪ/ *n.* схо́дство.

similarly /ˈsɪmɪləlɪ/ *adv.* так же.

simile /ˈsɪmɪlɪ/ *n.* сравне́ние.

simmer /ˈsɪmə(r)/ *v.i.* кипе́ть (*impf.*) на ме́дленном огне́; (*fig.*): **~ with indignation** кипе́ть (*impf.*) негодова́нием; **~ down** (*fig.*) успок|а́иваться, -о́иться.

simper /ˈsɪmpə(r)/ *n.* жема́нная улы́бка.
■ *v.i.* жема́нно улыб|а́ться, -ну́ться.

simple /ˈsɪmp(ə)l/ *adj.* (**simpler, simplest**)
1 просто́й.
2 (*easy*) лёгкий.

simpleton /ˈsɪmp(ə)lt(ə)n/ *n.* проста́к.

simplicity /sɪmˈplɪsɪtɪ/ *n.* простота́.

simplification /sɪmplɪfɪˈkeɪʃ(ə)n/ *n.* упроще́ние.

simplify /ˈsɪmplɪfaɪ/ *v.t.* упро|ща́ть, -сти́ть.

simplistic /sɪmˈplɪstɪk/ *adj.* (чрезме́рно) упрощённый.

simply /ˈsɪmplɪ/ *adv.* про́сто; **the weather was ~ dreadful** пого́да была́ про́сто ужа́сная.

simulate /'sɪmjʊleɪt/ *v.t.* (*feeling etc.*) изобра|жа́ть, -зи́ть, симули́ровать (*impf., pf.*); (*leather, stone*) и|мити́ровать, сы-; (*conditions*) модели́ровать, с-.

simulation /sɪmjʊ'leɪʃ(ə)n/ *n.* имита́ция; (*of conditions*) модели́рование.

simulator /'sɪmjʊleɪtə(r)/ *n.* (*person*) симуля́нт, притво́рщик; (*device*) модели́рующее/имити́рующее устро́йство; **flight ~** пилота́жный тренажёр.

simultaneous /sɪməl'teɪnɪəs/ *adj.* одновре́ме́нный.

sin /sɪn/ *n.* грех.
■ *v.i.* (**sinned, sinning**) греши́ть, со-.

since /sɪns/ *adv.* с тех пор; **the house has ~ been rebuilt** с тех пор (*or* поздне́е) дом перестро́или.
■ *prep.* с + *g.*; **nothing has happened ~ Christmas** с Рождества́ ничего́ не произошло́; **~ yesterday** со вчера́шнего дня.
■ *conj.* [1] (*from, during the time when*): **how long is it ~ we last met?** ско́лько вре́мени прошло́ с на́шей после́дней встре́чи?; **I have moved house ~ I saw you** с тех пор как мы с ва́ми (после́дний раз) ви́делись, я перее́хал.
[2] (*seeing that*) так как, поско́льку; **~ you ask** е́сли хоти́те знать.

sincere /sɪn'sɪə(r)/ *adj.* (**sincerer, sincerest**) и́скренний; **yours ~ly** и́скренне Ваш.

sincerity /sɪn'serɪtɪ/ *n.* и́скренность.

sinew /'sɪnju:/ *n.* сухожи́лие.

sinful /'sɪnfʊl/ *adj.* гре́шный.

sing /sɪŋ/ *v.t.* (*past* **sang;** *p.p.* **sung**) петь, с-; (*fig.*): **~ s.o.'s praises** восхваля́ть (*impf.*) кого́-н.
■ *v.i.* (*past* **sang;** *p.p.* **sung**) петь, с-.

Singapore /sɪŋə'pɔ:(r)/ *n.* Сингапу́р.

Singaporean /sɪŋə'pɔ:rɪən/ *n.* сингапу́р|ец (*fem.* -ка).
■ *adj.* сингапу́рский.

singe /sɪndʒ/ *v.t.* (**singeing**) пали́ть, о-; (*slightly*) подпа́л|ивать, -и́ть.

singer /'sɪŋə(r)/ *n.* пев|е́ц (*fem.* -и́ца).

singing /'sɪŋɪŋ/ *n.* пе́ние.

single /'sɪŋg(ə)l/ *n.* (*Br., ticket*) биле́т в оди́н коне́ц; (*CD, vinyl*) сингл; (*pl., of tennis etc.*) одино́чная игра́; одино́чный разря́д.
■ *adj.* [1] (*one*) оди́н; (*only one*) еди́нственный, еди́ный; **in ~ file** гусько́м; (*for or involving one person*): **~ bed** односпа́льная крова́ть; **~ room** (*in hotel*) одноме́стный но́мер.
[2] (*unmarried*) одино́кий; (*man*) холосто́й; (*woman*) незаму́жняя; **~ mother** мать-одино́чка; **~ parent** роди́тель-одино́чка.
■ *v.t.*: **~ out**: **he was ~d out** его́ вы́делили.
■ *cpds.* **~-handed** *adj. & adv.* без посторо́нней по́мощи; **~-minded** *adj.* целеустремлённый; **~-sex** *adj.*: **~-sex school** шко́ла разде́льного обуче́ния.

singlet /'sɪŋglɪt/ *n.* (*Br.*) ма́йка.

singular /'sɪŋgjʊlə(r)/ *n.* (*gram.*) еди́нственное число́.
■ *adj.*: **~ noun** существи́тельное в еди́нственном числе́.

sinister /'sɪnɪstə(r)/ *adj.* злове́щий.

sink /sɪŋk/ *n.* (*in kitchen etc.*) ра́ковина.
■ *v.t.* (*past* **sank** *or* **sunk;** *p.p.* **sunk**)
[1]: **~ a ship** топи́ть, по-/за- су́дно.
[2] (*plunge*) вби|ва́ть, -ть; (*fig.*): **the dog sank its teeth into his leg** соба́ка вонзи́ла зу́бы ему́ в но́гу.
[3] (*excavate*): **~ a well** рыть, вы́- коло́дец.
■ *v.i.* (*past* **sank** *or* **sunk;** *p.p.* **sunk** *or as adj.* **sunken**)
[1] (*in water etc.*) тону́ть, у-; (*of objects*) тону́ть, за-; **the ship sank** су́дно затону́ло.
[2] (*below the horizon*) за|ходи́ть, -йти́; **the sun ~s in the west** со́лнце захо́дит на за́паде.
[3] (*subside, of water*) спа|да́ть, -сть; (*of building or soil*) ос|еда́ть, -е́сть.
[4] (*get lower*) па́дать, упа́сть; **his voice sank** он пони́зил го́лос.
[5] (*fall*): **I sank into a deep sleep** я погрузи́лся в глубо́кий сон; (*fig.*): **my heart sank** (*with a sudden shock*) у меня́ се́рдце оборвало́сь; **his heart sank when he saw how much he had to do** ему́ ста́ло ду́рно, когда́ он уви́дел, ско́лько ему́ предстоя́ло сде́лать.
[6] (*penetrate*) впи́т|ываться, -а́ться; (*fig.*): **his words sank in** его́ слова́ дошли́ до меня́ (*и т. п.*).

sinner /'sɪnə(r)/ *n.* гре́шни|к (*fem.* -ца).

sinus /'saɪnəs/ *n.* па́зуха.

sinusitis /saɪnə'saɪtɪs/ *n.* (*med.*) синуси́т.

sip /sɪp/ *n.* глото́к.
■ *v.t.* (**sipped, sipping**) потя́гивать (*impf.*).

siphon, syphon /'saɪf(ə)n/ *n.* сифо́н (*трубка для переливания жидкостей*).
■ *v.t.*: **~ off, out** выка́чивать, вы́качать сифо́ном.

sir /sɜ:(r)/ *n.* (*form of address; title*) сэр, господи́н; **Dear S~** (*in letters*) Уважа́емый господи́н.

siren /'saɪərən/ *n.* сире́на.

sirloin /'sɜ:lɔɪn/ *n.* филе́ (*nt. indecl.*) (*говядины*).

sister /'sɪstə(r)/ *n.* сестра́; (*Br., nursing ~*) ста́ршая медици́нская сестра́.
■ *cpd.* **~-in-law** *n.* (*brother's wife*) неве́стка; (*husband's sister*) золо́вка; (*wife's sister*) своя́ченица.

sisterly /'sɪstəlɪ/ *adj.* се́стринский.

sit /sɪt/ *v.t.* (**sitting;** *past and p.p.* **sat**) (*Br.*): **~ an examination** сдава́ть (*impf.*) экза́мен.
■ *v.i.* (**sitting;** *past and p.p.* **sat**)
[1] (*take a seat*) сади́ться, сесть.
[2] (*be seated*) сиде́ть (*impf.*); **he can't ~ still** ему́ не сиди́тся (на ме́сте); **~ on a committee** быть чле́ном комите́та; **~ting duck, target** (*fig.*) лёгкая добы́ча/мише́нь.
[3] (*pose*): **~ for an artist** пози́ровать (*impf.*) худо́жнику; **~ for one's photograph** фотографи́роваться, с-.
[4] (*be in session*) заседа́ть (*impf.*); **the committee ~s at 10** заседа́ние комите́та начина́ется в 10 (часо́в).
■ *with advs.*: **~ down** *v.i.* сади́ться, сесть; **~ in** *v.i.*: **~ in on a meeting** прису́тствовать (*impf.*) на собра́нии; **~ up** *v.i.* (*from lying position*): **he sat up in bed** он приподня́лся и сел в посте́ли/крова́ти; (*straighten one's back*) сиде́ть (*impf.*) пря́мо.

sitcom /'sɪtkɒm/ *n.* (*coll.*) коме́дия положе́ний (*комедийный сериал с участием одних и тех же героев в разных ситуациях*).

site /saɪt/ *n.* (*place*) ме́сто; (*position*) положе́ние; (*location*) местоположе́ние.

sitter /'sɪtə(r)/ *n.*
1 (*person sitting for portrait*) моде́ль; **she was his ~ many times** она́ мно́го раз ему́ пози́ровала; (*paid one*) нату́рщи|к (*fem.* -ца).
2 (*baby~*) ≈ приходя́щая ня́ня.

sitting /'sɪtɪŋ/ *n.* (*of assembly*) заседа́ние; (*for serving meals*) сме́на.
■ *cpd.* **~ room** *n.* (*Br.*) гости́ная.

situate /'sɪtjʊeɪt/ *v.t.* распол|ага́ть, -ожи́ть.

situation /sɪtjʊ'eɪʃ(ə)n/ *n.*
1 (*place*) ме́сто; (*position*) местоположе́ние.
2 (*circumstances*) положе́ние, ситуа́ция; **what is the ~?** каково́ положе́ние дел?
3 (*job*): **~s vacant** (*Br.*, *as column heading*) вака́нтные до́лжности.

six /sɪks/ *n.* (число́/но́мер) шесть; (*~ people*) ше́стеро, шесть челове́к; (*figure; thing numbered 6; group of ~*) шестёрка.
■ *adj.* шесть + *g. pl.*

sixteen /sɪks'ti:n/ *n.* & *adj.* шестна́дцать (+ *g. pl.*).

sixteenth /sɪks'ti:nθ/ *n.* (*date*) шестна́дцатое (число́); (*fraction*) одна́ шестна́дцатая.
■ *adj.* шестна́дцатый.

sixth /sɪksθ/ *n.* (*date*) шесто́е (число́); (*fraction*) одна́ шеста́я.
■ *adj.* шесто́й; **in the ~ form** (*Br.*) в ста́ршем кла́ссе; **~ sense** шесто́е чу́вство.
■ *cpd.* **~-form college** *n.* (*Br.*) шко́ла со ста́ршими кла́ссами.

sixtieth /'sɪkstɪɪθ/ *n.* одна́ шестидеся́тая.
■ *adj.* шестидеся́тый.

sixt|y /'sɪkstɪ/ *n.* шестьдеся́т; **he is in his ~ies** ему́ за шестьдеся́т (*лет*); **in the ~ies** (*decade*) в шестидеся́тых года́х; в шестидеся́тые го́ды.
■ *adj.* шестьдеся́т + *g. pl.*

sizable /'saɪzəb(ə)l/ = **siz(e)able**

size /saɪz/ *n.*
1 (*dimension*) разме́р; величина́; **these books are all the same ~** все э́ти кни́ги одного́ форма́та; **cut s.o. down to ~** (*coll.*) ста́вить, по- кого́-н. на ме́сто.
2 (*of clothes etc.*): **I take ~ 12** я ношу́/у меня́ двена́дцатый разме́р; **I take ~ 10 in shoes** я ношу́ о́бувь деся́того разме́ра.
■ *v.t.*: **~ s.o. up** сост|авля́ть, -а́вить о ком-н. мне́ние; **~ up the situation** оц|е́нивать, -ени́ть обстано́вку.

siz(e)able /'saɪzəb(ə)l/ *adj.* значи́тельного разме́ра.

sizzle /'sɪz(ə)l/ *v.i.* шипе́ть (*impf.*).

skate[1] /skeɪt/ *n.* (*ice ~*) конёк; (**roller ~**) ро́лик; (*in sg. usu.*) боти́нок.
■ *v.i.* (*on ice*) ката́ться/бе́гать (*both indet.*) на конька́х; (*on roller-~s*) ката́ться (*indet.*) на ро́ликах.
■ *cpds.* **~board** *n.* скейтбо́рд; **~boarder** *n.* скейтборди́ст (*fem.* -ка); **~boarding** *n.* скейтбо́рдинг.

skate[2] /skeɪt/ *n.* (*fish*) скат.

skater /'skeɪtə(r)/ *n.* (*figure-skater*) фигури́ст (*fem.* -ка).

skating /'skeɪtɪŋ/ *n.* (*figure-~*) ката́ние на конька́х.
■ *cpd.* **~ rink** *n.* като́к.

skeleton /'skelɪt(ə)n/ *n.*
1 скеле́т.
2 (*attr.*): **~ key** отмы́чка.

skeptic /'skeptɪk/, **-al** /'skeptɪk(ə)l/ (*US*) = **sceptic, -al**

skepticism /'skeptɪsɪz(ə)m/ (*US*) = **scepticism**

sketch /sketʃ/ *n.*
1 (*artistic*) эски́з, набро́сок, зарисо́вка.
2 (*brief outline*) кра́ткое описа́ние; (*of plan*) о́бщее представле́ние.
3 (*play*) скетч.
■ *v.t.* (*draw*) набр|а́сывать, -оса́ть; (*fig. also*) опи́с|ывать, -а́ть в о́бщих черта́х.
■ *v.i.* де́лать, с- эски́з/зарисо́вку.
■ *cpd.* **~book** *n.* альбо́м для эски́зов/рисова́ния.

sketchy /'sketʃɪ/ *adj.* (**sketchier, sketchiest**) пове́рхностный.

skewer /'skju:ə(r)/ *n.* ве́ртел.
■ *v.t.* наса́|живать, -ди́ть на ве́ртел.

ski /ski:/ *n.* (*pl.* **~s**) лы́жа.
■ *v.i.* (**skis, skied** /ski:d/; **skiing**) (*cross-country*) ходи́ть (*indet.*) на лы́жах; (*downhill*) ката́ться (*impf.*) на лы́жах.
■ *cpds.* **~ boots** *n. pl.* лы́жные боти́нки (*m. pl.*); **~ jumping** *n.* прыжки́ (*m. pl.*) на лы́жах с трампли́на; **~ lift** *n.* (горнолы́жный) подъёмник.

skid /skɪd/ *n.* (*of car*) скольже́ние; юз, зано́с; **the car went into a ~** маши́ну занесло́.
■ *v.i.* (**skidded, skidding**) (*of car, wheels*) пойти́ (*pf.*) ю́зом.

skier /'ski:ə(r)/ *n.* лы́жник.

skiing /'ski:ɪŋ/ *n.* ката́ние на лы́жах.

skilful /'skɪlfʊl/ (*US* **skillful**) *adj.* иску́сный, уме́лый.

skill /skɪl/ *n.* мастерство́, иску́сство; (*specific ability*) на́вык.

skilled /skɪld/ *adj.* (*skilful*) иску́сный; (*trained*) квалифици́рованный.

skillet /'skɪlɪt/ *n.* (*US*) сковорода́.

skim /skɪm/ *v.t.* (**skimmed, skimming**)
1: **~ a liquid** сн|има́ть, -ять на́кипь/пе́нку с жи́дкости; **~med milk** обезжи́ренное молоко́.
2 (*move lightly over*) лете́ть (*det.*) над са́мой пове́рхностью + *g.*
3 (*scan through*) бегло́ просм|а́тривать, -отре́ть.

skimp /skɪmp/ *v.i.* скупи́ться, эконо́мить (*both impf.*).

skimpy /'skɪmpɪ/ *adj.* (**skimpier, skimpiest**) (*meagre*) ску́дный; (*of clothes*) те́сный, у́зкий.

skin /skɪn/ *n.*
1 ко́жа; **I got soaked to the ~** я промо́к до ни́тки; **escape by the ~ of one's teeth** чу́дом спас|а́ться, -ти́сь.
2 (*of animal*) шку́ра.
3 (*of fruit*) кожура́.
■ *v.t.* (**skinned, skinning**) (*remove ~ from*) сн|има́ть, -ять шку́ру с + *g.*; свежева́ть, о-.
■ *cpds.* **~-deep** *adj.* пове́рхностный; **~ diving** *n.* подво́дное пла́вание (с аквала́нгом); **~flint** *n.* скря́га (*c.g.*); **~head** *n.* (*Br.*) «бритоголо́вый», скинхе́д; **~tight**

adj.: **~tight trousers** брю́ки в обтя́жку.

skinny /ˈskɪnɪ/ *adj.* (**skinnier, skinniest**) то́щий.

skint /skɪnt/ *adj.* (*Br. coll.*): **I'm ~** я без копе́йки, я на мели́, я пусто́й (*sl.*).

skip¹ /skɪp/ *n.* скачо́к, прыжо́к.
■ *v.t.* (**skipped, skipping**) (*lesson etc.*) пропус|ка́ть, -ти́ть.
■ *v.i.* (**skipped, skipping**) (*use ~ping rope*) скака́ть/пры́гать (*impf.*) (че́рез скака́лку); **~ping rope** (*Br.*) скака́лка; (*jump*): **she ~ped for joy** она́ подпры́гнула от ра́дости.

skip² /skɪp/ (*Br., builders'*) конте́йнер для (перево́зки) му́сора.

skipper /ˈskɪpə(r)/ *n.* (*captain*) шки́пер, капита́н.

skirmish /ˈskɜːmɪʃ/ *n.* схва́тка.

skirt /skɜːt/ *n.* ю́бка.
■ *v.t.* (*go round*) об|ходи́ть, -ойти́; **we ~ed the town** мы обошли́ го́род; (*form border of*): **the road ~s the forest** доро́га обрамля́ет лес; **~ing board** (*Br.*) пли́нтус.

skittish /ˈskɪtɪʃ/ *adj.* (*of horse etc.*) норови́стый; (*of person*) капри́зный.

skittle /ˈskɪt(ə)l/ *n.* ке́гля; (*pl., game*) ке́гли (*f. pl.*).

skive /skaɪv/ *v.i.* (*Br. coll.*) сачкова́ть (*impf.*) (*sl.*).

skiver /ˈskaɪvə(r)/ *n.* (*Br. coll.*) сачо́к (*coll.*).

skulduggery /skʌlˈdʌgərɪ/ *n.* надува́тельство.

skulk /skʌlk/ *v.i.* зата́иваться (*impf.*).

skull /skʌl/ *n.* че́реп.

skunk /skʌŋk/ *n.* скунс.

sky /skaɪ/ *n.* не́бо.
■ *cpds.* **~diving** *n.* затяжны́е прыжки́ с парашю́том; **~-high** *adv.* (*fig.*) до небе́с; **~light** *n.* фона́рь (*m.*); **~line** *n.* (*horizon*) горизо́нт; (*silhouette against the sky*) силуэ́т (на фо́не не́ба); **~ marshal** *n.* сотру́дник слу́жбы безопа́сности, сопровожда́ющий возду́шные ре́йсы; **~scraper** *n.* небоскрёб.

slab /slæb/ *n.* (*of stone etc.*) плита́; (*of cake etc.*) кусо́к.

slack /slæk/ *adj.*
1 (*slow*) ме́дленный.
2 (*negligent*) небре́жный.
3 (*loose*): **~ rope** прови́сшая верёвка.
4 (*quiet*): **~ season, period** мёртвый сезо́н.
■ *v.i.* (*Br.*) ло́дырничать (*impf.*); **we ~ed off towards five** к пяти́ часа́м мы сба́вили темп (рабо́ты).

slacken /ˈslækən/ *v.t.*
1 (*rope, rein*) отпус|ка́ть, -ти́ть.
2 (*diminish*): **~ speed** сб|авля́ть, -а́вить ско́рость.
■ *v.i.* 1 (*of rope*) пров|иса́ть, -и́снуть; (*of screw, nut*) слабе́ть, о-.
2 (*die down*): **demand is ~ing** спрос уменьша́ется.

slag /slæg/ *v.i.* (**slagged, slagging**): **~ off** (*Br. coll.*) (*criticize*) разн|оси́ть, -ести́.
■ *cpd.* **~ heap** *n.* гру́да шла́ка.

slain /sleɪn/ *p.p. of* ▸ **slay**

slalom /ˈslɑːləm/ *n.* сла́лом.

slam /slæm/ *v.t.* (**slammed, slamming**)
1 (*shut with a bang*): **~ a door** хло́п|ать, -нуть две́рью.
2 (*other violent action*): **he ~med the brakes on** он ре́зко нажа́л на тормоза́.
■ *v.i.* (**slammed, slamming**) (*of door etc.*) захло́п|ываться, -нуться.

slander /ˈslɑːndə(r)/ *n.* клевета́.
■ *v.t.* клевета́ть, о- (*кого*), на- (*на кого*); **he ~ed me** он оклевета́л меня́, он наклевета́л на меня́.

slanderous /ˈslɑːndərəs/ *adj.* клеветни́ческий.

slang /slæŋ/ *n.* жарго́н; сленг.

slant /slɑːnt/ *n.* (*oblique position*) накло́н; укло́н.
■ *v.t.* (*incline*) наклон|я́ть, -и́ть.
■ *v.i.*: **his handwriting ~s to the right** он пи́шет с накло́ном впра́во.

slap /slæp/ *n.* шлепо́к; **~ in the face** (*lit., fig.*) пощёчина.
■ *adv.* (*exactly*) пря́мо.
■ *v.t.* (**slapped, slapping**) шлёпать, от-; **~ s.o.'s face** да|ва́ть, -ть кому́-н. пощёчину.
■ *cpd.* **~dash** *adj.* небре́жный.

slash /slæʃ/ *n.* (*slit*) разре́з; (*oblique mark; also, forward ~*) кося́я черта́; **back~** обра́тная кося́я черта́.
■ *v.t.* 1 (*wound with knife etc.*) ра́нить, по-.
2 (*cut slits in*) разр|еза́ть, -е́зать.
3 (*reduce*): **~ prices** ре́зко сн|ижа́ть, -и́зить це́ны.

slat /slæt/ *n.* пла́нка; (*of blind*) пласти́нка (жалюзи́).

slate /sleɪt/ *n.*
1 (*material*) сла́нец.
2 (*piece of ~ for roofing*) ши́ферная пли́тка.
3 (*fig.*): **wipe the ~ clean** поко́нчить (*pf.*) с про́шлым.
■ *v.t.* 1 (*cover with ~s*) крыть, по- ши́фером.
2 (*Br., criticize*) разн|оси́ть, -ести́.

slaughter /ˈslɔːtə(r)/ *n.* избие́ние, резня́; (*of animals*) убо́й.
■ *v.t.* 1 (*kill animals, people*) ре́зать, за-.
2 (*coll., defeat heavily*) разб|ива́ть, -и́ть в пух и прах.
■ *cpd.* **~house** *n.* (ското)бо́йня.

Slav /slɑːv/ *n.* слав|яни́н (*fem.* -я́нка).
■ *adj.* славя́нский.

slave /sleɪv/ *n.* раб (*fem.* -ы́ня).
■ *v.i.* (*also* **~ away**) рабо́тать (*impf.*) как раб.

slavery /ˈsleɪvərɪ/ *n.* ра́бство.

Slavic /ˈslɑːvɪk/ *adj.* славя́нский.

slavish /ˈsleɪvɪʃ/ *adj.* ра́бский.

Slavonic /sləˈvɒnɪk/ *adj.* славя́нский.

slay /sleɪ/ *v.t.* (*past* **slew;** *p.p.* **slain**) (*liter.*) умер|щвля́ть, -тви́ть.

sleazy /ˈsliːzɪ/ *adj.* (**sleazier, sleaziest**) (*coll.*) (*squalid*) захуда́лый, убо́гий.

sled /sled/ (*US*) (**sledded, sledding**) = **sledge**

sledge /sledʒ/ *n.* са́н|и (*pl., g.* -е́й).
■ *v.i.* ката́ться (*indet.*) на саня́х.

sledgehammer /ˈsledʒhæmə(r)/ *n.* кува́лда.

sleek /sliːk/ *adj.* (*of animal*) гла́дкий, лосня́щийся; (*of person's hair*) прили́занный.

sleep /sliːp/ *n.* сон; **have a ~** поспа́ть (*pf.*); **go to ~** зас|ыпа́ть, -ну́ть, усну́ть (*pf.*); **send to ~** усып|ля́ть, -и́ть; **we had our dog put to ~** нам пришло́сь усыпи́ть соба́ку.
■ *v.i.* (*past and p.p.* **slept**) спать (*impf.*); **~**

like a log спать (*impf.*) как убитый; **I can't ~** я не могу заснуть; **~ on a decision** откладывать, отложить решение до утра.
■ *with advs.*: **~ around** *v.i.* спать (*impf.*) с кем попало; **~ in** *v.i.* (*intentionally*) поспать (*pf.*) всласть; (*oversleep*) прос|ыпать, -пать; **~ with** (*have sex*) спать, пере- с + *i.*
■ *cpds.* **~walk** *v.i.* ходить (*impf.*) во сне; **~walker** *n.* лунатик.

sleeper /ˈsliːpə(r)/ *n.* (*person*): **he is a light/heavy ~** он чутко/крепко спит; (*Br., rail support*) шпала; (*sleeping car*) спальный вагон.

sleeping /ˈsliːpɪŋ/ *cpds.* **~ bag** *n.* спальный мешок; **~ pill** *n.* снотворная таблетка.

sleepless /ˈsliːplɪs/ *adj.* бессонный.

sleepy /ˈsliːpɪ/ *adj.* (**sleepier, sleepiest**) (*lit., fig.*) сонный; сонливый; **I feel ~** мне хочется (*or* я хочу) спать.

sleet /sliːt/ *n.* мокрый снег.
■ *v.i.*: **it is ~ing** идёт мокрый снег.

sleeve /sliːv/ *n.*
1 рукав; **have sth. up one's ~** (*fig.*) иметь (*impf.*) что-н. про запас.
2 (*record cover*) конверт (*пластинки*).

sleeveless /ˈsliːvlɪs/ *adj.* без рукавов.

sleigh /sleɪ/ *n.* сан|и (*pl., g.* -ей).

sleight of hand /slaɪt/ *n.* ловкость рук.

slender /ˈslendə(r)/ *adj.* (**slenderer, slenderest**)
1 (*thin*) тонкий; (*of person, slim*) стройный.
2 (*scanty*) скудный; **~ means** скудные средства.

slept /slept/ *past and p.p. of* ▸ **sleep**

sleuth /sluːθ/ *n.* сыщик.

slew /sluː/ *past of* ▸ **slay**

slice /slaɪs/ *n.*
1 (*of bread, meat*) ломоть (*m.*); (*of cake*) кусок; (*of fruit*) кусок, доля.
2 (*share*) часть, доля.
■ *v.t.* нар|езать, -езать ломтями/ломтиками; **~d bread** (предварительно) нарезанный хлеб.

slick /slɪk/ *adj.* (*skilful*) ловкий, бойкий; (*smooth, also fig.*) гладкий; (*slippery*) скользкий.

slid|e /slaɪd/ *n.*
1 (*chute*) спуск, жёлоб.
2 (*of microscope*) предметное стекло.
3 (*for projection on screen*) слайд, диапозитив.
4 (*Br., hair~e*) заколка.
■ *v.t.* (*past and p.p.* **slid** /slɪd/): **~e a drawer into place** задв|игать, -инуть ящик на место.
■ *v.i.* (*past and p.p.* **slid** /slɪd/)
1 скользить (*impf.*); **~ing door** раздвижная дверь; **the papers ~ off my lap** бумаги соскользнули у меня с колен.
2: **~ing scale** (*econ.*) скользящая шкала.
■ *cpds.* **~ projector** *n.* проектор; **~e rule** *n.* логарифмическая линейка.

slight[1] /slaɪt/ *n.* (*offence*) обида.
■ *v.t.* об|ижать, -идеть.

slight[2] /slaɪt/ *adj.*
1 (*slender*) тонкий.
2 (*not serious*) лёгкий; **she has a ~ cold** у неё лёгкая простуда.
3 (*small*): **there is a ~ risk of infection** есть некоторая опасность заражения.
4: **~est** малейший.

slightly /ˈslaɪtlɪ/ *adv.* слегка; **I know them ~** я с ними немного знаком; **~ younger** немного/чуть моложе.

slim /slɪm/ *adj.* (**slimmer, slimmest**) тонкий, худой.
■ *v.i.* (**slimmed, slimming**) худеть, по-.

slime /slaɪm/ *n.* (*mud*) ил; (*viscous substance*) слизь.

slimy /ˈslaɪmɪ/ *adj.* (**slimier, slimiest**)
1 слизистый, скользкий.
2 (*fig., coll., of person*) неискренний.

sling /slɪŋ/ *n.* перевязь.
■ *v.t.* (*past and p.p.* **slung**) швыр|ять, -нуть.

slink /slɪŋk/ *v.i.* (*past and p.p.* **slunk**): **~ off, away** (*stealthily*) выскальзывать, выскользнуть; (*in a guilty way*) уходить, уйти поджав хвост.

slinky /ˈslɪŋkɪ/ *adj.* (**slinkier, slinkiest**): **a ~ dress** облегающее платье.

slip /slɪp/ *n.*
1 (*error*) ошибка (по небрежности); **~ of the tongue/pen** оговорка/описка.
2 (*petticoat*) комбинация (*женское бельё*).
3 (*of paper*) полоска.
■ *v.t.* (**slipped, slipping**)
1 (*slide; pass covertly*): **he ~ped the ring on to her finger** он надел ей на палец кольцо; **I ~ped the waiter a coin** я сунул официанту монету.
2 (*escape from*) выскальзывать, выскользнуть из + *g.*; **his name ~ped my memory/mind** его имя выскочило у меня из памяти/головы.
■ *v.i.* (**slipped, slipping**)
1 (*slide*) скользить (*impf.*); (*fall over*) поскользнуться (*pf.*); **she ~ped on the ice** она поскользнулась на льду; **~ped disc** смещённый межпозвоночный диск.
2 (*move quickly*) выскальзывать, выскользнуть; **she ~ped out of the room** она выскользнула из комнаты; **I'll ~ into another dress** я (быстренько) переоденусь; **~ through** проск|альзывать, -ользнуть (через + *a.*).
■ *with adv.*: **~ up** *v.i.*: **he ~ped up and hurt his back** он поскользнулся и повредил себе спину; **I ~ped up in my calculations** я ошибся в подсчётах; (*fig.*) я просчитался.
■ *cpds.* **~ road** *n.* (*Br.*) подъездная дорога; **~shod** *adj.* (*fig.*) небрежный; **~-up** *n.* (*coll.*) ошибка.

slipper /ˈslɪpə(r)/ *n.* тапочка.

slippery /ˈslɪpərɪ/ *adj.* (*also fig.*) скользкий.

slit /slɪt/ *n.* (*cut*) разрез; (*slot*) щель, щёлка.
■ *v.t.* (**slitting;** *past and p.p.* **~**): **~ open an envelope** вскр|ывать, -ыть/раз|рывать, -орвать конверт; **~ s.o.'s throat** перер|езать, -езать кому-н. горло.

slither /ˈslɪðə(r)/ *v.i.*: **~ about in the mud** скользить (*impf.*) по грязи.

sliver /ˈslɪvə(r)/ *n.* (*of glass*) осколок; (*of cake, cheese*) кусочек.

slob /slɒb/ *n.* (*sl.*) недотёпа (*c.g.*).

slobber /ˈslɒbə(r)/ *v.i.* (*lit., fig.*) распус|кать, -тить слюни.

slog /slɒg/ *n.* (*coll., arduous work*) тяжёлая работа.
■ *v.i.* (**slogged, slogging**): (*work hard*)

S

вка́лывать (*impf.*) (*coll.*); **he was ~ging along the road** он упо́рно шага́л по доро́ге; **he is ~ging away at Latin** он корпи́т над лати́нью (*coll.*).

slogan /'sləʊgən/ *n.* (*advertising*) сло́ган; (*political*) ло́зунг.

slop /slɒp/ *n.* (*pl., waste liquid*) помо́|и (*pl., g.* -ев).
■ *v.t.* (**slopped, slopping**) : **~ beer over the table** расплёск|ивать, -а́ть пи́во по столу́.

slope /sləʊp/ *n.* (*area of land*) склон; (*of 90 degrees etc.*) укло́н, накло́н.
■ *v.i.*: **~ back(wards)/forwards** коси́ться, по- наза́д/вперёд; **~ down** спуска́ться (*impf.*); **~ up(wards)** поднима́ться (*impf.*).

sloping /'sləʊpɪŋ/ *adj.* (*roof, shoulders*) пока́тый; (*surface, handwriting*) накло́нный; (*ground*) понижа́ющийся.

sloppy /'slɒpɪ/ *adj.* (**sloppier, sloppiest**)
1 (*careless*) неря́шливый.
2 (*sentimental*) сентимента́льный.

slot /slɒt/ *n.*
1 (*slit*) паз; (*aperture*) отве́рстие.
2 (*in timetable*) специа́льно отведённое время; временно́й интерва́л.
■ *v.t.* (**slotted, slotting**)
1 : **~ together** соедин|я́ть, -и́ть на шипа́х.
2 : **~ in** вст|авля́ть, -а́вить.
■ *cpd.* **~ machine** *n.* (*Br., vending machine*) торго́вый автома́т; (*fruit machine*) игрово́й автома́т.

sloth /sləʊθ/ *n.*
1 (*zool.*) лени́вец.
2 (*idleness*) ле́ность.

slothful /'sləʊθfʊl/ *adj.* лени́вый.

slouch /slaʊtʃ/ *v.i.* суту́литься (*impf.*); **he sat ~ed in a chair** он сиде́л развали́вшись в кре́сле.

Slovak /'sləʊvæk/ *n.* (*person*) слова́|к (*fem.* -чка); (*language*) слова́цкий язы́к.
■ *adj.* слова́цкий.

Slovakia /slə'vækɪə/ *n.* Слова́кия.

Sloven|e /'sləʊvi:n/, **-ian** /slə'vi:nɪən/ *nn.* (*person*) слове́н|ец (*fem.* -ка); (*language*) слове́нский язы́к.
■ *adj.* слове́нский.

Slovenia /slə'vi:nɪə/ *n.* Слове́ния.

slovenly /'slʌvənlɪ/ *adj.* неря́шливый.

slow /sləʊ/ *adj.*
1 ме́дленный; **in ~ motion** в заме́дленном де́йствии.
2 (*of clock*): **my watch is 10 minutes ~** мои́ часы́ отстаю́т на де́сять мину́т.
3 (*dull-witted*) тупо́й.
4 (*not lively*): **business is ~** дела́ иду́т вя́ло.
■ *adv.* ме́дленно.
■ *v.t.* (*also* **~ down, ~ up**) зам|едля́ть, -е́длить.
■ *v.i.* (*also* **~ down, ~ up**) зам|едля́ться, -е́длиться.
■ *cpd.* **~-moving** *adj.* ме́дленный.

sludge /slʌdʒ/ *n.* грязь.

slug /slʌg/ *n.* (*zool.*) слизня́к.

sluggish /'slʌgɪʃ/ *adj.*
1 : **~ market** вя́лый ры́нок; (*slow-moving*) ме́дленный.
2 (*lazy*) лени́вый.

sluice /slu:s/ *n.* (*also* **~ gate**) шлюз.

slum /slʌm/ *n.* трущо́ба.

slumber /'slʌmbə(r)/ *n.* дремо́та; **disturb s.o.'s ~s** нар|уша́ть, -у́шить чей-н. сон.
■ *v.i.* дрема́ть, за-.

slump /slʌmp/ *n.* (*fall in prices etc.*) паде́ние; (*trade recession*) упа́док.
■ *v.i.* 1 (*of person*) сва́л|иваться, -и́ться.
2 (*of price, trade*) ре́зко па́дать, упа́сть.

slung /slʌŋ/ *past and p.p. of* ▶ **sling**

slunk /slʌŋk/ *past and p.p. of* ▶ **slink**

slur /slə:(r)/ *n.* пятно́.
■ *v.t.* (**slurred, slurring**) (*pronounce indistinctly*) говори́ть, сказа́ть невня́тно.

slush /slʌʃ/ *n.*
1 сля́коть.
2 : **~ fund** де́ньги для по́дкупа госуда́рственных чино́вников.

slushy /'slʌʃɪ/ *adj.* (**slushier, slushiest**) сля́котный, мо́крый; (*sentimental*) сентимента́льный.

slut /slʌt/ *n.* (*sloven*) неря́ха (*coll.*); (*loose woman*) шлю́ха, потаску́ха (*both vulg.*).

sly /slaɪ/ *adj.* (**slyer, slyest**) хи́трый; **on the ~** укра́дкой, потихо́ньку.

smack[1] /smæk/ *n.*
1 (*sound*) хлопо́к.
2 (*slap*) шлепо́к; **~ in the face** пощёчина.
■ *v.t.* хло́п|ать, -нуть; шлёпать, от-.

smack[2] /smæk/ *v.i.*: **~ of** (*lit., fig.*) отдава́ть (*impf.*) + *i.*

small /smɔ:l/ *n.*: **~ of the back** поясни́ца.
■ *adj.* 1 ма́ленький, небольшо́й, ма́лый; (*of eggs, berries, stones etc.*) ме́лкий; **~ change** ме́лкие де́ньги, ме́лочь; **~ print** ме́лкий шрифт; (*not big enough*): **this coat is too ~ for me** э́то пальто́ мне мало́; **make s.o. look ~** (*fig.*) ун|ижа́ть, -и́зить кого́-н.; **I felt very ~** я (по)чу́вствовал себя́ соверше́нно уничто́женным.
2 (*unimportant, of ~ value*) ме́лкий, незначи́тельный; **~ talk** све́тский разгово́р.
■ *adv.*: **chop sth. up ~** ме́лко наруб|а́ть, -и́ть что-н.
■ *cpds.* **~ ad** *n.* коро́ткое объявле́ние; **~-scale** *adj.* (*map, drawing*) маломасшта́бный.

smarmy /'smɑ:mɪ/ *adj.* (**smarmier, smarmiest**) (*coll.*) льсти́вый.

smart[1] /smɑ:t/ *v.i.*
1 (*of wound*) жечь (*impf.*); **my eyes are ~ing** у меня́ глаза́ щи́плет.
2 (*of person*) страда́ть (*impf.*).

smart[2] /smɑ:t/ *adj.*
1 (*sharp*) ре́зкий, суро́вый, о́стрый.
2 (*brisk*): **he walked off at a ~ pace** он удали́лся бы́стрым ша́гом.
3 (*clever*) сообрази́тельный.
4 (*elegant*): **a ~ hat** элега́нтная шля́па; **you look ~** вы вы́глядите про́сто превосхо́дно.
■ *cpd.* **~ card** *n.* пла́стиковая ка́рточка со встро́енным микропроце́ссором; смарт-ка́рта.

smarten /'smɑ:t(ə)n/ *v.t.* (*also* **~ up**): **~ o.s. up** прихора́шиваться (*impf.*) (*coll.*); (*a room, house, ship etc.*) прив|оди́ть, -ести́ в поря́док.
■ *v.i.*: **~ up** (*in appearance*): **he has ~ed up** он привёл себя́ в поря́док.

smash /smæʃ/ *n.*

1 (*sound*) грóхот; (*collision*) столкновéние.
2 (*at tennis etc.*) смэш.
3 : **~ hit** (*coll.*) суперхи́т; **be a ~ hit** имéть (*impf.*) оглуши́тельный успéх.
■ *v.t.* 1 (*shatter*) разб|ивáть, -и́ть.
2 (*drive with force*): **he ~ed the ball over the net** си́льным удáром он послáл мяч чéрез сéтку.
■ *v.i.* 1 (*be broken*) разб|ивáться, -и́ться.
2 (*crash*) вр|езáться, -éзаться; **the car ~ed into a wall** маши́на врéзалась в стéну.

smashing /'smæʃɪŋ/ *adj.* (*Br. coll.*): **a ~ film** замечáтельный/потрясáющий фильм.

smattering /'smætərɪŋ/ *n.*: **he has a ~ of German** он чуть-чуть знáет немéцкий.

smear /smɪə(r)/ *n.*
1 (*blotch*) пятнó; **~ test** мазóк с шéйки мáтки.
2 (*coll., slander*) клеветá; **~ campaign** клеветни́ческая кампáния.
■ *v.t.* мáзать, на-; размáз|ывать, -ать; **he ~ed grease paint on his face** он наложи́л грим (себé) на лицó.

smell /smel/ *n.*
1 (*faculty*) обоня́ние.
2 (*odour*) зáпах.
■ *v.t.* (*past and p.p.* **smelt** *or* **smelled**)
1 (*perceive ~ of*) чýвствовать, по- зáпах + *g.*; **I ~ something burning** я чýвствую зáпах гáри; (*of animals; also fig.*) чýять (*impf.*).
2 (*sniff*) ню́хать, по-; **~ing salts** ню́хательная соль.
■ *v.i.* (*past and p.p.* **smelt** *or* **smelled**) (*emit ~*) пáхнуть (*impf.*); (*pleasantly*) издавáть (*impf.*) аромáт; **the soup ~s good** суп хорошó/вкýсно пáхнет; **the room smelt of cigarettes** в кóмнате пáхло табакóм; (*unpleasantly*) дýрно/плóхо пáхнуть (*impf.*).

smelly /'smelɪ/ *adj.* (**smellier, smelliest**) дýрно пáхнущий, вонючий.

smelt /smelt *past and p.p. of*/ ▸ **smell**

smidgen /'smɪdʒ(ə)n/ *n.* (*coll.*) чутóк, немнóго.

smile /smaɪl/ *n.* улы́бка.
■ *v.i.* улыб|áться, -нýться; **~ on** (*fig.*): **fortune ~ed on him** счáстье емý улыбáлось.

smirk /smə:k/ *n.* самодовóльная улы́бка, ухмы́лка.
■ *v.i.* ухмыл|я́ться, -ьнýться.

smith /smɪθ/ *n.* **(black~)** кузнéц.

smithereens /smɪðə'ri:nz/ *n.* (*coll.*): **to ~** вдребезги.

smithy /'smɪðɪ/ *n.* кýзница.

smock /smɒk/ *n.* плáтье/блýзка со сбóрками.

smog /smɒg/ *n.* смог.

smoke /sməʊk/ *n.* дым.
■ *v.t.* 1 (*preserve with ~*) копти́ть, за-; **~d fish** копчёная ры́ба.
2 (*tobacco etc.*) кури́ть, вы́-.
■ *v.i.* 1 (*of person*) кури́ть (*impf.*).
2 (*of chimney etc.*) дыми́ться (*impf.*).
■ *cpd.* **~screen** *n.* (*lit., fig.*) дымовáя завéса.

smokeless /'sməʊklɪs/ *adj.* безды́мный; **~ zone** (*Br.*) безды́мная городскáя зóна.

smoker /'sməʊkə(r)/ *n.* курящий; кури́льщи|к (*fem.* -ца).

smoking /'sməʊkɪŋ/ *n.* курéние; **No S~** кури́ть воспрещáется; не кури́ть.

smoky /'sməʊkɪ/ *adj.* (**smokier, smokiest**) ды́мный.

smolder /'sməʊldə(r)/ (*US*) = **smoulder**

smooch /smu:tʃ/ *v.i.* (*coll.*)
1 (*kiss and cuddle*) обнимáться, целовáться, прижимáться (*coll.*), ти́скаться (*coll.*) (*all impf.*).
2 (*Br.*) (*dance in close embrace*) обнимáться, прижимáться (*coll.*) (*both impf.*) в тáнце (*or* танцýя).

smooth /smu:ð/ *adj.*
1 (*even, level*) глáдкий, рóвный; **a ~ paste** тéсто без комкóв.
2 (*not harsh*): **~ wine** нетéрпкое винó.
3 (*suave*) галáнтный.
■ *v.t.* 1 (*make level*) вырáвнивать, вы́ровнять.
2 (*flatten*) приглá|живать, -дить.
3 (*make easy*) смягч|áть, -и́ть.
■ *with advs.*: **~ away** *v.t.*: **he ~ed away our difficulties** он устрани́л нáши трýдности; **~ over** *v.t.* смягч|áть, -и́ть; **~ things over** улá|живать, -дить дéло.

smother /'smʌðə(r)/ *v.t.*
1 (*suffocate*) души́ть, за-; **~ a fire** туши́ть, по- огóнь.
2 (*cover*) покр|ывáть, -ы́ть.
3 (*suppress, conceal*) подав|ля́ть, -и́ть.

smoulder /'sməʊldə(r)/ (*US also* **smolder**) *v.i.* (*lit., fig.*) тлеть (*impf.*); **~ing hatred** затаённая нéнависть.

SMS (*abbr. of* ***Short Message/Messaging Service***): **~ message** SMS/CMC-сообщéние, (*coll.*) SMS (*pr.* эс-эм-э́с).

smudge /smʌdʒ/ *n.* пятнó.
■ *v.t.* смáз|ывать, -ать.

smug /smʌg/ *adj.* (**smugger, smuggest**) самодовóльный.

smuggle /'smʌg(ə)l/ *v.t.* пров|ози́ть, -езти́ контрабáндой; (*fig.*) **he was ~d into the house** егó тайкóм провели́ в дом.

smuggler /'smʌglə(r)/ *n.* контрабанди́ст (*fem.* -ка).

smuggling /'smʌglɪŋ/ *n.* контрабáнда.

smutty /'smʌtɪ/ *adj.* (**smuttier, smuttiest**): **~ face** грязное/запáчканное лицó; **~ joke** грязный/похáбный (*coll.*) анекдóт.

snack /snæk/ *n.* закýска; **have a ~** перекýс|ывать, -и́ть.
■ *cpd.* **~ bar** *n.* закýсочная, буфéт.

snag /snæg/
1 (*obstacle*) препя́тствие; (*difficulty*) затруднéние.
2 (*tear*) разры́в.

snail /sneɪl/ *n.* ули́тка.

snake /sneɪk/ *n.* змея́.

snap /snæp/ *n.*
1 (*noise*) щелчóк, щёлканье; (*of sth. breaking*) треск.
2 (*coll., photograph*) сни́мок.
■ *adj.*: **~ decision** внезáпное решéние.
■ *v.t.* (**snapped, snapping**)
1 (*make ~ping noise with*) щёлк|ать, -нуть + *i.*
2 (*break*) разл|áмывать, -омáть; **he ~ped the stick in two** он разломáл пáлку нáдвое.
3 (*coll., photograph*) сн|имáть, -ять.
■ *v.i.* (**snapped, snapping**)
1 (*make biting motion*): **~ at** огрыз|áться, -нýться на + *a.*; (*speak sharply*) груби́ть, на- (**at:** + *d.*); **don't ~ at me!** не груби́те (мне)!

S

2 (*break*) тре́снуть, слома́ться (*both pf.*).
■ *with advs.*: ~ **off** *v.t.*: ~ **s.o.'s head off** (*coll.*) набр|а́сываться, -о́ситься на кого́-н.; ~ **up** *v.t.* (*buy eagerly*) расхва́т|ывать, -а́ть.
■ *cpd.* ~**shot** *n.* (люби́тельский) сни́мок.

snappy /'snæpɪ/ *adj.* (**snappier, snappiest**): **make it ~!** жи́во!

snare /sneə(r)/ *n.* западня́, лову́шка.

snarl /snɑ:l/ *v.t.* & *i.* рыча́ть, за-.

snatch /snætʃ/ *n.* обры́вок, отры́вок.
■ *v.t.* хвата́ть, схвати́ть; ~ **sth. from s.o.** вырыва́ть, вы́рвать что-н. у кого́-н.
■ *v.i.* хвата́ть (*impf.*); ~ **at sth.** хвата́ться, схвати́ться за что-н.

sneak /sni:k/ *v.i.* (*past and p.p.* **sneaked** *or US coll.* **snuck**) кра́сться (*impf.*); ~ **into a room** прокра́|дываться, -сться в ко́мнату; ~ **out of a room** выска́льзывать, вы́скользнуть из ко́мнаты.

sneakers /'sni:kəz/ *n.* (*US*) кроссо́вки (*f. pl.*).

sneaking /'sni:kɪŋ/ *adj.*: ~ **feeling** сму́тное подозре́ние.

sneaky /'sni:kɪ/ *adj.*
1 (*person*) хи́трый.
2 = **sneaking**

sneer /snɪə(r)/ *n.* презри́тельная усме́шка.
■ *v.i.* усмех|а́ться, -ну́ться.

sneeze /sni:z/ *n.* чиха́нье.
■ *v.i.* чих|а́ть, -ну́ть.

snide /snaɪd/ *adj.* (*coll.*) ехи́дный.

sniff /snɪf/ *n.* вдох.
■ *v.t.* (*inhale*) вд|ыха́ть, -охну́ть; (*smell at*) ню́хать, по-.
■ *v.i.* шмы́г|ать, -ну́ть (но́сом) (*coll.*).

sniffle /'snɪf(ə)l/ *n.* сопе́ние; (*pl.*) на́сморк.
■ *v.i.* шмы́г|ать, -ну́ть (но́сом).

snigger /'snɪgə(r)/ *v.i.* хихи́к|ать, -нуть.

snip /snɪp/ *v.t.* (**snipped, snipping**) подр|еза́ть, -е́зать.

sniper /'snaɪpə(r)/ *n.* сна́йпер.

snippet /'snɪpɪt/ *n.* (*pl., of news etc.*) обры́вки (*m. pl.*).

snivel /'snɪv(ə)l/ *v.i.* (**snivelled, snivelling;** *US* **sniveled, sniveling**) хны́кать (*impf.*).

snob /snɒb/ *n.* сноб.

snobbery /'snɒbərɪ/ *n.* снобизм.

snobbish /'snɒbɪʃ/ *adj.* снобистский.

snog /snɒg/ *v.i.* (**snogged, snogging**) (*Br. coll.*) лиза́ться (*impf., coll.*).

snooker /'snu:kə(r)/ *n.* сну́кер (*игра на бильярде*).

snoop /snu:p/ *v.i.* (*coll.*) подгл|я́дывать, -яде́ть чужи́е та́йны.

snooty /'snu:tɪ/ *adj.* (**snootier, snootiest**) (*coll.*) наду́тый, зазна́вшийся.

snooze /snu:z/ (*coll.*) *n.*: **have, take a ~** вздремну́ть (*pf.*).
■ *v.i.* дрема́ть (*impf.*).

snore /snɔ:(r)/ *n.* храп.
■ *v.i.* храпе́ть, за-.

snorkel /'snɔ:k(ə)l/ *n.* (дыха́тельная) тру́бка (*для подводного плавания*).

snort /snɔ:t/ *v.i.* фы́рк|ать, -нуть.

snout /snaʊt/ *n.* (*of animal*) мо́рда; (*of pig*) ры́ло.

snow /snəʊ/ *n.* снег.
■ *v.i.*: **it is ~ing** идёт снег.
■ *with advs.*: ~ **in** *v.t.*: **we were ~ed in** наш дом занесло́ сне́гом; ~ **under** *v.t.* (*fig.*): **we are ~ed under with work** мы зава́лены рабо́той.
■ *cpds.* ~**ball** *n.* снежо́к; *v.i.* (*fig., increase*) расти́ (*impf.*) как сне́жный ком; ~**board** *n.* сноубо́рд; ~**boarding** *n.* сноубо́рдинг; ~**drift** *n.* сугро́б; ~**drop** *n.* подсне́жник; ~**fall** *n.* снегопа́д; ~**flake** *n.* снежи́нка; (*pl., large*) (сне́жные) хло́пья; ~**man** *n.* сне́жная ба́ба; ~**plough** *n.* снегоубо́рочная маши́на.

snowy /'snəʊɪ/ *adj.* (**snowier, snowiest**): ~ **weather** сне́жная пого́да; ~ **roofs** занесённые кры́ши.

snub /snʌb/ *n.* (*rebuff*) оби́да.
■ *v.t.* (**snubbed, snubbing**) ун|ижа́ть, -и́зить.

snuck /snʌk/ *US colloq. past and p.p. of* ▸ **sneak**

snuff /snʌf/ *n.* ню́хательный таба́к; **pinch of ~** поню́шка; **take ~** ню́хать, по- таба́к.
■ *cpd.* ~**box** *n.* табаке́рка.

snug /snʌg/ *adj.* (**snugger, snuggest**) ую́тный.

snuggle /'snʌg(ə)l/ *v.i.*: ~ **down in bed** свёр|тываться, -ну́ться в посте́ли; ~ **up to s.o.** приж|има́ться, -а́ться к кому́-н.

so /səʊ/ *adv.*
1 так; **is that ~?** э́то так?; (э́то) пра́вда?; **that being ~** раз так; **I'm ~ glad to see you** я так рад вас ви́деть; **would you be ~ kind as to visit her?** бу́дьте так добры́, навести́те её; **he is not ~ silly as to ask her** он не насто́лько глуп, что́бы проси́ть её; **he was ~ overworked that ...** он был так до тако́й сте́пени загру́жен рабо́той, что...; ~ **far** (*up to now*) до сих пор, пока́; ~ **far as I know** наско́лько я зна́ю; **and ~ forth, on** и так да́лее; ~ **long as** (*provided that*) е́сли то́лько; ~ **many** сто́лько + *g.*, так мно́го + *g.*; **thank you ~ much!** большо́е (вам) спаси́бо!; ~ **much the worse/better** тем ху́же/лу́чше; ~ **to say, speak** так сказа́ть; ~ **what** ну и что?
2 (*also*) то́же; **(and) ~ do I** и я то́же.
3 (*consequently, accordingly*) поэ́тому, так что; ита́к, зна́чит; **he is ill, (and) ~ he can't come** он нездоро́в, поэ́тому не мо́жет прийти́; ~ **you did see him after all** зна́чит/ита́к, вы всё-таки его́ ви́дели.
4 (*that the foregoing is true or will happen*): **I suppose/hope ~** я ду́маю/наде́юсь, что да; **do you think ~?** вы так ду́маете?
5 : ~ **as to** (*in order to*) для того́, что́бы; (*in such a way as to*) так, что́бы.
6 (*thereabouts*): **there were 100 or ~ people there** там бы́ло приме́рно сто челове́к (*or* о́коло ста челове́к).
■ *cpds.* ~**-called** *adj.* так называ́емый; ~**-so** *adj.* & *adv.* ничего́; так себе́.

soak /səʊk/ *v.t.*
1 (*wet*) зам|а́чивать, -очи́ть; выма́чивать, вы́мочить; **she ~s the laundry overnight** она́ зама́чивает бельё на́ ночь.
2 (*wet through*): **the shower ~ed me to the skin** дождь промочи́л меня́ до ни́тки/насквозь.
■ *v.i.* 1 (*remain immersed*) мо́кнуть (*impf.*).
2 (*drain*) впит|ываться, -а́ться; **the rain**

~ed into the ground дождь пропита́л по́чву; **the water ~ed through my shoes** вода́ просочи́лась мне в ту́фли.
■ *with adv.*: ~ **up** *v.t.* (*lit., fig.*) впит|ывать, -а́ть.

soaking /'səʊkɪŋ/ *adj.* & *adv.*: **you are ~ (wet)** вы промо́кли насквозь.

soap /səʊp/ *n.* мы́ло.
■ *cpds.* ~ **opera** *n.* мы́льная о́пера, телесериа́л; ~ **powder** *n.* стира́льный порошо́к.

soapy /'səʊpɪ/ *adj.* (**soapier, soapiest**)
1 (*covered with soap*) мы́льный, намы́ленный.
2 (*resembling, containing, consisting of soap*) мы́льный.

soar /sɔ:(r)/ *v.i.*
1 (*of birds*) высоко́ взлет|а́ть, -е́ть.
2 (*fig.*): **her spirits ~ed** она́ испыта́ла душе́вный подъём.
3 (*of prices*) (ре́зко) пов|ыша́ться, -ы́ситься.
4 (*of mountains, buildings*) возвыша́ться (*impf.*).

sob /sɒb/ *n.* всхлип, всхли́пывание.
■ *v.i.* (**sobbed, sobbing**) всхли́п|ывать, -нуть.

sober /'səʊbə(r)/ *adj.* (**soberer, soberest**)
1 (*not drunk, not fanciful*) тре́звый.
2 (*of colour*) споко́йный.
■ *v.t.* (*usu.* ~ **up**) отрезв|ля́ть, -и́ть.
■ *v.i.*: ~ **up** протрезв|ля́ться, -и́ться.

sobriety /sə'braɪɪtɪ/ *n.* тре́звость.

soccer /'sɒkə(r)/ *n.* футбо́л; ~ **match** футбо́льный матч; ~ **player** футболи́ст.

sociable /'səʊʃəb(ə)l/ *adj.* общи́тельный.

social /'səʊʃ(ə)l/ *adj.*
1 (*pert. to the community*) обще́ственный, социа́льный; **S~ Democrat** социа́л-демокра́т; ~ **sciences** обще́ственные нау́ки; ~ **security** (*system*) социа́льное обеспе́чение; (*money received*) посо́бие; ~ **services** систе́ма социа́льного обеспе́чения; ~ **worker** социа́льный рабо́тник.
2 (*convivial*): ~ **gathering** дру́жеская встре́ча.

socialism /'səʊʃəlɪz(ə)m/ *n.* социали́зм.

socialist /'səʊʃəlɪst/ *n.* социали́ст (*fem.* -ка).
■ *adj.* социалисти́ческий.

socialite /'səʊʃəlaɪt/ *n.* све́тская знамени́тость.

socialize /'səʊʃəlaɪz/ *v.i.* обща́ться (*impf.*).

society /sə'saɪətɪ/ *n.* о́бщество; (*association*) о́бщество, объедине́ние, организа́ция.

sociological /səʊsɪə'lɒdʒɪk(ə)l/ *adj.* социологи́ческий.

sociologist /səʊsɪ'ɒlədʒɪst/ *n.* социо́лог.

sociology /səʊsɪ'ɒlədʒɪ/ *n.* социоло́гия.

sock /sɒk/ *n.* носо́к.

socket /'sɒkɪt/ *n.*
1 (*anat.*) впа́дина; **eye ~** глазна́я впа́дина, глазни́ца.
2 (*for plug*) розе́тка; (*slot for connecting electrical device*) разъём; (*for bulb*) патро́н.

sod /sɒd/ (*Br.*) *n.* (*sl.*) сво́лочь (*f.*).
■ *v.i.*: ~ **(it)!** чёрт возьми́!; ~ **off**: **I told him to ~ off** я его́ посла́л; ~ **off!** иди́ на́ фиг!

soda /'səʊdə/ *n.*
1 со́да; **washing ~** стира́льная/кристалли́ческая со́да.
2 (*also* ~ **water**) со́довая (вода́).

sodden /'sɒd(ə)n/ *adj.* промо́кший.

sodium /'səʊdɪəm/ *n.* на́трий.

sofa /'səʊfə/ *n.* дива́н; ~ **bed** дива́н-крова́ть.

Sofia /'səʊfɪə/ *n.* Софи́я.

soft /sɒft/ *adj.*
1 мя́гкий; ~ **toy** мя́гкая игру́шка; ~ **drink** безалкого́льный напи́ток; ~ **drugs** лёгкие нарко́тики; ~ **sign** (*gram.*) мя́гкий знак.
2 (*compassionate*) мя́гкий; отзы́вчивый; **have a ~ spot for s.o.** пита́ть (*impf.*) сла́бость к кому́-н.; (*indulgent*) мя́гкий, нестро́гий; **she is too ~ with her children** она́ недоста́точно строга́ с детьми́.
■ *cpd.* **~ware** *n.* (*comput.*) програ́ммное обеспе́чение.

soften /'sɒf(ə)n/ *v.t.* смягч|а́ть, -и́ть.
■ *v.i.* смягч|а́ться, -и́ться.
■ *with adv.*: ~ **up** *v.t.*: ~ **s.o. up** (*fig.*) осл|абля́ть, -а́бить чьё-н. сопротивле́ние.

soggy /'sɒgɪ/ *adj.* (**soggier, soggiest**) сыро́й, вла́жный.

soil[1] /sɔɪl/ *n.* по́чва.

soil[2] /sɔɪl/ *v.t.* па́чкать, за-/ис-/вы́-; **~ed linen** гря́зное бельё.

soirée /'swɑ:reɪ/ *n.* зва́ный ве́чер.

sojourn /'sɒdʒ(ə)n/ (*liter.*) *n.* (вре́менное) пребыва́ние.
■ *v.i.* пребыва́ть, (вре́менно) жить, прожива́ть (*all impf.*).

solace /'sɒləs/ *n.* утеше́ние, отра́да.

solar /'səʊlə(r)/ *adj.* со́лнечный; ~ **system** Со́лнечная систе́ма.

sold /səʊld/ *past and p.p. of* ▶ **sell**

solder /'səʊldə(r)/ *v.t.* пая́ть (*impf.*); ~ **sth. to sth.** припа́|ивать, -я́ть что-н. к чему́-н; ~ **together** спая́ть (*pf.*).

soldier /'səʊldʒə(r)/ *n.* солда́т.
■ *v.i.*: ~ **on** (*fig., persevere doggedly*) не сдава́ться (*impf.*).

sole[1] /səʊl/ *n.* (*pl.* ~) (*fish*) морско́й язы́к (*род камбалы*).

sole[2] /səʊl/ *n.* (*of foot*) ступня́, подо́шва (*coll.*); (*of shoe*) подо́шва, подмётка.

sole[3] /səʊl/ *adj.* (*only*) еди́нственный; ~ **agent** еди́нственный представи́тель; (*exclusive*) исключи́тельный.

solecism /'sɒlɪsɪz(ə)m/ *n.* (*of language*) солеци́зм; гру́бая (языкова́я) оши́бка; (*of behaviour*) гру́бая вы́ходка, гру́бость.

solely /'səʊllɪ/ *adv.* то́лько, еди́нственно, исключи́тельно.

solemn /'sɒləm/ *adj.* торже́ственный; (*serious*) серьёзный, ва́жный.

solemnity /sə'lemnɪtɪ/ *n.* торже́ственность; (*gravity*) ва́жность; (*of appearance*) серьёзность.

solicit /sə'lɪsɪt/ *v.t.* (**solicited, soliciting**) (*petition*): ~ **s.o.'s help** проси́ть, по- кого́-н. о по́мощи.
■ *v.i.* (**solicited, soliciting**) (*of prostitute*) пристава́ть (*impf.*) к мужчи́нам.

solicitor /sə'lɪsɪtə(r)/ *n.* (*Br.*) адвока́т.

solicitous /sə'lɪsɪtəs/ *adj.* забо́тливый, внима́тельный; **she is ~ for, about your safety** она́ забо́тится о ва́шей безопа́сности.

solicitude /sə'lɪsɪtju:d/ *n.* забо́тливость.

S

solid /ˈsɒlɪd/ *n.* (*phys.*) твёрдое тéло.
■ *adj.* (**solider, solidest**)
1 (*not liquid*) твёрдый; **become ~** твердéть, за-.
2 (*not hollow*) цéльный.
3 (*homogeneous*): **~ silver** чи́стое серебрó.
4 (*unbroken*): **a ~ line** сплошнáя чертá; **it rained for 3 ~ days** дождь лил три дня подря́д.
5 (*firmly built*) прóчный.
6 (*sound, reliable*) соли́дный; надёжный.
solidarity /sɒlɪˈdærɪtɪ/ *n.* солидáрность.
solidify /səˈlɪdɪfaɪ/ *v.i.* твердéть, за-.
solidity /səˈlɪdɪtɪ/ *n.* твёрдость; (*sturdiness*) прóчность; (*reliability*) надёжность; (*soundness*) основáтельность.
soliloquy /səˈlɪləkwɪ/ *n.* монолóг.
solitary /ˈsɒlɪtərɪ/ *adj.* (*secluded*) уединённый; (*lonely*) одинóкий; **~ confinement** одинóчное заключéние; (*single*) едини́чный, еди́нственный.
solitude /ˈsɒlɪtjuːd/ *n.* уединéние, одинóчество.
solo /ˈsəʊləʊ/ *n.* (*mus.*) сóло (*nt. indecl.*).
■ *adj.* сóльный; (*aeron.*) самостоя́тельный.
soloist /ˈsəʊləʊɪst/ *n.* соли́ст (*fem.* -ка).
solstice /ˈsɒlstɪs/ *n.* солнцестоя́ние.
soluble /ˈsɒljʊb(ə)l/ *adj.* раствори́мый.
solution /səˈluːʃ(ə)n/ *n.*
1 (*result of dissolving*) раствóр.
2 (*solving, answer*) решéние.
solve /sɒlv/ *v.t.*: **~ an equation/problem** реш|áть, -и́ть уравнéние/задáчу; **~ a mystery** раскр|ывáть, -ы́ть тáйну.
solvent /ˈsɒlv(ə)nt/ *n.* раствори́тель (*m.*); **~ abuse** токсикомáния.
■ *adj.* (*fin.*) платёжеспосóбный.
Somali /səˈmɑːlɪ/ *n.* (*pl.* **~** *or* **~s**) (*person*) сомали́|ец (*fem.* -йка); (*language*) сомали́ (*m. indecl.*).
■ *adj.* сомали́йский.
Somalia /səˈmɑːlɪə/ *n.* Сомали́ (*nt. indecl.*).
sombre /ˈsɒmbə(r)/ (*US also* **somber**) *adj.* угрю́мый.
some /sʌm/ *pron.*
1 (*of persons*) нéкоторые, одни́; **~ left and others stayed** одни́ ушли́, други́е остáлись; **~ of these girls** нéкоторые/кое-кто из э́тих дéвушек.
2 (*of things*) (*an indefinite number*) нéсколько; **can I have ~?** мóжно (мне) взять нéсколько?; (*an indefinite amount*): **have ~ more!** возьми́те ещё!
3 (*a part*) часть; **I agree with ~ of what you said** части́чно я соглáсен с вáшими словáми.
■ *adj.* 1 (*definite though unspecified*) какóй-то; **~ fool has locked the door** какóй-то дурáк зáпер дверь; **~ day/time** когдá-нибудь.
2 (*no matter what*) какóй-нибудь, какóй-либо.
3 (*one or two*) кóе-каки́е (*pl.*); (*a certain amount*: *may be expr. by g.*): **I bought ~ milk** я купи́л молокá; (*a certain number*) нéсколько (*or untranslated*): **I bought ~ envelopes** я купи́л конвéрты; **for ~ time now** с нéкоторого врéмени.
4 (*approximately*) примéрно, óколо.
somebody /ˈsʌmbədɪ/ *pron.* (*also* **someone**) (*in particular*) ктó-то; **there is ~ in the cellar** в пóгребе ктó-то есть; (*only in nom.*) нéкто; (*no matter who*) ктó-нибудь, ктó-либо; **~ else can do it** ктó-нибудь другóй мóжет э́то сдéлать.
somehow /ˈsʌmhaʊ/ *adv.* (*no matter how*) кáк-нибудь; так и́ли инáче; **we shall manage ~** мы кáк-нибудь спрáвимся; (*in some unspecified way*) кáк-то, каки́м-то óбразом; **he found out my name ~** он каки́м-то óбразом узнáл, как меня́ зову́т; (*for some reason*): **~ I never liked him** он мне почему́-то никогдá не нрáвился.
someone /ˈsʌmwʌn/ = **somebody**
someplace /ˈsʌmpleɪs/ (*US*) = **somewhere 1**
somersault /ˈsʌməsɒlt/ *n.* (*in the air*) сáльто (*nt. indecl.*); (*on the ground*) кувырóк.
■ *v.i.* кувырк|áться, -ну́ться; дéлать, с- сáльто.
something /ˈsʌmθɪŋ/ *pron.* (*definite*) чтó-то; (*only in nom.*) нéчто; (*indefinite*) чтó-нибудь, чтó-либо; **I must get ~ to eat** я дóлжен чтó-нибудь поéсть; **she lectures in ~ or other** онá читáет лéкции по какóму-то (там) предмéту; **there is ~ about him** в нём чтó-то такóе есть; **she has a cold or ~** у неё простýда и́ли чтó-то в э́том рóде.
■ *adv.*: **he left ~ like a million** он остáвил чтó-то поря́дка миллиóна.
sometime /ˈsʌmtaɪm/ *adv.* когдá-нибудь, когдá-либо; **~ soon** кáк-нибудь, скóро.
sometimes /ˈsʌmtaɪmz/ *adv.* иногдá.
somewhat /ˈsʌmwɒt/ *adv.* кáк-то, нéсколько, довóльно.
somewhere /ˈsʌmweə(r)/ *adv.*
1 (*US also* **someplace**) (*place, specific*) гдé-то; (*place, anywhere*) гдé-нибудь, гдé-либо; (*motion, specific*) кудá-то; (*motion, anywhere*) кудá-нибудь, кудá-либо.
2 (*approximately*) óколо + *g.*
son /sʌn/ *n.* сын.
■ *cpd.* **~-in-law** *n.* зять (*m.*) (*муж дочери*).
sonata /səˈnɑːtə/ *n.* сонáта.
song /sɒŋ/ *n.* пéсня.
sonic /ˈsɒnɪk/ *adj.* звуковóй.
sonnet /ˈsɒnɪt/ *n.* сонéт.
sonorous /ˈsɒnərəs/ *adj.* звýчный.
soon /suːn/ *adv.*
1 (*in a short while*) скóро, вскóре; **write ~!** напиши́те (по)скорée!; **as ~ as possible** как мóжно скорée.
2 (*early*) рáно; **~er or later** рáно и́ли пóздно.
3 : **as ~ as** как тóлько; **as ~ as I saw him, I recognized him** я узнáл егó, как тóлько уви́дел.
4 (*willingly*): **I would ~er die than permit it** я скорée умрý, чем допущý э́то; **what would you ~er do: go now or wait?** что вы предпочитáете: уйти́ и́ли подождáть?
soot /sʊt/ *n.* сáжа, кóпоть.
soothe /suːð/ *v.t.* (*calm*) успок|áивать, -óить; (*relieve*) облегч|áть, -и́ть.
soothing /suːðɪŋ/ *adj.* (*tone*) утеши́тельный; (*cream*) успокои́тельный.
sooty /ˈsʊtɪ/ *adj.* (**sootier, sootiest**) (*blackened with soot*) закопчённый, закоптéлый; (*black as soot*) чёрный как сáжа;

(*containing soot*): ~ **deposit** слой са́жи.

sophisticated /sə'fɪstɪkeɪtɪd/ *adj.*
1 (*complicated*): ~ **techniques** сло́жная те́хника.
2 (*refined*): ~ **taste** утончённый вкус.

sophistication /səfɪstɪ'keɪʃ(ə)n/ *n.* (*refinement*) утончённость, искушённость.

soporific /sɒpə'rɪfɪk/ *adj.* снотво́рный, усыпля́ющий.

soppy /'sɒpɪ/ *adj.* (**soppier, soppiest**) (*Br. coll.*) (*sentimental*) сентимента́льный.

soprano /sə'prɑːnəʊ/ *n.* (*pl.* **~s**) (*singer*) сопра́но (*f. indecl.*); (*voice*) сопра́но (*nt. indecl.*).

sorbet /'sɔːbeɪ/ *n.* шербе́т.

sorcerer /'sɔːsərə(r)/ *n.* колду́н, волше́бник.

sorceress /'sɔːsərɪs/ *n.* колду́нья, волше́бница.

sorcery /'sɔːsərɪ/ *n.* колдовство́, волшебство́.

sordid /'sɔːdɪd/ *adj.* (*squalid*) убо́гий; (*morally bad*) гну́сный.

sore /sɔː(r)/ *n.* боля́чка, я́зва.
■ *adj.* : **a ~ tooth** больно́й зуб; **I have a ~** (*grazed*) **knee** я ссади́л себе́ коле́но; **he has a ~ throat** у него́ боли́т го́рло; **it is a ~ point with him** э́то у него́ больно́е ме́сто.

sorrow /'sɒrəʊ/ *n.* (*sadness*) печа́ль, го́ре; (*in pl.*) го́рести (*pl., f.*).

sorrowful /'sɒrəʊfʊl/ *adj.* печа́льный, го́рестный.

sorry /'sɒrɪ/ *adj.* (**sorrier, sorriest**)
1 (*regretful*): **be ~ for sth.** сожале́ть (*impf.*) о чём-н., жале́ть, по- о чём-н.; **we were ~ to hear of your father's death** мы с гру́стью узна́ли о сме́рти ва́шего отца́; **~!** винова́т!; прости́те!; извини́те!; **say you're ~!** (по)проси́ проще́ния!; **~, I'm busy** извини́те, но я за́нят; **I'm ~ I came** я жале́ю, что пришёл.
2 (*expr. pity, sympathy*): **I feel ~ for you** мне жа́лко/жаль тебя́; **it's the children I feel ~ for** кого́ мне жа́лко/жаль — так э́то дете́й; **feel ~ for o.s.** жале́ть (*impf.*) себя́.
3 (*wretched*) жа́лкий; **in a ~ state** в жа́лком состоя́нии.

sort /sɔːt/ *n.*
1 (*kind, species*) род, сорт, разря́д, вид; **he is not the ~ (of person) to complain** он не из тех, кто жа́луется; **what ~ of man is he?** что он за челове́к?; **what ~ of music do you like?** каку́ю му́зыку вы лю́бите?; **people of all ~s** са́мые ра́зные лю́ди.
2 : **~ of** (*coll.*) вро́де, как бы; в о́бщем-то; **he ~ of suggested I took him with me** он как бы дал мне поня́ть, что хо́чет пойти́ со мной.
3 : **out of ~s** (*Br.*) не в ду́хе.
■ *v.t.* раз|бира́ть, -обра́ть; **they ~ed themselves into groups of six** они́ разби́лись на гру́ппы по шесть челове́к; (*letters etc.; also comput.*) сортирова́ть, рас-.
■ *with adv.*: **~ out** *v.t.* (*select*) от|бира́ть, -обра́ть; (*separate*) отдел|я́ть, -и́ть; (*arrange*) раз|бира́ть, -обра́ть; (*fig., put in order*): **I have to go home to ~ things out** мне ну́жно пойти́ домо́й и во всём разобра́ться.

sortie /'sɔːtɪ/ *n.* (*sally*) вы́лазка (*also fig.*); (*flight*) вы́лет.

SOS *n.* (*pl.* **~s**) (радио)сигна́л бе́дствия.

sought /sɔːt/ *past and p.p. of* ▶ **seek**

soul /səʊl/ *n.*
1 душа́.
2 (*music*) со́ул.

soulful /'səʊlfʊl/ *adj.* проникнове́нный, задуше́вный.

soulless /'səʊllɪs/ *adj.* безду́шный.

sound[1] /saʊnd/ *n.*
1 звук; (*of rain, sea, wind etc.*) шум; **~ barrier** звуково́й барье́р; **~ effects** звуково́е сопровожде́ние, шумовы́е эффе́кты.
2 : **I don't like the ~ of it** мне э́то (что́-то) не нра́вится.
■ *v.t.*: **they ~ed the bell** они́ позвони́ли в ко́локол; **~ the alarm** бить, за- трево́гу.
■ *v.i.* 1 (*emit sound*) звуча́ть, про-.
2 (*give impression*) каза́ться, по-; **it ~s like thunder** похо́же на гром; **the statement ~s improbable** э́то заявле́ние ка́жется маловероя́тным.
■ *cpds.* **~ card** *n.* (*comput.*) звукова́я ка́рта; **~proof** *adj.* звуконепроница́емый; **~track** *n.* саундтре́к.

sound[2] /saʊnd/ *n.* (*strait*) проли́в.

sound[3] /saʊnd/ *v.t.* (*fig.*): **~ (out) s.o. (***or* **s.o.'s intentions, opinions)** зонди́ровать, про- кого́-н.

sound[4] /saʊnd/ *adj.*
1 (*healthy*) здоро́вый; **of ~ mind** в здра́вом уме́; (*in good condition*) испра́вный.
2 (*thorough*) хоро́ший; **he slept ~ly** он кре́пко спал; **he was ~ly thrashed** его́ си́льно изби́ли.

soup /suːp/ *n.* суп.
■ *cpds.* **~ kitchen** *n.* беспла́тная столо́вая для нужда́ющихся.

sour /'saʊə(r)/ *adj.*
1 (*of fruit etc.*) ки́слый.
2 (*of milk*) проки́сший, ски́сший; **go, turn ~** ск|иса́ть, -и́снуть.
3 (*of person*) мра́чный, озло́бленный.

source /sɔːs/ *n.*
1 (*of stream etc.*) исто́к.
2 (*fig.*) исто́чник.

south /saʊθ/ *n.* юг; (*naut.*) зюйд; **in the ~** на ю́ге; **from the ~** с ю́га; **to the ~ of** к ю́гу от + *g.*
■ *adj.* ю́жный; **~ wind** ю́жный ве́тер; **S~ Pole** Ю́жный по́люс.
■ *adv.*: **the ship sailed due ~** су́дно шло пря́мо на юг; **our village is ~ of London** на́ша дере́вня нахо́дится к ю́гу от Ло́ндона.
■ *cpds.* **~-east** *n.* ю́го-восто́к; *adj.* (*also* **~-easterly, ~-eastern**) ю́го-восто́чный; **~-east wind** зюйд-о́ст; *adv.* на ю́го-восто́к; **~-west** *n.* ю́го-за́пад; *adj.* (*also* **~-westerly, ~-western**) ю́го-за́падный; *adv.* на ю́го-за́пад; **~-west wind** зюйд-ве́ст; *adv.* на ю́го-за́пад.

South Africa /saʊθ 'æfrɪkə/ *n.* Ю́жная А́фрика.

South African /saʊθ 'æfrɪkən/ *n.* южноафрика́н|ец (*fem.* -ка).
■ *adj.* южноафрика́нский.

South America /saʊθ ə'merɪkə/ *n.* Ю́жная Аме́рика.

South American /saʊθ ə'merɪkən/ *n.* южноамерика́н|ец (*fem.* -ка).
■ *adj.* южноамерика́нский.

southerly /'sʌðəlɪ/ *n.* (*wind*) ю́жный ве́тер.

■ *adj.* южный.
southern /ˈsʌð(ə)n/ *adj.* южный.
southerner /ˈsʌðənə(r)/ *n.* южа́н|ин (*fem.* -ка).
southward /ˈsaʊθwəd/ *adj.* южный.
■ *adv.* (*also* **~s**) на юг; к югу, в южном направле́нии.
souvenir /suːvəˈnɪə(r)/ *n.* сувени́р.
sovereign /ˈsɒvrɪn/ *n.* (*monarch*) госуда́р|ь (*fem.* -ыня); (*coin*) соверéн.
■ *adj.* суверéнный.
sovereignty /ˈsɒvrɪntɪ/ *n.* суверенитéт.
Soviet /ˈsəʊvɪət/ (*hist.*) *n.* совéт.
■ *adj.* совéтский; **the ~ Union** Совéтский Сою́з.
sow[1] /saʊ/ *n.* (*pig*) свинья́ (*самка*).
sow[2] /səʊ/ *v.t.* (*past* **sowed** /səʊd/; *p.p.* **sown** *or* **sowed**)
1 (*seed*) сéять, по-.
2 (*ground*): зас|éивать, -éять.
soya /ˈsɔɪə/ *n.* (*also* **soy**) сóя.
■ *adj.* сóевый; **~ sauce** сóевый сóус.
sozzled /ˈsɒz(ə)ld/ *adj.* (*sl.*) пья́ный вдрéбзги.
spa /spɑː/ *n.* вóды (*f. pl.*), курóрт с минера́льными истóчниками.
space /speɪs/ *n.*
1 (*expanse*) простра́нство, простóр.
2 (*outer ~*) кóсмос; (*attr.*) косми́ческий.
3 (*distance, interval*) расстоя́ние.
4 (*of time, distance*) промежу́ток/периóд врéмени; **in the ~ of a hour** за час; в течéние ча́са.
5 (*area*) мéсто; **blank ~** пустóе мéсто.
■ *v.t.* (*also* **~ out**): **the posts were ~d six feet apart** столбы́ бы́ли располóжены на расстоя́нии шести́ фу́тов друг от дру́га.
■ *cpds.* **~craft** (*also* **~ship**) *nn.* косми́ческий корáбль; **~suit** *n.* скафа́ндр (*космонавта*).
spacious /ˈspeɪʃəs/ *adj.* простóрный.
spade /speɪd/ *n.*
1 (*tool*) лопа́та.
2 (*cards*) пи́ка; **queen of ~s** пи́ковая да́ма, да́ма пик.
spaghetti /spəˈgetɪ/ *n.* спагéтти (*nt. and pl. indecl.*).
Spain /speɪn/ *n.* Испа́ния.
span[1] /spæn/ *n.*
1 (*distance between supports*) пролёт.
2 (*of time*) промежу́ток/периóд врéмени.
3 : **wing ~** разма́х кры́льев.
■ *v.t.* (**spanned, spanning**) перекр|ыва́ть, -ы́ть; (*fig.*): **the movement ~s almost two centuries** э́то движéние охва́тывает почти́ два столéтия.
span[2] /spæn/ *past of* ▸ **spin**
span[3] /spæn/ *see* ▸ **spick**
Spaniard /ˈspænjəd/ *n.* испа́н|ец (*fem.* -ка).
spaniel /ˈspænj(ə)l/ *n.* спаниéль (*m.*).
Spanish /ˈspænɪʃ/ *n.*
1 (*language*) испа́нский (язы́к).
2 : **the ~** (*collect.*) испа́нцы (*m. pl.*).
■ *adj.* испа́нский.
spank /spæŋk/ *v.t.* шлёпать, от-.
spanner /ˈspænə(r)/ *n.* (*Br.*) гáечный ключ.
spar /spɑː(r)/ *v.i.* (**sparred, sparring**) бокси́ровать (*impf.*).
spare /speə(r)/ *n.*
1 (**~ part**) запасна́я часть, запча́сть.
2 (*~ wheel*) запаснóе колесó.
■ *adj.* (*extra*) ли́шний; **~ room** кóмната для гостéй; **~ time** свобóдное врéмя; (*additional, reserve*) запаснóй, резéрвный.
■ *v.t.* 1 (*withhold use of*) жалéть, по-.
2 (*dispense with, do without*) об|ходи́ться, -ойти́сь без + *g.*; **we cannot ~ him** мы не мóжем обойти́сь без негó.
3 (*afford*): **can you ~ a cigarette?** у вас не найдётся сигарéты?; **I can ~ you only a few minutes** я могу́ удели́ть вам тóлько нéсколько мину́т.
4 **to ~** (*available, left over*): **I have no time to ~** у меня́ нет ли́шнего врéмени; **we got there with an hour to ~** когда́ мы приéхали туда́, у нас остава́лся цéлый час в запáсе.
5 (*show leniency to*) щади́ть, по-; **I tried to ~ his feelings** я стара́лся щади́ть егó чу́вства.
6 (*save from*) изб|авля́ть, -а́вить (*кого от чего*); **I will ~ you the trouble of replying** я изба́влю вас от необходи́мости отвеча́ть.
spark /spɑːk/ *n.* и́скра (*also fig.*).
■ *v.t.* (*also* **~ off:** *cause*) вызыва́ть, вы́звать; (*friendship*) да|ва́ть, -ть нача́ло + *d.*
■ *cpd.* **~ plug** *n.* свеча́ зажига́ния, запа́льная свеча́.
sparkle /ˈspɑːk(ə)l/ *n.* сверка́ние, блеск, блиста́ние; блёстка, и́скорка.
■ *v.i.* сверка́ть, за-; (*flash*) блестéть, за-; **sparkling wine** шипу́чее/игри́стое винó.
sparkler /ˈspɑːklə(r)/ *n.* (*firework*) бенга́льский огóнь.
sparrow /ˈspærəʊ/ *n.* воробéй.
sparse /spɑːs/ *adj.* рéдкий; (*scattered*) разбрóсанный; **~ly populated** малонаселённый.
Spartan /ˈspɑːt(ə)n/ *n.* спарта́н|ец (*fem.* -ка).
■ *adj.* спарта́нский.
spasm /ˈspæz(ə)m/ *n.* (*of muscles*) спа́зм; (*mental or physical reaction*) при́ступ, припа́док.
spasmodic /spæzˈmɒdɪk/ *adj.* спазмати́ческий.
spastic /ˈspæstɪk/ *n.* (спасти́ческий) парали́тик.
■ *adj.* спасти́ческий, спазмати́ческий.
spat /spæt/ *past and p.p. of* ▸ **spit**[2]
spate /speɪt/ *n.* (*Br., sudden flood*) разли́в; (*fig.*) потóк.
spatial /ˈspeɪʃ(ə)l/ *adj.* простра́нственный.
spatter /ˈspætə(r)/ (*also* **splatter**) *v.t.* & *i.* бры́з|гать, -нуть; забры́згать (*pf.*); **~ed with mud** забры́зганный гря́зью.
spatula /ˈspætjʊlə/ *n.* (*med.*) шпа́тель (*m.*); (*cul.*) лопа́точка.
speak /spiːk/ *v.t.* (*past* **spoke;** *p.p.* **spoken**)
1 (*say*) говори́ть, сказа́ть; произн|оси́ть, -ести́; (*express*): **~ one's mind** выска́зывать, вы́сказать своё мнéние.
2 (*converse in*) говори́ть (*impf.*); **he ~s Russian well** он хорошó говори́т по-ру́сски.
■ *v.i.* (*past* **spoke;** *p.p.* **spoken**) говори́ть (*impf.*); (*converse*) говори́ть, по-; разгова́ривать (*impf.*); вести́ (*indet.*) разговóр; (*make a speech*) выступа́ть, вы́ступить; произн|оси́ть, -ести́ речь; **'Smith ~ing'** (*on telephone*) «(с ва́ми) говори́т Смит»; **roughly, broadly ~ing**

грубо говоря; в общих чертах; **strictly ~ing** строго говоря; **~ of** (*mention, refer to*) упом|инать, -януть о + *p*.
■ *with advs.*: **~ out** *v.i.* (*express o.s. plainly*) высказываться, высказаться (откровенно); **~ up** *v.i.* (*~ louder*) говорить (*impf.*) громче; (*express support*): **~ up for s.o.** поддерж|ивать, -ать кого-н.

speaker /'spi:kə(r)/ *n.*
1 : **the ~ was a man of about 40** говорящему было лет сорок.
2 : **a Russian ~** человек, владеющий русским языком.
3 (*public ~*) оратор, докладчик, выступающий.
4 **(loud~)** громкоговоритель (*m.*).
5 (*parl.*) спикер.

spear /'spɪə(r)/ *n.* копьё, дротик.
■ *cpd.* **~head** *v.t.*: **~head a movement** возгл|авлять, -авить движение.

spec[1] /spek/ *n.* (*coll.*): **he went there on ~** он пошёл туда наудачу.

spec[2] /spek/ *n.* (*coll., specification*) спецификация.

special /'speʃ(ə)l/ *adj.*
1 (*exceptional*) особый, особенный; (*for a particular purpose*) специальный.
2 (*extraordinary*) специальный, экстренный; **~ delivery** срочная доставка.
■ *cpd.* **~ effect** *n.* спецэффект.

specialist /'speʃəlɪst/ *n.* специалист (*fem.* -ка) (**in:** по + *d.*).

speciality /speʃɪ'ælɪtɪ/ (*US* **specialty**) *n.*
1 (*pursuit*) специальность, специализация.
2 (*product, recipe etc.*): **~ of the house** фирменное блюдо.

specialize /'speʃəlaɪz/ *v.i.* специализироваться (*impf., pf.*) (**in:** по + *d.*; в/на + *p.*).

specially /'speʃəlɪ/ *adv.*
1 (*for specific purpose*) специально.
2 (*exceptionally*) особенно, исключительно; **be ~ careful** быть особенно осторожным.

specialty /'speʃəltɪ/ (*US*) = **speciality**

species /'spi:ʃɪz/ *n.* (*pl.* ~) (биологический) вид.

specific /spə'sɪfɪk/ *adj.* определённый.

specifically /spə'sɪfɪkəlɪ/ *adv.* (*exactly*) определённо; (*specially*) специально.

specification /spesɪfɪ'keɪʃ(ə)n/ *n.* (*tech.*) спецификация; (*pl.*) технические характеристики (*f. pl.*).

specify /'spesɪfaɪ/ *v.t.* определ|ять, -ить.

specimen /'spesɪmən/ *n.* (*of rock, handwriting*) образец; (*of plant, animal*) экземпляр; **~ of urine** моча для анализа.

speck /spek/ *n.* (*of dirt*) пятнышко; **~ of dust** пылинка.

specs /speks/ *n. pl.* (*coll.*) = **spectacle 2**

spectacle /'spektək(ə)l/ *n.*
1 (*public show; sight*) зрелище.
2 (*Br., pl., glasses*) очк|и (*pl., g.* -ов).

spectacular /spek'tækjʊlə(r)/ *adj.* эффектный, впечатляющий.

spectator /spek'teɪtə(r)/ *n.* зритель (*fem.* -ница).

spectre /'spektə(r)/ (*US* **specter**) *n.* привидение, призрак.

spectrum /'spektrəm/ *n.* спектр.

speculate /'spekjʊleɪt/ *v.i.*
1 (*meditate*) размышлять (*impf.*) (*о чем*); (*conjecture*) гадать (*impf.*).
2 (*risk, invest money*) спекулировать (*impf.*), играть (*impf.*) на бирже; **he ~s in oil shares** он спекулирует акциями нефтяных компаний.

speculation /spekjʊ'leɪʃ(ə)n/ *n.* (*meditation*) размышление; (*conjecture*) догадка; (*investment*) спекуляция.

speculative /'spekjʊlətɪv/ *adj.* (*investment*) спекулятивный.

speculator /'spekjʊleɪtə(r)/ *n.* спекулянт (*fem.* -ка).

sped /sped/ *past and p.p. of* ▸ **speed** *v.i.* **1**

speech /spi:tʃ/ *n.* речь; **make a ~** произн|осить, -ести речь; **~ therapist** логопед.

speechless /'spi:tʃlɪs/ *adj.*: **I was ~ with surprise** я онемел от удивления.

speed /spi:d/ *n.* (*rapidity*) быстрота, скорость; (*rate*) скорость; **at full, top ~** на полной скорости.
■ *v.t.* (*past and p.p.* **speeded**) (*also* **~ up**) уск|орять, -орить.
■ *v.i.* 1 (*past and p.p.* **sped**) (*move quickly*) мчаться (*impf.*), нестись (*impf.*).
2 (*past and p.p.* **speeded**) (*go too fast*): **he was fined for ~ing** его оштрафовали за превышение скорости.
3 : **~ up** (*past and p.p.* **speeded**) уск|оряться, -ориться.
■ *cpd.* **~boat** *n.* быстроходный катер; **~ camera** *n.* камера-радар, спид-камера (*фиксирует скорость автомобиля для последующего доказательства превышения скорости*); **~ dating** *n.* экспресс-знакомства (*nt. pl.*).

speedometer /spi:'dɒmɪtə(r)/ *n.* спидометр.

speedy /'spi:dɪ/ *adj.* (**speedier, speediest**) (*rapid*) скорый, быстрый; (*hasty*) поспешный; (*prompt, undelayed*) скорый, немедленный.

spell[1] /spel/ *n.* (*magical formula*) чар|ы (*pl., g.* —); колдовство; **cast a ~ over** заколдов|ывать, -ать.
■ *cpd.* **~bound** *adj.* очарованный, зачарованный.

spell[2] /spel/ *n.* (*interval*) период; промежуток времени; **we're in for a ~ of fine weather** ожидается полоса хорошей погоды.

spell[3] /spel/ *v.t.* (*past and p.p.* **spelled** *or esp. Br.* **spelt**)
1 (*write or name letters in sequence*) произн|осить, -ести (*or* писать, на-) по буквам; **how do you ~ your name?** как пишется ваша фамилия?; **he cannot ~ his own name** он не может правильно написать свою фамилию.
2 (*fig., signify*) означать (*impf.*); **these changes ~ disaster** эти перемены сулят несчастье.
■ *v.i.* (*past and p.p.* **spelled** *or esp. Br.* **spelt**) писать (*impf.*) правильно/грамотно.
■ *cpd.* **~checker** *n.* (*comput.*) программа проверки орфографии.

spelling /'spelɪŋ/ *n.* правописание, орфография.

spelt /spelt/ *past and p.p. of* ▸ **spell**[3]

spend /spend/ *v.t.* (*past and p.p.* **spent**) [1] (*pay out*) тра́тить, ис-; расхо́довать, из-. [2] (*pass*) пров|оди́ть, -ести́; **how do you ~ your leisure?** как вы прово́дите свой досу́г? ■ *v.i.* (*past and p.p.* **spent**) (~ *money*) тра́титься, по-; **they went on a ~ing spree** они́ пошли́ транжи́рить де́ньги.

spent /spent/ *past and p.p. of* ▸ **spend**

sperm /spə:m/ *n.* (*pl.* ~ *or* ~**s**) спе́рма; (~ **whale**) кашало́т.

spew /spju:/ *v.t.* (*coll., vomit*) выблёвывать, вы́блевать (*sl.*); (*lit., fig.*) изрыга́ть (*impf.*); **a machine gun ~ing out bullets** пулемёт, полива́ющий (неприя́теля) огнём. ■ *v.i.* (*coll., vomit*) блева́ть (*impf.*) (*sl.*).

sphere /sfɪə(r)/ *n.* сфе́ра; ~ **of influence** сфе́ра влия́ния.

spherical /ˈsferɪk(ə)l/ *adj.* сфери́ческий.

sphinx /sfɪŋks/ *n.* сфинкс.

spice /spaɪs/ *n.* [1] спе́ция, пря́ность, припра́ва. [2] (*fig., piquancy*) острота́.

spick /spɪk/ *adj.*: ~ **and span** (*clean, tidy*) сверка́ющий чистото́й.

spicy /ˈspaɪsɪ/ *adj.* (**spicier, spiciest**) пря́ный; (*fig.*) пика́нтный.

spider /ˈspaɪdə(r)/ *n.* пау́к; **~'s web** паути́на.

spike /spaɪk/ *n.* остриё.

spiky /ˈspaɪkɪ/ *adj.* (**spikier, spikiest**) остроконе́чный; ~ **hair** ёжик.

spill /spɪl/ *v.t.* (*past and p.p.* **spilt** *or* **spilled**) (*liquid*) прол|ива́ть, -и́ть; (*powder etc.*) расс|ыпа́ть, -ы́пать. ■ *v.i.* (*past and p.p.* **spilt** *or* **spilled**) (*of liquids*) разл|ива́ться, -и́ться; (*of salt etc.*) расс|ыпа́ться, -ы́паться. ■ *with adv.*: ~ **over** *v.i.* перел|ива́ться, -и́ться (че́рез край).

spin /spɪn/ *n.* [1] (*whirl*) круже́ние, враще́ние. [2] (*of ball*) враще́ние; **put ~ on a ball** закру́|чивать, -ти́ть мяч. [3] (*outing*): **go for a ~ in the car** прокати́ться/поката́ться (*both pf.*) на маши́не. [4] (*bias*) пристра́стие. ■ *v.t.* (**spinning;** *past* **spun** *or* **span;** *p.p.* **spun**) [1] (*yarn, wool etc.*) прясть, с-; **the spider ~s its web** пау́к плетёт паути́ну. [2] (*cause to revolve*) верте́ть, за-; крути́ть, за-; кружи́ть, за-; ~ **a coin** подбр|а́сывать, -о́сить моне́ту. ■ *v.i.* (**spinning;** *past* **spun** *or* **span;** *p.p.* **spun**) верте́ться, за-; крути́ться, за-; кружи́ться, за-; (*of wheel*) бы́стро враща́ться/крути́ться (*impf.*); (*of person*): **my head is ~ning** у меня́ голова́ идёт кру́гом. ■ *with advs.*: ~ **out** *v.t.*: ~ **out a story** растя́|гивать, -ну́ть расска́з; ~ **round** *v.t.* & *i.* бы́стро пов|ора́чивать(ся), -ерну́ть(ся) (круго́м). ■ *cpds.* ~ **doctor** *n.* (*pol.*) политтехно́лог; ~ **dryer** *n.* (*Br.*) суши́лка, суши́льный автома́т; **~-off** *n.* (*coll.*) побо́чный результа́т.

spina bifida /ˈspaɪnə ˈbɪfɪdə/ *n.* расщепле́ние позвоно́чника.

spinach /ˈspɪnɪdʒ/ *n.* шпина́т.

spinal /ˈspaɪn(ə)l/ *adj.* спинно́й, позвоно́чный; ~ **column** позвоно́чный столб; ~ **cord** спинно́й мозг.

spindle /ˈspɪnd(ə)l/ *n.* (*axis, rod*) ось, шпи́ндель (*m.*).

spine /spaɪn/ *n.* [1] (*backbone*) позвоно́чник, спинно́й хребе́т. [2] (*of hedgehog, plant*) игла́. [3] (*of book*) корешо́к.

spineless /ˈspaɪnlɪs/ *adj.* (*fig.*) бесхребе́тный, бесхара́ктерный.

spinster /ˈspɪnstə(r)/ *n.* (*old maid*) ста́рая де́ва; (*leg., unmarried woman*) незаму́жняя же́нщина.

spiral /ˈspaɪər(ə)l/ *n.* спира́ль. ■ *adj.* спира́льный; ~ **staircase** винтова́я ле́стница. ■ *v.i.* (**spiralled, spiralling;** *US* **spiraled, spiraling**): **the crime rate is ~ling (upwards)** престу́пность (*or* у́ровень престу́пности) растёт бы́стрыми те́мпами.

spire /ˈspaɪə(r)/ *n.* (*of church etc.*) шпиль (*m.*).

spirit /ˈspɪrɪt/ *n.* [1] (*soul*) душа́; духо́вное нача́ло. [2] (*courage*) хра́брость; **show some ~** проявл|я́ть, -и́ть му́жество/хара́ктер. [3] (*pl., humour*) настрое́ние; **he was in high ~s** он был в приподня́том настрое́нии; **keep one's ~s up** мужа́ться (*impf.*); не па́дать (*impf.*) ду́хом. [4] (*pl., Br., alcoholic drink*) спиртно́й напи́ток. ■ *cpd.* ~ **level** *n.* ватерпа́с.

spirited /ˈspɪrɪtɪd/ *adj.* живо́й; **a ~ reply** бо́йкий отве́т; **a ~ horse** горя́чий конь.

spiritual /ˈspɪrɪtʃʊəl/ *adj.* духо́вный.

spiritualism /ˈspɪrɪtʃʊəlɪz(ə)m/ *n.* спирити́зм.

spiritualist /ˈspɪrɪtʃʊəlɪst/ *n.* спири́т (*fem.* -ка)

spirituality /spɪrɪtʃʊˈælɪtɪ/ *n.* одухотворённость.

spit[1] /spɪt/ *n.* (*for roasting*) ве́ртел.

spit[2] /spɪt/ *n.* [1] (*spittle*) слюна́. [2]: **the ~ting image of his father** то́чная ко́пия своего́ отца́. ■ *v.t.* (**spitting;** *past and p.p.* **spat** *or* ~) (*also* ~ **out**) выплёвывать, вы́плюнуть. ■ *v.i.* (**spitting;** *past and p.p.* **spat** *or* ~) [1] пл|ева́ть, -ю́нуть; (*of cat etc.*) фы́рк|ать, -нуть. [2] (*of fire*) сы́пать (*impf.*) и́скрами. [3] (*Br. coll., rain*) накра́пывать (*impf.*).

spite /spaɪt/ *n.* [1] (*ill will*) зло́ба, злость. [2]: **in ~ of** несмотря́ на + *a.* ■ *v.t.*: **he does it to ~ me** он де́лает э́то мне назло́.

spiteful /ˈspaɪtfʊl/ *adj.* зло́бный, злора́дный.

spitefulness /ˈspaɪtfʊlnɪs/ *n.* зло́бность, злора́дство.

spittle /ˈspɪt(ə)l/ *n.* плево́к; слюна́.

splash /splæʃ/ *n.* [1] (*sound*) вспле́ск, плеск. [2] (*liquid*) бры́зги (*m. pl.*); **I felt a ~ of rain** на меня́ упа́ли ка́пли дождя́. [3] (*of blood, mud etc.*) пятно́; **a ~ of colour** кра́сочное пятно́.

■ *v.t.* бры́з|гать, -нуть (*чем на что*); забры́згать (*pf.*) (*что чем*); **he ~ed paint on her dress** он забры́згал ей пла́тье кра́ской.
■ *v.i.* 1 (*of liquid etc.*) разбры́зг|иваться, -аться; (*of waves*) плеска́ться (*impf.*).
2 (*move or fall with ~*): **the ducks ~ed about in the pond** у́тки плеска́лись в пруду́; (*Br. coll., fig.*): **they ~ed out on a new carpet** они́ разори́лись на но́вый ковёр.

splatter /ˈsplætə(r)/ *v.t. & i.* = **spatter**

splay /spleɪ/ *v.t.*: **~ one's legs** раски́|дывать, -нуть но́ги.

spleen /spliːn/ *n.* (*anat.*) селезёнка.

splendid /ˈsplendɪd/ *adj.* (*excellent*) прекра́сный, отли́чный; **what a ~ idea** замеча́тельная/прекра́сная мысль!

splendour /ˈsplendə(r)/ (*US* **splendor**) *n.* великоле́пие, пы́шность.

splice /splaɪs/ *v.t.*
1 (*rope*) ср|а́щивать, -асти́ть.
2 (*tape*) скле́и|вать, -ть.

splint /splɪnt/ *n.* (*for broken bone*) ши́на, лубо́к.

splinter /ˈsplɪntə(r)/ *n.*
1 (*of wood*) лучи́на, ще́пка.
2 (*fig.*): **~ group** отколо́вшаяся фра́кция.
■ *v.t. & i.* расщеп|ля́ть(ся), -и́ть(ся).

split /splɪt/ *n.*
1 (*crack, fissure*) тре́щина, щель, расще́лина.
2 (*fig., schism*) раско́л.
3 : **do the ~s** (*Br.*) де́лать, с- шпага́т.
■ *v.t.* (**splitting;** *past and p.p.* **~**)
1 коло́ть, рас-; расщеп|ля́ть, -и́ть; (*crack open*) раск|а́лывать, -оло́ть.
2 (*divide*) раздел|я́ть, -и́ть; (*share*) дели́ть, по-.
3 (*cause dissension in*) раск|а́лывать, -оло́ть; **~ second** до́ля секу́нды.
■ *v.i.* (**splitting;** *past and p.p.* **~**)
1 (*of hard substance*) раск|а́лываться, -оло́ться; тре́снуть (*pf.*); (*divide*) раздел|я́ться, -и́ться.
2 (*become disunited*) разъедин|я́ться, -и́ться; раск|а́лываться, -оло́ться.
■ *with adv.*: **~ up** *v.t. & i.* (*separate*) ра|сходи́ться, -зойти́сь; **we ~ up into two groups** мы разби́лись на две гру́ппы; **he and his wife ~ up** они́ с жено́й разошли́сь.

splutter /ˈsplʌtə(r)/ *v.t. & i.* (*of person*) говори́ть (*impf.*) захлёбываясь; (*of fire*) шипе́ть (*impf.*).

spoil /spɔɪl/ *v.t.* (*past and p.p.* **spoilt** (*esp. Br.*) *or* **spoiled**)
1 (*impair, ruin*) по́ртить, ис-; **the rain ~t our holiday** дождь испо́ртил нам о́тпуск.
2 (*overindulge*) балова́ть, из-; **a ~t child** избало́ванный ребёнок.
■ *v.i.* (*past and p.p.* **spoilt** (*esp. Br.*) *or* **spoiled**) (*go bad etc.*) по́ртиться, ис-.
■ *cpd.* **~sport** *n.* тот, кто по́ртит удово́льствие други́м.

spoilt /spɔɪlt/ *past and p.p. of* ▸ **spoil**

spoke[1] /spəʊk/ *n.* (*of wheel*) спи́ца.

spoke[2] /spəʊk/ *past of* ▸ **speak**

spoken /ˈspəʊkən/ *p.p. of* ▸ **speak**

spokesman /ˈspəʊksmən/ *n.* представи́тель (*m.*).

spokesperson /ˈspəʊkspəːs(ə)n/ = **spokesman** *or* **spokeswoman**

spokeswoman /ˈspəʊkswʊmən/ *n.* представи́тельница.

sponge /spʌndʒ/ *n.*
1 (*zool.; toilet article*) гу́бка.
2 (*cake*) бискви́т.
■ *v.t.* (**sponging** *or* **spongeing**): обт|ира́ть, -ере́ть гу́бкой.
■ *v.i.* (**sponging** *or* **spongeing**) (*fig.*): **he ~s on his brother** он сиди́т на ше́е у бра́та.
■ *cpds.* **~ bag** *n.* (*Br.*) су́мка для туале́тных принадле́жностей; **~ cake** *n.* бискви́т.

sponsor /ˈspɒnsə(r)/ *n.*
1 (*guarantor*) поручи́тель (*fem.* -ница); (*of new member etc.*) рекоменда́тель (*fem.* -ница).
2 (*providing finance*) спо́нсор.
■ *v.t.* руча́ться, поручи́ться за + *a.*; рекомендова́ть (*impf., pf.*); (*on TV etc.*) финанси́ровать (*impf., pf.*).

sponsorship /ˈspɒnsəʃɪp/ *n.* поручи́тельство, пору́ка; спо́нсорство.

spontaneity /spɒntəˈneɪɪtɪ/ *n.* спонта́нность, стихи́йность, непосре́дственность.

spontaneous /spɒnˈteɪnɪəs/ *adj.* спонта́нный, стихи́йный.

spoof /spuːf/ (*coll.*) *n.* паро́дия.

spook /spuːk/ *n.* (*joc.*) привиде́ние, при́зрак.

spooky /ˈspuːkɪ/ *adj.* (*coll.*) (**spookier, spookiest**) злове́щий; **~ house** дом с привиде́ниями.

spool /spuːl/ *n.* шпу́лька, кату́шка.

spoon /spuːn/ *n.* ло́жка.

spoonful /ˈspuːnfʊl/ *n.* (по́лная) ло́жка (*чего*).

sporadic /spəˈrædɪk/ *adj.* споради́ческий, едини́чный, отде́льный.

sport /spɔːt/ *n.*
1 (*outdoor pastime(s)*) спорт; (*pl.*) спорт, ви́ды (*m. pl.*) спо́рта; **~s car** спорти́вный автомоби́ль.
2 (*pl., Br., athletic events*) спорти́вные и́гры (*f. pl.*).
3 (*coll., person*) молодчи́на (*m.*).

sporting /ˈspɔːtɪŋ/ *adj.*
1 (*connected with, fond of sport*) спорти́вный.
2 (*sportsmanlike*) че́стный, поря́дочный.

sportsman /ˈspɔːtsmən/ *n.* спортсме́н.

sportswoman /ˈspɔːtswʊmən/ *n.* спортсме́нка.

sporty /ˈspɔːtɪ/ *adj.* (**sportier, sportiest**) (*person, clothing*) спорти́вный.

spot /spɒt/ *n.*
1 (*patch*) пятно́; (*speck*) пя́тнышко, кра́пинка; **come out in ~s** (*rash*) покр|ыва́ться, -ы́ться сы́пью.
2 (*stain*) пятно́.
3 (*pimple*) прыщ(ик).
4 (*place*) ме́сто; **the police were on the ~ within minutes** поли́ция прибыла́ на ме́сто (уже́) че́рез не́сколько мину́т; **we were in a (tight) ~** нам пришло́сь ту́го; **~ check** вы́борочная прове́рка.
5 (*Br. coll., small amount*): **I have a ~ of work to do** мне ну́жно немно́го порабо́тать; **~ of bother** небольша́я неприя́тность.
6 : **~ on** (*Br. coll., exactly right*) в са́мую то́чку.
■ *v.t.* (**spotted, spotting**)

1 (*stain*) пáчкать, за-; (*with liquid*) закáпать (*pf.*); (*p.p., covered, decorated with* ~*s*): **a ~ted tie** гáлстук в крáпинку.
2 (*coll., notice*) зам|ечáть, -éтить; (*catch sight of*) увúдеть (*pf.*).
■ *cpd.* **~light** *n.* осветúтельный прожéктор; (*fig.*): **turn the ~light on sth.** привл|екáть, -éчь внимáние к чемý-н.; **be in the ~light** быть в цéнтре внимáния.

spotless /ˈspɒtlɪs/ *adj.* сверкáющий чистотóй; без едúного пя́тнышка.

spotty /ˈspɒtɪ/ *adj.* (**spottier, spottiest**) (*of colour*) пятнúстый; (*Br., pimply*) прыщевáтый.

spouse /spaʊs/ *n.* супрýг (*fem.* -a).

spout /spaʊt/ *n.* нóсик.
■ *v.t.* 1: **a whale ~s water** кит выбрáсывает струю́ воды́.
2 (*coll., declaim*) говорúть (*impf.*) о + *p.*; **~ poetry** декламúровать, про- стихú.
■ *v.i.* 1 бить (*impf.*); лúться (*impf.*) потóком.
2 (*fig., coll., make speeches*) разглагóльствовать (*impf.*).

sprain /spreɪn/ *n.* растяжéние.
■ *v.t.*: **~ one's wrist/ankle** раст|я́гивать, -янýть запя́стье/лоды́жку.

sprang /spræŋ/ *past of* ▸ **spring²**

sprat /spræt/ *n.* шпрóт(а), кúлька.

sprawl /sprɔːl/ *n.*: **urban ~** беспоря́дочный рост гóрода.
■ *v.i.* 1 (*person*) раст|я́гиваться, -янýться.
2 (*buildings*) раскú|дываться, -нуться.

spray /spreɪ/ *n.*
1 (*water droplets*) бры́зг|и (*pl., g.* —).
2 (*liquid preparation, e.g. fly spray*) жúдкость (для пульверизáции).
3 (*device for ~ing*) спрей; **~ can** аэрозóль (*m.*), спрей.

spread /spred/ *n.*
1 (*dissemination, expansion*) распространéние.
2 (*span*) размáх.
3 (*cul.*) пáста (*на хлеб*).
■ *v.t.* (*past and p.p.* ~)
1 (*extend*) распростран|я́ть, -úть; (*unfold*) ра|склáдывать, -зложúть; (*cover*) расст|илáть, -елúть (*or* разостлáть); **~ butter on bread** (*or* **bread with butter**) намáз|ывать, -ать мáсло на хлеб (*or* хлеб мáслом); **the bird ~ its wings** птúца распрáвила кры́лья; **~ (out) a map** ра|склáдывать, -зложúть кáрту.
2 (*diffuse*) распростран|я́ть, -úть.
■ *v.i.* (*past and p.p.* ~) распростран|я́ться, -úться; расстилáться (*impf.*); **the news soon ~** нóвость/весть бы́стро распространúлась; **the fire is ~ing** пожáр разрастáется.
■ *cpds.* **~eagle** *v.t.*: **lie ~eagled** лежáть (*impf.*) распластáвшись; **~sheet** *n.* (*comput.*) (электрóнная) таблúца.

spree /spriː/ *n.* (*coll.*) весéлье.

sprig /sprɪg/ *n.* вéточка.

sprightly /ˈspraɪtlɪ/ *adj.* (**sprightlier, sprightliest**) живóй, бóйкий.

spring¹ /sprɪŋ/ *n.* (*season*) веснá; **in ~** веснóй; (*attr.*) весéнний; **~ onion** (*Br.*) зелёный лук.
■ *cpds.* **~-clean** *v.t.* & *i.* произв|одúть, -естú генерáльную убóрку; **~time** *n.* веснá, весéнняя порá.

spring² /sprɪŋ/ *n.*
1 (*leap*) прыжóк, скачóк.
2 (*elasticity*) упрýгость, эластúчность.
3 (*elastic device*) пружúна.
4 (*of water*) истóчник, ключ, роднúк.
■ *v.t.* (*past* **sprang** *or US* **sprung;** *p.p.* **sprung**) (*produce suddenly*): **~ a surprise on s.o.** заст|игáть, -úчь когó-н. врасплóх; **~ a leak** да|вáть, -ть течь.
■ *v.i.* (*past* **sprang** *or US* **sprung;** *p.p.* **sprung**)
1 (*leap*) пры́г|ать, -нуть; скак|áть, -нýть; **~ out of bed** вск|áкивать, -очúть с постéли.
2 (*come into being*) (**~ up**) появ|ля́ться, -úться; возн|икáть, -úкнуть; **a breeze sprang up** поднялся лёгкий ветерóк.
■ *cpd.* **~board** *n.* (*lit., fig.*) трамплúн.

sprinkle /ˈsprɪŋk(ə)l/ *v.t.*: **~ sth. with water, ~ water on sth.** кропúть, о-/обры́зг|ивать, -ать что-н. водóй; **~ sth. with salt/sand, ~ salt/sand on sth.** пос|ыпáть, -ы́пать что-н. сóлью/пескóм.

sprinkler /ˈsprɪŋklə(r)/ *n.* разбры́згиватель (*m.*), пульверизáтор; (*in fire safety*) сприн́клер.

sprint /sprɪnt/ *n.* спринт.
■ *v.t.* & *i.* бежáть (*det.*) с максимáльной скóростью.

sprinter /ˈsprɪntə(r)/ *n.* сприн́тер.

sprocket /ˈsprɒkɪt/ *n.*
1 звёздочка (цéпи).
2 (*also* **~ wheel**) цепнóе/зубчáтое колесó; (*in film, tape*) зубчáтый барабáн.

sprout /spraʊt/ *n.* (*pl.,* **Brussels ~s**) брюссéльская капýста.
■ *v.i.* (*of plant*) пус|кáть, -тúть росткú; (*of seed*) прораст|áть, -ú.

spruce¹ /spruːs/ *n.* (*tree*) ель.

spruce² /spruːs/ *adj.* опря́тный, наря́дный.
■ *v.t.*: **~ up** нав|одúть, -естú красотý/блеск на + *a.*; **~ o.s. up** прихорáшиваться (*impf.*).

sprung /sprʌŋ/ *p.p. and US past of* ▸ **spring²**

spun /spʌn/ *past and p.p. of* ▸ **spin**

spur /spɜː(r)/ *n.*
1 (*on rider's heel*) шпóра.
2 (*fig.*) побуждéние, стúмул; **on the ~ of the moment** в сиюминýтном поры́ве.
■ *v.t.* (**spurred, spurring**) (*fig.*) побу|ждáть, -дúть; под|гоня́ть, -огнáть; **~red on by ambition** подгоня́емый честолю́бием.

spurious /ˈspjʊərɪəs/ *adj.* поддéльный.

spurn /spɜːn/ *v.t.* отв|ергáть, -éргнуть.

spurt¹ /spɜːt/ *n.* (*sudden effort*) поры́в; (*in race*) рывóк; **put on a ~** рванýться (*pf.*).

spurt² /spɜːt/ *n.* (*jet*) струя́.
■ *v.i.* бить (*impf.*) струёй; хлы́нуть (*pf.*).

sputnik /ˈspʊtnɪk/ *n.* (искýсственный) спýтник.

spy /spaɪ/ *n.* шпиóн.
■ *v.t.* (*liter., discern*) разгля́д|ывать, -éть.
■ *v.i.* (*engage in espionage*) шпиóнить (*impf.*); **~ on s.o.** подгля́дывать (*impf.*) за кем-н.

spying /ˈspaɪɪŋ/ *n.* шпионáж.

squabble /ˈskwɒb(ə)l/ *v.i.* пререкáться (*impf.*) (*с кем*); вздóрить, по-.

squad /skwɒd/ *n.*
1 (*mil.*) грýппа, комáнда, отделéние.
2 (*gang, group*) отря́д; рабóчая бригáда; **~ car** полицéйская патрýльная (авто)машúна.

squadron /ˈskwɒdrən/ *n.* (*aeron.*) эскадрúлья; (*mil.*) эскадрóн; (*nav.*) эскáдра.

squalid /ˈskwɒlɪd/ *adj.* ни́зкий, ни́зменный, гну́сный.

squall /skwɔːl/ *n.* шквал; поры́вистый ве́тер.

squalor /ˈskwɒlə(r)/ *n.* убо́жество; (*sordidness*) ни́зость, гну́сность.

squander /ˈskwɒndə(r)/ *v.t.* пром|а́тывать, -ота́ть; растра́|чивать, -тить.

square /skweə(r)/ *n.*
1 (*shape*) квадра́т.
2 (*on chessboard etc.*) кле́тка; **we are back to ~ one** (*fig.*) мы верну́лись в исхо́дное положе́ние.
3 (*open space in town*) пло́щадь.
■ *adj.* 1 (*geom., math.; shape*) квадра́тный; **~ metre** квадра́тный метр; **~ root (of)** квадра́тный ко́рень (из + *g.*); (*right-angled*) прямоуго́льный.
2 (*even*) то́чный; в поря́дке; **we are all ~** мы кви́ты.
■ *adv.* 1 (*at right angles*) перпендикуля́рно.
2 (*straight*) пря́мо.
3 : **ten feet ~** де́сять фу́тов в ширину́ и де́сять в длину́.
■ *v.t.* 1 (*straighten*) выпрямля́ть, вы́прямить; **~ one's shoulders** распр|авля́ть, -а́вить пле́чи.
2 (*settle*) ула́|живать, -дить.
3 (*math.*) возв|оди́ть, -ести́ в квадра́т; **3 ~d is 9** три в квадра́те равно́ девяти́.
■ *v.i.* 1 (*agree*) согласо́в|ываться, -а́ться; **~ with** сходи́ться (*impf.*) с + *i.*; **this statement does not ~ with the facts** э́то заявле́ние расхо́дится с фа́ктами.
2 : **~ up** (*settle accounts*) **with s.o.** поквита́ться (*pf.*) с кем-н.

squash[1] /skwɒʃ/ *n.* (*crush*) да́вка; (*Br., drink*) фрукто́вый напи́ток; **(~ rackets)** сквош.
■ *v.t.* (*crush*) дави́ть, раз-; (*compress*) сж|има́ть, -ать; **I ~ed the fly against the wall** я раздави́л му́ху на стене́; **the tomatoes were ~ed** помидо́ры помя́лись.
■ *v.i.* (*crowd*) потесни́ться (*pf.*); **they ~ed up to make room for me** они́ потесни́лись, что́бы дать мне ме́сто.

squash[2] /skwɒʃ/ *n.* (*pl.* **~** *or* **~es**) (*bot.*) (*winter* ~) ты́ква; (*summer* ~) кабачо́к.

squat /skwɒt/ *adj.* (**squatter, squattest**) призе́мистый.
■ *v.i.* (**squatted, squatting**)
1 (*be crouching*) сиде́ть (*impf.*) на ко́рточках.
2 (*occupy building illegally*) незако́нно всел|я́ться, -и́ться в чужо́й дом.

squatter /ˈskwɒtə(r)/ *n.* (*illegal occupant*) челове́к, незако́нно всели́вшийся в (чужо́й) дом.

squawk /skwɔːk/ *v.i.* пронзи́тельно крича́ть, за-.

squeak /skwiːk/ *n.*
1 (*of mouse etc.*) писк.
2 (*of hinge etc.*) скрип, визг.
■ *v.i.* 1 (*of person or animal*) пища́ть, пи́скнуть.
2 (*of object*) скрипе́ть, скри́пнуть.

squeaky /ˈskwiːkɪ/ *adj.* (**squeakier, squeakiest**) пискли́вый, визгли́вый; скрипу́чий.

squeal /skwiːl/ *v.i.* визжа́ть, за-.

squeamish /ˈskwiːmɪʃ/ *adj.* брезгли́вый; **feel ~** чу́вствовать, по- тошноту́.

squeeze /skwiːz/ *n.*
1 (*pressure*) сжа́тие, пожа́тие.
2 (*crush*) теснота́, да́вка; **we got in, but it was a tight ~** нам удало́сь вти́снуться, но бы́ло о́чень те́сно.
3 (*fin.*) ограниче́ние креди́та.
■ *v.t.* 1 (*compress*) сж|има́ть, -ать; сда́в|ливать, -и́ть; (*to extract moisture etc.*) выжима́ть, вы́жать; (*extort*): **~ a confession from s.o.** вынужда́ть, вы́нудить призна́ние у кого́-н.
2 (*force, cram*) вти́с|кивать, -нуть.
■ *v.i.* проти́с|киваться, -нуться.

squid /skwɪd/ *n.* кальма́р.

squiggle /ˈskwɪg(ə)l/ *n.* загогу́лина, кара́кул|я (*g. pl.* -ей *and* -ь).

squint /skwɪnt/ *n.* косогла́зие; **she has a ~ in her right eye** она́ коси́т на пра́вый глаз.
■ *v.i.* 1 коси́ть (*impf.*).
2 (*half-shut one's eyes*) щу́риться (*impf.*); прищу́ри|ваться, -ться.
3 : **~ at sth.** смотре́ть, по- и́скоса на что-н.

squirm /skwɜːm/ *n.* извива́ться (*impf.*); ко́рчиться (*impf.*); **he made me ~ with embarrassment** он меня́ так смути́л, что я не знал, куда́ де́ться.

squirrel /ˈskwɪr(ə)l/ *n.* бе́лка.

squirt /skwɜːt/ *v.t.* пры́с|кать, -нуть; **~ water in the air** пус|ка́ть, -ти́ть струю́ воды́ в во́здух; **~ scent from an atomizer** бры́згать, по- духа́ми из пульвериза́тора.
■ *v.i.* бить (*impf.*) струёй; разбры́зг|иваться, -аться.

Sri Lanka /ʃriː ˈlæŋkə/ *n.* Шри-Ланка́.

St. *abbr. of*
1 ***street*** ул. (у́лица).
2 **(St) *Saint*** св., Св. (свят|о́й, -а́я).

stab /stæb/ *n.*
1 уда́р (о́стрым ору́жием); **~ in the back** (*fig.*) нож/уда́р в спи́ну.
2 (*fig., sharp pain*) внеза́пная о́страя боль; уко́л.
■ *v.t.* (**stabbed, stabbing**): **~ s.o. in the chest with a knife** нан|оси́ть, -ести́ кому́-н. уда́р в грудь ножо́м.

stability /stəˈbɪlɪtɪ/ *n.* стаби́льность, усто́йчивость.

stabilize /ˈsteɪbɪlaɪz/ *v.t.* стабилизи́ровать (*impf., pf.*).

stable[1] /ˈsteɪb(ə)l/ *n.* коню́шня.

stable[2] /ˈsteɪb(ə)l/ *adj.* (**stabler, stablest**) усто́йчивый, стаби́льный.

staccato /stəˈkɑːtəʊ/ *n.* (*pl.* **~s**) & *adv.* стакка́то (*nt. indecl.*).
■ *adj.* отры́вистый.

stack /stæk/ *n.*
1 (*of hay etc.*) стог; скирда́.
2 (*pile*): **~ of wood** поле́нница, шта́бель (*m.*) дров; **~ of papers** ки́па/сто́пка бума́г; **~ of plates** стопа́/сто́пка таре́лок.
3 (*coll., usu. pl., large amount*) ма́сса, ку́ча, гру́да.
■ *v.t.*: **~ books on the floor** скла́дывать, сложи́ть кни́ги сто́пками на полу́.

stadium /ˈsteɪdɪəm/ *n.* стадио́н.

staff /stɑːf/ *n.* (*employees*) штат; **teaching ~** преподава́тельский соста́в; **~ room** (*Br., at school*) учи́тельская; **~ meeting** педагоги́ческий сове́т.

■ *v.t.* укомплектов|ывать, -ать (*что or* штат *чего*).

stag /stæg/ *n.* (*deer*) олéнь(*m.*)-самéц.
■ *cpd.* ~ **party** *n.* (*coll.*) мальчи́шник.

stage /steɪdʒ/ *n.*
1 (*theatr.*) сцéна, подмóстки; (*as profession*) теáтр, сцéна; **go on the ~** идти́, пойти́ на сцéну.
2 (*phase*) стáдия, фáза, этáп; **the war reached a critical ~** войнá вступи́ла в крити́ческую фáзу; **I shall do it in ~s** я сдéлаю э́то постепéнно.
■ *v.t.*: ~ **a play** стáвить, по- пьéсу; (*organize*) устр|áивать, -óить; организовáть (*impf., pf.*).
■ *cpds.* ~ **manager** *n.* постанóвщик.

stagger /'stægə(r)/ *v.t.*
1 (*disconcert*) потряс|áть, -ти́; порa|жáть, -зи́ть; ошелом|ля́ть, -и́ть; **~ing success** потрясáющий успéх.
2 : ~ **working hours, holidays** *etc.* распредел|я́ть, -и́ть часы́ рабóты, отпускá *и т. п.*
■ *v.i.* шатáться (*impf.*); пошáтываться (*impf.*).

stagnant /'stægnənt/ *adj.* (*water*) стоя́чий; (*pond*) застоя́вшийся.

stagnate /stæg'neɪt/ *v.i.* заст|áиваться, -оя́ться.

stagnation /stæg'neɪʃ(ə)n/ *n.* застóй.

staid /steɪd/ *adj.* степéнный.

stain /steɪn/ *n.*
1 пятнó.
2 (*for colouring*) краси́тель (*m.*).
■ *v.t.* 1 (*soil*) пáчкать, за-/ис-.
2 (*colour*) окрá|шивать, -сить; **~ed glass** цветнóе cтеклó; **~ed-glass window** витрáж; ~ **wood** мори́ть, за- дéрево.

stainless /'steɪnlɪs/ *adj.*: ~ **steel** нержавéющая сталь.

stair /steə(r)/ *n.*
1 (*step*) ступéнька.
2 (*pl. or* **~case**) лéстница; **he ran up the ~s** он взбежáл по лéстнице.
■ *cpds.* **~case, ~way** *nn.* лéстница; лéстничная клéтка.

stake /steɪk/ *n.*
1 (*post*) столб, кол (*pl.* кóлья).
2 (*wager*) стáвка, заклáд.
3 (*share in a business*) дóля; (*an interest*) заинтересóванность.
4 : **his reputation was at ~** егó репутáция былá постáвлена на кáрту.
■ *v.t.* 1 (*support with* ~) укреп|ля́ть, -и́ть колóм.
2 (*wager*) стáвить, по-; (*risk, gamble*) рисковáть (*impf.*) + *i.*
■ *with adv.*: ~ **out** *v.t.*: ~ **out a boundary** отм|ечáть, -éтить вéхами грани́цу.

stalactite /'stæləktaɪt/ *n.* сталакти́т.

stalagmite /'stæləgmaɪt/ *n.* сталагми́т.

stale /steɪl/ *adj.* (**staler, stalest**) несвéжий; ~ **bread** чёрствый хлеб; (*of air*) спёртый, зáтхлый.

stalemate /'steɪlmeɪt/ *n.* (*chess*) пат; (*fig., impasse*) тупи́к, безвы́ходное положéние.

stalk[1] /stɔːk/ *n.* (*stem*) стéбель (*m.*); черешóк.

stalk[2] /stɔːk/
1 (*pursue stealthily*) выслéживать, вы́следить.
2 (*persecute obsessively*) преслéдовать (*impf.*).

stalker /'stɔːkə(r)/ *n.* человéк, патологи́чески преслéдующий предмéт своегó внимáния; навя́зчивый преслéдователь.

stall[1] /stɔːl/ *n.*
1 (*for animal*) стóйло.
2 (*in market etc.*) прилáвок, стóйка; **book ~** киóск.
3 (*pl., Br., theatr.*) партéр, крéсла (*nt. pl.*).
■ *v.i.* (*of engine*) глóхнуть, за-.
■ *cpd.* **~holder** *n.* (*Br.*) владéлец палáтки (*на ры́нке*).

stall[2] /stɔːl/ *v.i.* (*play for time*) тянýть, затя́гивать (*both impf.*) врéмя.

stallion /'stæljən/ *n.* жеребéц.

stalwart /'stɔːlwət/ *adj.*: ~ **supporter** я́р|ый сторóнни|к (*fem.* -ая -ца), стóйкий привéрженец.

stamina /'stæmɪnə/ *n.* выносливость.

stammer /'stæmə(r)/ *n.* заикáние.
■ *v.i.* заикáться (*impf.*).

stamp /stæmp/ *n.*
1 (*instrument*) штамп, печáть, клеймó.
2 (*mark*) печáть, клеймó; (*postage etc.*) мáрка.
■ *v.t.* 1 (*imprint*) штамповáть, про-; стáвить, по- штамп/печáть на + *a.*
2 (*beat on ground*): ~ **one's feet** тóпать (*impf.*) ногáми.
■ *v.i.* (*feet*) тóп|ать, -нуть.
■ *with adv.*: ~ **out** *v.t.* (*lit.*): ~ **out a fire** зат|áптывать, -оптáть огóнь; (*exterminate, destroy*) уничт|ожáть, -óжить; (*suppress*) подав|ля́ть, -и́ть (*восстáние*).
■ *cpds.* ~ **collecting** *n.* коллекциони́рование мáрок; ~ **duty** *n.* гéрбовый сбор.

stampede /stæm'piːd/ *n.* бéгство.
■ *v.i.* разбе|гáться, -жáться врассыпнýю.

stance /stɑːns/ *n.* пози́ция.

stand /stænd/ *n.*
1 (*support*) подстáвка.
2 (*stall*) стóйка; (*Br., for display*) стенд.
3 (*for spectators*) трибýна.
4 (*for taxis etc.*) стоя́нка.
5 (*position*) мéсто; (*fig.*): **take a firm ~** зан|имáть, -я́ть твёрдую пози́цию; **make a ~ against s.o./sth.** окáз|ывать, -áть сопротивлéние комý-н./чемý-н.
■ *v.t.* (*past and p.p.* **stood**)
1 (*place, set*) стáвить, по-; **he stood the ladder against the wall** он пристáвил лéстницу к стенé.
2 (*bear*) терпéть, вы́-; выноси́ть, вы́нести; перен|оси́ть, -ести́; **she can't ~ him** онá егó не выно́сит (*or* терпéть не мóжет).
■ *v.i.* (*past and p.p.* **stood**)
1 (*be or stay in upright position*) стоя́ть (*impf.*)
2 (*remain*): **our house will ~ for another fifty years** наш дом простои́т ещё пятьдеся́т лет.
3 (*hold good*) ост|авáться, -áться в си́ле.
4 (*be situated*) стоя́ть (*impf.*); находи́ться (*impf.*).
5 (*find o.s., be*): **I shall leave the text as it ~s** я оставля́ю текст, как он есть; **as matters ~** при дáнном положéнии вещéй; **how do we ~ for money?** как у нас (обстои́т) с деньгáми?
6 (*rise to one's feet*) встa|вáть, -ть.
7 (*assume or move to specified position*): **I'll ~**

here я ста́ну сюда́; **we had to ~ in a queue** (*Br.*), **in line** (*US*) нам пришло́сь постоя́ть в о́череди; **~ back!** (отступи́те) наза́д!
■ *with preps.*: **we will ~ by** (*support*) **you** мы вас подде́ржим; **I ~ by what I said** я не отступа́юсь от свои́х слов; **~ for office** (*Br.*) выставля́ть, вы́ставить свою́ кандидату́ру; **~ for Parliament** (*Br.*) баллоти́роваться (*impf.*) в парла́мент; **we ~ for freedom** мы стои́м за свобо́ду; **'Mg' ~s for magnesium** Mg обознача́ет ма́гний; **I will not ~ for such impudence** я не потерплю́ тако́й на́глости; **he ~s to win/lose £1,000** его́ ждёт вы́игрыш/про́игрыш в ты́сячу фу́нтов.
■ *with advs.*: **~ about, ~ around** *vv.i.* стоя́ть (*impf.*) без де́ла; **~ aside** *v.i.* стоя́ть (*impf.*) в стороне́; **~ back** *v.i.* (*also fig.*) от|ходи́ть, -ойти́ в сто́рону; **~ by** *v.i.* (*be ready*) быть/стоя́ть (*impf.*) наготове; **~ down** *v.i.* : **he stood down in favour** (*Br.*), **favor** (*US*) **of his brother** он снял свою́ кандидату́ру в по́льзу бра́та; (*of minister etc.*) под|ава́ть, -а́ть в отста́вку; **~ in** *v.i.* (*substitute*): **~ in for s.o. else** замен|я́ть, -и́ть кого́-н. друго́го; **~ out** *v.i.* (*be prominent*) выделя́ться (*impf.*); выдава́ться (*impf.*); **~ up** *v.t.*: **he stood his bicycle up against the wall** он прислони́л свой велосипе́д к стене́; (*coll.*): **his girlfriend stood him up** его́ подру́га не пришла́ на свида́ние; *v.i.*: **he stood up as I entered** он встал, когда́ я вошёл; **he ~s up for his rights** он отста́ивает свои́ права́; **he stood up bravely to his opponent** он оказа́л му́жественное сопротивле́ние проти́внику.
■ *cpds.* **~-alone** *adj.* (*comput.*) автоно́мный; **~by** *n.* (*state of readiness*) гото́вность; (*dependable thing or person*) надёжная опо́ра; испы́танное сре́дство; **~-in** *n.* замести́тель (*fem.* -ница); **~point** *n.* то́чка зре́ния; **~still** *n.*: **come to a ~still** остан|а́вливаться, -ови́ться; засто́пориться (*pf.*) (*coll.*); **at a ~still** на мёртвой то́чке; **many factories are at a ~still** мно́го фа́брик безде́йствует/проста́ивает.

standard /ˈstændəd/ *n.*
[1] (*flag*) зна́мя, штанда́рт.
[2] (*norm*) станда́рт; (*level*) у́ровень (*m.*); **come up to ~** соотве́тствовать (*impf.*) тре́буемому у́ровню; **~ of living** жи́зненный у́ровень, у́ровень жи́зни.
■ *adj.* [1] станда́ртный.
[2] (*model, basic*) нормати́вный, образцо́вый; (*general*) типово́й.
[3] : **~ lamp** (*Br.*) напо́льная ла́мпа, торше́р.

standardize /ˈstændədaɪz/ *v.t.* стандартизи́ровать (*impf., pf.*).

standing /ˈstændɪŋ/ *n.*
[1] (*rank*) положе́ние; (*reputation*) репута́ция.
[2] (*duration*) продолжи́тельность; **a custom of long ~** стари́нный обы́чай.
■ *adj.*: **~ army** регуля́рная/постоя́нная а́рмия; **~ invitation** приглаше́ние приходи́ть в любо́е вре́мя; **~ order** (*Br.*) (*to banker*) прика́з о регуля́рных платежа́х.

stank /stæŋk/ *past of* ▸ **stink**

stanza /ˈstænzə/ *n.* строфа́.

staple¹ /ˈsteɪp(ə)l/ *n.* (*for papers*) ско́бка (*для степлера*).
■ *v.t.*: **~ papers together** скреп|ля́ть, -и́ть бума́ги сте́плером.

staple² /ˈsteɪp(ə)l/ *n.*
[1] (*principal commodity*) основно́й това́р/проду́кт.
[2] (*chief material*) осно́ва.
■ *adj.* основно́й, гла́вный.

stapler /ˈsteɪplə(r)/ *n.* (*for paper*) сте́плер.

star /stɑː(r)/ *n.*
[1] звезда́; **five-~ hotel** пятизвёздочная гости́ница.
[2] (*famous actor etc.*) звезда́; **film ~** кинозвезда́.
[3] (*asterisk*) звёздочка.
■ *v.i.* (**starred, starring**): **~ in a film** игра́ть (*impf.*) гла́вную роль в фи́льме.
■ *cpds.* **~fish** *n.* морска́я звезда́; **~ sign** *n.* знак зодиа́ка; **~-studded** *adj.* (*fig.*) с уча́стием мно́жества звёзд.

starboard /ˈstɑːbəd/ *n.* пра́вый борт.
■ *adj.* пра́вый; **~ side** пра́вый борт; **~ wind** ве́тер с пра́вого бо́рта.

starch /stɑːtʃ/ *n.* крахма́л.

stardom /ˈstɑːdəm/ *n.*: **rise to ~** ста|нови́ться, -ть звездо́й.

stare /steə(r)/ *n.* при́стальный взгляд.
■ *v.i.* глазе́ть (*impf.*); **~ at s.o.** при́стально смотре́ть/гляде́ть (*impf.*) на кого́-н.

stark /stɑːk/ *adj.*
[1] (*desolate*) го́лый.
[2] (*sharply evident*) я́вный; **be in ~ contrast to** ре́зко контрасти́ровать (*impf.*) с + *i.*
■ *adv.*: **~ naked** соверше́нно го́лый; в чём мать родила́ (*coll.*).

starling /ˈstɑːlɪŋ/ *n.* скворе́ц.

start /stɑːt/ *n.*
[1] (*sudden movement*) вздра́гивание, содрога́ние; **he woke with a ~** он вздро́гнул и просну́лся.
[2] (*beginning*) нача́ло; (*of journey*) отправле́ние; (*of race*) старт.
■ *v.t.* [1] (*begin*) нач|ина́ть, -а́ть; **it is ~ing to rain** начина́ется дождь; **we ~ed our journey** мы отпра́вились в путь; **she ~ed crying** она́ начала́ пла́кать/распла́калась; *with many vv., the pf. formed with* за- *means* '*to start …ing*'.
[2] (*set in motion*): **~ an engine** зав|оди́ть, -ести́ (*or* запус|ка́ть, -ти́ть) мото́р/дви́гатель.
[3] (*initiate*): **~ (up) a business** осно́в|ывать, -а́ть (*or* нач|ина́ть, -а́ть) би́знес/де́ло; **~ a family** зав|оди́ть, -ести́ семью́.
■ *v.i.* [1] (*make sudden movement*) вздр|а́гивать, -о́гнуть; содрог|а́ться, -ну́ться.
[2] (*begin*) нач|ина́ться, -а́ться; (*arise*) появ|ля́ться, -и́ться; возн|ика́ть, -и́кнуть; **it ~ed raining** пошёл/начался́ дождь; **we had to ~ again from scratch** пришло́сь нача́ть всё с нача́ла; **there were 12 of us to ~ with** снача́ла/сперва́ нас бы́ло 12 (челове́к); **to ~ with, you should write to him** пре́жде всего́ (*or* для нача́ла) вы должны́ написа́ть ему́; **~ing price** нача́льная/ста́ртовая цена́.
[3] (*set out*) отпр|авля́ться, -а́виться.
[4] (*of engine etc.*): **the car ~ed without any trouble** маши́на завела́сь без пробле́м.
■ *with advs.*: **~ off** *v.i.* (*leave*) пойти́, пое́хать (*both pf.*); **she ~ed off by apologizing for**

being late она́ начала́ с извине́ний за своё опозда́ние; **~ out** *v.i.* (*leave*) отпр|авля́ться, -а́виться; пойти́, пое́хать (*both pf.*); **~ over** *v.i.* (*US*) нач|ина́ть, -а́ть сно́ва; **~ up** *v.t.*: **~ up an engine** зав|оди́ть, -ести́ (*or* запус|ка́ть, -ти́ть) мото́р; **~ up a business** осн|о́вывать, -ова́ть би́знес/де́ло.

starter /'stɑ:tə(r)/ *n.* (*Br., first course*) заку́ска.

startle /'stɑ:t(ə)l/ *v.t.* (*scare*) пуга́ть, ис-; вспу́г|ивать, -ну́ть.

startling /'stɑ:tlɪŋ/ *adj.* порази́тельный, потряса́ющий.

starvation /stɑ:'veɪʃ(ə)n/ *n.* го́лод, голода́ние; **die of ~** ум|ира́ть, -ере́ть от го́лода (*or* с го́лоду).

starv|e /stɑ:v/ *v.t.* мори́ть, у-/за- (го́лодом); (*fig.*): **the child was ~ed of affection** ребёнок страда́л от отсу́тствия любви́.
■ *v.i.* (*go hungry*) голода́ть (*impf.*); **I'm ~ing** я ужа́сно проголода́лся!; я го́лоден как волк!

stash /stæʃ/ *n.* скры́тый запа́с.
■ *v.t.* (*coll.*): **he has £1,000 ~ed away** у него́ припря́тана ты́сяча фу́нтов.

state[1] /steɪt/ *n.*
1 (*condition*) состоя́ние, положе́ние.
2 (*country, government*) госуда́рство; (*attr.*) госуда́рственный; **United S~s** Соединённые Шта́ты (Аме́рики) (*abbr.* США); **S~ Department** (*US*) госуда́рственный департа́мент, министе́рство иностра́нных дел.
3 (*pomp*): **~ apartments** пара́дные поко́и (*m. pl.*); **~ visit** госуда́рственный визи́т.
■ *cpds.* **~-aided** *adj.* получа́ющий дота́цию/субси́дию от госуда́рства; **~-of-the-art** *adj.* ультрасовреме́нный, нове́йший.

state[2] /steɪt/ *v.t.* (*declare; say clearly*) заяв|ля́ть, -и́ть о + *p.*; сказа́ть (*pf.*), что; утвержда́ть (*impf.*), что; сообщ|а́ть, -и́ть о + *p.*; (*indicate*) ука́з|ывать, -а́ть.

stateless /'steɪtlɪs/ *adj.* не име́ющий гражда́нства.

stately /'steɪtlɪ/ *adj.* (**statelier, stateliest**) вели́чественный, велича́вый; **~ home** (*Br.*) дом-дворе́ц.

statement /'steɪtmənt/ *n.* (*declaration*) заявле́ние; (*fin.*) отчёт.

statesman /'steɪtsmən/ *n.* госуда́рственный де́ятель.

static /'stætɪk/ *n.*
1 (**~** *electricity*) стати́ческое электри́чество.
2 (*as radio interference*) (атмосфе́рные) поме́хи (*f. pl.*).
■ *adj.* 1 (*stationary*) неподви́жный, стациона́рный.
2 (*opp. dynamic*) стати́ческий, стати́чный.

station /'steɪʃ(ə)n/ *n.*
1 (*base, headquarters*) ста́нция; **police ~** полице́йский уча́сток; (*in Russia*) отделе́ние мили́ции.
2 (*rail.*) ста́нция; (*large, mainline* **~**) вокза́л.
■ *v.t.* распол|ага́ть, -ожи́ть; **~ a guard at the gate** выставля́ть, вы́ставить карау́л у воро́т; (*mil.*) разме|ща́ть, -сти́ть; дислоци́ровать (*impf., pf.*).
■ *cpd.* **~ wagon** *n.* (*US*) универса́л (*coll.*) (*тип кузова*).

stationary /'steɪʃənərɪ/ *adj.* неподви́жный.

stationery /'steɪʃənərɪ/ *n.* канцеля́рские принадле́жности (*f. pl.*)/това́ры (*m. pl.*).

statistical /stə'tɪstɪk(ə)l/ *adj.* статисти́ческий.

statistician /stætɪ'stɪʃ(ə)n/ *n.* стати́стик.

statistics /stə'tɪstɪks/ *n.* статисти́ческие да́нные.

statue /'stætju:/ *n.* ста́туя.

statuesque /stætjʊ'esk/ *adj.* велича́вый, вели́чественный.

statuette /stætjʊ'et/ *n.* статуэ́тка.

stature /'stætʃə(r)/ *n.*
1 (*height*) рост.
2 (*fig.*) масшта́б, кали́бр.

status /'steɪtəs/ *n.*
1 ста́тус.
2: **~ quo** ста́тус-кво́ (*m. & nt. indecl.*).

statute /'stætju:t/ *n.* стату́т; (*law*) зако́н.

statutory /'statjʊtərɪ/ *adj.* предусмо́тренный зако́ном.

staunch /stɔ:ntʃ/ *adj.* (*loyal*) лоя́льный; (*devoted*): **a ~ socialist** непрекло́нный/убеждённый социали́ст.

stave /steɪv/ *n. v.t.*: **~ off** предотвра|ща́ть, -ти́ть.

stay /steɪ/ *n.*
1 (*sojourn*) пребыва́ние.
2: **~ of execution** отсро́чка исполне́ния.
■ *v.i.* 1 (*stop, put up*) (*at a place*) остан|а́вливаться, -ови́ться; (*with s.o.*) гости́ть (*impf.*); остан|а́вливаться, -ови́ться; **we are** (*sc. at present*) **~ing with friends** мы останови́лись/гости́м у друзе́й.
2 (*remain*) ост|ава́ться, -а́ться; не уходи́ть (*impf.*); **~ at home** сиде́ть (*impf.*) до́ма; **I ~ed away from work** я не пошёл/вы́шел на рабо́ту; **can you ~ for, to tea?** вы мо́жете оста́ться на чай?; **I am ~ing in today** сего́дня я не выхожу́ (*or* я сижу́ до́ма); **he ~ed on at the university** он оста́лся при университе́те; **she is allowed to ~ out till midnight** ей разреша́ют не приходи́ть домо́й до 12 часо́в но́чи; **~ up late** не ложи́ться (*impf.*) (спать) допоздна́.
3 (*endure in race etc.*): **he has no ~ing power** у него́ нет никако́й выно́сливости.

STD (*abbr. of* ***sexually transmitted disease***) заболева́ние, передава́емое половы́м путём.

stead /sted/ *n.*: **stand s.o. in good ~** сослужи́ть (*pf.*) кому́-н. хоро́шую слу́жбу.

steadfast /'stedfɑ:st/ *adj.* (*reliable*) надёжный; (*unwavering*) непоколеби́мый.

steady /'stedɪ/ *adj.* (**steadier, steadiest**)
1 (*firmly fixed*) про́чный, усто́йчивый, твёрдый; **keep the camera ~!** не дви́гайте фотоаппара́т!; (*unfaltering*): **a ~ gaze** твёрдый взгляд.
2 (*even*) ро́вный; (*constant*) постоя́нный; **he works steadily** он упо́рно рабо́тает; **~ demand** постоя́нный спрос.
■ *v.t.* (*strengthen*): **the doctor gave him sth. to ~ his nerves** до́ктор дал ему́ лека́рство для укрепле́ния не́рвов.

steak /steɪk/ *n.* (*of beef*) бифште́кс (натура́льный).

steal /sti:l/ *v.t.* (*past* **stole;** *p.p.* **stolen**)
1 ворова́ть (*impf.*); красть, у-; **I had my handbag stolen** у меня́ укра́ли су́мку.

2 (*fig.*): **~ a glance at s.o.** взглянýть (*pf.*) укрáдкой на когó-н.
■ *v.i.* (*past* **stole;** *p.p.* **stolen**)
1 (*thieve*) воровáть (*impf.*).
2 (*move secretly or silently*) крáсться (*impf.*); **he stole round to the back door** он прокрáлся к зáдней двéри.

stealth /stelθ/ *n.*: **by ~** тайкóм, укрáдкой, втихомóлку (*coll.*).

stealthy /'stelθɪ/ *adj.* (**stealthier, stealthiest**): **~ glance** взгляд укрáдкой; **~ tread** крадýщаяся похóдка.

steam /sti:m/ *n.* пар; **let off ~** (*lit.*) выпускáть, вы́пустить пáры́; (*fig.*) да|вáть, -ть вы́ход чýвствам; **run out of ~** (*fig.*) выдыхáться, вы́дохнуться.
■ *v.t.* 1 (*cook with ~*) пáрить (*impf.*); **~ed fish** ры́ба, приготóвленная на парý.
2 (*cover with ~*): **the carriage windows were ~ed up** вагóнные óкна запотéли.
■ *v.i.* выделя́ть (*impf.*) пар/испарéния; пус|кáть, -ти́ть пар.
■ *cpds.* **~ engine** *n.* паровóз; **~roller** *n.* паровóй катóк.

steamer /'sti:mə(r)/ *n.* (*ship*) парохóд.

steamy /'sti:mɪ/ *adj.* (**steamier, steamiest**) (*full of steam*) пóлный пáра; (*humid*) (*coll.*) дýшный.

steed /sti:d/ *n.* (*poet.*) конь (*m.*).

steel /sti:l/ *n.* сталь; (*attr.*) стальнóй.
■ : **~ o.s.** (*pluck up courage*) соб|ирáться, -рáться с дýхом.
■ *cpd.* **~works** *n.* сталеплави́льный завóд.

steely /'sti:lɪ/ *adj.* (**steelier, steeliest**) (*fig.*, *unyielding*) желéзный, непреклóнный; (*stern*) сурóвый.

steep[1] /sti:p/ *adj.*
1 крутóй; (*fig.*): **there has been a ~ decline in trade** в торгóвле произошёл рéзкий спад.
2 (*coll.*, *excessive*) чрезмéрный, непомéрный; **we had to pay a ~ price** нам э́то влетéло в копéечку.

steep[2] /sti:p/ *v.t.* (*soak*) зам|áчивать, -очи́ть.

steeple /'sti:p(ə)l/ *n.* (*bell tower*) колокóльня; (*spire*) шпиль (*m.*).
■ *cpd.* **~chase** *n.* сти́пль-чéз; скáчки (*f. pl.*)/бег с препя́тствиями.

steer[1] /stɪə(r)/ *n.* (*animal*) вол.

steer[2] /stɪə(r)/ *v.t.*
1 (*ship, vehicle etc.*) управля́ть (*impf.*) + *i.*
2 (*person, activity etc.*) вести́ (*det.*); напр|авля́ть, -áвить.
■ *v.i.* 1 (*of steersman*) управля́ть/прáвить (*both impf.*) рулём.
2 (*of person*): **~ clear of** избегáть (*impf.*) + *g.*

steering wheel /'stɪərɪŋ wi:l/ *n.* (*of car*) руль (*m.*).

stem[1] /stem/ *n.*
1 (*bot.*) стéбель (*m.*).
2 (*of wine glass*) нóжка.
3 (*gram.*) оснóва.
■ *cpd.* **~ cell** *n.* (*biol.*) стволовáя клéтка.

stem[2] /stem/ *v.t.* (**stemmed, stemming**) (*lit., fig., check, stop*) остан|áвливать, -ови́ть.

stench /stentʃ/ *n.* вонь.

stencil /'stensɪl/ *n.* трафарéт.
■ *v.t.* (**stencilled, stencilling;** *US* **stenciled, stenciling**) распи́с|ывать, -áть при пóмощи трафарéта.

step /step/ *n.*
1 (*movement, distance, sound, manner of ~ping*) шаг.
2 (*fig., action*) шаг, мéра; **take ~s towards** предприн|имáть, -я́ть шаги́ к + *d.*
3 (*raised surface*) ступéнь; (*of staircase etc.*) ступéнька.
4 (*pl., Br.; also* **~ladder**) стремя́нка.
■ *v.i.* (**stepped, stepping**) шаг|áть, -нýть; ступ|áть, -и́ть; **~ping stone** кáмень для перехóда (*через ручей и т. п.*); (*fig.*) трампли́н; **a ~ping stone to success** ступéнь к успéху; **someone ~ped on my foot** ктó-то наступи́л мне нá ногу.
■ *with advs.*: **~ aside** *v.i.* сторони́ться, по-; (*fig.*) уступ|áть, -и́ть (дорóгу) другóму; **~ back** *v.i.* отступ|áть, -и́ть; **~ down** *v.i.*: **he ~ped down off the ladder** он спусти́лся/сошёл с лéстницы; **he ~ped down in favour of a more experienced man** он уступи́л мéсто бóлее óпытному человéку; **~ in** *v.i.* (*intervene*) вмéш|иваться, -áться; (*replace s.o.*): **thanks for ~ping in** спаси́бо, что вы́ручили; **~ up** *v.t.* (*increase*) пов|ышáть, -ы́сить; уси́ли|вать, -ть.
■ *cpds.* **~-by-~** *adj.* постепéнный; **~ladder** *n.* = **~** *n.* **4**

step|- /step/ *comb. form*: **~brother** *n.* свóдный брат; **~child** *n.* (*boy*) пáсынок; (*girl*) пáдчерица; **~daughter** *n.* пáдчерица; **~father** *n.* óтчим; **~mother** *n.* мáчеха; **~sister** *n.* свóдная сестрá; **~son** *n.* пáсынок.

steppe /step/ *n.* степь.

stereo /'sterɪəʊ/ *n.* (*pl.* **~s**) (**~***phonic system*) стереосистéма; **personal ~** плéер.

stereotype /'sterɪəʊtaɪp/ *n.* стереоти́п; (*attr.*) стереоти́пный.

stereotypical /sterɪəʊ'tɪpɪk(ə)l/ *adj.* стереоти́пный.

sterile /'steraɪl/ *adj.*
1 (*of land*) неплодорóдный; (*of person or animal*) бесплóдный.
2 (*germ-free*) стери́льный.

sterility /stə'rɪlɪtɪ/ *n.* бесплóдие.

sterilize /'sterɪlaɪz/ *v.t.* стерилизовáть (*impf., pf.*).

sterling /'stə:lɪŋ/ *n.* стéрлинг; фунт стéрлингов.

stern[1] /stə:n/ *n.* (*of ship*) кормá.

stern[2] /stə:n/ *adj.* (*severe*) сурóвый.

stern|um /'stə:nəm/ *n.* (*pl.* **~ums** *or* **~a**) груди́на.

steroid /'stɪerɔɪd/ *n.* стерóид.

stethoscope /'steθəskəʊp/ *n.* стетоскóп.

stew /stju:/ *n.* рагý (*nt. indecl.*).
■ *v.t.* (*meat, fish, vegetables*) туши́ть, по-; (*fruit*) вари́ть (*impf.*); **~ed fruit** компóт.

steward /'stju:əd/ *n.* (*of estate, club etc.*) управля́ющий, экономóм, стю́ард; (*of race meeting*) распоряди́тель (*m.*); (*on ship*) стю́ард; (*on train*) проводни́к; (*on plane*) бортпроводни́к, стю́ард.

stewardess /stju:ə'des/ *n.* (*on plane*) стюардéсса, бортпроводни́ца.

stick[1] /stɪk/ *n.*
1 (*for support, punishment*) пáлка; (**walking**

~) трость; (**hockey** ~ *etc.*) клю́шка.
[2] (~ *shaped object*): ~ **of chalk** мело́к; ~ **of celery/rhubarb** сте́бель (*m.*) сельдере́я/ревеня́; ~ **of dynamite** динами́тная ша́шка.

stick² /stɪk/ *v.t.* (*past and p.p.* **stuck**)
[1] (*insert point of*) втыка́ть, воткну́ть; **I stuck a pin in the map** я воткну́л була́вку в ка́рту.
[2] (*cause to adhere*) прикле́и|вать, -ть (*что к чему*); накле́и|вать, -ть (*что на что*); (*affix*): ~ **a notice on the door** ве́шать, пове́сить объявле́ние на дверь.
[3] (*coll., put*): ~ **that book on the shelf** су́ньте э́ту кни́гу на по́лку; **he stuck his head round the door** он просу́нул го́лову в дверь.
[4] (*Br. coll., endure*) терпе́ть, вы́-.
[5] (*coll. uses of pass. with preps.*): **get stuck into sth.** (*Br., make serious start on*) прин|има́ться, -я́ться за что-н. всерьёз.
■ *v.i.* (*past and p.p.* **stuck**)
[1] (*be implanted*): **a dagger** ~**ing in his back** кинжа́л, торча́щий у него́ в спине́.
[2] (*remain attached, adhere*) прил|ипа́ть, -и́пнуть (*к чему*); прикле́и|ваться, -ться; **these pages have stuck (together)** э́ти страни́цы скле́ились; ~**ing plaster** (*Br.*) лейкопла́стырь (*m.*), ли́пкий пла́стырь.
[3] (*cling, cleave*): ~ **to the point** не отступа́ть (*impf.*) от те́мы; ~ **to one's principles** ост|ава́ться, -а́ться ве́рным свои́м при́нципам; **the accused stuck to his story** обвиня́емый упо́рно стоя́л на своём.
[4] (*also* **be stuck, get stuck:** *become embedded, fixed*) застр|ева́ть, -я́ть; **the drawer** ~**s** я́щик застря́л; **can you help with this problem? I'm stuck** помоги́те мне, пожа́луйста, с э́той зада́чей — я запу́тался вконе́ц; **one thing** ~**s in my mind** одно́ у меня́ засе́ло в па́мяти.
■ *with advs.*: ~ **around** *v.i.* (*coll.*) не уходи́ть (*impf.*); ~ **down** *v.t.* (*seal*): **have you stuck the envelope down?** вы закле́или конве́рт?; ~ **on** *v.t.* (*affix*) прикле́и|вать, -ть; ~ **out** *v.t.*: ~ **one's tongue out** высо́вывать, вы́сунуть язы́к; ~ **one's head out** высо́вываться, вы́сунуться; *v.i.* (*project*) торча́ть (*impf.*); **his ears** ~ **out** у него́ торча́т у́ши; ~ **together** *v.t.* (*with glue*) скле́и|вать, -ть; *v.i.*: **good friends** ~ **together** настоя́щие друзья́ стоя́т друг за дру́га (горо́й); ~ **up** (*coll.*) *v.i.* (*protrude upwards*) торча́ть (*impf.*); ~ **up for** (*coll.*) (*defend*) заступ|а́ться, -и́ться за *кого.*

sticker /ˈstɪkə(r)/ *n.* накле́йка.

sticky /ˈstɪkɪ/ *adj.* (**stickier, stickiest**) кле́йкий, ли́пкий.

stiff /stɪf/ *adj.*
[1] (*not flexible or soft*) жёсткий.
[2] (*not working smoothly*) туго́й; ~ **hinges** туги́е пе́тли.
[3] (*of person or parts of body*) онеме́лый, окостене́лый; **I have a** ~ **neck** у меня́ ше́я онеме́ла; **he has a** ~ **leg** у него́ нога́ пло́хо сгиба́ется; **I feel** ~ я не могу́ ни согну́ться, ни разогну́ться.
[4] (*forceful*) си́льный; **a** ~ **drink** хоро́ший глото́к спиртно́го.
[5] (*difficult*) тру́дный, тяжёлый; **a** ~ **examination** тру́дный экза́мен; (*severe*) суро́вый; **he got a** ~ **sentence** ему́ вы́несли суро́вый пригово́р.
[6] (*constrained*) натя́нутый, чо́порный.
[7] (*pred., coll.*): **he was scared** ~ он перепуга́лся до́ смерти; **I was bored** ~ я чуть не у́мер со ску́ки.

stiffen /ˈstɪf(ə)n/ *v.t.* прид|ава́ть, -а́ть жёсткость + *d.*
■ *v.i.* (*become rigid*) де́латься, с- жёстким; (*of body*) кочене́ть, о-/костене́ть, о-.

stifl|e /ˈstaɪf(ə)l/ *v.t.*
[1] (*smother, suffocate*) души́ть, за-; **it is** ~**ing in here** здесь ду́шно.
[2] (*e.g. rebellion, feelings*) подав|ля́ть, -и́ть.

stigma /ˈstɪgmə/ *n.* позо́р, пятно́.

stigmatize /ˈstɪgmətaɪz/ *v.t.* клейми́ть, за-.

stile /staɪl/ *n.* (*steps*) перела́з (*ступеньки у забора, стены*).

stiletto /stɪˈletəʊ/ *n.* (*pl.* ~**s**): ~ **heels** шпи́льки (*f. pl.*); гво́здики (*m. pl.*).

still /stɪl/ *adj.*
[1] (*quiet, calm*) ти́хий.
[2] (*motionless*) неподви́жный; **sit/stand** ~ сиде́ть/стоя́ть (*impf.*) споко́йно; ~ **life** (*art*) натюрмо́рт.
[3] (*Br., not fizzy*) негазиро́ванный.
■ *adv.* [1] (*even now, then; as formerly*) (всё) ещё; до сих пор; по-пре́жнему.
[2] (*nevertheless*) тем не ме́нее, всё-таки, всё равно́.
[3] (*with comp.: even, yet*) ещё.

stilt /stɪlt/ *n.*
[1] ходу́ля; **walk on** ~**s** ходи́ть (*indet.*) на ходу́лях.
[2] (*supporting a building*) сва́я.

stilted /ˈstɪltɪd/ *adj.* (*of style etc.*) высокопа́рный.

stimulant /ˈstɪmjʊlənt/ *n.* (*med.*) стимули́рующее сре́дство.

stimulate /ˈstɪmjʊleɪt/ *v.t.*
[1] (*rouse, incite*) побу|жда́ть, -ди́ть (**s.o. to (do) sth.:** *кого + inf. or* + к + *d.*); стимули́ровать (*impf., pf.*).
[2] (*excite, arouse*) возбу|жда́ть, -ди́ть; **the story** ~**ed my curiosity** расска́з возбуди́л моё любопы́тство.

stimul|us /ˈstɪmjʊləs/ *n.* (*pl.* ~**li** /-laɪ/) (*incentive*) сти́мул, побужде́ние.

sting /stɪŋ/ *n.*
[1] (*of insect etc.*) жа́ло.
[2] (*by insect*) уку́с.
■ *v.t.* (*past and p.p.* **stung**)
[1] (*of insect etc.*) жа́лить, у-; куса́ть, укуси́ть; (*of plant*) обж|ига́ть, -е́чь; жечь (*impf.*); ~**ing nettle** (жгу́чая) крапи́ва.
[2] (*of pain, smoke etc.*) обж|ига́ть, -е́чь.
■ *v.i.* (*past and p.p.* **stung**)
[1] (*of insect etc.*) жа́литься (*impf.*); куса́ться (*impf.*).
[2] (*feel pain*) жечь (*impf.*); **the smoke made my eyes** ~ дым ел мне глаза́.

stingy /ˈstɪndʒɪ/ *adj.* (**stingier, stingiest**) скупо́й.

stink /stɪŋk/ *n.* вонь.
■ *v.i.* (*past* **stank** *or* **stunk;** *p.p.* **stunk**) воня́ть (*impf.*); **the room** ~**s of onions** в ко́мнате воня́ет лу́ком.

stint /stɪnt/ *n.* уро́к.
■ *v.t.*: **he did not** ~ **on his praise** он не скупи́лся на похвалы́.

stipend /ˈstaɪpend/ *n.* (*of clergyman*) жáлованье; (*of student*) стипéндия.

stipulate /ˈstɪpjʊleɪt/ *v.t.* обуслóв|ливать, -ить.

stir /stəː(r)/ *n.*: **the news caused a ~** это извéстие надéлало мнóго шýма.
■ *v.t.* (**stirred, stirring**): **the wind ~s the trees** вéтер колы́шет дерéвья; **~ one's tea** размéш|ивать, -áть чай; **~ the soup** мешáть, по- суп.
■ *v.i.* (**stirred, stirring**) шевели́ться, за-.
■ *with adv.*: **~ up** *v.t.* (*arouse*): **~ up rebellion** сéять (*impf.*) смýту.

stirrup /ˈstɪrəp/ *n.* стрéмя (*nt.*).

stitch /stɪtʃ/ *n.*
1 (*sewing*) стежóк; (*knitting*) петля́.
2 (*med.*) шов.
3 (*pain in side*) кóлик|и (*pl.*, *g.* —) в бокý.
■ *v.t.* (*sew together*) сши|вáть, -ть; (*esp. med.*) защ|ивáть, -и́ть.

stoat /stəʊt/ *n.* горностáй (в лéтнем мехý).

stock /stɒk/ *n.*
1 (*store, supply*) запáс, инвентáрь (*m.*); **in ~** в ассортимéнте; **take ~ of** (*fig., appraise*) крити́чески оцéн|ивать, -и́ть.
2 (*lineage*) семья́, происхождéние.
3 (*of farm*): **(live) ~** скот, поголóвье скотá.
4 (*cul.*) (крéпкий) бульóн.
5 (*comm.*) áкции (*f. pl.*); фóнды (*m. pl.*); **S~ Exchange** фóндовая би́ржа.
■ *adj.* (*regularly used*) обы́чный, шаблóнный.
■ *v.t.* 1 (*equip with ~*) снаб|жáть, -ди́ть (*что чем*); оборýдовать (*impf., pf.*).
2 (*keep in ~*) держáть (*impf.*); имéть (*impf.*) в нали́чии.
■ *v.i.*: **~ up: we ~ed up with fuel for the winter** мы запасли́сь тóпливом нá зиму.
■ *cpds.* **~broker** *n.* биржевóй мáклер; **~ cube** *n.* бульóнный кýбик; **~ market** *n.* фóндовая би́ржа; **~pile** *v.t.* запас|áть, -ти́ + *a. or g.*; **~-still** *adv.* неподви́жно; **~taking** *n.* инвентаризáция.

Stockholm /ˈstɒkhəʊm/ *n.* Стокгóльм.

stocking /ˈstɒkɪŋ/ *n.* чулóк.

stockist /ˈstɒkɪst/ *n.* (*Br.*) рóзничный продавéц (*определённых товаров*).

stocky /ˈstɒkɪ/ *adj.* (**stockier, stockiest**) коренáстый, приземи́стый.

stodgy /ˈstɒdʒɪ/ *adj.* (**stodgier, stodgiest**) (*Br., of food*) тяжёлый.

stoic /ˈstəʊɪk/ *n.* (*of either sex*) стóик.
■ *adj.* стои́ческий.

stoical /ˈstəʊɪk(ə)l/ *adj.* стои́ческий.

stoicism /ˈstəʊɪsɪz(ə)m/ *n.* стоици́зм.

stoke /stəʊk/ *v.t.* (*also* **~ up**) (*put more fuel on*) загру|жáть, -зи́ть (*топку*).

stole /stəʊl/ *past of* ▸ **steal**

stolen /ˈstəʊlən/ *p.p. of* ▸ **steal**

stomach /ˈstʌmək/ *n.*
1 (*internal organ*) желýдок.
2 (*external part of body; belly*) живóт, брю́хо.
■ *v.t.* (*fig., tolerate*): **I can't ~ him** я егó не переношý; я егó терпéть не могý.
■ *cpd.* **~ ache** *n.* кóлик|и (*pl.*, *g.* —) в животé.

stomp /stɒmp/ *v.i.* (*coll., tread heavily*) тóпать, про-.

stone /stəʊn/ *n.* (*sense 4*: *pl.* ~)
1 кáмень (*m.*).
2 (*rock, material*): **built of local ~** пострóенный из мéстного кáмня; **S~ Age** кáменный век; **~ circle** крóмлех.
3 (*of plum etc.*) кóсточка.
4 (*Br., weight*) стóун (*6,35 кг*).
■ *v.t.* 1 (*pelt with ~s*) поб|ивáть, -и́ть камня́ми.
2 : **~ cherries** оч|ищáть, -и́стить ви́шни от кóсточек.
3 : **~d** (*drunk*) пья́ный вдрéбезги (*coll.*); (*with drugs*) обдóлбанный (*sl.*).
■ *cpds.* **~ cold** *adj.* холóдный как лёд; **~-deaf** *adj.* совершéнно глухóй; **~mason** *n.* кáменщик.

stony /ˈstəʊnɪ/ *adj.* (**stonier, stoniest**) камени́стый; (*fig., unfeeling*) кáменный.

stood /stʊd/ *past and p.p. of* ▸ **stand**

stooge /stuːdʒ/ (*sl.*) *n.* (*comedian's foil*) партнёр кóмика; (*deputy of low standing*) подставнóе лицó.

stool /stuːl/ *n.* табурéт(ка).

stoop /stuːp/ *n.* сутýлость; **he walks with a ~** он сутýлится при ходьбé.
■ *v.i.* 1 (*of posture*) сутýлиться, с-; (*bend down*) наг|ибáться, -нýться; сгибáться, согнýться.
2 (*lower o.s.*): **he never ~ed to lying** он никогдá не унижáлся до лжи.

stop /stɒp/ *n.*
1 (*halt, halting place*) остановка; **come to a ~** остан|áвливаться, -ови́ться; **put a ~ to** положи́ть (*pf.*) конéц + *d.*
2 (*Br., punctuation mark*) знак препинáния; **full ~** (*in telegram*) тóчка (*abbr.* тчк).
■ *v.t.* (**stopped, stopping**)
1 (*also* **~ up:** *close, plug*) закр|ывáть, -ы́ть; зат|ыкáть, -кнýть; задéл|ывать, -ать.
2 (*arrest motion of*) остан|áвливать, -ови́ть; **he ~ped the car** он останови́л маши́ну.
3 (*arrest progress of; bring to an end*) остан|áвливать, -ови́ть; задéрж|ивать, -áть; прекра|щáть, -ти́ть; **rain ~ped play** дождь сорвáл игрý; **I ~ped the cheque** (*Br.*), **check** (*US*) я приостанови́л платёж по э́тому чéку; (*cut off, disallow, ~ provision of*): **my father ~ped my allowance** отéц перестáл выделя́ть мне дéньги.
4 (*prevent*): **~ s.o. from** удéрж|ивать, -áть когó-н. от + *g.*; не да|вáть, -ть *кому* + *inf.*; **I tried to ~ him (from) telling her** я пытáлся помешáть емý сказáть ей.
5 (*with gerund: discontinue, leave off*) перест|авáть, -áть + *inf.*; прекра|щáть, -ти́ть + *n. obj.* **~ teasing the cat!** перестáньте дразни́ть кóшку!; **they ~ped talking when I came in** когдá я вошёл, они́ умóлкли.
■ *v.i.* (**stopped, stopping**)
1 (*come to a halt*) остан|áвливаться, -ови́ться.
2 (*in speaking*) зам|олкáть, -óлкнуть; замолчáть (*pf.*).
3 (*cease activity*) перест|авáть, -áть; кончáть, кóнчить.
4 (*come to an end*) прекра|щáться, -ти́ться; кончáться, кóнчиться; перест|авáть, -áть; **the rain ~ped** дождь кóнчился/перестáл; **the road ~ped suddenly** неожи́данно дорóга кóнчилась.
■ *with advs.*: **~ by** *v.i.* за|ходи́ть, -йти́; (*in a vehicle*) за|езжáть, -éхать; **~ off, ~ over**

vv.i. остан|а́вливаться, -ови́ться.
■ *cpds.* **~gap** *n.* (*person*) вре́менная заме́на; (*thing*) заты́чка; вре́менная ме́ра; **~-off, ~over** *nn.* остано́вка (в пути́); **~watch** *n.* секундоме́р.

stoppage /ˈstɒpɪdʒ/ *n.* (*strike*) забасто́вка; (*stopping, discontinuing*) прекраще́ние.

stopper /ˈstɒpə(r)/ *n.* (*of bottle etc.*) про́бка.

storage /ˈstɔːrɪdʒ/ *n.* (*storing*) хране́ние; (*in warehouse*) склади́рование.
■ *cpd.* **~ heater** *n.* (*Br.*) электрообогрева́тель, аккумули́рующий тепло́.

store /stɔː(r)/ *n.*
1 (*stock, reserve*) запа́с, резе́рв, припа́сы (*m. pl.*); **he has a surprise in ~ for you** у него́ для вас припасён сюрпри́з.
2 (*pl., supplies*) припа́сы (*m. pl.*), резе́рвы (*m. pl.*).
3 (*US, shop*) магази́н, ла́вка; **department ~** универма́г.
■ *v.t.* 1 (*keep*) храни́ть (*impf.*).
2: **~ up** запас|а́ть, -ти́.
3 (*deposit in ~*) сда|ва́ть, -ть на хране́ние.
■ *cpds.* **~keeper** *n.* ла́вочни|к (*fem.* -ца); **~room** *n.* кладова́я.

storey /ˈstɔːrɪ/ *n.* (*US* **story**) эта́ж.

stork /stɔːk/ *n.* а́ист.

storm /stɔːm/ *n.* бу́ря; (*thunder ~*) гроза́.
■ *v.t.* (*mil.*) штурмова́ть (*impf.*); брать, взять шту́рмом/при́ступом.
■ *v.i.*: **he ~ed out of the room** он в гне́ве вы́бежал из ко́мнаты.
■ *cpd.* **~ cloud** *n.* грозова́я ту́ча.

stormy /ˈstɔːmɪ/ *adj.* (**stormier, stormiest**) бу́рный (*also fig.*).

story[1] /ˈstɔːrɪ/ *n.*
1 (*tale, account*) расска́з, исто́рия; (*fairy tale*) ска́зка; **short ~** расска́з, нове́лла.
2 (*newspaper report*) отчёт, статья́.
■ *cpds.* **~book** *n.* сбо́рник расска́зов; **~teller** *n.* расска́зчи|к (*fem.* -ца).

story[2] /ˈstɔːrɪ/ *US* = **storey**

stout /staʊt/ *n.* (*beer*) тёмное пи́во.
■ *adj.* 1 (*strong*) кре́пкий, про́чный.
2 (*corpulent*) по́лный, доро́дный.

stove /stəʊv/ *n.* печь, пе́чка; (*for cooking*) плита́.

stow /stəʊ/ *v.t.* укла́дывать, уложи́ть.
■ *cpd.* **~away** *n.* безбиле́тный пассажи́р, «за́яц».

St Petersburg /sənt ˈpiːtəzbəːg/ *n.* Санкт-Петербу́рг.

straddle /ˈstræd(ə)l/ *v.t.* охва́т|ывать, -и́ть.

straggl|e /ˈstræg(ə)l/ *v.i.*: **the children ~ed home from school** де́ти бре́ли/тащи́лись из шко́лы домо́й; **a ~ing line of houses** беспоря́дочный ряд домо́в.

straggler /ˈstræglə(r)/ *n.* отста́вший.

straggly /ˈstræglɪ/ *adj.* (**stragglier, straggliest**) (*hair*) всклоко́ченный, растрёпанный; (*plants*) увя́дший.

straight /streɪt/ *n.* (*of racecourse*): **home ~** фи́нишная пряма́я.
■ *adj.* 1 прямо́й; **in a ~ line** пря́мо в ряд; **she had ~ hair** у неё бы́ли прямы́е во́лосы; **I couldn't keep a ~ face** я не мог удержа́ться от улы́бки.
2 (*level*) ро́вный; (*neat, in order*) у́бранный, приведённый в поря́док; **put the record ~** (*fig.*) вн|оси́ть, -ести́ я́сность; **let's get this ~** дава́йте внесём определённость в э́тот вопро́с.
3 (*direct*) прямо́й, че́стный.
4 (*orthodox*): **~ play** (*theatr.*) (чи́стая) дра́ма; (*heterosexual*) гетеросексуа́льный.
5 (*undiluted*) неразба́вленный.
■ *adv.* 1 пря́мо; **sit (up) ~!** сиди́(те) пря́мо!; **keep ~ on!** иди́те пря́мо!; (*directly*): **I am going ~ to Paris** я е́ду пря́мо в Пари́ж; **I told him ~ (out)** я сказа́л ему́ пря́мо.
2: **~ away, off** сра́зу, то́тчас.
■ *cpd.* **~forward** *adj.* (*frank*) прямо́й; (*uncomplicated*) просто́й.

straighten /ˈstreɪt(ə)n/ *v.t.*
1 выпрямля́ть, вы́прямить; распрям|ля́ть, -и́ть; **he ~ed his back** он вы́прямился; он распрями́л спи́ну.
2 (*put in order*) прив|оди́ть, -ести́ в поря́док; ула́|живать, -дить; **I will try to ~ things out** я постара́юсь всё ула́дить.

strain /streɪn/ *n.*
1 (*tension*) натяже́ние; (*wearing effect*): **the ~s of modern life** напряжённость/стресс совреме́нной жи́зни; (*muscular ~*) растяже́ние (мы́шцы).
2 (*of animals, plants*) поро́да.
■ *v.t.* 1 (*exert*) напр|яга́ть, -я́чь; **I ~ed my ears to catch his words** я напря́г слух, что́бы улови́ть его́ слова́.
2 (*overexert*): **~ one's eyes** переутом|ля́ть, -и́ть глаза́; по́ртить, ис- зре́ние; **~ o.s.** над|рыва́ться, -орва́ться.
3 (*overtax*): **~ s.o.'s patience** испы́тывать (*impf.*) чьё-н. терпе́ние.
4 (*filter, also* **~ off**) проце́|живать, -ди́ть; отце́|живать, -ди́ть; сце́|живать, -ди́ть.
■ *v.i.* (*exert o.s.*) напр|яга́ться, -я́чься.

strainer /ˈstreɪnə(r)/ *n.* си́то; (*tea ~*) си́течко.

strait /streɪt/ *n.*
1 (*of water*) проли́в.
2: **in dire ~s** в отча́янном положе́нии.
■ *cpds.* **~jacket** *n.* смири́тельная руба́шка; **~-laced** *adj.* (*fig.*) пурита́нский.

straitened /ˈstreɪtənd/ *adj.*: **~ circumstances** стеснённые обстоя́тельства.

strand[1] /strænd/ *v.t.* сажа́ть, посади́ть на мель; **I was ~ed in Paris** я застря́л в Пари́же.

strand[2] /strænd/ *n.* (*fibre, thread*) прядь, нить.

strange /streɪndʒ/ *adj.*
1 (*unfamiliar*) незнако́мый, неизве́стный.
2 (*remarkable*) стра́нный, необыкнове́нный, необы́чный; **~ to say (*or* ~ly enough) he loves her** как (э́то) ни стра́нно, он лю́бит её.

strangeness /ˈstreɪndʒnɪs/ *n.* (*remarkableness*) стра́нность; (*unfamiliarity*) непривы́чность.

stranger /ˈstreɪndʒə(r)/ *n.*
1 (*unknown person*) незнако́м|ец (*fem.* -ка); посторо́нний (челове́к).
2 (*foreigner*): **I am a ~ here** я здесь чужо́й.

strangle /ˈstræŋg(ə)l/ *v.t.* души́ть, за-; удави́ть (*pf.*).

■ *cpd.* **~hold** *n.* (*lit., fig.*) заси́лье.
strap /stræp/ *n.* реме́нь (*m.*); (*of dress*) брете́лька.
■ *v.t.* (**strapped, strapping**) стя́|гивать, -ну́ть ремнём.
strapless /ˈstræplɪs/ *adj.* без брете́лек.
strapping /ˈstræpɪŋ/ *adj.* ро́слый, здоро́вый (*coll.*).
Strasbourg /ˈstræzbəːg/ *n.* Стра́сбург.
strata /ˈstrɑːtə/ *pl. of* ▶ **stratum**
stratagem /ˈstrætədʒəm/ *n.* уло́вка.
strategic /strəˈtiːdʒɪk/ *adj.* стратеги́ческий.
strategist /ˈstrætɪdʒɪst/ *n.* страте́г.
strategy /ˈstrætədʒɪ/ *n.* страте́гия.
stratif|y /ˈstrætɪfaɪ/ *v.t.* (*arrange in strata*) насл|а́ивать, -о́ить; (*deposit in strata*) напласто́в|ывать, -а́ть; **~ied rock** слои́стый ка́мень.
stratosphere /ˈstrætəsfɪə(r)/ *n.* стратосфе́ра.
strat|um /ˈstrɑːtəm/ *n.* (*pl.* **~a**) слой.
straw /strɔː/ *n.*
1 (*collect.*) соло́ма; (*attr.*) соло́менный.
2 (*single* ~) соло́минка; **clutch at ~s** (*fig.*) хвата́ться, схвати́ться за соло́минку; **that was the last ~** э́то бы́ло после́дней ка́плей; **~ poll,** (*US*) **vote** (неофициа́льный) опро́с; голосова́ние.
strawberry /ˈstrɔːbərɪ/ *n.* (*pl., collect.*) клубни́ка; (*wild*) земляни́ка.
stray /streɪ/ *adj.*
1 (*wandering, lost*) заблуди́вшийся, бездо́мный; **~ dog** бездо́мная соба́ка.
2 (*sporadic*): **a ~ bullet** шальна́я пу́ля.
■ *v.i.* 1 (*wander*) заблуди́ться (*pf.*); сбива́ться, сби́ться с пути́; **we must not ~ too far from the path** мы не должны́ отклоня́ться сли́шком далеко́ от тропи́нки.
2 (*of thoughts, affections*) блужда́ть (*impf.*).
streak /striːk/ *n.*
1 поло́ска, прожи́лка; **~ of lightning** вспы́шка мо́лнии.
2 (*fig., trace, tendency*) черта́, накло́нность.
■ *v.t.*: **~ed with red** с кра́сными поло́сками.
■ *v.i.* (*coll., move rapidly*) прон|оси́ться, -ести́сь.
stream /striːm/ *n.*
1 (*brook*) руче́й; (*rivulet*) ре́чка.
2 (*flow*) пото́к, тече́ние; **~ of abuse** пото́к руга́тельств (*nt. pl.*)/бра́ни.
■ *v.i.* течь, струи́ться, ли́ться (*all impf.*); **tears ~ed down her cheeks** слёзы струи́лись/лили́сь/текли́ у неё по щека́м; **light ~ed in at the window** свет струи́лся в окно́; **her eyes were ~ing** у неё из глаз лили́сь слёзы.
■ *cpds.* **~line** *v.t.* прид|ава́ть, -а́ть обтека́емую фо́рму + *d.*; (*fig.*) упро|ща́ть, -сти́ть; **~lined** *adj.* стро́йный; упрощённый.
streamer /ˈstriːmə(r)/ *n.* руло́н бума́жной ле́нты; (*flag*) вы́мпел.
street /striːt/ *n.* у́лица; **he lives in the next ~ (to us)** он живёт на сосе́дней у́лице.
■ *cpds.* **~car** *n.* (*US*) трамва́й; **~ credibility** (*coll.* **~ cred**) *n.* и́мидж; **~ lamp** *n.* у́личный фона́рь; **~wise** *adj.* (*coll.*) о́пытный, зна́ющий, у́шлый.
strength /streŋkθ/ *n.*
1 си́ла; (*of structure, material, beam*) про́чность; (*of wine, solution*) кре́пость; (*of a colour*) усто́йчивость.
2 (*basis*): **on the ~ of** на основа́нии + *g.*
strengthen /ˈstreŋkθ(ə)n/ *v.t.* укреп|ля́ть, -и́ть; уси́ли|вать, -ть.
strenuous /ˈstrenjʊəs/ *adj.* (*requiring effort*) напряжённый; (*energetic*) уси́ленный, интенси́вный.
stress /stres/ *n.*
1 (*tension*) напряже́ние; (*pressure*) давле́ние, нажи́м; (*psych.*) стресс.
2 (*emphasis*) ударе́ние; **lay ~ on** (*lit., fig.*) де́лать, с- ударе́ние на + *p.*
■ *v.t.* 1 (*subject to* ~) напр|яга́ть, -я́чь; **I'm ~ed out** я живу́ в постоя́нном стре́ссе/напряже́нии.
2 (*emphasize*) подчёрк|ивать, -ну́ть; де́лать, с- упо́р на + *a.*
stressful /ˈstresfʊl/ *adj.* стре́ссовый.
stretch /stretʃ/ *n.*
1 (*elasticity*) растяжи́мость, эласти́чность; **~ fabric** эласти́чная мате́рия.
2 (*expanse*) простра́нство.
3 (*of time*) отре́зок; **he works 8 hours at a ~** он рабо́тает во́семь часо́в подря́д.
■ *v.t.* 1 (*lengthen*) вытя́гивать, вы́тянуть; (*broaden*) растя́|гивать, -ну́ть.
2 (*pull to fullest extent*): **~ a rope between two posts** натя́|гивать, -ну́ть верёвку ме́жду двумя́ столба́ми; **~ o.s.** потя́|гиваться, -ну́ться; **~ one's legs** разм|ина́ть, -я́ть но́ги.
3 (*strain, exert*): **~ the truth** преувели́чи|вать, -ть.
■ *v.i.* 1 (*be elastic*) растя́гиваться (*impf.*).
2 (*extend*) прост|ира́ться, -ере́ться; (*of time*) дли́ться, про-.
3 (~ *o.s.*) потя́|гиваться, -ну́ться.
stretcher /ˈstretʃə(r)/ *n.*носи́л|ки (*pl., g.* -ок).
strew /struː/ *v.t.* (*p.p.* **strewn** *or* **strewed**) разбр|а́сывать, -оса́ть.
stricken /ˈstrɪkən/ *adj.* (*lit.*) ра́неный; (*fig.*) поражённый.
strict /strɪkt/ *adj.*
1 (*precise*) стро́гий, то́чный.
2 (*stringent*): **in ~ confidence** в строжа́йшей та́йне.
3 (*stern*) стро́гий, взыска́тельный.
stride /straɪd/ *n.* (широ́кий) шаг; **he took the exam in his ~** он с лёгкостью сдал экза́мен; **science has made great ~s** нау́ка доби́лась больши́х успе́хов.
■ *v.i.* (*past* **strode;** *p.p.* **stridden** /ˈstrɪd(ə)n/) шага́ть (*impf.*).
strident /ˈstraɪd(ə)nt/ *adj.* ре́зкий, пронзи́тельный.
strife /straɪf/ *n.* борьба́, вражда́.
strike /straɪk/ *n.*
1 (*of workers*) забасто́вка; **be on ~** бастова́ть (*impf.*); **go on ~** забастова́ть (*pf.*).
2 (*attack; blow*) нападе́ние; уда́р; налёт.
■ *v.t.* (*past* **struck;** *p.p.* **struck** *or arch.* **stricken**)
1 (*hit*) уд|аря́ть, -а́рить (*чем по чему; что обо что; кого чем*); **the ship struck a rock** кора́бль наскочи́л на скалу́.
2 (*fig., impress*) пора|жа́ть, -зи́ть; каза́ться, по- + *d.*; **he was struck by her beauty** он

был поражён её красотой; **the idea ~s me as a good one** эта мысль кажется мне удачной.
3 (*fig., discover*) нап|адать, -асть на + *a.*; на|ходить, -йти; откр|ывать, -ыть; **they struck oil** они открыли нефтяное месторождение.
4 : **~ a match** чирк|ать, -нуть спичкой.
5 (*of bell, clock etc.*) бить (*impf.*), проб|ивать, -ить; **the clock struck midnight** часы пробили полночь.
6 (*arrive at*): **~ a bargain** заключ|ать, -ить сделку; **~ a balance** подв|одить, -ести баланс/итоги; (*fig.*) на|ходить, -йти компромисс.
■ *v.i.* (*past* **struck;** *p.p.* **struck** *or* (*arch.*) **stricken**)
1 (*hit*) уд|арять, -арить.
2 (*of clock etc.*) бить, про-.
3 (*go on* ~) бастовать (*impf.*) (**for:** чтобы добиться + *g.*).
■ *with advs.*: **~ down** *v.t.* (*fell*) сби|вать, -ть с ног; сра|жать, -зить; (*of illness etc.*) свал|ивать, -ить; сра|жать, -зить; **~ off** *v.t.*: **~ s.o. (*or* s.o.'s name) off** (*list etc.*) вычёркивать, вычеркнуть кого-н. (*or* чьё-н. имя) (из списка *и т. п.*); **~ out** *v.t.* (*delete*) вычёркивать, вычеркнуть; **~ up** *v.t. & i.*: **~ up an acquaintance** завяз|ывать, -ать знакомство; *v.i.* (*begin playing/singing*) заиграть, запеть (*both pf.*).

striker /'straɪkə(r)/ *n.*
1 (*person on strike*) забастовщи|к (*fem.* -ца).
2 (*sport*) нападающий.

striking /'straɪkɪŋ/ *adj.* поразительный, замечательный.

string /strɪŋ/ *n.*
1 верёвка, бечёвка; **pull ~s** наж|имать, -ать на все кнопки.
2 (*of mus. instrument, racket*) струна; **the ~s** (*of orchestra*) струнные инструменты (*m. pl.*); **~ quartet** струнный квартет.
3 (*set of objects*): **~ of pearls** нитка жемчуга; **~ of onions/sausages** связка лука/сосисок; **~ of boats/houses** ряд лодок/домов.
■ *v.t. & i.* (*past and p.p.* **strung**): **~ along** *v.t.* (*coll., deceive*) водить (*impf.*) за нос; *v.i.*: **~ along with s.o.** (*coll., accompany*) тащиться, по- за кем-н.

stringent /'strɪndʒ(ə)nt/ *adj.* строгий, точный.

strip[1] /strɪp/ *n.* полоса; (*of cloth*) полоска, лента; **~ of land** полоска земли; **~ cartoon** рассказ в картинках; **~ lighting** (*Br.*) неоновое освещение.

strip[2] /strɪp/ *v.t.* (**stripped, stripping**)
1 (*tear off*) сдирать, содрать.
2 (*denude*) разд|евать, -еть; **the room was ~ped bare** из комнаты вынесли всю мебель; **~ (down) a machine/weapon** раз|бирать, -обрать (*or* демонтировать (*impf., pf.*)) машину/оружие.
■ *v.i.* (**stripped, stripping**): **~ (naked), ~ off** разд|еваться, -еться (донага).

stripe /straɪp/ *n.* полоса, полоска.

striped /straɪpt/ *adj.* полосатый.

stripling /'strɪplɪŋ/ *n.* юнец.

stripper /'strɪpə(r)/ *n.* стриптизёр (*fem.* -ка/-ша).

strive /straɪv/ *v.i.* (*past* **strove** *or* **strived;** *p.p.* **striven** /'strɪv(ə)n/ *or* **strived**) стремиться (*impf.*) (**after, for:** к + *d.*).

strode /strəʊd/ *past of* ▸ **stride**

stroke[1] /strəʊk/ *n.*
1 удар; **at a ~** (*fig.*) одним ударом/махом.
2 (*paralytic attack*) удар, инсульт.
3 (*in swimming*) стиль (*m.*).
4 (*single instance*): **~ of genius** гениальная мысль; **~ of luck** (неожиданная) удача; везение.
5 (*with pen etc.*) штрих; (*with brush*) мазок.

stroke[2] /strəʊk/ *v.t.* гладить, по-.

stroll /strəʊl/ *n.* прогулка.
■ *v.i.* гулять (*impf.*); прогул|иваться, -яться.

stroller /'strəʊlə(r)/ *n.* (*US, for child*) прогулочная коляска.

strong /strɒŋ/ *adj.* (**stronger** /'strɒŋgə(r)/; **strongest** /'strɒŋgɪst/)
1 (*powerful*) сильный, крепкий; **~ measures** крутые меры; **~ argument** веский аргумент; **~ evidence** убедительное доказательство.
2 (*tough; durable*) крепкий; прочный; **~ cloth** крепкая материя; **~ walls** прочные стены.
3 (*robust*) крепкий, здоровый.
4 : (*of faculties*) **oratory is his ~ point** его сила в красноречии.
5 (*of smell, taste etc.*): **~ flavour** (*Br.*), **flavor** (*US*) острый/резкий привкус.
6 (*concentrated*): **~ drink** крепкий напиток; **a ~ cup of tea** чашка крепкого чая.
7 (*sharply defined*): **~ light** резкий свет; **~ accent** сильный акцент.
■ *adv.*: **going ~** в прекрасной форме.
■ *cpds.* **~hold** *n.* крепость, твердыня; **~-willed** *adj.* решительный, волевой.

strongly /'strɒŋlɪ/ *adv.* сильно, крепко; (*fig.*) твёрдо; **I ~ believe that** я твёрдо убеждён, что; **I feel ~ about** я твёрдо уверен в *чём* (*or* в том, что); **I am ~ opposed to** я (настроен) решительно против + *g.*

stroppy /'strɒpɪ/ *adj.* (**stroppier, stroppiest**) (*Br. coll.*) несговорчивый, сварливый, строптивый.

strove /strəʊv/ *past of* ▸ **strive**

struck /strʌk/ *past and p.p. of* ▸ **strike**

structural /'strʌktʃər(ə)l/ *adj.*: **~ defects** дефекты (в) конструкции; **~ engineer** инженер-строитель (*m.*).

structure /'strʌktʃə(r)/ *n.*
1 (*abstr.*) структура.
2 (*concr.*) строение, сооружение; (*building*) здание.
■ *v.t.* строить, по-; организов|ывать, -ать.

struggle /'strʌg(ə)l/ *n.* (*lit., fig.*) борьба; (*tussle*) схватка, потасовка.
■ *v.i.* 1 (*fight*) бороться (*impf.*); биться (*impf.*).
2 (*try hard*) бороться (*impf.*); **he ~d to make himself heard** он изо всех сил пытался перекричать других; **he ~d for breath** он хватал ртом воздух; **he ~d to his feet** он с трудом поднялся на ноги.

strum /strʌm/ *v.t. & i.* (**strummed, strumming**) бренчать (*impf.*) (на + *p.*).

strung /strʌŋ/ *past and p.p. of* ▸ **string**

strut[1] /strʌt/ *v.i.* (**strutted, strutting**) ходить (*indet.*) с важным видом.

strut² /strʌt/ *n.* (*support*) стóйка, распóрка, подпóрка.

stub /stʌb/ *n.* (*of pencil*) огры́зок; (*of cigarette*) окýрок; (*of cheque etc.*) корешóк.
■ *v.t.* (**stubbed, stubbing**)
1: **~ (out) a cigarette** гаси́ть, по- папирóсу.
2: **~ one's toe on sth.** спот|ыкáться, -кнýться о(бо) что-н.

stubble /ˈstʌb(ə)l/ *n.* жнивьё, стерня́ (*сжатое поле с остатками соломы на корню*); (*of beard*) щети́на.

stubborn /ˈstʌbən/ *adj.* упря́мый.

stuck /stʌk/ *past and p.p. of* ▶ **stick²**

stuck-up /ˈstʌkˈʌp/ *adj.* (*coll., conceited*) высокомéрный.

stud¹ /stʌd/ *n.* (*of horses*) кóнный завóд.

stud² /stʌd/ *n.* (*metal decoration*) кнóпка; (*on boots*) шип; (*collar ~*) зáпонка.

student /ˈstju:d(ə)nt/ *n.* студéнт (*fem.* -ка); (*attr.*) студéнческий; (*pupil*) учени́|к (*fem.* -ца), учáщ|ийся (*fem.* -аяся); **~ teacher** учи́тель-практикáнт (*fem.* учи́тельница-практикáнтка).

studio /ˈstju:dɪəʊ/ *n.* (*pl.* **~s**)
1 (*of artist etc.*) мастерскáя, стýдия, ателье́ (*nt. indecl.*).
2 (*broadcasting ~*) (*radio*) радиостýдия; (*TV*) телестýдия.
3 (*cin.*) киностýдия.

studious /ˈstju:dɪəs/ *adj.* усéрдный.

stud|y /ˈstʌdɪ/ *n.*
1 (*learning*) изучéние, учёба, наýка; **~ies** заня́тия (*nt. pl.*).
2 (*room*) кабинéт.
■ *v.t.* изуч|áть, -и́ть; исслéдовать (*impf., pf.*).
■ *v.i.* учи́ться (*impf.*).

stuff /stʌf/ *n.*
1 (*substance*) материáл, веществó, вещь.
2 (*coll., things*) вéщи (*f. pl.*).
■ *v.t.* 1 (*pack*) наб|ивáть, -и́ть (*что чем*); (*cul.*) фаршировáть, за-; начин|я́ть, -и́ть.
2 (*cram*) запи́х|ивать, -áть/-нýть (*что во что*).

stuffing /ˈstʌfɪŋ/ *n.*
1 (*of cushion etc.*) наби́вка.
2 (*cul.*) начи́нка, фарш.

stuffy /ˈstʌfɪ/ *adj.* (**stuffier, stuffiest**) (*of room*) дýшный; (*of person*) чóпорный.

stultify /ˈstʌltɪfaɪ/ *v.t.* (*deaden*) притуп|ля́ть, -и́ть.

stumbl|e /ˈstʌmb(ə)l/ *v.i.*
1 (*miss one's footing*) оступ|áться, -и́ться; спот|ыкáться, -кнýться; **~ing block** кáмень (*m.*) преткновéния.
2 (*speak haltingly*) зап|инáться, -нýться; спот|ыкáться, -кнýться.
3: **~e across, upon** (*find by chance*) нат|áлкиваться, -олкнýться на + *a.*

stump /stʌmp/ *n.* (*of tree*) пень (*m.*); (*of limb*) культя́, обрýбок; (*of pencil*) огры́зок.
■ *v.t.*: **I was ~ed by the question** э́тот вопрóс постáвил меня́ в тупи́к.

stun /stʌn/ *v.t.* (**stunned, stunning**)
1 (*knock unconscious*) оглуш|áть, -и́ть.
2 (*amaze*) пора|жáть, -зи́ть; **a ~ning dress** потрясáющее плáтье.

stung /stʌŋ/ *past and p.p. of* ▶ **sting**

stunk /stʌŋk/ *past and p.p. of* ▶ **stink**

stunt /stʌnt/ *n.* трюк, нóмер; **~ man** (*cin.*) каскадёр.
■ *v.t.*: **~ growth** задéрж|ивать, -áть рост; **~ed trees** низкорóслые дерéвья.

stupefy /ˈstju:pɪfaɪ/ *v.t.* ошелом|ля́ть, -и́ть.

stupendous /stju:ˈpendəs/ *adj.* изуми́тельный; (*in size*) огрóмный, колоссáльный.

stupid /ˈstju:pɪd/ *adj.* (**stupider, stupidest**) глýпый.

stupidity /stju:ˈpɪdɪtɪ/ *n.* глýпость.

stupor /ˈstju:pə(r)/ *n.* остолбенéние, стýпор.

sturdy /ˈstə:dɪ/ *adj.* (**sturdier, sturdiest**) (*person*) крéпкий; (*thing*) прóчный.

sturgeon /ˈstə:dʒ(ə)n/ *n.* осётр; (*as food*) осётр, осетри́на.

stutter /ˈstʌtə(r)/ *n.* заикáние.
■ *v.i.* заикáться (*impf.*).

sty, stye /staɪ/ *n.* (*on eye*) ячмéнь (*m.*).

style /staɪl/ *n.*
1 (*manner*) стиль (*m.*), манéра.
2 (*elegance*): **she has ~** у неё есть вкус; **live in ~** жить (*impf.*) широкó.
3 (*fashion*) мóда, фасóн.
■ *v.t.*: **she had her hair ~d** она́ сдéлала себé причёску.

stylish /ˈstaɪlɪʃ/ *adj.* (*fashionable*) мóдный; (*smart*) элегáнтный, сти́льный.

stylishness /ˈstaɪlɪʃnɪs/ *n.* элегáнтность.

stylist /ˈstaɪlɪst/ *n.* стили́ст; **hair ~** парикмáхер-модельéр.

stylistic /staɪˈlɪstɪk/ *adj.* стилисти́ческий.

stylize /ˈstaɪlaɪz/ *v.t.* стилизовáть (*impf., pf.*).

stymie /ˈstaɪmɪ/ *v.t.* (**stymies, stymied, stymying** *or* **stymieing**) (*fig.*) мешáть (*impf.*) + *d.*; препя́тствовать (*impf.*) + *d.*

suave /swɑ:v/ *adj.* обходи́тельный, учти́вый.

subconscious /sʌbˈkɒnʃəs/ *n.* (*the ~*) подсознáние.
■ *adj.* подсознáтельный.

subcontinent /sʌbˈkɒntɪnənt/ *n.* субконтинéнт.

subcontract /sʌbkənˈtrækt/ *v.t.*: **the work was ~ed out** рабóту óтдали субподря́дчику.

subcontractor /sʌbkənˈtræktə(r)/ *n.* субподря́дчик.

subculture /ˈsʌbkʌltʃə(r)/ *n.* субкультýра.

subdivide /ˈsʌbdɪvaɪd/ *v.t. & i.* подраздел|я́ть(ся), -и́ть(ся).

subdivision /ˈsʌbdɪvɪʒ(ə)n/ *n.* подразделéние.

subdue /səbˈdju:/ *v.t.* (**subdues, subdued, subduing**)
1 (*subjugate*) подав|ля́ть, -и́ть.
2 (*soften*) смягч|áть, -и́ть; **~d light** мя́гкий свет.
3 (*restrain*): **he seems ~d today** он сегóдня что-то притих.

subedit /ˈsʌbedɪt/ *v.t.* (**subedited, subediting**) (*Br.*) редакти́ровать, от- пéред набóром; готóвить, под- к набóру.

subeditor /ˈsʌbedɪtə(r)/ *n.* (*Br.*) помóщник редáктора; техни́ческий редáктор (*abbr.* техрéд (*coll.*)).

subhuman /sʌbˈhju:mən/ *n.* недочеловéк.

S

■ *adj.* нечелове́ческий.

subject[1] /'sʌbdʒɪkt/ *n.*
1 (*pol.*) по́дданный.
2 (*gram.*) подлежа́щее.
3 (*theme*) те́ма, предме́т; **change the ~** перев|оди́ть, -ести́ разгово́р на другу́ю те́му.
4 (*branch of study*) предме́т.
■ *adj.* 1 (*subordinate*) подчинённый; **all citizens are ~ to the law** зако́н распространя́ется на всех гра́ждан.
2 (*liable*): **he is ~ to changes of mood** он подве́ржен (бы́стрым) сме́нам настрое́ния; **trains are ~ to delay** возмо́жны опозда́ния поездо́в.
3 : **~ to** (*conditional upon*) подлежа́щий + *d.*; **the treaty is ~ to ratification** догово́р подлежи́т ратифика́ции.
■ *cpd.* **~ matter** *n.* содержа́ние, предме́т (*чего*).

subject[2] /səb'dʒekt/ *v.t.* (*expose*) подв|ерга́ть, -е́ргнуть (*кого/что чему*); **he was ~ed to insult** его́ подве́ргли оскорбле́нию.

subjective /səb'dʒektɪv/ *adj.* субъекти́вный.

subjectivity /sʌbdʒek'tɪvɪtɪ/ *n.* субъекти́вность.

sub judice /sʌb 'dʒu:dɪsɪ/ *adj.* находя́щийся на рассмотре́нии (суда́).

subjugate /'sʌbdʒʊgeɪt/ *v.t.* покор|я́ть, -и́ть.

subjunctive /səb'dʒʌŋktɪv/ *n.* сослага́тельное наклоне́ние.

sublet /'sʌblet/ (**-letting;** *past and p.p.* **~let**) перед|ава́ть, -а́ть в субаре́нду.

sublime /sə'blaɪm/ *adj.* (**sublimer, sublimest**) возвы́шенный.

subliminal /səb'lɪmɪn(ə)l/ *adj.* подсозна́тельный.

submachine gun /sʌbmə'ʃi:n gʌn/ *n.* автома́т (*оружие*).

submarine /sʌbmə'ri:n/ *n.* подво́дная ло́дка.

submerge /səb'mə:dʒ/ *v.t.* & *i.* погру|жа́ть(ся), -зи́ть(ся).

submission /səb'mɪʃ(ə)n/ *n.*
1 (*subjection*) подчине́ние.
2 (*presentation*) представле́ние, предъявле́ние.

submissive /səb'mɪsɪv/ *adj.* поко́рный, смире́нный.

submit /səb'mɪt/ *v.t.* (**submitted, submitting**) (*present*) предст|авля́ть, -а́вить.
■ *v.i.* (**submitted, submitting**) подчин|я́ться, -и́ться.

subordinate /sə'bɔ:dɪnət/ *n.* подчинённый.
■ *adj.* подчинённый.

subpoena /sə'pi:nə/ *v.t.* (*past and p.p.* **subpoenaed** *or* **subpoena'd**) вызыва́ть, вы́звать в суд.

subscribe /səb'skraɪb/ *v.i.*: **~ to a journal** подпи́с|ываться, -а́ться на журна́л; **I cannot ~ to that view** я не могу́ согласи́ться с э́тим мне́нием.

subscriber /səb'skraɪbə(r)/ *n.* подпи́счик.

subscription /səb'skrɪpʃ(ə)n/ *n.* (*fee*) взнос; **~ to a newspaper** подпи́ска на газе́ту.

subsequent /'sʌbsɪkwənt/ *adj.* после́дующий, сле́дующий; **~ly** впосле́дствии.

subservience /səb'sə:vɪəns/ *n.* раболе́пие, послуша́ние.

subservient /səb'sə:vɪənt/ *adj.* раболе́пный.

subset /'sʌbset/ *n.* гру́ппа (*в составе чего-л.*).

subside /səb'saɪd/ *v.i.*
1 (*of ground or building*) ос|еда́ть, -е́сть.
2 (*of water*) спа|да́ть, -сть.
3 (*of fever*) па́дать, упа́сть; (*of wind, storm etc.*) ут|иха́ть, -и́хнуть.

subsidence /səb'saɪd(ə)ns/ *n.* (*of ground*) оседа́ние, оса́дка.

subsidiary /səb'sɪdɪərɪ/ *n.* (*comm.*) филиа́л.
■ *adj.* вспомога́тельный, второстепе́нный; (*of company*) доче́рний.

subsidize /'sʌbsɪdaɪz/ *v.t.* субсиди́ровать (*impf., pf.*).

subsidy /'sʌbsɪdɪ/ *n.* субси́дия.

subsist /səb'sɪst/ *v.i.* существова́ть (*impf.*).

subsistence /səb'sɪst(ə)ns/ *n.* существова́ние.

substance /'sʌbst(ə)ns/ *n.*
1 (*essential elements*) суть.
2 (*type of matter*) вещество́.
3 (*solidity*): **a piece of writing that lacks ~** сочине́ние, лишённое содержа́ния; **there is no ~ in the rumour** (*Br.*), **rumor** (*US*) э́тот слух ниче́м не подкреплён.

substandard /sʌb'stændəd/ *adj.* нестанда́ртный, низкока́чественный.

substantial /səb'stænʃ(ə)l/ *adj.*
1 (*solid*) кре́пкий; **a ~ building** соли́дное зда́ние; **a ~ dinner** сы́тный обе́д.
2 (*considerable*): **a ~ sum** поря́дочная су́мма; **a ~ improvement** значи́тельное/заме́тное улучше́ние.

substantiate /səb'stænʃɪeɪt/ *v.t.* обосно́в|ывать, -а́ть.

substitute /'sʌbstɪtju:t/ *n.* (*person*) заме́на, замести́тель (*m.*); (*in sport*) запасно́й (*игрок*).
■ *v.t.* (*use instead*) испо́льзовать (*impf., pf.*) (**for:** вме́сто + *g.*).
■ *v.i.*: **~ for** заме|ща́ть, -сти́ть; подмен|я́ть, -и́ть; (*sport*) замен|я́ть, -и́ть (*игрока*).

substitution /sʌbstɪ'tju:ʃ(ə)n/ *n.* заме́на, замеще́ние, подме́на.

subsume /səb'sju:m/ *v.t.* включ|а́ть, -и́ть в каку́ю-н. катего́рию; отн|оси́ть, -ести́ к како́й-н. катего́рии, гру́ппе *и т. п.*

subterfuge /'sʌbtəfju:dʒ/ *n.* уло́вка.

subterranean /sʌbtə'reɪnɪən/ *adj.* подзе́мный.

subtitles /'sʌbtaɪt(ə)lz/ *n. pl.* (*cin.*) субти́тры (*m. pl.*).

subtle /'sʌt(ə)l/ *adj.* (**subtler, subtlest**) (*fine, perceptive*) то́нкий; (*refined*) утончённый.

subtlety /'sʌtəltɪ/ *n.* то́нкость; утончённость.

subtotal /'sʌbtəʊt(ə)l/ *n.* промежу́точный ито́г.

subtract /səb'trækt/ *v.t.* вычита́ть, вы́честь.

subtraction /səb'trækʃ(ə)n/ *n.* вычита́ние.

subtropical /sʌb'trɒpɪk(ə)l/ *adj.* субтропи́ческий.

suburb /'sʌbə:b/ *n.* при́город.

suburban /sə'bə:bən/ *adj.* при́городный.

suburbia /sə'bə:bɪə/ *n.* (*collect.*) при́городы (*m. pl.*).

subversion /səb'və:ʃ(ə)n/ *n.* подрывна́я де́ятельность.

subversive /səb'və:sɪv/ *adj.* подрывно́й.

subway /'sʌbweɪ/ *n.* (*Br., passage under road*) подзе́мный перехо́д; (*US, railway*) метро́ (*nt. indecl.*), подзе́мка (*coll.*).

sub-zero /sʌb'zɪərəʊ/ *adj.*: **~ temperatures** минусовы́е температу́ры.

succeed /sək'si:d/ *v.t.* (*as heir*) насле́довать (*impf., pf.*) + *d.*; (*as replacement*) смен|я́ть, -и́ть. ■ *v.i.* (*be, become successful*) преусп|ева́ть, -е́ть; доб|ива́ться, -и́ться успе́ха/своего́; **he ~ed in tricking us all** ему́ удало́сь всех нас обману́ть.

success /sək'ses/ *n.* успе́х, уда́ча; **my holidays were not a ~ this year** мои́ кани́кулы в э́том году́ бы́ли неуда́чными.

successful /sək'sesfʊl/ *adj.* успе́шный, уда́чный; **I tried to persuade him, but was not ~** я пыта́лся убеди́ть его́, но мне э́то не удало́сь.

succession /sək'seʃ(ə)n/ *n.*
1 (*sequence*) после́довательность; **in ~** подря́д.
2 (*series*) ряд, цепь.
3 (*succeeding to office etc.*) насле́дство, насле́дование (*о порядке передачи*).

successive /sək'sesɪv/ *adj.* после́довательный; **on three ~ occasions** три ра́за подря́д.

successor /sək'sesə(r)/ *n.* прее́мни|к (*fem.* -ца), насле́дни|к (*fem.* -ца).

succinct /sək'sɪŋkt/ *adj.* сжа́тый.

succulent /'sʌkjʊlənt/ *adj.* со́чный.

succumb /sə'kʌm/ *v.i.* уступ|а́ть, -и́ть; подд|ава́ться, -а́ться; **they ~ed to the enemy's superior force** они́ уступи́ли превосходя́щей си́ле проти́вника; **she did not ~ to temptation** она́ не поддала́сь искуше́нию.

such /sʌtʃ/ *adj.*
1 (*of the kind mentioned; of this, that kind*) тако́й; **~ places** таки́е места́; **I have never seen ~ a sight** я никогда́ не ви́дел подо́бного зре́лища; **I said no ~ thing** я ничего́ подо́бного не говори́л; **some ~ thing** что́-то в э́том ро́де; **how could you do ~ a thing?** как вы могли́ так поступи́ть?
2: **~ as** (*of a kind ...*): **~ grapes as you never saw** тако́й виногра́д, како́го вы в жи́зни не ви́дели; **I am not ~ a fool as to believe him** я не тако́й дура́к, что́бы пове́рить ему́; (*like*): **a picture ~ as that is valuable** тако́го ро́да карти́ны высоко́ це́нятся.
■ *cpds.* **~-and-~** *adj.* тако́й-то; **~like** *pron.* & *adj.* подо́бный; **theatres, cinemas and ~like** теа́тры, кино́ и тому́ подо́бное.

suck /sʌk/ *v.t.*
1 соса́ть (*impf.*); (**~ in**, *imbibe*) вс|а́сывать, -оса́ть; тяну́ть (*impf.*) (*через соломинку и т. п.*).
2 (*squeeze or dissolve in mouth*) соса́ть (*impf.*).
■ *with adv.*: **~ up** *v.t.* выса́сывать, вы́сосать; *v.i.*: **~ up to s.o.** (*coll.*) подли́з|ываться, -а́ться к кому́-н.

sucker /'sʌkə(r)/ *n.*
1 (*organ, device*) присо́ска, присо́сок.
2 (*bot.*) отро́сток, боково́й побе́г.
3 (*sl., gullible person*) проста́|к (*fem.* -чка), лох (*sl.*).

suction /'sʌkʃ(ə)n/ *n.* вса́сывание.

Sudan /su:'dɑ:n/ *n.* Суда́н.

Sudanese /su:də'ni:z/ *n.* (*pl.* ~) суда́н|ец (*fem.* -ка).
■ *adj.* суда́нский.

sudden /'sʌd(ə)n/ *n.*: **(all) of a ~** внеза́пно, вдруг.
■ *adj.* (*unexpected*) внеза́пный, неожи́данный.

suddenly /'sʌd(ə)nlɪ/ *adv.* внеза́пно, вдруг.

suddenness /'sʌd(ə)nnɪs/ *n.* внеза́пность, неожи́данность.

suds /sʌdz/ *n. pl.* мы́льная пе́на.

sue /sju:/ *v.t.* (**sues, sued, suing**) возбу|жда́ть, -ди́ть иск/де́ло про́тив + *g.*; (**for libel** за клевету́; **for damages** о возмеще́нии убы́тков).
■ *v.i.* под|ава́ть, -а́ть в суд (на + *a.*).

suede /sweɪd/ *n.* за́мша; (*attr.*) за́мшевый.

suet /'su:ɪt/ *n.* нутряно́е са́ло; по́чечный жир.

suffer /'sʌfə(r)/ *v.t.* испы́т|ывать, -а́ть; претерп|ева́ть, -е́ть; (*defeat*) терпе́ть, по-.
■ *v.i.* страда́ть (*impf.*) (от + *g.*); **he ~s from shyness** он (о́чень) засте́нчив; **he is ~ing from measles** он боле́ет ко́рью; у него́ корь.

sufferance /'sʌfərəns/ *n.*: **on ~** из ми́лости; с молчали́вого согла́сия.

sufferer /'sʌfrə(r)/ *n.* страда́лец.

suffering /'sʌfrɪŋ/ *n.* страда́ние.

suffice /sə'faɪs/ *v.i.* быть доста́точным; хват|а́ть, -и́ть.

sufficient /sə'fɪʃ(ə)nt/ *adj.* доста́точный.

suffix /'sʌfɪks/ *n.* су́ффикс.

suffocat|e /'sʌfəkeɪt/ *v.t.* души́ть, за-; **he was ~ed by poisonous fumes** он задохну́лся от ядови́того ды́ма; **~ing heat** уду́шливая жара́.
■ *v.i.* зад|ыха́ться, -охну́ться.

suffocation /sʌfə'keɪʃ(ə)n/ *n.* удуше́ние, уду́шье.

suffrage /'sʌfrɪdʒ/ *n.* избира́тельное пра́во.

sugar /'ʃʊgə(r)/ *n.* са́хар.
■ *cpds.* **~ beet** *n.* са́харная свёкла; **~ cane** *n.* са́харный тростни́к; **~ lump** *n.* кусо́(че)к са́хара.

sugary /'ʃʊgərɪ/ *adj.*
1 са́харный, са́хари́стый.
2 (*fig., of tone, smile etc.*) сла́дкий, слаща́вый.

suggest /sə'dʒest/ *v.t.* предл|ага́ть, -ожи́ть; сове́товать, по-; **I ~ you try again** я сове́тую вам попро́бовать ещё раз(о́к).

suggestion /sə'dʒestʃ(ə)n/ *n.*
1 (*proposal*) предложе́ние, сове́т.
2 (*implication*) намёк, до́ля; (*tinge*) отте́нок.

suggestive /sə'dʒestɪv/ *adj.* непристо́йный.

suicidal /su:ɪ'saɪd(ə)l/ *adj.* (*person*) скло́нный к самоуби́йству; (*action*) самоуби́йственный.

suicide /'su:ɪsaɪd/ *n.*
1 (*also fig.*) самоуби́йство; **commit ~** конча́ть, (по)ко́нчить с собо́й.
2 (*person*) самоуби́йца (*c.g.*).

suit /sju:t/ *n.*
1 (*of clothes*) костю́м.
2 (*leg.*) иск, де́ло.
3 (*of cards*) масть.
■ *v.t.* 1 (*be convenient for*) под|ходи́ть, -ойти́ + *d.*; устр|а́ивать, -о́ить; **would Sunday ~ you?** воскресе́нье вам подойдёт (*or* вас устро́ит)?

S

2 (*be appropriate or good for*) под|ходи́ть, -ойти́ + *d.*; **the role does not ~ him** э́та роль ему́ не подхо́дит; **they are ~ed to one another** они́ подхо́дят друг дру́гу.
3 (*please*): **he tries to ~ everybody** он стара́ется всем угоди́ть.
4 (*enhance*): **that hat ~s her** э́та шля́па ей идёт.
■ *cpd.* **~case** *n.* чемода́н.

suitable /'sju:təb(ə)l/ *adj.* подходя́щий, го́дный.

suitably /'sju:təblɪ/ *adv.* соотве́тственно, пра́вильно.

suite /swi:t/ *n.* (*set*): **~ of furniture** ме́бельный гарниту́р; (*in hotel*) (но́мер) люкс.

suitor /'sju:tə(r)/ *n.* (*wooer*) жени́х, покло́нник.

sulf- /'sʌlf/ (*US*) = **sulph-**

sulk /sʌlk/ *v.i.* быть в дурно́м настрое́нии.

sulky /'sʌlkɪ/ *adj.* (**sulkier, sulkiest**) (*person*) наду́тый, мра́чный.

sullen /'sʌlən/ *adj.* (*sulky*) наду́тый; (*sombre*) мра́чный.

sulphur /'sʌlfə(r)/ (*US* **sulfur**) *n.* се́ра.

sulphuric /sʌl'fjʊərɪk/ (*US* **sulfuric**) *adj.*: **~ acid** се́рная кислота́.

sultana /sʌl'tɑ:nə/ *n.* изю́минка; (*collect.*) кишми́ш (*об изюме*).

sultry /'sʌltrɪ/ *adj.* (**sultrier, sultriest**) зно́йный.

sum /sʌm/ *n.*
1 (*total*) ито́г.
2 (*amount*) су́мма.
3 (*calculation*) (арифмети́ческая) зада́ча.
■ *v.t.* (**summed, summing**) (*usu.* **~ up**) сумми́ровать (*impf., pf.*); подв|оди́ть, -ести́ ито́ги + *g.*
■ *v.i.* (**summed, summing**): **~ up** сумми́ровать (*impf., pf.*).

summarize /'sʌməraɪz/ *v.t.* сумми́ровать (*impf., pf.*); резюми́ровать (*impf., pf.*).

summary /'sʌmərɪ/ *n.* резюме́ (*nt. indecl.*), сво́дка.

summer /'sʌmə(r)/ *n.* ле́то; **in ~** ле́том; (*attr.*) ле́тний; **~ school** ле́тний университе́т.
■ *cpds.* **~house** *n.* бесе́дка; **~time** *n.* ле́тняя пора́.

summery /'sʌmərɪ/ *adj.*: **~ weather** ле́тняя/тёплая пого́да; **~ clothes** лёгкая/ле́тняя оде́жда.

summit /'sʌmɪt/ *n.* (*lit., fig.*) верши́на, верх; **~ (meeting)** са́ммит, встре́ча в верха́х.

summon /'sʌmən/ *v.t.*
1 (*send for*) приз|ыва́ть, -ва́ть; (*also leg.*) вызыва́ть, вы́звать.
2 : **~ up one's energy/courage** соб|ира́ться, -ра́ться с си́лами/ду́хом.

summons /'sʌmənz/ *n.* (*pl.* **~es**) вы́зов; (*leg.*) суде́бная пове́стка, вы́зов в суд.
■ *v.t.* вызыва́ть, вы́звать в суд.

sumptuous /'sʌmptjʊəs/ *adj.* роско́шный.

sun /sʌn/ *n.* со́лнце; (*astron.*) Со́лнце; **lie in the ~** лежа́ть (*impf.*) на со́лнце.
■ *cpds.* **~bathe** *v.i.* загора́ть (*impf.*); **~bed** *n.* (*Br.*) (*lounger*) шезло́нг; (*for acquiring tan*) соля́рий; **~burn** *n.* (*inflammation*) со́лнечный ожо́г; **~burnt** *adj.* (*tanned*) загоре́лый; (*inflamed*) обожжённый со́лнцем; **~dial** *n.* со́лнечные часы́ (*m. pl.*); **~flower** *n.* подсо́лнечник; **~glasses** *n. pl.* солнцезащи́тные очки́; **~ hat** *n.* шля́па от со́лнца; **~lamp** *n.* ква́рцевая ла́мпа; **~light** *n.* со́лнечный свет; **~rise** *n.* восхо́д (со́лнца); **at ~rise** на заре́; **~roof** *n.* (*of car*) раздвижна́я кры́ша; **~set** *n.* захо́д со́лнца, зака́т; **at ~set** на зака́те; **~shade** *n.* (со́лнечный) зо́нтик; **~shine** *n.* со́лнечный свет; **~stroke** *n.* со́лнечный уда́р; **~tan** *n.* зага́р; **~tan lotion** крем для зага́ра.

Sunday /'sʌndeɪ/ *n.* воскресе́нье.

sundries /'sʌndrɪz/ *n.* ра́зное.

sundry /'sʌndrɪ/ *adj.* ра́зный, разли́чный; **all and ~** всё и вся; все без исключе́ния.

sung /sʌŋ/ *p.p. of* ▸ **sing**

sunk /sʌŋk/ *past and p.p. of* ▸ **sink**

sunken /'sʌŋkən/ *adj.* (*of cheeks etc.*) впа́лый; (*submerged*) подво́дный.

Sunni /'sʊnɪ/ *n.* сунни́т.

sunny /'sʌnɪ/ *adj.* (**sunnier, sunniest**) со́лнечный; **a ~ disposition** жизнера́достный хара́ктер.

super /'su:pə(r)/ *adj.* замеча́тельный, превосхо́дный.

superb /su:'pə:b/ *adj.* превосхо́дный, великоле́пный.

supercilious /su:pə'sɪlɪəs/ *adj.* высокоме́рный.

superficial /su:pə'fɪʃ(ə)l/ *adj.* пове́рхностный.

superficiality /su:pəfɪʃɪ'ælɪtɪ/ *n.* пове́рхностность.

superfluous /su:'pə:flʊəs/ *adj.* изли́шний.

superhuman /su:pə'hju:mən/ *adj.* сверхчелове́ческий.

superimpose /su:pərɪm'pəʊz/ *v.t.* на|кла́дывать, -ложи́ть (*что на что*).

superintendent /su:pərɪn'tend(ə)nt/ *n.* (*manager*) заве́дующий; (*of police*) нача́льник; (*US, of a building*) коменда́нт.

superior /su:'pɪərɪə(r)/ *n.* ста́рший, нача́льник.
■ *adj.* 1 (*of higher rank*) ста́рший, вы́сший.
2 (*better*) превосхо́дный, превосходя́щий.
3 (*supercilious*): **a ~ smile** презри́тельная улы́бка; **don't look so ~!** бро́сьте э́ту ва́шу высокоме́рную мане́ру!

superiority /su:pɪərɪ'ɒrɪtɪ/ *n.* старшинство́.

superlative /su:'pə:lətɪv/ *n.* (*gram.*) превосхо́дная сте́пень.
■ *adj.* велича́йший, высоча́йший.

superman /'su:pəmæn/ *n.* (*pl.* **supermen**) сверхчелове́к, суперме́н.

supermarket /'su:pəmɑ:kɪt/ *n.* суперма́ркет.

supermodel /'su:pəmɒd(ə)l/ *n.* супермоде́ль.

supernatural /su:pə'nætʃər(ə)l/ *n.*: **a belief in the ~** ве́ра в сверхъесте́ственное.
■ *adj.* сверхъесте́ственный.

superpower /'su:pəpaʊə(r)/ *n.* сверхдержа́ва.

supersede /su:pə'si:d/ *v.t.* смен|я́ть, -и́ть.

supersonic /su:pə'sɒnɪk/ *adj.* сверхзвуково́й.

superstar /'su:pəstɑ:(r)/ *n.* суперзвезда́.
superstition /su:pə'stɪʃ(ə)n/ *n.* суеве́рие.
superstitious /su:pə'stɪʃəs/ *adj.* суеве́рный.
superstore /'su:pəstɔ:(r)/ *n.* гиперма́ркет.
superstructure /'su:pəstrʌktʃə(r)/ *n.* надстро́йка.
supervise /'su:pəvaɪz/ *v.t.* надзира́ть (*impf.*) за + *i.*
supervision /su:pə'vɪʒ(ə)n/ *n.* надсмо́тр/надзо́р (за + *i.*).
supervisor /'su:pəvaɪzə(r)/ *n.* надсмо́трщи|к (*fem.* -ца); (*acad.*) (нау́чный) руководи́тель.
supervisory /'su:pəvaɪzərɪ/ *adj.* контро́льный, надзира́ющий; ~ **body** контро́льный о́рган; ~ **duties** обя́занности по надзо́ру.
supine /'su:paɪn/ *adj.* (*face up*) лежа́щий на́взничь; (*fig.*) безде́ятельный, ине́ртный, вя́лый.
supper /'sʌpə(r)/ *n.* у́жин; **have** ~ у́жинать, по-.
supplant /sə'plɑ:nt/ *v.t.* (*replace*) вытесня́ть, вы́теснить; (*oust*) выжива́ть, вы́жить.
supple /'sʌp(ə)l/ *adj.* (**suppler, supplest**) ги́бкий.
supplement[1] /'sʌplɪmənt/ *n.*
1 (*dietary*) доба́вка.
2 (*of book etc.*) дополне́ние.
3 (*surcharge*) допла́та.
supplement[2] /'sʌplɪment/ *v.t.* доп|олня́ть, -о́лнить.
supplementary /sʌplɪ'mentərɪ/ *adj.* дополни́тельный, доба́вочный.
supplier /sə'plaɪə(r)/ *n.* поставщи́|к (*fem.* -ца).
suppl|y /sə'plaɪ/ *n.*
1 (*providing*) снабже́ние (*чем*).
2 (*thing supplied, stock*) запа́с; **take, lay in a** ~**y of sth.** запас|а́ться, -ти́сь чем-н.; **bread is in short** ~**y** хлеб в дефици́те; ~**ies** (*mil.*) (бое)припа́сы (*m. pl.*).
3 (*econ.*) предложе́ние; ~**y and demand** спро́с и предложе́ние.
4 : ~**y teacher** (*Br.*) внешта́тн|ый учи́тель, рабо́тающ|ий (*fem.* -ая, -ница, -ая) по замеще́нию.
■ *v.t.* 1 (*furnish, equip*) снаб|жа́ть, -ди́ть; обеспе́чи|вать, -ть (*both кого/что чем*); пита́ть (*impf.*).
2 (*give, yield*) да|ва́ть, -ть; дост|авля́ть, -а́вить (*что кому/чему*); **cows** ~**y milk** коро́вы даю́т молоко́.
support /sə'pɔ:t/ *n.* подде́ржка; **give, lend** ~ ока́з|ывать, -а́ть подде́ржку + *d.*; **in** ~ **of** в подде́ржку + *g.*
■ *v.t.* 1 (*hold up*) подде́рж|ивать, -а́ть; подп|ира́ть, -ере́ть; (*fig., assist*): **which party do you** ~**?** каку́ю па́ртию вы подде́рживаете?; ~**ing actor** акт|ёр (*fem.* -ри́са) второ́го пла́на.
2 (*provide subsistence for*) содержа́ть (*impf.*); **he cannot** ~ **a family** он не в состоя́нии содержа́ть семью́.
3 (*confirm*) подкреп|ля́ть, -и́ть.
4 (*a particular sports team*) боле́ть (*impf.*) за + *a.*
supporter /sə'pɔ:tə(r)/ *n.* (*of cause, motion etc.*) сторо́нни|к (*fem.* -ца), приве́рженец; (*Br., of sports team*) боле́льщи|к (*fem.* -ца).
supportive /sə'pɔ:tɪv/ *adj.* подде́рживающий, лоя́льный.
suppose /sə'pəʊz/ *v.t.*
1 (*assume*) предпол|ага́ть, -ожи́ть; допус|ка́ть, -ти́ть; **supposing he came, what would you say?** е́сли бы он пришёл, что бы вы сказа́ли?; ~ **they find out?** а вдруг они узна́ют?
2 (*imagine, believe*): **he is** ~**d to be rich** счита́ется/говоря́т, что он бога́т.
3 (*pass., be expected*): **this is** ~**d to help you sleep** э́то должно́ помо́чь вам засну́ть; **he is** ~**d to wash the dishes** ему́ поло́жено мыть посу́ду.
supposedly /sə'pəʊzɪdlɪ/ *adv.* предположи́тельно.
supposition /sʌpə'zɪʃ(ə)n/ *n.* предположе́ние, гипо́теза, дога́дка.
suppository /sə'pɒzɪtərɪ/ (*med.*) *n.* суппозито́рий, све́чка.
suppress /sə'pres/ *v.t.*
1 подав|ля́ть, -и́ть; сдер́ж|ивать, -а́ть.
2 (*conceal*) скры|ва́ть, -ть; **they succeeded in** ~**ing the truth** им удало́сь скрыть пра́вду.
suppression /sə'preʃ(ə)n/ *n.* (*restraining*) подавле́ние, сде́рживание; (*banning*) запреще́ние; (*silencing*) зама́лчивание.
supremacy /su:'preməsɪ/ *n.* господ́ство, превосхо́дство.
supreme /su:'pri:m/ *adj.*
1 (*of authority*) верхо́вный.
2 (*greatest*): **he made the** ~ **sacrifice** он поже́ртвовал (свое́й) жи́знью.
surcharge /'sə:tʃɑ:dʒ/ *n.* допла́та, припла́та.
sure /ʃɔ:(r)/ *adj.*
1 (*certain, confident*) уве́ренный, убеждённый; **he is very** ~ **of himself** он о́чень уве́рен в себе́; **I'm** ~ **you are right** я уве́рен (*or* не сомнева́юсь), что вы пра́вы; **I'm not** ~ **whether to go or not** я не зна́ю, пойти́ или нет.
2 (*safe*) ве́рный, надёжный; **there can be no** ~ **proof** абсолю́тных доказа́тельств не мо́жет быть.
3 (*with inf, certain, to be relied on*): **he is** ~ **to come** он непреме́нно придёт; **it is** ~ **to be wet** наверняка́ бу́дет дождли́во.
4 : **for** ~ несомне́нно, непреме́нно; то́чно, наверняка́.
5 : **make** ~ (*convince, satisfy o.s.*) убе|жда́ться, -ди́ться; удостов|еря́ться, -е́риться (*all в чём*).
6 : **I made** ~ (*ensured*) **that he would come** я позабо́тился о том, что́бы он (обяза́тельно) пришёл.
■ *adv.*: ~ **enough** действи́тельно, коне́чно.
■ *cpd.* ~**-fire** *adj.* (*coll.*) ве́рный, надёжный.
surely /'ʃɔ:lɪ/ *adv.*
1 (*without doubt*) несомне́нно, ве́рно, наверняка́.
2 (*expr. strong hope or belief*): ~ **I have met you before** я уве́рен, что мы с ва́ми встреча́лись.
surf /sə:f/ *n.* прибо́й.
■ *v.i.* занима́ться (*impf.*) сёрфингом.
■ *v.t.*: ~ **the Internet** путеше́ствовать (*impf.*)

по Интернéту.
■ *cpd.* **~board** *n.* доскá для сёрфинга.
surface /'sə:fɪs/ *n.*повéрхность; **his politeness is only on the ~** егó вéжливость чи́сто внéшняя/показнáя.
■ *v.t.*: **~ a road** покр|ывáть, -ы́ть дорóгу асфáльтом *и т. п.*
■ *v.i.* вспл|ывáть, -ы́ть на повéрхность.
surfeit /'sə:fɪt/ *n.* (*excess of eating etc.*) изли́шество, избы́ток; (*repletion, satiety; also fig.*) пресыщéние.
■ *v.t.* (**surfeited, surfeiting**) (*satiate*) прес|ыщáть, -ы́тить.
surfer /'sə:fə(r)/ *n.* сёрфинги́ст (*fem.* -ка); человéк, занимáющийся сёрфингом.
surfing /'sə:fɪŋ/ *n.* сёрфинг.
surge /sə:dʒ/ *n.* (*of waves, water*) вóлны (*f. pl.*); вал; (*of crowd, emotion etc.*) волнá, прили́в; (*of elec. current*) и́мпульс.
■ *v.i.* 1 (*of waves, water*) вздымáться (*impf.*).
2 (*of crowd*): **the crowd ~d forward** толпá подалáсь вперёд.
3 (*of emotions*) нахлы́нуть (*pf.*).
surgeon /'sə:dʒ(ə)n/ *n.* хиру́рг.
surgery /'sə:dʒərɪ/ *n.*
1 (*operation*) оперáция.
2 (*Br., office*) приёмная/кабинéт (врачá); **the doctor holds a ~ every morning** врач принимáет кáждое у́тро.
surgical /'sə:dʒɪk(ə)l/ *adj.* хирурги́ческий; **~ spirit** (*Br.*) медици́нский спирт.
surly /'sə:lɪ/ *adj.* (**surlier, surliest**) непривéтливый.
surmise /sə'maɪz/ *n.* (*conjecture*) догáдка; (*supposition*) предположéние.
■ *v.t.* предпол|агáть, -ожи́ть.
■ *v.i.* догáд|ываться, -áться.
surmount /sə'maʊnt/ *v.t.* (*overcome*) преодол|евáть, -éть.
surmountable /sə'maʊntəb(ə)l/ *adj.* преодоли́мый.
surname /'sə:neɪm/ *n.* фами́лия.
surpass /sə'pɑ:s/ *v.t.* прев|осходи́ть, -зойти́.
surplice /'sə:plɪs/ *n.* стихáрь (*m.*) (*дли́нное одеяние с широкими рукавами, надеваемое священниками на время службы*).
surplus /'sə:pləs/ *n.* изли́шек.
■ *adj.* изли́шний, избы́точный.
surprise /sə'praɪz/ *n.*
1 (*astonishment*) удивлéние.
2 (*unexpected news, gift etc.*) неожи́данность, сюрпри́з.
3 (*unexpected action*): **catch, take s.o. by ~** заст|игáть, -и́чь когó-н. врасплóх.
■ *v.t.* 1 (*astonish*) удив|ля́ть, -и́ть; **I was ~d to hear you had been ill** я с удивлéнием узнáл, что вы бы́ли больны́.
2 (*capture by ~*) захвáт|ывать, -и́ть врасплóх; **we ~d him in the act of stealing** мы поймáли егó с поли́чным на воровствé (*or* при совершéнии крáжи).
surprising /sə'praɪzɪŋ/ *adj.* удиви́тельный, порази́тельный; **he eats ~ly little** он удиви́тельно/на удивлéние мáло ест.
surreal /sə'rɪəl/ *adj.* сюрреалисти́ческий.
surrealism /sə'rɪəlɪz(ə)m/ *n.* сюрреали́зм.
surrealist /sə'rɪəlɪst/ *n.* сюрреали́ст.
■ *adj.* сюрреалисти́ческий.
surrender /sə'rendə(r)/ *n.* (*handing over*) сдáча; (*giving up*) откáз (от + *g.*); (*capitulation*) капитуля́ция.
■ *v.t.* 1 (*yield*) сда|вáть, -ть.
2 (*give up*) откáз|ываться, -áться от + *g.*
■ *v.i.* сд|авáться, -áться; капитули́ровать (*impf., pf.*).
surreptitious /sʌrəp'tɪʃəs/ *adj.* тáйный.
surrogate /'sʌrəgət/ *n.* суррогáт; **~ mother** суррогáтная мать.
surround /sə'raʊnd/ *v.t.* окруж|áть, -и́ть; **the ~ing countryside** окрéстности (*f. pl.*).
surroundings /sə'raʊndɪŋz/ *n.* мéстность, окрéстности (*f. pl.*); обстанóвка.
surveillance /sə:'veɪləns/ *n.* надзóр; **~ camera** кáмера скры́того наблюдéния.
survey[1] /'sə:veɪ/ *n.*
1 (*inspection, investigation*) исслéдование, обслéдование; (*Br., of building*) оцéнка состоя́ния дóма/здáния; (*by asking questions*) опрóс.
2 (*of land*) съёмка, промéр.
survey[2] /sə'veɪ/ *v.t.*
1 (*view*) обозр|евáть, -éть.
2 (*inspect*) осм|áтривать, -отрéть.
3 (*land etc.*) межевáть (*impf.*); произв|оди́ть, -ести́ съёмку + *g.*
surveyor /sə'veɪə(r)/ *n.*
1 (*Br., of houses*) строи́тельный инспéктор.
2 (*of land etc.*) землемéр.
survival /sə'vaɪv(ə)l/ *n.* выживáние.
survive /sə'vaɪv/ *v.t.*
1 (*outlive*) пережи|вáть, -и́ть (*во времени*).
2 (*come alive through*): **~ an illness** перен|оси́ть, -ести́ болéзнь.
■ *v.i.* выживáть, вы́жить; (*be preserved*): сохрани́ться, уцелéть (*both pf.*); **the custom still ~s** э́тот обы́чай ещё сохрани́лся.
survivor /sə'vaɪvə(r)/ *n.* остáвшийся в живы́х, уцелéвший.
susceptible /sə'septɪb(ə)l/ *adj.*: **~ to** восприи́мчивый к + *d.*; **he is ~ to colds** он подвéржен простýде.
suspect[1] /'sʌspekt/ *n.* подозревáемый.
■ *adj.* подозри́тельный; не внушáющий довéрия.
suspect[2] /sə'spekt/ *v.t.*
1 подозревáть (*impf.*); **I ~ed him to be lying** я подозревáл, что он лжёт.
2 (*doubt*) сомневáться, усомни́ться в + *p.*
suspend /sə'spend/ *v.t.*
1 (*hang up*) подвé|шивать, -сить.
2 (*stop for a time*) приостан|áвливать, -ови́ть; **~ed sentence** услóвное осуждéние.
3 (*from office etc.*) врéменно отстран|я́ть, -и́ть.
suspender /sə'spendə(r)/ *n.* (*US, pl., braces*) подтя́ж|ки (*pl., g.* -ек).
■ *cpd.* **~ belt** *n.* (*Br.*) (жéнский) пóяс с подвя́зками.
suspense /sə'spens/ *n.* напряжéние, напряжённость; **keep s.o. in ~** держáть (*impf.*) когó-н. в неизвéстности.
suspension /sə'spenʃ(ə)n/ *n.*
1 (*stoppage*) приостановлéние.
2 (*from office etc.*) отстранéние.
suspicion /sə'spɪʃ(ə)n/ *n.* подозрéние;

arouse ~ возбу|ждать, -дить подозрения.

suspicious /sə'spɪʃəs/ *adj.*
1 (*mistrustful*) подозрительный, недоверчивый (к + *d.*).
2 (*arousing suspicion*) подозрительный.

suss /sʌs/ *v.t.* (*Br. coll.*): **she's got him ~ed** она его раскусила; **he ~ed out the best route** он разузнал лучший маршрут.

sustain /sə'steɪn/ *v.t.*
1 (*lit., fig., support*) поддерж|ивать, -ать.
2 (*suffer*) нести, по-; **the enemy ~ed heavy losses** противник понёс тяжёлые потери; **~ an injury** перен|осить, -ести травму; получ|ать, -ить увечье.
3 (*maintain*): **~ one's efforts** не ослаблять (*impf.*) усилий.

sustenance /'sʌstɪnəns/ *n.* питание, пища.

suture /'su:tʃə(r)/ *n.* (*med.*) шов.

swab /swɒb/ *n.* (*med.*) тампон.

swagger /'swægə(r)/ *v.i.* расхаживать (*impf.*) с важным видом.

Swahili /swə'hi:lɪ/ *n.* (*pl.* **~**) (*language, people*) суахили (*m. indecl.*).

swallow¹ /'swɒləʊ/ *n.* (*bird*) ласточка.

swallow² /'swɒləʊ/ *n.* (*gulp*) глоток.
■ *v.t.* прогл|атывать, -отить; загл|атывать, -отить; **he had to ~ his pride** ему пришлось поступиться своим самолюбием.
■ *v.i.* глотать (*impf.*).

swam /swæm/ *past of* ▸ **swim**

swamp /swɒmp/ *n.* болото.
■ *v.t.* 1 (*with water*) зал|ивать, -ить.
2 (*fig., overwhelm*): **we were ~ed with applications** мы были завалены заявлениями.

swampy /'swɒmpɪ/ *adj.* (**swampier, swampiest**) болотистый.

swan /swɒn/ *n.* лебедь (*m.*).

swank /swæŋk/ (*coll.*) *n.* показуха.
■ *v.i.*: **~ about sth.** хвастать (*impf.*) чем-н.

swanky /'swæŋkɪ/ *adj.* (**swankier, swankiest**) шикарный.

swap, swop /swɒp/ *n.* обмен.
■ *v.t.* (**swapped, swapping; swopped, swopping**) (*exchange for sth. else*) менять, по- (**for:** на + *a.*); **he ~ped his car for a motorbike** он поменял машину на мотоцикл; (*exchange with s.o. else*) меняться, по- + *i.* (**with s.o.:** с + *i.*); **will you ~ places with me?** вы не поменяетесь со мной местами?

swarm /swɔ:m/ *n.*: **~ of ants/bees** муравьиный/пчелиный рой.
■ *v.i.* 1 (*of bees, ants etc.*) роиться (*impf.*).
2 (*of people*): **children ~ed around him** дети столпились вокруг него.
3 (*teem*) кишеть (*impf.*) + *i.*; **the town is ~ing with tourists** город наводнён туристами.

swarthy /'swɔ:ðɪ/ *adj.* (**swarthier, swarthiest**) смуглый.

swastika /'swɒstɪkə/ *n.* свастика.

swat /swɒt/ *v.t.* (**swatted, swatting**) (*an insect*) прихлопнуть (*pf.*).

swathe /sweɪð/ *v.t.* (*wrap*): **~d in bandages** обмотанный бинтами; **~d in blankets** закутанный одеялами.

sway /sweɪ/ *n.*: **have, hold ~ over s.o.** держать (*impf.*) кого-н. в подчинении.
■ *v.t.* 1 (*rock*) кач|ать, -нуть.
2 (*influence*) влиять, по-; колебать, по-.
■ *v.i.* качаться, качнуться.

swear /sweə(r)/ *v.t.* & *i.* (*past* **swore;** *p.p.* **sworn**)
1 (*promise*) клясться, по-; **they swore eternal friendship** они поклялись в вечной дружбе.
2 (*bind by an oath*) прив|одить, -ести к присяге; **the jury was sworn in** присяжных привели к присяге; **he was sworn to secrecy** с него взяли клятву о неразглашении тайны; **sworn enemies** заклятые враги.
■ *v.i.* (*past* **swore;** *p.p.* **sworn**)
1 (*take an oath*) клясться, по-; (*fig.*): **he ~s by aspirin** он (безгранично) верит в пользу аспирина.
2 (*curse*) браниться (*impf.*); ругаться (*impf.*).
■ *cpd.* **~ word** *n.* ругательство.

swearing /'sweərɪŋ/ *n.* брань, ругань.

sweat /swet/ *n.*
1 пот, испарина.
2 (*state of* **~ing**) потение, пот; **a cold ~** холодный пот.
■ *v.i.* (*past and p.p.* **sweated** *or US* **~**) потеть, вс-.
■ *cpd.* **~shirt** *n.* хлопчатобумажный (спортивный) свитер, толстовка.

sweater /'swetə(r)/ *n.* свитер.

sweaty /'swetɪ/ *adj.* (**sweatier, sweatiest**): **~ hands** потные руки.

Swede /swi:d/ *n.* (*person*) швед (*fem.* -ка); (*s~: Br., vegetable*) брюква.

Sweden /'swi:dən/ *n.* Швеция.

Swedish /'swi:dɪʃ/ *n.* (*language*) шведский язык.
■ *adj.* шведский.

sweep /swi:p/ *n.*
1 (*with broom etc.*): **give a room a good ~** хорошенько подме|тать, -сти комнату.
2 (**~ing** *movement*) взмах, размах.
3 (*long flowing curve*) изгиб.
4 (**chimney ~**) трубочист.
■ *v.t.* (*past and p.p.* **swept**)
1 (*rush over*): **the waves swept the shore** волны набегали на берег.
2 (*carry forcefully*): **a wave swept him overboard** его смыло волной (за борт); **he swept her off her feet** (*fig.*) он вскружил ей голову.
3 (*clean, brush*) подме|тать, -сти; чистить, вы-; **he swept the litter into a corner** он замёл мусор в угол; **~ a chimney** проч|ищать, -истить трубу; (*fig.*): **~ sth. under the carpet** заме|тать, -сти что-н. под ковёр.
■ *v.i.* (*past and p.p.* **swept**)
1 (*rush, dash*) прон|оситься, -естись; **rain swept across the country** дождь прошёл по всей стране; **fear swept over him** страх охватил его.
2 (*walk majestically*): **she swept into the room** она гордо вошла в комнату.
3 (*brush*) мести, под-; подме|тать, -сти.
■ *with advs.*: **~ aside** *v.t.*: **he swept aside my protestations** он не стал слушать моих

возражéний; ~ **away** *v.t.* смe|тáть, -сти́; **the storm swept everything away** бу́ря всё смелá; ~ **up** *v.t.*: **be sure and ~ up all the dirt** смотри́те, вы́метите весь му́сор как слéдует; *v.i.*: **I had to ~ up after them** мне пришло́сь пóсле них убирáть.

sweeping /'swi:pɪŋ/ *adj.* (*comprehensive*) всеобъéмлющий; ~ **changes** радикáльные изменéния; (*too general*): **a ~ statement** огу́льное утверждéние.

sweet /swi:t/ *n.*
1 (*Br., piece of confectionary*) конфéта.
2 (*Br., dessert*) слáдкое, трéтье.
■ *adj.* 1 (*to taste*) слáдкий; **my brother has a ~ tooth** мой брат — сладкоéжка (*c.g.*).
2 (*fragrant*) слáдкий, души́стый; **how ~ the roses smell!** как слáдко пáхнут рóзы!
3 (*coll., charming, nice*) ми́лый; **a ~ little dog** симпати́чная собáчка.
■ *cpds.* **~-and-sour** *adj.* ки́сло-слáдкий; **~corn** *n.* (столо́вая) кукуру́за; **~heart** *n.* возлю́бленн|ый (*fem.* -ая); (*as form of address*) дорого́й, ми́лый, люби́мый; ~ **talk** (*coll.*) *n.* лесть; **~-talk** (*coll.*) *v.t.* загов|áривать, -ори́ть комý-н. зу́бы.

sweeten /'swi:t(ə)n/ *v.t.* подслá|щивать, -сти́ть.

sweetener /'swi:tənə(r)/ *n.* (*sugar substitute*) замени́тель (*m.*) сáхара; (*Br., bribe*) взя́тка.

swell /swel/ *n.* (*of sea*) зыбь.
■ *v.t.* (*p.p.* **swollen** *or* **swelled**)
1 (*increase size of*) разд|увáть, -у́ть; **my finger is swollen** у меня́ пáлец опу́х/распу́х.
2 (*increase number of*) увели́чи|вать, -ть.
■ *v.i.* (*p.p.* **swollen** *or* **swelled**)
1 (*expand, dilate: also* ~ **up**) над|увáться, -у́ться; (*of part of body*) оп|ухáть, -у́хнуть.
2 (*increase in size or volume*) вырастáть, вы́расти; **the crowd ~ed to over six thousand** толпá увели́чилась до шести́ с ли́шним ты́сяч (человéк).

swelling /'swelɪŋ/ *n.* о́пухоль.

sweltering /'sweltərɪŋ/ *adj.* нестерпи́мо жáркий.

swept /swept/ *past and p.p. of* ▸ **sweep**

swerve /swə:v/ *v.i.* (кру́то) пов|орáчиваться, -ерну́ться.

swift /swɪft/ *n.* (*bird*) стриж.
■ *adj.* (*rapid*) бы́стрый; (*prompt*) скóрый.

swig /swɪg/ (*coll.*) *n.* глото́к.
■ *v.t.* (**swigged, swigging**) хлебáть (*impf.*).

swill /swɪl/ *n.* (*lit., fig.*) по́йло; (*pig food*) помо́|и (*pl., g.* -ев).
■ *v.t.* 1 (*Br., wash, rinse*) мыть, вы́-; полоскáть, вы́-.
2 (*drink heavily*) лакáть, вы́-, хлебáть, вы́-, хлестáть, вы́- (*all coll.*).

swim /swɪm/ *n.*: **have, go for a ~** купáться, ис-.
■ *v.t.* (**swimming;** *past* **swam;** *p.p.* **swum**)
1 (*cross by ~ming*) перепл|ывáть, -ы́ть.
2 (*cover by ~ming*): ~ **a mile** пропл|ывáть, -ы́ть ми́лю.
■ *v.i.* (**swimming;** *past* **swam;** *p.p.* **swum**)
1 плáвать (*indet.*), плыть (*det.*), по-.
2 (*fig., swirl*): **everything was ~ming before my eyes** всё поплы́ло у меня́ пéред глазáми.
■ *cpd.* **~suit** *n.* купáльник.

swimmer /'swɪmə(r)/ *n.* плов|éц (*fem.* -чи́ха).

swimming /'swɪmɪŋ/ *n.* плáвание.
■ *cpds.* ~ **bath** (*Br.*), ~ **pool** *nn.* (плáвательный) бассéйн; ~ **cap** купáльная шáпочка; ~ **costume** *n.* (*Br.*) купáльник; ~ **trunks** *n. pl.* плáв|ки (*pl., g.* -ок).

swindle /'swɪnd(ə)l/ *n.* мошéнничество.
■ *v.t.* обмáн|ывать, -у́ть; ~ **money out of s.o.** выма́нивать, вы́манить у когó-н. дéньги.

swindler /'swɪndlə(r)/ *n.* мошéнник.

swine /swaɪn/ *n.* (*pl.* **~;** *fig. also* **~s**) (*lit., fig.*) свинья́.

swing /swɪŋ/ *n.*
1 (*movement*) качáние, колебáние; **in full ~** (*fig.*) в (пóлном) разгáре.
2 (*shift*): **the polls showed a ~ to the left** вы́боры показáли рéзкое увеличéние популя́рности «лéвых».
3 (*of rhythm*) ритм; **I couldn't get into the ~ of things** я никáк не мог включи́ться в дéло.
4 (*seat on rope*) качéл|и (*pl., g.* -ей).
■ *v.t.* (*past and p.p.* **swung**)
1 (*apply circular motion to*): ~ **one's arms** размáхивать (*impf.*) рукáми.
2 (*cause to turn*) пов|орáчивать, -ерну́ть; разв|орáчивать, -ерну́ть.
■ *v.i.* (*past and p.p.* **swung**)
1 (*sway*) качáться (*impf.*), колебáться (*impf.*); (*dangle*) висéть, свисáть, болтáться (*all impf.*).
2 (*turn*) пов|орáчиваться, -ерну́ться; вращáться (*impf.*); **the door swung open in the wind** дверь распахну́лась от вéтра.
■ *cpd.* ~ **doors** (*US* **swinging doors**) *n. pl.* свобо́дно распáхивающаяся (двуствóрчатая) дверь.

swingeing /'swɪndʒɪŋ/ *adj.* (*Br.*): **a ~ blow** ошеломля́ющий удáр; **a ~ majority** подавля́ющее большинствó; **a ~ fine** громáдный/огрóмный штраф.

swipe /swaɪp/ *v.t.* (*hit*) с си́лой уд|аря́ть, -áрить по + *d.*; (*steal*) стащи́ть (*pf.*) (*coll.*).
■ *cpd.* ~ **card** *n.* магни́тная кáрточка.

swirl /swə:l/ *v.i.* (*of water*) крути́ться (*impf.*) в водоворóте; (*of snow*) ви́хриться (*impf.*); (*of leaves etc.*) кружи́ться, за-.

Swiss /swɪs/ *n.* (*pl.* ~) швейцáр|ец (*fem.* -ка).
■ *adj.* швейцáрский.

switch /swɪtʃ/ *n.*
1 (*elec.*) выключáтель (*m.*), переключáтель (*m.*).
2 (*change*) поворóт, перемéна.
■ *v.t.* (*transfer*) перев|оди́ть, -ести́; переключ|áть, -и́ть.
■ *v.i.*: **he ~ed from one extreme to the other** он перешёл/брóсился из одно́й крáйности в другу́ю.
■ *with advs.*: ~ **off** *v.t.* выключáть, вы́ключить; ~ **off a lamp** гаси́ть, по- лáмпу; ~ **on** *v.t.* включ|áть, -и́ть; (*light*) заж|игáть, -éчь.
■ *cpd.* **~board** *n.* коммутáтор; **~board operator** телефони́ст (*fem.* -ка).

Switzerland /'swɪtsələnd/ *n.* Швейцáрия.

swivel /'swɪv(ə)l/ *v.t. & i.* (**swivelled, swivelling;** *US* **swiveled, swiveling**)

пов|ора́чивать(ся), -ерну́ть(ся) (на шарни́рах).
swollen /ˈswəʊlən/ *p.p. of* ▸ **swell**
swoop /swuːp/ *v.i.* (*aeron.*) пики́ровать, с-; **the eagle ~ed (down) on its prey** орёл стреми́тельно упа́л на свою́ же́ртву; **the enemy ~ed on the town** неприя́тель соверши́л внеза́пный налёт на го́род.
swop /swɒp/ = **swap**
sword /sɔːd/ *n.* (*cutting weapon*) меч; (*light thrust weapon*) шпа́га.
swore /swɔː/ *past of* ▸ **swear**
sworn /swɔːn/ *p.p. of* ▸ **swear**
swot /swɒt/ (*Br.*) *n.* зубри́ла (*c.g.*). ■ *v.i.* (**swotted, swotting**) зубри́ть (*impf.*).
swum /swʌm/ *p.p. of* ▸ **swim**
swung /swʌŋ/ *past and p.p. of* ▸ **swing**
sycamore /ˈsɪkəmɔː(r)/ *n.* я́вор.
sycophantic /sɪkəˈfæntɪk/ *adj.* подхали́мский, льсти́вый.
Sydney /ˈsɪdnɪ/ *n.* Си́дней.
syllable /ˈsɪləb(ə)l/ *n.* слог.
syllabus /ˈsɪləbəs/ *n.* програ́мма (*уче́бная*).
symbiosis /sɪmbaɪˈəʊsɪs/ *n.* симбио́з.
symbol /ˈsɪmb(ə)l/ *n.* си́мвол; (*sign, e.g. math.*) знак.
symbolic(al) /sɪmˈbɒlɪk(əl)/ *adj.* символи́ческий, символи́чный.
symbolism /ˈsɪmbəlɪz(ə)m/ *n.* символи́зм.
symbolize /ˈsɪmbəlaɪz/ *v.t.* символизи́ровать (*impf., pf.*).
symmetrical /sɪˈmetrɪk(ə)l/ *adj.* симметри́чный.
symmetry /ˈsɪmɪtrɪ/ *n.* симме́трия.
sympathetic /sɪmpəˈθetɪk/ *adj.*
1 (*compassionate*) сочу́вственный.
2 (*supportive*): **I am ~ towards his ideas** его́ иде́и мне близки́.
sympathize /ˈsɪmpəθaɪz/ *v.i.* сочу́вствовать (*impf.*) (**with:** + *d.*).
sympathizer /ˈsɪmpəθaɪzə(r)/ *n.* сторо́нни|к (*fem.* -ца).
sympathy /ˈsɪmpəθɪ/ *n.* (*compassion*) сочу́вствие, сострада́ние; (*agreement*) согла́сие; **the power workers came out in ~** рабо́тники электроста́нции забастова́ли в знак солида́рности.
symphony /ˈsɪmfənɪ/ *n.* симфо́ния; **~ orchestra/concert** симфони́ческий орке́стр/конце́рт.
symposi|um /sɪmˈpəʊzɪəm/ *n.* (*pl.* **~a** *or* **~ums**) симпо́зиум.
symptom /ˈsɪmptəm/ *n.* симпто́м.
symptomatic /sɪmptəˈmætɪk/ *adj.* симптомати́чный, симптомати́ческий.
synagogue /ˈsɪnəgɒg/ *n.* синаго́га.
sync /sɪŋk/ *n.* (*coll.*): **out of ~** несинхро́нный.
synchronize /ˈsɪŋkrənaɪz/ *v.t.* синхронизи́ровать (*impf., pf.*); **~d swimming** синхро́нное пла́вание.
syncopation /sɪŋkəˈpeɪʃ(ə)n/ *n.* синко́па.
syndicate /ˈsɪndɪkət/ *n.* синдика́т.
syndrome /ˈsɪndrəʊm/ *n.* синдро́м.
synonym /ˈsɪnənɪm/ *n.* сино́ним.
synonymous /sɪˈnɒnɪməs/ *adj.* (*fig.*) равнозна́чный (**with:** + *d.*).
synopsis /sɪˈnɒpsɪs/ *n.* (*pl.* **synopses** /-siːz/) резюме́ (*nt. indecl.*).
syntax /ˈsɪntæks/ *n.* си́нтаксис.
synthesis /ˈsɪnθɪsɪs/ *n.* (*pl.* **syntheses** /-siːz/) си́нтез.
synthe|size /ˈsɪnθɪsaɪz/ *v.t.* синтези́ровать (*impf., pf.*).
synthesizer /ˈsɪnθɪsaɪzə(r)/ *n.* синтеза́тор.
synthetic /sɪnˈθetɪk/ *adj.* синтети́ческий. ■ *n.* (*usu. pl.*) синте́тика (*collect.*).
syphilis /ˈsɪfɪlɪs/ *n.* си́филис.
Syria /ˈsɪrɪə/ *n.* Си́рия.
Syrian /ˈsɪrɪən/ *n.* сири́|ец (*fem.* -йка). ■ *adj.* сири́йский.
syringe /sɪˈrɪndʒ/ *n.* шприц.
syrup /ˈsɪrəp/ *n.* (*juice*) сиро́п; (*treacle*) па́тока; **golden ~** све́тлая па́тока.
system /ˈsɪstəm/ *n.*
1 (*complex; method*) систе́ма; **~s analysis/analyst** систе́мный ана́лиз/анали́тик.
2 (*network*) сеть.
3 (*body as a whole*) органи́зм; **get sth. out of one's ~** (*fig.*) изб|авля́ться, -а́виться от чего́-н.
systematic /sɪstəˈmætɪk/ *adj.* системати́ческий.
systemic /sɪˈstemɪk/ *adj.* относя́щийся ко всему́ органи́зму, сомати́ческий; **~ poison** общеядови́тое отравля́ющее вещество́.

Tt

tab /tæb/ *n.*
1 (*projecting flap*) ушко́.
2 (*coll., check*): **the police are keeping ~s on him** поли́ция присма́тривает за ним.
table /ˈteɪb(ə)l/ *n.*
1 стол.
2 (*arrangement of data*) табли́ца.
■ *v.t.* 1 (*Br., present for discussion*) ста́вить, по- на обсужде́ние.
2 (*US, postpone*) от|кла́дывать, -ложи́ть.
■ *cpds.* **~cloth** *n.* ска́терть; **~ mat** *n.* (*Br.*) подста́вка (*под таре́лку и т. п.*); **~spoon** *n.* столо́вая ло́жка; **~ tennis** *n.* насто́льный те́ннис, пинг-по́нг.
tablet /ˈtæblɪt/ *n.* табле́тка.
tabloid /ˈtæblɔɪd/ *n.* табло́ид; **the ~s** бульва́рная пре́сса.
taboo /təˈbuː/ *n.* (*lit., fig.*) табу́ (*nt. indecl.*).

tacit /'tæsɪt/ *adj.* молчали́вый (*согласие, одобрение*).

taciturn /'tæsɪtə:n/ *adj.* неразгово́рчивый, молчали́вый.

taciturnity /tæsɪ'tə:nɪtɪ/ *n.* неразгово́рчивость, молчали́вость.

tack /tæk/ *n.*
1 (*small nail*) гво́здик.
2 (*fig.*): **he is on the wrong ~** он на ло́жном пути́.
■ *v.t.* 1 (*fasten*) прикреп|ля́ть, -и́ть гво́здиками.
2 (*stitch*) намёт|ывать, -а́ть.
3 : **~ on** (*fig., add*) доб|авля́ть, -а́вить.

tackle /'tæk(ə)l/ *n.*
1 (*football*) блокиро́вка.
2 : **fishing ~** рыболо́вные сна́сти (*f. pl.*).
■ *v.t.* (*grapple with*) бра́ться, взя́ться за + *a.*; **I ~d him on the subject** я по́днял э́тот вопро́с в разгово́ре с ним; (*football*) блоки́ровать (*impf., pf.*).

tacky[1] /'tækɪ/ *adj.* (**tackier, tackiest**) (*sticky*) ли́пкий, кле́йкий.

tacky[2] /'tækɪ/ *adj.* (**tackier, tackiest**) (*coll., tasteless*) безвку́сный (*вульгарный*).

tact /tækt/ *n.* такт.

tactful /'tæktfʊl/ *adj.* такти́чный.

tactical /'tæktɪk(ə)l/ *adj.* такти́ческий.

tactician /tæk'tɪʃ(ə)n/ *n.* та́ктик.

tactic(s) /'tæktɪks/ *n.* та́ктика.

tactile /'tæktaɪl/ *adj.* осяза́тельный, такти́льный.

tactless /'tæktlɪs/ *adj.* беста́ктный.

tadpole /'tædpəʊl/ *n.* голова́стик.

tag /tæg/ *n.* ярлы́к.
■ *v.i.* (**tagged, tagging**) (*follow*): **the children ~ged along behind** де́ти тащи́лись сза́ди; **to ~ along with s.o.** увя́з|ываться, -а́ться за кем-н.

Tahiti /tə'hi:tɪ/ *n.* Таити (*m. indecl.*).

t'ai chi (ch'uan) /taɪ 'tʃi: ('tʃwɑ:n)/ *n.* тайцзицюа́нь (*f. indecl.*).

tail /teɪl/ *n.*
1 (*of animal*) хвост.
2 (*of a coin*) ре́шка.
3 : **~s** (*coat*) фрак.
■ *v.i.* уб|ыва́ть, -ы́ть; **the attendance figures ~ed off** посеща́емость упа́ла; **his voice ~ed away into silence** его́ го́лос (постепе́нно) зати́х.
■ *cpd.* **~back** *n.* (*Br.*) дли́нная верени́ца автомоби́лей в про́бке; многокилометро́вая про́бка.

tailor /'teɪlə(r)/ *n.* портно́й.
■ *v.t.* (*fig.*) приспос|а́бливать, -о́бить; **his speech was ~ed to the situation** его́ речь была́ соста́влена с учётом ситуа́ции.
■ *cpd.* **~-made** *adj.* (*clothes*) сде́ланный на зака́з; (*fig.*) подходя́щий.

taint /teɪnt/ *v.t.* по́ртить, ис-; **~ed money** гря́зные де́ньги; **~ed reputation** подмо́ченная репута́ция.

Taiwan /taɪ'wɑ:n/ *n.* Тайва́нь (*m.*).

Tajik /tɑ:'dʒi:k/ *n.*
1 (*person*) таджи́|к (*fem.* -чка).
2 (*language*) таджи́кский язы́к.
■ *adj.* таджи́кский.

Tajikistan /tədʒi:kɪ'stɑ:n/ *n.* Таджикиста́н.

take /teɪk/ *n.* (*cin.*) дубль (*m.*), монта́жный кадр.
■ *v.t.* (*past* **took;** *p.p.* **taken** /'teɪk(ə)n/)
1 (*pick up, grasp*) брать, взять; **he took her by the hand** он взял её за́ руку; **she took a coin out of her purse** она́ вы́нула моне́ту из кошелька́; **the last mile took it out of me** на после́дней ми́ле я вы́дохся.
2 (*capture*) брать, взять; **he was ~n captive** его́ взя́ли в плен; (*assume*) прин|има́ть, -я́ть на себя́; **you must ~ the initiative** вы должны́ взять на себя́ инициати́ву; **he took control** он взял управле́ние в свои́ ру́ки; (*win*) выи́грывать, вы́играть; **she took first prize** она́ получи́ла пе́рвый приз.
3 (*acquire*): **these seats are ~n** э́ти места́ за́няты; (*in payment*): **they took £50 in one evening** они́ вы́ручили 50 фу́нтов за оди́н ве́чер; (*by enquiry or examination*): определ|я́ть, -и́ть; **the doctor took my temperature** врач изме́рил мне температу́ру; (*unlawfully*): **the thieves took all her jewellery** во́ры забра́ли все её драгоце́нности.
4 (*avail o.s. of*): **please ~ a seat** пожа́луйста, сади́тесь; (*travel by*): **let's ~ a taxi** дава́йте возьмём такси́.
5 (*accept*) прин|има́ть, -я́ть; **will you ~ a cheque?** вы при́мете чек?; **will you ~ £50 for it?** вы отдади́те э́то за 50 фу́нтов?; **~ my advice!** послу́шайте меня́!; **I ~ responsibility** я беру́ на себя́ отве́тственность; **can't you ~ a joke?** вы что, шу́ток не понима́ете?; (*receive*) брать (*impf.*); **she ~s lessons in Spanish** она́ берёт уро́ки испа́нского языка́; (*submit to*): **when do you ~ your exams?** когда́ вы сдаёте экза́мены?
6 (*use regularly*) прин|има́ть, -я́ть; **he has begun to ~ drugs** он на́чал принима́ть нарко́тики; **do you ~ sugar in your tea?** вы пьёте чай с са́харом?; (*of size in clothes*): **I ~ a ten in shoes** у меня́ деся́тый разме́р о́буви.
7 (*make or obtain from original source*): **may I ~ your photograph?** позво́льте мне вас сфотографи́ровать?
8 (*convey*) (*on foot*) отн|оси́ть, -ести́; (*by transport*) отв|ози́ть, -езти́; брать, взять; перед|ава́ть, -а́ть; **he was ~n to hospital** его́ отвезли́ в больни́цу.
9 (*require*): **the job will ~ a long time** рабо́та займёт мно́го вре́мени; **how long does it ~ to get there?** ско́лько (вре́мени) туда́ добира́ться?; **it took us 3 hours to get there** нам потре́бовалось три часа́, что́бы добра́ться туда́; **he's got what it ~s** (*coll.*) у него́ есть для э́того все зада́тки.
■ *v.i.* (*past* **took;** *p.p.* **taken** /'teɪk(ə)n/)
1 (*~ effect; succeed*): **the vaccination has not ~n** вакци́на не привила́сь.
2 **~ after** (*resemble*): **he ~s after his father** он похо́ж на (своего́) отца́.
3 : **~ to** (*resort to*) приб|ега́ть, -е́гнуть к + *d.*; **she took to her bed** она́ слегла́; **he took to drink** он за́пил; **he has ~n to getting up early** он стал ра́но встава́ть; (*feel well-disposed towards*): **I took to him from the start** он мне сра́зу понра́вился.
■ *with advs.*: **~ apart** *v.t.* (*dismantle*)

раз|бира́ть, -обра́ть; **~ away** *v.t.* (*remove*) уб|ира́ть, -ра́ть; заб|ира́ть, -ра́ть; **the police took his gun away** поли́ция отобрала́ у него́ пистоле́т; **he was ~n away to prison** его́ отвезли́ в тюрьму́; (*subtract*) вычита́ть, вы́честь; **~ back** *v.t.* (*return*) верну́ть (*pf.*); (*retract*): **I ~ back everything I said** я беру́ наза́д всё, что сказа́л; **~ down** *v.t.* (*remove*) сн|има́ть, -ять; (*lengthen*): **she took her dress down an inch** она́ отпусти́ла пла́тье на дюйм; (*dismantle*) сн|оси́ть, -ести́; **the shed was ~n down** сара́й снесли́; (*write down*) запи́с|ывать, -а́ть; **~ in** *v.t.* (*lit.*) вн|оси́ть, -ести́; (*give shelter to*): **they took him in when he was starving** они́ приюти́ли его́, когда́ он голода́л; (*let accommodation to*): **she ~s in lodgers** она́ берёт постоя́льцев; (*make smaller*): **she took in her dress** она́ ушила пла́тье; (*comprehend*) усв|а́ивать, -о́ить; (*deceive*) обма́н|ывать, -у́ть; **~ off** *v.t.* (*remove*) сн|има́ть, -ять; (*deduct from price*): **I will ~ 10 off for cash** е́сли вы пла́тите нали́чными, я сбро́шу 10; (*Br. coll., mimic*) имити́ровать (*impf.*), копи́ровать (*impf.*); *v.i.* (*become airborne*) взлет|а́ть, -е́ть; **~ on** *v.t.* (*hire*) брать, взять; (*undertake*) брать, взять на себя́; **he took on too much** он взял на себя́ сли́шком мно́го; (*assume*) приобре|та́ть, -сти́; **~ out** *v.t.* (*extract*) вынима́ть, вы́нуть; **he took out his wallet** он вы́нул бума́жник; **he had all his teeth ~n out** ему́ удали́ли все зу́бы; **he took his girlfriend out to dinner** он повёл свою́ подру́гу в рестора́н; (*vent one's feelings*) срыва́ть, сорва́ть; **he took it out on his wife** он сорва́л всё на свое́й жене́; **~ over** *v.t.* & *i.* (*assume control* (*of*)) прин|има́ть, -я́ть руково́дство (+ *i.*); *v.i.* (*replace s.o.*): **let me ~ over!** я вас сменю́!; **~ up** *v.t.* (*lift*) подн|има́ть, -я́ть; (*accept*) прин|има́ть, -я́ть; **will he ~ up the challenge?** он при́мет вы́зов?; (*shorten*): **she had to ~ up her dress** ей пришло́сь укороти́ть пла́тье; (*occupy*) зан|има́ть, -я́ть; (*pursue*): **I shall ~ the matter up with the Minister** я обращу́сь с э́тим де́лом к мини́стру; (*accept challenge or offer*): **I'll ~ you up on that!** (я) ловлю́ вас на сло́ве; (*interest o.s. in*) бра́ться, взя́ться за + *a.*; *v.i.* (*consort*) свя́з|ываться, -а́ться с + *i.*

■ *cpds.* **~away** (*Br.*) *n.* рестора́н, продаю́щий еду́ на вы́нос; *adj.*: **a ~away meal** еда́ на вы́нос; **~-home** *adj.*: **~-home pay** чи́стый за́работок; **~-off** *n.* (*impersonation*) подража́ние, паро́дия; (*of aircraft; also fig.*) взлёт; **~out** (*US*) = **~away**; **~over** *n.* (*comm.*) поглоще́ние (*како́й-н. компа́нии друго́й компа́нией*).

taking /ˈteɪkɪŋ/ *n.* взя́тие; овладе́ние; **the money was there for the ~** де́ньги текли́ пря́мо в ру́ки; (*pl., money taken*) (*business*) вы́ручка; (*from concert etc.*) сбор; **the ~s were lower than expected** сбор оказа́лся ме́ньше, чем рассчи́тывали.

■ *adj.* привлека́тельный.

takings /ˈteɪkɪŋz/ *n.pl.* (*money taken*) вы́ручка.

talcum /ˈtælkəm/ *n.*: **~ powder** тальк.

tale /teɪl/ *n.*

1 расска́з, по́весть.

2 (*malicious or idle report*): **tell ~s (about)** я́бедничать, на- (на + *a.*).

talent /ˈtælənt/ *n.* тала́нт, дар.

talented /ˈtæləntɪd/ *adj.* тала́нтливый.

talisman /ˈtælɪzmən/ *n.* (*pl.* **~s**) талисма́н.

talk /tɔːk/ *n.*

1 (*speech, conversation*) разгово́р, бесе́да; **~ show** ток-шо́у (*nt. indecl.*).

2 (*lecture*) ле́кция; докла́д; **give a ~** чита́ть, про- ле́кцию.

3 (*discussion; usu. pl.*) перегово́ры (*m. pl.*).

■ *v.t.* 1 (*express*) говори́ть (*impf.*); **you are ~ing nonsense** вы говори́те чепуху́.

2 (*discuss*) обсу|жда́ть, -ди́ть; **they were ~ing politics** они́ говори́ли о поли́тике.

3 (*bring or make by ~ing*): **he ~ed me into it** он уговори́л меня́ сде́лать э́то; **I tried to ~ her out of it** я пыта́лся отговори́ть её от э́того.

■ *v.i.* говори́ть (*impf.*) (**about:** о + *p.*); **a ~ing parrot** говоря́щий попуга́й.

■ *with adv.*: **~ over** *v.t.* (*discuss*) обсу|жда́ть, -ди́ть.

talkative /ˈtɔːkətɪv/ *adj.* разгово́рчивый, болтли́вый.

talking-to /ˈtɔːkɪŋ/ *n.* (*coll.*) вы́говор.

tall /tɔːl/ *adj.* высо́кий, высо́кого ро́ста; **how ~ are you?** како́го вы ро́ста?; **six feet ~** ро́стом в шесть фу́тов.

Tallinn /ˈtælɪn/ *n.* Та́ллин.

tally /ˈtælɪ/ *n.* счёт.

■ *v.i.* соотве́тствовать (*impf.*).

talon /ˈtælən/ *n.* ко́готь (*m.*).

tambourine /tæmbəˈriːn/ *n.* бу́бен.

tame /teɪm/ *adj.* (*domesticated*) ручно́й, дома́шний; (*submissive*) послу́шный; (*dull*) пре́сный.

■ *v.t.* прируч|а́ть, -и́ть; (*of savage animals*) укро|ща́ть, -ти́ть.

Tamil /ˈtæmɪl/ *n.* (*person*) тами́л (*fem.* -ка); (*language*) тами́льский язы́к.

■ *adj.* тами́льский.

tamper /ˈtæmpə(r)/ *v.i.*: **~ with** (*meddle in*) вме́ш|иваться, -а́ться в + *a.*

tampon /ˈtæmpɒn/ *n.* тампо́н.

tan /tæn/ *n.* (*colour*) (желтова́то-/рыжева́то-)кори́чневый цвет; (*tint of skin*) зага́р; **he went to Spain to get a ~** он пое́хал загора́ть в Испа́нию.

■ *adj.* (желтова́то-/рыжева́то-)кори́чневый.

■ *v.t.* (**tanned, tanning**) (*make brown*): **a ~ned face** загоре́лое лицо́.

■ *v.i.* (**tanned, tanning**): **she ~s easily** она́ бы́стро загора́ет.

tangent /ˈtændʒ(ə)nt/ *n.* (*geom.*) каса́тельная; (*fig.*): **he went off at a ~** он отклони́лся от те́мы.

tangerine /ˈtændʒəriːn/ *n.* мандари́н, танжери́н.

tangible /ˈtændʒɪb(ə)l/ *adj.* осяза́емый.

tangle /ˈtæŋg(ə)l/ *n.* сплете́ние.

■ *v.t.* спу́т|ывать, -ать; **the wool had got ~d up** ни́тки спу́тались.

■ *v.i.* (*coll.*) свя́з|ываться, -а́ться.

tango /ˈtæŋgəʊ/ *n.* (*pl.* **tangos**) та́нго (*nt. indecl.*).

■ *v.i.* (**tangoes, tangoed**) танцева́ть, с- та́нго.

tangy /'tæŋɪ/ *adj.* (**tangier, tangiest**) óстрый, тéрпкий.

tank /tæŋk/ *n.*
[1] (*container*) бак, цистéрна; **petrol ~** бензобáк; **water ~** бак для воды́.
[2] (*armoured vehicle*) танк.

tankard /'tæŋkəd/ *n.* высóкая пивнáя крýжка.

tanker /'tæŋkə(r)/ *n.* (*ship*) тáнкер; (*vehicle*) автоцистéрна.

tantalize /'tæntəlaɪz/ *v.t.* (*tease*) дразни́ть (*impf.*).

tantamount /'tæntəmaʊnt/ *adj.*: **~ to** равноси́льный + *d.*

tantrum /'tæntrəm/ *n.* вспы́шка раздражéния; **the child is in a ~** ребёнок капри́зничает.

Tanzania /tænzə'ni:ə/ *n.* Танзáния.

Tanzanian /tænzə'ni:ən/ *n.* танзани́|ец (*fem.* -йка).
■ *adj.* танзани́йский.

tap¹ /tæp/ *n.* кран.
■ *v.t.* (**tapped, tapping**) (*fig.*): **the line is being ~ped** разговóр подслýшивают.

tap² /tæp/ *n.* (*light blow*) стук.
■ *v.t.* (**tapped, tapping**) легкó уд|аря́ть, -áрить; стучáть, по-.
■ *v.i.* (**tapped, tapping**) стучáться, по-; **he ~ped on the door** он постучáлся в дверь.
■ *cpds.* **~dance, ~-dancing** *nn.* чечётка.

tape /teɪp/ *n.* (*strip of fabric etc.*) тесьмá, лéнта; **adhesive ~** ли́пкая лéнта; (*magnetic ~*) (магнитофóнная) лéнта/плёнка.
■ *v.t.* [1] (*bind with ~*) свя́з|ывать, -áть тесьмóй.
[2] (*record*) запи́с|ывать, -áть (на плёнку).
■ *cpds.* **~ measure** *n.* рулéтка, (санти)мéтр; **~ recorder** *n.* магнитофóн; **~worm** *n.* лéнточный червь.

taper /'teɪpə(r)/ *v.t.* & *i.* сужáть(ся), сýзить(ся).

tapestry /'tæpɪstrɪ/ *n.* гобелéн.

tar /tɑ:(r)/ *n.* дёготь (*m.*).

tarantula /tə'ræntjʊlə/ *n.* тарáнтул.

tardy /'tɑ:dɪ/ *adj.* (**tardier, tardiest**) (*slow-moving*) медли́тельный; (*late in coming, belated*) запоздáвший, запоздáлый.

target /'tɑ:gɪt/ *n.* (*for shooting etc.*) мишéнь (*also fig.*), цель; (*objective*) цель.
■ *v.t.* (**targeted, targeting**)
[1] (*select as object*) дéлать, с- мишéнью.
[2] (*aim*) напр|авля́ть, -áвить.

tariff /'tærɪf/ *n.* (*duty*) тари́ф.

tarmac /'tɑ:mæk/ *n.* (*propr.*) гудрóн, асфáльт; (*aeron.*) бетони́рованная площáдка.

tarnish /'tɑ:nɪʃ/ *v.t.*: **~ed by damp** потускнéвший от влáги; **he has a ~ed reputation** он запятнáл свою́ репутáцию.
■ *v.i.* тускнéть, по-.

tarpaulin /tɑ:'pɔ:lɪn/ *n.* брезéнт.

tarragon /'tærəgən/ *n.* эстрагóн, тархýн.

tart¹ /tɑ:t/ *n.* (*flat pie*) откры́тый пирóг с фрýктами/я́годами.
■ *v.t.*: **~ up** (*Br. coll., embellish*) приукрá|шивать, -сить; **she was all ~ed up** онá былá разодéта с головы́ до ног.

tart² /tɑ:t/ *adj.* (*of taste*) ки́слый.

tartan /'tɑ:t(ə)n/ *n.* (*fabric*) шотлáндка (*клетчатая ткань*).

Tartar /'tɑ:tə(r)/ *n.* (*hist.*) татáро(-)монгóл.
■ *adj.* (*hist.*) татáро(-)монгóльский.

Tashkent /tæʃ'kent/ *n.* Ташкéнт.

task /tɑ:sk/ *n.* задáча, задáние; **~ force** (*mil.*) операти́вная грýппа.
■ *cpd.* **~master** *n.*: **he is a hard ~master** он из тебя́ все сóки выжимáет.

Tasmania /tæz'meɪnɪə/ *n.* Тасмáния.

tassel /'tæs(ə)l/ *n.* ки́сточка (*украшение*).

taste /teɪst/ *n.* (*sense; flavour*) вкус; (*act of tasting; small portion for tasting*): **have a ~ of this!** попрóбуйте/отвéдайте э́того!; (*fig., liking*): **she has expensive ~s in clothes** онá лю́бит носи́ть дороги́е вéщи; (*fig., discernment*) вкус; **he is a man of ~** он человéк со вкýсом; **bad ~** дурнóй вкус.
■ *v.t.* [1] (*perceive flavour of*) чýвствовать, по-; **can you ~ the garlic?** вы чýвствуете чеснóк?
[2] (*eat small amount of*) есть, по-.
[3] (*experience*) вку|шáть, -си́ть; извéд|ывать, -ать.
■ *v.i.*: **the meat ~s horrible** у мя́са отврати́тельный вкус; **~ of** имéть (*impf.*) при́вкус + *g.*

tasteful /'teɪstfʊl/ *adj.* изя́щный; со вкýсом.

tasteless /'teɪstlɪs/ *adj.* (*insipid; showing no taste*) безвкýсный; (*behaviour*) бестáктный.

tasty /'teɪstɪ/ *adj.* (**tastier, tastiest**) вкýсный, лáкомый.

Tatar /'tɑ:tə(r)/ (*inhabitant of Tatarstan etc.*) татáр|ин (*fem.* -ка).
■ *adj.* татáрский.

tattered /'tætəd/ *adj.* пóрванный, разóрванный.

tatters /'tætəz/ *n.* клóчь|я (*pl., g.* -ев), лохмóть|я (*pl., g.* -ев).

tattoo /tæ'tu:/ *n.* (*pl.* **~s**) (*on skin*) татуирóвка.
■ *v.t.* (**tattoos, tattooed**) татуи́ровать (*impf., pf.*).

tatty /'tætɪ/ *adj.* (**tattier, tattiest**) (*coll.*) потрёпанный.

taught /tɔ:t/ *past and p.p. of* ▶ **teach**

taunt /tɔ:nt/ *v.t.* дразни́ть (*impf.*).

Taurus /'tɔ:rəs/ *n.* (*astron.*) Телéц.

taut /tɔ:t/ *adj.* (*tight*) тугóй, тýго натя́нутый.

tautological /tɔ:tə'lɒdʒɪk(ə)l/ *adj.* тавтологи́ческий.

tautology /tɔ:'tɒlədʒɪ/ *n.* тавтолóгия.

tavern /'tæv(ə)n/ *n.* (*arch.*) тавéрна.

tawdry /'tɔ:drɪ/ *adj.* (**tawdrier, tawdriest**) кричáщий, безвкýсный.

tax /tæks/ *n.* налóг.
■ *v.t.* обл|агáть, -ожи́ть налóгом; (*fig.*): **he ~es my patience** он испы́тывает моё терпéние.
■ *cpds.* **~ collector** *n.* сбóрщик налóгов; **~ disc** *n.* (*Br.*) наклéйка об уплáте дорóжного налóга; **~-free** *adjs.* не облагáемый налóгом; **~ haven** *n.* странá с ни́зкими налóгами; **~payer** *n.* налогоплатéльщик.

taxable /'tæksəb(ə)l/ *adj.* подлежáщий обложéнию налóгом.

taxation /tæk'seɪʃ(ə)n/ *n.* налогообложéние.

taxi /'tæksɪ/ *n.* (*pl.* **taxis**) такси́ (*nt. indecl.*).
■ *v.i.* (**taxies, taxied, taxiing**) (*of aircraft*) рули́ть (*impf.*).

■ *cpds.* **~ rank** (*US* **~ stand**) *n.* стоянка такси.

taxidermist /'tæksɪdə:mɪst/ *n.* таксидерми́ст, наби́вщик чу́чел.

taxidermy /'tæksɪdə:mɪ/ *n.* таксидерми́я, наби́вка чу́чел.

taxonomic /tæksə'nɒmɪk/ *adj.* таксономи́ческий.

taxonomy /tæk'sɒnəmɪ/ *n.* система́тика, таксоно́мия.

TB (*abbr. of* ***tuberculosis***) туберкулёз.

Tbilisi /təbɪ'li:sɪ/ *n.* Тбили́си (*m. indecl.*).

tea /ti:/ *n.* (*plant, beverage*) чай; (*Br., meal*) по́лдник; **make (the) ~** зава́р|ивать, -и́ть чай; **have ~** пить, вы- чай/ча́я/ча́ю.
■ *cpds.* **~ bag** *n.* паке́тик ча́я, ча́йный паке́тик; **~ break** *n.* (*Br.*) переры́в на чай; **~cup** *n.* ча́йная ча́шка; **~pot** *n.* ча́йник (для зава́рки); **~ shop** *n.* кафе́ (*nt. indecl.*); **~spoon** *n.* ча́йная ло́жечка; **~spoonful** *n.* одна́/це́лая ча́йная ло́жка; **~-strainer** *n.* ча́йное си́течко; **~time** *n.* (*Br.*) ра́нний ве́чер, вре́мя (вече́рнего) чаепи́тия; **~ towel** *n.* (*Br.*) ку́хонное/посу́дное полоте́нце.

teach /ti:tʃ/ *v.t.* (*past and p.p.* **taught**)
1 (*instruct*) учи́ть, на-; обуч|а́ть, -и́ть; **she taught me Russian** она́ учи́ла меня́ ру́сскому языку́.
2 (*v.t. & i., give instruction*) (*school etc.*) учи́ть (*impf.*); (*university etc.*) преподава́ть (*impf.*); **~ing staff** преподава́тельский соста́в.
3 (*ellipt.*): **that will ~ you!** э́то бу́дет вам уро́ком!; **I'll ~ you (a lesson)!** я вас проучу́!

teacher /'ti:tʃə(r)/ *n.* учи́тель (*fem.* -ница); педаго́г; **~ training college** педагоги́ческий институ́т.

teaching /'ti:tʃɪŋ/ *n.* преподава́ние.

teak /ti:k/ *n.* (*wood*) тик; (*tree*) тик, ти́ковое де́рево.

team /ti:m/ *n.* (*games*) кома́нда; (*of workers etc.*) брига́да.
■ *cpds.* **~ spirit** *n.* коллективи́зм; (*sport*) кома́ндный дух; **~work** *n.* коллекти́вная рабо́та.

tear[1] /tɪə(r)/ *n.* **(~drop)** слеза́; **burst into ~s** распла́каться (*pf.*).
■ *cpd.* **~ gas** *n.* слезоточи́вый газ.

tear[2] /teə(r)/ *n.* (*rent*) разры́в, дыра́.
■ *v.t.* (*past* **tore;** *p.p.* **torn**)
1 (*rip*) раз|рыва́ть, -орва́ть; рвать, по-; **I tore my shirt on a nail** я порва́л руба́шку о гвоздь; **he tore open the envelope** он разорва́л/вскры́л конве́рт.
2 (*remove by force*) от|рыва́ть, -орва́ть; срыва́ть, сорва́ть.
■ *v.i.* (*past* **tore;** *p.p.* **torn**)
1 (*become torn*) рва́ться, по-.
2 (*rush*) мча́ться, по-; нести́сь, по-.
■ *with advs.*: **I could not ~ myself away** я не мог оторва́ться; **several pages had been torn out** не́сколько страни́ц бы́ло вы́рвано; **the letter was torn up** письмо́ разорва́ли.

tearful /'tɪəfʊl/ *adj.* запла́канный.

tease /ti:z/ *v.t.* дразни́ть (*impf.*).

teat /ti:t/ *n.* сосо́к.

technical /'teknɪk(ə)l/ *adj.* техни́ческий; **~ term** специа́льный те́рмин.

technicality /teknɪ'kælɪtɪ/ *n.* техни́ческая дета́ль.

technician /tek'nɪʃ(ə)n/ *n.* те́хник.

technique /tek'ni:k/ *n.* (*skill*) те́хника; (*method*) приём.

technocrat /'teknəkræt/ *n.* технокра́т.

technological /teknə'lɒdʒɪk(ə)l/ *adj.* техни́ческий.

technologist /tek'nɒlədʒɪst/ *n.* те́хник; (*in particular area*) техно́лог.

technology /tek'nɒlədʒɪ/ *n.* те́хника; (*in particular area*) техноло́гия.

teddy (bear) /'tedɪ/ *n.* (плю́шевый) ми́шка.

tedious /'ti:dɪəs/ *adj.* ну́дный.

teem /ti:m/ *v.i.*: **the house is ~ing with ants** дом киши́т муравья́ми.

teen /ti:n/ *n.*: **he is in his ~s** ему́ ещё нет двадцати́ (лет); он подро́сток.
■ *cpds.* **~age** *adj.* (*characteristic of teenagers*) подростко́вый, ю́ношеский; (*girl, boy*) несовершенноле́тний; **~ager** *n.* подро́сток, ю́ноша (*m.*)/де́вушка до двадцати́ лет; тине́йджер.

teeter /'ti:tə(r)/ *v.i.* кача́ться (*impf.*).

teeth /ti:θ/ *pl. of* ▶**tooth**

teeth|e /ti:ð/ *v.i.*: **baby is ~ing** у ребёнка ре́жутся зу́бы; **~ing troubles** (*fig.*) «де́тские боле́зни» (*f. pl.*).

teetotal /ti:'təʊt(ə)l/ *adj.* непью́щий.

TEFL /'tef(ə)l/ (*abbr. of* ***teaching of English as a foreign language***) преподава́ние англи́йского языка́ как иностра́нного.

Teh(e)ran /teə'rɑ:n/ *n.* Тегера́н.

Tel Aviv /'tel ə'vi:v/ *n.* Тель-Ави́в.

telecommunications /telɪkəmju:nɪ'keɪʃ(ə)nz/ *n. pl.* телекоммуника́ции (*f. pl.*).

teleconference /'telɪkɒnfərəns/ *n.* телеконфере́нция.

telegram /'telɪgræm/ *n.* телегра́мма.

telegraph /'telɪgrɑ:f, -græf/ *n.* телегра́ф.
■ *v.t. & i.* телеграфи́ровать (*impf., pf.*).
■ *cpd.* **~ pole** *n.* телегра́фный столб.

telepathic /telɪ'pæθɪk/ *adj.* телепати́ческий.

telepathy /tɪ'lepəθɪ/ *n.* телепа́тия.

telephone /'telɪfəʊn/ *n.* телефо́н; **he is (talking) on the ~** (*Br.*) он разгова́ривает по телефо́ну; **someone wants you on the ~** вас про́сят к телефо́ну; **he picked up the ~** он по́днял тру́бку; **~ booth, box** (*Br.*) телефо́нная бу́дка; **~ directory** телефо́нный спра́вочник; **~ call** телефо́нный звоно́к; **~ number** телефо́нный но́мер, (*coll.*) телефо́н; **~ operator** телефони́ст (*fem.* -ка); **public ~** телефо́н-автома́т.
■ *v.t. & i.* звони́ть, по- (*кому*) по телефо́ну.

telephonist /tɪ'lefənɪst/ *n.* (*Br.*) телефони́ст (*fem.* -ка).

telesales /'telɪseɪlz/ *n. pl.* прода́жа по телефо́ну.

telescope /'telɪskəʊp/ *n.* телеско́п.

telescopic /telɪ'skɒpɪk/ *adj.*
1 (*of or constituting a telescope*) телескопи́ческий; **~ lens** телескопи́ческий объекти́в.
2 (*visible by telescope*) ви́димый посре́дством телеско́па.
3 (*consisting of retracting and extending*

sections) складнóй, выдвижнóй; **~ aerial** выдвижнáя антéнна.

teletext /'telıtekst/ *n.* телетéкст.

televise /'telıvaız/ *v.t.* покáз|ывать, -áть по телевúдению.

television /'telıvıʒ(ə)n, -'vıʒ(ə)n/ *n.* (*system, process*) телевúдение; **what's on ~?** что покáзывают по телевúдению?; (*apparatus*) (*also* **~ set)** телевúзор; **~ camera** телекáмера; **~ programme** телевизиóнная передáча, телепередáча, телепрогрáмма; **~ studio** телестýдия.

tell /tel/ *v.t.* (*past and p.p.* **told**)
1 (*relate; inform of; make known*) расскáз|ывать, -áть; сообщ|áть, -úть; укáз|ывать, -áть; **~ me all about it!** расскажúте мне всё как есть/бы́ло.
2 (*speak, say*) говорúть, сказáть; **are you ~ing the truth?** вы говорúте прáвду?
3 (*decide, know*) определ|я́ть, -úть; узн|авáть, -áть; **can she ~ the time yet?** онá ужé умéет определя́ть врéмя?; **you never can ~** никогдá не знáешь.
4 (*distinguish*) отлич|áть, -úть; различ|áть, -úть; **I can't ~ them apart** я не могý их различúть.
5 (*instruct*) прикáз|ывать, -áть; говорúть, сказáть; **he was told to wait outside** емý сказáли/велéли подождáть за двéрью; **~ him not to wait** скажúте емý, чтóбы он не ждал.
6 (*predict*) предскáз|ывать, -áть; **I told you so!** я вам говорúл!
■ *v.i.* (*past and p.p.* **told**)
1 (*give information*) расскáз|ывать, -áть; **he told of his adventures** он рассказáл о своúх приключéниях; **don't ~ on me!** (*coll.*) не выдавáй меня́!; **he promised not to ~** (*divulge secret*) он обещáл молчáть.
2 (*have an effect*) скáз|ываться, -áться.
■ *with adv.*: **~ off** (*coll., reprove*) отчúт|ывать, -áть.
■ *cpd.* **~tale** *n.* сплéтник, я́беда (*c.g.*); (*attr.*) предáтельский.

telling /'telıŋ/ *adj.* сúльный; **a ~ argument** убедúтельный дóвод; **a ~ example** нагля́дный примéр; **a ~ blow** ощутúмый удáр.

telly /'telı/ *n.* (*Br.*) тéлик (*coll.*).

temerity /tı'merıtı/ *n.* смéлость.

temp /temp/ *n.* (*coll.*) рабóтающ|ий (*fem.* -ая) врéменно.
■ *v.i.* рабóтать (*impf.*) врéменно.

temper /'tempə(r)/ *n.*
1 (*disposition*) нрав; (*mood*) настроéние; **he lost his ~** он вы́шел из себя́.
2 (*anger*) вспы́льчивость; несдéржанность; **he has a quick ~** он вспы́льчив(ый); **he flew into a ~** он вспылúл; **he left in a ~** он разозлúлся и ушёл.
■ *v.t.* 1 (*metall.*) закáл|ивать, -úть.
2 (*mitigate*) ум|еря́ть, -éрить.

temperament /'temprəmənt/ *n.* темперáмент.

temperamental /temprə'ment(ə)l/ *adj.* капрúзный.

temperate /'tempərət/ *adj.* умéренный.

temperature /'temprıtʃə(r)/ *n.* температýра; (*fever*) жар; **he has (*or* is running) a ~** у негó температýра/жар.

tempest /'tempıst/ *n.* (*lit., fig.*) бýря.

tempestuous /tem'pestjʊəs/ *adj.* бýрный.

tempi /'tempi:/ *pl. of* ▸ **tempo**

template /'templeıt/ *n.* модéль; (*comput.*) шаблóн.

temple[1] /'temp(ə)l/ *n.* (*relig.*) храм, святúлище.

temple[2] /'temp(ə)l/ *n.* (*anat.*) висóк.

tempo /'tempəʊ/ *n.* (*pl.* **tempos** *or* **tempi**) темп.

temporal /'tempər(ə)l/ *adj.* (*of time*) временнóй; (*of this life; secular*) мирскóй, свéтский; (*anat.*) висóчный.

temporarily /'tempərərılı/ *adv.* врéменно.

temporary /'tempərərı/ *adj.* врéменный.

tempt /tempt/ *v.t.* соблазн|я́ть, -úть; иску|шáть, -сúть; **I was ~ed to agree with him** я был склóнен с ним согласúться; **~ing** соблазнúтельный.

temptation /temp'teıʃ(ə)n/ *n.* соблáзн, искушéние.

temptress /'temptrıs/ *n.* искусúтельница, соблазнúтельница.

ten /ten/ *n.* дéсять; (*figure; thing numbered 10; group of ~*) десятка.
■ *adj.* дéсять + *g. pl.*
■ *cpds.* **~pin bowling** *n.*, (*US*) **~pins** *n. pl.* кéгл|и (*pl., g.* -ей).

tenable /'tenəb(ə)l/ *adj.*
1 (*defensible*) разýмный, здрáвый; **a ~ argument** разýмный дóвод.
2 (*to be held*): **the office is ~ for three years** срок полномóчий — три гóда.

tenacious /tı'neıʃəs/ *adj.* настóйчивый.

tenacity /tı'næsıtı/ *n.* цéпкость; настóйчивость.

tenancy /'tenənsı/ *n.* наём помещéния.

tenant /'tenənt/ *n.* (*one renting from landlord*) (*private individual*) жилéц, квартирáнт; (*company*) арендáтор.

tend[1] /tend/ *v.t.* (*look after*) присм|áтривать, -отрéть за + *i.*

tend[2] /tend/ *v.i.* (*be inclined*) склоня́ться (*impf.*) (*к чему*); **he ~s to get excited** он легкó возбуждáется.

tendency /'tendənsı/ *n.* склóнность; **he has a ~ to forget** он забы́вчив(ый).

tender[1] /'tendə(r)/ *n.* (*comm.*) предложéние.
■ *v.t.* предл|агáть, -ожúть; **he ~ed his resignation** он пóдал заявлéние об отстáвке.

tender[2] /'tendə(r)/ *adj.* (**tenderer, tenderest**)
1 (*sensitive, loving*) нéжный; **my finger is still ~** мой пáлец всё ещё болúт.
2 (*not tough*): **a ~ steak** мя́гкий бифштéкс.

tenderness /'tendənıs/ *n.* нéжность; (*of meat etc.*) мя́гкость.

tendon /'tend(ə)n/ *n.* сухожúлие.

tendril /'tendrıl/ *n.* ýсик (*растения*).

tenement /'tenımənt/ *n.* (*block of flats*) многоквартúрный дом; (*flat*) квартúра.

tenet /'tenıt/ *n.* дóгмат, прúнцип.

tenner /'tenə(r)/ *n.* (*Br. coll.*) десятка (*10-фунтовая банкнота; сумма в 10 фунтов*).

tennis /'tenıs/ *n.* тéннис.
■ *cpds.* **~ court** *n.* тéннисный корт; **~**

player *n.* теннисист (*fem.* -ка).
tenor /ˈtenə(r)/ *n.* (*mus.*) тéнор.
tense[1] /tens/ *n.* (*gram.*) врéмя (*nt.*).
tense[2] /tens/ *adj.* натя́нутый, напряжённый.
■ *v.t.* натя́|гивать, -нýть; напр|ягáть, -я́чь.
tension /ˈtenʃ(ə)n/ *n.* (*stretching; mental strain*) напряжéние; (*stretched state*) натяжéние.
tent /tent/ *n.* палáтка.
tentacle /ˈtentək(ə)l/ *n.* щýпальце.
tentative /ˈtentətɪv/ *adj.* осторóжный.
tenterhooks /ˈtentəhʊks/ *n.*: **I was on ~** я сидéл как на игóлках.
tenth /tenθ/ *n.*
[1] (*date*) деся́тое числó.
[2] (*fraction*) деся́тая часть; **one ~** однá деся́тая.
■ *adj.* деся́тый.
tenuous /ˈtenjʊəs/ *adj.* слáбый.
tenure /ˈtenjə(r)/ *n.* (*holding of office*) пребывáние в дóлжности; (*period of office*) срок полномóчий; (*of property*) услóвия (*nt. pl.*) владéния имýществом; (*security of ~*) постоя́нная штáтная дóлжность.
tepid /ˈtepɪd/ *adj.* теплова́тый.
tera- /ˈterə/ *comb. form* тера…; **~byte** терабáйт; **~watt** теравáтт.
term /tɜːm/ *n.*
[1] (*fixed or limited period*) перúод; **~ of office** срок полномóчий; (*in school etc.*) тримéстр, учéбная чéтверть.
[2] (*expression*) тéрмин; **in ~s of** с тóчки зрéния + *g.*; в смы́сле + *g.*
[3] (*pl., conditions*) услóвия (*nt. pl.*); **they came to ~s** они́ пришли́ к соглашéнию.
[4] (*pl., relations*) отношéния (*nt. pl.*); **I kept on good ~s with him** я поддéрживал с ним хорóшие отношéния.
■ *v.t.* наз|ывáть, -вáть.
terminal /ˈtɜːmɪn(ə)l/ *n.*
[1] (*of transport*) конéчный пункт; (*rail*) вокзáл; **air ~** (*in city*) (городскóй) аэровокзáл.
[2] (*at airport*) терминáл.
[3] (*elec.*) клéмма, зажи́м.
[4] (*comput.; where oil/gas are stored*) терминáл.
■ *adj.* (*coming to or forming the end point*) конéчный; **~ illness** смертéльная болéзнь.
terminate /ˈtɜːmɪneɪt/ *v.t.* заверш|áть, -и́ть.
■ *v.i.* зак|áнчиваться, -óнчиться.
termination /tɜːmɪˈneɪʃ(ə)n/ *n.* завершéние; конéц; **~ of pregnancy** прекращéние берéменности.
terminology /tɜːmɪˈnɒlədʒɪ/ *n.* терминолóгия, номенклатýра.
terminus /ˈtɜːmɪnəs/ *n.* (*Br.*) конéчный пункт.
terrace /ˈterəs/ *n.* (*raised area*) террáса; (*Br., row of houses*) ряд однотúпных домóв, примыкáющих друг к дрýгу.
terraced /ˈterəst/ *adj.* (*of land, a garden*) террáсный; (*of house*) стоя́щий в ряду́ однотúпных домóв.
terracotta /terəˈkɒtə/ *n.* терракóта (*жёлтая/красная обожжённая гончарная глина*); (*attr.*) терракóтовый (*из такой глины; цвет*).
terrain /teˈreɪn/ *n.* мéстность.
terrapin /ˈterəpɪn/ *n.* пресновóдная черепáха.
terrestrial /təˈrestrɪəl/ *adj.* земнóй.
terrible /ˈterɪb(ə)l/ *adj.* стрáшный.
terribly /ˈterɪblɪ/ *adv.* ужáсно, стрáшно.
terrier /ˈterɪə(r)/ *n.* терьéр.
terrific /təˈrɪfɪk/ *adj.* (*coll., huge*) колоссáльный; (*coll., marvellous*) потрясáющий.
terrify /ˈterɪfaɪ/ *v.t.* ужас|áть, -нýть.
territorial /terɪˈtɔːrɪəl/ *adj.* территориáльный.
territory /ˈterɪtərɪ/ *n.* территóрия.
terror /ˈterə(r)/ *n.* ýжас, страх.
terrorism /ˈterərɪz(ə)m/ *n.* террори́зм.
terrorist /ˈterərɪst/ *n.* террори́ст (*fem.* -ка).
terrorize /ˈterəraɪz/ *v.t.* терроризи́ровать (*impf., pf.*).
terse /tɜːs/ *adj.* (**terser, tersest**) крáткий, сжáтый.
terseness /ˈtɜːsnɪs/ *n.* крáткость, сжáтость.
tertiary /ˈtɜːʃərɪ/ *adj.* (*geol. etc.*) трети́чный.
test /test/ *n.* испытáние, провéрка; **~ case** показáтельный слýчай; (*leg.*) дéло-прецедéнт; **his promises were put to the ~** егó обещáния подвéрглись провéрке на дéле; (*examination*) (*in school*) контрóльная рабóта; (*at college*) зачёт; (*oral*) опрóс, зачёт; **blood ~** анáлиз крóви.
■ *v.t.* [1] (*make trial of*) подв|ергáть, -éргнуть испытáнию; пров|еря́ть, -éрить.
[2] (*subject to ~s*) пров|еря́ть, -éрить.
■ *cpds.* **T~ match** *n.* (*cricket, rugby*) междунарóдный матч; **~ pilot** лётчик-испытáтель (*m.*); **~ tube** *n.* проби́рка; **~-tube baby** ребёнок «из проби́рки» (*зачатый вне материнского чрева*).
testament /ˈtestəmənt/ *n.* (*clear sign*) свидéтельство; (*bibl.*): **the Old/New T~** Вéтхий/Нóвый Завéт.
testicle /ˈtestɪk(ə)l/ *n.* (*anat.*) яи́чко.
testify /ˈtestɪfaɪ/ *v.i.*
[1] (*affirm*) свидéтельствовать (*impf.*).
[2]: **~ to** (*be evidence of*) свидéтельствовать (*impf.*) о + *p.*
testimonial /testɪˈməʊnɪəl/ *n.* рекомендáция.
testimony /ˈtestɪmənɪ/ *n.* (*statement*) показáния (*nt. pl.*); (*evidence*) доказáтельство.
testosterone /teˈstɒstərəʊn/ *n.* тестостерóн.
tetanus /ˈtetənəs/ *n.* (*med.*) столбня́к.
tetchy /ˈtetʃɪ/ *adj.* (**tetchier, tetchiest**) раздражи́тельный; оби́дчивый.
tête-à-tête /teɪtɑːˈteɪt/ *n.* тет-а-тéт.
■ *adv.* (*to talk*) тет-а-тéт; с глáзу на глáз; (*to dine*) вдвоём.
tether /ˈteðə(r)/ *n.* при́вязь; (*fig.*): **he was at the end of his ~** он дошёл до рýчки (*coll.*).
■ *v.t.* привя́з|ывать, -áть.
Teutonic /tjuːˈtɒnɪk/ *adj.* тевтóнский, германский.
text /tekst/ *n.* текст.
■ *v.t.* пос|ылáть, -лáть SMS (*pron.* эс-эм-эс) *кому-н.*
■ *cpds.* **~book** *n.* учéбник; **~ message**

SMS/СМС-сообще́ние.

textile /'tekstaɪl/ *n.* ткань.

textual /'tekstjʊəl/ *adj.* текстово́й; ~ **criticism** текстоло́гия.

texture /'tekstʃə(r)/ *n.* (*of fabric*): **this cloth has a smooth** ~ э́та ткань мя́гкая на о́щупь.

Thai /taɪ/ *n.* (*pl.* ~ *or* ~**s**) таила́нд|ец (*fem.* -ка).
■ *adj.* таила́ндский.

Thailand /'taɪlænd/ *n.* Таила́нд.

Thames /temz/ *n.* Те́мза.

than /ðæn/ *conj.* чем; **he's got more money** ~ **me** у него́ бо́льше де́нег, чем у меня́; **he is taller** ~ **I** он вы́ше меня́; **the visitor was no other** ~ **his father** посети́телем был не кто ино́й, как его́ оте́ц.

thank /θæŋk/ *v.t.* благодари́ть, по-; (*by returning favour*) отблагодари́ть (*pf.*); ~ **you (very much)** (большо́е) спаси́бо; ~ **God you are safe** сла́ва бо́гу, вы в безопа́сности.
■ *cpd.* ~ **you** *n.*: **he left without as much as a** ~ **you** он ушёл, да́же не сказа́в спаси́бо; *adj.*: ~**-you letter** благода́рственное письмо́.

thankful /'θæŋkfʊl/ *adj.* благода́рный.

thankless /'θæŋklɪs/ *adj.* неблагода́рный.

thanks /θæŋks/ *n. pl.* благода́рность; ~ **for everything** спаси́бо за всё; ~ **to** благодаря́ + *d.*
■ *cpd.* ~**giving** *n.*: **T**~**giving (Day)** День благодаре́ния.

that /ðæt/ *pron.* (*pl.* **those**)
1 (*demonstrative*) э́то; **those were the days!** вот э́то бы́ли времена́!; **what is** ~**?** что э́то (тако́е)?; **who is** ~ кто э́то?; ~**'s a nice hat!** кака́я краси́вая шля́пка!; ~**'s it!** (*sc. the point*) вот и́менно!; (*sc. right*) пра́вильно!; так!; ~ **is how the war began** вот как начала́сь война́; ~**'s right!** пра́вильно!; ве́рно!; ~**'s all** э́то всё; вот и всё!; **I'm going, and** ~**'s** ~ я ухожу́: всё; ~ **is (to say)** то́ есть.
2 (*rel.*) кото́рый; **the book** ~ **I am talking about** кни́га, о кото́рой я говорю́; **he was the best man** ~ **I ever knew** он был са́мым лу́чшим челове́ком, како́го я когда́-л. знал.
■ *adj.* (*pl.* **those**) э́тот, тот; **I'll take** ~ **one** я возьму́ (вот) э́тот; **at** ~ **time** в то вре́мя.
■ *adv.*: **I can't walk** ~ **far** я не могу́ так мно́го ходи́ть; **it is not all** ~ **cold** не так уж (и) хо́лодно.

■ *conj.* что; **I think** ~ **you're wrong** я ду́маю, что вы непра́вы; (*expr. wish*) что́бы; **I with** ~ **he would go away** я хочу́, что́бы он ушёл.

thatch /θætʃ/ *n.* (*straw*) соло́ма; (*reeds*) тростни́к.
■ *v.t.* крыть, по- соло́мой/тростнико́м; **a** ~**ed roof** соло́менная/тростнико́вая кры́ша.

thatched /θætʃt/ *adj.* соло́менный.

thaw /θɔ:/ *n.* (*also fig.*) о́ттепель.
■ *v.t.* (*ground, river*) отта́|ивать, -ять; (*food*) размор|а́живать, -о́зить.
■ *v.i.* (*of ground, river*) отта́|ивать, -ять; (*of food*) размор|а́живаться, -о́зиться; (*fig.*) смягч|а́ться, -и́ться.

the /ðə, ði:/ *def. art., usu. untranslated*; (*if more emphatic*) э́тот, тот (са́мый); ~ **one with** ~ **blue handle** тот, что с голубо́й ру́чкой; **he is** ~ **man for** ~ **job** он са́мый подходя́щий челове́к для э́той рабо́ты.
■ *adv.*: ~ **more** ~ **better** чем бо́льше, тем лу́чше; **he was none** ~ **worse (for it)** он (при э́том) нисколько не пострада́л.

theatre /'θɪətə(r)/ (*US* **theater**) *n.* теа́тр.
■ *cpd.* ~**goer** *n.* театра́л.

theatrical /θɪ'ætrɪk(ə)l/ *adj.* театра́льный.

theft /θeft/ *n.* кра́жа.

their /ðeə(r)/ *adj.* их; (*referring to gram. subject*) свой; **they want a house of** ~ **own** они́ хотя́т име́ть (свой) со́бственный дом.

theirs /ðeəz/ *pron.* их, свой; **the money was** ~ **by right** де́ньги принадлежа́ли им по пра́ву; **it is a habit of** ~ у них така́я привы́чка.

them /ðem/ *obj. of* ▸ **they**

thematic /θɪ'mætɪk/ *adj.* темати́ческий.

theme /θi:m/ *n.* те́ма; ~ **park** темати́ческий парк; ~ **song, tune** лейтмоти́в.

themselves /ðəm'selvz/ *pron.*
1 (*refl.*) себя́; -сь (*suff.*); **they blamed** ~ они́ вини́ли себя́; **they were proud of** ~ они́ горди́лись собо́й; **they hurt** ~ они́ ушиблись; **they live by** ~ они́ живу́т одни́; **they did it by** ~ они́ сде́лали э́то са́ми; **they have only** ~ **to blame** они́ са́ми винова́ты.
2 (*emph.*): **they did the work** ~ они́ сде́лали э́ту рабо́ту са́ми.

then /ðen/ *n.*: **before** ~ до э́того/того́ вре́мени; **by** ~ к э́тому/тому́ вре́мени; **since** ~ с тех пор.
■ *adv.* 1 (*at that time*) тогда́.
2 (*next*) да́льше, да́лее.
3 (*furthermore*) кро́ме того́; опя́ть-таки (*coll.*).
4 (*in that case*) тогда́; ~ **what *do* you want?** чего́ же вы тогда́ (*or* в тако́м слу́чае) хоти́те?

thence /ðens/ *adv.* отту́да.

theologian /θɪə'ləʊdʒ(ə)n/ *n.* богосло́в, тео́лог.

theological /θɪə'lɒdʒɪk(ə)l/ *adj.* богосло́вский, теологи́ческий.

theology /θɪ'ɒlədʒɪ/ *n.* богосло́вие, теоло́гия.

theorem /'θɪərəm/ *n.* теоре́ма.

theoretical /θɪə'retɪk(ə)l/ *adj.* теорети́ческий.

theorist /'θɪərɪst/ *n.* теоре́тик.

theorize /'θɪəraɪz/ *v.i.* теоретизи́ровать (*impf.*).

theory /'θɪərɪ/ *n.* тео́рия; **in** ~ в тео́рии; теорети́чески.

therapeutic /θerə'pju:tɪk/ *adj.* терапевти́ческий, лече́бный.

therapist /'θerəpɪst/ *n.* терапе́вт.

therapy /'θerəpɪ/ *n.* терапи́я, лече́ние.

there /ðeə(r)/ *adv.*
1 (*in or at that place*) там; вон (*coll.*); вон та́м; **that man** ~ **is my uncle** (вот) тот челове́к — мой дя́дя.
2 (*to that place*) туда́.
3 (*at that point*) тут, здесь.
4 (*demonstrative*): ~ **you go again!** опя́ть вы за своё!; ~ **you are, take it!** вот вам, держи́те!; **oh,** ~ **you are: I was looking for you** вот и вы! А я вас иска́л.

5 (*with v. 'to be', expr. presence, availability etc.*): **~'s a fly in my soup** у меня́ в су́пе му́ха; **is ~ a doctor here?** тут есть врач?; **~ seems to have been a mistake** тут, ка́жется, произошла́ оши́бка; **~ was plenty to eat** еды́ бы́ло полно́.
■ *int.*: **~! what did I tell you?** ну вот! что я вам говори́л?

thereabouts /ðeərə'baʊts/ *adv.* (*nearby*) поблизости; (*approximately*) о́коло э́того; приблизи́тельно.

thereby /ðeə'baɪ/ *adv.* э́тим.

therefore /'ðeəfɔ:(r)/ *adv.* поэ́тому, сле́довательно.

thereupon /ðeərə'pɒn/ *adv.* за э́тим.

thermal /'θə:m(ə)l/ *n.* (*aeron.*) восходя́щий пото́к тёплого во́здуха.
■ *adj.*: **~ capacity** теплоёмкость; **~ reactor** (я́дерный) реа́ктор на тепловы́х нейтро́нах, теплово́й я́дерный реа́ктор; **~ springs** горя́чие исто́чники.

thermodynamics /θə:məʊdaɪ'næmɪks/ *n.* термодина́мика.

thermometer /θə'mɒmɪtə(r)/ *n.* термо́метр.

Thermos /'θə:məs/ *n.* (*propr.*) (*in full* **~ flask)** те́рмос.

thermostat /'θə:məstæt/ *n.* термоста́т.

thesaurus /θɪ'sɔ:rəs/ *n.* теза́урус.

these /ði:z/ *pl. of* ▸ **this**

thesis /'θi:sɪs/ *n.* (*pl.* **theses** /-si:z/) (*dissertation*) диссерта́ция; (*contention*) те́зис.

thespian /'θespɪən/ *n.* (*joc.*) акт|ёр (*fem.* -ри́са).

they /ðeɪ/ *pron.* (*obj.* **them;** *poss.* **their, theirs**) они́; **~ who ...** те, кото́рые/кто...; **both of them** они́ о́ба.

thick /θɪk/ *n.*: **in the ~ of the crowd** в гу́ще толпы́; **in the ~ of the fighting** в са́мом пе́кле бо́я.
■ *adj.* 1 (*of solid substance*) то́лстый; (*of liquid*) густо́й.
2 (*dense*) густо́й.
3 (*coll., stupid*) тупо́й.
■ *adv.* гу́сто, ча́сто; **the blows came ~ and fast** уда́ры сы́пались оди́н за други́м.
■ *cpds.* **~set** *adj.* корена́стый; **~-skinned** *adj.* (*lit., fig.*) толстоко́жий.

thicken /'θɪkən/ *v.t.* сгу|ща́ть, -сти́ть; де́лать, с- бо́лее густы́м.
■ *v.i.* (*liquid*) де́латься, с- бо́лее густы́м; (*fog*) сгу|ща́ться, -сти́ться.

thicket /'θɪkɪt/ *n.* за́росл|и (*pl., g.* -ей).

thickness /'θɪknɪs/ *n.* толщина́, густота́; (*layer*) слой.

thief /θi:f/ *n.* (*pl.* **thieves**) вор.

thieve /θi:v/ *v.i.* красть, у-; ворова́ть, (*coll. pf.*) с-.

thieves /θi:vz/ *pl. of* ▸ **thief**

thigh /θaɪ/ *n.* бедро́.

thimble /'θɪmb(ə)l/ *n.* напёрсток.

thin /θɪn/ *adj.* (**thinner, thinnest**)
1 (*not fat; of person*) худо́й; (*of body, parts of body*) то́нкий; **she has got ~** она́ похуде́ла.
2 (*not thick; of paper, blanket*) то́нкий.
3 (*not dense; of hair*) ре́дкий.
4 (*of liquids*) жи́дкий.
■ *adv.* то́нко.
■ *v.t.* (**thinned, thinning**) (*liquid*) разб|авля́ть, -а́вить.
■ *v.i.* (**thinned, thinning**): **the crowd ~ned (out)** толпа́ пореде́ла; **his hair is ~ning** у него́ реде́ют во́лосы.

thing /θɪŋ/ *n.*
1 (*object*) вещь, предме́т.
2 (*pl., belongings*) иму́щество; ве́щи (*f. pl.*).
3 (*pl., equipment*) принадле́жности (*f. pl.*).
4 (*matter*) де́ло; вещь; **for one ~, he's too old** начнём с того́, что он сли́шком стар; **how are ~s?** как дела́?; **all ~s considered** принима́я во внима́ние всё.
5 (*act*) де́йствие; посту́пок; **that was a silly ~ to do** э́то был глу́пый посту́пок.
6 (*event*): **what a terrible ~ to happen!** како́е ужа́сное несча́стье!
7 (*remark*): **what a ~ to say!** как мо́жно сказа́ть тако́е!
8 (*issue*): **the ~ is, can you afford it?** хва́тит ли у вас на э́то де́нег? — вот в чём де́ло.
9 (**a ~:** *something; with neg.: nothing*): **I can't see a ~** я ничего́ не ви́жу.
10 (*of persons or animals*) созда́ние; **poor ~** бедня́га (*c.g.*).

think /θɪŋk/ *v.t.* & *i.* (*past and p.p.* **thought**) (*opine*) ду́мать, по-; полага́ть (*impf.*); счита́ть (*impf.*); **I ~** (я) ду́маю; мне ка́жется; **I don't ~ so** не ду́маю; **yes, I ~ so** да, пожа́луй; **I ~ I'll go** я, пожа́луй, пойду́; (*judge*) ду́мать, счита́ть, полага́ть (*all impf.*); **do you ~ she's pretty?** вы ду́маете она хоро́шенькая?/вы счита́ете её хоро́шенькой?; (*reflect*) ду́мать, по-; мы́слить (*impf.*); (*expect*) ду́мать (*impf.*); предполага́ть (*impf.*); (*imagine*): **I can't ~ how he does it** я не могу́ себе́ предста́вить, как он э́то де́лает; (*with preps.* **about, of**): **I have other things to ~ about** у меня́ мно́го други́х забо́т; **have you thought about going to the police?** вы не ду́мали пойти́ в поли́цию?; **I couldn't ~ of his name** я не мог вспо́мнить, как его́ зову́т; **who first thought of the idea?** кому́ пе́рвому пришла́ в го́лову э́та иде́я?
■ *with advs.*: **~ it over!** обду́майте э́то!; **he never ~s his answers through** он никогда́ не проду́мывает свои́ отве́ты (до конца́); **~ up** (*devise*) приду́м|ывать, -ать; (*invent*) выду́мывать, вы́думать.
■ *cpd.* **~ tank** *n.* (*coll.*) мозгово́й центр.

thinker /'θɪŋkə(r)/ *n.* мысли́тель (*m.*); **he is a quick ~** он бы́стро соobража́ет.

thinking /'θɪŋkɪŋ/ *n.*
1 (*process of thought*) размышле́ние.
2 (*opinion*) мне́ние; **to my way of ~** на мой взгляд.

third /θə:d/ *n.*
1 (*date*) тре́тье (число́); **my birthday is on the ~** мой день рожде́ния тре́тьего (числа́).
2 (*fraction*) треть; **two ~s** две тре́ти.
■ *adj.* тре́тий; **~ party** (*leg. etc.*) тре́тья сторона́; **the T~ World** тре́тий мир.
■ *cpd.* **~-class** *adj.* тре́тьего кла́сса; **~-generation** *adj.* тре́тьего поколе́ния (*технология*).

thirdly /'θə:dlɪ/ *adv.* в-тре́тьих.

thirst /θə:st/ *n.* жа́жда; **~ for knowledge** жа́жда зна́ний.

thirsty /'θə:stɪ/ *adj.* (**thirstier, thirstiest**)

t

испы́тывающий жа́жду; **I am/feel ~** мне хо́чется (*or* я хочу́) пить.

thirteen /θəː'tiːn/ *n.* трина́дцать.
■ *adj.* трина́дцать + *g. pl.*

thirteenth /θəː'tiːnθ/ *n.* (*date*) трина́дцатое число́; (*fraction*) одна́ трина́дцатая.
■ *adj.* трина́дцатый.

thirtieth /'θəːtɪɪθ/ *n.* (*date*) тридца́тое число́; (*fraction*) одна́ тридца́тая.
■ *adj.* тридца́тый.

thirt|y /'θəːtɪ/ *n.* три́дцать; **in the ~ies** в тридца́тых года́х; **he is in his ~ies** ему́ за три́дцать.
■ *adj.* три́дцать + *g. pl.*

this /ðɪs/ *pron.* (*pl.* **these**) э́то; **~ is what I think** вот, что я ду́маю; **are these your shoes?** э́то ва́ши ту́фли?; **we talked of ~ and that** мы (по)говори́ли о том, о сём.
■ *adj.* (*pl.* **these**) э́тот; да́нный; **~ book here** вот э́та кни́га; **come here ~ minute!** иди́ сюда́ сию́ же мину́ту!; **these days** (*nowadays*) в настоя́щее вре́мя, в на́ши дни.
■ *adv.*: **about ~ high** приме́рно тако́й высоты́.

thistle /'θɪs(ə)l/ *n.* чертополо́х.

thong /θɒŋ/ *n.*
1 реме́нь (*m.*).
2 (*garment*) тру́сик|и (*pl.*, *g.* -ов) «та́нга», та́нга (*pl. indecl.*), стри́нг|и (*pl.*, *g.* -ов).

thorn /θɔːn/ *n.* колю́чка, шип.

thorny /'θɔːnɪ/ *adj.* (**thornier, thorniest**) колю́чий; (*fig.*): **a ~ problem** сло́жная пробле́ма.

thorough /'θʌrə/ *adj.* (*search, investigation*) тща́тельный, всесторо́нний; (*person*) скрупулёзный.
■ *cpds.* **~bred** *n.* чистопоро́дное живо́тное; *adj.* чистокро́вный, чистопоро́дный; **~fare** *n.* тра́нспортная магистра́ль; **'No T~fare'** «прохо́да/прое́зда нет».

thoroughly /'θʌrəlɪ/ *adv.* (*satisfied, ashamed*) соверше́нно; (*study*) тща́тельно.

thoroughness /'θʌrənɪs/ *n.* тща́тельность; основа́тельность; скрупулёзность.

those /ðəʊz/ *pl. of* ▸ **that**

though /ðəʊ/ *adv.* & *conj.* хотя́, хоть; несмотря́ на то, что...; **even ~ it's late** пусть уже́ по́здно, но...; **he said he would come; he didn't, ~** он сказа́л, что придёт; одна́ко же не пришёл; **as ~** как бу́дто бы; **it looks as ~ he will lose** похо́же на то, что он проигра́ет.

thought[1] /θɔːt/ *n.*
1 (*thinking*) мысль; **modern scientific ~** совреме́нная нау́чная мысль.
2 (*reflection*) размышле́ние; **deep in ~** погружённый в размышле́ния; **on second ~s** поду́мав.
3 (*idea, opinion*) мысль, иде́я, соображе́ние.
■ *cpd.* **~-provoking** *adj.* заставля́ющий (серьёзно) заду́маться.

thought[2] /θɔːt/ *past and p.p. of* ▸ **think**

thoughtful /'θɔːtfʊl/ *adj.*
1 (*well-considered*): **a ~ essay** вду́мчивое/содержа́тельное эссе́.
2 (*considerate*) внима́тельный, чу́ткий.

thoughtless /'θɔːtlɪs/ *adj.* (*careless*) неосмотри́тельный; (*inconsiderate*) невнима́тельный.

thousand /'θaʊz(ə)nd/ *n.* & *adj.* (*pl.* **~s** *or* (*with numeral or qualifying word*) **~**) ты́сяча.

thousandth /'θaʊzəndθ/ *n.* ты́сячная часть.
■ *adj.* ты́сячный.

thrash /θræʃ/ *v.t.* (*beat*) изб|ива́ть, -и́ть; (*fig., defeat*) побе|жда́ть, -ди́ть.
■ *v.i.*: **the swimmer ~ed about in the water** плове́ц изо всех сил колоти́л рука́ми и нога́ми по воде́; **he ~ed about in bed** он мета́лся в посте́ли.
■ *with adv.*: **~ out** *v.t.* (*fig.*) обстоя́тельно обсу|жда́ть, -ди́ть; **let us ~ out this problem** дава́йте разберём э́тот вопро́с по пу́нктам.

thread /θred/ *n.*
1 (*spun fibre*) нить, ни́тка; **he lost the ~ of his argument** он потеря́л нить рассужде́ний.
2 (*of a screw etc.*) резьба́.
■ *v.t.* прод|ева́ть, -е́ть ни́тку в + *a.*; нани́з|ывать, -а́ть.
■ *cpd.* **~bare** *adj.* потёртый.

threat /θret/ *n.* угро́за.

threaten /'θret(ə)n/ *v.t.* & *i.* грози́ть, при- + *d.*; **he ~ed to leave** он угрожа́л, что уйдёт; он грози́лся уйти́.

three /θriː/ *n.* (число́/но́мер) три; (**~** *people*) тро́е; (*figure, thing numbered 3; group of* **~**) тро́йка.
■ *adj.* три + *g. sg.*
■ *cpds.* **~-cornered** *adj.* треуго́льный; **~-dimensional** *adj.* (*lit.*) трёхме́рный; **~fold** *adv.* втро́е; **~-piece** *adj.*: **~-piece suit** (костю́м-)тро́йка; **~-piece suite** дива́н с двумя́ кре́слами; **~-year-old** *adj.* трёхле́тний.

threshold /'θreʃhəʊld/ *n.* поро́г.

threw /θruː/ *past of* ▸ **throw**

thrift /θrɪft/ *n.* бережли́вость, эконо́мность.

thrifty /'θrɪftɪ/ *adj.* (**thriftier, thriftiest**) бережли́вый, эконо́мный.

thrill /θrɪl/ *n.* (*physical sensation*) дрожь, тре́пет; (*excitement*) восто́рг, восхище́ние.
■ *v.t.* восхи|ща́ть, -ти́ть; **a ~ing finish** захва́тывающий коне́ц.

thriller /'θrɪlə(r)/ *n.* три́ллер.

thrive /θraɪv/ *v.i.* (*prosper*) процвета́ть (*impf.*); (*grow vigorously*) разраст|а́ться, -и́сь.

throat /θrəʊt/ *n.* го́рло; **I have a sore ~** у меня́ боли́т го́рло.

throb /θrɒb/ *v.i.* (**throbbed, throbbing**) стуча́ть (*impf.*).

thrombosis /θrɒm'bəʊsɪs/ *n.* (*pl.* **thromboses** /-siːz/) (*med.*) тромбо́з.

throne /θrəʊn/ *n.* (*lit., fig.*) трон, престо́л.

throng /θrɒŋ/ *n.* толпа́.
■ *v.i.* ст|ека́ться, -е́чься.

throttle /'θrɒt(ə)l/ *v.t.* души́ть, за-.

through /θruː/ *adj.*
1 прямо́й; сквозно́й; **no ~ road** (*as notice*) прое́зда нет; **a ~ train** прямо́й по́езд.
2 (*various pred. uses*): **you must wait till I'm ~** (*finished*) **with the paper** вам придётся подожда́ть, пока́ я дочита́ю газе́ту; **she told him she was ~ with him** она́ ему́ сказа́ла, что ме́жду ни́ми всё ко́нчено.
■ *adv.* (*from beginning to end; completely*) до конца́; **have you read it ~?** вы всё

прочита́ли?; **you will get wet ~** вы промо́кнете наскво́зь; **the whole night ~** всю ночь напролёт; (*all the way*): **the train goes ~ to Paris** по́езд идёт пря́мо до Пари́жа.
■ *prep.* 1 че́рез + *a.*; **he came ~ the window** он влез че́рез окно́; (*esp. suggesting difficulty*) сквозь + *a.*; (*into, in*) в + *a.*; **look ~ the window!** посмотри́(те) в окно́!; (*via*): **we drove ~ Germany** мы е́хали че́рез Герма́нию.
2 (*during*) в тече́ние + *g.*
3 (*from, because of*) из-за + *g.*; по + *d.*; **~ laziness** из-за ле́ни; **~ stupidity** по глу́пости; (*of desirable result*) благодаря́ + *d.*
4 (*US, up to and including*): **from Monday ~ Saturday** с понеде́льника по суббо́ту (включи́тельно).
5 (*over the area of*): **the news quickly spread ~ the town** весть бы́стро распространи́лась по го́роду.
■ *cpd.* **~way** *n.* (*US*) автостра́да.

throughout /θruːˈaʊt/ *adv.* (*in every part*) везде́; повсю́ду; (*in all respects*) во всём.
■ *prep.* (*from end to end of*) че́рез + *a.*; **~ the country** по всей стране́; (*for the duration of*): **~ the 20th century** на протяже́нии всего́ XX/двадца́того ве́ка; **it rained ~ the night** всю ночь шёл дождь.

throw /θrəʊ/ *n.*
1 (*act of ~ing*) броса́ние, мета́ние.
2 (*in wrestling*) бросо́к.
■ *v.t.* (*past* **threw;** *p.p.* **thrown**)
1 бр|оса́ть, -о́сить; кида́ть, ки́нуть; **his horse threw him** ло́шадь сбро́сила его́; **the news threw me** (*coll.*) изве́стие потрясло́ меня́.
2 (*organize*) устр|а́ивать, -о́ить; **let's ~ a party** дава́йте устро́им вечери́нку.
■ *with advs.*: **~ away** *v.t.* (*discard*) выбра́сывать, вы́бросить; (*forgo*) упус|ка́ть, -ти́ть; **~ back** *v.t.* отбр|а́сывать, -о́сить наза́д; **~ in** *v.t.* вбр|а́сывать, -о́сить; (*fig.*) (*include*) доб|авля́ть, -а́вить; (*contribute*): **may I ~ in a suggestion?** разреши́те мне внести́ предложе́ние?; **~ off** *v.t.* сбр|а́сывать, -о́сить; **he threw off his clothes** он сбро́сил с себя́ оде́жду; **~ on** *v.t.*: **he threw on a coat** он набро́сил пальто́; **~ out** *v.t.* выбра́сывать, вы́бросить; (*reject*) отклон|я́ть, -и́ть; (*expel*) исключ|а́ть, -и́ть; выбра́сывать, вы́бросить; **~ together** *v.t.* (*compile*) сост|авля́ть, -а́вить; (*bring into contact*) соб|ира́ть, -ра́ть вме́сте; **~ up** *v.t.* подбр|а́сывать, -о́сить; *v.i.* (*vomit*): **he threw up** его́ вы́рвало.
■ *cpds.* **~away** *adj.* разового по́льзования; **~-in** *n.* вбра́сывание (мяча́) (*в футболе и регби*).

thrown /θrəʊn/ *p.p. of* ▸ **throw**

thrush¹ /θrʌʃ/ *n.* (*bird*) дрозд.

thrush² /θrʌʃ/ *n.* (*disease*) моло́чница.

thrust /θrʌst/ *n.* толчо́к.
■ *v.t.* (*past and p.p.* **thrust**) толк|а́ть, -ну́ть; **he ~ a note into my hand** он су́нул мне в ру́ку запи́ску.

thud /θʌd/ *n.* глухо́й звук; стук.
■ *v.i.* (**thudded, thudding**) глу́хо уд|аря́ться, -а́риться.

thug /θʌg/ *n.* банди́т, головоре́з.

thuggery /ˈθʌgərɪ/ *n.* банди́тизм, хулига́нство.

thuggish /ˈθʌgɪʃ/ *adj.* хулига́нский.

thumb /θʌm/ *n.* большо́й па́лец (руки́); **~s down** знак неодобре́ния; **~s up** знак одобре́ния; **he is completely under her ~** он по́лностью у неё под каблуко́м.
■ *v.t.* 1 : **~ through** перели́ст|ывать, -а́ть.
2 : **~ a lift** (*coll.*) голосова́ть (*impf.*).
■ *cpd.* **~tack** *n.* (*US*) кно́пка.

thump /θʌmp/ *n.* (*blow*) тяжёлый уда́р; (*noise*) глухо́й стук/шум.
■ *v.t.* бить (*impf.*); колоти́ть (*impf.*).
■ *v.i.* би́ться (*impf.*); колоти́ться (*impf.*).

thunder /ˈθʌndə(r)/ *n.* гром.
■ *v.i.*: **it is ~ing** гром греми́т.
■ *cpds.* **~bolt** *n.* уда́р мо́лнии; **~clap** *n.* уда́р гро́ма; **~storm** *n.* гроза́; **~struck** *adj.* (*fig.*) ошеломлённый.

Thursday /ˈθəːzdeɪ/ *n.* четве́рг.

thus /ðʌs/ *adv.* (*in this way*) таки́м о́бразом; (*accordingly*) сле́довательно, таки́м о́бразом.

thwart /θwɔːt/ *v.t.* меша́ть, по- + *d.*; **~ s.o.'s plans** расстр|а́ивать, -о́ить чьи-н. пла́ны.

thyme /taɪm/ *n.* тимья́н.

thyroid /ˈθaɪrɔɪd/ *n.* **(~ gland)** щитови́дная железа́.

tiara /tɪˈɑːrə/ *n.* тиа́ра, диаде́ма.

Tibet /tɪˈbet/ *n.* Тибе́т.

Tibetan /tɪˈbet(ə)n/ *n.* тибе́т|ец (*fem.* -ка).
■ *adj.* тибе́тский.

tick¹ /tɪk/ *n.*
1 (*of clock etc.*) ти́канье; **~-tock** тик-та́к.
2 (*checking mark*) га́лочка, пти́чка.
■ *v.i.* ти́кать (*impf.*).
■ *v.t.* отм|еча́ть, -е́тить га́лочкой.
■ *with adv.*: **~ off** (*coll., reprove*) отчи́т|ывать, -а́ть; (*mark with ~*): **she ~ed off the items** она́ отмеча́ла предме́ты га́лочками.

tick² /tɪk/ *n.* (*parasite*) клещ.

ticket /ˈtɪkɪt/ *n.* (*for travel, seating etc.*) биле́т; (*tag*) ярлы́к; (*US, list of election candidates*) спи́сок кандида́тов на вы́борах; (*printed notice of offence*): **he got a ~ for speeding** он получи́л штраф за превыше́ние ско́рости.
■ *cpd.* **~ office** *n.* биле́тная ка́сса.

tickle /ˈtɪk(ə)l/ *v.t.* щекота́ть, по-.

ticklish /ˈtɪklɪʃ/ *adj.*: **she is ~** она́ бои́тся щеко́тки; (*tricky*) щекотли́вый.

tidal /ˈtaɪd(ə)l/ *adj.* прили́вный; **~ wave** прили́вная волна́.

tidbit /ˈtɪdbɪt/ *n.* (*US*) = **titbit**

tide /taɪd/ *n.* (*rise*) морско́й прили́в; (*fall*) морско́й отли́в; (*fig.*) волна́, тече́ние; **the rising ~ of excitement** уси́ливающееся возбужде́ние.

tidiness /ˈtaɪdɪnɪs/ *n.* аккура́тность, опря́тность.

tidings /ˈtaɪdɪŋz/ *n.* (*liter. and joc.*) ве́сти (*f. pl.*), но́вости (*f. pl.*).

tidy /ˈtaɪdɪ/ *adj.* (**tidier, tidiest**) (*neat*) опря́тный, аккура́тный; (*considerable*): **a ~ sum** прили́чная су́мма.
■ *v.t.* (*also* **~ up**) прив|одить, -ести́ в поря́док; приб|ира́ть, -ра́ть.
■ *v.i.*: **~ up** нав|оди́ть, -ести́ поря́док.

tie /taɪ/ *n.*

1 (*also* **neck ~**) гáлстук.
2 (*part that fastens or connects*) завя́зка, связь; шнурóк.
3 (*fig., bond*) ýз|ы (*pl., g.* —).
4 (*fig., restriction*) обýза.
5 (*equal score*) ничья́; **the match ended in a ~** матч закóнчился ничьéй/вничью́.
■ *v.t.* (**tying**)
1 (*fasten*) свя́з|ывать, -áть; привя́з|ывать, -áть.
2 (*arrange in bow or knot*) перевя́з|ывать, -áть; завя́з|ывать, -áть; шнуровáть, за-.
■ *v.i.* (**tying**)
1 (*fasten*) завя́з|ываться, -áться.
2 (*make equal score*) равня́ть, с- счёт; игрáть, сыгрáть вничью́.
■ *with advs.*: **~ back** *v.t.*: **she wore her hair ~d back** онá завя́зывала вóлосы сзáди; **~ down** *v.t.* (*lit.*) привя́з|ывать, -áть; (*fig., restrict*) свя́з|ывать, -áть; **~ in (with)** *v.i.* соотвéтствовать (*impf.*) (+ *d.*); согласóв|ываться, -áться (с + *i.*); **~ up** *v.t.* (*lit.*) привя́з|ывать, -áть; свя́з|ывать, -áть; (*fig.*): **I'm ~d up this week** на э́той недéле у меня́ дел под завя́зку; **his capital is ~d up** его́ капитáл инвести́рован.
■ *cpd.* **~breaker** *n.* решáющая игрá (*после ничьей*).

tier /tɪə(r)/ *n.* ряд; я́рус.

tiff /tɪf/ *n.* размóлвка.

tiger /'taɪgə(r)/ *n.* тигр.

tight /taɪt/ *adj.*
1 (*with no slack*) тугóй; (*close-fitting*) тéсный; (*of clothes*) облегáющий; **my shoes are too ~** мои́ тýфли жмут.
2 (*strict*) стрóгий.
3 (*under pressure*): **I have a ~ schedule** у меня́ жёсткое расписáние.
■ *adv.* (*fitting*) тéсно, плóтно; (*screwed*) крéпко; (*stretched*) тýго; **hold ~!** держи́тесь крéпко!; **shut your eyes ~!** крéпко зажмýрьте глазá!
■ *cpds.* **~-fisted** *adj.* скупóй, прижи́мистый; **~(ly)-fitting** *adj.* плóтно облегáющий; **~rope** *n.* натя́нутый канáт.

tighten /'taɪt(ə)n/ *v.t.* (*grip*) сж|имáть, -ать; (*bonds*) закреп|ля́ть, -и́ть; (*screw, belt*) зат|я́гивать, -янýть.

tights /taɪts/ *n.* (*Br.*) колгóт|ки (*pl., g.* -ок).

tigress /'taɪgrɪs/ *n.* тигри́ца.

tile /taɪl/ *n.* (*for roof*) черепи́ца; (*for floor etc.*) пли́тка.
■ *v.t.* (*roof*) крыть, по- черепи́цей; (*walls*) крыть, по- пли́ткой.

till[1] /tɪl/ *n.* кácca.

till[2] /tɪl/ (*see also* ▸ **until**) *prep.* до + *g.*; **he will not come ~ after dinner** он придёт тóлько пóсле ýжина.
■ *conj.* покá... (не); до тех пор покá (не); **don't go ~ I come back** не ухóдите, покá я не вернýсь.

tilt /tɪlt/ *v.t.* наклон|я́ть, -и́ть.
■ *v.i.* (*slope*) наклон|я́ться, -и́ться.

timber /'tɪmbə(r)/ *n.* (*wood*) древеси́на; (*trees*) лес; (*beam*) бáлка.

timbre /'tæmbə(r)/ *n.* тембр.

time /taɪm/ *n.*
1 врéмя (*nt.*); **in ~, with ~** с течéнием врéмени; **~ will tell** врéмя покáжет.
2 (*duration, period, opportunity*): **after a ~** чéрез нéкоторое врéмя; **all the ~** всё врéмя, всегдá; **all in good ~** всемý своё врéмя; **in no ~ (at all)** моментáльно; **I haven't seen him for a long ~** я егó давнó не ви́дел; **take your ~!** не торопи́тесь!
3 (*experience*): **have a good ~!** желáю вам прия́тно провести́ врéмя; **we had the ~ of our lives** мы отли́чно провели́ врéмя.
4 (*~ of day or night*) час, врéмя; **what's the ~?** котóрый час?, скóлько врéмени?; **what ~ do you make it?** скóлько на вáших (часáх)?; **the ~ is 8 o'clock** сейчáс 8 часóв; **at that ~** (*hour*) в э́тот час; **what ~ do you go to bed?** в котóром часý вы ложи́тесь спать?
5 (*moment*) врéмя; **I was away at the ~** меня́ тогдá (*or* в то врéмя) нé было; **at ~s** инoгдá, временáми; **at all ~s** всегдá; во всех слýчаях; **by the ~ I got back he had gone** (к томý врéмени,) когдá я вернýлся, егó ужé нé было; **from ~ to ~** инoгдá, врéмя от врéмени; **it's ~ for bed** порá спать; **the train was on ~** пóезд пришёл вóвремя.
6 (*occasion*) раз; **nine ~s out of ten** в девяти́ слýчаях из десяти́; **another ~** когдá-нибудь; в другóй раз; **one at a ~!** по одномý; не все срáзу!; **the first ~ I saw him** когдá я впервы́е (*or* в пéрвый раз) уви́дел егó.
7 (*in multiplication*): **6 ~s 2 is 12** 6 (умнóжить) на 2 — 12; шéстью два — двенáдцать.
8 (*period*) врéмя, временá (*nt. pl.*), эпóха.
9 (*mus.*) такт, ритм; **in ~ with the music** в такт мýзыке.
■ *v.t.* 1 (*do at a chosen ~*) выбирáть, вы́брать врéмя для + *g.*
2 (*measure ~ of or for*) зас|екáть, -éчь врéмя + *g.*
3 (*schedule*): **the train was ~d to leave at 6** пóезд дóлжен был отойти́ в 6 часóв.
■ *cpds.* **~ bomb** *n.* бóмба замéдленного дéйствия; **~-consuming** *adj.* трéбующий мнóго врéмени; **~ limit** *n.* предéльный срок; **~ off** *n.* óтпуск; **~share** *n.* тáймшер, совмéстное владéние курóртным помещéнием; **~table** *n.* расписáние; грáфик; **~ zone** *n.* часовóй пóяс.

timeless /'taɪmlɪs/ *adj.* вéчный.

timely /'taɪmlɪ/ *adj.* (**timelier, timeliest**) своеврéменный.

timer /'taɪmə(r)/ *n.* тáймер, часовóй механи́зм.

timid /'tɪmɪd/ *adj.* (**timider, timidest**) застéнчивый.

timing /'taɪmɪŋ/ *n.* (*choosing of appropriate ~*) вы́бор (наибóлее подходя́щего) врéмени.

timpani, tympani /'tɪmpənɪ/ *n.* литáвры (*f. pl.*).

timpanist, tympanist /'tɪmpənɪst/ *n.* литаври́ст.

tin /tɪn/ *n.*
1 (*metal*) óлово; **~ can** (*for paint etc.*) жестянáя бáнка; (*for food*) консéрвная бáнка.
2 (*Br.*) (*~ can*) бáнка; (*for biscuits*) (металли́ческая) корóбка; (*for baking cakes*) фóрма; (*for roasting*) прóтивень (*m.*).
■ *v.t.* (**tinned, tinning**) консерви́ровать, за-; **~ned goods** консерви́рованные продýкты.
■ *cpds.* **~foil** *n.* фольгá; **~-opener** *n.* (*Br.*)

консе́рвный нож.

tinge /tɪndʒ/ *n.* отте́нок.
■ *v.t.* (**tinging** *or* **tingeing**) слегка́ окра́|шивать, -сить; (*fig.*): **her voice was ~d with regret** в её го́лосе звуча́ло лёгкое сожале́ние.

tingl|e /ˈtɪŋg(ə)l/, **-ing** /ˈtɪŋglɪŋ/ *nn.* пощи́пывание; (*of pleasure etc.*) тре́пет.
■ *v.i.*: **a ~ing sensation** ощуще́ние пощи́пывания; **they were ~ing with excitement** они́ дрожа́ли от возбужде́ния.

tinker /ˈtɪŋkə(r)/ *v.i.* (*meddle etc.*) вози́ться (*impf.*) (*с чем*).

tinkle /ˈtɪŋk(ə)l/ *n.* (*sound*) звон; звя́канье.
■ *v.i.*: **the bell ~d** колоко́льчик зазвене́л.

tinsel /ˈtɪns(ə)l/ *n.* блёст|ки (*pl.*, *g.* -ок).

tint /tɪnt/ *n.* отте́нок; тон.
■ *v.t.*: **~ed glasses** тёмные очки́.

tiny /ˈtaɪnɪ/ *adj.* (**tinier, tiniest**) кро́шечный.

tip¹ /tɪp/ *n.* (*pointed end*) ко́нчик; верху́шка; (*part attached, e.g. of arrow*) наконе́чник; **the ~s of my fingers are freezing** у меня́ мёрзнут ко́нчики па́льцев.
■ *cpd.* **~toe** *n.*: **on ~toe(s)** на цы́почках; *v.i.* ходи́ть (*indet.*) на цы́почках.

tip² /tɪp/ *n.* (*Br., for rubbish*) сва́лка.
■ *v.t.* (**tipped, tipping**)
1 (*tilt*) наклон|я́ть, -и́ть.
2 (*overturn*) выва́ливать, вы́валить; опорожн|я́ть, -и́ть.
■ *with adv.*: **~ over** *v.t.* & *i.* опроки́|дывать(ся), -нуть(ся); **the boat ~ped over** ло́дка переверну́лась.

tip³ /tɪp/ *n.*
1 (*piece of advice*) сове́т; намёк.
2 (*gratuity*) чаев|ы́е (*pl.*, *g.* -ы́х).
■ *v.t.* (**tipped, tipping**)
1 (*Br., predict*): **the horse was ~ped to win** предска́зывали, что победи́т э́та ло́шадь.
2 (*remunerate*) да|ва́ть, -ть на чай + *d.*
■ *with adv.*: **~ off** (*coll.*) предупре|жда́ть, -ди́ть.
■ *cpd.* **~-off** *n.*: **the police had a ~-off** поли́цию предупреди́ли.

Tipp-Ex, Tippex /ˈtɪpeks/ *n.* (*Br. propr.*) корректи́рующая жи́дкость.

tipple /ˈtɪp(ə)l/ *n.* напи́ток, питьё.
■ *v.i.* выпива́ть (*impf.*).

tipster /ˈtɪpstə(r)/ *n.* (*at races*) «жучо́к» (*на скачках*).

tipsy /ˈtɪpsɪ/ *adj.* (**tipsier, tipsiest**) подвы́пивший; (*pred.*) навеселе́.

tirade /taɪˈreɪd/ *n.* тира́да.

tire¹ /ˈtaɪə(r)/ (*US*) = **tyre**

tire² /ˈtaɪə(r)/ *v.t.* утом|ля́ть, -и́ть.
■ *v.i.* утом|ля́ться, -и́ться; уст|ава́ть, -а́ть.

tired /ˈtaɪəd/ *adj.* уста́лый; **she's ~** она́ уста́ла; **I'm ~ out** я соверше́нно вы́мотался (*coll.*); **you will soon get ~ of him** вы ско́ро от него́ уста́нете.

tireless /ˈtaɪəlɪs/ *adj.* неутоми́мый.

tiresome /ˈtaɪəsəm/ *adj.* надое́дливый, ну́дный.

tissue /ˈtɪʃuː/ *n.* (*handkerchief*) салфе́тка; (*text., biol.*) ткань; **~ paper** то́нкая обёрточная бума́га.

tit¹ /tɪt/ *n.* (*bird*) сини́ца.

tit² /tɪt/ *n.* (*vulg., breast*) си́ська (*coll.*).

titbit /ˈtɪtbɪt/ (*US* **tidbit** /ˈtɪdbɪt/) *n.* ла́комый кусо́чек; (*fig.*): **a ~ of news** пика́нтная но́вость.

titillate /ˈtɪtɪleɪt/ *v.t.* (*tickle*) щекота́ть (*impf.*); (*excite*) прия́тно возбу|жда́ть, -ди́ть.

titivate /ˈtɪtɪveɪt/ *v.i.* прихора́шиваться (*impf.*).

title /ˈtaɪt(ə)l/ *n.*
1 (*of book etc.*) назва́ние.
2 (*of rank etc.*) ти́тул.
■ *cpds.* **~-holder** *n.* чемпио́н; **~ role** *n.* загла́вная роль.

titter /ˈtɪtə(r)/ *n.* хихи́канье.
■ *v.i.* хихи́кать (*impf.*).

tiz(zy) /ˈtɪz(ɪ)/ *n.* (*coll.*) возбужде́ние, ажиота́ж; **she got into a ~** она́ пришла́ в стра́шное возбужде́ние.

to /tuː/ *adv.*
1 **pull the door ~!** закро́й дверь!
2 : **~ and fro** взад и вперёд; **he went ~ and fro in his search for a compromise** он колеба́лся в своём вы́боре, ища́ компроми́ссное реше́ние.
■ *prep.* 1 (*expr. ind. obj., recipient*): *usu. expr. by d. case*; **a letter ~ my wife** письмо́ мое́й жене́; **~ me that is absurd** по-мо́ему, э́то глу́по; (*expr. support*): **here's ~ our victory** за на́шу побе́ду (*тост*).
2 (*expr. destination*) (*with place names, countries etc.*) в + *a.*; **~ Moscow** в Москву́; **~ Russia** в Росси́ю; **~ the theatre** (*Br.*), **theater** (*US*) в теа́тр; (*expr. direction*): **the road ~ London** доро́га в Ло́ндон; (*with islands, planets, left and right etc.*) на + *a.*; **~ Cyprus** на Кипр; **back ~ Earth** обра́тно на Зе́млю; **turn ~ the right!** поверни́те напра́во!; **~ a concert** на конце́рт; **~ war** на войну́; **~ the factory** на заво́д/фа́брику; **~ the station** на ста́нцию; (*with persons*) к + *d.*; **he went ~ his parents'** он пое́хал к роди́телям; (*towards*) к + *d.*
3 (*up to, as far as*) до + *g.*; на + *a.*; по + *a.*; **is it far ~ town?** до го́рода далеко́?; **~ the bottom** на са́мое дно; **from 10 ~ 4** с десяти́ до четырёх; **from morning ~ night** с утра́ до́ ночи; **ten (minutes) ~ six** (*Br.*) без десяти́ (мину́т) шесть; **from April to June** с апре́ля по ию́нь.
4 (*expr. end state*): **smash ~ pieces** разби|ва́ть, -ть на куски́; **from bad ~ worse** всё ху́же и ху́же.
5 (*expr. response*) на + *a.*; к + *d.*; **an answer ~ my letter** отве́т на моё письмо́.
6 (*expr. result or reaction*) к + *d.*; **~ my surprise** к моему́ удивле́нию.
7 (*expr. attachment, suitability*) к + *d.*; от + *g.*; в + *a.*; **the key ~ the door** ключ от две́ри.
8 (*expr. reference or relationship*): **he is good ~ his employees** он хорошо́ отно́сится к свои́м сотру́дникам; **attention ~ detail** внима́ние к деталя́м.
9 (*expr. ratio or proportion*): **ten ~ one he won't succeed** де́сять про́тив одного́, что ему́ э́то не уда́стся.
10 (*expr. score*) на + *a.*; **we won by six goals ~ four** мы вы́играли со счётом 6:4.
11 (*expr. position*): **~ my right** спра́ва от меня́; **~ the south of Minsk** к ю́гу от Ми́нска.

t

■ *particle with v. forming inf.*
1 (*as subj. or obj. of v.*): **~ err is human** человéку свóйственно ошибáться; **he learnt ~ swim** он научи́лся плáвать.
2 (*as extension of adj.*): **this book is easy ~ read** э́та кни́га легкó читáется; **too hot ~ touch** такóй горя́чий, что не дотрóнуться.
3 (*expr. purpose*) (с тем *or* для тогó), чтóбы...; (*with inf. only*): **I came ~ help** я пришёл(, чтóбы) помóчь; (*expr. request*): **I asked him ~ help** я попроси́л егó помóчь; (*expr. result, sequel*): **I arrived only ~ find him gone** когдá я приéхал, оказáлось, что егó ужé нет.
4 (*as substitute for complete inf.*): **I was going ~ write but I forgot ~** я собирáлся написáть, но забы́л.

toad /təʊd/ *n.* жáба.
■ *cpd.* **~stool** *n.* погáнка.

toady /ˈtəʊdɪ/ *n.* лизоблю́д, подхали́м.
■ *v.i.* подли́зываться (*impf.*) (*к кому*).

toast[1] /təʊst/ *n.* (*toasted bread*) тост, грéнка.
■ *v.t.* поджáри|вать, -ть.

toast[2] /təʊst/ *n.*: **drink a ~ to sth.** пить, вы́- за что-н.
■ *v.t.* пить, вы́- за (*чьё-н.*) здорóвье.

toaster /ˈtəʊstə(r)/ *n.* тóстер.

tobacco /təˈbækəʊ/ *n.* (*pl.* **~s**) табáк.

tobacconist /təˈbækənɪst/ *n.* (*Br.*) торгóвец табáчными издéлиями.

toboggan /təˈbɒɡən/ *n.* сáн|и (*pl., g.* -éй); тобóгган, тобогáн.

today /təˈdeɪ/ *adv.* & *n.* сегóдня; сегóдняшний день; **what's ~?** какóй сегóдня день?; **~'s newspaper** сегóдняшняя газéта; (*fig., the present time*) настоя́щее врéмя, сегóдня; **young people of ~** совремéнная молодёжь.

toddler /ˈtɒdlə(r)/ *n.* ребёнок, начинáющий ходи́ть.

toe /təʊ/ *n.*
1 (*of foot*) пáлец (ноги́); **big ~** большóй пáлец (ноги́); **little ~** мизи́нец (ноги́).
2 (*of shoe or sock*) носóк.
■ *v.t.* (**toes, toed, toeing**): **~ the line** (*fig., conform*) ходи́ть (*indet.*) по стру́нке (*coll.*).
■ *cpd.* **~nail** *n.* нóготь (*m.*) на пáльце ноги́.

toffee /ˈtɒfɪ/ *n.* ири́ска.

together /təˈɡeðə(r)/ *adv.*
1 (*in company*) вмéсте; **~ with** (*in addition to*) вмéсте с + *i.*
2 (*simultaneously*) одноврéмéнно.

toggle /ˈtɒɡ(ə)l/ *n.* (*comput.*) ту́мблер.

toil /tɔɪl/ *v.i.* (*work hard*) труди́ться (*impf.*).

toilet /ˈtɔɪlɪt/ *n.* туалéт.
■ *cpd.* **~ paper** *n.* туалéтная бумáга.

toiletries /ˈtɔɪlɪtrɪz/ *n. pl.* туалéтные принадлéжности.

token /ˈtəʊkən/ *n.*
1 (*sign*) знак.
2 (*substitute for coin*) жетóн.
3 (*attr.*) символи́ческий.

Tokyo /ˈtəʊkjəʊ/ *n.* Тóкио (*m. indecl.*).

told /təʊld/ *past and p.p. of* ▸ **tell**

tolerable /ˈtɒlərəb(ə)l/ *adj.* терпи́мый.

tolerance /ˈtɒlərəns/ *n.* (*forbearance*) терпи́мость; (*resistance to hard conditions etc.*) выно́сливость.

tolerant /ˈtɒlərənt/ *adj.* терпи́мый.

tolerate /ˈtɒləreɪt/ *v.t.* (*endure*) терпéть (*impf.*); (*permit*) допус|кáть, -ти́ть.

toll[1] /təʊl/ *n.* (*tax*) пóшлина, сбор; **~ call** (*US*) междугорóдный разговóр.

toll[2] /təʊl/ *n.* (*of bell*) колокóльный звон.
■ *v.i.* звони́ть (*impf.*).

tom /tɒm/: *cpds.* **~boy** *n.* девчóнка-сорванéц; **~cat** *n.* кот.

tomato /təˈmɑːtəʊ/ *n.* (*pl.* **~es**) помидóр; **~ paste/purée** томáтная пáста; **~ sauce/juice** томáтный сóус/сок.

tomb /tuːm/ *n.* моги́ла.
■ *cpd.* **~stone** *n.* (*standing*) надгрóбный пáмятник; (*laid over*) надгрóбная плитá.

tome /təʊm/ *n.* (*liter.*) том.

tomorrow /təˈmɒrəʊ/ *adv.* & *n.* зáвтра; **~ morning** зáвтра у́тром; **the day after ~** послезáвтра; **~ week** (*Br.*) чéрез 8 дней.

ton /tʌn/ *n.* тóнна; (*fig.*): **he has ~s of money** у негó ку́ча дéнег.

tone /təʊn/ *n.*
1 (*quality of sound, colour*) тон; (*teleph.*) гудóк.
2 (*character*) харáктер.
■ *with advs.*: **~ down** *v.t.* смягч|áть, -и́ть; **~ in** *v.i.* гармони́ровать (*impf.*); **~ up** *v.t.* укреп|ля́ть, -и́ть.
■ *cpd.* **~-deaf** *adj.* лишённый музыкáльного слу́ха.

toner /ˈtəʊnə(r)/ *n.* (*xerographic*) тóнер.

tongs /tɒŋz/ *n.* щипц|ы́ (*pl., g.* -óв).

tongue /tʌŋ/ *n.*
1 (*lit., and as food*) язы́к; **put, stick one's ~ out** высóвывать, вы́сунуть язы́к.
2 (*fig., article so shaped*) язы́к, язычóк.
3 (*language*) язы́к; **mother/native ~** роднóй язы́к.
■ *cpds.* **~-tied** *adj.* лиши́вшийся дáра рéчи; **~-twister** *n.* скороговóрка.

tonic /ˈtɒnɪk/ *n.*
1 (*medicine*) тонизи́рующее срéдство; (*fig.*) поддéржка.
2 (**~ water**) тóник.

tonight /təˈnaɪt/ *adv.* & *n.* (*this evening*) сегóдня вéчером; (*this night*) сегóдня нóчью.

tonne /tʌn/ *n.* (метри́ческая) тóнна.

tonsil /ˈtɒns(ə)l/ *n.* миндáлина.

tonsillitis /tɒnsɪˈlaɪtɪs/ *n.* тонзилли́т, анги́на.

too /tuː/ *adv.*
1 (*also*) тáкже, тóже.
2 (*excessively*) сли́шком; **it's ~ cold for swimming** сли́шком хóлодно, чтóбы купáться; **that is ~ much!** э́то уж сли́шком!

took /tʊk/ *past of* ▸ **take**

tool /tuːl/ *n.* инструмéнт, ору́дие.
■ *cpd.* **~bar** *n.* (*comput.*) панéль инструмéнтов.

tooth /tuːθ/ *n.* (*pl.* **teeth**) зуб.
■ *cpds.* **~ache** *n.* зубнáя боль; **~brush** *n.* зубнáя щётка; **~paste** *n.* зубнáя пáста; **~pick** *n.* зубочи́стка.

toothless /ˈtuːθlɪs/ *adj.* беззу́бый.

top[1] /tɒp/ *n.*
1 (*summit; highest part*) верх (*pl.* -и́); верху́шка, верши́на; (*of hill, tree, head*) маку́шка (*coll.*); **at the ~ of the hill** на верши́не холмá; **at the ~ of the page** в начáле страни́цы; **she cleaned the house**

from ~ to bottom она́ тща́тельно убрала́ дом.
2 (*fig., highest rank, foremost place*) веду́щее положе́ние; пе́рвое ме́сто; **he came ~ of the class** он стал пе́рвым в кла́ссе.
3 (*fig., utmost degree*) верх; **at the ~ of his voice** во весь го́лос.
4 (*upper surface*) пове́рхность; верх; **on ~** (*lit.*) наверху́; (*fig.*): **I feel on ~ of the world** я чу́вствую себя́ на седьмо́м не́бе; **on ~ of everything I caught a cold** вдоба́вок ко всему́ я ещё (и) простуди́лся.
5 (*lid*) верх; кры́шка.
6 (*attr.*): **~ hat** цили́ндр; **~ secret** соверше́нно секре́тный; **at ~ speed** на максима́льной ско́рости.
■ *v.t.* (**topped, topping**)
1 (*serve as ~ to*) венча́ть, у-.
2 (*be higher than; exceed*) прев|ыша́ть, -ы́сить.
■ *with adv.*: **~ up** *v.t.* дол|ива́ть, -и́ть; **may I ~ you up?** вам доли́ть?
■ *cpds.* **~-heavy** *adj.* неусто́йчивый; **~-up** *n.* (*Br.*): **can I give you a ~?** вам доли́ть?

top² /tɒp/ *n.* (*toy*) волчо́к.
topaz /'təʊpæz/ *n.* топа́з; (*attr.*) топа́зовый.
topiary /'təʊpɪərɪ/ *adj.*: **the ~ art** фигу́рная стри́жка кусто́в.
topic /'tɒpɪk/ *n.* те́ма.
topical /'tɒpɪk(ə)l/ *adj.* актуа́льный.
topicality /tɒpɪ'kælɪtɪ/ *n.* актуа́льность.
topless /'tɒplɪs/ *adj.* с обнажённой гру́дью.
■ *adv.* то́плес(с).
topmost /'tɒpməʊst/ *adj.* (*highest*) са́мый ве́рхний; (*most important*) са́мый ва́жный.
topographical /tɒpə'græfɪk(ə)l/ *adj.* топографи́ческий.
topography /tə'pɒgrəfɪ/ *n.* топогра́фия; (*features*) релье́ф.
topping /'tɒpɪŋ/ *n.* (*cul.*) ве́рхний слой; (*sauce*) подли́вка.
topple /'tɒp(ə)l/ *v.t.* вали́ть, с-.
■ *v.i.* вали́ться, с-.
topsy-turvy /tɒpsɪ'tɜːvɪ/ *adj.* перевёрнутый вверх дном (*coll.*).
■ *adv.* вверх дном.
Torah /'tɔːrɑː/ *n.* (*relig.*) То́ра.
torch /tɔːtʃ/ *n.* (*flaming*) фа́кел; (*Br.*, **electric ~**) (электри́ческий) фона́рь.
tore /tɔː(r)/ *past of* ▸ **tear²**
torment¹ /'tɔːment/ *n.* муче́ние.
torment² /tɔː'ment/ *v.t.* му́чить (*impf.*).
tormentor /tɔː'mentə(r)/ *n.* мучи́тель (*fem.* -ница).
torn /tɔːn/ *p.p. of* ▸ **tear²**
tornado /tɔː'neɪdəʊ/ *n.* (*pl.* **~es** *or* **~s**) смерч.
torpedo /tɔː'piːdəʊ/ *n.* (*pl.* **~es**) торпе́да.
torpid /'tɔːpɪd/ *adj.* вя́лый, апати́чный; (*in hibernation*) находя́щийся в состоя́нии спя́чки.
torp|idity /tɔː'pɪdɪtɪ/, **-or** /'tɔːpə(r)/ *nn.* вя́лость, апа́тия.
torrent /'tɒrənt/ *n.* (*lit., fig.*) пото́к.
torrential /tə'renʃ(ə)l/ *adj.*: **~ rain** проливно́й дождь.
torrid /'tɒrɪd/ *adj.* жа́ркий; (*passionate*) стра́стный.
torso /'tɔːsəʊ/ *n.* ту́ловище, торс.
tortoise /'tɔːtəs/ *n.* черепа́ха.
tortuous /'tɔːtjʊəs/ *adj.* изви́листый.
torture /'tɔːtʃə(r)/ *n.* (*physical*) пы́тка; (*mental*) му́ки (*f. pl.*).
■ *v.t.* пыта́ть (*impf.*); му́чить (*impf.*).
torturer /'tɔːtʃərə(r)/ *n.* мучи́тель (*m.*), пала́ч.
Tory /'tɔːrɪ/ *n.* (*coll.*) то́ри (*m. indecl.*).
toss /tɒs/ *n.* бросо́к.
■ *v.t.* 1 (*throw*) бр|оса́ть, -о́сить; **they ~ed a coin to decide** они́ подки́нули моне́ту, что́бы реши́ть исхо́д де́ла.
2 (*agitate*) швыр|я́ть, -ну́ть.
■ *v.i.* мета́ться (*impf.*); **the child ~ed in its sleep** ребёнок мета́лся во сне.
■ *with advs.*: **~ off** *v.t.* (*do quickly*) де́лать, с- на́спех; **~ up** *v.i.*: **shall we ~ up to see who goes?** дава́йте бро́сим жре́бий, кому́ идти́.
tot¹ /tɒt/ *n.* (*Br., of liquor*) глото́к.
tot² /tɒt/: **~ up** (*Br.*) *v.t.* (**totted, totting**) сост|авля́ть, -а́вить (*су́мму*); сумми́ровать (*impf., pf.*); **he ~ted up the figures** он подвёл ито́г.
total /'təʊt(ə)l/ *n.* су́мма, ито́г.
■ *adj.* (*whole*) о́бщий; **the ~ figure** о́бщая ци́фра; (*complete*) **~ failure** по́лный прова́л.
■ *v.t.* (**totalled, totalling;** *US* **totaled, totaling**) (*also* **~ up**) подсчи́т|ывать, -а́ть.
totalitarian /təʊtælɪ'teərɪən/ *adj.* тоталита́рный.
totalitarianism /təʊtælɪ'teərɪənɪz(ə)m/ *n.* тоталитари́зм.
totality /təʊ'tælɪtɪ/ *n.* (*sum total*) вся су́мма, о́бщее коли́чество; (*the whole of sth.*) (по́лная) совоку́пность; **totality of sth.** что́-л. в по́лном объёме; **in sth.'s totality** в це́лом, в совоку́пности, во всей полноте́; (*astron.*) вре́мя по́лного затме́ния.
totally /'təʊtəlɪ/ *adv.* соверше́нно, абсолю́тно.
totter /'tɒtə(r)/ *v.i.* ковыля́ть (*impf.*).
touch /tʌtʃ/ *n.*
1 (*light pressure*) прикоснове́ние.
2 (*sense*) осяза́ние.
3 (*of pen or brush*) штрих.
4 (*tinge*) чу́точка, отте́нок, налёт; **a ~ of frost in the air** лёгкий моро́зец.
5 (*style*) стиль (*m.*); **you must have lost your ~** вы я́вно утра́тили (былу́ю) хва́тку.
6 (*communication*) конта́кт, обще́ние; **we must keep in ~** мы должны́ подде́рживать конта́кт друг с дру́гом; **how can I get in ~ with you?** как мо́жно с ва́ми связа́ться?; **we lost ~ with him** мы потеря́ли с ним конта́кт/связь.
7 (*football*) пло́щадь за боковы́ми ли́ниями по́ля; **to kick a ball into ~** выбива́ть, вы́бить мяч за боковую́ (ли́нию).
■ *v.t.* 1 (*contact physically*) тро́|гать, -нуть; каса́ться, косну́ться + *g.*; **he ~ed her (on the) arm** он косну́лся её руки́; **it was ~ and go** исхо́д был неизве́стен до са́мого конца́.
2 (*reach*) дост|ава́ть, -а́ть до + *g.*; дост|ига́ть, -и́гнуть + *g.*
3 (*approach in excellence*) равня́ться (*impf.*) с + *i.*; сравни́ться (*pf.*) с + *i.*; идти́ (*det.*) в сравне́ние с + *i.*

4 (*affect*) тро́|гать, -нуть; волнова́ть, вз-.
5 (*taste*) прик|аса́ться, -осну́ться к + *d.*; **I never ~ a drop** (*of alcohol*) я не прикаса́юсь к спиртно́му.
6 (*concern*) каса́ться (*impf.*) + *g.*
7 (*treat lightly*; *also v.i. with prep.* **on**) затр|а́гивать, -о́нуть; каса́ться, косну́ться + *g.*
■ *v.i.* соприк|аса́ться, -осну́ться.
■ *cpds.* **~down** *n.* (*aeron.*) поса́дка; (*rugby*) попы́тка; (*American football*) тачда́ун; **~line** *n.* бокова́я ли́ния (*поля*); **~-type** *v.i.* печа́тать (*impf.*) вслепу́ю/слепы́м ме́тодом.

touched /tʌtʃt/ *adj.* тро́нутый.

touching /'tʌtʃɪŋ/ *adj.* тро́гательный.

touchy /'tʌtʃɪ/ *adj.* (**touchier, touchiest**) оби́дчивый.

tough /tʌf/ *adj.*
1 (*of meat*) жёсткий.
2 (*strong, hardy*) кре́пкий; (*person*) выно́сливый.
3 (*difficult*) тру́дный; (*stubborn*) упря́мый.
4 (*coll., severe*) крутой; жёсткий.

toughen /'tʌfən/ *v.t.* де́лать, с- жёстким; (*body, character*) де́лать, с- выно́сливым.

toughness /'tʌfnɪs/ *n.* (*of food etc.*) жёсткость; (*strength*; *hardiness*) про́чность; выно́сливость; (*uncompromising nature*) несгово́рчивость; упря́мство.

toupee /'tu:peɪ/ *n.* небольшо́й пари́к, накла́дка.

tour /tʊə(r)/ *n.*
1 (*extended visit*) путеше́ствие; (*short*) пое́здка; (*of museum, garden*) экску́рсия.
2 (*of performer, sports team, politician*) турне́ (*nt. indecl.*), тур; (*of performer*) гастро́ли (*f. pl.*); **to be on ~** быть в турне́/на гастро́лях; гастроли́ровать (*impf.*).
■ *v.t. & i.* соверш|а́ть, -и́ть экску́рсию (по + *d.*).
■ *cpd.* **~ operator** (*company*) турфи́рма, туропера́тор.

tourism /'tʊərɪz(ə)m/ *n.* тури́зм.

tourist /'tʊərɪst/ *n.* тури́ст.

tournament /'tʊənəmənt/ *n.* турни́р.

tousled /'taʊzəld/ *adj.*: **~ hair** взъеро́шенные во́лосы.

tow /təʊ/ *n.*: **can I give you a ~?** взять вас на букси́р?
■ *v.t.* букси́ровать (*impf.*); **they ~ed the car away** маши́ну отбуксировали.

toward(s) /tə'wɔ:d(z)/ *prep.*
1 (*in the direction of*) к + *d.*; на + *a.*; по направле́нию к + *d.*
2 (*in relation to*) к + *d.*; по отноше́нию к + *d.*; относи́тельно + *g.*; **they seemed friendly ~ us** каза́лось, что они́ бы́ли располо́жены к нам дру́жески.
3 (*for the purpose of*) для + *g.*
4 (*near*) к + *d.*; о́коло + *g.*; **~ evening** к ве́черу, под ве́чер.

towel /'taʊəl/ *n.* полоте́нце.

tower /'taʊə(r)/ *n.* ба́шня; (*fig.*): **a ~ of strength** опло́т; надёжная опо́ра.
■ *v.i.* вы́ситься, возвыша́ться (*both impf.*).
■ *cpd.* **~ block** *n.* (*Br.*) многоэта́жный/высо́тный дом, высо́тка.

town /taʊn/ *n.*
1 го́род; **go to ~** (*coll.*) разверну́ться (*pf.*) вовсю́.
2 (*attr.*) городско́й; **~ council** мэ́рия; **~ hall** мэ́рия; ра́туша; **~ planning** градострои́тельство.

township /'taʊnʃɪp/ *n.*
1 (*hist., in South Africa*) негритя́нский кварта́л.
2 (*US*) райо́н.

toxic /'tɒksɪk/ *adj.* ядови́тый.

toxicologist /tɒksɪ'kɒlədʒɪst/ *n.* токсико́лог.

toxicology /tɒksɪ'kɒlədʒɪ/ *n.* токсиколо́гия.

toxin /'tɒksɪn/ *n.* токси́н.

toy /tɔɪ/ *n.* игру́шка; **~ boy** (*coll.*) молодо́й любо́вник.
■ *v.i.*: **he ~ed with his pencil** он верте́л в рука́х каранда́ш; **he ~ed with her affections** он игра́л её чу́вствами.
■ *cpd.* **~shop** *n.* магази́н игру́шек.

trace /treɪs/ *n.* след.
■ *v.t.* 1 (*delineate*) черти́ть, на-; (*with transparent paper*) перев|оди́ть, -ести́; **tracing paper** ка́лька.
2 (*follow the tracks of*) высле́живать, вы́следить; **the thief was ~d to London** следы́ во́ра вели́ в Ло́ндон.
3 (*discover by search*) устан|а́вливать, -ови́ть.

traceable /'treɪsəb(ə)l/ *adj.* просле́живаемый.

trachea /trə'ki:ə/ *n.* (*pl.* **tracheae** /-'ki:i:/ *or* **tracheas**) (*anat.*) трахе́я.

tracheotomy /trækɪ'ɒtəmɪ/ *n.* трахеотоми́я.

track /træk/ *n.*
1 (*mark*) след; **we lost ~ of him** мы потеря́ли его́ след.
2 (*path*) путь (*m.*), тра́сса.
3 (*for racing etc.*) (бегова́я) доро́жка; (*for bicycle and motor racing*) трек.
4 (*rail*) путь.
5 (*of tank etc.*) гу́сеница.
6 (*on tape, record*) доро́жка.
■ *v.t.* следи́ть за + *i.*; высле́живать, вы́следить.
■ *with adv.*: **~ down** *v.t.* (*person*) высле́живать, вы́следить; (*object*) оты́ск|ивать, -а́ть.
■ *cpd.* **~suit** *n.* трениро́вочный костю́м.

tracker /'trækə(r)/ *n.* (*hunter*) охо́тник; **~ dog** соба́ка-ище́йка.

tract /trækt/ *n.* (*region*) уча́сток, райо́н.

traction /'trækʃ(ə)n/ *n.* тя́га; **~ engine** тя́говый дви́гатель (*m.*); тяга́ч.

tractor /'træktə(r)/ *n.* тра́ктор.

trade /treɪd/ *n.*
1 (*business*) ремесло́; профе́ссия; **he is a builder by ~** он по профе́ссии строи́тель.
2 (*commerce*) торго́вля; **~ secret** профессиона́льный секре́т.
■ *v.t.* (*exchange*) меня́ть (*impf.*); **they ~d furs for food** они́ меня́ли меха́ на проду́кты.
■ *v.i.* торгова́ть (*impf.*); **he ~s in sables** он торгу́ет соболя́ми.
■ *with adv.*: **~ in** *v.t.*: **I ~d in my old car for a new one** я о́тдал ста́рую маши́ну в счёт поку́пки но́вой.
■ *cpds.* **~mark** *n.* това́рный знак; **~ name** *n.* назва́ние фи́рмы; **~-off** *n.* компроми́сс; **~sman** *n.* торго́вец; **~smen's entrance** чёрный ход; **~(s) union** *n.* профсою́з.

trader /'treɪdə(r)/ *n.* торго́вец.

tradition /trə'dɪʃ(ə)n/ *n.* тради́ция.

traditional /trə'dɪʃən(ə)l/ *adj.* традицио́нный.

traditionalist /trə'dɪʃənəlɪst/ *n.* традиционали́ст.

traffic /'træfɪk/ *n.*
1 (*movement of vehicles etc.*) (доро́жное) движе́ние, тра́нспорт; **heavy ~** большо́е движе́ние; **~ jam** про́бка; **~ lights** светофо́р; **~ warden** (*Br.*) инспе́ктор, контроли́рующий соблюде́ние пра́вил парко́вки и стоя́нки (*в черте города*).
2 (*trade*) торго́вля.
■ *v.i.* (**trafficked, trafficking**) торгова́ть (*чем*).

trafficker /'træfɪkə(r)/ *n.* (*pej.*) деле́ц, торго́вец; **drug ~** наркоде́лец.

tragedy /'trædʒɪdɪ/ *n.* (*lit. fig.*) траге́дия.

tragic /'trædʒɪk/ *adj.* траги́ческий.

trail /treɪl/ *n.* (*path*) доро́жка, тропи́нка; (*mark left*) след; **the storm left a ~ of destruction** бу́ря оста́вила по́сле себя́ полосу́ разруше́ния.
■ *v.t.* 1 (*draw or drag behind*) тащи́ть (*impf.*); волочи́ть (*impf.*).
2 (*pursue*) идти́ (*det.*) по сле́ду + *g.*
■ *v.i.* 1 (*be drawn or dragged*) тащи́ться (*impf.*); волочи́ться (*impf.*).
2 (*straggle*) плести́сь (*impf.*).
3 (*grow or hang loosely*) све́шиваться (*impf.*).

trailer /'treɪlə(r)/ *n.*
1 (*vehicle*) прице́п; (*US, caravan*) жило́й автоприце́п, тре́йлер.
2 (*cin., TV*) ано́нс.

train /treɪn/ *n.*
1 (*rail*) по́езд; **I came by ~** я прие́хал по́ездом.
2 (*procession*) проце́ссия; карава́н; (*mil.*) обо́з.
3 (*fig.*) ряд, цепь; **I don't follow your ~ of thought** мне тру́дно улови́ть ход ва́ших мы́слей.
4 (*of dress etc.*) шлейф.
■ *v.t.* 1 (*give instruction to*) учи́ть, об-/обуч|а́ть, -и́ть (**in:** + *d.*); (*prepare for a career*) гото́вить (*impf.*); (*sportsman*) тренирова́ть (*impf.*); (*animals*) дрессирова́ть (*impf.*).
2 (*direct*) нав|оди́ть, -ести́.
■ *v.i.* (*learn skill*) учи́ться, об-/обуч|а́ться, -и́ться; (*undertake preparation*) гото́виться (*impf.*); (*of sportsman*) тренирова́ться (*impf.*); **she is ~ing to be a teacher** она́ гото́вится стать учи́телем.
■ *cpd.* **~ driver** *n.* машини́ст.

trainee /treɪ'ni:/ *n.* стажёр; учени́|к (*fem.* -ца).

trainer /'treɪnə(r)/ *n.*
1 тре́нер; (*of horses etc.*) дрессиро́вщи|к (*fem.* -ца).
2 (*Br., sports shoe*) кроссо́вка.

training /'treɪnɪŋ/ *n.*
1 (*instruction*) подгото́вка, обуче́ние.
2 (*physical preparation*) трениро́вка.

traipse /treɪps/ *v.i.* (*coll.*) таска́ться (*impf.*) (*по улицам и т. п.*).

trait /treɪt/ *n.* осо́бенность, сво́йство.

traitor /'treɪtə(r)/ *n.* преда́тель (*m.*), изме́нник; (*fem.*) преда́тельница, изме́нница.

trajectory /trə'dʒektərɪ/ *n.* траекто́рия.

tram /træm/ *n.* (*Br.*) трамва́й.

tramp /træmp/ *n.* бродя́га.

trample /'træmp(ə)l/ *v.t.* топта́ть, по-, раст|а́птывать, -опта́ть.
■ *v.i.* тяжело́ ступа́ть (*impf.*); (*fig.*): **he ~d on everyone's feelings** он не счита́лся ни с чьи́ми чу́вствами.

trampoline /træmpə'li:n/ *n.* бату́т.

trance /trɑ:ns/ *n.* транс.

tranquil /'træŋkwɪl/ *adj.* споко́йный, ми́рный.

tranquillity /træŋ'kwɪlɪtɪ/ *n.* споко́йствие.

tranquillizer /'træŋkwɪlaɪzə(r)/ (*US* **tranquilizer**) *n.* успокои́тельное сре́дство, транквилиза́тор.

transaction /træn'zækʃ(ə)n/ *n.* сде́лка.

transatlantic /trænzət'læntɪk/ *adj.* трансатланти́ческий.

transcend /træn'send/ *v.t.* прев|ыша́ть, -ы́сить.

transcendental /trænsen'dent(ə)l/ *adj.* (*phil.*) трансцендента́льный.

transcontinental /trænzkɒntɪ'nent(ə)l/ *adj.* трансконтинента́льный.

transcribe /træn'skraɪb/ *v.t.* перепи́с|ывать, -а́ть.

transcript /'trænskrɪpt/ *n.* ко́пия.

transcription /træn'skrɪpʃ(ə)n/ *n.* перепи́сывание; ко́пия, транскри́пция; **phonetic ~** фонети́ческая транскри́пция.

transfer[1] /'trænsfə:(r)/ *n.* (*of object*) перенесе́ние, перено́с; (*of worker, money*) перево́д; (*of footballer*) перехо́д; (*conveyance, handing over*) переда́ча.

transfer[2] /træns'fə:(r)/ *v.t.* (**transferred, transferring**)
1 (*object*) перен|оси́ть, -ести́.
2 (*hand over*) перед|ава́ть, -а́ть.
3 (*footballer, worker, money*) перев|оди́ть, -ести́.
■ *v.i.* (**transferred, transferring**) (*of footballer, worker*) пере|ходи́ть, -йти́; (*to another vehicle*) перес|а́живаться, -е́сть.

transferable /træns'fə:rəb(ə)l/ *adj.* (*ticket, vote*) тот, кото́рый мо́жет быть пе́редан друго́му лицу́; (*skills*) универса́льный, приго́дный в любо́й ситуа́ции.

transference /'trænsfərəns/ *n.* перенесе́ние; перево́д; **thought ~** переда́ча мы́сли на расстоя́ние.

transfix /træns'fɪks/ *v.t.* прико́в|ывать, -а́ть к ме́сту; **he was ~ed with horror** он оцепене́л от у́жаса.

transform /træns'fɔ:m/ *v.t.* преобразо́в|ывать, -а́ть.

transformation /trænsfə'meɪʃ(ə)n/ *n.* преобразова́ние.

transformer /træns'fɔ:mə(r)/ *n.* (*elec.*) трансформа́тор.

transfusion /træns'fju:ʒ(ə)n/ *n.* перелива́ние (кро́ви).

transgress /trænz'gres/ *v.t. & i.* (*infringe*) пере|ходи́ть, -йти́ грани́цы + *g.*; нар|уша́ть, -у́шить (*закон и т. п.*).

transgression /trænz'greʃ(ə)n/ *n.* (*infringement*) просту́пок; (*offence*) наруше́ние; (*sin*) грех.

transience /'trænzɪəns/ *n.* быстроте́чность; мимолётность.

transient /'trænzɪənt/ *adj.* (*impermanent*)

вре́менный; (*brief*) мимолётный.

transistor /træn'zɪstə(r)/ *n.* транзи́стор.

transit /'trænzɪt/ *n.* транзи́т, перево́зка; **lost in ~** поте́рянный при перево́зке; **~ camp** транзи́тный ла́герь; **in ~** транзи́том.

transition /træn'zɪʃ(ə)n/ *n.* перехо́д.

transitional /træn'zɪʃənəl/ *adj.* перехо́дный; промежу́точный.

transitive /'trænsɪtɪv/ *adj.* перехо́дный.

transitory /'trænsɪtərɪ/ *adj.* преходя́щий, мимолётный.

translate /trænz'leɪt/ *v.t.* & *i.* перев|оди́ть, -ести́; **these poems do not ~ well** э́ти стихи́ не поддаю́тся перево́ду.

translation /trænz'leɪʃ(ə)n/ *n.* перево́д.

translator /trænz'leɪtə(r)/ *n.* перево́дчи|к (*fem.* -ца).

transliterate /trænz'lɪtəreɪt/ *v.t.* транслитери́ровать (*impf.*, *pf.*).

translucence /trænz'lu:s(ə)ns/ *n.* просве́чиваемость, полупрозра́чность.

translucent /trænz'lu:s(ə)nt/ *adj.* просве́чивающий, полупрозра́чный.

transmission /trænz'mɪʃ(ə)n/ *n.* переда́ча, трансми́ссия.

transmit /trænz'mɪt/ *v.t.* & *i.* перед|ава́ть, -а́ть.

transmitter /trænz'mɪtə(r)/ *n.* переда́тчик.

transparency /træns'pærənsɪ/ *n.*
1 прозра́чность.
2 (*picture*) транспара́нт.

transparent /træns'pærənt/ *adj.* прозра́чный.

transpire /træn'spaɪə(r)/ *v.i.* (*come to be known*) обнару́жи|ваться, -ться; (*coll.*, *happen*) случ|а́ться, -и́ться.

transplant[1] /'trænsplɑ:nt/ *n.* переса́дка.

transplant[2] /træns'plɑ:nt/ *v.t.* (*hort.*, *med.*) перес|а́живать, -ади́ть.

transplantation /trænsplɑ:n'teɪʃ(ə)n/ *n.* переса́дка, трансплanта́ция; (*fig.*) переселе́ние.

transport[1] /'trænspɔ:t/ *n.* тра́нспорт; **public ~** обще́ственный тра́нспорт.

transport[2] /træn'spɔ:t/ *v.t.* перев|ози́ть, -езти́; транспорти́ровать (*impf.*, *pf.*).

transportation /trænspɔ:'teɪʃ(ə)n/ *n.* (*of goods etc.*) перево́зка, транспортиро́вка.

transpose /træns'pəʊz/ *v.t.* перест|авля́ть, -а́вить.

transsexual /trænz'seksjʊəl/ *n.* транссексуа́л.

Trans-Siberian /trænzsaɪ'bɪərɪən/ *adj.*: **~ Railway** (*Br.*), **Railroad** (*US*) Транссиби́рская магистра́ль.

transvestite /trænz'vestaɪt/ *n.* трансвести́т.

trap /træp/ *n.*
1 (*for animals etc.*) западня́.
2 (*light vehicle*) рессо́рная двуко́лка.
■ *v.t.* (**trapped, trapping**) лови́ть, пойма́ть в лову́шку/капка́н; (*fig.*, *catch*): **his fingers were ~ped in the door** он защеми́л па́льцы две́рью.
■ *cpd.* **~door** *n.* люк.

trapeze /trə'pi:z/ *n.* трапе́ция (*цирковая*).

trapezi|um /trə'pi:zɪəm/ *n.* (*pl.* **~a** *or* **~ums**) (*geom.*) трапе́ция.

trapper /'træpə(r)/ *n.* охо́тник(, ста́вящий капка́ны) на пушно́го зве́ря.

trappings /'træpɪŋz/ *n.* (*harness*) сбру́я; (*fig.*): **the ~ of office** вне́шние атрибу́ты (*m. pl.*) вла́сти.

trash /træʃ/ *n.* му́сор.
■ *cpd.* **~ can** *n.* (*US*) му́сорное ведро́; (*outside*) му́сорный бак.

trauma /'trɔ:mə/ *n.* (*pl.* **~s**) тра́вма.

traumatic /trɔ:'mætɪk/ *adj.* (*distressing*) тя́жкий; (*of physical injury*) травмати́ческий.

traumatize /'trɔ:mətaɪz/ *v.t.* травми́ровать (*impf.*, *pf.*).

travel /'træv(ə)l/ *n.* путеше́ствие, пое́здка; **~ agency** туристи́ческое аге́нтство, тураге́нтство; **~ agent** туристи́ческий аге́нт.
■ *v.t.* (**travelled, travelling;** *US usu.* **traveled, traveling**) путеше́ствовать (*impf.*) по + *d.*; е́здить (*indet.*) по + *d.*
■ *v.i.* (**travelled, travelling;** *US usu.* **traveled, traveling**) путеше́ствовать (*impf.*); е́здить, съ-; (*move*) дви́гаться (*impf.*); перемеща́ться (*impf.*).
■ *cpd.* **~-sickness** *n.* тошнота́ при езде́.

traveller /'trævələ(r)/ (*US* **traveler**) *n.* путеше́ственник; **~'s cheque** (*US* **check**) доро́жный чек.

travelling /'trævəlɪŋ/ *n.* путеше́ствие.
■ *adj.* путеше́ствующий; **~ salesman** коммивояжёр.

traverse /'trævəs/ *v.t.* перес|ека́ть, -е́чь.

travesty /'trævɪstɪ/ *n.* паро́дия (**of:** на + *a.*).

trawl /trɔ:l/ *n.* (**~ net**) трал, тра́ловая сеть; до́нный не́вод.
■ *v.t.* & *i.* тра́лить (*impf.*); лови́ть (*impf.*) ры́бу тра́лом; **the fishermen ~ed their nets** рыбаки́ тащи́ли се́ти по дну; **they ~ed for herring** они́ тра́лили сельдь; (*fig.*, *search thoroughly*) проч|ёсывать, -еса́ть.

trawler /'trɔ:lə(r)/ *n.* тра́улер.

tray /treɪ/ *n.* подно́с.

treacherous /'tretʃərəs/ *adj.* преда́тельский.

treachery /'tretʃərɪ/ *n.* преда́тельство.

treacle /'tri:k(ə)l/ *n.* (*Br.*) па́тока.

tread /tred/ *n.*
1 (*manner or sound of walking*) похо́дка.
2 (*of tyre*) проте́ктор.
■ *v.t.* (*past* **trod;** *p.p.* **trodden** *or* **trod**) ступа́ть (*impf.*) по + *d.*; шага́ть (*impf.*) по + *d.*
■ *v.i.* (*past* **trod;** *p.p.* **trodden** *or* **trod**): **~ on that cockroach!** растопчи́те/раздави́те э́того тарака́на!; **don't ~ on the grass!** по газо́нам не ходи́ть!
■ *cpd.* **~mill** *n.* бегова́я доро́жка; (*fig.*) однообра́зная рабо́та.

treason /'tri:z(ə)n/ *n.* (госуда́рственная) изме́на.

treasonable /'tri:zənəb(ə)l/ *adj.* изме́ннический.

treasure /'treʒə(r)/ *n.* сокро́вище.
■ *v.t.* (*store up*) храни́ть, со-; **~d memories** дороги́е воспомина́ния; (*value highly*) высоко́ цени́ть (*impf.*).

treasurer /'treʒərə(r)/ *n.* казначе́й.

treasury /'treʒərɪ/ *n.* (*public department*) казна́.

treat /triːt/ *n.* удово́льствие; **it's my ~!** я угоща́ю!
■ *v.t.* 1 (*behave towards*) обраща́ться (*impf.*) с + *i.*; **he ~s me like a child** он обраща́ется со мной, как с ребёнком.
2 (*regard*) рассма́тривать (*impf.*); отн|оси́ться, -ести́сь к + *d.*
3 (*deal with; discuss*) осве|ща́ть, -ти́ть; рассм|а́тривать, -отре́ть; **he ~ed the subject in detail** он подро́бно освети́л те́му.
4 (*give medical care to*) лечи́ть (*impf.*).
5 (*apply chemical process to*) обраб|а́тывать, -о́тать.
6 (*give s.o. sth. at one's own expense*) уго|ща́ть, -сти́ть; **he ~ed me to a whisky** он угости́л меня́ ви́ски; **I shall ~ myself to a holiday** я устро́ю себе́ о́тпуск.

treatise /ˈtriːtɪs/ *n.* тракта́т; нау́чный труд.

treatment /ˈtriːtmənt/ *n.*
1 (*handling*) обраще́ние; рассмотре́ние.
2 (*chem. etc.*) обрабо́тка.
3 (*med.*) лече́ние; (*session of therapy*) процеду́ра.

treaty /ˈtriːtɪ/ *n.* догово́р.

treble /ˈtreb(ə)l/ *adj.* тройно́й.
■ *v.t. & i.* утр|а́ивать(ся), -о́ить(ся).

tree /triː/ *n.* де́рево.

trek /trek/ *n.* перехо́д.
■ *v.i.* (**trekked, trekking**) соверш|а́ть, -и́ть дли́тельный похо́д.

trellis /ˈtrelɪs/ *n.* шпале́ра.

tremble /ˈtremb(ə)l/ *v.i.* дрожа́ть (*impf.*); трясти́сь (*impf.*).

tremendous /trɪˈmendəs/ *adj.* (*huge*) огро́мный; (*coll., splendid*) замеча́тельный.

tremor /ˈtremə(r)/ *n.* (*quivering*) содрога́ние, дрожь; (*thrill*) тре́пет; **there was a ~ in his voice** его́ го́лос дрожа́л; **earth ~** подзе́мный толчо́к.

tremulous /ˈtremjʊləs/ *adj.* (*trembling*) дрожа́щий.

trench /trentʃ/ *n.* ров, кана́ва; (*mil.*) транше́я.

trend /trend/ *n.* направле́ние, тенде́нция; **set a ~** вв|оди́ть, -ести́ мо́ду (**for:** на + *a.*).

trendy /ˈtrendɪ/ *adj.* (**trendier, trendiest**) (*coll.*) мо́дный.

trepidation /trepɪˈdeɪʃ(ə)n/ *n.* тре́пет, дрожь; **in ~** трепеща́.

trespass /ˈtrespəs/ *v.i.* вт|орга́ться, -о́ргнуться в чужи́е владе́ния.

trespasser /ˈtrespəsə(r)/ *n.* лицо́, вторга́ющееся в чужи́е владе́ния; **~s will be prosecuted** наруши́тели бу́дут пресле́доваться.

trial /ˈtraɪəl/ *n.*
1 (*test*) испыта́ние, про́ба; **I discovered the truth by ~ and error** я пришёл к и́стине путём проб и оши́бок; **he took the car on a week's ~** он взял автомаши́ну на неде́льное испыта́ние.
2 (*attr.*) про́бный; **~ run** испыта́тельный пробе́г.
3 (*judicial examination*) суде́бный проце́сс; **he went on ~ for murder** его́ суди́ли за уби́йство.

triangle /ˈtraɪæŋg(ə)l/ *n.* треуго́льник.

triangular /traɪˈæŋgjʊlə(r)/ *adj.* треуго́льный; **a ~ argument** спор ме́жду тремя́ ли́цами.

triathlon /traɪˈæθlən/ *n.* троебо́рье.

tribal /ˈtraɪb(ə)l/ *adj.* племенно́й.

tribe /traɪb/ *n.* пле́мя (*nt.*).

tribulation /trɪbjʊˈleɪʃ(ə)n/ *n.* страда́ние, беда́.

tribunal /traɪˈbjuːn(ə)l/ *n.* трибуна́л.

tributary /ˈtrɪbjʊtərɪ/ *n.* прито́к.

tribute /ˈtrɪbjuːt/ *n.* дань; **he paid ~ to his wife's help** он вы́разил благода́рность свое́й жене́ за по́мощь.

trice /traɪs/ *n.*: **in a ~** вмиг, ми́гом.

trick /trɪk/ *n.*
1 (*dodge*) приём, хи́трость; **he knows all the ~s of the trade** он зна́ет все ходы́ и вы́ходы.
2 (*deception*) обма́н, трюк; (*prank*) шу́тка; **he is always playing ~s on me** он всегда́ надо мной подшу́чивает.
3 (*feat*) шту́ка; **that will do the ~** э́то срабо́тает наверняка́.
4 (*knack*) хва́тка.
5 (*at cards*) взя́тка.
■ *v.t.* обма́н|ывать, -у́ть; над|ува́ть, -у́ть; **they ~ed him out of a fortune** они́ вы́манили у него́ ма́ссу де́нег.

trickery /ˈtrɪkərɪ/ *n.* обма́н, надува́тельство.

trickle /ˈtrɪk(ə)l/ *n.* стру́йка.
■ *v.t.* ка́пать (*impf.*).
■ *v.i.* сочи́ться (*impf.*); ка́пать (*impf.*); (*fig.*): **the crowd began to ~ away** толпа́ ста́ла постепе́нно расходи́ться.

tricky /ˈtrɪkɪ/ *adj.* (**trickier, trickiest**) (*awkward*) сло́жный, мудрёный; (*crafty*) хи́трый, кова́рный.

tricycle /ˈtraɪsɪk(ə)l/ *n.* трёхколёсный велосипе́д.

trifle /ˈtraɪf(ə)l/ *n.*
1 (*thing of small value*) пустя́к, ме́лочь.
2 (*Br., sweet dish*) бискви́т со взби́тыми сли́вками.
■ *v.i.* относи́ться (*impf.*) несерьёзно к + *d.*; **he ~d with her affections** он игра́л её чу́вствами.

trifling /ˈtraɪflɪŋ/ *adj.* пустяко́вый; незначи́тельный.

trigger /ˈtrɪgə(r)/ *n.* куро́к.
■ *v.t.* (*usu.* **~ off**) вызыва́ть, вы́звать.

trigonometry /trɪgəˈnɒmɪtrɪ/ *n.* тригономе́трия.

trilby /ˈtrɪlbɪ/ *n.* (*Br.*) мя́гкая фе́тровая шля́па.

trill /trɪl/ *n.* трель.
■ *v.i.*: **the birds were ~ing** пти́цы залива́лись тре́лями.

trilogy /ˈtrɪlədʒɪ/ *n.* трило́гия.

trim /trɪm/ *n.*
1 (*order, fitness*) поря́док; состоя́ние гото́вности; **we must get into ~ before the race** нам ну́жно набра́ть фо́рму пе́ред соревнова́нием.
2 (*light cut*) подре́зка, стри́жка.
■ *adj.* (**trimmer, trimmest**) аккура́тный, опря́тный.
■ *v.t.* (**trimmed, trimming**)
1 (*cut to desired shape*) подр|еза́ть, -е́зать; подр|а́внивать, -овня́ть.

2 (*decorate*) отде́л|ывать, -ать; **a hat ~med with fur** ша́пка, отде́ланная ме́хом.

trimming /'trɪmɪŋ/ *n.* (*on dress etc.*) отде́лка; (*coll.*, *accessory*) гарни́р.

trinity /'trɪnɪtɪ/ *n.* Тро́ица; **T~ Sunday** день Свято́й Тро́ицы.

trinket /'trɪŋkɪt/ *n.* безделу́шка.

trio /'tri:əʊ/ *n.* (*pl.* **trios**) (*group of three*) тро́йка; (*mus.*) три́о (*nt. indecl.*).

trip /trɪp/ *n.* (*excursion*) пое́здка; (*longer one*) путеше́ствие.
■ *v.t.* (**tripped, tripping**) (*cause to stumble*; *also* **~ up**) ста́вить, по- подно́жку + *d.*; (*fig.*) запу́т|ывать, -ать, сби|ва́ть, -ть с то́лку.
■ *v.i.* (**tripped, tripping**)
1 (*run lightly*): **she came ~ping down the stairs** она́ легко́ сбежа́ла вниз по ле́стнице.
2 (*stumble*; *also* **~ up**) спот|ыка́ться, -кну́ться.

tripartite /traɪ'pɑ:taɪt/ *adj.* трёхсторо́нний.

tripe /traɪp/ *n.* (*offal*) требуха́; (*coll.*, *rubbish*) чепуха́, вздор.

triple /'trɪp(ə)l/ *adj.* тройно́й, утро́енный; **~ jump** (*sport*) тройно́й прыжо́к.

triplet /'trɪplɪt/ *n.*: **~s** (*children*) тро́йня (*sg.*).

triplicate /'trɪplɪkət/ *n.*: **in ~** в трёх экземпля́рах.

tripod /'traɪpɒd/ *n.* трено́га.

trite /traɪt/ *adj.* бана́льный, изби́тый.

triumph /'traɪʌmf/ *n.* (*joy at success*) торжество́; (*success*) триу́мф.
■ *v.i.* побе|жда́ть, -ди́ть; восторжествова́ть (*pf.*); **he ~ed over adversity** он преодоле́л все невзго́ды.

triumphant /traɪ'ʌmf(ə)nt/ *adj.* (*victorious*) победоно́сный; (*exultant*) торжеству́ющий.

trivia /'trɪvɪə/ *n.* ме́лочи (*f. pl.*).

trivial /'trɪvɪəl/ *adj.* (*trifling*) ме́лкий, незначи́тельный; (*everyday*) обы́денный.

triviality /trɪvɪ'ælɪtɪ/ *n.* незначи́тельность, тривиа́льность.

trivialize /'trɪvɪəlaɪz/ *v.t.* оп|ошля́ть, -о́шлить.

trod /trɒd/ *past and p.p. of* ▸ **tread**

trodden /'trɒd(ə)n/ *p.p. of* ▸ **tread**

trolley /'trɒlɪ/ *n.* (*pl.* **~s**) (*Br.*, *for luggage, purchases*) теле́жка; (*US*, *streetcar*) трамва́й.
■ *cpds.* **~bus** *n.* тролле́йбус; **~ car** *n.* (*US*) трамва́й.

trombone /trɒm'bəʊn/ *n.* тромбо́н.

trombonist /trɒm'bəʊnɪst/ *n.* тромбони́ст.

troop /tru:p/ *n.*
1 (*mil. unit*) батаре́я.
2 (*pl.*, *soldiers*) войск|а́ (*pl.*, *g.* —).

trooper /'tru:pə(r)/ *n.*
1 (*soldier*) (*in armoured unit*) танки́ст; (*in cavalry*) кавалери́ст.
2 (*US*, *policeman*) полице́йский.

trophy /'trəʊfɪ/ *n.* трофе́й.

tropic /'trɒpɪk/ *n.* тро́пик; **in the ~s** в тро́пиках.

tropical /'trɒpɪk(ə)l/ *adj.* тропи́ческий.

trot /trɒt/ *n.* рысь; **on the ~** (*Br.*) подря́д.
■ *v.i.* (**trotted, trotting**) (*of a horse*) идти́ (*det.*) ры́сью; (*of person*) семени́ть (*impf.*).
■ *with adv.* **~ out** *v.t.* (*coll.*): **he ~ted out the usual excuses** он, как обы́чно, привёл свои́ ста́рые отгово́рки.

trouble /'trʌb(ə)l/ *n.*
1 (*anxiety*) волне́ние, трево́га; беспоко́йство; (*misfortune*) го́ре, беда́, несча́стье.
2 (*difficulties*) хло́п|оты (*pl.*, *g.* -о́т), тру́дности (*f. pl.*); (*difficulty*) затрудне́ние; **money ~s** де́нежные затрудне́ния; **I am having ~ with the car** у меня́ непола́дки (*f. pl.*) с маши́ной; **what's the ~?** в чём де́ло?
3 (*predicament*) неприя́тность; **he's always getting into ~** он ве́чно попада́ет в исто́рии.
4 (*inconvenience*): **he saved me the ~** он изба́вил меня́ от э́той необходи́мости.
5 (*care, effort*) забо́та, труд, хло́п|оты (*pl.*, *g.* -о́т); **she took a lot of ~ over the cake** она́ приложи́ла нема́ло стара́ний, что́бы пригото́вить э́тот торт.
6 (*unrest*) волне́ния (*nt. pl.*); **~ spot** горя́чая то́чка.
■ *v.t.* 1 (*worry*) трево́жить (*impf.*); волнова́ть (*impf.*); **don't let it ~ you** не принима́йте э́то бли́зко к се́рдцу.
2 (*afflict*) беспоко́ить (*impf.*); му́чить (*impf.*); **he is ~d with a cough** его́ му́чит ка́шель.
3 (*put to inconvenience*) беспоко́ить, по-, затрудн|я́ть, -и́ть; **don't ~ yourself** не беспоко́йтесь; **sorry to ~ you!** прости́те за беспоко́йство!
■ *cpds.* **~-free** *adj.* (*reliable*) надёжный, безотка́зный; **~maker** *n.* смутья́н (*fem.* -ка); **~shooter** *n.* специали́ст по разреше́нию конфли́ктных/кри́зисных ситуа́ций (*в компании и т. п.*).

troublesome /'trʌb(ə)lsəm/ *adj.* тру́дный; хло́потный.

trough /trɒf/ *n.*
1 (*food ~*) корму́шка; (*drinking ~*) по́илка.
2 (*dip*) впа́дина.

troupe /tru:p/ *n.* тру́ппа.

trousers /'traʊzəz/ *n.* штан|ы́ (*pl.*, *g.* -о́в), брю́к|и (*pl.*, *g.* —); **a pair of ~** па́ра брюк.

trout /traʊt/ *n.* форе́ль.

trowel /'traʊəl/ *n.* (*for bricklaying etc.*) мастеро́к; (*for gardening*) (садо́вый) сово́к, лопа́тка.

truancy /'tru:ənsɪ/ *n.* прогу́л.

truant /'tru:ənt/ *n.* прогу́льщик; **did you ever play ~?** вы когда́-нибудь прогу́ливали уро́ки?

truce /tru:s/ *n.* переми́рие.

truck /trʌk/ *n.* (*Br.*, *railway wagon*) откры́тая грузова́я платфо́рма; (*lorry*) грузови́к; (*barrow*) теле́жка.

trucker /'trʌkə(r)/ *n.* води́тель (*m.*) грузовика́.

truculent /'trʌkjʊlənt/ *adj.* агресси́вный, драчли́вый.

trudge /trʌdʒ/ *v.i.* тащи́ться (*impf.*).

true /tru:/ *adj.* (**truer, truest**)
1 (*in accordance with fact*) ве́рный, правди́вый; **is it ~ that ...?** (э́то) пра́вда, что...? **a ~ story** правди́вый расска́з; **all my dreams came ~** все мои́ мечты́ сбыли́сь/осуществи́лись.
2 (*in accordance with reason*; *genuine*) правди́вый; настоя́щий; и́стинный.
3 (*conforming accurately*) ве́рный, пра́вильный; **~ to life** правди́вый.

4 (*loyal; dependable*) пре́данный, ве́рный; надёжный.

truffle /ˈtrʌf(ə)l/ *n.* (*fungus, candy*) трю́фель (*m.*).

truism /ˈtru:ɪz(ə)m/ *n.* изби́тая и́стина, трюи́зм; **it is a ~ that** общеизве́стно, что… .

truly /ˈtru:lɪ/ *adv.*
1 (*truthfully*) и́скренне; (*accurately*) правди́во.
2 (*sincerely*) и́скренне; **yours ~** (*at end of letter*) пре́данный Вам.

trump /trʌmp/ *n.* **(~ card)** ко́зырь (*m.*); **the weather turned up ~s** (*Br.*) нам (неожи́данно) повезло́ с пого́дой.

trumpet /ˈtrʌmpɪt/ *n.* труба́; **blow one's own ~** (*fig.*) хвали́ться (*impf.*).

trumpeter /ˈtrʌmpɪtə(r)/ *n.* труба́ч.

truncate /trʌŋˈkeɪt/ *v.t.* ус|ека́ть, -е́чь; **a ~d cone** усечённый ко́нус; **his speech was ~d** его́ ре́чь уре́зали.

truncheon /ˈtrʌntʃ(ə)n/ *n.* (*Br.*) (полице́йская) дуби́нка.

trundle /ˈtrʌnd(ə)l/ *v.t.* & *i.* кати́ть(ся) (*impf.*).

trunk /trʌŋk/ *n.*
1 (*of tree*) ствол.
2 (*of body*) ту́ловище.
3 (*box*) сунду́к.
4 (*of elephant*) хо́бот.
5 (*pl., garment*) пла́в|ки (*pl., g.* -ок).
6 (*US, boot of car*) бага́жник.
■ *cpd.* **~ road** *n.* (*Br.*) магистра́ль.

trust /trʌst/ *n.*
1 (*confidence*) дове́рие; ве́ра.
2 (*leg.*) довери́тельная со́бственность; **~ fund** целево́й фонд.
■ *v.t.* 1 (*have confidence in, rely on*) дов|еря́ть, -е́рить + *d.*
2 (*entrust*) вв|еря́ть, -е́рить.
■ *v.i.* 1 (*have faith, confidence*) дов|еря́ться, -е́риться (**in:** + *d.*); **she ~ed in God** она́ отдала́сь на во́лю Бо́жью.
2 (*commit o.s. with confidence*) дов|еря́ться, -е́риться (**to:** + *d.*); **he ~ed to luck** он дове́рился уда́че.

trustee /trʌsˈti:/ *n.* довери́тельный со́бственник; опеку́н.

trusting /ˈtrʌstɪŋ/ *adj.* дове́рчивый.

trustworthiness /ˈtrʌstwə:ðɪnɪs/ *n.* надёжность.

trustworthy /ˈtrʌstwə:ðɪ/ *adj.* надёжный.

trusty /ˈtrʌstɪ/ *adj.* (**trustier, trustiest**) ве́рный, надёжный.

truth /tru:θ/ *n.* пра́вда; (*verity*) и́стина.

truthful /ˈtru:θfʊl/ *adj.* (*of person*) правди́вый; (*of statement etc.*) правди́вый, ве́рный, то́чный.

truthfulness /ˈtru:θfʊlnɪs/ *n.* правди́вость; ве́рность, то́чность.

try /traɪ/ *n.*
1 (*attempt*) попы́тка.
2 (*test*): **why not give it a ~?** почему́ бы не попро́бовать?
3 (*rugby*) прохо́д с мячо́м в зачётное по́ле сопе́рника, попы́тка.
■ *v.t.* 1 (*attempt*) пыта́ться, по-; стара́ться, по-; **he tried his best** он стара́лся изо всех сил; **he tried hard** он о́чень стара́лся.
2 (*sample*) про́бовать, по-; (*taste*) отве́д|ывать, -ать; (*experiment with*) **have you tried aspirin?** вы про́бовали аспири́н?
3 (*leg.*) (*a person*) суди́ть (*impf.*).
4 (*subject to strain*): **he tries my patience** он испы́тывает моё терпе́ние; **a ~ing situation** тру́дное положе́ние.
5 (*test*) испы́т|ывать, -а́ть; пров|еря́ть, -е́рить.
■ *v.i.*: **~ harder next time!** в сле́дующий раз приложи́те бо́льше уси́лий!; **I tried for a prize** я добива́лся при́за; я претендова́л на приз.
■ *with advs.*: **~ on** *v.t.* прим|еря́ть, -е́рить; **~ out** *v.t.* испы́т|ывать, -а́ть; опро́бовать (*pf.*).

tsar, tzar /zɑ:(r)/ *n.* царь (*m.*).

T-shirt /ˈti:ʃə:t/ *n.* футбо́лка.

tsunami /tsuˈnɑ:mɪ/ *n.* цуна́ми (*nt. indecl.*).

tub /tʌb/ *n.*
1 ка́дка; бо́чка.
2 (*bath*) ва́нна.
3 (*of margarine*) упако́вка; (*of ice cream, yogurt*) стака́нчик.

tuba /ˈtju:bə/ *n.* ту́ба.

tubby /ˈtʌbɪ/ *adj.* (**tubbier, tubbiest**) (*of person*) коротконо́гий и то́лстый.

tube /tju:b/ *n.*
1 (*of metal, glass etc.*) труба́, тру́бка.
2 (*of toothpaste etc.*) тю́бик.
3 (*of tyre*) ка́мера (ши́ны).
4 (*in the body*) труба́.
5 (*Br. coll., underground railway*) метро́ (*nt. indecl.*).

tuberculosis /tjʊbə:kjʊˈləʊsɪs/ *n.* туберкулёз.

tuck[1] /tʌk/ *v.t.* (*stow*) пря́тать, с-; под|бира́ть, -обра́ть.
■ *with advs.*: **~ away** *v.t.* запря́т|ывать, -ать; **~ in** *v.t.* запр|авля́ть, -а́вить; **~ your shirt in!** запра́вьте руба́шку!; **~ up** *v.t.*: **he ~ed up his sleeves** он засучи́л рукава́; **they ~ed the children up (in bed)** дете́й уложи́ли в крова́ть и укры́ли одея́лом.

tuck[2] /tʌk/ *v.i.*: **they ~ed into their supper** они́ уплета́ли у́жин за о́бе щёки; **~ in!** налета́й(те)! (*на еду*).

Tuesday /ˈtju:zdeɪ/ *n.* вто́рник.

tuft /tʌft/ *n.* (*of grass, hair etc.*) пучо́к.

tug /tʌg/ *n.*
1 (*pull*) рыво́к, дёрганье.
2 (*boat*) букси́р.
■ *v.t.* (**tugged, tugging**) тащи́ть (*impf.*).
■ *v.i.* (**tugged, tugging**) дёр|гать, -нуть; **he ~ged at my sleeve** он дёрнул меня́ за рука́в.
■ *cpd.* **~ of war** *n.* перетя́гивание кана́та.

tuition /tju:ˈɪʃ(ə)n/ *n.* обуче́ние.

tulip /ˈtju:lɪp/ *n.* тюльпа́н.

tumble /ˈtʌmb(ə)l/ *n.*
1 (*fall*) паде́ние; **take a ~** упа́сть (*pf.*).
2 (*acrobatic feat*) кувыро́к.
■ *v.i.* сва́л|иваться, -и́ться.
■ *with adv.*: **the house seemed about to ~ down** дом, каза́лось, вот-во́т разва́лится.
■ *cpd.* **~ dryer** *n.* (*Br.*) электри́ческая суши́лка для белья́.

tumbler /ˈtʌmblə(r)/ *n.* (*glass*) стака́н.

tummy /ˈtʌmɪ/ *n.* (*coll.*) живо́т(ик).

tumour /ˈtju:mə(r)/ (*US* **tumor**) *n.* о́пухоль.

tumult /ˈtju:mʌlt/ *n.* сумато́ха.

tumultuous /tjʊˈmʌltjʊəs/ *adj.* шу́мный,

беспоко́йный; **he received a ~ welcome** ему́ устро́или бу́рную встре́чу.

tuna /'tju:nə/ *n.* туне́ц.

tundra /'tʌndrə/ *n.* ту́ндра.

tune /tju:n/ *n.*
[1] (*melody*) мело́дия; моти́в.
[2] (*correct pitch*): **you are not singing in ~** вы фальши́вите; **he plays out of ~** он игра́ет фальши́во; **the piano is out of ~** фортепиа́но расстро́ено.
■ *v.t.* [1] (*mus., bring to right pitch*) настр|а́ивать, -о́ить; **tuning fork** камерто́н.
[2] (*adjust running of*) настр|а́ивать, -о́ить; регули́ровать, от-.
■ *with adv.*: **~ in** *v.t.* & *i.* настр|а́ивать(ся), -о́ить(ся); **he ~d in to the BBC** он настро́ил приёмник на Би-би-си́.

tuneful /'tju:nfʊl/ *adj.* музыка́льный, мелоди́чный.

tuneless /'tju:nlɪs/ *adj.* немузыка́льный, немелоди́чный.

tuner /'tju:nə(r)/ *n.* (*of pianos etc.*) настро́йщик; (*radio component*) тю́нер; (*receiver*) (радио)приёмник.

tunic /'tju:nɪk/ *n.* (*ancient garment*) туни́ка; (*part of uniform*) ки́тель (*m.*).

Tunisia /tju:'nɪzɪə/ *n.* Туни́с.

Tunisian /tju:'nɪzɪən/ *n.* туни́с|ец (*fem.* -ка).
■ *adj.* туни́сский.

tunnel /'tʌn(ə)l/ *n.* тонне́ль (*m.*), тунне́ль (*m.*).
■ *v.t.* (**tunnelled, tunnelling;** *US* **tunneled, tunneling**): **they ~led their way out (of prison)** они́ сде́лали подко́п и сбежа́ли (из тюрьмы́).
■ *v.i.* (**tunnelled, tunnelling;** *US* **tunneled, tunneling**) про|кла́дывать, -ложи́ть тонне́ль.

turban /'tə:bən/ *n.* тюрба́н.

turbine /'tə:baɪn/ *n.* турби́на.

turbulence /'tə:bjʊləns/ *n.* бу́рность; (*aeron.*) турбуле́нтность; (*fig.*) суета́, сумато́ха.

turbulent /'tə:bjʊlənt/ *adj.* бу́рный; (*fig.*) беспоко́йный.

turf /tə:f/ *n.* (*pl.* **turfs** *or* **turves**) (*grassy topsoil*) дёрн; (*peat*) торф.
■ *v.t.* [1] (*cover with ~; also* **~ over**) покр|ыва́ть, -ы́ть дёрном.
[2] **~ out** (*Br. coll., eject*) выбра́сывать, вы́бросить.

turgid /'tə:dʒɪd/ *adj.* (*fig.*) напы́щенный.

Turk /tə:k/ *n.* ту́р|ок (*fem.* -ча́нка).

Turkey /'tə:kɪ/ *n.*
[1] (*country*) Ту́рция.
[2] (**t~:** *bird*) (*pl.* **~s**) инд|ю́к (*fem.* -е́йка); (*as food*) инде́йка, индю́шка.

Turkish /'tə:kɪʃ/ *n.* туре́цкий язы́к.
■ *adj.* туре́цкий; **~ delight** раха́т-луку́м.

Turkmen /'tə:kmən/ *n.* (*pl.* **~** *or* **~s**) (*person*) туркме́н (*fem.* -ка); (*language*) туркме́нский язы́к.
■ *adj.* туркме́нский.

Turkmenistan /tə:kmenɪ'stɑ:n/ *n.* Туркмениста́н.

turmeric /'tə:mərɪk/ *n.* курку́ма (*азиатская пряность*).

turmoil /'tə:mɔɪl/ *n.* беспоря́док; смяте́ние.

turn /tə:n/ *n.*
[1] (*rotation*) поворо́т, оборо́т.
[2] (*change of direction*) поворо́т; **I took a right ~** я поверну́л напра́во.
[3] (*change in condition*) переме́на; поворо́т; **his condition took a ~ for the worse** его́ состоя́ние ухудши́лось.
[4] (*chance of doing sth. in proper order*) о́чередь; **it's your ~ next** вы сле́дующий; **they all spoke in ~ (***or* **took ~s to speak)** они́ говори́ли по о́череди.
[5] (*service*) услу́га; **he did me a good ~** он оказа́л мне до́брую услу́гу.
[6] (*performance*) но́мер.
[7] (*coll., shock*) потрясе́ние; **you gave me quite a ~** вы меня́ поря́дком испуга́ли.
■ *v.t.* [1] (*cause to move round*) пов|ора́чивать, -ерну́ть; **he ~ed his head** он поверну́л го́лову; он оберну́лся; **she ~ed the pages** она́ перелиста́ла страни́цы.
[2] (*direct*) напр|авля́ть, -а́вить; **he can ~ his hand to anything** он всё уме́ет; (*incline*): **~ s.o. against s.o./sth.** настр|а́ивать, -о́ить кого́-н. про́тив + *g.*
[3] (*pass round or beyond*) пов|ора́чивать, -ерну́ть за + *a.*; **slow down as you ~ the corner** повора́чивая за́ угол, сба́вьте ско́рость; **it has ~ed two o'clock** уже́ два часа́; **he has ~ed fifty** ему́ испо́лнилось 50 лет.
[4] (*transform*) превра|ща́ть, -ти́ть; **he ~ed the water into wine** он обрати́л во́ду в вино́.
[5] (*cause to become*): **the shock ~ed his hair white** он поседе́л от потрясе́ния.
[6] (*send forcibly*) прог|оня́ть, -на́ть; **he was ~ed out of the house** его́ вы́гнали из до́ма/и́з дому.
■ *v.i.* [1] (*move round*) пов|ора́чиваться, -ерну́ться; враща́ться (*impf.*); **the key won't ~** ключ не повора́чивается; (*fig.*): **everything ~s on his answer** всё зави́сит от его́ отве́та; (*revolve*): **the discussion ~ed upon the meaning of democracy** спор враща́лся вокру́г по́длинного значе́ния демокра́тии.
[2] (*change direction*) свора́чиваться, сверну́ться; направля́ться (*impf.*); **right ~!** напра́во!; **who can I ~ to?** к кому́ я могу́ обрати́ться?; **he ~ed on his attackers** он бро́сился на свои́х оби́дчиков.
[3] (*change*) превра|ща́ться, -ти́ться; **the tadpoles ~ed into frogs** голова́стики преврати́лись в лягу́шек; **he ~ed into a miser** он стал скрягой.
[4] (*become*) ста|нови́ться, -ть; де́латься, с-; **she ~ed pale** она́ побледне́ла; **it has ~ed warm** потепле́ло.
■ *with advs.*: **~ away** *v.t.* (*refuse admittance to*) прог|оня́ть, -на́ть; не пус|ка́ть, -ти́ть; *v.i.*: **she ~ed away in disgust** она́ с отвраще́нием отверну́лась; **~ back** *v.t.* (*repel*) от|сыла́ть, -осла́ть наза́д; **we were ~ed back at the frontier** нас верну́ли с грани́цы; (*return to former position*): **we cannot ~ the clock back** (*fig.*) мы не мо́жем поверну́ть вре́мя вспять; *v.i.* пов|ора́чивать, -ерну́ть наза́д; пойти́ (*pf.*) обра́тно; **~ down** *v.t.* (*reduce by ~ing*) уб|авля́ть, -а́вить; **~ the volume down!** (*TV etc.*) уба́вьте звук!; (*reject*) отв|ерга́ть, -е́ргнуть; отка́з|ываться, -а́ться от + *g.*; **my offer was ~ed down** моё предложе́ние

было отвéргнуто; **~ in** *v.t.*: (*hand over*) сда|вáть, -ть; **he ~ed himself in to the police** он сдáлся поли́ции; **~ off** *v.t.* (*e.g. light, engine*) выключáть, вы́ключить; гаси́ть, по-; (*tap*) закр|ывáть, -ы́ть; *v.i.* (*make a diversion*) св|орáчивать, -ернýть; **~ on** *v.t.* (*e.g. light, engine, radio*) включ|áть, -и́ть; (*tap*) откр|ывáть, -ы́ть; (*fig.*): **this music ~s me on** (*coll.*) э́та мýзыка заводит меня́; **~ out** *v.t.* (*expel*) прог|оня́ть, -нáть; исключ|áть, -и́ть; (*switch off*) гаси́ть, по-; туши́ть, по-; (*produce*) выпускáть, вы́пустить; произв|оди́ть, -ести́; (*empty*) вывора́чивать, вы́вернуть; *v.i.* (*prove*) окáз|ываться, -áться; **let us see how things ~ out** посмóтрим, какóй оборóт при́мут делá; **he ~ed out to be a liar** он оказáлся лжецóм; **it ~ed out that he was right** получи́лось, что он был прав; (*assemble*) соб|ирáться, -рáться; **~ over** *v.t.* (*overturn*) перев|орáчивать, -ернýть; опроки́|дывать, -нуть; (*reverse position of*): **I ~ed over the page** я переверну́л страни́цу; (*hand over*) перед|авáть, -áть; *v.i.* (*overturn*) перев|орáчиваться, -ернýться; (*change position*) перев|орáчиваться, -ернýться; (*revolve*): **is the engine ~ing over?** дви́гатель вращáется?; **~ round** *v.t.* (*change or reverse position of*) перев|орáчивать, -ернýть; **he ~ed his car round** он разверну́л маши́ну; *v.i.* (*change position*): **he ~ed round to look** он оберну́лся, чтóбы посмотрéть; (*revolve*) вращáться (*impf.*); **~ up** *v.t.* (*increase flow of*) приб|авля́ть, -áвить; уси́ли|вать, -ть; *v.i.* (*arrive*) появ|ля́ться, -и́ться; (*be found*; *occur*) окáз|ываться, -áться; подв|ёртываться, -ернýться; (*happen*; *become available*) подвернýться (*pf.*).
■ *cpds.* **~around** *n.* (*reversal of policy, opinion etc.*) поворóт на 180 грáдусов; **~-off** *n.* поворóт, боковáя дорóга; (*repulsive thing*) что-н. отврати́тельное; **~out** *n.* (*assembly*): **there was a very good ~out** собрáлось óчень мнóго нарóду; **~over** *n.* (*in business*) оборóт (капитáла); (*of staff*) текýчесть; **~pike** *n.* (*US, tolled highway*) плáтная автомагистрáль; **~stile** *n.* турникéт; **~-up** *n.* (*Br.*) (*of trouser*) манжéта, отворóт.

turner /ˈtə:nə(r)/ *n.* тóкарь (*m.*).

turning /ˈtə:nɪŋ/ *n.* поворóт.
■ *cpd.* **~ point** *n.* (*fig.*) кри́зис, перелóм; **it was a ~ point in his career** э́то был поворóтный момéнт в егó карьéре.

turnip /ˈtə:nɪp/ *n.* рéпа.

turquoise /ˈtə:kwɔɪz/ *n.* бирюзóвый цвет.

turret /ˈtʌrɪt/ *n.* бáшенка; (*on a tank, warship, etc.*) бáшня.

turtle /ˈtə:t(ə)l/ *n.* черепáха.

tusk /tʌsk/ *n.* клык, би́вень (*m.*).

tussle /ˈtʌs(ə)l/ *n.* дрáка.

tutor /ˈtju:tə(r)/ *n.* (*private teacher*) репети́тор; (*university teacher*) преподавáтель (*fem., coll.* -ница).

tutorial /tju:ˈtɔ:rɪəl/ *n.* ≈ семинáр.

tutu /ˈtu:tu:/ *n.* пáчка (*балерины*).

tuxedo /tʌkˈsi:dəʊ/ *n.* (*pl.* **~s** *or* **~es**) (*US*) смóкинг.

TV (*abbr. of* **television**) ТВ (телеви́дение); (*set*) телеви́зор, (*coll.*) тéлик, я́щик.

twang /twæŋ/ *n.* (*of plucked string*) звеня́щий звук натя́нутой струны́; (*nasal voice*) гнусáвый гóлос.

tweak /twi:k/ *v.t.* ущипнýть (*pf.*).

tweed /twi:d/ *n.* твид; **a ~ jacket** тви́довый пиджáк.

tweezers /ˈtwi:zəz/ *n. pl.* пинцéт.

twelfth /twelfθ/ *n.* (*date*) двенáдцатое числó; (*fraction*) однá двенáдцатая.
■ *adj.* двенáдцатый.

twelve /twelv/ *n.* двенáдцать.
■ *adj.* двенáдцать + *g. pl.*

twentieth /ˈtwentɪɪθ/ *n.* (*date*) двадцáтое числó; (*fraction*) однá двадцáтая.
■ *adj.* двадцáтый.

twent|y /ˈtwentɪ/ *n.* двáдцать; **she is still in her ~ies** ей ещё нет тридцати́; **the ~ies** (*decade*) двадцáтые гóды.
■ *adj.* двáдцать + *g. pl.*

twice /twaɪs/ *adv.* (*two times*) двáжды, два рáза; (*doubly*) вдвóе, в два рáза; **~ a day** двáжды (*or* два рáза) в день; **he is ~ my age** он вдвóе стáрше меня́; **~ as much** в два рáза (*or* вдвóе) бóльше.

twiddl|e /ˈtwɪd(ə)l/ *v.t.* вертéть (*impf.*); крути́ть (*impf.*); **he sat there ~ing his thumbs** он бил баклýши; он бездéльничал.

twig /twɪg/ *n.* (*on tree*) вéтка; (*when cut*) прут.

twilight /ˈtwaɪlaɪt/ *n.* сýмер|ки (*pl., g.* -ек).

twin /twɪn/ *n.* близнéц; (*pl.*) близнецы́, двóйня (*f. sg.*).
■ *adj.* одинáковый; **they are ~ brothers** они́ (брáтья-)близнецы́; **~ beds** две односпáльные кровáти.
■ *v.t.* (**twinned, twinning**) (*fig.*) соедин|я́ть, -и́ть.

twine /twaɪn/ *n.* бечёвка, шнурóк.

twinge /twɪndʒ/ *n.* при́ступ óстрой бóли; (*fig.*) мýка; **~s of conscience** угрызéния сóвести.

twinkle /ˈtwɪŋk(ə)l/ *v.i.* мерцáть (*impf.*); сверкáть (*impf.*); **his eyes ~d with amusement** егó глазá вéсело блестéли.

twirl /twə:l/ *n.* вращéние.
■ *v.t.* вертéть (*impf.*); крути́ть (*impf.*).

twist /twɪst/ *n.*
1 (*sharp turning motion*) кручéние.
2 (*sharp change of direction*) изги́б, поворóт; **a ~ in the plot** крутóй поворóт сюжéта.
3 (*sth. ~ed or spiral in shape*) петля́; ýзел.
■ *v.t.* 1 (*screw round*) крути́ть (*or* скрýчивать), с-; **I ~ed my ankle** я подвернýл нóгу.
2 (*contort*) искрив|ля́ть, -и́ть; (*fig.*) иска|жáть, -зи́ть.
3 (*wind*) обв|ивáть, -и́ть; обм|áтывать, -отáть.
■ *v.i.* 1 (*wriggle*) кóрчиться (*impf.*); извивáться (*impf.*).
2 (*twine*) обв|ивáться, -и́ться; **the tendrils ~ed round their support** побéги растéния вили́сь вокрýг жёрдочки.
■ *with adv.*: **~ off** *v.t.* открý|чивать, -ти́ть.

twisted /ˈtwɪstɪd/ *adj.* (*perverted*) извращённый.

twit /twɪt/ *n.* (*Br.*) óлух (*coll.*).

twitch /twɪtʃ/ *n.* подёргивание, сýдорога.
■ *v.t.* 1 (*jerk*) дёргать (*impf.*).
2 (*move spasmodically*) подёргивать (*impf.*) + *i.*

■ *v.i.* дёргаться (*impf.*), подёргиваться (*impf.*).

twitter /ˈtwɪtə(r)/ *v.i.* (*chirp*) щебета́ть (*impf.*).

two /tu:/ *n.* (число́/но́мер) два; (~ *people*) дво́е; **~ each, in ~s, ~ at a time, ~ by ~** по́ два/дво́е; (*cut, divide*) **in ~** на́двое/попола́м; **the plate broke in ~** таре́лка разби́лась на две ча́сти; (*figure, thing numbered 2*) дво́йка; **I put ~ and ~ together** я сообрази́л, что к чему́; **that makes ~ of us** вот и я то́же.
■ *adj.* два + *g. sg.*; (*for m. nn. denoting people and pluralia tantum, also*) дво́е + *g. pl.*; **~ students** два студе́нта, дво́е студе́нтов; **~ children** дво́е дете́й; два ребёнка; **~ watches** дво́е часо́в.
■ *cpds.* **~-dimensional** *adj.* двухме́рный; **~-faced** *adj.* (*fig.*) двули́чный; **~fold** *adj.* двойно́й; *adv.* вдво́е; **~-seater** *n.* двухме́стный автомоби́ль/самолёт; **~-time** *v.t.* (*coll.*) обма́н|ывать, -у́ть; измен|я́ть, -и́ть (жене́/му́жу); **~-way** *adj.* (*e.g. traffic*) двусторо́нний; **~-way radio** одновре́менная двусторо́нняя радиосвя́зь.

tycoon /taɪˈku:n/ *n.* (*business magnate*) магна́т.

tying /ˈtaɪɪŋ/ *pres. part. of* ▶**tie**

tympan|i /ˈtɪmpənɪ/, **-ist** /ˈtɪmpənɪst/ = **timpan|i, -ist**

type /taɪp/ *n.*
1 (*class*) тип, род.
2 (*letters for printing*) шрифт.
■ *v.t.* (*write with ~writer*) печа́тать, на- (на маши́нке).
■ *v.i.* печа́тать (*impf.*) (на маши́нке); **typing** (*as n.*) маши́нопись.
■ *cpds.* **~cast** *adj.*: **he is ~cast as the butler** он всегда́ игра́ет роль дворе́цкого; **~face** *n.* шрифт; **~writer** *n.* пи́шущая маши́нка.

typhoid /ˈtaɪfɔɪd/ *n.* (*also* **~ fever**) брюшно́й тиф.

typhoon /taɪˈfu:n/ *n.* тайфу́н.

typical /ˈtɪpɪk(ə)l/ *adj.* типи́чный; **that is ~ of him** э́то сво́йственно ему́.

typify /ˈtɪpɪfaɪ/ *v.t.* быть типи́чным представи́телем + *g.*

typist /ˈtaɪpɪst/ *n.* (*fem.*) машини́стка.

typographic(al) /taɪpəˈgræfɪk, taɪpəˈgræfɪk(ə)l/ *adj.* типогра́фский.

typography /taɪˈpɒgrəfɪ/ *n.* (*art, process*) полиграфи́я; (*of books*) книгопеча́тание; (*appearance of printed matter*) оформле́ние (*книги и т. п.*).

tyrannical /tɪˈrænɪk(ə)l/ *adj.* тирани́ческий.

tyrannize /ˈtɪrənaɪz/ *v.t.* & *i.* тира́нить (*impf.*).

tyranny /ˈtɪrənɪ/ *n.* тирани́я.

tyrant /ˈtaɪərənt/ *n.* тира́н.

tyre /ˈtaɪə(r)/ (*US* **tire**) *n.* ши́на.

tzar /zɑ:(r)/ = **tsar**

Uu

UAE (*abbr. of* ***United Arab Emirates***) ОАЭ (Объединённые Ара́бские Эмира́ты).

ubiquitous /ju:ˈbɪkwɪtəs/ *adj.* вездесу́щий, повсеме́стный.

ubiquity /ju:ˈbɪkwɪˈtɪ/ *n.* вездесу́щность.

udder /ˈʌdə(r)/ *n.* вы́мя (*nt.*).

UEFA /ju:ˈi:fə/ (*abbr. of* ***Union of European Football Associations***) УЕФА́ (*m.* & *f. indecl.*).

UFO (*pl.* **UFOs**) (*abbr. of* ***unidentified flying object***) НЛО (*m. indecl.*) (неопо́знанный лета́ющий объе́кт).

Uganda /ju:ˈgændə/ *n.* Уга́нда.

Ugandan /ju:ˈgændən/ *n.* уганди́|ец (*fem.* -йка).
■ *adj.* уганди́йский.

ugly /ˈʌglɪ/ *adj.* (**uglier, ugliest**)
1 (*unsightly*) уро́дливый, безобра́зный; **~ duckling** га́дкий утёнок.
2 (*threatening*) опа́сный.

UK (*abbr. of* ***United Kingdom***) Соединённое Короле́вство (*Великобритании и Северной Ирландии*).
■ *adj.* (велико)брита́нский.

Ukraine /ju:ˈkreɪn/ *n.* Украи́на; **in (the) ~** в/на Украи́не.

Ukrainian /ju:ˈkreɪnɪən/ *n.* (*person*) украи́н|ец (*fem.* -ка); (*language*) украи́нский язы́к.
■ *adj.* украи́нский.

Ulan Bator /u:ˈlɑ:n ˈbɑ:tɔ:(r)/ *n.* Ула́н-Ба́тор.

ulcer /ˈʌlsə(r)/ *n.* я́зва.

ulcerate /ˈʌlsəreɪt/ *v.t.* изъязв|ля́ть, -и́ть.

Ulster /ˈʌlstə(r)/ *n.* О́льстер.

ulterior /ʌlˈtɪərɪə(r)/ *adj.* скры́тый, невы́раженный; **~ motive** скры́тый моти́в.

ultimate /ˈʌltɪmət/ *adj.* после́дний, оконча́тельный.

ultimately /ˈʌltɪmətlɪ/ *adv.* в конце́ концо́в.

ultimatum /ʌltɪˈmeɪtəm/ *n.* ультима́тум.

ultrasound /ˈʌltrəsaʊnd/ *n.* ультразву́к.

ultraviolet /ʌltrəˈvaɪələt/ *adj.* ультрафиоле́товый.

umbilical /ʌmˈbɪlɪk(ə)l/ *adj.*: **~ cord** пупови́на.

umbrage /ˈʌmbrɪdʒ/ *n.* оби́да; **take ~ (at)** об|ижа́ться, -и́деться (на + *a.*).

umbrella /ʌmˈbrelə/ *n.* зо́нтик, зонт.

umpire /ˈʌmpaɪə(r)/ *n.* (*arbitrator*) посре́дник; (*in games*) судья́ (*m.*).

umpteenth /ʌmpˈti:nθ/ *adj.* (*coll.*) э́нный; **I have told you for the ~ time** ско́лько раз я тебе́ говори́л!

UN (*abbr. of* ***United Nations (Organization)***): **the ~** ОО́Н (*f. indecl.*) (Организа́ция Объединённых На́ций).

un- /ʌn/ *neg. pref.*: *oft. expr. by pref.* не... (*e.g.* ▶**unable**) *or* без..., бес... (*e.g.* ▶**unashamed**).

unable /ʌn'eɪb(ə)l/ *adj.* неспосо́бный; **he is ~ to swim** он не уме́ет пла́вать; **I am ~ to say** я не могу́ сказа́ть.

unabridged /ʌnə'brɪdʒd/ *adj.* несокращённый, по́лный.

unacceptable /ʌnək'septəb(ə)l/ *adj.* неприе́млемый.

unaccompanied /ʌnə'kʌmpənɪd/ *adj.* нике́м не сопровожда́емый; (*mus.*) без аккомпанеме́нта.

unaccountable /ʌnə'kaʊntəb(ə)l/ *adj.* (*inexplicable*) необъясни́мый; (*irrational*) безотчётный; (*not obliged to render an account of o.s. or itself*): **~ to** не несу́щий отве́тственности пе́ред + *i.*

unaccounted for /ʌnə'kaʊntɪd/ *adj.* (*missing*): **two people were ~** не досчита́лись двух челове́к.

unaccustomed /ʌnə'kʌstəmd/ *adj.* непривы́кший; **~ as I am to public speaking** хотя́ я и не привы́к выступа́ть.

unacknowledged /ʌnək'nɒlɪdʒd/ *adj.* непризна́нный.

unadulterated /ʌnə'dʌltəreɪtɪd/ *adj.* настоя́щий, неподде́льный; **~ nonsense** чисте́йший/полне́йший вздор; **the ~ truth** чи́стая пра́вда.

unaffected /ʌnə'fektɪd/ *adj.* **1** (*without affectation*) непринуждённый. **2** (*not harmed or influenced*): **our plans were ~ by the weather** пого́да не измени́ла на́ших пла́нов.

unaided /ʌn'eɪdɪd/ *adj.* без посторо́нней по́мощи.

unalloyed /ʌnə'lɔɪd/ *adj.* нелеги́рованный, чи́стый (*о металле*); (*fig.*): **~ pleasure** ниче́м не омрачённая ра́дость.

unambiguous /ʌnæm'bɪgjʊəs/ *adj.* недвусмы́сленный.

unanimity /ju:nə'nɪmɪtɪ/ *n.* единоду́шие.

unanimous /ju:'nænɪməs/ *adj.* единоду́шный, единогла́сный; **the resolution was passed ~ly** резолю́ция была́ принята́ единогла́сно.

unannounced /ʌnə'naʊnst/ *adj.* (*to arrive, enter*) без докла́да.

unanswered /ʌn'ɑ:nsəd/ *adj.* оста́вшийся без отве́та.

unapologetic /ʌnəpɒlə'dʒetɪk/ *adj.* не прибега́ющий к оправда́ниям.

unappealing /ʌnə'pi:lɪŋ/ *adj.* неприя́тный.

unappreciative /ʌnə'pri:ʃ(ɪ)ətɪv/ *adj.* неблагода́рный.

unapproachable /ʌnə'prəʊtʃəb(ə)l/ *adj.* недосту́пный.

unarmed /ʌn'ɑ:md/ *adj.* невооружённый; **~ combat** самозащи́та без ору́жия.

unashamed /ʌnə'ʃeɪmd/ *adj.* бессты́дный.

unasked /ʌn'ɑ:skt/ *adj.* непро́шеный.

unassailable /ʌnə'seɪləb(ə)l/ *adj.*: **an ~ fortress** непристу́пная кре́пость; **an ~ argument** неопровержи́мый до́вод.

unassuming /ʌnə'sju:mɪŋ/ *adj.* непритяза́тельный.

unattached /ʌnə'tætʃt/ *adj.* не привя́занный/прикреплённый (**to:** к + *d.*); **she is ~** она́ одино́ка.

unattainable /ʌnə'teɪnəb(ə)l/ *adj.* недосяга́емый.

unattractive /ʌnə'træktɪv/ *adj.* непривлека́тельный.

unauthorized /ʌn'ɔ:θəraɪzd/ *adj.* неразрешённый; (*person*) посторо́нний.

unavailable /ʌnə'veɪləb(ə)l/ *adj.* недосту́пный; **he was ~** он был за́нят.

unavoidabl|e /ʌnə'vɔɪdəb(ə)l/ *adj.* (*sure to happen*) неизбе́жный; **I was ~y detained** я не мог освободи́ться (ра́ньше).

unaware /ʌnə'weə(r)/ *adj.* незна́ющий; **he was ~ of my presence** он не подозрева́л о моём прису́тствии; **I was ~ that he was married** я не знал, что он жена́т.

unawares /ʌnə'weəz/ *adv.* нечая́нно; **I was taken ~ by his question** его́ вопро́с засти́г меня́ враспло́х.

unbalanced /ʌn'bælənst/ *adj.* (*development*) неравноме́рный; (*report, views*) односторо́нний; (*mentally*) неуравнове́шенный, неусто́йчивый.

unbearable /ʌn'beərəb(ə)l/ *adj.* невыноси́мый.

unbeaten /ʌn'bi:t(ə)n/ *adj.* непревзойдённый.

unbeknown /ʌnbɪ'nəʊn/ (*coll.* **unbeknownst** /-'nəʊnst/) *adv.*: **he did it ~ to me** он сде́лал э́то без моего́ ве́дома.

unbelievable /ʌnbɪ'li:vəb(ə)l/ *adj.* (*coll., amazing*) невероя́тный.

unbias(s)ed /ʌn'baɪəst/ *adj.* беспристра́стный.

unblemished /ʌn'blemɪʃt/ *adj.* чи́стый; (*fig.*) незапя́тнанный.

unblock /ʌn'blɒk/ *v.t.*: **the plumber ~ed the drain** водопрово́дчик прочи́стил водосто́к.

unbolt /ʌn'bəʊlt/ *v.t.* (*door*) отп|ира́ть, -ере́ть.

unborn /ʌn'bɔ:n/ *adj.*: **her ~ child** её ещё не роди́вшийся ребёнок.

unbounded /ʌn'baʊndɪd/ *adj.* безме́рный.

unbridled /ʌn'braɪdəld/ *adj.* (*fig.*) необу́зданный.

unbroken /ʌn'brəʊkən/ *adj.*: **only one plate was ~** то́лько одна́ таре́лка уцеле́ла; **his spirit remained ~** его́ дух не́ был сло́млен; **an ~ record** непревзойдённый/непоби́тый реко́рд; **~ sleep** непреры́вный сон.

unburden /ʌn'bɜ:d(ə)n/ *v.t.*: **he ~ed his soul (*or* himself) to me** он изли́л мне ду́шу.

unbutton /ʌn'bʌt(ə)n/ *v.t.* расстёг|ивать, -ну́ть.

uncalled for /ʌn'kɔ:ldfɔ:(r)/ *adj.* неуме́стный.

uncanny /ʌn'kænɪ/ *adj.* (**uncannier, uncanniest**) стра́нный.

unceasing /ʌn'si:sɪŋ/ *adj.* беспреры́вный.

unceremonious /ʌnserɪ'məʊnɪəs/ *adj.* (*abrupt, discourteous*) бесцеремо́нный.

uncertain /ʌn'sɜ:t(ə)n/ *adj.* **1** (*hesitant, in doubt*) неуве́ренный; **he was ~ what to do** он не знал, что де́лать. **2** (*not clear*) нея́сный; **in no ~ terms** весьма́ недвусмы́сленно. **3** (*changeable, unreliable*): **the weather is ~**

погóда измéнчива; **my position is ~** (*shaky*) моё положéние неопределённо.

uncertainty /ʌn'sə:təntɪ/ *n.* [1] (*hesitation*) неувéренность. [2] (*unreliable nature*) измéнчивость.

unchanged /ʌn'tʃeɪndʒd/ *adj.* неизменúвшийся; **to remain ~** ост|авáться, -áться без изменéний.

uncharitable /ʌn'tʃærɪtəb(ə)l/ *adj.* жестóкий.

uncharted /ʌn'tʃɑ:tɪd/ *adj.* не отмéченный на кáрте; (*also fig.*) неисслéдованный, неизвéданный.

unchecked /ʌn'tʃekt/ *adj.*: **an ~ advance** (*mil.*) беспрепя́тственное продвижéние.

uncivilized /ʌn'sɪvɪlaɪzd/ *adj.* нецивилизóванный.

uncle /'ʌŋk(ə)l/ *n.* дя́дя (*m.*).

unclean /ʌn'kli:n/ *adj.* нечúстый.

uncomfortable /ʌn'kʌmftəb(ə)l/ *adj.* (*lit., fig.*) неудóбный; (*situation*) нелóвкий.

uncommon /ʌn'kɒmən/ *adj.* рéдкий.

uncommunicative /ʌnkə'mju:nɪkətɪv/ *adj.* неразговóрчивый.

uncomplimentary /ʌnkɒmplɪ'mentərɪ/ *adj.* нелéстный.

uncompromising /ʌn'kɒmprəmaɪzɪŋ/ *adj.* бескомпромúссный.

unconcealed /ʌnkən'si:ld/ *adj.* нескрывáемый.

unconcern /ʌnkən'sə:n/ *n.* беззабóтность, беспéчность; безразлúчие, равнодýшие.

unconcerned /ʌnkən'sə:nd/ *adj.* (*carefree*) беззабóтный; (*indifferent*) безразлúчный.

unconditional /ʌnkən'dɪʃən(ə)l/ *adj.* безуслóвный, безоговóрочный.

unconfirmed /ʌnkən'fə:md/ *adj.* неподтверждённый.

unconnected /ʌnkə'nektɪd/ *adj.* не свя́занный.

unconscious /ʌn'kɒnʃəs/ *n.*: **the ~** (*psych.*) подсознáние.
■ *adj.* [1] (*senseless*) потеря́вший сознáние; **he was ~** он был без сознáния/в óбмороке; **he was knocked ~** он потеря́л сознáние от удáра.
[2] (*unaware*) не сознаю́щий.
[3] (*unintentional*) невóльный.

unconsciousness /ʌn'kɒnʃəsnɪs/ *n.* (*physical*) бессознáтельное/óбморочное состоя́ние; (*unawareness*) отсýтствие (о)сознáния, неосóзнанность.

unconstitutional /ʌnkɒnstɪ'tju:ʃən(ə)l/ *adj.* неконституциóнный, противорéчащий конститýции.

uncontested /ʌnkən'testɪd/ *adj.* неоспорúмый.

uncontrollable /ʌnkən'trəʊləb(ə)l/ *adj.*: **an ~ temper** неукротúмый нрав; **an ~ child** неуправля́емый ребёнок.

unconventional /ʌnkən'venʃən(ə)l/ *adj.* нетрадициóнный; (*person, behaviour*) нешаблóнный.

unconvincing /ʌnkən'vɪnsɪŋ/ *adj.* неубедúтельный.

uncooked /ʌn'kʊkt/ *adj.* сырóй.

uncooperative /ʌnkəʊ'ɒpərətɪv/ *adj.* равнодýшный.

uncountable /ʌn'kaʊntəb(ə)l/ *adj.* (*gram.*) неисчисля́емый.

uncouth /ʌn'ku:θ/ *adj.* грýбый.

uncover /ʌn'kʌvə(r)/ *v.t.* (*take cover off*) сн|имáть, -ять покрóв с + *g.*; (*fig.*) раскр|ывáть, -ы́ть.

unctuous /'ʌŋktjʊəs/ *adj.* (*fig., oily*) елéйный (*liter.*), чрезмéрно угóдливый, слащáво-любéзный.

uncultivated /ʌn'kʌltɪveɪtɪd/ *adj.* (*of land*) необрабóтанный; (*of person*) некультýрный.

uncut /ʌn'kʌt/ *adj.* (*page, loop*) неразрéзанный; (*grass*) неподстрúженный; **the film was shown ~** фильм показáли в пóлной вéрсии.

undamaged /ʌn'dæmɪdʒd/ *adj.* неповреждённый.

undaunted /ʌn'dɔ:ntɪd/ *adj.* неустрашúмый.

undecided /ʌndɪ'saɪdɪd/ *adj.* (*not settled*) нерешённый; (*hesitating*) нерешúтельный.

undeniable /ʌndɪ'naɪəb(ə)l/ *adj.* неоспорúмый, я́вный.

under /'ʌndə(r)/ *adv.* вниз; **the ship went ~** корáбль затонýл.
■ *prep.* [1] под + *i.*; (*of motion*) под + *a.*; **(out) from ~** из-под + *g.*
[2] (*less than*) мéньше + *g.*; нúже + *g.*; **he earns ~ £400 a week** он зарабáтывает мéньше четырёхсóт фýнтов в недéлю; **children ~ 14** дéти молóже (*or* в вóзрасте до) четы́рнадцати лет.
[3] (*var. uses*): **you are ~ arrest** вы арестóваны; **~ the circumstances** при сложúвшихся обстоя́тельствах; **~ discussion** обсуждáемый; (*in progress*): **the investigation is ~ way** ведётся расслéдование.

underarm /'ʌndərɑ:m/ *adj.*: **an ~ deodorant** дезодорáнт для подмы́шек; **an ~ throw** бросóк снúзу; **serve ~** под|авáть, -áть снúзу.

undercarriage /'ʌndəkærɪdʒ/ *n.* (*of a plane*) шассú (*nt. indecl.*).

undercharge /ʌndə'tʃɑ:dʒ/ *v.t.* брать, взять с когó-н. недостáточно.

underclothes /'ʌndəkləʊðz/ *n.* нúжнее бельё.

undercoat /'ʌndəkəʊt/ *n.* (*of paint*) грунтóвка.

undercover /ʌndə'kʌvə(r)/ *adj.* тáйный.

undercurrent /'ʌndəkʌrənt/ *n.* подвóдное течéние; (*fig.*) скры́тая тендéнция.

undercut /ʌndə'kʌt/ *v.t.*: **he ~ his competitor** он назнáчил цéну нúже, чем егó конкурéнт.

underdeveloped /ʌndədɪ'veləpt/ *adj.* недорáзвитый; **~ countries** слаборáзвитые стрáны.

underdog /'ʌndədɒg/ *n.* (*sport*) побеждённая сторонá; (*downtrodden person*) неудáчник.

underdone /ʌndə'dʌn/ *adj.* (*of food*) недожáренный.

underestimate /ʌndər'estɪmeɪt/ *v.t.* недооцéн|ивать, -úть.

underfed /ʌndə'fed/ *adj.* недоедáющий; (*infant*) недокóрмленный.

underfoot /ʌndə'fʊt/ *adv.* под ногáми.

underfunded /ʌndəˈfʌndɪd/ *adj.*: **the project was ~** проéкт получи́л недостáточное финанси́рование.
undergo /ʌndəˈgəʊ/ *v.t.* испы́т|ывать, -áть; **he has to ~ an operation** емý предстои́т оперáция.
undergraduate /ʌndəˈgrædjʊət/ *n.* студéнт (*fem.* -ка).
underground /ˈʌndəgraʊnd/ *n.*
1 (*Br.*, *~ railway*) метрó (*indecl.*).
2 (*~ movement*) подпóлье.
■ *adj.* подзéмный; (*fig.*, *secret, subversive*) подпóльный.
■ *adv.* (*position*) под землёй; (*direction*) под зéмлю; (*fig.*) подпóльно.
undergrowth /ˈʌndəgrəʊθ/ *n.* подлéсок.
underhand /ˈʌndəhænd/ *adj.* (*secret, deceitful*) закули́сный, тáйный.
underlay /ˈʌndəleɪ/ *n.* (*fabric*) подклáдка, подсти́лка.
underl|ie /ʌndəˈlaɪ/ *v.t.* (*fig.*): **~ying causes** причи́ны, лежáщие в оснóве (*чего*).
underline /ʌndəˈlaɪn/ *v.t.* (*lit., fig.*) подч|ёркивать, -еркнýть.
underling /ˈʌndəlɪŋ/ *n.* мéлкий чинóвник.
undermine /ʌndəˈmaɪn/ *v.t.* подк|áпывать, -опáть; (*fig.*) разр|ушáть, -ýшить; **his authority is ~d** егó авторитéт подрывáют.
underneath /ʌndəˈniːθ/ *adv.* внизý, ни́же.
■ *prep.* под + *i.*; (*of motion*) под + *a.*
undernourished /ʌndəˈnʌrɪʃt/ *adj.* недоедáющий; (*infant*) недокóрмленный.
underpants /ˈʌndəpænts/ *n. pl.* (мужски́е) трус|ы́ (*pl.*, *g.* -óв).
underpass /ˈʌndəpɑːs/ *n.* проéзд под полотнóм желéзной дорóги.
underpay /ʌndəˈpeɪ/ *v.t.* (*worker*) недопл|áчивать, -ати́ть + *d.*
underpin /ʌndəˈpɪn/ *v.t.* подв|оди́ть, -ести́ фундáмент под + *a.*; (*fig.*) поддéрж|ивать, -áть.
underprivileged /ʌndəˈprɪvɪlɪdʒd/ *adj.* неимýщий.
underrate /ʌndəˈreɪt/ *v.t.* недооцéн|ивать, -и́ть.
underscore /ʌndəˈskɔː(r)/ *v.t.* подч|ёркивать, -еркнýть.
undersecretary /ʌndəˈsekrətərɪ/ *n.* замести́тель (*m.*)/помóщник мини́стра.
undersell /ʌndəˈsel/ *v.t.* (*another seller*) прод|авáть, -áть дешéвле (*кого*).
undershirt /ˈʌndəʃəːt/ *n.* (*US*) мáйка.
underside /ˈʌndəsaɪd/ *n.* низ; ни́жняя часть; (*fig., less favourable aspect*) непригля́дная сторонá.
understaffed /ʌndəˈstɑːft/ *adj.* неукомплектóванный.
understand /ʌndəˈstænd/ *v.t.*
1 (*comprehend*) пон|имáть, -я́ть; **he can make himself understood in English** он мóжет объясни́ться по-англи́йски; **he ~s children** он умéет обращáться с детьми́.
2 (*gather*): **I ~ you are leaving** я слы́шал, что вы уезжáете.
understandable /ʌndəˈstændəb(ə)l/ *adj.* поня́тный.
understanding /ʌndəˈstændɪŋ/ *n.*
1 (*intellect*) ум.
2 (*comprehension*) понимáние.
3 (*sympathy*) понимáние.
4 (*agreement*) соглашéние; **on the clear ~ that ...** тóлько при услóвии, что... .
■ *adj.* (*sympathetic*) отзы́вчивый, чýткий.
understatement /ˈʌndəsteɪtmənt/ *n.* преуменьшéние.
understudy /ˈʌndəstʌdɪ/ *n.* дублёр.
undertake /ʌndəˈteɪk/ *v.t.*
1 (*take on*) предприн|имáть, -я́ть.
2 (*promise*) обя́з|ываться, -áться.
undertaker /ˈʌndəteɪkə(r)/ *n.* завéдующий похорóнным бюрó.
undertaking /ˈʌndəteɪkɪŋ/ *n.* (*enterprise*) предприя́тие; (*pledge*) обязáтельство.
undertone /ˈʌndətəʊn/ *n.* полутóн; **in an ~** вполгóлоса; (*fig.*) оттéнок.
undervalue /ʌndəˈvæljuː/ *v.t.* недооцéн|ивать, -и́ть.
underwater /ʌndəˈwɔːtə(r)/ *adj.* подвóдный.
underwear /ˈʌndəweə(r)/ *n.* (ни́жнее) бельё.
underweight /ʌndəˈweɪt/ *adj.*: **she's ~** онá сли́шком худáя.
underworld /ˈʌndəwəːld/ *n.* (*criminal society*) престýпный мир.
underwriter /ˈʌndəraɪtə(r)/ *n.* (*insurer*) страхóвщик; (*guarantor*) гарáнт.
undeserved /ʌndɪˈzəːvd/ *adj.* незаслýженный.
undesirable /ʌndɪˈzaɪərəb(ə)l/ *adj.* нежелáтельный.
undetected /ʌndɪˈtektɪd/ *adj.* необнарýженный.
undeveloped /ʌndɪˈveləpt/ *adj.* неразвитóй; **an ~ country** слаборáзвитая странá; **~ land** необрабóтанная земля́.
undignified /ʌnˈdɪgnɪfaɪd/ *adj.* недостóйный.
undisciplined /ʌnˈdɪsɪplɪnd/ *adj.* недисциплини́рованный.
undiscovered /ʌndɪˈskʌvəd/ *adj.* неоткры́тый.
undiscriminating /ʌndɪˈskrɪmɪneɪtɪŋ/ *adj.* неразбóрчивый.
undisguised /ʌndɪsˈgaɪzd/ *adj.* незамаскирóванный.
undisputed /ʌndɪˈspjuːtɪd/ *adj.* неоспори́мый.
undisturbed /ʌndɪˈstəːbd/ *adj.* непотревóженный; **he seems to have been ~ by the news** кáжется, нóвость (ничýть) не встревóжила егó.
undivided /ʌndɪˈvaɪdɪd/ *adj.*: **~ attention** нераздéльное внимáние.
undo /ʌnˈduː/ *v.t.*
1 (*unfasten*) развя́з|ывать, -áть.
2 (*annul*) уничт|ожáть, -óжить; (*treaty, agreement*) аннули́ровать (*impf., pf.*).
undoubted /ʌnˈdaʊtɪd/ *adj.* несомнéнный; **you are ~ly right** вы, несомнéнно/безуслóвно, прáвы.
undress /ʌnˈdres/ *v.t. & i.* разд|евáть(ся), -éть(ся).
undrinkable /ʌnˈdrɪŋkəb(ə)l/ *adj.* непригóдный для питья́.
undue /ʌnˈdjuː/ *adj.* чрезмéрный.
undulat|e /ˈʌndjʊleɪt/ *v.i.* волновáться (*impf.*); колыхáться (*impf.*); **an ~ing landscape**

холми́стый пейза́ж.
undulating /ˈʌndjʊleɪtɪŋ/ *adj.* холми́стый.
unduly /ʌnˈdjuːlɪ/ *adv.* чрезме́рно.
undying /ʌnˈdaɪɪŋ/ *adj.* бессме́ртный.
unearned /ʌnˈɜːnd/ *adj.* незарабо́танный; **~ income** ре́нтный дохо́д, дохо́д от сбереже́ний, це́нных бума́г, недви́жимости.
unearth /ʌnˈɜːθ/ *v.t.* выка́пывать, вы́копать; **the body was ~ed** те́ло вы́копали; (*fig., discover*) раск|а́пывать, -опа́ть.
unearthly /ʌnˈɜːθlɪ/ *adj.*
1 (*supernatural*) неземно́й.
2 (*ghostly*) при́зрачный.
3 (*coll.*): **at this/that/some/an ~ hour** ни свет ни заря́; **don't call me again at that/this ~ hour!** не звони́ мне бо́льше в таку́ю рань!
unease /ʌnˈiːz/ *n.* нело́вкость, стеснённость; (*distress*) трево́га.
uneasiness /ʌnˈiːzɪnɪs/ *n.* нело́вкость (*смущение*).
uneasy /ʌnˈiːzɪ/ *adj.*
1 (*anxious*) беспоко́йный.
2 (*ill at ease*) стеснённый.
uneconomic /ʌniːkəˈnɒmɪk/ *adj.* неэконо́мный; нерента́бельный.
uneconomical /ʌniːkəˈnɒmɪk(ə)l/ *adj.* неэконо́мный.
uneducated /ʌnˈedjʊkeɪtɪd/ *adj.* необразо́ванный.
unemployable /ʌnɪmˈplɔɪəb(ə)l/ *adj.* нетрудоспосо́бный.
unemployed /ʌnɪmˈplɔɪd/ *adj.* безрабо́тный; (*as n.*: **the ~**) безрабо́тные (*pl.*).
unemployment /ʌnɪmˈplɔɪmənt/ *n.* безрабо́тица; **~ benefit** посо́бие по безрабо́тице.
unending /ʌnˈendɪŋ/ *adj.* бесконча́емый, бесконе́чный.
unenthusiastic /ʌnɪnθjuːzɪˈæstɪk/ *adj.* невосто́рженный.
unenviable /ʌnˈenvɪəb(ə)l/ *adj.* незави́дный.
unequal /ʌnˈiːkw(ə)l/ *adj.* нера́вный.
unequivocal /ʌnɪˈkwɪvək(ə)l/ *adj.* недвусмы́сленный; (*support*) определённый.
unerring /ʌnˈɜːrɪŋ/ *adj.* безоши́бочный.
UNESCO /juːˈneskəʊ/ *n.* (*abbr. of* ***United Nations Educational, Scientific, and Cultural Organization***) ЮНЕ́СКО (*f. indecl.*) (Организа́ция Объединённых На́ций по вопро́сам образова́ния, нау́ки и культу́ры).
unethical /ʌnˈeθɪk(ə)l/ *adj.* неэти́чный.
uneven /ʌnˈiːv(ə)n/ *adj.* неро́вный; неравноме́рный.
uneventful /ʌnɪˈventfʊl/ *adj.* ти́хий.
unexceptionable /ʌnɪkˈsepʃənəb(ə)l/ *adj.* безупре́чный.
unexceptional /ʌnɪkˈsepʃən(ə)l/ *adj.* неисключи́тельный, зауря́дный.
unexciting /ʌnɪkˈsaɪtɪŋ/ *adj.* ску́чный.
unexpected /ʌnɪkˈspektɪd/ *adj.* неожи́данный.
unfailing /ʌnˈfeɪlɪŋ/ *adj.* (*friend*) ве́рный; (*support*) неизме́нный.
unfair /ʌnˈfeə(r)/ *adj.* несправедли́вый; **~ advantage** незако́нное преиму́щество.
unfairness /ʌnˈfeənɪs/ *n.* несправедли́вость.
unfaithful /ʌnˈfeɪθfʊl/ *adj.* неве́рный; **his wife was ~ to him** жена́ ему́ измени́ла.
unfaithfulness /ʌnˈfeɪθfʊlnɪs/ *n.* неве́рность (**to:** + *d.*).
unfamiliar /ʌnfəˈmɪljə(r)/ *adj.* незнако́мый; **I am ~ with the district** я не зна́ю э́тот райо́н.
unfashionable /ʌnˈfæʃənəb(ə)l/ *adj.* немо́дный.
unfasten /ʌnˈfɑːs(ə)n/ *v.t.* откреп|ля́ть, -и́ть; (*untie*) отвя́з|ывать, -а́ть; (*unbutton, unclasp*) отстёг|ивать, -ну́ть; (*open*) откр|ыва́ть, -ы́ть.
unfavourable /ʌnˈfeɪvərəb(ə)l/ (*US* **unfavorable**) *adj.* неблагоприя́тный.
unfeeling /ʌnˈfiːlɪŋ/ *adj.* бесчу́вственный; жесто́кий.
unfinished /ʌnˈfɪnɪʃt/ *adj.* незако́нченный.
unfit /ʌnˈfɪt/ *adj.* неподходя́щий; **food ~ for (human) consumption** него́дная к употребле́нию пи́ща; **~ to rule** неспосо́бный пра́вить.
unflattering /ʌnˈflætərɪŋ/ *adj.* нele̍стный.
unfold /ʌnˈfəʊld/ *v.t.* развёр|тывать, -ну́ть; (*fig.*) раскр|ыва́ть, -ы́ть.
■ *v.i.* развёр|тываться, -ну́ться; **as the story ~s** по хо́ду повествова́ния.
unforeseeable /ʌnfɔːˈsiːəb(ə)l/ *adj.* непредви́денный.
unforeseen /ʌnfɔːˈsiːn/ *adj.* непредви́денный.
unforgettable /ʌnfəˈgetəb(ə)l/ *adj.* незабыва́емый.
unforgivable /ʌnfəˈgɪvəb(ə)l/ *adj.* непрости́тельный.
unforgiving /ʌnfəˈgɪvɪŋ/ *adj.* непроща́ющий.
unfortunate /ʌnˈfɔːtʃənət/ *adj.* (*person*) несча́стный; (*remark*) неуда́чный.
unfortunately /ʌnˈfɔːtʃənətlɪ/ *adv.* к сожале́нию; **~ for him** к несча́стью для него́.
unfounded /ʌnˈfaʊndɪd/ *adj.* необосно́ванный.
unfriendly /ʌnˈfrendlɪ/ *adj.* недружелю́бный.
unfulfilled /ʌnfʊlˈfɪld/ *adj.* неудовлетворённый.
unfurnished /ʌnˈfɜːnɪʃt/ *adj.* немеблиро́ванный, необста́вленный.
ungainly /ʌnˈgeɪnlɪ/ *adj.* нело́вкий, неуклю́жий.
ungodly /ʌnˈgɒdlɪ/ *adj.* (*coll.*) = **unearthly 3**
ungovernable /ʌnˈgʌvənəb(ə)l/ *adj.* неуправля́емый.
ungracious /ʌnˈgreɪʃəs/ *adj.* неве́жливый.
ungrammatical /ʌngrəˈmætɪk(ə)l/ *adj.* негра́мотный.
ungrateful /ʌnˈgreɪtfʊl/ *adj.* неблагода́рный.
unguarded /ʌnˈgɑːdɪd/ *adj.* (*e.g. town*) незащищённый; (*e.g. prisoner*) неохраня́емый; (*careless*) неосторо́жный.
unhappily /ʌnˈhæpɪlɪ/ *adv.*
1 (*without happiness*) несча́стливо.
2 (*unfortunately*) к несча́стью.
unhappiness /ʌnˈhæpɪnɪs/ *n.* несча́стье, грусть.
unhappy /ʌnˈhæpɪ/ *adj.* (*sorrowful*) несчастли́вый, несча́стный, гру́стный; (*unfortunate*) неуда́чный.

unharmed /ʌn'hɑ:md/ *adj.* невреди́мый; (*pred.*) цел и невреди́м.

unhealthy /ʌn'helθɪ/ *adj.*
1 (*in or indicating ill health*) нездоро́вый, боле́зненный.
2 (*coll., dangerous*) вре́дный.

unheard of /ʌn'hə:dɒv/ *adj.* никому́ не изве́стный.

unheeded /ʌn'hi:dɪd/ *adj.* незаме́ченный; **his advice went ~** к его́ сове́ту не прислу́шались.

unhelpful /ʌn'helpfʊl/ *adj.* бесполе́зный; (*person*) неотзы́вчивый.

unhinge /ʌn'hɪndʒ/ *v.t.* (*lit.*) сн|има́ть, -ять с пе́тель; (*fig.*) расстр|а́ивать, -о́ить; **the tragedy ~d his mind** от пе́режитой траге́дии он помеша́лся.

unhook /ʌn'hʊk/ *v.t.* расстёг|ивать, -ну́ть.

unhurried /ʌn'hʌrɪd/ *adj.* неторопли́вый.

unhurt /ʌn'hə:t/ *adj.* невреди́мый.

unhygienic /ʌnhaɪ'dʒi:nɪk/ *adj.* негигиени́чный.

unicorn /'ju:nɪkɔ:n/ *n.* единоро́г.

unidentified /ʌnaɪ'dentɪfaɪd/ *adj.* неопо́знанный.

unification /ju:nɪfɪ'keɪʃ(ə)n/ *n.* объедине́ние.

uniform /'ju:nɪfɔ:m/ *n.* фо́рма; (*esp. mil.*) мунди́р.
■ *adj.* однообра́зный; одина́ковый; станда́ртный.

uniformed /'ju:nɪfɔ:md/ *adj.* оде́тый в фо́рму; в мунди́ре.

uniformity /ju:nɪ'fɔ:mɪtɪ/ *n.* единообра́зие.

unify /'ju:nɪfaɪ/ *v.t.* объедин|я́ть, -и́ть.

unilateral /ju:nɪ'lætər(ə)l/ *adj.* односторо́нний.

unimaginable /ʌnɪ'mædʒɪnəb(ə)l/ *adj.* невообрази́мый.

unimaginative /ʌnɪ'mædʒɪnətɪv/ *adj.* прозаи́чный.

unimpeachable /ʌnɪm'pi:tʃəb(ə)l/ *adj.* безупре́чный, безукори́зненный.

unimpeded /ʌnɪm'pi:dɪd/ *adj.* беспрепя́тственный.

unimportant /ʌnɪm'pɔ:t(ə)nt/ *adj.* нева́жный, незначи́тельный.

unimpressed /ʌnɪm'prest/ *adj.*: **I was ~ by his threats** его́ угро́зы не произвели́ на меня́ никако́го впечатле́ния.

uninhabitable /ʌnɪn'hæbɪtəb(ə)l/ *adj.* неприго́дный для жилья́.

uninhabited /ʌnɪn'hæbɪtɪd/ *adj.* необита́емый.

uninhibited /ʌnɪn'hɪbɪtɪd/ *adj.* откры́тый, нестесни́тельный.

uninitiated /ʌnɪ'nɪʃɪeɪtɪd/ *adj.* непосвящённый.

uninjured /ʌn'ɪndʒəd/ *adj.* непострада́вший; **he was ~ by his fall** при паде́нии он не пострада́л.

unintelligible /ʌnɪn'telɪdʒɪb(ə)l/ *adj.* неразбо́рчивый.

unintended /ʌnɪn'tendɪd/ *adj.* ненаме́ренный; (*unforeseen*) непредусмо́тренный.

unintentional /ʌnɪn'tenʃən(ə)l/ *adj.* ненаме́ренный.

uninterested /ʌn'ɪntrestɪd/ *adj.* безразли́чный (**in:** к + *d.*).

uninteresting /ʌn'ɪntrestɪŋ/ *adj.* неинтере́сный.

uninvited /ʌnɪn'vaɪtɪd/ *adj.* незва́ный.

uninviting /ʌnɪn'vaɪtɪŋ/ *adj.* непривлека́тельный; **an ~ prospect** неприя́тная перспекти́ва.

union /'ju:njən/ *n.*
1 (*joining, uniting*) объедине́ние, сою́з.
2 (*association*) сою́з; **U~ Jack** госуда́рственный флаг Великобрита́нии; **students' ~** студе́нческий сою́з; (*building*) студе́нческий клуб.
3 **(trade ~)** профсою́з.

unique /ju:'ni:k/ *adj.* уника́льный, еди́нственный (в своём ро́де).

unisex /'ju:nɪseks/ *adj.*: **~ clothes** оде́жда, подходя́щая для обо́их поло́в; **~ hairdresser's** парикма́херская для мужчи́н и же́нщин.

unison /'ju:nɪs(ə)n/ *n.* (*fig.*) гармо́ния; **they acted in perfect ~** они́ де́йствовали в по́лном согла́сии.

unit /'ju:nɪt/ *n.*
1 (*single entity*) едини́ца; це́лое.
2 (*math., and of measurement*) едини́ца; **monetary ~** де́нежная едини́ца; **~ trust** (*Br.*) довери́тельный паево́й фонд.
3 (*mil.*) часть.
4 (*of furniture etc.*) се́кция.

unite /ju:'naɪt/ *v.t.* соедин|я́ть, -и́ть; **the U~d Nations** (*organization*) Организа́ция Объединённых На́ций; **the U~d Kingdom** Соединённое Короле́вство; **the U~d States** Соединённые Шта́ты.
■ *v.i.* соедин|я́ться, -и́ться; **~d front** еди́ный фронт.

unity /'ju:nɪtɪ/ *n.*
1 (*oneness; coherence*) еди́нство.
2 (*concord*) согла́сие.

universal /ju:nɪ'və:s(ə)l/ *adj.* всео́бщий, универса́льный.

universe /'ju:nɪvə:s/ *n.* вселе́нная.

university /ju:nɪ'və:sɪtɪ/ *n.* университе́т.

unjust /ʌn'dʒʌst/ *adj.* несправедли́вый.

unjustified /ʌn'dʒʌstɪfaɪd/ *adj.* неопра́вданный.

unkempt /ʌn'kempt/ *adj.* растрёпанный.

unkind /ʌn'kaɪnd/ *adj.* недо́брый, злой; (*unpleasant*) нелюбе́зный; **be ~ to s.o.** пло́хо обраща́ться (*impf.*) с кем-н.

unkindness /ʌn'kaɪndnɪs/ *n.* злость; нелюбе́зность.

unknown /ʌn'nəʊn/ *n.* неизве́стное.
■ *adj.* неизве́стный.

unlace /ʌn'leɪs/ *v.t.* расшнуро́в|ывать, -а́ть.

unlawful /ʌn'lɔ:fʊl/ *adj.* незако́нный.

unleaded /ʌn'ledɪd/ *adj.*: **~ petrol** неэтили́рованный бензи́н.

unleash /ʌn'li:ʃ/ *v.t.* спус|ка́ть, -ти́ть с при́вязи; (*fig.*) да|ва́ть, -ть во́лю + *d.*

unleavened /ʌn'lev(ə)nd/ *adj.* пре́сный (*хлеб*).

unless /ʌn'les/ *conj.* (*if not*) е́сли (то́лько) не; **I shall go ~ it rains** я пойду́, е́сли (то́лько) не бу́дет дождя́; (*until*) пока́ не; **I won't continue ~ he apologizes** я не бу́ду продолжа́ть, пока́ он не извини́тся; (*except if*) ра́зве (что/то́лько); **I don't know why he is late, ~ he has lost his way** не зна́ю, почему́ он опа́здывает — ра́зве что заблуди́лся.

unlike /ʌn'laɪk/ *adj.* & *prep.* (*different from*) непохо́жий, ра́зный; **he is ~ his sister** он не похо́ж на свою́ сестру́; **~ the others, he works hard** в отли́чие от други́х он рабо́тает усе́рдно.

unlikelihood /ʌn'laɪklɪhʊd/ *n.* неправдоподо́бие; маловероя́тность; невероя́тность.

unlikely /ʌn'laɪklɪ/ *adj.* (*tale*) неправдоподо́бный; (*not to be expected*): **it is ~ he will recover** маловероя́тно, что он попра́вится.

unlimited /ʌn'lɪmɪtɪd/ *adj.* неограни́ченный; (*expanse*) безграни́чный.

unlined /ʌn'laɪnd/ *adj.*
1: **~ paper** нелино́ванная бума́га.
2: **an ~ coat** пальто́ без подкла́дки.

unload /ʌn'ləʊd/ *v.t.* выгружа́ть, вы́грузить; разгру|жа́ть, -зи́ть; (*fig.*): **she ~ed her worries on to him** она́ облегчи́ла ду́шу, подели́вшись с ним свои́ми забо́тами.

unlock /ʌn'lɒk/ *v.t.* отп|ира́ть, -ере́ть (ключо́м).

unluckily /ʌn'lʌkɪlɪ/ *adv.* к несча́стью; **~ for him** к несча́стью для него́.

unlucky /ʌn'lʌkɪ/ *adj.* (*having bad luck*): **he is ~ at cards** ему́ не везёт в ка́ртах; (*causing bad luck*) несчастли́вый.

unmanageable /ʌn'mænɪdʒəb(ə)l/ *adj.* неуправля́емый.

unmarried /ʌn'mærɪd/ *adj.* (*man*) нежена́тый, холосто́й; (*woman*) незаму́жняя; **he is ~** он не жена́т; **she is ~** она́ не за́мужем.

unmask /ʌn'mɑːsk/ *v.t.* (*fig.*) разоблач|а́ть, -и́ть.

unmentionable /ʌn'menʃənəb(ə)l/ *adj.* неприли́чный, запре́тный.

unmistakable /ʌnmɪ'steɪkəb(ə)l/ *adj.* ве́рный, я́сный, очеви́дный.

unmitigated /ʌn'mɪtɪgeɪtɪd/ *adj.* по́лный.

unmoved /ʌn'muːvd/ *adj.* бесчу́вственный.

unnamed /ʌn'neɪmd/ *adj.* нена́званный; (*unidentified*) неизве́стный.

unnatural /ʌn'nætʃər(ə)l/ *adj.* неесте́ственный.

unnecessary /ʌn'nesəsərɪ/ *adj.* нену́жный; (*excessive*) изли́шний.

unnerve /ʌn'nɜːv/ *v.t.* обесси́ли|вать, -ть.

unnoticed /ʌn'nəʊtɪst/ *adj.* незаме́ченный.

unobservant /ʌnəb'zɜːv(ə)nt/ *adj.* ненаблюда́тельный.

unobstructed /ʌnəb'strʌktɪd/ *adj.* незагоро́женный.

unobtainable /ʌnəb'teɪnəb(ə)l/ *adj.* недосту́пный.

unobtrusive /ʌnəb'truːsɪv/ *adj.* скро́мный.

unoccupied /ʌn'ɒkjʊpaɪd/ *adj.* неза́нятый, свобо́дный; **an ~ house** пусто́й дом.

unofficial /ʌnə'fɪʃ(ə)l/ *adj.* неофициа́льный.

unorthodox /ʌn'ɔːθədɒks/ *adj.* неортодокса́льный, сме́лый.

unpack /ʌn'pæk/ *v.t.* & *i.* распако́в|ывать(ся), -а́ть(ся).

unpaid /ʌn'peɪd/ *adj.*
1 неопла́ченный; (*of debt, bill, etc.*) неупла́ченный.
2 (*of person, unsalaried*) не получа́ющий пла́ту/жа́лованье.

unpalatable /ʌn'pælətəb(ə)l/ *adj.* невку́сный; (*fig.*) неприя́тный; **an ~ truth** го́рькая пра́вда.

unparalleled /ʌn'pærəleld/ *adj.* несравни́мый.

unpatriotic /ʌnpætrɪ'ɒtɪk/ *adj.* (*behaviour*) непатриоти́ческий; (*person*) непатриоти́чный.

unperturbed /ʌnpə'tɜːbd/ *adj.* невозмути́мый.

unpick /ʌn'pɪk/ *v.t.* расп|а́рывать, -оро́ть (*шов*).

unplanned /ʌn'plænd/ *adj.* незаплани́рованный; (*unexpected*) неожи́данный.

unpleasant /ʌn'plez(ə)nt/ *adj.* неприя́тный.

unpleasantness /ʌn'plezəntnɪs/ *n.* неприя́тность.

unplug /ʌn'plʌg/ *v.t.* отключ|а́ть, -и́ть.

unpopular /ʌn'pɒpjʊlə(r)/ *adj.* непопуля́рный.

unpopularity /ʌnpɒpjʊ'lærɪtɪ/ *n.* непопуля́рность.

unprecedented /ʌn'presɪdentɪd/ *adj.* беспрецеде́нтный.

unpredictable /ʌnprɪ'dɪktəb(ə)l/ *adj.* непредсказу́емый.

unpremeditated /ʌnprɪ'medɪteɪtɪd/ *adj.* непреднаме́ренный.

unprepared /ʌnprɪ'peəd/ *adj.* неподгото́вленный; **his speech was ~** он произнёс свою́ речь экспро́мтом.

unprepossessing /ʌnpriːpə'zesɪŋ/ *adj.* нерасполага́ющий.

unpretentious /ʌnprɪ'tenʃəs/ *adj.* непретенцио́зный.

unprincipled /ʌn'prɪnsɪp(ə)ld/ *adj.* беспринци́пный.

unprintable /ʌn'prɪntəb(ə)l/ *adj.* нецензу́рный.

unproductive /ʌnprə'dʌktɪv/ *adj.* непродукти́вный.

unprofessional /ʌnprə'feʃən(ə)l/ *adj.* непрофессиона́льный; **~ conduct** наруше́ние профессиона́льной э́тики.

unprofitable /ʌn'prɒfɪtəb(ə)l/ *adj.* невы́годный.

unprompted /ʌn'prɒmptɪd/ *adj.* неподска́занный, спонта́нный.

unprotected /ʌnprə'tektɪd/ *adj.* незащищённый; **~ sex** незащищённый секс.

unprovoked /ʌnprə'vəʊkt/ *adj.* неспровоци́рованный.

unqualified /ʌn'kwɒlɪfaɪd/ *adj.*
1 (*without reservations*) безогово́рочный.
2 (*not competent*) некомпете́нтный; **I am ~ to judge this** я недоста́точно компете́нтен, что́бы суди́ть об э́том.

unquestionable /ʌn'kwestʃənəb(ə)l/ *adj.* (*undoubted*) несомне́нный; (*indisputable*) неоспори́мый.

unravel /ʌn'ræv(ə)l/ *v.t.* (**unravelled, unravelling;** *US* **unraveled, unraveling**) распу́т|ывать, -ать; (*fig.*) разга́д|ывать, -а́ть.

unreal /ʌn'rɪəl/ *adj.* (*imaginary*) нереа́льный; (*strange*) фантасти́ческий.

unrealistic /ʌnrɪə'lɪstɪk/ *adj.* нереа́льный.

unreasonable /ʌn'ri:zənəb(ə)l/ *adj.* не(благо)разу́мный; (*excessive*) чрезме́рный.

unrecognizable /ʌn'rekəgnaɪzəb(ə)l/ *adj.* неузнава́емый.

unrelated /ʌnrɪ'leɪtɪd/ *adj.* 1 (*not connected*) несвя́занный (**to:** с + *i.*). 2 (*not kin*): **he is ~ to me** он мне не ро́дственник.

unrelenting /ʌnrɪ'lentɪŋ/ *adj.* (*implacable*) неумоли́мый; (*ceaseless*) неослабева́ющий.

unreliable /ʌnrɪ'laɪəb(ə)l/ *adj.* (*person*) ненадёжный; (*information*) недостове́рный.

unremitting /ʌnrɪ'mɪtɪŋ/ *adj.* неосла́бный; (*incessant*) беспреста́нный.

unrequited /ʌnrɪ'kwaɪtɪd/ *adj.*: **~ love** неразделённая/безотве́тная любо́вь.

unreserved /ʌnrɪ'zə:vd/ *adj.* (*not set aside*) незаброни́рованый; (*open, frank*) открове́нный; (*wholehearted*) по́лный; **I agree with you ~ly** я по́лностью с ва́ми согла́сен.

unresolved /ʌnrɪ'zɒlvd/ *adj.* нереши́тельный.

unrest /ʌn'rest/ *n.* (*disquiet*) беспоко́йство; (*social, political*) волне́ния (*nt. pl.*).

unrestricted /ʌnrɪ'strɪktɪd/ *adj.* неограни́ченный.

unrewarding /ʌnrɪ'wɔ:dɪŋ/ *adj.* неблагода́рный.

unripe /ʌn'raɪp/ *adj.* неспе́лый, незре́лый (*also fig.*).

unrivalled /ʌn'raɪv(ə)ld/ (*US* **unrivaled**) *adj.* непревзойдённый.

unroll /ʌn'rəʊl/ *v.t.* & *i.* развёр|тывать(ся), -ну́ть(ся).

unruffled /ʌn'rʌf(ə)ld/ *adj.* (*fig.*) невозмути́мый.

unruly /ʌn'ru:lɪ/ *adj.* (**unrulier, unruliest**) непоко́рный.

unsafe /ʌn'seɪf/ *adj.* небезопа́сный.

unsaid /ʌn'sed/ *adj.*: **some things are better left ~** есть ве́щи, о кото́рых лу́чше умолча́ть.

unsatisfactory /ʌnsætɪs'fæktərɪ/ *adj.* неудовлетвори́тельный.

unsatisfied /ʌn'sætɪsfaɪd/ *adj.* неудовлетворённый.

unsavoury /ʌn'seɪvərɪ/ (*US* **unsavory**) *adj.* (*fig.*) сомни́тельный.

unscathed /ʌn'skeɪðd/ *adj.* цел и невреди́м.

unscheduled /ʌn'ʃedju:ld/ *adj.* незаплани́рованный; **an ~ flight** рейс вне расписа́ния.

unscrew /ʌn'skru:/ *v.t.* & *i.* отви́н|чивать(ся), -ти́ть(ся).

unscrupulous /ʌn'skru:pjʊləs/ *adj.* беспринци́пный.

unseasonable /ʌn'si:zənəb(ə)l/ *adj.* не по сезо́ну; **~ weather** пого́да не по сезо́ну; (*fig., untimely*) несвоевре́менный.

unseemly /ʌn'si:mlɪ/ *adj.* непристо́йный.

unseen /ʌn'si:n/ *adj.* неви́димый.

unselfish /ʌn'selfɪʃ/ *adj.* бескоры́стный.

unsettled /ʌn'set(ə)ld/ *adj.* неусто́йчивый.

unsettling /ʌn'setlɪŋ/ *adj.* трево́жный.

unshakeable /ʌn'ʃeɪkəb(ə)l/ *adj.* непоколеби́мый.

unshaken /ʌn'ʃeɪkən/ *adj.* (*resolute*) непоколеби́мый, непоколе́бленный.

unshaven /ʌn'ʃeɪv(ə)n/ *adj.* небри́тый.

unsightly /ʌn'saɪtlɪ/ *adj.* некраси́вый, непригля́дный.

unskilled /ʌn'skɪld/ *adj.* неквалифици́рованный; **~ labourer** (*Br.*), **laborer** (*US*) разнорабо́чий.

unsociable /ʌn'səʊʃəb(ə)l/ *adj.* необщи́тельный.

unsocial /ʌn'səʊʃ(ə)l/ *adj.* антиобще́ственный; **to work ~ hours** рабо́тать во вре́мя, отлича́ющееся от общепри́нятого.

unsolicited /ʌnsə'lɪsɪtɪd/ *adj.* (*not asked for*) непро́шеный; (*given, done voluntarily*) доброво́льный.

unsophisticated /ʌnsə'fɪstɪkeɪtɪd/ *adj.* (*person, approach*) просто́й, простоду́шный; (*thing, work*) безыску́сный.

unsound /ʌn'saʊnd/ *adj.* (*bad, rotten*) испо́рченный, гнило́й; (*unwholesome*) нездоро́вый; (*unstable*) непро́чный; **~ views** необосно́ванные взгля́ды; **of ~ mind** душевнобольно́й; **a man of ~ judgement** челове́к, лишённый здра́вого смы́сла.

unsparing /ʌn'speərɪŋ/ *adj.* (*merciless*) беспоща́дный, безжа́лостный; (*generous*) ще́дрый; (*diligent*) усе́рдный; **~ in his efforts** не щадя́щий сил.

unspeakable /ʌn'spi:kəb(ə)l/ *adj.* невырази́мый.

unspoil|ed /ʌn'spɔɪld/, **-t** /ʌn'spɔɪlt/ *adj.* неиспо́рченный; (*of person*) неизбало́ванный.

unspoken /ʌn'spəʊkən/ *adj.* невы́сказанный.

unstable /ʌn'steɪb(ə)l/ *adj.* неусто́йчивый, нестаби́льный.

unsteady /ʌn'stedɪ/ *adj.* нетвёрдый; **he was ~ on his legs** он нетвёрдо держа́лся на нога́х.

unstinting /ʌn'stɪntɪŋ/ *adj.* (*generous*) ще́дрый.

unstuck /ʌn'stʌk/ *adj.*: **the stamp came ~** ма́рка откле́илась; (*fig., coll.*): **my schemes came ~** мои́ пла́ны ру́хнули.

unsubstantiated /ʌnsəb'stænʃɪeɪtɪd/ *adj.* недока́занный.

unsuccessful /ʌnsək'sesfʊl/ *adj.* безуспе́шный, неуда́чный; **he was ~ in the exam** он не сдал экза́мен.

unsuitable /ʌn'sju:təb(ə)l/ *adj.* неподходя́щий.

unsung /ʌn'sʌŋ/ *adj.* (*not celebrated*) невоспе́тый; **an ~ hero** невоспе́тый геро́й.

unsure /ʌn'ʃɔ:(r)/ *adj.* (*not confident*) неуве́ренный; **he was ~ of his ground** он не чу́вствовал себя́ доста́точно компете́нтным; **~ of o.s.** не уве́ренный в себе́.

unsuspecting /ʌnsə'spektɪŋ/ *adj.* неподозрева́ющий.

unsweetened /ʌn'swi:t(ə)nd/ *adj.* неподслащённый.

unswerving /ʌn'swə:vɪŋ/ *adj.* (*fig.*) непоколеби́мый.

unsympathetic /ʌnsɪmpə'θetɪk/ *adj.* чёрствый, несочу́вствующий.

untangle /ʌn'tæŋg(ə)l/ *v.t.* распу́т|ывать, -ать.

untaxed /ʌn'tækst/ *adj.* не облага́емый нало́гом.

untenable /ʌn'tenəb(ə)l/ *adj.*: **~ arguments** неубеди́тельные до́воды; **an ~ position** (*mil.*) пози́ция, неприго́дная для оборо́ны; невы́годная пози́ция.

unthinkable /ʌn'θɪŋkəb(ə)l/ *adj.* немы́слимый.

unthinking /ʌn'θɪŋkɪŋ/ *adj.* (*thoughtless*) безду́мный; (*inadvertent*) нечá́янный; машина́льный.

untidiness /ʌn'taɪdɪnɪs/ *n.* неопря́тность, неаккура́тность.

untidy /ʌn'taɪdɪ/ *adj.* неопря́тный, неаккура́тный.

untie /ʌn'taɪ/ *v.t.* развя́з|ывать, -а́ть; отвя́з|ывать, -а́ть; расшнуро́в|ывать, -а́ть.

until /ən'tɪl/ = **till²**; **unless and ~** то́лько когда́/е́сли.

untimely /ʌn'taɪmlɪ/ *adj.* (*premature*) преждевре́менный; (*ill-timed*) неуме́стный.

untiring /ʌn'taɪərɪŋ/ *adj.* (*person*) неутоми́мый; (*work, efforts*) неуста́нный.

unto /'ʌntʊ/ (*arch.*) = **to**

untold /ʌn'təʊld/ *adj.*
1 (*suffering, delight*) невырази́мый.
2 (*damage*) неисчисли́мый; **~ wealth** несме́тные бога́тства.

untouchable /ʌn'tʌtʃəb(ə)l/ *n.* (*member of lowest-caste Hindu group*) неприкаса́емый.
■ *adj.* (*unattainable*) недосяга́емый, недосту́пный; (*impossible to compete with*) недосяга́емый.

untoward /ʌntə'wɔ:d/ *adj.*: **nothing ~ happened** ничего́ плохо́го не случи́лось.

untrained /ʌn'treɪnd/ *adj.* необу́ченный.

untranslatable /ʌntrænz'leɪtəb(ə)l/ *adj.* непереводи́мый.

untroubled /ʌn'trʌb(ə)ld/ *adj.* невозмути́мый.

untrue /ʌn'tru:/ *adj.* (*inaccurate*) неве́рный, ло́жный; (*unfaithful*) неве́рный.

untrustworthy /ʌn'trʌstwə:ðɪ/ *adj.* ненадёжный.

untruth /ʌn'tru:θ/ *n.* непра́вда.

untruthful /ʌn'tru:θfʊl/ *adj.* (*of thing*) неве́рный, ло́жный; (*of person or thing*) лжи́вый.

unused¹ /ʌn'ju:zd/ *adj.* (*not put to use*) неиспо́льзованный; **my ticket was ~** я не испо́льзовал свой биле́т.

unused² /ʌn'ju:st/ *adj.* (*unaccustomed*) непривы́кший (к + *d.*); **I am ~ to this** я к э́тому не привы́к.

unusual /ʌn'ju:ʒʊəl/ *adj.* необыкнове́нный, необы́чный; **~ly** осо́бенно, исключи́тельно.

unutterable /ʌn'ʌtərəb(ə)l/ *adj.* невырази́мый, несказа́нный.

unvarnished /ʌn'vɑ:nɪʃt/ *adj.* (*fig.*): **the ~ truth** неприкра́шенная/го́лая пра́вда.

unveil /ʌn'veɪl/ *v.t.* (*statue*) откр|ыва́ть, -ы́ть; (*plans*) изл|ага́ть, -ожи́ть.

unwanted /ʌn'wɒntɪd/ *adj.* нежела́нный; **they made me feel ~** они́ да́ли мне поня́ть, что я ли́шний среди́ них.

unwarranted /ʌn'wɒrəntɪd/ *adj.* необосно́ванный.

unwary /ʌn'weərɪ/ *adj.* неосторо́жный.

unwavering /ʌn'weɪvərɪŋ/ *adj.* непоколеби́мый.

unwelcome /ʌn'welkəm/ *adj.* неприя́тный.

unwell /ʌn'wel/ *adj.* нездоро́вый; **I felt ~** мне нездоро́вилось; **I have been ~** я был нездоро́в.

unwieldy /ʌn'wi:ldɪ/ *adj.* (**unwieldier, unwieldiest**) громо́здкий.

unwilling /ʌn'wɪlɪŋ/ *adj.* нежела́ющий; **he was ~ to agree** он не пожела́л согласи́ться.

unwillingness /ʌn'wɪlɪŋnɪs/ *n.* нежела́ние.

unwind /ʌn'waɪnd/ *v.t.* & *i.* разм|а́тывать(ся), -ота́ть(ся); (*fig.*): **the wine helped him to ~** вино́ помогло́ ему́ рассла́биться.

unwise /ʌn'waɪz/ *adj.* не(благо)разу́мный.

unwitting /ʌn'wɪtɪŋ/ *adj.* нечá́янный.

unworthy /ʌn'wə:ðɪ/ *adj.* недосто́йный (*кого/чего*).

unwrap /ʌn'ræp/ *v.t.* разв|ора́чивать (*or* разв|ёртывать), -ерну́ть.

unwritten /ʌn'rɪt(ə)n/ *adj.*: **an ~ law** непи́саный зако́н.

unzip /ʌn'zɪp/ *v.t.* (*coat*) расстёг|ивать, -ну́ть; (*bag*) раскр|ыва́ть, -ы́ть.

up /ʌp/ *n.*: **~s and downs** (*of fortune*) взлёты (*m. pl.*) и паде́ния (*nt. pl.*).
■ *adv.* 1 (*in a higher position*) вверху́, наверху́; **high ~ in the sky** высоко́ в не́бе; **'this side ~'** «верх!»; **the notice was ~ on the board** на доске́ висе́ло объявле́ние; **prices are ~** це́ны подняли́сь; (*advanced*): **he is 20 points ~ on his opponent** он на два́дцать очко́в впереди́ проти́вника; **he is well ~ in his subject** он прекра́сно зна́ет свой предме́т; (*with greater intensity*): **sing ~!/speak ~!** (по́йте)/(говори́те) гро́мче!
2 (*into a higher position*) вверх, наве́рх; **she carried the suitcases ~** она́ отнесла́ чемода́ны наве́рх; (**~wards**) вы́ше, бо́льше; **children from the age of twelve ~** де́ти от двена́дцати (лет) и ста́рше.
3 (*out of bed; standing; active*): **he was already ~ when I called** когда́ я пришёл, он уже́ встал; **she was soon ~ and about again** она́ вско́ре опра́вилась; **I was ~ late last night** я вчера́ о́чень по́здно лёг.
4 (*expr. completion or expiry*): **time's ~** вре́мя истекло́; **the game is ~!** ка́рта би́та!
5 (*coll., happening; amiss*): **what's ~?** в чём де́ло?; что тут происхо́дит?; **there's something ~ with the radio** (ра́дио)приёмник барахли́т.
6 **~ against** (*in contact with*): **the table was (right) ~ against the wall** стол стоя́л (пря́мо) у стены́ (*or* вплотну́ю к стене́); (*confronted by*): **you are ~ against stiff opposition** вы име́ете де́ло с упо́рным сопротивле́нием.
7 **~ to** (*equal to*): **I don't feel ~ to it** я не

чу́вствую себя́ в си́лах сде́лать э́то; (*as far as*) до + *g.*; **~ to, ~ till now** до сих пор; **I am ~ to chapter 3** я дочита́л до тре́тьей главы́; (*incumbent upon*): **it is ~ to us to help** э́то мы должны́ помо́чь; **it's ~ to you now** тепе́рь э́то/всё зави́сит от вас; (*occupied with*): **what is he ~ to?** чем он занима́ется?; **he is ~ to no good** он замы́слил что́-то недо́брое.
■ *prep.*: **they live ~ the hill** они́ живу́т на горе́/холме́; **he ran ~ the hill** он взбежа́л на́ гору, на холм; **the cat was ~ a tree** кот взобра́лся на де́рево; **he went ~ the stairs** он подня́лся по ле́стнице; **they live ~** (*further along*) **the street** они́ живу́т по/на э́той у́лице.

up-and-coming /ʌpən'kʌmɪŋ/ *adj.* многообеща́ющий.

upbeat /'ʌpbi:t/ *adj.* оптимисти́чный, бо́дрый.

upbringing /'ʌpbrɪŋɪŋ/ *n.* воспита́ние.

update /ʌp'deɪt/ *v.t.* (*one's wardrobe*) обнов|ля́ть, -и́ть; (*equipment*) модернизи́ровать (*impf.*, *pf.*); (*records*) испр|авля́ть, -а́вить.

upgrade /'ʌpgreɪd/ *v.t.* (*raise in rank*) пов|ыша́ть, -ы́сить в до́лжности; (*modernize*) модернизи́ровать (*impf.*, *pf.*).

upheaval /ʌp'hi:v(ə)l/ *n.* (*political*) потрясе́ния (*nt. pl.*); (*emotional*) потрясе́ние.

uphill /'ʌphɪl/ *adj.* иду́щий в го́ру; **an ~ task** тяжёлая зада́ча.
■ *adv.* в го́ру.

uphold /ʌp'həʊld/ *v.t.* (*support, lit., fig.*) подде́рж|ивать, -а́ть.

upholster /ʌp'həʊlstə(r)/ *v.t.* об|ива́ть, -и́ть; **an ~ed chair** кре́сло с мя́гкой оби́вкой.

upholsterer /ʌp'həʊlstərə(r)/ *n.* обо́йщик.

upholstery /ʌp'həʊlstərɪ/ *n.* оби́вка.

upkeep /'ʌpki:p/ *n.* содержа́ние.

uplift[1] /'ʌplɪft/ *n.* подъём; (*spiritual*) духо́вный подъём.

uplift[2] /ʌp'lɪft/ *v.t.* подн|има́ть, -я́ть.

upload /ʌp'ləʊd/ *v.t.* (*comput.*) загру|жа́ть, -зи́ть на друго́й (*удалённый*) компью́тер.

upmarket /ʌp'mɑ:kɪt/ *adj.* элита́рный, дорого́й.

upon /ə'pɒn/ *prep. see* ▶ **on**; **the holidays are ~ us** приближа́ются кани́кулы.

upper /'ʌpə(r)/ *adj.* ве́рхний; вы́сший; **he got the ~ hand** он одержа́л верх; **U~ House** (*in UK*) пала́та ло́рдов; (*in USA*) сена́т.
■ *cpds.* **~ class** *adj.* относя́щийся к вы́сшему о́бществу; **~most** *adj.* са́мый ве́рхний, вы́сший; **it was ~most in my mind** э́то бо́льше всего́ занима́ло мои́ мы́сли.

upright /'ʌpraɪt/ *adj.* (*erect*) вертика́льный; (*honourable*) че́стный.
■ *adv.*: **stand ~** стоя́ть (*impf.*) пря́мо.

uprising /'ʌpraɪzɪŋ/ *n.* (*rebellion*) восста́ние.

uproar /'ʌprɔ:(r)/ *n.* (*noise*) шум; (*confusion*) возмуще́ние.

uproarious /ʌp'rɔ:rɪəs/ *adj.* (*noisy*) шу́мный, бу́рный, бу́йный; (*funny*) ужа́сно/невозмо́жно смешно́й.

uproot /ʌp'ru:t/ *v.t.* вырыва́ть, вы́рвать с ко́рнем; (*fig., displace*) выселя́ть, вы́селить.

upset[1] /'ʌpset/ *n.*
[1] (*physical*) недомога́ние; **stomach ~** расстро́йство желу́дка.
[2] (*emotional shock*) огорче́ние.

upset[2] /ʌp'set/ *v.t.* (*knock over*) опроки́|дывать, -нуть; (*make unhappy*) расстр|а́ивать, -о́ить; (*food*): **rich food ~s my stomach** от жи́рной пи́щи у меня́ расстра́ивается желу́док.

upshot /'ʌpʃɒt/ *n.* развя́зка.

upside down /ʌpsaɪd 'daʊn/ *adv.* вверх дном, вверх нога́ми.

upstage /ʌp'steɪdʒ/ *v.t.* (*coll.*) затм|ева́ть, -и́ть.

upstairs /ʌp'steəz/ *adv.* (*position*) наверху́; (*direction*) наве́рх; **he ran ~** он побежа́л наве́рх; (*attr.*): **the ~ rooms** ве́рхние ко́мнаты.

upstanding /ʌp'stændɪŋ/ *adj.*
[1] (*honest*) че́стный, прямо́й.
[2] (*standing up*) стоя́щий; **be ~!** вста́ньте!

upstart /'ʌpstɑ:t/ *n.* вы́скочка (*c.g.*).

upstream /'ʌpstri:m/ *adv.* про́тив тече́ния; **~ of** вы́ше + *g.*

upsurge /'ʌpsə:dʒ/ *n.* (*of unrest, in production*) подъём; (*of feelings*) наплы́в.

uptake /'ʌpteɪk/ *n.*: **quick on the ~** (*coll.*) сообрази́тельный, бы́стро сообража́ющий.

uptight /ʌp'taɪt/ *adj.* (*coll., tense, angry*) напряжённый, нерво́зный.

up-to-date /ʌptə'deɪt/ *adj.* совреме́нный, нове́йший, (са́мый) после́дний.

upturn /'ʌptə:n/ *n.* (*fig.*) сдвиг (к лу́чшему); улучше́ние.

upward /'ʌpwəd/ *adj.* напра́вленный вверх; **an ~ trend in prices** тенде́нция к повыше́нию цен.
■ *adv.* (*also* **~s**) вверх.

Urals /'jʊər(ə)lz/ *n.* (*mountains*) Ура́льские го́ры (*f. pl.*), Ура́л.

uranium /jʊ'reɪnɪəm/ *n.* ура́н; (*attr.*) ура́новый.

Uranus /'jʊərənəs/ *n.* Ура́н.

urban /'ə:bən/ *adj.* городско́й.

urbane /ə:'beɪn/ *adj.* све́тский, учти́вый.

urchin /'ə:tʃɪn/ *n.* беспризо́рни|к (*fem.* -ца).

Urdu /'ʊədu:/ *n.* (язы́к) урду́ (*m. indecl.*).

urge /ə:dʒ/ *n.* побужде́ние, стремле́ние.
■ *v.t.* [1] (*impel*; *also* **~ on, ~ forward**) гнать (*impf.*); под|гоня́ть, -огна́ть.
[2] (*exhort*) угова́ривать (*impf.*).

urgency /'ə:dʒ(ə)nsɪ/ *n.* сро́чность, неотло́жность; **as a matter of ~** в сро́чном поря́дке.

urgent /'ə:dʒ(ə)nt/ *adj.* сро́чный, неотло́жный; **he is in ~ need of money** он кра́йне нужда́ется в деньга́х.

urinal /jʊə'raɪn(ə)l/ *n.* писсуа́р.

urinary /'jʊərɪnərɪ/ *adj.* мочево́й.

urinate /'jʊərɪneɪt/ *v.i.* мочи́ться, по-.

urine /'jʊərɪn/ *n.* моча́.

URL (*abbr. of* ***uniform/universal resource locator***) (*comput.*) URL-а́дрес.

urn /ə:n/ *n.* (*vase for ashes etc.*) у́рна, ва́за.

Uruguay /'jʊərəgwaɪ/ *n.* Уругва́й.

Uruguayan /jʊərə'gwaɪən/ *n.* уругва́|ец (*fem.* -йка).
■ *adj.* уругва́йский.

U

us /ʌs/ *obj. of* ▸ **we**

US(A) (*abbr. of* ***United States of America***) США (*pl., indecl.*) (Соединённые Шта́ты Аме́рики).
■ *adj.* америка́нский.

usable /ˈju:zəb(ə)l/ *adj.* примени́мый, (при)го́дный.

usage /ˈju:sɪdʒ/ *n.*
1 (*utilization*) употребле́ние, испо́льзование; по́льзование (**of:** + *i.*).
2 (*habitual process*) у́зус, пра́ктика, обыкнове́ние; **in accordance with general ~** согла́сно общепри́нятой пра́ктике; **a guide to English ~** уче́бник англи́йского словоупотребле́ния.

use¹ /ju:s/ *n.*
1 (*utilization*) употребле́ние, испо́льзование; по́льзование (**of:** + *i.*); **make good ~ of your time!** испо́льзуйте ва́ше вре́мя как сле́дует!; **he put his talents to good ~** он пра́вильно испо́льзовал свои́ спосо́бности.
2 (*purpose*) назначе́ние; примене́ние.
3 (*value*) по́льза, толк; **this machine is no longer (of) any ~** э́та маши́на бо́льше не годи́тся; **will this be of ~ to you?** вам э́то пригоди́тся?; **it's no ~ grumbling** что то́лку ворча́ть?
4 (*power of using*): **he lost the ~ of his legs** он утра́тил спосо́бность ходи́ть.
5 (*right to use*): **I gave him the ~ of my car** я разреши́л ему́ по́льзоваться мое́й маши́ной.

use² /ju:z/ *v.t.*
1 (*employ*) употреб|ля́ть, -и́ть; по́льзоваться, вос- + *i.*; испо́льзовать (*impf., pf.*); **a ~d car** подёржанная маши́на.
2 (**~ up:** *consume*) расхо́довать, из-; тра́тить, по-; испо́льзовать (*impf., pf.*); **this car ~s a lot of fuel** э́та маши́на расхо́дует мно́го бензи́на.
3 (*treat*) обраща́ться (*impf.*) с + *i.*; об|ходи́ться, -ойти́сь с + *i.*
4 (*exploit*): **I feel as if I have been ~d** я чу́вствую, что меня́ испо́льзовали в чьи́х-то це́лях.

use³ /ju:z/ *v.t.* & *i.*
1 (*accustom*): **get ~d to** прив|ыка́ть, -ы́кнуть к + *d.*; **he is ~d to it** он к э́тому привы́к; **he is ~d to dining late** он привы́к обе́дать по́здно.
2 (*be accustomed*): **he ~d to be a teacher** он ра́ньше был учи́телем; **I ~d not to like him** пре́жде он мне не нра́вился.

useful /ˈju:sfʊl/ *adj.* поле́зный.

useless /ˈju:slɪs/ *adj.* (*worthless*) неприго́дный; (*futile*) бесполе́зный; (*coll., incompetent*): **he is ~ at tennis** он никуды́шный тенниси́ст.

user /ˈju:zə(r)/ *n.* (*one who uses*) употребля́ющий; потреби́тель (*m.*); (*comput.*) по́льзователь (*m.*).
■ *cpd.* **~-friendly** *adj.* удо́бный в употребле́нии; (*comput.*) дру́жественный.

usher /ˈʌʃə(r)/ *v.t.* (*also* **~ in**) вв|оди́ть, -ести́.

usherette /ʌʃəˈret/ *n.* билетёрша (*coll.*).

USSR (*abbr. of* ***Union of Soviet Socialist Republics***) (*hist.*) СССР (*m. indecl.*) (Сою́з Сове́тских Социалисти́ческих Респу́блик).

usual /ˈju:ʒʊəl/ *adj.* обы́чный, обыкнове́нный; **it is ~ to remove one's hat** шля́пу при́нято снима́ть; **he is late as ~** он, как всегда́, опа́здывает; **the bus was fuller than ~** авто́бус был перепо́лнен бо́льше обы́чного.

usually /ˈju:ʒʊəlɪ/ *adv.* обы́чно.

usurp /jʊˈzə:p/ *v.t.* узурпи́ровать (*impf., pf.*).

usury /ˈju:ʒərɪ/ *n.* ростовщи́чество.

utensil /ju:ˈtens(ə)l/ *n.* инструме́нт; (*pl., collect.*) у́тварь.

uterus /ˈju:tərəs/ *n.* (*anat.*) ма́тка.

utilitarian /jʊtɪlɪˈteərɪən/ *n.* утилитари́ст (*fem.* -ка).
■ *adj.* утилита́рный.

utilit|y /ju:ˈtɪlɪtɪ/ *n.*
1 (*usefulness*) поле́зность, практи́чность, вы́годность.
2: **public ~ies** коммуна́льные услу́ги (*f. pl.*).
■ *cpd.* **~y room** *n.* кладова́я.

utilization /ju:tɪlaɪˈzeɪʃ(ə)n/ *n.* испо́льзование; утилиза́ция.

utilize /ˈju:tɪlaɪz/ *v.t.* испо́льзовать (*impf., pf.*).

utmost /ˈʌtməʊst/ *n.*: **he did his ~ to avoid defeat** он сде́лал всё возмо́жное, что́бы избежа́ть пораже́ния.
■ *adjs.* кра́йний.

Utopia /ju:ˈtəʊpɪə/ *n.* уто́пия.

Utopian /ju:ˈtəʊpɪən/ *adj.* утопи́ческий.

utter¹ /ˈʌtə(r)/ *adj.* по́лный, абсолю́тный, соверше́нный.

utter² /ˈʌtə(r)/ *v.t.* (*sound, cry*) изд|ава́ть, -а́ть; (*words*) произн|оси́ть, -ести́.

utterance /ˈʌtərəns/ *n.*
1 (*diction, speech*) произноше́ние, ди́кция; **defective ~** дефе́кт ре́чи.
2 (*expression*) выраже́ние; **he gave ~ to his anger** он вы́разил свой гнев.
3 (*pronouncement*) выска́зывание.

utterly /ˈʌtəlɪ/ *adv.* соверше́нно.

U-turn /ˈju:tə:n/ *n.* разворо́т; (*fig.*) ре́зкое измене́ние поли́тики.

UV (*abbr. of* ***ultraviolet***) ультрафиоле́товый.

Uzbek /ˈʊzbek/ *n.* (*person*) узбе́|к (*fem.* -чка); (*language*) узбе́кский язы́к.
■ *adj.* узбе́кский.

Uzbekistan /ʊzbekɪˈstɑ:n/ *n.* Узбекиста́н.

Vv

v. (*abbr. of* ***versus***) прóтив + *g.*

vacanc|y /ˈveɪkənsɪ/ *n.* (*job*) вакáнсия; (*place on course etc.*) мéсто; (*room*): **no ~ies** свобóдных кóмнат нет, «мест нет».

vacant /ˈveɪkənt/ *adj.*
1 (*unoccupied*) свобóдный; **a ~ post** вакáнтная дóлжность, вакáнсия.
2 (*of mind, expression etc.*) отсýтствующий.

vacate /veɪˈkeɪt/ *v.t.* освобо|ждáть, -дúть; **he will ~ the post in May** он уйдёт с дóлжности в мáе.

vacation /vəˈkeɪʃ(ə)n/ *n.*
1 (*at university*) канúкул|ы (*pl., g.* —); **long ~** лéтние канúкулы.
2 (*holiday*) óтпуск, óтдых; **on ~** в óтпуске.

vaccinate /ˈvæksɪneɪt/ *v.t.* дéлать, с- привúвку + *d.*; (**against:** от + *g.*).

vaccination /væksɪˈneɪʃ(ə)n/ *n.* привúвка.

vaccine /ˈvæksiːn/ *n.* вакцúна.

vacillate /ˈvæsɪleɪt/ *v.i.* колебáться (*impf.*).

vacuous /ˈvækjʊəs/ *adj.* пустóй.

vacuum /ˈvækjʊəm/ *n.*
1 (*empty place*) вáкуум; **~ flask** (*Br.*) тéрмос.
2 (*coll., also* **~ cleaner**) пылесóс.
■ *v.t. & i.* (*coll., clean with* **~ 2**) пылесóсить, про-.

vagabond /ˈvægəbɒnd/ *n.* (*vagrant*) бродя́га (*c.g.*), скитáлец.

vagary /ˈveɪgərɪ/ *n.* причýда, капрúз.

vagina /vəˈdʒaɪnə/ *n.* влагáлище.

vaginal /vəˈdʒaɪnəl/ *adj.* влагáлищный, вагинáльный.

vagrant /ˈveɪgrənt/ *n.* бродя́га (*c.g.*).

vague /veɪg/ *adj.* неопределённый, смýтный, нея́сный; **he was rather ~ about his plans** он был весьмá уклóнчив относúтельно своúх плáнов.

vagueness /ˈveɪgnɪs/ *n.* неопределённость, смýтность, нея́сность.

vain /veɪn/ *adj.*
1 (*unavailing; fruitless*) тщéтный, напрáсный; **they tried in ~ to get a seat** онú безуспéшно пытáлись найтú мéсто.
2 (*conceited*) тщеслáвный.

valedictory /vælɪˈdɪktərɪ/ *adj.* прощáльный; (*US, as n.*) речь на шкóльном вы́пуске.

valentine /ˈvæləntaɪn/ *n.* (*missive*) валентúнка, (анонúмное) любóвное послáние в день святóго Валентúна.

valet /ˈvæleɪ/ *n.* камердúнер, слугá (*m.*).

valiant /ˈvæljənt/ *adj.* дóблестный; (*of effort*) герóический.

valid /ˈvælɪd/ *adj.*
1 (*sound*) вéский, обоснóванный; **~ objections** убедúтельные возражéния.
2 (*leg.*) действúтельный; **a ticket ~ for 3 months** билéт, действúтельный в течéние трёх мéсяцев.

validate /ˈvælɪdeɪt/ *v.t.* утвер|ждáть, -дúть.

validation /vælɪˈdeɪʃ(ə)n/ *n.* утверждéние, подтверждéние.

valley /ˈvælɪ/ *n.* (*pl.* **~s**) долúна.

valour /ˈvælə(r)/ (*US* **valor**) *n.* дóблесть.

valuable /ˈvæljʊəb(ə)l/ *n.* (*usu. pl.*) цéнности (*f. pl.*).
■ *adj.* цéнный, полéзный, вáжный.

valuation /væljʊˈeɪʃ(ə)n/ *n.* оцéнка.

value /ˈvæljuː/ *n.*
1 (*worth*) цéнность, вáжность.
2 (*in money etc.*) цéнность, стóимость; **property is rising in ~** недвúжимое имýщество поднимáется в ценé; **the book is good ~ for money** (*Br.*) э́та кнúга — вы́годная покýпка.
3 (*pl., standards*) (*духовные и т. п.*) цéнности (*f. pl.*).
■ *v.t.* (**values, valued, valuing**)
1 (*estimate ~ of*) оцéн|ивать, -úть.
2 (*regard highly*) ценúть (*impf.*).

valuer /ˈvæljʊə(r)/ *n.* (*Br.*) оцéнщик.

valve /vælv/ *n.* клáпан.

vampire /ˈvæmpaɪə(r)/ *n.* вампúр.

van /væn/ *n.* фургóн.

vandal /ˈvænd(ə)l/ *n.* вандáл.

vandalism /ˈvændəlɪz(ə)m/ *n.* вандалúзм.

vandalize /ˈvændəlaɪz/ *v.t.* разр|ушáть, -ýшить.

vanguard /ˈvængɑːd/ *n.* авангáрд.

vanilla /vəˈnɪlə/ *n.* ванúль; (*attr.*) ванúльный.

vanish /ˈvænɪʃ/ *v.i.* исч|езáть, -éзнуть.

vanity /ˈvænɪtɪ/ *n.* тщеслáвие.

vanquish /ˈvæŋkwɪʃ/ *v.t.* побе|ждáть, -дúть; покор|я́ть, -úть.

vantage /ˈvɑːntɪdʒ/ *n.*: **~ point** вы́годная позúция.

vapour /ˈveɪpə(r)/ (*US* **vapor**) *n.*
1 (*steam*) пар.
2 (*gaseous manifestation*): **~ trail** инверсиóнный след.

variable /ˈveərɪəb(ə)l/ *n.* (*math.*) перемéнная (величинá).
■ *adj.* измéнчивый, непостоя́нный.

variance /ˈveərɪəns/ *n.*: **this is at ~ with what we heard** э́то противорéчит томý, что мы слы́шали.

variant /ˈveərɪənt/ *n.* вариáнт.

variation /veərɪˈeɪʃ(ə)n/ *n.*
1 (*fluctuation*) изменéние; колебáние; **~s of temperature** колебáния (*nt. pl.*) температýры.
2 (*divergence*) отклонéние.

varicose /ˈværɪkəʊs/ *adj.* варикóзный; **~ veins** варикóзные вéны.

varied /ˈveərɪd/ *adj.* разнообрáзный.

variegated /ˈveərɪgeɪtɪd/ *adj.* разноцвéтный, пёстрый.

variety /vəˈraɪətɪ/ *n.*
1 (*diversity*) разнообрáзие.
2 (*number of different things*) ряд; мнóжество; **for a ~ of reasons** по цéлому ря́ду

соображений, по ряду причин.
[3]: **~ show** эстрадное представление.
[4] (*type*) разновидность, вид, сорт.
varifocals /ˈveərɪfəʊk(ə)lz/ *n. pl.* (*spectacles*) очк|и́ (*pl.*, *g.* -о́в) с переменным фокусным расстоянием.
various /ˈveərɪəs/ *adj.*
[1] (*diverse*) различный, разный, разнообразный.
[2] (*with pl.*, *several*) многие (*pl.*); разные (*pl.*).
varnish /ˈvɑːnɪʃ/ *n.* лак; (*fig.*) лоск.
■ *v.t.* покр|ывать, -ыть лаком.
var|y /ˈveərɪ/ *v.t.* менять (*impf.*); измен|ять, -ить; разнообразить (*impf.*).
■ *v.i.* [1] (*change*) меняться (*impf.*); **the menu never ~ies** меню никогда не меняется.
[2] (*differ*) ра|сходиться, -зойтись; отлич|аться, -иться; **opinions ~y** мнения расходятся.
vase /vɑːz/ *n.* ваза.
vasectomy /vəˈsektəmɪ/ (*med.*) *n.* вазэктомия.
Vaseline /ˈvæsɪliːn/ *n.* (*propr.*) вазелин.
vast /vɑːst/ *adj.* обширный; огромный; (*grandiose*) грандиозный.
vastness /ˈvɑːstnɪs/ *n.* ширь; огромность; грандиозность.
VAT /viːeɪˈtiː, væt/ *n.* (*Br.*, *abbr. of* ***value added tax***) НДС (налог на добавленную стоимость).
vat /væt/ *n.* бочка, чан.
Vatican /ˈvætɪkən/ *n.* Ватикан.
vault[1] /vɔːlt/ *n.*
[1] (*arched roof*) свод.
[2] (*underground room*) подвал, погреб; (*of a bank*) хранилище.
vault[2] /vɔːlt/ *v.t.* & *i.* перепры́г|ивать, -нуть.
VCR (*abbr. of* ***video cassette recorder***) видеомагнитофон.
VD (*abbr. of* ***venereal disease***) венерическая болезнь.
VDU (*abbr. of* ***visual display unit***) (*Br.*) дисплей.
veal /viːl/ *n.* телятина.
veer /vɪə(r)/ *v.i.* измен|ять, -ить направление; пов|орачивать(ся), -ернуть(ся).
vegan /ˈviːgən/ *n.* строгий вегетарианец.
vegetable /ˈvedʒtəb(ə)l/ *n.* овощ.
■ *adj.* овощной; **~ oils** растительные масла.
vegetarian /vedʒɪˈteərɪən/ *n.* вегетариан|ец (*fem.* -ка).
■ *adj.* вегетарианский.
vegetate /ˈvedʒɪteɪt/ *v.i.* (*lit.*) расти; (*impf.*); (*fig.*) прозябать (*impf.*).
vegetation /vedʒɪˈteɪʃ(ə)n/ *n.* (*plant life*) растительность.
veggie burger /ˈvedʒɪ bɜːgə(r)/ *n.* вегетарианская котлета.
vehemence /ˈviːəməns/ *n.* сила, ярость.
vehement /ˈviːəmənt/ *adj.* сильный, яростный.
vehicle /ˈvɪək(ə)l/ *n.* транспортное средство.
veil /veɪl/ *n.* вуаль.
■ *v.t.*: **a ~ed threat** скрытая угроза.
vein /veɪn/ *n.*
[1] (*anat.*) вена, жила.
[2] (*fissure in rock*) жила.
[3] (*style*): **in the same ~** в том же духе/тоне/стиле.
Velcro /ˈvelkrəʊ/ *n.* (*propr.*): **~ fastener** застёжка «велкро», липучка.
velocity /vɪˈlɒsɪtɪ/ *n.* скорость; быстрота.
velvet /ˈvelvɪt/ *n.* бархат; **a ~ dress** бархатное платье.
velvety /ˈvelvɪtɪ/ *adj.* бархатный, бархатистый.
vendetta /venˈdetə/ *n.* вендетта.
vending machine /ˈvendɪŋ/ *n.* (торговый) автомат (*по продаже сигарет, напитков и т. п.*).
vendor /ˈvendə(r)/ *n.* продав|ец (*fem.* -щица).
veneer /vɪˈnɪə(r)/ *n.* шпон, фанера; (*fig.*) внешний лоск.
venerable /ˈvenərəb(ə)l/ *adj.*
[1] (*revered*) почтенный; **~ ruins** древние/священные развалины.
[2]: **V~** (*as title*) преподобный.
venerate /ˈvenəreɪt/ *v.t.* чтить (*impf.*); почитать (*impf.*); благоговеть (*impf.*) перед + *i.*
veneration /venəˈreɪʃ(ə)n/ *n.* почтение, благоговение.
venereal /vɪˈnɪərɪəl/ *adj.*: **~ disease** венерическая болезнь.
Venetian /vɪˈniːʃ(ə)n/ *n.* венециан|ец (*fem.* -ка).
■ *adj.* венецианский; **~ blinds** жалюзи (*pl. indecl.*).
Venezuela /venɪˈzweɪlə/ *n.* Венесуэла.
Venezuelan /venɪˈzweɪlən/ *n.* венесуэл|ец (*fem.* -ка).
■ *adj.* венесуэльский.
vengeance /ˈvendʒ(ə)ns/ *n.*
[1] месть; отмщение (*liter.*).
[2]: **with a ~** (*coll.*, *in a high degree*) вовсю, с лихвой.
vengeful /ˈvendʒfʊl/ *adj.* мстительный.
Venice /ˈvenɪs/ *n.* Венеция.
venison /ˈvenɪs(ə)n/ *n.* оленина.
venom /ˈvenəm/ *n.* яд; (*fig.*) яд, злоба.
venomous /ˈvenəməs/ *adj.* ядовитый.
vent /vent/ *n.* дымоход; **he gave ~ to his feelings** он дал волю своим чувствам.
■ *v.t.* (*fig.*) изл|ивать, -ить; да|вать, -ть выход + *d.*
ventilate /ˈventɪleɪt/ *v.t.* проветри|вать, -ть.
ventilation /ventɪˈleɪʃ(ə)n/ *n.* вентиляция.
ventilator /ˈventɪleɪtə(r)/ *n.* вентилятор (*also med.*).
ventriloquist /venˈtrɪləkwɪst/ *n.* чревовещатель (*m.*).
venture /ˈventʃə(r)/ *n.*
[1] (*risky undertaking*) рискованное предприятие.
[2] (*business enterprise*) (коммерческое) предприятие.
■ *v.t.* (*risk, bet*) риск|овать, -нуть + *i.*
■ *v.i.* (*dare*) осмели|ваться, -ться; **I ~ to suggest** осмелюсь предложить.
■ *cpd.* **~ capital** *n.* (*fin.*) венчурный капитал.
venue /ˈvenjuː/ *n.* место (проведения) (*концерта/соревнований*).
veracity /vəˈræsɪtɪ/ *n.* правдивость; достоверность.
veranda /vəˈrændə/ *n.* веранда.
verb /vɜːb/ *n.* глагол.

verbal /ˈvəːb(ə)l/ *adj.*
[1] (*of or in words*) слове́сный.
[2] (*oral*) у́стный.

verbalize /ˈvəːbəlaɪz/ *v.t.* (*put into words*) выража́ть, вы́разить слова́ми.

verbatim /vəːˈbeɪtɪm/ *adv.* досло́вно.

verbiage /ˈvəːbɪɪdʒ/ *n.* многосло́вие; пустосло́вие.

verbose /vəːˈbəʊs/ *adj.* многосло́вный.

verbosity /vəˈbɒsɪtɪ/ *n.* многосло́вие.

verdict /ˈvəːdɪkt/ *n.* (*leg.*) верди́кт, пригово́р; **the jury brought in a ~ of guilty/not guilty** суд прися́жных вы́нес обвини́тельный/оправда́тельный пригово́р; (*fig., judgement*) заключе́ние, пригово́р; **what's the ~?** како́в пригово́р?

verge /vəːdʒ/ *n.* край; (*Br., of road*) обо́чина; (*fig.*): **on the ~ of destruction** на краю́ ги́бели; **on the ~ of tears** на гра́ни слёз; **he was on the ~ of betraying his secret** он чуть не вы́дал свою́ та́йну.
■ *v.i.*: **it ~s on madness** э́то грани́чит с безу́мием.

verifiable /ˈverɪfaɪəb(ə)l/ *adj.* поддаю́щийся прове́рке.

verification /verɪfɪˈkeɪʃ(ə)n/ *n.* прове́рка; подтвержде́ние.

verify /ˈverɪfaɪ/ *v.t.* (*check accuracy of*) пров|еря́ть, -е́рить; (*confirm*) подтвер|жда́ть, -ди́ть.

veritable /ˈverɪtəb(ə)l/ *adj.* настоя́щий, су́щий.

vermicelli /vəːmɪˈtʃelɪ/ *n.* вермише́ль.

vermin /ˈvəːmɪn/ *n.*
[1] (*rats, foxes, etc.*) вреди́тели (*m. pl.*) (*в т. ч. хищники*).
[2] (*parasitic insects*) парази́ты (*m. pl.*).

vernacular /vəˈnækjʊlə(r)/ *n.*
[1] (*local language*) иско́нный язы́к; **Latin gave place to the ~** латы́нь уступи́ла ме́сто иско́нным языка́м.
[2] (*dialect*) диале́кт; наре́чие.
[3] (*jargon*) жарго́н, арго́ (*nt. indecl.*).
[4] (*colloquial speech*) просторе́чие.
■ *adj.* иско́нный, ме́стный; просторе́чный.

versatile /ˈvəːsətaɪl/ *adj.* (*person*) разносторо́нний; (*device*) универса́льный.

versatility /vəːsəˈtɪlɪtɪ/ *n.* разносторо́нность; универса́льность.

verse /vəːs/ *n.*
[1] (*stanza of poem, song*) строфа́; (*in Bible*) стих.
[2] (*sg. or pl., poetry, poems*) стихи́ (*m. pl.*); **he wrote in ~** он писа́л в стиха́х.

version /ˈvəːʃ(ə)n/ *n.*
[1] (*individual account*) ве́рсия, расска́з.
[2] (*form or variant of text etc.*) вариа́нт, текст.

verst /vəːst/ *n.* верста́.

versus /ˈvəːsəs/ *prep.* про́тив + *g.*

vertebra /ˈvəːtɪbrə/ *n.* (*pl.* **vertebrae** /-breɪ/) позвоно́к.

vertebrate /ˈvəːtɪbrət/ *n.* позвоно́чное (живо́тное).
■ *adj.* позвоно́чный.

vertical /ˈvəːtɪk(ə)l/ *adj.* вертика́льный; **a ~ cliff** отве́сный утёс.

vertigo /ˈvəːtɪgəʊ/ *n.* головокруже́ние.

verve /vəːv/ *n.* жи́вость, эне́ргия.

very /ˈverɪ/ *adj.*
[1] (*exact; identical*) тот са́мый; **this ~ day** сего́дня же.
[2] (*extreme*) са́мый; **at the ~ end** в са́мом конце́.
[3] (*in emphasis*): **the ~ idea of it** одна́ мысль об э́том.
■ *adv.* [1] (*exceedingly*) о́чень; **I don't feel ~ well** я чу́вствую себя́ нева́жно; **I can't sing ~ well** я дово́льно пло́хо пою́.
[2] (*emph., with superl. etc.*) са́мый; **the ~ best** са́мый лу́чший; наилу́чший; **the ~ next day** на сле́дующий же день; **you may keep it for your ~ own** мо́жете э́то взять (себе́) насовсе́м.

vessel /ˈves(ə)l/ *n.*
[1] (*receptacle*) сосу́д.
[2] (*ship*) су́дно, кора́бль (*m.*).
[3] (*anat.*) сосу́д; **blood ~** кровено́сный сосу́д.

vest[1] /vest/ *n.* (*Br., undergarment*) ма́йка; (*US, waistcoat*) жиле́т.

vest[2] /vest/ *v.t.*: **~ed interest** ли́чная заинтересо́ванность.

vestibule /ˈvestɪbjuːl/ *n.* вестибю́ль (*m.*).

vestige /ˈvestɪdʒ/ *n.* след.

vestment /ˈvestmənt/ *n.* (*eccl.*) облаче́ние, ри́за.

vestry /ˈvestrɪ/ *n.* (*eccl.*) (*room*) ри́зница.

vet[1] /vet/ *n.* (*coll., veterinary surgeon*) ветвра́ч, ветерина́р.
■ *v.t.* (**vetted, vetting**) (*coll., investigate*) пров|еря́ть, -е́рить.

vet[2] /vet/ *n.* (*US, coll, veteran*) ветера́н.

veteran /ˈvetərən/ *n.* (*lit., fig.*) ветера́н.
■ *adj.* многоо́пытный, старе́йший.

veterinarian /vetərɪˈneərɪən/ *n.* (*US*) ветерина́р.

veterinary /ˈvetərɪnərɪ/ *adj.*: **~ surgeon** (*Br.*) ветерина́рный врач.

veto /ˈviːtəʊ/ *n.* (*pl.* **vetoes**) ве́то (*indecl.*).
■ *v.t.* (**vetoes, vetoed**) нал|ага́ть, -ожи́ть ве́то на + *a.*

vex /veks/ *v.t.* доса|жда́ть, -ди́ть; раздраж|а́ть, -и́ть; **a ~ed question** больно́й вопро́с.

VHF (*abbr. of* ***very high frequency***) ОВЧ (о́чень высо́кая частота́).

via /ˈvaɪə/ *prep.* че́рез + *a.*

viable /ˈvaɪəb(ə)l/ *adj.* (*able to survive*) жизнеспосо́бный; (*coll., feasible*) осуществи́мый.

viaduct /ˈvaɪədʌkt/ *n.* виаду́к, путепрово́д.

vibes /vaɪbz/ *n.* (*coll.*) (*mus., vibraphone*) вибрафо́н; (*atmosphere*) флюи́ды (*m. pl.*).

vibrancy /ˈvaɪbrənsɪ/ *n.* (*liveliness*) жи́вость; (*of colours*) я́ркость.

vibrant /ˈvaɪbrənt/ *adj.* (*lively*) живо́й, по́лный жи́зни; (*of colours*) со́чный, я́ркий.

vibraphone /ˈvaɪbrəfəʊn/ *n.* вибрафо́н.

vibrate /vaɪˈbreɪt/ *v.i.* вибри́ровать, дрожа́ть (*both impf.*).

vibration /vaɪˈbreɪʃ(ə)n/ *n.* вибра́ция, дрожь.

vibrato /vɪˈbrɑːtəʊ/ *n.* & *adv.* (*mus.*) вибра́то (*nt. indecl.*).

vicar /ˈvɪkə(r)/ *n.* свяще́нник.

vicarage /ˈvɪkərɪdʒ/ *n.* дом свяще́нника.

vicarious /vɪˈkeərɪəs/ *adj.* ко́свенный; **feel ~ pleasure** пережива́ть (*impf.*) чужу́ю ра́дость.

vice[1] /vaɪs/ *n.* порóк.
vice[2] /vaɪs/ (*US* **vise**) *n.* (*tool*) тиск|и́ (*pl.*, *g.* -ов).
vice[3] /vaɪs/ *cpds.* **~ chairman** *n.* замести́тель (*m.*) председа́теля; **~ chancellor** *n.* (*Br.*) ре́ктор; **~-president** *n.* ви́це-президе́нт.
vice versa /vaɪsɪ'vɜ:sə/ *adv.* наоборóт.
vicinity /vɪ'sɪnɪtɪ/ *n.* окру́га, окре́стность; **in the ~ of** в райо́не + *g.*
vicious /'vɪʃəs/ *adj.*
1 (*spiteful*) злой.
2 : **a ~ circle** поро́чный круг.
viciousness /'vɪʃəsnɪs/ *n.* зло́бность.
vicissitude /vɪ'sɪsɪtju:d/ *n.* превра́тность.
victim /'vɪktɪm/ *n.* же́ртва; (*of accident*) пострада́вший.
victimization /vɪktɪmaɪ'zeɪʃ(ə)n/ *n.* пресле́дование.
victimize /'vɪktɪmaɪz/ *v.t.* подв|ерга́ть, -е́ргнуть пресле́дованию.
victor /'vɪktə(r)/ *n.* победи́тель (*m.*).
Victorian /vɪk'tɔ:rɪən/ *n.* викториа́н|ец (*fem.* -ка).
■ *adj.* викториа́нский; (*fig.*) старомо́дный.
victorious /vɪk'tɔ:rɪəs/ *adj.* победоно́сный, побе́дный.
victory /'vɪktərɪ/ *n.* побе́да (**over:** над + *i.*).
video /'vɪdɪəʊ/ *n.* (*pl.* **videos**) (*a ~ recorder* (*Br.*), *film*, *cassette*) ви́део (*indecl.*); **~ camera** видеока́мера; **~ cassette** видеокассе́та; **~ (cassette) recorder** видеомагнитофо́н; **~ clip** (видео)кли́п; **~ conference** видеоконфере́нция; **~ game** видеоигра́; **~phone** видеотелефо́н; **~tape** видеоле́нта; видеоплёнка.
■ *v.t.* (**videoes, videoed**) запи́с|ывать, -а́ть на ви́део.
vie /vaɪ/ *v.i.* (**vying**) состяза́ться (*impf.*); сопе́рничать (*impf.*); **they ~d with each other for first place** они́ состяза́лись за пе́рвое ме́сто.
Vienna /vɪ'enə/ *n.* Ве́на.
Vietnam /vjet'næm/ *n.* Вьетна́м.
Vietnamese /vɪetnə'mi:z/ *n.* (*pl.* ~) (*person*) вьетна́м|ец (*fem.* -ка); (*language*) вьетна́мский язы́к.
■ *adj.* вьетна́мский.
view /vju:/ *n.*
1 (*scene, prospect*) вид; пейза́ж; **you get a good ~ from here** отсю́да хоро́ший вид.
2 (*sight; field of vision*) вид; **in full ~ of the audience** на виду́ у пу́блики.
3 (*fig.*): **look at it from my point of ~** посмотри́те на э́то с мое́й то́чки зре́ния.
4 (*inspection*) смотр, просмо́тр; **private ~(ing)** закры́тый просмо́тр.
5 (*mental attitude or opinion*) взгляд, мне́ние; (*pl.*) взгля́ды (*m. pl.*), убежде́ния (*nt. pl.*); **in my ~** по-мо́ему; по моему́ мне́нию.
6 (*intention*) наме́рение; **I am saving with a ~ to buying a house** я коплю́ де́ньги, что́бы купи́ть дом.
7 (*consideration*): **in ~ of** ввиду́ + *g.*; **in ~ of recent developments** в све́те после́дних происше́ствий.
■ *v.t.* 1 (*survey; gaze on*) смотре́ть, по- на + *a.*; рассм|а́тривать, -отре́ть.
2 (*inspect*) осм|а́тривать, -отре́ть.
3 (*fig., consider*) рассм|а́тривать, -отре́ть; оце́н|ивать, -и́ть.
■ *cpds.* **~finder** *n.* видоиска́тель (*m.*); **~point** *n.* то́чка зре́ния.
viewer /'vju:ə(r)/ *n.* (*of TV*) (теле)зри́тель (*fem.* -ница).
vigil /'vɪdʒɪl/ *n.* бде́ние.
vigilance /'vɪdʒɪləns/ *n.* бди́тельность.
vigilant /'vɪdʒɪlənt/ *adj.* бди́тельный.
vigilante /vɪdʒɪ'læntɪ/ *n.* ≈ дружи́нник.
vigorous /'vɪgərəs/ *adj.* энерги́чный, бо́дрый.
vigour /'vɪgə(r)/ (*US* **vigor** *n.*) эне́ргия, бо́дрость.
Viking /'vaɪkɪŋ/ *n.* ви́кинг.
vile /vaɪl/ *adj.* гну́сный, ни́зкий.
vilify /'vɪlɪfaɪ/ *v.t.* поноси́ть (*impf.*); черни́ть, о-.
villa /'vɪlə/ *n.* ви́лла.
village /'vɪlɪdʒ/ *n.* дере́вня; (*larger*) село́.
villager /'vɪlɪdʒə(r)/ *n.* дереве́нск|ий/ се́льск|ий жи́тель (*fem.* -ая -ница).
villain /'vɪlən/ *n.*
1 (*man of base character*) злоде́й.
2 (*criminal*) престу́пник, злоде́й.
Vilnius /'vɪlnɪəs/ *n.* Ви́льнюс.
vinaigrette /vɪnɪ'gret/ *n.* сала́тная запра́вка из у́ксуса, оли́вкового ма́сла и спе́ций.
vindicate /'vɪndɪkeɪt/ *v.t.* опра́вд|ывать, -а́ть.
vindication /vɪndɪ'keɪʃ(ə)n/ *n.* оправда́ние.
vindictive /vɪn'dɪktɪv/ *adj.* мсти́тельный.
vindictiveness /vɪn'dɪktɪvnɪs/ *n.* мсти́тельность.
vine /vaɪn/ *n.* (*grape~*) виногра́дная лоза́; (*climbing or trailing plant*) выю́щееся/ ползу́чее расте́ние.
vinegar /'vɪnɪgə(r)/ *n.* у́ксус.
vineyard /'vɪnjɑ:d/ *n.* виногра́дник.
vintage /'vɪntɪdʒ/ *n.*
1 (*year of wine production*): **the 1950 ~** вино́ урожа́я ты́сяча девятьсо́т пятидеся́того го́да; **this is a good ~** э́то хоро́ший год (*о вине*); **~ wine** ма́рочное вино́.
2 (*fig.*): **a ~ car** (*Br.*) автомоби́ль (*m.*) ста́рой ма́рки.
vinyl /'vaɪnɪl/ *n.* вини́л; (*attr.*) вини́ловый.
viola /vɪ'əʊlə/ *n.* (*musical instrument*) альт.
violate /'vaɪəleɪt/ *v.t.*
1 (*infringe, transgress*) нар|уша́ть, -у́шить; преступ|а́ть, -и́ть.
2 (*profane*) осквер|ня́ть, -ни́ть.
violation /vaɪə'leɪʃ(ə)n/ *n.* наруше́ние; оскверне́ние.
violence /'vaɪələns/ *n.* си́ла, наси́лие; **he resorted to ~** он прибе́г(нул) к наси́лию.
violent /'vaɪələnt/ *adj.*
1 (*strong, forceful*) си́льный, неи́стовый, я́ростный.
2 (*using or involving force*): **he became ~** он на́чал бу́йствовать.
violet /'vaɪələt/ *n.* (*bot.*) фиа́лка; (*colour*) фиоле́товый цвет.
■ *adj.* (*of colour*) фиоле́товый.
violin /vaɪə'lɪn/ *n.* скри́пка.
violinist /vaɪə'lɪnɪst/ *n.* скрипа́ч (*fem.* -ка).
VIP (*abbr. of* ***very important person***)

высокопоста́вленное лицо́, высо́кий гость, VIP-гость.

viper /ˈvaɪpə(r)/ *n.* гадю́ка.

viral /ˈvaɪər(ə)l/ *adj.* ви́русный.

virgin /ˈvɜːdʒɪn/ *n.* (*female*) де́вственница; (*male*) де́вственник; **~ forest** де́вственный лес.

virginal /ˈvɜːdʒɪn(ə)l/ *adj.* де́вственный; непоро́чный.

virginity /vəˈdʒɪnɪtɪ/ *n.* де́вственность, неви́нность, непоро́чность; **lose one's ~** теря́ть, по- неви́нность, лиш|а́ться, -и́ться де́вственности.

Virgo /ˈvɜːɡəʊ/ *n.* (*pl.* **~s**) Де́ва.

virile /ˈvɪraɪl/ *adj.* му́жественный.

virility /vɪˈrɪlɪtɪ/ *n.* (*sexual potency*) мужска́я си́ла, полова́я поте́нция; (*manliness*) му́жественность.

virologist /vaɪˈrɒlədʒɪst/ *n.* вирусо́лог.

virology /vaɪˈrɒlədʒɪ/ *n.* вирусоло́гия.

virtual /ˈvɜːtjʊəl/ *adj.*
1 факти́ческий; **we remained ~ strangers** факти́чески мы остава́лись соверше́нно незнако́мыми людьми́.
2 (*comput.*, *phys.*) виртуа́льный.
■ *cpd.* **~ reality** *n.* (*comput.*) виртуа́льная реа́льность.

virtually /ˈvɜːtjʊəlɪ/ *adv.* факти́чески, практи́чески; **the dress was ~ new** э́то бы́ло факти́чески/практи́чески но́вое пла́тье; **it's ~ impossible** э́то факти́чески/практи́чески невозмо́жно.

virtue /ˈvɜːtjuː/ *n.*
1 (*moral excellence*) доброде́тель.
2 (*good quality, advantage*) досто́инство, преиму́щество.
3 (*consideration*): **by ~ of his long service** на основа́нии его́ многоле́тней слу́жбы.

virtuosity /vɜːtjuːˈɒsɪtɪ/ *n.* виртуо́зность.

virtuoso /vɜːtjʊˈəʊsəʊ/ *n.*: **a ~ performance** виртуо́зное исполне́ние.

virtuous /ˈvɜːtjʊəs/ *adj.* доброде́тельный.

virulence /ˈvɪrʊləns/ *n.* (*of poison*) си́ла, смерте́льность; (*of disease*) тя́жесть; (*of bacteria*) вируле́нтность; (*of temper, speech etc.*) зло́ба, я́рость.

virulent /ˈvɪrʊlənt/ *adj.* (*of poison*) сильноде́йствующий; смерте́льный; (*of disease*) тяжёлый; (*of bacteria*) вируле́нтный; (*of temper, words etc.*) зло́бный, я́ростный.

virus /ˈvaɪərəs/ *n.* (*also comput.*) ви́рус.

visa /ˈviːzə/ *n.* ви́за.

viscount /ˈvaɪkaʊnt/ *n.* вико́нт.

viscountess /ˈvaɪkaʊntɪs/ *n.* виконте́сса.

viscous /ˈvɪskəs/ *adj.* вя́зкий, ли́пкий.

vise /vaɪs/ (*US*) = **vice**[2]

visibility /vɪzɪˈbɪlɪtɪ/ *n.* ви́димость.

visibl|e /ˈvɪzɪb(ə)l/ *adj.*
1 (*perceptible by eye*) ви́димый.
2 (*apparent; obvious*) я́вный, очеви́дный; **she was ~y annoyed** она́ была́ заме́тно раздражена́.

vision /ˈvɪʒ(ə)n/ *n.*
1 (*faculty of sight*) зре́ние.
2 (*imaginative insight*) проница́тельность.
3 (*apparition*) при́зрак; привиде́ние.
4 (*sth. imagined or dreamed of*) мечта́.

visionary /ˈvɪʒənərɪ/ *n.* прови́д|ец (*fem.* -ица).
■ *adj.* дальнови́дный, му́дрый.

visit /ˈvɪzɪt/ *n.* (*call*) визи́т, посеще́ние; (*trip, stay*) пое́здка, пребыва́ние; **make, pay a ~ to s.o.** посе|ща́ть, -ти́ть (*or* наве|ща́ть, -сти́ть) кого́-н.
■ *v.t.* (**visited, visiting**) (*place*) посе|ща́ть, -ти́ть; (*person*) наве|ща́ть, -сти́ть; **he ~ed Europe** он побыва́л в Евро́пе; он съе́здил в Евро́пу; **I have never ~ed New York** я никогда́ не быва́л в Нью-Йо́рке; **~ing card** (*Br.*) визи́тная ка́рточка; **~ing hours** приёмные часы́; часы́ посеще́ния.
■ *v.i.* (*US*): **~ with** (*go to see*) вида́ться, по-.

visitor /ˈvɪzɪtə(r)/ *n.* гость (*m.*), посети́тель (*m.*).

visor /ˈvaɪzə(r)/ *n.* (*of helmet*) щито́к; (*of windscreen*) солнцезащи́тный щито́к.

vista /ˈvɪstə/ *n.* перспекти́ва, вид.

visual /ˈvɪʒʊəl/ *adj.* зри́тельный; визуа́льный; **~ arts** изобрази́тельные иску́сства; **~ aids** нагля́дные посо́бия.

visualize /ˈvɪʒʊəlaɪz/ *v.t.* предст|авля́ть, -а́вить себе́.

vital /ˈvaɪt(ə)l/ *adj.*
1 (*concerned with life*) жи́зненный; **~ statistics** (*joc., woman's measurements*) объём груди́, та́лии и бёдер.
2 (*essential*) насу́щный; **it is of ~ importance** э́то вопро́с/де́ло первостепе́нной ва́жности.
3 (*lively*) живо́й.

vitality /vaɪˈtælɪtɪ/ *n.* жи́вость.

vitamin /ˈvɪtəmɪn/ *n.* витами́н; **~ C** витами́н С (*pr.* це).

viticulture /ˈvɪtɪkʌltʃə(r)/ *n.* виногра́дарство.

vitriolic /vɪtrɪˈɒlɪk/ *adj.* ядови́тый (*комментарий и т. п.*).

viva /ˈvaɪvə/ (*Br.*) у́стный экза́мен.

vivacious /vɪˈveɪʃəs/ *adj.* живо́й, оживлённый.

vivacity /vɪˈvæsɪtɪ/ *n.* жи́вость, оживле́ние.

vivid /ˈvɪvɪd/ *adj.*
1 (*bright*) я́ркий.
2 (*lively*) живо́й, пы́лкий; **a ~ imagination** пы́лкое воображе́ние.
3 (*clear and distinct*) чёткий, я́сный.

vividness /ˈvɪvɪdnɪs/ *n.* я́ркость, жи́вость; чёткость.

vivisection /vɪvɪˈsekʃ(ə)n/ *n.* вивисе́кция.

vixen /ˈvɪks(ə)n/ *n.* лиси́ца(-са́мка).

viz. /vɪz/ *adv.* а и́менно.

vocabulary /vəˈkæbjʊlərɪ/ *n.* (*of an individual*) слова́рный запа́с; (*of a language*) слова́рный соста́в.

vocal /ˈvəʊk(ə)l/ *adj.*
1 (*of or using the voice*) голосово́й, речево́й.
2 (*eloquent*) красноречи́вый.
■ *n.* (*usu. pl.*) вока́льная па́ртия.

vocalist /ˈvəʊkəlɪst/ *n.* вокали́ст (*fem.* -ка).

vocation /vəˈkeɪʃ(ə)n/ *n.* призва́ние.

vocational /vəˈkeɪʃən(ə)l/ *adj.* профессиона́льный.

vociferous /vəˈsɪfərəs/ *adj.* шу́мный.

vodka /ˈvɒdkə/ *n.* во́дка.

vogue /vəʊɡ/ *n.* мо́да; **in ~** в мо́де.

voice /vɔɪs/ *n.* го́лос; **he shouted at the top of his ~** он крича́л во весь го́лос; **I lost my ~** я потеря́л го́лос.
■ *v.t.* выража́ть, вы́разить.
■ *cpds.* **~ mail** *n.* голосова́я по́чта; **~-over** *n.* (*TV etc.*) го́лос за ка́дром; зака́дровый коммента́рий.

void /vɔɪd/ *n.* пустота́.
■ *adj.* 1 (*empty*) пусто́й; лишённый (*чего*).
2 (*invalid*) недействи́тельный.

volatile /'vɒlətaɪl/ *adj.* (*of person*) непостоя́нный, изме́нчивый.

volcanic /vɒl'kænɪk/ *adj.* вулкани́ческий.

volcano /vɒl'keɪnəʊ/ *n.* (*pl.* **~es**) вулка́н.

Volga /'vɒlgə/ *n.* Во́лга.

volley /'vɒlɪ/ *n.* (*pl.* **~s**)
1 (*simultaneous discharge*) залп; (*fig.*): **a ~ of oaths** пото́к бра́ни.
2 (*tennis etc.*) уда́р с лёта.
■ *v.t.* (**volleys, volleyed**) уд|аря́ть, -а́рить с лёта.

volleyball /'vɒlɪbɔːl/ *n.* волейбо́л.

volt /vəʊlt/ *n.* вольт.

voltage /'vəʊltɪdʒ/ *n.* напряже́ние, вольта́ж.

volume /'vɒljuːm/ *n.*
1 (*tome*) том.
2 (*of sound*) гро́мкость; **~ control** регуля́тор гро́мкости.

voluminous /və'luːmɪnəs/ *adj.* огро́мный; **~ folds** пы́шные скла́дки; **a ~ work** объёмистое произведе́ние; **a ~ writer** плодови́тый писа́тель.

voluntary /'vɒləntərɪ/ *adj.* доброво́льный; **~ redundancy** доброво́льный ухо́д с рабо́ты; **~ work** обще́ственная рабо́та.

volunteer /vɒlən'tɪə(r)/ *n.* доброво́льный помо́щник; (*in army*) доброво́лец.
■ *v.t.* предл|ага́ть, -ожи́ть; де́лать, с- доброво́льно.
■ *v.i.* вызыва́ться, вы́зваться сде́лать что-н; **no one ~ed** жела́ющих не нашло́сь.

voluptuous /və'lʌptjʊəs/ *adj.* чу́вственный.

vomit /'vɒmɪt/ *n.* рво́та.
■ *v.i.* (**vomited, vomiting**): **he ~ed** его́ вы́рвало.

voracious /və'reɪʃəs/ *adj.* прожо́рливый.

vote /vəʊt/ *n.*
1 (*act of voting*) голосова́ние.
2 (*~ cast*) го́лос.
3 (*affirmation*) во́тум; **a ~ of confidence** во́тум дове́рия.
4 (*right to ~*) пра́во го́лоса.
■ *v.i.* голосова́ть, про-; **they are voting on the resolution** они́ голосу́ют резолю́цию.
■ *with adv.*: **they were ~d in by a large majority** их избра́ли большинство́м голосо́в.

voter /'vəʊtə(r)/ *n.* избира́тель (*m.*).

voting /'vəʊtɪŋ/ *n.* голосова́ние; уча́стие в вы́борах (*об избирателях*).

vouch /vaʊtʃ/ *v.i.* руча́ться, поручи́ться; **I can ~ for his honesty** я гото́в поручи́ться за его́ че́стность.

voucher /'vaʊtʃə(r)/ *n.* тало́н.

vow /vaʊ/ *n.* обе́т, кля́тва; **he broke his marriage ~s** он нару́шил бра́чный обе́т.
■ *v.t.* кля́сться, по-; **he ~ed** (*resolved*) **never to return** он покля́лся никогда́ не возвраща́ться.

vowel /'vaʊəl/ *n.* гла́сный (*звук*).

voyage /'vɔɪɪdʒ/ *n.* (*by sea*) (морско́е) путеше́ствие; пла́вание.

voyeur /vwɑː'jɜː(r)/ *n.* вуайери́ст.

vs *abbr.* (*of* **versus**) про́тив + *g.*

V-sign /'viːsaɪn/ *n.*
1 (*Br., gesture of contempt*) ≈ фи́га (*жест*).
2 (*for victory*) знак побе́ды.

vulgar /'vʌlgə(r)/ *adj.* вульга́рный, по́шлый, гру́бый.

vulgarity /vʌl'gærɪtɪ/ *n.* вульга́рность, по́шлость, гру́бость.

vulnerable /'vʌlnərəb(ə)l/ *adj.* уязви́мый.

vulture /'vʌltʃə(r)/ *n.* гриф (*птица*).

vulva /'vʌlvə/ *n.* (*pl.* **~s**) (*anat.*) ву́льва.

Ww

wacky /'wækɪ/ *adj.* (**wackier, wackiest**) (*coll.*) сумасше́дший, чо́кнутый.

wad /wɒd/ *n.*
1 (*pad*) комо́к.
2 (*of papers, banknotes*) па́чка.

waddle /'wɒd(ə)l/ *v.i.* ходи́ть (*indet.*) вразва́л(оч)ку (*coll.*).

wade /weɪd/ *v.i.* проб|ира́ться, -ра́ться; (*fig.*): **I have ~d through all his novels** я (с трудо́м) одоле́л все его́ рома́ны.

wafer /'weɪfə(r)/ *n.* (*cul.*) ва́фля.

waffle[1] /'wɒf(ə)l/ *n.* (*cul.*) ва́фля.

waffle[2] /'wɒf(ə)l/ (*coll.*) *n.* (*Br., verbiage*) вода́ (*в речи, в статье*).
■ *v.i.* (*also* **~ on**) (*Br.*) занима́ться (*impf.*) болтовнёй.

waft /wɒft/ *v.t.* дон|оси́ть, -ести́.
■ *v.i.* дон|оси́ться, -ести́сь.

wag /wæg/ *v.t.* (**wagged, wagging**) (*one's tail*) вил|я́ть, -ьну́ть + *i.*
■ *v.i.* (**wagged, wagging**) (*of dog's tail*) вил|я́ть, -ьну́ть; **this will set tongues ~ging** э́то даст по́вод к спле́тням.

wage[1] /weɪdʒ/ *n.* (*also* **wages**) за́работная пла́та; зарпла́та; **a living ~** прожи́точный ми́нимум.
■ *cpd.* **~ earner** *n.* наёмный рабо́чий; (*breadwinner*) корми́л|ец (*fem.* -ица).

wage[2] /weɪdʒ/ *v.t.* (*war*) вести́ (*impf.*); (*campaign*) пров|оди́ть, -ести́.

wager /'weɪdʒə(r)/ *n.* пари́ (*nt. indecl.*); **lay a**

~ держа́ть (*impf.*) пари́.

waggle /ˈwæg(ə)l/ *v.t.* & *i.* (*ears, toes*) шевели́ть, по- + *i.*

■ *v.i.* (*of ears, toes*) шевели́ться, по-; (*shake slightly*) пока́чиваться (*impf.*).

wagon /ˈwægən/ *n.*

1 (*horse-drawn*) пово́зка; (*with cover*) фурго́н.

2 (*Br., on railway*) ваго́н-платфо́рма.

3 : **he is on the ~** (*fig., not drinking alcohol*) он бро́сил пить.

wail /weɪl/ *n.* (*cry, howl*) вопль (*m.*); (*fig., of the wind, sirens*) вой.

■ *v.i.* вопи́ть (*impf.*); выть (*impf.*).

waist /weɪst/ *n.* та́лия.

■ *cpd.* **~coat** *n.* (*Br.*) жиле́т.

wait /weɪt/ *n.*

1 (*act or time of ~ing*) ожида́ние; **we had a long ~ for the bus** мы до́лго жда́ли авто́буса.

2 (*ambush*): **the robbers lay in ~ for their victim** граби́тели подстерега́ли свою́ же́ртву.

■ *v.t.*: **you must ~ your turn** вы должны́ дожда́ться свое́й о́череди.

■ *v.i.* 1 (*refrain from action*) ждать (*impf.*), подожда́ть (*pf.*); **we must ~ and see what happens** подождём — посмо́трим, что бу́дет да́льше; **I could hardly ~ to ...** я сгора́л от нетерпе́ния + *inf.*; **I ~ed for the rain to stop** я ждал, когда́ ко́нчится дождь; **~ing list** спи́сок (*кандидатов, очередников*); о́чередь; **~ing room** (*doctor's etc.*) приёмная; (*on station*) зал ожида́ния.

2 (*act as servant*): **she ~s on him hand and foot** она́ его́ по́лностью обслу́живает; **he ~ed at table** он прислу́живал за столо́м.

3 **~ up: she ~ed up for him** она́ не ложи́лась (спать) до его́ прихо́да.

waiter /ˈweɪtə(r)/ *n.* официа́нт.

waitress /ˈweɪtrɪs/ *n.* официа́нтка.

waive /weɪv/ *v.t.* (*forgo*) отка́з|ываться, -а́ться от + *g.*; (*claims*) возде́рж|иваться, -а́ться от + *g.*; (*rules*) не соблю|да́ть, -сти́ + *g.*

waiver /ˈweɪvə(r)/ *n.* отка́з (от + *g.*).

wake[1] /weɪk/ *v.t.* (*past* **woke;** *p.p.* **woken**) буди́ть, раз-.

■ *v.i.* (*past* **woke;** *p.p.* **woken**) (*also* **~ up**) прос|ыпа́ться, -ну́ться; **~ up!** (*lit., fig.*) просни́тесь!

wake[2] /weɪk/ *n.* (*of vessel*) кильва́тер; (*fig.*): **there was havoc in the ~ of the storm** бу́ря оста́вила по́сле себя́ многочи́сленные разруше́ния.

wakeful /ˈweɪkfʊl/ *adj.* (*person*) бо́дрствующий; **we had a ~ night** мы провели́ бессо́нную ночь.

waken /ˈweɪkən/ *v.t.* буди́ть, раз-; (*fig.*) буди́ть, про-.

Wales /weɪlz/ *n.* Уэ́льс.

walk /wɔːk/ *n.*

1 (*action of ~ing*) ходьба́; **a short ~ away** в не́скольких шага́х отсю́да/отту́да.

2 (*excursion*) (пе́шая) прогу́лка; (*long-distance*) похо́д; **I'm going for a ~** я пойду́ прогуля́юсь/погуля́ю; **I went on a ten-mile ~** я был в десятими́льном похо́де.

3 (*~ing pace*) шаг.

4 (*gait*) похо́дка, по́ступь.

5 (*route for ~ing*): **there are some pleasant ~s round here** здесь есть прия́тные места́ для прогу́лок.

6 (*path*) тропа́.

7 (*contest*): **long-distance ~** (спорти́вная) ходьба́ на дли́нную диста́нцию.

■ *v.t.* (*take for a ~*) выгу́ливать, вы́гулять; гуля́ть, по- с + *i.*; (*cause to ~*): **he ~ed his horse up the hill** он пусти́л ло́шадь ша́гом в го́ру; (*accompany*) сопрово|жда́ть, -ди́ть; **he offered to ~ her home** он вы́звался проводи́ть её домо́й.

■ *v.i.* 1 (*move on foot*) ходи́ть (*indet.*), идти́ (*det.*); (*stroll about*) прогу́ливаться (*impf.*); **I ~ed ten miles** я прошёл де́сять миль; **I ~ed into a shop** я вошёл в магази́н; **they ~ed into an ambush** они́ попа́ли в заса́ду.

2 (*opp. ride*) ходи́ть (*indet.*), идти́ (*det.*) пешко́м.

3 (*opp. run*): **he ~ed the last 100 metres** после́дние сто ме́тров он прошёл ша́гом.

4 (*take exercise etc. on foot*) ходи́ть (*indet.*) пешко́м; (*stroll*) гуля́ть (*impf.*); **I spent 2 weeks ~ing in Scotland** я броди́л две неде́ли по Шотла́ндии.

■ *with advs.*: **~ away** *v.i.* уходи́ть, уйти́; **he ~ed away with several prizes** он без труда́ завоева́л/получи́л не́сколько призо́в; **~ in** *v.i.* входи́ть, войти́; **~ off** *v.t.* (*annul by ~ing*): **he was ~ing off a heavy lunch** он соверша́л прогу́лку по́сле сы́тного обе́да; *v.i.* уходи́ть, уйти́; **someone ~ed off with my hat** кто́-то унёс мою́ шля́пу; **~ on** *v.i.* (*continue ~ing*) продолжа́ть (*impf.*) идти́; **~ out** *v.i.* выходи́ть, вы́йти; **the men are threatening to ~ out** (*strike*) рабо́чие грозя́т забасто́вкой; **~ up** *v.i.* (*approach*) под|ходи́ть, -ойти́; **I ~ed up to him** я подошёл к нему́.

■ *cpds.* **~over** *n.* лёгкая побе́да; **~way** *n.* перехо́д (*сооружение*).

walker /ˈwɔːkə(r)/ *n.* челове́к, соверша́ющий пе́шие/пешехо́дные прогу́лки; пе́ший тури́ст; **a popular route for ~s** популя́рный пешехо́дный маршру́т.

walkie-talkie /wɔːkɪˈtɔːkɪ/ *n.* ра́ция.

walking /ˈwɔːkɪŋ/ *n.* ходьба́; **~ shoes** о́бувь для ходьбы́.

■ *cpd.* **~ stick** *n.* трость.

Walkman /ˈwɔːkmən/ *n.* (*propr.*) плéер.

wall /wɔːl/ *n.* (*lit., fig.*) стена́, сте́нка; (*attr.*) насте́нный.

■ *v.t.*: **~ed garden** обнесённый стено́й сад.

■ *cpd.* **~paper** *n.* обо́|и (*pl., g.* -ев); *v.t.* обкле́и|вать, -ть обо́ями.

wallaby /ˈwɒləbɪ/ *n.* кенгуру́-валла́би (*m. indecl.*).

wallet /ˈwɒlɪt/ *n.* бума́жник.

wallop /ˈwɒləp/ *v.t.* (**walloped, walloping**) (*coll.*) дуба́сить, от- (*coll.*).

wallow /ˈwɒləʊ/ *v.i.* (*in mud, water*) валя́ться (*impf.*); (*fig.*) купа́ться (*impf.*) (*в чём*); **~ in grief** упива́ться (*impf.*) свои́м го́рем.

walnut /ˈwɔːlnʌt/ *n.* гре́цкий оре́х; (*wood*) оре́х.

walrus /ˈwɔːlrəs/ *n.* морж.

waltz /wɔːls/ *n.* вальс.

■ *v.i.* танцева́ть (*impf.*) вальс.

wan /wɒn/ *adj.* (**wanner, wannest**)

бле́дный, изнурённый; **a ~ light** сла́бый/ ту́склый свет; **a ~ smile** сла́бая улы́бка.

wand /wɒnd/ *n.* волше́бная па́лочка.

wander /ˈwɒndə(r)/ *v.t.* броди́ть, стра́нствовать, скита́ться (*all impf.*) по + *d.*
■ *v.i.* 1 (*go aimlessly*) броди́ть (*impf.*); **his mind was ~ing** (*absent-mindedly*) его́ мы́сли блужда́ли; (*in delirium*) он бре́дил.
2 (*stray*) заблуди́ться (*pf.*); (*lit., fig.*) отклон|я́ться, -и́ться; **we ~ed from the track** мы сби́лись с пути́; **don't let your attention ~** не отвлека́йтесь.
■ *with advs.*: **~ about** *v.i.* броди́ть (*impf.*); **~ off** *v.i.* брести́, по- куда́-н.

wanderer /ˈwɒndərə(r)/ *n.* стра́нник, скита́лец.

wane /weɪn/ *v.i.* (*of the moon*) убыва́ть (*impf.*); (*fig., decline*) ослабева́ть (*impf.*).

wangle /ˈwæŋg(ə)l/ *v.t.* заполучи́ть (*pf.*) хи́тростью; **he ~d £5 out of me** он вы́клянчил (*coll.*) у меня́ 5 фу́нтов.

wannabe /ˈwɒnəbɪ/ *n.* (*sl.*) челове́к, мечта́ющий стать (*кем-н.*).

want /wɒnt/ *n.*
1 (*lack*) недоста́ток, отсу́тствие; **for ~ of** за неиме́нием + *g.*
2 (*need*) нужда́.
■ *v.t.* 1 (*need; require*) нужда́ться (*impf.*) в + *p.*; **I don't ~ any bread today** сего́дня мне хлеб не ну́жен; **he is ~ed by the police** его́ разы́скивает поли́ция; **you're ~ed on the telephone** вас (про́сят) к телефо́ну.
2 (*desire*) хоте́ть (*impf.*) + *g. or a. or inf.*; жела́ть (*impf.*) + *g. or inf.*; **what do you ~?** что вы хоти́те?; что вам ну́жно?; **she ~s to go away** она́ хо́чет уе́хать/уйти́; **she ~s me to go away** она́ хо́чет, что́бы я уе́хал/ ушёл.

wanting /ˈwɒntɪŋ/ *adj.* недоста́точный; **he was tried and found ~** он не вы́держал испыта́ния.

wanton /ˈwɒnt(ə)n/ *adj.* (*wilful*) своенра́вный; **~ cruelty** бессмы́сленная жесто́кость.

war /wɔː(r)/ *n.*
1 война́; **make, wage ~ on** вести́ (*det.*) войну́ с + *i.*
2 (*attr.*) вое́нный.
■ *cpds.* **~ game** *n.* (*pl., military exercises*) (вое́нные) уче́ния; (*leisure activity*) вое́нная игра́; **~head** *n.* боеголо́вка; **~like** *adj.* (*martial*) вои́нственный; **~ship** *n.* вое́нный кора́бль; **~time** *n.* вое́нное вре́мя.

ward /wɔːd/ *n.*
1 (*person under guardianship*) подопе́чный.
2 (*urban division*) о́круг.
3 (*in hospital etc.*) пала́та.
■ *v.t.*: **~ off** (*a blow*) отра|жа́ть, -зи́ть; **~ off danger** отвра|ща́ть, -ти́ть опа́сность.

warden /ˈwɔːd(ə)n/ *n.*
1 (*Br., of hostel*) коменда́нт.
2 : **traffic ~** (*Br.*) инспе́ктор, контроли́рующий соблюде́ние пра́вил парко́вки и стоя́нки (*в черте города*).

warder /ˈwɔːdə(r)/ *n.* (*Br.*) (*in prison*) надзира́тель (*m.*).

wardrobe /ˈwɔːdrəʊb/ *n.*
1 гардеро́б.
2 (*theatr.*) костюме́рная.

warehouse /ˈweəhaʊs/ *n.* (това́рный) склад.

wares /weəz/ *n. pl.* това́ры (*m. pl.*).

warfare /ˈwɔːfeə(r)/ *n.* война́.

warm /wɔːm/ *adj.* тёплый.
■ *v.t.* греть (*impf.*); (*food, water*) подогр|ева́ть, -е́ть; нагр|ева́ть, -е́ть; **~ o.s. at the fire** гре́ться (*impf.*) у ками́на/огня́.
■ *v.i.* гре́ться (*impf.*); (*of objects*) нагр|ева́ться, -е́ться; (*of people, room*) согр|ева́ться, -е́ться; (*fig.*): **he ~ed to the subject as he went on** по ме́ре расска́за он всё бо́льше воодушевля́лся; **I ~ed to(wards) him as I got to know him** чем лу́чше я его́ узнава́л, тем бо́льше расположе́ния он вызыва́л у меня́.
■ *with adv.*: **~ up** *v.t.* разогр|ева́ть, -е́ть; согр|ева́ть, -е́ть; **a fire will ~ up the room** ками́н обогре́ет ко́мнату; *v.i.* согр|ева́ться, -е́ться; **it** (*sc. the weather*) **is ~ing up** тепле́ет; **he ~ed up before the race** он сде́лал разми́нку пе́ред нача́лом соревнова́ния.
■ *cpds.* **~-hearted** *adj.* серде́чный; **~-up** *n.* разми́нка.

warmth /wɔːmθ/ *n.* теплота́.

warn /wɔːn/ *v.t.* (*caution*) предупре|жда́ть, -ди́ть; (*of danger etc.*) предостер|ега́ть, -е́чь.

warning /ˈwɔːnɪŋ/ *n.* предупрежде́ние, предостереже́ние; **give ~ of** предупре|жда́ть, -ди́ть о + *p.*
■ *adj.* предупрежда́ющий; предостерега́ющий.

warp /wɔːp/ *v.t.*
1 (*distort*) коро́бить, по-; искрив|ля́ть, -и́ть.
2 (*fig.*) иска|жа́ть, -зи́ть; **a ~ed sense of humour** (*Br.*), **humor** (*US*) извращённое чу́вство ю́мора.
■ *v.i.* коро́биться, по-.

warrant /ˈwɒrənt/ *n.* о́рдер; суде́бное распоряже́ние.
■ *v.t.* опра́вд|ывать, -а́ть.

warranty /ˈwɒrəntɪ/ *n.* гара́нтия.

warren /ˈwɒrən/ *n.* (*rabbits'*) кро́личья нора́; (*fig.*) лабири́нт.

warrior /ˈwɒrɪə(r)/ *n.* во́ин.

Warsaw /ˈwɔːsɔː/ *n.* Варша́ва.

wart /wɔːt/ *n.* борода́вка.

wary /ˈweərɪ/ *adj.* (**warier, wariest**) осторо́жный; **be ~ of** остерега́ться (*impf.*) + *g.*

was /wɒz/ *1st and 3rd pers. sg. past of* ▶ **be**

wash /wɒʃ/ *n.*
1 (*act of ~ing*) мытьё; **I must have a ~** мне на́до помы́ться/умы́ться; **she gave the floor a good ~** она́ тща́тельно вы́мыла пол.
2 (*laundry*) сти́рка.
3 (*motion of water etc.*) прибо́й.
■ *v.t.* (*cleanse with water etc.*) мыть, по-/вы́-; (*hands, face, child*) ум|ыва́ть, -ы́ть; (*clothes*) стира́ть, по-/вы́-; **~ one's hands and face** мыть, по-/вы́- ру́ки и лицо́; **~ dishes** мыть, по-/вы́- посу́ду.
■ *v.i.* (**~ o.s.**) мы́ться, по-/вы́-.
■ *with advs.*: **~ away** *v.t.* (*carry off*) см|ыва́ть, -ыть; **~ out** *v.t.* (*of colour*): **you look ~ed out** у вас утомлённый вид; **~ up** *v.t. & i.* (*Br., dishes*) мыть, по-/вы́- (посу́ду); (*US, have a wash*) мы́ться, по-/вы́-; (*on to shore*) выбра́сывать, вы́бросить на бе́рег.
■ *cpds.* **~basin, ~bowl** *nn.* ра́ковина;

~cloth *n.* (*US*) махро́вая салфе́тка для лица́; **~out** *n.* прова́л, неуда́ча.

washable /ˈwɒʃəb(ə)l/ *adj.* мо́ющийся.

washer /ˈwɒʃə(r)/ *n.* (*tech.*) прокла́дка.

washing /ˈwɒʃɪŋ/ *n.*
1 (*action*) мытьё, умыва́ние, сти́рка.
2 (*clothes*) бельё.
■ *cpds.* **~ machine** *n.* стира́льная маши́на; **~ powder** *n.* (*Br.*) стира́льный порошо́к; **~-up** *n.* (*Br.*): **do the ~-up** мыть, по-/вы́-посу́ду; **~-up liquid** *n.* (*Br.*) сре́дство для мытья́ посу́ды.

Washington /ˈwɒʃɪŋt(ə)n/ *n.* Вашингто́н.

wasp /wɒsp/ *n.* оса́.

waspish /ˈwɒspɪʃ/ *adj.* язви́тельный, ко́лкий.

wastage /ˈweɪstɪdʒ/ *n.* убы́ток, уте́чка.

waste /weɪst/ *n.*
1 (*extravagant use; failure to use*) (рас)тра́та, растра́чивание; **~ of money** пуста́я тра́та де́нег; **go, run to ~** пропада́ть (*impf.*) да́ром.
2 (*refuse, superfluous material*) отхо́ды (*m. pl.*), отбро́сы (*m. pl.*), му́сор.
■ *adj.* 1 (*superfluous*) ли́шний, нену́жный; (*rejected*) брако́ванный; **~ products** отхо́ды (*m. pl.*); **~ paper** макулату́ра.
2 (*of land*): **~ ground** невозде́ланная земля́; **~land** пусты́рь (*m.*), пу́стошь; **lay ~** опустош|а́ть, -и́ть.
■ *v.t.* 1 (*make no use of, squander*) тра́тить, ис-/по- да́ром/зря/впусту́ю; растра́|чивать, -тить; **~ one's chance** упус|ка́ть, -ти́ть слу́чай.
2 (*wear away*) изнур|я́ть, -и́ть.
■ *cpds.* **~basket** *n.* (*US*) му́сорная корзи́на; **~-paper basket** (*Br.*) *n.* корзи́на для бума́г; **~ pipe** *n.* сливна́я/водоотво́дная труба́.

wasteful /ˈweɪstfʊl/ *adj.* расточи́тельный.

waster /ˈweɪstə(r)/ *n.* (*wasteful person*) расточи́тель (*m.*); (*coll., good-for-nothing*) никуды́шный/никчёмный челове́к; безде́льник.

watch[1] /wɒtʃ/ *n.* (*alert state*) надзо́р, присмо́тр, наблюде́ние; **keep ~** (*guard*) наблюда́ть (*impf.*) (**on:** за + *i.*); **the dog keeps ~ on, over the house** соба́ка карау́лит/сторожи́т дом.
■ *v.t.* 1 (*look at*) смотре́ть (*impf.*); **he was ~ing TV** он смотре́л телеви́зор; **I ~ed him draw** я смотре́л, как он рису́ет.
2 (*keep under observation*) следи́ть (*impf.*) за + *i.*; смотре́ть (*impf.*) за + *i.*; (*be careful of*) следи́ть (*impf.*) за + *i.*; **~ your step!** (*fig.*; *also, coll.*, **~ it!**) бу́дьте осторо́жны!
3 (*guard*) сторожи́ть (*impf.*).
■ *v.i.* 1 смотре́ть, наблюда́ть, следи́ть (*all impf.*); **he ~ed for the postman** он поджида́л почтальо́на; **he ~ed over her interests** он стоя́л на стра́же её интере́сов.
2 (*be careful*): **~ how you cross the street** бу́дьте осторо́жны (*or* смотри́те) при перехо́де у́лицы.
■ *with adv.*: **~ out** *v.i.* (*beware*) остерега́ться (+ *g.*).
■ *cpds.* **~dog** *n.* (*lit.*) сторожева́я соба́ка; (*fig.*) наблюда́тель (*m.*); **~man** *n.* сто́рож; **~word** *n.* деви́з.

watch[2] /wɒtʃ/ *n.* (*timepiece*) час|ы́ (*pl., g.*, -о́в).
■ *cpds.* **~band** (*US*), **~ strap** (*Br.*) *nn.* ремешо́к для часо́в.

watchful /ˈwɒtʃfʊl/ *adj.* бди́тельный.

water /ˈwɔːtə(r)/ *n.*
1 вода́.
2 (*attr.*): **~ sports** во́дные ви́ды спо́рта.
■ *v.t.* 1 (*plants*) пол|ива́ть, -и́ть водо́й.
2 (*animals*) пои́ть, на-.
■ *v.i.* (*of eyes*) слези́ться (*impf.*); **his eyes were ~ing with the wind** от ве́тра у него́ слези́лись глаза́; **the sight of food made my mouth ~** при ви́де еды́ у меня́ потекли́ слю́нки.
■ *with adv.*: **~ down** *v.t.* (*lit.*) разб|авля́ть, -а́вить; (*fig.*) смягч|а́ть, -и́ть.
■ *cpds.* **~colour** (*US* **~color**) *n.* (*paint*) акваре́ль, акваре́льные кра́ски (*f. pl.*); (*painting*) акваре́ль, акваре́льный рису́нок; **~course** *n.* ру́сло; **~cress** *n.* кресс водяно́й; **~fall** *n.* водопа́д; **~ feature** *n.* (*in gardening*) элеме́нт аквадиза́йна (*искусственный пруд, фонтан*); **~ level** *n.* у́ровень (*m.*) воды́; **~ lily** *n.* кувши́нка; **~logged** *adj.* заболо́ченный; **~ main** *n.* водопрово́дная магистра́ль; **~mark** *n.* водяно́й знак; **~melon** *n.* арбу́з; **~proof** *adj.* непромока́емый; *n.* (*Br.*) непромока́емый плащ; **~skiing** *n.* воднолы́жный спо́рт; **~skis** *n. pl.* во́дные лы́жи (*f. pl.*); **~tight** *adj.* (*lit.*) водонепроница́емый; (*fig., of argument etc.*) неопровержи́мый; **~way** *n.* фарва́тер; **~works** *n. pl.* водопрово́дная ста́нция.

watering /ˈwɔːtərɪŋ/ *n.* поли́вка.
■ *cpd.* **~ can** *n.* ле́йка.

watery /ˈwɔːtərɪ/ *adj.* водяни́стый, жи́дкий; **~ eyes** слезя́щиеся глаза́.

watt /wɒt/ *n.* ватт.

wattage /ˈwɒtɪdʒ/ *n.* мо́щность в ва́ттах.

wave /weɪv/ *n.*
1 (*ridge of water*) волна́.
2 (*fig., temporary increase*) подъём, волна́; **crime ~** ре́зкий рост престу́пности.
3 (*phys.*) волна́; **short/medium/long ~s** коро́ткие/сре́дние/дли́нные во́лны.
4 (*undulation*): **her hair has a natural ~** у неё (от приро́ды) вью́щиеся во́лосы.
5 (*gesture*) взмах.
■ *v.t.* 1 (*move to and fro or up and down*) маха́ть, по- + *i.*; разма́хивать (*impf.*) + *i.*
2 (*express by hand-waving*): **~ goodbye** маха́ть, по- (руко́й) на проща́ние.
■ *v.i.* 1 (*move to and fro or up and down*) развева́ться (*impf.*); кача́ться (*impf.*).
2 (**~** *one's hand*) маха́ть, по-; **~ at s.o.** маха́ть, по- кому́-н.
■ *cpds.* **~band** *n.* диапазо́н волн; **~length** *n.* длина́ волны́; **he and I are on the same ~length** (*fig.*) мы с ним легко́ нахо́дим о́бщий язы́к.

waver /ˈweɪvə(r)/ *v.i.*
1 (*falter*) дрожа́ть, за-; дро́гнуть (*pf.*).
2 (*hesitate*) колеба́ться (*impf.*).

wavy /ˈweɪvɪ/ *adj.* (**wavier, waviest**) волни́стый; **~ hair** вью́щиеся во́лосы.

wax[1] /wæks/ *n.* воск; (*in the ears*) се́ра.
■ *cpds.* **~work** *n.* (*dummy*) восково́я фигу́ра; **~works** *n.* (*museum*) галере́я восковы́х фигу́р.

wax² /wæks/ *v.i.* (*of moon*) прибыва́ть (*impf.*).

waxy /'wæksɪ/ *adj.* (**waxier, waxiest**) восково́й.

way /weɪ/ *n.*
[1] (*road, path*) доро́га, путь (*m.*); (*track*) тропа́.
[2] (*route, journey*) путь (*m.*); **which is the best ~ to London?** как лу́чше прое́хать в Ло́ндон?; **we made our ~ to the dining room** мы прошли́ в столо́вую; (*with preps.*): **by ~ of London** че́рез Ло́ндон; **by the ~** (*incidentally*) кста́ти; ме́жду про́чим; **on the ~** по доро́ге; на/по пути́; **he was on his ~ to the bank** он шёл в банк; **he went out of his ~ to help me** он прояви́л нема́лое усе́рдие, что́бы помо́чь мне; **out of the ~** (*remote*) в стороне́; далеко́; (*with adv. indicating direction*): **~ back** обра́тная доро́га; **~ in** вход; **~ out** (*lit., fig.*) вы́ход.
[3] (*direction*) сторона́, направле́ние; **which ~ did they go?** в каку́ю сто́рону они́ пошли́?; **this ~** сюда́; **you can't have it both ~s** ли́бо одно́, ли́бо друго́е; что́-нибудь одно́.
[4] (*of reversible things*): **his hat is on the wrong ~ round** он наде́л шля́пу за́дом наперёд; **the picture is the wrong ~ up** карти́на пове́шена вверх нога́ми; **is the flag the right ~ up?** флаг пове́шен пра́вильно?
[5] (*distance, time*) расстоя́ние; **a long ~ off** (*away*) далеко́; **it is only a little ~ to the shop** до магази́нов совсе́м недалеко́; **all the ~** всю доро́гу; (*fig.*) по́лностью.
[6] (*a long ~*) далеко́; **~ back** (*long ago*) давны́м-давно́; **~ ahead of the others** намно́го впереди́ остальны́х.
[7] (*clear passage*) прое́зд, прохо́д; **get in the ~** меша́ть, по- (*кому*); **get out of the ~!** (прочь) с доро́ги!; **make ~ for the President!** доро́гу президе́нту!; **you are standing in the ~** вы загора́живаете доро́гу; **give ~** (*fail to resist*) подд|ава́ться, -а́ться; (*collapse*) прова́л|иваться, -и́ться; раз|рыва́ться, -орва́ться; ру́хнуть (*pf.*); **his legs gave ~** у него́ подкоси́лись но́ги; (*make concessions*) уступ|а́ть, -и́ть; (*allow precedence*) уступ|а́ть, -и́ть доро́гу.
[8] (*means*) сре́дство, ме́тод, приём.
[9] (*manner*) сре́дство, спо́соб, о́браз, ме́тод, приём; **in this ~** таки́м о́бразом; **one ~ or another** так и́ли ина́че; **in the same ~** (то́чно) так же; **I love the ~ he smiles** мне о́чень нра́вится, как он улыба́ется; **try to see it my ~** попыта́йтесь встать на моё ме́сто; **let's put it this ~** ска́жем так; **either ~** (*in either fashion*) любы́м из двух спо́собов; (*in either case*) в обо́их слу́чаях, в любо́м слу́чае; **whichever ~ you look at it** с како́й стороны́ (на э́то) ни посмотре́ть; **by ~ of an apology** в ка́честве извине́ния; (*preference*): **have it your own ~!** будь/пусть бу́дет по-ва́шему!; **have, get one's own ~** доб|ива́ться, -и́ться своего́.

[10] (*custom*) обы́чай, привы́чка; **~ of life** о́браз жи́зни; **he has a ~ of not paying his bills** у него́ есть привы́чка не плати́ть по счета́м; **that's the ~ of the world** так уж заведено́/во́дится на све́те; **mend one's ~s** испр|авля́ться, -а́виться.
[11] (*state*) положе́ние, состоя́ние.
[12] (*sense*) смысл, отноше́ние; **in a ~** в не́котором смы́сле/отноше́нии; **in some ~s** в не́которых отноше́ниях; **in no ~** ничу́ть, нико́им о́бразом; **were you involved in any ~?** бы́ли ли вы каки́м-нибудь о́бразом в э́том заме́шаны?
[13] (*scale, degree*): **in a big ~** в широ́ком/большо́м масшта́бе.
■ *cpds.* **~lay** *v.t.* подстер|ега́ть, -е́чь; **~-out** *adj.* (*coll.*) замеча́тельный, бесподо́бный; **~side** *n.* обо́чина (доро́ги); (*attr.*) придоро́жный; **fall by the ~side** (*fig.*) выбыва́ть, вы́быть из стро́я.

wayward /'weɪwəd/ *adj.* своенра́вный.

waywardness /'weɪwədnɪs/ *n.* своенра́вие.

WC (*abbr. of* **water closet**) (*Br.*) туале́т (*уборная*).

we /wi:/ *pron.* (*obj.* **us;** *poss.* **our, ours**) мы; **~ lawyers** мы, адвока́ты.

weak /wi:k/ *adj.* сла́бый.
■ *cpd.* **~-willed** *adj.* слабово́льный.

weaken /'wi:kən/ *v.t.* осл|абля́ть, -а́бить.
■ *v.i.* слабе́ть, о-.

weakling /'wi:klɪŋ/ *n.* хи́лый челове́к.

weakness /'wi:knɪs/ *n.* сла́бость, хи́лость.

wealth /welθ/ *n.* бога́тство, состоя́ние; (*fig., profusion*) оби́лие; **a ~ of detail** мно́жество подро́бностей; **a ~ of experience** богате́йший о́пыт.

wealthy /'welθɪ/ *adj.* (**wealthier, wealthiest**) бога́тый, состоя́тельный.

wean /wi:n/ *v.t.* отн|има́ть, -я́ть от груди́; (*fig.*) отуч|а́ть, -и́ть (*от чего*).

weapon /'wepən/ *n.* ору́жие; (*piece of artillery*) ору́дие.
■ *cpd.* **~s of mass destruction** *n. pl.* ору́жие ма́ссового пораже́ния/уничтоже́ния.

weaponry /'wepənrɪ/ *n.* ору́жие.

wear /weə(r)/ *n.*
[1] (*articles or type of clothing*) оде́жда, пла́тье; **beach ~** пля́жная оде́жда; (*~ing of clothes*): **a suit for everyday ~** бу́дничный/повседне́вный костю́м.
[2] (*continued use*) изно́с; **this material stands up to hard ~** э́тот материа́л прекра́сно но́сится.
■ *v.t.* (*past* **wore;** *p.p.* **worn**)
[1] (*garments or accessories*) носи́ть (*indet.*); (*put on*) над|ева́ть, -е́ть; **what shall I ~?** что мне наде́ть?; (*of hair*): **~ one's hair long** носи́ть (*indet.*) дли́нные во́лосы; **~ one's hair short** ко́ротко стри́чься (*impf.*); (*fig.*): **~ing a smile** с улы́бкой (на лице́); **~ing a frown** нахму́рившись.
[2] (*damage surface of*) ст|ира́ть, -ере́ть; (*damage by use*) трепа́ть, ис-, изн|а́шивать, -оси́ть; (*clothing*) прот|ира́ть, -ере́ть.
[3] (*produce by friction*): **you've worn a hole in your trousers** вы протёрли брю́ки до дыр.
■ *v.i.* (*past* **wore;** *p.p.* **worn**): **~ thin** изн|а́шиваться, -оси́ться; (*fig.*): **his patience wore thin** его́ терпе́ние бы́ло на исхо́де.
■ *with advs.*: **~ away** *v.t.* & *i.* ст|ира́ть(ся), -ере́ть(ся); **weather had worn away the inscription** ве́тры и дожди́ стёрли на́дпись; **the cliffs were worn away in places** ска́лы места́ми вы́ветрились; **~ down** *v.t.* & *i.* изн|а́шивать(ся), -оси́ть(ся); (*fig.*): **they wore down the enemy's resistance** они́ сломи́ли сопротивле́ние проти́вника; **~ off**

v.t. & i. ст|ира́ть(ся), -ере́ть(ся); (*fig.*) (постепе́нно) проходи́ть (*impf.*); **the novelty soon wore off** вско́ре новизна́ прошла́; **~ out** *v.t. & i.* изн|а́шивать(ся), -оси́ть(ся); (*fig.*) утом|ля́ть(ся), -и́ть(ся).

weariness /ˈwɪərɪnɪs/ *n.* утомле́ние; (*boredom*) ску́ка.

wearing /ˈweərɪŋ/ *adj.* надое́дливый.

weary /ˈwɪərɪ/ *adj.* (**wearier, weariest**)
1 (*tired*) уста́лый; **the journey made him ~** путеше́ствие его́ утоми́ло.
2 : **~ of** (*fed up with*) уста́вший от *чего*.
■ *v.t. & i.* утом|ля́ть(ся), -и́ть(ся).

weasel /ˈwiːz(ə)l/ *n.* ла́ска (*хищное животное*); **~ words** (*fig.*) двусмы́сленные слова́, двусмы́сленности (*f. pl.*).
■ *v.t.* (**weaselled, weaselling;** *US* **weaseled, weaseling**) (*insinuate*): **she ~led her way (***or* **herself) into my confidence** она́ вкра́лась/втёрлась (*coll.*) ко мне в дове́рие.

weather /ˈweðə(r)/ *n.* пого́да; **what's the ~ like?** кака́я сего́дня пого́да?; **be, feel under the ~** (*fig.*) нева́жно себя́ чу́вствовать (*impf.*); **~ forecast** прогно́з пого́ды.
■ *v.t.* (*survive*) выде́рживать, вы́держать.
■ *cpds.* **~-beaten** *adj.* обве́тренный; **~proof** *adj.* погодоусто́йчивый.

weave /wiːv/ *v.t.* (*past* **wove;** *p.p.* **woven** *or* **wove**)
1 (*thread, flowers etc.*) плести́, с-; спле|та́ть, -сти́.
2 (*make basket etc. by weaving*) плести́, с-; (*cloth*) ткать, со-.
■ *v.i.* (*past* **wove;** *p.p.* **woven** *or* **wove**) петля́ть (*impf.*), идти́ (*det.*) непрямы́м путём.

weaver /ˈwiːvə(r)/ *n.* ткач (*fem.* -и́ха).

web /web/ *n.*
1 (*also* **spider's ~**) паути́на; (*fig.*) сеть, паути́на, сплете́ние.
2 (*the Web*) (*comput.*) Всеми́рная паути́на, Сеть, Интерне́т.
■ *cpds.* **~-footed** *adj.* перепо́нчатый; **~log** *n.* (*comput.*) сетево́й журна́л, блог; **~logger** *n.* (*comput.*) бло́ггер; **~ page** *n.* (*comput.*) веб-страни́ца, страни́ца в Интерне́те; **~site** *n.* (*comput.*) сайт, веб-са́йт.

webbed /webd/ *adj.* перепо́нчатый.

wedding /ˈwedɪŋ/ *n.* сва́дьба, бракосочета́ние; (*in church*) венча́ние; **~ anniversary** годовщи́на сва́дьбы.
■ *cpds.* **~ day** *n.* день (*m.*) сва́дьбы; **~ dress** *n.* сва́дебное пла́тье; **~ ring** *n.* обруча́льное кольцо́.

wedge /wedʒ/ *n.* клин; **it's the thin end of the ~** ≈ э́то ещё (то́лько) цвето́чки(, а я́годки (бу́дут) впереди́); **a ~ of cake** кусо́к то́рта.
■ *v.t.* закреп|ля́ть, -и́ть кли́ном; **~ in** вкли́н|ивать, -ить.

Wednesday /ˈwenzdeɪ/ *n.* среда́.

weed /wiːd/ *n.* сорня́к; (*in water*) во́доросль.
■ *v.t.* (*clear of ~s*) поло́ть, вы́-.
■ *with adv.*: **~ out** *v.t.* устран|я́ть, -и́ть.
■ *cpd.* **~killer** *n.* гербици́д.

weedy /ˈwiːdɪ/ *adj.* (**weedier, weediest**) (*Br.*) (*weak-looking*) то́щий.

week /wiːk/ *n.* неде́ля; **the ~ before last** позапро́шлая неде́ля; **the ~ after next** че́рез одну́ неде́лю; **a ~ today** ро́вно че́рез неде́лю; **(on) Monday ~** (*Br.*) че́рез понеде́льник; **~ in, ~ out** (це́лыми) неде́лями; **three times a ~** три ра́за в неде́лю; **working ~** рабо́чая неде́ля.
■ *cpds.* **~day** *n.* бу́дний/рабо́чий день; **~end** *n.* коне́ц неде́ли, уи́к-э́нд/уике́нд, суббо́та и воскресе́нье.

weekly /ˈwiːklɪ/ *n.* еженеде́льник.
■ *adj.* еженеде́льный.
■ *adv.* еженеде́льно.

weep /wiːp/ *v.i.* (*past and p.p.* **wept**)
1 (*shed tears*) пла́кать, за-; (*profusely*) рыда́ть (*impf.*).
2 (*of a wound*) мо́кнуть (*impf.*).

weigh /weɪ/ *v.t.*
1 (*find or test weight of*) взве́|шивать, -сить; **~ o.s.** взве́|шиваться, -ситься; (*fig., consider, compare*) взве́|шивать, -сить.
2 (*of ~ed object: amount to*) ве́сить (*impf.*); **what do you ~?** ско́лько вы ве́сите?; како́й у вас вес?
■ *v.i.*: **~ on** дави́ть (*impf.*) на + *a.*, угнета́ть (*impf.*).
■ *with advs.*: **~ down** *v.t.* (*burden*) отяго|ща́ть, -ти́ть; **the branches were ~ed down with, by fruit** ве́тви гну́лись под тя́жестью плодо́в; (*fig., be burdensome to*) угнета́ть (*impf.*); **~ in** *v.i.* (*be ~ed before contest*) взве́|шиваться, -ситься пе́ред соревнова́нием; **~ out** *v.t.* отве́|шивать, -сить; **~ up** *v.t.* (*lit., fig.*) взве́|шивать, -сить.

weight /weɪt/ *n.*
1 (*heaviness*) вес; **3 lbs in ~** ве́сом (в) три фу́нта; **gain, put on ~** приб|авля́ть, -а́вить в ве́се; **lose ~** теря́ть, по- в ве́се; **pull one's ~** (*fig.*) выполня́ть, вы́полнить свою́ до́лю рабо́ты; **throw one's ~ about** (*fig.*) распоряжа́ться (*impf.*), ва́жничать (*impf.*).
2 (*load*) тя́жесть, груз; (*fig.*) бре́мя (*nt.*); **it was a great ~ off my mind** у меня́ сло́вно ка́мень с души́ свали́лся.
3 (*object for weighing or ~ing*) ги́ря.
4 (*importance; influence*) вес; влия́ние; авторите́т; **his opinion carries great ~** с его́ мне́нием о́чень счита́ются.
■ *v.t.* утяжел|я́ть, -и́ть.
■ *cpds.* **~lifter** *n.* штанги́ст; **~lifting** *n.* подня́тие тя́жестей.

weightlessness /ˈweɪtlɪsnɪs/ *n.* невесо́мость.

weighty /ˈweɪtɪ/ *adj.* (**weightier, weightiest**) (*heavy*) тяжёлый; (*important*) ва́жный.

weir /wɪə(r)/ *n.* плоти́на.

weird /wɪəd/ *adj.*
1 (*unearthly*) таи́нственный.
2 (*strange*) стра́нный.

weirdness /ˈwɪədnɪs/ *n.* таи́нственность; стра́нность.

welcome /ˈwelkəm/ *n.* приём; **they gave us a warm ~** они́ нас раду́шно при́няли.
■ *adj.* 1 (*gladly received*) жела́нный; **this is ~ news** э́то прия́тное изве́стие; **make s.o. (feel) ~** ока́з|ывать, -а́ть кому́-н. раду́шный приём.
2 (*pred., ungrudgingly permitted*): **you are ~ to take it** пожа́луйста, бери́те!; **you're ~ to try** пожа́луйста, (по)про́буйте; **you're ~!** (*no thanks are required*) пожа́луйста!; не́ за что!

W

■ *v.t.* приве́тствовать (*impf.*); **a welcoming smile** приве́тливая улы́бка; **I would ~ the opportunity** я был бы рад (тако́му) слу́чаю.
■ *int.* добро́ пожа́ловать!

weld /weld/ *v.t.* & *i.* сва́р|ивать(ся), -и́ть(ся).

welder /ˈweldə(r)/ *n.* сва́рщик.

welding /ˈweldɪŋ/ *n.* сва́рка.

welfare /ˈwelfeə(r)/ *n.* (*well-being*) благополу́чие; (*organized provision for social needs*) социа́льное обеспе́чение; (*US, social security*) посо́бие (по безрабо́тице *и т. п.*); **the W~ State** госуда́рство всео́бщего благосостоя́ния/благоде́нствия; ≈ социа́льное госуда́рство.

well¹ /wel/ *n.* (*for water*) коло́дец; (*for oil*) нефтяна́я сква́жина.

well² /wel/ *adj.* (**better, best**) (*usu. pred.*)
1 (*in good health*) здоро́вый; **I haven't been ~** мне нездоро́вилось, я был нездоро́в; **you don't look ~** вы пло́хо вы́глядите.
2 (*right, satisfactory*): **all's ~** всё хорошо́/прекра́сно; всё в поря́дке.
3 (*as n.*): **leave ~** (*US also* **~ enough**) **alone** от добра́ добра́ не и́щут.
4 : **(just) (as) ~** (*advisable*): **it would be (as) ~ to ask** не меша́ло бы спроси́ть.
■ *adv.* (**better, best**)
1 (*satisfactorily*) хорошо́; **I did not sleep ~** я пло́хо спал; **~ done!** здо́рово!; молоде́ц!
2 (*very, thoroughly; properly*) о́чень, весьма́; **I am ~ aware of it** я э́то прекра́сно зна́ю; **the picture was ~ worth £2,000** э́та карти́на вполне́ сто́ила двух ты́сяч фу́нтов.
3 (*considerably: esp. with advs. & preps.*) гора́здо; далеко́; **~ past 40** далеко́ за со́рок.
4 (*favourably*): **~ off** бога́тый; **I wish him ~** я жела́ю ему́ благополу́чия.
5 (*successfully*) уда́чно, благополу́чно; **all went ~** всё прошло́ благополу́чно.
6 (*wisely*) разу́мно, пра́вильно; **you would be ~ advised to stay** с ва́шей стороны́ бы́ло бы благоразу́мно оста́ться.
7 (*indeed*): **it may ~ be true** (э́то) вполне́ возмо́жно.
8 : **as ~** (*in addition*) то́же; та́кже; вдоба́вок; сверх того́; **there was meat as ~ as fish** там была́ не то́лько ры́ба, но и мя́со.
■ *int.* ну; ну а; (*expr. surprise*) ну!; вот те ра́з!; **~, ~!** ну и ну!; (*expr. expectation*): **~ then?** ну как?; (*impatient interrogation*): **~, what do you want?** ну, так чего́ вы хоти́те?; (*agreement*): **very ~, I'll do it** хорошо́, я сде́лаю э́то; (*concession*): **~, you can come if you like** что ж(е), е́сли хоти́те, приходи́те; (*resignation*): **oh ~, it can't be helped** (ну) что ж, ничего́ не поде́лаешь; (*summing up*) ну вот; **~ then** (ну) так вот.
■ *cpds.* **~-balanced** *adj.* уравнове́шенный; **a ~-balanced diet** сбаланси́рованная дие́та; **~-behaved** *adj.* (благо)воспи́танный; **~-being** *n.* благополу́чие; **~-disposed** *adj.* благожела́тельный; **~-dressed** *adj.* хорошо́ оде́тый; **~-educated** *adj.* хорошо́ образо́ванный; **~-fed** *adj.* сы́тый; (*of animals*) отко́рмленный; **~-heeled** *adj.* (*coll.*) состоя́тельный; **~-informed** *adj.* зна́ющий; **~-kept** *adjs.* содержа́щийся в поря́дке; **~-known** *adj.* (*of person*) изве́стный; (*of facts*) (обще)изве́стный; **~-made** *adj.* хорошо сде́ланный; **~-mannered** *adj.* воспи́танный; **~-meaning** *adj.* де́йствующий из лу́чших побужде́ний; **~-off** *adj.* состоя́тельный; **~-paid** *adj.* хорошо́ опла́чиваемый; **~-read** *adj.* начи́танный; **~-thought-out** *adj.* проду́манный; **~-timed** *adj.* то́чно/хорошо́ рассчи́танный; (*words/act*) ска́занный/сде́ланный кста́ти; **~-to-do** *adj.* состоя́тельный; **~-wisher** *n.* доброжела́тель (*fem.* -ница); **~-worn** *adj.* (*lit.*) поно́шенный; (*fig., trite*) изби́тый.

wellington /ˈwelɪŋt(ə)n/ *n.* (*also* **~ boot**) (*Br.*) рези́новый сапо́г.

Welsh /welʃ/ *n.*
1 : **the ~** (*pl., people*) валли́йцы (*m. pl.*), у́льсцы (*m. pl.*).
2 (*language*) валли́йский язы́к.
■ *adj.* валли́йский, у́льский.

wench /wentʃ/ *n.* (*arch. or joc.*) де́вка.

wend /wend/ *v.t.*: **~ one's way** держа́ть (*impf.*) путь.

went /went/ *past of* ▸ **go**

wept /wept/ *past and p.p. of* ▸ **weep**

were /wɜː/ *2nd pers. sg. past, pl. past, and past subj. of* ▸ **be**

weren't /wɜːnt/ *neg. of* ▸ **were**

west /west/ *n.* за́пад; **to the ~ of** к за́паду от + *g.*; **the W~** (*pol.*) За́пад.
■ *adv.* на за́пад; к за́паду.
■ *adj.* за́падный; **W~ Germany** (*hist.*) За́падная Герма́ния; **W~ Indian** *adj.* вест-и́ндский; *n.* вы́ходец из (*or* жи́тель (*m.*)) стран(– острово́в) Кари́бского бассе́йна; **W~ Indies** *n. pl.* Вест-И́ндия.

westerly /ˈwestəlɪ/ (*wind*) за́падный ве́тер.
■ *adj.* за́падный.

western /ˈwest(ə)n/ *n.* ве́стерн.
■ *adj.* за́падный.

westerner /ˈwestənə(r)/ *n.* жи́тель (*m.*) (*fem.* -ница) за́пада.

westernize /ˈwestənaɪz/ *v.t.* внедр|я́ть, -и́ть за́падный о́браз жи́зни в + *a.*, подв|ерга́ть, -е́ргнуть вестерниза́ции.

westward /ˈwestwəd/ *adj.* за́падный.
■ *adv.* (*also* **~s**) на запад; к за́паду, в за́падном направле́нии.

wet /wet/ *adj.* (**wetter, wettest**)
1 (*soaked*) мо́крый; **~ through** промо́кший наскво́зь/до ни́тки; **get ~** пром|ока́ть, -о́кнуть; **~ suit** гидрокостю́м.
2 (*rainy*) дождли́вый.
3 (*damp*) сыро́й, вла́жный; **~ paint** све́жая кра́ска.
4 (*Br. coll., inept*) вя́лый.
■ *v.t.* (**wetting;** *past and p.p.* **~** *or* **wetted**) (*make* **~**) мочи́ть, на-; **the child ~ itself** ребёнок обмочи́лся/опи́сался (*coll.*); **the child ~ its bed** ребёнок описал посте́ль.
■ *cpd.* **~ blanket** *n.* (*fig., coll.*) зану́да (*c.g.*), ну́дный челове́к.

whack /wæk/ *n.* (*blow*) уда́р.
■ *v.t.* (*coll., hit*) бить, по-; **I feel ~ed** (*Br., exhausted*) я чу́вствую себя́ вконе́ц разби́тым.

whale /weɪl/ *n.*
1 кит.
2 : **we had a ~ of a time** мы потряса́юще/здо́рово провели́ вре́мя.

whaler /ˈweɪlə(r)/ *n.* (*man*) китобо́й; (*ship*)

китобо́ец, китобо́йное су́дно.

wharf /wɔ:f/ *n.* (*pl.* **wharves** *or* **wharfs**) при́стань.

what /wɒt/ *pron.*
[1] (*interrog.*) что?; **~'s that?** что э́то (тако́е)?; **~ (did you say)?** что (вы сказа́ли)?; что?; **~ is it?; ~'s the matter?** в чём де́ло?; **~ is she like?** (*in appearance*) как она́ вы́глядит?; (*in character*) кака́я она́?; **~'s the date?** како́е сего́дня число́?; **~ is his name?** как его́ зову́т?; **~ do you think?** как вы ду́маете?; **~ about money?** а де́ньги?; **~ about a walk?** не пройти́сь ли нам?; **~ for?** заче́м?; **~ are you talking about?** о чём вы говори́те?; **~ if ...?** а что, е́сли...?
[2] (*rel.*) (то), что; **and, ~ is more ...** к тому́ же...; **he is sorry for ~ happened** он жале́ет о случи́вшемся; **tell me ~ you remember** расскажи́те мне всё, что по́мните; **(do) you know ~?;** зна́ете что?; **I'll tell you ~!** вот что я вам скажу́!; **~ with one thing and another** то из-за одного́, то из-за друго́го.
[3] (*whatever*): **I will do ~ I can** я сде́лаю (всё), что могу́.
■ *adj.* [1] (*interrog.*) како́й; како́в?; **~ colour are his eyes?** како́го цве́та у него́ глаза́?; **~ kind of (a)** како́й; **~ time is it?** кото́рый час?; **~'s the use?** како́й смысл?
[2] (*rel.*): **~ little he published** то немно́гое, что он опубликова́л; **I gave him ~ money I had** я о́тдал ему́ все де́ньги, каки́е у меня́ бы́ли.
[3] (*exclamatory*): **~ a fool he is!** како́й дура́к!; **~ a pity/shame!** кака́я жа́лость/доса́да; **~ lovely soup!** како́й прекра́сный суп.
■ *cpds.* **~-d'ye-call-it, ~'s it** *nn.* как его́; э́то са́мое... .

whatever /wɒt'evə(r)/ *pron.*
[1] (*anything that*): **do ~ you like** де́лайте, что хоти́те.
[2] (*no matter what*): **~ happens** что бы ни случи́лось.
[3] (*what ever*): **~ are you doing?** что вы там де́лаете?
■ *adj.* [1] (*any*): **he took ~ food he could find** он забра́л всю еду́, каку́ю то́лько мог найти́.
[2] (*no matter what*) како́й/како́в бы ни.
[3] (*emphasising neg. or interrog.*): **there is no doubt ~ of his guilt** в его́ вино́вности нет ни мале́йшего сомне́ния.

wheat /wi:t/ *n.* пшени́ца.

wheedle /'wi:d(ə)l/ *v.t.*: **~ sth. out of s.o.** выпра́шивать, вы́просить что-н. у кого́-н.

wheel /wi:l/ *n.* колесо́; (*steering* **~**) руль (*m.*); **he was at the ~** (*driving*) **for 12 hours** он сиде́л за рулём 12 часо́в; (*potter's* **~**) круг.
■ *v.t.* ката́ть, вози́ть (*both indet.*); кати́ть (*det.*), везти́ (*det.*).
■ *v.i.* кружи́ть(ся) (*impf.*); **he ~ed round to face me** он кру́то поверну́лся ко мне.
■ *cpds.* **~barrow** *n.* та́чка; **~chair** *n.* инвали́дная коля́ска.

wheeler-dealer /'wi:lə(r)/ *n.* (*coll.*) махина́тор.

wheeze /wi:z/ *v.i.* сопе́ть (*impf.*).

wheezy /'wi:zɪ/ *adj.* хри́плый.

whelk /welk/ *n.* (*mollusc*) брюхоно́гий моллю́ск.

when /wen/ *adv.*
[1] (*interrog.*) когда́; **say ~!** (*to s.o. pouring a drink*) скажи́те, когда́ дово́льно.
[2] (*rel.*): **there have been occasions ~** бы́ли слу́чаи, когда́...; **the day ~ I met you** день, когда́ я вас встре́тил.
■ *with preps.*: **~ do you have to be there by** к како́му часу вам ну́жно там быть?; **~ does it date from?** к како́му вре́мени э́то отно́сится?; **since ~?** как давно́?; **till, until ~?** до каки́х пор?
■ *conj.* когда́; как (то́лько); по́сле того́ как; тогда́, когда́; (*by the time that*) пока́; **~ she saw him, she ...** когда́ она́ уви́дела его́, она́...; (*and then*) и тогда́; как (вдруг); да вдруг; (*although*) хотя́; **they won ~ everyone thought they would lose** они́ вы́играли, хотя́ все ду́мали, что они́ проигра́ют.

whence /wens/ *adv. & conj.* (*liter.*) (*interrog.*) (*also* **from ~**) отку́да; **~ this confusion?** отчего́ тако́е смяте́ние?; (*rel.*): **return it ~ it came** верни́те э́то по принадле́жности.

whenever /wen'evə(r)/ *adv. & conj.*
[1] (*at whatever time*) когда́; **come ~ you like** приходи́те, когда́ уго́дно.
[2] (*on every occasion when*) ка́ждый/вся́кий раз, когда́.

where /weə(r)/ *adv.*
[1] (*direct or indirect question*) где; (*whither*) куда́; **~ did he hit you?** куда́ он вас уда́рил?
[2] (*rel.*) где; **the hotel ~ we stopped** гости́ница, в кото́рой мы останови́лись; (*without antecedent*) там, где; **that's ~ you're wrong** вот где вы ошиба́етесь.
■ *with prep.*: **~ does he come from?** отку́да он (ро́дом)?

whereabouts /'weərəbaʊts/ *n.* местонахожде́ние.
■ *adv.* где; **~ did you find it?** где вы э́то нашли́?; (*whither*) куда́.

whereas /weər'æz/ *conj.* тогда́ как; а.

whereby /weə'baɪ/ *adv.* (*liter.*) (*by means of which*) посре́дством кото́рого; (*according to which*): **there is a rule ~ ...** существу́ет пра́вило, согла́сно кото́рому... .

whereupon /weərə'pɒn/ *adv.* (*and then*) по́сле чего́; всле́дствие чего́; тогда́.

wherever /weər'evə(r)/ *adj. & conj.* где; куда́; **sit ~ you like** сади́тесь, куда́ уго́дно; **~ he goes he makes friends** где бы он ни оказа́лся, он приобрета́ет друзе́й.

whet /wet/ *v.t.* (**whetted, whetting**) (*fig.*) возбу|жда́ть, -ди́ть.

whether /'weðə(r)/ *conj.*
[1] (*introducing indirect question*) ли; **I asked ~ he was coming with us** я спроси́л, пойдёт ли он с на́ми; **the question is ~ to go or stay** вопро́с в том — идти́ и́ли остава́ться.
[2] (*introducing alternative hypotheses*): **~ you like it or not, I shall go** нра́вится вам э́то и́ли нет, а я пойду́.

which /wɪtʃ/ *pron.*
[1] (*interrog.*) како́й, кото́рый; (*of person*) кто; **~ is the right answer?** како́й отве́т

пра́вильный?; ~ **of these bags is the heavier?** какая из этих сумок тяжелее?; **I cannot tell ~ is ~** (*of persons*) я никак не могу разобраться, кто из них кто.
2 (*rel.*) который; **the book (~) I was reading has gone** книга, которую я читал, пропала.
■ *adj.* 1 (*direct or indirect question*) какой; ~ **shoes are yours?** какие (тут) туфли ваши?; ~ **film do you mean?** какой фильм вы имеете в виду?
2 (*rel.*) какой; который; **ten years, during ~ time he spoke to nobody** десять лет, в течение которых он ни с кем не говорил.

whichever /wɪtʃ'evə(r)/ *pron.* & *adj.* какой бы ни, какой угодно; **take ~ book you like** берите какую угодно книгу; ~ **way you go, you'll have plenty of time** какой бы дорогой вы ни пошли, вы вполне успеете; ~ **way you look at it** с какой стороны (на это) ни посмотреть.

whiff /wɪf/ *n.* дуновение; (*pleasant smell*) лёгкий аромат; (*Br., unpleasant smell*) душок.

while /waɪl/ *n.* (какое-то) время; **after a ~** через некоторое время; **I am going away for a ~** я уезжаю на некоторое время; **a long, good ~ ago** давным-давно; **a short ~ ago, back** недавно; **it may take some (*or* quite a) ~** возможно, что это будет не скоро; **once in a ~** изредка; **it was well worth ~** это стоило затраченного времени/труда; **I will make it worth his ~** я постараюсь, чтобы он не разочаровался.
■ *v.t.*: ~ **away** коротать, с- (*время*).
■ *conj.* (*also* **whilst**)
1 (*during the time that*) пока; в то время, как; **be good ~ I'm away!** веди себя хорошо, пока меня нет дома; ~ **asleep** во сне; ~ **in Paris I visited the Louvre** во время (моего) пребывания в Париже, я посетил Лувр.
2 (*whereas*) а; тогда как.

whilst /waɪlst/ = **while** *conj.*

whim /wɪm/ *n.* прихоть, каприз.

whimper /'wɪmpə(r)/ *n.* (*of person*) хныканье; (*of dog*) поскуливание.
■ *v.i.* (*of person*) хныкать (*impf.*); (*of dog*) скулить (*impf.*).

whimsical /'wɪmzɪk(ə)l/ *adj.* (*fanciful*) причудливый; (*capricious*) капризный.

whine /waɪn/ *v.i.* скулить (*impf.*) (*also fig.*).

whinge /wɪndʒ/ *v.i.* (**whingeing**) (*Br. coll.*) скулить (*impf.*) (*жаловаться*).

whinny /'wɪnɪ/ *n.* (*gentle*) тихое ржание; (*joyful*) радостное ржание.
■ *v.i.* (*gently*) тихо ржать, за-; (*joyfully*) радостно ржать, за-.

whip /wɪp/ *n.*
1 (*short*) плеть, плётка; (*long*) кнут.
2 (*party official*) секретарь (*m.*) парламентской фракции.
■ *v.t.* (**whipped, whipping**)
1 (*flog*) пороть, вы-; хлестать, от-; сечь, вы-.
2 (*beat into froth*) взб|ивать, -ить; **~ped cream** взбитые сливки.
3 (*coll., move rapidly*): **as I entered he ~ped the papers into a drawer** когда я вошёл, он быстро сунул бумаги в ящик (стола).
■ *with adv.*: ~ **up** *v.t.* (*beat into froth*) взб|ивать, -ить; (*fig., stimulate*): ~ **up enthusiasm** возбу|ждать, -дить энтузиазм; (*coll., improvise*) делать, с- на скорую руку.
■ *cpds.* **~lash** *n.* (*injury*) травма шеи в результате резкого движения (*чаще всего в автоаварии*); **~-round** *n.* (*Br. coll., collection*) сбор денег (на благотворительные цели).

whir /wɜː(r)/ = **whir(r)**

whirl /wɜːl/ *n.*
1 (*revolving movement*) кружение; (*fig.*) смятение; **my head is in a ~** у меня голова идёт кругом.
2 (*bustling activity*) водоворот, вихрь (*m.*).
■ *v.t.* & *i.* вертеть(ся) (*impf.*); кружить(ся) (*impf.*).
■ *cpds.* **~pool** *n.* водоворот; **~wind** *n.* вихрь (*m.*).

whir(r) /wɜː(r)/ *v.i.* (**whirred, whirring**) жужжать (*impf.*).

whisk /wɪsk/ *n.* мутовка.
■ *v.t.* взб|ивать, -ить.
■ *v.i.* (*move briskly*) мчаться, по-.
■ *with advs.*: ~ **away,** ~ **off** *vv.t.* (*carry off quickly*) быстро ун|осить, -ести; (*lead off quickly*) быстро ув|одить, -ести.

whisker /'wɪskə(r)/ *n.* (*pl., facial hair*) бакенбард|ы (*pl., g.* —); (*of animal*) усы (*m. pl.*).

whisky /'wɪskɪ/ (*US* **whiskey**) *n.* виски (*nt. indecl.*).

whisper /'wɪspə(r)/ *n.* шёпот; **he spoke in a ~** он говорил шёпотом.
■ *v.i.* шептаться (*impf.*).
■ *v.t.* шептать, про-.

whistle /'wɪs(ə)l/ *n.*
1 (*sound*) свист.
2 (*instrument*) свисток.
■ *v.t.* (*tune*) насв|истывать, -истеть.
■ *v.i.* свистеть, про-, свистнуть; **the train ~d as it entered the tunnel** при входе в туннель поезд дал гудок.
■ *cpd.* **~-blower** *n.* доносчи|к (*fem.* -ца).

Whit /wɪt/ *adj.*: ~ **Monday** Духов день; ~ **Sunday** = **Whitsun**

white /waɪt/ *n.*
1 (*colour*) белый цвет; белизна.
2 (*of the eyes, an egg*) белок.
3 (*racial type*) белокожий, белый.
■ *adj.* белый; **grow ~** белеть, по-; ~ **coffee** (*Br.*) кофе с молоком; ~ **goods** (*domestic appliances*) бытовые электроприборы; **the W~ House** Белый дом; **a ~ lie** ложь во спасение.
■ *cpds.* **~-collar** *adj.*: **~-collar worker** *n.* служащий; **~wash** *n.* побелка; (*fig.*) обеление, оправдание; *v.t.* белить, по-; (*fig.*) обел|ять, -ить; оправд|ывать, -ать; **~-water rafting** *n.* сплав вниз по горному потоку.

whiten /'waɪt(ə)n/ *v.t.* белить, по-.

Whitsun /'wɪts(ə)n/ *n.* (*Whit Sunday*) Троицын день; Троица; *see also* ▸ **Whit**

whittle /'wɪt(ə)l/ *v.t.* (*wood*) строгать, вы-.
■ *with adv.*: ~ **away** *v.t.* (*fig.*) ум|еньшать, -еньшить; **his savings were ~d away** его сбережения постепенно иссякли.

whiz(z) /wɪz/ *v.i.* (**whizzed, whizzing**) прон|оситься, -естись со свистом.
■ *cpd.* **~-kid** *n.* (*coll.*) ≈ восходящая звезда

W

(*о молодом человеке*).

who /hu:/ *pron.* (*obj.* **whom** *or informally* **who;** *poss.* **whose**)
1 (*interrog.*) кто; **~ is he?** кто он (такой)?
2 (*rel.*) который, какой, кто; **people ~ live in the city** люди, которые живут в городе; **those ~** те, кто/которые; **anyone ~** всякий, кто; **Mr. X, ~ is my uncle** г-н X, мой дядя.

whoever /hu:'evə(r)/ *pron.*
1 (*anyone who*) кто бы ни, кто угодно; **~ comes will be welcome** кто бы ни пришёл, будет желанным гостем.
2 (*who ever*) кто только; **~ would have thought it?** кто бы мог подумать?

whole /həʊl/ *n.* (*single entity*) целое; (*totality*) все, всё; **taken as a ~** в целом; **on the ~** в общем (и целом); в основном.
■ *adj.* 1 (*intact; undamaged*) целый, невредимый.
2 (*in one piece*) целиком.
3 (*complete*) весь, целый, цельный; **he ate a ~ chicken** он съел целого цыплёнка; **the ~ world** весь мир.
■ *cpds.* **~hearted** *adj.* беззаветный; **~heartedly** *adv.* от всей души; **~sale** *n.* оптовая торговля; *adj.* оптовый; (*fig.*) массовый; *adv.* оптом; (*fig.*) в массовом масштабе; **~saler** *n.* оптовик.

wholesome /'həʊlsəm/ *adj.*
1 (*promoting health*) полезный.
2 (*sound*) здравый.

wholly /'həʊllɪ/ *adv.* полностью; целиком.

whom /hu:m/ *obj. of* ▶ **who**

whopper /'wɒpə(r)/ *n.* (*coll.*) громадина.

whopping /'wɒpɪŋ/ (*coll.*) *adj.* (*also* **~ great**) огромный.

whore /hɔ:(r)/ *n.* (*coll.*) шлюха.

whose /hu:z/ *pron.* (*interrog.*) чей; **~ partner are you?** чей вы партнёр?; (*rel.*) которого; **the people ~ house we bought** люди, у которых мы купили дом.

why /waɪ/ *adv., conj.* (*for what reason?*) почему; (*for what purpose?*) зачем; **~ do you ask?** почему вы спрашиваете? **why hurry?** зачем спешить? **why not?** а почему бы нет?; **I don't know why he's late** я не знаю, почему он опаздывает; **the reasons ~ ...** причины, по которым... .

wick /wɪk/ *n.* фитиль (*m.*).

wicked /'wɪkɪd/ *adj.* (*depraved*) грешный; (*roguish*) лукавый.

wicker /'wɪkə(r)/ *adj.*: **~ chair** плетёное кресло.
■ *cpd.* **~work** *n.* плетение.

wicket /'wɪkɪt/ *n.*
1 **(~ gate)** калитка.
2 (*at cricket*) ворот|ца (*pl., g.* -ец).
■ *cpd.* **~keeper** *n.* ловящий мяч за воротцами (*в крикете*).

wide /waɪd/ *adj.*
1 широкий; (*in measuring*) шириной в + *a.*, **the table is 3 feet ~** ширина стола 3 фута.
2 (*extensive*) широкий, обширный; **~ interests** широкий круг интересов.
3 (*off target*): **his answer was ~ of the mark** он попал пальцем в небо.
■ *adv.* 1 (*to full extent*): **open the door ~!** откройте дверь настежь!; **he is ~ awake** у него сна ни в одном глазу; **his mouth was ~ open** рот его был широко раскрыт.
2 (*off target*) мимо цели.
■ *cpds.* **~-angle** *adj.*: **~-angle lens** широкоугольный объектив; **~-eyed** *adj.* (*surprised*) изумлённый; (*naive*) наивный; **~ open** *adj.* открытый; **~-ranging** *adj.* (*intellect etc.*) разносторонний; **~screen** *adj.*: **~screen film** широкоэкранный фильм; **~spread** *adj.* (широко) распространённый.

widely /'waɪdlɪ/ *adv.*
1 (*to a large extent*) широко; **~ differing opinions** резко расходящиеся мнения.
2 (*over a large area*) далеко; **~ scattered** разбросанный; **it is ~ believed that ...** многие считают, что... .

widen /'waɪd(ə)n/ *v.t.* & *i.* расш|ирять(ся), -ирить(ся).

widow /'wɪdəʊ/ *n.* вдова.
■ *v.t.* делать, с- вдовой.

widower /'wɪdəʊə(r)/ *n.* вдовец.

width /wɪtθ/ *n.* ширина.

wield /wi:ld/ *v.t.* (*hold*) держать (*impf.*) в руках; **~ authority** пользоваться (*impf.*) властью.

wife /waɪf/ *n.* (*pl.* **wives**) жена.

wig /wɪg/ *n.* парик.

wiggle /'wɪg(ə)l/ *v.t.* (*ears, toes*) шевелить, по- + *i.*; **she ~s her hips** она покачивает бёдрами.

wiggly /'wɪglɪ/ *adj.* (**wigglier, wiggliest**): **a ~ line** волнистая линия; **a ~ tooth** шатающийся зуб.

wigwam /'wɪgwæm/ *n.* вигвам.

wild /waɪld/ *n.*
1 (**~** *state*): **this animal is not found in the ~** это животное не встречается в дикой природе.
2 (*pl., uncultivated tract*) дикое место; **in the ~s of Africa** на диких просторах Африки.
■ *adj.* 1 (*not domesticated; not cultivated*) дикий; **~ boar** кабан; **~ flower** дикорастущий цветок; **~ goose chase** (*fig.*) бессмысленное предприятие.
2 (*not civilized*) дикий.
3 (*of scenery: desolate*) дикий.
4 (*unrestrained, disorderly*) необузданный, бурный; **she lets her children run ~** она разрешает детям бегать без присмотра; **he let the garden run ~** он запустил сад.
5 (*tempestuous*) бурный, буйный.
6 (*excited, passionate*) вне себя; **they were ~ about him** они были в (диком) восторге от него.
7 (*reckless; ill-considered*) безумный; **a ~ scheme** безумная затея.
■ *cpds.* **~ card** *n.* (*comput.*) универсальный символ; **~fire** *n.*: **the news spread like ~fire** новость распространилась с молниеносной быстротой.

wilderness /'wɪldənɪs/ *n.* дикая местность; пустыня.

wildlife /'waɪldlaɪf/ *n.* живая природа; **~ sanctuary** заповедник.

wiles /waɪlz/ *n. pl.* ухищрения (*nt. pl.*).

wilful /'wɪlfʊl/ (*US* **willful**) *adj.*
1 (*of person*) своенравный, своевольный.
2 (*intentional*) умышленный.

wilfulness /'wɪlfʊlnɪs/ (*US* **willfulness**) *n.*

своенра́вие, своево́лие; преднаме́ренность.

will[1] /wɪl/ *n.*
1 (*faculty; determination, desire*) во́ля; **free ~** свобо́да во́ли; **against my ~** про́тив моего́ жела́ния; **the ~ to live** во́ля к жи́зни.
2 (*document of bequeathal*) завеща́ние.
■ *v.t.* 1 (*compel*) заст|авля́ть, -а́вить; **he ~ed himself to stay awake** (уси́лием во́ли) он заста́вил себя́ бо́дрствовать.
2 : **God ~ing** е́сли на то бу́дет во́ля Бо́жья.
■ *cpd.* **~power** *n.* си́ла во́ли.

will[2] /wɪl/ *v.t. & i.* (*3rd pers. sg. pres.* **will**) (*see also* ▸ **would**)
1 (*expr. future*): **he ~ be president** он бу́дет президе́нтом; **he said he would be back by 3** он сказа́л, что вернётся к трём; **I won't do it again** я бо́льше не бу́ду.
2 (*expr. willingness*): **I ~ come with you** я пойду́ с ва́ми; **he won't help me** он не хо́чет мне помо́чь; **the window won't open** окно́ (ника́к) не открыва́ется; **pass the salt, ~ (*or* would) you?** бу́дьте любе́зны, переда́йте соль.
3 (*expr. inevitability*): **boys ~ be boys** ма́льчики есть ма́льчики; **accidents ~ happen** вся́кое быва́ет.
4 (*expr. habit*): **he would often come to see me** он ча́сто заходи́л ко мне.
5 (*expr. surmise, probability*): **she would have been about 60 when she died** ей бы́ло, должно́ быть, о́коло шести́десяти, когда́ она́ умерла́.

willing /ˈwɪlɪŋ/ *adj.*
1 (*readily disposed*) скло́нный, располо́женный; **I am ~ to admit ...** я гото́в призна́ть... .
2 (*readily given or shown*) доброво́льный.

willingness /ˈwɪlɪŋnɪs/ *n.* гото́вность, жела́ние.

willow /ˈwɪləʊ/ *n.* и́ва.

willy /ˈwɪlɪ/ *n.* (*Br. coll.*) (мужско́й) член.

willy-nilly /wɪlɪˈnɪlɪ/ *adv.* во́лей-нево́лей.

wilt /wɪlt/ *v.i.* (*lit., fig.*) ни́кнуть, по-.

wily /ˈwaɪlɪ/ *adj.* (**wilier, wiliest**) хи́трый.

wimp /wɪmp/ *n.* (*coll.*) слизня́к.

win /wɪn/ *n.* (*gain*) вы́игрыш; (*victory*) побе́да.
■ *v.t.* (**winning;** *past and p.p.* **won**)
1 (*be victorious in*) выи́грывать, вы́играть; **the Allies won the war** сою́зники вы́играли войну́; **who won the election?** кто победи́л на вы́борах?; **~ a race** побе|жда́ть, -ди́ть в забе́ге.
2 (*gain*) выи́грывать, вы́играть; **he won £50 from me** он вы́играл у меня́ 50 фу́нтов; **~ a medal** завоёв|ывать, -а́ть меда́ль; **~ s.o.'s confidence** заслу́ж|ивать, -и́ть чьё-н. дове́рие.
■ *v.i.* (**winning;** *past and p.p.* **won**): **~ by 4 goals to 1** вы́играть (*pf.*) со счётом 4:1.
■ *with advs.*: **~ back** *v.t.* оты́гр|ывать, -а́ть; **~ over, ~ round** *vv.t.* угов|а́ривать, -ори́ть.

wince /wɪns/ *v.i.* содрог|а́ться, -ну́ться.

winch /wɪntʃ/ *n.* лебёдка.
■ *v.t.* подн|има́ть, -я́ть с по́мощью лебёдки.

wind[1] /wɪnd/ *n.*
1 ве́тер.
2 (*breath*) дыха́ние; **get back one's ~** отдыша́ться (*pf.*); **knock the ~ out of s.o.** (*fig.*) ошелом|ля́ть, -и́ть кого́-н.
3 (*Br., in bowels etc.*) га́зы (*m. pl.*) (*в желу́дке/кише́чнике*); **break ~** по́ртить, ис- во́здух.
4 (**~** *instruments*) духовы́е (инструме́нты) (*m. pl.*).
■ *v.t.* (*deprive of breath*): **the blow ~ed him** от уда́ра у него́ дух перехвати́ло.
■ *cpds.* **~fall** *n.* (*of money*) непредви́денный дохо́д; **~ farm** *n.* райо́н обслу́живания ветряны́х электроста́нций; **~mill** *n.* ветряна́я ме́льница; **~pipe** *n.* дыха́тельное го́рло; **~screen** (*US* **~shield**) *nn.* лобово́е/ветрово́е стекло́; **~screen wiper** стеклоочисти́тель (*m.*), «дво́рник»; **~swept** *adj.* (*of terrain*) откры́тый ве́тру; (*of hair etc.*) растрёпанный.

wind[2] /waɪnd/ *v.t.* (*past and p.p.* **wound**)
1 (*cause to encircle, curve or curl*): **she wound the wool into a ball** она́ смота́ла шерсть в клубо́к; **a rope was wound round the pole** на шест была́ намо́тана верёвка.
2 (*fold, wrap*) уку́т|ывать, -ать.
3 (*rotate*) верте́ть (*impf.*).
4 : **~ a clock** зав|оди́ть, -ести́ часы́.
■ *v.i.* (*past and p.p.* **wound**) (*twist*) ви́ться (*impf.*); извива́ться (*impf.*); **the path ~s up the hill** доро́жка/тропи́нка зме́йкой поднима́ется в го́ру; **~ing staircase** винтова́я ле́стница.
■ *with advs.*: **~ down** *v.t.* опус|ка́ть, -ти́ть; **~ up** *v.t.*: **~ up a clock** зав|оди́ть, -ести́ часы́; (*Br., tease*) дразни́ть (*impf.*); (*fig., settle*) заверш|а́ть, -и́ть; **I am ~ing up my affairs** я свора́чиваю свои́ дела́; (*fig., terminate*) зак|а́нчивать, -о́нчить.

window /ˈwɪndəʊ/ *n.*
1 окно́; (*dim., also cashier's etc.*) око́шко; **(shop ~)** витри́на; (*in full* **~ of opportunity**) (ре́дкая) возмо́жность.
2 (*comput.*) окно́.
■ *cpds.* **~ box** *n.* (нару́жный) я́щик для цвето́в; **~ cleaner** *n.* мо́йщик о́кон; **~ ledge** *n.* (нару́жный) подоко́нник; **~pane** *n.* око́нное стекло́; **~ seat** *n.* дива́н у окна́; **~-shopping** *n.* рассма́тривание/разгля́дывание витри́н; **~ sill** *n.* подоко́нник.

windsurfer /ˈwɪndsɜːfə(r)/ *n.* виндсёрфинги́ст.

windsurfing /ˈwɪndsɜːfɪŋ/ *n.* виндсёрфинг.

windy /ˈwɪndɪ/ *adj.* (**windier, windiest**)
1 (*characterized by wind*) ве́треный.
2 (*exposed to wind*) обдува́емый ве́тром.

wine /waɪn/ *n.* (виногра́дное) вино́.
■ *cpds.* **~ bar** *n.* ви́нный бар; **~ glass** *n.* бока́л, рю́мка; **~grower** *n.* виноде́л; **~-growing** *n.* виноде́лие; *adj.* виноде́льческий; **~ list** *n.* ка́рта вин; **~ tasting** *n.* дегуста́ция вин.

wing /wɪŋ/ *n.*
1 (*of bird, building, organization, car*) крыло́.
2 (*pl., of stage*) кули́сы (*f. pl.*); **wait in the ~s** (*fig.*) ждать (*impf.*) своего́ ча́са.

winger /ˈwɪŋə(r)/ *n.* (*player*) кра́йний напада́ющий.

wink /wɪŋk/ *n.* мига́ние; (*as signal, joke*) подми́гивание; **I didn't sleep a ~** я всю ночь не сомкну́л глаз.
■ *v.i.*: **~ at s.o.** подми́г|ивать, -ну́ть кому́-н.;

W

(*of star, light etc.*) мигáть (*impf.*).

winner /'wɪnə(r)/ *n.* победи́тель (*fem.* -ница); (*successful thing*) вéрное дéло.

winning /'wɪnɪŋ/ *adj.*
1 (*victorious*) вы́игравший.
2 (*bringing about a win*) вы́игрышный.
3 (*attractive*) привлекáтельный.
■ *cpd.* **~ post** *n.* фи́нишный столб.

winnings /'wɪnɪŋz/ *n. pl.* вы́игрыш (*деньги*).

winter /'wɪntə(r)/ *n.* зимá; **in ~** зимóй; (*attr.*) зи́мний.
■ *v.i.* зимовáть, пере-.
■ *cpd.* **~time** *n.* зимá.

wintry /'wɪntrɪ/ *adj.* (**wintrier, wintriest**) зи́мний, морóзный; (*fig.*) холóдный.

wipe /waɪp/ *v.t.*
1 (*rub clean or dry*) вытирáть, вы́тереть; (*~ surface of*) обт|ирáть, -ерéть; **~ s.o.'s nose** вытирáть, вы́тереть комý-н. нос; **~ one's eyes** вытирáть, вы́тереть слёзы; **~ your shoes on the mat!** вы́трите боти́нки о кóврик!
2 (*erase*) ст|ирáть, -ерéть.
■ *with advs.*: **~ away** *v.t.* ст|ирáть, -ерéть; (*tears*) вытирáть, вы́тереть; **~ down** *v.t.* прот|ирáть, -ерéть; **~ off** *v.t.* ст|ирáть, -ерéть; **~ out** *v.t.* (*destroy*) уничт|ожáть, -óжить; **the disease ~d out the entire population** эпидéмия пóлностью уничтóжила всё населéние; **~ up** *v.t.* подт|ирáть, -ерéть.

wire /'waɪə(r)/ *n.*
1 прóволока.
2 (*elec.*) прóвод.
3 (*coll., telegram*) телегрáмма.
■ *v.t.* 1 (*elec.*): **they ~d the house** они́ сдéлали провóдку в дóме.
2 (*coll., send telegram to*) телеграфи́ровать (*impf., pf.*) + *d.*

wiring /'waɪərɪŋ/ *n.* (*elec.*) (электро)провóдка.

wiry /'waɪərɪ/ *adj.* (**wirier, wiriest**) (*of person*) жи́листый; (*of hair*) жёсткий.

wisdom /'wɪzdəm/ *n.* мýдрость; (*prudence*) благоразýмие; **~ tooth** зуб мýдрости.

wise /waɪz/ *adj.*
1 (*sage*) мýдрый.
2 (*sensible*) благоразýмный; **you were ~ not to attempt it** вы прáвильно сдéлали, что не стáли прóбовать.
3 (*well-informed*) осведомлённый; **now that you've told me I am none the ~r** дáже пóсле вáшего объяснéния я мáло что понимáю; **~ guy** (*US sl.*) ýмник.

wish /wɪʃ/ *n.*
1 (*desire*) желáние; (*request*) прóсьба; **make a ~!** загадáйте желáние!; **you acted against my ~es** вы поступи́ли прóтив моéй вóли.
2 (*on another's behalf*) пожелáние; **with best ~es!** с наилýчшими пожелáниями.
■ *v.t.* 1 (*want, require*) желáть (*impf.*); хотéть (*impf.*) (*both + a. or g., inf. or* чтóбы).
2 (*expr. unfulfilled desire*): **I ~ I knew everything** éсли бы (тóлько) я всё знал; как бы я хотéл всё знать; **I ~ you'd be quiet** нельзя́ ли не шумéть (*or* поти́ше)?; **I ~ he hadn't left so soon** как жаль, что он ушёл так рáно; **I ~ he were alive** éсли бы тóлько он был жив.
3 (*with double object*): **I ~ him well** я желáю емý добрá; **I ~ you many happy returns** поздравля́ю вас с днём рождéния.
■ *v.i.*: **~ for** мечтáть о + *p.*

wishful /'wɪʃfʊl/ *adj.*: **~ thinking** самообольщéние; приня́тие желáемого за действи́тельное.

wisp /wɪsp/ *n.*: **a ~ of hair** прядь волóс; **a ~ of smoke** стрýйка ды́ма.

wispy /'wɪspɪ/ *adj.* (**wispier, wispiest**): **~ hair** рéдкие вóлосы.

wist|aria /wɪ'steərɪə/, **-eria** /wɪ'stɪərɪə/ *n.* (*bot.*) глици́ния.

wistful /'wɪstfʊl/ *adj.* тоскли́вый.

wit /wɪt/ *n.*
1 (*also* **~s**; *intelligence*) ум, рáзум.
2 (*wittiness*) остроýмие.
3 (*person*) остря́|к (*fem. coll.* -чка).

witch /wɪtʃ/ *n.* вéдьма.
■ *cpds.* **~craft** *n.* чёрная мáгия; **~ doctor** *n.* знáхарь (*m.*); **~-hunt** *n.* (*fig.*) охóта на вéдьм.

with /wɪð/ *prep.*
1 (*in the company of*) *usu.* с + *i.*; **come ~ me!** пойдёмте со мной!; **he is ~ the manager** он у завéдующего; **the boy was left ~ his aunt** мáльчика остáвили у тётки (*or* с тёткой); (*denoting host*) у + *g.*; **we stayed ~ our friends** мы жи́ли у друзéй.
2 (*denoting means*): **I am writing ~ a pen** я пишý рýчкой; **he walks ~ a stick** он хóдит с пáл(оч)кой.
3 (*expr. antagonism or separation*): **don't argue ~ me** не спóрьте со мной; **at war ~** в состоя́нии войны́ с + *i.*
4 (*denoting cause*) от + *g.*; **she was shaking ~ fright** онá дрожáла от стрáха.
5 (*denoting characteristic*): **a girl ~ blue eyes** дéвушка с голубы́ми глазáми; **a suit ~ grey stripes** костю́м в сéрую полóску.
6 (*denoting manner etc.*): **~ pleasure** с удовóльствием; **~ care** осторóжно.
7 (*in the same direction or degree as; at the same time as*): **one must move ~ the times** нáдо идти́ в нóгу со врéменем; **~ the approach of spring** с наступлéнием весны́.
8 (*denoting attendant circumstance*): **a holiday ~ all expenses paid** пóлностью оплáченный óтпуск; **~ your permission** с вáшего разрешéния.

withdraw /wɪð'drɔː/ *v.t.* (*past* **withdrew;** *p.p.* **withdrawn**) отн|имáть, -я́ть; **~ an offer** брать, взять обрáтно/назáд предложéние; **~ money from the bank** сн|имáть, -ять дéньги со счёта (в бáнке); **~ troops** выводи́ть, вы́вести войскá; **a ~n character** зáмкнутый человéк.
■ *v.i.* (*past* **withdrew;** *p.p.* **withdrawn**) удал|я́ться, -и́ться; **~ into o.s.** зам|ыкáться, -кнýться в себé; (*mil.*) уходи́ть, уйти́.

withdrawal /wɪð'drɔːəl/ *n.* (*of a product from the market*) изъя́тие; (*of a person from an election*) сня́тие; (*of troops*) вы́вод; **~ symptoms** абстинéнтный синдрóм.

withdrawn /wɪð'drɔːn/ *p.p. of* ▸ **withdraw**

withdrew /wɪð'druː/ *past of* ▸ **withdraw**

wither /'wɪðə(r)/ *v.t.*
1 иссуш|áть, -и́ть.
2 (*fig.*) губи́ть, по-; **a ~ing glance**

испепеля́ющий взгляд.
■ *v.i.* вя́нуть, за-.

withhold /wɪð'həʊld/ *v.t.* (*past and p.p.* **withheld** /-'held/) отка́з|ывать, -а́ть в *чём*; ~ **one's consent** не да|ва́ть, -ть согла́сия; ~ **payment** заде́рж|ивать, -а́ть опла́ту.

within /wɪ'ðɪn/ *adv.* внутри́; **from** ~ изнутри́.
■ *prep.* 1 (*inside*) в + *p.*; внутри́ + *g.*; ~ **these walls** в э́тих стена́х.
2 (*not farther than; accessible to*) в преде́лах + *g.*; **the library is** ~ **walking distance** до библиоте́ки мо́жно дойти́ пешко́м.
3 (*of time*) в тече́ние + *g.*; ~ **three days** в тече́ние трёх дней; **I can finish the job** ~ **a week** я могу́ (за)ко́нчить э́ту рабо́ту за неде́лю.
4 (~ *limits of*) в преде́лах/ра́мках + *g.*; **live** ~ **one's income** жить (*impf.*) по сре́дствам.

without /wɪ'ðaʊt/ *prep.* без + *g.*; ~ **doubt** без сомне́ния; ~ **fail** непреме́нно; **it goes** ~ **saying** само́ собо́й разуме́ется; (*with gerund*): ~ **thinking** не ду́мая; не поду́мав.

withstand /wɪð'stænd/ *v.t.* (*past and p.p.* **withstood** /-'stʊd/) усто́ять (*pf.*) пе́ред + *i.*; выде́рживать, вы́держать.

witness /'wɪtnɪs/ *n.* свиде́тель (*fem.* -ница); **bear** ~ свиде́тельствовать (*impf.*).
■ *v.t.* 1 (*event*) быть свиде́телем + *g.*; **no one** ~**ed the accident** никто́ не ви́дел, как произошла́ катастро́фа.
2 (*signature*) зав|еря́ть, -е́рить.
■ *cpd.* ~ **box** *n.* (*US* ~ **stand**) ме́сто для да́чи свиде́тельских показа́ний.

witticism /'wɪtɪsɪz(ə)m/ *n.* остро́та.

witty /'wɪtɪ/ *adj.* (**wittier, wittiest**) остроу́мный.

wives /waɪvz/ *pl. of* ▶ **wife**

wizard /'wɪzəd/ *n.* волше́бник.

WMD (*abbr. of* ***weapons of mass destruction***) ОМП (*оружие массового поражения*).

wobble /'wɒb(ə)l/ *v.t.* (*also* ~ **about**) шата́ть (*impf.*).
■ *v.i.* (*also* ~ **about**) (*sway*) шата́ться, кача́ться (*both impf.*); (*fig., vacillate*) колеба́ться (*impf.*).

wobbly /'wɒblɪ/ *adj.* (**wobblier, wobbliest**) (*lit., fig.*) ша́ткий, неусто́йчивый.

woe /wəʊ/ *n.*
1 (*grief*) го́ре.
2 (*pl., troubles*) бе́ды (*f. pl.*).

woeful /'wəʊfʊl/ *adj.* ско́рбный, го́рестный; (*pathetic*) жа́лкий; (*dull*) уны́лый; **a** ~ **countenance** ско́рбное лицо́; ~ **ignorance** вопию́щее неве́жество.

wok /wɒk/ *n.* сковорода́ (с вы́пуклым дни́щем) (*в китайской кухне*).

woke /wəʊk/ *past of* ▶ **wake**[1]

woken /'wəʊk(ə)n/ *p.p. of* ▶ **wake**[1]

wolf /wʊlf/ *n.* (*pl.* **wolves**) (*animal*) волк; **cry** ~ (*fig.*) подн|има́ть, -я́ть ло́жную трево́гу.
■ *v.t.* (*coll., also* ~ **down**) прогл|а́тывать, -оти́ть с жа́дностью.
■ *cpd.* ~ **whistle** *n.* (*coll.*) свист при ви́де краси́вой де́вушки.

woman /'wʊmən/ *n.* (*pl.* **women**)
1 же́нщина.
2: ~ **doctor** же́нщина-врач; ~ **friend** подру́га, прия́тельница.

womanize /'wʊmənaɪz/ *v.i.* (*coll., philander*) пу́таться (*impf.*) с ба́бами (*coll.*); гоня́ться (*impf.*) за ю́бками.

womanizer /'wʊmənaɪzə(r)/ *n.* ба́бник (*coll.*).

womanly /'wʊmənlɪ/ *adj.* (*figure*) же́нственный; (*virtues*) же́нский.

womb /wu:m/ *n.* ма́тка.

women /'wɪmɪn/ *pl. of* ▶ **woman**

won /wʌn/ *past and p.p. of* ▶ **win**

wonder /'wʌndə(r)/ *n.*
1 (*miracle, marvel*) чу́до; (*surprising thing*): **it's a** ~ **that...** удиви́тельно, что...; **no** ~ **he was angry!** неудиви́тельно, что он рассерди́лся!
2 (*amazement*) изумле́ние, восхище́ние.
■ *v.t.* (*desire to know; deliberate*): **I** ~ **who that was** интере́сно/любопы́тно, кто бы э́то мог быть; **he** ~**ed if she was coming** он гада́л, придёт она́ и́ли нет; **I was** ~**ing whether to invite him** я не мог реши́ть, приглаша́ть его́ и́ли нет.
■ *v.i.* 1 (*feel surprised*) удив|ля́ться, -и́ться (*чему*); пора|жа́ться, -зи́ться (*чему*).
2 (*feel curiosity*) интересова́ться (*impf.*); **I was** ~**ing about that** я и сам разду́мывал об э́том; **'Why do you ask?' — 'I just** ~**ed'** «Почему́ вы спра́шиваете?» — «Про́сто так».

wonderful /'wʌndəfʊl/ *adj.* (*pleasing*) чуде́сный, чу́дный; **what** ~ **weather!** кака́я чу́дная пого́да!

wonky /'wɒŋkɪ/ *adj.* (**wonkier, wonkiest**) (*Br. sl.*) (*unstable*) ша́ткий; (*crooked*) криво́й.

wont /wəʊnt/ (*arch. or liter.*) *n.*: **as is his** ~ по своему́ обыкнове́нию.
■ *adj.*: **as he was** ~ **to say** как он люби́л говори́ть.

won't /wəʊnt/ *neg. of* ▶ **will**[2]

woo /wu:/ *v.t.* (**woos, wooed**) (*arch.*) уха́живать (*impf.*) за + *i.*

wood /wʊd/ *n.*
1 (*in sing. or pl.*) (*forest*) лес; ~**ed country** леси́стая ме́стность; (*fig.*) **we're not out of the** ~ **yet** ещё не все опа́сности/тру́дности позади́.
2 (*substance*) де́рево; **touch** (*US* **knock on**) ~ тьфу, тьфу! чтоб не сгла́зить!
3 (*as fuel*) дров|а́ (*pl., g.* —).
■ *cpds.* ~**land** *n.* леси́стая ме́стность; ~**pecker** *n.* дя́тел; ~**wind** *n.* (*collect.*) деревя́нные духовы́е инструме́нты (*m. pl.*); ~**work** *n.* (*Br., carpentry*) столя́рная рабо́та; (*articles*) деревя́нные изде́лия; ~**worm** *n.* личи́нка древото́чца.

wooden /'wʊd(ə)n/ *adj.* (*also fig.*) деревя́нный.

woody /'wʊdɪ/ *adj.* (**woodier, woodiest**) (*wooded*) леси́стый; (*of or like wood*) деревя́нный.

woof /wʊf/ *n.* (*dog's bark*) га́вканье, лай.
■ *v.t.* га́вкать (*impf.*); ла́ять (*impf.*); ~! гав!

wool /wʊl/ *n.* шерсть; **pull the** ~ **over s.o.'s eyes** (*fig.*) пус|ка́ть, -ти́ть пыль в глаза́ кому́-н.

woollen /'wʊlən/ (*US* **woolen**) *adj.* шерстяно́й.

woolly /'wʊlɪ/ *adj.* (**woollier, woolliest**)
1 (*bearing or covered with wool*) шерсти́стый.
2 (*fig., lacking definition*) нея́сный.

word /wɜ:d/ *n.*
1 слóво; **I couldn't get a ~ in (edgeways)** мне не удалóсь встáвить ни слóва; **he never has a good ~ for anyone** он ни о ком дóброго слóва не скáжет; **may I have a ~ with you?** мóжно вас на пáру слов?; **in a ~** (однúм) слóвом; **in other ~s** инáче говоря́, другúми словáми; **a man of few ~s** немногослóвный человéк; **put in a good ~ for s.o.** замóлвить (*pf.*) словéчко за когó-н.; **~ for ~** слóво в слóво; **translate ~ for ~** перев|одúть, -естú дослóвно/буквáльно.
2 (*pl., quarrel*): **they had ~s** онú поссóрились.
3 (*pl., text set to music*) текст, словá (*nt. pl.*).
4 (*news*) извéстие, сообщéние; **he sent ~ that he was not coming** он передáл, что не смóжет прийтú; **the ~ got round that ...** стáло извéстно, что... .
5 (*promise*) слóво, обещáние; **give one's ~** да|вáть, -ть слóво; обещáть (*impf., pf.*); **keep one's ~** держáть, с- слóво; **he was as good as his ~** он сдержáл слóво; **you must take my ~ for it** вам придётся повéрить мне нá слово.
6 (*command*) слóво, прикáз; **just say the ~!** тóлько скажúте/прикажúте!
■ *v.t.* формулúровать, с-.
■ *cpds.* **~ processing** *n.* редактúрование тéкста; **~ processor** *n.* тéкстовый редáктор.

wording /ˈwɜ:dɪŋ/ *n.* редáкция (*текста, статьи*).

wore /wɔ:(r)/ *past of* ▶ **wear**

work /wɜ:k/ *n.*
1 (*labour, task*) рабóта, труд; (*official, professional*) рабóта, слýжба; (*school etc.*) занятия (*nt. pl.*); **he is at ~** он сейчáс рабóтает; **she is at ~ on a dictionary** онá рабóтает над словарём; **get to ~ on** нач|инáть, -áть рабóту над + *i.*; **get down to ~** прин|имáться, -я́ться/брáться, взя́ться за рабóту/дéло.
2 (*employment*) рабóта, слýжба; **it is hard to find ~** трýдно найтú рабóту; **in ~** рабóтающий; **out of ~** без рабóты.
3 (*literary or artistic composition*) произведéние, сочинéние; (*publication*) издáние; **the ~s of Chopin** произведéния Шопéна; **a ~ of art** произведéние искýсства.
4 (*pl., parts of machine*) механúзм.
5 (*pl., Br., factory*) завóд, фáбрика, предприя́тие; **steel ~s** сталелитéйный завóд.
■ *v.t.* (*past and p.p.* **worked**)
1 (*cause to ~*): **he ~s his men hard** он заставля́ет людéй мнóго рабóтать; **he ~ed himself to death** он извёл себя́ рабóтой.
2 (*set in motion*) прив|одúть, -естú в движéние/дéйствие; **how do you ~ this machine?** как управля́ть э́той машúной?
3 (*effect*): **~ wonders** творúть (*impf.*) чудесá.
4 (*achieve by ~ing*): **he ~ed his way through university** все гóды студéнчества он сам зарабáтывал себé на жизнь; **he ~ed his way up to the rank of manager** он пробúлся в директорá.
5 (*excite*) возбу|ждáть, -дúть; **he ~ed the crowd into a frenzy** он довёл толпý до неúстовства.
■ *v.i.* 1 (*be employed*) рабóтать (*над чем*), трудúться, служúть (*all impf.*); **he ~ed for 6 hours** он рабóтал 6 часóв; **~ with s.o.** сотрýдничать (*impf.*) с кем-н.
2 (*operate*) рабóтать (*impf.*); дéйствовать (*impf.*); **the brakes won't ~** тормозá отказáли.
3 (*produce desired effect*): **the plan ~ed** план удáлся; **the medicine ~ed** лекáрство помоглó/подéйствовало.
4 (*exert influence*) рабóтать, дéйствовать (*both impf.*); **~ against** мешáть, по- + *d.*
5 (*move gradually*): **a screw ~ed loose** винт ослáб.
■ *with advs.*: **~ off** *v.t.*: **he ran round the house to ~ off some of his energy** он пробежáлся вокрýг дóма, чтóбы дать вы́ход своéй энéргии; **I shall never be able to ~ off this debt** я никогдá не смогý отрабóтать э́тот долг; **~ out** *v.t.* (*devise*) разрабá|тывать, -óтать; (*calculate*) вычисля́ть, вы́числить; (*solve*) разреш|áть, -úть; *v.i.* (*turn out*) окáз|ываться, -áться; (*turn out well*) об|ходúться, -ойтúсь; **everything ~ed out** всё обошлóсь; **the expenses ~ out at £70** расхóды составля́ют 70 фýнтов; (*train, of an athlete*) тренировáться (*impf.*); **~ up** *v.t.* (*develop*): **I can't ~ up any interest in economics** я никáк не могý пробудúть в себé интерéс к эконóмике; (*pred.*): **I'm~ed up** (*excited*) я взволнóван; (*worried*) я расстрóен.
■ *cpds.* **~bench** *n.* верстáк; **~ experience** *n.* (*Br.*) произвóдственная прáктика (*для школьников*); **~force** *n.* рабóчая сúла; **~load** *n.* нагрýзка; **~man** *n.* рабóтник; **~manship** *n.* мастерствó; **~out** *n.* тренирóвка; **~shop** *n.* (*small*) мастерскáя; (*large*) цех; **~station** *n.* (*comput.*) рабóчая стáнция; **~top** *n.* (*Br.*) вéрхняя панéль; **~-to-rule** *n.* (*Br.*) ≈ итальянская забастóвка (*работа строго по правилам*).

workable /ˈwɜ:kəb(ə)l/ *adj.*
1 (*of mine etc.*) рентáбельный.
2 (*feasible*) выполнúмый.

workaholic /wɜ:kəˈhɒlɪk/ *n.* трудогóлик.

worker /ˈwɜ:kə(r)/ *n.* рабóтник, трудя́щийся; **office ~** слýжащий.

working /ˈwɜ:kɪŋ/ *n.*
1 (*usu. pl.; operation*) рабóта, дéйствие.
2 (*attr., pert. to work*) рабóчий; **~ capital** оборóтный капитáл; **~ conditions** услóвия трудá; **in ~ order** в исправности.
■ *adj.* рабóчий; **~ class** рабóчий класс.
■ *cpd.* **~-class** *adj.* рабóчий; **~-class families** сéмьи рабóчих.

world /wɜ:ld/ *n.*
1 (*universe*) мир; **out of this ~** (*coll., stupendous*) потрясáющий; **in this ~** на э́том свéте.
2 (*fig. uses*): **what in the ~ has happened?** да что же, наконéц, случúлось?; **why in the ~ didn't you tell me?** ну почемý же вы мне не сказáли?; **I wouldn't hurt him for the ~** я егó ни за что (на свéте) не стал бы обижáть; **the boss thinks the ~ of him** он у хозя́ина на óчень высóком счетý; **I felt on top of the ~** я был

на седьмо́м не́бе от сча́стья.
[3] (*infinite amount*) мно́го, у́йма (*coll.*); **a ~ of difference** огро́мная ра́зница; **it will do him a ~ of good** э́то пойдёт ему́ на по́льзу.
[4] (*geog.; the earth's countries and peoples*) мир, свет; **(all) over the ~** по всему́ све́ту; **go round the ~** объ|езжа́ть, -е́хать весь свет; **W~ Bank** Всеми́рный банк; **~ champion** чемпио́н ми́ра; **W~ Cup** Ку́бок ми́ра по футбо́лу; **a ~ power** вели́кая держа́ва; **~ record** мирово́й реко́рд; **~ war** мирова́я война́.
[5] (*human affairs*) жизнь; **go up in the ~** де́лать, с- карье́ру; **go down in the ~** утра́|чивать, -тить было́е положе́ние.
[6] (*domain*) мир; сфе́ра; **the ~ of nature** ца́рство приро́ды.
■ *cpds.* **~-famous** *adj.* всеми́рно изве́стный; **~ view** *n.* мировоззре́ние; **~wide** *adj.* всеми́рный, мирово́й; *adv.* по всему́ све́ту/ми́ру; **W~ Wide Web** *n.* Всеми́рная паути́на, Интерне́т, Сеть.

worldly /ˈwəːldlɪ/ *adj.* (**worldlier, worldliest**)
[1] (*material*) земно́й, материа́льный.
[2]: **a ~ person** о́пытный челове́к.
■ *cpd.* **~-wise** *adj.* о́пытный.

worm /wəːm/ *n.* червь (*m.*).
■ *v.t.* (*extract*) вытя́гивать, вы́тянуть.

worn /wɔːn/ *p.p. of* ▸ **wear**

worried /ˈwʌrɪd/ *adj.* обеспоко́енный, озабо́ченный.

worrier /ˈwʌrɪə(r)/ *n.*: **he's a ~** он ве́чно беспоко́ится.

worr|y /ˈwʌrɪ/ *n.*
[1] (*anxiety*) трево́га, забо́та.
[2] (*sth. causing anxiety*) неприя́тность, забо́та; **he is a ~y to me** он доставля́ет мне мно́го беспоко́йства/забо́т/хлопо́т; **financial ~ies** фина́нсовые пробле́мы (*f. pl.*).
■ *v.t.* [1] (*cause anxiety to*) беспоко́ить (*impf.*); **what is ~ying you?** что вас беспоко́ит?; чем вы озабо́чены?; **I'm ~ied about my son** я беспоко́юсь о сы́не.
[2] (*bother*) надоеда́ть (*impf.*) + *d.*; **the noise doesn't ~y me** шум не меша́ет мне.
■ *v.i.* беспоко́иться, волнова́ться, расстра́иваться (*all impf.*); **don't ~y!** не беспоко́йтесь!; **you are ~ying over nothing** вы напра́сно расстра́иваетесь/волну́етесь.

worse /wəːs/ *n.* ху́дшее; **there is ~ to come** ху́дшее ещё впереди́; **a change for the ~** переме́на к ху́дшему; **things went from bad to ~** положе́ние станови́лось всё ху́же и ху́же.
■ *adj.* ху́дший; **you will only make matters ~** вы то́лько уху́дшите положе́ние; **~ luck!** к сожале́нию; (*as pred.*) ху́же; **the patient is ~ today** больно́му сего́дня ху́же; **his work is getting ~** его́ рабо́та стано́вится ху́же; **they are ~ off than we** они́ в ху́дшем положе́нии, чем мы; (*financially*) они́ ме́нее состоя́тельны, чем мы.
■ *adv.* ху́же; **we played ~ than ever** мы игра́ли как никогда́ пло́хо; **you might do ~ than accept** мо́жет быть, и сто́ит приня́ть.

worsen /ˈwəːs(ə)n/ *v.t. & i.* ух|удша́ться, -у́дшиться.

worship /ˈwəːʃɪp/ *n.* поклоне́ние.
■ *v.t. & i.* (**worshipped, worshipping;** *US* **worshiped, worshiping**) поклоня́ться (*impf.*) + *d.*; **~ God** моли́ться (*impf.*) Бо́гу; (*attend ~*) моли́ться (*impf.*); (*adore*) боготвори́ть (*impf.*).

worshipper /ˈwəːʃɪpə(r)/ (*US* **worshiper**) *n.* моля́щийся.

worst /wəːst/ *n.* наиху́дшее; са́мое плохо́е; **the ~ is over** ху́дшее позади́; **the ~ of it is that ...** ху́же всего́ то, что...; **if the ~ comes to the ~** в са́мом ху́дшем слу́чае; **you saw him at his ~** вы ви́дели его́ с наиху́дшей стороны́; **at (the) ~ you may have to pay a fine** в кра́йнем слу́чае вам придётся уплати́ть штраф.
■ *adj.* наиху́дший; са́мый плохо́й; **you came at the ~ possible time** вы пришли́ в са́мое неподходя́щее вре́мя.
■ *adv.* (*of objects*) ху́же всего́; (*of people*) ху́же всех.

worth /wəːθ/ *n.* (*value*) це́нность; (*merit*) досто́инство; **of great ~** значи́тельный; (*quantity of specified value*): **give me a pound's ~ of sweets** да́йте мне конфе́т на (оди́н) фунт.
■ *pred. adj.* [1] (*of value equal to*): **it's ~ about £1** э́то сто́ит о́коло (одного́) фу́нта; **what is your house ~?** во ско́лько оце́нивается ваш дом?; **it's ~ a lot to me** для меня́ э́то о́чень це́нно/ва́жно.
[2] (*deserving of*) сто́ящий, заслу́живающий; **it's not ~ the trouble of asking** не сто́ит спра́шивать; **it is ~ while** сто́ит; **it's hardly ~ mentioning** об э́том вряд ли сто́ит упомина́ть; **well ~ having** о́чень сто́ящий/поле́зный.
[3] (*possessed of*): **he is ~ 3 billion** его́ ли́чное состоя́ние оце́нивается в 3 миллиа́рда; (*fig.*): **he ran for all he was ~** он мча́лся во весь дух.
■ *cpd.* **~while** *adj.* це́нный, сто́ящий.

worthless /ˈwəːθlɪs/ *adj.* (*goods*) ничего́ не сто́ящий; (*person, contribution*) ничто́жный.

worthy /ˈwəːðɪ/ *adj.* (**worthier, worthiest**)
[1] (*deserving respect*) досто́йный, почте́нный; **a ~ cause** досто́йное де́ло.
[2] (*deserving*) досто́йный, заслу́живающий + *g.*; **~ of note** досто́йный внима́ния; **~ of a place in the team** досто́йный быть чле́ном кома́нды.
[3] (*appropriate*) подоба́ющий + *d.*; **~ of the occasion** подоба́ющий слу́чаю.

would /wʊd/ *v. aux.* (*see also* ▸ **will**[2])
[1] (*conditional*): **he ~ be angry if he knew** он бы рассерди́лся, е́сли (бы) узна́л.
[2] (*expr. wish*): **I ~ like to know** я хоте́л бы знать; **I ~ rather** я бы предпочёл.
[3] (*of typical action etc.*): **you ~ do that!** с тебя́ ста́нется!; **of course he ~ say that** ну коне́чно, он э́то ска́жет.
[4] (*of habitual action*): *see* ▸ **will**[2] **4**
■ *cpd.* **~-be** *adj.*: **a ~-be writer** начина́ющий писа́тель.

wouldn't /ˈwʊd(ə)nt/ *neg. of* ▸ **would**

wound[1] /wuːnd/ *n.* ра́на, ране́ние.
■ *v.t.* ра́нить (*impf., pf.*); **he was ~ed in the leg** его́ ра́нило в но́гу; **there were many ~ed** бы́ло мно́го ра́неных.

wound[2] /waʊnd/ *past and p.p. of* ▸ **wind**[2]

wove /wəʊv/ *past of* ▶ **weave**
woven /ˈwəʊv(ə)n/ *p.p. of* ▶ **weave**
wow /waʊ/ *int.* здóрово!; вот э́то да́!; ух!
■ *v.t.* (*sl.*) прив|оди́ть, -ести́ в восто́рг.
WPC (*abbr. of* ***woman police constable***) (*Br.*) же́нщина-полице́йский.
wrangle /ˈræŋg(ə)l/ *n.* ссо́ра.
■ *v.i.* ссо́риться (*impf.*).
wrap /ræp/ *n.*
1 (*lit.*) (*shawl*) шаль, плато́к; (*rug*) плед.
2 (*fig.*): **under ~s** (*fig.*) в та́йне.
■ *v.t.* (**wrapped, wrapping**)
1 (*cover*) зав|ора́чивать, -ерну́ть; заку́т|ывать, -ать; (*parcel*) об|ора́чивать, -ерну́ть; **they were ~ping presents** они́ завора́чивали пода́рки; **~ o.s. in a blanket** зав|ора́чиваться, -ерну́ться в одея́ло.
2 (*wind as a covering*) об|ора́чивать, -ерну́ть; **we ~ sacking round the pipes in winter** зимо́й мы обора́чиваем тру́бы мешкови́ной; **he ~ped his arms around her** он заключи́л её в объя́тия; он о́бнял её.
■ *with adv.*: **~ up** *v.t.* (*cover up*) зав|ора́чивать, -ерну́ть; (*conclude*) свора́чивать, сверну́ть (*coll.*); (*summarize*) кра́тко сумми́ровать (*impf., pf.*); (*pass., be engrossed*) погру|жа́ться, -зи́ться (**in:** в + *a.*); *v.i.* (*put on extra clothes*) заку́т|ываться, -аться.
wrapper /ˈræpə(r)/ *n.* обёртка.
wrapping /ˈræpɪŋ/ *n.* обёртка, упако́вка.
■ *cpd.* **~ paper** *n.* обёрточная бума́га.
wrath /rɒθ/ *n.* гнев.
wrathful /ˈrɒθfʊl/ *adj.* гне́вный, я́ростный.
wreak /ri:k/ *v.t.*: **~ havoc (on)** нан|оси́ть, -ести́ уще́рб (+ *d.*).
wreath /ri:θ/ *n.* вено́к.
wreck /rek/ *n.*
1 (*~ed ship*) затону́вший кора́бль.
2 (*damaged vehicle, building, person etc.*) разва́лина.
■ *v.t.* 1 (*ship*): **the ship was ~ed** су́дно потерпе́ло круше́ние; **the ship was ~ed on the cliffs** кора́бль разби́лся о ска́лы.
2 (*car*) разб|ива́ть, -и́ть; (*building*) разр|уша́ть, -у́шить; (*equipment*) лома́ть, с-.
3 (*hope, life*) разб|ива́ть, -и́ть; (*weekend*) по́ртить, ис-.
wreckage /ˈrekɪdʒ/ *n.* (*remains*) обло́мки (*m. pl.*) (круше́ния *и т. п.*).
wren /ren/ *n.* крапи́вник (*птица*).
wrench /rentʃ/ *n.*
1 (*fig.*) тоска́, боль.
2 (*tool*) га́ечный ключ.
■ *v.t.*: **he ~ed the door open** он ре́зко рвану́л дверь на себя́; **he ~ed the paper out of my hand** он вы́рвал у меня́ бума́гу из рук.
wrestle /ˈres(ə)l/ *v.i.* боро́ться (*impf.*); (*fig.*): **~ with a problem** би́ться (*impf.*) над зада́чей; **he ~d with his conscience** он боро́лся со свое́й со́вестью.
wrestler /ˈreslə(r)/ *n.* боре́ц.
wrestling /ˈreslɪŋ/ *n.* борьба́.
wretch /retʃ/ *n.* негодя́й.
wretched /ˈretʃɪd/ *adj.* (**wretcheder, wretchedest**) (*miserable*) несча́стный; (*unpleasant*) скве́рный; (*damned*) прокля́тый.
wriggle /ˈrɪg(ə)l/ *n.* изги́б, изви́в.
■ *v.t.* (*also* **~ about**): **~ one's toes** шевели́ть (*impf.*) па́льцами ног; **he ~d free** он вы́вернулся/вы́скользнул.
■ *v.i.* (*also* **~ about**) извива́ться (*impf.*); **the baby ~d out of my arms** ребёнок вы́скользнул у меня́ из рук; **~ out of a responsibility** увил|ивать, -ьну́ть от отве́тственности.
wring /rɪŋ/ *v.t.* (*past and p.p.* **wrung**)
1 (*s.o.'s hand*) пож|има́ть, -а́ть; **he wrung his hands in despair** он в отча́янии лома́л себе́ ру́ки; (*squeeze out by twisting*) выжима́ть, вы́жать; **~ clothes dry** отж|има́ть, -а́ть бельё до́суха; (*chicken's neck*) свора́чивать, сверну́ть.
2 (*fig., extract by force*) вырыва́ть, вы́рвать; **I wrung a promise from him** я вы́рвал у него́ обеща́ние.
■ *with adv.*: **~ out** *v.t.*: (*clothes*) отж|има́ть, -жа́ть; (*water*) отж|има́ть, -а́ть.
wrinkle /ˈrɪŋk(ə)l/ *n.* (*on skin*) морщи́на.
■ *v.t.*: **~ one's nose** мо́рщить, с- нос.
■ *v.i.* мя́ться, по-/из-.
wrist /rɪst/ *n.* запя́стье.
■ *cpds.* **~watch** *n.* нару́чные час|ы́ (*pl., g.* -о́в).
writ /rɪt/ *n.* (*written injunction*) суде́бный прика́з; (*summons*) пове́стка; **serve a ~ on s.o.** вруч|а́ть, -и́ть кому́-н. суде́бный прика́з.
write /raɪt/ *v.t.* (*past* **wrote;** *p.p.* **written**)
1 писа́ть, на-.
2: **~ a cheque** (*Br.*), **check** (*US*) выпи́сывать, вы́писать чек.
3 (*compose*) писа́ть, на-; сочин|я́ть, -и́ть.
■ *v.i.* (*past* **wrote;** *p.p.* **written**)
1 писа́ть (*impf.*).
2 (*compose*) сочин|я́ть, -и́ть; писа́ть, на-.
■ *with advs.*: **~ away, ~ off** *vv.i.*: **he wrote away, off for a catalogue** он вы́писал катало́г; **~ back** *v.i.* отв|еча́ть, -е́тить (письмо́м); **~ down** *v.t.* (*make a note of*) запи́с|ывать, -а́ть; **~ off** *v.t.* (*cancel*): **~ off a debt** спи́с|ывать, -а́ть долг; (*recognize loss of*): **~ off £500 for depreciation** спи́с|ывать, -а́ть 500 фу́нтов на амортиза́цию; **the car had to be written off** маши́ну пришло́сь списа́ть; *v.i.* = **~ away**; **~ out** *v.t.* выпи́сывать, вы́писать.
■ *cpds.* **~-off** *n.*: **the car was a ~-off** маши́ну списа́ли; **~-up** *n.* (*account*) отчёт; (*review*) о́тзыв, реце́нзия.
writer /ˈraɪtə(r)/ *n.*
1 (*person writing*) а́втор.
2 (*author*) писа́тель (*fem.* -ница); **~'s block** отсу́тствие вдохнове́ния.
writhe /raɪð/ *v.i.* ко́рчиться (*impf.*).
writing /ˈraɪtɪŋ/ *n.*
1 (*ability, art*) письмо́, гра́мота.
2 (*written words; inscription*) на́дпись; **in ~** пи́сьменно; в пи́сьменной фо́рме.
3 (*handwriting*) по́черк.
4 (*literary composition*) произведе́ние.
■ *cpds.* **~ pad** *n.* блокно́т; **~ paper** *n.* пи́счая бума́га.
written /ˈrɪt(ə)n/ *p.p. of* ▶ **write**
wrong /rɒŋ/ *n.*
1 (*moral ~*) зло; (*action*) дурно́й посту́пок.
2 (*unjust action or its result*) несправедли́вость, оби́да.

[3] (*state of error*): **you are in the ~** вы непра́вы/винова́ты.

■ *adj.* [1] (*sinful*) гре́шный; (*reprehensible*) дурно́й; **it is ~ to steal** ворова́ть нехорошо́.
[2] (*mistaken*) непра́вый; **you are ~** вы непра́вы/ошиба́етесь; **he proved them ~** он доказа́л, что они́ ошиба́лись.
[3] (*incorrect*) непра́вильный, неве́рный, оши́бочный; (*unsuitable*) неподходя́щий; **take the ~ turning** (*lit.*) св|ора́чивать, -ерну́ть не туда́; **my food went down the ~ way** пи́ща попа́ла не в то го́рло; **that's the ~ way to go about it** э́то де́лается не так; **this shirt is the ~ size/colour** э́та руба́шка не того́ разме́ра/цве́та; **the clock is ~** часы́ иду́т непра́вильно; **you have the ~ number** вы не туда́ попа́ли (*по телефону*).
[4] (*out of order; causing concern*) нела́дный; **what's ~?** что случи́лось?; **what's ~ with you?** что с тобо́й?; **there's something ~ with my car** с мое́й маши́ной что́-то не в поря́дке; **to go ~** срыва́ться, сорва́ться; **our plans went ~** на́ши пла́ны спу́тались; **where did we go ~** (*make a mistake*)**?** в чём мы ошибли́сь?
[5] (*of health*): **the doctor asked me what was ~** врач спроси́л, на что я жа́луюсь; **he found nothing ~ with me** он не нашёл у меня́ никаки́х боле́зней.

■ *adv.* (*incorrectly*) непра́вильно, не так; (*reprehensibly*) пло́хо; **you did ~ to shout at the child** ты пло́хо сде́лал, что накрича́л на ребёнка.

■ *v.t.* (*treat unjustly*) быть несправедли́вым к + *d.*

■ *cpds.* **~doer** *n.* (*sinner*) гре́шни|к (*fem.* -ца); (*offender*) правонаруши́тель (*fem.* -ница); **~-foot** *v.t.* (*Br.*) заст|ига́ть, -и́гнуть врасплóх.

wrongful /ˈrɒŋfʊl/ *adj.* несправедли́вый.

wrongly /ˈrɒŋlɪ/ *adv.* (*reprehensibly*) ду́рно; (*incorrectly*) непра́вильно; (*by mistake*) по оши́бке.

wrote /rəʊt/ *past of* ▸ **write**

wrought /rɔːt/ *adj.*: **~ iron** ко́ваное/сва́рочное желе́зо.

wrung /rʌŋ/ *past and p.p. of* ▸ **wring**

wry /raɪ/ *adj.* криво́й.

WWW (*abbr. of* ***World Wide Web***) Всеми́рная паути́на, Интерне́т, Сеть.

WYSIWYG /ˈwɪzɪwɪg/ (*abbr. of* ***what you see is what you get***) (*comput.*) режи́м по́лного соотве́тствия (*печатного изображения и изображения на экране*).

X /eks/ *n.* (*unknown quantity or person*) X, икс; **~ marks the spot where the body was found** кресто́м обозна́чено ме́сто, где был на́йден труп; **an X film** фильм катего́рии X (*только для взрослых*).

■ *cpd.* **~-ray** *n.* (*pl.*) рентге́новские лучи́ (*m. pl.*); (*sg., picture*) рентге́новский сни́мок; *v.t.* просве́|чивать, -ти́ть рентге́новскими луча́ми.

xenophobia /zenəˈfəʊbɪə/ *n.* ксенофо́бия.

xenophobic /zenəˈfəʊbɪk/ *adj.* отлича́ющийся ксенофо́бией, ксенофо́бский.

xerox /ˈzɪərɒks/ *v.t.* ксерокопи́ровать (*impf., pf.*); ксери́ть, от- (*coll.*).

Xmas /ˈeksməs/ = **Christmas**

xylophone /ˈzaɪləfəʊn/ *n.* (*mus.*) ксилофо́н.

Yy

yacht /jɒt/ *n.* я́хта.

■ *cpds.* **~sman** *n.* яхтсме́н; **~swoman** *n.* яхтсме́нка.

yachting /ˈjɒtɪŋ/ *n.* па́русный спорт.

Yank /jæŋk/ (*coll.*) *n.* я́нки (*m. indecl.*).

yank /jæŋk/ *n.* рыво́к.

■ *v.t.* дёр|гать, -нуть.

■ *with adv.*: **~ off** *v.t.* срыва́ть, сорва́ть.

yap /jæp/ *n.* тя́вканье.

■ *v.i.* (**yapped, yapping**) тя́вк|ать, -нуть.

yard[1] /jɑːd/ *n.* (*unit of measure*) ярд (*0,9144 м*).

■ *cpd.* **~stick** *n.* (*fig.*) мери́ло, крите́рий.

yard[2] /jɑːd/ *n.*
[1] (*Br., of house*; **court~**) двор.
[2] (*for industrial purposes*): **timber ~** склад пиломатериа́лов; **builder's ~** склад стройматериа́лов.
[3] (*US, garden*) са́д(ик).

yarn /jɑːn/ *n.*
[1] (*spun thread*) пря́жа.
[2] (*coll., story*) расска́з.

yawn /jɔːn/ *n.* зево́к.

■ *v.i.* зев|а́ть, -ну́ть; (*fig., of chasm*) зия́ть (*impf.*).

yeah /jeə/ *adv.* (*coll.*) да; ага́.

year /jɪə(r)/ *n.*
1 год; **I have known him for ten ~s** я его́ зна́ю уже де́сять лет; **~ in, ~ out** из го́да в год; **all the ~ round** кру́глый год; **he's in the third year** (*as school pupil*) он в тре́тьем кла́ссе; **he is in his third ~** (*as college student*) он на тре́тьем ку́рсе.
2 (*pl., a long time*): **it is ~s since I saw him** я его́ це́лую ве́чность не ви́дел.
3 (*pl., age*) лета́; **he looks young for his ~s** он мо́лодо вы́глядит для свои́х лет; **he is getting on in ~s** он (уже́) в во́зрасте.

yearly /ˈjɪəlɪ/ *adj.* (*happening once a year*) ежего́дный; (*pert. to a year*): **~ income** годово́й дохо́д.
■ *adv.* (*once a year*) раз в год; (*every year*) ка́ждый год.

yearn /jəːn/ *v.i.*
1: **~ for** тоскова́ть (*impf.*) по + *d.*; жа́ждать (*impf.*) + *g.*
2: **~ to** жажда́ть (*impf.*) + *inf.*; мечта́ть (*impf.*) + *inf.*

yearning /ˈjəːnɪŋ/ *n.* тоска́ (**for:** по + *d.*); жа́жда (**for:** + *g.*).

yeast /jiːst/ *n.* дро́жж|и (*pl., g.* -е́й).

yell /jel/ *n.* (пронзи́тельный) крик.
■ *v.t.* & *i.* вопи́ть, за-; кр|ича́ть, -и́кнуть.

yellow /ˈjeləʊ/ *n.* желтизна́; жёлтый цвет.
■ *adj.* жёлтый; **go, turn ~** желте́ть, по-; **Y~ Pages** (*propr.*) «Жёлтые страни́цы».
■ *v.i.* желте́ть, по-.

yellowish /ˈjeləʊɪʃ/ *adj.* желтова́тый.

yelp /jelp/ *n.* визг.
■ *v.i.* визжа́ть, взви́згнуть.

Yemen /ˈjemən/ *n.* Йе́мен.

Yemeni /ˈjemənɪ/ *n.* йе́мен|ец (*fem.* -ка).
■ *adj.* йе́менский.

yen /jen/ *n.* (*pl.* **~**) (*currency*) ие́на.

yes /jes/ *adv.* да; (*in reply to neg. statement or command*) нет; **~, please** да, спаси́бо.

yesterday /ˈjestədeɪ/ *n.* вчера́ (*indecl.*), вчера́шний день; **~'s paper** вчера́шняя газе́та; **since ~** со вчера́шнего дня; **the day before ~** позавчера́.
■ *adv.* вчера́; **~ morning/evening** вчера́ у́тром/ве́чером.

yet /jet/ *adv.*
1 (*so far, up to now*) до сих пор; пока́ ещё; **as ~** пока́; (*with neg.*) ещё; **he has not read the book ~** он ещё не чита́л э́ту кни́гу; (*with interrog.*) уже́, ещё; **has the post arrived ~?** по́чта ещё не пришла́?; по́чта уже́ пришла́?
2 (*some day, before all is over*) ещё; **he will win ~** он ещё победи́т.
3 (*still*) ещё; **he has ~ to learn of the disaster** он ещё не зна́ет о катастро́фе.
4 (*so early*) уже́; **need you go ~?** вам уже́ пора́ (идти́)?; **shall we go? Not just ~** пойдёмте? Не сейча́с/Чуть по́зже.
5 (*with comp., even*) да́же, ещё; **this book is ~ more interesting** э́та кни́га ещё интере́снее.
6 (*again, in addition*) ещё; **there is ~ another reason** есть ещё и друга́я причи́на.
7 (*nevertheless*) тем не ме́нее; всё-таки; всё же.
■ *conj.* одна́ко.

yew /juː/ *n.* (*tree, wood*) тис.

Yiddish /ˈjɪdɪʃ/ *n.* и́диш, евре́йский язы́к.
■ *adj.*: **a ~ newspaper** газе́та на и́дише.

yield /jiːld/ *n.*
1 (*crop*) урожа́й.
2 (*return*) дохо́д.
3 (*quantity produced*) вы́ход.
■ *v.t.* 1 (*bring in; produce*) прин|оси́ть, -ести́; произв|оди́ть, -ести́; да|ва́ть, -ть.
2 (*give up*) уступ|а́ть, -и́ть; **~ ground** сда|ва́ть, -ть террито́рию; (*fig.*) сда|ва́ть, -ть (свои́) пози́ции.
■ *v.i.* уступ|а́ть, -и́ть; подд|ава́ться, -а́ться; **he would not ~ to persuasion** он не поддава́лся никаки́м угово́рам; (*of a door*) под|ава́ться, -а́ться.

yob /ˈjɒb/ *n.* (*Br. coll.*) хулига́н.

yobbish /ˈjɒbɪʃ/ *adj.* (*Br. coll.*) хулига́нский.

yoga /ˈjəʊgə/ *n.* йо́га.

yog(h)urt /ˈjɒgət/ *n.* йо́гурт.

yoke /jəʊk/ *n.* (*sense 3: pl.* **~** *or* **~s**)
1 (*fitted to oxen etc.*) ярмо́, хому́т.
2 (*fig.*) и́го, ярмо́; **the Tartar ~** (*hist.*) тата́рское и́го; **shake off the ~** сбр|а́сывать, -о́сить и́го/ярмо́.
3: **~ oxen** (*pair*) упря́жка воло́в.
4 (*for carrying pails etc.*) коромы́сло.
5 (*of dress*) коке́тка (*ве́рхняя* (*плечева́я/набе́дренная*) *часть пла́тья/ю́бки, к кото́рой пришива́ется основна́я их часть*).
■ *v.t.* (*lit.*) впря|га́ть, -чь в ярмо́; (*fig., link*) соедин|я́ть, -и́ть; сочета́ть (*impf., pf.*).

yokel /ˈjəʊk(ə)l/ *n.* дереве́нщина (*c.g.*).

yolk /jəʊk/ *n.* желто́к.

you /juː/ *pron.* (*obj.* **you**; *poss.* **your, yours**)
1 (*familiar sg.*) ты; (*pl. and polite sg.*) вы; **~ and I** ты и я; мы с тобо́й/ва́ми; **~ and he** ты/вы и он; вы с ним; **this is for ~** э́то для тебя́/вас, э́то тебе́/вам.
2 (*one, anyone*): **~ never can tell** никогда́ не зна́ешь; кто его́ зна́ет(?).
■ *cpd.* **~-know-who** *n.* (*coll.*) сам зна́ешь, кто; э́тот са́мый.

young /jʌŋ/ *n.*: **the ~** молодёжь; (**~** *animals*) детёныши (*m. pl.*); (*birds*) птенцы́ (*m. pl.*).
■ *adj.* (**younger** /ˈjʌŋgə/, **youngest** /ˈjʌŋgɪst/) молодо́й, ю́ный; **~ children** ма́ленькие де́ти; **~ people** молодёжь; **he is ~er than I** он моло́же меня́.

youngish /ˈjʌŋɪʃ/ *adj.* дово́льно молодо́й.

youngster /ˈjʌŋstə(r)/ *n.* (*boy*) ма́льчик; (*girl*) де́вочка; (*child*) ребёнок.

your /jɔː(r)/ *adj.* (*familiar sg.*) твой; (*pl. and polite sg.*) ваш; (*referring to subj. of clause*) свой.

yours /jɔːz/ *pron.* (*familiar sg.*) твой; (*pl. and polite sg.*) ваш; (*referring to subj. of clause*) свой; **a friend of ~** оди́н из ва́ших прия́телей; **my teacher and ~** (*2 people*) на́ши с ва́ми учителя́; (*1 person*) наш с ва́ми учи́тель; **here is my hat — have you found ~?** вот моя́ шля́па, а вы свою́ нашли́?

yourself /jɔːˈself/ *pron.* (*pl.* **yourselves**)
1 (*refl.*) себя́; -ся/-сь; **don't deceive ~!** не обма́нывайте себя́!; не обма́нывайтесь!
2 (*emph.*) сам; **you wrote to him ~** вы

сáми емý писáли.
3 (*after preps.*): **why are you sitting by ~?** почемý вы сидúте в одинóчестве?; **did you do it all by ~?** вы э́то сдéлали сáми?
4 : **you don't look ~ today** вы невáжно вы́глядите сегóдня.
youth /juːθ/ *n.*
1 (*state or period*) мóлодость, ю́ность; **in my ~** в мóлодости.
2 (*young man*) ю́ноша (*m.*).
3 (*young people*) молодёжь; **~ club** молодёжный клуб; **~ hostel** молодёжная (тур)бáза/гостúница.
youthful /'juːθfʊl/ *adj.* ю́ный, ю́ношеский; (*of face, person etc.*) молодóй, ю́ный.
youthfulness /'juːθfʊlnɪs/ *n.* мóлодость; (*of appearance*) моложáвость.
yuan /jʊ'ɑːn/ *n.* (*pl.* **~**) юáнь (*m.*).
yucca /'jʌkə/ *n.* ю́кка.
Yugoslav /'juːgəslɑːv/, **-ian** /juːgə'slɑːvɪən/ *adj.* (*hist.*) югослáвский.
Yugoslavia /juːgə'slɑːvɪə/ *n.* (*hist.*) Югослáвия.
yule /juːl/ *n.* (*arch.*) Рождествó; Свя́т|ки (*pl., g.* -ок).
yummy /'jʌmɪ/ *adj.* (**yummier, yummiest**) (*coll.*) вкýсный.
yuppie /'jʌpɪ/ *n.* (*coll. pej.*) я́ппи (*m. indecl.*) (*преуспевающий молодой человек*).

Zz

Zagreb /'zɑːgreb/ *n.* Зáгреб.
Zambia /'zæmbɪə/ *n.* Зáмбия.
Zambian /'zæmbɪən/ *n.* замбú|ец (*fem.* -йка).
■ *adj.* замбúйский.
zany /'zeɪnɪ/ *adj.* (**zanier, zaniest**) смешнóй.
zap /zæp/ (*sl.*) *v.t.* (**zapped, zapping**) (*kill, destroy*) мочúть, за- (*sl.*); (*comput., delete*) стирáть, стерéть.
■ *v.i.* (**zapped, zapping**) (*move quickly*) мчáться (*impf.*).
zeal /ziːl/ *n.* рвéние.
zealot /'zelət/ *n.* фанáт|ик (*fem.* -úчка).
zealous /'zeləs/ *adj.* рéвностный.
zebra /'zebrə/ *n.* зéбра; **~ crossing** (*Br.*) «зéбра» (*пешеходный переход*).
zenith /'zenɪθ/ *n.* (*lit., fig.*) зенúт.
zero /'zɪərəʊ/ *n.* (*pl.* **~s**) ноль (*m.*), нуль (*m.*); **ten degrees below ~** мúнус дéсять грáдусов; **~ hour** час «Ч».
■ *v.i.* (**zeroes, zeroed**): **~ in on a target** пристрéл|иваться, -я́ться.
zest /zest/ *n.* пыл; энтузиáзм; **~ for life** жизнерáдостность.
zigzag /'zɪgzæg/ *n.* зигзáг.
■ *adj.* зигзагообрáзный.
■ *v.i.* (**zigzagged, zigzagging**) дéлать (*impf.*) зигзáги.
Zimbabwe /zɪm'bɑːbwɪ/ *n.* Зимбáбве (*indecl.*).
Zimbabwean /zɪm'bɑːbwɪən/ *n.* зимбабвú|ец (*fem.* -йка).
■ *adj.* зимбабвúйский.
zinc /zɪŋk/ *n.* цинк.
Zionism /'zaɪənɪz(ə)m/ *n.* сионúзм.
Zionist /'zaɪənɪst/ *n.* сионúст (*fem.* -ка).
zip /zɪp/ *n.*
1 (*also* **~per**) (застёжка-)мóлния.
2 (*coll., energy*) пыл, энéргия.
3 : **Z~ code** (*US*) (почтóвый) úндекс.
■ *v.t.* (**zipped, zipping**) (*usu.* **~ up**) застёг|ивать, -нýть (на мóлнию).
■ *v.i.* (**zipped, zipping**) (*rush*) мчáться (*impf.*).
zit /zɪt/ *n.* (*US coll., pimple*) пры́щик.
zodiac /'zəʊdɪæk/ *n.* зодиáк.
zombie /'zɒmbɪ/ *n.* (*fig., coll.*) вя́лый/ апатúчный человéк.
zone /zəʊn/ *n.* зóна, пóяс.
zoo /zuː/ *n.* зоопáрк.
zoological /zəʊə'lɒdʒɪk(ə)l/ *adj.* зоологúческий; **~ gardens** зоопáрк, зоологúческий сад.
zoologist /zəʊ'ɒlədʒɪst/ *n.* зоóлог.
zoology /zəʊ'ɒlədʒɪ/ *n.* зоолóгия.
zoom /zuːm/ *n.* (*attr.*): **~ lens** объектúв с перемéнным фóкусным расстоя́нием.
■ *v.i.* 1 (*move quickly*): **cars ~ed past** машúны проносúлись мúмо.
2 (*phot., cin.*): **~ in on** да|вáть, -ть крýпный план + *g.*
zucchini /zʊ'kiːnɪ/ *n.* (*pl.* **~** *or* **~s**) (*US*) кабачóк.
Zurich /'zjʊərɪk/ *n.* Цю́рих.

Contents

Glossary of grammatical terms **868**

Russian declensions and conjugations ... **878**

Spelling rules 878

Nouns 878

Verbs 882

Adjectives 884

Numbers 886

Russian verbs **887**

Заметки об английской грамматике **896**

Существительные 896

Прилагательные 899

Притяжательные прилагательные 901

Наречия 902

Местоимения 903

Глаголы 907

Английские неправильные глаголы **917**

The Russian alphabet **920**

Английский алфавит **920**

Glossary of grammatical terms

NB: Items in **bold** type refer the user to a separate entry in the glossary.

Accusative: In Russian, the **case** used to express the **direct object** of a **transitive verb**; also, the case used after certain prepositions.

Active: In an active **clause**, the **subject** of the verb performs the action, e.g. '*Sam* (subject) *identified* (verb) *the suspect*' (as opposed to the passive construction 'the suspect was identified by Sam', where *the suspect* is the subject but is not doing the identifying). Cf. **Passive**.

Adjectival noun: An adjective that functions as a noun, e.g. 'the *empties*' (= empty bottles), '*mobile*' (= mobile phone), 'the *Greens*' (= environmentalists), Russian *столóвая* 'dining room', *морóженое* 'ice cream'.

Adjective: A word that describes a **noun** or **pronoun**, giving information about its shape, colour, size, etc., e.g. *triangular, red, large, beautiful* in 'a *triangular* sign', 'the *red* dress', 'it is *large*', 'they are *beautiful*'.

Adverb: A word expressing the manner, frequency, time, place, or extent of an action, e.g. *slowly* and *often* in 'Sue walked *slowly*', 'He *often* stumbled'. Adverbs can also **modify clauses**, e.g. 'Sue *probably* went home', **adjectives**, e.g. 'Sue is *very* tall', and other adverbs, e.g. 'Sue left *extremely* early'.

Affirmative: An affirmative **sentence** or **clause** is a positive statement that explicitly asserts a state of affairs, e.g. *The taxi is waiting*. Cf. **Negative**.

Agree: Words are said to agree when they are put in the correct form in relation to another word. In Standard English and in Russian, a singular noun or pronoun has to have a singular verb, e.g. '*he goes*' (Russian *он идёт*), and a plural noun or pronoun has to have a plural verb, e.g. '*they go*' (Russian *онú идýт*). **Demonstratives** also agree in **number** with the **nouns** they modify, e.g. '*this table*' (Russian *э́тот стол*), '*these tables*' (Russian *э́ти столы́*). In Russian, adjectives, pronouns, and most declined numerals are in the same **case** as the noun they modify, and adjectives, nouns, and verbs have the same **gender** and **number**.

Animate accusative rule: A convention in Russian, whereby in some contexts the form of the accusative is identical with that of the genitive case. This applies **(a)** to masculine singular animate nouns: *Я вúжу мáльчика* 'I see the boy', **(b)** to all plural animate nouns: *Я вúжу мáльчиков/дéвочек/живóтных* 'I see the boys/girls/animals', **(c)** to pronouns, adjectives, and participles that agree with the nouns listed under (a) and (b): *Я знáю э́тих нóвых учителéй* 'I know these new teachers', and **(d)** to the numerals *одúн, два/две, три, четы́ре*, and to *óба/óбе* (also all the collective numerals): *Онá приглосúла трёх подрýг* 'She invited three friends', *Он смотрéл на обóих брáтьев* 'He was looking at both brothers'.

Animate noun: A noun denoting a living being, e.g. *captain, elephant* (Russian *капитáн, слон*).

Antecedent: An earlier word, phrase, or clause to which another word (especially a following **relative pronoun**) refers back, e.g. '*The man* (whom) I know' (Russian *Человéк*, котóрого я знáю).

Article: see **Definite article**, **Indefinite article**.

Glossary of grammatical terms

Aspect: A grammatical category of the verb that expresses the nature of an action or process, viewing it either as continuous or habitual (imperfective aspect), or as completed (perfective aspect). Cf. **Submeanings of the aspects**.

Attributive adjective: An **adjective** placed in front of the noun it modifies, e.g. *empty* in 'the *empty* house' (Russian *пусто́й дом*). Cf. **Predicative adjective**.

Auxiliary verb: In English, a verb which functions together with another verb to form a particular **tense** of the other verb, or to form the **passive**, a question, a **negative**, or an **imperative**. In Russian, the future of the verb *быть* 'to be' combines, as an auxiliary verb, with the infinitive of imperfective verbs to form the future of those verbs, e.g. *Я бу́ду рабо́тать* 'I will work', while the past and future tenses and the conditional mood of *быть* combine with the short forms of perfective passive participles to express past, future, and conditional meanings, e.g. *он был назна́чен* 'he was appointed', *он бу́дет назна́чен* 'he will be appointed', *он был бы назна́чен* 'he would be/would have been appointed'.

Case: In Russian, the form of a noun, pronoun, adjective, or numeral that shows its function within the **clause** (e.g. whether it is the **subject** or **object**). Russian has six cases (**nominative**, **accusative**, **genitive**, **dative**, **instrumental**, and **prepositional**).

Clause: A sentence, or part of a sentence, consisting of a **subject** and a **verb**, e.g. *Mike snores*, or a structure containing **participles** or **infinitives** (with no subject), e.g. '*While waiting* for a bus, I fell asleep' or 'I asked her *to call a taxi*'.

Collective: A term applied to nouns that denote a group of beings or objects, e.g. *herd* (Russian *ста́до*), *clientele* (Russian *клиенту́ра*), *luggage* (Russian *бага́ж*). In Russian, there are also collective numerals (for the numbers from two to ten), which denote a group of individuals, e.g. *дво́е* ('two'), *тро́е* ('three'), *де́сятеро* ('ten'), or combine with **plural-only nouns**.

Comparative: The form of an **adjective** or **adverb** used when comparing one thing with another, to express a greater degree of a quality, e.g. *cheaper*, *more expensive, more accurately* in 'this book is *cheaper*', 'a *more expensive* holiday ', 'he described it *more accurately*'. Cf. **Superlative**.

Compound: A word or phrase created by putting two or more existing forms together. In English and Russian, compounds are sometimes written as one word, sometimes as two, and sometimes hyphenated, e.g. *motorway* (Russian *автостра́да*), *good-humoured* (Russian *доброду́шный*), *drawing board* (Russian *чертёжная доска́*), *bow tie* (Russian *га́лстук-ба́бочка*).

Conditional: A verb form which expresses what would happen, or would have happened, if something else (had) occurred. English normally uses *if* with a form of the **auxiliary verb** *would* to express this notion: *If I won the lottery I would buy a car* | *If I had won... I would have bought*.... Russian uses the particle *бы*: *Я поéхал бы, éсли бы бы́ло врéмя* 'I *would* have gone if there had been time'.

Conjugate: To list the different forms or **inflections** of a verb as they vary according to tense, number, person, or voice, e.g. the verb 'to read' is conjugated in the present tense as follows: (I) *read*, (you) *read*, (he/she/it) *reads*, (we) *read*, (you) *read*, (they) *read*. Cf. the equivalent Russian conjugation of *чита́ть*: (я) *чита́ю*, (ты) *чита́ешь*, (он/она́/оно́) *чита́ет*, (мы) *чита́ем*, (вы) *чита́ете*, (они́) *чита́ют*.

Conjugation: In inflected languages, a class to which a verb is assigned according to how it is **conjugated**. In Russian, *чита́ть* belongs to the first (or

-e-) conjugation and *говори́ть* belongs to the second (or -и-) conjugation.

Conjunction: A word whose function is to join single words, **clauses**, or **phrases**. Coordinating conjunctions (notably *and* and *or*) join words, clauses, or phrases, e.g. 'John *and* Mary', 'I'll go to the cinema *or* meet my friend for dinner'. Subordinating conjunctions (e.g. *that, because, while*) join clauses, e.g. 'I think *that* he is wrong', 'They left *because* it was late', 'I'll push *while* you lift'. Correlative conjunctions consist of words corresponding to each other and regularly used together, e.g. *both ... and, either ... or*.

Consonant: A speech sound that is produced with some restriction on the flow of air, e.g. *b, ch, r.* It can be combined with a **vowel** to form a **syllable**.

Consonant mutation: The change in a consonant when it occurs adjacent to another sound.

Continuous: A verb form indicating that an action or process is or was ongoing, e.g. 'He *is waiting*', 'She *was laughing*'. Also known as *progressive*.

Dative: In Russian, the **case** used to express the **indirect object** of a **verb**; also, the case used after certain prepositions and certain verbs.

Declension: In inflected languages, the class to which a noun is assigned according to how it is **declined**. Russian has three declensions. The first affects masculine nouns (except for those ending in *-а* or *-я*) and neuter nouns, the second feminine nouns (except for those ending in a soft sign), and the third feminine soft-sign nouns.

Decline: To list the different forms or **inflections** of a noun, adjective, pronoun, or numeral as they vary according to **case**. In English, only pronouns can really be said to decline, e.g. *he, him*.

Definite article: In English, the word *the*, which introduces a noun phrase and implies that the thing mentioned has already been mentioned or is common knowledge, e.g. '*the* book on *the* table'. Russian has no definite article, but achieves the same effect through word order (with the thing which has already been mentioned in first position in the sentence, e.g. *Кни́га* на столе́ '*The* book is on the table'), or by using words such as *э́тот* 'this'. Cf. **Indefinite article**.

Delimitation: A process by which the meaning of an adjective is limited to a particular sphere, e.g. Страна́ бога́та *ле́сом* 'The country is rich *in forest*'.

Demonstrative: A word indicating the person or thing referred to, e.g. *this, that, these, those* in '*this* book' (Russian *э́та* кни́га), '*that* house' (Russian *тот* дом), '*these* books' (Russian *э́ти* кни́ги), '*those* people' (Russian *те* лю́ди).

Direct object: A word or phrase **governed** by a verb, e.g. *dogs* in 'She loves *dogs*' (Russian Она́ лю́бит *соба́к*). In an **active** sentence, the person or thing affected by the action is the direct object. In Russian, the direct object is usually expressed by the accusative case. Cf. **Indirect object**.

Direct speech: In direct speech, the speaker's words or thoughts are presented unchanged, using quotation marks, e.g. '"*The shops are still open,*" said Jill'. Russian uses « » (known as guillemets) to show direct speech. Cf. **Indirect speech**.

Emphatic pronoun: The pronouns *myself, himself, themselves*, etc., used for emphasis or to personalize, e.g. 'I did it *myself*'. Russian uses *сам*: Я *сам* сде́лал э́то.

Ending: A letter or letters added to the stem of a word when it is declined or conjugated, e.g. (in English) dog*s*, laugh*ed*, (in Russian) вод*а́* 'water', на стол*е́* 'on the table', зелён*ыми* (instrumental plural) 'green', пиш*у́* 'I write', писа́ла 'she was writing').

Feminine: see **Gender**.

Finite: A verb form which has a specific **tense**, **number**, and **person**, e.g. *rings* in 'She *rings* the doctor' (Russian Она́ *звони́т* врачу́). Here, *rings*/*звони́т* is the third-person singular present tense of the verb *to ring*/*звони́ть*. A **clause** with a finite verb is called a finite clause. Cf. **Non-finite**.

Fleeting vowel: A vowel (*е*, *ё*, or *о*) that appears in some forms of a Russian word, but not in others, e.g. *е* in *бо́лен* (masculine short form of *больно́й* 'sick'), *ё* in *сестёр* (genitive plural of *сестра́* 'sister'), *о* in *сон* 'sleep' (genitive singular *сна*), *разобью́* (first-person singular of *разби́ть* 'to smash').

Future: The future **tense** is used when the time of the event described has not yet happened. English uses the auxiliary verbs *shall* and *will*, the present continuous, and *going to*, to express this notion: '*I shall meet* you in the restaurant', '*They will be* pleased', '*We're leaving* at six', '*I'm going to buy* a new car'. To express **imperfective** future meaning, Russian uses the future tense of *быть* + imperfective infinitive, e.g. Я *бу́ду рабо́тать*, 'I *shall work*' or 'I *shall be working*'. To express **perfective** future meaning, Russian uses conjugated forms of the perfective verb, e.g. Я *спрошу́* 'I *shall ask*'. Cf. **Aspect**.

Gender: In some languages, nouns and pronouns are divided into grammatical classes called genders. The gender of a noun or pronoun can affect the form of words such as verbs or adjectives that accompany them and may need to **agree** with them in gender. Russian has three genders, **masculine**, **feminine**, and **neuter**. The gender of a Russian noun can usually be identified from its ending: nouns ending in a consonant or *-й* are masculine (e.g. *стул* 'chair', *край* 'edge'); most nouns ending in *-а* or *-я* are feminine (e.g. *я́ма* 'hole', *шея́* 'neck'), and nouns ending in *-о* or *-е* are neuter (e.g. *окно́* 'window', *мо́ре* 'sea'). Gender in Russian applies in the singular only. Plural nouns and pronouns do not exhibit gender.

Genitive: In Russian, the **case** used to express possession; also, the case used after most cardinal numerals and after **indefinite numerals**, certain prepositions, and certain verbs.

Gerund: In English, a verb form in *-ing* that functions like a noun, e.g. *running* in 'She loves *running*' (cf. the Russian use of the **infinitive** in this meaning: Она́ лю́бит *бе́гать*). By contrast, the Russian gerund is a verbal adverb that replaces a clause. The imperfective gerund usually ends in *-я* (e.g. Он стои́т, *куря́* 'He stands, *smoking*'), the perfective in *-в* (e.g. *Поу́жинав*, он встал '*Having dined*, he got up').

Govern: A word requiring a noun or pronoun to be in a particular **case** is said to govern the noun or pronoun (e.g. the Russian verb *владе́ть* 'to own' governs the instrumental case, and the preposition *че́рез* 'across' governs the accusative case).

Hard consonant: A consonant that appears at the end of a word (e.g. final *-т* in *нет* 'no'), or is followed by *а*, *ы*, *о*, *у*, or (rarely) *э* (e.g. *г* and *т* in *газе́та* 'newspaper', *н* in *чёрный* 'black', *л* and *в* in *сло́во* 'word', *д* and *м* in *ду́ма* 'duma'). Exceptions are the consonants ч and щ which are always soft even if at the end of a word or followed by the above-listed vowels, and ж, ц, and ш which are always hard. Cf. **Soft consonant**.

Historic present: Use of the present tense in order to make the description of a past event more vivid, e.g. 'Suddenly he *breaks* into a run'.

Imperative: The form of the verb used to express a command, e.g. *come* in

'*Come* here!'

Imperfective: see **Aspect**.

Impersonal construction: A construction in which an action or state does not involve a specific person or thing as the grammatical subject, e.g. *Стемнéло* 'It grew dark', *Как тебя́ зову́т?* 'What is your name?'

Inanimate noun: A noun denoting a non-living thing, e.g. *hall, happiness* (Russian *зал, сча́стье*).

Indeclinable: A term applied to a noun, pronoun, or adjective that has no **inflections**. In English, the pronoun *you* is indeclinable (whereas *I, he, she*, and *they* change to *me, him, her*, and *them* in the object case, e.g. the dog bit *me*/you/*him*/*her*/*them*). In Russian, many **loanwords** are indeclinable (e.g. *такси́* 'taxi', *беж adj.* 'beige'), as are the possessive pronouns *его́*, 'his/its', *её* 'her(s)/its', *их* 'their(s)'.

Indefinite adverb: An adverb that does not refer to any place, time, manner, etc. in particular, e.g. *somewhere, sometime, somehow* (Russian *где́-то, когда́-то, ка́к-то*).

Indefinite article: In English, the word *a*/*an*, which introduces a noun phrase and implies that the thing mentioned is non-specific, e.g. 'she bought *a* book'. Russian has no indefinite article, but achieves the same effect through word order (with an object mentioned for the first time appearing at the end of the sentence, e.g. На столé лежи́т *ка́рта* '*A* map is lying on the table'). Cf. **Definite article**.

Indefinite numeral: In Russian, a numeral that denotes an indefinite quantity, e.g. *мно́го* 'much, many', *нéсколько* 'several'.

Indefinite pronoun: A pronoun that does not refer to any person or thing in particular, e.g. *someone* (Russian *кто́-то*), *something* (Russian *что́-то*), *anyone* (Russian *кто́-нибудь*), *anything* (Russian *что́-нибудь*).

Indicative: The form of a verb used to express a simple statement of fact, when an event is considered to be definitely taking place or to have taken place, e.g. 'He *is asleep*' (Russian Он *спит*), 'He *fell asleep*' (Russian Он *засну́л*). Cf. **Subjunctive**.

Indirect object: A word or phrase referring to the person who receives the **direct object**, e.g. *the driver* in the sentences 'She gave the ticket to *the driver*' or 'She gave *the driver* the ticket'. In Russian, the indirect object is usually expressed by the dative case, e.g. Она́ подари́ла часы́ *сы́ну* 'She gave the watch *to her son*'. Cf. **Direct object**.

Indirect speech: In indirect speech, the speaker's words or thoughts are reported in a subordinate clause using a reporting verb. In English a change of tense and person is needed, e.g. 'He said "*I want* a drink"' (direct speech) becomes 'He said *he wanted* a drink'. In Russian, only the person changes, not the tense, e.g. Он сказа́л: «*Я го́лоден*» 'He said "I'm hungry"' becomes Он сказа́л, что *он го́лоден* 'He said that *he was* hungry'.

Infinitive: The basic form of the verb, e.g. *laugh, damage, be*. It is not bound to a particular subject or tense and in English is often preceded by *to* or by another verb, e.g. 'I want *to see* her', 'She came *to see* me', 'Let me *see*'. Russian infinitives end in *-ть*, *-ти*, or *-чь* (e.g. *писа́ть* 'to write', *вести́* 'to lead', *мочь* 'to be able').

Inflection: A change in the form of a word (usually the ending), to express tense, gender, number, or case, etc., e.g. the English plural ending *-s* in 'car*s*' or the past tense inflection *-ed* in 'I visit*ed* my uncle'. Russian is a highly-inflected language in which nouns, pronouns, adjectives, and numerals decline, and verbs conjugate. Cf. **Case, Conjugate, Conjugation, Declension**, and **Decline**.

Instrumental: In Russian, the **case**

used to express the means by which something is done; also, the case used after certain prepositions and certain verbs.

Interrogative adverb: An adverb used to ask questions, e.g. *how* in '*How* are you?' (Russian *Как* (вы) пожива́ете?) or *when* in '*When* will they arrive?' (Russian *Когда́* они́ прие́дут?).

Interrogative pronoun: A pronoun used to ask questions, e.g. *which* in '*Which* do you want?' (Russian *Како́й* вы хоти́те?).

Intonation: The use of the pitch of the voice to convey meaning, e.g. *Well? Did you ask her?* (rising intonation) and *Well! I've never been so insulted!* (falling intonation). Different languages have different intonation patterns.

Intransitive verb: A verb not taking a **direct object**, e.g. slept in 'He slept soundly' (Russian Он кре́пко *спал*), and read in 'He can't read' (Russian Он не уме́ет *чита́ть*). Cf. **Transitive verb**.

Invariable: another term for **indeclinable** (when referring to nouns, adjectives, and pronouns). Adverbs and gerunds are also invariable in Russian.

Irregular verb: In English, a verb such as 'sing' whose **inflections** do not follow one of the usual **conjugation** patterns of the language (past sang by contrast with the usual past tense suffix *-ed*, e.g. walk*ed*). In Russian, the only truly irregular verbs are *бежа́ть* 'to run', *дать* 'to give', *есть* 'to eat', and *хоте́ть* 'to want'. Cf. **Regular verb**.

Loanword: A word borrowed from another language, e.g. Russian *ко́фе* 'coffee'.

Locative case: A term used as an alternative to the prepositional case to describe prepositional phrases that denote location and are introduced by *в* 'in' or *на* 'on': *в до́ме* 'in the house', *на столе́* 'on the table'. Some nouns have special locative forms in stressed *у*, *ю*, or *и*: *в лесу́* 'in the forest', *на краю́* 'on the edge', *на двери́* 'on the door'.

Main clause: In a **sentence** with more than one **clause**, the clause which is not **subordinate** to any of the others is known as the main clause, e.g. 'Peter stopped' in 'When it got too dark to see where he was going, Peter stopped'. A main clause can stand alone as a sentence. Cf. **Subordinate clause**.

Masculine: see **Gender**.

Mobile stress: A feature of some Russian words whereby the stressed syllable changes in one or more forms of the word's declension or conjugation, etc. Stress may move from the stem onto the ending, e.g. *стол* 'table', genitive singular *стола́*; *сло́во* 'word', nominative plural *слова́*; *печь* 'stove', locative singular *печи́*; masculine short form *до́рог* 'is dear', feminine *дорога́*; *пять* 'five', genitive *пяти́*. It may also move from the ending onto the stem, e.g. *река́* 'river', accusative singular *ре́ку* (also *реку́*) ; *окно́* 'window', nominative plural *о́кна*. In conjugation, stress shift occurs only from the ending onto the stem, e.g. *пишу́* 'I write', *пи́шет* 'he writes'.

Modify: A word or phrase modifies another word or phrase when it provides additional information about it. Modifying expressions include **adjectives**, e.g. *slow* in 'A *slow* train', and **adverbs**, e.g. *slowly* in 'The train moved *slowly*'.

Negative: A negative **sentence** or **clause** asserts that something is not the case, using a negative **particle**, e.g. '*The taxi is not waiting*'. Similarly, a negative **adverb** (*nowhere*, *never*) or negative **pronoun** (*nobody*, *nothing*). Cf. **Affirmative**.

Neuter: see **Gender**.

Nominative: In Russian, the **case** used to express the **subject** of a clause.

Non-finite: A term applied to a verb form which has no specific **tense**,

number, or **person**, e.g. *waiting* in 'While *waiting* for a bus, Peter read the paper'. Russian uses a **gerund** in such contexts, e.g. *Ожидáя* автóбус, Пи́тер читáл газéту. Cf. **Finite**.

Noun: A word that identifies a person, e.g. *milkman*, *girl*, *uncle*, a physical object, e.g. *cup*, *book*, *building*, or an abstract notion, e.g. *beauty*, *health*, *unpleasantness*.

Noun phrase: A group of words including a noun, which functions in a sentence as subject, object, or prepositional object.

Number: A grammatical classification whereby a word is either **singular** or **plural**.

Numeral: A word expressing a number. Members of the series of numbers *one, two*, etc. are referred to as cardinal numbers or cardinal numerals. Members of the series *first, second*, etc. are referred to as ordinal numbers or ordinal numerals. Russian also has a series of collective numerals, e.g. *двóе* in *двóе* детéй 'two children', *трóе* in *трóе* сáнок 'three sledges'.

Object: see **Direct object**, **Indirect object**.

Oblique cases: All **cases** other than the **nominative**.

Participle: In English, a word formed from a verb and used as an adjective or as a noun, or to form compound verb forms. The English present participle ends in *-ing*, e.g. '*Thinking* I was late, I hurried'(Russian uses a **gerund** in such contexts: *Дýмая*, что я опáздываю, я торопи́лся), and the past participle ends in *-ed*, e.g. 'I have *finished*' (Russian uses a **finite verb** in such contexts: Я *кóнчил*). Russian has four participles, present active, past active, present passive, and past passive, which either replace **relative clauses**, e.g. Дéвочка, *читáющая*/*читáвшая*/ *прочитáвшая* кни́гу 'the girl *who is reading*/*who was reading*/*who has read* the book', мотóр, *провéренный* механи́ками 'an engine *which has been checked* by the mechanics', or (using the short form of the past passive participle) function as **predicates**, e.g. Дом *прóдан* 'The house *has been sold*'.

Particle: In Russian, a word or a part of a word that invests other words or phrases with expressive nuances of meaning, e.g. *Не* я оши́бся! 'I'm not the one who got it wrong!', *Ну* и проголодáлся же я! 'Am I hungry!'

Partitive genitive: The genitive case used to denote a part, as opposed to the whole, of a substance, e.g. мнóго *молокá* 'a lot of milk', кусóк *мя́са* 'a piece of meat'. Some nouns have special partitive genitive forms in *-у* or *-ю*: тарéлка сýп*у* 'a plate of soup', Хóчешь чá*ю*? 'Would you like some tea?'

Part of speech: Any of the classes into which words are categorized for grammatical purposes. The main ones are **Noun**, **Adjective**, **Pronoun**, **Verb**, **Adverb**, **Preposition**, and **Conjunction**.

Passive: The form of the **clause** used when the individual referred to by the **subject** undergoes (rather than performs) the action, e.g. '*The soldier was nominated* for an award' (Russian *Солдáт был представлен* к наградé). Cf. **Active**.

Past: The past **tense** is used when the time of the event described precedes the time of utterance, e.g. 'Peter *lived* in London'. Cf. **Present**.

Perfect: A verb form indicating an action or process seen as completed, e.g. 'She *has paid* the bill'. In Russian this is rendered by a perfective past form of the verb, e.g. Онá *оплати́ла* счёт.

Perfective: see **Aspect**.

Person: Person forms are the grammatical forms (especially **pronouns**) that refer to or agree with the speaker and other individuals addressed or mentioned, e.g. *I, we* (first-person pronouns, Russian *я, мы*), *you* (second-person pronoun, Russian *ты*, *вы*), *he*, *she*, *it*, *they* (third-person pronouns, Russian *он*, *она́*, *оно́*, *они́*).

Personal pronoun: A **pronoun** that refers to a person or to people known to the speaker, e.g. *I*, *he*, *she*, *it*, *they* (Russian *я*, *он*, *она́*, *оно́*, *они́*).

Phrase: A group of words that function together in a **clause**, e.g. *The courier* is a (noun) phrase within the clause '*The courier* will go there'.

Plural: A word or form referring to more than one person or object, e.g. *children*, *books*, *we*, *are*. Cf. **Singular**.

Plural-only noun: A noun that has the form of a plural but can refer to a singular object or a number of like objects, e.g. *са́нки* 'sledge, sledges'.

Possessive: A pronoun indicating possession, e.g. Russian *мой* 'my, mine', *твой* 'your, yours', *его́* 'his, its', *её* 'her, hers, its', *наш* 'our, ours', *ваш* 'your, yours', *их* 'their, theirs'. Possessives are used both adjectivally (e.g. *наш дом* 'our house') and pronominally (e.g. *Э́тот дом — наш* 'This house is ours').

Predicate: The part of a clause that states something about the **subject**, e.g. *closed the door softly* in 'Mary *closed the door softly*', or *went home* in 'We *went home*'. Cf. **Subject**.

Predicative adjective: An **adjective** that appears in a separate **phrase** from the noun it modifies, often following the verb 'to be', e.g. *empty* in 'The house was *empty*'. Russian often uses a short-form adjective in such contexts: Дом был *пуст*. Cf. **Attributive adjective**.

Predicative adverb: In Russian, an adverb that is used as a predicate, e.g. *Ве́село* 'It's fun', Ему́ *гру́стно* 'He feels sad'.

Prefix: An element that is added to the beginning of a word to change its meaning or grammatical form, e.g. *mis-* and *re-* in '*mis*understand', '*re*consider', Russian *при-* in *при*ба́вить 'to add' and *от-* in *от*плати́ть 'to pay back'. Cf. **Suffix**.

Preposition: A word governing and usually preceding a noun or pronoun, expressing its relationship to another word in the sentence, e.g. 'She arrived *after* dinner', 'What did you do it *for*?' This relationship can be spatial, e.g. 'The book is *on* the table' (Russian Кни́га *на* столе́), temporal, e.g. 'He arrived *in* March' (Russian Он прие́хал *в* ма́рте), causal, e.g. 'She blushed *with* shame' (Russian Она́ покрасне́ла *от* стыда́), etc. A Russian preposition governs one of the **oblique cases**.

Prepositional: In Russian, the **case** used after certain prepositions, mainly to express location. See also **Locative case**.

Present: The present **tense** is used when the time of the event described includes the time of utterance, e.g. *lives* in 'Peter *lives* in London'. Cf. **Past**.

Progressive: another term for **Continuous**.

Pronoun: A word that substitutes for a noun or noun phrase, e.g. *them* in 'Children don't like *them*' (instead of 'Children don't like *vegetables*'). Cf. Russian Де́ти не лю́бят *их* (instead of *овоще́й*).

Reflexive pronoun: A pronoun that is the object of the verb, but refers back to the subject of the clause in denoting the same individual, e.g. *herself* in: 'She blamed *herself*'. Russian uses the declinable reflexive pronoun *себя́* in such contexts, e.g. Он смо́трит на *себя́* 'He looks at *himself*', Он купи́л *себе́* мотоци́кл, 'He bought *himself* a motorcycle', Она́ дово́льна *собо́й* 'She is pleased with *herself*'. Cf. also **Reflexive verb**.

Reflexive verb: In Russian, a verb that ends in the reflexive particle *-ся*/ *-сь*, e.g. Он одева́ет*ся* 'He dresses (*himself*)', Я мо́юсь 'I wash (*myself*)'.

Regular verb: A verb such as *laugh* whose **inflections** follow one of the usual **conjugation** patterns. In English, this involves (among other things) forming the **past tense** by adding *-ed* to the infinitive, e.g. laugh*ed* in 'They *laughed* at me'. Cf. **Irregular verb**.

Relative clause: A clause that is introduced by a **relative pronoun**.

Relative pronoun: A pronoun (*who*, *whose*, *which*, or *that*) used to introduce a subordinate clause and referring back to a person or thing in the preceding clause, e.g. 'Peter lost the book *that*/*which* he bought', 'The man *who* is waiting is my brother', or 'Have you met the man *whose* sister got married?' Russian uses the relevant forms of *кото́рый*.

Reported speech: another term for **Indirect speech**.

Sentence: A structure with at least one **finite** verb, and consisting of one or more **clauses**, e.g. '*John laughed*', '*John sat down and waited*', '*While waiting for the bus, John saw an accident*'.

Singular: A word or form referring to just one person or thing, e.g. *child, book, I, is*. Cf. **Plural**.

Soft consonant: In Russian, a consonant followed by a soft sign (e.g. *т* in *мать*), or by the vowels *я, е, и, ё*, or *ю* (e.g. *п* in *пять*, *н* in *не́бо*, *п* in *пи́во*, л in *лёд*, *т* in *утю́г*). The consonants ч and щ are always pronounced soft, while *ж*, *ц*, and *ш* are always pronounced hard. Cf. **Hard consonant**.

Spelling rules: In Russian, the following rules:

(a) *ы* is replaced by *и* after г, к, х, ж, ч, ш, and щ.

(b) unstressed *о* is replaced by *е* after ж, ч, ш, щ, and ц.

(c) *ю* and *я* are replaced by *у* and *а* after г, к, х, ж, ч, ш, and щ.

(d) the preposition *о* 'about, concerning' is spelt *об* before words beginning *а*, *э*, *и*, *о*, and *у*, and *обо* before *мне* and *всём*/*всех*: *обо мне* 'about me', *обо всём* 'about everything', *обо всех* 'about everyone'.

Stem: The base form or root of the word to which **endings**, **prefixes**, and **suffixes** may be added, e.g. *box* in *box*es, *consider* in 're*consider*' and *understand* in '*understand*ing'. Cf. Russian *книг-* in *кни́г*а 'book', *говор-* in *говор*и́ть 'to speak', and *-ход* in вос*хо́д* 'rising', *студе́нт-* in *студе́нт*ка 'female student'.

Stress: The **syllable** of a word receiving relatively greater force or emphasis than the other(s) is said to receive stress or to be the stressed syllable, e.g. *wíndow*, *ка́рта* 'map' (stressed on the first syllable), *dedúction*, *доро́га* 'road' (stressed medially), *suppóse*, *страна́* 'country'(stressed on the final syllable).

Subject: The part of the **clause** referring to the individual of whom or the object of which the **predicate** is asserted, e.g. *Anna* in: '*Anna* closed the door' or *The picture* in '*The picture* hangs on the wall'. In Russian, the subject usually appears in the nominative case, e.g. *А́нна* закры́ла дверь, *Карти́на* виси́т на стене́. Cf. **Predicate**.

Subjunctive: The form of the verb used in some languages when no claim is being made that the action or event actually takes (or took) place. The subjunctive is not often used in English, but can still be seen in expressions like *if I were you*. In Russian, the subjunctive is the structure used when an action is desired. It is formed using *что́бы* + past tense, e.g. Она́ хо́чет, *что́бы я ушёл* ('She wants me *to go away*'). Cf. **Indicative**.

Submeanings of the aspects: Aspectual meanings other than those that denote continuous or habitual action or process (imperfective), and those that denote completion (perfective). Submeanings describe intermittent action or process (imperfective *побáливает* 'hurts on and off'), inception (perfective *заплáкать* 'to burst into tears'), and short duration (perfective *поспáть* 'to have a nap'). Cf. **Aspect**.

Subordinate clause: A clause that cannot normally stand alone without a **main clause** and is usually introduced by a **conjunction**, e.g. *when it rang* in 'She answered the phone *when it rang*', or *because he is ill* in 'He is not at work *because he is ill*'. Cf. **Main clause**.

Suffix: An element that is added to the end of a word or **stem** to change its meaning or grammatical form, e.g. *-ing* and *-ness* in 'understand*ing*', 'kind*ness*', Russian *-ка* in *студéнтка* 'female student', *-инá* in *глубинá* 'depth'. Cf. **Prefix**.

Superlative: The form of an **adjective** or **adverb** used when comparing one thing with another to express the greatest degree of a quality, e.g. *cheapest* (Russian *сáмый дешёвый*), *most beautiful* (Russian *сáмый красúвый*), *least desirable* (Russian *наимéнее желáтельный*). Cf. **Comparative**.

Syllable: A unit of pronunciation that is normally less than a word but greater than a single sound, e.g. *abracadabra* has five syllables: *ab-ra-ca-dab-ra*, as does Russian *путеводúтель* ('guide'): *пу-те-во-дú-тель*.

Tense: The relationship between the time of utterance and the time of an event described in the clause is expressed by verb tense forms or **inflections**, e.g. 'Anna *waits*' (present tense, Russian Áнна *ждёт*), 'Anna *waited*' (past tense, Russian Áнна *ждалá*).

Transitive verb: A verb taking a **direct object**, e.g. *read* in 'She *was reading* a book' (Russian Онá *читáла* кнúгу). Cf. **Intransitive verb**.

Verb: A word that expresses an action, process, or state of affairs, e.g. 'He closed the door' (Russian Он *закры́л* дверь), 'She laughs' (Russian Онá *смеётся*), 'They were at home' (Russian Онú *бы́ли* дóма).

Verbal noun: In Russian, a noun derived from a verb stem and describing the action of the verb from which it derives, e.g. *развúтие* 'development', *приготовлéние* 'preparation', *обрабóтка* 'processing'.

Verbs of motion: In Russian, a series of fourteen pairs of imperfective verbs that denote various types of motion, one in each pair (the 'unidirectional') describing movement in one direction (*Он идёт домóй* 'He is on his way home'), the other (the 'multidirectional') describing movement in general (*Онá хóдит бы́стро* 'She walks fast'), movement in various directions (*Он хóдит взад и вперёд* 'He is walking up and down'), or habitual movement (*Я чáсто хожу́ в кинó* 'I often go to the cinema').

Vocative: In Russian, the form of a noun used in addressing someone. The nominative case usually fulfils this function: *Сергéй Пáвлович!* 'Sergei Pavlovich!', but some truncated forms are used in colloquial Russian, e.g. *мам!* 'Mum!', *Вань!* 'Vanya!' *Бóже* in *Бóже* мой! 'My God!' is a relic of the former vocative case (the nominative form being *Бог*).

Voiced and voiceless consonants: Consonants pronounced, respectively, with and without vibration of the vocal cords. In Russian, the voiceless consonants are к, п, с, т, ф, х, ц, ч, ш, and щ. The other consonants are voiced.

Vowel: A basic speech sound that is produced by the unrestricted flow of air, e.g. *a* in h*a*t, *ee* in f*ee*t, or *ow* in h*ow*. A vowel forms the nucleus of a **syllable**. Cf. **Consonant**.

Russian declensions and conjugations

The following is a comprehensive but not exhaustive guide to Russian declension and conjugation.

The vertical line | shows the division between the stem and the ending of a word.

When using these tables, the reader should bear in mind the Spelling Rules (see below), e.g. the nominative plural of кни́га noun 7 is кни́ги, and the Notes on the Declensions of Nouns (after Table 17 below).

Spelling Rules

The following Spelling Rules are important because they affect the endings of many nouns, adjectives, and verbs.

1. Unstressed o does not follow ж, ц, ч, ш, or щ; instead, e is used, e.g. с му́жем, шесть, ме́сяцев, с касси́ршей, хоро́шее пальто́.
2. ю and я do not follow г, к, ж, х, ц, ч, ш, or щ; they become у and a, e.g. держа́ть; я держу́, они́ де́ржат; слы́шать: я слы́шу, они́ слы́шат.
3. ы does not follow г, к, ж, х, ч, ш, or щ; it becomes и, e.g. две кни́ги, больши́е дома́.

Nouns

Masculine Nouns

TABLE 1

	Singular	Plural
Nominative	**авто́бус**	**авто́бус|ы**
Accusative	**авто́бус**	**авто́бус|ы**
Genitive	**авто́бус|а**	**авто́бус|ов**
Dative	**авто́бус|у**	**авто́бус|ам**
Instrumental	**авто́бус|ом**	**авто́бус|ами**
Prepositional	**авто́бус|е**	**авто́бус|ах**

This declension, comprising nouns ending in a hard consonant, is the most common declension for masculine nouns in Russian.

TABLE 2

	Singular	Plural
Nominative	**трамва́|й**	**трамва́|и**
Accusative	**трамва́|й**	**трамва́|и**
Genitive	**трамва́|я**	**трамва́|ев**
Dative	**трамва́|ю**	**трамва́|ям**
Instrumental	**трамва́|ем**	**трамва́|ями**
Prepositional	**трамва́|е**	**трамва́|ях**

This declension consists of nouns ending in -ай, -ей, -ой, or -уй.

Other common Russian words belonging to this declension are май, сара́й, слу́чай, урожа́й, чай; клей, руче́й, хокке́й, юбиле́й; бой, геро́й; поцелу́й.

TABLE 3

	Singular	Plural
Nominative	**репорта́ж**	**репорта́ж|и**
Accusative	**репорта́ж**	**репорта́ж|и**
Genitive	**репорта́ж|а**	**репорта́ж|ей**
Dative	**репорта́ж|у**	**репорта́ж|ам**
Instrumental	**репорта́ж|ем**	**репорта́ж|ами**
Prepositional	**репорта́ж|е**	**репорта́ж|ах**

This declension consists of nouns ending in -ж, -ш, or -щ, which are not stressed on the last syllable in declension in the singular.

Other nouns of this declension are пейза́ж, пляж, фарш, о́вощ, and това́рищ.

TABLE 4

	Singular	Plural
Nominative	**эта́ж**	**этаж|и́**
Accusative	**эта́ж**	**этаж|и́**
Genitive	**этаж|а́**	**этаж|е́й**
Dative	**этаж|у́**	**этаж|а́м**
Instrumental	**этаж|о́м**	**этаж|а́ми**
Prepositional	**этаж|е́**	**этаж|а́х**

These nouns differ from those in Table 3 by being stressed on the last syllable in all cases; in the instrumental singular they end in -ом instead of -ем.

Other such nouns are бага́ж, борщ, каранда́ш, нож, and плащ.

TABLE 5

	Singular	Plural
Nominative	**сцена́ри|й**	**сцена́ри|и**
Accusative	**сцена́ри|й**	**сцена́ри|и**
Genitive	**сцена́ри|я**	**сцена́ри|ев**
Dative	**сцена́ри|ю**	**сцена́ри|ям**
Instrumental	**сцена́ри|ем**	**сцена́ри|ями**
Prepositional	**сцена́ри|и**	**сцена́ри|ях**

Nouns belonging to this declension tend to be obscure or technical terms. One fairly common word is ге́ний, meaning ‘genius’.

TABLE 6

	Singular	Plural
Nominative	**спекта́кл|ь**	**спекта́кл|и**
Accusative	**спекта́кл|ь**	**спекта́кл|и**
Genitive	**спекта́кл|я**	**спекта́кл|ей**
Dative	**спекта́кл|ю**	**спекта́кл|ям**
Instrumental	**спекта́кл|ем**	**спекта́кл|ями**
Prepositional	**спекта́кл|е**	**спекта́кл|ях**

Masculine nouns ending in a soft sign belong to this declension. Other common words belonging to this group are автомоби́ль, апре́ль (and other names of months), Кремль, портфе́ль, рубль, and слова́рь.

Feminine nouns

TABLE 7

	Singular	Plural
Nominative	**газе́т|а**	**газе́т|ы**
Accusative	**газе́т|у**	**газе́т|ы**
Genitive	**газе́т|ы**	**газе́т**
Dative	**газе́т|е**	**газе́т|ам**
Instrumental	**газе́т|ой**	**газе́т|ами**
Prepositional	**газе́т|е**	**газе́т|ах**

This is the most common declension for feminine nouns in Russian. A few masculine nouns, e.g. де́душка, мужчи́на, and па́па, also belong to this declension.

Remember the Spelling Rules, whereby ы and unstressed o do not follow certain letters (see p. 878), e.g. кни́ги (*books*), афи́ши (*posters*), с учени́цей (*with the pupil*).

TABLE 8

Singular	Plural	
Nominative	**неде́л|я**	**неде́л|и**
Accusative	**неде́л|ю**	**неде́л|и**
Genitive	**неде́л|и**	**неде́л|ь**
Dative	**неде́л|е**	**неде́л|ям**
Instrumental	**неде́л|ей**	**неде́л|ями**
Prepositional	**неде́л|е**	**неде́л|ях**

This declension is for feminine nouns ending in a consonant + -я. A few masculine nouns also belong to this declension, e.g. дя́дя, судья́. Other feminine nouns of this declension are ба́шня, дере́вня, пе́сня, спа́льня, and ту́фля. Some nouns of this declension have a genitive plural form ending in -ей, e.g. дя́дя, семья́, and тётя. This is indicated at the dictionary entries.

TABLE 9

	Singular	Plural
Nominative	**ста́нци|я**	**ста́нци|и**
Accusative	**ста́нци|ю**	**ста́нци|и**
Genitive	**ста́нци|и**	**ста́нци|й**
Dative	**ста́нци|и**	**ста́нци|ям**
Instrumental	**ста́нци|ей**	**ста́нци|ями**
Prepositional	**ста́нци|и**	**ста́нци|ях**

This declension consists of feminine nouns ending in -ия. Other nouns of this declension are а́рмия, исто́рия, ли́ния, организа́ция, фами́лия, and the names of most countries.

TABLE 10

	Singular	Plural
Nominative	**галере́|я**	**галере́|и**
Accusative	**галере́|ю**	**галере́|и**
Genitive	**галере́|и**	**галере́|й**
Dative	**галере́|е**	**галере́|ям**
Instrumental	**галере́|ей**	**галере́|ями**
Prepositional	**галере́|е**	**галере́|ях**

This declension consists of feminine nouns ending in -ея or -уя. Other such nouns are алле́я, батаре́я, иде́я, ше́я, and ста́туя.

TABLE 11

	Singular	Plural
Nominative	**бол|ь**	**бо́л|и**
Accusative	**бол|ь**	**бо́л|и**
Genitive	**бо́л|и**	**бо́л|ей**
Dative	**бо́л|и**	**бо́л|ям**
Instrumental	**бо́л|ью**	**бо́л|ями**
Prepositional	**бо́л|и**	**бо́л|ях**

This declension is for feminine nouns ending in -ь. Other such nouns are жизнь, крова́ть, ме́бель, пло́щадь, посте́ль, тетра́дь, and the numbers ending in -ь.

Neuter Nouns

TABLE 12

	Singular	Plural
Nominative	**чу́вств|о**	**чу́вств|а**
Accusative	**чу́вств|о**	**чу́вств|а**
Genitive	**чу́вств|а**	**чувств**
Dative	**чу́вств|у**	**чу́вств|ам**
Instrumental	**чу́вств|ом**	**чу́вств|ами**
Prepositional	**чу́вств|е**	**чу́вств|ах**

This declension is for neuter nouns ending in -о. Other such nouns are блю́до, ма́сло, молоко́, пи́во, and сло́во.

TABLE 13

	Singular	Plural
Nominative	**учи́лищ|е**	**учи́лищ|а**
Accusative	**учи́лищ|е**	**учи́лищ|а**
Genitive	**учи́лищ|а**	**учи́лищ**
Dative	**учи́лищ|у**	**учи́лищ|ам**
Instrumental	**учи́лищ|ем**	**учи́лищ|ами**
Prepositional	**учи́лищ|е**	**учи́лищ|ах**

This declension is for neuter nouns ending in -ще or -це. Other nouns of this declension are кла́дбище, полоте́нце, and со́лнце.

TABLE 14

	Singular	Plural
Nominative	**зда́ни|е**	**зда́ни|я**
Accusative	**зда́ни|е**	**зда́ни|я**
Genitive	**зда́ни|я**	**зда́ни|й**
Dative	**зда́ни|ю**	**зда́ни|ям**
Instrumental	**зда́ни|ем**	**зда́ни|ями**
Prepositional	**зда́ни|и**	**зда́ни|ях**

This declension is for neuter nouns ending in -ие. Other such nouns are внима́ние, путеше́ствие, and удивле́ние.

TABLE 15

	Singular	Plural
Nominative	**воскресе́н|ье**	**воскресе́н|ья**
Accusative	**воскресе́н|ье**	**воскресе́н|ья**
Genitive	**воскресе́н|ья**	**воскресе́н|ий**
Dative	**воскресе́н|ью**	**воскресе́н|ьям**
Instrumental	**воскресе́н|ьем**	**воскресе́н|ьями**
Prepositional	**воскресе́н|ье**	**воскресе́н|ьях**

This declension is for neuter nouns ending in -ье or -ьё. Other such nouns are варе́нье, сиде́нье, and сча́стье.

TABLE 16

	Singular	Plural
Nominative	**мо́р|е**	**мор|я́**
Accusative	**мо́р|е**	**мор|я́**
Genitive	**мо́р|я**	**мор|е́й**
Dative	**мо́р|ю**	**мор|я́м**
Instrumental	**мо́р|ем**	**мор|я́ми**
Prepositional	**мо́р|е**	**мор|я́х**

This declension is for neuter nouns ending in a consonant + -е, but not -ще or -це. In practice, the only other two nouns of this declension are го́ре and по́ле.

TABLE 17

	Singular	Plural
Nominative	**вре́м|я**	**врем|ена́**
Accusative	**вре́м|я**	**врем|ена́**
Genitive	**вре́м|ени**	**врем|ён**
Dative	**вре́м|ени**	**врем|ена́м**
Instrumental	**вре́м|енем**	**врем|ена́ми**
Prepositional	**вре́м|ени**	**врем|ена́х**

This declension is for a small number of neuter nouns ending in -мя. Others belonging to this group are и́мя, пла́мя, and се́мя.

Notes on the declension of nouns

The accusative ending for masculine singular animate and all plural animate nouns (those denoting living beings) coincides with the genitive ending, e.g.

он уви́дел большо́го чёрного во́лка (he saw a big black wolf)
мы попроси́ли свои́х друзе́й помо́чь (we asked our friends to help)

Some masculine nouns take the ending -у́ or -ю́ in the prepositional singular after в and на, e.g. в лесу́, на мосту́; some feminine nouns ending in -ь take -и́, e.g. в тени́. They are said to be in the locative case.Where this happens it is shown at the dictionary entry.

Some masculine nouns have the ending -а in the nominative plural, e.g. па́спорт, бе́рег. Others have the ending -ья, e.g. брат, стул. Where this happens it is shown at the dictionary entry.

Some nouns are indeclinable. They usually end in a vowel, are neuter, and have been borrowed into Russian from another language. Examples are кафе́, ра́дио, такси́.

Many nouns change their stress in declension. This is shown in the individual dictionary entries.

Verbs

The -e- conjugation

чита́|ть:

TABLE 18

	Singular	Plural
1st person	**чита́|ю**	**чита́|ем**
2nd person	**чита́|ешь**	**чита́|ете**
3rd person	**чита́|ет**	**чита́|ют**

сия́|ть:

TABLE 19

	Singular	Plural
1st person	**сия́|ю**	**сия́|ем**
2nd person	**сия́|ешь**	**сия́|ете**
3rd person	**сия́|ет**	**сия́|ют**

Verbs of this type differ from those belonging to Table 18 only by having a я at the end of the stem, instead of an a.

про́б|овать:

TABLE 20

	Singular	Plural
1st person	**про́б|ую**	**про́б|уем**
2nd person	**про́б|уешь**	**про́б|уете**
3rd person	**про́б|ует**	**про́б|уют**

The verbs of this conjugation are not stressed on the suffix -овать.

рис|ова́ть:

TABLE 21

	Singular	Plural
1st person	**рис|у́ю**	**рис|у́ем**
2nd person	**рис|у́ешь**	**рис|у́ете**
3rd person	**рис|у́ет**	**рис|у́ют**

Verbs of this conjugation differ from those belonging to Table 20 only in having the stress on the suffix rather than on the stem.

Note: The conjugation of other -e- conjugation verbs (those ending in -ать, -еть, -нуть, and -ять) is given in the dictionary entries.

The -i- conjugation

говор|и́ть:

TABLE 22

	Singular	Plural
1st person	**говор|ю́**	**говор|и́м**
2nd person	**говор|и́шь**	**говор|и́те**
3rd person	**говор|и́т**	**говор|я́т**

стро́|ить:

TABLE 23

	Singular	Plural
1st person	**стро́|ю**	**стро́|им**
2nd person	**стро́|ишь**	**стро́|ите**
3rd person	**стро́|ит**	**стро́|ят**

Verbs of this conjugation differ from those belonging to Table 22 by ending in a vowel + -ить. Other examples are кле́ить, сто́ить.

Note: The conjugation of other -i- conjugation verbs (those ending in -ать, -еть, and -ять) is given in the dictionary entries.

In addition, where the stem of a verb ends in б, п, м, в, or ф, and an л is inserted before the ending of the first person singular, this is shown in the dictionary entries (e.g. люби́ть: я люблю́; спать: я сплю).

Also, where the consonant at the end of the stem changes in the first person singular, this is shown in the dictionary entries (e.g. ви́деть: я ви́жу; плати́ть: я плачу́; спроси́ть: я спрошу́).

Adjectives

TABLE 24a

	Singular			Plural
	Masculine	Feminine	Neuter	
Nominative	**краси́в|ый**	**краси́в|ая**	**краси́в|ое**	**краси́в|ые**
Accusative	**краси́в|ый**	**краси́в|ую**	**краси́в|ое**	**краси́в|ые**
Genitive	**краси́в|ого**	**краси́в|ой**	**краси́в|ого**	**краси́в|ых**
Dative	**краси́в|ому**	**краси́в|ой**	**краси́в|ому**	**краси́в|ым**
Instrumental	**краси́в|ым**	**краси́в|ой**	**краси́в|ым**	**краси́в|ыми**
Prepositional	**краси́в|ом**	**краси́в|ой**	**краси́в|ом**	**краси́в|ых**

Note: The words кото́рый and како́й decline like краси́вый, as do the ordinal numbers пе́рвый, второ́й, etc. Note that тре́тий has 'soft' endings and inserts a soft sign (-тья, -тье, -тьи).

Soft Adjectives

TABLE 24b

	Singular			Plural
	Masculine	Feminine	Neuter	
Nominative	**си́н|ий**	**си́н|яя**	**си́н|ее**	**си́н|ие**
Accusative	**си́н|ий**	**си́н|юю**	**си́н|ее**	**си́н|ие**
Genitive	**си́н|его**	**си́н|ей**	**си́н|его**	**си́н|их**
Dative	**си́н|ему**	**си́н|ей**	**си́н|ему**	**си́н|им**
Instrumental	**си́н|им**	**си́н|ей**	**си́н|им**	**си́н|ими**
Prepositional	**си́н|ем**	**си́н|ей**	**си́н|ем**	**си́н|их**

Determiners/pronouns

мой (and similarly **твой, свой**):

TABLE 25

	Singular			Plural
	Masculine	Feminine	Neuter	
Nominative	**мой**	**моя́**	**моё**	**мои́**
Accusative	**мой**	**мою́**	**моё**	**мои́**
Genitive	**моего́**	**мое́й**	**моего́**	**мои́х**
Dative	**моему́**	**мое́й**	**моему́**	**мои́м**
Instrumental	**мои́м**	**мое́й**	**мои́м**	**мои́ми**
Prepositional	**моём**	**мое́й**	**моём**	**мои́х**

наш (and similarly **ваш**)

	Singular			Plural
	Masculine	Feminine	Neuter	
Nominative	**наш**	**на́ша**	**на́ше**	**на́ши**
Accusative	**наш**	**на́шу**	**на́ше**	**на́ши**
Genitive	**на́шего**	**на́шей**	**на́шего**	**на́ших**
Dative	**на́шему**	**на́шей**	**на́шему**	**на́шим**
Instrumental	**на́шим**	**на́шей**	**на́шим**	**на́шими**
Prepositional	**на́шем**	**на́шей**	**на́шем**	**на́ших**

The other possessive determiners, его́, её, and их, are indeclinable.

э́тот:

TABLE 26

	Singular			Plural
	Masculine	**Feminine**	**Neuter**	
Nominative	**э́тот**	**э́та**	**э́то**	**э́ти**
Accusative	**э́тот**	**э́ту**	**э́то**	**э́ти**
Genitive	**э́того**	**э́той**	**э́того**	**э́тих**
Dative	**э́тому**	**э́той**	**э́тому**	**э́тим**
Instrumental	**э́тим**	**э́той**	**э́тим**	**э́тими**
Prepositional	**э́том**	**э́той**	**э́том**	**э́тих**

сам, the emphatic pronoun, declines like **э́тот** and is stressed on the final syllable.

тот:

	Singular			Plural
	Masculine	**Feminine**	**Neuter**	
Nominative	**тот**	**та**	**то**	**те**
Accusative	**тот**	**ту**	**то**	**те**
Genitive	**того́**	**той**	**того́**	**тех**
Dative	**тому́**	**той**	**тому́**	**тем**
Instrumental	**тем**	**той**	**тем**	**те́ми**
Prepositional	**том**	**той**	**том**	**тех**

весь:

TABLE 27

	Singular			Plural
	Masculine	**Feminine**	**Neuter**	
Nominative	**весь**	**вся**	**всё**	**все**
Accusative	**весь**	**всю**	**всё**	**все**
Genitive	**всего́**	**всей**	**всего́**	**всех**
Dative	**всему́**	**всей**	**всему́**	**всем**
Instrumental	**всем**	**всей**	**всем**	**все́ми**
Prepositional	**всём**	**всей**	**всём**	**всех**

Numbers

TABLE 28

Cardinal Numbers		Ordinal Numbers	
one	**оди́н/одна́/одно́**	first	**пе́рвый**
two	**два/две**	second	**второ́й**
three	**три**	third	**тре́тий**
four	**четы́ре**	fourth	**четвёртый**
five	**пять**	fifth	**пя́тый**
six	**шесть**	sixth	**шесто́й**
seven	**семь**	seventh	**седьмо́й**
eight	**во́семь**	eighth	**восьмо́й**
nine	**де́вять**	ninth	**девя́тый**
ten	**де́сять**	tenth	**деся́тый**
eleven	**оди́ннадцать**	eleventh	**оди́ннадцатый**
twelve	**двена́дцать**	twelfth	**двена́дцатый**
thirteen	**трина́дцать**	thirteenth	**трина́дцатый**
fourteen	**четы́рнадцать**	fourteenth	**четы́рнадцатый**
fifteen	**пятна́дцать**	fifteenth	**пятна́дцатый**
sixteen	**шестна́дцать**	sixteenth	**шестна́дцатый**
seventeen	**семна́дцать**	seventeenth	**семна́дцатый**
eighteen	**восемна́дцать**	eighteenth	**восемна́дцатый**
nineteen	**девятна́дцать**	nineteenth	**девятна́дцатый**
twenty	**два́дцать**	twentieth	**двадца́тый**
twenty-one	**два́дцать оди́н/одна́/одно́**	twenty-first	**два́дцать пе́рвый**
twenty-two	**два́дцать два/две**	twenty-second	**два́дцать второ́й**
twenty-three	**два́дцать три**	twenty-third	**два́дцать тре́тий**
thirty	**три́дцать**	thirtieth	**тридца́тый**
forty	**со́рок**	fortieth	**сороково́й**
fifty	**пятьдеся́т**	fiftieth	**пятидеся́тый**
sixty	**шестьдеся́т**	sixtieth	**шестидеся́тый**
seventy	**се́мьдесят**	seventieth	**семидеся́тый**
eighty	**во́семьдесят**	eightieth	**восьмидеся́тый**
ninety	**девяно́сто**	nintieth	**девяно́стый**
hundred	**сто**	hundredth	**со́тый**
hundred and one	**сто оди́н/одна́/одно́**	hundred-and-first	**сто пе́рвый**
two hundred	**две́сти**	two-hundredth	**двухсо́тый**
three hundred	**три́ста**	three-hundredth	**трёхсо́тый**
four hundred	**четы́реста**	four-hundredth	**четырёхсо́тый**
five hundred	**пятьсо́т**	five-hundredth	**пятисо́тый**
six hundred	**шестьсо́т**	six-hundredth	**шестисо́тый**
thousand	**ты́сяча**	thousandth	**ты́сячный**
million	**миллио́н**	millionth	**миллио́нный**

оди́н:

TABLE 29

	Singular			Plural
	Masculine	Feminine	Neuter	
Nominative	**оди́н**	**одна́**	**одно́**	**одни́**
Accusative	**оди́н**	**одну́**	**одно́**	**одни́**
Genitive	**одного́**	**одно́й**	**одного́**	**одни́х**
Dative	**одному́**	**одно́й**	**одному́**	**одни́м**
Instrumental	**одни́м**	**одно́й**	**одни́м**	**одни́ми**
Prepositional	**одно́м**	**одно́й**	**одно́м**	**одни́х**

For the declension of other numbers, see the dictionary entries.

Russian verbs

(a) The verb list contains examples of:

(i) verbs in **-чь** (e.g. бере́чь)

(ii) verbs in **-ти** (e.g. вести́)

(iii) verbs in **-сть** (e.g. сесть)

(iv) verbs in **-оть** (e.g. боро́ться)

(v) verbs in **-ереть** (e.g. запере́ть)

(vi) verbs in **-овать** and **-евать** (e.g. бесе́довать, воева́ть)

(vii) verbs (first conjugation) with consonant change (e.g. писа́ть)

(viii) verbs (second conjugation) with consonant change (e.g. бро́сить)

(ix) second-conjugation verbs in **-ать**/**-ять** (e.g. стуча́ть, стоя́ть)

(x) first- and second-conjugation verbs in **-еть** (e.g. име́ть, горе́ть)

(xi) monosyllabic verbs (e.g. брать)

(xii) irregular verbs (e.g. хоте́ть)

(b) Most verbs listed are non-derivative (e.g. дать). Compound verbs are not normally given when a root verb is available (дать 'to give' appears, but not прода́ть 'to sell' or зада́ть 'to ask [a question]'). Some compounds have no commonly-used root verb, in which case a hyphenated root is given (e.g. -казать).

(c) Also listed are verbs that have no -л in the masculine past (e.g. везти́ 'to convey', masculine past вёз).

(d) The pattern of presentation is:

(i) for all verbs: present or future conjugation, and meaning; the verb's other aspect (if available)

(ii) for selected verbs: the past tense; the government of the verb; the imperative; short forms of the perfective passive participle.

Note: Absence of a first-person singular form indicates that none exists, or that none exists in the meaning given (see, for example, греме́ть 'to thunder').

бежа́ть/по- 'to run': бегу́ бежи́шь бежи́т бежи́м бежи́те бегу́т; беги́!

бере́чь/по- 'to take care of': берегу́ бережёт берегу́т; берёг берегла́; береги́!

бесе́довать 'to converse': бесе́дую бесе́дует бесе́дуют

бить/по 'to strike': бью бьёт бьют; бей!

бледне́ть/по- 'to grow pale': бледне́ю бледне́ет бледне́ют

блесте́ть 'to shine': блещу́ блести́т блестя́т; pf. **блесну́ть**

боле́ть (+ i.) 'to be ill (with)': боле́ю боле́ет боле́ют

боле́ть 'to hurt' (intrans.): боли́т боля́т

боро́ться (за + a.) 'to struggle (for)': борю́сь бо́рется бо́рются; бори́сь!

боя́ться (+ g.) 'to fear': бою́сь бои́тся боя́тся; (не) бо́йся!

брать 'to take': беру́ берёт беру́т; брал брала́ бра́ло; бери́!; pf. **взять**

бри́ться/по- 'to shave' (intrans.): бре́юсь бре́ется бре́ются

бро́сить 'to throw': бро́шу бро́сит бро́сят; брось!; бро́шен; impf. **броса́ть**

буди́ть/раз- 'to awaken' (trans.): бужу́ бу́дит бу́дят; буди́!; разбу́жен

быть 'to be': бу́ду бу́дет бу́дут; был была́ бы́ло; будь!

везти́ 'to convey': везу́ везёт везу́т; вёз везла́

ве́сить 'to weigh' : ве́шу ве́сит ве́сят

вести́ 'to lead': веду́ ведёт веду́т; вёл вела́

взять 'to take': возьму́ возьмёт возьму́т; взял взяла́ взя́ло; возьми́!; взят взята́ взя́то; impf. **брать**

ви́деть/у- 'to see': ви́жу ви́дит ви́дят

висе́ть 'to hang' (intrans.): вишу́ виси́т вися́т

владе́ть (+ i.) 'to own': владе́ю владе́ет владе́ют

влечь 'to attract': влеку́ влечёт влеку́т; влёк влекла́; -влечён -влечена́ (in compounds)

води́ть 'to lead': вожу́ во́дит во́дят

воева́ть 'to wage war': вою́ю вою́ет вою́ют

возврати́ться 'to return' (intrans.): возвращу́сь возврати́тся возвратя́тся; impf. **возвраща́ться**

вози́ть 'to convey': вожу́ во́зит во́зят

возни́кнуть 'to arise': возни́кну возни́кнет возни́кнут; возни́к возни́кла; impf. **возника́ть**

волнова́ться/вз- 'to be excited': волну́юсь волну́ется волну́ются; (не) волнуйся!

врать/на- and **со-** 'to tell lies': вру врёт врут; врал врала́ вра́ло; (не) ври!

встава́ть 'to get up, stand up': встаю́ встаёт встаю́т; встава́й!; pf. **встать**

встать 'to get up, stand up': вста́ну вста́нет вста́нут; встань!; impf. **встава́ть**

встре́тить 'to meet': встре́чу встре́тит встре́тят; impf. **встреча́ть**

вы́глядеть (+ i.) 'to look, appear': вы́гляжу вы́глядит вы́глядят

вы́разить 'to express': вы́ражу вы́разит вы́разят; вы́ражен; impf. **выража́ть**

вяза́ть/с- 'to tie': вяжу́ вя́жет вя́жут; -вя́зан (in compounds)

гаси́ть/за- or **по-** 'to extinguish': гашу́ га́сит га́сят; зага́шен/пога́шен

ги́бнуть/по- 'to perish': ги́бну ги́бнет ги́бнут; гиб/ги́бнул ги́бла

гла́дить/вы- or **по-** 'to iron': гла́жу гла́дит гла́дят; вы́глажен

гляде́ть (на + a.) 'to look (at)': гляжу́ гляди́т глядя́т; pf. **гля́нуть**

гна́ться (за + i.) 'to chase (after)':

гоню́сь го́нится го́нятся; гна́лся гнала́сь

годи́ться (в + a.) 'to be fit (for)': гожу́сь годи́тся годя́тся

голосова́ть/про- (за + a.) 'to vote (for)': голосу́ю голосу́ет голосу́ют

горди́ться (+ i.) 'to be proud of': горжу́сь горди́тся гордя́тся; горди́сь!

горе́ть/с- 'to burn' (intrans.): гори́т горя́т

гото́вить/при- 'to prepare': гото́влю гото́вит гото́вят; гото́вь!; пригото́влен

греме́ть/про- 'to thunder': греми́т гремя́т

греть 'to heat': гре́ю гре́ет гре́ют; -грет (in compounds)

грози́ть/при- (+ d.) 'to threaten': грожу́ грози́т грозя́т

грузи́ть/по- 'to load': гружу́ гру́зит гру́зят; погру́жен

дава́ть 'to give': даю́ даёт даю́т; дава́й!; pf. **дать**

дави́ть (на + a.) 'to press (upon)': давлю́ да́вит да́вят; -давлен (in compounds)

дать 'to give': дам дашь даст дади́м дади́те даду́т; дал дала́ да́ло; дай!; дан дана́; impf. **дава́ть**

де́йствовать 'to act': де́йствую де́йствует де́йствуют; де́йствуй!

держа́ть 'to hold': держу́ де́ржит де́ржат; держи́!; -держан (in compounds)

доба́вить 'to add': доба́влю доба́вит доба́вят; доба́вь!; доба́влен; impf. **добавля́ть**

дости́гнуть (+ g.) 'to achieve': дости́гну дости́гнет дости́гнут; дости́г дости́гла; дости́гнут; impf. **достига́ть**

дрема́ть 'to doze': дремлю́ дре́млет дре́млют

дрожа́ть 'to tremble': дрожу́ дрожи́т дрожа́т; pf. **дро́гнуть**

дуть 'to blow': ду́ю ду́ет ду́ют; pf. **ду́нуть**

дыша́ть 'to breathe': дышу́ ды́шит ды́шат

е́здить 'to travel': е́зжу е́здит е́здят; е́зди!

есть/съ- 'to eat': ем ешь ест еди́м еди́те едя́т; ешь!; съе́ден

е́хать/по- 'to travel': е́ду е́дет е́дут; поезжа́й!

жале́ть/по- 'to pity': жале́ю жале́ет жале́ют

жа́ловаться/по- (на + a.) 'to complain (of, about)': жа́луюсь жа́луется жа́луются

жать 'to press, squeeze': жму жмёт жмут; жми!; -жат (in compounds)

ждать/подо- (+ a./g.) 'to wait (for)': жду ждёт ждут; ждал ждала́ жда́ло; жди!

жева́ть 'to chew': жую́ жуёт жую́т

же́ртвовать/по- (+ i.) 'to sacrifice': же́ртвую же́ртвует же́ртвуют

жечь/с- 'to burn' (trans.): жгу жжёт жгут; жёг жгла; жги!; -жжён -жжена́ (in compounds)

жить 'to live': живу́ живёт живу́т; жил жила́ жи́ло

забо́титься/по- (о + p.) 'to care about': забо́чусь забо́тится забо́тятся

забы́ть 'to forget': забу́ду забу́дет забу́дут; (не) забу́дь!; забы́т; impf. **забыва́ть**

заве́довать (+ i.) 'to be in charge of': заве́дую заве́дует заве́дуют

зави́довать/по- (+ d.) 'to envy': зави́дую зави́дует зави́дуют

зави́сеть (от + g.) 'to depend (on)': зави́шу зави́сит зави́сят

закры́ть 'to shut': закро́ю закро́ет закро́ют; закро́й!; закры́т; impf.

закрывáть

замёрзнуть 'to freeze' (intrans.): замёрзну замёрзнет замёрзнут; замёрз замёрзла; impf. **замерзáть**

замéтить 'to notice': замéчу замéтит замéтят; замéчен; impf. **замечáть**

заня́ть 'to occupy': займу́ займёт займу́т; зáнял занялá зáняло; займи́!; зáнят занятá зáнято; impf. **занимáть**

заперéть 'to lock': запру́ запрёт запру́т; зáпер заперлá зáперло; запри́!; зáперт запертá зáперто; impf. **запирáть**

запрети́ть 'to forbid': запрещу́ запрети́т запретя́т; запрещён запрещенá; impf. **запрещáть**

заряди́ть 'to load, charge': заряжу́ заряди́т зарядя́т; заряжён заряженá; impf. **заряжáть**

захвати́ть 'to seize': захвачу́ захвáтит захвáтят; захвáчен; impf. **захвáтывать**

защити́ть (от + g.) 'to defend (from)': защищу́ защити́т защитя́т; защищён защищенá; impf. **защищáть**.

заяви́ть 'to declare': заявлю́ зая́вит зая́вят; зая́влен; impf. **заявля́ть**

звать/по- 'to call': зову́ зовёт зову́т; звал звалá звáло; зови́!; -зван (in compounds)

звучáть 'to sound': звучи́т звучáт

знакóмиться/по- (с + i.) 'to become acquainted (with)': знакóмлюсь знакóмится знакóмятся; знакóмься!

идти́ 'to go': иду́ идёт иду́т; шёл шла; иди́!

изобрести́ 'to invent': изобрету́ изобретёт изобрету́т; изобрёл изобрелá; изобретён изобретенá; impf. **изобретáть**

имéть 'to have': имéю имéет имéют

интересовáться (+ i.) 'to be interested in': интересу́юсь интересу́ется интересу́ются

искáть (+ a./g.) 'to look for': ищу́ и́щет и́щут; ищи́!

испóльзовать 'to use' (impf. and pf.): испóльзую испóльзует испóльзуют; испóльзуй!; испóльзован

исслéдовать 'to investigate' (impf. and pf.): исслéдую исслéдует исслéдуют; исслéдован

исчéзнуть 'to disappear': исчéзну исчéзнет исчéзнут; исчéз исчéзла; impf. **исчезáть**

-казáть (only in compounds): -кажу́ -кáжет -кáжут; -кажи́!; -кáзан; impf. **-кáзывать**

казáться/по- (+ i.) 'to seem': кажу́сь кáжется кáжутся

кати́ть 'to roll' (trans.): качу́ кáтит кáтят

кáшлять 'to cough': кáшляю кáшляет кáшляют; pf. **кáшлянуть**

кипéть/вс- 'to boil' (intrans.): киплю́ (in figurative sense only) кипи́т кипя́т

класть 'to place': кладу́ кладёт кладу́т; клади́!; pf. **положи́ть**

колебáться/по- 'to hesitate': колéблюсь колéблется колéблются

комáндовать (+ i.) 'to command': комáндую комáндует комáндуют

корми́ть/на- 'to feed': кормлю́ кóрмит кóрмят; накóрмлен

крáсить/вы- or **по-** 'to paint': крáшу крáсит крáсят; вы́крашен

краснéть/по- 'to blush': краснéю краснéет краснéют

красть/у- 'to steal': краду́ крадёт краду́т; укрáден

крéпнуть/о- 'to get stronger': крéпну крéпнет крéпнут; креп крéпла

кричáть 'to shout': кричу́ кричи́т кричáт; кричи́!; pf. **кри́кнуть**

купи́ть 'to buy': куплю́ ку́пит ку́пят; купи́!; ку́плен; impf. **покупа́ть**

ла́зить 'to climb': ла́жу ла́зит ла́зят; (не) лазь!

лгать/со- or **на-** 'to tell lies': лгу лжёт лгут; лгал, лгала́, лга́ло; (не) лги!

лежа́ть 'to lie': лежу́ лежи́т лежа́т

лезть 'to climb': ле́зу ле́зет ле́зут; лез ле́зла; лезь!

лете́ть 'to fly': лечу́ лети́т летя́т

лечь 'to lie down': ля́гу ля́жет ля́гут; лёг легла́; ляг!; impf. **ложи́ться**

лиза́ть 'to lick': лижу́ ли́жет ли́жут; pf. **лизну́ть**

лить 'to pour': лью льёт льют; лил лила́ ли́ло; лей!; -лит (in compounds)

лови́ть 'to catch': ловлю́ ло́вит ло́вят; pf. **пойма́ть**

люби́ть 'to like, love': люблю́ лю́бит лю́бят

любова́ться/по- (+ i. or на + a.) 'to admire': любу́юсь любу́ется любу́ются

маха́ть (+ i.) 'to wave': машу́ ма́шет ма́шут; pf. **махну́ть**

мести́/под- 'to sweep': мету́ метёт мету́т; мёл мела́; подметён подметена́

молча́ть 'to be silent': молчу́ молчи́т молча́т; молчи́!

мочь/с- 'to be able': могу́ мо́жет мо́гут; мог могла́

мча́ться 'to race': мчусь мчи́тся мча́тся; мчись!

мы́ться/вы- or **по-** 'to wash' (intrans.): мо́юсь мо́ется мо́ются; мо́йся!

награди́ть (за + a.) 'to reward (for)': награжу́ награди́т наградя́т; награждён награждена́; impf. **награжда́ть**

наде́ть 'to put on': наде́ну наде́нет наде́нут; наде́нь!; impf. **надева́ть**

наде́яться/по- (на + a.) 'to hope (for)': наде́юсь наде́ется наде́ются

назва́ть 'to name': назову́ назовёт назову́т; назва́л назвала́ назва́ло; на́зван; impf. **называ́ть**

найти́ 'to find': найду́ найдёт найду́т; нашёл нашла́; на́йден; impf. **находи́ть**

напа́сть (на + a.) 'to attack': нападу́ нападёт нападу́т; impf. **напада́ть**

находи́ть 'to find': нахожу́ нахо́дит нахо́дят; pf. **найти́**

находи́ться 'to be situated': нахожу́сь нахо́дится нахо́дятся

нача́ть 'to begin' (trans.): начну́ начнёт начну́т; на́чал начала́ на́чало; начни́!; на́чат начата́ на́чато; impf. **начина́ть**

нача́ться 'to begin' (intrans.): начнётся начну́тся; начался́ начала́сь; impf. **начина́ться**

ненави́деть 'to hate': ненави́жу ненави́дит ненави́дят

нести́ 'to carry': несу́ несёт несу́т; нёс несла́; неси́!

носи́ть 'to carry': ношу́ но́сит но́сят

ночева́ть/пере- 'to spend the night': ночу́ю ночу́ет ночу́ют

нра́виться/по- (+ d.) 'to please': нра́влюсь нра́вится нра́вятся

оби́деть 'to offend': оби́жу оби́дит оби́дят; оби́жен; impf. **обижа́ть**

обня́ть 'to embrace': обниму́ обни́мет обни́мут; о́бнял обняла́ о́бняло; обними́!; impf. **обнима́ть**

обогна́ть 'to overtake, outstrip': обгоню́ обго́нит обго́нят; обогна́л обогнала́ обогна́ло; impf. **обгоня́ть**

образова́ть 'to form' (impf. and pf.): образу́ю образу́ет образу́ют; образо́ван; impf. also **образо́вывать**

обрати́ться (к + d.) 'to turn (to)': обращу́сь обрати́тся обратя́тся; обрати́сь!; impf. **обраща́ться**

обсуди́ть 'to discuss': обсужу́ обсу́дит обсу́дят; обсуждён обсуждена́; impf. **обсужда́ть**

оде́ться 'to dress' (intrans.): оде́нусь оде́нется оде́нутся; оде́нься! impf. **одева́ться**

организова́ть 'to organize' (impf. and pf.): организу́ю организу́ет организу́ют; организо́ван

освети́ть 'to illuminate': освещу́ освети́т осветя́т; освещён освещена́; impf. **освеща́ть**

освободи́ть 'to free': освобожу́ освободи́т освободя́т; освобождён освобождена́; impf. **освобожда́ть**

остава́ться 'to remain': остаю́сь остаётся остаю́тся; остава́йся!; pf. **оста́ться**

останови́ться 'to stop' (intrans.): остановлю́сь остано́вится остано́вятся; останови́сь!; impf. **остана́вливаться**

оста́ться 'to remain': оста́нусь оста́нется оста́нутся; оста́нься! impf. **остава́ться**

отве́тить (на + a.) 'to answer': отве́чу отве́тит отве́тят; отве́ть!; impf. **отвеча́ть**

откры́ть 'to open' (trans.): откро́ю откро́ет откро́ют; откро́й!; откры́т; impf. **открыва́ть**

отня́ть 'to take away': отниму́ отни́мет отни́мут; о́тнял отняла́ о́тняло; отними́!; impf. **отнима́ть**

отпере́ть 'to unlock': отопру́ отопрёт отопру́т; отопри́!; о́тпер отперла́ о́тперло; о́тперт отперта́ о́тперто; impf. **отпира́ть**

ошиби́ться 'to make a mistake': ошибу́сь ошибётся ошибу́тся; оши́бся оши́блась; impf. **ошиба́ться**

па́хнуть (+ i.) 'to smell (of)': па́хнет па́хнут; пах па́хла

перестава́ть 'to stop' (intrans.): перестаю́ перестаёт перестаю́т; pf. **переста́ть**

переста́ть 'to stop' (intrans.): переста́ну переста́нешь переста́нут; переста́нь!; impf. **перестава́ть**

петь/с- 'to sing': пою́ поёт пою́т; пой!

печь/ис- to bake': пеку́ печёт пеку́т; пёк пекла́; испечён испечена́

писа́ть/на- 'to write': пишу́ пи́шет пи́шут; пиши́!; напи́сан

пить/вы́- 'to drink': пью пьёт пьют; пил, пила́, пи́ло; пей!; вы́пит

пла́кать 'to weep': пла́чу пла́чет пла́чут; (не) плачь!

плати́ть/за- (за + a.) 'to pay (for)': плачу́ пла́тит пла́тят; плати́!; запла́чен

плева́ть 'to spit': плюю́ плюёт плюю́т; pf. **плю́нуть**

плыть 'to swim': плыву́ плывёт плыву́т; плыл плыла́ плы́ло

победи́ть 'to win': победи́т победя́т; побеждён побеждена́; impf. **побежда́ть**

подве́ргнуть (+ d.) 'to subject (to)': подве́ргну подве́ргнет подве́ргнут; подве́рг подве́ргла; подве́ргнут; impf. **подверга́ть**

пове́сить 'to hang' (trans.): пове́шу пове́сит пове́сят; пове́сь!; пове́шен; impf. **ве́шать**

подня́ть 'to lift': подниму́ подни́мет подни́мут; по́днял подняла́ по́дняло; подними́!; по́днят поднята́ по́днято; impf. **поднима́ть**

подтверди́ть 'to confirm': подтвержу́ подтверди́т подтвердя́т; подтверждён подтверждена́; impf. **подтвержда́ть**

поздра́вить (с + i.) 'to congratulate (on)': поздра́влю поздра́вит поздра́вят; поздра́вь!; impf. **поздравля́ть**

покры́ть 'to cover': покро́ю покро́ет покро́ют; покро́й!; покры́т; impf. **покрыва́ть**

ползти́ 'to crawl': ползу́ ползёт ползу́т; полз ползла́

по́льзоваться/вос- (+ i.) 'to use': по́льзуюсь по́льзуется по́льзуются

помо́чь (+ d.) 'to help': помогу́ помо́жет помо́гут; помо́г помогла́; помоги́!; impf. **помога́ть**

пони́зить 'to lower': пони́жу пони́зит пони́зят; пони́жен; impf. **понижа́ть**

поня́ть 'to understand': пойму́ поймёт пойму́т; по́нял поняла́ по́няло; пойми́!; по́нят понята́ по́нято; impf. **понима́ть**

по́ртить/ис- 'to spoil': по́рчу по́ртит по́ртят; испо́рчен

посади́ть 'to plant, seat': посажу́ поса́дит поса́дят; поса́жен; impf. **сажа́ть**

посвяти́ть (+ d.) 'to dedicate (to)': посвящу́ посвяти́т посвятя́т; посвящён посвящена́; impf. **посвяща́ть**

посети́ть 'to visit': посещу́ посети́т посетя́т; посещён посещена́; impf. **посеща́ть**

пра́вить (+ i.) 'to rule, govern': пра́влю пра́вит пра́вят

пра́здновать/от- 'to celebrate': пра́здную пра́зднует пра́зднуют

преврати́ть (в + a.) 'to transform (into)': превращу́ преврати́т превратя́т; превращён превращена́; impf. **превраща́ть**

предупреди́ть 'to warn': предупрежу́ предупреди́т предупредя́т; предупреждён предупреждена́; impf. **предупрежда́ть**

прекрати́ть 'to stop, curtail': прекращу́ прекрати́т прекратя́т; прекрати́!; прекращён прекращена́; impf. **прекраща́ть**

преодоле́ть 'to overcome': преодоле́ю преодоле́ет преодоле́ют; преодолён преодолена́; impf. **преодолева́ть**

прибли́зиться (к + d.) 'to approach': прибли́жусь прибли́зится прибли́зятся; impf. **приближа́ться**

привы́кнуть (к + d.) 'to get used (to)': привы́кну привы́кнет привы́кнут; привы́к привы́кла; impf. **привыка́ть**

пригласи́ть 'to invite': приглашу́ пригласи́т приглася́т; пригласи́!; приглашён приглашена́; pf. **приглаша́ть**

признава́ться (в + p.) 'to confess (to)': признаю́сь признаётся признаю́тся; pf. **призна́ться**

приня́ть 'to accept': приму́ при́мет при́мут; при́нял приняла́ при́няло; прими́!; при́нят принята́ при́нято; impf. **принима́ть**

про́бовать/по- 'to test, try': про́бую про́бует про́буют; про́буй!

проси́ть/по- (+ a./g.) 'to request': прошу́ про́сит про́сят; проси́!

прости́ть (за + a.) 'to forgive (for)': прощу́ прости́т простя́т; прости́!; прощён прощена́; impf. **проща́ть**

прости́ться (с + i.) 'to say goodbye (to)': прощу́сь прости́тся простя́тся; impf. **проща́ться**

простуди́ться 'to catch cold': простужу́сь просту́дится просту́дятся; impf. **простужа́ться**

пря́тать/с- 'to hide': пря́чу пря́чет пря́чут; прячь!; спря́тан

пусти́ть 'to let go': пущу́ пу́стит пу́стят; пу́щен; impf. **пуска́ть**

ра́доваться/об- (+ d.) 'to rejoice (at)': ра́дуюсь ра́дуется ра́дуются

разби́ть 'to smash': разобью́ разобьёт разобью́т; разбе́й! разби́т; impf. **разбива́ть**

разви́ться 'to develop' (intrans.): разовью́сь разовьётся разовью́тся; разви́лся развила́сь; impf. **развива́ться**

разде́ться 'to get undressed': разде́нусь разде́нется разде́нутся; разде́нься!; impf. **раздева́ться**

расста́ться (с + i.) 'to part (with)': расста́нусь расста́нется расста́нутся; impf. **расстава́ться**

расти́/вы- 'to grow' (intrans.): расту́ растёт расту́т; рос росла́

рвать 'to tear': рву рвёт рвут; рвал рвала́ рва́ло

ре́зать/раз- 'to cut': ре́жу ре́жет ре́жут; режь!; разре́зан

рисова́ть/на- 'to draw': рису́ю рису́ет рису́ют; нарисо́ван

руби́ть 'to chop': рублю́ ру́бит ру́бят; -рублен (in compounds)

руководи́ть (+ i.) 'to manage': руковожу́ руководи́т руководя́т

сади́ться 'to sit down': сажу́сь сади́тся садя́тся; сади́сь!; pf. **сесть**

свисте́ть 'to whistle': свищу́ свисти́т свистя́т; сви́стнуть

серди́ться/рас- 'to get angry': сержу́сь се́рдится се́рдятся; (не) серди́сь!

сесть 'to sit down': ся́ду ся́дет ся́дут; сядь!; impf. **сади́ться**

се́ять/по- 'to sow': се́ю се́ет се́ют; посе́ян

сиде́ть 'to sit': сижу́ сиди́т сидя́т; сиди́!

сказа́ть 'to say': скажу́ ска́жет ска́жут; скажи́!; ска́зан; impf. **говори́ть**

скрыть 'to conceal': скро́ю скро́ет скро́ют; скрой!; скрыт; impf. **скрыва́ть**

слать 'to send': шлю шлёт шлют; шли!

следи́ть (за + i.) 'to track': слежу́ следи́т следя́т

сле́довать/по- (за + i.) 'to follow': сле́дую сле́дует сле́дуют

слы́шать/у- 'to hear': слы́шу слы́шит слы́шат; услы́шан

сметь/по- 'to dare': сме́ю сме́ет сме́ют

смея́ться/по- (над + i.) 'to laugh (at)': смеюсь смеётся смеются; (не) сме́йся!

смотре́ть/по- (на + a.) 'to look (at)': смотрю́ смо́трит смо́трят; смотри́!

снять 'to take off': сниму́ сни́мет сни́мут; снял сняла́ сня́ло; сними́!; снят снята́ сня́то; impf. **снима́ть**

сове́товать/по- (+ d.) 'to advise': сове́тую сове́тует сове́туют

согласи́ться (на + a./с + i.) 'to agree (to something/with someone)': соглашу́сь согласи́тся согладя́тся; impf. **соглаша́ться**

спасти́ 'to save': спасу́ спасёт спасу́т; спас спасла́; спасён спасена́; impf. **спаса́ть**

спать 'to sleep': сплю спит спят; спал спала́ спа́ло; спи!

спроси́ть 'to ask': спрошу́ спро́сит спро́сят; спроси́!; impf. **спра́шивать**

ста́вить/по- 'to put, stand' (trans.): ста́влю ста́вит ста́вят; ставь!; поста́влен

стать 'to become': ста́ну ста́нет ста́нут; стань!; impf. **станови́ться**

стере́ть 'to erase': сотру́ сотрёт сотру́т; стёр стёрла; сотри́!; стёрт; impf. **стира́ть**

стоя́ть 'to stand' (intrans.): стою́ стои́т стоя́т; стой!

стричь/о- 'to cut (hair or nails)': стригу́ стрижёт стригу́т; стриг стри́гла; остри́жен

ступи́ть 'to step': ступлю́ сту́пит сту́пят; impf. **ступа́ть**

стуча́ть/по- (в + a.) 'to knock (at)': стучу́ стучи́т стуча́т

суди́ть 'to judge': сужу́ су́дит су́дят

танцева́ть/с- 'to dance': танцу́ю

танцу́ет танцу́ют

та́ять/рас- 'to melt' (intrans.): та́ет та́ют

темне́ть/по- 'to grow dark': темне́ет темне́ют

тере́ть 'to rub': тру трёт трут; тёр тёрла; три!

терпе́ть 'to bear, tolerate': терплю́ те́рпит те́рпят

течь 'to flow': течёт теку́т; тёк текла́

топи́ть 'to heat': топлю́ то́пит то́пят; -топлен (in compounds)

торгова́ть (+ i.) 'to trade (in)': торгу́ю торгу́ет торгу́ют

торопи́ться/по- 'to hurry': тороплю́сь торо́пится торо́пятся; торопи́сь!

тра́тить/ис- (на + a.) 'to expend (on)': тра́чу тра́тит тра́тят; трать!; истра́чен

тре́бовать/по- (+ g./a.) 'to demand': тре́бую тре́бует тре́буют

труди́ться 'to labour': тружу́сь тру́дится тру́дятся; труди́сь!

трясти́ 'to shake' (trans.): трясу́ трясёт трясу́т; тряс трясла́; pf. **тряхну́ть**

убеди́ть 'to convince': убеди́т убедя́т; убеждён убеждена́; impf. **убежда́ть**

удиви́ться (+ d.) 'to be surprised (at)': удивлю́сь удиви́тся удивя́тся; impf. **удивля́ться**

укрепи́ть 'to strengthen': укреплю́ укрепи́т укрепя́т; укреплён укреплена́; impf. **укрепля́ть**

умере́ть 'to die': умру́ умрёт умру́т; у́мер умерла́ у́мерло; impf. **умира́ть**

уме́ть 'to know how': уме́ю уме́ет уме́ют

упа́сть 'to fall': упаду́ упадёт упаду́т; impf. **па́дать**

употреби́ть 'to use': употреблю́ употреби́т употребя́т; употреблён употреблена́; impf. **употребля́ть**

успе́ть 'to have time': успе́ю успе́ет успе́ют; impf. **успева́ть**

установи́ть 'to establish': установлю́ устано́вит устано́вят; устано́влен; impf. **устана́вливать**

уча́ствовать (в + p.) 'to participate in': уча́ствую уча́ствует уча́ствуют

уче́сть 'to take account of': учту́ учтёт учту́т; учёл учла́; учти́!; учтён учтена́; impf. **учи́тывать**

ходи́ть 'to go': хожу́ хо́дит хо́дят; ходи́!

хоте́ть/за- 'to want': хочу́ хо́чешь хо́чет хоти́м хоти́те хотя́т

худе́ть/по- 'to lose weight': худе́ю худе́ет худе́ют

цвести́ 'to flower': цветёт цвету́т; цвёл цвела́

чеса́ть/по- 'to scratch': чешу́ че́шет че́шут

чи́стить/вы́- or по- 'to clean': чи́щу чи́стит чи́стят; вы́чищен/очи́щен

чу́вствовать 'to feel': чу́вствую чу́вствует чу́вствуют

шепта́ть 'to whisper': шепчу́ ше́пчет ше́пчут; pf. **шепну́ть**

шить/с- 'to sew': шью шьёт шьют; шей!

шуме́ть 'to make a noise': шуми́т шумя́т

шути́ть/по- 'to joke': шучу́ шу́тит шу́тят

эконо́мить/с- 'to economize': эконо́млю эконо́мит эконо́мят; сэконо́млен

яви́ться (+ i. 'to be'): явлю́сь я́вится я́вятся; impf. **явля́ться**

Заметки об английской грамматике

Существительные

Артикли

Неопределённый артикль

Неопределённый артикль **a** стоит перед словами, начинающимися на согласный или на сочетания, содержащие звук /j/:

a ball мяч
a girl девочка
a union союз

Перед гласным или перед непроизносимым /h/ неопределённый артикль принимает форму **an**:

an apple яблоко
an hour час

Неопределённый артикль обычно употребляется с исчисляемыми существительными. Рассмотрим следующие случаи употребления:

- с названиями профессий:
  She is a doctor Она врач
  He is an engineer Он инженер
- после предлогов:
  She works as a tour guide Она работает гидом/экскурсоводом
  Anna has gone without an umbrella Анна ушла без зонта
- в обобщающих высказываниях:
  A whale is larger than a frog Кит больше лягушки

Определённый артикль

Определённый артикль **the** употребляется с существительными единственного и множественного числа:

the cat кошка
the owls совы

Определённый артикль не употребляется с существительными, обозначающими:

- учреждения:
  I don't go to church Я не хожу в церковь
  He's starting school next week Он пойдёт в школу на следующей неделе

Но когда определённый артикль обозначает здания, а не учреждения, он употребляется:

Turn right at the school У школы поверните направо

- время еды:
  Breakfast is at 8.30 Завтрак в 8:30
  Dinner is ready Обед готов

- время суток, после предлогов (за исключением **in** и **during**):

I am never out at night	Вечером я всегда дома
They left in the morning	Они уехали утром

- абстрактные понятия:

Hatred is a destructive force	Ненависть — разрушительная сила
The book is on English grammar	Это книга об английской грамматике

- болезни:

She's got tonsillitis	У неё ангина

- времена года:

Spring is here!	Наступила весна
It's like winter today	Сегодня совсем зима

- страны:

Russia	Россия
England	Англия

- улицы, парки и т. д.:

a concert in Hyde Park	концерт в Гайд-парке
I work on Baker Street	Я работаю на Бейкер-стрит

Определённый артикль, однако, употребляется в предложениях, в которых рассматриваются конкретные примеры:

The breakfast he served was awful	Завтрак, который он подал, был ужасным
The winter of 2004 was very mild	Зима 2004 года была очень мягкая

Следующие классы существительных всегда употребляются с определённым артиклем:

- географические названия во множественном числе:

the Netherlands	Нидерланды
the United States	Соединённые Штаты
the Alps	Альпы

- названия рек, морей и океанов:

the Thames	Темза
the Black Sea	Чёрное море
the Pacific	Тихий океан

- названия гостиниц, пабов, театров, музеев и проч.:

the Hilton	Хилтон
the Fox and Hounds	Лиса и гончие
the New Theatre	Новый театр
the British Museum	Британский музей

Множественное число

Множественное число существительных обычно образуется прибавлением к слову окончания **-s**:

dog — dogs	**tape — tapes**

К словам, оканчивающимся на **-s**, **-ss**, **-sh**, **-ch**, **-x**, **-zz**, следует добавлять окончание **-es**:

dress — dresses	**box — boxes**

Такое же окончание появляется в словах, оканчивающихся на *согласный* + **y**.

Причём конечный **-y** становится **-i-**:

baby — babies

Подобного не происходит у существительных, оканчивающихся на сочетание *гласный* + **y**:

valley — valleys

Существительные, оканчивающиеся на **-o**, получают во множественном числе или **-s**, или **-es**:

potato — potatoes **tomato — tomatoes**
solo — solos **zero — zeros**

У существительных, оканчивающихся на **-f(e)**, возможны три варианта окончания множественного числа:

life — lives **dwarf — dwarfs/dwarves**
roof — roofs

Ниже приводится список наиболее часто встречающихся нерегулярных форм множественного числа:

child — children **foot — feet**
man — men **mouse — mice**
tooth — teeth **woman — women**

Субстантивные словосочетания

Данные сочетания строятся по следующим образцам:

существительное + существительное:

summer dress летнее платье
tennis shoes теннисные туфли
record collection коллекция пластинок

существительное + герундий:

disco dancing танцы на дискотеке
dressmaking швейное дело

герундий + существительное:

parking meter паркинговый автомат
writing course писательские курсы
boarding card посадочный талон

Множественное число таких сочетаний образуется прибавлением окончания множественного числа только к основному в смысловом отношении слову:

a record collection — record collections
a photo album — photo albums

Женский род

Категория рода у неодушевлённых существительных отсутствует в английском языке. Так, существительные **cousin**, **friend**, **doctor** могут называть лиц и мужского, и женского пола. Поэтому, если при обозначении профессии или степени родства, требуется указать на род, то используются описательные конструкции типа **a male student**, **a woman doctor**.

Родительный (притяжательный) падеж

Родительный (притяжательный) падеж оформляется сочетанием **s** с апострофом, который стоит или перед **s** или после него (**'s/s'**).

's добавляется к существительным единственного числа:

the boy's book	книга мальчика

Апостроф без **s** добавляется к существительным, оканчивающимся во множественном числе на **-s**:

the boys' room	комната мальчиков
the boys' books	книги мальчиков

Если существительное относится к нерегулярной группе, и его множественное число не оканчивается на **-s**, то в родительном (притяжательном) падеже множественного числа употребляется **-'s**:

the children's toys	игрушки детей

В родительном (притяжательном) падеже имён собственных, оканчивающихся на **-s**, может встречаться и **'s**, и **s'** (вариант с **s'** более употребительный): **Keats's poetry** или **Keats' poetry** (**поэзия Китса**). С греческими и римскими именами, оканчивающимися на **-s**, как правило, употребляется только апостроф: **Socrates' death** (**смерть Сократа**), **Catullus' poetry** (**поэзия Катулла**).

Родительный (притяжательный) падеж употребляется с существительными, обозначающими людей, животных (в особенности домашних), а также с названиями стран:

Andrew's house	дом Эндрю
the lion's den	логово льва
America's foreign policy	внешняя политика Америки

Родительный (притяжательный) падеж может выражать следующие отношения:

We are going to Anne's	Мы идём к Анне (домой)
We are going to Peter and Anne's	Мы идём к Питеру и Анне (домой)

(форма **Peter's and Anne's** неупотребительна, если **Peter** и **Anne** рассматриваются как смысловая пара)

Jane Austen's and George Orwell's novels	Романы Джейн Остин и Джорджа Оруэлла

(Джейн Остин и Джордж Оруэлл рассматриваются здесь по отдельности)

I got it at the baker's/chemist's	Я купил это в булочной/аптеке

(дословно: **at the baker's shop/at the chemist's shop**)

В разговорном языке довольно часто встречается форма двойного родительного падежа:

He is a friend of my brother's	Он друг моего брата
It was an idea of Anne's	Это было идеей Анны/Это была идея Анны

Прилагательные

Прилагательные в английском языке имеют только одну форму. Они не согласуются с существительным ни в роде, ни в числе, ни в падеже:

an old man	пожилой мужчина
five old women	пять пожилых женщин

Положение прилагательных в предложении

Прилагательные могут стоять перед определяемым существительным: **a long story** (**длинная история**), или после него: **This story is long** (**Эта история длинная**). Однако некоторые прилагательные употребляются только после существительных: **The girl is upset** (**Девочка расстроена**). Нельзя сказать **the upset girl**.

Сравнительная и превосходительная форма

Существует три степени сравнения: положительная, сравнительная и превосходная.

Односложные прилагательные образуют сравнительную и превосходную степени добавлением **-(e)r** и **-(e)st** соответственно:

dull	скучный
duller	скучнее
dullest	скучнейший
big	большой
bigger	больше
biggest	самый большой

(Обратите внимание на удвоение конечного согласного.)

nice	хороший
nicer	лучше
nicest	самый лучший

Многосложные прилагательные образуют сравнительную и превосходную степень при помощи вспомогательных слов **more** и **most**:

generous	щедрый
more generous	более щедрый, щедрее
most generous	самый щедрый, щедрейший

По такому же образцу образуются сравнительная и превосходная степени некоторых двусложных прилагательных, например, **useful** (**полезный**).

Однако в большинстве своём двусложные прилагательные не подчиняются одному определённому правилу. С большой долей вероятности можно только утверждать, что прилагательные, оканчивающиеся на **-y**, **-le**, **-ow**, **-er**, образуют сравнительную и превосходную степени при помощи окончаний **-er**/**-est**. Например:

pretty (**-y** меняется на **-i-**)	милый
prettier	милее, более милый
prettiest	милейший, самый милый
narrow	узкий
narrower	уже, более узкий
narrowest	самый узкий
curious	любопытный
more curious	любопытнее, более любопытный
most curious	любопытнейший, самый любопытный

Сравнительная и превосходная степень прилагательных, образованных от действительных и страдательных причастий, образуется при помощи вспомогательных слов **more** и **most**:

boring скучный
more boring скучнее, более скучный
most boring скучнейший, самый скучный

Most также употребляется в значении «чрезвычайно», «очень»:

That was a most interesting story Это была очень интересная/интереснейшая история

Ниже приводится список наиболее употребительных нерегулярных прилагательных:

bad плохой
worse хуже, более плохой
worst самый плохой/наихудший

good хороший
better лучше, более хороший
best лучший, самый лучший

little маленький
less меньше, меньший
least меньше всего

many/much много
more больше
most больше всего

far далёкий
farther более далёкий
farthest самый далёкий (только о расстоянии)

old старший
elder старше
eldest самый старший

При этом регулярные формы (**old, older, oldest — старый, старее, самый старый**) описывают и людей, и предметы.

Отрицательная форма сравнительной степени образуется при помощи слов **less/least**:

far далёкий
less far менее далёкий
least far наименее далёкий

Прилагательные могут употребляться в функции существительных, особенно, когда они обозначают группу людей:

the young молодые, молодёжь
the old старые, старики
the unemployed безработные

Притяжательные прилагательные

К притяжательным прилагательным относятся:

my	мой
our	наш
your	твой
your	ваш
his, her, its	его (м. р.), её (ж. р.), его (ср. р.)
their	их

Род этих прилагательных зависит от рода обладателя предмета, а не от рода самого предмета:

his mother	его мать
her mother	её мать
their mother	их мать

Притяжательные прилагательные не согласуются с определяемым существительным в числе:

my cat	моя кошка
my cats	мои кошки

Наречия

Наречия определяют:

- прилагательные:

  The job was extremely dangerous — Работа была чрезвычайно опасной

- глаголы:

  He finished quickly — Он быстро закончил

- другие наречия:

  very quickly — очень быстро

Extremely, **quickly**, **very** являются наречиями.

Большинство наречий образуется прибавлением **-ly** к прилагательному:

sad — sadly	(печальный — печально)
brave — bravely	(храбрый — храбро)
beautiful — beautifully	(красивый — красиво)

При образовании наречий по такой модели возможны некоторые изменения в орфографии:

true — truly	(верный — верно)
due — duly	(должный — должно)
whole — wholly	(цельный — целиком)

Другие важные орфографические изменения:

конечный **-y** меняется на **-i-**:	**ready — readily**
конечное **-le** на **-ly**:	**gentle — gently**

Некоторые наречия совпадают по форме с соответствующими им прилагательными:

back (задний, назад), **early** (ранний, рано), **far** (далеко, далёкий), **fast** (быстрый, быстро), **left** (левый, налево), **little** (маленький, мало), **long** (длинный, длинно), **only** (единственный, только), **right** (правый, направо), **still** (спокойный, спокойно), **straight** (прямой, прямо), **well** (хороший, хорошо), **wrong** (неправильный, неправильно):

a wrong answer	неправильный ответ
He did it wrong	Он сделал это неправильно
an early summer	раннее лето
Summer arrived early	Лето наступило рано
a straight road	прямая дорога
He came straight to the point	Он перешёл прямо к делу

Местоимения

Личные местоимения

Именительный падеж		Косвенный падеж	
I	(я)	**me**	(меня, мне, мной)
you	(ты)	**you**	(тебя, тебе, тобой)
he	(он)	**him**	(его, ему, им)
she	(она)	**her**	(её, ей, ею)
it	(оно)	**it**	(его, ему, им)
we	(мы)	**us**	(нас, нам, нами)
you	(вы)	**you**	(вас, вам, вами)
they	(они)	**them**	(их, им, ими)

В английском языке глагольные формы не выражают лица. Поэтому русская глагольная форма **иду** должна переводиться на английский язык сочетанием **I go**, а не отдельной формой **go**.

Местоимения в косвенных падежах являются в предложении:

- прямыми дополнениями:

  Mary loves him Мэри любит его

- косвенными дополнениями без предлога:

  John gave me a lift Джон подвёз меня

- косвенными дополнениями с предлогом:

  The book is from her Книга от неё

Другие функции личных местоимений

he, she

Эти местоимения иногда обозначают животных, особенно домашних:

Poor Whiskers, we had to take him to the vet's	Бедный Уискерс. Нам пришлось отнести его к ветеринару

it употребляется:

- в безличных конструкциях:

It's sunny	Солнечно
It's hard to know what to do	Трудно понять, что надо делать
It looks as though they were right	Кажется, они были правы

в конструкциях, выражающих время и пространство:

It's five o'clock	Сейчас 5 часов
It's January the sixth	Сегодня 6 января
How far is it to Edinburgh?	Как далеко до Эдинбурга?

It's является сокращённой формой конструкции **it is**. Её не следует путать с притяжательным местоимением **its**.

you

Данное местоимение не имеет вежливой формы.

You употребляется в обобщённом значении, для обозначения людей вообще.

You never know; it might be sunny this week	Как знать. Может быть, на этой неделе будет солнечно
You can't buy cars like that any more	Таких машин уже не купить

they

- употребляется в обобщённом значении для обозначения неопределённой группы людей, особенно, если они обладают какой-либо властью, силой или умением:

They don't make cars like that any more	Таких машин уже не делают
They will have to find the murderer first	Вначале им надо будет найти убийцу
You'll have to get them to repair the car	Тебе надо будет заставить их отремонтировать машину

- употребляется вместо **he** или **she** (**он, она**):

The person appointed will be answerable to the director. They will be responsible for...	Человек, назначенный на эту должность, будет подчиняться директору. Он будет отвечать за...
A personal secretary will assist them (= him/her)	Им будет помогать персональный секретарь

- соотносится с неопределёнными местоимениями **somebody, someone** (**кто-то**); **anybody, anyone** (**кто-нибудь**); **everybody, everyone** (**всякий, все**); **nobody, no one** (**никто**):

If anyone has seen my pen, will they please tell me?	Если кто-нибудь видел мою ручку, пусть он мне скажет

one

One, так же, как **you**, употребляется в обобщённом значении, но является более литературным:

One needs to get a clear picture of what one wants.	Человек должен точно знать, что он хочет

Следует избегать чрезмерного употребления в речи **one**.

Возвратные местоимения

myself (себя, сам)	**ourselves** (себя, сами)
yourself (себя, сам, сама)	**yourselves** (себя, сами)
himself, herself, itself (себя, сам, сама, само)	**themselves** (себя, сами)

примеры употребления:

I always buy myself a Christmas present (косвенное дополнение)	Я всегда покупаю себе рождественский подарок
She talks to herself (предложное дополнение)	Она разговаривает сама с собой
Do it yourself (эмфатическая конструкция)	Сделай это сам
He burned himself badly (прямое дополнение)	Он сильно обжёгся

Притяжательные местоименные существительные

mine	мой
yours	твой
his, hers	его, её
ours	наш
yours	ваш
theirs	их

Род этих слов зависит от рода их обладателя, а не от рода самого предмета:

Whose book is it? — It's hers	Чья эта книга?—Её
Whose shoes are these? — They are hers	Чьи эти туфли?—Её
Whose car is that? — It's theirs	Чья та машина?—Их

Вопросительные местоимения и прилагательные

who	кто
whom	кому
whose	чей
which	который, какой
what	что

Who употребляется для обозначения одушевлённого подлежащего:

Who is it? Кто это?

Whom употребляется для обозначения одушевлённого дополнения:

To whom did you send the letter?	Кому ты послал письмо?
Whom did you see?	Кого ты видел?

Whom является литературной формой и часто заменяется местоимением who:

Who did you send the letter to?	Кому ты послал письмо?
Who did you see?	Кого ты видел?

Whose является родительным падежом **who**:

Whose are these?	Это чьи?
Whose socks are these?	Чьи это носки?

Which может относиться и к одушевлённым, и к неодушевлённым предметам, а также обозначать подлежащее:

Which of you are going?	Кто из вас идёт?
Which is bigger?	Какой/который больше?
Which box is bigger?	Какой из ящиков больше?

Дополнение:

Which of the singers do you prefer?	Какого певца ты предпочитаешь?
Which of the pictures do you prefer?	Какую картину ты предпочитаешь?

What относится только к неодушевлённым предметам и может обозначать подлежащее:

What is this?	Что это?
What type of bird is that?	Какой это вид птиц?

дополнение:

What are you going to do?	Что ты собираешься делать?
What sort of books do you like?	Какие книги тебе нравятся?

What используется в более широких и менее определённых толкованиях, нежели **which**.

Относительные местоимения

who, whom	который, которого, которому
that	который
which	который
whose	чей, который

Относительные местоимения обычно отсылают к предмету, который уже упоминался в речи (антецедент). Так, в предложении **She phoned the man who had contacted her earlier** (**Она позвонила мужчине, который обращался к ней ранее**) относительное местоимение **who** относится к слову **the man**.

антецедент	подлежащее	дополнение
люди	**who/that**	**whom/who/that**
предметы	**which/that**	**which/that**

люди: подлежащее

В данной функции употребляется относительное местоимение **who**, хотя возможно и употребление **that**:

There is a prize for the student who/that gets the highest mark
Студент, который наберёт самый высокий балл, получит приз

Whom является более литературной формой и часто заменяется местоимением **who** или **that**.

Относительное местоимение может опускаться:

The man she met last night was a spy
Мужчина, которого она вчера встретила, был шпионом

предметы: подлежащее

The book which is on the table was a present
Книга, которая лежит на столе, была мне подарена

John gave me the book which/that is on the table
Джон подарил мне книгу, которая лежит на столе

предметы: дополнение

The film, which we went to see last week, was excellent
Фильм, который мы смотрели на прошлой неделе, был прекрасным

В последнем примере относительное местоимение может опускаться:

The film we went to see last week was excellent

Whose является формой родительного падежа:

This is the boy whose dog has been killed Это мальчик, чью собаку убили

Форма **of which** употребляется в литературной или специальной речи и относится к неодушевлённым предметам:

Water, the boiling point of which is 100˚C, is a colourless liquid
Вода является бесцветной жидкостью, точка кипения которой — 100 ˚C

Запомните, что сочетание **who's** является сокращённой формой сочетания **who is**. Его не следует путать с относительным местоимением **whose** (**чей**).

Неопределённые местоимения и прилагательные

some/any	немного

Как прилагательные эти слова употребляются с существительными во множественном числе и с неисчисляемыми существительными:

Take some apples	Возьми немного яблок
Take some jam	Возьми немного варенья
Have you got any apples?	У вас есть яблоки?
Have you any jam?	У вас есть варенье?

Эти местоимения могут заменять существительные во множественном числе и неисчисляемые существительные:

I'd like some jam. — We haven't got any	Мне хочется варенья. — У нас его нет

Some (как прилагательное и как местоимение) употребляется:

- в утвердительных высказываниях:

He bought some	Он купил немного
He bought some jam	Он купил немного варенья
He bought some apples	Он купил немного яблок

- в вопросах, которые предполагают положительный ответ:

Can you lend me some money?	Ты можешь одолжить мне немного денег?

- в предложениях и в просьбах:

Would you like some?	Хотите немного?
Could you buy some onions for me?	Купите мне, пожалуйста, немного лука

Any (как прилагательное и как местоимение) употребляется:

- в высказываниях с отрицанием:

I haven't got any brothers or sisters	У меня нет ни братьев, ни сестёр

- в вопросах:

Have you got any bananas?	У вас есть бананы?

Слова, производные от **some** и **any**, употребляются аналогичным образом:

I saw something really strange today	Сегодня я видел нечто очень странное
Did you meet anyone you know?	Ты видел каких-нибудь (своих) знакомых?
We didn't see anything interesting	Мы не видели ничего интересного

Глаголы

Инфинитив является основной формой глагола. Полная форма инфинитива включает частицу **to**:

to live (жить), **to die** (умереть) и т. д.

Список неправильных глаголов приводится на стр. 917.

Правильные глаголы спрягаются по следующему образцу:

инфинитив

want	**love (1)**	**stop (2)**	**prefer (3)**

настоящее время

wants	**loves**	**stops**	**prefers**

причастие настоящего времени/герундий

wanting **loving** **stopping** **preferring**

простое прошедшее время/причастие прошедшего времени

wanted **loved** **stopped** **preferred**

в таблице показаны следующие типы глаголов:

(1) инфинитив оканчивается на **-e**;

(2) односложный инфинитив оканчивается сочетанием *гласный + согласный*;

(3) инфинитив оканчивается сочетанием *ударный гласный + согласный*.

Герундий может употребляться как существительное:

I do not like dancing	Мне не нравится танцевать
Dancing is fun	Танцевать — весело

Времена

Настоящее время

to be (быть)	**to have** (иметь)
I am	**I have**
you are	**you have**
he/she/it is	**he/she/it has**
we are	**we have**
you are	**you have**
they are	**they have**

У остальных глаголов форма инфинитива и настоящего времени совпадает во всех лицах, за исключением 3 лица единственного числа, где к глаголу присоединяется окончание **-s**:

to want (хотеть)	**I want, you want, he/she/it wants, we want, you want, they want**
to love (любить)	**I love, you love, he/she/it loves, we love, you love, they love**

У глаголов, оканчивающихся в инфинитиве на **-s**, **-ss**, **-sh**, **-ch**, **-x**, **-zz**, в 3 лице единственного числа прибавляется окончание **-es**:

to watch (смотреть)	**he/she/it watches**
to kiss (целовать)	**he/she/it kisses**

Настоящее время выражает:

- повторяющиеся действия, общепринятые истины, фактические утверждения:

He takes the 8 o'clock train to work	Он едет на работу 8-часовым поездом
The Earth rotates around the Sun	Земля вращается вокруг Солнца
I work in publishing	Я работаю в издательстве

- вкусы и мнения:

I hate Mondays	Я ненавижу понедельник
He doesn't believe in God	Он не верит в Бога

- чувственные восприятия:

The pie smells delicious	Пирог вкусно пахнет

Простое прошедшее время

Простое прошедшее время правильных глаголов образуется прибавлением окончания **-ed** к основе глагола:

I/you/he/she/it/we/you/they wanted

Неправильные глаголы имеют особые формы, которые следует заучивать. Таблица неправильных глаголов приводится на стр. 917.

Данное время служит для выражения законченных в прошлом действий или событий:

He flew to America last week	На прошлой неделе он улетел в Америку

Настоящее совершённое время

Данное время образуется при помощи вспомогательного глагола **to have** в форме настоящего времени и причастия прошедшего времени:

I/you have loved
he/she/it has loved
we/you/they have loved

Данное время служит для выражения действий, законченных в прошлом, но имеющих какую-либо связь с настоящим.

Разница между настоящим совершённым временем и простым прошедшим временем обнаруживается при сравнении следующих примеров:

Have you seen Peter this morning?	Ты видел Питера утром? (действие происходит утром)
Did you see Peter this morning?	Ты видел Питера сегодня утром? (действие происходит днём или вечером)

Прошедшее совершённое время

Данное время образуется при помощи вспомогательного глагола **to have** в форме прошедшего времени и причастия прошедшего времени:

I/you/he/she/it/we/you/they had wanted

Данное время служит для выражения действий, которые предшествовали другим действиям в прошлом:

She had already left home when I arrived	Когда я пришёл, она уже ушла из дома

Длительные времена

Данная группа времён образуется при помощи вспомогательного глагола **to be** и причастия настоящего времени.

Настоящее длительное время

I am singing	я пою
you are singing	ты поёшь
he is singing	он поёт

и т. д.

Настоящее длительное время описывает события, происходящие в момент речи, при этом любые действия рассматриваются, прежде всего, как процесс:

What are you doing? — I am trying to fix the television	Что ты делаешь? — Я пытаюсь починить телевизор
He always interrupts when I am reading to the children	Он всегда мне мешает, когда я читаю детям

Прошедшее длительное время

I was singing	я пел
you were singing	ты пел
he was singing	он пел

и т. д.

Прошедшее длительное время описывает события, которые происходили одновременно с другими событиями в прошлом.

He rushed into my office while I was talking to the director	Он ворвался в мой офис, когда я разговаривал с директором

Настоящее совершённое и прошедшее совершённое могут употребляться в длительной форме: I have been writing (я писал), I had been writing (я писал), I will be writing (я буду писать).

Будущее время

В английском языке существует несколько способов выражения будущего времени:

■ вспомогательный глагол **will/shall** сочетается с инфинитивом.
Will употребляется для всех лиц в единственном и множественном числе.
Shall употребляется только в 1-м лице единственного и множественного числа:

I will/shall go	я пойду
we will/shall go	мы пойдём
you will go	ты пойдёшь
you will go	вы пойдёте
he/she/it will go	он/она/оно пойдёт
they will go	они пойдут

Will и отрицательные формы **will not** и **shall not** могут употребляться в сокращённой форме:

You'll be angry	Ты будешь сердиться
We won't/shan't stay long	Мы останемся там ненадолго

■ конструкция **going to**
Данная конструкция чаще всего употребляется для выражения намерения или предположения:

I am going to go to London tomorrow	Завтра я еду в Лондон
The boss is going to be furious when he hears	Босс будет в ярости, когда услышит об этом

Конструкцию **going to** в большинстве случаев можно заменить сочетанием с **will**:

The boss will be furious when he hears	Босс будет в ярости, когда услышит об этом
I wonder whether the car is going to/will start	Интересно, машина заведётся?

■ настоящее время в значении будущего
Настоящее время может употребляться в значении будущего, если событие должно произойти в определённый момент в будущем. Например, когда речь идет о событиях, предусмотренных расписанием или планом:

When does term finish?	Когда заканчивается семестр?
The train for London leaves at 10 o'clock	Поезд на Лондон отходит в 10 часов

- настоящее длительное время

Подобно конструкции с **going to**, данное время может выражать намерение:

I am spending Christmas in Paris	Рождество я проведу в Париже
Where are you going for your holidays?	Куда вы поедете в отпуск?

Повелительное наклонение

Для выражения приказов и просьб употребляется основная форма глагола (инфинитив):

Go home!	Иди домой!
Shut the door!	Закрой дверь!

Отрицательная форма повелительного наклонения образуется при помощи вспомогательного глагола **do not** или, чаще, его сокращённой формы don't:

Don't forget to phone Alan!	Не забудь позвонить Алану!

Конструкция **let's** употребляется в 1-м лице множественного числа для выражения побуждений, предложений:

Let's go!	Давайте пойдём!/Идёмте!
Don't let's go!	Давайте не пойдём!
Let's not go!	Давайте не пойдём!

Вопросительная форма

Для образования настоящего и прошедшего времени данной формы используется вспомогательный глагол **do**, который согласуется с подлежащим в лице и числе:

Do you live here?	Ты здесь живёшь?
Did you live here?	Ты здесь жил?

Если предложение содержит вспомогательный глагол (**to have**, **to be**) или модальный глагол, то вопросительная форма образуется посредством изменения порядка слов, и сказуемое ставится перед подлежащим:

Are they going to get married?	Они собираются пожениться?
Have they seen us?	Они видели нас?
Can John come at eight?	Джон может прийти в восемь?

Если предложение содержит вопросительное местоимение, то вопросительные формы имеют следующий вид:

Who came?	Кто пришёл?
Who fed the cat?	Кто кормил кошку?
What have they done to you?	Что они с тобой сделали?
What shall we write about?	О чём мы будем писать?

В отрицательных предложениях частица **not**, если она употребляется в полной форме, ставится после подлежащего:

Did they not say they would come?/ Didn't they say they would come?	Разве они не сказали, что они придут?
Will the director not be there?/ Won't the director be there?	Разве директора там не будет?

В разговорной речи порядок слов в вопросительном предложении может быть таким же, как и в утвердительном, а сам вопрос обозначается повышением голоса (восходящей интонацией):

He told you to leave?	Он велел тебе уйти?
He left without saying a word?	Он ушёл, не сказав ни слова?

Присоединённые вопросы

В английском языке присоединёнными вопросами называются особые конструкции, употребляемые в конце предложения и побуждающие собеседника к подтверждению сказанного.

Положительное утверждение обычно сопровождается отрицательным присоединённым вопросом:

You smoke, don't you?	Ты куришь, не правда ли?/не так ли?

Вспомогательный глагол **don't** заменяет в присоединённом вопросе глагол smoke.

Отрицательное утверждение обычно сопровождается положительным присоединённым вопросом:

You don't smoke, do you?	Ты не куришь, не правда ли?

Если в (главном) предложении содержится вспомогательный или модальный глагол, то он повторяется и в присоединённом вопросе:

You aren't going, are you?	Ты не идёшь, не правда ли?
You will come, won't you?	Ты придёшь, не правда ли?
You shouldn't say that, should you?	Ты не должен так говорить, не правда ли?

Обратите внимание на форму глагола в присоединённом вопросе в случаях, когда в главном предложении употреблено сказуемое **am**:

I am lucky, aren't I?	Мне везёт, не правда ли?

Сказуемое в присоединённом вопросе употребляется в том же времени, что и сказуемое в главном предложении:

You wanted to go home, didn't you?	Ты хотел пойти домой, не правда ли?

Неполные предложения

Давая положительные или отрицательные ответы на вопросы, не обязательно повторять полную форму глагола. Достаточно употребить соответствующий вспомогательный глагол (**to be**, **to have**, **to do**) или модальный глагол, фигурирующий в вопросе:

Is it raining? — Yes, it is/No, it isn't	Дождь идёт? — Да, идёт/Нет, не идёт
Do you like fish? — Yes, I do/No, I don't	Ты любишь рыбу? — Да, люблю/Нет, не люблю
Can you drive? — Yes, I can/No, I can't	Ты умеешь водить машину? — Да, умею/Нет, не умею

Отрицательные предложения

Отрицательные предложения образуются при помощи вспомогательного глагола **do**, согласованного с подлежащим, и отрицательной частицы **not**. Сокращённые формы данной конструкции в настоящем времени выглядят следующим образом: **do + not = don't**, **does + not = doesn't**, **did + not = didn't**. Например:

They do not/don't understand English	Они не понимают по-английски
They did not/didn't go anywhere yesterday	Вчера они никуда не ходили

В эмфатических предложениях сказуемое употребляется в полной форме:

I do not approve!	Я (э)того не одобряю!

Модальные глаголы

can, could; may, might; shall, should; will, would; must; ought to

Модальные глаголы не изменяются по лицам и числам:

I can, you can, he can

Вопросительные формы образуются посредством изменения порядка слов, при этом сказуемое ставится перед подлежащим:

Can I go now?	Мне можно идти?

Модальные глаголы часто употребляются в сокращённой форме:

will и **shall** сокращаются до формы **'ll**: **I'll be going** (Я пойду)

would сокращается до формы **'d**: **I'd like a cup of tea** (Мне хочется чаю)

Отрицательная форма модальных глаголов образуется при помощи частицы **not** (**would not**, **might not** и т. д.). Отрицательная форма глагола **can** — **cannot** (в британском варианте английского языка пишется как одно слово).

Сокращённые формы отрицательных конструкций с модальными глаголами выглядят так: **can't**, **couldn't**, **mightn't**, **shan't**, **shouldn't**, **won't**, **wouldn't**, **mustn't**, **oughtn't**. (Форма **mayn't** малоупотребительна.)

can выражает:

■ разрешение:

Can I leave the table, please?	Можно мне встать из-за стола?
I can have another sweet: daddy said so	Мне можно съесть ещё одну конфету: папа разрешил

■ способность:

He can count to hundred	Он умеет считать до ста
Can he drive?	Он умеет водить машину?

■ возможность:

Accidents can happen	Неприятности случаются

■ просьбу:

Can you help me, please?	Вы можете мне помочь?

could

Could является прошедшим временем **can**. В число его значений входят:

■ разрешение, способность, возможность, просьба, относящиеся к прошлому:

Daddy said I could have another sweet	Папа сказал, что я могу съесть ещё одну конфету
By the time he was three, he could count to a hundred	К трём годам, он уже умел считать до ста
She asked if he could help her	Она спросила, может ли он ей помочь

■ вежливые, официальные просьбы:

Could I leave a message, please?	Могу ли я оставить записку?

■ возможность:

I don't know where John is; I suppose he could be at Anne's	Я не знаю, где Джон; возможно, (что) он у Анны

■ возмущение:

You could have warned me!	Ты мог бы меня предупредить!

may

■ разрешение и вежливая просьба:

May I use your phone, please?	Могу ли я воспользоваться вашим телефоном?
You may not leave the examination hall until I give the sign.	Вы не можете покинуть экзаменационный зал, пока я не дам вам разрешения

■ возможность:

We may get an extra day's holiday	У нас может быть дополнительный выходной (день)
They may have left	Возможно, (что) они уехали

might

■ возможность:

Might, в отличие от **may**, предполагает, что указанная возможность маловероятна:

We might get a pay rise	Может быть нам повысят зарплату (= маловероятно, что это произойдёт)

Данная форма используется и в прошедшем времени:

He was afraid he might have arrived late	Он боялся, вдруг он опоздал

Might может также выражать:

■ разрешение или вежливую просьбу:

Do you think I might have another whisky?	Вы позволите мне ещё одно виски?

■ возмущение:

You might have phoned!	Мог бы и позвонить!

shall

Об употреблении **shall** в будущем времени см. стр. 910. **Shall** употребляется также для выражения:

■ вопросов, которые предполагают получение совета или рекомендации:

Where shall we put the shopping?	Куда нам положить покупки?
What time shall I set the alarm for?	На какое время мне поставить будильник?

■ предложения:

Shall I make you a cup of tea?	Сделать тебе чаю?
Shall we meet outside the station?	Давайте встретимся у вокзала

should

Should является прошедшим временем **shall**. Помимо этого **should** обозначает:

■ правила и условности:

You shouldn't tell lies	Лгать нельзя
What do you think we should do?	Как, по-твоему, нам следует поступить?

■ вероятность:

Once this job is finished, we should have more spare time	Когда мы закончим эту работу, у нас должно быть больше (свободного) времени
They should be here by now	Они должны были уже приехать

The key should be in that drawer	Ключ должен быть в этом ящике
That's where I left them	Я их там оставил

will

Об употреблении **will** в будущем времени см. стр. 910. Об употреблении **will** в условных предложениях см. стр. 916.

Кроме того, **will** выражает:

- свойства и внутренние характеристики:

Hot air will rise	Тёплый воздух поднимается
The stadium will seat 4,000 people	Стадион вмещает 4000 человек

- намерение, желание, одобрение:

Will you see to the post for me?	Вы займётесь почтой?
I'll do what I can to help him	Я помогу ему всем, чем могу

- предложение:

Will you have another slice of cake?	Не хотите ли ещё пирога?

- высокую степень вероятности:

There's someone at the door. That will be Anne	Кто-то стучит в дверь. Это должно быть Анна

- приказ:

You will go and wash your hands immediately	Немедленно/сейчас же идите и вымойте руки

would

Would является прошедшим временем **will**. Об употреблении **would** в условных предложениях см. стр. 916. Кроме того, **would** выражает:

- будущее прошедшее время:

He told me he would do it soon	Он сказал мне, что сделает это скоро
They said they wouldn't wait for me	Они сказали мне, что не будут ждать меня

- повторяющиеся действия в прошлом:

He would always get up at 6 a.m.	Он всегда вставал в 6 утра

must

- обязанность:

You must make sure you lock up	Вы обязательно должны запереть дверь
I must check whether my neighbour is all right	Я должен проверить, всё ли в порядке у соседа

Запомните, что **mustn't** выражает запрет:

You mustn't park there	Там нельзя парковаться (= это запрещено)

Если вы хотите сказать, что в совершении каких-либо действий нет необходимости, вы можете употребить конструкции **don't have to**, **needn't**, **don't need to**:

You don't have to eat that/You needn't eat that/You don't need to eat that	Вам не надо это есть

- возможность:

They must be there by now	Они, наверное, уже там
You must have been annoyed by the decision	Должно быть, это решение рассердило вас

ought

- обязанность:

You ought to be leaving	Вам надо уходить
They ought to kick him out	Они должны выдворить его

- вероятность, предположение:

They ought to be there by now	Они должны быть уже там
Two kilos of potatoes. That ought to be enough	Два килограмма картофеля. Этого должно хватить

Условные предложения с *if*

Существует три основных типа условных предложений с ***if***:

if + настоящее время, главное предложение с **will** (для выражения реально осуществимых предположений):

> **If we hurry, we'll catch the train/We'll catch the train if we hurry**
> Если мы поторопимся, мы успеем на поезд

if + простое прошедшее, главное предложение с **would** (для выражения маловероятных предположений):

> **If I won the lottery, I would buy a new house/I would buy a new house if I won the lottery**
> Если бы я выиграл в лотерее, я бы купил новый дом

if + прошедшее совершённое, главное предложение с **would have** (для выражения невыполнимых предположений, относящихся к прошлому):

> **If Mike hadn't lost the tickets, we would have arrived on time/ We would have arrived on time if Mike hadn't lost the tickets**
> Мы бы приехали вовремя, если бы Майк не потерял билеты

Глагольные сочетания

В английском языке многие глаголы образуют устойчивые сочетания с предлогами (т. н. фразовые глаголы), в которых присоединяемый предлог — аналогично глагольным приставкам в русском языке — меняет значение глагола:

to take (брать)

John took a book	Джон взял книгу

to take off (**1.** снять **2.** взлететь)

He took off his boots/ He took his boots off	Он снял ботинки
The plane took off	Самолёт взлетел

to take after (походить на, быть похожим на)

He takes after his mother	Он походит/похож на свою мать

Обратите внимание на то, что дополнение может появляться в двух позициях: после предлога или между предлогом и глаголом (см. вышеприведённые примеры с глаголом **take off**).

Однако если в качестве дополнения выступает местоимение, то оно может стоять только между глаголом и предлогом:

He looked it up in the dictionary	Он посмотрел это в словаре
They have put it off	Они это отложили

Английские неправильные глаголы

Вариантные формы глаголов даются через запятую, например формы простого прошедшего времени глагола forbid: forbade, forbad.

* звёздочкой обозначаются вариантные формы, которые используются только в определённом значении (значениях) глагола, подробнее о них см. словарные статьи к соответствующим глаголам, например: *cost, costed.

Инфинитив	Простое прошедшее время	Причастие прошедшего времени
arise	arose	arisen
awake	awoke	awoken
be	was *sg.*, were *pl.*	been
bear	bore	borne, born
beat	beat	beaten
become	became	become
befall	befell	befallen
beget	begot, (*arch.*) begat	begotten
begin	began	begun
behold	beheld	beheld
bend	bent	bent
beseech	besought, beseeched	besought, beseeched
beset	beset	beset
bet	bet, betted	bet, betted
bid	bid	bid
bind	bound	bound
bite	bit	bitten
bleed	bled	bled
blow	blew	blown
break	broke	broken
breed	bred	bred
bring	brought	brought
broadcast	broadcast	broadcast
build	built	built
burn	burnt, burned	burnt, burned
burst	burst	burst
bust	bust, busted	bust, busted
buy	bought	bought
cast	cast	cast
catch	caught	caught
choose	chose	chosen
cling	clung	clung
come	came	come
cost	*cost, costed	*cost, costed
creep	crept	crept

Инфинитив	Простое прошедшее время	Причастие прошедшего времени
cut	cut	cut
deal	dealt	dealt
dig	dug	dug
dive	dived, (*US*) dove	dived, (*US*) dove
do	did	done
draw	drew	drawn
dream	dreamt, dreamed	dreamt, dreamed
drink	drank	drunk
drive	drove	driven
dwell	dwelled, dwelt	dwelled, dwelt
eat	ate	eaten
fall	fell	fallen
feed	fed	fed
feel	felt	felt
fight	fought	fought
find	found	found
flee	fled	fled
fling	flung	flung
floodlight	floodlit	floodlit
fly	flew	flown
forbid	forbade, forbad	forbidden
forecast	forecast forecasted	forecast forecasted
for(e)go	for(e)went	for(e)gone
foresee	foresaw	foreseen
forget	forgot	forgotten, (*US*) forgot
forgive	forgave	forgiven
forsake	forsook	forsaken
freeze	froze	frozen
get	got	got, (*US*) gotten
give	gave	given
go	went	gone
grind	ground	ground

Инфинитив	Простое прошедшее время	Причастие прошедшего времени
grow	grew	grown
hang	*hung, hanged	*hung, hanged
have	had	had
hear	heard	heard
heave	heaved, (*naut.*) hove	heaved, (*naut.*) hove
hide	hid	hidden
hit	hit	hit
hold	held	held
hurt	hurt	hurt
inlay	inlaid	inlaid
keep	kept	kept
kneel	knelt, (*esp. US*) kneeled	knelt, (*esp. US*) kneeled
knit	knitted, knit	knitted, knit
know	knew	known
lay[2]	laid	laid
lead[2]	led	led
lean	leaned, (*esp. Br.*) leant	leaned, (*esp. Br.*) leant
leap	leapt, leaped	leapt, leaped
learn	learnt (*esp. Br*), learned	learnt (*esp. Br*), learned
leave	left	left
lend	lent	lent
let[2]	let	let
lie[2]	lay	lain
light[1]	*lit, lighted	*lit, lighted
lose	lost	lost
make	made	made
mean	meant	meant
meet	met	met
mislay	mislaid	mislaid
mislead	misled	misled
mistake	mistook	mistaken
mow	mowed	mown, mowed
offset	offset	offset
OK	OK'd	OK'd
pay	paid	paid
prove	proved	proved, proven
put	put	put
quit	quitted, quit	quitted, quit
read	read	read

Инфинитив	Простое прошедшее время	Причастие прошедшего времени
rid	rid	rid
ride	rode	ridden
ring[2]	rang	rung
rise	rose	risen
run	ran	run
saw	sawed	sawn, sawed
say	said	said
see	saw	seen
seek	sought	sought
sell	sold	sold
send	sent	sent
set	set	set
sew	sewed	sewn, sewed
shake	shook	shaken
shave	shaved	*shaved, shaven
shear	sheared	shorn, sheared
shed	shed	shed
shine	*shone, shined	*shone, shined
shoe	shod	shod
shoot	shot	shot
show	showed	shown, showed
shrink	shrank	*shrunk, shrunken
shut	shut	shut
sing	sang	sung
sink	sank, sunk	*sunk, sunken
sit	sat	sat
slay	slew	slain
sleep	slept	slept
slide	slid	slid
sling	slung	slung
slink	slunk	slunk
slit	slit	slit
smell	smelt, smelled	smelt, smelled
sneak	sneaked, (*US coll.*) snuck	sneaked, (*US coll.*) snuck
sow	sowed	sown, sowed
speak	spoke	spoken
speed	*sped, speeded	*sped, speeded
spell	spelled, (*esp. Br.*) spelt	spelled, (*esp. Br.*) spelt
spend	spent	spent

Инфинитив	Простое прошедшее время	Причастие прошедшего времени
spill	spilt, spilled	spilt, spilled
spin	spun, span	spun
spit[2]	spat, spit	spat, spit
split	split	split
spoil	spoiled, (*esp. Br.*) spoilt	spoiled, (*esp. Br.*) spoilt
spread	spread	spread
spring[2]	sprang, (*US*) sprung	sprung
stand	stood	stood
steal	stole	stolen
stick[2]	stuck	stuck
sting	stung	stung
stink	stank, stunk	stunk
strew	strewed	strewed, strewn
stride	strode	stridden
strike	struck	struck, (*arch.*) stricken
string	strung	strung
strive	strove, strived	striven, strived
sublet	sublet	sublet
subpoena	subpoenaed, subpoena'd	subpoenaed, subpoena'd
swear	swore	sworn
sweat	sweated, (*US*) sweat	sweated, (*US*) sweat
sweep	swept	swept

Инфинитив	Простое прошедшее время	Причастие прошедшего времени
swell	swelled	swollen, swelled
swim	swam	swum
swing	swung	swung
take	took	taken
teach	taught	taught
tear[2]	tore	torn
tell	told	told
think	thought	thought
throw	threw	thrown
thrust	thrust	thrust
tread	trod	trodden, trod
understand	understood	understood
undo	undid	undone
unwind	unwound	unwound
upset[2]	upset	upset
wake	woke	woken
wear	wore	worn
weave	wove	woven, wove
weep	wept	wept
wet	wet, wetted	wet, wetted
win	won	won
wind[2]	wound	wound
withdraw	withdrew	withdrawn
withhold	withheld	withheld
withstand	withstood	withstood
wring	wrung	wrung
write	wrote	written

The Russian alphabet

Capital letters	Lower-case letters	Letter names	Capital letters	Lower-case letters	Letter names
А	а	а	Р	р	эр
Б	б	бэ	С	с	эс
В	в	вэ	Т	т	тэ
Г	г	гэ	У	у	у
Д	д	дэ	Ф	ф	эф
Е	е	е	Х	х	ха
Ё	ё	ё	Ц	ц	цэ
Ж	ж	жэ	Ч	ч	че
З	з	зэ	Ш	ш	ша
И	и	и	Щ	щ	ща
Й	й	и кра́ткое	Ъ	ъ	твёрдый знак
К	к	ка	Ы	ы	ы
Л	л	эль	Ь	ь	мя́гкий знак
М	м	эм	Э	э	э
Н	н	эн	Ю	ю	ю
О	о	о	Я	я	я
П	п	пэ			

Английский алфавит

Прописные буквы	Строчные буквы	Названия букв	Прописные буквы	Строчные буквы	Названия букв
A	a	/eɪ/	N	n	/en/
B	b	/biː/	O	o	/əʊ/
C	c	/siː/	P	p	/piː/
D	d	/diː/	Q	q	/kjuː/
E	e	/iː/	R	r	/ɑː(r)/
F	f	/ef/	S	s	/es/
G	g	/dʒiː/	T	t	/tiː/
H	h	/eɪtʃ/	U	u	/juː/
I	i	/aɪ/	V	v	/viː/
J	j	/dʒeɪ/	W	w	/ˈdʌb(ə)ljuː/
K	k	/keɪ/	X	x	/eks/
L	l	/el/	Y	y	/waɪ/
M	m	/em/	Z	z	/zed/